CHILTON'S™
AUTO REPAIR MANUAL
1996-00

President	Dean F. Morgantini, S.A.E.
Vice President–Finance	Barry L. Beck
Vice President–Sales	Glenn D. Potere
Executive Editor	Kevin M. G. Maher, A.S.E.
Manager–Consumer Automotive	Richard Schwartz, A.S.E.
Manager–Marine/Recreation	James R. Marotta, A.S.E.
Production Specialists	Brian Hollingsworth, Melinda Possinger
Project Managers	Will Kessler, A.S.E., S.A.E., Thomas A. Mellon, A.S.E., S.A.E., Richard J. Rivele, Todd W. Stidham, A.S.E., Ron Webb
Project Editors	David R. Back, A.S.E., Tim Crain, A.S.E., David N. Gaunt, A.S.E., Richard T. Smith
Editors	Christopher Bishop, A.S.E., Joseph D'Orazio, A.S.E., Scott A. Freeman, Eric Michael Mihalyi, A.S.E., S.A.E., S.T.S., Christopher G. Ritchie, A.S.E., S.T.S., Christine L. Sheeky, S.A.E.

CHILTON™ Automotive Books

PUBLISHED BY **W. G. NICHOLS, INC.**

Manufactured in USA
© 1999 W. G. Nichols
1020 Andrew Drive
West Chester, PA 19380
ISBN 0-8019-9300-8
Library of Congress Catalog Card No. 99-72324
1234567890 8765432109

™Chilton is a registered trademark of Cahners Business Information, a division of Reed Elsevier, Inc., and has been licensed to W. G. Nichols, Inc.

www.chiltononline.com

Table of Contents

Unit Repair Sections

Table of Contents

Car Sections

Model Index

HOW TO USE THIS MANUAL

Specifications

Specifications charts for all models covered in this book are located in Section 1. They include: Vehicle and Engine Identification, General Engine Specifications, Engine Tune-Up Specifications, Capacities, Valve Specifications, Crankshaft & Connecting Rod Specifications, Piston & Ring Specifications and Engine Fastener Torque Specifications. Specifications charts for brake systems can be found in Section 6.

Unit Repair Sections

The Unit Repair Sections (URS's) are written to cover all applicable 1996-00 models for the specific URS system or component, unless specifically noted otherwise. The procedures covered in the 10 URS's are not repeated in the model specific sections; therefore, refer to the URS's for the service procedures for the applicable systems or components. Refer to the Table of Contents for URS coverage.

Model Specific Sections

The model specific sections are grouped by manufacturer and arranged in alphabetical order. The text and illustrations that comprise the service procedures in each model specific section are arranged in the following order of systems and components: Engine Repair (Gasoline, then Diesel if applicable), Fuel System (Gasoline, then Diesel if applicable), Drive Train, Steering and Suspension.

All illustrations are located as close as possible to the applicable procedure. Procedures are for all models in the particular section unless specifically noted otherwise.

Locating Information

The Table of Contents, located at the front of the book, lists each Unit Repair Section (URS) and model specific section in this manual.

To find where a particular model specific section is located in the book, you need only look in the Table of Contents. Once you have found the proper section, you may wish to find where specific procedures are located in that section. Turn to the Index at the front of the model specific section. At the upper left-hand side is a listing of the main topics within that section and the page number on which they may be found. Following the main topics is an alphabetical listing of all of the procedures within the section and their page numbers.

The Model Index, located just after the Table of Contents in the beginning of this manual, may also be used to locate the specific section for any vehicle model covered in this manual.

Safety Notice

Proper service and repair procedures are vital to the safe, reliable operation of all motor vehicles, as well as the personal safety of those performing the repairs. This manual outlines procedures for servicing and repairing vehicles using safe effective methods. The procedures contain many NOTES, WARNINGS and CAUTIONS which should be followed along with standard safety procedures to eliminate the possibility of personal injury or improper service which could damage the vehicle or compromise its safety.

It is important to note that repair procedures and techniques, tools and parts for servicing vehicles, as well as the skill and experience of the individual performing the work vary widely. It is not possible to anticipate all of the conceivable ways or conditions under which vehicles may be serviced, or to provide cautions as to all of the possible hazards that may result. Standard and accepted safety precautions and equipment should be used when handling toxic or flammable fluids, and safety goggles or other protection should be used during cutting, grinding, chiseling, prying, or any other process that can cause material removal or projectiles.

Some procedures require the use of tools specially designed for a specific purpose. Before substituting another tool or procedure, you must be completely satisfied that neither your personal safety, nor the performance of the vehicle will be endangered.

Although information in this manual is based on industry sources and is as complete as possible at the time of publication, the possibility exists that some vehicle manufacturers made later changes which could not be included here. Information on very late models may not be available in some circumstances. While striving for total accuracy, Chilton cannot assume responsibility for any errors, changes, or omissions that may occur in the compilation of this data.

Part Numbers

Part numbers listed in this book are not recommendations by Chilton for any product by brand name. They are references that can be used with interchange manuals and aftermarket supplier catalogs to locate each brand supplier's discrete part number.

Special Tools

Special tools are recommended by the vehicle manufacturer to perform their specific job. Use has been kept to a minimum, but where absolutely necessary, they are referred to in the text by the part number of the tool manufacturer. These tools may be purchased, under the appropriate part number, from your local dealer or regional distributor, or an equivalent tool can be purchased locally from a tool supplier or parts outlet. Before substituting any tool for the one recommended, read the previous Safety Notice.

Acknowledgments

This publication contains material that is reproduced and distributed under a license from Ford Motor Company. No further reproduction or distribution of the Ford Motor Company material is allowed without the expressed written permission from Ford Motor Company.

Portions of the material contained herein have been reprinted with permission of General Motors Corporation, Service Technology Group.

Chilton would also like to thank all manufacturers involved in the production of this book. A special thanks goes to Lincoln Automotive Products, 1 Lincoln Way, St. Louis, MO 63120, for providing the professional shop equipment used in our tear-down facility, including jacks, engine stands, fluid and lubrication tools, and shop presses.

Copyright Notice

SPECIFICATIONS

1

CHRYSLER CORP.
Chrysler 300M • Concorde • LHS • New Yorker •
Dodge Intrepid • Eagle Vision

ENGINE AND VEHICLE IDENTIFICATION

Engine							Model Year	
Code ①	Liters (cc)	Cu. In.	Cyl.	Fuel Sys.	Engine Type	Eng. Mfg.	Code ②	Year
F	3.5 (3518)	215	V6	MFI	SOHC	Chrysler	T	1996
G	3.5 (3518)	215	V6	MFI	SOHC	Chrysler	V	1997
J	3.2 (3231)	195	V6	MFI	SOHC	Chrysler	W	1998
R	2.7 (2736)	167	V6	MFI	DOHC	Chrysler	X	1999
T	3.3 (3301)	201	V6	MFI	OHV	Chrysler	Y	2000

MFI - Multi-point Fuel Injection
DOHC - Double Overhead Camshafts
SOHC - Single Overhead Camshaft
OHV - Overhead Valve
① 8th position of the Vehicle Identification Number (VIN)
② 10th position of VIN

93001C01

GENERAL ENGINE SPECIFICATIONS
All measurements are given in inches.

Year	Model	Engine Displacement Liters (cc)	Engine Series (ID/VIN)	Fuel System	Net Horsepower @ rpm	Net Torque @ rpm (ft. lbs.)	Bore x Stroke (in.)	Compression Ratio	Oil Pressure @ rpm
1996	Concorde	3.3 (3301)	T	MFI	161@5300	181@3200	3.66x3.19	8.9:1	30-80@3000
	Concorde	3.5 (3518)	F	MFI	214@5800	221@3100	3.78x3.19	9.6:1	25-80@3000
	Intrepid	3.3 (3300)	T	MFI	161@5300	181@3200	3.66x3.19	8.9:1	30-80@3000
	Intrepid	3.5 (3518)	F	MFI	214@5800	221@3100	3.78x3.19	9.6:1	25-80@3000
	LHS	3.5 (3518)	F	MFI	214@5800	221@3100	3.78x3.19	9.6:1	25-80@3000
	New Yorker	3.5 (3518)	F	MFI	214@5800	221@3100	3.78x3.19	9.6:1	25-80@3000
	Vision	3.3 (3301)	T	MFI	161@5300	181@3200	3.66x3.19	8.9:1	30-80@3000
	Vision	3.5 (3518)	F	MFI	214@5800	221@3100	3.78x3.19	9.6:1	25-80@3000
1997	Concorde	3.5 (3518)	F	MFI	214@5800	221@3100	3.78x3.19	9.6:1	25-80@3000
	Intrepid	3.3 (3300)	T	MFI	161@5300	181@3200	3.66x3.19	8.9:1	30-80@3000
	Intrepid	3.5 (3518)	F	MFI	214@5800	221@3100	3.78x3.19	9.6:1	25-80@3000
	LHS	3.5 (3518)	F	MFI	214@5800	221@3100	3.78x3.19	9.6:1	25-80@3000
	Vision	3.5 (3518)	F	MFI	214@5800	221@3100	3.78x3.19	9.6:1	25-80@3000
1998	Concorde	2.7 (2736)	R	MFI	200@5800	190@4850	3.39x3.09	9.6:1	25-105@3000
	Concorde	3.2 (3231)	J	MFI	225@6300	225@3800	3.62x3.19	9.5:1	25-105@3000
	Intrepid	2.7 (2736)	R	MFI	200@5800	190@4850	3.39x3.09	9.6:1	25-105@3000
	Intrepid	3.2 (3231)	J	MFI	225@6300	225@3800	3.62x3.19	9.5:1	25-105@3000
1999-00	300M	2.7 (2736)	R	MFI	200@5800	190@4850	3.39x3.09	9.6:1	25-105@3000
	300M	3.5 (3518)	G	MFI	214@5800	221@3100	3.78x3.19	9.6:1	25-105@3000
	Concorde	2.7 (2736)	R	MFI	200@5800	190@4850	3.39x3.09	9.6:1	25-105@3000
	Concorde	3.2 (3231)	J	MFI	225@6300	225@3800	3.62x3.19	9.5:1	25-105@3000
	Intrepid	2.7 (2736)	R	MFI	200@5800	190@4850	3.39x3.09	9.6:1	25-105@3000
	Intrepid	3.2 (3231)	J	MFI	225@6300	225@3800	3.62x3.19	9.5:1	25-105@3000
	LHS	3.5 (3518)	G	MFI	214@5800	221@3100	3.78x3.19	9.6:1	25-105@3000

MFI - Multi-point Fuel Injection

93001C02

ENGINE TUNE-UP SPECIFICATIONS

Year	Engine Displacement Liters (cc)	Engine ID/VIN	Spark Plug Gap (in.)	Ignition Timing (deg.)	Fuel Pump (psi) ①	Idle Speed (rpm)	Valve Clearance Intake	Valve Clearance Exhaust
1996	3.3 (3301)	T	0.048-0.053	②	55	600-840	HYD	HYD
	3.5 (3518)	F	0.033-0.038	②	48	750-1100	HYD	HYD
1997	3.3 (3301)	T	0.048-0.053	②	55	600-840	HYD	HYD
	3.5 (3518)	F	0.033-0.038	②	48	750-1100	HYD	HYD
1998	2.7 (2736)	R	0.048-0.053	②	49	600-840	HYD	HYD
	3.2 (3231)	J	0.048-0.053	②	49	600-840	HYD	HYD
	3.5 (3518)	G	0.048-0.053	②	49	750-1100	HYD	HYD
1999-00	2.7 (2736)	R	0.048-0.053	②	49	600-840	HYD	HYD
	3.2 (3231)	J	0.048-0.053	②	49	600-840	HYD	HYD
	3.5 (3518)	G	0.048-0.053	②	49	750-1100	HYD	HYD

NOTE: The Vehicle Emission Control Information label often reflects specification changes made during production. The label figures must be used if they differ from those in this chart.

HYD - Hydraulic

① This reading measured with vacuum hose disconnected from fuel pressure regulator

② Basic ignition timing is not adjustable

93001C03

CAPACITIES

Year	Model	Engine Displacement Liters (cc)	Engine ID/VIN	Engine Oil with Filter (qts.)	Auto. Transmission (pts.) ①	Front Drive Axle (pts.)	Fuel Tank (gal.)	Cooling System (qts.)
1996	Concorde	3.3 (3301)	T	5.0	19.8	2.0	18.0	10.2
	Concorde	3.5 (3518)	F	5.5	19.7	2.0	18.0	11.8
	Intrepid	3.3 (3300)	T	5.0	19.8	2.0	18.0	10.2
	Intrepid	3.5 (3518)	F	5.5	19.8	2.0	18.0	11.8
	LHS	3.5 (3518)	F	5.5	19.8	2.0	18.0	11.8
	New Yorker	3.5 (3518)	F	5.5	19.8	2.0	18.0	11.8
	Vision	3.3 (3301)	T	5.0	19.8	2.0	18.0	10.2
	Vision	3.5 (3518)	F	5.5	19.8	2.0	18.0	11.8
1997	Concorde	3.5 (3518)	F	5.5	19.7	2.0	18.0	11.8
	Intrepid	3.3 (3300)	T	5.0	19.8	2.0	18.0	10.2
	Intrepid	3.5 (3518)	F	5.5	19.8	2.0	18.0	11.8
	LHS	3.5 (3518)	F	5.5	19.8	2.0	18.0	11.8
	Vision	3.3 (3301)	T	5.0	19.8	2.0	18.0	10.2
1998	300M	3.5 (3518)	G	5.5	19.8	2.0	18.0	11.8
	Concorde	2.7 (2736)	R	5.0	19.8	2.0	18.0	8.0
	Concorde	3.2 (3231)	J	5.0	19.8	2.0	18.0	8.0
	Intrepid	2.7 (2736)	R	5.0	19.8	2.0	18.0	8.0
	Intrepid	3.2 (3231)	J	5.0	19.8	2.0	18.0	8.0
1999-00	300M	3.5 (3518)	G	5.5	19.8	2.0	18.0	11.8
	Concorde	2.7 (2736)	R	5.0	19.8	2.0	18.0	8.0
	Concorde	3.2 (3231)	J	5.0	19.8	2.0	18.0	8.0
	Intrepid	2.7 (2736)	R	5.0	19.8	2.0	18.0	8.0
	Intrepid	3.2 (3231)	J	5.0	19.8	2.0	18.0	8.0
	LHS	3.5 (3518)	G	5.5	19.8	2.0	18.0	11.8

NOTE: All capacities are approximate. Add fluid gradually and ensure a proper fluid level is obtained.

① Overhaul fill capacity with torque converter empty
Estimated service fill: 9 pts.

93001C04

VALVE SPECIFICATIONS

Year	Engine Displacement Liters (cc)	Engine ID/VIN	Seat Angle (deg.)	Face Angle (deg.)	Spring Test Pressure (lbs. @ in.)	Spring Installed Height (in.)	Stem-to-Guide Clearance (in.) Intake	Stem-to-Guide Clearance (in.) Exhaust	Stem Diameter (in.) Intake	Stem Diameter (in.) Exhaust
1996	3.5 (3518)	F	45-45.5	44.5-45	①	1.496	0.0009-0.0026	0.0020-0.0037	0.2730-0.2737	0.2719-0.2726
	3.3 (3301)	T	45-45.5	44.5-45	②	1.622-1.681	0.0010-0.0100	0.0020-0.0060	0.3120-0.3130	0.3112-0.3119
1997	3.5 (3518)	F	45-45.5	44.5-45	①	1.496	0.0009-0.0026	0.0020-0.0037	0.2730-0.2737	0.2719-0.2726
	3.3 (3301)	T	45-45.5	44.5-45	②	1.622-1.681	0.0010-0.0100	0.0020-0.0060	0.3120-0.3130	0.3112-0.3119
1998	3.5 (3518)	G	45-45.5	44.5-45	①	1.496	0.0009-0.0026	0.0020-0.0037	0.2730-0.2737	0.2719-0.2726
	3.2 (3231)	J	45-45.5	44.5-45	③	1.496	0.0009-0.0026	0.0020-0.0037	0.2730-0.2737	0.2719-0.2726
	2.5 (2736)	R	45-45.5	44.5-45	④	1.496	0.0009-0.0026	0.0020-0.0033	0.2337-0.2344	0.2326-0.2333
1999-00	3.5 (3518)	G	45-45.5	44.5-45	①	1.496	0.0009-0.0026	0.0020-0.0037	0.2730-0.2737	0.2719-0.2726
	3.2 (3231)	J	45-45.5	44.5-45	③	1.496	0.0009-0.0026	0.0020-0.0037	0.2730-0.2737	0.2719-0.2726
	2.5 (2736)	R	45-45.5	44.5-45	④	1.496	0.0009-0.0026	0.0020-0.0033	0.2337-0.2344	0.2326-0.2333

① Intake: 201.7-218.3 lbs. @ 1.1752 in.
   Exhaust: 158.5-171.5 lbs. @ 1.239 in.

② Intake: 95-100 lbs. @ 1.570 in. valve closed
   Exhaust: 207-229 lbs. @ 1.169 in. valve closed

③ Intake: 69.5-80.5 lbs. @ 1.496 in. valve closed
   Intake: 188.0-204.0 lbs. @ 1.1594 in. valve opened
   Exhaust: 56-64 lbs. @ 1.4961 in. valve closed
   Exhaust: 124-136 lbs. @ 1.239 in. valve opened

④ 56-64 lbs. @ 1.496 in. valve closed
   Intake: 147.9-162.1 lbs. @ 1.1417 in. valve opened
   Exhaust: 138.0-150.8 lbs. @ 1.811 in. valve opened

93001C05

CRANKSHAFT AND CONNECTING ROD SPECIFICATIONS
All measurements are given in inches.

Year	Engine Displacement Liters (cc)	Engine ID/VIN	Crankshaft Main Brg. Journal Dia.	Crankshaft Main Brg. Oil Clearance	Crankshaft Shaft End-play	Crankshaft Thrust on No.	Connecting Rod Journal Diameter	Connecting Rod Oil Clearance	Connecting Rod Side Clearance
1996	3.3 (3300)	T	2.5190-2.5200	0.0007-0.0028	0.0040-0.0120	2	2.2830-2.2840	0.0008-0.0034	0.0050-0.0150
	3.5 (3518)	F	2.5185-2.5195	0.0007-0.0022	0.0040-0.0120	2	2.2830-2.2840	0.0008-0.0030	0.0050-0.0150
1997	3.3 (3300)	T	2.5190-2.5200	0.0007-0.0028	0.0040-0.0120	2	2.2830-2.2840	0.0008-0.0034	0.0050-0.0150
	3.5 (3518)	F	2.5185-2.5195	0.0007-0.0022	0.0040-0.0120	2	2.2830-2.2840	0.0008-0.0030	0.0050-0.0150
1998	2.7 (2736)	R	2.4997-2.5004	0.0014-0.0021	0.017 max.	3	2.1067-2.1060	0.001-0.0026	0.0052-0.0150
	3.5 (3518)	J	2.5190-2.5200	0.0007-0.0028	0.0040-0.0170	2	2.2820-2.2830	0.0008-0.0034	0.0050-0.0157
1999-00	2.7 (2736)	R	2.4997-2.5004	0.0014-0.0021	0.017 max.	3	2.1067-2.1060	0.001-0.0026	0.0052-0.0150
	3.2 (3231)	J	2.5190-2.5200	0.0007-0.0034	0.0040-0.0170	2	2.2830-2.2840	0.0008-0.0034	0.0050-0.0150
	3.5 (3518)	G	2.5190-2.5200	0.0004-0.0022	0.0040-0.0090	2	2.2830-2.2840	0.0008-0.0026	0.0050-0.0150

93001C06

PISTON AND RING SPECIFICATIONS
All measurements are given in inches.

Year	Engine Displacement Liters (cc)	Engine ID/VIN	Piston Clearance	Ring Gap			Ring Side Clearance		
				Top Compression	Bottom Compression	Oil Control	Top Compression	Bottom Compression	Oil Control
1996	3.3 (3300)	T	0.0009-0.0022	0.012-0.022	0.012-0.022	0.010-0.040	0.0012-0.0037	0.0012-0.0037	0.0005-0.0089
	3.5 (3518)	F	0.0007-0.0020	0.012-0.018	0.012-0.022	0.010-0.030	0.0012-0.0031	0.0012-0.0031	0.0019-0.0077
1997	3.3 (3300)	T	0.0009-0.0022	0.012-0.022	0.012-0.022	0.010-0.040	0.0012-0.0037	0.0012-0.0037	0.0005-0.0089
	3.5 (3518)	F	0.0007-0.0020	0.012-0.018	0.012-0.022	0.010-0.030	0.0012-0.0031	0.0012-0.0031	0.0019-0.0077
1998	2.7 (2736)	R	0.0001-0.0016	0.008-0.014	0.0146-0.0249	0.010-0.030	0.0016-0.0031	0.0016-0.0031	0.0025-0.0082
	3.2 (3231)	J	0.0003-0.0018	0.008-0.014	0.0091-0.0197	0.010-0.030	0.0014-0.0034	0.0014-0.0034	0.0015-0.0073
1999-00	2.7 (2736)	R	0.0001-0.0016	0.008-0.014	0.0146-0.0249	0.010-0.030	0.0016-0.0031	0.0016-0.0031	0.0025-0.0082
	3.2 (3231)	J	0.0003-0.0018	0.008-0.014	0.0091-0.0197	0.010-0.030	0.0014-0.0034	0.0014-0.0034	0.0015-0.0073
	3.5 (3518)	G	0.0003-0.0018	0.008-0.014	0.0091-0.0197	0.010-0.030	0.0014-0.0034	0.0014-0.0034	0.0015-0.0073

93001C07

TORQUE SPECIFICATIONS
All readings in ft. lbs.

Year	Engine Displacement Liters (cc)	Engine ID/VIN	Cylinder Head Bolts	Main Bearing Bolts	Rod Bearing Bolts	Crankshaft Damper Bolts	Flywheel Bolts	Manifold		Spark Plugs	Lug Nuts
								Intake	Exhaust		
1996	3.5 (3518)	F	①	②	③	85	75	21	17	20	100
	3.3 (3301)	T	④	⑤	③	40	75	17	17	20	100
1997	3.5 (3518)	F	①	②	③	85	75	21	17	20	100
	3.3 (3301)	T	④	⑤	③	40	75	17	17	20	100
1998	3.5 (3518)	G	①	②	③	85	75	⑥	17	20	100
	3.2 (3231)	J	①	⑦	③	75	75	17	17	20	100
	2.7 (2736)	R	⑧	⑨	⑧	125	75	⑩	17	15	100
1999-00	3.5 (3518)	G	①	②	③	85	75	⑥	⑥	20	100
	3.2 (3231)	J	①	⑧	③	75	75	17	17	20	100
	2.7 (2736)	R	⑨	⑩	⑧	125	75	⑩	17	15	100

① Step 1: 45 ft. lbs.
Step 2: 65 ft. lbs.
Step 3: 65 ft. lbs.
Step 4: Plus 1/4 turn
Final torque should be over 90 ft. lbs.

② Main cap bolts: 30 ft. lbs. plus 1/4 turn
Main cap tie bolts: 40 ft. lbs.

③ Step 1: 40 ft. lbs.
Step 2: Plus 1/4 turn

④ Step 1: 45 ft. lbs.
Step 2: 65 ft. lbs.
Step 3: 65 ft. lbs.
Step 4: Plus 1/4 turn
Torque small bolt in rear of cylinder head to 25 ft. lbs.

⑤ Step 1: 30 ft. lbs.
Step 2: Plus 1/4 turn

⑥ M8 bolts: 250 inch lbs.
M6 bolts: 105 inch lbs.

⑦ Main cap inside bolts: 15 ft. lbs. plus 1/4 turn
Main cap outside bolts: 20 ft. lbs. plus 1/4 turn
Main cap tie bolts: 250 inch lbs.

⑧ Step 1: 35 ft. lbs.
Step 2: 55 ft. lbs.
Step 3: 55 ft. lbs.
Step 4: Plus 90 degrees
Step 5: M8 bolts (3 front) 250 inch lbs.

⑨ Main cap tie bolts: 250 in. lbs.
Main cap inner bolts: 15 ft. lbs. plus 1/4 turn
Main cap outer bolts: 20 ft. lbs. plus 1/4 turn

⑩ Step 1: 20 ft. lbs.
Step 2: Plus 1/4 turn

93001C08

Timing chain and gear service is covered in the model specific sections of this manual

SCHEDULED MAINTENANCE INTERVALS
(CHRYSLER STRATUS & SEBRING CONVERTIBLE, DODGE CIRRUS, PLYMOUTH BREEZE)

TO BE SERVICED	TYPE OF SERVICE	VEHICLE MILEAGE INTERVAL (x1000)												
		7.5	15	22.5	30	37.5	45	52.5	60	67.5	75	82.5	90	97.5
Engine oil & filter	R	✓	✓	✓	✓	✓	✓	✓	✓	✓	✓	✓	✓	✓
Brake hoses	S/I	✓	✓	✓	✓	✓	✓	✓	✓	✓	✓	✓	✓	✓
Coolant level, hoses & clamps	S/I	✓	✓	✓	✓	✓	✓	✓	✓	✓	✓	✓	✓	✓
CV joints & front suspension components	S/I	✓	✓	✓	✓	✓	✓	✓	✓	✓	✓	✓	✓	✓
Exhaust system	S/I	✓	✓	✓	✓	✓	✓	✓	✓	✓	✓	✓	✓	✓
Rotate tires	S/I	✓	✓	✓	✓	✓	✓	✓	✓	✓	✓	✓	✓	✓
Accessory drive belts	S/I		✓		✓		✓		✓		✓		✓	
Brake linings	S/I				✓		✓			✓			✓	
Air filter element	R					✓			✓				✓	
Spark plugs ①	R					✓			✓				✓	
Lubricate front & rear ball joints	S/I					✓			✓				✓	
Engine coolant	R						✓				✓			
PCV valve	S/I								✓				✓	
Ignition cables ②	R								✓					
Camshaft timing belt ③	R													

① 4-cylinder shown; 6-cylinder = 100,000 miles.

② 4-cylinder 60,000 miles, 6-cylinder 100,000 miles.

③ Replace at 105,000 miles for normal service; replace at 102,000 miles for servere service

R - Replace   S/I - Service or Inspect

FREQUENT OPERATION MAINTENANCE (SEVERE SERVICE)

If a vehicle is operated under any of the following conditions it is considered severe service:

- Extremely dusty areas.

- 50% or more of the vehicle operation is in 32°C (90°F) or higher temperatures, or constant
  operation in temperatures below 0°C (32°F).

- Prolonged idling (vehicle operation in stop and go traffic).

- Frequent short running periods (engine does not warm to normal operating temperatures).

- Police, taxi, delivery usage or trailer towing usage.

Oil & oil filter change - change every 3000 miles.

Rotate tires every 6000 miles.

Brake linings - check every 12,000 miles.

Air filter element - change every 15,000 miles.

Automatic transaxle fluid - service or inspect every 15,000 miles.

PCV valve - check every 30,000 miles.

Engine coolant, replace at 36,000, 51,000 & 81,000 miles.

93001C09

SCHEDULED MAINTENANCE INTERVALS
CHRYSLER CORPORATION
CHRYSLER CONCORDE, LHS, NEW YORKER, 300M
DODGE INTREPID, EAGLE VISION

The following should be used as a guide when determining the amount of work required for a particular service.
In estimating how long a particular Scheduled Maintenance Service should take, please observe the following:

- **Chilton Time** is time based on field research and data supplied by the vehicle manufacturer.
  - Labor time operations are given in hours and tenths of an hour.
    - All labor operations, are to be used as a guide.

Mechanic Skill Level Codes:
(A) PRECISION: Really skilled with multiple certification.
(B) GENERAL: Normally skilled with certification.
(C) MAINTENANCE: Semi-skilled working on certification.

	Chilton Time		Chilton Time		Chilton Time
7500 Mile Service (C)		**45000 Mile Service (B)**		**67500 Mile Service (C)**	
All Models	1.3	All Models	2.4	All Models	1.8
15000 Mile Service (C)		**52500 Mile Service (C)**		**75000 Mile Service (C)**	
All Models	1.9	All Models	1.3	All Models	1.9
22500 Mile Service (C)		**60000 Mile Service (B)**		**82500 Mile Service (C)**	
All Models	1.8	All Models	3.7	All Models	1.3
30000 Mile Service (B)		Replace timing belt add	3.6	**90000 Mile Service (B)**	
All Models	2.8			All Models	3.5
37500 Mile Service (C)				**97500 Mile Service (C)**	
All Models	1.3			All Models	1.3

93001C00

Ignition system service is covered in the model specific sections of this manual

CHRYSLER CORP.
Chrysler Cirrus • Sebring Convertible •
Dodge Stratus • Plymouth Breeze

ENGINE AND VEHICLE IDENTIFICATION

Engine							Model Year	
Code ①	Liters (cc)	Cu. In.	Cyl.	Fuel Sys.	Engine Type	Eng. Mfg.	Code ②	Year
C	2.0 (1996)	122	I4	MFI	SOHC	Chrysler	T	1996
H	2.5 (2497)	152	V6	MFI	SOHC	Mitsubishi	V	1997
X	2.4 (2429)	148	I4	MFI	DOHC	Chrysler	W	1998
							X	1999
							Y	2000

MFI - Multi-point Fuel Injection

SOHC - Single Overhead Camshaft

DOHC - Double Overhead Camshaft

① 8th position of VIN

② 10th position of VIN

93001C11

GENERAL ENGINE SPECIFICATIONS
All measurements are given in inches.

Year	Model	Engine Displacement Liters (cc)	Engine Series (ID/VIN)	Fuel System	Net Horsepower @ rpm	Net Torque @ rpm (ft. lbs.)	Bore x Stroke (in.)	Compression Ratio	Oil Pressure @ rpm
1996	Breeze	2.0 (1996)	C	MFI	132@6000	129@5000	3.44x3.26	9.8:1	25-80@3000
	Cirrus	2.4 (2429)	X	MFI	150@5200	167@4000	3.44x3.98	9.4:1	25-80@3000
	Cirrus	2.5 (2497)	H	MFI	168@5800	170@4350	3.29x2.99	9.4:1	25-80@3000
	Sebring Convertible	2.4 (2429)	X	MFI	150@5200	167@4000	3.44x3.98	9.4:1	25-80@3000
	Sebring Convertible	2.5 (2497)	H	MFI	168@5800	170@4350	3.29x2.99	9.4:1	25-80@3000
	Stratus	2.0 (1996)	C	MFI	132@6000	129@5000	3.44x3.26	9.8:1	25-80@3000
	Stratus	2.4 (2429)	X	MFI	150@5200	167@4000	3.44x3.98	9.4:1	25-80@3000
	Stratus	2.5 (2497)	H	MFI	168@5800	170@4350	3.29x2.99	9.4:1	25-80@3000
1997	Breeze	2.0 (1996)	C	MFI	132@6000	129@5000	3.44x3.26	9.8:1	25-80@3000
	Cirrus	2.4 (2429)	X	MFI	150@5200	167@4000	3.44x3.98	9.4:1	25-80@3000
	Cirrus	2.5 (2497)	H	MFI	168@5800	170@4350	3.29x2.99	9.4:1	25-80@3000
	Sebring Convertible	2.4 (2429)	X	MFI	150@5200	167@4000	3.44x3.98	9.4:1	25-80@3000
	Sebring Convertible	2.5 (2497)	H	MFI	168@5800	170@4350	3.29x2.99	9.4:1	25-80@3000
	Stratus	2.0 (1996)	C	MFI	132@6000	129@5000	3.44x3.26	9.8:1	25-80@3000
	Stratus	2.4 (2429)	X	MFI	150@5200	167@4000	3.44x3.98	9.4:1	25-80@3000
	Stratus	2.5 (2497)	H	MFI	168@5800	170@4350	3.29x2.99	9.4:1	25-80@3000
1998	Breeze	2.0 (1996)	C	MFI	132@6000	129@5000	3.44x3.26	9.8:1	25-80@3000
	Cirrus	2.4 (2429)	X	MFI	150@5200	167@4000	3.44x3.98	9.4:1	25-80@3000
	Cirrus	2.5 (2497)	H	MFI	168@5800	170@4350	3.29x2.99	9.4:1	25-80@3000
	Sebring Convertible	2.4 (2429)	X	MFI	150@5200	167@4000	3.44x3.98	9.4:1	25-80@3000
	Sebring Convertible	2.5 (2497)	H	MFI	168@5800	170@4350	3.29x2.99	9.4:1	25-80@3000
	Stratus	2.0 (1996)	C	MFI	132@6000	129@5000	3.44x3.26	9.8:1	25-80@3000
	Stratus	2.4 (2429)	X	MFI	150@5200	167@4000	3.44x3.98	9.4:1	25-80@3000
	Stratus	2.5 (2497)	H	MFI	168@5800	170@4350	3.29x2.99	9.4:1	25-80@3000
1999-00	Breeze	2.0 (1996)	C	MFI	132@6000	129@5000	3.44x3.26	9.8:1	25-80@3000
	Cirrus	2.4 (2429)	X	MFI	150@5200	167@4000	3.44x3.98	9.4:1	25-80@3000
	Cirrus	2.5 (2497)	H	MFI	168@5800	170@4350	3.29x2.99	9.4:1	25-80@3000
	Sebring Convertible	2.4 (2429)	X	MFI	150@5200	167@4000	3.44x3.98	9.4:1	25-80@3000
	Sebring Convertible	2.5 (2497)	H	MFI	168@5800	170@4350	3.29x2.99	9.4:1	25-80@3000
	Stratus	2.0 (1996)	C	MFI	132@6000	129@5000	3.44x3.26	9.8:1	25-80@3000
	Stratus	2.4 (2429)	X	MFI	150@5200	167@4000	3.44x3.98	9.4:1	25-80@3000
	Stratus	2.5 (2497)	H	MFI	168@5800	170@4350	3.29x2.99	9.4:1	25-80@3000

MFI - Multi-point Fuel Injectiom

93001C12

GASOLINE ENGINE TUNE-UP SPECIFICATIONS

Year	Engine Displacement Liters (cc)	Engine ID/VIN	Spark Plug Gap (in.)	Ignition Timing (deg.)		Fuel Pump (psi) ①	Idle Speed (rpm)		Valve Clearance	
				MT	AT		MT	AT	In.	Ex.
1996	2.0 (1996)	C	0.035	②	②	48	③	③	HYD	HYD
	2.4 (2429)	X	0.050	—	②	49	—	③	HYD	HYD
	2.5 (2497)	H	0.038-0.043	—	②	49	—	500-1100	HYD	HYD
1997	2.0 (1996)	C	0.035	②	②	48	③	③	HYD	HYD
	2.4 (2429)	X	0.050	—	②	49	—	③	HYD	HYD
	2.5 (2497)	H	0.038-0.043	—	②	49	—	500-1100	HYD	HYD
1998	2.0 (1996)	C	0.035	②	②	48	③	③	HYD	HYD
	2.4 (2429)	X	0.050	—	②	49	—	③	HYD	HYD
	2.5 (2497)	H	0.038-0.043	—	②	49	—	500-1100	HYD	HYD
1999-00	2.0 (1996)	C	0.035	②	②	48	③	③	HYD	HYD
	2.4 (2429)	X	0.050	—	②	49	—	③	HYD	HYD
	2.5 (2497)	H	0.038-0.043	—	②	49	—	500-1100	HYD	HYD

NOTE: The Vehicle Emission Control Information label often reflects specification changes made during production. The label figures must be used if they differ from those in this chart.

HYD - Hydraulic

① This reading measured with vacuum hose disconnected from fuel pressure regulator.

② Ignition timing cannot be adjusted. Base engine timing is set at TDC during assembly.

③ Refer to the Vehicle Emission Control Information label for correct specifications.

93001C13

CAPACITIES

Year	Model	Engine Displacement Liters (cc)	Engine ID/VIN	Engine Oil with Filter (qts.)	Transmission (pts.) 5-Spd	Transmission (pts.) Auto.		Fuel Tank (gal.)	Cooling System (qts.)
1996	Breeze	2.0 (1996)	C	4.5	①	8.0		16.0	7.4
	Cirrus	2.4 (2429)	X	5.0	—	18.2	②	16.0	9.0
	Cirrus	2.5 (2497)	H	4.5	—	18.2	②	16.0	10.5
	Sebring Convertible	2.4 (2429)	X	4.5	—	18.2	②	16.0	9.0
	Sebring Convertible	2.5 (2497)	H	4.5	—	18.2	②	16.0	10.5
	Stratus	2.0 (1996)	C	4.5	4.4 ①	—		16.0	7.4
	Stratus	2.4 (2429)	X	4.5	—	8.0		16.0	9.0
	Stratus	2.5 (2497)	H	4.5	—	8.0		16.0	10.5
1997	Breeze	2.0 (1996)	C	4.5	①	8.0		16.0	7.4
	Cirrus	2.4 (2429)	X	5.0	—	18.2	②	16.0	9.0
	Cirrus	2.5 (2497)	H	4.5	—	18.2	②	16.0	10.5
	Sebring Convertible	2.4 (2429)	X	4.5	—	18.2	②	16.0	9.0
	Sebring Convertible	2.5 (2497)	H	4.5	—	18.2	②	16.0	10.5
	Stratus	2.0 (1996)	C	4.5	4.4 ①	—		16.0	7.4
	Stratus	2.4 (2429)	X	4.5	—	8.0		16.0	9.0
	Stratus	2.5 (2497)	H	4.5	—	8.0		16.0	10.5
1998	Breeze	2.0 (1996)	C	4.5	①	8.0		16.0	7.4
	Cirrus	2.4 (2429)	X	5.0	—	18.2	②	16.0	9.0
	Cirrus	2.5 (2497)	H	4.5	—	18.2	②	16.0	10.5
	Sebring Convertible	2.4 (2429)	X	4.5	—	18.2	②	16.0	9.0
	Sebring Convertible	2.5 (2497)	H	4.5	—	18.2	②	16.0	10.5
	Stratus	2.0 (1996)	C	4.5	4.4 ①	—		16.0	7.4
	Stratus	2.4 (2429)	X	4.5	—	8.0		16.0	9.0
	Stratus	2.5 (2497)	H	4.5	—	8.0		16.0	10.5
1999-00	Breeze	2.0 (1996)	C	4.5	①	8.0		16.0	7.4
	Cirrus	2.4 (2429)	X	5.0	—	18.2	②	16.0	9.0
	Cirrus	2.5 (2497)	H	4.5	—	18.2	②	16.0	10.5
	Sebring Convertible	2.4 (2429)	X	4.5	—	18.2	②	16.0	9.0
	Sebring Convertible	2.5 (2497)	H	4.5	—	18.2	②	16.0	10.5
	Stratus	2.0 (1996)	C	4.5	4.4 ①	—		16.0	7.4
	Stratus	2.4 (2429)	X	4.5	—	8.0		16.0	9.0
	Stratus	2.5 (2497)	H	4.5	—	8.0		16.0	10.5

NOTE: All capacities are approximate. Add fluid gradually and ensure a proper fluid level is obtained.

① Fill to bottom of fill hole.

② Overhaul fill capacity with torque converter empty.

93001C14

VALVE SPECIFICATIONS

Year	Engine Displacement Liters (cc)	Engine ID/VIN	Seat Angle (deg.)	Face Angle (deg.)	Spring Test Pressure (lbs. @ in.)	Spring Installed Height (in.)	Stem-to-Guide Clearance (in.) Intake	Stem-to-Guide Clearance (in.) Exhaust	Stem Diameter (in.) Intake	Stem Diameter (in.) Exhaust
1996	2.0 (1996)	C	44.5-45	45-45.5	75@1.54	1.540	0.0018-0.0025	0.0029-0.0037	0.2340	0.2330
	2.4 (2429)	X	45-45.5	44.5-45	76@1.50	1.496	0.0018-0.0025	0.0029-0.0037	0.2340	0.2330
	2.5 (2497)	H	44-44.5	45-45.5	60@1.74	1.740	0.0008-0.0020	0.0016-0.0028	0.2360	0.2360
1997	2.0 (1996)	C	44.5-45	45-45.5	75@1.54	1.540	0.0018-0.0025	0.0029-0.0037	0.2340	0.2330
	2.4 (2429)	X	45-44.5	45-45.5	76@1.50	1.496	0.0018-0.0025	0.0029-0.0037	0.2340	0.2330
	2.5 (2497)	H	45-44.5	45-45.5	60@1.74	1.740	0.0008-0.0020	0.0016-0.0028	0.2360	0.2360
1998	2.0 (1996)	C	44.5-45	45-45.5	75@1.54	1.540	0.0018-0.0025	0.0029-0.0037	0.2340	0.2330
	2.4 (2429)	X	45-44.5	45-45.5	76@1.50	1.496	0.0018-0.0025	0.0029-0.0037	0.2340	0.2330
	2.5 (2497)	H	45-44.5	45-45.5	60@1.74	1.740	0.0008-0.0020	0.0016-0.0028	0.2360	0.2360
1999-00	2.0 (1996)	C	44.5-45	45-45.5	75@1.54	1.540	0.0018-0.0025	0.0029-0.0037	0.2340	0.2330
	2.4 (2429)	X	45-44.5	45-45.5	76@1.50	1.496	0.0018-0.0025	0.0029-0.0037	0.2340	0.2330
	2.5 (2497)	H	45-44.5	45-45.5	60@1.74	1.740	0.0008-0.0020	0.0016-0.0028	0.2360	0.2360

93001C15

Refer to the model specific sections for engine mechanical service procedures

CRANKSHAFT AND CONNECTING ROD SPECIFICATIONS
All measurements are given in inches.

Year	Engine Displacement Liters (cc)	Engine ID/VIN	Crankshaft				Connecting Rod		
			Main Brg. Journal Dia.	Main Brg. Oil Clearance	Shaft End-play	Thrust on No.	Journal Diameter	Oil Clearance	Side Clearance
1996	2.0 (1996)	C	2.0469-2.0475	0.0008-0.0024	0.0035-0.0094	3	1.8894-1.8900	0.0010-0.0023	0.0050-0.0150
	2.4 (2429)	X	2.3610-2.3630	0.0006-0.0027	0.0035-0.0094	3	1.9670-1.9685	0.0009-0.0027	0.0130-0.0150
	2.5 (2497)	H	2.3620	0.0008-0.0016	0.0020-0.0160	3	1.9690	0.0008-0.0016	0.0040-0.0160
1997	2.0 (1996)	C	2.0469-2.0475	0.0008-0.0024	0.0035-0.0094	3	1.8894-1.8900	0.0010-0.0023	0.0050-0.0150
	2.4 (2429)	X	2.3610-2.3625	0.0006-0.0027	0.0035-0.0095	3	1.9670-1.9685	0.0009-0.0027	0.0051-0.0150
	2.5 (2497)	H	2.3620	0.0008-0.0016	0.0020-0.0160	3	1.9690	0.0008-0.0016	0.0040-0.0160
1998	2.0 (1996)	C	2.0469-2.0475	0.0008-0.0024	0.0035-0.0094	3	1.8894-1.8900	0.0010-0.0023	0.0050-0.0150
	2.4 (2429)	X	2.3610-2.3625	0.0006-0.0027	0.0035-0.0095	3	1.9670-1.9685	0.0009-0.0027	0.0051-0.0150
	2.5 (2497)	H	2.3620	0.0008-0.0016	0.0020-0.0160	3	1.9690	0.0008-0.0016	0.0040-0.0160
1999-00	2.0 (1996)	C	2.0469-2.0475	0.0008-0.0024	0.0035-0.0094	3	1.8894-1.8900	0.0010-0.0023	0.0050-0.0150
	2.4 (2429)	X	2.3610-2.3625	0.0006-0.0027	0.0035-0.0095	3	1.9670-1.9685	0.0009-0.0027	0.0051-0.0150
	2.5 (2497)	H	2.3620	0.0008-0.0016	0.0020-0.0160	3	1.9690	0.0008-0.0016	0.0040-0.0160

93001C16

PISTON AND RING SPECIFICATIONS
All measurements are given in inches.

| Year | Engine Displacement Liters (cc) | Engine ID/VIN | Piston Clearance | Ring Gap | | | Ring Side Clearance | | |
				Top Compression	Bottom Compression	Oil Control	Top Compression	Bottom Compression	Oil Control
1996	2.0 (1996)	C	0.0004- ① 0.0017	0.009- 0.020	0.019- 0.031	0.009- 0.026	0.0010- 0.0026	0.0010- 0.0026	0.0002- 0.007
	2.4 (2429)	X	0.0009- ② 0.0022	0.010- 0.020	0.010- 0.018	0.010- 0.025	0.0011- 0.0031	0.0011- 0.0031	0.0004- 0.0070
	2.5 (2497)	H	0.0008- 0.0016	0.010- 0.031	0.016- 0.031	0.006- 0.039	0.0012- 0.0040	0.0007- 0.0040	NA
1997	2.0 (1996)	C	0.0004- ① 0.0017	0.009- 0.020	0.019- 0.031	0.009- 0.026	0.0010- 0.0026	0.0010- 0.0026	0.0002- 0.007
	2.4 (2429)	X	0.0009- ② 0.0022	0.010- 0.020	0.010- 0.018	0.010- 0.025	0.0011- 0.0031	0.0011- 0.0031	0.0004- 0.0070
	2.5 (2497)	H	0.0008- 0.0016	0.010- 0.031	0.016- 0.031	0.006- 0.039	0.0012- 0.0040	0.0007- 0.0040	NA
1998	2.0 (1996)	C	0.0004- ① 0.0017	0.009- 0.020	0.019- 0.031	0.009- 0.026	0.0010- 0.0026	0.0010- 0.0026	0.0002- 0.007
	2.4 (2429)	X	0.0009- ② 0.0022	0.010- 0.020	0.010- 0.018	0.010- 0.025	0.0011- 0.0031	0.0011- 0.0031	0.0004- 0.0070
	2.5 (2497)	H	0.0008- 0.0016	0.010- 0.031	0.016- 0.031	0.006- 0.039	0.0012- 0.0040	0.0007- 0.0040	NA
1999-00	2.0 (1996)	C	0.0004- ① 0.0017	0.009- 0.020	0.019- 0.031	0.009- 0.026	0.0010- 0.0026	0.0010- 0.0026	0.0002- 0.007
	2.4 (2429)	X	0.0009- ② 0.0022	0.010- 0.020	0.010- 0.018	0.010- 0.025	0.0011- 0.0031	0.0011- 0.0031	0.0004- 0.0070
	2.5 (2497)	H	0.0008- 0.0016	0.010- 0.031	0.016- 0.031	0.006- 0.039	0.0012- 0.0040	0.0007- 0.0040	NA

NA - Not Available

① Clearance at 11/16 inch from bottom of skirt

② Clearance at 9/16 inch from bottom of skirt

93001C17

Refer to the model specific sections for fuel system service procedures

TORQUE SPECIFICATIONS
All readings in ft. lbs.

Year	Engine Displacement Liters (cc)	Engine ID/VIN	Cylinder Head Bolts	Main Bearing Bolts	Rod Bearing Bolts	Crankshaft Damper Bolts	Flywheel Bolts	Manifold Intake	Manifold Exhaust	Spark Plug	Lug Nut
1996	2.0 (1996)	C	①	②	③	105	70	17	17	20	95
	2.4 (2429)	X	①	②	③	100	70	17	17	20	95
	2.5 (2497)	H	80	60	37	134	70	16	22	18	95
1997	2.0 (1996)	C	①	②	③	105	70	17	17	20	95
	2.4 (2429)	X	①	②	③	100	70	17	17	20	95
	2.5 (2497)	H	80	60	37	134	70	16	22	18	95
1998	2.0 (1996)	C	①	②	③	105	70	17	17	20	95
	2.4 (2429)	X	①	②	③	100	70	17	17	20	95
	2.5 (2497)	H	80	60	37	134	70	16	22	18	95
1999-00	2.0 (1996)	C	①	②	③	105	70	17	17	20	95
	2.4 (2429)	X	①	②	③	100	70	17	17	20	95
	2.5 (2497)	H	80	60	37	134	70	16	22	18	95

① Step 1: 25 ft. lbs.
Step 2: 50 ft. lbs.
Step 3: 50 ft. lbs.
Step 4: Plus 1/4 turn

② Step 1: 30 ft. lbs
Step 2: Plus 1/4 turn

③ Step 1: 20 ft. lbs.
Step 2: Plus 1/4 turn

93001C18

SCHEDULED MAINTENANCE INTERVALS
(CHRYSLER STRATUS & SEBRING CONVERTIBLE, DODGE CIRRUS, PLYMOUTH BREEZE)

TO BE SERVICED	TYPE OF SERVICE	VEHICLE MILEAGE INTERVAL (x1000)												
		7.5	15	22.5	30	37.5	45	52.5	60	67.5	75	82.5	90	97.5
Engine oil & filter	R	✓	✓	✓	✓	✓	✓	✓	✓	✓	✓	✓	✓	✓
Brake hoses	S/I	✓	✓	✓	✓	✓	✓	✓	✓	✓	✓	✓	✓	✓
Coolant level, hoses & clamps	S/I	✓	✓	✓	✓	✓	✓	✓	✓	✓	✓	✓	✓	✓
CV joints & front suspension components	S/I	✓	✓	✓	✓	✓	✓	✓	✓	✓	✓	✓	✓	✓
Exhaust system	S/I	✓	✓	✓	✓	✓	✓	✓	✓	✓	✓	✓	✓	✓
Rotate tires	S/I	✓	✓	✓	✓	✓	✓	✓	✓	✓	✓	✓	✓	✓
Accessory drive belts	S/I		✓		✓		✓		✓		✓		✓	
Brake linings	S/I			✓			✓			✓			✓	
Air filter element	R				✓				✓				✓	
Spark plugs ①	R				✓				✓				✓	
Lubricate front & rear ball joints	S/I				✓				✓				✓	
Engine coolant	R						✓				✓			
PCV valve	S/I								✓				✓	
Ignition cables ②	R								✓					
Camshaft timing belt ③	R													

① 4-cylinder shown; 6-cylinder = 100,000 miles.

② 4-cylinder 60,000 miles, 6-cylinder 100,000 miles.

③ Replace at 105,000 miles for normal service; replace at 102,000 miles for servere service

R - Replace   S/I - Service or Inspect

FREQUENT OPERATION MAINTENANCE (SEVERE SERVICE)

If a vehicle is operated under any of the following conditions it is considered severe service:

- Extremely dusty areas.
- 50% or more of the vehicle operation is in 32°C (90°F) or higher temperatures, or constant operation in temperatures below 0°C (32°F).
- Prolonged idling (vehicle operation in stop and go traffic).
- Frequent short running periods (engine does not warm to normal operating temperatures).
- Police, taxi, delivery usage or trailer towing usage.

Oil & oil filter change - change every 3000 miles.

Rotate tires every 6000 miles.

Brake linings - check every 12,000 miles.

Air filter element - change every 15,000 miles.

Automatic transaxle fluid - service or inspect every 15,000 miles.

PCV valve - check every 30,000 miles.

Engine coolant, replace at 36,000, 51,000 & 81,000 miles.

93001C19

Refer to the model specific sections for engine electrical system service procedures

SCHEDULED MAINTENANCE INTERVALS
CHRYSLER CORPORATION
CHRYSLER CIRRUS, SEBRING CONVERTIBLE
DODGE STRATUS, PLYMOUTH BREEZE

The following should be used as a guide when determining the amount of work required for a particular service.
In estimating how long a particular Scheduled Maintenance Service should take, please observe the following:

- **Chilton Time** is time based on field research and data supplied by the vehicle manufacturer.
  - Labor time operations are given in hours and tenths of an hour.
    - All labor operations, are to be used as a guide.

Mechanic Skill Level Codes:
(A) PRECISION: Really skilled with multiple certification.
(B) GENERAL: Normally skilled with certification.
(C) MAINTENANCE: Semi-skilled working on certification.

	Chilton Time			Chilton Time			Chilton Time
7500 Mile Service (C)			**45000 Mile Service (B)**			**67500 Mile Service (C)**	
All Models	1.3		All Models	2.1		All Models	1.6
15000 Mile Service (C)			**52500 Mile Service (C)**			**75000 Mile Service (C)**	
All Models	1.4		All Models	1.3		All Models	1.9
22500 Mile Service (C)			**60000 Mile Service (B)**			**82500 Mile Service (C)**	
All Models	1.6		All Models	3.6		All Models	1.3
30000 Mile Service (B)						**90000 Mile Service (B)**	
All Models	2.6					All Models	3.1
37500 Mile Service (C)						**97500 Mile Service (C)**	
All Models	1.3					All Models	1.3

93001C20

CHRYSLER CORP.
Chrysler Sebring Coupe • Dodge Avenger

ENGINE AND VEHICLE IDENTIFICATION

		Engine						Model Year	
Code ①	Liters (cc)	Cu. In.	Cyl.	Fuel Sys.	Engine Type	Eng. Mfg.		Code ②	Year
N	2.5 (2497)	152	V6	MFI	SOHC	Mitsubishi		T	1996
Y	2.0 (1996)	122	I4	MFI	DOHC	Chrysler		V	1997
								W	1998
								X	1999
								Y	2000

MFI - Multi-port Fuel Injection

DOHC - Double Overhead Camshaft

SOHC - Single Overhead Camshaft

① 8th position of the Vehicle Identification Number (VIN).

② 10th position of VIN.

93001C21

GENERAL ENGINE SPECIFICATIONS
All measurements are given in inches.

Year	Model	Engine Displacement Liters (cc)	Engine Series (ID/VIN)	Fuel System	Net Horsepower @ rpm	Net Torque @ rpm (ft. lbs.)	Bore x Stroke (in.)	Com-pression Ratio	Oil Pressure @ rpm
1996	Avenger	2.5 (2497)	N	MFI	155@5500	161@4400	3.29 x 2.99	9.4:1	35-75@3000
		2.0 (1996)	Y	MFI	140@6000	130@4800	3.44 x 3.27	9.6:1	25-80@3000
	Sebring	2.5 (2497)	N	MFI	155@5500	161@4400	3.29 x 2.99	9.4:1	35-75@3000
		2.0 (1996)	Y	MFI	140@6000	130@4800	3.44 x 3.27	9.6:1	25-80@3000
1997	Avenger	2.5 (2497)	N	MFI	155@5500	161@4400	3.29 x 2.99	9.4:1	35-75@3000
		2.0 (1996)	Y	MFI	140@6000	130@4800	3.44 x 3.27	9.6:1	25-80@3000
	Sebring Coupe	2.5 (2497)	N	MFI	155@5500	161@4400	3.29 x 2.99	9.4:1	35-75@3000
		2.0 (1996)	Y	MFI	140@6000	130@4800	3.44 x 3.27	9.6:1	25-80@3000
1998	Avenger	2.5 (2497)	N	MFI	155@5500	161@4400	3.29 x 2.99	9.4:1	35-75@3000
		2.0 (1996)	Y	MFI	140@6000	130@4800	3.44 x 3.27	9.6:1	25-80@3000
	Sebring Coupe	2.5 (2497)	N	MFI	155@5500	161@4400	3.29 x 2.99	9.4:1	35-75@3000
		2.0 (1996)	Y	MFI	140@6000	130@4800	3.44 x 3.27	9.6:1	25-80@3000
1999-00	Avenger	2.5 (2497)	N	MFI	155@5500	161@4400	3.29 x 2.99	9.4:1	35-75@3000
		2.0 (1996)	Y	MFI	140@6000	130@4800	3.44 x 3.27	9.6:1	25-80@3000
	Sebring Coupe	2.5 (2497)	N	MFI	155@5500	161@4400	3.29 x 2.99	9.4:1	35-75@3000
		2.0 (1996)	Y	MFI	140@6000	130@4800	3.44 x 3.27	9.6:1	25-80@3000

MFI - Multi-port Fuel Injection

93001C22

For accessory drive belt replacement procedures see the model specific sections of this manual

ENGINE TUNE-UP SPECIFICATIONS

Year	Engine Displacement Liters (cc)	Engine ID/VIN	Spark Plug Gap (in.)	Ignition Timing (deg.)	Fuel Pump (psi)		Idle Speed (rpm)		Valve Clearance	
							MT	AT	In.	Ex.
1996	2.0 (1996)	Y	0.033-0.038	①	47-50		800	800	HYD	HYD
	2.5 (2497)	N	0.039-0.043	①	47-50	②	—	700	HYD	HYD
1997	2.0 (1996)	Y	0.033-0.038	①	47-50		800	800	HYD	HYD
	2.5 (2497)	N	0.039-0.043	①	47-50	②	—	750	HYD	HYD
1998	2.0 (1996)	Y	0.033-0.038	①	47-50		800	800	HYD	HYD
	2.5 (2497)	N	0.039-0.043	①	47-50	②	—	750	HYD	HYD
1999-00	2.0 (1996)	Y	0.033-0.038	①	47-50		800	800	HYD	HYD
	2.5 (2497)	N	0.039-0.043	①	47-50	②	—	750	HYD	HYD

NOTE: The Vehicle Emission Control Information label often reflects specification changes made during production. The label figures must be used if they differ from those in this chart.
HYD - Hydraulic

① Basic ignition timing is not adjustable.

② This reading measured with the vacuum hose disconnected from the fuel pressure regulator.

93001C23

CAPACITIES

Year	Model	Engine Displacement Liters (cc)	Engine ID/VIN	Engine Oil with Filter (qts.)	Transmission (pts.)		Fuel Tank (gal.)	Cooling System (qts.)
					Manual	Auto.①		
1996	Avenger	2.0 (1996)	Y	4.5	4.2	18.0	16.9	7.4
		2.5 (2497)	N	4.5	—	18.0	16.9	7.4
	Sebring Coupe	2.0 (1996)	Y	4.5	4.2	18.2	16.9	7.4
		2.5 (2497)	N	4.5	—	18.2	16.9	7.4
1997	Avenger	2.0 (1996)	Y	4.5	4.2	18.0	16.9	7.4
		2.5 (2497)	N	4.5	—	18.0	16.9	7.4
	Sebring Coupe	2.0 (1996)	Y	4.5	4.2	18.2	16.9	7.4
		2.5 (2497)	N	4.5	—	18.2	16.9	7.4
1998	Avenger	2.0 (1996)	Y	4.5	4.2	18.0	16.9	7.4
		2.5 (2497)	N	4.5	—	18.0	16.9	7.4
	Sebring Coupe	2.0 (1996)	Y	4.5	4.2	18.2	16.9	7.4
		2.5 (2497)	N	4.5	—	18.2	16.9	7.4
1999-00	Avenger	2.0 (1996)	Y	4.5	4.2	18.0	16.9	7.4
		2.5 (2497)	N	4.5	—	18.0	16.9	7.4
	Sebring Coupe	2.0 (1996)	Y	4.5	4.2	18.2	16.9	7.4
		2.5 (2497)	N	4.5	—	18.2	16.9	7.4

NOTE: All capacities are approximate. Add fluid gradually and ensure a proper fluid level is obtained.

① Overhaul fill capacity with torque converter empty

93001C24

VALVE SPECIFICATIONS

Year	Engine Displacement Liters (cc)	Engine ID/VIN	Seat Angle (deg.)	Face Angle (deg.)	Spring Test Pressure (lbs. @ in.)	Spring Installed Height (in.)	Stem-to-Guide Clearance (in.)		Stem Diameter (in.)	
							Intake	Exhaust	Intake	Exhaust
1996	2.0 (1996)	Y	44.5-45	45-45.5	123-137@ 1.153	1.496	0.0019-0.0030	0.0029-0.0040	0.2336-0.2343	0.2325-0.2332
	2.5 (2497)	N	44-44.5	45-45.5	60@1.740	1.740	0.0008-0.0040	0.0016-0.0060	0.2360	0.2360
1997	2.0 (1996)	Y	44.5-45	45-45.5	123-137@ 1.153	1.496	0.0019-0.0030	0.0029-0.0040	0.2336-0.2343	0.2325-0.2332
	2.5 (2497)	N	44-44.5	45-45.5	60@1.740	1.740	0.0008-0.0040	0.0016-0.0060	0.2360	0.2360
1998	2.0 (1996)	Y	44.5-45	45-45.5	123-137@ 1.153	1.496	0.0019-0.0030	0.0029-0.0040	0.2336-0.2343	0.2325-0.2332
	2.5 (2497)	N	44-44.5	45-45.5	60@1.740	1.740	0.0008-0.0040	0.0016-0.0060	0.2360	0.2360
1999-00	2.0 (1996)	Y	44.5-45	45-45.5	123-137@ 1.153	1.496	0.0019-0.0030	0.0029-0.0040	0.2336-0.2343	0.2325-0.2332
	2.5 (2497)	N	44-44.5	45-45.5	60@1.740	1.740	0.0008-0.0040	0.0016-0.0060	0.2360	0.2360

93001C25

CRANKSHAFT AND CONNECTING ROD SPECIFICATIONS
All measurements are given in inches.

Year	Engine Displacement Liters (cc)	Engine ID/VIN	Crankshaft				Connecting Rod		
			Main Brg. Journal Dia.	Main Brg. Oil Clearance	Shaft End-play	Thrust on No.	Journal Diameter	Oil Clearance	Side Clearance
1996	2.0 (1996)	Y	2.0469-2.0475	0.0009-0.0024	0.0035-0.0094	3	1.8894-1.8900	0.0010-0.0150	0.0051-0.0150
	2.5 (2497)	N	2.3600	0.0008-0.0039	0.0020-0.0160	3	1.9700	0.0008-0.0039	0.0039-0.0157
1997	2.0 (1996)	Y	2.0469-2.0475	0.0009-0.0024	0.0035-0.0150	3	1.8894-1.8900	0.0010-0.0030	0.0051-0.0150
	2.5 (2497)	N	2.3600	0.0008-0.0040	0.0020-0.0120	3	1.9700	0.0008-0.0040	0.0039-0.0157
1998	2.0 (1996)	Y	2.0469-2.0475	0.0009-0.0024	0.0035-0.0150	3	1.8894-1.8900	0.0010-0.0030	0.0051-0.0150
	2.5 (2497)	N	2.3600	0.0008-0.0040	0.0020-0.0120	3	1.9700	0.0008-0.0040	0.0039-0.0157
1999-00	2.0 (1996)	Y	2.0469-2.0475	0.0009-0.0024	0.0035-0.0150	3	1.8894-1.8900	0.0010-0.0030	0.0051-0.0150
	2.5 (2497)	N	2.3600	0.0008-0.0040	0.0020-0.0120	3	1.9700	0.0008-0.0040	0.0039-0.0157

93001C26

For brake related suspension and axle service, refer to the model specific sections of this manual

PISTON AND RING SPECIFICATIONS
All measurements are given in inches.

Year	Engine Displacement Liters (cc)	Engine ID/VIN	Piston Clearance	Ring Gap			Ring Side Clearance		
				Top Compression	Bottom Compression	Oil Control	Top Compression	Bottom Compression	Oil Control
1996	2.0 (1996)	Y	0.0005- 0.0017 ①	0.009- 0.310	0.019- 0.039	0.009- 0.039	0.0010- 0.0040	0.0010- 0.0040	0.0002- 0.0070
	2.5 (2497)	N	0.0008- 0.0016	0.010- 0.031	0.016- 0.031	0.006- 0.039	0.0012- 0.0040	0.0008- 0.0040	NA
1997	2.0 (1996)	Y	0.0005- 0.0017 ①	0.009- 0.031	0.019- 0.039	0.009- 0.039	0.0010- 0.0040	0.0010- 0.0040	0.0002- 0.0070
	2.5 (2497)	N	0.0008- 0.0016	0.010- 0.031	0.016- 0.031	0.006- 0.039	0.0012- 0.0040	0.0008- 0.0040	NA
1998	2.0 (1996)	Y	0.0005- 0.0017 ①	0.009- 0.031	0.019- 0.039	0.009- 0.039	0.0010- 0.0040	0.0010- 0.0040	0.0002- 0.0070
	2.5 (2497)	N	0.0008- 0.0016	0.010- 0.031	0.016- 0.031	0.006- 0.039	0.0012- 0.0040	0.0008- 0.0040	NA
1999-00	2.0 (1996)	Y	0.0005- 0.0017 ①	0.009- 0.031	0.019- 0.039	0.009- 0.039	0.0010- 0.0040	0.0010- 0.0040	0.0002- 0.0070
	2.5 (2497)	N	0.0008- 0.0016	0.010- 0.031	0.016- 0.031	0.006- 0.039	0.0012- 0.0040	0.0008- 0.0040	NA

NA - Not Available

① Clearance at 11/16 inch from the bottom of the skirt

93001C27

TORQUE SPECIFICATIONS
All readings in ft. lbs.

Year	Engine Displacement Liters (cc)	Engine ID/VIN	Cylinder Head Bolts	Main Bearing Bolts	Rod Bearing Bolts	Crankshaft Damper Bolts	Flywheel Bolts	Manifold		Spark Plugs	Lug Nuts
								Intake	Exhaust		
1996	2.0 (1996)	Y	①	55 ②	③	105	70	17	17	20	65-80
	2.5 (2497)	N	80	69	37	134	70	16	22	18	65-80
1997	2.0 (1996)	Y	①	55 ②	③	105	70	17	17	20	88-103
	2.5 (2497)	N	80	69	37	134	70	16	22	18	88-103
1998	2.0 (1996)	Y	①	55 ②	③	105	70	17	17	20	88-103
	2.5 (2497)	N	80	69	37	134	70	16	22	18	88-103
1999-00	2.0 (1996)	Y	①	55 ②	③	105	70	17	17	20	88-103
	2.5 (2497)	N	80	69	37	134	70	16	22	18	88-103

① Step 1: Fasteners 1 through 6 to 24 ft. lbs.
   Fasteners 7 through 10 to 20 ft. lbs.
   Step 2: Fasteners 1 through 6 to 48 ft. lbs.
   Fasteners 7 through 10 to 20 ft. lbs.
   Step 3: Fasteners 1 through 6 to 48 ft. lbs.
   Fasteners 7 throught 10 to 20 ft. lbs.
   Step 4: Tighten all fasteners 1/4 turn

② Tighten side bolts to 21 ft. lbs.

③ Step 1: 20 ft. lbs.
   Step 2: 1/4 turn

93001C29

SCHEDULED MAINTENANCE INTERVALS
(CHRYSLER SEBRING, DODGE AVENGER)

TO BE SERVICED	TYPE OF SERVICE	VEHICLE MILEAGE INTERVAL (x1000)												
		7.5	15	22.5	30	37.5	45	52.5	60	67.5	75	82.5	90	97.5
Engine oil & filter	R	✓	✓	✓	✓	✓	✓	✓	✓	✓	✓	✓	✓	✓
Coolant level, hoses & clamps	S/I	✓	✓	✓	✓	✓	✓	✓	✓	✓	✓	✓	✓	✓
Rotate tires	S/I	✓	✓	✓	✓	✓	✓	✓	✓	✓	✓	✓	✓	✓
Automatic transaxle fluid level	S/I		✓		✓		✓		✓		✓		✓	
Brake hoses & disc brake pads	S/I		✓		✓				✓		✓		✓	
Drive shaft boots & front suspension components	S/I		✓		✓		✓		✓		✓		✓	
Air filter element	R				✓				✓				✓	
Engine coolant	R				✓				✓				✓	
Spark plugs (DOHC)	R				✓				✓				✓	
Spark plugs (SOHC) ①	R				✓				✓				✓	
Accessory drive belts	S/I				✓				✓				✓	
Ball joints & steering linkage seals	S/I				✓				✓				✓	
Exhaust system	S/I				✓				✓				✓	
Fuel hoses	S/I				✓				✓				✓	
Manual transaxle oil	S/I				✓				✓				✓	
PCV valve	S/I				✓				✓				✓	
Rear drum brake lining & rear wheel cylinders	S/I				✓				✓				✓	
Camshaft timing belt	R								✓					
Ignition cables	R								✓					
Distributor cap & rotor	S/I								✓					
EVAP system	S/I								✓					
Fuel system	S/I								✓					

① Spark plugs - replace every 100,000 miles.

R - Replace   S/I - Service or Inspect

FREQUENT OPERATION MAINTENANCE (SEVERE SERVICE)

If a vehicle is operated under any of the following conditions it is considered severe service:

- Extremely dusty areas.
- 50% or more of the vehicle operation is in 32°C (90°F) or higher temperatures, or constant operation in temperatures below 0°C (32°F).
- Prolonged idling (vehicle operation in stop and go traffic).
- Frequent short running periods (engine does not warm to normal operating temperatures).
- Police, taxi, delivery usage or trailer towing usage.

Oil & oil filter change - change every 3000 miles.

Disc brake pads - check every 6000 miles.

Air filter element - change every 15,000 miles.

Automatic transaxle fluid - change every 15,000 miles.

Rear drum brake linings & rear wheel cylinders - check every 15,000 miles.

Spark plugs - change every 15,000 miles.

93001C30

Refer to the model specific sections for driveline service procedures

SCHEDULED MAINTENANCE INTERVALS
CHRYSLER CORPORATION
CHRYSLER SEBRING COUPE
DODGE AVENGER

The following should be used as a guide when determining the amount of work required for a particular service.
In estimating how long a particular Scheduled Maintenance Service should take, please observe the following:

- **Chilton Time** is time based on field research and data supplied by the vehicle manufacturer.
  - Labor time operations are given in hours and tenths of an hour.
    - All labor operations, are to be used as a guide.

Mechanic Skill Level Codes:
(A) PRECISION: Really skilled with multiple certification.
(B) GENERAL: Normally skilled with certification.
(C) MAINTENANCE: Semi-skilled working on certification.

	Chilton Time		Chilton Time		Chilton Time
7500 Mile Service (C)		**45000 Mile Service (C)**		**75000 Mile Service (C)**	
All Models	1.3	All Models	1.7	All Models	1.7
15000 Mile Service (C)		**52500 Mile Service (C)**		**82500 Mile Service (C)**	
All Models	1.6	All Models	1.3	All Models	1.3
22500 Mile Service (C)		**60000 Mile Service (B)**			
All Models	1.3	All Models	6.1	**90000 Mile Service (B)**	
30000 Mile Service (B)		**67500 Mile Service (C)**		All Models	3.3
All Models	3.3	All Models	1.3	**97500 Mile Service (C)**	
37500 Mile Service (C)				All Models	1.3
All Models	1.3				

93001C31

CHRYSLER CORP.
Dodge/Plymouth Neon

ENGINE AND VEHICLE IDENTIFICATION

		Engine					Model Year	
Code ①	Liters	Cu. In. (cc)	Cyl.	Fuel Sys.	Engine Type	Eng. Mfg.	Code ②	Year
C	2.0	122 (1996)	4	MFI	SOHC	Chrysler	T	1996
Y	2.0	122 (1996)	4	MFI	DOHC	Chrysler	V	1997
							W	1998
							X	1999
							Y	2000

MFI - Multi-point Fuel Injection

SOHC - Single Overhead Camshaft

DOHC - Double Overhead Camshaft

① 8th position of VIN

② 10th position of VIN

93001C32

GENERAL ENGINE SPECIFICATIONS
All measurements are given in inches.

Year	Model	Engine Displacement Liters (cc)	Engine Series (ID/VIN)	Fuel System	Net Horsepower @ rpm	Net Torque @ rpm (ft. lbs.)	Bore x Stroke (in.)	Com-pression Ratio	Oil Pressure @ rpm
1996	Neon	2.0 (1996)	C	MFI	132@6000	129@5000	3.44x3.26	9.8:1	25-80@3000
	Neon	2.0 (1996)	Y	MFI	150@4400	NA	3.44x3.26	9.6:1	25-80@3000
1997	Neon	2.0 (1996)	C	MFI	132@6000	129@5000	3.44x3.26	9.8:1	25-80@3000
	Neon	2.0 (1996)	Y	MFI	150@4400	NA	3.44x3.26	9.6:1	25-80@3000
1998	Neon	2.0 (1996)	C	MFI	132@6000	129@5000	3.44x3.26	9.8:1	25-80@3000
	Neon	2.0 (1996)	Y	MFI	150@4400	NA	3.44x3.26	9.6:1	25-80@3000
1999-00	Neon	2.0 (1996)	C	MFI	132@6000	129@5000	3.44x3.26	9.8:1	25-80@3000
	Neon	2.0 (1996)	Y	MFI	150@4400	NA	3.44x3.26	9.6:1	25-80@3000

NA - Not available

MFI - Multi-point Fuel Injection

SOHC - Single Overhead Camshaft

DOHC - Double Overhead Camshaft

93001C33

ENGINE TUNE-UP SPECIFICATIONS

Year	Engine Displacement Liters (cc)	Engine ID/VIN	Spark Plugs Gap (in.)	Ignition Timing (deg.) MT	AT	Fuel Pump (psi)	Idle Speed (rpm) MT	AT	Valve Clearance In.	Ex.
1996	2.0 (1996)	C	0.035	①	①	48	②	②	HYD	HYD
	2.0 (1996)	Y	0.035	①	①	48	②	②	HYD	HYD
1997	2.0 (1996)	C	0.035	①	①	48	②	②	HYD	HYD
	2.0 (1996)	Y	0.035	①	①	48	②	②	HYD	HYD
1998	2.0 (1996)	C	0.035	①	①	48	②	②	HYD	HYD
	2.0 (1996)	Y	0.035	①	①	48	②	②	HYD	HYD
1999-00	2.0 (1996)	C	0.035	①	①	48	②	②	HYD	HYD
	2.0 (1996)	Y	0.035	①	①	48	②	②	HYD	HYD

NOTE: The Vehicle Emission Control Information label often reflects specification changes made during production. The label figures must be used if they differ from those in this chart.

HYD - Hydraulic

① Refer to the Vehicle Emission Control Information label for correct timing specifications with a range of +/- 2 degrees

   Ignition timing cannot be adjusted. Base engine timing is set at TDC during assembly.

② Refer to Vehicle Emissions Control Information label for proper specification

93001C34

For exhaust manifold replacement procedures, see the model specific sections of this manual

CAPACITIES

Year	Model	Engine Displacement Liters (cc)	Engine ID/VIN	Engine Oil with Filter (qts.)	Transmission (pts.) 5-Spd	Transmission (pts.) Auto.	Fuel Tank (gal.)	Cooling System (qts.)
1996	Neon	2.0 (1996)	C	4.5	①	8.0	11.0	7.4
	Neon	2.0 (1996)	Y	4.5	①	8.0	11.0	7.4
1997	Neon	2.0 (1996)	C	4.5	①	8.0	11.0	7.4
	Neon	2.0 (1996)	Y	4.5	①	8.0	11.0	7.4
1998	Neon	2.0 (1996)	C	4.5	①	8.0	11.0	7.4
	Neon	2.0 (1996)	Y	4.5	①	8.0	11.0	7.4
1999-00	Neon	2.0 (1996)	C	4.5	①	8.0	11.0	7.4
	Neon	2.0 (1996)	Y	4.5	①	8.0	11.0	7.4

NOTE: All capacities are approximate. Add fluid gradually and ensure a proper fluid level is obtained.

① Fill to bottom of fill hole

93001C35

VALVE SPECIFICATIONS

Year	Engine Displacement Liters (cc)	Engine ID/VIN	Seat Angle (deg.)	Face Angle (deg.)	Spring Test Pressure (lbs. @ in.)	Spring Installed Height (in.)	Stem-to-Guide Clearance (in.) Intake	Stem-to-Guide Clearance (in.) Exhaust	Stem Diameter (in.) Intake	Stem Diameter (in.) Exhaust
1996	2.0 (1996)	C	44.5-45	45-45.5	75@1.54	1.540	0.0018-0.0025	0.0029-0.0037	0.2340	0.2330
	2.0 (1996)	Y	44.5-45	45-45.5	55-60@1.49	1.490	0.0018-0.0025	0.0029-0.0037	0.2340	0.2330
1997	2.0 (1996)	C	44.5-45	45-45.5	75@1.54	1.540	0.0018-0.0025	0.0029-0.0037	0.2340	0.2330
	2.0 (1996)	Y	44.5-45	45-45.5	55-60@1.49	1.490	0.0018-0.0025	0.0029-0.0037	0.2340	0.2330
1998	2.0 (1996)	C	44.5-45	45-45.5	75@1.54	1.540	0.0018-0.0025	0.0029-0.0037	0.2340	0.2330
	2.0 (1996)	Y	44.5-45	45-45.5	55-60@1.49	1.490	0.0018-0.0025	0.0029-0.0037	0.2340	0.2330
1999-00	2.0 (1996)	C	44.5-45	45-45.5	75@1.54	1.540	0.0018-0.0025	0.0029-0.0037	0.2340	0.2330
	2.0 (1996)	Y	44.5-45	45-45.5	55-60@1.49	1.490	0.0018-0.0025	0.0029-0.0037	0.2340	0.2330

93001C36

CRANKSHAFT AND CONNECTING ROD SPECIFICATIONS
All measurements are given in inches.

| Year | Engine Displacement Liters (cc) | Engine ID/VIN | Crankshaft | | | | Connecting Rod | | |
			Main Brg. Journal Dia.	Main Brg. Oil Clearance	Shaft End-play	Thrust on No.	Journal Diameter	Oil Clearance	Side Clearance
1996	2.0 (1996)	C	2.0469-2.0475	0.0008-0.0024	0.0035-0.0094	3	1.8894-1.8900	0.0010-0.0023	0.0050-0.0150
	2.0 (1996)	Y	2.0469-2.0475	0.0009-0.0024	0.0035-0.0094	3	1.8894-1.8900	0.0010-0.0023	0.0051-0.0150
1997	2.0 (1996)	C	2.0469-2.0475	0.0008-0.0024	0.0035-0.0094	3	1.8894-1.8900	0.0010-0.0023	0.0050-0.0150
	2.0 (1996)	Y	2.0469-2.0475	0.0009-0.0024	0.0035-0.0094	3	1.8894-1.8900	0.0010-0.0023	0.0051-0.0150
1998	2.0 (1996)	C	2.0469-2.0475	0.0008-0.0024	0.0035-0.0094	3	1.8894-1.8900	0.0010-0.0023	0.0050-0.0150
	2.0 (1996)	Y	2.0469-2.0475	0.0009-0.0024	0.0035-0.0094	3	1.8894-1.8900	0.0010-0.0023	0.0051-0.0150
1999-00	2.0 (1996)	C	2.0469-2.0475	0.0008-0.0024	0.0035-0.0094	3	1.8894-1.8900	0.0010-0.0023	0.0050-0.0150
	2.0 (1996)	Y	2.0469-2.0475	0.0009-0.0024	0.0035-0.0094	3	1.8894-1.8900	0.0010-0.0023	0.0051-0.0150

93001C37

PISTON AND RING SPECIFICATIONS
All measurements are given in inches.

| Year | Engine Displacement Liters (cc) | Engine ID/VIN | Piston Clearance | Ring Gap | | | Ring Side Clearance | | |
				Top Compression	Bottom Compression	Oil Control	Top Compression	Bottom Compression	Oil Control
1996	2.0 (1996)	C	0.0004-0.0017	0.0090-0.0200	0.0190-0.0310	0.009-0.026	0.0010-0.0026	0.0010-0.0026	0.0002-0.0070
	2.0 (1996)	Y	0.0005-0.0017	0.0090-0.0200	0.0190-0.0310	0.009-0.026	0.0010-0.0026	0.0010-0.0026	0.0002-0.0070
1997	2.0 (1996)	C	0.0004-0.0017	0.0090-0.0200	0.0190-0.0310	0.009-0.026	0.0010-0.0026	0.0010-0.0026	0.0002-0.0070
	2.0 (1996)	Y	0.0005-0.0017	0.0090-0.0200	0.0190-0.0310	0.009-0.026	0.0010-0.0026	0.0010-0.0026	0.0002-0.0070
1998	2.0 (1996)	C	0.0004-0.0017	0.0090-0.0200	0.0190-0.0310	0.009-0.026	0.0010-0.0026	0.0010-0.0026	0.0002-0.0070
	2.0 (1996)	Y	0.0005-0.0017	0.0090-0.0200	0.0190-0.0310	0.009-0.026	0.0010-0.0026	0.0010-0.0026	0.0002-0.0070
1999-00	2.0 (1996)	C	0.0004-0.0017	0.0090-0.0200	0.0190-0.0310	0.009-0.026	0.0010-0.0026	0.0010-0.0026	0.0002-0.0070
	2.0 (1996)	Y	0.0005-0.0017	0.0090-0.0200	0.0190-0.0310	0.009-0.026	0.0010-0.0026	0.0010-0.0026	0.0002-0.0070

93001C38

Refer to the model specific sections for cooling system service procedures

TORQUE SPECIFICATIONS
All readings in ft. lbs.

Year	Engine Displacement Liters (cc)	Engine ID/VIN	Cylinder Head Bolts	Main Bearing Bolts	Rod Bearing Bolts	Crankshaft Damper Bolts	Flywheel Bolts	Manifold		Spark Plugs	Lug Nut
								Intake	Exhaust		
1996	2.0 (1996)	C	①	②	③	105	70	17	17	20	95
	2.0 (1996)	Y	④	②	③	105	70	17	17	20	95
1997	2.0 (1996)	C	①	②	③	105	70	17	17	20	95
	2.0 (1996)	Y	④	②	③	105	70	17	17	20	95
1998	2.0 (1996)	C	①	②	③	105	70	17	17	20	95
	2.0 (1996)	Y	④	②	③	105	70	17	17	20	95
1999-00	2.0 (1996)	C	①	②	③	105	70	17	17	20	95
	2.0 (1996)	Y	④	②	③	105	70	17	17	20	95

① Step 1: 25 ft. lbs.
Step 2: 50 ft. lbs.
Step 3: 50 ft. lbs.
Step 4: plus 90 degrees

② Step 1: 30 ft. lbs.
Step 2: plus 90 degrees

③ Step 1: 20 ft. lbs.
Step 2: plus 90 degrees

④ Step 1:
Bolts 1-6: 25 ft. lbs.
Bolts 7-10: 20 ft. lbs.
Step 2:
Bolts 1-6: 50 ft. lbs.
Bolts 7-10: 20 ft. lbs.
Step 3:
Bolts 1-6: 50 ft. lbs.
Bolts 7-10: 20 ft. lbs.
Step 4: plus 90 degrees

93001C39

SCHEDULED MAINTENANCE INTERVALS
(DODGE NEON, PLYMOUTH NEON)

TO BE SERVICED	TYPE OF SERVICE	VEHICLE MILEAGE INTERVAL (x1000)												
		7.5	15	22.5	30	37.5	45	52.5	60	67.5	75	82.5	90	97.5
Engine oil & filter	R	✓	✓	✓	✓	✓	✓	✓	✓	✓	✓	✓	✓	✓
Brake hoses	S/I	✓	✓	✓	✓	✓	✓	✓	✓	✓	✓	✓	✓	✓
Coolant level, hoses & clamps	S/I	✓	✓	✓	✓	✓	✓	✓	✓	✓	✓	✓	✓	✓
CV joints & front suspension components	S/I	✓	✓	✓	✓	✓	✓	✓	✓	✓	✓	✓	✓	✓
Exhaust system	S/I	✓	✓	✓	✓	✓	✓	✓	✓	✓	✓	✓	✓	✓
Manual transaxle oil	S/I	✓	✓	✓	✓	✓	✓	✓	✓	✓	✓	✓	✓	✓
Rotate tires	S/I	✓	✓	✓	✓	✓	✓	✓	✓	✓	✓	✓	✓	✓
Accessory drive belts	S/I		✓		✓		✓		✓		✓		✓	
Brake linings	S/I			✓			✓			✓			✓	
Air filter element	R				✓				✓				✓	
Spark plugs	R				✓				✓				✓	
Lubricate ball joints	S/I				✓				✓				✓	
Engine coolant	R						✓				✓			
PCV valve	S/I								✓				✓	
Ignition cables	R								✓					
Camshaft timing belt ①	R													

① Camshaft timing belt - replace at 105,000 miles.

R - Replace   S/I - Service or Inspect

FREQUENT OPERATION MAINTENANCE (SEVERE SERVICE)

If a vehicle is operated under any of the following conditions it is considered severe service:

- Extremely dusty areas.
- 50% or more of the vehicle operation is in 32°C (90°F) or higher temperatures, or constant operation in temperatures below 0°C (32°F).
- Prolonged idling (vehicle operation in stop and go traffic).
- Frequent short running periods (engine does not warm to normal operating temperatures).
- Police, taxi, delivery usage or trailer towing usage.

Oil & oil filter change - change every 3000 miles.

Rotate tires every 6000 miles.

Brake linings - inspect every 12,000 miles.

Air filter element - service or inspect every 15,000 miles.

Automatic transaxle - change fluid & adjust bands every 15,000 miles.

Manual transaxle fluid - replace every 15,000 miles.

Engine coolant - replace at 36,000 miles, and every 30,000 miles thereafter.

93001C40

SCHEDULED MAINTENANCE INTERVALS
CHRYSLER CORPORATION
DODGE NEON
PLYMOUTH NEON

The following should be used as a guide when determining the amount of work required for a particular service.
In estimating how long a particular Scheduled Maintenance Service should take, please observe the following:

- **Chilton Time** is time based on field research and data supplied by the vehicle manufacturer.

- Labor time operations are given in hours and tenths of an hour.

- All labor operations, are to be used as a guide.

Mechanic Skill Level Codes:
(A) PRECISION: Really skilled with multiple certification.
(B) GENERAL: Normally skilled with certification.
(C) MAINTENANCE: Semi-skilled working on certification.

	Chilton Time
7500 Mile Service (C)	
All Models	1.4
15000 Mile Service (C)	
All Models	1.5
22500 Mile Service (C)	
All Models	1.7
30000 Mile Service (B)	
All Models	2.3

	Chilton Time
37500 Mile Service (C)	
All Models	1.4
45000 Mile Service (B)	
All Models	2.3
52500 Mile Service (C)	
All Models	1.4
60000 Mile Service (B)	
All Models	2.9
67500 Mile Service (C)	
All Models	1.7

	Chilton Time
75000 Mile Service (C)	
All Models	2.0
82500 Mile Service (C)	
All Models	1.4
90000 Mile Service (B)	
All Models	2.8
97500 Mile Service (C)	
All Models	1.4

93001C41

CHRYSLER CORP.
Dodge Stealth

ENGINE AND VEHICLE IDENTIFICATION

			Engine					Model Year	
Code ①	Liters (cc)	Cu. In.	Cyl.	Fuel Sys.	Type	Eng. Mfg.		Code ②	Year
6G72/H	3.0 (2972)	181	6	MFI	SOHC	Mitsubishi		T	1996
6G72/J	3.0 (2972)	181	6	MFI	DOHC	Mitsubishi			
6G72/K	3.0 (2972)	181	6	MFI-Turbo	DOHC	Mitsubishi			

MFI - Multiport fuel injection

SOHC - Single overhead camsh;

DOHC - Double overhead camshafts

① Engine ID / 8th digit of the VIN

② 10th digit of the VIN

93001C42

GENERAL ENGINE SPECIFICATIONS

Year	Model	Engine Displacement Liters (cc)	Engine ID/VIN	Fuel System Type	Net Horsepower @ rpm	Net Torque @ rpm (ft. lbs.)	Bore x Stroke (in.)	Compression Ratio	Oil Pressure @ rpm
1996	Stealth	3.0 (2972)	6G72/H	MFI	175@5500	185@3000	3.59x2.99	8.9:1	30-80@2000
	Stealth	3.0 (2972)	6G72/J	MFI	202@6000	201@3500	3.59x2.99	10.0:1	30-80@2000
	Stealth AWD	3.0 (2972)	6G72/K	MFI	320@6000	315@2500	3.59x2.99	8.0:1	30-80@2000

93001C43

ENGINE TUNE-UP SPECIFICATIONS

Year	Engine Displacement Liters (cc)	Engine ID/VIN	Spark Plugs Gap (in.)	Ignition Timing (deg.) MT	Ignition Timing (deg.) AT	Fuel Pump (psi)	Idle Speed (rpm) MT	Idle Speed (rpm) AT	Valve Clearance In.	Valve Clearance Ex.
1996	3.0 (2972)	6G72/H	0.039-0.043	5B	5B	38	600-800	600-800	HYD	HYD
	3.0 (2972)	6G72/J	0.039-0.043	5B	5B	38	600-800	600-800	HYD	HYD
	3.0 (2972)	6G72/K	0.039-0.043	5B	5B	34	600-800	600-800	HYD	HYD

NOTE: The Vehicle Emission Control Information label often reflects specification changes made during production. The label figures must be used if they differ from those in this chart.

B - Before top dead center

HYD - Hydraulic

93001C44

Timing chain and gear service is covered in the model specific sections of this manual

CAPACITIES

| Year | Model | Engine Displacement Liters (cc) | Engine ID/VIN | Engine Oil with Filter | Transmission (pts.) | | Transfer Case (pts.) | Drive Axle | | Fuel Tank (gal.) | Cooling System (qts.) |
					5 or 6-Spd	Auto.		Front (pts.)	Rear (pts.)		
1996	Stealth	3.0 (2972)	6G72/H	4.5	4.8	15.8	①	—	—	19.8	8.5
	Stealth	3.0 (2972)	6G72/J	4.5	4.8	15.8	①	—	—	19.8	8.5
	Stealth AWD	3.0 (2972)	6G72/K	4.5	5.0	15.8	①	—	2.3	19.8	8.5

① M/T: 0.58 pts.
A/T: 0.64 pts.

93001C45

VALVE SPECIFICATIONS

| Year | Engine Displacement Liters (cc) | Engine ID/VIN | Seat Angle (deg.) | Face Angle (deg.) | Spring Test Pressure (lbs. @ in.) | Spring Installed Height (in.) | Stem-to-Guide Clearance (in.) | | Stem Diameter (in.) | |
							Intake	Exhaust	Intake	Exhaust
1996	3.0 (2972)	6G72/H	44.5-45	45-45.5	40.4@1.591	1.591	0.0012-0.0024	0.0020-0.0035	0.315	0.311
	3.0 (2972)	6G72/J	44.5-45	45-45.5	37.9@1.492	1.492	0.0008-0.0020	0.0020-0.0035	0.260	0.256
	3.0 (2972)	6G72/K	44.5-45	45-45.5	37.9@1.492	1.492	0.0008-0.0020	0.0020-0.0035	0.260	0.256

93001C46

CRANKSHAFT AND CONNECTING ROD SPECIFICATIONS
All measurements are given in inches.

| Year | Engine Displacement Liters (cc) | Engine ID/VIN | Crankshaft | | | | Connecting Rod | | |
			Main Brg. Journal Dia.	Main Brg. Oil Clearance	Shaft End-play	Thrust on No.	Journal Diameter	Oil Clearance	Side Clearance
1996	3.0 (2972)	6G72/H	2.3614-2.3622	0.0008-0.0040	0.0020-0.0120	3	2.1646-2.1654	0.0008-0.0040	0.0039-0.0160
	3.0 (2972)	6G72/J	2.3613-2.3620	0.0008-0.0040	0.0020-0.0120	3	2.1646-2.1654	0.0008-0.0040	0.0039-0.0160
	3.0 (2972)	6G72/K	2.3613-2.3620	0.0008-0.0040	0.0020-0.0120	3	2.1646-2.1654	0.0008-0.0040	0.0039-0.0160

93001C47

PISTON AND RING SPECIFICATIONS
All measurements are given in inches.

Year	Engine Displacement Liters (cc)	Engine ID/VIN	Piston Clearance	Ring Gap			Ring Side Clearance		
				Top Compression	Bottom Compression	Oil Control	Top Compression	Bottom Compression	Oil Control
1996	3.0 (2972)	6G72/H	0.0008-0.0020	0.0118-0.0310	0.0177-0.0310	0.0079-0.0390	0.0012-0.0040	0.0008-0.0040	NA
	3.0 (2972)	6G72/J	0.0008-0.0020	0.0118-0.0310	0.0177-0.0310	0.0079-0.0390	0.0012-0.0040	0.0008-0.0040	NA
	3.0 (2972)	6G72/K	0.0008-0.0020	0.0118-0.0310	0.0177-0.0310	0.0079-0.0390	0.0012-0.0040	0.0008-0.0040	NA

93001C48

TORQUE SPECIFICATIONS
All readings in ft. lbs.

Year	Engine Displacement Liters (cc)	Engine ID/VIN	Cylinder Head Bolts	Main Bearing Bolts	Rod Bearing Bolts	Crankshaft Damper Bolts	Flywheel Bolts	Manifold		Spark Plugs	Lug Nut
								Intake	Exhaust		
1996	3.0 (2972)	6G72/H	①	57	38	136	54	13	13	18	95
	3.0 (2972)	6G72/J	①	67	38	136	54	16	22	18	95
	3.0 (2972)	6G72/K	②	54	38	136	54	16	③	18	95

① Step 3: Tighen all bolts in 3 steps to 80 ft. lbs.
② Step 1: Tighten all bolts in 3 steps to 91 ft. lbs.
   Step 2: Loosen all bolts to 0 ft. lbs.
   Step 3: Tighen all bolts in 3 steps to 91 ft. lbs.
③ Step 1: Tighten 5 inner nuts to 22 ft. lbs.
   Step 2: Tighten 2 outer nuts to 36 ft. lbs.
   Step 3: Loosen 2 outer nuts to 7 ft. lbs.
   Step 4: Tighten 2 outer nuts to 22 ft. lbs.

93001C49

Ignition system service is covered in the model specific sections of this manual

SCHEDULED MAINTENANCE INTERVALS
(DODGE STEALTH)

TO BE SERVICED	TYPE OF SERVICE	VEHICLE MILEAGE INTERVAL (x1000)												
		7.5	15	22.5	30	37.5	45	52.5	60	67.5	75	82.5	90	97.5
Engine oil & filter (Non-turbo) ①	R	✓	✓	✓	✓	✓	✓	✓	✓	✓	✓	✓	✓	✓
Coolant level, hoses & clamps	S/I	✓	✓	✓	✓	✓		✓	✓	✓	✓	✓	✓	✓
Rotate tires	S/I	✓	✓	✓	✓	✓	✓	✓	✓	✓	✓	✓	✓	✓
Brake hoses	S/I		✓		✓		✓		✓		✓		✓	
Driveshaft boots & front suspension components	S/I		✓		✓		✓		✓		✓		✓	
Brake linings	S/I		✓		✓		✓		✓		✓		✓	
Air filter element	R				✓				✓				✓	
Automatic transaxle fluid & filter	R				✓				✓				✓	
Differential fluid (AWD)	R				✓				✓				✓	
Engine coolant	R				✓				✓				✓	
Spark plugs (Non-platinum)	R				✓				✓				✓	
Accessory drive belts	S/I				✓								✓	
Ball joints & steering linkage seals	S/I				✓				✓				✓	
Exhaust system	S/I				✓				✓				✓	
Fuel hoses	S/I				✓				✓				✓	
Manual transaxle oil (including transfer)	S/I				✓				✓				✓	
PCV valve	S/I				✓				✓				✓	
Spark plugs (Platinum)	R								✓					
Camshaft timing belt	R								✓					
Ignition cables	R								✓					
EVAP system	S/I								✓					
Distributor cap & rotor	S/I								✓					
Fuel system	S/I								✓					

① Engine oil & filter (Turbo) - change every 5000 miles.
R - Replace   S/I - Service or Inspect

FREQUENT OPERATION MAINTENANCE (SEVERE SERVICE)
If a vehicle is operated under any of the following conditions it is considered severe service:
- Extremely dusty areas.
- 50% or more of the vehicle operation is in 32°C (90°F) or higher temperatures, or constant operation in temperatures below 0°C (32°F).
- Prolonged idling (vehicle operation in stop and go traffic).
- Frequent short running periods (engine does not warm to normal operating temperatures).
- Police, taxi, delivery usage or trailer towing usage.

CV joints & front suspension components - check every 3000 miles.
Oil & oil filter change - change every 3000 miles.
Brake linings - check every 6000 miles.
Air filter element - service or inspect every 7500 miles.
Automatic transaxle fluid - change every 15,000 miles.
Differential fluid - change every 15,000 miles.
Manual transaxle (including transfer) - change every 15,000 miles.
Spark plugs - change every 15,000 miles.
Tie rod ends & steering linkage - lubricate every 15,000 miles.

93001C50

SCHEDULED MAINTENANCE INTERVALS
CHRYSLER CORPORATION
DODGE STEALTH

The following should be used as a guide when determining the amount of work required for a particular service.
In estimating how long a particular Scheduled Maintenance Service should take, please observe the following:

- **Chilton Time** is time based on field research and data supplied by the vehicle manufacturer.
- Labor time operations are given in hours and tenths of an hour.
- All labor operations, are to be used as a guide.

Mechanic Skill Level Codes:
(A) PRECISION: Really skilled with multiple certification.
(B) GENERAL: Normally skilled with certification.
(C) MAINTENANCE: Semi-skilled working on certification.

	Chilton Time		Chilton Time		Chilton Time
7500 Mile Service (C)		**45000 Mile Service (C)**		**67500 Mile Service (C)**	
All Models	1.0	All Models	1.6	All Models	1.0
15000 Mile Service (C)		**52500 Mile Service (C)**		**75000 Mile Service (C)**	
All Models	1.7	All Models	1.0	All Models	1.7
22500 Mile Service (C)		**60000 Mile Service (B)**		**82500 Mile Service (C)**	
All Models	1.0	All Models	6.8	All Models	1.0
30000 Mile Service (B)				**90000 Mile Service (B)**	
All Models	3.3			All Models	3.3
37500 Mile Service (C)				**97500 Mile Service (C)**	
All Models	1.0			All Models	1.0

93001C51

CHRYSLER CORP.
Eagle Talon

ENGINE AND VEHICLE IDENTIFICATION

			Engine					Model Year	
Code ①	Liters (cc)	Cu. In.	Cyl.	Fuel Sys.	Engine Type	Eng. Mfg.		Code ②	Year
F	2.0 (1999)	122	4	MFI Turbo	DOHC	Mitsubsihi		T	1996
Y	2.0 (1996)	122	4	MFI	DOHC	Chrysler		V	1997
								W	1998

MFI - Multi-port Fuel Injection

DOHC - Double Overhead Camshaft

① 8th digit of the Vehicle Identification Number (VIN)

② 10th digit of the VIN

93001C52

GENERAL ENGINE SPECIFICATIONS
All measurements are given in inches.

Year	Engine Displacement Liters (cc)	Engine Series (ID/VIN)	Fuel System	Net Horsepower @ rpm	Net Torque @ rpm (ft. lbs.)	Bore x Stroke (in.)	Compression Ratio	Oil Pressure @ rpm
1996	2.0 (1997)	F	MFI-Turbo	①	②	3.35x3.46	8.5:1	③
	2.0 (1996)	Y	MFI	140@6000	131@4800	3.44x3.27	9.6:1	④
1997	2.0 (1997)	F	MFI-Turbo	①	②	3.35x3.46	8.5:1	③
	2.0 (1996)	Y	MFI	140@6000	131@4800	3.44x3.27	9.6:1	④
1998	2.0 (1997)	F	MFI-Turbo	①	②	3.35x3.46	8.5:1	③
	2.0 (1996)	Y	MFI	140@6000	131@4800	3.44x3.27	9.6:1	④

MFI - Multi-port Fuel Injection

① Automatic: 205@6000
   Manual: 210@6000

② Automatic: 220@3000
   Manual: 214@3000

③ 11.4 psi or more at curb idle speed

④ 4 psi or more at curb idle speed

93001C53

ENGINE TUNE-UP SPECIFICATIONS

Year	Engine Displacement Liters (cc)	Engine ID/VIN	Spark Plug Gap (in.)	Ignition Timing (deg.)		Fuel Pump (psi) ①	Idle Speed (rpm)		Valve Clearance	
				MT	AT		MT	AT	In.	Ex.
1996	2.0 (1997)	F	0.028-0.030	5B	5B	33	750	750	HYD	HYD
	2.0 (1996)	Y	0.033-0.038	②	②	38	800	800	HYD	HYD
1997	2.0 (1997)	F	0.028-0.030	5B	5B	33	750	750	HYD	HYD
	2.0 (1996)	Y	0.033-0.038	②	②	38	800	800	HYD	HYD
1998	2.0 (1997)	F	0.028-0.030	5B	5B	33	750	750	HYD	HYD
	2.0 (1996)	Y	0.033-0.038	②	②	38	800	800	HYD	HYD

NOTE: The Vehicle Emission Control Information label often reflects specification changes made during production. The label figures must be used if they differ from those in this chart.

HYD - Hydraulic

① Pressure at idle with vacuum applied to fuel pressure regulator

② Basic ignition timing is not adjustable

93001C54

CAPACITIES

Year	Engine Displacement Liters (cc)	Engine ID/VIN	Engine Oil with Filter (qts.)	Transmission (pts.)		Drive Axle (qts.)	Fuel Tank	Cooling System
				5-Spd	Auto.			
1996	2.0 (1997)	F	4.6	①	14.2	1.8	16.0	7.4
	2.0 (1996)	Y	4.5	4.2	18.2	—	16.0	7.4
1997	2.0 (1997)	F	4.6	①	14.2	1.8	16.0	7.4
	2.0 (1996)	Y	4.5	4.2	18.2	—	16.0	7.4
1998	2.0 (1997)	F	4.6	①	14.2	1.8	16.0	7.4
	2.0 (1996)	Y	4.5	4.2	18.2	—	16.0	7.4

NOTE: All capacities are approximate. Add fluid gradually and ensure a proper fluid level is obtained.

① 2WD: 4.6
4WD: 4.8

93001C55

VALVE SPECIFICATIONS

Year	Engine Displacement Liters (cc)	Engine ID/VIN	Seat Angle (deg.)	Face Angle (deg.)	Spring Test Pressure (lbs. @ in.)	Spring Installed Height (in.)	Stem-to-Guide Clearance (in.)		Stem Diameter (in.)	
							Intake	Exhaust	Intake	Exhaust
1996	2.0 (1997)	F	44-44.5	45-45.5	54@1.570	1.570	0.0008-0.0040	0.0020-0.0060	0.2600	0.2560
	2.0 (1996)	Y	45	44.5-45	123-137@1.153	1.496	0.0019-0.0030	0.0029-0.0040	0.2336-0.2343	0.2325-0.2332
1997	2.0 (1997)	F	44-44.5	45-45.5	54@1.570	1.570	0.0008-0.0040	0.0020-0.0060	0.2600	0.2560
	2.0 (1996)	Y	45	44.5-45	123-137@1.153	1.496	0.0019-0.0030	0.0029-0.0040	0.2336-0.2343	0.2325-0.2332
1998	2.0 (1997)	F	44-44.5	45-45.5	54@1.570	1.570	0.0008-0.0040	0.0020-0.0060	0.2600	0.2560
	2.0 (1996)	Y	45	44.5-45	123-137@1.153	1.496	0.0019-0.0030	0.0029-0.0040	0.2336-0.2343	0.2325-0.2332

93001C56

CRANKSHAFT AND CONNECTING ROD SPECIFICATIONS
All measurements are given in inches.

Year	Engine Displacement Liters (cc)	Engine ID/VIN	Crankshaft				Connecting Rods		
			Main Brg. Journal Dia.	Main Brg. Oil Clearance	Shaft End-play	Thrust on No.	Journal Diameter	Oil Clearance	Side Clearance
1996	2.0 (1997)	F	2.2400	0.0008-0.0016	0.0020-0.0071	3	1.7700	0.0008-0.0020	0.0039-0.0098
	2.0 (1996)	Y	2.0469-2.0475	0.0009-0.0024	0.0035-0.0094	3	1.8894-1.8900	0.0010-0.0023	0.0051-0.0150
1997	2.0 (1997)	F	2.2400	0.0008-0.0016	0.0020-0.0071	3	1.7700	0.0008-0.0020	0.0039-0.0098
	2.0 (1996)	Y	2.0469-2.0475	0.0009-0.0024	0.0035-0.0094	3	1.8894-1.8900	0.0010-0.0023	0.0051-0.0150
1998	2.0 (1997)	F	2.2400	0.0008-0.0016	0.0020-0.0071	3	1.7700	0.0008-0.0020	0.0039-0.0098
	2.0 (1996)	Y	2.0469-2.0475	0.0009-0.0024	0.0035-0.0094	3	1.8894-1.8900	0.0010-0.0023	0.0051-0.0150

93001C57

Refer to the model specific sections for engine mechanical service procedures

PISTON AND RING SPECIFICATIONS
All measurements are given in inches.

Year	Engine Displacement Liters (cc)	Engine ID/VIN	Piston Clearance	Ring Gap			Ring Side Clearance		
				Top Compression	Bottom Compression	Oil Control	Top Compression	Bottom Compression	Oil Control
1996	2.0 (1997)	F	0.0012-0.0020	0.0098-0.0138	0.0157-0.0217	0.0039-0.0157	0.0016-0.0031	0.0008-0.0024	0.0005-0.0089
	2.0 (1996)	Y	0.0005-0.0017	0.0090-0.0200	0.0190-0.0310	0.0090-0.0260	0.0010-0.0026	0.0010-0.0026	0.0002-0.0070
1997	2.0 (1997)	F	0.0012-0.0020	0.0098-0.0138	0.0157-0.0217	0.0039-0.0157	0.0016-0.0031	0.0008-0.0024	0.0005-0.0089
	2.0 (1996)	Y	0.0005-0.0017	0.0090-0.0200	0.0190-0.0310	0.0090-0.0260	0.0010-0.0026	0.0010-0.0026	0.0002-0.0070
1998	2.0 (1997)	F	0.0012-0.0020	0.0098-0.0138	0.0157-0.0217	0.0039-0.0157	0.0016-0.0031	0.0008-0.0024	0.0005-0.0089
	2.0 (1996)	Y	0.0005-0.0017	0.0090-0.0200	0.0190-0.0310	0.0090-0.0260	0.0010-0.0026	0.0010-0.0026	0.0002-0.0070

93001C58

TORQUE SPECIFICATIONS
All readings in ft. lbs.

Year	Engine Displacement Liters (cc)	Engine ID/VIN	Cylinder Head Bolts	Main Bearing Bolts	Rod Bearing Bolts	Crankshaft Damper Bolts	Flywheel Bolts	Manifold		Spark Plugs	Lug Nuts
								Intake	Exhaust		
1996	2.0 (1997)	F	①	②	③	94	94-101	14	18-22	18	65-80
	2.0 (1996)	Y	④	55	⑤	105	—	17	17	20	65-80
1997	2.0 (1997)	F	①	②	③	94	94-101	14	18-22	18	65-80
	2.0 (1996)	Y	④	55	⑤	105	—	17	17	20	65-80
1998	2.0 (1997)	F	①	②	③	94	94-101	14	18-22	18	65-80
	2.0 (1996)	Y	④	55	⑤	105	—	17	17	20	65-80

① Step 1: 58 ft. lbs.
Step 2: Fully loosen
Step 3: 15 ft. lbs.
Step 4: Plus 90 degrees
Step 5: Repeat Step 4

② Step 1: 18 ft. lbs.
Step 2: Plus 90 degrees

③ 14.5 ft. lbs. plus 90 degrees

④ Step 1:
Bolts 1-6: 24 ft. lbs.
Bolts 7-10: 20 ft. lbs.
Step 2:
Bolts 1-6: 49 ft. lbs.
Bolts 7-10: 20 ft. lbs.
Step 3: Plus 90 degrees.

⑤ 20 ft. lbs. plus 90 degrees

93001C59

SCHEDULED MAINTENANCE INTERVALS
(EAGLE TALON)

TO BE SERVICED	TYPE OF SERVICE	VEHICLE MILEAGE INTERVAL (x1000)												
		7.5	15	22.5	30	37.5	45	52.5	60	67.5	75	82.5	90	97.5
Engine oil & filter (Non-turbo) ①	R	✓	✓	✓	✓	✓	✓	✓	✓	✓	✓	✓	✓	✓
Coolant level, hoses & clamps	S/I	✓	✓	✓	✓	✓	✓	✓	✓	✓	✓	✓	✓	✓
Rotate tires	S/I	✓	✓	✓	✓	✓	✓	✓	✓	✓	✓	✓	✓	✓
Automatic transaxle fluid level	S/I		✓		✓		✓		✓		✓		✓	
Brake hoses & disc brake pads	S/I		✓		✓		✓		✓		✓		✓	
Driveshaft boots & front suspension components	S/I		✓		✓		✓		✓		✓		✓	
Air filter element	R				✓				✓				✓	
Automatic transaxle fluid & filter ②	R				✓				✓				✓	
Engine coolant	R				✓				✓				✓	
Spark plugs	R				✓				✓				✓	
Accessory drive belts	S/I				✓				✓				✓	
Ball joints & steering linkage seals	S/I				✓				✓				✓	
Exhaust system	S/I				✓				✓				✓	
Fuel hoses	S/I				✓				✓				✓	
Manual transaxle oil (including transfer)	S/I				✓				✓				✓	
Rear axle oil (AWD)	S/I				✓				✓				✓	
Camshaft timing belt	R								✓					
Ignition cables	R								✓					
EVAP & fuel system	S/I								✓					

① Engine oil & filter (Turbo) - change every 5000 miles.

② Turbo w/ A/T only.
R - Replace   S/I - Service or Inspect

FREQUENT OPERATION MAINTENANCE (SEVERE SERVICE)

If a vehicle is operated under any of the following conditions it is considered severe service:
- Extremely dusty areas.
- 50% or more of the vehicle operation is in 32°C (90°F) or higher temperatures, or constant operation in temperatures below 0°C (32°F).
- Prolonged idling (vehicle operation in stop and go traffic).
- Frequent short running periods (engine does not warm to normal operating temperatures).
- Police, taxi, delivery usage or trailer towing usage.

Oil & filter change - change every 3000 miles.
Air filter element - service or inspect every 7500 miles.
Automatic transaxle fluid - change every 15,000 miles.
Spark plugs - change every 15,000 miles.
Disc brake pads - check more frequently than every 7500 miles.

93001C60

Refer to the model specific sections for fuel system service procedures

SCHEDULED MAINTENANCE INTERVALS
CHRYSLER CORPORATION
EAGLE TALON

The following should be used as a guide when determining the amount of work required for a particular service. In estimating how long a particular Scheduled Maintenance Service should take, please observe the following:

- **Chilton Time** is time based on field research and data supplied by the vehicle manufacturer.
  - Labor time operations are given in hours and tenths of an hour.
  - All labor operations, are to be used as a guide.

Mechanic Skill Level Codes:
(A) PRECISION: Really skilled with multiple certification.
(B) GENERAL: Normally skilled with certification.
(C) MAINTENANCE: Semi-skilled working on certification.

	Chilton Time		Chilton Time		Chilton Time
7500 Mile Service (C)		**45000 Mile Service (B)**		**67500 Mile Service (C)**	
All models	1.0	All models	1.3	All models	1.0
15000 Mile Service (B)		**52500 Mile Service (C)**		**75000 Mile Service (C)**	
All models	1.3	All models	1.0	All models	1.3
22500 Mile Service (C)		**60000 Mile Service (B)**		**82500 Mile Service (C)**	
All models	1.0	All models	7.5	All models	1.0
30000 Mile Service (B)				**90000 Mile Service (B)**	
All models	4.0			All models	4.0
37500 Mile Service (C)				**97500 Mile Service (C)**	
All models	1.0			All models	1.0

93001C61

FORD MOTOR CO.
Ford Contour • Mercury Mystique • 1999–00 Cougar

ENGINE AND VEHICLE IDENTIFICATION

	Engine							Model Year	
Code ①	Liters (cc)	Cu. In.	Cyl.	Fuel Sys.	Engine Type	Eng. Mfg.		Code ②	Year
3	2.0 (1999)	122	4	SFI	DOHC	Ford		T	1996
L	2.5 (2507)	153	6	SFI	DOHC	Ford		V	1997
								W	1998
								X	1999
								Y	2000

SFI - Sequential Fuel Injection

DOHC - Double Overhead Camshaft

① 8th digit of VIN

② 10th digit of VIN

93001C62

GENERAL ENGINE SPECIFICATIONS

Year	Model	Engine Displacement Liters (cc)	Engine ID/VIN	Fuel System Type	Net Horsepower @ rpm	Net Torque @ rpm (ft. lbs.)	Bore x Stroke (in.)	Compression Ratio	Oil Pressure @ rpm
1996	Contour	2.0 (1999)	3	SFI	125@6000	130@4500	3.39x3.46	9.6:1	20-45@1500
		2.5 (2507)	L	SFI	170@6200	165@4200	3.25x3.13	9.7:1	25-45@1500
	Mystique	2.0 (1999)	3	SFI	125@5500	130@4000	3.39x3.46	9.6:1	20-45@1500
		2.5 (2507)	L	SFI	170@6200	165@4200	3.25x3.13	9.7:1	20-45@1500
1997	Contour	2.0 (1999)	3	SFI	125@6000	130@4500	3.39x3.46	9.6:1	20-45@1500
		2.5 (2507)	L	SFI	170@6200	165@4200	3.25x3.13	9.7:1	25-45@1500
	Mystique	2.0 (1999)	3	SFI	125@5500	130@4000	3.39x3.46	9.6:1	20-45@1500
		2.5 (2507)	L	SFI	170@6200	165@4200	3.25x3.13	9.7:1	20-45@1500
1998	Contour	2.0 (1999)	3	SFI	125@6000	130@4500	3.39x3.46	9.6:1	20-45@1500
		2.5 (2507)	L	SFI	170@6200	165@4200	3.25x3.13	9.7:1	25-45@1500
	Mystique	2.0 (1999)	3	SFI	125@5500	130@4000	3.39x3.46	9.6:1	20-45@1500
		2.5 (2507)	L	SFI	170@6200	165@4200	3.25x3.13	9.7:1	20-45@1500
1999-00	Contour	2.0 (1999)	3	SFI	125@6000	130@4500	3.39x3.46	9.6:1	20-45@1500
		2.5 (2507)	L	SFI	170@6200	165@4200	3.25x3.13	9.7:1	25-45@1500
	Cougar	2.0 (1999)	3	SFI	125@6000	130@4500	3.39x3.46	9.6:1	20-45@1500
		2.5 (2507)	L	SFI	170@6200	165@4200	3.25x3.13	9.7:1	25-45@1500
	Mystique	2.0 (1999)	3	SFI	125@5500	130@4000	3.39x3.46	9.6:1	20-45@1500
		2.5 (2507)	L	SFI	170@6200	165@4200	3.25x3.13	9.7:1	20-45@1500

SFI - Sequential Fuel Injection

93001C63

Refer to the model specific sections for engine electrical system service procedures

ENGINE TUNE-UP SPECIFICATIONS

Year	Engine Displacement Liters (cc)	Engine ID/VIN	Spark Plug Gap (in.)	Ignition Timing (deg.) MT	Ignition Timing (deg.) AT	Fuel Pump (psi) ①	Idle Speed (rpm) MT	Idle Speed (rpm) AT	Valve Clearance Intake	Valve Clearance Exhaust
1996	2.0 (1999)	3	0.050	10B	10B	37-41	②	②	HYD	HYD
	2.5 (2507)	L	0.054	10B	10B	37-41	②	②	HYD	HYD
1997	2.0 (1999)	3	0.050	10B	10B	37-41	②	②	HYD	HYD
	2.5 (2507)	L	0.054	10B	10B	37-41	②	②	HYD	HYD
1998	2.0 (1999)	3	0.050	10B	10B	37-41	②	②	HYD	HYD
	2.5 (2507)	L	0.054	10B	10B	37-41	②	②	HYD	HYD
1999-00	2.0 (1999)	3	0.050	10B	10B	37-41	②	②	HYD	HYD
	2.5 (2507)	L	0.054	10B	10B	37-41	②	②	HYD	HYD

NOTE: The Vehicle Emission Control Information label often reflects specification changes made during production. The label figures must be used if they differ from those in this chart.

B - Before Top Dead Center

HYD - Hydraulic

① Fuel pressure with engine running, pressure regulator vacuum hose connected

② Refer to Vehicle Emission Control Information (VECI) label

93001C64

CAPACITIES

Year	Model	Engine Displacement Liters (cc)	Engine ID/VIN	Engine Oil with Filter (qts.)	Transaxle (pts.) Manual	Transaxle (pts.) Auto. ①	Front Drive Axle (pts.)	Fuel Tank (gal.)	Cooling System (qts.)
1996	Contour	2.0 (1999)	3	4.5	5.5	18.0	②	14.5	③
		2.5 (2507)	L	5.8	5.5	20.6	②	14.5	④
	Mystique	2.0 (1999)	3	4.5	5.5	18.0	②	14.5	③
		2.5 (2507)	L	5.8	5.5	20.6	②	14.5	④
1997	Contour	2.0 (1999)	3	4.5	5.5	18.0	②	14.5	③
		2.5 (2507)	L	5.8	5.5	20.6	②	14.5	④
	Mystique	2.0 (1999)	3	4.5	5.5	18.0	②	14.5	③
		2.5 (2507)	L	5.8	5.5	20.6	②	14.5	④
1998	Contour	2.0 (1999)	3	4.5	5.5	18.0	②	14.5	③
		2.5 (2507)	L	5.8	5.5	20.6	②	14.5	④
	Mystique	2.0 (1999)	3	4.5	5.5	18.0	②	14.5	③
		2.5 (2507)	L	5.8	5.5	20.6	②	14.5	④
1999-00	Contour	2.0 (1999)	3	4.5	5.5	18.0	②	14.5	③
		2.5 (2507)	L	5.8	5.5	20.6	②	14.5	④
	Cougar	2.0 (1999)	3	4.5	5.5	18.0	②	14.5	④
		2.5 (2507)	L	5.8	5.5	20.6	②	14.5	④
	Mystique	2.0 (1999)	3	4.5	5.5	18.0	②	14.5	③
		2.5 (2507)	L	5.8	5.5	20.6	②	14.5	④

NOTE: All capacities are approximate. Add fluid gradually and ensure a proper fluid level is obtained.

① Includes torque converter

② Included in transaxle capacity

③ Automatic transaxle: 7.5 qts.
   Manual transaxle: 7.0 qts.

④ Automatic transaxle: 9.1 qts.
   Manual transaxle: 8.9 qts.

93001C65

VALVE SPECIFICATIONS

Year	Engine Displacement Liters (cc)	Engine ID/VIN	Seat Angle (deg.)	Face Angle (deg.)	Spring Test Pressure (lbs. @ in.)	Spring Installed Height (in.)	Stem-to-Guide Clearance (in.)		Stem Diameter (in.)	
							Intake	Exhaust	Intake	Exhaust
1996	2.0 (1999)	3	45	45	NA	1.346	0.0007- 0.0025	0.0014- 0.0032	0.2373- 0.2379	0.2366- 0.2372
	2.5 (2507)	L	44.75	45.5	153@1.18	1.570	0.0007- 0.0027	0.0017- 0.0037	0.2350- 0.2358	0.2343- 0.2350
1997	2.0 (1999)	3	45	45	NA	1.346	0.0007- 0.0025	0.0014- 0.0032	0.2373- 0.2379	0.2366- 0.2372
	2.5 (2507)	L	44.75	45.5	153@1.18	1.570	0.0007- 0.0027	0.0017- 0.0037	0.2350- 0.2358	0.2343- 0.2350
1998	2.0 (1999)	3	45	45	NA	1.346	0.0007- 0.0025	0.0014- 0.0032	0.2373- 0.2379	0.2366- 0.2372
	2.5 (2507)	L	44.75	45.5	153@1.18	1.570	0.0007- 0.0027	0.0017- 0.0037	0.2350- 0.2358	0.2343- 0.2350
1999-00	2.0 (1999)	3	45	45	NA	1.346	0.0007- 0.0025	0.0014- 0.0032	0.2373- 0.2379	0.2366- 0.2372
	2.5 (2507)	L	44.75	45.5	153@1.18	1.570	0.0007- 0.0027	0.0017- 0.0037	0.2350- 0.2358	0.2343- 0.2350

93001C66

CRANKSHAFT AND CONNECTING ROD SPECIFICATIONS
All measurements are given in inches.

Year	Engine Displacement Liters (cc)	Engine ID/VIN	Crankshaft				Connecting Rod		
			Main Brg. Journal Dia.	Main Brg. Oil Clearance	Shaft End-play	Thrust on No.	Journal Diameter	Oil Clearance	Side Clearance
1996	2.0 (1999)	3	2.2827- 2.2835	0.0008- 0.0017	0.0035- 0.0100	3	1.8425- 1.8504	0.0006- 0.0028	0.0035- 0.0126
	2.5 (2507)	L	2.4670- 2.4790	0.0009- 0.0019	0.0040- 0.0090	4	1.9670- 1.9680	0.0010- 0.0025	0.0039- 0.0118
1997	2.0 (1999)	3	2.2827- 2.2835	0.0008- 0.0017	0.0035- 0.0100	3	1.8425- 1.8504	0.0006- 0.0028	0.0035- 0.0126
	2.5 (2507)	L	2.4670- 2.4790	0.0009- 0.0019	0.0040- 0.0090	4	1.9670- 1.9680	0.0010- 0.0025	0.0039- 0.0118
1998	2.0 (1999)	3	2.2827- 2.2835	0.0008- 0.0017	0.0035- 0.0100	3	1.8425- 1.8504	0.0006- 0.0028	0.0035- 0.0126
	2.5 (2507)	L	2.4670- 2.4790	0.0009- 0.0019	0.0040- 0.0090	4	1.9670- 1.9680	0.0010- 0.0025	0.0039- 0.0118
1999-00	2.0 (1999)	3	2.2827- 2.2835	0.0008- 0.0017	0.0035- 0.0100	3	1.8425- 1.8504	0.0006- 0.0028	0.0035- 0.0126
	2.5 (2507)	L	2.4670- 2.4790	0.0009- 0.0019	0.0040- 0.0090	4	1.9670- 1.9680	0.0010- 0.0025	0.0039- 0.0118

93001C67

For accessory drive belt replacement procedures see the model specific sections of this manual

PISTON AND RING SPECIFICATIONS
All measurements are given in inches.

Year	Engine Displacement Liters (cc)	Engine ID/VIN	Piston Clearance	Ring Gap			Ring Side Clearance		
				Top Compression	Bottom Compression	Oil Control	Top Compression	Bottom Compression	Oil Control
1996	2.0 (1999)	3	0.0008-0.0016	0.008-0.010	0.012-0.020	0.016-0.055	0.0016-0.0028	0.0008-0.0021	Snug
	2.5 (2507)	L	0.0005-0.0009	0.004-0.010	0.011-0.017	0.006-0.026	0.0015-0.0029	0.0015-0.0033	Snug
1997	2.0 (1999)	3	0.0008-0.0016	0.008-0.010	0.012-0.020	0.016-0.055	0.0016-0.0028	0.0008-0.0021	Snug
	2.5 (2507)	L	0.0005-0.0009	0.004-0.010	0.011-0.017	0.006-0.026	0.0015-0.0029	0.0015-0.0033	Snug
1998	2.0 (1999)	3	0.0008-0.0016	0.008-0.010	0.012-0.020	0.016-0.055	0.0016-0.0028	0.0008-0.0021	Snug
	2.5 (2507)	L	0.0005-0.0009	0.004-0.010	0.011-0.017	0.006-0.026	0.0015-0.0029	0.0015-0.0033	Snug
1999-00	2.0 (1999)	3	0.0008-0.0016	0.008-0.010	0.012-0.020	0.016-0.055	0.0016-0.0028	0.0008-0.0021	Snug
	2.5 (2507)	L	0.0005-0.0009	0.004-0.010	0.011-0.017	0.006-0.026	0.0015-0.0029	0.0015-0.0033	Snug

93001C68

TORQUE SPECIFICATIONS
All readings in ft. lbs.

Year	Engine Displacement Liters (cc)	Engine ID/VIN	Cylinder Head Bolts	Main Bearing Bolts	Rod Bearing Bolts	Crankshaft Damper Bolts	Flywheel Bolts	Manifold		Spark Plugs	Lug Nuts
								Intake	Exhaust		
1996	2.0 (1999)	3	①	55-66	②	81-89	80-87	12-15	13-16	9-13	63
	2.5 (2507)	L	③	④	⑤	⑥	54-64	6-9	13-16	7-15	63
1997	2.0 (1999)	3	①	55-66	②	81-89	80-87	12-15	13-16	9-13	63
	2.5 (2507)	L	③	④	⑤	⑥	54-64	6-9	13-16	7-15	63
1998	2.0 (1999)	3	①	55-66	②	81-89	80-87	12-15	13-16	9-13	63
	2.5 (2507)	L	③	④	⑤	⑥	54-64	6-9	13-16	7-15	63
1999-00	2.0 (1999)	3	①	55-66	②	81-89	80-87	12-15	13-16	9-13	63
	2.5 (2507)	L	③	④	⑤	⑥	54-64	6-9	13-16	7-15	63

NOTE: Always follow proper torque patterns. Stretch bolts are used in all procedures that require rotating the fastener a certain number of degrees. The bolts stretch and cannot be reused. For reassembly, replace with new fastners.

① Step 1: 15-22 ft. lbs.
　Step 2: 30-37 ft. lbs.
　Step 3: Tighten 90-120 degrees

② Step 1: 22-25 ft. lbs.
　Step 2: Tighten each bolt 85-95 degrees

③ Step 1: 27-32 ft. lbs.
　Step 2: Tighten 85-95 degrees
　Step 3: Loosen bolts then repeat Step 1
　Step 4: Tighten 85-95 degrees
　Step 5: Repeat Step 4

④ Step 1: 2.0-3.6 ft. lbs.
　Step 2: Push crankshaft rearward.
　Lightly seat crankshaft washer forward
　Step 3: Outer cap bolts: 16-21 ft. lbs.
　Step 4: Inner cap bolts: 27-32 ft. lbs.
　Step 5: Tighten inner and outer cap bolts 85-95 degrees
　Step 6: Remaining bolts: 15-22 ft. lbs.

⑤ 26-33 ft. lbs. plus 90-120 degrees

⑥ Step 1: 89 ft. lbs.
　Step 2: Loosen bolt
　Step 3: 35-39 ft. lbs.
　Step 4: Tighten 85-95 degrees

93001C69

SCHEDULED MAINTENANCE INTERVALS
(FORD CONTOUR, MERCURY COUGAR MYSTIQUE)

TO BE SERVICED	TYPE OF SERVICE	VEHICLE MILEAGE INTERVAL (x1000)												
		5	10	15	20	25	30	35	40	45	50	55	60	65
Engine oil & filter	R	✓	✓	✓	✓	✓	✓	✓	✓	✓	✓	✓	✓	✓
Rotate tires	S/I	✓		✓		✓		✓		✓		✓		✓
Front & rear brakes	S/I		✓		✓		✓		✓		✓		✓	
Cooling system, hoses, clamps & coolant strength	S/I			✓			✓			✓			✓	
Passenger compartment air filter	R				✓				✓				✓	
Air cleaner element	R						✓						✓	
Automatic transaxle fluid & filter (1995)	R						✓						✓	
Automatic transaxle fluid & filter (1996-99)	S/I												✓	
Exhaust heat shields	S/I						✓						✓	
Accessory drive belt(s)	S/I						✓						✓	
Fuel lines & hoses	S/I						✓						✓	
Crankcase emission filter (2.0L)	R						✓							
Engine coolant ①	R										✓			
Spark plugs ②	R												✓	
PCV valve	R												✓	

① Change initially at 50,000 miles & every 30,000 miles thereafter.

② 2.0L shown; 2.5L - replace every 100,000 miles.

R - Replace   S/I - Service or Inspect

FREQUENT OPERATION MAINTENANCE (SEVERE SERVICE)

If a vehicle is operated under any of the following conditions it is considered severe service:
- Extremely dusty areas.
- 50% or more of the vehicle operation is in 32°C (90°F) or higher temperatures, or constant operation in temperatures below 0°C (32°F).
- Prolonged idling (vehicle operation in stop and go traffic).
- Frequent short running periods (engine does not warm to normal operating temperatures).
- Police, taxi, delivery usage or trailer towing usage.

Oil & filter change - change every 3000 miles.
Front & rear brakes - check every 9000 miles.
Rotate tires at 6000 miles & every 9000 miles thereafter.
Air cleaner element - check every 15,000 miles.
Passenger compartment air filter - change every 18,000 miles.
Automatic transaxle fluid & filter - change every 30,000 miles.
Spark plugs - replace every 60,000 miles.

93001C70

For brake related suspension and axle service, refer to the model specific sections of this manual

SCHEDULED MAINTENANCE INTERVALS
FORD MOTOR COMPANY
FORD CONTOUR
MERCURY MYSTIQUE, COUGAR

The following should be used as a guide when determining the amount of work required for a particular service.
In estimating how long a particular Scheduled Maintenance Service should take, please observe the following:

- **Chilton Time** is time based on field research and data supplied by the vehicle manufacturer.
  - Labor time operations are given in hours and tenths of an hour.
    - All labor operations, are to be used as a guide.

Mechanic Skill Level Codes:
(A) PRECISION: Really skilled with multiple certification.
(B) GENERAL: Normally skilled with certification.
(C) MAINTENANCE: Semi-skilled working on certification.

	Chilton Time			Chilton Time			Chilton Time
5000 Mile Service (C)			**30000 Mile Service (B)**			**50000 Mile Service (B)**	
All Models	.9		All Models	1.7		All Models	1.2
10000 Mile Service (C)			**35000 Mile Service (C)**			**55000 Mile Service (C)**	
All Models	.7		All Models	.9		All Models	.7
15000 Mile Service (C)			**40000 Mile Service (C)**			**60000 Mile Service (B)**	
All Models	1.0		All Models	1.0		All Models	3.4
20000 Mile Service (C)			**45000 Mile Service (C)**			*Renew auto. trans. fluid & filter add*	.6
All Models	1.0		All Models	1.0		**65000 Mile Service (C)**	
25000 Mile Service (C)						All Models	.9
All Models	.9						

93001C71

FORD MOTOR CO.
Ford Aspire

ENGINE AND VEHICLE IDENTIFICATION

Engine							Model Year	
Code ①	Liters (cc)	Cu. In.	Cyl.	Fuel Sys.	Engine Type	Eng. Mfg.	Code ②	Year
H	1.3 (1319)	81	4	SFI	SOHC	Kia Motors	T	1996
							V	1997

SFI - Sequential Fuel Injection
SOHC - Single Overhead Camshaft
① 8th digit of the Vehicle Identification Number (VIN)
② 10th digit of VIN

93001C72

GENERAL ENGINE SPECIFICATIONS
All measurements are given in inches.

Year	Model	Engine Displacement Liters (cc)	Engine Series (ID/VIN)	Fuel System	Net Horsepower @ rpm	Net Torque @ rpm (ft. lbs.)	Bore x Stroke (in.)	Com- pression Ratio	Oil Pressure @ rpm
1996	Aspire	1.3 (1319)	H	SFI	63@5000	73@3000	2.79x3.29	9.7:1	50-64@3000
1997	Aspire	1.3 (1319)	H	SFI	63@5000	73@3000	2.79x3.29	9.7:1	50-64@3000

SFI - Sequential Fuel Injection

93001C73

ENGINE TUNE-UP SPECIFICATIONS

Year	Engine Displacement Liters (cc)	Engine ID/VIN	Spark Plug Gap (in.)	Ignition Timing (deg.) MT	Ignition Timing (deg.) AT	Fuel Pump (psi)	Idle Speed (rpm) MT	Idle Speed (rpm) AT	Valve Clearance Intake	Valve Clearance Exhaust
1996	1.3 (1319)	H	0.040	10B	10B	30-38 ①	700	750	HYD	HYD
1997	1.3 (1319)	H	0.040	10B	10B	30-38 ①	700	750	HYD	HYD

NOTE: The Vehicle Emission Control Information label often reflects specification changes made during production. The label figures must be used if they differ from those in this chart.
HYD - Hydraulic

① Fuel pressure with engine running, pressure regulator vacuum hose connected.

93001C74

CAPACITIES

Year	Model	Engine Displacement Liters (cc)	Engine ID/VIN	Engine Oil with Filter (qts.)	Transmission (pts.) Manual	Transmission (pts.) Auto. ①	Front Drive Axle (pts.)	Fuel Tank (gal.)	Cooling System (qts.)
1996	Aspire	1.3 (1319)	H	3.6	5.2	12.0	②	10.0	6.3
1997	Aspire	1.3 (1319)	H	3.6	5.2	12.0	②	10.0	6.3

NOTE: All capacities are approximate. Add fluid gradually and ensure a proper fluid level is obtained.

① Includes torque converter

② Included in transaxle capacity

93001C75

VALVE SPECIFICATIONS

Year	Engine Displacement Liters (cc)	Engine ID/VIN	Seat Angle (deg.)	Face Angle (deg.)	Spring Test Pressure (lbs. @ in.)	Spring Free-Length (in.)	Stem-to-Guide Clearance (in.) Intake	Stem-to-Guide Clearance (in.) Exhaust	Stem Diameter (in.) Intake	Stem Diameter (in.) Exhaust
1996	1.3 (1319)	H	45	45	NA	1.717	0.0010-0.0024	0.0012-0.0026	0.2744-0.2750	0.2742-0.2748
1997	1.3 (1319)	H	45	45	NA	1.717	0.0010-0.0024	0.0012-0.0026	0.2744-0.2750	0.2742-0.2748

NA - Not Avaliable

93001C76

CRANKSHAFT AND CONNECTING ROD SPECIFICATIONS
All measurements are given in inches.

Year	Engine Displacement Liters (cc)	Engine ID/VIN	Crankshaft Main Brg. Journal Dia.	Crankshaft Main Brg. Oil Clearance	Crankshaft Shaft End-play	Crankshaft Thrust on No.	Connecting Rod Journal Diameter	Connecting Rod Oil Clearance	Connecting Rod Side Clearance
1996	1.3 (1319)	H	1.9661-1.9688	0.0007-0.0014	0.0031-0.0111	4	1.5724-1.5731	0.0009-0.0017	0.0120
1997	1.3 (1319)	H	1.9661-1.9688	0.0007-0.0014	0.0031-0.0111	4	1.5724-1.5731	0.0009-0.0017	0.0120

93001C77

PISTON AND RING SPECIFICATIONS
All measurements are given in inches.

Year	Engine ID/VIN	Engine Displacement Liters (cc)	Piston Clearance	Ring Gap			Ring Side Clearance		
				Top Compression	Bottom Compression	Oil Control	Top Compression	Bottom Compression	Oil Control
1996	H	1.3 (1319)	0.0060	0.006-0.012	0.006-0.012	0.008-0.028	0.001-0.003	0.001-0.003	Snug
1997	H	1.3 (1319)	0.0060	0.006-0.012	0.006-0.012	0.008-0.028	0.001-0.003	0.001-0.003	Snug

93001C78

TORQUE SPECIFICATIONS
All readings in ft. lbs.

Year	Engine Displacement Liters (cc)	Engine ID/VIN	Cylinder Head Bolts	Main Bearing Bolts	Rod Bearing Bolts	Crankshaft Damper Bolts	Flywheel Bolts	Manifold		Spark Plugs	Lug Nuts
								Intake	Exhaust		
1996	1.3 (1319)	H	①	40-43	②	③	71-76	14-20	12-17	15-22	76
1997	1.3 (1319)	H	①	40-43	②	③	71-76	14-20	12-17	15-22	76

NOTE: Always follow proper torque patterns, and stretch bolts are used in all procedures that require rotating the fastener a certain number of degrees. The bolts stretch and cannot be reused. For reassembly, replace with new fastners.

① Step 1: 35-40 ft. lbs.
Step 2: 56-60 ft. lbs.

② Step 1: 11-13 ft. lbs.
Step 2: 22-25 ft. lbs.

③ Pulley bolts: 9-13 ft. lbs.
Sprocket bolt: 80-87 ft. lbs.

93001C79

For exhaust manifold replacement procedures, see the model specific sections of this manual

SCHEDULED MAINTENANCE INTERVALS
(FORD ASPIRE)

TO BE SERVICED	TYPE OF SERVICE	VEHICLE MILEAGE INTERVAL (x1000)												
		5	10	15	20	25	30	35	40	45	50	55	60	65
Engine oil & filter	R	✓	✓	✓	✓	✓	✓	✓	✓	✓	✓	✓	✓	✓
Rotate tires	S/I	✓		✓		✓		✓		✓		✓		✓
Air cleaner element & engine coolant	R						✓						✓	
Spark plugs	R						✓						✓	
Automatic transaxle fluid & filter	R						✓						✓	
Exhaust heat shields	S/I						✓						✓	
Disc brake pads & rotors, brake linings, drum, brake lines, hoses & connections	S/I						✓						✓	
Accessory drive belt(s)	S/I						✓						✓	
Fuel lines, hoses & idle speed	S/I						✓						✓	
Cooling system, hoses, clamps & coolant strength	S/I						✓						✓	
Clutch pedal operation	S/I						✓						✓	
Front wheel driveshaft joint boots	S/I						✓						✓	
Front suspension ball joints, steering operation & linkage	S/I						✓						✓	
Timing belt/chain & fuel filter	R												✓	
Fuel lines & tubes (emission)	S/I												✓	
Ignition timing	S/I												✓	
Repack front & rear wheel bearings	S/I												✓	

R – Replace   S/I – Service or Inspect

FREQUENT OPERATION MAINTENANCE (SEVERE SERVICE)

If a vehicle is operated under any of the following conditions it is considered severe service:
- Extremely dusty areas.
- 50% or more of the vehicle operation is in 32°C (90°F) or higher temperatures, or constant operation in temperatures below 0°C (32°F).
- Prolonged idling (vehicle operation in stop and go traffic).
- Frequent short running periods (engine does not warm to normal operating temperatures).
- Police, taxi, delivery usage or trailer towing usage.

Oil & oil filter – change every 3000 miles.
Rotate tires at 6000 miles & every 9000 miles thereafter.
Air cleaner element - service or inspect every 15,000 miles.
Automatic transaxle fluid & filter - change every 21,000 miles.

79221CA7

SCHEDULED MAINTENANCE INTERVALS
FORD MOTOR COMPANY
FORD ASPIRE

The following should be used as a guide when determining the amount of work required for a particular service.
In estimating how long a particular Scheduled Maintenance Service should take, please observe the following:

- **Chilton Time** is time based on field research and data supplied by the vehicle manufacturer.
  - Labor time operations are given in hours and tenths of an hour.
  - All labor operations, are to be used as a guide.

Mechanic Skill Level Codes:
(A) PRECISION: Really skilled with multiple certification.
(B) GENERAL: Normally skilled with certification.
(C) MAINTENANCE: Semi-skilled working on certification.

	Chilton Time		Chilton Time		Chilton Time
5000 Mile Service (C)		**30000 Mile Service (B)**		**45000 Mile Service (C)**	
All Models	.9	All Models	3.0	All Models	.9
10000 Mile Service (C)		**35000 Mile Service (C)**		**50000 Mile Service (C)**	
All Models	.4	All Models	.9	All Models	.4
15000 Mile Service (C)		**40000 Mile Service (C)**		**55000 Mile Service (C)**	
All Models	.9	All Models	.4	All Models	.9
20000 Mile Service (C)				**60000 Mile Service (B)**	
All Models	.4			All Models	6.1
25000 Mile Service (C)				**65000 Mile Service (C)**	
All Models	.9			All Models	.9

93001C80

Refer to the model specific sections for cooling system service procedures

FORD MOTOR CO.
Ford Crown Victoria • Lincoln Town Car • Mercury Grand Marquis

ENGINE AND VEHICLE IDENTIFICATION

Engine							Model Year	
Code ①	Liters (cc)	Cu. In.	Cyl.	Fuel Sys.	Type	Eng. Mfg.	Code ②	Year
W	4.6 (4593)	281	8	SFI	SOHC	Ford	T	1996
							V	1997
							W	1998
							X	1999
							Y	2000

SFI - Sequential Fuel Injection

SOHC - Single Overhead Camshaft

① 8th digit of the Vehicle Identification Number (VIN)

② 10th digit fo the Vehicle Identification Number (VIN)

93001C81

GENERAL ENGINE SPECIFICATIONS

Year	Model	Engine Displacement Liters (cc)	Engine ID/VIN	Fuel System Type	Net Horsepower @ rpm	Net Torque @ rpm (ft. lbs.)	Bore x Stroke (in.)	Compression Ratio	Oil Pressure @ rpm
1996	Crown Victoria	4.6 (4593)	W	SFI	①	②	3.55x3.54	③	20-45@1500
	Grand Marquis	4.6 (4593)	W	SFI	①	②	3.55x3.54	9.0:1	20-45@1500
	Town Car	4.6 (4593)	W	SFI	210@4250	275@3250	3.55x3.54	9.0:1	20-45@1500
1997	Crown Victoria	4.6 (4593)	W	SFI	①	②	3.55x3.54	③	20-45@1500
	Grand Marquis	4.6 (4593)	W	SFI	①	②	3.55x3.54	9.0:1	20-45@1500
	Town Car	4.6 (4593)	W	SFI	210@4250	275@3250	3.55x3.54	9.0:1	20-45@1500
1998	Crown Victoria	4.6 (4593)	W	SFI	①	②	3.55x3.54	③	20-45@1500
	Grand Marquis	4.6 (4593)	W	SFI	①	②	3.55x3.54	9.0:1	20-45@1500
	Town Car	4.6 (4593)	W	SFI	210@4250	275@3250	3.55x3.54	9.0:1	20-45@1500
1999-00	Crown Victoria	4.6 (4593)	W	SFI	①	②	3.55x3.54	③	20-45@1500
	Grand Marquis	4.6 (4593)	W	SFI	①	②	3.55x3.54	9.0:1	20-45@1500
	Town Car	4.6 (4593)	W	SFI	210@4250	275@3250	3.55x3.54	9.0:1	20-45@1500

SFI - Sequential Fuel Injection

① Single exhaust: 190@4250

Dual exhaust: 210@4250

Crown Victoria with natural gas: 178@4500

② Single exhaust: 265@3250

Dual exhaust: 275@3250

Crown Victoria with natural gas: 237@3500

③ Base engine: 9.0:1

Crown Victoria with natural gas: 10.0:1

93001C82

ENGINE TUNE-UP SPECIFICATIONS

Year	Engine Displacement Liters (cc)	Engine ID/VIN	Spark Plug Gap (in.)	Ignition Timing (deg.)	Fuel Pump (psi) ①	Idle Speed (rpm)	Valve Clearance Intake	Valve Clearance Exhaust
1996	4.6 (4593)	W	0.054	10B	35-45	②	HYD	HYD
1997	4.6 (4593)	W	0.054	10B	35-45	②	HYD	HYD
1998	4.6 (4593)	W	0.054	10B	35-45	②	HYD	HYD
1999-00	4.6 (4593)	W	0.054	10B	35-45	②	HYD	HYD

NOTE: The Vehicle Emission Control Information label often reflects specification changes made during production. The label figures must be used if they differ from those in this chart.

B - Before Top Dead Center

HYD - Hydraulic

① Fuel pressure with engine running, pressure regulator vacuum hose connected

② Refer to Vehicle Emission Control Information label

93001C83

CAPACITIES

Year	Model	Engine Displacement Liters (cc)	Engine ID/VIN	Engine Oil with Filter (qts.)	Automatic Transmission (pts.) ①	Rear Drive Axle (pts.) ②	Fuel Tank (gal.)	Cooling System (qts.)
1996	Crown Victoria	4.6 (4593)	W	5.0	27.2	3.75	20.0	14.1
	Grand Marquis	4.6 (4593)	W	5.0	28.2	3.75	20.0	15.1
	Town Car	4.6 (4593)	W	5.0	28.2	3.75	20.0	15.1
1997	Crown Victoria	4.6 (4593)	W	5.0	27.2	3.75	20.0	14.1
	Grand Marquis	4.6 (4593)	W	5.0	28.2	3.75	20.0	15.1
	Town Car	4.6 (4593)	W	5.0	28.2	3.75	20.0	15.1
1998	Crown Victoria	4.6 (4593)	W	5.0	27.2	3.75	20.0	14.1
	Grand Marquis	4.6 (4593)	W	5.0	28.2	3.75	20.0	15.1
	Town Car	4.6 (4593)	W	5.0	28.2	3.75	20.0	15.1
1998-99	Crown Victoria	4.6 (4593)	W	5.0	27.2	3.75	20.0	14.1
	Grand Marquis	4.6 (4593)	W	5.0	28.2	3.75	20.0	15.1
	Town Car	4.6 (4593)	W	5.0	28.2	3.75	20.0	15.1

NOTE: All capacities are approximate. Add fluid gradually and ensure a proper fluid level is obtained.

① Includes torque converter

② 7.50" axle: 3.0 pts.
   8.80" axle: 3.25 pts.

93001C84

VALVE SPECIFICATIONS

Year	Engine Displacement Liters (cc)	Engine ID/VIN	Seat Angle (deg.)	Face Angle (deg.)	Spring Test Pressure (lbs. @ in.)	Spring Installed Height (in.)	Stem-to-Guide Clearance (in.)		Stem Diameter (in.)	
							Intake	Exhaust	Intake	Exhaust
1996	4.6 (4593)	W	45	45.5	132@1.10	1.570	0.0008-0.0027	0.0018-0.0037	0.2746-0.2754	0.2736-0.2744
1997	4.6 (4593)	W	45	45.5	132@1.10	1.570	0.0008-0.0027	0.0018-0.0037	0.2746-0.2754	0.2736-0.2744
1998	4.6 (4593)	W	45	45.5	132@1.10	1.570	0.0008-0.0027	0.0018-0.0037	0.2746-0.2754	0.2736-0.2744
1999-00	4.6 (4593)	W	45	45.5	132@1.10	1.570	0.0008-0.0027	0.0018-0.0037	0.2746-0.2754	0.2736-0.2744

93001C85

CRANKSHAFT AND CONNECTING ROD SPECIFICATIONS
All measurements are given in inches.

Year	Engine Displacement Liters (cc)	Engine ID/VIN	Crankshaft				Connecting Rod		
			Main Brg. Journal Dia.	Main Brg. Oil Clearance	Shaft End-play	Thrust on No.	Journal Diameter	Oil Clearance	Side Clearance
1996	4.6 (4593)	W	2.6500-2.6570	0.0009-0.0026	0.0051-0.0119	5	2.0870-2.8670	0.0009-0.0026	0.0006-0.0177
1997	4.6 (4593)	W	2.6500-2.6570	0.0009-0.0026	0.0051-0.0119	5	2.0870-2.8670	0.0009-0.0026	0.0006-0.0177
1998	4.6 (4593)	W	2.6500-2.6570	0.0009-0.0026	0.0051-0.0119	5	2.0870-2.8670	0.0009-0.0026	0.0006-0.0177
1999-00	4.6 (4593)	W	2.6500-2.6570	0.0009-0.0026	0.0051-0.0119	5	2.0870-2.8670	0.0009-0.0026	0.0006-0.0177

93001C86

PISTON AND RING SPECIFICATIONS
All measurements are given in inches.

| Year | Engine Displacement Liters (cc) | Engine ID/VIN | Piston Clearance ① | Ring Gap | | | Ring Side Clearance | | |
				Top Compression	Bottom Compression	Oil Control	Top Compression	Bottom Compression	Oil Control
1996	4.6 (4593)	W	0.0002-0.0010	0.005-0.012	0.012-0.022	0.006-0.026	②	0.008-0.0024	0.0010-0.0077
1997	4.6 (4593)	W	0.0002-0.0010	0.005-0.012	0.012-0.022	0.006-0.026	②	0.008-0.0024	0.0010-0.0077
1998	4.6 (4593)	W	0.0002-0.0010	0.005-0.012	0.012-0.022	0.006-0.026	②	0.008-0.0024	0.0010-0.0077
1999-00	4.6 (4593)	W	0.0002-0.0010	0.005-0.012	0.012-0.022	0.006-0.026	②	0.008-0.0024	0.0010-0.0077

① Measured 1.96 in. (43mm) from the top
② On 10:1 engines: 0.0012 - 0.0028 in.
   On 9:1 engines: 0.0008 - 0.0024 in.

93001C87

TORQUE SPECIFICATIONS
All readings in ft. lbs.

| Year | Engine Displacement Liters (cc) | Engine ID/VIN | Cylinder Head Bolts | Main Bearing Bolts | Rod Bearing Bolts | Crankshaft Damper Bolts | Flywheel Bolts | Manifold | | Spark Plugs | Lug Nuts |
								Intake	Exhaust		
1996	4.6 (4593)	W	①	②	③	114-121	54-64	15-22	13-16	7-15	95
1997	4.6 (4593)	W	①	②	③	114-121	54-64	15-22	13-16	7-15	95
1998	4.6 (4593)	W	①	②	③	114-121	54-64	15-22	13-16	7-15	95
1999-00	4.6 (4593)	W	①	②	③	114-121	54-64	15-22	13-16	7-15	95

NOTE: Stretch bolts are used in all procedures that require rotating the fastener a certain number of degrees. The bolts stretch and cannot be reused. For reassembly, replace with new fasteners.

① Step 1: 22-30 ft. lbs.
   Step 2: Rotate each bolt 85-95 degrees
   Step 3: Repeat Step 2

② Step 1: Main bearing cap bolts: 22-25 ft. lbs.
   Step 2: Rotate each bolt 85-95 degrees
   Step 3: Main bearing cap adjusting screws: 44 inch lbs. then 80-90 inch lbs.
   Step 4: Main bearing cap side bolts: 7 ft. lbs. then 14-17 ft. lbs.

③ Step 1: 8 ft. lbs.
   Step 2: 12 ft. lbs.
   Step 3: 25-34 ft. lbs.
   Step 4: Rotate 85-95 degrees

93001C88

Timing chain and gear service is covered in the model specific sections of this manual

SCHEDULED MAINTENANCE INTERVALS
(FORD CROWN VICTORIA, LINCOLN TOWN CAR, MERCURY GRAND MARQUIS)

TO BE SERVICED	TYPE OF SERVICE	VEHICLE MILEAGE INTERVAL (x1000)												
		5	10	15	20	25	30	35	40	45	50	55	60	65
Engine oil & filter	R	✓	✓	✓	✓	✓	✓	✓	✓	✓	✓	✓	✓	✓
Rotate tires	S/I	✓		✓		✓		✓		✓		✓		✓
Cooling system, hoses, clamps & coolant strength	S/I			✓			✓			✓			✓	
Lubricate steering linkage (Crown Victoria, Grand Marquis)	S/I			✓			✓			✓			✓	
Air cleaner element	R						✓						✓	
Automatic transaxle fluid & filter	R						✓						✓	
Spark plugs②	R													
Exhaust heat shields	S/I						✓						✓	
Fuel filter (NGV Crown Victoria) ③	R					✓					✓			
Lubricate steering linkage (Town Car)	S/I						✓						✓	
Front & rear brakes	S/I						✓						✓	
Lubricate suspension (Town Car)	S/I						✓						✓	
Engine coolant ①	R										✓			
PCV valve	R												✓	
Accessory drive belt(s)	S/I												✓	

① Change initially at 50,000 miles & thereafter every 30,000 miles.

② Replace every 100,000 miles.

③ Also drain coalescer. Perform every 24,000 miles for severe service.

R - Replace   S/I - Service or Inspect

FREQUENT OPERATION MAINTENANCE (SEVERE SERVICE)

If a vehicle is operated under any of the following conditions it is considered severe service:
- Extremely dusty areas.
- 50% or more of the vehicle operation is in 32°C (90°F) or higher temperatures, or constant operation in temperatures below 0°C (32°F).
- Prolonged idling (vehicle operation in stop and go traffic).
- Frequent short running periods (engine does not warm to normal operating temperatures).
- Police, taxi, delivery usage or trailer towing usage.

Oil & filter change - change every 3000 miles.
Rotate tires at 6000 miles & every 9000 miles thereafter.
Automatic transmission fluid & filter - change every 21,000 miles.

93001C89

SCHEDULED MAINTENANCE INTERVALS
FORD MOTOR COMPANY
FORD CROWN VICTORIA, MERCURY GRAND MARQUIS
LINCOLN TOWN CAR

The following should be used as a guide when determining the amount of work required for a particular service.
In estimating how long a particular Scheduled Maintenance Service should take, please observe the following:

- **Chilton Time** is time based on field research and data supplied by the vehicle manufacturer.
  - Labor time operations are given in hours and tenths of an hour.
    - All labor operations, are to be used as a guide.

Mechanic Skill Level Codes:
(A) PRECISION: Really skilled with multiple certification.
(B) GENERAL: Normally skilled with certification.
(C) MAINTENANCE: Semi-skilled working on certification.

	Chilton Time
5000 Mile Service (C)	
All Models	.8
10000 Mile Service (C)	
All Models	.3
15000 Mile Service (C)	
All Models	.9
20000 Mile Service (C)	
All Models	.3
25000 Mile Service (C)	
All Models	.8

	Chilton Time
30000 Mile Service (B)	
1996-00 Crown Victoria	1.5
1996-00 Grand Marquis	1.5
1996-00 Town Car	1.7
Replace auto. trans. fluid & filter add	.5
35000 Mile Service (C)	
All Models	.8
40000 Mile Service (C)	
All Models	.3
45000 Mile Service (C)	
All Models	.9
50000 Mile Service (B)	
All Models	1.4
Replace engine coolant add	.5

	Chilton Time
55000 Mile Service (C)	
All Models	.8
60000 Mile Service (B)	
1996-00 Crown Victoria	1.5
1996-00 Grand Marquis	1.5
1996-00 Town Car	1.7
Replace auto. trans. fluid & filter add	.5
65000 Mile Service (C)	
All Models	.8

93001C90

Ignition system service is covered in the model specific sections of this manual

FORD MOTOR CO.
Ford Escort • Escort ZX2 • Mercury Tracer

ENGINE AND VEHICLE IDENTIFICATION

Engine							Model Year	
Code ①	Liters (cc)	Cu. In.	Cyl.	Fuel Sys.	Type	Eng. Mfg.	Code ②	Year
3	2.0 (1990)	121	4	SFI	DOHC	Ford	T	1996
8	1.8 (1844)	112	4	MFI	DOHC	Mazda	V	1997
J	1.9 (1901)	116	4	SFI	SOHC	Ford	W	1998
P	2.0 (1999)	121	4	SFI	SOHC	Ford	X	1999
							Y	2000

MFI - Multi-point Fuel Injection

SFI - Sequential Fuel Injection

DOHC - Double Overhead Camshafts

SOHC - Single Overhead Camshaft

① 8th digit of the VIN

② 10th digit of the VIN

93001C91

GENERAL ENGINE SPECIFICATIONS

Year	Model	Engine Displacement Liters (cc)	Engine ID/VIN	Fuel System Type	Net Horsepower @ rpm	Net Torque @ rpm (ft. lbs.)	Bore x Stroke (in.)	Compression Ratio	Oil Pressure @ rpm
1996	Escort	1.8 (1844)	8	MFI	127@6500	114@4500	3.27x3.35	9.0:1	28-43@1000
	Escort	1.9 (1901)	J	SFI	88@4400	108@3800	3.23x3.35	9.0:1	35-65@2000
	Tracer	1.8 (1844)	8	MFI	127@6500	114@4500	3.27x3.35	9.0:1	28-43@1000
	Tracer	1.9 (1901)	J	SFI	88@4400	108@3800	3.23x3.35	9.0:1	35-65@2000
1997	Escort	2.0 (1999)	P	SFI	110@5000	125@3750	3.34x3.46	9.2:1	35-65@2000
	Tracer	2.0 (1999)	P	SFI	110@5000	125@3750	3.34x3.46	9.2:1	35-65@2000
1998	Escort	2.0 (1999)	P	SFI	110@5000	125@3750	3.34x3.46	9.2:1	35-65@2000
	Escort ZX2	2.0 (1999)	3	SFI	125@5500	130@4000	3.34x3.46	10.0:1	35-65@2000
	Tracer	2.0 (1999)	P	SFI	110@5000	125@3750	3.34x3.46	9.2:1	35-65@2000
1999-00	Escort	2.0 (1999)	P	SFI	110@5000	125@3750	3.34x3.46	9.2:1	35-65@2000
	Escort ZX2	2.0 (1999)	3	SFI	125@5500	130@4000	3.34x3.46	10.0:1	35-65@2000
	Tracer	2.0 (1999)	P	SFI	110@5000	125@3750	3.34x3.46	9.2:1	35-65@2000

MFI - Multi-point Fuel Injection

SFI - Sequential Fuel Injection

93001C92

ENGINE TUNE-UP SPECIFICATIONS

Year	Engine Displacement Liters (cc)	Engine ID/VIN	Spark Plug Gap (in.)	Ignition Timing (deg.) MT	Ignition Timing (deg.) AT	Fuel Pump (psi)	Idle Speed (rpm) MT	Idle Speed (rpm) AT	Valve Clearance In.	Valve Clearance Ex.
1996	1.8 (1844)	8	0.039-0.043	10B	10B	31-38 ①	750	750	HYD	HYD
	1.9 (1901)	J	0.052-0.056	10B	10B	38-45 ①	②	②	HYD	HYD
1997	2.0 (1999)	P	0.052-0.056	10B	10B	38-45 ①	②	②	HYD	HYD
1998	2.0 (1999)	3	0.052-0.056	10B	10B	31-38 ①	②	②	HYD	HYD
	2.0 (1999)	P	0.052-0.056	10B	10B	38-45 ①	②	②	HYD	HYD
1999-00	2.0 (1999)	3	0.052-0.056	10B	10B	31-38 ①	②	②	HYD	HYD
	2.0 (1999)	P	0.052-0.056	10B	10B	38-45 ①	②	②	HYD	HYD

NOTE: The Vehicle Emission Control Information label often reflects specification changes made during production. The label figures must be used if they differ from those in this chart.

B - Before Top Dead Center

HYD - Hydraulic

① Fuel pressure with engine running, pressure regulator vacuum hose connected

② Refer to Vehicle Emission Control Information label

93001C93

CAPACITIES

Year	Model	Engine Displacement Liters (cc)	Engine ID/VIN	Oil with Filter (qts.)	Transmission (pts.) Manual	Transmission (pts.) Auto. ①	Front Axle (pts.)	Fuel Tank (gal.)	Cooling System (qts.)
1996	Escort	1.8 (1944)	8	4.0	6.7	13.4	②	13.2	6.3
	Escort	1.9 (1901)	J	4.0	5.7	13.4	②	11.9	③
	Tracer	1.8 (1944)	8	4.0	6.7	13.4	②	13.2	6.3
	Tracer	1.9 (1901)	J	4.0	5.7	13.4	②	11.9	③
1997	Escort	2.0 (1999)	P	4.0	6.7	13.4	②	13.2	④
	Tracer	2.0 (1999)	P	4.0	5.7	13.4	②	11.9	④
1998	Escort	2.0 (1999)	P	4.0	5.7	13.4	②	11.9	④
	Escort ZX2	2.0 (1999)	3	4.0	6.7	13.4	②	13.2	⑤
	Tracer	2.0 (1999)	P	4.0	5.7	13.4	②	11.9	④
1999-00	Escort	2.0 (1999)	P	4.0	5.7	13.4	②	11.9	④
	Escort ZX2	2.0 (1999)	3	4.0	6.7	13.4	②	13.2	⑤
	Tracer	2.0 (1999)	P	4.0	5.7	13.4	②	11.9	④

Note: All capacities are approximates. Add fluid gradually and ensure a proper fluid level is obtained.

① Includes torque converter

② Included in transaxle capacity

③ Manual transaxle: 5.3 qts.
   Automatic transaxle: 6.3 qts.

④ Manual transaxle 7.9
   Automatic transaxle 5.8

⑤ Manual transaxle 7.0
   Automatic transaxle 7.5

93001C94

VALVE SPECIFICATIONS

Year	Engine Displacement Liters (cc)	Engine ID/VIN	Seat Angle (deg.)	Face Angle (deg.)	Spring Test Pressure (lbs. @ in.)	Spring Installed Height (in.)	Stem-to-Guide Clearance (in.)		Stem Diameter (in.)	
							Intake	Exhaust	Intake	Exhaust
1996	1.8 (1844)	8	45	45	NA	①	0.0010-0.0024	0.0012-0.0026	0.2350-0.2356	0.2348-0.2354
	1.9 (1901)	J	45	45.6	200@1.09	1.440-1.480	0.0008-0.0027	0.0018-0.0037	0.3159-0.3167	0.3149-0.3156
1997	2.0 (1999)	P	45	45.6	200@1.09	1.420-1.540	0.0008-0.0027	0.0018-0.0037	0.3159-0.3167	0.3149-0.3156
1998	2.0 (1999)	3	45	45	NA	1.346	0.0007-0.0025	0.0014-0.0032	0.2373-0.2379	0.2366-0.2372
	2.0 (1999)	P	45	45.6	200@1.09	1.420-1.540	0.0008-0.0027	0.0018-0.0037	0.3159-0.3167	0.3149-0.3156
1999-00	2.0 (1999)	3	45	45	NA	1.346	0.0007-0.0025	0.0014-0.0032	0.2373-0.2379	0.2366-0.2372
	2.0 (1999)	P	45	45.6	200@1.09	1.420-1.540	0.0008-0.0027	0.0018-0.0037	0.3159-0.3167	0.3149-0.3156

① Spring height measured unloaded
Minimum length: 1.821 in.

93001C95

CRANKSHAFT AND CONNECTING ROD SPECIFICATIONS
All measurements are given in inches.

Year	Engine Displacement Liters (cc)	Engine ID/VIN	Crankshaft				Connecting Rod		
			Main Brg. Journal Dia.	Main Brg. Oil Clearance	Shaft End-play	Thrust on No.	Journal Diameter	Oil Clearance	Side Clearance
1996	1.8 (1844)	8	1.9661-1.9668	0.0008-0.0026	0.0009-0.0012	4	1.7692-1.7699	0.0030	0.0045-0.0103
	1.9 (1901)	J	2.2827-2.2835	0.0008-0.0026	0.0040-0.0080	3	1.8460-1.8468	0.0008-0.0015	0.0045-0.0103
1997	2.0 (1999)	P	2.2827-2.2835	0.0008-0.0026	0.0040-0.0120	3	1.7279-1.7287	0.0008-0.0026	0.0040-0.0110
1998	2.0 (1999)	3	2.2827-2.2835	0.0008-0.0026	0.0040-0.0120	3	1.8461-1.8500	0.0006-0.0028	0.0040-0.0110
	2.0 (1999)	P	2.2827-2.2835	0.0008-0.0026	0.0040-0.0120	3	1.7279-1.7287	0.0008-0.0026	0.0040-0.0110
1999-00	2.0 (1999)	3	2.2827-2.2835	0.0008-0.0026	0.0040-0.0120	3	1.8461-1.8500	0.0006-0.0028	0.0040-0.0110
	2.0 (1999)	P	2.2827-2.2835	0.0008-0.0026	0.0040-0.0120	3	1.7279-1.7287	0.0008-0.0026	0.0040-0.0110

93001C96

PISTON AND RING SPECIFICATIONS

All measurements are given in inches.

Year	Engine Displacement Liters (cc)	Engine ID/VIN	Piston Clearance	Ring Gap			Ring Side Clearance		
				Top Compression	Bottom Compression	Oil Control	Top Compression	Bottom Compression	Oil Control
1996	1.8 (1844)	8	0.0015-0.0020	0.006-0.012	0.006-0.012	0.008-0.028	0.0012-0.0026	0.0012-0.0028	—
	1.9 (1901)	J	0.0012-0.0028	0.010-0.030	0.010-0.030	0.016-0.066	0.0015-0.0032	0.0015-0.0035	—
1997	2.0 (1999)	P	0.0008-0.0027	0.010-0.030	0.010-0.030	0.016-0.066	0.0015-0.0032	0.0015-0.0035	—
1998	2.0 (1999)	3	0.0004-0.0012	0.0118-0.0197	0.0118-0.0197	0.0158-0.0551	0.0015-0.0032	0.0015-0.0035	—
	2.0 (1999)	P	0.0008-0.0027	0.010-0.030	0.010-0.030	0.016-0.066	0.0015-0.0032	0.0015-0.0035	—
1999-00	2.0 (1999)	3	0.0010-0.0022	0.012-0.022	0.012-0.022	0.010-0.039	0.0015-0.0032	0.0015-0.0035	—
	2.0 (1999)	P	0.0008-0.0027	0.010-0.030	0.010-0.030	0.016-0.066	0.0015-0.0032	0.0015-0.0035	—

93001C97

TORQUE SPECIFICATIONS

All readings in ft. lbs.

Year	Engine Displacement Liters (cc)	Engine ID/VIN	Cylinder Head Bolts	Main Bearing Bolts	Rod Bearing Bolts	Crankshaft Damper Bolts	Flywheel Bolts	Manifold		Spark Plugs	Lug Nut
								Intake	Exhaust		
1996	1.8 (1844)	8	50-60	40-43	35-37	80-87	71-76	14-19	28-34	11-17	76
	1.9 (1901)	J	①	67-80	26-30	81-96	54-67	12-15	15-20	8-15	76
1997	2.0 (1999)	P	①	66-79	26-30	80-87	71-76	15-22	15-17	12-15	76
1998	2.0 (1999)	3	②	55-65	③	80-87	71-76	11-12	10-12	10-12	76
	2.0 (1999)	P	①	66-79	26-30	80-87	71-76	15-22	15-17	12-15	76
1999-00	2.0 (1999)	3	②	55-65	③	80-87	71-76	11-12	10-12	10-12	76
	2.0 (1999)	P	①	66-79	26-30	80-87	71-76	15-22	15-17	12-15	76

NOTE: Always follow proper torque patterns

NOTE: Stretch bolts are used in all procedures that require rotating the fastener a certain number of degrees. The bolts stretch and cannot be reused. For reassembly, replace with new fastners.

① Do not reuse cylinder head bolts.
    Step 1: Tighten bolts, in sequence, to 44 ft. lbs.
    Step 2: Loosen bolts approx. two turns,
        retighten in sequence to 44 ft. lbs.
    Step 3: Turn all bolts, in sequence, +90 degrees
    Step 4: Repeat Step 3

② Step 1: 15-22 ft. lbs.
    Step 2: 30-37 ft. lbs.
    Step 3: Rotate 90-120 degrees

③ Step 1: 22-25 ft. lbs.
    Step 2: Rotate each bolt 85-95 degrees

93001C98

Refer to the model specific sections for engine mechanical service procedures

SCHEDULED MAINTENANCE INTERVALS
(FORD ESCORT, MERCURY TRACER (1996))

TO BE SERVICED	TYPE OF SERVICE	VEHICLE MILEAGE INTERVAL (x1000)												
		5	10	15	20	25	30	35	40	45	50	55	60	65
Engine oil & filter	R	✓	✓	✓	✓	✓	✓	✓	✓	✓	✓	✓	✓	✓
Rotate tires	S/I	✓		✓		✓		✓		✓		✓		✓
Cooling system, hoses, clamps & coolant strength (1.9L)	S/I			✓			✓			✓			✓	
Air cleaner element, automatic transmission fluid & filter	R						✓						✓	
Crankcase emission filter (1.9L)	R						✓						✓	
Engine coolant (1.8L)	R						✓						✓	
Engine coolant (1.9L 1996) ①	R										✓			
Accessory drive belt(s) (1.8L)	S/I						✓						✓	
Bolts & nuts on chassis & body	S/I						✓						✓	
Idle speed (1.8L)	S/I						✓						✓	
Clutch pedal operation, brake lines, hoses & connections	S/I						✓						✓	
Cooling system, hoses, clamps & coolant strength (1.8L)	S/I						✓						✓	
Exhaust heat shields, front & rear brakes	S/I						✓						✓	
Front suspension lower arm ball joints, steering operation & linkage, & front wheel driveshaft joint boots	S/I						✓						✓	
Fuel lines & hoses (1.8L)	S/I						✓						✓	
Fuel filter (1.8L)	R												✓	
PCV valve (1.9L)	R												✓	
Spark plugs (1.8L)	R						✓						✓	
Spark plugs (1.9L)	R												✓	

93001C99

SCHEDULED MAINTENANCE INTERVALS
(FORD ESCORT, MERCURY TRACER (1996) (Cont.)

TO BE SERVICED	TYPE OF SERVICE	VEHICLE MILEAGE INTERVAL (x1000)												
		5	10	15	20	25	30	35	40	45	50	55	60	65
Timing belt (1.8L)	R												✓	
Accessory drive belt(s) (1.9L)	S/I												✓	
Evaporative emission hose for emissions (1.8L)	S/I												✓	

① Change initially at 50,000 miles & every 30,000 miles thereafter.

R - Replace   S/I - Service or Inspect

FREQUENT OPERATION MAINTENANCE (SEVERE SERVICE)

If a vehicle is operated under any of the following conditions it is considered severe service:
- Extremely dusty areas.
- 50% or more of the vehicle operation is in 32°C (90°F) or higher temperatures, or constant operation in temperatures below 0°C (32°F).
- Prolonged idling (vehicle operation in stop and go traffic).
- Frequent short running periods (engine does not warm to normal operating temperatures).
- Police, taxi, delivery usage or trailer towing usage.

Oil & oil filter - change every 3000 miles.
Air cleaner element - check every 15,000 miles.
Front & rear brakes - check every 15,000 miles.
Nuts & bolts on chassis & body - check every 15,000 miles.
Automatic transaxle fluid & filter - change every 21,000 miles.

93001CA1

Refer to the model specific sections for fuel system service procedures

SCHEDULED MAINTENANCE INTERVALS
FORD MOTOR COMPANY
FORD ESCORT
MERCURY TRACER

The following should be used as a guide when determining the amount of work required for a particular service. In estimating how long a particular Scheduled Maintenance Service should take, please observe the following:

- **Chilton Time** is time based on field research and data supplied by the vehicle manufacturer.
- Labor time operations are given in hours and tenths of an hour.
- All labor operations, are to be used as a guide.

Mechanic Skill Level Codes:
(A) PRECISION: Really skilled with multiple certification.
(B) GENERAL: Normally skilled with certification.
(C) MAINTENANCE: Semi-skilled working on certification.

	Chilton Time
5000 Mile Service (C)	
All Models	.9
10000 Mile Service (C)	
All Models	.4
15000 Mile Service (C)	
All Models	
1.8L	.9
1.9L	1.0
2.0L	1.1
20000 Mile Service (C)	
All Models	.4
25000 Mile Service (C)	
All Models	.9
30000 Mile Service (B)	
All Models	
1.8L	2.0
1.9L	2.6
2.0L	1.3

	Chilton Time
35000 Mile Service (C)	
All Models	.9
40000 Mile Service (C)	
All Models	.4
45000 Mile Service (C)	
All Models	
1.8L	.9
1.9L	1.0
2.0L	1.1
50000 Mile Service (C)	
All Models	
1.8L	.4
1.9L	.9
2.0L	.7
55000 Mile Service (C)	
All Models	.9
60000 Mile Service (B)	
All Models	
1.8L	5.9
1.9L	2.8
2.0L	1.6

	Chilton Time
65000 Mile Service (C)	
All Models	.9
70000 Mile Service (C)	
1997-99	.4
75000 Mile Service (C)	
1997-99	1.1
80000 Mile Service (C)	
1997-99	.7
85000 Mile Service (C)	
1997-99	.8
90000 Mile Service (C)	
1997-99	1.3
95000 Mile Service (C)	
1997-99	.9
100000 Mile Service (C)	
All Models	.4

93001CA2

FORD MOTOR CO.
Ford Mustang • Thunderbird • Lincoln Mark VIII • Mercury 1996–97 Cougar

ENGINE AND VEHICLE IDENTIFICATION

		Engine						Model Year	
Code ①	Liters (cc)	Cu. In.	Cyl.	Fuel Sys.	Engine Type	Eng. Mfg.		Code ②	Year
4	3.8 (3802)	232	6	SFI	OHV	Ford		T	1996
V	4.6 (4593)	281	8	SFI	DOHC	Ford		V	1997
W	4.6 (4593)	281	8	SFI	SOHC	Ford		W	1998
X	4.6 (4593)	281	8	SFI	SOHC	Ford		X	1999
								Y	2000

OHV - Overhead Valve

SOHC - Single Overhead Camshaft

DOHC - Double Overhead Camshaft

SFI - Sequential Fuel Injection

① 8th position of VIN

② 10th position of VIN

93001CA3

GENERAL ENGINE SPECIFICATIONS
All measurements are given in inches.

Year	Model	Engine Displacement Liters (cc)	Engine Series (ID/VIN)	Fuel System	Net Horsepower @ rpm	Net Torque @ rpm (ft. lbs.)	Bore x Stroke (in.)	Compression Ratio	Oil Pressure @ rpm
1996	Cougar	3.8 (3802)	4	SFI	145@4000	215@2750	3.81x3.39	9.0:1	40-60@2500
	Cougar	4.6 (4593)	W	SFI	205@4250	280@3000	3.55x3.54	9.0:1	20-45@1500
	Mark VIII	4.6 (4593)	V	SFI	①	②	3.55x3.54	9.85:1	20-45@1500
	Mustang	3.8 (3802)	4	SFI	150@4000	215@2750	3.81x3.39	9.0:1	40-60@2500
	Mustang	4.6 (4593)	V	SFI	305@5800	300@4800	3.55x3.54	9.5:1	20-45@1500
	Mustang	4.6 (4593)	W	SFI	215@4400	285@3500	3.55x3.54	9.0:1	20-45@1500
	Thunderbird	3.8 (3802)	4	SFI	145@4000	215@2750	3.81x3.39	9.0:1	40-60@2500
	Thunderbird	4.6 (4593)	W	SFI	205@4250	280@3000	3.55x3.54	9.0:1	20-45@1500
1997	Cougar	3.8 (3802)	4	SFI	145@4000	215@2750	3.81x3.39	9.0:1	40-60@2500
	Cougar	4.6 (4593)	W	SFI	205@4250	280@3000	3.55x3.54	9.0:1	20-45@1500
	Mark VIII	4.6 (4593)	V	SFI	①	②	3.55x3.54	9.85:1	20-45@1500
	Mustang	3.8 (3802)	4	SFI	150@4000	215@2750	3.81x3.39	9.0:1	40-60@2500
	Mustang	4.6 (4593)	V	SFI	305@5800	300@4800	3.55x3.54	9.5:1	20-45@1500
	Mustang	4.6 (4593)	W	SFI	215@4400	285@3500	3.55x3.54	9.0:1	20-45@1500
	Thunderbird	3.8 (3802)	4	SFI	145@4000	215@2750	3.81x3.39	9.0:1	40-60@2500
	Thunderbird	4.6 (4593)	W	SFI	205@4250	280@3000	3.55x3.54	9.0:1	20-45@1500
1998	Mark VIII	4.6 (4593)	V	SFI	①	②	3.55x3.54	9.85:1	20-45@1500
	Mustang	3.8 (3802)	4	SFI	150@4000	215@2750	3.81x3.39	9.0:1	40-60@2500
	Mustang	4.6 (4593)	V	SFI	305@5800	300@4800	3.55x3.54	9.5:1	20-45@1500
	Mustang	4.6 (4593)	X	SFI	215@4400	285@3500	3.55x3.54	9.0:1	20-45@1500
1999-00	Mustang	3.8 (3802)	4	SFI	150@4000	215@2750	3.81x3.39	9.0:1	40-60@2500
	Mustang	4.6 (4593)	V	SFI	305@5800	300@4800	3.55x3.54	9.5:1	20-45@1500
	Mustang	4.6 (4593)	X	SFI	215@4400	285@3500	3.55x3.54	9.0:1	20-45@1500

SFI - Sequential Fuel Injection

① Mark VIII without LSC package: 280@5500
   Mark VIII with LSC package: 290@5750

② Mark VIII without LSC package: 285@4500
   Mark VIII with LSC package: 292@4500

93001CA4

Refer to the model specific sections for engine electrical system service procedures

ENGINE TUNE-UP SPECIFICATIONS

Year	Engine Displacement Liters (cc)	Engine ID/VIN	Spark Plug Gap (in.)	Ignition Timing (deg.) MT	Ignition Timing (deg.) AT	Fuel Pump (psi) ①	Idle Speed (rpm) MT	Idle Speed (rpm) AT	Valve Clearance Intake	Valve Clearance Exhaust
1996	3.8 (3802)	4	0.054	②	②	28-54	②	②	HYD	HYD
	4.6 (4593)	V	0.054	10B	—	35-45	②	—	HYD	HYD
	4.6 (4593)	W	0.054	10B	10B	35-45	②	②	HYD	HYD
1997	3.8 (3802)	4	0.054	②	②	28-54	②	②	HYD	HYD
	4.6 (4593)	V	0.054	10B	—	35-45	②	—	HYD	HYD
	4.6 (4593)	W	0.054	10B	10B	35-45	②	②	HYD	HYD
1998	3.8 (3802)	4	0.054	②	②	28-54	②	②	HYD	HYD
	4.6 (4593)	V	0.054	10B	—	35-45	②	—	HYD	HYD
	4.6 (4593)	X	0.054	10B	10B	35-45	②	②	HYD	HYD
1999-00	3.8 (3802)	4	0.054	②	②	28-54	②	②	HYD	HYD
	4.6 (4593)	V	0.054	10B	—	35-45	②	—	HYD	HYD
	4.6 (4593)	X	0.054	10B	10B	35-45	②	②	HYD	HYD

NOTE: The Vehicle Emission Control Information label often reflects specification changes made during production. The label figures must be used if they differ from those in this chart.

B - Before Top Dead Center

HYD - Hydraulic

① Fuel pressure with engine running, pressure regulator vacuum hose connected

② Refer to Vehicle Emission Control Information label

93001CA5

CAPACITIES

Year	Model	Engine Displacement Liters (cc)	Engine ID/VIN	Engine Oil with Filter (qts.)	Transmission (pts) Manual	Transmission (pts) Auto. ①	Drive Axle Rear (pts.)	Fuel Tank (gal.)	Cooling System (qts.)
1996	Cougar	3.8 (3802)	4	5.0	—	27.8	②	18.0	12.6
	Cougar	4.6 (4593)	W	5.3	—	27.8	②	18.0	14.1
	Mark VIII	4.6 (4593)	V	6.0	—	25.6	3.00	18.0	16.0
	Mustang	3.8 (3802)	4	5.0	5.6	27.8	3.50	15.4	11.8
	Mustang	4.6 (4593)	V	6.0	6.5	27.8	3.75	15.4	14.1
	Mustang	4.6 (4593)	W	③	6.5	25.6	3.75	15.4	14.1
	Thunderbird	3.8 (3802)	4	5.0	—	27.8	②	18.0	12.6
	Thunderbird	4.6 (4593)	W	5.3	—	27.8	②	18.0	14.1
1997	Cougar	3.8 (3802)	4	5.0	—	27.8	②	18.0	12.6
	Cougar	4.6 (4593)	W	5.3	—	27.8	②	18.0	14.1
	Mark VIII	4.6 (4593)	V	6.0	—	25.6	3.00	18.0	16.0
	Mustang	3.8 (3802)	4	5.0	5.6	27.8	3.50	15.4	11.8
	Mustang	4.6 (4593)	V	6.0	6.5	27.8	3.75	15.4	14.1
	Mustang	4.6 (4593)	W	③	6.5	25.6	3.75	15.4	14.1
	Thunderbird	3.8 (3802)	4	5.0	—	27.8	②	18.0	12.6
	Thunderbird	4.6 (4593)	W	5.3	—	27.8	②	18.0	14.1
1998	Mark VIII	4.6 (4593)	V	6.0	—	25.6	3.00	18.0	16.0
	Mustang	3.8 (3802)	4	5.0	5.6	27.8	3.50	15.4	11.8
	Mustang	4.6 (4593)	V	6.0	6.5	27.8	3.75	15.4	14.1
	Mustang	4.6 (4593)	X	③	6.5	25.6	3.75	15.4	14.1
1999-00	Mustang	3.8 (3802)	4	5.0	5.6	27.8	3.50	15.7	11.8
	Mustang	4.6 (4593)	V	6.0	6.5	27.8	3.75	15.7	14.1
	Mustang	4.6 (4593)	X	③	6.5	25.6	3.75	15.7	14.1

NOTE: All capacities are approximate. Add fluid gradually and ensure a proper fluid level is obtained.

① Includes torque converter

② 7.50" limited slip axle: 2.75 pts.

7.50" standard axle: 3.0 pts.

8.80" axle: 3.25 pts.

③ If equipped with an automatic transmission: 6.7 qts.

If equipped with a manual transmission: 6.4 qts.

93001CA6

VALVE SPECIFICATIONS

Year	Engine Displacement Liters (cc)	Engine ID/VIN	Seat Angle (deg.)	Face Angle (deg.)	Spring Test Pressure (lbs. @ in.)	Spring Installed Height (in.)	Stem-to-Guide Clearance (in.) Intake	Stem-to-Guide Clearance (in.) Exhaust	Stem Diameter (in.) Intake	Stem Diameter (in.) Exhaust
1996	3.8 (3802)	4	44.5	45.8	220@1.18	1.650	0.0010-0.0027	0.0015-0.0032	0.3415-0.3423	0.3410-0.3418
	4.6 (4593)	V	45	45.5	160@1.10	1.425	0.0008-0.0027	0.0018-0.0037	0.2746-0.2754	0.2736-0.2744
	4.6 (4593)	W	45	45.5	132@1.10	1.570	0.0008-0.0027	0.0018-0.0037	0.2746-0.2754	0.2736-0.2744
1997	3.8 (3802)	4	44.5	45.8	220@1.18	1.650	0.0010-0.0027	0.0015-0.0032	0.3415-0.3423	0.3410-0.3418
	4.6 (4593)	V	45	45.5	160@1.10	1.425	0.0008-0.0027	0.0018-0.0037	0.2746-0.2754	0.2736-0.2744
	4.6 (4593)	W	45	45.5	132@1.10	1.570	0.0008-0.0027	0.0018-0.0037	0.2746-0.2754	0.2736-0.2744
1998	3.8 (3802)	4	44.5	45.8	220@1.18	1.650	0.0010-0.0027	0.0015-0.0032	0.3415-0.3423	0.3410-0.3418
	4.6 (4593)	V	45	45.5	160@1.10	1.425	0.0008-0.0027	0.0018-0.0037	0.2746-0.2754	0.2736-0.2744
	4.6 (4593)	X	45	45.5	132@1.10	1.570	0.0008-0.0027	0.0018-0.0037	0.2746-0.2754	0.2736-0.2744
1999-00	3.8 (3802)	4	44.7	45.7	224@1.16	1.620	0.0450-0.0900	0.0015-0.0033	0.2738-0.2751	0.2728-0.2741
	4.6 (4593)	V	45	45.5	160@1.03	1.660	0.0008-0.0027	0.0018-0.0037	0.2746-0.275	0.2736-0.2744
	4.6 (4593)	X	45	45.5	161@1.03	1.570	0.0008-0.0027	0.0018-0.0037	0.2746-0.2754	0.2736-0.2744

93001CA7

For accessory drive belt replacement procedures see the model specific sections of this manual

CRANKSHAFT AND CONNECTING ROD SPECIFICATIONS
All measurements are given in inches.

Year	Engine Displacement Liters (cc)	Engine ID/VIN	Crankshaft Main Brg. Journal Dia.	Crankshaft Main Brg. Oil Clearance	Crankshaft Shaft End-play	Thrust on No.	Connecting Rod Journal Diameter	Connecting Rod Oil Clearance	Connecting Rod Side Clearance
1996	3.8 (3802)	4	①	0.0010-0.0014	0.0040-0.0080	3	2.3103-2.3111	0.0010-0.0014	0.0047-0.0144
	4.6 (4593)	V	2.6567-2.6577	0.0001-0.0018	0.0051-0.0119	5	2.0859-2.0867	0.0011-0.0027	0.0006-0.0177
	4.6 (4593)	W	2.6569-2.6576	0.0011-0.0026	0.0051-0.0119	5	2.0861-2.0867	0.0011-0.0027	0.0006-0.0177
1997	3.8 (3802)	4	①	0.0010-0.0014	0.0040-0.0080	3	2.3103-2.3111	0.0010-0.0014	0.0047-0.0144
	4.6 (4593)	V	2.6567-2.6577	0.0001-0.0018	0.0051-0.0119	5	2.0859-2.0867	0.0011-0.0027	0.0006-0.0177
	4.6 (4593)	W	2.6569-2.6576	0.0011-0.0026	0.0051-0.0119	5	2.0861-2.0867	0.0011-0.0027	0.0006-0.0177
1998	3.8 (3802)	4	①	0.0010-0.0014	0.0040-0.0080	3	2.3103-2.3111	0.0010-0.0014	0.0047-0.0144
	4.6 (4593)	V	2.6567-2.6577	0.0001-0.0018	0.0051-0.0119	5	2.0859-2.0867	0.0011-0.0027	0.0006-0.0177
	4.6 (4593)	X	2.6569-2.6576	0.0011-0.0026	0.0051-0.0119	5	2.0861-2.0867	0.0011-0.0027	0.0006-0.0177
1999-00	3.8 (3802)	4	①	0.0010-0.0014	0.0040-0.0080	3	2.3103-2.3111	0.0010-0.0014	0.0047-0.0144
	4.6 (4593)	V	2.6567-2.6577	0.0001-0.0018	0.0051-0.0119	5	2.0859-2.0867	0.0011-0.0027	0.0006-0.0177
	4.6 (4593)	X	2.6569-2.6576	0.0011-0.0026	0.0051-0.0119	5	2.0861-2.0867	0.0011-0.0027	0.0006-0.0177

① Journals 1, 2, 3: 2.5194-2.5186 in.
  Journal 4: 2.5100-2.5092 in.

93001CA8

PISTON AND RING SPECIFICATIONS
All measurements are given in inches.

Year	Engine Displacement Liters (cc)	Engine ID/VIN	Piston Clearance	Ring Gap			Ring Side Clearance		
				Top Compression	Bottom Compression	Oil Control	Top Compression	Bottom Compression	Oil Control
1996	3.8 (3802)	4	0.0014-0.0022	0.011-0.012	0.009-0.020	0.015-0.058	0.0016-0.0034	0.0016-0.0034	SNUG
	4.6 (4593)	V	0.0000-0.0010	0.010-0.020	0.009-0.019	0.006-0.026	0.0003-0.0009	0.0012-0.0031	SNUG
	4.6 (4593)	W	0.0005-0.0010	0.009-0.019	0.009-0.019	0.006-0.026	0.0016-0.0035	0.0018-0.0031	SNUG
1997	3.8 (3802)	4	0.0014-0.0022	0.011-0.012	0.009-0.020	0.015-0.058	0.0016-0.0034	0.0016-0.0034	SNUG
	4.6 (4593)	V	0.0000-0.0010	0.010-0.020	0.009-0.019	0.006-0.026	0.0003-0.0009	0.0012-0.0031	SNUG
	4.6 (4593)	W	0.0005-0.0010	0.009-0.019	0.009-0.019	0.006-0.026	0.0016-0.0035	0.0018-0.0031	SNUG
1998	3.8 (3802)	4	0.0014-0.0022	0.011-0.012	0.009-0.020	0.015-0.058	0.0016-0.0034	0.0016-0.0034	SNUG
	4.6 (4593)	V	0.0000-0.0010	0.010-0.020	0.009-0.019	0.006-0.026	0.0003-0.0009	0.0012-0.0031	SNUG
	4.6 (4593)	X	0.0005-0.0010	0.009-0.019	0.009-0.019	0.006-0.026	0.0016-0.0035	0.0018-0.0031	SNUG
1999-00	3.8 (3802)	4	0.0007-0.0017	0.011-0.012	0.009-0.020	0.015-0.058	0.0016-0.0034	0.0016-0.0034	SNUG
	4.6 (4593)	V	0.0000-0.0010	0.010-0.020	0.009-0.019	0.006-0.026	0.0003-0.0009	0.0012-0.0031	SNUG
	4.6 (4593)	X	0.0005-0.0010	0.009-0.019	0.009-0.019	0.006-0.026	0.0016-0.0035	0.0018-0.0031	SNUG

93001CA9

For brake related suspension and axle service, refer to the model specific sections of this manual

TORQUE SPECIFICATIONS
All readings in ft. lbs.

Year	Engine Displacement Liters (cc)	Engine ID/VIN	Cylinder Head Bolts	Main Bearing Bolts	Rod Bearing Bolts	Crankshaft Damper Bolts	Flywheel Bolts	Manifold		Spark Plugs	Lug Nuts
								Intake	Exhaust		
1996	3.8 (3802)	4	①	65-81	31-36	103-132	54-64	②	15-22	7-15	95
	4.6 (4593)	V	③	④	⑤	114-121	54-64	⑥	13-16	7-15	95
	4.6 (4593)	W	③	⑦	⑧	114-121	54-64	15-22	15-22	7-15	95
1997	3.8 (3802)	4	①	65-81	31-36	103-132	54-64	②	15-22	7-15	95
	4.6 (4593)	V	③	④	⑤	114-121	54-64	⑥	13-16	7-15	95
	4.6 (4593)	W	③	⑦	⑧	114-121	54-64	15-22	15-22	7-15	95
1998	3.8 (3802)	4	①	65-81	31-36	103-132	54-64	②	15-22	7-15	95
	4.6 (4593)	V	③	④	⑤	114-121	54-64	⑥	13-16	7-15	95
	4.6 (4593)	X	③	⑦	⑧	114-121	54-64	15-22	15-22	7-15	95
1999-00	3.8 (3802)	4	①	⑨	⑩	118	54-64	②	15-22	7-15	95
	4.6 (4593)	V	⑪	④	⑤	114-121	54-64	⑥	13-16	7-15	95
	4.6 (4593)	X	③	⑦	⑧	114-121	54-64	15-22	15-22	7-15	95

① Do not reuse cylinder head bolts.
Step 1: 15 ft. lbs.
Step 2: 29 ft. lbs.
Step 3: 37 ft. lbs.
Step 4: Loosen bolts one at a time and retorque as follows:
Long bolts: 11-18 ft. lbs.
Short bolts: 7-15 ft. lbs.
Step 5: Tighten 85-95 degrees

② Upper intake manifold bolts:
Step 1: 8 ft. lbs.
Step 2: 15 ft. lbs.
Step 3: 24 ft. lbs
Lower intake manifold bolts:
Step 1: 13 ft. lbs.
Step 2: 16 ft. lbs.

③ Do not reuse cylinder head bolts.
Step 1: 27-32 ft. lbs.
Step 2: Tighten each bolt 85-95 degrees
Step 3: Repeat Step 2

④ Step 1: Main bearing cap bolts: 6-9 ft. lbs.
Step 2: Main bearing cap bolts, outer: 16-21 ft. lbs.
Step 3: Main bearing cap bolts, inner: 27-32 ft. lbs.
Step 4: Tighten main bearing cap bolts 85-95 degrees
Step 5: Main cap adjusting screws: 4 ft. lbs. then 7.5 ft. lbs.
Step 6: Main cap side bolts: 7 ft. lbs. then 14-17 ft. lbs.

⑤ Step 1: 5 ft. lbs.
Step 2: 10 ft. lbs.
Step 3: 18-25 ft. lbs.
Step 4: Tighten 85-95 degrees

⑥ Step 1: Four inside short bolts: 9-11 ft. lbs.
Step 2: All other bolts: 13-16 ft. lbs.
Step 3: Tighten 85-95 degrees

⑦ Do not reuse main cap bolts.
Step 1: Main bearing cap bolts: 22-25 ft. lbs.
Step 2: Tighten each bolt 85-95 degrees
Step 3: Main bearing cap adjust screws: 4 ft. lbs. then 6-8 ft. lbs.
Step 4: Main bearing cap side bolts: 7 ft. lbs. then 14-17 ft. lbs.

⑧ Do not reuse rod bolts.
Step 1: 12 ft. lbs.
Step 2: Tighten 85-95 degrees

⑨ Step 1: 37 ft. lbs.
Step 2: Tighten 115-125 degrees

⑩ Step 1: 18 ft. lbs.
Step 2: 33 ft. lbs.
Step 3: Tighten 90-120 degrees

⑪ Step 1: 30 ft. lbs.
Step 2: Tighten 90 degrees
Step 3: Loosen all bolts one (1) turn
Step 4: 30 ft. lbs.
Step 5: Tighten 90 degrees
Step 6: Tighten an additional 90 degrees

93001CA0

SCHEDULED MAINTENANCE INTERVALS
(FORD MUSTANG, THUNDERBIRD, LINCOLN MARK VIII, MERCURY COUGAR)

TO BE SERVICED	TYPE OF SERVICE	VEHICLE MILEAGE INTERVAL (x1000)												
		5	10	15	20	25	30	35	40	45	50	55	60	65
Engine oil & filter	R	✓	✓	✓	✓	✓	✓	✓	✓	✓	✓	✓	✓	✓
Adjust clutch pedal by lifting pedal	S/I	✓	✓	✓	✓	✓	✓	✓	✓	✓	✓	✓	✓	✓
Rotate tires	S/I	✓		✓		✓		✓		✓		✓		✓
Cooling system, hoses, clamps & coolant strength	S/I			✓			✓			✓			✓	
Lubricate steering linkage (T-Bird/Cougar)	S/I			✓			✓			✓			✓	
Air cleaner element	R						✓						✓	
Automatic transmission fluid & filter	R						✓						✓	
Engine coolant ①	R						✓						✓	
Spark plugs (Mark VIII) ②	R													
Spark plugs (T-Bird & Cougar)	R												✓	
Spark plugs (Mustang) -	R													
Accessory drive belt(s)	S/I						✓						✓	
Brake lines, hoses & connections	S/I						✓						✓	
Clutch fluid level (T-Bird)	S/I						✓						✓	
Exhaust heat shields	S/I						✓						✓	
Front & rear brakes	S/I						✓						✓	
PCV valve	R												✓	
Rear axle lubricant ②	R													
Supercharger fluid level	S/I												✓	

① Engine coolant - change engine coolant at 48,000 to 50,000 miles and thereafter every 30,000 miles.

② Replace every 100,000 miles.

R - Replace   S/I - Service or Inspect

93001CB1

Refer to the model specific sections for driveline service procedures

SCHEDULED MAINTENANCE INTERVALS
FORD MOTOR COMPANY
FORD MUSTANG, THUNDERBIRD
LINCOLN MARK VIII, MERCURY COUGAR (1996-97)

The following should be used as a guide when determining the amount of work required for a particular service.
In estimating how long a particular Scheduled Maintenance Service should take, please observe the following:

- **Chilton Time** is time based on field research and data supplied by the vehicle manufacturer.
- Labor time operations are given in hours and tenths of an hour.
- All labor operations, are to be used as a guide.

Mechanic Skill Level Codes:
(A) PRECISION: Really skilled with multiple certification.
(B) GENERAL: Normally skilled with certification.
(C) MAINTENANCE: Semi-skilled working on certification.

	Chilton Time
5000 Mile Service (C)	
All Models	1.0
10000 Mile Service (C)	
All Models	.5
15000 Mile Service (C)	
All Models	1.2
20000 Mile Service (C)	
All Models	.5
25000 Mile Service (C)	
All Models	1.0

	Chilton Time
30000 Mile Service (B)	
1996-00 Mustang	3.3
1996-98 Mark VIII	3.5
1996-97 Thunderbird	3.7
1996-97 Cougar	3.5
35000 Mile Service (C)	
All Models	1.0
40000 Mile Service (C)	
All Models	.5
45000 Mile Service (C)	
1996-00 Mustang	1.2
50000 Mile Service (C)	
All Models	.5

	Chilton Time
55000 Mile Service (C)	
1996-00 Mustang	1.0
60000 Mile Service (B)	
1996-00 Mustang	3.8
1996-98 Mark VIII	4.0
1996-97 Thunderbird	3.7
1996-97 Cougar	3.5
65000 Mile Service (C)	
All Models	1.0

93001CB2

FORD MOTOR CO.
Ford Probe

ENGINE AND VEHICLE IDENTIFICATION

		Engine Code						Model Year	
Code ①	Liters (cc)	Cu. In.	Cyl.	Fuel Sys.	Engine Type	Eng. Mfg.		Code ②	Year
A	2.0 (1993)	122	4	MFI	DOHC	Mazda		T	1996
B	2.5 (2501)	153	6	MFI	DOHC	Mazda		V	1997

MFI - Multi-point Fuel Injection

DOHC - Double Overhead Camshafts

① 8th digit of the VIN

② 10th digit of the VIN

93001CB3

GENERAL ENGINE SPECIFICATIONS
All measurements are given in inches.

Year	Model	Engine Displacement Liters (cc)	Engine (ID/VIN)	Fuel System	Net Horsepower @ rpm	Net Torque @ rpm (ft. lbs.)	Bore x Stroke (in.)	Compression Ratio	Oil Pressure @ rpm
1996	Probe	2.0 (1993)	A	SFI	118 @ 5500	127 @ 4500	3.27x3.62	9.0:1	57-71 @ 2000
	Probe	2.5 (2501)	B	SFI	①	②	3.33x2.92	9.2:1	49-71 @ 3000
1997	Probe	2.0 (1993)	A	SFI	118 @ 5500	127 @ 4500	3.27x3.62	9.0:1	57-71 @ 2000
	Probe	2.5 (2501)	B	SFI	①	②	3.33x2.92	9.2:1	49-71 @ 3000

SFI - Sequential Fuel Injection

① California: 160 @ 5500
   Except California: 164 @ 5600

② California: 156 @ 5000
   Except California: 160 @ 4800

93001CB4

ENGINE TUNE-UP SPECIFICATIONS

Year	Engine Displacement Liters (cc)	Engine ID/VIN	Spark Plug Gap (in.)	Ignition Timing (deg.) MT	Ignition Timing (deg.) AT	Fuel Pump (psi) ①	Idle Speed (rpm) MT	Idle Speed (rpm) AT	Valve Clearance In.	Valve Clearance Ex.
1996	2.0 (1993)	A	0.041	10B	12B	30-38	700	700	HYD	HYD
	2.5 (2501)	B	0.041	10B	10B	30-36	700	700	HYD	HYD
1997	2.0 (1993)	A	0.041	10B	12B	30-38	700	700	HYD	HYD
	2.5 (2501)	B	0.041	10B	10B	30-36	700	700	HYD	HYD

NOTE: The Vehicle Emission Control Information label often reflects specification changes made during production. The label figures must be used if they differ from those in this chart.

HYD - Hydraulic

① Fuel pressure with engine running, pressure regulator vacuum hose connected.

93001CB4A

For exhaust manifold replacement procedures, see the model specific sections of this manual

CAPACITIES

Year	Model	Engine Displacement Liters (cc)	Engine ID/VIN	Engine Oil with Filter (qts.)	Transaxle (pts)		Drive Axle (pts.)	Fuel Tank (gal.)	Cooling System (qts.)
					Manual	Automatic ①			
1996	Probe	2.0 (1993)	A	3.7	5.8	17.6	②	15.5	7.4
	Probe	2.5 (2501)	B	4.2	5.8	14.4	②	15.5	7.9
1997	Probe	2.0 (1993)	A	3.7	5.8	17.6	②	15.5	7.4
	Probe	2.5 (2501)	B	4.2	5.8	14.4	②	15.5	7.9

NOTE: All capacities are approximate. Add fluid gradually and ensure a proper fluid level is obtained.

① Includes torque converter

② Included in transaxle capacity

93001CB5

VALVE SPECIFICATIONS

Year	Engine Displacement Liters (cc)	Engine ID/VIN	Seat Angle (deg.)	Face Angle (deg.)	Spring Out-of-Square (in.)	Spring Free-Length (in.)	Stem-to-Guide Clearance (in.)		Stem Diameter (in.)	
							Intake	Exhaust	Intake	Exhaust
1996	2.0 (1993)	A	45	45	0.061	1.732	0.0010-0.0024	0.0012-0.0026	0.2350-0.2356	0.2348-0.2354
	2.5 (2501)	B	45	45	0.642	①	0.0010-0.0023	0.0012-0.0026	0.2351-0.2356	0.2349-0.2354
1997	2.0 (1993)	A	45	45	0.061	1.732	0.0010-0.0024	0.0012-0.0026	0.2350-0.2356	0.2348-0.2354
	2.5 (2501)	B	45	45	0.642	①	0.0010-0.0023	0.0012-0.0026	0.2351-0.2356	0.2349-0.2354

① Spring-free length: Intake: 1.729, Exhaust: 1.847

93001CB6

CRANKSHAFT AND CONNECTING ROD SPECIFICATIONS
All measurements are given in inches.

Year	Engine Displacement Liters (cc)	Engine ID/VIN	Crankshaft				Connecting Rod		
			Main Brg. Journal Dia.	Main Brg. Oil Clearance	Shaft End-play	Thrust on No.	Journal Diameter	Oil Clearance	Side Clearance
1996	2.0 (1993)	A	2.2022-2.2029	①	0.0031-0.0111	4	1.8874-1.8880	0.0005-0.0015	0.0043-0.0103
	2.5 (2501)	B	2.4385-2.4392	0.0015-0.0022	0.0032-0.0111	4	2.0841-2.0848	0.0009-0.0017	0.0070-0.0130
1997	2.0 (1993)	A	2.2022-2.2029	①	0.0031-0.0111	4	1.8874-1.8880	0.0005-0.0015	0.0043-0.0103
	2.5 (2501)	B	2.4385-2.4392	0.0015-0.0022	0.0032-0.0111	4	2.0841-2.0848	0.0009-0.0017	0.0070-0.0130

① No. 1, 2, 4 & 5: 0.0009-0.0020 in.
No. 3: 0.0012-0.0022 in.

93001CB7

PISTON AND RING SPECIFICATIONS
All measurements are given in inches.

Year	Engine Displacement Liters (cc)	Engine ID/VIN	Piston Clearance	Ring Gap			Ring Side Clearance		
				Top Compression	Bottom Compression	Oil Control	Top Compression	Bottom Compression	Oil Control
1996	2.0 (1993)	A	0.0015-0.0020	0.006-0.012	0.006-0.012	0.008-0.028	0.0014-0.0026	0.0014-0.0026	SNUG
	2.5 (2501)	B	0.0012-0.0022	0.0060-0.0118	0.010-0.015	0.008-0.027	0.0008-0.0026	0.0010-0.0015	SNUG
1997	2.0 (1993)	A	0.0015-0.0020	0.006-0.012	0.006-0.012	0.008-0.028	0.0014-0.0026	0.0014-0.0026	SNUG
	2.5 (2501)	B	0.0012-0.0022	0.0060-0.0118	0.010-0.015	0.008-0.027	0.0008-0.0026	0.0010-0.0015	SNUG

93001CB8

TORQUE SPECIFICATIONS
All readings in ft. lbs.

Year	Engine Displacement Liters (cc)	Engine ID/VIN	Cylinder Head Bolts	Main Bearing Bolts	Rod Bearing Bolts	Crankshaft Damper Bolts	Flywheel Bolts	Manifold		Spark Plugs	Lug Nut
								Intake	Exhaust		
1996	2.0 (1993)	A	①	②	③	116-123	70-75	14-19	14-21	11-17	85
	2.5 (2501)	B	①	④	③	116-123	45-49	14-18	14-18	11-16	85
1997	2.0 (1993)	A	①	②	③	116-123	70-75	14-19	14-21	11-17	85
	2.5 (2501)	B	①	④	③	116-123	45-49	14-18	14-18	11-16	85

NOTE: Always follow proper torque patterns. Stretch bolts are used in all procedures that require rotating the fastener a certain number of degrees.

The bolts stretch and cannot be reused. For reassembly, replace with new fastners.

① Step 1: 8-10 ft. lbs.
  Step 2: 13-16 ft. lbs.
  Step 3: Tighten 90 degrees
  Step 4: Repeat Step 3

② Step 1: 12 ft. lbs.
  Step 2: Tighten each bolt 85-95 degrees

③ 16-19 ft. lbs. plus 90 degrees

④ Step 1: Inner main bolts: 10-12 ft. lbs.
  Step 2: Inner main bolts: 17-19 ft. lbs.
  Step 3: Outer main bolts: 6-8 ft. lbs.
  Step 4: Outer main bolts: 13-15 ft. lbs.
  Step 5: Tighten inner bolts 75 degrees
  Step 6: Tighten outer bolts 60 degrees
  Step 7: Repeat Steps 5 and 6
  Step 8: Outer cylinder block bolts: 14-15 ft. lbs.

93001CB9

Refer to the model specific sections for cooling system service procedures

SCHEDULED MAINTENANCE INTERVALS
(FORD PROBE)

TO BE SERVICED	TYPE OF SERVICE	VEHICLE MILEAGE INTERVAL (x1000)												
		5	10	15	20	25	30	35	40	45	50	55	60	65
Engine oil & filter	R	✓	✓	✓	✓	✓	✓	✓	✓	✓	✓	✓	✓	✓
Rotate tires	S/I	✓		✓		✓		✓		✓		✓		✓
Air cleaner element	R						✓						✓	
Spark plugs	R						✓						✓	
Automatic transmission fluid & filter	R						✓						✓	
Exhaust heat shields	S/I						✓						✓	
Front & rear brakes	S/I						✓						✓	
Accessory drive belt(s)	S/I						✓						✓	
Fuel lines & hoses	S/I						✓						✓	
Cooling system, hoses, clamps & coolant strength	S/I						✓						✓	
Front wheel driveshaft joint boots	S/I						✓						✓	
Brake lines, hoses & connections	S/I						✓						✓	
Front suspension ball joints, steering operation & linkage	S/I						✓						✓	
Idle speed	S/I						✓						✓	
Bolts & nuts on chassis & body	S/I						✓						✓	
Engine coolant	R										✓			
Timing belt/chain & fuel filter	R												✓	
Fuel lines & tubes (emission)	S/I												✓	

R – Replace   S/I – Service or Inspect

FREQUENT OPERATION MAINTENANCE (SEVERE SERVICE)

If a vehicle is operated under any of the following conditions it is considered severe service:
- Extremely dusty areas.
- 50% or more of the vehicle operation is in 32°C (90°F) or higher temperatures, or constant operation in temperatures below 0°C (32°F).
- Prolonged idling (vehicle operation in stop and go traffic).
- Frequent short running periods (engine does not warm to normal operating temperatures).
- Police, taxi, delivery usage or trailer towing usage.

Oil & oil filter – change every 3000 miles.
Air cleaner element - check every 15,000 miles.
Bolts & nuts on chassis & body - check every 15,000 miles.
Front & rear brakes - check every 15,000 miles.
Automatic transaxle fluid & filter - change every 21,000 miles.

79221CC7

SCHEDULED MAINTENANCE INTERVALS
FORD MOTOR COMPANY
FORD PROBE

The following should be used as a guide when determining the amount of work required for a particular service.
In estimating how long a particular Scheduled Maintenance Service should take, please observe the following:

- **Chilton Time** is time based on field research and data supplied by the vehicle manufacturer.
- Labor time operations are given in hours and tenths of an hour.
- All labor operations, are to be used as a guide.

Mechanic Skill Level Codes:
(A) PRECISION: Really skilled with multiple certification.
(B) GENERAL: Normally skilled with certification.
(C) MAINTENANCE: Semi-skilled working on certification.

	Chilton Time			Chilton Time			Chilton Time
5000 Mile Service (C)			**25000 Mile Service (C)**			**50000 Mile Service (C)**	
All Models	.9		All Models	.9		All Models	1.1
10000 Mile Service (C)			**30000 Mile Service (B)**			**55000 Mile Service (C)**	
All Models	.4		All Models	3.3		All Models	.9
15000 Mile Service (C)			**35000 Mile Service (C)**			**60000 Mile Service (B)**	
All Models	.9		All Models	.9		All Models	5.4
20000 Mile Service (C)			**40000 Mile Service (C)**			**65000 Mile Service (C)**	
All Models	.4		All Models	.4		All Models	.9
			45000 Mile Service (C)				
			All Models	.9			

93001CC1

For complete service labor times order Chilton's Labor Guide Manual

FORD MOTOR CO.
Ford Taurus • Taurus SHO • Lincoln Continental • Mercury Sable

ENGINE AND VEHICLE IDENTIFICATION

Engine							Model Year	
Code ①	Liters (cc)	Cu. In.	Cyl.	Fuel Sys.	Engine Type	Eng. Mfg.	Code ②	Year
N	3.4 (3393)	207	8	SFI	DOHC	Yamaha	T	1996
S	3.0 (3049)	182	6	SFI	DOHC	Ford	V	1997
U	3.0 (2982)	181	6	SFI	OHV	Ford	W	1998
V	4.6 (4593)	281	8	SFI	DOHC	Ford	X	1999
							Y	2000

OHV - Overhead Valves

DOHC - Double Overhead Camshafts

SFI - Sequential Fuel Injection

① 8th digit of the Vehicle Identification Number (VIN)

② 10th digit of the Vehicle Identification Number (VIN)

93001CC2

GENERAL ENGINE SPECIFICATIONS

Year	Model	Engine Displacement Liters (cc)	Engine ID/VIN	Fuel System Type	Net Horsepower @ rpm	Net Torque @ rpm (ft. lbs.)	Bore x Stroke (in.)	Compression Ratio	Oil Pressure @ rpm
1996	Continental	4.6 (4593)	V	SFI	260@5750	265@4750	3.55x3.54	9.8:1	33@1500
	Sable	3.0 (2982)	U	SFI	145@5250	170@3250	3.50x3.15	9.3:1	40-60@2500
	Sable	3.0 (2998)	S	SFI	200@5750	200@4500	3.50x3.13	10.0:1	20-45@1500
	Taurus	3.0 (2982)	U	SFI	145@5250	170@3250	3.50x3.15	9.3:1	40-60@2500
	Taurus	3.0 (2998)	S	SFI	200@5750	200@4500	3.50x3.13	10.0:1	20-45@1500
	Taurus SHO	3.4 (3393)	N	SFI	235@6100	230@4800	3.25x3.13	10.0:1	20-45@1500
1997	Continental	4.6 (4593)	V	SFI	260@5750	265@4750	3.55x3.54	9.8:1	33@1500
	Sable	3.0 (2982)	U	SFI	145@5250	170@3250	3.50x3.15	9.3:1	40-60@2500
	Sable	3.0 (2998)	S	SFI	200@5750	200@4500	3.50x3.13	10.0:1	20-45@1500
	Taurus	3.0 (2982)	U	SFI	145@5250	170@3250	3.50x3.15	9.3:1	40-60@2500
	Taurus	3.0 (2998)	S	SFI	200@5750	200@4500	3.50x3.13	10.0:1	20-45@1500
	Taurus SHO	3.4 (3393)	N	SFI	235@6100	230@4800	3.25x3.13	10.0:1	20-45@1500
1998	Continental	4.6 (4593)	V	SFI	260@5750	270@3000	3.55x3.54	9.8:1	33@1500
	Sable	3.0 (2982)	U	SFI	145@5250	170@3250	3.50x3.15	9.3:1	40-60@2500
	Sable	3.0 (2998)	S	SFI	200@5750	200@4500	3.50x3.13	10.0:1	20-45@1500
	Taurus	3.0 (2982)	U	SFI	145@5250	170@3250	3.50x3.15	9.3:1	40-60@2500
	Taurus	3.0 (2998)	S	SFI	200@5750	200@4500	3.50x3.13	10.0:1	20-45@1500
	Taurus SHO	3.4 (3393)	N	SFI	235@6100	230@4800	3.25x3.13	10.0:1	20-45@1500
1999-00	Continental	4.6 (4593)	V	SFI	260@5750	270@3000	3.55x3.54	9.8:1	33@1500
	Sable	3.0 (2982)	U	SFI	145@5250	170@3250	3.50x3.15	9.3:1	40-60@2500
	Sable	3.0 (2998)	S	SFI	200@5750	200@4500	3.50x3.13	10.0:1	20-45@1500
	Taurus	3.0 (2982)	U	SFI	145@5250	170@3250	3.50x3.15	9.3:1	40-60@2500
	Taurus	3.0 (2998)	S	SFI	200@5750	200@4500	3.50x3.13	10.0:1	20-45@1500
	Taurus SHO	3.4 (3393)	N	SFI	235@6100	230@4800	3.25x3.13	10.0:1	20-45@1500

SFI - Sequential Fuel Injection

93001CC3

ENGINE TUNE-UP SPECIFICATIONS

Year	Engine Displacement Liters (cc)	Engine ID/VIN	Spark Plug Gap (in.)	Ignition Timing (deg.)	Fuel Pump (psi) ①	Idle Speed (rpm)	Valve Clearance	
							Intake	**Exhaust**
1996	3.0 (2982)	U	0.042-0.046	10B	30-45	②	HYD	HYD
	3.0 (2998)	S	0.052-0.056	10B	30-45	②	HYD	HYD
	3.4 (3393)	N	0.042-0.046	10B	35-45	②	0.006-0.010	0.010-0.014
	4.6 (4593)	V	0.052-0.056	10B	30-45	②	HYD	HYD
1997	3.0 (2982)	U	0.042-0.046	10B	30-45	②	HYD	HYD
	3.0 (2998)	S	0.052-0.056	10B	30-45	②	HYD	HYD
	3.4 (3393)	N	0.042-0.046	10B	35-45	②	0.006-0.010	0.010-0.014
	4.6 (4593)	V	0.052-0.056	10B	30-45	②	HYD	HYD
1998	3.0 (2982)	U	0.042-0.046	10B	30-45	②	HYD	HYD
	3.0 (2998)	S	0.052-0.056	10B	30-45	②	HYD	HYD
	3.4 (3393)	N	0.042-0.046	10B	35-45	②	0.006-0.010	0.010-0.014
	4.6 (4593)	V	0.052-0.056	10B	30-45	②	HYD	HYD
1999-00	3.0 (2982)	U	0.042-0.046	10B	26-45	②	HYD	HYD
	3.0 (2998)	S	0.052-0.056	10B	26-45	②	HYD	HYD
	3.4 (3393)	N	0.042-0.046	NA	35-45	②	0.006-0.010	0.010-0.014
	4.6 (4593)	V	0.052-0.056	10B	30-45	②	HYD	HYD

NOTE: The Vehicle Emission Control Information label often reflects specification changes made during production. The label figures must be used if they differ from those in this chart.

B - Before Top Dead Center

HYD - Hydraulic

NA - Not Adjustable

① Fuel pressure with engine running, pressure regulator vacuum hose connected

② Refer to Vehicle Emission Control Information label

93001CC4

Timing chain and gear service is covered in the model specific sections of this manual

CAPACITIES

Year	Model	Engine Displacement Liters (cc)	Engine ID/VIN	Engine Oil with Filter (qts.)	Transaxle (pts.) Auto. ①	Drive Axle (pts.)	Fuel Tank (gal.)	Cooling System (qts.)
1996	Continental	4.6 (4593)	V	6.0	27.4	②	17.8	14.3
	Sable	3.0 (2982)	U	4.5	24.5	②	③	11.6
	Sable	3.0 (2998)	S	5.8	27.0	②	③	10.5
	Taurus	3.0 (2982)	U	4.5	24.5	②	③	11.6
	Taurus	3.0 (2998)	S	5.8	27.0	②	③	10.5
	Taurus SHO	3.4 (3393)	N	5.8	27.0	②	③	10.8
1997	Continental	4.6 (4593)	V	6.0	27.4	②	17.8	14.3
	Sable	3.0 (2982)	U	4.5	24.5	②	③	11.6
	Sable	3.0 (2998)	S	5.8	27.0	②	③	10.5
	Taurus	3.0 (2982)	U	4.5	24.5	②	③	11.6
	Taurus	3.0 (2998)	S	5.8	27.0	②	③	10.5
	Taurus SHO	3.4 (3393)	N	5.8	27.0	②	③	10.8
1998	Continental	4.6 (4593)	V	6.0	27.4	②	17.8	14.3
	Sable	3.0 (2982)	U	4.5	24.5	②	③	11.6
	Sable	3.0 (2998)	S	5.8	27.0	②	③	10.5
	Taurus	3.0 (2982)	U	4.5	24.5	②	③	11.6
	Taurus	3.0 (2998)	S	5.8	27.0	②	③	10.5
	Taurus SHO	3.4 (3393)	N	5.8	27.0	②	③	10.8
1999-00	Continental	4.6 (4593)	V	6.0	27.4	②	17.8	14.3
	Sable	3.0 (2982)	U	4.5	24.5	②	③	11.6
	Sable	3.0 (2998)	S	5.8	27.0	②	③	10.5
	Taurus	3.0 (2982)	U	4.5	24.5	②	③	11.6
	Taurus	3.0 (2998)	S	5.8	27.0	②	③	10.5
	Taurus SHO	3.4 (3393)	N	6.7	27.0	②	③	10.8

NOTE: All capacities are approximate. Add fluid gradually and ensure a proper fluid level is obtained.

① Includes torque converter

② Included in transaxle capacity

③ Standard tank: 16.0 gals.

    Optional extended range tank: 18.6 gals.

93001CC5

VALVE SPECIFICATIONS

Year	Engine Displacement Liters (cc)	Engine ID/VIN	Seat Angle (deg.)	Face Angle (deg.)	Spring Test Pressure (lbs. @ in.)	Spring Installed Height (in.)	Stem-to-Guide Clearance (in.)		Stem Diameter (in.)	
							Intake	Exhaust	Intake	Exhaust
1996	3.0 (2982)	U	45	44	180@1.16	1.580	0.0001-0.0028	0.0015-0.0033	0.3126-0.3134	0.3121-0.3129
	3.0 (2998)	S	44.75	45.5	153@1.18	1.570	0.0007-0.0027	0.0017-0.0037	0.2350-0.2358	0.2343-0.2350
	3.4 (3393)	N	45	45.5	89@1.00	1.360	0.0010-0.0023	0.0012-0.0025	0.2346-0.2352	0.2344-0.2350
	4.6 (4593)	V	45	45.5	160@1.103	1.425	0.0008-0.0027	0.0018-0.0037	0.2746-0.2754	0.2736-0.2744
1997	3.0 (2982)	U	45	44	180@1.16	1.580	0.0001-0.0028	0.0015-0.0033	0.3126-0.3134	0.3121-0.3129
	3.0 (2998)	S	44.75	45.5	153@1.18	1.570	0.0007-0.0027	0.0017-0.0037	0.2350-0.2358	0.2343-0.2350
	3.4 (3393)	N	45	45.5	89@1.00	1.360	0.0010-0.0023	0.0012-0.0025	0.2346-0.2352	0.2344-0.2350
	4.6 (4593)	V	45	45.5	160@1.103	1.425	0.0008-0.0027	0.0018-0.0037	0.2746-0.2754	0.2736-0.2744
1998	3.0 (2982)	U	45	44	180@1.16	1.580	0.0001-0.0027	0.0015-0.0033	0.3126-0.3134	0.3121-0.3129
	3.0 (2998)	S	44.75	45.5	153@1.18	1.570	0.0007-0.0027	0.0017-0.0037	0.2350-0.2358	0.2343-0.2350
	3.4 (3393)	N	45	45.5	89@1.00	1.360	0.0010-0.0023	0.0012-0.0025	0.2346-0.2352	0.2344-0.2350
	4.6 (4593)	V	45	45.5	160@1.103	1.425	0.0008-0.0027	0.0018-0.0037	0.2746-0.2754	0.2736-0.2744
1999-00	3.0 (2982)	U	45	44	180@1.16	1.580	0.0010-0.0028	0.0015-0.0033	0.3126-0.3134	0.3121-0.3129
	3.0 (2998)	S	44.75	45.5	153@1.18	1.570	0.0007-0.0027	0.0017-0.0037	0.2350-0.2358	0.2343-0.2350
	3.4 (3393)	N	45	45.5	89@1.00	1.360	0.0010-0.0023	0.0012-0.0025	0.2346-0.2352	0.2344-0.2350
	4.6 (4593)	V	45	45.5	160@1.103	1.425	0.0008-0.0027	0.0018-0.0045	0.2746-0.2754	0.2736-0.2744

93001CC6

Ignition system service is covered in the model specific sections of this manual

CRANKSHAFT AND CONNECTING ROD SPECIFICATIONS
All measurements are given in inches.

Year	Engine Displacement Liters (cc)	Engine ID/VIN	Crankshaft				Connecting Rod		
			Main Brg. Journal Dia.	Main Brg. Oil Clearance	Shaft End-play	Thrust on No.	Journal Diameter	Oil Clearance	Side Clearance
1996	3.0 (2982)	U	2.5190-2.5198	0.0009 0.0030	0.0040 0.0080	3	2.1253-2.1261	0.0009 0.0030	0.0060 0.0140
	3.0 (2998)	S	2.4670-2.4790	0.0009-0.0018	0.0040 0.0090	4	1.9670-1.9680	0.0010-0.0025	0.0039-0.0118
	3.4 (3393)	N	2.4794-2.4803	0.0004-0.0012	0.0024-0.0103	3	1.9765-1.9685	0.0009-0.0023	0.0060-0.0120
	4.6 (4593)	V	2.6580-2.6576	0.0010-0.0018	0.0051-0.0119	5	2.0859-2.0867	0.0011-0.0027	0.0059-0.0177
1997	3.0 (2982)	U	2.5190-2.5198	0.0009 0.0030	0.0040 0.0080	3	2.1253-2.1261	0.0009 0.0030	0.0060 0.0140
	3.0 (2998)	S	2.4670-2.4790	0.0009-0.0018	0.0040 0.0090	4	1.9670-1.9680	0.0010-0.0025	0.0039-0.0118
	3.4 (3393)	N	2.4794-2.4803	0.0004-0.0012	0.0024-0.0103	3	1.9765-1.9685	0.0009-0.0023	0.0060-0.0120
	4.6 (4593)	V	2.6580-2.6576	0.0010-0.0018	0.0051-0.0119	5	2.0859-2.0867	0.0011-0.0027	0.0059-0.0177
1998	3.0 (2982)	U	2.5190-2.5198	0.0009 0.0030	0.0040 0.0080	3	2.1253-2.1261	0.0009 0.0030	0.0060 0.0140
	3.0 (2998)	S	2.4670-2.4790	0.0009-0.0018	0.0040-0.0090	4	1.9670-1.9680	0.0010-0.0025	0.0039-0.0118
	3.4 (3393)	N	2.4794-2.4803	0.0004-0.0012	0.0024-0.0103	3	1.9765-1.9685	0.0009-0.0023	0.0060-0.0120
	4.6 (4593)	V	2.6580-2.6576	0.0010-0.0018	0.0051-0.0119	5	2.0859-2.0867	0.0011-0.0027	0.0059-0.0177
1999-00	3.0 (2982)	U	2.5190-2.5198	0.0009 0.0027	0.0040 0.0080	3	2.1253-2.1261	0.0009 0.0027	0.0060 0.0140
	3.0 (2998)	S	2.4670-2.4790	0.0009-0.0018	0.0040 0.0090	4	1.9670-1.9680	0.0010 0.0025	0.0039-0.0118
	3.4 (3393)	N	2.4794-2.4803	0.0004-0.0012	0.0024-0.0103	3	1.9675-1.9685	0.0009-0.0023	0.0060 0.0120
	4.6 (4593)	V	2.6580-2.6576	0.0010-0.0018	0.0051-0.0119	5	2.0859-2.0867	0.0011-0.0027	0.0059 0.0177

93001CC7

PISTON AND RING SPECIFICATIONS
All measurements are given in inches.

| Year | Engine Displacement Liters (cc) | Engine ID/VIN | Piston Clearance | Ring Gap | | | Ring Side Clearance | | |
				Top Compression	Bottom Compression	Oil Control	Top Compression	Bottom Compression	Oil Control
1996	3.0 (2982)	U	0.0014-0.0022	0.010-0.020	0.010-0.020	0.010-0.049	0.0012 0.0031	0.0012 0.0031	SNUG
	3.0 (2998)	S	0.0005-0.0009	0.004-0.010	0.011-0.017	0.005-0.026	0.0015-0.0029	0.0015-0.0033	SNUG
	3.4 (3393)	N	0.0008-0.0016	0.008-0.014	0.008-0.014	0.008-0.028	0.0018-0.0031	0.0012-0.0028	0.0024-0.0059
	4.6 (4593)	V	0.0007-0.0018	0.010-0.020	0.010-0.020	0.006-0.026	0.0004-0.0009	0.0012-0.0032	SNUG
1997	3.0 (2982)	U	0.0014-0.0022	0.010-0.020	0.010-0.020	0.010-0.049	0.0012 0.0031	0.0012 0.0031	SNUG
	3.0 (2998)	S	0.0005-0.0009	0.004-0.010	0.011-0.017	0.005-0.026	0.0015-0.0029	0.0015-0.0033	SNUG
	3.4 (3393)	N	0.0008-0.0016	0.008-0.014	0.008-0.014	0.008-0.028	0.0018-0.0031	0.0012-0.0028	0.0024-0.0059
	4.6 (4593)	V	0.0007-0.0018	0.010-0.020	0.010-0.020	0.006-0.026	0.0004-0.0009	0.0012-0.0032	SNUG
1998	3.0 (2982)	U	0.0014-0.0022	0.010-0.020	0.010-0.020	0.010-0.049	0.0012 0.0031	0.0012 0.0031	SNUG
	3.0 (2998)	S	0.0005-0.0009	0.004-0.010	0.011-0.017	0.005-0.026	0.0015-0.0029	0.0015-0.0033	SNUG
	3.4 (3393)	N	0.0008-0.0016	0.008-0.014	0.008-0.014	0.008-0.028	0.0018-0.0031	0.0012-0.0028	0.0024-0.0059
	4.6 (4593)	V	0.0007-0.0018	0.010-0.020	0.010-0.020	0.006-0.026	0.0004-0.0009	0.0012-0.0032	SNUG
1999-00	3.0 (2982)	U	0.0014-0.0022	0.010-0.020	0.010-0.020	0.010-0.049	0.0012 0.0031	0.0012 0.0031	SNUG
	3.0 (2998)	S	0.0005-0.0009	0.004-0.010	0.011-0.017	0.006-0.026	0.0015-0.0029	0.0015-0.0033	SNUG
	3.4 (3393)	N	0.0008-0.0016	0.008-0.014	0.008-0.014	0.008-0.028	0.0018-0.0031	0.0012-0.0028	0.0024-0.0059
	4.6 (4593)	V	0.0007-0.0018	0.010-0.020	0.010-0.020	0.006-0.026	0.0004-0.0009	0.0012-0.0032	SNUG

93001CC8

TORQUE SPECIFICATIONS
All readings in ft. lbs.

Year	Engine Displacement Liters (cc)	Engine ID/VIN	Cylinder Head Bolts	Main Bearing Bolts	Rod Bearing Bolts	Crankshaft Damper Bolts	Flywheel Bolts	Manifold		Spark Plugs	Lug Nuts
								Intake	Exhaust		
1996	3.0 (2982)	U	①	56-62	23-28	93-121	54-64	15-22	15-18	7-15	95
	3.0 (2998)	S	③	④	⑤	⑥	54-64	⑦	13-16	7-15	95
	3.4 (3393)	N	⑧	⑨	⑩	⑥	54-64	14-20	11-19	11-15	95
	4.6 (4593)	V	⑪	⑫	⑬	⑥	54-64	⑭	⑯	7-15	95
1997	3.0 (2982)	U	①	56-62	23-28	93-121	54-64	15-22	15-18	7-15	95
	3.0 (2998)	S	③	④	⑤	⑥	54-64	⑦	13-16	7-15	95
	3.4 (3393)	N	⑧	⑨	⑩	⑥	54-64	14-20	11-19	11-15	95
	4.6 (4593)	V	⑪	⑫	⑬	⑥	54-64	⑭	⑯	7-15	95
1998	3.0 (2982)	U	①	56-62	23-28	93-121	54-64	②	15-18	7-15	95
	3.0 (2998)	S	③	④	⑤	⑥	54-64	⑦	13-16	7-15	95
	3.4 (3393)	N	⑧	⑨	⑩	⑥	54-64	14-20	11-19	11-15	95
	4.6 (4593)	V	⑮	⑫	⑬	⑥	54-64	⑭	⑰	7-15	95
1999-00	3.0 (2982)	U	⑱	56-62	23-28	93-121	54-64	②	15-18	7-15	95
	3.0 (2998)	S	③	④	⑤	⑥	54-64	⑦	13-16	7-15	95
	3.4 (3393)	N	⑧	⑨	⑩	⑥	55-61	14-20	11-19	11-15	95
	4.6 (4593)	V	⑮	⑫	⑬	⑥	54-64	⑭	⑰	7-15	95

① Step 1: 52-66 ft.lbs
  Step 2: Loosen one turn
  Step 3: 34-40 ft. lbs.
  Step 4: 63-73 ft. lbs.

② Upper intake: 15-22 ft. lbs.
  Lower Intake:
  Step 1: 15-22 ft. lbs.
  Step 2: 20-23 ft. lbs.

③ Step 1: 28-31 ft. lbs.
  Step 2: Rotate 85-95 degrees
  Step 3: Loosen one turn
  Step 4: 28-31 ft. lbs.
  Step 5: Rotate 85-95 degrees
  Step 6: Repeat Step 5

④ Step 1: Cap bolts 1-8 (outer) 17-20 ft. lbs.
  Step 2: Cap bolts 9-16 (inner) 28-31 ft. lbs.
  Step 3: Rotate bolts 1-16, 85-95 degrees
  Step 4: Bolts 17-22; 15-22 ft. lbs.

⑤ Step 1: 30-33 ft. lbs.
  Step 2: Rotate 90-120 degrees

⑥ Step 1: 88 ft. lbs
  Step 2: Loosen 360 degrees
  Step 3: Tighten to 35-39 ft. lbs.
  Step 4: Rotate 85-95 degrees

⑦ 71-106 inch lbs.

⑧ Step 1: 20-23 ft. lbs.
  Step 2: Rotate 85-95 degrees

⑨ Step 1: Cap bolts 1-10 (outer) 17-20 ft. lbs.
  Step 2: Cap bolts 11-20 (inner) 28-31 ft. lbs.
  Step 3: Rotate bolts 1-20, 85-95 degrees
  Step 4: Bolts 21-31, 15-22 ft. lbs.

⑩ Step 1: 30-33 ft. lbs.
  Step 2: Rotate 90-120 degrees

⑪ Step 1: 27-32 ft. lbs.
  Step 2: Rotate 85-95 degrees
  Step 3: Repeat Step 2

⑫ Step 1: Main bearing cap bolts: 6-9 ft. lbs.
  Step 2: Main bearing cap bolts, outer: 16-21 ft. lbs.
  Step 3: Main bearing cap bolts, inner: 27-32 ft. lbs.
  Step 4: Rotate main bearing cap bolts 85-95 degrees
  Step 5: Main cap adjusting screws 4 ft. lbs. then 7.5 ft. lbs.
  Step 6: Main cap side bolts: 7 ft. lbs. then 14-17 ft. lbs.

⑬ Step 1: 5 ft. lbs.
  Step 2: 10 ft. lbs.
  Step 3: 18-25 ft. lbs.
  Step 4: Rotate 85-95 degrees

⑭ Step 1: Four inside short bolts: 9-11 ft. lbs.
  Step 2: All other bolts: 13-16 ft. lbs.
  Step 3: Rotate all fasteners 85-95 degrees

⑮ Step 1: 28-31 ft. lbs.
  Step 2: Rotate 85-95 degrees
  Step 3: Loosen all bolts 360 degrees
  Step 4: Repeat Step 1
  Step 5: Repeat Step 2
  Step6: Repeat Step 5

⑯ Studs: 15-22 ft. lbs.
  Nuts: 14-16 ft .lbs.

⑰ Studs: 8-9 ft. lbs.
  Nuts: 14-16 ft .lbs.

⑱ Step 1: 35-39 ft. lbs.
  Step 2: Loosen one turn
  Step 3: 20-24 ft. lbs.
  Step 4: Rotate 85-95 degrees
  Step 5: Repeat Step 4

93001CC9

SCHEDULED MAINTENANCE INTERVALS
(FORD TAURUS, LINCOLN CONTINENTAL, MERCURY SABLE)

TO BE SERVICED	TYPE OF SERVICE	VEHICLE MILEAGE INTERVAL (x1000)												
		5	10	15	20	25	30	35	40	45	50	55	60	65
Engine oil & filter	R	✓	✓	✓	✓	✓	✓	✓	✓	✓	✓	✓	✓	✓
Rotate tires	S/I	✓		✓		✓		✓		✓		✓		✓
Engine coolant protection, hoses & clamps	S/I						✓			✓			✓	
Pass. compartment air filter (Continental)	R			✓			✓			✓			✓	
Pass. compartment air filter (Taurus, Sable)	R				✓				✓				✓	
Air cleaner filter	R						✓						✓	
Automatic transaxle fluid & filter	R						✓						✓	
Brake lines & connections	S/I						✓						✓	
Exhaust heat shields	S/I						✓						✓	
Front and rear disc brake pads & rotors	S/I						✓						✓	
Accessory drive belt(s)	S/I												✓	
Engine coolant ①	R										✓			
Spark plugs exc. 3.0L FF) ②	R													
Spark plugs exc. 3.0L FF)	R						✓						✓	
PCV valve (except 3.0L 4-valve)	R												✓	
PCV valve (except 3.0L 4-valve) ③	R													

① Engine coolant - change initially at 50,000 miles & thereafter every 30,000 miles.

② Platinum tip spark plugs - change every 100,000 miles.

③ Replace every 100,000 miles.

R - Replace   S/I - Service or Inspect

FREQUENT OPERATION MAINTENANCE (SEVERE SERVICE)

If a vehicle is operated under any of the following conditions it is considered severe service:
- Extremely dusty areas.
- 50% or more of the vehicle operation is in 32°C (90°F) or higher temperatures, or constant operation in temperatures below 0°C (32°F).
- Prolonged idling (vehicle operation in stop and go traffic).
- Frequent short running periods (engine does not warm to normal operating temperatures).
- Police, taxi, delivery usage or trailer towing usage.

Oil & filter change - change every 3000 miles.
Rotate tires at 6000 miles & every 9000 miles thereafter.
Air cleaner element - service or inspect every 15,000 miles.
Automatic transaxle fluid & filter - change every 21,000 miles.

93001CC0

Refer to the model specific sections for engine mechanical service procedures

SCHEDULED MAINTENANCE INTERVALS
FORD MOTOR COMPANY
FORD TAURUS, MERCURY SABLE
LINCOLN CONTINENTAL

The following should be used as a guide when determining the amount of work required for a particular service.
In estimating how long a particular Scheduled Maintenance Service should take, please observe the following:

- **Chilton Time** is time based on field research and data supplied by the vehicle manufacturer.
  - Labor time operations are given in hours and tenths of an hour.
  - All labor operations, are to be used as a guide.

Mechanic Skill Level Codes:
(A) PRECISION: Really skilled with multiple certification.
(B) GENERAL: Normally skilled with certification.
(C) MAINTENANCE: Semi-skilled working on certification.

	Chilton Time		Chilton Time		Chilton Time
5000 Mile Service (C)		**30000 Mile Service (B)**		**50000 Mile Service (C)**	
All Models	1.0	All Models	3.2	All Models	1.0
		Replace auto. trans. fluid &		**55000 Mile Service (C)**	
0000 Mile Service (C)		*filter add*	.6	All Models	1.0
All Models	.5	*Replace engine coolant add*	.6		
5000 Mile Service (C)		**35000 Mile Service (C)**		**60000 Mile Service (B)**	
All Models	1.3	All Models	1.0	All Models	3.4
				Replace auto. trans. fluid &	
0000 Mile Service (C)		**40000 Mile Service (C)**		*filter add*	.6
All Models	.7	All Models	.7	*Replace engine coolant add*	.6
5000 Mile Service (C)		**45000 Mile Service (C)**		**65000 Mile Service (C)**	
All Models	1.0	All Models	1.1	All Models	1.0

93001CD1

GENERAL MOTORS A-BODY
Buick Century • Oldsmobile Cutlass Ciera • Cutlass Cruiser

ENGINE AND VEHICLE IDENTIFICATION

		Engine						Model Year	
Code ①	Liters (cc)	Cu. In.	Cyl.	Fuel Sys.	Engine Type	Eng. Mfg.		Code ②	Year
4	2.2 (2195)	134	4	MFI	OHV	BOC		T	1996
M	3.1 (3130)	191	6	MFI	OHV	BOC			

MFI - Multi-point Fuel Injection

BOC - Buick/Oldsmobile/Cadillac

OHV - Overhead Valves

① 8th position of VIN

② 10th position of VIN

93001CD2

GENERAL ENGINE SPECIFICATIONS

Year	Model	Engine Displacement Liters (cc)	Engine Series (ID/VIN)	Fuel System	Net Horsepower @ rpm	Net Torque @ rpm (ft. lbs.)	Bore x Stroke (in.)	Com-pression Ratio	Oil Pressure @ rpm
1996	Century	2.2 (2195)	4	MFI	120@5200	130@4000	3.50x3.46	8.85:1	56@3000
	Century	3.1 (3130)	M	MFI	160@5200	185@4000	3.50x3.31	9.5:1	15@1100
	Cutlass Ciera	2.2 (2195)	4	MFI	120@5200	130@4000	3.50x3.46	8.85:1	56@3000
	Cutlass Ciera	3.1 (3130)	M	MFI	160@5200	185@4000	3.50x3.31	9.5:1	15@1100
	Cutlass Cruiser	3.1 (3130)	M	MFI	160@5200	185@4000	3.50x3.31	9.5:1	15@1100

MFI - Multi-point Fuel Injection

93001CD3

ENGINE TUNE-UP SPECIFICATIONS

Year	Engine Displacement Liters (cc)	Engine ID/VIN	Spark Plug Gap (in.)	Ignition Timing (deg.)		Fuel Pump (psi)	Idle Speed (rpm)		Valve Clearance	
				MT	AT		MT	AT	Intake	Exhaust
1996	2.2 (2195)	4	0.060	①	①	41-47	②	②	HYD	HYD
	3.1 (3130)	M	0.060	①	①	41-47	②	②	HYD	HYD

NOTE: The Vehicle Emission Control Information (VECI) label often reflects specification changes made during production. The label figures must be used if they differ from those in this chart.

HYD - Hydraulic

① DIS Ignition System timing not adjustable.

② Idle speed maintained by ECM and is not adjustable.

93001CD4

Refer to the model specific sections for fuel system service procedures

CAPACITIES

Year	Model	Engine Displacement Liters (cc)	Engine ID/VIN	Engine Oil with Filter (qts.)	Transaxle (pts.) 3 - speed	Transaxle (pts.) 4 - speed	Fuel Tank (gal.)	Cooling System (qts.)
1996	Century	2.2 (2195)	4	4.0	8.0	12.0	16.5	8.7
	Century	3.1 (3130)	M	4.0	8.0	12.0	16.5	11.6
	Cutlass Ciera	2.2 (2195)	4	4.0	8.0	12.0	16.5	8.7
	Cutlass Ciera	3.1 (3130)	M	4.0	8.0	12.0	16.5	11.6
	Cutlass Cruiser	3.1 (3130)	M	4.0	8.0	12.0	16.5	11.6

NOTE: All capacities are approximate. Add fluid gradually and ensure a proper fluid level is obtained.

93001CD5

VALVE SPECIFICATIONS

Year	Engine Displacement Liters (cc)	Engine ID/VIN	Seat Angle (deg.)	Face Angle (deg.)	Spring Test Pressure (lbs. @ in.)	Spring Installed Height (in.)	Stem-to-Guide Clearance (in.) Intake	Stem-to-Guide Clearance (in.) Exhaust	Stem Diameter (in.) Intake	Stem Diameter (in.) Exhaust
1996	2.2 (2195)	4	46	45	220-236 @ 1.278	1.710	0.0010-0.0027	0.0014-0.0031	NA	NA
	3.1 (3130)	M	45	45	230 @ 1.260	1.701	0.0010-0.0027	0.0010-0.0027	NA	NA

NA - Not Available

93001CD6

CRANKSHAFT AND CONNECTING ROD SPECIFICATIONS
All measurements are given in inches.

Year	Engine Displacement Liters (cc)	Engine ID/VIN	Crankshaft Main Brg. Journal Dia.	Crankshaft Main Brg. Oil Clearance	Crankshaft Shaft End-play	Crankshaft Thrust on No.	Connecting Rod Journal Diameter	Connecting Rod Oil Clearance	Connecting Rod Side Clearance
1996	2.2 (2195)	4	2.4945-2.4954	0.0006-0.0019	0.0020-0.0070	3	1.9983-1.9994	0.0010-0.0031	0.0039-0.0149
	3.1 (3130)	M	2.6473-2.6383	0.0008- ① 0.0025	0.0024-0.0083	3	1.9987-1.9994	0.0007-0.0024	0.0070-0.0170

NA: Not available

① Thrust bearing: 0.0012 - 0.0030

93001CD7

PISTON AND RING SPECIFICATIONS
All measurements are given in inches.

Year	Engine Displacement Liters (cc)	Engine ID/VIN	Piston Clearance	Ring Gap			Ring Side Clearance		
				Top Compression	Bottom Compression	Oil Control	Top Compression	Bottom Compression	Oil Control
1996	2.2 (2195)	4	0.0007-0.0017	0.010-0.020	0.0100-0.0200	0.0100-0.0500	0.0019-0.0027	0.0019-0.0027	0.0019-0.0082
	3.1 (3130)	M	0.0013-0.0027	0.006-0.014	0.0197-0.0280	0.0098-0.0500	0.0020-0.0033	0.0020-0.0035	0.0080

93001CD8

TORQUE SPECIFICATIONS
All readings in ft. lbs.

Year	Engine Displacement Liters (cc)	Engine ID/VIN	Cylinder Head Bolts	Main Bearing Bolts	Rod Bearing Bolts	Crankshaft Damper Bolts	Flywheel Bolts	Manifold		Spark Plugs	Lug Nuts
								Intake	Exhaust		
1996	2.2 (2195)	4	①	70	38	77	55	24	10	②	100
	3.1 (3130)	M	③	④	⑤	76	59	⑥	12	②	100

① Short bolts: 43 ft. lbs. plus 90 degrees
Long bolts: 46 ft. lbs. plus 90 degrees

② New cylinder first-time installation: 21 ft. lbs.
All others: 11 ft. lbs.

③ Coat threads with sealer
Tighten to 37 ft. lbs.
Tighten an additional 1/4 turn (90 degrees)

④ 37 ft. lbs. plus 75 degrees

⑤ 15 ft. lbs. plus 75 degrees

⑥ Tighten all bolts to 15 ft. lbs.,
Retighten to 24 ft. lbs.

93001CD9

Refer to the model specific sections for engine electrical system service procedures

SCHEDULED MAINTENANCE INTERVALS
(GM A BODY - BUICK CENTURY, OLDSMOBILE CUTLASS CIERA & CUTLASS CRUISER)

TO BE SERVICED	TYPE OF SERVICE	VEHICLE MILEAGE INTERVAL (x1000)												
		7.5	15	22.5	30	37.5	45	52.5	60	67.5	75	82.5	90	97.5
Engine oil & filter	R	✓	✓	✓	✓	✓	✓	✓	✓	✓	✓	✓	✓	✓
Brake hoses	S/I	✓	✓	✓	✓	✓	✓	✓	✓	✓	✓	✓	✓	✓
Chassis lubrication	S/I	✓	✓	✓	✓	✓	✓	✓	✓	✓	✓	✓	✓	✓
Coolant level, hoses & clamps	S/I	✓	✓	✓	✓	✓	✓	✓	✓	✓	✓	✓	✓	✓
Driveshaft boots & front suspension components	S/I	✓	✓	✓	✓	✓	✓	✓	✓	✓	✓	✓	✓	✓
Exhaust system	S/I	✓	✓	✓	✓	✓	✓	✓	✓	✓	✓	✓	✓	✓
Lubricate transaxle shift linkage, parking brake cable guides, underbody contact points & linkage	S/I	✓	✓	✓	✓	✓	✓	✓	✓	✓	✓	✓	✓	✓
Rotate tires	S/I	✓		✓		✓		✓		✓		✓		✓
Brake linings	S/I	✓		✓		✓		✓		✓		✓		✓
Air filter element	R				✓				✓				✓	
Engine coolant ②	R				✓				✓				✓	
Spark plugs ①	R				✓				✓				✓	
Accessory drive belt(s)	S/I				✓				✓				✓	
EGR & fuel systems	S/I				✓				✓				✓	
PCV valve & filter	S/I				✓				✓				✓	
Ignition cables	S/I				✓				✓				✓	
Automatic transaxle fluid & filter ③	R													
Throttle body mount bolt torque	S/I	✓												

① Platinum tip spark plugs - replace every 100,000 miles.

② Engine coolant - replace every 100,000 miles. Use O.E. specified (DEX-COOL™) coolant only. If any silicate coolant is used, the service interval is every 30,000 miles.

③ Replace fluid & filter every 100,000 miles.

R - Replace S/I - Service or Inspect

FREQUENT OPERATION MAINTENANCE (SEVERE SERVICE)

If a vehicle is operated under any of the following conditions it is considered severe service:
- Extremely dusty areas.
- 50% or more of the vehicle operation is in 32°C (90°F) or higher temperatures, or constant operation in temperatures below 0°C (32°F).
- Prolonged idling (vehicle operation in stop and go traffic).
- Frequent short running periods (engine does not warm to normal operating temperatures).
- Police, taxi, delivery usage or trailer towing usage.

Engine oil & filter change - change every 3000 miles.
Inspect CV joints & front suspension components - check every 3000 miles.
Throttle body mount bolt torque - tighten at 6000 miles.
Rotate tires at 6000 miles, then every 12,000 miles.
Brake linings - check every 9000 miles.
Air filter element - service or inspect ever 15,000 miles.
Automatic transaxle fluid & filter - change every 50,000 miles.

93001CD0

SCHEDULED MAINTENANCE INTERVALS
GENERAL MOTORS CORPORATION
A BODY
BUICK CENTURY, OLDSMOBILE CUTLASS CIERA, CUTLASS CRUISER

The following should be used as a guide when determining the amount of work required for a particular service.
In estimating how long a particular Scheduled Maintenance Service should take, please observe the following:

- **Chilton Time** is time based on field research and data supplied by the vehicle manufacturer.
  - Labor time operations are given in hours and tenths of an hour.
  - All labor operations, are to be used as a guide.

Mechanic Skill Level Codes:
(A) PRECISION: Really skilled with multiple certification.
(B) GENERAL: Normally skilled with certification.
(C) MAINTENANCE: Semi-skilled working on certification.

	Chilton Time			Chilton Time			Chilton Time
7500 Mile Service (C)			**45000 Mile Service (C)**			**67500 Mile Service (C)**	
All Models	1.5		All Models	.8		All Models	1.5
15000 Mile Service (C)			**52500 Mile Service (C)**			**75000 Mile Service (C)**	
All Models	.8		All Models	1.5		All Models	.8
22500 Mile Service (C)			**60000 Mile Service (B)**			**82500 Mile Service (C)**	
All Models	1.5		All Models	4.0		All Models	1.5
30000 Mile Service (B)						**90000 Mile Service (B)**	
All Models	4.0					All Models	4.0
37500 Mile Service (C)						**97500 Mile Service (C)**	
All Models	1.5					All Models	1.5

93001CE1

For accessory drive belt replacement procedures see the model specific sections of this manual

GENERAL MOTORS B-BODY
Buick Roadmaster • Cadillac Fleetwood Brougham • Chevrolet Caprice • Impala SS

ENGINE AND VEHICLE IDENTIFICATION

Engine							Model Year	
Code ①	Liters (cc)	Cu. In.	Cyl.	Fuel Sys.	Engine Type	Eng. Mfg.	Code ②	Year
P	5.7 (5737)	350	8	MFI	OHV	CPC	T	1996
W	4.3 (4294)	265	8	MFI	OHV	CPC		

CPC - Chevrolet/Pontiac/Canada

MFI - Multi-point Fuel Injection

OHV - Overhead Valves

① 8th position of VIN

② 10th position of VIN

93001CE2

GENERAL ENGINE SPECIFICATIONS

Year	Model	Engine Displacement Liters (cc)	Engine Series (ID/VIN)	Fuel System	Net Horsepower @ rpm	Net Torque @ rpm (ft. lbs.)	Bore x Stroke (in.)	Compression Ratio	Oil Pressure @ rpm
1996	Caprice	5.7 (5737)	P	MFI	260@5000	330@3200	4.00x3.48	10.25:1	18@2000
	Caprice	4.3 (4294)	W	MFI	200@5200	245@2400	3.74x3.48	9.93:1	18@2000
	Fleetwood	5.7 (5733)	P	MFI	260@5000	330@3200	4.00x3.48	10.25:1	18@2000
	Impala SS	5.7 (5737)	P	MFI	260@5000	330@3200	4.00x3.48	10.25:1	18@2000
	Roadmaster	5.7 (5737)	P	MFI	260@5000	330@3200	4.00x3.48	10.25:1	18@2000

MFI - Multi-point Fuel Injection

93001CE3

ENGINE TUNE-UP SPECIFICATIONS

Year	Engine Displacement Liters (cc)	Engine ID/VIN	Spark Plug Gap (in.)	Ignition Timing (deg.)	Fuel Pump (psi)	Idle Speed (rpm) AT	Valve Clearance Intake	Valve Clearance Exhaust
1996	5.7 (5737)	P	0.035	①	41-47	①	HYD	HYD
	4.3 (4294)	W	0.050	①	6-24	①	HYD	HYD

NOTE: The Vehicle Emission Control Information label often reflects specification changes made during production. The label figures must be used if they differ from those in this chart.

HYD - Hydraulic

① Refer to the Vehicle Emission Control Information (VECI) label.

93001CE4

CAPACITIES

Year	Model	Engine Displacement Liters (cc)	Engine ID/VIN	Engine Oil with Filter (qts.)	Transmission (pts.)		Drive Axle (pts.)	Fuel Tank (gal.)	Cooling System (qts.)
1996	Caprice	5.7 (5737)	P	5.0	7.0	①	②	22.0	14.6
	Caprice	4.3 (4294)	W	4.5	7.0	①	②	23.0	12.6
	Fleetwood	5.7 (5733)	P	5.0	10.0	③	②	23.0	14.6
	Impala SS	5.7 (5737)	P	5.0	7.0	①	②	22.0	14.6
	Roadmaster	5.7 (5733)	P	5.0	10.0		②	22.0	16.4

NOTE: All capacities are approximate. Add fluid gradually and ensure a proper fluid level is obtained.

① With std. cooling: 14.40
   With heavy duty cooling: 15.10

② Fill the differential to the bottom of the filler plug.

③ Fluid change with filter

93001CE5

VALVE SPECIFICATIONS

Year	Engine Displacement Liters (cc)	Engine ID/VIN	Seat Angle (deg.)	Face Angle (deg.)	Spring Test Pressure (lbs. @ in.)	Spring Installed Height (in.)	Stem-to-Guide Clearance (in.)		Stem Diameter (in.)	
							Intake	Exhaust	Intake	Exhaust
1996	4.3 (4294)	W	46	45	187-203@ 1.27	1.70	0.0009- 0.0027	0.0009- 0.0027	NA	NA
	5.7 (5737)	P	46	45	187-203@ 1.27	1.70	0.0009- 0.0027	0.0009- 0.0027	NA	NA

NA - Not Available

93001CE6

CRANKSHAFT AND CONNECTING ROD SPECIFICATIONS
All measurements are given in inches.

Year	Engine Displacement Liters (cc)	Engine ID/VIN	Crankshaft				Connecting Rod		
			Main Brg. Journal Dia.	Main Brg. Oil Clearance	Shaft End-play	Thrust on No.	Journal Diameter	Oil Clearance	Side Clearance
1996	4.3 (4294)	W	2.4485- 2.4491	0.0009- 0.0020	0.0020- 0.0080	5	2.0978- 2.0998	0.0013- 0.0035	0.0060- 0.0140
	5.7 (5737)	P	①	②	0.0020- 0.0080	5	2.0978- 2.0998	0.0013- 0.0035	0.0060- 0.0140

① Journal number 1: 2.4484 - 2.4493

Journal numbers 2, 3, 4: 2.4481 - 2.4490

Journal number 5: 2.4479 - 2.4488

② Journal number 1: 0.0007 - 0.0021

Journal numbers 2, 3, 4: 0.0009 - 0.0024

Journal number 5: 0.0010 - 0.0027

93001CE7

For brake related suspension and axle service, refer to the model specific sections of this manual

PISTON AND RING SPECIFICATIONS

All measurements are given in inches.

Year	Engine Displacement Liters (cc)	Engine ID/VIN	Piston Clearance	Ring Gap			Ring Side Clearance		
				Top Compression	Bottom Compression	Oil Control	Top Compression	Bottom Compression	Oil Control
1996	4.3 (4294)	W	0.0010-0.0027	0.010-0.016	0.018-0.026	0.010-0.030	0.0012-0.0029	0.0012-0.0029	0.002-0.007
	5.7 (5737)	P	0.0010-0.0027	0.010-0.016	0.018-0.026	0.010-0.030	0.0019-0.0035	0.0019-0.0035	0.002-0.007

93001CE8

TORQUE SPECIFICATIONS

All readings in ft. lbs.

Year	Engine Displacement Liters (cc)	Engine ID/VIN	Cylinder Head Bolts	Main Bearing Bolts	Rod Bearing Bolts	Crankshaft Damper Bolts	Flywheel Bolts	Manifold		Spark Plugs	Lug Nuts
								Intake	Exhaust		
1996	4.3 (4294)	W	65	78	47	60	74	①	35	11	100
	5.7 (5737)	P	65	78	47	60	74	①	35	11	100

① Step 1: 71 inch lbs.
Step 2: 35 ft. lbs.

93001CE9

SCHEDULED MAINTENANCE INTERVALS
(GM B BODY-BUICK ROADMASTER, CADILLAC FLEETWOOD, CHEVROLET CAPRICE & IMPALA SS)

TO BE SERVICED	TYPE OF SERVICE	VEHICLE MILEAGE INTERVAL (x1000)												
		7.5	15	22.5	30	37.5	45	52.5	60	67.5	75	82.5	90	97.5
Engine oil & filter	R	✓	✓	✓	✓	✓	✓	✓	✓	✓	✓	✓	✓	✓
Automatic transmission fluid & filter	S/I	✓	✓	✓	✓	✓	✓	✓	✓	✓	✓	✓	✓	✓
Brake hoses	S/I	✓	✓	✓	✓	✓	✓	✓	✓	✓	✓	✓	✓	✓
Engine coolant level, hoses & clamps	S/I	✓	✓	✓	✓	✓	✓	✓	✓	✓	✓	✓	✓	✓
Exhaust system & throttle linkage	S/I	✓	✓	✓	✓	✓	✓	✓	✓	✓	✓	✓	✓	✓
Front suspension components	S/I	✓	✓	✓	✓	✓	✓	✓	✓	✓	✓	✓	✓	✓
Lubricate chassis, suspension, steering linkage, transmission shift linkage, parking brake cable guides, underbody contact points & linkage	S/I	✓	✓	✓	✓	✓	✓	✓	✓	✓	✓	✓	✓	✓
Brake linings & rotate tires	S/I	✓		✓		✓		✓		✓		✓		✓
Air filter element	R				✓				✓				✓	
Engine coolant ②	R				✓				✓				✓	
Spark plugs ①	R				✓				✓				✓	
Front wheel bearings	S/I				✓				✓				✓	
Ignition cables, EGR & fuel systems	S/I				✓				✓				✓	
Serpentine drive belt	S/I				✓				✓				✓	
Thermostatically controlled air cleaner	S/I				✓				✓				✓	
Rear axle oil (Limited slip)	R	✓												
Throttle body mount bolt torque	S/I	✓												

① Platinum tip spark plugs - replace every 100,000 miles.

② Engine coolant - replace every 100,000 miles. Use O.E. specified (DEX-COOL™) coolant only. If any silicate coolant is used, the service interval is every 30,000 miles.

R - Replace   S/I - Service or Inspect

93001CE0

Refer to the model specific sections for driveline service procedures

SCHEDULED MAINTENANCE INTERVALS
GENERAL MOTORS CORPORATION
B BODY
BUICK ROADMASTER, CADILLAC FLEETWOOD BROUGHAM
CHEVROLET CAPRICE, IMPALA SS

The following should be used as a guide when determining the amount of work required for a particular service.
In estimating how long a particular Scheduled Maintenance Service should take, please observe the following:

- **Chilton Time** is time based on field research and data supplied by the vehicle manufacturer.
  - Labor time operations are given in hours and tenths of an hour.
    - All labor operations, are to be used as a guide.

Mechanic Skill Level Codes:
(A) PRECISION: Really skilled with multiple certification.
(B) GENERAL: Normally skilled with certification.
(C) MAINTENANCE: Semi-skilled working on certification.

	Chilton Time
7500 Mile Service (B)	
All Models	2.3
15000 Mile Service (C)	
All Models	1.1
22500 Mile Service (C)	
All Models	1.8
30000 Mile Service (B)	
All Models	3.3

	Chilton Time
37500 Mile Service (C)	
All Models	1.8
45000 Mile Service (C)	
All Models	1.1
52500 Mile Service (C)	
All Models	1.8
60000 Mile Service (B)	
All Models	3.3
67500 Mile Service (C)	
All Models	1.8

	Chilton Time
75000 Mile Service (C)	
All Models	1.1
82500 Mile Service (C)	
All Models	1.8
90000 Mile Service (B)	
All Models	3.3
97500 Mile Service (C)	
All Models	1.8

93001CF1

GENERAL MOTORS C- & H-BODIES
Buick LeSabre • Park Avenue • Oldsmobile Eighty-Eight •
Ninety-Eight • LSS • Regency • Pontiac Bonneville

ENGINE AND VEHICLE IDENTIFICATION

Engine							Model Year	
Code ①	Liters (cc)	Cu. In.	Cyl.	Fuel Sys.	Engine Type	Eng. Mfg.	Code ②	Year
1 ③	3.8 (3785)	231	6	MFI	OHV	BOC	T	1996
K	3.8 (3785)	231	6	MFI	OHV	BOC	V	1997
							W	1998
							X	1999
							Y	2000

MFI - Multi-point Fuel Injection

BOC - Buick/Oldsmobile/Cadillac

OHV - Overhead Valves

① 8th position of VIN

② 10th position of VIN

③ Supercharged engine

93001CF2

For exhaust manifold replacement procedures, see the model specific sections of this manual

GENERAL ENGINE SPECIFICATIONS

Year	Model	Engine Displacement Liters (cc)	Engine Series (ID/VIN)		Fuel System	Net Horsepower @ rpm	Net Torque @ rpm (ft. lbs.)	Bore x Stroke (in.)	Compression Ratio	Oil Pressure @ rpm
1996	Bonneville	3.8 (3785)	1	①	MFI	225@5000	275@3200	3.80x3.40	9.0:1	60@1850
	Bonneville	3.8 (3785)	K		MFI	205@5200	230@4000	3.80x3.40	9.4:1	60@1850
	Eighty-Eight	3.8 (3786)	K		MFI	205@5200	230@4000	3.80x3.40	9.4:1	60@1850
	Eighty-Eight/LSS	3.8 (3785)	1	①	MFI	225@5000	275@3200	3.80x3.40	9.0:1	60@1850
	LeSabre	3.8 (3785)	K		MFI	205@5200	230@4000	3.80x3.40	9.4:1	60@1850
	Ninety-Eight	3.8 (3786)	K		MFI	205@5200	230@4000	3.80x3.40	9.4:1	60@1850
	Park Avenue	3.8 (3785)	K		MFI	205@5200	230@4000	3.80x3.40	9.4:1	60@1850
	Park Avenue Ultra	3.8 (3785)	1	①	MFI	225@5000	275@3200	3.80x3.40	9.0:1	60@1850
1997	Bonneville	3.8 (3785)	1	①	MFI	225@5000	275@3200	3.80x3.40	9.0:1	60@1850
	Bonneville	3.8 (3785)	K		MFI	205@5200	230@4000	3.80x3.40	9.4:1	60@1850
	Eighty-Eight	3.8 (3786)	K		MFI	205@5200	230@4000	3.80x3.40	9.4:1	60@1850
	LeSabre	3.8 (3785)	K		MFI	205@5200	230@4000	3.80x3.40	9.4:1	60@1850
	LSS	3.8 (3785)	1	①	MFI	225@5000	275@3200	3.80x3.40	9.0:1	60@1850
	LSS	3.8 (3786)	K		MFI	205@5200	230@4000	3.80x3.40	9.4:1	60@1850
	Park Avenue	3.8 (3785)	1	①	MFI	225@5000	275@3200	3.80x3.40	9.0:1	60@1850
	Park Avenue	3.8 (3785)	K		MFI	205@5200	230@4000	3.80x3.40	9.4:1	60@1850
	Regency	3.8 (3786)	K		MFI	205@5200	230@4000	3.80x3.40	9.4:1	60@1850
1998	Bonneville	3.8 (3785)	1	①	MFI	225@5000	275@3200	3.80x3.40	9.0:1	60@1850
	Bonneville	3.8 (3785)	K		MFI	205@5200	230@4000	3.80x3.40	9.4:1	60@1850
	Eighty-Eight	3.8 (3786)	K		MFI	205@5200	230@4000	3.80x3.40	9.4:1	60@1850
	LeSabre	3.8 (3785)	K		MFI	205@5200	230@4000	3.80x3.40	9.4:1	60@1850
	LSS	3.8 (3786)	K		MFI	205@5200	230@4000	3.80x3.40	9.4:1	60@1850
	Park Avenue	3.8 (3785)	1	①	MFI	225@5000	275@3200	3.80x3.40	9.0:1	60@1850
	Park Avenue	3.8 (3785)	K		MFI	205@5200	230@4000	3.80x3.40	9.4:1	60@1850
	Regency	3.8 (3786)	K		MFI	205@5200	230@4000	3.80x3.40	9.4:1	60@1850
1999-00	Bonneville	3.8 (3785)	1	①	MFI	225@5000	275@3200	3.80x3.40	9.0:1	60@1850
	Bonneville	3.8 (3785)	K		MFI	205@5200	230@4000	3.80x3.40	9.4:1	60@1850
	Eighty-Eight	3.8 (3786)	K		MFI	205@5200	230@4000	3.80x3.40	9.4:1	60@1850
	LeSabre	3.8 (3785)	K		MFI	205@5200	230@4000	3.80x3.40	9.4:1	60@1850
	LSS	3.8 (3786)	K		MFI	205@5200	230@4000	3.80x3.40	9.4:1	60@1850
	Park Avenue	3.8 (3785)	1	①	MFI	225@5000	275@3200	3.80x3.40	9.0:1	60@1850
	Park Avenue	3.8 (3785)	K		MFI	205@5200	230@4000	3.80x3.40	9.4:1	60@1850
	Regency	3.8 (3786)	K		MFI	205@5200	230@4000	3.80x3.40	9.4:1	60@1850

MFI - Multi-point Fuel Injection

① Supercharged engine

93001CF3

ENGINE TUNE-UP SPECIFICATIONS

Year	Engine Displacement Liters (cc)	Engine ID/VIN	Spark Plug Gap (in.)	Ignition Timing (deg.)	Fuel Pump (psi)②	Idle Speed (rpm)	Valve Clearance	
							Intake	Exhaust
1996	3.8 (3786)	1	0.060	①	41-47	③	HYD	HYD
	3.8 (3785)	K	0.060	①	41-47	③	HYD	HYD
1997	3.8 (3786)	1	0.060	①	41-47	③	HYD	HYD
	3.8 (3785)	K	0.060	①	41-47	③	HYD	HYD
1998	3.8 (3786)	1	0.060	①	41-47	③	HYD	HYD
	3.8 (3785)	K	0.060	①	41-47	③	HYD	HYD
1999-00	3.8 (3786)	1	0.060	①	41-47	③	HYD	HYD
	3.8 (3785)	K	0.060	①	41-47	③	HYD	HYD

NOTE: The Vehicle Emission Control Information label often reflects specification changes made during production. The label figures must be used if they differ from those in this chart.

HYD - Hydraulic

① DIS Ignition System timing not adjustable

② Pressure at fuel pump

③ Idle speed maintained by ECM. There is no recommended adjustment procedure

93001CF4

Refer to the model specific sections for cooling system service procedures

CAPACITIES

Year	Model	Engine Displacement Liters (cc)	Engine ID/VIN	Engine Oil with Filter (qts.)	Transmission (pts.)	Fuel Tank (gal.)	Cooling System (qts.)
1996	Bonneville	3.8 (3785)	1	4.5	12.0	18.0	13.0
	Bonneville	3.8 (3785)	K	4.5	12.0	18.0	13.0
	Eighty-Eight	3.8 (3785)	K	4.5	12.0	18.0	13.0
	Eighty-Eight/LSS	3.8 (3785)	1	4.5	12.0	18.0	13.0
	LeSabre	3.8 (3785)	K	4.5	12.0	18.0	13.0
	Ninety-Eight	3.8 (3785)	K	4.5	12.0	18.0	13.0
	Park Avenue	3.8 (3785)	K	4.5	12.0	18.0	13.0
	Park Avenue Ultra	3.8 (3785)	1	4.5	12.0	18.0	13.0
1997	Bonneville	3.8 (3785)	1	4.5	12.0	18.0	13.0
	Bonneville	3.8 (3785)	K	4.5	12.0	18.0	13.0
	Eighty-Eight	3.8 (3785)	K	4.5	12.0	18.0	13.0
	LeSabre	3.8 (3785)	K	4.5	12.0	18.0	13.0
	LSS	3.8 (3785)	1	4.5	12.0	18.0	13.0
	LSS	3.8 (3785)	K	4.5	12.0	18.0	13.0
	Park Avenue	3.8 (3785)	1	4.5	12.0	18.0	13.0
	Park Avenue	3.8 (3785)	K	4.5	12.0	18.0	13.0
	Regency	3.8 (3785)	K	4.5	12.0	18.0	13.0
1998	Bonneville	3.8 (3785)	1	4.5	12.0	18.0	13.0
	Bonneville	3.8 (3785)	K	4.5	12.0	18.0	13.0
	Eighty-Eight	3.8 (3785)	K	4.5	12.0	18.0	13.0
	LeSabre	3.8 (3785)	K	4.5	12.0	18.0	13.0
	LSS	3.8 (3785)	K	4.5	12.0	18.0	13.0
	Park Avenue	3.8 (3785)	1	4.5	12.0	18.0	13.0
	Park Avenue	3.8 (3785)	K	4.5	12.0	18.0	13.0
	Regency	3.8 (3785)	K	4.5	12.0	18.0	13.0
1999-00	Bonneville	3.8 (3785)	1	4.5	12.0	18.0	13.0
	Bonneville	3.8 (3785)	K	4.5	12.0	18.0	13.0
	Eighty-Eight	3.8 (3785)	K	4.5	12.0	18.0	13.0
	LeSabre	3.8 (3785)	K	4.5	12.0	18.0	13.0
	LSS	3.8 (3785)	K	4.5	12.0	18.0	13.0
	Park Avenue	3.8 (3785)	1	4.5	12.0	18.0	13.0
	Park Avenue	3.8 (3785)	K	4.5	12.0	18.0	13.0
	Regency	3.8 (3785)	K	4.5	12.0	18.0	13.0

NOTE: All capacities are approximate. Add fluid gradually and ensure a proper fluid level is obtained.

93001CF5

VALVE SPECIFICATIONS

Year	Engine Displacement Liters (cc)	Engine ID/VIN	Seat Angle (deg.)	Face Angle (deg.)	Spring Test Pressure (lbs. @ in.)	Spring Installed Height (in.)	Stem-to-Guide Clearance (in.) Intake	Stem-to-Guide Clearance (in.) Exhaust	Stem Diameter (in.) Intake	Stem Diameter (in.) Exhaust
1996	3.8 (3785)	1	45	45	80@1.750	1.690-1.720	0.0015-0.0032	0.0015-0.0032	NA	NA
	3.8 (3785)	K	45	45	80@1.750	1.690-1.720	0.0015-0.0032	0.0015-0.0032	NA	NA
1997	3.8 (3785)	1	45	45	80@1.750	1.690-1.720	0.0015-0.0032	0.0015-0.0032	NA	NA
	3.8 (3785)	K	45	45	80@1.750	1.690-1.720	0.0015-0.0032	0.0015-0.0032	NA	NA
1998	3.8 (3785)	1	45	45	80@1.750	1.690-1.720	0.0015-0.0032	0.0015-0.0032	NA	NA
	3.8 (3785)	K	45	45	80@1.750	1.690-1.720	0.0015-0.0032	0.0015-0.0032	NA	NA
1999-00	3.8 (3785)	1	45	45	80@1.750	1.690-1.720	0.0015-0.0032	0.0015-0.0032	NA	NA
	3.8 (3785)	K	45	45	80@1.750	1.690-1.720	0.0015-0.0032	0.0015-0.0032	NA	NA

NA - Not Available

93001CF6

CRANKSHAFT AND CONNECTING ROD SPECIFICATIONS
All measurements are given in inches.

Year	Engine Displacement Liters (cc)	Engine ID/VIN	Crankshaft Main Brg. Journal Dia.	Crankshaft Main Brg. Oil Clearance	Crankshaft Shaft End-play	Crankshaft Thrust on No.	Connecting Rod Journal Diameter	Connecting Rod Oil Clearance	Connecting Rod Side Clearance
1996	3.8 (3786)	1	2.4988-2.4998	①	0.0030-0.0110	2	2.2487-2.2499	0.0005-0.0026	0.0040-0.0200
	3.8 (3786)	K	2.4988-2.4998	①	0.0030-0.0110	2	2.2487-2.2499	0.0005-0.0026	0.0040-0.0200
1997	3.8 (3786)	1	2.4988-2.4998	①	0.0030-0.0110	2	2.2487-2.2499	0.0005-0.0026	0.0040-0.0200
	3.8 (3786)	K	2.4988-2.4998	①	0.0030-0.0110	2	2.2487-2.2499	0.0005-0.0026	0.0040-0.0200
1998	3.8 (3786)	1	2.4988-2.4998	①	0.0030-0.0110	2	2.2487-2.2499	0.0005-0.0026	0.0040-0.0200
	3.8 (3786)	K	2.4988-2.4998	①	0.0030-0.0110	2	2.2487-2.2499	0.0005-0.0026	0.0040-0.0200
1999-00	3.8 (3786)	1	2.4988-2.4998	①	0.0030-0.0110	2	2.2487-2.2499	0.0005-0.0026	0.0040-0.0200
	3.8 (3786)	K	2.4988-2.4998	①	0.0030-0.0110	2	2.2487-2.2499	0.0005-0.0026	0.0040-0.0200

① Journal 1: 0.0007 - 0.0016
  Journals 2 and 3: 0.0010 - 0.0020
  Journal 4: 0.0009 - 0.0018

93001CF7

PISTON AND RING SPECIFICATIONS
All measurements are given in inches.

| Year | Engine Displacement Liters (cc) | Engine ID/VIN | Piston Clearance | Ring Gap | | | Ring Side Clearance | | |
				Top Compression	Bottom Compression	Oil Control	Top Compression	Bottom Compression	Oil Control
1996	3.8 (3786)	1	0.0004-0.0020	0.012-0.022	0.030-0.040	0.010-0.030-	0.0013-0.0031	0.0013-0.0031	0.0009-0.0079
	3.8 (3786)	K	0.0004-0.0020	0.012-0.022	0.030-0.040	0.010-0.030-	0.0013-0.0031	0.0013-0.0031	0.0009-0.0079
1997	3.8 (3786)	1	0.0004-0.0020	0.012-0.022	0.030-0.040	0.010-0.030-	0.0013-0.0031	0.0013-0.0031	0.0009-0.0079
	3.8 (3786)	K	0.0004-0.0020	0.012-0.022	0.030-0.040	0.010-0.030-	0.0013-0.0031	0.0013-0.0031	0.0009-0.0079
1998	3.8 (3786)	1	0.0004-0.0020	0.012-0.022	0.030-0.040	0.010-0.030-	0.0013-0.0031	0.0013-0.0031	0.0009-0.0079
	3.8 (3786)	K	0.0004-0.0020	0.012-0.022	0.030-0.040	0.010-0.030-	0.0013-0.0031	0.0013-0.0031	0.0009-0.0079
1999-00	3.8 (3786)	1	0.0004-0.0020	0.012-0.022	0.030-0.040	0.010-0.030-	0.0013-0.0031	0.0013-0.0031	0.0009-0.0079
	3.8 (3786)	K	0.0004-0.0020	0.012-0.022	0.030-0.040	0.010-0.030-	0.0013-0.0031	0.0013-0.0031	0.0009-0.0079

93001CF9

TORQUE SPECIFICATIONS
All readings in ft. lbs.

| Year | Engine Displacement Liters (cc) | Engine ID/VIN | Cylinder Head Bolts | Main Bearing Bolts | Rod Bearing Bolts | Crankshaft Damper Bolts | Flywheel Bolts | Manifold | | Spark Plugs | Lug Nuts |
								Intake	Exhaust		
1996	3.8 (3786)	1	①	②	③	④	⑤	⑦	22	11	100
	3.8 (3786)	K	①	⑥	③	④	⑤	11	38	11	100
1997	3.8 (3786)	1	①	②	③	④	⑤	⑦	22	11	100
	3.8 (3786)	K	①	⑥	③	④	⑤	11	38	11	100
1998	3.8 (3786)	1	①	②	③	④	⑤	⑦	22	11	100
	3.8 (3786)	K	①	⑥	③	④	⑤	11	38	11	100
1999-00	3.8 (3786)	1	①	②	③	④	⑤	⑦	22	11	100
	3.8 (3786)	K	①	⑥	③	④	⑤	11	38	11	100

① Step 1: Tighten all bolts to 35 ft. lbs.
   Step 2: Turn all bolts 130 degrees
   Step 3: Rotate four center bolts an additional 30 degrees

② Step 1: Tighten caps in equal increments to 52 ft. lbs.
   Step 2: Loosen 360 degrees
   Step 3: 15 ft. lbs.
   Step 4: 54 ft. lbs.
   Step 5: Plus three turns of 35 degrees for a total of 105 degrees

③ 20 ft. lbs. plus 50 degrees

④ 111 ft. lbs. plus 76 degrees

⑤ 11 ft. lbs. plus 50 degrees

⑥ 26 ft. lbs. plus 50 degrees

⑦ Upper manifold: 8 ft. lbs.
   Lower manifold: 11 ft. lbs.

93001CF0

SCHEDULED MAINTENANCE INTERVALS
(GM C & H BODIES-BUICK LESABRE, PARK AVENUE, OLDSMOBILE LSS, REGENCY & EIGHTY-EIGHT, NINETY-EIGHT, PONTIAC BONNEVILLE)

TO BE SERVICED	TYPE OF SERVICE	VEHICLE MILEAGE INTERVAL (x1000)												
		7.5	15	22.5	30	37.5	45	52.5	60	67.5	75	82.5	90	97.5
Engine oil & filter	R	✓	✓	✓	✓	✓	✓	✓	✓	✓	✓	✓	✓	✓
Exhaust system & brake hoses	S/I	✓	✓	✓	✓	✓	✓	✓	✓	✓	✓	✓	✓	✓
Drive shaft boots & front suspension components	S/I	✓	✓	✓	✓	✓	✓	✓	✓	✓	✓	✓	✓	✓
Lubricate chassis, suspension, steering linkage, transaxle shift linkage, parking brake cable guides, underbody contact points & linkage	S/I	✓	✓	✓	✓	✓	✓	✓	✓	✓	✓	✓	✓	✓
Coolant level, hoses & clamps	S/I	✓	✓	✓	✓	✓	✓	✓	✓	✓	✓	✓	✓	✓
Throttle linkage	S/I	✓	✓	✓	✓	✓	✓	✓	✓	✓	✓	✓	✓	✓
Brake linings & rotate tires	S/I	✓		✓		✓		✓		✓		✓		✓
Accessory drive belts supercharger oil	S/I				✓				✓				✓	
Engine coolant ②	R													
Spark plugs ①	R				✓				✓				✓	
Air filter element	R				✓				✓				✓	
PCV filter	R				✓				✓				✓	
Ignition cables	S/I				✓				✓				✓	
EGR & fuel systems	S/I				✓				✓				✓	
Automatic transaxle fluid & filter	R													✓
Throttle body mount bolt torque	S/I	✓												

① Platinum tip spark plugs - replace every 100,000 miles.

② Engine coolant - replace every 100,000 miles. Use O.E. specified (DEX-COOL™) coolant only. If any silicate coolant is used, the service interval is every 30,000 miles.

R - Replace   S/I - Service or Inspect

93001CG1

Timing chain and gear service is covered in the model specific sections of this manual

SCHEDULED MAINTENANCE INTERVALS
GENERAL MOTORS CORPORATION
C & H BODIES
BUICK LESABRE, PARK AVENUE, OLDSMOBILE EIGHTY-EIGHT, NINETY-EIGHT, LSS, REGENCY, PONTIAC BONNEVILLE

The following should be used as a guide when determining the amount of work required for a particular service. In estimating how long a particular Scheduled Maintenance Service should take, please observe the following:

- **Chilton Time** is time based on field research and data supplied by the vehicle manufacturer.
  - Labor time operations are given in hours and tenths of an hour.
  - All labor operations, are to be used as a guide.

Mechanic Skill Level Codes:
(A) PRECISION: Really skilled with multiple certification.
(B) GENERAL: Normally skilled with certification.
(C) MAINTENANCE: Semi-skilled working on certification.

	Chilton Time		Chilton Time		Chilton Time
7500 Mile Service (C)		**45000 Mile Service (C)**		**67500 Mile Service (C)**	
All Models	1.5	All Models	.9	All Models	1.5
15000 Mile Service (C)		**52500 Mile Service (C)**		**75000 Mile Service (C)**	
All Models	.9	All Models	1.5	All Models	.9
22500 Mile Service (C)		**60000 Mile Service (B)**		**82500 Mile Service (C)**	
All Models	1.5	All Models	3.8	All Models	1.5
30000 Mile Service (B)				**90000 Mile Service (B)**	
All Models	3.8			All Models	3.8
37500 Mile Service (C)				**97500 Mile Service (B)**	
All Models	1.5			All Models	2.0

93001CG2

GENERAL MOTORS E- & K-BODIES
Cadillac DeVille • DeVille Concours • Eldorado • Seville

ENGINE AND VEHICLE IDENTIFICATION

Engine							Model Year	
Code ①	Liters (cc)	Cu. In.	Cyl.	Fuel Sys.	Engine Type	Eng. Mfg.	Code ②	Year
9	4.6 (4573)	279	8	MFI	DOHC	Cadillac	T	1996
Y	4.6 (4573)	279	8	MFI	DOHC	Cadillac	V	1997
DOHC - Double Overhead Camshafts							W	1998
MFI - Multi-point Fuel Injection							X	1999
① 8th position of VIN							Y	2000
② 10th position of VIN								

93001CG3

GENERAL ENGINE SPECIFICATIONS

Year	Model	Engine Displacement Liters (cc)	Engine Series (ID/VIN)	Fuel System	Net Horsepower @ rpm	Net Torque @ rpm (ft. lbs.)	Bore x Stroke (in.)	Compression Ratio	Oil Pressure @ rpm
1996	DeVille	4.6 (4573)	Y	MFI	275@5600	300@4000	3.66x3.31	10.3:1	35@2000
	DeVille Concours	4.6 (4573)	9	MFI	300@6000	290@4400	3.66x3.31	10.3:1	35@2000
	Eldorado	4.6 (4573)	Y	MFI	275@5600	300@4000	3.66x3.31	10.3:1	35@2000
	Eldorado ETC	4.6 (4573)	9	MFI	300@6000	290@4400	3.66x3.31	10.3:1	35@2000
	Seville SLS	4.6 (4573)	Y	MFI	275@5600	300@4000	3.66x3.31	10.3:1	35@2000
	Seville STS	4.6 (4573)	9	MFI	300@6000	290@4400	3.66x3.31	10.3:1	35@2000
1997	DeVille	4.6 (4573)	Y	MFI	275@5600	300@4000	3.66x3.31	10.3:1	35@2000
	DeVille Concours	4.6 (4573)	9	MFI	300@6000	290@4400	3.66x3.31	10.3:1	35@2000
	Eldorado	4.6 (4573)	Y	MFI	275@5600	300@4000	3.66x3.31	10.3:1	35@2000
	Eldorado ETC	4.6 (4573)	9	MFI	300@6000	290@4400	3.66x3.31	10.3:1	35@2000
	Seville SLS	4.6 (4573)	Y	MFI	275@5600	300@4000	3.66x3.31	10.3:1	35@2000
	Seville STS	4.6 (4573)	9	MFI	300@6000	290@4400	3.66x3.31	10.3:1	35@2000
1998	DeVille	4.6 (4573)	Y	MFI	275@5600	300@4000	3.66x3.31	10.3:1	35@2000
	DeVille Concours	4.6 (4573)	9	MFI	300@6000	290@4400	3.66x3.31	10.3:1	35@2000
	Eldorado	4.6 (4573)	Y	MFI	275@5600	300@4000	3.66x3.31	10.3:1	35@2000
	Eldorado ETC	4.6 (4573)	9	MFI	300@6000	290@4400	3.66x3.31	10.3:1	35@2000
	Seville SLS	4.6 (4573)	Y	MFI	275@5600	300@4000	3.66x3.31	10.3:1	35@2000
	Seville STS	4.6 (4573)	9	MFI	300@6000	290@4400	3.66x3.31	10.3:1	35@2000
1999-00	DeVille	4.6 (4573)	Y	MFI	275@5600	300@4000	3.66x3.31	10.3:1	35@2000
	DeVille Concours	4.6 (4573)	9	MFI	300@6000	290@4400	3.66x3.31	10.3:1	35@2000
	Eldorado	4.6 (4573)	Y	MFI	275@5600	300@4000	3.66x3.31	10.3:1	35@2000
	Eldorado ETC	4.6 (4573)	9	MFI	300@6000	290@4400	3.66x3.31	10.3:1	35@2000
	Seville SLS	4.6 (4573)	Y	MFI	275@5600	300@4000	3.66x3.31	10.3:1	35@2000
	Seville STS	4.6 (4573)	9	MFI	300@6000	290@4400	3.66x3.31	10.3:1	35@2000

MFI - Multi-point Fuel Injection

93001CG4

Ignition system service is covered in the model specific sections of this manual.

ENGINE TUNE-UP SPECIFICATIONS

Year	Engine Displacement Liters (cc)	Engine ID/VIN	Spark Plug Gap (in.)	Ignition Timing (deg.)	Fuel Pump (psi)	Idle Speed (rpm)	Valve Clearance	
							Intake	Exhaust
1996	4.6 (4573)	9	0.050	①	40-50	①	HYD	HYD
	4.6 (4573)	Y	0.050	①	40-50	①	HYD	HYD
1997	4.6 (4573)	9	0.050	①	40-50	①	HYD	HYD
	4.6 (4573)	Y	0.050	①	40-50	①	HYD	HYD
1998	4.6 (4573)	9	0.050	①	40-50	①	HYD	HYD
	4.6 (4573)	Y	0.050	①	40-50	①	HYD	HYD
1999-00	4.6 (4573)	9	0.050	①	40-50	①	HYD	HYD
	4.6 (4573)	Y	0.050	①	40-50	①	HYD	HYD

NOTE: The Vehicle Emission Control Information label often reflects specification changes made during production. The label figures must be used if they differ from those in this chart.

HYD - Hydraulic

① Refer to Vehicle Emission Control Information label

93001CG5

CAPACITIES

Year	Model	Engine Displacement Liters (cc)	Engine ID/VIN	Engine Oil with Filter (qts.)	Transmission (pts.) ①	Fuel Tank (gal.)	Cooling System (qts.) ②
1996	DeVille	4.6 (4573)	Y	7.5	16.0	20.0	12.3
	DeVille Concours	4.6 (4573)	9	7.5	16.0	18.0	12.3
	Eldorado	4.6 (4573)	Y	7.5	16.0	20.0	12.3
	Eldorado ETC	4.6 (4573)	9	7.5	16.0	20.0	12.3
	Seville SLS	4.6 (4573)	Y	7.5	16.0	20.0	12.3
	Seville STS	4.6 (4573)	9	7.5	16.0	20.0	12.3
1997	DeVille	4.6 (4573)	Y	7.5	16.0	20.0	12.3
	DeVille Concours	4.6 (4573)	9	7.5	16.0	18.0	12.3
	Eldorado	4.6 (4573)	Y	7.5	16.0	20.0	12.3
	Eldorado ETC	4.6 (4573)	9	7.5	16.0	20.0	12.3
	Seville SLS	4.6 (4573)	Y	7.5	16.0	20.0	12.3
	Seville STS	4.6 (4573)	9	7.5	16.0	20.0	12.3
1998	DeVille	4.6 (4573)	Y	7.5	16.0	20.0	12.3
	DeVille Concours	4.6 (4573)	9	7.5	16.0	18.0	12.3
	Eldorado	4.6 (4573)	Y	7.5	16.0	20.0	12.3
	Eldorado ETC	4.6 (4573)	9	7.5	16.0	20.0	12.3
	Seville SLS	4.6 (4573)	Y	7.5	16.0	20.0	12.3
	Seville STS	4.6 (4573)	9	7.5	16.0	20.0	12.3
1999-00	DeVille	4.6 (4573)	Y	7.5	16.0	20.0	12.3
	DeVille Concours	4.6 (4573)	9	7.5	16.0	18.0	12.3
	Eldorado	4.6 (4573)	Y	7.5	16.0	20.0	12.3
	Eldorado ETC	4.6 (4573)	9	7.5	16.0	20.0	12.3
	Seville SLS	4.6 (4573)	Y	7.5	16.0	20.0	12.3
	Seville STS	4.6 (4573)	9	7.5	16.0	20.0	12.3

① Bottom pan and side cover

② Dex-Cool engine coolant and three pellets of P/N 1052753 or equivalent
   (Do not mix with ethylene glycol base)

93001CG6

VALVE SPECIFICATIONS

Year	Engine Displacement Liters (cc)	Engine ID/VIN	Seat Angle (deg.)	Face Angle (deg.)	Spring Test Pressure (lbs. @ in.)	Spring Installed Height (in.)	Stem-to-Guide Clearance (in.)		Stem Diameter (in.)	
							Intake	Exhaust	Intake	Exhaust
1996	4.6 (4573)	9	46	45	53@1.190	1.190	0.0010-0.0030	0.0020-0.0040	0.2331-0.2339	0.2331-0.2339
	4.6 (4573)	Y	46	45	46@1.190	1.190	0.0010-0.0030	0.0020-0.0040	0.2331-0.2339	0.2331-0.2339
1997	4.6 (4573)	9	46	45	53@1.190	1.190	0.0010-0.0030	0.0020-0.0040	0.2331-0.2339	0.2331-0.2339
	4.6 (4573)	Y	46	45	46@1.190	1.190	0.0010-0.0030	0.0020-0.0040	0.2331-0.2339	0.2331-0.2339
1998	4.6 (4573)	9	46	45	53@1.190	1.190	0.0010-0.0030	0.0020-0.0040	0.2331-0.2339	0.2331-0.2339
	4.6 (4573)	Y	46	45	46@1.190	1.190	0.0010-0.0030	0.0020-0.0040	0.2331-0.2339	0.2331-0.2339
1999-00	4.6 (4573)	9	46	45	53@1.190	1.190	0.0010-0.0030	0.0020-0.0040	0.2331-0.2339	0.2331-0.2339
	4.6 (4573)	Y	46	45	46@1.190	1.190	0.0010-0.0030	0.0020-0.0040	0.2331-0.2339	0.2331-0.2339

93001CG7

CRANKSHAFT AND CONNECTING ROD SPECIFICATIONS
All measurements are given in inches.

Year	Engine Displacement Liters (cc)	Engine ID/VIN	Crankshaft				Connecting Rod		
			Main Brg. Journal Dia.	Main Brg. Oil Clearance	Shaft End-play	Thrust on No.	Journal Diameter	Oil Clearance	Side Clearance
1996	9	4.6 (4573)	2.5335-2.5337	0.0006-0.0025	0.0020-0.0200	3	2.1239-2.1235	0.001-0.003	0.0080-0.0200
	Y	4.6 (4573)	2.5335-2.5337	0.0006-0.0025	0.0020-0.0200	3	2.1239-2.1235	0.001-0.003	0.0080-0.0200
1997	9	4.6 (4573)	2.5335-2.5337	0.0006-0.0025	0.0020-0.0200	3	2.1239-2.1235	0.001-0.003	0.0080-0.0200
	Y	4.6 (4573)	2.5335-2.5337	0.0006-0.0025	0.0020-0.0200	3	2.1239-2.1235	0.001-0.003	0.0080-0.0200
1998	9	4.6 (4573)	2.5335-2.5337	0.0006-0.0025	0.0020-0.0200	3	2.1239-2.1235	0.001-0.003	0.0080-0.0200
	Y	4.6 (4573)	2.5335-2.5337	0.0006-0.0025	0.0020-0.0200	3	2.1239-2.1235	0.001-0.003	0.0080-0.0200
1999-00	9	4.6 (4573)	2.5335-2.5337	0.0006-0.0025	0.0020-0.0200	3	2.1239-2.1235	0.001-0.003	0.0080-0.0200
	Y	4.6 (4573)	2.5335-2.5337	0.0006-0.0025	0.0020-0.0200	3	2.1239-2.1235	0.001-0.003	0.0080-0.0200

93001CG8

PISTON AND RING SPECIFICATIONS

All measurements are given in inches.

Year	Engine Displacement Liters (cc)	Engine ID/VIN	Piston Clearance	Ring Gap			Ring Side Clearance		
				Top Compression	Bottom Compression	Oil Control	Top Compression	Bottom Compression	Oil Control
1996	4.6 (4573)	9	0.0008-0.0020	0.010-0.016	0.014-0.020	0.010-0.030	0.0016-0.0037	0.0016-0.0037	①
	4.6 (4573)	Y	0.0008-0.0020	0.010-0.016	0.014-0.020	0.010-0.030	0.0016-0.0037	0.0016-0.0037	①
1997	4.6 (4573)	9	0.0008-0.0020	0.010-0.016	0.014-0.020	0.010-0.030	0.0016-0.0037	0.0016-0.0037	①
	4.6 (4573)	Y	0.0008-0.0020	0.010-0.016	0.014-0.020	0.010-0.030	0.0016-0.0037	0.0016-0.0037	①
1998	4.6 (4573)	9	0.0008-0.0020	0.010-0.016	0.014-0.020	0.010-0.030	0.0016-0.0037	0.0016-0.0037	①
	4.6 (4573)	Y	0.0008-0.0020	0.010-0.016	0.014-0.020	0.010-0.030	0.0016-0.0037	0.0016-0.0037	①
1999-00	4.6 (4573)	9	0.0008-0.0020	0.010-0.016	0.014-0.020	0.010-0.030	0.0016-0.0037	0.0016-0.0037	①
	4.6 (4573)	Y	0.0008-0.0020	0.010-0.016	0.014-0.020	0.010-0.030	0.0016-0.0037	0.0016-0.0037	①

① Side sealing

93001CG9

SCHEDULED MAINTENANCE INTERVALS
(GM E & K BODIES-CADILLAC DEVILLE, DEVILLE CONCOURS, ELDORADO, SEVILLE)

TO BE SERVICED	TYPE OF SERVICE	VEHICLE MILEAGE INTERVAL (x1000)												
		7.5	15	22.5	30	37.5	45	52.5	60	67.5	75	82.5	90	97.5
Engine oil & filter	R	✓	✓	✓	✓	✓	✓	✓	✓	✓	✓	✓	✓	✓
Coolant level, hoses & clamps	S/I	✓	✓	✓	✓	✓	✓	✓	✓	✓	✓	✓	✓	✓
Drive shaft boots & front suspension components	S/I	✓	✓	✓	✓	✓	✓	✓	✓	✓	✓	✓	✓	✓
Exhaust system, brake hoses & throttle linkage	S/I	✓	✓	✓	✓	✓	✓	✓	✓	✓	✓	✓	✓	✓
Lubricate chassis, suspension, steering linkage, transaxle shift linkage, parking brake cable guides, underbody contact points & linkage	S/I	✓	✓	✓	✓	✓	✓	✓	✓	✓	✓	✓	✓	✓
Throttle body mount bolt torque	S/I	✓												
Brake linings	S/I	✓		✓		✓		✓		✓		✓		✓
Rotate tires	S/I	✓		✓		✓		✓		✓		✓		✓
Inspect throttle body bore & throttle plate for deposits	S/I		✓				✓				✓		✓	
Air filter element	R				✓				✓				✓	
Engine coolant ②	R													
PCV valve	R				✓				✓				✓	
Spark plugs ①	R				✓				✓				✓	
Accessory drive belt(s)	S/I				✓				✓				✓	
Automatic transaxle fluid & filter	S/I				✓				✓				✓	
EGR & fuel systems	S/I				✓				✓				✓	
Ignition cables	S/I				✓				✓				✓	

① Platinum tip spark plugs - replace every 100,000 miles.

② Engine coolant - replace every 100,000 miles. Use O.E. specified (DEX-COOL™) coolant only. If any silicate coolant is used, the service interval is every 30,000 miles.

R - Replace   S/I - Service or Inspect

FREQUENT OPERATION MAINTENANCE (SEVERE SERVICE)
If a vehicle is operated under any of the following conditions it is considered severe service:
- Extremely dusty areas.
- 50% or more of the vehicle operation is in 32°C (90°F) or higher temperatures, or constant operation in operation in temperatures below 0°C (32°F).
- Prolonged idling (vehicle operation in stop and go traffic).
- Frequent short running periods (engine does not warm to normal operating temperatures).
- Police, taxi, delivery usage or trailer towing usage.

CV joints & front suspension components - service or inspect every 3000 miles.
Engine oil & filter change - change every 3000 miles.
Brake linings - check every 6000 miles.
Chassis lubrication - lubricate every 6000 miles.
Suspension, steering linkage, transaxle shift linkage, parking cable guides, underbody contact points - lubricate every 6000 miles.
Throttle body mount bolt torque - tighten at 6000 miles.
Air filter element - service or inspect every 15,000 miles.
Automatic transaxle fluid - change every 50,000 miles (1996-97).
Inspect throttle body bore & throttle plate for deposits - clean as required every 15,000 miles.
Rotate tires at 6000 miles, then every 15,000 miles.

93001CH1

Refer to the model specific sections for engine mechanical service procedures

SCHEDULED MAINTENANCE INTERVALS
GENERAL MOTORS CORPORATION
E & K BODIES
CADILLAC DEVILLE, DEVILLE CONCOURS
ELDORADO, SEVILLE

The following should be used as a guide when determining the amount of work required for a particular service.
In estimating how long a particular Scheduled Maintenance Service should take, please observe the following:

- **Chilton Time** is time based on field research and data supplied by the vehicle manufacturer.
  - Labor time operations are given in hours and tenths of an hour.
  - All labor operations, are to be used as a guide.

Mechanic Skill Level Codes:
(A) PRECISION: Really skilled with multiple certification.
(B) GENERAL: Normally skilled with certification.
(C) MAINTENANCE: Semi-skilled working on certification.

	Chilton Time			Chilton Time			Chilton Time
7500 Mile Service (C)			**45000 Mile Service (C)**			**67500 Mile Service (C)**	
All Models	1.6		All Models	1.0		All Models	1.5
15000 Mile Service (C)			**52500 Mile Service (C)**			**75000 Mile Service (C)**	
All Models	.9		All Models	1.5		All Models	1.0
22500 Mile Service (C)			**60000 Mile Service (B)**			**82500 Mile Service (C)**	
All Models	1.5		All Models	3.9		All Models	1.5
30000 Mile Service (B)						**90000 Mile Service (B)**	
All Models	3.9					All Models	4.1
37500 Mile Service (C)						**97500 Mile Service (C)**	
All Models	1.5					All Models	1.5

93001CH2

GENERAL MOTORS F-BODY
Chevrolet Camaro • Pontiac Firebird

ENGINE AND VEHICLE IDENTIFICATION

			Engine					Model Year
Code ①	Liters (cc)	Cu. In.	Cyl.	Fuel Sys.	Engine Type	Eng. Mfg.	Code ②	Year
G	5.7 (5665)	350	8	MFI	OHV	CPC	T	1996
K	3.8 (3785)	231	6	MFI	OHV	CPC	V	1997
P	5.7 (5737)	350	8	MFI	OHV	CPC	W	1998
							X	1999
							Y	2000

MFI - Multi-point Fuel Injection

CPC - Chevrolet/Pontiac/Canada

OHV - Overhead Valve

① 8th position of VIN

② 10th position of VIN

93001CH3

GENERAL ENGINE SPECIFICATIONS

Year	Model	Engine Displacement Liters (cc)	Engine Series (ID/VIN)	Fuel System	Net Horsepower @ rpm	Net Torque @ rpm (ft. lbs.)	Bore x Stroke (in.)	Com-pression Ratio	Oil Pressure @ rpm
1996	Camaro	3.8 (3785)	K	MFI	160@4600	200@3600	3.80x3.40	9.4:1	60@1850
		5.7 (5737)	P	MFI	275@5000	325@2400	4.00x3.48	10.25:1	18@2000
	Firebird	3.8 (3785)	K	MFI	160@4600	200@3600	3.80x3.40	9.4:1	60@1850
		5.7 (5737)	P	MFI	275@5000	325@2400	4.00x3.48	10.25:1	18@2000
1997	Camaro	3.8 (3785)	K	MFI	160@4600	200@3600	3.80x3.40	9.4:1	60@1850
		5.7 (5737)	P	MFI	275@5000	325@2400	4.00x3.48	10.25:1	18@2000
	Firebird	3.8 (3785)	K	MFI	160@4600	200@3600	3.80x3.40	9.4:1	60@1850
		5.7 (5737)	P	MFI	275@5000	325@2400	4.00x3.48	10.25:1	18@2000
1998	Camaro	5.7 (5665)	G	MFI	305@5200	335@4000	3.89x3.62	10.0:1	18@2000
		3.8 (3785)	K	MFI	200@5200	225@4000	3.80x3.40	9.4:1	60@1850
	Firebird	5.7 (5665)	G	MFI	305@5200	335@4000	3.89x3.62	10.0:1	18@2000
		3.8 (3785)	K	MFI	200@5200	225@4000	3.80x3.40	9.4:1	60@1850
1999-00	Camaro	5.7 (5665)	G	MFI	305@5200	335@4000	3.89x3.62	10.0:1	18@2000
		3.8 (3785)	K	MFI	200@5200	225@4000	3.80x3.40	9.4:1	60@1850
	Firebird	5.7 (5665)	G	MFI	305@5200	335@4000	3.89x3.62	10.0:1	18@2000
		3.8 (3785)	K	MFI	200@5200	225@4000	3.80x3.40	9.4:1	60@1850

MFI - Multi-point Fuel Injection

93001CH4

Refer to the model specific sections for fuel system service procedures

ENGINE TUNE-UP SPECIFICATIONS

Year	Engine Displacement Liters (cc)	Engine ID/VIN	Spark Plug Gap (in.)	Ignition Timing (deg.) MT	Ignition Timing (deg.) AT	Fuel Pump (psi)	Idle Speed (rpm) MT	Idle Speed (rpm) AT	Valve Clearance Intake	Valve Clearance Exhaust
1996	3.8 (3785)	K	0.045	①	①	41-47	①	①	HYD	HYD
	5.7 (5737)	P	0.035	—	①	41-47	—	①	HYD	HYD
1997	3.8 (3785)	K	0.045	①	①	41-47	①	①	HYD	HYD
	5.7 (5737)	P	0.035	—	①	41-47	—	①	HYD	HYD
1998	3.8 (3785)	K	0.045	①	①	41-47	①	①	HYD	HYD
	5.7 (5665)	G	0.060	①	①	48-55	①	①	HYD	HYD
1999-00	5.7 (5665)	G	0.060	①	①	48-55	①	①	HYD	HYD
	3.8 (3785)	K	0.045	①	①	41-47	①	①	HYD	HYD

NOTE: The Vehicle Emission Control Information label often reflects specification changes made during production. The label figures must be used if they differ from those in this chart.

HYD - Hydraulic

① Refer to Vehicle Emission Control Information label

93001CH5

CAPACITIES

Year	Model	Engine Displacement Liters (cc)	Engine ID/VIN	Engine Oil with Filter (qts.) ①	Transmission (pts.) 5-Spd	Transmission (pts.) Auto.	Drive Axle (pts.)	Fuel Tank (gal.)	Cooling System (qts.)
1996	Camaro	3.8 (3785)	K	4.5	5.9	10.0	3.5	15.5	12.5
		5.7 (5737)	P	4.5	②	10.0	3.5	15.5	15.2
	Firebird	3.8 (3785)	K	4.5	5.9	10.0	3.5	15.5	12.5
		5.7 (5737)	P	4.5	②	10.0	3.5	15.5	15.2
1997	Camaro	3.8 (3785)	K	4.5	5.9	10.0	3.5	15.5	12.5
		5.7 (5737)	P	4.5	②	10.0	3.5	15.5	15.2
	Firebird	3.8 (3785)	K	4.5	5.9	10.0	3.5	15.5	12.5
		5.7 (5737)	P	4.5	②	10.0	3.5	15.5	15.2
1998	Camaro	3.8 (3785)	K	4.5	5.9	10.0	3.5	15.5	④
		3.8 (3785)	K	4.5	5.9	10.0	3.5	15.5	④
	Firebird	5.7 (5665)	G	4.5	②	10.0	3.5	15.5	③
		5.7 (5665)	G	4.5	②	10.0	3.5	15.5	③
1999-00	Camaro	3.8 (3785)	K	4.5	5.9	10.0	3.5	15.5	④
		3.8 (3785)	K	4.5	5.9	10.0	3.5	15.5	④
	Firebird	5.7 (5665)	G	4.5	②	10.0	3.5	15.5	③
		5.7 (5665)	G	4.5	②	10.0	3.5	15.5	③

NOTE: All capacities are approximate. Add fluid gradually and ensure a proper fluid level is obtained.

① With vehicle on level surface, check oil level. Add as required to fill.

② ZF 6 speed transmission: 4.4 pts.

③ With mauual transmission: 12.5 qts.
   With automatic transmission: 12.3 qts.

④ With manual transmission: 15.3 qts.
   With automatic transmission: 15.1 qts.

93001CH6

VALVE SPECIFICATIONS

Year	Engine Displacement Liters (cc)	Engine ID/VIN	Seat Angle (deg.)	Face Angle (deg.)	Spring Test Pressure (lbs. @ in.) ①	Spring Installed Height (in.)	Stem-to-Guide Clearance (in.)		Stem Diameter (in.)	
							Intake	Exhaust	Intake	Exhaust
1996	3.8 (3785)	K	45	45	210@1.32	1.69-1.72	0.0015-0.0035	0.0015-0.0032	NA	NA
	5.7 (5737)	P	46	45	245-265@1.33	1.78	0.0009-0.0027	0.0009-0.0027	NA	NA
1997	3.8 (3785)	K	45	45	210@1.32	1.69-1.72	0.0015-0.0035	0.0015-0.0032	NA	NA
	5.7 (5737)	P	46	45	245-265@1.33	1.78	0.0009-0.0027	0.0009-0.0027	NA	NA
1998	3.8 (3785)	K	45	45	228@1.277	1.69-1.72	0.0015-0.0035	0.0015-0.0032	NA	NA
	5.7 (5665)	G	46	45	220@1.32	1.80	0.0010-0.0026	0.0010-0.0026	0.0313-0.0314	0.0313-0.0314
1999-00	3.8 (3785)	K	45	45	228@1.277	1.69-1.72	0.0015-0.0035	0.0015-0.0032	NA	NA
	5.7 (5665)	G	46	45	220@1.32	1.80	0.0010-0.0026	0.0010-0.0026	0.0313-0.0314	0.0313-0.0314

NA - Not Available

① With valve open

93001CH7

Refer to the model specific sections for engine electrical system service procedures

CRANKSHAFT AND CONNECTING ROD SPECIFICATIONS

All measurements are given in inches.

Year	Engine Displacement Liters (cc)	Engine ID/VIN	Crankshaft				Connecting Rod		
			Main Brg. Journal Dia.	Main Brg. Oil Clearance	Shaft End-play	Thrust on No.	Journal Diameter	Oil Clearance	Side Clearance
1996	3.8 (3786)	K	2.4988-2.4998	①	0.0030-0.0110	2	2.2487-2.2499	0.0005-0.0026	0.0040-0.0200
	5.7 (5737)	P	②	③	0.002-0.0080	5	2.0978-2.0998	0.0013-0.0035	0.0060-0.0240
1997	3.8 (3786)	K	2.4988-2.4998	①	0.0030-0.0110	2	2.2487-2.2499	0.0005-0.0026	0.0040-0.020
	5.7 (5737)	P	②	③	0.002-0.0080	5	2.0978-2.0998	0.0013-0.0035	0.0060-0.0240
1998	3.8 (3786)	K	2.4988-2.4998	①	0.0030-0.0110	2	2.2487-2.2499	0.0005-0.0026	0.0040-0.0200
	5.7 (5665)	G	2.5590	0.0007-0.0021	0.0015-0.0078	3	2.0990	0.0006-0.0030	0.0043-0.0200
1999-00	3.8 (3786)	K	2.4988-2.4998	①	0.0030-0.0110	2	2.2487-2.2499	0.0005-0.0026	0.0040-0.020
	5.7 (5665)	G	2.5590	0.0007-0.0021	0.0015-0.0078	3	2.0990	0.0006-0.0030	0.00433-0.0200

① Journal 1: 0.0007 - 0.0016
   Journals 2 and 3: 0.0010 - 0.0020
   Journal 4: 0.0009 - 0.0018
② Journal 1: 2.4484 - 2.4493
   Journals 2, 3 and 4: 2.4481 - 2.4491
   Journal 5: 2.4479 - 2.4491
③ Journal 1: 0.0007 - 0.0021
   Journals 2, 3 and 4: 0.0009 - 0.0024
   Journal 5: 0.0010 - 0.0027

93001CH8

PISTON AND RING SPECIFICATIONS

All measurements are given in inches.

Year	Engine Displacement Liters (cc)	Engine ID/VIN	Piston Clearance	Ring Gap			Ring Side Clearance		
				Top Compression	Bottom Compression	Oil Control	Top Compression	Bottom Compression	Oil Control
1996	3.8 (3786)	K	0.0004-0.0020	0.012-0.022	0.0300-0.0400	0.010-0.030-	0.0013-0.0031	0.0013-0.0031	0.0009-0.0079
	5.7 (5737)	P	0.0010-0.0027	0.010-0.016	0.0180-0.0260	0.010-0.030	0.0019-0.0035	0.0019-0.0035	0.0020-0.0070
1997	3.8 (3786)	K	0.0004-0.0020	0.012-0.022	0.0300-0.0400	0.010-0.030-	0.0013-0.0031	0.0013-0.0031	0.0009-0.0079
	5.7 (5737)	P	0.0010-0.0027	0.010-0.016	0.0180-0.0260	0.010-0.030	0.0019-0.0035	0.0019-0.0035	0.0020-0.0070
1998	3.8 (3786)	K	0.0004-0.0020	0.012-0.022	0.0300-0.0400	0.010-0.030-	0.0013-0.0031	0.0013-0.0031	0.0009-0.0079
	5.7 (5665)	G	0.0007-0.0021	0.009-0.015	0.0017-0.0025	0.007-0.027	0.0016-0.0034	0.0016-0.0032	0.0004-0.0087
1999-00	3.8 (3786)	K	0.0004-0.0020	0.012-0.022	0.0300-0.0400	0.010-0.030-	0.0013-0.0031	0.0013-0.0031	0.0009-0.0079
	5.7 (5665)	G	0.0007-0.0021	0.009-0.015	0.0017-0.0025	0.007-0.027	0.0016-0.0034	0.0016-0.0032	0.0004-0.0087

93001CH9

For accessory drive belt replacement procedures see the model specific sections of this manual

TORQUE SPECIFICATIONS
All readings in ft. lbs.

Year	Engine Displacement Liters (cc)	Engine ID/VIN	Cylinder Head Bolts	Main Bearing Bolts	Rod Bearing Bolts	Crankshaft Damper Bolts	Flywheel Bolts	Manifold Intake	Manifold Exhaust	Spark Plugs	Lug Nuts
1996	3.8 (3785)	K	①	②	20	③	④	⑤	18	23	100
	5.7 (5737)	P	65	78	47	60	74	35	22	11	100
1997	3.8 (3785)	K	①	②	20	③	④	⑤	18	23	100
	5.7 (5737)	P	65	78	47	60	74	35	22	11	100
1998	3.8 (3785)	K	①	②	20	③	④	⑤	18	23	100
	5.7 (5665)	G	⑥	⑦	⑧	⑨	⑩	⑪	⑫	12	100
1999-00	3.8 (3785)	K	⑤	②	20	③	④	⑤	18	23	100
	5.7 (5665)	G	⑥	⑦	⑧	⑨	⑩	⑪	⑫	12	100

NA - Not Available

① Step 1: 37 ft. lbs. plus 130 degrees

   Step 2: Turn center bolts an additional 30 degrees

② Step 1: Tighten to 52 ft. lbs. to fully seat caps

   Step 2: Loosen bearing cap 360 degrees counter-clockwise

   Step 3: Tighten caps 15 ft. lbs., then 30 ft. lbs., then 35 degrees,

   then an additional 35 degrees plus 40 degrees -- for a total of 110 degrees

③ 111 ft. lbs. plus 76 degrees

④ 11 ft. lbs. plus 50 degrees

⑤ Upper manifold: 18 ft. lbs.

   Lower manifold bolt/nut: 22 ft. lbs.

   Upper manifold studs: 89 inch lbs.

⑥ Step 1: 22 ft. lbs.

   Step 2: Rotate 76 degrees

   Step 3: Repeat Step 2

   Step 3: Rotate 34 degrees

   Step 4: Tighten inner (M8) bolts to 22 ft. lbs

⑦ Step 1: Inner bolts: 15 ft. lbs.

   Step 2: Inner bolts: Rotate 80 degrees

   Step 3: Outer side studs: 18 ft. lbs.

   Step 4: Outer side studs: Rotate 53 degrees

⑧ Step 1: 15 ft. lbs.

   Step 2: Rotate 60 degrees

⑨ Step 1: Ensure damper is instll fully, tighten old bolt 240 ft. lbs.

   Step 1: Ensure damper is instll fully, tighten old bolt 240 ft. lbs.

   Step 3: Rotate 120 degrees

⑩ Step 1: 15 ft. lbs.

   Step 2: 37 ft. lbs.

   Step 3: 74 ft. lbs.

⑪ Step 1: 44 inch lbs.

   Step 2: 74 inch lbs

⑫ Step 1: 11 ft. lbs.

   Step 2: 18 ft. lbs

93001CH0

SCHEDULED MAINTENANCE INTERVALS
(GM F BODY - CHEVROLET CAMARO, PONTIAC FIREBIRD)

TO BE SERVICED	TYPE OF SERVICE	VEHICLE MILEAGE INTERVAL (x1000)												
		7.5	15	22.5	30	37.5	45	52.5	60	67.5	75	82.5	90	97.5
Engine oil & filter	R	✓	✓	✓	✓	✓	✓	✓	✓	✓	✓	✓	✓	✓
Coolant level, hoses & clamps	S/I	✓	✓	✓	✓	✓	✓	✓	✓	✓	✓	✓	✓	✓
Exhaust system, brake hoses & throttle linkage	S/I	✓	✓	✓	✓	✓	✓	✓	✓	✓	✓	✓	✓	✓
Lubricate chassis, suspension, steering linkage, transaxle shift linkage, parking brake cable guides, underbody contact points & linkage	S/I	✓	✓	✓	✓	✓	✓	✓	✓	✓	✓	✓	✓	✓
Brake hoses & brake linings	S/I	✓		✓		✓		✓		✓		✓		✓
Rotate tires ③	S/I	✓		✓		✓		✓		✓		✓		✓
Automatic transmission fluid & filter ⑤	S/I													
Air filter element & PCV filter	R				✓				✓				✓	
Engine coolant ②	R													
Spark plugs ①	R				✓				✓				✓	
Ignition cables, EGR & fuel systems	S/I				✓				✓				✓	
Serpentine drive belt	S/I				✓				✓				✓	
Rear axle oil (Limited slip) ④	R	✓												

① Platinum tip spark plugs - replace every 100,000 miles.

② Engine coolant - replace every 100,000 miles. Use O.E. specified (DEX-COOL™) coolant only. If any silicate coolant is used, the service interval is every 30,000 miles.

③ For models with P245/50ZR16 tires, rotate front-to-rear only, & be sure that the tires roll in the direction indicated by the arrows on the side walls.

④ If the vehicle is used to tow a trailer, change the rear axle fluid every 7500 miles in either type of differential.

⑤ Automatic transmission fluid & filter - replace every 100,000 miles.

R - Replace   S/I - Service or Inspect

FREQUENT OPERATION MAINTENANCE (SEVERE SERVICE)

If a vehicle is operated under any of the following conditions it is considered severe service:
- **Extremely dusty areas.**
- **50% or more of the vehicle operation is in 32°C (90°F) or higher temperatures, or constant operation in operation in temperatures below 0°C (32°F).**
- **Prolonged idling (vehicle operation in stop and go traffic).**
- **Frequent short running periods (engine does not warm to normal operating temperatures).**
- **Police, taxi, delivery usage or trailer towing usage.**

Oil & oil filter - change every 3000 miles.
Chassis lubrication - lubricate every 6000 miles.
Automatic transmission fluid & filter - change every 15,000 miles.
Air filter element - service or inspect every 15,000 miles.
Rotate tires at 6000 miles, then every 15,000 miles. ®

93001CI1

For brake related suspension and axle service, refer to the model specific sections of this manual

SCHEDULED MAINTENANCE INTERVALS
GENERAL MOTORS CORPORATION
F BODY
CHEVROLET CAMARO
PONTIAC FIREBIRD, TRANS AM

The following should be used as a guide when determining the amount of work required for a particular service. In estimating how long a particular Scheduled Maintenance Service should take, please observe the following:

- **Chilton Time** is time based on field research and data supplied by the vehicle manufacturer.
  - Labor time operations are given in hours and tenths of an hour.
    - All labor operations, are to be used as a guide.

Mechanic Skill Level Codes:
(A) PRECISION: Really skilled with multiple certification.
(B) GENERAL: Normally skilled with certification.
(C) MAINTENANCE: Semi-skilled working on certification.

	Chilton Time		Chilton Time		Chilton Time
7500 Mile Service (C)		**37500 Mile Service (C)**		**75000 Mile Service (C)**	
All Models	1.8	All Models	1.5	All Models	.9
15000 Mile Service (C)		**45000 Mile Service (C)**		**82500 Mile Service (C)**	
All Models	.9	All Models	.9	All Models	1.5
22500 Mile Service (C)		**52500 Mile Service (C)**		**90000 Mile Service (B)**	
All Models	1.5	All Models	1.5	All Models	2.9
30000 Mile Service (B)		**60000 Mile Service (B)**		**97500 Mile Service (C)**	
All Models	2.9	All Models	2.9	All Models	1.5
		67500 Mile Service (C)			
		All Models	1.5		

93001CI2

GENERAL MOTORS G-BODY
Buick Riviera • Oldsmobile Aurora

ENGINE AND VEHICLE IDENTIFICATION

	Engine							Model Year	
Code ①	Liters (cc)	Cu. In.	Cyl.	Fuel Sys.	Engine Type	Eng. Mfg.		Code ②	Year
1 ③	3.8 (3785)	231	6	MFI	OHV	BOC		T	1996
C	4.0 (3995)	244	8	MFI	DOHC	BOC		V	1997
K	3.8 (3785)	231	6	MFI	OHV	BOC		W	1998
								X	1999
								Y	2000

DOHC - Double Overhead Camshafts

OHV - Overhead Valves

MFI - Multi-point Fuel Injection

BOC - Buick/Oldsmobile/Cadillac

① 8th position of VIN

② 10th position of VIN

③ Supercharged Engine

93001CI3

GENERAL ENGINE SPECIFICATIONS

Year	Model	Engine Displacement Liters (cc)		Engine Series (ID/VIN)	Fuel System	Net Horsepower @ rpm	Net Torque @ rpm (ft. lbs.)	Bore x Stroke (in.)	Com-pression Ratio	Oil Pressure @ rpm
1996	Aurora	4.0 (3995)		C	MFI	250@5600	245@4400	3.43x3.31	10.2:1	30@2000
	Riviera	3.8 (3785)	①	1	MFI	225@5000	275@3200	3.80x3.40	9.0:1	60@1850
		3.8 (3785)		K	MFI	205@5200	230@4000	3.80x3.40	9.4:1	60@1850
1997	Aurora	4.0 (3995)		C	MFI	250@5600	245@4400	3.43x3.31	10.2:1	30@2000
	Riviera	3.8 (3785)	①	1	MFI	225@5000	275@3200	3.80x3.40	9.0:1	60@1850
		3.8 (3785)		K	MFI	205@5200	230@4000	3.80x3.40	9.4:1	60@1850
1998	Aurora	4.0 (3995)		C	MFI	250@5600	245@4400	3.43x3.31	10.2:1	30@2000
	Riviera	3.8 (3785)	①	1	MFI	225@5000	275@3200	3.80x3.40	9.0:1	60@1850
		3.8 (3785)		K	MFI	205@5200	230@4000	3.80x3.40	9.4:1	60@1850
1999-00	Aurora	4.0 (3995)		C	MFI	250@5600	245@4400	3.43x3.31	10.2:1	30@2000

MFI - Multi-point Fuel Injection

① Supercharged Engine

93001CI4

Refer to the model specific sections for driveline service procedures

ENGINE TUNE-UP SPECIFICATIONS

Year	Engine Displacement Liters (cc)	Engine ID/VIN	Spark Plug Gap (in.)	Ignition Timing (deg.)	Fuel Pump (psi)	Idle Speed (rpm)	Valve Clearance Intake	Valve Clearance Exhaust
1996	3.8 (3785)	1	0.060	①	40-47	②	HYD	HYD
	3.8 (3785)	K	0.060	①	40-47	②	HYD	HYD
	4.0 (3995)	C	0.050	①	41-47	②	HYD	HYD
1997	3.8 (3785)	1	0.060	①	40-47	②	HYD	HYD
	3.8 (3785)	K	0.060	①	40-47	②	HYD	HYD
	4.0 (3995)	C	0.050	①	41-47	②	HYD	HYD
1998	3.8 (3785)	1	0.060	①	40-47	②	HYD	HYD
	3.8 (3785)	K	0.060	①	40-47	②	HYD	HYD
	4.0 (3995)	C	0.050	①	41-47	②	HYD	HYD
1999-00	4.0 (3995)	C	0.050	①	41-47	②	HYD	HYD

NOTE: The Vehicle Emission Control Information label often reflects specification changes made during production. The label figures must be used if they differ from those in this chart.

HYD - Hydraulic

① DIS Ignition System timing is not adjustable

② Idle speed is maintained by the ECM. There is no recommended adjustment procedure

93001CI5

CAPACITIES

Year	Model	Engine Displacement Liters (cc)	Engine ID/VIN	Engine Oil with Filter (qts.)	Transmission (pts.)	Fuel Tank (gal.)	Cooling System (qts.)
1996	Aurora	4.0 (3995)	C	7.0	6.5	20.0	13.0
	Riviera	3.8 (3785)	1	5.0	13.2	20.0	13.0
		3.8 (3785)	K	5.0	13.2	20.0	13.0
1997	Aurora	4.0 (3995)	C	7.5	6.5	20.0	13.0
	Riviera	3.8 (3785)	1	5.0	12.0	20.0	13.0
		3.8 (3785)	K	4.5	12.0	20.0	13.0
1998	Aurora	4.0 (3995)	C	7.5	6.5	20.0	13.0
	Riviera	3.8 (3785)	1	5.0	12.0	20.0	13.0
		3.8 (3785)	K	4.5	12.0	20.0	13.0
1999-00	Aurora	4.0 (3995)	C	7.5	6.5	20.0	13.0

NOTE: All capacities are approximate. Add fluid gradually and ensure a proper fluid level is obtained.

93001CI6

VALVE SPECIFICATIONS

Year	Engine Displacement Liters (cc)	Engine ID/VIN	Seat Angle (deg.)	Face Angle (deg.)	Spring Test Pressure (lbs. @ in.)	Spring Installed Height (in.)	Stem-to-Guide Clearance (in.)		Stem Diameter (in.)	
							Intake	Exhaust	Intake	Exhaust
19'96	3.8 (3785)	1	45	45	210@1.315	1.690-1.720	0.0015-0.0035	0.0015-0.0032	NA	NA
	3.8 (3785)	K	45	45	210@1.315	1.690-1.720	0.0015-0.0035	0.0015-0.0032	NA	NA
	4.0 (3995)	C	46	45	92@0.854	1.190	0.0010-0.0030	0.0020-0.0040	NA	NA
1997	3.8 (3785)	1	45	45	210@1.315	1.690-1.720	0.0015-0.0035	0.0015-0.0032	NA	NA
	3.8 (3785)	K	45	45	210@1.315	1.690-1.720	0.0015-0.0035	0.0015-0.0032	NA	NA
	4.0 (3995)	C	46	45	92@0.854	1.190	0.0010-0.0030	0.0020-0.0040	NA	NA
1998	3.8 (3785)	1	45	45	210@1.315	1.690-1.720	0.0015-0.0035	0.0015-0.0032	NA	NA
	3.8 (3785)	K	45	45	210@1.315	1.690-1.720	0.0015-0.0035	0.0015-0.0032	NA	NA
	4.0 (3995)	C	46	45	92@0.854	1.190	0.0010-0.0030	0.0020-0.0040	NA	NA
1999-00	4.0 (3995)	C	46	45	92@0.854	1.190	0.0010-0.0030	0.0020-0.0040	NA	NA

NA - Not Available

93001CI7

For exhaust manifold replacement procedures, see the model specific sections of this manual

CRANKSHAFT AND CONNECTING ROD SPECIFICATIONS
All measurements are given in inches.

Year	Engine Displacement Liters (cc)	Engine ID/VIN	Crankshaft				Connecting Rod		
			Main Brg. Journal Dia.	Main Brg. Oil Clearance	Shaft End-play	Thrust on No.	Journal Diameter ①	Oil Clearance	Side Clearance
1996	3.8 (3785)	1	2.4988-2.4998	0.0008-0.0022	0.0030-0.0110	2	2.3738-2.3745	0.0005-0.0026	0.0030-0.0150
	3.8 (3785)	K	2.4988-2.4998	0.0008-0.0022	0.0030-0.0110	2	2.3738-2.3745	0.0005-0.0026	0.0030-0.0150
	4.0 (3995)	C	2.5335-2.5337	0.0006-0.0025	0.0020-0.0200	2	2.2490	0.0010-0.0030	0.0080-0.0200
1997	3.8 (3785)	1	2.4988-2.4998	0.0008-0.0022	0.0030-0.0110	2	2.3738-2.3745	0.0005-0.0026	0.0030-0.0150
	3.8 (3785)	K	2.4988-2.4998	0.0008-0.0022	0.0030-0.0110	2	2.3738-2.3745	0.0005-0.0026	0.0030-0.0150
	4.0 (3995)	C	2.5335-2.5337	0.0006-0.0025	0.0020-0.0200	2	2.2490	0.0010-0.0030	0.0080-0.0200
1998	3.8 (3785)	1	2.4988-2.4998	0.0008-0.0022	0.0030-0.0110	2	2.3738-2.3745	0.0005-0.0026	0.0030-0.0150
	3.8 (3785)	K	2.4988-2.4998	0.0008-0.0022	0.0030-0.0110	2	2.3738-2.3745	0.0005-0.0026	0.0030-0.0150
	4.0 (3995)	C	2.5335-2.5337	0.0006-0.0025	0.0020-0.0200	2	2.2490	0.0010-0.0030	0.0080-0.0200
1999-00	4.0 (3995)	C	2.5335-2.5337	0.0006-0.0025	0.0020-0.0200	2	2.2490	0.0010-0.0030	0.0080-0.0200

① Large end of connecting rod ID

93001CI8

PISTON AND RING SPECIFICATIONS
All measurements are given in inches.

Year	Engine ID/VIN	Engine Displacement Liters (cc)	Piston Clearance	Ring Gap			Ring Side Clearance		
				Top Compression	Bottom Compression	Oil Control	Top Compression	Bottom Compression	Oil Control
1996	3.8 (3785)	1	0.0004-0.0020	0.012-0.022	0.030-0.040	0.010-0.030	0.0013-0.0031	0.0013-0.0031	0.0009-0.0079
	3.8 (3785)	K	0.0004-0.0020	0.012-0.022	0.030-0.040	0.010-0.030	0.0013-0.0031	0.0013-0.0031	0.0009-0.0079
	4.0 (3995)	C	0.0008-0.0020	0.010-0.016	0.014-0.020	0.010-0.030	0.0016-0.0037	0.0016-0.0037	side-sealing
1997	3.8 (3785)	1	0.0004-0.0020	0.012-0.022	0.030-0.040	0.010-0.030	0.0013-0.0031	0.0013-0.0031	0.0009-0.0079
	3.8 (3785)	K	0.0004-0.0020	0.012-0.022	0.030-0.040	0.010-0.030	0.0013-0.0031	0.0013-0.0031	0.0009-0.0079
	4.0 (3995)	C	0.0008-0.0020	0.010-0.016	0.014-0.020	0.010-0.030	0.0016-0.0037	0.0016-0.0037	side-sealing
1998	3.8 (3785)	1	0.0004-0.0020	0.012-0.022	0.030-0.040	0.010-0.030	0.0013-0.0031	0.0013-0.0031	0.0009-0.0079
	3.8 (3785)	K	0.0004-0.0020	0.012-0.022	0.030-0.040	0.010-0.030	0.0013-0.0031	0.0013-0.0031	0.0009-0.0079
	4.0 (3995)	C	0.0008-0.0020	0.010-0.016	0.014-0.020	0.010-0.030	0.0016-0.0037	0.0016-0.0037	side-sealing
1999-00	4.0 (3995)	C	0.0008-0.0020	0.010-0.016	0.014-0.020	0.010-0.030	0.0016-0.0037	0.0016-0.0037	side-sealing

93001CI9

TORQUE SPECIFICATIONS
All readings in ft. lbs.

Year	Engine Displacement Liters (cc)	Engine ID/VIN	Cylinder Head Bolts	Main Bearing Bolts	Rod Bearing Bolts	Crankshaft Damper Bolts	Flywheel Bolts	Manifold Intake	Manifold Exhaust	Spark Plugs	Lug Nuts
1996	3.8 (3785)	1	①	②	③	④	⑤	7	38	11	100
	3.8 (3785)	K	①	②	③	④	⑤	7	38	11	100
	4.0 (3995)	C	⑦	⑧	⑨	⑩	⑤	89	18	⑥	100
1997	3.8 (3786)	1	①	⑪	③	④	⑤	⑬	22	11	100
	3.8 (3786)	K	①	⑫	③	④	⑤	11	38	11	100
	4.0 (3995)	C	⑦	⑧	⑨	⑩	⑤	89	18	⑥	100
1998	3.8 (3786)	1	①	⑪	③	④	⑤	⑬	22	11	100
	3.8 (3786)	K	①	⑫	③	④	⑤	11	38	11	100
	4.0 (3995)	C	⑦	⑧	⑨	⑩	⑤	89	18	⑥	100
1999-00	4.0 (3995)	C	⑦	⑧	⑨	⑩	⑤	89	18	⑥	100

① Step 1: 36 ft. lbs.
　Step 2: 130 degrees
　Step 3: Plus 30 degrees additional on four center bolts
　(NOTE: Must use new bolts)
② 26 ft. lbs. plus 50 degrees
③ 20 ft. lbs. plus 50 degrees
④ 110 ft. lbs. plus 76 degrees
⑤ Step 1: 11 ft. lbs.
　Step 2: Plus 50 degrees
⑥ New cylinder head 1st-time installation: 20 ft. lbs.
　All others: 11 ft. lbs.
⑦ Step 1: Torque to 22 ft. lbs. then 90 degrees.
　Step 2: Retorque an additional 75 degrees.
⑧ 15 ft. lbs. plus 65 degrees
⑨ 18 ft. lbs. plus 90 degrees
⑩ 44 ft. lbs. plus 120 degrees
⑪ Step 1: Tighten caps in equal increments to 52 ft. lbs.
　Step 2: Loosen 360 degrees
　Step 3: 15 ft. lbs.
　Step 4: 54 ft. lbs.
　Step 5: Plus three turns of 35 degrees-total of 105 degrees
⑫ 26 ft. lbs. plus 90 degrees
⑬ Upper manifold: 8 ft. lbs.
　Lower manifold: 11 ft. lbs.

93001CI0

Refer to the model specific sections for cooling system service procedures

SCHEDULED MAINTENANCE INTERVALS
(GM G BODY - BUICK RIVIERA, OLDSMOBILE AURORA)

TO BE SERVICED	TYPE OF SERVICE	7.5	15	22.5	30	37.5	45	52.5	60	67.5	75	82.5	90	97.5
		VEHICLE MILEAGE INTERVAL (x1000)												
Engine oil & filter	R	✓	✓	✓	✓	✓	✓	✓	✓	✓	✓	✓	✓	✓
Coolant level, hoses & clamps	S/I	✓	✓	✓	✓	✓	✓	✓	✓	✓	✓	✓	✓	✓
Drive shaft boots & front suspension components	S/I													
Exhaust system & brake hoses	S/I	✓	✓	✓	✓	✓	✓	✓	✓	✓	✓	✓	✓	✓
Lubricate chassis, suspension, steering linkage, transaxle shift linkage, parking brake cable guides, underbody contact points & linkage	S/I	✓	✓	✓	✓	✓	✓	✓	✓	✓	✓	✓	✓	✓
Throttle linkage	S/I	✓	✓	✓	✓	✓	✓	✓	✓	✓	✓	✓	✓	✓
Brake linings	S/I	✓			✓			✓			✓			✓
Rotate tires	S/I	✓		✓		✓		✓		✓		✓		✓
Air filter element	R				✓				✓				✓	
Engine coolant ②	R													
Spark plugs ①	R				✓				✓				✓	
Accessory drive belt(s)	S/I				✓				✓				✓	
Automatic transaxle fluid & filter	S/I				✓				✓				✓	
Fuel system	S/I				✓				✓				✓	
Ignition cables	R				✓				✓				✓	
Inspect throttle body bore & throttle plate for deposits (Oldsmobile)	S/I		✓				✓				✓			
Supercharger oil	S/I				✓				✓				✓	
Throttle body mounting torque	S/I	✓												

① Platinum tip spark plugs - replace every 100,000 miles.

② Engine coolant - replace every 100,000 miles. Use O.E. specified (DEX-COOL™) coolant only. If any silicate coolant is used, the service interval is every 30,000 miles.

R - Replace   S/I - Service or Inspect

FREQUENT OPERATION MAINTENANCE (SEVERE SERVICE)

If a vehicle is operated under any of the following conditions it is considered severe service:
- Extremely dusty areas.
- 50% or more of the vehicle operation is in 32°C (90°F) or higher temperatures, or constant operation in operation in temperatures below 0°C (32°F).
- Prolonged idling (vehicle operation in stop and go traffic).
- Frequent short running periods (engine does not warm to normal operating temperatures).
- Police, taxi, delivery usage or trailer towing usage.

CV joints & front suspension components - service or inspect every 3000 miles.
Engine oil & filter change - change every 3000 miles.
Brake linings - check every 6000 miles.
Chassis lubrication - lubricate every 6000 miles.
Suspension, steering linkage, transaxle shift linkage, parking cable guides, underbody contact points - lubricate every 6000 miles.
Throttle body mount bolt torque - tighten at 6000 miles.
Air filter element - service or inspect every 15,000 miles.
Automatic transaxle fluid - change every 50,000 miles (1996-97).
Inspect throttle body bore & throttle plate for deposits - clean as required every 15,000 miles.
Rotate tires at 6000 miles, then every 15,000 miles.

93001CJ1

SCHEDULED MAINTENANCE INTERVALS
GENERAL MOTORS CORPORATION
G BODY
BUICK RIVIERA, OLDSMOBILE AURORA

The following should be used as a guide when determining the amount of work required for a particular service.
In estimating how long a particular Scheduled Maintenance Service should take, please observe the following:

- **Chilton Time** is time based on field research and data supplied by the vehicle manufacturer.
  - Labor time operations are given in hours and tenths of an hour.
  - All labor operations, are to be used as a guide.

Mechanic Skill Level Codes:
(A) PRECISION: Really skilled with multiple certification.
(B) GENERAL: Normally skilled with certification.
(C) MAINTENANCE: Semi-skilled working on certification.

	Chilton Time
7500 Mile Service (B)	
All Models	1.8
15000 Mile Service (C)	
All Models	.9
Inspect throttle body for deposits add	.1
22500 Mile Service (B)	
All Models	1.6
30000 Mile Service (B)	
All Models	2.8
37500 Mile Service (B)	
All Models	1.6

	Chilton Time
45000 Mile Service (C)	
All Models	.9
Inspect throttle body for deposits add	.1
52500 Mile Service (B)	
All Models	1.6
60000 Mile Service (B)	
All Models	2.8

	Chilton Time
67500 Mile Service (B)	
All Models	1.6
75000 Mile Service (C)	
All Models	.9
Inspect throttle body for deposits add	.1
82500 Mile Service (B)	
All Models	1.6
90000 Mile Service (B)	
All Models	2.8
97500 Mile Service (B)	
All Models	1.6

93001CJ2

GENERAL MOTORS J-BODY
Chevrolet Cavalier • Pontiac Sunfire

ENGINE AND VEHICLE IDENTIFICATION CHART

Code ①	Liters (cc)	Cu. In.	Cyl.	Fuel Sys.	Engine Type	Eng. Mfg.
4	2.2 (2180)	133	4	MFI	OHV	CUS
T	2.4 (2392)	146	4	MFI	DOHC	CUS

Code ②	Year
T	1996
V	1997
W	1998
X	1999
Y	2000

CUS - Chevrolet/United States

MFI - Multi-point Fuel Injection

OHV - Overhead Valves

DOHC - Double Overhead Camshafts

① 8th position of VIN

② 10th position of VIN

93001CJ3

ENGINE TUNE-UP SPECIFICATIONS

Year	Engine Displacement Liters (cc)	Engine ID/VIN	Spark Plug Gap (in.)	Ignition Timing (deg.)	Fuel Pump (psi)	Idle Speed (rpm)	Valve Clearance Intake	Valve Clearance Exhaust
1996	2.2 (2180)	4	0.060	①	41-47	①	HYD	HYD
	2.4 (2392)	T	0.060	①	41-47	①	HYD	HYD
1997	2.2 (2180)	4	0.060	①	41-47	①	HYD	HYD
	2.4 (2392)	T	0.060	①	41-47	①	HYD	HYD
1998	2.2 (2180)	4	0.060	①	41-47	①	HYD	HYD
	2.4 (2392)	T	0.060	①	41-47	①	HYD	HYD
1999-00	2.2 (2180)	4	0.060	①	41-47	①	HYD	HYD
	2.4 (2392)	T	0.060	①	41-47	①	HYD	HYD

NOTE: The Vehicle Emission Control Information label often reflects specification changes made during production. The label figures must be used if they differ from those in this chart.

HYD - Hydraulic

① Refer to Vehicle Emission Control Information label

93001CJ4

GENERAL ENGINE SPECIFICATIONS

Year	Model	Engine Displacement Liters (cc)	Engine Series (ID/VIN)	Fuel System	Net Horsepower @ rpm	Net Torque @ rpm (ft. lbs.)	Bore x Stroke (in.)	Compression Ratio	Oil Pressure @ rpm
1996	Cavalier	2.2 (2180)	4	MFI	120@5200	130@3200	3.50x3.46	9.0:1	56@3000
		2.4 (2392)	T	MFI	150@6000	155@4400	3.54x3.70	9.5:1	30@3000
	Sunfire	2.2 (2180)	4	MFI	120@5200	130@3200	3.50x3.46	9.0:1	56@3000
		2.4 (2392)	T	MFI	150@6000	155@4400	3.54x3.70	9.5:1	30@3000
1997	Cavalier	2.2 (2180)	4	MFI	120@5200	130@3200	3.50x3.46	9.0:1	56@3000
		2.4 (2392)	T	MFI	150@6000	155@4400	3.54x3.70	9.5:1	30@3000
	Sunfire	2.2 (2180)	4	MFI	120@5200	130@3200	3.50x3.46	9.0:1	56@3000
		2.4 (2392)	T	MFI	150@6000	155@4400	3.54x3.70	9.5:1	30@3000
1998	Cavalier	2.2 (2180)	4	MFI	120@5200	130@3200	3.50x3.46	9.0:1	56@3000
		2.4 (2392)	T	MFI	150@6000	155@4400	3.54x3.70	9.5:1	30@3000
	Sunfire	2.2 (2180)	4	MFI	120@5200	130@3200	3.50x3.46	9.0:1	56@3000
		2.4 (2392)	T	MFI	150@6000	155@4400	3.54x3.70	9.5:1	30@3000
1999-00	Cavalier	2.2 (2180)	4	MFI	120@5200	130@3200	3.50x3.46	9.0:1	56@3000
		2.4 (2392)	T	MFI	150@6000	155@4400	3.54x3.70	9.5:1	30@3000
	Sunfire	2.2 (2180)	4	MFI	120@5200	130@3200	3.50x3.46	9.0:1	56@3000
		2.4 (2392)	T	MFI	150@6000	155@4400	3.54x3.70	9.5:1	30@3000

MFI - Multi-point Fuel Injection

93001CJ5

CAPACITIES

Year	Model	Engine Displacement Liters (cc)	Engine ID/VIN	Engine Oil with Filter (qts.)	Transmission (pts.) Manual	Transmission (pts.) Auto.	Fuel Tank (gal.)	Cooling System (qts.)
1996	Cavalier	2.2 (2180)	4	4.5	4.0	14.0	15.2	10.5
		2.4 (2392)	T	4.5	4.0	14.0	15.2	10.5
	Sunfire	2.2 (2180)	4	4.5	4.0	14.0	15.2	10.5
		2.4 (2392)	T	4.5	4.0	14.0	15.2	10.5
1997	Cavalier	2.2 (2180)	4	4.5	4.0	14.0	15.2	10.5
		2.4 (2392)	T	4.5	4.0	14.0	15.2	10.5
	Sunfire	2.2 (2180)	4	4.5	4.0	14.0	15.2	10.5
		2.4 (2392)	T	4.5	4.0	14.0	15.2	10.5
1998	Cavalier	2.2 (2180)	4	4.5	4.0	14.0	15.2	10.5
		2.4 (2392)	T	4.5	4.0	14.0	15.2	10.5
	Sunfire	2.2 (2180)	4	4.5	4.0	14.0	15.2	10.5
		2.4 (2392)	T	4.5	4.0	14.0	15.2	10.5
1999-00	Cavalier	2.2 (2180)	4	4.5	4.0	14.0	15.2	10.5
		2.4 (2392)	T	4.5	4.0	14.0	15.2	10.5
	Sunfire	2.2 (2180)	4	4.5	4.0	14.0	15.2	10.5
		2.4 (2392)	T	4.5	4.0	14.0	15.2	10.5

NOTE: All capacities are approximate. Add fluid gradually and ensure a proper fluid level is obtained.

93001CJ6

Timing chain and gear service is covered in the model specific sections of this manual

VALVE SPECIFICATIONS

Year	Engine Displacement Liters (cc)	Engine ID/VIN	Seat Angle (deg.)	Face Angle (deg.)	Spring Test Pressure (lbs. @ in.)	Spring Installed Height (in.)	Stem-to-Guide Clearance (in.) Intake	Stem-to-Guide Clearance (in.) Exhaust	Stem Diameter (in.) Intake	Stem Diameter (in.) Exhaust
1996	2.2 (2180)	4	46	45	225-233@1.25	1.640	0.0011-0.0026	0.0014-0.0031	NA	NA
	2.4 (2392)	T	45	46	50-55@1.44	1.437	0.0009-0.0025	0.0016-0.0032	0.2331-0.2339	0.2326-0.2334
1997	2.2 (2180)	4	46	45	75-81@1.71	1.710	0.0010-0.0027	0.0014-0.0031	NA	NA
	2.4 (2392)	T	45	46	50-55@1.44	1.437	0.0009-0.0025	0.0016-0.0032	0.2331-0.2339	0.2326-0.2334
1998	2.2 (2180)	4	46	45	75-81@1.71	1.710	0.0010-0.0027	0.0014-0.0031	NA	NA
	2.4 (2392)	T	45	46	50-55@1.44	1.437	0.0009-0.0025	0.0016-0.0032	0.2331-0.2339	0.2326-0.2334
1999-00	2.2 (2180)	4	46	45	75-81@1.71	1.710	0.0010-0.0027	0.0014-0.0031	NA	NA
	2.4 (2392)	T	45	46	50-55@1.44	1.437	0.0009-0.0025	0.0016-0.0032	0.2331-0.2339	0.2326-0.2334

NA - Not Available

93001CJ7

CRANKSHAFT AND CONNECTING ROD SPECIFICATIONS
All measurements are given in inches.

Year	Engine Displacement Liters (cc)	Engine ID/VIN	Crankshaft Main Brg. Journal Dia.	Crankshaft Main Brg. Oil Clearance	Crankshaft Shaft End-play	Crankshaft Thrust on No.	Connecting Rod Journal Diameter	Connecting Rod Oil Clearance	Connecting Rod Side Clearance
1996	2.2 (2180)	4	2.4945-2.4954	0.0006-0.0019	0.0020-0.0070	4	1.9983-1.9994	0.0010-0.0030	0.0040-0.0150
	2.4 (2392)	T	2.3634-2.3636	0.0005-0.0030	0.0034-0.0095	3	1.8887-1.8897	0.0005-0.0020	0.0060-0.0180
1997	2.2 (2180)	4	2.4945-2.4954	0.0006-0.0019	0.0020-0.0070	4	1.9983-1.9994	0.0010-0.0030	0.0040-0.0150
	2.4 (2392)	T	2.3634-2.3636	0.0005-0.0030	0.0034-0.0095	3	1.8887-1.8897	0.0005-0.0020	0.0060-0.0180
1998	2.2 (2180)	4	2.4945-2.4954	0.0006-0.0019	0.0020-0.0070	4	1.9983-1.9994	0.0010-0.0030	0.0040-0.0150
	2.4 (2392)	T	2.3634-2.3636	0.0005-0.0030	0.0034-0.0095	3	1.8887-1.8897	0.0005-0.0020	0.0060-0.0180
1999-00	2.2 (2180)	4	2.4945-2.4954	0.0006-0.0019	0.0020-0.0070	4	1.9983-1.9994	0.0010-0.0030	0.0040-0.0150
	2.4 (2392)	T	2.3634-2.3636	0.0005-0.0030	0.0034-0.0095	3	1.8887-1.8897	0.0005-0.0020	0.0060-0.0180

① Large end of connecting rod ID

93001CJ8

PISTON AND RING SPECIFICATIONS
All measurements are given in inches.

Year	Engine Displacement Liters (cc)	Engine ID/VIN	Piston Clearance	Ring Gap			Ring Side Clearance		
				Top Compression	Bottom Compression	Oil Control	Top Compression	Bottom Compression	Oil Control
1996	2.2 (2180)	4	0.0007-0.0017	0.0100-0.0200	0.0100-0.0200	0.0100-0.0400	0.0019-0.0027	0.0019-0.0027	0.0019-0.0082
	2.4 (2392)	T	0.0006-0.0018	0.0060-0.0120	0.0120-0.0160	①	0.0016-0.0031	0.0012-0.0028	①
1997	2.2 (2180)	4	0.0007-0.0017	0.0100-0.0200	0.0100-0.0200	0.0100-0.0400	0.0019-0.0027	0.0019-0.0027	0.0019-0.0082
	2.4 (2392)	T	0.0006-0.0018	0.0060-0.0120	0.0120-0.0160	①	0.0016-0.0031	0.0012-0.0028	①
1998	2.2 (2180)	4	0.0007-0.0017	0.0100-0.0200	0.0100-0.0200	0.0100-0.0400	0.0019-0.0027	0.0019-0.0027	0.0019-0.0082
	2.4 (2392)	T	0.0006-0.0018	0.0060-0.0120	0.0120-0.0160	①	0.0016-0.0031	0.0012-0.0028	①
1999-00	2.2 (2180)	4	0.0007-0.0017	0.0100-0.0200	0.0100-0.0200	0.0100-0.0400	0.0019-0.0027	0.0019-0.0027	0.0019-0.0082
	2.4 (2392)	T	0.0006-0.0018	0.0060-0.0120	0.0120-0.0160	①	0.0016-0.0031	0.0012-0.0028	①

① Oil rail gap 0.0098 - 0.0256
Oil ring gap 0.0157 - 0.0551
Oil ring width 0.0196 - 0.0206

93001CJ9

TORQUE SPECIFICATIONS
All readings in ft. lbs.

Year	Engine Displacement Liters (cc)	Engine ID/VIN	Cylinder Head Bolts	Main Bearing Bolts	Rod Bearing Bolts	Crankshaft Damper Bolts	Flywheel Bolts	Manifold		Spark Plugs	Lug Nuts
								Intake	Exhaust		
1996	2.2 (2180)	4	①	77	38	85 ②	52-55	18	6-13	13	100
	2.4 (2392)	T	③	④	⑤	⑥	⑦	⑧	⑨	13	100
1997	2.2 (2180)	4	①	70	38	77 ②	52-55	24	18	13	100
	2.4 (2392)	T	③	④	⑤	⑥	⑦	⑧	⑨	13	100
1998	2.2 (2180)	4	①	70	38	77 ②	52-55	24	18	13	100
	2.4 (2392)	T	③	④	⑤	⑥	⑦	⑧	⑨	13	100
1999-00	2.2 (2180)	4	①	70	38	77 ②	52-55	24	18	13	100
	2.4 (2392)	T	③	④	⑤	⑥	⑦	⑧	⑨	13	100

NA - Not Available

① Step 1: 41 ft. lbs.
Step 2: Tighten an additional 45 degrees
Step 3: Tighten an additional 45 degrees
Step 4: Long bolts 1, 4-5, 8-9 an additional 20 degrees
Step 5: Short bolts 2-3, 6-7, 10 an additional 10 degrees

② Center bolt spec shown; Pulley-to-hub bolts: 37 ft. lbs.

③ Cylinder head bolts: 40 ft. lbs.
plus 90 degrees

④ 15 ft. lbs. plus 90 degrees

⑤ 18 ft. lbs. plus 80 degrees

⑥ 74 ft. lbs. plus 90 degrees

⑦ 22 ft. lbs. plus 45 degrees

⑧ Nuts: 18 ft. lbs.
Studs: 96 inch lbs.

⑨ Bolts: 27 ft. lbs.
Studs: 106 inch lbs.

93001CJ0

Ignition system service is covered in the model specific sections of this manual

SCHEDULED MAINTENANCE INTERVALS
(GM J BODY - CHEVROLET CAVALIER, PONTIAC SUNFIRE)

TO BE SERVICED	TYPE OF SERVICE	VEHICLE MILEAGE INTERVAL (x1000)												
		7.5	15	22.5	30	37.5	45	52.5	60	67.5	75	82.5	90	97.5
Engine oil & filter	R	✓	✓	✓	✓	✓	✓	✓	✓	✓	✓	✓	✓	✓
Exhaust system & brake hoses	S/I	✓	✓	✓	✓	✓	✓	✓	✓	✓	✓	✓	✓	✓
Drive shaft boots & front suspension components	S/I	✓	✓	✓	✓	✓	✓	✓	✓	✓	✓	✓	✓	✓
Coolant level, hoses & clamps	S/I	✓	✓	✓	✓	✓	✓	✓	✓	✓	✓	✓	✓	✓
Throttle linkage	S/I	✓	✓	✓	✓	✓	✓	✓	✓	✓	✓	✓	✓	✓
Lubricate chassis, suspension, steering linkage, transaxle shift linkage, parking brake cable guides, underbody contact points & linkage	S/I	✓	✓	✓	✓	✓	✓	✓	✓	✓	✓	✓	✓	✓
Brake linings & rotate tires	S/I	✓		✓		✓		✓		✓		✓		✓
Automatic transmission fluid & filter ③	S/I													
Air filter element & PCV filter	R				✓				✓				✓	
Engine coolant ②	R													
Spark plugs ①	R				✓				✓				✓	
Accessory drive belt(s)	R				✓				✓				✓	
EGR & fuel systems	S/I				✓				✓				✓	
Ignition cables	S/I				✓				✓				✓	
Throttle body mount bolt torque	S/I	✓												

① Platinum tip spark plugs - replace every 100,000 miles.

② Engine coolant - replace every 100,000 miles. Use O.E. specified (DEX-COOL™) coolant only. If any silicate coolant is used, the service interval is every 30,000 miles.

③ Automatic transaxle fluid & filter - replace at 100,000 miles (if not changed previously).

R - Replace   S/I - Service or Inspect

93001CK1

SCHEDULED MAINTENANCE INTERVALS
GENERAL MOTORS CORPORATION
J BODY
CHEVROLET CAVALIER, PONTIAC SUNFIRE

The following should be used as a guide when determining the amount of work required for a particular service. In estimating how long a particular Scheduled Maintenance Service should take, please observe the following:

- **Chilton Time** is time based on field research and data supplied by the vehicle manufacturer.
  - Labor time operations are given in hours and tenths of an hour.
    - All labor operations, are to be used as a guide.

Mechanic Skill Level Codes:
(A) PRECISION: Really skilled with multiple certification.
(B) GENERAL: Normally skilled with certification.
(C) MAINTENANCE: Semi-skilled working on certification.

	Chilton Time			Chilton Time			Chilton Time
7500 Mile Service (B)			**37500 Mile Service (C)**			**67500 Mile Service (C)**	
All Models	2.0		All Models	1.7		All Models	1.7
15000 Mile Service (C)			**45000 Mile Service (C)**			**75000 Mile Service (C)**	
All Models	.9		All Models	.9		All Models	.9
22500 Mile Service (C)			**52500 Mile Service (C)**			**82500 Mile Service (C)**	
All Models	1.7		All Models	1.7		All Models	1.7
30000 Mile Service (B)			**60000 Mile Service (B)**			**90000 Mile Service (B)**	
All Models	2.5		All Models	2.5		All Models	2.5

93001CK2

GENERAL MOTORS L-BODY
Chevrolet Corsica • Beretta

ENGINE AND VEHICLE IDENTIFICATION

Engine							Model Year	
Code ①	Liters (cc)	Cu. In.	Cyl.	Fuel Sys.	Engine Type	Eng. Mfg.	Code ②	Year
4	2.2 (2180)	133	4	MFI	OHV	CUS	T	1996
M	3.1 (3130)	191	6	MFI	OHV	CPC		

CUS - Chevrolet/United States
CPC - Chevrolet/Pontiac/Canada
MFI - Multi-point Fuel Injection
OHV - Overhead Valves

① 8th position of VIN

② 10th position of VIN

93001CK3

GENERAL ENGINE SPECIFICATIONS

Year	Model	Engine Displacement Liters (cc)	Engine Series (ID/VIN)	Fuel System	Net Horsepower @ rpm	Net Torque @ rpm (ft. lbs.)	Bore x Stroke (in.)	Compression Ratio	Oil Pressure @ rpm
1996	Beretta	2.2 (2180)	4	MFI	120@5200	130@3200	3.50x3.46	9.0:1	56@3000
	Beretta	3.1 (3130)	M	MFI	155@5200	185@4000	3.50x3.31	9.5:1	15@1100
	Corsica	2.2 (2180)	4	MFI	120@5200	130@3200	3.50x3.46	9.0:1	56@3000
	Corsica	3.1 (3130)	M	MFI	155@5200	185@4000	3.50x3.31	9.5:1	15@1100

MFI - Multi-point Fuel Injection

93001CK4

ENGINE TUNE-UP SPECIFICATIONS

Year	Engine Displacement Liters (cc)	Engine ID/VIN	Spark Plugs Gap (in.)	Ignition Timing (deg.)		Fuel Pump (psi)	Idle Speed (rpm)		Valve Clearance	
				MT	AT		MT	AT	In.	Ex.
1996	2.2 (2180)	4	0.045	①	①	41-47	①	①	HYD	HYD
	3.1 (3130)	M	0.045	①	①	41-47	①	①	HYD	HYD

NOTE: The Vehicle Emission Control Information label often reflects specification changes made during production. The label figures must be used if they differ from those in this chart.
HYD - Hydraulic

① Refer to Vehicle Emission Control Information label

93001CK5

CAPACITIES

Year	Model	Engine Displacement Liters (cc)	Engine ID/VIN	Engine Oil with Filter (qts.)	Transmission (pts.)		Fuel Tank (gal.)	Cooling System (qts.)
					5-Spd	Auto ①		
1996	Beretta	2.2 (2180)	4	4.5	4.0	14.0	15.6	9.5
	Beretta	3.1 (3130)	M	4.5	4.0	14.0	15.6	②
	Corsica	2.2 (2180)	4	4.5	4.0	14.0	15.6	9.5
	Corsica	3.1 (3130)	M	4.5	4.0	14.0	15.6	②

NOTE: All capacities are approximate. Add fluid gradually and ensure a proper fluid level is obtained.

① Drain and refill figure, overhaul: 16.0 pts.

② Automatic transmission: 12.4 qts.
Manual transmission: 11.8 qts.

93001CK6

VALVE SPECIFICATIONS

Year	Engine Displacement Liters (cc)	Engine ID/VIN	Seat Angle (deg.)	Face Angle (deg.)	Spring Test Pressure (lbs. @ in.)	Spring Installed Height (in.)	Stem-to-Guide Clearance (in.)		Stem Diameter (in.)	
							Intake	Exhaust	Intake	Exhaust
1996	2.2 (2195)	4	46	45	75-81@1.71	1.71	0.0010-0.0027	0.0014-0.0031	NA	NA
	3.1 (3136)	M	45	45	80@1.71	1.71	0.0010-0.0027	0.0010-0.0027	NA	NA

NA - Not Available

93001CK7

CRANKSHAFT AND CONNECTING ROD SPECIFICATIONS
All measurements are given in inches.

Year	Engine Displacement Liters (cc)	Engine ID/VIN	Crankshaft				Connecting Rod		
			Main Brg. Journal Dia.	Main Brg. Oil Clearance	Shaft End-play	Thrust on No.	Journal Diameter	Oil Clearance	Side Clearance
1996	2.2 (2195)	4	2.4945-2.4954	0.0006-0.0019	0.0020-0.0070	3	1.9983-1.9994	0.00098-0.00310	0.0039-0.0149
	3.1 (3130)	M	2.6473-2.6383	0.0008-0.0025 ①	0.0024-0.0083	3	1.9987-1.9994	0.0007-0.0024	0.0070-0.0170

① Thrust bearing: 0.0012 - 0.0030

93001CK8

Refer to the model specific sections for engine mechanical service procedures

PISTON AND RING SPECIFICATIONS
All measurements are given in inches.

Year	Engine Displacement Liters (cc)	Engine ID/VIN	Piston Clearance	Ring Gap			Ring Side Clearance		
				Top Compression	Bottom Compression	Oil Control	Top Compression	Bottom Compression	Oil Control
1996	2.2 (2195)	4	0.0007-0.0017	0.0100-0.0200	0.0100-0.0200	0.0100-0.0500	0.0019-0.0027	0.0019-0.0027	0.0019-0.0082
	3.1 (3130)	M	0.0013-0.0027	0.0060-0.0140	0.0197-0.0280	0.0098-0.0500	0.0020-0.0033	0.0020-0.0035	0.0080-0.0120

93001CK9

TORQUE SPECIFICATIONS
All readings in ft. lbs.

Year	Engine Displacement Liters (cc)	Engine ID/VIN	Cylinder Head Bolts	Main Bearing Bolts	Rod Bearing Bolts	Crankshaft Damper Bolts	Flywheel Bolts	Manifold		Spark Plugs	Lug Nut
								Intake	Exhaust		
1996	2.2 (2180)	4	①	70	38	77 ②	52-55	24	18	11	100
	3.1 (3130)	M	③	④	37	76	61	⑤	12	11	100

① Step 1: 41 ft. lbs.
  Step 2: Tighten an additional 45 degrees
  Step 3: Tighten an additional 45 degrees
  Step 4: Long bolts 1, 4-5, 8-9 an additional 20 degrees
  Step 4: Short bolts 2-3, 6-7, 10 an additional 10 degrees

② Center bolt spec shown; Pulley-to-hub bolts: 37 ft. lbs.

③ 33 ft. lbs. plus 90 degrees

④ 37 ft. lbs. plus 75 degrees

⑤ 115 inch lbs.

93001CK0

SCHEDULED MAINTENANCE INTERVALS
(GM L BODY - CHEVROLET CORSICA & BERETTA)

TO BE SERVICED	TYPE OF SERVICE	7.5	15	22.5	30	37.5	45	52.5	60	67.5	75	82.5	90	97.5
							VEHICLE MILEAGE INTERVAL (x1000)						
Engine oil & filter	R	✓	✓	✓	✓	✓	✓	✓	✓	✓	✓	✓	✓	✓
Automatic transaxle fluid & filter ④	S/I	✓	✓	✓	✓	✓	✓	✓	✓	✓	✓	✓	✓	✓
Brake hoses	S/I	✓	✓	✓	✓	✓	✓	✓	✓	✓	✓	✓	✓	✓
Chassis lubrication	S/I	✓	✓	✓	✓	✓	✓	✓	✓	✓	✓	✓	✓	✓
Coolant level, hoses & clamps	S/I	✓	✓	✓	✓	✓	✓	✓	✓	✓	✓	✓	✓	✓
Drive shaft boots & front suspension components	S/I	✓	✓	✓	✓	✓	✓	✓	✓	✓	✓	✓	✓	✓
Exhaust system	S/I	✓	✓	✓	✓	✓	✓	✓	✓	✓	✓	✓	✓	✓
Lubricate chassis, suspension, steering linkage, transaxle shift linkage, parking brake cable guides, underbody contact points & linkage	S/I	✓	✓	✓	✓	✓	✓	✓	✓	✓	✓	✓	✓	✓
Manual transaxle oil	S/I	✓	✓	✓	✓	✓	✓	✓	✓	✓	✓	✓	✓	✓
Throttle linkage	S/I	✓	✓	✓	✓	✓	✓	✓	✓	✓	✓	✓	✓	✓
Brake linings	S/I	✓		✓		✓		✓		✓		✓		✓
Rotate tires ③	S/I	✓		✓		✓		✓		✓		✓		✓
Air filter element	R				✓				✓				✓	
Engine coolant ②	R													
PCV filter	R				✓				✓				✓	
Spark plugs ①	R				✓				✓				✓	
Accessory drive belt(s)	S/I				✓				✓				✓	
EGR & fuel systems	S/I				✓				✓				✓	
Ignition cables	S/I				✓				✓				✓	
Throttle body mount bolt torque	S/I	✓												

① Platinum tip spark plugs - replace every 100,000 miles.

② Engine coolant - replace every 100,000 miles. Use O.E. specified (DEX-COOL™) coolant only. If any silicate coolant is used, the service interval is every 30,000 miles.

③ Rotate tires front-to-rear only on Beretta GTZ and Z26.

④ Automatic transaxle fluid & filter - replace at 100,000 miles (if not changed previously).

R - Replace   S/I - Service or Inspect

93001CL1

Refer to the model specific sections for fuel system service procedures

SCHEDULED MAINTENANCE INTERVALS
GENERAL MOTORS CORPORATION
L BODY
CHEVROLET CORSICA, BERETTA

The following should be used as a guide when determining the amount of work required for a particular service.
In estimating how long a particular Scheduled Maintenance Service should take, please observe the following:

- **Chilton Time** is time based on field research and data supplied by the vehicle manufacturer.
  - Labor time operations are given in hours and tenths of an hour.
  - All labor operations, are to be used as a guide.

Mechanic Skill Level Codes:
(A) PRECISION: Really skilled with multiple certification.
(B) GENERAL: Normally skilled with certification.
(C) MAINTENANCE: Semi-skilled working on certification.

	Chilton Time		Chilton Time		Chilton Time
7500 Mile Service (B)		**37500 Mile Service (B)**		**75000 Mile Service (C)**	
All Models	2.1	All Models	2.0	All Models	1.3
15000 Mile Service (C)		**45000 Mile Service (C)**		**82500 Mile Service (B)**	
All Models	1.2	All Models	1.3	All Models	2.0
22500 Mile Service (B)		**52500 Mile Service (B)**		**90000 Mile Service (B)**	
All Models	2.0	All Models	2.0	All Models	3.0
30000 Mile Service (B)		**60000 Mile Service (B)**		**97500 Mile Service (B)**	
All Models	3.0	All Models	3.0	All Models	2.0
		67500 Mile Service (B)			
		All Models	2.0		

93001CL2

GENERAL MOTORS L/N-BODY
Chevrolet Malibu • Oldsmobile Cutlass

ENGINE AND VEHICLE IDENTIFICATION

Engine							Model Year	
Code ①	Liters (cc)	Cu. In.	Cyl.	Fuel Sys.	Engine Type	Eng. Mfg.	Code ②	Year
M	3.1 (3130)	191	6	MFI	OHV	BOC	V	1997
T	2.4 (2392)	146	4	MFI	DOHC	CUS	W	1998
							X	1999
							Y	2000

BOC - Buick/Oldsmobile/Cadillac

CUS - Chevrolet/United States

MFI - Multi-point Fuel Injection

① 8th position of VIN

② 10th position of VIN

93001CR2

GENERAL ENGINE SPECIFICATIONS

Year	Model	Engine Displacement Liters (cc)	Engine Series (ID/VIN)	Fuel System	Net Horsepower @ rpm	Net Torque @ rpm (ft. lbs.)	Bore x Stroke (in.)	Compression Ratio	Oil Pressure @ rpm
1997	Cutlass	3.1 (3130)	M	MFI	160@5200	185@4000	3.50x3.31	9.5:1	15@1100
	Malibu	3.1 (3130)	M	MFI	160@5200	185@4000	3.50x3.31	9.5:1	15@1100
	Malibu	2.4 (2392)	T	MFI	150@6000	150@5600	3.54x3.70	9.5:1	30@3000
1998	Cutlass	3.1 (3130)	M	MFI	160@5200	185@4000	3.50x3.31	9.5:1	15@1100
	Malibu	3.1 (3130)	M	MFI	160@5200	185@4000	3.50x3.31	9.5:1	15@1100
	Malibu	2.4 (2392)	T	MFI	150@6000	150@5600	3.54x3.70	9.5:1	30@3000
1999-00	Cutlass	3.1 (3130)	M	MFI	160@5200	185@4000	3.50x3.31	9.5:1	15@1100
	Malibu	3.1 (3130)	M	MFI	160@5200	185@4000	3.50x3.31	9.5:1	15@1100
	Malibu	2.4 (2392)	T	MFI	150@6000	150@5600	3.54x3.70	9.5:1	30@3000

MFI - Multi-point Fuel Injection

93001CR3

ENGINE TUNE-UP SPECIFICATIONS

Year	Engine Displacement Liters (cc)	Engine ID/VIN	Spark Plug Gap (in.)	Ignition Timing (deg.) MT	AT	Fuel Pump (psi)	Idle Speed (rpm) MT	AT	Valve Clearance In.	Ex.
1997	2.4 (2392)	T	0.035	①	①	41-47	①	①	HYD	HYD
	3.1 (3130)	M	0.060	①	①	41-47	①	①	HYD	HYD
1998	2.4 (2392)	T	0.035	①	①	41-47	①	①	HYD	HYD
	3.1 (3130)	M	0.060	①	①	41-47	①	①	HYD	HYD
1999-00	2.4 (2392)	T	0.035	①	①	41-47	①	①	HYD	HYD
	3.1 (3130)	M	0.060	①	①	41-47	①	①	HYD	HYD

NOTE: The Vehicle Emission Control Information label often reflects specification changes made during production. The label figures must be used if they differ from those in this chart.

HYD - Hydraulic

① Refer to Vehicle Emission Control Information label

93001CR4

Refer to the model specific sections for engine electrical system service procedures

CAPACITIES

Year	Model	Engine Displacement Liters (cc)	Engine ID/VIN	Engine Oil with Filter (qts.)	Transmission (pts.)	Fuel Tank (gal.)	Cooling System (qts.)
1997	Cutlass	3.1 (3130)	M	4.0	15	15.2	13.6
	Malibu	3.1 (3130)	M	4.0	15	15.2	13.6
	Malibu	2.4 (2392)	T	4.0	15	15.2	11.3
1998	Cutlass	3.1 (3130)	M	4.0	15	15.2	13.6
	Malibu	3.1 (3130)	M	4.0	15	15.2	13.6
	Malibu	2.4 (2392)	T	4.0	15	15.2	11.3
1999-00	Cutlass	3.1 (3130)	M	4.0	15	15.2	13.6
	Malibu	3.1 (3130)	M	4.0	15	15.2	13.6
	Malibu	2.4 (2392)	T	4.0	15	15.2	11.3

NOTE: All capacities are approximate. Add fluid gradually and ensure a proper fluid level is obtained.

93001CR5

VALVE SPECIFICATIONS

Year	Engine Displacement Liters (cc)	Engine ID/VIN	Seat Angle (deg.)	Face Angle (deg.)	Spring Test Pressure (lbs. @ in.)	Spring Installed Height (in.)	Stem-to-Guide Clearance (in.) Intake	Stem-to-Guide Clearance (in.) Exhaust	Stem Diameter (in.) Intake	Stem Diameter (in.) Exhaust
1997	2.4 (2392)	T	45	46	50-55@ 1.437	1.437	0.0009-0.0025	0.0016-0.0032	0.2331-0.2339	0.2326-0.2334
	3.1 (3130)	M	45	45	250@1.239	1.710	0.0010-0.0027	0.0010-0.0027	NA	NA
1998	2.4 (2392)	T	45	46	50-55@ 1.437	1.437	0.0009-0.0025	0.0016-0.0032	0.2331-0.2339	0.2326-0.2334
	3.1 (3130)	M	45	45	250@1.239	1.710	0.0010-0.0027	0.0010-0.0027	NA	NA
1999-00	2.4 (2392)	T	45	46	50-55@ 1.437	1.437	0.0009-0.0025	0.0016-0.0032	0.2331-0.2339	0.2326-0.2334
	3.1 (3130)	M	45	45	250@1.239	1.710	0.0010-0.0027	0.0010-0.0027	NA	NA

NA - Not Available

93001CR6

CRANKSHAFT AND CONNECTING ROD SPECIFICATIONS
All measurements are given in inches.

Year	Engine Displacement Liters (cc)	Engine ID/VIN	Crankshaft Main Brg. Journal Dia.	Crankshaft Main Brg. Oil Clearance	Crankshaft Shaft End-play	Crankshaft Thrust on No.	Connecting Rod Journal Diameter	Connecting Rod Oil Clearance	Connecting Rod Side Clearance
1997	2.4 (2392)	T	2.3622-2.3631	0.0004-0.0023	0.0034-0.0095	3	1.8887-1.8897	0.0004-0.0026	0.0059-0.0177
	3.1 (3130)	M	2.6473-2.6383	0.0008-0.0025 ①	0.0024-0.0083	3	1.9987-1.9994	0.0007-0.0024	0.0070-0.0170
1998	2.4 (2392)	T	2.3622-2.3631	0.0004-0.0023	0.0034-0.0095	3	1.8887-1.8897	0.0004-0.0026	0.0059-0.0177
	3.1 (3130)	M	2.6473-2.6383	0.0008-0.0025 ①	0.0024-0.0083	3	1.9987-1.9994	0.0007-0.0024	0.0070-0.0170
1999-00	2.4 (2392)	T	2.3622-2.3631	0.0004-0.0023	0.0034-0.0095	3	1.8887-1.8897	0.0004-0.0026	0.0059-0.0177
	3.1 (3130)	M	2.6473-2.6383	0.0008-0.0025 ①	0.0024-0.0083	3	1.9987-1.9994	0.0007-0.0024	0.0070-0.0170

① Thrust bearing: 0.0012 - 0.0030

93001CR7

PISTON AND RING SPECIFICATIONS
All measurements are given in inches.

Year	Engine Displacement Liters (cc)	Engine ID/VIN	Piston Clearance	Ring Gap Top Compression	Ring Gap Bottom Compression	Ring Gap Oil Control	Ring Side Clearance Top Compression	Ring Side Clearance Bottom Compression	Ring Side Clearance Oil Control
1997	2.4 (2392)	T	0.0006-0.0015	0.006-0.012	0.010-0.016	0.010-0.030	0.0016-0.0031	0.0012-0.0028	0.0005-0.0089
	3.1 (3130)	M	0.0013-0.0027	0.006-0.014	0.0197-0.0280	0.0098-0.0500	0.002-0.0033	0.002-0.0035	0.008
1998	2.4 (2392)	T	0.0006-0.0015	0.006-0.012	0.010-0.016	0.010-0.030	0.0016-0.0031	0.0012-0.0028	0.0005-0.0089
	3.1 (3130)	M	0.0013-0.0027	0.006-0.014	0.0197-0.0280	0.0098-0.0500	0.002-0.0033	0.002-0.0035	0.008
1999-00	2.4 (2392)	T	0.0006-0.0015	0.006-0.012	0.010-0.016	0.010-0.030	0.0016-0.0031	0.0012-0.0028	0.0005-0.0089
	3.1 (3130)	M	0.0013-0.0027	0.006-0.014	0.0197-0.0280	0.0098-0.0500	0.002-0.0033	0.002-0.0035	0.008

93001CR8

For accessory drive belt replacement procedures see the model specific sections of this manual

TORQUE SPECIFICATIONS
All readings in ft. lbs.

Year	Engine Displacement Liters (cc)	Engine ID/VIN	Cylinder Head Bolts	Main Bearing Bolts	Rod Bearing Bolts	Crankshaft Damper Bolts	Flywheel Bolts	Manifold Intake	Manifold Exhaust	Spark Plug	Lug Nut
1997	2.4 (2392)	T	①	②	③	④	⑤	19	31	16	100
	3.1 (3130)	M	⑥	⑦	⑧	76	59	⑨	12	⑩	100
1998	2.4 (2392)	T	①	②	③	④	⑤	19	31	16	100
	3.1 (3130)	M	⑥	⑦	⑧	76	59	⑨	12	⑩	100
1999-00	2.4 (2392)	T	①	②	③	④	⑤	19	31	16	100
	3.1 (3130)	M	⑥	⑦	⑧	76	59	⑨	12	⑩	100

NA - Not Available

① Bolts 1-8: 30 ft. lbs.
  Bolts 9-10: 26 ft. lbs.
  Tighten all bolts an additional 90 degrees

② 15 ft. lbs. plus 90 degrees

③ 18 ft. lbs. plus 80 degrees

④ 129 ft. lbs. plus 90 degrees

⑤ 22 ft. lbs. plus 45 degrees

⑥ Coat threads with sealer torque to 37 ft. lbs.,
  then turn 1/4 turn (90 degrees)

⑦ 37 ft. lbs. plus 75 degrees

⑧ 15 ft. lbs. plus 75 degrees

⑨ Torque all bolts to 15 ft. lbs.,
  Retorque to 24 ft. lbs.

⑩ New cylinder first-time installation: 21 ft. lbs.
  All others: 11 ft. lbs.

93001CR9

SCHEDULED MAINTENANCE INTERVALS
(GM L/N BODY—CHEVROLET MALIBU, OLDSMOBILE CUTLASS)

TO BE SERVICED	TYPE OF SERVICE	VEHICLE MILEAGE INTERVAL (x1000)																	
		7.5	15	22.5	30	37.5	45	52.5	60	67.5	75	82.5	90	97.5	100	105	112.5	120	150
Accessory drive belts	S/I								✓									✓	
Air cleaner element	R				✓				✓				✓					✓	
Cooling system	S/I ①																		✓
Cooling system hoses	S/I																		✓
Engine coolant	R																		✓
Engine oil and filter	R	✓	✓	✓	✓	✓	✓	✓	✓	✓	✓	✓	✓	✓		✓		✓	✓
Fuel tank, cap and lines	S/I				✓				✓				✓					✓	
Radiator, condenser, pressure cap and neck	C																		✓
Spark plug wires	S/I														✓				
Spark plugs	R														✓				
Tires and wheels	S/I ②	✓	✓	✓	✓	✓	✓	✓	✓	✓	✓	✓	✓	✓		✓	✓	✓	

① Pressure test the cooling system and pressure cap.

② This includes rotating the tires.

R - Replace   S/I - Inspect and service, if needed   L - Lubricate   A - Adjust   C - Clean

FREQUENT OPERATION MAINTENANCE (SEVERE SERVICE) ADDITIONS

If a vehicle is operated under any of the following conditions it is considered severe service:

- Towing a trailer or using a camper or car-top carrier.
- Repeated short trips of less than 5 miles in temperatures below freezing, or trips of less than 10 miles in any temperature.
- Extensive idling or low-speed driving for long distances as in heavy commercial use, such as delivery, taxi or police cars.
- Operating on rough, muddy or salt-covered roads.
- Operating on unpaved or dusty roads.
- Driving in extremely hot (over 90°) conditions.

Engine oil and filter - change every 3,000 miles or 3 months, whichever occurs first.

Tires and wheels - inspect and rotate every 6,000 miles.

Air cleaner element - inspect every 15,000 miles, and replace or clean as needed. Replace it at least every 30,000 miles.

Transaxle fluid and filter - replace every 50,000 miles.

79221CN4

For brake related suspension and axle service, refer to the model specific sections of this manual

SCHEDULED MAINTENANCE INTERVALS
GENERAL MOTORS CORPORATION
L/N BODY
CHEVROLET MALIBU, OLDSMOBILE CUTLASS

The following should be used as a guide when determining the amount of work required for a particular service.
In estimating how long a particular Scheduled Maintenance Service should take, please observe the following:

- **Chilton Time** is time based on field research and data supplied by the vehicle manufacturer.
  - Labor time operations are given in hours and tenths of an hour.
    - All labor operations, are to be used as a guide.

Mechanic Skill Level Codes:
(A) PRECISION: Really skilled with multiple certification.
(B) GENERAL: Normally skilled with certification.
(C) MAINTENANCE: Semi-skilled working on certification.

	Chilton Time			Chilton Time			Chilton Time
7500 Mile Service (C)			**52500 Mile Service (C)**			**97500 Mile Service (C)**	
All Models	1.0		All Models	1.0		All Models	1.0
15000 Mile Service (C)			**60000 Mile Service (B)**			**100000 Mile Service (C)**	
All Models	1.0		All Models	1.5		All Models	
22500 Mile Service (C)			**67500 Mile Service (C)**			*Replace Spark Plugs*	1.0
All Models	1.0		All Models	1.0		*Replace Spark Plug Wires*	1.1
30000 Mile Service (B)			**75000 Mile Service (C)**			**105000 Mile Service (C)**	
All Models	1.4		All Models	1.0		All Models	1.0
37500 Mile Service (C)			**82500 Mile Service (C)**			**112500 Mile Service (C)**	
All Models	1.0		All Models	1.0		All Models	1.0
45000 Mile Service (C)			**90000 Mile Service (B)**			**120000 Mile Service (B)**	
All Models	1.0		All Models	1.4		All Models	1.5

93001CR0

GENERAL MOTORS N-BODY
Buick Skylark • Oldsmobile Achieva • Alero • Pontiac Grand Am

ENGINE AND VEHICLE IDENTIFICATION

		Engine						Model Year	
Code ①	Liters (cc)	Cu. In. (cc)	Cyl.	Fuel Sys.	Engine Type	Eng. Mfg.		Code ②	Year
E	3.4 (3350)	207	4	MFI	OHV	BOC		T	1996
M	3.1 (3130)	191	6	MFI	OHV	BOC		V	1997
T	2.4 (2392)	146	4	MFI	DOHC	CUS		W	1998
								X	1999
								Y	2000

BOC - Buick/Oldsmobile/Cadillac

CUS - Chevrolet/United States

MFI - Multi-point Fuel Injection

① 8th position of VIN

② 10th position of VIN

93001CL3

GENERAL ENGINE IDENTIFICATION

Year	Model	Engine Displacement Liters (cc)	Engine Series (ID/VIN)	Fuel System	Net Horsepower @ rpm	Net Torque @ rpm (ft. lbs.)	Bore x Stroke (in.)	Com- pression Ratio	Oil Pressure @ rpm
1996	Achieva	3.1 (3130)	M	MFI	160@5200	185@4000	3.50x3.31	9.5:1	15@1100
	Achieva	2.4 (2392)	T	MFI	150@6000	150@4400	3.54x3.70	9.5:1	30@3000
	Grand Am	3.1 (3130)	M	MFI	160@5200	185@4000	3.50x3.31	9.5:1	15@1100
	Grand Am	2.4 (2392)	T	MFI	150@6000	150@4400	3.54x3.70	9.5:1	30@3000
	Skylark	3.1 (3130)	M	MFI	160@5200	185@4000	3.50x3.31	9.5:1	15@1100
	Skylark	2.4 (2392)	T	MFI	150@6000	150@4400	3.54x3.70	9.5:1	30@3000
1997	Achieva	3.1 (3130)	M	MFI	160@5200	185@4000	3.50x3.31	9.5:1	15@1100
	Achieva	2.4 (2392)	T	MFI	150@6000	150@4400	3.54x3.70	9.5:1	30@3000
	Grand Am	3.1 (3130)	M	MFI	160@5200	185@4000	3.50x3.31	9.5:1	15@1100
	Grand Am	2.4 (2392)	T	MFI	150@6000	150@4400	3.54x3.70	9.5:1	30@3000
	Skylark	3.1 (3130)	M	MFI	160@5200	185@4000	3.50x3.31	9.5:1	15@1100
	Skylark	2.4 (2392)	T	MFI	150@6000	150@4400	3.54x3.70	9.5:1	30@3000
1998	Achieva	3.1 (3130)	M	MFI	160@5200	185@4000	3.50x3.31	9.5:1	15@1100
	Achieva	2.4 (2392)	T	MFI	150@6000	150@4400	3.54x3.70	9.5:1	30@3000
	Grand Am	3.1 (3130)	M	MFI	160@5200	195@4000	3.50x3.31	9.5:1	15@1100
	Grand Am	2.4 (2392)	T	MFI	150@6000	150@4400	3.54x3.70	9.5:1	30@3000
1999-00	Alero	2.4 (2392)	T	MFI	150@6000	150@4400	3.54x3.70	9.5:1	30@3000
	Alero	3.4 (3934)	E	MFI	170@5200	195@4000	3.62x3.31	9.5:1	15@1100
	Grand Am	2.4 (2392)	T	MFI	150@6000	150@4400	3.54x3.70	9.5:1	30@3000
	Grand Am	3.1 (3130)	M	MFI	160@5200	185@4000	3.50x3.31	9.5:1	15@1100
	Grand Am	3.4 (3934)	E	MFI	170@5200	195@4000	3.62x3.31	9.5:1	15@1100

MFI - Multi-point Fuel Injection

93001CL4

Refer to the model specific sections for driveline service procedures

ENGINE TUNE-UP SPECIFICATIONS

Year	Engine Displacement Liters (cc)	Engine ID/VIN	Spark Plugs Gap (in.)	Ignition Timing (deg.) MT	Ignition Timing (deg.) AT	Fuel Pump (psi)	Idle Speed (rpm) MT	Idle Speed (rpm) AT	Valve Clearance In.	Valve Clearance Ex.
1996	2.4 (2392)	T	0.060	①	①	41-47	①	①	HYD	HYD
	3.1 (3130)	M	0.060	①	①	41-47	①	①	HYD	HYD
1997	2.4 (2392)	T	0.060	①	①	41-47	①	①	HYD	HYD
	3.1 (3130)	M	0.060	①	①	41-47	①	①	HYD	HYD
1998	2.4 (2392)	T	0.060	①	①	41-47	①	①	HYD	HYD
	3.1 (3130)	M	0.060	①	①	41-47	①	①	HYD	HYD
1999-00	2.4 (2392)	T	0.060	①	①	41-47	①	①	HYD	HYD
	3.1 (3130)	M	0.060	①	①	41-47	①	①	HYD	HYD
	3.4 (3934)	E	0.060	①	①	41-47	①	①	HYD	HYD

NOTE: The Vehicle Emission Control Information label often reflects specification changes made during production. The label figures must be used if they differ from those in this chart.

HYD - Hydraulic

① Refer to Vehicle Emission Control Information label

93001CL5

CAPACITIES

Year	Model	Engine Displacement Liters (cc)	Engine ID/VIN	Engine Oil with Filter (qts.)	Transmission (pts.) Manual	Transmission (pts.) Auto.	Fuel Tank (gal.)	Cooling System (qts.)
1996	Achieva	2.4 (2392)	T	4.0 ①	4.0	②	15.2	10.4
	Achieva	3.1 (3130)	M	4.0 ①	4.0	②	15.2	10.8
	Grand Am	2.4 (2392)	T	4.5	4.0	8.0 ③	15.2	10.4
	Grand Am	3.1 (3130)	M	4.5	4.0	8.0 ③	15.2	13.1
	Skylark	2.4 (2392)	T	4.0 ①	12.0	8.0 ③	15.2	10.4
	Skylark	3.1 (3130)	M	4.0 ①	12.0	8.0 ③	15.2	13.1
1997	Achieva	2.4 (2392)	T	4.0 ①	4.0	②	15.2	10.4
	Achieva	3.1 (3130)	M	4.0 ①	4.0	②	15.2	10.8
	Grand Am	2.4 (2392)	T	4.5	4.0	8.0 ③	15.2	10.4
	Grand Am	3.1 (3130)	M	4.5	4.0	8.0 ③	15.2	13.1
	Skylark	2.4 (2392)	T	4.0 ①	12.0	8.0 ③	15.2	10.4
	Skylark	3.1 (3130)	M	4.0 ①	12.0	8.0 ③	15.2	13.1
1998	Achieva	2.4 (2392)	T	4.0 ①	4.0	②	15.2	10.4
	Achieva	3.1 (3130)	M	4.0 ①	4.0	④	15.2	10.8
	Grand Am	2.4 (2392)	T	4.5	4.0	8.0 ③	15.2	10.4
	Grand Am	3.1 (3130)	M	4.5	4.0	8.0 ③	15.2	13.1
1999-00	Alero	2.4 (2392)	T	4.0 ①	4.0	②	15.2	10.4
	Alero	3.4 (3934)	E	4.0 ①	4.0	②	15.2	10.4
	Grand Am	2.4 (2392)	T	4.5	4.0	8.0 ③	15.2	10.4
	Grand Am	3.1 (3130)	M	4.5	4.0	8.0 ③	15.2	13.1
	Grand Am	3.4 (3934)	E	4.0 ①	4.0	②	15.2	10.4

NOTE: All capacities are approximate. Add fluid gradually and ensure a proper fluid level is obtained.

① Capacity is without filter replacement; Additional oil may be required

② 3 speed: 8.0
4 speed: 12

③ With 4T60E transaxle: 12.0 pts.

④ 3 speed: 8.0
4 speed: 12

93001CL6

VALVE SPECIFICATIONS

Year	Engine Displacement Liters (cc)	Engine ID/VIN	Seat Angle (deg.)	Face Angle (deg.)	Spring Test Pressure (lbs. @ in.)	Spring Installed Height (in.)	Stem-to-Guide Clearance (in.) Intake	Stem-to-Guide Clearance (in.) Exhaust	Stem Diameter (in.) Intake	Stem Diameter (in.) Exhaust
1996	2.4 (2392)	T	45	46	50-55@ 1.437	1.437	0.0009- 0.0025	0.0016- 0.0032	0.2331- 0.2339	0.2326- 0.2334
	3.1 (3130)	M	45	45	250@ 1.239	1.710	0.0010- 0.0027	0.0010- 0.0027	NA	NA
1997	2.4 (2392)	T	45	46	50-55@ 1.437	1.437	0.0009- 0.0025	0.0016- 0.0032	0.2331- 0.2339	0.2326- 0.2334
	3.1 (3130)	M	45	45	250@ 1.239	1.710	0.0010- 0.0027	0.0010- 0.0027	NA	NA
1998	2.4 (2392)	T	45	46	50-55@ 1.437	1.437	0.0009- 0.0025	0.0016- 0.0032	0.2331- 0.2339	0.2326- 0.2334
	3.1 (3130)	M	45	45	250@ 1.239	1.710	0.0010- 0.0027	0.0010- 0.0027	NA	NA
1999-00	2.4 (2392)	T	45	46	50-55@ 1.437	1.437	0.0009- 0.0025	0.0016- 0.0032	0.2331- 0.2339	0.2326- 0.2334
	3.1 (3130)	M	45	45	250@ 1.239	1.710	0.0010- 0.0027	0.0010- 0.0027	NA	NA
	3.4 (3934)	E	45	45	75@ 1.701	1.701	0.0010- 0.0027	0.0010- 0.0027	NA	NA

NA - Not available

93001CL7

CRANKSHAFT AND CONNECTING ROD SPECIFICATIONS
All measurements are given in inches.

Year	Engine Displacement Liters (cc)	Engine ID/VIN	Crankshaft Main Brg. Journal Dia.	Crankshaft Main Brg. Oil Clearance	Crankshaft Shaft End-play	Crankshaft Thrust on No.	Connecting Rod Journal Diameter	Connecting Rod Oil Clearance	Connecting Rod Side Clearance
1996	2.4 (2392)	T	2.3622- 2.3631	0.0004- 0.0023	0.0034- 0.0095	3	1.8887- 1.8897	0.0004- 0.0026	0.0059- 0.0177
	3.1 (3130)	M	2.6473- 2.6383	0.0008- 0.0025 ①	0.0024- 0.0083	3	1.9987- 1.9994	0.0007- 0.0024	0.0070- 0.0170
1997	2.4 (2392)	T	2.3622- 2.3631	0.0004- 0.0023	0.0034- 0.0095	3	1.8887- 1.8897	0.0004- 0.0026	0.0059- 0.0177
	3.1 (3130)	M	2.6473- 2.6383	0.0008- 0.0025 ①	0.0024- 0.0083	3	1.9987- 1.9994	0.0007- 0.0024	0.0070- 0.0170
1998	2.4 (2392)	T	2.3622- 2.3631	0.0004- 0.0023	0.0034- 0.0095	3	1.8887- 1.8897	0.0004- 0.0026	0.0059- 0.0177
	3.1 (3130)	M	2.6473- 2.6383	0.0008- 0.0025 ①	0.0024- 0.0083	3	1.9987- 1.9994	0.0007- 0.0024	0.0070- 0.0170
1999-00	2.4 (2392)	T	2.3622- 2.3631	0.0004- 0.0023	0.0034- 0.0095	3	1.8887- 1.8897	0.0004- 0.0026	0.0059- 0.0177
	3.1 (3130)	M	2.6473- 2.6383	0.0008- 0.0025 ①	0.0024- 0.0083	3	1.9987- 1.9994	0.0007- 0.0024	0.0070- 0.0170
	3.4 (3934)	E	2.6473- 2.6383	0.0008- 0.0025 ①	0.0024- 0.0083	3	1.9987- 1.9994	0.0007- 0.0024	0.0070- 0.0170

① Thrust bearing: 0.0012 - 0.0030

93001CL8

For exhaust manifold replacement procedures, see the model specific sections of this manual

PISTON AND RING SPECIFICATIONS
All measurements are given in inches.

Year	Engine Displacement Liters (cc)	Engine ID/VIN	Piston Clearance	Ring Gap			Ring Side Clearance		
				Top Compression	Bottom Compression	Oil Control	Top Compression	Bottom Compression	Oil Control
1996	T	2.4 (2392)	0.0006-0.0015	0.006-0.012	0.010-0.016	0.010-0.030	0.0016-0.0031	0.0012-0.0028	0.0005-0.0089
	M	3.1 (3130)	0.0013-0.0027	0.006-0.014	0.0197-0.0280	0.0098-0.0500	0.002-0.0033	0.002-0.0035	0.008
1997	T	2.4 (2392)	0.0006-0.0015	0.006-0.012	0.010-0.016	0.010-0.030	0.0016-0.0031	0.0012-0.0028	0.0005-0.0089
	M	3.1 (3130)	0.0013-0.0027	0.006-0.014	0.0197-0.0280	0.0098-0.0500	0.002-0.0033	0.002-0.0035	0.008
1998	T	2.4 (2392)	0.0006-0.0015	0.006-0.012	0.010-0.016	0.010-0.030	0.0016-0.0031	0.0012-0.0028	0.0005-0.0089
	M	3.1 (3130)	0.0013-0.0027	0.006-0.014	0.0197-0.0280	0.0098-0.0500	0.002-0.0033	0.002-0.0035	0.008
1999-00	T	2.4 (2392)	0.0006-0.0015	0.006-0.012	0.010-0.016	0.010-0.030	0.0016-0.0031	0.0012-0.0028	0.0005-0.0089
	M	3.1 (3130)	0.0013-0.0027	0.006-0.014	0.0197-0.0280	0.0098-0.0500	0.002-0.0033	0.002-0.0035	0.008
	E	3.4 (3934)	0.0013-0.0027	0.006-0.014	0.0197-0.0280	0.0098-0.0500	0.002-0.0033	0.002-0.0035	0.008

93001CL9

TORQUE SPECIFICATIONS
All readings in ft. lbs.

Year	Engine Displacement Liters (cc)	Engine ID/VIN	Cylinder Head Bolts	Main Bearing Bolts	Rod Bearing Bolts	Crankshaft Damper Bolts	Flywheel Bolts	Manifold		Spark Plug	Lug Nut
								Intake	Exhaust		
1996	2.4 (2392)	T	①	②	③	④	⑤	19	31	16	100
	3.1 (3130)	M	⑥	⑦	⑧	76	59	⑨	12	20	100
1997	2.4 (2392)	T	①	②	③	④	⑤	19	31	16	100
	3.1 (3130)	M	⑥	⑦	⑧	76	59	⑨	12	20	100
1998	2.4 (2392)	T	①	②	③	④	⑤	19	31	16	100
	3.1 (3130)	M	⑥	⑦	⑧	76	59	⑨	12	20	100
1999-00	2.4 (2392)	T	①	②	③	④	⑤	19	31	16	100
	3.1 (3130)	M	⑥	⑦	⑧	76	59	⑨	12	20	100
	3.4 (3934)	E	⑩	⑪	⑧	76	59	⑫	12	20	100

① Nos. 1-8: 30 ft. lbs.
   Nos. 9-10: 26 ft. lbs.
   Tighten all bolts an additional 90 degrees

② 15 ft. lbs. plus 90 degrees

③ 18 ft. lbs. plus 80 degrees

④ 129 ft. lbs. plus 90 degrees

⑤ 22 ft. lbs. plus 45 degrees

⑥ Coat threads with sealer torque to 37 ft. lbs., then turn 1/4 turn (90 degrees)

⑦ 37 ft. lbs. plus 75 degrees

⑧ 15 ft. lbs. plus 75 degrees

⑨ Torque all bolts to 15 ft. lbs., retorque to 24 ft. lbs.

⑩ 33 ft. lbs. plus 90 degrees

⑪ 37 ft. lbs. plus 77 degrees

⑫ Lower - 115 inch lbs.
   Upper - 18 ft. lbs.

93001CL0

SCHEDULED MAINTENANCE INTERVALS
(GM N BODY - BUICK SKYLARK, OLDSMOBILE ACHIEVA, PONTIAC GRAND AM)

TO BE SERVICED	TYPE OF SERVICE	7.5	15	22.5	30	37.5	45	52.5	60	67.5	75	82.5	90	97.5
		VEHICLE MILEAGE INTERVAL (x1000)												
Engine oil & filter	R	✓	✓	✓	✓	✓	✓	✓	✓	✓	✓	✓	✓	✓
Automatic transaxle fluid & filter ③	S/I	✓	✓	✓	✓	✓	✓	✓	✓	✓	✓	✓	✓	✓
Brake hoses	S/I	✓	✓	✓	✓	✓	✓	✓	✓	✓	✓	✓	✓	✓
Chassis lubrication	S/I	✓	✓	✓	✓	✓	✓	✓	✓	✓	✓	✓	✓	✓
Coolant level, hoses & clamps	S/I	✓	✓	✓	✓	✓	✓	✓	✓	✓	✓	✓	✓	✓
Drive shaft boots & front suspension components	S/I	✓	✓	✓	✓	✓	✓	✓	✓	✓	✓	✓	✓	✓
Exhaust system	S/I	✓	✓	✓	✓	✓	✓	✓	✓	✓	✓	✓	✓	✓
Lubricate chassis, suspension, steering linkage, transaxle shift linkage, parking brake cable guides, underbody contact points & linkage	S/I	✓	✓	✓	✓	✓	✓	✓	✓	✓	✓	✓	✓	✓
Manual transaxle oil	S/I	✓	✓	✓	✓	✓	✓	✓	✓	✓	✓	✓	✓	✓
Throttle linkage	S/I	✓	✓	✓	✓	✓	✓	✓	✓	✓	✓	✓	✓	✓
Brake linings	S/I	✓		✓		✓		✓		✓		✓		✓
Rotate tires	S/I	✓		✓		✓		✓		✓		✓		✓
Air filter element & PCV filter	R				✓				✓				✓	
Engine coolant ②	R													
Spark plugs ①	R				✓				✓				✓	
Accessory drive belt(s)	S/I				✓				✓				✓	
EGR & fuel systems	S/I				✓				✓				✓	
Ignition cables	S/I				✓				✓				✓	
Throttle body mount bolt torque	S/I	✓												

① Platinum tip spark plugs - replace every 100,000 miles.

② Engine coolant - replace every 100,000 miles. Use O.E. specified (DEX-COOL™) coolant only. If any silicate coolant is used, the service interval is every 30,000 miles.

③ Automatic transaxle fluid & filter - replace at 100,000 miles (if not changed previously).

R - Replace   S/I - Service or Inspect

93001CM1

Refer to the model specific sections for cooling system service procedures

SCHEDULED MAINTENANCE INTERVALS
GENERAL MOTORS CORPORATION
N BODY
BUICK SKYLARK, OLDSMOBILE ACHIEVA
PONTIAC GRAND AM

The following should be used as a guide when determining the amount of work required for a particular service. In estimating how long a particular Scheduled Maintenance Service should take, please observe the following:

- **Chilton Time** is time based on field research and data supplied by the vehicle manufacturer.
  - Labor time operations are given in hours and tenths of an hour.
  - All labor operations, are to be used as a guide.

Mechanic Skill Level Codes:
(A) PRECISION: Really skilled with multiple certification.
(B) GENERAL: Normally skilled with certification.
(C) MAINTENANCE: Semi-skilled working on certification.

	Chilton Time			Chilton Time			Chilton Time
7500 Mile Service (B)			**37500 Mile Service (C)**			**75000 Mile Service (C)**	
All Models	2.0		All Models	1.8		All Models	1.1
15000 Mile Service (C)			**45000 Mile Service (C)**			**82500 Mile Service (C)**	
All Models	1.1		All Models	1.2		All Models	1.8
22500 Mile Service (C)			**52500 Mile Service (C)**			**90000 Mile Service (B)**	
All Models	1.8		All Models	1.8		All Models	2.8
30000 Mile Service (B)			**60000 Mile Service (B)**			**97500 Mile Service (C)**	
All Models	2.8		All Models	2.8		All Models	1.8
			67500 Mile Service (C)				
			All Models	1.8			

93001CM2

GENERAL MOTORS V-BODY
Cadillac Catera

ENGINE AND VEHICLE IDENTIFICATION

			Engine					Model Year	
Code ①	Liters (cc)	Cu. In.	Cyl.	Fuel Sys.	Engine Type	Eng. Mfg.		Code ②	Year
R	3.0 (2972)	181	V6	SMFI	DOHC	Opel		V	1997
								W	1998
								X	1999
								Y	2000

SMFI - Sequential Multi-port Fuel Injection

DOHC - Double Overhead Camshaft

① 8th position of VIN

② 10th position of VIN

93001CM3

GENERAL ENGINE SPECIFICATIONS

Year	Model	Engine Displacement Liters (cc)	Engine Series (ID/VIN)	Fuel System	Net Horsepower @ rpm	Net Torque @ rpm (ft. lbs.)	Bore x Stroke (in.)	Compression Ratio	Oil Pressure @ rpm
1997	Catera	3.0 (2972)	R	MFI	200@6000	192@3600	3.38x3.34	10.0:1	22@900
1998	Catera	3.0 (2972)	R	MFI	200@6000	192@3600	3.38x3.34	10.0:1	22@900
1999-00	Catera	3.0 (2972)	R	MFI	200@6000	192@3600	3.38x3.34	10.0:1	22@900

MFI - Multi-point Fuel Injection

93001CM4

ENGINE TUNE-UP SPECIFICATIONS

Year	Engine Displacement Liters (cc)	Engine ID/VIN	Spark Plug Gap (in.)	Ignition Timing (deg.) AT	Fuel Pump (psi)	Idle Speed (rpm) AT	Valve Clearance In.	Valve Clearance Ex.
1997	3.0 (2972)	R	0.034 - 0.043	①	41-47	①	HYD	HYD
1998	3.0 (2972)	R	0.034 - 0.043	①	41-47	①	HYD	HYD
1999-00	3.0 (2972)	R	0.034 - 0.043	①	41-47	①	HYD	HYD

NOTE: The Vehicle Emission Control Information label often reflects specification changes made during production. The label figures must be used if they differ from those in this chart.

HYD - Hydraulic

① Refer to Vehicle Emission Control Information label

93001CM5

CAPACITIES

Year	Model	Engine Displacement Liters (cc)	Engine ID/VIN	Engine Oil with Filter (qts.)	Transmission (pts.)	Drive Axle Rear (pts.)	Fuel Tank (gal.)	Cooling System (qts.)
1997	Catera	3.0 (2972)	R	6.0	14	3.5	18	10
1998	Catera	3.0 (2972)	R	6.0	14	3.5	18	10
1999-00	Catera	3.0 (2972)	R	6.0	14	3.5	18	10

NOTE: All capacities are approximate. Add fluid gradually and ensure a proper fluid level is obtained.

93001CM6

VALVE SPECIFICATIONS

Year	Engine Displacement Liters (cc)	Engine ID/VIN	Seat Angle (deg.)	Face Angle (deg.)	Spring Test Pressure (lbs. @ in.)	Spring Installed Height (in.)	Stem-to-Guide Clearance (in.) Intake	Stem-to-Guide Clearance (in.) Exhaust	Stem Diameter (in.) Intake	Stem Diameter (in.) Exhaust
1997	3.0 (2972)	R	①	45	56.6@1.338	1.543	0.0012-0.0022	0.0016-0.0026	0.2344-0.2350	0.2341-0.2346
1998	3.0 (2972)	R	①	45	56.6@1.338	1.543	0.0012-0.0022	0.0016-0.0026	0.2344-0.2350	0.2341-0.2346
1999-00	3.0 (2972)	R	①	45	56.6@1.338	1.543	0.0012-0.0022	0.0016-0.0026	0.2344-0.2350	0.2341-0.2346

① 45 degrees 20 minutes

93001CM7

CRANKSHAFT AND CONNECTING ROD SPECIFICATIONS
All measurements are given in inches.

Year	Engine Displacement Liters (cc)	Engine ID/VIN	Crankshaft Main Brg. Journal Dia.	Crankshaft Main Brg. Oil Clearance	Crankshaft Shaft End-play	Crankshaft Thrust on No.	Connecting Rod Journal Diameter	Connecting Rod Oil Clearance	Connecting Rod Side Clearance
1997	3.0 (2972)	R	①	0.0006-0.0017	0.0004-0.0300	2	②	0.0005-0.0024	0.0027-0.0110
1998	3.0 (2972)	R	①	0.0006-0.0017	0.0004-0.0300	2	②	0.0005-0.0024	0.0027-0.0110
1999-00	3.0 (2972)	R	①	0.0006-0.0017	0.0004-0.0300	2	②	0.0005-0.0024	0.0027-0.0110

① Green 2.6763 - 2.6766
Brown 26766 - 2.6770
Green/Blue 2.6665 - 2.6668
Brown/Blue 2.6668 - 2.6671
Green/White 2.6566 - 2.6570
Brown/White 2.6570 - 2.6573
② Undersize 0.25; 1.918 - 1.919
Undersize 0.50; 1.908 - 1.909

93001CM8

PISTON AND RING SPECIFICATIONS
All measurements are given in inches.

Year	Engine Displacement Liters (cc)	Engine ID/VIN	Piston Clearance	Ring Gap			Ring Side Clearance		
				Top Compression	Bottom Compression	Oil Control	Top Compression	Bottom Compression	Oil Control
1997	3.0 (2972)	R	0.0010-0.0018	0.0118-0.0196	0.0118-0.0196	0.0157-0.0551	0.0008-0.0015	0.0008-0.0015	0.0004-0.0012
1998	3.0 (2972)	R	0.0010-0.0018	0.0118-0.0196	0.0118-0.0196	0.0157-0.0551	0.0008-0.0015	0.0008-0.0015	0.0004-0.0012
1999-00	3.0 (2972)	R	0.0010-0.0018	0.0118-0.0196	0.0118-0.0196	0.0157-0.0551	0.0008-0.0015	0.0008-0.0015	0.0004-0.0012

93001CM9

TORQUE SPECIFICATIONS
All readings in ft. lbs.

Year	Engine Displacement Liters (cc)	Engine ID/VIN	Cylinder Head Bolts	Main Bearing Bolts	Rod Bearing Bolts	Crankshaft Damper Bolts	Flywheel Bolts	Manifold		Spark Plugs	Lug Nut
								Intake	Exhaust		
1997	3.0 (2972)	R	①	②	③	④	⑤	15	15	19	100
1998	3.0 (2972)	R	①	②	③	④	⑤	15	15	19	100
1999-00	3.0 (2972)	R	①	②	③	④	⑤	15	15	19	100

① Step 1: 18 ft. lbs.
Step 2: Rotate 90 degrees
Step 3: Rotate 90 degrees
Step 4: Rotate 90 degrees
Step 5: Rotate 15 degrees

② Step 1: 37 ft. lbs.
Step 2: Rotate 60 degrees
Step 3: Rotate 15 degrees

③ Step 1: 26 ft. lbs.
Step 2: Rotate 45 degrees
Step 3: Rotate 15 degrees

④ Step 1: 184 ft. lbs.
Step 2: Rotate 45 degrees
Step 3: Rotate 15 degrees
Step 4: Harmonic balancer 15 ft. lbs.

⑤ Step 1: 48 ft. lbs.
Step 2: Rotate 30 degrees
Step 3: Rotate 15 degrees

93001CM0

Timing chain and gear service is covered in the model specific sections of this manual

GENERAL MOTORS W-BODY
Buick Regal • 1998–00 Century • Chevrolet Lumina • Monte Carlo •
Oldsmobile Cutlass Supreme • Intrigue • Pontiac Grand Prix

ENGINE AND VEHICLE IDENTIFICATION

Engine Code								Model Year		
Code ①	Liters (cc)	Cu. In.	Cyl.	Fuel Sys.	Engine Type	Eng. Mfg.		Code ②		Year
1	3.8 (3785)	231	6	MFI	OHV	BOC		T		1996
K	3.8 (3785)	231	6	MFI	OHV	CPC		V		1997
H	3.5 (3475)	212	6	MFI	DOHC	BOC		W		1998
M	3.1 (3130)	191	6	MFI	OHV	BOC		X		1999
X	3.4 (3393)	207	6	MFI	OHV	CPC		Y		2000

MFI - Multi-point Fuel Injection
BOC - Buick/Oldsmobile/Cadillac
CPC - Chevrolet/Pontiac/Canada
① 8th position of VIN
② 10th position of VIN

93001CN1

GENERAL ENGINE SPECIFICATIONS

Year	Model	Engine Displacement Liters (cc)	Engine Series (ID/VIN)	Fuel System	Net Horsepower @ rpm	Net Torque @ rpm (ft. lbs.)	Bore x Stroke (in.)	Compression Ratio	Oil Pressure @ rpm
1996	Cutlass Supreme	3.1 (3130)	M	MFI	160@5200	185@4000	3.50x3.31	9.5:1	15@1100
	Cutlass Supreme	3.4 (3393)	X	MFI	210@5200	215@4000	3.62x3.31	9.25:1	15@1100
	Grand Prix	3.1 (3130)	M	MFI	160@5200	185@4000	3.50x3.31	9.5:1	15@1100
	Grand Prix	3.4 (3393)	X	MFI	210@5200	215@4000	3.62x3.31	9.25:1	15@1100
	Lumina	3.1 (3130)	M	MFI	160@5200	185@4000	3.50x3.31	9.5:1	15@1100
	Lumina	3.4 (3393)	X	MFI	210@5200	215@4000	3.62x3.31	9.25:1	15@1100
	Monte Carlo	3.1 (3130)	M	MFI	160@5200	185@4000	3.50x3.31	9.5:1	15@1100
	Monte Carlo	3.4 (3393)	X	MFI	210@5200	215@4000	3.62x3.31	9.25:1	15@1100
	Regal	3.8 (3785)	K	MFI	205@5200	230@4000	3.80x3.40	9.4:1	60@1850
	Regal	3.1 (3130)	M	MFI	160@5200	185@4000	3.50x3.31	9.5:1	15@1100
1997	Cutlass Supreme	3.1 (3130)	M	MFI	160@5200	185@4000	3.50x3.31	9.5:1	15@1100
	Grand Prix	3.8 (3785)	1	MFI	240@5200	280@3200	3.80x3.40	9.0:1	60@1850
	Grand Prix	3.8 (3785)	K	MFI	205@5200	230@4000	3.80x3.40	9.4:1	60@1850
	Grand Prix	3.1 (3130)	M	MFI	160@5200	185@4000	3.50x3.31	9.5:1	15@1100
	Lumina	3.1 (3130)	M	MFI	160@5200	185@4000	3.50x3.31	9.5:1	15@1100
	Lumina	3.4 (3393)	X	MFI	210@5200	215@4000	3.62x3.31	9.25:1	15@1100
	Monte Carlo	3.1 (3130)	M	MFI	160@5200	185@4000	3.50x3.31	9.5:1	15@1100
	Monte Carlo	3.4 (3393)	X	MFI	210@5200	215@4000	3.62x3.31	9.25:1	15@1100
	Regal	3.8 (3785)	1	MFI	240@5200	280@3200	3.80x3.40	9.0:1	60@1850
	Regal	3.8 (3785)	K	MFI	205@5200	230@4000	3.80x3.40	9.4:1	60@1850
	Regal	3.1 (3130)	M	MFI	160@5200	185@4000	3.50x3.31	9.5:1	15@1100
1998	Century	3.1 (3130)	M	MFI	160@5200	185@4000	3.50x3.31	9.5:1	15@1100
	Grand Prix	3.8 (3785)	1	MFI	240@5200	280@3200	3.80x3.40	9.0:1	60@1850
	Grand Prix	3.8 (3785)	K	MFI	205@5200	230@4000	3.80x3.40	9.4:1	60@1850
	Grand Prix	3.1 (3130)	M	MFI	160@5200	185@4000	3.50x3.31	9.5:1	15@1100
	Intrigue	3.8 (3785)	K	MFI	205@5200	230@4000	3.80x3.40	9.4:1	60@1850
	Lumina	3.8 (3785)	K	MFI	205@5200	230@4000	3.80x3.40	9.4:1	60@1850
	Lumina	3.1 (3130)	M	MFI	160@5200	185@4000	3.50x3.31	9.5:1	15@1100
	Monte Carlo	3.8 (3785)	K	MFI	205@5200	230@4000	3.80x3.40	9.4:1	60@1850
	Monte Carlo	3.1 (3130)	M	MFI	160@5200	185@4000	3.50x3.31	9.5:1	15@1100
	Regal	3.8 (3785)	1	MFI	240@5200	280@3200	3.80x3.40	9.0:1	60@1850
	Regal	3.8 (3785)	K	MFI	205@5200	230@4000	3.80x3.40	9.4:1	60@1850
	Regal	3.1 (3130)	M	MFI	160@5200	185@4000	3.50x3.31	9.5:1	15@1100
1999-00	Century	3.1 (3130)	M	MFI	160@5200	185@4000	3.50x3.31	9.5:1	15@1100
	Grand Prix	3.8 (3785)	1	MFI	240@5200	280@3200	3.80x3.40	9.0:1	60@1850
	Grand Prix	3.8 (3785)	K	MFI	205@5200	230@4000	3.80x3.40	9.4:1	60@1850
	Grand Prix	3.1 (3130)	M	MFI	160@5200	185@4000	3.50x3.31	9.5:1	15@1100
	Intrigue	3.5 (3475)	H	MFI	215@5600	230@4400	3.52x3.62	9.3:1	29@2000
	Lumina	3.8 (3785)	K	MFI	205@5200	230@4000	3.80x3.40	9.4:1	60@1850
	Lumina	3.1 (3130)	M	MFI	160@5200	185@4000	3.50x3.31	9.5:1	15@1100
	Monte Carlo	3.8 (3785)	K	MFI	205@5200	230@4000	3.80x3.40	9.4:1	60@1850
	Monte Carlo	3.1 (3130)	M	MFI	160@5200	185@4000	3.50x3.31	9.5:1	15@1100
	Regal	3.8 (3785)	1	MFI	240@5200	280@3200	3.80x3.40	9.0:1	60@1850
	Regal	3.8 (3785)	K	MFI	205@5200	230@4000	3.80x3.40	9.4:1	60@1850
	Regal	3.1 (3130)	M	MFI	160@5200	185@4000	3.50x3.31	9.5:1	15@1100

MFI - Multi-point Fuel Injection

93001CN2

Ignition system service is covered in the model specific sections of this manual

ENGINE TUNE-UP SPECIFICATIONS

Year	Engine Displacement Liters (cc)	Engine ID/VIN	Spark Plug Gap (in.)	Ignition Timing (deg.)	Fuel Pump (psi)	Idle Speed (rpm)	Valve Clearance In.	Ex.
1996	3.1 (3130)	M	0.060	①	41-47	②	HYD	HYD
	3.4 (3393)	X	0.045	①	41-47	②	HYD	HYD
	3.8 (3785)	K	0.060	①	41-47	②	HYD	HYD
1997	3.1 (3130)	M	0.060	①	41-47	②	HYD	HYD
	3.4 (3393)	X	0.045	①	41-47	②	HYD	HYD
	3.8 (3785)	1	0.060	①	41-47	②	HYD	HYD
	3.8 (3785)	K	0.060	①	41-47	②	HYD	HYD
1998	3.1 (3130)	M	0.060	①	41-47	②	HYD	HYD
	3.8 (3785)	1	0.060	①	41-47	②	HYD	HYD
	3.8 (3785)	K	0.060	①	41-47	②	HYD	HYD
1999-00	3.1 (3130)	M	0.060	①	41-47	②	HYD	HYD
	3.5 (3475)	H	0.050	①	41-47	②	HYD	HYD
	3.8 (3785)	1	0.060	①	41-47	②	HYD	HYD
	3.8 (3785)	K	0.060	①	41-47	②	HYD	HYD

NOTE: The Vehicle Emission Control Information label often reflects specification changes made during production. The label figures must be used if they differ from those in this chart.

HYD - Hydraulic

① Distributorless Ignition System (DIS) timing is not adjustable

② Idle speed is maintained by the Engine Control Module (ECM). There is no recommended adjustment procedure

93001CN3

CAPACITIES

Year	Model	Engine Displacement Liters (cc)	Engine ID/VIN	Engine Oil with Filter (qts.)		Transmission (pts.)	Fuel Tank (gal.)	Cooling System (qts.)
1996	Cutlass Supreme	3.1 (3130)	M	4.5		②	16.0	12.6
	Cutlass Supreme	3.4 (3393)	X	5.0		②	16.5	12.7
	Grand Prix	3.1 (3130)	M	4.5		②	16.0	12.6
	Grand Prix	3.4 (3393)	X	5.0		②	16.5	12.7
	Lumina	3.1 (3130)	M	4.5		②	16.0	12.6
	Lumina	3.4 (3393)	X	5.0		②	16.5	12.7
	Monte Carlo	3.1 (3130)	M	4.5		②	16.5	12.6
	Monte Carlo	3.4 (3393)	X	5.0		②	16.5	12.7
	Regal	3.8 (3785)	K	4.0	①	②	17.1	11.1
	Regal	3.1 (3130)	M	4.0	①	②	17.1	12.5
1997	Cutlass Supreme	3.1 (3130)	M	4.5		②	16.0	12.6
	Grand Prix	3.8 (3785)	1	5.0		②	16.5	12.7
	Grand Prix	3.8 (3785)	K	5.0		②	16.5	12.7
	Grand Prix	3.1 (3130)	M	4.5		②	16.0	12.6
	Lumina	3.1 (3130)	M	4.5		②	16.0	12.6
	Lumina	3.4 (3393)	X	5.0		②	16.5	12.7
	Monte Carlo	3.1 (3130)	M	4.5		②	16.5	12.6
	Monte Carlo	3.4 (3393)	X	5.0		②	16.5	12.7
	Regal	3.8 (3785)	1	5.0		②	16.5	12.7
	Regal	3.8 (3785)	K	5.0		②	17.1	11.1
	Regal	3.1 (3130)	M	4.5		②	17.1	12.5
1998	Century	3.1 (3130)	M	4.5		②	16.0	12.6
	Grand Prix	3.8 (3785)	1	5.0		②	16.5	12.7
	Grand Prix	3.8 (3785)	K	5.0		②	16.5	12.7
	Grand Prix	3.1 (3130)	M	4.5		②	16.0	12.6
	Intrigue	3.8 (3785)	K	5.0		②	16.5	12.7
	Lumina	3.8 (3785)	K	5.0		②	16.5	12.7
	Lumina	3.1 (3130)	M	4.5		②	16.0	12.6
	Monte Carlo	3.8 (3785)	K	5.0		②	16.5	12.7
	Monte Carlo	3.1 (3130)	M	4.5		②	16.5	12.6
	Regal	3.8 (3785)	1	5.0		②	16.5	12.7
	Regal	3.8 (3785)	K	5.0		②	17.1	11.1
	Regal	3.1 (3130)	M	4.5		②	17.1	12.5
1999-00	Century	3.1 (3130)	M	4.5		②	16.0	12.6
	Grand Prix	3.8 (3785)	1	5.0		②	16.5	12.7
	Grand Prix	3.8 (3785)	K	5.0		②	16.5	12.7
	Grand Prix	3.1 (3130)	M	4.5		②	16.0	12.6
	Intrigue	3.5 (3475)	H	6.0		②	18.0	9.6
	Lumina	3.8 (3785)	K	5.0		②	16.5	12.7
	Lumina	3.1 (3130)	M	4.5		②	16.0	12.6
	Monte Carlo	3.8 (3785)	K	5.0		②	16.5	12.7
	Monte Carlo	3.1 (3130)	M	4.5		②	16.5	12.6
	Regal	3.8 (3785)	1	5.0		②	16.5	12.7
	Regal	3.8 (3785)	K	5.0		②	17.1	11.1
	Regal	3.1 (3130)	M	4.5		②	17.1	12.5

NOTE: All capacities are approximate. Add fluid gradually and ensure a proper fluid is obtained.

① Capacity is without filter replacement; Additional oil may be required

② 3T40 trans.: 8.0 pts.
4T60 trans.: 12.0 pts.
4T60E trans.: 14.8 pts.
4T65E trans.: 14.8 pts.

93001CN4

Please visit our web site at www.chiltononline.com

VALVE SPECIFICATIONS

Year	Engine Displacement Liters (cc)	Engine ID/VIN	Seat Angle (deg.)	Face Angle (deg.)	Spring Test Pressure (lbs. @ in.)	Spring Installed Height (in.)	Stem-to-Guide Clearance (in.)		Stem Diameter (in.)	
							Intake	Exhaust	Intake	Exhaust
1996	3.1 (3130)	M	45	45	250@1.239	1.710	0.0001-0.0027	0.0010-0.0027	NA	NA
	3.4 (3393)	X	46	45	75@1.40	1.400	0.0011-0.0026	0.0014-0.0031	NA	NA
	3.8 (3785)	K	45	45	210@1.32	1.690-1.720	0.0015-0.0035	0.0015-0.0032	NA	NA
1997	3.1 (3130)	M	45	45	250@1.239	1.710	0.0001-0.0027	0.0010-0.0027	NA	NA
	3.4 (3393)	X	46	45	75@1.40	1.400	0.0011-0.0026	0.0014-0.0031	NA	NA
	3.8 (3785)	1	45	45	80@1.750	1.690-1.720	0.0015-0.0032	0.0015-0.0032	NA	NA
	3.8 (3785)	K	45	45	210@1.32	1.690-1.720	0.0015-0.0035	0.0015-0.0032	NA	NA
1998	3.1 (3130)	M	45	45	250@1.239	1.710	0.0001-0.0027	0.0010-0.0027	NA	NA
	3.8 (3785)	1	45	45	80@1.750	1.690-1.720	0.0015-0.0032	0.0015-0.0032	NA	NA
	3.8 (3785)	K	45	45	210@1.32	1.690-1.720	0.0015-0.0035	0.0015-0.0032	NA	NA
1999-00	3.1 (3130)	M	45	45	250@1.239	1.710	0.0001-0.0027	0.0010-0.0027	NA	NA
	3.5 (3475)	H	45.75	45	130-142@0.964	1.377	0.0010-0.0030	0.0020-0.0040	0.233-0.234	0.233-0.234
	3.8 (3785)	1	45	45	80@1.750	1.690-1.720	0.0015-0.0032	0.0015-0.0032	NA	NA
	3.8 (3785)	K	45	45	210@1.32	1.690-1.720	0.0015-0.0035	0.0015-0.0032	NA	NA

NA - Not Available

93001CN5

CRANKSHAFT AND CONNECTING ROD SPECIFICATIONS
All measurements are given in inches.

Year	Engine Displacement Liters (cc)	Engine ID/VIN	Crankshaft				Connecting Rod		
			Main Brg. Journal Dia.	Main Brg. Oil Clearance	Shaft End-play	Thrust on No.	Journal Diameter	Oil Clearance	Side Clearance
1996	3.1 (3130)	M	2.6473-2.6383	0.0008- ① 0.0025	0.0024-0.0083	3	1.9987-1.9994	0.0007-0.0024	0.0070-0.0170
	3.4 (3393)	X	2.6472-2.6479	0.0008-0.0025	0.0024-0.0083	3	1.9987-1.9994	0.0007-0.0024	0.0070-0.0170
	3.8 (3785)	K	2.4988-2.4998	0.0008-0.0022	0.0030-0.0110	2	2.3738-2.3745	0.0005-0.0026	0.0030-0.0150
1997	3.1 (3130)	M	2.6473-2.6383	0.0008- ① 0.0025	0.0024-0.0083	3	1.9987-1.9994	0.0007-0.0024	0.0070-0.017
	3.4 (3393)	X	2.6472-2.6479	0.0008-0.0025	0.0024-0.0083	3	1.9987-1.9994	0.0007-0.0024	0.0070-0.0170
	3.8 (3785)	1	2.4988-2.4998	0.0008-0.0022	0.0030-0.011	2	2.3738-2.3745	0.0005-0.0026	0.0030-0.0150
	3.8 (3785)	K	2.4988-2.4998	0.0008-0.0022	0.0030-0.0110	2	2.3738-2.3745	0.0005-0.0026	0.0030-0.0150
1998	3.1 (3130)	M	2.6473-2.6383	0.0008- ① 0.0025	0.0024-0.0083	3	1.9987-1.9994	0.0007-0.0024	0.0070-0.0170
	3.8 (3785)	1	2.4988-2.4998	0.0008-0.0022	0.0030-0.011	2	2.3738-2.3745	0.0005-0.0026	0.0030-0.0150
	3.8 (3785)	K	2.4988-2.4998	0.0008-0.0022	0.0030-0.0110	2	2.3738-2.3745	0.0005-0.0026	0.003-0.015
1999-00	3.1 (3130)	M	2.6473-2.6383	0.0008- ① 0.0025	0.0024-0.0083	3	1.9987-1.9994	0.0007-0.0024	0.0070-0.0170
	3.5 (3475)	H	2.755-2.756	0.0006-0.0021	0.0050-0.0200	3	2.1829-2.1835	0.0009-0.0025	0.0040-0.0130
	3.8 (3785)	1	2.4988-2.4998	0.0008-0.0022	0.0030-0.011	2	2.3738-2.3745	0.0005-0.0026	0.0030-0.0150
	3.8 (3785)	K	2.4988-2.4998	0.0008-0.0022	0.0030-0.0110	2	2.3738-2.3745	0.0005-0.0026	0.0030-0.0150

① Thrust bearing: 0.0012 - 0.0030

93001CN6

Refer to the model specific sections for engine mechanical service procedures

PISTON AND RING SPECIFICATIONS

All measurements are given in inches.

Year	Engine Displacement Liters (cc)	Engine ID/VIN	Piston Clearance	Ring Gap			Ring Side Clearance		
				Top Compression	Bottom Compression	Oil Control	Top Compression	Bottom Compression	Oil Control
1996	3.1 (3130)	M	0.0010-0.0018	0.0118-0.0196	0.0118-0.0196	0.0157-0.0551	0.0008-0.0015	0.0008-0.0015	0.0004-0.0012
	3.4 (3393)	X	0.0008-0.0020	0.0080-0.0180	0.0220-0.0320	0.0098-0.0229	0.0013-0.0031	0.0013-0.0031	0.0011-0.0081
	3.8 (3785)	K	0.0004-0.0020	0.0120-0.0220	0.0300-0.0400	0.0100-0.0300	0.0013-0.0031	0.0013-0.0031	0.0009-0.0079
1997	3.1 (3130)	M	0.0010-0.0018	0.0118-0.0196	0.0118-0.0196	0.0157-0.0551	0.0008-0.0015	0.0008-0.0015	0.0004-0.0012
	3.4 (3393)	X	0.0008-0.0020	0.0080-0.0180	0.0220-0.0320	0.0098-0.0229	0.0013-0.0031	0.0013-0.0031	0.0011-0.0081
	3.8 (3785)	1	0.0004-0.0020	0.0120-0.0220	0.0300-00.040	0.0100-0.0300	0.0013-0.0031	0.0013-0.0031	0.0009-0.0079
	3.8 (3785)	K	0.0004-0.0020	0.0120-0.0220	0.0300-0.0400	0.0100-0.0300	0.0013-0.0031	0.0013-0.0031	0.0009-0.0079
1998	3.1 (3130)	M	0.0010-0.0018	0.0118-0.0196	0.0118-0.0196	0.0157-0.0551	0.0008-0.0015	0.0008-0.0015	0.0004-0.0012
	3.8 (3785)	1	0.0004-0.0020	0.0120-0.0220	0.0300-00.040	0.0100-0.0300	0.0013-0.0031	0.0013-0.0031	0.0009-0.0079
	3.8 (3785)	K	0.0004-0.0020	0.0120-0.0220	0.0300-0.0400	0.0100-0.0300	0.0013-0.0031	0.0013-0.0031	0.0009-0.0079
1999-00	3.1 (3130)	M	0.0010-0.0018	0.0118-0.0196	0.0118-0.0196	0.0157-0.0551	0.0008-0.0015	0.0008-0.0015	0.0004-0.0012
	3.5 (3475)	H	0.0010-0.0025	0.0080-0.0180	0.0140-0.0200	0.0100-0.0300	0.0016-0.0037	0.0016-0.0037	side-sealing
	3.8 (3785)	1	0.0004-0.0020	0.0100-0.0160	0.0300-00.040	0.0100-0.0300	0.0013-0.0031	0.0013-0.0031	0.0009-0.0079
	3.8 (3785)	K	0.0004-0.0020	0.0120-0.0220	0.0300-0.0400	0.0100-0.0300	0.0013-0.0031	0.0013-0.0031	0.0009-0.0079

93001CN7

TORQUE SPECIFICATIONS
All readings in ft. lbs.

Year	Engine Displacement Liters (cc)	Engine ID/VIN	Cylinder Head Bolts	Main Bearing Bolts	Rod Bearing Bolts	Crankshaft Damper Bolts	Flywheel Bolts	Manifold Intake	Manifold Exhaust	Spark Plug	Lug Nut
1996	3.1 (3130)	M	①	②	③	76	61	④	10	⑤	100
	3.4 (3393)	X	⑥	②	39	78	61	18	⑦	11	100
	3.8 (3785)	K	⑧	⑬	20	⑪	⑫	⑭	18	11	100
1997	3.1 (3130)	M	①	②	③	76	61	④	10	⑤	100
	3.4 (3393)	X	⑥	②	39	78	61	18	⑦	11	100
	3.8 (3785)	1	⑧	⑬	20	⑪	⑫	⑯	22	11	100
	3.8 (3785)	K	⑧	⑬	20	⑪	⑫	⑭	38	11	100
1998	3.1 (3130)	M	①	②	③	76	61	④	10	⑩	100
	3.8 (3785)	1	⑧	⑬	⑮	⑪	⑫	⑯	22	11	100
	3.8 (3785)	K	⑧	⑬	⑮	⑪	⑫	⑭	38	11	100
1999-00	3.1 (3130)	M	①	②	③	76	61	④	10	⑩	100
	3.5 (3475)	H	⑨	⑰	⑱	⑲	⑳	5	18	15	100
	3.8 (3785)	1	⑧	⑬	⑮	⑪	⑫	⑯	22	11	100
	3.8 (3785)	K	⑧	⑬	⑮	⑪	⑫	⑭	38	11	100

① Coat threads with sealer torque to 33 ft. lbs., then turn 1/4 turn (90 degrees)

② 37 ft. lbs. plus 77 degrees

③ 15 ft. lbs. plus 75 degrees

④ Torque all bolts to 15 ft. lbs. Retorque to 24 ft. lbs.

⑤ New cylinder head:
   1st-time installation: 20 ft. lbs.
   All other installations: 11 ft. lbs.

⑥ 37 ft. lbs. plus 90 degrees

⑦ 115 inch lbs.

⑧ Step 1: 35 ft. lbs.
   Step 2: 130 degrees
   Step 3: Rotate four center bolts an additional 30 degrees

⑨ Step 1: 22 ft. lbs.
   Step 2: 60 degrees
   Step 3: 60 degrees
   Step 4: 80 degrees

⑩ 20 ft. lbs. plus 50 degrees

⑪ 110 ft. lbs. plus 76 degrees

⑫ 11 ft. lbs. plus 50 degrees

⑬ 30 ft. lbs. plus 110 degrees
   Side bolts: 11 ft. lbs. plus 45 degrees

⑭ Upper manifold: 18 ft. lbs.
   Lower manifold bolt/nut: 22 ft. lbs.
   Upper manifold studs: 89 in. lbs.

⑮ 20 ft. lbs. plus 50 degrees

⑯ Upper manifold: 8 ft. lbs.
   Lower manifold: 11 ft. lbs.

⑰ Cap bolts
   Step 1: 15 ft. lbs.
   Step 2: 70 degrees
   Perimeter bolts: 22 ft. lbs.

⑱ Step 1: 22 ft. lbs.
   Step 2: Loosen completely
   Step 3: 18 ft. lbs.
   Step 4: 110 degrees

⑲ Step 1: 37 ft. lbs.
   Step 2: 150 degrees

⑳ Step 1: 11 ft. lbs.
   Step 2: 50 degrees

93001CN8

Refer to the model specific sections for fuel system service procedures

SCHEDULED MAINTENANCE INTERVALS
(GM W BODY - BUICK CENTURY & REGAL, CHEVROLET LUMINA & MONTE CARLO, OLDSMOBILE INTRIGUE & CUTLASS SUPREME, PONTIAC GRAND PRIX)

TO BE SERVICED	TYPE OF SERVICE	VEHICLE MILEAGE INTERVAL (x1000)												
		7.5	15	22.5	30	37.5	45	52.5	60	67.5	75	82.5	90	97.5
Engine oil & filter	R	✓	✓	✓	✓	✓	✓	✓	✓	✓	✓	✓	✓	✓
Automatic transaxle fluid & filter ③	S/I	✓	✓	✓	✓	✓	✓	✓	✓	✓	✓	✓	✓	✓
Brake hoses	S/I	✓	✓	✓	✓	✓	✓	✓	✓	✓	✓	✓	✓	✓
Coolant level, hoses & clamps	S/I	✓	✓	✓	✓	✓	✓	✓	✓	✓	✓	✓	✓	✓
Drive shaft boots & front suspension components	S/I	✓	✓	✓	✓	✓	✓	✓	✓	✓	✓	✓	✓	✓
Exhaust system & throttle linkage	S/I	✓	✓	✓	✓	✓	✓	✓	✓	✓	✓	✓	✓	✓
Lubricate chassis, suspension, steering linkage, transaxle shift linkage, parking brake cable guides, underbody contact points & linkage	S/I	✓	✓	✓	✓	✓	✓	✓	✓	✓	✓	✓	✓	✓
Rotate tires	S/I	✓		✓		✓		✓		✓		✓		✓
Air filter element	R				✓				✓				✓	
Engine coolant ②	R				✓				✓				✓	
PCV filter	R				✓				✓				✓	
Spark plugs ①	R				✓				✓				✓	
Accessory drive belt(s)	S/I				✓				✓				✓	
Ignition cables, EGR & fuel systems	S/I				✓				✓				✓	
Camshaft timing belt	R								✓					
Throttle body mount bolt torque	S/I	✓												

① Platinum tip spark plugs - replace every 100,000 miles.

② Engine coolant - replace every 100,000 miles. Use O.E. specified (DEX-COOL™) coolant only. If any silicate coolant is used, the service interval is every 30,000 miles.

③ Automatic transaxle fluid & filter - replace at 100,000 miles (if not changed previously).

R - Replace   S/I - Service or Inspect

FREQUENT OPERATION MAINTENANCE (SEVERE SERVICE)

If a vehicle is operated under any of the following conditions it is considered severe service:
- Extremely dusty areas.
- 50% or more of the vehicle operation is in 32°C (90°F) or higher temperatures, or constant operation in operation in temperatures below 0°C (32°F).
- Prolonged idling (vehicle operation in stop and go traffic).
- Frequent short running periods (engine does not warm to normal operating temperatures).
- Police, taxi, delivery usage or trailer towing usage.

Oil & oil filter - change every 3000 miles
Chassis lubrication - lubricate every 6000 miles.
Rotate tires at 6000 miles, then every 12,000 miles.
Throttle body mount bolt torque - tighten at 6000 miles.
Air filter element - service or inspect every 15,000 miles.
Camshaft timing belt - change every 60,000 miles.

93001CN9

SCHEDULED MAINTENANCE INTERVALS
GENERAL MOTORS CORPORATION
W BODY
BUICK REGAL, CENTURY (1997-00), CHEVROLET LUMINA, MONTE CARLO
OLDSMOBILE CUTLASS SUPREME, OLDSMOBILE INTRIGUE, PONTIAC GRAND PRIX

The following should be used as a guide when determining the amount of work required for a particular service.
In estimating how long a particular Scheduled Maintenance Service should take, please observe the following:

- **Chilton Time** is time based on field research and data supplied by the vehicle manufacturer.
- Labor time operations are given in hours and tenths of an hour.
- All labor operations, are to be used as a guide.

Mechanic Skill Level Codes:
(A) PRECISION: Really skilled with multiple certification.
(B) GENERAL: Normally skilled with certification.
(C) MAINTENANCE: Semi-skilled working on certification.

	Chilton Time		Chilton Time		Chilton Time
7500 Mile Service (C)		**45000 Mile Service (C)**		**67500 Mile Service (C)**	
All Models	1.5	All Models	.8	All Models	1.3
15000 Mile Service (C)		**52500 Mile Service (C)**		**75000 Mile Service (C)**	
All Models	.8	All Models	1.3	All Models	.8
22500 Mile Service (C)		**60000 Mile Service (B)**		**82500 Mile Service (C)**	
All Models	1.3	All Models	3.1	All Models	1.3
30000 Mile Service (B)		*Add for timing belt R&R.*		**90000 Mile Service (B)**	
All Models	3.1			All Models	3.1
37500 Mile Service (C)				**97500 Mile Service (C)**	
All Models	1.3			All Models	1.3

93001C01

Refer to the model specific sections for engine electrical system service procedures

GENERAL MOTORS Y-BODY
Chevrolet Corvette

ENGINE AND VEHICLE IDENTIFICATION

			Engine					Model Year	
Code ①	Liters (cc)	Cu. In.	Cyl.	Fuel Sys.	Engine Type	Eng. Mfg.		Code ②	Year
5	5.7 (5737)	350	8	MFI	DOHC	CPC		T	1996
G	5.7 (5665)	350	8	MFI	OHV	CPC		V	1997
P	5.7 (5737)	350	8	MFI	OHV	CPC		W	1998
								X	1999
								Y	2000

CPC - Chevrolet/Pontiac/Canada

MFI - Multi-point Fuel Injection

OHC - Over Head Camshaft

DOHC - Dual Overhead Camshaft

① 8th position of VIN

② 10th position of VIN

93001C02

GENERAL ENGINE SPECIFICATIONS

Year	Model	Engine Displacement Liters (cc)	Engine Series (ID/VIN)	Fuel System	Net Horsepower @ rpm	Net Torque @ rpm (ft. lbs.)	Bore x Stroke (in.)	Compression Ratio	Oil Pressure @ rpm
1996	Corvette	5.7 (5737)	5	MFI	375@5800	370@4800	3.90x3.66	11.0:1	40@2000
	Corvette	5.7 (5737)	P	MFI	300@5000	340@3600	4.00x3.48	10.25:1	18@2000
1997	Corvette	5.7 (5665)	G	MFI	345@5600	350@4400	3.89x3.62	10.1:1	18@2000
1998	Corvette	5.7 (5665)	G	MFI	345@5600	350@4400	3.89x3.62	10.1:1	18@2000
1999-00	Corvette	5.7 (5665)	G	MFI	345@5600	350@4400	3.89x3.62	10.1:1	18@2000

MFI - Multi-point Fuel Injection

93001C03

ENGINE TUNE-UP SPECIFICATIONS

Year	Engine Displacement Liters (cc)	Engine ID/VIN	Spark Plug Gap (in.)	Ignition Timing (deg.) MT	Ignition Timing (deg.) AT	Fuel Pump (psi)	Idle Speed (rpm) MT	Idle Speed (rpm) AT	Valve Clearance In.	Valve Clearance Ex.
1996	5.7 (5737)	5	0.035	①	①	48-55	①	①	HYD	HYD
	5.7 (5737)	P	0.035	—	①	41-47	—	①	HYD	HYD
1997	5.7 (5665)	G	0.060	①	①	48-55	①	①	HYD	HYD
1998	5.7 (5665)	G	0.060	①	①	48-55	①	①	HYD	HYD
1999-00	5.7 (5665)	G	0.060	①	①	48-55	①	①	HYD	HYD

NOTE: The Vehicle Emission Control Information label often reflects specification changes made during production. The label figures must be used if they differ from those in this chart.

HYD - Hydraulic

① Refer to Vehicle Emission Control Information label

93001C04

CAPACITIES

Year	Model	Engine Displacement Liters (cc)	Engine ID/VIN	Engine Oil with Filter (qts.)	Transmission (pts.) 6-Spd	Transmission (pts.) Auto.	Drive Axle (pts.)	Fuel Tank (gal.)	Cooling System (qts.)
1996	Corvette	5.7 (5737)	5	7.6	①	②	3.8	20.0	14.7
	Corvette	5.7 (5737)	P	5.0	①	②	3.8	20.0	17.8
1997	Corvette	5.7 (5737)	G	6.5	①	②	3.8	20.0	14.7
1998	Corvette	5.7 (5737)	G	6.5	①	②	3.8	20.0	14.7
1999-00	Corvette	5.7 (5737)	G	6.5	①	②	3.8	20.0	14.7

NOTE: All capacities are approximate. Add fluid gradually and ensure a proper fluid level is obtained.

① ZF 6 speed trans.: 4.4 pts.
 MM 6 speed trans.: 4.1 pts.

② 440T4 trans.: 13.0 pts.
 125C trans.: 8.0 pts.
 4L60E trans.: 10.0 pts.

93001C05

VALVE SPECIFICATIONS

Year	Engine Displacement Liters (cc)	Engine ID/VIN	Seat Angle (deg.)	Face Angle (deg.)	Spring Test Pressure (lbs. @ in.)	Spring Installed Height (in.)	Stem-to-Guide Clearance (in.) Intake	Stem-to-Guide Clearance (in.) Exhaust	Stem Diameter (in.) Intake	Stem Diameter (in.) Exhaust
1996	5.7 (5737)	5	44	45	147-166@ 0.95	1.34	0.0012- 0.0026	0.0014- 0.0030	NA	NA
	5.7 (5737)	P	46	45	81-89@1.78	1.78	0.0009- 0.0027	0.0009- 0.0027	NA	NA
1997	5.7 (5665)	G	46	45	76@1.80	1.80	0.0010- 0.0026	0.0010- 0.0026	NA	NA
1998	5.7 (5665)	G	46	45	76@1.80	1.80	0.0010- 0.0026	0.0010- 0.0026	NA	NA
1999-00	5.7 (5665)	G	46	45	76@1.80	1.80	0.0010- 0.0026	0.0010- 0.0026	NA	NA

NA - Not Available

93001C06

For accessory drive belt replacement procedures see the model specific sections of this manual

CRANKSHAFT AND CONNECTING ROD SPECIFICATIONS

All measurements are given in inches.

Year	Engine Displacement Liters (cc)	Engine ID/VIN	Crankshaft				Connecting Rod		
			Main Brg. Journal Dia.	Main Brg. Oil Clearance	Shaft End-play	Thrust on No.	Journal Diameter	Oil Clearance	Side Clearance
1996	5.7 (5737)	P	①	②	0.0020-0.0080	5	2.0978-2.0998	0.0013-0.0030	0.0060-0.0240
	5.7 (5737)	5	2.4485-2.4491	0.0010-0.0020	0.0020-0.0080	5	2.0978-2.0998	0.0010-0.0030	0.0060-0.0140
1997	5.7 (5665)	G	2.558-2.559	0.0007-0.0021	0.0015-0.0078	5	2.0987	0.0006-0.0025	0.0043-0.0200
1998	5.7 (5665)	G	2.558-2.559	0.0007-0.0021	0.0015-0.0078	5	2.0987	0.0006-0.0025	0.0043-0.0200
1999-00	5.7 (5665)	G	2.558-2.559	0.0007-0.0021	0.0015-0.0078	5	2.0987	0.0006-0.0025	0.0043-0.0200

① No. 1: 2.4484 - 2.4493
   Nos. 2, 3, 4: 2.4481 - 2.4490
   No. 5: 2.4479 - 2.4488
② No.1: 0.0007 - 0.0021
   Nos. 2, 3, 4: 0.0009 - 0.0024
   No. 5: 0.0010 - 0.0027

93001C07

PISTON AND RING SPECIFICATIONS

All measurements are given in inches.

Year	Engine Displacement Liters (cc)	Engine ID/VIN	Piston Clearance	Ring Gap			Ring Side Clearance		
				Top Compression	Bottom Compression	Oil Control	Top Compression	Bottom Compression	Oil Control
1996	5.7 (5737)	P	0.0010-0.0027	0.010-0.016	0.018-0.026	0.010-0.030	0.0019-0.0035	0.0019-0.0035	0.0020-0.0070
	5.7 (5737)	5	0.0010-0.0027	0.010-0.016	0.018-0.026	0.010-0.030	0.0019-0.0035	0.0019-0.0035	0.0020-0.0070
1997	5.7 (5665)	G	0.0007-0.0021	0.009-0.015	0.017-0.025	0.007-0.027	0.0016-0.0033	0.0016-0.0031	0.0004-0.0087
1998	5.7 (5665)	G	0.0007-0.0021	0.009-0.015	0.017-0.025	0.007-0.027	0.0016-0.0033	0.0016-0.0031	0.0004-0.0087
1999-00	5.7 (5665)	G	0.0007-0.0021	0.009-0.015	0.017-0.025	0.007-0.027	0.0016-0.0033	0.0016-0.0031	0.0004-0.0087

93001C08

TORQUE SPECIFICATIONS
All readings in ft. lbs.

Year	Engine Displacement Liters (cc)	Engine ID/VIN	Cylinder Head Bolts	Main Bearing Bolts	Rod Bearing Bolts	Crankshaft Damper Bolts	Flywheel Bolts	Manifold Intake	Manifold Exhaust	Spark Plugs	Lug Nut
1996	5.7 (5737)	P	65	78	47	60	74	35	30	11	100
	5.7 (5737)	5	①	②	③	148	66	④	⑤	15	100
1997	5.7 (5665)	G	⑥	⑦	⑧	⑨	⑩	⑪	⑫	11	100
1998	5.7 (5665)	G	⑥	⑦	⑧	⑨	⑩	⑪	⑫	11	100
1999-00	5.7 (5665)	G	⑥	⑦	⑧	⑨	⑩	⑪	⑫	11	100

NA - Not Available

① Step 1: 45 ft. lbs.
  Step 2: 74 ft. lbs.
  Step 3: 118 ft. lbs.

② Step 1: 15 ft. lbs.
  Step 2: Inner: 65-70 degrees
  Step 3: Outer: 80-85 degrees

③ 22 ft. lbs. plus 80-85 degrees

④ Injector housing and fuel rail bolts: 20 ft. lbs.

⑤ Studs: 22 ft. lbs.
  Bolts: 18 ft. lbs.

⑥ Step 1: 22 ft. lbs.
  Step 2: Rotate 76 degrees
  Step 3: Repeat Step 2 except for the medium
    length bolts at the front and rear.
  Step 4: Rotate the medium bolts at the front
    and rear of each head 34 degrees

⑦ Step 1: Inner bolts 15 ft. lbs.
  Step 2: Inner bolts rotate 80 degrees
  Step 3: Side bolts 18 ft. lbs.
  Step 4: Outer studs 15 ft. lbs.
  Step 5: Outer studs rotate 53 degrees

⑧ Step 1: 15 ft. lbs.
  Step 2: Rotate 60 degrees

⑨ Step 1: 240 ft. lbs.
  Step 2: Loosen bolt and retighten to 37 ft. lbs.
  Step 3: Rotate 120 degrees

⑩ Step 1: 15 ft. lbs.
  Step 2: 37 ft. lbs.
  Step 3: 74 ft. lbs.

⑪ Step 1: 44 inch lbs.
  Step 2: 74 inch lbs.

⑫ Step 1: 11 ft. lbs.
  Step 2: 18 ft. lbs.

93001C09

For brake related suspension and axle service, refer to the model specific sections of this manual

SCHEDULED MAINTENANCE INTERVALS
(GM Y BODY - CHEVROLET CORVETTE)

TO BE SERVICED	TYPE OF SERVICE	VEHICLE MILEAGE INTERVAL (x1000)												
		7.5	15	22.5	30	37.5	45	52.5	60	67.5	75	82.5	90	97.5
Engine oil & filter ③	R	✓	✓	✓	✓	✓	✓	✓	✓	✓	✓	✓	✓	✓
Brake hoses & brake lining	S/I	✓	✓	✓	✓	✓	✓	✓	✓	✓	✓	✓	✓	✓
Coolant level, hoses & clamps	S/I	✓	✓	✓	✓	✓	✓	✓	✓	✓	✓	✓	✓	✓
Exhaust system & throttle linkage	S/I	✓	✓	✓	✓	✓	✓	✓	✓	✓	✓	✓	✓	✓
Lubricate chassis, suspension, steering linkage, transaxle shift linkage, parking brake cable guides, underbody contact points & linkage	S/I	✓	✓	✓	✓	✓	✓	✓	✓	✓	✓	✓	✓	✓
Rear axle fluid level	S/I	✓	✓	✓	✓	✓	✓	✓	✓	✓	✓	✓	✓	✓
Automatic transaxle fluid & filter ④	S/I		✓		✓		✓		✓		✓		✓	
Air filter element	R				✓				✓				✓	
Engine coolant ②	R				✓				✓				✓	
Ignition cables, EGR & fuel systems	S/I				✓				✓				✓	
Serpentine drive belt	S/I				✓				✓				✓	
Spark plugs ①	R													

① Platinum tip spark plugs - replace every 100,000 miles.

② Engine coolant - replace every 100,000 miles. Use O.E. specified (DEX-COOL™) coolant only. If any silicate coolant is used, the service interval is every 30,000 miles.

③ Corvette engines require a special oil meeting GM Standard 4718M.

④ Automatic transaxle fluid & filter - replace at 100,000 miles (if not changed previously).

R - Replace   S/I - Service or Inspect

FREQUENT OPERATION MAINTENANCE (SEVERE SERVICE)

If a vehicle is operated under any of the following conditions it is considered severe service:
- Extremely dusty areas.
- 50% or more of the vehicle operation is in 32°C (90°F) or higher temperatures, or constant operation in operation in temperatures below 0°C (32°F).
- Prolonged idling (vehicle operation in stop and go traffic).
- Frequent short running periods (engine does not warm to normal operating temperatures).
- Police, taxi, delivery usage or trailer towing usage.

Engine oil & oil filter - change every 3000 miles ®

Chassis lubrication - lubricate every 6000 miles.

Lubricate suspension, parking brake cable guides, underbody contact points & linkage - lubricate every 6000 miles.

Air filter element - service or inspect every 15,000 miles.

Automatic transmission fluid & filter - change every 15,000 miles.

93001C00

SCHEDULED MAINTENANCE INTERVALS
GENERAL MOTORS CORPORATION
Y BODY
CHEVROLET CORVETTE

The following should be used as a guide when determining the amount of work required for a particular service.
In estimating how long a particular Scheduled Maintenance Service should take, please observe the following:

- **Chilton Time** is time based on field research and data supplied by the vehicle manufacturer.
  - Labor time operations are given in hours and tenths of an hour.
    - All labor operations, are to be used as a guide.

Mechanic Skill Level Codes:
(A) PRECISION: Really skilled with multiple certification.
(B) GENERAL: Normally skilled with certification.
(C) MAINTENANCE: Semi-skilled working on certification.

	Chilton Time		Chilton Time		Chilton Time
7500 Mile Service (C)		**37500 Mile Service (C)**		**75000 Mile Service (C)**	
All Models	1.2	All Models	1.2	All Models	1.3
15000 Mile Service (C)		**45000 Mile Service (C)**		**82500 Mile Service (C)**	
All Models	1.3	All Models	1.3	All Models	1.2
22500 Mile Service (C)		**52500 Mile Service (C)**		**90000 Mile Service (B)**	
All Models	1.2	All Models	1.2	All Models	2.0
30000 Mile Service (B)		**60000 Mile Service (B)**		**97500 Mile Service (C)**	
All Models	2.0	All Models	2.0	All Models	1.2
		67500 Mile Service (C)			
		All Models	1.2		

93001CP1

Refer to the model specific sections for driveline service procedures

GEO/CHEVROLET
Metro • Prizm

ENGINE AND VEHICLE IDENTIFICATION

			Engine					Model Year	
Code ①	Liters (cc)	Cu. In.	Cyl.	Fuel Sys.	Engine Type	Eng. Mfg.		Code ②	Year
6	1.0 (993)	(61)	3	TFI	SOHC	Suzuki		T	1996
6	1.6 (1590)	(97)	4	MFI	SOHC	Suzuki		V	1997
8	1.8 (1803)	(110)	4	MFI	DOHC	Toyota		W	1998
9	1.3 (1300)	(79)	4	TFI	DOHC	Suzuki		X	1999
								Y	2000

TBI - Throttle body Fuel Injection

MFI - Multi-point Fuel Injection

① 8th position of VIN

② 10th position of VIN

93001CP2

GENERAL ENGINE SPECIFICATIONS

Year	Model	Engine Displacement Liters (cc)	Engine Series (ID/VIN)	Fuel System	Net Horsepower @ rpm	Net Torque @ rpm (ft. lbs.)	Bore x Stroke (in.)	Compression Ratio	Oil Pressure @ rpm
1996	Metro	1.0 (993)	6	TFI	55@5700	58@3300	2.91x3.03	9.5:1	54@3000
	Metro	1.3 (1300)	9	TFI	70@5500	74@3500	2.91x3.03	9.5:1	54@3000
	Prism	1.6 (1590)	6	MFI	105@5800	100@4800	3.20x3.00	9.5:1	36-71@3000
	Prizm	1.8 (1803)	8	MFI	115@5200	117@2800	3.20x3.40	9.5:1	36-71@3000
1997	Metro	1.0 (993)	6	TFI	55@5700	58@3300	2.91x3.03	9.5:1	54@3000
	Metro	1.3 (1300)	9	TFI	70@5500	74@3500	2.91x3.03	9.5:1	54@3000
	Prism	1.6 (1590)	6	MFI	105@5800	100@4800	3.20x3.00	9.5:1	36-71@3000
	Prizm	1.8 (1803)	8	MFI	115@5200	117@2800	3.20x3.40	9.5:1	36-71@3000
1998	Metro	1.0 (993)	6	TFI	55@5700	58@3300	2.91x3.03	9.5:1	54@3000
	Metro	1.3 (1300)	9	TFI	70@5500	74@3500	2.91x3.03	9.5:1	54@3000
	Prism	1.8 (1803)	8	MFI	115@5200	117@2800	3.20x3.40	9.5:1	36-71@3000
1999-00	Metro	1.0 (993)	6	TFI	55@5700	58@3300	2.91x3.03	9.5:1	54@3000
	Metro	1.3 (1300)	9	TFI	70@5500	74@3500	2.91x3.03	9.5:1	54@3000
	Prizm	1.8 (1803)	8	MFI	115@5200	117@2800	3.20x3.40	9.5:1	36-71@3000

TFI - Throttle body Fuel Injection

MFI - Multi-point Fuel Injection

93001CP3

TUNE-UP SPECIFICATIONS

Year	Engine Displacement Liters (cc)	Engine ID/VIN	Spark Plug Gap (in.)	Ignition Timing (deg.) MT		Ignition Timing (deg.) AT		Fuel Pump (psi)	Idle Speed (rpm) MT	Idle Speed (rpm) AT	Valve Clearance Intake	Valve Clearance Exhaust
1996	1.0 (993)	6	0.041	5B	①	5B	①	23-30	800	850	HYD	HYD
	1.3 (1300)	9	0.041	5B	①	5B	①	23-30	800	850	HYD	HYD
	1.6 (1590)	6	0.031	10B	②	10B	②	31-37	700-750	700-750	0.0060-0.010	0.0100-0.0140
	1.8 (1803)	8	0.031	10B	②	10B	②	31-37	700-750	700-750	0.0060-0.010	0.0100-0.0140
1997	1.0 (993)	6	0.041	5B	①	5B	①	23-30	800	850	HYD	HYD
	1.3 (1300)	9	0.041	5B	①	5B	①	23-30	800	850	HYD	HYD
	1.6 (1590)	6	0.031	10B	②	10B	②	31-37	700-750	700-750	0.0060-0.010	0.0100-0.0140
	1.8 (1803)	8	0.031	10B	②	10B	②	31-37	700-750	700-750	0.0060-0.010	0.0100-0.0140
1998	1.0 (993)	6	0.041	5B	①	5B	①	23-30	800	850	HYD	HYD
	1.3 (1300)	9	0.041	5B	①	5B	①	23-30	800	850	HYD	HYD
	1.8 (1803)	8	0.031	10B	②	10B	②	31-37	700-750	700-750	0.0060-0.010	0.0100-0.0140
1999-00	1.0 (993)	6	0.041	5B	①	5B	①	23-30	800	850	HYD	HYD
	1.3 (1300)	9	0.041	5B	①	5B	①	23-30	800	850	HYD	HYD
	1.8 (1803)	8	0.031	10B	②	10B	②	31-37	700-750	700-750	0.0060-0.010	0.0100-0.0140

NOTE: The Vehicle Emission Control Information label often reflects specification changes made during production. The label figures must be used if they differ from those in this chart.

B - Before top dead center

HYD - Hydraulic

① Connect a fused jumper from Duty Check cavity 4 to cavity 5 for fixed timing (DLC connector located at left strut tower)

② Insert jumper wire between terminals in DLC connector E1 and TE1

93001CP4

For exhaust manifold replacement procedures, see the model specific sections of this manual

CAPACITIES

Year	Model	Engine ID/VIN	Engine Displacement Liters (cc)	Engine Oil with Filter	Transmission (pts.)		Drive Axle (pts.)	Fuel Tank (gal.)	Cooling System (qts.)
					5-Spd	Auto.			
1995	Metro	6	1.0 (993)	3.7	5.0	10.1 ①	—	10.6	4.2
	Metro	9	1.3 (1300)	3.7	5.0	10.4 ①	—	10.6	4.9
	Prizm	6	1.6 (1590)	3.2	3.0	6.6	3.0 ②	13.2	6.7
	Prizm	8	1.8 (1803)	3.9	3.0	6.6	3.0 ②	13.2	6.7
1996	Metro	6	1.0 (993)	3.7	5.0	10.1 ①	—	10.6	4.2
	Metro	9	1.3 (1300)	3.7	5.0	10.1 ①	—	10.6	4.9
	Prizm	6	1.6 (1590)	3.2	4.0	6.6	3.0 ②	13.2	6.7
	Prizm	8	1.8 (1803)	3.9	4.0	6.6	3.0 ②	13.2	6.7
1997	Metro	6	1.0 (993)	3.7	5.0	10.1 ①	—	10.6	4.2
	Metro	9	1.3 (1300)	3.7	5.0	10.1 ①	—	10.6	4.9
	Prizm	6	1.6 (1590)	3.2	4.0	6.6	3.0 ②	13.2	6.7
	Prizm	8	1.8 (1803)	3.9	4.0	6.6	3.0 ②	13.2	6.7
1998	Metro	6	1.0 (993)	3.7	5.0	10.1 ①	—	10.6	4.2
	Metro	9	1.3 (1300)	3.7	5.0	10.1 ①	—	10.6	4.9
	Prizm	8	1.8 (1803)	3.9	4.0	6.6	3.0 ②	13.2	6.7
199-00	Metro	6	1.0 (993)	3.7	5.0	10.1 ①	—	10.6	4.2
	Metro	9	1.3 (1300)	3.7	5.0	10.1 ①	—	10.6	4.9
	Prizm	8	1.8 (1803)	3.9	4.0	6.6	3.0 ②	13.2	6.7

NOTE: All capacities are approximate. Add fluid gradually and ensure a proper fluid level is obtained.

① Automatic transmission - Specification is after complete overhaul. Drain and fill will be less

② 3 speed automatic only

93001CP5

VALVE SPECIFICATIONS

Year	Engine Displacement Liters (cc)	Engine ID/VIN	Seat Angle (deg.)	Face Angle (deg.)	Spring Test Pressure (lbs. @ in.)	Spring Installed Height (in.)	Stem-to-Guide Clearance (in.)		Stem Diameter (in.)	
							Intake	Exhaust	Intake	Exhaust
1996	1.0 (993)	6	45	45	46.1-51.8@ 1.28	1.28	0.0008- 0.0022	0.0018- 0.0028	0.2148- 0.2157	0.2142- 0.2148
	1.3 (1300)	9	45	45	54.7-64.3@ 1.63	1.63	0.0008- 0.0019	0.0014- 0.0025	0.2742- 0.2748	0.2737- 0.2742
	1.6 (1590)	6	45	45.5	37.3@1.25	1.25	0.0010- 0.0024	0.0012- 0.0026	0.2350- 0.2356	0.2348- 0.2354
	1.8 (1803)	8	45	45.5	37.3@1.25	1.25	0.0010- 0.0024	0.0012- 0.0026	0.2350- 0.2356	0.2348- 0.2354
1997	1.0 (993)	6	45	45	46.1-51.8@ 1.28	1.28	0.0008- 0.0022	0.0018- 0.0028	0.2148- 0.2157	0.2142- 0.2148
	1.3 (1300)	9	45	45	54.7-64.3@ 1.63	1.63	0.0008- 0.0019	0.0014- 0.0025	0.2742- 0.2748	0.2737- 0.2742
	1.6 (1590)	6	45	45.5	37.3@1.25	1.25	0.0010- 0.0024	0.0012- 0.0026	0.2350- 0.2356	0.2348- 0.2354
	1.8 (1803)	8	45	45.5	37.3@1.25	1.25	0.0010- 0.0024	0.0012- 0.0026	0.2350- 0.2356	0.2348- 0.2354
1998	1.0 (993)	6	45	45	46.1-51.8@ 1.28	1.28	0.0008- 0.0022	0.0018- 0.0028	0.2148- 0.2157	0.2142- 0.2148
	1.3 (1300)	9	45	45	54.7-64.3@ 1.63	1.63	0.0008- 0.0019	0.0014- 0.0025	0.2742- 0.2748	0.2737- 0.2742
	1.8 (1803)	8	45	45.5	37.3@1.25	1.25	0.0010- 0.0024	0.0012- 0.0026	0.2350- 0.2356	0.2348- 0.2354
1999-00	1.0 (993)	6	45	45	46.1-51.8@ 1.28	1.28	0.0008- 0.0022	0.0018- 0.0028	0.2148- 0.2157	0.2142- 0.2148
	1.3 (1300)	9	45	45	54.7-64.3@ 1.63	1.63	0.0008- 0.0019	0.0014- 0.0025	0.2742- 0.2748	0.2737- 0.2742
	1.8 (1803)	8	45	45.5	37.3@1.25	1.25	0.0010- 0.0024	0.0012- 0.0026	0.2350- 0.2356	0.2348- 0.2354

93001CP6

Refer to the model specific sections for cooling system service procedures

CRANKSHAFT AND CONNECTING ROD SPECIFICATIONS

All measurements are given in inches.

Year	Engine Displacement Liters (cc)	Engine ID/VIN	Crankshaft				Connecting Rod		
			Main Brg. Journal Dia.	Main Brg. Oil Clearance	Shaft End-play	Thrust on No.	Journal Diameter	Oil Clearance	Side Clearance
1996	1.0 (993)	6	①	0.00008-0.00015	0.0044-0.0122	NA	1.6529-1.6535	0.0012-0.0019	0.0039-0.0078
	1.3 (1300)	9	①	0.00008-0.00015	0.0044-0.0122	NA	1.6529-1.6535	0.0012-0.0019	0.0039-0.0078
	1.6 (1590)	6	②	0.0006-0.0013	0.0006-0.0087	3	1.5742-1.5748	0.0008-0.0020	0.0050-0.0150
	1.8 (1803)	8	②	0.0006-0.0013	0.0006-0.0087	3	1.8893-1.8898	0.0008-0.0019	0.0050-0.0150
1997	1.0 (993)	6	①	0.00008-0.00015	0.0044-0.0122	NA	1.6529-1.6535	0.0012-0.0019	0.0039-0.0078
	1.3 (1300)	9	①	0.00008-0.00015	0.0044-0.0122	NA	1.6529-1.6535	0.0012-0.0019	0.0039-0.0078
	1.6 (1590)	6	②	0.0006-0.0013	0.0006-0.0087	3	1.5742-1.5748	0.0008-0.0020	0.0050-0.0150
	1.8 (1803)	8	②	0.0006-0.0013	0.0006-0.0087	3	1.8893-1.8898	0.0008-0.0019	0.0050-0.0150
1998	1.0 (993)	6	①	0.00008-0.00015	0.0044-0.0122	NA	1.6529-1.6535	0.0012-0.0019	0.0039-0.0078
	1.3 (1300)	9	①	0.00008-0.00015	0.0044-0.0122	NA	1.6529-1.6535	0.0012-0.0019	0.0039-0.0078
	1.8 (1803)	8	②	0.0006-0.0013	0.0006-0.0087	3	1.8893-1.8898	0.0008-0.0019	0.0050-0.0150
1999-00	1.0 (993)	6	①	0.00008-0.00015	0.0044-0.0122	NA	1.6529-1.6535	0.0012-0.0019	0.0039-0.0078
	1.3 (1300)	9	①	0.00008-0.00015	0.0044-0.0122	NA	1.6529-1.6535	0.0012-0.0019	0.0039-0.0078
	1.8 (1803)	8	②	0.0006-0.0013	0.0006-0.0087	3	1.8893-1.8898	0.0008-0.0019	0.0050-0.0150

① 1 Stamping: 1.7714-1.7716
  2 Stamping: 1.7712- 1.7714
  3 Stamping: 1.7710- 1.7712

② 0 Stamping: 1.8895-1.8898
  1 Stamping: 1.8893- 1.8895
  2 Stamping: 1.8891- 1.8893

93001CP7

PISTON AND RING SPECIFICATIONS

All measurements are given in inches.

Year	Engine Displacement Liters (cc)	Engine ID/VIN	Piston Clearance	Ring Gap			Ring Side Clearance		
				Top Compression	Bottom Compression	Oil Control	Top Compression	Bottom Compression	Oil Control
1996	1.0 (993)	6	0.0008-0.0015	0.0079-0.0118	0.0079-0.0118	0.0079-0.0275	0.0012-0.0027	0.0008-0.0023	—
	1.3 (1300)	9	0.0008-0.0015	0.0079-0.0118	0.0079-0.0012	0.0079-0.0275	0.0014-0.0027	0.0008-0.0023	—
	1.6 (1590)	6	0.0033-0.0041	0.0098-0.0138	0.0138-0.0197	0.0039-0.0157	0.0018-0.0033	0.0012-0.0028	—
	1.8 (1803)	8	0.0033-0.0041	0.0098-0.0138	0.0138-0.0197	0.0039-0.0157	0.0018-0.0033	0.0012-0.0028	—
1997	1.0 (993)	6	0.0008-0.0015	0.0079-0.0118	0.0079-0.0118	0.0079-0.0275	0.0012-0.0027	0.0008-0.0023	—
	1.3 (1300)	9	0.0008-0.0015	0.0079-0.0118	0.0079-0.0012	0.0079-0.0275	0.0014-0.0027	0.0008-0.0023	—
	1.6 (1590)	6	0.0033-0.0041	0.0098-0.0138	0.0138-0.0197	0.0039-0.0157	0.0018-0.0033	0.0012-0.0028	—
	1.8 (1803)	8	0.0033-0.0041	0.0098-0.0138	0.0138-0.0197	0.0039-0.0157	0.0018-0.0033	0.0012-0.0028	—
1998	1.0 (993)	6	0.0008-0.0015	0.0079-0.0118	0.0079-0.0118	0.0079-0.0275	0.0012-0.0027	0.0008-0.0023	—
	1.3 (1300)	9	0.0008-0.0015	0.0079-0.0118	0.0079-0.0012	0.0079-0.0275	0.0014-0.0027	0.0008-0.0023	—
	1.8 (1803)	8	0.0033-0.0041	0.0098-0.0138	0.0138-0.0197	0.0039-0.0157	0.0018-0.0033	0.0012-0.0028	—
1999-00	1.0 (993)	6	0.0008-0.0015	0.0079-0.0118	0.0079-0.0118	0.0079-0.0275	0.0012-0.0027	0.0008-0.0023	—
	1.3 (1300)	9	0.0008-0.0015	0.0079-0.0118	0.0079-0.0012	0.0079-0.0275	0.0014-0.0027	0.0008-0.0023	—
	1.8 (1803)	8	0.0033-0.0041	0.0098-0.0138	0.0138-0.0197	0.0039-0.0157	0.0018-0.0033	0.0012-0.0028	—

93001CP8

TORQUE SPECIFICATIONS
All readings in ft. lbs.

Year	Engine Displacement Liters (cc)	Engine ID/VIN	Cylinder Head Bolts	Main Bearing Bolts	Rod Bearing Bolts	Crankshaft Damper Bolt	Flywheel Bolts	Manifold		Spark Plugs	Lug Nuts
								Intake	Exhaust		
1996	1.0 (993)	6	54	40	26	81 ①	52	17	17	21	44
	1.3 (1300)	9	54	40	26	79 ①	45	17	17	21	44
	1.6 (1590)	6	②	44	②	87 ①	③	14	25	21	76
	1.8 (1803)	8	②	44	18 ⑤	87 ①	③	14	25	21	76
1997	1.0 (993)	6	54	40	26	81 ①	52	17	17	21	44
	1.3 (1300)	9	54	40	26	79 ①	45	17	17	21	44
	1.6 (1590)	6	②	44	②	87 ①	③	14	25	21	76
	1.8 (1803)	8	②	44	18 ⑤	87 ①	③	14	25	21	76
1998	1.0 (993)	6	54	40	26	81 ①	52	17	17	21	44
	1.3 (1300)	9	54	40	26	79 ①	45	17	17	21	44
	1.8 (1803)	8	②	44	18 ⑤	87 ①	③	14	25	21	76
1999-00	1.0 (993)	6	54	40	26	81 ①	52	17	17	21	44
	1.3 (1300)	9	54	40	26	79 ①	45	17	17	21	44
	1.8 (1803)	8	②	44	18 ⑤	87 ①	③	14	25	21	76

① Crankshaft timing belt sprocket
② Step 1: 22 ft. lbs.
　　Step 2: Plus 90 degrees
③ Manual transaxle: 58 ft. lbs.
　　Automatic transaxle: 47 ft. lbs.
④ Step 1: 26 ft. lbs.
　　Step 2: 41 ft. lbs.
　　Step 3: 52 ft. lbs.
⑤ Tighten an additional 90 degrees

93001CP9

SCHEDULED MAINTENANCE INTERVALS
(GEO METRO & PRIZM)

TO BE SERVICED	TYPE OF SERVICE	VEHICLE MILEAGE INTERVAL (x1000)												
		7.5	15	22.5	30	37.5	45	52.5	60	67.5	75	82.5	90	97.5
Engine oil & filter	R	✓	✓	✓	✓	✓	✓	✓	✓	✓	✓	✓	✓	✓
Chassis lubrication (Metro)	S/I	✓	✓	✓	✓	✓	✓	✓	✓	✓	✓	✓	✓	✓
Locking front hubs (Metro)	S/I	✓	✓	✓	✓	✓	✓	✓	✓	✓	✓	✓	✓	✓
Lubricate parking brake cable guides, underbody contact points & linkage	S/I	✓	✓	✓	✓	✓	✓	✓	✓	✓	✓	✓	✓	✓
Rotate tires	S/I	✓	✓	✓	✓	✓	✓	✓	✓	✓	✓	✓	✓	✓
Brake system	S/I	✓		✓		✓		✓		✓		✓		✓
Engine idle speed (Prizm)	S/I	✓		✓		✓		✓		✓		✓		✓
Exhaust system	S/I	✓		✓		✓		✓		✓		✓		✓
Chassis lubrication (Prizm)	S/I		✓			✓	✓		✓		✓		✓	
Fuel tank, cap & lines (Metro)	S/I		✓			✓	✓		✓		✓		✓	
Fuel tank, cap & lines (Prizm)	S/I				✓				✓				✓	
Valve clearance (Prizm)	S/I								✓					
Air cleaner filter	R				✓				✓				✓	
Engine coolant	R				✓				✓				✓	
Fuel filter (Metro)	R				✓				✓				✓	
Fuel tank cap gasket (Prizm)	R				✓				✓				✓	
Manual transaxle oil	R				✓				✓				✓	
Spark plugs	R				✓				✓				✓	
Accessory drive belt(s) (Prizm)	S/I								✓		✓		✓	✓
Accessory drive belt(s) (except Prizm)	S/I				✓				✓				✓	

93001CP0

Timing chain and gear service is covered in the model specific sections of this manual

SCHEDULED MAINTENANCE INTERVALS
(GEO METRO & PRIZM) (Cont.)

TO BE SERVICED	TYPE OF SERVICE	VEHICLE MILEAGE INTERVAL (x1000)												
		7.5	15	22.5	30	37.5	45	52.5	60	67.5	75	82.5	90	97.5
Cooling system (Metro)	S/I				✓				✓				✓	
Cooling system (Prizm)	S/I						✓				✓			
Automatic transaxle fluid & filter	S/I				✓				✓				✓	
EGR system	S/I				✓				✓				✓	
Engine timing (Metro)	S/I								✓					
Ignition cables	S/I								✓					
PCV system	S/I				✓				✓				✓	
Brake fluid (Metro)	R								✓					
PCV valve (Metro) ①	R													
Timing belt	R								✓					
EVAP canister (Prizm)	S/I								✓					
Throttle body unit mount bolt torque	S/I	✓												

① PCV valve - replace at 50,000 miles.

R - Replace   S/I - Service or Inspect

FREQUENT OPERATION MAINTENANCE (SEVERE SERVICE)

If a vehicle is operated under any of the following conditions it is considered severe service:
- Extremely dusty areas.
- 50% or more of the vehicle operation is in 32°C (90°F) or higher temperatures, or constant operation in operation in temperatures below 0°C (32°F).
- Prolonged idling (vehicle operation in stop and go traffic).
- Frequent short running periods (engine does not warm to normal operating temperatures).
- Police, taxi, delivery usage or trailer towing usage.

Oil & oil filter (Metro & Prizm) - change every 3000 miles.
Chassis lubrication (Metro & Prizm) - lubricate every 6000 miles.
Throttle body mount bolt torque - torque at 6000 miles.
Air cleaner filter - service or inspect every 15,000 miles.
Differential fluid (Prizm) - replace every 15,000 miles.
Rotate tires - rotate at 6000 miles and then every 15,000 miles thereafter.
Automatic transaxle fluid & filter (Prizm) - replace every 15,000 miles.
Automatic transaxle fluid & filter (Metro) - replace every 50,000 miles.

93001CQ1

SCHEDULED MAINTENANCE INTERVALS
GENERAL MOTORS CORPORATION
GEO/CHEVROLET
METRO & PRIZM

The following should be used as a guide when determining the amount of work required for a particular service. In estimating how long a particular Scheduled Maintenance Service should take, please observe the following:

- **Chilton Time** is time based on field research and data supplied by the vehicle manufacturer.
- Labor time operations are given in hours and tenths of an hour.
- All labor operations, are to be used as a guide.

Mechanic Skill Level Codes:
(A) PRECISION: Really skilled with multiple certification.
(B) GENERAL: Normally skilled with certification.
(C) MAINTENANCE: Semi-skilled working on certification.

	Chilton Time
7500 Mile Service (C)	
All Models	1.8
Inspect locking hubs (Metro) add	.1
15000 Mile Service (C)	
All Models	.7
Inspect locking hubs (Metro) add	.1
Rotate tires add	.5
22500 Mile Service (C)	
All Models	1.6
Inspect locking hubs (Metro) add	.1
30000 Mile Service (B)	
All Models	2.7
Inspect locking hubs (Metro) add	.1
Rotate tires add	.5

	Chilton Time
37500 Mile Service (C)	
All Models	1.6
Inspect locking hubs (Metro) add	.1
45000 Mile Service (C)	
All Models	.7
Inspect locking hubs (Metro) add	.1
Rotate tires add	.5
52500 Mile Service (C)	
Metro	1.6
Inspect locking hubs (Metro) add	.1
60000 Mile Service (B)	
Metro	5.2
Inspect locking hubs (Metro) add	.1
Replace brake fluid (Metro) add	.5
Prizm	4.9
67500 Mile Service (C)	
All Models	1.6
Inspect locking hubs (Metro) add	.1

	Chilton Time
75000 Mile Service (C)	
All Models	.7
Inspect locking hubs (Metro) add	.1
82500 Mile Service (C)	
All Models	1.6
Inspect locking hubs (Metro) add	.1
90000 Mile Service (B)	
All Models	2.8
Inspect locking hubs (Metro) add	.1
97500 Mile Service (C)	
All Models	1.6
Inspect locking hubs (Metro) add	.1

93001CQ2

Ignition system service is covered in the model specific sections of this manual

SATURN
SC1 • SC2 • SL • SL1 • SL2 • SW1 • SW2

ENGINE AND VEHICLE IDENTIFICATION

			Engine					Model Year	
Code ①	Liters (cc)	Cu. In.	Cyl.	Fuel Sys.	Engine Type	Eng. Mfg.		Code ②	Year
7	1.9 (1901)	116	4	MFI	DOHC	Saturn		T	1996
8	1.9 (1901)	116	4	MFI	SOHC	Saturn		V	1997
								W	1998
								X	1999
								Y	2000

MFI - Multi-point Fuel Injection
DOHC - Double Overhead Camshafts
SOHC - Single Overhead Camshaft
① 8th digit of VIN
② 10th digit of VIN

93001CQ3

GENERAL ENGINE SPECIFICATIONS

Year	Model	Engine Displacement Liters (cc)	Engine ID/VIN	Fuel System Type	Net Horsepower @ rpm	Net Torque @ rpm (ft. lbs.)	Bore x Stroke (in.)	Com- pression Ratio	Oil Pressure @ rpm
1996	Coupe	1.9 (1901)	7	MFI	124@5600	122@4800	3.23x3.54	9.5:1	29@2000
	Coupe	1.9 (1901)	8	MFI	100@5000	114@2400	3.23x3.54	9.3:1	36@2000
	Sedan	1.9 (1901)	7	MFI	124@5600	122@4800	3.23x3.54	9.5:1	29@2000
	Sedan	1.9 (1901)	8	MFI	100@5000	114@2400	3.23x3.54	9.3:1	36@2000
	Wagon	1.9 (1901)	7	MFI	124@5600	122@4800	3.23x3.54	9.5:1	29@2000
	Wagon	1.9 (1901)	8	MFI	100@5000	114@2400	3.23x3.54	9.3:1	36@2000
1997	Coupe	1.9 (1901)	7	MFI	124@5600	122@4800	3.23x3.54	9.5:1	29@2000
	Coupe	1.9 (1901)	8	MFI	100@5000	114@2400	3.23x3.54	9.3:1	36@2000
	Sedan	1.9 (1901)	7	MFI	124@5600	122@4800	3.23x3.54	9.5:1	29@2000
	Sedan	1.9 (1901)	8	MFI	100@5000	114@2400	3.23x3.54	9.3:1	36@2000
	Wagon	1.9 (1901)	7	MFI	124@5600	122@4800	3.23x3.54	9.5:1	29@2000
	Wagon	1.9 (1901)	8	MFI	100@5000	114@2400	3.23x3.54	9.3:1	36@2000
1998	Coupe	1.9 (1901)	7	MFI	124@5600	122@4800	3.23x3.54	9.5:1	29@2000
	Coupe	1.9 (1901)	8	MFI	100@5000	114@2400	3.23x3.54	9.3:1	36@2000
	Sedan	1.9 (1901)	7	MFI	124@5600	122@4800	3.23x3.54	9.5:1	29@2000
	Sedan	1.9 (1901)	8	MFI	100@5000	114@2400	3.23x3.54	9.3:1	36@2000
	Wagon	1.9 (1901)	7	MFI	124@5600	122@4800	3.23x3.54	9.5:1	29@2000
	Wagon	1.9 (1901)	8	MFI	100@5000	114@2400	3.23x3.54	9.3:1	36@2000
1999-00	Coupe	1.9 (1901)	7	MFI	124@5600	122@4800	3.23x3.54	9.5:1	29@2000
	Coupe	1.9 (1901)	8	MFI	100@5000	114@2400	3.23x3.54	9.3:1	36@2000
	Sedan	1.9 (1901)	7	MFI	124@5600	122@4800	3.23x3.54	9.5:1	29@2000
	Sedan	1.9 (1901)	8	MFI	100@5000	114@2400	3.23x3.54	9.3:1	36@2000
	Wagon	1.9 (1901)	7	MFI	124@5600	122@4800	3.23x3.54	9.5:1	29@2000
	Wagon	1.9 (1901)	8	MFI	100@5000	114@2400	3.23x3.54	9.3:1	36@2000

MFI - Multi-port Fuel Injection

93001CQ4

ENGINE TUNE-UP SPECIFICATIONS

Year	Engine Displacement Liters (cc)	Engine ID/VIN	Spark Plug Gap (in.)	Ignition Timing (deg.)		Fuel Pump (psi) ①	Idle Speed (rpm)		Valve Clearance	
				MT	AT		MT ②	AT ②	In.	Ex.
1996	1.9 (1901)	7	0.040	③	③	31-36	850	750	HYD	HYD
	1.9 (1901)	8	0.040	③	③	26-31	750	650	HYD	HYD
1997	1.9 (1901)	7	0.040	③	③	31-36	850	750	HYD	HYD
	1.9 (1901)	8	0.040	③	③	31-36	750	650	HYD	HYD
1998	1.9 (1901)	7	0.040	③	③	31-36	850	750	HYD	HYD
	1.9 (1901)	8	0.040	③	③	31-36	750	650	HYD	HYD
1999-00	1.9 (1901)	7	0.040	③	③	31-36	850	750	HYD	HYD
	1.9 (1901)	8	0.040	③	③	31-36	750	650	HYD	HYD

NOTE: The Vehicle Emission Control Information label often reflects specification changes made during production. The label figures must be used if they differ from those in this chart.

HYD - Hydraulic

① Pressure measured at idle.

② Idle speed measured with manual transmission in Neutral; automatic transmission in D (drive).

③ Engines equipped with Distributorless Ignition System (DIS). Ignition timing is not adjustable.

93001CQ5

CAPACITIES

Year	Model	Engine Displacement Liters (cc)	Engine ID/VIN	Engine Oil with Filter (qts.)	Transaxle (pts.)		Fuel Tank (gal.)	Cooling System (qts.)
					Manual	Auto. ①		
1996	Coupe	1.9 (1901)	7	4.0	5.2	7.5	12.8	7.0
	Coupe	1.9 (1901)	8	4.0	5.2	7.5	12.8	7.0
	Sedan	1.9 (1901)	7	4.0	5.2	7.5	12.8	7.0
	Sedan	1.9 (1901)	8	4.0	5.2	7.5	12.8	7.0
	Wagon	1.9 (1901)	7	4.0	5.2	7.5	12.8	7.0
	Wagon	1.9 (1901)	8	4.0	5.2	7.5	12.8	7.0
1997	Coupe	1.9 (1901)	7	4.0	5.2	7.5	12.8	7.0
	Coupe	1.9 (1901)	8	4.0	5.2	7.5	12.8	7.0
	Sedan	1.9 (1901)	7	4.0	5.2	7.5	12.8	7.0
	Sedan	1.9 (1901)	8	4.0	5.2	7.5	12.8	7.0
	Wagon	1.9 (1901)	7	4.0	5.2	7.5	12.8	7.0
	Wagon	1.9 (1901)	8	4.0	5.2	7.5	12.8	7.0
1998	Coupe	1.9 (1901)	7	4.0	5.2	7.5	12.8	7.0
	Coupe	1.9 (1901)	8	4.0	5.2	7.5	12.8	7.0
	Sedan	1.9 (1901)	7	4.0	5.2	7.5	12.8	7.0
	Sedan	1.9 (1901)	8	4.0	5.2	7.5	12.8	7.0
	Wagon	1.9 (1901)	7	4.0	5.2	7.5	12.8	7.0
	Wagon	1.9 (1901)	8	4.0	5.2	7.5	12.8	7.0
1999-00	Coupe	1.9 (1901)	7	4.0	5.2	7.5	12.1	7.0
	Coupe	1.9 (1901)	8	4.0	5.2	7.5	12.1	7.0
	Sedan	1.9 (1901)	7	4.0	5.2	7.5	12.1	7.0
	Sedan	1.9 (1901)	8	4.0	5.2	7.5	12.1	7.0
	Wagon	1.9 (1901)	7	4.0	5.2	7.5	12.1	7.0
	Wagon	1.9 (1901)	8	4.0	5.2	7.5	12.1	7.0

NOTE: All capacities are approximate. Add fluid gradually and ensure a proper fluid level is obtained.

① Specification is for overhaul. 8.4 pts. with fluid and filter change

93001CQ6

VALVE SPECIFICATIONS

Year	Engine Displacement Liters (cc)	Engine ID/VIN	Seat Angle (deg.)	Face Angle (deg.)	Spring Test Pressure (lbs. @ in.)	Spring Free-Length (in.)	Stem-to-Guide Clearance (in.)		Stem Diameter (in.)	
							Intake	Exhaust	Intake	Exhaust
1996	1.9 (1901)	7	44.5-45.4	45-45.5	163-180@ 0.984	1.6100	0.0010- 0.0025	0.0015- 0.0032	0.2736- 0.2740	0.2729- 0.2736
	1.9 (1901)	8	44.5-45.4	45-45.5	202-211@ 1.280	1.8898- 1.9134	0.0010- 0.0025	0.0015- 0.0032	0.2736- 0.2741	0.2736- 0.2740
1997	1.9 (1901)	7	44.5-45.4	45-45.5	163-180@ 0.984	1.6100	0.0010- 0.0025	0.0015- 0.0032	0.2736- 0.2740	0.2729- 0.2736
	1.9 (1901)	8	44.5-45.4	45-45.25	202-211@ 1.280	1.8898- 1.9134	0.0010- 0.0025	0.0015- 0.0032	0.2736- 0.2741	0.2736- 0.2740
1998	1.9 (1901)	7	44.5-45.4	45-45.5	163-180@ 0.984	1.6100	0.0010- 0.0025	0.0015- 0.0032	0.2736- 0.2740	0.2729- 0.2736
	1.9 (1901)	8	44.5-45.4	45-45.25	202-211@ 1.280	1.8898- 1.9134	0.0010- 0.0025	0.0015- 0.0032	0.2736- 0.2741	0.2736- 0.2740
1999-00	1.9 (1901)	7	44.5-45.4	45-45.5	163-180@ 0.984	1.6100	0.0010- 0.0025	0.0015- 0.0032	0.2736- 0.2740	0.2729- 0.2736
	1.9 (1901)	8	44.5-45.4	45-45.25	202-211@ 1.280	1.8898- 1.9134	0.0010- 0.0025	0.0015- 0.0032	0.2736- 0.2741	0.2736- 0.2740

93001CQ7

CRANKSHAFT AND CONNECTING ROD SPECIFICATIONS
All measurements are given in inches.

Year	Engine Displacement Liters (cc)	Engine ID/VIN	Crankshaft				Connecting Rod		
			Main Brg. Journal Dia.	Main Brg. Oil Clearance	Shaft End-play	Thrust on No.	Journal Diameter	Oil Clearance	Side Clearance
1996	1.9 (1901)	7	2.2438- 2.2444	0.0002- 0.0020	0.0020- 0.0079	3	1.9761- 1.9767	0.0001- 0.0021	0.0065- 0.0171
	1.9 (1901)	8	2.2438- 2.2444	0.0002- 0.0020	0.0020- 0.0079	3	1.9761- 1.9767	0.0001- 0.0021	0.0065- 0.0171
1997	1.9 (1901)	7	2.2438- 2.2444	0.0002- 0.0020	0.0020- 0.0079	3	1.9761- 1.9767	0.0001- 0.0021	0.0065- 0.0171
	1.9 (1901)	8	2.2438- 2.2444	0.0002- 0.0020	0.0020- 0.0079	3	1.9761- 1.9767	0.0001- 0.0021	0.0065- 0.0171
1998	1.9 (1901)	7	2.2438- 2.2444	0.0002- 0.0020	0.0020- 0.0079	3	1.9761- 1.9767	0.0001- 0.0021	0.0065- 0.0171
	1.9 (1901)	8	2.2438- 2.2444	0.0002- 0.0020	0.0020- 0.0079	3	1.9761- 1.9767	0.0001- 0.0021	0.0065- 0.0171
1999-00	1.9 (1901)	7	2.2438- 2.2444	0.0002- 0.0020	0.0020- 0.0079	3	1.9761- 1.9767	0.0001- 0.0021	0.0065- 0.0171
	1.9 (1901)	8	2.2438- 2.2444	0.0002- 0.0020	0.0020- 0.0079	3	1.9761- 1.9767	0.0001- 0.0021	0.0065- 0.0171

93001CQ8

PISTON AND RING SPECIFICATIONS
All measurements are given in inches.

Year	Engine Displacement Liters (cc)	Engine ID/VIN	Piston Clearance	Ring Gap			Ring Side Clearance		
				Top Compression	Bottom Compression	Oil Control	Top Compression	Bottom Compression	Oil Control
1996	1.9 (1901)	7	①	0.0098-0.0157	0.0098-0.0197	0.0098-0.0429	0.0016-0.0032	0.0012-0.0031	SNUG
	1.9 (1901)	8	①	0.0098-0.0157	0.0098-0.0197	0.0098-0.0429	0.0016-0.0032	0.0012-0.0031	SNUG
1997	1.9 (1901)	7	①	0.0098-0.0157	0.0098-0.0197	0.0098-0.0429	0.0016-0.0032	0.0012-0.0031	SNUG
	1.9 (1901)	8	①	0.0098-0.0157	0.0098-0.0197	0.0098-0.0429	0.0016-0.0032	0.0012-0.0031	SNUG
1998	1.9 (1901)	7	①	0.0098-0.0157	0.0098-0.0197	0.0098-0.0429	0.0016-0.0032	0.0012-0.0031	SNUG
	1.9 (1901)	8	①	0.0098-0.0157	0.0098-0.0197	0.0098-0.0429	0.0016-0.0032	0.0012-0.0031	SNUG
1999-00	1.9 (1901)	7	①	0.0098-0.0157	0.0098-0.0197	0.0098-0.0429	0.0016-0.0032	0.0012-0.0031	SNUG
	1.9 (1901)	8	①	0.0098-0.0157	0.0098-0.0197	0.0098-0.0429	0.0016-0.0032	0.0012-0.0031	SNUG

① Piston No. 1, 2, and 3: 0.0002-0.0017
Piston No. 4: 0.0002-0.0021

93001CQ9

Refer to the model specific sections for engine mechanical service procedures

TORQUE SPECIFICATIONS
All readings in ft. lbs.

Year	Engine Displacement Liters (cc)	Engine ID/VIN	Cylinder Head Bolts	Main Bearing Bolts	Rod Bearing Bolts	Crankshaft Damper Bolts	Flywheel Bolts	Manifold Intake	Manifold Exhaust	Spark Plugs	Lug Nuts
1996	1.9 (1901)	7	①	37	33	159	59 ②	22 ③	22 ③	20	103
	1.9 (1901)	8	④	37	33	159	59 ②	22 ③	22 ③	20	103
1997	1.9 (1901)	7	①	37	33	159	59 ②	22 ③	19 ③	20	103
	1.9 (1901)	8	④	37	33	159	59 ②	22 ③	16 ③	20	103
1998	1.9 (1901)	7	①	37	33	159	59 ②	22 ③	19 ③	20	103
	1.9 (1901)	8	④	37	33	159	59 ②	22 ③	16 ③	20	103
1999-00	1.9 (1901)	7	①	37	33	159	59 ②	22 ③	19 ③	20	103
	1.9 (1901)	8	④	37	33	159	59 ②	22 ③	16 ③	20	103

① Step 1: 22 ft. lbs.
   Step 2: 37 ft. lbs.
   Step 3: 90 degrees
② Flexplate specification: 44 ft. lbs.
③ Studs: 106 inch lbs.
④ Step 1: 22 ft. lbs.
   Step 2: 33 ft. lbs.
   Step 3: 90 degrees

93001CQ0

SCHEDULED MAINTENANCE INTERVALS
(SATURN SC, SC1, SC2, SL, SL1, SL2, SW1, & SW2)

TO BE SERVICED	TYPE OF SERVICE	VEHICLE MILEAGE INTERVAL (x1000)												
		3	6	9	12	15	18	21	24	27	30	33	36	39
Engine oil & filter	R		✓		✓		✓		✓		✓		✓	
Lubricate chassis, suspension, steering linkage, transmission shift linkage, parking brake cable guides, underbody contact points & linkage	S/I		✓		✓		✓		✓		✓		✓	
Drive shaft boots, suspension bushings & ball joint seals	S/I		✓		✓		✓		✓		✓		✓	
Exhaust system & throttle linkage	S/I		✓		✓		✓		✓		✓		✓	
Rotate tires	S/I		✓				✓				✓			
Brake hoses & brake lining	S/I		✓				✓				✓			
Accessory drive belt(s)	S/I						✓						✓	
Engine coolant level, hoses & clamps	S/I						✓						✓	
Air filter element	R										✓			
Engine coolant	R												✓	
Manual transaxle oil	R		✓											
Spark plugs①	R										✓			
Automatic transaxle fluid & filter	R										✓			
Ignition cables & fuel systems	S/I										✓			
Vacuum line/hose	S/I										✓			
Fuel filter②	R													

① Platinum tip spark plugs - replace every 100,000 miles.
② Replace every 60,000 miles.
R – Replace   S/I – Service or Inspect

FREQUENT OPERATION MAINTENANCE (SEVERE SERVICE)
If a vehicle is operated under any of the following conditions it is considered severe service:
- Extremely dusty areas.
- 50% or more of the vehicle operation is in 32°C (90°F) or higher temperatures, or constant operation in temperatures below 0°C (32°F).
- Prolonged idling (vehicle operation in stop and go traffic).
- Frequent short running periods (engine does not warm to normal operating temperatures).
- Police, taxi, delivery usage or trailer towing usage.
Engine oil & oil filter - change every 3000 miles.

79221CT9

Refer to the model specific sections for fuel system service procedures

SCHEDULED MAINTENANCE INTERVALS
SATURN
SC1, SC2, SL, SL1, SL2
SW1, SW2

The following should be used as a guide when determining the amount of work required for a particular service. In estimating how long a particular Scheduled Maintenance Service should take, please observe the following:

- **Chilton Time** is time based on field research and data supplied by the vehicle manufacturer.
  - Labor time operations are given in hours and tenths of an hour.
  - All labor operations, are to be used as a guide.

Mechanic Skill Level Codes:
(A) PRECISION: Really skilled with multiple certification.
(B) GENERAL: Normally skilled with certification.
(C) MAINTENANCE: Semi-skilled working on certification.

	Chilton Time			Chilton Time			Chilton Time
6000 Mile Service (B)			**18000 Mile Service (C)**			**30000 Mile Service (B)**	
All Models	1.8		All Models	1.5		All Models	3.1
12000 Mile Service (C)			**24000 Mile Service (C)**			**36000 Mile Service (C)**	
All Models	.9		All Models	.9		All Models	1.6

93001CR1

MAINTENANCE LIGHT RESETTING AND DTC RETRIEVAL

2

MAINTENANCE INDICATOR LIGHT (MIL) RESETTING

This section describes reset procedures for maintenance indicator lights. Maintenance indicator lights are used to indicate to the operator that some type of routine maintenance should be performed. Unlike a Check Engine light that will be displayed when there is a fault with the engine management system, the maintenance light will be displayed when an engine or transmission oil change is recommended according to driving conditions. Also, the light will be displayed to indicate when the emission control system is in need of maintenance service.

Ford Motor Co.

RESETTING

1996–97 Mark VIII

The 1996–97 Mark VIII continues to use the CHANGE OIL SOON or OIL CHANGE REQUIRED light. When the oil life left is between 5% and 0%, CHANGE OIL SOON will be displayed on the message center. When oil life reaches 0%, the OIL CHANGE REQUIRED message will be displayed. The message center indicator will indicate the percentage of oil life left during the System Check (during start

up). This percentage is based on the driver's driving history and the amount of time since the last oil change. In order to ensure oil life

The electronic message center control button locations—1996–97 Mark VIII

left indications, the driver should only perform the OIL CHANGE RESET procedure after every oil change. Reset the system by pressing the **OIL CHANGE RESET** switch and hold for 5 seconds. After a successful reset the message center will display oil life indicators. The CHANGE OIL SOON or OIL CHANGE REQUIRED message will disappear after the 5 second interval.

General Motors

RESETTING

B Body Vehicles

The General Motors B body class designation includes the Caprice, the Impala, the Roadmaster and the Fleetwood.

After changing the engine oil, reset the engine oil life indicator whether the CHANGE OIL warning/indicator lamp illuminated or not.

1. Reset the engine oil life monitor as follows:

a. Turn the ignition switch to the **ON** position, but don't start the engine.

b. Depress the accelerator pedal to the Wide Open Throttle (WOT) position and release it 3 times within 5 seconds.

c. If the CHANGE OIL warning/indicator lamp blinks twice, then goes out, the system has been reset. If the CHANGE OIL warning/indicator lamp does not reset, turn the ignition switch to the **OFF** position and repeat the procedure.

C & H and G Body Vehicles

The General Motors C & H body class designations include the LeSabre, the Park Ave., the Eighty Eight, the Ninety Eight, the Bonneville, the Regency and the LSS. The G body designation refers to the Riviera and the Aurora.

These vehicles may be equipped with an ENGINE OIL LIFE INDEX (EOLI) in the display located on the Drivers Information Center (DIC). The Powertrain Control Module (PCM) determines approximately when the engine oil should be changed by calculating information based on vehicle speed, coolant temperature and engine RPM. Once the PCM determines it is time to change the engine oil, it will illuminate the CHANGE OIL SOON light on the

DIC. This indicates that the remaining oil life is below 10%, (not to be confused with oil level). On a new vehicle, or one that has just been reset, the oil life is 100%. This percentage will slowly decrease based on inputs the PCM receives. When oil life reaches the 0% mark, the PCM will illuminate the CHANGE OIL NOW light on the DIC. At this time both messages will be displayed accompanied by a slow 5 second audible chime. The reset button must be pressed to acknowledge each of these messages. If a steady CHANGE OIL SOON light persists, Diagnostic Trouble Code (DTC) 61 has been set, indicating a possible shorted switch. Remaining oil life percentage can be displayed by pressing the **OIL** button on the DIC and advancing through the messages until the oil life index is displayed. The oil life index will not detect abnormal conditions, such as excessively dusty conditions or engine malfunctions that could otherwise affect engine oil life.

Reset the EOLI as follows:

1. Acknowledge all diagnostic messages in the Drivers Information Center by pressing the **RESET** button.

2. Press the **SEL** button on the left to select OIL. Press the **SEL** button on the right, if necessary, to display oil life.

Driver Information Center (DIC) display—most General Motors vehicles

Instrument cluster warning/indicator lights, showing the location of the CHANGE OIL lamp—B Body vehicles

3. Press and hold the **RESET** button for about 5 seconds. Once the oil life index has been reset, a RESET message will be displayed, then oil life will change to 100%. Be careful not reset the oil life accidentally at any time other than when the oil has just been changed. It can not be reset accurately until the next oil change.

E & K Body Vehicles

ENGINE OIL

The General Motors E & K body class designations include the deVille, the Eldorado, the Seville, and the deVille Concours.

These vehicles are equipped with an Engine Oil Life Index (EOLI) feature as part of the Driver Information Center (DIC) display. Engine oil life is displayed through engine data as the EOLI and as a CHANGE ENGINE OIL message. The EOLI is displayed following a number between 0 (zero) and 100. This is the percentage of oil life remaining, based on driving conditions, engine oil temperature, and mileage driven since the last time the oil life indicator was reset. When the oil life index reaches 10% or less a CHANGE OIL SOON message will appear as a reminder to schedule an oil change. When the oil life index reaches 0, the CHANGE ENGINE OIL message will appear indicating that the oil should be changed within the next 200 miles (320 km). After the oil has been changed, display the EOLI message by pressing the **INFORMATION** button several times. Press and hold the **RESET** button until the display shows 100. This will reset the oil life index. The CHANGE ENGINE OIL message will remain off until the next oil change is needed. The percentage of oil life remaining may be checked at any time by pressing the **INFORMATION** button several times until the EOLI appears.

TRANSAXLE FLUID

➡This procedure is only applicable for 1996 models. Also, a scan tool is necessary to reset the CHANGE TRANS FLUID indicator.

All Cadillacs with 4.6L Northstar engines and 4T80-E transaxles are equipped with a transaxle fluid change indicator. A CHANGE TRANS FLUID message will display on the Information Center when the Powertrain Control Module (PCM) monitors actual operating conditions and displays the CHANGE TRANS FLUID message due either to calculations based on those conditions, or at the 100,000 mile (160,000 km) mark. Change the fluid by removing the lower pan and the side-cover drain plug. Change both the transmission fluid and the filter every 15,000 miles (25,000 km), if the vehicle is mainly driven under one or more of these conditions:

- In heavy city traffic where outside temperatures regularly reach 90°F (32°C) or higher.
- On high or mountain terrain.
- Frequent trailer pulling.
- Used for delivery service.

If the vehicle is not used under any of the preceding conditions, change both the fluid and filter (or service the screen) every 100,000 miles (160,000 km).

1. Reset the indicator as follows:
    a. When the CHANGE TRANS FLUID message appears, change the fluid in both the pan and side cover.
    b. To reset the transaxle oil life indicator it requires the use of a scan tool. Set the scan tool to the MISC TEST, then perform the OIL LIFE RESET followed by the TRANS OIL ST. The system is now reset.

Y Body Vehicles

The General Motors Y body class designation refers to the Corvette.

1996 VEHICLES

1. Turn the key to the **ON** position, but do not start the engine.
2. Press the **ENG MET** button on the trip monitor and release. Press the button again within 5 seconds.
3. Within 5 seconds of pressing the button the second time, press and hold the **GAUGES** button on the trip monitor. The CHANGE OIL light will flash.
4. Hold the **GAUGES** button until the CHANGE OIL light stops flashing and extinguishes. The monitor is reset at this point. Repeat this procedure if the light does not go out.

1997–99 VEHICLES

The 1997–99 Corvette is equipped with an Oil Life Monitor. The Oil Life Monitor is used to inform the driver when the next service is required. A scan tool can be used to monitor and display the amount of oil life left (shown as a percentage).

➡Repair any Throttle Position (TP) or Accelerator Pedal Position (APP) sensor diagnostic trouble codes before resetting the oil life monitor.

1. Turn the ignition **ON** but do not start the engine.
2. Depress the accelerator pedal to the Wide Open Throttle (WOT) position and release it 3 times within 5 seconds.
3. If the Oil Life Monitor is not reset, perform this procedure again.
4. Change the oil and the filter.

OBD II DIAGNOSTIC TROUBLE CODES

General Information

For years, vehicles have been capable of storing diagnostic trouble codes. Codes prior to the 1996 OBD II legislation have been proprietary to the vehicle manufacturer. In some cases, the codes are specific to the individual make and model.

Furthermore, some manufacturers have developed specialized devices to read their codes. This complicates code reading and clearing.

Chrysler Corp.

SELF-DIAGNOSTICS

The Chrysler fuel injection systems combine electronic spark advance and fuel control. At the center of these systems is a digital, pre-programmed computer, known as a Powertrain Control Module (PCM). The PCM can also be referred to as the Single Module

Engine Controller (SMEC) or as the Single Board Engine Controller (SBEC). The PCM regulates ignition timing, air-fuel ratio, emission control devices, cooling fan, charging system idle speed and speed control. It has the ability to update and revise its commands to meet changing operating conditions.

Various sensors provide the input necessary for PCM to correctly regulate fuel flow at the injectors. These include the Manifold Absolute Pressure (MAP), Throttle Position Sensor (TPS), oxygen sensor, coolant temperature sensor, charge temperature sensor, and vehicle speed sensors.

In addition to the sensors, various switches are used to provide important information to the PCM. These include the neutral safety switch, air conditioning clutch switch, brake switch and speed control switch. These signals cause the PCM to change either the fuel flow at the injectors or the ignition timing or both.

The PCM is designed to test it's own input and output circuits, If a fault is found in a major system, this information is stored in the PCM for eventual display to the technician. Information on this fault can be displayed to the technician by means of the instrument panel CHECK ENGINE light or by connecting a diagnostic read-out tester and reading a numbered display code, which directly relates to a general fault. Some inputs and outputs are checked continuously and others are checked under certain conditions. If the problem is repaired or no longer exists, the PCM cancels the fault code after approximately 50 key **ON/OFF** cycles.

When a fault code is detected, it appears as either a flash of the CHECK ENGINE light on the instrument panel or by watching the Diagnostic Readout Box version II (ORB-II). This indicates that an abnormal signal in the system has been recognized by the PCM. Fault codes do indicate the presence of a failure but they don't identify the failed component directly.

Fault Codes

Fault codes are 2 digit numbers that tell the technician which circuit is bad. Fault codes do indicate the presence of a failure but they don't identify the failed component directly. Therefore a fault code a result and not always the reason for the problem.

Indicator Codes

Indicator codes are 2 digit numbers that tell the technician if particular sequences or conditions have occurred. Such a condition where the indicator code will be displayed is at the beginning or the end of a diagnostic test. Indicator codes will not generate a CHECK ENGINE light or engine running test code.

Actuator Test Mode (ATM) Codes

Starting in 1985, ATM test codes are 2 digit numbers that identify the various circuits used by the technician during the diagnosis procedure. In 1989 the PCM and test equipment changed design. The actuator test functions where expanded, but access to these functions may have changed, dependent on vehicle or test equipment being used.

Engine Running Test Codes

Engine running test codes where introduced on fuel injected vehicles. These are 2 digit numbers. The codes are used to access sensor readouts while the engine is running and place the engine in particular operating conditions for diagnosis. Feedback carburetor system does not offer engine running sensor test mode.

Check Engine Light

This is possibly the most critical step of diagnosis. A detailed examination of connectors, wiring and vacuum hoses can often lead to a repair without further diagnosis. A careful inspector will check the undersides of hoses as well as the integrity of hard-to-reach hoses blocked by the air cleaner or other component. Wiring should be checked carefully for any sign of strain, burning, crimping, or terminals pulled-out from a connector. Checking connectors at components or in harnesses is required; usually, pushing them together will reveal a loose fit.

The CHECK ENGINE or Maintenance Indicator Lamp (MIL) light has 2 modes of operation: diagnostic mode and switch test mode.

If a ORB-II diagnostic tester is not available, the PCM can show the technician fault codes by flashing the CHECK ENGINE light on the instrument panel in the diagnostic mode. In the switch test mode, after all codes are displayed, switch function can be confirmed. The light will turn on and off when a switch is turned ON and OFF.

Even though the light can be used as a diagnostic tool, it cannot do the following:

Once the light starts to display fault codes, it cannot be stopped. If the technician loses count, he must start the test procedure again. The light cannot display all of the codes or any blank displays.

The light cannot tell the technician if the oxygen feed-back system is lean or rich and if the idle motor and detonation systems are operational. The light cannot perform the actuation test mode, sensor test mode or engine running test mode.

➡ Be advised that the CHECK ENGINE light can only perform a limited amount of functions and is not to be used as a substitute for a diagnostic tester. All diagnostic procedure described herein are intended for use with a Diagnostic Readout Box II (DRB-II) or equivalent tool.

Limp-In Mode

The limp-in mode is the attempt by the PCM to compensate for the failure of certain components by substituting information from other sources. If the PCM senses incorrect data or no data at all from the MAP sensor, throttle position sensor or coolant temperature sensor, the system is placed into limp-in mode and the CHECK ENGINE light on the instrument panel is activated. This mode will keep the vehicle drive able until the customer can get it to a service facility.

Test Modes

There are 5 modes of testing required for the proper diagnosis of the system. They are as follows:

Diagnostic Test Mode This mode is used to access the fault codes from the PCM's memory.

Circuit Actuation Test Mode (ATM Test) This mode is used to turn a certain circuit on and off in order to test it. ATM test codes are used in this mode.

Switch Test Mode This mode is used to determine if specific switch inputs are being received by the PCM.

Sensor Test Mode This mode looks at the output signals of certain sensors as they are received by the PCM when the engine is not running. Sensor access codes are read in this mode. Also this mode is used to clear the PCM memory of stored codes.

Engine Running Test Mode This mode looks at sensor output signals as seen by the PCM when the engine is running. Also this mode is used to determine some specific running conditions necessary for diagnosis.

READING CODES

Obtaining Trouble Codes

Entering the Jeep or Eagle self-diagnostic system requires the use of a special adapter that connects with the Diagnostic Readout Box II (DRB-II). These systems require the adapter because all of the system diagnosis is done Off-Board instead of On-Board like most vehicles. The adapter, which is a computer module itself, measures signals at the diagnostic connector and converts the signals into a form which the ORBII can use to perform tests. On vehicles other than Jeep and Eagle the following procedures will obtain stored Diagnostic Trouble Codes (DTC).

USING THE CHECK ENGINE LAMP

Codes display on vehicles built before 1989 are displayed in numerical order, after 1989 codes are displayed in order of occurrence.

1. Connect the readout box to the diagnostic connector located in the engine compartment near PCM.
2. Start the engine, if possible, cycle the transmission selector and the A/C switch if applicable. Shut off the engine.
3. Turn the ignition switch ON—OFF, ON—OFF, ON -OFF, ON within 5 seconds.
4. Observe the CHECK ENGINE light on the instrument panel.
5. Just after the last ON cycle, the dash warning (MIL) lamp will begin flashing the stored codes.
6. The codes are transmitted as two digit flashes.
7. Example would be Code 21 will be displayed as a FLASH FLASH pause FLASH.
8. Be ready to write down the codes as they appear; the only way to repeat the codes is to start over at the beginning.

SCAN TOOL

The scan tool is the preferred choice for fault recovery and system diagnosis. Some hints on using the ORB-II include:
- To use the HELP screen, press and hold F3 at any time.

Typical view of the Chrysler data link connector

- To restart the ORB-II at any time, hold the MODE button and press ATM at the same time.
- Pressing the up or down arrows will move forward or backward one item within a menu.
- To select an item, either press the number of the item or move the cursor arrow to the selection, then press ENTER.
- To return to the previous display (screen), press ATM.
- Some test screens display multiple items. To view only one, move the cursor arrow to the desired item, then press ENTER.

To read stored faults with the ORB-II:

1. With the ignition switch OFF, connect the tool to the diagnostic connector near the engine controller under the hood. On some 1988 and earlier models, cycling the ignition key ON-OFF three times may be necessary to enter the diagnostics. On 1989 and newer models, simply turn the ignition switch ON to access the read fault code data.
2. Start the engine if possible. Cycle the transmission from Park to a forward gear, then back to Park. Cycle the air conditioning ON and OFF. Turn the ignition switch OFF.
3. Turn the ignition switch ON but do not start the engine. The ORB-II will begin its power-up sequence; do not touch any keys on the scan tool during this sequence.
4. Reading faults must be selected from the FUEL/IGN MENU. To reach this menu on the ORB-II:

Cycle the ignition switch ON-OFF three times to enter the diagnostic mode

```
----- FUEL/IGN FAULTS -----
NO FAULTS DETECTED

X STARTS SINCE ERS
```

```
1 OF X FAULTS
[message
appears here]
X STARTS SINCE SET
```

Example of the DRB-II display screen while reading the trouble codes

---

Ignition system service is covered in the model specific sections of this manual

a. When the initial menu is displayed after the power-up sequence, use the down arrow to display choice 4) SELECT SYSTEM and select this choice.

b. Once on the—SELECT SYSTEM—screen, choose 1) ENGINE. This will enter the engine diagnostics section of the program.

c. The screen will momentarily display the engine family and SBEC identification numbers. After a few seconds the screen displays the choices 1) With A/C and 2) Without A/C. Select and enter the correct choice for the vehicle.

d. When the—ENGINE SYSTEM—screen appears, select 1) FUEL/IGNITION from the menu.

e. On the next screen, select 2) READ FAULTS.

5. If any faults are stored, the display will show how many are stored (1 of 4 faults, etc.) and issue a text description of the problem, such as COOLANT SENSOR VOLTAGE TOO LOW. The last line of the display shows the number of engine starts since the code was set. If the number displayed is 0 starts, this indicates a hard or current fault. Faults are displayed in reverse order of occurrence; the first fault shown is the most current and the last fault shown is the oldest.

6. Press the down arrow to read each fault after the first. Record the screen data carefully for easy reference.

7. If no faults are stored in the controller, the display will state NO FAULTS DETECTED and show the number of starts since the system memory was last erased.

8. After all faults have been read and recorded, press ATM.

9. Refer to the appropriate diagnostic chart for a diagnostic path. Remember that the fault message identifies a circuit problem, not a component. Use of the charts is required to sequentially test a circuit and identify the fault.

SWITCH TEST

The PCM only recognizes 2 switch input states—HI and LOW. For this reason the PCM cannot tell the difference between a selected switch position and an open circuit, short circuit or an open switch. However, if one of the switches is toggled, the controller does have the ability to respond to the change of state in the switch. If the change is displayed, it can be assumed that entire switch circuit to the PCM is operational.

1988 AND EARLIER MODELS:
After all codes have been shown and has indicated Code 55 end of message, actuate the following component switches. The digital display must change its numbers between 00 and 88 and the CHECK ENGINE light will blink when the following switches are activated and released:
- Brake pedal
- Gear shift selector
- A/C switch
- Electric defogger switch (1984)

1989 AND NEWER MODELS:
To enter the switch test mode, activate read input states or equivalent function on the readout box for the following switch tests:
- Z1 Voltage Sense
- Speed Control Set
- Speed Control ON/OFF
- Speed Control Resume
- A/C Switch Sense
- Brake Switch
- Park/neutral Switch

SCAN TOOL FUNCTIONS

> ※※ CAUTION
>
> **Always apply the parking brake and block the wheels before performing any diagnostic procedures with the engine running. Failure to do so may result in personal injury and/or property damage.**

After stored faults have been read and recorded, the scan tool may be used to investigate states and functions of various components. This ability compliments but does not replace the use of diagnostic charts. The ORB-II functions are useful in identifying circuits which are or are not operating correctly as well as checking component function or signal.

When diagnosing an emissions-related problem, keep in mind that the SBEC system only enters closed loop mode under certain conditions. The single most important criteria for entry into closed loop operation is that the engine be at normal operating temperature; i.e., fully warmed up. The engine is considered to be at normal operating temperature if any of the following are true: the electric cooling fan cycles on at least once or the upper radiator hose is hot to the touch or the heater is able to deliver hot air.

In open loop operation, the signal from the oxygen sensor is ignored by the engine controller and the fuel injection is controlled by pre-programmed values within the computer. Once closed loop operation is begun, the signal from the oxygen sensor is used by the engine controller to constantly adjust the fuel injection to maintain the proper air/fuel ratio. The system will switch in and out of closed loop operation depending on sensor signals and driver input. In most cases, the system will be in closed loop operation during normal driving, acceleration or deceleration and idle. Wide open throttle will cause the system to momentarily switch to open loop operation. Additionally, some engine control systems will momentarily switch to open loop under hard acceleration or deceleration until the MAP sensor signal stabilizes.

The ORB-II may be operated in the following diagnostic modes from the FUEL/IGN MENU screen.

Sensors

This function displays current data being transmitted from the fuel and ignition sensors to the engine controller. Examples of sensor data available include MAP voltage, throttle position sensor voltage and percentage, RPM, coolant temperature, voltage sensor, total spark advance, and vehicle speed. Many other sensors may be monitored depending on engine/transmission combinations.

Data for each sensor is displayed in the appropriate units, such as volts, mph, in. Hg, degrees F, etc.

1988 AND EARLIER MODELS

1. Put the system into the diagnostic test mode and wait for Code 55 to appear on the display screen.

2. Press the ATM button on the diagnostic tool to activate the display. If a specific sensor read test is desired, hold the ATM button down until the desired test code appears.

3. Slide the READ/HOLD switch to the HOLD position to display the corresponding sensor output.

Sensor Read Test Display codes:

Code 01 Battery temperature sensor; display voltage divided by 10 equals sensor temperature

Code 02 Oxygen sensor voltage; display number divided by 10 equals sensor voltage

Code 03 Charge temperature sensor voltage; display number divided by 10 equals sensor voltage

Code 04 Engine coolant temperature sensor; display number multiplied by 10 equals degrees of engine coolant sensor

Code 05 Throttle position sensor voltage; display number divided by 10 equals sensor voltage or temperature

Code 06 Peak knock sensor voltage; display number is sensor voltage

Code 07 Battery voltage; display number is battery voltage

Code 08 Map sensor voltage; display number divided by 10 equals sensor voltage

Code 09 Speed control switches:
- Display is blank—Cruise OFF
- Display shows 00—Cruise ON
- Display shows 10- Cruise SET
- Display shows 01—Cruise RESUME

Code 10 Fault code erase routine; display will flash 0's for 4 seconds

The State Display programs allow the operator to view the present conditions in the SBEC system. These choices are displayed on the FUEL IGN STATE screen and offer the choices of MODULE INFO, SENSORS, INPUTS/OUTPUTS or MONITORS. Viewing system data through these windows can be helpful in observing the effects of repairs or to compare the problem vehicle to a known-good vehicle.

1989 AND NEWER MODELS

To enter the sensor test mode, activate read sensor voltage or read sensor values or equivalent functions on the readout box for the following sensor displays:
Read Sensor Voltage
- Battery temperature sensor
- Oxygen sensor input
- Throttle body temperature sensor
- Coolant temperature sensor
- Throttle position
- Minimum throttle
- Battery voltage
- MAP sensor voltage

Read Sensor Values
- Throttle body temperature
- Coolant temperature
- MAP gauge reading
- AIS motor position
- Added adaptive fuel
- Adaptive fuel factor
- Barometric pressure
- Engine speed
- Module spark advance
- Vehicle speed
- Oxygen sensor state

Engine Running Test Mode

1988 AND EARLIER MODELS

The Engine Running Test Mode monitors the sensors on the vehicle which check operating conditions while the engine is running. The engine running test mode can be performed with the engine idling in NEUTRAL and with parking brake set or under actual driving conditions. With the diagnostic readout box

READ/HOLD switch in the READ position, the engine running test mode is initiated after the engine is started.

Select a test code by switching the READ/HOLD switch to the READ position and pressing the actuator button until the desired code appears. Release actuator button and switch the READ/HOLD switch to the HOLD position. The logic module will monitor that system test and results will be displayed.

Only fuel injected engines offer this function. The Feedback carburetor system does not offer engine running sensor test mode.

ENGINE RUNNING TEST DISPLAY CODES:
Code 61 Battery temperature sensor; display number divided by 10 equals voltage

Code 62 Oxygen sensor; display number divided by 10 equals voltage

Code 63 Fuel injector temperature sensor; display number divided by 10 equals voltage

Code 64 Engine coolant temperature sensor; display number multiplied by 10 equals degrees F

Code 65 Throttle position sensor; display number divided by 10 equals voltage

Code 67 Battery voltage sensor; display is voltage

Code 68 Manifold vacuum sensor; display is in. Hg code 69—Minimum throttle position sensor; display number divided by 10 equals voltage

Code 70 Minimum airflow idle speed sensor; display number multiplied by 10 equals rpm (see minimum air flow check procedure)

Code 71 Vehicle speed sensor; display is mph Code 72—Engine speed sensor; display number multiplied by 10 equals rpm

FUEL/IGNITION INPUT/OUTPUT:
The engine controller recognizes only two states of electrical signals, voltage high or low. In some cases this corresponds to a switch or circuit being on or off; in other circuits a voltage signal may change from low voltage to higher voltage as a sensor opens. The controller cannot recognize the difference between a selected switch position and an open or shorted circuit.

In this test mode, the change in the circuit may be viewed as the switch is operated. For example, if the BRAKE SWITCH state is selected, the display should change from Low to High as the brake pedal is pressed. If a change in a circuit is displayed as the switch is used, it may be reasonably assumed that the entire switch circuit into the engine controller is operating correctly.

Depending on the engine/transmission in the vehicle, some of the switch states which may be checked include the air conditioning switch, brake switch, park/neutral switch, fuel flow signal, air conditioning clutch relay, radiator fan relay, CHECK ENGINE lamp, overdrive solenoid(s), lock-up solenoid and the speed control vent or vacuum solenoids. The scan tool will recognize the correct choices for each vehicle and only offer the appropriate systems on the screen.

MONITORS

On vehicles built before 1991, this display is called ENGINE PARAMETERS. 1991 and newer vehicles name the screen MONITORS. This display allows close observation of groups of related signals. For example, if RPM is chosen, the screen will display data for many of the factors affecting the rpm such as throttle position sensor, advance, air conditioning status, park/neutral status, AIS status and coolant temperature.

One of the screens within this test is NO START. When this display is selected, the screen shows the initial data sent to the engine controller during cranking. Using this screen to identify missing or unusual signals can shorten diagnostic time.

Actuator Tests

The purpose of the circuit actuation mode test is to check for proper operation of the output circuits that the PCM cannot internally recognize. The PCM can attempt to activate these outputs and allow the technician to affirm proper operation. Most of the tests performed in this mode issue an audible click or visual indication of component operation (click of relay contacts, injector spray, etc.). Except for intermittent conditions, if a component functions properly when it is tested, it can be assumed that the component, attendant wiring and driving circuit are functioning properly.

1988 AND EARLIER MODELS

The Actuator Test Mode 10 Code number was introduced in 1985. In 1983–84 ATM function only provided 3 ignition sparks, 2 AIS motor cycles and 1 injector pulse.

1. Put the system into the diagnostic test mode and wait for Code 55 to appear on the display screen.

2. Press ATM button on the tool to activate the display. If a specific ATM test is desired, hold the ATM button down until the desired test code appears.

3. The computer will continue to turn the selected circuit on and off for as long as 5 minutes or until the ATM button is pressed again or the ignition switch is turned to the OFF position.

4. If the ATM button is not pressed again, the computer will continue to cycle the selected circuit for 5 minutes and then shut the system off. Turning the ignition to the OFF position will also turn the test mode off.

ACTUATOR TEST DISPLAY CODES:

Code 01 Spark activation—once every 2 seconds

Code 02 Injector activation—once every 2 seconds

Code 03 AIS activation—one step open, one step closed every 4 seconds

Code 04 Radiator fan relay—once every 2 seconds code 05-A/C WOT cutout relay—once every 2 seconds Code 06—ASD relay activation—once every 2 seconds code 07- Purge solenoid activation—one toggle every 2 seconds (The A/C fan will run continuously and the A/C switch must be in the ON position to allow for actuation)

Code 08 Speed control activation—speed control vent and vacuum every 2 seconds (Speed control switch must be in the ON position to allow for activation)

Code 09 Alternator control field activation—one toggle every 2 seconds

Code 10 Shift indicator activation—one toggle every 2 seconds

Code 11 EGR diagnosis solenoid activation—one toggle every 2 seconds

1989 AND NEWER MODELS

This family of tests is chosen from the FUEL/IGN MENU screen. The actuator tests allow the operation of the output circuits not recognized by the engine controller to be checked by energizing them on command. Testing in this fashion is necessary because the controller does not recognize the function of all the external components. If an output to a relay is triggered, and the relay is heard to click, it may be reasonably assumed that both the output circuit and the relay are operating properly. In this mode, most of the tests cause a response that may be seen or heard, although close attention may be necessary to notice the change.

Once selected, the ACTUATOR TEST screen offers a choice of items to be activated. Depending on engine and fuel system, some of the choices include:

- Stop all tests
- Engine rpm
- Ignition coil
- Fuel injector
- Fuel system
- Solenoid/relay
- AIS motor

The engine speed may be set to a desired level through the ENGINE RPM screen. Once a system is chosen, related screens will appear allowing detailed selection of which relay, injector or component is to be operated.

Exiting Diagnostic Test

By turning the ignition switch to the OFF position, the test mode system is exited. With a Diagnostic Readout Box attached to the system and the ATM control button not pressed, the computer will continue to cycle the selected circuits for 5 minutes and then automatically shut the system down.

Clearing Codes

Stored faults should only be cleared by use of the ORB-II or similar scan tool. Disconnecting the battery will clear codes but is not recommended as doing so will also clear all other memories on the vehicle and may affect drive ability. Disconnecting the PCM connector will also clear codes, but on newer models it may store a power loss code and will affect driveability until the vehicle is driven and the PCM can relearn it's drive ability memory.

The—ERASE—screen will appear when ATM is pressed at the end of the stored faults. Select the desired action from ERASE or DON'T ERASE. If ERASE is chosen, the display asks ARE YOU SURE? Pressing ENTER erases stored faults and displays the message FAULTS ERASED. After the faults are erased, press ATM to return the FUEL/IGN MENU.

DOMESTIC VEHICLE SELF-DIAGNOSTICS

Chrysler Domestic Built Fuel Injection System

Code 88 Display used for start of test

Code 11 Camshaft signal or Ignition signal—no reference signal detected during engine cranking

Code 12 Memory to controller has been cleared within 50-100 engine starts

Code 13 MAP sensor pneumatic signal—no variation in MAP sensor signal is detected or no difference is recognized between the engine MAP reading and the stored barometric pressure reading

Code 14 MAP voltage too high or too low

Code 15 Vehicle speed sensor signal—no distance sensor signal detected during road load conditions

Code 16 Knock sensor circuit—Open or short has been detected in the knock sensor circuit

Code 16 Battery input sensor—battery voltage sensor input below 4 volts with engine running

Code 17 Low engine temperature—engine coolant temperature remains below normal operating temperature during vehicle travel; possible thermostat problem

Code 21 Oxygen sensor signal—neither rich or lean condition is detected from the oxygen sensor input

Code 22 Coolant voltage low—coolant temperature sensor input below the minimum acceptable voltage/Coolant voltage high—coolant temperature sensor input above the maximum acceptable voltage

Code 23 Air Charge or Throttle Body temperature voltage HIGH/LOW—charge air temperature sensor input is above or below the acceptable voltage limits

Code 24 Throttle Position sensor voltage high or low. Code 25 - Automatic Idle Speed (AIS) motor driver circuit—short or open detected in 1 or more of the AIS control circuits

Code 26 Injectors No. 1, 2, or 3 peak current not reached, high resistance in circuit

Code 27 Injector control circuit—bank output driver stage does not respond properly to the control signal

Code 27 Injectors No. 1, 2, or 3 control circuit and peak current not reached

Code 31 Purge solenoid circuit—open or short detected in the purge solenoid circuit

Code 32 Exhaust Gas Recirculation (EGR) solenoid circuit—open or short detected in the EGR solenoid circuit EGR system failure—required change in fuel/air ratio not detected during diagnostic test

Code 32 Surge valve solenoid—open or short in turbocharger surge valve circuit—some 1993 vehicles

Code 33 Air conditioner clutch relay circuit—open or short detected in the air conditioner clutch relay circuit. If vehicle doesn't have air conditioning ignore this code

Code 34 Speed control servo solenoids or MUX speed control circuit HIGH/LOW—open or short detected in the vacuum or vent solenoid circuits or speed control switch input above or below allowable voltage

Code 35 Radiator fan control relay circuit—open or short detected in the radiator fan relay circuit

Code 35 Idle switch shorted—switch input shorted to ground—some 1993 vehicles

Code 36 Wastegate solenoid—open or short detected in the turbocharger wastegate control solenoid circuit

Code 37 Part Throttle Unlock (PTU) circuit for torque converter clutch—open or short detected in the torque converter part throttle unlock solenoid circuit

Code 37 Baro Reed Solenoid—solenoid does not turn off when it should

Code 37 Shift indicator circuit (manual transaxle)

Code 37 Transaxle temperature out of range—some 1993 models

Code 41 Charging system circuit—output driver stage for generator field does not respond properly to the voltage regulator control signal

Code 42 Fuel pump or no Auto shut-down (ASD) relay voltage sense at controller

Code 43 Ignition control circuit—peak primary circuit current not respond properly with maximum dwell time

Code 43 Ignition coil #1, 2, or 3 primary circuits—peak primary was not achieved within the maximum allowable dwell time

Code 44 Battery temperature voltage—problem exists in the PCM battery temperature circuit or there is an open or short in the engine coolant temperature circuit

Code 44 Fused J2 circuit in not present in the logic board; used on the single engine module controller system

Code 45 Turbo boost limit exceeded—MAP sensor detects overboost

Code 44 Overdrive solenoid circuit—open or short in overdrive solenoid circuit

Code 46 Battery voltage too high—battery voltage sense input above target charging voltage during engine operation

Code 47 Battery voltage too low—battery voltage sense input below target charging voltage

Code 51 Air/fuel at limit—oxygen sensor signal input indicates LEAN air/fuel ratio condition during engine operation

Code 52 Air/fuel at limit—oxygen sensor signal input indicates RICH air/fuel ratio condition during engine operation

Code 52 Logic module fault—1984 vehicles. Code 53—Internal controller failure—internal engine controller fault condition detected during self test

Code 54 Camshaft or (distributor sync.) reference circuit—No camshaft position sensor signal detected during engine rotation

Code 55 End of message

Code 61 Baro read solenoid—open or short detected in the baro read solenoid circuit

Code 62 EMR mileage not stored—unsuccessful attempt to update EMR mileage in the controller EEPROM

Code 63 EEPROM write denied—unsuccessful attempt to write to an EEPROM location by the controller

Code 64 Flex fuel sensor—Flex fuel sensor signal out of range—(new in 1993)- CNG Temperature voltage out of range—CN gas pressure out of range

Code 65 Manifold tuning valve—an open or short has been detected in the manifold tuning valve solenoid circuit (3.3L and 3.5L LH-Platform)

Code 66 No CCO messages or no BODY CCO messages or no EATX CCO messages—messages from the CCO bus or the BODY CCD or the EATX CCO were not received by the PCM

Code 76 Ballast bypass relay—open or short in fuel pump relay circuit

Code 77 Speed control relay—an open or short has been detected in the speed control relay

Code 88 Display used for start of test

Code Error Fault code error—Unrecognized fault 10 received by ORBII

➡ **This list is for reference and does not mean that a component is defective. The code identifies the circuit and component that require further testing.**

Chrysler Domestic Built Feedback Carburetor System

Code 88 Display used for start of test—must appear or other codes aren't valid

Code 11 Carburetor oxygen solenoid

Code 12 Transmission unlock relay—3.7L and 5.2L

Code 13 Air switching solenoid—3.7L and 5.2L—or Vacuum operated secondary control solenoid—2.2L

Code 14 Battery feed to computer disconnected with 20–40 engine starts

Code 16 Ignore

Code 17 Electronic throttle control solenoid

Code 18 EGR or Purge control solenoid

Code 21 Distributor pick-up signal

Code 22 Oxygen feedback stays rich or lean too long -3.7L and 5.2L—or Oxygen feedback is LEAN too long—2.2L

Code 23 Oxygen feedback is RICH too long—2.2L

Code 24 Vacuum transducer signal problem

Code 25 Charge temperature switch signal—3.7L and 5.2L engine—or Radiator fan temperature switch signal—2.2L engine

Code 26 Charge temperature sensor signal—3.7L and 5.2L engine—or Engine temperature sensor signal—2.2L

Code 28 Speed sensor circuit (if equipped)

Code 31 Battery feed to computer

Code 32 Computer can't enter diagnostics

Code 33 Computer can't enter diagnostics

Code 55 End of message

Code 88 Display used for start of test

Code 00 Diagnostic readout box is powered up and waiting for codes

➡This list is for reference and does not mean that a component is defective. The code identifies the circuit and component that require further testing.

Chrysler Import Built Fuel Systems

1984–1988 COLT, VISTA, SUMMIT AND D50

Code 1 Oxygen sensor

Code 2 Crank angle sensor—or Ignition signal

Code 3 Air flow sensor

Code 4 Barometric pressure sensor

Code 5 Throttle Position Sensor (TPS)

Code 6 Motor Position Sensor (MPS)—or Idle Speed Control (ISC) position sensor

Code 7 Engine Coolant Temperature Sensor

Code 8 No. 1 cylinder TDC Sensor—or Vehicle speed sensor

➡Some 1988 Multi-Point injected vehicles use 1989 2-digit codes.

1988–93 COLT, SUMMIT, VISTA, LASER, TALON, STEALTH AND D50

Code 11 Oxygen sensor

Code 12 Air flow sensor

Code 13 Intake Air Temperature Sensor

Code 14 Throttle Position Sensor (TPS)

Code 15 SC Motor Position Sensor (MPS)

Code 21 Engine Coolant Temperature Sensor

Code 22 Crank angle sensor

Code 23 No. 1 cylinder TOC (Camshaft position) Sensor

Code 24 Vehicle speed sensor

Code 25 Barometric pressure sensor

Code 31 Knock (KS) sensor

Code 32 Manifold pressure sensor

Code 36 Ignition timing adjustment signal

Code 39 Oxygen sensor (rear—turbocharged)

Code 41 Injector

Code 42 Fuel pump

Code 43 EGR-California

Code 44 Ignition Coil—power transistor unit (No. 1 and No. 4 cylinders) on 3.0L Stealth

Code 52 Ignition Coil—power transistor unit (No. 2 and No. 5 cylinders) on 3.0L Stealth

Code 53 Ignition coil, power transistor unit (No. 3 and No. 6 cylinders)

Code 55 IAC valve position sensor

Code 59 Heated oxygen sensor

Code 61 Transaxle control unit cable (automatic transmission)

Code 62 Warm up control valve position sensor (non-turbo)

Jeep and Eagle Built Fuel Systems

1988–90 2.5L, 3.0L AND 4.0L ENGINE

Code 1000 Ignition line low

Code 1001 Ignition line high

Code 1002 Oxygen heater line

Code 1004 Battery voltage low

Code 1005 Sensor ground line out of limits

Code 1010 Diagnostic enable line low

Code 1011 Diagnostic enable line high

Code 1012 MAP line low

Code 1013 MAP line high

Code 1014 Fuel pump line low

Code 1015 Fuel pump line high

Code 1016 Charge air temperature sensor low

Code 1017 Charge air temperature sensor high

Code 1018 No serial data from the ECU

Code 1021 Engine failed to start due to mechanical, fuel, or ignition problem

Code 1022 Start line low

Code 1024 ECU does not see start signal

Code 1025 Wide open throttle circuit low

Code 1027 ECU sees wide open throttle

Code 1028 ECU does not see wide open throttle

Code 1031 ECU sees closed throttle

Code 1032 ECU does not see closed throttle

Code 1033 Idle speed increase line low

Code 1034 Idle speed increase line high

Code 1035 Idle speed decrease line low

Code 1036 Idle speed decrease line high

Code 1037 Throttle position sensor reads low

Code 1038 Park/Neutral line high

Code 1040 Latched B+ line low

Code 1041 Latched B+ line high

Code 1042 No Latched B+ 1/2 volt drop

Code 1047 Wrong ECU

Code 1048 Manual vehicle equipped with automatic ECU

Code 1949 Automatic vehicle equipped with manual ECU

Code 1050 Idle RPM less than 500

Code 1051 Idle RPM greater than 2000

Code 1052 MAP sensor out of limits

Code 1053 Change in MAP reading out of limits

Code 1054 Coolant temperature sensor line low

Code 1055 Coolant temperature sensor line high

Code 1056 Inactive coolant temperature sensor

Code 1057 Knock circuit shorted

Code 1058 Knock value out of limits

Code 1059 A/C request line low

Code 1060 A/C request line high

Code 1061 A/C select line low

Code 1062 A/C select line high

Code 1063 A/C clutch line low

Code 1064 A/C clutch line high

Code 1065 Oxygen reads rich

Code 1066 Oxygen reads lean

Code 1067 Latch relay line low

Code 1068 Latch relay line high

Code 1070 A/C cutout line low

Code 1071 A/C cutout line high

Code 1073 ECU does not see speed sensor signal

Code 1200 ECU defective

Code 1202 Injector shorted to ground

Code 1209 Injector open

Code 1218 No voltage at ECU from power latch relay
Code 1220 No voltage at ECU from EGR solenoid
Code 1221 No injector voltage
Code 1222 MAP not grounded
Code 1223 No ECU tests run

➡ **Prior to 1988 vehicles used an Off-Board Diagnostic system which required special diagnostic equipment to read codes. After 1991 Jeep and Eagle vehicles used the Chrysler Domestic Built Engine Control system. The code list for Chrysler Built Domestic Fuel injection System also covers 1991 and newer Jeep and Eagle vehicles.**

Ford Motor Co.

INTRODUCTION TO FORD SELF-DIAGNOSTICS

The engine control systems are used in conjunction with either a throttle body (CFI) injection or multi-point (EFI and SEFI) injection fuel delivery system or feedback carburetor systems depending on the year, model and powertrain. Although the individual system components vary slightly, the electronic control system operation is basically the same. The major difference is the number and type of output devices being controlled by the ECA.

Automotive manufacturers have developed on-board computers to control engines, transmissions and many other components. These on-board computers with dozens of sensors and actuators have become almost impossible to test without the help of electronic test equipment.

One of these electronic test devices has become the on-board computer itself. The Powertrain Control Modules (PCM), sometimes called the Electronic Control Assembly (ECA), used on toadies vehicles has a built in self testing system. This self test ability is called self-diagnosis. The self-diagnosis system will test many or all of the sensors and controlled devices for proper function. When a malfunction is detected this system will store a fault code in memory that's related to that specific circuit. You can access the computer to obtain fault codes recorded in memory by using an analog voltmeter or special diagnostic scan tool. This will help narrow down what area to begin testing.

Fault code meanings can vary from year to year even on the same model. It is extremely important after retrieving a fault code to verify its meaning with a proper manual. Servicing a fault code incorrectly will not only lead to the wrong conclusion but could also cause damage if tested or serviced incorrectly. There is a list of general code descriptions provide later in this manual.

What System Is On My Car?

There are 3 electronic fuel control systems used by Ford Motor Company. These systems all operate using similar components and on-board computers. Self-Diagnostic on these systems will vary, but, the basic fuel control operation is the same. Ford uses the following systems:

• **EEC-IV and EEC-V** engine control system: used on most domestic built Ford vehicles since 1984.
• **Non-NAAO EEC** engine control system: used on import built Ford vehicles, referred to as Non-NAAO cars.
• **MCU** feedback carburetor system: used on most Ford vehicles before 1984 and some later model vehicles equipped with a V8 engine and feedback carburetor.

Most Ford vehicles made after 1983 except for Capri, Festiva, Probe, Escort and Tracer use the 4th generation Electronic Engine Control system, commonly designated EEC-IV.

If you own a Capri, Festiva, Probe 2.0L, 2.2L, or 2.SL, an Escort or Tracer with a 1 .6L or 1 .8L engine, then the fuel control system is referred to as NON-NAAO (Not North American Automotive Operations produced vehicles) system. The fuel system used on these vehicles is called Electronic Engine Control (EEC). This Non-NAAO EEC system components and operation are basically the same as the EEC-IV system. The self-diagnostic function on the EEC system differs from the EEC-VI system and is covered under NON-NAAO vehicle.

Most 1984–94 Ford domestic built vehicles employ the 4th generation Electronic Engine Control system, commonly called EEC-IV, to manage fuel, ignition and emissions on vehicle engines. In 1994 the EEC-V system was introduced on some models. The diagnostic system on EEC-V provides 3 digit codes in place of 2 digit codes, and it is capable of monitoring more inputs and outputs.

If your vehicle was made before 1984, or has a feedback carburetor equipped V8 engine, then it probably uses the Microprocessor Control Unit (MCU). The MCU system was used on most 1981-83 carburetor equipped vehicles, and 1984 and newer V8 engines with feedback carburetors. The MCU system uses a large six sided connector, identical to the one used with EEC-IV systems. The MCU system does NOT use the small single wire connector, like the EEC-IV system. The MCU system is covered in greater detail later in this manual.

EEC-IV AND EEC-V DIAGNOSTIC SYSTEMS

This system includes all Ford Motor Company vehicles with the exception of imported vehicles like the Capri, Festiva, Probe 2.0L, 2.2L and 2.SL engine and the Escort and Tracer equipped with the 1 .8L engine.

Most 1984–94 Ford domestic built vehicles employ the 4th generation Electronic Engine Control system, commonly designated EEC-IV, to manage fuel, ignition and emissions on vehicle engines. In 1994 the EEC-V system was introduced on some models. The diagnostic system on EEC-V provides 3 digit codes in place of 2 digit codes and monitors more components.

Engine Control System

The Powertrain Control Modules (PCM), usually referred to as the Electronic Control Assembly (ECA) by Ford, is given responsibility for the operation of the emission control devices, cooling fans, ignition and advance and in some cases, automatic transmission functions. Because the EEC-IV oversees both the ignition timing and the fuel injector operation, a precise air/fuel ratio will be maintained under all operating conditions. The ECA is a microprocessor or small computer which receives electrical inputs from several sensors, switches and relays on and around the engine.

Based on combinations of these inputs, the ECA controls outputs to various devices concerned with engine operation and emissions. The engine control assembly relies on the signals to form a correct picture of current vehicle operation. If any of the input signals is incorrect, the ECA reacts to what ever picture is painted for it. For example, if the coolant temperature sensor is inaccurate and reads too low, the ECA may see a picture of the engine never warming up. Consequently, the engine settings will be maintained as if the engine were cold. Because so many inputs can affect one output, correct diagnostic procedures are essential on these systems.

One part of the ECA is devoted to monitoring both input and output functions within the system. This ability forms the core of the self-diagnostic system. If a problem is detected within a circuit, the controller will recognize the fault, assign it an identification code, and store the code in a memory section. Depending on the year and model, the fault code(s) may be represented by two or three digit numbers. The stored code(s) may be retrieved during diagnosis.

When the term Powertrain Control Module (PCM) is used in this manual it will refer to the engine control computer regardless that it may also be called an Electronic Control Assembly (ECA).

While the EEC-IV system is capable of recognizing many internal faults, certain faults will not be recognized. Because the computer system sees only electrical signals, it cannot sense or react to mechanical or vacuum faults affecting engine operation. Some of these faults may affect another component which will set a code. For example, the ECA monitors the output signal to the fuel injectors, but cannot detect a partially clogged injector. As long as the output driver responds correctly, the computer will read the system as functioning correctly. However, the improper flow of fuel may result in a lean mixture. This would, in turn, be detected by the oxygen sensor and noticed as a constantly lean signal by the ECA. Once the signal falls outside the pre-programmed limits, the engine control assembly would notice the fault and set an identification code.

Additionally, the EEC-IV system employs adaptive fuel logic. This process is used to compensate for normal wear and variability within the fuel system. Once the engine enters steady-state operation, the engine control assembly watches the oxygen sensor signal for a bias or tendency to run slightly rich or lean. If such a bias is detected, the adaptive logic corrects the fuel delivery to bring the air/fuel mixture towards a centered or 14.7:1 ratio. This compensating shift is stored in a non-volatile memory which is retained by battery power even with the ignition switched off. The correction factor is then available the next time the vehicle is operated.

➡️**If the battery is disconnected for longer than 5 minutes, the adaptive fuel factor will be lost. After repair it will be necessary to drive the car at least 10 miles to allow the processor to relearn the correct factors. The driving period should include steady-throttle open road driving if possible. During the drive, the vehicle may exhibit driveability symptoms not noticed before. These symptoms should clear as the ECA computes the correction factor. The ECA will also store Code 19 indicating loss of power to the controller.**

FAILURE MODE EFFECTS MANAGEMENT (FMEM)

The engine controller assembly contains back-up programs which allow the engine to operate if a sensor signal is lost. If a sensor input is seen to be out of range—either high or low—the FMEM program is used. The processor substitutes a fixed value for the missing sensor signal. The engine will continue to operate, although performance and driveability may be noticeably reduced. This function of the controller is sometimes referred to as the limp-in or fail-safe mode. If the missing sensor signal is restored, the FMEM system immediately returns the system to normal operation. The dashboard warning lamp will be lit when FMEM is in effect.

HARDWARE LIMITED OPERATION STRATEGY (HLOS)

This mode is only used if the fault is too extreme for the FMEM circuit to handle. In this mode, the processor has ceased all computation and control; the entire system is run on fixed values. The vehicle may be operated but performance and driveability will be greatly reduced. The fixed or default settings provide minimal cali-

bration, allowing the vehicle to be carefully driven in for service. The dashboard warning lamp will be lit when HLOS is engaged. Codes cannot be read while the system is operating in this mode.

Dashboard Warning Lamp

The CHECK ENGINE or SERVICE ENGINE SOON dashboard warning lamp is referred to as the Malfunction Indicator Lamp (MIL). The lamp is connected to the engine control assembly and will alert the driver to certain malfunctions within the EEC-IV system. When the lamp is lit, the ECA has detected a fault and stored an identity code in memory. The engine control system will usually enter either FMEM or HLOS mode and driveability will be impaired.

The light will stay on as long as the fault causing it is present. Should the fault self-correct, the MIL will extinguish but the stored code will remain in memory.

Under normal operating conditions, the MIL should light briefly when the ignition key is turned ON. As soon as the ECA receives a signal that the engine is cranking, the lamp will be extinguished. The dash warning lamp should remain out during the entire operating cycle.

➡️**On Continental, the CHECK ENGINE message is displayed on the message center. When a fault is detected, the message is accompanied by a 1 second tone every 5 seconds. The tone stops after 1 minute. When the Continental system enters HLOS, the additional message CHECK DCL is displayed. DCL refers to the Data Communications Link running between the engine controller and the message center.**

EEC-IV AND EEC-V SCAN TOOL FUNCTIONS

Although stored codes may be read by using a analog voltmeter, the use of hand-held scan tools such as Ford's Self-Test Automatic Readout (STAR) tester or the second generation SUPER STAR II tester or their equivalent is recommended. There are many manufacturers of these tools; the purchaser must be certain that the tool is proper for the intended use.

Both the STAR and SUPER STAR testers are designed to communicate directly with the EEC-IV system and interpret the electrical signals. The SUPER STAR tester may be used to read either 2 or 3 digit codes; the original STAR tester will not read the 3 digit codes used on many 1990 and newer vehicles.

The scan tool allows any stored faults to be read from the engine controller memory. Use of the scan tool provides additional data during troubleshooting but does not eliminate the use of the charts. The scan tool makes collecting information easier; the data must be correctly interpreted by an operator familiar with the system.

Electrical Tools

The most commonly required electrical diagnostic tool is the Digital Multimeter, allowing voltage, resistance and amperage to be read by one instrument. Many of the diagnostic charts require the use of a volt or ohmmeter during diagnosis.

The multimeter must be a high impedance unit, with 10 megohms of impedance in the voltmeter. This type of meter will not place an additional load on the circuit it is testing; this is extremely important in low voltage circuits. The multimeter must be of high quality in all respects. It should be handled carefully and protected from impact or damage. Replace the batteries frequently in the unit.

Additionally, an analog (needle type) voltmeter may be used to read stored fault codes if the STAR tester is not available. The codes are transmitted as visible needle sweeps on the face of the instrument.

Almost all diagnostic procedures will require the use of the Break-out Box, a device which connects into the EEC-IV harness and provides testing ports for the 60 wires in the harness. Direct testing of the harness connectors at the terminals or by back-probing is not recommended; damage to the wiring and terminals is almost certain to occur.

Other necessary tools include a quality tachometer with inductive (clip-on) pickup, a fuel pressure gauge with system adapters and a vacuum gauge with an auxiliary source of vacuum.

EEC-IV AND EEC-V SELF-DIAGNOSTICS

Diagnosis of a driveability problem requires attention to detail and following the diagnostic procedures in the correct order. Resist the temptation to begin extensive testing before completing the preliminary diagnostic steps. The preliminary or visual inspection must be completed in detail before diagnosis begins. In many cases this will shorten diagnostic time and often cure the problem without electronic testing.

Visual Inspection

This is possibly the most critical step of diagnosis. A detailed examination of all connectors, wiring and vacuum hoses can often lead to a repair without further diagnosis. Performance of this step relies on the skill of the technician performing it; a careful inspector will check the undersides of hoses as well as the integrity of hard-to-reach hoses blocked by the air cleaner or other components. Wiring should be checked carefully for any sign of strain , burning, crimping or terminal pull-out from a connector.

Checking connectors at components or in harnesses is required; usually, pushing them together will reveal a loose fit. Pay particular attention to ground circuits, making sure they are not loose or corroded. Remember to inspect connectors and hose fittings at components not mounted on the engine, such as the evaporative canister or relays mounted on the fender aprons. Any component or wiring in the vicinity of a fluid leak or spillage should be given extra attention during inspection.

Additionally, inspect maintenance items such as belt condition and tension, battery charge and condition and the radiator cap carefully. Any of these very simple items may affect the system enough to set a fault.

Diagnostic Connector Location

The Diagnostic Link Connectors (DLC) are located a 6 basic locations:
- Near the bulkhead (right or left side of vehicle)
- Near the wheel well (right or left side of vehicle)

Typical diagnostic link connector locations. Locations will vary depending on the year or model

• Near the front corner of the engine compartment (right or left side of vehicle)

EEC-IV AND EEC-V READING CODES

The EEC-IV system may be interrogated for stored codes using the Quick Test procedures. These tests will reveal faults immediately present during the test as well as any intermittent codes set within the previous 80 warm up cycles. If a code was set before a problem self-corrected (such as a momentarily loose connector), the code will be erased if the problem does not reoccur within 80 warm-up cycles.

The Quick Test procedure is divided into 2 sections, Key On Engine Off (KOEO) and Key On Engine Running (KOER). These 2 procedures must be performed correctly if the system is to run the internal self-checks and provide accurate fault codes. Codes will be output and displayed as numbers on the hand scan tool, i.e. 23. Code 23 would be displayed as 2 needle sweeps and pause and 3 more needle sweeps. For codes being read on an analog voltmeter, the needle sweeps indicate the code digits in the same manner as the lamp flashes on other systems.

In all cases, the codes 11 or 111 are used to indicate PASS during testing. Note that the PASS code may appear, followed by other stored codes. These are codes from the continuous memory and may indicate intermittent faults, even though the system does not presently contain the fault. The PASS designation only indicates the system passes all internal tests at the moment.

Once the Quick Test has been performed and all fault codes recorded, refer to the code charts. The charts direct the use of specific pinpoint tests for the appropriate circuit and will allow complete circuit testing.

✳✳ CAUTION

To prevent injury and/or property damage, always block the drive wheels, firmly apply the parking brake, place the transmission in Park or Neutral and turn all electrical loads off before performing the Quick Test procedures.

Reading Codes With Analog Voltmeter

➡ **There are inexpensive tools available at auto parts stores that make reading and clear Ford engine codes very easy. Reading the voltmeter needle sweeps is sometimes difficult. Always check the code more than once to make certain it was read correctly.**

In the absence of a scan tool, an analog voltmeter may be used to retrieve stored fault codes. Set the meter range to read DC 0–15 volts. Connect the positive (+) lead of the meter to the battery posi-

Connect an analog voltmeter as shown to read diagnostic trouble codes

tive terminal and connect the negative (-) lead of the meter to the self-test output pin of the diagnostic connector.

Follow the directions given for performing the KOEO and KOER tests. To activate the tests, use a jumper wire to connect the signal return pin on the diagnostic connector to the self-test input connector. The self-test input line is the separate wire and connector with or near the diagnostic connector.

The codes will be transmitted as groups of needle sweeps. This method may be used to read either 2 or 3 digit codes. The Continuous Memory codes are separated from the KOEO codes by 6 seconds, a single sweep and another 6 second delay.

KEY ON ENGINE OFF (KOEO) TEST

1. Connect the scan tool to the self-test connectors. Make certain the test button is unlatched or up.

2. Start the engine and run it until normal operating temperature is reached.

3. Turn the engine OFF for 10 seconds.

4. Activate the test button on the STAR tester.

5. Turn the ignition switch ON but do not start the engine. For vehicles with 4.9L engines, depress the clutch during the entire test. For vehicles with the 7.3L diesel engine, hold the accelerator to the floor during the test.

6. The KOEO codes will be transmitted. Six to nine seconds after the last KOEO code, a single separator pulse will be transmitted. Six to nine seconds after this pulse, the codes from the Continuous Memory will be transmitted.

Code transmission during KOEO test. Note the continuous memory codes are transmitted after a pause and a separator pulse

Example of STAR tester display screen. the colon must be present before the codes can be retrieved

7. Record all service codes displayed. Do not depress the throttle on gasoline engines during the test.

KEY ON ENGINE RUNNING (KOER) TEST

1. Make certain the self-test button is released or de-activated on the STAR tester.

2. Start the engine and run it at 2000 rpm for two minutes. This action warms up the oxygen sensor.

3. Turn the ignition switch OFF for 10 seconds.

4. Activate or latch the self-test button on the scan tool.

5. Start the engine. The engine identification code will be transmitted. This is a single digit number representing ½ the number of cylinders in a gasoline engine. On the STAR tester, this number may appear with a zero, i.e., 20 = 2. For 7.3L diesel engines, the 10 code is 5. The code is used to confirm that the correct processor is installed and that the self-test has begun.

6. If the vehicle is equipped with a Brake On/Off (BOO) switch, the brake pedal must be depressed and released after the 10 code is transmitted.

7. If the vehicle is equipped with a Power Steering Pressure Switch (PSPS), the steering wheel must be turned at least 1/2 turn and released within 2 seconds after the engine 10 code is transmitted.

8. If the vehicle is equipped with the E400 transmission, the Overdrive Cancel Switch (OCS) must be cycled after the engine 10 code is transmitted.

9. Certain Ford vehicles will display a Dynamic Response code 6–20 seconds after the engine 10 code. This will appear as one

Example of code display pattern using an analog voltmeter

Example of the Continental message panel screen

pulse on a meter or as a 10 on the STAR tester. When this code appears, briefly take the engine to wide open throttle. This allows the system to test the throttle position, MAF and MAP sensors.

10. All relevant codes will be displayed and should be recorded. Remember that the codes refer only to faults present during this test cycle. Codes stored in Continuous Memory are not displayed in this test mode.

11. Do not depress the throttle during testing unless a dynamic response code is displayed.

TESTING WITH CONTINENTAL MESSAGE CENTER:

The stored fault codes may be displayed on the electronic message screen in Continentals so equipped. To perform the KOEO test, press all 3 buttons on the electronic instrument cluster (GAUGE SELECT, ENGLISH/METRIC, SPEED ALARM or SELECT, RESET and SYSTEM CHECK) simultaneously. Turn the ignition switch ON and release the buttons; stored codes will be displayed on the screen.

To perform the KOER test:

12. Hold in all 3 buttons, start the engine and release the buttons.

13. Press the SELECT or GAUGE SELECT button 3 times. The message DEALER 4 should appear at the bottom of the message panel.

14. Initiate the test by using a jumper wire to connect the signal return pin on the diagnostic connector to the self-test input connector. The self-test input line is the separate wire and connector with or near the diagnostic connector.

15. The stored codes will be output to the vehicle display.

16. To exit the test, turn the ignition switch OFF and disconnect the jumper wire.

Advanced Test Modes

CONTINUOUS MONITOR OR WIGGLE TEST MODE

Once entered, this mode allows the technician to attempt to recreate intermittent faults by wiggling or tapping components, wiring or connectors. The test may be performed during either KOEO or KOER procedures. The test requires the use of either an analog voltmeter or a hand scan tool.

To enter the continuous monitor mode during KOEO testing, turn the ignition switch ON. Activate the test, wait 10 seconds, then deactivate and reactivate the test; the system will enter the continuous monitor mode. Tap, move or wiggle the harness, component or connector suspected of causing the problem; if a fault is detected, the code will store in the memory. When the fault occurs, the dash warning lamp will illuminate, the STAR tester will light a red indicator (and possibly beep) and the analog meter needle will sweep once.

To enter this mode in the KOER test:

1. Start the engine and run it at 2000 rpm for two minutes. This action warms up the oxygen sensor.

Ignition system service is covered in the model specific sections of this manual

2. Turn the ignition switch OFF for 10 seconds.

3. Start the engine.

4. Activate the test, wait 10 seconds, then deactivate and reactivate the test; the system will enter the continuous monitor mode.

5. Tap, move or wiggle the harness, component or connector suspected of causing the problem; if a fault is detected, the code will store in the memory.

6. When the fault occurs, the dash warning lamp will illuminate, the STAR tester will light a red indicator (and possibly beep) and the analog meter needle will sweep once.

OUTPUT STATE CHECK

This testing mode allows the operator to energize and de-energize most of the outputs controlled by the EEC-IV system. Many of the outputs may be checked at the component by listening for a click or feeling the item move or engage by a hand placed on the case. To enter this check:

1. Enter the KOEO test mode.

2. When all codes have been transmitted, depress the accelerator all the way to the floor and release it.

3. The output actuators are now all ON. Depressing the throttle pedal to the floor again switches the all the actuator outputs OFF.

4. This test may be performed as often as necessary, switching between ON and OFF by depressing the throttle.

5. Exit the test by turning the ignition switch OFF, disconnecting the jumper at the diagnostic connector or releasing the test button on the scan tool.

CYLINDER BALANCE TEST

This test is only for SEFI engines. On SEFI engine the EEC-IV system allows a cylinder balance test to be performed on engines equipped with the Sequential Electronic Fuel Injection system. Cylinder balance testing identifies a weak or non-contributing cylinder.

Enter the cylinder balance test by depressing and releasing the throttle pedal within 2 minutes of the last code output in the KOER test. The idle speed will become fixed and engine mm is recorded for later reference. The engine control assembly will shut off the fuel to the highest numbered cylinder (4, 6 or 8), allow the engine to stabilize and then record the rpm. The injector is turned back on and the next one shut off and the process continues through cylinder No. 1.

The controller selects the highest rpm drop from all the cylinders tested, multiplies it by a percentage and arrives at an rpm drop value for all cylinders. For example, if the greatest drop for any cylinder was 150 rpm, the processor applies a multiple of 65% and arrives at 98 mm. The processor then checks the recorded rpm drops, checking that each was at least 98 rpm. If all cylinders meet the criteria, the test is complete and the ECA outputs Code 90 indicating PASS.

If one cylinder did not drop at least this amount, then the cylinder number is output instead of the 90 code. The cylinder number will be followed by a zero, so 30 indicates cylinder No. 3 did not meet the minimum rpm drop.

The test may be repeated a second time by depressing and releasing the throttle pedal within 2 minutes of the last code output. For the second test, the controller uses a lower percentage (and thus a lower rpm) to determine the minimum acceptable rpm drop. Again, either Code 90 or the number of the weak cylinder will be output.

Performing a third test causes the ECA to select an even lower percentage and rpm drop. If a cylinder is shown as weak in the third test, it should be considered non-contributing. The tests may be repeated as often as needed if the throttle is depressed within two minutes of the last code output. Subsequent tests will use the percentage from the third test instead of selecting even lower values.

Continuous Memory Codes

These codes are retained in memory for 80 warm-up cycles. To clear the codes for the purposes of testing or confirming repair, perform the KOEO test. When the fault codes begin to be displayed, deactivate the test by either disconnecting the jumper wire (meter, MIL or message center) or releasing the test button on the hand scanner. Stopping the test during code transmission will erase the Continuous Memory. Do not disconnect the negative battery cable to clear these codes; the Keep Alive memory will be cleared and a new code, 19, will be stored for loss of ECA power.

KEEP ALIVE MEMORY

The Keep Alive Memory (KAM) contains the adaptive factors used by the processor to compensate for component tolerances and wear. It should not be routinely cleared during diagnosis. If an emissions related part is replaced during repair, the KAM must be cleared. Failure to clear the KAM may cause severe driveability problems since the correction factor for the old component will be applied to the new component.

To clear the Keep Alive Memory, disconnect the negative battery cable for at least 5 minutes. After the memory is cleared and the battery reconnected, the vehicle must be driven at least 10 miles so that the processor may relearn the needed correction factors. The distance to be driven depends on the engine and vehicle, but all drives should include steady-throttle cruise on open roads. Certain driveability problems may be noted during the drive because the adaptive factors are not yet functioning.

To prevent the replacement of good components, remember that the EEC-IV system has no control over the following items:
- Fuel quantity and quality
- Damaged or faulty ignition components
- Internal engine condition—rings, valves, timing belt, etc.
- Starter and battery circuit
- Dual Hall sensor
- TFI or DIS module
- Distributor condition or function
- Camshaft sensor
- Crankshaft sensor
- Ignition or DIS coil
- Engine governor module Any of these systems can cause erratic engine behavior easily mistaken for an EEC-IV problem.

NON-NAAO DIAGNOSTIC SYSTEM

The Capri, Festiva, Probe 2.0L, 2.2L and 2.5L engine, Escort and Tracer with 1.8L engine diagnostic system vehicles are referred to by Ford Motor Company as NON-NAAO, indicating the vehicles and/or their engines originate outside North American Automotive Operations. Note that some of the models also contain North American engines, such as the Probe with 3.0L engine, Escort or Tracer with 1.9L engine.

Although these vehicles share many similarities in their engine control systems, differences must also be considered. While the fault codes are almost standardized (i.e., Code 14 indicates the barometric pressure sensor), not all engines use the same components so a code may be unique to a particular engine or family. These procedures encompass both turbocharged and non-turbocharged engines.

Beside the engine diagnostic function, these procedures will also display codes related to the 4-speed Electronically-controlled Automatic Transaxle (4EAT) used in these vehicles. Note that the 4EAT codes are displayed by these procedures even though retrieving the engine fault codes may require the North American procedures described at the beginning of this section. The Probe with 3.0L engine, Escort and Tracer with 1.9L engine are examples of this situation.

Engine Control System

These vehicles employ the Electronic Engine Control system, commonly designated EEC, to manage fuel, ignition and emissions on vehicle engines. This system is not EEC-IV, but does share some similarities.

The engine control assembly (ECA) is given responsibility for the operation of the emission control devices, cooling fans, ignition and advance and in some cases, automatic transmission functions. Because the EEC oversees both the ignition timing and the fuel injector operation, a precise air/fuel ratio will be maintained under all operating conditions. The ECA is a microprocessor or small computer which receives electrical in-puts from several sensors, switches and relays on and around the engine.

Based on combinations of these inputs, the ECA controls outputs to various devices concerned with engine operation and emissions. The engine control assembly relies on the signals to form a correct picture of current vehicle operation. If any of the input signals is incorrect, the ECA reacts to what ever picture is painted for it. For example, if the coolant temperature sensor is inaccurate and reads too low, the ECA may see a picture of the engine never warming up. Consequently, the engine settings will be maintained as if the engine were cold. Because so many inputs can affect one output, correct diagnostic procedures are essential on these systems.

One part of the ECA is devoted to monitoring both input and out-put functions within the system. This ability forms the core of the self-diagnostic system. If a problem is detected within a circuit, the controller will recognize the fault, assign it an identification code, and store the code in a memory section. Most NON-NAAO vehicles use two-digit codes for both engine and 4EAT transaxle faults. The stored code(s) may be retrieved during diagnosis.

➡**When the term Powertrain Control Module (PCM) is used in this manual it will refer to the engine control computer regardless that it may also be called an Electronic Control Assembly (ECA).**

While the EEC system is capable of recognizing many internal faults, certain faults will not be recognized. Because the computer system sees only electrical signals, it cannot sense or react to mechanical or vacuum faults affecting engine operation. Some of these faults may affect another component which will set a code. For example, the ECA monitors the output signal to the fuel injectors, but cannot detect a partially clogged injector. As long as the output driver responds correctly, the computer will read the system as functioning correctly. However, the improper flow of fuel may result in a lean mixture. This would, in turn, be detected by the oxygen sensor and noticed as a constantly lean signal by the ECA. Once the signal falls outside the pre-programmed limits, the engine control assembly would notice the fault and set an identification code.

Dashboard Warning Lamp

The CHECK ENGINE dashboard warning lamp is referred to as the Malfunction Indicator Lamp (MIL). The lamp is connected to the engine control assembly and will alert the driver to certain malfunc-tions within the EEC system. When the lamp is lit, the ECA has detected a fault and stored an identity code in memory.

The light will stay on as long as the fault causing it is present.

Should the fault self-correct, the MIL will extinguish but the stored code will remain in memory.

Under normal operating conditions, the MIL should light briefly when the ignition key is turned ON. As soon as the ECA receives a sig-nal that the engine is running, the lamp will be extinguished. The dash warning lamp should remain out during the entire operating cycle.

Vehicles with a 4EAT transaxle (except 1.8L and 1.9L engines) also provide a manual shift light, indicating when the transmission is in manual shift mode. On 2.2L turbocharged engines, this lamp will light to advise the driver of certain electronic malfunctions.

NON-NAAO SCAN TOOL FUNCTIONS

Although stored codes may be read by using an analog voltmeter by counting the needle sweeps, the use of hand-held scan tools such as Ford's second generation SUPER STAR II tester or equivalent is recommended. There are many manufacturers of these tools; the pur-chaser must be certain that the tool is proper for the intended use.

➡**The engine and 4EAT fault codes on NON-NAAO vehicles may only be read with the SUPER STAR II or its equivalent. The regular STAR tester or voltmeter may be capable not retrieve the stored codes.**

The SUPER STAR II tester is designed to communicate directly with the EEC system and interpret the electrical signals. The scan tool allows any stored faults to be read from the engine controller memory. Use of the scan tool provides additional data during trou-bleshooting but does not eliminate the use of the charts. The scan tool makes collecting information easier; the data must be correctly interpreted by an operator familiar with the system.

An adapter cable will be required to connect the scan tool to the vehicle; the adapter(s) may differ depending on the vehicle being tested.

Electrical Tools

The most commonly required electrical diagnostic tool is the Digital Multimeter, allowing voltage, resistance and amperage to be read by one instrument. Many of the diagnostic charts require the use of a voltmeter or ohmmeter during diagnosis.

The multimeter must be a high impedance unit, with 10 megohms of impedance in the voltmeter. This type of meter will not place an additional load on the circuit it is testing; this is extremely important in low voltage circuits. The multimeter must be of high quality in all respects. It should be handled carefully and protected from impact or damage. Replace the batteries fre-quently in the unit.

Additionally, an analog (needle type) voltmeter may be used to read stored fault codes if the SUPER STAR II tester is not available. The codes are transmitted as visible needle sweeps on the face of the instrument.

Almost all diagnostic procedures will require the use of the Breakout Box, a device which connects into the EEC harness and provides testing ports for the 60 wires in the harness. Direct testing of the harness connectors at the terminals or by backprobing is not recommended; damage to the wiring and terminals is almost certain to occur.

Other necessary tools include a quality tachometer with inductive (clip-on) pickup, a fuel pressure gauge with system adapters and a vacuum gauge with an auxiliary source of vacuum.

NON-NAAO SELF-DIAGNOSTICS

Diagnosis of a driveability problem requires attention to detail and following the diagnostic procedures in the correct order. Resist the temptation to begin extensive testing before completing the preliminary diagnostic steps. The preliminary or visual inspection must be completed in detail before diagnosis begins. In many cases this will shorten diagnostic time and often cure the problem without electronic testing.

Keep in mind that all the things that previously went wrong with vehicles, before the age of electronics, can still go wrong and are still the cause of the majority of the driveability problems. The best diagnosis starts with a list of symptoms and possible causes, followed by careful checking of those causes in the most likely order. Eliminate all the possible mechanical causes before considering electrical faults.

Visual Inspection

This is possibly the most critical step of diagnosis. A detailed examination of all connectors, wiring and vacuum hoses can often lead to a repair without further diagnosis. Performance of this step relies on the skill of the technician performing it; a careful inspector will check the undersides of hoses as well as the integrity of hard-to-reach hoses blocked by the air cleaner or other components. Wiring should be checked carefully for any sign of strain , burning, crimping or terminal pull-out from a connector.

Checking connectors at components or in harnesses is required; usually, pushing them together will reveal a loose fit. Pay particular attention to ground circuits, making sure they are not loose or corroded. Remember to inspect connectors and hose fittings at components not mounted on the engine, such as the evaporative canister or relays mounted on the fender aprons. Any component or wiring in the vicinity of a fluid leak or spillage should be given extra attention during inspection.

Additionally, inspect maintenance items such as belt condition and tension, battery charge and condition and the radiator cap carefully. Any of these very simple items may affect the system enough to set a fault.

NON-NAAO READING CODES

The EEC system may be interrogated for stored codes using the Quick Test procedures. If a code was set before a problem self-corrected (such as a momentarily loose connector), the code will remain in memory until cleared.

The Quick Test procedure is divided into 3 sections, Key On Engine Off (KOEO), Key On Engine Running (KOER) and the Switch Monitor test. These 3 procedures must be performed correctly if the system is to run the internal self-checks and provide accurate fault codes. Codes will be output and displayed as numbers on the hand scan tool, i.e. 23. If the codes are being read by an analog voltmeter, the codes will be displayed as groups of needle sweeps separated by pauses.

Code 23 would be shown as two sweeps, a pause and three more sweeps. A longer pause will occur between codes. Unlike the EEC-IV system, the EEC system does not broadcast a PASS designator or code. If no fault codes are stored, the display screen of the hand scanner will remain blank. Additionally, the EEC system does not operate switches or sensors during KOEO or KOER testing.

Once the Quick Test has been performed and all fault codes

recorded, refer to the service code charts. The charts direct the use of specific pinpoint tests for the appropriate circuit and will allow complete circuit testing.

The EEC diagnostic connector is located at the left rear corner of the engine compartment on most vehicles except when equipped with the 1 .6L engine. The 1 .6L diagnostic connector is in the right rear corner of the engine compartment. When connecting the test equipment and adapters, note that the Self-Test Input (STI) connector is separate from the main diagnostic connector on all NON-NAAO engines except for the 1 .8L engine. The Self-Test Output (STO) connector is contained within the main diagnostic connector.

✳✳ CAUTION

To prevent injury and/or property damage, always block the drive wheels, firmly apply the parking brake, place the transmission in Park or Neutral and turn all electrical loads off before performing the Quick Test procedures.

Reading Codes With Analog Voltmeter

In the absence of a scan tool, an analog voltmeter may be used to retrieve stored fault codes. Set the meter range to read DC 0–20 volts. Connect the + lead of the meter to the STO pin in the diagnostic connector and connect the—lead of the meter to the negative battery terminal or a good engine ground.

Follow the directions given for performing the KOEO and KOER tests. To activate the tests, use a jumper wire to connect the STI connector to ground. The codes will be transmitted as groups of needle sweeps.

Code display patterns on an analog voltmeter

KEY ON ENGINE OFF (KOEO) TEST

1. Make certain the scan tool is OFF; connect it to the self-test connectors. Switch the scan tool to the MECS position. Except on 1 .8L engines, make certain the adapter ground cable is connected to the negative battery terminal. On the 1 .8L engine, make certain the switch on the adapter is set to EEC or ECA if engine codes are to be retrieved. The other switch position will retrieve codes from the 4EAT.

2. Make certain the scan tool test button is ON or latched down.

3. For all engine or 4EAT codes except 1 .8L and 1 .9L engines, turn the ignition switch ON but do not start the engine, then turn the scan tool ON. On 1 .8L and 1 .9L engines, turn the scan tool ON first, then turn the ignition switch ON.

4. Once energized, the tester should display 888 and beep for 2 seconds. Release the test button; 00 should appear, signifying the tool is ready to read codes.

5. Re-engage the test button.

6. The KOEO codes will be transmitted.

7. Record all service codes displayed.

8. After all codes are received, release the test button to review all the codes retained in tester memory.

9. Make sure all codes displayed are recorded. Clear the ECA memory and perform the KOEO test again. This will isolate hard faults from intermittent ones. Any hard faults will cause the code(s) to be repeated in the 2nd test. An intermittent which is not now present will not set a new code.

10. Record all codes from the 2nd test. After repairs are made on hard fault items, the intermittent ones must be recreated by tapping suspect sensors, wiggling wires or connectors or reproducing circumstances on a test drive.

➡**For both KOEO and KOER tests, the message STO LO always displayed on the screen indicates that the system cannot initiate the Self-Test. The message STI LO displayed with an otherwise blank screen indicates Pass or No Codes Stored.**

KEY ON ENGINE RUNNING (KOER) TEST

1. Make certain the self-test button is released or de-activated on the SUPER STAR II tester and that the tester is properly connected.

2. Start the engine and run it at 2000 rpm for 2 minutes. This action warms up the oxygen sensor.

3. Turn the ignition switch OFF.

4. Turn the ignition switch ON for 10 seconds but do not start the engine.

5. Start the engine and run it at idle.

6. Activate or latch the self-test button on the scan tool.

7. All relevant codes will be displayed and should be recorded.

SWITCH MONITOR TESTS

This test mode allows the operator to check the input signal from individual switches to the ECA. All switches to be tested must be OFF at the time the test begins; if one switch is on, it will affect the testing of another. The test must begin with the engine cool. The tests may be performed with either the SUPER STAR II tester or an analog voltmeter. When using the scan tool, the small LED on the

Switch	1.3L	1.8L	2.2L	2.2L Turbo	SUPER STAR II Tester LED or Analog VOM Indications
Clutch engage Switch/ Neutral Gear Switch (CES/NGS) (MTX only)	X	X	X	X	LED on or 12V in gear and clutch pedal released
Manual Lever Position Switch (MLP) (ATX Only)	X	X	X		LED on or 12V in P or N
Idle Switch (IDL)	X	X	X	X	LED on or 12V with accelerator pedal depressed
Brake On-Off Switch (BOO)	X	X MTX	X	X	LED on or 12V with brake pedal depressed
Headlamps Switch (HLDT)	X	X	X	X	LED on or 12V with headlamp switch on
Blower Motor Switch (BLMT)	X	X	X	X	LED on or 12V with blower switch at 2nd or above position
A/C Switch (ACS)	X	X			LED on or 12V with A/C switch on and blower on
Defrost Switch (DEF)	X	X	X	X	LED on or 12V with defrost switch on
Coolant Temperature Switch (CTS)	X	X		X	LED on or 12V with cooling fan on
Wide Open Throttle Switch (WOT)	X	X MTX			LED off or 0V with accelerator pedal fully depressed

79222G15

Switch tests for 1990 and early Ford Non-NAAO vehicles

Refer to the model specific sections for fuel system service procedures

Switch	1.3L	1.6L	1.8L	2.2L	2.2L Turbo	SUPER STAR II Tester LED or Analog VOM Indications
Clutch engage Switch/ Neutral Gear Switch (CES/NGS) (MTX only)	X	X	X	X	X	LED on or less than 1.5V in gear and clutch pedal released
Manual Lever Position Switch (MLP) (ATX Only)	X	X	X	X	X	LED on or less than 1.5V in P or N
Idle Switch (IDL)	X	X	X	X	X	LED on or less than 1.5V with accelerator pedal depressed
Brake On-Off Switch (BOO)	X	X	X MTX		X	LED on or less than 1.5V with brake pedal depressed (not fully)
Headlamps Switch (HLDT)	X	X	X	X	X	LED on or less than 1.5V with headlamp switch on
Blower Motor Switch (BLMT)	X	X	X	X	X	LED on or less than 1.5V with blower switch at 2nd or above position
A/C Switch (ACS)	X	X	X	X	X	LED on or less than 1.5V with A/C switch on and blower on
Defrost Switch (DEF)	X	X	X	X	X	LED on or less than 1.5V with defrost switch on
Coolant Temperature Switch (CTS)	X	X	X	X	X	LED on or less than 1.5V with cooling fan on
Wide Open Throttle Switch (WOT)	X		X			LED off or 0V with accelerator pedal fully depressed
Knock Control (KC)					X	LED on or less than 1.5V while tapping on engine

79222G16

Switch tests for 1991 and newer Ford Non-NAAO vehicles

adapter cable will light to show that the ECA has received the switch signal. If the voltmeter is used, the voltage will change when the switch is engaged or disengaged.

1. The engine must be off and cooled. Place the transmission in Park or Neutral.

2. Turn all accessories OFF.

3. If using the SUPER STAR II, connect it properly. If using an analog voltmeter, use a jumper to ground the STI terminal. Connect the positive (+) voltmeter lead to the SML terminal of the diagnostic connector and connect the negative (-) lead to a good engine ground.

4. Turn the ignition switch **ON**. Engage the center button on the SUPER STAR II. Most switches can be exercised without starting the engine.

5. Operate each switch according to the test chart and note the response either on the LED or the volt scale. Remember that an improper response means the ECA did not see the switch operation; check circuitry and connectors before assuming the switch is faulty.

6. Turn the ignition switch **OFF** when testing is complete.

Clearing Codes

Codes stored within the memory must be erased when repairs are completed. Additionally, erasing codes during diagnosis can separate hard faults from intermittent ones.

To erase stored codes, disconnect the negative battery cable, then depress the brake pedal for at least 10 seconds. Reconnect the battery cable and recheck the system for any remaining or newly-set codes.

MCU CARBURETED DIAGNOSTIC SYSTEM

The Microprocessor Control Unit (MCU) system was used on most 1981–83 carburetor equipped vehicles, and 1984 and newer V8 engines with feedback carburetors. The MCU system uses a large six sided connector, identical to the one used with EEC-IV systems. The MCU system does NOT use the small single wire connector, like the EEC-IV system.

This system has limited ability to diagnose a malfunction within itself. Through the use of trouble codes, the system will indicate where to test. When an analog voltmeter or special tester is connected to the diagnostic link connector and the system is triggered, the self-test simulates a variety of engine operating conditions and evaluates all the responses received from the various MCU components, so any abnormal operating conditions can be detected.

MCU CARBURETED SELF-DIAGNOSTICS

Diagnosis of a driveability problem requires attention to detail and following the diagnostic procedures in the correct order. Resist the temptation to begin extensive testing before completing the preliminary diagnostic steps. The preliminary or visual inspection must be completed in detail before diagnosis begins. In many cases this will shorten diagnostic time and often cure the problem without electronic testing.

Visual Inspection

This is possibly the most critical step of diagnosis. A detailed examination of all connectors, wiring and vacuum hoses can often lead to a repair without further diagnosis. Performance of this step relies on the skill of the technician performing it; a careful inspector will check the undersides of hoses as well as the integrity of hard-to-reach hoses blocked by the air cleaner or other components. Wiring should be checked carefully for any sign of strain , burning, crimping or terminal pull-out from a connector.

Checking connectors at components or in harnesses is required; usually, pushing them together will reveal a loose fit. Pay particular attention to ground circuits, making sure they are not loose or corroded. Remember to inspect connectors and hose fittings at components not mounted on the engine, such as the evaporative canister or relays mounted on the fender aprons. Any component or wiring in the vicinity of a fluid leak or spillage should be given extra attention during inspection.

Additionally, inspect maintenance items such as belt condition and tension, battery charge and condition and the radiator cap carefully. Any of these very simple items may affect the system enough to set a fault.

MCU CARBURETED READING CODES

Preparation For Reading Codes

1. Turn OFF all electrical equipment and accessories in vehicle.
2. Follow all safety precautions during testing.
3. Make sure all fluids are at proper levels.
4. Perform `Visual Inspection' as detailed in EEC-IV system testing, earlier in this section.
5. Start the engine and let it idle, until the engine reaches normal operating temperature. This is when the upper radiator hose is Hot and engine RPM has dropped to its normal warm idle speed.
6. Turn ignition switch OFF.

✵✵ CAUTION

Always operate the vehicle in a well ventilated area. Exhaust gases are very poisonous.

INLINE 4 AND 6 CYLINDER ENGINES

On Inline 4- and 6-cylinder engines with canister control valves, remove the hose that goes to the carbon canister (this simulates a clean carbon canister). Do NOT plug this hose for the remainder of the test procedure. Make certain the throttle linkage is off of the high choke cam setting.

The 2.3L engines with GK code, you must remove the cap from the anti-backfire vacuum switch tee during testing. The switch is near the rear of the MCU module. On 2.3L engines with an EGR vacuum load control (wide open throttle) valve, you must cover the atmospheric vent holes with a piece of tape.

During testing, disconnect the hose to the canister purge valve

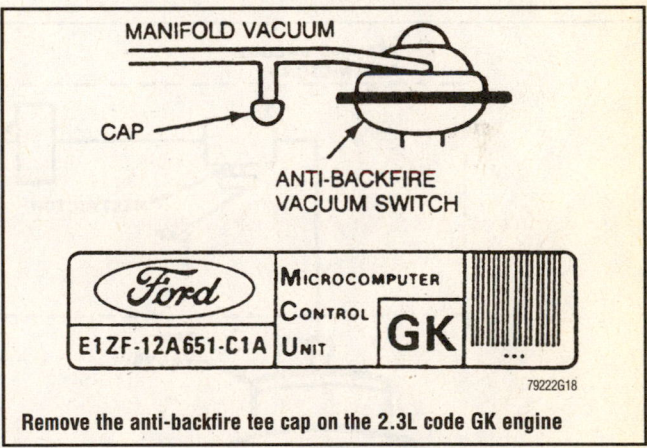

Remove the anti-backfire tee cap on the 2.3L code GK engine

Cover the EGR control valve vent holes with tape–2.3L engine

Refer to the model specific sections for engine electrical system service procedures

V6 AND V8 ENGINES

On V6 and V8 engines, remove the PCV valve from breather cap on valve cover. On the 4.2L and 5.8L engines with vacuum delay valves, uncap the restrictor on the thermactor vacuum control line. On the V6 4.2L engine the vacuum cap is on the TAD line on the 5.8L engine the vacuum cap is on the TAB line.

➡**Remember to replace vacuum lines, tee caps and return all components to original condition after testing is complete.**

After you have performed any special procedures for your vehicle, have a pencil and paper nearby to write down codes. Now you are ready to perform the KOEO test.

Using an Analog Voltmeter

KEY ON ENGINE OFF (KOEO) TEST

1. With the ignition switch in the **OFF** position, connect a jumper wire between circuits 60 and 201 on the self-test connector.

2. Connect the analog voltmeter from the battery positive post to the self-test output connector.

3. Self the voltmeter scale to 0-15 volt range.

4. Turn the ignition switch **ON**, but do NOT start the engine. One quick initialization pulse may occur. The output codes will follow in about 5 seconds.

5. Count the voltmeter sweeps, to determine which codes are being transmitted.

Connecting the analog voltmeter to the MCU diagnostic link connector

6. The MCU system uses 2-digit codes with the pause between each digit being about 2 seconds long. The pause between the two different codes is about 4 seconds long. The code group is sent twice. This allows you to check the accuracy of the codes as you record them.

7. Once this test has been performed and all fault codes recorded, you can refer to the `Code Descriptions' in this manual for

Remove the TAB or TAD tee vacuum cap—V6 and V8 engines

the meaning of the fault code(s). For more detailed code retrieval information and to repair faults refer to your specific vehicle service manual.

KEY ON ENGINE RUNNING (KOER) TEST

1. Turn OFF all electrical equipment and accessories in vehicle.
2. Follow all safety precautions during testing.
3. Make sure all fluids are at the proper levels.
4. Perform `Visual Inspection' as detailed earlier in this manual.

> ⚙ **CAUTION**
>
> **The following steps involve servicing the engine with the engine running. Observe safety precautions.**

- Apply the parking brake.
- Put the shift lever in P (automatic transmission) or NEUTRAL (manual transmission).
- Block the drive wheels.
- Always operate vehicle in well ventilated area. Exhaust gases are very poisonous.
- Stay clear of hot and moving engine parts.

5. The engine should be at normal operating temperature for this test. If not, start the engine and let it idle, until the engine reaches normal operating temperature. This is when the upper radiator hose is Hot and engine RPM has dropped to its normal warm idle speed and repeat Key ON Engine OFF test again.
6. If engine is warm, after codes have been retrieved, Start the engine.

> ⚙ **CAUTION**
>
> **Always operate the vehicle in a well ventilated area. Exhaust gases are very poisonous.**

7. To extract the fault codes:
   Inline 4- and 6-cylinder engines: Start the engine and raise the idle to 3000 RPM within 20 seconds of starting vehicle. Hold at 3000 RPM until codes are sent. When codes are sent release throttle and let engine return to idle speed.
   V6 and V8 engines: Start the engine are raise to 2000 RPM for 2 minutes and turn OFF ignition. Immediately re-start engine and allow to idle. Some engines equipped with throttle kicker will increase idle during the testing, this is normal.

8. If your vehicle is equipped with a knock sensor perform the following test, if not skip to Step 10.
   Simulate a spark knock by placing a 4 inch socket extension (or similar tool) on the manifold near the base of knock sensor. Tap on the end of extension lightly with a 2-6 oz. hammer for approximately 15 seconds. Do NOT hit on the knock sensor itself. Count the voltmeter sweeps to determine which codes are being sent.

9. The first series of sweeps should be the engine ID code, ignore any sweeps that last any longer than 1 second. The engine ID code will be ½ the number of cylinders. For example, a 4 cylinder would appear as 2 sweeps and a 6 cylinder as 3 sweeps and an 8 cylinder as 4 sweeps.

10. If no sweeps occur repeat KOER test procedures, starting with Step 1. If the meter still does not sweep, you have a problem which must be repaired before proceeding. Refer to your specific vehicle service manual.

11. Count the sweeps on the meter to find out which codes are being sent. All codes are 2-digits long and will appear the same way as in KOEO Self-Test. Ignore any sweeps lasting more than 1 second. Write codes down on a piece of paper, codes will be sent twice so you can check your list for accuracy. Write codes down in the order they appear. Turn the ignition switch OFF when codes are finished and remove jumper wire.

DIAGNOSTIC TROUBLE CODES (DTC'S)

MCU System

The code definitions listed are general for Ford Vehicles using the Microprocessor Control Unit (MCU) engine control system. Most Ford vehicles up to 1983 and feedback carburetor equipped V8 engines into the 1990's use the MCU engine control system. For a specific code definition or component test procedure consult service manual for your vehicle. A diagnostic code does not mean the component is defective. For example a Code 44 is an oxygen sensor code (rich oxygen sensor signal). This code may set if a carburetor is flooding or has a very restricted air cleaner. Replacing the oxygen sensor would not fix the problem.

➡**When the term Powertrain Control Module (PCM) is used in this manual it will refer to the engine control computer regardless that it may be a Powertrain Control Module (PCM) or Electronic Control Module (ECM) or Electronic Control Assembly (ECA).**

Code 11 System Pass—Except High Altitude—or Altitude (ALT) circuit is open—High Altitude

Code 12 RPM out of specification (throttle kicker system)

Code 25 Knock Sensor (KS) signal is not detected during Key On Engine Running (KOER) Self-Test

Code 33 Key On Engine Running (KOER) Self-Test not initiated

Code 41 Oxygen sensor voltage signal always Lean (low value)—does not switch

Code 42 Oxygen sensor voltage signal always Rich (high value) -does not switch

Code 44 Oxygen sensor signal indicates Rich—excessive fuel, restricted air intake—or Inoperative Thermactor System

Code 45 Thermactor Air flow is always upstream (going into exhaust manifold)

Code 46 Thermactor Air System unable to bypass air (vent to atmosphere)

Code 51 Low or Mid Temperature vacuum switch circuit is open when engine is hot on Inline 4 and 6 cylinder engines—or HI or HI/LOW vacuum switch circuit is always open on V6 or V8 engines

Code 52 Idle Tracking Switch (ITS) voltage does not change from closed to open throttle (Closed throttle checked during KOEO condition. Open throttle checked during KOER conditions) on 4 cylinder car—or Idle/Decel Vacuum switch circuit always open -on 4 cylinder truck—or Wide Open Throttle vacuum switch circuit always open—on Inline 6 cylinder engine

Code 53 Wide Open Throttle vacuum switch circuit always open on 4 cylinder engine—or Crowd vacuum switch circuit is always open—on Inline 6 cylinder engine—or Dual temperature switch circuit is always open -on V6 and V8 engines

Code 54 Mid temperature switch circuit is always open

Code 55 Road load vacuum switch circuit is always open—on 4 cylinder engine—or Mid vacuum switch circuit is always open—on V6 and V8 engines

Code 56 Closed throttle vacuum switch circuit is always open

Code 61 Hi/Low Vacuum switch circuit is always closed

Code 62 Idle Tracking Switch (ITS) circuit is closed at idle—or Idle/Decel vacuum switch circuit is always closed—on 4 cylinder car -or Wide Open Throttle vacuum switch circuit always closed—on 4 cylinder truck—or System Pass—High Altitude; Altitude (ALT) circuit is open except High Altitude on V6 and V8 engines

Code 63 Wide Open Throttle (WOT) vacuum switch circuit is always closed—on 4 cylinder engine—or Crowd vacuum switch circuit is always closed -on 6 cylinder engine

Code 65 System pass—on 4 cylinder engine (High Altitude)—or Altitude (ALT) circuit is open—4 cylinder engine (except High Altitude)—or Mid vacuum circuit is always closed—V6 and V8 engines

Code 66 Closed Throttle Vacuum switch circuit is always closed

➡This list is for reference and does not mean a specific component is defective. NOTE: High Altitude refers to vehicles with computer adjusted for operation at high elevations as in mountain regions.

EEC-IV System

The code definitions listed general 2-digit codes for Ford Vehicles using the Ford EEC-IV engine control system. In 1991 Ford started introducing vehicles that use 3-digit codes. The code definitions for both the 2 and 3-digit codes are found in this section. For a specific code definition or component test procedure consult your `Chilton Total Car Care' manual for your vehicle. A diagnostic code does not mean the component is defective. For example a Code 29 is a vehicle speed sensor code. This does not mean the sensor is defective, but to check the sensor and related components. A defective speedometer cable or transmission problem will also set this code.

➡'When the term Powertrain Control Module (PCM) is used in this manual it will refer to the engine control computer regardless that it may be a PCM or Electronic Control Module (ECM) or Electronic Control Assembly (ECA).

2-DIGIT DTC'S

1981–94 PASSENGER CARS AND 1984–94 LIGHT TRUCKS:

Code 11 System Pass

Code 12 (R) Idle control fault—RPM Unable To Reach Upper Limit Self-Test

Code 13 (C) DC Motor Did Follow Dashpot

Code 13 (O) DC Motor Did Not Move

Code 13 (R) Idle control fault—Cannot control RPM during Self-Test low RPM check

Code 14(C)—Engine RPM signal fault—Profile Ignition Pickup (PIP) circuit failure or RPM sensor.

Code 15 (C) EEC Processor, power to Keep Alive Memory (KAM) interrupted or test failed

Code 15 (O) Power Interrupted To Processor or EEC Processor ROM Test failure

Code 16 (O,R) RPM too low to perform Exhaust Gas Oxygen (EGO) sensor test or fuel control error.

Code 1 (O)7 CFI Fuel Control System fault—Rich/Lean condition indicated; 3.8L V-6/5.0LV-8 (1984).

Code 17 (R) RPM Below Self-Test Limit, Set Too Low. Code 18 (C)—Ignition diagnostic monitor (1DM) circuit failure, loss of RPM signal or SPOUT circuit grounded

Code 18 (O)—Ignition Diagnostic Monitor (1DM) circuit

Code 18 (R) SPOUT or SAW circuit open

Code 19 (C) Cylinder Identification (CID) Sensor Input failure

Code 19 (O) Failure in EEC Processor internal voltage. Code 19 (R)—Erratic RPM During EGR Test or RPM Too Low During ISC Off Test

Code 21 Engine Coolant Temperature (ECT) out of Self-Test range

Code 22 (O, R) Manifold Absolute Pressure (MAP)/Barometric Pressure (BP/BARO) Sensor circuit out of Self-Test range

Code 23 Throttle Position (TP) Sensor out of Self-Test range

Code 24 (O, R) Air Charge (ACT) or Intake Air (IAT) Temperature out of Self-Test range

Code 25 (R) Knock not sensed during dynamic response test

Code 26 (O, R) Transmission Fluid Temp (TFT) out of Self-Test range

Code 26 (O, R) Vane Air (VAF) or Mass Air (MAF) sensor out of self-test range

Code 28 (C) Loss Of Primary Tach, Right Side. Code 29 (C)—Insufficient input from Vehicle Speed Sensor (VSS) or Programmable Speedometer/Odometer Module (PSOM)

Code 31 EGR valve position sensor circuit below minimum voltage

Code 32 EGR Valve Position (EVP) sensor circuit voltage below closed limit

Code 33 (C) Throttle Position (TP) sensor noisy/harsh on line

Code 33 (R, C) EGR valve position sensor circuit, EGR valve opening not detected

Code 34 EGR valve circuit out of self-test range or valve not closing

Code 35 EGR valve circuit above maximum voltage -except 2.3L HSC with Feedback Carburetor System—or—Throttle Kicker on 2.3L HSC with Feedback Carburetor System.

Code 38 (C) Idle Track Switch Circuit Open. Code 39 (C)—AXOD Torque Converter or Bypass Clutch Not Applying Properly

Code 41 (R,C) Oxygen Sensor circuit indicates system always lean

Code 42 (R,C) Oxygen Sensor circuit indicates system always rich, right side if 2 sensors used

Code 43 (C) Oxygen Sensor Out Of Test Range—on 1992 and earlier vehicles—or—Throttle Position Sensor failure—on 1993 and newer vehicles

Code 43 (R) Exhaust Gas Oxygen (EGO) sensor cool down has occurred during testing—2.3L HSC and 2.8L FBC truck

Code 44 (R) Air injection control system failure (right side cylinders, if a split system)

Code 45 (C) Coil 1 primary circuit failure

Code 45 (R) Air injection control system air flow misdirected

Code 46 (C) Coil Primary Circuit failure

Code 46 (R) Thermactor air not bypassed during Self-Test

Code 47 (C) 4x4 switch is closed—on Truck.

Code 47 (R) Airflow low at idle—on fuel injected engines—or—4 x 4 switch is closed—on Truck—or—Fuel control system/Exhaust Gas Oxygen (EGO) Sensor fault—on 2.3L HSC and 2.8L FBC truck

Code 48 (C) Coil Primary Circuit failure; Except 2.3L Truck—or—Loss Of Secondary Tach, Left Side—with 2.3L Truck engine

Code 48 Airflow high at base idle

Code 49 (C) El˽ electronic Transmission Shift Error—on Truck and 1992 and later cars—or—SPOUT Signal Defaulted To 10 Degrees BTDC or SPOUT Open—Up to 1991 passenger cars

Code 51 (O, C) Engine Coolant Temperature (ECT) circuit open or out of range during self-test

Code 52 (O) Power Steering Pressure Switch (PSPS) circuit open

Code 52 (R) Power Steering Pressure Switch (PSPS) circuit did not change states

Code 53 (O, C) Throttle Position (TP) circuit above maximum voltage

Code 54 (O, C) Air Charge (ACT) or Intake Air (IAT) Temperature circuit open

Code 55 (R) Key Power Input To Processor—open circuit

Code 56 (O, C) Mass Air (MAF) or Vane Air (VAF) Flow circuit above maximum voltage—Port fuel injected engines—or—Transmission oil temperature (TOT) circuit open—on vehicles with automatic transaxle

Code 57 (C) AXOD Circuit failure—on vehicles with automatic overdrive transaxle—or—Octane Adjust Circuit failure—on some 1992 and newer cars

Code 58 (R) Idle Tracking Switch circuit fault.

Code 59 (C) Automatic Transmission Shift Error—on 1991 and newer—or—AXOD 4/3 or Neutral Pressure Switch Failed Open—on 3.0L EFI and 3.8L AXOD—vehicles with automatic overdrive transaxle

Code 59 (O) AXOD 4/3 Pressure Switch Failed Closed -on 3.8L engine AXOD—vehicles with automatic transaxle—or—Idle Adjust Service Pin In Use—on 2.9L EFI engine—or—Low Speed Fuel Pump Circuit failure—on 3.0L SHO engine

Code 61 (O, C) Engine Coolant Temperature (ECT) circuit grounded

Code 62 (C) Converter clutch error

Code 62 (O) Electronic Transmission Shift Error. Code 63 (O, C)—Throttle Position (TP) circuit below minimum voltage

Code 64 (O, C) Air Charge (ACT) or Intake Air (IAT) Temperature circuit grounded

Code 65 (C) Fuel System Failed To Enter Closed Loop Mode or key power

Code 65 (O) Key Power Check—Possible Charging System overvoltage condition

Code 65 (R) Overdrive Cancel Switch (OCS) circuit did not switch

Code 66 (C) Mass Air (MAF) or Vane Air (VAF) Flow circuit below minimum voltage—engine with Port fuel injection—or—Transmission Oil Temperature (TOT) circuit grounded—vehicles with automatic transaxle

Code 67 (O, C) Manual Lever Position (MLP) sensor out of range and A/C ON

Code 67 (O, C) Neutral/Drive Switch (NDS) circuit open/A/C on during Self-Test

Code 67 (O, R) Neutral Drive Circuit Failed or A/C Input High -or—Clutch Switch Circuit failed—on vehicles with manual transaxle -or—Manual Lever Position Sensor out of range—on vehicles with automatic transaxle

Code 68 (C) Transmission Fluid Temp (TFT) transmission over temp (over heated)

Code 68 (O) Idle Tracking Switch circuit—on 2.8L FBC truck only—or—Air temperature sensor—except FBC truck.

Code 68 (R,C) Air Temperature Sensor Circuit failure -on 1.9L EFI engine—or—Idle Tracking Switch Circuit failure—on CFI engine—or—Transmission Temperature Circuit

Code 69 (O, C) Transmission Shift Error

Code 70 (C) Data Communications Link Circuit failure

Code 71(C) Software Re-Initialization Detected—on 1 .9L EFI and 2.3L Turbo—or—Idle Tracking Switch failure—on CFI

engine—or -Message Center Control Circuit failure—on vehicles with Message Center Control Center—or—Power Interrupt Detected—except vehicles with 3.8L AXOD (automatic overdrive transaxle)

Code 72 (R) Insufficient Manifold Absolute Pressure (MAP) change during Dynamic Response Test

Code 73 (R) Insufficient Throttle Position (TP) change during Dynamic Response Test

Code 74 (R,C) Brake On/Off (BOO) circuit open/not actuated during Self-Test

Code 75 (R) Brake On/Off (BOO) circuit closed/EEC processor input open

Code 76 (R) Insufficient Airflow Output Change During Test

Code 77 (R) Brief Wide Open Throttle (WOT) not sensed during Self-Test/operator error (Dynamic Response/Cylinder Balance Tests)

Code 78 (C) Power Interrupt Detected

Code 79 (O) A/C on/Defrost on during Self-Test

Code 81(C) MAP Sensor Has Not Changing Normally

Code 81(O) Air Management Circuit failure

Code 82 (O) Supercharger Bypass Circuit failure, 3.8L SC engine—or—Air Management Circuit failure, Except 3.8L SC engine—or -EGR Solenoid Circuit failure, 2.3L OHC engine

Code 83 OIC—Low speed fuel pump relay circuit failure

Code 83 (O) High Speed Electro Drive Fan Circuit failure, Except 2.3L OHC and 3.0L SHO engine—or—Low Speed Fuel Pump Relay Circuit failure, 3.0L SHO engine

Code 84 (O) EGR Vacuum Regulator (EVR) circuit failure

Code 84 (R) EGR Solenoid Circuit failure

Code 85 (C) Adaptive Lean Limit Reached

Code 85 (O) Canister Purge (CANP) circuit failure

Code 86 (C) Adaptive Rich Limit Reached

Code 86 (O) Shift Solenoid (SS) circuit failure—or—Wide Open Throttle (WOT) A/C Cutoff Solenoid circuit—on Carbureted engine

Code 87 Fuel Pump circuit fault

Code 88 (C) Loss Of Dual Plug Input control

Code 88 (O) Electro Drive Fan Circuit failure—fuel injected engine—or—Throttle Kicker, feedback carburetor system

Code 89 (O) Transmission solenoid circuit failure. **Code 89 (O)** Clutch Converter Override (CCO) circuit failure—or—Exhaust Heat Control (EHC) Solenoid circuit—3.8L CFI engine

Code 91(C) No Heated Exhaust Gas Oxygen (HEGO) sensor switching detected—left HEGO

Code 91(O) Shift Solenoid 1 (SS1) circuit failure.

Code 91(R) Heated Exhaust Gas Oxygen (H EGO) sensor circuit indicates system lean—left HEGO

Code 92 (O) Shift Solenoid Circuit failure

Code 92 (R) Oxygen Sensor Circuit failure

Code 93 (O) Throttle Position Sensor (TPS) input low at maximum DC motor extension—OR—Shift solenoid circuit failure

Code 93 (O) Coast Clutch Solenoid (CCS) circuit failure

Code 94 (O) Torque Converter Clutch (TCC) solenoid circuit failure

Code 94 (O) Converter Clutch Control (CCC) Solenoid circuit failure

Code 94 (R) Thermactor Air System inoperative, left side

Code 95 (O, C) Fuel Pump secondary circuit failure/Fuel Pump circuit open—EEC processor to motor ground

Code 96 (O, C) Fuel Pump secondary circuit failure/Fuel Pump circuit open—battery to EEC processor

Ignition system service is covered in the model specific sections of this manual

Code 97 (O) Overdrive Cancel Indicator Light (OCIL) circuit failure

Code 98 (R) Electronic control assembly failure

Code 98 (O)—Electronic Pressure Control (EPC) Driver open in EEC processor

Code 98 (R) Hard fault is present—FMEM mode

Code 99 (0,C) Electronic Pressure Control (EPC) circuit failure

Code 92 (O) Shift Solenoid 2 (SS2) circuit failure

Code 92 (R) Heated Exhaust Gas Oxygen (HEGO) sensor circuit indicates system rich—left HEGO

Code 93 (O) Throttle Position Sensor Input Low At Max DC Motor Extension, CFI engine—or—Shift Solenoid Circuit failure—Except CFI engine

Code 94 (O) Converter Clutch Solenoid Circuit failure

Code 94 (R) Thermactor Air System Inoperative

Code 95 (O, C) Fuel Pump Circuit failure, ECA To ground

Code 96 (O, C) Fuel Pump Circuit failure

Code 97 (O) Transmission Indicator Circuit failure

Code 98 (O) Electronic Pressure Control Circuit failure

Code 98 (R) Electronic Control Assembly failure

Code 99 (O, C) Electronic Pressure Control Circuit or Transmission Shift failure

Code 99 (R) EEC System Has Not Learned To Control Idle: Ignore Codes 12 & 13

No Code–Unable to Run Self Test or Output Codes, or list does not apply to vehicle tested, refer to service manual.

➡**This list is to be used as a reference for testing and does not mean a specific component Is defective.**

(O)—Key On, Engine Off
(R)—Engine running
(C)—Continuous Memory

3-DIGIT DTC'S

1991–95 VEHICLES:
Code 111 System pass
Code 112 Intake Air Temperature (IAT) Sensor circuit below minimum voltage
Code 113 Intake Air Temperature (IAT) Sensor circuit above maximum voltage
Code 114 Intake Air Temperature (IAT) higher or lower than expected
Code 116 Engine Coolant Temperature (ECT) higher or lower than expected
Code 117 Engine Coolant Temperature (ECT) Sensor circuit below minimum voltage
Code 118 Engine Coolant Temperature (ECT) Sensor circuit above maximum voltage
Code 121 Closed throttle voltage higher or lower than expected
Code 121 Indicates Throttle Position voltage inconsistent with Mass Air Flow (MAF) Sensor
Code 122 Throttle Position (TP) Sensor circuit below minimum voltage
Code 123 Throttle Position (TP) Sensor circuit above maximum voltage
Code 124 Throttle Position (TP) Sensor circuit voltage higher than expected
Code 125 Throttle Position (TP) Sensor circuit voltage lower than expected
Code 126 Manifold Absolute Pressure/Barometric Pressure (MAP/BARO) Sensor higher or lower than expected

Code 128 Manifold Absolute Pressure (MAP) Sensor vacuum hose damaged/disconnected

Code 129 Insufficient Manifold Absolute Pressure (MAP)/Mass Air Flow (MAF) change during Dynamic Response Test-KOER

Code 136 Lack of Heated Oxygen Sensor (HO2S-2) switches during KOER, indicates lean—Bank # 2

Code 137 Lack of Heated Oxygen Sensor (HO2S-2) switches during KOER, indicates rich—Bank # 2

Code 138 Cold Start Injector (CSI) flow insufficient—KOER

Code 139 No Heated Oxygen Sensor (HO2S-2) switches detected—Bank # 2

Code 141 Fuel system indicates lean

Code 144 No Heated Oxygen Sensor (HO2S-1) switches detected—Bank # 1

Code 157 Mass Air Flow (MAF) Sensor circuit below minimum voltage

Code 158 Mass Air Flow (MAF) Sensor circuit above maximum voltage

Code 159 Mass Air Flow (MAF) higher or lower than expected

Code 167 Insufficient Throttle Position (TP) change during Dynamic Response Test—KOER

Code 171 Fuel system at adaptive limits, Heated Oxygen Sensor (HO2S-I) unable to switch—Bank # 1

Code 172 Lack of Heated Oxygen Sensor (HO2S-1) switches, indicates lean—Bank # 1

Code 173 Lack of Heated Oxygen Sensor (HO2S-1) switches, indicates rich—Bank # 1

Code 174 Heated Oxygen Sensor (HO2S) switching time is slow—Right side—1992 vehicles only

Code 175 Fuel system at adaptive limits, Heated Oxygen Sensor (HO2S-2) unable to switch—Bank # 2

Code 176 Lack of Heated Oxygen Sensor (HO2S-2) switches, indicates lean—Bank # 2

Code 177 Lack of Heated Oxygen Sensor (HO2S-2) switches, indicates rich—Bank # 2

Code 178 Heated Oxygen Sensor (HO2S) switching time is slow—Left side—1992 vehicles only

Code 179 Fuel system at lean adaptive limit at part throttle, system rich—Bank # 1

Code 181 Fuel system at rich adaptive limit at part throttle, system lean—Bank # 1

Code 182 Fuel system at lean adaptive limit at idle, system rich—Right side—1992 vehicles only

Code 183 Fuel system at rich adaptive limit at idle, system lean—Right side—1992 vehicles only

Code 184 Mass Air Flow (MAF) higher than expected

Code 185 Mass Air Flow (MAF) lower than expected

Code 186 Injector pulse width higher or Mass Air Flow (MAF) lower than expected (without BARO Sensor)

Code 187 Injector pulse width lower than expected (with BARO Sensor)

Code 187 Injector pulse width lower or Mass Air Flow (MAF) higher than expected (without BARO Sensor)

Code 188 Fuel system at lean adaptive limit at part throttle, system rich—Bank # 2

Code 189 Fuel system at rich adaptive limit at part throttle, system lean—Bank # 2

Code 191 Adaptive fuel lean limit is reached at idle -Left side—1992 vehicles only

Code 192 Adaptive fuel rich limit is reached at idle—Left side—1992 vehicles only

Code 193 Flexible Fuel (FF) Sensor circuit failure

Code 211 Profile Ignition Pickup (PIP) circuit failure

Code 212 Loss of Ignition Diagnostic monitor (1DM) input to Powertrain Control Module (PCM)/SPOUT circuit grounded

Code 213 SPOUT circuit open

Code 214 Cylinder Identification (CID) circuit failure

Code 215 Powertrain Control Module (PCM) detected Coil 1 Primary circuit failure (EI)

Code 216 Powertrain Control Module (PCM) detected Coil 2 Primary circuit failure (EI)

Code 217 Powertrain Control Module (PCM) detected Coil 3 Primary circuit failure (EI)

Code 218 Loss of Ignition Diagnostic Monitor (1DM) signal left side (dual plug EI)

Code 219 Spark Timing defaulted to 10 degrees -SPOUT circuit open (EI)

Code 221 Spark Timing error (EI)

Code 222 Loss of Ignition Diagnostic Monitor (1DM) signal - right side (dual plug EI)

Code 223 Loss of Dual Plug Inhibit (DPI) control (Dual Plug EI)

Code 224 Powertrain Control Module (PCM) detected Coil 1,2,3,or 4 Primary circuit failure (Dual Plug EI)

Code 225 Knock not sensed during Dynamic Response Test—KOER

Code 226 Ignition Diagnostic Monitor (1DM) signal not received (EI)

Code 232 Powertrain Control Module (PCM) detected Coil 1,2,3,or 4 Primary circuit failure (EI)

Code 238 Powertrain Control Module (PCM) detected Coil 4 Primary circuit failure (EI)

Code 241 Ignition Control Module (1CM) to Powertrain Control Module (PCM) Ignition Diagnostic Monitor (1DM) Pulse Width Transmission error (EI)

Code 244 Cylinder Identification (CID) circuit fault present when Cylinder Balance Test requested

Code 311 Secondary Air Injection (AIR) system inoperative during KOER Bank # 1 with dual HO$_2$S

Code 312 Secondary Air Injection (AIR) misdirected during KOER

Code 313 Secondary Air Injection (AIR) not bypassed during KOER

Code 314 Secondary Air Injection (AIR) system inoperative during KOER—Bank # 2 with dual HO$_2$S

Code 326 EGR (PFE/DPFE) circuit voltage lower than expected

Code 327 EGR (EVP/PFE/DPFE) circuit below minimum voltage

Code 328 EGR (EVP) closed valve voltage lower than expected

Code 332 Insufficient EGR flow detected/EGR Valve opening not detected (EVP/PFE/DPFE)

Code 334 EGR (EVP) closed valve voltage higher than expected

Code 335 EGR (PFE/DPFE) Sensor voltage higher or lower than expected during KOEO

Code 336 Exhaust pressure high/EGR (PFE/DPFE) circuit voltage higher than expected

Code 337 EGR (EVP/PFE/DPFE) circuit above maximum voltage

Code 338 Engine Coolant Temperature (ECT) lower than expected (thermostat test)

Code 339 Engine Coolant Temperature (ECT) higher than expected (thermostat test)

Code 341 Octane Adjust service pin open

Code 411 Cannot control RPM during KOER low rpm check

Code 412 Cannot control RPM during KOER high rpm check

Code 415 Idle Air Control (IAC) system at maximum adaptive lower limit

Code 416 Idle Air Control (IAC) system at upper adaptive learning limit

Code 452 Insufficient input from Vehicle Speed Sensor (VSS) to PCM

Code 453 Servo leaking down (KOER IVSC test)

Code 454 Servo leaking up (KOER IVSC test)

Code 455 Insufficient RPM increase (KOER IVSC test)

Code 456 Insufficient RPM decrease (KOER IVSC test)

Code 457 Speed Control Command Switch(s) circuit not functioning (KOEO IVSC test)

Code 458 Speed Control Command Switch(s) stuck/circuit grounded (KOEO IVSC test)

Code 459 Speed Control ground circuit open (KOEO IVSC test)

Code 511 Powertrain Control Module (PCM) Read Only Memory (ROM) test failure (KOEO)

Code 512 Powertrain Control Module (PCM) Keep Alive Memory (KAM) test failure

Code 513 Powertrain Control Module (PCM) internal voltage failure (KOEO)

Code 519 Power Steering Pressure (PSP) Switch circuit open—KOEO

Code 521 Power Steering Pressure (PSP) Switch circuit did not change states—KOER

Code 522 Vehicle not in park or neutral during KOEO/Park/Neutral Position (PNP) Switch circuit open

Code 524 Low speed Fuel Pump circuit open—battery to PCM

Code 525 Indicates vehicle in gear/A/C on

Code 526 Neutral Pressure Switch (NPS) circuit closed; A/C on -1992 vehicles only

Code 527 Park/Neutral Position (PNP) Switch open—A/C on, KOEO

Code 528 Clutch Pedal Position (CPP) switch circuit failure

Code 529 Data Communications Link (DCL) or PCM circuit failure

Code 532 Cluster Control Assembly (CCA) circuit failure

Code 533 Data Communications Link (DCL) or Electronic Instrument Cluster (EIC) circuit failure

Code 536 Brake On/Off (BOO) circuit failure/not actuated during KOER

Code 538 Insufficient RPM change during KOER Dynamic Response Test

Code 538 Invalid Cylinder Balance Test due to throttle movement during test—SFI only

Code 538 Invalid Cylinder Balance test due to Cylinder Identification (CID) circuit failure

Code 539 A/C on/Defrost on during Self-Test

Code 542 Fuel Pump secondary circuit failure

Code 543 Fuel Pump secondary circuit failure

Code 551 Idle Air Control (IAC) circuit failure—KOEO

Code 552 Secondary Air Injection Bypass (AIRB) circuit failure -KOEO

Code 553 Secondary Air Injection Diverter (AIRD) circuit failure—KOEO

Code 554 Fuel Pressure Regulator Control (FPRC) circuit failure

Code 556 Fuel Pump Relay primary circuit failure

Code 557 Low speed Fuel Pump primary circuit failure

Code 558 EGR Vacuum Regulator (EVR) circuit failure -KOEO

Code 559 Air Conditioning On (ACON) Relay circuit failure-KOEO

Code 563 High Fan Control (HFC) circuit failure—KOEO

Code 564 Fan Control (FC) circuit failure—KOEO

Code 565 Canister Purge (CANP) circuit failure—KOEO

Code 566 3-4 Shift Solenoid circuit failure, A4LD transmission -KOEO

Code 567 Speed Control Vent (SCVNT) circuit failure -KOEO IVSC test

Code 568 Speed Control Vacuum (SCVAC) circuit failure—KOEO IVSC test

Code 569 Auxiliary Canister Purge (CANP2) circuit failure-KOEO

Code 571 EGRA solenoid circuit failure KOEO

Code 572 EGRV solenoid circuit failure KOEO

Code 578 A/C Pressure Sensor circuit shorted (VCRM) mode

Code 579 Insufficient A/C pressure change (VCRM) mode

Code 581 Power to fan circuit over current (VCRM) mode

Code 582 Fan circuit open (VCRM) mode

Code 583 Power to Fuel Pump over current (VCRM) mode

Code 584 Power ground circuit open (Pin 1) (VCRM) mode

Code 585 Power to A/C Clutch over current (VCRM) mode

Code 586 A/C Clutch circuit open (VCRM) mode

Code 587 Variable Control Relay Module (VCRM) communication failure

Code 593 Heated Oxygen Sensor Heater (HO$_2$S HTR)

Code 617 1-2 Shift error

Code 618 2-3 Shift error

Code 619 3-4 Shift error

Code 621 Shift Solenoid 1 (SS1) circuit failure—KOEO

Code 622 Shift Solenoid 2 (SS2) circuit failure—KOEO

Code 623 Transmission Control Indicator Lamp (TCIL) circuit failure

Code 624 Electronic Pressure Control (EPC) circuit failure

Code 625 Electronic Pressure Control (EPC) driver open in PCM

Code 626 Coast Clutch Solenoid (CCS) circuit failure—KOEO

Code 627 Torque Converter Clutch (TCC) solenoid circuit failure

Code 628 Excessive Converter Clutch slippage

Code 629 Torque Converter Clutch (TCC) solenoid circuit failure

Code 631 Transmission Control Indicator Lamp (TCIL) circuit failure—KOEO

Code 632 Transmission Control Switch (TCS) circuit did not change states during KOER

Code 633 4 x 4L Switch closed during KOEO

Code 634 Manual Lever Position (MLP) voltage higher or lower than expected/ error in Transmission Select Switch (TSS) circuit(s)

Code 636 Transmission Oil Temperature (TOT) higher or lower than expected

Code 637 Transmission Oil Temperature (TOT) Sensor circuit above maximum voltage/circuit open

Code 638 Transmission Oil Temperature (TOT) Sensor circuit below minimum voltage/circuit shorted

Code 639 Insufficient input from Transmission Speed Sensor (TSS)

Code 641 Shift Solenoid 3 (SS3) circuit failure

Code 643 Torque Converter Clutch (TCC) circuit failure

Code 645 Incorrect gear ratio obtained for first gear

Code 646 Incorrect gear ratio obtained for second gear

Code 647 Incorrect gear ratio obtained for third gear

Code 648 Incorrect gear ratio obtained for fourth gear

Code 649 Electronic Pressure Control (EPC) higher or lower than expected

Code 651 Electronic Pressure Control (EPC) circuit failure

Code 652 Torque Converter Clutch (TCC) Solenoid circuit failure

Code 654 Manual Lever Position (MLP) Sensor not indicating park during KOEO

Code 655 Manual Lever Position (MLP) Sensor indicating not in neutral during Self-Test

Code 656 Torque Converter Clutch (TCC) continuous slip error

Code 657 Transmission Over Temperature condition occurred

Code 659 High vehicle speed in park indicated

Code 667 Transmission Range sensor circuit voltage below minimum voltage

Code 668 Transmission Range sensor circuit voltage above maximum voltage

Code 675 Transmission Range sensor circuit voltage out of range

Code 691 4x4 Low switch open or short circuit

Code 692 Transmission state does not match calculated ratio

Code 998 Hard fault present—FMEM Mode

➡️If specific cylinder banks or sides are referred to in any of the above codes, but the vehicle code is being obtained from has a 4 cylinder engine, or only one Oxygen Sensor, disregard the bank side reference, but the code definition and components it pertains to is always the same.

EEC-V System

1994 PASSENGER CARS AND LIGHT TRUCKS

DTC P0102 Mass Air Flow (MAF) Sensor circuit low input

DTC P0103 Mass Air Flow (MAF) Sensor circuit high input

DTC P0112 Intake Air Temperature (IAT) Sensor circuit low input

DTC P0113 Intake Air Temperature (IAT) Sensor high input

DTC P0117 Engine Coolant Temperature (ECT) low input

DTC P0118 Engine Coolant Temperature (ECT) Sensor circuit high input

DTC P0122 Throttle Position (TP) Sensor circuit low input

DTC P0123 Throttle Position (TP) Sensor high input

DTC P0125 Insufficient coolant temperature to enter closed loop fuel control

DTC P0132 Upstream Heated Oxygen Sensor (HO$_2$S 11) circuit high voltage (Bank #1)

DTC P0135 Heated Oxygen Sensor Heater (HTR 11) circuit malfunction

DTC P0138 Downstream Heated Oxygen Sensor (HO$_2$S 12) circuit high voltage (Bank #1)

DTC P0140 Heated Oxygen Sensor (HO$_2$S 12) circuit no activity detected (Bank #1)

DTC P0141 Heated Oxygen Sensor Heater (HTR 12) circuit malfunction

DTC P0152 Upstream Heated Oxygen Sensor (HO$_2$S 21) circuit high voltage (Bank #2)

DTC P0155 Heated Oxygen Sensor Heater (HTR 21) circuit malfunction

DTC P0158 Downstream Heated Oxygen Sensor (HO$_2$S 22) circuit high voltage (Bank #2)

DTC P0160 Heated Oxygen Sensor (HO$_2$S 12) circuit no activity detected (Bank #2)

DTC P0161 Heated Oxygen Sensor Heater (HTR 22) circuit malfunction

DTC P0171 System (adaptive fuel) too lean (Bank #1)

DTC P0172 System (adaptive fuel) too lean (Bank #1)

DTC P0174 System (adaptive fuel) too lean (Bank #1)

DTC P0175 System (adaptive fuel) too lean (Bank #1)

DTC P0300 Random misfire detected

DTC P0301 Cylinder #1 misfire detected

DTC P0302 Cylinder #2 misfire detected

DTC P0303 Cylinder #3 misfire detected

DTC P0304 Cylinder #4 misfire detected

DTC P0305 Cylinder #5 misfire detected

DTC P0306 Cylinder #6 misfire detected

DTC P0307 Cylinder #7 misfire detected

DTC P0308 Cylinder #8 misfire detected

DTC P0320 Ignition engine speed (Profile Ignition Pickup) input circuit malfunction

DTC P0340 Camshaft Position (CMP) sensor circuit malfunction (CID)

DTC P0402 Exhaust Gas Recirculation (EGR) excess flow detected (valve open at idle)

DTC P0420 Catalyst system efficiency below threshold (Bank #1)

DTC P0430 Catalyst system efficiency below threshold (Bank #2)

DTC P0443 Evaporative emission control system Canister Purge (CANP) Control Valve circuit malfunction

DTC P0500 Vehicle Speed Sensor (VSS) malfunction

DTC P0505 Idle Air Control (IAC) system malfunction

DTC P0605 Powertrain Control Module (PCM)—Read Only Memory (ROM) test error

DTC P0703 Brake On/Off (BOO) switch input malfunction

DTC P0707 Manual Lever Position (MLP) sensor circuit low input

DTC P0708 Manual Lever Position (MLP) sensor circuit high input

DTC P0720 Output Shaft Speed (OSS) sensor circuit malfunction

DTC P0741 Torque Converter Clutch (TCC) system incorrect mechanical performance

DTC P0743 Torque Converter Clutch (TCC) system electrical failure

DTC P0750 Shift Solenoid #1(SS1) circuit malfunction

DTC P0751 Shift Solenoid #1(SS1) performance

DTC P0755 Shift Solenoid #2 (SS2) circuit malfunction

DTC P0756 Shift Solenoid #2 (SS2) performance

DTC P1000 OBD II Monitor Testing not complete

DTC P1100 Mass Air Flow (MAF) sensor intermittent

DTC P1101 Mass Air Flow (MAF) sensor out of Self-Test range

DTC P1112 Intake Air Temperature (IAT) sensor intermittent

DTC P1116 Engine Coolant Temperature (ECT) sensor out of Self-Test range

DTC P1117 Engine Coolant Temperature (ECT) sensor intermittent

DTC P1120 Throttle Position (TP) sensor out of range low

DTC P1121 Throttle Position (TP) sensor inconsistent with MAF sensor

DTC P1124 Throttle Position (TP) sensor out of Self-Test range

DTC P1125 Throttle Position (TP) sensor circuit intermittent

DTC P1130 Lack of HO$_2$S 11 switch, adaptive fuel at limit

DTC P1131 Lack of HO$_2$S 11 switch, sensor indicates lean (Bank #1)

DTC P1132 Lack of HO$_2$S 11 switch, sensor indicates rich (Bank #1)

DTC P1137 Lack of HO$_2$S 12 switch, sensor indicates lean (Bank #1)

DTC P1138 Lack of HO$_2$S 12 switch, sensor indicates rich (Bank #1)

DTC P1150 Lack of HO$_2$S 21 switch, adaptive fuel at limit

DTC P1151 Lack of HO$_2$S 21 switch, sensor indicates lean (Bank #2)

DTC P1152 Lack of HO$_2$S 21 switch, sensor indicates rich (Bank #2)

DTC P1157 Lack of HO$_2$S 22 switch, sensor indicates lean (Bank #2)

DTC P1158 Lack of HO$_2$S 22 switch, sensor indicates rich (Bank #2)

DTC P1351 Ignition Diagnostic Monitor (1DM) circuit input malfunction

DTC P1352 Ignition coil A primary circuit malfunction

DTC P1353 Ignition coil B primary circuit malfunction

DTC P1354 Ignition coil C primary circuit malfunction

DTC P1355 Ignition coil D primary circuit malfunction

DTC P1364 Ignition coil primary circuit malfunction

DTC P1390 Octane Adjust (OCT ADJ) out of Self-Test range

DTC P1400 Differential Pressure Feedback Electronic (DPFE) sensor circuit low voltage detected

DTC P1401 Differential Pressure Feedback Electronic (DPFE) sensor circuit high voltage detected

DTC P1403 Differential Pressure Feedback Electronic (DPFE) sensor hoses reversed

DTC P1405 Differential Pressure Feedback Electronic (DPFE) sensor upstream hose off or plugged

DTC P1406 Differential Pressure Feedback Electronic (DPFE) sensor downstream hose off or plugged

DTC P1407 Exhaust Gas Recirculation (EGR) no flow detected (valve stuck closed or inoperative)

DTC P1408 Exhaust Gas Recirculation (EGR) flow out of Self-Test range

DTC P1473 Fan Secondary High with fan(s) off

DTC P1474 Low Fan Control primary circuit malfunction

DTC P1479 High Fan Control primary circuit malfunction

DTC P1480 Fan Secondary low with low fan on

DTC P1481 Fan Secondary low with high fan on

DTC P1500 Vehicle Speed Sensor (VSS) circuit intermittent

DTC P1505 Idle Air Control (IAC) system at adaptive clip

DTC P1605 Powertrain Control Module (PCM)—Keep Alive Memory (KAM) test error

DTC P1703 Brake On/Off (BOO) switch out of Self-Test range

DTC P1705 Manual Lever Position (MLP) sensor out of Self-Test range

DTC P1711 Transmission Fluid Temperature (TFT) sensor out of Self-Test range

DTC P1742 Torque Converter Clutch (TCC) solenoid mechanically failed (turns MIL on)

DTC P1743 Torque Converter Clutch (TCC) solenoid mechanically failed (turns TCIL on)

DTC P1744 Torque Converter Clutch (TCC) system mechanically stuck in off position

Refer to the model specific sections for fuel system service procedures

DTC P1746 Electronic Pressure Control (EPC) solenoid circuit low input (open circuit)

DTC P1747 Electronic Pressure Control (EPC) solenoid circuit high input (short circuit)

DTC P1751 Shift Solenoid #1(SS1) performance

DTC P1756 Shift Solenoid #2 (SS2) performance

DTC P1780 Transmission Control Switch (TCS) circuit out of Self-Test range

1995 PASSENGER CARS AND LIGHT TRUCKS

DTC P0102 Mass Air Flow (MAF) Sensor circuit low input

DTC P0103 Mass Air Flow (MAF) Sensor circuit high input

DTC P0112 Intake Air Temperature (IAT) Sensor circuit low input

DTC P0113 Intake Air Temperature (IAT) Sensor high input

DTC P0117 Engine Coolant Temperature (ECT) low input

DTC P0118 Engine Coolant Temperature (ECT) Sensor circuit high input

DTC P0121 In range operating Throttle Position (TP) sensor circuit failure

DTC P0122 Throttle Position (TP) Sensor circuit low input

DTC P0123 Throttle Position (TP) Sensor high input

DTC P0125 Insufficient coolant temperature to enter closed loop fuel control

DTC P0126 Insufficient coolant temperature for stable operation

DTC P0131 Upstream Heated Oxygen Sensor (HO2S 11) circuit out of range low voltage (bank #1)

DTC P0132 Upstream Heated Oxygen Sensor (HO2S 11) circuit high voltage (Bank #1)

DTC P0133 Upstream Heated Oxygen Sensor (HO2S 11) circuit slow response (Bank #1)

DTC P0135 Heated Oxygen Sensor Heater (HTR 11) circuit malfunction

DTC P0136 Downstream Heated Oxygen Sensor (HO2S 12) circuit malfunction (Bank #1

DTC P0138 Downstream Heated Oxygen Sensor (HO2S 12) circuit high voltage (Bank #1)

DTC P0140 Heated Oxygen Sensor (HO2S 12) circuit no activity detected (Bank #1)

DTC P0141 Heated Oxygen Sensor Heater (HTR 12) circuit malfunction

DTC P0151 Upstream Heated Oxygen Sensor (HO2S 21) circuit out of range low voltage (Bank #2)

DTC P0152 Upstream Heated Oxygen Sensor (HO2S 21) circuit high voltage (Bank #2)

DTC P0153 Upstream Heated Oxygen Sensor (HO2S 21) circuit slow response (Bank #2)

DTC P0155 Heated Oxygen Sensor Heater (HTR 21) circuit malfunction

DTC P0156 Downstream Heated Oxygen Sensor (HO2S 22) circuit malfunction (Bank #2)

DTC P0158 Downstream Heated Oxygen Sensor (HO2S 22) circuit high voltage (Bank #2)

DTC P0160 Heated Oxygen Sensor (HO2S 12) circuit no activity detected (Bank #2)

DTC P0161 Heated Oxygen Sensor Heater (HTR 22) circuit malfunction

DTC P0171 System (adaptive fuel) too lean (Bank #1)

DTC P0172 System (adaptive fuel) too rich (Bank #1)

DTC P0174 System (adaptive fuel) too lean (Bank #2)

DTC P0175 System (adaptive fuel) too rich (Bank #2)

DTC P0222 Throttle Position Sensor B (TP-B) circuit low input

DTC P0223 Throttle Position Sensor B (TP-B) circuit high input

DTC P0230 Fuel pump primary circuit malfunction

DTC P0231 Fuel pump secondary circuit low

DTC P0232 Fuel pump secondary circuit high

DTC P0300 Random misfire detected

DTC P0301 Cylinder #1 misfire detected

DTC P0302 Cylinder #2 misfire detected

DTC P0303 Cylinder #3 misfire detected

DTC P0304 Cylinder #4 misfire detected

DTC P0305 Cylinder #5 misfire detected

DTC P0306 Cylinder #6 misfire detected

DTC P0307 Cylinder #7 misfire detected

DTC P0308 Cylinder #8 misfire detected

DTC P0320 Ignition engine speed (Profile Ignition Pickup) input circuit malfunction

DTC P0340 Camshaft Position (CMP) sensor circuit malfunction (CID)

DTC P0350 Ignition Coil primary circuit malfunction

DTC P0351 Ignition Coil A primary circuit malfunction

DTC P0352 Ignition Coil B primary circuit malfunction

DTC P0353 Ignition Coil C primary circuit malfunction

DTC P0354 Ignition Coil D primary circuit malfunction

DTC P0400 Exhaust Gas Recirculation (EGR) flow malfunction

DTC P0401 Exhaust Gas Recirculation (EGR) flow insufficient detected

DTC P0402 Exhaust Gas Recirculation (EGR) excess flow detected (valve open at idle)

DTC P0411 Secondary Air Injection system incorrect flow detected

DTC P0412 Secondary Air Injection system control valve malfunction

DTC P0420 Catalyst system efficiency below threshold (Bank #1)

DTC P0430 Catalyst system efficiency below threshold (Bank #2)

DTC P0443 Evaporative emission control system Canister Purge (CANP) Control Valve circuit malfunction

DTC P0500 Vehicle Speed Sensor (VSS) malfunction

DTC P0505 Idle Air Control (IAC) system malfunction

DTC P0603 Powertrain Control Module (PCM)—Keep Alive Memory (KAM) test error

DTC P0605 Powertrain Control Module (PCM)—Read Only Memory (ROM) test error

DTC P0704 Clutch Pedal Position (CPP) switch input circuit malfunction

DTC P0703 Brake On/Off (BOO) switch input malfunction

DTC P0707 Manual Lever Position (MLP) sensor circuit low input

DTC P0708 Manual Lever Position (MLP) sensor circuit high input

DTC P0712 Transmission Fluid Temperature (TFT) sensor circuit low input

DTC P0713 Transmission Fluid Temperature (TFT) sensor circuit high input

DTC P0715 Turbine Shaft Speed (TSS) sensor circuit malfunction

DTC P0720 Output Shaft Speed (OSS) sensor circuit malfunction

DTC P0731 Incorrect ratio for first gear

DTC P0732 Incorrect ratio for second gear

DTC P0733 Incorrect ratio for third gear

DTC P0734 Incorrect ratio for fourth gear

DTC P0736 Reverse incorrect gear

DTC P0741 Torque Converter Clutch (TCC) system incorrect mechanical performance

DTC P0746 Electronic Pressure Control (EPC) solenoid performance

DTC P0743 Torque Converter Clutch (TCC) system electrical failure

DTC P0750 Shift Solenoid #1(SS1) circuit malfunction

DTC P0751 Shift Solenoid #1(SS1) performance

DTC P0755 Shift Solenoid #2 (SS2) circuit malfunction

DTC P0756 Shift Solenoid #2 (SS2) performance

DTC P0760 Shift Solenoid #3 (SS3) circuit malfunction

DTC P0761 Shift Solenoid #3 (SS3) performance

DTC P0781 1 to 2 shift error

DTC P0782 2 to 3 shift error

DTC P0783 3 to 4 shift error

DTC P0784 4 to 5 shift error

DTC P1000 OBD II Monitor Testing not complete

DTC U1039 OBD II Monitor not complete

DTC UIOS1 Brake switch signal missing or incorrect

DTC P1100 Mass Air Flow (MAF) sensor intermittent

DTC P1101 Mass Air Flow (MAF) sensor out of Self-Test range

DTC P1112 Intake Air Temperature (IAT) sensor intermittent

DTC P1116 Engine Coolant Temperature (ECT) sensor out of Self-Test range

DTC P1117 Engine Coolant Temperature (ECT) sensor intermittent

DTC P1120 Throttle Position (TP) sensor out of range low

DTC P1121 Throttle Position (TP) sensor inconsistent with MAF sensor

DTC P1124 Throttle Position (TP) sensor out of Self-Test range

DTC P1125 Throttle Position (TP) sensor circuit intermittent

DTC P1130 Lack of HO_2S 11 switch, adaptive fuel at limit

DTC P1131 Lack of HO_2S 11 switch, sensor indicates lean (Bank #1)

DTC P1132 Lack of HO_2S 11 switch, sensor indicates rich (Bank #1)

DTC U1135 Ignition switch signal missing or incorrect

DTC P1137 Lack of HO_2S 12 switch, sensor indicates lean (Bank #1)

DTC P1138 Lack of HO_2S 12 switch, sensor indicates rich (Bank #1)

DTC P1150 Lack of HO_2S 21 switch, adaptive fuel at limit

DTC P1151 Lack of HO_2S 21 switch, sensor indicates lean (Bank #2)

DTC P1152 Lack of HO_2S 21 switch, sensor indicates rich (Bank #2)

DTC P1157 Lack of HO_2S 22 switch, sensor indicates lean (Bank #2)

DTC P1158 Lack of HO_2S 22 switch, sensor indicates rich (Bank #2)

DTC P1220 Series Throttle Control malfunction

DTC P1224 Throttle Position Sensor (TP-B) out of Self-test range

DTC P1233 Fuel Pump driver Module off-line

DTC P1234 Fuel Pump driver Module off-line

DTC P1235 Fuel Pump control out of range

DTC P1236 Fuel Pump control out of range

DTC P1237 Fuel Pump secondary circuit malfunction

DTC P1238 Fuel Pump secondary circuit malfunction

DTC P1260 THEFT detected—engine disabled

DTC P1270 Engine RPM or vehicle speed limiter reached

DTC P1351 Ignition Diagnostic Monitor (1DM) circuit input malfunction

DTC P1352 Ignition coil A primary circuit malfunction

DTC P1353 Ignition coil B primary circuit malfunction

DTC P1354 Ignition coil C primary circuit malfunction

DTC P1355 Ignition coil D primary circuit malfunction

DTC P1358 Ignition Diagnostic Monitor (1DM) signal out of Self-Test range

DTC P1359 Spark output circuit malfunction

DTC P1364 Ignition coil primary circuit malfunction

DTC P1390 Octane Adjust (OCT ADJ) out of Self-Test range

DTC P1400 Differential Pressure Feedback Electronic (DPFE) sensor circuit low voltage detected

DTC P1401 Differential Pressure Feedback Electronic (DPFE) sensor circuit high voltage detected

DTC P1403 Differential Pressure Feedback Electronic (DPFE) sensor hoses reversed

DTC P1405 Differential Pressure Feedback Electronic (DPFE) sensor upstream hose off or plugged

DTC P1406 Differential Pressure Feedback Electronic (DPFE) sensor downstream hose off or plugged

DTC P1407 Exhaust Gas Recirculation (EGR) no flow detected (valve stuck closed or inoperative)

DTC P1408 Exhaust Gas Recirculation (EGR) flow out of Self-Test range

DTC P1409 Electronic Vacuum Regulator (EVR) control circuit malfunction

DTC P1414 Secondary Air Injection system monitor circuit high voltage

DTC P1443 Evaporative emission control system—vacuum system purge control solenoid or purge control valve malfunction

DTC P1444 4- Purge Flow Sensor (PFS) circuit low input

DTC P1445 Purge Flow Sensor (PFS) circuit high input

DTC U1451 Lack of response from Passive Anti-Theft system (PATS) module—engine disabled

DTC P1460 Wide Open Throttle Air Conditioning Cut-off (WAC) circuit malfunction

DTC P1461 Air Conditioning Pressure (ACP) sensor circuit low input

DTC P1462 Air Conditioning Pressure (ACP) sensor circuit high input

DTC P1463 Air Conditioning Pressure (ACP) sensor insufficient pressure change

DTC P1469 Low air conditioning cycling period

DTC P1473 Fan Secondary High with fan(s) off

DTC P1474 Low Fan Control primary circuit malfunction

DTC P1479 High Fan Control primary circuit malfunction

DTC P1480 Fan Secondary low with low fan on

DTC P1481 Fan Secondary low with high fan on

DTC P1500 Vehicle Speed Sensor (VSS) circuit intermittent

DTC P1505 Idle Air Control (IAC) system at adaptive clip

DTC P1506 Idle Air control (IAC) over speed error

DTC P1518 Intake Manifold Runner Control (IMRC) malfunction (stuck open)

DTC P1519 Intake Manifold Runner Control (IMRC) malfunction (stuck closed)

DTC P1520 Intake Manifold Runner Control (IMRC) circuit malfunction

Refer to the model specific sections for engine electrical system service procedures

2-32 **MAINTENANCE LIGHT RESETTING AND DTC RETRIEVAL**
FORD MOTOR CO.

GENERAL MOTORS

DTC P1507 Idle Air control (IAC) under speed error
DTC P1605 Powertrain Control Module (PCM)—Keep Alive Memory (KAM) test error
DTC P1650 Power steering Pressure (PSP) switch out of Self-Test range
DTC P1651 Power steering Pressure (PSP) switch input malfunction
DTC P1701 Reverse engagement error
DTC P1703 Brake On/Off (BOO) switch out of Self-Test range
DTC P1705 Manual Lever Position (MLP) sensor out of Self-Test range
DTC P1709 Park or Neutral Position (PNP) switch out of Self-test range
DTC P1729 4X4 Low switch error
DTC P1711 Transmission Fluid Temperature (TFT) sensor out of Self-Test range
DTC P1741 Torque Converter Clutch (TOG) control error
DTC P1742 Torque Converter Clutch (TOO) solenoid mechanically failed (turns MIL on)
DTC P1743 Torque Converter Clutch (TOO) solenoid mechanically failed (turns TOIL on)
DTC P1744 Torque Converter Clutch (TOO) system mechanically stuck in off position
DTC P1748 Electronic Pressure Control (EPC) solenoid circuit low input (open circuit)
DTO P1747 Electronic Pressure Control (EPC) solenoid circuit high input (short circuit)
DTC P1749 Electric Pressure Control (EPC) solenoid failed low
DTC P1751 Shift Solenoid #1(SS1) performance
DTC P1756 Shift Solenoid #2 (SS2) performance
DTC P1780 Transmission Control Switch (TCS) circuit out of Self-Test range

EEC NON-NAAO System

The Capri, Festiva, Probe, Escort and Tracer are referred to as NON-NAAO (Not North American Automotive Operations) produced vehicles. The fuel system used on these vehicles is called Electronic Engine Control (EEC). This EEC system components and operation are basically the same as the EEC-IV system. The self-diagnostic function on the EEC system differs from the EEC-VI system and is covered under NON-NAAO vehicle.

The Non-NAAO EEC system self-diagnostics and code retrieval many be different than domestic built Ford engines. The code descriptions are mostly the same for all of the NON NAAO vehicles. Take note that not all vehicles use all codes. The transaxle codes were introduced in 1992 some Capri, Escort, Probe and Tracer models. Late model Probe and Escort may be equipped with EEC-IV fuel control system, the diagnostic link connector (DLC) will be of the EEC-IV design.

The code definitions listed general 2-digit codes for Ford Vehicles using the Ford EEC engine control system. For a specific code definition or component test procedure consult a vehicle service manual for your vehicle. A diagnostic code does not mean the component is defective. For example a Code 6 is a vehicle speed sensor code. This does not mean the sensor is defective, but to check the sensor and related components. A defective speedometer cable or transmission problem will also set this code.

➡**When the term Powertrain Control Module (PCM) is used in this manual it will refer to the engine control computer regardless that it may be a Powertrain Control Module (PCM) or Electronic Control Module (ECM) or Electronic Control Assembly (ECA).**

Code 02 Crankshaft position sensor
Code 03 Cylinder identification sensor #1, 1.6L engine
Code 06 Vehicle speed sensor, 1.6L engine
Code 08 Air flow signal
Code 09 Engine coolant temperature sensor
Code 10 Air temperature sensor
Code 12 Throttle position sensor, 1.6L engine
Code 14 Barometric pressure sensor
Code 15 Oxygen sensor, signal LEAN
Code 16 EGR position valve, 2.2L engine
Code 17 Oxygen sensor, signal RICH
Code 25 Fuel pressure regulator solenoid, 1.6L engine
Code 26 Canister purge solenoid
Code 34 Idle speed control solenoid
Code 41 High speed inlet air control solenoid
Code 55 Pulse generator, transaxle code
Code 57 Down shift signal, transaxle code
Code 60 1-2 Shift solenoid, transaxle code
Code 61 2-3 Shift solenoid, transaxle code
Code 62 3-4 Shift solenoid, transaxle code
Code 63 Lock-up control, transaxle code

➡**This list is to be used as a reference for testing and does not mean a specific component is defective.**

No Code Unable to Run Self Test or Output Codes, or list does not apply to vehicle tested, refer to specific vehicle service manual

General Motors

SELF-DIAGNOSTICS

Automotive manufacturers have developed on-board computers to control engines, transmissions and many other components. These on-board computers with dozens of sensors and actuators have become almost impossible to test without the help of electronic test equipment.

One of these electronic test devices has become the on-board computer itself. The Powertrain Control Modules (PCM), sometimes called the Electronic Control Module (ECM), used on toadies vehicles has a built in self testing system. This self test ability is called self-diagnosis. The self-diagnosis system will test many or all of the sensors and controlled devices for proper function. When a malfunction is detected this system will store a code in memory that's related to that specific circuit. The computer can later be accessed to obtain fault codes recorded in memory using the procedures for Reading Codes. This helps narrow down what area to begin testing.

Fault code meanings can vary from year to year even on the same model. It is extremely important after retrieving a fault code to verify its meaning with a proper manual. Servicing a code incorrectly will not only lead to the wrong conclusion but could also cause damage if tested or serviced incorrectly.

Since the control module is programmed to recognize the presence and value of electrical inputs, it will also note the lack of a signal or a radical change in values. It will, for example, react to the loss of signal from the vehicle speed sensor or note that engine coolant temperature has risen beyond acceptable (programmed) limits. Once a fault is recognized, a numeric code is assigned and held in memory. The dashboard warning lamp—CHECK ENGINE or SERVICE ENGINE SOON—will illuminate to advise the operator that the system has detected a fault.

More than one code may be stored. Although not every engine

uses every code and the same code may carry different meanings relative to each engine or engine family. For example, on the 3.3L (VIN N), Code 46 indicates a fault found in the power steering pressure switch circuit. The same code on the 5.7L (VIN F) engine indicates a fault in the VATS anti-theft system. The list of codes and descriptions can be found in the `Code Descriptions' section of the manual.

In the event of an PCM failure, the system will default to a pre-programmed set of values. These are compromise values which allow the engine to operate, although possibly at reduced efficiency. This is also known as the default, limp-in or back-up mode. Driveability is almost always affected when the PCM enters this mode.

Service Precautions

- Protect the on-board solid-state components from rough handling or extremes of temperature.
- Always turn the ignition OFF when connecting or disconnecting battery cables, jumper cables, or a battery charger. Failure to do this can result in PCM or other electronic component damage.
- Remove the PCM before any arc welding is performed to the vehicle
- Electronic components are very susceptible to damage caused by electrostatic discharge (static electricity). To prevent electronic component damage, do not touch the control module connector pins or soldered components on the control module circuit board.

Visual Inspection

This is possibly the most critical step of diagnosis. A detailed examination of all connectors, wiring and vacuum hoses can often lead to a repair without further diagnosis. Also, take into consideration if the vehicle has been serviced recently? Sometimes things get reconnected in the wrong place, or not at all. A careful inspector will check the undersides of hoses as well as the integrity of hard-to-reach hoses blocked by the air cleaner or other components. Correct routing for vacuum hoses can be obtained from your specific vehicle service manual or Vehicle Emission Control Information (VECI) label in the engine compartment of the vehicle. Wiring should be checked carefully for any sign of strain, burning, crimping or terminals pulled-out from a connector.

Checking connectors at components or in harnesses is required; usually, pushing them together will reveal a loose fit. Also, check electrical connectors for corroded, bent, damaged, improperly seated pins, and bad wire crimps to terminals. Pay particular attention to ground circuits, making sure they are not loose or corroded. Remember to inspect connectors and hose fittings at components not mounted on the engine, such as the evaporative canister or relays mounted on the fender aprons. Any component or wiring in the vicinity of a fluid leak or spillage should be given extra attention during inspection.

➡**There are many problems with connectors on electronic engine control systems. Due to the low voltage signals that these systems use any dirt, corrosion or damage will affect their operation. Note that some connectors use a special grease on the contacts to prevent corrosion. Do not wipe this grease off, it is a special type for this purpose. You can obtain this grease from your vehicle dealer.**

Additionally, inspect maintenance items such as belt condition and tension, battery charge and condition and the radiator cap carefully. Any of these very simple items may affect the system enough to set a fault.

Dashboard Warning Lamp

The primary function of the dash warning lamp is to advise the operator that a fault has been detected, and, in most cases, a code stored. Under normal conditions, the dash warning lamp will illuminate when the ignition is turned ON. Once the engine is started and running, the PCM will perform a system check and extinguish the warning lamp if no fault is found.

Additionally, the dash warning lamp can be used to retrieve stored codes after the system is placed in the Diagnostic Mode. Codes are transmitted as a series of flashes with short or long pauses. When the system is placed in the Field Service Mode (available on fuel injected model) the dash lamp will indicate open loop or closed loop function.

The Check Engine or Service Engine Soon (MIL) lamp is used for reading trouble codes

Intermittent Problems

If a fault occurs intermittently, such as a loose connector pin breaking contact as the vehicle hits a bump, the PCM will note the fault as it occurs and energize the dash warning lamp. If the problem self-corrects, as with the terminal pin again making contact, the dash lamp will extinguish after 10 seconds but a code will remain stored in the PCM memory. When an unexpected code appears during an intermittent failure that self-corrected; the codes are still useful in diagnosis and should not be discounted.

Diagnostic Connector Location

The Assembly Line Communication Link (ALCL) or Assembly Line Diagnostic Link (ALDL) is a Diagnostic Link Connector (DLC) located in the passenger compartment. It has terminals which are used in the assembly plant to check that the engine is operating properly before it leaves the plant.

On most vehicles, the diagnostic link connector is located under the instrument panel

For OBD I, the diagnostic link connector (DLC) is a notched, 12 pin connector

This DLC is where you connect you jumper the terminals to place the engine control computer into self-diagnostic mode. The standard term DLC is sometimes referred to as the ALCL or the ALDL in different manuals. Either way it is referred to, they all still perform the same function.

READING & CLEARING CODES

Reading Codes (Except Cadillac)

Since the inception of electronic engine management systems on General Motors vehicles, there has been a variety of connectors provided to the technician for retrieving Diagnostic Trouble Codes (DTC)s. Additionally, there have been a number of different names given to these connectors over the years; Assembly Line Communication Link (ALCL), Assembly Line Diagnostic Link (ALDL), Data Link Connector (DLC). Actually when the system was initially introduced to the 49 states in 1979, early 1980, there was no connector used at all. On these early vehicles there was a green spade terminal taped to the ECM harness and connected to the diagnostic enable line at the computer. When this terminal was grounded with the key ON, the system would flash any stored diagnostic trouble codes. The introduction of the ALOL was found to be a much more convenient way of retrieving fault codes. This connector was located underneath the instrument panel on most GM vehicles, however on some models it will not be found there. On early Corvettes the ALOL is located underneath the ashtray, it can be found in the glove compartment of some early FWD Oldsmobiles, and between the seats in the Pontiac Fiero. The connector was first introduced as a square

connector with four terminals, then progressed to a flat five terminal connector, and finally to what is still used in 1993, a 12 terminal double row connector. To access stored Diagnostic Trouble Codes (DTC) from the square connector, turn the ignition ON and identify the diagnostic enable terminal (usually a white wire with a black tracer) and ground it. The flat five terminal connector is identified from left to right as A, B, C, D, and E. There is a space between terminal D and E which permits a spade to be inserted for the purposes of diagnostics when the ignition key is ON. On this connector terminal D is the diagnostic enable line, and E is a ground. The 12 terminal double row connector has been continually expanded through the years as vehicles acquired more on-board electronic systems such as Anti-lock Brakes. Despite this the terminals used for engine code retrieval have remained the same. The 12 terminal connector is identified from right-to-left on the top row A-F, and on the bottom row from left-to-right, G-L. To access engine codes turn the ignition ON and insert a jumper between terminals A and B. Terminal A is a ground, and terminal B is the diagnostic request line. Stored trouble codes can be read through the flashing of the Check Engine Light or on later vehicles the Service Engine Soon lamp. Trouble codes are identified by the timed flash of the indicator light. When diagnostics are first entered the light will flash once, pause; then two quick flashes.

This reads as DTC 12 which indicates that the diagnostic system is working. This code will flash indefinitely if there are no stored trouble codes. If codes are stored in memory, Code 12 will flash three times before the next code appears. Codes are displayed in the next highest numerical sequence. For example, Code 13 would be displayed next if it was stored in memory and would read as follow: flash, pause, flash, flash, flash, long pause, repeat twice. This sequence will continue until all codes have been displayed, and then start all over again with Code 12.

Clearing Codes (Except Cadillac)

EXCEPT RIVIERA, TORONADO AND TROFEO

To clear any Diagnostic Trouble Codes (DTC's) from the PCM memory, either to determine if the malfunction will occur again or because repair has been completed, power feed must be disconnected for at least 30 seconds. Depending on how the vehicle is equipped, the system power feed can be disconnected at the positive battery terminal pigtail, the inline fuseholder that originates at the positive connection at the battery, or the ECM/PCM fuse in the fuse block. The negative battery terminal may be disconnected but other on-board memory data such as preset radio tuning will also be lost. To prevent system damage, the ignition switch must be in the OFF position when disconnecting or reconnecting power.

When using a Diagnostic Computer such as Tech 1, or equivalent scan tool to read the diagnostic trouble codes, clearing the codes is done in the same manner. On some systems, OTC's may be cleared through the Tech 1, or equivalent scan tool.

On Riviera, Toronado and Trofeo, clearing codes is part of the dashboard display menu or diagnostic routine. Because of the amount of electronic equipment on these vehicles, clearing codes by disconnecting the battery is not recommended.

RIVIERA, TORONADO AND TROFEO (NON-CRT/DID VEHICLES)

USING THE ON-BOARD DIAGNOSTIC DISPLAY SYSTEM:

First turn the ignition to the ON position. On Riviera depress the OFF and TEMP buttons on the ECCP at the same time and hold

DIAGNOSTIC CODE DISPLAY

Example of a code 12 displayed on the check engine lamp

until all display segments light. This is known as the Segment Check. On Toronado and Trofeo follow the same procedure, however, depress the OFF and WARMER buttons on the ECOP instead. After diagnostics is entered, any OTC's stored in computer memory will be displayed. Codes may be stored for the PCM, BCM, PC or SIR systems. Following the display of OTC's, the first available system for testing will be displayed. For example, `EC?' would be displayed on Riviera for EOM testing, while on Toronado and Trofeo the message `ECM?' will appear. The message is more clear on these vehicles due to increased character space in the IPO display area.

1. Depress the `FAN UP' button on the ECCP until the message `DATA EC?' appears on the display for Riviera, or `ECM DATA?' is displayed on Toronado and Trofeo.

2. Depress the `FAN DOWN' button on the ECCP until the message `CLR E CODE' appears on the display for Riviera, or `ECM CLEAR CODES?' is displayed on Toronado and Trofeo.

3. Depressing the `FAN UP' button on the ECCP will result in the message `E CODE CLR' or `E NOT CLR' on Riviera, `EOM CODES CLEAR' or `ECM CODES NOT CLEAR' on Toronado and Trofeo. This message will appear for 3 seconds. After 3 seconds the display will automatically return to the next available test type for the selected system. It is a good idea to either cycle the ignition once or test drive the vehicle to ensure the code(s) do not reset.

TORONADO AND TROFEO (CRT/DID EQUIPPED)

USING THE ON-BOARD DIAGNOSTIC DISPLAY SYSTEM:

First turn the ignition switch to the ON position. Depress the `OFF' hard key and `WARM' soft key on the CRT/DID at the same time and hold until all display segments light. This is the `Segment Check.' During diagnostic operation, all information will be displayed on the Driver Information Center (DIC) located in the Instrument Panel Cluster (IPC). Because of the limited space available single letter identifiers are often used for each of the major computer systems. These are: E for ECM, B for 6CM, I for IPC and R for SIR. After diagnostics is entered, any OTC's stored in computer memory will be displayed. Codes may be stored for the PCM, BCM, PC or SIR systems. Following the display of OTC's, the first available system for testing will be displayed. This will be displayed as 'ECM?'.

1. Depress the `YES' soft key until the display reads `ECM DATA?'.

2. Depress the `NO' soft key until the display reads `ECM CLEAR CODES?'.

3. Depressing the `YES' soft key will result in either the message `ECM CODES CLEAR' or `ECM CODES NOT CLEAR' being displayed, indicating whether or not the codes were successfully cleared. This message will appear for 3 seconds. After 3 seconds the display will automatically return to the next available test type for the selected system. It is a good idea to either cycle the ignition once or test drive the vehicle to ensure the code(s) do not reset.

Reading and Clearing Cadillac Engine Codes

➡**The Cadillac Cimmaron used the 12 terminal DLC and codes can be accessed in the conventional manner as all other General Motors vehicles. The rear wheel drive Cadillac equipped with either the 4.1L V6, 5.0L V8, or the 5.7L V8 all can also be accessed in the conventional manner using the DLC.**

1980–1983 DIGITAL FUEL INJECTION

1. Turn the ignition switch **ON**.

2. Depress the OFF and WARMER buttons on the Electronic Climate Control (ECO) panel simultaneously and hold until .. is displayed.

3. The numerals 88 should then appear indicating that all display segments are functional. Diagnosis should not be attempted unless the entire 88 is displayed or misdiagnosis will result.

4. If trouble codes are present they will appear on the digital ECO panel as follows:

   a. The lowest numbered code will be displayed for approximately two seconds.

   b. Progressively higher numbered codes, if present, will be displayed consecutively for two second intervals until the highest code has been displayed.

   c. 88 is again displayed.

   d. Parts A, B, and C will be repeated a second time.

   e. After the trouble codes have been displayed Code 70 will then appear. 70 indicates that the ECM is prepared for the switch test procedure.

5. If no trouble codes are stored in memory, 88 will appear for a longer time, and then the ECM will display Code 70.

CLEARING CODES:

While still in the diagnostic mode, press the OFF and HIGH buttons simultaneously until 00 appears. Trouble codes are now removed from the system memory.

➡**The fuel data panel will go blank when the system is displaying in the diagnostic mode.**

1984 DIGITAL FUEL INJECTION

1. Turn the ignition switch ON.

2. Depress the OFF and WARMER buttons on the Electronic Climate Control (ECC) panel simultaneously and hold until .. is displayed.

3. —1.8.8 should then appear indicating that all display segments are functional. Diagnosis should not be attempted unless the entire -1.8.8 is displayed or misdiagnosis will result.

4. If trouble codes are present they will appear on the digital ECO panel as follows:

   a. The lowest numbered code will be displayed for approximately two seconds.

   b. Progressively higher numbered codes, if present, will be displayed consecutively for two second intervals until the highest code has been displayed.

   c. 88 is again displayed.

   d. Parts A, B, and C will be repeated a second time.

   e. After the trouble codes have been displayed Code 70 will then appear. 70 indicates that the ECM is prepared for the switch test procedure.

5. If no trouble codes are stored in memory, —1.8.8 will appear for a longer time, and then the ECM will display Code 70.

CLEARING CODES:

While still in the diagnostic mode, press the OFF and HIGH buttons simultaneously until .0.0 appears. Trouble codes are now removed from the system memory.

➡**The fuel data panel will go blank when the system is displaying in the diagnostic mode.**

Ignition system service is covered in the model specific sections of this manual

1985–1986 DIGITAL FUEL INJECTION

1. Turn the ignition switch **ON**.
2. Depress the OFF and WARMER buttons on the Climate Control Panel (CCP) simultaneously and hold until –188 is displayed.
3. –188 should then appear indicating that all display segments are functional. Diagnosis should not be attempted unless the entire –188 is displayed or misdiagnosis will result.
4. If trouble codes are present they will appear on the Fuel Data Center (FDC) panel as follows:

   a. Display of trouble codes will begin with an 8.8.8 on the FDC panel for approximately one second. . . . E will then be displayed which indicates beginning of the ECM stored trouble codes. The initial pass of ECM codes includes all the detected malfunctions whether or not they are currently present. If no ECM codes are stored the . . . E display will be bypassed.

   b. Following the display of . . . E the lowest numbered ECM code will be displayed for approximately two seconds. All ECM codes will be prefixed with an E (i.e. E12, E13, etc.).

   c. Progressively higher numbered codes, if present, will be displayed consecutively for two second intervals until the highest code has been displayed.

   d. .E.E is again displayed which indicates the start of the second pass of ECM trouble codes. On the second pass only current faults (hard codes) will be displayed. Codes displayed on the first pass are history failures or (soft codes). If all displayed codes were history codes the .E.E will be bypassed.

   e. When all ECM codes have been displayed, BCM codes will appear with the prefix F in the same manner as the ECM did.

   f. After the display of all codes, or if no codes were stored, Code .7.0 will appear indicating the start of the switch tests.

CLEARING CODES:
While still in the diagnostic mode, press the OFF and HIGH buttons simultaneously until E.0.0 appears. Trouble codes are now removed from the ECM memory.

1987–1993 DEVILLE AND FLEETWOOD

1. Turn the ignition switch **ON**.
2. Depress the OFF and WARMER buttons on the Climate Control Panel (CCP) simultaneously and hold until -188 is displayed.
3. -188 should then appear indicating that all display segments are functional. Diagnosis should not be attempted unless the entire -188 is displayed or misdiagnosis will result.
4. If trouble codes are present they will appear on the Fuel Data Center (FDC) panel as follows:

   a. Display of trouble codes will begin with an 8.8.8 on the FDC panel for approximately one second. . . . E will then be displayed which indicates beginning of the ECM stored trouble codes. The initial pass of ECM codes includes all the detected malfunctions whether or not they are currently present. If no ECM codes are stored the . . . E display will be bypassed.

   b. Following the display of . . . E the lowest numbered ECM code will be displayed for approximately two seconds. All ECM codes will be prefixed with an E (i.e. E12, E13, etc.).

   c. Progressively higher numbered codes, if present, will be displayed consecutively for two second intervals until the highest code has been displayed.

   d. .E.E is again displayed which indicates the start of the second pass of ECM trouble codes. On the second pass only current faults (hard codes) will be displayed. Codes displayed on the first pass are history failures or (soft codes). If all displayed codes were history codes the .E.E will be bypassed.

   e. When all ECM codes have been displayed, BCM codes will appear with the prefix F in the same manner as the ECM did.

5. After the display of all codes, or if no codes were stored, Code .7.0 will appear indicating the start of the switch tests.

CLEARING CODES:
While still in the diagnostic mode, press the OFF and HIGH buttons simultaneously until E.0.0 appears. Trouble codes are now removed from the ECM memory.

1987–1993 ALLANTE, ELDORADO AND SEVILLE

1. Turn the ignition switch **ON**.
2. Depress the OFF and WARMER buttons on the Climate Control Panel (CCP) simultaneously and hold until the segment check appears on the Instrument Panel Cluster (IPC) and the Climate Control Driver Information Center (CODIC).
3. Diagnosis should not be attempted unless all of the segments of the vacuum fluorescent display are working as this could lead to misdiagnosis. On the PC however the turn signal indicators do not light during this check.
4. After the service mode is entered, any trouble codes stored in the computer memory will be displayed, starting with ECM codes prefixed with an E.
5. If no trouble codes are present, the message NO ECM CODES will be displayed. Some later systems will display NO X CODES present, with X representing the system selected such as ECM, BOM, SIR, etc.

CLEARING CODES:
6. While still in the service mode, and the ECM diagnostic code display has been completed press the HI button on the CCP.
7. This action should cause the display to read `ECM DATA?'.
8. Press the LO button on the COP until the display reads 'ECM CLEAR CODES?'.
9. Press the HI button on the CCP and the display should read `ECM CODES CLEAR'.
10. After approximately 3 seconds, all stored ECM codes will be erased.

➡The Cadillac Cimmaron used the 12 terminal DLC and codes can be accessed in the conventional manner. The rear wheel drive Cadillacs equipped with either the 4.1 L V6, 5.0L V8, or the 5.7L V8 all can be accessed in the conventional manner using the DLC.

DIAGNOSTIC TROUBLE CODES

Except Front Wheel Drive Cadillac

Code 12 No engine RPM reference pulses—System Normal
Code 13 Oxygen Sensor (02S) circuit open—left side on 2 sensor system
Code 14 Engine Coolant Temperature (ECT) sensor -possible circuit high or shorted sensor
Code 15 Engine Coolant Temperature (ECT) sensor -circuit low or open circuit
Code 16 Direct ignition system (DIS), fault line circuit or Distributor ignition system (low resolution pulse) or Missing 2x reference circuit or OPTI-Spark ignition timing system (low resolution pulse) or System voltage out of range
Code 17 Camshaft Position Sensor (OPS) or spark reference circuit error

"F" SERIES

2.8L (173 CID) V6   RPO: LC1/LL1 H.O.   V.I.N. CODE: 1/L

COMPUTER SYSTEM

- **C1** Electronic Control Module (ECM)
- **C2** ALCL Connector
- **C3** "CHECK ENGINE" Light
- **C4** System Power
- **C5** System Ground
- **C6** Fuse Panel
- **C7** Lamp Driver
- **C8** Computer Control Harness

AIR/FUEL SYSTEM

- **1** Mixture Control
- **2** Idle Speed Solenoid
- **4** Heated Grid EFE

TRANSMISSION CONVERTER CLUTCH CONTROL SYSTEM

- **5** Trans. Conv. Clutch Connector

IGNITION SYSTEM

- **6** Electronic Spark Timing Connector

AIR INJECTION SYSTEM

- **8** Air Injection Pump
- **9** Air Control Solenoid Valve (Divert)
- **10** Air Switching Solenoid Valve

EXHAUST GAS RECIRCULATION CONTROL SYSTEM

- **11** Exhaust Gas Recirculation Valve
- **12** Exhaust Gas Recirculation Solenoid Valve

FUEL VAPOR CONTROL SYSTEM

- **13** Canister Purge Solenoid Valve
- **14** From Fuel Tank
- **15** Vapor Canister

SEM S/SWITCHES

- **A** Differential Pressure Sensor
- **B** Exhaust Oxygen Sensor
- **C** Throttle Position Sensor
- **D** Coolant Sensor
- **E** Barometric Pressure Sensor
- **F** Vehicle Speed Sensor

79222G26

Example of component locator on a vehicle with electronic engine controls—2.8L Firebird shown

Code 18 Crank/Cam error

Code 19 Crankshaft Position Sensor (CPS) circuit

Code 21 Throttle Position (TP) sensor circuit—signal voltage out of range, probably high

Code 22 Throttle Position (TP) sensor circuit—signal voltage low

Code 23 Intake Air Temperature (IAT or MAT) sensor circuit temperature out of range, low or Open or grounded M/C solenoid Feedback Carburetor system

Code 24 Vehicle Speed Sensor (VSS) circuit

Code 25 Intake Air Temperature (IAT or MAT) sensor circuit temperature out of range, high

Code 26 Quad-Driver Module #1 circuit or Transaxle gear switch circuit

Code 27 Quad-Driver Module circuit or Transaxle gear switch, probably 2nd gear switch circuit

Code 28 Quad-Driver Module (QDM) #2 circuit or Transaxle gear switch, probably 3rd gear switch circuit

Code 29 Transaxle gear switch, probably 4th gear switch circuit

Code 31 Camshaft sensor circuit fault or Park/Neutral Position (PNP) switch circuit or Wastegate circuit signal

Code 32 Exhaust Gas Recirculation (EGR) circuit fault or Barometric Pressure Sensor circuit low Feedback Carburetor system

Code 33 Manifold Absolute Pressure (MAP) sensor—signal voltage out of range, high or Mass Air Flow (MAE) sensor—signal voltage out of range, probably high

Code 34—Manifold Absolute Pressure (MAP) sensor—circuit out of range voltage, low or Mass Air Flow (MAF) sensor circuit (gm/sec low)

Code 35—Idle Air Control (IAC) or idle speed error or Idle Speed Control (ISO) circuit throttle switch shorted Feedback Carburetor system

Code 36 Ignition system circuit error or Transaxle shift problem—4T60E Transaxle

Code 38 Brake input circuit fault—Torque converter clutch signal

Code 39 Clutch input circuit fault—Torque converter clutch signal

Code 41 Cam sensor or cylinder select circuit fault ignition control (IC) reference pulse system fault or Electronic Spark Timing (EST) circuit open or shorted

Code 42 Electronic Spark Timing (EST) circuit grounded or Ignition Control (IC) circuit grounded or faulty bypass line

Code 43 Knock Sensor (KS) or Electronic Spark Control (ESC) circuit fault

Code 44 Oxygen Sensor (02S), left side on 2 sensor system lean exhaust indicated

Code 45 Oxygen Sensor (02S), left side on 2 sensor system rich exhaust indicated

Code 46 Personal Automotive Security System (PASSKey II) circuit or Power Steering Pressure Switch (PSPS) circuit

Code 47 PCM-BCM data circuit

Code 48 Misfire diagnosis

Code 51 Calibration error, faulty MEM-CAL, ECM or EEPROM failure

Code 52 Engine oil temperature sensor circuit, low temperature indicated or Fuel Calpac missing or Over voltage condition or EGR Circuit fault

Code 53 Battery voltage error or EGR problem or Personal Automotive Security System (PASS-Key) circuit

Code 54 EGR #2 problem or Fuel pump circuit (low voltage) or Shorted mixture control solenoid circuit Feedback Carburetor system

Code 55 A/D Converter error, PCM error or not grounded, EGR #3 problem, Fuel lean monitor, Grounded voltage reference, faulty oxygen sensor or fuel lean Feedback Carburetor system

Code 56 Quad-Driver Module (QDM) #2 circuit or Secondary air inlet valve actuator vacuum sensor circuit signal high 5.7L (VIN J)

Code 57 Boost control problem

Code 58 Vehicle Anti-theft System fuel enable circuit

Code 61 A/C system performance or Cruise vent solenoid circuit fault or Oxygen Sensor (02S) degraded signal or Secondary port throttle valve system fault 5.7L (VIN J) or Transaxle gear switch signal

Code 62 Cruise vacuum solenoid circuit fault or Engine oil temperature sensor, high temperature indicated or Transaxle gear switch signal circuit fault

Code 63 Oxygen Sensor (02S), right side circuit open or Cruise system problem (speed error) or Manifold Absolute Pressure (MAP) sensor circuit out of range

Code 64 Oxygen Sensor (02S), right side—lean exhaust indicated

Code 65 Oxygen Sensor (02S), right side—rich exhaust indicated or Cruise servo position circuit or Fuel injector circuit low current

Code 66 A/C pressure sensor circuit fault, probably low pressure or Engine power switch, voltage high or low or PCM fault 5.7L (VIN J)

Code 67 A/C pressure sensor circuit, sensor or A/C clutch circuit failure or Cruise switch circuit fault

Code 68 A/C compressor relay (shorted circuit) or Cruise system fault

Code 69 A/C clutch circuit or head pressure high

Code 70 A/C refrigerant pressure sensor circuit (high pressure)

Code 71 A/C evaporator temperature sensor circuit (low temperature)

Code 72 Gear selector switch circuit

Code 73 A/C evaporator temperature sensor circuit (high temperature)

Code 75 Digital EGR #1 solenoid error

Code 76 Digital EGR #2 solenoid error

Code 77 Digital EGR #3 solenoid error

Code 79 Vehicle Speed Sensor (VSS) circuit signal high

Code 80 Vehicle Speed Sensor (VSS) circuit signal low

Code 81 Brake input circuit fault—Torque converter clutch signal

Code 82 Ignition Control (IC) 3X signal error

Code 85 PROM error

Code 86 Analog/Digital ECM error

Code 87 EEPROM error

Code 99 Power management

➡**This list is for reference and does not mean a specific component is defective.**

Front Wheel Drive Cadillac

Cadillac Codes may start with an `E', `EO', `P or `P0' dependent on model or type of code display. This prefix has been left off the following code description list.

Code 12 No spark reference from ignition control module or distributor

Code 13 Oxygen sensor No.1 not ready

Code 14 Engine Coolant Temperature (ECT) sensor circuit shorted

Code 15 Engine Coolant Temperature (ECT) sensor circuit open
Code 16 System voltage out of range
Code 17 Oxygen sensor No.2 not ready
Code 19 Fuel pump circuit shorted
Code 20 Fuel pump circuit open
Code 21 Throttle Position Sensor (TPS) circuit shorted
Code 22 Throttle Position Sensor (TPS) circuit open
Code 23 Electronic Spark Timing (EST) circuit fault or Ignition Control (IC) circuit problem
Code 24 Vehicle Speed Sensor (VSS) circuit problem
Code 26 Throttle Position (TP) switch circuit shorted
Code 27 Throttle Position (TP) switch circuit open
Code 28 Transaxle pressure switch problem
Code 29 Transaxle shift `B' solenoid problem
Code 30 Idle Speed Control (ISO) RPM out of range
Code 31 Manifold Absolute Pressure (MAP) sensor circuit shorted
Code 32 Manifold Absolute Pressure (MAP) sensor circuit open
Code 33 Extended travel brake switch input circuit problem
Code 34 Manifold Absolute Pressure (MAP) sensor signal too high
Code 35 Ignition ground voltage out of range
Code 36 EGR valve pintle position out of range
Code 37 Intake Air Temperature (IAT) Manifold Air Temperature (MAT) circuit shorted
Code 38 Intake Air Temperature (IAT) sensor, Manifold Air Temperature (MAT) circuit open
Code 39 Torque Converter Clutch (TCC) engagement problem
Code 40 Power Steering Pressure Switch (PSPS) open
Code 41 Cam sensor circuit fault
Code 42 Oxygen sensor No.1 LEAN exhaust signal
Code 43 Oxygen sensor No.1 RICH exhaust signal
Code 44 Oxygen sensor No.2 LEAN exhaust signal
Code 45 Oxygen sensor No.2 RICH exhaust signal
Code 46 Bank-to-bank fueling difference
Code 47 ECM Body Control Module (BCM) or IPC/PCM data fault
Code 48 EGR control system fault
Code 50 2nd gear pressure circuit fault
Code 51 MEM-CAL error or PROM checksum mismatch
Code 52 ECM memory reset indicator or PCM keep alive memory reset
Code 53 Spark reference signal interrupt from Ignition Control (IC) module
Code 55 Closed throttle angle out of range or Throttle Position Sensor (TPS) misadjusted
Code 56 Transaxle input speed sensor circuit problem
Code 57 Shorted transaxle temperature sensor circuit
Code 58 Personal Automotive Security System (PASS) control fault
Code 59 Open transaxle temperature sensor circuit
Code 60 Cruise transaxle not in drive
Code 61 Cruise vent solenoid circuit fault

Code 62 Cruise vacuum solenoid circuit fault
Code 63 Cruise vehicle speed and set speed difference
Code 64 Cruise vehicle acceleration too high
Code 65 Cruise servo position sensor failure
Code 66 Cruise engine RPM too high
Code 67 Cruise set/coast or resume/accel input shorted
Code 68 Cruise Control Command (CCC) fault or servo position out of range
Code 69 Traction control active in cruise
Code 70 Intermittent Throttle Position (TP) sensor signal
Code 71 Intermittent Manifold Absolute Pressure (MAP) sensor signal
Code 73 Intermittent Engine Coolant Temperature (ECT) sensor signal
Code 74 Intermittent Intake Air Temperature (IAT) sensor signal
Code 75 Vehicle Speed Sensor (VSS) signal intermittent
Code 76 Transaxle pressure control solenoid circuit malfunction
Code 80 Fuel system rich or TP Sensor/idle learn not complete
Code 81 Cam to 4X reference correlation problem
Code 83 24X Reference signal high
Code 85 Idle throttle angle too high, Throttle body service required
Code 86 Undefined gear ratio
Code 88 Torque Converter Clutch (TOO) not disengaging
Code 89 Long shift and maximum adapt
Code 90 Viscous Converter Clutch (VOC) brake switch input fault
Code 91 Park/neutral switch fault
Code 92 Heated windshield fault
Code 93 Traction control system PWM link failure
Code 94 Transaxle shift `A' solenoid problem
Code 95 Engine stall detected
Code 96 Torque converter overstress
Code 97 Park/neutral to drive/reverse at high throttle angle
Code 98 High RPM P/N to D/R shift under Idle Speed Control (ISO)
Code 99 Cruise control servo not applied in cruise
Code P102 Shorted Brake Booster Vacuum (BBV) sensor
Code P103 Open Brake Booster Vacuum (BBV) sensor
Code P105 Brake Booster Vacuum (BBV) too low
Code P106 Stop lamp switch input circuit problem
Code P107 PCM/BCM data link problem
Code P108 PROM checksum mismatch
Code P109 POM keep alive memory reset
Code P110 Generator L-terminal circuit problem
Code P112 Total EEPROM failure
Code P117 Shift `A/Shift `B' circuit output open or shorted
Code P131 Active Knock Sensor (KS) failure
Code P132 Knock Sensor (KS) circuit failure
Code P137 Loss of ABS/TCS data
This list is for reference and does not mean a specific component is defective.

Refer to the model specific sections for fuel system service procedures

OBD II DIAGNOSTIC TROUBLE CODES

Introduction

To comply with On-Board Diagnostics Second Generation (OBD II) regulations, the Control Module is equipped with software designed to allow it to monitor vehicle emission control systems and components. Once the ignition is turned on or the engine is started, and certain test conditions are met, the PCM runs a series of monitors to test the emission control systems and components. Test conditions include different inputs such as time since startup, run-time, engine speed and temperature, transaxle gear position, and the engine open or closed loop status. Once the monitor is started, the control module attempts to run it to completion. If a particular monitor fails a test, a code is set and operating conditions at that time are recorded in memory. If the same component or system fails twice in succession, the Malfunction Indicator Lamp (MIL) is activated.

Monitors are divided into 2 types: Main Monitors and the Comprehensive Component Monitors.

- Catalyst Monitor
- EGR Monitor
- EVAP Monitor
- Fuel System Monitor
- Misfire Monitor
- Oxygen Sensor Monitor
- Oxygen Sensor Heater Monitor

Certain monitors, in particular the fuel system and misfire monitors, have limitations that are different from any of the other monitors. The first time either of these monitors fail, the MIL is activated, and engine conditions at the time of the fault are recorded. In order for the control module to turn off an MIL related to these 2 monitors, it must determine that no faults are present with engine operating conditions similar to when it detected the fault. To qualify, the engine must be operated within a specified speed range, engine load range and temperature range.

A warm-up cycle is considered to be vehicle operation after the engine has been turned off for a period of time, with the ECT input rising a specified amount and reaching normal operating temperature. When the MIL is turned off because a fault is no longer present, most OBD II codes will be erased after a minimum of 40 warm-up cycles. Misfire and fuel system codes require a minimum of 80 warm-up cycles before they clear.

OBD II Systems use a standardized test connector, called the Data Link Connector (DLC). It is located under the left side of the instrument panel. The DLC is located out of the line of sight of vehicle passengers, but is easily viewable from a kneeling position outside the vehicle. The connector is rectangular in design and contains up to 16 terminals. It has keying features to allow for easy connection. Both the DLC and Scan Tool connectors have latching features that ensure the scan tool will remain properly connected.

Some common uses of the Scan Tool are to identify and clear Diagnostic Trouble Codes (DTC's) and to read control module freeze frame.

The Malfunction Indicator Lamp (MIL) looks similar to the "Check Engine" lamp. However, on OBD II Systems, it is controlled under a strict set of guidelines that dictate when the MIL is illuminated. If any of the control module monitors detects a fault that could impact vehicle emissions, a fault code is set. A One-Trip Monitor requires that a test fail once, a Two-Trip Monitor requires a test fail twice in succession, and a Three-Trip Monitor requires that a test fail 3 times in succession to activate the MIL.

The MIL is mounted in the instrument panel and has 2 functions: To act as a bulb check at key On and to inform the driver that an emissions fault has occurred.

Once the engine is started, if no faults are detected, the control module should extinguish the MIL after a few seconds. If the MIL remains On or flashes with the engine running a driveability symptom is present.

Federal law required all vehicle manufacturers to meet On Board Diagnostics, Second Generation or OBD II standards by 1996. In order to meet this standard, the automobile's on-board computer must monitor and perform diagnostic tests on vehicle emissions to ensure that the vehicle is operating at an acceptable (legal) emission level. The maximum allowable emission level is set by the Federal Test Procedure (FTP).

All 1996–00 vehicles are OBD II compliant. All OBD II vehicles have the same 16-pin diagnostic connector or DLC. This eliminates the need to have a manufacturer specific connector to plug a scan tool into your vehicle.

TROUBLE CODE DESCRIPTION

In the past, trouble code numbers varied between manufacturers, years, makes and models. OBD II requires that all vehicle manufacturers use a common Diagnostic Trouble Code (DTC) numbering system. Since the generic listing was not specific enough, most manufacturers came up with their own DTC listings which are called manufacturer specific codes. Both generic and manufacturer specific codes are 5 digits. The numbers can be decoded as follows:

The first digit is a letter which identifies the function of the device or circuit which has the fault. This digit can be either:

- P—Powertrain
- B—Body
- C—Chassis
- U—Network or data link code

The second digit is either a 0 or 1 and indicates whether the code is generic or manufacturer specific.

- 0—Generic
- 1—Manufacturer Specific

The third digit represents the specific vehicle circuit or system that has the fault. Listed below are the number identifiers for the powertrain system.

- 1—Fuel and Air Metering
- 2—Fuel and Air Metering (Injector Circuit Malfunctions Only)
- 3—Ignition System or Misfire
- 4—Auxiliary Emission Control

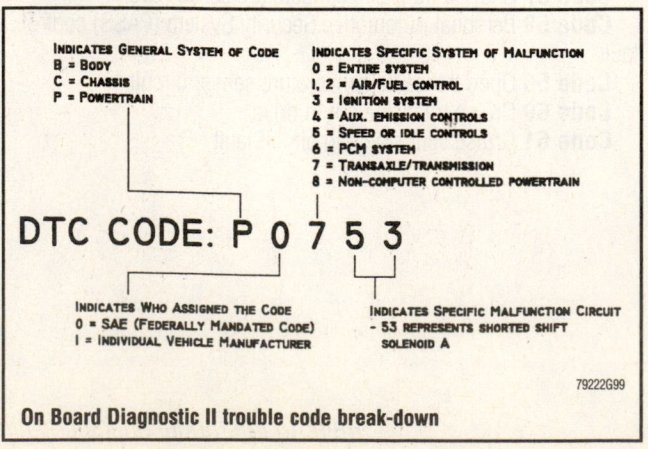

On Board Diagnostic II trouble code break-down

- 5—Vehicle Speed Control and Idle Control System
- 6—Computer and Auxiliary Outputs
- 7—Transmission
- 8—Transmission

The last 2 digits indicate the specific trouble code.

On OBD II vehicles there are 2 different types of DTC's: Stored and Pending. For a DTC to become Stored, certain malfunction conditions must occur. The condition(s) required to Store codes are different for every DTC and vary by vehicle manufacturer.

In order for some DTC's to become Stored, a malfunction condition has to happen more than once. If the malfunction conditions are required to occur more than once, the potential malfunction is called a Pending DTC. The DTC remains pending until the malfunction condition occurs the required number of times to make the code stored. If the malfunction condition does not occur again after a set time the pending DTC will be cleared.

Chrysler Corp.

READING CODES

With Scan Tool

Reading the control module memory is one of the first steps in OBD II system diagnostics. This step should be initially performed to determine the general nature of the fault. Subsequent readings will determine if the fault has been cleared.

Reading codes can be performed by any of the methods below:
- Read the control module memory with the Generic Scan Tool (GST)
- Read the control module memory with the vehicle manufacturer's specific tester

To read the fault codes, connect the scan tool or tester according to the manufacturer's instructions. Follow the manufacturer's specified procedure for reading the codes.

Without Scan Tool

On all 1996–97 vehicles, as well as the 1998 Sebring coupe and Avenger models with a 2.0L engine, DTC's can be accessed by observing the 2-digit number (referred to as an OBD II Equivalent code) displayed by the Malfunction Indicator Lamp (MIL). The MIL is shown on the instrument panel as the Check Engine lamp. This method should be used as a "quick test" only; always use a scan tool to get the most detailed information.

➡Be advised that the MIL can only perform a limited number of functions and it is a good idea to have the system checked with a scan tool to double check the circuit function.

Within a period of 5 seconds, cycle the ignition key **ON— OFF—ON—OFF—ON**.

1. Count the number of times the MIL (check engine lamp) on the instrument panel flashes on and off.

The number of flashes represents the trouble code. There is a short pause between the flashes representing the 1st and 2nd digits of the code. Longer pauses are used to separate individual 2-digit trouble codes.

An example of a flashed DTC is as follows:
- Lamp flashes 4 times, pauses, then flashes 6 more times. This denotes a DTC number 46.

- Lamp flashes 5 times, pauses, then flashes 5 more times. This indicates a DTC number 55.

DTC 55 will always be the last code to be displayed.

CLEARING CODES

With Scan Tool

Control module reset procedures are a very important part of OBD II System diagnostics. This step should be done at the end of any fault code repair and at the end of any driveability repair.

Clearing codes can be performed by any of the methods below:
- Clear the control module memory with the Generic Scan Tool (GST)
- Clear the control module memory with the vehicle manufacturer's specific tester
- Turn the ignition OFF and remove the negative battery cable for at least 1 minute.

Removing the negative battery cable may cause other systems in the vehicle to loose their memory. Prior to removing the cable, ensure you have the proper reset codes for radios and alarms.

➡The MIL will may also be de-activated for some codes if the vehicle completes 3 consecutive trips without a fault detected with vehicle conditions similar to those present during the fault.

Without Scan Tool

Control module reset procedures are a very important part of OBD II System diagnostics. This step should be done at the end of any fault code repair and at the end of any driveability repair.

Clearing codes can be performed by turning the ignition OFF and removing the negative battery cable for at least 1 minute. Removing the negative battery cable may cause other systems in the vehicle to loose their memory. Prior to removing the cable, ensure you have the proper reset codes for radios and alarms.

➡The MIL will may also be de-activated for some codes if the vehicle completes 3 consecutive trips without a fault detected with vehicle conditions similar to those present during the fault.

OBD II TROUBLE CODES

P0100 Mass or Volume Air Flow Circuit Malfunction
P0101 Mass or Volume Air Flow Circuit Range/Performance Problem
P0102 Mass or Volume Air Flow Circuit Low Input
P0103 Mass or Volume Air Flow Circuit High Input
P0104 Mass or Volume Air Flow Circuit Intermittent
P0105 Manifold Absolute Pressure/Barometric Pressure Circuit Malfunction
P0106 Manifold Absolute Pressure/Barometric Pressure Circuit Out Of Range
P0107 Manifold Absolute Pressure/Barometric Pressure Circuit Low Input
P0108 Manifold Absolute Pressure/Barometric Pressure Circuit High Input
P0109 Manifold Absolute Pressure/Barometric Pressure Circuit Intermittent

P0110 Intake Air Temperature Circuit Malfunction
P0111 Intake Air Temperature Circuit Range/Performance Problem
P0112 Intake Air Temperature Circuit Low Input
P0113 Intake Air Temperature Circuit High Input
P0114 Intake Air Temperature Circuit Intermittent
P0115 Engine Coolant Temperature Circuit Malfunction
P0116 Engine Coolant Temperature Circuit Range/Performance Problem
P0117 Engine Coolant Temperature Circuit Low Input
P0118 Engine Coolant Temperature Circuit High Input
P0119 Engine Coolant Temperature Circuit Intermittent
P0120 Throttle/Pedal Position Sensor/Switch "A" Circuit Malfunction
P0121 Throttle/Pedal Position Sensor/Switch "A" Circuit Range/Performance Problem
P0122 Throttle/Pedal Position Sensor/Switch "A" Circuit Low Input
P0123 Throttle/Pedal Position Sensor/Switch "A" Circuit High Input
P0124 Throttle/Pedal Position Sensor/Switch "A" Circuit Intermittent
P0125 Insufficient Coolant Temperature For Closed Loop Fuel Control
P0126 Insufficient Coolant Temperature For Stable Operation
P0130 O_2Circuit Malfunction (Bank #1 Sensor #1)
P0131 O_2Sensor Circuit Low Voltage (Bank #1 Sensor #1)
P0132 O_2Sensor Circuit High Voltage (Bank #1 Sensor #1)
P0133 O_2Sensor Circuit Slow Response (Bank #1 Sensor #1)
P0134 O_2Sensor Circuit No Activity Detected (Bank #1 Sensor #1)
P0135 O_2Sensor Heater Circuit Malfunction (Bank #1 Sensor #1)
P0136 O_2Sensor Circuit Malfunction (Bank #1 Sensor #2)
P0137 O_2Sensor Circuit Low Voltage (Bank #1 Sensor #2)
P0138 O_2Sensor Circuit High Voltage (Bank #1 Sensor #2)
P0139 O_2Sensor Circuit Slow Response (Bank #1 Sensor #2)
P0140 O_2Sensor Circuit No Activity Detected (Bank #1 Sensor #2)
P0141 O_2Sensor Heater Circuit Malfunction (Bank #1 Sensor #2)
P0142 O_2Sensor Circuit Malfunction (Bank #1 Sensor #3)
P0143 O_2Sensor Circuit Low Voltage (Bank #1 Sensor #3)
P0144 O_2Sensor Circuit High Voltage (Bank #1 Sensor #3)
P0145 O_2Sensor Circuit Slow Response (Bank #1 Sensor #3)
P0146 O_2Sensor Circuit No Activity Detected (Bank #1 Sensor #3)
P0147 O_2Sensor Heater Circuit Malfunction (Bank #1 Sensor #3)
P0150 O_2Sensor Circuit Malfunction (Bank #2 Sensor #1)
P0151 O_2Sensor Circuit Low Voltage (Bank #2 Sensor #1)
P0152 O_2Sensor Circuit High Voltage (Bank #2 Sensor #1)
P0153 O_2Sensor Circuit Slow Response (Bank #2 Sensor #1)
P0154 O_2Sensor Circuit No Activity Detected (Bank #2 Sensor #1)
P0155 O_2Sensor Heater Circuit Malfunction (Bank #2 Sensor #1)
P0156 O_2Sensor Circuit Malfunction (Bank #2 Sensor #2)
P0157 O_2Sensor Circuit Low Voltage (Bank #2 Sensor #2)
P0158 O_2Sensor Circuit High Voltage (Bank #2 Sensor #2)
P0159 O_2Sensor Circuit Slow Response (Bank #2 Sensor #2)
P0160 O_2Sensor Circuit No Activity Detected (Bank #2 Sensor #2)

P0161 O_2Sensor Heater Circuit Malfunction (Bank #2 Sensor #2)
P0162 O_2Sensor Circuit Malfunction (Bank #2 Sensor #3)
P0163 O_2Sensor Circuit Low Voltage (Bank #2 Sensor #3)
P0164 O_2Sensor Circuit High Voltage (Bank #2 Sensor #3)
P0165 O_2Sensor Circuit Slow Response (Bank #2 Sensor #3)
P0166 O_2Sensor Circuit No Activity Detected (Bank #2 Sensor #3)
P0167 O_2Sensor Heater Circuit Malfunction (Bank #2 Sensor #3)
P0170 Fuel Trim Malfunction (Bank #1)
P0171 System Too Lean (Bank #1)
P0172 System Too Rich (Bank #1)
P0173 Fuel Trim Malfunction (Bank #2)
P0174 System Too Lean (Bank #2)
P0175 System Too Rich (Bank #2)
P0176 Fuel Composition Sensor Circuit Malfunction
P0177 Fuel Composition Sensor Circuit Range/Performance
P0178 Fuel Composition Sensor Circuit Low Input
P0179 Fuel Composition Sensor Circuit High Input
P0180 Fuel Temperature Sensor "A" Circuit Malfunction
P0181 Fuel Temperature Sensor "A" Circuit Range/Performance
P0182 Fuel Temperature Sensor "A" Circuit Low Input
P0183 Fuel Temperature Sensor "A" Circuit High Input
P0184 Fuel Temperature Sensor "A" Circuit Intermittent
P0185 Fuel Temperature Sensor "B" Circuit Malfunction
P0186 Fuel Temperature Sensor "B" Circuit Range/Performance
P0187 Fuel Temperature Sensor "B" Circuit Low Input
P0188 Fuel Temperature Sensor "B" Circuit High Input
P0189 Fuel Temperature Sensor "B" Circuit Intermittent
P0190 Fuel Rail Pressure Sensor Circuit Malfunction
P0191 Fuel Rail Pressure Sensor Circuit Range/Performance
P0192 Fuel Rail Pressure Sensor Circuit Low Input
P0193 Fuel Rail Pressure Sensor Circuit High Input
P0194 Fuel Rail Pressure Sensor Circuit Intermittent
P0195 Engine Oil Temperature Sensor Malfunction
P0196 Engine Oil Temperature Sensor Range/Performance
P0197 Engine Oil Temperature Sensor Low
P0198 Engine Oil Temperature Sensor High
P0199 Engine Oil Temperature Sensor Intermittent
P0200 Injector Circuit Malfunction
P0201 Injector Circuit Malfunction—Cylinder #1
P0202 Injector Circuit Malfunction—Cylinder #2
P0203 Injector Circuit Malfunction—Cylinder #3
P0204 Injector Circuit Malfunction—Cylinder #4
P0205 Injector Circuit Malfunction—Cylinder #5
P0206 Injector Circuit Malfunction—Cylinder #6
P0207 Injector Circuit Malfunction—Cylinder #7
P0208 Injector Circuit Malfunction—Cylinder #8
P0209 Injector Circuit Malfunction—Cylinder #9
P0210 Injector Circuit Malfunction—Cylinder #10
P0211 Injector Circuit Malfunction—Cylinder #11
P0212 Injector Circuit Malfunction—Cylinder #12
P0213 Cold Start Injector #1 Malfunction
P0214 Cold Start Injector #2 Malfunction
P0215 Engine Shutoff Solenoid Malfunction
P0216 Injection Timing Control Circuit Malfunction
P0217 Engine Over Temperature Condition
P0218 Transmission Over Temperature Condition
P0219 Engine Over Speed Condition
P0220 Throttle/Pedal Position Sensor/Switch "B" Circuit Malfunction

P0221 Throttle/Pedal Position Sensor/Switch "B" Circuit Range/Performance Problem

P0222 Throttle/Pedal Position Sensor/Switch "B" Circuit Low Input

P0223 Throttle/Pedal Position Sensor/Switch "B" Circuit High Input

P0224 Throttle/Pedal Position Sensor/Switch "B" Circuit Intermittent

P0225 Throttle/Pedal Position Sensor/Switch "C" Circuit Malfunction

P0226 Throttle/Pedal Position Sensor/Switch "C" Circuit Range/Performance Problem

P0227 Throttle/Pedal Position Sensor/Switch "C" Circuit Low Input

P0228 Throttle/Pedal Position Sensor/Switch "C" Circuit High Input

P0229 Throttle/Pedal Position Sensor/Switch "C" Circuit Intermittent

P0230 Fuel Pump Primary Circuit Malfunction
P0231 Fuel Pump Secondary Circuit Low
P0232 Fuel Pump Secondary Circuit High
P0233 Fuel Pump Secondary Circuit Intermittent
P0234 Engine Over Boost Condition
P0261 Cylinder #1 Injector Circuit Low
P0262 Cylinder #1 Injector Circuit High
P0263 Cylinder #1 Contribution/Balance Fault
P0264 Cylinder #2 Injector Circuit Low
P0265 Cylinder #2 Injector Circuit High
P0266 Cylinder #2 Contribution/Balance Fault
P0267 Cylinder #3 Injector Circuit Low
P0268 Cylinder #3 Injector Circuit High
P0269 Cylinder #3 Contribution/Balance Fault
P0270 Cylinder #4 Injector Circuit Low
P0271 Cylinder #4 Injector Circuit High
P0272 Cylinder #4 Contribution/Balance Fault
P0273 Cylinder #5 Injector Circuit Low
P0274 Cylinder #5 Injector Circuit High
P0275 Cylinder #5 Contribution/Balance Fault
P0276 Cylinder #6 Injector Circuit Low
P0277 Cylinder #6 Injector Circuit High
P0278 Cylinder #6 Contribution/Balance Fault
P0279 Cylinder #7 Injector Circuit Low
P0280 Cylinder #7 Injector Circuit High
P0281 Cylinder #7 Contribution/Balance Fault
P0282 Cylinder #8 Injector Circuit Low
P0283 Cylinder #8 Injector Circuit High
P0284 Cylinder #8 Contribution/Balance Fault
P0285 Cylinder #9 Injector Circuit Low
P0286 Cylinder #9 Injector Circuit High
P0287 Cylinder #9 Contribution/Balance Fault
P0288 Cylinder #10 Injector Circuit Low
P0289 Cylinder #10 Injector Circuit High
P0290 Cylinder #10 Contribution/Balance Fault
P0291 Cylinder #11 Injector Circuit Low
P0292 Cylinder #11 Injector Circuit High
P0293 Cylinder #11 Contribution/Balance Fault
P0294 Cylinder #12 Injector Circuit Low
P0295 Cylinder #12 Injector Circuit High
P0296 Cylinder #12 Contribution/Balance Fault
P0300 Random/Multiple Cylinder Misfire Detected

P0301 Cylinder #1—Misfire Detected
P0302 Cylinder #2—Misfire Detected
P0303 Cylinder #3—Misfire Detected
P0304 Cylinder #4—Misfire Detected
P0305 Cylinder #5—Misfire Detected
P0306 Cylinder #6—Misfire Detected
P0307 Cylinder #7—Misfire Detected
P0308 Cylinder #8—Misfire Detected
P0309 Cylinder #9—Misfire Detected
P0310 Cylinder #10—Misfire Detected
P0311 Cylinder #11—Misfire Detected
P0312 Cylinder #12—Misfire Detected
P0320 Ignition/Distributor Engine Speed Input Circuit Malfunction

P0321 Ignition/Distributor Engine Speed Input Circuit Range/Performance

P0322 Ignition/Distributor Engine Speed Input Circuit No Signal

P0323 Ignition/Distributor Engine Speed Input Circuit Intermittent

P0325 Knock Sensor #1—Circuit Malfunction (Bank #1 or Single Sensor)

P0326 Knock Sensor #1—Circuit Range/Performance (Bank #1 or Single Sensor)

P0327 Knock Sensor #1—Circuit Low Input (Bank #1 or Single Sensor)

P0328 Knock Sensor #1—Circuit High Input (Bank #1 or Single Sensor)

P0329 Knock Sensor #1—Circuit Input Intermittent (Bank #1 or Single Sensor)

P0330 Knock Sensor #2—Circuit Malfunction (Bank #2)
P0331 Knock Sensor #2—Circuit Range/Performance (Bank #2)
P0332 Knock Sensor #2—Circuit Low Input (Bank #2)
P0333 Knock Sensor #2—Circuit High Input (Bank #2)
P0334 Knock Sensor #2—Circuit Input Intermittent (Bank #2)
P0335 Crankshaft Position Sensor "A" Circuit Malfunction
P0336 Crankshaft Position Sensor "A" Circuit Range/Performance
P0337 Crankshaft Position Sensor "A" Circuit Low Input
P0338 Crankshaft Position Sensor "A" Circuit High Input
P0339 Crankshaft Position Sensor "A" Circuit Intermittent
P0340 No Camshaft Position Sensor Signal At PCM
P0341 Camshaft Position Sensor Circuit Range/Performance
P0342 Camshaft Position Sensor Circuit Low Input
P0343 Camshaft Position Sensor Circuit High Input
P0344 Camshaft Position Sensor Circuit Intermittent
P0350 Ignition Coil Primary/Secondary Circuit Malfunction
P0351 Ignition Coil "1" Primary/Secondary Circuit Malfunction
P0352 Ignition Coil "2" Primary/Secondary Circuit Malfunction
P0353 Ignition Coil "3" Primary/Secondary Circuit Malfunction
P0354 Ignition Coil "4" Primary/Secondary Circuit Malfunction
P0355 Ignition Coil "5" Primary/Secondary Circuit Malfunction
P0356 Ignition Coil "6" Primary/Secondary Circuit Malfunction
P0357 Ignition Coil "7" Primary/Secondary Circuit Malfunction
P0358 Ignition Coil "8" Primary/Secondary Circuit Malfunction
P0359 Ignition Coil "9" Primary/Secondary Circuit Malfunction
P0360 Ignition Coil "10" Primary/Secondary Circuit Malfunction
P0361 Ignition Coil "11" Primary/Secondary Circuit Malfunction
P0362 Ignition Coil "12" Primary/Secondary Circuit Malfunction
P0370 Timing Reference High Resolution Signal "A" Malfunction

P0371 Timing Reference High Resolution Signal "A" Too Many Pulses

P0372 Timing Reference High Resolution Signal "A" Too Few Pulses

P0373 Timing Reference High Resolution Signal "A" Intermittent/Erratic Pulses

P0374 Timing Reference High Resolution Signal "A" No Pulses

P0375 Timing Reference High Resolution Signal "B" Malfunction

P0376 Timing Reference High Resolution Signal "B" Too Many Pulses

P0377 Timing Reference High Resolution Signal "B" Too Few Pulses

P0378 Timing Reference High Resolution Signal "B" Intermittent/Erratic Pulses

P0379 Timing Reference High Resolution Signal "B" No Pulses

P0380 Glow Plug/Heater Circuit "A" Malfunction

P0381 Glow Plug/Heater Indicator Circuit Malfunction

P0382 Glow Plug/Heater Circuit "B" Malfunction

P0385 Crankshaft Position Sensor "B" Circuit Malfunction

P0386 Crankshaft Position Sensor "B" Circuit Range/Performance

P0387 Crankshaft Position Sensor "B" Circuit Low Input

P0388 Crankshaft Position Sensor "B" Circuit High Input

P0389 Crankshaft Position Sensor "B" Circuit Intermittent

P0400 Exhaust Gas Recirculation Flow Malfunction

P0401 Exhaust Gas Recirculation Flow Insufficient Detected

P0402 Exhaust Gas Recirculation Flow Excessive Detected

P0403 Exhaust Gas Recirculation Circuit Malfunction

P0404 Exhaust Gas Recirculation Circuit Range/Performance

P0405 Exhaust Gas Recirculation Sensor "A" Circuit Low

P0406 Exhaust Gas Recirculation Sensor "A" Circuit High

P0407 Exhaust Gas Recirculation Sensor "B" Circuit Low

P0408 Exhaust Gas Recirculation Sensor "B" Circuit High

P0410 Secondary Air Injection System Malfunction

P0411 Secondary Air Injection System Incorrect Flow Detected

P0412 Secondary Air Injection System Switching Valve "A" Circuit Malfunction

P0413 Secondary Air Injection System Switching Valve "A" Circuit Open

P0414 Secondary Air Injection System Switching Valve "A" Circuit Shorted

P0415 Secondary Air Injection System Switching Valve "B" Circuit Malfunction

P0416 Secondary Air Injection System Switching Valve "B" Circuit Open

P0417 Secondary Air Injection System Switching Valve "B" Circuit Shorted

P0418 Secondary Air Injection System Relay "A" Circuit Malfunction

P0419 Secondary Air Injection System Relay "B" Circuit Malfunction

P0420 Catalyst System Efficiency Below Threshold (Bank #1)

P0421 Warm Up Catalyst Efficiency Below Threshold (Bank #1)

P0422 Main Catalyst Efficiency Below Threshold (Bank #1)

P0423 Heated Catalyst Efficiency Below Threshold (Bank #1)

P0424 Heated Catalyst Temperature Below Threshold (Bank #1)

P0430 Catalyst System Efficiency Below Threshold (Bank #2)

P0431 Warm Up Catalyst Efficiency Below Threshold (Bank #2)

P0432 Main Catalyst Efficiency Below Threshold (Bank #2)

P0433 Heated Catalyst Efficiency Below Threshold (Bank #2)

P0434 Heated Catalyst Temperature Below Threshold (Bank #2)

P0440 Evaporative Emission Control System Malfunction

P0441 Evaporative Emission Control System Incorrect Purge Flow

P0442 Evaporative Emission Control System Leak Detected (Small Leak)

P0443 Evaporative Emission Control System Purge Control Valve Circuit Malfunction

P0444 Evaporative Emission Control System Purge Control Valve Circuit Open

P0445 Evaporative Emission Control System Purge Control Valve Circuit Shorted

P0446 Evaporative Emission Control System Vent Control Circuit Malfunction

P0447 Evaporative Emission Control System Vent Control Circuit Open

P0448 Evaporative Emission Control System Vent Control Circuit Shorted

P0449 Evaporative Emission Control System Vent Valve/Solenoid Circuit Malfunction

P0450 Evaporative Emission Control System Pressure Sensor Malfunction

P0451 Evaporative Emission Control System Pressure Sensor Range/Performance

P0452 Evaporative Emission Control System Pressure Sensor Low Input

P0453 Evaporative Emission Control System Pressure Sensor High Input

P0454 Evaporative Emission Control System Pressure Sensor Intermittent

P0455 Evaporative Emission Control System Leak Detected (Gross Leak)

P0460 Fuel Level Sensor Circuit Malfunction

P0461 Fuel Level Sensor Circuit Range/Performance

P0462 Fuel Level Sensor Circuit Low Input

P0463 Fuel Level Sensor Circuit High Input

P0464 Fuel Level Sensor Circuit Intermittent

P0465 Purge Flow Sensor Circuit Malfunction

P0466 Purge Flow Sensor Circuit Range/Performance

P0467 Purge Flow Sensor Circuit Low Input

P0468 Purge Flow Sensor Circuit High Input

P0469 Purge Flow Sensor Circuit Intermittent

P0470 Exhaust Pressure Sensor Malfunction

P0471 Exhaust Pressure Sensor Range/Performance

P0472 Exhaust Pressure Sensor Low

P0473 Exhaust Pressure Sensor High

P0474 Exhaust Pressure Sensor Intermittent

P0475 Exhaust Pressure Control Valve Malfunction

P0476 Exhaust Pressure Control Valve Range/Performance

P0477 Exhaust Pressure Control Valve Low

P0478 Exhaust Pressure Control Valve High

P0479 Exhaust Pressure Control Valve Intermittent

P0480 Cooling Fan #1 Control Circuit Malfunction

P0481 Cooling Fan #2 Control Circuit Malfunction

P0482 Cooling Fan #3 Control Circuit Malfunction

P0483 Cooling Fan Rationality Check Malfunction

P0484 Cooling Fan Circuit Over Current

P0485 Cooling Fan Power/Ground Circuit Malfunction

P0500 Vehicle Speed Sensor Malfunction

P0501 Vehicle Speed Sensor Range/Performance

P0502 Vehicle Speed Sensor Circuit Low Input

P0503 Vehicle Speed Sensor Intermittent/Erratic/High

P0505 Idle Control System Malfunction

P0506 Idle Control System RPM Lower Than Expected
P0507 Idle Control System RPM Higher Than Expected
P0510 Closed Throttle Position Switch Malfunction
P0520 Engine Oil Pressure Sensor/Switch Circuit Malfunction
P0521 Engine Oil Pressure Sensor/Switch Range/Performance
P0522 Engine Oil Pressure Sensor/Switch Low Voltage
P0523 Engine Oil Pressure Sensor/Switch High Voltage
P0530 A/C Refrigerant Pressure Sensor Circuit Malfunction
P0531 A/C Refrigerant Pressure Sensor Circuit Range/Performance
P0532 A/C Refrigerant Pressure Sensor Circuit Low Input
P0533 A/C Refrigerant Pressure Sensor Circuit High Input
P0534 A/C Refrigerant Charge Loss
P0550 Power Steering Pressure Sensor Circuit Malfunction
P0551 Power Steering Pressure Sensor Circuit Range/Performance
P0552 Power Steering Pressure Sensor Circuit Low Input
P0553 Power Steering Pressure Sensor Circuit High Input
P0554 Power Steering Pressure Sensor Circuit Intermittent
P0560 System Voltage Malfunction
P0561 System Voltage Unstable
P0562 System Voltage Low
P0563 System Voltage High
P0565 Cruise Control On Signal Malfunction
P0566 Cruise Control Off Signal Malfunction
P0567 Cruise Control Resume Signal Malfunction
P0568 Cruise Control Set Signal Malfunction
P0569 Cruise Control Coast Signal Malfunction
P0570 Cruise Control Accel Signal Malfunction
P0571 Cruise Control/Brake Switch "A" Circuit Malfunction
P0572 Cruise Control/Brake Switch "A" Circuit Low
P0573 Cruise Control/Brake Switch "A" Circuit High
P0574 Through P0580 Reserved for Cruise Codes
P0600 Serial Communication Link Malfunction
P0601 Internal Control Module Memory Check Sum Error
P0602 Control Module Programming Error
P0603 Internal Control Module Keep Alive Memory (KAM) Error
P0604 Internal Control Module Random Access Memory (RAM) Error
P0605 Internal Control Module Read Only Memory (ROM) Error
P0606 PCM Processor Fault
P0608 Control Module VSS Output "A" Malfunction
P0609 Control Module VSS Output "B" Malfunction
P0620 Generator Control Circuit Malfunction
P0621 Generator Lamp "L" Control Circuit Malfunction
P0622 Generator Field "F" Control Circuit Malfunction
P0650 Malfunction Indicator Lamp (MIL) Control Circuit Malfunction
P0654 Engine RPM Output Circuit Malfunction
P0655 Engine Hot Lamp Output Control Circuit Malfunction
P0656 Fuel Level Output Circuit Malfunction
P0700 Transmission Control System Malfunction
P0701 Transmission Control System Range/Performance
P0702 Transmission Control System Electrical
P0703 Torque Converter/Brake Switch "B" Circuit Malfunction
P0704 Clutch Switch Input Circuit Malfunction
P0705 Transmission Range Sensor Circuit Malfunction (PRNDL Input)
P0706 Transmission Range Sensor Circuit Range/Performance

P0707 Transmission Range Sensor Circuit Low Input
P0708 Transmission Range Sensor Circuit High Input
P0709 Transmission Range Sensor Circuit Intermittent
P0710 Transmission Fluid Temperature Sensor Circuit Malfunction
P0711 Transmission Fluid Temperature Sensor Circuit Range/Performance
P0712 Transmission Fluid Temperature Sensor Circuit Low Input
P0713 Transmission Fluid Temperature Sensor Circuit High Input
P0714 Transmission Fluid Temperature Sensor Circuit Intermittent
P0715 Input/Turbine Speed Sensor Circuit Malfunction
P0716 Input/Turbine Speed Sensor Circuit Range/Performance
P0717 Input/Turbine Speed Sensor Circuit No Signal
P0718 Input/Turbine Speed Sensor Circuit Intermittent
P0719 Torque Converter/Brake Switch "B" Circuit Low
P0720 Output Speed Sensor Circuit Malfunction
P0721 Output Speed Sensor Circuit Range/Performance
P0722 Output Speed Sensor Circuit No Signal
P0723 Output Speed Sensor Circuit Intermittent
P0724 Torque Converter/Brake Switch "B" Circuit High
P0725 Engine Speed Input Circuit Malfunction
P0726 Engine Speed Input Circuit Range/Performance
P0727 Engine Speed Input Circuit No Signal
P0728 Engine Speed Input Circuit Intermittent
P0730 Incorrect Gear Ratio
P0731 Gear #1 Incorrect Ratio
P0732 Gear #2 Incorrect Ratio
P0733 Gear #3 Incorrect Ratio
P0734 Gear #4 Incorrect Ratio
P0735 Gear #5 Incorrect Ratio
P0736 Reverse Incorrect Ratio
P0740 Torque Converter Clutch Circuit Malfunction
P0741 Torque Converter Clutch Circuit Performance or Stuck Off
P0742 Torque Converter Clutch Circuit Stuck On
P0743 Torque Converter Clutch Circuit Electrical
P0744 Torque Converter Clutch Circuit Intermittent
P0745 Pressure Control Solenoid Malfunction
P0746 Pressure Control Solenoid Performance or Stuck Off
P0747 Pressure Control Solenoid Stuck On
P0748 Pressure Control Solenoid Electrical
P0749 Pressure Control Solenoid Intermittent
P0750 Shift Solenoid "A" Malfunction
P0751 Shift Solenoid "A" Performance or Stuck Off
P0752 Shift Solenoid "A" Stuck On
P0753 Shift Solenoid "A" Electrical
P0754 Shift Solenoid "A" Intermittent
P0755 Shift Solenoid "B" Malfunction
P0756 Shift Solenoid "B" Performance or Stuck Off
P0757 Shift Solenoid "B" Stuck On
P0758 Shift Solenoid "B" Electrical
P0759 Shift Solenoid "B" Intermittent
P0760 Shift Solenoid "C" Malfunction
P0761 Shift Solenoid "C" Performance Or Stuck Off
P0762 Shift Solenoid "C" Stuck On
P0763 Shift Solenoid "C" Electrical

Ignition system service is covered in the model specific sections of this manual

P0764 Shift Solenoid "C" Intermittent
P0765 Shift Solenoid "D" Malfunction
P0766 Shift Solenoid "D" Performance Or Stuck Off
P0767 Shift Solenoid "D" Stuck On
P0768 Shift Solenoid "D" Electrical
P0769 Shift Solenoid "D" Intermittent
P0770 Shift Solenoid "E" Malfunction
P0771 Shift Solenoid "E" Performance Or Stuck Off
P0772 Shift Solenoid "E" Stuck On
P0773 Shift Solenoid "E" Electrical
P0774 Shift Solenoid "E" Intermittent
P0780 Shift Malfunction
P0781 1–2 Shift Malfunction
P0782 2–3 Shift Malfunction
P0783 3–4 Shift Malfunction
P0784 4–5 Shift Malfunction
P0785 Shift/Timing Solenoid Malfunction
P0786 Shift/Timing Solenoid Range/Performance
P0787 Shift/Timing Solenoid Low
P0788 Shift/Timing Solenoid High
P0789 Shift/Timing Solenoid Intermittent
P0790 Normal/Performance Switch Circuit Malfunction
P0801 Reverse Inhibit Control Circuit Malfunction
P0803 1–4 Upshift (Skip Shift) Solenoid Control Circuit Malfunction
P0804 1–4 Upshift (Skip Shift) Lamp Control Circuit Malfunction
P1195 1/1 O_2Sensor Slow During Catalyst Monitor
P1196 2/1 O_2Sensor Slow During Catalyst Monitor
P1197 1/2 O_2Sensor Slow During Catalyst Monitor
P1198 Radiator Temp Sensor Voltage Too High
P1199 Radiator Temp Sensor Voltage Too Low
P1281 Engine Is Cold Too Long
P1282 Fuel Pump Relay Control Circuit
P1288 Intake Manifold Short Runner Solenoid Circuit
P1289 Manifold Tune Valve Solenoid Circuit
P1290 CNG Fuel System Pressure Too High—3.3L CNG vehicles only
P1291 No Temp Rise Seen From Intake Air Heaters
P1292 CNG Pressure Sensor Voltage Too High—3.3L CNG vehicles only
P1293 CNG Pressure Sensor Voltage Too Low—3.3L CNG vehicles only
P1294 Target Idle Not Reached
P1295 No 5-Volts To TP Sensor
P1296 No 5-Volts To MAP Sensor
P1297 No Change In MAP From Start To Run
P1298 Lean Operation At Wide Open Throttle
P1299 Vacuum Leak Found (IAC Fully Seated)
P1388 ASD Relay Control Circuit
P1389 No ASD Relay Output Voltage At PCM
P1390 Timing Belt Skipped 1 Tooth or More
P1391 Intermittent Loss Of CMP Or CKP
P1398 Misfire Adaptive Numerator At Limit (Possible Defective Crank Sensor)
P1399 Wait To Start Lamp Circuit
P1403 No 5-Volts to EGR Sensor
P1476 Too Little Secondary Air
P1477 Too Much Secondary Air
P1478 Battery Temp Sensor Volts Out of Limits
P1479 Transmission Fan Relay Circuit
P1480 PCV Solenoid Circuit

P1482 Catalyst Temp Sensor Circuit Shorted Low
P1483 Catalyst Temp Sensor Circuit Shorted High
P1484 Catalytic Converter Overheat Detected
P1485 Air Injection Solenoid Circuit
P1486 EVAP Leak Monitor Pinched Hose Or Obstruction Found
P1487 High Speed Rad Fan CTRL Circuit
P1488 Auxiliary 5-Volt Supply Output Too Low
P1489 High Speed Fan CTRL Relay Circuit
P1490 Low Speed Rad Fan CTRL Circuit
P1491 Radiator Fan Control Relay Circuit
P1492 Battery Temp Sensor Voltage Too High
P1493 Battery Temp Sensor Voltage Too Low
P1494 Leak Detection Pump Pressure Switch Or Mechanical Fault
P1495 Leak Detection Pump Solenoid Circuit
P1496 5-Volt Supply, Output Too Low
P1498 Auxiliary 5-Volt Supply Output Too Low
P1594 Charging System Voltage Too High
P1595 Speed Control Solenoid Circuits
P1596 Speed Control Switch Always High
P1597 Speed Control Switch Always Low
P1598 A/C Pressure Sensor Voltage Too High
P1599 A/C Pressure Sensor Voltage Too Low
P1680 Clutch Release Switch Circuit
P1681 No I/P Cluster CCD/J1850 Messages Received
P1682 Charging System Voltage Too Low
P1683 Speed Control Power Relay or Driver Circuit
P1684 Battery Has Been Disconnected Within the Last 50 Starts
P1685 (SKIM) Smart Key Immobilizer Module Invalid Key
P1686 No SKIM Bus Messages Received
P1697 PCM Failure SRI Mile Not Stored
P1698 PCM Failure EEPROM Write Denied
P1756 Governor Pressure Not Equal To Target @ 15–20 PSI
P1757 Governor Pressure Above 3 PSI In Gear With 0 MPH
P1762 Governor Pressure Sensor Offset Volts Too Low Or High
P1763 Governor Pressure Sensor Volts Too High
P1764 Governor Pressure Sensor Volts Too Low
P1765 Trans 12-Volt Supply Relay Control Circuit
P1899 P/N Switch Stuck In Park Or In Gear

OBD II TROUBLE CODE EQUIVALENTS

11 No crank reference signal at PCM
11 Timing belt skipped 1 tooth or more
11 Intermittent loss of CMP or CKP
11 Misfire adaptive numerator at limit
12 Battery disconnect
13 Slow change in idle MAP sensor signal (VIN N engine)
13 No change in MAP from start to run
14 MAP sensor voltage too low
14 MAP sensor voltage too high
14 No 5-volts to MAP sensor
15 5-volt supply output too low
16 No vehicle speed sensor signal
16 Knock sensor signal
17 Engine cold too long
17 Closed loop temperature not reached
21 Front O_2S shorted to voltage
21 Front O_2S stays at center
21 Rear O_2S shorted to voltage
21 Rear O_2S stays at center
21 Upstream O_2S shorted to ground

21 Upstream O$_2$S shorted to voltage
21 Upstream O$_2$S response
21 Upstream O$_2$S stays at center
21 Upstream O$_2$S heater failure
21 Downstream O$_2$S shorted to ground
21 Downstream O$_2$S shorted to voltage
21 Downstream O$_2$S response
21 Downstream O$_2$S signal inactive
21 Downstream O$_2$S heater failure
21 Front bank upstream O$_2$S shorted to ground (6-cylinder)
21 Front bank upstream O$_2$S shorted to voltage (6-cylinder)
21 Front bank upstream O$_2$S slow response 6-cylinder)
21 Front bank upstream O$_2$S stays at center (6-cylinder)
21 Front bank upstream O$_2$S heater failure (6-cylinder)
21 Front bank downstream O$_2$S shorted to ground (6-cylinder)
21 Front bank downstream O$_2$S shorted to voltage (6-cylinder)
21 Front bank downstream O$_2$S stays at center (6-cylinder)
21 Front bank downstream O$_2$S heater failure (6-cylinder)
22 ECT sensor voltage too low
22 ECT sensor voltage too high
23 Intake air temperature voltage low
23 Intake air temperature voltage high
24 TPS voltage does not agree with MAP
24 Throttle position sensor voltage low
24 Throttle position sensor voltage high
24 No 5-volts to TPS
25 Idle air control motor circuits
25 Target idle not reached
25 Vacuum leak found (IAC fully seated)
27 Injector #1 control circuit
27 Injector #2 control circuit
27 Injector #3 control circuit
27 Injector #4 control circuit
27 Injector #5 control circuit (6-cylinder)
27 Injector #6 control circuit (6-cylinder)
31 EVAP purge flow monitor failure
31 EVAP system small leak
31 EVAP solenoid circuit
31 EVAP system large leak
31 EVAP leak monitor pinched hose
31 Leak detection pump pressure switch
31 EVAP emission vent solenoid switch or mechanical failure
31 Leak detection pump solenoid circuit
31 EVAP emission vent solenoid circuit
31 High speed radiator fan ground control relay circuit
32 EGR system failure
32 EGR solenoid circuit
33 A/C pressure sensor volts too high
33 A/C pressure sensor volts too low
33 A/C clutch relay circuit
34 Speed control switch always low
34 Speed control switch always high
34 Speed control solenoid circuit
35 High speed condenser fan control relay circuit
35 High fan and high fan ground control relay circuit
35 High speed radiator fan control relay circuit
35 High speed fan control relay circuit
35 Low speed fan control relay circuit
37 Park/Neutral switch failure
41 Alternator field not switching properly

42 Auto shutdown relay circuit
42 No ASD relay output voltage at PCM
42 Fuel level sending unit volts too low
42 Fuel level sending unit volts too high
42 Fuel level unit no change over miles
42 Fuel pump relay control circuit
43 Multiple cylinder misfire
43 Cylinder #1 misfire
43 Cylinder #2 misfire
43 Cylinder #3 misfire
43 Cylinder #4 misfire
43 Cylinder #5 misfire
43 Cylinder #6 misfire
43 Ignition coil #1 primary circuit
43 Ignition coil #2 primary circuit
44 Ambient temperature sensor
44 Battery temperature sensor volts out of limit
44 Battery temperature sensor voltage too high
44 Battery temperature sensor voltage too low
45 Transaxle fault present
46 Charging system voltage too high
47 Charging system voltage too low
51 Fuel system lean (4-cylinder)
51 Rear bank fuel system lean (6-cylinder)
51 Front bank fuel system lean (6-cylinder)
52 Fuel system rich (4-cylinder)
52 Rear bank fuel system rich (6-cylinder)
52 Front bank fuel system rich (6-cylinder)
53 Internal controller failure
53 PCM failure SPI communications
53 Internal controller failure
53 PCM failure SPI communications
54 No cam signal at PCM
55 Completion or fault code display on Check Engine Lamp
62 PCM failure SRI mile not stared
63 PCM failure EEPROM write denied
64 Catalytic converter efficiency failure
64 Rear bank catalytic converter efficiency failure
65 Power steering switch failure
65 Brake switch performance circuit
66 No CCD message from body controller
66 No CCD message from TCM
71 5-volt output low speed control power circuit
72 Catalytic Converter efficiency failure
72 Front bank catalytic converter efficiency failure
77 Malfunction detected with power feed to speed control servo

Ford Motor Co.

READING CODES

Reading the control module memory is one of the first steps in OBD II system diagnostics. This step should be initially performed to determine the general nature of the fault. Subsequent readings will determine if the fault has been cleared.

Reading codes can be performed by any of the methods below:
• Read the control module memory with the Generic Scan Tool (GST).

• Read the control module memory with the vehicle manufacturer's specific tester.

To read the fault codes, connect the scan tool or tester according to the manufacturer's instructions. Follow the manufacturer's specified procedure for reading the codes.

CLEARING CODES

Control module reset procedures are a very important part of OBD II System diagnostics. This step should be done at the end of any fault code repair and at the end of any driveability repair.

Clearing codes can be performed by any of the methods below:

• Clear the control module memory with the Generic Scan Tool (GST).

• Clear the control module memory with the vehicle manufacturer's specific tester.

• Turn the ignition OFF and remove the negative battery cable for at least 1 minute.

Removing the negative battery cable may cause other systems in the vehicle to loose their memory. Prior to removing the cable, ensure you have the proper reset codes for radios and alarms.

➡**The MIL may also be de-activated for some codes if the vehicle completes 3 consecutive trips without a fault detected with vehicle conditions similar to those present during the fault.**

OBD II TROUBLE CODES

P0000 No Failures
P0100 Mass or Volume Air Flow Circuit Malfunction
P0101 Mass or Volume Air Flow Circuit Range/Performance Problem
P0102 Mass or Volume Air Flow Circuit Low Input
P0103 Mass or Volume Air Flow Circuit High Input
P0104 Mass or Volume Air Flow Circuit Intermittent
P0105 Manifold Absolute Pressure/Barometric Pressure Circuit Malfunction
P0106 Manifold Absolute Pressure/Barometric Pressure Circuit Range/Performance Problem
P0107 Manifold Absolute Pressure/Barometric Pressure Circuit Low Input
P0108 Manifold Absolute Pressure/Barometric Pressure Circuit High Input
P0109 Manifold Absolute Pressure/Barometric Pressure Circuit Intermittent
P0110 Intake Air Temperature Circuit Malfunction
P0111 Intake Air Temperature Circuit Range/Performance Problem
P0112 Intake Air Temperature Circuit Low Input
P0113 Intake Air Temperature Circuit High Input
P0114 Intake Air Temperature Circuit Intermittent
P0115 Engine Coolant Temperature Circuit Malfunction
P0116 Engine Coolant Temperature Circuit Range/Performance Problem
P0117 Engine Coolant Temperature Circuit Low Input
P0118 Engine Coolant Temperature Circuit High Input
P0119 Engine Coolant Temperature Circuit Intermittent
P0120 Throttle/Pedal Position Sensor/Switch "A" Circuit Malfunction
P0121 Throttle/Pedal Position Sensor/Switch "A" Circuit Range/Performance Problem

P0122 Throttle/Pedal Position Sensor/Switch "A" Circuit Low Input
P0123 Throttle/Pedal Position Sensor/Switch "A" Circuit High Input
P0124 Throttle/Pedal Position Sensor/Switch "A" Circuit Intermittent
P0125 Insufficient Coolant Temperature For Closed Loop Fuel Control
P0126 Insufficient Coolant Temperature For Stable Operation
P0130 O_2 Circuit Malfunction (Bank #1 Sensor #1)
P0131 O_2 Sensor Circuit Low Voltage (Bank #1 Sensor #1)
P0132 O_2 Sensor Circuit High Voltage (Bank #1 Sensor #1)
P0133 O_2 Sensor Circuit Slow Response (Bank #1 Sensor #1)
P0134 O_2 Sensor Circuit No Activity Detected (Bank #1 Sensor #1)
P0135 O_2 Sensor Heater Circuit Malfunction (Bank #1 Sensor #1)
P0136 O_2 Sensor Circuit Malfunction (Bank #1 Sensor #2)
P0137 O_2 Sensor Circuit Low Voltage (Bank #1 Sensor #2)
P0138 O_2 Sensor Circuit High Voltage (Bank #1 Sensor #2)
P0139 O_2 Sensor Circuit Slow Response (Bank #1 Sensor #2)
P0140 O_2 Sensor Circuit No Activity Detected (Bank #1 Sensor #2)
P0141 O_2 Sensor Heater Circuit Malfunction (Bank #1 Sensor #2)
P0142 O_2 Sensor Circuit Malfunction (Bank #1 Sensor #3)
P0143 O_2 Sensor Circuit Low Voltage (Bank #1 Sensor #3)
P0144 O_2 Sensor Circuit High Voltage (Bank #1 Sensor #3)
P0145 O_2 Sensor Circuit Slow Response (Bank #1 Sensor #3)
P0146 O_2 Sensor Circuit No Activity Detected (Bank #1 Sensor #3)
P0147 O_2 Sensor Heater Circuit Malfunction (Bank #1 Sensor #3)
P0150 O_2 Sensor Circuit Malfunction (Bank #2 Sensor #1)
P0151 O_2 Sensor Circuit Low Voltage (Bank #2 Sensor #1)
P0152 O_2 Sensor Circuit High Voltage (Bank #2 Sensor #1)
P0153 O_2 Sensor Circuit Slow Response (Bank #2 Sensor #1)
P0154 O_2 Sensor Circuit No Activity Detected (Bank #2 Sensor #1)
P0155 O_2 Sensor Heater Circuit Malfunction (Bank #2 Sensor #1)
P0156 O_2 Sensor Circuit Malfunction (Bank #2 Sensor #2)
P0157 O_2 Sensor Circuit Low Voltage (Bank #2 Sensor #2)
P0158 O_2 Sensor Circuit High Voltage (Bank #2 Sensor #2)
P0159 O_2 Sensor Circuit Slow Response (Bank #2 Sensor #2)
P0160 O_2 Sensor Circuit No Activity Detected (Bank #2 Sensor #2)
P0161 O_2 Sensor Heater Circuit Malfunction (Bank #2 Sensor #2)
P0162 O_2 Sensor Circuit Malfunction (Bank #2 Sensor #3)
P0163 O_2 Sensor Circuit Low Voltage (Bank #2 Sensor #3)
P0164 O_2 Sensor Circuit High Voltage (Bank #2 Sensor #3)
P0165 O_2 Sensor Circuit Slow Response (Bank #2 Sensor #3)
P0166 O_2 Sensor Circuit No Activity Detected (Bank #2 Sensor #3)
P0167 O_2 Sensor Heater Circuit Malfunction (Bank #2 Sensor #3)
P0170 Fuel Trim Malfunction (Bank #1)
P0171 System Too Lean (Bank #1)
P0172 System Too Rich (Bank #1)
P0173 Fuel Trim Malfunction (Bank #2)
P0174 System Too Lean (Bank #2)

P0175 System Too Rich (Bank #2)
P0176 Fuel Composition Sensor Circuit Malfunction
P0177 Fuel Composition Sensor Circuit Range/Performance
P0178 Fuel Composition Sensor Circuit Low Input
P0179 Fuel Composition Sensor Circuit High Input
P0180 Fuel Temperature Sensor "A" Circuit Malfunction
P0181 Fuel Temperature Sensor "A" Circuit Range/Performance
P0182 Fuel Temperature Sensor "A" Circuit Low Input
P0183 Fuel Temperature Sensor "A" Circuit High Input
P0184 Fuel Temperature Sensor "A" Circuit Intermittent
P0185 Fuel Temperature Sensor "B" Circuit Malfunction
P0186 Fuel Temperature Sensor "B" Circuit Range/Performance
P0187 Fuel Temperature Sensor "B" Circuit Low Input
P0188 Fuel Temperature Sensor "B" Circuit High Input
P0189 Fuel Temperature Sensor "B" Circuit Intermittent
P0190 Fuel Rail Pressure Sensor Circuit Malfunction
P0191 Fuel Rail Pressure Sensor Circuit Range/Performance
P0192 Fuel Rail Pressure Sensor Circuit Low Input
P0193 Fuel Rail Pressure Sensor Circuit High Input
P0194 Fuel Rail Pressure Sensor Circuit Intermittent
P0195 Engine Oil Temperature Sensor Malfunction
P0196 Engine Oil Temperature Sensor Range/Performance
P0197 Engine Oil Temperature Sensor Low
P0198 Engine Oil Temperature Sensor High
P0199 Engine Oil Temperature Sensor Intermittent
P0200 Injector Circuit Malfunction
P0201 Injector Circuit Malfunction—Cylinder #1
P0202 Injector Circuit Malfunction—Cylinder #2
P0203 Injector Circuit Malfunction—Cylinder #3
P0204 Injector Circuit Malfunction—Cylinder #4
P0205 Injector Circuit Malfunction—Cylinder #5
P0206 Injector Circuit Malfunction—Cylinder #6
P0207 Injector Circuit Malfunction—Cylinder #7
P0208 Injector Circuit Malfunction—Cylinder #8
P0209 Injector Circuit Malfunction—Cylinder #9
P0210 Injector Circuit Malfunction—Cylinder #10
P0213 Cold Start Injector #1 Malfunction
P0214 Cold Start Injector #2 Malfunction
P0215 Engine Shutoff Solenoid Malfunction
P0216 Injection Timing Control Circuit Malfunction
P0217 Engine Over Temperature Condition
P0218 Transmission Over Temperature Condition
P0219 Engine Over Speed Condition
P0220 Throttle/Pedal Position Sensor/Switch "B" Circuit Malfunction
P0221 Throttle/Pedal Position Sensor/Switch "B" Circuit Range/Performance Problem
P0222 Throttle/Pedal Position Sensor/Switch "B" Circuit Low Input
P0223 Throttle/Pedal Position Sensor/Switch "B" Circuit High Input
P0224 Throttle/Pedal Position Sensor/Switch "B" Circuit Intermittent
P0225 Throttle/Pedal Position Sensor/Switch "C" Circuit Malfunction
P0226 Throttle/Pedal Position Sensor/Switch "C" Circuit Range/Performance Problem
P0227 Throttle/Pedal Position Sensor/Switch "C" Circuit Low Input

P0228 Throttle/Pedal Position Sensor/Switch "C" Circuit High Input
P0229 Throttle/Pedal Position Sensor/Switch "C" Circuit Intermittent
P0230 Fuel Pump Primary Circuit Malfunction
P0231 Fuel Pump Secondary Circuit Low
P0232 Fuel Pump Secondary Circuit High
P0233 Fuel Pump Secondary Circuit Intermittent
P0234 Engine Over Boost Condition
P0261 Cylinder #1 Injector Circuit Low
P0262 Cylinder #1 Injector Circuit High
P0263 Cylinder #1 Contribution/Balance Fault
P0264 Cylinder #2 Injector Circuit Low
P0265 Cylinder #2 Injector Circuit High
P0266 Cylinder #2 Contribution/Balance Fault
P0267 Cylinder #3 Injector Circuit Low
P0268 Cylinder #3 Injector Circuit High
P0269 Cylinder #3 Contribution/Balance Fault
P0270 Cylinder #4 Injector Circuit Low
P0271 Cylinder #4 Injector Circuit High
P0272 Cylinder #4 Contribution/Balance Fault
P0273 Cylinder #5 Injector Circuit Low
P0274 Cylinder #5 Injector Circuit High
P0275 Cylinder #5 Contribution/Balance Fault
P0276 Cylinder #6 Injector Circuit Low
P0277 Cylinder #6 Injector Circuit High
P0278 Cylinder #6 Contribution/Balance Fault
P0279 Cylinder #7 Injector Circuit Low
P0280 Cylinder #7 Injector Circuit High
P0281 Cylinder #7 Contribution/Balance Fault
P0282 Cylinder #8 Injector Circuit Low
P0283 Cylinder #8 Injector Circuit High
P0284 Cylinder #8 Contribution/Balance Fault
P0285 Cylinder #9 Injector Circuit Low
P0286 Cylinder #9 Injector Circuit High
P0287 Cylinder #9 Contribution/Balance Fault
P0288 Cylinder #10 Injector Circuit Low
P0289 Cylinder #10 Injector Circuit High
P0290 Cylinder #10 Contribution/Balance Fault
P0300 Random/Multiple Cylinder Misfire Detected
P0301 Cylinder #1—Misfire Detected
P0302 Cylinder #2—Misfire Detected
P0303 Cylinder #3—Misfire Detected
P0304 Cylinder #4—Misfire Detected
P0305 Cylinder #5—Misfire Detected
P0306 Cylinder #6—Misfire Detected
P0307 Cylinder #7—Misfire Detected
P0308 Cylinder #8—Misfire Detected
P0309 Cylinder #9—Misfire Detected
P0310 Cylinder #10—Misfire Detected
P0320 Ignition/Distributor Engine Speed Input Circuit Malfunction
P0321 Ignition/Distributor Engine Speed Input Circuit Range/Performance
P0322 Ignition/Distributor Engine Speed Input Circuit No Signal
P0323 Ignition/Distributor Engine Speed Input Circuit Intermittent
P0325 Knock Sensor #1—Circuit Malfunction (Bank #1 or Single Sensor)
P0326 Knock Sensor #1—Circuit Range/Performance (Bank #1 or Single Sensor)

Refer to the model specific sections for fuel system service procedures

P0327 Knock Sensor #1—Circuit Low Input (Bank #1 or Single Sensor)

P0328 Knock Sensor #1—Circuit High Input (Bank #1 or Single Sensor)

P0329 Knock Sensor #1—Circuit Input Intermittent (Bank #1 or Single Sensor)

P0330 Knock Sensor #2—Circuit Malfunction (Bank #2)

P0331 Knock Sensor #2—Circuit Range/Performance (Bank #2)

P0332 Knock Sensor #2—Circuit Low Input (Bank #2)

P0333 Knock Sensor #2—Circuit High Input (Bank #2)

P0334 Knock Sensor #2—Circuit Input Intermittent (Bank #2)

P0335 Crankshaft Position Sensor "A" Circuit Malfunction

P0336 Crankshaft Position Sensor "A" Circuit Range/Performance

P0337 Crankshaft Position Sensor "A" Circuit Low Input

P0338 Crankshaft Position Sensor "A" Circuit High Input

P0339 Crankshaft Position Sensor "A" Circuit Intermittent

P0340 Camshaft Position Sensor Circuit Malfunction

P0341 Camshaft Position Sensor Circuit Range/Performance

P0342 Camshaft Position Sensor Circuit Low Input

P0343 Camshaft Position Sensor Circuit High Input

P0344 Camshaft Position Sensor Circuit Intermittent

P0350 Ignition Coil Primary/Secondary Circuit Malfunction

P0351 Ignition Coil "A" Primary/Secondary Circuit Malfunction

P0352 Ignition Coil "B" Primary/Secondary Circuit Malfunction

P0353 Ignition Coil "C" Primary/Secondary Circuit Malfunction

P0354 Ignition Coil "D" Primary/Secondary Circuit Malfunction

P0355 Ignition Coil "E" Primary/Secondary Circuit Malfunction

P0356 Ignition Coil "F" Primary/Secondary Circuit Malfunction

P0357 Ignition Coil "G" Primary/Secondary Circuit Malfunction

P0358 Ignition Coil "H" Primary/Secondary Circuit Malfunction

P0359 Ignition Coil "I" Primary/Secondary Circuit Malfunction

P0360 Ignition Coil "J" Primary/Secondary Circuit Malfunction

P0361 Ignition Coil "K" Primary/Secondary Circuit Malfunction

P0362 Ignition Coil "L" Primary/Secondary Circuit Malfunction

P0370 Timing Reference High Resolution Signal "A" Malfunction

P0371 Timing Reference High Resolution Signal "A" Too Many Pulses

P0372 Timing Reference High Resolution Signal "A" Too Few Pulses

P0373 Timing Reference High Resolution Signal "A" Intermittent/Erratic Pulses

P0374 Timing Reference High Resolution Signal "A" No Pulses

P0375 Timing Reference High Resolution Signal "B" Malfunction

P0376 Timing Reference High Resolution Signal "B" Too Many Pulses

P0377 Timing Reference High Resolution Signal "B" Too Few Pulses

P0378 Timing Reference High Resolution Signal "B" Intermittent/Erratic Pulses

P0379 Timing Reference High Resolution Signal "B" No Pulses

P0380 Glow Plug/Heater Circuit "A" Malfunction

P0381 Glow Plug/Heater Indicator Circuit Malfunction

P0382 Glow Plug/Heater Circuit "B" Malfunction

P0385 Crankshaft Position Sensor "B" Circuit Malfunction

P0386 Crankshaft Position Sensor "B" Circuit Range/Performance

P0387 Crankshaft Position Sensor "B" Circuit Low Input

P0388 Crankshaft Position Sensor "B" Circuit High Input

P0389 Crankshaft Position Sensor "B" Circuit Intermittent

P0400 Exhaust Gas Recirculation Flow Malfunction

P0401 Exhaust Gas Recirculation Flow Insufficient Detected

P0402 Exhaust Gas Recirculation Flow Excessive Detected

P0403 Exhaust Gas Recirculation Circuit Malfunction

P0404 Exhaust Gas Recirculation Circuit Range/Performance

P0405 Exhaust Gas Recirculation Sensor "A" Circuit Low

P0406 Exhaust Gas Recirculation Sensor "A" Circuit High

P0407 Exhaust Gas Recirculation Sensor "B" Circuit Low

P0408 Exhaust Gas Recirculation Sensor "B" Circuit High

P0410 Secondary Air Injection System Malfunction

P0411 Secondary Air Injection System Incorrect Flow Detected

P0412 Secondary Air Injection System Switching Valve "A" Circuit Malfunction

P0413 Secondary Air Injection System Switching Valve "A" Circuit Open

P0414 Secondary Air Injection System Switching Valve "A" Circuit Shorted

P0415 Secondary Air Injection System Switching Valve "B" Circuit Malfunction

P0416 Secondary Air Injection System Switching Valve "B" Circuit Open

P0417 Secondary Air Injection System Switching Valve "B" Circuit Shorted

P0418 Secondary Air Injection System Relay "A" Circuit Malfunction

P0419 Secondary Air Injection System Relay "B" Circuit Malfunction

P0420 Catalyst System Efficiency Below Threshold (Bank #1)

P0421 Warm Up Catalyst Efficiency Below Threshold (Bank #1)

P0422 Main Catalyst Efficiency Below Threshold (Bank #1)

P0423 Heated Catalyst Efficiency Below Threshold (Bank #1)

P0424 Heated Catalyst Temperature Below Threshold (Bank #1)

P0430 Catalyst System Efficiency Below Threshold (Bank #2)

P0431 Warm Up Catalyst Efficiency Below Threshold (Bank #2)

P0432 Main Catalyst Efficiency Below Threshold (Bank #2)

P0433 Heated Catalyst Efficiency Below Threshold (Bank #2)

P0434 Heated Catalyst Temperature Below Threshold (Bank #2)

P0440 Evaporative Emission Control System Malfunction

P0441 Evaporative Emission Control System Incorrect Purge Flow

P0442 Evaporative Emission Control System Leak Detected (Small Leak)

P0443 Evaporative Emission Control System Purge Control Valve Circuit Malfunction

P0444 Evaporative Emission Control System Purge Control Valve Circuit Open

P0445 Evaporative Emission Control System Purge Control Valve Circuit Shorted

P0446 Evaporative Emission Control System Vent Control Circuit Malfunction

P0447 Evaporative Emission Control System Vent Control Circuit Open

P0448 Evaporative Emission Control System Vent Control Circuit Shorted

P0449 Evaporative Emission Control System Vent Valve/Solenoid Circuit Malfunction

P0450 Evaporative Emission Control System Pressure Sensor Malfunction

P0451 Evaporative Emission Control System Pressure Sensor Range/Performance

P0452 Evaporative Emission Control System Pressure Sensor Low Input

P0453 Evaporative Emission Control System Pressure Sensor High Input

P0454 Evaporative Emission Control System Pressure Sensor Intermittent

P0455 Evaporative Emission Control System Leak Detected (Gross Leak)

P0460 Fuel Level Sensor Circuit Malfunction

P0461 Fuel Level Sensor Circuit Range/Performance

P0462 Fuel Level Sensor Circuit Low Input

P0463 Fuel Level Sensor Circuit High Input

P0464 Fuel Level Sensor Circuit Intermittent

P0465 Purge Flow Sensor Circuit Malfunction

P0466 Purge Flow Sensor Circuit Range/Performance

P0467 Purge Flow Sensor Circuit Low Input

P0468 Purge Flow Sensor Circuit High Input

P0469 Purge Flow Sensor Circuit Intermittent

P0470 Exhaust Pressure Sensor Malfunction

P0471 Exhaust Pressure Sensor Range/Performance

P0472 Exhaust Pressure Sensor Low

P0473 Exhaust Pressure Sensor High

P0474 Exhaust Pressure Sensor Intermittent

P0475 Exhaust Pressure Control Valve Malfunction

P0476 Exhaust Pressure Control Valve Range/Performance

P0477 Exhaust Pressure Control Valve Low

P0478 Exhaust Pressure Control Valve High

P0479 Exhaust Pressure Control Valve Intermittent

P0480 Cooling Fan #1 Control Circuit Malfunction

P0481 Cooling Fan #2 Control Circuit Malfunction

P0482 Cooling Fan #3 Control Circuit Malfunction

P0483 Cooling Fan Rationality Check Malfunction

P0484 Cooling Fan Circuit Over Current

P0485 Cooling Fan Power/Ground Circuit Malfunction

P0500 Vehicle Speed Sensor Malfunction

P0501 Vehicle Speed Sensor Range/Performance

P0502 Vehicle Speed Sensor Circuit Low Input

P0503 Vehicle Speed Sensor Intermittent/Erratic/High

P0505 Idle Control System Malfunction

P0506 Idle Control System RPM Lower Than Expected

P0507 Idle Control System RPM Higher Than Expected

P0510 Closed Throttle Position Switch Malfunction

P0520 Engine Oil Pressure Sensor/Switch Circuit Malfunction

P0521 Engine Oil Pressure Sensor/Switch Range/Performance

P0522 Engine Oil Pressure Sensor/Switch Low Voltage

P0523 Engine Oil Pressure Sensor/Switch High Voltage

P0530 A/C Refrigerant Pressure Sensor Circuit Malfunction

P0531 A/C Refrigerant Pressure Sensor Circuit Range/Performance

P0532 A/C Refrigerant Pressure Sensor Circuit Low Input

P0533 A/C Refrigerant Pressure Sensor Circuit High Input

P0534 A/C Refrigerant Charge Loss

P0550 Power Steering Pressure Sensor Circuit Malfunction

P0551 Power Steering Pressure Sensor Circuit Range/Performance

P0552 Power Steering Pressure Sensor Circuit Low Input

P0553 Power Steering Pressure Sensor Circuit High Input

P0554 Power Steering Pressure Sensor Circuit Intermittent

P0560 System Voltage Malfunction

P0561 System Voltage Unstable

P0562 System Voltage Low

P0563 System Voltage High

P0565 Cruise Control On Signal Malfunction

P0566 Cruise Control Off Signal Malfunction

P0567 Cruise Control Resume Signal Malfunction

P0568 Cruise Control Set Signal Malfunction

P0569 Cruise Control Coast Signal Malfunction

P0570 Cruise Control Accel Signal Malfunction

P0571 Cruise Control/Brake Switch "A" Circuit Malfunction

P0572 Cruise Control/Brake Switch "A" Circuit Low

P0573 Cruise Control/Brake Switch "A" Circuit High

P0574 **Through P0580** Reserved for Cruise Codes

P0600 Serial Communication Link Malfunction

P0601 Internal Control Module Memory Check Sum Error

P0602 Control Module Programming Error

P0603 Internal Control Module Keep Alive Memory (KAM) Error

P0604 Internal Control Module Random Access Memory (RAM) Error

P0605 Internal Control Module Read Only Memory (ROM) Error

P0606 PCM Processor Fault

P0608 Control Module VSS Output "A" Malfunction

P0609 Control Module VSS Output "B" Malfunction

P0620 Generator Control Circuit Malfunction

P0621 Generator Lamp "L" Control Circuit Malfunction

P0622 Generator Field "F" Control Circuit Malfunction

P0650 Malfunction Indicator Lamp (MIL) Control Circuit Malfunction

P0654 Engine RPM Output Circuit Malfunction

P0655 Engine Hot Lamp Output Control Circuit Malfunction

P0656 Fuel Level Output Circuit Malfunction

P0700 Transmission Control System Malfunction

P0701 Transmission Control System Range/Performance

P0702 Transmission Control System Electrical

P0703 Torque Converter/Brake Switch "B" Circuit Malfunction

P0704 Clutch Switch Input Circuit Malfunction

P0705 Transmission Range Sensor Circuit Malfunction (PRNDL Input)

P0706 Transmission Range Sensor Circuit Range/Performance

P0707 Transmission Range Sensor Circuit Low Input

P0708 Transmission Range Sensor Circuit High Input

P0709 Transmission Range Sensor Circuit Intermittent

P0710 Transmission Fluid Temperature Sensor Circuit Malfunction

P0711 Transmission Fluid Temperature Sensor Circuit Range/Performance

P0712 Transmission Fluid Temperature Sensor Circuit Low Input

P0713 Transmission Fluid Temperature Sensor Circuit High Input

P0714 Transmission Fluid Temperature Sensor Circuit Intermittent

P0715 Input/Turbine Speed Sensor Circuit Malfunction

P0716 Input/Turbine Speed Sensor Circuit Range/Performance

P0717 Input/Turbine Speed Sensor Circuit No Signal

P0718 Input/Turbine Speed Sensor Circuit Intermittent

P0719 Torque Converter/Brake Switch "B" Circuit Low

P0720 Output Speed Sensor Circuit Malfunction

P0721 Output Speed Sensor Circuit Range/Performance

P0722 Output Speed Sensor Circuit No Signal

P0723 Output Speed Sensor Circuit Intermittent

Refer to the model specific sections for engine electrical system service procedures

P0724 Torque Converter/Brake Switch "B" Circuit High
P0725 Engine Speed Input Circuit Malfunction
P0726 Engine Speed Input Circuit Range/Performance
P0727 Engine Speed Input Circuit No Signal
P0728 Engine Speed Input Circuit Intermittent
P0730 Incorrect Gear Ratio
P0731 Gear #1 Incorrect Ratio
P0732 Gear #2 Incorrect Ratio
P0733 Gear #3 Incorrect Ratio
P0734 Gear #4 Incorrect Ratio
P0735 Gear #5 Incorrect Ratio
P0736 Reverse Incorrect Ratio
P0740 Torque Converter Clutch Circuit Malfunction
P0741 Torque Converter Clutch Circuit Performance or Stuck Off
P0742 Torque Converter Clutch Circuit Stuck On
P0743 Torque Converter Clutch Circuit Electrical
P0744 Torque Converter Clutch Circuit Intermittent
P0745 Pressure Control Solenoid Malfunction
P0746 Pressure Control Solenoid Performance or Stuck Off
P0747 Pressure Control Solenoid Stuck On
P0748 Pressure Control Solenoid Electrical
P0749 Pressure Control Solenoid Intermittent
P0750 Shift Solenoid "A" Malfunction
P0751 Shift Solenoid "A" Performance or Stuck Off
P0752 Shift Solenoid "A" Stuck On
P0753 Shift Solenoid "A" Electrical
P0754 Shift Solenoid "A" Intermittent
P0755 Shift Solenoid "B" Malfunction
P0756 Shift Solenoid "B" Performance or Stuck Off
P0757 Shift Solenoid "B" Stuck On
P0758 Shift Solenoid "B" Electrical
P0759 Shift Solenoid "B" Intermittent
P0760 Shift Solenoid "C" Malfunction
P0761 Shift Solenoid "C" Performance Or Stuck Off
P0762 Shift Solenoid "C" Stuck On
P0763 Shift Solenoid "C" Electrical
P0764 Shift Solenoid "C" Intermittent
P0765 Shift Solenoid "D" Malfunction
P0766 Shift Solenoid "D" Performance Or Stuck Off
P0767 Shift Solenoid "D" Stuck On
P0768 Shift Solenoid "D" Electrical
P0769 Shift Solenoid "D" Intermittent
P0770 Shift Solenoid "E" Malfunction
P0771 Shift Solenoid "E" Performance Or Stuck Off
P0772 Shift Solenoid "E" Stuck On
P0773 Shift Solenoid "E" Electrical
P0774 Shift Solenoid "E" Intermittent
P0780 Shift Malfunction
P0781 1–2 Shift Malfunction
P0782 2–3 Shift Malfunction
P0783 3–4 Shift Malfunction
P0784 4–5 Shift Malfunction
P0785 Shift/Timing Solenoid Malfunction
P0786 Shift/Timing Solenoid Range/Performance
P0787 Shift/Timing Solenoid Low
P0788 Shift/Timing Solenoid High
P0789 Shift/Timing Solenoid Intermittent
P0790 Normal/Performance Switch Circuit Malfunction
P0801 Reverse Inhibit Control Circuit Malfunction
P0803 1–4 Upshift (Skip Shift) Solenoid Control Circuit Malfunction

P0804 1–4 Upshift (Skip Shift) Lamp Control Circuit Malfunction
P1000 OBD II Monitor Testing Not Complete More Driving Required
P1001 Key On Engine Running (KOER) Self-Test Not Able To Complete, KOER Aborted
P1100 Mass Air Flow (MAF) Sensor Intermittent
P1101 Mass Air Flow (MAF) Sensor Out Of Self-Test Range
P1111 System Pass 49 State Except Econoline
P1112 Intake Air Temperature (IAT) Sensor Intermittent
P1116 Engine Coolant Temperature (ECT) Sensor Out Of Self-Test Range
P1117 Engine Coolant Temperature (ECT) Sensor Intermittent
P1120 Throttle Position (TP) Sensor Out Of Range (Low)
P1121 Throttle Position (TP) Sensor Inconsistent With MAF Sensor
P1124 Throttle Position (TP) Sensor Out Of Self-Test Range
P1125 Throttle Position (TP) Sensor Circuit Intermittent
P1127 Exhaust Not Warm Enough, Downstream Heated Oxygen Sensors HO_2S) Not Tested
P1128 Upstream Heated Oxygen Sensors (HO_2S) Swapped From Bank To Bank
P1129 Downstream Heated Oxygen Sensors (HO_2S) Swapped From Bank To Bank
P1130 Lack Of Upstream Heated Oxygen Sensor (HO_2S 11) Switch, Adaptive Fuel At Limit (Bank #1)
P1131 Lack Of Upstream Heated Oxygen Sensor (HO_2S 11) Switch, Sensor Indicates Lean (Bank #1)
P1132 Lack Of Upstream Heated Oxygen Sensor (HO_2S 11) Switch, Sensor Indicates Rich (Bank #1)
P1137 Lack Of Downstream Heated Oxygen Sensor (HO_2S 12) Switch, Sensor Indicates Lean (Bank #1)
P1138 Lack Of Downstream Heated Oxygen Sensor (HO_2S 12) Switch, Sensor Indicates Rich (Bank #1)
P1150 Lack Of Upstream Heated Oxygen Sensor (HO_2S 21) Switch, Adaptive Fuel At Limit (Bank #2)
P1151 Lack Of Upstream Heated Oxygen Sensor (HO_2S 21) Switch, Sensor Indicates Lean (Bank #2)
P1152 Lack Of Upstream Heated Oxygen Sensor (HO_2S 21) Switch, Sensor Indicates Rich (Bank #2)
P1157 Lack Of Downstream Heated Oxygen Sensor (HO_2S 22) Switch, Sensor Indicates Lean (Bank #2)
P1158 Lack Of Downstream Heated Oxygen Sensor (HO_2S 22) Switch, Sensor Indicates Rich (Bank #2)
P1169 (HO_2S 12) Signal Remained Unchanged For More Than 20 Seconds After Closed Loop
P1170 (HO_2S 11) Signal Remained Unchanged For More Than 20 Seconds After Closed Loop
P1173 Feedback A/F Mixture Control (HO_2S 21) Signal Remained Unchanged For More Than 20 Seconds After Closed Loop
P1184 Engine Oil Temp Sensor Circuit Performance
P1195 Barometric (BARO) Pressure Sensor Circuit Malfunction (Signal Is From EGR Boost Sensor)
P1196 Starter Switch Circuit Malfunction
P1209 Injection Control Pressure (ICP) Peak Fault
P1210 Injection Control Pressure (ICP) Above Expected Level
P1211 Injection Control Pressure (ICP) Not Controllable— Pressure Above/Below Desired
P1212 Injection Control Pressure (ICP) Voltage Not At Expected Level
P1218 Cylinder Identification (CID) Stuck High

P1219 Cylinder Identification (CID) Stuck Low

P1220 Series Throttle Control Malfunction (Traction Control System)

P1224 Throttle Position Sensor "B" (TP-B) Out Of Self-Test Range (Traction Control System)

P1230 Fuel Pump Low Speed Malfunction

P1231 Fuel Pump Secondary Circuit Low With High Speed Pump On

P1232 Low Speed Fuel Pump Primary Circuit Malfunction

P1233 Fuel Pump Driver Module Off-line (MIL DTC)

P1234 Fuel Pump Driver Module Disabled Or Off-line (No MIL)

P1235 Fuel Pump Control Out Of Range (MIL DTC)

P1236 Fuel Pump Control Out Of Range (No MIL)

P1237 Fuel Pump Secondary Circuit Malfunction (MIL DTC)

P1238 Fuel Pump Secondary Circuit Malfunction (No DMIL)

P1250 Fuel Pressure Regulator Control (FPRC) Solenoid Malfunction

P1260 THEFT Detected—Engine Disabled

P1261 High To Low Side Short—Cylinder #1 (Indicates Low side Circuit Is Shorted To B+ Or To The High Side Between The IDM And The Injector)

P1262 High To Low Side Short—Cylinder #2 (Indicates Low side Circuit Is Shorted To B+ Or To The High Side Between The IDM And The Injector)

P1263 High To Low Side Short—Cylinder #3 (Indicates Low side Circuit Is Shorted To B+ Or To The High Side Between The IDM And The Injector)

P1264 High To Low Side Short—Cylinder #4 (Indicates Low side Circuit Is Shorted To B+ Or To The High Side Between The IDM And The Injector)

P1265 High To Low Side Short—Cylinder #5 (Indicates Low side Circuit Is Shorted To B+ Or To The High Side Between The IDM And The Injector)

P1266 High To Low Side Short—Cylinder #6 (Indicates Low side Circuit Is Shorted To B+ Or To The High Side Between The IDM And The Injector)

P1267 High To Low Side Short—Cylinder #7 (Indicates Low side Circuit Is Shorted To B+ Or To The High Side Between The IDM And The Injector)

P1268 High To Low Side Short—Cylinder #8 (Indicates Low side Circuit Is Shorted To B+ Or To The High Side Between The IDM And The Injector)

P1270 Engine RPM Or Vehicle Speed Limiter Reached

P1271 High To Low Side Open—Cylinder #1 (Indicates A High To Low Side Open Between The Injector And The IDM)

P1272 High To Low Side Open—Cylinder #2 (Indicates A High To Low Side Open Between The Injector And The IDM)

P1273 High To Low Side Open—Cylinder #3 (Indicates A High To Low Side Open Between The Injector And The IDM)

P1274 High To Low Side Open—Cylinder #4 (Indicates A High To Low Side Open Between The Injector And The IDM)

P1275 High To Low Side Open—Cylinder #5 (Indicates A High To Low Side Open Between The Injector And The IDM)

P1276 High To Low Side Open—Cylinder #6 (Indicates A High To Low Side Open Between The Injector And The IDM)

P1277 High To Low Side Open—Cylinder #7 (Indicates A High To Low Side Open Between The Injector And The IDM)

P1278 High To Low Side Open—Cylinder #8 (Indicates A High To Low Side Open Between The Injector And The IDM)

P1280 Injection Control Pressure (ICP) Circuit Out Of Range Low

P1281 Injection Control Pressure (ICP) Circuit Out Of Range High

P1282 Injection Control Pressure (ICP) Excessive

P1283 Injection Pressure Regulator (IPR) Circuit Failure

P1284 Injection Control Pressure (ICP) Failure—Aborts KOER Or CCT Test

P1285 Cylinder Head Temperature (CHT) Over Temperature Sensed

P1288 Cylinder Head Temperature (CHT) Sensor Out Of Self-Test Range

P1289 Cylinder Head Temperature (CHT) Sensor Circuit Low Input

P1290 Cylinder Head Temperature (CHT) Sensor Circuit High Input

P1291 IDM To Injector High Side Circuit #1 (Right Bank) Short To GND Or B+

P1292 IDM To Injector High Side Circuit #2 (Right Bank) Short To GND Or B+

P1293 IDM To Injector High Side Circuit Open Bank #1 (Right Bank)

P1294 IDM To Injector High Side Circuit Open Bank #2 (Left Bank)

P1295 Multiple IDM/Injector Circuit Faults On Bank #1 (Right)

P1296 Multiple IDM/Injector Circuit Faults On Bank #2 (Left)

P1297 High Sides Shorted Together

P1298 IDM Failure

P1299 Engine Over Temperature Condition

P1309 Misfire Detection Monitor Is Not Enabled

P1316 Injector Circuit/IDM Codes Detected

P1320 Distributor Signal Interrupt

P1336 Crankshaft Position Sensor (Gear)

P1345 No Camshaft Position Sensor Signal

P1351 Ignition Diagnostic Monitor (IDM) Circuit Input Malfunction

P1351 Indicates Ignition System Malfunction

P1352 Indicates Ignition System Malfunction

P1353 Indicates Ignition System Malfunction

P1354 Indicates Ignition System Malfunction

P1355 Indicates Ignition System Malfunction

P1356 PIPs Occurred While IDM Pulse width Indicates Engine Not Turning

P1357 Ignition Diagnostic Monitor (IDM) Pulse width Not Defined

P1358 Ignition Diagnostic Monitor (IDM) Signal Out Of Self-Test Range

P1359 Spark Output Circuit Malfunction

P1364 Spark Output Circuit Malfunction

P1390 Octane Adjust (OCT ADJ) Out Of Self-Test Range

P1391 Glow Plug Circuit Low Input Bank #1 (Right)

P1392 Glow Plug Circuit High Input Bank #1 (Right)

P1393 Glow Plug Circuit Low Input Bank #2 (Left)

P1394 Glow Plug Circuit High Input Bank #2 (Left)

P1395 Glow Plug Monitor Fault Bank #1

P1396 Glow Plug Monitor Fault Bank #2

P1397 System Voltage Out Of Self Test Range

P1400 Differential Pressure Feedback EGR (DPFE) Sensor Circuit Low Voltage Detected

P1401 Differential Pressure Feedback EGR (DPFE) Sensor Circuit High Voltage Detected/EGR Temperature Sensor

P1402 EGR Valve Position Sensor Open Or Short

P1403 Differential Pressure Feedback EGR (DPFE) Sensor Hoses Reversed

P1405 Differential Pressure Feedback EGR (DPFE) Sensor Upstream Hose Off Or Plugged

P1406 Differential Pressure Feedback EGR (DPFE) Sensor Downstream Hose Off Or Plugged

P1407 Exhaust Gas Recirculation (EGR) No Flow Detected (Valve Stuck Closed Or Inoperative)

P1408 Exhaust Gas Recirculation (EGR) Flow Out Of Self-Test Range

P1409 Electronic Vacuum Regulator (EVR) Control Circuit Malfunction

P1410 Check That Fuel Pressure Regulator Control Solenoid And The EGR Check Solenoid Connectors Are Not Swapped

P1411 Secondary Air Injection System Incorrect Downstream Flow Detected

P1413 Secondary Air Injection System Monitor Circuit Low Voltage

P1414 Secondary Air Injection System Monitor Circuit High Voltage

P1442 Evaporative Emission Control System Small Leak Detected

P1443 Evaporative Emission Control System—Vacuum System, Purge Control Solenoid Or Purge Control Valve Malfunction

P1444 Purge Flow Sensor (PFS) Circuit Low Input

P1445 Purge Flow Sensor (PFS) Circuit High Input

P1449 Evaporative Emission Control System Unable To Hold Vacuum

P1450 Unable To Bleed Up Fuel Tank Vacuum

P1455 Evaporative Emission Control System Control Leak Detected (Gross Leak)

P1460 Wide Open Throttle Air Conditioning Cut-Off Circuit Malfunction

P1461 Air Conditioning Pressure (ACP) Sensor Circuit Low Input

P1462 Air Conditioning Pressure (ACP) Sensor Circuit High Input

P1463 Air Conditioning Pressure (ACP) Sensor Insufficient Pressure Change

P1464 Air Conditioning (A/C) Demand Out Of Self-Test Range/A/C On During KOER Or CCT Test

P1469 Low Air Conditioning Cycling Period

P1473 Fan Secondary High, With Fan(s) Off

P1474 Low Fan Control Primary Circuit Malfunction

P1479 High Fan Control Primary Circuit Malfunction

P1480 Fan Secondary Low, With Low Fan On

P1481 Fan Secondary Low, With High Fan On

P1483 Power To Fan Circuit Over current

P1484 Open Power/Ground To Variable Load Control Module (VLCM)

P1485 EGR Control Solenoid Open Or Short

P1486 EGR Vent Solenoid Open Or Short

P1487 EGR Boost Check Solenoid Open Or Short

P1500 Vehicle Speed Sensor (VSS) Circuit Intermittent

P1501 Vehicle Speed Sensor (VSS) Out Of Self-Test Range/Vehicle Moved During Test

P1502 Invalid Self Test—Auxiliary Powertrain Control Module (APCM) Functioning

P1504 Idle Air Control (IAC) Circuit Malfunction

P1505 Idle Air Control (IAC) System At Adaptive Clip

P1506 Idle Air Control (IAC) Over-speed Error

P1507 Idle Air Control (IAC) Under-speed Error

P1512 Intake Manifold Runner Control (IMRC) Malfunction (Bank #1 Stuck Closed)

P1513 Intake Manifold Runner Control (IMRC) Malfunction (Bank #2 Stuck Closed)

P1516 Intake Manifold Runner Control (IMRC) Input Error (Bank #1)

P1517 Intake Manifold Runner Control (IMRC) Input Error (Bank #2)

P1518 Intake Manifold Runner Control (IMRC) Malfunction (Stuck Open)

P1519 Intake Manifold Runner Control (IMRC) Malfunction (Stuck Closed)

P1520 Intake Manifold Runner Control (IMRC) Circuit Malfunction

P1521 Variable Resonance Induction System (VRIS) Solenoid #1 Open Or Short

P1522 Variable Resonance Induction System (VRIS) Solenoid #2 Open Or Short

P1523 High Speed Inlet Air (HSIA) Solenoid Open Or Short

P1530 Air Condition (A/C) Clutch Circuit Malfunction

P1531 Invalid Test—Accelerator Pedal Movement

P1536 Parking Brake Applied Failure

P1537 Intake Manifold Runner Control (IMRC) Malfunction (Bank #1 Stuck Open)

P1538 Intake Manifold Runner Control (IMRC) Malfunction (Bank #2 Stuck Open)

P1539 Power To Air Condition (A/C) Clutch Circuit Over-current

P1549 Problem In Intake Manifold Tuning (IMT) Valve System

P1550 Power Steering Pressure (PSP) Sensor Out Of Self-Test Range

P1601 Serial Communication Error

P1605 Powertrain Control Module (PCM)—Keep Alive Memory (KAM) Test Error

P1608 PCM Internal Circuit Malfunction

P1609 PCM Internal Circuit Malfunction (2.5L Only)

P1625 B+ Supply To Variable Load Control Module (VLCM) Fan Circuit Malfunction

P1626 B+ Supply To Variable Load Control Module (VLCM) Air Conditioning (A/C) Circuit

P1650 Power Steering Pressure (PSP) Switch Out Of Self-Test Range

P1651 Power Steering Pressure (PSP) Switch Input Malfunction

P1660 Output Circuit Check Signal High

P1661 Output Circuit Check Signal Low

P1662 Injection Driver Module Enable (IDM EN) Circuit Failure

P1663 Fuel Delivery Command Signal (FDCS) Circuit Failure

P1667 Cylinder Identification (CID) Circuit Failure

P1668 PCM—IDM Diagnostic Communication Error

P1670 EF Feedback Signal Not Detected

P1701 Reverse Engagement Error

P1701 Fuel Trim Malfunction (Villager)

P1703 Brake On/Off (BOO) Switch Out Of Self-Test Range

P1704 Digital Transmission Range (TR) Sensor Failed To Transition State

P1705 Transmission Range (TR) Sensor Out Of Self-Test Range

P1705 TP Sensor (AT) Villager

P1705 Clutch Pedal Position (CPP) Or Park Neutral Position (PNP) Problem

P1706 High Vehicle Speed In Park

P1709 Park Or Neutral Position (PNP) Or Clutch Pedal Position (CPP) Switch Out Of Self-Test Range

P1709 Throttle Position (TP) Sensor Malfunction (Aspire 1.3L, Escort/ Tracer 1.8L, Probe 2.5L)

P1711 Transmission Fluid Temperature (TFT) Sensor Out Of Self-Test Range

P1714 Shift Solenoid "A" Inductive Signature Malfunction

P1715 Shift Solenoid "B" Inductive Signature Malfunction

P1716 Transmission Malfunction

P1717 Transmission Malfunction

P1719 Transmission Malfunction

P1720 Vehicle Speed Sensor (VSS) Circuit Malfunction

P1727 Coast Clutch Solenoid Inductive Signature Malfunction

P1728 Transmission Slip Error—Converter Clutch Failed

P1729 4x4 Low Switch Error

P1731 Improper 1–2 Shift

P1732 Improper 2–3 Shift

P1733 Improper 3–4 Shift

P1734 Improper 4–5 Shift

P1740 Torque Converter Clutch (TCC) Inductive Signature Malfunction

P1741 Torque Converter Clutch (TCC) Control Error

P1742 Torque Converter Clutch (TCC) Solenoid Failed On (Turns On MIL)

P1743 Torque Converter Clutch (TCC) Solenoid Failed On (Turns On TCIL)

P1744 Torque Converter Clutch (TCC) System Mechanically Stuck In Off Position

P1744 Torque Converter Clutch (TCC) Solenoid Malfunction (2.5L Only)

P1746 Electronic Pressure Control (EPC) Solenoid Open Circuit (Low Input)

P1747 Electronic Pressure Control (EPC) Solenoid Short Circuit (High Input)

P1748 Electronic Pressure Control (EPC) Malfunction

P1749 Electronic Pressure Control (EPC) Solenoid Failed Low

P1751 Shift Solenoid #1 (SS1) Performance

P1754 Coast Clutch Solenoid (CCS) Circuit Malfunction

P1756 Shift Solenoid #2 (SS2) Performance

P1760 Overrun Clutch SN

P1761 Shift Solenoid #3 (SS3) Performance

P1762 Transmission Malfunction

P1765 3–2 Timing Solenoid Malfunction (2.5L Only)

P1779 TCIL Circuit Malfunction

P1780 Transmission Control Switch (TCS) Circuit Out Of Self-Test Range

P1781 4x4 Low Switch, Out Of Self-Test Range

P1783 Transmission Over Temperature Condition

P1784 Transmission Malfunction

P1785 Transmission Malfunction

P1786 Transmission Malfunction

P1787 Transmission Malfunction

P1788 3–2 Timing/Coast Clutch Solenoid (3–2/CCS) Circuit Open

P1789 3–2 Timing/Coast Clutch Solenoid (3–2/CCS) Circuit Shorted

P1792 Idle (IDL) Switch (Closed Throttle Position Switch) Malfunction

P1794 Loss Of Battery Voltage Input

P1795 EGR Boost Sensor Malfunction

P1797 Clutch Pedal Position (CPP) Switch Or Neutral Switch Circuit Malfunction

P1900 Cooling Fan

U1021 SCP Indicating The Lack Of Air Conditioning (A/C) Clutch Status Response

U1039 Vehicle Speed Signal (VSS) Missing Or Incorrect

U1051 Brake Switch Signal Missing Or Incorrect

U1073 SCP Indicating The Lack Of Engine Coolant Fan Status Response

U1131 SCP Indicating The Lack Of Fuel Pump Status Response

U1135 SCP Indicating The Ignition Switch Signal Missing Or Incorrect

U1256 SCP Indicating A Communications Error

U1451 Lack Of Response From Passive Anti-Theft System (PATS) Module—Engine Disabled

General Motors Corporation

READING CODES

Reading the diagnostic trouble codes is one of the first steps in OBD II system diagnostics. This step should be initially performed to determine the general nature of the fault. Subsequent readings will determine if the fault has been cleared.

Reading codes can be performed by any of the methods below:

- Read the control module memory with the Generic Scan Tool (GST)
- Read the control module memory with the vehicle manufacturer's specific tester

To read the fault codes, connect the scan tool or tester according to the manufacturer's instructions. Follow the manufacturer's specified procedure for reading the codes.

CLEARING CODES

Control module reset procedures are a very important part of OBD II System diagnostics. This step should be done at the end of any fault code repair and at the end of any driveability repair.

Clearing codes can be performed by any of the methods below:

- Clear the control module memory with the Generic Scan Tool (GST)
- Clear the control module memory with the vehicle manufacturer's specific tester
- Turn the ignition OFF and remove the negative battery cable for at least 1 minute.

Removing the negative battery cable may cause other systems in the vehicle to loose their memory. Prior to removing the cable, ensure you have the proper reset codes for radios and alarms.

➡**The MIL will may also be de-activated for some codes if the vehicle completes 3 consecutive trips without a fault detected with vehicle conditions similar to those present during the fault.**

OBD II TROUBLE CODES

P0100 Mass or Volume Air Flow Circuit Malfunction

P0101 Mass or Volume Air Flow Circuit Range/Performance Problem

P0102 Mass or Volume Air Flow Circuit Low Input

P0103 Mass or Volume Air Flow Circuit High Input

P0104 Mass or Volume Air Flow Circuit Intermittent

Ignition system service is covered in the model specific sections of this manual

P0105 Manifold Absolute Pressure/Barometric Pressure Circuit Malfunction

P0106 Manifold Absolute Pressure/Barometric Pressure Circuit Range/Performance Problem

P0107 Manifold Absolute Pressure/Barometric Pressure Circuit Low Input

P0108 Manifold Absolute Pressure/Barometric Pressure Circuit High Input

P0109 Manifold Absolute Pressure/Barometric Pressure Circuit Intermittent

P0110 Intake Air Temperature Circuit Malfunction

P0111 Intake Air Temperature Circuit Range/Performance Problem

P0112 Intake Air Temperature Circuit Low Input

P0113 Intake Air Temperature Circuit High Input

P0114 Intake Air Temperature Circuit Intermittent

P0115 Engine Coolant Temperature Circuit Malfunction

P0116 Engine Coolant Temperature Circuit Range/Performance Problem

P0117 Engine Coolant Temperature Circuit Low Input

P0118 Engine Coolant Temperature Circuit High Input

P0119 Engine Coolant Temperature Circuit Intermittent

P0120 Throttle/Pedal Position Sensor/Switch "A" Circuit Malfunction

P0121 Throttle/Pedal Position Sensor/Switch "A" Circuit Range/Performance Problem

P0122 Throttle/Pedal Position Sensor/Switch "A" Circuit Low Input

P0123 Throttle/Pedal Position Sensor/Switch "A" Circuit High Input

P0124 Throttle/Pedal Position Sensor/Switch "A" Circuit Intermittent

P0125 Insufficient Coolant Temperature For Closed Loop Fuel Control

P0126 Insufficient Coolant Temperature For Stable Operation

P0130 O_2 Circuit Malfunction (Bank #1 Sensor #1)

P0131 O_2 Sensor Circuit Low Voltage (Bank #1 Sensor #1)

P0132 O_2 Sensor Circuit High Voltage (Bank #1 Sensor #1)

P0133 O_2 Sensor Circuit Slow Response (Bank #1 Sensor #1)

P0134 O_2 Sensor Circuit No Activity Detected (Bank #1 Sensor #1)

P0135 O_2 Sensor Heater Circuit Malfunction (Bank #1 Sensor #1)

P0136 O_2 Sensor Circuit Malfunction (Bank #1 Sensor #2)

P0137 O_2 Sensor Circuit Low Voltage (Bank #1 Sensor #2)

P0138 O_2 Sensor Circuit High Voltage (Bank #1 Sensor #2)

P0139 O_2 Sensor Circuit Slow Response (Bank #1 Sensor #2)

P0140 O_2 Sensor Circuit No Activity Detected (Bank #1 Sensor #2)

P0141 O_2 Sensor Heater Circuit Malfunction (Bank #1 Sensor #2)

P0142 O_2 Sensor Circuit Malfunction (Bank #1 Sensor #3)

P0143 O_2 Sensor Circuit Low Voltage (Bank #1 Sensor #3)

P0144 O_2 Sensor Circuit High Voltage (Bank #1 Sensor #3)

P0145 O_2 Sensor Circuit Slow Response (Bank #1 Sensor #3)

P0146 O_2 Sensor Circuit No Activity Detected (Bank #1 Sensor #3)

P0147 O_2 Sensor Heater Circuit Malfunction (Bank #1 Sensor #3)

P0150 O_2 Sensor Circuit Malfunction (Bank #2 Sensor #1)

P0151 O_2 Sensor Circuit Low Voltage (Bank #2 Sensor #1)

P0152 O_2 Sensor Circuit High Voltage (Bank #2 Sensor #1)

P0153 O_2 Sensor Circuit Slow Response (Bank #2 Sensor #1)

P0154 O_2 Sensor Circuit No Activity Detected (Bank #2 Sensor #1)

P0155 O_2 Sensor Heater Circuit Malfunction (Bank #2 Sensor #1)

P0156 O_2 Sensor Circuit Malfunction (Bank #2 Sensor #2)

P0157 O_2 Sensor Circuit Low Voltage (Bank #2 Sensor #2)

P0158 O_2 Sensor Circuit High Voltage (Bank #2 Sensor #2)

P0159 O_2 Sensor Circuit Slow Response (Bank #2 Sensor #2)

P0160 O_2 Sensor Circuit No Activity Detected (Bank #2 Sensor #2)

P0161 O_2 Sensor Heater Circuit Malfunction (Bank #2 Sensor #2)

P0162 O_2 Sensor Circuit Malfunction (Bank #2 Sensor #3)

P0163 O_2 Sensor Circuit Low Voltage (Bank #2 Sensor #3)

P0164 O_2 Sensor Circuit High Voltage (Bank #2 Sensor #3)

P0165 O_2 Sensor Circuit Slow Response (Bank #2 Sensor #3)

P0166 O_2 Sensor Circuit No Activity Detected (Bank #2 Sensor #3)

P0167 O_2 Sensor Heater Circuit Malfunction (Bank #2 Sensor #3)

P0170 Fuel Trim Malfunction (Bank #1)

P0171 System Too Lean (Bank #1)

P0172 System Too Rich (Bank #1)

P0173 Fuel Trim Malfunction (Bank #2)

P0174 System Too Lean (Bank #2)

P0175 System Too Rich (Bank #2)

P0176 Fuel Composition Sensor Circuit Malfunction

P0177 Fuel Composition Sensor Circuit Range/Performance

P0178 Fuel Composition Sensor Circuit Low Input

P0179 Fuel Composition Sensor Circuit High Input

P0180 Fuel Temperature Sensor "A" Circuit Malfunction

P0181 Fuel Temperature Sensor "A" Circuit Range/Performance

P0182 Fuel Temperature Sensor "A" Circuit Low Input

P0183 Fuel Temperature Sensor "A" Circuit High Input

P0184 Fuel Temperature Sensor "A" Circuit Intermittent

P0185 Fuel Temperature Sensor "B" Circuit Malfunction

P0186 Fuel Temperature Sensor "B" Circuit Range/Performance

P0187 Fuel Temperature Sensor "B" Circuit Low Input

P0188 Fuel Temperature Sensor "B" Circuit High Input

P0189 Fuel Temperature Sensor "B" Circuit Intermittent

P0190 Fuel Rail Pressure Sensor Circuit Malfunction

P0191 Fuel Rail Pressure Sensor Circuit Range/Performance

P0192 Fuel Rail Pressure Sensor Circuit Low Input

P0193 Fuel Rail Pressure Sensor Circuit High Input

P0194 Fuel Rail Pressure Sensor Circuit Intermittent

P0195 Engine Oil Temperature Sensor Malfunction

P0196 Engine Oil Temperature Sensor Range/Performance

P0197 Engine Oil Temperature Sensor Low

P0198 Engine Oil Temperature Sensor High

P0199 Engine Oil Temperature Sensor Intermittent

P0200 Injector Circuit Malfunction

P0201 Injector Circuit Malfunction—Cylinder #1

P0202 Injector Circuit Malfunction—Cylinder #2

P0203 Injector Circuit Malfunction—Cylinder #3

P0204 Injector Circuit Malfunction—Cylinder #4

P0205 Injector Circuit Malfunction—Cylinder #5

P0206 Injector Circuit Malfunction—Cylinder #6

P0207 Injector Circuit Malfunction—Cylinder #7

P0208 Injector Circuit Malfunction—Cylinder #8

P0209 Injector Circuit Malfunction—Cylinder #9

P0210 Injector Circuit Malfunction—Cylinder #10

P0211 Injector Circuit Malfunction—Cylinder #11
P0212 Injector Circuit Malfunction—Cylinder #12
P0213 Cold Start Injector #1 Malfunction
P0214 Cold Start Injector #2 Malfunction
P0215 Engine Shutoff Solenoid Malfunction
P0216 Injection Timing Control Circuit Malfunction
P0217 Engine Over Temperature Condition
P0218 Transmission Over Temperature Condition
P0219 Engine Over Speed Condition
P0220 Throttle/Pedal Position Sensor/Switch "B" Circuit Malfunction
P0221 Throttle/Pedal Position Sensor/Switch "B" Circuit Range/Performance Problem
P0222 Throttle/Pedal Position Sensor/Switch "B" Circuit Low Input
P0223 Throttle/Pedal Position Sensor/Switch "B" Circuit High Input
P0224 Throttle/Pedal Position Sensor/Switch "B" Circuit Intermittent
P0225 Throttle/Pedal Position Sensor/Switch "C" Circuit Malfunction
P0226 Throttle/Pedal Position Sensor/Switch "C" Circuit Range/Performance Problem
P0227 Throttle/Pedal Position Sensor/Switch "C" Circuit Low Input
P0228 Throttle/Pedal Position Sensor/Switch "C" Circuit High Input
P0229 Throttle/Pedal Position Sensor/Switch "C" Circuit Intermittent
P0230 Fuel Pump Primary Circuit Malfunction
P0231 Fuel Pump Secondary Circuit Low
P0232 Fuel Pump Secondary Circuit High
P0233 Fuel Pump Secondary Circuit Intermittent
P0234 Engine Over Boost Condition
P0261 Cylinder #1 Injector Circuit Low
P0262 Cylinder #1 Injector Circuit High
P0263 Cylinder #1 Contribution/Balance Fault
P0264 Cylinder #2 Injector Circuit Low
P0265 Cylinder #2 Injector Circuit High
P0266 Cylinder #2 Contribution/Balance Fault
P0267 Cylinder #3 Injector Circuit Low
P0268 Cylinder #3 Injector Circuit High
P0269 Cylinder #3 Contribution/Balance Fault
P0270 Cylinder #4 Injector Circuit Low
P0271 Cylinder #4 Injector Circuit High
P0272 Cylinder #4 Contribution/Balance Fault
P0273 Cylinder #5 Injector Circuit Low
P0274 Cylinder #5 Injector Circuit High
P0275 Cylinder #5 Contribution/Balance Fault
P0276 Cylinder #6 Injector Circuit Low
P0277 Cylinder #6 Injector Circuit High
P0278 Cylinder #6 Contribution/Balance Fault
P0279 Cylinder #7 Injector Circuit Low
P0280 Cylinder #7 Injector Circuit High
P0281 Cylinder #7 Contribution/Balance Fault
P0282 Cylinder #8 Injector Circuit Low
P0283 Cylinder #8 Injector Circuit High
P0284 Cylinder #8 Contribution/Balance Fault
P0285 Cylinder #9 Injector Circuit Low
P0286 Cylinder #9 Injector Circuit High

P0287 Cylinder #9 Contribution/Balance Fault
P0288 Cylinder #10 Injector Circuit Low
P0289 Cylinder #10 Injector Circuit High
P0290 Cylinder #10 Contribution/Balance Fault
P0300 Random/Multiple Cylinder Misfire Detected
P0301 Cylinder #1—Misfire Detected
P0302 Cylinder #2—Misfire Detected
P0303 Cylinder #3—Misfire Detected
P0304 Cylinder #4—Misfire Detected
P0305 Cylinder #5—Misfire Detected
P0306 Cylinder #6—Misfire Detected
P0307 Cylinder #7—Misfire Detected
P0308 Cylinder #8—Misfire Detected
P0309 Cylinder #9—Misfire Detected
P0310 Cylinder #10—Misfire Detected
P0320 Ignition/Distributor Engine Speed Input Circuit Malfunction
P0321 Ignition/Distributor Engine Speed Input Circuit Range/Performance
P0322 Ignition/Distributor Engine Speed Input Circuit No Signal
P0323 Ignition/Distributor Engine Speed Input Circuit Intermittent
P0325 Knock Sensor #1—Circuit Malfunction (Bank #1 or Single Sensor)
P0326 Knock Sensor #1—Circuit Range/Performance (Bank #1 or Single Sensor)
P0327 Knock Sensor #1—Circuit Low Input (Bank #1 or Single Sensor)
P0328 Knock Sensor #1—Circuit High Input (Bank #1 or Single Sensor)
P0329 Knock Sensor #1—Circuit Input Intermittent (Bank #1 or Single Sensor)
P0330 Knock Sensor #2—Circuit Malfunction (Bank #2)
P0331 Knock Sensor #2—Circuit Range/Performance (Bank #2)
P0332 Knock Sensor #2—Circuit Low Input (Bank #2)
P0333 Knock Sensor #2—Circuit High Input (Bank #2)
P0334 Knock Sensor #2—Circuit Input Intermittent (Bank #2)
P0335 Crankshaft Position Sensor "A" Circuit Malfunction
P0336 Crankshaft Position Sensor "A" Circuit Range/Performance
P0337 Crankshaft Position Sensor "A" Circuit Low Input
P0338 Crankshaft Position Sensor "A" Circuit High Input
P0339 Crankshaft Position Sensor "A" Circuit Intermittent
P0340 Camshaft Position Sensor Circuit Malfunction
P0341 Camshaft Position Sensor Circuit Range/Performance
P0342 Camshaft Position Sensor Circuit Low Input
P0343 Camshaft Position Sensor Circuit High Input
P0344 Camshaft Position Sensor Circuit Intermittent
P0350 Ignition Coil Primary/Secondary Circuit Malfunction
P0351 Ignition Coil "A" Primary/Secondary Circuit Malfunction
P0352 Ignition Coil "B" Primary/Secondary Circuit Malfunction
P0353 Ignition Coil "C" Primary/Secondary Circuit Malfunction
P0354 Ignition Coil "D" Primary/Secondary Circuit Malfunction
P0355 Ignition Coil "E" Primary/Secondary Circuit Malfunction
P0356 Ignition Coil "F" Primary/Secondary Circuit Malfunction
P0357 Ignition Coil "G" Primary/Secondary Circuit Malfunction
P0358 Ignition Coil "H" Primary/Secondary Circuit Malfunction
P0359 Ignition Coil "I" Primary/Secondary Circuit Malfunction
P0360 Ignition Coil "J" Primary/Secondary Circuit Malfunction
P0361 Ignition Coil "K" Primary/Secondary Circuit Malfunction

P0362 Ignition Coil "L" Primary/Secondary Circuit Malfunction
P0370 Timing Reference High Resolution Signal "A" Malfunction
P0371 Timing Reference High Resolution Signal "A" Too Many Pulses
P0372 Timing Reference High Resolution Signal "A" Too Few Pulses
P0373 Timing Reference High Resolution Signal "A" Intermittent/Erratic Pulses
P0374 Timing Reference High Resolution Signal "A" No Pulses
P0375 Timing Reference High Resolution Signal "B" Malfunction
P0376 Timing Reference High Resolution Signal "B" Too Many Pulses
P0377 Timing Reference High Resolution Signal "B" Too Few Pulses
P0378 Timing Reference High Resolution Signal "B" Intermittent/Erratic Pulses
P0379 Timing Reference High Resolution Signal "B" No Pulses
P0380 Glow Plug/Heater Circuit "A" Malfunction
P0381 Glow Plug/Heater Indicator Circuit Malfunction
P0382 Glow Plug/Heater Circuit "B" Malfunction
P0385 Crankshaft Position Sensor "B" Circuit Malfunction
P0386 Crankshaft Position Sensor "B" Circuit Range/Performance
P0387 Crankshaft Position Sensor "B" Circuit Low Input
P0388 Crankshaft Position Sensor "B" Circuit High Input
P0389 Crankshaft Position Sensor "B" Circuit Intermittent
P0400 Exhaust Gas Recirculation Flow Malfunction
P0401 Exhaust Gas Recirculation Flow Insufficient Detected
P0402 Exhaust Gas Recirculation Flow Excessive Detected
P0403 Exhaust Gas Recirculation Circuit Malfunction
P0404 Exhaust Gas Recirculation Circuit Range/Performance
P0405 Exhaust Gas Recirculation Sensor "A" Circuit Low
P0406 Exhaust Gas Recirculation Sensor "A" Circuit High
P0407 Exhaust Gas Recirculation Sensor "B" Circuit Low
P0408 Exhaust Gas Recirculation Sensor "B" Circuit High
P0410 Secondary Air Injection System Malfunction
P0411 Secondary Air Injection System Incorrect Flow Detected
P0412 Secondary Air Injection System Switching Valve "A" Circuit Malfunction
P0413 Secondary Air Injection System Switching Valve "A" Circuit Open
P0414 Secondary Air Injection System Switching Valve "A" Circuit Shorted
P0415 Secondary Air Injection System Switching Valve "B" Circuit Malfunction
P0416 Secondary Air Injection System Switching Valve "B" Circuit Open
P0417 Secondary Air Injection System Switching Valve "B" Circuit Shorted
P0418 Secondary Air Injection System Relay "A" Circuit Malfunction
P0419 Secondary Air Injection System Relay "B" Circuit Malfunction
P0420 Catalyst System Efficiency Below Threshold (Bank #1)
P0421 Warm Up Catalyst Efficiency Below Threshold (Bank #1)
P0422 Main Catalyst Efficiency Below Threshold (Bank #1)
P0423 Heated Catalyst Efficiency Below Threshold (Bank #1)
P0424 Heated Catalyst Temperature Below Threshold (Bank #1)
P0430 Catalyst System Efficiency Below Threshold (Bank #2)
P0431 Warm Up Catalyst Efficiency Below Threshold (Bank #2)
P0432 Main Catalyst Efficiency Below Threshold (Bank #2)

P0433 Heated Catalyst Efficiency Below Threshold (Bank #2)
P0434 Heated Catalyst Temperature Below Threshold (Bank #2)
P0440 Evaporative Emission Control System Malfunction
P0441 Evaporative Emission Control System Incorrect Purge Flow
P0442 Evaporative Emission Control System Leak Detected (Small Leak)
P0443 Evaporative Emission Control System Purge Control Valve Circuit Malfunction
P0444 Evaporative Emission Control System Purge Control Valve Circuit Open
P0445 Evaporative Emission Control System Purge Control Valve Circuit Shorted
P0446 Evaporative Emission Control System Vent Control Circuit Malfunction
P0447 Evaporative Emission Control System Vent Control Circuit Open
P0448 Evaporative Emission Control System Vent Control Circuit Shorted
P0449 Evaporative Emission Control System Vent Valve/Solenoid Circuit Malfunction
P0450 Evaporative Emission Control System Pressure Sensor Malfunction
P0451 Evaporative Emission Control System Pressure Sensor Range/Performance
P0452 Evaporative Emission Control System Pressure Sensor Low Input
P0453 Evaporative Emission Control System Pressure Sensor High Input
P0454 Evaporative Emission Control System Pressure Sensor Intermittent
P0455 Evaporative Emission Control System Leak Detected (Gross Leak)
P0460 Fuel Level Sensor Circuit Malfunction
P0461 Fuel Level Sensor Circuit Range/Performance
P0462 Fuel Level Sensor Circuit Low Input
P0463 Fuel Level Sensor Circuit High Input
P0464 Fuel Level Sensor Circuit Intermittent
P0465 Purge Flow Sensor Circuit Malfunction
P0466 Purge Flow Sensor Circuit Range/Performance
P0467 Purge Flow Sensor Circuit Low Input
P0468 Purge Flow Sensor Circuit High Input
P0469 Purge Flow Sensor Circuit Intermittent
P0470 Exhaust Pressure Sensor Malfunction
P0471 Exhaust Pressure Sensor Range/Performance
P0472 Exhaust Pressure Sensor Low
P0473 Exhaust Pressure Sensor High
P0474 Exhaust Pressure Sensor Intermittent
P0475 Exhaust Pressure Control Valve Malfunction
P0476 Exhaust Pressure Control Valve Range/Performance
P0477 Exhaust Pressure Control Valve Low
P0478 Exhaust Pressure Control Valve High
P0479 Exhaust Pressure Control Valve Intermittent
P0480 Cooling Fan #1 Control Circuit Malfunction
P0481 Cooling Fan #2 Control Circuit Malfunction
P0482 Cooling Fan #3 Control Circuit Malfunction
P0483 Cooling Fan Rationality Check Malfunction
P0484 Cooling Fan Circuit Over Current
P0485 Cooling Fan Power/Ground Circuit Malfunction
P0500 Vehicle Speed Sensor Malfunction
P0501 Vehicle Speed Sensor Range/Performance
P0502 Vehicle Speed Sensor Circuit Low Input

P0503 Vehicle Speed Sensor Intermittent/Erratic/High
P0505 Idle Control System Malfunction
P0506 Idle Control System RPM Lower Than Expected
P0507 Idle Control System RPM Higher Than Expected
P0510 Closed Throttle Position Switch Malfunction
P0520 Engine Oil Pressure Sensor/Switch Circuit Malfunction
P0521 Engine Oil Pressure Sensor/Switch Range/Performance
P0522 Engine Oil Pressure Sensor/Switch Low Voltage
P0523 Engine Oil Pressure Sensor/Switch High Voltage
P0530 A/C Refrigerant Pressure Sensor Circuit Malfunction
P0531 A/C Refrigerant Pressure Sensor Circuit Range/Performance
P0532 A/C Refrigerant Pressure Sensor Circuit Low Input
P0533 A/C Refrigerant Pressure Sensor Circuit High Input
P0534 A/C Refrigerant Charge Loss
P0550 Power Steering Pressure Sensor Circuit Malfunction
P0551 Power Steering Pressure Sensor Circuit Range/Performance
P0552 Power Steering Pressure Sensor Circuit Low Input
P0553 Power Steering Pressure Sensor Circuit High Input
P0554 Power Steering Pressure Sensor Circuit Intermittent
P0560 System Voltage Malfunction
P0561 System Voltage Unstable
P0562 System Voltage Low
P0563 System Voltage High
P0565 Cruise Control On Signal Malfunction
P0566 Cruise Control Off Signal Malfunction
P0567 Cruise Control Resume Signal Malfunction
P0568 Cruise Control Set Signal Malfunction
P0569 Cruise Control Coast Signal Malfunction
P0570 Cruise Control Accel Signal Malfunction
P0571 Cruise Control/Brake Switch "A" Circuit Malfunction
P0572 Cruise Control/Brake Switch "A" Circuit Low
P0573 Cruise Control/Brake Switch "A" Circuit High
P0574 **Through P0580** Reserved for Cruise Codes
P0600 Serial Communication Link Malfunction
P0601 Internal Control Module Memory Check Sum Error
P0602 Control Module Programming Error
P0603 Internal Control Module Keep Alive Memory (KAM) Error
P0604 Internal Control Module Random Access Memory (RAM) Error
P0605 Internal Control Module Read Only Memory (ROM) Error
P0606 PCM Processor Fault
P0608 Control Module VSS Output "A" Malfunction
P0609 Control Module VSS Output "B" Malfunction
P0620 Generator Control Circuit Malfunction
P0621 Generator Lamp "L" Control Circuit Malfunction
P0622 Generator Field "F" Control Circuit Malfunction
P0650 Malfunction Indicator Lamp (MIL) Control Circuit Malfunction
P0654 Engine RPM Output Circuit Malfunction
P0655 Engine Hot Lamp Output Control Circuit Malfunction
P0656 Fuel Level Output Circuit Malfunction
P0700 Transmission Control System Malfunction
P0701 Transmission Control System Range/Performance
P0702 Transmission Control System Electrical
P0703 Torque Converter/Brake Switch "B" Circuit Malfunction
P0704 Clutch Switch Input Circuit Malfunction
P0705 Transmission Range Sensor Circuit Malfunction (PRNDL Input)

P0706 Transmission Range Sensor Circuit Range/Performance
P0707 Transmission Range Sensor Circuit Low Input
P0708 Transmission Range Sensor Circuit High Input
P0709 Transmission Range Sensor Circuit Intermittent
P0710 Transmission Fluid Temperature Sensor Circuit Malfunction
P0711 Transmission Fluid Temperature Sensor Circuit Range/Performance
P0712 Transmission Fluid Temperature Sensor Circuit Low Input
P0713 Transmission Fluid Temperature Sensor Circuit High Input
P0714 Transmission Fluid Temperature Sensor Circuit Intermittent
P0715 Input/Turbine Speed Sensor Circuit Malfunction
P0716 Input/Turbine Speed Sensor Circuit Range/Performance
P0717 Input/Turbine Speed Sensor Circuit No Signal
P0718 Input/Turbine Speed Sensor Circuit Intermittent
P0719 Torque Converter/Brake Switch "B" Circuit Low
P0720 Output Speed Sensor Circuit Malfunction
P0721 Output Speed Sensor Circuit Range/Performance
P0722 Output Speed Sensor Circuit No Signal
P0723 Output Speed Sensor Circuit Intermittent
P0724 Torque Converter/Brake Switch "B" Circuit High
P0725 Engine Speed Input Circuit Malfunction
P0726 Engine Speed Input Circuit Range/Performance
P0727 Engine Speed Input Circuit No Signal
P0728 Engine Speed Input Circuit Intermittent
P0730 Incorrect Gear Ratio
P0731 Gear #1 Incorrect Ratio
P0732 Gear #2 Incorrect Ratio
P0733 Gear #3 Incorrect Ratio
P0734 Gear #4 Incorrect Ratio
P0735 Gear #5 Incorrect Ratio
P0736 Reverse Incorrect Ratio
P0740 Torque Converter Clutch Circuit Malfunction
P0741 Torque Converter Clutch Circuit Performance or Stuck Off
P0742 Torque Converter Clutch Circuit Stuck On
P0743 Torque Converter Clutch Circuit Electrical
P0744 Torque Converter Clutch Circuit Intermittent
P0745 Pressure Control Solenoid Malfunction
P0746 Pressure Control Solenoid Performance or Stuck Off
P0747 Pressure Control Solenoid Stuck On
P0748 Pressure Control Solenoid Electrical
P0749 Pressure Control Solenoid Intermittent
P0750 Shift Solenoid "A" Malfunction
P0751 Shift Solenoid "A" Performance or Stuck Off
P0752 Shift Solenoid "A" Stuck On
P0753 Shift Solenoid "A" Electrical
P0754 Shift Solenoid "A" Intermittent
P0755 Shift Solenoid "B" Malfunction
P0756 Shift Solenoid "B" Performance or Stuck Off
P0757 Shift Solenoid "B" Stuck On
P0758 Shift Solenoid "B" Electrical
P0759 Shift Solenoid "B" Intermittent
P0760 Shift Solenoid "C" Malfunction
P0761 Shift Solenoid "C" Performance Or Stuck Off
P0762 Shift Solenoid "C" Stuck On
P0763 Shift Solenoid "C" Electrical

Refer to the model specific sections for fuel system service procedures

P0764 Shift Solenoid "C" Intermittent
P0765 Shift Solenoid "D" Malfunction
P0766 Shift Solenoid "D" Performance Or Stuck Off
P0767 Shift Solenoid "D" Stuck On
P0768 Shift Solenoid "D" Electrical
P0769 Shift Solenoid "D" Intermittent
P0770 Shift Solenoid "E" Malfunction
P0771 Shift Solenoid "E" Performance Or Stuck Off
P0772 Shift Solenoid "E" Stuck On
P0773 Shift Solenoid "E" Electrical
P0774 Shift Solenoid "E" Intermittent
P0780 Shift Malfunction
P0781 1–2 Shift Malfunction
P0782 2–3 Shift Malfunction
P0783 3–4 Shift Malfunction
P0784 4–5 Shift Malfunction
P0785 Shift/Timing Solenoid Malfunction
P0786 Shift/Timing Solenoid Range/Performance
P0787 Shift/Timing Solenoid Low
P0788 Shift/Timing Solenoid High
P0789 Shift/Timing Solenoid Intermittent
P0790 Normal/Performance Switch Circuit Malfunction
P0801 Reverse Inhibit Control Circuit Malfunction
P0803 1–4 Upshift (Skip Shift) Solenoid Control Circuit Malfunction
P0804 1–4 Upshift (Skip Shift) Lamp Control Circuit Malfunction
P1106 MAP Sensor Voltage Intermittently High
P1107 MAP Sensor Voltage Intermittently Low
P1111 IAT Sensor Circuit Intermittent High Voltage
P1112 IAT Sensor Circuit Intermittent Low Voltage
P1114 ECT Sensor Circuit Intermittent Low Voltage
P1115 ECT Sensor Circuit Intermittent High Voltage
P1121 TP Sensor Voltage Intermittently High
P1122 TP Sensor Voltage Intermittently Low
P1133 HO$_2$S Insufficient Switching Bank #1, Sensor #1
P1134 HO$_2$S Transition Time Ratio Bank #1, Sensor #1
P1153 HO$_2$S Insufficient Switching Sensor Bank #2, Sensor #1
P1154 HO$_2$S Transition Time Ratio Bank #2, Sensor #1
P1171 Fuel system lean during acceleration
P1200 Injector control circuit
P1222 Injector control circuit intermittent

P1345 Crankshaft/Camshaft (CKP/CMP) Correlation
P1350 Ignition Control (IC) Circuit Malfunction
P1351 Ignition Control (IC) Circuit High Voltage
P1361 Ignition Control (IC) Circuit Not Toggling
P1361 Ignition Control (IC) Circuit Low Voltage
P1374 3X Reference circuit
P1380 Electronic Brake Control Module (EBCM) DTC Detected Rough Road Data Unusable
P1381 Misfire Detected, No EBCM/PCM/VCM Serial Data
P1406 EGR Pintle Position Circuit Fault
P1415 AIR System Bank #1
P1416 AIR System Bank #2
P1441 EVAP Control System Flow During Non-Purge
P1442 EVAP Vacuum Switch Circuit
P1450 Barometric Pressure Sensor Circuit Fault
P1451 Barometric Pressure Sensor Performance
P1460 Cooling Fan Control System Fault
P1500 Starter Signal Circuit Fault
P1510 Back-up Power Supply Fault
P1508 IAC System Low RPM
P1509 IAC System High RPM
P1520 PNP Circuit
P1530 Ignition Timing Adjustment Switch Circuit
P1554 Cruise control status circuit
P1600 PCM Battery Circuit Fault
P1626 Theft Deterrent System Fuel Enable Circuit
P1629 Theft Deterrent Crank Signal Malfunction
P1635 5-Volt Reference "A" Circuit
P1639 5-Volt Reference "B" Circuit
P1641 MIL Control Circuit
P1642 FC Relay 2 and Relay 3 Control Circuit
P1643 Engine Speed Output Circuit
P1651 Fan #1 Relay Control Circuit
P1652 Fan #2 Relay Control Circuit
P1654 A/C Relay Control
P1655 EVAP Purge Solenoid Control Circuit
P1657 Skip Shift Solenoid Control Circuit
P1661 MIL Control Circuit
P1662 Cruise Control Inhibit Control Circuit
P1664 Skip Shift Lamp Control Circuit
P1667 Reverse Inhibit Solenoid Control Circuit
P1672 Low Engine Oil Level Light Control Circuit

FIRING ORDERS

3

FIRING ORDERS

On every vehicle manufactured between 1996 and 2000, there are essentially only two basic methods for distributing the ignition system spark to the spark plugs: distributor system and Distributorless Ignition System (DIS). The distributor system uses a rotating rotor within a distributor cap to dispense the system's spark to the applicable spark plug. DIS systems use one of three general set-ups for spark distribution: remote coil pack(s), waste spark system, and direct ignition system (also often referred to as DIS). All DIS systems are controlled by the engine control computer, which computes the proper ignition timing based upon incoming reference signals from engine sensors.

The remote coil pack set-up uses one or more coil packs connected to the spark plugs via plug wires. The waste spark system is actually a sub-type of the remote coil pack system. The only difference being that two spark plugs are fired simultaneously because they share one coil. Many waste spark systems are designed as a hybrid of a direct ignition system and a remote coil pack system, because a coil is mounted directly on top of one spark plug and attached to another spark plug via a plug wire. Direct ignition does away with the spark plug wires completely and uses a single coil pack mounted directly on top of the spark plug for each cylinder.

Firing orders are most important for vehicles equipped with distributor ignition systems because the distributor can be rotated (which can lead to confusion as to which plug tower is what). If the

distributor is rotated and the spark plug wires are installed on the original cap towers, the ignition timing will be adversely affected. DIS systems are not adjustable in the same manner as distributor systems. Therefore, if you connect the wires (when applicable) to the proper coil pack towers, the ignition timing will always be correct. Thus, if the vehicle is equipped with a DIS system and the firing order illustration does not contain a specific firing order, simply attach the wires to the proper coil pack towers and the ignition system will function properly.

➡**The coil packs used on DIS systems are often labeled with the cylinder number of their corresponding spark plugs.**

If the vehicle is equipped with a distributor which is not keyed for installation with only one orientation, it could have been removed previously and rewired. The resultant wiring would hold the correct firing order, but could change the relative placement of the plug towers in relation to the engine. For this reason it is imperative that all wires be labeled before disconnecting any of them. Also, before removal, compare the current wiring with the accompanying illustrations. If the current wiring does not match, make notes in your book to reflect how your engine is wired.

➡**To avoid confusion, remove and tag the spark plug wires one at a time, for replacement.**

FIRING ORDER INDEX

MANUFACTURER ENGINE	FIGURE
Chrysler Corp.	
2.0L (VIN C) Engines	1
2.0L (VIN F) Engines	2
2.0L (VIN Y) Engines	3
2.4L (VIN X) Engines	3
2.5L (VIN H) Engines	4
2.5L (VIN N) Engines	5
2.7L Engines	6
3.0L Engine	7
3.2L Engines	6
3.3L Engines	8
3.5L Engines	8
Ford Motor Co.	
1.3L Engines	9
1.8L Engines	10
1.9L Engines	11
2.0L (VIN A) Engines	12
2.0L (VIN P and 3) Engines	13
2.0L (VIN 3) Engines	14
2.5L (VIN B) Engines	15
2.5L (VIN L) Engines	16
3.0L (VIN U) 1996-97 Engines	17
3.0L (VIN S) Engines	18
3.4L Engines	19
3.8L (VIN 4) Engines	
1996-98 Models	20
1999-00 Models	21
4.6L (VIN V) Engines	22
4.6L (VIN X) Engines	23
4.6L (VIN W) Engines	24
General Motors	
2.2L Engines	25
2.4L Engines	26
3.0L Engines	27
3.1L Engines	28
3.4L (VIN E) Engines	29
3.4L (VIN X) Engines	30
3.8L (VIN 1 and L) Engines	31
3.8L (VIN K) Engines	32
4.0L Engines	33
4.3L (VIN W) Engines	34
4.6L Engines	
1996-97 Models	35
1998-00 Models	36
5.7L (VIN G) Engines	37

FIRING ORDER INDEX

MANUFACTURER ENGINE	FIGURE
General Motors (cont)	
5.7L (VIN P) Engines	34
Geo/Chevrolet	
1.0L Engines	38
1.3L Engines	39
1.6L Engines	40
1.8L Engines	40
Saturn	
1.9L Engine	41

93003G07

Front
of the
Vehicle

79223G34

Fig. 1 Chrylser 2.0L (VIN C) Engine
Firing order: 1–3–4–2
Distributorless ignition system

79223G16

Fig. 2 Chrysler 2.0L (VIN F) Engine
Firing order: 1–3–4–2
Distributorless ignition system

IGNITION COIL   CONNECTOR

FRONT OF ENGINE

79223G13

Fig. 3 Chrysler 2.0L (VIN Y) and 2.4L (VIN X) Engines
Firing order: 1–3–4–2
Distributorless ignition system

For complete service labor times order Chilton's Labor Guide Manual

Fig. 4 Chrysler 2.5L (VIN H) Engine
Firing order: 1–2–3–4–5–6
Distributor rotation: Counterclockwise

79223G04

Fig. 6 Chrysler 2.7L and 3.2L Engines
Firing order: 1–2–3–4–5–6
Distributorless ignition system (One coil on each cylinder)

79223G01

Fig. 5 Chrysler 2.5L (VIN N) Engine
Firing order: 1–2–3–4–5–6
Distributor rotation: Counterclockwise

79223G29

Fig. 7 Chrysler 1996 3.0L (VIN K) Engine
Firing order: 1–2–3–4–5–6
Distributor rotation: Counterclockwise

79233G26

Fig. 8 Chrysler 3.3L and 3.5L Engines
Firing order: 1–2–3–4–5–6
Distributorless ignition system

Fig. 9 Ford 1996–97 1.3L Engine
Firing order: 1–3–4–2
Distributor rotation: Counterclockwise

Fig. 10 Ford 1996 1.8L Engine
Firing order: 1–3–4–2
Distributor rotation: Counterclockwise

Ignition system service is covered in the model specific sections of this manual

FRONT OF
ENGINE

FRONT OF
ENGINE

79223G19

Fig. 11 Ford 1996 1.9L Engine
Firing order: 1–3–4–2
Distributorless ignition system

FRONT OF CAR

Fig. 12 Ford 1996–97 2.0L (VIN A) Engine
Firing order: 1–3–4–2
Distributor rotation: Clockwise

Front of the Vehicle

Fig. 13 Ford 2.0L (VIN P and 3) Engines
Firing order: 1–3–4–2
Distributorless ignition system

FRONT OF VEHICLE

Fig. 14 Ford 2.0L (VIN 3) Engine
Firing order: 1–3–4–2
Distributorless ignition system

Fig. 15 Ford 1996–97 2.5L (VIN B) Engine
Firing order: 1–2–3–4–5–6
Distributor rotation: Counterclockwise

Fig. 18 Ford 3.0L (VIN S) Engine
Firing order: 1–4–2–5–3–6
Distributorless ignition system

Fig. 16 Ford 2.5L (VIN L) Engine
Firing order: 1–4–2–5–3–6
Distributorless ignition system

Fig. 19 Ford 3.4L (VIN N) Engine
Firing order: 1–5–4–2–6–3–7–8
Distributorless ignition system (one coil on each cylinder)

Fig. 17 Ford 3.0L (VIN U) Engines
Firing order: 1–4–2–5–3–6
Distributorless ignition system

Fig. 20 Ford 1996–98 3.8L (VIN 4) Engine
Firing order: 1–4–2–5–3–6
Distributor rotation: Counterclockwise

Fig. 21 Ford 1999–00 3.8L (VIN 4) Engine
Firing order: 1–4–2–5–3–6
Distributorless ignition system

93003G01

FRONT OF VEHICLE

Fig. 24 Ford 4.6L (VIN W) Engine
Firing order: 1–3–7–2–6–5–4–8
Distributorless ignition system

79223G28

FRONT

Fig. 22 Ford 4.6L (VIN V) Engine
Firing order: 1–3–7–2–6–5–4–8
Distributorless ignition system (One coil on each cylinder)

93003G03

Fig. 25 GM 2.2L Engine
Firing order: 1–3–4–2
Distributorless ignition system

79223G36

FRONT

Fig. 23 Ford 4.6L (VIN X) Engine
Firing order: 1–3–7–2–6–5–4–8
Distributorless ignition system (One coil on each cylinder)

93003G02

FRONT OF CAR

Fig. 26 GM 2.4L Engines
Firing order: 1–3–4–2
Distributorless ignition system

79223G12

Refer to the model specific sections for engine electrical system service procedures

Fig. 27 GM 3.0L Engine
Firing order: 1–2–3–4–5–6
Distributorless ignition system

Fig. 30 GM 1996–97 3.4L (VIN X) Engine
Firing order: 1–2–3–4–5–6
Distributorless ignition system

Fig. 28 GM 3.1L Engine
Firing order: 1–2–3–4–5–6
Distributorless ignition system

Fig. 31 GM 3.8L (VIN 1 and L) Engines
Firing order: 1–6–5–4–3–2
Distributorless ignition system

Fig. 29 GM 1999–00 3.4L (VIN E) Engine
Firing order: 1–2–3–4–5–6
Distributorless ignition system

Fig. 32 GM 3.8L (VIN K) Engines
Firing order: 1–6–5–4–3–2
Distributorless ignition system

Fig. 33 GM 4.0L Engine
Distributorless ignition system

79223G38

Front
of the
Vehicle

79223G37

Fig. 36 GM 1998–00 4.6L (VIN 9 and Y) Engines
Firing order: 1–2–7–3–4–5–6–8
Distributorless ignition system

FRONT OF CAR

79223G33

Fig. 34 GM 1996 4.3L (VIN W) and 1996–97 5.7L (VIN P) Engines
Firing order: 1–8–4–3–6–5–7–2
Distributor rotation: Clockwise

79223G17

Fig. 35 GM 1996–97 4.6L (VIN 9 and Y) Engines
Firing order: 1–2–7–3–4–5–6–8
Distributorless ignition system

Front
of the
Vehicle

79223G40

Fig. 37 GM 1998–00 5.7L (VIN G) Engine
Firing order: 1–8–4–3–6–5–7–2
Distributorless ignition system (one coil on each cylinder)

For complete service labor times order Chilton's Labor Guide Manual

FIRING ORDER 1-3-2

79223G20

Fig. 38 GEO 1.0L Engine
Firing order: 1–3–2
Distributor rotation: Counterclockwise

FIRING ORDER 1-3-4-2

79223G21

Fig. 39 GEO 1.3L Engine
Firing order: 1–3–4–2
Distributor rotation: Counterclockwise

FRONT OF ENGINE

Front of car

79223G22

Fig. 40 GEO 1.6L (1996–97) and 1.8L Engines
Firing order: 1–3–4–2
Distributor rotation: Counterclockwise

79223G14

Fig. 41 Saturn 1.9L Engine
Firing order: 1–3–4–2
Distributorless ignition system

ACCESSORY DRIVE BELTS

4

ACCESSORY DRIVE BELTS

Accessory drive belts are usually divided into two basic types: V-belts (conventional, cogged and flat multi-ribbed) and serpentine (multi-ribbed) belts. The flat multi-ribbed V-belt actually resembles a serpentine belt, however, unlike a serpentine belt, only the inner surface of the belt makes contact with the components' pulleys. (Rarely, the back of multi-ribbed V-belts may ride against an idler or tensioner pulley, however.) V-belts ride in pulleys with V-shaped groove(s) to rotate various accessories, such as the power steering pump, air conditioner compressor, alternator/generator, water pump, and air pump. Only the inside of a V-belt is used, unlike a serpentine belt which utilizes both sides. V-belts typically operate one or two accessories per belt, whereas a single serpentine belt can drive all of the accessories. V-belts and a few serpentine belts require periodic adjustment because the belts are under tension and stretch over time. Most serpentine belts utilize an automatic belt tensioner that constantly provides the proper tension to the belt.

V-Belts

INSPECTION

Although different maintenance intervals are given by each manufacturer, it is a good rule of thumb to inspect the drive belts every 15,000 miles (24,000 km) or 12 months (whichever occurs first). Determine the belt tension at a point half-way between the pulleys by pressing on the belt with moderate thumb pressure. The belt

CONVENTIONAL "V" BELT

COGGED "V" BELT

"V" RIBBED BELT

TCCS1218

Typical accessory drive belts found on vehicles today

should deflect about ¼–½ in. (6–13mm) at this point. Note that "deflection" is not play, but the ability of the belt, under actual tension, to stretch slightly and give.

Inspect the belts for the following signs of damage or wear: glazing, cracking, fraying, crumbling or missing chunks. A glazed belt will be perfectly smooth from slippage, while a good belt will have a slight texture of fabric visible. Cracks will usually start at the inner edge of the belt and run outward. A belt that is fraying will have the fabric backing de-laminating itself from the belt. A belt that is crumbling or missing chunks will have voids in the cross-section of the belt, some times the section missing chunks will be in the pulley groove and not easily seen. All worn or damaged drive belts should be replaced immediately. It is best to replace all drive belts at one time, as a preventive maintenance measure.

Although it is generally easier on the component to have the belt too loose than too tight, a very loose belt may place a high impact load on a bearing due to the whipping or snapping action of the belt. A belt that is slightly loose may slip, especially when component loads are high. This slippage may be hard to identify. For

The cover of this belt is worn, exposing the critical reinforcing cords to excessive wear

An example of a healthy drive belt

Installing too wide a belt can result in serious belt wear and/or breakage

example, the generator belt may run okay during the day, then slip at night when headlights are turned on. Slipping belts wear quickly not only due to the direct effect of slippage but also because of the heat the slippage generates. Extreme slippage may even cause a belt to burn. A very smooth, glazed appearance on the belt's sides, as opposed to the obvious pattern of a fabric cover, indicates that the belt has been slipping.

ADJUSTMENT

> **✳✳ CAUTION**
>
> **On vehicles with an electric cooling fan, disable the power to the fan by disengaging the fan motor wiring connector or removing the negative battery cable before replacing or adjusting the drive belts. Otherwise, the fan may engage even though the ignition is OFF.**

Belt tension can be checked by pressing on the belt at the center point of its longest straight span. The belt should give approximately

Deep cracks in this belt will cause flex, building up heat that will eventually lead to belt failure

¼ – ½ in. (6–13mm). If the belt is loose it will slip, whereas if the belt is too tight it will damage the bearings in the driven unit.

For the purposes of V-belt tensioning, there are generally three types of mounting for the various components driven by the drive belt. The first method, referred to as pivoting type without adjuster, is designed so that the component is secured by at least 2 bolts. One of the bolts is a pivoting bolt and the other is the lockbolt. When both bolts are loosened so that the component may move, the component pivots on the pivoting bolt. The lockbolt passes through the component and a slotted bracket, so that when the lockbolt's nut is tightened the component is held in that position. There are not automatic adjusting mechanisms used with this type of mounting.

The second method of component mounting, referred to as pivoting type with adjuster, is almost identical except for the addition of an adjuster of some sort. Usually the adjuster is composed of a bracket attached to the component and a threaded adjusting bolt. After loosening the pivoting and lockbolts, the adjusting bolt can be tightened or loosened to increase or decrease the drive belt's ten-

sion. With this type of mounting, you do not have to hold the component in a tensioned position and tighten the pivoting and lockbolts; the adjusting bolt does the job for you.

Some versions of this method of mounting use an adjuster which is built into one of the components mounting braces. The brace attaches the component to the engine and incorporates a threaded adjuster in its mid-span, so that when the threaded adjuster is turned the brace shortens or lengthens. This in turn increases or decreases the amount of tension on the component.

The third type of mounting, referred to as stationary type, is designed so that the component is mounted on its brackets. There are no pivoting or lockbolts, and the component is not designed to be moved. Rather, this type of mounting uses an extra tensioner idler pulley assembly. The drive belt is tensioned by adjusting the position of the idler pulley, usually accomplished by turning the adjuster bolt on the idler mechanism.

Pivoting Type

WITHOUT ADJUSTER

1. Disconnect the negative battery cable.
2. Loosen the component's lockbolt and pivoting bolt only enough for the component to move.
3. Using a strong wooden, plastic or metal prytool, move the component either closer to, or farther away from, the engine to provide the correct tension on the belt.

> ※※ **WARNING**
>
> **If using a metal prytool, always wrap the end with a rag or towel to prevent accidentally damaging the component from undue stress.**

4. Once the proper amount of tension is applied to the drive belt, hold the prytool with one hand while tightening the lockbolt securely with the other hand.
5. Release the pressure from the prytool and tighten the pivoting bolt securely.
6. Double check the drive belt's tension, in case the component moved slightly while tightening the bolts.
7. Connect the negative battery cable.

WITH ADJUSTER

This type of drive belt is tensioned by a tensioner, which makes precise tension adjustment easy.
1. Disconnect the negative battery cable.
2. Loosen the component's pivot and lockbolts.
3. Inspect the tensioner assembly on the component; the tensioner adjusting bolt may use a locknut or screw to prevent it from loosening over time. On the type of adjuster with a threaded mounting brace, there may be two jam nuts used on either side of the threaded coupling. If such locking fasteners are found, loosen them.
4. Turn the tensioner adjusting bolt or threaded coupling to increase or decrease the amount of tension on the drive belt, as necessary.
5. When the belt tension is correct, tighten the lockbolt and the pivot bolt.
6. If equipped, tighten the tension adjusting bolt locknut or screw to prevent the adjuster from slowly loosening over time. If equipped, tighten the two jam nuts.
7. Connect the negative battery cable.

A typical pivoting accessory with an adjusting bolt

An accessory that is fixed will have an adjustable pulley—notice the square slot to aid the adjustment

For complete service labor times order Chilton's Labor Guide Manual

Stationary Type

IDLER PULLEY WITH ADJUSTING BOLT

1. Loosen the idler bracket pivot bolt and locking bolts.
2. Adjust the belt tension by inserting the proper size ratchet in the square slot of the idler bracket and rotating the bracket until tension is applied.
3. While holding the tension on the belt with the ratchet, tighten the locking bolts, then the pivot bolt.

IDLER PULLEY WITHOUT ADJUSTING BOLT

1. Loosen the mounting/pivot bolt behind the idler pulley.
2. Swivel the idler pulley with a pair of pliers or a wrench on the bearing mounting until the proper tension is achieved.
3. While holding the idler pulley, at the proper tension, tighten the mounting/pivot bolt.

REMOVAL & INSTALLATION

If a belt must be replaced, the driven unit or idler pulley must be loosened and moved to its extreme loosest position, generally by moving it toward the center of the motor. After removing the old belt, check the pulleys for dirt or built-up material which could affect belt contact. Carefully install the new belt, remembering that it is new and unused; it may appear to be just a little too small to fit over the pulley flanges. Fit the belt over the largest pulley (usually the crankshaft pulley at the bottom center of the motor) first, then work on the smaller one(s). Gentle pressure in the direction of rotation is helpful. Some belts run around a third, or idler pulley, which acts as an additional pivot in the belt's path. It may be possible to loosen the idler pulley as well as the main component, making your job much easier. Depending on which belt(s) you are changing, it may be necessary to loosen or remove other interfering belts to get at the one(s) you want.

When buying replacement belts, remember that the fit is critical according to the length of the belt ("diameter"), the width of the belt, the depth of the belt and the angle or profile of the V shape or the ribs. The belt shape should match the shape of the pulley exactly; belts that are not an exact match can cause noise, slippage and premature failure.

After the new belt is installed, draw tension on it by moving the driven unit or idler pulley away from the motor and tighten its mounting bolts. This is sometimes a three or four-handed job; you may find an assistant helpful. Be sure that all the bolts you loosened get retightened and that any other loosened belts also have the correct tension. A new belt can be expected to stretch a bit after installation so be prepared to readjust your new belt, if needed, within the first two hundred miles of use.

Pivoting Type

> ### ❊❊ CAUTION
>
> **On vehicles with an electric cooling fan, disable the power to the fan by disengaging the fan motor wiring connector or removing the negative battery cable before replacing or adjusting the drive belts. Otherwise, the fan may engage even though the ignition is OFF.**

WITHOUT ADJUSTER

1. Disconnect the negative battery cable.
2. Loosen the accessory's slotted adjusting bracket bolt. If the hinge bolt is excessively tight, it too will have to be loosened.
3. Push the component toward the engine to provide enough slack in the belt so that it will slide over one of the accessory drive pulleys. Remove the drive belt from the accessory drive pulleys and from the vehicle.

To install:
4. Position the new drive belt over the component pulleys. Be sure that it is routed correctly.
5. Adjust the tension of the belt, as described earlier in this section.
6. Connect the negative battery cable.

WITH ADJUSTER

1. Disconnect the negative battery cable.
2. Loosen the component's pivot and lockbolts.
3. Inspect the tensioner assembly on the component; the tensioner adjusting bolt may use a locknut or screw to prevent it from loosening over time. On the type of adjuster with a threaded mounting brace, there may be two jam nuts used on either side of the threaded coupling. If such locking fasteners are found, loosen them.
4. Turn the tensioner adjusting bolt or threaded coupling to relieve all tension from the drive belt until the most possible slack is gained from the component.
5. Slip the belt off of the accessory pulley, then remove it from the other pulleys. Remove the belt from the vehicle.

To install:
6. Route the new belt on the component pulleys. Make certain that it is routed correctly; incorrect routing could cause a components to spin backward, possibly damaging it.
7. Once the belt is correctly positioned on all of the pulleys, adjust the tension as described earlier in this section.
8. Connect the negative battery cable.

Stationary Type

IDLER PULLEY WITH ADJUSTING BOLT

1. Disconnect the negative battery cable.
2. Loosen the idler bracket pivot bolt and locking bolts.
3. Move the idler pulley until the most amount of slack is gained.
4. Remove the drive belt from the accessory pulley, then from the other applicable pulleys.

To install:
5. Position the new belt over the crankshaft pulley, the idler pulley and the accessory pulley. Make certain that it is correctly routed, otherwise it could cause the accessory to be rotated backwards. This could cause damage to the accessory.
6. Adjust the belt tension, as described earlier in this section.
7. While holding the tension on the belt with the ratchet, tighten the locking bolts, then the pivot bolt.
8. Connect the negative battery cable.

IDLER PULLEY WITHOUT ADJUSTING BOLT

1. Disconnect the negative battery cable.
2. Loosen the mounting/pivot bolt behind the idler pulley.
3. Remove the drive belt from the accessory pulley, then from the other applicable pulleys.

To install:
4. Position the new belt over the crankshaft pulley, the idler pulley and the accessory pulley. Make certain that it is correctly routed, otherwise it could cause the accessory to be rotated backwards. This could cause damage to the accessory.

5. Swivel the idler pulley with a pair of pliers or a wrench on the bearing mounting until the proper tension is achieved.

6. While holding the idler pulley, at the proper tension, tighten the mounting/pivot bolt.

7. Connect the negative battery cable.

Serpentine Belts

INSPECTION

Although many manufacturers recommend that the drive belt(s) be inspected every 30,000 miles (48,000 km) or more, it is really a good idea to check them at least once a year, or at every major fluid change. Whichever interval you choose, the belts should be checked for wear or damage. Obviously, a damaged drive belt can cause problems should it give way while the vehicle is in operation. But, improper length belts (too short or long), as well as excessively worn belts, can also cause problems. Loose accessory drive belts can lead to poor engine cooling and diminished output from the alternator, air conditioning compressor or power steering pump. A belt that is too tight places a severe strain on the driven unit and can wear out bearings quickly.

Serpentine drive belts should be inspected for rib chunking (pieces of the ribs breaking off), severe glazing, frayed cords or other visible damage. Any belt which is missing sections of 2 or more adjacent ribs which are ½ in. (13mm) or longer must be replaced. You might want to note that serpentine belts do tend to form small cracks across the backing. If the only wear you find is in the form of one or more cracks are across the backing and NOT parallel to the ribs, the belt is still good and does not need to be replaced.

Typical wear patterns for a serpentine drive belt

ADJUSTMENT

Periodic drive belt tensioning is not necessary, because an automatic spring-loaded tensioner is used with these belts to maintain proper adjustment at all times. The tensioner is also useful as a wear indicator. When the belt is properly installed, the arrow on the

Typical drive belt automatic tensioner wear indicator

tensioner housing must point within the acceptable range lines on the tensioner's face. If the arrow falls outside the range, either an improper belt has been installed or the belt is worn beyond its useful life span. In either case, a new belt must be installed immediately to assure proper engine operation and to prevent possible accessory damage.

REMOVAL & INSTALLATION

Because serpentine belts use a spring loaded tensioner for adjustment, belt replacement tends to be somewhat easier than it used to be on engines where accessories were pivoted and bolted in place for tension adjustment. Basically, all belt replacement involves is to pivot the tensioner to loosen the belt, then slide the belt off of the pulleys. The two most important points are to pay CLOSE attention to the proper belt routing (since serpentine belts tend to be "snaked" all different ways through the pulleys) and to be sure the V-ribs are properly seated in all the pulleys.

Often the underhood label will display the serpentine drive belt routing

Troubleshooting the Serpentine Drive Belt

Problem	Cause	Solution
Tension sheeting fabric failure (woven fabric on outside circumference of belt has cracked or separated from body of belt)	• Grooved or backside idler pulley diameters are less than minimum recommended • Tension sheeting contacting (rubbing) stationary object • Excessive heat causing woven fabric to age • Tension sheeting splice has fractured	• Replace pulley(s) not conforming to specification • Correct rubbing condition • Replace belt • Replace belt
Noise (objectional squeal, squeak, or rumble is heard or felt while drive belt is in operation)	• Belt slippage • Bearing noise • Belt misalignment • Belt-to-pulley mismatch • Driven component inducing vibration • System resonant frequency inducing vibration	• Adjust belt • Locate and repair • Align belt/pulley(s) • Install correct belt • Locate defective driven component and repair • Vary belt tension within specifications. Replace belt.
Rib chunking (one or more ribs has separated from belt body)	• Foreign objects imbedded in pulley grooves • Installation damage • Drive loads in excess of design specifications • Insufficient internal belt adhesion	• Remove foreign objects from pulley grooves • Replace belt • Adjust belt tension • Replace belt
Rib or belt wear (belt ribs contact bottom of pulley grooves)	• Pulley(s) misaligned • Mismatch of belt and pulley groove widths • Abrasive environment • Rusted pulley(s) • Sharp or jagged pulley groove tips • Rubber deteriorated	• Align pulley(s) • Replace belt • Replace belt • Clean rust from pulley(s) • Replace pulley • Replace belt
Longitudinal belt cracking (cracks between two ribs)	• Belt has mistracked from pulley groove • Pulley groove tip has worn away rubber-to-tensile member	• Replace belt • Replace belt
Belt slips	• Belt slipping because of insufficient tension • Belt or pulley subjected to substance (belt dressing, oil, ethylene glycol) that has reduced friction • Driven component bearing failure • Belt glazed and hardened from heat and excessive slippage	• Adjust tension • Replace belt and clean pulleys • Replace faulty component bearing • Replace belt
"Groove jumping" (belt does not maintain correct position on pulley, or turns over and/or runs off pulleys)	• Insufficient belt tension • Pulley(s) not within design tolerance • Foreign object(s) in grooves	• Adjust belt tension • Replace pulley(s) • Remove foreign objects from grooves

TCCS3C09

Troubleshooting the Serpentine Drive Belt

Problem	Cause	Solution
"Groove jumping" (belt does not maintain correct position on pulley, or turns over and/or runs off pulleys)	• Excessive belt speed • Pulley misalignment • Belt-to-pulley profile mismatched • Belt cordline is distorted	• Avoid excessive engine acceleration • Align pulley(s) • Install correct belt • Replace belt
Belt broken (Note: identify and correct problem before replacement belt is installed)	• Excessive tension • Tensile members damaged during belt installation • Belt turnover • Severe pulley misalignment • Bracket, pulley, or bearing failure	• Replace belt and adjust tension to specification • Replace belt • Replace belt • Align pulley(s) • Replace defective component and belt
Cord edge failure (tensile member exposed at edges of belt or separated from belt body)	• Excessive tension • Drive pulley misalignment • Belt contacting stationary object • Pulley irregularities • Improper pulley construction • Insufficient adhesion between tensile member and rubber matrix	• Adjust belt tension • Align pulley • Correct as necessary • Replace pulley • Replace pulley • Replace belt and adjust tension to specifications
Sporadic rib cracking (multiple cracks in belt ribs at random intervals)	• Ribbed pulley(s) diameter less than minimum specification • Backside bend flat pulley(s) diameter less than minimum • Excessive heat condition causing rubber to harden • Excessive belt thickness • Belt overcured • Excessive tension	• Replace pulley(s) • Replace pulley(s) • Correct heat condition as necessary • Replace belt • Replace belt • Adjust belt tension

TCCS3C10

Although belt routing diagrams have been included in this section, the first places you should check for proper belt routing are the labels in your engine compartment. These should include a belt routing diagram which may reflect changes made during a production run.

1. Disconnect the negative battery cable for safety. This will help assure that no one mistakenly cranks the engine over with your hands between the pulleys, and that the cooling fan cannot activate while servicing the belt(s).

➡ **Take a good look at the installed belt and make a note of the routing. Before removing the belt, be sure the routing matches that of the belt routing label or one of the diagrams in this book. If for some reason a diagram does not match (you may not have the original engine or it may have been modified), carefully note the changes on a piece of paper.**

2. For tensioners equipped with a ½ in. (13mm) square hole, insert the drive end of a large breaker bar into the hole. Use the breaker bar to pivot the tensioner away from the drive belt. For tensioners not equipped with this hole, use the proper-sized socket and breaker bar (or a large handled wrench) on the tensioner idler pulley center bolt to pivot the tensioner away from the belt. This will loosen the belt sufficiently so it can be pulled off of one or more of

the pulleys. It is usually easiest to carefully pull the belt out from under the tensioner pulley itself.

3. Once the belt is off one of the pulleys, gently pivot the tensioner back into position. DO NOT allow the tensioner to snap back, as this could damage the tensioner's internal parts.

4. Now finish removing the belt from the other pulleys and remove it from the engine.

To install:

5. While referring to the proper routing diagram (which you identified earlier), begin to route the belt over the pulleys, leaving whichever pulley you first released it from for last.

6. Once the belt is mostly in place, carefully pivot the tensioner and position the belt over the final pulley. As you begin to allow the tensioner back into contact with the belt, run your hand around the pulleys and be sure the belt is properly seated in the ribs. If not, release the tension and seat the belt.

7. Once the belt is installed, take another look at all the pulleys to double check your installation.

8. Connect the negative battery cable, then start and run the engine to check belt operation.

9. Once the engine has reached normal operating temperature, turn the ignition **OFF** and check that the belt tensioner arrow is within the proper adjustment range.

Refer to the model specific sections for engine mechanical service procedures

Relieve the belt tension by pivoting the automatic tensioner away from the belt, then remove the belt

88231P44

Verifying serpentine belt alignment in the pulley

79244G60

ACCESSORY DRIVE BELT ROUTING INDEX

MANUFACTURER

ENGINES	DESCRIPTION	FIGURE
Chrysler Corp.		
2.0L (VIN C, Y) Neon engine	Accessory drive belt routing	1
2.0L (VIN Y) except Neon engine	Accessory drive belt routing	2
2.0L (VIN F) turbo engine	Accessory drive belt routing	3
2.4L engine	Accessory drive belt routing	4
2.5L engine	Accessory drive belt routing	5
2.7L engine	Accessory drive belt routing	6
3.0L (VIN H) SOHC engine	Accessory drive belt routing	7
3.0L (VIN J, K) DOHC engines	Accessory drive belt routing	8
3.2L engine	Accessory drive belt routing	9
3.3L engine	Accessory drive belt routing	10
3.5L engine	Accessory drive belt routing	11
Ford Motor Co.		
1.3L Aspire engine	Accessory drive belt routing	12
1.8L engine	Accessory drive belt routing	13
1.9L engine	Serpentine accessory drive belt routing	14
2.0L Probe engine	Accessory drive belt routing	15
2.0L (VIN 3) engine	Accessory drive belt routing	16
2.0L (VIN P) Escort/Tracer engine with A/C	Accessory drive belt routing	17
2.0L (VIN P) Escort/Tracer engine without A/C	Accessory drive belt routing	18
2.0L (VIN 3) 1998-00 Escort/Tracer engine	Accessory drive belt routing	19
2.5L (VIN B) Probe engine without A/C	Alternator drive belt routing	20
2.5L (VIN B) Probe engine with A/C	Alternator drive belt routing	21
2.5L (VIN B) Probe engine	Power steering and water pump drive belts	22
2.5L (VIN L) engine	Water pump drive belt routing	23
2.5L (VIN L) engine with A/C	Accessory drive belt routing	24
2.5L (VIN L) engine without A/C	Accessory drive belt routing	25
3.0L (VIN U) OHV engine	Serpentine drive belt routing	26
3.0L (VIN S) DOHC engine	Serpentine drive belt routing	27
3.4L SHO engine	Serpentine drive belt routing	28
3.4L SHO engine	Water pump drive belt routing	29
3.8L (VIN 4) engine	Accessory drive belt routing	30
3.8L supercharged engine	Accessory drive belt routing	31
4.6L (VIN W) engine	Serpentine drive belt routing	32
4.6L (VIN V) Continental engine	Serpentine drive belt routing	33
4.6L (VIN X) Mustang engine	Serpentine drive belt routing	34

93004G07

ACCESSORY DRIVE BELT ROUTING INDEX

MANUFACTURER ENGINES	DESCRIPTION	FIGURE
General Motors		
2.2L engines		
A body models	Serpentine drive belt routing	35
Except A body models		
1996-97 engines	Serpentine drive belt routing	36
1998-00 engines with A/C	Serpentine drive belt routing	37
1998-00 engines without A/C	Serpentine drive belt routing	38
2.4L engines	Serpentine drive belt routing	39
3.1L engines		
A body models	Serpentine drive belt routing	40
Except A and L/N body models	Serpentine drive belt routing	41
L/N body models	Serpentine drive belt routing	42
3.4L engines		
Except F body models	Serpentine drive belt routing	43
F body models	Serpentine drive belt routing	44
3.8L engines		
C & H bodies 3.8L (VIN K) engines	Serpentine drive belt routing	45
C & H bodies 3.8L (VIN 1) engines	Serpentine drive belt routing	46
F body models	Serpentine drive belt routing	47
G body 3.8L (VIN 1) engines	Serpentine drive belt routing	48
G body 3.8L (VIN K) engines	Serpentine drive belt routing	49
W body models	Serpentine drive belt routing	50
4.0L engines	Serpentine drive belt routing	51
4.3L engines	Serpentine drive belt routing	52
4.6L engines	Serpentine drive belt routing	53
5.7L engines		
5.7L (VIN P) except B or F body engines	Serpentine drive belt routing	54
5.7L (VIN G) except B or F body engines	Serpentine drive belt routing	55
5.7L B body engines	Serpentine drive belt routing	52
5.7L 1996-97 F body engines	Serpentine drive belt routing	56
5.7L 1998-00 F body engines	Serpentine drive belt routing	57
5.7L 1998-00 F body engines	A/C drive belt routing	58
Geo/Chevrolet		
All engines	Accessory drive belt routing	59
Saturn		
All engines	Serpentine drive belt routing	60

93004G08

Fig. 1 Accessory drive belt routing—Chrysler Neon 2.0L (VIN C, Y) engine

79224G08

Fig. 2 Accessory drive belt routing—Chrysler 2.0L (VIN Y) engine except Neon

79224G05

Refer to the model specific sections for engine electrical system service procedures

Fig. 3 Accessory drive belt routing—Chrysler 2.0L (VIN F) turbo engine

Fig. 4 Accessory drive belt routing—Chrysler 2.4L engine

Fig. 6 Accessory belt routing—Chrysler 2.7L engine

Fig. 5 Accessory drive belt routing—Chrysler 2.5L engine

A: Crankshaft pulley
B: Power steering pump pulley
C: Tension pulley
D: Generator pulley
F: Air conditioning compressor pulley

Fig. 7 Accessory drive belt routing—Chrysler 3.0L SOHC engines—Stealth

<DOHC without air conditioning>

<DOHC with air conditioning>

A: Crankshaft pulley
B: Power steering pump pulley
C: Tension pulley
D: Generator pulley
E: Idler pulley
F: Air conditioning compressor pulley

93004G02

Fig. 8 Accessory drive belt routing—Chrysler 3.0L DOHC engines—Stealth

Fig. 10 Accessory drive belt routing—Chrysler 3.3L engine

79224G01

79224G03

Fig. 9 Accessory drive belt routing—Chrysler 3.2L engine

79224G02

Fig. 11 Accessory drive belt routing—Chrysler 3.5L engine

For accessory drive belt replacement procedures see the model specific sections of this manual

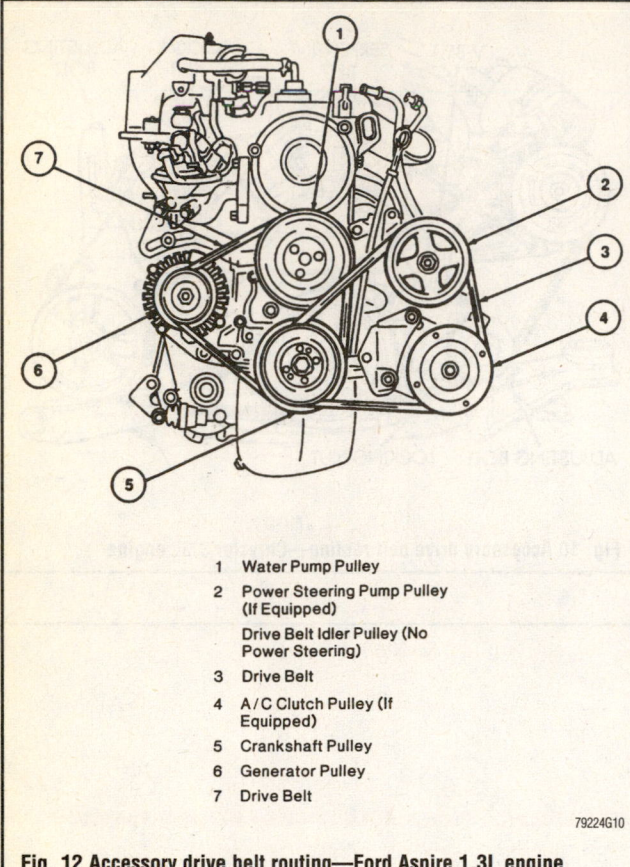

1 Water Pump Pulley
2 Power Steering Pump Pulley
   (If Equipped)
   Drive Belt Idler Pulley (No
   Power Steering)
3 Drive Belt
4 A/C Clutch Pulley (If
   Equipped)
5 Crankshaft Pulley
6 Generator Pulley
7 Drive Belt

79224G10

Fig. 12 Accessory drive belt routing—Ford Aspire 1.3L engine

WATER PUMP
PULLEY

POWER STEERING
PUMP PULLEY

ALTERNATOR
PULLEY

ALTERNATOR AND
WATER PUMP BELT

CRANKSHAFT
PULLEY

A/C COMPRESSOR
PULLEY

POWER STEERING
PUMP AND A/C
COMPRESSOR BELT

79224G28

Fig. 13 Accessory drive belt routing—Ford 1.8L engine

1.9L DRIVE BELT ROUTING

A/C, POWER STEERING, GENERATOR

GENERATOR ONLY

POWER STEERING, GENERATOR

79224G27

Fig. 14 Serpentine accessory drive belt routing—Ford 1.9L engine

POWER STEERING
PUMP PULLEY

WATER PUMP
PULLEY

GENERATOR
PULLEY

CRANKSHAFT
PULLEY

A/C PULLEY

79224G11

Fig. 15 Accessory drive belt routing—Ford Probe 2.0L engine

Pulley, Routing—2.0L Engine

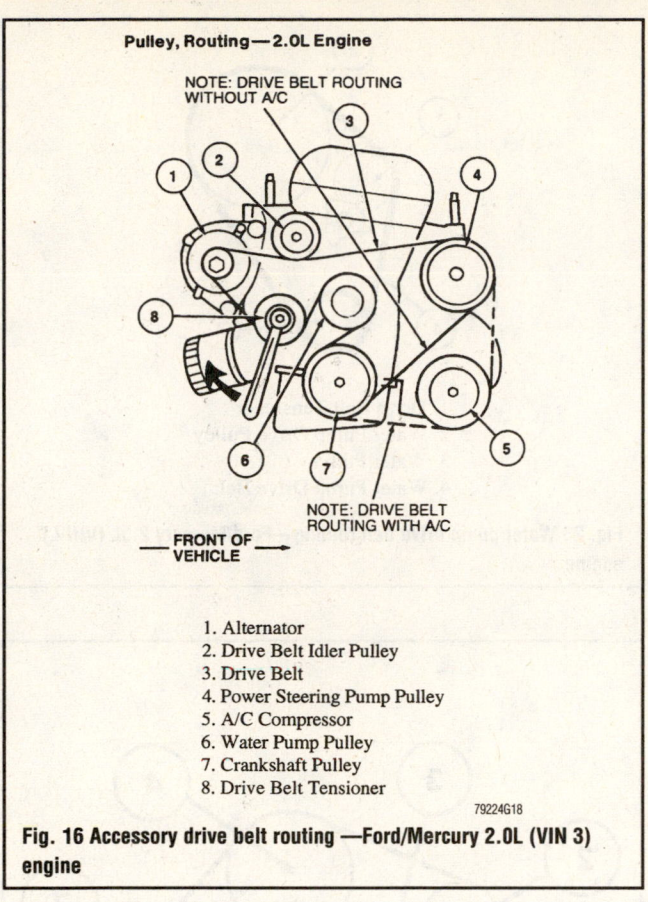

NOTE: DRIVE BELT ROUTING WITHOUT A/C

NOTE: DRIVE BELT ROUTING WITH A/C

FRONT OF VEHICLE

1. Alternator
2. Drive Belt Idler Pulley
3. Drive Belt
4. Power Steering Pump Pulley
5. A/C Compressor
6. Water Pump Pulley
7. Crankshaft Pulley
8. Drive Belt Tensioner

79224G18

Fig. 16 Accessory drive belt routing —Ford/Mercury 2.0L (VIN 3) engine

1	Belt tensioner
2	Generator pulley
3	Belt
4	Power steering pump pulley
5	Crankshaft damper

93004G04

Fig. 18 Accessory drive belt routing —Ford/Mercury 2.0L (VIN P) SOHC engine without A/C—1997–00 Escort/Tracer

1	Belt tensioner
2	Generator pulley
3	Belt
4	Power steering pump pulley
5	Belt idler pulley
6	A/C clutch pulley
7	Crankshaft damper

93004G03

Fig. 17 Accessory drive belt routing —Ford/Mercury 2.0L (VIN P) SOHC engine with A/C—1997–00 Escort/Tracer

1	Generator pulley
2	Belt idler pulley
3	Power steering pump pulley
4	Water pump pulley
5	Belt tensioner
6	A/C clutch pulley
7	Crankshaft pulley damper
8	Belt idler pulley
9	Drive belt

93004G05

Fig. 19 Accessory drive belt routing —Ford/Mercury 2.0L (VIN 3) DOHC engine—1998–00 Escort/Tracer

Refer to the model specific sections for cooling system service procedures

Fig. 20 Alternator drive belt routing—Ford Probe 2.5L (VIN B) engine without A/C

Fig. 21 Alternator drive belt routing—Ford Probe 2.5L (VIN B) engine with A/C

Fig. 22 Power steering and water pump drive belt routing —Ford Probe 2.5L (VIN B) engine

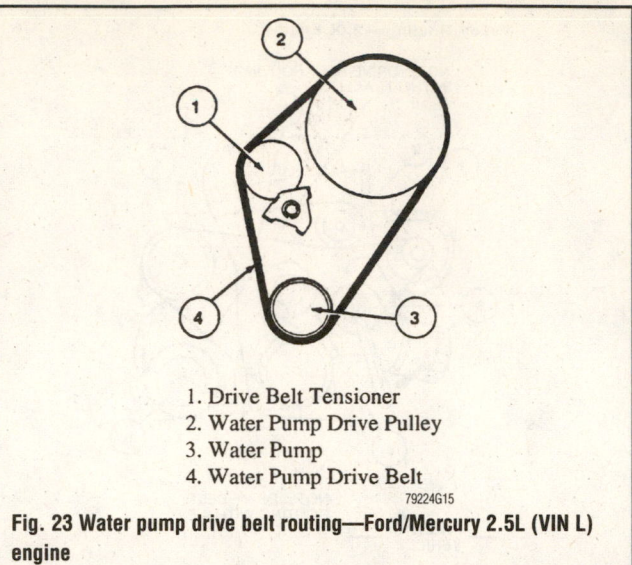

1. Drive Belt Tensioner
2. Water Pump Drive Pulley
3. Water Pump
4. Water Pump Drive Belt

Fig. 23 Water pump drive belt routing—Ford/Mercury 2.5L (VIN L) engine

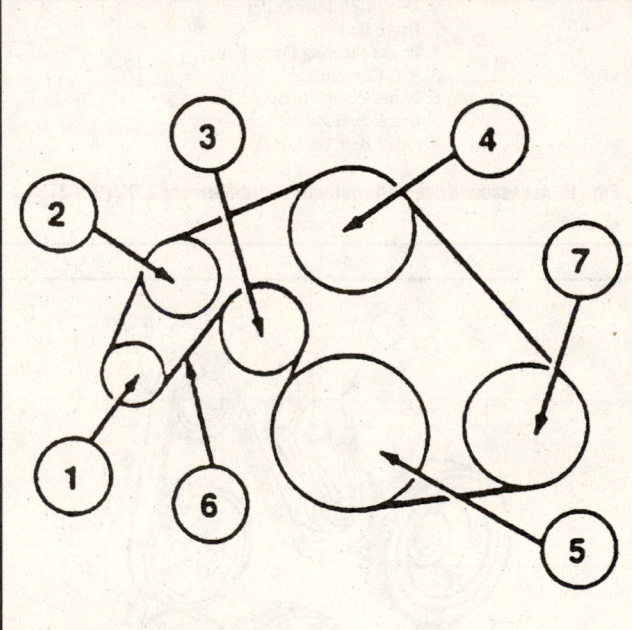

1. Alternator
2. Idler Pulley
3. Tensioner
4. Power Steering Pulley
5. Crankshaft Pulley
6. Drive Belt
7. A/C Compressor

Fig. 24 Accessory drive belt routing—Ford/Mercury 2.5L (VIN L) engine with A/C

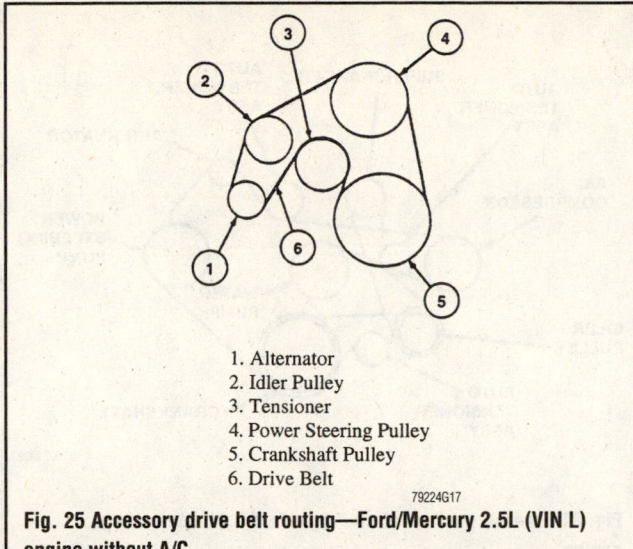

1. Alternator
2. Idler Pulley
3. Tensioner
4. Power Steering Pulley
5. Crankshaft Pulley
6. Drive Belt

79224G17

Fig. 25 Accessory drive belt routing—Ford/Mercury 2.5L (VIN L) engine without A/C

1. Generator
2. Drive belt tensioner
3. Power steering pump
4. A/C compressor
5. Crankshaft pulley
6. Idler pulley
7. Water pump
8. Drive belt

79224G24

Fig. 26 Serpentine accessory drive belt routing—Ford 3.0L (VIN U) engines

1. Power steering pump
2. Water pump
3. A/C compressor
4. Drive belt
5. Crankshaft pulley
6. Drive belt tensioner
7. Generator

79224G25

Fig. 27 Serpentine accessory drive belt routing—Ford 3.0L (VIN S) engine

1. Power Steering Pump Pulley
2. Drive Belt Idler Pulley (RH)
3. A/C Compressor
4. Drive Belt
5. Crankshaft Pulley
6. Drive Belt Tensioner
7. Alternator
8. Drive Belt Idler Pulley (LH)
9. Drive Belt Idler Pulley (Center)

79224G20

Fig. 28 Serpentine accessory drive belt routing—Ford 3.4L SHO engine

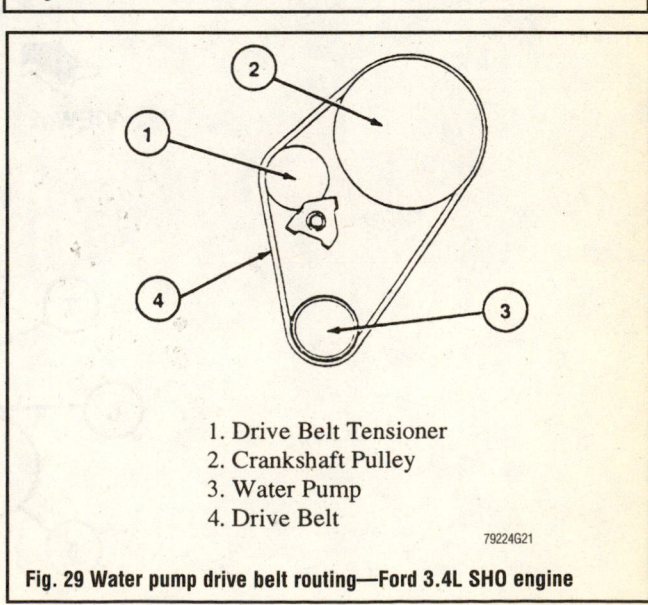

1. Drive Belt Tensioner
2. Crankshaft Pulley
3. Water Pump
4. Drive Belt

79224G21

Fig. 29 Water pump drive belt routing—Ford 3.4L SHO engine

For complete service labor times order Chilton's Labor Guide Manual

1. Tensioner
2. A/C compressor or idler pulley
3. Idler pulley
4. Alternator
5. Power steering pump
6. Crankshaft
7. Water pump

79224G31

Fig. 30 Accessory drive belt routing—Ford 3.8L (VIN 4) engine

79224G32

Fig. 31 Accessory drive belt routing—Ford 3.8L supercharged engine

1. Alternator
2. Water pump
3. Power steering pump
4. Crankshaft
5. A/C compressor
6. Drive belt
7. Tensioner
8. Idler pulley

VIEW A

FRONT OF ENGINE

VIEW A

79224G30

Fig. 32 Accessory drive belt routing—Ford 4.6L (VIN W) engine

Drive Belt Routing

FRONT OF ENGINE

1. Generator
2. Water pump pulley
3. Belt idler pulley
4. Drive belt tensioner
5. Power steering pump
6. Drive belt
7. A/C compressor
8. Crankshaft pulley

79224G26

Fig. 33 Serpentine accessory drive belt routing— 4.6L (VIN V) engine—1999–00 Mustang and Lincoln Continental

1	Generator pulley
2	Drive belt
3	Water pump pulley
4	Power steering pump pulley
5	Crankshaft vibration damper
6	A/C clutch pulley
7	Drive belt tensioner
8	Belt idler pulley
9	Belt idler pulley

93004G06

Fig. 34 Accessory drive belt routing—Ford 4.6L (VIN X) engine— 1999–00 Mustang

FRT

1 GENERATOR
2 PUMP, COOLANT
3 COMPRESSOR, A.C
4 CRANKSHAFT, ENGINE
5 BELT, SERPENTINE DRIVE
6 TENSIONER, SERPENTINE DRIVE BELT
7 PUMP, POWER STEERING

79224G34

Fig. 35 Serpentine drive belt routing—GM "A" Bodies 2.2L engine

WITHOUT A/C

WITH A/C

1 POWER STEERING PUMP
2 GENERATOR
3 WATER PUMP
4 A/C COMPRESSOR
5 CRANKSHAFT
6 TENSIONER

79224G49

Fig. 36 Serpentine drive belt routing—GM 1996–97 2.2L engine

Fig. 37 Serpentine drive belt routing with A/C—GM 1998–00 2.2L engine

Fig. 38 Serpentine drive belt routing without A/C—GM 1998–00 2.2L engine

A ROTATE TENSIONER IN DIRECTION OF ARROW TO REMOVE OR INSTALL BELT.

Fig. 39 Serpentine drive belt routing—GM 2.4L engine

23 BALANCER, CRANKSHAFT
39 PUMP ASSEMBLY, WATER
45 TENSIONER, SERPENTINE DRIVE BELT
302 COMPRESSOR ASSEMBLY, AIR CONDITIONING
304 SHIELD, SERPENTINE DRIVE BELT
305 BOLT/SCREW, SERPENTINE DRIVE BELT SHIELD
307 PUMP ASSEMBLY, POWER STEERING
308 BELT, SERPENTINE DRIVE
309 GENERATOR ASSEMBLY

Fig. 40 Serpentine drive belt routing—GM "A" Bodies 3.1L engine

1 GENERATOR
2 POWER STEERING
3 TENSIONER, SERPENTINE DRIVE BELT
4 COOLANT PUMP
5 CRANKSHAFT
6 A/C COMPRESSOR
7 SERPENTINE DRIVE BELT
8 SERPENTINE DRIVE BELT ROTATION

Fig. 41 Serpentine drive belt routing—GM 3.1L engine except L/N bodies

Fig. 42 Serpentine drive belt routing—GM 3.1L engine L/N bodies

1 BELT, SERPENTINE
2 TENSIONER, DRIVE BELT

Fig. 43 Serpentine drive belt routing—GM 3.4L (VIN X) engine

POWER STEERING PUMP PULLEY

GENERATOR ASSEMBLY

WATER PUMP PULLEY

A

AIR CONDITIONING COMPRESSOR ASSEMBLY OR DRIVE BELT IDLER PULLEY ASSEMBLY

DRIVE BELT TENSIONER ASSEMBLY

CRANKSHAFT PULLEY

Fig. 44 Serpentine drive belt routing—GM "F" Bodies 3.4L (VIN E) engine

Refer to the model specific sections for engine mechanical service procedures

Fig. 45 Serpentine drive belt routing—GM "C and H" Bodies 3.8L (VIN K) engine

1 ACCESSORY DRIVE BELT
2 SUPERCHARGER BELT

Fig. 46 Serpentine drive belt routing—GM "C and H" Bodies 3.8L (VIN 1) engine

WITHOUT AIR CONDITIONING

WITH AIR CONDITIONING

A   INDICATOR MARK
B   MINIMUM TOLERANCE BELT READING
C   MAXIMUM TOLERANCE BELT READING
1   PULLEY, GENERATOR
2   PULLEY, DRIVE BELT IDLER
3   PULLEY, AIR CONDITINING COMPRESSOR
4   TENSIONER, DRIVE BELT
5   PULLEY, CRANKSHAFT
6   PULLEY, POWER STEERING PUMP
7   PULLEY, WATER PUMP
8   BELT, SERPENTINE DRIVE

Fig. 47 Serpentine drive belt routing—GM "F" Bodies 3.8L engine

Fig. 48 Serpentine drive belt routing—GM "G" Bodies 3.8L (VIN 1) engine

Fig. 50 Serpentine drive belt routing—GM "W" body 3.8L engine

Fig. 49 Serpentine drive belt routing—GM "G" Bodies 3.8L (VIN K) engine

Fig. 51 Serpentine drive belt routing—GM "G" Body 4.0L engine

Refer to the model specific sections for engine electrical system service procedures

A COOLING SYSTEM WITHOUT MECHANICAL FAN
B COOLING SYSTEM WITH MECHANICAL FAN
C INDICATOR MARK
D ACCEPTABLE OPERATING RANGE
E UNACCEPTABLE OPERATING RANGE
40 TENSIONER ASSEMBLY, DRIVE BELT (WITH MECHANICAL FAN)
41 PULLEY, FAN
42 BALANCER ASSEMBLY, CRANKSHAFT

- 46 PUMP ASSEMBLY, POWER STEERING
- 47 GENERATOR ASSEMBLY
- 48 BELT, SERPENTINE DRIVE
- 49 COMPRESSOR ASSEMBLY, AIR CONDITIONING
- 92 PULLEY, CRANKSHAFT
- 98 BELT, FAN
253 TENSIONER ASSEMBLY, DRIVE BELT

79224G35

Fig. 52 Serpentine drive belt routing—GM "B" Bodies 4.3L and 5.7L engine

1 POWER STEERING PUMP PULLEY
2 TENSIONER PULLEY
3 CRANKSHAFT PULLEY
4 A/C COMPRESSOR PULLEY
5 GENERATOR PULLEY
6 IDLER PULLEY

79224G40

Fig. 53 Serpentine drive belt routing—GM "E and K" Bodies 4.6L engine

VIEW A

A MINIMUM BELT LENGTH MARK
B MAXIMUM BELT LENGTH MARK
C BELT REPLACEMENT MARK
D MOVABLE INDICATOR
42 BALANCER ASSEMBLY, CRANKSHAFT
145 TENSIONER ASSEMBLY, DRIVE BELT
146 PUMP ASSEMBLY, POWER STEERING
147 GENERATOR ASSEMBLY
148 BELT, SERPENTINE DRIVE
149 COMPRESSOR ASSEMBLY, AIR CONDITIONING
150 PULLEY, DRIVE BELT IDLER

79224G58

Fig. 54 Serpentine drive belt routing—GM 1996 5.7L (VIN P) engine

79224G60

Fig. 55 Serpentine drive belt routing—GM 5.7L (VIN G) engine

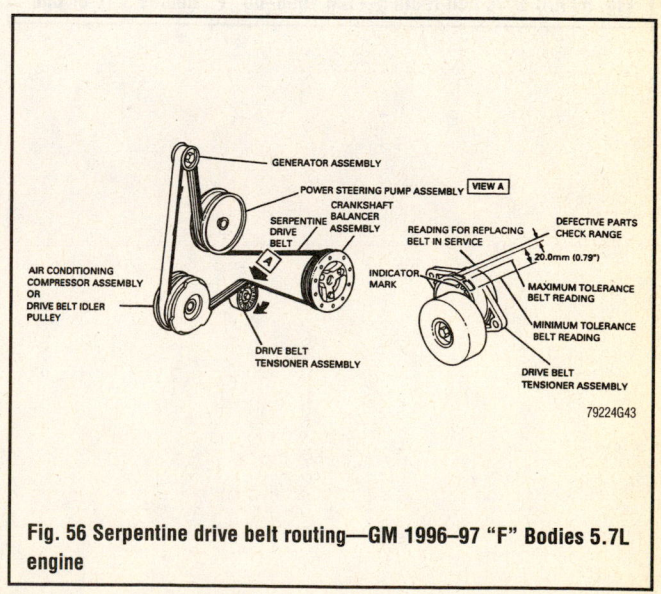

79224G43

Fig. 56 Serpentine drive belt routing—GM 1996–97 "F" Bodies 5.7L engine

For accessory drive belt replacement procedures see the model specific sections of this manual

Fig. 57 Serpentine drive belt routing—GM 1998–00 "F" Bodies 5.7L engine

1 POWER STEERING PUMP PULLEY
2 COMPRESSOR CLUTCH PULLEY
3 TENSIONER PULLEY
4 CRANKSHIFT PULLEY
5 GENERATOR PULLY
6 COOLANT PUMP PULLEY
A 10KG (22 LB) THUMB PRESSURE
B DEFLECTION: 8–10MM (0.30–0.40)

Fig. 59 Accessory drive belt—GEO/Chevrolet engines

Fig. 58 A/C drive belt routing—GM 1998–00 "F" Bodies 5.7L engine

SOHC (LKO)   DOHC (LLO)

Fig. 60 Serpentine drive belt routing—Saturn engines

TIMING BELTS

GENERAL INFORMATION

Timing belts are typically only used on overhead camshaft engines. Timing belts are used to synchronize the crankshaft with the camshaft, similar to a timing chain on an overhead valve (pushrod) engine. Unlike a timing belt, a timing chain will normally last the life of the engine without needing service or replacement. Timing belts use raised teeth to mesh with sprockets to operate the valvetrain of an overhead camshaft engine.

Whenever a vehicle with an unknown service history comes into your repair facility or is recently purchased, here are some points that should be asked to help prevent costly engine damage:

• Does the owner know if or when the belt was replaced?

• If the vehicle purchased is used or the condition and mileage of the last timing belt replacement are unknown, it is recommended to inspect, replace or at least inform the owner that the vehicle is equipped with a timing belt.

• Note the mileage of the vehicle. The average replacement interval for a timing belt is approximately 60,000 miles (96,000 km).

Interference Engines

Engines, chain- or belt-driven, can be classified as either free-running or interference, depending on what would happen if the piston-to-valve timing is disrupted. A free-running engine is designed with enough clearance between the pistons and valves to allow the crankshaft to rotate (pistons still moving) while the camshaft stays in one position (several valves fully open). If this condition occurs normally, no internal engine damage will result. In an interference engine, there is not enough clearance between the pistons and valves to allow the crankshaft to turn without the camshaft being in time.

An interference engine can suffer extensive internal damage if a timing belt fails. The piston design does not allow clearance for the valve to be fully open and the piston to be at the top of its stroke. If the belt fails, the piston will collide with the valve and will bend or break the valve, damage the piston, and/or bend a connecting rod. When this type of failure occurs, the engine will need to be replaced or disassembled for further internal inspection; either choice costing many times that of replacing the timing belt.

TIMING BELT SERVICE

Inspection

➡ **For manufacturer's recommended service interval, refer to the maintenance interval chart located in this manual.**

The average replacement interval for a timing belt is approximately 60,000 miles (96,000km). If, however, the timing belt is inspected earlier or more frequently than suggested, and shows signs of wear or defects, the belt should be replaced at that time.

※※ WARNING

Never allow antifreeze, oil or solvents to come into with a timing belt. If this occurs immediately wash the solution from the timing belt. Also, never excessive bend or twist the timing belt; this can damage the belt so that its lifetime is severely shortened.

Inspect both sides of the timing belt. Replace the belt with a new one if any of the following conditions exist:

• Hardening of the rubber—back side is glossy without resilience and leaves no indentation when pressed with a fingernail
• Cracks on the rubber backing
• Cracks or peeling of the canvas backing
• Cracks on rib root
• Cracks on belt sides
• Missing teeth or chunks of teeth
• Abnormal wear of belt sides—the sides are normal if they are sharp, as if cut by a knife.

If none of these conditions exist, the belt does not need replacement unless it is at the recommended interval. The belt MUST be replaced at the recommended interval.

TCCS1242

Never bend or twist a timing belt excessively, and do not allow solvents, antifreeze, gasoline, acid or oil to come into contact with the belt

TCCS1245

Back surface worn or cracked from a possible overheated engine or interference with the belt cover

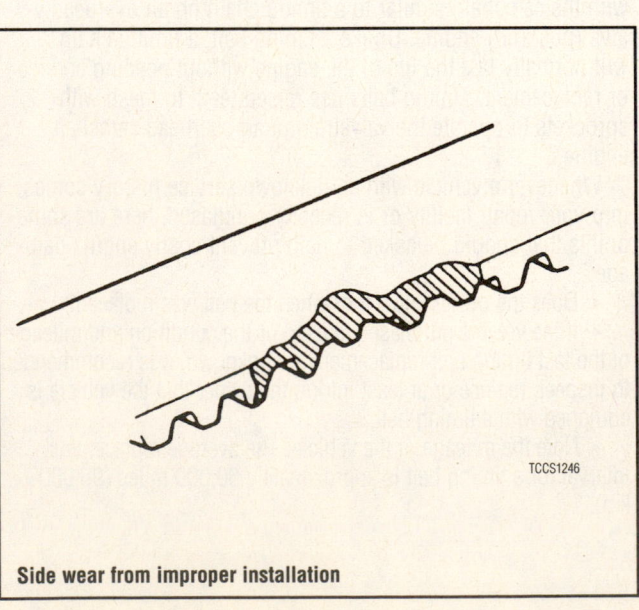

TCCS1244

Broken tooth may be due to a damaged pulley

TCCS1246

Side wear from improper installation

Worn teeth from excessive belt tension, camshaft or distributor not turning properly or fluid leaking on the belt

✳✳ WARNING

On interference engines, it is very important to replace the timing belt at the recommended intervals, otherwise expensive engine damage will likely result if the belt fails.

Removal & Installation

CHRYSLER CORPORATION

2.0L (VIN C) SOHC Engine

1. On Cirrus, Stratus, Breeze, and Sebring Convertible models, disconnect the negative battery cable from the left strut tower. The ground cable is equipped with a insulator grommet which should be placed on the stud to prevent the negative battery cable from accidentally grounding.
2. On Neon models, disconnect the negative battery cable.
3. Remove the drive belts and accessories.
4. Raise and safely support the vehicle.
5. Remove the right inner splash-shield.
6. Remove the crankshaft damper.
7. Remove the right engine mount.
8. Place a support under the engine.
9. Remove the engine mount bracket.
10. Remove the timing belt cover.
11. Loosen the timing belt tensioner bolts.
12. Remove the timing belt and the tensioner.

➡**When tensioner is removed from the engine it is necessary to compress the plunger into the tensioner body.**

13. Place the tensioner in a soft-jawed vise to compress the tensioner.
14. After compressing the tensioner place a pin (⅝₄ in. Allen wrench will work) into the plunger side hole to retain the plunger until installation.
   To install:
15. Set the crankshaft sprocket to Top Dead Center (TDC) by

TDC alignment for timing belt installation—2.0L (VIN C) SOHC Engine

aligning the notch on the sprocket with the arrow on the oil pump housing, then back off the sprocket three notches before TDC.
16. Set the camshaft to align the timing marks.
17. Move the crankshaft to ½ notch before TDC.
18. Install the timing belt starting at the crankshaft, around the water pump, then around the camshaft last.
19. Move the crankshaft to TDC to take up the belt slack.
20. Reinstall the tensioner to the block but do not tighten it.
21. Using a torque wrench apply 250 inch lbs. (28 Nm) of torque to the tensioner pulley.
22. With torque being applied to the tensioner pulley, move the tensioner up against the tensioner bracket and tighten the fasteners to 275 inch lbs. (31 Nm).
23. Remove the tensioner plunger pin, the tension is correct when the plunger pin can be removed and replaced easily.
24. Rotate the crankshaft two revolutions and recheck the timing marks.
25. Reinstall the timing belt cover.
26. Reinstall the engine mount bracket.
27. Reinstall the right engine mount.
28. Remove the engine support.
29. Reinstall the crankshaft damper and tighten to 105 ft. lbs. (142 Nm).
30. Reinstall the drive belts and accessories.
31. Reinstall the right inner splash-shield.
32. Perform the crankshaft and camshaft relearn alignment procedure using the DRB scan tool or equivalent.

2.0L (VIN F) Engine

1. Disconnect the negative battery cable.
2. Remove the engine undercover.

3. Remove the engine mount bracket.

4. Remove the drive belts.

5. Remove the belt tensioner pulley.

6. Remove the water pump pulleys.

7. Remove the crankshaft pulley.

8. Remove the stud bolt from the engine support bracket and remove the timing belt covers.

9. Rotate the crankshaft clockwise to align the camshaft timing marks. Always turn the crankshaft in the forward direction only.

10. Loosen the tension pulley center bolt.

➡**If the timing belt is to be reused, mark the direction of rotation on the flat side of the belt with an arrow.**

11. Move the tension pulley towards the water pump and remove the timing belt.

12. Remove the crankshaft sprocket center bolt using special tool MB990767 to hold the crankshaft sprocket while removing the center bolt. Then, use MB998778 or equivalent puller to remove the sprocket.

13. Mark the direction of rotation on the timing belt "B" with a arrow.

14. Loosen the center bolt on the tensioner and remove the belt.

15. To remove the camshaft sprocket, remove the cylinder head cover. Use a wrench to hold the hexagonal part of the camshaft and remove the sprocket mounting bolt.

❊❊ WARNING

Do not rotate the camshafts or the crankshaft while the timing belt is removed.

Notice the timing mark on the oil pump drive sprocket—Chrysler 2.0L (VIN F) engines

Timing belt "B" timing marks locations—Chrysler 2.0L (VIN F) engines

To install:

16. Use a wrench to hold the camshaft, then install the sprocket and mounting bolt. Tighten the bolt(s) to 65 ft. lbs. (88 Nm).

17. Install the cylinder head cover.

18. Place the crankshaft sprocket on the crankshaft. Use tool MB990767 (or equivalent) to hold the crankshaft sprocket while tightening the center bolt. Tighten the center bolt to 80–94 ft. lbs. (108–127 Nm).

19. Align the timing marks on the crankshaft sprocket "B" and the balance shaft.

20. Install timing belt "B" on the sprockets. Position the center of the tensioner pulley to the left and above the center of the mounting bolt.

21. Push the pulley clockwise toward the crankshaft to apply tension to the belt and tighten the mounting bolt to 14 ft. lbs. (19 Nm). Do not let the pulley turn when tightening the bolt because it will cause excessive tension on the belt. The belt should deflect 0.20–0.28 in. (5–7mm) when finger pressure is applied between the pulleys.

22. Install the crankshaft sensing blade and the crankshaft sprocket. Apply engine oil to the mounting bolt and tighten the bolt to 80–94 ft. lbs. (108–127 Nm).

23. Use a press or vise to compress the auto tensioner pushrod. Insert a set pin when the holes are aligned.

❊❊ WARNING

Do not compress the pushrod too quickly, damage to the pushrod can occur.

24. Install the auto tensioner on the engine.

25. Align the timing marks on the camshaft sprocket, crankshaft sprocket and the oil pump sprocket.

26. After aligning the mark on the oil pump sprocket, remove the cylinder block plug and insert a Phillips screwdriver in the hole to check the position of the counter balance shaft. The screwdriver should go in at least 2.36 in. or more. If not, rotate the oil pump sprocket once and realign the timing mark so the screwdriver goes in. Do not remove the screwdriver until the timing belt is installed.

27. Install the timing belt on the intake camshaft and secure it with a clip.

28. Install the timing belt on the exhaust camshaft. Align the timing marks with the cylinder head top surface using two wrenches. Secure the belt with another clip.

29. Install the belt around the idler pulley, oil pump sprocket, crankshaft sprocket and the tensioner pulley.

30. Turn the tension pulley so the pinholes are at the bottom. Press the pulley lightly against the timing belt.

31. Screw the special tool into the left engine support bracket until it contacts the tensioner arm, then screw the tool in a little more and remove the pushrod pin from the auto tensioner. Remove the special tool and tighten the center bolt to 35 ft. lbs. (48 Nm).

32. Turn the crankshaft ¼ turn counterclockwise, then clockwise until the timing marks are aligned.

33. Loosen the center bolt. Install special tool MD998767 or equivalent on the tension pulley. Turn the tension pulley counterclockwise with a torque of 2.6 ft. lbs. (3.5 Nm) and tighten the center bolt to 35 ft. lbs. (48 Nm). Do not let the tension pulley turn with the bolt.

34. Turn the crankshaft two revolutions to the right and align the timing marks. After 15 minutes, measure the protrusion of the pushrod on the auto tensioner. The standard measurement is 0.150–0.177 in. (3.8–4.5mm). If the protrusion is out of specification, loosen the tension pulley, apply the proper torque to the belt and retighten the center bolt.

35. Install the crankshaft pulley. Tighten the mounting bolts to 18 ft. lbs. (25 Nm).

36. Install the water pump. Tighten the mounting bolts to 6.5 ft. lbs. (8.8 Nm).

37. Install and adjust the drive belts.

38. Install the engine mount bracket.

39. Install the engine undercover.

40. Connect the negative battery cable.

2.0L (VIN Y) Engine

Valve timing is critical to engine operation. Use care when servicing the timing belt. There are a number of timing marks that must be properly aligned or engine damage will result. If the timing belt has not broken or jumped teeth, it is recommended that the crankshaft be turned by hand (clockwise) to Top Dead Center (TDC) No.1 cylinder compression stroke (firing position) before beginning work. This should align all the timing marks and serve as a reference for later work. Some technicians will apply a small amount of white paint to all timing marks. This helps make them more visible under the low-light conditions found underhood.

1. Disconnect the negative battery cable.

2. Remove the accessory drive belts.

3. Using C 3281 or equivalent crankshaft holding tool, remove the crankshaft pulley center retaining bolt.

4. Using puller tools 1026 and 6827 or equivalent, remove the crankshaft pulley.

5. Remove the power steering pump from the bracket and position it aside. Do not disconnect the hoses.

6. Remove the power steering pump bracket from the engine.

7. Use a floor jack with a piece of wood on it and raise the engine to take the weight off of the engine mount.

8. Remove the engine mount and bracket.

9. Remove the front timing belt cover.

10. If not done so previously, align the timing marks. Loosen the timing belt tensioner and remove the belt.

Do not rotate the crankshaft or camshafts after removing the timing belt or valvetrain components may be damaged. Always align the timing marks before removing the timing belt.

11. For 1996–97 models:

a. If the timing belt tensioner is to be replaced, remove the retaining bolts and remove the timing belt tensioner. When the timing belt tensioner is removed from the engine, it is necessary to compress the plunger into the tensioner body.

b. Place the tensioner in a vise and slowly compress the plunger.

➡Position the tensioner in the vise the same way it will be installed on the engine. This is to ensure proper pin orientation for when the tensioner is installed on the engine.

Install the timing belt by starting at the crankshaft sprocket and working around the other pulleys in a counterclockwise direction—Chrysler 2.0L (VIN Y) engine

Wrench position for properly locking the tensioner on 1998–00 Chrysler 2.0L (VIN Y) engine

Timing chain and gear service is covered in the model specific sections of this manual

c. When the plunger is compressed into the tensioner body, install a pin through the body and plunger to hold the plunger in place until the tensioner is installed.

12. For 1998–00 models:

a. Place an 8mm Allen wrench into the belt tensioner, then using the long end of a ⅛ in. (3mm) Allen wrench, rotate the tensioner counterclockwise until it slides into the locking hole.

13. Remove the timing belt.

To install:

14. Check that all timing marks are still aligned. Bring the crankshaft sprocket to ½ a notch before TDC.

15. Install the timing belt. Starting at the crankshaft, route the belt around the water pump sprocket, idler pulley, camshaft sprockets, then around the tensioner pulley.

16. Move the crankshaft to TDC to take up the slack in the belt. Install the tensioner to the block but do not tighten the retaining bolts.

17. For 1996–97 models:

a. Using a torque wrench on the tensioner pulley, apply 21 ft. lbs. (28 Nm) of torque to the pulley.

b. With the torque being applied to the tensioner pulley, move the tensioner up against the tensioner pulley bracket and tighten the retaining bolts to 23 ft. lbs. (31 Nm).

c. Remove the tensioner plunger pin. Pretension is correct when the pin can be removed and installed.

18. For 1998–00 models, remove the wrenches from the tensioner.

19. Rotate the crankshaft two revolutions and check the timing marks. If the timing marks are not properly aligned, remove the belt and reinstall it as described.

20. Install the front timing belt cover.

21. Lower the engine enough to install the engine mount bracket.

22. Install the bracket and remove the floor jack.

23. Install the power steering pump bracket and pump.

24. Install the crankshaft pulley using C-4685-C or an equivalent pulley installer.

25. Tighten the mounting bolt to 105 ft. lbs. (142 Nm).

26. Install the accessory drive belts.

27. Connect the negative battery cable.

28. Start the engine. Check for leaks and proper engine operation.

2.4L (VIN X) Engine

1. Disconnect the negative battery cable from the left strut tower. The ground cable is equipped with a insulator grommet which should be placed on the stud to prevent the negative battery cable from accidentally grounding.

2. Remove the right inner splash-shield.

3. Remove the accessory drive belts.

4. Remove the crankshaft damper.

5. Remove the right engine mount.

6. Place a suitable floor jack under the vehicle to support the engine.

7. Remove the engine mount bracket.

8. Remove the timing belt cover.

➡ **Do not rotate the crankshaft or the camshafts after the timing belt has been removed. Damage to the valve components may occur. Before removing the timing belt, always align the timing marks.**

Timing belt cover bolt locations—2.4L (VIN X) Engine

Crankshaft and camshaft alignment marks—2.4L (VIN X) Engine

9. Align the timing marks of the timing belt sprockets to the timing marks on the rear timing belt cover and oil pump cover. Loosen the timing belt tensioner bolts.

10. Remove the timing belt and the tensioner.

11. Remove the camshaft timing belt sprockets.

12. Remove the crankshaft timing belt sprocket using special removal tool No. 6793 or equivalent.

13. Place the tensioner into a soft-jawed vise to compress the tensioner.

14. After compressing the tensioner, place a pin (⅝₄ in. Allen wrench will work) into the plunger side hole to retain the plunger until installation.

To install:

15. Using special tool No. 6792 or its equivalent, install the crankshaft timing belt sprocket onto the crankshaft.

16. Install the camshaft sprockets onto the camshafts. Install and tighten the camshaft sprocket bolts to 75 ft. lbs. (101 Nm).

17. Set the crankshaft sprocket to Top Dead Center (TDC) by aligning the notch on the sprocket with the arrow on the oil pump housing.

18. Set the camshafts to align the timing marks on the sprockets.

19. Move the crankshaft to ½ notch before TDC.

20. Install the timing belt starting at the crankshaft, then around the water pump sprocket, idler pulley, camshaft sprockets and the tensioner pulley.

21. Move the crankshaft sprocket to TDC to take up the belt slack.

22. Reinstall the tensioner to the block but do not tighten it at this time.

23. Using a torque wrench on the tensioner pulley, apply 250 inch lbs. (28 Nm) of torque to the tensioner pulley.

24. With torque being applied to the tensioner pulley, move the tensioner up against the tensioner pulley bracket and tighten the fasteners to 275 inch lbs. (31 Nm).

25. Remove the tensioner plunger pin, the tension is correct when the plunger pin can be removed and replaced easily.

26. Rotate the crankshaft two revolutions and recheck the timing marks. Wait several minutes, then recheck that the plunger pin can easily be removed and installed.

27. Reinstall the front timing belt cover.

28. Reinstall the engine mount bracket.

29. Reinstall the right engine mount.

30. Remove the floor jack from under the vehicle.

31. Install the crankshaft damper and tighten to 105 ft. lbs. (142 Nm).

32. Install and adjust the accessory drive belts.

33. Install the right inner splash-shield.

34. Reconnect the negative battery cable.

35. Perform the crankshaft and camshaft relearn alignment procedure using the DRB scan tool or equivalent.

2.5L (VIN H) Engine

1. Disconnect the negative battery cable from the left strut tower. The ground cable is equipped with a insulator grommet which should be placed on the stud to prevent the negative battery cable from accidentally grounding.

2. Raise and safely support the vehicle. Remove the right inner splash-shield.

3. Remove the accessory drive belts.

4. Remove the crankshaft damper.

5. Remove the right engine mount.

6. Place a suitable floor jack under the vehicle to support the engine.

7. Remove the right engine mount bracket.

8. Remove the timing belt upper left cover, upper right cover and lower cover.

9. Loosen the timing belt tensioner bolts.

➤Before removing timing belt, be sure to align the sprocket timing marks to the timing marks on the rear timing belt cover.

10. If the present timing belt is going to be reused, mark the running direction of the timing belt for installation. Remove the timing belt and the tensioner.

11. Remove the camshaft timing belt sprockets from the camshaft, if necessary.

12. Remove the crankshaft timing belt sprocket and key.

13. Place the tensioner into a soft-jawed vise to compress tensioner.

Timing belt engine sprocket timing—2.5L (VIN H) Engine

14. After compressing the tensioner place a pin into the plunger side hole to retain the plunger until installation.

To install:

15. If removed, reinstall the camshaft sprockets onto the camshaft. Install the camshaft sprocket bolt and tighten to 65 ft. lbs. (88 Nm).

16. If removed, reinstall the crankshaft timing belt sprocket and key onto the crankshaft.

17. Set the crankshaft sprocket to Top Dead Center (TDC) by aligning the notch on the sprocket with the arrow on the oil pump housing, then back off the sprocket three notches before TDC.

18. Set the camshafts to align the timing marks on the sprockets with the marks on the rear timing belt cover.

19. Install the belt on the rear camshaft sprocket first.

20. Install a binder clip on the belt to the sprocket so it won't slip out of position.

21. Keeping the belt taut, install it under the water pump pulley and around the front camshaft sprocket.

22. Install a binder on the front sprocket and belt.

23. Rotate the crankshaft to TDC.

24. Continue routing the belt by the idler pulley and around the crankshaft sprocket to the tensioner pulley.

25. Move the crankshaft sprocket clockwise to TDC to take up the belt slack. Check that all timing marks are in alignment.

26. Reinstall the tensioner to the block but do not tighten it at this time.

27. Using special tool No. MD998767 (or equivalent) and a torque wrench on the tensioner pulley, apply 39 inch lbs. (4.4 Nm) of torque to the tensioner. Tighten the tensioner pulley bolt to 35 ft. lbs. (48 Nm).

28. With torque being applied to the tensioner pulley, move the tensioner up against the tensioner bracket and tighten the fasteners to 17 ft. lbs. (23 Nm).

29. Remove the tensioner plunger pin, the tension is correct when the plunger pin can be removed and replaced easily.

30. Rotate the crankshaft two revolutions clockwise and recheck the timing marks. Check to be sure the tensioner plunger pin can be easily installed and removed. If the pin does not remove and install easily, perform the procedure again.

31. Reinstall the timing belt cover.
32. Reinstall the engine mount bracket.
33. Reinstall the right engine mount.
34. Remove the engine support.
35. Install the crankshaft damper and tighten to 134 ft. lbs. (182 Nm).
36. Reinstall the accessory drive belts and adjust them.
37. Reinstall the right inner splash-shield.
38. Perform the crankshaft and camshaft relearn alignment procedure using the DRB scan tool or equivalent.

2.5L (VIN N) Engine

1. Disconnect the negative battery cable.
2. Remove the accessory drive belts.
3. Using Crankshaft Holding Tools MB990767 and MB998754 or their equivalents, remove the crankshaft bolt and remove the pulley.
4. Remove the heated oxygen sensor connection.
5. Remove the power steering pump with the hose attached and position it aside.
6. Remove the power steering pump bracket.
7. Place a floor jack under the engine oil pan, with a block of wood in between, and raise the engine so that the weight of the engine is no longer being applied to the engine support bracket.
8. Remove the upper engine mount. Spraying lubricant, slowly remove the reamer (alignment) bolt and remaining bolts and remove the engine support bracket.

➡ **The reamer bolt is sometimes heat-seized on the engine support bracket.**

9. Remove the front timing belt covers.
10. If the timing belt is to be reused, draw an arrow indicating the direction of rotation on the back of the belt for reinstallation.
11. Align the timing marks by turning the crankshaft with MD998769 Crankshaft Turning tool or its equivalent. Loosen the center bolt on the timing belt tensioner pulley and remove the belt.

⁜⁜ **WARNING**

Do not rotate the crankshaft or camshaft after removing the timing belt or valvetrain components may be damaged. Always align the timing marks before removing the timing belt.

12. Check the belt tensioner for leaks and check the pushrod for cracks.
13. If the timing belt tensioner is to be replaced, remove the retaining bolts and remove the timing belt tensioner. When the timing belt tensioner is removed from the engine, it is necessary to compress the plunger into the tensioner body.
14. Place the tensioner in a vise and slowly compress the plunger. Take care not to damage the pushrod.

➡ **Position the tensioner in the vise the same way it will be installed on the engine. This is to ensure proper pin orientation for when the tensioner is installed on the engine.**

15. When the plunger is compressed into the tensioner body, install a pin through the body and plunger to hold the plunger in place until the tensioner is installed.

To install:
16. Install the timing belt tensioner and tighten the retaining bolts to 17 ft. lbs. (24 Nm), but do not remove the pin at this time.
17. Check that all timing marks are still aligned.
18. Use bulldog clips (large paper binder clips) or other suitable tool to secure the timing belt and to prevent it from slacking. Install the timing belt. Starting at the crankshaft, go around the idler pulley, then the front camshaft sprocket, the water pump pulley, the rear camshaft sprocket and the tensioner pulley.
19. Be sure the belt is tight between the crankshaft and front camshaft sprocket, between the camshaft sprockets and the water pump. Gently raise the tensioner pulley, so that the belt does not sag, and temporarily tighten the center bolt.
20. Move the crankshaft ¼ turn counterclockwise, then turn it clockwise to the position where the timing marks are aligned.
21. Loosen the center bolt of the tensioner pulley. Using MD998767 or equivalent tensioner tool, and a torque wrench apply 3.3 ft. lbs. (4.4 Nm) tensional torque to the timing belt and tighten the center bolt to 35 ft. lbs. (48 Nm). When tightening the bolt, be sure that the tensioner pulley shaft does not rotate with the bolt.
22. Remove the tensioner plunger pin. Pretension is correct when the pin can be removed and installed easily. If the pin cannot be easily removed and installed it is still satisfactory as long as it is within its standard value.
23. Check that the tensioner pushrod is within the standard value. When the tensioner is engaged the pushrod should measure 0.149–0.177 in. (3.8–4.5mm).
24. Rotate the crankshaft two revolutions and check the timing marks. If the timing marks are not properly aligned remove the belt and repeat Steps 17 through 23.
25. Install the timing belt covers.
26. Install the engine mounting bracket.
27. Lower the engine enough to install the engine mount onto bracket and remove the floor jack.
28. Install the power steering pump bracket and pump.
29. Install the crankshaft pulley and tighten the retaining bolt to 13 ft. lbs. (18 Nm).
30. Install the accessory drive belts.
31. Properly fill the cooling system.
32. Connect the negative battery cable.
33. Check for leaks and proper engine and cooling system operation.

Camshaft and crankshaft alignment marks—Chrysler 2.5L (VIN N) engines

79225G02

3.2L (VIN J) and 3.5L (VIN F) Engines

Use care when servicing a timing belt. Valve timing is absolutely critical to engine performance. If the valve timing marks on all drive sprockets are not properly aligned, engine damage will result. If only the belt and tensioner are being serviced, do not loosen the camshaft drive sprockets unless they are to be replaced. The sprockets have oversized openings and can be rotated several degrees in each direction on their shafts. This means the sprockets must be retimed, requiring some special tools.

❄❄ CAUTION

Fuel injection systems remain under pressure, even after the engine has been turned off. The fuel system pressure must be relieved before disconnecting any fuel lines. Failure to do so may result in fire and/or personal injury.

1. Disconnect the negative battery cable.
2. Rotate the engine to Top Dead Center (TDC) on the compression stroke for cylinder No. 1.
3. Release the fuel system pressure using the recommended procedure.
4. Place a pan under the radiator and drain the coolant.
5. Remove the radiator and cooling fan assemblies.
6. Remove the accessory drive belts.
7. Remove the upper radiator hose.
8. Remove the crankshaft damper with a quality puller tool gripping the inside of the pulley.
9. Remove the stamped steel cover. Do not remove the sealer on the cover; it may be reusable.
10. Remove the left side cast cover. If necessary, remove the lower belt cover, located behind the crankshaft damper.
11. If the timing belt is to be reused, mark the timing belt with the running direction for installation.
12. Align the camshaft sprockets with the marks on the rear covers.
13. Remove the timing belt and tensioner.
14. If it is necessary to service the camshaft sprockets, use the following procedure:

ALIGN CAMSHAFT SPROCKET TIMING MARK BETWEEN MARKS ON REAR TIMING BELT COVER

CRANKSHAFT AT TDC

79225G01

Timing belt alignment marks—Chrysler 3.2L and 3.5L engines

a. Hold the camshaft sprocket with a 36mm box end wrench, loosen and remove the sprocket retaining bolt and washer.

➡**To remove the camshaft sprocket retainer bolt while the engine is in the vehicle, it may be necessary to raise that side of the engine due to the length of the retainer bolt. The right bolt is 8 ⅜ in. (213mm) long, while the left bolt is 10 in. (254mm) long. These bolts are not interchangeable and their original location during removal should be noted.**

b. Remove the camshaft sprocket from the camshaft. The camshaft sprockets are not interchangeable from side-to-side.
c. Remove the crankshaft sprocket using Puller L-4407A or equivalent.

To install:

15. If it was necessary to remove the camshaft sprockets, use the following procedure:

➡**This procedure can only be used when the camshaft sprockets have been loosened or removed from the camshafts. Each sprocket has a D shaped hole that allows it to be rotated several degrees in each direction on its shaft. This design must be timed with the engine to ensure proper performance.**

a. Install the crankshaft sprocket, using tool C-4685-C1, thrust bearing, washer and 12mm bolt.
b. When the camshaft sprockets are loosened or removed, the camshafts must be timed to the engine. Install the Camshaft Alignment tools 6642-A or their exact equivalents, to the rear of the cylinder heads. These tools lock the camshafts in the proper position.
16. Preload the belt tensioner as follows:
a. Place the tensioner in a vise the same way it is mounted on the engine.
b. Slowly compress the plunger into the tensioner body.
c. When the plunger is compressed into the tensioner body, install a pin through the body and plunger to retain the plunger in place until the tensioner is installed.
17. Install both camshaft sprockets to the appropriate shafts. The left camshaft sprocket has the DIS pick-up as part of the sprocket.

➡**The right bolt is 8 ⅜ in. (213mm) long, while the left bolt is 10 in. (254mm) long. These bolts are not interchangeable.**

18. Apply Loctite®271 or equivalent, to the threads of the camshaft sprocket retainer bolts and install to the appropriate shafts. Do not tighten the bolts at this time.
19. Align the camshaft sprockets between the marks on the rear belt covers.
20. Align the crankshaft sprocket with the TDC mark on the oil pump cover.
21. Install the timing belt, starting at the crankshaft sprocket and going in a counterclockwise direction. After the belt is installed on the right sprocket, keep tension on the belt until it is past the tensioner pulley.
22. Holding the tensioner pulley against the belt, install the timing belt tensioner into the housing and tighten to 21 ft. lbs. (28 Nm).
23. When the tensioner is in place, pull the retainer pin out to allow tensioner to extend to the pulley bracket.

Refer to the model specific sections for engine mechanical service procedures

➡**Be sure that the timing marks on the cam sprockets are still between the marks on the rear cover.**

24. Remove the spark plug in the No.1 cylinder and install a dial indicator to check for Top Dead Center (TDC) of the piston. Rotate the crankshaft until the piston is exactly at TDC.

25. Hold the camshaft sprocket hex with a 36mm wrench and tighten the right camshaft sprocket bolt to 75 ft. lbs. (102 Nm) plus an additional 90 degree turn. Tighten the left camshaft sprocket bolt to 85 ft. lbs. (115 Nm) plus an additional 90 degree turn.

26. Remove the dial indicator. Install the spark plug and tighten to 20 ft. lbs. (28 Nm).

27. Remove the camshaft alignment tools from the back of the cylinder heads and install the cam covers with new O-rings.

28. Tighten the fasteners to 20 ft. lbs. (27 Nm). Repeat this procedure on the other camshaft.

29. Rotate the crankshaft sprocket two revolutions and check for proper alignment of the timing marks on the camshaft and the crankshaft. If the timing marks do not align, repeat the procedure.

30. Before installing, inspect the sealer on the stamped steel cover. If some sealer is missing, use MOPAR Silicone Rubber Adhesive sealant or equivalent to replace the missing sealer.

31. Install the lower belt cover behind the crankshaft damper, if necessary.

32. Install the stamped steel cover and the left side cast cover. Tighten the 6mm bolts to 105 inch lbs. (12 Nm), the 8mm bolts to 250 inch lbs. (28 Nm) and the 10mm bolts to 40 ft. lbs. (54 Nm).

33. Install the crankshaft damper using special tool L-4524, a 5.9 in. long bolt, thrust bearing and washer or equivalent damper installation tools. Tighten the center bolt to 85 ft. lbs. (115 Nm).

34. Install the upper radiator hose.

35. Install the accessory drive belts and adjust them to the proper tension.

36. Install the radiator and cooling fan assemblies.

37. Refill and bleed the cooling system.

38. Connect the negative battery cable.

39. With the radiator cap off so coolant can be added, run the engine. Watch for leaks and listen for unusual engine noises.

3.0L (VIN H) SOHC Engine

1. Position the engine so the No. 1 cylinder is at Top Dead Center (TDC) of its compression stroke.

✳✳ CAUTION

Wait at least 90 seconds after the negative battery cable is disconnected to prevent possible deployment of the air bag.

2. Remove all necessary components for access to the timing belt covers, then remove the covers from the engine.

3. If the same timing belt will be reused, mark the direction of the timing belt's rotation for installation in the same direction. Be sure the engine is positioned so the No. 1 cylinder is at the TDC of it's compression stroke and the timing marks are aligned with the engine's timing mark indicators.

4. Loosen the timing belt tensioner bolt and remove the belt. If the tensioner is not being removed, position it as far away from the center of the engine as possible and tighten the bolt.

5. If the tensioner is being removed, mark the outside of the spring to ensure that it is not installed backwards. Unbolt the tensioner and remove it along with the spring.

Align the sprockets properly before removing or installing the timing belt—Chrysler Stealth with the 3.0L (VIN H) SOHC engine

❋❋ WARNING

Do not rotate the camshafts when the timing belt is removed from the engine. Turning the camshaft when the timing belt is removed could cause the valves to interfere with the pistons thus causing severe internal engine damage.

To install:

6. Install the tensioner, if removed, and hook the upper end of the spring to the water pump pin and the lower end to the tensioner in exactly the same position as originally installed.

7. Ensure both camshafts are still positioned so the timing marks align with those on the rear timing covers. Rotate the crankshaft so the timing mark aligns with the mark on the front cover.

8. Install the timing belt on the crankshaft sprocket and while keeping the belt tight on the tension side, install the belt on the front (left) camshaft sprocket.

9. Install the belt on the water pump pulley, then the rear (right) camshaft sprocket and the tensioner.

10. Loosen the bolt that secures the adjustment of the tensioner and lightly press the tensioner against the timing belt.

11. Check that the timing marks are in alignment.

12. Rotate the crankshaft 2 full turns in the clockwise direction only, then realign the timing marks.

13. Tighten the bolt that secures the tensioner to 19 ft. lbs. (26 Nm).

14. Install the lower and the upper timing belt covers, along with all other applicable components.

3.0L (VIN J and K) DOHC Engine

1. Position the engine so the No. 1 cylinder is at Top Dead Center (TDC) of its compression stroke.

2. Remove all necessary components for access to the timing belt covers, then remove the covers from the engine.

❋❋ CAUTION

Be sure to disconnect the negative battery cable. Wait at least 90 seconds after the negative battery cable is disconnected to prevent possible deployment of the air bag.

3. If the same timing belt will be reused, mark the direction of the timing belt's rotation for installation in the same direction. Be sure the engine is positioned so the No. 1 cylinder is at the TDC of it's compression stroke and the timing marks are aligned with the engine's timing mark indicators on the rear timing covers.

❋❋ WARNING

Turning the camshaft sprocket when the timing belt is removed could cause the valves to contact with the pistons, resulting in severe engine damage.

4. Remove the bolts that secure the auto-tensioner to the engine block and remove the tensioner.

To install:

➡ **The auto-tensioner assembly must be reset to correctly adjust belt tension.**

Sprocket alignment for timing belt installation— Chrysler Stealth with the 3.0L (VIN J and K) DOHC engine

79235G65

For accessory drive belt replacement procedures see the model specific sections of this manual

5. Loosen the center bolt of tensioner pulley to provide timing belt slack. Remove the timing belt assembly.

6. Position the auto-tensioner into a vise with soft jaws. The plug at the rear of tensioner protrudes, be sure to use a washer as a spacer to protect the plug from contacting vise jaws.

7. Slowly push the rod into the tensioner until the set hole in rod is aligned with set hole in the auto-tensioner.

8. Insert a 0.055 in. (1.4mm) wire into the aligned set holes. Unclamp the tensioner from the vise and install it on the engine. Tighten tensioner mounting bolts to 17 ft. lbs. (24 Nm).

❊❊❊ WARNING

DO NOT rotate or turn the camshafts when removing the sprockets or severe engine damage will result from internal component interference.

9. Align the mark on the crankshaft sprocket with the mark on the front case. Then, move the crankshaft sprocket 1 tooth counterclockwise.

10. Align the timing marks of the camshafts with the marks on the rear covers.

11. Using large paper clips to secure the timing belt to the sprockets, install the timing belt in the following order. Be sure camshafts-to-cylinder heads and crankshaft-to-front cover timing marks are aligned. Install the timing belt around the pulleys in the following order:
   a. Exhaust camshaft sprocket (front bank).
   b. Intake camshaft sprocket (front bank).
   c. Water pump pulley.
   d. Intake camshaft sprocket (rear bank).
   e. Exhaust camshaft sprocket (rear bank).
   f. Tensioner pulley.
   g. Crankshaft pulley.
   h. Idler pulley.

➡**Since the camshaft sprockets turn easily, secure them with box wrenches when installing the timing belt.**

12. Align all timing mark on the crankshaft and raise tensioner pulley against belt to remove slack, snug tensioner bolt.

13. Check the alignment of all the timing marks and remove the clips that secure the timing belt to the camshaft sprockets.

14. Rotate the engine ¼ turn counterclockwise, then rotate the engine clockwise to align the timing marks. Check that all the timing marks are in alignment.

15. Loosen the center bolt on the tensioner pulley. Using tool MD998752 or equivalent and a torque wrench, apply 84 inch lbs. (10 Nm) to the tool on the tensioner. Tighten the tensioner bolt to 35 ft. lbs. (49 Nm) and be sure the tensioner does not rotate with the bolt.

16. Rotate the crankshaft two complete turns clockwise and let it sit for approximately five minutes. Then, check that the set pin can easily be inserted and removed from the hole in the auto-tensioner.

17. Remove the set wire attached to the auto-tensioner.

18. Measure the auto-tensioner protrusion (the distance between the tensioner arm and auto-tensioner body) to ensure that it is within 0.15–0.18 in. (3.8–4.5mm). If out of specification, repeat adjustment procedure until the specified value is obtained.

19. Check again that the timing marks on all sprockets are in proper alignment.

20. Install the timing belt covers and all other applicable components.

FORD MOTOR COMPANY

1.3L (VIN H) Engine

1. Disconnect the negative battery cable.

2. Remove the accessory drive belts.

3. Remove the three water pump pulley attaching bolts and remove the water pump pulley.

4. Raise and safely support the vehicle on jackstands.

5. Remove the right front wheel and tire assembly and the right inner fender panel.

6. Remove the four attaching bolts and the screws from the crankshaft pulley. Remove the spacer and outer pulley, if equipped. Remove the inner spacer, inner pulley and the baffle or guide plates, as required.

7. Remove the attaching bolts and the upper and lower covers.

8. Rotate the crankshaft until the sprocket timing marks are aligned.

9. Remove the timing belt tensioner spring, spring cover and timing belt tensioner bolt. Remove the timing belt.

➡**If the timing belt is to be reused, mark the direction of rotation on the belt, using a crayon, so the belt can be reinstalled in the same direction.**

10. If the camshaft sprocket requires removal, proceed as follows:
   a. Hold the camshaft stationary with an open end wrench and remove the camshaft sprocket retaining bolt.
   b. Pull the camshaft sprocket with the dowel pin off of the camshaft. Use care not to drop the dowel pin.

11. If the crankshaft sprocket requires removal, proceed as follows:
   a. Remove the crankshaft pulley retaining bolt.
   b. Pull the crankshaft pulley hub, sprocket and key from the crankshaft. Be sure not to drop the crankshaft key.

Before removing or installing the timing belt, be sure the crankshaft and both camshaft matchmarks are aligned as shown—Ford 1.3L (VIN H) engine

To install:

12. If removed, install the crankshaft sprocket as follows:

   a. Install the sprocket with the key onto the crankshaft.

   b. Install the crankshaft pulley hub.

   c. Clean the threads of the crankshaft pulley bolt and coat with a non-hardening sealer.

   d. Install the bolt and tighten to 80–85 ft. lbs. (108–118 Nm).

13. If removed, install the camshaft sprocket as follows:

   a. Position the sprocket and dowel pin to the camshaft and install the retaining bolt.

   b. Hold the camshaft stationary with an open end wrench and tighten the retaining bolt to 36–45 ft. lbs. (49–61 Nm).

14. Align the camshaft and crankshaft timing marks with the marks located on the cylinder head and oil pump housing.

15. If reusing the original timing belt, install the timing belt with the mark made indicating the direction of rotation.

16. Install the timing belt tensioner spring and cover on the tensioner. Position the tensioner and spring assembly on the engine and install the attaching bolt. Do not tighten the bolt at this time.

17. Rotate the crankshaft two turns in the direction of normal rotation and align the timing marks. Ensure all marks are still correctly aligned.

18. Reconnect the free end of the spring to the spring anchor. Tighten the tensioner bolt to 14–19 ft. lbs. (19–26 Nm).

19. Install the upper and lower covers. Install the attaching bolts and tighten to 71–97 inch lbs. (8–11 Nm).

20. Install the crankshaft pulley baffle with the curved lip facing outward or install the large guide plate, then the small guide plate, as required.

21. Install the inner pulley with the deep recess facing outward. Install the spacer, then the outer pulley, spacer and screws. Install the pulley bolts and tighten to 109–152 inch lbs. (12–17 Nm).

22. Install the inner fender panel.

23. Install the wheel and tire assembly. Tighten the lug bolts to 65–87 ft. lbs. (88–118 Nm).

24. Lower the vehicle.

25. Install the water pump pulley and tighten the bolts to 36–45 ft. lbs. (49–61 Nm).

26. Install the accessory drive belts.

27. Connect the negative battery cable.

28. Run the engine and check for proper operation.

1.8L (VIN 8) Engine

1. Disconnect the negative battery cable.

2. Remove the timing belt upper cover and gasket.

3. Remove the accessory drive belts.

4. Remove the water pump pulley bolts and remove the pulley.

5. Raise and safely support the vehicle on jackstands.

6. Remove the right front wheel and tire assembly.

7. Remove the right upper and lower splash-shields.

8. Remove the timing belt middle and lower covers along with the gaskets.

9. Remove the crankshaft pulley hub bolt and hub.

10. Rotate the crankshaft and align the timing marks located on the camshaft sprockets and seal plate.

11. Check that the crankshaft sprocket and the oil pump are aligned.

➡**If the timing belt is to be reused, mark an arrow on the belt to indicate it's rotational direction for installation reference.**

12. Loosen the timing belt tensioner bolt.

13. Turn the timing belt tensioner counterclockwise and hand-tighten the tensioner bolt to relieve the tension on the timing belt.

14. Remove the timing belt.

15. If the camshaft sprockets are to be removed, continue as follows:

   a. Disconnect and tag the ignition wires and vacuum lines blocking the removal of the cylinder head cover.

   b. Remove the cylinder head cover retaining bolts and remove the cover and gasket.

   c. While holding the camshaft with a wrench, remove the camshaft sprocket retaining bolt.

   d. Remove the camshaft sprocket.

   e. If removing both camshaft sprockets, tag the sprockets for identification at reassembly.

16. If removing the crankshaft sprocket, remove the crankshaft pulley bolt and hub, if not already done. Slide the crankshaft sprocket off the crankshaft.

Camshaft timing alignment marks—Ford 1.8L (VIN 8) engines

Crankshaft timing mark position—Ford 1.8L (VIN 8) engines

17. Inspect the timing belt tensioner and spring, replace if necessary.

To install:

18. If the crankshaft sprocket was removed, install the crankshaft key with the tapered end facing the oil pump. Install the crankshaft sprocket onto the crankshaft while making sure to match the alignment grooves.

19. If removed, install the camshaft sprockets as follows

a. Turn the camshaft until the dowel pins face straight up.

b. Install the camshaft sprocket with the **I** mark straight up for the intake camshaft or with the **E** mark straight up for the exhaust camshaft.

c. Align the camshaft sprockets with the timing marks on the seal plate.

d. While holding each camshaft with a wrench, install the camshaft sprocket retaining bolts. Tighten the bolts to 36–45 ft. lbs. (49–61 Nm).

e. Install a new cylinder head cover gasket onto the cylinder head.

f. Place the cylinder head cover into its mounting position and install the retaining bolts. Tighten the cylinder head cover bolts to 43–78 inch lbs. (4.9–8.8 Nm).

g. Install the ignition wires to the spark plugs and connect the vacuum hoses to the cylinder head cover.

20. Temporarily secure the timing belt tensioner in the far left position.

21. Verify that the timing marks on the crankshaft sprocket and the oil pump are aligned.

22. Verify that the timing marks on the camshaft sprockets and the seal plate are aligned.

23. Install the timing belt in a counterclockwise motion. Be sure there is no looseness on the idler side of the timing belt or between the camshaft sprockets.

➡️**If using the old timing belt, be sure to install the belt in the same direction of travel as it was removed.**

24. Loosen the timing belt tensioner bolt. Allow the tensioner spring to apply tension to the timing belt.

25. Rotate the crankshaft 1 ⅚ turns clockwise and align the timing belt pulley mark with the tension set mark which is located at approximately the 10 o'clock position.

26. Turn the crankshaft two turns clockwise and align the crankshaft sprocket with the tension set mark on the oil pump.

27. Verify that all timing marks are aligned. If not, remove the timing belt and repeat the installation procedures.

28. Apply tension to the timing belt tensioner and tighten the tensioner lockbolt to 27–38 ft. lbs. (37–52 Nm).

29. Rotate the crankshaft 2 ⅙ (780 degrees) turns clockwise and verify that the camshaft and crankshaft timing marks are aligned.

30. Measure the timing belt deflection by applying 22 lbs. (98 N) of pressure on the timing belt between the camshaft sprockets. The timing belt deflection should be 0.35–0.45 in. (9–11.5mm). If necessary to adjust the timing belt deflection, rotate the crankshaft two turns clockwise and ensure that the timing marks are still aligned. If the timing marks are not aligned, repeat the installation procedure.

31. Install the crankshaft pulley hub and tighten the retaining bolt to 80–87 ft. lbs. (108–118 Nm).

32. Install the crankshaft pulley and washer. Install the retaining bolts and tighten to 109–152 inch lbs. (12–17 Nm).

33. Install the timing belt middle and lower covers with the gaskets. Tighten the middle and lower timing belt cover retaining bolts to 65–95 inch lbs. (7.8–11 Nm).

34. Install the power steering drive belt.

35. Install the water pump pulley and retaining bolts. Tighten the bolts to 69–95 inch lbs. (7.8–11.0 Nm).

36. Install the alternator/water pump drive belt.

37. Install the splash-shields. Tighten the bolts to 69–95 inch lbs. (7.8–11.0 Nm).

38. Install the right wheel and tire assembly. Tighten the lug nuts to 65–87 ft. lbs. (88–118 Nm).

39. Lower the vehicle.

40. Install the timing belt upper cover and gasket. Tighten the bolts to 69–95 inch lbs. (7.8–11.0 Nm).

41. Connect the negative battery cable.

42. Run the engine and check for leaks.

43. Road test the vehicle and check for proper engine operation.

1.9L (VIN J) Engine

1. Disconnect the negative battery cable.

2. Remove the accessory drive belt automatic tensioner and the accessory drive belt.

3. Remove the timing belt cover.

4. Align the timing mark on the camshaft sprocket with the timing mark on the cylinder head.

5. Confirm that the timing mark on the crankshaft sprocket is aligned with the timing mark on the oil pump housing.

6. Loosen the belt tensioner attaching bolt, pry the tensioner away from the timing belt and retighten the bolt.

7. Remove the spark plugs. Remove the right engine mount.

8. Raise and safely support the vehicle on jackstands.

9. Remove the right side splash-shield.

10. Remove the flywheel inspection shield.

1. Cylinder head timing mark
2. Camshaft sprocket timing pointer
3. Tension check point
4. Oil pump timing mark
5. Crankshaft timing pointer
6. Crankshaft sprocket
7. Timing belt
8. Water pump sprocket
9. Timing belt tensioner bolt
10. Timing belt tensioner
11. Camshaft sprocket

View of timing belt and alignment positions—Ford 1.9L (VIN J) Engine

79225G98

11. Use a suitable tool to hold the flywheel in place.

12. Remove the crankshaft damper bolt and washer and remove the bolt.

13. Remove the timing belt.

➡**With the timing belt removed and the No. 1 piston at Top Dead Center (TDC), do not rotate the camshaft. If the camshaft must be rotated, align the crankshaft damper 90 degrees BTDC.**

To install:

14. Install the timing belt over the sprockets in a counterclockwise direction starting at the crankshaft. Keep the belt span from the crankshaft to the camshaft tight while installing over the remaining sprocket.

15. Loosen the belt tensioner attaching bolt, allowing the tensioner to snap against the belt.

16. Rotate the crankshaft clockwise two complete revolutions, stopping at TDC. This will allow the tensioner spring to load the timing belt.

➡**Do not turn the engine counterclockwise to align the timing marks. Do not rotate the crankshaft with the spark plugs installed.**

17. Recheck the camshaft and crankshaft timing marks for alignment, to be sure the timing belt has not skipped a tooth during rotation. Repeat the procedure if the timing marks are not aligned.

18. Tighten the tensioner attaching bolt to 17–22 ft. lbs. (23–30 Nm).

19. Install the crankshaft dampener and the bolt and washer. Tighten the bolt to 81–96 ft. lbs. (110–130 Nm).

20. Install the flywheel inspection shield.

21. Install the splash-shield and lower the vehicle.

22. Install the right engine mount. Install the spark plugs.

23. Install the timing belt cover.

24. Install the accessory drive belt automatic tensioner and the accessory drive belt.

25. Connect the negative battery cable.

2.0L (VIN 3) Engine

When installing a timing belt, tensioner spring (6L277) and retaining bolt (W700001-S309) must be purchased and properly installed on the engine. First, check to see if these parts are already installed. The tensioner spring will adjust the timing belts tension and should not require further adjustments.

1. Disconnect the negative battery cable.

2. Remove the engine air intake resonators.

3. Label and remove the ignition wires from the spark plugs. Move the ignition wires aside.

4. Remove the spark plugs.

5. Manually rotate the crankshaft to Top Dead Center (TDC) for the No. 1 piston on its compression stroke. Be sure to align the timing marks.

6. Disconnect the retaining bracket for the power steering pressure hose from the engine lifting eye.

7. Install the Three Bar Engine Support D88L-6000-A or equivalent, onto the engine lifting eyes and slightly raise the engine.

8. Remove the upper camshaft timing belt cover retaining bolts and the cover from the engine.

➡**Mark the location of the upper front engine support bracket before removing it from the engine support bracket.**

9. Remove the upper front engine support bracket retainer nuts, the bracket and the upper front engine support insulator.

10. If equipped, remove the wiring harness connector from the low coolant level sensor at the radiator coolant recovery reservoir.

11. Remove the radiator coolant recovery reservoir retainers and move the reservoir aside.

12. Remove the upper front engine support insulator.

13. Set the coolant recovery reservoir back into position temporarily.

14. Loosen the water pump pulley retaining bolts. Do not remove the bolts completely.

15. Remove the accessory drive belt.

16. Remove the drive belt idler pulley retaining bolt and pulley from the alternator mounting bracket.

17. Finish removing the water pump retaining bolts and remove the water pump pulley.

18. Remove the center camshaft timing belt cover retaining bolts and the cover from the engine.

19. Raise and safely support the vehicle on jackstands.

20. Remove the crankshaft pulley.

21. Remove the lower camshaft timing belt cover bolts and the cover from the engine.

22. Remove the valve cover as follows:

   a. Disconnect the crankcase ventilation tube from the valve cover.

   b. Remove the retaining bolt and nut for the power steering pressure hose retaining bracket and move the hose aside.

   c. Remove the valve cover retaining bolts in a standard removal sequence starting from the outside of the valve cover and working toward the inside of the valve cover.

   d. Remove the valve cover and gasket from the engine.

23. Place Camshaft Alignment Timing Tool T94P-6256-CH or equivalent, into the slots of both camshafts at the rear of the cylinder head to lock the camshafts into position.

24. Loosen the camshaft timing belt tensioner pulley retaining

Crankshaft alignment position—Ford 2.0L (VIN 3) engines

CRANKSHAFT PULLEY

OIL PAN

ALIGN CRANKSHAFT TIMING MARKS

79225G09

Timing chain and gear service is covered in the model specific sections of this manual

EXHAUST CAMSHAFT   INTAKE CAMSHAFT

CAMSHAFT
ALIGNMENT
TIMING
TOOL

79225G10

Placement of Camshaft Alignment Timing Tool T94P-6256-CH or equivalent—Ford 2.0L (VIN 3) engines

bolt and move the tensioner pulley to relieve the tension on the timing belt.

25. Temporarily tighten the tensioner in this position.

➡**If the timing belt is to be reused, mark the belt for the direction of rotation before removing to prevent premature wear or failure.**

26. Remove the timing belt.

27. If required, remove the sprockets as follows:

    a. Hold the camshaft with the Camshaft Sprocket Holding Tool T74P-6256-B or equivalent.

    b. Loosen and remove the camshaft sprocket retaining bolt.

    c. Remove the sprocket from the camshaft.

    d. Repeat the procedure for the 2nd camshaft sprocket.

    e. Remove the crankshaft sprocket.

To install:

28. Slide the crankshaft sprocket onto the crankshaft aligning the keyway.

29. Align the camshafts using the Camshaft Alignment Timing Tool T94P-6256-CH.

30. Reinstall the sprockets onto the camshafts and loosely install the camshaft retaining bolts.

31. Tighten the camshaft sprocket retaining bolts to 47–53 ft. lbs. (64–72 Nm).

32. Loosely install the crankshaft pulley to verify that the engine is at TDC. Realign the marks if they have moved.

33. Verify that the camshafts are aligned.

➡**It is recommended to purchase a tensioner spring and retaining bolt through the dealer parts to apply the proper tension for used or new belt installations. The spring is bolted to the tensioner assembly and becomes a part of the engine. Ignore this notice if the tensioner spring is already installed.**

34. Reinstall the retaining bolt (W700001-S309) into the hole provided in the cylinder block and place the tensioner spring (6L277) between the bolt and the camshaft timing belt tensioner pulley.

35. Tighten the retainer bolt to 71–97 inch lbs. (8–11 Nm).

36. Remove the crankshaft pulley and install the timing belt onto the crankshaft sprocket, then onto the camshaft sprockets working in a counterclockwise direction.

37. Tighten the camshaft sprocket retaining bolts to 47–53 ft. lbs. (64–72 Nm).

38. Be sure that the span of the camshaft timing belt between the crankshaft sprocket and the exhaust camshaft sprocket is not loose.

39. Be sure that the camshaft timing belt is securely aligned on all sprockets.

40. Reinstall the lower timing belt cover and tighten the retaining bolts to 53–71 inch lbs. (6–8 Nm).

41. Apply silicone sealer to the keyway of the crankshaft pulley and install. Tighten the retaining bolt to 81–89 ft. lbs. (110–120 Nm).

42. Inspect the timing mark on the crankshaft pulley to verify that the engine is still at TDC.

43. Loosen the camshaft timing belt tensioner pulley retaining bolt and allow the tensioner spring attached to the pulley to draw the tensioner pulley against the camshaft timing belt.

44. Remove the camshaft alignment timing tool from the camshafts at the rear of the engine.

45. Turn the crankshaft two revolutions in a clockwise direction.

46. Tighten the camshaft timing belt tensioner pulley retaining bolt to 26–30 ft. lbs. (35–40 Nm).

47. Recheck that the crankshaft timing mark is at TDC for the No. 1 piston, and that both camshafts are in alignment using the camshaft alignment timing tool.

➡**A slight adjustment of the camshafts to allow the insertion of the camshaft alignment timing tool is permissible as long as the crankshaft stays at the TDC location.**

48. Camshaft Sprocket Holding Tool T74P-6256-b can be used to move the camshaft sprocket(s) if a slight adjustment is required.

49. If a camshaft is not properly aligned, perform the following procedure:

    a. Loosen the retaining bolt securing the sprocket to the camshaft while holding the camshaft sprocket from turning with the sprocket holding tool.

    b. Turn the camshaft until the camshaft alignment timing tool can be installed.

    c. Verify that the crankshaft timing mark is at TDC for the No. 1 cylinder.

    d. While holding the camshaft sprocket with the camshaft sprocket holding tool, tighten the retaining bolt to 47–53 ft. lbs. (64–72 Nm).

    e. Remove the tool and rotate the crankshaft two revolutions (clockwise).

    f. Verify that the camshafts are aligned and that the crankshaft is at TDC for the No. 1 cylinder.

50. Reinstall the valve cover as follows:

    a. Clean the gasket sealing surfaces.

    b. Inspect the valve cover gasket and O-rings; replace as required.

    c. Reinstall the valve cover retaining bolts and tighten them in a standard sequence starting from the center and working towards the outside of the valve cover to 53–71 inch lbs. (6–8 Nm).

    d. Reinstall the power steering hose retaining bracket and the power steering hose.

    e. Reinstall the crankcase ventilation tube to the valve cover.

51. Position the center camshaft timing belt cover.

52. Reinstall the center camshaft timing belt cover retaining bolts and tighten them to 53–71 inch lbs. (6–8 Nm).

53. Reinstall the water pump pulley and the retaining bolts. Reinstall the bolts, finger-tight.

54. Reinstall the drive belt idler pulley.

55. Reinstall the drive belt idler pulley retaining bolt and tighten it to 35 ft. lbs. (48 Nm).

56. Reinstall the accessory drive belt.

57. Tighten the water pump pulley retaining bolts to 89–124 inch lbs. (10–14 Nm).

58. Move the radiator coolant recovery reservoir aside.

59. Reinstall the upper front engine support insulator.

60. Position the radiator coolant recovery reservoir and install the retainers.

61. If equipped, install the wiring harness to the low coolant level sensor on the coolant recovery reservoir.

62. Reinstall the upper front engine support bracket to the engine and the upper front engine support insulator using the mark made during the removal procedure for reference.

63. Install the upper camshaft timing belt cover.

64. Reinstall the upper camshaft timing belt cover retaining bolts and tighten to 27–44 inch lbs. (3–5 Nm).

65. Remove the engine support.

66. Reinstall the retaining bracket for the power steering pressure hose to the engine lifting eye.

67. Reinstall the spark plugs and the ignition wires.

68. Reinstall the engine air intake resonators.

69. Replace the engine oil.

70. Reconnect the negative battery cable.

71. Run the engine and check for leaks and proper operation.

2.0L (VIN A) Engine

1. Disconnect the negative battery cable.

2. Label and disconnect the spark plug wires and clips from the cylinder head cover. Remove the ignition distributor with wiring and set it aside.

3. Remove the power steering hose brackets from the cylinder head cover. If necessary disconnect the crankshaft position sensor.

4. Disconnect the breather tube and PCV valve from the cylinder head cover.

5. Loosen the cylinder head cover bolts in 2–3 steps. Remove the cylinder head cover.

6. Remove the power steering belt shield. Loosen the power steering adjusting bolt, lockbolt and through-bolt and remove the power steering belt.

7. Loosen the alternator adjusting bolt and upper mounting bolt. Remove the alternator belt.

8. Support the engine with Engine Support Tool 014–00750 or equivalent. Raise the engine slightly with a jack and remove the right side engine support insulator (mount).

9. Remove the oil level indicator bolt and four upper timing belt cover bolts and remove the upper timing belt cover.

10. Raise and safely support the vehicle.

11. Remove the splash-shields. Using Holder Tool T92C-6316-AH or equivalent, hold the crankshaft pulley and remove the pulley bolt. Use a suitable puller to remove the pulley, then remove the guide plate.

12. Remove the four lower timing belt cover bolts and remove the lower timing belt cover.

13. Temporarily install the crankshaft pulley bolt.

14. Turn the crankshaft until the timing mark on the crankshaft sprocket aligns with the timing mark on the oil pump and the

Be sure that the intake and exhaust camshaft timing marks align so that they face each other—Ford 2.0L (VIN A) engines

camshaft sprocket timing marks, **E** and **I**, align on the camshaft sprockets.

15. Lower the vehicle.

16. Insert camshaft sprocket holding tool T92C-6256-AH or equivalent, between the camshaft sprockets.

17. Turn the timing belt tensioner with an Allen wrench and remove the tensioner spring from the tensioner spring pin.

18. If the timing belt is to be reused, mark the direction of rotation on the timing belt. Remove the timing belt.

19. If necessary to remove the sprockets, remove the camshaft sprocket holding tool. Hold the camshaft by placing a suitable wrench on the hexagon which is cast into the camshaft. Place another wrench onto the camshaft sprocket retaining bolt and loosen the bolt.

➡**Before removing the camshaft sprocket(s), be sure that the camshafts are still in alignment and tag each sprocket to the camshaft from which it was removed.**

20. Remove the camshaft sprocket bolt and the camshaft sprocket from the camshaft.

21. Repeat the camshaft sprocket removal procedure for the opposite camshaft if required.

22. Raise and safely support the vehicle.

23. Slide off the crankshaft sprocket and remove the crankshaft key.

To install:

24. Install the crankshaft key and slide the crankshaft sprocket into position.

25. Lower the vehicle.

26. Install the camshaft sprocket onto the proper camshaft, making sure to align the dowel pin.

27. Be sure that the **I** and **E** are in alignment.

28. Install the camshaft sprocket bolt. Hold the hexagon on the camshaft with a suitable wrench and tighten the sprocket bolt to 35–48 ft. lbs. (47–65 Nm). Be sure the camshaft sprockets are still properly aligned and reinstall the sprocket holding tool.

29. Be sure the timing marks on the camshaft and crankshaft sprockets are still aligned.

30. Install the timing belt. If reusing the original timing belt, be sure it is installed in the same direction of rotation.

31. Turn the tensioner clockwise with an Allen wrench and install the tensioner spring. Remove the holding tool from between the camshaft sprockets.

32. Rotate the crankshaft clockwise two turns and align the timing marks. Be sure all marks are still correctly aligned.

➡**The timing chain tensioner automatically adjusts the tension on the timing belt.**

33. Raise and safely support vehicle on jackstands.

34. Install the timing belt lower cover and tighten the four bolts to 71–88 inch lbs. (8–10 Nm).

35. Install the guide plate, crankshaft pulley and pulley bolt. Secure the pulley with the holder tool and tighten the bolt to 116–123 ft. lbs. (157–167 Nm).

36. Install the splash-shields and lower the vehicle.

37. Raise the engine slightly with the jack and install the right side engine mount. Tighten the mount through-bolt to 63–86 ft. lbs. (86–116 Nm) and the mount attaching nuts to 54–75 ft. lbs. (74–103 Nm). Remove the engine support tool.

38. Install the upper timing belt cover and tighten the bolts to 71–88 inch lbs. (8–10 Nm).

39. Clean the cylinder head and valve cover mating surfaces thoroughly.

40. Apply silicone sealant to the cylinder head surface in the area adjacent to the front camshaft bearing caps. Apply sealant to a new gasket and install it on the cylinder head cover.

41. Install the cylinder head cover and tighten the bolts.

42. Install the power steering hose brackets and tighten the bolts to 71–88 inch lbs. (8–10 Nm). Connect the spark plug wires and wire clips. Connect the breather tube and PCV valve. If necessary, connect the crankshaft position sensor.

43. Install the alternator belt and adjust the tension. Tighten the upper mounting bolt to 14–18 ft. lbs. (19–25 Nm) and the lower through-bolt to 27–38 ft. lbs. (37–52 Nm).

44. Install the power steering belt and adjust the tension. Tighten the through-bolt to 32–45 ft. lbs. (43–61 Nm) and the lockbolt to 23–34 ft. lbs. (31–46 Nm). Install the power steering belt shield and tighten the bolts to 61–86 inch lbs. (7–9 Nm).

45. Connect the negative battery cable.

46. Run the engine and check for leaks and proper engine operation.

2.0L (VIN P) Engine

1. Unfasten the three nuts and three bolts from the timing belt cover.

2. Remove the cover.

3. Raise and safely support the vehicle.

4. Remove the right-hand splash shield and the crankshaft pulley.

5. Align the timing marks as illustrated in the accompanying illustration.

6. Refer to the accompanying illustration and remove the timing belt as follows:

   a. Loosen the timing belt tensioner bolt (1).

   b. Use an 8mm Allen wrench, and turn the tensioner (2) counterclockwise ¼ turn.

   c. Insert a ⅛ inch drill bit in the hole (3) to lock the belt tensioner in place.

   d. Remove the timing belt (4).

   e. Inspect the belt for damage and signs of oil leakage.

To install:

➡**Install the timing belt over the sprocket in a counterclockwise direction starting at the crankshaft. Keep the belt span between the crankshaft and camshaft tight when installing the belt over the camshaft.**

7. Install the timing belt and remove the drill bit.

8. Tighten the tensioner bolt to 15–22 ft. lbs. (20–30 Nm).

9. Rotate the engine two complete revolutions and make sure the timing marks are aligned.

10. Install the timing belt cover and tighten the nuts and bolts to 71–97 inch lbs. (8–11 Nm).

93005G01

The timing marks on both the camshaft and crankshaft pulleys must be aligned like this before removing or installing the timing belt—2.0L (VIN P) SOHC engines

93005G02

Remove the timing belt by following these 4 numbered steps (refer to the text for an explanation)—2.0L (VIN P) SOHC engine

11. Install the pulley and the bolt. Tighten the bolt to 81–98 ft. lbs. (110–120 Nm).

12. Install the splash shield(s).

13. Lower the vehicle and install the drive belt.

14. Connect the negative battery cable.

15. Start the vehicle and check for proper operation.

2.5L (VIN B) Engine

1. Disconnect the negative battery cable.

2. Label and disengage the electrical connectors from the coolant elbow. Label and remove the electrical connectors from the knock sensor (if required) and crankshaft position sensor.

3. Loosen the drive belt tensioner locknuts and adjusting bolts. Remove the accessory drive belts.

4. Raise and safely support the vehicle on jackstands.

5. Remove the lower bolt from the A/C and alternator tensioner bracket.

6. Remove the right wheel and splash-shields.

7. Hold the crankshaft pulley (damper) with Holder Tool T92C-6316-AH or equivalent, and remove the crankshaft pulley bolt. Remove the crankshaft pulley, using a puller if needed.

8. Remove the 5 front timing belt cover bolts.

9. Hold the water pump pulley with Holder Tool T92C-6312-AH or equivalent, remove the four bolts and the water pump pulley.

10. Hold the power steering pump pulley with Strap Wrench D85L-6000-A or equivalent and remove the power steering pump pulley nut and pulley.

11. Lower the vehicle.

12. Remove the upper bolt from the belt idler bracket and remove the bracket.

13. Remove the engine oil dipstick tube retaining bolt and the tube.

14. Remove the 8 rear timing belt cover retaining bolts and remove the timing belt covers.

15. Temporarily reinstall the crankshaft pulley bolt.

16. Remove the three nuts and through-bolt from the right-hand engine support insulator and remove the support insulator. Remove the support insulator bracket.

17. Raise and safely support the vehicle on jackstand.

18. Turn the crankshaft to Top Dead Center (TDC) No. 1 cylinder in the direction of normal rotation. Be sure that the timing mark on the crankshaft sprocket aligns with the timing mark on the oil pump.

19. Remove the two bolts from the timing belt tensioner arm, removing the lower bolt first.

20. Remove the timing belt tensioner arm.

21. If the timing belt is to be reused, mark the direction of rotation on the timing belt.

22. Loosen the Allen bolt on the timing belt tensioner.

23. Remove the timing belt.

24. If the timing belt sprockets are to be removed, proceed as follows:

   a. Remove the intake manifold.

   b. Label and disconnect the necessary hoses from the cylinder head covers.

   c. Label and disconnect the spark plug wires from the spark plugs.

   d. Remove the cylinder head cover retaining bolts and remove the cylinder head covers.

   e. Hold the camshaft using a suitable wrench on the hexagon

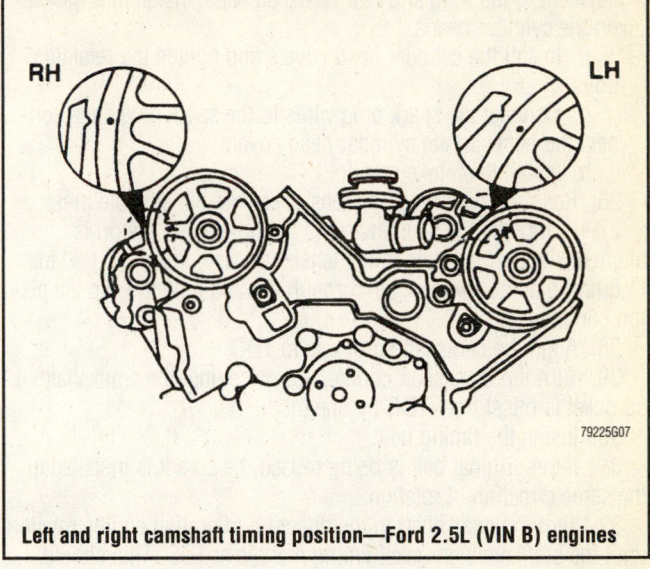

Left and right camshaft timing position—Ford 2.5L (VIN B) engines

TDC alignment for the crankshaft—Ford 2.5L (VIN B) engines

cast into the camshaft. Remove the camshaft sprocket bolts and the camshaft sprockets.

   f. Use Crankshaft Damper Puller T74P-6316-A or equivalent, to remove the crankshaft sprocket. Remove the crankshaft sprocket key.

To install:

25. If the timing belt sprockets were removed, proceed as follows:

   a. Install the crankshaft sprocket key and crankshaft sprocket.

   b. Install the camshaft sprockets on the camshafts with the retaining bolts.

   c. Hold the camshaft using a suitable wrench on the hexagon cast into the camshaft. Tighten the camshaft sprocket bolts to 90–103 ft. lbs. (123–140 Nm).

   d. Be sure the cylinder head cover and cylinder head contact surfaces are clean and free of dirt, oil and old sealant and gasket material.

   e. Apply silicone sealant to the cylinder heads in the area

adjacent to the front and rear camshaft caps. Install new gaskets on the cylinder heads.

f. Install the cylinder head covers and tighten the retaining bolts.

g. Connect the spark plug wires to the spark plugs and connect the hoses to the cylinder head covers.

h. Install the intake manifold.

26. Position the timing belt tensioner arm in a suitable press.

27. Compress the tensioner until the hole in the piston is aligned with the 2nd hole in the tensioner case. Insert a 0.060 in. (1.6mm) diameter wire or pin through the 2nd hole to keep the piston compressed.

28. Align the camshaft sprockets to TDC.

29. Turn the crankshaft counterclockwise until the crankshaft sprocket is offset from TDC by one tooth.

30. Install the timing belt.

31. If the original belt is being reused, be sure it is installed in the same direction of rotation.

32. Turn the crankshaft in the direction of normal engine rotation until the crankshaft sprocket timing mark is at TDC. This should place all of the belt slack in the timing belt tensioner portion of the timing belt.

33. Install the timing belt tensioner arm and two bolts. Tighten the bolts to 14–18 ft. lbs. (19–25 Nm).

34. Remove the wire or pin from the tensioner.

➡When properly timed, the crankshaft timing marks will align and the crankshaft sprocket timing mark will no longer be one tooth off.

35. Rotate the crankshaft two complete turns in the direction of normal rotation and align the timing marks. Be sure all marks are still correctly aligned. This will also set the timing belt tension.

➡The timing belt tensioner will automatically adjust the timing belt tension.

36. Tighten the timing belt tensioner Allen bolt to 28–32 ft. lbs. (35–51 Nm).

37. Install the right-hand engine support insulator. Tighten the three nuts to 54–76 ft. lbs. (74–103 Nm) and the through-bolt to 50–68 ft. lbs. (67–93 Nm).

38. Remove the crankshaft damper bolt.

39. Install the timing belt covers with the rear 8 bolts. Tighten to 71–88 inch lbs. (8–10 Nm).

40. Install the engine oil dipstick tube and retaining nut.

41. Install the belt idler bracket and the upper retaining bolt.

42. Raise and safely support the vehicle on jackstands.

43. Install the power steering pump pulley and nut. Tighten the nut to 36–43 ft. lbs. (49–59 Nm) while holding the pulley with a strap wrench.

44. Install the water pump pulley and four bolts. Secure the pulley with the holder tool and tighten the bolts to 71–88 inch lbs. (8–10 Nm).

45. Install the 5 front timing belt cover bolts and tighten to 71–88 inch lbs. (8–10 Nm).

46. Install the crankshaft pulley (damper) with the bolt. Hold the crankshaft pulley with the holding tool and tighten to 116–122 ft. lbs. (157–166 Nm).

47. Install the splash-shields.

48. Install the wheel and tighten the lug nuts to 65–87 ft. lbs. (88–118 Nm).

49. Install the lower bolt into the A/C and alternator tensioner bracket.

50. Lower the vehicle.

51. Install the accessory drive belts and adjust the tension.

52. Engage the electrical connectors to the sensors at the coolant elbow and the knock sensor and crankshaft position sensor.

53. Connect the negative battery cable.

54. Run the engine and check for leaks and proper engine operation.

GENERAL MOTORS

1.0L (VIN 6) and 1.3 (VIN 9) Engines

➡Timing belts must always be completely free of dirt, grease, fluids and lubricants. This includes the sprockets and contact surfaces on which the belt rides. The belt must never be crimped, twisted or bent. Never use tools to pry or wedge the belt.

1. Disconnect the negative battery cable.
2. Raise and safely support the vehicle.
3. Remove the clips and right side splash-shield.
4. Remove the lower alternator cover plate.
5. Remove the alternator drive belt, if equipped, the A/C drive belt.
6. Remove the water pump pulley.

➡It is not necessary to remove the crankshaft timing sprocket bolt (center bolt) to remove the crankshaft pulley.

7. Remove the crankshaft pulley bolts and crankshaft pulley.
8. Remove the retaining bolts and nut from the timing belt outside cover.
9. Remove the timing belt outside cover.
10. Turn the crankshaft to align the timing marks. The mark on the crankshaft sprocket should align with the arrow mark on the oil pump housing. The mark on the camshaft sprocket should align with the V mark on the timing belt inner cover or cylinder head cover.
11. If the timing belt is to be reused, mark the direction of rotation on the belt.
12. Remove the timing belt tensioner, tensioner plate, tensioner spring, spring damper and timing belt.

➡Never turn the camshaft or crankshaft independently after the timing belt has been removed. Interference may occur between the pistons and valves, and parts may be damaged.

13. Inspect the timing belt for wear or cracks, and replace as necessary. Check the tensioner for smooth rotation.
14. If the timing belt sprockets are to be removed, proceed as follows:

a. Using a 0.39 in. (10mm) rod inserted into the camshaft, hold the camshaft and remove the retaining bolt and camshaft sprocket.

✺ WARNING

Be careful not to damage the cylinder head or cylinder head cover mating surfaces. Place a clean shop cloth between the rod and cylinder head. Do not bump the rod hard against the cylinder head when loosening the bolt.

b. Raise and safely support the vehicle on jackstands.

c. If equipped with a manual transaxle, lock the crankshaft in position by inserting a suitable flat-bladed tool into the hole in the bottom of the bell housing to engage the flywheel teeth.

d. If equipped with an automatic transaxle, lock the crankshaft

1 CAMSHAFT TIMING PULLEY	5 SLOT NO. 1
2 TIMING MARK	6 SLOT NO. 2
3 "V" MARK	7 PULLEY PIN
4 BELT INSIDE COVER	

79225G16

Upper timing pulley position—GM 1.0L (VIN 6) and 1.3L (VIN 9) engines

A	**ARROW MARK ON OIL PUMP CASE**
B	**PUNCH MARK ON CRANKSHAFT TIMING GEAR**
674	**CRANKSHAFT PULLEY TIMING GEAR BOLT**
6021	**CRANKSHAFT TIMING GEAR**

79225G17

Crankshaft timing mark—GM 1.0L (VIN 6) and 1.3L (VIN 9) engines

in position by inserting a suitable flat-bladed tool between the flywheel teeth and against the engine block.

    e. Remove the crankshaft sprocket bolt and crankshaft sprocket.

To install:

15. If the timing belt sprockets were removed, proceed as follows:

    a. Install the crankshaft sprocket, aligning the keyway. Lock the crankshaft in place and tighten the crankshaft sprocket bolt to 81 ft. lbs. (110 Nm).

    b. Lower the vehicle.

    c. Install the camshaft sprocket and retaining bolt. Lock the camshaft in place using the rod, and tighten the bolt to 44 ft. lbs. (60 Nm). Remove the locking rod.

16. Install the tensioner plate to the tensioner.

17. Insert the lug of the tensioner plate into the hole of the tensioner.

18. Install the tensioner, tensioner plate and spring. Do not fully tighten the tensioner bolt and stud at this time.

19. Move the tensioner plate in a counterclockwise direction. This should cause the tensioner to move in the same direction. If it does not, remove the tensioner and tensioner plate, and reinsert the tensioner plate lug in the timing plate tensioner hole.

20. Check that the camshaft timing marks are aligned. If not, align the two marks by turning the camshaft.

21. Check that the punch mark on the crankshaft timing belt sprocket is aligned with the arrow mark on the oil pump case. If not, align the two marks by turning the crankshaft.

22. With the timing marks aligned, install the timing belt on the two sprockets. If the old belt is being reused, be sure to install it running in the same direction of original rotation.

23. Install the tensioner spring and spring damper. Turn the timing belt two rotations clockwise after installing the tensioner spring and damper to remove any belt slack. Tighten the tensioner stud to 8 ft. lbs. (11 Nm), then the tensioner bolt to 20 ft. lbs. (27 Nm).

➡**Confirm that both sets of timing marks are aligned properly.**

24. Using a new seal, install the timing belt cover and tighten the bolts and nut to 97 inch lbs. (11 Nm).

25. Install the crankshaft pulley. Fit the keyway on the pulley to the crankshaft timing belt sprocket and tighten the bolts to 8–12 ft. lbs. (11–16 Nm).

26. Install the alternator drive belt, if equipped, A/C drive belt.

27. Install the lower alternator cover plate. Tighten the bolts to 89 inch lbs. (10 Nm).

28. Install the right side splash-shield and clips.

29. Lower the vehicle and connect the negative battery cable.

30. Run the engine. Check for leaks.

1.6L (VIN 6) and 1.8L (VIN 8) Engines

1. Disconnect the negative battery cable.

2. Remove the windshield washer reservoir from the engine compartment.

3. If equipped with cruise control, proceed as follows:

    a. Remove the cruise control actuator cover.

    b. Disconnect the cruise control harnesses.

    c. Disconnect the control cable.

    d. Remove the bolts and actuator from the vehicle.

4. Raise and safely support the vehicle on jackstands.

5. Remove the right front wheel.

6. Remove the bolts and plastic clips and the right front wheel housing.

7. Remove the alternator/water pump drive belt.

8. Lower the vehicle.

9. If equipped with A/C, proceed as follows:

    a. Remove the A/C compressor drive belt.

    b. Disconnect the compressor harness.

    c. Remove the bolts and compressor, without disconnecting the refrigerant lines. Suspend the compressor aside.

    d. Remove the compressor mounting bracket.

10. Remove the power steering pump drive belt.

11. Disconnect the wiring from the alternator and oil pressure switch.

12. Remove the engine wiring harness cover.

13. Remove the wiring harness from the cylinder head cover.

14. Disconnect the ignition wires from the spark plugs, then remove the spark plugs.

15. Remove the PCV hoses from the valve cover.

For accessory drive belt replacement procedures see the model specific sections of this manual

16. Remove the cap nuts, the seal washers and the cylinder head cover with the gasket.

17. Turn the crankshaft to align the timing mark on the crankshaft pulley at **0**, setting the piston in the No. 1 cylinder at Top Dead Center (TDC) on the compression stroke. Check that the valve lash adjusters on the No. 1 cylinder are loose. If not, turn the crankshaft pulley one complete revolution (360 degrees).

18. Remove the engine ground wire from the right fender apron.

19. Install a suitable support under the engine and remove the engine mount.

20. Remove the water pump pulley.

21. Remove the crankshaft pulley using a suitable puller.

22. Remove the 9 retaining bolts and the timing belt covers.

23. Slide the timing belt guide from the crankshaft.

24. Be sure the timing belt sprockets are properly aligned.

✳✳ WARNING

Do not turn the crankshaft or camshaft independently after removal of the timing belt; binding or damage to

620   CAMSHAFT TIMING GEAR

79225G18

Aligning the camshaft timing marks—GM 1.6L (VIN 6) and 1.8L (VIN 8) engines

693   CRANKSHAFT TIMING GEAR

79225G19

Crankshaft pulley alignment indicator—GM 1.6L (VIN 6) and 1.8L (VIN 8) engines

engine components could result. If the timing belt is to be reused, mark the belt with an arrow showing the direction of engine revolution.

25. Remove the timing belt tensioner bolt, tensioner and tension spring.

26. Remove the timing belt from the sprockets. Inspect the timing belt for cracked or damaged teeth. Replace as necessary.

✳✳ WARNING

Do not bend, twist or turn the timing belt.

27. If the camshaft sprocket is to be removed, hold the camshaft stationary using a wrench positioned on the hexagon cast into the camshaft, and remove the sprocket retaining bolt and sprocket.

✳✳ WARNING

Be careful not to damage the cylinder head when holding the camshaft in place.

28. If the crankshaft sprocket is to be removed, pry it from the crankshaft using two flat-bladed prybars.

To install:

29. Align the camshaft key with the groove on the sprocket and slide the sprocket on. Hold the camshaft with the wrench at the hexagonal portion of the camshaft, and tighten the camshaft timing sprocket bolt to 43 ft. lbs. (59 Nm).

30. Be sure the sprocket is still properly aligned.

31. Install the crankshaft timing sprocket. Align the crankshaft key with the groove on the sprocket and slide it on.

32. Reinstall the timing belt tensioner and the tension spring. Pry the tensioner to the left as far as it will go and temporarily tighten the retaining bolt.

33. Install the timing belt. If installing the old belt, observe the matchmarks made during removal.

34. Loosen the retaining bolt for the timing belt tensioner and allow it to tension the belt.

35. Temporarily install the crankshaft pulley bolt and turn the crankshaft clockwise two full revolutions. Be sure each timing mark realigns exactly.

36. Tighten the timing belt tensioner bolt to 27 ft. lbs. (37 Nm).

37. Measure the timing belt deflection. Correct deflection should be 0.20–0.24 in. (5–6mm) at 4 lbs. (20 Nm) of pressure. If the deflection is not correct, adjust it with the timing belt tensioner.

38. Install the timing belt guide, with the cup side facing outward.

39. Install the timing belt covers, installing the bottom one first. Tighten the 9 cover bolts to 62 inch lbs. (7 Nm).

40. Install the crankshaft pulley after aligning the pulley key with the slot on the pulley. Hold the pulley with tool J-8614-01 or equivalent, and tighten the pulley bolt to 87 ft. lbs. (118 Nm).

41. Temporarily install the water pump pulley.

42. Raise and safely support the vehicle on jackstands.

43. Install the engine mount.

44. Install or connect the remaining components.

45. If equipped with A/C, proceed as follows:

　a. Install the compressor mounting bracket and tighten the bolts to 35 ft. lbs. (47 Nm).

　b. Install the compressor and tighten the bolts to 18 ft. lbs. (25 Nm).

　c. Engage the compressor wiring connector.

　d. Install the compressor drive belt and adjust the tension.

46. If equipped with cruise control, proceed as follows:

a. Install the cruise control actuator and tighten the bolts to 89 inch lbs. (10 Nm).
b. Connect the cruise control cable.
c. Install the cruise control actuator cover.
47. Connect the negative battery cable.
48. Start the engine and check vehicle operation.

3.0L (VIN R) Engine

➡**The steps in this procedure are critical in preventing catastrophic engine damage, adhering to this sequence is imperative. There are special tools needed to perform this** procedure. **It is a good idea to read this procedure several times before attempting to perform this job. This is an interference engine.**

Always turn the crankshaft in the direction of rotation (clockwise), never against engine rotation. Never remove the timing belt without first setting the camshaft gears and crankshaft drive gear to Top Dead Center (TDC) and locking them in place with tool J42069 or equivalent.

The "Timing Belt Installation and Adjustment Table" provides an overview of the steps needed to properly install and adjust the timing belt. Use this table as a reference, not as a substitution, for the steps in this procedure.

TIMING BELT INSTALLATION AND ADJUSTMENT TABLE

Step	Action	Value	Yes	No
1	Install the timing belt and align marks on the belt with the marks on the camshaft gears and the crankshaft gear. Check the timing belt deflection between the idler pulley for camshafts 3 & 4 and camshaft number 4. Is the timing belt installed, the marks aligned and the timing belt deflection adjusted?	1 cm (0.4 in) maximum	Go to Step 2	—
2	Set the initial timing belt tension at the timing belt tensioner. Is the initial timing belt tension set?	—	Go to Step 3	—
3	Rotate the engine two complete revolutions and secure the crankshaft at Top Dead Center (TDC) with the J 42069-10. Has the engine been rotated and the crankshaft secured to TDC?	—	Go to Step 4	—
4	Starting with camshafts 3 and 4, check the alignment of the marks on the camshaft gears with the marks on the J 42069-20 checking gauge. Do the marks on the camshaft gears align exactly with the marks on J 42069-20?	—	Go to Step 5	Go to Step 6
5	Check the alignment of the marks on camshafts gears 1 and 2 with the marks on the J 42069-20 checking gauge. Do the marks on the camshaft gears align exactly with the marks on J 42069-20?	—	Go to Step 14	Go to Step 10
6	Do the camshaft gear marks line up to the left (BTDC) of the marks on the J 42069-20 checking gauge?	—	Go to Step 8	Go to Step 7
7	Do the camshaft gear marks line up to the right (ATDC) of the marks on the J 42069-20 checking gauge?	—	Go to Step 9	—
8	Turn the idler pulley eccentric, for camshafts 3 and 4, counterclockwise until the marks on the camshaft gear align exactly with the marks on J 42069-20. Rotate the engine two complete revolutions, lock the crankshaft at TDC with J 42069-10 and recheck the alignment of the camshaft gear marks to the marks on J 42069-20. Do the marks on the camshaft gears align exactly with the marks on J 42069-20?	—	Go to Step 5	Go to Step 6
9	Turn the idler pulley eccentric, for camshafts 3 and 4, clockwise until the marks on the camshaft gear align exactly with the marks on J 42069-20. Rotate the engine two complete revolutions, lock the crankshaft at TDC with J 42069-10 and recheck the alignment of the camshaft gear marks to the marks on J 42069-20. Do the marks on the camshaft gears align exactly with the marks on J 42069-20?	—	Go to Step 5	Go to Step 6

79225G35

Timing belt installation and adjustment table—GM 3.0L (VIN R) engine

Step	Action	Value	Yes	No
10	Do the camshaft gear marks line up to the left (BTDC) of the marks on the J 42069-20 checking gauge?	—	Go to Step 12	Go to Step 11
11	Do the camshaft gear marks line up to the right (ATDC) of the marks on the J 42069-20 checking gauge?	—	Go to Step 13	—
12	Turn the idler pulley eccentric, for camshafts 1 and 2, counterclockwise until the marks on the camshaft gear align exactly with the marks on J 42069-20. Rotate the engine two complete revolutions, lock the crankshaft at TDC with J 42069-10 and recheck the alignment of the camshaft gear marks to the marks on J 42069-20. Do the marks on the camshaft gears align exactly with the marks on J 42069-20?	—	Go to Step 14	Go to Step 10
13	Turn the idler pulley eccentric, for camshafts 1 and 2, clockwise until the marks on the camshaft gear align exactly with the marks on J 42069-20. Rotate the engine two complete revolutions, lock the crankshaft at TDC with J 42069-10 and recheck the alignment of the camshaft gear marks to the marks on J 42069-20. Do the marks on the camshaft gears align exactly with the marks on J 42069-20?	—	Go to Step 14	Go to Step 10
14	Set the final timing belt tension at the timing belt tensioner. Is the final timing belt tension set?	—	Go to Step 15	—
15	Again, rotate the engine two complete revolutions and lock the crankshaft at TDC. Do a final inspection of the camshaft gear marks' relationship to the J 42069-20 marks. The marks must align exactly. Do the marks on the camshaft gears align exactly with the marks on the J 42069-20?	—	Go to Step 16	Go to Step 2
16	Remove all checking tools and ensure all idler pulleys and the tensioner locking nut are tightened to specifications. Continue with re-assembly of the engine.	—	—	—

79225G36

Timing belt installation and adjustment table (continued)—GM 3.0L (VIN R) engine

1. Disconnect the negative battery cable.
2. Remove the resonance chamber.
3. Remove the front timing belt cover.

Crankshaft alignment to 60 degrees BTDC—GM 3.0L (VIN R) engine

79225G30

4. Remove the harmonic balancer from the crankshaft.
5. Rotate the crankshaft clockwise to 60 degrees BTDC.
6. Install J42069-10 (or equivalent) to the crankshaft drive gear with knurled bolt.
7. Turn the engine clockwise, with J42098 or equivalent, until the lever of J42069-10 or equivalent firmly contacts the water pump pulley flange. Secure the lever to the water pump.

➡**Be sure the engine is not 180 degrees off. The camshaft marks must align with the rear timing cover.**

8. Lock the camshaft gears, using J42069-1 or equivalent and J42069-2 or equivalent. It may be necessary to loosen the relevant idler pulley to lock the gears, then tighten the idler pulley bolt to 30 ft. lbs. (40 Nm).
9. Loosen the timing belt tensioner and remove the belt.

✳✳ WARNING

With the belt removed, do not rotate the camshaft or crankshaft or remove the locking tools, because the pistons may contact the valves and cause internal engine damage.

To install:
10. Remove J42069-10 or equivalent.

Securing the crankshaft—GM 3.0L (VIN R) engine

Using the tool to pin the timing belt—GM 3.0L (VIN R) engine

Locking the camshaft—GM 3.0L (VIN R) engine

11. Raise and safely support the vehicle securely on jackstands.

12. Install the timing belt, starting at the crankshaft gear and aligning the double dash (TDC) mark on the belt with the oil pump and belt drive gear.

13. Using J42069-30 or equivalent, secure the belt to prevent the splines from jumping.

14. Lower the vehicle.

15. Route the belt between the idler pulley for camshafts 3 and 4, then between the gears for 3 and 4.

16. If the dash marks on the belt do not align with the camshaft and rear timing cover marks, loosen the idler pulley or move the cam gears slightly, with the camshaft gears still locked in place, until the timing belt can be properly installed. Temporally tighten the idler pulley locking bolt; the locking bolt will be tightened to specification after final adjustments are made.

➡The timing belt deflection must be no more than 0.4 in. (10mm) between camshaft gear 4 and the idler pulley. To adjust the deflection, rotate the timing belt idler pulley for camshafts 3 and 4 counterclockwise with tool J42069-40 or equivalent.

17. Route the belt between the idler pulley for camshafts 1 and 2, then between gears for 1 and 2.

18. If the dash marks on the belt do not align with the camshaft and rear timing cover marks, loosen the idler pulley or move the cam gears slightly, with the camshaft gears still locked in place, until the timing belt can be installed. Temporally tighten the idler pulley; the locking bolt will be tightened to specification after final adjustments are made.

19. Apply tension to the belt to keep it from slipping off the gears by turning the timing belt idler pulley for camshafts 1 and 2 counterclockwise with J42069-40 or equivalent. Temporally tighten the idler pulley; the locking bolt will be tightened to specification after final adjustments are made.

20. Complete the routing of the timing belt through the belt tensioner.

21. Apply initial tension by turning the timing belt tensioner counterclockwise, with a 5mm Allen wrench, until the marks are set as shown in the initial timing belt adjustment illustration.

22. Tighten the tensioner locking nut to 15 ft. lbs. (20 Nm).

23. Ensure that the alignment marks are at their specific reference points.

24. Remove J42069-30, J42069-1 and J42069-2.

25. Rotate the engine two revolutions clockwise, stopping at 60 degrees BTDC.

26. Install J42069-10 to the crankshaft gear with the knurled bolt.

27. Turn the engine clockwise, with J42098 or equivalent, until the lever of J42069-10 or equivalent firmly contacts the water pump pulley flange. Secure the lever to the water pump.

➡The alignment marks on the timing belt will no longer match the marks on the camshaft gears after one or more revolutions. The marks on the camshaft gears must align with the notches on the rear timing cover, and the crankshaft drive gear and the oil pump housing should match up to their mark.

28. If timing belt adjustment is necessary, first adjust camshafts 3 and 4.

Timing chain and gear service is covered in the model specific sections of this manual

79225G34

Initial timing belt tension adjustment—GM 3.0L (VIN R) engine

29. Check the alignment of camshafts 3 and 4, 1 and 2 with gauge J42069-20.

30. If alignment is OK, then set final belt tension as follows:

   a. Loosen the timing belt tensioner locking nut.

   b. Adjust the timing belt tensioner by turning the eccentric cam, with a 5mm hex wrench, until the marks are set.

31. Tighten the tensioner locking nut to 15 ft. lbs. (20 Nm).

32. Remove J42069-10 and J42069-20.

33. Rotate the engine clockwise two revolutions, stopping at 60 degrees BTDC.

34. If further adjustment is needed, then repeat the applicable steps.

35. Tighten the idler pulley bolts for the camshafts to 30 ft. lbs. (40 Nm).

36. Be sure all tools are removed from the engine.

37. Install the harmonic balancer and tighten the bolts to 15 ft. lbs. (20 Nm).

38. Install the timing belt covers.

39. Install the resonance chamber.

40. Connect the negative battery cable, and reprogram applicable accessories.

3.4L (VIN X) Engine

The 3.4L (VIN X) engine uses a timing chain and camshaft timing belts.

1. Disconnect the negative battery cable.

2. Disconnect and remove the power steering pump from the pump mounting bracket.

3. Remove the left, right and center timing belt covers.

4. Rotate the engine clockwise to align the timing marks, TDC on the No.1 exhaust stroke, on the camshaft sprockets and intermediate shaft.

5. Loosely clamp the two camshaft sprockets on each side of the engine together using clamping pliers or the equivalent. Secure the belt to the right side cam sprocket with a C-clamp and a wide pad on the belt.

➡When clamping the sprockets no deflection should be noticed. If any deflection is noticed, loosen the clamping devices. DO NOT mar the camshaft sprockets with the clamping device.

6. Remove the tensioner side plate retaining bolts from the tensioner and remove the side plate from the actuator and base.

7. Rotate the actuator assembly around the arm pivot and out of the base. Removal of the tensioner from the base allows it to extend to its maximum travel.

8. Set the actuator aside on a table in a vertical position to allow the oil to drain into the boot end. The tensioner should be allowed to sit for 5 minutes prior to refilling with oil.

9. Reset the timing belt actuator as follows:

   a. Straighten out a paper clip or a piece of stiff wire 0.032 in. (0.75mm) diameter to a minimum straight length of 1.85 in. (47mm). Form a double loop in the remaining end.

   b. Remove the rubber end plug from the rear of the tensioner assembly. This will aid in allowing the oil in the tensioner to escape.

   c. Hold the tensioner in your hand with the rubber boot end of the tensioner pointing down.

   d. DO NOT remove the vent plug. Push the paper clip through the center hole in the vent plug and into the pilot hole.

   e. Insert a small screwdriver into the screw slot inside the end of the tensioner.

   f. Retract the tensioner by rotating the tensioner plunger in a clockwise direction while pushing the rod tip against a table top.

   g. Align the screw slot to align with the vent hole, and push the straight section of the wire into the screw slot to retain the plunger in the retracted position.

   h. If tensioner oil has been lost, fill the tensioner with SAE 5W30 Mobil 1®. Fill the tensioner to the bottom of the plug. The tensioner **MUST** be fully retracted before being filled with oil.

10. If the belt is being reused, mark the direction of rotation on the belt.

11. Remove the timing belt tensioner pulley mounting bolt and pulley.

12. Remove the timing belt after first removing the C-clamp retaining the belt to the right side camshaft sprocket.

13. Remove the Torx® head bolts securing the idler pulleys, if the idlers need to be replaced.

14. Remove the intermediate shaft sprocket using the following procedure:

   a. Use a suitable tool to hold the engine from turning.

   b. Remove the intermediate shaft sprocket mounting bolt and washer.

   c. Using J-38616 or an equivalent sprocket puller, remove the sprocket from the intermediate shaft.

15. If the camshaft sprockets need to be removed, proceed as follows:

   a. Remove the camshaft carrier cover(s).

   b. Remove the camshaft sprocket clamping pliers.

   c. Rotate the camshaft being serviced so the flats on the camshaft are face up.

   d. Install a camshaft hold-down tool J-38613 or equivalent, and tighten to 22 ft. lbs. (30 Nm).

   e. Remove the camshaft sprocket mounting bolt and washer while holding the camshaft from turning with J-38613 and J-38614 or the equivalent

   f. Using J-38616 or an equivalent sprocket puller, remove the sprocket from the camshaft.

   g. Repeat for each camshaft sprocket as necessary.

16. Drain the cooling system.

17. Disconnect the lower radiator hose from water pump inlet pipe.

18. If equipped with a manual transaxle, disconnect the front AIR hose from the AIR pipe.

19. Disconnect the heater hose at the front cover.

20. Remove the heater pipe bracket mounting bolts at the frame.
21. Raise and safely support the vehicle on jackstands. Remove the right front tire and wheel assembly and the right inner fender splash-shield.
22. Remove the crankshaft pulley mounting bolts and remove the pulley from the damper.
23. Remove the crankshaft damper as follows:
    a. While holding the crankshaft from turning using a suitable tool, remove the damper mounting bolt and washer.
    b. Install tool J-24420-B or equivalent, and remove the damper from the crankshaft.
24. Place an oil catch pan under the oil filter and remove the oil filter.
25. Remove the A/C compressor mounting bracket bolts.
26. Remove the lower front cover bolts.
27. On automatic transaxle vehicles, remove the halfshaft following the recommended procedure.
28. Remove the rear alternator bracket.
29. Disconnect and remove the starter following the recommended procedure.
30. Lower the vehicle.
31. Remove the intermediate shaft drive belt sprocket retaining bolt and remove the intermediate shaft drive belt sprocket using J38616 or an equivalent puller.
32. Remove the upper alternator mounting bolts.
33. Remove the forward light relay center screws and position the relay center aside.
34. Disconnect the oil cooler hose from the front cover.
35. Remove the water pump pulley.
36. Remove the upper front cover bolts and remove the front cover.
37. Mark the intermediate shaft sprocket, chain link, crankshaft sprocket and cylinder block for assembly reference. The marks should be made with paint so they won't be lost when the components are removed.
38. Retract the timing chain tensioner shoe as follows:
    a. Insert tool J-33875 or equivalent, on both sides of the tensioner.
    b. Pull on the through-pin in the tensioner arm to retract the spring located in the tensioner arm.

    c. While compressing the spring, use a suitable tool, a cotter pin or nail, and insert the pin in the hole in the tensioner assembly to hold the tensioner compressed. The tool used must be strong enough to hold the tensioner compressed.

➡️ **The timing chain, crankshaft sprocket and intermediate shaft sprocket will be removed at the same time. If, when removing the assembly, the intermediate shaft sprocket does not easily come off the intermediate shaft, rotate the crankshaft back and forth to loosen the intermediate shaft sprocket.**

39. Install a suitable puller, J-38611 and J-8433 or their equivalents.
40. Tighten the bolt on the puller and slowly pull the crankshaft sprocket off the crankshaft. Be sure the intermediate shaft sprocket is moving along with the crankshaft sprocket.
41. Remove the timing chain and sprockets.
42. Remove the tensioner mounting bolts and remove the tensioner assembly.
To install:
43. Install the tensioner assembly and tensioner assembly mounting bolts finger-tight first. Tighten the bolt in the slotted hole first to 18 ft. lbs. (25 Nm), then tighten the remainder of the bolts to 18 ft. lbs. (25 Nm).
44. Check to ensure that the crankshaft key is fully seated in the crankshaft cutout and the tensioner assembly is fully retracted.
45. Assemble the timing chain, intermediate shaft sprocket and crankshaft sprocket on a work bench. The timing marks made should be in alignment. The large chamfer and counterbore of the crankshaft sprocket are installed facing toward the engine and the intermediate shaft spline sockets are installed facing away from the engine.
46. Install the sprocket and chain assembly onto the engine. As the sprockets are installed, parallel alignment must be maintained.
47. The crankshaft sprocket will have to be pressed on the final 0.31 in. (8mm). This can be done using J-38612 or an equivalent puller.
48. Ensure timing was maintained.
49. Remove the retaining pin from tensioner. Clean all gasket surfaces completely.
50. Apply GM Sealer 1052080 or equivalent, to the lower edges

A   LOCATION OF TIMING MARKS WITH CAM HOLD DOWN TOOLS J 38613 INSTALLED (#4 TDC COMPRESSION STROKE)
B   FRONT COVER TIMING MARK
C   LOCATION OF TIMING MARKS WITH DRIVE BELT INSTALLED
D   LOCATION WHERE CAM HOLD DOWN TOOLS ARE INSTALLED
1   RH EXHAUST CAMSHAFT SPROCKET
2   RH INTAKE CAMSHAFT SPROCKET
3   LH INTAKE CAMSHAFT SPROCKET
4   LH EXHAUST CAMSHAFT SPROCKET
5   PERMANENT MARKS PAINTED DOTS REMOVE PREVIOUS MARKS IF TIMING IS BEING CHANGED AND MARKS AGAIN IN THESE LOCATIONS
6   CRANKSHAFT BALANCER
7   INTERMEDIATE SHAFT SPROCKET

NOTE: CAMSHAFT BELT REMOVED. CAM FLATS UP. ORIGINAL TIMING MARKS STILL ON.

Timing marks with hold-down tool in place—GM 3.4L (VIN X) engines

of the sealing surface of the front cover. Install a new gasket on the front cover.

51. Install the front cover on the engine. Apply thread sealant to the large bolts and tighten the bolts enough to pull the front cover against the engine block.

52. Install the water pump pulley.

53. Connect the oil cooler hose to the front cover.

54. Position the forward light relay center and install the mounting screws.

55. Install the upper alternator mounting bolt and tighten it to 22 ft. lbs. (30 Nm).

56. Install the intermediate shaft drive belt sprocket. The sprocket must lock into the intermediate shaft timing chain sprocket. Install the mounting bolt and washer. While holding the engine from turning, tighten the bolt to 95 ft. lbs. (130 Nm).

57. Raise and safely support vehicle on jackstands.

58. Connect and install the starter. Tighten the starter mounting bolts to 32 ft. lbs. (43 Nm).

59. Install the halfshaft following the recommended procedure.

60. Install the rear alternator bracket. Tighten the mounting bolt to 22 ft. lbs. (30 Nm) and the mounting stud to 41 ft. lbs. (55 Nm) and the lower bolt to 61 ft. lbs. (83 Nm).

61. Install the lower front cover bolts and tighten the small bolts to 18 ft. lbs. (25 Nm).

62. Install the A/C compressor mounting bolts and tighten the mounting bolts to 37 ft. lbs. (50 Nm).

63. Install a new oil filter.

64. Install the crankshaft damper as follows:

    a. Coat the seal contact area on the damper with clean engine oil.

    b. Align the notch inside the damper with the crankshaft key and slide the damper on until the key is started into the notch.

    c. Using J-29113 or an equivalent puller, press the damper into position on the crankshaft.

    d. Install the crankshaft pulley and pulley mounting bolts. Tighten the pulley mounting bolts to 37 ft. lbs. (50 Nm).

    e. Install the crankshaft damper mounting bolt and washer, and tighten to 78 ft. lbs. (105 Nm).

65. Install the right side inner fender splash-shield.

66. Install the tire and wheel assembly.

67. Lower the vehicle.

68. Tighten the upper front cover small bolts to 18 ft. lbs. (25 Nm) and the large bolts to 35 ft. lbs. (47 Nm).

69. Connect the heater hose to the front cover.

70. Install the heater pipe bracket mounting bolts.

71. If equipped with a manual transaxle, connect the front AIR hose to the AIR pipe.

72. Connect the lower radiator hose to the water pump.

73. Install the right side cooling fan. Install the upper radiator support.

74. Position the torque strut mounting bracket and install the mounting bolts and tighten to 52 ft. lbs. (70 Nm).

75. Install the front engine lift hook and tighten the mounting bolt to 52 ft. lbs. (70 Nm).

76. To install the camshaft sprockets, proceed as follows:

    a. Wipe the camshaft noses with clean engine oil.

    b. Install the camshaft sprocket onto the nose of the camshaft.

    c. Install the lockring and shim ring.

    d. Install, but DO NOT tighten, the camshaft sprocket mounting bolts at this time.

77. Install the intermediate shaft sprocket as follows:

    a. Lubricate the seal contact area on the intermediate shaft sprocket with clean engine oil.

b. Slide the sprocket through the intermediate shaft sprocket seal and engage the locking tangs into the sockets of the chain sprocket.

c. Lightly lubricate the shaft seal and place it in position on the end of the intermediate shaft.

d. Install the intermediate shaft sprocket mounting bolt and washer. Tighten the bolt to 96 ft. lbs. (130 Nm) while holding the crankshaft from turning.

78. Install the timing belt idler pulleys and tighten the Torx® bolts to 37 ft. lbs. (50 Nm).

79. Install the actuator assembly and side plate. Tighten the actuator mounting bracket bolts to 37 ft. lbs. (50 Nm).

80. Install the belt, taking note of direction of rotation if the old belt was used.

81. Install the tensioner pulley to the mounting base. Tighten the bolt to 37 ft. lbs. (50 Nm).

82. Rotate the tensioner pulley counterclockwise into the belt using the cast square lug on the body and engage the ball end of the actuator into the socket on the pulley arm.

83. Remove the tensioner lockpin allowing the tensioner shaft to extend and the pulley to move into the belt.

84. Rotate the tensioner pulley counterclockwise, applying 14 ft. lbs. (18 Nm) of torque.

85. Rotate the engine clockwise three times to seat the belt. Align the crankshaft reference marks during the final rotation to TDC. Do not allow the crankshaft to spring back or reverse its direction of rotation.

➡️**The timing flats on the camshafts should be 180 degrees apart from the left side to the right side. Both camshafts on the same side should be the same.**

86. To perform the camshaft timing procedure, proceed as follows:

    a. Rotate the camshaft flats up on the right side camshafts and install a camshaft hold-down tool J-38613 or equivalent, and tighten to 22 ft. lbs. (30 Nm).

    b. Seat the lockring on the right exhaust and intake camshaft sprockets by threading in the mounting bolt and washer.

    c. Hold the sprocket from turning using tool J-38614 or equivalent.

➡️**Running torque of the bolts before seating should be 55 ft. lbs. (75 Nm).**

    d. If less torque is required, replace the shim ring and lockring.

    e. If more torque is required, replace the shim ring and lockring and inspect the bolts for burrs.

    f. Seating of the lockring is accomplished when the edge is flush with the sprocket hub.

    g. With the lockring seated tighten the bolt to final torque of 81 ft. lbs. (110 Nm).

    h. Remove J-38613 or equivalent.

    i. Rotate the engine clockwise one full revolution or any number of odd revolutions. **DO NOT** rotate the engine backward.

    j. Be sure the timing mark on the damper aligns with the mark on the front cover.

    k. Repeat Substeps **a** through **i** for the left side.

87. Install the camshaft carrier covers.

88. Install timing the belt left, right and center covers and retaining bolts.

89. Connect the negative battery cable.

90. Start the engine and verify proper operation and engine performance.

BRAKES

6

CHRYSLER CORP.

Caliper

REMOVAL & INSTALLATION

**Chrysler Concorde, New Yorker, LHS
Dodge Intrepid
Eagle Vision**

FRONT

1. Raise and support the vehicle safely.
2. Remove the appropriate wheel and tire assemblies.
3. Remove the 2 caliper guide pin bolts and remove the caliper assembly. If the caliper is not being removed from the vehicle as during brake pad renewal, simply hang the caliper with a piece of wire to take the weight off the brake hose. If the caliper is being removed for rebuild or replacement, continue to Step 5.
4. Remove the bolt retaining the brake hose to the caliper. Be sure to plug the end of the brake hose or cover it with a plastic bag to prevent contamination from entering the hydraulic system. Remove the caliper from the vehicle.

To install:
5. Reconnect the brake hose to the caliper, if removed, using new sealing washers.

6. If new linings are being installed, the caliper pistons must be pushed back into their bore to accommodate the thickness of the new lining. Special tools are available for pushing the piston back although a large C-clamp can often be used. It is good practice to remove some (⅓–½) brake fluid from the master cylinder reservoir. This prevents overflow caused by brake fluid being forced through the lines as the piston is pushed back.

Front brake caliper and related components—Concorde, New Yorker, LHS, Intrepid, Vision

7. Install the brake pads into the caliper.

8. Install the caliper to the steering knuckle in the correct position. Lightly lubricate the machined areas that support the caliper with high-temperature grease.

9. Install and torque the caliper guide pin bolts. Use care not to cross the threads of the caliper pin bolts. Torque the guide pin bolts to 15 ft. lbs. (20 Nm).

10. Torque the brake hose fittings to 35 ft. lbs. (48 Nm).

11. Be sure to bleed the brake system.

12. Install the wheels and lug nuts. Torque the wheel lug nuts in a star pattern sequence to 95–100 ft. lbs. (129–135 Nm).

13. Lower the vehicle.

14. Before attempting to move the vehicle, pump the brake pedal to seat the pads against the rotors. Make sure the vehicle has a firm brake pedal. Check the level of the brake fluid and add DOT 3 brake fluid, if necessary.

15. Road test the vehicle and make several stops to wear off any foreign material on the brakes and to seat the brake linings, if replaced.

REAR

1. Raise and support the vehicle safely.

2. Remove the appropriate wheel and tire assemblies.

3. Remove the 2 caliper guide pin bolts and remove the caliper assembly. If the caliper is not being removed from the vehicle as during brake pad renewal, simply hang the caliper with a piece of wire to take the weight off the brake hose. If the caliper is being removed for rebuild or replacement, continue to Step 5.

4. Remove the bolt retaining the brake hose to the caliper. Be sure to plug the end of the brake hose or cover it with a plastic bag to prevent contamination from entering the hydraulic system. Remove the caliper from the vehicle.

To install:

5. Reconnect the brake hose to the caliper, if removed, using new sealing washers.

6. If new linings are being installed, the caliper pistons must be pushed back into their bore to accommodate the thickness of the new lining. Special tools are available for this, although a large C-clamp can often be used. It is good practice to remove some brake fluid from the master cylinder reservoir. This prevents overflow caused by brake fluid being forced through the lines as the piston is pushed back.

7. Install the brake pads into the caliper.

8. Install the brake caliper to the caliper adapter. Lightly lubricate machined areas that support the caliper with high-temperature grease.

9. Install and tighten the caliper guide pin bolts. Use care not to cross the threads of the caliper pin bolts. Torque the guide pin bolts to 17 ft. lbs. (22 Nm).

10. Torque the brake hose fittings to 35 ft. lbs. (48 Nm).

11. Be sure to bleed the brake system.

12. Install the wheels and lug nuts. Torque the wheel lug nuts in a star pattern sequence to 95–100 ft. lbs. (129–135 Nm).

13. Lower the vehicle.

14. Before attempting to move the vehicle, pump the brake pedal to seat the pads against the rotors. Make sure the vehicle has a firm brake pedal.

15. Check the level of the brake fluid and add DOT 3 brake fluid, if necessary.

16. Road test the vehicle and make several stops to wear off any foreign material on the brakes and to seat the brake linings, if replaced.

Dodge Stealth

FRONT OR REAR

1. Disconnect the negative battery cable.

✳✳ CAUTION

Wait at least 90 seconds after the negative battery cable is disconnected to prevent possible deployment of the air bag.

2. Raise and safely support the vehicle.

3. Remove appropriate wheel assembly.

4. Disconnect the brake hose.

5. Remove the caliper lock pins holding the caliper to the caliper support and remove the caliper.

To install:

6. Install the brake caliper on the caliper support and torque the bolts to 65 ft. lbs. (90 Nm).

7. Reconnect the brake hose and torque to 11 ft. lbs. (15 Nm).

8. Make sure the brake hose is not twisted after installation. Refill the brake fluid as required and bleed the brakes.

Chrysler Sebring
Dodge Avenger

FRONT

1. Remove about half of the brake fluid from the master cylinder.

2. Raise and safely support the vehicle and remove the wheel assembly.

3. Position a C-clamp, or other suitable tool, over the caliper. Smoothly apply pressure, forcing the caliper piston into the caliper bore until it bottoms. Remove the C-clamp, if used.

4. If the caliper is to be completely removed from the vehicle, remove the brake hose attaching bolt, disconnect the brake hose from the caliper and plug the hose to prevent fluid contamination or loss.

5. Remove the caliper mounting bolts and lift the caliper off of the support bracket.

6. Remove the caliper from the vehicle. If the caliper is only removed for access to other components, support the caliper, with

1. Pad & wear indicator assembly
2. Pad assembly
3. Clip
4. Outer shim (stainless)
5. Outer shim (coated with rubber)
6. Inner shim (stainless)
7. Inner shim (coated with rubber)

93006G02

Exploded view of the front brake pads and related components— Sebring, Avenger

the brake hose attached, so that there is no strain on the brake hose.

To install:

7. Position the caliper to the steering knuckle. Lubricate and install the mounting bolts. Torque the bolts to 54 ft. lbs. (74 Nm).

8. If removed, unplug and install the brake line hose to the caliper and torque the inlet fitting bolt to 22 ft. lbs. (29 Nm).

9. Fill the master cylinder with fresh brake fluid and, if the brake hose was removed, bleed the brake system.

10. Install the wheel assembly and lower the vehicle.

11. Depress the brake pedal 3–4 times to seat the brake linings and to restore pressure in the system.

❋❋ CAUTION

Do not move the vehicle until a firm pedal is obtained.

REAR

Unlike many rear disc brake designs, this system does not incorporate the parking brake system, into the rear brake caliper. The rear brake system is serviced the same as the front system.

1. Remove about half of the brake fluid from the master cylinder.

2. Raise and safely support the vehicle and remove the wheel assembly.

3. Position a C-clamp, or other suitable tool, over the caliper. Smoothly apply pressure, forcing the caliper piston into the caliper bore until it bottoms. Remove the C-clamp, if used.

4. If the caliper is to be completely removed from the vehicle, remove the brake hose attaching bolt, disconnect the brake hose from the caliper and plug the hose to prevent fluid contamination or loss.

5. Remove the caliper mounting bolts and lift the caliper off of the support bracket.

6. Remove the caliper from the vehicle. If the caliper is only removed for access to other components, support the caliper, with the brake hose attached, so that there is no strain on the brake hose.

To install:

7. Position the caliper on the support bracket, lubricate and install the mounting bolts. Torque the bolts to 54 ft. lbs. (74 Nm).

8. If removed, unplug and install the brake line hose to the caliper and torque the inlet fitting bolt to 22 ft. lbs. (29 Nm).

9. Fill the master cylinder with fresh brake fluid and, if the brake hose was removed, bleed the brake system.

10. Install the wheel assembly and lower the vehicle.

11. Depress the brake pedal 3–4 times to seat the brake linings and to restore pressure in the system.

❋❋ CAUTION

Do not move the vehicle until a firm pedal is obtained.

Eagle Talon

FRONT

1. Raise the vehicle and support safely.

2. Remove the appropriate tire and wheel assembly.

3. To disconnect the front brake hose, hold the nut on the brake

Caliper locking pin and guide pin description—Talon

93006G82

hose side and loosen the flared brake line nut. Remove the brake hose from the caliper.

4. Remove the caliper guide and lock pins and lift the caliper assembly from the caliper support.

To install:

5. Position caliper onto the caliper support. Install the guide pin and lock pin. Torque guide and locking pins to 54 ft. lbs. (75 Nm).

6. Reconnect the brake hose.

7. Bleed the brake system.

8. Apply brake pedal and inspect system. Ensure proper operation and no leakage.

9. Reinstall tire and wheel assembly. Torque lug nuts to 87–101 ft. lbs. (120–140 Nm).

REAR

1. Disconnect the battery negative cable.

2. Raise the vehicle and support safely.

3. Remove the appropriate tire and wheel assemblies. Loosen the parking brake cable adjustment from inside the vehicle.

4. Disconnect the parking brake cable end installed to the rear brake caliper assembly.

5. Remove the caliper lock and guide pins. Lift the caliper assembly from the caliper support.

6. Remove the rear brake hose from the caliper. Remove the caliper from the vehicle.

To install:

7. Install the rear brake hose onto the caliper with new washers in place. If equipped with brake hose retainer bolt, torque bolt to 25 ft. lbs. (35 Nm) torque. If no bolt is used, torque the brake hose fitting to 12 ft. lbs. (17 Nm).

8. Install the caliper over the brake pads. Lubricate and install the lock pin and torque to 23 ft. lbs. (32 Nm). Reinstall the guide pin and torque to 23 ft. lbs. (32 Nm).

9. Bleed the brake system.

10. Inspect the brake system for leaks and ensure proper operation.

11. Install tire and wheel assemblies. Torque wheels to 87–101 ft. lbs. (120–140 Nm).

12. Properly adjust parking brake cable.

Dodge/Plymouth Neon

1. On 1999–00 models, isolate the master cylinder as follows:

a. Use a brake pedal holding tool and depress the brake pedal past its first one inch of travel and hold it in this position. (This will keep brake fluid from draining from the master cylinder).

2. Raise and safely support the vehicle. Remove the front wheels.

3. Remove the 2 caliper guide pin bolts.

4. Disconnect the brake hose from the caliper.

5. Remove the caliper from the steering spindle.

To install:

6. Reconnect the brake hose to the caliper and torque to 35 ft. lbs. (48 Nm).

7. Reinstall the caliper to the steering spindle.

8. Reinstall the caliper guide pin bolts and torque to 16 ft. lbs. (22 Nm).

9. Properly bleed the brake system.

10. Reinstall the front wheels and lower the vehicle.

11. Pump the brake pedal to seat the front brake pads before moving the vehicle.

12. Road test the vehicle and check for proper operation.

Chrysler Cirrus, Sebring
Dodge Stratus
Plymouth Breeze

1. Raise and safely support the vehicle.

2. Remove the front wheels.

3. Remove the 2 caliper-to-steering knuckle guide pin bolts.

4. If the caliper is to be removed from the vehicle completely, for example, for overhaul perform the following procedure.

a. Disconnect the brake hose from the caliper.

b. Cover the opening of the brake hose so the hydraulic system does not become contaminated.

5. Remove the caliper from the steering knuckle.

To install:

6. Clean and lubricate both steering knuckle abutments with a coating of multipurpose grease.

7. Position the caliper and brake pad assembly over the brake rotor. Be sure to properly install the caliper assembly into the abutments of the steering knuckle. Be sure the caliper guide pin bolts, rubber bushings and sleeves are clear of the steering knuckle bosses.

8. Reinstall the caliper guide pin bolts and torque to 16 ft. lbs. (22 Nm). On Sebring and Avenger models, torque the caliper guide pin bolts to 54 ft. lbs. (74 Nm).

9. If removed, connect the brake hose to the caliper and torque to 35 ft. lbs. (48 Nm).

10. Properly bleed the brake system.

11. Reinstall the wheel and tire and torque the lug nuts in a star pattern sequence to half specification. Repeat the tightening procedure to full specified torque of 95–100 ft. lbs. (129–135 Nm).

12. Pump the brake pedal to seat the front brake pads before moving the vehicle.

13. Road test the vehicle and check for proper operation.

Disc Brake Pads

REMOVAL & INSTALLATION

Chrysler Concorde, New Yorker, LHS
Dodge Intrepid
Eagle Vision

FRONT AND REAR

1. Remove some of the fluid from the master cylinder.

2. Raise the vehicle and support safely. Remove the appropriate wheels.

3. Remove the 2 caliper guide pin bolts. Remove the caliper assembly by swinging the top part of the caliper away from the brake rotor edge, then lift the caliper assembly up.

4. Prevent strain or other damage to the brake hose by supporting the caliper assembly with a strong piece of wire hanging from the strut.

5. Remove the outboard brake pad by prying the brake pad retaining clip over raised area on the caliper. Then slide the pad down and off the caliper.

6. Before removing the inboard brake pad, use a large C-clamp to press the piston back into the caliper. This will prevent possible damage to the caliper piston. It is good practice to remove some (⅓–½) of the brake fluid from the reservoir. This is because as the caliper piston is pushed back into the caliper, brake fluid will be pushed back through the lines, back into the master cylinder and fluid reservoir, possibly causing the reservoir to overflow.

7. Remove the inboard brake pad by pulling away from piston until the retainer clip is free from the cavity in the piston.

To install:

8. Lubricate both the caliper mating surface and the machined abutment surfaces with multi-purpose lubricant.

9. Before brake pad installation, be sure to lightly coat the outer backing plate surface of the new brake pads with a disc brake pad anti-squeal lubricant, usually a gel-like material that deadens any high-frequency vibration that can be the source of disc brake squeal.

10. Install brake pads into the caliper assembly making sure both pads are seated securely onto the caliper.

11. Install the caliper assembly back into position over the brake rotor and install the caliper guide pin bolts. Torque the front and rear caliper guide pin bolts to 17 ft. lbs. (23 Nm).

12. Install the wheels and lug nuts. Torque the lug nuts, in a star pattern sequence, to 95–100 ft. lbs. (129–135 Nm).

13. Lower the vehicle.

14. Top off the master cylinder to the appropriate level, using Dot 3 type brake fluid only.

15. Before moving the vehicle, pump the brakes until a firm pedal is obtained. Road test the vehicle to make sure the brake operation is normal.

Dodge Stealth

FRONT AND REAR

1. Remove approximately ⅓ of the brake fluid from the master cylinder to prevent overflow of the fluid when the caliper pistons are compressed.

2. Disconnect the negative battery cable.

1. Clip
2. Pad pin
3. Cross spring
4. Pad assembly
5. Shim A
6. Shim B
7. Inner pad
   (with wear indicator)

93006G03

Front disc brake pads—all wheel drive Stealth

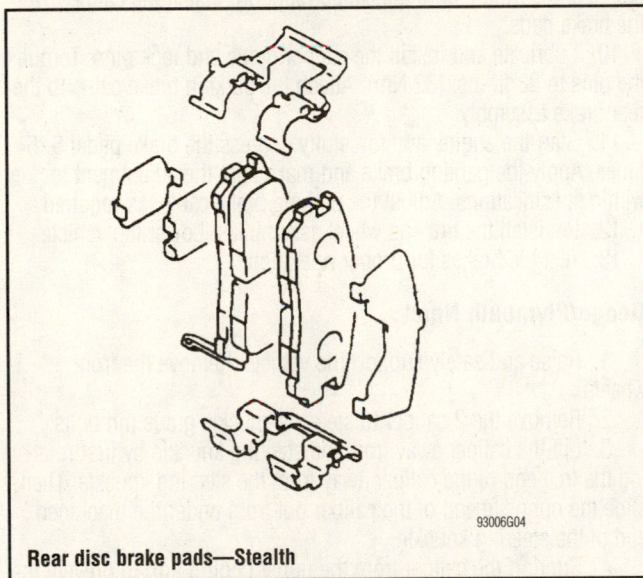

93006G04

Rear disc brake pads—Stealth

✻✻ CAUTION

Wait at least 90 seconds after the negative (–) battery cable is disconnected to prevent possible deployment of the air bag.

3. Raise the vehicle and support it safely.
4. Remove the appropriate wheel assembly.
5. On the front of All Wheel Drive (AWD) vehicles, remove the pad retaining pins and pull the pads out of the caliper body.
6. On others, remove the lock pin and swing the caliper upward and support it with a wire. Take note of the clips, pins, anti-squeal shims and other parts for reference at assembly.

To install:

7. Use a large C-clamp to compress the piston(s) back into the caliper bore.
8. Install the pads and all other small parts.
9. On AWD front disc brakes, apply a small amount of multipurpose grease to the inner pad shims.

10. Reinstall the caliper to the caliper support. Make sure the brake hose is not twisted after installation if both guide pins were removed.
11. Reinstall the tire and wheel assembly and torque to 87–101 ft. lbs. (120–140 Nm).
12. Reconnect the negative battery cable.
13. Refill the master cylinder if needed and pump the brake pedal until firm before putting transaxle in gear or moving vehicle.

Chrysler Sebring
Dodge Avenger

FRONT

1. Remove some of the brake fluid from the master cylinder reservoir. The reservoir should be no more than ½ full. When the pistons are depressed into the calipers, excess fluid will flow up into the reservoir.
2. Raise and safely support the vehicle.
3. Remove the appropriate tire and wheel assemblies.
4. Remove the caliper guide and lock pins and lift the caliper assembly from the caliper support. Tie the caliper out of the way using wire. Do not allow the caliper to hang by the brake line.

➡ **On some models the caliper can be flipped up by leaving the upper pin in place, using it as a pivot point.**

5. Remove the brake pads, spring clip and shims. Take note of positioning to aid installation.
6. Install the wheel lug nuts onto the studs and lightly tighten. This is done to hold the disc on the hub.

To install:

7. Use a large C-clamp to compress the piston(s) back into the caliper bore.
8. Lubricate the slide points and install the brake pads, shims and spring clip onto the caliper support. Install the caliper over the brake pads.
9. Lubricate and install the caliper guide and lock pins in their original positions. Torque guide and locking pins to 54 ft. lbs. (74 Nm).
10. Install the tire and wheel assemblies. Lower the vehicle.

✻✻ CAUTION

Pump brake pedal several times, until firm, before attempting to move the vehicle.

11. Road test the vehicle and check brakes for proper operation.

REAR

Unlike many rear disc brake designs, this system does not incorporate the parking brake system, into the rear brake caliper, therefore, the rear brake system is serviced the same as the front system.

1. Remove some of the brake fluid from the master cylinder reservoir. The reservoir should be no more than ½ full. When the pistons are depressed into the calipers, excess fluid will flow up into the reservoir.
2. Raise and safely support the vehicle.
3. Remove the appropriate tire and wheel assemblies.
4. Remove the caliper guide and lock pins and lift the caliper assembly from the caliper support. Tie the caliper out of the way using wire. Do not allow the caliper to hang by the brake hose.

➡️**On some models, the caliper can be flipped up by leaving the upper pin in place, using it as a pivot point.**

5. Remove the brake pads, spring clip and shims. Take note of positioning to aid installation.

6. Install the wheel lug nuts onto the studs and lightly tighten. This is done to hold the brake disc on the hub.

To install:

7. Use a large C-clamp to compress the piston(s) back into the caliper bore.

8. Lubricate the slide points and install the brake pads, shims and spring clip onto the caliper support. Install the caliper over the brake pads.

9. Lubricate and install the caliper guide and lock pins in their original positions. Torque guide and locking pins to 54 ft. lbs. (74 Nm).

10. Install the tire and wheel assemblies. Lower the vehicle.

❈ CAUTION

Pump brake pedal several times, until firm, before attempting to move the vehicle.

11. Road test the vehicle and check brakes for proper operation.

Eagle Talon

FRONT

1. Remove some of the brake fluid from the master cylinder reservoir. The reservoir should be no more than half full. When the pistons are pressed into the calipers, excess fluid will flow up into the reservoir.

2. Raise the vehicle and support safely.

3. Remove the appropriate tire and wheel assemblies.

4. Remove the caliper guide and lock pins and lift the caliper assembly from the caliper support. Tie the caliper out of the way using wire. Do not allow the caliper to hang by the brake line.

➡️**On some vehicles, the caliper can be flipped up by leaving the upper pin in place and using it as a pivot point.**

5. Remove the brake pads, spring clip and shims. Take note of positioning to aid installation.

6. Install the wheel lug nuts onto the studs and lightly tighten. This is done to hold the disc on the hub.

To install:

7. Use a large C-clamp to compress piston(s) back into caliper bore. On 2 piston calipers both pistons will have to be retracted together.

8. Lubricate slide points and install the brake pads, shims and spring clip onto the caliper support. Install the caliper over the brake pads.

9. Lubricate and install the caliper guide and lock pins in their original positions. Torque guide and locking pins to 54 ft. lbs. (75 Nm).

10. Reinstall the tire and wheel assemblies. Lower the vehicle.

➡️**Pump brake pedal several times, until firm, before attempting to move vehicle.**

11. Road test the vehicle and check brakes for proper operation.

REAR

1. Remove some of the brake fluid from the master cylinder reservoir. The reservoir should be no more than half full. When the pistons are depressed into the calipers, excess fluid will flow up into the reservoir.

2. Raise the vehicle and support safely.

3. Remove the appropriate tire and wheel assemblies. Loosen the parking brake cable adjustment from inside the vehicle.

4. Disconnect the parking brake cable end installed to the rear brake caliper assembly.

5. Remove the caliper lock and guide pins and lift the caliper assembly from the caliper support. Tie the caliper out of the way using wire. Do not allow the caliper to hang by the brake line.

6. Remove the outer shim, brake pads and spring clips from the caliper support. Take note of positioning of each to aid in installation.

7. Reinstall the wheel lug nuts onto the studs and lightly tighten. This is done to hold the disc on the hub.

8. Clean the caliper piston. Using rear disc brake driver tool MB990652, or equivalent, thread the piston into the caliper bore. Be sure, at this point, that the stopper groove of the piston correctly fits into the projection on the replacement brake pads rear surface.

To install:

9. Lubricate all sliding and pivot points. Install the brake pads, shims and spring clip to the caliper support. Install the caliper over the brake pads.

10. Lubricate and install the caliper guide and lock pins. Torque the pins to 23 ft. lbs. (32 Nm). Attach the parking brake cable to the rear brake assembly.

11. Start the engine and forcefully depress the brake pedal 5–6 times. Apply the parking brake and make sure the adjustment is within specifications. Adjust the parking brake cable, as required.

12. Reinstall the tire and wheel assemblies. Lower the vehicle.

13. Test the brakes for proper operation.

Dodge/Plymouth Neon

1. Raise and safely support the vehicle. Remove the front wheels.

2. Remove the 2 caliper to steering knuckle guide pin bolts.

3. Lift the caliper away from the steering knuckle by first rotating the free end of the caliper away from the steering knuckle. Then, slide the opposite end of the caliper out from under the machined end of the steering knuckle.

4. Support the caliper from the upper control arm to prevent the weight of the caliper from being supported by the brake flex hose that will damage the hose.

5. Remove the brake pads from the caliper. Remove the outboard brake pad by prying the pad retaining clip over the raised area on the caliper. Then, slide the pad down and off the caliper. Pull the inboard brake pad away from the piston until the retaining clip is free from the cavity in the piston.

6. If required, the rotor can be removed by pulling it straight off the wheel mounting studs.

To install:

7. Clean all parts well. Inspect the caliper for piston seal leaks (brake fluid in and around the boot area and inboard lining) and for any ruptures of the piston dust boot. If the boot is damaged or fluid leak is visible, disassemble the caliper and install a new seal and boot (and piston, if scored).

8. Inspect the caliper pin bushings. Replace if damaged, dry or brittle.

9. Completely compress the piston into the caliper using a large C-clamp or other suitable tool.

10. Lubricate the area on the steering knuckle where the caliper slides with high temperature grease.

Disc brake pad identification—Neon

Disc brake pad identification—Cirrus, Sebring, Stratus, Breeze

11. Reinstall the rotor if removed.

12. Reinstall the brake pads into the caliper. Note that the inboard and outboard pads are different. Make sure the inboard brake shoe assembly is positioned squarely against the face of the caliper piston.

➡ **Be sure to remove the noise suppression gasket paper cover if the pads come so equipped.**

13. Carefully position the caliper and brake shoe assemblies over the rotor by hooking the lower end of the caliper over the steering knuckle. Then, rotate the caliper into position at the top of the steering knuckle. Make sure the caliper guide pin bolts, bushings and sleeves are clear of the steering knuckle bosses.

14. Reinstall the caliper guide pin bolts and torque to 16 ft. lbs. (22 Nm).

15. Reinstall the wheels and torque the mounting bolts to 100 ft. lbs. (135 Nm).

16. Lower the vehicle.

17. Pump the brake pedal until the brake pads are seated and a firm pedal is achieved before attempting to move the vehicle.

18. Road test the vehicle for proper operation.

Chrysler Cirrus, Sebring
Dodge Stratus
Plymouth Breeze

1. Raise and safely support the vehicle.
2. Remove the front wheels.
3. Remove the 2 caliper-to-steering knuckle guide pin bolts.
4. Lift the caliper away from the steering knuckle by first rotating the free end of the caliper away from the steering knuckle. Then slide the opposite end of the caliper out from under the machined end of the steering knuckle.
5. Support the caliper from the upper control arm to prevent the weight of the caliper from being supported by the brake flex hose which will damage the hose.
6. Remove the brake pads from the caliper. Remove the outboard brake pad by prying the pad retaining clip over the raised area on the caliper. Then slide the pad down and off the caliper. Pull the inboard brake pad away from the piston until the retaining clip is free from the cavity in the piston.

To install:

7. Completely depress the piston into the caliper using a large C-clamp or other suitable tool.

8. Lubricate the area on the steering knuckle where the caliper slides with high temperature grease.

9. Install the new inboard brake pad into the caliper piston by firmly pressing into the piston bore. Install the brake pads into the caliper. Note that the inboard and outboard pads are different. Make sure the inboard brake pad assembly is positioned squarely against the face of the caliper piston.

➡ **Be sure to remove the noise suppression gasket paper cover if the pads come so equipped.**

10. Install the new outboard brake pad onto the caliper assembly.

11. Carefully position the caliper and brake pad assemblies over the rotor by hooking the lower end of the caliper over the steering knuckle. Then rotate the caliper into position at the top of the steering knuckle. Make sure the caliper guide pin bolts, bushings and sleeves are clear of the steering knuckle bosses.

12. Reinstall the caliper guide pin bolts and torque to 16 ft. lbs. (22 Nm). On Sebring and Avenger models, torque the caliper guide pin bolts to 54 ft. lbs. (74 Nm).

13. Reinstall the wheel and tire. Torque the lug nuts in 2 steps, in a star pattern sequence to 95–100 ft. lbs. (129–135 Nm).

14. Lower the vehicle.

15. Pump the brake pedal until the brake pads are seated and a firm pedal is achieved before attempting to move the vehicle.

16. Road test the vehicle to check for proper operation.

Brake Drums

REMOVAL & INSTALLATION

Chrysler Concorde, New Yorker, LHS
Dodge Intrepid
Eagle Vision

1. Raise the vehicle and support safely.
2. Remove the rear wheels.
3. Remove the brake drum from the rear hub and bearing

For brake related suspension and axle service, refer to the model specific sections of this manual

assembly. If the drum is difficult to remove, increase the clearance between the brake shoes and the drum as follows:

  a. Remove the rubber plug from the top of the brake support plate.

  b. Rotate the automatic shoe adjuster screw with an upward motion using a medium size flat tipped tool.

4. Remove the brake drum from the rear hub and bearing.

5. Inspect the brake shoe linings and drums for wear, contamination and scoring.

To install:

6. Install the rear brake drum onto the rear hub and bearing assembly.

7. Adjust the brake shoes as follows:

  a. Rotate the automatic shoe adjuster in a downward motion using a medium size flat tip tool. Turn the adjuster until there is a slight drag felt while turning the drum.

  b. Install the rubber plug back into the top part of the brake support plate.

8. Install the rear wheels and lug nuts. Torque the lug nuts in a star pattern sequence to 95–100 ft. lbs. (129–135 Nm).

Chrysler Sebring
Dodge Avenger

1. Raise and safely support the vehicle.

2. Remove the wheel assembly.

3. Remove the brake drum detent (retaining) screw and remove the drum from the axle.

4. If difficulty is encountered in removing the drum:

  a. Verify the parking brake is released.

  b. Loosen the parking brake cable.

  c. Remove the access hole plug from the backing plate and move the parking brake lever until the lever stop rests on the brake shoe.

  d. If necessary, turn the adjuster so that it draws in to allow more clearance between the shoe and drum.

To install:

5. Inspect all parts. Check the drum for cracks or excessive wear.

6. Turn the adjuster until it is drawn all the way in to the stop. Check that the adjuster turns freely. The nut must NOT lock at the end of the adjuster. Check that the parking brake lever stops are against the edge of the shoe web.

7. Install the brake drum and detent screw.

8. Install the wheel assembly, then lower the vehicle.

9. Apply the foot brake at least 10 times until clicking of the adjustment actuator can no longer be heard. This procedure will automatically adjust the clearance between the shoe and drum.

Dodge/Plymouth Neon

1. Raise and safely support the vehicle. Remove the rear wheels.

  a. Locate and remove the rubber plug from the top of the brake support plate (backing plate).

  b. Insert a small prying tool through the adjuster access hole and engage the teeth on the adjuster wheel.

  c. Rotate the adjuster wheel so it is moved toward the front of the vehicle. This will back off the adjustment of the rear brake shoes.

  d. Continue moving the adjuster wheel toward the front of the vehicle until it stops moving.

2. Remove the rear brake drum from the hub assembly.

To install:

3. Inspect the brake drums for cracks or signs of overheating. Measure the drum runout and diameter. If not to specification, resurface the drum. Runout should not exceed 0.006 inch (0.152mm). The diameter variation (oval shape) of the drum braking surface must not exceed either 0.0025 inch (0.0635mm) in 30° or 0.0035 inch (0.089mm) in 360°. All brake drums are marked with the maximum allowable brake drum diameter on the face of the drum.

4. Install the rear brake drum onto the hub assembly.

5. Reinstall the wheels and properly adjust the brakes. Lower the vehicle.

6. Road test vehicle to check brake operation.

Chrysler Cirrus, Sebring
Dodge Stratus
Plymouth Breeze

All vehicles except Sebring Convertible, are equipped with rear wheel, 2-shoe leading/trailing, internal expanding type of drum brakes with automatic self-adjuster mechanisms. The automatic self-adjuster mechanisms used on these vehicles are new designs and function differently than the screw type adjusters used in the past. These new self-adjusters are still actuated each time the vehicle's service brakes are applied. The new adjusters are located directly below the wheel cylinders.

The Sebring Convertible's rear wheel drum brake is a 2-shoe leading/trailing internal expanding type with an automatic self-adjuster mechanism. The automatic self-adjuster mechanism used on this vehicle is the screw type adjuster. The self-adjuster mechanism is actuated each time the vehicle service brakes are applied. Generally, drum brakes with a self-adjusting mechanism do not require manual brake shoe adjustment. Although, in the event that the brake shoes are replaced, it is advisable to make the initial adjustment manually to speed up the initial adjustment time. The initial adjustment procedure must be done prior to driving the vehicle.

1. Raise and safely support the vehicle.

2. Remove the rear wheel assembly.

3. For all vehicles, except Sebring Convertible, use the following procedure:

  a. Locate and remove the rubber plug from the brake support plate (backing plate).

  b. Insert a brake adjuster tool or similarly shaped prytool through the automatic adjuster access hole and engage the teeth on the adjuster wheel. Rotate the adjuster wheel so it is moved

Automatic self-adjuster mechanism—Cirrus, Sebring Coupe, Stratus, Breeze

LUBRICATE THIS SURFACE BETWEEN QUADRANT AND STRUT OF ADJUSTER MECHANISM

KNURLED PIN

AUTOMATIC SELF ADJUSTER MECHANISM

STRUT

SPRING

QUADRANT

93006G07

Rear brake shoe automatic self-adjuster mechanism and actuating lever—Sebring Convertible

Kelsey Hayes rear brake assembly—Sebring Convertible

toward the front of the vehicle. Continue moving the adjuster until it stops; this will back off the adjustment of the rear brake shoes.

4. For the Sebring Convertible, use the following procedure for releasing the self-adjusting mechanism:

   a. Locate and remove the rubber plug from the brake support plate (backing plate).

   b. Insert a brake adjuster tool or similarly shaped prytool through the automatic adjuster access hole and carefully push the adjuster actuating lever out of engagement with the adjuster starwheel. While holding the lever away from the starwheel, insert a second prytool through the access hole and engage the teeth on the adjuster wheel. Rotate the adjuster wheel upward away from the ground; this will back off the adjustment of the rear brake shoes.

5. Remove the rear brake drum from the hub assembly.

To install:

6. Inspect the brake drums for cracks or signs of overheating. Measure the drum run-out and diameter. If not to specification, resurface the drum. Run-out should not exceed 0.006 in. (0.15mm). The diameter variation (oval shape) of the drum braking surface must not exceed either 0.0025 in. (0.064mm) in 30 degrees rotation, or 0.0035 in. (0.089mm) in 360 degrees rotation. All brake drums are marked with the maximum allowable brake drum diameter on the face of the drum.

7. Install the rear brake drum onto the hub assembly.

8. Reinstall the wheel and tire. Torque the lug nuts in a star pattern sequence to about 45 ft. lbs. (61 Nm); then, repeat the pattern and final torque to 95–100 ft. lbs. (129–135 Nm).

9. Properly adjust the rear brakes.
10. Lower the vehicle.
11. Road test vehicle to check for proper brake operation.

Brake Shoes

REMOVAL & INSTALLATION

Chrysler Concorde, New Yorker, LHS
Dodge Intrepid
Eagle Vision

1. Raise the vehicle and support safely.
2. Remove the rear wheels and brake drums.
3. Remove the dust cap from the rear hub and bearing assembly.
4. Remove the cotter pin, nut retainer and wave washer. Discard the old cotter pin.
5. Remove the rear hub and bearing assembly retainer nut and washer. Remove the rear hub and bearing assembly from the spindle.
6. Remove the automatic adjuster spring from the adjuster lever.
7. Rotate the automatic adjuster starwheel enough so both shoes move out far enough to be free of the wheel cylinder boots.
8. Disconnect the parking brake cable from the actuating lever. Disconnect parking brake cable one side at a time.
9. Remove the both lower brake shoe to anchor springs.
10. Remove the 2 brake shoe hold-down springs from the brake shoes.
11. Remove the brake shoes, upper shoe-to-shoe return spring, automatic adjuster and automatic adjuster lever from the backing plate as an assembly.
12. Separate the brake shoes from the automatic adjuster mechanism.
13. Remove the brake shoe automatic adjuster lever from the leading brake shoe.

To install:

14. Thoroughly clean and dry the backing plate. To prepare the backing plate, lubricate the bosses, anchor pin and parking brake actuating lever pivot surface lightly with lithium based grease.
15. Remove, clean and dry all parts still on the old shoes. Lubricate the starwheel shaft threads with anti-seize lubricant.
16. Assemble both brake shoes, the top shoe to shoe return spring, automatic adjuster and automatic adjuster lever before mounting on vehicle. Make sure the ends of the automatic adjusters are positioned above the extruded pins in the webbing of the brake shoes prior to installation.
17. Install the brake shoe assembly onto the brake support plate and install the hold-down springs.
18. Install the lower anchor springs and reconnect the parking brake cable to the park brake lever of the trailing brake shoe.
19. Rotate the serrated adjuster nut to remove the free-play from the adjuster assembly.
20. Install the automatic adjuster lever spring on the lead brake shoe assembly and the automatic adjuster lever.
21. Install the rear hub and bearing assembly. Install washer and retainer nut and torque to 124 ft. lbs. (168 Nm).
22. Install the wave washer, nut retainer and a new cotter pin onto the spindle. Install dust cap.

23. Adjust brake shoes so not to interfere with brake drum installation. Install the rear brake drum.

➡**After installing the brake drums, pump the brake pedal several times to partially adjust the brake shoes. To verify proper operation of the self-adjusting parking brake, be sure that both rear brakes are not dragging when the parking brake pedal is released.**

24. Install the rear wheels and lug nuts. Torque the lug nuts, in a star pattern sequence, to 95 ft. lbs. (129 Nm).

25. Road test the vehicle. The automatic adjusters will continue brake adjustment during the road test of the vehicle.

Chrysler Sebring
Dodge Avenger

1. Raise and safely support the vehicle and remove the wheel assembly.

2. Remove the detent screw and brake drum. If difficulty is encountered in removing the drum:
   a. Verify the parking brake is released.
   b. Loosen the parking brake cable.
   c. Remove the access hole plug from the backing plate and move the parking brake lever until the lever stop rests on the brake shoe.
   d. If necessary, turn the adjuster so that it draws in to allow more clearance between the shoe and drum.

➡**Note the location of all springs and clips for proper reassembly.**

Opening the retainer clip—Sebring, Avenger

3. Remove the shoe-to-lever spring and remove the adjuster lever.

4. Remove the auto adjuster assembly.

5. Remove the retainer spring.

6. Remove the hold-down springs, washers and pins.

7. Remove the shoe-to-shoe spring.

8. Remove the brake shoes from the backing plate.

9. Using a flat-tipped tool, open up the parking brake lever retaining clip. Remove the clip and washer from the pin on the shoe assembly and remove the shoe from the lever assembly.

1. Brake drum
2. Shoe-to-lever spring
3. Adjuster lever
4. Auto adjuster assembly
5. Retainer spring
6. Shoe hold-down cup
7. Shoe hold-down spring
8. Shoe hold-down cup
9. Shoe-to-shoe spring
10. Shoe and lining assembly
11. Shoe and lever assembly

12. Retainer
13. Wave washer
14. Parking lever
15. Shoe and lining assembly
16. Shoe hold-down pin
17. Brake pipe connection
18. Wheel cylinder
19. Bleeder screw
20. Snap ring
21. Rear hub assembly
22. Backing plate

Exploded view of the drum brake assembly—Sebring, Avenger

Adjusting nut and nut holder—Sebring, Avenger

To install:

10. Thoroughly clean and dry the backing plate. Lubricate the backing plate at the brake shoe contact points.

11. Lubricate backing plate bosses, anchor pin, and parking brake actuating mechanism with a lithium-based grease.

12. Install the parking brake lever assembly on the lever pin. Install the wave washer and a new retaining clip. Use pliers or the like to install the retainer on the pin. If removed, connect the parking brake lever to the parking brake cable and verify that the cable is properly routed.

13. Clean and lubricate the adjuster assembly. Make sure the nut-adjuster is drawn all the way to the stop, but the nut must NOT lock firmly at the end of the assembly.

14. Install the brake shoes on the backing plate with the hold-down springs, washers and pins.

15. Install the shoe-to-shoe spring.

16. Install the retainer spring.

17. Install the auto adjuster assembly and install the adjuster lever and the shoe-to-lever spring.

18. Pre-adjust the shoes so the drum slides on with a light drag and install the brake drum.

19. Adjust the rear brake shoes and install the rear wheels.

20. Adjust the parking brake cable.

21. Lower the vehicle and check for proper brake operation.

Dodge/Plymouth Neon

1. Raise and safely support the vehicle. Remove the rear wheels.

Kelsey Hayes rear brake assembly (left side shown)—Neon

2. Remove the drums.

3. Remove the automatic adjuster spring and lever.

4. Remove the hold-down clips and pins.

5. Rotate the automatic adjuster starwheel enough so both shoes move out far enough to be free of the wheel cylinder boots.

6. Disconnect the parking brake cable from the actuating lever.

7. Remove the lower shoe to shoe spring.

8. With the shoes held together by the upper shoe to shoe spring, remove them from the backing plate.

To install:

9. Thoroughly clean and dry the backing plate. To prepare the backing plate, lubricate the bosses, anchor pin and parking brake actuating lever pivot surface lightly with lithium based grease.

10. Remove, clean and dry all brake components. Lubricate the starwheel shaft threads with anti-seize lubricant and transfer all parts to their proper locations on the new shoes.

11. Reinstall the lower spring.

12. Reconnect the parking brake cable.

13. Reinstall the automatic adjuster lever and spring.

14. Adjust the starwheel.

15. Remove any grease from the linings and install the drum.

16. Reinstall the wheels and properly adjust the brakes. Lower the vehicle.

17. Check for proper brake system operation.

Chrysler Cirrus, Sebring Coupe
Dodge Stratus
Plymouth Breeze

All vehicles except Sebring Convertible, are equipped with rear wheel, 2 shoe leading/trailing, internal expanding type of drum brakes with automatic self-adjuster mechanisms. The automatic self-adjuster mechanisms used on these vehicles are new designs and function differently than the screw type adjusters used in the past. These new self-adjusters are still actuated each time the vehicles' service brakes are applied. The new adjusters are located directly below the wheel cylinders.

1. Raise and safely support the vehicle.

2. Remove the rear wheel assembly.

Varga rear wheel brake assembly (left side shown)—Cirrus, Sebring Coupe, Stratus, Breeze

a. Locate and remove the rubber plug from the top of the brake support plate (backing plate).

b. Insert a brake adjuster tool or similarly shaped prytool through the automatic adjuster access hole and engage the teeth on the adjuster quadrant. Then rotate the quadrant so the teeth of the quadrant are moved toward the front of the vehicle. This will back off the adjustment of the rear brake shoes.

c. Continue moving the quadrant toward the front of the vehicle until it stops moving.

3. Remove the drum from the hub assembly.

4. Remove the actuating spring from the adjuster mechanism and trailing brake shoe.

5. Remove the upper return spring from the brake shoes.

6. Remove the lower return spring from the brake shoes.

7. Remove the brake shoe retainer and pin attaching the leading brake shoe assembly to the brake support plate.

8. Remove the leading brake shoe and the adjuster mechanism as an assembly from the rear brake support plate. The adjuster mechanism cannot be separated from the leading brake shoe until the brake shoe and the adjuster mechanism is removed from the support plate.

9. Remove the trailing brake shoe retainer and pin attaching the trailing brake shoe assembly to the brake support plate. Remove the trailing brake shoe assembly.

➡ **On this vehicle, the parking brake actuating lever is permanently attached to the trailing brake shoe assembly. Do not attempt to remove it from the original brake shoe assembly or reuse the original actuating lever on a replacement brake shoe assembly. All replacement brake shoe assemblies for this vehicle must have the actuating lever as part of the trailing brake shoe assembly.**

10. Remove the parking brake cable from the parking brake lever. Do not remove the lever from the brake shoe.

11. Remove the automatic adjuster mechanism from the brake shoe by fully extending the adjuster and rotate the adjuster out to release from the brake shoe.

To inspect:

12. Thoroughly clean all parts. The brake lining should show contact across the entire width and from heel to toe; otherwise, replace. Clean and inspect the brake support plate and the automatic adjuster mechanism. Be sure the quadrant (toothed part) of the adjuster is free to rotate throughout its entire tooth contact range and is free to slide the full length of its mounting slot. Check the knurled pin. It should be securely attached to the adjuster mechanism and its teeth should be in good condition. If the adjuster is worn or damaged, replace it. If the adjuster is serviceable, lubricate lightly with high-temperature grease between the strut and the quadrant. Check the brake springs. Overheating indications are paint discoloration or distorted end coils. Replace parts as required.

13. Inspect the brake drums for cracks or signs of overheating. Measure the drum run-out and diameter. If not to specification, reface the drum. Run-out should not exceed 0.006 in. (0.15mm). The diameter variation (oval shape) of the drum braking surface must not exceed either 0.0025 in. (0.064mm) in 30 degrees rotation, or 0.0035 in. (0.089mm) in 360 degrees rotation. All brake drums are marked with the maximum allowable brake drum diameter on the face of the drum.

To install:

14. Lubricate the 8 brake shoe contact points with high-temperature grease.

➡ **The trailing brake shoe assemblies used on the rear brakes of this vehicle are unique to the left and right side of the vehicle. Care must be taken to ensure the brake shoes are properly installed in their correct side of the vehicle. When the trailing shoes are properly installed on their correct side of the vehicle, the park brake actuating lever will be positioned under the brake shoe web.**

15. Reinstall the parking brake cable onto the parking brake lever and install the trailing brake shoe and attaching pin.

16. Reinstall the automatic self-adjuster on the leading brake shoe by rotating it inward to attach. Install the leading shoe and adjuster assembly to the brake support plate.

17. Make sure the leading brake shoe is squarely seated on the brake support plate shoe contact areas, and install the brake retainer on the retainer pin.

18. Reinstall the lower return spring.

➡ **The upper brake shoe return spring and adjuster mechanism actuating spring are unique to the side of the vehicle they are used on. The springs are colored for identification. The left side springs are green and the right side springs are blue.**

19. Reinstall the upper return spring (blue, right side; green, left side) on the leading brake shoe first, then on the trailing brake shoe.

20. Reinstall the self-adjuster spring on the trailing brake shoe first then attach it to the adjuster.

21. Reinstall the rear brake drums.

22. Reinstall the wheel and tire. Torque the lug nuts in a star pattern sequence to about 45 ft. lbs. (61 Nm), then repeat the pattern and final torque to 95–100 ft. lbs. (129–135 Nm).

23. Lower the vehicle.

24. Adjust the rear brakes by depressing the brake pedal. Brake shoe adjustment will occur the first time the brake pedal is depressed, pushing the rear brake shoes against the braking surface of the rear brake drums. Brake shoes should now be correctly adjusted and will not require any type of manual adjustment.

25. Road test vehicle to check for proper brake operation.

Sebring Convertible

The Sebring Convertible's rear wheel drum brake is a 2-shoe leading/trailing internal expanding type with an automatic self-adjuster mechanism. The automatic self-adjuster mechanism used on this vehicle is the screw type adjuster. The self-adjuster mechanism is actuated each time the vehicle service brakes are applied. Generally, drum brakes with a self-adjusting mechanism do not require manual brake shoe adjustment. Although, in the event that the brake shoes are replaced, it is advisable to make the initial adjustment manually to speed up the initial adjustment time. The initial adjustment procedure must be done prior to driving the vehicle.

➡ **When removing the rear brake shoes, replace the brake shoes from only one side of the vehicle at a time. This is due to the automatic adjustment feature of the parking brake system. If the brake shoes are removed from both sides of the vehicle at the same time, the automatic adjuster will remove all slack from the parking brake cables, which will make brake shoe installation extremely difficult.**

1. Raise and safely support the vehicle.
2. Remove the rear wheel assembly.

a. Locate and remove the rubber plug from the brake support plate (backing plate).

b. Insert a brake adjuster tool or similarly shaped prytool through the automatic adjuster access hole and carefully push the adjuster actuating lever out of engagement with the adjuster starwheel. While holding the lever away from the starwheel, insert a second prytool through the access hole and engage the teeth on the adjuster wheel. Rotate the adjuster wheel upward away from the ground. This will back off the adjustment of the rear brake shoes.

3. Remove the drum from the hub assembly.

4. Remove the adjusting lever actuating spring from the leading brake shoe. Remove the automatic adjuster actuating lever from the leading brake shoe.

5. Thread the adjuster starwheel all the way into the adjuster, which will remove all tension from the adjuster.

6. Remove the upper and lower return springs from the brake shoes.

7. Remove the brake shoe hold-down spring and pin attaching the leading brake shoe assembly to the brake support plate.

8. Remove the leading brake shoe from the support plate.

9. Remove the automatic adjuster from the parking brake actuating lever and trailing brake shoe.

10. Remove the retaining clip securing the parking brake actuating lever to the trailing brake shoe.

11. Remove the trailing brake shoe hold-down spring and pin attaching the trailing brake shoe assembly to the brake support plate.

12. Remove the trailing brake shoe from the brake support plate and separate the shoe from the parking brake actuating lever.

To inspect:

13. Clean all parts well. The brake lining should show contact across the entire width and from heel to toe; otherwise, replace. Clean and inspect the brake support plate and the automatic adjuster mechanism. Be sure the adjuster is free to rotate throughout its entire range. If the adjuster is worn or damaged, replace it. If the adjuster is serviceable, lightly lubricate the threaded portion with high-temperature grease. Check the brake springs. Overheating indications are paint discoloration or distorted end coils. Replace parts as required.

14. Inspect the brake drums for cracks or signs of overheating. Measure the drum run-out and diameter. If not to specification, reface the drum. Run-out should not exceed 0.006 in. (0.15mm). The diameter variation (oval shape) of the drum braking surface must not exceed either 0.0025 in. (0.064mm) in 30° rotation, or 0.0035 in. (0.089mm) in 360° rotation. All brake drums are marked with the maximum allowable brake drum diameter on the face of the drum.

To install:

15. Lubricate the 6 brake shoe contact points and the brake shoe anchor points with high-temperature grease.

16. Reinstall the wave washer on the pivot pin of the parking brake actuating lever.

17. Install the trailing brake shoe onto the attaching pin of the parking brake actuating lever.

18. Position the trailing brake shoe onto the brake support plate and be sure the trailing brake shoe is squarely seated on the support plate shoe contact areas and install the brake shoe hold-down spring on the hold-down pin.

19. Reinstall the parking brake actuating lever-to-trailing brake shoe retaining clip.

20. Reinstall the automatic adjuster on the trailing brake shoe and the parking brake actuating lever.

21. Place the leading brake shoe onto the brake support plate in proper position and install the attaching pin and hold-down spring.

22. Reinstall the lower and upper return springs.

23. Reinstall the automatic adjuster actuating lever and spring onto the leading brake shoe.

24. Manually adjust the brake shoes to the furthest adjusted position but not so far as to interfere with the installation of the brake drum.

25. Reinstall the rear brake drums. Check and adjust the brake shoes as necessary.

26. Reinstall the wheel and tire. Torque the lug nuts in a star pattern sequence to about 45 ft. lbs. (61 Nm), then repeat the pattern and final torque to 100 ft. lbs. (135 Nm).

27. Lower the vehicle.

28. Road test vehicle to check for proper brake operation.

FORD MOTOR COMPANY

Brake Caliper

REMOVAL & INSTALLATION

Ford Aspire

1. Raise and safely support the vehicle.
2. Remove the wheel and tire assembly.
3. Remove the brake pads.
4. Remove the banjo bolt securing the brake hose to the caliper and plug the hose end. Discard the 2 copper sealing washers.
5. Remove the 2 caliper retaining bolts.
6. Remove the caliper and the anti-squeak caps from the vehicle.

To install:

7. Install the anti-squeak caps.
8. Position the caliper on the steering knuckle and install the 2 caliper retaining bolts. Torque the caliper retaining bolts to 29–36 ft. lbs. (39–49 Nm).

9. Connect the brake hose to the caliper using the banjo bolt and 2 new copper sealing washers. Torque the banjo bolt to 16–22 ft. lbs. (22–29 Nm).

10. Install the brake pads.
11. Bleed the brake system.
12. Install the wheel and tire assembly.
13. Lower the vehicle.
14. Apply the brake pedal several times to position the brake pads, before attempting to move the vehicle.
15. Check for proper brake operation.

Ford Probe

FRONT

1. Raise and safely support the vehicle.
2. Remove the wheel.

For brake related suspension and axle service, refer to the model specific sections of this manual

1	**Anti-Rattle Spring**
2	**Front Disc Plate Caliper**
	Anchor Plate Bolt (2 Req'd)
3	**Front Disc Brake Rotor**
4	**Shims**
5	**Brake Shoe and Lining**
6	**Front Disc Brake Caliper**
	Anchor Plate
7	**Clips**

8	**Front Disc Brake Caliper**
9	**Brake Caliper Bolt**
10	**Banjo Bolt**
11	**Front Brake Hose**

93006G15

Front brake caliper (exploded view)—Probe

3. Remove the banjo bolt attaching the brake hose to the caliper and discard the 2 sealing washers. Plug the hose to prevent fluid leakage.

4. Remove the caliper mounting bolt and pivot the caliper upward and off the brake pads.

5. Slide the caliper from the guide pin and remove from the vehicle.

To install:

6. Remove the guide pin bushing dust boots and push out the caliper guide pin bushing.

7. Lubricate the guide pin bushings with high temperature grease and install them in the caliper. Install the guide pin bushing dust boots.

8. Slide the caliper onto the guide pin and pivot the caliper down onto the brake pads. To provide the necessary clearance, it may be necessary to pull slightly outward on the caliper.

9. Install the caliper mounting bolt and torque to 33–36 ft. lbs. (44–49 Nm).

10. Install 2 new copper washers and the banjo bolt on the brake hose banjo fitting.

11. Position the brake hose on the caliper and install the banjo bolt. Torque the bolt to 16–22 ft. lbs. (22–29 Nm).

12. Bleed the brake system.

13. Install the wheel and torque the lug nuts to 65–87 ft. lbs. (80–118 Nm).

14. Lower the vehicle.

15. Check the brake system for proper operation.

REAR

1. Raise and safely support the vehicle.

2. Remove the wheel.

3. Remove the parking brake cable retaining clip.

4. Loosen the parking brake cable housing adjustment nut. Remove the cable housing from the bracket and the parking brake lever.

5. Remove the banjo bolt mounting the brake hose to the caliper.

6. Remove and discard the copper washers from the banjo fitting.

7. Remove the caliper mounting bolt.

1	Banjo Bolt
2	Brake Caliper Bolt
3	Rear Disc Brake Caliper
4	Anti-Rattle Spring
5	Rear Brake Shoe and Lining
6	Shim
7	Rear Disc Brake Rotor
8	Rear Disc Brake Caliper Anchor Plate
9	Wheel Hub

10	Parking Brake Rear Cable and Conduit
11	Rear Disc Brake Caliper Anchor Plate Bolt (2 Req'd)
12	Rear Wheel Brake Hose
13	Clip

93006G16

Rear brake caliper—Probe

8. Pivot the caliper off the brake pads and slide the caliper off the guide pin.

To install:

9. Lubricate the guide pin bushings with high temperature grease. Install the caliper onto the guide pin and pivot the caliper over the brake pads. Torque the caliper attaching bolt to 25–29 ft. lbs. (34–39 Nm).

10. Install new copper washers and the banjo bolt mounting the brake hose to the caliper. Torque the banjo bolt to 16–22 ft. lbs. (23–29 Nm).

11. Position the parking brake cable into the parking brake lever and bracket. Install the retaining clip.

12. Adjust the parking brake cable so there is no clearance between the cable end and the parking brake lever. Tighten the parking brake cable locknut.

13. Bleed the brake system.

14. Install the wheel and torque the lug nuts to 65–87 ft. lbs. (80–118 Nm).

15. Lower the vehicle.

16. Check the brake system for proper operation.

Ford Contour
Mercury Mystique

FRONT

1. Raise and safely support the vehicle.

2. Remove the wheel and tire assembly.

3. Remove the outer disc brake pad spring clip (anti-rattle clip).

4. Remove the 2 locator pin covers and remove the locator pins.

5. Free the hose from its mounting on the strut.

6. Lift the caliper off of the brake rotor.

7. Remove the inboard disc brake pad from the caliper.

8. If the brake caliper is to be removed from the vehicle, place a pan under the caliper to catch the brake fluid for proper disposal. Disconnect the brake hose at the caliper and allow to drain.

For complete service labor times order Chilton's Labor Guide Manual

Position of disc brake pad (brake shoe and lining) spring clip—Contour, Mystique

View of disc brake caliper locating pins—Contour, Mystique

View of inboard disc brake pad (brake shoe and lining)—Contour, Mystique

9. Remove the brake caliper.

10. If the caliper is not to be serviced, tie off the caliper to prevent strain on the brake hose.

To install:

11. If removed, install the brake hose onto the caliper. Torque the fitting to 10 ft. lbs. (14 Nm).

12. Position the inboard disc brake pad into the caliper.

13. Make sure that the outboard disc brake pad is positioned properly.

Positioning the outboard disc brake pad (brake shoe and lining)—Contour, Mystique

14. Reinstall the caliper over the brake rotor and position onto the caliper anchor plate.

15. Reinstall the 2 caliper locator pins and torque to 20 ft. lbs. (28 Nm).

16. Reinstall the caliper locator pin covers.

17. Reinstall the outer disc brake pad spring clip.

18. Reconnect the brake hose to the front strut.

19. Bleed the brake system of air. Top off the master cylinder when complete.

20. If the brake pedal feels spongy, repeat the brake bleeding procedure.

21. Reinstall the wheel and tire assembly. Torque the lug nuts to 62 ft. lbs. (85 Nm).

22. Lower the vehicle.

23. Pump the brake pedal several times to position the brake pads before attempting to move the vehicle.

24. Road test the vehicle and check for proper brake system operation.

REAR

1. Raise and safely support the vehicle.

2. Remove the wheel and tire assembly.

3. Remove the parking brake rear cable and conduit from the parking brake lever at the disc brake caliper, using a pair of pliers.

4. Remove the cotter pin and guide pin.

5. Remove the caliper locating pin cover and remove the locating pin.

6. Lift the rear disc brake caliper off of the anchor plate.

7. Place a pan under the caliper to catch any lost brake fluid. Dispose of properly.

Method of removing the parking brake cable—Contour, Mystique

8. Crack open the rear brake hose fitting and allow the brake fluid to drain.

9. Finish removing the rear brake hose and washers from the caliper. Discard the washers.

10. Remove the disc brake caliper.

To install:

11. Retract the piston fully into the caliper using service tool T87P–2588–A or equivalent.

12. Reconnect the rear brake hose to the caliper using new washers.

13. Fit the rear disc brake caliper over the rotor and position onto the anchor plate.

14. Reinstall the caliper locating pin and torque to 30 ft. lbs. (41 Nm).

15. Reinstall the caliper locating pin cover.

16. Reinstall the guide pin and the cotter pin.

17. Reinstall the parking brake rear cable and conduit onto the parking brake lever.

18. Adjust the parking brake by operating the parking brake control several times.

19. Properly bleed the brake system of air. Top off the master cylinder when complete.

20. If the brake pedal feels spongy, repeat the brake bleeding procedure.

21. Reinstall the wheel and tire assembly. Torque the lug nuts to 94 ft. lbs. (128 Nm).

22. Lower the vehicle.

23. Pump the brake pedal several times to position the brake pads before attempting to move the vehicle.

24. Road test the vehicle and check for proper brake system operation.

Ford Taurus
Lincoln Continental
Mercury Sable

✳✳ CAUTION

On Continentals, the air suspension switch, located in the left side of the luggage compartment, must be turned OFF before raising the vehicle. Failure to do so may result in unexpected inflation or deflation of the air springs that may result in shifting of the vehicle during service.

FRONT

1. Remove brake fluid from the brake master cylinder reservoir until the reservoir is ½ full.

2. For Continentals, turn the air suspension switch, located in the left side of the luggage compartment, to the **OFF** position.

3. Raise and safely support the vehicle. Remove the wheel and tire assembly.

4. Mark the disc brake caliper to ensure that it is reinstalled in the correct location.

5. Remove the hollow bolt connecting the brake hose to the disc brake caliper and plug the brake hose. Discard the 2 copper sealing washers.

6. Remove the caliper locating pins and lift the caliper off the rotor using a rotating motion.

To install:

7. Retract the disc brake caliper piston fully in the piston bore, using an old brake pad or block of wood and a C-clamp or equivalent.

➡**Make sure the clip-on insulators are attached to the brake pads.**

8. Install the disc brake pads to the caliper. Make sure the brake pad insulators are correctly attached to the brake pad plate.

9. Position the disc brake caliper and pad assembly above the rotor and install it with a rotating motion. Make sure the inner and outer pads are properly positioned and the outer anti-rattle spring is properly positioned.

10. Lubricate the locating pins and the inside of the insulators with silicone grease. Torque the locating pins to 25 ft. lbs. (34 Nm).

11. Remove the plug and install the brake hose to the disc brake caliper. Use 2 new copper washers and torque the hollow bolt to 30–40 ft. lbs. (41–54 Nm).

12. Bleed the brake system, filling the master cylinder as required.

13. Install the wheel and tire assembly; torque the nuts to 85–104 ft. lbs. (115–142 Nm).

14. Lower the vehicle.

15. Pump the brake pedal several times to position the brake pads prior to moving the vehicle.

16. For Continentals, turn the air suspension service switch to the **ON** position.

17. Road test the vehicle and check for proper brake system operation.

REAR

1. Remove brake fluid from the brake master cylinder reservoir until the reservoir is ½ full.

2. For Continentals, turn the air suspension switch, located in the left side of the luggage compartment, to the **OFF** position.

3. Raise and safely support the vehicle. Remove the wheel and tire assembly.

4. Remove the retaining bolt and disconnect the brake hose from the caliper assembly. Discard the copper sealing washers.

5. Remove the retaining clip from the parking brake at the caliper. Disengage the parking brake cable end from the lever arm.

6. Lift the rear disc brake caliper away from the rear disc support bracket.

7. Remove the disc brake caliper locating pins and boots from the rear disc support bracket.

To install:

8. Using rear caliper piston adjuster tool T87P-2588-A, or equivalent, rotate the rear disc brake piston and adjuster clockwise until fully seated.

➡**Make sure one of the 2 slots in the rear disc brake piston and adjuster face is positioned so it will engage the nib on the disc brake pad.**

9. Apply silicone dielectric compound or equivalent, to the inside of the slider pin boots and the slider pins.

10. Position the slider pins and boots in the support bracket. Position the caliper assembly on the support bracket. Make sure the brake pads are installed correctly.

11. Remove the residue from the pin retainer threads and apply 1 drop of threadlock and sealer. Install the pin retainers and torque to 23–26 ft. lbs. (31–35 Nm).

12. Attach the cable end to the parking brake lever. Install the cable retaining clip on the caliper assembly.

13. Using new washers, connect the brake flex hose to the caliper. Torque the retaining bolt to 40 ft. lbs. (54 Nm).

14. Bleed the brake system, filling the master cylinder as required.

15. Install the wheel and tire assembly; torque the nuts to 85–104 ft. lbs. (115–142 Nm).

16. Lower the vehicle.

17. Pump the brake pedal several times to position the brake pads prior to moving the vehicle.

18. For Continentals, turn the air suspension service switch to the **ON** position.

19. Road test the vehicle and check for proper brake system operation.

Ford Escort
Mercury Tracer

FRONT

1. Raise and safely support the vehicle.
2. Remove the wheel and tire assembly.
3. Remove the disc brake pads.
4. Remove the banjo bolt securing the brake hose to the brake caliper. Discard 2 copper sealing washers.
5. Remove 2 brake caliper retaining bolts and remove the brake caliper.

To install:

6. Place the brake caliper in position and install 2 brake caliper retaining bolts. Torque the bolts to 29–36 ft. lbs. (39–49 Nm).

7. Install the brake hose to the brake caliper and install the banjo bolt with 2 new copper sealing washers. Torque the banjo bolt to 16–22 ft. lbs. (22–29 Nm).

8. Install the disc brake pads.
9. Bleed the brake system.
10. Install the wheel and tire assembly. Torque the lug nuts to 65–87 ft. lbs. (88–118 Nm).
11. Lower the vehicle.
12. Pump the brake pedal several times to position the brake pads to the brake rotor.
13. Road test the vehicle and check the brake system for proper operation.

REAR

1. Raise and safely support the vehicle.
2. Remove the wheel and tire assembly.
3. Remove the disc brake pads.
4. Remove the parking brake cable bracket bolt and position the bracket aside.
5. Remove the parking brake cable from the operating lever.
6. Remove the banjo bolt securing the brake hose to the brake caliper. Discard 2 copper sealing washers.
7. Remove the upper brake caliper retaining bolt.
8. Slide the brake caliper off the mounting bracket and remove from the vehicle.

To install:

9. Place the brake caliper on the mounting bracket and slide into position.
10. Install the upper brake caliper retaining bolt. Torque the bolt to 33–43 ft. lbs. (45–59 Nm).
11. Install the brake hose to the brake caliper and secure with the banjo bolt using 2 new copper sealing washers. Torque the banjo bolt to 16–22 ft. lbs. (22–29 Nm).

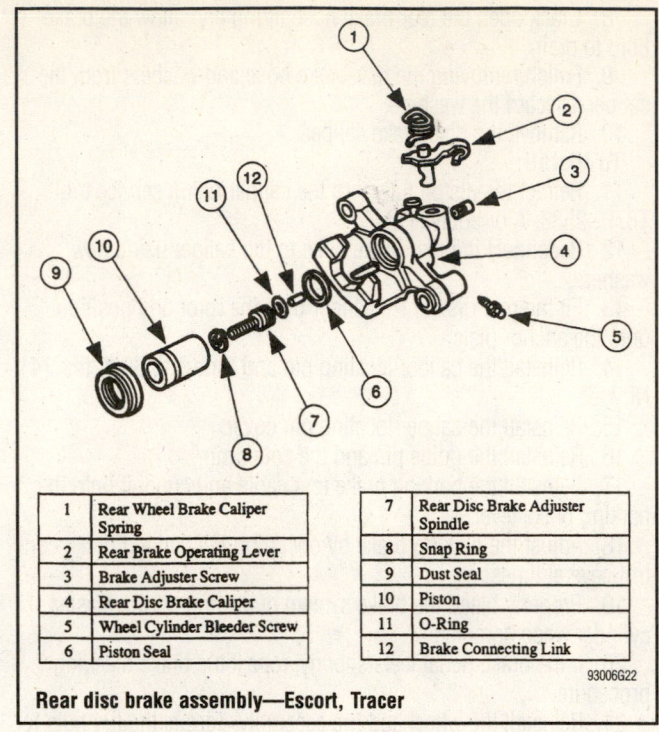

1	Rear Wheel Brake Caliper Spring		7	Rear Disc Brake Adjuster Spindle
2	Rear Brake Operating Lever		8	Snap Ring
3	Brake Adjuster Screw		9	Dust Seal
4	Rear Disc Brake Caliper		10	Piston
5	Wheel Cylinder Bleeder Screw		11	O-Ring
6	Piston Seal		12	Brake Connecting Link

93006G22

Rear disc brake assembly—Escort, Tracer

12. Connect the parking brake cable to the operating lever. Position the bracket and install the bracket bolt.

13. Install the disc brake pads.

14. Bleed the brake system.

15. Install the wheel and tire assembly. Torque the lug nuts to 65–87 ft. lbs. (88–118 Nm).

16. Lower the vehicle.

17. Pump the brake pedal several times to position the brake pads to the brake rotor.

18. Road test the vehicle and check the brake system for proper operation.

Ford Mustang

FRONT

1. Raise and safely support the vehicle.
2. Remove the wheel and tire assembly.
3. Mark the disc brake caliper to ensure that it will be installed to the same side if both calipers are being removed.
4. Remove the banjo bolt that connects the brake hose fitting to the disc brake caliper. Remove and plug the brake hose. Discard 2 copper sealing washers.
5. On single piston calipers, remove the lower brake caliper locating pin.
6. Rotate the brake caliper approximately 90° away from the anchor assembly.
7. Slide the brake caliper away from anchor assembly until the brake caliper disengages from the upper locating pin and remove from the vehicle.
8. On dual piston calipers, remove the clip and washer with the locating pin and remove the disc brake caliper.

To install:

9. If required, compress the caliper piston(s) using a C-clamp and an old disc brake pad or block of wood.
10. On single piston calipers, engage the upper disc brake caliper locating pin into the insulator.

11. Make sure the anti–rattle is properly installed on caliper.

12. Make sure the brake pads are properly installed.

13. Rotate the brake caliper assembly into place on the anchor plate.

➡ **New locating pins are recommended due to the thread locking compound on the threads.**

14. Install the lower disc brake caliper locating pin and torque to 23 ft. lbs. (31 Nm).

15. On dual piston calipers, place the disc brake caliper over the brake rotor with the brake pads installed and lower the caliper onto the brake rotor.

16. Install the disc brake caliper locating pin and clip by pressing the caliper down to compress the bias springs and the locating pin into position and secure with the washer and clip.

17. Unplug and install the brake hose to the disc brake caliper using 2 new copper sealing washers, 1 on each side of the fitting. Install the banjo bolt and torque to 30 ft. lbs. (40 Nm).

18. Bleed the brake system and check for leaks. Replace the bleeder screw rubber cap.

19. Install the wheel and tire assembly. Torque the lug nuts in a star pattern to 85–105 ft. lbs. (115–142 Nm).

20. Lower the vehicle.

21. Pump the brake pedal several times to position the brake pads before the vehicle is moved.

22. Road test the vehicle and check for proper brake system operation.

REAR

1. Raise and safely support the vehicle.

2. Remove the wheel and tire assembly.

3. Remove the banjo bolt securing the brake hose to the disc brake caliper. Separate the brake hose from the caliper and plug the hose. Discard 2 copper sealing washers.

4. Remove the retaining clip from the parking brake rear cable at the disc brake caliper. Release the tension from the parking brake cable and disengage the cable end from the parking brake lever on the brake caliper.

5. Hold the disc brake caliper locating pin hex-heads with an open-end wrench or equivalent and remove 2 brake pin retainer bolts.

6. Lift the disc brake caliper assembly away from the disc support bracket and remove the disc brake caliper from the vehicle.

7. Remove the brake caliper locating pins and boots from support bracket.

To install:

8. If required, use Caliper Piston Adjuster T87P-2588-A, or equivalent, to rotate the caliper piston into the caliper bore. Align the tool tips with the slots in the piston and rotate the tool clockwise until the piston is seated.

9. Apply a suitable silicone dielectric compound to the inside of the locating pin boots and the caliper locating pins.

10. Install the brake caliper locating pins and boots in the disc support bracket.

11. Properly install the disc brake pads and anti-rattle clips.

12. Apply a drop of suitable thread locking compound to the threads of the brake pin retainer bolts and install the brake pin retainers. Torque the brake pin retainer bolts to 23–26 ft. lbs. (31–35 Nm) while holding the brake caliper locating pins with an open-end wrench, or equivalent.

13. Attach the end of the parking brake cable to the parking brake lever on the disc brake caliper.

14. Unplug and install the brake hose to the disc brake caliper using 2 new copper sealing washers on the fitting. Insert the banjo bolt through both washers and the brake line fitting and torque to 30 ft. lbs. (40 Nm).

15. Properly bleed the brake system and check for leaks.

16. Install the wheel and tire assembly. Torque the lug nuts in a star pattern to 85–105 ft. lbs. (115–142 Nm).

17. Lower the vehicle.

18. Pump the brake pedal several times to position the brake pads before moving the vehicle.

19. Road test the vehicle and check the brake system for proper operation.

Ford Thunderbird
Lincoln Mark VIII
Mercury Cougar (up to 1998)

FRONT

1. Raise and safely support the vehicle.

2. Remove the wheel and tire assembly.

3. Loosen the brake line fitting that connects the brake hose to the brake line at the frame bracket. Plug the brake line. Remove the retaining clip from the hose and bracket and disengage the hose from the bracket.

4. Remove the hollow bolt attaching the brake hose to the caliper and remove the brake hose. Discard the sealing washers.

5. Disconnect the brake pad wear sensor connector (if equipped).

6. Remove the caliper locating pins and remove the caliper. If removing both calipers, mark the right and left sides so they may be reinstalled correctly.

To install:

7. Fully retract piston into caliper bore.

8. Install the caliper over the rotor with the outer brake pad against the rotor's braking surface. This prevents pinching the piston boot between the inner brake pad and the piston.

9. Lubricate the locating pins and the inside of the locating pin insulators with silicone dielectric grease. Install the caliper locating pins and thread them into the spindle/anchor plate assembly by hand. Torque the caliper locating pins to 45–65 ft. lbs. (61–88 Nm).

10. Connect brake pad wear sensor connector (if equipped).

11. Install new sealing washers on each side of the brake hose fitting outlet and install the hollow bolt through the hose fitting and into the caliper. Torque the bolt to 30 ft. lbs. (41 Nm).

12. Place the brake hose in the bracket and install the retaining clip. Make sure the hose is not twisted.

13. Remove the plug from the brake line, connect the brake line to the brake hose and torque the fitting nut to 10–18 ft. lbs. (13–24 Nm).

14. Bleed the brake system using clean DOT 3 or equivalent, brake fluid from a closed container.

15. Install the wheel and tire assembly. Torque the lug nuts to 85–105 ft. lbs. (115–142 Nm).

16. Lower the vehicle.

17. Apply the brake pedal several times before moving the vehicle, to position the brake pads.

18. Road test the vehicle and check for proper brake system operation.

For brake related suspension and axle service, refer to the model specific sections of this manual

REAR

1. Raise and safely support the vehicle.
2. Remove the wheel and tire assembly.
3. Disconnect brake pad wear sensor connector (if equipped).
4. Remove the brake fitting retaining bolt from the disc brake caliper and disconnect the flexible brake hose from the caliper. Plug the hose and the caliper fitting.
5. Release the tension from the parking brake cable. Disconnect the cable from the caliper.
6. Remove the disc brake caliper locating pins. Lift the caliper off the brake rotor and anchor plate using a rotating motion.
7. Remove the disc brake pads.

To install:

8. Place the Rear Caliper Piston Adjuster T87P-2588-A, or equivalent, in the caliper. Be sure the pins on the tool are meshed with the slots on the piston. Rotate the tool clockwise until the piston is seated in the caliper bore.
9. Install the disc pads in the support bracket. Make sure that the pads are on the correct side.
10. Place the disc brake caliper assembly above the brake rotor with the anti-rattle spring located on the lower adapter support arm. Install the caliper over the rotor with a rotating motion. Make sure the inner pad is properly positioned with the nub in the piston slot.
11. Apply a suitable thread-locking compound to the caliper locating pin threads and start them in by hand. Torque the locating pins to 19–26 ft. lbs. (26–35 Nm).
12. Install the brake hose on the disc brake caliper with a new gasket on each side of the fitting outlet. Insert the retaining bolt and torque to 30–40 ft. lbs. (40–54 Nm).
13. Connect the parking brake cable to the caliper and adjust the tension.
14. Connect the brake pad wear sensor connector (if equipped).
15. Bleed the brake system using clean DOT 3 or equivalent, brake fluid from a closed container.
16. Install the wheel and tire assembly. Torque the lug nuts to 85–105 ft. lbs. (115–142 Nm).
17. Lower the vehicle.
18. Apply the brake pedal several times before moving the vehicle, to position the brake pads.
19. Verify proper parking brake system operation.
20. Road test the vehicle and check for proper brake system operation.

**Ford Crown Victoria
Lincoln Town Car
Mercury Grand Marquis**

FRONT

➡ **Before continuing with this procedure, make sure to have available, 2 new disc brake caliper guide pin bolts and 2 banjo bolt sealing washers, per caliper. Once removed, these parts loose their torque holding ability or retention capability and must not be reused.**

1. If equipped with air suspension, the air suspension switch, located on the right-hand side of the luggage compartment, must be turned to the **OFF** position before raising the vehicle.
2. Raise and safely support the vehicle.
3. Remove the front wheel and tire assembly.
4. Loosen and remove the banjo bolt securing the brake hose from the disc brake caliper. Plug the brake hose. Discard the sealing washers.

5. Remove 2 disc brake caliper guide pin bolts and discard. If removing both calipers, mark the right and left sides so they may be reinstalled correctly.
6. Lift the disc brake caliper off of the anchor plate.

To install:

7. Retract the disc brake caliper piston fully in the piston bore, using an old brake pad or block of wood and a C-clamp, or equivalent.
8. Install the disc brake pads to the caliper. Make sure that the brake pad insulators are correctly attached to the brake pad plate.
9. Position the disc brake caliper onto the anchor plate. Make sure the inner and outer pads are properly positioned and the anti-rattle spring is properly positioned. The caliper bleed screw should be positioned on top of the caliper when assembled on the vehicle.
10. Install 2 new caliper guide pin bolts. Torque the bolts to 21–26 ft. lbs. (28–26 Nm).
11. Unplug and install the brake hose to the disc brake caliper using 2 new copper sealing washers on the banjo bolt. Torque the bolt to 30–40 ft. lbs. (41–54 Nm).
12. Bleed the brake system, filling the master cylinder as required. Only use clean DOT 3 or equivalent, brake fluid from a sealed container.
13. Install the wheel and tire assembly. Torque the lug nuts in a star pattern to 85–104 ft. lbs. (115–142 Nm).
14. Lower the vehicle.
15. If equipped with air suspension, turn the air suspension switch to the **ON** position.
16. Pump the brake pedal several times to position the brake pads prior to moving the vehicle.
17. Road test the vehicle and check for proper brake system operation.

REAR

➡ **Before continuing with this procedure, make sure to have available, 2 banjo bolt sealing washers, per caliper. Once removed, these parts loose their torque holding ability or retention capability and must not be reused.**

1. If equipped with air suspension, the air suspension switch, located on the right-hand side of the luggage compartment, must be turned to the **OFF** position before raising the vehicle.
2. Raise and safely support the vehicle.
3. Remove the rear wheel and tire assembly.
4. Loosen and remove the banjo bolt securing the brake hose to the disc brake caliper. Plug the brake hose and discard both sealing washers.
5. Remove 2 disc brake caliper locating bolts. Lift the disc brake caliper off the rotor and anchor plate using a rotating motion.

To install:

6. Retract the disc brake caliper piston fully in the piston bore, using an old brake pad or block of wood and a C-clamp or equivalent.
7. Install the disc brake pads on the caliper. Make sure that the pads are on the correct side.
8. Position the disc brake caliper assembly above the rotor with the anti-rattle spring located on the lower adapter support arm. Install the caliper over the rotor with a rotating motion.
9. Clean the inner surface of the caliper bushings and locating bolts. Lubricate the caliper locating bolts with a suitable silicone dielectric compound. Install and start the locating bolts by hand only. Torque both bolts to 16–20 ft. lbs. (22–27 Nm).
10. Unplug and install the brake hose to the disc brake caliper using 2 new copper sealing washers on the banjo bolt. Torque the bolt to 30–40 ft. lbs. (41–54 Nm).

11. Bleed the brake system, filling the master cylinder as required. Only use clean DOT 3 or equivalent, brake fluid from a sealed container.

12. Replace the rubber rear disc brake bleeder screw cap.

13. Install the wheel and tire assembly. Torque the lug nuts in a star pattern to 85–104 ft. lbs. (115–142 Nm).

14. Lower the vehicle.

15. If equipped with air suspension, turn the air suspension switch to the **ON** position.

16. Pump the brake pedal several times to position the brake pads prior to moving the vehicle.

17. Road test the vehicle and check for proper brake system operation.

Disc Brake Pads

REMOVAL & INSTALLATION

Ford Aspire

1. Remove brake fluid from the master cylinder reservoir to lower the level by approximately ⅓ preventing brake fluid overflow when the caliper piston is pressed back into its bore.

2. Raise and safely support the vehicle.

3. Remove the tire and wheel assembly.

4. Use the proper brake tool or a C-clamp to move the caliper piston into its bore approximately ⅛ in. (3mm) to allow removal of the disc brake pads.

5. Remove the brake pad anti-rattle clip. Disengage the M-shaped anti-rattle spring from the brake pads.

6. Remove the 2 disc brake caliper locating pins and the M-shaped anti-rattle spring.

7. Remove the brake pads and shims. Do not discard the shims found behind the brake pads.

To install:

8. Use the proper brake tool or a C-clamp and one of the old brake pads to push the caliper piston back into the caliper bore. Do not push directly against the caliper piston or damage to the piston may result.

9. Apply suitable grease, normally supplied with the brake pad set, to both surfaces of the inner shim and to the back of the brake pads. Be careful not to get grease on the friction surface of the brake pads.

10. Install the brake pads, making sure the shims are installed.

1	Anti-Squeak Caps
2	Disc Brake Caliper Locating Pins (2 Req'd)
3	Disc Brake Pad Anti-Rattle Clip
4	Brake Pad Shim
5	Brake Shoe and Lining
6	M-Shaped Anti-Rattle Spring
7	Disc Brake Caliper, Front

8	Brake Caliper Bolt (2 Req'd)
9	Banjo Bolt
10	Front Brake Hose
11	Brake Pad Shims (Part of 2001)
12	Brake Shoe and Lining

93006G23

Disc brake assembly—Aspire

For complete service labor times order Chilton's Labor Guide Manual

11. Install the 2 disc brake caliper locating pins and the M-shaped anti-rattle spring.

12. Install the disc brake pad anti-rattle clip.

13. Install the wheel and tire assembly. Torque the lug bolts to 65–87 ft. lbs. (88–118 Nm).

14. Lower the vehicle.

15. Apply the brake pedal several times to seat the pads, before moving the vehicle. Check the brake fluid level in the master cylinder and add fluid as necessary.

16. Check for proper brake operation.

Ford Probe

FRONT

1. Remove brake fluid from the master cylinder reservoir until the reservoir is approximately ½ full. Discard the removed fluid.

2. Raise and safely support the vehicle.

3. Remove the wheel.

4. If necessary, clean the brake assembly with brake cleaner and allow it to dry.

5. Using an appropriate tool, pry the caliper outboard.

6. Remove the caliper mounting bolt. Pivot the caliper upward on the fixed guide pin and secure it out of the way.

7. Remove the 2 anti-rattle springs.

8. Remove the shims. Tag the shims so they can be reinstalled in their original position.

9. Remove the brake pads and retaining clips from the caliper anchor.

10. Inspect the disc brake rotor for wear and/or damage. Machine or replace, as necessary. If machining, observe the minimum thickness specification.

   To install:

11. Install the retaining clips.

12. Install the brake pads into the caliper anchor. The pad with the wear indicator is the inboard pad.

13. Install the shims in their original position.

14. Compress the caliper piston into its bore using a large C-clamp and one of the old brake pads. Do not allow the clamp to push directly on the caliper piston.

15. Pivot the caliper down over the brake pads. Install the anti-rattle springs. Install the caliper mounting bolt and torque the bolt to 33–36 ft. lbs. (44–49 Nm).

16. Install the wheel. Torque the lug nuts to 65–87 ft. lbs. (80–118 Nm).

17. Lower the vehicle.

18. Pump the brake pedal several times to position the caliper piston.

19. Check the fluid level in the master cylinder reservoir and add fluid as necessary.

20. Road test the vehicle for proper brake operation.

REAR

1. Remove brake fluid from the master cylinder reservoir until the reservoir is approximately ½ full. Discard the removed fluid.

2. Raise and safely support the vehicle.

3. Remove the wheel.

4. Remove the parking brake cable retaining clip.

5. Loosen the parking brake cable housing adjusting nut. Remove the cable housing from the bracket and the parking brake lever.

6. Insert an Allen wrench into the back of the caliper and turn the manual adjustment gear counterclockwise to pull the caliper piston inward. Turn the gear until it stops.

7. Remove the caliper mounting bolt and pivot the caliper to clear the brake pads. Remove the caliper and suspend it with wire from the rear strut.

8. Remove the anti-rattle spring from the disc brake pads. Remove the disc brake pads, the shims and retaining clips. If the brake pads and shims are to be reused, tag them so they can be installed in their original positions.

9. Inspect the disc brake rotor for wear and/or damage. Machine or replace, as necessary. If machining, observe the minimum thickness specification.

   To install:

10. Install the retaining clips. Position the shims on the disc brake pads and install the pads into the caliper anchor bracket.

11. Install the anti-rattle spring onto the disc brake pads.

12. Lightly lubricate the guide pin bushings with high temperature grease and install the caliper onto the guide pin. Pivot the caliper over the disc brake pads.

Front disc brake pads—Probe

93006G24

Rear disc brake pads—Probe

93006G25

13. Install the caliper mounting bolt and torque to 25–29 ft. lbs. (34–39 Nm).

14. Install the parking brake cable into the parking brake lever and bracket. Install the parking brake cable retaining clip.

15. Adjust the cable so there is no clearance between the cable end and the parking brake lever. Tighten the parking brake cable locknut.

16. Turn the caliper manual adjustment gear clockwise with an Allen wrench until the brake pads just touch the rotor, then back off ⅓ turn.

17. Install the wheel and torque the lug nuts to 65–87 ft. lbs. (80–118 Nm).

18. Lower the vehicle.

19. Pump the brake pedal several times to position the caliper piston. Check the fluid level in the master cylinder reservoir and add clean brake fluid, if necessary.

20. Road test and check for proper brake operation.

Ford Contour
Mercury Mystique
Mercury Cougar (1999)

FRONT

1. Remove ½ of the brake fluid from the master cylinder reservoir.

2. Raise and safely support the vehicle.

3. Remove the wheel and tire assembly.

4. Remove the outer disc brake pad spring clip (anti-rattle clip).

5. Remove the 2 locating pin covers and remove the locating pins.

6. Free the hose from its mounting on the strut.

7. Lift the caliper off of the brake rotor and tie it off to prevent damage to the brake hose.

8. Remove the outboard disc brake pad from the anchor plate.

9. Remove the inboard disc brake pad from the brake caliper.

To install:

10. If installing new disc brake pads, use a C-clamp or similar tool to push the caliper piston into the caliper bore. This will allow room for the new pads.

11. Place the inboard disc brake pad into the caliper.

12. Place the outboard disc brake pad into position in the anchor plate.

13. Position the disc brake caliper onto the rotor.

14. Reinstall the 2 locating pins and torque to 20 ft. lbs. (28 Nm).

15. Reinstall the caliper locating pin covers.

16. Secure the brake hose to its support on the strut.

17. Reinstall the disc brake pad spring clip.

18. Reinstall the wheel and tire assembly. Torque the lug nuts to 62 ft. lbs. (85 Nm).

19. Lower the vehicle.

20. Pump the brake pedal several times to achieve a good pedal before attempting to move the vehicle.

21. Check the brake fluid level in the master cylinder fluid reservoir and add fluid as necessary.

22. Road test the vehicle and check for proper brake system operation.

REAR

1. Remove ½ of the brake fluid from the master cylinder reservoir.

2. Raise and safely support the vehicle.

3. Remove the wheels.

4. Remove the cotter pin and guide pin.

5. Remove the caliper locating pin cover and remove the locating pin.

6. Swing the rear disc brake caliper away from the brake rotor and anchor plate. There is no need to remove the parking brake cable or brake hose.

7. Remove the inner and outer disc brake pads.

To install:

8. If installing new disc brake pads, use rear caliper piston adjuster T87P-2588-A or similar tool, to rotate the rear disc brake

1	Rear Disc Brake Rotor
2	Rear Disc Brake Caliper Anchor Plate
3	Guide Pin
4	Anti-Rattle Clip
5	Parking Brake Lever

93006G26

Rear disc brake components—Contour, Mystique

ALIGN NIBS ON TOOL WITH SLOTS IN PISTON

1	Rear Disc Brake Caliper
2	Rear Caliper Piston Adjuster
3	Nibs (Part of T87P-2588-A)
4	Piston Adjuster Slots (Part of 2B588)
5	Rear Disc Brake Caliper Piston and Adjuster

93006G27

Diagram of rear caliper piston and the adjuster tool—Contour, Mystique

piston clockwise, retracting the caliper piston. This will allow room for the new brake pads.

9. Install the inner and outer disc brake pads.

10. Swing the rear disc brake caliper back into position over the disc brake pads.

11. Clean the locating pin threads and apply 1 drop of a thread locking agent or similar sealer.

12. Apply a small amount of disc brake caliper slide grease to the shaft of the locating pin.

13. Reinstall the locating pin and torque to 30 ft. lbs. (41 Nm).

14. Reinstall the guide pin and the cotter pin.

15. Adjust the parking brake by operating the parking brake control several times.

16. Reinstall the wheel and tire assembly. Torque the lug nuts to 62 ft. lbs. (85 Nm).

17. Lower the vehicle.

18. Adjust the parking brake by operating the parking brake control several times.

19. Pump the brake pedal several times to achieve a good pedal before attempting to move the vehicle.

20. Check the brake fluid level in the master cylinder fluid reservoir and add fluid as necessary.

21. Road test the vehicle and check for proper brake system operation.

Ford Taurus
Lincoln Continental
Mercury Sable

⁂ CAUTION

For Continentals, the air suspension switch, located in the left side of the luggage compartment, must be turned OFF before raising the vehicle. Failure to do so may result in unexpected inflation or deflation of the air springs that may result in shifting of the vehicle during service.

FRONT

1. Remove the master cylinder reservoir cap and check the fluid level in the reservoir. Remove brake fluid until the reservoir is ½ full. Discard the removed fluid.

2. On Continentals, turn the air suspension switch, located in the left side of the luggage compartment, to the **OFF** position.

3. Raise and safely support the vehicle. Remove the wheel and tire assembly.

4. Remove the disc brake caliper locating pins. Lift the caliper assembly from the anchor plate and rotor using a rotating motion.

5. Suspend the caliper inside the fender housing with wire. Do not allow the caliper to hang from the brake hose.

6. Remove the inner and outer brake pads. Inspect the rotor braking surfaces for scoring and machine as necessary.

To install:

7. Use a C-clamp and an old brake pad or block of wood to seat the caliper piston in its bore.

8. Remove any rust buildup from the inside of the caliper in the brake pad contact area.

9. Install the inner pad in the caliper piston.

10. Install the outer pad onto the anchor plate. Make sure the clips are properly seated.

➡**Make sure the insulators are installed on the brake pads.**

Front disc brake caliper, pads and related components—Taurus, Continental, Sable

93006G28

11. Install the disc brake caliper onto the anchor plate.

12. Install caliper locating pins and torque to 23–28 ft. lbs. (31–38 Nm).

13. Install wheel and tire assembly and torque lugs nuts to 85–104 ft. lb. (115–142 Nm)

14. Lower the vehicle.

15. Pump the brake pedal several times prior to moving the vehicle to position the brake pads to the rotor.

16. Refill the master cylinder reservoir as necessary, using only clean DOT 3 or equivalent brake fluid from a closed container.

17. On Continentals, turn the air suspension service switch to the **ON** position.

18. Road test the vehicle and check the brake system for proper operation.

REAR

1. Remove the master cylinder reservoir cap and check the fluid level in the reservoir. Remove brake fluid until the reservoir is ½ full. Discard the removed fluid.

2. On Continentals, turn the air suspension switch, located in the left side of the luggage compartment, to the **OFF** position.

3. Raise and safely support the vehicle. Remove the wheel and tire assembly.

4. Remove the screw retaining the brake hose bracket to the frame side rail.

5. Remove the retaining clip from the parking brake cable at the disc brake caliper. Remove the cable end from the parking brake lever.

6. Remove the upper disc brake caliper locating pin at the support bracket. Rotate the caliper away from the rotor.

7. Remove the disc brake pads.

8. Inspect the rotor braking surfaces for scoring and machine as necessary.

To install:

9. Using Rear Caliper Piston Adjuster T87P-2588-A, or equivalent, rotate the piston clockwise until it is fully seated. Make sure one of the slots in the piston face is positioned so it will engage the nib on the brake pad.

10. Install the brake pads in the support bracket. Rotate the caliper assembly over the rotor into position on the support bracket. Make sure the brake pads are installed correctly.

11. Remove the residue from the rear brake pin retainer bolt threads

and apply 1 drop of a suitable threadlock sealer. Install and torque the disc brake caliper locating pin to 23–26 ft. lbs. (31–35 Nm).

12. Attach the cable end to the parking brake lever. Install the cable retaining clip on the caliper assembly. Position the brake flex hose and bracket assembly to the side rail, and install the retaining screw. Torque to 11 ft. lbs. (16 Nm).

13. Install the wheel and tire assembly and torque lug nuts to 85–104 ft. lbs. (115–142 Nm).

14. Lower the vehicle.

15. Pump the brake pedal several times prior to moving the vehicle, to position the brake pads to the rotor.

16. Refill the master cylinder reservoir if necessary, using only clean DOT 3 or equivalent brake fluid from a closed container.

17. On Continentals, turn the air suspension service switch to the **ON** position.

18. Road test the vehicle and check the brake system for proper operation.

Ford Escort
Mercury Tracer

FRONT

1. Remove the master cylinder reservoir cap and check the fluid level in the reservoir. Remove brake fluid until the reservoir is ½ full. Discard the removed fluid.

2. Raise and safely support the vehicle.

3. Remove the wheel and tire assembly.

4. Remove the W-spring.

5. Remove 2 disc brake pad locating pins and remove the M-spring.

6. Remove the brake pads and shims from the brake caliper.

7. Inspect the brake rotor. Resurface or replace if needed.

To install:

8. Use a suitable tool to push the piston into the brake caliper bore.

9. Apply a suitable grease between the shims and the disc brake pad guide plates and position the brake pads and shims to the brake caliper.

10. Install the W-spring and 2 brake pad locating pins.

11. Install the M-spring.

12. Install the wheel and tire assembly. Torque the lug nuts to 65–87 ft. lbs. (88–118 Nm).

13. Lower the vehicle.

14. Pump the brake pedal several times prior to moving the vehicle to position the brake pads.

Front disc brake pads—Escort, Tracer

15. Check the fluid level in the master cylinder reservoir and fill as needed.

16. Road test the vehicle and check for proper brake system operation.

REAR

1. Remove the master cylinder reservoir cap and check the fluid level in the reservoir. Remove brake fluid until the reservoir is ½ full. Discard the removed fluid.

2. Raise and safely support the vehicle.

3. Remove the wheel and tire assembly.

4. If necessary, remove the screw plug and turn the adjustment gear counterclockwise with an Allen® wrench to pull the piston fully inward.

5. Remove the lower brake caliper bolt.

6. Using a small prybar, pivot the caliper on its mounting bracket to access the brake pads. If the upper lock bolt requires lubrication or service, remove it and suspend the caliper with mechanics wire.

7. Remove the brake pads, shims, spring and guides.

8. Inspect the brake rotor. Resurface or replace if needed.

To install:

9. Apply an appropriate brake pad grease between the shims and the brake pads.

10. Pivot the caliper on its mounting bracket and position the brake pads, shims, spring and guides to the brake rotor.

11. Lubricate and install the lower caliper bolt. Tighten the bolt to 33–43 ft. lbs. (45–59 Nm).

12. Turn the adjustment gear clockwise with an Allen wrench until the brake pads just touch the rotor, then loosen the gear ⅓ of a turn. Install the screw plug and torque to 12 ft. lbs. (16 Nm).

13. Install the wheel and tire assembly. Torque the lug nuts to 65–87 ft. lbs. (88–118 Nm).

14. Lower the vehicle.

15. Pump the brake pedal several times prior to moving the vehicle to position the brake pads.

16. Check the brake fluid level in the master cylinder reservoir and fill if needed.

17. Road test the vehicle and check for proper brake system operation.

Mustang

FRONT WITH SINGLE PISTON CALIPER

1. Remove and discard ½ of the brake fluid from the brake master cylinder reservoir. Properly dispose of the used brake fluid.

2. Raise and safely support vehicle.

3. Remove the wheel and tire assembly.

4. Remove 2 anchor plate mounting bolts and lift the disc brake caliper from the anchor plate and rotor using a rotating motion. Hang the disc brake caliper from the body with wire. Do not let the disc brake caliper hang by the brake hose.

5. Remove the outer and inner disc brake pads and the anti-rattle clip from the disc brake caliper.

6. Clean any residue from the caliper anchor plate and disc brake pad contact areas.

7. Inspect the disc brake rotor for scoring and wear. Replace or machine, as necessary.

8. Inspect the piston boot and the caliper pin boots for damage. Replace as necessary.

For brake related suspension and axle service, refer to the model specific sections of this manual

NOTE: DO NOT REMOVE FOR CALIPER REPLACEMENT

1	Upper Caliper Brake Bolt
2	Front Caliper Sleeve
3	Insulator
4	Caliper Housing (Part of 2B119)
5	Disc Brake Pad Anti-Rattle Clip
6	Caliper Piston
7	Piston Seal
8	Dust Boot
9	Brake Shoe and Lining
10	Front Disc Brake Caliper Anchor Plate
11	Disc Brake Caliper Locating Pin
A	Tighten to 88 N·m (65 Lb-Ft)

93006G30

Disc brake pads and related components—Mustang with single piston caliper

To install:

9. Use a large C-clamp and a wood block or equivalent, to push the caliper piston back into its bore.

10. Remove the protective paper from the insulators on the back of the disc brake pads, if equipped.

11. Install the inner and outer disc brake pads and the anti-rattle clip in the disc brake caliper.

12. Install the disc brake caliper and pads over the rotor and onto the anchor plate using a rotating motion. Hand-start 2 anchor plate mounting bolts. Torque the bolts to 95 ft. lbs. (130 Nm).

13. Install the wheel and tire assembly and torque the lug nuts in a star pattern to 85–105 ft. lbs. (115–142 Nm).

14. Repeat the procedure for the opposite disc brake caliper assembly.

15. Lower the vehicle.

16. Pump the brake pedal prior to moving the vehicle to seat the brake pads.

17. Fill the brake master cylinder reservoir with clean DOT 3 or equivalent brake fluid from a closed container.

18. If the disc brake calipers were replaced or repaired, be sure to bleed the system.

19. Road test the vehicle and check the brake system for proper operation.

FRONT WITH DUAL PISTON CALIPER

1. Remove and discard ½ of the brake fluid from the brake master cylinder reservoir. Properly dispose of the used brake fluid.

2. Raise and safely support vehicle.

3. Remove the wheel and tire assembly.

4. Remove the clip, washer and disc brake caliper locating pin.

5. Remove the disc brake caliper from the brake rotor and the caliper anchor plate. Hang the disc brake caliper from the body with wire. Do not let the disc brake caliper hang by the brake hose.

6. Remove the outer and inner disc brake pads from the disc brake caliper.

7. Clean any residue from the caliper anchor plate and disc brake pad contact areas.

8. Inspect the disc brake rotor for scoring and wear. Replace or machine, as necessary.

9. Inspect the piston boots and the caliper pin boots for damage. Replace as necessary.

To install:

10. Use a large C-clamp and a wood block or equivalent, to push the caliper pistons back into their bores.

11. Remove the protective paper from the insulators on the back of the disc brake pads, if equipped.

12. Install the inner and outer disc brake pads in the disc brake caliper. Make sure the pads are seated properly.

13. Install the disc brake caliper and pads over the rotor and onto the anchor plate using a rotating motion. Make sure that the guiding surfaces of the disc brake pads and the anchor bracket are seating correctly.

14. Press the disc brake caliper down by hand to compress the bias spring and slide the disc brake caliper locating pin into position.

15. Install the washer and clip.

16. Install the wheel and tire assembly. Torque the lug nuts in a star pattern to 85–105 ft. lbs. (115–142 Nm).

17. Repeat the procedure for the opposite disc brake caliper assembly.

18. Lower the vehicle.

19. Pump the brake pedal prior to moving the vehicle to position the brake pads.

20. Fill the brake master cylinder reservoir with clean DOT 3 or equivalent brake fluid from a closed container.

21. If the disc brake calipers were replaced or repaired, be sure to bleed the system.

22. Road test the vehicle and check the brake system for proper operation.

REAR

1. Remove and discard ½ of the brake fluid from the brake master cylinder reservoir. Properly dispose of the used brake fluid.

2. Raise and safely support vehicle.

3. Remove the wheel and tire assembly.

4. Remove the screw retaining the brake hose bracket to the shock absorber bracket.

5. Remove the retaining clip from the parking brake cable at the disc brake caliper.

6. Release the tension from the parking brake cable and disen-

1	Caliper Housing
2	Piston Seal (2 Req'd)
3	Caliper Piston (2 Req'd)
4	Dust Boot (2 Req'd)
5	Front Brake Locating Pin
6	Brake Shoe and Lining

7	Front Disc Brake Caliper Anchor Plate
8	Clip
9	Washer
10	Anti-Rattle Clip and Insulator
11	Wheel Cylinder Bleeder Screw
12	Cover

93006G31

Disc brake pads and related components—Mustang with dual piston caliper

gage the parking brake cable end from the parking brake lever on the disc brake caliper.

7. Hold the disc brake caliper locating pin hex-head with an open-end wrench or equivalent. Remove the upper brake pin retainer.

8. Rotate the disc brake caliper away from the brake rotor.

9. Remove the inner and outer disc brake pads and the anti-rattle clip from the disc support bracket.

10. Inspect the disc brake rotor for scoring and wear. Replace or machine, as necessary.

To install:

11. Using Rear Caliper Piston Adjuster T87P-2588-A, or equivalent, rotate the caliper piston clockwise until the piston is fully seated.

➡**Ensure that one of the 2 slots in the rear brake piston face is positioned so it will engage the nib on the back of the inner brake pad.**

12. Install the disc brake pad anti-rattle clips and install the inner and outer disc brake pads on the rear disc support bracket.

13. Rotate the disc brake caliper over the brake rotor into position on the disc support bracket. Make sure the disc brake pads and anti-rattle clips are correctly installed.

14. Apply a suitable thread-locking compound to the threads of the upper brake pin retainer.

15. Install the brake pin retainer and tighten to 23–26 ft. lbs. (31–35 Nm) while holding the disc brake caliper locating pin with an open-end wrench, or equivalent.

16. Install the parking brake cable end to the parking brake lever

on the disc brake caliper. Install the retaining clip to the disc brake caliper.

17. Install the wheel and tire assembly. Torque the lug nuts in a star pattern to 85–105 ft. lbs. (115–142 Nm).

18. Repeat the procedure for the opposite disc brake caliper assembly.

19. Lower the vehicle.

20. Pump the brake pedal prior to moving the vehicle to position the brake pads.

21. Fill the brake master cylinder reservoir with clean DOT 3 or equivalent brake fluid from a closed container.

22. If the disc brake calipers were replaced or repaired, be sure to bleed the system.

23. Road test the vehicle and check the brake system for proper operation.

Ford Thunderbird
Mercury Cougar (up to 1998)

FRONT

1. If equipped with air suspension, the air suspension switch, located on the right-hand side of the luggage compartment, must be turned to the **OFF** position before raising the vehicle.

2. Remove and properly dispose ½ of the brake fluid from the master cylinder.

3. Raise and safely support vehicle.

4. Remove the front wheel and tire assembly.

5. Remove 2 disc brake caliper locating pins and remove the

caliper from the anchor plate and rotor. Suspend the caliper inside the fender housing with a length of wire. Do not let the caliper hang by the brake hose.

6. Remove the disc brake pads from the caliper.

7. Inspect the disc brake rotor for scoring and wear. Replace or machine as necessary. Observe the minimum thickness specification stamped on the rotor if machining is required.

To install:

8. Use a C-clamp and an old brake pad, wood block or equivalent, to seat the caliper piston in its bore. Do not allow metal or sharp objects to come into direct contact with the caliper piston surface or damage will result.

9. Install the correct inner disc brake pad to the caliper piston using care not to bend the anti-rattle clips.

10. Install the correct outer disc brake pad to the caliper making sure to properly install the anti-rattle clip. The outer pads are marked for left-hand or right-hand installation.

11. Install the disc brake caliper over the rotor with the outer brake pad against the rotor's braking surface. This prevents pinching the piston boot between the inner brake pad and the piston.

NOTE: DO NOT REMOVE FOR CALIPER REPLACEMENT

1	Brake Caliper Bolt
2	Front Caliper Sleeve
3	Insulator
4	Disc Brake Caliper
5	Disc Brake Pad Anti-Rattle Clip
6	Caliper Piston
7	Piston Seal
8	Dust Boot
9	Brake Shoe and Lining
10	Front Disc Brake Caliper Anchor Plate
11	Disc Brake Caliper Locating Pin
A	Tighten to 81 N·m (60 Lb-Ft)

93006G32

Front Disc brake pads and related components (15 inch wheel)— Thunderbird and Cougar

12. If worn, install 2 new locating pin insulators in the disc brake caliper by fabricating a tool for this purpose.

13. Lubricate the locating pins and the inside of the locating pin insulators with silicone dielectric grease, or equivalent. Install the caliper locating pins and thread them into the spindle/anchor plate assembly by hand.

14. Torque the caliper locating pins to 45–65 ft. lbs. (61–88 Nm).

15. Install the wheel and tire assembly. Torque the lug nuts in a star pattern to 85–104 ft. lbs. (115–142 Nm).

16. Lower the vehicle.

17. If equipped with air suspension, turn the air suspension switch to the **ON** position.

18. Pump the brake pedal prior to moving the vehicle to seat the brake pads.

19. If the disc brake calipers were replaced or repaired be sure to bleed the hydraulic brake system.

20. Fill the master cylinder reservoir with clean DOT 3 or equivalent brake fluid from a closed container.

21. Road test the vehicle and check for proper brake system operation.

REAR

1. If equipped with air suspension, the air suspension switch, located on the right-hand side of the luggage compartment, must be turned to the **OFF** position before raising the vehicle.

2. Remove and properly dispose ½ of the brake fluid from the master cylinder.

3. Raise and safely support vehicle.

4. Remove the rear wheel and tire assembly.

5. Release the tension from the parking brake cable and disconnect the parking brake cable from the disc brake caliper.

6. Remove 2 caliper locating pins. Lift the disc brake caliper off the rotor and anchor plate using a rotating motion.

7. Remove the inner and outer disc brake pads.

8. Inspect the disc brake rotor for scoring and wear. Replace or machine, as necessary. Observe the minimum thickness specification stamped on the rotor if machining is required.

To install:

9. Use a C-clamp and an old brake pad, wood block or equivalent, to seat the caliper piston in its bore. Do not allow metal or sharp objects to come into direct contact with the plastic caliper piston surface or damage will result.

10. Position Caliper Piston Tool T87P-2588-A or equivalent, on the rear disc brake caliper. Be sure the pins on the tool are meshed with the slots on the piston. Rotate the tool clockwise until the piston is seated in the caliper.

11. Install the inner and outer disc brake pads in the support bracket. Make sure the pads are on the correct sides.

12. Position the disc brake caliper above the rotor with the anti-rattle spring located on the lower adapter support arm. Install the caliper over the rotor with a rotating motion. Make sure the inner pad is properly positioned.

13. Insert 2 disc brake caliper locating pins and thread them in by hand. Torque the pins to 19–26 ft. lbs. (26–35 Nm).

14. Install the wheel and tire assembly. Torque the lug nuts in a star pattern to 85–104 ft. lbs. (115–142 Nm).

15. Lower the vehicle.

16. If equipped with air suspension, turn the air suspension switch to the **ON** position.

17. Pump the brake pedal prior to moving the vehicle to seat the brake pads.

18. If the disc brake caliper was repaired or replaced, make sure to bleed the hydraulic brake system.

19. Fill the master cylinder reservoir with clean DOT 3 or equivalent, brake fluid from a closed container.

20. Road test the vehicle and check for proper brake system operation.

Lincoln Mark VIII

FRONT

1. Remove and discard ½ of the brake fluid from the brake master cylinder.

2. Turn the air suspension service switch to the **OFF** position.

3. Raise and safely support vehicle.

4. Remove the wheel and tire assembly.

5. Remove the disc brake caliper pin retainers from the locating pins and remove the caliper from the anchor plate and disc brake rotor. Suspend the caliper inside the fender housing with a length of wire. Do not let the caliper hang by the brake hose.

6. Remove the outer, then inner disc brake pads from the caliper.

7. Inspect the disc brake rotor for scoring, runout and wear. Replace or machine as necessary. Do not exceed the minimum allowable thickness stamped on each disc brake rotor.

To install:

8. Using a C-clamp and a block of wood or equivalent, press the disc brake caliper piston into the caliper housing to allow for the new disc brake pads to fit the brake rotor.

9. Install the inner, then outer disc brake pads in the caliper.

10. Install the disc brake caliper over the rotor with the outer brake pad against the rotor's braking surface. This prevents pinching the piston boot between the inner brake pad and the piston.

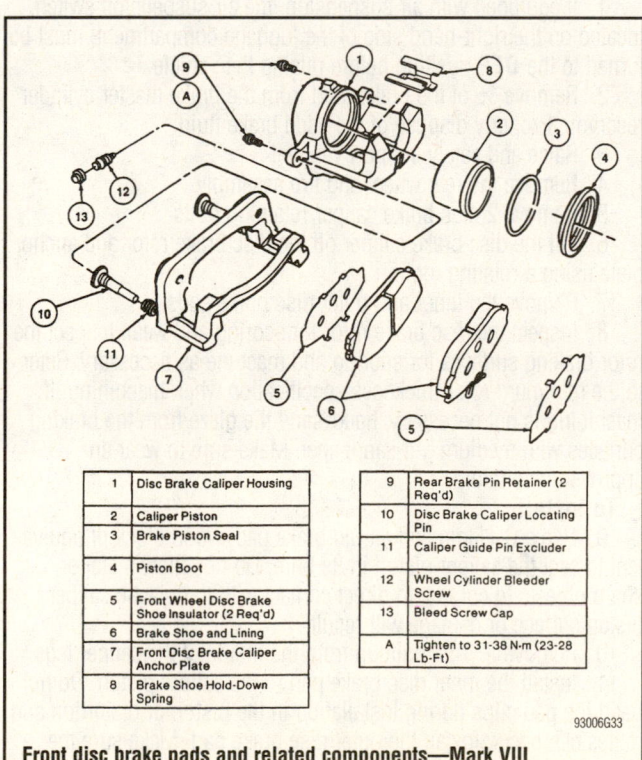

1	Disc Brake Caliper Housing	9	Rear Brake Pin Retainer (2 Req'd)
2	Caliper Piston	10	Disc Brake Caliper Locating Pin
3	Brake Piston Seal	11	Caliper Guide Pin Excluder
4	Piston Boot	12	Wheel Cylinder Bleeder Screw
5	Front Wheel Disc Brake Shoe Insulator (2 Req'd)	13	Bleed Screw Cap
6	Brake Shoe and Lining	A	Tighten to 31-38 N·m (23-28 Lb-Ft)
7	Front Disc Brake Caliper Anchor Plate		
8	Brake Shoe Hold-Down Spring		

93006G33

Front disc brake pads and related components—Mark VIII

11. Install the disc brake caliper pin retainers to the locating pins, by hand. Torque the caliper pin retainers to 16–23 ft. lbs. (22–32 Nm).

12. Install the wheel and tire assembly. Torque the lug nuts in a star pattern to 85–105 ft. lbs. (115–142 Nm).

13. Lower the vehicle.

14. Turn the air suspension service switch to the **ON** position.

15. Pump the brake pedal prior to moving the vehicle to seat the disc brake pads.

16. If the disc brake calipers were replaced or repaired, be sure to bleed the brake system.

17. Fill the brake master cylinder as needed with clean DOT 3 or equivalent brake fluid from a closed container.

18. Road test the vehicle and check for proper brake system operation.

REAR

1. Remove and discard ½ of the brake fluid from the brake master cylinder.

2. Verify that the parking brake control is released.

3. Turn the air suspension service switch to the **OFF** position.

4. Raise and safely support vehicle.

5. Remove the wheel and tire assembly.

6. Remove the retaining clip from the parking brake cable at the disc brake caliper.

7. Release the parking brake cable tension and disengage the cable end from the caliper lever.

8. Remove the disc brake caliper pin retainers securing the caliper to the locating pins.

9. Rotate the caliper away from the disc brake rotor.

10. Remove the inner and outer disc brake pads from the disc brake support bracket.

11. Inspect the disc brake rotor for scoring, runout and wear. Replace or machine as necessary. Do not exceed the minimum allowable thickness stamped on each disc brake rotor.

To install:

12. Using Caliper Piston Adjuster T87P-2588-A, or equivalent, rotate the disc brake caliper piston until it is fully seated in the caliper. Be sure the pins on the tool are meshed with the slots on the piston.

13. Install the inner and outer disc brake pads in the rear disc support bracket. Check to be sure the pads are on the correct sides, and that the nib on the inner disc brake pad is correctly installed to the slot in the caliper piston.

14. Rotate the disc brake caliper over the rotor into position on the support bracket. Install the caliper pin retainers to the caliper locating pins and thread them in by hand. Torque the pin retainers to 23–26 ft. lbs. (31–35 Nm).

15. Install the wheel and tire assembly. Torque the lug nuts in a star pattern to 85–105 ft. lbs. (115–142 Nm).

16. Lower the vehicle.

17. Turn the air suspension service switch to the **ON** position.

18. Pump the brake pedal prior to moving the vehicle to seat the disc brake pads.

19. If the disc brake calipers were replaced or repaired, be sure to bleed the brake system.

20. Fill the brake master cylinder as needed with clean DOT 3 or equivalent brake fluid from a closed container.

21. Road test the vehicle and check for proper brake system operation.

Ford Crown Victoria
Lincoln Town Car
Mercury Grand Marquis

➡ **Before continuing with this procedure, make sure to have available, 2 new disc brake caliper anchor bracket mounting bolts, per caliper. Once removed, these parts lose their torque holding ability or retention capability and must not be reused.**

FRONT

1. If equipped with air suspension, the air suspension switch, located on the right-hand side of the luggage compartment, must be turned to the **OFF** position before raising the vehicle.

2. Remove ½ of the brake fluid from the brake master cylinder reservoir. Properly dispose of the used brake fluid.

3. Raise and safely support vehicle.

4. Remove the front wheel and tire assembly.

5. Remove 2 disc brake caliper anchor bracket mounting bolts and discard. Lift the caliper assembly from the disc brake rotor using a rotating motion. Suspend the caliper inside the fender housing with wire. Do not allow the caliper to hang from the brake hose.

6. Remove the inner and outer disc brake pads. Inspect the rotor braking surfaces for scoring and machine as necessary. Refer to the minimum rotor thickness specification when machining. If

Item	Description
1	Bolt (2 Req'd)
2	Disc Brake Caliper
3	Rivet (3 Req'd)
4	Wheel Hub with ABS
5	Washer (2 Req'd)
6	Front Disc Brake Rotor
7	Wheel Hub Without ABS
8	Front Disc Brake Rotor Shield
9	Front Wheel Spindle
10	Front Disc Brake Caliper Anchor Plate Assembly

93006G83

Exploded view of the front disc assembly—Crown Victoria, Town Car, Grand Marquis

machining is not necessary, hand-sand the glaze from the braking surfaces with medium grit sandpaper. Make sure to wear an approved respirator.

To install:

7. Use a C-clamp and an old brake pad, wood block or equivalent to seat the caliper piston in its bore. Do not allow metal or sharp objects to come into direct contact with the plastic caliper piston surface or damage will result.

8. Remove all rust buildup from the inside of the caliper legs.

9. Make sure the anti-rattle spring is seated in the caliper lining inspection opening and that it is installed from the lining side.

10. Install the inner disc brake pad to the caliper piston. Do not bend the pad clips during installation in the piston or distortion and rattles can occur. Install the outer disc brake pad. Make sure the clips are properly seated.

11. Install the disc brake caliper over the rotor and install 2 new anchor bracket mounting bolts. Torque the bolts to 126–169 ft. lbs. (170–230 Nm).

12. Install the wheel and tire assembly. Torque the lug nuts in a star pattern to 85–104 ft. lbs. (115–142 Nm).

13. Lower the vehicle.

14. If equipped with air suspension, turn the air suspension switch to the **ON** position.

15. Pump the brake pedal prior to moving the vehicle to seat the brake pads.

16. Fill the master cylinder reservoir with clean DOT 3 or equivalent, brake fluid from a closed container.

17. If the disc brake calipers were replaced or repaired be sure to bleed the system.

18. Road test the vehicle and check for proper brake system operation.

REAR

1. If equipped with air suspension, the air suspension switch, located on the right-hand side of the luggage compartment, must be turned to the **OFF** position before raising the vehicle.

2. Remove ½ of the brake fluid from the brake master cylinder reservoir. Properly dispose of the used brake fluid.

3. Raise and safely support vehicle.

4. Remove the rear wheel and tire assembly.

5. Remove 2 disc brake caliper retaining bolts.

6. Lift the disc brake caliper off the disc brake rotor and anchor plate using a rotating motion.

7. Remove the inner and outer disc brake pads.

8. Inspect the disc brake rotor for scoring and wear. Inspect the rotor braking surfaces for scoring and machine as necessary. Refer to the minimum rotor thickness specification when machining. If machining is not necessary, hand-sand the glaze from the braking surfaces with medium grit sandpaper. Make sure to wear an approved respirator.

To install:

9. Use a C-clamp and an old brake pad, wood block or equivalent to seat the caliper piston in its bore. Do not allow metal or sharp objects to come into direct contact with the plastic caliper piston surface or damage will result.

10. Remove all rust buildup from the inside of the caliper legs.

11. Install the inner disc brake pad to the caliper piston. Do not bend the pad clips during installation in the piston or distortion and rattles can occur. Install the outer disc brake pad. Make sure the clips are properly seated.

➡ **Make sure the insulators are installed on the brake pads.**

12. Install the disc brake caliper over the disc brake rotor and install 2 caliper retaining bolts. Torque to 16–20 ft. lbs. (22–27 Nm).

13. Install the wheel and tire assembly. Torque the lug nuts in a star pattern to 85–104 ft. lbs. (115–142 Nm).

14. Lower the vehicle.

15. If equipped with air suspension, turn the air suspension switch to the **ON** position.

16. Pump the brake pedal prior to moving the vehicle to seat the disc brake pads.

17. Fill the master cylinder reservoir with clean DOT 3 or equivalent, brake fluid from a closed container.

18. If the disc brake calipers were replaced or repaired be sure to bleed the system.

19. Road test the vehicle and check for proper brake system operation.

Brake Drums

REMOVAL & INSTALLATION

Ford Aspire

1. Raise and safely support the vehicle.
2. Remove the tire and wheel assembly.
3. Remove the hub grease cap.
4. Remove the cotter pin and wheel bearing nut cover. Discard the cotter pin.
5. Remove the wheel bearing nut.

➡**A left-hand threaded locknut is used on the vehicle's right rear wheel spindle. Turn this locknut clockwise to loosen.**

6. Remove the brake drum, washer and bearings as an assembly. Be careful not to let the outer wheel bearing fall out of the hub during removal.

7. If the brake drum is to be machined or replaced, remove the inner wheel bearing and grease seal.

To install:

8. If removed, install the inner wheel bearing and a new grease seal.

9. Make sure the bearings and hub contain an adequate amount of clean wheel bearing grease.

10. Adjust the distance between the brake shoes to match the inner diameter of the brake drum if the brake drum has been machined or replaced.

11. Position the brake drum on the spindle. Keep the drum centered on the spindle to prevent damage to the grease seal and spindle threads.

12. Install the outer wheel bearing, washer and wheel bearing nut.

13. Properly adjust the wheel bearing preload.

14. Install the wheel bearing nut cover and a new cotter pin.

15. Install the tire and wheel assembly. Torque the lug bolts to 65–87 ft. lbs. (88–118 Nm).

16. Lower the vehicle.

17. Check the brake system for proper operation.

Ford Probe

1. Raise and safely support the vehicle.
2. Remove the wheel.

3. Remove the hub grease cap.

4. Remove the 2 brake drum screws and remove the brake drum.

5. Inspect the brake drum for wear, scoring, cracks or other damage. Machine or replace the drum, as necessary. If machining, observe the maximum drum diameter specification.

To install:

6. If the brake drum has been machined and/or the brake shoes replaced, measure the inside diameter of the brake drum using adjustment gauge D81L-1103-A or equivalent.

7. Insert a suitable tool into the knurled quadrant of the rear

Removing the brake drum—Probe

Measuring the drum with the brake adjustment gauge—Probe

Measuring the brake shoes with the brake adjustment gauge—Probe

For brake related suspension and axle service, refer to the model specific sections of this manual

Adjusting the brake shoes—Probe

brake strut and quadrant. Adjust the shoes to the same measurement as the brake drum.

8. Install the brake drum.

9. Install the brake drum screws and torque to 89–123 inch lbs. (10–14 Nm).

10. Install the hub grease cap.

11. Install the wheel and torque the lug nuts to 65–87 ft. lbs. (88–118 Nm).

12. Lower the vehicle. Complete the brake adjustment by sharply applying the brakes several times while driving the vehicle alternately forward and reverse.

Ford Contour
Mercury Mystique

1. Raise and safely support the vehicle.
2. Remove the wheel and tire assembly.
3. Remove the brake drum retainers, if installed.
4. Grasp the brake drum and remove.
5. If the drum will not slide off with light force, then the brake shoes will need to be backed off as follows:

   a. Remove the rubber plug on the backing plate and insert a screwdriver or small brake adjusting tool into the slot to contact the brake strut and quadrant.

   b. A forward motion of the tool will separate the quadrant from the knurled wheel and allow the brake shoes to retract.

   c. Remove the brake drum.

To install:

6. Make sure the brake drum and shoes are clean of any oils or protective coatings.

Positioning a screwdriver to release the brake shoes—Contour, Mystique

7. Position the brake drum onto the wheel hub.

8. Install new brake drum retainers if available.

9. Reinstall the wheel and tire assembly. Torque the lug nuts to 94 ft. lbs. (128 Nm).

10. Lower the vehicle.

11. Work the parking brake control several times to adjust the rear brake shoes.

12. Pump the brake pedal several times to assure a good pedal before attempting to move the vehicle.

13. Road test the vehicle and check for proper brake system operation.

Ford Taurus
Mercury Sable

1. Raise and safely support the vehicle. Remove the wheel and tire assembly.

2. Remove the brake drum.

➡️**If the brake drum cannot be removed easily, remove the brake tube-to-axle retention bracket and pry rubber plug from rear brake backing plate inspection hole. This will allow sufficient room for insertion of a screwdriver and brake tools to disengage brake shoe adjusting lever and back off the brake adjuster screw.**

3. Inspect the drum for scoring and/or other wear. Machine or replace, as necessary.

To install:

4. Measure the brake drum inside diameter using D81L-1103-A or equivalent brake adjustment gauge.

5. Using the brake adjustment gauge, adjust the brake shoes to the same dimensions as the brake drum.

6. Position the brake drum over the brake shoes on the axle hub.

7. Install the wheel and tire assembly. Torque the lug nuts to 85–104 ft. lbs. (115–141 Nm).

8. Lower the vehicle.

9. Pump the brake pedal several times to position the brake shoes and complete the adjustment.

10. Road test the vehicle and check for proper brake system operation.

Retracting the brake shoes to allow drum removal—Taurus and Sable

Ford Escort
Mercury Tracer

1. Raise and safely support the vehicle.
2. Remove the wheel and tire assembly.

3. Remove 2 brake drum retaining screws.

4. Pull the brake drum from the hub. Inspect the drum and refinish or replace, as necessary. If refinishing, check the maximum inside diameter specification.

To install:

5. If needed, adjust the brake shoes to fit the brake drum.

6. Place the brake drum on the hub.

7. Install 2 brake drum retaining screws. Torque to 89–123 inch lbs. (10–14 Nm).

8. Install the wheel and tire assembly. Torque the lug nuts to 73–100 ft. lbs. (100–135 Nm).

9. Lower the vehicle.

10. Check the brake system for proper operation.

Ford Mustang, Thunderbird Mercury Cougar

1. Raise and safely support the vehicle.

2. Remove the wheel and tire assembly.

3. Remove the drum retaining nuts, if equipped, and remove the brake drum.

4. Inspect the brake drum for scoring and wear. Replace or machine as necessary. If machining, observe the maximum diameter specification.

To install:

5. If a new brake drum is being installed, remove the protective coating from the drum using brake cleaner.

6. Adjust the brake shoes to the brake drum using Brake Adjusting Gauge D81L-1103-A, or equivalent.

7. Install the brake drum.

8. Install the wheel and tire assembly.

9. Lower the vehicle.

10. Complete the brake adjustment by carefully backing the vehicle up several times while applying the brakes with a minimum force of 25 lbs. (111 N).

11. Road test the vehicle and check the brake system for proper operation.

12. Check the drums for conditioning and wear. Replace or machine as necessary. If machining, observe the maximum diameter specification.

13. Installation is the reverse of removal.

Brake Shoes

REMOVAL & INSTALLATION

Ford Aspire

1. Raise and safely support the vehicle.

2. Remove the wheel and tire assembly.

3. Remove the brake drum.

4. Remove the brake shoe hold-down springs and pins.

5. Remove the brake shoe retracting springs and the right hand anti-rattle spring.

6. Pull the brake shoes away from the backing plate and remove.

To install:

7. Clean the brake backing plate.

8. Lubricate the backing plate shoe pads with a suitable high temperature grease.

9. Install the brake shoe upper retracting spring on the primary

Brake shoe hold-down spring and pin removal—Ford Aspire

Removing the secondary brake shoe—Ford Aspire

Lubricate the brake shoe pads with high temperature grease—Ford Aspire

brake shoe. Position the primary brake shoe on the backing plate and install the hold-down pin and spring.

10. Connect the upper retracting spring to the secondary brake shoe and position the shoe against the backing plate. Install the secondary brake shoe hold-down pin and spring.

11. Install the right hand anti-rattle spring and the lower brake shoe retracting spring.

12. Set the self adjuster to the fully released position. Place a suitable tool against the adjuster cam and push it to the released position.

Securing the primary brake shoe with the hold-down pin and spring—Ford Aspire

Installing the anti-rattle spring—Ford Aspire

Installing the lower brake shoe return spring—Ford Aspire

13. Install the brake drum and properly adjust the wheel bearing preload.

14. Lower the vehicle.

15. Push the brake pedal several times to set the self adjuster.

16. Check the brake system for proper operation.

Ford Probe

1. Raise and safely support the vehicle.

2. Remove the wheel and dust cap.

3. Unstake the hub locknut. Have an assistant apply the brakes to lock the hub, then remove the locknut.

4. Remove the brake drum and the hub.

5. Remove the brake shoe hold-down springs. Push the hold-down spring inward and twist the hold-down pin using needle-nose pliers until the head of the pin aligns with the slot in the spring. Release the spring and pin.

6. Remove the parking brake cable from the parking brake anchor plate.

7. Remove the brake shoe return springs and remove the brake shoes.

To install:

8. Clean the brake backing plate and brake hardware with suitable brake cleaner and air dry.

9. Inspect all components for wear and/or damage and replace, as necessary. Inspect the wheel cylinder for moisture which may indicate leakage. Verify that the rear wheel cylinder pistons move freely and that the wheel cylinder bolts are torqued to 84–108 inch lbs. (10–13 Nm).

10. Inspect the brake drum for wear, scoring cracks or other damage; machine or replace as necessary. If the drum is to be machined, be sure to observe the maximum drum diameter specification.

11. Using high temperature grease, lubricate the 6 shoe contact pads on the brake backing plate.

1	Brake Shoe Retracting Spring, Upper
2	Brake Shoe Hold Down Spring Pin
3	Trailing Brake Shoe and Lining
4	Brake Shoe Retracting Spring, Lower
5	Brake Shoe Hold-Down Spring
6	Leading Brake Shoe and Lining

Brake shoes and related components—Ford Probe

Removing the parking brake cable from the parking brake lever— Ford Probe

Removing the trailing brake shoe—Ford Probe

Apply lubricant to the brake backing plate at these locations—Ford Probe

12. Position the trailing brake shoe in the parking brake strut and install the rear hold-down pin and spring.

13. Position the leading brake shoe against the parking brake strut and backing plate and install the hold-down pin and spring.

14. Install the brake shoe return springs. Connect the parking brake cable.

15. Measure the drum inside diameter using gauge tool D81L-1103-A or equivalent. Insert a small prybar or screwdriver into the

knurled quadrant of the parking brake strut and adjust the brake shoes to the same measurement as the brake drum. The brake shoes should just touch the brake drum when properly adjusted.

16. Install the hub and the brake drum. Install a new locknut and torque to 130–174 ft. lbs. (177–235 Nm). Stake the locknut using a dull bladed chisel. Install the dust cap.

17. Install the wheel and torque the lug nuts to 65–87 ft. lbs. (88–118 Nm).

18. Lower the vehicle.

19. Complete the brake adjustment by sharply applying the brakes several times while driving the vehicle alternately forward and reverse.

Ford Contour
Mercury Mystique

1. Raise and safely support the vehicle.
2. Remove the rear wheel and tire assembly.
3. Remove the brake drum retainers, if equipped.
4. Grasp the brake drum and remove.
5. If the drum will not slide off with light force, then the brake shoes will need to be backed off:
   a. Remove the rubber plug on the backing plate and insert a screwdriver or small brake adjusting tool into the slot to contact the brake strut and quadrant.
   b. A forward motion of the screwdriver will separate the quadrant from the knurled wheel and allow the brake shoes to retract.
   c. Remove the brake drum.
6. Remove the brake shoe hold down springs and the brake shoe hold down pins.

1	Rear Brake Strut and Quadrant
2	Rear Wheel Cylinder
3	Rear Brake Shoe and Lining
4	Brake Shoe Retracting Spring
5	Parking Brake Return Spring
6	Brake Shoe Hold Down Spring
7	Anchor Block
8	Brake Shoe Hold Down Spring Pin
9	Rear Brake Backing Plate

Location of brake components—Contour/Mystique

Removal of parking brake cable—Contour/Mystique

Lubricating points on backing plate—Contour/Mystique

Measuring the brake drum inner diameter—Contour/Mystique

Adjusting the brake shoes to fit the drum—Contour/Mystique

Measuring the brake shoe adjustment—Contour/Mystique

7. Remove the brake shoe retracting springs.

8. Disengage the parking brake cable and conduit from the parking brake lever.

9. Remove the brake shoes.

10. Disengage the rear brake strut and quadrant from the rear brake shoe.

11. Remove the parking brake rear cable and conduit from the parking brake cable anchor on the trailing brake shoe.

To install:

12. Lubricate the rear brake shoe contact points on the backing plate with an appropriate grease.

13. Engage the parking brake rear cable and conduit into the parking brake cable anchor on the trailing brake shoe.

14. Position the trailing brake shoe on the backing plate.

15. Engage the rear brake strut and quadrant.

16. Reinstall the parking brake rear spring.

17. Reinstall the brake shoe hold down spring pin and the hold down spring.

18. Insert the leading brake shoe into the slot on the rear brake strut and quadrant.

19. Reinstall the brake shoe hold down pin and hold down spring.

20. Reinstall the brake shoe retracting springs.

21. Adjust the brake shoes by first measuring the inside drum diameter with an appropriate brake adjustment gauge.

22. Insert a small screwdriver or similar tool into the knurled quadrant of the brake strut and quadrant to adjust the brake shoes to the same measurement of the brake drum by expanding the brake strut and quadrant.

23. Trial fit the brake drum. The shoes should just contact the drum surface when properly adjusted.

24. Make sure that the brake drum and brake shoes are clean of any oils or protective coatings.

25. Reinstall the brake drum.

26. Reinstall new drum retainers, if available.

27. Reconnect the parking brake rear cable and conduit to the parking brake lever. It may be necessary to back off on the parking brake cable adjustment to allow for the new brake shoes.

28. Reinstall the wheel and tire assembly. Torque the lug nuts to 62 ft. lbs. (85 Nm).

29. Lower the vehicle.

30. Work the parking brake control several times to complete the brake shoe adjustment and to check the parking brake adjustment as well.

31. Pump the brake pedal several times to assure a good pedal.

32. Road test the vehicle and check for proper brake system operation.

Ford Taurus
Mercury Sable

1. Raise and safely support the vehicle. Remove the wheel and tire assembly.

2. Remove the brake drum.

3. Remove the parking brake cable from the parking brake lever.

4. Remove the 2 brake shoe hold-down springs and pins.

5. Lift the brake shoes, springs and adjuster assembly off the backing plate and wheel cylinder assembly. When removing the assembly, be careful not to bend the adjusting lever.

6. Remove the retracting springs from the lower brake attachments and upper shoe-to-adjusting lever attachment points.

7. Remove the horseshoe retaining clip and spring washer and slide the lever off the parking brake lever pin on the trailing shoe. Discard the horseshoe clip.

To install:

8. Apply a light coating of disc brake caliper slide grease at the points where the brake shoes contact the backing plate.

9. Apply a thin coat of lubricant to the adjuster screw threads and socket end of the adjusting screw. Install the stainless steel washer over the socket end of the adjusting screw and install the socket. Turn the adjusting screw into the adjusting pivot nut to the limit of the threads and then back off ½ turn.

10. Assemble the parking brake lever to the trailing shoe by installing the spring washer and a new horseshoe retaining clip. Crimp the clip until it retains the lever to the shoe securely.

11. Position the trailing shoe on the backing plate and attach the rear parking brake cable.

12. Position the leading shoe on the backing plate and attach the lower brake shoe adjusting spring to the brake shoes.

13. Install the adjuster assembly in the slots on the brake shoes. The wide slot on the dual slotted end must fit into the leading shoe. The narrow slot on the dual slotted end fits into the shoe adjusting lever. The single slotted side of the adjuster assembly must fit into the slots on the trailing shoe and the rear parking brake cable bracket.

➡ **The adjuster socket blade is marked R for the right or L for the left brake assemblies. The adjuster blade must be installed with the letter R or L in the upright position, facing the wheel cylinder. Make sure the adjuster socket fits into the parking brake lever.**

14. Complete the installation by reversing the removal procedures.

15. Pump the brake pedal several times to position the brake shoes and finish the brake shoe adjustment.

16. Road test the vehicle and check the brake system for proper operation.

1	Boot
2	Spring Expander
3	Rear Wheel Cylinder
4	Piston and Insert
5	Shoe Adjustment Access Hole
6	Wheel Cylinder Retaining Bolt (2 Req'd)
7	Brake Adjusting Hole Cover
8	Brake Shoe Hold-Down Spring Pin
9	Rear Brake Backing Plate
10	Trailing Shoe and Lining
11	Brake Shoe Hold-Down Spring
12	Brake Shoe Retracting Spring
13	Parking Brake Lever
14	Parking Brake Lever Pin (Inner)
15	Brake Shoe Adjusting Screw Socket
16	Brake Shoe Adjusting Lever
17	Parking Brake Lever Pin
18	Leading Shoe and Lining
19	Brake Shoe Adjusting Screw Spring
20	Cup
21	Washer
22	Brake Adjuster Screw
23	Washer
24	Parking Brake Lever Pin Retainer
25	Adjusting Pivot Nut
A	Tighten to 12-18 N·m (107-159 Lb-In)

93006G56

Brake shoes and related components—Taurus and Sable

For brake related suspension and axle service, refer to the model specific sections of this manual

Ford Escort
Mercury Tracer

1. Raise and safely support the vehicle.
2. Remove the wheel and tire assembly.
3. Remove 2 brake drum retaining screws and remove the brake drum.
4. Remove 2 brake shoe return springs.
5. Remove the right-hand anti-rattle spring.
6. Push and turn to release 2 brake shoe hold-down springs and remove the springs.
7. Remove the leading and trailing shoes from the brake backing plate.

To install:

8. Use a suitable high temperature grease to lightly lubricate the brake shoe contact points on the backing plate.
9. Position the trailing brake shoe on the backing plate and install one of the brake shoe hold-down springs.
10. Position the leading brake shoe on the backing plate and install the other brake shoe hold-down spring.
11. Install the right-hand anti-rattle spring.
12. Install 2 brake shoe return springs.
13. Using a brake adjusting gauge, measure the inside diameter of the brake drum.
14. Compare the brake drum measurement to the brake shoes.
15. Adjust the brake shoes by inserting a screwdriver into the knurled quadrant of the rear quad operating lever and adjust the shoes to the same measurement as the brake drum.

16. Install the brake drum.
17. Install 2 brake drum retaining screws.
18. Install the wheel and tire assembly. Torque the lug nuts to 65–87 ft. lbs. (88–118 Nm).
19. Lower the vehicle.
20. Complete the brake shoe adjustment by sharply applying the brakes several times while driving the vehicle alternating between forward and reverse gears.
21. Check the brake system operation by making several stops while driving forward.

93006G58

Checking the adjustment of the brake shoes—Escort/Tracer

1	Parking Brake Link Spring
2	Brake Shoe Hold-Down Spring Pin
3	Rear Brake Backing Plate
4	Rear Wheel Cylinder
5	Right Hand Anti-Rattle Spring
6	Rear Brake Shoe and Lining

7	Brake Shoe Hold-Down Spring
8	Brake Drum Screw (2 Req'd)
9	Brake Drum
10	Brake Shoe Retracting Spring
11	Parking Brake Lever
12	Parking Brake Return Spring
13	Brake Adjusting Hole Cover

93006G57

Brake shoes and related components—Escort/Tracer

Ford Thunderbird
Mercury Cougar (Up to 1998)

1. Raise and safely support the vehicle.
2. Remove the wheel and tire assembly.
3. Remove the brake drum.
4. Disconnect the parking brake rear cable from the parking brake lever.
5. Remove 2 brake shoe hold-down retainers, brake shoe hold-down springs and hold-down pins.
6. Lift the brake shoes, springs and adjuster off of the brake backing plate as an assembly using care not to bend the brake shoe adjusting lever.
7. Remove the brake shoe adjusting screw spring.
8. Separate the brake shoes by removing the brake shoe retracting springs.
9. Remove the parking brake lever pin retainer and spring washer, then remove the brake shoe adjusting lever from the adapter.

To install:

10. Apply a light coating of caliper slide grease or equivalent, to the brake backing plate brake shoe contact areas as well as the adjuster screw threads.
11. Assemble the adjuster screw and the brake shoe adjusting screw socket and washer. Turn the brake shoe adjusting screw socket all the way down, then back off ½ turn.
12. Install the parking brake lever to the trailing shoe with the spring washer and a new parking brake lever pin retainer. Crimp the retainer to securely retain the parking brake lever.

13. Place the trailing shoe on the brake backing plate and attach the parking brake cable.
14. Install the brake shoe hold-down pin, spring and retainers on the trailing brake shoe.
15. Place the leading shoe on the brake backing plate and attach the lower brake shoe retracting spring between both brake shoes.
16. Install the leading brake shoe hold-down pin, spring and retainers.
17. Install the brake adjuster assembly to the slots between the brake shoes. The brake shoe adjusting screw socket end must fit into the slot in the leading shoe and the adjuster nut end must fit into the slots of the trailing brake shoe and parking brake lever.
18. Install the brake shoe adjusting lever on the pin of the leading shoe and to the slot in the brake shoe adjusting screw socket.
19. Install the upper brake shoe retracting spring in the slot on the trailing shoe and the slot in the brake shoe adjusting lever. Verify that the brake shoe adjusting lever is contacting the starwheel on the adjuster assembly.
20. Adjust the brake shoes to the brake drum.
21. Install the brake drum.
22. Install the wheel and tire assembly. Using a torque wrench, torque the lug nuts in a star pattern to 85–105 ft. lbs. (115–142 Nm).
23. Lower the vehicle.
24. Apply the brakes several times while backing up the vehicle. After each stop, the vehicle must be moved forward.
25. Road test the vehicle and check for proper brake system operation by making several stops from varying forward speeds.

GENERAL MOTORS

Brake Caliper

REMOVAL & INSTALLATION

GM A-Body:
Buick Century
Oldsmobile Cutlass Ciera, Cutlass Cruiser

FRONT

1. Raise and safely support the vehicle.
2. Remove the wheel assembly.
3. If the caliper is to be removed from the vehicle for bench unit repair, disconnect the brake hose from the caliper. Cap the brake hose to avoid leakage and/or contamination. If caliper removal is to service other components, leave the brake hose connected and after caliper removal, hang the caliper out of the way on a stiff piece of wire. Do not allow the caliper to hang by the brake hose.
4. Remove the caliper mounting bolts.
5. Install 2 wheel nuts to hold the rotor in place when the caliper is removed.
6. Remove the caliper from the steering knuckle.

To install:

7. Install the caliper on the steering knuckle and torque the mounting bolts to 63 ft. lbs. (85 Nm).
8. If removed, connect the brake hose to the caliper and torque the mounting bolt to 40 ft. lbs. (54 Nm).

9. Measure the caliper clearance at the top and bottom of the caliper. The clearance should be 0.005–0.0012 inch (0.13–0.30mm).
10. Remove the nuts securing the rotor.
11. Install the tire and wheel assembly and tighten the wheel nuts to specification.
12. Lower the vehicle.
13. If the brake hose had been disconnected, bleed the brake system following the recommended procedure.

2. MOUNTING BOLT
12. CALIPER
13. INLET FITTING

93006G59

Front caliper mounting bolts—Century, Cutlass Ciera, Cutlass Cruiser

GM B-Body:
Buick Roadmaster
Cadillac Fleetwood Brougham
Chevrolet Caprice, Impala SS

1. Remove ⅔ of the brake fluid from the master cylinder assembly.

2. Raise and support the vehicle safely.

3. Mark the relationship of the wheel to the hub for reinstallation, then remove the tire and wheel assembly.

4. Position a C-clamp over the outboard shoe and lining and the caliper housing, then slowly tighten the C-clamp in order to bottom the piston into the caliper bore.

5. If removing the caliper from the vehicle for service or replacement, remove the bolt, copper washers and inlet fitting from the caliper housing. Plug the openings to prevent system contamination or excessive fluid loss and discard the used copper washers.

6. Remove the mounting bolts and the sleeves, then remove the caliper from the rotor. If the caliper is not being completely removed from the vehicle, it must be suspended from the suspension using a hook, string or wire. Never allow the caliper to hang by the brake line or damage could occur.

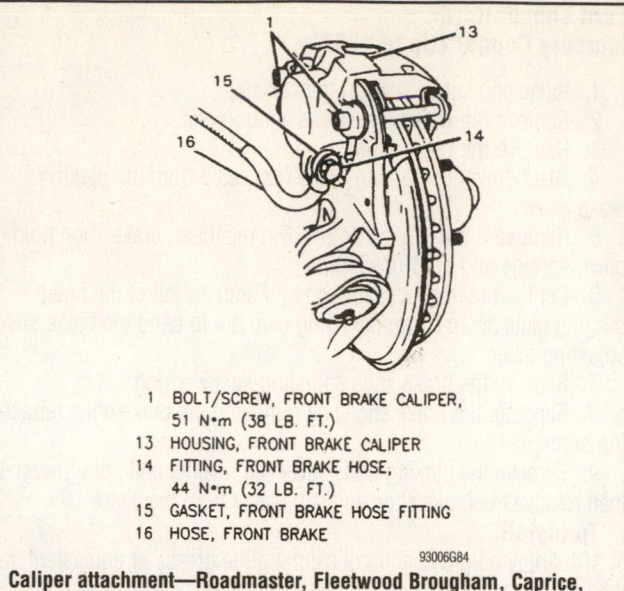

1 BOLT/SCREW, FRONT BRAKE CALIPER,
   51 N•m (38 LB. FT.)
13 HOUSING, FRONT BRAKE CALIPER
14 FITTING, FRONT BRAKE HOSE,
   44 N•m (32 LB. FT.)
15 GASKET, FRONT BRAKE HOSE FITTING
16 HOSE, FRONT BRAKE

93006G84

Caliper attachment—Roadmaster, Fleetwood Brougham, Caprice, Impala SS

A WEAR SENSOR
1 BOLT/SCREW, FRONT BRAKE
   CALIPER, 51 N•m (38 LB. FT.)
2 SLEEVE, FRONT BRAKE CALIPER BOLT
3 BUSHING, FRONT BRAKE CALIPER BOLT INNER
4 BUSHING, FRONT BRAKE CALIPER BOLT OUTER
5 PAD, FRONT DISC BRAKE OUTER
6 PAD, FRONT DISC BRAKE INNER
8 SPRING, FRONT DISC BRAKE INNER PAD RETAINER
9 BOOT, FRONT BRAKE CALIPER PISTON
10 PISTON, FRONT BRAKE CALIPER
11 SEAL, FRONT BRAKE CALIPER PISTON
12 VALVE, FRONT BRAKE CALIPER BLEEDER, 13 N•m
   (115 LB. IN.)
13 HOUSING, FRONT BRAKE CALIPER
19 CAP, FRONT BRAKE CALIPER BLEEDER VALVE

93006G85

Exploded view of the front caliper assembly—Roadmaster, Fleetwood Brougham, Caprice, Impala SS

A CALIPER BORE
6 VALVE, REAR BRAKE CALIPER BLEEDER
7 CAP, REAR BRAKE CALIPER BLEEDER VALVE
13 BOLT/SCREW, REAR BRAKE CALIPER GUIDE PIN UPPER
14 HOUSING, REAR BRAKE CALIPER
15 PIN, REAR BRAKE CALIPER GUIDE
16 BOOT, REAR BRAKE CALIPER GUIDE PIN
17 BRACKET, REAR BRAKE CALIPER ANCHOR
18 SEAL, REAR BRAKE CALIPER PISTON
19 PISTON, REAR BRAKE CALIPER
20 BOOT, REAR BRAKE CALIPER PISTON
29 PAD, REAR DISC BRAKE INNER
30 PAD, REAR DISC BRAKE OUTER
52 BOLT/SCREW, REAR BRAKE CALIPER GUIDE PIN LOWER
53 INSULATOR, REAR DISC BRAKE OUTER PAD

93006G86

Exploded view of the rear caliper—Roadmaster, Fleetwood Brougham, Caprice, Impala SS

To install:

7. Lubricate the sleeves and bushings with silicone grease, then insert the sleeves into caliper housing.

8. Position the caliper assembly onto the rotor and knuckle assembly.

9. Insert the mounting bolts and torque to 38 ft. lbs. (51 Nm).

10. Measure the distance between the caliper housing and the stops on the knuckle assembly. There should be 0.005–0.012 in. (0.13–0.30mm) of clearance. If necessary, remove the caliper assembly and file the ends of the stops on the knuckle to increase clearance. Excessive clearance requires replacement of the caliper and/or steering knuckle.

11. If removed for service or replacement, bolt new copper washers and the inlet fitting to the caliper housing, then torque to 32 ft. lbs. (44 Nm).

12. Align the marks on the wheel and hub, then install the wheel assembly.

13. Lower the vehicle.

14. Fill the master cylinder to the proper level.

15. If the line was disconnected, bleed the entire brake system following the proper procedures.

REAR

1. Raise and safely support vehicle.

2. Remove wheel and tire assembly.

3. Remove the brake hose fitting from the caliper and discard the 2 copper washers.

4. Cap the brake hose to avoid leakage and/or contamination.

5. Remove the upper and lower guide pin bolts.

6. Remove the caliper from the anchor bracket

To install:

7. Place caliper onto anchor bracket making sure that the brake pads and clips are properly seated.

8. Install the upper and lower guide pin bolts. Torque the bolts to 23 ft. lbs. (31 Nm).

9. Attach the brake hose to the caliper using 2 new copper washers. Torque the hose bolt to 20 ft. lbs. (27 Nm).

10. Bleed the entire brake system following the proper procedures.

11. Install the wheel and tire assembly and torque to specifications.
12. Lower the vehicle.
13. Check and fill the master cylinder as needed.

GM C- and H-Bodies:
Buick LeSabre, Park Avenue
Oldsmobile Eighty Eight Royale, Ninety Eight, Regency
Pontiac Bonneville

➡**The Bosch 2U ABS system cannot increase brake pressure above master cylinder pressure applied by during braking. There is no need to depressurize the system prior to service.**

1. Remove brake fluid from the master cylinder reservoir until the reservoir is approximately ⅓ full.
2. Raise and safely support the vehicle.
3. Remove the front wheel. Mark the position of the wheel to the wheel studs, prior to removal, for installation reference.
4. Install 2 lug nuts to retain the rotor once the caliper is removed.
5. Using a large C-clamp, bottom the piston in the caliper bore by positioning the C-clamp on the outboard pad and on the round portion of the brake caliper where the piston is housed.
6. Remove the banjo bolt that fastens the brake hose to the brake caliper. Discard the gaskets.
7. Cap the brake line to avoid excessive fluid loss or fluid contamination.
8. Remove the rubber dust boots from the caliper mounting bolt heads (if equipped).
9. Remove the caliper mounting bolts.
10. Remove the caliper from the vehicle.
11. Remove the brake pads.

To install:
12. Install the brake pads. Lubricate the slides where the caliper mounts on the steering knuckle with silicone grease.
13. Install the caliper over the rotor.
14. Install the caliper mounting bolts. Torque the mounting bolts to 38 ft. lbs. (51 Nm).
15. Install the rubber dust boots over the caliper mounting bolt heads (if equipped).
16. Check the clearance between the brake caliper and caliper bracket stops. If the clearance is too tight, check the caliper leading and trailing edges for build up. File down as necessary.
17. Connect the brake hose to the caliper. Install the brake hose banjo bolt, using new gaskets, and torque to 33 ft. lbs. (45 Nm).
18. Remove the lug nuts used to secure the rotor.
19. Install the wheel, aligning the reference marks made during removal, and torque the lug nuts to 100 ft. lbs. (140 Nm).

BRACKET

CLEARANCE BETWEEN CALIPER AND BRACKET STOPS SHALL BE 0.13-0.30 MM (0.005-0.012 IN.) TWO PLACES

CALIPER

93006G60

Measuring the caliper clearance—LeSabre, Park Avenue, Eighty Eight Royale, Ninety Eight, Regency, Bonneville

20. Lower the vehicle.
21. Refill the master cylinder and bleed the brake system using the recommended procedure.
22. Road test the vehicle and check for proper braking performance.

GM E-, K- and V-Bodies:
Cadillac deVille, Eldorado, Seville

FRONT

1. Disconnect the negative battery cable.
2. Remove ⅔ of the brake fluid from the master cylinder.
3. Raise and safely support the vehicle.
4. Remove the front wheel. Mark the relationship between the wheel and the wheel stud for re-installation purposes.
5. Install 2 wheel nuts to keep the rotor in place.
6. Using a large C-clamp against the inboard pad, compress the caliper piston into the caliper to provide clearance during removal.
7. Place a catch pan under the caliper.
8. Disconnect the brake hose from the caliper. Cap the line to prevent excessive fluid loss or contamination.
9. Remove the caliper mounting bolts and remove the caliper from the vehicle.
10. Inspect the mounting bolts; sleeves and boots for wear and/or damage. Replace parts as necessary.

To install:
11. Before installing the caliper, make sure the piston is fully seated in the bore and the brake pads are properly seated.
12. Lubricate the mounting bolt shafts and inner diameter of the sleeves with silicone grease.
13. Install the caliper in the caliper mounting bracket and install the mounting bolts. Torque the mounting bolts to 38 ft. lbs. (51 Nm).
14. Connect the brake hose with the bolt and new gaskets. Torque the brake hose bolt to 33 ft. lbs. (45 Nm).
15. Refill the master cylinder and bleed the brake system.
16. Remove the 2 wheel nuts securing the rotor.
17. Install the wheel and tire assembly.
18. Lower the vehicle.
19. Connect the negative battery cable.
20. Road test the vehicle for proper brake system operation.

REAR

1. Disconnect the negative battery cable.
2. Remove ⅔ of the brake fluid from the master cylinder.
3. Raise and safely support the vehicle.
4. Remove the rear wheel.
5. Install 2 wheel nuts to keep the rotor in place.
6. Place a catch pan under the caliper.
7. Disconnect the brake hose from the caliper. Cap the line to prevent fluid loss or contamination.
8. Loosen the tension on the parking brake at the equalizer.
9. Remove the parking brake cable mounting lever, and remove the cable end by lifting up and disengaging the end.
10. Remove the caliper sleeve bolt.
11. Lift the caliper up and slide the caliper inboard off of the pin sleeve to remove the caliper from the vehicle.
12. Use a suitable tool in the caliper piston slots to turn the piston and thread it into the caliper. After bottoming the piston, lift the inner edge of the boot next to the piston and press out any trapped air the boot must lay flat.

To install:
13. Inspect the pin boot, bolt boot and sleeve boot for cuts, tears or deterioration and replace as necessary.

14. Inspect the bolt sleeve and pin sleeve for corrosion or damage. Pull the boots to gain access to the sleeves for inspection or replacement. Replace corroded or damaged sleeves; do not try to polish away corrosion.

15. If not replaced, remove the pin boot from the caliper and install the small end over the pin sleeve (installed on caliper support) until the boot seats in the pin groove. This prevents cutting the pin boot when sliding the caliper onto the pin sleeve.

16. Hold the caliper in the position as removed and start it over the end of the pin sleeve. As the caliper approaches the pin boot, work the large end of the pin boot in the caliper groove, then push the caliper fully onto the pin.

17. Pivot the caliper down, being careful not to damage the piston boot on the inboard disc brake pad. Compress the sleeve boot by hand as the caliper moves into position to prevent boot damage.

18. After the caliper is in position, recheck the position of the pad clips. If necessary, use a small prybar to reseat or enter the pad clips on the bracket abutments.

19. Install the sleeve bolt and torque to 20 ft. lbs. (27 Nm).

20. Install the parking brake cable bracket, with the cable attached, and torque the bolt to 32 ft. lbs. (43 Nm).

21. Install the parking brake cable onto the parking brake lever and the retaining clip onto the parking brake cable.

22. Connect the brake hose with the bolt and new gaskets and torque the bolt to 32 ft. lbs. (43 Nm).

23. Adjust the parking brake cable.

24. Refill the master cylinder and bleed the brake system.

25. Remove the wheel nuts retaining the rotor and install the wheel. Lower the vehicle.

26. Connect the negative battery cable.

27. Road test the vehicle for proper brake system operation.

GM F-BODY:
Chevrolet Camaro
Pontiac Firebird

FRONT W/SINGLE PISTON

1. Remove ⅔ of the brake fluid from the master cylinder.
2. Raise and support the vehicle safely.
3. Matchmark the relationship between the wheel and hub, then remove the wheel and tire assembly.
4. Reinstall 2 of the lug nuts in order to retain the rotor.
5. Position a C-clamp over the outboard brake pad and the caliper housing, then use the C-clamp to bottom the piston into the caliper bore.
6. If completely removing the caliper from the vehicle for replacement or service, remove the brake hose bolt from the caliper housing and discard the copper washers.
7. Plug the openings in the inlet fitting and caliper housing to prevent system contamination or excessive fluid loss.
8. Remove the caliper mounting bolts.
9. Remove the caliper assembly from the rotor and bracket. If the caliper is not being completely removed, it must be suspended from the vehicle using a wire hook in order to prevent damage to the brake lines.

To install:

10. Inspect the mounting bolts and sleeves for damage or corrosion and replace as necessary. Do not attempt to polish away corrosion. Ensure all caliper-to-bracket contact points are rust free and clean. Check the inlet fitting bolt for blockage.

11. Lubricate the sleeves, bushings and slide points with a suitable silicone grease.

12. Install the sleeves into the caliper housing, then install the caliper assembly onto the rotor and bracket assembly. Install the mounting bolts and torque to 38 ft. lbs. (51 Nm).

13. Attach brake hose to caliper using new copper washers. Torque the bolt to 32 ft. lbs. (44 Nm).

14. Replace the brake fluid in the master cylinder and, if the caliper was removed, bleed the caliper.

15. Align the marks made earlier and install the wheel and tire assembly.

16. Lower the vehicle, then with the engine running pump the brake pedal slowly and firmly 3 times to seat then brake pads.

FRONT W/DUAL PISTON

1. Remove ⅔ of the brake fluid from the master cylinder.
2. Raise and support the vehicle safely.
3. Matchmark the relationship of the wheel and hub, then remove the wheel and tire assembly.
4. If completely removing the caliper from the vehicle for replacement or service, remove the bolt, inlet fitting and 2 gaskets from the caliper housing. Plug the openings in the caliper housing and inlet fitting to prevent system contamination or excessive fluid loss.
5. Remove the circlip and retainer pin.
6. Remove the caliper housing from the rotor and mounting bracket. If the caliper is not being completely removed, it must be suspended from the vehicle using a wire hook in order to prevent damage to the brake lines.

To install:

7. Check the inlet fitting bolt for blockage, clear or replace as necessary.
8. Install the caliper housing over the rotor and onto the mounting bracket. Ensure the guiding surfaces on the inboard and outboard disc brake pads and mounting bracket are seated correctly.
9. Press the caliper housing down to compress the bias springs. Slide a new retainer pin into position and install a new circlip.
10. If removed, install the inlet fitting, bolt and 2 new gaskets. Torque the bolt to 30 ft. lbs. (40 Nm).
11. Fill the master cylinder and bleed the brake system.
12. Align the matchmarks made earlier and install the wheel and tire assembly.
13. Lower the vehicle, then with the engine running pump the brake pedal slowly and firmly 3 times to seat then brake pads.

REAR

1. Raise and safely support the vehicle.
2. Matchmark the relationship between the wheel and hub, then remove the wheel and tire assembly. Install 2 wheel nuts to retain the rotor.
3. If completely removing the caliper from the vehicle for replacement or service, remove the brake hose bolt inlet fitting and 2 gaskets from the caliper housing.
4. Plug the openings in the caliper housing and inlet fitting to prevent system contamination or excessive fluid loss.
5. The following steps are for are for 1996 and earlier models:
   a. Disconnect the cable assembly at the equalizer.
   b. Disconnect the parking brake cable from the caliper lever and bracket.
   c. Remove the caliper lever return spring only if it is defective. Discard the spring if the coils are opened.

For brake related suspension and axle service, refer to the model specific sections of this manual

d. If necessary remove the vibration damper nut from the parking brake cable bracket.

6. Remove the 2 caliper guide pin bolts.

7. Remove the caliper housing from the rotor and mounting bracket. If the caliper is not being completely removed, it must be suspended from the vehicle using a wire hook in order to prevent damage to the brake lines.

To install:

8. Inspect the guide pins and boots and replace if corroded, worn or damaged. Check the inlet fitting bolt for blockage, clear or replace as necessary.

9. Install the caliper housing over the rotor and into the mounting bracket.

10. Install 2 caliper guide pin bolts starting with the upper pin and torque the bolts to 27 ft. lbs. (37 Nm).

11. Attach the brake hose to the caliper using 2 new copper gaskets. Torque the bolt to 22 ft. lbs. (30 Nm).

12. The following steps are for 1996 and earlier models:

a. Install the caliper lever return spring, if removed.

b. Connect the parking brake cable to the caliper bracket and caliper lever.

13. If the hose fitting was removed, bleed the entire brake system.

14. Lower the vehicle sufficiently and cycle the parking brake.

15. Raise and safely support the vehicle.

16. Inspect the caliper parking brake levers and ensure they are against the stops on the caliper housing. If the levers are not on their stops, check the parking brake adjustment.

17. Remove the 2 nuts securing the rotor, then align the match-marks made earlier and install the wheel assembly.

18. Lower the vehicle, then with the engine running pump the brake pedal slowly and firmly 3 times to seat then brake pads.

19. Check the hydraulic system for leaks.

GM G-BODY:
Buick Riviera
Oldsmobile Aurora

FRONT

1. Siphon ⅔ of the brake fluid out of the master cylinder reservoir.

2. Raise and safely support the vehicle.

3. Remove the tire and wheel assembly.

4. Install 2 wheel nuts loosely to secure the rotor when the caliper is removed.

5. Remove the bolts securing the brake hose to the caliper and disconnect the brake hose from the caliper.

6. Plug the hose to prevent excessive fluid loss and possible fluid contamination.

7. Compress the piston into the caliper bore to provide clearance for removal.

8. Remove the caliper mounting bolts.

9. Remove the caliper from the anchor bracket.

10. If the caliper is being replaced remove the brake pads from the caliper or anchor bracket.

To install:

11. Coat the inside of the caliper bushings with silicone grease (1996 and earlier).

12. Seat the caliper piston fully in its bore.

13. Install the brake pads in the caliper or anchor bracket.

14. Install the caliper on the anchor bracket and install the mounting bolts.

15. Torque the caliper mounting bolts to 38 ft. lbs. (51 Nm). On 1997 and newer models, torque the mounting bolts to 63 ft. lbs. (85 Nm).

16. Reconnect the brake hose to the caliper using new washers. Torque the fitting bolt to 33 ft. lbs. (45 Nm).

(1) Pin Bolts
(2) Outboard Pad
(3) Caliper Boot
(4) Inboard Pad
(5) Piston Seal
(6) Piston
(7) Anchor bracket
(8) Bleeder Valve
(9) Caliper Housing
(10) Caliper Anchor Bracket

93006G87

Front caliper and brake pad components—Riviera, Aurora

Compressing the front caliper piston—Riviera, Aurora

17. Remove the 2 lug nuts securing the brake rotor.
18. Install the wheel and tire assembly and torque the wheel nuts to 100 ft. lbs. (140 Nm).
19. Refill the master cylinder with fluid and bleed the brake system.
20. Pump the brake pedal several times to seat the brake pads against the rotor. Verify no hydraulic leaks and a good firm brake pedal.

REAR

1. Siphon ⅔ of the brake fluid out of the master cylinder reservoir.
2. Raise and safely support the vehicle.
3. Remove the tire and wheel assembly.
4. Install 2 wheel nuts loosely to secure the rotor when the caliper is removed.

Caliper mounting bolt and sleeve lubrication points—Riviera, Aurora

1	SLEEVE BOLT	12	PISTON BOOT
2	OUTBOARD SHOE & LINING	13	PISTON ASSEMBLY
3	INBOARD SHOE & LINING	14	PISTON SEAL
4	PAD CLIP	15	BLEEDER VALVE CAP
5	WEAR SENSOR	16	BLEEDER VALVE
6	PIN BOOT	17	LEVER RETURN SPRING
7	BOLT BOOT	18	BOLT AND WASHER
8	SLEEVE BOLT	19	CABLE SUPPORT BRACKET
9	BOLT SLEEVE	20	CALIPER BODY ASSEMBLY
10	PIN BOLT	21	CALIPER SUPPORT
11	PIN SLEEVE		

Rear caliper and brake pad components—Riviera, Aurora

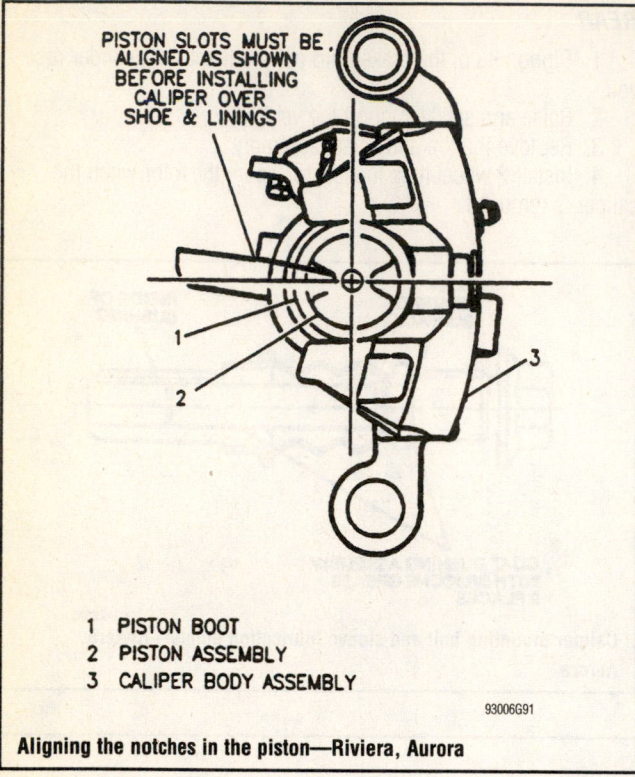

1 PISTON BOOT
2 PISTON ASSEMBLY
3 CALIPER BODY ASSEMBLY

93006G91

Aligning the notches in the piston—Riviera, Aurora

5. Remove the bolt securing the brake hose to the caliper and disconnect the brake hose from the caliper.

6. Plug the hose to prevent excessive fluid loss and possible fluid contamination.

7. The following steps are required for 1997 and earlier models:

   a. Compress the parking brake actuator lever on the caliper and disconnect the parking brake cable.

   b. Remove the bolt and washer securing the parking brake cable bracket to the caliper.

   c. Remove the lower caliper mounting bolt.

   d. Pivot the caliper upwards until it clears the brake rotor. Push the caliper inward to remove it from the upper mounting pin.

8. For 1998 and later models, remove upper and lower caliper bolts and lift caliper from mounting bracket.

To install:

9. Seat the caliper piston fully in its bore.

10. Make sure the notches in the caliper piston are at 6 and 12 o'clock.

11. The following steps are required for 1997 and earlier models:

   a. Install the caliper onto the upper pivot pin. Turn the caliper downward until it is seated over the rotor.

   b. Reinstall the sleeve bolt and torque to 20 ft. lbs. (27 Nm).

   c. Reinstall the parking brake cable bracket and torque the mounting bolt to 32 ft. lbs. (43 Nm).

   d. Pivot the parking brake actuator lever and connect the cable end to the actuator arm.

12. On 1998 and later models, mount caliper onto anchor bracket. Install the 2 mounting bolts and torque bolts to 63 ft. lbs. (85 Nm)

13. Reconnect the brake hose to the caliper using new copper washers. Torque the mounting bolt to 33 ft. lbs. (45 Nm).

14. Remove the wheel nuts securing the rotor.

15. Reinstall the tire and wheel assembly and torque the wheel nuts to 100 ft. lbs. (140 Nm).

16. Refill the master cylinder with fluid and bleed the brake system.

17. Pump the brake pedal several times to seat the brake pads against the rotor. Verify no hydraulic leaks and a good firm brake pedal.

GM J-BODY:
Chevrolet Cavalier
Pontiac Sunfire

1. Siphon ⅔ of the brake fluid out of the master cylinder.

2. Raise and safely support the vehicle.

3. Remove the tire and wheel assembly.

4. Compress the caliper piston back into the caliper bore using a large pair of pliers, C-clamp or special piston retracting tool.

5. If the caliper is to be completely removed from the vehicle for bench service, disconnect and cap the brake line from the caliper. Discard the old washers.

6. Remove the caliper mounting bolts and sleeves.

7. Remove the caliper from the knuckle.

8. Remove the brake pads from the caliper, if caliper is being replaced.

To install:

9. Install the brake pads in the caliper.

10. Install the caliper on the steering knuckle.

11. Install the mounting bolts and sleeves and torque to 40 ft. lbs. (51 Nm).

12. If the caliper brake line was disconnected, uncap and connect the brake hose to the caliper using new copper washers. Torque the mounting bolt to 35 ft. lbs. (44 Nm).

13. Refill the master cylinder and bleed the brake system.

14. Install the tire and wheel assembly and tighten to specification.

15. Lower the vehicle. Verify correct brake operation.

GM L-BODY:
Chevrolet Corsica, Beretta

1. Drain ⅔ of the brake fluid from the master cylinder.

2. Raise and safely support the vehicle.

3. Remove the tire and wheel assembly.

4. Compress the caliper piston, using a suitable tool (C-clamp or large pliers).

5. Remove the brake hose mounting bolt and discard the copper washers.

6. Plug the hose to prevent excessive fluid loss and possible fluid contamination.

7. Remove the caliper mounting bolts and remove the caliper from the vehicle.

8. If the caliper is being replaced remove the brake pads from the caliper.

To install:

9. Before installing the caliper make sure the piston is full seated in the bore and the brake pads are properly installed.

10. Install the caliper onto the steering knuckle.

11. Install the mounting bolt and sleeve assembly. Torque the mounting bolts to 38 ft. lbs. (51 Nm).

12. Attach the brake hose to the caliper using 2 new copper washers. Torque the brake hose bolt to 33 ft. lbs. (45 Nm).

13. Refill and bleed the brake system.

14. Install the wheel and tire assembly.

15. Lower the vehicle.

16. Pump the brake pedal to verify firm and correct brake pedal feel. Road test the vehicle to verify correct braking action.

GM L/N and N-BODY
Buick Skylark
Chevrolet Malibu
Oldsmobile Achieva, Cutlass
Pontiac Grand Am

1. Siphon ⅔ of the brake fluid out of the master cylinder.

2. Raise and safely support the vehicle. Remove the tire and wheel assembly.

3. Compress the caliper piston back into the caliper bore using a large pair of pliers, C-clamp or special piston retracting tool.

4. Remove the brake hose from the caliper and discard the copper washers.

5. Plug the hose to prevent excessive fluid loss and possible fluid contamination.

6. Remove the caliper mounting bolts and remove the caliper from the knuckle.

7. Remove the brake pads from the caliper, if the caliper is being replaced.

To install:

8. Inspect the condition of the caliper support for rust and corrosion that will hinder the travel of the caliper.

9. Inspect the caliper mounting hardware. New bolts are usually recommended.

10. Lubricate the mounting bushings and sleeves with silicone grease as required.

11. Install the brake pads in the caliper.

12. Install the caliper on the steering knuckle.

13. Install the mounting bolts and torque to 40 ft. lbs. (51 Nm).

14. Connect the brake hose to the caliper using new copper washers and torque the mounting bolt to 35 ft. lbs. (44 Nm).

15. Refill the master cylinder and bleed the brake system.

16. Install the tire and wheel assembly.

17. Lower the vehicle. Verify correct brake operation.

GM W-BODY:
Buick Century, Regal
Chevrolet Lumina, Monte Carlo
Oldsmobile Cutlass Supreme, Intrigue
Pontiac Grand Prix

FRONT

1. Remove ⅔ of the brake fluid from the master cylinder assembly.

2. Raise and safely support the vehicle.

3. Remove the tire and wheel assembly. Mark a relationship between the wheel and the wheel stud for re-installation purposes.

4. Install 2 wheel nuts to retain the rotor on the vehicle.

5. Install a large C-clamp over top of the caliper housing and against the back of the outboard shoe. Slowly tighten the C-clamp until the piston(s) are pushed into the caliper bore.

6. Disconnect the bolt attaching the brake hose fitting to the brake caliper.

Slide bolts lubrication points—Century, Regal, Lumina, Monte Carlo, Cutlass Supreme, Intrigue, Grand Prix

7. Plug the opening in the caliper housing and brake line to prevent brake fluid loss and contamination.

8. Remove the caliper mounting bolts.

9. Remove the brake caliper housing from the rotor and mounting bracket.

10. If the caliper is to be replaced or repaired remove the brake pads from the caliper or mounting bracket.

To install:

11. Fully inspect the brake caliper bushing assemblies for cuts, tears or deterioration and replace parts as needed.

12. Inspect the slide bolts for corrosion. If corrosion is found, replace the slide bolts and bushings before installing the brake caliper assembly.

13. Before installing the caliper, make sure the piston(s) are seated in the bore, and that the brake pads are correctly installed.

14. Lubricate the caliper slide bolts with silicone grease. Do not lubricate the bolt threads.

15. Install brake pads onto caliper or mounting bracket.

16. Install the caliper bolts and torque the bolts to 63 ft. lbs. (85 Nm).

17. Install the brake hose inlet fitting to the caliper and torque the bolt to 24 ft. lbs. (32 Nm).

18. Remove wheel nuts securing the brake rotor to the hub.

19. Install the tire and wheel assembly.

20. Safely lower the vehicle.

21. Fill the master cylinder to the proper level.

22. Bleed the brake system.

23. Verify correct brake operation.

REAR

1. Remove ⅔ of the brake fluid from the master cylinder assembly.

2. Raise and safely support the vehicle.

3. Remove the tire and wheel assembly. Mark a relationship between the wheel and the wheel stud for re-installation purposes.

4. Install 2 wheel nuts to retain the rotor.

5. Remove the brake hose from the caliper and discard the copper washers.

6. Plug the openings in the caliper and the brake hose to prevent brake fluid loss and contamination.

7. The following steps are for models with the park brake cable attached to the caliper:

    a. Disconnect the parking brake cable from the parking brake

1	CALIPER SLIDE BOLT	9	PISTON SEAL
2	OUTBOARD SHOE & LINING	10	CAP
3	INBOARD SHOE & LINING	11	BLEEDER
4	BUSHING ASSEMBLY	12	CALIPER HOUSING
7	CALIPER BOOT	13	BRACKET
8	PISTON	14	WEAR SENSOR

93006G62

Caliper attachments—Century, Regal, Lumina, Monte Carlo, Cutlass Supreme, Intrigue, Grand Prix

lever on the caliper. Lift up one end of the cable spring clip free end of the cable from the lever.

b. Remove the bolt and washer attaching the cable support bracket to the caliper body assembly.

c. Remove the caliper sleeve bolts.

8. For all others, remove the two caliper mounting bolts.

9. Remove the caliper body assembly from the vehicle. Pivot the caliper assembly up to clear the rotor and then slide it inboard off the pin sleeve.

To install:

10. Inspect the caliper bolt boots, pins and sleeve bolt for cuts, tears or deterioration. Replace as necessary.

11. Lubricate the mounting surfaces and the mounting sleeves.

12. Hold the caliper body assembly in the position from which it was removed, and start it over the end of the pin sleeve.

13. As the caliper body assembly approaches the pin boot, work the large end of the pin boot in the caliper body groove. Push the caliper body fully onto the pin.

14. Pivot the caliper body assembly down, using care not to damage the piston boot on the inboard shoe. Compress the sleeve boot by hand as the caliper body moves into position to prevent boot damage.

15. After installing the caliper assembly into position, recheck

the installation of the pad clips. If necessary, use a small prying tool to reset or center the pad clips.

16. Install the brake caliper sleeve bolts and torque to 20 ft. lbs. (27 Nm).

17. On models without caliper mounted park brake cable, torque caliper mounting bolts to 32 ft. lbs. (43 Nm)

18. To install the park brake cable, the following steps apply (some models).

a. Install the cable support bracket with the cable attached. Torque bolt to 32 ft. lbs. (43 Nm).

b. Lift up on the end of the cable spring clip and work the end of the parking brake cable into the notch of the parking brake lever.

19. Connect the brake hose to the brake caliper and torque the bolt to 32 ft. lbs. (44 Nm).

20. Remove the wheel nuts securing the rotor to the hub and bearing assembly.

21. Install the tire and wheel assembly.

22. Safely lower the vehicle.

23. Fill the master cylinder to the proper level with clean brake fluid.

24. Bleed the brake system using the recommended procedure.

25. Apply approximately 175 lbs. (79 kg) of force, 3 times, to properly seat the brake shoe and linings against the rotor.

26. Adjust the parking brake cable as necessary (some models).

GM Y-BODY:
Chevrolet Corvette

FRONT

1. Disconnect the negative battery cable and remove ⅔ of the brake fluid from the master cylinder reservoir.

2. Raise and support the vehicle safely.

3. Mark the relationship between the wheel and axle flange, then remove the tire and wheel assembly.

4. Install 2 wheel nuts to retain the brake rotor.

5. Depress the caliper pistons into the caliper bores in order to provide clearance between the pads and the rotor.

6. Disconnect the brake hose fitting at the caliper by removing the bolt. Discard the 2 copper washers.

7. Plug all openings to prevent fluid contamination or loss.

➡**Do not allow the fluid to come into contact with the front transverse spring, as damage to the spring may occur.**

8. For 1996 Corvette, remove the circlip and the retainer pin.

9. For 1997 and later Corvette, remove the 2 caliper mounting bolts.

10. Remove the caliper housing from the rotor and the caliper mounting bracket.

To install:

11. Install the caliper over the brake rotor and into the caliper mounting bracket. Make sure the shoe lining guiding surfaces are correctly seated in the bracket.

➡**For 1996 Corvette, there are 2 sets of retainer pins in most repair kits. One set is for base calipers and the other is for heavy duty calipers. Make certain the correct retainer pins are installed.**

12. Compress the bias springs by applying pressure to the mounting bracket, then install the new retainer pin and circlip (1996 Corvette).

13. Connect the brake hose inlet fitting using 2 new copper washers and the inlet fitting bolt. Torque the bolt to 30 ft. lbs. (40 Nm).

14. Properly bleed the entire brake system.

15. Remove the wheel nuts retaining the rotor, align the marks made earlier and install the tire and wheel assembly.

16. Lower the vehicle.

17. Check the brake fluid and add as necessary.

18. Connect the negative battery cable, start the engine and pump the brake pedal slowly and firmly 3 times to seat the shoe and lining assemblies.

REAR

1. On 1996 models, disengage the parking brake automatic adjuster as follows:

   a. Remove the drivers seat cushion.

   b. Remove the parking brake lever cover and screws.

   c. Using a suitable offset tool, disengage and hold the drive pawl from the drive sector.

   d. Insert a nail or drift through the hole in the anchor plate to retain the drive pawl in the disengaged position.

   e. Move the parking brake lever until it aligns with the lock pawl.

   f. Depress the button on the lever and move the lever to the down position.

   g. Verify the anchor plate is against the stud on the parking brake lever, if not as specified, repeat the procedure.

2. Raise and support the vehicle safely.

3. Mark the relationship between the wheel and axle flange, then remove the tire and wheel assembly.

4. Install 2 wheel nuts to retain the brake rotor.

5. Disconnect the brake line fitting at the caliper and discard the 2 copper gaskets.

6. Plug all openings to prevent fluid contamination or loss.

1	CAP, BLEEDER SCREW	7	PIN, RETAINER
2	SCREW, BLEEDER	8	PAD, INBOARD BRAKE
3	HOUSING, CALIPER	9	PAD, OUTBOARD BRAKE
4	SEAL	10	BRACKET, CALIPER MOUNTING
5	PISTON, CALIPER	11	CIRCLIP
6	BOOT	12	SPRING, BIAS

93006G63

Exploded view of the front caliper assembly—Corvette

For brake related suspension and axle service, refer to the model specific sections of this manual

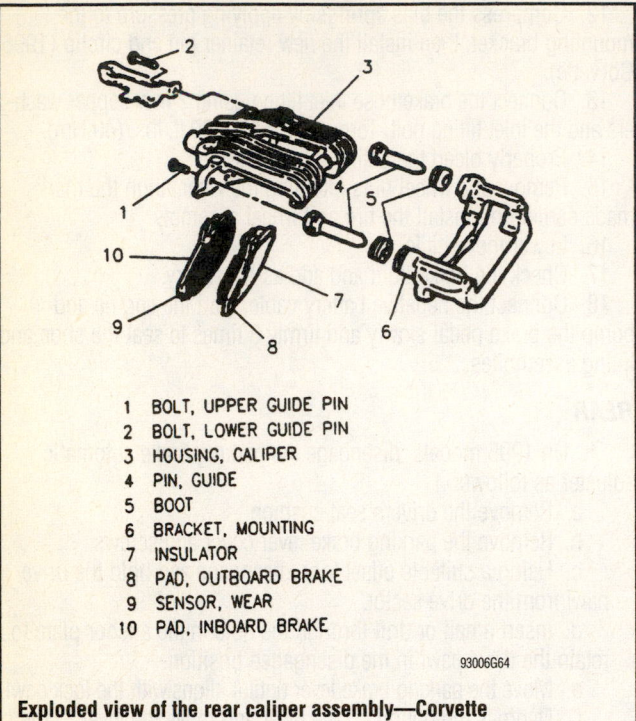

1	BOLT, UPPER GUIDE PIN
2	BOLT, LOWER GUIDE PIN
3	HOUSING, CALIPER
4	PIN, GUIDE
5	BOOT
6	BRACKET, MOUNTING
7	INSULATOR
8	PAD, OUTBOARD BRAKE
9	SENSOR, WEAR
10	PAD, INBOARD BRAKE

93006G64

Exploded view of the rear caliper assembly—Corvette

➡**Do not remove the lever return spring unless the parking brake cable automatic adjuster has been properly disabled (1996 models).**

7. Remove the lever return spring. Discard the spring if the coils are opened.

8. Disconnect the brake cable from the lever and bracket.

9. Remove the 2 guide pins bolts and discard.

10. Remove the caliper housing from the brake rotor and caliper mounting bracket.

To install:

11. Inspect the guide pins for free movement and replace the pins or boots if damaged or corroded.

12. Install the caliper over the brake rotor and into the mounting bracket.

13. For 1997 and later models, install the caliper mounting bolts and torque to 23 ft. lbs. (31 Nm).

14. For 1996 models, install 2 new guide pin bolts. Torque the upper bolt to 26 ft. lbs. (35 Nm) and the lower bolt to 16 ft. lbs. (22 Nm).

15. Install the cable to the bracket and parking brake lever, then install the lever return spring (1996 models).

16. Connect the brake line fitting using 2 new copper washers and the inlet fitting bolt. Torque the bolt to 30 ft. lbs. (40 Nm).

17. Properly bleed the entire hydraulic brake system.

18. For 1996 models, enable the parking brake automatic adjuster in the reverse order of the disable procedure and make sure the levers are against the stops on the caliper housing.

19. Remove the 2 nuts securing the rotor to the hub.

20. Align the marks made earlier and install the tire and wheel assembly.

21. Lower the vehicle.

22. Check the brake fluid level.

23. Connect the negative battery cable, start the engine and pump the brake pedal slowly and firmly 3 times to seat the shoe and lining assemblies.

GEO Metro

1. Siphon a sufficient quantity of brake fluid from the master cylinder reservoir to prevent the brake fluid from overflowing the master cylinder when removing or installing the calipers. This is necessary, as the piston must be forced into the cylinder bore to provide sufficient clearance to install the caliper.

2. Raise and safely support the vehicle.

3. Remove the wheel and tire assembly.

4. Install 2 lug nuts finger tight to hold the disc in place.

5. Disconnect the brake hose fitting at the caliper and discard the 2 copper washers. Use a pan to catch any spilled fluid and immediately plug the disconnected hose.

6. Remove the 2 caliper mounting bolts and then remove the caliper from the mounting bracket.

To install:

7. Use a caliper compressor, a C-clamp or large pair of pliers to slowly press the caliper piston back into the caliper.

8. Apply a thin, even coating of anti-seize compound to the sliding surfaces. Don't use grease or spray lubricants; they will not hold up under the extreme temperatures generated by the brakes.

9. Install the caliper assembly to the mounting plate.

10. Install caliper mounting bolts and torque to 22 ft. lbs. (30 Nm).

11. Install the brake hose to the caliper using 2 new copper washers. Torque the bolt to 17 ft. lbs. (23 Nm).

12. Bleed the brake system.

13. Remove the 2 lugs holding the disc in place and install the wheel and tire assembly.

14. Lower the vehicle.

15. Check the level of the brake fluid in the master cylinder reservoir; it should be at least to the middle of the reservoir.

GEO Prizm

FRONT

1. Raise and safely support the vehicle.

2. Siphon a sufficient quantity of brake fluid from the master cylinder reservoir to prevent the brake fluid from overflowing the master cylinder when removing or installing the calipers. This is necessary, as the piston must be forced into the cylinder bore to provide sufficient clearance to install the caliper.

84229044

Using a large C-clamp to compress the piston back into the caliper bore

3. Remove the wheel and tire assembly.

4. Install 2 lug nuts finger tight to hold the brake rotor in place.

5. Disconnect the brake hose at the caliper and discard the 2 copper washers. Use a pan to catch any spilled fluid and immediately plug the disconnected hose.

6. Remove the 2 caliper mounting bolts and then remove the caliper from the mounting bracket.

To install:

7. Use a caliper compressor, a C-clamp or large pair of pliers to slowly press the caliper piston back into the caliper.

8. Apply a thin, even coating of anti-seize compound to the sliding surfaces. Don't use grease or spray lubricants; they will not hold up under the extreme temperatures generated by the brakes.

9. Install the caliper assembly to the mounting plate.

10. Install the caliper mounting bolts and torque to 25 ft. lbs. (34 Nm).

11. Install the brake hose to the caliper using 2 new copper washers. Torque the brake hose bolt to 22 ft. lbs. (30 Nm).

12. Bleed the brake system.

13. Remove the 2 lugs holding the disc in place and install the wheel.

14. Lower the vehicle to the ground.

15. Check the level of the brake fluid in the master cylinder reservoir; it should be at least to the middle of the reservoir.

Saturn

FRONT

1. Raise and safely support the vehicle.

2. Remove the front wheel and tire assembly.

3. Disconnect the brake hose from the caliper and discard the 2 copper washers.

4. Plug the openings to prevent system contamination or excessive fluid loss.

5. Remove the lock pin and guide pin from the caliper.

6. Remove the caliper from the support, being careful not to damage the pin boots.

7. Remove the pin boots from the caliper support and inspect for damage.

To install:

8. If necessary, bottom the caliper piston by hand, or by using a C-clamp.

9. If removed, install the brake pads and clips to the caliper support.

10. Lubricate the pin boots and guide pins with silicone grease.

11. Install the pin boots into the caliper support, using the pin to assure that the boot passes all the way through the support.

12. Position the caliper onto the support and over the brake pads.

13. Lubricate the non-threaded portion of the guide and lock pins with silicone grease.

14. Install the pins through the caliper and torque to 27 ft. lbs. (36 Nm).

➡**Make sure the brake line is properly routed with loop to the rear and that the hose is not twisted.**

15. Install the brake hose using 2 new copper washers. Torque the fitting bolt to 36 ft. lbs. (49 Nm).

16. Properly bleed the hydraulic brake system.

17. Install the wheel and tire assembly.

18. Lower the vehicle.

REAR

1. Raise and safely support the vehicle.

2. Remove the rear wheel and tire assembly.

3. Disconnect the brake hose from the caliper and discard the 2 copper washers.

4. Plug the openings to prevent system contamination or excessive fluid loss.

5. Slip the end of the parking cable off the parking brake lever.

6. Remove the cable outer housing from the cable bracket with SA9151BR, or an equivalent cable release tool.

7. Remove the lock pin and guide pin.

8. Remove the caliper from the support, being careful not to damage the pin boots.

9. Remove the pin boots from the caliper support for inspection and lubrication.

To install:

10. Make sure the piston is bottomed in the bore. Do not compress the piston using a C-clamp; instead the piston must be rotated into the caliper on its threads using a piston driver tool.

11. If removed, install the brake pads and clips to the caliper support.

12. Lubricate the pin boots and guide pins with silicone grease.

13. Install the pin boots into the caliper support, using the pin to assure that the boot passes all the way through the support.

14. Position the caliper onto the caliper support.

15. Lubricate the non-threaded portion of the guide and lock pins. Install the pins and torque to 27 ft. lbs. (36 Nm).

16. Install the brake hose using new copper washers and torque the fitting bolt to 36 ft. lbs. (49 Nm).

17. Connect the parking brake cable.

18. Properly bleed the hydraulic brake system.

19. Install the wheel and tire assembly.

20. Lower the vehicle.

Disc Brake Pads

REMOVAL & INSTALLATION

GM A-BODY:
Buick Century
Oldsmobile Cutlass Ciera, Cutlass Cruiser

FRONT W/LIGHT DUTY BRAKES

1. Siphon ⅔ of the brake fluid out of the master cylinder reservoir.

2. Raise and safely support the vehicle.

3. Remove the tire and wheel assembly.

4. Install 2 wheel nuts to secure the rotor in place when the caliper is removed.

5. Unstake the outboard pads using a hammer and chisel.

6. Remove the caliper mounting bolt and sleeve assemblies.

7. Remove the caliper from the steering knuckle and support on a wire. DO NOT disconnect the brake hose or allow the brake hose to support the weight of the caliper.

8. Remove the outboard pad from the caliper.

2   MOUNTING BOLT & SLEEVE ASSEMBLY
3   BUSHING
4   BLEEDER VALVE CAP
5   OUTBOARD SHOE & LINING
6   WEAR SENSOR
7   INBOARD SHOE & LINING
8   BOOT
9   PISTON
10 PISTON SEAL
11 BLEEDER VALVE
12 CALIPER HOUSING

93006G65

Brake components w/light duty front brakes—Century, Cutlass Ciera, Cutlass Cruiser

7. INBOARD SHOE & LINING
12 CALIPER HOUSING
17 SHOE RETAINER SPRING

93006G66

Installing the inboard pad into the caliper—Century, Cutlass Ciera, Cutlass Cruiser

9. Pull the top of the inboard pad out from the caliper to disengage the spring clip and remove the pad.

10. Using a suitable C-Clamp compress the caliper piston fully into the caliper bore.

To install:

11. Install the inboard pad with a new spring clip into the caliper piston. Locking the bottom edge of the spring clip into the piston, and pushing the top of the pad back will lock the pad into position.

12. Install the outboard pad into the caliper.

13. Install the caliper on the steering knuckle.

14. Torque the mounting to 38 ft. lbs. (51 Nm).

15. Pump up the brake pedal until the pads seat against the rotor.

16. Using a suitable tool lock the brake pedal down keeping the front wheels locked.

17. Using a hammer and punch, stake the pad ears down until they are flat against the caliper. The pad ears must hold the pad firmly in place.

18. Remove the 2 wheel nuts securing the rotor.

19. Install the tire and wheel assembly and torque to specification.

20. Lower the vehicle.

21. Check and fill the master cylinder with clean brake fluid.

FRONT W/HEAVY DUTY BRAKES

1. Siphon ⅔ of the brake fluid out of the master cylinder reservoir.

2. Raise and safely support the vehicle.

3. Remove the tire and wheel assembly.

4. Install 2 wheel nuts to secure the rotor in place when the caliper is removed.

5. Remove the caliper mounting bolts.

6. Remove the caliper from the steering knuckle and support on a wire. DO NOT disconnect the brake hose from the caliper or allow the caliper to hang by the brake hose unsupported.

7. Remove the outboard pad by pushing the pad inward to unseat the pad from the caliper. Once the pad alignment dowels are clear of the caliper body push the pad out of the caliper.

8. Pull the top of the inboard pad out from the caliper to disengage the spring clip securing the inboard pad and remove the pad.

9. Using a suitable C-Clamp or large pliers, compress the caliper piston fully into the caliper bore.

To Install:

10. Install the inboard pad with a new spring clip into the caliper piston. Locking the bottom edge of the spring clip into the piston, and pushing the top of the pad back will lock the pad into position.

11. Install the outboard pad into the caliper making sure the dowels in the brake pad seat in the holes in the caliper.

12. Install the caliper on the steering knuckle and install the mounting bolts.

13. Torque the mounting bolts to 38 ft. lbs. (51 Nm).

14. Remove the 2 wheel nuts securing the brake rotor.

15. Install the tire and wheel assembly and torque to specification.

16. Lower the vehicle.

17. Pump the brake pedal several times to seat the pads against the rotor.

18. Check and fill the master cylinder.

GM B-BODY:
Buick Roadmaster
Cadillac Fleetwood Brougham
Chevrolet Caprice, Impala SS

1. Raise and safely support the vehicle.
2. Mark the relationship of the wheel to the hub for reinstallation, then remove the tire and wheel assembly.
3. Position a C-clamp over the outboard shoe and lining and the caliper housing, then slowly tighten the C-clamp in order to bottom the piston into the caliper bore.
4. Remove the caliper mounting bolts.
5. Remove the caliper from the bracket and support the caliper with wire. Do not let the caliper hang by the brake hose.
6. Remove the inner and outer brake pads from the caliper.
7. Remove the bushings and sleeves from the grooves in the caliper housing.
8. Remove the shoe retainer spring from the inboard pad.

To install:

9. If not done during removal, bottom the piston in the caliper bore using a large C-clamp.
10. Lift the inner edge of the piston boot and press out any trapped air.
11. Clean and then lubricate the bushings and sleeves with silicone grease, then install the bushings and sleeves into the grooves of the caliper housing.
12. Install the shoe retainer spring onto the back of the inboard pad and position the pad into the piston.
13. Be sure to seat the shoe retainer spring in the piston and check that the pad is flat against the piston. Also, the boot and inner pad must not be in contact. If necessary, reseat or reposition the boot.

➡ **The wear sensor should be at the leading edge of the inboard pad during forward wheel rotation.**

14. Install the outboard pad with the back of the pad flat against the housing.
15. Install the caliper assembly onto the mounting bracket. Torque the mounting bolts to 38 ft. lbs. (51 Nm).
16. Clinch the pad tabs using a chisel or wedge tool between the tab and caliper casting, then using a brass punch to drive the tab down against the caliper.
17. Install the tire and wheel assembly.
18. Lower the vehicle.
19. Apply the brake pedal 3 times to seat the pads and to achieve a firm brake pedal.

REAR

1. Raise and safely support vehicle.
2. Remove wheel and tire assembly.
3. Position a C-clamp over the outboard shoe and lining and the caliper housing, then slowly tighten the C-clamp in order to bottom the piston into the caliper bore.
4. Remove the upper guide pin bolt.
5. Rotate the caliper in a downward motion. Use caution not to strain the brake hose or cable conduit.
6. Remove the brake pads from the anchor bracket.

To install:

7. Place the brake pads and shims into the anchor bracket.
8. Rotate the caliper upward onto anchor bracket. Make sure that the brake pads and clips are properly seated.

9. Install the upper guide pin bolt. Torque the bolt to 23 ft. lbs. (31 Nm).
10. Install the wheel and tire assembly and torque to specifications.
11. Lower the vehicle.
12. Pump the brake pedal several times to seat the brake pads.
13. Check and fill the master cylinder as needed.

GM C- and H-BODIES:
Buick LeSabre, Park Avenue
Oldsmobile Eighty Eight Royale, Ninety Eight, Regency
Pontiac Bonneville

1. Remove brake fluid from the master cylinder reservoir until the reservoir is approximately ⅓ full. Discard the removed fluid.
2. Raise and safely support the vehicle.
3. Remove the front wheel. Mark the position of the wheel to the wheel studs, prior to removal, for installation reference.
4. Install 2 lug nuts to retain the rotor once the caliper is removed.
5. Remove the caliper mounting sleeve bolts. Support the caliper out of the way using wire. DO NOT disconnect the brake hose or allow the caliper to hang from the brake hose.
6. Remove the outboard pad by pushing it in toward the piston until the mounting tabs clear the holes in the caliper body. With the tabs clear of the holes, push the pad out the bottom of the caliper.
7. Remove the inboard pad from the piston by pulling the top of the pad out to disengage the retainer spring.

To install:

8. Before installing the pads in the caliper, the piston must be fully seated in the bore. A large C-clamp can be used to compress the piston.
9. Install the inboard pad in the caliper by inserting the top pad ears in first, then sliding the bottom of the pad into place until the spring clip snaps into place. Make sure the inboard pad seats flush against the caliper piston.
10. Install the outboard pad by lining up the tabs on the rear of the pad with the mounting holes in the caliper body. Press the pad firmly down into the caliper until the tabs snap into the mounting holes.
11. Clean and lubricate the caliper bolt and sleeve assemblies and install them into the caliper. Lubricate the caliper slides and mountings.
12. Install the caliper over the rotor and torque the mounting bolts to 38 ft. lbs. (51 Nm).
13. Remove the 2 lug nuts used to secure the rotor in place.
14. Install the wheel, aligning the marks made during removal, and torque the lug nuts to 100 ft. lbs. (140 Nm).
15. Lower the vehicle.
16. Pump the brake pedal several times to seat the pads against the rotor.
17. Refill the master cylinder using DOT 3 brake fluid only and road test to verify proper brake operation.

GM E-, K- and V-BODIES:
Cadillac deVille, Eldorado, Seville

FRONT

1. Remove ⅔ of the brake fluid from the master cylinder reservoir.
2. Raise and safely support the vehicle.
3. Remove the front wheel.
4. Remove the caliper mounting bolts.

5. Remove the caliper from the steering knuckle without disconnecting the brake hose.

6. Suspend the caliper from the coil spring with wire. Do not let the caliper hang from the brake hose.

7. The following steps apply to 1997 and earlier models:

a. Remove the outboard pad by pushing in enough to unseat the back of the pad from the caliper housing. Once the button on the back of the pad is clear of the caliper, push the pad out the bottom of the caliper.

b. Remove the inboard pad by unsnapping the shoe spring from the piston.

8. On 1998 and later models, remove brake pads from anchor bracket.

Supporting the front caliper—deVille, Eldorado, Seville

7. Inboard Shoe & Lining
12. Caliper Housing
17. Shoe Retainer Spring

Installing the inboard disc brake pad into the front caliper—deVille, Eldorado, Seville

5. Outboard Shoe & Lining
6. Wear Sensor
12. Caliper Housing

Installing the outboard disc brake pad in the front caliper—deVille, Eldorado, Seville

To install:

9. Fully seat the caliper piston into the bore using a large C-clamp.

10. Lubricate the brake caliper mounting surfaces.

11. The following steps apply to 1997 and earlier models:

a. Install the inboard pad by snapping the pad retainer spring into the caliper piston. The pad must lie flat against the piston.

b. Install the outer pad by pushing the pad straight in from the bottom of the caliper. A click will be heard when the button on the back of the pad seats in the recess in the caliper. Take care when installing the new pad, not to distort the spring clip on the outside of the pad. Make sure the wear indicator is at the trailing edge of the pad during forward wheel rotation.

c. Install the caliper on the steering knuckle and install the bolts. Torque the mounting bolts to 38 ft. lbs. (51 Nm).

12. 1998 and later models:

a. Install the brake pads onto the anchor bracket using new shims and clips.

b. Place the caliper onto the anchor bracket and install mounting bolts.

c. Torque the mounting bolts to 63 ft. lbs. (85 Nm).

13. Install the wheel and tire assembly and torque to specification.

14. Lower the vehicle.

15. Pump the brake pedal several times to seat the brake pads.

16. Check the fluid level in the master cylinder and fill as necessary.

17. Road test the vehicle for proper brake operation.

REAR

1. Remove ⅔ of the brake fluid from the master cylinder reservoir.

2. Raise and safely support the vehicle.

3. Remove the rear wheel.

4. Remove the park brake cable from the caliper.

➡**Some models use a brake pad wear sensor. Disconnect the sensor connector from the vehicle harness.**

5. Remove the caliper mounting bolts and position and suspend the caliper from the strut with a wire. Do not let the caliper hang from the brake hose.

6. Remove the inboard and the outboard brake pads from the caliper mounting bracket.

To install:

7. Lubricate mounting surfaces and install new brake pad clips.

8. The caliper piston must be fully seated in the bore. A spanner type tool can be used to bottom the piston into its bore by turning it in. Make sure the slots in the piston are straight across from each other so the notches on the brake pad will seat.

9. Install the inboard pad by inserting the pad into the straight tabs on the retainer, then pressing down and snapping the pad under the S-shaped tabs. The pad should lay flat against the rotor. Make sure the D-shaped notches are in line with the buttons on the back of the pad lining. If they are not in alignment, rotate the piston until the D-shaped notches face the caliper mounting bolt holes.

10. Install the outer pad into the brake pad clips. Make sure the wear indicator is at the leading edge of the pad during forward wheel rotation.

11. Install the caliper on the mounting bracket and install the bolts. Torque the mounting bolts to 63 ft. lbs. (85 Nm).

12. Install the parking brake cable onto the caliper.

13. Install the wheel and tire assembly and torque to specification.

14. Lower the vehicle.

1 PISTON BOOT
2 PISTON ASSEMBLY
3 CALIPER BODY ASSEMBLY

93006G70

Aligning the slots on the rear caliper—deVille, Eldorado, Seville

15. Fill the master cylinder reservoir to the FULL mark and pump the brake pedal several times to seat the brake pads.

16. Check the fluid level in the master cylinder again and fill as necessary.

17. Road test the vehicle for proper brake operation.

GM F-BODY:
Chevrolet Camaro
Pontiac Firebird

FRONT

1. Remove the caliper assembly from the rotor and mounting bracket without disconnecting the brake line, then position aside. Do not allow the caliper to hang by the brake hose, suspend it with a length of wire or a fabricated hook.

2. Remove the outer pad assembly using a small prytool, if necessary, to disengage the show buttons from the caliper assembly.

3. Remove the inner pad.

To install:

4. If not done already, bottom the piston into the caliper using a large C-clamp positioned on the housing and inside the piston well.

5. With the piston bottomed in the caliper bore, lift the inner edge of the boot next to the piston and press out any trapped air. Make sure the boot is flat.

6. Install the inner pad assembly by positioning the retainer spring into the piston. The pad must lay flat against the piston and the boot must not touch the pad. If the boot and pad are in contact, remove the pad and reposition the boot.

7. Install the outer pad assembly, making sure the back of the pad is flat against the caliper. The wear sensor should be at the trailing lower edge of the outer pad during forward wheel rotation or the outer pad has been installed on the wrong side.

8. Install the caliper assembly to the rotor and mounting bracket.

REAR

1. Remove ⅔ of the brake fluid from the master cylinder reservoir.

2. Raise and safely support the vehicle.

3. Matchmark the relationship of the wheel to the axle flange, then remove the wheel and tire assembly. Install 2 wheel nuts to retain the rotor.

4. Position a C-clamp and tighten until the piston bottoms in the base of the caliper housing. Make sure 1 end of the C-clamp rests on the inlet fitting bolt and the other against the outboard disc brake pad.

➡️It is not necessary to remove the parking brake caliper lever return spring to replace the disc brake pads.

5. Remove the upper caliper guide pin bolt and discard.

6. Rotate the caliper housing on the lower caliper mounting bolt. Be careful not to strain the hose or cable conduit. It may be necessary to loosen the lower caliper guide pin slightly.

7. Remove the disc brake pads and discard the shim.

To install:

8. Clean all residue from the pad guide surfaces on the mounting bracket and caliper housing. Inspect the guide pins for free movement in the mounting bracket. Replace the guide pins or boots, if they are corroded or damaged.

9. Install a new shim, then install the disc brake pads. The outboard pad with insulator is installed toward the caliper housing. The inboard pad with the wear sensor is installed nearest the caliper piston. The wear sensor must be on the leading edge with forward wheel rotation or the pad has been installed on the wrong side.

10. Rotate the caliper housing into its operating position. The springs on the outboard brake pad must not stick through the inspection hole in the caliper housing. If the springs are sticking through the inspection hole in the caliper housing, lift the caliper housing and make the necessary corrections to the outboard brake pad positions.

A WEAR SENSOR
8 BRACKET, PARKING BRAKE CABLE
9 BOLT/SCREW, LOWER CALIPER GUIDE PIN
10 SHIM
13 BOLT/SCREW, UPPER CALIPER GUIDE PIN
14 HOUSING, REAR BRAKE CALIPER
15 PIN, REAR BRAKE CALIPER GUIDE
16 BOOT, REAR BRAKE CALIPER GUIDE PIN
17 BRACKET, REAR BRAKE CALIPER ANCHOR
29 PAD, REAR DISC BRAKE INNER
30 PAD, REAR DISC BRAKE OUTER
40 DAMPENER, REAR BRAKE VIBRATION
41 NUT, REAR BRAKE VIBRATION DAMPENER

93006G92

Exploded view of the rear caliper assembly—Camaro, Firebird

For brake related suspension and axle service, refer to the model specific sections of this manual

11. Install a new upper caliper guide pin bolt and torque to 27 ft. lbs. (37 Nm). Ensure that the lower caliper guide bolt is torqued to 27 ft. lbs. (37 Nm).

12. With the engine running, pump the brake pedal slowly and firmly to seat the brake pads.

13. Check the caliper parking brake levers to make sure they are against the stops on the caliper housing. If the levers are not on their stops, check the parking brake adjustment.

14. Remove the 2 wheel nuts from the rotor, then align the marks and install the wheel assembly.

15. Lower the vehicle, check the master cylinder fluid level and road test the vehicle.

GM G-BODY:
Buick Riviera
Oldsmobile Aurora

FRONT

1. Siphon ⅔ of the brake fluid from the master cylinder.
2. Raise and safely support the vehicle.
3. Remove the tire and wheel assembly.
4. Install 2 wheel nuts to secure the rotor on the hub.
5. Remove the caliper mounting bolts and sleeves.
6. Remove the caliper from the mounting bracket and support the caliper. DO NOT allow the caliper to hang unsupported from the brake hose.
7. Remove the outboard brake pad from the caliper by pushing the pad inward toward the piston to unseat the buttons on the back of pad from the holes in the caliper. Once the buttons are unseated push the pad out of the caliper.
8. Remove the inboard pad from the caliper by pulling the top of the pad away from the piston and disengaging the spring clip from the caliper.
9. Compress the piston back into the bore using a C-Clamp.

To install:

10. Install the inboard pad into the caliper so the spring clip seats in the piston. Make sure lower edge of the spring clip is engaged in the piston and the pad is even against the base of the piston. Push the pad flat against caliper piston.

11. Install the outboard pad into the caliper so the wear indicator is at the trailing edge of the pad during forward wheel rotation. Push the pad the straight down into the caliper so the spring clips rode along the outside of the caliper. The buttons on the pad will snap into the mounting holes when the pad is correctly installed.

12. Reinstall the caliper onto the steering knuckle and torque the mounting bolts to 38 ft. lbs. (51 Nm).

5	CALIPER HOUSING
9	INBOARD SHOE AND LINING
10	OUTBOARD SHOE AND LINING

93006G93

Removing the outboard front pad—Riviera, Aurora

5	CALIPER HOUSING
9	INBOARD SHOE AND LINING
14	SHOE RETAINER SPRING

93006G94

Installing the inboard front pad—Riviera, Aurora

5	CALIPER HOUSING
10	OUTBOARD SHOE AND LINING
11	WEAR SENSOR

93006G95

Installing the outboard front pad—Riviera, Aurora

13. Remove the 2 wheel nuts securing the rotor.
14. Reinstall the tire and wheel assembly and torque the wheel nuts to 100 ft. lbs. (140 Nm).
15. Lower the vehicle.
16. Refill the master cylinder. Pump the brake pedal several times to seat the pads against the rotor.
17. Check the master cylinder level and add fluid as necessary.

REAR

1. Siphon ⅔ of the brake fluid from the master cylinder.
2. Raise and safely support the vehicle.
3. Remove the tire and wheel assembly.
4. Install 2 wheel nuts to secure the rotor on the hub.
5. Pivot the parking brake actuator level and disconnect the parking brake cable from the lever.
6. Remove the mounting bolt securing the parking brake cable bracket to the caliper and position the cable and bracket out of the way.
7. Remove the lower caliper mounting bolt.
8. Pivot the caliper upward and secure the caliper in a position over the mounting bracket. DO NOT remove the caliper from the upper pivot pin.
9. Remove the inboard and outboard pads from the caliper bracket.
10. Remove the brake pad clips from the mounting bracket.

To install:

11. Spin the caliper piston back into the bore. Make sure the piston notches are at 6 and 12 o'clock after the piston is compressed.
12. Install new brake pad clips in the caliper mounting bracket.
13. Install the inboard and outboard pads in the mounting bracket.
14. Pivot the caliper down over the pads.

15. Reinstall the lower mounting bolt and torque to 20 ft. lbs. (27 Nm).

16. Reinstall the parking brake cable bracket on the caliper and torque the mounting bolt to 32 ft. lbs. (43 Nm).

17. Pivot the actuator lever and connect the cable end to the actuator.

18. Remove the 2 wheel nuts securing the rotor.

19. Reinstall the tire and wheel assembly and torque the wheel nuts to 100 ft. lbs. (140 Nm).

20. Lower the vehicle.

21. Refill the master cylinder. Pump the brake pedal several times to seat the pads against the rotor.

22. Check the master cylinder level and add fluid as necessary.

GM J-BODY:
Chevrolet Cavalier
Pontiac Sunfire

1. Siphon ⅔ of the brake fluid out of the master cylinder reservoir.

2. Raise and safely support the vehicle.

3. Remove the tire and wheel assembly.

4. Compress the caliper piston back into the caliper bore using a large pair of pliers, C-clamp or special caliper piston retracting tool.

5. Remove the caliper mounting bolts and sleeves.

6. Remove the caliper from the steering knuckle without disconnecting the brake hose. Do not allow the caliper to hang from the brake hose. Support the caliper with a piece of wire.

7. Remove the outboard pad by pushing in on the outside edge of the pad to release the mounting dowel from the hole in the caliper. When both dowels are unseated, push the pad out the bottom of the caliper.

8. Remove the inboard pad from the caliper by pulling it out of the caliper.

To install:

9. Inspect the caliper for any signs of leakage. If the caliper is leaking, new brake pads will be damaged. Also inspect the condition of the caliper support for rust and corrosion which will hinder the travel on the caliper.

10. Inspect the caliper mounting hardware. New bolts are usually recommended. Clean all parts well. Lubricate the mounting bushings and sleeves with silicone grease as required.

11. Install the inboard pad in the caliper so the spring clip on the pad back engages in the caliper piston.

12. Install the outboard pad over the caliper end until the mounting dowels snap into the mounting holes in the caliper.

13. Install the caliper over the rotor onto the steering knuckle.

14. Install the mounting bolts and sleeves and torque to 40 ft. lbs. (51 Nm).

15. Install the tire and wheel assembly.

16. Lower the vehicle.

17. Pump the brake pedal several times to seat the pads against the rotor before attempting to move the vehicle.

18. Check the master cylinder level and add fluid as necessary.

GM L-BODY:
Chevrolet Corsica, Beretta

1. Siphon ⅔ of the brake fluid out of the master cylinder reservoir.

2. Raise and safely support the vehicle. Remove the tire and wheel assembly.

3. Remove the caliper from the vehicle.

2	MOUNTING BOLT & SLEVE ASSEMBLY	9	PISTON
3	BUSHING	10	PISTON SEAL
5	OUTBOARD SHOE & LINING	11	BLEEDER VALVE
6	WEAR SENSOR	12	CALIPER HOUSING
7	INBOARD SHOE & LINING	20	BLEEDER VALVE CAP
8	BOOT		

93006G96

Exploded view of the brake caliper—Corsica, Beretta

4. Remove the outboard pad by pushing in on the outside edge of the pad to release the mounting dowel from the hole in the caliper. When both dowels are unseated push the pad out the bottom of the caliper.

5. Remove the inboard pad from the caliper by pulling it out of the caliper.

To install:

6. Install the inboard pad in the caliper so the spring clip on the pad back engages in the caliper piston.

7. Install the outboard pad over the caliper end until the mounting dowels snap into the mounting holes in the caliper.

8. Install the caliper over the rotor onto the steering knuckle.

9. Install the mounting bolts and sleeves and torque to 38 ft. lbs. (51 Nm).

10. Install the tire and wheel assembly. Lower the vehicle.

11. Pump the brake pedal several times to seat the pads against the rotor.

12. Check the master cylinder level and add fluid as necessary.

13. Verify a firm brake pedal before attempting to move the vehicle.

GM L/N and N-BODY:
Buick Skylark
Chevrolet Malibu
Oldsmobile Achieva, Cutlass
Pontiac Grand Am

1. Siphon ⅔ of the brake fluid out of the master cylinder reservoir.

2. Raise and safely support the vehicle. Remove the tire and wheel assembly.

3. Remove the caliper from the steering knuckle without disconnecting the brake hose. DO NOT allow the caliper to hang from the brake hose. Support the caliper with a piece of wire.

4. Remove the outboard pad by pushing in on the outside edge of the pad to release the mounting dowel from the hole in the caliper. When both dowels are unseated push the pad out the bottom of the caliper.

5. Remove the inboard pad from the caliper by pulling it out of the caliper.

To install:

6. Install the inboard pad in the caliper so the spring clip on the pad back engages in the caliper piston.

7. Install the outboard pad over the caliper end until the mounting dowels snap into the mounting holes in the caliper.

8. Install the caliper over the rotor onto the steering knuckle. Install the mounting bolts and sleeves and torque to 40 ft. lbs. (51 Nm).

9. Install the tire and wheel assembly. Lower the vehicle.

10. Pump the brake pedal several times to seat the pads against the rotor before attempting to move the vehicle.

11. Check the master cylinder level and add fluid as necessary.

GM W-BODY:
Buick Century, Regal
Chevrolet Lumina, Monte Carlo
Oldsmobile Cutlass Supreme, Intrigue
Pontiac Grand Prix

FRONT

1. Siphon ⅔ of the brake fluid out of the master cylinder.

2. Raise and safely support the vehicle.

3. Mark the relationship of the wheel to the wheel stud for re-installation purposes. Remove the tire and wheel assembly.

4. Install 2 lug nuts to secure the rotor in place when the caliper is removed.

5. Install a large C-clamp over the top of the caliper housing and against the back of the outboard shoe. Slowly tighten the C-clamp until the caliper pistons are pushed into the caliper bore enough to slide the caliper assembly off the rotor. Use care not to tighten the C-clamp too far or the outboard shoe retaining spring will be deformed and require replacement.

6. Remove the caliper mounting bolts and remove the brake caliper from the mounting bracket.

7. DO NOT disconnect the brake hose from the caliper or allow the brake hose to support the weight of the caliper. Support the caliper on a piece of wire out of the way.

8. Remove the outer brake pad from the caliper using a suitable prying tool to lift the outboard shoe retaining spring so that it will clear the caliper center lug and pull the brake pad out of the caliper.

9. Remove the inner brake pad by unsnapping the shoe springs from the piston.

To install:

10. Clean all parts well. If the brake pads were worn so badly that the brake rotor is damaged, it must be replaced. Light scoring of the rotor surfaces not exceeding 0.060 inch (1.5mm) in depth is not harmful to brake operation and may result from normal use. Brake rotors may be refinished. Do not use a rotor that, after refinishing, will not meet the thickness specification cast in the rotor. Always replace with a new rotor.

11. If not done at removal, now use a C-clamp and clamp both pistons at the same time with a metal plate or wooden block across the face of both pistons. Take care not to damage the pistons or caliper boots.

➡ **After bottoming the pistons into the caliper bore, lift the inner edge of each caliper boot next to the piston and press out any trapped air. Make sure each boot convolution is tucked back into place. Boots must lay flat.**

12. Inspect the caliper bushings for wear. Replace as necessary. Carefully inspect the slide bolts for corrosion. If corrosion if found, use new parts including the bushing assemblies when installing the

(1) Caliper Housing
(2) Inboard Pad
(3) Outboard Pad
(4) Wear Sensor

Front brake pads and caliper—Century, Regal, Lumina, Monte Carlo, Cutlass Supreme, Intrigue, Grand Prix

93006G71

caliper. Do not attempt to polish away corrosion. Lubricate caliper slide bolts with silicone grease.

13. Install the new inner disc brake pad in the caliper by snapping the shoe retainer springs into the piston making sure both sets of locking tabs are seated in the caliper pistons. The pad must seat flat against the pistons.

14. Install the outer pad into the caliper by snapping the outboard shoe retaining spring over the caliper center lug and into the housing slot. The pad will slide up onto the caliper and the retaining ring will lock into place on the groove in the caliper.

15. The outer pad wear sensor should be at the trailing edge of the shoe during forward wheel rotation.

16. Install the caliper mounting bolts and torque to 80 ft. lbs. (108 Nm).

17. Remove the 2 nuts temporarily securing the rotor.

18. Install the tire and wheel assembly and tighten to specification.

19. Lower the vehicle.

20. Pump the brake pedal several times to seat the pads against the rotor.

21. Check the brake fluid level and top off as necessary.

22. Road test the vehicle to ensure the proper brake performance.

REAR

1. Siphon ⅔ of the brake fluid out of the master cylinder.
2. Raise and safely support the vehicle.
3. Remove the tire and wheel assembly.
4. Install 2 lug nuts to secure the rotor in place when the caliper is removed.
5. Remove bolt and washer attaching cable support bracket to caliper body assembly. It is not necessary to disconnect the parking brake lever or disconnect the brake hose.
6. Remove the caliper retaining bolt.
7. Pivot the caliper body assembly up from the rotor and remove from the bracket. Do not completely remove the caliper assembly body.
8. Remove the outboard and inboard shoe and linings from the caliper support assembly.
9. Remove 2 brake lining clips from the caliper support.

To install:

➡️**In order for the rear pads to seat in the caliper properly, the cut outs in the caliper piston must be at the 6 and 12 o'clock positions. Failure to align the piston correctly can lead to brake drag, premature brake wear and possible brake failure.**

10. Using a suitable type spanner tool turn the piston in to bottom the piston fully into the caliper bore. Once the caliper is fully seated make sure the cutouts in the piston are at the 6 and 12 o'clock positions.

11. After bottoming the piston into the caliper bore, lift the inner edge of boot next to the piston assembly and press out any trapped air.

12. Install 2 pad clips in the caliper support.

13. Lubricate the inner pad where it contacts the piston and mounting surfaces.

14. Install outboard and inboard shoe and linings in caliper support. Position the wear sensors downward at the leading edge of the rotor during forward wheel rotation.

PISTON SLOTS MUST BE ALIGNED AS SHOWN BEFORE INSTALLING CALIPER OVER SHOE & LININGS

13	PISTON BOOT
14	PISTON ASSEMBLY
21	CALIPER BODY ASSEMBLY

93006G72

Positioning rear caliper piston slots—Century, Regal, Lumina, Monte Carlo, Cutlass Supreme, Intrigue, Grand Prix

15. Hold the metal shoe edge against the spring end of clips in the caliper support. Push brake pad in towards the hub, bending spring ends slightly and engage shoe notches with support abutments.

16. Pivot the caliper body assembly down over the brake pad. Compress the sleeve boot by hand as the caliper body moves into position to prevent boot damage.

➡️**After the caliper body assembly is in position, recheck installation of the brake pad clips. If necessary, use a small prying tool to reseat or center the pad clip on the support abutments.**

17. Install the sleeve bolts and torque bolt to 20 ft. lbs. (27 Nm).

18. Install the cable support bracket with the cable attached and bolt washer. Torque bolt to 32 ft. lbs. (43 Nm).

19. Remove the 2 lug nuts securing the rotor.

20. Install the tire and wheel assembly and tighten to specification.

21. Lower the vehicle.

22. Pump the brake pedal several times to seat the pads against the rotor.

23. Check the brake fluid level and top off as necessary.

24. Adjust parking brake as necessary.

25. Road test the vehicle for proper brake performance.

GM Y-BODY:
Chevrolet Corvette

FRONT

1. Disconnect the negative battery cable.
2. Remove the caliper from the mounting bracket but do not disconnect the brake hose and inlet fitting assembly.
3. Suspend the caliper from the upper control arm with wire to avoid damage to the brake hose.
4. Remove the pad and lining assemblies from the caliper.

To install:

5. Clean all residue from the pad and lining assembly guiding surfaces on the caliper housing and the mounting bracket.

6. Install the outboard pad with the insulator to the caliper hous-

ing and the inboard pad with the wear sensor into the caliper pistons. Press the pads firmly until they are they are fully seated.

7. Remove the support and install the caliper to the mounting bracket.

8. Connect the negative battery cable.

REAR

1. Disconnect the negative battery cable and remove ⅔ of the brake fluid from the master cylinder reservoirs.

2. Raise and support the vehicle safely.

3. Mark the relationship between the wheel to the axle flange.

4. Remove the tire and wheel assembly. Install 2 wheel nuts to retain the brake rotor.

5. Use a C-clamp to depress the caliper pistons into the caliper bores to provide clearance between the pads and the rotor. Make sure 1 end of the clamp rests on the inlet fitting bolt while the other end rests on the outboard pad.

6. Remove the caliper upper guide pin bolt and discard, then rotate the caliper on the lower guide pin to access the pad linings. Be careful not to strain the cable conduit or the hoses.

7. Remove the pads from the caliper.

To install:

8. Install the outboard pad with the insulator to the caliper housing and the inboard pad with the wear sensor nearest the caliper pistons. The wear sensor must be in the trailing position during forward wheel rotation. Press the pads firmly until they are they are fully seated.

9. Rotate the caliper housing into position, then install a new upper guide pin bolt and torque 26 ft. lbs. (35 Nm).

10. Remove the wheel nuts securing the rotor to the hub and install the tire and wheel assembly.

11. Lower the vehicle and fill the master cylinder to the proper level with clean brake fluid.

12. Connect the negative battery cable, start the engine and pump the brake pedal slowly and firmly 3 times to seat the shoe and lining assemblies.

GEO Metro

1. Raise and safely support the front of the vehicle. Set the parking brake and block the rear wheels.

2. Siphon a sufficient quantity of brake fluid from the master cylinder reservoir to prevent the brake fluid from overflowing from the master cylinder when removing or installing the brake pads. This is necessary, as the piston must be forced into the cylinder bore to provide sufficient clearance to install the pads.

3. Remove the wheel, then reinstall 2 lug nuts finger tight to hold the disc in place.

4. Remove the 2 caliper mounting bolts and then remove the caliper from the mounting bracket. Position the caliper out of the way and support it with wire so it doesn't hang by the brake line.

5. Remove the brake pads, the wear indicators, the anti-squeal shims, the support plates and the anti squeal springs (if so equipped). Disassemble slowly and take note of how the parts fit together. This will save much time during reassembly.

6. Inspect the brake disc for scoring or gouging. Measure the disc for both thickness and run-out.

7. Inspect the pads for remaining thickness and condition. Any sign of uneven wear, cracking, heat checking or spotting is cause for replacement. Compare the wear of the inner pad to the outer pad. While they will not wear at exactly the same rate, the remaining thickness should be about the same on both pads. If one is heavily

Front disc brake assembly

84249014

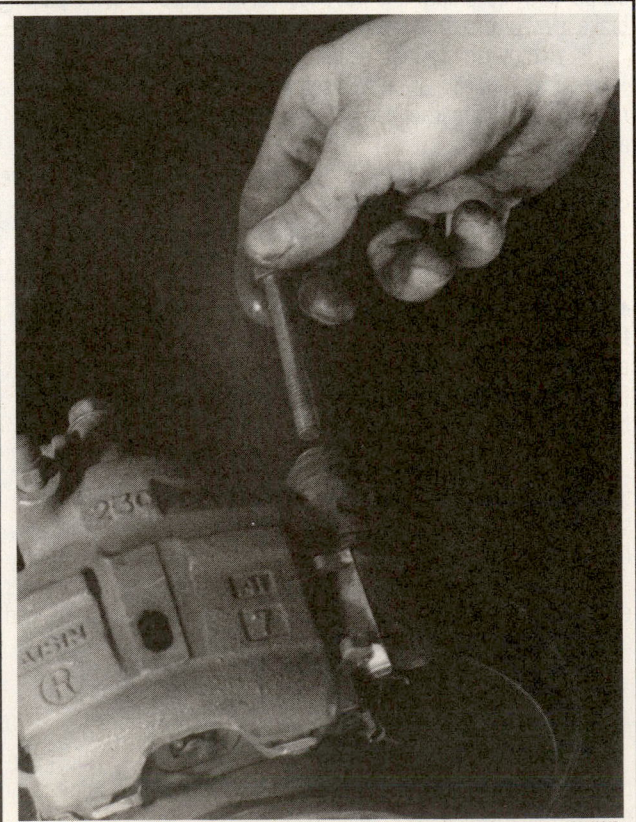

Removing caliper mounting bolts

84249015

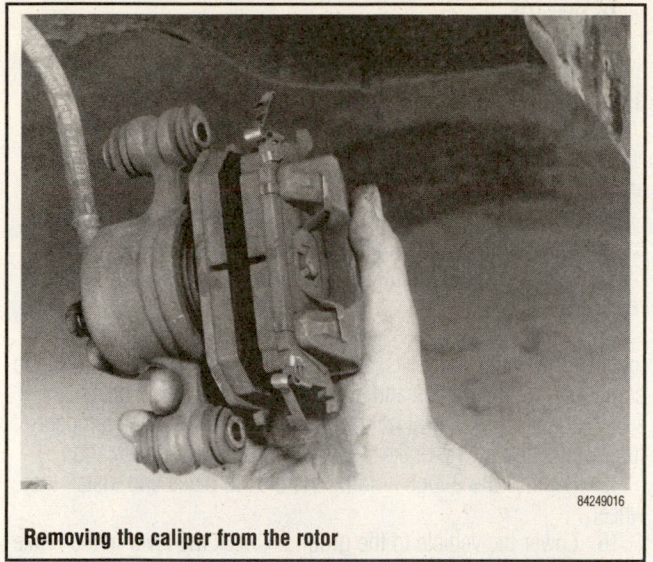

Removing the caliper from the rotor

The inside brake pad is attached to the caliper piston with a spring clip

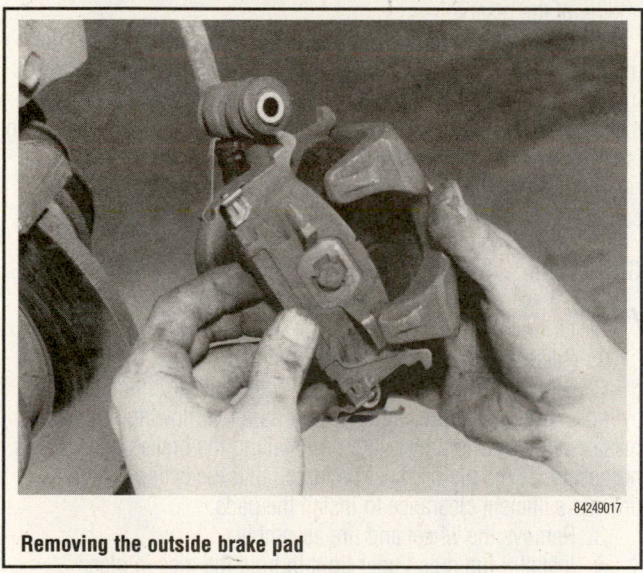

Removing the outside brake pad

Inside pad is at top and outside pad is on bottom. Note wear indicator springs protruding from sides of outside pad

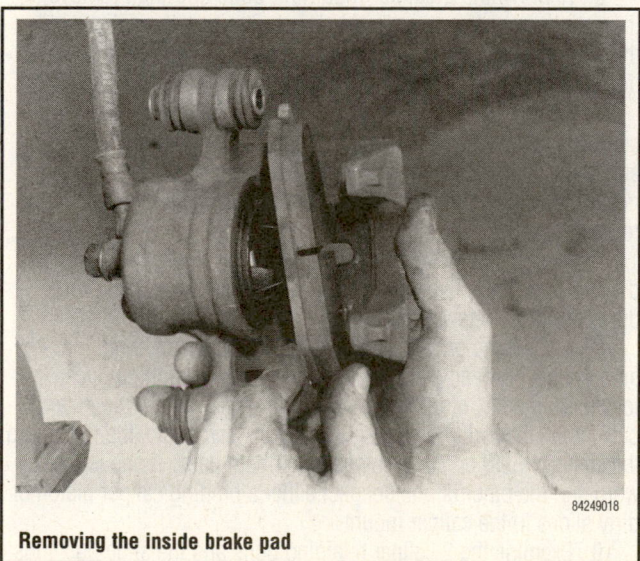

Removing the inside brake pad

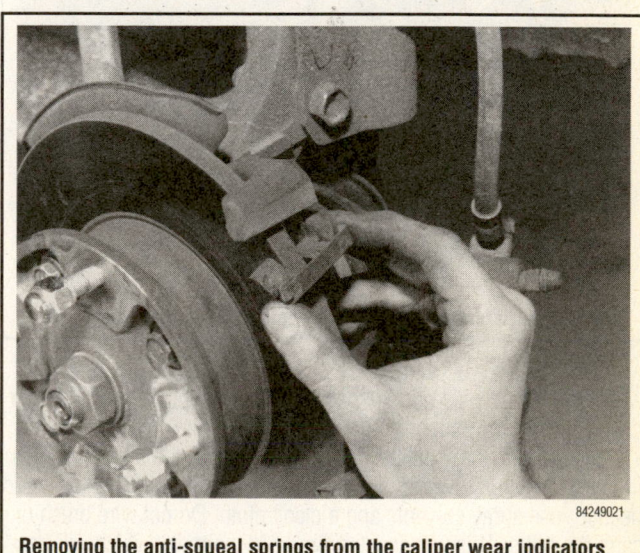

Removing the anti-squeal springs from the caliper wear indicators

For brake related suspension and axle service, refer to the model specific sections of this manual

Using a C-clamp to compress the caliper piston

Coat the caliper mounting bolts with anti-seize during installation

worn and the other is not, suspect either a binding caliper piston or dirty slides in the caliper mount.

8. Examine the 2 caliper retaining bolts and the slide bushings in which they run. Everything should be clean and dry. If cleaning is needed, use spray solvents and a clean cloth. Do not wire brush or sand the bolts. This will cause grooves in the metal which will trap more dirt. Check the condition of the rubber dust boots and replace them if damaged.

To install:

9. Install the pad support plates onto the mounting bracket.

10. Install new pad wear indicators onto each pad, making sure the arrow on the tab points in the direction of disc rotation.

11. Install new anti-squeal pads to the back of the pads.

12. Install the pads into the mounting bracket and install the anti-squeal springs.

13. Use a caliper compressor, or a C-clamp to slowly press the caliper piston back into the caliper. If the piston is frozen, or if the caliper is leaking hydraulic fluid, the caliper must be overhauled or replaced.

14. Install the caliper assembly to the mounting plate. Before installing the retaining bolts, apply a thin, even coating of anti-seize compound to the threads and slide surfaces. Don't use grease or spray lubricants; they will not hold up under the extreme temperatures generated by the brakes. Torque the bolts to specification.

15. Remove the 2 lugs holding the disc in place and install the wheel.

16. Lower the vehicle to the ground. Check the level of the brake fluid in the master cylinder reservoir; it should be at least to the middle of the reservoir.

17. Depress the brake pedal several times and make sure that the movement feels normal. The first brake pedal application may result in a very "long" pedal due to the pistons being retracted. Always make several brake applications before starting the vehicle. Bleeding is not usually necessary after pad replacement.

18. Recheck the fluid level and add to the **MAX** line if necessary.

GEO Prizm

FRONT

1. Raise and safely support the vehicle.

2. Siphon a sufficient quantity of brake fluid from the master cylinder reservoir to prevent the brake fluid overflowing from the master cylinder when removing or installing the brake pads. This is necessary, as the piston must be forced into the cylinder bore to provide sufficient clearance to install the pads.

3. Remove the wheel and tire assembly.

4. Install 2 lug nuts finger tight to hold the disc in place.

5. Remove the 2 caliper mounting bolts and then remove the caliper from the mounting bracket. Position the caliper out of the way and support it with wire so it doesn't hang by the brake line.

6. Remove the 2 brake pads, the 2 wear indicators, the 4 anti-squeal shims, the 4 support plates (anti-rattle springs) and the 2 anti squeal springs, if so equipped. Disassemble slowly and take note of how the parts fit together. This will save much time during reassembly.

7. Inspect the brake disc for scoring or gouging. Measure the disc for both thickness and run-out. Complete inspection procedures are given later in this section.

8. Inspect the pads for remaining thickness and condition. Any sign of uneven wear, cracking, heat checking or spotting is cause for replacement. Compare the wear of the inner pad to the outer pad. While they will not wear at exactly the same rate, the remaining thickness should be about the same on both pads. If one is heavily worn and the other is not, suspect either a binding caliper piston or dirty slides in the caliper mount.

9. Examine the 2 caliper retaining bolts and the slide bushings in which they run. Everything should be clean and dry. If cleaning is needed, use spray solvents and a clean cloth. Do not wire brush or

sand the bolts. This will cause grooves in the metal which will trap more dirt. Check the condition of the rubber dust boots and replace them if damaged.

To install:

10. Install the 4 pad support plates (anti-rattle springs) onto the mounting bracket.

11. Install new pad wear indicators onto each pad, making sure the arrow on the tab points in the direction of disc rotation.

12. Install new anti-squeal pads to the back of the pads.

13. Install the pads into the mounting bracket and install the anti-squeal springs, if so equipped.

14. Use a caliper compressor, a C-clamp or large pair of pliers to slowly press the caliper piston back into the caliper. If the piston is frozen, or if the caliper is leaking hydraulic fluid, the caliper must be overhauled or replaced.

15. Install the caliper assembly to the mounting plate. Before installing the retaining bolts, apply a thin, even coating of anti-seize compound to the threads and slide surfaces. Don't use grease or spray lubricants; they will not hold up under the extreme temperatures generated by the brakes. Torque the bolts to 25 ft. lbs. (34 Nm).

16. Remove the 2 lugs holding the disc in place and install the wheel.

17. Lower the vehicle to the ground. Check the level of the brake fluid in the master cylinder reservoir; it should be at least to the middle of the reservoir.

Carefully remove the caliper assembly from the rotor

You will need a short extension to remove the front caliper mounting bracket bolts

Suspend the caliper assembly out of the way to avoid hanging from the hose

For complete service labor times order Chilton's Labor Guide Manual

Removing the outer brake pad from the caliper assembly

Correct placement of the support plates (anti-rattle springs)

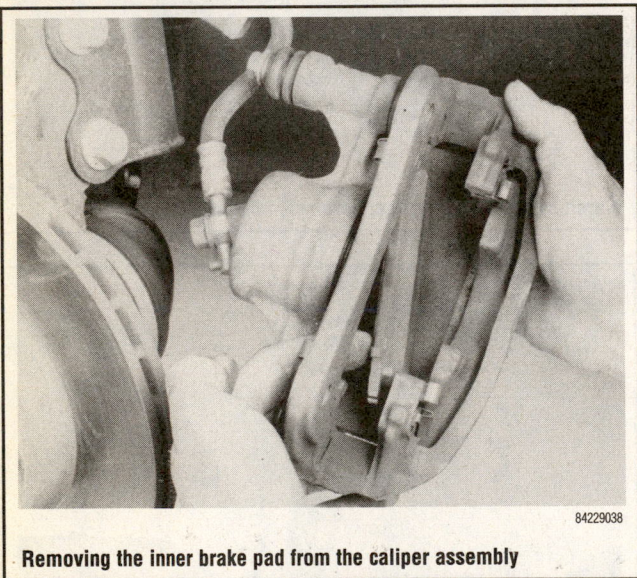

Removing the inner brake pad from the caliper assembly

Make certain the brake wear indicators are correctly installed

18. Depress the brake pedal several times and make sure that the movement feels normal. The first brake pedal application may result in a very "long" pedal due to the pistons being retracted. Always make several brake applications before starting the vehicle. Bleeding is not usually necessary after pad replacement.

19. Recheck the fluid level and add to the "MAX" line if necessary.

REAR

1. Raise and safely support the rear of the vehicle on jackstands. Block the front wheels.

2. Siphon a sufficient quantity of brake fluid from the master cylinder reservoir to prevent the brake fluid from overflowing the master cylinder when removing or installing the brake pads. This is necessary, as the piston must be forced into the cylinder bore to provide sufficient clearance to install the pads.

3. Remove the wheel, then reinstall 2 lug nuts finger tight to hold the disc in place.

4. Remove the lower mounting bolt from the mounting bracket. Do not remove the caliper main (upper) pin.

Note the correct position support plates (anti-rattle springs)

Brake Hose — Union Bolt — Main Pin Boot

Bleeder Plug — Gasket

Rotor Disc

Cable Support Bracket

Sliding Bushing

Brake Cylinder

Parking Brake Crank

Torque Plate

Spring

Stopper Pin

Parking Brake Strut

Sliding Bushing

Adjusting Bolt

Dust Boot

Adjusting Bolt Spring Plate

Anti-Squeal Shim

O-Ring

Spring

Snap Ring

Piston Seal

Anti-Rattle Spring

Adjusting Bolt Stopper

Pad

Adjusting Bolt Spring Retainer

Set Ring

Pad Guide Plate

Anti-Squeal Shim

Piston

Pad

Cylinder Boot

84229065

Rear disc brake components

5. Lift the caliper from the bottom so that it hinges upward on the upper pin. Use a piece of wire to hold the caliper up. Do not allow the brake hose to become twisted or kinked during this operation.

6. Remove the brake pads with their shims, springs and support plates.

7. Check the rotor thickness.

8. Install new pad support plates to the lower sides of the mounting bracket.

9. Install new anti-rattle springs to the upper side of the mounting bracket.

To install:

10. Install a new anti-squeal shim to the back of each pad and install the pads onto the mounting bracket. Install the pads so that the wear indicators are on the uppermost side.

11. Use GM tool J-37149, or equivalent, to turn the caliper piston clockwise while pressing it into the caliper bore. Proceed until it locks.

12. Lower the caliper so that the pad protrusion fits into the piston stopper groove. Install the mounting bolts and torque to 14 ft. lbs. Install the rear wheel.

13. Depress the brake pedal until a firm pedal is obtained.

14. Repeat this procedure on the remaining caliper.

15. Pump the brakes until a firm pedal is felt. Lower the vehicle and fill the master cylinder reservoir to the correct level.

84229066

Correct method for raising the rear caliper to gain access to the pads

Installing support plates and anti-rattle shims

Using the GM tool to retract the rear caliper piston

Align the stopper groove with the pad protrusion

Saturn

FRONT

1. Raise and support the vehicle safely and remove the front wheels.
2. Remove the caliper lower lock pins.
3. Either pivot the caliper up on the guide pin or remove the upper guide pin and support the caliper from the strut using a coat hanger or length of wire.
4. Remove the 2 brake pads and the pad clips from the caliper support. Discard the old pad clips.
5. Check the caliper pins, pin boots and the piston boot for deterioration or damage.

To install:

6. By hand or using a C-clamp, bottom the piston all the way into the caliper bore.

7. Carefully lift the inner edge of the piston boot by hand to release any trapped air.
8. Install new pad clips into the caliper support.
9. Install the inner and outer brake pads into the support. If installed, remove the temporary support wire from the caliper.
10. Pivot or place the caliper body on the support and upper guide pin into position. Compress the boots by hand as the caliper is positioned onto the support.
11. Lubricate the smooth ends of the removed pin(s) with silicone grease, then install the pin(s) and torque to 27 ft. lbs. (36 Nm). Do not get grease on the pin threads.
12. Install the wheels, then lower the vehicle.
13. Prior to operating the vehicle, depress the brake pedal a few times until the brake pads are seated against the rotor.

REAR

1. Raise and support the vehicle safely, then remove the rear wheels.
2. Remove the caliper lock and guide pins.
3. Remove the caliper from the support, being careful not to damage the pin boots and suspend the caliper from a wire.
4. Remove the brake pads from the support.

To install:

5. Using SA91110NE, or an equivalent piston driver tool, bottom the piston by rotating it clockwise into the caliper bore; do not use a C-clamp to press the piston into the bore.
6. Align the piston slots so they are perpendicular to the brake pads.
7. Carefully lift the inner edge of the piston boot to release any trapped air. The boot must lie flat below the level of the piston face.
8. Install new pad clips into the caliper support.
9. Install the inner and outer brake pads into the clips on the support. The pad with the wear sensor should be located outboard. The piston indentation slots should be positioned to correctly accept the brake pads.
10. Position the caliper body onto the support. Lubricate the non-threaded portion of the guide and lock pins, then install the pins and torque to 27 ft. lbs. (36 Nm).
11. Check the position of the pad clips. If necessary, use a small suitable tool to re-seat or center the pad clips on the support. Repeat the procedure for the opposite side brake pads.
12. Install the rear wheel assemblies and lower the vehicle.
13. Prior to operating the vehicle, depress the brake pedal a few times until the brake pads are seated against the rotor.

Brake Drums

REMOVAL & INSTALLATION

GM A-BODY:
Buick Century
Oldsmobile Cutlass Ciera, Cutlass Cruiser

1. Raise and safely support the vehicle.
2. Remove the tire and wheel assembly.
3. Mark the relationship of the brake drum to the axle flange so that, it the drum is reused, it can be installed in its original location. Remove the brake drum from the vehicle. Do not pry against the splash shield that surrounds the backing plate in an attempt to free the drum. This will bend the splash shield. If difficulty is encountered in removing the brake drum, try the following.

a. Make sure the parking brake is released.

b. Back off the parking brake cable adjustment.

c. Remove the access hole plug from the backing plate.

d. Use a small brake spoon to reach in and back off the adjusting screw (sometimes called a starwheel).

e. After loosening the adjustment, install the access hole plug to keep out dirt and debris.

f. Use a small amount of penetrating oil applied around the drum pilot hole (on the face of the drum where the end of the axle shaft hub comes through the center of the brake drum).

To install:

4. Clean all parts well. Inspect the drum for cracks or excessive wear. If in doubt, replace the drum.

5. If it is suspected that the self-adjusters are not working, disassemble the brakes far enough to remove the adjuster. Soak the adjuster in penetrating oil and disassemble the adjuster, Clean the threads and lubricate with GM lubricant 1052196, or equivalent, anti-seize compound to the adjuster screw threads, the inside diameter of the adjuster socket and the socket face.

6. Pre-adjust the brake shoes and install the brake drum(s).

7. Properly adjust the brakes.

8. Install the tire and wheel assembly and torque to specification.

9. Lower the vehicle.

10. Road test the vehicle and verify proper brake operation.

GM B-BODY:
Buick Roadmaster
Cadillac Fleetwood Brougham
Chevrolet Caprice, Impala SS

1. Raise and support the vehicle safely, then remove the rear wheel assembly.

2. Mark the relationship of the drum to the axle flange.

3. Make sure the parking brake is released and carefully slide the drum from the axle flange studs.

4. If there is difficulty removing the rotor, use a rubber mallet to tap gently on the outer rim of the drum and/or the inner drum diameter by the spindle. If necessary, remove the adjusting hole or knockout plate from the backing plate and back off the adjusting screw with a suitable tool.

To install:

5. Adjust the brake shoes. The outside diameter of the shoe and linings should be 0.050 in. (1.27mm) less than the inside diameter of the brake drum on each wheel.

6. Position the drum on the axle flange, aligning the marks made earlier.

7. Install the rear tire and wheel assembly.

8. Adjust the parking brake, then lower vehicle.

GM C- and H-BODIES:
Buick LeSabre, Park Avenue
Oldsmobile Eighty Eight Royale, Ninety Eight, Regency
Pontiac Bonneville

1. Raise and safely support the vehicle.

2. Remove the rear wheel. Mark the position of the wheel on the wheel studs, prior to removal, for installation reference.

3. Remove the brake drum from the hub. Mark the position of the drum on the wheel studs, prior to removal, for installation reference.

4. If the brake drum is difficult to remove, check the following:

a. Make sure that the parking brake is released.

b. Back off on the parking brake cable adjustment.

c. Use a hammer and a small metal punch to bend in the backing plate knockout to provide access to the park brake lever.

d. Insert a screwdriver through the hole and press in to push the park brake lever off its stop. This lets the brake shoes retract slightly.

e. Apply a small amount of penetrating oil around the drum pilot hole.

5. Remove the brake drum from the vehicle.

6. Inspect the wheel cylinder for leakage and inspect the brake shoes for wear; replace as necessary.

7. Inspect the brake drum for scoring, cracks or other wear; machine or replace as necessary. If machining, observe the maximum diameter specification.

To install:

8. Measure the inside diameter of the brake drum using clearance gauge J 21177-A, or equivalent.

9. Turn the starwheel on the adjusting screw assembly until the brake shoe diameter is 0.050 in. (1.27mm) less than the drum inside diameter.

10. Install the brake drum onto the wheel hub, aligning the marks made during removal.

11. Install the wheel, aligning the marks made during removal. Torque the lug nuts to 100 ft. lbs. (140 Nm).

12. Lower the vehicle.

13. Road test the vehicle and check brake operation.

GM F-BODY:
Chevrolet Camaro
Pontiac Firebird

1. Raise and support the vehicle safely.

2. Matchmark the relationship of the wheel to the axle flange, then remove the wheel and tire assembly.

3. Matchmark the relationship of the drum to the axle flange and remove the brake drum. If the brake drum is difficult to remove, try the following:

a. Ensure the parking brake is released.

b. Back off the parking brake cable adjustment.

c. Remove the adjusting hole cover or knockout plate from the backing plate. Back off the adjustment screw, using suitable brake adjusting tools.

d. Use a rubber mallet to tap gently on the outer rim of the drum and/or around the inner drum diameter by the spindle. Be careful not to deform the drum by excessive use of force.

To install:

4. Adjust the brake shoes. The outside diameter of the shoe and linings should be 0.050 inch (1.27mm) less than the inside diameter of the brake drum on each wheel.

5. Install the drum, aligning the marks on the drum and the axle flange.

6. Install the wheel and tire assembly, aligning the marks on the wheel and axle flange. Lower the vehicle.

GM J-BODY:
Chevrolet Cavalier
Pontiac Sunfire

1. Raise and safely support the vehicle.

2. Remove the wheel and tire assembly.

For brake related suspension and axle service, refer to the model specific sections of this manual

3. Pull the brake drum off. It may be necessary to gently tap the rear edge of the drum to start it off the studs. If extreme resistance to removal is encountered, it will be necessary to retract the brake shoe self-adjuster screw, sometimes called the starwheel. Knock out the access hole in the brake drum and turn the adjuster to retract the linings from the drum. Install a replacement hole cover before reinstalling the drum.

➡Do not hammer on the brake drum to remove it.

To install:

4. Inspect the inside of the brake drum. If worn, heavily grooved or if the opening is distorted, the drum should be refinished or replaced. If refinishing, observe the maximum drum diameter specification.

5. Inspect the wheel cylinder for signs of brake fluid leakage. Inspect the brake shoe springs and self-adjuster mechanism. The adjuster should usually be disassembled, cleaned and lubricated when the drum is removed for brake service.

6. Install the drum over the brake shoes.
7. Install the wheel and tire assembly.
8. Adjust the brakes.
9. Lower the vehicle. Check brake operation.

GM L-BODY:
Chevrolet Corsica, Beretta

1. Raise and safely support the vehicle. Remove the tire and wheel assembly.
2. Remove the brake drum by sliding it off the hub bearing assembly. It may be necessary to back off the brake adjuster to remove the drum.
3. If the adjuster is backed off and the drum won't come off tap lightly around the edge of the drum with a soft hammer.

To install:

4. Install the drum onto the hub assembly.
5. Install the tire and wheel assembly and torque to specification.
6. Adjust the rear brakes.
7. Lower the vehicle.

GM L/N and N-BODY:
Buick Skylark
Chevrolet Malibu
Oldsmobile Achieva, Cutlass
Pontiac Grand Am

1. Raise and safely support the vehicle.
2. Remove the wheel.
3. Pull the brake drum off. It may be necessary to gently tap the rear edge of the drum to start it off the studs. If extreme resistance to removal is encountered, it will be necessary to retract the brake shoe self-adjuster screw, sometimes called the starwheel. Knock out the access hole in the brake drum and turn the adjuster to retract the linings from the drum. Install a replacement hole cover before reinstalling the drum.

➡DO NOT hammer on the brake drum to remove it.

To install:

4. Inspect the inside of the brake drum. If worn, heavily grooved or if the opening is distorted, the drum should be refinished or replaced. If refinishing, observe the maximum drum diameter specification.

5. Inspect the wheel cylinder for signs of brake fluid leakage.

1 ADJUSTER SOCKET
2 ADJUSTER SCREW
3 PIVOT NUT

93006G73

Brake adjuster—Skylark, Malibu, Achieva, Cutlass, Grand Am

Inspect the brake shoe springs and self-adjuster mechanism. The adjuster should usually be disassembled, cleaned and lubricated when the drum is removed for brake service.

6. Install the drum over the brake shoes.
7. Install the wheel. Adjust the brakes.
8. Lower the vehicle. Check brake operation.

GM W-BODY:
Buick Century, Regal
Chevrolet Lumina, Monte Carlo
Oldsmobile Cutlass Supreme, Intrigue
Pontiac Grand Prix

1. Raise and safely support the vehicle.
2. Mark the relationship of the wheel to the axle flange to help maintain wheel balance after assembly.
3. Remove the tire and wheel assembly.
4. Mark the relationship of the brake drum to the axle flange.
5. If difficulty is encountered in removing the brake drum, the following steps may be of assistance.
   a. Make sure the parking brake is released.
   b. Back off the parking brake cable adjustment.
   c. Remove the access hole plug from the backing plate.
   d. Using a screwdriver, back off the adjusting screw.
   e. Install the access hole plug to prevent dirt or contamination from entering the drum brake assembly.
   f. Use a small amount of penetrating oil applied around the brake drum pilot hole.
   g. Carefully remove the brake drum from the vehicle.
6. After removing the brake drum it should be checked for the following:
   a. Inspecting for cracks and deep grooves.
   b. Inspect for out of round and taper.
   c. Inspecting for hot spots (black in color).

To install:

7. Install the brake drum onto the vehicle aligning the reference marks on the axle flange.
8. Install the tire and wheel assembly, torquing it to specifications.
9. Lower the vehicle and road test for proper brake operation.

GEO Metro

1. Make sure the parking brake is fully released.
2. Raise and safely support the vehicle.

3. Remove the rear wheels.

4. Without ABS, perform the following:

a. Remove the dust cap. Using a hammer and punch, unstake the spindle nut.

b. Remove the spindle nut and washer. Discard the spindle nut.

5. If equipped with ABS, perform the following:

a. Remove the 2 brake drum retaining screws.

b. Install 2, 8mm screws in the 2 opposite threaded holes on the brake drum.

c. Alternately rotate each screw slowly until the 2 screws pull the drum from the hub and wheel studs.

6. Remove the drum from the vehicle. Remove the 2, 8mm screws from the drum.

7. Remove the rear brake drum assembly from the vehicle.

8. Remove the brake drum. If the drum is frozen on the hub, tap the drum with a rubber mallet or wooden hammer handle to loosen it.

9. Inspect the brake shoes for wear and/or damage; replace as necessary. Inspect the wheel cylinder for signs of brake fluid leakage; replace as necessary.

10. Inspect the drum for cracks, scoring or other wear; machine or replace as necessary. If machining, observe the maximum drum diameter specification.

To install:

11. Install the brake drum assembly onto the spindle.

12. On non-ABS equipped models;

a. Install the washer and a new spindle nut.

b. Torque the spindle nut to 74 ft. lbs. (100 Nm).

c. Stake the spindle nut.

d. Install the dust cap.

13. On ABS equipped models, install the brake drum and tighten the brake drum retaining screws.

14. Install the wheel. Lower the vehicle.

15. To adjust the brakes, depress the brake pedal 3–5 times with approximately 66 lbs. (30 kg) of pressure.

16. Road test and check brake operation.

GEO Prizm

1. Make sure the parking brake is fully released.

2. Raise and safely support the vehicle.

3. Remove the rear wheel.

4. Without ABS, perform the following:

a. Remove the dust cap. Using a hammer and punch, unstake the spindle nut.

b. Remove the spindle nut and washer. Discard the spindle nut.

5. If equipped with ABS, perform the following:

a. Remove the 2 brake drum retaining screws.

b. Install 2, 8mm screws in the 2 opposite threaded holes on the brake drum.

c. Alternately rotate each screw slowly until the 2 screws pull the drum from the hub and wheel studs.

6. Remove the drum from the vehicle. Remove the 2, 8mm screws from the drum.

7. Remove the rear brake drum assembly from the vehicle.

8. Mark the position of 1 wheel lug stud in relation to a hole in the drum. This will allow the drum to be reinstalled in the original position.

Backing off the rear brake adjuster—Prizm

9. Remove the brake drum. If the drum is frozen on the hub, tap the drum with a rubber mallet or wooden hammer handle to loosen it.

10. Inspect the brake shoes for wear and/or damage and replace as necessary. Inspect the wheel cylinder for signs of brake fluid leakage; replace as necessary.

11. Inspect the drum for cracks, scoring or other wear; machine or replace as necessary. If machining, observe the maximum drum diameter specification.

To install:

12. Install the brake drum assembly onto the spindle.

13. On non-ABS equipped models;

a. Install the washer and a new spindle nut.

b. Torque the spindle nut to 74 ft. lbs. (100 Nm).

c. Stake the spindle nut.

d. Install the dust cap.

14. On ABS equipped models, install the brake drum and tighten the brake drum retaining screws.

15. Install the drum, observing the matchmarks made earlier. Keep the drum straight while installing it, or it could damage the brake shoes.

16. Install the wheel. Lower the vehicle.

17. To adjust the brakes, depress the brake pedal 3–5 times with approximately 66 lbs. (30 kg) of pressure.

18. Road test and check brake operation.

Saturn

1. Raise and support the vehicle safely.

2. Remove the rear wheel and tire assembly.

3. Remove the brake drum.

4. If necessary, turn the starwheel of the brake adjuster assembly to loosen the brake shoes and allow for drum removal.

To install:

5. Install brake drum over brake shoes and onto hub.

6. Install tire and wheel assembly. Torque to the proper specification.

7. Adjust brakes following the proper procedure.

8. Lower vehicle.

9. Road test for braking operation.

Brake Shoes

REMOVAL & INSTALLATION

GM A-BODY:
Buick Century
Oldsmobile Cutlass Ciera, Cutlass Cruiser

1. Raise and safely support vehicle.
2. Remove the tire and wheel assembly.
3. Remove the brake drum. If the drum is difficult to remove, remove the access plug from the backing plate and back off the adjusting screw.
4. Remove the return springs from the anchor using appropriate brake spring pliers.
5. Remove the hold-Down springs and retaining pins. Remove the lever pivot, actuator link, actuator lever, actuator pivot and lever return spring, parking brake strut and strut spring.
6. Remove the brake shoes, then disconnect the parking brake cable.
7. Remove the adjusting screw assembly and spring. Note position of adjusting spring.

➡ **Do not interchange the adjusting screws or adjusting screw springs from right to left brake assembly**

8. Remove the retaining ring, pin and parking brake lever from the secondary shoe.
To install:
9. Lubricate the shoe contact surfaces on the backing plate and adjusting screw assembly.
10. Install the parking brake lever on the secondary shoe with the pin and retaining ring.
11. Install the adjusting screw assembly and spring.
12. Install the shoe and lining assemblies after attaching the parking brake cable.
13. Install the parking brake strut and spring by spreading the shoes apart. Ensure the strut is properly positioned. The end with the spring engages the primary shoe and the end without the spring engages the parking brake lever.
14. Install the actuator pivot, actuator lever and return spring.
15. Install the actuator link in the shoe retainer.
16. Install the link into the lever while holding up on the lever.
17. Install the hold-down pins, lever pivot and hold-down spring.
18. Install the shoe return springs.
19. Install the brake drum, wheel and tire assembly, then lower vehicle. Apply the brake pedal several times to seat the brake shoes. Check and adjust the parking brake, as required.
20. Check the master cylinder reservoir and add fluid if required.

1 ACTUATOR SPRING
2 ADJUSTER ACTUATOR
6 ADJUSTER SHOE & LINING
7 PARK BRAKE LEVER
8 PARK BRAKE SHOE & LINING
9 RETRACTOR SPRING
13 BACKING PLATE ASSEMBLY
14 ACCESS HOLE PLUG
15 ADJUSTING SCREW ASSEMBLY

93006G75

Rear drum brake components—Century, Cutlass Ciera, Cutlass Cruiser

GM B-BODY:
Buick Roadmaster
Cadillac Fleetwood Brougham
Chevrolet Caprice, Impala SS

1. Raise and support the vehicle safely.
2. Remove the tire and wheel assemblies.

3. Remove the brake drums. If the brake drum cannot be removed, try the following:
   a. Make sure the parking brake is released.
   b. Back off the parking brake cable adjustment.
   c. Remove the adjusting hole knockout plate from the backing plate and back off the adjusting screw.

A	CONTACT SURFACE
B	ANCHOR PIN
C	STANDARD BRAKE (9.5 INCH DRUM)
D	HEAVY – DUTY BRAKE (11 INCH DRUM)
1	SPRING, REAR BRAKE SHOE RETURN
2	SPRING, REAR BRAKE SHOE RETURN
3	SPRING, REAR BRAKE SHOE HOLD-DOWN
4	PIVOT, REAR BRAKE SHOE ADJUST ACTUATOR
5	PIN, REAR BRAKE SHOE
6	LINK, REAR BRAKE SHOE ADJUST ACTUATOR
7	ACTUATOR, REAR BRAKE SHOE ADJUST
8	PAWL, REAR BRAKE SHOE ADJUST
9	SPRING, REAR BRAKE SHOE ADJUST PAWL
10	GUIDE, REAR BRAKE SHOE
11	STRUT, REAR PARKING BRAKE LEVER
12	SPRING, REAR PARKING BRAKE LEVER STRUT
13	SHOE, REAR BRAKE PRIMARY
14	SHOE, REAR BRAKE SECONDARY
15	SPRING, REAR BRAKE SHOE ADJUST
16	SOCKET, REAR BRAKE SHOE ADJUST
17	WASHER, REAR BRAKE SHOE ADJUST THRUST
18	NUT, REAR BRAKE SHOE ADJUST
19	ADJUSTER, REAR BRAKE SHOE
20	LEVER, REAR PARKING BRAKE
21	PUSHROD, REAR WHEEL CYLINDER
22	BOLT/SCREW, REAR WHEEL CYLINDER
23	BOOT, REAR WHEEL CYLINDER PISTON
24	PISTON, REAR WHEEL CYLINDER
25	SEAL, REAR WHEEL CYLINDER PISTON
26	SPRING, REAR WHEEL CYLINDER PISTON
27	VALVE, REAR BRAKE BLEEDER
28	BODY, REAR WHEEL CYLINDER
29	PLATE, REAR BRAKE BACKING
30	CYLINDER, REAR WHEEL
31	ADJUSTER ASSEMBLY, REAR BRAKE SHOE

93006G76

Rear drum brake components—Roadmaster, Fleetwood Brougham, Caprice, Impala SS

d. Use a rubber mallet to tap on the outer rim of the drum and around the inner drum diameter by the spindle.

4. Remove the return springs.

5. Remove the hold-down pins and springs.

6. Remove the actuator lever pivot.

7. Lift up on the actuator lever to remove the actuator link. Remove the lever, pawl if equipped, and lever return spring.

8. Remove the shoe guide, the parking brake strut and spring.

9. Remove the brake shoes from the backing plate and the parking brake cable.

10. Remove the adjusting screw assembly and spring from the brake shoes.

11. Remove the parking brake lever by unhooking the lever tab from the slot in the brake shoe.

To install:

12. Clean the adjusting screw with a wire brush and then clean all components with brake cleaner or denatured alcohol.

13. Using 1052196 or equivalent, lubricate the adjusting screw threads, inside diameter of the socket and the socket face, for smooth rotation.

14. Install the parking brake lever by hooking lever tab into slot in primary or secondary shoe lining.

15. Install the adjusting screw assembly and the adjusting screw spring.

16. Connect the primary/secondary shoes to the parking brake cable and the brake backing plate.

17. Install the strut and spring by spreading the shoes and inserting the components, then install the shoe guide.

18. Install the pawl, if equipped, the actuator lever and the lever return spring.

19. Install the hold-down pins, pivot and springs.

20. Connect the actuator link to the actuator pin. Install the actuator link into actuator lever while holding up on actuator lever.

21. Install the return springs with suitable a tool.

22. Repeat the procedure for the opposite rear wheel.

23. Adjust the brake shoes. The outside diameter of both shoe and linings should be 0.050 in. (1.27mm) less than the inside diameter of the brake drum on each wheel.

24. Install the brake drums.

25. Install the tire and wheel assembly.

26. Lower the vehicle.

27. Be sure to adjust the parking brake cable, if the parking brake adjuster was loosened to remove the drums.

GM C- and H-BODIES:
Buick LeSabre, Park Avenue
Oldsmobile Eighty Eight Royale, Ninety Eight, Regency
Pontiac Bonneville

1. Raise and safely support the vehicle.

2. Remove the rear wheel. Mark the position of the wheel to the wheel studs, prior to removal, for installation reference.

3. Remove the brake drum. Mark the position of the brake drum to the wheel studs, prior to removal, for installation reference.

4. Using tool J 38400, or an equivalent brake spanner tool and remover, remove the actuator spring from the adjuster lever. Use care not to distort the spring when removing it.

5. Lift the end of the retractor spring from the adjuster shoe assembly. Insert the hook end of the J-38400 between the retractor spring and the shoe. Pry slightly to remove the spring end from the hole in the shoe.

6. Pry the end of the retractor spring toward the axle with the flat end of the tool until the spring snaps down off the shoe web onto the backing plate.

7. Remove the one brake shoe and remove the adjuster assembly.

8. Disconnect the parking brake lever from the shoe. DO NOT

A ACCESS HOLE PLUG.	4 RETRACTOR SPRING	9 BACKING PLATE
	5 ADJUSTER SHOE AND LINING	10 PARK BRAKE SHOE AND LINING
1 ADJUSTER SOCKET	6 WHEEL CYLINDER	11 PARK BRAKE LEVER
2 ADJUSTER SCREW	7 BLEEDER VALVE	12 ACTUATOR SPRING
3 PIVOT NUT	8 BOLT	13 ADJUSTER ACTUATOR

93006G77

Exploded view of the drum brake components—LeSabre, Park Avenue, Eighty Eight, Royale, Ninety Eight, Regency, Bonneville

remove the parking brake lever from the cable end unless it is being replaced.

9. Using J 38400, or equivalent, lift the end of the retractor spring from the adjuster shoe assembly. Insert the hook end of the tool between the retractor spring and the shoe. Pry slightly to remove the spring end from the hole in the shoe. Pry the end of the retractor spring toward the axle with the flat end of the tool, until the spring snaps down off the shoe web onto the backing plate. Leave the spring there. Do not remove it.

10. Remove the brake shoe.

To install:

11. Check the backing plate attaching bolts to make sure that they are tight. Use fine emery cloth to clean all rust and dirt from the shoe contact surfaces on the plate and lubricate with high temperature grease. Check the wheel cylinder for signs of leakage.

12. Clean all parts completely in brake solvent and air dry.

13. Clean the backing plate shoe contact points.

14. Inspect the inside of the brake drum. If worn, heavily grooved or if the opening is distorted, the drum should be machined or replaced. If machining, observe the maximum drum diameter specification.

15. Disassemble, clean and lubricate the adjuster screw.

16. Position the brake shoe that connects to the parking brake lever, on the backing plate. Using J-38400 or equivalent, pull the end of the retractor spring up to rest on the web of the shoe. Pull the end of the retractor spring up until it snaps into the slot in the brake shoe.

17. Connect the parking brake lever.

18. Install the remaining shoe and the adjuster screw assembly.

19. Position the brake shoe using J-38400 or equivalent, and pull the end of the retractor spring up to rest on the web of the shoe. Pull the end of the retractor spring up until it snaps into the slot in the brake shoe.

20. Using J-38400, or equivalent, spread the brake shoes and work the adjuster screw into position.

21. Install the actuator spring with the U-shaped end going through the web.

22. Measure the inside diameter of the brake drum using clearance gauge J 21177-A or equivalent.

23. Turn the starwheel on the adjusting screw assembly until the brake shoe diameter is 0.050 in. (1.27mm) less than the drum inside diameter.

24. Install the brake drum onto the wheel hub, aligning the marks made during removal.

25. Install the wheel, aligning the marks made during removal. Torque the lug nuts to 100 ft. lbs. (140 Nm).

26. Repeat the procedure for the brake shoe assembly on the opposite side of the vehicle.

27. Lower the vehicle.

28. Apply and release the brake pedal 30–35 times with normal pedal force. Pause about 1 second between applications.

29. Road test the vehicle and check brake operation.

GM F-BODY:
Chevrolet Camaro
Pontiac Firebird

1. Raise and support the vehicle safely.

2. Matchmark the relationship of the wheel to the axle flange, then remove the wheel and tire assembly.

3. Matchmark the relationship of the drum to the axle flange and remove the brake drum.

4. Remove the return springs using a suitable tool.

5. Remove the hold-down springs and pins. Remove the actuator pivot.

6. Remove the actuator link while lifting up on the actuator.

7. Remove the actuator lever and lever return spring.

8. Remove the shoe guide, parking brake strut and strut spring.

9. Remove the brake shoes and disconnect the parking brake lever from the appropriate shoe.

10. Remove the adjusting screw assembly and spring.

To install:

11. Install the parking brake lever on the appropriate shoe by hooking the lever tab into the slot.

12. Install the adjusting screw and spring. Lubricate the adjusting screw with suitable brake grease.

13. Clean and lubricate the contact points of the backing plate, then install the brake shoe assemblies and the parking brake cable to the backing plate.

14. Install the parking brake strut and strut spring by spreading the shoes apart. The strut end with the spring engages the parking brake lever and shoe. The other end engages the opposite shoe.

15. Install the shoe guide, actuator lever and lever return spring.

16. Install the hold-down pins, actuator pivot and springs.

17. Install the actuator link on the anchor pin. Install the actuator link into the actuator lever while holding up on the lever.

18. Install the shoe return springs and adjust the brakes. When properly adjusted, the brake shoe linings will be approximately 0.050 inch (1.27mm) less than the inner diameter of the brake drum.

19. Align and install the brake drum, then the wheel and tire assembly.

20. Lower the vehicle.

GM J-BODY:
Chevrolet Cavalier
Pontiac Sunfire

1. Raise and safely support the vehicle.

2. Remove the tire and wheel assembly.

3. Remove the brake drum. It may be necessary to gently tap the rear edge of the drum to start it off the studs. If extreme resistance to removal is encountered, it will be necessary to retract the brake shoe self-adjuster screw, sometime called the starwheel. Turn the adjuster to retract the linings from the drum.

➠**Do not hammer on the brake drum to remove it.**

4. Remove the upper return springs from the shoes using tool J-8057, or the equivalent brake spring tool.

5. Remove the hold-down springs using J-8049, or the equivalent brake spring tool.

6. Remove the shoe hold-down pins from behind the brake backing plate.

7. Lift up the actuator lever for the self-adjusting mechanism and remove the actuating link. Remove the actuator lever, pivot, and the pivot return spring.

8. Spread the shoes apart to clear the wheel cylinder pistons, then remove the parking brake strut and spring.

9. Disconnect the parking brake cable from the lever. Remove the shoes, still connected by their adjusting screw spring.

10. With the shoes removed, note the position of the adjusting spring and remove the spring and adjusting screw.

For brake related suspension and axle service, refer to the model specific sections of this manual

1	RETURN SPRING	11	PRIMARY SHOE AND LINING	21	BOLT
2	RETURN SPRING	12	SECONDARY SHOE AND LINING	22	BOOT
3	HOLD DOWN SPRING	13	ADJUSTING SCREW SPRING	23	PISTON
4	BEARING SLEEVE	14	SOCKET	24	SEAL
5	HOLD–DOWN PIN	15	PIVOT NUT	25	SPRING ASSEMBLY
6	ACTUATOR LINK	16	ADJUSTING SCREW	26	WHEEL CYLINDER
7	ACTUATOR LEVER	17	RETAINING RING	27	BACKING PLATE
8	LEVER RETURN SPRING	18	PIN	30	SHOE RETAINER
9	PARKING BRAKE STRUT	19	PARKING BRAKE LEVER	32	ANCHOR PIN
10	STRUT SPRING	20	BLEEDER VALVE	33	SHOE PADS

93006G97

Exploded view of drum brake components—Cavalier, Sunfire

11. Remove the C-clip from the parking brake lever and remove the lever from the secondary shoe.

12. Use a damp cloth to remove all dirt and dust from the backing plate and brake parts.

To install:

13. Check the backing plate attaching bolts to make sure they are tight. Use fine emery cloth to clean all rust and dirt from the shoe contact surfaces on the plate and lubricate with brake grease. Check the wheel cylinder for signs of leakage.

14. Clean all parts completely in brake solvent and air dry.

15. Clean the backing plate shoe contact points.

16. Inspect the inside of the brake drum. If worn, heavily grooved or if the opening is distorted, the drum should be refinished or replaced.

17. Inspect the brake shoe springs and self-adjuster mechanism. Disassemble the adjuster mechanism and clean the threads and coat with grease. Make sure the adjuster assembly turns freely before installing in the vehicle.

18. Install the parking brake lever on the secondary shoe and secure with C-clip.

19. Install the adjusting screw and spring on the shoes, connecting them together. The coils of the spring must not be over the starwheel on the adjuster. The left and right hand springs are not interchangeable.

20. Spread the shoe assemblies apart and connect the parking brake cable. Install the shoes on the backing plate, engaging the shoes at the top temporarily with the wheel cylinder pistons. Make sure the starwheel on the adjuster is lined up with the adjusting hole in the backing plate, if equipped.

21. Spread the shoes apart slightly and install the parking brake strut and spring. Make sure the end of the strut without the spring engages the parking brake lever. The end with the spring engages the primary shoe (the one with the shorter lining).

22. Install the actuator pivot, lever and return spring. Install the actuating link in the shoe retainer. Lift up the actuator lever and hook the link into the lever.

23. Install the hold-down pins through the back of the plate using J-8057, or the equivalent. Install the lever pivots and hold-down springs. Install the shoe return springs using J-8049, or the equivalent. Be careful not to stretch or distort the springs.

24. Make sure the linings are in the right place, the self-adjusting mechanism is correctly installed, and the parking brake parts are hooked up.

25. Measure the distance from the edge of the primary lining to the edge secondary lining, then measure the inside width of the drum. Adjust the linings by means of the adjuster so the drum will fit onto the linings.

26. Install the hub and bearing assembly onto the axle if removed. Torque the retaining bolts to 35 ft. lbs. (55 Nm).

27. Install the drum.

28. Install the wheel and tire assembly.

29. Adjust the brakes. Install a rubber hole cover in the adjustment knock-out hole after the adjustment is complete. Adjust the parking brake.

30. Lower the car.

31. Road test the vehicle and verify proper brake operation.

GM L-BODY:
Chevrolet Corsica, Beretta

1. Raise and safely support the vehicle. Remove the tire and wheel assembly.

2. Remove the brake drum.

3. Remove the upper return springs from the shoes with brake spring tool J-8049, or equivalent.

4. Remove the hold-down springs by gripping them with special tool J-8056, or equivalent then pressing down and turning 90° (¼ turn).

5. Remove the shoe hold-down pins from behind the brake backing plate. They will simply slide out once the hold-down spring tension is relieved.

6. Lift up the actuator lever for the self-adjusting mechanism and remove the actuating link. Remove the actuator lever, pivot and the pivot return spring.

1	RETURN SPRING	11	PRIMARY SHOE AND LINING	21	BOLT
2	RETURN SPRING	12	SECONDARY SHOE AND LINING	22	BOOT
3	HOLD DOWN SPRING	13	ADJUSTING SCREW SPRING	23	PISTON
4	BEARING SLEEVE	14	SOCKET	24	SEAL
5	HOLD-DOWN PIN	15	PIVOT NUT	25	SPRING ASSEMBLY
6	ACTUATOR LINK	16	ADJUSTING SCREW	26	WHEEL CYLINDER
7	ACTUATOR LEVER	17	RETAINING RING	27	BACKING PLATE
8	LEVER RETURN SPRING	18	PIN	30	SHOE RETAINER
9	PARKING BRAKE STRUT	19	PARKING BRAKE LEVER	32	ANCHOR PIN
10	STRUT SPRING	20	BLEEDER VALVE	33	SHOE PADS

93006G98

Exploded view of the drum brake assembly—Corsica, Beretta

7. Spread the shoes apart to clear the wheel cylinder pistons, then remove the parking brake strut and spring.

8. Spread the shoes far enough apart to clear the hub and bearing assembly.

9. Disconnect the parking brake cable from the lever. Remove the shoes, still connected by their adjusting screw spring, from the car.

10. With the shoes removed, note the position of the adjusting spring, then remove the spring and adjusting screw.

11. Remove the C-clip from the parking brake lever and the lever from the secondary shoe.

To install:

12. Use a damp cloth to remove all dirt and dust from the backing plate and brake parts.

13. Lubricate the fulcrum end of the parking brake lever with brake grease specially made for the purpose. Install the lever on the secondary shoe and secure with the C-clip.

14. Install the adjusting screw and spring on the shoes, connecting them together. The coils of the spring must not be over the star-wheel on the adjuster. The left and right hand springs are not interchangeable.

15. Lubricate the shoe contact surfaces on the backing plate with the brake grease.

16. Spread the shoe assemblies apart and connect the parking brake cable. Install the shoes on the backing plate, engaging the shoes at the top temporarily with the wheel cylinder pistons.

17. Spread the shoes apart slightly and install the parking brake strut and spring. Make sure the end of the strut without the spring engages the parking brake lever. The end with the spring engages the primary shoe (the one with the shorter lining).

18. Install the actuator pivot, lever and return spring. Install the actuating link in the shoe retainer. Lift up the actuator lever and hook the link into the lever.

19. Install the hold-down pins and hold-down springs. Install the shoe return springs with J-8049, or equivalent.

20. Install the brake drum.

21. Install the tire and wheel assembly and torque to specification.

22. Adjust the brakes. Be sure to install a rubber hole cover in the knock-out hole after the adjustment is complete.

23. Adjust the parking brake.

GM L/N and N-BODY:
Buick Skylark
Chevrolet Malibu
Oldsmobile Achieva, Cutlass
Pontiac Grand Am

1. Raise and safely support the vehicle. Remove the tire and wheel assembly. Remove the brake drum.

2. Remove the upper return springs from the shoes using tool J-8057, or the equivalent brake spring tool.

3. Remove the hold-down springs using J-8049, or the equivalent brake spring tool.

4. Remove the shoe hold-down pins from behind the brake backing plate.

5. Lift up the actuator lever for the self-adjusting mechanism and remove the actuating link. Remove the actuator lever, pivot, and the pivot return spring.

6. Spread the shoes apart to clear the wheel cylinder pistons and remove the parking brake strut and spring.

7. Disconnect the parking brake cable from the lever. Remove the shoes, still connected by their adjusting screw spring.

8. With the shoes removed, note the position of the adjusting spring and remove the spring and adjusting screw.

9. Remove the C-clip from the parking brake lever and the lever from the secondary shoe.

10. Use a damp cloth to remove all dirt and dust from the backing plate and brake parts.

To install:

11. Check the backing plate attaching bolts to make sure they are tight. Use fine emery cloth to clean all rust and dirt from the shoe contact surfaces on the plate and lubricate with brake grease. Check the wheel cylinder for signs of leakage.

12. Clean all parts completely in brake solvent and air dry. Clean the backing plate shoe contact points.

13. Inspect the inside of the brake drum. If worn, heavily grooved or if the opening is distorted, the drum should be refinished or replaced.

14. Inspect the brake shoe springs and self-adjuster mechanism. Disassemble the adjuster mechanism and clean the threads and coat with grease. Make sure the adjuster assembly turns freely before installing in the vehicle.

15. Install the parking brake lever on the secondary shoe and secure with C-clip.

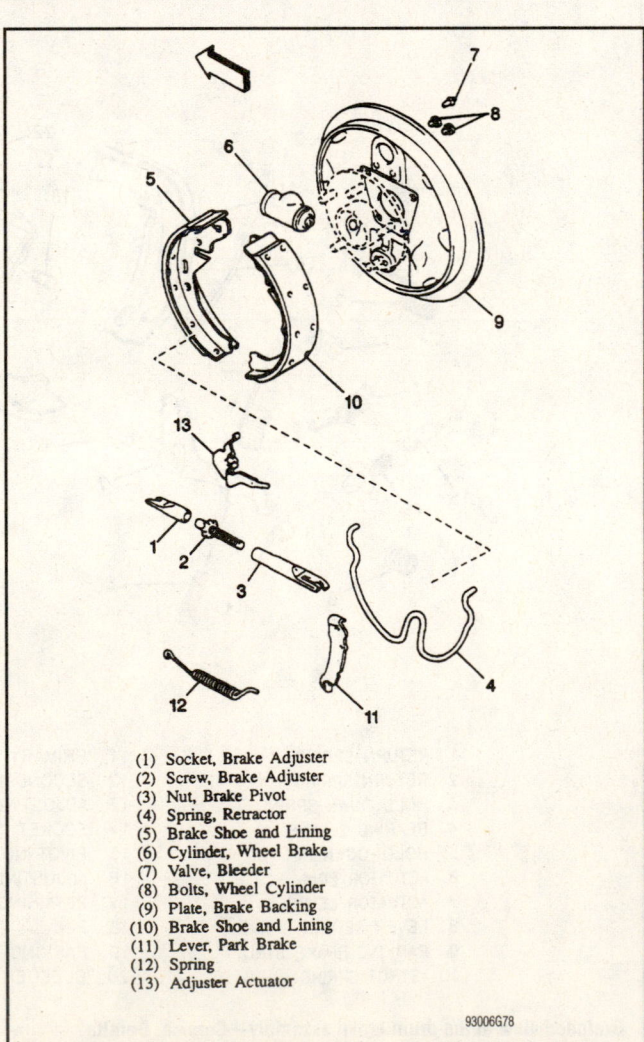

(1) Socket, Brake Adjuster
(2) Screw, Brake Adjuster
(3) Nut, Brake Pivot
(4) Spring, Retractor
(5) Brake Shoe and Lining
(6) Cylinder, Wheel Brake
(7) Valve, Bleeder
(8) Bolts, Wheel Cylinder
(9) Plate, Brake Backing
(10) Brake Shoe and Lining
(11) Lever, Park Brake
(12) Spring
(13) Adjuster Actuator

93006G78

Drum brake components, exploded view—Skylark, Malibu, Achieva, Cutlass, Grand Am

16. Install the adjusting screw and spring on the shoes, connecting them together. The coils of the spring must not be over the star-wheel on the adjuster. The left and right hand springs are not interchangeable.

17. Spread the shoe assemblies and connect the parking brake cable. Install the shoes on the backing plate, engaging the shoes at the top temporarily with the wheel cylinder pistons. Make sure the starwheel on the adjuster is lined up with the adjusting hole in the backing plate, if equipped.

18. Spread the shoes slightly and install the parking brake strut and spring. Make sure the end of the strut without the spring engages the parking brake lever. The end with the spring engages the primary shoe (the one with the shorter lining).

19. Install the actuator pivot, lever and return spring. Install the actuating link in the shoe retainer. Lift up the actuator lever and hook the link into the lever.

20. Install the hold-down pins through the back of the plate using J-8057, or the equivalent. Install the lever pivots and hold-down springs. Install the shoe return springs using J-8049, or the equivalent. Be careful not to stretch or distort the springs.

21. Make sure the linings are in the right place, the self-adjusting mechanism is correctly installed, and the parking brake parts are hooked up.

22. Measure the distance from the edge of the primary lining to the edge secondary lining, then measure the inside width of the drum. Adjust the linings by means of the adjuster so the drum will fit onto the linings.

23. Install the hub and bearing assembly onto the axle if removed. Torque the retaining bolts to 35 ft. lbs. (55 Nm).

24. Install the drum and the wheels.

25. Adjust the brakes. Install a rubber hole cover in the adjustment knock-out hole after the adjustment is complete. Adjust the parking brake.

26. Lower the vehicle. Road test the vehicle and verify proper brake operation.

GM W-BODY:
Buick Century, Regal
Chevrolet Lumina, Monte Carlo
Oldsmobile Cutlass Supreme, Intrigue
Pontiac Grand Prix

1. Raise and safely support the vehicle.
2. Remove the tire and wheel assembly.
3. Remove the brake drum.
4. Using tool J-38400, or an equivalent brake spanner and remover, remove the actuator spring from the adjuster lever. Use care not to distort the spring when removing it.

❊❊ CAUTION

During the following steps when removing the retractor spring from either shoe and lining assembly, do not over stretch the spring. This will reduce its effectiveness. Keep fingers away from retractor spring to prevent fingers from being pinched between the spring and shoe web or spring and the backing plate.

5. Lift the end of the retractor spring from the adjuster shoe assembly. Insert the hook end of the J-38400, or equivalent, between the retractor spring and the shoe. Pry slightly to remove the spring end from the hole in the shoe.

6. Pry the end of the retractor spring toward the axle with the flat end of the tool until the spring snaps down off the shoe web onto the backing plate.

7. Remove the one brake shoe and remove the adjuster assembly.

8. Disconnect the parking brake lever from the shoe. DO NOT remove the parking brake lever from the cable end unless it is being replaced.

9. Using J-38400, or the equivalent, lift the end of the retractor spring from the adjuster shoe assembly. Insert the hook end of the J-38400, or the equivalent between the retractor spring and the shoe. Pry

1 SPRING, ACTUATOR
2 ACTUATOR, ADJUSTER
6 SHOE AND LINING, ADJUSTER
7 LEVER, PARKING BRAKE
8 SHOE AND LINING, PARKING BRAKE
9 SPRING, RETRACTOR
13 PLATE ASSEMBLY, BACKING
14 PLUG, ACCESS HOLE
15 BOLT/SCREW ASSEMBLY, ADJUSTING

93006G79

Rear brake assembly component alignment—Century, Regal, Lumina, Monte Carlo, Cutlass Supreme, Intrigue, Grand Prix

slightly to remove the spring end from the hole in the shoe. Pry the end of the retractor spring toward the axle with the flat end of the tool until the spring snaps down off the shoe web onto the backing plate.

10. Remove the brake shoe.

To install:

11. Clean all the brake spring completely with brake solvent and allow to air dry.

12. Disassemble, clean and lubricate the adjuster screw. Once lubricated, reassemble.

13. Clean the backing plate and after it is dry apply a thin coat of brake grease to the brake shoe contact points on the backing plate.

14. Position the brake shoe that connects to the parking brake lever, on the backing plate. Using J-38400, or the equivalent, pull the end of the retractor spring up to rest on the web of the shoe. Pull the end of the retractor spring up until it snaps into the slot in the brake shoe.

15. Connect the parking brake lever.

16. Install the remaining shoe and the adjuster screw assembly.

17. Position the brake shoe, using J-38400, or the equivalent, pull the end of the retractor spring up to rest on the web of the shoe. Pull the end of the retractor spring up until it snaps into the slot in the brake shoe.

18. Using J-38400, or the equivalent, spread the brake shoes and work the adjuster screw into position.

19. Install the actuator spring with the U-shaped end going through the web.

20. Install the brake drum.

21. Install the tire and wheel assembly.

22. Adjust the brakes.

23. Lower the vehicle and road test for proper brake operation.

GEO Metro

1. Raise and safely support the vehicle.

2. Remove the rear wheels.

3. Remove the brake drum.

4. Remove the upper and lower return springs from the brake shoes.

5. Remove the anti-rattle spring and brake shoe adjustment strut.

6. Remove the primary and secondary brake shoe hold-down springs by pressing in and turning the hold-down pins.

7. Remove the parking brake cable.

8. Inspect all parts for wear and/or damage and replace as necessary.

1 HOLD-DOWN SPRINGS
2 HOLD-DOWN PINS

93006G80

Removing the shoe hold-down springs—Metro

9. Clean the brake backing plate and all parts to be reused with suitable brake parts cleaner and allow it to dry.

To install:

10. Lubricate all contact points on the backing plate with grease.

11. Install the hold-down pins on the backing plate.

12. Install the brake cable.

13. Install the primary and secondary brake shoes to the vehicle and secure with the hold-down springs.

14. Install the brake adjustment strut and anti-rattle spring.

15. Install the upper and lower return springs to the primary and secondary brake shoes.

16. Install the brake drum.

17. Install the rear wheels.

18. Lower the vehicle.

19. Press the brake pedal 3–5 times with approximately 66 lbs. (30 kg) pressure to adjust the brake shoe clearance.

20. Check to ensure the brake drum is free from dragging and proper braking is obtained.

GEO Prizm

1. Raise and safely support the vehicle.

2. Remove the rear wheels.

3. Remove the brake drum. Inspect the drum for wear and/or damage. Replace or machine the drum as necessary.

4. Remove the upper return spring.

5. Remove the front brake shoe hold-down spring, retainers and pin.

6. Remove the anchor spring from the front brake shoe and remove the front brake shoe.

7. Remove the rear brake shoe hold-down spring, retainers and pin.

8. Remove the automatic adjusting lever spring and the adjuster.

9. Remove the parking brake cable.

10. Use a suitable tool to spread the C-clips and remove the automatic adjuster lever and parking brake lever from the rear brake shoe.

11. Clean all parts and the brake backing plate with an approved brake parts cleaner.

To install:

12. Before reinstallation, apply grease to the contact points on the backing plate and pivot points on the adjuster lever.

13. Install the parking brake and automatic adjuster levers to the rear brake shoe.

14. Install new C-clips and use pliers to install them. Do not bend more than necessary to hold in place.

15. Check the clearance between the parking brake lever and the brake shoe using a feeler gauge. The clearance must be at least 0.0138 in. (0.35mm). If the clearance is not as specified, replace the shim between the lever and shoe.

16. Connect the parking brake cable.

17. Install the adjuster and the lever spring.

18. Install the rear brake shoe on the backing plate with the end of the shoe inserted in the wheel cylinder and the adjuster in place. Install the hold-down spring, retainer and pin.

19. Install the anchor spring between the front and rear shoe.

20. Install the front brake shoe with the end of the shoe inserted in the wheel cylinder and the adjuster in place.

21. Install the hold-down spring, retainers and pin.

22. Connect the return spring.

23. Adjust the brake shoes. When adjusted properly, the outside diameter of the brake shoes will be approximately 0.024 in. (0.6mm) less than the inner diameter of the brake drum.

24. Install the brake drum and the wheel.
25. Lower the vehicle.
26. Road test and check for proper brake operation.

Saturn

1. Raise and support the vehicle, then remove the wheels and brake drums.
2. Remove the lower return and adjuster springs using a universal brake spring remover. Do not over extend the springs or they will damaged and will need to be replaced.
3. Compress the leading brake shoe hold-down cup and spring while removing the pin from the rear of the backing plate. Release spring compression, then remove the hold-down cup and spring.
4. Pull the leading shoe towards the front of the vehicle and remove the adjuster assembly and lever. It may be necessary to turn the adjuster starwheel to shorten the adjuster's length.
5. Remove the leading shoe by twisting the shoe out of engagement with the upper return spring.
6. Remove the upper return spring from the park brake shoe, then remove the park brake shoe hold-down cup, spring and pin assembly.
7. Push the park brake shoe lever into the cable spring while disengaging the cable from the end lever and remove the parking brake shoe, lever and cable spring from the vehicle.
8. Remove the retainer and wave washer, then remove the park brake lever from the shoe.
9. Disassemble the brake adjuster socket, screw and nut, then clean the components in denatured alcohol. Inspect the assembly, making sure the screw threads smoothly into the adjusting nut over the full threaded length.
10. Inspect the wheel cylinder for signs of leakage and for cut or damaged boots. Do not attempt to repair a damaged cylinder, the assembly must be replaced.

To install:

11. Lubricate the adjuster assembly, the 6 backing plate raised shoe contact pads, the brake lever pin and surfaces which contact brake shoe webs with brake lubricant.
12. Install the park brake lever onto the pin on the brake shoe and secure with the wave washer and retainer clip. Crimp the ends of the retainer to secure the brake lever.
13. Install the cable spring into the cage on the park brake lever, then install the cable through the spring and onto the lever.
14. Install the park brake shoe using the hold-down cup assembly; use a universal spring cup remover/installer tool. Make sure the shoe is correctly engaged into the wheel cylinder (top) and the anchor (bottom).
15. Install the long straight end of the upper return spring into the back hole in the park brake shoe, position the other brake shoe and install the other end of the spring into the back of the leading shoe.

Rear brake shoe and adjuster installation—Saturn

16. Pull the lead shoe toward the front of the vehicle and install the adjuster between the park and leading brake shoes. Verify that the adjuster notches properly engage the brake shoe notches and that the shoe is properly aligned in the wheel cylinder and anchor.
17. Install the adjuster lever and adjuster spring. Make sure the notch on the lever engages the pin on the park shoe and the notch on the adjusting socket. The lower leg of the lever should engage the teeth of the starwheel adjuster assembly.
18. Secure the leading brake shoe using the hold-down cup assembly.
19. Install the adjuster spring to the upper side of the brake shoes with the short end to the lead shoe and the long end to the adjuster lever. Then install the lower return spring into the lower holes of the shoes.
20. Verify the correct location of all brake components, if necessary, use the other side brake assembly for comparison.
21. Using a suitable drum clearance gauge, measure the inner diameter of the brake drum and adjust the outside diameter of the brake shoes to 0.02 inch (0.50mm) less than the inner diameter of the drum.
22. Repeat the procedure for the opposite brake shoes and install the brake drums.
23. If the wheel cylinders have been replaced, bleed the hydraulic brake system.
24. Install the rear wheels and lower the vehicle.
25. Apply and release the brake pedal 20 times to allow the adjuster to properly position the brake shoes.
26. Check and adjust the parking brake cable, as necessary.

For brake related suspension and axle service, refer to the model specific sections of this manual

BRAKE SPECIFICATIONS
CHRYSLER 300M, CONCORD, LHS, NEW YORKER, DODGE INTREPID, EAGLE VISION
All measurements in inches unless noted

Year	Model		Master Cylinder Bore	Brake Disc Original Thickness	Brake Disc Minimum Thickness	Brake Disc Maximum Runout	Brake Drum Diameter Original Inside Diameter	Brake Drum Diameter Max. Wear Limit	Brake Drum Diameter Maximum Machine Diameter	Minimum Lining Thickness	Brake Caliper Mounting Bolts (ft. lbs.)
1996	Concorde	F	0.874	0.945	0.882	0.003	—	—	—	0.310	17
		R	—	0.468	0.409	0.003	—	—	—	0.280	17
	Intrepid	F	0.937	0.945	0.882	0.005	—	—	—	0.310	17
		R	—	0.468	0.409	0.003	8.00	①	①	0.280	17
	LHS	F	0.874	0.945	0.882	0.003	—	—	—	0.310	17
		R	—	0.468	0.409	0.003	—	—	—	0.280	17
	Vision	F	0.937	0.945	0.882	0.003	—	—	—	0.312	17
		R	—	0.468	0.409	0.003	8.00	①	—	0.281	17
1997	Concorde	F	0.874	0.945	0.882	0.003	—	—	—	0.310	17
		R	—	0.468	0.409	0.003	—	—	—	0.280	17
	Intrepid	F	0.937	0.945	0.882	0.005	—	—	—	0.310	17
		R	—	0.468	0.409	0.003	8.00	①	①	0.280	17
	LHS	F	0.874	0.945	0.882	0.003	—	—	—	0.310	17
		R	—	0.468	0.409	0.003	—	—	—	0.280	17
	Vision	F	0.937	0.945	0.882	0.003	—	—	—	0.312	17
		R	—	0.468	0.409	0.003	8.00	①	—	0.281	17
1998	300M	F	0.937	1.019	0.882	0.003	—	—	—	0.310	17
		R	—	0.468	0.409	0.003	—	—	—	0.281	17
	Concorde	F	0.937	1.019	0.882	0.003	—	—	—	0.310	17
		R	—	0.468	0.409	0.003	—	—	—	0.280	17
	Intrepid	F	0.937	1.019	0.882	0.005	—	—	—	0.310	17
		R	—	0.468	0.409	0.003	—	—	—	0.280	17
	LHS	F	0.937	1.019	0.882	0.003	—	—	—	0.310	17
		R	—	0.468	0.409	0.003	—	—	—	0.280	17
1999-00	300M	F	0.937	1.019	0.882	0.003	—	—	—	0.310	17
		R	—	0.468	0.409	0.003	—	—	—	0.281	17
	Concorde	F	0.937	1.019	0.882	0.003	—	—	—	0.310	17
		R	—	0.468	0.409	0.003	—	—	—	0.280	17
	Intrepid	F	0.937	1.019	0.882	0.005	—	—	—	0.310	17
		R	—	0.468	0.409	0.003	—	—	—	0.280	17
	LHS	F	0.937	1.019	0.882	0.003	—	—	—	0.310	17
		R	—	0.468	0.409	0.003	—	—	—	0.280	17

F - Front

R - Rear

① Maximum diameter is stamped on drum

93006C01

BRAKE SPECIFICATIONS
CHRYSLER CIRRUS, SEBRING CONVERTIBLE, DODGE STRATUS, PLYMOUTH BREEZE
All measurements in inches unless noted

Year	Model		Master Cylinder Bore	Brake Disc Original Thickness	Brake Disc Minimum Thickness	Brake Disc Maximum Run-out	Brake Drum Diameter Original Inside Diameter	Brake Drum Diameter Max. Wear Limit	Brake Drum Diameter Maximum Machine Diameter	Minimum Lining Thickness	Brake Caliper Guide Pin Bolts (ft. lbs.)
1996	Breeze	F	0.874	0.911	0.843	0.003	—	—	—	0.035	16
		R	—	0.360	0.285	0.005	NA	①	①	②	16
	Cirrus	F	0.874	0.911	0.843	0.005	—	—	—	0.035	16
		R	—	0.360	0.285	0.005	NA	①	①	②	16
	Sebring Convertible	F	0.874	0.911	0.843	0.005	—	—	—	0.035	16
		R	—	0.360	0.285	0.005	NA	①	①	②	16
	Stratus	F	0.874	0.911	0.843	0.003	—	—	—	0.035	16
		R	—	0.360	0.285	0.005	NA	①	①	②	16
1997	Breeze	F	0.874	0.911	0.843	0.003	—	—	—	0.035	16
		R	—	0.360	0.285	0.005	NA	①	①	②	16
	Cirrus	F	0.874	0.911	0.843	0.005	—	—	—	0.035	16
		R	—	0.360	0.285	0.005	NA	①	①	②	16
	Sebring Convertible	F	0.874	0.911	0.843	0.005	—	—	—	0.035	16
		R	—	0.360	0.285	0.005	NA	①	①	②	16
	Stratus	F	0.874	0.911	0.843	0.003	—	—	—	0.035	16
		R	—	0.360	0.285	0.005	NA	①	①	②	16
1998	Breeze	F	0.874	0.911	0.843	0.003	—	—	—	0.035	16
		R	—	0.360	0.285	0.005	NA	①	①	②	16
	Cirrus	F	0.874	0.911	0.843	0.005	—	—	—	0.035	16
		R	—	0.360	0.285	0.005	NA	①	①	②	16
	Sebring Convertible	F	0.874	0.911	0.843	0.005	—	—	—	0.035	16
		R	—	0.360	0.285	0.005	NA	①	①	②	16
	Stratus	F	0.874	0.911	0.843	0.003	—	—	—	0.035	16
		R	—	0.360	0.285	0.005	NA	①	①	②	16
1999-00	Breeze	F	0.874	0.911	0.843	0.003	—	—	—	③	16
		R	—	0.360	0.285	0.005	NA	①	①	②	16
	Cirrus	F	0.874	0.911	0.843	0.005	—	—	—	③	16
		R	—	0.360	0.285	0.005	NA	①	①	②	16
	Sebring Convertible	F	0.874	0.911	0.843	0.005	—	—	—	③	16
		R	—	0.360	0.285	0.005	NA	①	①	②	16
	Stratus	F	0.874	0.911	0.843	0.003	—	—	—	③	16
		R	—	0.360	0.285	0.005	NA	①	①	②	16

NA - Not Available

① Maximum diameter is stamped on drum

② Disc brake lining and backing total thickness = 9/32 inch

Drum brake shoe lining and backing total thickness = 1/8 inch

③ Disc brake lining and backing = 3/8 inch

93006C02

BRAKE SPECIFICATIONS
CHRYSLER SEBRING COUPE, DODGE AVENGER
All measurements in inches unless noted

Year	Model		Master Cylinder Bore	Brake Disc Original Thickness	Minimum Thickness	Maximum Run-out	Brake Drum Diameter Original Inside Diameter	Max. Wear Limit	Maximum Machine Diameter	Min. Lining Thickness	Brake Caliper Bracket Bolts (ft. lbs.)	Mounting Bolts (ft. lbs.)
1996	Avenger	F	0.937	0.940	0.880	0.003	—	—	—	0.080	65	54
		R	—	0.390	0.330	0.003	④	①	①	⑤	—	38
	Sebring	F	0.937 ②	0.940	0.880	0.003	—	—	—	0.080	65	54
		R	—	0.390	0.330	0.003	④	①	①	⑤	—	38
1997	Avenger	F	0.937	0.940	0.880	0.003	—	—	—	0.080	65	54
		R	—	0.390	0.330	0.003	④	①	①	⑤	—	38
	Sebring	F	1.000	0.940	0.880	0.003	—	—	—	0.080	65	54
	Coupe	R	—	0.390 ⑥	0.330 ⑦	0.003	④	①	①	⑤	—	38
1998	Avenger	F	0.937	0.940	0.880	0.003	—	—	—	0.080	65	54
		R	—	0.390	0.330	0.003	④	①	①	⑤	—	38
	Sebring	F	1.000	0.940	0.880	0.003	—	—	—	0.080	65	54
	Coupe	R	—	0.390 ⑥	0.330 ⑦	0.003	④	①	①	⑤	—	38
1999-00	Avenger	F	0.937	0.940	0.880	0.003	—	—	—	0.080	65	54
		R	—	0.390	0.330	0.003	④	①	①	⑤	—	38
	Sebring	F	1.000	0.940	0.880	0.003	—	—	—	0.080	66	54
	Coupe	R	—	0.390 ⑥	0.330 ⑦	0.003	④	①	①	⑤	—	38

F - Front

R - Rear

① Maximum diameter is stamped on drum

② Equipped with ABS: 1.000

③ Solid rear disc

④ Minimum diameter: 9.00 in.

⑤ 0.039 in. with drum brakes
   0.080 in. with disc brakes

⑥ Vented rear disc: 0.790

⑦ Vented rear disc: 0.720

93006C03

DODGE/PLYMOUTH NEON
All measurements in inches unless noted

Year	Model		Master Cylinder Bore	Brake Disc Original Thickness	Minimum Thickness	Maximum Runout	Brake Drum Diameter Original Inside Diameter	Max. Wear Limit	Maximum Machine Diameter	Minimum Lining Thickness	Brake Caliper Bracket Bolts (ft. lbs.)	Mounting Bolts (ft. lbs.)
1996	Neon	F	①	0.792	0.724	0.005	—	—	—	0.313	55	16
		R	—	0.364	0.285	0.005	7.88	NA	②	③	45	16
1997	Neon	F	①	0.792	0.724	0.005	—	—	—	0.300	55	16
		R	—	0.364	0.285	0.005	7.88	NA	②	③	45	16
1998	Neon	F	①	0.792	0.724	0.005	—	—	—	0.300	55	16
		R	—	0.364	0.285	0.005	7.88	NA	②	③	45	16
1999-00	Neon	F	①	0.792	0.724	0.005	—	—	—	0.300	55	16
		R	—	0.364	0.285	0.005	7.88	NA	②	③	45	16

NA - Not Available

① If equipped with rear drum brakes: 0.827
   If equipped with rear disc brakes: 0.875

② Stamped on the outer edge of drum

③ Disc brake pad total thickness - 0.281
   Brake shoe lining thickness - 0.0625

93006C04

BRAKE SPECIFICATIONS
DODGE STEALTH
All measurements in inches unless noted

Year	Model		Master Cylinder Bore	Brake Disc			Brake Drum Diameter			Minimum Lining Thickness		Brake Caliper	
				Original Thickness	Minimum Thickness	Maximum Runout	Original Inside Diameter	Max. Wear Limit	Maximum Machine Diameter	Front	Rear	Caliper-to-Adapter Bolts (ft. lbs.)	Adapter-to-Hub Bolts (ft. lbs.)
1996	Stealth	F	1.000	0.940	0.880	0.003	—	—	—	0.079	—	54	65
		R	—	0.710	0.650	0.003	—	—	—	—	0.079	20	36-43
	Stealth ①	F	1.060	1.180	1.120	0.003	—	—	—	0.079	—	54	65
		R	—	0.790	0.720	0.003	—	—	—	—	0.079	20	36-43
	Stealth AWD	F	1.060	1.180	1.120	0.003	—	—	—	0.079	—	54	65
		R	—	0.790	0.720	0.003	—	—	—	—	0.079	20	36-43

① With ABS

93006C05

BRAKE SPECIFICATIONS
EAGLE TALON
All measurements in inches unless noted

Year	Model		Master Cylinder Bore	Brake Disc Original Thickness	Brake Disc Minimum Thickness	Brake Disc Maximum Runout	Minimum Lining Thickness	Bake Caliper Bracket Bolts (ft.bs.)	Bake Caliper Mounting Bolts (ft.bs.)
1996	Talon	F	①	0.940	0.882	0.003	0.080	65	54
		R	①	0.390	0.331	0.003	0.080	—	38
1997	Talon	F	①	0.940	0.882	0.003	0.080	65	54
		R	①	0.390	0.331	0.003	0.080	—	38
1998	Talon	F	①	0.940	0.882	0.003	0.080	65	54
		R	①	0.390	0.331	0.003	0.080	—	38

① Non-turbocharged: 0.938
FWD turbocharged: 0.938
AWD turbocharged: 1.000

93006C06

BRAKE SPECIFICATIONS
FORD CONTOUR, MERCURY MYSTIQUE, COUGAR (1999-00)
All measurements in inches unless noted

| Year | Model | | Brake Disc | | | Brake Drum | | | Minimum Lining Thickness | Brake Caliper Mounting Bolts (ft. lbs.) |
			Original Thickness	Minimum Thickness	Maximum Run-out	Original Inside Diameter	Max. Wear Limit	Maximum Machine Diameter		
1996	Contour	F	0.950	0.870	0.006	—	—	—	0.125	20
		R	0.790	0.710	0.006	8.00	NA	8.04	0.125	30
	Mystique	F	0.950	0.870	0.006	—	—	—	0.125	20
		R	0.790	0.710	0.006	8.00	NA	8.04	0.125	30
1997	Contour	F	0.950	0.870	0.006	—	—	—	0.125	20
		R	0.790	0.710	0.006	8.00	NA	8.04	0.125	30
	Mystique	F	0.950	0.870	0.006	—	—	—	0.125	20
		R	0.790	0.710	0.006	8.00	NA	8.04	0.125	30
1998	Contour	F	0.950	0.870	0.006	—	—	—	0.125	20
		R	0.790	0.710	0.006	8.00	NA	8.04	0.125	30
	Mystique	F	0.950	0.870	0.006	—	—	—	0.125	20
		R	0.790	0.710	0.006	8.00	NA	8.04	0.125	30
1999-00	Contour	F	0.950	0.870	0.006	—	—	—	0.125	20
		R	0.790	0.710	0.006	8.00	NA	8.04	0.125	30
	Cougar	F	0.950	0.870	0.006	—	—	—	0.125	20
		R	0.790	0.710	0.006	8.00	NA	8.04	0.125	30
	Mystique	F	0.950	0.870	0.006	—	—	—	0.125	20
		R	0.790	0.710	0.006	8.00	NA	8.04	0.125	30

NOTE: Follow specifications stamped on rotor or drum if figures differ from those in this chart.

NA - Not Available

F - Front

R - Rear

93006C07

For brake related suspension and axle service, refer to the model specific sections of this manual

BRAKE SPECIFICATIONS
FORD ASPIRE
All measurements in inches unless noted

Year	Model		Master Cylinder Bore	Brake Disc			Brake Drum Diameter			Minimum Lining Thickness		Brake Caliper Mounting Bolts (ft. lbs.)
				Original Thickness	Minimum Thickness	Maximum Run-out	Original Inside Diameter	Max. Wear Limit	Maximum Machine Diameter	Front	Rear	
1996	Aspire	①	②	0.710	0.630	0.004	7.87	7.93	NA	0.080	0.040	29-36
		③	②	0.860	0.780	0.004	7.87	7.93	NA	0.080	0.040	29-36
1997	Aspire	①	②	0.710	0.630	0.004	7.87	7.93	NA	0.080	0.040	29-36
		③	②	0.860	0.780	0.004	7.87	7.93	NA	0.080	0.040	29-36

NOTE: Follow specifications stamped on rotor or drum if figures differ from those in this chart.

NA - Not Available

F - Front

R - Rear

① Manual transaxle

② Without ABS: 0.810
   With ABS: 0.870

③ Automatic transaxle

93006C08

BRAKE SPECIFICATIONS
FORD CROWN VICTORIA, LINCOLN TOWN CAR, MERCURY GRAND MARQUIS
All measurements in inches unless noted

Year	Model	Master Cylinder Bore	Front Brake Disc			Rear Brake Disc			Minimum Lining Thickness	Brake Caliper Bracket Bolts (ft. lbs.)	Mounting Bolts (ft. lbs.)
			Original Thickness	Minimum Thickness	Maximum Run-out	Original Thickness	Minimum Thickness	Maximum Run-out			
1996	Crown Victoria	1.000	1.024	0.974	0.002	0.550	0.510	0.002	0.125	125-169	21-26
	Grand Marquis	1.000	1.024	0.974	0.002	0.550	0.510	0.002	0.125	125-169	21-26
	Town Car	1.000	1.024	0.974	0.002	0.550	0.510	0.002	0.125	125-169	21-26
1997	Crown Victoria	1.000	1.024	0.974	0.002	0.550	0.510	0.002	0.125	125-169	21-26
	Grand Marquis	1.000	1.024	0.974	0.002	0.550	0.510	0.002	0.125	125-169	21-26
	Town Car	1.000	1.024	0.974	0.002	0.550	0.510	0.002	0.125	125-169	21-26
1998	Crown Victoria	1.000	1.024	0.974	0.002	0.550	0.510	0.002	0.125	125-169	21-26
	Grand Marquis	1.000	1.024	0.974	0.002	0.550	0.510	0.002	0.125	125-169	21-26
	Town Car	1.000	1.024	0.974	0.002	0.550	0.510	0.002	0.125	125-169	21-26
1999-00	Crown Victoria	1.000	1.024	0.974	0.002	0.550	0.510	0.002	0.125	125-169	21-26
	Grand Marquis	1.000	1.024	0.974	0.002	0.550	0.510	0.002	0.125	125-169	21-26
	Town Car	1.000	1.024	0.974	0.002	0.550	0.510	0.002	0.125	125-169	21-26

NOTE: Follow specifications stamped on rotor or drum if figures differ from those in this chart.

93006C09

For complete service labor times order Chilton's Labor Guide Manual

BRAKE SPECIFICATIONS
FORD ESCORT, ESCORT ZX2, MERCURY TRACER
All measurements in inches unless noted

Year	Model		Master Cylinder Bore	Brake Disc			Brake Drum Diameter			Minimum Lining Thickness	Brake Caliper Mounting Bolts (ft. lbs.)
				Original Thickness	Minimum Thickness	Maximum Runout	Original Inside Diameter	Max. Wear Limit	Maximum Machine Diameter		
1996	Escort	F	0.875	0.870	0.790	0.004	—	—	—	0.080	35
		R	—	0.350	0.280	0.004	7.87	7.95	7.91	0.040	—
	Tracer	F	0.875	0.870	0.790	0.004	—	—	—	0.080	35
		R	—	0.350	0.280	0.004	7.87	7.95	7.91	0.040	—
1997	Escort	F	0.875	0.870	0.790	0.004	—	—	—	0.080	36-43
		R	—	0.350	0.280	0.004	7.87	7.95	7.91	0.040	—
	Tracer	F	0.875	0.870	0.790	0.004	—	—	—	0.080	36-43
		R	—	0.350	0.280	0.004	7.87	7.95	7.91	0.040	—
1998	Escort	F	0.875	0.870	0.790	0.004	—	—	—	0.080	36-43
		R	—	0.350	0.280	0.004	7.87	7.95	7.91	0.040	—
	Escort ZX2	F	0.875	0.870	0.790	0.004	—	—	—	0.080	36-43
		R	—	0.350	0.280	0.004	7.87	7.95	7.91	0.040	—
	Tracer	F	0.875	0.870	0.790	0.004	—	—	—	0.080	36-43
		R	—	0.350	0.280	0.004	7.87	7.95	7.91	0.040	—
1999-00	Escort	F	0.875	0.870	0.790	0.004	—	—	—	0.080	36-43
		R	—	0.350	0.280	0.004	7.87	7.95	7.91	0.040	—
	Escort ZX2	F	0.875	0.870	0.790	0.004	—	—	—	0.080	36-43
		R	—	0.350	0.280	0.004	7.87	7.95	7.91	0.040	—
	Tracer	F	0.875	0.870	0.790	0.004	—	—	—	0.080	36-43
		R	—	0.350	0.280	0.004	7.87	7.95	7.91	0.040	—

NOTE: Follow specifications stamped on rotor or drum if figures differ from those in this chart.

NA - Not Available

F - Front

R - Rear

93006C00

BRAKE SPECIFICATIONS
FORD MARK VIII, MUSTANG, THUNDERBIRD, MERCURY COUGAR (1996-97)
All measurements in inches unless noted

Year	Model			Master Cylinder Bore	Brake Disc Original Thickness	Brake Disc Minimum Thickness	Brake Disc Maximum Run-out	Brake Drum Diameter Original Inside Diameter	Brake Drum Diameter Max. Wear Limit	Brake Drum Diameter Maximum Machine Diameter	Minimum Lining Thickness	Brake Caliper Mounting Bolts (ft. lbs.)
1996	Cougar		F	0.938	1.025	0.974	0.002	—	—	—	0.125	60
			R	—	0.710	0.657	—	9.80	NA	9.90	0.125	26
	Mark VIII		F	1.000	1.024	0.974	0.003	—	—	—	0.125	60
			R	—	0.709	0.657	0.002	—	—	—	0.125	26
	Mustang	①	F	1.060	1.030	0.970	0.001	—	—	—	0.125	64
		②	F	1.000	1.030	0.970	0.002	—	—	—	0.125	64
		③	F	1.000	1.100	1.040	0.001	—	—	—	0.125	64
			R	—	0.550	0.500	0.002	—	—	—	0.123	26
		③	R	—	0.710	0.660	0.002	—	—	—	0.123	26
	Thunderbird		F	0.938	1.025	0.974	0.002	—	—	—	0.125	60
			R	—	0.710	0.657	—	9.80	NA	9.90	0.125	26
1997	Cougar		F	0.938	1.025	0.974	0.002	—	—	—	0.125	60
			R	—	0.710	0.657	—	9.80	NA	9.90	0.125	26
	Mark VIII		F	1.000	1.024	0.974	0.003	—	—	—	0.125	60
			R	—	0.709	0.657	0.002	—	—	—	0.125	26
	Mustang	①	F	1.060	1.030	0.970	0.001	—	—	—	0.125	64
		②	F	1.000	1.030	0.970	0.002	—	—	—	0.125	64
		③	F	1.000	1.100	1.040	0.001	—	—	—	0.125	64
			R	—	0.550	0.500	0.002	—	—	—	0.123	26
		③	R	—	0.710	0.660	0.002	—	—	—	0.123	26
	Thunderbird		F	0.938	1.025	0.974	0.002	—	—	—	0.125	60
			R	—	0.710	0.657	—	9.80	NA	9.90	0.125	26
1998	Mark VIII		F	1.000	1.024	0.974	0.003	—	—	—	0.125	60
			R	—	0.709	0.657	0.002	—	—	—	—	26
	Mustang	①	F	1.060	1.030	0.970	0.001	—	—	—	0.125	64
		②	F	1.000	1.030	0.970	0.002	—	—	—	0.125	64
		③	F	1.000	1.100	1.040	0.001	—	—	—	0.125	64
			R	—	0.550	0.500	0.002	—	—	—	0.123	26
		③	R	—	0.710	0.660	0.002	—	—	—	0.123	26
1999-00	Mustang	①	F	1.060	1.030	0.970	0.001	—	—	—	0.125	64
		②	F	1.000	1.030	0.970	0.002	—	—	—	0.125	64
		③	F	1.000	1.100	1.040	0.001	—	—	—	0.125	64
			R	—	0.550	0.500	0.002	—	—	—	0.123	26
		③	R	—	0.710	0.660	0.002	—	—	—	0.123	26

NOTE: Follow specifications stamped on rotor or drum if figures differ from those in this chart.

NA - Not Available

F - Front

R - Rear

① 3.8L engine

② 4.6L except Cobra

③ Cobra

93006C11

Please visit our web site at www.chiltononline.com

BRAKE SPECIFICATIONS
FORD PROBE
All measurements in inches unless noted

| Year | | Model | Master Cylinder Bore | Brake Disc | | | Minimum Lining Thickness | Brake Caliper | |
				Original Thickness	Minimum Thickness	Maximum Run-out	Front	Bracket Bolts (ft. lbs.)	Mounting Bolts (ft. lbs.)
1996	F	Probe	0.937	0.890	0.860	0.004	0.040	58-74	33-36
	R	Probe	—	0.345	0.315	0.004	0.040	33-49	25-29
1997	F	Probe	0.937	0.890	0.860	0.004	0.040	58-74	33-36
	R	Probe	—	0.345	0.315	0.004	0.040	33-49	25-29

NOTE: Follow specifications stamped on rotor or drum if figures differ from those in this chart.

93006C12

BRAKE SPECIFICATIONS
FORD TAURUS, LINCOLN CONTINENTAL, MERCURY SABLE
All measurements in inches unless noted

Year	Model		Master Cylinder Bore	Brake Disc			Brake Drum			Minimum Lining Thickness	Brake Caliper	
				Original Thickness	Minimum Thickness	Maximum Run-out	Original Inside Diameter	Max. Wear Limit	Maximum Machine Diameter		Bracket Bolts (ft. lbs.)	Mounting Bolts (ft. lbs.)
1996	Continental	F	NA	1.020	0.974	0.003	—	—	—	0.039	65-87	25
		R	—	0.550	0.502	0.001	—	—	—	0.039	—	25
	Sable	F	1.000	1.020	0.974	0.002	—	—	—	0.039	65-85	23-28
		R	—	0.550	0.500	0.004	8.86	0.06	8.92	0.039	65-87	23-25
	Taurus ①	F	1.000	1.020	0.974	0.002	—	—	—	0.039	65-85	23-28
		R	—	0.940	0.500	0.002	8.86	0.06	8.92	0.039	65-87	23-25
1997	Continental	F	NA	1.020	0.974	0.003	—	—	—	0.039	65-87	25
		R	—	0.550	0.502	0.001	—	—	—	0.039	—	25
	Sable	F	1.000	1.020	0.974	0.002	—	—	—	0.039	65-85	23-28
		R	—	0.550	0.500	0.004	8.86	0.06	8.92	0.039	65-87	23-25
	Taurus ①	F	1.000	1.020	0.974	0.002	—	—	—	0.039	65-85	23-28
		R	—	0.940	0.500	0.002	8.86	0.06	8.92	0.039	65-87	23-25
1998	Continental	F	NA	1.020	0.974	0.003	—	—	—	0.039	65-87	25
		R	—	0.550	0.502	0.001	—	—	—	0.039	—	25
	Sable	F	1.000	1.020	0.974	0.002	—	—	—	0.039	65-85	23-28
		R	—	0.550	0.500	0.004	8.86	0.06	8.92	0.039	65-87	23-25
	Taurus ①	F	1.000	1.020	0.974	0.002	—	—	—	0.039	65-85	23-28
		R	—	0.940	0.500	0.002	8.86	0.06	8.92	0.039	65-87	23-25
1999-00	Continental	F	NA	1.020	0.974	0.003	—	—	—	0.039	65-87	25
		R	—	0.550	0.502	0.001	—	—	—	0.039	—	25
	Sable	F	1.000	1.020	0.974	0.002	—	—	—	0.039	65-85	23-28
		R	—	0.550	0.500	0.004	8.85	0.05	8.92	0.039	65-87	23-25
	Taurus ①	F	1.000	1.020	0.974	0.002	—	—	—	0.039	65-85	23-28
		R	—	0.940	0.500	0.002	8.85	0.05	8.92	0.039	65-87	23-25

NOTE: Follow specifications stamped on rotor or drum if figures differ from those in this chart.

NA - Not Available

F - Front

R - Rear

① SHO models: 1.090 inch

93006C13

For brake related suspension and axle service, refer to the model specific sections of this manual

BRAKE SPECIFICATIONS
GM A BODY
BUICK CENTURY, OLDSMOBILE CUTLASS CIERA AND CUTLASS CRUISER
All measurements in inches unless noted

Year	Model	Master Cylinder Bore	Brake Disc			Brake Drum			Minimum Lining Thickness		Brake Caliper Mounting Bolts (ft. lbs.)
			Original Thickness	Minimum Thickness	Maximum Run-out	Original Inside Diameter	Max. Wear Limit	Maximum Machine Diameter	Front	Rear	
1996	Century	0.944	1.028	0.957	0.002	8.863	8.909	8.920	0.030	0.031	38
	Cutlass Ciera	0.944	1.028	0.957	0.002	8.863	8.909	8.920	0.030	0.031	38
	Cutlass Cruiser	0.944	1.028	0.957	0.002	8.863	8.909	8.920	0.030	0.031	38

93006C14

BRAKE SPECIFICATIONS
GM B BODY
BUICK ROADMASTER, CADILLAC FLEETWOOD, CHEVROLET CAPRICE AND IMPALA SS

All measurements in inches unless noted

Year	Model	Master Cylinder Bore	Brake Disc			Brake Drum Diameter			Minimum Lining Thickness		Brake Caliper Mounting Bolts
			Original Thickness	Minimum Thickness	Maximum Runout	Original Inside Diameter	Max. Wear Limit	Maximum Machine Diameter	Front	Rear	(ft. lbs.)
1996	Caprice	1.125	1.043	0.980	0.004	11.00	11.09	11.06	0.030	0.030	38
	Impala SS	1.125	1.043	0.980	0.004	11.00	11.09	11.06	0.030	0.030	38
	Fleetwood	1.125	1.125	1.043	0.004	11.00	11.09	11.06	0.030	0.030	38
	Roadmaster	1.125	1.043	0.965	0.004	9.500	9.590	9.560	0.030	①	38

① 0.030 over rivet head; If bonded lining, use 0.062 from shoe

93006C15

BRAKE SPECIFICATIONS
GM C & H BODIES
BUICK LeSABRE, PARK AVENUE, OLDSMOBILE EIGHTY-EIGHT, LSS, PONTIAC BONNEVILLE
All measurements in inches unless noted

| Year | Model | Master Cylinder Bore | Brake Disc | | | Brake Drum Diameter | | | Minimum Lining Thickness | | Brake Caliper Mounting Bolts |
			Original Thickness	Minimum Thickness	Maximum Runout	Original Inside Diameter	Max. Wear Limit	Maximum Machine Diameter	Front	Rear	(ft. lbs.)
1996	Bonneville	1.000	1.260	1.209	0.002	8.860	8.909	8.920	0.030	0.030	38
	Eighty-Eight	1.000	1.276	1.209	0.004	8.860	8.909	8.800	0.030	①	38
	LeSabre	1.000	1.260	1.209	0.002	8.863	8.909	8.920	0.030	①	38
	Ninety-Eight	1.000	1.276	1.209	0.004	8.860	8.909	8.800	0.030	①	38
	Park Avenue	1.000	1.260	1.209	0.002	8.863	8.909	8.920	0.030	①	38
1997	Bonneville	1.000	1.260	1.209	0.002	8.860	8.909	8.920	0.030	0.030	38
	Eighty-Eight	1.000	1.276	1.209	0.004	8.860	8.909	8.800	0.030	①	38
	LeSabre	1.000	1.260	1.209	0.002	8.863	8.909	8.920	0.030	①	38
	LSS	1.000	1.276	1.209	0.004	8.860	8.909	8.800	0.030	①	38
	Park Avenue	1.000	1.260	1.209	0.002	8.863	8.909	8.920	0.030	①	38
	Regency	1.000	1.276	1.209	0.004	8.860	8.909	8.800	0.030	①	38
1998	Bonneville	1.000	1.260	1.209	0.002	8.860	8.909	8.920	0.030	0.030	38
	Eighty-Eight	1.000	1.276	1.209	0.004	8.860	8.909	8.800	0.030	①	38
	LeSabre	1.000	1.260	1.209	0.002	8.863	8.909	8.920	0.030	①	38
	LSS	1.000	1.276	1.209	0.004	8.860	8.909	8.800	0.030	①	38
	Park Avenue	1.000	1.260	1.209	0.002	8.863	8.909	8.920	0.030	①	38
	Regency	1.000	1.276	1.209	0.004	8.860	8.909	8.800	0.030	①	38
1999-00	Bonneville	1.000	1.260	1.209	0.002	8.860	8.909	8.920	0.030	0.030	38
	Eighty-Eight	1.000	1.276	1.209	0.004	8.860	8.909	8.800	0.030	①	38
	LeSabre	1.000	1.260	1.209	0.002	8.863	8.909	8.920	0.030	①	38
	LSS	1.000	1.276	1.209	0.004	8.860	8.909	8.800	0.030	①	38
	Park Avenue	1.000	1.260	1.209	0.002	8.863	8.909	8.920	0.030	①	38
	Regency	1.000	1.276	1.209	0.004	8.860	8.909	8.800	0.030	①	38

① 0.030 over rivet head; If bonded lining, use 0.062 from shoe

93006C16

BRAKE SPECIFICATIONS
GM E & K BODIES
CADILLAC DEVILLE, ELDORADO AND SEVILLE
All measurements in inches unless noted

Year	Model		Master Cylinder Bore	Brake Disc Original Thickness	Brake Disc Minimum Thickness	Brake Disc Maximum Runout	Minimum Lining Thickness	Brake Caliper Mounting Bolts (ft. lbs.)
1996	DeVille	F	1.000	1.268	1.209	0.002	0.030	38
		R	—	0.433	0.374	0.002	0.030	20
	DeVille Concours	F	1.000	1.268	1.209	0.002	0.030	38
		R	—	0.433	0.374	0.002	0.030	20
	Eldorado	F	1.000	1.268	1.209	0.002	0.030	38
		R	—	0.433	0.374	0.002	0.030	20
	Eldorado ETC	F	1.000	1.268	1.209	0.002	0.030	38
		R	—	0.433	0.374	0.002	0.030	20
	Seville SLS	F	1.000	1.268	1.209	0.002	0.030	38
		R	—	0.433	0.374	0.002	0.030	20
	Seville STS	F	1.000	1.268	1.209	0.002	0.030	38
		R	—	0.433	0.374	0.002	0.030	20
1997	DeVille	F	1.000	1.268	1.209	0.002	0.030	38
		R	—	0.433	0.374	0.002	0.030	20
	DeVille Concours	F	1.000	1.268	1.209	0.002	0.030	38
		R	—	0.433	0.374	0.002	0.030	20
	Eldorado	F	1.000	1.268	1.209	0.002	0.030	38
		R	—	0.433	0.374	0.002	0.030	20
	Eldorado ETC	F	1.000	1.268	1.209	0.002	0.030	38
		R	—	0.433	0.374	0.002	0.030	20
	Seville SLS	F	1.000	1.268	1.209	0.002	0.030	38
		R	—	0.433	0.374	0.002	0.030	20
	Seville STS	F	1.000	1.268	1.209	0.002	0.030	38
		R	—	0.433	0.374	0.002	0.030	20
1998	DeVille	F	1.000	1.268	1.209	0.002	0.030	38
		R	—	0.433	0.374	0.002	0.030	20
	DeVille Concours	F	1.000	1.268	1.209	0.002	0.030	38
		R	—	0.433	0.374	0.002	0.030	20
	Eldorado	F	1.000	1.268	1.209	0.002	0.030	38
		R	—	0.433	0.374	0.002	0.030	20
	Eldorado ETC	F	1.000	1.268	1.209	0.002	0.030	38
		R	—	0.433	0.374	0.002	0.030	20
	Seville SLS	F	1.000	1.268	1.209	0.002	0.030	38
		R	—	0.433	0.374	0.002	0.030	20
	Seville STS	F	1.000	1.268	1.209	0.002	0.030	38
		R	—	0.433	0.374	0.002	0.030	20
1999-00	DeVille	F	1.000	1.268	1.209	0.002	0.030	38
		R	—	0.433	0.374	0.002	0.030	20
	DeVille Concours	F	1.000	1.268	1.209	0.002	0.030	38
		R	—	0.433	0.374	0.002	0.030	20
	Eldorado	F	1.000	1.268	1.209	0.002	0.030	38
		R	—	0.433	0.374	0.002	0.030	20
	Eldorado ETC	F	1.000	1.268	1.209	0.002	0.030	38
		R	—	0.433	0.374	0.002	0.030	20
	Seville SLS	F	1.000	1.268	1.209	0.002	0.030	38
		R	—	0.433	0.374	0.002	0.030	20
	Seville STS	F	1.000	1.268	1.209	0.002	0.030	38
		R	—	0.433	0.374	0.002	0.030	20

93006C17

BRAKE SPECIFICATIONS
GM F BODY
CHEVROLET CAMARO, PONTIAC FIREBIRD
All measurements in inches unless noted

Year	Model		Master Cylinder Bore	Brake Disc			Brake Drum Diameter			Minimum Lining Thickness	Brake Caliper	
				Original Thickness	Minimum Thickness	Maximum Runout	Original Inside Diameter	Max. Wear Limit	Maximum Machine Diameter		Bracket Bolt (ft. lbs.)	Mounting Bolt (ft. lbs.)
1996	Camaro	F	①	1.043	0.980	0.005	—	—	—	0.030	160	38
		R		0.795	0.744	0.005	9.50	9.59	9.56	0.030	160	27
	Firebird	F	①	1.043	0.980	0.005	—	—	—	0.030	160	38
		R		0.795	0.744	0.005	9.50	9.59	9.56	0.030	160	27
1997	Camaro	F	①	1.043	0.980	0.005	—	—	—	0.030	160	38
		R		0.795	0.744	0.005	9.50	9.59	9.56	0.030	160	27
	Firebird	F	①	1.043	0.980	0.005	—	—	—	0.030	160	38
		R		0.795	0.744	0.005	9.50	9.59	9.56	0.030	160	27
1998	Camaro	F	①	1.260	1.223	0.005	—	—	—	0.030	160	23
		R		—	0.985	0.005	—	—	—	0.030	160	27
	Firebird	F	①	1.260	1.223	0.005	—	—	—	0.030	160	23
		R		—	0.985	0.005	—	—	—	0.030	160	27
1999-00	Camaro	F	①	1.260	1.223	0.005	—	—	—	0.030	160	23
		R		—	0.985	0.005	—	—	—	0.030	160	27
	Firebird	F	①	1.260	1.223	0.005	—	—	—	0.030	160	23
		R		—	0.985	0.005	—	—	—	0.030	160	27

NA - Not Available

F - Front

R - Rear

① Rear drum: 0.945; Rear disc: 1.00

93006C18

BRAKE SPECIFICATIONS
GM G BODY
BUICK RIVIERA AND OLDSMOBILE AURORA
All measurements in inches unless noted

Year	Model		Master Cylinder Bore	Brake Disc			Minimum Lining Thickness	Brake Caliper Mounting Bolt (ft. lbs.)
				Original Thickness	Minimum Thickness	Maximum Run-out		
1996	Aurora	F	1.000	1.260	1.209	0.002	0.030	38
		R		0.433	0.374	0.002	0.030	20
	Riviera	F	1.000	1.260	1.209	0.002	0.030	38
		R		0.433	0.374	0.002	0.030	20
1997	Aurora	F	1.000	1.260	1.209	0.002	0.030	38
		R		0.433	0.374	0.002	0.030	20
	Riviera	F	1.000	1.260	1.209	0.002	0.030	38
		R		0.433	0.374	0.002	0.030	20
1998	Aurora	F	1.000	1.260	1.209	0.002	0.030	38
		R		0.433	0.374	0.002	0.030	20
	Riviera	F	1.000	1.260	1.209	0.002	0.030	38
		R		0.433	0.374	0.002	0.030	20
1999-00	Aurora	F	1.000	1.260	1.209	0.002	0.030	38
		R		0.433	0.374	0.002	0.030	20

F - Front
R - Rear

93006C19

For brake related suspension and axle service, refer to the model specific sections of this manual

BRAKE SPECIFICATIONS
GM J BODY
CHEVROLET CAVALIER AND PONTIAC SUNFIRE
All measurements in inches unless noted

| Year | Model | Master Cylinder Bore | Brake Disc | | | Brake Drum | | | Minimum Lining Thickness | | Brake Caliper Mounting Bolts (ft. lbs.) |
			Original Thickness	Minimum Thickness	Maximum Run-out	Original Inside Diameter	Max. Wear Limit	Maximum Machine Diameter	Front	Rear	
1996	Cavalier	0.874	0.806	0.736	0.003	7.880	7.930	7.900	0.030	0.030	40
	Sunfire	0.874	0.786	0.736	0.003	7.870	7.930	7.900	0.030	0.030	40
1997	Cavalier	0.874	0.806	0.736	0.003	7.880	7.930	7.900	0.030	0.030	40
	Sunfire	0.874	0.786	0.736	0.003	7.870	7.930	7.900	0.030	0.030	40
1998	Cavalier	0.874	0.806	0.736	0.003	7.880	7.930	7.900	0.030	0.030	40
	Sunfire	0.874	0.786	0.736	0.003	7.870	7.930	7.900	0.030	0.030	40
1999-00	Cavalier	0.874	0.806	0.736	0.003	7.880	7.930	7.900	0.030	0.030	40
	Sunfire	0.874	0.786	0.736	0.003	7.870	7.930	7.900	0.030	0.030	40

93006C20

BRAKE SPECIFICATIONS
GM L BODY
CHEVROLET BERETTA AND CORSICA
All measurements in inches unless noted

Year	Model	Master Cylinder Bore	Brake Disc			Brake Drum			Minimum Lining Thickness		Brake Caliper Mounting Bolts
			Original Thickness	Minimum Thickness	Maximum Run-out	Original Inside Diameter	Max. Wear Limit	Maximum Machine Diameter	Front	Rear	(ft. lbs.)
1996	Beretta	0.945	0.885	0.830	0.004	7.879	7.929	7.899	0.030	0.030	38
	Corsica	0.945	0.885	0.830	0.004	7.879	7.929	7.899	0.030	0.030	38

93006C21

BRAKE SPECIFICATIONS
GM L/N BODY
All measurements in inches unless noted

Year	Model	Master Cylinder Bore	Brake Disc			Brake Drum Diameter			Minimum Lining Thickness		Brake Caliper	
			Original Thickness	Minimum Thickness	Maximum Runout	Original Inside Diameter	Max. Wear Limit	Maximum Machine Diameter	Front	Rear	Bracket Bolts (ft. lbs.)	Mounting Bolts (ft. lbs.)
1997	Cutlass	0.874	1.031	0.987	0.003	8.900 8.909	8.920	8.909	0.030	①	85	40
	Malibu	0.874	1.031	0.987	0.003	8.900 8.909	8.920	8.909	0.030	①	85	40
1998	Cutlass	0.874	1.031	0.987	0.003	8.900 8.909	8.920	8.909	0.030	①	85	40
	Malibu	0.874	1.031	0.987	0.003	8.900 8.909	8.920	8.909	0.030	①	85	40
1999-00	Cutlass	0.874	1.031	0.987	0.003	8.900 8.909	8.920	8.909	0.030	①	85	40
	Malibu	0.874	0.806	0.736	0.003	8.900 8.909	8.920	8.909	0.030	①	85	40

① 0.030 over rivet head; If bonded lining, use 0.062 from shoe

93006C28

BRAKE SPECIFICATIONS
GM N BODY
All measurements in inches unless noted

Year	Model	Master Cylinder Bore	Brake Disc Original Thickness	Brake Disc Minimum Thickness	Brake Disc Maximum Runout	Brake Drum Diameter Original Inside Diameter	Brake Drum Diameter Max. Wear Limit	Brake Drum Diameter Maximum Machine Diameter	Minimum Lining Thickness Front	Minimum Lining Thickness Rear	Brake Caliper Bracket Bolts (ft. lbs.)	Brake Caliper Mounting Bolts (ft. lbs.)
1996	Achieva	0.874	0.806	0.736	0.003	7.874-7.890	7.930	7.899	0.030	①	—	38
	Grand Am	0.874	0.806	0.736	0.003	7.874	7.930	7.900	0.030	0.030	—	38
	Skylark	0.874	0.806	0.736	0.003	7.874-7.890	7.929	7.899	0.030	①	—	38
1997	Achieva	0.874	0.806	0.736	0.003	7.874-7.890	7.930	7.899	0.030	①	—	38
	Grand Am	0.874	0.806	0.736	0.003	7.874	7.930	7.900	0.030	0.030	—	38
	Skylark	0.874	0.806	0.736	0.003	7.874-7.890	7.929	7.899	0.030	①	—	38
1998	Achieva	0.874	0.806	0.736	0.003	7.874-7.890	7.930	7.899	0.030	①	—	38
	Grand Am	0.874	0.806	0.736	0.003	7.874	7.930	7.900	0.030	0.030	—	38
1999-00	Alero	1.000	②	③	④	8.86	8.920	8.909	0.030	①	85	⑤
	Grand Am	1.000	②	③	④	8.86	8.920	8.909	0.030	①	85	⑤

NA - Not available

① 0.030 over rivet head; If bonded lining, use 0.062 from shoe

② Front - 1.031
Rear - 0.430

③ Front - 0.972
Rear - 0.410

④ Front - 0.003
Rear - NA

⑤ Front - 23 ft. lbs.
Rear - 81 ft. lbs.

93006C22

BRAKE SPECIFICATIONS
GM V BODY
All measurements in inches unless noted

Year	Model		Master Cylinder Bore	Brake Disc			Minimum Lining Thickness		Brake Caliper	
				Original Thickness	Minimum Thickness	Maximum Runout			Bracket Bolts (ft. lbs.)	Mounting Bolts (ft. lbs.)
1997	Catera	F	1.000	1.102	0.984	0.001	0.315	①	137	63
		R	—	0.472	0.393	0.004	NA		92	32
1998	Catera	F	1.000	1.102	0.984	0.001	0.315	①	137	63
		R	—	0.472	0.393	0.004	NA		92	32
1999-00	Catera	F	1.000	1.102	0.984	0.001	0.315	①	137	63
		R	—	0.472	0.393	0.004	NA		92	32

F - Front

R - Rear

NA - Not available

① Total thickness of lining and backing plate

93006C23

BRAKE SPECIFICATIONS
GM W BODY
All measurements in inches unless noted

Year	Model		Master Cylinder Bore	Brake Disc Original Thickness	Brake Disc Minimum Thickness	Brake Disc Maximum Runout	Brake Drum Diameter Original Inside Diameter	Brake Drum Diameter Max. Wear Limit	Brake Drum Diameter Maximum Machine Diameter	Minimum Lining Thickness Front	Minimum Lining Thickness Rear	Brake Caliper Bracket Bolts (ft. lbs.)	Brake Caliper Mounting Bolts (ft. lbs.)
1996	Cutlass Sup.	F	1.000	1.039	0.972	0.003	—	—	—	0.030	0.030	148	80
		R	—	0.492	0.429	0.003	8.863	8.920	8.909	0.030	0.030	81	20
	Grand Prix	F	0.944	1.039	0.972	0.004	—	—	—	0.030	0.030	148	80
		R	—	0.492	0.429	0.004	8.863	8.920	8.909	0.030	0.030	81	20
	Lumina	F	0.945	1.040	0.972	0.004	—	—	—	0.030	0.030	148	80
		R	—	0.492	0.429	0.004	8.863	8.920	8.909	0.030	0.030	81	20
	Monte Carlo	F	0.945	1.040	0.972	0.004	—	—	—	0.030	0.030	148	80
		R	—	0.492	0.429	0.004	8.863	8.920	8.909	0.030	0.030	81	20
	Regal	F	0.945	1.039	0.972	0.003	—	—	—	0.030	0.030	148	80
		R	—	0.492	0.429	0.003	8.863	8.920	8.909	0.030	0.030	81	20
1997	Cutlass Sup.	F	1.000	1.039	0.972	0.003	—	—	—	0.030	0.030	148	80
		R	—	0.492	0.429	0.003	8.863	8.920	8.909	0.030	0.030	81	20
	Grand Prix	F	0.944	1.039	0.972	0.004	—	—	—	0.030	0.030	137	63
		R	—	0.492	0.429	0.004	8.863	8.920	8.909	0.030	0.030	92	33
	Lumina	F	0.945	1.040	0.972	0.004	—	—	—	0.030	0.030	148	80
		R	—	0.492	0.429	0.004	8.863	8.920	8.909	0.030	0.030	81	20
	Monte Carlo	F	0.945	1.040	0.972	0.004	—	—	—	0.030	0.030	148	80
		R	—	0.492	0.429	0.004	8.863	8.920	8.909	0.030	0.030	81	20
	Regal	F	0.945	1.039	0.972	0.003	—	—	—	0.030	0.030	137	63
		R	—	0.492	0.429	0.003	8.863	8.920	8.909	0.030	0.030	92	33
1998	Century	F	1.000	1.039	0.972	0.003	—	—	—	0.030	0.030	137	63
		R	—	0.492	0.429	0.003	8.863	8.920	8.909	0.030	0.030	92	33
	Grand Prix	F	1.000	1.039	0.972	0.003	—	—	—	0.030	0.030	137	63
		R	—	0.492	0.429	0.003	—	—	—	0.030	0.030	92	33
	Intrigue	F	1.000	1.039	0.972	0.003	—	—	—	0.030	0.030	137	63
		R	—	0.492	0.429	0.003	—	—	—	0.030	0.030	92	33
	Lumina	F	0.945	1.040	0.972	0.004	—	—	—	0.030	0.030	148	80
		R	—	0.492	0.429	0.004	8.863	8.920	8.909	0.030	0.030	81	20
	Monte Carlo	F	0.945	1.040	0.972	0.004	—	—	—	0.030	0.030	148	80
		R	—	0.492	0.429	0.004	8.863	8.920	8.909	0.030	0.030	81	20
	Regal	F	1.000	1.039	0.972	0.003	—	—	—	0.030	0.030	137	63
		R	—	0.492	0.429	0.003	8.863	8.920	8.909	0.030	0.030	92	33
1999-00	Century	F	1.000	1.039	0.972	0.003	—	—	—	0.030	0.030	137	63
		R	—	0.492	0.429	0.003	8.863	8.920	8.909	0.030	0.030	92	33
	Grand Prix	F	1.000	1.039	0.972	0.003	—	—	—	0.030	0.030	137	63
		R	—	0.492	0.429	0.003	—	—	—	0.030	0.030	92	33
	Intrigue	F	1.000	1.039	0.972	0.003	—	—	—	0.030	0.030	137	63
		R	—	0.492	0.429	0.003	—	—	—	0.030	0.030	92	33
	Lumina	F	0.945	1.040	0.972	0.004	—	—	—	0.030	0.030	148	80
		R	—	0.492	0.429	0.004	8.863	8.920	8.909	0.030	0.030	81	20
	Monte Carlo	F	0.945	1.040	0.972	0.004	—	—	—	0.030	0.030	148	80
		R	—	0.492	0.429	0.004	8.863	8.920	8.909	0.030	0.030	81	20
	Regal	F	1.000	1.039	0.972	0.003	—	—	—	0.030	0.030	137	63
		R	—	0.492	0.429	0.003	8.863	8.920	8.909	0.030	0.030	92	33

F - Front
R - Rear

93006C24

For brake related suspension and axle service, refer to the model specific sections of this manual

BRAKE SPECIFICATIONS
GM Y BODY
All measurements in inches unless noted

| Year | Model | Master Cylinder Bore | Brake Disc | | | Minimum Lining Thickness | | Brake Caliper | |
			Original Thickness	Minimum Thickness	Maximum Runout	Front	Rear	Bracket Bolts (ft. lbs.)	Mounting Bolts (ft. lbs.)
1996	Corvette	NA	①	②	0.006	0.030	0.030	—	③
1997	Corvette	NA	①	②	0.006	0.030	0.030	—	③
1998	Corvette	NA	①	②	0.006	0.030	0.030	—	③
1999-00	Corvette	NA	①	②	0.006	0.030	0.030	—	③

NA - Not Available

① Heavy duty: 1.110; Std.: 0.795

② Heavy duty: 1.059; Std.: 0.744

③ Front: NA, Rear: upper 26 ft. lbs., lower 16 ft. lbs.

93006C25

BRAKE SPECIFICATIONS
GEO/CHEVROLET
All measurements in inches unless noted

Year	Model	Master Cylinder Bore	Brake Disc Original Thickness	Brake Disc Minimum Thickness	Brake Disc Maximum Runout	Brake Drum Diameter Original Inside Diameter	Brake Drum Diameter Max. Wear Limit	Brake Drum Diameter Maximum Machine Diameter	Minimum Lining Thickness Front ②	Minimum Lining Thickness Rear ②	Brake Caliper Bracket Bolts (ft. lbs.)	Brake Caliper Mounting Bolts (ft. lbs.)
1996	Metro	NA	0.670	0.590	0.004	①	①	①	0.236	0.111	—	18
	Prizm	NA	0.866	0.787	0.003	7.87	7.91	7.91	0.390	0.390	—	③
1997	Metro	NA	0.670	0.590	0.004	①	①	①	0.236	0.111	—	18
	Prizm	NA	0.866	0.787	0.003	7.87	7.91	7.91	0.390	0.390	—	③
1998	Metro	NA	0.670	0.590	0.004	①	①	①	0.236	0.111	—	18
	Prizm	NA	0.866	0.787	0.003	7.87	7.91	7.91	0.390	0.390	—	③
1999-00	Metro	NA	0.670	0.590	0.004	①	①	①	0.236	0.111	—	18
	Prizm	NA	0.866	0.787	0.003	7.87	7.91	7.91	0.390	0.390	—	③

NA - Not Available

① 2 door: 7.09
  4 door: 7.87

② Minimum lining thickness includes pad/shoe backing

③ Front: 18 ft. lbs.
  Rear: 14 ft. lbs.

93006C26

BRAKE SPECIFICATIONS
SATURN COUPES, SEDANS, WAGONS
All measurements in inches unless noted

Year	Model	Brake Disc			Brake Drum			Minimum Lining Thickness		Brake Caliper	
		Original Thickness	Minimum Thickness	Maximum Run-out	Original Inside Diameter	Max. Wear Limit	Maximum Machine Diameter	Pads	Shoes	Bracket Bolts (ft. lbs.)	Mounting Bolts (ft. lbs.)
1996	Coupe	①	②	0.0024	7.87	7.93	7.91	0.080	0.040	③	27
	Sedan	①	②	0.0024	7.87	7.93	7.91	0.080	0.040	③	27
	Wagon	①	②	0.0024	7.87	7.93	7.91	0.080	0.040	③	27
1997	Coupe	①	②	0.0024	7.87	7.93	7.91	0.080	0.040	③	27
	Sedan	①	②	0.0024	7.87	7.93	7.91	0.080	0.040	③	27
	Wagon	①	②	0.0024	7.87	7.93	7.91	0.080	0.040	③	27
1998	Coupe	①	②	0.0024	7.87	7.93	7.91	0.080	0.040	③	27
	Sedan	①	②	0.0024	7.87	7.93	7.91	0.080	0.040	③	27
	Wagon	①	②	0.0024	7.87	7.93	7.91	0.080	0.040	③	27
1999-00	Coupe	①	②	0.0024	7.87	7.93	7.91	0.080	0.040	③	27
	Sedan	①	②	0.0024	7.87	7.93	7.91	0.080	0.040	③	27
	Wagon	①	②	0.0024	7.87	7.93	7.91	0.080	0.040	③	27

① Front: 0.710
Rear: 0.430

② Front: 0.633
Rear: 0.370

③ Front: 81 ft. lbs.
Rear: 63 ft. lbs

93006C27

WINDSHIELD WIPER SYSTEMS

7

CHRYSLER CORPORATION

Avenger, Breeze, Cirrus, Sebring, Stealth, Stratus and Talon

GENERAL DESCRIPTION

Front Windshield Wiper and Washer

When the wiper switch is placed in the **LO** position with the ignition switch in the **ACC** or **ON** position, wipers operate continuously at low speed. Placing the wiper switch in the **HI** position causes the wipers to operate at high speed.

When the wiper switch is placed in the **OFF** position, the cam contacts of the wiper motor causing current to flow through the auto wiper stop circuit, allowing the wiper blades to cycle before they reach the stop position.

When the wiper switch is placed in the **INT** position, with the ignition switch in **ACC** or **ON** position, the intermittent wiper relay is energized, causing the intermittent wiper relay contacts to close and open repeatedly. When the contacts are closed, the wiper motor is energized. When the wiper motor is energized, the relay contacts open; however the cam contacts keep the wiper motor energized until the wiper blades return to the **PARK** position.

When the washer switch is turned **ON**, the intermittent wiper relay contacts close causing the wipers to cycle 2–3 times.

Rear Window Wiper and Washer

When the rear wiper switch is placed in the **ON** position with the ignition switch in the **ACC** or **ON** position, the wiper will operate continuously at low speed.

When the rear wiper switch is placed in the **OFF** position, the cam closes the contacts of the wiper motor causing current to flow through the auto wiper stop circuit, allowing the wiper blade to cycle before reaching the **PARK** position.

When the rear window wiper switch is placed in the **INT** position, with the ignition switch in the **ACC** or **ON** position, the rear intermittent wiper relay is energized causing the rear intermittent wiper relay contacts to close and open repeatedly. When the contacts are closed, the wiper motor is energized. When the rear wiper motor is energized, the rear intermittent wiper relay contacts open. However, the cam contacts keep the rear wiper motor energized until the wiper blades return to their **PARK** position.

TROUBLESHOOTING

Front Windshield Wiper/Washer System

1. Neither wipers nor washer operate.
- Check fuse.
- Check for good ground.
2. Only **LOW** or **HIGH** inoperative.
- Check for problem in switch.
3. Wipers do not stop.
- Check the wiper motor.
- Check the intermittent wiper relay.
- Check the wiper switch.
4. Intermittent wiper inoperative. The intermittent relay is built into the switch
- Check the voltage of steering-column combination switch, ter-

minal **7** for Talon, Stratus, Cirrus, Sebring and Avenger with the intermittent relay energized.
- If 0 volts, check wiper relay or switch.
- If 12 volts, steadily, check intermittent wiper relay.
- If 0–12 volts, alternating, this is normal operation.
5. Length of intermittent pause cannot be varied.
- Check the variable intermittent wiper control switch.
- Check the intermittent wiper relay, built into the switch.
6. Washer is inoperative but wipers operate when washer switch is engaged.
- Check the washer motor.
7. Washer is inoperative and wipers do not engage when washer switch is operated.
- Check the washer switch.
8. Washer-wiper operation is inoperative.
- Check the intermittent wiper relay, built into the switch.

Rear Window Wiper/Washer System

1. Neither wipers nor washer operate.
- Check the fuse.
- Check for a good ground.
2. Only **LOW** inoperative.
- Check for a problem in rear wiper switch.
3. Wipers do not stop.
- Check the wiper motor.
- Check the intermittent wiper relay
- Check the rear wiper switch. Intermittent relay is built into the switch
4. Intermittent wiper inoperative.
- Check terminal voltage of terminal **2** or **8** (except Talon, Cirrus, Stratus, Sebring and Avenger) or terminal **6** (Talon, Sebring and Avenger) of the rear intermittent wiper relay which is behind the rear trim panel, with the intermittent relay energized, except Stealth. Check the intermittent wiper relay terminal voltage for Stealth.
  a. If 0 volts, check rear intermittent wiper relay or rear wiper switch.
  b. If 12 volts, check intermittent wiper relay.
  c. If 0–12 volts, alternating, this is normal operation.
5. Washer is inoperative.
- Check washer motor.
- Check washer switch.

TESTING

Front Wiper and Washer System

FRONT WIPER MOTOR—EXCEPT STEALTH

1. Check the wiper motor after first disconnecting the wiring harness connector and with the wiper motor remaining installed to the body. Inspect the wiring connector. With the notch at the top, note that there are either 4 or 6 terminals.
2. Using jumper wires, connect battery voltage to the upper left terminal. The motor, still installed, should complete the ground circuit. The motor should run at low speed.
3. Using jumper wires, connect battery voltage to the upper right terminal on the 4 terminal version, or to the upper middle terminal on the 6 terminal versions. The motor, still installed, should complete the ground circuit. The motor should run at high speed.
4. Run the motor at low speed, disconnect the jumper wire from

Inspection while operating

Low speed   High speed   Battery

Inspection while stopped

Low speed   Battery
Automatic stop

8838XG01

Wiper motor testing—Talon, Sebring and Avenger

the battery and stop the motor. Using jumper wires, connect the battery to the lower left terminal and bridge the upper left to the lower right terminal (4 terminal version) or to the lower middle terminal (6 terminal versions). The motor should start turning at low speed, then stop at the automatic stop position.

5. If the motor does not pass these tests, replace it.

FRONT WIPER MOTOR—STEALTH

1. Check the wiper motor after first disconnecting the wiring harness connector and with the wiper motor remaining installed to the body. Inspect the wiring connector. With the notch at the top, note that there are 4 terminals.

2. Using jumper wires, connect battery voltage to the upper left terminal. The motor, still installed, should complete the ground circuit. The motor should run at low speed.

3. Using jumper wires, connect battery voltage to the upper right terminal. The motor, still installed, should complete the ground circuit. The motor should run at high speed.

4. Run the motor at low speed, disconnect the jumper wire from the battery and stop the motor. Using jumper wires, connect the battery to the lower left terminal and bridge the upper left to the lower right terminal. The motor should start turning at low speed, then stop at the automatic stop position.

5. If the motor does not pass these tests, replace it.

In addition to the preceding front wiper motor testing procedure, troubleshooting the Stealth windshield wiper system can be aided by accessing the ETACS electronic control unit. After performing the previous testing procedure, use a voltmeter to check whether or not the input signals from each switch are input to the electronic control unit as follows:

6. Connect the voltmeter to the diagnosis connector located at the right side of the junction block.

7. Check the movement of the voltmeter needle when each switch or sensor is activated.

If the needle moves, the input signal is being input to the electronic control unit; the switch or sensor can be considered to be functioning normally. If the needle does not move, there is a problem with that switch or sensor or in the wiring which needs to be checked.

Areas to check if a problem is indicated are: the ignition switch, wiper switch, intermittent variable switch and washer switch.

WIPER/WASHER SWITCH

1. Remove the lower dash panel and the steering column cover.

2. Disconnect the wiper/washer switch connector and check for continuity between the terminals.

3. If continuity checks are not as specified, replace the wiper/washer switch.

Switch position		Terminal				
		5	6	7	8	9
Wiper switch	OFF		○—	—○		
	1 (LO)			○—		—○
	2 (HI)				○—	—○
Washer switch	ON	○—				—○

8838XG02

Front wiper and washer switch testing—Talon, Sebring and Avenger

Switch position		3	4	5	6	7	8	9	10
Wiper switch	OFF				○—				—○
	INT	○—			○—		—○		
	LO			○—	—○				
	HI			○—		—○			
Variable intermittent wiper control switch			○—				—○		
Washer switch			○—			—○			

NOTE
○—○ denotes that there is continuity between the terminals.

8470V006

1	2	⊠		3	4	
5	6	7	8	9	10	11

Front wiper and washer switch testing—Stealth

WIPER RELAY—STEALTH

The wiper relay is an integral part of the column switch.

1. Disconnect the column switch connector. Using an ohmmeter, check for continuity between terminals **5** and **11** and between terminals **6** and **10**. Make sure that there is no continuity between terminals **6** and **11**.

2. Connect the positive terminal of the battery to terminal **5** and the negative terminal to terminal **11** to check that the battery voltage is available at terminal **6**.

3. If continuity or voltage checks are not as specified, replace the relay.

Wiper relay testing—Stealth

WASHER MOTOR

1. Prior to testing the washer motor, make sure it is mounted on the washer tank and that the washer tank is filled.

2. Disconnect the wiring harness connector from the washer motor.

3. Connect a jumper wire from the positive battery post to the lower of the two washer motor terminals (with the locking tab of the connector being on top), then connect a jumper wire from the negative battery post to the other washer motor terminal.

4. The washer motor should pump water out. If not, replace the washer pump.

Rear Wiper and Washer System

WIPER MOTOR

1. Check the wiper motor after first disconnecting the wiring harness connector and with the wiper motor remaining installed to the body. Inspect the wiring connector. With the notch at the top, note that there are 3 terminals.

2. Using a jumper wire, connect battery voltage to the left terminal. The motor, still installed, should complete the ground circuit. The motor should run at low speed.

3. Run the motor at low speed, then disconnect the jumper wire from the battery and stop the motor.

4. Using jumper wires, connect battery voltage to the right terminal. Connect a 2nd jumper wire to the left and center terminals. The motor, still installed, should complete the ground circuit. The motor should start turning, then stop at the automatic **PARK** position.

5. If the motor is defective, remove and replace.

6. On Talon, fill the tank. With the notch of the connector on top, connect battery voltage to the left terminal and ground the right ter-

minal. The washer motor should run and water should spray from the nozzle at the top of the liftgate glass.

WIPER AND WASHER SWITCH

1. Remove the wiper/washer switch.

2. Check for continuity between the terminals.

3. If continuity checks are not as specified, replace the wiper/washer switch.

	Terminal	2	4	5	6	7	8	3	1
Switch position									
Wiper switch	OFF		o—o						
	ON			o—o	o—o				
	INT		o—o	o				o—o	
Washer switch					o—o	o—o			Illumination light

NOTE
o—o indicates that there is continuity between the terminals.

8470V009

Rear wiper and washer switch testing—Talon, Sebring and Avenger

	Terminal	2	4	5	6	7	8	1	3
Switch position									
Wiper switch	OFF	o—o							
	INT	o—o			o—o			ILL	
	ON			o—o					
Washer switch	OFF								
	ON	o		o—o					

NOTE
o—o denotes that there is continuity between the terminals.

8470V010

Rear wiper and washer switch testing—Stealth

INTERMITTENT WIPER RELAY

1. On Stealth, remove the left rear quarter trim.

2. With the wiper relay connected to the wire harness connector, operate the intermittent wipers.

3. Using a voltmeter, check the voltage at terminal **2**.
   a. With the wiper stationary, there should be 0 volts.
   b. With the wiper operating, there should be 12 volts.

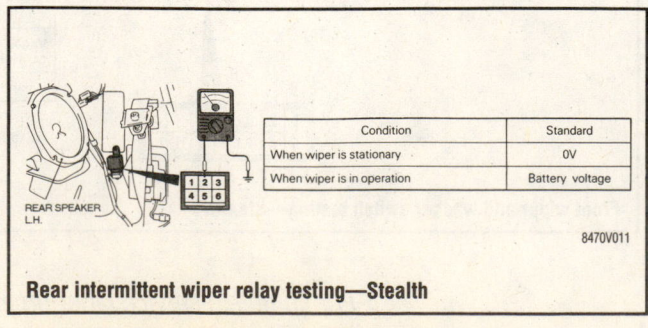

Condition	Standard
When wiper is stationary	0V
When wiper is in operation	Battery voltage

8470V011

Rear intermittent wiper relay testing—Stealth

WASHER MOTOR

1. Prior to testing the washer motor, make sure it is mounted on the washer tank and that the washer tank is filled.
2. Disconnect the wiring harness connector from the washer motor.
3. Connect the positive and negative battery leads to the washer motor terminals.
4. The washer motor should pump water out. If not, replace the washer pump.

REMOVAL & INSTALLATION

Front Washer Reservoir and Pump

TALON, SEBRING AND AVENGER—NON-TURBO MODELS

1. Disconnect the negative battery cable.
2. On non-turbo models, remove the brake fluid reservoir mounting bolt to gain access to the washer tank bolts.
3. Disconnect the fluid hose and electrical connector from the washer motor.
4. Remove the washer fluid tank mounting bolts.
5. Remove the washer tank from the vehicle.
6. Remove the washer pump motor from the washer tank.
To install:
7. Installation is the reverse of the removal procedure.

STEALTH

1. Remove the negative and positive battery cables.
2. Remove the hold-down and battery.
3. Remove the 4 nuts and the battery tray.
4. Disconnect the electrical connector from the pump.
5. Remove the hose from the washer pump and drain the reservoir.
6. Disconnect the washer fluid level sensor from the reservoir.
7. Disconnect the filler tube from the reservoir.
8. Remove the reservoir and pump assembly.
9. Remove the pump from the reservoir.
To install:
10. Installation is the reverse of the installation procedure.

Rear Washer Reservoir and Pump

TALON, SEBRING AND AVENGER

1. Remove the rear side trim panel.
2. Remove the washer cap.
3. Disconnect the electrical connector from the pump.
4. Disconnect the hose and drain the reservoir.
5. Remove the 3 nuts and the reservoir and pump assembly.
6. Remove the pump from the reservoir.
To install:
7. Installation is the reverse of the removal procedure.

STEALTH

1. Remove the rear side trim panel.
2. Remove the washer cap.
3. Disconnect the electrical connector from the pump.
4. Disconnect the hose and drain the reservoir.
5. Remove the 3 bolts and the reservoir and pump assembly.
6. Remove the pump from the reservoir.

To install:
7. Installation is the reverse of the removal procedure.

Concorde, Intrepid, Vision and New Yorker

GENERAL DESCRIPTION

The windshield wipers will only operate with the ignition switch in the **ACC** or **IGN** position. A fuse, located in the fuse block, protects the circuitry of the wiper system and the vehicle.

The wiper motor has permanent magnet fields. The speeds are determined by current flow to the appropriate set of brushes.

The intermittent wiper system, in addition to low and high speed, has a delay mode. The delay mode has a range of ½–18 seconds. The wiper delay will double to a range of 1–36 seconds when the vehicle speed is less than 10 MPH. The delay is performed by a variable resistor in the wiper switch and 2 relays. One relay operates the **ON/OFF** and the other changes the speeds.

The wiper system completes the wipe cycle when the switch is turned **OFF.** The blades park in the lowest portion of the wiping pattern.

TROUBLESHOOTING

Wiper and Washer System

WIPER MOTOR WILL NOT RUN IN ANY SWITCH POSITION

1. Check fuse **10** in the junction block and fuse **C** in the power distribution center.
  - If the fuse(s) are good, go to Step 2.
  - If the fuse(s) are defective, replace them and check the wiper motor operation in all switch positions.
  - If the motor is still inoperative and fuses do not blow, go to Step 2.
  - If the fuse blows, go to Step 11.
2. Disconnect the wiper motor connector.
3. Check the wiper motor low speed. Connect a jumper wire from the positive battery terminal to terminal **3** of the motor connector. Connect a 2nd jumper wire from terminal **2** to a suitable ground. Check the wiper motor high speed. Move the grounded jumper wire from terminal **2** to terminal **4**.
  - If motor runs; go to Step 5.
  - If motor does not run in high or low speed, go to Step 4.
4. Using an ohmmeter, check for a good ground at terminal **4** of the wiper motor wire harness connector.
  - If OK, replace the motor.
  - If not, repair the ground as necessary.
5. Using a voltmeter, check for battery voltage at terminal **D** of the intermittent wiper relay in the power distribution center.
  - If no voltage is found, check fuse **C**.
  - If OK, go to Step 6.
6. Using an ohmmeter, check from terminal **D** to the **HI-LO** wiper relay to terminal **2** of the wiper motor wiring harness connector for continuity. Check from terminal **E** of the **HI-LO** wiper relay to terminal **3** of the wiper motor wiring harness connector for continuity.
  - If OK, go to Step 7.
  - If not, repair as necessary.
7. Using an ohmmeter, check for continuity from terminal **B** of the **HI-LO** wiper relay to terminal **B** of the intermittent wiper relay.

Inspection while operating

Low speed   High speed   Battery

Inspection while stopped

Low speed   Automatic stop   Battery

8838XG01

Wiper motor wire harness connector—Concorde, Intrepid, Vision, and New Yorker

- If OK, check for faulty relays.
- If not, repair as necessary.

8. Disconnect the connector from the body controller located on the right lower kick panel behind the trim panel.

9. Using an ohmmeter, check for continuity between terminal **1** of the body controller connector and terminal **C** of the intermittent wiper relay.
- If OK, go to Step 10.
- If not, repair as necessary.

10. Using a voltmeter, with the wiper switch connected, connect the positive lead to terminal **1** of the wiper switch. Turn the ignition switch to the **ON** position. Slowly move the wiper switch from the **OFF** position through each position to **HIGH**.
- If no voltage is present, replace the wiper switch.
- If OK, check for continuity between terminal **1** of the wiper switch and terminal **16** of the body controller connector.

11. Turn the ignition switch **OFF**. Using an ohmmeter, check for continuity between fuse **10** and terminal **1** and **18** of the body controller connector.
- If there is no continuity; check the **HI-LO** and intermittent relays.
- If OK, repair the wiring as necessary.
- If voltage increased from 0 to approximately 10 volts in the **HIGH** position, replace the body controller.

MOTOR RUNS SLOWLY AT ALL SPEEDS

1. Disconnect the wiper motor connector from the motor. Remove the wiper arms and blades. Disconnect the wiper motor drive link from the motor. Connect an ammeter from the positive battery terminal to terminal **3** of the wiper motor connector. Connect a ground wire from terminal **4** of the wiper motor connector to a suitable ground.
- If the wiper motor runs and the average ammeter reading is more than 6 amps, go to Step 2.

- If the wiper motor runs and the average ammeter reading is less than 6 amps, go to Step 3.

2. Using an ohmmeter, check the high and low circuits for a short to ground.

3. Check to see if the wiper linkage or pivots are binding or caught.

MOTOR WILL RUN AT HIGH SPEED, BUT NOT LOW; MOTOR WILL RUN AT LOW SPEED, BUT NOT HIGH

1. Disconnect the wiper motor electrical connector.

2. If the wiper motor will not run on **LOW** speed, connect a jumper wire from the positive battery terminal to terminal **3** of the motor connector. Connect a 2nd jumper wire from terminal **4** of the motor connector to a suitable ground.
- If the motor runs, go to Step 3.
- If the motor does not run, replace the motor.

3. If the motor will not run on **HIGH** speed, connect a jumper wire from the positive battery terminal to terminal **2** of the motor connector. Connect a 2nd jumper wire from terminal **4** of the motor connector to a suitable ground.
- If the motor runs, go to Step 4.
- If the motor does not run, replace the motor.

4. If the motor will not run at **LOW** speed, check for an open circuit using an ohmmeter. Check between terminal **E** of the **HI-LO** wiper relay and terminal **3** of the wiper motor wire harness for continuity.
- If OK, go to Step 5.
- If no continuity, repair wiring as necessary.

5. If the motor will not run at **LOW** speed, check for an open circuit using an ohmmeter. Check between terminal **D** of the **HI-LO** wiper relay and terminal **2** of the wiper motor wire harness for continuity.
- If OK, go to Step 6.
- If no continuity, repair wiring as necessary.

6. Check for **HI-LO** wiper relay malfunction.

WIPERS WILL OPERATE AT HIGH SPEED WITH THE SWITCH IN THE LOW POSITION; WIPERS WILL OPERATE IN INTERMITTENT MODE, BUT EACH WIPING CYCLE IS IN HIGH SPEED

1. Disconnect the wiper motor connector.

2. Connect a jumper wire from the positive battery terminal to terminal **3** of the wiper motor wire harness connector. Connect a 2nd jumper wire from the negative battery terminal to terminal **4** of the wiper motor wire harness connector.
- If wiper motor runs at **LOW** speed, go to Step 3.
- If the motor runs at **HIGH** speed, check for crossed wires in the wiper motor pigtail connector.

3. Check for a faulty **HI-LO** wiper relay.
- If faulty, replace it.
- If OK, go to Step 4.

4. Check for crossed wires in the harness from the **HI-LO** relay to the motor.
- If crossed, repair the circuit.
- If OK, go to Step 5.

5. Disconnect the connector from the body controller and remove the intermittent wiper relay and check for a short to ground.
- If short is found, repair it.
- If OK, go to Step 6.

6. If none of the above malfunctions are present, replace the body controller.

WIPERS RUN AT LOW SPEED WITH THE SWITCH IN THE HIGH SPEED POSITION

1. Check for a faulty **HI-LO** wiper relay.
- If faulty, replace the relay.
- If OK, go to Step 2.
2. Using an ohmmeter, check for an open circuit between terminal **C** of the **HI-LO** wiper relay and terminal **18** of the body controller 24–way connector.
- If OK, go to Step 3.
- If open circuit is found; repair as necessary.
3. Check the wiper switch.

MOTOR WILL KEEP RUNNING WITH THE SWITCH IN THE OFF POSITION

1. Check the wiper motor wiring harness for shorts between the low speed motor feed terminal **3** or high speed motor feed terminal **2** and the battery or ignition switch.
- If short is found, repair it.
- If OK, go to Step 2.
2. Check for a faulty **HI-LO** or intermittent relay.
- If faulty, replace the relay.
- If OK, go to Step 3.
3. Check the circuit from terminal **C** of the intermittent relay and terminal **B** of the **HI-LO** relay to the battery or ignition.
- If no voltage is found at the relay, repair the short.
- If OK, go to Step 4.
4. Disconnect the connector from the body controller. Check the circuit from terminal **1** of the connector to terminal **C** of the intermittent wiper relay for a short to ground.
- If short is found, repair the circuit.
- If OK, go to Step 5.
5. Using a voltmeter, connect the positive lead to terminal **16** of the body controller connector. Connect the negative lead to ground.
- If the voltmeter reads greater than 0 volts, check the wiper switch and wiring.
- If no voltage is found, go to Step 6.
6. Using a voltmeter, connect the positive lead to terminal **10** of the body controller connector.
- If the voltmeter reads 10–15 volts, check the circuit for a short to the battery or ignition.
- If the voltmeter reads 0 volts, replace the body controller.

WIPERS WILL RUN CONTINUOUSLY WITH THE SWITCH IN THE INTERMITTENT POSITION; WHEN THE SWITCH IS TURNED OFF, WIPERS STOP WHEREVER THEY ARE WITHOUT GOING TO THE PARK POSITION

1. Check for ground at the wiper motor wire connector terminal **4**.
2. Using an ohmmeter, with the wiper motor in the **PARK** position, check for continuity between terminal **1** and terminal **4** of the motor connector.
- If OK, go to Step 3.
- If no continuity is found; replace the wiper motor.
3. Check for continuity between terminal **1** of the wiper motor harness connector and terminal **2** of the body controller connector.
- If continuity is not found, check for a short between the battery or ignition feed in the circuit.

WIPERS DO NOT OPERATE WHEN THE WASHER MOTOR IS ENGAGED

1. Disconnect the connector from the body controller.
2. Using a voltmeter, connect the positive lead to terminal **10** of the body controller connector.
3. Engage the washer switch so the washer motor runs continuously.
- If voltage is 0, check the wiring between the washer motor and the body controller.
- If the voltage is 10–15 volts, replace the body controller.

TESTING

Intermittent Wiper Switch Test

❈❈ CAUTION

If equipped with the air bag restraint system, follow the manufacturer's instructions when removing the steering wheel or column.

Disconnect the wires from the body wiring in the steering column. Using an ohmmeter, test for continuity between the terminals of the switch. For test purposes, the 1st position is the **OFF** position, the next 6 are for the delay wiping, 7th is the **LOW** position and 8th is the **HIGH** position. In any wiping mode, if the knob is pushed all the way in, the washer circuit will be completed.

SWITCH POSITION		TERMINALS	RESISTANCE VALUE
OFF		PIN I to M	OPEN ≥ 300 K OHMS
DELAY LEVEL	1	PIN I to M	9.72 K OHMS
	2	PIN I to M	8.22 K OHMS
	3	PIN I to M	6.61 K OHMS
	4	PIN I to M	5.12 K OHMS
	5	PIN I to M	3.67 K OHMS
	6	PIN I to M	2.22 K OHMS
LOW		PIN I to M	1.02 K OHMS
HIGH		PIN I to M	0.51 K OHMS
WASH		PIN I to W	OPEN
RESISTANCE AT MAXIMUM DELAY POSITION SHOULD BE			9,720 K OHMS
RESISTANCE AT MINIMUM DELAY POSITION SHOULD BE			2,220 K OHMS

8470V015

Intermittent wiper switch testing—Concorde, Intrepid, Vision, and New Yorker

REMOVAL & INSTALLATION

Washer Reservoir and Pump

1. Disconnect the hose from the washer pump and drain the system.
2. Disconnect the negative and positive battery cables.
3. Remove the battery heat shield, battery and tray.
4. Remove the 2 mounting nuts and the screw retaining the reservoir.
5. Disconnect the electrical connectors from the pump and float sensor.
6. Remove the reservoir.
7. Pry the pump away from the reservoir and out of the grommet. Care must be taken not to puncture the reservoir.

To install:

8. Installation is the reverse of the removal procedure.
9. Torque the mounting nuts and the screw to 80–124 inch lbs. (9–14 Nm).

Washer Fluid Level Sensor

1. Raise and support the vehicle safely.
2. Disconnect the electrical connector from the sensor.
3. Press the sensor lock upwards and remove the sensor.

➡ **There will be no fluid loss because there is no hole in the housing.**

To install:

4. Clean the connector and seal.
5. Slide the sensor in until it locks.
6. Connect the electrical connector.

Neon

GENERAL DESCRIPTION

The windshield wipers will only operate with the ignition switch in the **ACC** or **IGN** position. A fuse, located in the fuse block and a circuit breaker located in the wiper motor, protects the circuitry of the wiper system and the vehicle.

The wiper motor has permanent magnet fields. The speeds are determined by current flow to the appropriate set of brushes.

The intermittent wiper system (if equipped), in addition to low and high speed, has a delay mode. The delay mode has a range of 1–15 seconds. Pulse wipe is accomplished by momentarily moving the stalk lever into the **WASH** position while the wiper switch is in either **OFF** or **DELAY** positions.

The intermittent wiper function is integral to the wiper switch. All electronics and relay are contained within the switch assembly. The wiper system completes the wipe cycle when the switch is turned **OFF**. The blades park in the lowest portion of the wiping pattern.

TROUBLESHOOTING

Wiper and Washer System

WIPER MOTOR WILL NOT RUN IN ANY SWITCH POSITION

1. Check fuse **15** in the fuse block.
- If the fuse(s) are good, go to Step 2.

SWITCH POSITION	CONTINUITY BETWEEN
OFF	PIN P2 and PIN L
LOW	PIN P1 and PIN L
HIGH	PIN P1 and PIN H
WASH	PIN P1 and PIN W
INTERMITTENT	CANNOT BE CHECKED

8838XG05

Wiper motor wire harness connector—Neon

- If the fuse(s) are defective, replace them and check the wiper motor operation in all switch positions.
- If the motor is still inoperative and fuses do not blow, go to Step 2.
- If the fuse blows, go to Step 10.
2. Disconnect the wiper motor connector.
3. Check the wiper motor low speed. Connect a jumper wire from the positive battery terminal to terminal **2** of the motor connector. Connect a 2nd jumper wire from ground to motor ground strap. Check the wiper motor high speed. Connect the positive wire to **1** and other to ground strap.
- If motor runs; go to Step 5.
- If motor does not run in high or low speed, go to Step 4.
4. Using an ohmmeter, check for a good ground at the ground strap connector.
- If OK, replace the motor.
- If not, repair the ground as necessary.
5. Using an ohmmeter, check at terminal **E** and ground for continuity. If OK, go to next Step. If not OK, repair ground circuit.
6. Using a voltmeter, with the switch connected, connect a negative lead to motor ground and connect positive lead to terminal **P1** of the switch connector.
- If no voltage, repair wiring.
- If OK, go to next step.
7. Check switch low speed by connecting voltmeter positive lead to terminal **L** of switch connector. Move stalk to **LOW**. If no voltage, replace switch.
8. Check switch high speed by connecting voltmeter positive lead to terminal **H** of switch connector. Move stalk to **HIGH**. If no voltage, replace switch.
9. Disconnect motor connector and replace fuse 15.
- If fuse does not blow, replace motor.
- If fuse blows, disconnect switch and replace fuse. If fuse does not blow, replace switch. If fuse blows, repair wiring.

MOTOR RUNS SLOWLY AT ALL SPEEDS

Disconnect the wiper motor connector from the motor. Remove the wiper arms and blades. Disconnect the wiper motor drive link from the motor. Connect an ammeter from the positive battery terminal to terminal **4** of the wiper motor connector. Connect a ground wire from to ground strap.

TERMINAL 4   AMMETER

+ BATTERY −

8838XG06

Wiper motor ammeter testing—Neon

- If the wiper motor runs and the average ammeter reading is more than 6 amps, check the high and low circuits for a short to ground.
- If the wiper motor runs and the average ammeter reading is less than 6 amps, check to see if the linkage is not binding.

MOTOR WILL RUN AT HIGH SPEED WITH SWITCH IN LOW SPEED POSITION, OR WIPERS RUN AT LOW SPEED WITH SWITCH IN HIGH SPEED POSITION

Check for crossed wires in the motor pigtail or switch connectors.

WIPERS WILL OPERATE CONTINUOUSLY WITH SWITCH IN THE INTERMITTENT POSITION; WHEN WIPER SWITCH IS TURNED OFF, WIPERS STOP WHEREVER THEY ARE, WITHOUT RETURNING TO PARK POSITION

1. Check motor ground strap connection.
2. Turn the ignition **OFF**. Using an ohmmeter, with the motor in **PARK** position, check for continuity between terminal **3** and ground strap. If continuity, replace switch. If no continuity, repair wiring.

WIPERS DO NOT OPERATE WHEN WASHER MOTOR IS ENGAGED, OR WIPERS DO NOT OPERATE IN INTERMITTENT POSITION

1. 2-speed wiper–check for ground at motor strap. If OK, replace switch.
2. Intermittent wiper–check for ground at motor strap and terminal **E** of switch. If OK, replace switch. If not, repair wiring.

TESTING

Intermittent Wiper Switch Test

❋❋ **CAUTION**

If equipped with the air bag restraint system, follow the manufacturer's instructions when removing the steering wheel or column.

Disconnect the wires from the body wiring in the steering column. Using an ohmmeter, test for continuity between the terminals of the switch.

REMOVAL & INSTALLATION

Washer Reservoir and Pump

1. Disconnect the hose from the washer pump and drain the system.
2. Disconnect the negative and positive battery cables.
3. Remove the mounting nuts and the screw retaining the reservoir.
4. Disconnect the electrical connectors from the pump. Care must be taken not to puncture the reservoir.
5. Remove the reservoir.
6. Pry the pump away from the reservoir and out of the grommet.
   To install:
7. Installation is the reverse of the removal procedure.
8. Torque the mounting screws to 20–29 inch lbs. (2–3 Nm).

Wiper Switch

1. Disconnect the negative battery cable and wait 90 seconds.
2. Remove the upper half of steering column shroud.
3. Remove mounting screw and switch. Disconnect the harness.
4. Installation is the reverse of removal.

Wiper Module

1. Disconnect the negative battery cable and wait 90 seconds.
2. Remove the wiper arms and blades.
3. Remove the rear hood seal with cowl top plastic screen.
4. Disconnect the motor connector and remove the mounting screws and module.
5. Installation is the reverse of removal. Torque the screws to 60–80 inch lbs. (7–9 Nm).

Wiper Motor

1. Disconnect the negative battery cable and wait 90 seconds.
2. Remove the wiper module assembly as previously outlined.
3. Remove the linkage from motor crank. Insert suitable prybar between crank and linkage then twist and lift straight up.
4. Installation is the reverse of removal. Add Unilube®grease to the socket. Torque the motor screws to 45–55 inch lbs. (5–6 Nm) and drive link nut to 98–106 inch lbs. (11–12 Nm).

FORD MOTOR COMPANY

Wiper and Washer System

GENERAL DESCRIPTION

Continental, Crown Victoria, Grand Marquis, Mark VIII, Taurus, Town Car and Sable, Cougar, Mustang and Thunderbird

The wiper motor is located under the wiper assembly. A drive link connects the motor directly to the lever of the right hand pivot shaft.

The 2-speed, permanent magnet, 3 brush electric windshield wiper motor has a brush rigging that permits a selection of low or high speeds. When the control lever is in the **LO** position, the common brush and blue/orange wire brushes are used. When the control lever is in the **HI** position, the common brush and white wire brushes are used. Current bypasses a portion of the armature winding, causing the motor to run faster. When the control lever is moved to the **OFF** position, the motor will continue to run at low speed until the motor switch outer contacts open, signaling the motor to park and activates the depressed park mechanism which is part of the output arm.

Escort, Tempo, Tracer and Topaz

The wiper motor is located under the wiper assembly. A drive link connects the motor directly to the lever of the right hand pivot shaft.

The 2-speed, permanent magnet, 3 brush electric windshield wiper motor has a brush rigging that permits a selection of low or high speeds. When the control lever is in the **LO** position, the common brush and white wire brushes are used. When the control lever is in the **HI** position, the common brush and blue/orange wire brushes are used. Current bypasses a portion of the armature winding, causing the motor to run faster. When the control lever is moved to the **OFF** position, the motor will continue to run at low speed until the motor switch grounds the low speed brush, stopping the motor in the park position.

Aspire and Probe

The windshield wipers are operated by an electric motor mounted in the left rear corner of the engine compartment. The motor is attached to an access plate that is in turn attached to the dash panel. To prevent metal-to-metal contact and transmissions to the body, the motor is mounted on rubber insulators.

The rotary motion of the motor is transferred to the wiper arms through a linkage and pivot assembly. The wiper arm pivots extend through the cowl sheet metal and are held in position with attaching nuts. The ends of the pivot shafts are serrated and cone shaped to prevent the wiper arm from slipping on the shaft.

DIAGNOSTIC TESTING

• On all vehicles, when trouble shooting the wiper system, test the motor first, then work back towards the switch to test the interval governor or module (depending on the vehicle), power circuits and the switch itself.

• In most of the tests, a volt-ohmmeter is required, although a test light can also be useful. For testing the motor, a 0–15 amp DC ammeter is required.

• When the test calls for a voltage check, the ignition switch must be in the **ON** position.

• When testing for continuity or resistance values, turn the ignition switch to the **OFF** position and/or disconnect the negative battery cable.

• Improper or careless testing can cause permanent damage to the vehicle's electronic circuits and to test equipment. Carefully follow the test equipment manufacturer's instructions.

TESTING

Wiper Motor Operation

EXCEPT ASPIRE AND PROBE

The motors in these vehicles contain permanent magnets made of ceramic, which can shatter like glass if the motor is dropped or hit with a hammer. When removing the wiper motor, handle with care.

1. Remove the wiper motor linkage and electrical connectors from the windshield wiper motor.

➡**If the electrical connector is not accessible, the motor may need to be removed.**

2. Using a suitable charging tester, connect the power lead of the tester to the positive battery terminal.
3. Connect a jumper wire from the negative battery terminal to the circuit as follows:
   a. Taurus, Sable, Cougar and Thunderbird, Grand Marquis, Crown Victoria, and Town Car—**61**
   b. Mustang and Continental, Mark VIII, Contour and Mystique—**HI or LO**
4. Connect the other power lead from the charging tester to circuit **56** or **COMMON**, the motor should operating at low speed, note the draw. Remove the red lead from circuit **56** and connect it to circuit **58**, the motor should begin operating at high speed, note the draw.
5. The draw should be no more than 3.5 amps at either speed. Repairs to the motor itself are not possible.

PROBE

Connect the 12 volt power source to the motor electrical connections to check for proper motor operation. Repairs to the motor itself are not possible.

ASPIRE

On this motor, the blue wire is a common 12 volts and is powered whenever the ignition switch is **ON**. The blue/white and blue/red wires are ground circuits for the low and high speeds. The blue/black wire connects to the motor's internal park switch and, when the wipers are in the **PARK** position, should have continuity with the blue wire terminal on the motor to feed 12 volts to the wiper switch.

1. To test the motor, turn the ignition switch **OFF** and unplug the wiper motor connector.
2. Carefully use a jumper wire to feed 12 volts to the blue wire terminal on the motor plug.
3. Use a jumper wire to carefully ground the blue/white wire terminal to check for **LOW** speed operation.

Wiper/washer schematic (interval wipers)—Probe

8838XG18

INTERIOR FUSE JUNCTION PANEL

Pin	Circuit	Circuit Function
1B	42 (BK/GN)	START/ON Power
2B	40 (BK/W)	START/ON Power
3B	71 (BL)	ON Power
4B	73 (BL/BK)	ACC/ON Power
5B	303 (BL/Y)	Ignition Key Reminder Switch Signal
6B	304 (PK)	Ignition/Door Lock Cylinder Illumination Ground
7B	80 (O)	Instrument Illumination Power
8B	117 (GN/W)	Right Front Turn Signal Lamp
9B	116 (GN/BK)	Left Front Turn Signal Lamp
10B	84G (BL/R)	Hot At All Times Power

INTERIOR FUSE JUNCTION PANEL

Pin	Circuit	Circuit Function
1C	117 (GN/W)	Right Rear Turn Signal
2C	80 (O)	Instrument Illumination Power
3C	116 (GN/BK)	Left Rear Turn Signal
4C	41E (BK/Y)	START/ON Power
5C	73 (BL/BK)	ACC/ON Power
6C	307 (BR/BK)	Safety Belt Warning Indicator
7C	31 (BL/W)	ACC/ON Power
8C	85 (GN/R)	Hot At All Times Power
9C	81 (BR)	Hot At All Times Power
10C	—	NOT USED

Pin	Circuit	Circuit Function
11C	84D (BL/R)	Hot At All Times Power
12C	70 (BL/GN)	ON Power
13C	300A (R/W)	Door Ajar Warning Indicator
14C	108 (R/BK)	Backup Lamps

**TURN SIGNAL AND
WINDSHIELD WIPER SWITCH**

Pin	Circuit	Circuit Function
1A	84J (BL/R)	Ignition Switch Lock Cylinder Illumination Power
2A	79 (LG)	Parking Lamp Relay Control
3A	50C (BK)	Headlamp Switch Ground
4A	127 (BL/BK)	Intermittent Mode Output
5A	124 (BL/O)	Windshield Washer Pump Output
6A	115 (GN/R)	Hazard Flasher Switch Power
7A	304 (PK)	Ignition Switch Lock Cylinder Illumination Control
8A	262 (W/R)	Headlamp Switch Power
9A	42 (BK/GN)	Turn Signal Switch Power
10A	50D (BK)	Windshield Wiper/Washer Switch Ground
11A	71 (BL)	Windshield Wiper/Washer Switch Power
12A	126 (R)	High-Speed Output
13A	125 (BL/W)	Low-Speed Output
14A	50F (BK)	Hazard Flasher Switch Ground

8838XG19

Wiper/washer connector description—Probe

8470V032

Wiper motor testing—Type C—Cougar and Thunderbird, Crown Victoria, Grand Marquis, Sable, Taurus, and Town Car

8838XG07

Wiper motor testing—Type E—Continental, Mark VIII and Mustang

STARTING AND
CHARGING TESTER
078-00005

+FEED TO
COMMON
TERMINAL
FOR TEST.
GROUND
HI OR LO
TO RUN

GREEN

RED

BATTERY

5
4
3
2
1

8838XG08

Wiper motor testing—Type F—Contour and Mystique

4. Disconnect the jumper from the blue/white wire and ground the blue/red wire to check for **HIGH** speed operation.

5. With 12 volts to the blue wire terminal and only the motor case grounded, the motor should go to **PARK**. In **PARK**, there should be 12 volts between the blue/black terminal and ground.

Wiper Motor Parking

EXCEPT ESCORT, MARK VIII, CONTINENTAL, MUSTANG, CONTOUR AND MYSTIQUE

1. Connect a jumper wire from the positive battery terminal to terminal **63**.

2. Connect terminals **G1** and **G2** to a suitable body ground with jumper wires.

3. The wipers should complete 1 cycle and return to **PARK**.

4. If the wipers do not **PARK**, replace the motor.

ESCORT

1. Stop the wipers, when they are not in the **PARK** position, by turning the ignition switch to the **OFF** position.

2. Disconnect the electrical connector from the wiper motor.

3. Using a jumper wire, connect the black and white connectors on the wiper motor harness.

4. Using a 2nd jumper wire, connect the red connector of the wiper motor harness to the positive battery terminal.

5. The motor should complete 1 full cycle and return to the **PARK** position.

6. If the wiper motor does not **PARK** or does not complete a full cycle, replace the motor.

MARK VIII, CONTINENTAL AND MUSTANG

1. Unplug connector at motor and check ground circuit **57 (BLK)**.

2. Turn ignition switch to **RUN** and multi-function switch **OFF**. Check battery voltage between circuits **65 (DARK GREEN)** and **57 (BLK)** at the motor connector. Should be voltage.

3. With multi-function switch **OFF**, check for continuity between circuit **28 (BK/PK)** and **56 (DB/O)** and circuits **61 (Y/R)** and **63**

(R) or **57 (BK)** from the motor-to-wiper control module. If present, replace the wiper control module.

4. Check that the mounting arm and pivot shaft and linkage is not bent, cracked or misaligned.

CONTOUR AND MYSTIQUE

1. With wiper and ignition switch **OFF**, check for short to ground at motor harness circuit **32 (W/BK)** and ground. Resistance should be greater then 10K ohms.

2. Disconnect fuse junction panel connector **K**. Check for open in circuit **32** between wiper connector pin 4 and fuse panel connector pin **K4**. The resistance should be less than 3 ohms.

3. Measure circuit **14 (P)** resistance between wiper motor connector pin 5 and fuse panel connector pin **K8**. Resistance should be less than 3 ohms.

4. Remove the central timer module from fuse panel. Measure resistance from timer module pin S13 and fuse panel connector pin **K4**. Resistance should be less than 1 ohm.

5. Connect fuse panel connector **K**. Turn ignition switch to **RUN** and measure voltage at motor connector pin 5. Should be voltage.

6. With ignition in **RUN** position, measure voltage between motor connector pins **3** and **5**. Should be battery voltage.

7. The resistance through motor connector pin **3** and **5** should be 3 ohms or less.

Circuit Breaker

Some vehicles have an 8.25 amp circuit breaker located in the fuse panel. Two separate tests are necessary to check for correct circuit breaker operation.

1. Remove the circuit breaker from the fuse panel.

2. Using a suitable volt-amp tester, touch the test leads together and adjust the current draw until it equals the circuit breaker rating.

3. Connect the test leads to the circuit breaker, hold the current reading on the ammeter at the rated current and leave it connected for 10 minutes.

4. If the circuit breaker opens during the 10 minutes, replace the circuit breaker.

5. Touch the testers leads together and adjust the current draw until it is twice the rated current.

6. Connect the circuit breaker to the tester and hold the current rating on twice the rated current.

7. The current reading on the ammeter should drop to 0 within 30 seconds.

8. If it takes longer than 30 seconds for the ammeter to drop to 0 (circuit breaker to open), replace the circuit breaker.

Washer Pump Draw

1. Connect a suitable volt-amp tester to the washer pump.

2. Run the washer pump using the column switch.

3. The current draw should not exceed 4 amps nor indicate below 2 amps while in use.

Wiper Switch

On all vehicles, the switch can be tested independently using a powered test light to check for continuity. Interval systems must be tested with an ohmmeter. Locate the correct schematic and follow the switch testing procedure indicated. A defective switch or interval governor cannot be repaired and must be replaced.

Refer to the model specific sections for engine electrical system service procedures

TO TEST	Connect Self-Powered Test Light or Ohmmeter to Terminals	Move Switch to These Positions	A Good Switch Will Indicate
Washer Switch Circuit	590, 590 (DB/W) *and* 993, 993 (BR/W)	With Wiper Switch OFF: Push washer switch in Release washer switch	Closed Circuit 103.3K ohm
Wiper Switch Circuit	589, 589 (O) *and* 993, 993 (BR/W)	OFF INT LO HI	47.6K ohm 11.33K ohm 4.08K ohm Closed Circuit
Interval Time Adjust	590, 590 (DB/W) *and* 993, 993 (BR/W)	INT and OFF	Rotate Control toward OFF; Ohmmeter will show smoothly increasing resistance from 3.3K ohm min. to 103.3K ohm max.
		LO and HI	3.3K ohm

8470V020

Wiper switch test—Continental, Crown Victoria, Grand Marquis, Mark VIII, Sable, Taurus, Mustang and Town Car

TO TEST	Connect Self-Powered Test Lamp or Ohmmeter to Terminals	Move Switch to These Positions	A Good Switch Will Indicate
Wiper Speed "LO"	C225 (Pin J) *and* C225 (Pin N)	Off Lo Hi	Open Circuit Open Circuit Closed Circuit
Wiper Speed "HI"	C225 (Pin J) *and* C225 (Pin L)	Off Lo Hi	Open Circuit Closed Circuit Open Circuit
Park Switch Circuit	C225 (Pin N) *and* C225 (Pin K)	Off Lo Hi	Closed Circuit Open Circuit Open Circuit

TO TEST	Connect Self-Powered Test Lamp or Ohmmeter to Terminals	Move Switch to These Positions	A Good Switch Will Indicate
Wiper Speed "LO"	C225 (Pin J) *and* C225 (Pin N)	Off Int Lo Hi	Open Circuit Open Circuit Closed Circuit Open Circuit
Wiper Speed "HI"	C225 (Pin J) *and* C225 (Pin L)	Off Int Lo Hi	Open Circuit Open Circuit Open Circuit Closed Circuit
Park Switch Circuit	C225 (Pin N) *and* C225 (Pin K)	Off Int Lo Hi	Closed Circuit Closed Circuit Open Circuit Open Circuit
"MIST" Circuit	C225 (Pin J) *and* C225 (Pin L)	Mist Switch On Mist Switch Off	Closed Circuit Open Circuit

8470V026

Wiper switch test—Probe

Pin Number	Circuit	Circuit Function
1	32 (W/GN)	Wiper Motor Low Speed Output
2	32 (W/BK)	Wiper Motor High Speed Output
3	—	Not Used
4	32 (W/BK)	Wiper Motor Intermittent Timer Input
5	8 (W/BK)	Wiper Motor Intermittent Timer Reference Signal
6	8 (W)	Wiper Motor Intermittent Timer Signal
7	—	Not Used
8	14 (P/O)	Switch Supply
9	33 (Y/BK)	Washer Timer Input
10	31 (BK)	Ground
11	14 (P·W)	Washer Motor Output

8838XG09

Wiper switch test—Contour and Mystique

MALFUNCTION CHART

When troubleshooting wiper problems, first visually inspect the components. Check for a blown 20 amp fuse or 8.25 circuit breaker (depending on the vehicle), loose or corroded connections, damaged wiring harness, damaged wiper motor or switch. Also check for binding wiper arms or linkage.

To aid in troubleshooting, turn the ignition switch **ON**, place the wiper switch in each position and observe if the wiper is functioning. If the problem, such as damaged wires or broken linkage is not evident, use the following list of conditions with their possible causes to start troubleshooting.

Aspire

WINDSHIELD WASHER INOPERATIVE

1. Turn the ignition **OFF**. Disconnect the windshield washer pump connector. Apply 12V to the **BL/O** wire terminal on the windshield washer pump. Apply 12V to the **BK** wire terminal on the windshield washer pump.
   a. If the windshield washer pump operates, go to Step 2.
   b. If the windshield washer pump does not operate, replace the windshield washer pump.
2. Turn the ignition **OFF**. Disconnect the windshield washer pump connector. Measure resistance of **BK** wire between the windshield washer pump connector and ground.
   a. If the resistance is less than 5 ohms, go to Step 3.
   b. If the resistance is greater than 5 ohms, service the **BK** wire.
3. Turn the ignition **OFF**. Disconnect the turn signal/windshield wiper switch connector.
   a. Measure resistance of the following wire terminals of the turn signal/windshield wiper switch under the following conditions:
   • With the switch in the **OFF** position, the resistance of terminals 1-to-5 should be less than 5 ohms.

Electrical schematic—Front wiper/washer system (with interval function)—Aspire

• With the switch in the **INT** position, the resistance of terminals 1-to-5 should be less than 5 ohms.
• With the switch in the **LO** position, the resistance of terminals 15-to-5 should be less than 5 ohms.
• With the switch in the **HIGH** position, the resistance of terminals 15-to-4 should be less than 5 ohms.
• With the switch in the **MIST** position, the resistance of terminals 15-to-4 should be less than 5 ohms.
• With the switch in the **WASH** position, the resistance of terminals 15-to-3 should be less than 5 ohms.
• The resistance of all other terminals not listed under the conditions should be greater than 10,000 ohms.
   b. If the switch's resistance requirements are:
• Okay, service the **BL/O** wire.
• Not okay, replace the turn signal/windshield wiper switch.

REAR WINDOW WASHER INOPERATIVE

1. Turn the ignition **OFF**. Disconnect the rear window washer pump connector. Apply 12V to the **BL/GN** wire terminal on the rear window washer pump. Apply ground to the **BL/Y** wire terminal on the rear window washer pump.
   a. If the windshield washer pump operates, go to Step 2.
   b. If the windshield washer pump does not operate, replace the rear window washer pump.

TURN SIGNAL AND WINDSHIELD
WIPER SWITCH

Pin	Circuit	Circuit Function
1	231 (BL · W)	Windshield Wiper Motor Park Input
2	500 (BK)	Ground
3	734 (BL / O)	Windshield Washer Motor Output
4	233 (BL / R)	High Speed Wiper Output
5	232 (BL / BK)	Low Speed Wiper Output
6	50K (BK)	Ground
7	387 (GN)	Left Turn Signal Output
8	388 (Y)	Right Turn Signal Output
9	160H (BK / Y)	Power Supply
10	13 (R/W)	Parking Lamp Relay Control

Pin	Circuit	Circuit Function
11	388 (O)	Hazard Flasher Switch Output
12	227 (BL / Y)	Rear Window Washer Motor Control
13	50E (BK)	Ground
14	226 (BK / BL)	Rear Window Wiper Motor Control
15	230A (BL)	ACC / ON Power
16	12 (R / GN)	Headlamp Relay Input
17	7 (R)	Hot At All Times Power
18	281 (R / W)	High Beam Output
19	282 (R / BL)	Low Beam Output
20	11 (R / BL)	Headlamp Relay Control
21	50V (BK)	Ground

8838XG11

Wiper switch connector description—Aspire

2. Turn the ignition **OFF**. Disconnect the rear window washer pump connector. Turn the ignition **ON**. Measure the voltage on the **BL/GN** wire at the rear window washer pump connector. Apply ground to the **BL/Y** wire terminal on the rear window washer pump.

   a. If the voltage is greater than 10 volts, go to Step 3.

   b. If the voltage is less than 10 volts, service the **BL/GN** wire.

3. Turn the ignition **OFF**. Disconnect the turn signal/windshield wiper switch connector.

   a. Measure the resistance between the **BL/Y** and **BK** wire terminals on the turn signal/windshield wiper switch connector under the following conditions:

   • With the switch in the **ON** position, the resistance should be less than 5 ohms.

   • With the switch in the **OFF** position, the resistance should be greater than 10,000 ohms.

   b. Measure the resistance between the **BL/Y** and **BK** wire terminals on the turn signal/windshield wiper switch connector under the following conditions:

   • If the resistances meet specifications, go to Step 4.

   • If the resistances do not meet specifications, replace the turn signal/windshield wiper switch.

4. Turn the ignition **OFF**. Disconnect the turn signal/windshield wiper switch connector. Measure the resistance between the **BK** wire terminal between the turn signal/windshield wiper switch connector and ground:

   a. If the resistance is less than 5 ohms, service the **BL/Y** wire terminal between the rear window washer pump and the turn signal/windshield wiper switch.

   b. If the resistance is greater than 5 ohms, service the **BK** wire.

WINDSHIELD WIPERS INOPERATIVE IN ALL SWITCH POSITIONS

1. Turn the ignition **OFF**. In the interior fuse panel, check the **20A WIPER** fuse.

   a. If the fuse is okay, go to Step 4.

   b. If the fuse is not okay, go to Step 2.

2. Turn the ignition **OFF**. In the interior fuse panel, install the **20A WIPER** fuse. Turn the ignition **ON**.

   a. If the fuse is okay, go to Step 4.

   b. If the fuse is not okay, go to Step 3.

3. Turn the ignition **OFF**. Remove the **20A WIPER** fuse. Disconnect the windshield wiper motor connector and the turn signal/windshield wiper switch connector. Measure the resistance of the **BL** wire between the bottom terminal of the **20A WIPER** fuse holder and ground:

   a. If the resistance is less than 5 ohms, service the **BL** wire.

   b. If the resistance is greater than 5 ohms, replace the **20A WIPER** fuse and go the Step 4.

4. Turn the ignition **OFF**. Disconnect the windshield wiper motor connector and the turn signal/windshield wiper switch connector. Turn the ignition **ON**. Measure the voltage of the **BL** wire at the windshield wiper motor connector and the turn signal/windshield wiper switch connector:

   a. If the voltage is less than 10 volts, service the **BL** wire.

   b. If the voltage is greater than 10 volts, go the Step 5.

5. Turn the ignition **OFF**. Disconnect the windshield wiper motor connector. Apply 12 volts to terminal **2** of the windshield wiper motor; the wiper should operate at low speed.

6. Apply 12 volts to terminal **1** of the windshield wiper motor; the wiper should operate at high speed.

   a. To check the interval park switch, measure the resistance between the wire terminals **3** and **4** of the windshield wiper motor, under the following conditions:

   • With the wipers in the park position, the resistance should be less than 5 ohms.

   • With the wipers not in the park position, the resistance should be greater than 10,000 ohms.

   b. If the windshield wiper motor test are:

- Okay, go to Step 6.
- Not okay, replace the windshield wiper motor.

7. Turn the ignition **OFF**. Disconnect the turn signal/windshield wiper switch connector.

a. Measure resistance of the following wire terminals of the turn signal/windshield wiper switch under the following conditions:

- With the switch in the **OFF** position, the resistance of terminals 1-to-5 should be less than 5 ohms.
- With the switch in the **INT** position, the resistance of terminals 1-to-5 should be less than 5 ohms.
- With the switch in the **LO** position, the resistance of terminals 15-to-5 should be less than 5 ohms.
- With the switch in the **HIGH** position, the resistance of terminals 15-to-4 should be less than 5 ohms.
- With the switch in the **MIST** position, the resistance of terminals 15-to-4 should be less than 5 ohms.
- With the switch in the **WASH** position, the resistance of terminals 15-to-3 should be less than 5 ohms.
- The resistance of all other terminals not listed under the conditions should be greater than 10,000 ohms.

b. If the switch's resistance requirements are:

- Okay, service the **BL/W**, **BL/R** and/or **BL/BK** wires between the turn signal/windshield wiper switch and the windshield wiper motor.
- Not okay, replace the turn signal/windshield wiper switch.

WINDSHIELD WIPERS INOPERATIVE AT HIGH SPEED

1. Turn the ignition **OFF**. Disconnect the windshield wiper motor connector. Apply 12 volts to terminal **2** of the windshield wiper motor; the wiper should operate at low speed. Apply 12 volts to terminal **1** of the windshield wiper motor; the wiper should operate at high speed.

a. To check the interval park switch, measure the resistance between the wire terminals **3** and **4** of the windshield wiper motor, under the following conditions:

- With the wipers in the park position, the resistance should be less than 5 ohms.
- With the wipers not in the park position, the resistance should be greater than 10,000 ohms.

b. If the windshield wiper motor test are:

- Okay, go to Step 2.
- Not okay, replace the windshield wiper motor.

2. Turn the ignition **OFF**. Disconnect the turn signal/windshield wiper switch connector.

a. Measure resistance of the following wire terminals of the turn signal/windshield wiper switch under the following conditions:

- With the switch in the **OFF** position, the resistance of terminals 1-to-5 should be less than 5 ohms.
- With the switch in the **INT** position, the resistance of terminals 1-to-5 should be less than 5 ohms.
- With the switch in the **LO** position, the resistance of terminals 15-to-5 should be less than 5 ohms.
- With the switch in the **HIGH** position, the resistance of terminals 15-to-4 should be less than 5 ohms.
- With the switch in the **MIST** position, the resistance of terminals 15-to-4 should be less than 5 ohms.
- With the switch in the **WASH** position, the resistance of terminals 15-to-3 should be less than 5 ohms.

- The resistance of all other terminals not listed under the conditions should be greater than 10,000 ohms.

b. If the switch's resistance requirements are:

- Okay, service the **BL/R** wire between the turn signal/windshield wiper switch and the windshield wiper motor.
- Not okay, replace the turn signal/windshield wiper switch.

WINDSHIELD WIPERS INOPERATIVE AT LOW SPEED

1. Turn the ignition **OFF**. Disconnect the windshield wiper motor connector. Apply 12 volts to terminal **2** of the windshield wiper motor; the wiper should operate at low speed. Apply 12 volts to terminal **1** of the windshield wiper motor; the wiper should operate at high speed.

a. To check the interval park switch, measure the resistance between the wire terminals **3** and **4** of the windshield wiper motor, under the following conditions:

- With the wipers in the park position, the resistance should be less than 5 ohms.
- With the wipers not in the park position, the resistance should be greater than 10,000 ohms.

b. If the windshield wiper motor test are:

- Okay, go to Step 2.
- Not okay, replace the windshield wiper motor.

2. Turn the ignition **OFF**. Disconnect the turn signal/windshield wiper switch connector.

a. Measure resistance of the following wire terminals of the turn signal/windshield wiper switch under the following conditions:

- With the switch in the **OFF** position, the resistance of terminals 1-to-5 should be less than 5 ohms.
- With the switch in the **INT** position, the resistance of terminals 1-to-5 should be less than 5 ohms.
- With the switch in the **LO** position, the resistance of terminals 15-to-5 should be less than 5 ohms.
- With the switch in the **HIGH** position, the resistance of terminals 15-to-4 should be less than 5 ohms.
- With the switch in the **MIST** position, the resistance of terminals 15-to-4 should be less than 5 ohms.
- With the switch in the **WASH** position, the resistance of terminals 15-to-3 should be less than 5 ohms.

- The resistance of all other terminals not listed under the conditions should be greater than 10,000 ohms.

b. If the switch's resistance requirements are:

- Okay, service the **BL/BK** wire between the turn signal/windshield wiper switch and the windshield wiper motor.
- Not okay, replace the turn signal/windshield wiper switch.

WINDSHIELD WIPERS WILL NOT PARK BELOW WINDSHIELD

1. Turn the ignition **OFF**. Disconnect the windshield wiper motor connector. Apply 12 volts to terminal **2** of the windshield wiper motor; the wiper should operate at low speed. Apply 12 volts to terminal **1** of the windshield wiper motor; the wiper should operate at high speed.

a. To check the interval park switch, measure the resistance between the wire terminals **3** and **4** of the windshield wiper motor, under the following conditions:

- With the wipers in the park position, the resistance should be less than 5 ohms.
- With the wipers not in the park position, the resistance should be greater than 10,000 ohms.

b. If the windshield wiper motor test are:

- Okay, go to Step 2.
- Not okay, replace the windshield wiper motor.

2. Turn the ignition **OFF**. Disconnect the turn signal/windshield wiper switch connector. Disconnect the windshield wiper motor connector. Measure resistance of the **BL/W** wire between the turn signal/windshield wiper switch connector and the windshield wiper motor connector.

   a. If the resistance is less than 5 ohms, replace the turn signal/windshield wiper switch.

   b. If the resistance is greater than 5 ohms, service the **BL/W** wire.

WINDSHIELD WIPERS WILL NOT TURN OFF

1. Turn the ignition **OFF**. Disconnect the turn signal/windshield wiper switch connector.

2. Measure resistance of the following wire terminals of the turn signal/windshield wiper switch under the following conditions:

- With the switch in the **OFF** position, the resistance of terminals 1-to-5 should be less than 5 ohms.
- With the switch in the **INT** position, the resistance of terminals 1-to-5 should be less than 5 ohms.
- With the switch in the **LO** position, the resistance of terminals 15-to-5 should be less than 5 ohms.
- With the switch in the **HIGH** position, the resistance of terminals 15-to-4 should be less than 5 ohms.
- With the switch in the **MIST** position, the resistance of terminals 15-to-4 should be less than 5 ohms.
- With the switch in the **WASH** position, the resistance of terminals 15-to-3 should be less than 5 ohms.
- The resistance of all other terminals not listed under the conditions should be greater than 10,000 ohms.

3. If the switch's resistance requirements are:
- Okay, replace the windshield wiper motor.
- Not okay, replace the turn signal/windshield wiper switch.

REAR WINDOW WIPER INOPERATIVE

1. Turn the ignition **OFF**. In the interior fuse panel, check the **15A R.WIPER** fuse.

   a. If the fuse is okay, go to Step 4.

   b. If the fuse is not okay, go to Step 2.

2. Turn the ignition **OFF**. In the interior fuse panel, install the **15A R.WIPER** fuse. Turn the ignition **ON**.

   a. If the fuse is okay, go to Step 4.

   b. If the fuse is not okay, go to Step 3.

3. Turn the ignition **OFF**. Remove the **15A WIPER** fuse. Disconnect the rear window wiper motor connector and the rear window washer motor connector. Measure the resistance of the **BL/GN** wire between the bottom terminal of the **15A R.WIPER** fuse holder and ground:

   a. If the resistance is less than 5 ohms, service the **BL/GN** wire.

   b. If the resistance is greater than 5 ohms, replace the **15A R.WIPER** fuse and go the Step 4.

4. Turn the ignition **OFF**. Disconnect the rear window wiper motor connector. Turn the ignition **ON**.

5. Measure the voltage of the **BL/GN** wire at the rear window wiper motor connector:

   a. If the voltage is less than 10 volts, service the **BL/GN** wire.

   b. If the voltage is greater than 10 volts, go the Step 5.

6. Turn the ignition **OFF**. Disconnect the rear window wiper motor connector. Apply 12 volts to the **BL/GN** terminal of the rear window wiper motor. Apply ground to the **BK/BL** wire terminal of the rear window wiper motor.

   a. If the rear window wiper motor operates, go to Step 6.

   b. If the rear window wiper motor does not operate, replace the rear window wiper motor.

7. Turn the ignition **OFF**. Disconnect the turn signal/windshield wiper switch connector.

   a. Measure resistance between the **BK/BL** and **BK** wire terminals of the turn signal/windshield wiper switch under the following conditions:

- With the rear wiper switch in the **ON** position, the resistance should be less than 5 ohms.
- With the rear wiper switch in the **OFF** position, the resistance should be greater than 10,000 ohms.

   b. If the switch's resistance requirements are:
- Okay, go to Step 7.
- Not okay, replace the turn signal/windshield wiper switch.

8. Turn the ignition **OFF**. Disconnect the turn signal/windshield wiper switch connector. Measure the resistance of the **BK** wire between pin **13** of the turn signal/windshield wiper switch connector and ground:

   a. If the resistance is less than 5 ohms, service the **BK/BL** wire between the turn signal/windshield wiper switch and the rear window wiper motor.

   b. If the resistance is greater than 5 ohms, service the **BK** wire.

REAR WINDOW WIPER WILL NOT TURN OFF

1. Turn the ignition **OFF**. Disconnect the turn signal/windshield wiper switch connector.

2. Measure resistance between the **BK/BL** and **BK** wire terminals of the turn signal/windshield wiper switch under the following conditions:

- With the rear wiper switch in the **ON** position, the resistance should be less than 5 ohms.
- With the rear wiper switch in the **OFF** position, the resistance should be greater than 10,000 ohms.

3. If the switch's resistance requirements are:
- Okay, service the **BK/BL** wire between the turn signal/windshield wiper switch and the rear window wiper motor.
- Not okay, replace the turn signal/windshield wiper switch.

Escort and Tracer

WINDSHIELD WASHER INOPERATIVE

1. Turn the key to the **OFF** position. Disconnect the turn signal/windshield wiper switch connector.

   a. Measure the resistance between the turn signal/windshield wiper switch terminals under the following conditions:

- With the switch in the **HI** position, terminals **BL**-to-**R** should be less than 5 ohms.
- With the switch in the **LO** position, terminals **BL**-to-**BL/W** should be less than 5 ohms.
- With the switch in the **MIST (OFF and pushed)** position, terminals **BL**-to-**R** should be less than 5 ohms.
- With the switch in the **WASH (pulled)** position, terminals **BL**-to-**BL/O** should be less than 5 ohms.
- With the switch in the **OFF** position, terminals **BL/Y**-to-**BL/W** should be less than 5 ohms.

   b. Perform the following procedures:
- If the resistances are okay, go to Step 2.
- If the resistances are not okay, replace the turn signal/windshield wiper switch.

2. Check power to windshield washer pump. Turn the key to the

OFF position. Disconnect the windshield washer pump connector. Turn the key to the **ON** position. Turn the washer **ON**. Measure the voltage on the **BL/O** wire at the windshield wiper/washer pump connector:

    a. If the voltage is greater than 10 volts, go to Step 3.

    b. If the voltage is less than 10 volts, service the **BL/O** wire.

  3. Check the windshield washer pump ground. Turn the key to the **OFF** position. Disconnect the windshield washer pump connector. Measure the resistance on the **BK** wire between the windshield washer pump connector and ground:

    a. If the resistance is less than 5 ohms, replace the windshield washer pump.

    b. If the resistance is greater than 5 ohms, service the **BK** wire.

REAR WINDOW WASHER INOPERATIVE

  1. Turn the key to the **OFF** position. Disconnect the rear window wiper/washer switch connector.

    a. Measure the resistance of the rear window wiper/washer switch terminals, under the following conditions:

• With the switch in the **REST** position, check terminals **BK**-to-**BL/BK**; the resistance should be greater than 10,000 ohms.

• With the switch in the **REST** position, check terminals **BK**-to-**O**; the resistance should be greater than 10,000 ohms.

• With the switch in the **WIPER ON** position, check terminals **BK**-to-**BL/BK**; the resistance should be less than 5 ohms.

• With the switch in the **WIPER ON** position, check terminals **BK**-to-**O**; the resistance should be greater than 10,000 ohms.

• With the switch in the **WASHER ON** position, check terminals **BK**-to-**BL/BK**; the resistance should be less than 5 ohms.

• With the switch in the **WASHER ON** position, check terminals **BK**-to-**O**; the resistance should be less than 5 ohms.

    b. Perform the following procedures:

• If the resistances are okay, go to Step 2.

• If the resistances are not okay, replace the rear window wiper/washer switch.

  2. Check rear window washer pump. Turn the key to the **OFF** position. Disconnect the rear window washer pump connector. Apply 12 volts to the **BL/GN** wire at the rear window washer pump. Ground the **O** wire terminal at the rear window washer pump; the pump should operate:

    a. If the tests are okay, go to Step 3.

    b. If the tests are not okay, replace the rear window washer pump.

  3. Check power to rear window washer pump. Turn the key to the **OFF** position. Disconnect the rear window washer pump connector. Turn the key to the **ON** position. Measure the voltage on the **BL/GN** wire at the rear window washer pump connector:

    a. If the voltage is greater than 10 volts, go to Step 4.

    b. If the voltage is less than 10 volts, service the **BL/GN** wire.

  4. Check rear window wiper/washer switch ground. Turn the key to the **OFF** position. Disconnect the rear window wiper/washer pump connector. Measure the resistance on the **BK** wire between the rear window wiper/washer pump connector and ground:

    a. If the resistance is less than 5 ohms, service the **O** wire between the rear window wiper/washer pump and rear window wiper/washer pump connector.

    b. If the resistance is greater than 5 ohms, service the **BK** wire.

WINDSHIELD WIPERS INOPERATIVE IN ALL SWITCH POSITIONS

  1. Turn the key to the **OFF** position. Check **20A WIPER** fuse.

    a. If fuse is okay, go to Step 4.

    b. If fuse is bad, go to Step 2.

  2. Turn the key to the **OFF** position. Install and confirm fuse is good. Turn ignition switch **ON** and check that **20A WIPER** fuse does not blow.

    a. If fuse is okay, go to Step 4.

    b. If fuse is bad, go to Step 3.

  3. Check for short to ground. Turn ignition switch **OFF**. Disconnect the interior fuse junction panel, the wiper motor switch and the wiper motor connectors. Measure the resistance of the **BL** wire between the interior fuse junction panel connector and ground.

    a. If resistance is greater then 5 ohms, install the interior fuse junction panel connector and go to Step 4.

    b. If resistance is less than 5 ohms, service the **BL** wire.

  4. Check washer switch. Turn the key to the **OFF** position. Disconnect the turn signal/windshield wiper switch connector.

    a. Measure the resistance between the turn signal/windshield wiper switch terminals under the following conditions:

• With the switch in the **HI** position, terminals **BL**-to-**R** should be less than 5 ohms.

• With the switch in the **LO** position, terminals **BL**-to-**BL/W** should be less than 5 ohms.

• With the switch in the **MIST (OFF and pushed)** position, terminals **BL**-to-**R** should be less than 5 ohms.

• With the switch in the **WASH (pulled)** position, terminals **BL**-to-**BL/O** should be less than 5 ohms.

• With the switch in the **OFF** position, terminals **BL/Y**-to-**BL/W** should be less than 5 ohms.

  5. Perform the following procedures:

• If the resistances are okay, go to Step 5.

• If the resistances are not okay, replace the turn signal/windshield wiper switch.

  6. Check windshield wiper motor. Turn the key to the **OFF** position. Disconnect the windshield wiper motor connectors.

    a. To check for **LO** wiper operation, perform the following procedures:

• Apply 12 volts to terminal **BL** of one connector and **BL/W** of the other connector.

• Apply ground to terminal **BK** of one connector and **BK** of the other connector.

• The wiper should operate in **LO** speed.

    b. To check for **HI** wiper operation, perform the following procedures:

• Apply 12 volts to terminal **BL** of one connector and **R** of the other connector.

• Apply ground to terminal **BK** of one connector and **BK** of the other connector.

• The wiper should operate in **HI** speed.

    c. Perform the following procedure:

• If the motor tests okay, go to Step 6.

• If the motor does not test okay, replace the windshield wiper motor.

  7. Check power to turn signal/windshield wiper switch. Turn the key to the **OFF** position. Disconnect the turn signal/windshield wiper switch connector. Turn the key to the **ON** position. Measure

---

the voltage on the **BL** wire at the turn signal/windshield wiper switch connector:

    a. If the voltage is greater than 10 volts, go to Step 7.

    b. If the voltage is less than 10 volts, service the **BL** wire.

8. Check turn signal/windshield wiper switch ground. Turn the key to the **OFF** position. Disconnect the turn signal/windshield wiper switch connector. Measure the resistance on the **BK** wire between the turn signal/windshield wiper switch connector and ground:

    a. If the resistance is less than 5 ohms, go to Step 8.

    b. If the resistance is greater than 5 ohms, service the **BK** wire.

9. Check windshield wiper motor power feed. Turn the key to the **OFF** position. Disconnect the windshield wiper motor connectors. Turn the key to the **ON** position. Measure the voltage on the **BL** wire at the windshield wiper motor connector:

    a. If the voltage is greater than 10 volts, service the **BK** wire(s) between the windshield wiper motor and ground.

    b. If the voltage is less than 10 volts, service the **BL** wire.

WINDSHIELD WIPERS INOPERATIVE AT HIGH SPEED

1. Turn the key to the **OFF** position. Disconnect the turn signal/windshield wiper switch connector.

    a. Measure the resistance between the turn signal/windshield wiper switch terminals under the following conditions:

• With the switch in the **HI** position, terminals **BL**-to-**R** should be less than 5 ohms.

• With the switch in the **LO** position, terminals **BL**-to-**BL/W** should be less than 5 ohms.

• With the switch in the **MIST (OFF and pushed)** position, terminals **BL**-to-**R** should be less than 5 ohms.

• With the switch in the **WASH (pulled)** position, terminals **BL**-to-**BL/O** should be less than 5 ohms.

• With the switch in the **OFF** position, terminals **BL/Y**-to-**BL/W** should be less than 5 ohms.

    b. Perform the following procedures:

• If the resistances are okay, go to Step 2.

• If the resistances are not okay, replace the turn signal/windshield wiper switch.

2. Check the windshield wiper motor high speed input, Turn the key to the **OFF** position. Disconnect the windshield wiper motor connector. Turn the key to the **ON** position and place the wipers on **HI**. Measure the voltage on the **R** wire at the windshield wiper motor connector:

    a. If the voltage is greater than 10 volts, replace windshield wiper motor.

    b. If the voltage is less than 10 volts, service the **R** wire.

WINDSHIELD WIPERS INOPERATIVE AT LOW SPEED

1. Turn the key to the **OFF** position. Disconnect the turn signal/windshield wiper switch connector.

    a. Measure the resistance between the turn signal/windshield wiper switch terminals under the following conditions:

• With the switch in the **HI** position, terminals **BL**-to-**R** should be less than 5 ohms.

• With the switch in the **LO** position, terminals **BL**-to-**BL/W** should be less than 5 ohms.

• With the switch in the **MIST (OFF and pushed)** position, terminals **BL**-to-**R** should be less than 5 ohms.

• With the switch in the **WASH (pulled)** position, terminals **BL**-to-**BL/O** should be less than 5 ohms.

• With the switch in the **OFF** position, terminals **BL/Y**-to-**BL/W** should be less than 5 ohms.

    b. Perform the following procedures:

• If the resistances are okay, go to Step 2.

• If the resistances are not okay, replace the turn signal/windshield wiper switch.

2. Check the windshield wiper motor low speed input. Turn the key to the **OFF** position. Disconnect the windshield wiper motor connector. Turn the key to the **ON** position and place the wipers on **LO**. Measure the voltage on the **BL/W** wire at the windshield wiper motor connector:

    a. If the voltage is greater than 10 volts, replace windshield wiper motor.

    b. If the voltage is less than 10 volts, service the **BL/W** wire.

WINDSHIELD WIPERS INOPERATIVE AT INTERVAL SETTING

1. Turn the key to the **OFF** position. Disconnect the turn signal/windshield wiper switch connector.

2. Measure the resistance between the turn signal/windshield wiper switch terminals under the following conditions:

• With the switch in the **HI** position, terminals **BL**-to-**R** should be less than 5 ohms.

• With the switch in the **LO** position, terminals **BL**-to-**BL/W** should be less than 5 ohms.

• With the switch in the **MIST (OFF and pushed)** position, terminals **BL**-to-**R** should be less than 5 ohms.

• With the switch in the **WASH (pulled)** position, terminals **BL**-to-**BL/O** should be less than 5 ohms.

• With the switch in the **OFF** position, terminals **BL/Y**-to-**BL/W** should be less than 5 ohms.

3. Perform the following procedures:

• If the resistances are okay, service the **BL/Y** wire.

• If the resistances are not okay, replace the turn signal/windshield wiper switch.

WINDSHIELD WIPERS WILL NOT TURN OFF

1. Turn the key to the **OFF** position. Disconnect the turn signal/windshield wiper switch connector.

2. Measure the resistance between the turn signal/windshield wiper switch terminals under the following conditions:

• With the switch in the **HI** position, terminals **BL**-to-**R** should be less than 5 ohms.

• With the switch in the **LO** position, terminals **BL**-to-**BL/W** should be less than 5 ohms.

• With the switch in the **MIST (OFF and pushed)** position, terminals **BL**-to-**R** should be less than 5 ohms.

• With the switch in the **WASH (pulled)** position, terminals **BL**-to-**BL/O** should be less than 5 ohms.

• With the switch in the **OFF** position, terminals **BL/Y**-to-**BL/W** should be less than 5 ohms.

3. Perform the following procedures:

• If the resistances are okay, replace the windshield wiper motor.

• If the resistances are not okay, replace the turn signal/windshield wiper switch.

REAR WINDOW WIPER INOPERATIVE

1. Turn the key to the **OFF** position. Check **10A REAR WIPER** fuse.

    a. If fuse is okay, go to Step 4.

    b. If fuse is bad, go to Step 2.

2. Check the system. Turn the key to the **OFF** position. Install and confirm fuse is good. Turn ignition switch **ON** and check that **10A REAR WIPER** fuse does not blow.

    a. If fuse is okay, go to Step 4.

    b. If fuse is bad, go to Step 3.

3. Check for short to ground. Turn ignition switch **OFF**. Disconnect the interior fuse junction panel, the rear window washer pump and the rear window wiper motor connectors. Measure the resistance of the **BL/GN** wire between the interior fuse junction panel connector and ground.

   a. If resistance is greater then 10,000 ohms, install the interior fuse junction panel connector and go to Step 4.

   b. If resistance is less than 10,000 ohms, service the **BL/GN** wire.

4. Check the rear window wiper switch. Turn the key to the **OFF** position. Disconnect the rear window wiper/washer switch connector.

   a. Measure the resistance of the rear window wiper/washer switch terminals, under the following conditions:

   • With the switch in the **REST** position, check terminals **BK**-to-**BL/BK**; the resistance should be greater than 10,000 ohms.

   • With the switch in the **REST** position, check terminals **BK**-to-**O**; the resistance should be greater than 10,000 ohms.

   • With the switch in the **WIPER ON** position, check terminals **BK**-to-**BL/BK**; the resistance should be less than 5 ohms.

   • With the switch in the **WIPER ON** position, check terminals **BK**-to-**O**; the resistance should be greater than 10,000 ohms.

   • With the switch in the **WASHER ON** position, check terminals **BK**-to-**BL/BK**; the resistance should be less than 5 ohms.

   • With the switch in the **WASHER ON** position, check terminals **BK**-to-**O**; the resistance should be less than 5 ohms.

   b. Perform the following procedures:

   • If the resistances are okay, go to Step 5.

   • If the resistances are not okay, replace the rear window wiper/washer switch.

5. Check the rear window wiper motor. Turn the key to the **OFF** position. Disconnect the rear window wiper motor connector. Apply 12 volts to terminal **BL/GN** wire terminal at the rear window wiper motor. Ground the **BL/BK** terminal of at the rear window wiper motor. Perform the following procedure:

   a. If the motor tests okay, go to Step 6.

   b. If the motor does not test okay, replace the rear window wiper motor.

6. Check the rear window wiper motor power supply. Turn the key to the **OFF** position. Disconnect the rear window wiper motor connector. Turn the key to the **ON** position. Measure the voltage on the **BL/GN** wire at the rear window wiper motor connector:

   a. If the voltage is greater than 10 volts, go to Step 7.

   b. If the voltage is less than 10 volts, service the **BL/GN** wire.

7. Check the rear window wiper switch ground. Turn the key to the **OFF** position. Disconnect the rear window wiper/washer switch. Measure the resistance on the **BK** wire between the rear window wiper/washer switch connector and ground:

   a. If the resistance is less than 5 ohms, service the **BL/BK** wire between the rear window wiper motor and rear window wiper/washer switch.

   b. If the resistance is greater than 5 ohms, service the **BK** wire.

REAR WINDOW WIPER WILL NOT SHUT OFF

1. Turn the key to the **OFF** position. Disconnect the rear window wiper/washer switch connector.

2. Measure the resistance of the rear window wiper/washer switch terminals, under the following conditions:

   • With the switch in the **REST** position, check terminals **BK**-to-**BL/BK**; the resistance should be greater than 10,000 ohms.

   • With the switch in the **REST** position, check terminals **BK**-to-**O**; the resistance should be greater than 10,000 ohms.

   • With the switch in the **WIPER ON** position, check terminals **BK**-to-**BL/BK**; the resistance should be less than 5 ohms.

   • With the switch in the **WIPER ON** position, check terminals **BK**-to-**O**; the resistance should be greater than 10,000 ohms.

   • With the switch in the **WASHER ON** position, check terminals **BK**-to-**BL/BK**; the resistance should be less than 5 ohms.

   • With the switch in the **WASHER ON** position, check terminals **BK**-to-**O**; the resistance should be less than 5 ohms.

3. Perform the following procedures:

   • If the resistances are okay, service the **BL/BK** wire between the rear window wiper motor and the rear window wiper/washer switch.

   • If the resistances are not okay, replace the rear window wiper/washer switch.

Probe

WINDSHIELD WASHER INOPERATIVE

1. Check the front wiper fuse. Turn the ignition switch **OFF**.

2. Check the **20A WIPER** fuse.

   a. If the fuse is okay, go the Step 4

   b. If the fuse is not okay, go the Step 2

3. Check system. Turn the ignition switch **OFF**. Install the **20A WIPER** fuse.

   a. If the fuse is okay, go the Step 4

   b. If the fuse is not okay, go the Step 3

4. Check the short to ground check. Turn the ignition switch **OFF**. Disconnect the turn signal/windshield wiper switch, the windshield wiper motor and the interior fuse junction panel connectors. Measure the resistance of the **BL** wire between the fuse junction panel and ground:

   a. If the resistance is less than 5 ohms, service the **BL** wire.

   b. If the resistance is greater than 5 ohms, replace the **20A WIPER** fuse and go the Step 4.

5. Check the windshield washer switch power supply. Turn the ignition switch **OFF**. Reconnect the windshield wiper motor and the interior fuse junction panel connectors. Disconnect the turn signal/windshield wiper switch (harness side). Turn the ignition switch **ON**. Measure the voltage of the **BL** wire at the turn signal/windshield wiper switch connector:

   a. If the voltage is less than 10 volts, service the **BL** wire.

   b. If the voltage is greater than 10 volts, go the Step 5.

6. Check the windshield wiper/washer switch. Turn the ignition switch **OFF**. Reconnect the turn signal/windshield wiper switch connector. Turn the ignition switch **ON**. Depress the windshield washer switch. Measure the voltage of the **BL/O** wire at the turn signal/windshield wiper switch connector. Release the windshield washer switch. Measure the voltage of the **BL/O** wire at the turn signal/windshield wiper switch connector:

   a. If the voltage is less than 10 volts with the switch depressed and/or greater than 1 volt with the switch released, replace the turn signal/windshield wiper switch.

   b. If the voltage is greater than 10 volts with the switch depressed and less than 1 volt with the switch released, go the Step 6.

7. Check the windshield wiper/washer switch and windshield washer pump wire. Turn the ignition switch **OFF**. Disconnect the turn signal/windshield wiper switch and the windshield washer

pump connector. Measure the resistance of the **BL/O** wire between the turn signal/windshield wiper switch connector and the windshield washer pump connector. Measure the resistance of the **BL/O** wire between the turn signal/windshield wiper switch connector and ground:

    a. If the resistance is less than 5 ohms between the turn signal/windshield wiper switch connector and the windshield washer pump connector and greater than 10,000 ohms between the turn signal/windshield wiper switch connector and ground, go the Step 7.

    b. If the resistance is greater than 5 ohms between the turn signal/windshield wiper switch connector and the windshield washer pump connector and less than 10,000 ohms between the turn signal/windshield wiper switch connector and ground, service the **BL/O** wire.

8. Check the windshield washer pump ground. Turn the ignition switch **OFF**. Disconnect the windshield washer pump connector. Measure the resistance of the **BK** wire between the windshield washer pump connector and ground:

    a. If the resistance is less than 5 ohms, replace the windshield washer pump.

    b. If the resistance is greater than 5 ohms, service the **BK** wire.

REAR WINDOW WASHER INOPERATIVE

1. Check the rear wiper fuse. Turn the ignition switch **OFF**. Check the **15A REAR WIPER** fuse.

    a. If the fuse is okay, go the Step 4.

    b. If the fuse is not okay, go the Step 2.

2. Check the system. Turn the ignition switch **OFF**. Install the **15A REAR WIPER** fuse. Turn the ignition switch **ON**.

    a. If the fuse is okay, go the Step 3.

    b. If the fuse is not okay, go the Step 4.

3. Check the short to ground. Turn the ignition switch **OFF**. Disconnect the rear window washer switch, the rear window wiper motor and the interior fuse junction panel connectors. Measure the resistance of the **BL/GN** wire between the fuse junction panel and ground:

    a. If the resistance is less than 5 ohms, service the **BL/GN** wire.

    b. If the resistance is greater than 5 ohms, replace the **15A REAR WIPER** fuse and go the Step 4.

4. Check the rear window washer pump power supply. Turn the ignition switch **OFF**. Reconnect the rear window wiper motor and the interior fuse junction panel connectors. Disconnect the rear window washer pump connector. Turn the ignition switch **ON**. Measure the voltage of the **BL/GN** wire at the rear window washer pump connector:

    a. If the voltage is less than 10 volts, service the **BL/GN** wire.

    b. If the voltage is greater than 10 volts, go the Step 5.

5. Check the rear window washer pump ground. Turn the ignition switch **OFF**. Disconnect the rear window washer pump connector. Depress the rear window washer switch. Measure the resistance of the **BL/Y** wire between the rear window washer pump connector and ground. Release the rear window washer switch. Measure the resistance of the **BL/Y** wire between the rear window washer pump connector and ground:

    a. If the resistance is less than 5 ohms with the rear window washer switch depressed and greater than 10,000 ohms with the rear window washer switch released, replace the rear window washer switch.

    b. If the resistance is greater than 5 ohms with the rear win-

dow washer switch depressed and less than 1 ohm with the rear window washer switch released, go the Step 6.

6. Check the rear window washer switch and pump wire. Turn the ignition switch **OFF**. Disconnect the rear window washer pump and the rear window washer switch connectors. Measure the resistance of the **BL/Y** wire between the rear window washer pump connector and the rear window washer switch connectors. Measure the resistance of the **BL/Y** wire between the rear window washer pump connector and ground:

    a. If the resistance is less than 5 ohms between the rear window washer pump and the rear window washer switch and greater than 10,000 ohms between the rear window washer pump and ground, go the Step 7.

    b. If the resistance is greater than 5 ohms between the rear window washer pump and the rear window washer switch and less than 10,000 ohms between the rear window washer pump and ground, service the **BL/O** wire.

7. Check the rear window washer switch. Turn the ignition switch **OFF**. Disconnect the rear window washer switch connector. Depress the rear window washer switch. Measure the resistance between the **BL/Y** wire terminal and the **BK** wire terminal on the rear window washer switch. Release the rear window washer switch. Measure the resistance between the **BL/Y** wire terminal and the **BK** wire terminal on the rear window washer switch:

    a. If the resistance is less than 5 ohms with the rear window washer switch depressed and greater than 10,000 ohms with rear window washer switch released, service the **BK** wire.

    b. If the resistance is greater than 5 ohms with the rear window washer switch depressed and/or less than 10,000 ohms with rear window washer switch released, replace the rear window washer switch.

WINDSHIELD WIPERS INOPERATIVE IN ALL SWITCH POSITIONS

1. Check the fuse. Turn the ignition switch **OFF**. Check the **20A WIPER** fuse.

    a. If the fuse is okay, go the Step 4.

    b. If the fuse is not okay, go the Step 2.

2. Check the system. Turn the ignition switch **OFF**. Install the **20A WIPER** fuse. Turn the ignition switch **ON**.

    a. If the fuse is okay, go the Step 4.

    b. If the fuse is not okay, go the Step 3.

3. Check for the short to ground. Turn the ignition switch **OFF**. Disconnect the turn signal/windshield wiper switch, the windshield wiper motor and the interior fuse junction panel connectors. Measure the resistance of the **BL** wire between the fuse junction panel and ground:

    a. If the resistance is less than 5 ohms, service the **BL** wire.

    b. If the resistance is greater than 5 ohms, replace the **20A WIPER** fuse and go the Step 4.

4. Check the windshield wiper motor and turn signal/windshield wiper switch power supply. Turn the ignition switch **OFF**. Reconnect the interior fuse junction panel connectors. Disconnect the turn signal/windshield wiper switch and the windshield wiper motor connectors. Turn the ignition switch **ON**. Measure the voltage of the **BL** wire at the turn signal/windshield wiper switch connector and the voltage of the **BL** wire at the windshield wiper motor connector:

    a. If the voltages are less than 10 volts, service the **BL** wire.

    b. If the voltages are greater than 10 volts, go the Step 5.

5. Check the windshield wiper/washer switch. Turn the ignition switch **OFF**. Disconnect the turn signal/windshield wiper switch connector.

6. Measure the resistance of the wire terminals at the switch side of the turn signal/windshield wiper switch connector:

- With the switch in the **OFF** position, the resistance between terminals **BL/BK**-to-**BL/W** should be 5 ohms.
- With the switch in the **INT** position, the resistance between terminals **BL/BK**-to-**BL/W** should be 5 ohms.
- With the switch in the **LO** position, the resistance between terminals **BL**-to-**BL/W** should be 5 ohms.
- With the switch in the **HI** position, the resistance between terminals **BL**-to-**R** should be 5 ohms.
- With the switch in the **MIST** position, the resistance between terminals **BL**-to-**R** should be 5 ohms.
- With the switch in the **WASH** position, the resistance between terminals **BL**-to-**BL/O** should be 5 ohms.

7. Perform the following procedures:

- If the resistances meet the specifications, go the Step 6.
- If the resistances do not meet the specifications, replace the turn signal/windshield wiper switch.

8. Check the windshield wiper/washer switch and windshield washer motor wire. Turn the ignition switch **OFF**. Disconnect the turn signal/windshield wiper switch and the windshield washer motor connector. Measure the resistances between the turn signal/windshield wiper switch connector and the windshield washer motor connector wires: **BL/BK**, **R** and **BL/W**. Measure the resistances between the turn signal/windshield wiper switch connector and ground wires: **BL/BK**, **R** and **BL/W**. Perform the following procedures:

   a. If the resistance is less than 5 ohms between the turn signal/windshield wiper switch connector and the windshield washer motor connector and greater than 10,000 ohms between the turn signal/windshield wiper switch connector and ground, check the **BK** wire between the windshield wiper motor case and ground. If okay, replace the windshield wiper motor.

   b. If the resistance is greater than 5 ohms between the turn signal/windshield wiper switch connector and the windshield washer motor connector and/or less than 10,000 ohms between the turn signal/windshield wiper switch connector and ground, service the wires in question.

WINDSHIELD WIPERS INOPERATIVE AT HIGH SPEED

1. Turn the ignition switch **OFF**. Disconnect the turn signal/windshield wiper switch connector.

   a. Measure the resistance of the wire terminals at the switch side of the turn signal/windshield wiper switch connector:

- With the switch in the **OFF** position, the resistance between terminals **BL/BK**-to-**BL/W** should be 5 ohms.
- With the switch in the **INT** position, the resistance between terminals **BL/BK**-to-**BL/W** should be 5 ohms.
- With the switch in the **LO** position, the resistance between terminals **BL**-to-**BL/W** should be 5 ohms.
- With the switch in the **HI** position, the resistance between terminals **BL**-to-**R** should be 5 ohms.
- With the switch in the **MIST** position, the resistance between terminals **BL**-to-**R** should be 5 ohms.
- With the switch in the **WASH** position, the resistance between terminals **BL**-to-**BL/O** should be 5 ohms.

   b. Perform the following procedures:

- If the resistances meet the specifications, go the Step 2.
- If the resistances do not meet the specifications, replace the turn signal/windshield wiper switch.

2. Check the circuit. Turn the ignition switch **OFF**. Disconnect the windshield wiper motor connector. Turn the windshield wiper switch to **HIGH**. Measure the voltage of the **R** wire at the windshield wiper motor connector:

- If the voltage is less than 10 volts, service the **R** wire.
- If the voltage is greater than 10 volts, service the windshield motor.

WINDSHIELD WIPERS INOPERATIVE AT LOW SPEED

1. Turn the ignition switch **OFF**. Disconnect the turn signal/windshield wiper switch connector.

   a. Measure the resistance of the wire terminals at the switch side of the turn signal/windshield wiper switch connector:

- With the switch in the **OFF** position, the resistance between terminals **BL/BK**-to-**BL/W** should be 5 ohms.
- With the switch in the **INT** position, the resistance between terminals **BL/BK**-to-**BL/W** should be 5 ohms.
- With the switch in the **LO** position, the resistance between terminals **BL**-to-**BL/W** should be 5 ohms.
- With the switch in the **HI** position, the resistance between terminals **BL**-to-**R** should be 5 ohms.
- With the switch in the **MIST** position, the resistance between terminals **BL**-to-**R** should be 5 ohms.
- With the switch in the **WASH** position, the resistance between terminals **BL**-to-**BL/O** should be 5 ohms.

   b. Perform the following procedures:

- If the resistances meet the specifications, go the Step 2.
- If the resistances do not meet the specifications, replace the turn signal/windshield wiper switch.

2. Check the circuit. Turn the ignition switch **OFF**. Disconnect the windshield wiper motor connector. Turn the ignition switch to **ON**. Turn the windshield wiper switch to **LOW**. Measure the voltage of the **BL/W** wire at the windshield wiper motor connector:

   a. If the voltage is less than 10 volts, service the **BL/W** wire.

   b. If the voltage is greater than 10 volts, service the windshield motor.

WINDSHIELD WIPERS INOPERATIVE AT INTERVAL SETTINGS

1. Turn the ignition switch **OFF**. Disconnect the windshield wiper motor connector. Measure the resistance between the windshield wiper motor case and ground to ensure the resistance is less than 5 ohms. Apply 12 volts to terminal **BL/W** of the windshield wiper motor; **LO** speed wiper operation should result. Apply 12 volts to terminal **R** of the windshield wiper motor; **HI** speed wiper operation should result. Perform the following procedures:

2. If the testing specifications are met, replace the turn signal/windshield wiper switch.

3. If the testing specifications are not met, replace the windshield wiper motor.

WINDSHIELD WIPERS WILL NOT PARK BELOW THE GLASS

1. Turn the ignition switch **OFF**. Disconnect the windshield wiper motor connector. Turn the ignition switch to **ON**. Measure the voltage of the **BL** wire at the windshield wiper motor connector:

   a. If the voltage is less than 10 volts, service the **BL** wire.

   b. If the voltage is greater than 10 volts, go to Step 2.

2. Check the windshield wiper motor. Turn the ignition switch

OFF. Disconnect the windshield wiper motor connector. Measure the resistance between the windshield wiper motor case and ground to ensure the resistance is less than 5 ohms. Apply 12 volts to terminal **BL/W** of the windshield wiper motor; **LO** speed wiper operation should result. Apply 12 volts to terminal **R** of the windshield wiper motor; **HI** speed wiper operation should result. Perform the following procedures:

　　a. If the testing specifications are met, go to Step 3.

　　b. If the testing specifications are not met, replace the windshield wiper motor.

3. Check the windshield wiper/washer switch and windshield washer motor wire. Turn the ignition switch **OFF**. Disconnect the turn signal/windshield wiper switch and the windshield washer motor connector. Measure the resistance of the **BL/BK** wire between the turn signal/windshield wiper switch connector and the windshield washer motor connector wires. Measure the resistance of the **BL/BK** wire between the turn signal/windshield wiper switch connector and ground wires. Perform the following procedures:

　　a. If the resistance is less than 5 ohms between the turn signal/windshield wiper switch connector and the windshield washer motor connector and greater than 10,000 ohms between the turn signal/windshield wiper switch connector and ground, replace the turn signal/windshield wiper switch.

　　b. If the resistance is greater than 5 ohms between the turn signal/windshield wiper switch connector and the windshield washer motor connector and/or less than 10,000 ohms between the turn signal/windshield wiper switch connector and ground, service the **BL/BK** wire.

WINDSHIELD WIPERS WILL NOT TURN OFF

1. Turn the ignition switch **OFF**. Disconnect the turn signal/windshield wiper switch connector.

2. Measure the resistance of the wire terminals at the switch side of the turn signal/windshield wiper switch connector:

● With the switch in the **OFF** position, the resistance between terminals **BL/BK**-to-**BL/W** should be 5 ohms.

● With the switch in the **INT** position, the resistance between terminals **BL/BK**-to-**BL/W** should be 5 ohms.

● With the switch in the **LO** position, the resistance between terminals **BL**-to-**BL/W** should be 5 ohms.

● With the switch in the **HI** position, the resistance between terminals **BL**-to-**R** should be 5 ohms.

● With the switch in the **MIST** position, the resistance between terminals **BL**-to-**R** should be 5 ohms.

● With the switch in the **WASH** position, the resistance between terminals **BL**-to-**BL/O** should be 5 ohms.

3. Perform the following procedures:

● If the resistances meet the specifications, service the **R** or **BL/W** wire between the turn signal/windshield wiper switch and windshield motor for short.

● If the resistances do not meet the specifications, replace turn signal/windshield wiper switch.

REAR WINDOW WIPER INOPERATIVE

1. Turn the ignition switch **OFF**. Check the **15A REAR WIPER** fuse.

　　a. If the fuse is okay, go the Step 4.

　　b. If the fuse is not okay, go the Step 2.

2. Check the system. Turn the ignition switch **OFF**. Install the **15A REAR WIPER** fuse. Turn the ignition switch **ON**.

　　a. If the fuse is okay, go the Step 4.

　　b. If the fuse is not okay, go the Step 3.

3. Check the short to ground. Turn the ignition switch **OFF**. Disconnect the rear window wiper pump, the rear window wiper motor and the interior fuse junction panel connectors. Measure the resistance of the **BL/GN** wire between the fuse junction panel and ground:

　　a. If the resistance is less than 5 ohms, service the **BL/GN** wire.

　　b. If the resistance is greater than 5 ohms, replace the **15A REAR WIPER** fuse and go the Step 4.

4. Check the rear window wiper motor power supply. Turn the ignition switch **OFF**. Disconnect the fuse junction panel connector. Disconnect the rear window wiper motor connector. Turn the ignition switch to **ON**. Measure the voltage of the **BL/GN** wire at the rear window wiper motor connector:

　　a. If the voltage is less than 10 volts, service the **BL/GN** wire.

　　b. If the voltage is greater than 10 volts, go to Step 5.

5. Check the rear window wiper motor ground. Turn the ignition switch **OFF**. Disconnect the rear window wiper motor switch. Depress the rear window wiper motor connector. Measure the resistance of the **BK/BL** wire between the rear window wiper motor connector and ground. Perform the following procedures:

　　a. If the resistance is less than 5 ohms with the rear window wiper motor switch depressed and greater than 10,000 ohms with the rear window wiper motor switch released, replace the rear window wiper motor.

　　b. If the resistance is greater than 5 ohms with the rear window wiper motor switch depressed and/or less than 10,000 ohms with the rear window wiper motor switch released, go to Step 6.

6. Check the rear window wiper motor-to-rear window switch wire. Turn the ignition switch **OFF**. Disconnect the rear window wiper motor switch connector and the rear window wiper motor connector. Measure the resistance of the **BK/BL** wire between the rear window wiper motor connector and the rear window wiper motor switch connector. Measure the resistance of the **BK/BL** wire between the rear window wiper motor connector and ground. Perform the following procedures:

　　a. If the resistance is less than 5 ohms between the rear window wiper motor and the rear window wiper motor switch and greater than 10,000 ohms between the rear window wiper motor and ground, go to Step 7.

　　b. If the resistance is greater than 5 ohms between the rear window wiper motor and the rear window wiper motor switch and/or less than 10,000 ohms between the rear window wiper motor and ground, service, the **BK/BL** wire.

7. Check the rear window wiper switch. Turn the ignition switch **OFF**. Disconnect the rear window wiper switch connector.

8. Depress the rear window wiper switch. Measure the resistance of the **BK/BL** wire terminal and the **BK** wire terminal on the rear window wiper switch. Release the rear window wiper switch. Measure the resistance of the **BK/BL** wire terminal and the **BK** wire terminal on the rear window wiper switch. Perform the following procedures:

　　a. If the resistance is less than 5 ohms with the rear window wiper switch depressed and greater than 10,000 ohms with the rear window wiper switch released, service the **BK** wire between the rear window wiper switch connector and ground.

　　b. If the resistance is greater than 5 ohms with the rear window wiper switch depressed and/or less than 10,000 ohms with the rear window wiper switch released, replace the rear window wiper switch.

REAR WINDOW WIPER WILL NOT PARK

1. Turn the ignition switch **ON**. Turn the rear window wiper **ON**. Turn the ignition switch **OFF** when the rear window wiper is not in the park position. Disconnect the rear window wiper switch connector. Measure the resistance between the **BK/BL** wire terminal at the rear window wiper motor connector and the rear window wiper motor ground terminal. Perform the following procedures:

　　a. If the resistance is less than 5 ohms with the rear window wiper out of the park position, go to Step 2.

　　b. If the resistance is greater than 5 ohms with the rear window wiper out of the park position, replace the rear window wiper motor.

2. Check the rear window wiper park position. Turn the ignition switch **OFF**. Reconnect the rear window wiper motor connector. Turn the ignition switch **ON**. Turn the ignition switch **OFF** when the rear window wiper reaches the park position. Disconnect the rear window wiper motor connector. Measure the resistance between the **BK/BL** wire terminal at the rear window wiper motor connector and the rear window wiper motor ground terminal. Perform the following procedures:

　　a. If the resistance is less than 10,000 ohms with the rear window wiper in the park position, replace the rear window wiper motor.

　　b. If the resistance is greater than 10,000 ohms with the rear window wiper in the park position, service the rear window wiper motor ground wire and/or the rear window wiper motor ground wire terminal.

REAR WINDOW WIPER WILL NOT TURN OFF

1. Turn the ignition switch **OFF**. Disconnect the rear window wiper switch connector. Depress the rear window wiper switch. Measure the resistance of the **BK/BL** wire terminal and the **BK** wire terminal on the rear window wiper switch. Release the rear window wiper switch. Measure the resistance of the **BK/BL** wire terminal and the **BK** wire terminal on the rear window wiper switch. Perform the following procedures:

　　a. If the resistance is less than 5 ohms with the rear window wiper switch depressed and greater than 10,000 ohms with the rear window wiper switch released, go to Step 2.

　　b. If the resistance is greater than 5 ohms with the rear window wiper switch depressed and/or less than 10,000 ohms with the rear window wiper switch released, replace the rear window wiper switch.

2. Check the circuit. Turn the ignition switch **OFF**. Disconnect the rear window wiper motor connector. Measure the resistance the **BK/BL** wire between the rear window wiper motor connector and ground. Perform the following procedures:

　　a. If the resistance is less than 10,000 ohms, service the **BK/BL** wire.

　　b. If the resistance is greater than 10,000 ohms, replace the rear window wiper motor.

Cougar and Thunderbird

WINDSHIELD WASHERS DO NOT OPERATE

1. Check the fluid level of the windshield washer reservoir.
　　a. If empty, fill the reservoir.
　　b. If OK, go to Step 2.

2. Activate the turn signal/windshield wiper switch and check the washer pump operation.

　　a. If the windshield washer pump will squirt fluid, go to Step 11.

　　b. If the windshield washer pump will not squirt fluid, go to Step 3.

3. Activate the turn signal/windshield wiper switch and check the washer operation.

　　a. If the windshield washer runs and will squirt fluid, go to Step 4.

　　b. If the windshield washer runs but will not squirt fluid, go to Step 9.

4. Check windshield washer hoses and nozzles for kinks or blockage.

　　a. If the hoses and nozzles are kinked or blocked, clean, repair or replace as necessary.

　　b. If the hoses and nozzles are OK, go to Step 5.

5. Check the washer hose at the windshield washer pump outlet for blockage.

　　a. If the washer pump is blocked, remove the washer pump from reservoir and clean or replace it.

　　b. If the washer pump is not blocked, replace the windshield washer pump.

6. Using an voltmeter or test lamp, check for voltage at the windshield washer pump by operating the turn signal/windshield washer switch.

　　a. If voltage is found, go to Step 7.

　　b. If no voltage is found, go to Step 8.

7. Using an ohmmeter, check the ground at the windshield washer pump.

　　a. If ground is found, replace the pump.

　　b. If no ground is found, repair the wiring.

8. Check the power at the switch by operating the turn signal/windshield wiper switch.

　　a. If wipers operate, go to Step 9.

　　b. If wipers do not operate, go to Step 10.

9. Using an voltmeter or test lamp, activate the turn signal/windshield washer switch and check for voltage at terminal **BK/W** (circuit **941**) of the wiper switch.

　　a. If voltage is found, go to Step 11.

　　b. If voltage is not found, go to Step 12.

10. Activate the heater blower.

　　a. If the heater blower motor runs, go to Step 11.

　　b. If the heater blower motor will not run, service the open circuit in the power feed wiring.

11. Check the windshield wiper/washer fuse.

　　a. If the circuit breaker is operational, go to Step 12.

　　b. If the circuit breaker is not operational, replace the fuse.

12. Check the turn signal/windshield wiper switch.

　　a. If the turn signal/windshield wiper switch circuits are functional, go to Step 13.

　　b. If the turn signal/windshield wiper switch circuits are not functional, replace the turn signal/windshield wiper switch.

13. Using an ohmmeter, perform the following tests on the windshield wiper switch:

• With the wash switch turned **OFF**, the resistance of pin **4**-to-**2** should be 3.3 kilo-ohms.

• With the wash switch turned **ON**, the resistance is closed to pin **4**-to-**2**.

• With the wiper switch turned **OFF** and the wash switch turned

Windshield wiper test—terminal identification—Cougar and Thunderbird

OFF, the resistance of pin **4**-to-**2** should be 103.3 kilo-ohms and the resistance of pin **4**-to-**6** should be 47.6 kilo-ohms.

• With the wiper interval switch at **MAX** delay (closest position to OFF) to **MIN** delay (closest position to **LO**), the resistance is of pin **4**-to-**2** should be 11.33 kilo-ohms and linearly decreasing from 103.3 kilo-ohms to 3.3 kilo-ohms.

• With the wiper switch turned **LO** and the wash switch turned **OFF**, the resistance of pin **4**-to-**2** should be 3.3 kilo-ohms and the resistance of pin **4**-to-**6** should be 4.08 kilo-ohms.

• With the wiper switch turned **HI** and the wash switch turned **OFF**, the resistance of pin **4**-to-**2** should be 3.3 kilo-ohms and closed to pin **4**-to-**6**.

 a. If the switch test are OK, service the wiper/washer wiring and connectors.

 b. If the switch test are not OK, service the switch.

WIPERS DO NOT WORK IN ANY SWITCH POSITION

1. Unplug the wiper motor connector, set the turn signal/windshield wiper switch on **HIGH**, and check for battery voltage at circuits **65 (DG)** and **56 (DB/O)**.

 a. If voltage is found, go to Step 2.

 b. If no voltage is found:

• Check for a malfunctioning turn signal/windshield wiper switch.

• Check for an open connector.

• Check for an open wire in circuit **56 (DB/O)** or **65 (DG)**.

2. Check the wiper motor current draw:

• Disconnect the windshield wiper mounting arm and pivot shaft from the windshield wiper motor.

• Disconnect the electrical connector from the wiper motor.

• Connect the green lead from the test equipment to the battery positive **(+)** post.

• Connect the positive **(R)** lead from the tester to the common brush terminal (circuit **61**).

• Attach a ground first to the low speed connection (circuit **56**) and then to the high speed connection (circuit **58**) at the connector plug.

• In either case, the current draw should not exceed 3.5 amps.

 a. If the tests are performed OK, check the linkage for binding and service as necessary.

 b. If the tests are not performed OK, repair motor as necessary.

WIPERS DO NOT WORK IN HIGH SPEED SWITCH POSITION

1. Turn the turn signal/windshield wiper switch to **LOW**.

 a. If the low speed works, go to Step 4.

 b. If the low speed does not work, go to Step 2.

2. Turn the ignition switch **ON** and the turn signal/windshield wiper switch to **HI**. Unplug the windshield wiper motor connector. Check the battery voltage at circuits **65 (DG)**.

 a. If battery voltage is found, go to Step 3.

 b. If no voltage is found:

• Check for an open circuit breaker in the fuse junction panel.

• Check for an open connector.

• Check for an open wire in circuit **65 (DG)**.

• Check for poor ground connection, service as required.

3. Check the battery voltage at circuit **65 (DG)** pin 5 of the connector at the fuse junction panel.

 a. If battery voltage is present, go to Step 4.

 b. If battery voltage is not present:

• Service an open in the power feed to malfunction indicator lamp control.

• Check for an open unseated connector.

• Check for an open wire in circuit **65 (DG)**.

4. Turn the ignition switch to the **RUN** position. Turn the turn signal/windshield wiper switch to **HI**. Disconnect windshield wiper motor connector. Check the battery voltage at circuit **61 (Y/R)** and **58 (W)**.

 a. If battery voltage is present, go to Step 7.

 b. If battery voltage is not present, go to Step 5.

5. Check for battery voltage between the malfunction indicator lamp control and pin **2** of the fuse junction panel.

 a. If battery voltage is present, check for an open wire, an open connector and/or an unseated connector, service as necessary.

 b. If battery voltage is not present, go to Step 6.

6. Disconnect the malfunction indicator lamp control connector. Measure the resistance between circuits **993 (BR/W)** and **589 (O)**.

 a. If the resistance is less than 1.0 ohm, replace the malfunction indicator lamp control.

 b. If the resistance is greater than 1.0 ohm:

• Check for an open wire between the turn signal/windshield wiper switch and the malfunction indicator lamp control.

• Check for a damaged turn signal/windshield wiper switch, service as required.

7. Disconnect the turn signal/windshield wiper switch connector. Measure the resistance between circuits **993 (BR/W)** and **589 (O)**.

 a. If the resistance is less than 1.0 ohm, go to Step 8.

 b. If the resistance is greater than 1.0 ohm, check for a damaged turn signal/windshield wiper switch, service as required.

8. Check the wiper motor current draw:

• Disconnect the windshield wiper mounting arm and pivot shaft from the windshield wiper motor.

• Disconnect the electrical connector from the wiper motor.

• Connect the green lead from the test equipment to the battery positive **(+)** post.

• Connect the positive **(R)** lead from the tester to the common brush terminal (circuit **61**).

• Attach a ground first to the low speed connection (circuit **56**) and then to the high speed connection (circuit **58**) at the connector plug.

• In either case, the current draw should not exceed 3.5 amps.

 a. If the tests are performed OK, check the linkage for binding and service as necessary.

 b. If the tests are not performed OK, repair motor as necessary.

WIPERS DO NOT WORK IN LOW SPEED SWITCH POSITION

1. Turn the turn signal/windshield wiper switch to **HIGH**.
   a. If the low speed works, go to Step 4.
   b. If the low speed does not work, go to Step 2.
2. Turn the ignition switch to the **RUN** position and the turn signal/windshield wiper switch to **HI**. Unplug the windshield wiper motor connector. Check the battery voltage at circuits **65 (DG)**.
   a. If battery voltage is found, go to Step 3.
   b. If no voltage is found:
   • Check for an open circuit breaker in the fuse junction panel.
   • Check for an open connector.
   • Check for an open wire in circuit **65 (DG)**.
   • Check for poor ground connection, service as required.
3. Check the battery voltage at circuit **65 (DG)** pin 5 of the connector at the fuse junction panel.
   a. If battery voltage is present, go to Step 4.
   b. If battery voltage is not present:

• Service an open in the power feed to malfunction indicator lamp control.
• Check for an open unseated connector.
• Check for an open wire in circuit **65 (DG)**.
4. Turn the ignition switch to the **RUN** position. Turn the turn signal/windshield wiper switch to **LO**. Disconnect windshield wiper motor connector. Check the battery voltage at circuit **56 (DB/O)** and **58 (W)**.
   a. If battery voltage is present, go to Step 7.
   b. If battery voltage is not present, go to Step 5.
5. Check for battery voltage between circuit **56 (DB/O)** and **58 (W)** of the malfunction indicator lamp control connector.
   a. If battery voltage is present, check for an open wire in circuit **56 (DB/O)** or **58 (W)**, an open connector and/or an unseated connector, service as necessary.
   b. If battery voltage is not present, go to Step 6.
6. Disconnect the malfunction indicator lamp control connector. Measure the resistance between circuits **993 (BR/W)** and **589 (O)**.

Windshield wiper/washer system—Cougar and Thunderbird

8838XG23

MALFUNCTION INDICATOR LAMP
CONTROL 12-PIN LC-12 CONNECTOR

Pin Number	Circuit	Circuit Function
1	296 (W/P)	ACC-RUN
2	54 (LG/Y)	+Battery
3	53 (BK/LB)	Courtesy Lamps
4	640 (R/Y)	RUN-START
5	65 (DG)	ACC-RUN

MALFUNCTION INDICATOR LAMP CONTROL
8 PIN S CONNECTOR

Pin Number	Circuit	Circuit Function
1	56 (W)	Wiper Motor—HI
2	705 (LG/O)	Engine Compartment Lamp
3	705 (LG/O)	+Battery
4	705 (LG/O)	Glove Compartment Lamp
5	28 (BK/PK)	Wiper PARK—RUN Switch
6	941 (BK/WH)	Washer Motor
7	56 (DB/O)	Wiper Motor—LO
8	—	Not Used

Pin Number	Circuit	Circuit Function
1	993 (BR/W)	Wiper Switch Return
2	57 (BK)	Ground
3	—	Not Used
4	159 (R/PK)	Driver's Door Switch
5	85 (BR/LB)	Seat Belt Switch
6	450 (DG/LG)	Seat Belt Warning Lamp
7	590 (DB/W)	Wiper Switch—Delay
8	589 (O)	Wiper Switch—Mode
9	482 (P)	MIL Warning
10	465 (W/LB)	Door Handle Switch
11	257 (W/R)	Headlamp Switch
12	158 (BK/PK)	Key in Switch

MALFUNCTION INDICATOR LAMP CONTROL
5-PIN J/B CONNECTOR

TURN SIGNAL AND WINDSHIELD
WIPER SWITCH CONNECTOR

8838XG24

**Description and identification of the electrical connectors—Cougar
and Thunderbird**

a. If the resistance is between 3.5–4.5 ohms, replace the malfunction indicator lamp control.

b. If the resistance is not between 3.5–4.5 ohms:

• Check for an open wire between the turn signal/windshield wiper switch and the malfunction indicator lamp control.

• Check for a damaged turn signal/windshield wiper switch, service as required.

7. Disconnect the turn signal/windshield wiper switch connector. Measure the resistance between circuits **993 (BR/W)** and **589 (O)**.

a. If the resistance is between 3.5–4.5 ohms, go to Step 8.

b. If the resistance is not between 3.5–4.5 ohms, check for a damaged turn signal/windshield wiper switch, service as required.

8. Check the wiper motor current draw:

• Disconnect the windshield wiper mounting arm and pivot shaft from the windshield wiper motor.

• Disconnect the electrical connector from the wiper motor.

• Connect the green lead from the test equipment to the battery positive **(+)** post.

• Connect the positive **(R)** lead from the tester to the common brush terminal (circuit **61**).

• Attach a ground first to the low speed connection (circuit **56**) and then to the high speed connection (circuit **58**) at the connector plug.

• In either case, the current draw should not exceed 3.5 amps.

a. If the tests are performed OK, check the linkage for binding and service as necessary.

b. If the tests are not performed OK, repair motor as necessary.

Pin Number	Circuit	Circuit Function
1	196 (DB/O)	Supply-Hot At All Times
2	590 (DB/W)	Wiper Switch-Delay
3	12 (LG/BK)	High Beam Feed
4	993 (BR/W)	Wiper Switch Return
5	13 (R/BK)	Low Beam Feed
6	589 (O)	Wiper Switch-Mode
7	15 (R/Y)	Feed-Headlamps ON

VEHICLE MAINTENANCE
MONITOR CONNECTOR

WINDSHIELD
WIPER MOTOR

Pin Number	Circuit	Circuit Function
1	57 (BK)	Ground Circuit
2	28 (BK/PK)	Windshield Wiper Switch to Windshield Wiper Motor
3	65 (DG)	Windshield Wiper Switch to Windshield Wiper Motor
4	57 (BK)	Ground Circuit
5	56 (DB/O)	Windshield Wiper Switch to Windshield Wiper Motor
6	58 (W)	Windshield Wiper Switch to Windshield Wiper Motor

Pin Number	Circuit	Circuit Function
1	57 (BK)	Ground
2	—	Not Used
3	—	Not Used
4	29 (Y/W)	Fuel Level
5	—	Not Used
6	82 (PK/Y)	Washer Fluid Level
7	794 (LB)	Coolant Level Sensor
8	419 (DG/LG)	Firm Ride ON Input
9	627 (BK/O)	Door Ajar Input
10	960 (BK/LB)	Traction ON Indicator Input
11	298 (P/O)	Ignition Power
12	959 (G/Y)	Traction Assist Switch Output

8838XG25

Description and identification of the electrical connectors—Cougar and Thunderbird, Cont.

WIPERS DO NOT WORK AT INTERVAL SETTING POSITIONS

1. Set the wiper switch to interval.
   a. If the slow(s) speed work(s), go to Step 2.
   b. If the slow(s) speed do not work(s), go to Wipers do not Work in Low Speed Position procedure.
2. Disconnect the connector from the malfunction indicator lamp control. Measure the resistance between terminals for circuits **993 (BR/W)** and **589 (O)**.
   a. If the resistance is between 10.5 kilo-ohms and 12.0 kilo-ohms, go to Step 4.
   b. If the resistance is not between 10.5 kilo-ohms and 12.0 kilo-ohms, go to Step 3.
3. Disconnect the connector from the turn signal/windshield wiper switch. Measure the resistance between circuits **993 (BR/W)** and **589 (O)**.
   a. If the resistance is between 10.5 kilo-ohms and 12.0 kilo-ohms, check for an open wire between the turn signal/windshield wiper switch and the windshield wiper governor, service as required.
   b. If the resistance is not between 10.5 kilo-ohms and 12.0 kilo-ohms, check for a damaged turn signal/windshield wiper switch, service as required.
4. Rotate the interval control on the turn signal/windshield wiper switch from **S** to **F**. Measure the resistance between circuits **993 (BR/W)** and **590 (DB/W)**.
   a. If the resistance is between 3.3–103.3 kilo-ohms, replace the windshield wiper governor.
   b. If the resistance is not between 3.3–103.3 kilo-ohms, go to Step 5.
5. Disconnect the harness from the turn signal/windshield wiper switch. Rotate the interval control on the turn signal/windshield wiper switch from **S** to **F**. Measure the resistance between terminals of circuits **993 (BR/W)** and **590 (DB/W)**.
   a. If the resistance is between 3.3–103.3 kilo-ohms, check for open wires between turn signal/windshield wiper switch and windshield wiper governor, serviced as required.
   b. If the resistance is not between 3.3–103.3 kilo-ohms, check for a damaged turn signal/windshield wiper switch, serviced as required.

WIPERS WILL NOT PARK AT PROPER POSITION

1. Turn the ignition switch to the **OFF** position and the turn signal/windshield wiper switch to **OFF**. Unplug the windshield wiper motor connector. Check for continuity between circuits **28 (BK/PK)** and **56 (DB/O)**.
   a. If continuity is found, go to Step 4.
   b. If continuity is not found, go to Step 2.
2. Locate the malfunction indicator lamp control at the fuse junction panel and disconnect its electrical connector. Check for continuity between pins **7** and **8**.
   a. If continuity is found, check for an unseated connector or an open circuit between the malfunction indicator lamp control and the windshield wiper motor, service as required.
   b. If continuity is not found, go to Step 3.
3. Measure the resistance between circuits **993 (BR/W)** and **589 (O)**.
   a. If the resistance is between 45 kilo-ohms and 50 kilo-ohms, replace the malfunction indicator lamp control.

   b. If the resistance is not between 45 kilo-ohms and 50 kilo-ohms:
   • Check for a damaged turn signal/windshield wiper switch, service as required.
   • Check for an open unseated turn signal/windshield wiper switch connector.
   • Check for an open wire in circuit **993 (BR/W)** and **589 (O)**.
4. Turn the ignition switch to the **RUN** position. Disconnect the windshield wiper motor connector. Using a voltmeter, connect 1 lead to a good ground and the other lead to circuit **65 (DG)**; then, read the voltage.
   a. If battery voltage is present, go to Step 5.
   b. If battery voltage is not present, service circuit **65 (DG)**, restore vehicle and retest system.
5. Using a voltmeter at the windshield wiper motor connector, connect 1 lead to circuit **65 (DG)** and the other lead to circuit **57 (BK)**; then, read the voltage.
   a. If battery voltage is present, go to Step 6.
   b. If battery voltage is not present, service circuit **57 (BK)**, restore vehicle and retest system.
6. Connect its electrical connector to the windshield wiper motor. Using an ohmmeter at the windshield wiper motor connector, connect 1 lead to circuit **28 (BK/PK)** and the other lead to the ground terminal; then, read the ohmmeter.
   a. If continuity is found, go to Step 7.
   b. If continuity is not found, replace the windshield wiper motor, restore vehicle and retest system.
7. Inspect the windshield wiper mounting arm and pivot shaft.
   a. If the windshield wiper mounting arm is bent or cracked, service as required, restore vehicle and retest system.
   b. If the windshield wiper mounting arm is not bent or cracked, go to Step 8.
8. Using an ohmmeter, perform the following tests on the windshield wiper switch:
   • With the wash switch turned **OFF**, the resistance of pin **4**-to-**2** should be 3.3 kilo-ohms.
   • With the wash switch turned **ON**, the resistance is closed to pin **4**-to-**2**.
   • With the wiper switch turned **OFF** and the wash switch turned **OFF**, the resistance of pin **4**-to-**2** should be 103.3 kilo-ohms and the resistance of pin **4**-to-**6** should be 47.6 kilo-ohms.
   • With the wiper interval switch at **MAX** delay (closest position to **OFF**) to **MIN** delay (closest position to **LO**), the resistance is of pin **4**-to-**2** should be 11.33 kilo-ohms and linearly decreasing from 103.3 kilo-ohms to 3.3 kilo-ohms.
   • With the wiper switch turned **LO** and the wash switch turned **OFF**, the resistance of pin **4**-to-**2** should be 3.3 kilo-ohms and the resistance of pin **4**-to-**6** should be 4.08 kilo-ohms.
   • With the wiper switch turned **HI** and the wash switch turned **OFF**, the resistance of pin **4**-to-**2** should be 3.3 kilo-ohms and closed to pin **4**-to-**6**.
   a. If the switch test are OK, replace the malfunction indicator lamp control, restore the vehicle and retest the system.
   b. If the switch test are not OK, replace the turn signal/windshield wiper switch, restore the vehicle and retest the system.

WIPERS RUN WHEN SWITCH IS TURNED OFF

1. Disconnect the electrical connector from the windshield wiper motor and the wires at the malfunction indicator lamp control. Check for continuity of circuit **28 (BK/PK)**.

a. If continuity is found, go to Step 2.

b. If continuity is not found, check for an unseated component or a damaged windshield wiper motor, service as required.

2. Measure the continuity of circuits **28 (BK/PK)** and **56 (DB/O)** at the malfunction indicator lamp control.

a. If continuity is found, check for an open circuit between the malfunction indicator lamp control and windshield wiper motor, service as required.

b. If continuity is not found, go to Step 3.

3. Measure the resistance between circuits **589 (O)** and **993 (BR/W)** at the wiper switch.

a. If resistance is between 45 kilo-ohms and 50 kilo-ohms, replace the malfunction indicator lamp control.

b. If resistance is not between 45 kilo-ohms and 50 kilo-ohms, check for and open circuit at **589 (O)** or **993 (BR/W)** between the turn signal/windshield wiper switch and malfunction indicator lamp control or a damaged turn signal/windshield wiper switch. Service as required.

Crown Victoria, Grand Marquis and Town Car

WINDSHIELD WIPERS INOPERATIVE

1. Check the fluid level in the reservoir.

a. If the fluid level is OK, go to Step 2.

b. If the fluid level is low, fill the reservoir.

2. Activate the turn signal/windshield wiper switch and check the washer pump operation.

a. If the washer pump squirts fluid, go to Step 11.

b. If the washer pump does not squirt fluid, go to Step 3.

3. Activate the turn signal/windshield wiper switch and check the washer pump operation.

a. If the washer pump runs but not squirt fluid, go to Step 9.

b. If the washer pump and squirts fluid, go to Step 4.

4. Turn the ignition switch **ON**, depress the turn signal/windshield wiper switch and check for battery voltage at circuit **941 (BK/W)** at the windshield wiper motor.

a. If the battery voltage is present, go to Step 8.

Windshield wiper/washer electrical schematic—Continental, Crown Victoria, Grand Marquis and Town Car—Continental, Mark VIII, Sable and Taurus are similar

Wire Harness Connector End View

WINDSHIELD WIPER GOVERNOR

Pin Number	Circuit	Circuit Function
1	589 (O)	Turn Signal and Windshield Wiper Switch
2	65 (DG)	Hot in ACC or RUN
3	57 (BK)	Ground
4	941 (BK/W)	Windshield Washer Pump
5	57 (BK)	Ground
6	28 (BK/PK)	Windshield Wiper Motor
7	993 (BR/W)	Windshield Wiper Governor to Turn Signal and Windshield Wiper Switch

Pin Number	Circuit	Circuit Function
8	56 (DB/O)	Windshield Wiper Motor-Lo
9	590 (DB/W)	Interval Switch
10	—	Not Used
11	—	Not Used
12	61 (Y/R)	Windshield Wiper Motor Switch-Parked Position
13	63 (R)	Turn Signal and Windshield Wiper Switch
14	58 (W)	Windshield Wiper Motor-Hi

8838XG27

Windshield wiper governor electrical terminal description—Continental, Crown Victoria, Mark VIII, Grand Marquis and Town Car

b. If the battery voltage is not present, go to Step 5.

5. Check for battery voltage at circuit **65 (DG)** at the windshield wiper governor pin **J1-2**.

a. If battery voltage is present, go to Step 6.

b. If battery voltage is not present, check for an open circuit breaker, an open connector and/or an open wire circuit **65 (DG)**, service as required.

6. Disconnect the windshield wiper governor connector, depress the turn signal/windshield wiper switch and measure the resistance between circuits **993 (BR/W)** and **590 (DB/W)**.

a. If there is continuity, go to Step 7.

b. If there is no continuity:

• Check for an open wire between the turn signal/windshield wiper switch and the windshield wiper governor.

• Check for a damaged turn signal/windshield wiper switch, service or replace as required.

7. Connect the windshield wiper governor connector, turn the ignition switch to **RUN**, depress the turn signal/windshield wiper switch and measure the voltage at circuit **58 (W)** at the windshield wiper governor connector.

a. If battery voltage is present, check for an open circuit **58 (W)** between the windshield wiper governor and windshield wiper motor.

b. If battery voltage is not present, replace the damaged windshield wiper governor.

8. Using an ohmmeter, check the ground at the windshield washer pump.

a. If the ground is functional, replace the windshield washer pump.

b. If the ground is functional, service the ground.

9. Inspect window washer hose and windshield washer nozzle jet and bracket for blockage or window washer hose kinks.

a. If the window washer hose is bent or kinked, clean, repair or replace as necessary.

b. If the window washer hose is not bent or kinked, go to Step 10.

10. Disconnect window washer hose at windshield washer reservoir and check for blockage at the windshield washer pump outlet.

a. If the window washer hose is blocked at the washer pump outlet, remove the windshield washer pump from the windshield washer reservoir and clean.

b. If the window washer hose is not blocked, replace the windshield washer pump.

11. Disconnect windshield wiper motor connector, turn the ignition switch to **RUN**, depress and release the turn signal/windshield wiper switch; then, check for battery voltage between circuits **58 (W)** and **61 (Y/R)**.

a. If battery voltage is present, perform the windshield wiper motor current draw test, service as required.

b. If battery voltage is not present, go to Stop 12.

12. Turn the ignition switch to **RUN**, depress and release the turn signal/windshield wiper switch; then, check for battery voltage between circuits **58 (W)** and **61 (Y/R)** at the windshield wiper governor connector.

a. If battery voltage is present, check for an unseated connector. Check for an open circuit **58 (W)** between the windshield wiper governor and the windshield wipe motor.

b. If battery voltage is not present, replace the windshield wiper governor.

WINDSHIELD WIPERS INOPERATIVE IN ALL SWITCH POSITIONS

1. Turn the ignition switch to **RUN** and the turn signal/windshield wiper switch to **HI**. Unplug the windshield wiper motor and check for battery voltage at circuit **65 (DG)**.

a. If battery voltage is present, go to Step 2.

b. If battery voltage is not present;

• Check for an open circuit breaker in the fuse junction panel.

• Check for an open connector.

• Check for an open wire circuit **65 (DG)**.

• Check for poor ground connection, service as required.

Refer to the model specific sections for engine electrical system service procedures

2. Check for battery voltage at circuit **65 (DG)** pin **2** of the connector.

    a. If battery voltage is present, go to Step 3.

    b. If battery voltage is not present, service the open in the power feed to windshield wiper governor;

- Check for an open unseated connector.
- Check for an open wire circuit **65 (DG)**.

3. Turn the ignition switch to **RUN** and the turn signal/windshield wiper switch to **HI.** Disconnect the connector from the windshield washer pump. Check for battery voltage between circuits **61 (Y/R)** and **58 (W)**.

    a. If battery voltage is present, go to Step 6.

    b. If battery voltage is not present, go to Step 4.

4. Check for battery voltage between pin **12**, circuit **61 (Y/R)** and pin **14,** circuit **58 (W)** of the windshield wiper governor connector.

    a. If battery voltage is not present, go to Step 5.

    b. If battery voltage is present;

- Check for an unseated connector.
- Check for an open connector.
- Check for an open wire circuits **58 (W)** or **61 (Y/R)**.

5. Disconnect the connector from the windshield wiper governor. Measure the resistance between circuits **993 (BR/W)** and circuit **589 (O)**.

    a. If resistance is present, replace the windshield wiper governor.

    b. If resistance is not present;

- Check for damaged turn signal/windshield wiper switch, service as required.
- Check for an open wire between the turn signal/windshield wiper switch and windshield wiper governor.

6. Disconnect the connector from the turn signal/windshield wiper switch. Check the resistance between terminals for circuits **993 (BR/W)** and circuit **589 (O)**.

    a. If resistance is less than 1.0 ohm, check for an open wire between the turn signal/windshield wiper switch and the windshield wiper windshield wiper governor, then, go to Step 7.

    b. If resistance is greater than 1.0 ohm, check for a damaged turn signal/windshield wiper switch, service as required.

7. Check the wiper motor current draw:

- Disconnect the windshield wiper mounting arm and pivot shaft from the windshield wiper motor.
- Disconnect the electrical connector from the wiper motor.
- Connect the green lead from the test equipment to the battery positive **(+)** post.
- Connect the positive **(R)** lead from the tester to the common brush terminal (circuit **61**).
- Attach a ground first to the high speed connection (circuit **58**) and then to the low speed connection (circuit **56**) at the connector plug.
- In either case, the current draw should not exceed 3.5 amps.

    a. If the tests are performed OK, check the linkage for binding and service as necessary.

    b. If the tests are not performed OK, repair motor as necessary.

WINDSHIELD WIPERS INOPERATIVE AT HIGH SPEED

1. Check the windshield wiper operation.

    a. If the low speed works, go to Step 4.

    b. If the low speed does not work, go to Step 2.

2. Turn the ignition switch **ON** and the turn signal/windshield

wiper switch to **HI.** Unplug the windshield wiper motor and check for battery voltage at circuit **65 (DG)**.

    a. If battery voltage is present, go to Step 3.

    b. If battery voltage is not present;

- Check for an open circuit breaker in the fuse junction panel.
- Check for an open connector.
- Check for an open wire circuit **65 (DG)**.
- Check for poor ground connection, service as required.

3. Check for battery voltage at circuit **65 (DG)** pin **2** of the connector.

    a. If battery voltage is present, go to Step 4.

    b. If battery voltage is not present, service the open in the power feed to windshield wiper governor;

- Check for an open unseated connector.
- Check for an open wire circuit **65 (DG)**.

4. Turn the ignition switch to **RUN** and the turn signal/windshield wiper switch to **HI.** Disconnect the connector from the windshield wiper motor. Check for battery voltage between circuits **61 (Y/R)** and **56 (DB/O)**.

    a. If battery voltage is present, go to Step 7.

    b. If battery voltage is not present, go to Step 5.

5. Check for battery voltage between pin **12**, circuit **61 (Y/R)** and pin **14,** circuit **56 (DB/O)** of the windshield wiper governor connector.

    a. If battery voltage is not present, go to Step 6.

    b. If battery voltage is present;

- Check for an unseated connector.
- Check for an open connector.
- Check for an open wire circuits **56 (DB/O)** or **61 (Y/R)**.

6. Disconnect the connector from the windshield wiper governor. Measure the continuity between circuits **993 (BR/W)** and circuit **589 (O)**.

    a. If continuity is present, replace the windshield wiper governor.

    b. If continuity is not present;

- Check for damaged turn signal/windshield wiper switch, service as required.
- Check for an open wire between the turn signal/windshield wiper switch and windshield wiper governor.

7. Disconnect the connector from the turn signal/windshield wiper switch. Check the continuity between terminals for circuits **993 (BR/W)** and circuit **589 (O)**.

    a. If continuity is present, go to Step 8.

    b. If continuity is not present, check for a damaged turn signal/windshield wiper switch, service as required.

8. Check the wiper motor current draw:

- Disconnect the windshield wiper mounting arm and pivot shaft from the windshield wiper motor.
- Disconnect the electrical connector from the wiper motor.
- Connect the green lead from the test equipment to the battery positive **(+)** post.
- Connect the positive **(R)** lead from the tester to the common brush terminal (circuit **61**).
- Attach a ground first to the high speed connection (circuit **58**) and then to the low speed connection (circuit **56**) at the connector plug.
- In either case, the current draw should not exceed 3.5 amps.

    a. If the tests are performed OK, check the linkage for binding and service as necessary.

    b. If the tests are not performed OK, service the windshield wiper motor as necessary.

WINDSHIELD WIPERS INOPERATIVE AT LOW SPEED

1. Check the windshield wiper operation.
   a. If the high speed works, go to Step 4.
   b. If the high speed does not work, go to Step 2.
2. Turn the ignition switch **ON** and the turn signal/windshield wiper switch to **HI**. Unplug the windshield wiper motor and check for battery voltage at circuit **65 (DG)**.
   a. If battery voltage is present, go to Step 3.
   b. If battery voltage is not present;
   • Check for an open circuit breaker in the fuse junction panel.
   • Check for an open connector.
   • Check for an open wire circuit **65 (DG)**.
   • Check for poor ground connection, service as required.
3. Check for battery voltage at circuit **65 (DG)** pin **2** of the connector.
   a. If battery voltage is present, go to Step 4.
   b. If battery voltage is not present, service the open in the power feed to windshield wiper governor;
   • Check for an open unseated connector.
   • Check for an open wire circuit **65 (DG)**.
4. Turn the ignition switch to **RUN** and the turn signal/windshield wiper switch to **LO**. Disconnect the connector from the windshield wiper motor. Check for battery voltage between circuits **61 (Y/R)** and **58 (W)**.
   a. If battery voltage is present, go to Step 7.
   b. If battery voltage is not present, go to Step 5.
5. Check for battery voltage between pin **12**, circuit **61 (Y/R)** and pin **8**, circuit **58 (W)** of the windshield wiper governor connector.
   a. If battery voltage is not present, go to Step 6.
   b. If battery voltage is present;
   • Check for an unseated connector.
   • Check for an open connector.
   • Check for an open wire circuits **58 (W)** or **61 (Y/R)**.
6. Disconnect the connector from the windshield wiper governor. Measure the resistance between circuit **993 (BR/W)** and circuit **589 (O)**.
   a. If resistance is 4.08 kilo-ohms, replace the windshield wiper governor.
   b. If resistance is not 4.08 kilo-ohms;
   • Check for damaged turn signal/windshield wiper switch, service as required.
   • Check for an open wire between the turn signal/windshield wiper switch and windshield wiper governor.
7. Disconnect the connector from the turn signal/windshield wiper switch. Measure the resistance between circuit **993 (BR/W)** and circuit **589 (O)**.
   a. If resistance is 4.08 kilo-ohms, go to Step 8.
   b. If resistance is not 4.08 kilo-ohms, service the damaged turn signal/windshield wiper switch.
8. Check the wiper motor current draw:
   • Disconnect the windshield wiper mounting arm and pivot shaft from the windshield wiper motor.
   • Disconnect the electrical connector from the wiper motor.
   • Connect the green lead from the test equipment to the battery positive **(+)** post.
   • Connect the positive **(R)** lead from the tester to the common brush terminal (circuit **61**).
   • Attach a ground first to the high speed connection (circuit **58**) and then to the low speed connection (circuit **56**) at the connector plug.

• In either case, the current draw should not exceed 3.5 amps.
   a. If the tests are performed OK, check the linkage for binding and service as necessary.
   b. If the tests are not performed OK, service the windshield wiper motor as necessary.

WINDSHIELD WIPERS INOPERATIVE AT INTERVAL SETTING

1. Check the windshield wiper operation.
   a. If the low speed works, go to Step 2.
   b. If the low speed does not work, go to Windshield Wipers Inoperative at Low Speed.
2. Disconnect the connector from the windshield wiper governor. Measure the resistance between circuit **993 (BR/W)** and circuit **589 (O)**.
   a. If resistance is 11.3 kilo-ohms, go to Step 4.
   b. If resistance is not 11.3 kilo-ohms, go to Step 3.
3. Disconnect the connector from the turn signal/windshield wiper switch. Measure the resistance between circuit **993 (BR/W)** and circuit **589 (O)**.
   a. If resistance is 11.3 kilo-ohms, check for an open wire between the turn signal/windshield wiper switch and the windshield wiper governor.
   b. If resistance is not 11.3 kilo-ohms, check for a damaged turn signal/windshield wiper switch, service as required.
4. Rotate the interval control on the turn signal/windshield wiper switch. Measure the resistance between circuit **993 (BR/W)** and circuit **590 (DB/W)**.
   a. If resistance is 3.3 kilo-ohms to 11.3 kilo-ohms, replace the windshield wiper governor.
   b. If resistance is not 3.3 kilo-ohms to 11.3 kilo-ohms, go to Step 5.
5. Disconnect the connector from the turn signal/windshield wiper switch. Rotate the interval control on the turn signal/windshield wiper switch from **MIN** to **MAX**. Measure the resistance between terminals of the turn signal/windshield wiper switch for circuit **993 (BR/W)** and circuit **590 (DB/W)**.
   a. If resistance is 3.3 kilo-ohms to 11.3 kilo-ohms, check for an open wire(s) between the turn signal/windshield wiper switch and the windshield wiper governor.
   b. If resistance is not 3.3 kilo-ohms to 11.3 kilo-ohms, check for a damaged turn signal/windshield wiper switch, service as required.

WINDSHIELD WIPERS WILL NOT PARK

1. Turn the turn signal/windshield wiper switch to **OFF** position. Unplug the windshield wiper motor and check for continuity between circuit **28 (BK/PK)** and circuit **58 (W)**.
   a. If continuity is present, perform the windshield wiper motor parking test.
   b. If continuity is not present, go to Step 2.
2. Turn the ignition switch to **OFF** position. Unplug the windshield wiper governor and check for continuity between pin **J1-6** and **J1-8** of the windshield wiper governor.
   a. If continuity is present:
   • Check for unseated connectors.
   • Check for an open circuit between the windshield wiper governor and windshield wiper motor, service as required.
   b. If continuity is not present, go to Step 3.
3. Turn the turn signal/windshield wiper switch to **OFF** position. Measure the resistance between circuit **589 (O)** and circuit **993 (BR/W)**.

a. If resistance is not approximately 47.6 kilo-ohms:
• Check for open circuit **589 (O)** or **993 (BR/W)**.
• Check for a damaged turn signal/windshield wiper switch, service as required.
• Check for an unseated turn signal/windshield wiper switch connector.
  b. If resistance is approximately 47.6 kilo-ohms, replace the windshield wiper governor.

WINDSHIELD WIPERS WILL NOT TURN OFF

1. Disconnect the connector from the windshield wiper motor. Turn the ignition switch to **RUN** position and the turn signal/windshield wiper switch to **OFF** position. Measure the continuity between circuits **28 (BK/PK)** and between circuits **61 (Y/R)** and **63 (R)**.
   a. If continuity is present:
• Check for unseated connectors.
• Check for a damaged windshield wiper motor, service as required.
   b. If continuity is not present, go to Step 2.
2. Measure the continuity between circuits **28 (BK/PK)** and **58**

(W) and between circuits **61 (Y/R)** and **63 (R)** at the windshield wiper governor.
   a. If continuity is present, service the open circuit between the windshield wiper governor and windshield wiper motor.
   b. If continuity is not present, go to Step 3.
3. Measure the resistance between circuit **589 (O)** and circuit **993 (BR/W)**.
   a. If resistance is not approximately 47.6 kilo-ohms:
• Check for open circuit **589 (O)** or **993 (BR/W)** between turn signal/windshield wiper switch and the windshield wiper governor.
• Check for a damaged turn signal/windshield wiper switch, service as required.
   b. If resistance is approximately 47.6 kilo-ohms, replace the windshield wiper governor.

Mustang

WINDSHIELD WASHER INOPERATIVE

1. Check the fluid level in the reservoir.
   a. If the level is OK, go to Step 2.

Windshield wiper electrical schematic—Mustang

8838XG28

Connector End Views

WINDSHIELD WIPER MOTOR

WINDSHIELD WIPER CONTROL MODULE

Pin Number	Circuit	Circuit Function
1	57 (BK)	Wiper Motor Ground (Park)
2	28 (BK/PK)	Wiper Module to Wiper Motor (Park Switch)
3	65 (DG)	Wiper Motor Power (Park Feed)
4	61 (Y/R)	Wiper Motor Common (RUN)
5	56 (DB/O)	Wiper Motor LO
6	58 (W)	Wiper Motor HI

Pin Number	Circuit	Circuit Function
1	58 (W)	Windshield Wiper Motor HI
2	28 (BK/PK)	Windshield Wiper Motor Park Switch
3	—	Not Used
4	65 (DG)	Power (Hot in ACC or RUN)
5	61 (Y/R)	Windshield Wiper Motor Connector
6	590 (DB/W)	Interval Wiper / Washer Reference Voltage
7	56 (DB/O)	Windshield Wiper Motor LO
8	993 (BR/W)	Interval Wiper / Washer Reference Voltage
9	—	Not Used
10	57 (BK)	Ground
11	941 (BK/W)	Windshield Washer Pump Motor
12	57 (BK)	Ground
13	65 (DG)	Power (Hot in ACC or RUN)
14	589 (O)	Windshield Wiper Switch

8838XG29

Windshield wiper motor terminal identification—Mustang

b. If the level is not OK, fill the reservoir.

2. Turn the windshield washer switch **ON**. Check the fluid level in the reservoir.

    a. If the windshield washer pump runs, go to Step 3.

    b. If the windshield washer pump does not run, go to Step 6.

3. Inspect the windshield washer nozzle jet and bracket for blockage.

    a. If the windshield washer nozzle jet and bracket are blocked, clean and replace the windshield washer nozzle jet and bracket.

    b. If the windshield washer nozzle jet and bracket are not blocked, go to Step 4.

4. Inspect the windshield washer hose, filter and/or check valve for blockage or kinks.

    a. If blockage or kinks are present, clean, service or replace as necessary.

    b. If blockage or kinks are not present, go to Step 5.

5. Inspect the windshield washer pump outlet for blockage.

    a. If the windshield washer pump outlet is blockage or obstructed, remove and clean the washer pump.

    b. If windshield washer pump outlet is not blockage or obstructed, Replace the washer pump and retest the system.

6. Using a voltmeter, actuate the turn signal/windshield wiper switch and check for voltage at the windshield washer pump.

    a. If battery voltage is present, go to Step 7.

    b. If battery voltage is not present, go to Step 8.

7. Using an ohmmeter, check for ground at the pump connector.

    a. If the connector is properly grounded, replace the windshield washer pump.

    b. If the connector is not properly grounded, service the ground.

8. Turn the windshield wiper **ON** and check the operation.

    a. If wipers operate, go to Step 9.

    b. If wipers do not operate, go to Windshield Wipers Inoperative in All Switch Positions.

9. Disconnect the connector from the windshield wiper control module. Depress the washer switch on the end of the turn signal/windshield wiper switch. Check the continuity between circuits **993 (BR/W)** and **590 (DB/W)**.

   a. If continuity is present, go to Step 11.

   b. If continuity is not present, go to Step 10.

10. Disconnect the connector from the windshield wiper switch. Depress the turn signal/windshield wiper switch. Check the continuity between terminated **B** and **W**.

   a. If continuity is present, service for an open circuit between the turn signal/windshield wiper switch and the wiper control module.

   b. If continuity is not present, service the turn signal/windshield wiper switch.

11. Check the continuity of circuit **941 (BK/W)** from the wiper control module to the windshield washer pump.

   a. If continuity is present, replace the wiper control module.

   b. If continuity is not present, service for an open circuit.

WINDSHIELD WIPERS INOPERATIVE IN ALL SWITCH POSITIONS

1. Turn the ignition switch **RUN** and the turn signal/windshield wiper switch to **HI**. Unplug the windshield wiper motor. Check for battery voltage at circuit **65 (DG)**.

   a. If battery voltage is present, go to Step 2.

   b. If battery voltage is not present, go to Step 3.

2. Check for battery voltage at circuit **65 (DG)** pin **2** of the connector.

   a. If battery voltage is present, go to Step 4.

   b. If battery voltage is not present, service circuit **65 (DG)** for an open circuit, restore vehicle and retest the system.

3. Using a test lamp, check for battery voltage at fuse **2** (30 amp).

   a. If voltage is present on both sides of the circuit breaker, service the circuit **65 (DG)** for an open circuit, restore vehicle and retest the system.

   b. If voltage is not present, replace the fuse.

4. Turn the ignition switch **RUN** and the turn signal/windshield wiper switch to **HI**. Unplug the windshield wiper motor. Check for battery voltage between circuits **61 (Y/R)** and **58 (W)**.

   a. If battery voltage is present, go to Step 8.

   b. If battery voltage is not present, go to Step 5.

5. Check for battery voltage between pin **10**, circuit **61 (Y/R)** and pin **14**, circuit **58 (W)** of the windshield wiper control module connector with the turn signal/windshield wiper switch in the **HI** position.

   a. If battery voltage is present, service circuit **61 (Y/R)** or circuit **58 (W)** for an open circuit, restore the vehicle and retest the system.

   b. If battery voltage is not present, go to Step 6.

6. Disconnect the connector from the windshield wiper control module. Measure the resistance between circuits **993 (BR/W)** and **589 (O)** with the turn signal/windshield wiper switch in the **HI** position.

   a. If resistance is less than 1.0 ohm, replace the windshield wiper control module, restore the vehicle and retest the system.

   b. If resistance is greater than 1.0 ohm, go to Step 7.

7. Disconnect the connector from the turn signal/windshield wiper switch. Check the continuity between terminals for circuits **993 (BR/W)** and **589 (O)** with the turn signal/windshield wiper switch in the **HI** position.

   a. If resistance is less than 1.0 ohm, service circuits **993 (BR/W)** or **589 (O)** for an open circuit, restore the vehicle and retest the system.

   b. If resistance is greater than 1.0 ohm, replace the turn signal/windshield wiper switch, restore the vehicle and retest the system.

8. Check the wiper motor current draw:

• Disconnect the starter relay cable from the battery.

• Disconnect the windshield wiper mounting arm and pivot shaft from the windshield wiper motor.

• Disconnect the electrical connector from the wiper motor.

• Connect the green lead from the test equipment to the battery positive **(+)** post.

• Attach a battery ground wire to pin **4** (circuit **61**) of the wiper motor.

• Connect the positive **(R)** lead from the tester to pin **5** (circuit **56**) or pin **6** (circuit **58**) of the wiper motor.

• In either case, the current draw should not exceed 3.0 amps.

   a. If the tests are performed OK, check the linkage for binding, restore the vehicle and retest the system.

   b. If the tests are not performed OK, replace the windshield wiper motor, restore the vehicle and retest the system.

WINDSHIELD WIPERS INOPERATIVE AT LOW SPEED

1. Turn the ignition switch to the **RUN** position and the turn signal/windshield wiper switch to the **LO** position. Unplug the windshield wiper motor connector. Check for battery voltage between circuits **61 (Y/R)** and **56 (DB/O)**.

   a. If battery voltage is present, go to Step 5.

   b. If battery voltage is not present, go to Step 2.

2. Check for battery voltage between pin **10**, circuit **61 (Y/R)** and pin **8**, circuit **56 (DB/O)** of the windshield wiper control module connector.

   a. If battery voltage is present, service circuit **61 (Y/R)** or circuit **56 (DB/O)** for an open circuit, restore the vehicle and retest the system.

   b. If battery voltage is not present, go to Step 3.

3. Disconnect the connector from the windshield wiper control module. Measure the resistance between circuits **993 (BR/W)** and **589 (O)** with the turn signal/windshield wiper switch in the **LO** position.

   a. If the resistance is between 3.5 kilo-ohms and 4.5 kilo-ohms, replace the windshield wiper control module, restore the vehicle and retest the system.

   b. If the resistance is not between 3.5 kilo-ohms and 4.5 kilo-ohms, go to Step 4.

4. Disconnect the connector from the turn signal/windshield wiper switch. Measure the continuity between terminals for circuits **993 (BR/W)** and **589 (O)** with the turn signal/windshield wiper switch in the **LO** position.

   a. If the resistance is between 3.5 kilo-ohms and 4.5 kilo-ohms, service circuits **993 (BR/W)** or **589 (O)** for an open circuit, restore the vehicle and retest the system.

   b. If the resistance is not between 3.5 kilo-ohms and 4.5 kilo-ohms, replace the damaged turn signal/windshield wiper switch, restore the vehicle and retest the system.

5. Check the wiper motor current draw:

• Disconnect the starter relay cable from the battery.

• Disconnect the windshield wiper mounting arm and pivot shaft from the windshield wiper motor.

• Disconnect the electrical connector from the wiper motor.

- Connect the green lead from the test equipment to the battery positive **(+)** post.
- Attach a battery ground wire to pin **4** (circuit **61**) of the wiper motor.
- Connect the positive **(R)** lead from the tester to pin **5** (circuit **56**) or pin **6** (circuit **58**) of the wiper motor.
- In either case, the current draw should not exceed 3.0 amps.
    a. If the tests are performed OK, check the linkage for binding, restore the vehicle and retest the system.
    b. If the tests are not performed OK, replace the windshield wiper motor, restore the vehicle and retest the system.

WINDSHIELD WIPERS INOPERATIVE AT INTERVAL SETTING

1. Disconnect the connector from the wiper control module. Measure the resistance between circuit **993 (BR/W)** and circuit **589 (O)** with the turn signal/windshield wiper switch at the interval setting.
    a. If the resistance is between 10.5 kilo-ohms and 12.0 kilo-ohms, go to Step 3.
    b. If the resistance is not between 10.5 kilo-ohms and 12.0 kilo-ohms, go to Step 2
2. Disconnect the connector from the turn signal/windshield wiper switch. Measure the resistance between terminals for circuits **993 (BR/W)** and **589 (O)** with the turn signal/windshield wiper switch at the interval setting.
    a. If the resistance is between 10.5 kilo-ohms and 12.0 kilo-ohms, service circuit **993 (BR/W)** or circuit **589 (O)** for an open circuit, restore the vehicle and retest the system.
    b. If the resistance is not between 10.5 kilo-ohms and 12.0 kilo-ohms, replace the damaged wiper/washer switch, restore the vehicle and retest the system.
3. Rotate the interval control on the turn signal/windshield wiper switch from **MIN** to **MAX**. Measure the resistance between circuits **993 (BR/W)** and circuit **590 (DB/W)**.
    a. If the resistance is less than 104 kilo-ohms, replace the wiper control module, restore the vehicle and retest the system.
    b. If the resistance is greater than 104 kilo-ohms, go to Step 4.
4. Disconnect the connector from the turn signal/windshield wiper switch. Rotate the interval control on the turn signal/windshield wiper switch from **MIN** to **MAX**. Measure the resistance between terminals of the wiper switch for circuits **993 (BR/W)** and circuit **590 (DB/W)**.
    a. If the resistance is less than 104 kilo-ohms, service circuit **993 (BR/W)** or circuit **589 (O)** for an open circuit, restore the vehicle and retest the system.
    b. If the resistance is greater than 104 kilo-ohms, replace the damaged wiper/washer switch, restore the vehicle and retest the system.

WINDSHIELD WIPERS WILL NOT PARK AT PROPER POSITION

1. Unplug the wiper motor connector. Check for ground at circuit **57 (BK)**.
    a. If ground is okay, go to Step 2.
    b. If ground is not okay, service the open circuit.
2. Turn the ignition switch to the **RUN** position and the wiper switch to the **OFF** position. Check for battery voltage between circuit **65 (DG)** and **57 (BK)**.

    a. If battery voltage is present, go to Step 3.
    b. If battery voltage is not present, service the open circuits.
3. Turn the wiper switch to the **OFF** position. Check for continuity of circuit **28 (BK/PK)** to **56 (DB/O)** and circuit **61 (Y/R)** to **57 (BK)**.
    a. If continuity is okay, go to Step 5.
    b. If continuity is not okay, go to Step 4.
4. Check continuity of circuits **28 (BK/PK)**, **56 (DB/O)**, **61 (Y/R)** and **57 (BK)** from the wiper motor to the wiper control module.
    a. If continuity is okay, replace the wiper control module.
    b. If continuity is not okay, service the open circuits.
5. Check that the wiper linkage is not bent, cracked or out of position from the motor shaft.
    a. If the linkage is okay, replace the wiper motor.
    b. If the linkage is not okay, service linkage.

WIPERS WILL NOT STOP IN INTERVAL OR STOP MODE

1. Check that the wiper motor and the wiper control module connectors are fully seated.
    a. If connections are is okay, go to Step 2.
    b. If connections are not okay, service as required and recheck the system.
2. Disconnect the connector from the wiper motor. Turn the wiper switch to the **OFF** position. Check the continuity of circuits **28 (BK/PK)** to **56 (DB/O)** and between circuits **61 (Y/R)** and **57 (BK)** at the motor connector.
    a. If the continuity exists, replace the damaged wiper motor.
    b. If the continuity does not exist, go to Step 3.
3. Check the continuity of circuits **28 (BK/PK)**, **56 (DB/O)**, **61 (Y/R)** and **57 (BK)** from the wiper motor to wiper control module.
    a. If the continuity is okay, go to Step 4.
    b. If the continuity is not okay, service circuit as required.
4. Turn the wiper switch to the **OFF** position. Measure the resistance between circuits **589 (O)** and **933 (BR/W)** at the wiper control module.
    a. If resistance is between 45 kilo-ohms and 50 kilo-ohms, replace the wiper control module.
    b. If resistance is not between 45 kilo-ohms and 50 kilo-ohms:, go to Step 5
5. Check the continuity of circuits **589 (O)** and **993 (BR/W)** between the wiper switch and wiper control module.
    a. If the continuity is okay, replace the wiper switch.
    b. If the continuity is not okay, service open circuit(s).

Mark VIII, Sable and Taurus

WINDSHIELD WASHERS INOPERATIVE IN ALL SWITCH POSITIONS

1. Check the fluid level in the reservoir.
    a. If the level is OK, go to Step 2.
    b. If the level is not OK, fill the reservoir.
2. Activate the washer switch. Check the fluid level in the reservoir.
    a. If the motor is inoperative, go to Step 3.
    b. If the motor operates but fluid will not squirt, go to Step 8.
    c. If fluid squirts but the wipers do not operate, go to Step 10.
3. Turn the ignition switch **ON**. Depress the washer switch. Check for battery voltage at circuit **941 (BK/W)** at the washer pump.

Refer to the model specific sections for engine electrical system service procedures

GROUND JUMPER TO NEGATIVE BATTERY POST

58 (HI)
56 (LO)
61 (COM)
57 (G)
63 (GR)
28 (PR)
65 (PF)

8838XG31

Windshield wiper motor terminal identification and motor testing—Mark VIII, Sable and Taurus

a. If battery voltage is present, go to Step 7.

b. If battery voltage is not present, go to Step 4.

4. Check for battery voltage at circuits **65 (DG)** of the wiper control module.

   a. If battery voltage is present, go to Step 5.

   b. If battery voltage is not present:

• Check for circuit breakers.

• Check for an open connector.

• Check for an open wire circuit **65 (DG)**, service as required.

5. Disconnect the connector from the windshield control module. Depress the washer switch. Measure the resistance between circuit **993 (BR/W)** and between circuit **590 (DB/W)**.

   a. If continuity is present, go to Step 6.

   b. If continuity is not present:

• Check for an open wire between the wiper switch and the wiper control module.

• Check for a damaged windshield wiper/washer switch, service as required.

6. Connect the connector to the wiper control module. Turn the ignition switch to the **RUN** position. Depress the washer switch.

WINDSHIELD WIPER SWITCH CONNECTOR ON 14401 WIRING ASSY

Pin Number	Circuit	Circuit Function
1	590 (DB W)	Interval Switch
2	993 (BR W)	Interval Wiper Reference Voltage
3	589 (O)	Windshield Wiper Switch
4	196 (DB O)	Supply
5	12 (LG BK)	Headlamps Hi Beam
6	13 (R BK)	Autolamp Auto Dimmer Control
7	15 (R Y)	Hot with Headlamps ON

WINDSHIELD WIPER MOTOR FOUR PIN CONNECTOR ON 14401 WIRING HARNESS

Pin Number	Circuit	Circuit Function
1	28 (BK PK)	Wiper Motor Switch
2	65 (DG)	Supply
3	63 (R)	Wiper Motor Switch
4	57 (BK)	Ground

WINDSHIELD WIPER MOTOR 3-PIN CONNECTOR ON 14401 WIRING HARNESS

Pin Number	Circuit	Circuit Function
1	61 (Y R)	Motor Common
2	56 (DB O)	Motor Low Speed Supply
3	58 (W)	Motor High Speed Supply

Washer

WINDSHIELD WIPER GOVERNOR

WINDSHIELD WASHER PUMP

WINDSHIELD WASHER RESERVOIR FLUID LEVEL SENSOR

INSTRUMENT CLUSTER

LOW WASHER FLUID LEVEL INDICATOR

8838XG32

Windshield wiper motor and switch connectors terminal identification and washer electrical schematic—Continental

Pin Number	Circuit	Circuit Function
1	589 (O)	Turn Signal and Windshield Wiper Switch
2	65 (DG)	Power (Hot in ACC or RUN)
3	26 (W/P)	Ground
4	941 (BK/W)	Windshield Washer Pump
5	57 (BK)	Ground
6	28 (BK/PK)	Turn Signal and Windshield Wiper Switch
7	993 (BR/W)	Windshield Wiper Governor to Turn Signal and Windshield Wiper Switch
8	56 (DB/O)	Windshield Wiper Motor—LO
9	590 (DB/W)	Windshield Wiper Governor to Turn Signal and Windshield Wiper Switch
10	—	Not Used
11	—	Not Used
12	61 (Y/R)	Windshield Wiper Motor Common
13	63 (R)	Turn Signal and Windshield Wiper Switch
14	58 (W)	Windshield Wiper Motor—HI

8838XG33

Windshield wiper interval governor connector terminal identification—Sable and Taurus

Measure the voltage at circuit **56 (DB/O)** at the wiper control module connector.

  a. If battery voltage is present, check for an open circuit **56 (DB/O)** between the wiper control module and wiper motor.

  b. If continuity is not present, replace the damaged wiper control module.

7. Using an ohmmeter, check the ground at the pump.

  a. If the ground is functional, replace the washer pump.

  b. If the ground is not functional, service the ground.

8. Inspect the washer hose and nozzle for blockage or hose kinks.

  a. If the hose is blocked or kinked, clean, replace or service the nozzle of hoses.

  b. If the hose is not blocked or kinked, go to Step 9.

9. Disconnect the hose at the reservoir and check for blockage at the washer pump outlet.

  a. If the hose is blocked at the washer outlet, remove and clean the nozzle water pump.

  b. If the hose is not blocked at the washer outlet, replace the washer pump.

10. Disconnect the connector from the wiper motor. Turn the ignition switch to the **RUN** position. Depress and release the washer switch. Check for battery voltage between circuit **56 (DB/O)** and **61 (Y/R)**.

  a. If battery voltage is present, perform the wiper motor current draw test, service as required.

  b. If battery voltage is not present, go to Step 11.

11. Turn the ignition switch to the **RUN** position. Depress and release the washer switch. Check for battery voltage between cir-cuit **56 (DB/O)** and **61 (Y/R)** at the wiper control module connector.

  a. If battery voltage is present:

• Check for an unseated connector.

• Check for an open circuit **56 (DB/O)** between the wiper control module and wiper motor.

  b. If battery voltage is not present, replace the wiper control module.

WINDSHIELD WIPERS INOPERATIVE AT HIGH SPEED

1. Check the low speed operation.

  a. If the low speed works, go to Step 4.

  b. If the low speed does not work, go to Step 2.

2. Turn the ignition switch to the **ON** position and the wiper switch to the **HI** position. Unplug the wiper motor connector. Check for battery voltage at circuit **65 (DG)**.

  a. If battery voltage is present, go to Step 3.

  b. If battery voltage is not present:

• Check for an open circuit breaker in the fuse panel.

• Check for an open wire circuit **65 (DG)**.

• Check for an open wire connector.

• Check for a poor ground connection, service as required.

3. Check for battery voltage at circuit **65 (DG)** pin **2** of the connector.

  a. If battery voltage is present, go to Step 4.

  b. If battery voltage is not present, service the open in the power feed to module:

- Check for an open in circuit **65 (DG)**.
- Check for an open unseated connector.

4. Turn the ignition switch to the **RUN** position and the wiper switch to the **HI** position. Disconnect the connector from the wiper motor. Check for battery voltage between circuit **58 (W)** and **61 (Y/R)**.

    a. If battery voltage is present, go to Step 7.
    b. If battery voltage is not present, go to Step 5.

5. Check for battery voltage between pin **12** circuit **61 (Y/R)** and pin **14** circuit **58 (W)** of the wiper control module connector.

    a. If battery voltage is present:

- Check for open wire circuits **58 (W)** or **61 (Y/R)**.
- Check for an unseated connector.
- Check for an open unseated connector.

    b. If battery voltage is not present, go to Step 6.

6. Disconnect the connector from the wiper control module. Measure the resistance between circuit **993 (BR/W)** and circuit **589 (O)**.

    a. If the resistance is less than 1.0 ohm, replace the wiper control module.
    b. If the resistance is greater than 1.0 ohm:

- Check for an open wire between the wiper switch and the wiper control module.
- Check for a damaged wiper/washer switch, service as required.

7. Disconnect the connector from the wiper switch. Measure the resistance between terminals for circuit **993 (BR/W)** and circuit **589 (O)**.

    a. If the resistance is less than 1.0 ohm, check for an open wire between the switch and the wiper control module.
    b. If the resistance is greater than 1.0 ohm, check for a damaged wiper/washer switch, service as required.

8. Check the wiper motor current draw:

- Disconnect the windshield wiper mounting arm and pivot shaft from the windshield wiper motor.
- Disconnect the electrical connector from the wiper motor.
- Connect the green lead from the test equipment to the battery positive **(+)** post.
- Connect the positive **(R)** lead from the tester to the common brush terminal (circuit **61**).
- Attach a ground first to the low speed connection (circuit **56**) and then to the high speed connection (circuit **58**) at the connector plug.
- In either case, the current draw should not exceed 3.5 amps.

    a. If the tests are performed OK, check the linkage for binding and service as necessary.
    b. If the tests are not performed OK, service the wiper motor as necessary.

WINDSHIELD WIPERS INOPERATIVE AT LOW SPEED

1. Check the high speed operation.
    a. If the high speed works, go to Step 4.
    b. If the high speed does not work, go to Step 2.

2. Turn the ignition switch to the **ON** position and the wiper switch to the **HI** position. Unplug the wiper motor connector. Check for battery voltage at circuit **65 (DG)**.

    a. If battery voltage is present, go to Step 3.
    b. If battery voltage is not present:

- Check for an open circuit breaker in the fuse panel.
- Check for an open wire circuit **65 (DG)**.
- Check for an open connector.
- Check for a poor ground connection, service as required.

3. Check for battery voltage at circuit **65 (DG)** pin **2** of the connector.

    a. If battery voltage is present, go to Step 4.
    b. If battery voltage is not present, service the open in the power feed to module:

- Check for an open wire in circuit **65 (DG)**.
- Check for an open unseated connector.

4. Turn the ignition switch to the **RUN** position and the wiper switch to the **LO** position. Disconnect the connector from the wiper motor. Check for battery voltage between circuit **56 (DB/O)** and **61 (Y/R)**.

    a. If battery voltage is present, go to Step 7.
    b. If battery voltage is not present, go to Step 5.

5. Check for battery voltage between pin **12** circuit **61 (Y/R)** and pin **8** circuit **56 (DB/O)** of the wiper control module connector.

    a. If battery voltage is present:

- Check for open wire circuits **56 (DB/O)** or **61 (Y/R)**.
- Check for an unseated connector.
- Check for an open connector.

    b. If battery voltage is not present, go to Step 6.

6. Disconnect the connector from the wiper control module. Measure the resistance between circuit **993 (BR/W)** and circuit **589 (O)**.

    a. If the resistance is between 3.5–4.5 kilo-ohms, replace the wiper control module.
    b. If the resistance is not between 3.5–4.5 kilo-ohms:

- Check for an open wire between the wiper switch and the wiper control module.
- Check for a damaged wiper/washer switch, service as required.

7. Disconnect the connector from the wiper switch. Measure the resistance between terminals for circuit **993 (BR/W)** and circuit **589 (O)**.

    a. If the resistance is between 3.5–4.5 kilo-ohms, check for an open wire between the switch and the wiper control module.
    b. If the resistance is not between 3.5–4.5 kilo-ohms, check for a damaged wiper/washer switch, service as required.

8. Check the wiper motor current draw:

- Disconnect the windshield wiper mounting arm and pivot shaft from the windshield wiper motor.
- Disconnect the electrical connector from the wiper motor.
- Connect the green lead from the test equipment to the battery positive **(+)** post.
- Connect the positive **(R)** lead from the tester to the common brush terminal (circuit **61**).
- Attach a ground first to the low speed connection (circuit **56**) and then to the high speed connection (circuit **58**) at the connector plug.
- In either case, the current draw should not exceed 3.5 amps.

    a. If the tests are performed OK, check the linkage for binding and service as necessary.
    b. If the tests are not performed OK, service the wiper motor as necessary.

WINDSHIELD WIPERS INOPERATIVE AT SLOW SPEED INTERVAL

1. Check the slow speed operation.
    a. If the slow(s) speed works, go to Step 2.
    b. If the slow(s) speed does not work, go to Windshield Wipers Inoperative at High Speed.

2. Disconnect the connector from the wiper control module. Measure the resistance between circuit **993 (BR/W)** and circuit **589 (O)**.

a. If the resistance is between 10.5 kilo-ohms and 12.0 kilo-ohms, go to Step 4.

b. If the resistance is not between 10.5 kilo-ohms and 12.0 kilo-ohms, go to Step 3

3. Disconnect the connector from the wiper switch. Measure the resistance between terminals for circuit **993 (BR/W)** and circuit **589 (O)**.

a. If the resistance is between 10.5 kilo-ohms and 12.0 kilo-ohms, check for an open wire between the switch and the wiper control module.

b. If the resistance is not between 10.5 kilo-ohms and 12.0 kilo-ohms, check for a damaged wiper/washer switch, service as required.

4. Rotate the interval control on the wiper switch from **S** to **F**. Measure the resistance between circuit **993 (BR/W)** and circuit **590 (DB/W)**.

a. If the resistance is between 3.3 kilo-ohms and 104 kilo-ohms, replace the wiper control module.

b. If the resistance is not between 3.3 kilo-ohms and 104 kilo-ohms, go to Step 5

5. Disconnect the connector from the wiper switch. Rotate the interval control on the wiper switch from **S** to **F**. Measure the resistance between terminals of the wiper switch for circuit **993 (BR/W)** and circuit **590 (DB/W)**.

a. If the resistance is between 3.3 kilo-ohms and 104 kilo-ohms, check for open wires between the wiper switch and the wiper control module.

b. If the resistance is not between 3.3 kilo-ohms and 104 kilo-ohms, Check for a damaged wiper switch, service as required.

WINDSHIELD WIPERS WILL NOT PARK

1. Turn the wiper switch to the **OFF** position. Unplug the wiper motor connector. Check for continuity between circuit **28 (BK/PK)** and **56 (DB/O)**.

a. If continuity is present, perform the motor parking test.

b. If continuity is not present, go to Step 2.

2. Turn the ignition switch to the **OFF** position. Unplug the wiper control module. Check for continuity between pin **6** and pin **8** of the wiper control module.

a. If continuity is present:

• Check for an open circuit breaker between the wiper control module and the wiper motor.

• Check for an open unseated connector.

b. If continuity is not present, go to Step 3.

3. Turn the wiper switch to the **OFF** position. Measure the resistance between circuit **589 (O)** and **993 (BR/W)**.

a. If resistance is between 45 kilo-ohms to 50 kilo-ohms, replace the wiper control module.

b. If resistance is not between 45 kilo-ohms to 50 kilo-ohms:

• Check for an unseated wiper switch connector.

• Check for an open circuit **589 (O)** and **993 (BR/W)**.

• Check for a damaged wiper switch, service as required.

WIPERS WILL NOT STOP IN INTERVAL OR STOP MODE

1. Disconnect the connector from the wiper motor. Turn the ignition switch to the **RUN** position and the wiper switch to the **OFF** position. Measure the continuity between circuits **28 (BK/PK)** and between circuits **61 (Y/R)** and **63 (R)**.

a. If the continuity exists, check for an unseated component and/or a damaged wiper motor, service as required.

b. If the continuity does not exist, go to Step 2.

2. Measure the continuity between circuits **28 (BK/PK)** and **56 (DB/O)** and between circuits **61 (Y/R)** and **63 (R)** at the wiper control module connector.

a. If the continuity exists, check open circuit between the wiper control module and the wiper motor.

b. If the continuity does not exist, go to Step 3.

3. Measure the resistance between circuit **589 (O)** and **993 (BR/W)**.

a. If resistance is between 45 kilo-ohms and 50 kilo-ohms, replace the wiper control module.

b. If resistance is not between 45 kilo-ohms and 50 kilo-ohms:

• Check for an open circuit **589 (O)** and **993 (BR/W)** between the wiper switch and the wiper control module.

• Check for a damaged wiper switch, service as required.

REAR WINDSHIELD WIPER DIAGNOSIS

1. Locate the interior fuse junction panel. Check the 10 amp window wiper motor fuse.

a. If the fuse is OK, go to Step 4.

b. If the fuse is not OK, go to Step 2.

2. Replace the fuse. Turn the ignition switch to the **RUN** position. Check the 10 amp window wiper motor fuse.

a. If the fuse is OK, go to Step 3.

b. If the fuse is not OK, service the **DB/DG** wire for a short to ground.

3. Turn the ignition switch to the **RUN** position and the window wiper motor to the **ON** position. Check the 10 amp window wiper motor fuse.

a. If the fuse is OK, the system is OK.

b. If the fuse is not OK, replace the window wiper motor.

4. Disconnect the connector from the wiper motor. Turn the ignition switch to the **ON** position. Measure the voltage on the **DB/DG** wire.

a. If the voltage is greater than 10 volts, go to Step 5.

b. If the voltage is less than 10 volts, service the **DB/DG** wire.

5. Connect the connector to the wiper motor. Disconnect the connector from the wiper switch. Turn the ignition switch to the **ON** position. Measure the voltage on the **DB/BK** wire at the rear window wiper/washer switch connector.

a. If the voltage is greater than 10 volts, go to Step 6.

b. If the voltage is less than 10 volts, service the **DB/BK** wire.

6. Turn the ignition switch to the **OFF** position. Measure resistance between the **BK** wire at the rear window wiper/washer switch connector and ground.

a. If the resistance is greater than 5 ohms, service the **BK** wire.

b. If the resistance is less than 5 ohms, go to Step 7.

7. Disconnect the connector from the rear window wiper switch. Jumper the **DB/BK** wire at the rear window wiper switch connector to ground. Turn the ignition switch to the **ON** position.

a. If the rear window wiper switch operates, replace the rear wiper switch.

b. If the rear window wiper switch operates, replace the rear window wiper motor.

Continental

WINDSHIELD WASHER INOPERATIVE

1. Make sure fluid level is full. If pump runs but no spray, check for clogged hoses or nozzles.

2. Check for voltage and ground at washer pump when activating switch.

3. Check for voltage at switch by operating the wiper motor.

4. Unplug connector from wiper control module, depress washer switch and check continuity between circuits **993 (BR/W and 590 (DB/W)**.

5. Unplug switch connector and depress switch. Check continuity between terminals **C2-4** and **C2-6**. If not continuity, replace switch. If continuity, repair open in circuit.

6. Check continuity of circuit **941 (BK/W)** from control module to washer pump. If continuity, replace control module. If not, repair open circuit.

WINDSHIELD WIPERS INOPERATIVE AT ALL SWITCH POSITIONS

1. Turn ignition switch to **RUN** and wiper switch to **HI**. Unplug wiper motor and check for voltage at circuit **65 (DG)**. If not, check circuit breaker, open connector, open **65 (DG)** or **297 (BK/LG)** circuits.

2. Unplug control module connector and check for voltage at circuit **65 (DG)** pin 13. If not, repair open circuit.

3. Turn ignition switch to **RUN** and wiper switch to **HI**. Check for voltage between circuits **61 (Y/R)** and **58 (W)**. If voltage, check for motor current draw or go to next step.

4. Check for voltage between **pins 3** and **1** of control module connector with switch in **HI** position. If voltage, check for opens in circuits**58 (W)** and **61 (Y/R)**. If not, go to next step.

5. Disconnect connector from control module. Measure resistance between circuits **993 (BR/W)** and **589 (O)** with switch on **HI**. If resistance is less than 5 ohms, replace control module. If greater, go to next step.

6. Disconnect harness from switch and check continuity between terminals **C2-4** and **C2-1** with switch on **HI**. If less than 1 ohm, check for open wire. If greater, replace switch.

WINDSHIELD WIPERS INOPERATIVE AT LOW SPEED

1. Check for voltage at motor connector circuits **61 (Y/R)** and **56 (DB/O)**. If present, check motor current draw. If not, go to next step.

2. Check for voltage at wiper control module. Place switch on **LOW** and check circuits **61 (Y/R)** and **56 (DB/O)** of module connector for battery voltage. If voltage, check for opens. If not, go to next step.

3. Disconnect control module and measure resistance between circuits **993 (BR/W)** and **589 (O)** with switch on **LOW**. If resistance is 3.5–4.5 ohms, replace control module. If not, go to next step.

4. Disconnect switch and check continuity between switch terminals **993 (BR/W)** and **589 (O)** with switch on **LOW**. If resistance is 3.5–4.5 ohms, service open between switch and control module. If not, replace switch.

WINDSHIELD WIPERS INOPERATIVE AT INTERVAL SETTINGS

1. Disconnect control module connector and measure resistance between circuits **993 (BR/W)** and **589 (O)** with switch at **INTERVAL**. If resistance is 10.5–12.0 kilo-ohms, check interval select input signal at switch (step 3). If not, go to next step.

2. Disconnect wiper switch and measure resistance between circuits **993 (BR/W)** and **589 (O)**. If resistance is 10.5–12.0 kilo-ohms, check for open circuit. If not, check for defective switch.

3. Disconnect wiper switch and rotate interval control counterclockwise. Measure resistance between switch terminal circuits **590 (DB/W)** and **993 (BR/W)**. If resistance is 3.3–103.3 kilo-ohms, check for opens. If not, check for defective switch.

4. Check continuity of circuits **590 (DB/W)** and **993 (BR/W)**. If continuity, replace control module. If not, repair opens.

Contour and Mystique

WINDSHIELD WASHER INOPERATIVE

1. Make sure fluid level is full. If pump runs but no spray, check for clogged hoses or nozzles.

2. Check for voltage and ground at washer pump when activating switch.

3. Check for voltage at switch by operating the wiper motor.

4. Unplug connector from wiper switch and measure resistance of circuits **32 (W/R)** to washer pump connector **W/BK**. If circuit **32** resistance is less than 5 ohms, go to next step. If not, repair circuit **32**.

5. Remove circuit breaker in **F20** position of fuse block and check continuity. If not, replace circuit breaker.

6. Disconnect connector **N** from fuse panel and measure resistance of circuits **14 (P/O)** pin 1 and **pin 8** (wiper switch). Resistance should be less than 3 ohms. If not, repair circuit **14**.

7. Check for voltage at connector **N, pin N1** with ignition on **RUN**. If voltage, install new switch. If not, install new fuse and retest.

8. Press washer switch, disconnect switch connector and measure resistance of circuit **31 (BK)** between **pin 10** of switch connector and ground. Resistance should be 5 ohms or less. If so, go to next step. If not, repair circuit **31**.

9. Disconnect fuse panel connector **N**, measure resistance between circuit **33 (Y/BK)** from **pin 9** of switch to **pin N10**. Go to next step if resistance is less than 3 ohms. If not, repair circuit **33**.

10. Disconnect central timer module from fuse panel and measure resistance between **pin N10** and **pin 3** of timer module. If resistance is less than 3 ohms, replace timer module. If not, install new fuse.

WINDSHIELD WIPERS INOPERATIVE AT ALL SWITCH POSITIONS

1. Turn ignition switch to **RUN** and wiper switch to **HI**. Unplug wiper motor and check for voltage at circuit **32 (W/BK)**. If not, go to step 3. If voltage, check wiper motor current draw.

2. Disconnect wiper switch connector and measure resistance of circuit **32 (W/BK)** from switch connector **pin 2** to motor connector **pin 1**. If resistance is less than 3 ohms, go to next step. If not, service circuit **32**.

3. Disconnect switch and place ignition switch to **RUN**. Check for voltage of **pin 8** of switch connector. If present, install new switch. If not, go to next step.

4. Remove circuit breaker **F20** from fuse panel and check continuity. If OK, reinstall and go to next step. If not, replace circuit breaker.

5. Disconnect connector **N** from fuse panel and measure resistance of circuits **14 (P/O)** from **pin 1** of connector **N** to **pin 8** of wiper switch connector. If less than 3 ohms, go to next step. If not, repair circuit **14**.

6. At connector **N** and ignition in **RUN** position, measure voltage from pin **N1** to ground. If voltage, install new switch. If not, install new fuse.

WINDSHIELD WIPERS INOPERATIVE AT HIGH SPEED

1. Turn ignition switch **ON**, wiper switch to **HIGH** and disconnect wiper motor. Check for voltage at circuit **32 (W/BK)**. If voltage, check motor draw. If not, go to next step.

2. Disconnect switch connector and measure resistance of circuit **32 (W/BK)** from switch connector **pin 2** to motor connector **pin 1**. If circuit resistance is less than 3 ohms, go to next step. If not, repair circuit **32**.

3. Disconnect wiper switch and turn ignition to **RUN**. Check

voltage on **pin 8** of switch connector. If voltage, install new switch. If not, go to next step.

4. Check **F20** circuit breaker in the fuse block for continuity. If not, replace circuit breaker. If continuity, install and go to next step.

5. Disconnect connector **N** from fuse panel and measure resistance between circuit **14 (P/O)** from **pin 1** of connector **N** to **pin 8** of switch connector. If resistance is less than 3 ohms, go to next step. If not, repair circuit **14**.

6. Disconnect connector **N** from fuse panel and place ignition switch to **RUN**. Measure voltage from **pin N1** to ground. If voltage at pin **N1**, install new switch. If not, install new fuse.

WINDSHIELD WIPERS INOPERATIVE AT LOW SPEED

1. Check for voltage at motor connector circuits **32 (W/GN)**. If present, check motor current draw. If not, go to next step.

2. Disconnect switch connector and measure resistance of circuit **32 (W/BK)** from switch connector **pin 1** to motor connector **pin 2**. If circuit resistance is less than 3 ohms, go to next step. If not, repair circuit **32**.

3. Disconnect wiper switch and turn ignition to **RUN**. Check voltage on **pin 8** of switch connector. If voltage, install new switch. If not, go to next step.

4. Check **F20** circuit breaker in the fuse block for continuity. If not, replace circuit breaker. If continuity, install and go to next step.

5. Disconnect connector **N** from fuse panel and measure resistance between circuit **14 (P/O)** from **pin 1** of connector **N** to **pin 8** of switch connector. If resistance is less than 3 ohms, go to next step. If not, repair circuit **14**.

6. Disconnect connector **N** from fuse panel and place ignition switch to **RUN**. Measure voltage from **pin N1** to ground. If voltage at pin **N1**, install new switch. If not, install new fuse.

WINDSHIELD WIPERS INOPERATIVE AT INTERVAL SETTINGS

1. With ignition switch **OFF**, disconnect timer module at fuse panel. Connect ohmmeter to timer module **pin S14** and **S17**. Set ohmmeter to 20K range and go from **SLOW** to **FAST** while observing meter. Resistance should be 10–12 kilo-ohms. If within range, check wiper relay output. If not, go to next step.

2. Does ohmmeter read an open in the previous step? If yes, go to next step. If no, check for short circuit between connector **N** terminals **N3** and **N4**.

3. Disconnect wiper switch and measure resistance from **pin S17** to **pin 6**. If less than 3 ohms, go to step after next. If not, go to next step.

4. Check fuse pins **S17** and **N3** for continuity. If less than 1 ohm, service open circuit **8 (W)**. If not, install new fuse.

5. Measure resistance between **pin S14** and **pin 5** of switch connector. If less than 3 ohms, go to step after next. If not, go to next step.

6. Check fuse pins **S14** and **N4** for continuity. If less than 1 ohm, service open circuit **8 (W/BK)**. If not, install new fuse.

7. Measure resistance between fuse panel **pin N4** and **pin 4** of switch connector. If less than 3 ohms, go to next step. If not, repair open circuit **32 (W/GN)**.

8. Remove wiper relay from fuse panel and connect ohmmeter between terminals as shown in illustration. Replace relay if necessary.

9. Disconnect fuse panel connector **N** and check for a short circuit between **N3** and **N4**. If yes, repair short circuit. If no, install new wiper switch.

Relay Terminal	Relay Energized	Relay Not Energized
3 and 5	Closed	Open
3 and 6	Open	Closed

8838XG36

Wiper relay terminal schematic—Contour and Mystique

REMOVAL & INSTALLATION

Front Washer Reservoir and Pump

COUGAR AND THUNDERBIRD

1. Drain the reservoir.
2. Remove the bolts and the reservoir.
3. Disconnect the washer hose and the electrical connector.
4. Remove the pump from the reservoir.

To install:

5. Install the pump into the reservoir.
6. Connect the hose and electrical connector to the pump.
7. Position the reservoir and torque the bolts to 48–60 inch lbs. (5.4–6.8 Nm).
8. Fill the reservoir and check for proper operation.

CROWN VICTORIA, GRAND MARQUIS AND TOWN CAR

1. Remove the left front wheel well apron shield.
2. Remove the air cleaner.
3. Remove the retaining screws from the reservoir and disconnect the reservoir from the apron.
4. Disconnect the washer hose from the pump and drain the system.
5. Disconnect the electrical connector from the pump.
6. Carefully pry the pump from the reservoir.
7. Remove the seal/filter and inspect for damage.

To install:

8. Insert the seal into the reservoir.
9. Lubricate the inside diameter of the seal with soapy water and insert the pump until it is firmly seated.
10. Installation of the reservoir is the reverse of the removal procedure.
11. Fill the washer system slowly to avoid an air lock.
12. Check for system leaks.

CONTOUR, MYSTIQUE, CONTINENTAL, TAURUS AND SABLE

1. On SHO, Contour and Mystique vehicles, remove the 2 reservoir retaining screws and the right front inner splash shield.

Refer to the model specific sections for engine electrical system service procedures

2. All others, remove the reservoir retaining screw.

3. Remove the left or right front wheel well apron shield.

4. Disconnect the hose from the washer pump and drain the reservoir.

5. Disconnect the electrical connector.

6. Carefully pry the pump from the reservoir.

7. Remove the seal/filter and inspect for damage.

To install:

8. Insert the seal into the reservoir.

9. Lubricate the inside diameter of the seal with soapy water and insert the pump until it is firmly seated.

10. Installation of the reservoir is the reverse of the removal procedure.

11. Fill the washer system slowly to avoid air lock.

12. Check for system leaks.

ESCORT AND TRACER—1.8L ENGINE

1. Disconnect the negative battery cable.

2. Remove the 2 power steering fluid reservoir bolts and position the reservoir to the side.

3. Loosen the 2 cruise control bracket mounting bolts and position the bracket to the side.

4. Remove the 2 washer reservoir mounting bolts.

5. Disconnect the electrical connector from the washer pump.

6. Disconnect the hose from the washer pump and drain the system.

7. Carefully pry the washer reservoir with the motor attached.

To install:

8. Installation is the reverse of the removal procedure.

9. Torque the washer reservoir mounting bolts to 61–87 inch lbs. (7–9 Nm).

ESCORT AND TRACER—1.9L ENGINE

1. Disconnect the negative battery cable.

2. Remove the 2 bolts and nut and the washer reservoir.

3. Disconnect the electrical connector from the washer pump.

4. Disconnect the hose from the washer pump and drain the system.

5. Carefully pry the washer reservoir with the motor attached.

To install:

6. Installation is the reverse of the removal procedure.

7. Torque the washer reservoir mounting bolts to 61–87 inch lbs. (7–9 Nm).

ASPIRE

1. Disconnect the negative battery cable.

2. Remove the filler neck-to-vehicle attaching bolt and the filler neck from the reservoir.

3. Raise and support the vehicle safely.

4. Remove the left front wheel and tire assembly.

5. Remove the left front fender splash shield and the front splash shield.

6. Remove the 2 washer reservoir bolts.

7. Disconnect the filler tube from the reservoir and remove the reservoir.

8. Disconnect the windshield washer electrical connector and hose.

9. Remove the washer pump.

To install:

10. Install the pump onto the reservoir. Connect the hose and electrical connector to the washer.

11. Install the reservoir and connect the filler neck to it,

12. Position the reservoir and tighten the 2 reservoir-to-vehicle bolts.

13. Install the left front splash shield and the front fender splash shield.

14. Install the tire and wheel assembly and torque the lug bolts to 65–87 ft. lbs. (88–118 Nm).

15. Lower the vehicle.

16. Install the filler neck to the reservoir and filler neck-to-vehicle attaching bolt.

17. Connect the negative battery cable.

18. Fill the system and check for leaks.

MUSTANG

1. Disconnect the negative battery cable.

2. Remove the left front inner fender splash shield.

3. Disconnect the lock-tab wire connector and hose.

4. Remove the screw and disconnect the reservoir and pump assembly from the fender apron.

5. Disconnect the washer hose from the pump and drain the reservoir.

6. Remove the reservoir and pump assembly.

7. Pry the washer pump retaining ring from the reservoir.

8. Remove the pump by carefully pulling it from the reservoir with pliers around 1 side of the electrical terminal wall.

➡ **If the impeller and seal come off during removal, reassemble them onto the pump.**

To install:

9. Clean the reservoir pump chamber thoroughly before installation.

10. Lubricate the outer diameter of the pump seal with a dry lubricant.

11. Align the projection of the motor end cap with the slot in the reservoir, and insert the pump so the seal seats against the bottom of the motor cavity.

12. Using a 1 inch 12 point socket or equivalent, press the pump retaining ring securely against the motor endplate.

13. Connect the hose and electrical connector to the pump.

14. Install the reservoir and tighten the mounting screw.

15. Install the splash shield.

16. Fill the reservoir and check for leaks.

MARK VIII

1. Disconnect the negative battery cable.

2. Remove the radiator sight shield.

3. Remove the reservoir filler tube support bracket bolt.

4. Raise and support the vehicle safely.

5. Open the access panel above the headlamp.

6. Remove the nuts attaching the cornering lamps to the grill.

7. Remove the screws attaching the lamps to the fender.

8. Disconnect the lamps from the body and bulbs from the lamps.

9. Remove the lamps.

10. Remove the 8 bolts and the upper radiator grill molding.

11. Remove the 6 screws (3 on each side) attaching the bumper cover to the fender splash shields at the front fender wheel opening.

12. Remove the 4 screws (2 on each side) attaching the bottom of the cover to the front fender splash shield.

13. Remove the 4 nuts (2 on each side) through the front cornering lamp opening attaching the front cover to the fenders.

14. Remove the 2 bolts attaching the grill support rods to the grill opening reinforcement.

15. Remove the screw attaching the cover to the "Z" brace.

16. Remove the 4 push pins attaching the bottom of the cover to the radiator support.

17. Carefully remove the cover and grille assembly.
18. Remove the power steering cooler and position it aside.
19. Remove the daytime running lamp and position it aside.
20. Disconnect the electrical connectors.
21. Remove the reservoir retaining screws.
22. Disconnect the pump supply hose and drain the system.
23. Remove the reservoir from the vehicle.
24. Carefully pry the pump from the reservoir.
25. Remove the seal/filter from the reservoir and inspect for damage.

To install:
26. Insert the seal into the reservoir.
27. Lubricate the inside diameter of the seal with soapy water and insert the pump until it is firmly seated.
28. Connect the hose and electrical connector to the assembly.
29. Install the reservoir and torque the screws to 41–55 inch lbs. (4.6–6.2 Nm).
30. Install the bumper cover onto the body.
31. Install the 4 push pins into the radiator support.
32. Connect the "Z" brace to the cover and torque the bolt to 12–15 inch lbs. (1.3–1.7 Nm).
33. Connect the grill support rods to the grill opening reinforcement and torque the bolts to 49–66 inch lbs. (5.5–7.4 Nm).
34. Install the 4 nuts connecting the cover to the fender and torque them to 5.8–8.2 inch lbs. (57–72 Nm).
35. Install the 4 screws connecting the cover to the splash shields and torque them to 12–15 inch lbs. (1.3–1.7 Nm).
36. Install the 6 screws connecting the cover to the splash shields and torque them to 12–15 inch lbs. (1.3–1.7 Nm).
37. Install the headlamp and grill mounding.
38. Install the radiator sight shield panel.
39. Install the bulbs into the cornering lamp sockets.
40. Install the lamps and torque the screws to 15–20 inch lbs. (1.6–2.2 Nm).
41. Install the lamp mounting nuts and torque them to 46–64 inch lbs. (5.2–7.2 Nm).
42. Lower the vehicle.
43. Install the filler neck support bracket bolt.
44. Fill the system and check for leaks.

PROBE
1. Disconnect the negative battery cable.
2. Remove the reservoir filler tube retaining bolt and tube.
3. Raise and support the vehicle safely.
4. Remove the screws and the right front inner fender splash shield.
5. Remove the 2 reservoir mounting bolts.
6. Disconnect the hose from the pump and drain the system.
7. Disconnect the pump and washer fluid lever sensor connectors.
8. Remove the reservoir and pump assembly.
9. Pry the pump away from the reservoir.

To install:
10. Installation is the reverse of the removal procedure.

Rear Washer Reservoir and Pump

ESCORT AND TRACER
1. Disconnect the negative battery cable.
2. Remove the right rear lower quarter trim panel.
3. Remove the 3 reservoir mounting bolts.
4. Disconnect the washer pump electrical connector.

5. Disconnect the hose from the pump and drain the reservoir.
6. Remove the reservoir.
7. Pry the pump from the reservoir.

To install:
8. Installation is the reverse of the removal procedure.

ASPIRE
1. Disconnect the negative battery cable.
2. Remove the right luggage compartment side cover.
3. Remove the right rear quarter trim panel.
4. Remove the 2 reservoir mounting bolts.
5. Remove the hose from the wire duct. Pull the reservoir away from the quarter panel.
6. Disconnect the washer pump electrical connector.
7. Disconnect the hose from the pump and drain the reservoir.
8. Remove the reservoir.
9. Remove the 2 washer pump-to-reservoir screws and the pump.

To install:
10. Installation is the reverse of the removal procedure.

➡ **When installing the filler neck, ensure that it is properly seated in the body grommet.**

11. Check for system leaks.

PROBE
1. Remove the left rear lower side trim panel.
2. Remove the filler cap.
3. Loosen the reservoir filler tube attaching clamp and remove the tube.
4. Lift the reservoir from the mounting bracket.
5. Disconnect the hose from the washer pump and drain the system.
6. Disconnect the electrical connector from the washer pump.
7. Remove the reservoir and pump assembly.
8. Pry the washer pump from the reservoir.

To install:
9. Installation is the reverse of the removal procedure.

TAURUS AND SABLE
1. Remove the right rear quarter panel trim.
2. Disconnect the electrical connector from the washer reservoir.
3. Disconnect the hose from the washer reservoir pump and the washer nozzle jet and the bracket; drain the system.
4. Remove the reservoir-to-vehicle screws and the reservoir/pump assembly.
5. Using a prybar, pry the washer pump from the reservoir; be careful not to damage the plastic housing.

To install:
6. Installation is the reverse of the removal procedure.
7. Inspect the seal/filter for damage.
8. Lubricate the inside seal with soapy water and insert the pump into the reservoir until firmly seated.
9. Connect the electrical connector and the hoses.
10. Install the reservoir and the screws.
11. Refill the reservoir and install the quarter trim panel.

Wiper Control Module (WCM)

CROWN VICTORIA, GRAND MARQUIS AND TOWN CAR
1. Disconnect the negative battery cable.

2. Remove the split steering column cover retaining screws and separate the 2 halves.

3. Disconnect the multiple connector at the rear of the wiper switch.

4. Disconnect the multiple connector at the main wiring loom.

5. Remove the **WCM** from the bracket.

To install:

6. Installation is the reverse of the removal procedure.

MARK VIII

➡The wiper control module is located on the far left side of the instrument panel and is attached to the lower panel flange.

1. Disconnect the negative battery cable.
2. Remove the left lower hush panel.
3. Remove the bolt and the **WCM** assembly.
4. Disconnect the electrical connector.

To install:

5. Installation is the reverse of the removal procedure.

6. Torque the bolt to 2.3–3.2 ft. lbs. (3.1–4.3 Nm).

MUSTANG

➡The wiper control module is located at the instrument panel fuse panel.

1. Disconnect the negative battery cable.
2. Disconnect the electrical harness connector.
3. Remove the **WCM** assembly from the bracket.

To install:

4. Installation is the reverse of the removal procedure.

TAURUS AND SABLE

➡On Taurus and Sable, the wiper control module is located on the right side of the steering column support bracket and is attached to a bracket.

1. Disconnect the negative battery cable.
2. Disconnect the harness connector.
3. Remove the both retaining screws and the **WCM** assembly.

To install:

4. Installation is the reverse of the removal procedure.
5. Torque the bolt to 2.3–3.2 ft. lbs. (3.1–4.3 Nm).

CONTINENTAL

➡The wiper control module is located on the left side of steering column support bracket.

1. Disconnect the negative battery cable.
2. Disconnect the harness connector.
3. Remove the both retaining screws and the **WCM** assembly.

To install:

4. Installation is the reverse of the removal procedure.
5. Torque the bolt to 2.3–3.2 ft. lbs. (3.1–4.3 Nm).

Central Timer Module

CONTOUR AND MYSTIQUE

The timer module is located in the fuse panel. It is removed by pulling straight out of the fuse panel.

GENERAL MOTORS CORPORATION MODELS WITH A 4-TERMINAL WIPER MOTOR

All Equipped Models

GENERAL INFORMATION

Models equipped with this type of wiper motor have 4 terminals and a roughly square-type cover, along with a separate, remote washer motor.

Based on the type of control switch used and whether an optional electronic printed circuit board is attached to the wiper cover, the system can serve as either a pulse-type wiper-washer system or a standard 2-speed type windshield wiper. Pulse timing and demand wash functions are controlled electronically on pulse windshield wipers.

Wiper System

This wiper motor is a 2-speed motor designed for a non-depressed wiper park system. It uses a permanent magnet positive park wiper motor with a dynamic brake and separate washer pump assembly.

When equipped for delay or pulse type operation, the pulse windshield wiper and washer system uses a turn signal type wiper/washer switch. The pulse and demand wash functions are controlled by a plug-in printed circuit board enclosed in the wiper's die-cast aluminum housing cover.

Internal parts such as field magnet, armature, drive gear, park switch actuator and brush holder assembly are enclosed in the aluminum housing. The cover is attached with rivets. A radio interference suppressor is located in the terminal connector on the wiper motor. A strap attached to one of the motor bolt hole grommets provides a ground for the suppressor. An automatic reset-type circuit breaker located on the motor brush holder assembly protects the motor while a fuse in the fuse block protects the vehicle wiring.

Power and control are through a 4-terminal connector. Use care when disconnecting the lock-type connectors that attach the vehicle wiring to the wiper.

The wiper motor has 3 brushes: common, low speed and high speed. When the ignition switch is **ON**, a 12V **(+)** circuit is applied to both the low and high speed fixed contacts in the multi-function lever. The low and high speed brushes are connected to the multi-function lever through terminals **C** and **D**. The armature is grounded through the common brush via the ground strap.

Washer System

The washer system consists of a solvent container, pump, washer hose and nozzle.

The fluid washer system is controlled by a small plastic element designed into the washer nozzle. As water is forced through this insert, the design of the mechanism creates an oscillating power stream, designed to more widely disperse the washer fluid for better cleaning. A correctly operating wiper-washer system has a spray pattern that cleans 75 percent of the wipe pattern within 10 wiper cycles.

If the nozzle becomes plugged, apply air pressure. If nozzle remains plugged, the nozzle must be replaced. If the spray pattern is too low or too high on the windshield, wedge-type adjustment shims can be used. Placement of a shim under the nozzle mounting bracket will raise the pattern about 3 degrees. Reverse installation of the same shim will lower the pattern 3 degrees.

WIPER AND WASHER OPERATION

The electronic printed circuit board controls all the timing and washer commands. When the wash button is pushed for more than

0.3 second, a demand wash is performed in 1½ second intervals for as long as the button is held, followed by approximately 6 seconds of dry wipes and a shut **OFF**.

Rotating the switch to either the **LOW** or **HIGH** speed position completes the respective brush circuit to 12V DC **(+)** at the multi-function lever and the wiper motor runs at that speed.

An instantaneous wipe can be obtained by rotating the switch to the mist position and a continuous wipe will be performed if the switch is held.

To have the blades stop in their normal **PARK** position and to have the wiper motor shut off properly when the wiper is turned **OFF** at the multi-function lever, the motor operates at low speed at the shut-down cycle. This is accomplished as follows: the low speed brush circuit is completed to 12V DC **(+)** at the multi-function lever through a park switch located on the brush assembly (terminals **A** and **B**). The park switch contacts are normally closed and this permits the wiper to continue running. When the blades reach the park position, a cam on the large gear moves the park switch actuator that opens the normally closed positive park switch and grounds the wiper motor. This accomplishes a reversal of the motor flux path which causes a no-coast positive park, shutting off the wiper.

The wiper motor can be operated only when the ignition switch is in the **RUN** or **ACCESSORY** position.

CIRCUIT OPERATION

In addition to the features of a conventional (non-pulse) wiper system, (2-speed, **LOW** and **HIGH**), the pulse-type wiper/washer system includes an operating mode in which the wipers make a single stroke with an adjustable time interval between stokes. The time interval is controlled by a solid state Pulse/Speed/Wash Control in the wiper motor assembly. The duration of the delay interval is determined by the delay rheostat in the wiper switch.

The wiper motor has a built-in self-resetting circuit breaker which opens to protect the motor when the wipers are blocked, as from ice on the windshield, for example. The circuit breaker will reset upon cooling.

Low Speed

In the **LOW** position, the wiper switch supplies voltage to the gray wire and the Pulse/Speed/Wash Control grounds the Park/Run relay which closes its contacts, supplying voltage to the low speed brush of the wiper motor. The wipers run at low speed.

High Speed

With the wiper switch in the **HIGH** position, battery voltage is supplied from the purple wire directly to a 2nd armature terminal of the wiper motor. The wipers run at high speed. When the wiper switch is turned to **OFF**, the wipers complete the last sweep at low speed and return to the **PARK** position.

Park

When the wiper switch is 1st turned to **OFF**, voltage is still applied to the wiper motor through contacts in the Park/Run relay. The wiper motor runs at low speed. When the wipers reach the park position, the Park/Run relay opens and shunts the wiper motor to stop it quickly. The wiper blades remain in the **PARK** position.

Mist

When the wiper switch is moved to **MIST** and released, the wipers make 1 sweep at low speed and return to **PARK**. The circuit operation is the same as **LOW** speed.

Pulse

With the wiper switch in **PULSE**, voltage is applied to the gray wire and the solid state Pulse/Speed/Wash control. The Pulse/Speed/Wash control momentarily supplies ground to the Park/Run relay which closes its contacts, applying voltage to the wiper motor. When the wipers return to park, the Park/Run switch opens and ground is removed from the Park/Run relay. The wipers remain in park until the Pulse/Speed/Wash control again supplies ground to the Park/Run relay to start another sweep. The delay time between sweeps is controlled by the variable resistor and can be adjusted from 0–20 seconds.

Washer

When the washer switch is depressed, voltage is applied to the Pulse/Speed/Wash control. The Pulse/Speed/Wash control supplies battery voltage to the washer pump through the orange and pink wires. It also starts the wiper cycle through the low speed brush of the wiper motor. The washer pump continues to run as long as the switch is held down. The Pulse/Speed/Wash control keeps the wipers on for approximately 6 seconds after the washer pump goes **OFF**. If the washer pump is switched **ON** during the pulse operation, the wipers run in low speed for 6 seconds. The wash cycle is completed before the wipers return to the pulse operation.

CHEVROLET Cavalier; PONTIAC Sunfire

TROUBLESHOOTING

Symptom Tests

The following procedures assume that the technician has checked the following:

1. Check fuse **14**. If open, check for short to ground through circuit **143** and replace fuse.
2. Continuity of all harness wires.
3. Wiper motor and wiper/washer switch connectors are mated correctly.
4. If the wiper motor operates but the wipers do not; check the wiper linkage and wiper motor crank arm.
5. Wiper motor-to-dash mounting screws tight for good ground.
6. Washer hoses clear, fluid in tank.

➡**Prior to starting the diagnosis procedure, it is very important to confirm the reported condition with a complete operational check including the washer system.**

WIPERS DO NOT OPERATE IN ANY MODE

1. With ignition to **RUN**, backprobe with test light to switch connector **C215** terminal **D** to ground. If light, go to next step. If not, repair open in circuit **243**. If fuse **A25** is blown, check for short in related circuits.
2. Wiper switch to **HI** and connect test light from connector **C215** terminal **G**. If light, go to next step. If not, check for poor connections at **C215** or open in pigtail **143**. If OK, replace wiper switch.

3. Disconnect wiper motor connector and test light connector terminal **C** to ground. If light, go to next step. If not, repair open in circuit **92** between connector **C215** and motor.

4. Connect test light from motor connector terminal **C** to ground. If light, go to next step. If not, repair open or poor connection in ground circuit **150**.

WIPERS RUN WHEN SWITCH IS IN "OFF" POSITION

1. Ignition switch to **RUN**, wiper switch **OFF** and disconnect wiper switch connector **C215**

2. If motor keeps running, use a voltmeter to measure voltage from connector **C215** terminal **E** to ground. If more than 1 volt, reconnect **C215**, disconnect motor connector and measure voltage from motor connector terminal **D** to ground. If more than 1 volt, repair battery connection to circuit **113**. If less than 1 volt, replace wiper motor cover assembly.

3. If motor parks, check for shorted wires in pigtail to wiper switch assembly. If OK, replace switch.

NO HIGH SPEED MODE

1. Ignition switch to **RUN**, wiper switch **HI**.
2. Do wipers operate at all with switch on **HI**. If not, replace switch.
3. If yes, test light between switch connector **C215** terminal **G** and ground. If light, go to next step. If not, repair open or poor connection in connector **215** or switch pigtail. If OK, replace switch.
4. Disconnect motor connector and test light between motor connector terminal **C** and ground. If light, check for poor connection to motor. If OK, replace motor. If no light, repair open in circuit **92**

LOW SPEED, PULSE DELAY AND MIST MODES INOPERATIVE (HIGH SPEED MODE OK)

1. Ignition switch to **RUN**, wiper switch **LO**. Measure voltage from wiper switch connector **C215** to ground. If more than 1 volt, go to next step. If not, check for poor connection at connector **C215** or open pigtail to switch. If OK, replace switch.

2. Disconnect motor connector and measure voltage from terminal **D** to ground. If more than 1 volt, replace motor cover. If less than 1 volt, repair open in circuit **113**.

PULSE DELAY OPERATES INCORRECTLY OR NOT AT ALL

1. Ignition switch **OFF**, disconnect wiper switch connector **C215**, wiper switch to **DELAY**. Measure resistance of switch connector **C215** terminal **D** to **F**. Move the delay button through the delay range, one notch at a time. The resistance should vary 39–680 kilo-ohms. If not, replace switch. If OK, go to next step.

2. Reconnect switch connector and disconnect motor connector. With ignition in **RUN**, measure voltage from motor connector terminal **E** to ground. If voltage, replace motor cover assembly. If not, check circuit **112**. If OK, replace motor cover.

WIPERS STOP RANDOMLY AND DO NOT PARK WHEN SWITCH IS MOVED TO "OFF"

1. Ignition switch **RUN**, disconnect wiper switch connector **C215**, wiper switch to **OFF**. Do wipers park?
2. If not, measure voltage from **C215** terminal **E** to ground. If more than 1 volt, go to next step. If less, replace motor cover assembly.
3. Reconnect switch and disconnect motor connector. Measure voltage from motor connector terminal **D** to ground. If more than 1 volt, repair short to battery in circuit **113**. If less, replace motor cover assembly.

WIPERS DO NOT OPERATE WHEN WASHER SWITCH IS ACTIVATED

Ignition switch **RUN**, connect test light between switch connector **C215** terminal **E** and ground. Activate washer switch. If light, check for open in circuit **113** or poor connection. If OK, replace motor cover assembly. If no light, check for open in switch. If OK, replace switch.

WASHER DOES NOT OPERATE

1. Disconnect pump connector and connect test light between terminals **A** and **B**. If no light, go to next step. If yes, check for poor connection to washer pump. If OK, replace pump.

2. Connect test light between pump connector terminal **A** and ground. If no light, go to next step. If light, repair open in circuit **150**.

3. Connect test light between switch connector terminal **H** and ground. If no light, check for poor connection at connector **C215** terminal **H**. If OK, replace switch. If light, check for open in circuit **228**.

REMOVAL & INSTALLATION

Repairs can be made to the wiper motor cover and pulse board only.

Wiper Motor Cover

1. Remove wiper motor from vehicle.
2. Remove the bolt or rivets.
3. Remove cover.
To assemble:
4. Install the cover and torque the bolt to 26 inch lbs. (3 Nm).
5. Install the wiper motor.

Pulse Circuit Board Replacement

1. Disconnect the negative battery cable and wait 90 seconds.
2. Remove wiper arms, 4 screws, 5 retainers and screen assembly.
3. Disconnect motor connector and remove wiper drive system.
4. Remove 3 screws and pulse circuit board and cover assembly.
5. Installation is the reverse of removal. Torque the cover screws to 18 inch lbs. (2 Nm).

BUICK Century, LeSabre, Park Avenue, Regal, CADILLAC deVille, Eldorado, Seville; CHEVROLET Lumina, Monte Carlo; OLDSMOBILE Cutlass Ciera, Cutlass Supreme, Eighty-Eight Royale, Ninety-Eight; PONTIAC Bonneville, Grand Prix

---

TROUBLESHOOTING

Diagnostic Tests

WIPERS DO NOT OPERATE IN ANY MODE

1. Disconnect the wiper/washer switch connector. Turn the ignition switch to the **RUN** position. Connect a test light between the connector's, white wire terminal and ground.
   a. If the test light is **ON**, go to Step 2.
   b. If the test light is **OFF**, check for an open in the wiper fuse

or in circuit **93 (WHITE)**. If okay, check for an open in the power feed circuit **4**.

2. Disconnect the wiper motor connector **C2**. Connect a test light between the connector, terminal **C (BLACK)** to the battery's positive **(+)** terminal.

    a. If the test light is **ON**, go to Step 3.

    b. If the test light is **OFF**, repair the open in the ground circuit **150**, **151** or **152**.

3. Connect the wiper/washer switch connector. Disconnect the wiper motor connector **C1**. Connect a test light between the connector terminal **C (DARK GREEN)** and ground.

    a. If the test light is **ON**, go to Step 4.

    b. If the test light is **OFF**, check for a poor connection at the wiper/washer switch connector or for an open in circuit **95 (DARK GREEN)**. If okay, replace the wiper/washer switch.

4. Turn the wiper switch to the **LO** position. Connect a test light between the connector **C1**, terminal **B (GREY)** and ground.

    a. If the test light is **ON**, go to Step 5.

    b. If the test light is **OFF**, check for a poor connection at the wiper/washer switch connector or for an open in circuit **91 (GREY)**. If okay, replace the wiper/washer switch.

5. Check for continuity between the wiper motor connector **C1**, terminal **A (YELLOW)** and connector **C2**, terminal **B (YELLOW)**.

    a. If there is continuity, go to Step 6.

    b. If there is no continuity, repair the open in circuit **196 (YELLOW)**.

6. Check for a poor connection at the wiper motor connectors.

    a. If okay, replace the wiper motor cover assembly.

    b. If trouble is not corrected, replace the wiper motor.

WIPERS RUN AT HIGH SPEED ONLY—LOW SPEED INOPERATIVE

1. Disconnect the wiper motor connector **C1**. Turn the ignition switch to the **RUN** position and the wiper switch to the **LO** position. Connect a test light between the connector **C1**, terminal **B (GREY)** and ground.

    a. If the test light is **ON**, go to Step 2.

    b. If the test light is **OFF**, check for an open in circuit **91 (GREY)** or a poor connection at the wiper/washer switch connector. If okay, replace the wiper/washer switch.

2. Connect a test light between the connector **C1**, terminal **C (DARK GREEN)** and ground.

    a. If the test light is **ON**, go to Step 3.

    b. If the test light is **OFF**, check circuit **95 (DARK GREEN)** for poor connections or open. If okay, replace the wiper/washer switch.

3. Check for continuity through circuit **196 (YELLOW)**.

    a. If there is continuity, go to Step 4.

    b. If there is no continuity, repair the open in circuit **196 (YELLOW)**.

4. Check for a poor connection at connector **C1**.

    a. If okay, replace the wiper motor cover assembly.

    b. If trouble is not corrected, replace the wiper motor.

WIPERS RUN AT LOW SPEED ONLY—HIGH SPEED INOPERATIVE

1. Disconnect the wiper motor connector **C2**. Turn the ignition switch to the **RUN** position and the wiper switch to the **HI** position. Connect a test light between the connector **C2**, terminal **A (PUR-PLE)** and ground.

    a. If the test light is **ON**, go to Step 2.

    b. If the test light is **OFF**, check for an open in circuit **92 (PURPLE)** or a poor connection at the wiper/washer switch connector. If okay, replace the wiper/washer switch.

2. Check for a poor connection at connector **C2**, terminal **A (PURPLE)**.

    a. If okay, replace the wiper motor cover assembly.

    b. If trouble is not corrected, replace the wiper motor.

WIPERS RUN INTERMITTENTLY IN LOW OR HIGH SPEED SETTINGS

1. Remove the wiper fuse and connect an ammeter (0–30 amp) across the fuse block terminals. Turn the ignition switch to the **RUN** position and the wiper switch to the **LO** position. Observe the lowest current draw while the wipers are running on dry glass (current draw will fluctuate).

    a. If the lowest current draw is less than 3.5 amps, replace the wiper motor.

    b. If the current draw is 3.5–6.5 amps, end test.

    c. If the lowest current draw is more than 6.5 amps, go to Step 2.

2. Replace the wiper blade elements and repeat the test.

    a. If the lowest current draw is still more than 6.5 amps, go to Step 3.

    b. If the lowest current draw is less than 6.5 amps, end test.

3. Disconnect the wiper transmission drive link from the wiper motor crank arm and repeat test.

    a. If the lowest current draw is still more than 6.5 amps, replace the wiper motor.

    b. If the lowest current draw is less than 6.5 amps, the wiper transmission assembly is binding, repair or replace as required.

8838XG41

Windshield wiper motor wiring harness electrical connectors—BUICK Century, LeSabre, Park Avenue, Regal; CADILLAC deVille, Eldorado, Seville; CHEVROLET Lumina, Monte Carlo; OLDSMOBILE Cutlass Ciera, Cutlass Supreme, Eighty-Eight Royale, Ninety-Eight; PONTIAC Bonneville, Grand Prix

Refer to the model specific sections for engine electrical system service procedures

WIPERS WILL NOT TURN OFF

1. Disconnect the wiper motor connector **C1**. Turn the ignition switch to the **RUN** position and the wiper switch to the **OFF** position. Using a digital multimeter, measure the voltage from connector **C1**, terminal **B (GREY)** to ground.

   a. If the voltage is 0 volts, go to Step 2.

   b. If battery voltage is present, check for a short to **B+** in circuit **91 (GREY)**. If okay, replace the wiper/washer switch.

2. Disconnect the wiper motor connector **C2**. Using a digital multimeter, measure the voltage from connector **C2**, terminal **A (PURPLE)** to ground.

   a. If the voltage is 0 volts, repair the short to **B+** in circuit **196 (YELLOW)**.

   b. If battery voltage is present, check for a short to **B+** in circuit **92 (PURPLE)**. If okay, replace the wiper/washer switch.

WIPERS CYCLE IN AND OUT OF PARK AFTER WIPERS ARE SHUT OFF

1. Turn the ignition switch to the **RUN** position. Operate the wiper switch and return it to the **OFF** position.

   a. If the wiper motor continues to operate in low speed, go to Step 2.

   b. If the wiper motor continues to operate in high speed, go to Wipers Run At High Speed Only chart.

2. Replace the park switch assembly.

   a. If the trouble is corrected, end test.

   b. If the trouble is not corrected, replace the wiper motor assembly.

PULSE DELAY OPERATES INCORRECTLY OR NOT AT ALL

1. Disconnect the wiper/washer switch connector. Turn the ignition switch to the **OFF** position and the wiper switch to the **DELAY** position. Using a digital multimeter, measure the resistance through the wiper/washer switch at connector, from white wire terminal to pink wire terminal; then, move the wiper switch through the entire **DELAY** range.

   a. If the resistance varies from 1.244 Mega-ohms to 0.024 Mega-ohms, go to Step 2.

   b. If the resistance does not vary from 1.244 Mega-ohms to 0.024 Mega-ohms, replace the wiper/washer switch assembly.

2. Measure the resistance through the wiper/washer switch at connector, from gray wire terminal to white wire terminal.

   a. If the resistance is less than 3 ohms, go to Step 3.

   b. If the resistance is greater than 3 ohm, replace the wiper/washer switch assembly.

3. Check circuits **91 (GREY)** and **94 (PINK)** for an open or poor connection. If okay, remove the wiper motor cover assembly.

   a. If the park switch pulse contacts are touching the pads on the circuit board, replace the wiper motor cover assembly.

   b. If the park switch pulse contacts are not touching the pads on the circuit board, replace the park switch spring contacts.

WASHER WILL NOT OPERATE

1. Disconnect the washer pump connector. Turn the ignition switch to the **RUN** position. Connect a test light between terminals **A (RED)** and **B (DARK BLUE)** of the washer pump connector; then, activate the washer switch while observing the test light.

   a. If the test light is **OFF**, go to Step 2.

   b. If the test light is **ON**, check for a poor connection at the washer pump connector. If okay, replace the washer pump.

2. Connect a test light between connector, terminal **A (RED)** and ground; then, activate the washer switch while observing the test light.

   a. If the test light is **OFF**, go to Step 3.

   b. If the test light is **ON**, check for a poor connection or open in circuit **227 (DARK BLUE)**. If okay, replace the wiper motor assembly (internal ground circuit open).

3. Connect a test light between wiper motor connector **C1**, terminal **D (RED)** and ground.

   a. If the test light is **OFF**, go to Step 4.

   b. If the test light is **ON**, check for a poor connection or open in circuit **228 (RED)**.

4. Turn the ignition switch to the **RUN** position. Using a digital multimeter, backprobe the wiper/washer switch connector, from pink wire terminal to ground; then, activate the washer switch while observing the digital multimeter.

   a. If 0 voltage is present, replace the wiper/washer switch assembly.

   b. If battery voltage is present, check for a poor connection at the wiper/washer switch connector(s) and wiper motor assembly; or open in circuit **94 (PINK)**. If okay, replace the wiper motor assembly.

WASHER WILL NOT SHUT OFF

1. Turn the ignition switch to the **RUN** position and the wiper switch to the **LO** position. Disconnect the wiper motor connector **C1**. Connect a test light between connector **C1**, terminal **F (PINK)** and ground at the wiper motor case. Momentarily, activate the washer switch while observing the test light.

2. If the test light is **OFF** when the washer switch is released, replace the wiper motor cover assembly.

3. If the test light is **ON** when the washer switch is released, replace the wiper/washer switch assembly.

REMOVAL & INSTALLATION

Wiper Motor Cover

1. Remove the wiper arm assemblies from the vehicle. Disconnect the negative battery cable from the battery. At the center or the cowl, remove the washer hose from the nipple.

➡ **The air inlet shroud is 2 pieces; be careful not to break it.**

2. Remove the screws and the air inlet shroud.

3. At the wiper motor cover's electrical connector, pull the retainer from the connector; then, disconnect the electrical connector from the wiper motor cover assembly.

4. Remove the wiper motor cover-to-wiper motor screws and the cover.

To install:

5. With the wiper motor in the park position, align the wiper motor cover's cam slot with the drive pin. Install the cover and torque the screws to 18 inch lbs. (2 Nm).

6. Install the electrical connector and secure with the retainer. Install the air inlet shroud.

7. Lubricate the washer hose and install onto the nipple. Connect the negative battery cable. Install the wiper arm assemblies.

Park Switch Assembly

1. Remove the wiper motor cover assembly.

➡ **If the wiper motor is in the park position, operate the motor (as required) to remove the pawl from the relay slot.**

2. Remove the screw and the park switch from the wiper motor assembly.

To install:

3. Install the park switch and screw onto the wiper motor assembly.

4. When the pawl is in the relay slot, operate the wiper motor back into the park position.

5. Install the wiper motor cover assembly.

Wiper Drive System Module

1. Remove the wiper arm assemblies from the vehicle. Disconnect the negative battery cable from the battery. At the center or the cowl, remove the washer hose from the nipple.

➡ **The air inlet shroud is 2 pieces; be careful not to break it.**

2. Remove the screws and the air inlet shroud.

3. At the wiper motor electrical connectors, pull the retainers from the connectors; then, disconnect the electrical connectors from the wiper motor assembly.

4. Remove the wiper drive system module-to-cowl screws and the module from the vehicle.

To install:

5. Install the wiper drive system module and torque the module-to-cowl screws to 106 inch lbs. (12 Nm).

6. Connect the electrical connectors to the wiper motor and secure with the retainers.

7. Install the air inlet shroud.

8. Lubricate the washer hose and install onto the nipple. Connect the negative battery cable. Install the wiper arm assemblies.

CHEVROLET Corsica and Beretta

TROUBLESHOOTING

Diagnostic Tests

WIPERS DO NOT OPERATE IN ANY MODE

1. Disconnect the wiper/washer switch connector **C1**. Turn the ignition switch to the **RUN** position. Connect a test light between the connector **C1**, terminal **G (WHITE)** and ground.

    a. If the test light is **ON,** go to Step 2.

    b. If the test light is **OFF,** check for an open in the wiper fuse **or in c10** or in circuit **93 (WHITE)**. If okay, check for an open in the power feed circuit **4**.

2. Disconnect the wiper motor connector **C2**. Connect a test light between the connector **C2**, terminal **C (BLACK)** to the battery's positive **(+)** terminal.

    a. If the test light is **ON,** go to Step 3.

    b. If the test light is **OFF,** repair the open in the ground circuit **150 (BLACK)**.

3. Connect the wiper/washer switch connector **C1**. Disconnect the wiper motor connector **C1**. Connect a test light between the connector **C1**, terminal **C (DARK GREEN)** and ground.

    a. If the test light is **ON,** go to Step 4.

    b. If the test light is **OFF,** check for a poor connection at the wiper/washer and defogger switch connector **C1** or for an open in circuit **91 (GREY)**. If okay, replace the wiper/washer and defogger switch.

4. Turn the wiper switch to the **LO** position. Connect a test light

between the connector **C1**, terminal **B (DARK GREEN)** and ground.

    a. If the test light is **ON,** go to Step 5.

    b. If the test light is **OFF,** check for an open in circuit **95 (DARK GREEN)**. If okay, replace the wiper/washer and defogger switch.

5. Check for continuity between the wiper motor connector **C1**, terminal **A (YELLOW)** and connector **C2**, terminal **B (YELLOW)**.

    a. If there is continuity, go to Step 6.

    b. If there is no continuity, repair the open in circuit **196 (YELLOW)**.

6. Check for a poor connection at the wiper motor connectors.

    a. If okay, replace the wiper motor cover assembly.

    b. If trouble is not corrected, replace the wiper motor.

WIPERS RUN AT HIGH SPEED ONLY—LOW SPEED INOPERATIVE

1. Disconnect the wiper motor connector **C1**. Turn the ignition switch to the **RUN** position and the wiper switch to the **LO** position. Connect a test light between the connector **C1**, terminal **B (DARK GREEN)** and ground.

    a. If the test light is **ON,** go to Step 2.

    b. If the test light is **OFF,** check for an open in circuit **95 (DARK GREEN)** or a poor connection at the wiper/washer switch connector **C1**. If okay, replace the wiper/washer and defogger switch.

2. Connect a test light between the connector **C1**, terminal **C (GREY)** and ground.

    a. If the test light is **ON,** go to Step 3.

    b. If the test light is **OFF,** check circuit **91 (GREY)** for poor connections or open. If okay, replace the wiper/washer and defogger switch.

3. Check for continuity through circuit **196 (YELLOW)**.

    a. If there is continuity, go to Step 4.

    b. If there is no continuity, repair the open in circuit **196 (YELLOW)**.

4. Check for a poor connection at connector **C1**.

    a. If okay, replace the wiper motor cover assembly.

    b. If trouble is not corrected, replace the wiper motor.

WIPERS RUN AT LOW SPEED ONLY—HIGH SPEED INOPERATIVE

1. Disconnect the wiper motor connector **C2**. Turn the ignition switch to the **RUN** position and the wiper switch to the **HI** position. Connect a test light between the connector **C2**, terminal **A (PURPLE)** and ground.

    a. If the test light is **ON,** go to Step 2.

    b. If the test light is **OFF,** check for an open in circuit **92 (PURPLE)** or a poor connection at the wiper/washer and defogger switch connector **C1**. If okay, replace the wiper/washer and defogger switch.

2. Check for a poor connection at connector **C2**, terminal **A (PURPLE)**.

    a. If okay, replace the wiper motor cover assembly.

    b. If trouble is not corrected, replace the wiper motor.

WIPERS RUN INTERMITTENTLY IN LOW OR HIGH SPEED SETTINGS

1. Remove the wiper fuse **fuse #1010** and connect an ammeter (0–30 amp) across the fuse block terminals. Turn the ignition

Windshield wiper motor wiring harness electrical connectors—Corsica and Beretta

switch to the **RUN** position and the wiper switch to the **LO** position. Observe the lowest current draw while the wipers are running on dry glass (current draw will fluctuate).

    a. If the lowest current draw is less than 3.5 amps, replace the wiper motor.

    b. If the current draw is 3.5–6.5 amps, end test.

    c. If the lowest current draw is more than 6.5 amps, go to Step 2.

2. Replace the wiper blade elements and repeat the test.

    a. If the lowest current draw is still more than 6.5 amps, go to Step 3.

    b. If the lowest current draw is less than 6.5 amps, end test.

3. Disconnect the wiper transmission from the wiper motor crank arm and repeat test.

    a. If the lowest current draw is still more than 6.5 amps, replace the wiper motor.

    b. If the lowest current draw is less than 6.5 amps, the wiper transmission assembly is binding, repair or replace as required.

WIPERS WILL NOT TURN OFF

1. Disconnect the wiper motor connector **C1**. Turn the ignition switch to the **RUN** position and the wiper switch to the **OFF** position. Using a digital multimeter, measure the voltage from connector **C1**, terminal **B (DARK GREEN)** to ground.

    a. If the voltage is 0 volts, go to Step 2.

    b. If battery voltage is present, check for a short to **B+** in circuit **95 (DARK GREEN)**. If okay, replace the wiper/washer and defogger switch.

2. Disconnect the wiper motor connector **C2**. Using a digital multimeter, measure the voltage from connector **C2**, terminal **A (YELLOW)** to ground.

    a. If the voltage is 0 volts, repair the short to **B+** in circuit **196 (YELLOW)**.

    b. If battery voltage is present, check for a short to **B+** in circuit **92 (PURPLE)**. If okay, replace the wiper/washer and defogger switch.

WIPERS CYCLE IN AND OUT OF PARK AFTER WIPERS ARE SHUT OFF

1. Turn the ignition switch to the **RUN** position. Operate the wiper switch and return it to the **OFF** position.

    a. If the wiper motor continues to operate in low speed, go to Step 2.

    b. If the wiper motor continues to operate in high speed, go to Wipers Run At High Speed Only chart.

2. Replace the park switch assembly.

    a. If the trouble is corrected, end test.

    b. If the trouble is not corrected, replace the wiper motor assembly.

PULSE DELAY OPERATES INCORRECTLY OR NOT AT ALL

1. Disconnect the wiper/washer and defogger switch connector **C1**. Turn the ignition switch to the **OFF** position and the wiper switch to the **DELAY** position. Using a digital multimeter, measure the resistance through the wiper/washer switch at connector **C1**, from terminal **G (WHITE)** to terminal **H (BROWN)**; then, move the wiper switch through the entire **DELAY** range.

    a. If the resistance varies from 1.244 Mega-ohms to 0.024 Mega-ohms, go to Step 2.

    b. If the resistance does not vary from 1.244 Mega-ohms to 0.024 Mega-ohms, replace the wiper/washer switch assembly.

2. Measure the resistance through the wiper/washer switch at connector **C1**, from terminal **F (DARK GREEN)** to terminal **G (WHITE)**.

    a. If the resistance is less than 3 ohms, go to Step 3.

    b. If the resistance is greater than 3 ohm, replace the wiper/washer and defogger switch assembly.

3. Check circuits **95 (DARK GREEN)** and **96 (BROWN)** for an open or poor connection. If okay, remove the wiper motor cover assembly.

    a. If the park switch pulse contacts are touching the pads on the circuit board, replace the wiper motor cover assembly.

    b. If the park switch pulse contacts are not touching the pads on the circuit board, replace the park switch spring contacts.

WASHER WILL NOT OPERATE

1. Disconnect the washer pump connector. Turn the ignition switch to the **RUN** position. Connect a test light between terminals **A (RED)** and **B (DARK BLUE)** of the washer pump connector; then, activate the washer switch while observing the test light.

    a. If the test light is **OFF,** go to Step 2.

    b. If the test light is **ON,** check for a poor connection at the washer pump connector. If okay, replace the washer pump.

2. Connect a test light between connector, terminal **A (RED)** and ground; then, activate the washer switch while observing the test light.

    a. If the test light is **OFF,** check for an open in circuit **228 (RED)**. If okay, replace the wiper/washer and defogger switch assembly.

    b. If the test light is **ON,** check for a poor connection at the wiper motor connector **C1**, terminal **E (DARK BLUE)** or open in circuit **227 (DARK BLUE)**. If okay, replace the wiper motor assembly (internal ground circuit open).

WASHER WILL NOT OPERATE

1. Disconnect the washer pump connector. Turn the ignition switch to the **RUN** position. Connect a test light between terminals **A (RED)** and terminal **B (DARK BLUE)** of the water pump connector. Momentarily, activate the washer switch while observing the test light.

    a. If the test light is **OFF,** go to Step 2.

    b. If the test light is **ON** when the washer switch is released, check for a poor connection at the washer pump connector. If okay, replace the washer pump.

2. Connect a test light between terminal **A (RED)** and ground. Momentarily, activate the washer switch while observing the test light.

    a. If the test light is **OFF,** check for an open in circuit **228**

(RED). If okay, replace the wiper/washer and defogger switch assembly.

b. If the test light is **ON** when the washer switch is released, check for a poor connection at the wiper motor connector **C1**, terminal **E (DARK BLUE)** or an open in circuit **227 (DARK BLUE)**. If okay, replace the wiper motor assembly (internal ground circuit open).

PULSE DELAY DOES NOT DECREASE WITH INCREASING VEHICLE SPEED

1. Disconnect the washer pump connector **C1**. Turn the ignition switch to the **RUN** position. Using a digital multimeter, measure voltage between connector **C1**, terminal **D (GREY)** and ground.

2. If 0 voltage is present, check circuit **817** for an open or poor connection at connector **C1**, terminal **D (GREY)**. If okay, see Vehicle Speed Sensor Electrical Diagnosis.

3. If battery voltage is present, replace the wiper motor cover assembly.

REMOVAL & INSTALLATION

Wiper Motor Cover

1. Disconnect the negative battery cable from the battery.
2. Disconnect the electrical connector from the wiper motor cover and the wiper motor.
3. Remove the wiper motor cover-to-wiper motor screws and the cover.
   #### To install:
4. With the wiper motor in the park position, align the wiper motor cover's cam slot with the drive pin. Install the cover and torque the screws to 18 inch lbs. (2 Nm).
5. Install the electrical connectors.
6. Connect the negative battery cable.

Park Switch Assembly

1. Remove the wiper motor assembly.
2. Remove the wiper motor cover assembly.

➡**If the wiper motor is in the park position, operate the motor (as required) to remove the pawl from the relay slot.**

3. Remove the screw and the park switch from the wiper motor assembly.
   #### To install:
4. Install the park switch and screw onto the wiper motor assembly.
5. When the pawl is in the relay slot, operate the wiper motor back into the park position.
6. Install the wiper motor cover assembly.
7. Install the wiper motor assembly.

Wiper Transmission Assembly

1. Remove the wiper arm/blade assemblies from the vehicle. Remove the cowl panel assembly.
2. Remove the transmission drive link from the wiper motor crank arm ball using tool J-39232.
3. Remove the wiper transmission-to-cowl screws. Remove the transmission assembly by guiding it through the access hole in the shroud's upper panel.

To install:
4. Loosen but do not remove the 2 transmission drive link adjusting nuts.

5. Position the transmission assembly in the plenum chamber through shroud's upper panel opening. Install the 6 transmission-to-cowl screws and torque the screws to 71 inch lbs. (8 Nm).

6. Using tool J-39529 or equivalent, install the transmission drive link socket to the crank arm ball of the wiper motor assembly; be sure the socket is fully seated and torque the nuts to 44 inch lbs. (5 Nm).

7. Install the cowl panel assembly. Install the wiper arm/blade assemblies.

CHEVROLET Corvette

TROUBLESHOOTING

Diagnostic Tests

WIPERS DO NOT OPERATE IN ANY MODE

1. Disconnect the wiper/washer switch connector **C236**. Turn the ignition switch to the **ACCY** or **RUN** position. Connect a test light between the connector **C236**, terminal **B (YELLOW)** and ground.
   a. If the test light is **ON**, go to Step 2.
   b. If the test light is **OFF**, check for an open in the wiper fuse or in circuit **143 (YELLOW)**. If okay, check for an open in the power feed circuit **4**.
2. Connect the wiper/washer switch connector **C1**. Disconnect all 3 wiper motor connectors. Connect a test light between the connector **C2**, terminal **C (GREY)** and ground.
   a. If the test light is **ON**, go to Step 3.
   b. If the test light is **OFF**, check for an open in circuit **91 (GREY)**. If okay, replace the wiper/washer switch.
3. Turn the wiper switch to the **LO** position. Connect a test light between the connector **C2**, terminal **B (LIGHT BLUE)** and ground.
   a. If the test light is **ON**, go to Step 4.
   b. If the test light is **OFF**, check for an open in circuit **97 (LIGHT BLUE)**. If okay, replace the wiper/washer switch.
4. Reconnect the wiper motor connectors **C1** and **C2**. With the wiper switch still in the **LO** position, connect a test light between connector **C3**, terminal **B (YELLOW)** and ground.
   a. If the test light is **ON**, go to Step 5.
   b. If the test light is **OFF**, check for an open in circuit **196 (GREY)**. If okay, replace the wiper motor assembly.
5. Connect a test light between connector **C3**, terminal **A (PURPLE)** and ground. Turn the wiper switch to the **HI** position.
   a. If there is continuity, check for an open or short to battery voltage in ground circuit **150**. If okay, replace the wiper motor assembly.
   b. If there is no continuity, check the open in circuit **92 (YELLOW)**. If okay, replace the wiper/washer switch.

WIPERS RUN AT HIGH SPEED ONLY—LOW SPEED INOPERATIVE

1. Disconnect the wiper motor connectors **C2** and **C3**. Turn the ignition switch to the **ACCY** or **RUN** position and the wiper switch to the **LO** position. Connect a test light between the connector **C2**, terminal **C (GREY)** and ground.

Windshield wiper/washer system electrical schematic—Corvette

a. If the test light is **ON,** go to Step 2.

b. If the test light is **OFF,** check for an open in circuit **91 (GREY).** If okay, replace the wiper/washer switch.

2. Connect a test light between the connector **C2,** terminal **B (LIGHT BLUE)** and ground.

a. If the test light is **ON,** go to Step 3.

b. If the test light is **OFF,** check for an open in circuit **97 (LIGHT BLUE).** If okay, replace the wiper/washer switch.

3. Reconnect connector **C2.** Connect a test light between the connector **C2,** terminal **B (LIGHT BLUE)** and ground.

a. If the test light is **ON,** replace the wiper motor.

b. If the test light is **OFF,** check for an open in circuit **196 (YELLOW).** If okay, replace the wiper motor.

WIPERS WILL NOT TURN OFF

1. Disconnect the 3 wiper motor connectors. Turn the ignition switch to the **ACCY** or **RUN** position and the wiper switch to the **OFF** position. Connect a test light between connector **C1,** terminal **A (BROWN)** to ground.

a. If the test light is **OFF,** go to Step 2.

b. If the test light is **ON,** check for an short to **B+** in circuit **96 (BROWN).** If okay, replace the wiper/washer switch.

2. Connect a test light between connector **C2,** terminal **B (LIGHT BLUE)** and ground.

a. If the test light is **OFF,** go to Step 3.

b. If the test light is **ON,** check for an short to **B+** in circuit **97 (LIGHT BLUE).** If okay, replace the wiper/washer switch.

3. Reconnect connectors **C1** and **C2.** Connect a test light between connector **C3,** terminal **B (YELLOW)** and ground.

a. If the test light is **OFF,** go to Step 4.

b. If the test light is **ON,** check for an short to **B+** in circuit **196 (YELLOW).** If okay, replace the wiper motor.

4. Connect a test light between connector **C3,** terminal **A (BROWN)** and ground.

a. If the test light is **OFF,** replace the wiper motor.

b. If the test light is **ON,** check for an short to **B+** in circuit **92 (PURPLE).** If okay, replace the wiper/washer switch.

WIPERS RUN AT LOW SPEED ONLY—HIGH SPEED INOPERATIVE

1. Disconnect the wiper motor connector **C3.** Turn the ignition switch to the **ACCY** or **RUN** position and the wiper switch to the **HI**

position. Connect a test light between the connector **C3,** terminal **A (PURPLE)** and ground.

2. If the test light is **ON,** replace the wiper motor.

3. If the test light is **OFF,** check for an open in circuit **92 (PURPLE).** If okay, replace the wiper/washer switch.

PULSE DELAY OPERATES INCORRECTLY OR NOT AT ALL

1. Disconnect the wiper motor connectors **C1** and **C2.** Turn the ignition switch to the **OFF** position and the wiper switch to the **LO** position. Using a digital multimeter, measure the resistance across connector **C1,** from terminal **A (BROWN)** and connector **C2,** terminal **B (LIGHT BLUE).**

a. If the resistance is more than 24 kilo-ohms, go to Step 2.

b. If the resistance is less than 24 kilo-ohms, check for an open in circuit **96 (BROWN)** or **97 (LIGHT BLUE).** If okay, replace the wiper/washer switch assembly.

2. Move the wiper switch through the entire pulse **DELAY** range and measure the resistance.

a. If the resistance increases to approximately 1.2 Mega-ohms, replace the wiper motor assembly.

b. If the resistance does not increase to approximately 1.2 Mega-ohms, replace the wiper/washer switch assembly.

WASHER WILL NOT OPERATE

1. Disconnect the washer pump connector. Turn the ignition switch to the **ACCY** or **RUN** position. Connect a test light between terminals **A (PINK)** and **B (BLACK)** of the washer pump connector; then, activate the washer switch while observing the test light.

a. If the test light is **OFF,** go to Step 2.

b. If the test light is **ON,** replace the washer pump.

2. Connect a test light between connector, terminal **A (PINK)** and ground; then, activate the washer switch while observing the test light.

a. If the test light is **OFF,** go to Step 3.

b. If the test light is **ON,** repair the open in circuit **150 (BLACK);** terminal of the pump connector.

3. Disconnect the wiper motor connectors **C1** and **C2.** Connect a test light between wiper motor connector **C1,** terminal **C (PINK)** and ground; then, activate the washer switch while observing the test light.

a. If the test light is **OFF,** go to Step 4.

b. If the test light is **ON,** repair the open in circuit **94 (PINK).**

4. Connect a test light between wiper motor connector **C1,** terminal **A (PINK)** and ground; then, activate the washer switch while observing the test light.

a. If the test light is **OFF,** check for an open in circuit **96 (BROWN).**

b. If the test light is **ON,** go to Step 5.

5. Connect a test light between wiper motor connector **C2,** terminal **B (LIGHT BLUE)** and ground; then, activate the washer switch while observing the test light.

a. If the test light is **OFF,** check for an open in circuit **97 (LIGHT BLUE).** If okay, replace the wiper/washer switch assembly.

b. If the test light is **ON,** replace the wiper motor.

REMOVAL & INSTALLATION

Wiper Motor Cover

1. Disconnect the negative battery cable from the battery.

2. Disconnect the electrical connector from the wiper motor cover and the wiper motor.

3. Remove the wiper motor cover-to-wiper motor screws and the cover.

To install:

4. With the wiper motor in the park position, align the wiper motor cover's cam slot with the drive pin. Install the cover and torque the screws to 18 inch lbs. (2 Nm).

5. Install the electrical connectors.

6. Connect the negative battery cable.

Park Switch Assembly

1. Remove the wiper motor assembly.

2. Remove the wiper motor cover assembly.

➡**If the wiper motor is in the park position, operate the motor (as required) to remove the pawl from the relay slot.**

3. Remove the screw and the park switch from the wiper motor assembly.

To install:

4. Install the park switch and screw onto the wiper motor assembly.

5. When the pawl is in the relay slot, operate the wiper motor back into the park position.

6. Install the wiper motor cover assembly.

7. Install the wiper motor assembly.

CHEVROLET Camaro; PONTIAC Firebird

TROUBLESHOOTING

Diagnostic Tests

WIPERS DO NOT OPERATE IN ANY MODE

1. Turn the ignition switch to the **RUN** position. Backprobe with a test light from the wiper/washer switch connector **C215**, terminal **D (YELLOW)** and ground.

   a. If the test light is **ON,** go to Step 2.

   b. If the test light is **OFF,** check for an open in circuit **143 (YELLOW)**. If fuse **14** is open, check for a short to ground in the related circuits.

2. Turn the wiper switch to the **HI** position. Connect a test light between the connector **C215**, terminal **G (PURPLE)** to ground.

   a. If the test light is **ON,** go to Step 3.

   b. If the test light is **OFF,** check for a poor connection at connector **C215**, terminal **D (YELLOW)** or an open in circuit **143 (YELLOW)** to the wiper/washer switch.

3. Disconnect the wiper motor connector. Connect a test light between the connector, terminal **C (PURPLE)** and ground.

   a. If the test light is **ON,** go to Step 4.

   b. If the test light is **OFF,** check for an open or a poor connection in circuit **92 (PURPLE)** between connector **C215** and the wiper motor.

4. Connect a test light between the wiper motor connector, terminal **C (PURPLE)** and terminal **A (BLACK)**.

   a. If the test light is **ON,** check for a poor connection to the wiper motor assembly. If okay, replace the wiper motor assembly.

   b. If the test light is **OFF,** repair the open or poor connection in the ground circuit **150 (BLACK)**.

WIPERS RUN WHEN SWITCH IS OFF

1. Turn the ignition switch to the **RUN** position and the wiper switch to the **OFF** position. Disconnect the wiper/washer switch connector **C215**.

   a. If the wiper motor keeps running, go to Step 2.

   b. If the wiper motor parks, check for shorted wires in the pigtail to the wiper/washer switch assembly. If okay, replace the wiper/washer switch assembly.

2. Using a digital multimeter, measure the voltage from connector **C215** (vehicle side), terminal **E (DARK GREEN)** to ground.

   a. If more than 1.0 volt is present, go to Step 3.

   b. If less than 1.0 volt is present (approx. 0 volts), go to Step 4.

3. Reconnect the wiper/washer switch connector **C215**. Disconnect the wiper motor connector. Using a digital multimeter, measure the voltage from the wiper motor connector, terminal **D (DARK GREEN)** to ground.

   a. If more than 1.0 volt is present, repair **B+** connection to circuit **113 (DARK GREEN)**.

   b. If less than 1.0 volt is present, replace the wiper motor cover assembly.

4. Reconnect the wiper/washer switch connector **C215**. Disconnect the wiper motor connector. Using a digital multimeter, measure the voltage from the wiper motor connector, terminal **C (PURPLE)** to ground.

   a. If 0 volts is present, replace the wiper motor cover assembly.

   b. If **B+** voltage is present, repair the short to the **B+** in circuit **92 (PURPLE)**.

NO HIGH SPEED MODE

1. Turn the ignition switch to the **RUN** position and the wiper/washer switch to the **HI** position.

   a. If the wipers work some, go to Step 2.

   b. If the do not work at all, replace the wiper/washer switch.

2. With the ignition switch in the **RUN** position and the wiper switch in the **HI** position. Connect a test light between the wiper/washer switch connector **C215**, terminal **G (PURPLE)** and ground.

   a. If the test light is **ON,** go to Step 3.

   b. If the test light is **OFF,** check for a poor connection at the wiper/washer switch connector **C215** or for an open in the pigtail to the wiper/washer switch assemble. If okay, replace the wiper/washer switch.

3. Disconnect the wiper motor connector. Connect a test light between the harness terminal **C (PURPLE)** and ground.

   a. If the test light is **ON,** check for a poor connection at the wiper motor assembly. If okay, replace the wiper motor cover assembly.

   b. If the test light is **OFF,** repair the open in circuit **92 (PURPLE)**.

LOW SPEED, PULSE DELAY AND MIST MODES INOPERATIVE—HIGH SPEED MODE OK

1. Turn the ignition switch to the **RUN** position and the wiper switch to the **LO** position. Using a digital multimeter, measure the voltage from the wiper/washer switch connector **C215**, terminal **E (DARK GREEN)** to ground.

   a. If more than 1.0 volt is present, go to Step 2.

Refer to the model specific sections for engine electrical system service procedures

A   BLK
B   YEL
C   PPL
D   DK GRN
E   GRY

8838XG47

Windshield wiper motor wiring harness electrical connector— Camaro and Firebird

b. If less than 1.0 volt is present (approx. 0 volt), check for a poor connection at the wiper/washer switch connector **C215** or for an open pigtail to the wiper/washer switch assembly. If okay, replace the wiper/washer switch.

2. Disconnect the wiper motor connector. Using a digital multi-meter, measure the voltage from the wiper motor connector, terminal **D (DARK GREEN)** to ground.

　　a. If more than 1.0 volt is present, replace the wiper motor cover assembly.

　　b. If less than 1.0 volt is present (approx. 0 volt), repair the open in circuit **113 (DARK GREEN)**.

PULSE DELAY OPERATES INCORRECTLY OR NOT AT ALL

1. Disconnect the wiper/washer switch connector **C215**. Turn the ignition switch to the **OFF** position and the wiper switch to the **DELAY** position. Using a digital multimeter, measure the resistance through the wiper/washer switch assembly from connector **C215**, terminal **D (YELLOW)** to terminal **F (GREY)**. Move the wiper switch through the entire **DELAY** range, one notch at a time.

　　a. If the resistance varies from 39 kilo-ohms to 680 kilo-ohms, go to Step 2.

　　b. If the resistance does not vary from 39 kilo-ohms to 680 kilo-ohms, replace the wiper/washer switch assembly.

2. Reconnect the wiper/washer switch connector **C215**. Disconnect the wiper motor connector. Turn the ignition switch to the **RUN** position. Using a digital multimeter, measure the voltage from the wiper motor connector, terminal **E (GREY)** to ground.

　　a. If **B+** is present, replace the wiper motor cover assembly.

　　b. If approx. 0 volts is present, check circuit **112 (GREY)** for an open or poor connection. If okay, replace the wiper motor cover assembly.

WIPERS STOP RANDOMLY AND DO NOT PARK WHEN SWITCH IS MOVED TO OFF

1. Turn the ignition switch to the **RUN** position and the wiper switch to the **OFF** position. Disconnect the wiper/washer switch connector **C215**.

　　a. If the wipers do not park, go to Step 2.

　　b. If the wipers park, replace the wiper/washer switch assembly.

2. Using a digital multimeter, measure the voltage from connector **C215** (vehicle side), terminal **E (GREY)** to ground.

a. If more than 1.0 volt is present, go to Step 3.

b. If less than 1.0 volt is present (approx. 0 volt), replace the wiper motor cover assembly.

3. Reconnect the wiper/washer switch connector **C215**. Disconnect the wiper motor connector. Using a digital multimeter, measure the voltage from connector, terminal **D (DARK GREEN)** to ground.

　　a. If more than 1.0 volt is present, repair the short to **B+** in circuit **113 (DARK GREEN)**.

　　b. If less than 1.0 volt is present (approx. 0 volt), replace the wiper motor cover assembly.

WIPERS DO NOT OPERATE WHEN WASHER SWITCH IS ACTIVATED

1. Turn the ignition switch to the **RUN** position. Connect a test light between the wiper/washer switch connector **C215**, terminal **E (DARK GREEN)** and ground; then activate the washer switch and observe the test light.

　　a. If the light turns **ON,** check for an open in circuit **113 (DARK GREEN)** or for a poor connection at connector **C215** or at the wiper motor assembly.

　　b. If the light does not turn **ON,** check for an open in the wiper/washer switch assembly pigtail and connection. If okay, replace the wiper/washer switch assembly.

2. Reconnect the wiper/washer switch connector **C215**. Disconnect the wiper motor connector. Turn the ignition switch to the **RUN** position. Using a digital multimeter, measure the voltage from the wiper motor connector, terminal **E (GREY)** to ground.

　　a. If **B+** is present, replace the wiper motor cover assembly.

　　b. If approx. 0 volts is present, check circuit **112 (GREY)** for an open or poor connection. If okay, replace the wiper motor cover assembly.

WASHER DOES NOT OPERATE

1. Disconnect the washer pump connector. Connect a test light between terminals **A (RED)** and **B (BLACK)** of the washer pump connector; then, activate the washer switch while observing the test light.

　　a. If the test light is **OFF,** go to Step 2.

　　b. If the test light is **ON,** check for a poor connection to the washer pump. If okay, replace the washer pump.

2. Connect a test light between the washer pump connector, terminal **A (RED)** and ground.

　　a. If the test light is **OFF,** go to Step 3.

　　b. If the test light is **ON,** repair the open in circuit **150 (BLACK)**; terminal of the pump connector.

3. Connect a test light between wiper/washer switch connector **C215**, terminal **H (PINK)** and ground.

　　a. If the test light is **OFF,** check for a poor connection at connector **C215**, terminal **H (PINK)**. If okay, replace the wiper/washer switch assembly.

　　b. If the test light is **ON,** check for an open in circuit **94 (PINK)**, circuit **228 (RED)** or isolation diode.

REMOVAL & INSTALLATION

Wiper Motor Cover

1. Disconnect the negative battery cable from the battery.

2. Disconnect the electrical connector from the wiper motor cover and the wiper motor.

3. Remove the wiper motor cover-to-wiper motor screws and the cover.

To install:

4. With the wiper motor in the park position, align the wiper motor cover's cam slot with the drive pin. Install the cover and torque the screws to 18 inch lbs. (2 Nm).

5. Install the electrical connectors.

6. Connect the negative battery cable.

PONTIAC Grand Am

TROUBLESHOOTING

Diagnostic Tests

WIPERS DO NOT OPERATE IN ANY MODE

1. Disconnect the wiper/washer switch connector. Turn the ignition switch to the **RUN** position. Connect a test light between the connector, terminal **B. (WHITE)** and ground.

   a. If the test light is **ON**, go to Step 2.

   b. If the test light is **OFF**, check for an open in the wiper fuse or in circuit **93 (WHITE)**. If okay, check for an open in the power feed circuit **4**.

2. Disconnect the wiper motor connector **C2**. Connect a test light between the connector, terminal **C (BLACK)** to the battery's positive **(+)** terminal.

   a. If the test light is **ON**, go to Step 3.

   b. If the test light is **OFF**, repair the open in the ground circuit **150**.

3. Connect the wiper/washer switch connector. Disconnect the wiper motor connector **C1**. Connect a test light between the connector, terminal **C (GREY)** and ground.

   a. If the test light is **ON**, go to Step 4.

   b. If the test light is **OFF**, check for an open in circuit **91 (GREY)**. If okay, replace the wiper/washer switch.

4. Turn the wiper switch to the **LOW** position. Connect a test light between the connector **C1**, terminal **B (BROWN)** and ground.

Windshield wiper/washer electrical schematic—Grand Am

8838XG48

a. If the test light is **ON**, go to Step 5.

b. If the test light is **OFF**, check for an open in circuit **96** (**BROWN**). If okay, replace the wiper/washer switch.

5. Check for continuity between the wiper motor connector **C1**, terminal **A** (**YELLOW**) and connector **C2**, terminal **B** (**YELLOW**).

a. If there is continuity, check for a poor connection at the wiper motor connectors. If okay, replace the wiper motor assembly.

b. If there is no continuity, repair the open in circuit **196** (**YELLOW**).

WIPERS RUN AT HIGH SPEED ONLY—LOW SPEED INOPERATIVE

1. Disconnect the wiper motor connector **C1**. Turn the ignition switch to the **RUN** position and the wiper switch to the **LOW** position. Connect a test light between the connector **C1**, terminal **B** (**BROWN**) and ground.

a. If the test light is **ON**, go to Step 2.

b. If the test light is **OFF**, check for an open in circuit **96** (**BROWN**). If okay, replace the wiper/washer switch.

2. Connect a test light between the connector **C1**, terminal **C** (**GREY**) and ground.

a. If the test light is **ON**, go to Step 3.

b. If the test light is **OFF**, check circuit **91** (**GREY**) for an open. If okay, replace the wiper/washer switch.

3. Check for continuity through circuit **196** (**YELLOW**).

a. If there is continuity, check for a poor connection at connector **C1**. If okay, replace the wiper motor cover assembly.

b. If there is no continuity, repair the open in circuit **196** (**YELLOW**).

WIPERS RUN AT LOW SPEED ONLY—HIGH SPEED INOPERATIVE

1. Disconnect the wiper motor connector **C2**. Turn the ignition switch to the **RUN** position and the wiper switch to the **HIGH** position. Connect a test light between the connector **C2**, terminal **A** (**PURPLE**) and ground.

2. If the test light is **ON**, check for a poor connection at connector **C2**, terminal **A** (**PURPLE**). If okay, replace the wiper motor assembly.

3. If the test light is **OFF**, check for an open in circuit **92** (**PURPLE**). If okay, replace the wiper/washer switch.

WIPERS RUN INTERMITTENTLY IN LOW OR HIGH SPEED SETTINGS

1. Remove the wiper fuse and connect an ammeter (0–30 amp) across the fuse block terminals. Turn the ignition switch to the **RUN** position and the wiper switch to the **LOW** position. Observe the lowest current draw while the wipers are running on dry glass (current draw will fluctuate).

a. If the lowest current draw is less than 3.5 amps, replace the wiper motor.

b. If the current draw is 3.5–6.5 amps, end test.

c. If the lowest current draw is more than 6.5 amps, go to Step 2.

2. Replace the wiper blade elements and repeat the test.

a. If the lowest current draw is still more than 6.5 amps, go to Step 3.

b. If the lowest current draw is less than 6.5 amps, end test.

3. Disconnect the wiper transmission drive link from the wiper motor crank arm and repeat test.

a. If the lowest current draw is still more than 6.5 amps, replace the wiper motor.

Windshield wiper motor wiring harness electrical connectors— Grand Am

b. If the lowest current draw is less than 6.5 amps, the wiper transmission assembly is binding, repair or replace as required.

WIPERS WILL NOT TURN OFF

1. Disconnect the wiper motor connector **C1**. Turn the ignition switch to the **RUN** position and the wiper switch to the **OFF** position. Using a digital multimeter, measure the voltage from connector **C1**, terminal **B** (**GREY**) to ground.

a. If the voltage is 0 volts, go to Step 2.

b. If battery voltage is present, check for a short to **B+** in circuit **96** (**BROWN**). If okay, replace the wiper/washer switch.

2. Disconnect the wiper motor connector **C2**. Using a digital multimeter, measure the voltage from connector **C2**, terminal **A** (**PURPLE**) to ground.

a. If the voltage is 0 volts, repair the short to **B+** in circuit **196** (**YELLOW**).

b. If battery voltage is present, check for a short to **B+** in circuit **92** (**PURPLE**). If okay, replace the wiper/washer switch.

WIPERS CYCLE IN AND OUT OF PARK AFTER WIPERS ARE SHUT OFF

1. Turn the ignition switch to the **RUN** position. Operate the wiper switch and return it to the **OFF** position.

a. If the wiper motor continues to operate in low speed, go to Step 2.

b. If the wiper motor continues to operate in high speed, go to Wipers Run At High Speed Only chart.

2. Replace the park switch assembly.

a. If the trouble is corrected, end test.

b. If the trouble is not corrected, replace the wiper motor assembly.

PULSE DELAY OPERATES INCORRECTLY OR NOT AT ALL

1. Disconnect the wiper/washer switch connector. Turn the ignition switch to the **OFF** position and the wiper switch to the **DELAY** position. Using a digital multimeter, measure the resistance through the wiper/washer switch at connector, from terminal **B** (**WHITE**) to terminal **F** (**PINK**); then, move the wiper switch through the entire **DELAY** range.

a. If the resistance varies from 1.244 Mega-ohms to 0.024 Mega-ohms, go to Step 2.

b. If the resistance does not vary from 1.244 Mega-ohms to 0.024 Mega-ohms, replace the wiper/washer switch assembly.

2. Measure the resistance through the wiper/washer switch at connector, from terminal **B** (**WHITE**) to terminal **E** (**BROWN**).

a. If the resistance is less than 3 ohms, go to Step 3.

b. If the resistance is greater than 3 ohm, replace the wiper/washer switch assembly.

3. Check circuits **96 (BROWN)** and **94 (PINK)** for an open or poor connection. If okay, remove the wiper motor cover assembly.

a. If the park switch pulse contacts are touching the pads on the circuit board, replace the wiper motor cover assembly.

b. If the park switch pulse contacts are not touching the pads on the circuit board, replace the park switch spring contacts.

WASHER WILL NOT OPERATE

1. Disconnect the washer pump connector. Turn the ignition switch to the **RUN** position. Connect a test light between terminals **A (RED)** and **B (DARK BLUE)** of the washer pump connector; then, activate the washer switch while observing the test light.

a. If the test light is **OFF**, go to Step 2.

b. If the test light is **ON,** check for a poor connection at the washer pump connector. If okay, replace the washer pump.

2. Connect a test light between connector, terminal **A (RED)** and ground; then, activate the washer switch while observing the test light.

a. If the test light is **OFF**, go to Step 3.

b. If the test light is **ON,** check for a poor connection or open in circuit **227 (DARK BLUE)**. If okay, replace the wiper motor assembly (internal ground circuit open).

3. Connect a test light between wiper motor connector **C1**, terminal **D (RED)** and ground.

a. If the test light is **OFF**, go to Step 4.

b. If the test light is **ON,** check for a poor connection or open in circuit **228 (RED)**.

4. Turn the ignition switch to the **RUN** position. Using a digital multimeter, backprobe the wiper/washer switch connector, from terminal **B (WHITE)** to ground; then, activate the washer switch while observing the digital multimeter.

a. If 0 voltage is present, replace the wiper/washer switch assembly.

b. If battery voltage is present, check for a poor connection at the wiper/washer switch and wiper motor assembly connectors; or open in circuit **94 (PINK)**. If okay, replace the wiper motor assembly.

WASHER WILL NOT SHUT OFF

1. Turn the ignition switch to the **RUN** position and the wiper switch to the **LOW** position. Disconnect the wiper motor connector **C1**. Connect a test light between connector **C1**, terminal **F (PINK)** and ground, at the wiper motor case. Momentarily, activate the washer switch while observing the test light.

2. If the test light is **OFF** when the washer switch is released, replace the wiper motor cover assembly.

3. If the test light is **ON** when the washer switch is released, replace the wiper/washer switch assembly.

REMOVAL & INSTALLATION

Wiper Motor Cover

1. Disconnect the negative battery cable from the battery. At the center or the cowl, remove the washer hose from the nipple.

2. At the wiper motor cover's electrical connector, pull the retainer from the connector; then, disconnect the electrical connector from the wiper motor cover assembly.

3. Remove the wiper motor cover-to-wiper motor screws and the cover.

To install:

4. With the wiper motor in the park position, align the wiper motor cover's cam slot with the drive pin. Install the cover and torque the screws to 18 inch lbs. (2 Nm).

5. Install the electrical connector and secure with the retainer.

6. Connect the negative battery cable.

Park Switch Assembly

1. Remove the wiper motor cover assembly.

➡**If the wiper motor is in the park position, operate the motor (as required) to remove the pawl from the relay slot.**

2. Remove the screw and the park switch from the wiper motor assembly.

To install:

3. Install the park switch and screw onto the wiper motor assembly.

4. When the pawl is in the relay slot, operate the wiper motor back into the park position.

5. Install the wiper motor cover assembly.

BUICK Riviera; OLDSMOBILE Aurora

TROUBLESHOOTING

Troubleshooting Hints

WIPERS DO NOT OPERATE IN ANY MODE

1. Disconnect the wiper switch connector **C202**, ignition switch to **RUN** and connect test light from connector terminal **E5** to ground. If light, go to next step. If no light, check for open in fuse, circuit **93** or power circuit **4**.

2. Disconnect motor connector **C2** and connect test light from terminal **C** to battery positive. If light go to next step. If no light, repair open in ground circuit **151**.

3. Reconnect switch connector and disconnect motor connector **C1**. Connect test light from **C1** terminal **C** and ground. If light, go to next step. If no light, check for open in circuit **95**. If OK, replace wiper switch.

4. Wiper switch to **LO** and connect test light from connector **C1** terminal **B** to ground. If light, go to next step. If no light, check for open in circuit **91**. If OK, replace wiper switch.

5. Check for continuity between motor connector **C1** terminal **A** and connector **C2** terminal **B**. If continuity, check for poor connec-

Windshield wiper motor harness connector—Aurora/Riviera

tions. If OK, replace wiper motor cover assembly. If still not corrected, replace motor assembly. If no continuity, repair open in circuit **196**.

WIPERS RUN AT HIGH SPEED ONLY (LOW SPEED INOPERATIVE)

1. Disconnect motor connector **C1**, ignition to **RUN**, wiper switch to **LO** and connect test light from **C1** terminal **B** to ground. If light, go to next step. If no light, check for open in circuit **91** or poor connection.

2. Connect test light from **C1** terminal **C** to ground. If light, check for continuity through circuit **196**. If no light, check for open in circuit **95**. If **95** OK, replace wiper switch.

3. If circuit **196** has continuity, check for poor connection at motor connector **C1**. If **(C1)** OK, replace wiper motor cover. If still not corrected, replace wiper motor. If circuit **95** is not OK, repair as needed.

WIPERS RUN AT LOW SPEED ONLY (HIGH SPEED INOPERATIVE)

1. Disconnect motor connector **C2**, ignition to **RUN**, wiper switch to **HI** and connect test light from **C2** terminal **A** to ground. If light, go to next step. If no light, check for open in circuit **92** or poor connection. If circuit **92** OK, replace wiper switch.

2. Check for poor connection at motor connector **C2** terminal **A**. If OK, replace wiper motor.

Windshield wiper/washer system electrical schematic (part 1 of 2)—Aurora/Riviera

Windshield wiper/washer system electrical schematic (part 2 of 2)—Aurora/Riviera

WIPERS RUN INTERMITTENTLY IN LOW OR HIGH SPEED

1. Remove wiper fuse and connect ammeter with 0–30 amps across fuse terminals. Ignition switch to **RUN** and wiper switch to **LO**. Observe lowest current draw while wipers are running on dry glass. If lowest current draw is less than 3.5 amps, replace wiper motor. If no, go to next step.

2. Is lowest current draw more than 6.5 amps? If no, end of test. If yes, replace worn blades and retest. If still more than 6.5 amps, disconnect wiper transmission from crank arm. If still more than 6.5 amps, replace motor. If below 6.5 amps, replace binding transmission.

WIPERS WILL NOT TURN OFF

1. Disconnect motor connector **C1**, ignition switch to **RUN**, wiper switch to **OFF**, measure voltage from **C1** terminal **B** to ground. If zero volts, go to next step. If voltage, check for short to battery in circuit **91**. If **91** OK, replace wiper switch.

2. Disconnect motor connector **C2** and measure voltage from **C2** terminal **A** to ground. If zero volts, repair short to battery in circuit **196**. If voltage, check for short to battery in circuit **92**. If **92** OK, replace wiper switch.

WIPERS CYCLE IN AND OUT OF PARK AFTER WIPERS ARE SHUT OFF

1. Does motor operate in **LO**? If yes, replace park switch. If no, refer to the "WIPERS RUN AT HIGH SPEED ONLY" test.

2. After replacing park switch, is not corrected, replace wiper motor.

PULSE DELAY OPERATES INCORRECTLY OR NOT AT ALL

1. With ignition switch **OFF**, disconnect wiper switch connector **C202**, wiper switch to **DELAY** measure resistance through connector **C202** terminals **E5** and **E9**. Move the switch through the delay range. If the resistance varies from 1.224–0.024 M ohms, go to next step. If not, replace switch.

Refer to the model specific sections for engine electrical system service procedures

2. Measure resistance through connector **C202** terminals **E5** and **E6**. If less than 3 ohms, go to next step. If not, replace wiper switch.

3. Check circuits **91** and **94** for opens or poor connections. If circuits OK, replace wiper motor cover. Replace park switch spring contacts if pulse terminals are not touching pads on circuit board.

WASHER WILL NOT OPERATE

1. Disconnect the washer pump connector. Turn the ignition switch to the **RUN** position. Connect a test light between terminals **A (RED)** and **B (DARK BLUE)** of the washer pump connector; then, activate the washer switch while observing the test light.

    a. If the test light is **OFF,** go to Step 2.

    b. If the test light is **ON,** check for a poor connection at the washer pump connector. If okay, replace the washer pump.

2. Connect a test light between connector, terminal **A (RED)** and ground; then, activate the washer switch while observing the test light.

    a. If the test light is **OFF,** go to Step 3.

    b. If the test light is **ON,** check for a poor connection or open in circuit **227 (DARK BLUE)**. If okay, replace the wiper motor assembly (internal ground circuit open).

3. Connect a test light between wiper motor connector **C1**, terminal **D (RED)** and ground.

    a. If the test light is **OFF,** go to Step 4.

    b. If the test light is **ON,** check for a poor connection or open in circuit **228 (RED)**.

4. Turn the ignition switch to the **RUN** position. Using a digital multimeter, backprobe the wiper/washer switch connector, from terminal **E9 (WHITE)** to ground; then, activate the washer switch while observing the digital multimeter.

    a. If 0 voltage is present, replace the wiper/washer switch assembly.

    b. If battery voltage is present, check for a poor connection at the wiper/washer switch and wiper motor assembly connectors; or open in circuit **94 (PINK)**. If okay, replace the wiper motor assembly.

WASHER WILL NOT SHUT OFF

1. Turn the ignition switch to the **RUN** position and the wiper switch to the **LOW** position. Disconnect the wiper motor connector

C1. Connect a test light between connector **C1**, terminal **F (PINK)** and ground, at the wiper motor case. Momentarily, activate the washer switch while observing the test light.

2. If the test light is **OFF** when the washer switch is released, replace the wiper motor cover assembly.

3. If the test light is **ON** when the washer switch is released, replace the wiper/washer switch assembly.

REMOVAL & INSTALLATION

Wiper Motor Cover

1. Disconnect the negative battery cable from the battery. At the center or the cowl, remove the washer hose from the nipple.

2. At the wiper motor cover's electrical connector, pull the retainer from the connector; then, disconnect the electrical connector from the wiper motor cover assembly.

3. Remove the wiper motor cover-to-wiper motor screws and the cover.

To install:

4. With the wiper motor in the park position, align the wiper motor cover's cam slot with the drive pin. Install the cover and torque the screws to 18 inch lbs. (2 Nm).

5. Install the electrical connector and secure with the retainer.

6. Connect the negative battery cable.

Park Switch Assembly

1. Remove the wiper motor cover assembly.

➡**If the wiper motor is in the park position, operate the motor (as required) to remove the pawl from the relay slot.**

2. Remove the screw and the park switch from the wiper motor assembly.

To install:

3. Install the park switch and screw onto the wiper motor assembly.

4. When the pawl is in the relay slot, operate the wiper motor back into the park position.

5. Install the wiper motor cover assembly.

GENERAL MOTORS CORPORATION MODELS WITH A 9-TERMINAL WIPER MOTOR

All Equipped Models

GENERAL INFORMATION

The basic 9-terminal windshield wiper/washer system is available with the washer pump mounted remotely on the solvent container.

Depending on the type of control switch used and whether an optional electronic printed circuit board is attached to the wiper cover, the system can serve as either a pulse-type wiper/washer system or a standard type 2-speed windshield wiper. Pulse timing and demand wash functions are controlled electronically on pulse windshield wipers.

Standard wound field (non-pulse) motors are about 4½ in. (114mm) in length. The wiper motor and gearbox assembly electrical leads (black and black with a pink stripe) are routed internally

through a cavity in the gearbox casting. These leads, formerly exposed on a past model design, are routed through a grommet in the motor casting.

Both standard system and multiplex pulse system styles use similar motors. Multiplex pulse wipers use a green pulse relay case. Multiplex pulse wipers can also be identified by a single electrical lead **(BLACK/PINK)** leading to the timing circuit.

The multiplex pulse wiper system provides a controlled wiping action. It uses a wound field motor and wiper blades that park below the hood line. The wiper switch in the **DELAY** mode can be turned from a **MIN** (minimum) to a **MAX** (maximum) position. Turning the control knob from the **MIN** to **MAX** position varies the amount of time the wiper will delay between each wipe. The delay ranges between 0–12 seconds depending on the position of the knob. Minimum delay or 0 seconds between wipes provides the equivalent of low speed continuous operation.

WIPER AND WASHER OPERATION

Standard Wiper/Washer System

The standard system is controlled by the multi-function lever switch and the wipers can be driven at 2 speeds, either **HIGH** or **LOW**. When pushed, the **WASH** switch on the lever energizes the washer motor to drive the pump and deliver washer fluid to the windshield as long as the switch is pressed.

Multiplex Pulse Wiper/Washer System

The dash switch is a combination of switches and a variable resistor controlled by a single knob and a wash button switch. Two relays control motor operation:
1. Parking relay (gearbox relay) located in the gearbox.
2. Pulse relay (part of the timing circuit) located on the washer pump frame.

Both relays must be energized to complete 12V DC circuit to the wiper motor windings.

> **BUICK Century, LeSabre, Park Avenue, Regal, Riviera, Skylark; CADILLAC deVille, Eldorado, Seville; CHEVROLET Beretta, Camaro, Corsica, Corvette, Lumina, Monte Carlo; OLDSMOBILE Achieva, Aurora, Cutlass Ciera, Cutlass Cruiser, Cutlass Supreme, Eighty-Eight Royale, Ninety-Eight; PONTIAC Bonneville, Firebird, Grand Am, Grand Prix**

TROUBLESHOOTING

Wiper Motor System Operation

To help find problems, it's important to understand normal operation. The following should be used as a guide:
1. With the ignition switch in **ACCY** or **RUN**, press the washer switch to **ON** for less than 1 second. Look for:
   a. Normal operation is for the washer to spray the windshield for approximately 2½ seconds.
   b. The wiper should run at low speed and continue to run at low speed until the washer button is released.
   c. After the button is released, wipers run for approximately 6 seconds and then return to park.
2. With the wiper switch turned to **PULSE** or **DELAY** Mode, look for:
   a. Wipers should make 1 complete stroke, then pause for 0–25 seconds before making the next stroke.
   b. The wait time should be adjustable by turning the wiper switch through the delay range.
3. With the wiper switch in **PULSE**, hold the washer switch **ON** for 1–2 seconds. Look for:
   a. Washer should spray windshield as long as washer button is held **ON**.
   b. Pulse function is overridden and the wipers run at low speed during the spray period.
   c. After the washer stops, the wipers continue to run for 6 seconds.
   d. Wipers return to Pulse operation.
4. With the wiper switch in **HIGH**, hold the washer switch for

1–2 seconds. Look for: Same operation at low speed wash except that wipers run at high speed.
5. Turn wiper switch to **LOW**. Look for: Wipers should run continuously at low speed.
6. Turn wiper switch to **HIGH**. Look for: Wipers should run continuously at high speed.
7. Turn wiper switch **OFF**. Look for: Wipers should return to the park position at **LOW** speed, then shut **OFF.**
8. Turn the wiper switch to **MIST**. Look for: Wipers should make 1 complete stroke and then park.
   In addition, check the following:
9. Check the wiper fuse.
10. Check that the wiper/washer switch connector and wiper/washer motor connectors are mated correctly.
11. If the washer does not operate check that:
    a. The washer reservoir is filled.
    b. The hoses are not pinched or kinked.
    c. The hoses are correctly attached.
    d. The nozzles are not clogged.
12. If the wipers cycle in and out of park position in **HIGH** but do not operate in **LOW, MIST** or **PULSE**, check the yellow wire of an open.
13. If the wiper motor runs but the wiper blades do not, check the wiper linkage at the wiper crank arm.

CIRCUIT OPERATION

In addition to the features of a conventional non-pulse wiper system (2-speed, low and high) the pulse-type windshield wiper/washer system includes an operating mode in which the wipers make a single stroke with an adjustable time interval between strokes. The time interval is controlled by a solid state timer in the wiper motor assembly. The duration of the delay interval is determined by the delay rheostat in the wiper switch assembly.

The wiper motor is protected by a circuit breaker. If the wipers are blocked (by snow or ice, for example) the circuit breaker will open the circuit. The circuit breaker resets automatically when it cools.

TESTING

Symptom Test—Wiper Motor: Pulse

1. Wipers do not operate in any mode.
   a. Perform Test A: Wiper/Washer Switch Voltage.
   b. Perform Test B: Wiper Motor Module Input Voltage.
   c. Perform Test E: Wiper Motor Module Current Draw.
2. Wipers run at **LOW** speed only (no **HIGH** speed). Perform Test B: Wiper Motor Module Input Voltage.
3. Wipers cycle in and out of park when in **HIGH**.
   a. Perform Test B: Wiper Motor Module Input Voltage.
   b. Perform Test C: Wiper Motor Module Resistance.
4. Wipers cycle in and out of park when in **OFF** and operate in **LOW**. Replace the Park Switch.
5. Wipers will not shut off. Perform Test B: Wiper Motor Module Input Voltage.
6. No delay in **PULSE** mode or **PULSE** mode does not operate correctly.
   a. Perform Test B: Wiper Motor Module Input Voltage.
   b. Perform Test D: Wiper/Washer Pulse Control Resistance.

7. Wipers operate very slowly or intermittently. Perform Test E: Wiper Motor Module Current Draw.

8. Wipers do not park. Perform Test F: Complete Mechanical Inspection.

9. Washer will not operate or runs continuously.
   a. Perform Test B: Wiper Motor Module Input Voltage.
   b. Perform Test G: Washer Motor Voltage.

10. Wipers stay in delay during wash cycle. Replace cover assembly.

TROUBLESHOOTING TESTS

Test A: Wiper/Washer Switch Voltage

1. Measure the voltage at the wiper/washer switch connector (disconnected).
2. Turn the ignition switch to **RUN**.
3. Measure the voltage between terminal **D (WHITE)** and ground. It should read battery voltage.
   a. If voltage is correct, recheck symptoms.
   b. If no voltage is present, check the white wire and the wiper fuse for an open.

Test B: Wiper Motor Module Input Voltage

1. Measure the voltage at the wiper motor module connectors **C1 (DARK BLUE)** and **C2 (BLACK)** disconnected.
2. Turn the ignition switch to **RUN**.
3. With the wiper switch in position **OFF**, connect between connector **C2 (BLACK)**, terminal **A (PURPLE)** and ground.
   a. There should be no voltage.
   b. If there is voltage, check the associated wiring for a short to voltage.
   c. If wiring is good, replace the wiper/washer switch.
4. With the wiper switch in position **OFF**, connect between connector **C1 (DARK BLUE)**, terminal **B (GREY)** and ground.
   a. There should be no voltage.
   b. If there is voltage, check the associated wiring for a short to voltage.
   c. If wiring is good, replace the wiper/washer switch.
5. With the wiper switch in position **OFF**, connect between connector **C1 (DARK BLUE)**, terminal **C (DARK GREEN)** and ground.
   a. There should be battery voltage.
   b. If there is no voltage, check the associated wiring to the wiper/washer switch for an open or short to ground.
   c. If the wiring is good, replace the wiper/washer switch.

SWITCH MODE / TERMINAL #		MIST	OFF	PULSE	LO	HI	WASH
PULSE	1	C TO 8	C TO 8	C TO 8	C TO 8	C TO 8	C TO 8
	2	B(+)	—	B(+)	B(+)	C TO 3	C TO 3
	3	B(+)	B(+)	—	B(+)	C TO 2	C TO 2
	4	—	—	—	—	—	—
	5	—	—	—	—	—	B(+)
	6	10-12V	10-12V	10-12V	10-12V	10-12V	B(+)
	7	GROUND	GROUND	GROUND	GROUND	GROUND	GROUND
	8	C TO 1	C TO 1	C TO 1	C TO 1	C TO 1	C TO 1
	9	—	—	—	—	B(+)	—
STANDARD	1	C TO 8	C TO 8		C TO 8	C TO 8	C TO 8
	2	B(+)	—		B(+)	C TO 3	C TO 3
	3	B(+)	B(+)		B(+)	C TO 2	C TO 2
	4	—	—		—	—	—
	5	—	—		—	—	B(+)
	6	—	—		—	—	—
	7	GROUND	GROUND		GROUND	GROUND	GROUND
	8	C TO 1	C TO 1		C TO 1	C TO 1	C TO 1
	9	—	—		—	B(+)	—

C = CONTINUITY

9-Terminal wiper motor wiper/washer switch check chart—General Motors except Buick Roadmaster, Cadillac Fleetwood, Chevrolet Caprice, Cavalier and Impala SS, Pontiac Sunbird and Sunfire

TERMINAL #1
TERMINAL #2
TERMINAL #3
TERMINAL #4
TERMINAL #5
TERMINAL #6
TERMINAL #7
TERMINAL #8
TERMINAL #9

9-Terminal wiper motor wiper terminal identification—General Motors except Buick Roadmaster, Cadillac Fleetwood, Chevrolet Caprice, Cavalier and Impala SS, Pontiac Sunbird and Sunfire

6. With the wiper switch in position **OFF**, connect between connector **C1 (DARK BLUE)**, terminal **F (PINK)** and ground.
   a. There should be battery voltage.
   b. If there is no voltage, check the associated wiring to the wiper/washer switch for an open or short to ground.
   c. If the wiring is good, replace the wiper/washer switch.
7. With the wiper switch in position **MIST**, connect between connector **C2 (BLACK)**, terminal **A (PURPLE)** and ground.
   a. There should be no voltage.
   b. If there is voltage, check the associated wiring for a short to voltage.
   c. If the wiring is good, replace the wiper/washer switch.
8. With the wiper switch in position **MIST**, connect between connector **C1 (DARK BLUE)**, terminal **B (GREY)** and ground.
   a. There should be battery voltage.
   b. If there is no voltage, check the associated wiring for an open or a short to ground.
   c. If the wiring is good, replace the wiper/washer switch.

BLACK C1

BLACK C2

9-Terminal wiper motor assembly electrical connectors—General Motors except Buick Roadmaster, Cadillac Fleetwood, Chevrolet Caprice, Cavalier and Impala SS, Pontiac Sunbird and Sunfire

9. With the wiper switch in position **MIST**, connect between connector **C1 (DARK BLUE)**, terminal **C (DARK GREEN)** and ground.

    a. There should be battery voltage.

    b. If there is no voltage, check the associated wiring for an open or a short to ground.

    c. If the wiring is good, replace the wiper/washer switch.

10. With the wiper switch in position **MIST**, connect between connector **C1 (DARK BLUE)**, terminal **F (PINK)** and ground.

    a. There should be battery voltage.

    b. If there is no voltage, check the associated wiring for an open or a short to ground.

    c. If the wiring is good, replace the wiper/washer switch.

11. With the wiper switch in position **PULSE**, connect between connector **C2 (BLACK)**, terminal **A (PURPLE)** and ground.

    a. There should be no voltage.

    b. If there is voltage, check the associated wiring for a short to voltage.

    c. If wiring is good, replace the wiper/washer switch.

12. With the wiper switch in position **PULSE**, connect between connector **C1 (DARK BLUE)**, terminal **B (GREY)** and ground.

    a. There should be battery voltage.

    b. If there is no voltage, check the associated wiring for an open or a short to ground.

    c. If the wiring is good, replace the wiper/washer switch.

13. With the wiper switch in position **PULSE**, connect between connector **C1 (DARK BLUE)**, terminal **C (DARK GREEN)** and ground.

    a. There should be no voltage.

    b. If there is voltage, check the associated wiring for a short to voltage.

    c. If wiring is good, replace the wiper/washer switch.

14. With the wiper switch in position **PULSE**, connect between connector **C1 (DARK BLUE)**, terminal **F (PINK)** and ground.

    a. There should be battery voltage.

    b. If there is no voltage, check the associated wiring for an open or a short to ground.

    c. If the wiring is good, replace the wiper/washer switch.

15. With the wiper switch in position **LOW**, connect between connector **C2 (BLACK)**, terminal **A (PURPLE)** and ground.

    a. There should be no voltage.

    b. If there is voltage, check the associated wiring for a short to voltage.

    c. If wiring is good, replace the wiper/washer switch.

16. With the wiper switch in position **LOW**, connect between connector **C1 (DARK BLUE)**, terminal **B (GREY)** and ground.

    a. There should be battery voltage.

    b. If there is no voltage, check the associated wiring for an open or a short to ground.

    c. If the wiring is good, replace the wiper/washer switch.

17. With the wiper switch in position **LOW**, connect between connector **C1 (DARK BLUE)**, terminal **C (DARK GREEN)** and ground.

    a. There should be battery voltage.

    b. If there is no voltage, check the associated wiring for an open or a short to ground.

    c. If the wiring is good, replace the wiper/washer switch.

18. With the wiper switch in position **LOW**, connect between connector **C1 (DARK BLUE)**, terminal **F (PINK)** and ground.

    a. There should be battery voltage.

    b. If there is no voltage, check the associated wiring for an open or a short to ground.

    c. If the wiring is good, replace the wiper/washer switch.

19. With the wiper switch in position **HIGH**, connect between connector **C2 (BLACK)**, terminal **A (PURPLE)** and ground.

    a. There should be battery voltage.

    b. If there is no voltage, check the associated wiring for an open or a short to ground.

    c. If the wiring is good, replace the wiper/washer switch.

20. With the wiper switch in position **HIGH**, connect between connector **C1 (DARK BLUE)**, terminal **B (GREY)** and ground.

    a. There should be no voltage.

    b. If there is voltage, check the associated wiring for a short to voltage.

    c. If wiring is good, replace the wiper/washer switch.

21. With the wiper switch in position **OFF** and washer switch **ON**, connect between connector **C2 (BLACK)**, terminal **A (PURPLE)** and ground.

    a. There should be no voltage.

    b. If there is voltage, check the associated wiring for a short to voltage.

    c. If wiring is good, replace the wiper/washer switch.

22. With the wiper switch in position **OFF** and washer switch **ON**, connect between connector **C1 (DARK BLUE)**, terminal **B (GREY)** and ground.

    a. There should be battery voltage.

    b. If there is no voltage, check the associated wiring for an open or a short to ground.

    c. If the wiring is good, replace the wiper/washer switch.

23. With the wiper switch in position **OFF** and washer switch **ON**, connect between connector **C1 (DARK BLUE)**, terminal **C (DARK GREEN)** and ground.

    a. There should be battery voltage.

    b. If there is no voltage, check the associated wiring for an open or a short to ground.

    c. If the wiring is good, replace the wiper/washer switch.

24. With the wiper switch in position **OFF** and washer switch **ON**, connect between connector **C1 (DARK BLUE)**, terminal **F (PINK)** and ground.

    a. There should be battery voltage.

    b. If there is no voltage, check the associated wiring for an open or a short to ground.

    c. If the wiring is good, replace the wiper/washer switch.

    d. If all measurements are correct and the wiper motor is **ON** all the time, replace the cover assembly. Otherwise, review symptoms.

Test C: Wiper Motor Module Resistance

1. Measure the resistance at the wiper motor assembly connectors **C1** and **C2** (disconnected).

2. Turn the ignition switch **OFF** and the wiper switch to **HIGH**. Measure the resistance between connector **C1**, terminal **C (DARK GREEN)** and terminal **B (GREY)**. It should read less than 0.5 ohms.

    a. If resistance is not as specified, check the dark green wire and gray wire for a short to ground, to each other or opens.

    b. If wires are okay, replace wiper switch assembly.

3. Turn the ignition switch **OFF**, and the wiper switch to **OFF, PULSE**. Measure the resistance between connector **C1**, terminal **C (DARK GREEN)** and terminal **B (GREY)**. It should read infinite resistance.

a. If resistance is not as specified, check the dark green wire and gray wire for a short to ground, to each other or opens.

b. If wires are okay, replace wiper switch assembly.

4. Turn the ignition switch **OFF** and the wiper switch to **OFF, PULSE**. Measure the resistance between connector **C1**, terminal **A (YELLOW)** which is a jumper between the connectors and connector **C2**, terminal **B** of the other end of the yellow wire. It should read less than 0.5 ohms. If resistance is not as specified, check the yellow wire an open.

5. Turn the ignition switch **OFF** and the wiper switch to **OFF, PULSE**. Measure the resistance between connector **C1**, terminal **A (YELLOW)** and ground. It should read infinite resistance. If resistance is not as specified, check the yellow wire for a short to ground.

Test D: Wiper/Washer Pulse Control Resistance

1. Measure the resistance at the wiper motor assembly connector **C1** (disconnected).

2. Turn the ignition switch **OFF**, disconnect the negative battery cable and turn the wiper switch to **LOW**. Measure the resistance between terminal **B (GREY)** and terminal **F (PINK)**. It should read approximately 24 kilo-ohms.

a. If resistance is not as specified, check the pink wire and gray wire for an open.

b. If the wires are okay, replace wiper switch assembly.

3. Turn the ignition switch **OFF**, disconnect the negative battery cable and turn the wiper switch through the delay range to the maximum delay position. Measure the resistance between terminal **B (GREY)** and terminal **F (PINK)**. It should read approximately 1.2 mega-ohms.

a. If resistance is not as specified, check the pink wire and gray wire for an open.

b. If the wires are okay, replace wiper switch assembly.

c. If both resistances are correct, but the pulse mode does not operate, replace the cover assembly.

Test E: Wiper Motor Module Current Draw

1. Remove the wiper fuse.

2. Connect an ammeter (30 amp range or higher) across fuse terminals.

3. Turn the ignition switch to **RUN**, wet the windshield and turn the wiper switch to **HIGH**.

4. Read the ammeter. Current will vary. Look for the lowest reading. If the lowest reading is less than 3.5 amps or if the reading cycles between any value and 0, check:

a. Motor grounds.

b. Brush/commutator condition.

c. Circuit breaker, which should be closed.

d. Armature.

5. If the ammeter reading is greater than 6.5 amps:

a. Replace the wiper blades.

b. Retest.

6. After replacing the wiper blades and retesting, if the reading is less then 6.5 amps system is okay. The wiper blades were causing the problem.

7. After replacing the wiper blades and retesting, if the reading is greater then 6.5 amps:

a. Disconnect the linkage from the motor crank.

b. Retest.

c. If current draw is still greater than 6.5 amps, remove the wiper motor assembly for repair.

d. If the current draw is now less than 6.5 amps, the linkage is binding. Remove and repair as required.

Test F: Mechanical Inspection

1. Remove the wiper motor cover.

2. Reconnect the motor without the cover.

3. Turn the wiper switch to **LOW**.

4. Observe the spring loaded latch arm and drive pawl which rotates with the big gear.

5. Turn the wiper switch **OFF**.

6. Does the latch arm spring out and catch drive pawl to shift to park?

a. If latch arm doesn't spring out, replace the park switch.

b. If latch arm does spring out, check for bent pawl or shaft end.

Test G: Washer Motor Voltage

1. Measure the voltage at the washer motor connector (disconnected).

2. Turn the ignition switch to **ACCY** and the washer switch to **ON** and hold.

3. Measure the voltage between terminal **A (RED)** and terminal **B (DARK BLUE)**. It should read battery voltage.

a. If measurement does not read battery voltage, check the red wire and dark blue wire for an open.

b. If the wires are okay, check the terminal control between the park switch and cover assembly.

c. If the contact is good, replace the cover assembly.

4. Turn the ignition switch to **ACCY** and turn the washer switch to **OFF**.

5. Measure the voltage between terminal **A (RED)** and terminal **B (DARK BLUE)**. It should read 0 voltage.

a. If voltage is present, check the red wire for a short to voltage.

b. If the wire is okay, replace the cover assembly.

c. If all voltage checks are okay and washer does not work, replace washer motor.

REMOVAL & INSTALLATION

Washer Pump (Standard Wiper Motor)

1. Remove the washer hoses from the pump.

2. Disconnect the wires from the pump relay.

3. Remove the plastic pump cover.

4. Remove the attaching screws securing the pump frame to the motor gearbox and remove the pump and frame.

To install:

5. Installation is the reverse of the removal procedure.

6. The wiper motor gear must be in park position to assemble the pump to the wiper motor.

7. Rotate the 4-lobe cam until the index hole in the cam is aligned with the hole in the pump mounting plate. Insert a pin through both holes to maintain cam in position.

8. Position the pump on the wiper so the slot in the 4-lobe cam fits over the gear drive pin which is part of the lock pawl. Secure the pump to gear housing and remove the locator pin. Temporarily connect the wiring connector.

9. Turn the wiper motor **ON** and use the washer pump to check pump operation. A loud knocking noise would indicate that the pump cam has not engaged the drive pin properly.

10. Install pump cover.

Multiplex Pulse Wiper Motor

1. Remove the complete wiper/washer assembly from the vehicle.
2. Pull the plastic cover off the mounting post.
3. Disconnect the green lead from terminal **1A**, the yellow and red leads from the pulse relay terminals and unsolder the black with pink stripe wire from the remaining relay terminal.
4. If just the pump assembly is being removed from the motor and gearbox (wiper motor still on vehicle), cut the black with pink stripe lead 4 in. from the motor grommet.

➡**Depending on the type of repair required, it will be necessary to splice this lead to the replacement relay lead or to the original relay lead after the pump is reinstalled.**

5. Remove the 3 screws that attach the pump to the gearbox.

To install:

6. Installation is the reverse of the removal procedure. Make sure the wiper gearbox is in the park position.
7. Install a locator pin in the pump mechanism through the hole in the 4-lobe cam.

➡**If it is necessary to rotate the cam to install the locator pin, be sure to turn the cam counterclockwise.**

8. Position the pump assembly on the gearbox and install the 3 attaching screws. Remove the locator pin.
9. Route and attach the leads. Solder the black and pink stripe wire back into place.
10. Position the cover on the washer pump and mechanism and snap it over the mounting pin.
11. Reinstall wiper in vehicle, attach wiring and hoses. Test system.

Relay Switch and Terminal Board Assembly (Multiplex Pulse Wiper Motor)

1. Remove the washer pump.
2. The wiper gear mechanism must be out of the park position to remove the relay switch and terminal board assembly. If the wiper gear mechanism is not in the park position, drive pawl away from the latch arm, use the following procedure:

   a. To move the wiper gear drive pawl out of the park position, manually trip the latch arm toward the coil and apply feed current to the center terminal of the relay switch and terminal board and ground the motor case. The wiper motor should turn the gear, moving the drive pawl out of the park position in the relay switch slot.

   b. If applying feed current to the center terminal does not energize the motor, it is possible to remove some of the insulation from the black with pink stripe wire between the motor and the relay switch and apply feed current at this point. Be sure to cover the exposed wire with tape after the repair is complete.

3. Remove the relay switch and terminal board attaching screw and carefully lift the assembly out of the gearbox. Unsolder leads as required.

To install:

4. Installation is the reverse of the removal procedure.
5. Resolder leads to relay switch and terminal board assembly as required.

   a. Solder the black wire to terminal 3 and the black with pink stripe wire to the fixed contact post.

   Use care to route the wires in such a manner as to avoid having them pinched between the relay switch and wiper housing.

6. Position the relay switch and terminal board assembly in the housing and attach with screw.
7. Install the washer pump to the wiper motor.
8. Install assembly into vehicle and test system.

Park Switch Replacement

1. Remove the wiper motor cover.
2. If the motor is in the park position, operate the motor as required to remove the pawl from the relay slot.
3. Remove the park switch assembly.

To install:

4. Installation is the reverse of the removal procedure.
5. Install the new park switch assembly.

➡**When installing the new wiper cover, always install the cover assembly with the wiper in the park position and the drive pin in the large angled open area of the cam. Do not try to put the drive pin in the slot of the cam. Place it in the open area only.**

6. Torque the cover screws to 18 inch lbs. (2 Nm).

Wiper Motor Replacement

1. Raise the hood and remove the cowl screen.
2. Loosen the transmission drive link-to-motor crank arm attaching nuts.
3. Remove the transmission drive link from the motor crank arm.
4. Disconnect the wiring and washer hoses.
5. Remove the 3 motor attaching screws.
6. Remove the motor while guiding crank arm through hole.

To install:

7. Installation is the reverse of the removal procedure.

➡**The motor must be in the park position before assembling the crank arm to the transmission.**

8. Connect wiring and hoses.

BUICK Roadmaster; CHEVROLET Caprice, Impala SS; CADILLAC Fleetwood RWD

GENERAL INFORMATION

The windshield wiper system used on these vehicles is similar to the system listed above. There are some differences in wiring color codes that will affect troubleshooting.

Before beginning troubleshooting, check fuse 10. If open, check for short to ground in the white wire that runs from the fuse block to the wiper/washer switch. Make sure all connectors are firmly mated.

If the washer does not operate, check that the washer reservoir is filled, the hoses correctly attached, hoses are not cut, kinked or pinches, the nozzles are not clogged and the connector seal at the washer motor is not damaged or missing.

If the washer does not operate and wipers run in **HIGH** only (low speed inoperative), check the gray wire that runs from the washer/wiper switch to the windshield wiper motor module for an open.

Other problem areas could be binding or broken wiper arm linkage or missing or damaged connector seal at the windshield wiper motor module.

CIRCUIT OPERATION

In addition to the features of a standard (non-pulse) wiper system (mist, low and high speed), the pulse-type wiper/washer system includes an operating mode in which the wipers make single strokes with an adjustable time interval between strokes. The time interval is controlled by a solid state timer in the wiper motor assembly, often referred to as the wiper motor module since it contains not only the wiper motor itself, but also the solid state electronic components that make up the delay timer as well as the park relay and self-resetting circuit breaker. The duration of the delay interval is determined by the pulse delay resistor in the windshield wiper/washer switch assembly.

Note that in the following information, connector **C1** and **C2** refers to the connectors at the wiper motor.

Pulse Operation

With the wiper/washer switch in **PULSE**, voltage is applied to the windshield wiper motor at connector **C1**, terminal **F** through the pink wire. Voltage is also applied to connector **C1**, terminal **B** through the gray wire.

The variable resistance seen through the pulse delay resistor is used by the wiper motor module to determine the delay time between sweeps.

Low Speed

In the **LOW** position, the wiper/washer switch applies battery voltage to the wiper motor module at connector **C1** terminal **C** through the dark green wire to connector **C1** terminal **B** through the gray wire. Voltage is also applied from a 24 kilo-ohm resistor inside the wiper/washer switch to connector **C1** terminal **F** through the pink wire.

The wiper motor assembly module supplies power through connector **C1** terminal **A** through the yellow jumper wire to connector **C2** terminal **B** to the wiper motor, which runs continuously.

High Speed

In the **HIGH** position, the wiper/washer switch applies battery voltage to the wiper motor assembly at connector **C1** terminal **C** through the dark green wire and to connector **C1** terminal **B** through the gray wire.

The wiper motor assembly supplies power from connector **C1** terminal **A** through the yellow jumper wire to connector **C2** terminal **B** to the wiper motor. The wiper motor also has voltage applied from the wiper/washer switch to connector **C2** terminal **A** through the purple wire to a separate armature brush for high speed operation.

Off (Park) Position

When turned **OFF** from any position, the wipers complete the last sweep and park. When the wiper/washer switch is **OFF,** the wiper motor assembly module has battery voltage applied through connector **C1**, terminal **C** through the dark green wire and connector **C1** terminal **F** through the pink wire. The wiper motor module controls power through the park relay to connector **C1** terminal **A** through the yellow jumper wire to connector **C2**, terminal **B** to the wiper motor, which runs until the park relay is opened.

The park relay is controlled both electronically and mechanically. The relay is held closed mechanically until the wipers reach the park position and the wiper request is no longer present. Whenever wiper request is present, the relay is held closed electronically.

Washer Operation

When the washer switch is turned **ON**, the wipers operate at low speed using the same circuit operation as low speed or the same as high speed only if **HIGH** speed is selected.

When the washer switch is held **ON**, the wiper motor assembly module will keep the washer motor **ON** only as long as the washer switch is held **ON**.

If the wipers had been in **PULSE, LOW** or **HIGH** they would return to that operation after the wash cycle. If not, they then return to the **PARK** position.

Mist

When the wiper/washer switch is moved to **MIST** and released, the wipers make 1 sweep at low speed and return to **PARK.** The circuit operation is the same as that of low speed.

TROUBLESHOOTING

Wiper Motor System Operation

To help find problems, it's important to understand normal operation. The following should be used as a guide:

1. With the ignition switch in **RUN**, turn the wiper/washer switch to **WASHER**. Normal operation is for the wipers to operate at low speed. The washer sprays the windshield as long as the washer switch is held in the **WASHER** position. After releasing the switch, the washer stops and the wipers return to park.

2. With the ignition switch in **RUN**, turn the wiper/washer switch to **PULSE**. Normal operation is for the wipers to make 1 complete stroke then pause for 1–25 seconds before making the next stroke. The pause time is adjusted by turning the wiper switch through the delay range.

3. With the ignition switch in **RUN**, turn the wiper/washer switch to **PULSE** and turn the washer switch to **ON**. Look for:

   a. Normal operation is for the washer to spray the windshield as long as the washer switch is held **ON.**

   b. Wipers run at low speed while spraying and continue until the washer switch is released. Wipers then return to pulse operation.

4. With the ignition switch in **RUN**, turn the wiper/washer switch to **LOW**. Normal operation is for the wipers to run continuously at low speed.

5. With the ignition switch in **RUN**, turn the wiper/washer switch to **HIGH**. Normal operation is for the wipers to run continuously at **HIGH** speed.

6. With the ignition switch in **RUN**, turn the wiper/washer switch **OFF**. Normal operation is for the wipers to run at low speed and return to **PARK**.

7. With the ignition switch in **RUN**, turn the wiper/washer switch to **MIST** and then release. Normal operation is for the wipers to make one complete stroke then return to the **PARK** position.

TESTING

Wipers Do Not Operate in Any Mode

1. Disconnect the washer/wiper switch connector. This connector is flat and gray in color and is located at the base of the steering column. Turn ignition switch to **RUN**. Connect test light to terminal **B** of the connector, **(YELLOW)**.

a. If test light is not **ON,** check for open fuse **fuse #1010** or open in yellow wire.

b. If test light is **ON,** go to Step 2.

2. Disconnect the windshield wiper motor module connector **C2.** Connect a test light from connector **C2,** terminal **C (BLACK)** to battery voltage.

a. If test light is not **ON,** repair open in ground circuit **(BLACK).**

b. If test light is **ON,** go to Step 3.

3. Reconnect the washer/wiper switch connector. Disconnect the windshield wiper motor connector **C1.** Connect a test light from connector **C1,** terminal **C (DARK GREEN)** to ground.

a. If test light is not **ON,** check for a poor connection at the wiper/washer switch or at the wiper motor or an open in the dark green wire between the switch and motor. If all are okay, replace the wiper/washer switch.

b. If test light is **ON,** go to Step 4.

4. Turn wiper switch to **LOW.** Connect a test light from connector **C1** terminal **B (GREY)** to ground.

a. If test light is not **ON,** check for a poor connection at the wiper/washer switch or an open in the gray wire between the switch and motor. If all are okay, replace the wiper/washer switch.

b. If test light is **ON,** go to Step 5.

5. Check for continuity from windshield wiper module connector **C1** terminal **A (YELLOW)** to connector **C2** terminal **B** (which is the other end of the yellow wire).

a. If there is continuity, check for poor connection at the windshield wiper motor connectors. If okay, replace windshield wiper motor cover assembly. If trouble is not corrected, replace the wiper motor assembly.

b. If there is no continuity, repair open in the yellow wire on the wiper motor assembly running from connector **C1** terminal **A** (yellow jumper wire) to connector **C2** terminal **B** (which is the other end of the yellow wire).

Wipers Run At High Speed Only (Low Speed Inoperative)

1. Disconnect wiper motor assembly connector **C1** (connector with red, pink, dark green, gray and yellow wire).

2. Turn the ignition switch to **RUN** and the wiper switch to **LOW.**

3. Connect a test light from the connector, terminal **B (GREY)** and to ground.

a. If test light is **ON,** go to Step 4.

b. If test light is not **ON,** check the gray wire for an open or poor connections. If okay, replace wiper/washer switch.

4. Connect a test light from connector **C1,** terminal **C (DARK GREEN)** to ground.

a. If the test light turns **ON,** go to Step 5.

b. If the test light does not turn **ON,** check the dark green wire for an open or poor connections. If okay, replace wiper/washer switch.

5. Check for continuity through the connector **C1,** terminal **A (YELLOW).**

a. If there is continuity, go to Step 6.

b. If there is no continuity, repair the open circuit **196 (YELLOW).**

6. Check for a poor connection at wiper motor cover assembly connector **C1.** If connection and wires are okay, replace wiper motor cover assembly. If trouble is not corrected, replace the wiper motor assembly.

Wipers Run At Low Speed Only (High Speed Inoperative)

1. Disconnect the wiper motor assembly connector **C2** (**Y/BLK/PRP**).

2. Turn the ignition switch to **RUN** and the wiper switch to **HIGH.**

3. Connect a test light from the connector **C2,** terminal **A (PURPLE)** and to ground.

a. If test light is **ON,** check for poor connection at connector **C2,** terminal **A (PURPLE)** of the wiper motor assembly. If connection and wires are okay, replace wiper motor assembly.

b. If test light is not **ON,** check for an open in connector **C2,** terminal **A (PURPLE).** If okay, replace wiper/washer switch.

Wiper Run Intermittently in Low or High Speed Settings

1. Remove the fuse **fuse #1010** and connect an ammeter (0–30 amp) across the fuse block terminals.

2. Turn the ignition switch to **RUN** and the wiper switch to **LO.**

3. Observe the lowest current draw while the wipers are running on dry glass (current draw will fluctuate).

a. If the current draw is less than 3.5 amps, replace the wiper motor assembly.

b. If the lowest current draw is greater than 6.5 amps, go to Step 4; otherwise, end test.

4. Replace the wiper blade elements and repeat the test.

a. If the lowest current draw is still greater than 6.5 amps, go to Step 5.

b. If the lowest current draw is not greater than 6.5 amps, end test.

5. Disconnect the wiper transmission from the wiper motor crank arm and repeat test.

a. If the lowest current draw is still greater than 6.5 amps, replace the wiper motor assembly.

b. If the lowest current draw is not greater than 6.5 amps; the wiper transmission assembly is binding, replace or repair, as required.

Wipers Will Not Turn Off

1. Disconnect windshield wiper motor assembly connector **C1** (red, pink, dark green, gray and yellow wires).

2. Turn the ignition switch to **RUN** and the wiper switch to **OFF.**

3. Using a digital voltmeter, measure the voltage from connector **C1,** terminal **B (GREY)** to ground.

a. If there is battery voltage, check for a short to voltage somewhere along the gray wire. If okay, replace the wiper/washer switch.

b. If there is no voltage, go to Step 4.

4. Disconnect the wiper motor assembly connector **C2** (purple, black and yellow wires). Using a digital voltmeter, measure the voltage from connector **C2** terminal **A (YELLOW)** to ground.

a. If there is battery voltage, check for a short to voltage somewhere along the purple wire. If okay, replace the wiper/washer switch.

b. If there is no voltage, repair the short in circuit **196 (YELLOW).**

Wipers Cycle In and Out of Park After Wipers Are Turned Off

1. Turn the wiper switch to **LO.**

a. If the wiper motor operates, go to Step 2.

b. If the wiper motor does not operate, perform Wipers Run at High Speed Only procedure.

2. Replace the park switch assembly.

   a. If the trouble is corrected, end of test.

   b. If the trouble is not corrected, replace the wiper motor assembly.

Pulse Delay Operates Incorrectly Or Not At All

1. Turn ignition switch **OFF** and disconnect the wiper/washer switch connector **C216**.

2. Turn the windshield wiper/washer switch to **DELAY**.

3. With a digital voltmeter set to the ohms scale, measure the resistance through the wiper/washer switch at the switch connector **C216**, from terminal **B (YELLOW)** to terminal **F (PINK)**. Move the wiper switch through the entire delay range.

   a. If the resistance varies from approximately 1.224–0.024 mega-ohms, go to Step 2.

   b. If the resistance does not vary from approximately 1.224–0.024 mega-ohms, replace the wiper/washer switch.

4. Measure the resistance through connector **C216**, from terminal **B (YELLOW)** to terminal **C (GREY)**.

   a. If the resistance is less than 3.0 ohms, go to Step 3.

   b. If the resistance is greater than 3.0 ohms, replace the wiper/washer switch.

5. Check circuits **91 (GREY)** and **94 (PINK)** for an open or a poor connection; if okay remove the wiper motor cover assembly

   a. If the park switch pulse contacts are touching the pads on the circuit board, replace the wiper motor cover assembly.

   b. If the park switch pulse contacts are not touching the pads on the circuit board, replace the park switch spring contacts.

Windshield wiper motor wiring harness electrical connectors—Cadillac Fleetwood (RWD)

Washer Will Not Operate

1. Disconnect the windshield washer pump connector.

2. Turn the ignition to **RUN**.

3. Connect a test light between terminal **A (RED)** and terminal **B (DARK BLUE)** of the windshield washer pump connector. Activate the washer switch with observing the test light.

   a. If the test light is not **ON,** go to Step 4.

   b. If the test light is **ON,** check for a poor connection at the washer pump connector. If okay, replace the windshield washer pump.

4. Connect a test light from the washer pump connector terminal **A (RED)** to ground. Activate the washer switch while observing the test light.

   a. If the test light is not **ON,** go to Step 5.

   b. If the test light is **ON,** check for a poor connection or an open in circuit **227 (DARK BLUE)**. If okay, replace the windshield wiper motor; it has an internal ground open.

5. Connect a test light from the washer motor connector **C1**, terminal **D (RED)** to ground.

   a. If the test light is not **ON,** go to Step 6.

   b. If the test light is **ON,** check for a poor connection or an open in circuit **228 (RED)**.

6. Turn the ignition to **RUN**. Using a digital voltmeter, back probe the windshield wiper/washer switch connector **C216**, from terminal **F (PINK)** to ground. Activate the washer switch while observing the voltmeter.

   a. If there is no voltage, replace the windshield wiper/washer switch.

   b. If there is battery voltage, check for a poor connection at the connector of the body harness and the windshield wiper motor. Also check for an open along the **(PINK)**. If all okay, replace the windshield wiper motor cover assembly.

REMOVAL & INSTALLATION

Washer Pump

1. Remove the washer solvent from the reservoir.

2. Disconnect the electrical connector and washer hose from washer pump.

3. Remove the washer pump from the reservoir.

To install:

4. Installation is the reverse of the removal procedure.

5. Install the washer pump to the reservoir.

➡ **The new washer pump must be pushed all the way into the solvent container recess and gasket.**

6. Connect the electric connector and the washer hose.

7. Refill with washer solvent and test system.

Wiper Motor Cover

1. Remove the wiper motor assembly.

2. Remove the wiper motor cover screws.

3. Remove the wiper motor cover. Note the position of the cam and the drive pin.

To install:

4. Installation is the reverse of the removal procedure.

➡ **When installing the new wiper cover, always install the cover assembly with the wiper in the PARK position and the drive pin in the large angled open area of the cam. Do not try to put the drive pin in the slot of the cam. Place it in the open area only.**

5. Tighten the cover screws to 18 inch lbs. (2 Nm).

Park Switch Replacement

1. Remove the wiper motor cover.

2. If the motor is in the **PARK** position, operate the motor as required to remove the pawl from the relay slot.

3. Remove the park switch assembly.

A Drive pin must be in area shown
B Pin, drive
C Wiper motor in park position
(pawl in relay slot)

8470V041

9-Terminal wiper motor drive pin assembly

To install:

4. Installation is the reverse of the removal procedure.
5. Install the new park switch assembly.

➡**When installing the new wiper cover, always install the cover assembly with the wiper in the PARK position and the drive pin in the large angled open area of the cam. Do not try to put the drive pin in the slot of the cam. Place it in the open area only.**

6. Tighten the cover screws to 18 inch lbs. (2 Nm).

Wiper Motor Replacement

1. Remove the right side wiper arm and hose.

To prevent possible windshield damage, the left side cowl vent screen must be removed before the right side cowl vent screen is removed.

2. Remove the left and right side cowl vent screens.
3. Remove the wiper linkage access hole cover screws and remove the cover.
4. Disconnect the wiper drive link from the motor crank arm.
5. Disconnect the electrical connectors, remove the motor attaching bolts and remove the wiper motor, guiding the crank arm through the hole.

To install:

6. Installation is the reverse of the removal procedure.

1. Screw
2. Cover assembly
3. Motor , wiper
4. Screw
5. Switch assembly, park
6. Arm, crank
7. Nut

8470V042

Exploded view of 9-terminal wiper motor

7. Install the wiper motor guiding the crank arm through the hole. Tighten the mounting bolts to 80 inch lbs. (9 Nm).
8. Install the electrical connectors.
9. Connect the motor drive link to the motor crank arm. Tighten the socket nuts to 27 inch lbs. (3 Nm).
10. Apply a suitable body sealer to the edges of the access hole cover and reinstall the cover. Tighten the cover screws to 18 inch lbs. (2 Nm).
11. Install the vent screens.

To avoid damage to the windshield, the right side cowl vent screen must be installed before the left side cowl vent screen.

12. Connect the right side wiper arm and hose.
13. Test system.

SATURN

General Information

Saturn uses single wiper motor which is located in the cowl (on the driver's side) attached to the wiper transmission. The wiper control module is attached to the wiper motor assembly. An underhood junction block is located in the engine compartment on the left wheel housing; it houses a 30 amp fuse that supplies power to the ignition switch. Power is directed from the ignition switch to an instrument panel junction block (located under the driver's side of the instrument panel); it houses a 25 amp fuse that directs power to the wiper control module and windshield wiper switch.

SYSTEM PERFORMANCE TEST

1. Turn the ignition switch to the **ACC** position the wiper switch to the **INTERMITTENT 1** position; the wipers should activate. On the **INTERMITTENT 1** position, the time interval between cycles

(1 cycle being 1 back/forth motion of the blades) should be 2 seconds.

- On the **INTERMITTENT 1** position, the time interval between cycles (1 cycle being 1 back/forth motion of the blades) should be 2 seconds.
- On the **INTERMITTENT 2** position, the time interval between cycles should be 7 seconds.
- On the **INTERMITTENT 3** position, the time interval between cycles should be 12 seconds.

2. Start the engine.

3. Place the wiper switch in the **LOW** speed position; the wipers should activate and the speed should be 42–52 cycles/min.

4. Place the wiper switch in the **HIGH** speed position; the wipers should activate (within 1 second) and the speed should be 61–73 cycles/min. on a wet windshield.

5. Push the wiper switch down to the **MIST** position; the wipers should cycle once as long as the switch is being held in that position.

6. Pull the wiper switch to the **WASH** position; the washer pump and wipers should both activate within 1 second. The wipers should cycle twice and the washer pump should remain **ON** as long as the switch lever is pulled into the position. The wipers will complete 2 cycles before parking after wash; do not operate the washer pump without fluid in the washer reservoir.

7. With the wipers on the **LOW** speed, crank the engine. The wipers should shop moving and start again once the ignition is back in the run position.

FRONT WIPER TROUBLESHOOTING

Wiper Switch

1. Disconnect the electrical connector from the wiper switch. Using an ohmmeter, measure the resistance of the switch between pins **C** and **A**.

   a. With column switch in the **OFF** position, the resistance should be open.

   b. With column switch in the **LOW** position, the resistance should be 300 ohms.

   c. With column switch in the **HIGH** position, the resistance should be 300 ohms.

   d. With column switch in the **MIST** position, the resistance should be 300 ohms.

   e. With column switch in the **INTERMITTENT 1** position, the resistance should be 2.09 kilo-ohms.

   f. With column switch in the **INTERMITTENT 2** position, the resistance should be 990 ohms.

   g. With column switch in the **INTERMITTENT 3** position, the resistance should be 560 ohms.

   h. With column switch in the **WASH** position, the resistance should be 130 ohms.

2. Using an ohmmeter, measure the continuity of the switch between pins **B** and **A**; there should be less than 1.0 ohms when the switch is in the **HIGH** position, and **OPEN** when the switch is in any other position.

Fuse Tests

- **IGN4 Fuse**: A 30 amp fuse located in the underhood junction block and feeds circuit **202**.

- **Wiper Fuse**: A 25 amp fuse located in the instrument panel junction block and feeds circuit **143**.

Ground Circuit Tests

Before checking the ground circuit from the faulty component all the way to the ground stud, check the circuit from the splice pack to ground by testing some of the other subsystems grounded by the same splice pack. If the other subsystems function properly, it is most likely that the path from the splice pack to ground is good.

INSTRUMENT PANEL SPLICE PACK #1

It is taped to the harness behind the instrument cluster. If subsystems Perf/Norm switch, instrument panel dimmer, cruise module, headlight switch or cigar lighter work properly, ground circuit is most likely OK.

RIGHT SIDE FORWARD LAMP SPLICE PACK

Located behind front right headlight. If subsystems coolant level switch, washer pump or right forward lights work properly, ground circuit is most likely OK.

INSTRUMENT PANEL SPLICE PACK #2

It is taped to the harness behind the instrument cluster. If subsystems fuel sensor, park brake switch, wiper motor or radio work properly, ground circuit is most likely OK.

CIRCUIT 350R

Connects the wiper module connector cavity **B** to instrument panel ground splice pack #2 cavity **G** (black 16 gauge wire). It provides ground for the wiper motor and control module.

CIRCUIT 350F

Connects the column switch connector cavity **A** to instrument panel ground splice pack #1 cavity **G** (black 22 gauge wire). It provides ground for the column switch.

CIRCUIT 150J

Connects the washer pump connector cavity **2** to forward light splice pack cavity **D** (black 20 gauge wire). It provides ground for the washer pump.

CIRCUIT 150Y

Connects the forward light ground splice pack cavity **K** to right forward light ground ring terminal (black **14** gauge wire). It provides ground for the fog light switch.

CIRCUIT 350Y

Connects the instrument panel ground splice pack #1 cavity **A** to chassis ground ring (black 18 gauge wire). It provides ground for the instrument panel ground splice pack #1.

CIRCUIT 350Z

Connects the instrument panel ground splice pack #2 cavity **A** to chassis ground ring (black 18 gauge wire). It provides ground for the instrument panel ground splice pack #2.

CIRCUIT 350AA

Connects the instrument panel ground splice pack #2 cavity **A** to ground splice pack #1 cavity **A** (black 18 gauge wire). It provides ground for the instrument panel ground splice pack #1 and 2.

Power Circuit Tests

CIRCUIT 202/4/143

The circuit provides power to the windshield wiper motor/control module through the ignition switch.

CIRCUIT 202

Connects the underhood junction block connector cavity **A** to ignition switch connector cavity **H** (red 12 gauge wire). Should have voltage at all times.

CIRCUIT 4

Connects the ignition switch cavity **G** to instrument panel junction connector cavity **F12** (brown **14** gauge wire). Should have voltage at ignition **ACC** or **RUN** positions.

CIRCUIT 143

Connects the instrument panel junction block connector cavity **E12** to wiper module cavity **E** (yellow 16 gauge wire). Should have voltage at ignition **ACC** or **RUN** positions.

CIRCUIT 92

Connects the wiper module connector cavity **C** to column switch cavity **F** (purple 22 gauge wire). Should have voltage at ignition **ACC** or **RUN** positions.

CIRCUIT 96

Connects the wiper module connector cavity **D** to column switch cavity **E** (brown 22 gauge wire). Should have voltage at ignition **ACC** or **RUN** positions.

CIRCUIT 94A/94

Power for washer pump. Connects the wiper module connector cavity **A** to underhood junction block connector cavity **C3** (pink 16 gauge wire). Should have voltage at ignition **ACC** or **RUN** positions with the column switch on **WASH**.

REAR WIPER TROUBLESHOOTING

Fuse Tests

- **SUN Fuse**: A 15 amp fuse located in the instrument panel junction block and feeds circuit **580**. This fuse powers the sunroof and rear wiper.
- **Power Convenience Fuse**: A 30 amp fuse located in the underhood junction block and feeds circuit **302**. This fuse powers the power windows, sunroof and rear wiper.

Ground Circuit Tests

Before checking the ground circuit from the faulty component all the way to the ground stud, check the circuit from the splice pack to ground by testing some of the other subsystems grounded by the same splice pack. If the other subsystems function properly, it is most likely that the path from the splice pack to ground is good.

REAR BODY SPLICE PACK

Located above left rear shock tower. It provides ground for the rear body, deck lid and hatch. If subsystems license, cargo lights, fuel pump, or washer pump work properly, ground circuit is most likely OK.

CIRCUIT 550EB

Connects rear wiper motor connector cavity **C** to inline connector cavity **E** (black 20 gauge wire). It provides ground for the rear wiper motor.

CIRCUIT 550AG

Connects inline connector cavity **E** to rear body ground (black 20 gauge wire). It provides ground for the rear wiper motor.

CIRCUIT 550AH

Connects rear washer pump connector cavity **2** to rear body ground splice pack cavity **E** (black 20 gauge wire). It provides ground for the rear washer pump.

CIRCUIT 550AS

Connects left rear body splice pack cavity **J** to left rear body ground ring terminal (black **14** gauge wire). It provides ground for the left rear body splice pack.

Power Circuit Tests

CIRCUIT 302

Connects underhood junction block connector cavity **A** to instrument panel junction block connector cavity **A10** (red **14** gauge wire). It provides power to the instrument panel junction block.

CIRCUIT 580A

Connects underhood junction block connector cavity **A2** to inline connector cavity **B** (orange/black 20 gauge wire). It provides power to the rear wiper motor.

CIRCUIT 580F

Connects inline connector cavity **B** to rear wiper motor connector cavity **A** (orange 20 gauge wire). It provides power to the rear wiper motor.

CIRCUIT 580D

Connects instrument panel junction block connector cavity **B** to rear wiper switch connector cavity **D** (orange 20 gauge wire). It provides power to the rear wiper switch.

CIRCUIT 393C

Connects inline connector cavity **C** to rear wiper motor connector cavity **B** (white 20 gauge wire). It provides power to the rear wiper motor.

CIRCUIT 393A

Connects rear wiper switch connector cavity **C** to instrument panel inline connector cavity **B** (white 20 gauge wire). It provides power to the rear wiper motor.

CIRCUIT 392A

Connects rear wiper switch connector cavity **B** to instrument panel body inline connector cavity **A** (dark green 20 gauge wire). It provides power to the rear washer pump.

Refer to the model specific sections for engine electrical system service procedures

CIRCUIT 392B

Connects instrument panel body inline connector cavity **A** to rear washer pump connector cavity **1** (dark green 20 gauge wire). It provides power to the rear washer pump.

CIRCUIT 393B

Connects instrument panel body inline connector cavity **B** to inline connector cavity **C** (white 20 gauge wire). It provides power to the rear wiper motor.

OXYGEN (O₂) SENSORS

8

OXYGEN (O₂) SENSORS

General Information

An Oxygen (O₂) sensor is an input device used by the engine control computer to monitor the amount of oxygen in the exhaust gas stream. This information is used by the computer, along with other inputs, to fine-tune the air/fuel mixture so that the engine can run with the greatest efficiency in all conditions. The O₂ sensor sends this information to the computer in the form of a 100–900 millivolt (mV) reference signal, which is actually created by the O₂ sensor itself through chemical interactions between the sensor tip material (zirconium dioxide in almost all cases) and the oxygen levels in the exhaust gas stream and ambient atmosphere gas. At operating temperatures, approximately 1100°F (600°C), the element becomes a semiconductor. Essentially, through the differing levels of oxygen in the exhaust gas stream and in the surrounding atmosphere, the sensor creates a voltage signal that is directly and consistently related to the concentration of oxygen in the exhaust stream. Typically, a higher than normal amount of oxygen in the exhaust stream indicates that not all of the available oxygen was used in the combustion process, because there was not enough fuel (lean condition) present. Inversely, a lower than normal concentration of oxygen in the exhaust stream indicates that a large amount was used in the combustion process, because a larger than neces-

sary amount of fuel was present (rich condition). Thus, the engine control computer can correct the amount of fuel introduced into the combustion chambers.

Since the control computer uses the O₂ sensor output voltage as an indication of the oxygen concentration, and the oxygen concentration directly affects O₂ sensor output, the signal voltage from the sensor to the computer fluctuates constantly. This fluctuation is caused by the nature of the interaction between the computer and the O₂ sensor, which follows a general pattern: detect, compare, compensate, detect, compare, compensate, etc. This means that when the computer detects a lean signal from the O₂ sensor, it compares the reading with known parameters stored within its memory. It calculates that there is too much oxygen present in the exhaust gases, so it compensates by adding more fuel to the air/fuel mixture. This, in turn, causes the O₂ sensor to send a rich signal to the computer, which then compares this new signal, and adjusts the air/fuel mixture again. This pattern constantly repeats itself: detect rich, compare, compensate lean, detect lean, compare, compensate rich, etc. Since the O₂ sensor fluctuates between rich and lean, and because the lean limit for sensor output is 100 mV and the rich limit is 900 mV, the proper voltage signal from a normally functioning O₂ sensor consistently fluctuates between 100–300 and 700–900 mV.

A cut away view of a heated oxygen sensor

O₂ sensor output voltage vs. mixture ratio

➡ **The sensor voltage may never quite reach 100 or 900 mV, but it should fluctuate from at least below 300 mV to above 700 mV, and the mid-point of the fluctuations should be centered around 500 mV.**

To improve O₂ sensor efficiency, newer O₂ sensors were designed with a built-in heating element, and were called Heated O₂ (HO₂) sensors. This heating element was incorporated into the sensor so that the sensor would reach optimal operating temperature quicker, meaning that the O₂ sensor output signal could be used by the engine control computer sooner. Because the sensor reaches optimal temperature quicker, modern vehicles enjoy improved driveability and fuel economy even before the engine reaches normal operating temperature.

On-Board Diagnostics second generation (OBD-II), an updated system based on the former OBD-I, calls for additional O₂ sensors to be used after the catalytic converter, so that catalytic converter efficiency can be measured by the vehicle's engine control computer. The O₂ sensors mounted in the exhaust system after the cat-alytic converters are not used to affect air/fuel mixture; they are used solely to monitor catalytic converter efficiency.

O₂ (Oxygen Sensors) Service

PRECAUTIONS

When testing or servicing an O₂ sensor you will need to start and warm the engine to operating temperature in order to either perform the necessary testing procedures or to easily remove the sensor from its fitting. This will create a situation in which you will be working around a **HOT** exhaust system. The following is a list of precautions to consider during this service:

• Do not pierce any wires when testing an O₂ sensor, as this can lead to wiring harness damage. Backprobe the connector, when necessary.

• While testing the sensor, be sure to keep out of the way of moving engine components, such as the cooling fan. Refrain from wearing loose clothing which may become tangled in moving engine components.

• Safety glasses must be worn at all times when working on or near the exhaust system. Older exhaust systems may be covered with loose rust particles which can shower you when disturbed. These particles are more than a nuisance and can injure your eye.

• Be cautious when working on and around the hot exhaust system. Painful burns will result if skin is exposed to the exhaust system pipes or manifolds.

• The O₂ sensor may be difficult to remove when the engine temperature is below 120°F (48°C). Excessive force may damage the threads in the exhaust manifold or pipe, therefore always start the engine and allow it to reach normal operating temperature prior to removal.

• Since O₂ sensors are usually designed with a permanently-attached wiring pigtail (this allows the wiring harness and sensor connectors to be positioned away from the hot exhaust system), it may be necessary to use a socket or wrench that is designed specifically for this purpose. Before purchasing such a socket, be sure that you can't save some money by using a box end wrench for sensor removal.

TESTING

The best, and most accurate method to test the operation of an O₂ sensor is with the use of either an oscilloscope or a Diagnostic Scan Tool (DST), following their specific instructions for testing. It is possible, however, to test whether the O₂ sensor is functioning properly within general parameters using a Digital Volt-Ohmmeter (DVOM), also referred to as a Digital Multi-Meter (DMM). Newer DMM's are often designed to perform many advanced diagnostic functions, and some are even constructed to be used as an oscilloscope. Two in-vehicle testing procedures, and one bench test procedure, will be provided for the common zirconium dioxide oxygen sensor. The first in-vehicle test makes use of a standard DVOM with a 10 megohm impedance, whereas the second in-vehicle test presented necessitates the usage of an advanced DMM with MIN/MAX/Average functions. Both of these in-vehicle test procedures are likely to set Diagnostic Trouble Codes (DTC's) in the engine control computer. Therefore, after testing, be sure to clear all DTC's before retesting the sensor, if necessary.

These are some of the common DTC's which may be set during testing:

- Open in the O₂ sensor circuit
- Constant low voltage in the O₂ sensor circuit
- Constant high voltage in the O₂ sensor circuit
- Other fuel system problems could set a O₂ sensor code

➡ **Because an improperly functioning fuel delivery and/or control system can adversely affect the O₂ sensor voltage output signal, testing only the O₂ sensor is an inaccurate method for diagnosing an engine driveability problem.**

If after testing the sensor, the sensor is thought to be defective because of high or low readings, be sure to check that the fuel delivery and engine management system is working properly before condemning the O₂ sensor. Otherwise, the new O₂ sensor may continue to register the same high or low readings.

Often, by testing the O₂ sensor, another problem in the engine control management system can be diagnosed. If the sensor appears to be defective while installed in the vehicle, perform the bench test. If the sensor functions properly during the bench test, chances are that there may be a larger problem in the vehicle's fuel delivery and/or control system.

Many things can cause an O₂ sensor to fail, including old age, antifreeze contamination, physical damage, prolonged exposure to overly-rich exhaust gases, and exposure to silicone sealant fumes.

Wiring schematic of typical 1-, 2-, 3- and 4-wire oxygen sensor circuits

79228G10

Be sure to remedy any such condition prior to installing a new sensor, otherwise the new sensor may be damaged as well.

➡ **Perform a visual inspection of the sensor. Black sooty deposits may indicate a rich air/fuel mixture, brown deposits may indicate an oil consumption problem, and white gritty deposits may indicate an internal coolant leak. All of these conditions can destroy a new sensor if not corrected before installation.**

O₂ Sensor Terminal Identification

The easiest method for determining sensor terminal identification is to use a wiring diagram for the vehicle and engine in question. However, if a wiring diagram is not available there is a method for determining terminal identification. Throughout the testing procedures, the following terms will be used for clarity:

• Vehicle harness connector—this refers to the connector on the wires which are attached to the vehicle; NOT the connector at the end of the sensor pigtail.

• Sensor pigtail connector—this refers to the connector attached to the sensor itself.

• O₂ circuit—this refers to the circuit in a Heated O₂ (HO₂) sensor which corresponds to the oxygen-sensing function of the sensor; NOT the heating element circuit.

• Heating circuit—this refers to the circuit in a HO₂ sensor which is designed to warm the HO₂ sensor quickly to improve driveability.

• Sensor Output (SOUT) terminal—this is the terminal which corresponds to the O₂ circuit output. This is the terminal which will register the millivolt signals created by the sensor based upon the amount of oxygen in the exhaust gas stream.

• Sensor Ground (SGND) terminal—when a sensor is so equipped, this refers to the O₂ circuit ground terminal. Many O₂ sensors are not equipped with a ground wire, rather they utilize the exhaust system for the ground circuit.

• Heating Power (HPWR) terminal—this terminal corresponds to the circuit which provides the O₂ sensor heating circuit with power when the ignition key is turned to the **ON** or **RUN** positions.

• Heating Ground (HGND) terminal—this is the terminal connected to the heating circuit ground wire.

1-WIRE SENSOR

1-wire sensors are by far the easiest to determine sensor terminal identification, but this is self-evident. On 1-wire O₂ sensors, the single wire terminal is the SOUT and the exhaust system is used to provide the sensor ground pathway. Proceed to the test procedures.

2-WIRE SENSOR

On 2-wire sensors, one of the connector terminals is the SOUT and the other is the SGND. To determine which one is which, perform the following:

1. Locate the O₂ sensor and its pigtail connector. It may be necessary to raise and safely support the vehicle to gain access to the connector.

2. Start the engine and allow it to warm up to normal operating temperature, then turn the engine **OFF**.

3. Using a DVOM set to read 100–900 mV (millivolts) DC, backprobe the positive DVOM lead to one of the unidentified terminals and attach the negative lead to a good engine ground.

While the engine is running, keep clear of all moving and hot components. Do not wear loose clothing. Otherwise severe personal injury or death may occur.

4. Have an assistant restart the engine and allow it to idle.

5. Check the DVOM for voltage.

6. If no voltage is evident, check your DVOM leads to ensure that they are properly connected to the terminal and engine ground. If still no voltage is evident at the first terminal, move the positive meter lead to backprobe the second terminal.

7. If voltage is now present, the positive meter lead is attached to the SOUT terminal. The remaining terminal is the SGND terminal. If still no voltage is evident, either the O₂ sensor is defective or the meter leads are not making adequate contact with the engine ground and terminal contacts; clean the contacts and retest. If still no voltage is evident, the sensor is defective.

8. Have your assistant turn the engine **OFF**.

9. Label the sensor pigtail SOUT and SGND terminals.

10. Proceed to the test procedures.

3-WIRE SENSOR

➡ **3-wire sensors are HO₂ sensors.**

On 3-wire sensors, one of the connector terminals is the SOUT, one of the terminals is the HPWR and the other is the HGND. The SGND is achieved through the exhaust system, as with the 1-wire O₂ sensor. To identify the 3 terminals, perform the following:

1. Locate the O₂ sensor and its pigtail connector. It may be necessary to raise and safely support the vehicle to gain access to the connector.

2. Disengage the sensor pigtail connector from the vehicle harness connector.

3. Using a DVOM set to read 12 volts, attach the DVOM ground lead to a good engine ground.

4. Have an assistant turn the ignition switch **ON** without actually starting the engine.

5. Probe all 3 terminals in the vehicle harness connector. One of the terminals should exhibit 12 volts of power with the ignition key **ON**; this is the HPWR terminal.

   a. If the HPWR terminal was identified, note which of the sensor harness connector terminals is the HPWR, then match the vehicle harness connector to the sensor pigtail connector. Label the corresponding sensor pigtail connector terminal with HPWR.

   b. If none of the terminals showed 12 volts of power, locate and test the heater relay or fuse. Then, perform Steps 3–6 again.

6. Start the engine and allow it to warm up to normal operating temperature, then turn the engine **OFF**.

7. Have your assistant turn the ignition **OFF**.

8. Using the DVOM set to measure resistance (ohms), attach one of the leads to the HPWR terminal of the sensor pigtail connector. Use the other lead to probe the 2 remaining terminals of the sensor pigtail connector, one at a time. The DVOM should show continuity with only one of the remaining unidentified terminals; this is the HGND terminal. The remaining terminal is the SOUT.

   a. If continuity was found with only 1 of the 2 unidentified terminals, label the HGND and SOUT terminals on the sensor pigtail connector.

b. If no continuity was evident, or if continuity was evident from both unidentified terminals, the O₂ sensor is defective.

9. All 3-wire terminals should now be labeled on the sensor pigtail connector. Proceed with the test procedures.

4-WIRE SENSOR

➡ **4-wire sensors are HO₂ sensors.**

On 4-wire sensors, one of the connector terminals is the SOUT, one of the terminals is the SGND, one of the terminals is the HPWR and the other is the HGND. To identify the 4 terminals, perform the following:

1. Locate the O₂ sensor and its pigtail connector. It may be necessary to raise and safely support the vehicle to gain access to the connector.

2. Disengage the sensor pigtail connector from the vehicle harness connector.

3. Using a DVOM set to read 12 volts, attach the DVOM ground lead to a good engine ground.

4. Have an assistant turn the ignition switch **ON** without actually starting the engine.

5. Probe all 4 terminals in the vehicle harness connector. One of the terminals should exhibit 12 volts of power with the ignition key **ON**; this is the HPWR terminal.

   a. If the HPWR terminal was identified, note which of the sensor harness connector terminals is the HPWR, then match the vehicle harness connector to the sensor pigtail connector. Label the corresponding sensor pigtail connector terminal with HPWR.

   b. If none of the terminals showed 12 volts of power, locate and test the heater relay or fuse. Then, perform Steps 2–6 again.

6. Have your assistant turn the ignition **OFF**.

7. Using the DVOM set to measure resistance (ohms), attach one of the leads to the HPWR terminal of the sensor pigtail connector. Use the other lead to probe the 3 remaining terminals of the sensor pigtail connector, one at a time. The DVOM should show continuity with only one of the remaining unidentified terminals; this is the HGND terminal.

   a. If continuity was found with only one of the 2 unidentified terminals, label the HGND terminal on the sensor pigtail connector.

   b. If no continuity was evident, or if continuity was evident from all unidentified terminals, the O₂ sensor is defective.

   c. If continuity was found at 2 of the other terminals, the sensor is probably defective. However, the sensor may not necessarily be defective, because it may have been designed with the 2 ground wires joined inside the sensor in case one of the ground wires is damaged; the other circuit could still function properly. Though, this is highly unlikely. A wiring diagram is necessary in this particular case to know whether the sensor was so designed.

8. Reattach the sensor pigtail connector to the vehicle harness connector.

9. Start the engine and allow it to warm up to normal operating temperature, then turn the engine **OFF**.

10. Using a DVOM set to read 100–900 mV (millivolts) DC, backprobe the negative DVOM lead to one of the unidentified terminals and the positive lead to the other unidentified terminal.

✷✷ CAUTION

While the engine is running, keep clear of all moving and hot components. Do not wear loose clothing. Otherwise severe personal injury or death may occur.

11. Have an assistant restart the engine and allow it to idle.

12. Check the DVOM for voltage.

   a. If no voltage is evident, check your DVOM leads to ensure that they are properly connected to the terminals. If still no voltage is evident at either of the terminals, either the terminals were accidentally marked incorrectly or the sensor is defective.

   b. If voltage is present, but the polarity is reversed (the DVOM will show a negative voltage amount), turn the engine **OFF** and swap the 2 DVOM leads on the terminals. Start the engine and ensure that the voltage now shows the proper polarity.

   c. If voltage is evident and is the proper polarity, the positive DVOM lead is attached to the SOUT and the negative lead to the SGND terminals.

13. Have your assistant turn the engine **OFF**.

14. Label the sensor pigtail SOUT and SGND terminals.

In-Vehicle Tests

✷✷ WARNING

Never apply voltage to the O₂ circuit of the sensor, otherwise it may be damaged. Also, never connect an ohmmeter (or a DVOM set on the ohm function) to both of the O₂ circuit terminals (SOUT and SGND) of the sensor pigtail connector; it may damage the sensor.

Test 1 makes use of a standard DVOM with a 10 megohm impedance, whereas Test 2 necessitates the usage of an advanced Digital Multi-Meter (DMM) with MIN/MAX/Average functions or a sliding bar graph function. Both of these in-vehicle test procedures are likely to set Diagnostic Trouble Codes (DTC's) in the engine control computer. Therefore, after testing, be sure to clear all DTC's before retesting the sensor, if necessary. The third in-vehicle test is designed for the use of a scan tool or oscilloscope. The 4th test (Heating Circuit Test) is designed to check the function of the heating circuit in a HO₂ sensor.

➡ **If the O₂ sensor being tested is designed to use the exhaust system for the SGND, excessive corrosion between the exhaust and the O₂ sensor may affect sensor functioning.**

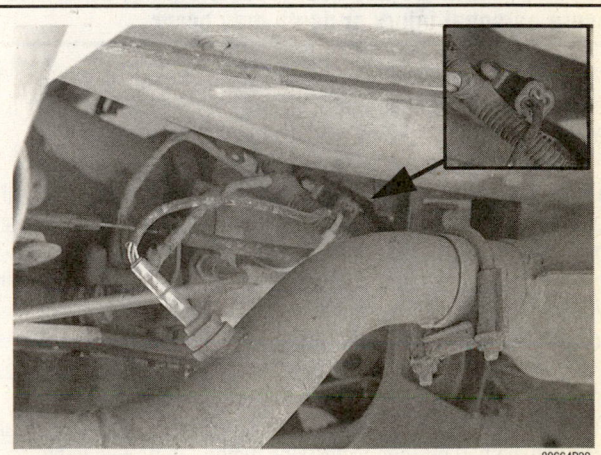

89664P30

To test the O₂ sensor, locate it and its connector (inset), which should be positioned away from the exhaust system to prevent heat damage.

The in-vehicle tests may be performed for O₂ sensors located in the exhaust system after the catalytic converter. However, the O₂ sensors located behind the catalytic converter will not fluctuate like the sensors mounted before the converter, because the converter, when functioning properly, emits a steady amount of oxygen. If the O₂ sensor mounted after the catalytic converter exhibits a fluctuating signal (like other O₂ sensors), the catalytic converter is most likely defective.

TEST 1—DIGITAL VOLT-OHMMETER

This test will not only verify proper sensor functioning, but is also designed to ensure the engine control computer and associated wiring is functioning properly as well.

1. Start the engine and allow it to warm up to normal operating temperature.

➡**If you are using the opening of the thermostat to gauge normal operating temperature, be forewarned: a defective thermostat can open too early and prevent the engine from reaching normal operating temperature. This can cause a slightly rich condition in the exhaust, which can throw the O₂ sensor readings off slightly.**

2. Turn the ignition switch **OFF**, then locate the O₂ sensor pigtail connector.

3. Perform a visual inspection of the connector to ensure it is properly engaged and all terminals are straight, tight and free from corrosion or damage.

4. Disengage the sensor pigtail connector from the vehicle harness connector.

5. On sensors equipped with a SGND terminal (sensors which do not use the exhaust system for the sensor ground pathway), connect a jumper wire to the SGND terminal and to a good, clean engine ground (preferably the negative terminal of the battery).

6. Using a DVOM set to read DC voltage, attach the positive lead to the SOUT terminal of the sensor pigtail connector, and the DVOM negative lead to a good engine ground.

✳✳ CAUTION

While the engine is running, keep clear of all moving and hot components. Do not wear loose clothing. Otherwise severe personal injury or death may occur.

7. Have an assistant start the engine and hold it at approximately 2000 rpm. Wait at least 1 minute before commencing with the test to allow the O₂ sensor to sufficiently warm up.

8. Using a jumper wire, connect the SOUT terminal of the **vehicle harness connector** to a good engine ground. This will fool the engine control computer into thinking it is receiving a lean signal from the O₂ sensor, and, therefore, the computer will enrichen the air/fuel ratio. With the SOUT terminal so grounded, the DVOM should register at least 800 mV, as the control computer adds additional fuel to the air/fuel ratio.

9. While observing the DVOM, disconnect the vehicle harness connector SOUT jumper wire from the engine ground. Use the jumper wire to apply slightly less than 1 volt to the SOUT terminal of the vehicle harness connector. One method to do this is by grasping and squeezing the end of the jumper between your forefinger and thumb of one hand while touching the positive terminal of the battery post with your other hand. This allows your body to act as a resistor for the battery positive voltage, and fools the engine control computer into thinking it is receiving a rich signal. Or, use a

mostly-drained AA battery by connecting the positive terminal of the AA battery to the jumper wire and the negative terminal of the battery to a good engine ground. (Another jumper wire may be necessary to do this.) The computer should lean the air/fuel mixture out. This lean mixture should register as 150 mV or less on the DVOM.

10. If the DVOM did not register millivoltages as indicated, the problem may be either the sensor, the engine control computer or the associated wiring. Perform the following to determine which is the defective component:

   a. Remove the vehicle harness connector SOUT jumper wire.

   b. While observing the DVOM, artificially enrich the air/fuel charge using propane. The DVOM reading should register higher than normal millivoltages. (Normal voltage for an ideal air/fuel mixture is approximately 450–550 mV DC). Then, lean the air/fuel intake charger by either disconnecting one of the fuel injector wiring harness connectors (to prevent the injector from delivering fuel) or by detaching 1 or 2 vacuum lines (to add additional non-metered air into the engine). The DVOM should now register lower than normal millivoltages. If the DVOM functioned as indicated, the problem lies elsewhere in the fuel delivery and control system. If the DVOM readings were still unresponsive, the O₂ sensor is defective; replace the sensor and retest.

➡**Poor wire connections and/or ground circuits may shift a normal O₂ sensor's millivoltage readings up into the rich range or down into the lean range. It is a good idea to check the wire condition and continuity before replacing a component which will not fix the problem. A voltage drop test between the sensor case and ground which reveals 14–16 mV or more, indicates a probable bad ground.**

11. Turn the engine **OFF**, remove the DVOM and all associated jumper wires. Reattach the vehicle harness connector to the sensor pigtail connector. If applicable, reattach the fuel injector wiring connector and/or the vacuum line(s).

12. Clear any DTC's present in the engine control computer memory, as necessary.

TEST 2—DIGITAL MULTI-METER

This test method is a more straight-forward O₂ sensor test, and does not test the engine control computer's response to the O₂ sensor signal. The use of a DMM with the MIN/MAX/Average function or sliding bar graph/wave function is necessary for this test. Don't forget that the O₂ sensor mounted after the catalytic converter (if equipped) will not fluctuate like the other O₂ sensor(s) will.

1. Start the engine and allow it to warm up to normal operating temperature.

➡**If you are using the opening of the thermostat to gauge normal operating temperature, be forewarned: a defective thermostat can open too early and prevent the engine from reaching normal operating temperature. This can cause a slightly rich condition in the exhaust, which can throw the O₂ sensor readings off slightly.**

2. Turn the ignition switch **OFF**, then locate the O₂ sensor pigtail connector.

3. Perform a visual inspection of the connector to ensure it is properly engaged and all terminals are straight, tight and free from corrosion or damage.

4. Backprobe the O₂ sensor connector terminals. Attach the DMM positive test lead to the SOUT terminal of the sensor pigtail connector and the negative lead to either the SGND terminal of the

sensor pigtail connector (if equipped—refer to the terminal identification procedures earlier in this section for clarification) or to a good, clean engine ground.

5. Activate the MIN/MAX/Average or sliding bar graph/wave function on the DMM.

✳ CAUTION

While the engine is running, keep clear of all moving and hot components. Do not wear loose clothing. Otherwise severe personal injury or death may occur.

6. Have an assistant start the engine and wait a few minutes before commencing with the test to allow the O₂ sensor to sufficiently warm up.

7. Read the minimum, maximum and average readings exhibited by the O₂ sensor or observe the bar graph/wave form. The average reading for a properly functioning O₂ sensor is be approximately 450–550 mV DC. The minimum and maximum readings should vary more than 300–600 mV. A typical O₂ sensor can fluctuate from as low as 100 mV to as high as 900 mV; if the sensor range of fluctuation is not large enough, the sensor is defective. Also, if the fluctuation range is biased up or down in the scale. For example, if the fluctuation range is 400 mV to 900 mV the sensor is defective, because the readings are pushed up into the rich range (as long as the fuel delivery system is functioning properly). The same goes for a fluctuation range pushed down into the lean range. The mid-point of the fluctuation range should be around 400–500 mV. Finally, if the O₂ sensor voltage fluctuates too slowly (usually the voltage wave should oscillate past the mid-way point of 500 mV several times per second) the sensor is defective. (Technician's refer to this state as "lazy.")

➡ Poor wire connections and/or ground circuits may shift a normal O₂ sensor's millivoltage readings up into the rich range or down into the lean range. It is a good idea to check the wire condition and continuity before replacing a component which will not fix the problem. A voltage drop test between the sensor case and ground which reveals 14–16 mV or more, indicates a probable bad ground.

8. Using the propane method, enrichen the air/fuel mixture and observe the DMM readings. The average O₂ sensor output signal voltage should rise into the rich range.

9. Lean the air/fuel mixture by either disconnecting a fuel injector wiring harness connector or by disconnecting a vacuum line. The O₂ sensor average output signal voltage should drop into the lean range.

10. If the O₂ sensor did not react as indicated, the sensor is defective and should be replaced.

11. Turn the engine **OFF**, remove the DMM and all associated jumper wires. Reattach the vehicle harness connector to the sensor pigtail connector. If applicable, reattach the fuel injector wiring connector and/or the vacuum line(s).

12. Clear any DTC's present in the engine control computer memory, as necessary.

TEST 3—OSCILLOSCOPE

This test is designed for the use of an oscilloscope to test the functioning of an O₂ sensor.

➡ This test is only applicable for O₂ sensors mounted in the exhaust system before the catalytic converter.

1. Start the engine and allow it to reach normal operating temperature.

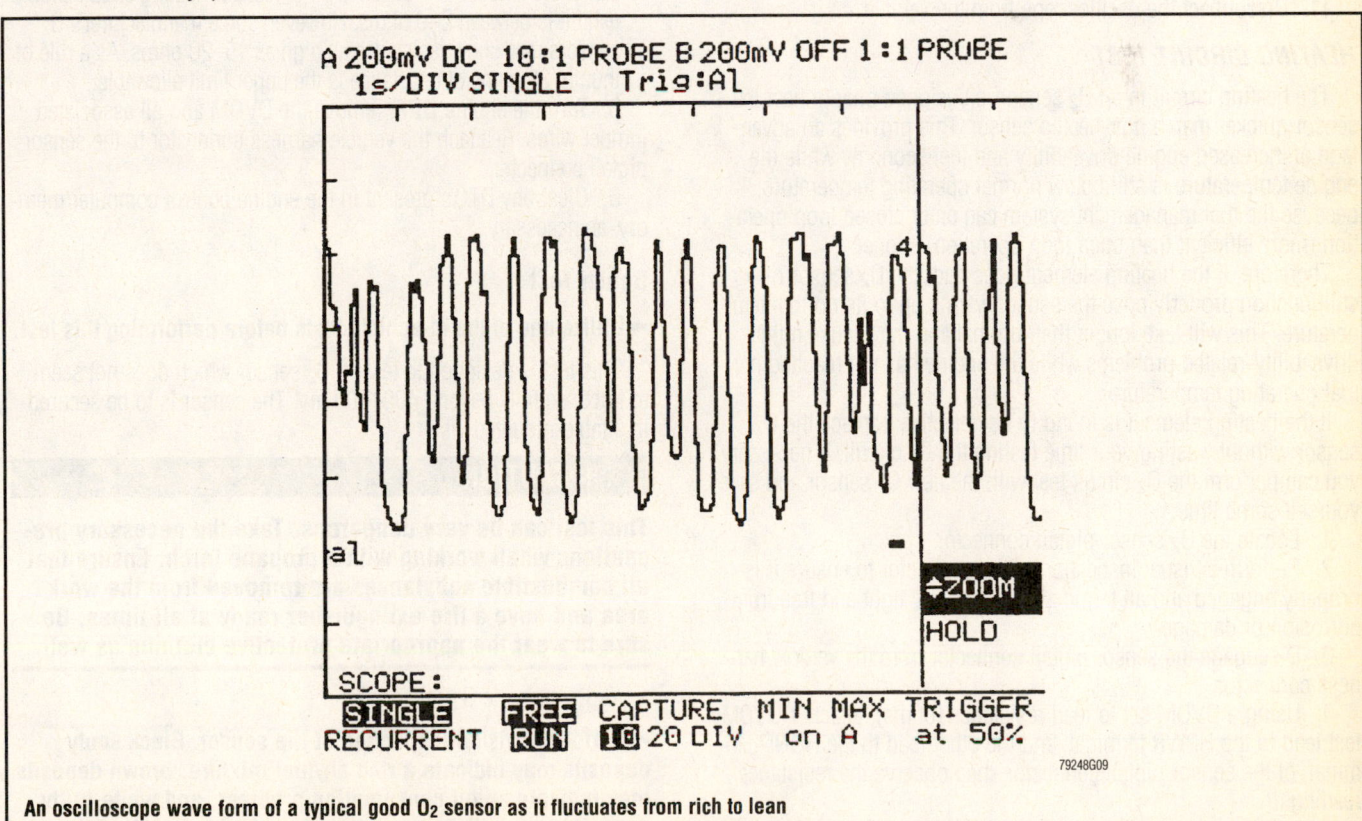

An oscilloscope wave form of a typical good O₂ sensor as it fluctuates from rich to lean

2. Turn the engine **OFF**, and locate the O₂ sensor connector. Backprobe the scope lead to the O₂ sensor connector SOUT terminal. Refer to the manufacturer's instructions for more information on attaching the scope to the vehicle.

3. Turn the scope ON.

4. Set the oscilloscope amplitude to 200 mV per division, and the time to 1 second per division. Use the 1:1 setting of the probe, and be sure to connect the scope's ground lead to a good, clean engine ground. Set the signal function to automatic or internal triggering.

5. Start the engine and run it at 2000 rpm.

6. The oscilloscope should display a wave form, representative of the O₂ sensor switching between lean (100–300 mV) and rich (700–900 mV). The sensor should switch between rich and lean, or lean and rich (crossing the mid-point of 500 mV) several times per second. Also, the range of each wave should reach at least above 700 mV and below 300 mV. However, an occasional low peak is acceptable.

7. Force the air/fuel mixture rich by introducing propane into the engine, then observe the oscilloscope readings. The fluctuating range of the O₂ sensor should climb into the rich range.

8. Lean the air/fuel mixture out by either detaching a vacuum line or by disengaging one of the fuel injector's wiring connectors. Watch the scope readings; the O₂ sensor wave form should drop toward the lean range.

9. If the O₂ sensor's wave form does not fluctuate adequately, is not centered around 500 mV during normal engine operation, does not climb toward the rich range when propane is added to the engine, or does not drop toward the lean range when a vacuum hose or fuel injector connector is detached, the sensor is defective.

10. Reattach the fuel injector connector or vacuum hose.

11. Disconnect the oscilloscope from the vehicle.

HEATING CIRCUIT TEST

The heating circuit in an O₂ sensor is designed only to heat the sensor quicker than a non-heated sensor. This provides an advantage of increased engine driveability and fuel economy while the engine temperature is still below normal operating temperature, because the fuel management system can enter closed loop operation (more efficient than open loop operation) sooner.

Therefore, if the heating element goes bad, the O₂ sensor may still function properly once the sensor warms up to its normal temperature. This will take longer than normal and may cause mild driveability-related problems while the engine has not reached normal operating temperature.

If the heating element is found to be defective, replace the O₂ sensor without wasting your time testing the O₂ circuit; if necessary, you can perform the O₂ circuit test with the new O₂ sensor and save yourself some time.

1. Locate the O₂ sensor pigtail connector.

2. Perform a visual inspection of the connector to ensure it is properly engaged and all terminals are straight, tight and free from corrosion or damage.

3. Disengage the sensor pigtail connector from the vehicle harness connector.

4. Using a DVOM set to read resistance (ohms), attach 1 DVOM test lead to the HPWR terminal, and the other lead to the HGND terminal, of the sensor pigtail connector, then observe the resistance readings.

   a. If there is no continuity between the HPWR and HGND terminals, the sensor is defective. Replace it with a new one and retest.

The heating circuit of the O₂ sensor can be tested with a DMM set to measure resistance

   b. If there is continuity between the 2 terminals, but the resistance is greater than approximately 20 ohms, the sensor is defective. Replace it with a new one and retest.

➡**For the following step, the HO₂ sensor should be approximately 75°F (23°C) for the proper resistance values.**

   c. If there is continuity between the 2 terminals and it is less than 20 ohms, the sensor is probably not defective. Because of the large diversity of engine control systems used in vehicles today, O₂ sensor heating circuit resistance specifications change often. Generally, the amount of resistance an O₂ sensor heating circuit should exhibit is between 2–9 ohms. However, some manufacturer's O₂ sensors may show resistance as high as 15–20 ohms. As a rule of thumb, 20 ohms of resistance is the upper limit allowable.

5. Turn the engine **OFF**, remove the DVOM and all associated jumper wires. Reattach the vehicle harness connector to the sensor pigtail connector.

6. Clear any DTC's present in the engine control computer memory, as necessary.

Bench Test

➡**Utilize one of the in-vehicle tests before performing this test.**

This test is designed to test an O₂ sensor which does not seem to fluctuate fully beyond 400–700 mV. The sensor is to be secured in a table-mounted vise.

✷✷ CAUTION

This test can be very dangerous. Take the necessary precautions when working with a propane torch. Ensure that all combustible substances are removed from the work area and have a fire extinguisher ready at all times. Be sure to wear the appropriate protective clothing as well.

1. Remove the O₂ sensor.

➡**Perform a visual inspection of the sensor. Black sooty deposits may indicate a rich air/fuel mixture, brown deposits may indicate an oil consumption problem, and white gritty deposits may indicate an internal coolant leak. All of these conditions can destroy a new sensor if not corrected before installation.**

2. Position the sensor in a vise so that the vise holds the sensor by the hex portion of its case.

3. Attach 1 lead of a DVOM set to read DC millivoltages to the sensor case and the other lead to the SOUT terminal of the sensor pigtail connector.

4. Carefully use a propane torch to heat the tip (and ONLY the tip) of the sensor. Once the sensor reaches close to normal operating temperature range, alternately heat the sensor up and allow it to cool down; the sensor output voltage signal should change with the temperature change.

➡ **This may also clean a sensor covered with a heavy coat of carbon.**

5. If the sensor voltage does not change with the fluctuation in temperature, replace the sensor with a new one. Install the new sensor and perform one of the in-vehicle tests to rule out additional fuel management system faults.

Disengage the sensor pigtail connector half from the vehicle harness connector half

Since sensor locations vary between vehicles, the first step in removal is to locate the O₂ sensors (arrows) . . .

For flange type sensors, loosen the hold-down fasteners . . .

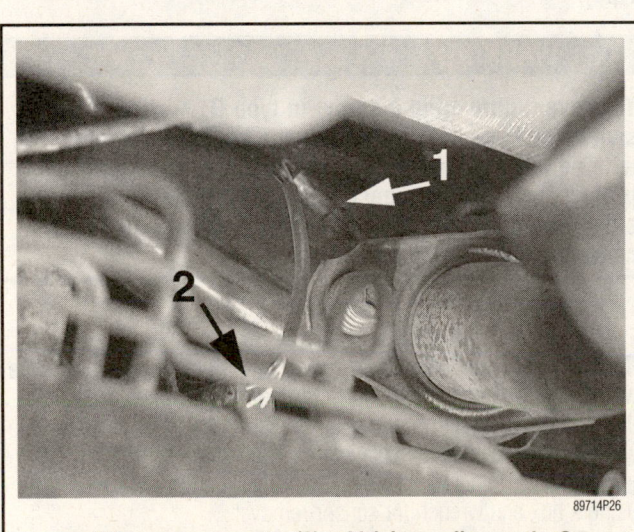

. . . and the sensor connector (2), which is usually near the O₂ sensor (1), but removed enough from the heat of the exhaust system

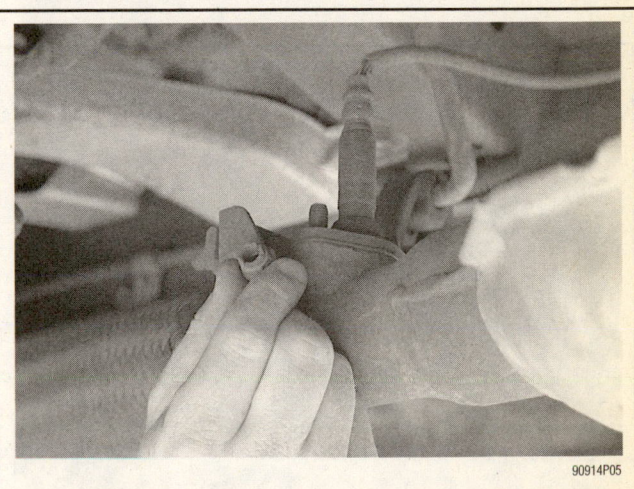

. . . which happen to be nuts in this particular case—some models may use bolts rather than nuts

For exhaust manifold replacement procedures, see the model specific sections of this manual

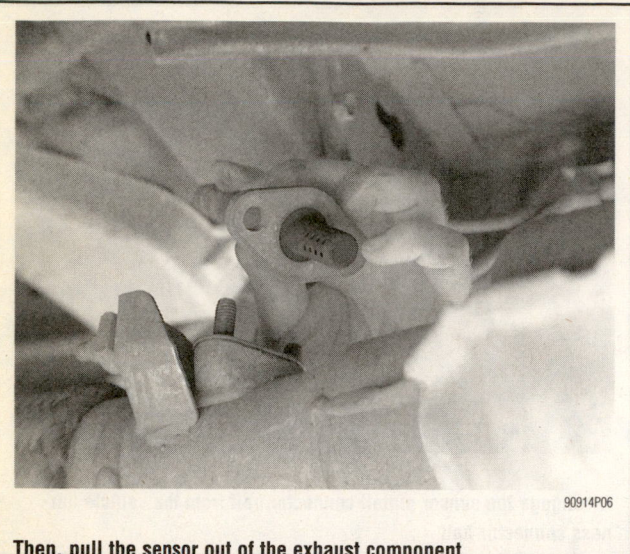

Then, pull the sensor out of the exhaust component

90914P06

For screw-in type sensors (arrow) . . .

89714P22

. . . either use a box end wrench to loosen the sensor or a socket designed expressly for this purpose . . .

89714P23

. . . then remove the sensor from the exhaust component

89714P24

REMOVAL & INSTALLATION

1. Start the engine and allow it to reach normal operating temperature, then turn the ignition switch **OFF**.
2. Disconnect the negative battery cable.
3. Open the hood and locate the O₂ sensor connector. It may be necessary to raise and safely support the vehicle for access to the sensor and its connector.

➡ **On a few models, it may be necessary to remove the passenger seat and lift the carpeting in order to access the connector for a downstream O₂ sensor.**

4. Disengage the O₂ sensor pigtail connector from the vehicle harness connector.

➡ **There are generally 2 methods used to mount an O₂ sensor in the exhaust system: either the O₂ sensor is threaded directly into the exhaust component (screw-in type) or the O₂ sensor is retained by a flange and 2 nuts or bolts (flange type).**

✳✳ WARNING

To prevent damaging a screw-in type O₂ sensor, if excessive force is needed to remove the sensor lubricate it with penetrating oil prior to removal. Also, be sure to protect the tip of the sensor; O₂ sensor tips are very sensitive and may be easily damaged if allowed to strike or come in contact with other objects.

5. Remove the sensor, as follows:
- Screw-in type sensors—Since O₂ sensors are usually designed with a permanently-attached wiring pigtail (this allows the wiring harness and sensor connectors to be positioned away from the hot exhaust system), it may be necessary to use a socket or wrench that is designed specifically for this purpose. Before purchasing such a socket, be sure that you can't save some money by using a box end wrench for sensor removal.
- Flange type sensors—Loosen the hold-down nuts or bolts and pull the sensor out of the exhaust component. Be sure to remove and discard the old sensor gasket, if equipped. You will need a new gasket for installation.

6. Perform a visual inspection of the sensor. Black sooty deposits may indicate a rich air/fuel mixture, brown deposits may indicate an oil consumption problem, and white gritty deposits may indicate an internal coolant leak. All of these conditions can destroy a new sensor if not corrected before installation.

To install:

7. Install the sensor, as follows:

➡**A special anti-seize compound is used on most screw-in type O₂ sensor threads, and is designed to ease O₂ sensor removal. New sensors usually have the compound already applied to the threads. However, if installing the old O₂ sensor or the new sensor did not come with compound, apply a thin coating of electrically-conductive anti-seize compound to the sensor threads.**

✳✳ WARNING

Be sure to prevent any of the anti-seize compound from coming in contact with the O₂ sensor tip. Also, take precautions to protect the sensor tip from physical damage during installation.

• Screw-in type sensors—Install the sensor in the mounting boss, then tighten it securely.

• Flange type sensors—Position a new sensor gasket on the exhaust component and insert the sensor. Tighten the hold-down fasteners securely and evenly.

8. Reattach the sensor pigtail connector to the vehicle harness connector.

9. Lower the vehicle.

10. Connect the negative battery cable.

11. Start the engine and ensure no Diagnostic Trouble Codes (DTC's) are set.

LOCATIONS

There are different locations in the exhaust system where O₂ sensors are positioned. The locations have been given numbers and will be used in the accompanying charts to identify the positions of O₂ sensors in most vehicles.

Due to mid-year production changes or factory inconsistencies, all models may not be covered. If a vehicle being serviced is not covered in the charts, inspect the exhaust system (while cold!) in the general locations to find the applicable O₂ sensors.

➡**If equipped with dual exhaust systems, there may be up to 4 or 5 O₂ sensors in the exhaust system. Be sure to locate all of them before commencing with any testing or service.**

UPSTREAM OXYGEN SENSOR

EXHAUST PIPE

79248G01

Location No. 1—down pipe or exhaust manifold

For complete service labor times order Chilton's Labor Guide Manual

Location No. 1—typical O$BSB2sensor located in the exhaust manifold

Location No. 4—outlet of the catalytic converter

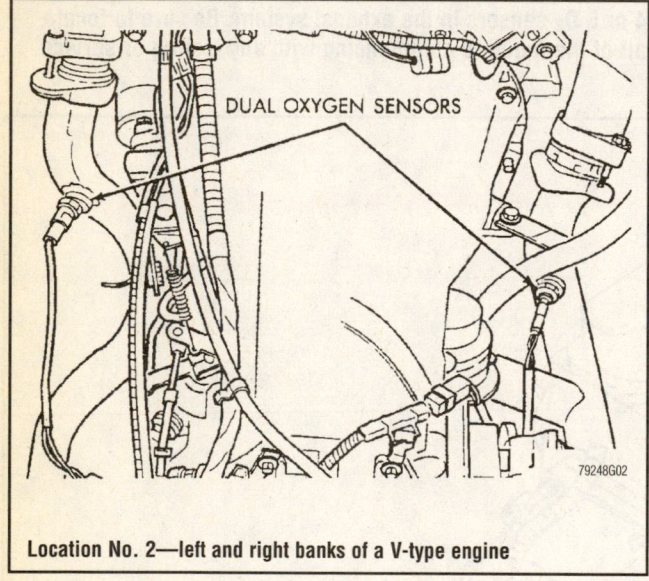

Location No. 2—left and right banks of a V-type engine

Location No. 5—inlet and outlet of the catalytic converter

Location No. 3—exhaust collector (where more than one pipe joins together)

Location No. 6—front, rear, left and right banks of a V-type engine

<Turbo>

Right bank heated oxygen sensor (front)

Right bank heated oxygen sensor (rear)

Left bank heated oxygen sensor (front)

Left bank heated oxygen sensor (rear)

93008G02

Location No. 7— front, rear, inlet and outlet of the catalytic converter

Ignition system service is covered in the model specific sections of this manual

OXYGEN SENSOR LOCATIONS

Manufacturer / Years	Engines	No. of Sensors	Location	Manufacturer / Years	Engines	No. of Sensors	Location
Chrysler LH Vehicles ①				**General Motors B Body**			
1996-00	ALL	4	2, 4	1996	4.3L	4	2, 4
Chrysler Avenger and Sebring Coupe					5.7L	4	2, 4
1996-00	2.0L	2	1, 4	**General Motors C & H Body**			
	2.5L	3	2, 4	1996-00	3.8L	2	1, 4
Dodge Stealth				**General Motors E & K Bodies**			
1996	3.0L	4	6, 7	1996-00	4.6L	4	1, 5
Eagle Talon				**General Motors F Body**			
1996-98	ALL	2	1, 4	1996-00	3.8L	3	5
Plymouth Neon					5.7L	4	5
1996-00	ALL	2	1, 4	**General Motors G Body**			
Chrysler JA/JX Vehicles ②				1996-00	3.8L	2	1, 4
1996-00	ALL	2	1, 4		4.0L	2	1, 4
Ford Aspire				**General Motors J Body**			
1996-97	1.3L	2	1, 4	1996-00	2.2L	2	5
Ford Probe					2.4L	2	5
1996-97	2.0L	2	1, 4	**General Motors L Body**			
	2.5L	4	2, 4	1996	2.2L	2	5
Ford Contour, Mystique and 1999-00 Cougar					3.1L	2	5
1996-00	2.0L	2	1, 4	**General Motors L/N Body**			
	2.5L	3	1, 4	1997-00	2.4L	2	1, 4
Ford Taurus and Sable					3.1L	2	1, 4
1996-00	ALL	4	2, 4	**General Motors N Body**			
Lincoln Continental				1996-00	2.4L	2	1, 4
1996-00	4.6L	4	5		3.1L	2	1, 4
Ford Escort, Tracer and ZX2				**General Motors V Body**			
1996-97	1.8L	2	1, 4	1997-00	3.0L	4	5
	1.9L	2	1, 4	**General Motors W Body**			
1998-00	2.0L	2	1, 4	1996-00	3.1L	2	5
Ford Mustang					3.4L	2	5
1996-00	ALL	4	2, 4		3.8L	2	5
Lincoln Mark VIII				**General Motors Y Body**			
1996-00	4.6L	4	5	1996-00	5.7L	4	5
Ford Cougar (1996-97)				**GEO/Chevrolet**			
1996-97	3.8L	2	1, 4	1996-00	ALL	2	1, 4
	4.6L	4	5	**Saturn**			
Ford Full-size				1996-00	1.9L	2	1, 4
1996-00	4.6L	4	5				
General Motors A Body							
1996	2.2L	2	1, 4				
	3.1L	2	1, 4				

① Chrysler LH class designation refers to the Chrysler 300M, Concorde, LHS, New Yorker, Dodge Intrepid and Eagle Vision.

② Chrysler JA class designation refers to the Chrysler Cirrus, Plymouth Breeze and Dodge Stratus.

Chrysler JX class designation refers to the Chrysler Sebring Convertible.

93008C01

ELECTRIC COOLING FANS

9

ELECTRIC COOLING FANS

General Information

A basic vehicle cooling system consists of a radiator, water pump, thermostat, electric or engine-driven cooling fan, and hoses. Electric cooling fans are common on today's vehicles due to engine compartment space limitations or engine layout. Electric cooling fans operate in either a pusher or a puller capacity. A pusher type fan is typically mounted on the front of the radiator assembly and forces air through the radiator, whereas a puller type fan is mounted on the engine side of the radiator and draws air through the grill and radiator assembly. Vehicles that utilize a transversely-mounted engine will always be equipped with at least one electric cooling fan (most having two), because none of the engine pulleys are inline with the radiator air-flow.

There are generally two types of electric cooling fans: primary cooling fans and secondary cooling fans. Primary cooling fans are typically of the puller style. Vehicles that do not incorporate an engine-driven mechanical cooling fan will utilize a primary cooling fan. The secondary cooling fan, also known as a A/C condenser fan or auxiliary cooling fan by certain manufacturers, could be of either a pusher or a puller style. Vehicles equipped with A/C will either utilize the radiator cooling fan or a separate fan as the A/C condenser cooling fan (which performs the same function as an auxiliary cooling fan on vehicles with a primary mechanical fan). The engine control computer that receives inputs from various sensors in the engine compartment commonly controls electric cooling fans. The engine control computer receives inputs from the engine coolant temperature sensors and A/C system pressure switches, then actuates the necessary cooling fan relays to engage the applicable cooling fan for the condition. On models equipped with only one electric primary cooling fan, the fan can operate at two speeds: low speed and high speed. The low speed condition is enabled when the engine begins to heat up or when the A/C is engaged. As the engine demands more cooling, the cooling fan will be stepped-up to high speed.

Electric Cooling Fan Service

Due to the wide variety of vehicle manufacturers and suppliers of electric cooling fans it is almost impossible to cover every specific combination of cooling fan and model. The following procedures will cover the most common types of mountings and troubleshooting techniques.

UNDER-HOOD
FUSE/RELAY BOX

CONDENSER
FAN RELAY

RADIATOR
FAN RELAY

RADIATOR FAN
CONTROL MODULE

RADIATOR FAN
SWITCH B

RADIATOR FAN
SWITCH A

CONDENSER
FAN MOTOR

RADIATOR FAN
MOTOR

79229G01

Typical dual fan set-up, showing common cooling fan system control components used on many vehicles with A/C

REMOVAL & INSTALLATION

Puller Type

➡**It may be simpler to remove the cooling fan(s) with the radiator as an assembly.**

1. Disconnect the negative battery cable.
2. Inspect the cooling fan and take note of any wires, hoses or A/C lines which may hamper fan removal. Also at this time, decide whether it is necessary to remove the fan along with the radiator or not.
3. Position aside all wires, hoses and A/C lines for fan removal. It may not always be possible to create enough clearance for fan removal by simply moving these obstructions aside; often they must be disconnected. If any cooling system lines must be disconnected, drain and recycle the engine coolant. If any of the A/C lines must be disconnected, the A/C system will need to be discharged and evacuated by a MVAC-trained technician using an approved recovery machine.
4. Disengage the cooling fan wiring harness connector.

5. If the fan can be removed without the radiator, perform the following:
   a. Loosen the mounting fasteners. Usually there are two nuts or bolts along the top edge of the cooling fan shroud and either two retaining clips or bolts along the bottom edge.
   b. Carefully lift the fan up and out of the engine compartment, making sure that no wires or hoses get hung up on it.
6. If it is necessary to remove the radiator for fan removal, perform the following:
   a. Disconnect all cooling system hoses from it after draining the cooling system.
   b. Locate all of the radiator mounting fasteners (usually two or more nuts or bolts along the top, possibly two along the bottom).

➡**Quite a few radiators are secured along the bottom by two posts which fit into rubber grommets. The rubber grommets help isolate the radiator from harsh vibrations in the frame. If no nuts or bolts can be located along the bottom of the radiator, chances are that the radiator is secured with the posts and grommets.**

Exploded view of a typical dual cooling fan set-up and related cooling system components

Labels in diagram:
- LOWER RADIATOR HOSE
- UPPER RADIATOR HOSE
- RADIATOR CAP
- RADIATOR
- ATF COOLER HOSES
- O-RING
- DRAIN PLUG
- FAN MOTOR
- RADIATOR FAN SHROUD
- RADIATOR FAN
- CONDENSER FAN SHROUD ASSEMBLY

79229G02

To remove a puller type cooling fan, first detach any braces (1), wires (2) or other obstructions . . .

89713P96

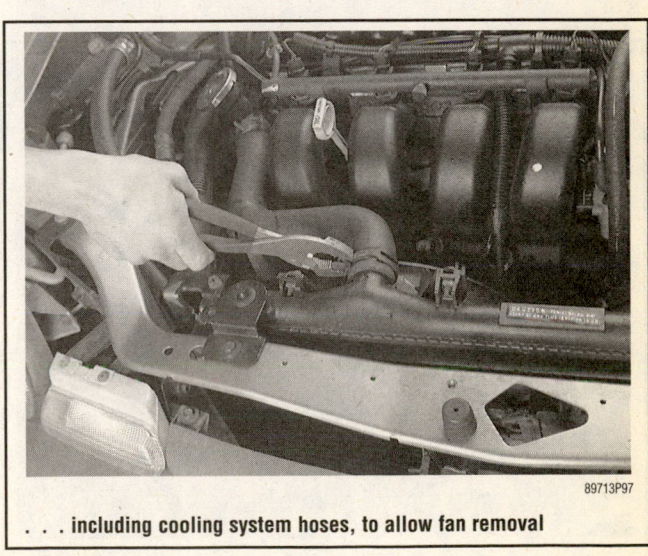

. . . including cooling system hoses, to allow fan removal

89713P97

For complete service labor times order Chilton's Labor Guide Manual

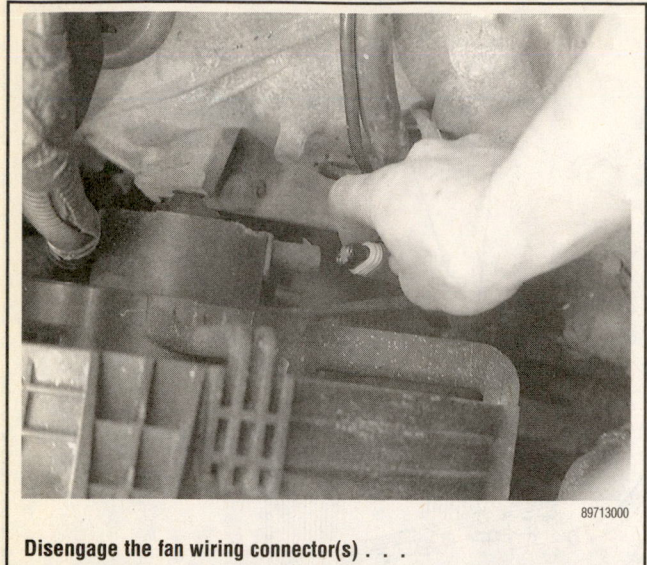

Disengage the fan wiring connector(s) . . .

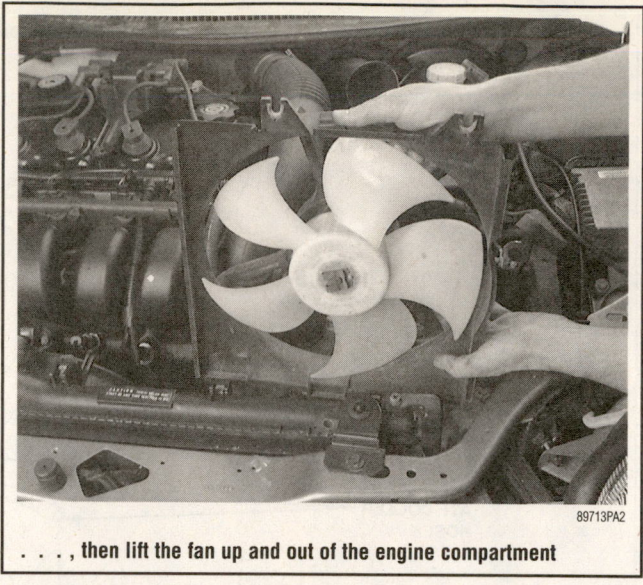

. . ., then lift the fan up and out of the engine compartment

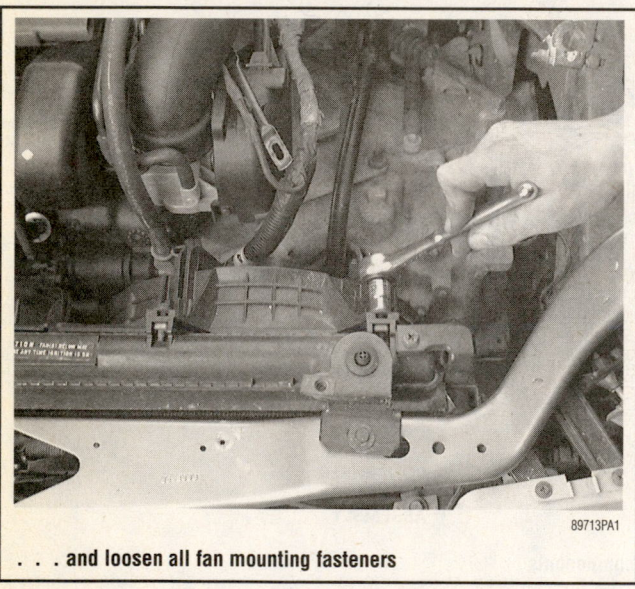

. . . and loosen all fan mounting fasteners

ELECTRICAL CONNECTOR **FASTENERS**

CLIPS

79249G09

Typical mounting of a puller type cooling fan assembly utilizing retaining clips and screws—note that this particular model uses a dual puller fan setup

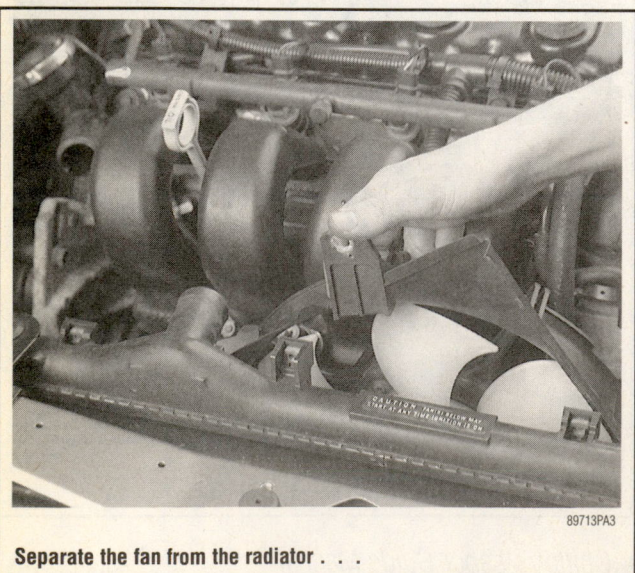

Separate the fan from the radiator . . .

1 FAN ASSEMBLY
2 BOLT
3 CLIP
4 INSULATOR, ENGINE COOLING FAN

79249G10

Notice the slots in the bottom of the radiator, in which the fan housing posts rest—common mounting of a puller type cooling fan.

This fan mounts to the fan shroud, then the shroud mounts to the radiator—molded clips in the radiator hold the bottom in place and screws at the top.

79249G11

Typically the cooling fan is rubber mounted to isolate vibration and noise—usually the rubber grommets are located at the mount, verify their position before installation

79249G12

c. Lift the radiator and cooling fan up and out of the engine compartment together.

d. Separate the cooling fan from the radiator by removing the attaching fasteners.

To install:

7. If applicable, install the cooling fan on the radiator.

8. Install the cooling fan and shroud assembly (also the radiator if necessary). Tighten the fan shroud mounting bolts.

9. Reattach all wires, hoses and A/C lines as applicable. If the A/C lines were detached, the system must be evacuated and recharged by a MVAC-trained technician.

10. If drained, refill and bleed the cooling system.

11. Reattach the cooling fan electrical harness connector.

12. Connect the negative battery cable.

13. Start the engine and check for leaks.

14. Verify the operation of the cooling fan(s).

Pusher Type

Vehicles that utilize the pusher type of electric cooling fan, may require the removal of the grilles and/or upper radiator shroud in order to gain access the fasteners that mount the fan assembly in the vehicle.

1. Disconnect the negative battery cable.

2. Access the cooling fan.

3. Label and disconnect the cooling fan electrical harness.

➡**It may be necessary to loosen the mounting bolts for the A/C condenser to the body**

4. Remove the fasteners that mount the cooling fan to the A/C condenser or radiator.

5. Lift the cooling fan out of the vehicle.

To install:

6. Insert the cooling fan into the vehicle.

7. Mount the cooling fan to the A/C condenser or radiator

8. Connect the cooling fan electrical harness.

1	Connector
2	Bolt
3	Condenser fan

79249G13

After removal of the grill assembly, the pusher type of cooling fan can be removed

1 J-CLIP
2 BOLT
3 COOLING FAN
4 BRACKET
5 ELECTRICAL CONNECTOR

VIEW A

79249G14

It may be necessary to remove the grill assembly to access the A/C condenser cooling fan—pusher type

9. If removed, install any shrouding or grills.
10. Connect the negative battery cable.

TROUBLESHOOTING

When diagnosing an inoperative cooling fan it may be necessary to use a diagnostic scan tool to monitor engine coolant temperature and the engine control computer.

1. Perform a visual inspection of the cooling fan. If the fan does not turn with ease, the fan motor is seized and needs to be replaced.
2. Check all the fuses and fusible links related to the cooling fan circuit.
3. Check the integrity of the electrical connections related to the cooling fan circuit.
4. Check the cooling fan motor.
5. Check the relays associated with the cooling fan circuit.
6. Using a scan tool, determine if the engine control computer is calling for the fan to activate.

Cooling Fan Motor

1. Disconnect the negative battery cable.
2. Disengage the cooling fan motor connector.

3. Identify and label the ground and the power terminals of the cooling fan connector using the wiring diagrams provided.
4. Using jumper leads with a fuse in series, apply battery voltage to the appropriate terminals of the cooling fan.
5. The cooling fan should operate. If not, replace the cooling fan.

If the cooling fan functions properly during this test, proceed to the cooling fan relay test.

Cooling Fan Relay

1. Turn the ignition **OFF**.
2. Remove the relay.
3. Locate the two terminals on the relay, which are connected to the coil windings. Check the relay coil for continuity. Connect the common meter lead to terminal 85 and positive meter lead to terminal 86. There should be continuity. If not, replace the relay.
4. Check the operation of the internal relay contacts.
   a. Connect the meter leads to terminals 30 and 87. Meter polarity does not matter for this step.
   b. Apply positive battery voltage to terminal 86 and ground to terminal 85. The relay should click as the contacts are drawn toward the coil and the meter should indicate continuity. Replace the relay if your results are different.

If the relay functions properly during this test, inspect the coolant temperature sensor and the cooling fan system wiring for defects.

79249G15

Use an ohmmeter to check for circuit continuity of the coil in the relay

79249G16

Terminal identification of the most common types of relays. Diodes and resistors in the relay prevent voltage spikes induced when the current is removed from the coil from damaging electronic components

COOLING FAN DIAGRAM INDEX

MANUFACTURER MODEL AND ENGINE	DIAGRAM
Chrysler Corp.	
Avenger, Sebring Coupe 2.0L	1
Avenger, Sebring Coupe 2.5L	2
Breeze, Cirrus, Sebring Convertible, Stratus 2.0L/ 2.4L/ 2.5L	
1996 Models	3
1997-00 Models	4
Concord, Intrepid, LHS, New Yorker, Vision 2.7L/ 3.2L/ 3.3L/ 3.5L	5
Neon 2.0L	
1996 Models	6
1997-00 Models	7
Talon 2.0L (Non-turbo)	
1996-97 Models with A/T	8
1996-97 Models with M/T	9
1998 Models	10
Talon 2.0L (Turbo)	
1996-98 Models with A/T	11
1996-98 Models with M/T	12
Ford Motor Co.	
Ford Aspire 1.3L	13
Ford Continental 4.6L	
1996 Models	14
1997-00 Models	15
Ford Contour, Mystique	
1996-00 Models 2.0L	16
1996-00 Models 2.5L	17
Ford Crown Victoria, Grand Marquis	
1996-00 Models 4.6L	18
Ford Escort, Tracer, ZX2	
1996 Models 1.8L/ 1.9L with A/T	19
1996 Models 1.8L/ 1.9L with M/T	20
1997-00 Models	21
Ford Mark VIII	
1996-00 Models 4.6L	22
Ford Mustang	
1996-00 Models 3.8L	23
1996-00 Models 4.6L	24
Ford Probe	
1996-97 Models 2.0L/ 2.5L	25
Ford Taurus, Sable	
1996-00 Models 3.0L/ 3.4L	26
Ford Thunderbird, Cougar - XR7	
1996-97 Models 3.8L/ 4.6L	27
Lincoln Town Car 4.6L	
1996-00 Models 4.6L	28
General Motors	
A Body (Century, Cutlass Ciera, Cruiser) 2.2L/ 3.1L	29
B Body (Caprice, Impala SS, Roadmaster) 4.3L/ 5.7L (w/o Mechanical Fan)	30

93009C01

Refer to the model specific sections for engine mechanical service procedures

COOLING FAN DIAGRAM INDEX

MANUFACTURER MODEL AND ENGINE	DIAGRAM
General Motors (cont.)	
B Body (Caprice, Impala SS, Roadmaster) 4.3L/ 5.7L (w/ Mechanical Fan)	31
B Body (Fleetwood) 5.7L (w/o Mechanical Fan)	32
B Body (Fleetwood) 5.7L (w/ Mechanical Fan)	33
C & H Bodies (Bonneville, Eighty-Eight, Ninety-Eight, Park Ave., Le Sabre, LSS) 3.8L	34
E & K Bodies (DeVille, Eldorado, Seville) 4.6L	
1996-97 Models	35
1998-00 Models	36
F Body (Camaro, Firebird) 3.8L	37
F Body (Camaro, Firebird) 5.7L	
1996-00 Models	37
1998-00 Models	38
G Body (Aurora, Riviera)	
1996 Models with 3.8L	39
1997-00 Models with 3.8L	40
1996-00 Models with 4.0L	41
J Body (Cavalier, Sunfire) 2.2L/ 2.3L/ 2.4L	42
L Body (Beretta, Corsica) 2.2L/ 3.1L	43
L/N Bodies (Cutlass, Malibu) 2.4L/ 3.1L	44
N Body (Acheiva, Grand Am, Skylark) 2.3L/ 2.4L/ 3.1L	45
V Body (Catera) 3.0L	46
W Body (Lumina, Monte Carlo, Grand Prix, Cutlass Supreme, Regal, Intrigue) 3.1L/ 3.4L/ 3.8L	
1996 Models (except Cutlass Supreme)	47
1996-97 Cutlass Supreme	47
1997-00 Models (except Cutlass Supreme and Intrigue)	48
1998-00 Models (Intrigue)	48
Y Body (Corvette) 5.7L	
1996 Models	49
1997-00 Models	50
Geo/Chevrolet	
Metro 1.0L/ 1.3L (w/o A/C)	51
Metro 1.0L/ 1.3L (w/ A/C)	52
Prism 1.6L/ 1.8L (w/ A/C)	53
Prism 1.6L/ 1.8L (w/o A/C)	54
Saturn	
1.9L	55

93009C02

HOT AT ALL TIMES
FUSE LINK
6 30A C5

HOT AT ALL TIMES

IGNITION SWITCH
START
RUN
ACCY
OFF LOCK
C12

HOT AT ALL TIMES
FUSE
8 20A C5

TO A/C SYSTEM

BL/R

RADIATOR FAN RELAY (HI2) C5
RADIATOR FAN RELAY (LOW) C5
RADIATOR FAN RELAY (HI1) C5
CONDENSER FAN RELAY (HI) C5
CONDENSER FAN RELAY (LOW) C5

BL/R
R/BL
R/B
BL/R
BL/R
BL/R
BL/W
BL/W
BL/W
G/O

G/O
W/L
W/B
G/B
G/Y
B
L/G
G/W
BL/W
BL
B

M RADIATOR FAN C1
G4

M CONDENSER FAN C3
B B
G4

POWERTRAIN CONTROL MODULE C5

93009G01

DIA. 1—1996–00 Chrysler Avenger/Sebring Coupe 2.0L

HOT AT ALL TIMES
FUSE LINK
6 30A C5

HOT AT ALL TIMES

IGNITION SWITCH
START
RUN
ACCY
OFF LOCK
C12

HOT AT ALL TIMES
FUSE
8 20A C5

TO AUTOMATIC COMPRESSOR ECM

B/W

BL/R

RADIATOR FAN RELAY (HI) C5
RADIATOR FAN RELAY (LOW) C5
CONDENSER FAN RELAY (HI) C5
CONDENSER FAN RELAY (LOW) C5

BL/R
R/BL
R/B
BL/R
BL/R
BL/W
BL/W
BL/W

G/O
W/L
W/B
G/B
G/O
BL/W
BL
B

NO CONNECTION
B

M RADIATOR FAN C1
B
G4

M CONDENSER FAN C3
B B
G4

POWERTRAIN CONTROL MODULE C5

93009G02

DIA. 2—1996–00 Chrysler Avenger/Sebring Coupe 2.5L

Refer to the model specific sections for cooling system service procedures

HOT AT ALL TIMES
FUSE 19 40A
(CIRRUS,STRATUS,BREEZE)
FUSE 17 40A
(SEBRING CNVT)

HOT IN RUN OR START
FUSE 9 10A

R/LG C5

LG/B C13

R/LG   LG/B   LOW SPEED RADIATOR FAN RELAY   C5

LG/B   R/LG   HIGH SPEED RADIATOR FAN RELAY   C5

DG/LG   DB/T   DB/PK   Y/V OR Y/R

POWERTRAIN CONTROL MODULE

RADIATOR FAN MOTOR ASSEMBLY   C2

M   M

B

RFI SUPP MODULE

G5

93009G03

DIA. 3—1996 Chrysler Breeze/Cirrus/Sebring Convertible/Stratus 2.0L/2.4L/2.5L

HOT AT ALL TIMES
FUSE 19 40A
(CIRRUS,STRATUS,BREEZE)
FUSE 17 40A
(SEBRING CNVT)

HOT IN RUN OR START
FUSE 9 10A

R/LG C5

LG/B C12

R/LG   LG/B   LOW SPEED RADIATOR FAN RELAY   C5

LG/B   R/LG   HIGH SPEED RADIATOR FAN RELAY   C5

DG/LG   DB/T   DB/PK   Y/V OR Y/R

RADIATOR FAN MOTOR   C1

M

B

POWERTRAIN CONTROL MODULE

RADIATOR FAN MOTOR   C3

M

B

B

G5

93009G04

DIA. 4—1997–00 Chrysler Breeze/Cirrus/Sebring Convertible/Stratus 2.0L/2.4L/2.5L

HOT IN RUN OR START

FUSE
20
10A

C13

LG/B

HOT AT ALL TIMES

FUSE
D
40A

C5

R/LG

R/LG · LG/B · LG/B · R/LG

LOW
SPEED
RADIATOR
FAN
RELAY

C5

HIGH
SPEED
RADIATOR
FAN
RELAY

C5

T · W · DB/PK · Y

POWERTRAIN CONTROL
MODULE

C8

RADIATOR
FAN
MOTOR
ASSEMBLY

M · M

C2

B

G1

93009G05

DIA. 5—1996–00 Chrysler Concorde/Intrepid/LHS/New Yorker/Vision 2.7L/3.2L/3.3L/3.5L

HOT AT ALL TIMES

FUSE
5
30A

C5

HOT IN RUN ONLY

FUSE
10
15A

C12

HOT AT ALL TIMES

FUSE
18
10A

C5

GY · NCA · NCA · R/B

RADIATOR
FAN
RELAY

C5

A/C
COMPRESSOR
CLUTH
FAN
RELAY

C5

LG · DB/PK · DBL/O · DBL/B

COOLING
FAN
MOTOR

M

C2

X#

TO
A/C
SYSTEM

POWERTRAIN
CONTROL MODULE

C5

93009G06

DIA. 6—1996 Chrysler Neon 2.0L

For complete service labor times order Chilton's Labor Guide Manual

HOT AT ALL TIMES
FUSE 5 30A
C5
GY

SOLID STATE FAN RELAY
C5

DG   LG   B

COOLING FAN MOTOR
C2

B

B
G1

LG

POWERTRAIN CONTROL MODULE
C5

93009G07

DIA. 7—1997–00 Chrysler Neon 2.0L

HOT AT ALL TIMES
FUSE LINK 7 30A   C4

HOT AT ALL TIMES
IGNITION SWITCH
START   ACCY
RUN   LOCK
OFF   C12

HOT AT ALL TIMES
FUSE 9 20A   C13

TO A/C SYSTEM

BL/R   R/BL   R/B   BL/R   B/V   BL/R   BL/V   BL/V   BL/V   G/O

RADIATOR FAN RELAY (HI2)   C5

RADIATOR FAN RELAY (LOW)   C5

CONDENSER FAN RELAY (HI)   C5

CONDENSER FAN RELAY (LOW)   C5

G/O   V/BL   V/B   G/B   G/O   BL/V   BL   B

RADIATOR FAN   C1

CONDENSER FAN   C5

B   B
G4

B   B
G4

POWERTRAIN CONTROL MODULE
C5

93009G08

DIA. 8—1996–97 Chrysler Neon 2.0L (Non-Turbo—A/T)

DIA. 9—1996–98 Chrysler Neon 2.0L (Non-Turbo—M/T)

DIA. 10—1998 Chrysler Neon 2.0L (Non-Turbo)

DIA. 11—1996–98 Chrysler Neon 2.0L (Turbo—A/T)

93009G11

DIA. 12—1996–98 Chrysler Neon 2.0L (Turbo—M/T)

93009G12

HOT IN RUN OR START

ENGINE
FUSE
10A
[C13]

HOT AT ALL TIMES

COOLING
FAN
FUSE
30A
[C5]

HOT IN RUN

WIPER
FUSE
20A
[C13]

B/W

W/B

W/B

BL

COOLING
FAN
RELAY
[C5]

CONDENSER
FAN
RELAY
[C4]

BR

Y

BL/B

LG

(M) COOLING
FAN
MOTOR
[C3]

CONDENSER
FAN
MOTOR (M)
[C1]

B

B

[G1]

[G1]

POWERTRAIN CONTROL MODULE
[C13]

93009G13

DIA. 13—1996–97 Ford Aspire 1.3L

HOT AT ALL TIMES

FUSE
LINK
2
60A
[C5]

BK/O

BK/O   BK/O   BK/O   BK/O

CONSTANT CONTROL RELAY MODULE
[C3]

R/O   R/O   R   LG/P   DBL   PK/Y GY/W B/Y   P   B

R/O

(M) COOLING
FAN
[C2]

POWERTRAIN
CONTROL
MODULE
[C2]

TO
AUTOMATIC
TEMPERATURE
CONTROL

B

[C5]

93009G14

DIA. 14—1996 Ford Continental 4.6L

Refer to the model specific sections for engine mechanical service procedures

DIA. 15—1997–00 Ford Continental 4.6L

DIA. 16—1996–00 Ford Contour/Mystique 2.0L

DIA. 17

HOT IN RUN
FUSE 4 20A
C13

HOT AT ALL TIMES
FUSE LINK 9 20A
C5

HOT AT ALL TIMES
FUSE LINK 2 60A
C5

PCM POWER RELAY
C5

G1

G1

HIGH SPEED COOLING FAN RELAY
C5

LOW SPEED COOLING FAN RELAY
C5

G1

COOLING FAN MOTOR #2
C2

COOLING FAN MOTOR #1
C2

COOLING FAN RESISTOR
C3

G1

POWERTRAIN CONTROL MODULE

93009G17

DIA. 17—1996–00 Ford Contour/Mystique 2.5L

DIA. 18

HOT AT ALL TIMES
COOLING FAN FUSE LINK 50A
C4

TO PCM RELAY

COOLING FAN RELAY
C4

COOLING FAN
C2

POWERTRAIN CONTROL MODULE
C5

G4

93009G18

DIA. 18—1996–00 Ford Crown Victoria/Grand Marquis 4.6L

Refer to the model specific sections for cooling system service procedures

HOT IN RUN OR START   HOT AT ALL TIMES   HOT IN RUN OR START

ENGINE
FUSE
15A
C13

COOLING
FAN
FUSE
LINK
30A
C5

ENGINE
FUSE
15A
C13

B/W   R/B   B/R   B/W

COOLING
FAN
RELAY
C5

COOLING
FAN
HIGH
SPEED
RELAY
C5

B/DG   Y   DBL   B/DG

B/DG → TO A/C SYSTEM

B/DG → TO A/C SYSTEM

B/DG → TO PCM

B/DG

COOLANT FAN
TEMPERATURE
SWITCH
C18

COOLING
FAN
M
C2

B

G5

B/DG

HI FAN
ENGINE
COOLANT
TEMPERATURE
SWITCH
C19

B

93009G19

DIA. 19—1996 Ford Escort/Tracer 1.8/1.9L A/T

HOT IN RUN OR START   HOT AT ALL TIMES

ENGINE
FUSE
15A
C13

COOLING
FAN
FUSE
LINK
30A
C5

B/W   B/R

COOLING
FAN
RELAY
C5

B/DG   Y

TO A/C SYSTEM ← B/DG

TO PCM ← B/DG

B/DG

COOLANT FAN
TEMPERATURE
SWITCH
C19

COOLING
FAN
M
C3

B

G3

93009G20

DIA. 20—1996 Ford Escort/Tracer 1.8/1.9L M/T

HOT AT ALL TIMES   HOT IN RUN OR START   HOT AT ALL TIMES   HOT AT ALL TIMES

COOLING
FAN
FUSE
LINK
40A
[C5]
B/O

ENGINE
FUSE
15A
[C12]

FUEL
INJ
FUSE
30A
[C5]

FUEL
PUMP
FUSE
30A
[C5]
TO
A/C-
HEATER
SYSTEM

B/O   B/O   B/W   W/G   W/G   BL/Y   BL/B   G/R

CONSTANT CONTROL RELAY MODULE   [C5]

G/Y   G/Y   Y   Y   PK/W   R/B   W/R   R/W   LG   B/PK   B   R   BL/W

G/Y   Y

(M)   B

COOLING
FAN
[C2]

ENGINE
CONTROLS

[G4]

TO
A/C-
HEATER
SYSTEM

PCM   [C11]

93009G21

DIA. 21—1997–00 Ford Escort/Tracer 1.8/1.9L

HOT AT ALL TIMES

COOL
FAN
FUSE
LINK
40A
[C5]

Y OR DBL   Y OR DBL   Y OR DBL

**VARIABLE CONTROL
RELAY MODULE**   [C2]

LBL   LBL

LBL

(M)   COOLING
FAN
[C2]

B

[G3]

93009G22

DIA. 22—1996–98 Ford Mark VIII 4.6L

For complete service labor times order Chilton's Labor Guide Manual

HOT IN RUN OR START HOT AT ALL TIMES HOT AT ALL TIMES

FUSE
18
20A
C10

EEC
FUSE
LINK
20A
C5

FAN
FUSE
LINK
60A
C5

R/LG   Y   Y   B/O

CONSTANT CONTROL RELAY MODULE

C4

R   R   DBL   R/O   R/O   B

C3

TO
ELECTRONIC
ENGINE
CONTROL

POWERTRAIN
CONTROL
MODULE
C9

R/O

M COOLING
FAN
MOTOR
C2

B

G1

93009G23

DIA. 23—1996–00 Ford Mustang 3.8L

HOT IN RUN OR START   HOT AT ALL TIMES   HOT AT ALL TIMES

FUSE
18
20A
C10

EEC
FUSE
LINK
20A
C5

FAN
FUSE
LINK
60A
C5

R/LG   Y   Y   B/O   B/O

CONSTANT CONTROL RELAY MODULE

C5

R   R   DBL   LG/P   R/O   R/O   O/LBL   O/LBL   B/W

G3

TO
ELECTRONIC
ENGINE
CONTROL

R

R

MASS AIR
FLOW
SENSOR

POWERTRAIN
CONTROL
MODULE
C9

R/O   O/LBL

M COOLING
FAN
MOTOR
C2

B

G3

93009G24

DIA. 24—1996–00 Ford Mustang 4.6L

HOT IN RUN OR START

FUSE
10
15A
C13

HOT AT ALL TIMES

FUSE
LINK
8
40A
C5

B/W

B/W

R

B/R

B/W

LOW
SPEED
COOLING
FAN
RELAY
C5

HIGH
SPEED
COOLING
FAN
RELAY
C5

BL/O

BL/Y

BL/B

BL/G

M COOLING
FAN
MOTOR
C3

B

G3

BL/G

TO
A/C
SYSTEM
(2.5L)

BL/G

POWERTRAIN CONTROL MODULE

C11

93009G25

DIA. 25—1996–97 Ford Probe 2.0L/2.5L

HOT AT ALL TIMES

COOLING
FAN
FUSE
LINK
40A
C3

DBL

POWERTRAIN CONTROL MODULE

C6

DBL

DBL

LG/P

T/O

R

LBL/O

CONSTANT CONTROL RELAY MODULE

C5

GY/R

C1

R/O

R/O

B

DG/W

GY/R

R/O

RESISTOR

C4

TO
A/C
SYSTEM

GY/R

GY/R

M COOLING
FAN
#2
C1

M COOLING
FAN
#1
C3

B

B

B

C4

93009G26

DIA. 26—1996–00 Ford Taurus/Sable 3.0L/3.4L

HOT AT ALL TIMES

FUSE LINK 5 60A [C5]

B/O

HOT AT ALL TIMES
FUSE LINK 15 20A [C5]
Y

HOT IN RUN OR START
FUSE LINK 3 20A [C5]
R/LG

HOT AT ALL TIMES
FUSE LINK 13 20A [C5]
B/Y

TO A/C-HEATER
PK/LBL   PK/Y

CONSTANT CONTROL RELAY MODULE

BR/O   BR/O   DBL   DBL   T/O   LG/P   B [G1]   R   R   LBL/O   PK/B   GY/V   B/Y

BR/O
COOLING FAN MOTOR [C2]   (M)   B   [G1]

DBL   POWERTRAIN CONTROL MODULE [C10]

TO ELECTRONIC ENGINE CONTROLS

TO A/C-HEATER

93009G27

DIA. 27—1996–97 Ford Thunderbird/Cougar—XR7 3.8L/4.6L

HOT AT ALL TIMES

FUSE P 30A [C4]
Y

TO PCM RELAY
R

COOLING FAN RELAY [C4]

R/O   DBL

COOLING FAN MOTOR [C2]   (M)   POWERTRAIN CONTROL MODULE [C5]

B   [G4]

93009G28

DIA. 28—1996–00 Lincoln Town Car 4.6L

PRECAUTIONS

Test Equipment

Never use jumper wires made from a thinner gauge wire than the circuit being tested. If the jumper wire is of too small a gauge, it may overheat and possibly melt. Never use jumpers to bypass high resistance loads in a circuit. Bypassing resistances, in effect, creates a short circuit. This may, in turn, cause damage and fire. Jumper wires should only be used to bypass lengths of wire or to simulate switches.

Do not use a test light to probe electronic ignition, spark plug or coil wires. Never use a pick-type test light to probe wiring on computer controlled systems unless specifically instructed to do so. Any wire insulation that is pierced by the test light probe should be taped and sealed with silicone after testing.

Never use an ohmmeter to check the resistance of a component or wire while there is voltage applied to the circuit.

A self-powered test light should not be used on any computer controlled system or component. The small amount of electricity transmitted by the test light is enough to damage many electronic automotive components.

Never disengage any sensor while the ignition is ON.

Always replace fuses, circuit breakers and fusible links with identically rated components. Under no circumstances should a component of higher or lower amperage rating be substituted.

Electronic Control Systems

Electronic control systems are very delicate and complicated. To save yourself aggravation, money and time, be sure to adhere to the following points when working on a vehicle's control system:

• Unless otherwise instructed, always disconnect the battery cables when servicing the electronic system.

• When disconnecting the battery, always be sure to detach the negative battery cable FIRST, then the positive cable. This simple practice will almost completely prevent the chance of arcing or shorting the system.

• Never pierce, or cut the insulation off of, a wire for testing purposes. Many of the control system's wires are designed to handle a precise amount of electrical resistance, and the computer expects to see a certain predetermined amount of resistance. If you pierce, or cut the insulation off of a wire, corrosion can build up in the wiring, leading to decreased control system efficiency, DTC storing or possibly even component damage.

• Never subject any control computer to excessive jolts (such as dropping).

• If welding on the vehicle, always disconnect the computer from the vehicle's wiring harness.

• Never detach a wiring harness connector when the ignition switch is turned ON.

Handling Electrostatic Discharge (ESD) Sensitive Parts

Electronic modules are very sensitive to Electrostatic Static Discharge (ESD). If the modules are exposed to these charges, they may be damaged. While most vehicles display a label informing you that their electronic components may be damaged by ESD, some do not have labels, but they may be damaged also. To avoid possible damage to any of these components, follow the steps outlined below.

1. Body movement produces an electrostatic charge. To discharge personal static electricity, touch a ground point (metal) on the vehicle. This should be performed any time you:
  • Slide across the vehicle seat
  • Sit down or get up
  • Do any walking
  • Touch an ESD sensitive part

2. Do not touch any exposed terminals on components or connectors with your fingers or any tools.

3. Never use jumper wires, ground a terminal on a component, use test equipment on any component or terminal unless instructed to in a diagnostic or testing procedure. When using test equipment, always connect the ground lead first.

4. Do not remove the part from its protective packing until it's time to install it.

5. Before removing the part from its protective packing, ground the packing to a known good ground on the vehicle.

Air Bags

When working on the air bag system or any components which require the removal of the air bag, adhere to all of the following precautions to minimize the risks of personal injury or component damage:

1. Before attempting to diagnose, remove or install air bag system components, you must first disconnect and isolate the negative (-) battery cable. Failure to do so could result in accidental deployment and possible personal injury.

2. When an undeployed air bag assembly is to be removed from the steering wheel, after disconnecting the negative battery cable, allow the system capacitor to discharge for two minutes before commencing with the air bag system component removal.

3. Replace the air bag system components only with specified replacement parts, or equivalent. Substitute parts may visually appear interchangeable, but internal differences may result in inferior occupant protection.

4. The fasteners, screws, and bolts originally used for the air bag system have special coatings and are specifically designed for the system. They must never be replaced with any substitutes. Anytime a new fastener is needed, replace with the correct fasteners provided in the service package or fasteners listed in the parts books.

HOW TO READ DIAGRAMS:

BLACK	B	PINK	PK
BROWN	BR	PURPLE	P
RED	R	GREEN	G
ORANGE	O	WHITE	W
YELLOW	Y	LIGHT BLUE	LBL
GRAY	GY	LIGHT GREEN	LG
BLUE	BL	DARK GREEN	DG
VIOLET	V	DARK BLUE	DBL
NO COLOR AVAILABLE			NCA

**WIRE COLOR
ABREVIATIONS**

**POWER
CONDITION**

**COMPONENT
NAMES**

**WIRE
COLORS**

**LOCATION MARKER
'C' FOR COMPONENTS
'G' FOR GROUNDS**

**SPLICE
OR
CONNECTOR**

**LOCATION MARKER
'C' FOR COMPONENTS
'G' FOR GROUNDS**

GROUND

**OTHER
SYSTEM
REFERENCE**

DIA. 6- 1997-99 WINDSTAR

DIA. #   **YEAR**   **MODEL**

HOT AT ALL TIMES

FUSIBLE
LINK F
C19
R

HOT IN RUN OR START

ENG-A/C
IN-LINE
FUSE
10A
C12
PK

R   PK

PK   R

PUSHER
COOLANT
FAN
RELAY
C1

PRIMARY
COOLANT
FAN
RELAY
C1

B   DBL   DG   LBL

PCM

PUSHER
COOLANT
FAN
C1

PRIMARY
COOLANT
FAN
C3

B   G19   B   G19

93009G29

DIA. 29—1996 Century/Cutlass Ciera/Cutlass Cruiser 2.2L/3.1L

HOT AT ALL TIMES

MAXI
FUSE
12
40A
C4

HOT IN RUN OR START

FUSE
7
10A
C4

FUSE
8
10A
C4

HOT AT ALL TIMES

MAXI
FUSE
13
40A
C4

R   BR   BR   R

PRIMARY
COOLING
FAN
RELAY
C4

SECOND-
ARY
COOLING
FAN
RELAY
C4

LBL   DG   DBL   B

PCM

RIGHT
PRIMARY
COOLING
FAN
MOTOR
C1

LEFT
SECONDARY
COOLING
FAN
MOTOR
C3

B   G1   B   G1

93009G30

DIA. 30—1996 Caprice/Impala SS/Roadmaster 4.3L/5.7L (w/o Mechanical Fan)

Refer to the model specific sections for engine mechanical service procedures

HOT IN RUN OR START

FUSE
8
10A
C4

HOT AT ALL TIMES

MAXI
FUSE
13
40A
C4

BR

R

SECOND-
ARY
COOLING
FAN
RELAY
C4

DBL

B

PCM

SECONDARY
COOLING
FAN
MOTOR
C2

B

G1

93009G31

DIA. 31—1996 Caprice/Impala SS/Roadmaster 4.3L/5.7L (w/ Mechanical Fan)

HOT AT ALL TIMES

MAXI
FUSE
8
40A
C4

HOT IN RUN OR START

FUSE
20
10A
C12

HOT AT ALL TIMES

FUSE
16
10A
C12

HOT AT ALL TIMES

MAXI
FUSE
7
40A
C4

R

BR

PRIMARY
COOLING
FAN
RELAY
C4

BR

R

SECOND-
ARY
COOLING
FAN
RELAY
C4

LBL

DG

DBL

B

PCM

RIGHT
PRIMARY
COOLING
FAN
MOTOR
C2

LEFT
SECONDARY
COOLING
FAN
MOTOR
C2

B

G15

B

G15

93009G32

DIA. 32—1996 Fleetwood 5.7L (w/o Mechanical Fan)

HOT IN RUN OR START

FUSE
16
10A
C12

HOT AT ALL TIMES

MAXI
FUSE
7
40A
C5

BR

R

SECOND-
ARY
COOLING
FAN
RELAY
C5

DBL

B

PCM

SECONDARY
COOLING
FAN
MOTOR
C2

B

G15

93009G33

DIA. 33—1996 Fleetwood 5.7L (w/ Mechanical Fan)

HOT AT ALL TIMES

FUSE
40A
C8

HOT IN RUN OR START

FUSE
5C
10A
C13

R

BR

BR

R

R

BR

HIGH
SPEED
COOLING
FAN
RELAY
C8

BR

R

LOW
SPEED
COOLING
FAN
RELAY
C8

B

DBL

DG

LBL

PCM

LBL

LEFT
COOLING
FAN
MOTOR
C3

LBL

RIGHT
COOLING
FAN
MOTOR
C1

B

G3

B

G3

93009G34

DIA. 34—1996–99 Bonneville/88/98/Le Sabre/LSS/Regency and 1996–00 Park Avenue 3.8L

Refer to the model specific sections for cooling system service procedures

DIA. 35—1996-97 DeVille/Eldorado/Seville 4.6L

DIA. 36—1998-00 DeVille/Eldorado/Seville 4.6L

HOT AT ALL TIMES
MAXI FUSE LINK
FUSE 40A C
(98-00 3.8L)
C3
R

HOT IN RUN OR START
COOLING A/C
FUSE FUSE 7
10A 20A (96 3.8L)
(98-00 3.8L) 25A (ALL OTHERS)
C3

COOLING FAN RELAY 1
C3

COOLING FAN RELAY 2
C3

COOLING FAN RELAY 3
C3

DG

LBL

LEFT COOLING FAN
C3

GY OR B

DBL

B

G3

DBL

DBL

V

V

RIGHT COOLING FAN
C1

V

B

G2

PCM
C5

DIA. 37—1996–00 Camaro/Firebird 3.8L/5.7L

93009G37

HOT AT ALL TIMES
MAXI FUSE 40A
C8
R

COOLING FUSE 10A
C5

R

COOLING FAN RELAY 1
C3

COOLING FAN RELAY 3
C3

COOLING FAN RELAY 2
C3

DG

LBL

LEFT COOLING FAN
C3

GY

DBL

B

V

DBL

DBL

V

V

RIGHT COOLING FAN
C1

V

B

G3

PCM
C3

DIA. 38—1998–00 Camaro/Firebird 5.7L

93009G38

For complete service labor times order Chilton's Labor Guide Manual

DIA. 39—1996 Aurora/Riviera 3.8L

DIA. 40—1997–00 Aurora/Riviera 3.8L

HOT AT ALL TIMES
COOLING FAN FUSE 60A
C8

HOT AT ALL TIMES
COOLING FAN RELAY FUSE
10A (98)
20A (96-97)
C9

R

O

D/B OR O

R

COOLING FAN RELAY 1 (LOW SPEED)
C7

D

COOLING FAN RELAY POSITION A
C3

D

R

HIGH SPEED COOLING FAN RELAY POSITION B
C3

DG

B

NCA

DBL

B

LBL

DBL

LBL

C3
LEFT COOLING FAN

M

LEFT COOLING FAN DIODE

V

NCA

A

DBL

LBL

RIGHT COOLING FAN

M

C1

B

G4

PCM

C9

93009G41

DIA. 41—1996–00 Aurora/Riviera 4.0L

HOT AT ALL TIMES

C3

COOLING FAN FUSE 30A

R

R

COOLANT FAN RELAY
C3

DG

LBL

C1

PCM

COOLANT FAN

M

C2

B

G25

93009G42

DIA. 42—1996–00 Cavalier/Sunfire 2.2L/2.3L/2.4L

DIA. 43—1996 Beretta/Corsica 2.2L/3.1L

DIA. 44—1997–00 Cutlass/Malibu 2.4L/3.1L

HOT AT ALL TIMES

ERLS
FUSE
20A

C12

R

COOLANT
FAN
RELAY

C5

DG

LBL

PCM

C10

COOLANT
FAN

C2

M

B

G4

93009G45

DIA. 45—1996–00 Achieva/Grand Am/Skylark 2.3L/2.4L/3.1L

HOT AT ALL TIMES

FUSE
10
10A

FUSE
40
30A

C12

C5

BR

BR

R

FAN
CONTROL
RELAY
K28

C5

BR/V

BR/V

R/V

A/C
PRES-
SURE
SWITCH

C4

R

TEMP-
ERATURE
SWITCH
#2

C2

B

HOT AT ALL TIMES

FUSE
42
40A

C5

B

BR

FAN
CONTROL
RELAY
K52

C5

R/V

BR/G

BR/V

AUX
COOLING
FAN 2

C3

B

AUX
COOLING
FAN 1

C1

R/V

G3

HOT AT ALL TIMES

FUSE
50
10A

C5

BR

FAN
CONTROL
RELAY
K67

C5

BR/V

R/V

R/V

COOLING
FAN

C2

M

B

G3

TEMP
SWITCH

G3

HOT AT ALL TIMES

FUSE
52
30A

C5

R

R

R

FAN
CONTROL
RELAY
K26

C5

BR/BL

R/V

R/BL

RESISTOR

R/V

TO
HVAC
CONTROLS

FAN
CON-
TROL
RELAY
K87

C5

G

B

G3

R/V

93009G46

DIA. 46—1997–00 Catera 3.0L

Refer to the model specific sections for engine mechanical service procedures

DIA. 47—1996 Lumina/Monte Carlo/Grand Prix/Cutlass Supreme/Regal and 1997 Cutlass Supreme 3.1L/3.4L

DIA. 48—1997-00 Century/Grand Prix/Regal and 1998-00 Intrigue 3.1L/3.8L

HOT AT ALL TIMES
PRIMARY
COOLING
FAN
FUSE 2
30A

HOT IN RUN OR START
FAN
FUSE
5A

HOT AT ALL TIMES
SECONDARY
COOLING
FAN
FUSE 5
40A

PK

PK

PK

PK

R

COOL
FAN 1
RELAY

B

PK

COOL
FAN 3
RELAY

PK

R

COOL
FAN 2
RELAY

DG

LBL

B

V

DBL

DBL

V

M ENGINE
COOLING
FAN
MOTOR
LEFT

V

M ENGINE
COOLING
FAN
MOTOR
RIGHT

DBL

B B

POWERTRAIN CONTROL MODULE

93009G49

DIA. 49—1996 Corvette 5.7L

HOT AT ALL TIMES
COOL
FAN
MAXI
FUSE
30A
[X#]

HOT IN RUN OR START
COOL
FAN 3
FUSE
10A
[X#]

HOT AT ALL TIMES
COOL
FAN 2
MAXI
FUSE
30A
[X#]

NCA

NCA

NCA

NCA

NCA

COOL
FAN 1
RELAY
[X#]

B

NCA

COOL
FAN 3
RELAY
[X#]

NCA

NCA

COOL
FAN 2
RELAY
[X#]

DG

LBL

B

V

DBL

DBL

V

M ENGINE
COOLING
FAN
MOTOR
[C1]

V

M ENGINE
COOLING
FAN
MOTOR
[C3]

DBL

B B

POWERTRAIN CONTROL MODULE [X#]

[X#]

93009G50

DIA. 50—1997-00 Corvette 5.7L

Refer to the model specific sections for cooling system service procedures

DIA. 51—1996–00 Metro 1.0L/1.3L (w/o A/C)

DIA. 52—1996–00 Metro 1.0L/1.3L (w/ A/C)

HOT AT ALL TIMES

A/C
FUSE
15A
C13

B/R

B/R

B/R   B/R

A/C
MG
RELAY
C3

BL/B   B/V

TO
A/C
AMPLIFIER

HOT IN RUN OR START

CDS
FUSE
LINK
30A
C3

B/R

BL

M A/C
   CONDENSER
   FAN
   MOTOR
   C1

B

V

A/C
FAN
NO 3
RELAY
C3

V/B   V/R

G3

G4   B

A/C
NO 2
RELAY
C3

BL/B   B/R

HOT IN RUN OR START

FAN
FUSE
LINK
30A
C3

G

RADIATOR
FAN
MOTOR
C3

BL

M

B

G3

HOT IN RUN OR START

ECU-IG
FUSE
15A
C13

B/Y

B/Y

FAN 1
RELAY
C3

BL/B

G/B

A/C
HIGH
PRESSURE
SWITCH
C1

LG

FAN
THERMO
SWITCH
C1

93009G53

DIA. 53—1996–00 Prism 1.6L/1.8L (w/ A/C)

HOT IN RUN OR START

FAN
FUSE
LINK
30A
C3

NCA

HOT IN RUN OR START

ECU-IG
FUSE
15A
C13

B/Y

COOLING
FAN
RELAY
C3

B/R

LG/B

M ENGINE
   COOLING
   FAN
   MOTOR
   C2

B

G3

FAN
THERMOSTAT
SWITCH
C18

93009G54

DIA. 54—1996–00 Prism 1.6L/1.8L (w/o A/C)

For complete service labor times order Chilton's Labor Guide Manual

HOT AT ALL TIMES

COOLING
FAN
FUSE
30 A
C3

R

NCA   NCA

COOLING
FAN
RELAY
C3

B/R OR LBL   DG/W

COOLING
FAN
MOTOR
C2   M   PCM   C8

B

G7

93009G55

(w/o A/C) DIA. 55—1996-00 Saturn 1.9L

STARTING AND CHARGING SYSTEMS

STARTING SYSTEM

General Information

The starting system includes the battery, starter motor, solenoid, ignition switch, and in some cases, a starter relay. An inhibitor (neutral safety) switch is included in the starting system circuit to prevent the vehicle from being started while in gear.

When the ignition key is turned to the **START** position, current flows and energizes the starter's solenoid coil. The energized coil becomes an electromagnet which pulls the plunger into the coil, the plunger closes a set of contacts which allow high current to reach the starter motor. On models where the solenoid is mounted on the starter, the plunger also serves to push the starter pinion to mesh with the teeth on the flywheel/flexplate.

To prevent damage to the starter motor when the engine starts, the pinion gear incorporates an over-running (1-way) clutch that is splined to the starter armature shaft. The rotation of the running engine may speed the rotation of the pinion but not the starter motor itself.

Some starting systems employ a starter relay in addition to the solenoid. This relay may be located under the instrument panel, in the kick panel or in the fuse/relay center under the hood. This relay is used to reduce the amount of current the starting (ignition) switch must carry.

PRECAUTIONS

To prevent damage to the on-board computer, alternator and regulator, the following precautionary measures must be taken when working with the electrical system.

• Always disconnect the negative battery cable before servicing the starter motor. Battery voltage is always present at the large (**B**) terminal on the solenoid. When removing the starter motor, be prepared to support its weight after the last bolt is removed because the starter motor is a fairly heavy component.

• Never operate the starter motor for more than 30 seconds at a time. Too much cranking will cause the starter motor to overheat, causing permanent damage. Allow the starter motor to cool for at least 2 minutes between starting attempts.

• Wear safety glasses when working on or near the battery.

• Don't wear a watch with a metal band when servicing the battery. Serious burns can result if the band completes the circuit between the positive battery terminal and ground.

• Be absolutely sure of the polarity of a booster battery before making connections. Connect the cables positive to positive, and negative to negative. Connect positive cables first and then make the last connection to ground on the body of the booster vehicle so that arcing cannot ignite hydrogen gas that may have accumulated

Before servicing the electrical system always disconnect the negative battery cable to prevent system damage

near the battery. Even momentary connection of a booster battery with the polarity reversed will damage the alternator diodes.

• Disconnect both vehicle battery cables before attempting to charge a battery.

• Be cautious when using metal tools around a battery to avoid creating a short circuit between the terminals.

• When installing a battery, make sure that the positive and negative cables are not reversed.

• When jump-starting the car, be sure that like terminals are connected. This also applies to using a battery charger. Reversed polarity will burn out the alternator and regulator in a matter of seconds.

• Always disconnect the battery (negative cable first) when charging it.

System Testing

➡A good quality digital multimeter with at least 10 megohms/volt impedance should be used when testing modern automotive circuits. These meters can accurately detect very small amounts of voltage, current and resistance. This type of meter also has a high internal resistance that will not load the circuit being tested. Loading the circuit causes inaccurate readings, and may cause damage to sensitive computer circuits. Although we are not testing computer circuits in this section, accuracy is very important.

WITH STARTER MOUNTED SOLENOID

1. Check the battery and clean the connections as follows:

a. If the battery cells have removable caps, check the water level. Add distilled water if low. Load test the battery and charge if necessary. See Battery Testing in this section for the procedure.

b. Remove the cables and clean them with a wire brush. Reconnect the cables.

2. Check the starter motor ground circuit with a voltage drop test as follows:

a. Set the meter to read DC voltage on the lowest possible scale.

b. Connect the negative lead of your multimeter to the negative terminal of the battery.

c. Connect the positive lead to the body of the starter. Make sure the starter mounting bolts are tight. The meter should read 0.2 volts or less. If the voltage reading is greater, remove and clean the negative battery connection on the engine block. The voltage reading should now be within specification: if not, replace the negative battery cable.

3. Check the motor feed circuit with a voltage drop test as follows:

a. Disconnect the coil wire or the fuel injector harness to prevent the engine from starting.

b. Connect the positive lead of your meter to the positive terminal of the battery.

Typical starter solenoid terminal identification

Starting system circuit used by most vehicles—the solenoid is usually mounted on the starter as indicated

Before testing the system, be sure that the battery is in good shape, which includes ensuring the cells are full

TCCA1P08

Also, disconnect both battery cables (negative first)

TCCA1P02

.. clean the cable terminals of all dirt and corrosion with a wire brush..

TCCA1P04

.. and apply petroleum jelly or multi-purpose grease to the terminals before reattaching the cables

TCCA1P06

c. Connect the negative meter lead to the motor feed terminal. The motor feed terminal comes out of the body of the starter motor and connects to the solenoid.

d. Turn the ignition key to the **START** position. The meter should read 0.2 volts or less. If the voltage reading is greater, remove and clean the positive battery connection on the starter solenoid. The voltage reading should now be within specification, if not replace the positive battery cable.

e. Connect the coil wire or fuel injector harness.

4. Check for battery voltage at the **S** terminal on the starter solenoid as follows:

a. Disconnect the coil wire or the fuel injector harness to prevent the engine from starting.

b. Set the meter to read battery voltage. Move it to the next higher range if set on the 2 volt scale.

c. Connect the positive lead to the **S** terminal on the starter solenoid and the negative lead to a good ground.

d. Turn the ignition key to the **START** position and crank the engine. The meter should read battery voltage. If battery voltage is not present, check the inhibitor (neutral safety) switch, fuse(s) and wiring between the ignition switch and starter solenoid. If battery voltage is present at the **S** terminal on the solenoid and the starter does not operate, replace the starter and solenoid assembly.

e. Connect the coil wire or fuel injector harness.

WITH EXTERNAL SOLENOID

➡Not all solenoids are mounted on the starter motor. Some models use a solenoid (relay) mounted on the inner fender or firewall. Both types of solenoids serve to make the connection between the battery and starter motor. Trace the wires for positive identification. The small wire comes from the ignition switch, one large cable from the battery and the other large cable to the starter. The terminals are S, B and M respectively.

1. Check the battery and clean the connections as follows:

a. If the battery cells have removable caps, check the water level. Add distilled water if low. Load test the battery and charge if necessary. See Battery Testing in this section for the procedure.

Always remove the negative battery cable first, and install it last.

   b. Remove the cables and clean them with a wire brush. Disconnect and clean the cables on the solenoid in the same manner. Reconnect the cables on the solenoid, then the battery.

2. Check the starter motor ground circuit with a voltage drop test as follows:

   a. Set the meter to read DC voltage on the lowest possible scale.

   b. Connect the negative lead of your multimeter to the negative terminal of the battery.

   c. Connect the positive lead to the body of the starter. Make sure the starter mounting bolts are tight. The meter should read 0.2 volts or less. If the voltage reading is greater, remove and clean the negative battery connection on the engine block. The voltage reading should now be within specification; if not, replace the negative battery cable.

3. Check the motor feed circuit with a voltage drop test as follows:

   a. Disconnect the coil wire or the fuel injector harness to prevent the engine from starting.

   b. Connect the positive lead of your meter to the positive terminal of the battery.

   c. Connect the negative meter lead to the motor feed terminal at the starter. This is the heavy cable on the starter. Turn the ignition key to the **START** position and crank the engine. The meter should read 0.2 volts or less. If the voltage reading is greater, remove and clean the positive battery connections on the starter and solenoid. The voltage reading should now be within specification; if not, replace the positive battery cable.

   d. Connect the coil wire or fuel injector harness.

4. Check for battery voltage at the **S** terminal on the starter solenoid as follows:

   a. Disconnect the coil wire or the fuel injector harness to prevent the engine from starting.

   b. Set the meter to read battery voltage. Move it to next higher range, if previously set on the 2 volt scale.

   c. Connect the positive lead to the **S** terminal on the starter solenoid and the negative lead to a good ground.

   d. Turn the ignition key to the **START** position. The meter should read battery voltage. If battery voltage is not present, check the inhibitor (neutral safety) switch, fuse(s) and wiring between the ignition switch and starter solenoid. If battery voltage is present at the **S** and **B** terminals but not at the motor feed terminal, replace the solenoid. If battery voltage is present at all 3 terminals and the starter does not operate, replace the starter motor.

   e. Connect the coil wire or fuel injector harness.

Starter Motor

REMOVAL & INSTALLATION

1. Disconnect the negative battery cable.

2. Remove all components necessary to gain access to the starter motor (such as exhaust pipes, air intake ducts, hoses, brackets and heat shields).

3. Disconnect the wiring from the starter. In some cases, the

To remove the starter, raise the vehicle if needed and loosen the starter mounting fasteners (arrows)..

.. then pull the starter out of the transmission bell housing..

.. and disconnect the starter motor wires, if not already done

Before installing the starter motor, be sure to inspect the gear teeth (arrow)..

89662P10

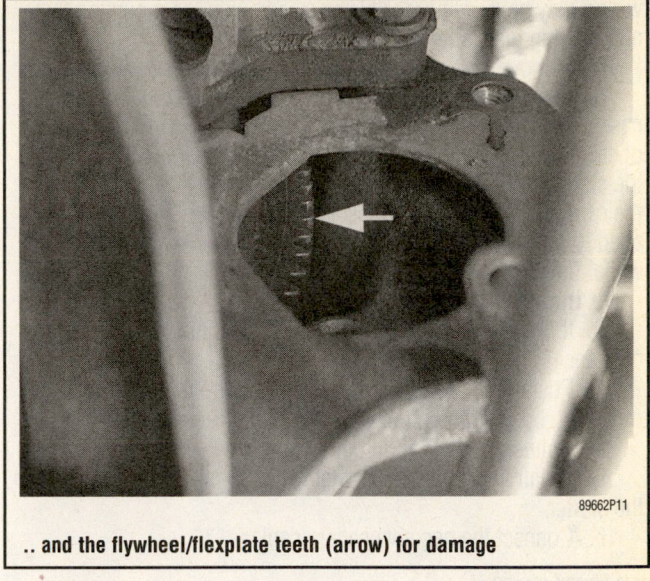

.. and the flywheel/flexplate teeth (arrow) for damage

89662P11

Typical starter motor mounting, with the bolts installed from the starter motor side

79240G22

Typical starter motor mounting, with the bolts installed from the bottom of the starter motor

79240G21

Typical starter motor mounting, with the bolts installed from the transmission side

79240G20

Ignition system service is covered in the model specific sections of this manual

wiring may be more accessible after removing the mounting bolts and moving the starter.

4. Remove the starter mounting bolts, if not already done.

5. Remove the starter assembly from the vehicle. In some cases, the starter will have to be turned to a different angle to clear obstructions. Don't loose any shims that may fall out from between the starter and the mounting boss, they will need to be returned to their original position when installing the starter. The shims are used to adjust the clearance between the starter pinion and flywheel/flexplate teeth.

To install:

6. If necessary, measure and adjust the pinion-to-ring gear clearance.

7. Position the shim (if any) and the starter motor on the mounting boss. Tighten the mounting bolts securely.

8. Connect the wiring, if not already done.

9. Install any components that were removed to gain access to the starter.

10. Connect the negative battery cable.

ADJUSTMENTS

Starter Pinion Depth

➡**This procedure is used to diagnose starter noise caused by incorrect clearance between the starter pinion and flywheel while the starter is engaged.**

1. Raise and safely support the front of the vehicle securely.

2. Remove the flywheel cover.

3. Inspect the flywheel for chipped or missing teeth, abnormal wear, cracks and warpage. Replace the damaged component, if any, and continue with the procedure.

4. Make sure the vehicle is in Park or Neutral. Apply the parking brake.

5. Have an assistant slowly and smoothly rotate the crankshaft in the normal direction of rotation.

6. Slowly move a piece of chalk toward the edge of the flywheel until it just touches, which will highlight the high spot of the ring gear.

7. Disconnect the negative battery cable.

8. Turn the high spot of the flywheel to the area of the starter drive pinion.

To adjust the pinion clearance, shims are placed between the starter motor mounting surface on the engine and the starter motor

9. Using a wire gauge, measure the clearance between the tip of the ring gear tooth and the bottom of the pinion gear teeth. Clearance should generally be 0.02–0.06 in. (0.5–1.5mm).

10. Add or remove shims to adjust the clearance, if needed.

11. Install the flywheel cover.

12. Lower the vehicle to the floor.

13. Connect the negative battery cable.

Generally, add shims if the starter whines after the engine starts, and remove shims if the starter whines only during cranking.

Starter Relay

➡**The starter relay is usually located in the fuse/relay panel. Depending on the manufacturer, it may be in the engine compartment, under the dash or behind a kick panel. Refer to the owner's manual for the location of the fuse/relay box.**

TESTING

➡**A good quality Digital Multimeter (DMM) with at least 10 megohms/volt impedance should be used when testing mod-**

Use a wire gauge (black dot) to measure the clearance between the tip of the flywheel tooth (top gear) to the bottom of the pinion teeth (bottom gear)

Use an ohmmeter to check for circuit continuity of the coil in the relay

Terminal identification of the most common types of relays. Diodes and resistors in the relay prevent voltage spikes, induced when the current is removed from the coil, from damaging electronic components

ern automotive circuits. These meters can accurately detect very small amounts of voltage, current and resistance. This type of meter also has a high internal resistance that will not load the circuit being tested. Loading the circuit gives inaccurate readings and may cause damage to sensitive computer circuits.

1. Turn the ignition **OFF**.
2. Remove the relay.
3. Locate the 2 terminals on the relay which are connected to the coil windings. Check the relay coil for continuity. Connect the negative meter lead to terminal **85** and positive meter lead to terminal **86**. There should be continuity. If not, replace the relay.
4. Check the operation of the internal relay contacts, as follows:

　a. Connect the meter leads to terminals **30** and **87**. Meter polarity does not matter for this step.

　b. Apply positive battery voltage to terminal **86** and ground to terminal **85**. The relay should click as the contacts are drawn toward the coil and the meter should indicate continuity. Replace the relay if your results are different.

Solenoid

TESTING

1. Disconnect the negative battery cable.
2. Remove the wire connections from the starter solenoid.
3. Using a self-powered test light or ohmmeter, check for continuity between the following:
- Solenoid **B** terminal and solenoid case or ground terminal—no continuity
- **S** terminal and solenoid case or ground terminal—continuity
- **S** terminal and **M** terminal—continuity
- **M** terminal and solenoid case or ground terminal—continuity

4. If the actual results of the test are different than indicated, replace the starter solenoid.

Testing the starter solenoid internal windings with a self-powered test light—starter mounted solenoid shown

Testing the starter solenoid internal windings with an ohmmeter—externally mounted solenoid shown

REMOVAL & INSTALLATION

→This procedure is for externally mounted starter solenoids only. For solenoids mounted on the starter, we recommend replacing the complete assembly.

1. Disconnect the negative battery cable.
2. Remove the wiring from the starter solenoid. Label the wires and the corresponding terminals if necessary for installation.

3. Remove the fasteners securing the solenoid to the fender or firewall.
4. Remove the solenoid.

To install:

5. Clean the solenoid mounting and the solenoid to ensure good electrical contact.
6. Install the solenoid.
7. Connect the wiring to the proper terminals.
8. Connect the negative battery cable.

CHARGING SYSTEM

General Information

A typical charging system contains an alternator (generator), drive belt, battery, voltage regulator and the associated wiring. The charging system, like the starting system is a series circuit with the battery wired in parallel. After the engine is started and running, the alternator takes over as the source of power and the battery then becomes part of the load on the charging system.

Some vehicle manufacturers use the term generator instead of alternator. Many years ago there used to be a difference, now they are one and the same. The alternator, which is driven by the belt, consists of a rotating coil of laminated wire called the rotor. Surrounding the rotor are more coils of laminated wire that remain stationary just inside the alternator case. This is how we get the name of stator. When current is passed through the rotor via the slip rings and brushes, the rotor becomes a rotating magnet with, of course, a magnetic field. When a magnetic field passes through a conductor (the stator), alternating current (A/C) is generated. This A/C current is rectified, turned into direct current (D/C), by the diodes located within the alternator.

The voltage regulator controls the alternator's field voltage by grounding one end of the field windings very rapidly. The frequency varies according to current demand. The more the field is grounded, the more voltage and current the alternator produces. Voltage is maintained at about 13.5–15 volts. During high engine speeds and low current demands, the regulator will adjust the voltage of the alternator field to lower the alternator output voltage. Conversely, when the vehicle is idling and the current demands may be high, the regulator will increase the field voltage, increasing the output of the alternator. Some vehicles actually turn the alternator off during periods of no load and/or wide open throttle. This was designed to reduce fuel consumption and increase power. Depending on the manufacturer, voltage regulators can be found in different locations, including inside or on the alternator, on the fender or firewall and even inside the PCM.

Drive belts are often overlooked when diagnosing a charging system failure. Check the belt tension on the alternator pulley and replace/adjust the belt. A loose belt will result in an undercharged battery and a no-start condition. This is especially true in wet weather conditions when the moisture causes the belt to become more slippery.

PRECAUTIONS

To prevent damage to the on-board computer, alternator and regulator, the following precautionary measures must be taken when working with the electrical system:

- Wear safety glasses when working on or near the battery.
- Don't wear a watch with a metal band when servicing the battery. Serious burns can result if the band completes the circuit between the positive battery terminal and ground.

- Be absolutely sure of the polarity of a booster battery before making connections. Connect the cables positive-to-positive, and negative-to-negative. Connect positive cables first, and then make the last connection to ground on the body of the booster vehicle so that arcing cannot ignite hydrogen gas that may have accumulated near the battery. Even momentary connection of a booster battery with the polarity reversed will damage alternator diodes.
- Disconnect both vehicle battery cables before attempting to charge a battery.
- Never ground the alternator or generator output or battery terminal. Be cautious when using metal tools around a battery to avoid creating a short circuit between the terminals.
- Never ground the field circuit between the alternator and regulator.
- Never run an alternator or generator without load unless the field circuit is disconnected.
- Never attempt to polarize an alternator.
- When installing a battery, make sure that the positive and negative cables are not reversed.
- When jump-starting the car, be sure that like terminals are connected. This also applies to using a battery charger. Reversed polarity will burn out the alternator and regulator in a matter of seconds.
- Never operate the alternator with the battery disconnected or on an otherwise uncontrolled open circuit.
- Do not short across or ground any alternator or regulator terminals.
- Do not try to polarize the alternator.
- Do not apply full battery voltage to the field (brown) connector.
- Always disconnect the battery ground cable before disconnecting the alternator lead.
- Always disconnect the battery (negative cable first) when charging it.
- Never subject the alternator to excessive heat or dampness. If you are steam cleaning the engine, cover the alternator.
- Never use arc-welding equipment on the car with the alternator connected.

SYSTEM TESTING

The charging system should be inspected if:
- A Diagnostic Trouble Code (DTC) is set relating to the charging system
- The charging system warning light is illuminated
- The voltmeter on the instrument panel indicates improper charging (either high or low) voltage
- The battery is overcharged (electrolyte level is low and/or boiling out)
- The battery is undercharged (insufficient power to crank the starter)

The starting point for all charging system problems begins with the inspection of the battery, related wiring and the alternator drive belt. The battery must be in good condition and fully charged before system testing. If a Diagnostic Trouble Code (DTC) is set, diagnose and repair the cause of the trouble code first.

If equipped, the charging system warning light will illuminate if the charging voltage is either too high or too low. The warning light should light when the key is turned to the **ON** position as a bulb check. When the alternator starts producing voltage due to the engine starting, the light should go out. A good sign of voltage that is too high are lights that burn out and/or burn very brightly. Overcharging can also cause damage to the battery and electronic circuits.

Alternator

TESTING

➡**Before testing, make sure all connections and mounting bolts are clean and tight. Many charging system problems are related to loose and corroded terminals or bad grounds. Don't overlook the engine ground connection to the body, or the tension of the alternator drive belt.**

Voltage Drop Test

➡**A good quality Digital Multimeter (DMM) with at least 10 megohms/volt impedance should be used when testing modern automotive circuits. These meters can accurately detect very small amounts of voltage, current and resistance. This type of meter also has a high internal resistance that will not load the circuit being tested. Loading the circuit gives inaccurate readings and may cause damage to sensitive computer circuits.**

1. Make sure the battery is in good condition and fully charged.
2. Perform a voltage drop test of the positive side of the circuit as follows:
   • Start the engine and allow it to reach normal operating temperature.
   • Turn the headlamps, heater blower motor and interior lights on.
   • Bring the engine to about 2,500 rpm and hold it there.
   • Connect the negative (-) voltmeter lead directly to the battery positive (+) terminal.
   • Touch the positive (+) voltmeter lead directly to the alternator **B+** output stud, not the nut. The meter should read no higher than about 0.5 volts. If it does, then there is higher than normal resistance between the positive side of the battery and the **B+** output at the alternator.
   • Move the positive (+) meter lead to the nut and compare the voltage reading with the previous measurement. If the voltage reading drops substantially, then there is resistance between the stud and the nut.

➡**The theory is to keep moving closer to the battery terminal one connection at a time in order to find the area of high resistance (bad connection).**

3. Perform a voltage drop test of the negative side of the circuit as follows:
   a. Start the engine and allow it to reach normal operating temperature.

b. Turn the headlamps, heater blower motor and interior lights ON.

c. Bring the engine to about 2,500 rpm and hold it there.

d. Connect the negative (-) voltmeter lead directly to the negative battery terminal.

e. Touch the positive (+) voltmeter lead directly to the alternator case or ground connection. The meter should read no higher than about 0.3 volts. If it does, then there is higher than normal resistance between the battery ground terminal and the alternator ground.

f. Move the positive (+) meter lead to the alternator mounting bracket, if the voltage reading drops substantially then you know that there is a bad electrical connection between the alternator and the mounting bracket.

➡**The theory is to keep moving closer to the battery terminal one connection at a time in order to find the area of high resistance (bad connection).**

Current Output Test

➡**A good quality Digital Multimeter (DMM) with at least 10 megohms/volt impedance should be used when testing modern automotive circuits. These meters can accurately detect very small amounts of voltage, current and resistance. This type of meter also has a high internal resistance that will not load the circuit being tested. Loading the circuit gives inaccurate readings and may cause damage to sensitive computer circuits.**

1. Perform a current output test as follows:

➡**The current output test requires the use of a volt/amp tester with battery load control and an inductive amperage pick-up. Follow the manufacturer's instructions on the use of the equipment.**

a. Start the engine and allow it to reach normal operating temperature.

b. Apply the parking brake and turn OFF all electrical accessories.

c. Connect the tester to the battery terminals and cable according to the instructions.

VAT-40 charging system tester. Many similar testers are available that perform equally as well

Refer to the model specific sections for engine electrical system service procedures

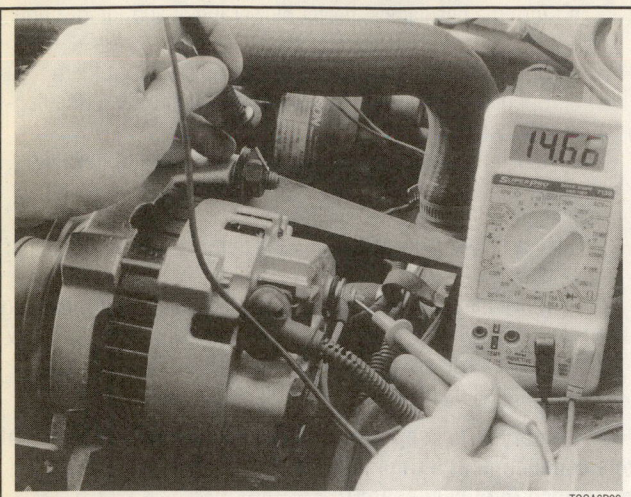

TCCA6P06

The output voltage of the alternator can be quickly measured by probing between the output terminal and a good ground

d. Bring the engine to about 2,500 rpm and hold it there.

e. Apply a load to the charging system with the rheostat on the tester. Do not let the voltage drop below 12 volts.

f. The alternator should deliver to within 10% of the rated output. If the amperage is not within 10% and all other components test good, replace the alternator.

Alternator Isolation Test

➡A good quality Digital Multimeter (DMM) with at least 10 megohms/volt impedance should be used when testing modern automotive circuits. These meters can accurately detect very small amounts of voltage, current and resistance. This type of meter also has a high internal resistance that will not load the circuit being tested. Loading the circuit gives inaccurate readings and may cause damage to sensitive computer circuits.

On some models it is possible to isolate the alternator from the regulator by grounding the **F** (field) terminal. Grounding the **F** terminal removes the regulator from the circuit and forces full alternator output. On alternators equipped with internal regulators, we recommend replacing the complete assembly if either the alternator or regulator is defective.

✳✳ WARNING

Do not allow the voltage to rise above 18 volts. Damage to electrical circuits may occur.

1. Connect a voltmeter across the battery terminals so the voltage can be monitored.

2. Start the engine and allow it reach normal operating temperature.

3. Connect a jumper lead to a good ground.

4. Locate the field terminal (negative) on the back of the alternator.

5. Momentarily connect the grounded jumper to the field terminal. If the alternator is OK, the voltage will climb rapidly. Disconnect the jumper before the output reaches 18 volts. If the voltage does not rise, replace the alternator. If the voltage rises, then the regulator is bad.

79240G12

Typical Motorcraft field terminal location on the back of the alternator

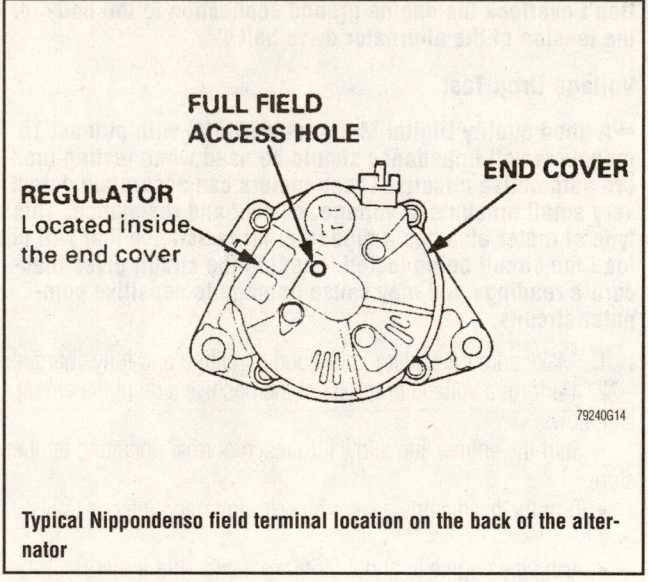

79240G14

Typical Nippondenso field terminal location on the back of the alternator

79240G15

Typical Mopar alternator terminal locations

➡Chrysler models have 2 field terminals, 1 positive and 1 negative. The positive (+) terminal will have battery voltage present and the negative (-) terminal will have 3–5 volts less. Ground the negative (-) terminal when testing this type of alternator.

REMOVAL & INSTALLATION

1. Disconnect the negative battery cable.
2. Remove the drive belt from the alternator pulley.

➡In some cases, it may be easier to disconnect the wiring after the alternator has been removed. Be sure to support the alternator by hand while removing the wiring.

3. Disconnect the wiring from the alternator.
4. Remove the alternator.

To install:

➡If necessary, attach the wiring to the alternator before installation.

When removing the mounting bolts, be sure to retain any washers, spacers or nuts for reassembly

To remove the alternator, first detach the wiring terminals from it (if possible)..

If not possible earlier, now disconnect any applicable wiring from the alternator

.. then loosen the alternator mounting bolts (arrows)

Finally, carefully remove the alternator from the engine compartment—although not shown here some alternators must be dropped out the bottom of the vehicle

For complete service labor times order Chilton's Labor Guide Manual

Example of the mounting of a typical alternator, which utilizes a serpentine belt

79240G23

Example of the mounting for a common alternator that uses a V-belt

79240G24

5. Install the alternator and attach the wiring if not already done.

6. Install the drive belt on the alternator pulley. Adjust the belt if necessary.

7. Connect the negative battery cable.

Battery

TESTING

❊❊ CAUTION

If the battery shows signs of freezing, cracking, leaking, loose posts or low electrolyte level, do not attempt to test, charge or jump start. Internal arcing may occur and cause the battery to explode. Always replace a battery that is physically damaged. If only the water level is low and the battery can be filled, add distilled water to the proper level. When charging, disconnect the battery cables, attach the connections to the battery first, then turn the charger ON. Never disconnect the battery cable(s) while the engine is running. Always wear safety glasses when servicing the battery.

Specific Gravity Test

The fluid (sulfuric acid solution) contained in the battery cells will tell you many things about the condition of the battery. Because the cell plates must be kept submerged below the fluid level in order to operate, maintaining the fluid level is extremely important. And, because the specific gravity of the acid is an indication of electrical charge, testing the fluid can be an aid in determining if the battery must be replaced. A battery in a vehicle with a properly operating charging system should require little maintenance, but careful, periodic inspection should reveal problems before they leave you stranded.

At least once a year, check the specific gravity of the battery. It should be between 1.20 and 1.26 in.Hg on the gravity scale. Most auto supply stores carry a variety of inexpensive battery testing hydrometers. These can be used on any non-sealed battery to test the specific gravity in each cell.

TCCA1P08

If the battery cells are low on fluid, top them up with distilled water

Draw some battery fluid into the hydrometer and read the specific gravity indicated by the float inside the tester

Draw some of the electrolyte from the battery into the hydrometer until the float is lifted from its seat. Read the specific gravity indicated by the position of the float. If the specific gravity is low in one or more cells, the battery should be slowly charged and checked again to see if the gravity has come up. Generally, if after charging, the specific gravity between any 2 cells varies more than 50 points (0.50), replace the battery, as it can no longer produce sufficient voltage to guarantee proper operation.

No Load Voltage Test

➡**A good quality Digital Multimeter (DMM) with at least 10 megohms/volt impedance should be used when testing modern automotive circuits. These meters can accurately detect very small amounts of voltage, current and resistance. This type of meter also has a high internal resistance that will not load the circuit being tested. Loading the circuit gives inaccurate readings and may cause damage to sensitive computer circuits.**

Use a high quality DMM to measure the battery voltage

| Open Circuit Voltage ||
Open Circuit Volts	Charge Percentage
11.7 volts or less	0%
12.0 volts	25%
12.2 volts	50%
12.4 volts	75%
12.6 volts or more	100%

Compare the actual voltage measured with these values to determine the percent of charge based on no load test results

1. Perform a no load voltage test to determine the state of charge by doing the following:

 a. If the battery has just been charged, remove the surface charge by turning on the headlamps for 15 seconds, then let the voltage stabilize for about 5 minutes before making any measurements.

 b. Disconnect the negative battery cable.

 c. Measure the battery voltage with a DMM.

 d. Compare the readings to the chart to determine the state of charge.

High Capacity Discharge Test

1. Perform a high capacity discharge test to determine the cranking capacity as follows:

 a. Fully charge the battery.

 b. Connect a VAT-40 or equivalent load tester to the battery.

| Load Test Temperature |||
| Minimum Voltage | Temperature ||
	°F	°C
9.6 volts	70° and above	21° and above
9.5 volts	60°	16°
9.4 volts	50°	10°
9.3 volts	40°	4°
9.1 volts	30°	-1°
8.9 volts	20°	-7°
8.7 volts	10°	-12°
8.5 volts	0°	-18°

High capacity discharge test minimum voltage/temperature chart

Ignition system service is covered in the model specific sections of this manual

c. Apply a load equal to ½ of the Cold Cranking Amp (CCA) rating of the battery for 15 seconds. The CCA is usually found on the battery label, if not, apply a load equal to 200 amps.

d. If the voltmeter reading falls below 9.6 volts at 70°F (21°C) or more, the battery should be replaced. The minimum battery voltage will be lower depending on the ambient temperature. Refer to the chart for testing in temperatures lower than 70°F (21°C).

Parasitic Draw Test

➡**A good quality Digital Multimeter (DMM) with at least 10 megohms/volt impedance should be used when testing modern automotive circuits. These meters can accurately detect very small amounts of voltage, current and resistance. This type of meter also has a high internal resistance that will not load the circuit being tested. Loading the circuit gives inaccurate readings and may cause damage to sensitive computer circuits.**

This test measures the amount of current that the vehicle draws while it is parked and not in use. A small amount of current should be flowing for such things as the on-board computer memory, automatic climate control, clock, and radio station presets. If there is a short in the vehicle electrical system or something has been left on, the excess current draw will eventually drain the battery and cause a no-start condition.

1. Be sure all accessories are turned **OFF**. Disconnect the negative battery cable.

2. Install a battery quick-disconnect switch (such as GM Parasitic Draw Test Switch J 38758) between the negative cable and the negative battery terminal. A battery disconnect switch will work in most cases.

3. Road test the vehicle while activating all accessories including the radio and air conditioning. Then, turn all accessories **OFF**.

4. Turn the vehicle **OFF** and open the hood.

5. If equipped, disable the underhood light.

6. Allow approximately 20 minutes for the vehicle computer system(s) to power down.

7. Connect one end of a jumper with a 10 amp fuse to the side of the quick-disconnect switch closest to the negative battery terminal. Be sure the jumper is on the metal part of the switch.

Before starting the parasitic draw test, install a battery disconnect switch between the negative battery cable and the battery terminal, as shown

79240G13

8. Connect the remaining end of the jumper to the other side of the switch closest to the negative battery cable.

✳✳ WARNING

Do not connect the multimeter to the circuit if more than 10 amps are flowing. Damage to the meter may occur.

9. Open the switch so all current flows through the jumper with the 10 amp fuse. If the fuse blows, there is more than 10 amps flowing in the circuit. This indicates that a component was left on (glove box light or other accessory) or there is a short in the electrical system. Find and correct the cause of the large current flow, then continue with this test.

10. If the fuse does not blow, close the disconnect switch and remove the jumper.

11. Set the multimeter to read 10 amps.

12. Connect the multimeter leads in place of the jumper used previously. When the switch is opened, current will flow through the meter.

13. The current draw should now be below 2 amps. If not, then something in the vehicle has been left on. Find the cause and correct it. When the current is less than 2 amps, set the meter to the 2 amp range. This will allow you to measure small amounts of current.

✳✳ WARNING

Do not open the door of the vehicle. The interior lights coming on will blow the fuse of the meter while on the 2 amp range.

14. Normal current draw should be less than ¼ of the reserve capacity of the battery. If the reserve capacity is unknown, normal current draw should be somewhere in the range of 0.005–0.040 amps depending on the type and amount of equipment on the vehicle.

➡**The reserve capacity is the amount of time, in minutes, it takes for the battery voltage to fall below 10.5 volts at a discharge rate of 25 amps at 80°F (26.7°C). In most cases, this number can be found on the battery label.**

15. If the current draw is higher than specified, pull fuses and/or disconnect components until the problem is found. Don't overlook the alternator connection.

REMOVAL & INSTALLATION

➡**Disconnecting the negative battery cable on some vehicles may interfere with the functioning of the on-board computer system, and may require the computer to undergo a relearning process once the negative battery cable is reconnected.**

1. Turn the ignition key to the **OFF** position.

2. Disconnect the negative battery cable first. On some vehicles, a cover or trim panel may have to be removed first.

3. Disconnect the positive battery cable.

4. Remove the battery hold-down.

➡**A battery strap or holding device can make removing or installing the battery much easier. In some cases it can be difficult to get your hands under the battery.**

To install:

5. Position the battery in the vehicle. Pay attention to the location of the terminals.

6. Install the battery hold-down. A loose battery may cause a vehicle fire or severe damage to the electrical system.

7. Clean the terminals and connect the positive battery cable first, then the negative cable.

8. If equipped, install the cover or trim panel.

JUMP STARTING A DEAD BATTERY

Whenever a vehicle is jump started, precautions must be followed in order to prevent the possibility of personal injury. Remember that batteries contain a small amount of explosive hydrogen gas which is a by-product of battery charging. Sparks should always be avoided when working around batteries, especially when attaching jumper cables. To minimize the possibility of accidental sparks, follow the procedure carefully.

❋❋ CAUTION

NEVER hook the batteries up in a series circuit or the entire electrical system will go up in smoke, including the starter!

Vehicles equipped with a diesel engine may utilize 2, 12 volt batteries. If so, the batteries are connected in a parallel circuit (positive terminal-to-positive terminal, negative terminal-to-negative terminal). Hooking the batteries up in parallel circuit increases battery cranking power without increasing total battery voltage output. Output remains at 12 volts. On the other hand, hooking 2, 12 volt batteries up in a series circuit (positive terminal-to-negative terminal, positive terminal-to-negative terminal) increases total battery output to 24 volts (12 volts plus 12 volts).

Jump Starting Precautions

To avoid personal injury and/or vehicle damage, please read all of the following precautions prior to jump starting a discharged battery:

• NEVER hook the batteries up in a series circuit or the entire electrical system will go up in smoke, including the starter!

• Be sure that both batteries are of the same voltage. Vehicles covered by this manual and most vehicles on the road today utilize a 12 volt charging system.

• Be sure that both batteries are of the same polarity (have the same terminal, in most cases NEGATIVE grounded).

• Be sure that the vehicles are not touching, otherwise a short could occur.

• On serviceable batteries, be sure the vent cap holes are not obstructed.

• Do not smoke or allow sparks anywhere near the batteries.

• In cold weather, make sure the battery electrolyte is not frozen. This can occur more readily in a battery that has been in a state of discharge.

• Do not allow electrolyte to contact your skin or clothing.

Jump Starting Procedure

1. Make sure that the voltages of the 2 batteries are the same. Most batteries and charging systems are of the 12 volt variety.

2. Pull the vehicle with the good battery into a position so the jumper cables can reach the dead battery and that vehicle's engine compartment. Make sure that the vehicles DO NOT touch.

➡ **Remote power terminals are usually provided on vehicles where the battery is located in the fender or other location that makes connecting jumper cables difficult. These power terminals are located in the engine compartment. If this is the situation, use the remote terminals instead of the terminals on the battery.**

3. Place the transmissions/transaxles of both vehicles in Neutral, manual transmissions, or P (park), automatic transmissions, as applicable, then firmly set their parking brakes.

➡ **If necessary for safety reasons, the hazard lights on both vehicles may be operated throughout the entire procedure without significantly increasing the difficulty of jumping the dead battery.**

4. Turn all lights and accessories OFF on both vehicles. Be sure the ignition switches on both vehicles are turned to the **OFF** position.

5. Cover the battery cell caps with a rag, but do not cover the terminals.

6. Make sure the terminals on both batteries are clean and free of corrosion, otherwise proper electrical connection will be impeded. If necessary, clean the battery terminals before proceeding.

7. Identify the positive (+) and negative (-) terminals on both batteries.

8. Connect the first jumper cable to the positive (+) terminal of the dead battery, then attach the other end of that cable to the positive (+) terminal of the booster (good) battery.

9. Connect the clamp of the negative jumper cable to the negative (-) terminal on the good battery and the final cable clamp to an engine bolt head, alternator bracket or other solid, metallic point on the engine with the dead battery. Try to pick a ground on the engine that is positioned away from the battery in order to minimize the possibility of explosion due to the sparks created when the last connection is made. DO NOT connect this clamp to the negative terminal of the bad battery.

❋❋ WARNING

Be very careful to keep the jumper cables away from moving parts (cooling fan, belts, etc.) on both engines.

10. Ensure the cables are routed away from any moving parts, then start the donor vehicle's engine. Run the engine at moderate speed for several minutes to allow the dead battery a chance to receive some initial charge.

11. With the donor vehicle's engine still running slightly above idle, try to start the vehicle with the dead battery. Crank the engine for no more than 10 seconds at a time and let the starter cool for at least 20 seconds between tries. If the vehicle does not start in 3 tries, it is likely that something else is also wrong, or that the battery needs additional time to charge.

12. Once the vehicle is started, allow it to run at idle for a few seconds to make sure that it is operating properly.

13. Turn ON the headlights, heater blower and, if equipped, the rear defroster of both vehicles in order to reduce the severity of voltage spikes and subsequent risk of damage to the vehicles' electrical systems when the cables are disconnected. This step is especially important to any vehicle equipped with computer control modules.

14. Carefully remove the cables in the reverse order of connection. Start with the negative cable that is attached to the engine ground, then the negative cable on the donor battery. Disconnect the positive cable from the donor battery, and finally disconnect the positive cable from the formerly dead battery. Be careful when disconnecting the cables from the positive terminals not to allow the alligator clips to touch any metal on either vehicle or a short and sparks will occur.

Voltage Regulator

TESTING

➡**Most regulators are integral (built in) to the alternator or Powertrain Control Module (PCM). If the regulator is found to be defective on these models, the alternator or PCM should be replaced.**

For voltage regulator testing, refer to the Alternator Isolation test.

REMOVAL & INSTALLATION

➡**The following procedure is only for voltage regulators mounted on the back (outside) of the alternator or elsewhere in the engine compartment.**

1. Disconnect the negative battery cable.
2. If equipped, remove the exterior alternator cover to expose the regulator. Do not disassemble the alternator case that houses the rotor and stator.
3. If equipped, disengage the electrical connector from the regulator.
4. Remove the regulator mounting screws and remove the regulator.

To install:
5. Position the regulator in its original position and install the mounting screws.
6. Connect any wiring that was removed from the regulator.
7. If equipped, install the cover.
8. Connect the negative battery cable.

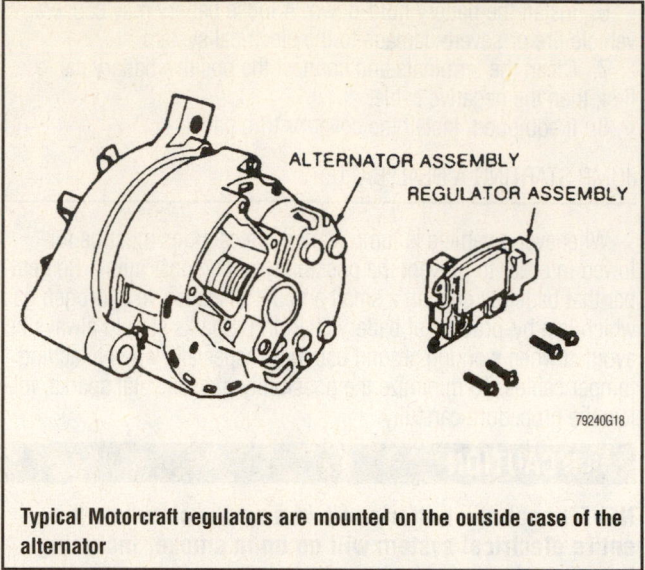

Typical Motorcraft regulators are mounted on the outside case of the alternator

The regulator on a common Bosch alternator is mounted under a cover on the rear of the alternator

PISTON, PISTON RING AND CONNECTING ROD POSITIONING

11

PISTON, PISTON RING AND CONNECTING ROD POSITIONING

When assembling the pistons, piston rings and connecting rods, and when installing these assemblies into the engine block, it is vitally important to ensure that these three components are properly positioned with respect to each other. Often times the engine block is designed so that if a connecting rod or piston is installed backwards, or in the wrong bank of cylinders, internal engine damage may occur once the engine is started. The piston ring end-gap spacing that is recommended by the engine manufacturer is often with the purpose of increased compression pressures during the engine break-in period. Failure to properly space the piston ring end-gaps may lead to increased oil consumption and extended break-in time. Therefore, always be sure to position the pistons, rings and connecting rods as shown in the accompanying illustrations.

✳ WARNING

Always be sure to matchmark the connecting rods and caps prior to disassembly so that they may be reassembled with their original counterparts. If the caps are not installed on their original connecting rods, the assemblies will most likely need machining to avoid bearing, connecting rod and/or crankshaft damage.

PISTON, PISTON RING AND CONNECTING ROD POSITIONING INDEX

MANUFACTURER

ENGINE	DESCRIPTION	FIGURE
Chrysler Corp.		
All engines	Connecting Rod And Cap Installation	1
	Piston Ring Identification Mark Locations	2
2.0L engines	Piston Ring Orientation	3
	Piston Ring End-Gap Spacing	5
	Piston Positioning	6
	Piston Positioning	8
	Piston Ring End-Gap Spacing	7
	Piston Positioning	9
2.4L engines	Piston Positioning	6
	Piston Ring End-Gap Spacing	5
	Piston Ring Orientation	3
2.5L engines	Piston Ring End-Gap Spacing	7
	Piston Ring Orientation	3
	Piston Positioning Mark Locations	10
	Piston Positioning	9
2.7L engines	Piston Positioning	11
	Piston Ring End-Gap Spacing	7
	Piston Ring Orientation	4
3.0L engines	Piston Positioning	12
	Piston Ring End-Gap Spacing	7
	Piston Ring Orientation	4
3.2L engines	Piston Positioning	9
	Piston Ring End-Gap Spacing	7
	Piston Ring Orientation	4
3.3L engines	Piston Positioning	13
	Piston Ring End-Gap Spacing	5
	Piston Ring Orientation	4
3.5L engines	Piston Positioning Mark Locations	14
	Piston Ring End-Gap Spacing	7
	Piston Ring Orientation	4
Ford Motor Co.		
All engines	Connecting Rod And Cap Installation	15
1.3L engines	Piston And Connecting Rod Assembly	18
	Piston Ring End-Gap Spacing	17
	Piston Ring Positioning	16
1.8L engines	Piston Ring End-Gap Spacing	19
	Piston Positioning	21
1.9L engines	Piston Ring End-Gap Spacing	20
	Piston Positioning	21
2.0L (VIN 3 and P) engines	Piston Ring Positioning, End-Gap Spacing And Piston Positioning	22
2.0L (VIN A) engines	Piston And Connecting Rod Assembly	18
	Piston Ring End-Gap Spacing	17
	Piston Ring Positioning	16

9300AC01

PISTON, PISTON RING AND CONNECTING ROD POSITIONING INDEX

9300AC02

For complete service labor times order Chilton's Labor Guide Manual

PISTON, PISTON RING AND CONNECTING ROD POSITIONING INDEX

9300AC03

Fig. 1 Chrysler engine connecting rod and cap installation—ensure to matchmark the cap and rod prior to disassembly

7922AG01

Fig. 3 Chrysler 2.0L, 2.4L and 2.5L engines—piston ring orientation

7922AG03

Fig. 2 Common Chrysler piston ring identification mark locations

7922AG02

Fig. 4 Chrysler 2.7L, 3.2L, 3.0L, 3.3L and 3.5L engines—piston ring orientation

7922AG04

Fig. 5 Chrysler 2.0L (VIN C and Y), 2.4L and 3.3L engines—piston ring end-gap spacing

Fig. 8 Chrysler 2.0L (VIN F) engine—piston positioning. The front mark on the top face of the piston must point toward the front of the engine

Fig. 6 Chrysler 2.0L (VIN C) and 2.4L engines—piston positioning. The arrow or weight marking (L or H) must face toward the timing belt side of the engine

Fig. 9 Chrysler 2.0L (VIN Y), 2.5L (VIN N) and 3.2L engines—piston positioning. The small arrows on the crown of the pistons must point toward the front of the engine

Fig. 7 Chrysler 2.0L (VIN F), 2.5L, 2.7L, 3.0L, 3.2L and 3.5L engines—piston ring end-gap spacing

Fig. 10 Chrysler 2.5L (VIN H) engine—piston positioning mark locations

Fig. 11 Chrysler 2.7L engine—piston positioning

1. Indicates left or right side of engine.
2. Should point toward front of engine.

Fig. 14 Chrysler 3.5L engine—piston positioning mark locations

Fig. 12 Chrysler 3.0L engine—piston-to-engine block mark locations

Fig. 15 Ford engine connecting rod and cap installation. Ensure to matchmark the cap and rod prior to disassembly

Fig. 13 Chrysler 3.3L engine—piston positioning. The notches on the crown of the pistons must be oriented toward the front of the engine

Fig. 16 Ford 1.3L and 2.0L (VIN A) engines—piston ring positioning

Fig. 17 Ford 1.3L and 2.0L (VIN A) engines—piston ring end-gap spacing

Fig. 18 Ford 1.3L and 2.0L (VIN A) engines—piston and connecting rod assembly

Fig. 19 Ford 1.8L engine—piston ring end-gap spacing

PISTON RING SPACING

1. Oil ring segment gap
2. Piston
3. 150 degrees (spacing)
4. Pin bore
5. Front of vehicle
A. Oil ring spacer gap
B. Compression ring gap
C. Compression ring(opposite placement)gap

Fig. 20 Ford 1.9L engine—piston ring end-gap spacing

Fig. 21 Ford 1.8L and 1.9L engines—piston positioning. Ensure that the notch on the top of the piston is oriented toward the front of the engine

Refer to the model specific sections for engine mechanical service procedures

Fig. 22 Ford 2.0L (VIN 3 and P) and 2.5L (VIN L) engines—piston ring positioning, end-gap spacing and piston positioning. The small directional arrow must face the front of the engine

1. Top ring end gap
2. Piston pin end gap
3. Second ring end gap
4. Oil ring lower rail end gap
5. Oil ring spacer end gap
6. Oil ring upper rail end gap

Fig. 23 Ford 2.5L (VIN B) engine—piston ring end-gap spacing

Fig. 24 Ford 2.5L (VIN B) engine—piston and connecting rod assembly

Fig. 25 Ford 3.0L (VIN S and U) and 3.8L engines—piston ring end-gap spacing

Fig. 26 Ford 3.0L (VIN S and U) and 3.8L engines—piston and connecting rod positioning

Fig. 27 Ford 3.4L engines—piston ring positioning

Fig. 28 Ford 3.4L engines—piston ring end-gap spacing

Fig. 29 Ford 3.4L engines—piston and connecting rod positioning

Fig. 30 Ford 4.6L (VIN V) engine—piston ring positioning

Fig. 31 Ford 4.6L (VIN V) engine—piston ring end-gap spacing and piston positioning

Fig. 34 Ford 5.0L engines—piston ring end-gap spacing

Fig. 32 Ford 4.6L (VIN W and X) engines—piston ring positioning

Fig. 35 Ford 5.0L engines—piston assembly positioning

Fig. 33 Ford 4.6L (VIN W and X) engines—piston ring end-gap spacing and piston positioning

Fig. 36 General Motors engine connecting rod and cap installation. Be sure to matchmark the cap and rod prior to disassembly, as shown

OIL RING ASSEMBLY GAP

120° TYPICAL

LOWER COMPRESSION RING GAP

PISTON

FRONT OF ENGINE

UPPER COMPRESSION RING GAP

7922AG50

Fig. 37 General Motors 2.4L engines—piston ring end-gap spacing

1. PISTON
2. ORIENTATION ARROW - TOWARDS FRONT OF ENGINE
3. CONNECTING ROD
4. OIL SQUIRT HOLE - TOWARDS EXHAUST SIDE
5. BEARING CONNECTING ROD
6. NUT, CONNECTING ROD CAP TO CONNECTING ROD
7. CAP, CONNECTING ROD

7922AG49

Fig. 38 General Motors 2.4L engines—piston and connecting rod assembly positioning

1. Oil rings
2. Top compression ring
3. Second compression ring
4. Expander

7922AG48

Fig. 39 General Motors 2.2L, 3.1L, 3.4L and 3.8L engines—piston ring positioning

A. OIL RING SPACER GAP
(TANG IN HOLE OR SLOT WITH ARC)

B. OIL RING RAIL GAPS

C. 2ND COMPRESSION RING GAP

D. TOP COMPRESSION RING GAP

7922AG46

Fig. 40 General Motors 2.2L, 3.1L, 3.4L and 3.8L engines—piston ring end-gap spacing

ARROW TOWARDS FRONT OF ENGINE

FRT

7922AG47

Fig. 41 General Motors 2.2L, 3.1L, 3.4L and 3.8L engines—piston positioning. Often the arrow is replaced by a notch, which also must face toward the front of the engine

(1) 1st Compression Ring End Gap Location
(2) 2nd Compression Ring End Gap Location
(3) Oil Control Ring Upper Ring End Gap Location
(4) Oil Control Ring Spacer End Gap Location
(5) Oil Control Ring Lower Ring End Gap Location

7922AG55

Fig. 42 General Motors 3.0L engine—piston ring end-gap spacing

1. Oil ring segment gap
2. Upper compression ring gap
3. Oil ring segment gap
4. Expander & lower compression ring gaps
5. Expander ring
6. Oil segment rings
7. Lower compression ring
8. Upper compression ring

7922AG52

Fig. 43 General Motors 4.0L and 4.6L engines—piston ring and ring end-gap positioning

LEFT BANK

◄FRT

B   A

RIGHT BANK

**BOTTOM VIEW
(PAN - SIDE UP)**

PISTON ARROW TOWARD
CHAINCASE ON BOTH SIDES

RIGHT BANK

3   5   7

1

◄FRT

2   4   6   8

LEFT BANK

**TOP VIEW
(PAN - SIDE DOWN)**

ROD CAPS

PISTON

◄FRT

LOCATOR LUGS
INDICATE PISTON
FRONT TOWARDS
ENGINE FRONT

ROD CAP

PISTON

ROD CAP

BEARING CAP NOTCHES
POINT TOWARD EACH
OTHER ON PAIRED RODS

BEARING CAP NOTCHES
POINT TOWARD EACH
OTHER ON PAIRED RODS

◄FRT

VIEW A

VIEW B

7922AG53

Fig. 44 General Motors 4.0L and 4.6L engines—piston and connecting rod assembly positioning

1. Piston
2. Upper compression piston ring
3. Lower compression piston ring
4. Oil control piston ring
5. Oil control ring spring w/spacer

7922AG43

Fig. 45 General Motors 4.3L and 5.7L engines—piston ring positioning

Refer to the model specific sections for engine mechanical service procedures

ENGINE LEFT   ENGINE FRONT   ENGINE RIGHT

A. Oil ring spacer gap
B. Oil ring rail gaps
C. 2nd compression ring gap
D. Top compression ring gap

7922AG42

Fig. 46 General Motors 4.3L and 5.7L engines—piston ring end-gap spacing

CONNECTING ROD CAP

CONNECTING ROD NUT

CRANKSHAFT ASSEMBLY

CONNECTING ROD BEARING

FRT

CONNECTING ROD ASSEMBLY

CONNECTING ROD BEARING

PISTON ASSEMBLY

CONNECTING ROD BEARING

ARROW TO BE ORIENTED TO FRONT OF ENGINE

PISTON ASSEMBLY

CRANKSHAFT ASSEMBLY

FLANGES OF CONNECTING RODS MUST FACE TO THE FRONT IN THE LEFT BANK AND TO THE REAR IN THE RIGHT BANK

FRT

VIEW A

VIEW B

7922AG45

Fig. 47 General Motors 4.3L and 5.7L (VIN 5 and P) engines—piston and connecting rod assembly positioning

NOTE: LARGE CHAMFERS ON CONNECTING RODS MUST FACE CRANKSHAFT COUNTERWEIGHTS.

1. Piston
2. Connecting rod LH
3. Connecting rod bearing
4. Connecting rod RH
5. Connecting rod bearing cap
6. Connecting rod bearing cap bolt
7. Crankshaft

7922AG44

Fig. 48 General Motors 5.7L (VIN G) engine—piston and connecting rod assembly positioning

A   45°
B   PISTON ARROW MARK
C   FIRST RING END GAP
D   SECOND RING END GAP
E   OIL RING END GAPS
F   OIL RING SPACER GAP
G   INTAKE SIDE
H   EXHAUST SIDE

7922AG39

Fig. 50 GEO/Chevrolet 1.0L, 1.3L, 1.6L and 1.8L engines—piston ring end-gap spacing

CRANKSHAFT PULLEY SIDE

A. Arrow mark
B. Oil hole (oil hole should come on intake side)
1. Piston
2. Connecting rod

7922AG41

Fig. 51 GEO/Chevrolet 1.0L, 1.3L, 1.6L and 1.8L engines—piston and connecting rod assembly positioning

A   "R" OR "T" MARK
B   OIL RING
C   UPPER COMPRESSION RING
D   LOWER COMPRESSION RING

7922AG40

Fig. 49 GEO/Chevrolet 1.0L, 1.3L, 1.6L and 1.8L engines—piston ring positioning

7922AG36

Fig. 52 Saturn 1.9L engines—piston ring end-gap spacing

Fig. 53 Saturn 1.9L engines—both upper rings (DOHC) or only the second ring (SOHC) have top marks; the top ring (SOHC only) can be installed both ways

7922AG38

Fig. 54 Saturn 1.9L engines—piston and connecting rod assembly positioning mark locations. The mark on the piston and the rod bearing tang slots must face the front of the engine

7922AG37

PRECAUTIONS

Before servicing any vehicle, please be sure to read all of the following precautions, which deal with personal safety, prevention of component damage, and important points to take into consideration when servicing a motor vehicle:

• Never open, service or drain the radiator or cooling system when the engine is hot; serious burns can occur from the steam and hot coolant.

• Observe all applicable safety precautions when working around fuel. Whenever servicing the fuel system, always work in a well ventilated area. Do not allow fuel spray or vapors to come in contact with a spark, open flame, or excessive heat (a hot drop light, for example). Keep a dry chemical fire extinguisher near the work area. Always keep fuel in a container specifically designed for fuel storage; also, always properly seal fuel containers to avoid the possibility of fire or explosion. Refer to the additional fuel system precautions later in this section.

• Fuel injection systems often remain pressurized, even after the engine has been turned **OFF**. The fuel system pressure must be relieved before disconnecting any fuel lines. Failure to do so may result in fire and/or personal injury.

• Brake fluid often contains polyglycol ethers and polyglycols. Avoid contact with the eyes and wash your hands thoroughly after handling brake fluid. If you do get brake fluid in your eyes, flush your eyes with clean, running water for 15 minutes. If eye irritation persists, or if you have taken brake fluid internally, IMMEDIATELY seek medical assistance.

• The EPA warns that prolonged contact with used engine oil may cause a number of skin disorders, including cancer! You should make every effort to minimize your exposure to used engine oil. Protective gloves should be worn when changing oil.

Wash your hands and any other exposed skin areas as soon as possible after exposure to used engine oil. Soap and water, or waterless hand cleaner should be used.

• All new vehicles are now equipped with an air bag system, often referred to as a Supplemental Restraint System (SRS) or Supplemental Inflatable Restraint (SIR) system. The system must be disabled before performing service on or around system components, steering column, instrument panel components, wiring and sensors. Failure to follow safety and disabling procedures could result in accidental air bag deployment, possible personal injury and unnecessary system repairs.

• Always wear safety goggles when working with, or around, the air bag system. When carrying a non-deployed air bag, be sure the bag and trim cover are pointed away from your body. When placing a non-deployed air bag on a work surface, always face the bag and trim cover upward, away from the surface. This will reduce the motion of the module if it is accidentally deployed. Refer to the additional air bag system precautions later in this section.

• Clean, high quality brake fluid from a sealed container is essential to the safe and proper operation of the brake system. You should always buy the correct type of brake fluid for your vehicle. If the brake fluid becomes contaminated, completely flush the system with new fluid. Never reuse any brake fluid. Any brake fluid that is removed from the system should be discarded. Also, do not allow any brake fluid to come in contact with a painted surface; it will damage the paint.

• Never operate the engine without the proper amount and type of engine oil; doing so WILL result in severe engine damage.

• Timing belt maintenance is extremely important! Many models utilize an interference-type, non-freewheeling engine. If the timing belt breaks, the valves in the cylinder head may strike the pistons, causing potentially serious (also time-consuming and

expensive) engine damage. Refer to the maintenance interval charts in the front of this manual for the recommended replacement interval for the timing belt, and to the timing belt section for belt replacement and inspection.

• Disconnecting the negative battery cable on some vehicles may interfere with the functions of the on-board computer system(s) and may require the computer to undergo a relearning process once the negative battery cable is reconnected.

• When servicing drum brakes, only disassemble and assemble one side at a time, leaving the remaining side intact for reference.

• Only an MVAC-trained, EPA-certified automotive technician should service the A/C system or its components.

ENGINE REPAIR

Ignition Timing

ADJUSTMENT

All models utilize a distributorless ignition system referred to as the Direct Ignition System (DIS). It is a fixed ignition timing system which means that basic ignition timing cannot be adjusted. All spark advance is permanently set by the Powertrain Control Module (PCM).

Engine Assembly

REMOVAL & INSTALLATION

1996–97 Models

1. Before servicing the vehicle, refer to the precautions in the beginning of this section.

2. Disconnect negative battery cable.

7922BG01

Engine front and side views—3.3L engines

7922BG02

Engine front and side views—1996–97 3.5L engines

3. Properly relieve the fuel system pressure.

4. Matchmark the hood and hinges and remove the hood assembly.

5. Drain the cooling system.

6. Remove the radiator and cooling fan assemblies.

7. Label and unplug all electrical connections.

8. Remove the coolant hoses from the engine.

9. Disconnect the fuel lines using the following procedure:

   a. At the fuel rail, push the quick-connect fitting toward the fuel tube while depressing the built-in disconnect tool with Quick-Connect Fitting Tool 6751 or equivalent.

   b. To disconnect the fitting from the fuel rail, slightly twist the fitting while maintaining downward pressure on tool 6751.

   c. Wrap shop towels around the fuel hoses to absorb any fuel spillage and be sure to cover the openings to prevent system contamination.

10. Disconnect the accelerator and cruise control cables from the throttle body.

11. Remove the air cleaner assembly. Raise and safely support the vehicle.

12. Drain the engine oil.

13. Remove the air conditioning compressor mounting bolts and position the compressor aside. It should not be necessary to disconnect the refrigerant lines from the compressor.

14. Disconnect the exhaust pipe from the exhaust manifold.

15. Remove the transaxle inspection cover and mark the flexplate for reference during installation.

16. Remove the screws holding the torque converter to the flexplate. Attach a C-clamp or some other restraint on the converter housing to prevent the torque converter from falling out during removal of the engine.

17. Remove the power steering pump mounting bolts and position the pump aside.

18. Remove the two lower transaxle-to-block screws. Remove the starter motor from the transaxle housing.

19. Lower the vehicle and disconnect the vacuum lines and ground strap. Support the transaxle with a jack.

20. Attach an engine lifting hoist to the engine and support it.

21. Remove the upper transaxle mounting bolts.

22. Remove the insulator mounting nuts from the engine mounts.

23. Lift the engine from the vehicle.

To install:

24. Lower the engine into the engine compartment. Align the engine mounts and install all nuts. Once all mount bolts are installed, tighten the fasteners to 45 ft. lbs. (61 Nm).

25. Install the transaxle to the engine block and tighten the bolts to 75 ft. lbs. (102 Nm).

26. Remove the engine hoist and the transaxle holding fixture.

27. Remove the C-clamp from the converter housing, if installed.

28. Align the flexplate to the converter using the marks made during removal. Install the converter mounting screws and tighten to 55 ft. lbs. (75 Nm).

29. Install the transaxle inspection cover.

30. Reconnect the exhaust system to the engine exhaust manifold and install the starter. Tighten the exhaust pipe-to-manifold bolts to 25 ft. lbs. (34 Nm).

31. Install the power steering pump and the air conditioning compressor to their mounting brackets and secure. Tighten the mounting bracket bolts to 30 ft. lbs. (41 Nm).

32. Lower the vehicle and reconnect all vacuum lines.

33. Attach all electrical connectors including the ground strap.

34. Reconnect the fuel lines to the fuel rail as follows:

   a. Be sure that the black plastic release ring in the quick-connect fitting is in the OUT position. Place Special Tool 6751 under the largest diameter of the quick-connect fitting.

   b. Pull Tool 6751 toward the fuel rail until the quick-connect fitting clicks into place.

   c. Place the special tool between the shoulder of the built-in disconnect tool and the top of the quick-connect fitting, then inspect the security of the fitting by applying a slight downward force against the fitting. It should be locked in place.

35. Reconnect the accelerator and cruise control cables to the throttle lever.

36. Install the radiator and cooling fan assemblies.

37. Refill the crankcase with the proper amount of engine oil and replace the oil filter, if necessary.

38. Refill and bleed the cooling system.

39. Install the hood onto the vehicle aligning the marks made during removal.

40. Check to be sure that all hoses, wiring connectors, cables, vacuum and fluid lines are reconnected.

41. Reconnect the negative battery cable. Check all fluid levels.

42. Start the engine and allow to idle until normal operating temperature is reached. Inspect all fluid systems for leaks and correct level.

43. Road test the vehicle. Adjust the transaxle linkage, as necessary.

1998–00 Models

2.7L ENGINE

1. Before servicing the vehicle, refer to the precautions in the beginning of this section.

2. Relieve the fuel system pressure.

3. Disconnect the negative battery cable at the remote terminal near the right strut tower.

4. Matchmark the hood hinges on the hood and remove the hood.

5. Drain the cooling system.

6. Remove the wiper arms, cowl covers and cowl support.

7. Remove the air intake duct and air cleaner assembly.

8. Remove the upper radiator crossmember.

9. Disconnect the hood release cable from the latch.

10. Remove the cooling fan assembly.

11. Remove the upper and lower radiator hoses.

12. Remove the fasteners attaching the A/C condenser to the radiator, then remove the radiator.

13. Remove the accessory drive belts.

14. Remove the power steering pump without disconnecting the lines and position the pump out of the way.

➥The generator can be removed with the engine.

15. Unbolt the A/C compressor the position it to the side without disconnecting the lines.

16. Remove the V-band clamps at the exhaust manifolds.

17. Disconnect the speed control and throttle cables from the throttle body.

18. Disconnect the heater hoses and the coolant hoses at the pressure bottle.

19. Disconnect all vacuum lines, electrical connectors and ground straps from the engine.

20. Raise the vehicle and drain the engine oil.

21. Remove the fasteners supporting the catalytic converter down pipes at the front of the rear mounts.

22. Remove the structural collar mounting bolts and the structural collar.

23. Matchmark the flexplate and torque converter, then remove the torque converter bolts.

24. Remove both transaxle cooler line brackets from the engine.

25. Remove the starter and the Crankshaft Position (CKP) sensor.

26. Remove the two lower transaxle-to-engine bolts.

27. Safely lower the vehicle.

28. Remove the EGR valve assembly.

29. Remove the fuel line and engine harness from the throttle body bracket.

30. Remove the following brackets from the double-ended transaxle-to-engine bolts:

- Wiring harness bracket
- Transaxle shift cable bracket
- Throttle body support bracket

31. Remove the upper transaxle-to-engine bolts.

32. Remove the fasteners attaching the right and left engine mount isolators to the engine mount brackets.

STRUCTURAL COLLAR

9300BG02

Removing the structural collar—2.7L engine

> ❊❊ **WARNING**

Do not damage the intake manifold or cylinder head covers while lifting the engine.

33. Attach an engine lifting fixture to the engine.

34. Support the transaxle with a jack and lift the engine from the vehicle.

To install:

35. Lower the engine into the vehicle.

36. Align the engine mounts and install the fasteners, but do not tighten them at this time.

> ❊❊ **WARNING**

Do not tighten the transaxle-to-engine bolts until all of the bolts have been hand-started and the engine is flush against the transaxle.

37. Install the transaxle-to-engine bolts. Tighten the bolts to 75 ft. lbs. (102 Nm).

38. Remove the engine support fixture.

39. Tighten the engine mount isolator-to-bracket fasteners to 45 ft. lbs. (61 Nm).

40. Raise the vehicle. Align the matchmarks and install the flexplate-to-torque converter bolts. Tighten the bolts to 55 ft. lbs. (75 Nm).

41. Install the starter and the crankshaft position sensor.

42. Install the structural collar using the following sub-steps:

   a. Install the vertical collar-to-oil pan bolts. Tighten the bolts to 10 inch lbs. (1.1 Nm).

   b. Install the collar-to-transaxle bolts. Tighten the bolts to 40 ft. lbs. (55 Nm).

   c. Tighten the center vertical bolt to 40 ft. lbs. (55 Nm) then tighten the remaining vertical bolts to the same torque.

43. The remainder of the installation is the reverse of removal. Keep the following in mind:

COWL SUPPORT   **WINDSHIELD**

SUPPORT FASTENERS

9300BG01

Remove the cowl support for clearance when removing the engine—2.7L engine

ENGINE LIFTING FIXTURE

REAR OF ENGINE

ATTACHING LOCATION

FRONT

FRONT OF ENGINE

ATTACHING LOCATION

9300BG03

Engine support fixture attaching points—2.7L engine

• Use new V-band clamps and tighten them to 100 inch lbs. (11 Nm)

• Tighten the A/C compressor and power steering pump fasteners to 250 inch lbs. (28 Nm).

• Refill the cooling system and the engine oil to the correct levels.

3.2L AND 3.5L ENGINES

1. Before servicing the vehicle, refer to the precautions in the beginning of this section.

2. Disconnect negative battery cable.

3. Properly relieve the fuel system pressure.

4. Matchmark the hood and hinges and remove the hood assembly.

5. Remove the wiper arms.

6. Remove the cowl covers and supports.

7. Disconnect and remove the air cleaner assembly and the air inlet duct.

8. Remove the upper radiator support and the hood release cable.

9. Remove the fan module.

10. Drain and recycle the engine coolant.

11. Remove the accessory drive belts.

12. Remove the upper and lower radiator hoses.

13. Disconnect the engine oil and transmission cooler lines at the radiator.

14. If necessary, label and disconnect the generator wiring harness, then remove the generator.

15. Remove the air conditioning compressor mounting bolts and position the compressor aside. It should not be necessary to disconnect the refrigerant lines from the compressor.

16. Remove the power steering pump mounting bolts and position the pump aside.

17. Loosen, then remove the V-band clamp at the right exhaust manifold.

18. Remove the right side bracket fasteners attaching the right catalytic converter down pipe.

19. Label and disconnect the fuel lines.

20. Disconnect the throttle and cruise control cables.

21. Label and disconnect all vacuum hoses.

22. Disconnect the ground straps at both cylinder heads.

❋❋ CAUTION

The intake manifold is a composite design, and should be removed

before lifting the engine or it will be damaged and have to be replaced.

23. Remove the upper intake manifold, and cover the openings to prevent debris from entering the engine.

24. Disconnect the heater hoses.

25. Remove the throttle body support brackets.

26. Remove the upper transaxle-to-engine mounting bolts.

27. Label and detach all electrical and vacuum hose connections.

28. Raise and safely support the vehicle.

29. Drain the engine oil into a suitable container.

30. Remove the structural collar, then matchmark the flexplate-to-torque converter position.

31. Remove the flexplate-to-torque converter mounting bolts.

32. Loosen and remove the left exhaust manifold V-band clamp, then the left catalytic converter support brackets.

33. Remove the starter.

34. Remove the left and right engine mounting bolts.

35. Remove the Crankshaft Position (CKP) sensor.

36. Remove the lower engine-to-transaxle mounting bolts.

37. Lower the vehicle.

38. Attach a suitable lifting device to the engine.

39. Support the transaxle using a floor jack with a small block of wood in between.

WINDSHIELD

LEFT COWL COVER

RIGHT COWL COVER

COWL SUPPORT

WINDSHIELD

SUPPORT FASTENERS

7922BG03

Be careful not to damage the windshield when removing the cowl covers and supports—1998–00 3.2L and 3.5L models

Timing belt service is covered in Section 5 of this manual

40. Slowly lift the engine from the vehicle.

To install:

41. Carefully lower the engine into the vehicle.

42. Align the engine mounts and install the fasteners, but do not tighten them until all of the mounting bolts have been installed.

43. Install the engine-to-transaxle mounting bolts and tighten to 75 ft. lbs. (102 Nm).

44. Remove the engine lifting device.

45. Raise and safely support the vehicle.

46. Tighten the engine mount nuts/bolts 45 ft. lbs. (61 Nm).

47. Align the flexplate-to-torque converter matchmarks and install the mounting bolts, then tighten to 55 ft. lbs. (75 Nm).

48. Install the CKP and the starter.

49. Install the left-side exhaust manifold V-band clamp and tighten to 100 inch lbs. (11 Nm).

50. Install the mounting bracket fasteners for the left-side catalytic converter.

51. Install the structural collar utilizing the following procedure:

   a. Install the vertical collar to the oil pan mounting bolts and tighten, temporarily to 10 inch lbs. (1.1 Nm).

   b. Install the collar-to-transaxle bolts and tighten to 40 ft. lbs. (55 Nm).

   c. Starting with the center vertical bolt and working outward, tighten the bolts to 40 ft. lbs. (55 Nm).

52. Lower the vehicle.

53. Install the throttle body support bracket.

54. Connect the heater hoses, all ground straps, and vacuum hoses.

55. Install the upper intake manifold.

56. Attach all engine wiring harnesses.

57. Connect and adjust the throttle and cruise control cables.

58. Connect the fuel lines.

59. Install the V-band clamp on the right exhaust manifold and tighten to 100 inch lbs. (11 Nm).

60. Install the mounting bracket fasteners for the right-side catalytic converter.

61. Install the air conditioning compressor, and tighten the mounting bolts to 250 inch lbs. (28 Nm).

62. If removed, install the generator and attach its wiring harness.

63. Install the radiator.

64. Install the power steering pump.

65. Connect the engine oil and transaxle cooler lines.

66. Connect the radiator hoses and install the accessory drive belt.

67. Fill the cooling system and the engine oil pan to the proper level.

68. Install the hood release cable and the upper radiator support.

69. Install the air cleaner and inlet hose.

70. Install the cowl covers and supports, then the wiper arms.

71. Line up the matchmarks and install the hood.

72. Connect the negative battery cable.

Water Pump

REMOVAL & INSTALLATION

The water pump has a die cast aluminum body and a stamped steel impeller. It bolts directly to the chain case cover using an O-ring for sealing. It is driven by the back side of the serpentine belt.

It is normal for a small amount of coolant to drip from the weep hole located on the water pump body (small black spot). If this condition exists, DO NOT replace the water pump. Only replace the water pump if a heavy deposit or steady flow of brown/green coolant is visible on the water pump body from the weep hole, which would indicate shaft seal failure. Before replacing the water pump, be sure to perform a thorough inspection. A defective pump will not be able to circulate heated coolant through the long heater hose.

2.7L Engine

1. Before servicing the vehicle, refer to the precautions in the beginning of this section.

2. Disconnect the negative battery cable.

3. Drain the coolant from the engine.

4. Remove the upper radiator crossmember.

5. Remove the fan module.

6. Remove the accessory drive belts.

➡**The water pump is driven by the primary timing chain.**

7. Remove the crankshaft damper, timing chain cover, timing chain, and all guides.

8. Remove the water pump mounting bolts.

9. Remove the water pump, then clean the mounting surface.

To install:

10. Install the water pump and gasket, then tighten the mounting bolts to 105 inch lbs. (12 Nm).

11. Install the all guides, timing chain, and timing chain cover.

12. Install the crankshaft damper and tighten the center bolt to 125 ft. lbs. (170 Nm).

13. Install the accessory drive belts.

14. Install the fan module and the upper radiator crossmember.

15. Fill the cooling system.

16. Connect the negative battery cable.

3.2L and 3.5L Engines

1. Before servicing the vehicle, refer to the precautions in the beginning of this section.

2. Disconnect the negative battery cable.

3. Drain the coolant from the engine.

❊❊ WARNING

Do not use pliers to open the plastic drain.

4. Remove the coolant pressure bottle cap and open the thermostat bleed valve.

5. Remove the timing belt using the recommended procedure. It is good practice to turn the crankshaft until the engine is at TDC No. 1 cylinder, compression stroke (firing position). This aligns all the timing marks and serves as a reference point for all the work that follows.

6. Remove the water pump mounting bolts and pump. Discard the O-ring seal.

7. Clean the gasket sealing surfaces. Do not scratch the aluminum surfaces.

To install:

8. Install a new O-ring and wet with clean coolant. Be sure to keep the new O-ring free of any oil or grease.

9. Install the water pump and O-ring to the engine block.

10. Install the retaining bolts and tighten to 105 inch lbs. (12 Nm).

11. Rotate the pump and check for freedom of movement.

12. Install the timing belt using the recommended procedure. Verify that all valve timing marks align. This is very important; an engine out-of-time will be seriously damaged when first started.

13. Be sure that the radiator drain is closed. Open the thermostat bleed valve. Install a ¼ in. (6mm) clear hose about 48 in. (1.2m) long to the end of the bleed valve and the other end into a clean container. The intent is to keep coolant off of the drive belt(s).

14. Slowly refill the coolant pressure bottle until a steady stream of coolant flows out of the thermostat bleed valve. Gently squeeze the upper radiator hose until all of the air is removed from the system.

15. Close the bleed valve and continue to fill up the coolant pressure bottle to the proper level. Install the cap back on the bottle and remove the hose from the bleed valve.

16. Reconnect the negative battery cable. Start the engine and allow to run until normal operating temperature is reached.

17. Check the cooling system for leaks and correct coolant level. Be sure that the thermostat bleed valve is closed once the cooling system has been bled of any trapped air.

3.3L Engines

1. Before servicing the vehicle, refer to the precautions in the beginning of this section.

2. Disconnect the negative battery cable.

3. Drain the coolant from the engine.

✳✳ WARNING

Do not use pliers to open the plastic drain.

4. Remove the coolant pressure bottle cap and open the thermostat bleed valve.

5. Remove the serpentine belt. If necessary, remove the right front lower fender shield.

6. Remove the water pump pulley bolts and pulley.

7. Remove the water pump mounting bolts and pump. Discard the O-ring seal.

8. Clean the gasket sealing surfaces. Do not scratch the aluminum surfaces.

To install:

9. Install a new O-ring into the O-ring groove and the water pump to the timing chain case. Be sure to keep the O-ring free of any oil or grease.

10. Install the retaining bolts and tighten to 105 inch lbs. (12 Nm).

11. Rotate the pump and check for freedom of movement.

12. Install the pump pulley and tighten the bolts to 250 inch lbs. (30 Nm).

13. Install the serpentine belt and right lower fender shield.

14. Be sure that that the radiator drain is closed. Open the thermostat bleed valve. Install a ¼ in. (6mm) diameter clear hose about 48 in. (1.2m) long to the end of the bleed valve and the other end into a clean container. The intent is to keep coolant off the drive belt(s).

15. Slowly refill the coolant pressure bottle until a steady stream of coolant flows out of the thermostat bleed valve. Gently squeeze the upper radiator hose until all of the air is removed from the system.

16. Close the bleed valve and continue to fill the coolant pressure bottle to the

proper level. Install the cap back on the bottle and remove the hose from the bleed valve.

17. Reconnect the negative battery cable. Start the engine and allow to run until normal operating temperature is reached.

18. Check the cooling system for leaks and correct coolant level. Be sure that the thermostat bleed valve is closed once the cooling system has been bled of any trapped air.

Cylinder Head

REMOVAL & INSTALLATION

2.7L Engine

1. Before servicing the vehicle, refer to the precautions in the beginning of this section.

2. Disconnect the negative battery cable.

3. Properly relieve the fuel system pressure.

4. Drain and recycle the engine coolant.

5. Remove the accessory drive belts.

6. Remove the crankshaft damper.

7. Remove the intake plenum, lower intake manifold, and exhaust manifold. Place shop rags in the openings to prevent debris from entering the engine.

8. Remove the valve and timing chain covers.

9. Remove the coolant connections for the cylinder heads.

10. Rotate the crankshaft until the crankshaft timing mark aligns with the timing mark on the oil pump.

11. Remove the primary timing chain.

12. Remove the camshaft bearing caps, gradually, in the reverse order of the tightening sequence.

13. Remove the camshafts from the cylinder heads.

✳✳ WARNING

Be sure the head bolts 9–11 are removed before attempting to remove the cylinder head, the head and/or block may be damaged.

14. Remove the cylinder head bolts in reverse order of installation starting with bolts 11–9, then 8–1.

15. Remove the cylinder head(s).

RIGHT CYLINDER HEAD   **LEFT CYLINDER HEAD**

FRONT

Cylinder head bolt tightening sequence—2.7L engines

7922BG04

FRONT ➤

Camshaft bolt tightening sequence—2.7L engines

7922BG05

To install:

16. Thoroughly clean and dry the mating surfaces of the head and block. Check the cylinder head for cracks, damage or engine coolant leakage. Remove scale, sealing compound and carbon. Clean the oil passages thoroughly.

17. Place a new head gasket on the cylinder block over the locating dowels.

18. Inspect the cylinder head bolts for necking (stretching) by holding a straight-edge against the threads of each bolt. If all of the threads are not contacting the straightedge, the bolt should be replaced. New head bolts are recommended.

❊❊ WARNING

Due to the cylinder head bolt torque method used, it is imperative that the threads of the bolts be inspected for necking (stretching) prior to installation. If the threads are necked down, the bolt should be replaced. Failure to do so may result in parts failure or damage.

19. Lubricate the bolt threads with clean engine oil, then install them.

20. Tighten the head bolts in the sequence as shown, utilizing the following steps and tightening values:

    a. Step 1. Bolts 1–8 to 35 ft. lbs. (48 Nm)

    b. Step 2. Bolts 1–8 to 55 ft. lbs. (75 Nm)

    c. Step 3. Bolts 1–8 to 55 ft. lbs. (75 Nm)

    d. Step 4. Bolts 1–8 plus an additional 90 degree turn. Do not use a torque wrench for this step.

    e. Step 5. Bolts 9–11 to 250 inch lbs. (28 Nm).

21. Install the camshafts, timing chain, and sprockets.

22. Install the water connections to the cylinder head.

23. Install the valve and timing chain covers.

24. Install the crankshaft damper and tighten the center bolt to 125 ft. lbs. (170 Nm)

25. Install the lower intake manifold and intake plenum.

26. Install the exhaust manifolds.

27. Install the accessory drive belts, then fill the cooling system.

28. Connect the negative battery cable.

3.2L and 3.5L Engines

1. Before servicing the vehicle, refer to the precautions in the beginning of this section.

This engine uses aluminum alloy cylinder heads. Use care when working with light alloy components. The heads are common to either cylinder bank, but in practice a cylinder head should be returned to the side of the engine from which it was removed. Removal of a cylinder head involves removal of the timing belt. Great care is required to install the belt, paying attention to all valve timing marks. Please note that camshaft removal on this engine does require the removal of the cylinder head.

2. Release the fuel system pressure using the recommended procedure.

3. Disconnect negative battery cable.

4. Drain the cooling system.

5. Remove the radiator and cooling fan assemblies.

6. Remove the air cleaner assembly and the intake manifold plenum. Cover the lower intake manifold during service.

7. Remove the accessory drive belts.

8. Remove the crankshaft damper using the proper puller.

9. Remove the engine valve covers.

10. Remove the timing belt covers.

11. Mark the timing belt running direction for installation. Align the camshaft sprockets with the marks on the rear covers. Remove the timing belt and tensioner.

12. Pre-load the timing belt tensioner as follows:

    a. Place tensioner in a vise the same way it is mounted on the engine.

    b. Slowly compress the plunger into the tensioner body.

7922BG09

Remove the rear timing belt cover-to-cylinder head bolts, noting the bolt locations—3.2L and 3.5L engines

7922BG10

Right side belt cover, water pump and O-rings—3.2L and 3.5L engines

7922BG11

Correct positioning for the head gaskets—3.2L and 3.5L engines

7922BG12

Cylinder head bolt tightening sequence—3.2L and 3.5L engines

c. When the plunger is compressed into the tensioner body, install a pin through the body and plunger to retain plunger in place until the tensioner is installed.

13. Hold the camshaft sprocket with a 36mm box wrench, loosen and remove the sprocket retaining bolt and washer.

➡ **To remove the camshaft sprocket retainer bolt while the engine is in the vehicle, it may be necessary to raise that side of the engine due to the length of the retainer bolt. The right bolt is 8.370 in. (212.6mm) long, while the left bolt is 10.0 in. (253mm) long. These bolts are not interchangeable and their original location during removal should be noted.**

14. Remove the camshaft sprocket from the camshaft. The camshaft sprockets are not interchangeable from side-to-side.

15. Remove the intake manifold assembly using the recommended procedure.

16. Remove the rear timing belt cover-to-cylinder head fasteners. If the right timing belt cover is to be removed, there are O-rings located behind it for the water pump passages.

17. Remove the cylinder head mounting bolts in the reverse order of the tightening sequence. Remove the cylinder head.

To install:

18. Thoroughly clean and dry the mating surfaces of the head and block.

➡ **When cleaning the cylinder head and block mating surfaces, do not use a metal scraper because the soft aluminum surfaces could be cut or damaged. Instead, use a scraper made of wood or plastic.**

19. Check the cylinder head for cracks, damage or engine coolant leakage. Check the head for flatness. End-to-end, the head should be within 0.002 in. (0.051mm) normally with 0.008 in. (0.203mm) the maximum allowed out of true. The resurface limit is 0.008 in. (0.203mm) maximum, the combined total dimension of stock removal from the cylinder head, if any, and block top surface.

20. Place a new head gasket on the cylinder block locating dowels, being sure the gasket is on the correct side.

21. Inspect the cylinder head bolts for necking (stretching) by holding a straightedge against the threads of each bolt. If all of the threads are not contacting the scale, the bolt should be replaced.

✴✴ WARNING

Due to the cylinder head bolt torque method used, it is imperative that the threads of the bolts be inspected for necking prior to installation. If the threads are necked down, the bolt should be replaced. Failure to do so may result in parts failure or damage. New bolts are always recommended.

22. Install the cylinder head into position on the engine block and over the dowels. Install the cylinder head bolts, lubricating the threads with clean engine oil prior to installation. Tighten the bolts following the proper sequence as listed below:

    a. Step 1—45 ft. lbs. (61 Nm).
    b. Step 2—65 ft. lbs. (88 Nm).
    c. Step 3—again, 65 ft. lbs. (88 Nm).
    d. Step 4—additional ¼ turn.

➡ **Do not use a torque wrench for Step 4. Inspect the bolt torque after tightening. The torque should be over 90 ft. lbs. (122 Nm). If not, replace the cylinder head bolt.**

23. Install the rear timing belt cover bolts and tighten as follows:
- M6 bolts—105 inch lbs. (12 Nm)
- M8 bolts—21 ft. lbs. (28 Nm)
- M10 bolts—40 ft. lbs. (54 Nm)

24. Install the intake manifold assembly and tighten the bolts following the proper sequence to 21 ft. lbs. (28 Nm).

➡ **The following procedure can only be used when the camshaft sprockets have been loosened or removed from the shafts.**

25. When the camshaft sprockets are loosened or removed, the camshafts must be timed to the engine. Install the Camshaft Alignment Tools 6642-A or exact equivalent, to the rear of the cylinder heads.

26. Install both camshaft sprockets to the appropriate shafts. The left camshaft sprocket has the DIS pick-up as part of the sprocket.

27. Apply thread locking compound to the threads of the camshaft sprocket retainer bolts and install to the appropriate shafts. The right bolt is 8.380 in. (21.3cm) long, while the left bolt is 10.0 in. (25.4cm) long. These bolts are not interchangeable. Do not tighten the bolts at this time. The camshaft marks should be positioned between the marks on the cover.

28. Place the crankshaft sprocket to the TDC mark on the oil pump housing. Install the timing belt starting at the crankshaft sprocket and working in a counterclockwise direction.

29. After the belt is installed around the last sprocket keep tension on the belt until it is past the tensioner pulley.

30. Holding the tensioner pulley against the belt, install the tensioner housing and tighten to 21 ft. lbs. (28 Nm).

31. When the tensioner is in place pull the retainer pin to allow the tensioner to extend to the pulley bracket.

32. Install a dial indicator in the spark plug hole of the No. 1 cylinder to check Top Dead Center (TDC) of the piston. Rotate the crankshaft until the piston is exactly at TDC.

33. Hold the right camshaft sprocket hex with a 36mm box wrench and tighten the right camshaft sprocket bolt to 75 ft. lbs. (102 Nm). Turn the sprocket bolt an additional 90 degrees.

34. Hold the left camshaft sprocket hex

with a 36mm box wrench and tighten the left camshaft sprocket bolt to 85 ft. lbs. (115 Nm). Turn the sprocket bolt an additional 90 degrees.

35. Remove the dial indicator.

36. Remove the camshaft alignment tools from the back of the cylinder heads and install the cam covers and new O-rings. Tighten the fasteners to 20 ft. lbs. (27 Nm). Repeat this procedure on the other camshaft.

37. Install the timing belt covers and crankshaft damper. Tighten the crankshaft damper bolt to 85 ft. lbs. (115 Nm).

38. Install the valve covers and tighten bolts to 105 inch lbs. (12 Nm).

39. Install the spark plug tube nut and O-ring. Tighten the nut to 60 inch lbs. (7 Nm). Install spark plugs and tighten to 20 ft. lbs. (28 Nm).

40. Install the air conditioning compressor to the mounting bracket. Tighten the mounting bracket bolts to 30 ft. lbs. (41 Nm).

41. Reconnect the spark plug wires to the correct spark plugs.

42. Install the accessory drive belts. Adjust to the proper tension.

43. Install the intake manifold plenum using the recommended procedure.

44. Install the air cleaner assembly.

45. Install the radiator and cooling fan assemblies.

46. Check to be sure that all hoses, wiring connectors, cables, fluid and vacuum lines are reconnected.

47. Change the engine oil and oil filter.

48. Refill and bleed the cooling system.

49. Reconnect the negative battery cable, run the vehicle with the radiator cap off so coolant can be added as required until the thermostat opens. Watch for leaks and for unusual engine noises. Fill the radiator completely as required.

50. Once the vehicle has cooled, recheck the coolant and oil level.

3.3L Engines

1. Before servicing the vehicle, refer to the precautions in the beginning of this section.

The cylinder heads on this engine are aluminum alloy, retained by nine bolts. Valve seats and guides are inserts. Use care when handling alloy parts. In addition, the cylinder head bolts are torque-to-yield type which stretch during the torque process. Head bolts must be checked carefully before reuse. New head bolts are recommended.

2. Release the fuel system pressure using the recommended procedure.

3. Disconnect negative battery cable.

4. Drain the cooling system.

5. Remove the intake manifold and throttle body assemblies using the recommended procedure. Use care when handling the intake manifold gasket. It is made of very thin metal and could cause cuts if carelessly handled.

6. Disconnect the coil wires, sending unit wire, heater hoses and bypass hose.

7. Remove the evaporation control system, closed ventilation system and the cylinder head covers.

8. Remove the exhaust manifold(s) from the engine.

When installing the end gasket, the markings on the gasket must be seen—3.3L engine

When reusing them, inspect the cylinder head bolts for necking (stretching). You can see a difference in these bolts—all models

Cylinder head bolt tightening sequence—3.3L engine

9. Remove rocker arm and shaft assemblies. Remove the pushrods and identify to assure installation in their original locations.

10. Loosen and remove the nine head bolts in the reverse order of the tightening sequence from the cylinder head.

11. Lift the head off the cylinder block.

To install:

12. Thoroughly clean and dry the mating surfaces of the head and block. Check the cylinder head for cracks, damage or engine coolant leakage. Remove scale, sealing compound and carbon. Clean the oil passages thoroughly. Check the head for flatness. End-to-end, the head should be within 0.002 in. (0.051mm) normally with 0.008 in. (0.203mm) the maximum allowed out of true. The total thickness allowed to be removed from the head and block is 0.008 in. (0.203mm) maximum.

13. Place a new head gasket on the cylinder block with the identification marks facing upward. Do not use sealer on factory type gaskets.

14. Inspect the cylinder head bolts for necking (stretching) by holding a straightedge against the threads of each bolt. If all of the threads are not contacting the straightedge, the bolt should be replaced. New head bolts are recommended.

✳✳ WARNING

Due to the cylinder head bolt torque method used, it is imperative that the threads of the bolts be inspected for necking (stretching) prior to installation. If the threads are necked down, the bolt should be replaced. Failure to do so may result in parts failure or damage.

15. Install the cylinder head bolts. Tighten bolts Nos. 1 through 8 following the proper sequence as listed below:

    a. Step 1—45 ft. lbs. (61 Nm)
    b. Step 2—65 ft. lbs. (88 Nm)
    c. Step 3— (again) 65 ft. lbs. (88 Nm)
    d. Step 4—additional ¼ -turn

➡**Do not use a torque wrench for Step 4. Inspect the bolt torque after tightening. The torque should be over 90 ft. lbs. (122 Nm). If not, replace the cylinder head bolt.**

16. Tighten bolt No. 9 to 25 ft. lbs. (33 Nm) only after bolts 1–8 have been tightened to specification.

17. Inspect the pushrods and replace worn or bent rods. Install the pushrods,

rocker arm and shaft assemblies with the stamped steel retainers in the forward positions. Tighten the rocker shaft retainers to 250 inch lbs. (28 Nm).

➡**The rocker arm shaft should be tightened down slowly, starting with the centermost bolts. Allow 20 minutes tappet bleed down time after installation of the rocker shafts before engine operation.**

18. Install the cylinder head covers with new gaskets in place. Tighten the retainers to 105 inch lbs. (12 Nm).

✳✳ CAUTION

The factory type intake manifold gasket is made of very thin metal and is very sharp. Handle with care or personal injury may occur.

19. Using all new gaskets, install the intake manifold, throttle body, air intake plenum and exhaust manifold, using the recommended procedure and following the proper torque sequences.

20. Connect all exhaust and fuel connections.

21. Reconnect the coil wires, sending unit wire, heater hoses and bypass hose.

22. Install the air intake hose.

23. Change the engine oil and oil filter.

24. Refill and bleed the cooling system.

25. Reconnect the negative battery cable and run the vehicle with the radiator cap off so coolant can be added as required until the thermostat opens. Watch for leaks and unusual engine noises that might indicate a problem. Fill the radiator completely.

26. Once the vehicle has cooled, recheck the coolant and oil level.

Rocker Arm/Shafts

REMOVAL & INSTALLATION

2.7L Engines

1. Before servicing the vehicle, refer to the precautions in the beginning of this section.

2. Disconnect the negative battery cable.

3. Remove the valve covers.

4. Position the camshaft so that the base circle (heel) is facing the rocker arm being serviced.

✳✳ WARNING

Depress the valve spring only enough to remove the rocker arm or damage to the spring may result.

5. Using Valve Spring tool 8215 and Adapter 8216, or their equivalent, depress the valve spring enough to release the tension on the rocker arm.

SPECIAL TOOL 8215

ADAPTOR 8216

7922BG59

Only depress the valve spring enough to remove the rocker arm—2.7L engine

For engine torque specifications, refer to Section 1 of this manual

6. If the rocker arms are to be reused, identify their positions for reassembly in their original positions.

7. Repeat this procedure for each rocker arm being removed.

To install:

8. Lubricate the rocker arms with clean engine oil, prior to installation.

9. Position the camshaft so that the base circle (heel) is facing the rocker arm being installed.

✳✳ WARNING

Depress the valve spring only enough to install the rocker arm or damage to the spring may result.

10. Using Valve Spring tool 8215 and Adapter 8216, or their equivalent, depress the valve spring enough to install the rocker arm.

11. Install the rocker arm in the original position (if reused) over the valve and lash adjuster.

➡**Inspect the rocker arm for proper engagement into the lash adjuster and valve tip.**

12. Release the tension on the valve spring and remove the tools.

13. Install the valve covers.

14. Connect the negative battery cable.

3.2L and 3.5L Engines

1. Before servicing the vehicle, refer to the precautions in the beginning of this section.

2. Disconnect the negative battery cable.

3. Relieve the fuel system pressure.

4. Remove the air cleaner assembly and the intake manifold plenum. Cover the lower intake manifold during service.

5. Remove the cylinder head covers.

6. Remove the rocker arm assembly mounting bolts and remove the assembly from the engine.

7. Inspect the rocker arms for wear or damage. Inspect the roller for scuffing or wear. Replace assembly as necessary.

➡**Do not remove the lash adjusters from the rocker arm assembly. The rocker arm and the adjuster are serviced as an assembly.**

8. Identify the rocker arm assemblies and rocker arms and disassemble the shaft as follows:

a. Thread a nut, washer and spacer onto a 4mm screw.

b. Insert and tighten the 4mm screw into the dowel pin on the shaft.

c. Loosen the nut on the screw. This will pull the dowel pin from the shaft support.

d. Remove the rocker arms and pedestals, keeping them in order.

e. Check the oil holes for restrictions with a small wire and clean as required.

To install:

9. Assemble the rocker shaft as follows:

a. Install the rocker arms and pedestals onto the shaft, keeping them in the original order.

b. Press the dowel pins into the pedestals until they bottom out in the pedestals.

10. Position the camshaft so that the timing mark on the right camshaft timing belt

sprocket aligns with the timing mark on the rear timing belt cover and the timing mark on the left sprocket is 45 degrees from the mark on the rear timing belt cover. There will be no load on the shaft during installation. Install the rocker shafts so the identification marks are facing toward the front of the engine.

11. Install the oil feed bolt in the correct location on the rocker shaft retainer. Tighten the bolts in proper sequence to 23 ft. lbs. (31 Nm).

12. Install the valve covers and tighten bolts to 105 inch lbs. (12 Nm).

Left bank rocker arm and shaft identification—3.2L and 3.5L engines

Remove the dowel pin using a 4mm screw, nut, spacer and washer installed into the pin—3.2L and 3.5L engines

RIGHT SIDE SHOWN

LEFT SIDE SHOWN

Proper torque sequence for the rocker arm and shaft assemblies—3.2L and 3.5L engines

13. Install the intake manifold plenum and the air cleaner assembly.

14. Reconnect the negative battery cable.

3.3L Engines

1. Before servicing the vehicle, refer to the precautions in the beginning of this section.

2. Disconnect negative battery cable.

3. Relieve the fuel system pressure.

4. Remove the upper intake manifold assembly.

5. Disconnect and label the spark plug wires from the plugs. Remove by first twisting, then pulling on the boot, in line with the spark plug.

6. Disconnect the closed crankcase ventilation system and the evaporative control system from the cylinder head cover.

7. Remove the cylinder head cover and gasket from the engine.

8. Remove the four rocker shaft bolts and retainers. Remove the rocker arms and shafts from the engine.

9. Inspect the rocker arm and components for wear or damage and replace as required. If the rocker shaft is disassembled for cleaning or replacement, be sure to install the components in their original locations.

To install:

10. Install the rocker arms and shaft assemblies with the stamped steel retainers in the four positions. Tighten the retainer bolts slowly to 21 ft. lbs. (28 Nm), in three even steps starting at the centermost bolts and working outward.

❋❋ WARNING

After installation, allow the tappets to bleed down for 20 minutes before operating the engine or damage to the valves may occur.

11. Clean the mating surfaces of the cylinder head cover gasket. Inspect the cylinder head cover and straighten out if distorted.

12. Install the cylinder head cover with new gasket in place. Tighten the fasteners to 105 inch lbs. (12 Nm).

13. Reconnect the closed crankcase ventilation system and the evaporative control system.

14. Reconnect the spark plug wires making sure that each wire is connected to the correct spark plug.

15. Install the upper intake manifold assembly and reconnect the negative battery cable.

Intake Manifold

REMOVAL & INSTALLATION

2.7L and 3.3L Engines

1. Before servicing the vehicle, refer to the precautions in the beginning of this section.

2. Disconnect the negative battery cable.

3. Remove the fuel filler cap. Release the fuel system pressure using the recommended procedure.

4. Drain the cooling system.

5. Disconnect the air tube from the air cleaner and the throttle body.

6. Hold the throttle lever in the wide-open position and remove the throttle cable and the speed control cable from the lever. Compress the locking tabs on the cables and remove them from the mounting brackets.

7. Unplug the electrical connector from the solenoid on the EGR valve transducer, Manifold Absolute Pressure (MAP) sensor, Throttle Position (TP) sensor and the Idle Air Control (IAC) motor.

8. Disconnect the vacuum hose from the PCV valve as well as the power brake booster at the intake manifold nipple. Disconnect the vacuum line at the fuel pressure regulator.

9. Disconnect the purge hose from the throttle body.

10. Unplug the electrical harnesses from the TP sensor and the IAC motor.

11. Remove the EGR tube mounting screws at the intake manifold plenum.

12. Remove the intake manifold plenum (upper part of the manifold) mounting bolts and remove the plenum from the engine. Cover the lower part of the intake manifold to prevent foreign material from entering the engine.

13. Disconnect the fuel supply and return tubes to the fuel rail at the rear of the intake manifold by pushing the quick-connect fitting toward the fuel tube while depressing the built-in disconnect tool with Quick-Connect Fitting Tool 6751. To disconnect the fitting from the fuel rail, slightly twist the fitting while maintaining downward pressure on tool 6751. Wrap shop towels around the fuel hoses to absorb any fuel spillage.

14. Cover the fuel line openings to prevent system contamination.

15. Remove the screw from the fuel clamp and separate the fuel tubes from the bracket.

16. Tag each connector for identification, then disconnect the electrical harness from the injectors and turn toward the center of the engine.

17. Remove the fuel rail mounting bolts and lift the fuel rail with the injectors attached straight up and off the engine. Cover the injector openings.

18. On the 3.3L engine, remove the upper radiator hose, heater hose and the rear intake manifold hose.

19. Remove the intake manifold bolts and the manifold from the engine.

20. Remove the intake manifold seal retainer screws and the intake manifold gasket. Clean all mating surfaces.

21. Inspect the manifold for damage, cracks or clogged passages. Repair, clean or replace the manifold as required.

To install:

22. Verify that all intake manifold and cylinder head sealing surfaces are clean. Place a drop of sealant onto each of the four corners of the intake manifold gasket, where the cylinder head meets the engine block. On the 3.3L engine, carefully install the intake manifold gasket and tighten the end seal retainers to 105 inch lbs. (12 Nm).

➡**The intake manifold gasket is made of very thin metal and can cause cuts if handled carelessly.**

23. Install the intake manifold and eight mounting bolts. Snug down evenly to just 10 inch lbs. (1.1 Nm).

24. On the 3.3L engine, tighten the lower intake manifold bolts in the proper

Loosening and tightening sequence for the intake manifold bolts—2.7L engine

7922BG19

For complete mechanical specifications, refer to Section 1 of this manual

sequence to 16 ft. lbs. (22 Nm). Once all bolts are tightened, repeat the sequence again tightening the bolts to 16 ft. lbs. (22 Nm). Inspect to be sure all seals are still in place.

25. On the 2.7L engine, tighten the lower intake manifold bolts in the proper sequence to 105 inch lbs. (12 Nm).

26. Apply a light coat of clean engine oil to the O-ring on the nozzle end of each injector.

27. Insert the fuel injector nozzles into the openings in the intake manifold. Seat the injectors in place and install the fuel rail mounting bolts, tightening to 16 ft. lbs. (22 Nm).

28. Attach the electrical connectors to each fuel injector. Rotate the injectors toward the cylinder head covers.

29. Reconnect the fuel supply and return tubes to the fuel rail. Be sure that the black plastic release ring to the quick-connect fitting is in the OUT position. Place special tool 6751 under the largest diameter of the quick-connect fitting.

30. Pull tool 6751 toward the fuel rail until the quick-connect fitting clicks into place. Place the special tool between the shoulder of the built-in disconnect tool and top of the quick-connect fitting, then inspect the security of the fitting by applying a slight downward force against the fitting. It should be locked in place.

31. Install the intake plenum with new

Tightening sequence for the intake plenum—2.7L engine

Loosening and tightening sequence for the intake manifold bolts—3.3L engine

Tightening sequence for the intake plenum—3.3L engine

gasket onto the intake manifold. Loosely install the mounting bolts.

32. Install the EGR tube to the manifold with a new gasket in place. Loosely install the mounting screws.

33. On the 3.3L engine, tighten the intake manifold plenum mounting bolts to 21 ft. lbs. (28 Nm) following the outlined sequence.

34. On the 2.7L engine, tighten the intake manifold plenum mounting bolts to

105 inch lbs. (12 Nm) following the out-lined sequence.

35. On the 2.7L engine, install the left and right support brackets to the manifold. Tighten the lower fasteners to 50 inch lbs. (6 Nm) and the upper fasteners to 105 inch lbs. (12 Nm).

36. Tighten the EGR tube mounting bolts.

37. Reconnect the PCV valve hose and power brake booster hose.

38. Attach the electrical connectors to the EGR transducer solenoid, idle air control motor, MAP and TP sensors.

39. Install the throttle cable and speed control cable to the mounting bracket and connect to the throttle body lever while holding lever in the wide-open position.

40. Reconnect the purge hose to the throttle body. Reconnect the air tube to the air cleaner and the throttle body.

41. Drain and replace the engine oil and oil filter.

42. Reconnect the negative battery cable. Refill the cooling system. Run the vehicle with the radiator cap removed until the thermostat opens, adding coolant as required. Watch for fuel and coolant leaks and for correct engine operation.

43. Once the vehicle has cooled, recheck the coolant level and add, if necessary.

3.2L and 3.5L Engines

1. Before servicing the vehicle, refer to the precautions in the beginning of this section.

2. Disconnect negative battery cable.

3. Remove the fuel filler cap. Release the fuel system pressure using the recommended procedure.

4. Drain the cooling system.

5. Remove the engine cover from the top of the intake manifold.

6. Remove the accelerator and the speed control cable from the throttle lever.

7. Unplug the electrical connector from the Idle Air Control (IAC) motor, Intake Air Temperature (IAT) sensor and the Manifold Absolute Pressure (MAP) sensor.

8. Remove the ground screw from the intake manifold. Unplug the electrical connector to the throttle position sensor.

9. Disconnect the vacuum hoses from the manifold tuning valve, PCV make-up air hose, IAC motor supply hose and the purge hose from the throttle bodies.

10. Disconnect the brake booster hose, PCV hose and the remaining vacuum hoses from the intake manifold. If required, label for proper installation.

11. Remove the mounting bolts for the EGR tube at the intake manifold plenum.

12. Remove the plenum support bracket mounting bolts on each side of the plenum. Remove the intake plenum mounting bolts.

➡ **The intake manifold plenum (upper half of the intake manifold assembly) uses two different length bolts. Take note of their position and be sure they are installed in the same location during installation.**

13. Remove the intake manifold plenum from the intake manifold. Discard the old gasket. Cover the intake manifold openings with tape to keep debris from entering the engine.

14. Remove the upper radiator hose from the thermostat housing and the heater hose from the rear of the intake manifold.

15. Remove the lower intake manifold retaining bolts and the manifold from the engine. Clean all gasket mating surfaces and inspect for distortion with a good straightedge.

To install:

16. Verify that all intake manifold and cylinder head sealing surfaces are clean. Carefully install the intake manifold gasket, then the lower manifold. Tighten the bolts in the proper sequence to 250 inch lbs. (28 Nm).

17. Reconnect the upper radiator hose to the thermostat housing and the heater hose to the rear of the intake manifold.

18. Ensure the ignition cables are routed out of the way of the intake plenum. Install the intake manifold plenum with a new gasket in place and tighten in sequence to 250 inch lbs. (28 Nm).

Note the positions of the four plenum bolts (they are two different sizes)—1996–97 3.5L engines

Upper intake manifold tightening and loosening sequence—1998–00 3.2L and 3.5L engines

Loosening and tightening sequence for the lower manifold bolts—3.2L and 3.5L engines

19. Install the intake manifold plenum with a new gasket in place. Tighten the mounting bolts, working from the center outward, to 250 inch lbs. (28 Nm). Do not overtighten bolts when working with light alloys.

20. Install and tighten the support bracket bolts.

21. Reconnect the electrical connectors to the MAP sensor, TP sensor, IAC motor and IAT sensor.

22. Reconnect the vacuum hose to the manifold tuning valve.

23. Install the EGR tube. Tighten the EGR tube-to-intake manifold plenum screws to 200 inch lbs. (22 Nm). Be sure that the insulation on the EGR tube aligns with and contacts the insulation on the vacuum harness at the rear of the engine. Rotate the throttle lever to the wide-open position and reconnect the speed control and throttle cables.

Please refer to Section 9 for electric cooling fan wiring schematics

24. Reconnect the PCV valve hose. Install the air cleaner plenum and reconnect the plenum hose.

25. Reconnect the ground wire to the intake manifold plenum. Reconnect the brake booster hose to the fitting on the intake manifold plenum.

26. Reconnect the throttle body purge tubes.

27. Install the cover on the intake manifold plenum.

28. Reconnect the negative battery cable. Fill and bleed the cooling system.

29. Raise and safely support the vehicle. Change the engine oil and filter.

30. Test run the engine, check for fuel and coolant leaks and verify correct engine operation.

Exhaust Manifold

REMOVAL & INSTALLATION

2.7L Engine

RIGHT MANIFOLD

1. Before servicing the vehicle, refer to the precautions in the beginning of this section.

2. Disconnect the negative battery cable.

3. Remove the air intake plenum and the air filter housing.

4. Remove the bolt holding the battery cable housing tube to the transaxle.

5. Remove the EGR valve and tube from the vehicle.

6. Disconnect the Oxygen (O2S) sensor wiring harness and remove.

7. Loosen and remove the V-band clamp from the manifold.

➡ **Do not reuse the V-band clamps.**

8. Remove the heat shield, then the manifold retaining bolts and remove the manifold.

9. Remove all traces of the old manifold gasket and clean both gasket mating surfaces.

To install:

10. Install the exhaust manifold and new gasket. Tighten the bolts to 200 inch lbs. (23 Nm) working from the center outward.

11. Install the heat shields and tighten the mounting bolts to 105 inch lbs. (12 Nm).

12. Install the new V-band clamp and tighten to 100 inch lbs. (11.3 Nm).

13. Install the O2S sensor and connect its wiring harness.

14. Install the EGR valve and tube, using new gaskets, then tighten to 95 inch lbs. (11 Nm).

15. Attach the battery cable tube to the transaxle and tighten the bolt to 75 ft. lbs. (101 Nm).

16. Connect the air inlet plenum and install the air filter housing.

17. Connect the negative battery cable.

LEFT MANIFOLD

1. Before servicing the vehicle, refer to the precautions in the beginning of this section.

2. Disconnect the negative battery cable.

3. Raise and safely support the vehicle.

4. Remove the exhaust system, then the V-band clamps and left catalytic converter.

➡ **Do not reuse the V-band clamps.**

5. Loosen and rotate the transaxle dipstick tube out of the way.

6. Lower the vehicle.

7. Remove the engine wiring harness support bracket from the cylinder head.

8. Disconnect the Oxygen (O2S) sensor wiring harness, then remove it from the manifold.

9. Remove the engine oil dipstick tube and the manifold heat shield.

10. Remove the manifold mounting bolts, then remove the manifold from the vehicle.

To install:

11. Remove all traces of the old manifold gasket and clean both gasket mating surfaces.

12. Install the exhaust manifold and new gasket. Tighten the bolts to 200 inch lbs. (23 Nm) working from the center outward.

13. Install the heat shields and tighten the mounting bolts to 105 inch lbs. (12 Nm).

14. Install the O2S sensor and connect its wiring harness.

15. Raise and safely support the vehicle.

16. Reposition the transaxle dipstick tube.

17. Replace the O-ring for the engine oil dipstick tube and install the tube.

18. Install the catalytic converter, then the new V-band clamp and tighten to 100 inch lbs. (10 Nm).

19. Install the engine wiring harness support bracket to the cylinder head.

20. Install the exhaust system, then lower the vehicle.

21. Connect the negative battery cable.

3.2L and 3.5L Engines

1. Before servicing the vehicle, refer to the precautions in the beginning of this section.

2. Disconnect the negative battery cable. Raise and safely support the vehicle.

3. Disconnect the exhaust pipes from the exhaust manifold.

4. Disconnect the Heated Oxygen (HO2S) sensor electrical wiring.

5. Lower the vehicle and remove the screws attaching the heat shield to the exhaust manifold.

6. Remove the manifold attaching bolts, then remove the manifold from the cylinder head.

7. Inspect the manifold for damage or cracks. Check for distortion against a straightedge or thickness gauge. Replace manifold if required.

8. Remove all traces of the old manifold gasket and clean both gasket mating surfaces.

To install:

9. Install the new manifold gasket and exhaust manifold to the cylinder head. Install the retainer bolts and tighten to 15 ft. lbs. (20 Nm).

10. Raise and safely support the vehicle.

11. Reconnect the exhaust pipe to the exhaust manifold and tighten the nuts to 21 ft. lbs. (28 Nm).

12. Lower the vehicle. Install the heat shield to the manifold and tighten the retaining screws to 11 ft. lbs. (15 Nm).

13. Reattach the electrical wiring on the HO2S sensor.

14. Connect the negative battery cable. Operate the vehicle and inspect for exhaust leaks.

3.3L Engines

1. Before servicing the vehicle, refer to the precautions in the beginning of this section.

2. Disconnect the negative battery cable.

3. Raise and safely support the vehicle. Disconnect the exhaust pipe from the exhaust manifold.

4. Disconnect the Heated Oxygen (HO2S) sensor lead wire and remove the EGR tube from the exhaust manifold.

5. Remove the screws attaching the heat shield to the exhaust manifold. Lower the vehicle, if necessary.

6. Remove the manifold attaching bolts and remove the manifold from the cylinder head.

7. These manifolds are thin-wall designs to save weight. Inspect the manifold carefully for cracks or other damage. Check for distortion against a straightedge or thickness gauge. Replace the manifold if required.

8. Remove all traces of the old manifold gasket and clean both gasket mating surfaces.

To install:

9. Install the exhaust manifold and a new manifold gasket to the cylinder head. Install the retainer bolts and tighten to 17 ft. lbs. (23 Nm).

10. Reconnect the exhaust pipe to the exhaust manifold and tighten the nuts to 21 ft. lbs. (28 Nm).

11. Install the EGR tube back onto the manifold.

12. Install the heat shield to the manifold. Lower the vehicle, if necessary.

13. Attach the electrical connector at the HO2S sensor.

14. Reconnect the negative battery cable. Operate the vehicle and inspect for exhaust leaks.

Front Crankshaft Seal

➤**The front crankshaft seal procedures are for timing belt equipped engines only. For engines which utilize timing chains, please refer to the applicable procedure later in this section.**

REMOVAL & INSTALLATION

3.2L and 3.5L Engines

Note that the timing belt must be removed from the vehicle to perform this service. Use care to be sure all valve timing marks are carefully aligned both before removing the belt and after belt installation and all service has been completed. It may be good practice to set the engine to TDC No. 1 cylinder compression stroke (firing position) and aligning all timing marks before removing the timing belt. This serves as a reference for all work that follows.

1. Before servicing the vehicle, refer to the precautions in the beginning of this section.

2. Disconnect negative battery cable.

3. Release the fuel system pressure using the recommended procedure.

4. Remove the radiator and cooling fan module assembly.

5. Remove the accessory drive belts.

6. Hold the crankshaft from turning and remove the crankshaft damper bolt. Use a balancer puller and remove the crankshaft damper.

7. Remove the stamped steel timing belt front cover.

➤**The sealer on the timing belt front cover may be reusable and should not be removed. Use silicone rubber adhe-**

Removing the timing belt sprocket dowel pin on the crankshaft—3.2L and 3.5L engines

sive sealant to replace any missing sealer.

8. Remove the timing belt and tensioner using the recommended procedure, located in the unit repair section in the front of this manual.

9. Remove the timing belt sprocket at the crankshaft using puller L-4407A or an equivalent puller.

10. Locate the small dowel pin in the crankshaft. With a small punch, carefully tap out the dowel from the end of the crankshaft.

11. Remove the crankshaft seal using tool 6341A or an equivalent seal puller, taking care not to nick the shaft seal surface or seal bore during removal.

To install:

12. Inspect the crankshaft seal lip surface for varnish and dirt. Polish the area using 400 grit sand paper to remove varnish as necessary.

13. Install the crankshaft seal using Seal Installer tool 6342 or equivalent seal driver.

14. Install the rear lower timing belt cover.

15. Install the dowel into the crankshaft so that it protrudes 0.047 in. (1.2mm).

16. Install the timing belt sprocket at the crankshaft using tool C-4685C1, thrust bearing, washer and 12mm bolt or an equivalent setup to pull the sprocket onto crankshaft. Do not hammer on the sprocket.

17. Verify that all valve timing marks are aligned.

18. Install the timing belt and tensioner using the recommended procedure.

19. Rotate the crankshaft two complete turns and recheck the timing marks on the camshafts and crankshaft. The marks must line up with their respective locations. If the marks do not line up, repeat the timing belt installation procedure. When correct valve timing has been verified, install the timing belt covers.

Installing the crankshaft oil seal—3.2L and 3.5L engines

20. Install the crankshaft damper. Hold the crankshaft damper using tool L-3281 or equivalent and tighten the crankshaft bolt to 85 ft. lbs. (115 Nm).

21. Install the accessory drive belts and adjust to the proper tension.

22. Install the radiator and cooling fan assemblies.

23. Refill and bleed the cooling system.

24. Connect the negative battery cable.

Camshaft and Valve Lifters

REMOVAL & INSTALLATION

2.7L Engine

1. Before servicing the vehicle, refer to the precautions in the beginning of this section.

❋❋ CAUTION

When the timing chain is removed and the cylinder heads are installed, DO NOT turn the crankshaft or camshaft without first locating the proper crankshaft position. Failure to do so will result in piston-to-valve contact.

2. Remove the primary timing chain.

3. Remove the second chain tensioner mounting bolts.

Camshaft bearing cap tightening sequence—2.7L engine

4. Slowly loosen the camshaft bearing cap retaining bolts in the reverse order of the tightening sequence.

5. Remove the bearing caps.

6. Remove the camshafts, secondary chain, and tensioner as an assembly.

TENSIONER BODY

GASKET

CHECK BALL ASSEMBLY

SPRING

LOWER CHAIN GUIDE FACE

THIS SIDE TOWARDS FRONT OF ENGINE

FRONT

7922BG61

Exploded view of the camshaft (secondary) chain tensioner, early build—2.7L engine

PLATED CHAIN LINKS

CAMSHAFT TIMING MARKS

7922BG63

Proper camshaft (secondary) chain alignment—2.7L engine

LOCK PIN

7922BG62

Fabricate a lockpin, as shown, to keep the tensioner compressed—2.7L engine

7. Remove the tensioner and chain from the crankshaft.

To install:

8. Assemble the chain on the camshafts. Ensure the plated links are facing toward the front. Align the plated links to the dots on the camshaft sprockets.

➡There are two different styles of camshaft (secondary) chain tensioners. The Early Build tensioners will separate into subcomponents, the Later Build tensioners will not. Compress the camshaft (secondary) chain as follows:

9. For Early Build vehicles,

a. Separate the tensioner cylinder from the tensioner housing.

b. Carefully drain the oil from the housing using care not to remove the internal tensioner components.

c. Assemble the tensioner housing as shown.

d. Using hand pressure, compress and lock the tensioner using a fabricated lockpin.

10. For Late Build vehicles,

a. Place the tensioner in a soft-jawed vise.

b. Slowly compress the tensioner until the fabricated lockpin can be installed.

c. Remove the compressed and locked tensioner from the vise.

11. Insert the compressed and locked camshaft chain tensioner in between the camshafts and chain.

12. Position the camshafts so that the plated links and dots are facing 12 o'clock.

13. Install the cams to the cylinder head. Ensure that the rocker arms are correctly seated and in proper positions.

14. Install the camshaft bearing caps in their original positions.

15. Tighten the camshaft bearing cap retaining bolts gradually in sequence, as shown, to 105 inch lbs. (12 Nm).

16. Install the secondary chain tensioner bolts and tighten to 105 inch lbs. (12 Nm).

17. Remove the lockpin from the secondary chain tensioner.

18. Install the primary timing chain.

19. Connect the negative battery cable.

3.2L and 3.5L Engines

1. Before servicing the vehicle, refer to the precautions in the beginning of this section.

Camshafts are serviced from the rear of the cylinder head. Although the engine does not need to be removed for camshaft service, the cylinder head must be removed from the vehicle. Note too, that the camshaft sprockets have a D-shaped hole that allows it to rotate several degrees in each direction on its shaft. When cam sprockets are loosened or removed, the camshafts must be timed to the engine to ensure proper performance of the engine.

2. Disconnect the negative battery cable.

3. Release the fuel system pressure. Drain the cooling system.

4. Remove the radiator/cooling fan assemblies and the accessory drive belts.

5. Remove the crankshaft damper and the timing belt covers.

6. Mark the timing belt rotation direction for installation. Align the timing belt sprockets with marks on the rear timing belt covers before removing the timing belt.

7. Remove the timing belt tensioner and timing belt.

8. Remove the timing belt sprockets at each camshaft.

9. Remove the intake manifold assembly using the recommended procedure.

10. Separate the exhaust manifold from the cylinder head assembly. Be sure to clean the gasket mating surfaces between the exhaust manifold and the cylinder head.

11. The rear timing belt cover must be

removed to remove the cylinder heads. Remove the rear timing belt cover-to-cylinder head bolts. Remove the rear timing belt covers.

➡**The right-hand side timing belt cover has O-rings located behind it for the water pump passages.**

12. Remove the cylinder head bolts and remove the cylinder head from the engine.

13. Mark the rocker arm assembly to note component locations prior to disassembly. Remove the rocker arm and shaft assemblies from the cylinder head.

14. Remove the rear camshaft cover and O-ring from the head.

15. Carefully remove the camshaft from the rear of the head taking care not to nick or scratch the journals.

16. Inspect camshaft journals for wear or damage. If wear is present, inspect the cylinder head for damage. Inspect the head oil holes for clogging. Replace the camshaft as required.

17. Measure the height of the cam using a micrometer. Measure in two places: the unworn area and in the wear zone. Subtract the figures to get cam wear. The standard specification is 0.001 in. (0.0254mm) with the wear limit being 0.010 in. (0.254mm). Replace the camshaft if it is worn beyond this specification.

To install:

18. Lubricate the camshaft journals and lobes with clean engine oil. Install the camshaft into the cylinder head.

19. Install the camshaft cover and O-ring to the head and tighten to 21 ft. lbs. (28 Nm).

20. Install the rocker arm assemblies in their original locations.

21. Install the cylinder head assembly to the engine block. New head bolts are recommended.

22. Install the rear timing belt covers and tighten the rear cover-to-cylinder head bolts.

23. Install the timing belt sprocket, timing belt and timing belt tensioner using the recommended procedure. Be sure that once they are all installed, the timing of the camshaft(s) is accurate.

24. Install the exhaust manifold, with a new manifold gasket, to the cylinder head.

25. Install the intake manifold assembly using the recommended procedure.

26. Install the timing belt covers and crankshaft damper. Install the accessory drive belts and set them to the proper tension.

27. Install the radiator and cooling fan assembly.

28. Refill and bleed the cooling system. An oil and filter change is recommended.

29. Reconnect the negative battery cable.

3.3L Engines

1. Before servicing the vehicle, refer to the precautions in the beginning of this section.

➡**To remove and replace the camshaft on this engine, the engine assembly must be removed from the vehicle.**

2. Disconnect the battery negative cable.

3. Raise and safely support the vehicle. Drain the engine oil and remove the oil filter.

4. Relieve the fuel system pressure using the recommended procedure.

5. Remove the radiator and cooling fan assemblies.

6. Remove the engine from the vehicle using the recommended procedure.

7. With the engine removed from the vehicle, remove the cylinder head covers, rocker arm and rocker arm shaft assemblies.

8. Remove the intake manifold assembly and cylinder heads from the engine.

9. Remove the harmonic balancer. Remove the timing chain case cover and timing chain from the engine.

10. Remove the pushrods and tappets. If any valvetrain components are to be reused, identify each part and its location so each can be installed in its original location.

➡**If the camshaft is being removed to replace it with a new one, new valve lifters MUST be installed. Installing used lifters on a new camshaft will quickly cause the camshaft to fail.**

11. Remove the camshaft thrust plate. Install a long bolt into the front of the camshaft to act as a handle and aid in removal. Remove the camshaft being careful not to damage the cam bearings with the cam lobes.

7922BG27

Rocker arm/shaft tightening sequence—3.2L and 3.5L engines

Timing belt service is covered in Section 5 of this manual

12. Inspect the bearing journals and the lobes on the shaft for wear, replace the camshaft if required. Remember, new lifters must be installed with a new camshaft.

To install:

13. Lubricate the camshaft lobes and the camshaft bearing journals. Inspect the bearing journals on the camshaft and install the shaft within 2 in. (5cm) of its final position in the cylinder block.

➡ **Chrysler recommends 1 pint (0.473L) of Chrysler Crankcase Conditioner or equivalent, be added to the crankcase when the camshaft has been replaced. This will aid during break-in. Leave the oil mixture in the engine for a minimum of 500 miles (804 km) and drain at the next normal oil change.**

14. Install the camshaft thrust plate with the two screws and tighten to 105 inch lbs. (12 Nm).

15. Rotate the crankshaft so the timing arrow is in the 12 o'clock position.

16. Position the camshaft sprocket so the timing arrow is at the 6 o'clock position. Place the timing chain around the camshaft sprocket aligning the dark colored link of the chain with the dot on the camshaft sprocket.

17. Place the timing chain around the crankshaft sprocket aligning the dot on the crankshaft sprocket with the dark colored link on the chain. Install the camshaft sprocket in position on the shaft.

18. Using a straightedge, check the alignment of the timing arrows. Install the camshaft bolt and washer and tighten to 40 ft. lbs. (54 Nm).

19. Rotate the crankshaft two revolutions in the direction of engine rotation. Check the alignment of the timing arrows, which should line up with each other.

   a. If they do not align, remove the camshaft sprocket and re-time the engine.

   b. Again, rotate the crankshaft two revolutions in the direction of rotation, and confirm alignment of the timing marks.

20. Check the camshaft end-play. With a new thrust plate the specification is 0.005–0.012 in. (0.0127–0.3040mm) or 0.012 in. (0.3040mm) for an old thrust plate. If not within specifications, replace the thrust plate.

21. Lubricate and install the valve lifters (tappets) in their original positions. If the camshaft was replaced, all lifters must be replaced with new parts.

22. Install the timing chain front cover using new seals and O-rings.

23. Install the cylinder heads and intake manifold assemblies onto the engine using the recommended procedures.

Sprocket, thrust plate and camshaft in the order of removal—3.3L engine

Using a straightedge, check the alignment of the timing arrows during timing chain installation—3.3L engine

24. Lubricate and install the pushrods in their original positions.

25. Install the rocker arm and rocker arm shaft assemblies. Install the cylinder head covers.

26. Tighten the oil pan drain plug and install a new oil filter.

27. Install the engine into the vehicle using the recommended procedure.

28. Install the radiator and cooling fan assemblies.

29. Be sure that all fluid lines, cables, hoses, and electrical connectors are attached and secured.

30. Refill the engine with the correct amount of clean SAE 5W-30 **OR** SAE 10W-30 engine oil only. Do not mix the two grades of oil.

31. Refill and bleed the cooling system.

32. Reconnect the negative battery cable. Start the engine and inspect for leaks. Test drive the vehicle.

33. Check engine fluid levels and top off if necessary.

Valve Lash

ADJUSTMENT

These engines use hydraulic roller lifters to take up the free-play in the valve train system, therefore no lash adjustments are necessary.

Oil Pan

REMOVAL & INSTALLATION

2.7L, 3.2L, and 1998–00 3.5L Engines

1. Before servicing the vehicle, refer to the precautions in the beginning of this section.

2. Disconnect the negative battery cable.

3. Remove the dipstick and housing.

4. Raise and safely support the vehicle, then drain the engine oil and remove the oil filter.

5. Remove the structural collar from the rear of the oil pan and transmission housing.

6. If equipped, remove the engine oil cooler lines from the oil pan.

7. If necessary, remove the transmission oil cooler line clips.

8. Remove the oil pan mounting bolts, then remove the oil pan and gasket.

9. Clean the oil pan and all gasket surfaces.

To install:

10. Apply a ⅛ in. (3mm) bead of sealer at the parting line of the oil pump body and the rear seal retainer.

11. Install the oil pan to the engine block and tighten the M8 nuts/bolts to 250 inch lbs. (28 Nm) and the M6 nuts/bolts to 105 inch lbs. (12 Nm).

12. Install the structural collar utilizing the following procedure:

   a. Install the vertical collar to the oil pan mounting bolts and tighten, temporarily to 10 inch lbs. (1.1 Nm).

   b. Install the collar-to-transaxle bolts and tighten to 40 ft. lbs. (55 Nm).

   c. Starting with the center vertical bolt and working outward, tighten the bolts to 40 ft. lbs. (55 Nm).

13. Lower the vehicle and install the dipstick and housing.

14. Refill the engine with the proper

To ensure a proper seal, apply sealer as shown—2.7L and 1998–00 3.5L engines

GASKET

OIL PAN

7922BG28

Exploded view of the oil pan removal and installation—2.7L and 1998–00 3.5L engines

amount of clean SAE 5W-30 **OR** SAE 10W-30 engine oil only. Do not mix the two grades of oil.

15. Connect the negative battery cable.
16. Start the engine and check for leaks.

3.3L Engines

1. Before servicing the vehicle, refer to the precautions in the beginning of this section.
2. Disconnect negative battery cable.
3. Remove the engine oil dipstick.
4. Raise and safely support the vehicle.
5. Place a drain pan underneath the vehicle and drain the engine oil. Remove the oil filter.
6. Disconnect the sway bar and move to the rear of the vehicle, if necessary.
7. Remove the transaxle support bracket and inspection cover.
8. Remove the oil pan bolts, then the oil pan.
9. Remove the oil pick-up tube, if necessary. Discard the old oil pick-up tube O-ring.

To install:
10. Thoroughly clean and dry the oil pan, cylinder block bolts and bolt holes.

Inspect the oil pan flange for bends or distortion. Straighten the flange if necessary. Clean the oil screen and pipe in clean solvent. Inspect the condition of the screen and replace if necessary.

11. Apply a ⅛ in. (3mm) bead of sealer at the parting line of the chain case cover and the rear seal retainer.
12. Install a new O-ring on the oil pick-up tube and install it into the pump body. Tighten the screws to 20 ft. lbs. (28 Nm), if removed.
13. Install a new oil pan gasket.
14. Install the oil pan and retaining bolts and tighten to 9 ft. lbs. (12 Nm).
15. Install the transaxle support bracket and inspection cover.
16. Reconnect the sway bar.
17. Tighten the oil pan drain plug and install a new oil filter.
18. Lower the vehicle and install the oil dipstick.
19. Refill the engine with the proper amount of clean SAE 5W-30 **OR** SAE 10W-30 engine oil only. Do not mix the two grades of oil.
20. Reconnect the negative battery cable.
21. Start the engine and check for leaks.

1996–97 3.5L Engines

1. Before servicing the vehicle, refer to the precautions in the beginning of this section.
2. Disconnect negative battery cable.
3. Remove the engine oil dipstick.
4. Raise and safely support the vehicle.
5. Drain the engine oil. Remove the oil filter.
6. Disconnect the sway bar and move to the rear of the vehicle, if necessary.
7. Remove the transaxle support bracket and inspection cover.
8. Remove the oil pan screws and remove the oil pan.
9. Remove the oil pick-up tube, if necessary and the windage tray/oil pan gaskets. The windage tray and oil pan gasket are integral. The silicone rubber gaskets are bonded directly to both sides of the windage tray. This assembly is reusable if it is not damaged upon removal. Discard the old oil pick-up tube O-ring.

➡**Any old sealant must be carefully removed if the gasket is going to be used again.**

To install:

10. Thoroughly clean and dry the oil pan, cylinder block bolts and bolt holes. Inspect the oil pan flange for bends or distortion. Straighten the flange if necessary. Clean the oil screen and pipe in clean solvent. Inspect the condition of the screen and replace if necessary.

11. Apply a ⅛ in. (3mm) bead of sealer at the parting line of the oil pump body and the rear seal retainer.

12. Install a new O-ring on the oil pick-up tube and install the tube into the pump body. Tighten the screws to 20 ft. lbs. (28 Nm), if removed.

13. Install the windage tray/oil pan gasket.

14. Install the oil pan and retaining bolts. Tighten the screws to 9 ft. lbs. (12 Nm).

15. Install the transaxle support bracket and inspection cover.

16. Reconnect the sway bar.

17. Tighten the oil pan drain plug and install a new oil filter.

18. Lower the vehicle and install the oil dipstick.

19. Refill the engine with the proper amount of clean SAE 5W-30 **OR** SAE 10W-30 engine oil only. Do not mix the two grades of oil.

20. Reconnect the negative battery cable.

21. Start the engine and check for leaks.

Oil Pump

REMOVAL & INSTALLATION

2.7L Engine

1. Before servicing the vehicle, refer to the precautions in the beginning of this section.

2. Remove the crankshaft damper, timing chain cover, timing chain, crankshaft sprocket, and oil pan.

3. Unbolt the oil pick-up tube and remove the O-ring.

4. Remove the oil pump mounting bolts, then remove the pump.

To install:

5. Fill the oil pump rotor cavity with clean engine oil.

6. Carefully install the oil pump over the crankshaft and into position.

7. Install the oil pump mounting bolts and tighten to 250 inch lbs. (28 Nm).

8. Lubricate the new pick-up tube O-ring with clean engine oil and tighten the pick-up tube mounting bolts to 250 inch lbs. (28 Nm).

9. Install the oil pan, crankshaft

Oil pump mounting bolt locations—2.7L engine

sprocket, timing chain, timing chain cover, and crankshaft damper.

10. Fill the crankcase with clean engine oil to the proper level.

3.2L and 3.5L Engines

Please note that the timing belt must be removed to access the oil pump behind the crankshaft drive sprocket. It is good practice to turn the crankshaft to TDC No. 1 cylinder compression stroke (firing position) before starting disassembly. This should align all timing marks and be a good point of reference for all work to follow.

1. Before servicing the vehicle, refer to the precautions in the beginning of this section.

2. Disconnect the negative battery cable.

3. The cooling system must be drained and the radiator removed for access to the timing belt covers and vibration damper. Use the following procedure.

   a. Place a drain pan under the radiator. Open the radiator drain fitting located at the lower right side of the radiator. DO NOT use pliers to open the plastic drain fitting.

   b. Remove the coolant pressure bottle cap and open the thermostat bleed valve.

   c. Remove the radiator hoses and radiator for access to the timing belt covers and crankshaft damper.

4. Remove the accessory drive belts.

5. Raise and safely support the vehicle. Place a drain pan under the vehicle and drain the engine oil.

6. Remove the oil filter. Remove the oil pan, oil pump pick-up tube and windage tray/oil pan gasket.

7. Lower the vehicle.

8. Remove the crankshaft damper using a suitable puller tool. Remove the timing belt covers.

9. Place marks on the timing belt to aid installation. Line up the marks on the camshaft sprockets to marks on the rear

timing belt covers before removing the timing belt using the recommended procedure.

10. Remove the timing belt. Inspect timing belt for cracks or excessive wear and replace if necessary.

11. Remove the crankshaft sprocket using a suitable puller tool.

12. Remove the oil pump mounting screws and the pump from the engine.

13. Remove the oil pump cover retaining screws and lift off the oil pump cover.

14. Remove the pump rotors. Wash all parts in solvent and inspect carefully for damage or wear.

To install:

15. Clean all parts well. There should be no traces of old gasket/sealer on any components.

16. Assemble the oil pump with new parts as required.

17. Install the pump cover and tighten the fasteners to 9 ft. lbs. (12 Nm).

18. Prime the oil pump prior to installation by filling the rotor cavity with clean engine oil.

19. Install the oil pump over the crankshaft and carefully into position. Tighten the retaining screws as follows:
- M8 screws—21 ft. lbs. (28 Nm)
- M10 screws—40 ft. lbs. (55 Nm)

20. Raise and safely support the vehicle. Tighten the oil pan drain plug and install a new oil filter.

21. Install the oil pump pick-up tube, windage tray/oil pan gasket and the oil pan. Tighten the oil pan fasteners to 9 ft. lbs. (12 Nm). Pay attention to sealing the oil pan gasket and its integral windage tray.

22. Lower the vehicle.

23. Install the crankshaft sprocket using tool C-4685C1, thrust bearing, washer and 12mm bolt to draw the sprocket onto the crankshaft.

24. Install the timing belt and set to the correct tension using the recommended procedure.

25. Install the timing belt covers and install the vibration damper using tool L-

Be sure to prime the oil pump before installation, because a dry pump will wear prematurely and cause low oil pressure— 3.2L and 3.5L engines

4524, thrust bearing and washer plate or equivalent damper installation tools.

26. Install the accessory drive belts and adjust to the correct tension.

27. Install the radiator into the vehicle. Install the radiator hoses.

28. Refill and bleed the cooling system.

29. Refill the engine with the correct amount of clean SAE 5W-30 **OR** SAE 10W-30 engine oil only. Do not mix the two grades of oil.

30. Reconnect the negative battery cable.

31. Run the engine. Check for leaks and proper oil pressure.

3.3L Engines

1. Before servicing the vehicle, refer to the precautions in the beginning of this section.

2. Disconnect the negative battery cable and drain the cooling system.

3. Remove the radiator assembly.

4. Raise and safely support the vehicle.

5. Drain the engine oil. Remove the oil filter.

6. Disconnect the sway bar and place it to the rear of the vehicle to gain access to the oil pan.

7. Remove the transmission support brackets and inspection cover.

8. Remove the oil pan and the oil pump pick-up tube.

9. Lower the vehicle.

10. Remove the accessory drive belts and tensioner pulley bracket.

11. Remove the power steering pump and set aside. Remove the air compressor mounting bolts and set compressor aside. Remove the compressor mounting bracket. It is not necessary to disconnect the refrigerant lines or evacuate the refrigerant from the air conditioning system.

12. Using an appropriate puller, remove the crankshaft pulley.

13. Remove the tensioner pulley bracket.

14. Remove the camshaft sensor from the chain case cover.

15. Remove the timing chain case cover mounting bolts and the cover from the front of the engine.

16. Clean the gasket material from the mating surfaces of the cover and the block.

17. Remove the oil pump cover retaining screws from the timing cover. Lift off the oil pump cover.

18. Remove the pump rotors. Wash all parts in solvent and inspect carefully for damage or wear.

To install:

19. Clean all parts well. Assemble the oil pump with new parts as required. Install the inner rotor with the chamfer facing the cast iron oil pump cover.

20. Install the pump cover and tighten the fasteners to 9 ft. lbs. (12 Nm).

21. Prime the oil pump prior to installation by filling the rotor cavity with clean engine oil.

22. Remove the crankshaft oil seal from the front cover.

23. Install a new cover gasket and O-ring onto the cover.

24. Rotate the crankshaft so the oil pump drive flats are vertical. Position the oil pump inner rotor so the mating flats are in the same position as the crankshaft drive flats.

25. Install the front cover making sure the pump is correctly engaged on the crankshaft, or severe damage may result.

26. Install the chain case cover screws and snug the two bottom screws and the top center screw. Ensure the cover is seated to the block, then tighten all screws to 20 ft. lbs. (27 Nm).

27. Install the oil seal and the crankshaft damper.

28. Install the tensioner pulley bracket and the cam sensor.

29. Install the air conditioning compressor to the mounting bracket.

30. Install the accessory drive belt.

31. Raise and safely support the vehicle. Tighten the oil pan drain plug and install a new oil filter.

32. Install the oil pump pick-up tube and oil pan. Install the transaxle inspection cover, if removed.

33. Fill the crankcase with clean engine oil to the proper level. Install a new oil filter.

34. Install the radiator assembly. Check the condition of the radiator hoses. Fill and bleed the cooling system.

35. Reconnect the negative battery cable. Run the engine and check for leaks. Verify correct oil pressure with a gauge.

Rear Main Seal

REMOVAL & INSTALLATION

1. Before servicing the vehicle, refer to the precautions in the beginning of this section.

2. Disconnect the negative battery cable.

3. Raise and support the vehicle.

4. Remove the transaxle inspection cover and flywheel/flexplate.

5. Using a small prytool, carefully pry out the rear oil seal. Be careful not to nick or damage the crankshaft flange seal surface or the retainer bore.

To install:

6. Place the Seal Pilot Tool C-4681 (or equivalent) onto the crankshaft.

7. Lightly coat the oil seal outside diameter with Loctite Stud N' Bearing Mount® or the equivalent.

8. Apply a light coating of engine oil to the entire circumference of the oil seal lip.

9. Place the seal over the special tool and tap the seal in place with a plastic mallet.

10. Install the flexplate or flywheel. Install the transaxle.

11. Lower the vehicle and connect the battery cable.

Timing Chain, Sprockets, Front Cover and Seal

REMOVAL & INSTALLATION

2.7L Engine

✳✳ WARNING

When aligning the timing marks, rotate the engine using the crankshaft, not the camshafts. DO NOT rotate the camshafts or crankshaft with the timing chain removed without locating the crankshaft position, piston and/or valve damage may occur.

1. Before servicing the vehicle, refer to the precautions in the beginning of this section.

2. Remove the upper intake manifold and valve covers.

3. Remove the upper radiator crossmember.

4. Remove the fan module.

5. Remove the accessory drive belts.

6. Using Crankshaft Damper Holder tool 8191, or equivalent, hold the crankshaft and remove the center bolt.

7. Remove the damper using a three jaw puller.

8. Remove the power steering pump, and position it aside without disconnecting the hydraulic lines.

9. Remove the accessory drive belt tensioner pulley.

Refer to Section 1 for engine rebuilding specifications

CHAIN
GUIDE

CAMSHAFT
DAMPER

ACCESS
PLUG

CHAIN
GUIDE

CAMSHAFT
SPROCKETS

CHAIN
TENSIONER

CHAIN
TENSIONER
ARM

PRIMARY
TIMING
CHAIN

CAMSHAFT
POSITION
SENSOR

CRANKSHAFT
SPROCKET

CHAIN
GUIDE

7922BG33

Exploded view of the timing chain drive assembly—2.7L engine

**SPECIAL TOOL
8191**

7922BG32

Removing the crankshaft center bolt using the Crankshaft Damper Holder tool—2.7L engine

10. Remove the timing chain cover mounting bolts.

11. Clean and inspect the sealing surfaces.

12. Align the crankshaft sprocket timing mark to the mark on the oil pump housing.

➡**The mark on the oil pump housing is 60° After Top Dead Center (ATDC).**

13. Remove the primary timing chain tensioner from the right cylinder head.

14. Remove the camshaft position sensor and the timing chain access plug from the left cylinder head.

➡**The camshafts will rotate clockwise, when the camshaft sprocket bolts are removed.**

15. Starting with the right camshaft, remove the sprocket mounting bolts, camshaft damper, and the sprocket.

16. Remove the left camshaft sprocket attaching bolts and sprocket.

17. Remove the lower timing chain guide and tensioner arm, then the primary timing chain.

To install:

➡**Lubricate the timing chain and guides with clean engine oil before installation.**

18. Verify that the crankshaft sprocket timing mark is aligned with the mark on the oil pump housing.

19. Place the left side primary timing chain sprocket onto the chain, while aligning the timing mark on the sprocket to the two plated links on the chain.

20. Lower the chain with the left

sprocket through the left cylinder head opening.

21. Loosely position the left camshaft sprocket over the camshaft hub.

22. Align the plated link to the crankshaft sprocket timing mark.

23. Position the timing chain around the water pump drive sprocket.

24. Align the right camshaft sprocket timing mark to the plated link on the timing chain and loosely position the sprocket over the camshaft hub.

25. Verify that all the plated links are aligned to their proper timing marks.

26. Install the left lower timing chain guide and tensioner, then tighten the bolts to 250 inch lbs. (28 Nm).

➡**Inspect the timing chain guide access plug O-rings before installing. Replace damaged O-rings as necessary.**

27. Install the timing chain guide access plug to the left cylinder head and tighten to 15 ft. lbs. (20 Nm).

➡**To reset the timing chain tensioner, oil will first need to be purged from the tensioner.**

28. Purge oil from the timing chain tensioner using the following procedure:

a. Remove the tensioner from the tensioner housing.

b. Place the check ball end of the tensioner into the shallow end of the Tensioner Resetting Special tool 8186 or equivalent.

c. Using hand pressure, slowly depress the tensioner until oil is purged from the cylinder.

d. Reinstall the tensioner into the tensioner housing.

29. Reset the timing chain tensioner using the following procedure:

a. Position the cylinder plunger into the deeper side of the Tensioner Resetting special tool 8186 or equivalent.

b. Apply a downward force until the tensioner is reset.

✳✳ CAUTION

Ensure that the tensioner is properly reset. The tensioner body must be bottomed against the top edge of the Tensioner Resetting Special tool 8186 or equivalent. Failure to properly perform the resetting procedure may cause tensioner jamming.

30. Install the chain tensioner into the right cylinder head.

31. Starting at the right cylinder head, insert a ⅜ in. square drive extension with a breaker bar into the intake camshaft drive hub. Rotate the camshaft until the camshaft

Using the Tensioner Resetting Special tool, or equivalent, to purge the oil from the tensioner—2.7L engine

hub aligns with the camshaft sprocket and damper attaching holes. Install the sprocket attaching bolts and tighten to 250 inch lbs. (28 Nm).

32. Turn the left camshaft by inserting a ⅜ in. square drive extension with a breaker bar into the intake camshaft drive hub. Rotate the camshaft until the camshaft hub aligns with the camshaft sprocket and damper attaching holes. Install the sprocket attaching bolts and tighten to 250 inch lbs. (28 Nm).

33. If necessary, rotate the engine slightly clockwise to remove any slack in the timing chain.

34. To arm the timing chain tensioner: Use a flat-bladed prytool to gently pry the tensioner arm towards the tensioner slightly. Then, release the tensioner arm. Verify the tensioner extends.

35. Inspect and replace the timing chain cover gasket and oil seal.

36. Apply a ⅛ in. (3mm) bead of sealer at the parting line of the oil pan and engine block.

➡ **When installing the timing cover, guide the seal over the crankshaft to prevent damage to the lip of the seal.**

37. Install the timing cover and gasket, then tighten the M10 bolts to 40 ft. lbs. (54

After the timing chain is installed, the timing marks should be aligned as shown—2.7L engine

For engine torque specifications, refer to Section 1 of this manual

Nm) and the M6 bolts to 105 inch lbs. (12 Nm).

38. Install the crankshaft damper.

39. Install the accessory drive belt tensioner pulley.

40. Install the power steering pump.

41. Install the crankshaft damper onto the crankshaft.

42. Utilizing tool 8191, tighten the crankshaft center bolt to 125 ft. lbs. (170 Nm).

43. Install the accessory drive belts.

44. Install the fan module and engage its electrical wiring harness.

45. Install the upper radiator crossmember.

46. Connect the negative battery cable.

3.3L Engines

1. Before servicing the vehicle, refer to the precautions in the beginning of this section.

2. Relieve the fuel system pressure using the recommended procedure.

3. Rotate the engine to Top Dead Center (TDC) on No. 1 cylinder. This provides a reference point.

4. Disconnect the negative battery cable.

5. Drain the cooling system. Remove the radiator and cooling fan assemblies.

6. Raise and safely support the vehicle. Place a drain pan under the engine oil pan and drain the engine oil.

7. Disconnect the sway bar and place it to the rear of the vehicle to gain access to the oil pan.

8. Remove the transaxle supports brackets and inspection cover.

9. Remove the engine oil pan and oil pump pick-up.

10. Remove the accessory drive belt(s).

11. Remove the power steering pump and set aside. It may be necessary to also remove the air conditioning compressor and set aside.

12. Remove the crankshaft damper using a puller to draw the damper from the crankshaft.

13. Remove the tensioner pulley bracket.

14. Remove the Camshaft Position (CMP) sensor from the chain case cover.

15. Remove the timing chain front cover and remove the front cover oil seal.

16. If the chain is found to be out of specification, remove the camshaft sprocket attaching bolt, and remove the timing chain with the camshaft sprocket.

17. Using a gear puller, remove the crankshaft sprocket. Be careful not to damage the crankshaft surface.

To install:

18. Position a new crankshaft sprocket onto the shaft, then install the sprocket with a suitably-sized socket and a rubber or plastic mallet. Be sure that the sprocket is seated in position.

19. Rotate the crankshaft, if needed, until the timing mark is in the 12 o'clock position.

20. Situate the timing chain on the camshaft sprocket and hold the camshaft sprocket so that the timing mark is in the 6 o'clock position.

21. Align the dark colored links with the dot on the camshaft sprocket, place the timing chain around the crankshaft sprocket with the dark colored link lined up with the dot on the sprocket and install the camshaft sprocket onto the end of the camshaft.

22. Using a straightedge, check the alignment of the crankshaft and camshaft timing marks.

23. Install the camshaft bolt and washer. Tighten the bolt to 40 ft. lbs. (54 Nm).

24. Rotate the crankshaft two full revolutions. The timing marks should line up. If the timing marks do not line up, remove the camshaft sprocket and realign it.

Using a straightedge to align the timing marks during installation—3.3L engine

Timing cover mounting bolt locations— 3.3L engine

25. Check the camshaft end-play. With a new thrust plate the specification is 0.005–0.012 in. (0.0127–0.304mm). The old thrust plate specification is 0.012 in. (0.31mm) maximum. If not within these limits install a new thrust plate.

26. Install the timing chain snubbers. Tighten the retaining screws to 9 ft. lbs. (12 Nm). Each model year of these engines may use different length bolts, therefore do not use bolts for this component from any other model year engine.

27. Clean all parts well. Use care to remove all old sealer and gasket material from the timing chain cover.

➡**The crankshaft oil seal must be removed to insure correct oil pump engagement.**

28. Remove the old oil seal from the timing case cover. Be sure that the mating surfaces for the timing chain cover gasket are clean and free of any burrs. Rotate the crankshaft so that the oil pump drive flats are vertical. Position the oil pump inner rotor so the mating flats are in the same position as the crankshaft drive flats. Install the timing chain front cover using new gasket and O-rings. Be sure the oil pump is engaged on the crankshaft correctly or severe damage may result.

29. Install the chain case cover screws. Snug down the two bottom screws and the top center screw. Be sure the cover is seated on the block, then tighten all the other screws to 20 ft. lbs. (27 Nm).

30. Install a new front cover oil seal.

31. Install the crankshaft damper and tighten the center bolt to 40 ft. lbs. (54 Nm).

32. Install the tensioner pulley bracket.

33. Install the CMP sensor.

34. Install the accessory drive belt(s) and adjust to the proper tension.

35. Install the oil pump pick-up tube and the oil pan.

36. Install the transaxle support brackets and inspection cover.

37. Install the power steering pump and air conditioning compressor, if removed.

38. Connect the front sway bar.

39. Install the radiator and cooling fan assemblies.

40. Refill the engine with the correct amount of clean SAE 5W-30 **OR** SAE 10W-30 engine oil only. Do not mix the two grades of oil. A filter change is recommended.

41. Refill and bleed the cooling system.

42. Reconnect the negative battery cable.

43. Test run the engine and check for leaks.

FUEL SYSTEM

Fuel System Service Precautions

Safety is the most important factor when performing not only fuel system maintenance but any type of maintenance. Failure to conduct maintenance and repairs in a safe manner may result in serious personal injury or death. Maintenance and testing of the vehicle's fuel system components can be accomplished safely and effectively by adhering to the following rules and guidelines:

• To avoid the possibility of fire and personal injury, always disconnect the negative battery cable unless the repair or test procedure requires that battery voltage be applied.

• Always relieve the fuel system pressure prior to disconnecting any fuel system component (injector, fuel rail, pressure regulator, etc.), fitting or fuel line connection. Exercise extreme caution whenever relieving fuel system pressure to avoid exposing skin, face and eyes to fuel spray. Please be advised that fuel under pressure may penetrate the skin or any part of the body that it contacts.

• Always place a shop towel or cloth around the fitting or connection prior to loosening to absorb any excess fuel due to spillage. Ensure that all fuel spillage (should it occur) is quickly removed from engine surfaces. Ensure that all fuel soaked cloths or towels are deposited into a suitable waste container.

• Always keep a dry chemical (Class B) fire extinguisher near the work area.

• Do not allow fuel spray or fuel vapors to come into contact with a spark or open flame.

• Always use a back-up wrench when loosening and tightening fuel line connection fittings. This will prevent unnecessary stress and torsion to fuel line piping.

• Always replace worn fuel fitting O-rings with new. Do not substitute fuel hose or equivalent, where fuel pipe is installed.

Before servicing the vehicle, also make sure to refer to the precautions in the beginning of this section as well.

Fuel System Pressure

RELIEVING

1. Before servicing the vehicle, refer to the precautions in the beginning of this section.

2. Disconnect the negative battery cable.
3. Remove the fuel filler cap.
4. Remove the safety cap from the fuel pressure test port located on the fuel rail.
5. Place the open end of the fuel pressure release hose tool C-4799-1 or equivalent, into a proper gasoline container.
6. Connect the other end of the hose to the fuel pressure test port.
7. The fuel pressure will bleed off through the hose into the container.

Fuel Filter

The fuel filter mounts to the frame rail in front of the fuel tank. The inlet and outlet ends of the filter are marked for installation purposes.

REMOVAL & INSTALLATION

1996–97 Vehicles

1. Before servicing the vehicle, refer to the precautions in the beginning of this section.
2. Relieve the fuel system pressure.
3. Raise and safely support the vehicle, then locate the filter.
4. Disengage the quick-connect fittings from the filter.
5. Remove the filter mounting bracket, then the filter.

To install:

➡ **The inlet and outlet sides of the filter are marked, install the filter with the inlet side to the fuel tank.**

6. Place the filter into the bracket. Place the bracket against the frame rail, tighten the mounting screw to 110 inch lbs. (12 Nm).
7. Apply a light coat of clean 30 weight engine oil to the fuel filter nipples. Install the fuel lines.

The fuel filter mounts to the frame rail in front of the fuel tank—1996–97 vehicles

8. Lower the vehicle.
9. Start the engine and check for leaks.

1998–00 Vehicles

➡ **The fuel filter is part of the fuel pressure regulator mounted on the fuel pump module.**

1. Before servicing the vehicle, refer to the precautions in the beginning of this section.
2. Properly relieve the fuel system pressure.
3. Disconnect the negative battery cable.
4. Raise and safely support the vehicle.
5. Lower the fuel tank and remove the purge and vent lines.
6. Remove the fuel line from the pressure regulator.
7. Remove the filter/regulator by pushing in the locking tab and turning the regulator to unlock it. Pull the regulator straight up.

To install:

8. Push the fuel filter/regulator into the fuel pump module and turn to lock it into position.
9. Connect the fuel lines and install the tank.
10. Lower the vehicle. Start the engine and check for leaks.

Cut away view of the fuel filter/pressure regulator—1998–00 vehicles

Fuel Pump

REMOVAL & INSTALLATION

1996–97 Vehicles

An electric fuel pump is used with fuel injection systems in order to provide higher and more uniform fuel pressures. It is located in the tank. To perform the testing or servicing, you will need a DRB III or equivalent scan tool.

1. Before servicing the vehicle, refer to the precautions in the beginning of this section.

2. Release the fuel system pressure.

3. Disconnect the negative battery cable.

4. Open the trunk lid, then remove the trunk liner.

5. Remove the access panel fasteners.

6. Remove the access panel and gasket. Inspect the gasket for damage. If necessary, replace the gasket.

7. Disconnect the electrical wiring from the top of the pump module.

8. Disconnect the fuel supply and return tubes from the fuel pump module.

9. Disconnect the hose from the pressure relief/rollover valve.

10. A band clamp fastens the pump module to the tank. The module rises up from the tank after loosening the clamp.

11. Loosen the band clamp until the pump module rises up from the tank.

※※ WARNING

The pump reservoir may contain fuel. Do not spill fuel while removing the module.

12. To absorb any possible spillage, place a shop towel around the access open-

Once the cover is removed, access to the pump is obtained—1996–97 vehicles

Note that the alignment marks must be aligned to install the pump correctly—1996–97 vehicles

ing. Without removing the module, tip it backwards to allow fuel in the reservoir to run down the side and back into the tank.

13. Remove the pump module and gasket from the tank.

➡ **The float arm of the sensor catches on the inside of the tank while removing the module. Tilt the module to the one side when removing it from the tank.**

14. Drain the remainder of fuel from the reservoir before servicing the pump module.

To install:

➡ **The fuel pump module and tank have alignment marks. The tank has two molded lines at the ten o'clock position. The fuel pump has a triangular alignment mark. Align the marks to correctly position the pump.**

15. With a new gasket, insert the pump straight into the tank to set the float on the bottom. Align the marks on the pump and tank.

16. Seat the pump to the tank by pushing the top downward. Be sure the gasket does not slip over the outside or inside edge of the tank lip. While holding the pump in the seated position, place the band clamp over the lip of the tank and edge of the pump. Tighten the band clamp to 31 inch lbs. (4 Nm). Do not overtighten.

17. Install the fuel tubes over the return and supply nipples on the module.

18. Connect the vent line to the pressure relief/rollover valve.

19. Attach the electrical wiring to the pump.

20. Using a DRB III or equivalent scan tool, pressurize the fuel system.

21. Check for leaks.

22. Install the access cover and gasket. Tighten the fasteners.

23. Install the trunk liner.

24. Connect the negative battery cable.

1998–00 Vehicles

The in-tank fuel pump module contains the fuel pump and pressure regulator which adjusts fuel system pressure to approximately 49 psi. (338 kPa). Voltage to the fuel pump is supplied through the fuel pump relay.

The fuel pump is serviced as part of the fuel pump module. The fuel pump module is installed in the top of the fuel tank and contains the electric fuel pump, fuel pump reservoir, inlet strainer fuel gauge sending unit, fuel supply and return line connections and the pressure regulator. The inlet

Using special tool 6856 or equivalent, remove the fuel pump module locknut—1998–00 vehicles

strainer, fuel pressure regulator and level sensor are the only serviceable items. If the fuel pump requires service, replace the fuel pump module. Use the following procedure.

1. Before servicing the vehicle, refer to the precautions in the beginning of this section.

2. Remove the fuel filler cap and properly relieve the fuel system pressure.

3. Disconnect and isolate the negative battery cable.

4. Drain and remove the fuel tank.

5. Clean the top of the tank to remove any loose dirt.

6. Disconnect the fuel lines from the fuel pump module by squeezing the quick-connect fitting with thumb and forefinger.

7. Disconnect the fuel pump module electrical connector from the top of the fuel pump module.

8. Using special tool 6856 or equivalent, remove the fuel pump locknut by turning it counterclockwise.

※※ CAUTION

The fuel reservoir of the fuel pump module does not empty out when the tank is drained. The fuel in the reservoir may spill out when the module is removed.

9. Remove the fuel pump and O-ring from the tank. Discard the O-ring.

To install:

10. Thoroughly clean all parts. Wipe the seal area of the tank clean. Place a new O-ring on the ledge between the tank threads and the pump module opening.

11. Position the fuel pump module in the tank. Be sure the alignment tab on the underside of the pump module flange sits in the corresponding notch in the fuel tank.

12. While holding the fuel pump module in place install the locking ring and tighten to 40 inch lbs. (5 Nm) using special tool 6856 or equivalent spanner-type tool.

13. Install the fuel tank assembly.

14. Connect fuel pump module electrical connector.

15. Reconnect the negative battery cable.

16. Fill the fuel tank with fuel. Install the fuel filler cap. Turn the ignition switch to the **ON** position to pressurize the system. Check the fuel system for leaks.

DRIVE TRAIN

Transaxle Assembly

REMOVAL & INSTALLATION

The 42LE four speed transaxle uses fully-adaptive controls. Adaptive controls are those which perform their functions based on real-time feedback sensor information. The transaxle is conventional in the use of hydraulically applied clutches to shift a planetary gear train. However, it uses electronics to control virtually all other functions. The following components are serviceable in the vehicle: valve body assembly, solenoid pack, manual valve lever position sensor, input and output speed sensors, transfer chain and sprockets, short (right side) stub shaft seal and the long (left side) stub shaft and ball bearing. Note that the factory recommends that before attempting any repair on the 42LE four-speed automatic transaxle, always check for proper shift linkage adjustment. Also check for diagnostic trouble codes with the Chrysler DRB scan tool (or equivalent).

Use MOPAR Type 7176 Automatic Transmission Fluid only. Do not substitute transaxle fluid. If the differential sump requires fluid, use 80W-90 petroleum based Hypoid gear lubricant. The transaxle can be removed without removing the engine. Use the following procedure.

1. Before servicing the vehicle, refer to the precautions in the beginning of this section.

2. Disconnect the negative battery cable.

3. Remove the engine air inlet tube.

4. The Crankshaft Position (CKP) sensor is located on the upper right side of the transaxle bell housing. Unplug the CKP sensor connector and remove the sensor.

5. Unplug the transaxle wiring connector block located on the right shock tower.

To free the connector from the harness, remove the wire ties.

6. Raise and safely support the vehicle.

7. Remove the front wheels.

8. Remove the strut-to-steering knuckle bolts on both sides of the vehicle. Disconnect the tie rod ends if required.

9. Remove the Anti-lock Brake System (ABS) wheel speed sensor, if equipped.

10. Remove the halfshafts from the transfer case by inserting a prybar between the halfshaft and the transaxle case and prying the shaft from the transaxle housing. Swing the shafts out of the way, keeping the joints straight and suspend using wire. Be careful not to damage the halfshaft seals.

➡**Do not let the halfshafts or CV-joints hang unsupported. Internal joint damage may result if allowed to hang free.**

11. Remove the engine-to-transaxle brackets and the transaxle bell housing cover.

12. Mark the driveplate to the torque converter and remove the torque converter bolts. The driveplate-to-torque converter bolts are not to be reused.

13. Unbolt and remove the starter assembly from the bell housing and allow the starter motor to sit between the engine and the frame.

14. Disconnect the oil cooler lines from the transaxle and plug to prevent excess fluid leakage.

15. Remove the transaxle dipstick.

16. Disconnect the gear selector cable from the transaxle.

17. Disconnect the exhaust pipe from the exhaust manifold and position out of the way. If the clearance will not allow for transaxle removal, remove the exhaust system from the vehicle.

18. Support the transaxle using a transmission jack. Raise the transaxle slightly to relieve the weight off the rear transaxle mount.

19. Remove the engine-to-transaxle brackets and the transaxle mount throughbolt.

20. Remove the rear crossmember mounting bolts. Pry the transaxle mount rearward to separate the mount from the transaxle. Remove the rear crossmember.

21. Lower the rear of the transaxle to gain access to the bell housing bolts. Remove the bell housing bolts.

22. Place a drain pan under the dipstick in the transaxle to catch transaxle fluid that will drain out of the case. Remove the dipstick tube from the transaxle and plug hole.

23. Remove the engine-to-transaxle

bolts and lower the transaxle from the vehicle.

➡**The driveplate-to-torque converter bolts and the driveplate-to-crankshaft bolts must not be reused. Install new bolts whenever these bolts are removed.**

24. Inspect the driveplate for cracks. If cracks are present, replace the driveplate.

To install:

➡**Apply a light coating of grease to the pilot hole of the crankshaft if the torque converter is being replaced.**

✳✳ WARNING

When installing the transaxle unit into the vehicle, be careful that the fuel tubes at the rear of the engine do not contact the following:

- Tie rod attachment plate at the power steering rack
- Exhaust Gas Recirculation (EGR) tube
- Transaxle wiring harness

25. Install the driveplate to the engine and secure using new fasteners. Tighten the fastener to 75 ft. lbs. (101 Nm).

26. Install the transaxle into the vehicle and install the engine-to-transaxle case mounting bolts. Tighten the bolts to 75 ft. lbs. (101 Nm).

27. Install the rear transaxle case mount and the rear crossmember in position and secure all fasteners.

28. Install the dipstick tube.

29. Reconnect the exhaust pipe to the engine exhaust manifold.

30. Reconnect the gear selector cable to the transaxle. Reconnect the transaxle oil cooler lines.

31. Install the starter assembly and secure with the mounting bolts tightened to 40 ft. lbs. (54 Nm). Be sure that the starter ground strap is installed correctly.

32. Position the torque converter so that the matchmarks made during disassembly are in alignment. Install new torque converter-to-driveplate bolts and tighten to 60 ft. lbs. (81 Nm).

33. Install the transaxle bell housing cover. Install the engine to transaxle brackets.

34. While pulling the top of the steering knuckle outward, install the inner CV-joint, with new retainer clip in place, into the transaxle.

35. Install the ABS wheel sensor, if removed. Install the strut-to-steering knuckle bolts and secure.

36. Install the front wheels and lug nuts.

Tighten the lug nuts, in a star pattern sequence, to 95–100 ft. lbs. (129–135 Nm).

37. Lower the vehicle to the ground. Install the transaxle dipstick.

38. Engage the transaxle wiring harness connector on the right shock tower.

39. Install and reconnect the CKP sensor.

40. Install the air inlet tube and reconnect the negative battery cable.

41. Start the engine and allow it to idle for two minutes. Apply the parking brake and move the selector through each gear position, ending in **N**. Recheck the fluid level and add if necessary. Be sure the vehicle is level when refilling the transaxle. Use Mopar Type 7176 Automatic Transmission Fluid (ATF) only. Do not substitute transaxle fluid. If the differential sump requires fluid, use 80W-90 petroleum based Hypoid gear lubricant.

42. Check the transaxle or proper operation. Adjust the shift linkage, if necessary. Be sure the reverse lamps come on when in reverse.

Halfshaft

REMOVAL & INSTALLATION

❋❋ WARNING

Allowing the CV-joint assemblies to dangle unsupported, or pulling or pushing the ends, can damage boots or CV-joints. Always support both ends of the halfshaft to prevent damage or disengagement of the Tripod joint.

1. Before servicing the vehicle, refer to the precautions in the beginning of this section.

2. Disconnect the negative battery cable.

3. Raise and support the vehicle safely.

4. Remove the front wheels.

5. Remove the front caliper assembly from the steering knuckle.

6. Remove the front brake rotor from the hub by pulling it straight off the wheel mounting studs.

7. Remove the speed sensor cable routing bracket from the strut assembly.

8. Remove the hub and bearing-to-stub axle retainer nut.

9. Install a puller tool onto the hub and bearing assembly and secure it into place using the wheel lug nuts.

10. Protect wheel stud threads by installing a wheel lug nut onto a wheel stud. Use a flat-bladed prying tool to prevent the

7922BG44

Removing the stub axle from the front hub/bearing assembly—halfshaft service

7922BG45

Be careful not to damage the threads for the axle nut when removing the outer CV joint from the steering knuckle—halfshaft service

hub from turning. Using the puller tool, force the halfshaft outer stub axle from the hub and bearing assembly.

11. Dislodge the inner Tripod joint from the stub shaft retaining snapring on the transaxle. To do this, insert a prybar between the transaxle case and the inner Tripod joint and pry on Tripod joint.

➡**Do not try to remove the inner Tripod joint from the transaxle stub shaft at this time. Only disengage the inner Tripod joint from the retainer snapring.**

12. Remove the strut assembly-to-steering knuckle attaching bolts from the strut assembly.

❋❋ WARNING

The strut assembly-to-steering knuckle bolts are serrated (toothed) where they go through the strut assembly and steering knuckle. When removing the bolts, turn the nuts off the bolt; do not turn the bolts in the steering knuckle or damage to the steering knuckle will result.

13. Separate the top of the steering knuckle from the lower end of the strut.

14. Hold the outer joint assembly with one hand. Grasp the steering knuckle with the other hand and rotate it out and to the rear of the vehicle, until the outer CV-joint clears the hub and bearing assembly.

❋❋ WARNING

When removing the outer CV-joint from the hub and bearing assembly, do not allow the flange disc on the hub and bearing assembly to become damaged. If this happens, dirt and water can enter the bearing which will cause premature bearing failure.

15. Remove the halfshaft inner joint from the transaxle stub shaft by grasping the inner Tripod joint and the interconnecting shaft and pulling both pieces at the same time. Take care not to pull on the interconnecting shaft to remove or separation of the spider assembly will occur.

To install:

16. Replace the inner Tripod joint retaining circlip and O-ring seal on the transaxle stub shaft. These components are not reusable and must be replaced whenever the halfshaft is removed.

17. Apply an even coat of grease on the splines of the inner Tripod joint, where the O-ring seats against the Tripod joint.

18. Install the halfshaft through the hole in the splash shield. Grasp the inner joint in 1 hand and interconnecting shaft in the other. Align the inner Tripod joint spline with the stub shaft spline on the transaxle. Use a rocking motion with the inner Tripod joint to get it past the circlip on the transaxle stub shaft.

19. Continue pushing the Tripod joint onto transaxle stub shaft until it stops moving. The O-ring on the stub shaft should not be visible when the inner Tripod joint is fully installed. Check that the inner Tripod joint is locked in position by grasping the inner joint and pulling. If locked in position, the joint will not move on the stub shaft.

20. Hold the outer CV-joint assembly with one hand. Grasp the steering knuckle with the other and rotate it out and to the rear of the vehicle. Install the outer CV-joint into the hub and bearing assembly.

21. Install the top of the steering knuckle into the strut assembly. Align the steering knuckle-to-strut assembly mounting holes.

22. Install the strut assembly-to-steering knuckle attaching bolts. Install the nuts to

the attaching bolts and while holding the bolt heads, tighten the nuts to 125 ft. lbs. (170 Nm). Turn the nuts on the bolts. DO NOT turn the bolts.

23. Install a new hub and bearing assembly-to-stub shaft retainer nut. Tighten but do not torque the nut at this time.

24. Install the speed sensor cable routing bracket and secure the attaching screw.

25. Install the brake rotor and the caliper assembly. Install the caliper guide pin bolts to the steering knuckle and tighten to 30 ft. lbs. (41 Nm).

26. Install the front wheels and lug nuts. Lower the vehicle to the ground. Pump the brakes until a firm pedal is obtained.

27. Apply the brakes and tighten the new stub shaft-to-hub and bearing assembly retainer nut to 120 ft. lbs. (163 Nm).

✳✳ WARNING

When tightening the stub shaft retaining nut, be careful not to exceed the maximum torque specification of 120 ft. lbs. (163 Nm). If this specification is exceeded, failure of the halfshaft could result.

28. Reconnect the negative battery cable. Road test the vehicle to check for noise or vibration.

STEERING AND SUSPENSION

Air Bag

✳✳ CAUTION

Some vehicles are equipped with an air bag system, also known as the Supplemental Inflatable Restraint (SIR) or Supplemental Restraint System (SRS). The system must be disabled before performing service on or around system components, steering column, instrument panel components, wiring and sensors. Failure to follow safety and disabling procedures could result in accidental air bag deployment, possible personal injury and unnecessary system repairs.

PRECAUTIONS

Several precautions must be observed when handling the inflator module to avoid accidental deployment and possible personal injury.

• Never carry the inflator module by the wires or connector on the underside of the module.

• When carrying a live inflator module, hold securely with both hands, and ensure that the bag and trim cover are pointed away.

• Place the inflator module on a bench or other surface with the bag and trim cover facing up.

• With the inflator module on the bench, never place anything on or close to the module which may be thrown in the event of an accidental deployment.

Before servicing the vehicle, also make sure to refer to the precautions in the beginning of this section as well.

DISARMING

✳✳ CAUTION

The Air Bag system must be disarmed before repair and/or removal of any component in its immediate area including the air bag itself. Failure to do so may cause accidental deployment of the air bag, resulting in unnecessary system repairs and/or personal injury.

1. Disconnect the negative battery cable and isolate the cable using an appropriate insulator (wrap with quality electrical tape).

2. Allow the system capacitor to discharge for two minutes before starting any repair on any air bag system or related components. This will disable the air bag system.

✳✳ CAUTION

Always wear safety goggles when working with, or around, the air bag system. When carrying a live air bag, be sure the bag and trim cover are pointed away from the body. In the unlikely event of an accidental deployment, the bag will, then deploy with minimal chance of injury. When placing a live air bag on a bench or other surface, always face the bag and trim cover up, away from the surface. This will reduce the motion of the module if it is accidentally deployed.

Power Rack and Pinion Steering Gear

REMOVAL & INSTALLATION

1996–97 Models

1. Before servicing the vehicle, refer to the precautions in the beginning of this section.

2. Disconnect the negative battery cable. Disarm the air bag system.

3. Raise and safely support the vehicle.

4. Remove the gear shift cable from the shifter lever on the transaxle.

5. Loosen the bolt at the gear shift cable-to-transaxle mount. Remove the cable from the transaxle.

6. Lower the vehicle.

7. If necessary, disconnect the throttle cable from the throttle body and remove the throttle cable bracket.

8. Remove both wiper arm assemblies from the wiper arm pivots. Remove the cowl closure panel and weather-stripping as an assembly from the cowl.

9. Disconnect the wiper module wiring harness from the vehicle wiring harness. Remove the wiper module assembly from the vehicle cowl panel.

10. Disconnect the air plenum from the throttle body, PCV make up air tube and the idle air control motor. Remove the plenum from the right side of the vehicle through the wiper module area.

11. Remove the vacuum connector from the power brake booster at the intake manifold.

12. Turn the front wheels to the full left position. Then, turn the wheels back in the other direction until the roll pin in the lower steering coupler is accessible. Turn the ignition key switch to the **LOCK** position to keep the steering column from rotating after the coupler is removed from the steering gear. If the steering column shaft rotates beyond the normal number of turns in either direction, the air bag clock spring will be damaged.

13. Using paint, mark the steering coupling and steering gear shaft for orientation. Using the correct size punch, remove the roll pin from the steering coupling.

14. If equipped with a brake pedal travel sensor, remove the pedal travel sensor from the brake booster as follows:

a. Pump the brake pedal approximately 20 times. This will bleed the vacuum stored in the booster.

b. Remove the wiring harness connector from the sensor.

c. Using a small flat-tipped tool, lift the retainer ring from the notch. Then, remove the retaining ring from the grommet.

d. Remove the pedal travel sensor from the brake booster by carefully pulling it straight out of its mounting grommet. Do not twist the sensor.

15. Loosen and remove the two nuts attaching the master cylinder to the brake booster. Remove the master cylinder with the brake lines connected, and position aside.

16. Remove the power steering pressure hose and return hose from the power steering gear.

17. Bend back the retaining tabs on the bolt attaching the tie rods to the steering gear and remove the bolts.

18. Lay the tie rods, bolts and plate as an assembly on the bell housing of the transaxle.

19. If the rack and pinion steering gear unit being removed is a speed proportional steering gear, disconnect the vehicle wiring harness from the solenoid control module.

20. Remove the four bolts attaching the steering gear assembly to the crossmember. Slide the steering gear forward in the vehicle to disengage the steering coupler from the steering gear shaft. After the gear is disengaged, do not rotate the steering gear shaft.

21. Remove the steering gear assembly from the vehicle through the area in the cowl from which the windshield wiper module was previously removed.

To install:

22. If a replacement rack is being installed, grasp the shaft of the steering gear and rotate it until the steering gear center take off is in a full left turn position. Install the steering gear into the vehicle through the wiper module opening in the cowl.

23. If the original gear is being installed, align the paint mark on the steering coupler with the mark on the steering gear shaft and install the steering gear shaft into the steering gear coupler.

24. If a replacement rack is being installed, the steering gear shaft and steering coupler must be aligned. Rotate the steering gear shaft back from the full left turn position until the master spline on the steering gear shaft is aligned with the master spline on the steering coupler. At this point, install the steering gear into the coupler.

25. Align the steering gear with the mounting holes in the crossmember and install the bolts. Be sure the brake line routing clip is installed under the left steering gear mounting bracket. Tighten the mounting bolts to 50 ft. lbs. (68 Nm).

26. Install the steering coupler-to-steering gear shaft retaining roll pin until it is flush with the top edge of the steering coupler.

27. If equipped with the 3.5L engine, correct orientation of the power steering pressure hose at the power steering pump must be maintained. Be sure the power steering hose is installed in the orientation clip at the power steering pump prior to tightening the tube fitting. Attach the power steering pressure and return lines onto the proper ports of the power steering gear. Tighten both fittings to 23 ft. lbs. (31 Nm).

28. Align the center take off on the steering gear with the tie rod assemblies. Install the tie rod attaching bolts and washers into the steering gear assembly. Be sure the washers are installed between the tie rods and the steering gear. Tighten the tie rod-to-steering gear attaching bolts to 55 ft. lbs. (75 Nm). Bend the retaining tabs against the heads of the bolts.

29. Install the pedal travel sensor retainer ring on the travel sensor grommet in the vacuum booster. The tab on the retaining ring should be located in the top notch of the mounting grommet.

30. Sparingly lubricate the pedal travel sensor O-ring with fresh brake fluid. Install the pedal travel O-ring into the pedal travel sensor mounting grommet. Coat the end of the sensor with fresh brake fluid and install it by pushing straight into the mounting grommet on the brake booster until the tab on the sensor is past the retaining ring on grommet.

31. Install the wiring harness connector to the pedal travel sensor.

32. Install the master cylinder and tighten the nuts to 250 inch lbs. (28 Nm).

33. Install the power booster vacuum hose to the intake manifold. Install the windshield wiper module to the cowl panel. Reconnect the electrical harness to the module.

34. If removed, install the air intake plenum and reconnect to the idle air control motor, PCV air tube and throttle body.

35. Install the windshield wiper module assembly into the vehicle cowl area and reconnect the wiring harness from the wiper module to the vehicle wiring harness.

36. Install the cowl closure panel and tighten the six mounting screws. Install the weather strip on the shock towers.

37. Install the windshield washer hoses on the wiper arms, then install arms on the windshield wiper pivots.

38. If removed, install the throttle cable to the bracket and install the bracket to the throttle body.

39. Reconnect the wiring harness from the solenoid control valve onto the solenoid control module. Be sure that the harness connector seal is in good condition before installation.

40. Raise and safely support the vehicle.

41. Install the gear shift cable onto the shift lever on the transaxle. Install the gear shift cable on the cable mounting bracket of the transaxle and securely tighten the bolt.

COUPLER
COUPLER BOLT
COUPLING BOLT PIN
INTERMEDIATE SHAFT

7922BG46

Matchmark the steering coupler to the intermediate shaft for proper alignment

ATTACHING BOLT = STEERING GEAR
CROSSMEMBER
LEFT MOUNT
ATTACHING BRACKET (2)
ATTACHING BOLT
RIGHT MOUNT

7922BG47

Steering rack-to-subframe attaching bolt locations—replace mounts if worn

42. Lower the vehicle. Connect the negative battery cable.

43. Refill the pump reservoir to the correct lever with Mopar Power Steering Fluid or equivalent. Do not use any type of automatic transmission fluid. Start the engine and turn the steering wheel several times from stop-to-stop to bleed air from the fluid in the system. Check and add fluid as required.

44. Adjust the front suspension toe setting.

1998–00 Models

1. Before servicing the vehicle, refer to the precautions in the beginning of this section.

2. Turn the front wheels to the straight ahead position.

3. Disconnect the negative battery cable.

4. Raise the vehicle just until the front wheels are off the floor.

5. Remove the wiper arms.

6. Remove the wiper module cover and cowl cover.

7. Remove the reinforcement from the strut towers and wiper module.

8. Remove the intake air duct and resonator from the throttle body.

9. Clamp the steering wheel in the center position with some type of holding device.

10. Remove the bolt and separate the intermediate shaft from the steering column coupler.

11. Remove both tie rods from the steering gear and place them on the transaxle bell housing.

12. Remove as much power steering fluid from the reservoir as possible with a siphon pump.

13. Disconnect the fluid lines from the steering gear.

14. If equipped with speed proportional steering, disconnect the wiring from the solenoid control valve on the end of the steering gear under the master cylinder.

15. Remove the master cylinder from the booster and position it to the side without disconnect the fluid lines.

16. Remove the vacuum hose from the booster and position it out of the way.

➥**It may be helpful to loosen the two bolts attaching the right mounting bracket to the steering gear in order the clear the A/C lines.**

17. Remove the four steering gear mounting bolts (two on each side).

The steering gear is removed or installed through the right side of the vehicle, as shown

18. Move the steering gear and intermediate shaft into the engine compartment to gain access to the roll pin.

➥**Special tools are commercially available for removing roll pins.**

19. Remove the roll pin and separate the intermediate shaft from the steering gear.

20. Raise the vehicle and remove the right front wheel.

21. Remove the tie rod end from the steering arm on the right strut.

➥**If equipped with a 2.7L engine, turn the left front tire towards the left as far as possible to provide clearance.**

22. Slide the right end of the steering gear out through the tie rod hole while raising the left end of the steering gear upward.

To install:

23. Position the tie rod attaching points at the center of the steering gear travel.

24. Install the steering gear in the vehicle by reversing the removal steps.

➥**If equipped with a 2.7L engine, turn the left front tire straight ahead.**

25. Install the right tie rod on the steering arm. Tighten the nut to 27 ft. lbs. (37 Nm).

26. Install the right front wheel. Tighten the nuts in sequence to half of the specified torque, then tighten the nuts in sequence again to 95 ft. lbs. (129 Nm).

27. Lower the vehicle so the front tires are just off the floor.

28. Connect the intermediate shaft to the steering gear using the roll pin. Be sure the pin is centered in the joint.

29. Install the four steering gear mounting bolts. Tighten the bolts to 43 ft. lbs. (58 Nm).

30. If the bracket bolts were loosened during removal, tighten them to 27 ft. lbs. (37 Nm).

Center the spacer block in the steering gear before installing the tie rods

Be sure to position the washers between the tie rods and the steering gear as shown

31. Connect the fluid lines to the steering gear. Tighten the tube nuts to 35 ft. lbs. (47 Nm).

32. Connect the solenoid valve if equipped with speed proportional steering.

✳✳ WARNING

Be sure the spacer block in the rack is centered before connecting the tie rods to the steering gear.

33. Install the tie rods to the steering gear with the washers between the rods and the steering gear. Tighten the bolts to 60 ft. lbs. (82 Nm).

34. Install the remaining components in the reverse order of the removal steps.

35. Connect the negative battery cable.

36. Add Mopar® power steering fluid to the reservoir and let it settle for at least two minutes. Start the engine for a few seconds and turn it **OFF**. Add fluid as necessary. Repeat this procedure until the fluid level remains constant.

37. Raise the front wheels off the floor and start the engine. Turn the steering from lock to lock several times. Do not hold the wheel in the locked position for more than two seconds at a time. Refill the reservoir as needed.

38. Lower the vehicle and repeat the procedure. If the fluid is extremely foamy, allow the vehicle to stand with the engine **OFF** for a few minutes, then repeat the procedure.

Strut

REMOVAL & INSTALLATION

Front

1. Before servicing the vehicle, refer to the precautions in the beginning of this section.

➡️ **Service of the coil spring requires the use of a coil spring compressor tool. It is required that 5 coils be captured within the jaws of the compressor tool.**

2. Disconnect the negative battery cable.
3. Raise and safely support the vehicle. Do not support the vehicle by placing supports under the suspension arms. The suspension arms must hang freely.
4. Remove the front wheel(s).
5. Remove the stabilizer bar attaching link at the strut assembly.
6. Loosen, but do not remove the outer tie rod end-to-strut assembly steering arm attaching nut. Then, remove the outer tie rod end from the steering arm using puller MB-990635 or equivalent.
7. If equipped with ABS, remove the speed sensor wiring harness mounting bracket from the strut.
8. Remove the brake caliper assembly. Support the caliper assembly from the vehicle frame with a strong piece of wire. Do not allow the assembly to hang by the brake hose. Remove the front brake rotor disc.

❊❊ WARNING

The strut assembly-to-steering knuckle bolts are serrated where they go through the strut and steering knuckle. Do not turn the bolts during removal. If the bolts are turned, damage to the steering knuckle will result.

9. The strut assembly-to-steering knuckle bolts must not be turned during strut removal. Hold the bolt head with a wrench and turn the nuts off the bolts.
10. Remove the three strut assembly upper mount-to-shock tower mounting nuts and washers. Remove the strut from the vehicle.
11. Securely mount the strut assembly into a vise. Using paint, mark the strut unit, lower spring isolator, spring and upper strut mount for indexing of the parts at assembly.
12. Position the spring compressor tool onto the strut. Compress the coil spring until all load is off the upper strut mount assembly.
13. Install Strut Rod Socket tool L-4558A on the strut shaft nut and a 10mm socket on the end of the strut shaft to prevent it from turning. Remove the strut shaft nut.
14. Remove the upper mount assembly, jounce bumper and seat bearing and dust shield as an assembly.
15. Remove the coil spring and compressor as an assembly from the strut. Remove the lower spring isolator from the strut assembly lower spring seat.
16. Inspect all components for abnormal wear, oil leakage or failure. Replace parts as required.

To install:

17. Inspect the strut assembly for signs of leakage. Actual leakage will be a stream of fluid running down the side and dripping off the lower end of the strut. A slight amount of seepage between the strut rod and strut shaft seal is not unusual and does not affect performance of the strut assembly.
18. Install the lower spring isolator on the strut unit. Install the compressed coil spring onto the strut assembly aligning the paint marks made during removal.
19. Install the strut bearing into the bearing seat. The bearing must be installed into the seat with the notches on the bearings facing down.
20. Lower the seat bearing and dust shield onto the strut and spring assembly. Align the paint marks made during removal.
21. Install the jounce bumper and upper mount on the strut shaft, aligning the paint marks.
22. Install the strut mount-to-shaft retainer nut. Inspect all alignment marks made during removal and align as required. While holding the strut shaft from turning with a 10mm socket, tighten the strut shaft nut to 70 ft. lbs. (94 Nm).
23. Equally loosen the spring compressor tool until all tension is released. Remove the spring compressor tool.
24. Install the front strut into the strut tower and install the three upper mount nuts and washers. Tighten the mounting nuts to 25 ft. lbs. (33 Nm).
25. Position the steering knuckle neck into the strut assembly. Install the strut assembly-to-steering knuckle bolts. Install the nuts onto the attaching bolts and tighten to 125 ft. lbs. (169 Nm). Do not turn the serrated bolt heads during installation. Turn only the nuts.

❊❊ WARNING

The strut assembly-to-steering knuckle bolts are serrated (toothed) where they go through the strut and steering knuckle. Do not turn the bolts during removal. If bolts are turned, damage to the steering knuckle will result

26. Install the brake rotor and the caliper assembly to the adapter. Tighten the caliper mounting bolts to 14 ft. lbs. (19 Nm).
27. Install the front speed sensor cable routing bracket onto the front strut, if equipped.
28. Install the outer tie rod on the steering arm and tighten the attaching nut to 27 ft. lbs. (37 Nm).
29. Install the stabilizer link assembly onto the strut assembly and tighten the attaching nut to 70 ft. lbs. (95 Nm).
30. Install the front wheel and lug nuts. Tighten the lug nuts, in sequence, to 95–100 ft. lbs. (129–135 Nm).
31. Lower the vehicle to the ground. Connect the negative battery cable.

Rear

1. Before servicing the vehicle, refer to the precautions in the beginning of this section.
   The rear strut assemblies support the weight of the vehicle using coil springs positioned around the struts. The coil springs are contained between the upper mount of the strut assembly and a lower spring seat on the body of the strut assembly. The strut is attached to the spindle by a split collar on the rear spindle with a pinch bolt to hold the spindle to the strut.
2. Raise and safely support the vehicle.
3. Remove the rear wheel and tire assembly.
4. If equipped with rear disc brakes, remove the caliper assembly and rotor from the hub. If equipped with rear drum brakes, disconnect the brake flex hose from the support bracket and wheel cylinder. Plug the brake flex hose to prevent system contamination. Do not allow the rear caliper to hang by the brake hose. Support the caliper off of the frame with a strong piece of wire.
5. If equipped with ABS, remove the speed sensor cable routing bracket and tube.
6. Remove the bolts attaching the lateral links to the rear spindle assembly.
7. Remove the rear strut assembly-to-

stabilizer bar attaching link at the stabilizer bar. Hold the hex on the attaching link stud while breaking the nut loose. The attaching link does not have to be removed from the strut.

➡**Service of the coil spring requires the use of a coil spring compressor tool. It is required that 5 coils be captured within the jaws of the compressor tool.**

8. Remove the rear spindle-to-strut assembly pinch bolt. Install a center punch in the hole on the spindle and tap the punch into the hole until jammed. This will spread the spindle casting allowing it to be removed from the strut.

9. Using a hammer, tap on the top surface of the spindle, driving the spindle down and off the end of the strut assembly. Let the spindle and assembled components hang from the trailing arm while the strut is being serviced.

10. Lower the vehicle. From inside the trunk of the vehicle, remove the three upper strut mounting bolts and remove the strut from the vehicle.

11. Securely mount the strut assembly into a vise. Using paint, mark the strut assembly, lower spring isolator, spring and upper strut mount for indexing of the parts at reassembly.

12. Position a spring compressor tool onto the coil spring. Compress the coil spring until all load is off of the upper strut mount assembly.

13. Install the strut rod socket tool L-4558 on the strut shaft nut and an 8mm Allen wrench on the end of the strut shaft to prevent it from turning. Remove the strut shaft nut.

14. Remove the upper strut mount assembly off of the strut shaft. Remove the coil spring and compressor tool as an assembly from the strut.

15. Remove the plate, dust shield and jounce bumper off of the strut unit.

16. Inspect all components for abnormal wear, oil leakage or failure. Replace parts as required.

To install:

17. Install the lower spring isolator on the strut unit.

18. Install the lower spring isolator on the strut unit. If it is the original isolator, align the paint marks.

19. Install the jounce bumper into the dust shield. Install the plate on top of the dust shield and into the jounce bumper.

20. Install the dust shield, jounce bumper and the top plate onto the strut unit as an assembly.

21. Install the coil spring and compressor tool onto the strut unit and align the paint marks on the spring to that of the strut unit.

22. Install the upper strut mount assembly onto the strut shaft. Align the paint marks and install the strut shaft retaining nut.

23. Using the strut rod socket tool L-4558 and the 8mm Allen wrench to prevent the strut shaft from turning, tighten the strut shaft nut to 70 ft. lbs. (95 Nm).

24. Equally loosen the spring compressor tool until all tension is released. Remove the spring compressor tool.

25. Position the strut in the vehicle and install the three upper mounting nuts to 20 ft. lbs. (28 Nm).

26. Install the spindle assembly onto the bottom of the strut. Push or tap the spindle assembly onto the strut until the notch in the spindle is tightly seated against the locating tap on the strut assembly. Remove the center punch from the hole in the spindle.

27. Install the strut-to-spindle pinch bolt and tighten to 40 ft. lbs. (55 Nm).

28. Install the lateral link to the spindle attaching bolt and tighten to 105 ft. lbs. (140 Nm).

29. Install the stabilizer bar attaching link onto the stabilizer bar and install the stabilizer link-to-stabilizer bar attaching nut. Tighten the attaching nut to 70 ft. lbs. (95 Nm), while holding the stabilizer link stud at the hex with a wrench.

30. If equipped with ABS, mount rear

Loosen, then remove the rear spindle-to-strut pinch bolt—rear strut service

Separate the lateral links from the spindle—rear strut service

Insert a center punch into the hole on the spindle and tap until the casting is spread—rear strut service

Remove the nut from the stabilizer-to-strut attaching link stud at the bar—rear strut service

Tap with a hammer on the surface of the spindle driving it down and off the end of the strut—rear strut service

Turn to Section 6 for brake system applications

Allow the components to hang from the trailing arm as shown—rear strut service

Access the three upper strut mounting nuts through the trunk—rear strut service

During reassembly, tap the spindle onto the strut until the notch in the spindle is tightly seated against the tab—rear strut service

speed sensor cable routing tube and bracket in position. Install rear disc brake rotor and caliper assembly to the adapter plate. Tighten the caliper mounting bolts to 16 ft. lbs. (22 Nm).

31. If equipped with rear drum brakes, install the rear brake flex hose to the wheel cylinder and support plate. The brake system will require bleeding.

32. Install the rear wheel(s) and lug nuts. Tighten the lug nuts, in sequence, to 95 ft. lbs. (129 Nm). Lower the vehicle. Bleed the brake system, if equipped with rear drum brakes.

33. Have the rear wheel toe set to specifications.

Coil Springs

REMOVAL & INSTALLATION

Front

Refer to the front strut removal and installation procedure for coil spring service information.

Rear

Refer to the rear strut removal and installation procedure for coil spring service information.

Lower Ball Joint

➡The lower ball joints on this vehicle are not serviced separately. The lower ball joints operate with no free-play. If defective, the entire lower control arm must be replaced.

Lower Control Arm

REMOVAL & INSTALLATION

The front lower control arm is a steel forging with two rubber bushings isolating the lower control arm from the front cradle assembly. The isolator bushings consist of a metal encased pivot bushing and a solid rubber tension strut bushing. The lower control arm is bolted to the cradle assembly using a pivot bolt through the center of the rubber pivot bushing at the tension strut isolator bushing. The ball joint is built into the lower control arm and is non-service-able. If the ball joint becomes worn, the entire lower control arm must be replaced. The ball joint seal, however, is replaceable as well as the lower control arm inner bushing. If the lower control arm is damaged, do not attempt to repair or straighten a broken or bent lower control arm.

1. Before servicing the vehicle, refer to the precautions in the beginning of this section.

2. Raise and safely support the vehicle.

3. Remove the front wheel(s).

4. Remove the ball joint stud-to-steering knuckle clamp nut and bolt.

5. Carefully insert a prybar between the lower control arm and the steering knuckle and separate ball joint from knuckle. Be sure the ball joint seal does not get damaged during separation.

✷✷ WARNING

Pulling the steering knuckle out from the vehicle after releasing from the ball joint can separate the inner CV-joint. Do not separate the inner CV-joint or it can be damaged.

6. Remove the tension strut-to-cradle attaching nut and washer from the end of the tension strut. When removing the nut, keep the strut from turning by holding the tension strut at the flats using an open end wrench. Discard the tension strut-to-cradle retainer nut. A new nut must be used during installation.

➡A new tension strut-to-cradle attaching nut must be used when installing the tension strut.

Remove the tension strut-to-cradle nut and washer—lower control arm service

Loosen the pivot bolt and remove it—lower control arm service

Inspect the control arm and tension strut for distortion—lower control arm service

7. Loosen and remove the lower control arm pivot bushing-to-cradle assembly pivot bolt.

8. Separate the lower control arm and tension strut from the cradle as an assembly by first removing the pivot bushing from the cradle, then sliding the tension strut out of the isolator bushing. Inspect the control arm and tension strut for distortion, check the rubber bushings for excessive wear or deterioration and replace these components, if necessary.

To install:

9. Install the tension strut and isolator bushing into the cradle first, then install lower control arm pivot bushing into bracket on the cradle.

10. Installing the lower control arm-to-cradle bracket attaching bolt. Do not tighten the bolt at this time.

11. Install the washer and new nut on the end of the tension strut. Tighten the tension strut-to-cradle bracket retainer nut to 110 ft. lbs. (150 Nm), while holding the tension strut flat with an open end wrench.

12. Inspect the ball joint seal and replace it if damaged. Install the lower ball joint stud into the steering knuckle and install the

clamp bolt and nut. Tighten the bolt to 40 ft. lbs. (55 Nm).

13. Install the front wheel and lug nuts. Tighten the lug nuts, in a star pattern, to 95–100 ft. lbs. (129–135 Nm). Lower the vehicle so the suspension is supporting the weight of the vehicle.

14. Tighten the lower control arm pivot bushing-to-cradle bracket attaching bolt to 90 ft. lbs. (123 Nm).

Wheel Bearings

ADJUSTMENT

These front wheel drive vehicles are equipped with permanently sealed front and rear wheel bearings. There is no periodic lubrication or maintenance recommended for these units.

REMOVAL & INSTALLATION

Front

1. Before servicing the vehicle, refer to the precautions in the beginning of this section.

2. Raise and support the vehicle safely.

3. Remove the front wheel.

4. Remove the front caliper assembly from the steering knuckle by removing the two guide pin bolts, then rotating the top of the caliper away from the knuckle and lifting the caliper off the machined abutment on the steering knuckle.

5. Suspend the caliper out of the way with a piece of wire.

6. Remove the front brake rotor from the hub by pulling it straight off of the wheel mounting stud.

7. Remove the hub and bearing-to-stub axle retainer nut.

➡**This hub nut is a torque prevailing retaining nut and can not be reused. A NEW retaining nut MUST be used when assembling the hub.**

8. Remove the three attaching bolts that mount the hub and bearing assembly to the steering knuckle assembly.

➡**If the metal seal on the hub and bearing assembly is seized to the steering knuckle and becomes dislodged on the hub and bearing during removal, the hub and bearing must be replaced. If the flinger disc becomes damaged during the removal procedure, the hub and bearing assembly must be replaced.**

9. Remove the hub and bearing assembly from the steering knuckle by sliding it straight out of the knuckle and off the ends of the stub shaft.

10. Gently pry the assembly out with a prybar or tap it out with a soft-faced hammer, if necessary. Be very careful not to damage the hub and bearing assembly.

To install:

11. Clean the hub and bearing mounting surfaces of dirt and be sure there are no nicks present.

12. Install the hub and bearing squarely onto the stub shaft and the steering knuckle.

13. Install the bearing assembly mounting bolts and tighten equally until the bearing assembly is seated squarely against the front of the steering knuckle. Tighten the mounting bolts to 80 ft. lbs. (110 Nm).

14. Install a new hub and bearing assembly-to-stub shaft retainer nut. A NEW retaining nut MUST be used when assembling the hub. Tighten but do not torque the nut at this time.

Carefully pry the front bearing/hub assembly away from the steering knuckle

15. Install the brake rotor and the caliper assembly. Tighten the brake caliper guide bolts to 16 ft. lbs. (22 Nm).

16. Install the wheel and lug nuts. Tighten the lug nuts in a star pattern to 95–100 ft. lbs. (129–135 Nm).

17. Lower the vehicle.

18. Pump the brakes until a firm pedal is obtained.

19. With the weight on the vehicle on its wheels, apply the brakes to keep the vehicle from moving. Tighten the hub and bearing assembly-to-stub shaft retaining nut to 120 ft. lbs. (163 Nm).

❊❊ WARNING

When tightening the hub and bearing assembly to stub shaft retaining nut, do not exceed the maximum torque of 120 ft. lbs. (163 Nm). If the maximum torque is exceeded this may result in a failure of the halfshaft.

20. Inspect the toe setting on the vehicle and adjust, if necessary.

Rear

1. Before servicing the vehicle, refer to the precautions in the beginning of this section.

2. Raise the vehicle and support safely. Remove the rear wheel.

3. Remove the brake caliper and rotor if equipped with rear disc brakes. Remove the brake drum if equipped with drum brakes.

4. Remove the bearing dust cap using a suitable prybar.

5. Remove the cotter pin, nut retainer, nut, washer and bearing/hub assembly from the spindle.

To install:

6. Install the bearing/hub assembly. Install the bearing/hub assembly washer and retaining nut. Tighten the nut to 124 ft. lbs. (168 Nm). Install the nut retainer and a new cotter pin.

7. Install the dust cap.

8. Install the brake drum or rotor and caliper assembly.

9. Install the rear wheel and tighten the lug nuts, in a star pattern, to 95–100 ft. lbs. (129–135 Nm). Lower the vehicle safely.

10. Road test the vehicle to verify no excessive noise from the rear wheel bearing area.

CHRYSLER CORPORATION

13

Chrysler-Sebring Coupe • **Dodge**-Avenger

PRECAUTIONS

Before servicing any vehicle, please be sure to read all of the following precautions, which deal with personal safety, prevention of component damage, and important points to take into consideration when servicing a motor vehicle:

• Never open, service or drain the radiator or cooling system when the engine is hot; serious burns can occur from the steam and hot coolant.

• Observe all applicable safety precautions when working around fuel. Whenever servicing the fuel system, always work in a well-ventilated area. Do not allow fuel spray or vapors to come in contact with a spark, open flame, or excessive heat (a hot drop light, for example). Keep a dry chemical fire extinguisher near the work area. Always keep fuel in a container specifically designed for fuel storage; also, always properly seal fuel containers to avoid the possibility of fire or explosion. Refer to the additional fuel system precautions later in this section.

• Fuel injection systems often remain pressurized, even after the engine has been turned **OFF**. The fuel system pressure must be relieved before disconnecting any fuel lines. Failure to do so may result in fire and/or personal injury.

• Brake fluid often contains polyglycol ethers and polyglycols. Avoid contact with the eyes and wash your hands thoroughly after handling brake fluid. If you do get brake fluid in your eyes, flush your eyes with clean, running water for 15 minutes. If eye irritation persists, or if you have taken brake fluid internally, IMMEDIATELY seek medical assistance.

• The EPA warns that prolonged contact with used engine oil may cause a number of skin disorders, including cancer! You should make every effort to minimize your exposure to used engine oil. Protective gloves should be worn when changing oil. Wash your hands and any other exposed skin areas as soon as possible after exposure to used engine oil. Soap and water, or waterless hand cleaner should be used.

• All new vehicles are now equipped with an air bag system, often referred to as a Supplemental Restraint System (SRS) or Supplemental Inflatable Restraint (SIR) system. The system must be disabled before performing service on or around system components, steering column, instrument panel components, wiring and sensors. Failure to follow safety and disabling procedures could result in accidental air bag deployment, possible personal injury and unnecessary system repairs.

• Always wear safety goggles when working with, or around, the air bag system. When carrying a non-deployed air bag, be sure the bag and trim cover are pointed away from your body. When placing a non-deployed air bag on a work surface, always face the bag and trim cover upward, away from the surface. This will reduce the motion of the module if it is accidentally deployed. Refer to the additional air bag system precautions later in this section.

• Clean, high quality brake fluid from a sealed container is essential to the safe and proper operation of the brake system. You should always buy the correct type of brake fluid for your vehicle. If the brake fluid becomes contaminated, completely flush the system with new fluid. Never reuse any brake fluid. Any brake fluid that is removed from the system should be discarded. Also, do not allow any brake fluid to come in contact with a painted surface; it will damage the paint.

• Never operate the engine without the proper amount and type of engine oil; doing so WILL result in severe engine damage.

• Timing belt maintenance is extremely important! Many models utilize an interfer-ence-type, non-freewheeling engine. If the timing belt breaks, the valves in the cylinder head may strike the pistons, causing potentially serious (also time-consuming and expensive) engine damage. Refer to the maintenance interval charts in the front of this manual for the recommended replacement interval for the timing belt, and to the timing belt section for belt replacement and inspection.

• Disconnecting the negative battery cable on some vehicles may interfere with the functions of the on-board computer system(s) and may require the computer to undergo a relearning process once the negative battery cable is reconnected.

• When servicing drum brakes, only disassemble and assemble one side at a time, leaving the remaining side intact for reference.

• Only an MVAC-trained, EPA-certified automotive technician should service the A/C system or its components.

ENGINE REPAIR

Distributor

REMOVAL

2.5L Engine

The 2.5L engine is equipped with a camshaft driven mechanical distributor. This engine uses a fixed ignition timing system, in which the basic ignition timing is not adjustable. The Powertrain Control Module (PCM) determines spark advance. The Crankshaft Position (CKP) sensor and Camshaft Position (CMP) sensor are Hall effect devices. The CKP sensor is mounted remotely from the distributor, while the

CMP sensor is mounted inside the distributor housing. Both sensors generate pulses which serve as inputs to the PCM; the PCM determines crankshaft position from these sensors, then calculates injector sequence and ignition timing, based on the data.

1. Before servicing the vehicle, refer to the precautions in the beginning of this section.

2. Disconnect the negative battery cable.

3. If necessary for access, perform the following:

   a. Remove the bolt attaching the air inlet resonator to the intake manifold.

   b. Loosen the clamps holding the air cleaner cover to the air cleaner housing.

   c. Remove the Positive Crankcase Vent (PCV) make-up air hose from the air inlet tube.

   d. Loosen the hose clamp at the throttle body.

   e. Remove the air cleaner cover, resonator and inlet tube.

   f. Remove the Exhaust Gas Recirculation (EGR) tube.

4. Mark for identification, if necessary, and remove the spark plug wires from the distributor cap.

5. Remove the distributor cap.

6. Matchmark the rotor-to-distributor and the distributor-to-engine positioning to help with installation.

7. Remove the rotor.

8. Unfasten the two electrical harness connections from the distributor.

9. Remove the two distributor hold-down nuts and washers.

10. If necessary, remove the spark plug cable mounting bracket.

11. Remove the transaxle dipstick tube.

12. Carefully remove the distributor from the engine.

INSTALLATION

2.5L Engine

TIMING NOT DISTURBED

1. Before servicing the vehicle, refer to the precautions in the beginning of this section.

2. Inspect the rotor for cracks or burned electrodes, and replace if defective. Install the rotor onto the distributor.

3. Inspect the O-ring seal. If nicked or cracked, replace with a new one. Be sure the O-ring is properly seated on the distributor.

4. Carefully engage the distributor drive with the slotted end of the camshaft. When

the distributor is installed properly, the rotor will be in line with the previously made mark.

5. Verify proper rotor and distributor alignment with the mark made at disassembly.

6. Reinstall the distributor hold-down nuts and washers. Tighten the nuts to 9 ft. lbs. (13 Nm).

7. Reinstall the spark plug cable bracket.

8. Reconnect the two distributor wiring connectors.

9. Reinstall the distributor cap.

10. Reinstall the spark plug cables, following the identification marks made at disassembly.

11. Reinstall the transaxle dipstick tube.

12. If removed earlier, install the following:

   a. Install the EGR tube and tighten the mounting bolts to 95 inch lbs. (11 Nm).

   b. Install the air cleaner cover, resonator and inlet tube.

   c. Tighten the hose clamp at the throttle body.

   d. Install the PCV hose.

   e. Tighten the clamps holding the cover to the air cleaner housing.

   f. Install the bolt attaching the air inlet resonator to the intake manifold.

13. Reconnect the negative battery cable.

Prior to installation, align the distributor shaft with the distributor housing—2.5L engine

TIMING DISTURBED

1. Rotate the crankshaft until the No. 1 piston is at Top Dead Center (TDC) of the compression stroke.

2. Align the mark on the rotor shaft with the mark on the distributor housing.

3. Position the distributor into place, engaging the distributor drive with the drive on the camshaft. With the distributor fully seated on the engine, the rotor should be

under the No. 1 terminal of the distributor cap.

4. Reinstall the distributor hold-down nuts and washers. Tighten the nuts to 9 ft. lbs. (13 Nm).

5. Reinstall the spark plug cable bracket.

6. Reconnect the two distributor wiring connectors.

7. Reinstall the distributor cap.

8. Reinstall the spark plug cables, following the identification marks made at disassembly.

9. Reinstall the transaxle dipstick tube.

10. If removed earlier, install the following:

   a. Install the EGR tube and tighten the mounting bolts to 95 inch lbs. (11 Nm).

   b. Install the air cleaner cover, resonator and inlet tube.

   c. Tighten the hose clamp at the throttle body.

   d. Install the PCV hose.

   e. Tighten the clamps holding the air cleaner cover to the air cleaner housing.

   f. Install the bolt attaching the air inlet resonator to the intake manifold.

11. Reconnect the negative battery cable.

Ignition Timing

Ignition timing is controlled by the Powertrain Control Module (PCM) and is not adjustable.

Engine Assembly

REMOVAL & INSTALLATION

1. Before servicing the vehicle, refer to the precautions in the beginning of this section.

➡**The transaxle must be removed before removing the engine. They will not come out as a unit.**

2. Disconnect the negative battery cable.

3. Drain the engine coolant.

4. Drain the engine oil and the transmission oil.

5. Safely relieve the pressure within the fuel injection system.

6. Matchmark the hood to the hinges and remove the hood.

7. Remove the engine under covering.

8. Remove the transaxle assembly using the recommended procedure.

9. Remove the radiator, disconnecting the hoses at the engine.

10. Disconnect the accelerator cable and remove the bracket.

11. Disconnect the heater hoses.

12. Disconnect the brake booster vacuum hose at the engine.

13. Label and disconnect the vacuum hoses running to the bulkhead.

14. Disconnect the high pressure fuel line and discard the O-ring. It is not reusable.

15. Remove the fuel return hose from the fuel supply rail.

16. Label and disengage the electrical

Exploded view of the right-side engine mount—2.0L engine

connectors to the engine components. All wires and connectors should be labeled at the time of engine removal. This will save time during assembly.

17. Remove the accessory drive belts. Remove the bolts holding the power steering pump to its bracket and hang the pump out of the way. Do not disconnect the hoses and do not allow the pump to hang by the hoses. Remove the power steering pump bracket.

18. Remove the air conditioning compressor from its mount and hang it from a stiff wire out of the way. Note that the hoses should be left still attached. Do not loosen them or discharge the system.

19. Remove the bolts at the exhaust system joint just below the manifold. Separate the exhaust pipes. Discard the gasket and the two nuts.

20. Raise and safely support the vehicle. Install the engine hoist equipment and make certain the attaching points on the engine are secure. Draw tension on the hoist just enough to support the engine's weight but no more. Do not disturb the placement of the vehicle on the stands.

21. Remove the through-bolt from the rear (bulkhead side) roll stopper. Remove the through-bolt from the front engine roll stopper.

22. Remove the nuts and bolts holding the upper (right-side) engine mount to the engine. Remove the through-bolt and the mount assembly. Also remove the support bracket below the mount.

23. Double check for any remaining cables, wires or hoses running to the engine. Elevate the hoist and remove the engine from the vehicle. Immediately place it on an engine stand or support it with wooden blocks. Do not allow it to rest on the oil pan or lie on its side. Do not leave the engine hanging from the hoist.

To install:

After repairs, make certain the engine is fully reassembled before installation. All components removed with the engine out of the vehicle should be in place before reinstallation.

24. Installation is the reverse of the removal procedure. Please note the following important steps:

a. Connect the exhaust system to the manifold, using a new gasket. Tighten the bolts to 33 ft. lbs. (44 Nm).

b. Tighten the engine mount nuts and bolts as follows:

• Nut and bolt holding the right-side mount to engine: 63 ft. lbs. (86 Nm)

• Right-side mount through-bolt: 71–85 ft. lbs. (98–118 Nm)

• Rear roll stopper through-bolt: 32 ft. lbs. (44 Nm)

• Front roll stopper through-bolt: 41 ft. lbs. (56 Nm)

➡ **Allow the mounts to support the engine weight before final tightening of the front roll stopper through-bolt.**

c. On the 2.0L engine, tighten the power steering pump bracket bolts to 16 ft. lbs. (22 Nm). On the 2.5L engine, tighten the power steering pump bracket bolts to 29 ft. lbs. (39 Nm).

d. Connect the wiring and harness connectors to the engine. Make certain each terminal is clean and the connector is firmly seated to its mate. Do not route wires near hot surfaces or moving parts.

e. Using a new O-ring lightly lubricated with clean engine oil, connect the high pressure fuel line and tighten the bolts to 1.8 ft. lbs. (2.5 Nm).

f. Check the engine oil drain plug and secure it if necessary. Install the proper amount of engine oil.

g. Check the transaxle drain plug, tightening it if needed, and install the proper amount of transmission oil.

h. Check the radiator and engine drain cocks, closing them if necessary and refill the coolant system.

1. Engine mount insulator mounting bolt
2. Engine mount bracket
3. Engine mount stopper
4. Dynamic damper

Exploded view of the right-side engine mount—2.5L engine

i. Double check all installation items, paying particular attention to loose hoses or hanging wires, loosened nuts, poor routing of hoses and wires (too tight or rubbing) and tools left in the engine area.

25. Connect the negative battery cable. Start the engine and check for leaks.

26. Attend to all leaks immediately, remembering that fluids and metal surfaces may be hot. Adjust the drive belts to the correct tension. Adjust all cables (transmission, throttle, shift selector) and check the fluid levels. Check the operation of all gauges and dashboard lights.

27. In a safe location at low speed, road test the vehicle for correct operation of steering, brakes, transaxle, clutch and speedometer.

Water Pump

REMOVAL & INSTALLATION

2.0L Engine

1. Before servicing the vehicle, refer to the precautions in the beginning of this section.

2. Disconnect the negative battery cable.

❋❋ WARNING

This procedure requires removing the engine timing belt and the auto-tensioner. The factory specifies that the timing marks should always be aligned before removing the timing belt. Set the engine at TDC on the No. 1 cylinder compression stroke. This should align all timing marks on the crankshaft sprocket and both camshaft sprockets.

3. Raise and safely support the vehicle to a level that allows access from above and beneath.

4. Remove the right inner splash shield.

5. Remove the accessory drive belts.

6. Drain the engine coolant.

7. Properly support the engine, then remove the right motor mount.

8. Remove the timing belt, tensioner and camshaft sprockets.

❋❋ WARNING

With the timing belt removed, DO NOT rotate the camshaft or crankshaft or damage to the engine could occur.

12 Nm
8.7 ft.lbs.

2

1

1. Water pump
2. O-ring

7922CG04

Exploded view of the water pump mounting—2.0L engine

9. Remove the rear timing belt cover to access the water pump.

10. Remove the water pump attaching bolts.

11. Remove the water pump.

To install:

12. Thoroughly clean all sealing surfaces. Replace the water pump if there are any cracks, signs of coolant leakage from the shaft seal, loose or rough turning bearings, damaged impeller or sprocket or loose or damaged sprocket flange.

13. Install a new rubber O-ring into the water pump.

❋❋ WARNING

Be sure the O-ring is properly seated in the water pump groove before tightening the screws. An improperly located O-ring may cause damage to the O-ring and cause a coolant leak.

14. Install the water pump and tighten the bolts to 105 inch lbs. (12 Nm).

15. Using a cooling system pressure tester, pressurize the cooling system to 15 psi (103 kPa) and check for leaks. If okay, release the pressure and continue the engine assembly process.

16. Rotate the water pump by hand to check for freedom of movement.

17. Install the rear timing belt cover.

18. Install the camshaft sprocket(s), timing belt and tensioner. DO NOT allow the camshafts to turn while the sprocket bolts are being tightened to maintain timing mark alignment.

❋❋ WARNING

Do not attempt to compress the tensioner plunger with the tensioner assembly installed in the engine. This will cause damage to the tensioner and other related components. The tensioner MUST be compressed in a vise.

19. Install the timing belt covers.

20. Install the right engine mount bracket and engine mount.

21. Remove the support from the engine.

22. Install the crankshaft damper.

23. Install the right inner splash shield.

24. Lower the vehicle.

25. Install and tension the accessory drive belts.

26. Refill the cooling system using the correct quantity and type of coolant. Bleed the cooling system.

27. Start the engine and check for proper operation.

28. Check and top off the cooling system, if necessary.

Timing belt service is covered in Section 5 of this manual

2.5L Engine

1. Before servicing the vehicle, refer to the precautions in the beginning of this section.

2. Disconnect the negative battery cable.

3. Drain the engine coolant.

➡This procedure requires removing the engine timing belt and the auto-tensioner. To help assure proper alignment at assembly, it may be helpful to set the engine at TDC on the No. 1 cylinder compression stroke. This should align all timing marks on the crankshaft sprocket and both camshaft sprockets.

4. Remove the accessory drive belts and crankshaft damper.

5. Remove the right engine mount. This requires safely supporting the engine so the mount can be removed.

6. Remove the timing belt covers.

7. Remove the timing belt and tensioner.

8. Remove the water pump mounting bolts.

9. Separate the water pump from the water inlet pipe and remove the pump.

To install:

10. Thoroughly clean all sealing surfaces. Inspect the pump for damage or cracks, signs of coolant leakage at the vent and excessive looseness or rough turning bearing. Any problems require a new pump.

11. Install a new O-ring on the water inlet pipe. Wet the O-ring with water to make installation easier. DO NOT use oil or grease on the O-ring.

12. Install a new gasket on the water pump and fit the pump inlet opening over the water pipe. Press the assembly together to force the pipe into the water pump.

13. Install the water pump-to-engine bolts and tighten to 20 ft. lbs. (27 Nm).

Exploded view of the water pump mounting—2.5L engine

14. Install the timing belt and timing belt tensioner. Set the timing belt tension.

15. Install the timing belt covers. Install the right engine mount. Remove the floor jack and engine block from underneath the engine.

16. Install the crankshaft damper.

17. Install the accessory drive belts and set to proper tension.

18. Connect the negative battery cable.

19. Fill and bleed the engine cooling system.

20. Start the engine and verify proper operation.

Cylinder Head

REMOVAL & INSTALLATION

2.0L Engine

1. Before servicing the vehicle, refer to the precautions in the beginning of this section.

2. Disconnect the negative battery cable from the left shock absorber tower. The ground cable is equipped with an insulator grommet which should be placed on the stud to prevent the negative battery cable from accidentally grounding.

3. Properly relieve the fuel system pressure.

4. Remove the air cleaner assembly.

5. Drain and properly contain the engine coolant.

6. Label and disengage all vacuum hoses, lines and wiring harness connections that are required for cylinder head removal.

7. Disconnect the fuel line.

8. Disconnect the throttle linkage.

9. Remove the accessory drive belt(s).

10. Remove the power steering pump and move aside.

11. Disconnect the coil pack wiring connector. Disconnect the spark plug wires from the spark plugs. Remove the ignition coil pack unit from the engine.

12. Remove the cylinder head cover.

13. Remove the intake and exhaust manifolds, if necessary.

14. Remove the timing belt cover, timing belt, camshaft sprocket and rear timing belt cover using the recommended procedure.

15. Remove the rocker arm/rocker arm shaft assemblies.

16. Remove the cylinder head bolts and remove the cylinder head.

To install:

➡The cylinder head bolts should be checked for stretching before reuse. If

Checking the cylinder head bolts for necking (stretching)—2.0L engine

*Location of 110 mm (4.330 in.) short bolts.

Cylinder head bolt tightening sequence—2.0L engine

the thread area of the bolt is necked down the bolts must be replaced with new. New head bolts are recommended.

17. Thoroughly clean all parts. Clean all sealing surfaces. Use care not to scratch the aluminum cylinder head sealing surface. Check the cylinder head for flatness using a feeler gauge and a straight-edge. The cylinder head must be flat within 0.004 in. (0.1mm).

18. Check the cylinder head for cracks or other damage.

19. Install a new gasket and the cylinder head to the engine block.

20. Be sure to oil the cylinder head bolt threads with clean engine oil. Install the four cylinder head bolts, the 4.330 in. (110mm) short bolts are to be installed in positions 7, 8, 9 and 10. Tighten the bolts in proper sequence.

21. Tighten the bolts in four steps as follows:

a. First: all bolts to 25 ft. lbs. (34 Nm).

b. Second: all bolts to 50 ft. lbs. (68 Nm).

c. Third: all bolts again to 50 ft. lbs. (68 Nm).

d. Fourth: all bolts an additional ¼ turn.

➡Do not use a torque wrench for the fourth step.

22. Install the rocker arm/rocker arm shaft assemblies.

23. Install the cylinder head cover.

24. Install the timing belt rear cover and camshaft sprocket. Install the timing belt.

25. Install the timing belt cover.

26. Install the intake and exhaust manifolds, if removed.

27. Install the ignition coil pack onto the engine. Reconnect the coil pack wiring connector and the spark plug wires to the correct spark plugs.

28. Install the power steering pump.

29. Install and adjust the accessory drive belts.

30. Connect the throttle linkage.

31. Ensure all ducts, hoses, fuel lines and wiring harness connectors have been properly engaged.

32. Install the air cleaner assembly.

33. Fill the cooling system with a ⁵⁰/₅₀ mixture of clean antifreeze and water. A complete oil and filter change is recommended.

34. Connect the negative battery cable.

35. Start the engine and check for leaks. Run the engine with the radiator cap off so as the engine warms and the thermostat opens, coolant can be added to the radiator. When satisfied that the cooling system is full, shut the engine **OFF**, install the radiator cap and allow the engine to cool.

36. With the engine cool, check all fluid levels. Add coolant and oil as required. Restart the engine and test drive vehicle to check for proper operation.

2.5L Engine

1. Before servicing the vehicle, refer to the precautions in the beginning of this section.

2. Release the fuel system pressure.

3. Disconnect the negative battery cable.

4. Drain the engine cooling system.

5. Remove the timing belt and camshaft sprockets.

6. Label and disengage any wiring harnesses, vacuum hoses and lines that would in some way inhibit removal of the cylinder head.

7. Remove the intake manifold assembly.

8. Remove the water pump inlet pipe retaining bolt on the inner rear part of the front cylinder head.

9. Remove the valve covers and rocker arm assemblies.

10. Remove the distributor assembly.

11. On the front cylinder head, remove the ground strap on the left-end of the head.

12. Remove the exhaust manifolds and crossover pipe.

13. Remove the cylinder head mounting bolts and place them in numbered order through holes made in a piece of cardboard.

14. Remove the cylinder head.

To install:

15. Thoroughly clean and dry the mating surfaces of the head and block. Check the cylinder head for cracks, damage or engine coolant leakage. Remove scale, sealing compound and carbon. Clean the oil passages thoroughly. Check the head for flatness. End-to-end, the head should be no more than 0.008 in. (0.2mm) out-of-true. If the service limit is exceeded, correct to meet specifications. Note that the maximum amount from stock allowed to be removed

Cylinder head bolt tightening sequence—2.5L engine

Install the head gasket with the identification mark at the front facing upward—2.5L engine

from the cylinder head and mating cylinder block is 0.0079 in. (0.2mm). If the cylinder head cannot be made serviceable by removing this amount, replace the head.

16. Check that the head gaskets have the proper identification marks for the engine. Lay the head gasket with the identification mark at the front top.

➡**Do not apply sealant to the head gasket or mating surfaces.**

17. Inspect the cylinder head bolts prior to installation. If the threads are necked down (stretched), the bolts should be replaced. Necking can be checked by holding a straightedge against the threads. If all of the threads do not contact the straightedge, the bolt should be replaced. All new head bolts are recommended.

18. Install the head straight down onto the block. Try to eliminate most of the side-to-side adjustments, as this may move the gasket out of position or damage the gasket. Before installing the bolts, the threads should be oiled with clean engine oil. Install the bolts and the special washers by hand and just start each bolt one or two turns on the threads.

➡**The washers must be installed correctly. The rounded shoulder of the washer denotes the face in contact with the bolt. The flat side of the washer contacts the head.**

19. Correct tightening of the head bolts requires three steps:

    a. Following the tightening sequence, tighten each bolt to 62 ft. lbs. (84 Nm).

    b. Follow the tightening sequence and tighten each bolt to 70 ft. lbs. (95 Nm).

    c. Follow the tightening sequence and tighten each bolt to 80 ft. lbs. (108 Nm).

20. Install the valve cover and gasket.

21. Install the exhaust manifolds and crossover pipe.

22. Install the distributor assembly.

23. Install the intake manifold assembly.

24. Ensure that all wiring harnesses, vacuum hoses and lines are all properly connected.

➡**Before proceeding, double check all installation items, paying particular attention to loose hoses or hanging wires, nuts not properly tightened, poor routing of hoses and wires (too tight or rubbing) and tools left in the engine area.**

25. Fill the cooling system with coolant. Changing the oil and filter is recommended

to eliminate pollutants such as coolant in the oil.

26. Connect the negative battery cable. With the radiator cap off, start the engine and check for leaks of fuel, vacuum, oil or coolant. Check the operation of all engine electrical systems as well as dashboard gauges and lights. Add coolant as the engine warms.

27. Perform necessary adjustments to the accelerator cable and drive belts. Allow the engine to cool and once again check and adjust the coolant level.

Rocker Arm/Shafts

REMOVAL & INSTALLATION

This procedure applies to the 2.5L engine only. On the 2.0L engine, the valves are actuated directly by the camshafts.

2.5L Engine

1. Before servicing the vehicle, refer to the precautions in the beginning of this section.

2. Disconnect the negative battery cable.

3. Properly relieve the fuel system pressure.

4. If removing the right (firewall) side rocker arm/shaft assembly, remove the upper intake manifold (air intake plenum), which is a 2-piece unit of aluminum alloy.

5. Remove the valve cover(s).

6. Identify the rocker arm shaft assemblies before removal.

7. Install the auto lash adjuster retainers Special Tool MD 998443 or equivalent to keep the auto lash adjusters from falling out of the rocker arms when the rocker arm assembly is removed.

8. Loosen the attaching fasteners and remove the rocker arm shaft assemblies from the cylinder head.

➡ **The hydraulic automatic lash adjusters are precision units installed in the machined openings in the rocker arm units. Do not disassemble the auto lash adjusters.**

To install:

9. The rocker arm shafts are hollow and used as a lubrication oil duct. Ensure all valvetrain parts are clean. Check the rocker arm mounting portion of the shafts for wear or damage. Replace if necessary. Check all oil holes for clogging with a small wire and clean as required. If any rockers were removed, lubricate and install on the shafts in their original positions.

10. Install the rocker arm and shaft

1. Rocker cover
2. Rocker cover gasket
3. Oil seal
4. Oil seal
5. Rocker arm and rocker arm shaft
6. Rocker arm and rocker arm shaft
7. Rocker shaft spring
8. Rocker arm A
9. Rocker arm B
10. Rocker arm shaft
11. Lash adjuster
12. Rocker arm C
13. Rocker arm shaft
14. Lash adjuster
15. Thrust case
16. O-ring
17. Camshaft

7922CG10

Exploded view of the cylinder head valvetrain assembly—2.5L engine

assemblies with the FLAT in the rocker arm shafts facing toward the timing belt side of the engine for the right cylinder head. For the left cylinder head install the rocker arm and shaft assembly with the FLAT in the rocker arm shaft facing toward the transaxle side of the engine. Install the retainers and spring clips in their original positions on the exhaust and intake shafts. Tighten the retainer bolts to 23 ft. lbs. (31 Nm) working from the center, outward. Remove the valve lash retainer tools that should have been installed at disassembly.

11. Inspect the spark plug tube seals located on the ends of each tube. These seals slide onto each tube to seal the cylinder head cover to the spark plug tube. If these seals show signs of hardness and/or cracks, they should be replaced.

12. Install the valve cover(s).

13. Install the upper intake manifold (plenum), if necessary.

14. Ensure all remaining electrical connectors have been reconnected. Tighten the air tube connections.

15. An oil and filter change is recommended.

16. Connect the negative battery cable. Start the engine and check for leaks, abnormal noises and vibrations.

Intake Manifold

REMOVAL & INSTALLATION

2.0L Engine

This engine uses a two-piece aluminum intake manifold. The upper half of the manifold (also called a plenum) mounts the throttle body. The lower half of the manifold contains the fuel rail and injectors. A non-reusable gasket joins the two halves. Use care when working with light alloy parts.

➡**Be sure to observe all cautions and warnings in the beginning of the section that may be related to this procedure.**

1. Relieve the fuel system pressure.
2. Disconnect the negative battery cable and drain the cooling system.
3. Disconnect the accelerator cable, breather hose and air intake hose.
4. Disengage the vacuum connection at the power brake booster and the Positive Crankcase Vent (PCV) valve. Disconnect all remaining vacuum hoses and pipes, as necessary. Tag for identification, if necessary, to save time at assembly.
5. Disconnect the fuel line(s), then remove the throttle control cable and brackets.

❊❊ CAUTION

Do not use conventional fuel filters, hoses or clamps when servicing fuel injection systems. They are not com-patible with the injection system and could fail, causing personal injury or damage to the vehicle. Use only hoses and clamps specifically designed for fuel injection.

6. Unplug the alternator wiring harness connection.
7. Disengage the Manifold Absolute Pressure (MAP) sensor and the Intake Air Temperature (IAT) sensor connectors.
8. Disengage the Throttle Position Sensor (TPS) connector and position the engine wiring harness aside.
9. Disengage the Exhaust Gas Recirculation (EGR) pipe connection.
10. Remove the intake manifold stay and the engine hanger. Disengage the fuel injector connectors.
11. Remove the throttle body assembly.
12. Remove the mounting bolts and remove the intake manifold plenum and gasket.
13. Remove the complete fuel rail assembly. Use care since the fuel injectors can drop out of the fuel rail as it is being removed.

14. Remove the mounting bolts, then remove the intake manifold and gasket from the engine.

To install:

15. Clean all gasket material from the cylinder head and intake manifold assembly. Check both surfaces for cracks or other damage. Check the intake manifold water passages and air passages for clogging. Clean if necessary. Check the gasket surface of the intake manifold for flatness using a straight edge and feeler gauge. It should be 0.006 in. (0.15mm) or less. The limit is 0.008 in. (0.20mm).
16. Install a new intake manifold gasket to the head and install the manifold. Tighten the manifold in a crisscross pattern, starting from the inside and working outwards to 17 ft. lbs. (23 Nm).
17. Apply a thin coat of clean engine oil to the fuel injector O-rings. Install the fuel rail, injector and pressure regulator assembly to the lower intake manifold.
18. Thoroughly clean the mating surfaces and install the intake manifold plenum with a new gasket.
19. Install the throttle body assembly.
20. Install the intake manifold stay and the engine hanger. Plug in the fuel injector connectors.
21. Attach the EGR pipe connection.
22. Engage the engine control electrical connectors.
23. Engage the generator wiring harness connection.
24. Connect the fuel line(s) and the throttle control cable brackets.
25. Connect the vacuum hose at the power brake booster and the PCV valve. Connect all remaining vacuum hoses and pipes.
26. Connect the accelerator cable, breather hose and air intake hose.
27. Connect the negative battery cable.
28. Start the engine and check for proper operation.

2.5L Engine

1. Before servicing the vehicle, refer to the precautions in the beginning of this section.
2. Disconnect the negative battery cable.
3. Properly relieve the fuel system pressure.
4. Disconnect the fuel line(s) from the fuel rail assembly. On quick-connect fittings, squeeze the fitting retainer tabs together and separate the connection.

1. Air intake hose
2. Breather hose
3. Accelerator cable connection
4. Clip
5. MAP sensor connector
6. Intake air temperature sensor connector
7. Vacuum hose connection
8. TPS connector
9. Idle air control motor connector
10. Control wiring harness
11. Generator wiring harness connection
12. PCV hose assembly
13. Vacuum hose
14. Vacuum hose connection
15. Brake booster vacuum hose connection
16. EGR pipe connection
17. Fuel return hose connection
18. High-pressure fuel hose connection
Ⓝ use new components

7922CG11

Intake manifold hose, cable and wire attachment identification—2.0L engine

3.9 Nm
2.9 ft.lbs.

3.9 Nm
2.9 ft.lbs.

2.5 Nm
1.8 ft.lbs.

8 Nm
6 ft.lbs.

Refer to Section 1 for engine rebuilding specifications

5. Loosen the throttle body air inlet hose clamp, then release the snaps holding the air cleaner housing cover to the housing. Remove the air cleaner cover and inlet hose from the engine.

6. Unplug the vacuum connection at the power brake booster and the Positive Crankcase Vent (PCV) valve. Disconnect all remaining vacuum hoses and pipes, as necessary. Tag for identification, if necessary, to save time at assembly.

➡It may be helpful to identify and tag each sensor connector and vacuum connection as it is being removed or disengaged. This may save time at assembly.

7. Disengage the connectors from the Manifold Absolute Pressure (MAP) sensor and the Intake Air Temperature (IAT) sensors.

8. If necessary, disengage the power steering pressure switch and oxygen sensor connectors.

9. Remove the plenum support bracket located to the rear of the MAP sensor.

10. Remove the control wiring harness mounting fasteners located on top of the upper plenum near the valve cover.

11. Disconnect the Throttle Position Sensor (TPS) and the Idle Air Control (IAC) motor electrical connections.

12. Remove the throttle body assembly.

13. Remove the throttle cable bracket.

14. Remove the Exhaust Gas Recirculation (EGR) tube from the engine intake manifold.

1. Air intake hose
2. TPS connector
3. Idle air control motor connector
4. Vacuum hose connection
5. Throttle body assembly
6. Power steering oil pressure switch connector
7. Heated oxygen sensor connector
8. Intake air temperature sensor connector
9. Injector connector
10. Control wiring harness
11. Accelerator cable connection
12. Vacuum hose connection
13. Brake booster vacuum hose connection
14. Vacuum hose connection
15. MAP sensor
16. Heated oxygen sensor harness
17. EGR pipe connection
18. EGR valve and EGR transducer assembly
19. Intake manifold plenum
20. Intake manifold plenum gasket

Exploded view of the plenum and intake manifold—2.5L engine

7922CG12

15. Remove the EGR valve and transducer assembly.

16. Remove the plenum support bracket located to the rear of the EGR tube.

17. Remove the seven bolts attaching the upper intake plenum to the lower manifold and remove the plenum. Remove the intake plenum-to-lower manifold gasket.

18. Disconnect the fuel injector electrical connectors.

19. Remove the four bolts attaching the fuel rail to the intake manifold. Use care, there are spacers under each fuel rail bolt. Remove the fuel rail.

➥It may be necessary to remove the power steering fluid reservoir and mounting bracket to access all of the lower intake manifold fasteners.

20. Remove the lower intake manifold attaching bolts.

21. Remove the intake manifold and discard the old gaskets.

To install:

22. Clean all gasket sealing surfaces. Check both surfaces for cracks or other damage. Check the intake manifold air passages for clogging. Clean if necessary.

23. Check upper and lower manifold gasket surfaces for flatness using a straight-edge and feeler gauge.

24. The surfaces must be flat within 0.006 in. (0.15mm) per 12 in. (30.5cm) of manifold length. The limit is 0.008 in. (0.20mm).

25. Properly position the new gaskets on the heads and install the lower intake manifold.

   a. Tighten the nuts on the front bank to 5 ft. lbs. (7 Nm).

   b. Tighten the nuts on the rear bank to 14–17 ft. lbs. (20–23 Nm).

   c. Tighten the nuts on the front bank to 14–17 ft. lbs. (20–23 Nm).

   d. Repeat Steps **b** and **c** again.

26. Apply a light coating of engine oil to the fuel injector O-rings.

27. Reinstall the fuel injectors into the engine.

28. Seat the injectors in place and tighten the fuel rail bolts to 8 ft. lbs. (12 Nm).

29. Engage the electrical connectors to the fuel injectors.

30. Reconnect the fuel line(s) to the fuel rail assembly. Exert a slight tug on the fuel line away from the fuel rail to verify positive engagement.

31. Install the upper intake plenum with new gaskets.

32. Tighten the plenum bolts to 13 ft. lbs. (18 Nm).

33. Reinstall the plenum support brackets and tighten to 13 ft. lbs. (18 Nm).

34. Install the EGR valve and transducer assembly.

35. Install the EGR tube and tighten the screws to 95 inch lbs. (11 Nm).

36. Install the throttle cable bracket.

37. Install the throttle body assembly.

38. Reconnect the TPS and IAC electrical connections.

39. Place the control wiring harness into correct position on the engine and tighten the mounting fasteners.

40. Engage the power steering pressure switch and oxygen sensor connectors, if previously disconnected.

41. Engage the MAP sensor and the IAT sensor connectors.

42. Connect the vacuum hose at the power brake booster and the PCV valve. Connect all remaining vacuum hoses and pipes.

43. Connect the remaining engine control system electrical connectors.

44. Reinstall the air cleaner cover and air inlet hose. Tighten the intake hose-to-throttle body hose clamp.

45. Reconnect the negative battery cable.

46. Start the engine and check for leaks.

Exhaust Manifold

REMOVAL & INSTALLATION

2.0L Engine

1. Before servicing the vehicle, refer to the precautions in the beginning of this section.

2. Disconnect the negative battery cable.

3. Remove the air intake hose and the small air hose connection.

4. Properly drain the engine coolant.

5. Disconnect the upper radiator hose from the thermostat housing.

6. Disengage the control wiring harness connection.

7. Remove the water pipe assembly and the engine oil level dipstick.

8. Remove the heat shield and the engine hanger.

9. Remove the pulsed secondary air injection valve, if equipped.

10. Raise and safely support the vehicle.

1. Air intake hose
2. Radiator upper hose connection
3. Air hose connection
4. Control wiring harness connection
5. Water pipe assembly
6. Engine oil level gauge
7. Heat protector
8. Engine hanger
9. Front exhaust pipe connection
10. Heat protector
11. Exhaust manifold
12. Exhaust manifold gasket

7922CG13

Exploded view of the exhaust manifold and related components—2.0L engine

11. Remove the exhaust pipe-to-exhaust manifold locknuts and separate the exhaust pipe. Discard the gasket.

12. Lower the vehicle.

13. Loosen the mounting fasteners, and remove the exhaust manifold.

To install:

14. Clean all gasket material from the mating surfaces and check the manifold for cracks or warpage.

15. Install a new gasket and install the manifold. Tighten the fasteners, in a criss-cross pattern to 17 ft. lbs. (23 Nm).

16. Raise and safely support the vehicle.

17. Install the exhaust pipe to the exhaust manifold with a new gasket and new locknuts. Tighten the nuts to 33 ft. lbs. (44 Nm).

18. Lower the vehicle.

19. Install the pulsed secondary air injection valve, if equipped.

20. Install the heat shield and the engine hanger.

21. Engage the control wiring harness connection.

22. Connect the upper radiator hose to the thermostat housing.

23. Properly fill the engine cooling system.

24. Install the air intake hose and the small air hose connection.

25. Connect the negative battery cable and check for exhaust leaks.

2.5L Engine

FRONT BANK

1. Before servicing the vehicle, refer to the precautions in the beginning of this section.

2. Disconnect the negative battery cable.

3. Remove the cooling fan motor assembly.

1. Condenser fan motor assembly
2. Dipstick guide assembly connection
3. Engine hanger
4. Exhaust manifold
5. Exhaust manifold stay
6. Exhaust manifold gasket
7. Intake manifold plenum
8. Intake manifold plenum stay
9. Heated oxygen sensor
10. Generator
11. EGR pipe assembly
12. Exhaust manifold stay
13. Exhaust manifold
14. Exhaust manifold gasket

Exploded view of the exhaust manifold assembly and related components—2.5L engine

7922CG14

4. Remove the engine oil level dipstick and tube.

5. Remove the engine hanger or lower heat shield, if equipped.

6. Raise and safely support the vehicle.

7. Remove the exhaust pipe-to-exhaust manifold locknuts and separate the exhaust pipe. Discard the gasket.

8. Lower the vehicle.

9. Remove the exhaust manifold mounting fasteners, the exhaust manifold stay (brace), the exhaust manifold and the gasket.

To install:

10. Clean all gasket material from the mating surfaces and check the manifold for cracks or warpage.

11. Install a new gasket and install the manifold and manifold stay (brace). Tighten the fasteners, in a crisscross pattern to 22 ft. lbs. (29 Nm).

12. Raise and safely support the vehicle.

13. Install the exhaust pipe to the exhaust manifold with a new gasket. Tighten the nuts to 33 ft. lbs. (44 Nm).

14. Lower the vehicle.

15. Install the engine hanger or lower heat shield, if equipped. Tighten the lower heat shield fasteners to 10 ft. lbs. (13 Nm).

16. Install the engine oil level dipstick and tube.

17. Install the cooling fan motor assembly.

18. Connect the negative battery cable and check for exhaust leaks.

REAR BANK

1. Before servicing the vehicle, refer to the precautions in the beginning of this section.

2. Disconnect the negative battery cable.

3. Remove the intake manifold plenum and the plenum stay.

4. Remove the Heated Oxygen (HO$_2$S) sensor.

5. Remove the alternator.

6. Remove the EGR pipe assembly.

7. Raise and safely support the vehicle.

8. Remove the exhaust pipe-to-exhaust manifold locknuts and separate the exhaust pipe. Discard the gasket.

9. Lower the vehicle.

10. If equipped, remove the manifold heat shield.

11. Remove the exhaust manifold mounting bolts, the exhaust manifold stay (brace), the exhaust manifold and the gasket.

To install:

12. Clean all gasket material from the mating surfaces and check the manifold for cracks or warpage.

13. Install a new gasket and install the manifold and manifold stay (brace). Tighten the nuts, in a crisscross pattern to 22 ft. lbs. (30 Nm).

14. Install the manifold heat shield, if equipped.

15. Raise and safely support the vehicle.

16. Install the exhaust pipe to the exhaust manifold with a new gasket. Tighten the nuts to 33 ft. lbs. (44 Nm).

17. Lower the vehicle.

18. Install the EGR pipe assembly.

19. Install the alternator and the HO$_2$S sensor.

20. Install the intake manifold plenum and the plenum stay (brace).

21. Connect the negative battery cable and check for exhaust leaks.

Front Crankshaft Seal

REMOVAL & INSTALLATION

2.0L Engine

1. Before servicing the vehicle, refer to the precautions in the beginning of this section.

2. Disconnect the negative battery cable.

3. Remove the accessory drive belts.

4. Raise and safely support the vehicle. Drain the engine oil.

5. Remove the crankshaft damper/pulley.

6. Remove the timing belt cover.

7. Remove the timing belt.

8. Remove the crankshaft sprocket.

✳✳ WARNING

Be careful not to nick the seal surface of the crankshaft or the seal bore.

9. Remove the front crankshaft seal using a seal puller tool. Be careful not to damage the seal contact area of the crankshaft.

To install:

10. Apply a light coating of clean engine oil to the lip of the new oil seal. Install the new front crankshaft oil seal by using oil seal installer tool No. 6780–1 or equivalent seal tool.

11. Place a new oil seal into the opening with the seal spring facing the inside of the engine. Be sure the oil seal is installed flush with the front cover.

12. Install the crankshaft timing belt sprocket.

13. Install the timing belt.

14. Install the timing belt cover.

15. Install the crankshaft damper/pulley.

16. Lower the vehicle.

17. Reinstall the accessory drive belts. Adjust the belts to the proper tension.

18. Refill the engine with the correct amount of clean engine oil. A filter change is recommended.

19. Reconnect the negative battery cable. Start the engine and check for leaks.

2.5L Engine

1. Before servicing the vehicle, refer to the precautions in the beginning of this section.

2. Disconnect the negative battery cable.

3. Drain the engine oil.

4. Remove the accessory drive belts.

5. Remove the crankshaft damper/pulley.

6. Remove the front timing belt covers.

7. Remove the timing belt.

8. Remove the crankshaft sprocket and key.

9. Remove the front crankshaft seal by prying it out with a flat tipped prytool. Be sure to cover the end of the prytool tip with a shop towel.

✳✳ WARNING

Be careful not to nick the seal surface of the crankshaft or the seal bore.

To install:

10. Apply a light coating of clean engine oil to the lip of the new oil seal. Install the new front crankshaft oil seal into the oil pump housing by using oil seal installer tool No. MD998717 or an equivalent seal installer. Be sure the oil seal is installed flush with the oil pump cover.

11. Install the crankshaft timing belt sprocket and key.

12. Install the timing belt.

13. Install the timing belt covers.

14. Install the crankshaft damper/pulley onto the crankshaft.

15. Install the accessory drive belts.

16. Fill the engine with the correct amount of clean engine oil.

17. Connect the negative battery cable. Start the engine and check for leaks.

Camshaft and Valve Lifters

REMOVAL & INSTALLATION

2.0L Engine

1. Before servicing the vehicle, refer to the precautions in the beginning of this section.

2. Disconnect the negative battery cable.

3. Properly relieve the fuel system pressure.

4. Label and disconnect the spark plug wires from the spark plugs.

5. Remove the ignition coil pack and spark plug wires.

6. Remove the cylinder head cover retaining fasteners and remove the cover from the cylinder head. Discard the old cover gasket.

7. Remove the ground strap.

8. Remove the timing belt covers, timing belt and camshaft sprockets using the recommended procedure.

9. Take note that the camshaft bearing caps are numbered for correct location during installation. Remove the outer bearing caps first.

10. Loosen, but do not remove, the camshaft bearing cap retaining fasteners in the correct sequence, inside working outward. Perform this step on one camshaft at a time.

11. Identify the camshafts, if they are to be reused, for later installation. The camshafts are not interchangeable. Remove the camshaft bearing caps and remove the camshafts.

12. Remove the camshaft followers. Any components that are to be reused must be installed in their original locations. Use care

Camshaft bearing cap identification—2.0L engine

to identify and mark the positions of any removed valvetrain components so they may be reinstalled correctly.

13. Inspect the camshaft bearing oil feed holes in the cylinder head for clogging. Inspect the camshaft bearing journals for wear or scoring. Check the cam surface for abnormal wear and damage. A visible worn groove in the roller path or on the cam lobes is cause for replacement.

To install:

14. Thoroughly clean all camshaft and related parts.

15. If the fit and condition of the camshafts are acceptable, remove the camshafts for installation of the cam followers.

16. The hydraulic valve lash adjusters are inside the roller cam followers. Be sure they are clean, well-lubricated with clean engine oil and properly positioned. Install the cam followers in their original positions on the hydraulic adjuster and valve stem.

❋❋ WARNING

To avoid valve to piston contact, be sure NONE of the pistons are at Top Dead Center when installing the camshafts.

17. Lubricate the camshaft bearing journals and cam followers with clean engine oil and install the camshafts. Install right and left camshaft bearing caps No. 2 through No. 5 and right side No. 6. Tighten the M6 fasteners to 105 inch lbs. (12 Nm) in correct sequence.

18. Apply Mopar® Gasket Maker or equivalent sealer to the No. 1 and left-side No. 6 bearing caps. Install the bearing caps and tighten the M8 fasteners to 250 inch lbs. (28 Nm). The end caps must be installed before the seals may be installed.

19. Install the camshaft end seals.

20. Reinstall the camshaft sprockets, if removed. Install the timing belt using care to be sure all timing marks are properly

aligned, using the recommended procedure. Install the timing belt covers.

❋❋ WARNING

Verify that all timing marks are correct. If the timing belt or sprockets are incorrectly installed, engine damage will occur. Take time to be sure all timing marks are correctly aligned.

21. Clean all sealing surfaces. Make certain the rails are flat.

22. Install new cylinder head cover gaskets. Use care; DO NOT allow oil or solvents to contact the timing belt as they can deteriorate the rubber and cause tooth skipping. Apply Mopar Silicone Rubber Adhesive Sealant, or equivalent, at the camshaft cap corners and at the top edge of the ½ round seal.

➡**Inspect the spark plug well seals for cracking and/or swelling and replace if necessary.**

23. Install the cylinder head cover assembly to the head and tighten the fasteners in sequence using the following three steps:

a. Tighten all cylinder head cover fasteners to 40 inch lbs. (4.5 Nm).

b. Tighten all fasteners to 80 inch lbs. (9 Nm).

c. Tighten all fasteners to 105 inch lbs. (12 Nm).

24. Install the ignition coil pack and connect the spark plug wiring to the correct spark plugs. Tighten the coil pack retaining fasteners to 105 inch lbs. (12 Nm).

25. Reconnect the ground strap.

26. Ensure all vacuum lines and remaining wiring have been reconnected.

➡**An oil and filter change is recommended to wash out any sealant or gasket material that may have fallen into the engine.**

27. Reconnect the negative battery cable and test run the vehicle. Check for leaks and for proper operation.

2.5L Engine

➡**For camshaft service, the cylinder head must be removed.**

1. Disconnect the negative battery cable.

2. Relieve the fuel system pressure.

3. Place a large drain pan under the radiator drain plug. Drain the cooling system.

4. Remove the timing belt covers, tim-

Camshaft bearing cap retaining bolt removal sequence—2.0L engine

Camshaft bearing cap retaining bolt tightening sequence—2.0L engine

ing belt and camshaft sprockets using the recommended procedure.

5. The intake manifold is a two-piece unit. The upper part is a large air intake plenum of aluminum alloy. Use care working with light alloy parts. Remove the air intake plenum first, then remove the lower intake manifold.

6. Remove the cylinder head bolts and remove the cylinder head from the vehicle.

7. Remove the thrust case from the left head assembly and remove the camshaft from the rear of the head. If not already done, remove the distributor from the right cylinder head and remove the camshaft from the rear of the head.

To install:

8. Lubricate the camshaft journals and carefully install the camshaft into the cylinder head. Install the thrust case and tighten the fasteners to 9 ft. lbs. (13 Nm).

9. Apply a light coating of engine oil to the camshaft oil seal lip and install the camshaft seal. The camshaft must be installed before installing the seal. Be sure the seal is installed flush with the cylinder head surface. Install the camshaft sprocket and tighten to 65 ft. lbs. (88 Nm).

10. Install the cylinder head.

11. Install the lower intake manifold using new gaskets.

12. Install the rocker arm and shaft assemblies.

1. Breather hose connection
2. Blow-by hose
3. Fuel hose assembly connection
4. Vacuum pipe connection
5. Spark plug cable
6. Rocker cover
7. Distributor
8. Camshaft sprocket
9. Cylinder head assembly
10. Rocker arm and rocker shaft assembly
11. Camshaft
12. Camshaft oil seal

7922CG18

Exploded view of the rear cylinder head and camshaft mounting—2.5L engine

1. Blow-by hose
2. PCV valve and hose assembly connection
3. Spark plug cable
4. Vacuum pipe and hose asembly
5. Rocker cover
6. Relay box bracket assembly
7. Control module and bracket assembly
8. Thrust case
9. Camshaft sprocket
10. Rocker arm and rocker shaft assembly
11. Camshaft
12. Camshaft oil seal

7922CG19

Exploded view of the front cylinder head and camshaft mounting—2.5L engine

13. Install the timing belt.

14. Inspect the spark plug tube seals located on the ends of each tube. These seals slide onto each tube to seal the cylinder head cover to the spark plug tube. If these seals show signs of hardness and/or cracks, they should be replaced.

15. Install the cylinder head cover. Reconnect the spark plug wires.

16. Install the intake manifold plenum.

17. Connect the throttle and speed control cables.

18. Install the air inlet resonator, air inlet hose and the air cleaner housing cover.

19. Ensure all remaining electrical connectors have been reconnected. Tighten the air tube connections.

20. Refill the cooling system. An oil and filter change is recommended whenever a cylinder head has been removed since coolant can get into the oil system.

21. Reconnect the negative battery cable. Start the engine and check for leaks, abnormal noises and vibrations. Bleed the cooling system.

Valve Lash

ADJUSTMENT

The engines in these vehicles do not require periodic valve lash adjustment.

Oil Pan

REMOVAL & INSTALLATION

2.0L Engine

1. Before servicing the vehicle, refer to the precautions in the beginning of this section.

2. Disconnect the negative battery cable.

3. Raise and safely support the vehicle.

4. Remove the oil pan drain plug and drain the engine oil.

5. Remove the oil dipstick and tube.

6. Remove the front plate.

7. Remove the front exhaust pipe.

8. Remove the oil pan retaining bolts and carefully remove the oil pan.

To install:

9. Inspect the oil pan for damage and cracks. Replace if faulty. While the pan is removed, inspect the oil screen for clogging, damage and cracks. Clean and/or replace if faulty.

10. Thoroughly clean the mating surfaces of the cylinder block and the oil pan.

11. Apply sealant to the seams between the oil pump and the engine block.

12. Install the oil pan onto the cylinder block and tighten the retaining bolts to 9 ft. lbs. (12 Nm).

13. Install the front exhaust pipe.

14. Install the oil dipstick and tube.

15. Install the oil drain plug and tighten to 25 ft. lbs. (34 Nm).

16. Lower the vehicle and fill the crankcase to the proper level with clean engine oil.

17. Connect the negative battery cable. Start the engine and check for leaks.

2.5L Engine

1. Before servicing the vehicle, refer to the precautions in the beginning of this section.

2. Disconnect the negative battery cable.

3. Raise and safely support the vehicle.

4. Place a large drain pan under the oil pan drain plug and drain the oil from the engine.

5. Disconnect and lower the front exhaust pipe.

6. Remove the center member.

Please refer to Section 9 for electric cooling fan wiring schematics

Exploded view of the engine lubricating components—2.0L engine

7. Remove the engine oil dipstick tube and dipstick.

8. Remove the starter motor.

9. Remove the front and rear plates.

10. Remove the transaxle inspection cover.

11. Remove the oil pan attaching bolts.

12. Remove the oil pan. If necessary, use a rubber-faced mallet, or a hammer with a block of wood to separate the oil pan from the engine block.

To install:

13. Thoroughly clean and dry the oil pan, cylinder block and cylinder block bolts and bolt holes.

14. Apply a continuous 0.157 in. (4mm) bead of MOPAR® Silicone Adhesive Sealant or equivalent, to the oil pan gasket surface. Be sure to circle all mounting bolt holes as well. Install the oil pan within a 10–15 minute period of applying the gasket material to ensure proper sealing.

15. Install the oil pan to the engine.

16. Tighten the oil pan attaching bolts to 53 inch lbs. (6 Nm).

17. Install transaxle inspection cover.

18. Install the front and rear plates and tighten the bolts to 80 ft. lbs. (108 Nm).

19. Install the starter motor.

20. Install the engine oil dipstick tube and dipstick.

21. Install the center member. Tighten the mounting bolts to 65 ft. lbs. (88 Nm).

22. Connect the front exhaust pipe.

23. Reinstall the oil pan drain plug and gasket. Tighten the drain plug to 29 ft. lbs. (40 Nm).

24. Lower the vehicle.

25. Refill the engine with fresh oil to the proper level. An oil filter change is recommended.

26. Reconnect the negative battery cable. Start the engine and check for leaks.

Oil Pump

REMOVAL & INSTALLATION

2.0L Engine

1. Before servicing the vehicle, refer to the precautions in the beginning of this section.

2. Disconnect the negative battery cable.

3. Remove the timing belt.

4. Remove the oil pan.

5. Using a suitable puller, draw the crankshaft sprocket from the front of the crankshaft.

6. Remove the oil pump pick-up tube and O-ring.

7. Remove the oil pump and front crankshaft seal. The front cover/oil pump mounting bolts may be different sizes and must be reinstalled in their original locations. Remove and tag the front cover mounting bolts.

8. Inspect the oil pump case for damage and remove the rear cover.

9. Remove the pump rotors and inspect the inside of the case for excessive wear.

10. Check that the oil relief plunger

To ensure a leak-free seal, apply sealer as shown and tighten the bolts following the specified sequence—2.5L engine

slides smoothly and check for a broken spring.

To install:

11. Clean all parts well. Be sure the block and pump surfaces are clean and free of old sealer.

12. Assemble the pump using new parts as required with clean oil. Align the marks on the inner and outer rotors when assembling.

13. Install the pump back cover and tighten the screws to 88 inch lbs. (10 Nm).

14. Reinstall the pump relief valve, spring, gasket and valve cap. Tighten the valve cap to 30–33 ft. lbs. (41–44 Nm).

15. Apply gasket maker to the engine block mounting surface of the oil pump body.

16. Install the oil ring into the discharge passage of the pump body.

17. Prime the oil pump before installation by filling the rotor cavity with clean engine oil.

18. Align the flats of the oil pump rotor with the flats on the crankshaft as you install the pump to the engine block.

19. Install and tighten the oil pump-to-engine block mounting bolts to 17–21 ft. lbs. (23–28 Nm).

20. Install a new front oil seal.

21. Install the crankshaft sprocket.

22. Install the oil pump pick-up tube and O-ring. Tighten the oil pump pick-up tube mounting screw to 21 ft. lbs. (28 Nm).

23. Install the oil pan.

24. Install the timing belt and covers.

25. Install the crankshaft damper.

26. Install a new oil filter.

27. Refill the engine with new, clean engine oil and coolant.

28. Test run the vehicle to check for leaks. An oil pressure gauge should be installed to verify proper engine oil pressure.

2.5L Engine

1. Before servicing the vehicle, refer to the precautions in the beginning of this section.

2. Disconnect the negative battery cable.

3. Remove the drive belts and accessories.

4. Drain the engine coolant.

5. Raise and safely support the vehicle. Drain the engine oil.

6. Remove the crankshaft damper.

7. Remove the timing belt upper and lower covers.

8. Loosen the timing belt and crankshaft sprocket from the crankshaft.

9. Remove the five bolts that attach the oil pump to the block and remove the oil pump.

10. Inspect the oil pump case for damage and remove the rear cover.

11. Remove the pump rotors and inspect the inside of the case for excessive wear.

12. Check that the oil relief plunger slides smoothly and check for a broken spring.

To install:

13. Clean all parts well. Be sure the block and pump surfaces are clean and free of old sealer.

14. Assemble the pump using new parts as required with clean oil. Align the marks on the inner and outer rotors when assembling.

15. Install the pump back cover and

tighten the screws to 88 inch lbs. (10 Nm).

16. Reinstall the pump relief valve, spring, gasket and valve cap. Tighten the valve cap to 30–33 ft. lbs. (41–44 Nm).

17. Prime the pump before installation by filling the rotor cavity with clean engine oil.

18. Apply gasket maker or equivalent sealer to the pump. Install the O-ring into the counterbore on the pump body discharge passage. Position the pump onto the crankshaft until seated on the block. Tighten the size M8 fasteners to 10 ft. lbs. (14 Nm) and size M10 fasteners to 30 ft. lbs. (41 Nm).

19. Install the timing belt and crankshaft sprocket.

20. Install the timing belt cover.

21. Install the crankshaft damper.

22. Install the drive belts and accessories.

1. Oil pressure switch
2. Oil pressure gauge unit
3. Oil filter
4. Oil filter bracket
5. Oil filter bracket gasket
6. Drain plug
7. Drain plug gasket
8. Oil pan
9. Oil screen
10. Oil screen gasket
11. Plug
12. Relief spring
13. Relief plunger
14. Crankshaft oil seal
15. Oil pump case
16. O-ring
17. Oil pump cover
18. Oil pump outer rotor
19. Oil pump inner rotor

Exploded view of the oil pan and pump assembly—2.5L engine

7922CG20

23. Refill the cooling system. Install a new oil filter and refill the engine with oil.

24. Road test the vehicle. Check for proper operation as well as leaks.

Rear Main Seal

REMOVAL & INSTALLATION

2.0L Engine

➡ **Be sure to observe all cautions and warnings in the beginning of the section that may be related to this procedure.**

1. Remove the transaxle and flexplate/flywheel.
2. Remove the rear crankshaft oil seal from the oil seal housing using a suitable flat bladed prying tool.

To install:

➡ **When installing seal there is no need to lubricate sealing surface.**

3. Install seal into housing using a suitable installation tool.
4. Install the flexplate/flywheel, and tighten the bolts to 68 ft. lbs. (92 Nm).
5. Install the transaxle.

2.5L Engine

1. Before servicing the vehicle, refer to the precautions in the beginning of this section.
2. Remove the transaxle and flexplate/flywheel.
3. Remove the five rear seal housing mounting bolts.
4. Remove the housing from the engine.
5. Remove the rear crankshaft oil seal from the oil seal housing using a suitable flat bladed prying tool.

To install:

➡ **When installing the seal there is no need to lubricate sealing surface.**

6. Install the seal into the housing using a suitable seal and bearing driver.
7. Apply silicone rubber adhesive sealant to the mating surface of the seal housing.
8. Apply a light coating of engine oil to the entire oil seal lip circumference.
9. Install the oil seal and housing to the engine cylinder block. Install and tighten the mounting bolts to 96 inch lbs. (11 Nm).
10. Install the flexplate/flywheel, and tighten the bolts to 68 ft. lbs. (92 Nm).
11. Install the transaxle.

FUEL SYSTEM

Fuel System Service Precautions

Safety is the most important factor when performing not only fuel system maintenance but any type of maintenance. Failure to conduct maintenance and repairs in a safe manner may result in serious personal injury or death. Maintenance and testing of the vehicle's fuel system components can be accomplished safely and effectively by adhering to the following rules and guidelines.

• To avoid the possibility of fire and personal injury, always disconnect the negative battery cable unless the repair or test procedure requires that battery voltage be applied.

• Always relieve the fuel system pressure prior to disconnecting any fuel system component (injector, fuel rail, pressure regulator, etc.), fitting or fuel line connection. Exercise extreme caution whenever relieving fuel system pressure to avoid exposing skin, face and eyes to fuel spray. Please be advised that fuel under pressure may penetrate the skin or any part of the body that it contacts.

• Always place a shop towel or cloth around the fitting or connection prior to loosening to absorb any excess fuel due to spillage. Ensure that all fuel spillage (should it occur) is quickly removed from engine surfaces. Ensure that all fuel soaked cloths or towels are deposited into a suitable waste container.

• Always keep a dry chemical (Class B) fire extinguisher near the work area.

• Do not allow fuel spray or fuel vapors to come into contact with a spark or open flame.

• Always use a back-up wrench when loosening and tightening fuel line connection fittings. This will prevent unnecessary stress and torsion to fuel line piping.

• Always replace worn fuel fitting O-rings with new. Do not substitute fuel hose or equivalent, where fuel pipe is installed.

Fuel System Pressure

RELIEVING

1. Before servicing the vehicle, refer to the precautions in the beginning of this section.
2. Remove the fuel filler cap to release fuel tank pressure.

3. Remove the rear seat cushion.
4. At the fuel tank, disconnect the fuel pump harness connector.
5. Start the vehicle and allow it to run until it stalls from lack of fuel. Turn the key to the **OFF** position.
6. Disconnect the negative battery cable, then reconnect the fuel pump connector.
7. Install the rear seat cushion and the fuel filler cap.

✳✳ CAUTION

Always wrap shop towels around a fitting that is being disconnected to absorb residual fuel in the lines.

Fuel Filter

REMOVAL & INSTALLATION

A replaceable fuel filter is located in the engine compartment, on the bulkhead, next to the brake booster.

1. Before servicing the vehicle, refer to the precautions in the beginning of this section.
2. Following proper procedures, relieve the fuel system residual pressure.
3. Disconnect the negative battery cable.
4. Remove the air intake hose for access.
5. Hold the fuel filter housing securely with a wrench. Cover the hoses with shop towels and remove the eye bolt. Discard the gaskets.
6. Separate the flare nut connection at the bottom of the filter.
7. Remove the mounting bolts and the fuel filter from the vehicle.

✳✳ CAUTION

Do not use conventional fuel filters, hoses or clamps when servicing fuel injection systems. They are not compatible with the injection system and the high pressures in fuel injection

Exploded view of the fuel line-to-filter connection

systems and could cause substandard parts to fail, causing personal injury or damage to the vehicle. Use only hoses and clamps specifically designed for fuel injection.

To install:

8. Tighten the flare nut fitting by hand before mounting the filter to the bracket.

9. Install the filter to its bracket only finger-tight. Movement of the filter will ease attachment of the fuel lines.

10. Using new gaskets, connect the high pressure hose and eye bolt. While holding the fuel filter housing, tighten the eye bolt to 21 ft. lbs. (29 Nm). Tighten the flare nut to 27 ft. lbs. (36 Nm).

11. Tighten the filter mounting bolts fully.

12. Install the intake air hose.

13. Connect the negative battery cable, turn the key to the **ON** position to pressurize the fuel system and check for leaks.

14. If necessary, release the fuel pressure and repair leaks.

Fuel Pump

REMOVAL & INSTALLATION

1. Before servicing the vehicle, refer to the precautions in the beginning of this section.

Do not use conventional fuel filters, hoses or clamps when servicing fuel injection systems. They are not compatible with the injection system and could fail, causing personal injury or damage to the vehicle. Use only hoses and clamps specifically designed for fuel injection.

2. Relieve the fuel system pressure, using proper procedures. Disconnect negative battery cable.

Position the fuel pump for installation by aligning the seal projections (arrows) with the fuel pump holes

➡The rear seat cushion must be removed in order to gain access to the fuel pump.

3. Remove the rear seat cushion by pulling the seat stopper outward and lifting the lower cushion upward. There are two access covers underneath the seat. The panel on the far right-side is for the fuel pump.

4. Remove the access cover.

5. Disconnect the fuel pump wiring.

6. Disconnect the return hose and the high pressure fuel hose.

7. Remove the pump mounting nuts and remove the pump assembly.

To install:

8. Align the seal position projections with the holes in the fuel pump assembly and install the assembly in the tank. Tighten the retaining nuts to 22 inch lbs. (2.5 Nm).

9. Connect the high pressure hose, return hose and the fuel pump wiring.

10. Connect the negative battery cable.

11. Check the fuel pump for proper pressure and inspect the entire system for leaks.

12. Apply sealant to the access cover and install the cover.

13. Install the rear seat cushion.

14. Pressurize the fuel system by turning the ignition key to the **ON** position. Check for leaks. Start the engine to verify proper fuel pump performance.

DRIVE TRAIN

Transaxle Assembly

REMOVAL & INSTALLATION

Manual

1. Before servicing the vehicle, refer to the precautions in the beginning of this section.

2. Disconnect both battery cables, negative side first. Remove the battery and battery tray.

3. Remove the battery stay (brace).

4. Remove the air cleaner and intake hoses.

5. Drain the transaxle fluid.

6. Remove the cotter pin securing the select and shift cables and remove the cable ends from the transaxle.

7. Disconnect the back-up light switch harness and position it aside.

For transaxle removal, properly support the engine assembly as shown

Also, use a transmission jack to support the transaxle assembly

8. Disconnect the speedometer electrical connector, from the transaxle assembly.

9. Remove the starter motor and position it aside.

10. Using special tool 7137 or C-4852 or equivalent, support the engine assembly.

11. Remove the rear roll stopper mounting bracket.

12. Remove the transaxle mount bracket.

13. Remove the upper transaxle mounting bolts.

14. Raise and safely support the vehicle.

15. Remove the front wheel assemblies.

16. Remove the under cover.

17. Remove the cotter pin and disconnect the tie rod end, from the steering knuckle.

18. Disconnect the stabilizer bar link, from the damper fork.

19. Disconnect the damper fork, from the lateral lower control arm.

20. Disconnect the lateral lower arm, and the compression lower arm, lower ball joints, from the steering knuckle.

21. Pry the halfshafts from the transaxle, and secure aside.

22. Remove the connection for the clutch release cylinder and without disconnecting the hydraulic line, secure aside.

23. Remove the cover from the transaxle bell housing.

24. Remove the engine front roll stopper through-bolt.

25. Remove the centermember.

26. Support the transaxle, using a transmission jack, and remove the transaxle lower coupling bolt.

➡ **The coupling bolt threads from the engine side, into the transaxle, and is located just above the halfshaft opening.**

27. Slide the transaxle rearward and carefully lower it from the vehicle.

To install:

28. Install the transaxle to the engine and install the mounting bolts and tighten to 70 ft. lbs. (95 Nm).

29. Install the cover to the transaxle bell housing and tighten the mounting bolts to 7 ft. lbs. (9 Nm).

30. Install the centermember and tighten the front mounting bolts to 65 ft. lbs. (88 Nm) and the rear bolt to 54 ft. lbs. (73 Nm). Install the front engine roll stopper through-bolt and lightly tighten. Once the full weight of the engine is on the mounts, tighten the bolt to 42 ft. lbs. (57 Nm).

31. Connect the clutch release cylinder.

32. Install the halfshafts, using new circlips on the axle ends.

✳ WARNING

When installing the halfshaft, keep the inboard joint straight in relation to the axle, to avoid damaging the oil seal lip of the transaxle, with the serrated part of the halfshaft.

33. Connect the tie rod and ball joints to the steering knuckle. Tighten the ball joint self-locking nuts to 48 ft. lbs. (65 Nm). Tighten the tie rod end nut to 21 ft. lbs. (28 Nm) and secure with a new cotter pin.

34. Connect the damper fork to the lower control arm and tighten the through-bolt to 65 ft. lbs. (88 Nm).

35. Connect the stabilizer link to the damper fork, and tighten the self-locking nut to 29 ft. lbs. (39 Nm).

36. Install the under cover.

37. Install the wheels and lower the vehicle.

38. Install the transaxle mount bracket to the transaxle, and tighten the mounting nuts to 32 ft. lbs. (43 Nm).

39. Install the rear roll stopper mounting bracket.

40. Remove the engine support. Tighten the transaxle mount through-bolt to 51 ft. lbs. (69 Nm) and tighten the front engine roll stopper through-bolt.

41. Install the upper transaxle mounting bolts and tighten to 35 ft. lbs. (48 Nm).

42. Install the starter motor.

43. Connect the back-up light switch and the speedometer connector.

44. Connect the select and shift cables and install new cotter pins.

45. Install the air cleaner and the air intake hose.

46. Install the battery tray and battery.

47. Install the battery stay.

48. Be sure the vehicle is level, and refill the transaxle with Mopar® MS9417 MTX fluid, part number 4773167.

49. Check the transaxle for proper operation. Be sure the reverse lights come on when in reverse.

Automatic

1. Before servicing the vehicle, refer to the precautions in the beginning of this section.

2. Disconnect both battery cables, negative side first. Remove the battery and battery tray.

3. Remove the battery stay (brace).

4. Remove the air cleaner and intake hoses.

5. Drain the transaxle fluid into a suitable waste container.

6. Remove the nut securing the shifter lever to the transaxle. Remove the cable retaining clip and remove the cable from the transaxle.

7. Remove the shifter cable mounting bracket.

8. Disconnect and tag the electrical connectors for the speedometer, solenoid, neutral safety switch (inhibitor switch), the pulse generator, kickdown servo switch and oil temperature sensor.

9. Disconnect and tag the oil cooler lines, at the transaxle.

10. Remove the bolt securing the fluid dipstick tube, to the transaxle. Remove the dipstick and tube from the transaxle.

11. Remove the starter motor and position aside.

12. Using special tool 7137 or C-4852 or equivalent, support the engine assembly.

13. Remove the rear roll stopper mounting bracket.

14. Remove the transaxle mount bracket.

15. Remove the upper transaxle mounting bolts.

16. Raise and safely support the vehicle.

17. Remove the front wheels.

18. Remove the left-side undercover.

19. Remove the cotter pin and disconnect the tie rod end, from the steering knuckle.

20. Disconnect the stabilizer bar link, from the damper fork.

21. Disconnect the damper fork, from the lateral lower control arm.

22. Disconnect the lateral lower arm, and the compression lower arm, lower ball joints, from the steering knuckle.

23. Pry the halfshafts from the transaxle, and secure aside.

24. Remove the cover from the transaxle bell housing.

25. Remove the engine front roll stopper through-bolt.

26. Remove the centermember.

27. Remove the bolts holding the flexplate to the torque converter with a box wrench. Rotate the crankshaft to bring the bolts into a position for removal, one at a time.

28. To make installation easier, use chalk or paint to make matchmarks on the torque converter and flexplate. These marks will be used at assembly to realign the assembly, keeping these parts in balance. After removing the bolts, push the torque converter toward the transaxle. This will prevent the converter from remaining in contact with the engine, possibly damaging the converter.

29. Support the transaxle using a transmission jack (at the side of the case, NOT at the pan), and remove the transaxle lower coupling bolt.

➡ **The coupling bolt is inserted from the engine side into the transaxle, and is located just above the halfshaft opening.**

30. Slide the transaxle rearward and carefully lower it from the vehicle.

To install:

31. After the torque converter has been mounted on the transaxle, install the transaxle assembly to the engine. Install the mounting bolts and tighten to 70 ft. lbs. (95 Nm).

32. Align the balance matchmarks made at disassembly, connect the torque converter to the flexplate and tighten the bolts to 55 ft. lbs. (75 Nm).

33. Install the cover to the transaxle bell housing and tighten the mounting bolts to 9 ft. lbs. (12 Nm).

34. Install the centermember and tighten the front mounting bolts to 65 ft. lbs. (88 Nm) and the rear bolts to 51–58 ft. lbs. (69–78 Nm). Install the front engine roll stopper through-bolt and lightly tighten. Once the full weight of the engine is on the mounts, tighten the bolt to 42 ft. lbs. (56 Nm).

35. Install the halfshafts, using new circlips on the axle ends.

⁂ WARNING

When installing the halfshaft, keep the inboard joint straight in relation to the axle to avoid damaging the oil seal lip of the transaxle with the splined part of the halfshaft.

36. Connect the tie rod and ball joints to the steering knuckle. Tighten the ball joint self-locking nuts to 48 ft. lbs. (65 Nm). Tighten the tie rod end nut to 21 ft. lbs. (28 Nm) and secure with a new cotter pin.

37. Connect the damper fork to the lower control arm and tighten the through-bolt to 65 ft. lbs. (88 Nm).

38. Connect the stabilizer link to the damper fork, and tighten the self-locking nut to 29 ft. lbs. (39 Nm).

39. Install the left-side undercover.

40. Install the wheels and lower the vehicle.

41. Install the transaxle mount bracket, to the transaxle, and tighten the mounting nuts to 32 ft. lbs. (43 Nm).

42. Install the rear roll stopper mounting bracket.

43. Remove the engine support. Tighten the transaxle mount through-bolt to 51 ft. lbs. (69 Nm) and tighten the front engine roll stopper through-bolt.

44. Install the upper transaxle mounting bolts and tighten to 35 ft. lbs. (48 Nm).

45. Install the starter motor.

46. Install the dipstick tube and the dipstick.

47. Install the shifter cable mounting bracket.

48. Connect the shifter lever and tighten the retaining nut to 14 ft. lbs. (19 Nm).

49. Connect the oil cooler lines and secure with clamps.

50. Connect the electrical connectors for the speedometer, solenoid, neutral safety switch (inhibitor switch), the pulse generator, kickdown servo switch and oil temperature sensor.

51. Install the air cleaner and the air intake hose.

52. Install the battery tray and battery.

53. Be sure the vehicle is level, then refill the transaxle with MOPAR® ATF PLUS or equivalent transmission fluid. Start the engine and allow it to idle for two minutes. Apply the parking brake and move the selector through each gear position, ending in **N**. Recheck fluid level and add if necessary. Fluid level should be between the marks in the **HOT** range on the dipstick.

54. Check the transaxle for proper operation. Be sure the reverse lights come on when in reverse and the engine starts only in **P** or **N**.

Clutch

ADJUSTMENT

Pedal Height and Free-Play

1. Measure the clutch pedal height from the face of the pedal pad to the bulkhead. Compare the measured value with the desired distance of 7.0–7.09 in. (175–180mm).

2. Measure the clutch pedal clevis pin play at the face of the pedal pad. Press the pedal lightly until resistance is met, and measure this distance. The clutch pedal clevis pin play should be within 0.040–0.120 in. (1–3mm).

3. If the clutch pedal height or clevis pin play are not within the standard values, adjust as follows:

    a. For vehicles without cruise control, turn and adjust the stop bolt so the pedal height is the standard value, then tighten the locknut.

    b. For vehicles with auto-cruise control system, disconnect the clutch switch connector and turn the switch to obtain the standard clutch pedal height. Then, lock by tightening the locknut.

    c. Turn the pushrod to adjust the clutch pedal clevis pin play to agree with the standard value and secure the pushrod with the locknut.

➠**When adjusting the clutch pedal height or the clutch pedal clevis pin play, be careful not to push the pushrod toward the master cylinder.**

Clutch pedal height and free-play adjustment measurements

d. Check that when the clutch pedal is depressed all the way, the interlock switch switches over from **ON** to **OFF**.

4. Move the clutch pedal until the resistance begins to increase; measure between this point and the pedal resting point to determine the clutch pedal free-play. The clutch pedal free-play measurement should be between 0.240–0.510 in. (6–13mm). With the pedal fully disengaged, check the distance between the bulkhead and the top of the pedal pad. The measurement should be 2.760 in. (70mm) or more.

5. If the measurements are not within specification, bleed the clutch hydraulic system. If after bleeding the measurements are still not within specified range, there is a faulty component in the system, which must be replaced.

REMOVAL & INSTALLATION

1. Before servicing the vehicle, refer to the precautions in the beginning of this section.

2. Disconnect the negative battery cable.

3. Raise and safely support the vehicle.

4. Remove the transaxle assembly from the vehicle using the recommended procedure.

5. Remove the pressure plate attaching bolts, pressure plate and clutch disc. If the pressure plate is to be reused, loosen the bolts in a diagonal pattern, one or two turns at a time. This will prevent warping the clutch cover assembly.

6. Remove the return clip and the pressure plate release bearing. Do not use solvent to clean the bearing.

7. Inspect the clutch release fork and fulcrum for damage or wear. If necessary, remove the release fork and the fulcrum from the transaxle.

8. Carefully inspect the condition of the clutch components and replace any worn or damaged parts.

To install:

9. Inspect the flywheel for heat damage or cracks. Resurface or replace the flywheel as required. Install the flywheel using new bolts.

10. Install the fulcrum, if removed, and tighten. Install the release fork. Apply a coating of multi-purpose grease to the point of contact with the fulcrum and the point of contact with the release bearing. Apply a coating of multi-purpose grease to the end of the release cylinder's pushrod and the pushrod hole in the release fork.

1. Oil tube
2. Clutch release cylinder
3. Clutch & flywheel assembly
4. Clutch release bearing
5. Clutch release lever
6. Clutch control equip stud
7. Boot

75 Nm
55 ft.lbs.

Drive plate

Exploded view of the clutch assembly

➡ **When installing the clutch, apply grease to each part, but be careful not to apply excessive grease. Excessive grease will cause clutch slippage and shudder.**

11. Apply multi-purpose grease to the clutch release bearing. Pack the bearing inner surface and the groove with grease. Do not apply grease to the resin portion of the bearing. Place the bearing in position and install the return clip.

12. Apply a coating of grease to the clutch disc splines, then use a brush to rub it in the grooves. Using a universal clutch disc alignment tool, position the clutch disc on the flywheel. Install the retainer bolts and tighten a little at a time, in a diagonal sequence.

13. Install the transaxle assembly using the recommended procedure and check the fluid level.

14. Verify proper clutch operation.

Hydraulic Clutch System

BLEEDING

1. Before servicing the vehicle, refer to the precautions in the beginning of this section.

2. Fill the reservoir with clean DOT 3 or DOT 4 brake fluid.

3. Loosen the bleed screw, then have the clutch pedal pressed to the floor.

4. Tighten the bleed screw, then release the clutch pedal.

5. Repeat the procedure until the fluid is free of air bubbles.

➡ **It is suggested that a hose be attached to the bleed screw with the other end immersed in a container at least half full of brake fluid during the bleeding operation. Do not allow the reservoir to run out of fluid during bleeding.**

6. Refill the reservoir with clean brake fluid.

7. Check the clutch for proper operation.

Halfshaft

REMOVAL & INSTALLATION

✳✳ WARNING

If the vehicle is going to be rolled while the halfshafts are out of the vehicle, obtain two outer CV-joints or proper equivalent tools and install to the hubs. If the vehicle is rolled without the proper torque applied to the front wheel bearings, the bearings will no longer be usable.

1. Before servicing the vehicle, refer to the precautions in the beginning of this section.

2. Disconnect the negative battery cable.

3. Remove the cotter pin, halfshaft nut and washer.

4. Raise and safely support the vehicle.

5. Remove the wheel.

6. Using joint separation tool MB991113 or equivalent, disconnect the tie rod end from the steering knuckle.

✳✳ WARNING

Use of improper methods of joint separation can result in damage to the joint, leading to possible failure.

7. Disconnect the sway bar link from the damper fork.

8. Remove the damper fork lower through-bolts and upper pinch bolt. Remove the damper fork assembly.

9. Using a joint separation tool, disconnect the lateral arm and the compression arm from the steering knuckle.

10. Remove the halfshaft from the hub/knuckle by setting up a puller on the outside wheel hub and pushing the halfshaft from the front hub. After pressing the outer shaft, insert a prybar between the transaxle case and the halfshaft and pry the shaft from the transaxle.

✳✳ WARNING

Do not pull on the shaft. Doing so damages the inboard joint. Do not insert the prybar too far or the oil seal in the case may be damaged.

To install:

11. Inspect the halfshaft boot for damage or deterioration. Check the ball joints and splines for wear.

12. Replace the circlips on the ends of the halfshaft(s).

13. Insert the halfshaft into the transaxle. Be sure it is fully seated.

14. Pull the knuckle assembly outward and install the other end of the halfshaft into the hub.

15. Install the washer so the chamfered edge faces outward. Install the halfshaft nut and tighten temporarily.

16. Connect the lateral arm and the compression arm to the steering knuckle. Tighten the self-locking nuts to 43–52 ft. lbs. (59–71 Nm).

17. Install the damper fork. Tighten the lower through-bolt/nut to 65 ft. lbs. (88 Nm) and the upper pinch bolt to 76 ft. lbs. (103 Nm).

18. Connect the tie rod end to the steering knuckle. Tighten the retaining nut to 17–25 ft. lbs. (24–33 Nm) and install a new cotter pin.

19. Connect the sway bar link to the damper fork and tighten the link nut to 29 ft. lbs. (39 Nm).

20. Install the lockwasher and axle nut. Tighten the axle nut with the special tool MB990767 to hold the hub from turning. Tighten the nut to 145–188 ft. lbs. (200–260 Nm).

Removal steps

1. Cotter pin
2. Drive shaft nut
3. Tie rod end connection
4. Stabilizer link connection
5. Damper fork
6. Lateral lower arm connection
7. Compression lower arm connection
8. Harness clip
9. Bolt
10. Drive shaft and inner shaft (R.H.) <SOHC>
11. Drive shaft
12. Circlip

Caution
* : Indicates parts which should be temporarily tightened, and then fully tightened with the vehicle on the ground in the unladen condition.

7922CG29

Exploded view of the left and right halfshaft assemblies' mounting

➡**Before securely tightening the axle nut be sure there is no load on the wheel bearings.**

21. Install a new cotter pin and bend to secure.
22. Install the wheel.
23. Check the transaxle fluid level and top off, if necessary.
24. Connect the negative battery cable.
25. Test drive the vehicle and check for proper operation.

STEERING AND SUSPENSION

Air Bag

❄❄ CAUTION

Some vehicles are equipped with an air bag system, also known as the Supplemental Inflatable Restraint (SIR) system or Supplemental **Restraint System (SRS). The system must be disabled before performing service on or around system components, steering column, instrument panel components, wiring and sensors. Failure to follow safety and disabling procedures could result in accidental air bag deployment, possible personal injury and unnecessary system repairs.**

PRECAUTIONS

Several precautions must be observed when handling the inflator module to avoid accidental deployment and possible personal injury. Along with the precautions in the beginning of this section, observe the following:

• Never carry the inflator module by the wires or connector on the underside of the module.

• When carrying a live inflator module, hold securely with both hands, and ensure that the bag and trim cover are pointed away.

• Place the inflator module on a bench or other surface with the bag and trim cover facing up.

• With the inflator module on the bench, never place anything on or close to the module which may be thrown in the event of an accidental deployment.

1. Do not attempt to repair any of the air bag system wiring harness connectors. If any of the connectors or wires are faulty, replace that harness.

• Air bag components should not be subjected to heat over 200° F. Remove the SRS-ECU, the air bag modules themselves and the clock spring before drying or baking the vehicle after painting.

• After air bag system service, check the SRS warning light operation to be sure that the system functions properly.

• Make certain that the ignition switch is in the **OFF** position when a scan tool is connected or disconnected.

DO NOT use any electrical test equipment on or near any SRS components except those specified by Chrysler corporation:

• Use a digital multi-meter for which the maximum test current is 2mA or less at the minimum range of resistance measurement for use with the Chrysler SRS Check Harness when checking the SRS electrical circuitry.

• Chrysler special tool MB991613 SRS Check Harness acts like a "break-out box" for checking SRS wiring. There are other factory special tool wiring adapters that are available and may be used.

• DRB III or equivalent scan tool for reading and erasing air bag diagnostic codes.

NEVER ATTEMPT TO REPAIR THE FOLLOWING COMPONENTS:

• Air Bag Control Unit (SRS-ECU)
• Air Bag Modules
• If any of these components are diagnosed as faulty, they should only be replaced.

DISARMING

The Air Bag system (Chrysler also calls it the Supplemental Restraint System or SRS) is designed to supplement the driver's and passenger's seat belts to help reduce the risk or severity of injury to the driver and front passenger by activating and deploying both air bags in certain frontal collisions. The system consists of two air bag modules, one located in the center of the steering wheel and another located above the glove box, which contains the folded air bag and an inflator unit. The air bag Electronic Control Unit (SRS-ECU) located under the floor console assembly monitors the system and which contains a safing G sensor and analog G sensor. An SRS warning light is located on the instrument panel which indicates the status of the air bag system. A clock spring interconnection is located within the steering column.

To deploy the air bags, the SRS-ECU must respond to the output signal from the analog G sensor and the safing G sensor must be ON. The SRS-ECU, then causes the air bag modules to ignite and deploy.

Service technicians should use care when working around any vehicle equipped with an air bag system, to avoid injury to the technician by inadvertent deployment of the air bag or to the driver by rendering the air bag system inoperative.

The SRS-ECU not only controls the air bag system, it can provide diagnostic information. The SRS-ECU monitors the air bag system and stores data concerning any detected faults in the system. When the ignition key is turned to the **ON** or **START** position, the SRS warning light should illuminate for about 7 seconds, then turn off. That indicates that the SRS system is in operating condition. If the SRS warning light does not illuminate as described or stays on for more than 7 seconds or if the SRS light illuminates while driving, imme-

diate inspection is required. If the vehicle's SRS warning light is in any of these three conditions, the SRS system must be inspected, diagnosed and serviced.

To avoid injury from accidental deployment of the air bag during vehicle servicing, refer to all service precautions.

✳✳ CAUTION

The Air Bag system must be disarmed before removing many components. Failure to do so may cause accidental deployment of the air bag, resulting in unnecessary system repairs and/or personal injury.

1. Disarm the air bag system using the following procedure:

a. Position the front wheels in the straight-ahead position and place the key in the **LOCK** position. Remove the key from the ignition lock cylinder.

b. Disconnect the negative battery cable and insulate the cable end with high-quality electrical tape or similar non-conductive wrapping.

c. Wait at least one minute before working on the vehicle. The air bag system is designed to retain enough voltage to deploy the air bag for a short period of time even after the battery has been disconnected.

Power Rack and Pinion Steering Gear

REMOVAL & INSTALLATION

✳✳ CAUTION

Prior to removal of the steering rack and pinion unit, center the front wheels and remove the ignition key. Failure to do so may damage the SRS (air bag system) clock spring under the steering wheel and render SRS system inoperative, risking serious driver injury.

1. Before servicing the vehicle, refer to the precautions in the beginning of this section.

2. Drain the power steering fluid using the following procedure:

a. Disconnect the power steering return (low side) hose.

b. Connect a suitable container to the hose.

c. Properly disable the ignition system by removing the connector from the ignition coil.

d. While cranking the engine, turn the wheels, several times, from side-to-side, until the fluid is removed.

3. Disarm the SRS system.

4. Raise and safely support the vehicle.

5. Remove both front wheels.

6. Remove the bolt holding the lower steering column joint to the rack and pinion input shaft.

7. Remove the stabilizer bar and the washer tank.

8. Remove the cotter pins and using joint separator MB991113, disconnect the tie rod ends from the steering knuckles.

9. On vehicles equipped with Electronic Control Power steering (EPS), disconnect the wiring harness, from the solenoid connector.

10. Locate the two triangular braces near the crossmember and remove both.

11. Support the center crossmember. Remove the through-bolt from the front round roll stopper and remove the three bolts securing the center crossmember.

12. Remove the center crossmember.

13. Properly support the engine and remove the rear roll stopper through-bolt. Lower the engine slightly.

✳✳ WARNING

In order to prevent damage to the engine, when supporting and jacking the engine, place a block of wood between the jack and the oil pan.

14. Disconnect the power steering fluid pressure pipe and return hose from the rack fittings. Plug the fittings to prevent excessive fluid leakage.

15. Remove the clamp bolts and the two bolts securing the rack assembly to the chassis.

16. Remove the rack and pinion steering assembly and its rubber mounts.

➡ **When removing the rack and pinion assembly, tilt the assembly to the inner side of the compression lower arm, and remove from the left side of the vehicle. Use caution to avoid damaging the boots.**

To install:

17. Align the rack assembly so the splines are inserted into the steering column shaft.

18. Install the rack and the mounting bolts. Tighten the mounting bolts to 51 ft. lbs. (69 Nm).

19. Install the pinch bolt and tighten the bolt to 13 ft. lbs. (18 Nm).

20. Connect the power steering fluid lines to the rack and tighten the high side

1. Joint assembly and gear box connecting bolt
2. Power steering pipe connection
3. Cotter pin
4. Tie rod end and knuckle connection
5. Stay (L.H.)
6. Stay (R.H.)
7. Center member assembly
8. Clamp
9. Gear box assembly

Caution
The fasteners marked * should be temporarily tightened before they are finally tightened once the total weight of the engine has been placed on the vehicle body.

7922CG30

Exploded view of the power rack and pinion steering gear mounting

fitting to 11 ft. lbs. (15 Nm). Secure the low side hose with the clamp.

21. Raise the engine into position. Install the rear roll stopper through-bolt and tighten to 32 ft. lbs. (43 Nm).

22. Raise the crossmember into position. Install the center member mounting bolts and tighten the front bolts to 58–65 ft. lbs. (78–88 Nm) and the rear bolt to 51–58 ft. lbs. (69–78 Nm).

23. Install the front roll stopper bolt and tighten the nut to 32 ft. lbs. (43 Nm).

24. Install the two triangular braces and tighten the mounting bolts to 50–56 ft. lbs. (69–78 Nm).

25. Install the stabilizer bar.

26. Connect the tie rod ends and tighten the nuts to 20 ft. lbs. (27 Nm).

27. On vehicles equipped with EPS, connect the wiring harness to the solenoid connector.

28. Install the wheels and lower the vehicle.

29. Refill the reservoir with power steering fluid and properly bleed the power steering system.

30. Perform a front end alignment.

Shock Absorber

REMOVAL & INSTALLATION

Front

1. Before servicing the vehicle, refer to the precautions in the beginning of this section.

2. Disconnect the negative battery cable.

3. Raise and safely support the vehicle.

4. Remove the appropriate wheel assembly.

5. Disconnect the sway bar link from the damper fork.

6. Remove the damper fork lower through-bolt and upper pinch bolt. Remove the damper fork assembly.

7. Remove the shock absorber upper nuts and remove the shock absorber assembly from the vehicle. DO NOT remove the large center nut.

To install:

8. Install the shock to the vehicle and tighten the upper mounting nuts to 32 ft. lbs. (44 Nm).

7922CG31

Exploded view of the front shock absorber assembly mounting

Exploded view of the front shock absorber

1. Self-locking nut
2. Washer
3. Upper bushing A
4. Upper bracket assembly
5. Upper spring pad
6. Collar
7. Upper bushing B
8. Cup assembly
9. Bump rubber
10. Dust cover
11. Coil spring
12. Shock absorber assembly

7922CG32

9. Align the shock to the damper fork and install the damper fork. Tighten the lower through-bolt/nut to 65 ft. lbs. (88 Nm) and the upper pinch bolt to 76 ft. lbs. (103 Nm).

10. Connect the sway bar link to the damper fork and tighten the link nut to 29 ft. lbs. (39 Nm).

11. Install the wheel and tire assembly.

12. Perform a front end alignment.

Rear

➡**The shock absorber assembly is a load bearing component, therefore the vehicle chassis and axle weight must be supported separately, requiring the use of two separate lifting devices.**

The rear package shelf front cover(s) must be removed to access the top mounting nuts. Most connections are plastic clips. Use care when removing these components to avoid unnecessary damage.

1. Remove the rear shelf speaker covers.

2. Remove the rear shelf top assembly.

3. Remove the front cover(s) to access the shock absorber top mounting nuts.

4. Raise and support the vehicle chassis.

5. Raise and support lower control arm assembly slightly.

6. Remove the shock absorber upper mounting nuts.

Exploded view of the rear shock absorber assembly mounting

7922CG33

Exploded view of the rear shock absorber

1. Self-locking nut
2. Washer
3. Upper bushing A
4. Bracket
5. Spring pad
6. Upper bushing B
7. Collar
8. Cup
9. Dust cover
10. Bump rubber
11. Coil spring
12. Shock absorber assembly

7922CG34

7. Remove the shock absorber lower mounting bolt and remove the assembly from the vehicle.

To install:

8. Position the shock absorber assembly so that the lower mounting bolt can be installed and lightly tightened.

9. Use a jack to raise or lower the lower control arm, so that the top shock absorber

plate studs align through the body. Raise the jack to hold the shock absorber assembly in position.

10. Install the top plate nuts on the studs and tighten the mounting nuts to 32 ft. lbs. (44 Nm).

11. Tighten the lower mounting bolt to 71 ft. lbs. (98 Nm).

12. Install the interior trim pieces to complete shock absorber installation.

Coil Spring

REMOVAL & INSTALLATION

1. Before servicing the vehicle, refer to the precautions in the beginning of this section.

2. Place the shock absorber assembly in a MB991237 and MB991238 spring compressor assembly or equivalent. Tighten the compressor and compress the spring slowly. Make certain the compressor is properly engaged before tightening.

3. After tension has been removed from the shock absorber assembly and shock absorber plate, remove the piston rod nut and washer from the top of the shock absorber assembly.

4. If the spring is to be replaced, slowly release the tension on the spring compressor. Allow the spring to expand fully. If only the shock absorber is being replaced the spring may remain in the compressor assembly.

5. By hand, remove the upper shock absorber bearing, washer, mount and shock absorber shield. Remove the upper insulator ring, the spring, the bumper and lower insulator from the spring. Take notice to each components location for proper reassembly.

To install:

6. Install the lower insulator, the shock absorber bumper and the uncompressed spring. Install the upper spring insulator, shock absorber shield, mount and washer.

7. Install or align the spring compressor. Make certain the spring is correctly positioned relative to the upper and lower insulator rings. Smoothly compress the spring.

8. Install the washer and piston rod nut. Tighten the nut on the front strut to 18 ft. lbs. (25 Nm) or 16 ft. lbs. (22 Nm) on the rear strut. Install the dust cap.

9. Carefully release the spring compressor, watching the spring position as it seats. When the spring is properly seated, release/remove the compressor tools.

10. Reinstall the shock absorber assembly.

Upper Ball Joint

REMOVAL & INSTALLATION

The upper ball joint is an integrated part of the upper control arm assembly, and can not be serviced separately. A worn or damaged ball joint requires replacement of the upper control arm assembly.

Lower Ball Joint

REMOVAL & INSTALLATION

The front suspension is called a Multi-Link Suspension. There are two lower arms used in this front suspension; a curved arm called the Compression Lower Arm and also a straight arm called the Lateral Lower Arm. Both arms contain lower ball joints since there are two sockets in the steering knuckle. Ball joints and lower arms are removed and replaced as an assembly. A front end alignment is required after these procedures.

Upper Control Arm

REMOVAL & INSTALLATION

1. Before servicing the vehicle, refer to the precautions in the beginning of this section.
2. Raise and safely support the vehicle.
3. Remove the appropriate wheel.
4. Using the joint separation tool, MB991113 or equivalent, disconnect the ball joint stud from the steering knuckle.
5. The ball joint can be checked using the following procedure:
   a. An adapter (MB 990326) is available that fits onto the ball joint stud and adapts to an inch-pound torque wrench. If this tool is not available, a shop-made substitute can be fabricated.
   b. Turn the ball joint stud with the torque wrench. The factory standard for breakaway torque is 3–13 inch lbs. (0.34–1.45 Nm).
   c. If the ball joint stud is out of specification (turns too easily or is too stiff), continue with the ball joint/control arm assembly replacement. Note that the boot over the ball joint can be removed, and the joint greased. A new replacement ball joint boot is recommended.
6. Inside the engine compartment, at the shock absorber tower, locate the upper

86 Nm
62 ft.lbs.

57 Nm
41 ft.lbs.

57 Nm
41 ft.lbs.

28 Nm
20 ft.lbs.

1. Upper arm ball joint and knuckle connection
2. Self-locking nut for upper arm installation
3. Upper arm assembly
4. Upper arm shaft assembly

7922CG35

Exploded view of the upper control arm mounting

control arm mounting nuts. Remove the nuts and using the joint separation tool, separate the upper arm shafts from the shock absorber tower.
7. Remove the control arm assembly.
To install:
8. Align the upper control arm shafts to the shock absorber tower and secure it with the mounting nuts. Tighten the mounting nuts to 62 ft. lbs. (86 Nm).
9. Connect the ball joint to the knuckle and tighten the locking nut to 20 ft. lbs. (28 Nm).
10. Install the wheel and lower the vehicle.
11. Check the wheel alignment and adjust if necessary.

Lower Control Arm

REMOVAL & INSTALLATION

Lateral Lower Arm

1. Before servicing the vehicle, refer to the precautions in the beginning of this section.
2. Raise and safely support the vehicle.

3. Remove the appropriate wheel assembly.
4. Remove the stay bracket from the crossmember.
5. Using joint separator MB991113, disconnect the ball joint stud from the steering knuckle.
6. Remove the through-bolt, connecting the damper fork to the lower control arm.
7. Remove the mounting bolt connecting the lower control arm to the suspension crossmember.
8. Remove the lower control arm from the vehicle.
To install:
9. When installing the control arm, temporarily tighten the nuts and/or bolts securing the control arm to the suspension crossmember. Tighten them fully only after the vehicle is sitting on its wheels.
10. Connect the damper fork to the lower control arm and tighten the through-bolt to 64 ft. lbs. (88 Nm).
11. Connect the ball joint stud to the knuckle and tighten the nut to 65–80 ft. lbs. (88–108 Nm). Install a new cotter pin.

Turn to Section 6 for brake system applications

98 – 118 Nm
71 – 85 ft.lbs.

88 Nm
64 ft.lbs.

69 – 78 Nm
51 – 58 ft.lbs.

83 Nm
60 ft.lbs.

83 Nm
60 ft.lbs.

59 – 71 Nm
43 – 51 ft.lbs.

Lips

Dust cover

Grease: MOPAR Multi-mileage Lubricant
Part No. 2525035 or equivalent

1. Compression lower arm ball joint and knuckle connection
2. Compression lower arm mounting bolt
3. Compression lower arm assembly
4. Stay
5. Shock absorber lower mounting bolt and nut
6. Lateral lower arm ball joint and knuckle connection
7. Lateral lower arm mounting bolt and nut
8. Lateral lower arm assembly

Caution
*: Indicates parts which should be temporarily tightened, and then fully tightened with the vehicle on the ground in the unladen condition.

7922CG36

Exploded view of the lateral lower arm and the compression lower arm mounting

12. Connect the tension rod to the control arm and tighten the nuts to 80–94 ft. lbs. (108–127 Nm).

13. Connect the stay bracket to the crossmember and tighten the mounting bolts to 50–56 ft. lbs. (69–78 Nm).

14. Install the wheels and lower the vehicle to the floor.

15. Once the full weight of the vehicle is on the suspension, tighten the inner lower arm mounting bolt nut to 71–85 ft. lbs. (98–118 Nm).

16. Check the front end alignment and adjust as required.

Compression Lower Arm

1. Before servicing the vehicle, refer to the precautions in the beginning of this section.

2. Raise and support the vehicle safely.

3. Remove the appropriate wheel assembly.

4. Using joint separator MB991113, disconnect the ball joint stud from the steering knuckle.

5. Remove the mounting bolts connecting the lower control arm to the suspension crossmember.

To install:

6. Connect the control arm to the suspension crossmember, and tighten the bolts to 60 ft. lbs. (83 Nm).

7. Connect the ball joint stud to the knuckle and tighten the nut to 43–51 ft. lbs. (59–71 Nm).

8. Install the wheels and lower the vehicle to the floor.

9. Check the front end alignment and adjust as required.

Wheel Bearings

ADJUSTMENT

Front

To check hub and bearing assembly end-play, remove the caliper and rotor. Position a dial indicator to bear against the hub flange near the center ridge. Wiggle the hub back and forth. If end-play exceeds 0.002 in. (0.05mm), replace the front hub and bearing assembly.

Rear

The rear hub and wheel bearing assembly is designed for the life of the vehicle and requires no type of adjustment or periodic maintenance. The bearing is a sealed unit with the wheel hub and can only be removed and/or replaced as one unit.

REMOVAL & INSTALLATION

Front

1. Before servicing the vehicle, refer to the precautions in the beginning of this section.

2. Remove the cotter pin, halfshaft nut and washer.

3. Raise and safely support the vehicle.

4. Remove the appropriate wheel assembly.

5. If equipped with ABS, remove the Vehicle Speed Sensor (VSS),

6. Remove the caliper and brake pads. Support the caliper out of the way using wire.

7. Remove the brake rotor from the hub assembly.

8. Disconnect the upper ball joint from the steering knuckle using a press type tool and pull the knuckle outward.

✷✷ WARNING

Use of improper methods of joint separation can result in damage to joint, leading to possible failure. Never use wedge-type tools or the ball joint can be damaged.

9. From the back of the knuckle, remove the four bolts securing the hub to the knuckle.

10. Remove the hub and bearing assembly from the knuckle.

➡**The hub and wheel bearing assembly is not serviceable and should not be disassembled.**

To install:

11. Install the hub to the steering knuckle and tighten the mounting bolts to 65 ft. lbs. (88 Nm).

12. Connect the upper ball joint to the steering knuckle and tighten the self-locking nut to 21 ft. lbs. (28 Nm).

**88 Nm
65 ft.lbs.**

6

**28 Nm
21 ft.lbs.**

3

**88 Nm
65 ft.lbs.**

7

**196 – 255 Nm
145 – 188 ft.lbs.**

4

2

1

5

1. Cotter pin
2. Drive shaft nut
3. Front speed sensor <Vehicles with ABS>
4. Caliper assembly

5. Brake disc
6. Upper arm connection
7. Front hub assebly

**Caution
Do not disassemle the front hub assembly.**

7922CG37

Exploded view of the front hub assembly mounting and related components

13. Position the rotor on the hub. Install a couple of lug nuts and lightly tighten to hold the rotor on the hub.

14. Install the caliper holder and place the brake pads in the holder. Slide the caliper over the brake pads and install the guide pins. Once the caliper is secured, the lug nuts can be removed.

15. If equipped with ABS, install the VSS.

16. Install the wheel assembly and lower the vehicle.

17. Install the wheel and lower the vehicle to the floor. Examine the driveshaft (half-shaft) hub washer. Locate the chamfered side. This side is installed outward, away from the hub. Install the washer and hub nut. Tighten the axle nut with the brakes applied. Tighten the nut to 145–188 ft. lbs. (200–260 Nm).

18. Install a new cotter pin and bend to secure.

✳✳ WARNING

Pump the brake pedal until hard, before attempting to move the vehicle.

Rear

WITH DRUM BRAKES

1. Before servicing the vehicle, refer to the precautions in the beginning of this section.

2. Raise and safely support the vehicle.

3. Remove the appropriate wheel assembly.

4. If equipped with ABS, remove the Vehicle Speed Sensor (VSS).

5. Remove the brake drum from the hub assembly.

6. From the back of the knuckle, remove the four bolts securing the hub to the knuckle.

7. Remove the hub and bearing assembly from the knuckle.

➡**The hub assembly is not serviceable and should not be disassembled.**

8. If replacing the hub, use special socket MB991248 and a press, to remove the wheel sensor rotor from the hub.

To install:

9. Press the wheel sensor rotor onto the hub.

10. Install the hub to the knuckle and tighten the mounting bolts to 54–65 ft. lbs. (74–88 Nm).

11. Install the brake drum on the hub.

12. If equipped with ABS, install the VSS.

13. Install the wheel assembly and lower the vehicle.

WITH DISC BRAKES

1. Before servicing the vehicle, refer to the precautions in the beginning of this section.

2. Raise and safely support the vehicle.

3. Remove the appropriate wheel assembly.

4. If equipped with ABS, remove the Vehicle Speed Sensor (VSS).

5. Remove the caliper and brake pads. Support the caliper out of the way using wire.

6. Remove the brake rotor from the hub assembly.

7. Remove the parking brake shoes as follows:

   a. Remove the upper shoe-to-anchor springs.

<Vehicles with drum brakes>

74 – 88 Nm
54 – 65 ft.lbs.

<Vehicles with disc brakes>

74 – 88 Nm
54 – 65 ft.lbs.

49 – 59 Nm
36 – 43 ft.lbs.

1. Rear speed sensor
   <Vehicles with ABS>
2. Caliper assembly
3. Brake drum
4. Brake disc
5. Clip mounting bolt
6. Shoe and lining assembly
   <Drum in disc brake>
7. Rear hub assembly
8. ABS-rotor <Vehicles with ABS>

Caution
Do not disassemble the rear hub assembly.

7922CG38

Exploded view of the rear hub assembly mounting

b. Remove the lower shoe-to-shoe spring.

c. Remove the brake shoe hold-down springs.

d. Disconnect the parking brake cable from the actuating lever.

8. From the back of the knuckle, remove the four bolts securing the hub to the knuckle.

9. Remove the hub and bearing assembly from the knuckle.

➡**The hub assembly is not serviceable and should not be disassembled.**

10. If replacing the hub, use special socket MB991248 and a press, to remove the wheel sensor rotor from the hub.

To install:

11. Press the wheel sensor rotor onto the hub.

12. Install the hub to the knuckle and tighten the mounting bolts to 54–65 ft. lbs. (74–88 Nm).

13. Install the parking brake shoes.

14. Position the rotor on the hub. Install a couple of lug nuts and lightly tighten to hold rotor on hub.

15. Install the caliper holder and place brake pads in holder. Slide the caliper over brake pads and install guide pins. Once caliper is secured, lug nuts can be removed.

16. If equipped with ABS, install the VSS.

17. Install the wheel assembly and lower the vehicle.

PRECAUTIONS

Before servicing any vehicle, please be sure to read all of the following precautions, which deal with personal safety, prevention of component damage, and important points to take into consideration when servicing a motor vehicle:

• Never open, service or drain the radiator or cooling system when the engine is hot; serious burns can occur from the steam and hot coolant.

• Observe all applicable safety precautions when working around fuel. Whenever servicing the fuel system, always work in a well-ventilated area. Do not allow fuel spray or vapors to come in contact with a spark, open flame, or excessive heat (a hot drop light, for example). Keep a dry chemical fire extinguisher near the work area. Always keep fuel in a container specifically designed for fuel storage; also, always properly seal fuel containers to avoid the possibility of fire or explosion. Refer to the additional fuel system precautions later in this section.

• Fuel injection systems often remain pressurized, even after the engine has been turned **OFF**. The fuel system pressure must be relieved before disconnecting any fuel lines. Failure to do so may result in fire and/or personal injury.

• Brake fluid often contains polyglycol ethers and polyglycols. Avoid contact with the eyes and wash your hands thoroughly after handling brake fluid. If you do get brake fluid in your eyes, flush your eyes with clean, running water for 15 minutes. If eye irritation persists, or if you have taken brake fluid internally, IMMEDIATELY seek medical assistance.

• The EPA warns that prolonged contact with used engine oil may cause a number of skin disorders, including cancer! You should make every effort to minimize your exposure to used engine oil. Protective gloves should be worn when changing oil. Wash your hands and any other exposed skin areas as soon as possible after exposure to used engine oil. Soap and water, or waterless hand cleaner should be used.

• All new vehicles are now equipped with an air bag system, often referred to as a Supplemental Restraint System (SRS) or Supplemental Inflatable Restraint (SIR) system. The system must be disabled before performing service on or around system components, steering column, instrument panel components, wiring and sensors. Failure to follow safety and disabling procedures could result in accidental air bag deployment, possible personal injury and unnecessary system repairs.

• Always wear safety goggles when working with, or around, the air bag system. When carrying a non-deployed air bag, be sure the bag and trim cover are pointed away from your body. When placing a non-deployed air bag on a work surface, always face the bag and trim cover upward, away from the surface. This will reduce the motion of the module if it is accidentally deployed. Refer to the additional air bag system precautions later in this section.

• Clean, high quality brake fluid from a sealed container is essential to the safe and proper operation of the brake system. You should always buy the correct type of brake fluid for your vehicle. If the brake fluid becomes contaminated, completely flush the system with new fluid. Never reuse any brake fluid. Any brake fluid that is removed from the system should be discarded. Also,

do not allow any brake fluid to come in contact with a painted surface; it will damage the paint.

• Never operate the engine without the proper amount and type of engine oil; doing so WILL result in severe engine damage.

• Timing belt maintenance is extremely important! Many models utilize an interference-type, non-freewheeling engine. If the timing belt breaks, the valves in the cylinder head may strike the pistons, causing potentially serious (also time-consuming and expensive) engine damage. Refer to the maintenance interval charts in the front of this manual for the recommended replacement interval for the timing belt, and to the timing belt section for belt replacement and inspection.

• Disconnecting the negative battery cable on some vehicles may interfere with the functions of the on-board computer system(s) and may require the computer to undergo a relearning process once the negative battery cable is reconnected.

• When servicing drum brakes, only disassemble and assemble one side at a time, leaving the remaining side intact for reference.

• Only an MVAC-trained, EPA-certified automotive technician should service the A/C system or its components.

ENGINE REPAIR

Ignition Timing

It is not necessary to check the ignition timing, because the crankshaft position is detected directly and the ignition timing is controlled electronically.

Engine Assembly

REMOVAL & INSTALLATION

The following procedure can be used on all vehicles. Slight variations may occur due to extra connections, etc., but the basic procedure should cover all models.

1. Be sure to observe all cautions and warnings in the beginning of the section that may be related to this procedure.
2. Before servicing the vehicle, refer to the precautions in the beginning of this section.
3. Relieve the fuel system pressure.
4. Disconnect the negative battery cable.
5. If equipped, remove the engine undercover.
6. Matchmark the hood and hinges and remove the hood assembly. Remove the air cleaner assembly and all adjoining air intake duct work.
7. Drain the engine coolant into a suitable container, then remove the radiator assembly, coolant reservoir and intercooler.
8. Drain the engine oil.
9. If equipped with AWD, remove the transaxle and transfer case.
10. Tag and detach the following components: accelerator cable, heater hoses, brake vacuum hose, connection for vacuum hoses, high pressure fuel line, fuel return line, Oxygen (O_2S) sensor connection, coolant temperature gauge connection, coolant temperature sensor connector, connection for thermo switch sensor, if equipped with automatic transaxle, the connection for the idle speed control, motor position sensor connector, throttle position sensor connector, EGR temperature sensor connection (California vehicles), fuel injector connectors, power transistor connector, ignition coil connector, condenser and noise filter connector, distributor and control harness, connections for the alternator and oil pressure switch wires.
11. If equipped with A/C, remove the A/C drive belt and the compressor. Leave the A/C lines attached. DO NOT discharge the system. Wire the compressor aside.
12. Remove the power steering pump and wire aside.
13. Remove the exhaust manifold-to-head pipe nuts. Discard the gasket and replace with a new one during installation.
14. Attach a hoist to the engine and take up the engine weight. Remove the engine mount bracket. Remove any torque control

brackets (roll stoppers). Note that some engine mount pieces have arrows on them for proper assembly. Double check that all cables, hoses, harness connectors, etc., are disconnected from the engine. Lift the engine slowly from the engine compartment.

To install:

15. Install the engine and secure in position. The front lower mount through-bolt nut should not be tightened until the full weight of the engine is on the mount.
  a. Tighten the engine mount bolts to 50 ft. lbs. (69 Nm).
16. Install the exhaust pipe, power steering pump and A/C compressor.
17. Checking the tags installed during removal, attach all electrical and vacuum connections.
18. Install the transaxle in the vehicle and tighten the upper mounting bolts to 65 ft. lbs. (90 Nm). Install the starter assembly and tighten both mounting bolts to 54–65 ft. lbs. (75–90 Nm).
19. Install the radiator assembly and intercooler.
20. Install the air cleaner assembly. Install all control brackets, if not already done.

21. Fill the engine with the proper amount of engine oil. Connect the negative battery cable.
22. Refill the cooling system. Start the engine, and allow it to reach normal operating temperature. Check for leaks.
23. Check the ignition timing and adjust, if necessary.
24. Install the hood, making sure to align the matchmarks made during disassembly.
25. Road test the vehicle and check all functions for proper operation.

Water Pump

REMOVAL & INSTALLATION

1. Be sure to observe all cautions and warnings in the beginning of the section that may be related to this procedure.
2. Drain the engine coolant into a suitable container.
3. Remove the timing belt.
4. If necessary, remove the alternator brace from the water pump.
5. Unfasten the retainers, then remove any brackets for access to the rear cover.

12–15 Nm
8.7–11 ft.lbs.

12–15 Nm
8.7–11 ft.lbs.

24 Nm
17 ft.lbs.

12–15 Nm
8.7–11 ft.lbs.

12–15 Nm
8.7–11 ft.lbs.

Removal steps
1. Generator brace
2. Water pump
3. Water pump gasket
4. O-ring

8x25
(.31x.98)

8x22
(.31x.87)

8x65
(.31x2.56)

8x22
(.31x.87)

8x14
(.31x.55)

Bolt diameter x length: mm (in.)

7922DG01

Water pump mounting and bolt locations—2.0L (VIN F) engine

**12 Nm
8.7 ft.lbs.**

1. Water pump
2. O-ring

7922DG02

Exploded view of the water pump and O-ring mounting—2.0L (VIN Y) engine

6. If necessary, remove the timing belt rear cover.

7. Remove the water pump mounting bolts.

8. Remove the water pump, gasket and O-ring. Discard the gasket and O-ring and replace with new ones during installation.

To install:

9. Install a new O-ring on the water inlet pipe. Coat the O-ring with water or coolant. Do not allow oil or other grease to contact the O-ring.

10. Use a new gasket and install the water pump on the engine block. Tighten the mounting bolts to 8.7–11 ft. lbs. (12–15 Nm). Install the alternator brace on the water pump. Tighten the brace pivot bolt to 17 ft. lbs. (24 Nm).

11. If removed, install the timing belt rear cover.

12. Install the timing belt.

13. Install the remaining components.

14. Refill the engine with coolant.

15. Connect the negative battery cable, start the engine and check for leaks.

Cylinder Head

REMOVAL & INSTALLATION

2.0L (Vin F) Engine

1. Be sure to observe all cautions and warnings in the beginning of the section that may be related to this procedure.

2. Disconnect the negative battery cable.

3. Drain the engine coolant and engine oil into suitable containers.

4. Disconnect the accelerator cable and remove the mounting bracket.

5. Detach the intake air duct (hose) from the throttle body.

6. Tag and detach the electrical connectors from the following components: Idle Air Control (IAC) motor, knock sensor (ks), Heated Oxygen (HO$_2$S) sensor, engine coolant temperature gauge sender, Engine Coolant Temperature (ECT) sensor, ignition module (power transistor), Throttle Position (TP) sensor, condenser, manifold differential pressure sensor, fuel injectors, ignition coil, Camshaft Position (CMP) sensor, Crankshaft Position (CKP) sensor, A/C compressor, and engine control wiring harness

7. Remove the engine center cover. Tag and disconnect the spark plug wires.

8. Disconnect the brake booster vacuum hose.

9. Detach the fuel lines from the fuel supply rail.

10. Disconnect the bypass hose and the water hose connections.

11. Disconnect the vacuum hoses, breather hose and the PCV hose.

12. Remove the timing belt.

13. Remove the power steering pump.

14. Remove the cylinder head cover and the semi-circular packing.

15. Remove the heat protector.

16. Mark the position of the hose clamps on the hoses and disconnect the water hoses and the radiator hoses.

17. Remove the thermostat housing and the O-ring.

18. Remove the intake manifold stay.

19. Remove the turbocharger assembly from the exhaust manifold.

20. Gradually loosen the cylinder head bolts in two or three steps using the specified sequence and remove the bolts.

21. Remove the cylinder head and the gasket. Discard the gasket and replace with a new one during installation.

To install:

22. Thoroughly clean the deck surface of the engine block and the sealing surface of the cylinder head. Check the cylinder head for warpage.

23. Measure the length of the cylinder head bolts from below the head to the end; if the bolt measures more than 3.913 in. (9.94cm), replace the bolt.

24. Install a new gasket on the engine block with the identification mark facing upwards.

25. Carefully place the cylinder head on the engine. Apply clean engine oil to the bolts and install the bolts finger-tight.

26. Tighten the bolts in the proper sequence using the following procedure:

   a. Tighten the bolts in sequence to 58 ft. lbs. (78 Nm).

   b. Loosen the bolts completely in the reverse order.

   c. Tighten the bolts in sequence to 15 ft. lbs. (20 Nm).

   d. Make a paint mark on the head of each bolt and the cylinder head at the same spot. Tighten the bolt 90 degrees or ¼ turn from the mark.

   e. Tighten the bolt an additional 90 degrees or ¼ turn so that the mark on the head of the bolt is opposite the original mark on the cylinder head.

27. Use a new gasket and install the turbocharger on the exhaust manifold.

28. Install the intake manifold stay.

29. Install the thermostat housing and connect the hoses. Align the matchmarks and install the clamps.

30. Install the heat protector.

31. Apply sealant to the semi-circular packing and install it on the cylinder head.

32. Apply sealant at the front of the cylinder head where the camshaft oil seal retainer and the cylinder head come together and install the cylinder head cover using a new gasket.

33. Install the power steering pump.

34. Install the timing belt.

35. Connect the PCV, breather and vacuum hoses.

36. Connect the water hose and the bypass hose.

37. Use a new O-ring and connect the lines to the fuel supply rail. Apply a small amount of engine oil to the new O-ring.

38. Connect the brake booster vacuum hose.

Cylinder head bolt removal sequence—2.0L (VIN F and Y) engines

Cylinder head bolt tightening sequence—2.0L (VIN F and Y) engines

39. Connect the spark plug wires and install the center cover.

40. Attach all of the connectors, as tagged during removal.

41. Connect the intake air hose to the throttle body.

42. Connect and adjust the accelerator cable.

43. Refill the engine with coolant.

44. Replace the oil filter and refill the engine with the proper amount of oil.

45. Connect the negative battery cable, start the engine and check for fuel, coolant and oil leaks.

2.0L (Vin Y) Engine

1. Be sure to observe all cautions and warnings in the beginning of the section that may be related to this procedure.

2. Disconnect the negative battery cable.

3. Drain the engine coolant and oil into suitable containers.

4. Remove the air cleaner and air intake duct.

5. Tag and detach the connectors from the following components: A/C compressor, Power Steering Pressure (PSP) switch, Heated Oxygen (HO$_2$S) sensor, engine coolant temperature gauge sender, Engine Coolant Temperature (ECT) sensor, Manifold Absolute Pressure (MAP) sensor, Intake Air Temperature (IAT) sensor, Throttle Position (TP) sensor, Idle Air Control (IAC) motor, injector harness, ignition coil, Camshaft Position (CMP) sensor, and EGR solenoid valve.

6. Disconnect the accelerator cable from the throttle body.

7. Detach the heater hoses from the rear of the engine.

8. Disconnect the fuel lines from the fuel supply rail.

9. Detach the purge air hose and the brake booster vacuum hose connections.

10. Unfasten the overflow tube connection.

11. Mark the position of the clamp on the hose and disconnect the upper radiator hose and the water hose connections.

12. Remove the timing belt.

13. Remove the intake manifold stay.

14. Remove the intake and exhaust camshafts.

15. Disconnect the exhaust pipe connection from the exhaust manifold.

16. Unfasten the cylinder head mounting bolts, in the proper sequence, then remove the cylinder head from the vehicle.

To install:

17. Thoroughly clean the cylinder head and engine block sealing surfaces. Check the deck and the cylinder head for warpage.

18. Clean the cylinder head bolts and inspect them for stretching. If a bolt appears to be stretched, replace it.

19. Place a new head gasket on the engine block and carefully place the cylinder head on the engine.

20. Coat the threads of the bolts with clean engine oil and install the bolts finger-tight in the engine block. The short bolts go in the corners.

21. Tighten the cylinder head bolts in the proper sequence and in the following three steps:

  a. Tighten the center bolts 1 through 6 to 25 ft. lbs. (33 Nm), then tighten the outer bolts 7 through 10 to 20 ft. lbs. (27 Nm).

  b. Tighten the center bolts 1 through 6 to 50 ft. lbs. (67 Nm), then tighten the outer bolts 7 through 10 to 20 ft. lbs. (27 Nm).

  c. Retighten the center bolts 1 through 6 to 50 ft. lbs. (67 Nm), then retighten the outer bolts 7 through 10 to 20 ft. lbs. (27 Nm).

  d. Turn all fasteners 1 through 10 ¼ turn (90 degrees) more in sequence. Do not use a torque wrench for this step.

22. Use a new gasket and connect the front exhaust pipe to the exhaust manifold.

23. Install the camshafts.

24. Install the timing belts.

25. Install the intake manifold stay.

26. Connect the upper radiator hose. Install the clamp in the original position.

27. Attach the water hose to the water pipe.

28. Connect the overflow tube.

29. Attach the brake booster vacuum hose and purge air hose connection.

30. Use a new O-ring and connect the fuel lines to the fuel supply rail.

31. Connect the heater hose.

32. Attach all electrical connectors, as tagged during removal.

33. Install and adjust the accelerator cable.

34. Install the air intake duct and the air cleaner assembly.

35. Refill the engine with oil and coolant. Replace the oil filter.

36. Turn the ignition to the **ON** position and check for fuel leaks. Then, start the engine and check for coolant leaks and proper operation.

Rocker Arm/Shafts

REMOVAL & INSTALLATION

The DOHC engines do not use rocker arm shafts; the valves are directly actuated by rocker arms. To remove the arms, the camshaft must first be removed. It is recommended that all rocker arms and lash adjusters be replaced together. Refer the camshaft procedure for details.

Turbocharger

REMOVAL & INSTALLATION

1. Be sure to observe all cautions and warnings in the beginning of the section that may be related to this procedure.

2. Disconnect the negative battery cable.

3. Drain the engine oil, cooling system and remove the radiator. On vehicles equipped with A/C, remove the condenser fan assembly with the radiator.

4. Disconnect the Oxygen (O$_2$S) sensor connector and remove the sensor.

Timing belt service is covered in Section 5 of this manual

5. Remove the oil dipstick and tube.

6. Remove the air intake bellows hose, the wastegate vacuum hose, the connections for the air outlet hose, and the upper and lower heat shield.

7. Unbolt the power steering pump and bracket assembly and leaving the hoses connected, wire it aside.

8. Remove the self-locking exhaust manifold nuts, the triangular engine hanger bracket, the eyebolt and gaskets that connect the oil feed line to the turbo center section and the water cooling lines. The water line under the turbo has a threaded connection.

9. Remove the exhaust pipe nuts and gasket and lift off the exhaust manifold. Discard the gasket.

10. Remove the two through-bolts and two nuts that hold the exhaust manifold to the turbocharger.

11. Remove the two capscrews from the oil return line (under the turbo). Discard the gasket. Separate the turbo from the exhaust manifold. The two water pipes and oil feed line can still be attached.

12. Visually check the turbine wheel (hot side) and compressor wheel (cold side) for cracking or other damage. Check whether the turbine wheel and the compressor wheel

can be easily turned by hand. Check for oil leakage. Check whether or not the wastegate valve remains open. If any problem is found, replace the part. Inspect oil passages for restriction or deposits and clean as required.

13. The wastegate can be checked with a pressure tester. Apply approximately 9 psi (62 kPa) to the actuator and be sure the rod moves. Do not apply more than 10.3 psi (71 kPa) or the diaphragm in the wastegate may be damaged. Vacuum applied to the wastegate actuator should be maintained, replace if it leaks vacuum. Do not attempt to adjust the wastegate valve.

To install:

14. Prime the oil return line with clean engine oil. Replace all locking nuts. Before installing the threaded connection for the water inlet pipe, apply light oil to the inner surface of the pipe flange. Assemble the turbocharger and exhaust manifold.

15. Install the exhaust manifold using a new gasket.

16. Connect the water cooling lines, oil feed line and engine hanger.

17. If removed, install the power steering pump and bracket.

18. Install the heat shields, air outlet hose, wastegate hose and air intake bellows.

19. Install the oil dipstick tube and dipstick. Install the O_2S sensor.

20. Install the radiator assembly.

21. Fill the engine with fresh oil, fill the cooling system and reconnect the negative battery cable.

Intake Manifold

REMOVAL & INSTALLATION

2.0L (VIN F) Engine

1. Be sure to observe all cautions and warnings in the beginning of the section that may be related to this procedure.

2. Relieve the fuel system pressure.

3. Disconnect the negative battery cable.

4. Drain the cooling system.

5. Disconnect the accelerator cable, breather hose and air intake hose.

6. Disconnect the upper radiator hose, heater hose and water bypass hose.

7. Remove all vacuum hoses and pipes as necessary, including the brake booster vacuum line.

8. Disconnect the high pressure fuel line and the fuel return hose.

9. Tag and detach the electrical connectors from the Oxygen (O_2S) sensor, Engine Coolant Temperature (ECT) sensor, thermo switch, idle speed control, EGR temperature sensor and spark plug wires.

10. Remove the three bolts and the fuel rail with the injectors and pressure regulator still attached.

11. Remove the intake manifold bracket.

12. Disconnect the water hose at the throttle body, and the water inlet and heater connections.

13. Remove the thermostat housing, if necessary.

14. Disconnect the vacuum line from the power brake booster and PCV valve if connected.

15. Remove the intake manifold mounting bolts and remove the manifold.

To install:

16. Clean the gasket material from the intake mounting surface and manifold assembly. Check both surfaces for cracks or other damage. Check the intake manifold water passages and air passages for clogging. Clean if necessary.

17. Install a new gasket to the head, and install the manifold. Tighten the manifold in a crisscross pattern, starting from the inside and working outwards to 11–14 ft. lbs. (15–19 Nm).

18. Reinstall the fuel rail with injectors and pressure regulator, lubricating all seals

35–50 Nm
25–36 ft.lbs.

28–34 Nm
20–25 ft.lbs.

55–65 Nm
40–47 ft.lbs.

10–12 Nm
7–9 ft.lbs.

35–50 Nm
25–36 ft.lbs.

8–10 Nm
6–7 ft.lbs.

1. Oil return pipe
2. Gasket
3. Turbocharger
4. Eye bolt
5. Gasket
6. Water pipe B
7. Eye bolt
8. Gasket
9. Water pipe A
10. Eye bolt
11. Gasket
12. Oil pipe
13. Exhaust fitting
14. Gasket

7922DG06

Exploded view of the turbocharger assembly—2.0L (VIN F) engine

lightly with oil. Tighten the retaining bolts to 84–108 inch lbs. (10–13 Nm).

19. Reinstall the thermostat housing, if removed, intake manifold brace bracket, and throttle body bracket.

20. Attach or install all hoses, cables and electrical connectors that were removed.

21. Fill the system with coolant.

22. Reconnect the negative battery cable. Run the vehicle until the thermostat opens, fill the radiator completely. Check for leaks.

23. Adjust the accelerator cable. Check and adjust the ignition timing. Once the vehicle has cooled, recheck the coolant level.

2.0L (VIN Y) Engine

1. Be sure to observe all cautions and warnings in the beginning of the section that may be related to this procedure.

2. Properly relieve the fuel system pressure.

3. Disconnect the negative battery cable.

4. Drain the engine coolant.

5. Remove the vacuum reservoir, if equipped with cruise control.

6. Remove the air intake and breather hoses.

7. Remove the accelerator cable from the bracket.

8. Disconnect the engine harness retaining clips.

9. Disconnect the Manifold Absolute Pressure (MAP) sensor.

10. Disconnect the Charge Temperature (CT) sensor connector.

11. Disconnect the Throttle Position (TP) sensor and the Auto Idle Speed (AIS) motor connectors.

12. Position the engine control wiring harness out of the way.

13. Disconnect the alternator wiring harness.

14. Remove the PCV hose assembly.

15. Label and disconnect the vacuum hoses.

16. Detach the EGR pipe connection.

17. Disconnect the fuel lines from the fuel rail.

18. Remove the intake manifold stay and the engine hanger.

19. Remove the throttle body.

20. Remove the intake manifold plenum and gasket.

21. Disconnect the injector connectors.

22. Remove the fuel rail with the injectors.

23. Remove the intake manifold.

To install:

24. Use a new gasket and install the intake manifold.

25. Reinstall the fuel rail assembly and connect the injectors.

26. Use a new gasket and install the intake plenum.

27. Use a new gasket and install the throttle body.

28. Reinstall the intake manifold stay and the engine hanger.

29. Use a new O-ring and connect the fuel lines to the fuel rail.

30. Reconnect the EGR pipe.

31. Reconnect the vacuum hoses and the PCV hose assembly.

32. Reconnect the alternator wiring harness.

33. Reposition the engine control wiring harness and install the brackets and clips.

34. Reconnect the AIS motor and the TP sensor.

35. Reconnect the vacuum hose to the throttle body.

36. Reconnect the MAP and the CT sensor.

37. Reinstall the accelerator cable in the bracket and connect it to the throttle body.

38. Reconnect the breather hose and the air intake hose.

39. Reinstall the vacuum reservoir, if equipped.

40. Reconnect the negative battery cable.

41. Refill the engine with coolant.

42. Adjust the accelerator cable.

Exhaust Manifold

REMOVAL & INSTALLATION

2.0L (VIN F) Engine

1. Be sure to observe all cautions and warnings in the beginning of the section that may be related to this procedure.

2. Disconnect the battery negative cable. Drain the cooling system.

3. If equipped with A/C, remove the condenser cooling fan. Remove the power steering pump and place aside.

4. Disconnect the Oxygen (O2S) sensor harness.

5. Raise the vehicle and support safely.

6. Drain the oil and remove the dipstick tube.

7. Remove the exhaust pipe-to-turbocharger nuts and separate the exhaust pipe. Discard the gasket.

8. Lower the vehicle. Remove the air intake and vacuum hose connections.

9. Remove the exhaust manifold and turbocharger heat shields.

10. Remove the exhaust manifold-to-turbocharger attaching bolts and nut.

11. If applicable, remove the engine hanger, water and oil lines from the turbocharger.

12. Remove the exhaust manifold mounting nuts. Remove the exhaust manifold and gasket from the engine.

To install:

13. Clean all gasket material from the mating surfaces and check the manifold for damage.

14. Install new gaskets and install the manifold. Tighten the manifold-to-head nuts in a crisscross pattern to 18–22 ft. lbs. (25–30 Nm). Tighten the manifold-to-turbocharger nut and bolts to 40–47 ft. lbs. (55–65 Nm).

15. Reinstall the engine hanger, water and oil lines to the turbocharger.

16. Reinstall the heat shields.

17. Install the new gasket and connect the exhaust pipe.

18. Reinstall the condenser cooling fan and power steering pump. Reconnect the O2S sensor harness.

19. Reinstall the oil level indicator and tube replacing the O-ring as required.

20. Fill the crankcase with clean oil and refill the cooling system.

21. Reconnect the negative battery cable and run the engine until the thermostat opens.

22. Check for fluid and exhaust leaks. Top off the engine coolant.

2.0L (VIN Y) Engine

1. Be sure to observe all cautions and warnings in the beginning of the section that may be related to this procedure.

2. Disconnect the negative battery cable.

3. Drain the engine coolant.

4. Remove the air intake hose.

5. Disconnect the upper radiator hose from the water outlet.

6. Detach the air hose connection.

7. Remove the engine control wiring harness from the rear of the engine.

8. Remove the water pipe assembly.

9. Remove the oil dipstick.

10. Remove the upper heat shield.

11. Remove the engine hanger.

12. Disconnect the pulsed secondary air injection (PAIR) (check valve) valve from the exhaust pipe (manual transaxle only).

13. Disconnect the front exhaust pipe from the manifold.

14. Remove the lower heat shield.
15. Remove the exhaust manifold and gasket.

To install:

16. Use a new gasket and install the exhaust manifold. Tighten the nuts and bolts to 17 ft. lbs. (23 Nm).
17. Reinstall the lower heat shield.
18. Use a new gasket and connect the front exhaust pipe to the manifold.
19. On vehicles with manual transaxles, connect the pulsed secondary air injection valve to the exhaust pipe.
20. Reinstall the engine hanger.
21. Reinstall the upper heat shield.
22. Reinstall the dipstick and the water pipe.
23. Attach the engine wiring harness to the rear of the engine.
24. Reconnect the air hose and the upper radiator hose.
25. Reinstall the air intake hose.
26. Reconnect the negative battery cable.
27. Refill the engine with coolant, start the engine and check for leaks.

Front Crankshaft Seal

REMOVAL & INSTALLATION

2.0L (VIN F) Engine

1. Be sure to observe all cautions and warnings in the beginning of the section that may be related to this procedure.
2. Disconnect the negative battery cable.
3. Remove the timing belts.

➡If reusing the timing belt, be sure to mark the direction of rotation on the belt. This will ensure the same direction of rotation, thereby extending belt life.

4. Remove the crankshaft pulley.
5. Remove the timing belt crankshaft sprocket. If the sprocket is difficult to remove, an appropriate puller may be used.
6. Pry the seal from the bore using the proper tools.

To install:

7. Using a proper-sized driver, install a new seal.
8. Reinstall the crankshaft sprocket.
9. Reinstall the timing belt and remaining components.
10. Reinstall the engine undercover. Reconnect the negative battery cable, start the engine and check for leaks.

2.0L (VIN Y) Engine

1. Be sure to observe all cautions and warnings in the beginning of the section that may be related to this procedure.
2. Remove the timing belt.
3. Using Crankshaft Sprocket Removal tool MB995027 or equivalent, remove the crankshaft sprocket.
4. Using Crankshaft oil seal Removal tool MB995020 or equivalent, remove the oil seal. Be careful not the scratch the oil seal bore or the crankshaft sealing surface.

To prevent damaging the end of the crankshaft, use the proper sprocket removal tool—2.0L (VIN Y) engine

Using the special tool to remove the front crankshaft seal—2.0L (VIN Y) engine

To avoid damaging the front seal, use the front oil seal installer tool MB995022 or equivalent, as shown—2.0L (VIN Y) engine

Installing the front crankshaft sprocket using the Crankshaft Sprocket Installer tools MB995035 and MB995026 or equivalents—2.0L (VIN Y) engine

To install:

5. Apply clean engine oil to the oil seal. Using seal driver, install the oil seal.
6. Using Crankshaft Sprocket Installer tools MB995035 and MB995026 or equivalent, install the crankshaft sprocket.
7. Reinstall the timing belt.

Camshaft and Valve Lifters

REMOVAL & INSTALLATION

2.0L (VIN F) Engine

1. Be sure to observe all cautions and warnings in the beginning of the section that may be related to this procedure.
2. Disconnect the negative battery cable.
3. Disconnect the accelerator cable from the throttle body and remove the cable bracket from the intake plenum.
4. Remove the engine center cover.
5. Disconnect the spark plug cables from the spark plugs. Label them if necessary.
6. Disconnect the breather hose and the PCV hose from the rocker cover.
7. Remove the rocker cover.
8. Position the No. 1 piston at TDC on the compression stroke.
9. Remove the timing belt.
10. Use a wrench on the hex shaped part of the camshaft to hold the cam and remove the sprockets.
11. Loosen the bearing cap bolts in two or three steps and remove the bearing caps. If the bearing caps are hard to remove, tap the rear of the camshaft with a plastic hammer.

➡Bearing caps and rocker arms must be installed in the same location from which they were removed.

12. Remove the camshaft(s) and the seals.

Tap the camshaft with a plastic hammer to loosen the bearing caps—2.0L (VIN F) engine

Identifying the rocker arm shafts—notice the slits in the intake side

To install:

13. Apply engine oil or assembly lube to the camshafts and install them on the cylinder head with the dowels facing up.

✷✷ WARNING

If new camshaft(s) are being installed, remove the rocker arms and install the camshaft(s) and bearing caps. Be sure the camshaft(s) can be turned by hand. After checking, remove the camshafts and install the rocker arms.

For installation, position the camshafts with the dowels facing up, as shown—2.0L (VIN F) engine

14. Install the bearing caps and tighten the bolts evenly in two or three steps to 14 ft. lbs. (20 Nm).
15. Apply engine oil to the lip of the seal. Using MB998713 or a similar seal installer, install the front oil seal.
16. Install the camshaft sprockets.
17. Install the timing belt.
18. Apply sealant to the semi-circular packing and install it in the cylinder head.
19. Apply sealant to the lower part of the front and rear bearing caps where they meet the cylinder head. Use a new gasket and install the rocker cover.
20. Connect the PCV hose and the breather hose.
21. Connect the spark plug wires.
22. Install the center cover.
23. Install and adjust the accelerator cable.
24. Connect the negative battery cable.

2.0L (VIN Y) Engine

1. Be sure to observe all cautions and warnings in the beginning of the section that may be related to this procedure.
2. Disconnect the negative battery cable.
3. Remove the ignition coil pack.
4. Disconnect the PCV hose and the breather hose from the cylinder head cover.
5. Remove the semi-circular packing from the rear of the head.
6. Remove the Camshaft Position (CMP) sensor.
7. Remove the timing belt.
8. Use tool MB990767 and MB998719 or their equivalents to hold the camshaft sprockets and remove the sprocket mounting bolt and sprocket.
9. Remove the bracket and the rear timing belt cover.
10. Remove the outside camshaft bearing cap.
11. Gradually loosen the camshaft bearing caps in the reverse of the tightening sequence, one camshaft at a time, and remove the bearing caps.

➡**Keep the bearing caps in order. They must be installed in the location from which they were removed.**

12. Mark the camshafts for later identification and remove the camshafts. The camshafts are not interchangeable.

To install:

13. Apply engine oil or assembly lube to the camshaft and install the camshafts.
14. Install the bearing caps. Tighten the bolts evenly and in sequence.

Camshaft bearing cap bolt tightening sequence—2.0L (VIN Y) engine

Cylinder head cover bolt tightening sequence—2.0L (VIN Y) engine

15. Apply Loctite 518® to the outside camshaft bearing caps and install them.
16. Install the camshaft oil seal.
17. Install the rear timing belt cover and the bracket.
18. Use the special tools and install the camshaft sprockets.
19. Install the timing belt.
20. Apply Loctite 5699® or equivalent to the semi-circular packing and install it in the rear of the cylinder head.
21. Install the CMP sensor.
22. Install the cylinder head cover. Tighten the bolts in the proper sequence, evenly as follows:
    a. 40 inch lbs. (4.5 Nm).
    b. 80 inch lbs. (9.0 Nm).
    c. 106 inch lbs. (12 Nm).
23. Install the air, breather and PCV hoses.
24. Install the coil pack.
25. Connect the negative battery cable.

Valve Lash

ADJUSTMENT

Valve clearance is not adjustable. Proper valve clearance is maintained by the hydraulic lash adjusters.

Refer to Section 1 for engine rebuilding specifications

Oil Pan

REMOVAL & INSTALLATION

2.0L (VIN F) Engine

1. Be sure to observe all cautions and warnings in the beginning of the section that may be related to this procedure.
2. Disconnect the negative battery cable.
3. Raise the vehicle and support safely.
4. Remove the oil pan drain plug and drain the engine oil.
5. Disconnect and lower the exhaust pipe from the engine manifold.
6. On AWD models, remove the transfer assembly and right driveshaft.
7. Using the appropriate equipment, support the weight of the engine and remove the crossmember.
8. Disconnect the return pipe for the turbocharger from the side of the oil pan.
9. Remove the oil pan bolts. Tap a thin prytool between the engine block and the oil pan to break the seal.
10. Inspect the oil pan for damage and cracks. Replace if faulty. While the pan is removed, inspect the oil screen for clogging, damage and cracks. Replace if faulty.

To install:

11. Using a wire brush or other tool, clean all gasket surfaces of the cylinder block and the oil pan so that all loose material is removed. Clean sealing surfaces of all dirt and oil.
12. Apply sealant around the gasket surfaces of the oil pan in such a manner that all bolt holes are circled and there is a continuous bead of sealer around the entire perimeter of the oil pan.

➡ **The continuous bead of sealer should be applied in a bead approximately 0.16 in. (4mm) in diameter.**

13. Install the oil pan onto the cylinder block within 15 minutes after applying sealant. Reinstall the fasteners and tighten to 48–72 inch lbs. (6–8 Nm).
14. Reinstall the oil return pipe using a new gasket, if removed. Tighten the retainers to 62–88 inch lbs. (7–10 Nm).
15. Reinstall the crossmember and tighten the mounting bolts to 72 ft. lbs. (100 Nm).
16. Reinstall the left member and tighten the forward retainer bolts to 72 ft. lbs. (100 Nm). Tighten the rearward left member bolts to 58 ft. lbs. (80 Nm).
17. Reinstall the transfer assembly and right driveshaft.

18. Reconnect the exhaust pipe to the manifold with a new gasket. Tighten the exhaust pipe-to-manifold flange nuts to 43 ft. lbs. (60 Nm).
19. Reinstall the oil drain plug and tighten to 33 ft. lbs. (42 Nm).
20. Lower the vehicle and fill the crankcase to the proper level with clean engine oil.

❋❋ WARNING

Operating the engine without the proper amount and type of engine oil will result in severe engine damage.

21. Reconnect the negative battery cable. Start the engine and check for leaks.

2.0L (VIN Y) Engine

1. Be sure to observe all cautions and warnings in the beginning of the section that may be related to this procedure.
2. Disconnect the negative battery cable.
3. Raise and safely support the vehicle.
4. Drain the engine oil.
5. Remove the front exhaust pipe.
6. Remove the dipstick and tube assembly.
7. Remove the front plate.
8. Remove the oil pan mounting bolts.
9. Remove the oil pan and gasket.

To install:

10. Clean all traces of old gasket or sealer material from the oil pan and engine block mating surfaces.
11. Apply sealant at the point where the engine block meets the oil pump.
12. Use a new gasket and install the oil pan. Tighten the mounting bolts to 107 inch lbs. (12 Nm).
13. Reinstall the front plate.
14. Reinstall the front exhaust pipe.
15. Reinstall the dipstick and tube assembly.
16. Lower the vehicle.
17. Refill the crankcase with oil to the proper level.
18. Reconnect the negative battery cable.
19. Start the engine and check for leaks.

Oil Pump

REMOVAL & INSTALLATION

2.0L (VIN F) Engine

❋❋ WARNING

Whenever the oil pump is disassembled or the cover is removed, the gear cavity must be filled with petro-

leum jelly. This seals the pump and acts like a primer so the oil pump draws oil as soon as the engine turns. Do not use grease.

1. Be sure to observe all cautions and warnings in the beginning of the section that may be related to this procedure.
2. Disconnect the negative battery cable. Rotate the engine so that the No. 1 cylinder is at Top Dead Center (TDC) of its compression stroke. The timing marks should be aligned at this point.
3. Raise and safely support the vehicle.
4. Drain the engine oil. Lower the vehicle.
5. Using the proper equipment, support the weight of the engine. Remove the front engine mount bracket and accessory drive belts.
6. Remove timing belt upper and lower covers.
7. Remove the timing belt and crankshaft sprocket.
8. Detach the electrical connector from the oil pressure sending unit and remove the oil pressure sensor. Remove the oil filter and bracket.
9. Remove the oil pan, oil screen and gasket.
10. Using special plug removal tool MD998162, remove the plug cap in the engine front cover.
11. Remove the plug on the side of the engine block. Insert a suitable tool with a shaft diameter of 0.32 in. (8mm) into the plug hole. This will hold the silent shaft in position.
12. Remove the driven gear bolt that secures the oil pump driven gear to the silent shaft.
13. Remove and tag the front cover mounting bolts. Note the lengths of the mounting bolts as they are removed for proper installation.
14. Remove the front case cover and oil pump assembly. If necessary, the silent shaft can come out with the cover assembly.
15. Remove the oil pump cover, located on the back of the engine front cover. Remove the oil pump drive and driven gears.
16. After disassembling the oil pump, clean all components and remove all residual gasket material from the mating surfaces.
17. Assemble the oil pump gears into the front case and rotate it to ensure smooth movement and no looseness. Be sure there is no ridge wear on the contact surface between the front case and the gear surface of the oil pump front cover.

To install:

18. Align the timing mark on the oil pump drive gear with that on the driven gear and install them into the engine front case. Apply engine oil to the gears.

19. Reinstall the oil pump cover and tighten the retainer bolts to 13 ft. lbs. (18 Nm).

20. Using the appropriate driver, install a new crankshaft seal into the front case.

21. Position a new front case gasket in place. Set seal guide tool MD998285 or equivalent on the front end of the crankshaft to protect the seal from damage. Apply a thin coat of oil to the outer circumference of the seal pilot tool.

22. Reinstall the front case assembly through a new front case gasket and temporarily tighten the flange bolts.

23. Mount the oil filter on the bracket with a new oil filter bracket gasket in place. Reinstall the four bolts with washers and tighten to 25 ft. lbs. (34 Nm).

24. Insert a suitable tool into the hole in the left side of the engine block to lock the silent shaft in place.

25. Secure the oil pump drive gear onto the left silent shaft by installing and tightening the driven gear bolt to 29 ft. lbs. (40 Nm).

26. Install a new O-ring in the groove in the front case and install the plug cap. Using the special tool MD998162 or equivalent, tighten the cap to 20 ft. lbs. (27 Nm).

27. Reinstall the oil screen in position with a new gasket in place.

28. Clean both mating surfaces of the oil pan and the cylinder block. Apply sealant in the groove in the oil pan flange, keeping towards the inside of the bolt holes. The width of the sealant bead applied is to be about 0.16 in. (4mm) wide.

➡**Install the oil pan within 15 minutes of sealant application.**

Using the special tool to tighten the plug cap—2.0L (VIN F) engine

29. Install the oil pan to the engine and secure with the retainers. Tighten the bolts to 108 inch lbs. (12 Nm).

30. Reinstall the oil pressure gauge unit and the oil pressure switch. Reconnect the electrical harness.

31. Reinstall the oil cooler. Secure it with the oil cooler bolt tightened to 33 ft. lbs. (45 Nm).

32. Install new oil filter and refill the crankcase.

33. Reconnect the negative battery cable and start the engine. Verify oil pressure and inspect for leaks.

2.0L (VIN Y) Engine

1. Be sure to observe all cautions and warnings in the beginning of the section that may be related to this procedure.

2. Disconnect the negative battery cable.

3. Raise and safely support the vehicle.

4. Drain the engine oil.

5. Remove the rear plate.

6. Remove the oil filter and adapter.

7. Remove the oil pan.

8. Remove the oil pick-up tube.

9. Remove the timing belt.

10. Using the crankshaft sprocket Removal tool MB995027 or equivalent, remove the crankshaft sprocket.

✳✳ WARNING

Do not nick the crankshaft sealing surface or the seal bore.

11. Using crankshaft oil seal tool MB995020 or equivalent, remove the crankshaft oil seal.

12. Remove the oil pump mounting bolts.

13. Remove the oil pump.

To install:

14. Apply a bead of sealant to the sealing surface of the oil pump and install a new O-ring into the counterbore on the oil pump discharge passage.

15. Carefully install the oil pump on the crankshaft until seated to the engine block. Tighten the bolts to 17 ft. lbs. (23 Nm).

16. Install a new crankshaft oil seal in the oil pump.

17. Reinstall the crankshaft sprocket using the proper installation tools.

18. Reinstall the timing belt and related components.

19. Reinstall the oil pick-up tube.

20. Apply Loctite® 18718 or equivalent at the point where the oil pump meets the engine block.

21. Reinstall the oil pan using a new gasket. Tighten the mounting bolts to 108 inch lbs. (12 Nm).

22. Use a new O-ring and install the oil filter adapter onto the engine. Be sure the roll pin aligns with the hole. Tighten the assembly to 40 ft. lbs. (55 Nm).

23. Reinstall a new oil filter.

24. Reinstall the rear plate.

25. Safely lower the vehicle to the floor.

26. Refill the engine with the proper amount of oil.

✳✳ WARNING

Operating the engine without the proper amount and type of engine oil will result in severe engine damage.

27. Start the engine and check for leaks.

Rear Main Seal

REMOVAL & INSTALLATION

1. Be sure to observe all cautions and warnings in the beginning of the section that may be related to this procedure.

2. Disconnect the negative battery cable.

3. Remove the transaxle and transfer case, if equipped, from the vehicle.

4. If equipped with an automatic transaxle, remove the flywheel/ring gear assembly from the crankshaft.

5. If equipped with a manual transaxle, remove the rear engine plate and the bell housing cover.

6. If the crankshaft rear oil seal case is leaking, remove it. Otherwise, just remove the oil seal. Some engines have a separator that should also be removed.

To install:

7. Lubricate the inner diameter of the new seal with clean engine oil.

8. Install the oil seal in the crankshaft rear oil seal case using tool MD998376 or an equivalent seal installer. Press the seal all the way in without tilting it. Drive the oil separator into the oil seal case so the oil hole in the separator is downward.

9. Install the seal case on the crankshaft with a new gasket, if removed.

10. Install the flywheel or drive plate, transfer case and transaxle.

11. Connect the negative battery cable and check for leaks.

❊❊ WARNING

Operating the engine without the proper amount and type of engine oil will result in severe engine damage.

12. Fill the crankcase with clean oil to the proper level. Start the engine and check for leaks.

FUEL SYSTEM

Fuel System Service Precautions

Safety is an important factor when servicing the fuel system. Failure to conduct maintenance and repairs in a safe manner may result in serious personal injury. Maintenance and testing of the vehicle's fuel system components can be accomplished safely and effectively by adhering to the following rules and guidelines.

• To avoid the possibility of fire and personal injury, always disconnect the negative battery cable unless the repair or test procedure requires that battery voltage be applied.

• Always relieve the fuel system pressure prior to disconnecting any fuel system component (injector, fuel rail, pressure regulator, etc.), fitting or fuel line connection. Exercise extreme caution whenever relieving fuel system pressure to avoid exposing skin, face and eyes to fuel spray. Please be advised that fuel under pressure may penetrate the skin or any part of the body that it contacts.

• Always place a shop towel or cloth around the fitting or connection prior to loosening to absorb any excess fuel due to spillage. Ensure that all fuel spillage is quickly removed from engine surfaces. Ensure that all fuel soaked cloths or towels are deposited into a suitable waste container.

• Always keep a dry chemical (Class B) fire extinguisher near the work area.

• Do not allow fuel spray or fuel vapors to come into contact with a spark or open flame.

• Always use a back-up wrench when loosening and tightening fuel line connection fittings. This will prevent unnecessary stress and torsion to fuel line piping.

• Always replace worn fuel fitting O-rings. Do not substitute fuel hose where fuel pipe is installed.

Fuel System Pressure

RELIEVING

1. Be sure to observe all cautions and warnings in the beginning of the section that may be related to this procedure.
2. Remove the rear seat cushion.
3. Remove the protector, then detach the fuel pump connector.
4. Start the engine and allow it to run until it stops, due to lack of fuel. Turn the ignition switch to the **OFF** position.
5. Disconnect the negative battery cable.
6. Attach the fuel pump connector and install the protector.
7. Install the rear seat cushion.

Fuel Filter

REMOVAL & INSTALLATION

On most vehicles covered by this manual, the fuel filter is located in the engine compartment, mounted on the firewall. On some non-turbo engines, the fuel filter is mounted under the vehicle near the fuel tank.

❊❊ CAUTION

Do not use conventional fuel filters, hoses or clamps when servicing fuel injection systems. They are not compatible with the injection system and could fail, causing personal injury or damage to the vehicle. Use only hoses and clamps specifically designed for fuel injection systems.

1. Properly relieve the fuel system pressure.
2. If not already done, disconnect the negative battery cable.
3. On non-turbo engines, raise and safely support the vehicle to gain access to the filter.

➡**Wrap shop towels around the fitting that is being disconnected to absorb residual fuel in the lines.**

4. Cover the hose connection with shop towels to prevent any splash of fuel that could be caused by residual pressure in the fuel pipe line. Hold the fuel filter nut securely with a back-up wrench, then remove the eye bolt. Disconnect the high-pressure fuel line from the filter. Remove and discard the gaskets.

5. While holding the fuel filter nut securely with a back-up wrench, loosen the main pipe flare nut. Separate the flare nut

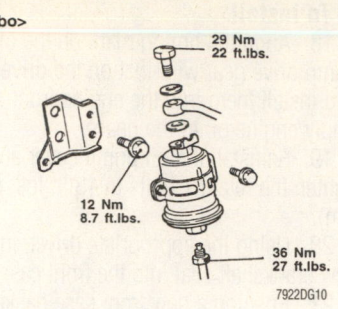

<Turbo>

29 Nm
22 ft.lbs.

12 Nm
8.7 ft.lbs.

36 Nm
27 ft.lbs.

7922DG10

Exploded view of the fuel filter mounting—2.0L (VIN F) engine

<Non-turbo>

29 Nm
22 ft.lbs.

29 Nm
22 ft.lbs.

29 Nm
22 ft.lbs.

36 Nm
27 ft.lbs.

7922DG11

Exploded view of the fuel filter mounting—2.0L (VIN Y) engine

connection from the filter. Remove and discard the gaskets.

6. If equipped with a fuel tank mounted filter, perform the following:
   a. Remove the eye bolt, gasket and connector.
   b. Remove the pressure regulator.

7. Remove the mounting bolts and remove the fuel filter. If necessary, remove the fuel filter bracket.

To install:

8. Install the filter in its bracket only finger-tight. Movement of the filter will ease attachment of the fuel lines.

➡**Be sure new O-rings are installed prior to assembly.**

9. Insert the main pipe at the connector part of the filter and manually screw in the main pipe's flare nut.

10. While holding the fuel filter nut with a back-up wrench, tighten the eye bolts to 22 ft. lbs. (30 Nm). Tighten the flare nut to 25 ft. lbs. (35 Nm), with a back-up wrench on the nut.

11. Tighten the filter mounting bolts to 10 ft. lbs. (14 Nm).

12. Connect the negative battery cable. Turn the key to the **ON** position to pressurize the fuel system and check for leaks.

13. If repairs of a leak are required, remember to release the fuel pressure before opening the fuel system.

Fuel Pump

REMOVAL & INSTALLATION

1. Be sure to observe all cautions and warnings in the beginning of the section that may be related to this procedure.
2. Relieve the fuel system pressure.
3. Disconnect the negative battery cable.
4. Remove the rear seat cushion by pulling the seat stopper near the floor and lifting the cushion up.
5. Remove the inspection cover on the right side of the vehicle.
6. Disconnect the harness connector and the fuel lines.
7. Remove the fuel pump assembly from the tank. Use Fuel Pump Locking Ring Removal tool MB991480 or equivalent to remove the locking ring on the AWD model.

To install:
8. Install the fuel pump in the tank.
9. Attach the hoses and the harness connector.
10. Reinstall the inspection cover.
11. Reinstall the rear seat.
12. Reconnect the negative battery cable.

7922DG22

To service the fuel pump on AWD vehicles, a Fuel Pump Locking Ring Removal tool MB991480 or equivalent is needed

DRIVE TRAIN

Transaxle Assembly

REMOVAL & INSTALLATION

Manual

1. Be sure to observe all cautions and warnings in the beginning of the section that may be related to this procedure.

2. Remove the battery and the air intake hoses.
3. Remove the battery tray and support.
4. If equipped with cruise control, remove the auto-cruise actuator and bracket.
5. Drain the transaxle and transfer case fluid, if equipped, into a suitable container.
6. Remove the charcoal canister and bracket.
7. Disconnect the shift and select cables from the transaxle.
8. Disconnect the back-up light switch and the Vehicle Speed Sensor (VSS).
9. Remove the starter assembly.
10. Attach a support fixture to the engine and remove the transaxle mounting bolts.
11. Remove the rear roll stopper bracket mounting bolts.
12. Remove the transaxle mounting bracket nuts.
13. Raise and safely support the vehicle and remove the engine undercover.
14. If equipped with all wheel drive (AWD), remove the transfer case assembly.

❊❊ WARNING

Do not remove or install the axle shaft nut when the vehicle is on the floor or damage to the bearings will occur.

15. Remove the axle shafts.
16. Remove the slave cylinder from the bell housing but do not disconnect the fluid line. Position it out of the way.
17. Remove the bell housing cover and the right-hand center member stay (support).
18. Remove the center member.
19. Place a transmission jack under the transaxle and remove the transaxle mounting bolt.
20. Remove the transaxle mount and lower the transaxle.

To install:
21. Raise the transaxle into position and install the transaxle mounting. Tighten the through-bolt to 50 ft. lbs. (69 Nm).
22. Reinstall the transaxle assembly mounting bolts. Tighten the bolts to 22–25 ft. lbs. (30–34 Nm).
23. Reinstall the center member assembly and the right-hand stay.
24. Reinstall the bell housing cover and the slave cylinder.
25. Reinstall the axle shafts. Be sure to install the washer in the proper direction.
26. Reinstall the engine undercover and lower the vehicle.

27. Reinstall the transfer case assembly, if removed.
28. Reinstall the transaxle mounting bracket nuts.
29. Reinstall the rear roll stopper bracket mounting bolts.
30. Reinstall the transaxle assembly mounting bolts. Tighten the mounting bolts to 35 ft. lbs. (48 Nm).
31. Remove the engine support fixture.
32. Reinstall the starter assembly.
33. Attach the VSS and the back-up light connectors.
34. Reinstall the cruise control actuator, if removed.
35. Reinstall the battery tray support and the tray.
36. Reinstall the charcoal canister bracket and the canister.
37. Reinstall the air duct and the air cleaner assembly.
38. Refill the transaxle. On turbocharged models, fill with gear oil of classification GL-4 or higher, SAE 75W-85W or 75W-90. On non-turbocharged models, fill with Mopar MS9417 MTX Fluid P/N 4773167 or equivalent.
39. Refill the transfer case with gear oil of classification GL-4 or higher, SAE 75W-85W or 75W-90.

Automatic

1. Be sure to observe all cautions and warnings in the beginning of the section that may be related to this procedure.
2. Disconnect the negative battery cable. Remove the battery and battery tray.
3. On vehicles equipped with auto-cruise, remove the control actuator and bracket.
4. Drain the transaxle fluid.
5. Remove the air cleaner assembly, intercooler and air hose, as required.
6. Mark the shift cable. Remove the adjusting nut and disconnect the shift cable.
7. Remove the dipstick and tube assembly.
8. Detach the electrical connectors for the solenoid, neutral safety switch (inhibitor switch), pulse generator kickdown servo switch and oil temperature sensor.
9. Disconnect the speedometer cable and oil cooler lines.
10. Disconnect the wires to the starter motor and remove the starter.
11. Remove the upper transaxle-to-engine bolts.
12. Support the transaxle and remove the transaxle mounting bracket.

13. Raise the vehicle and support safely. Remove the sheet metal undercover.

14. Disconnect the tie rod ends and ball joints from the steering knuckle.

15. Remove the halfshafts.

16. On AWD vehicles, disconnect the exhaust pipe and remove the transfer case.

17. Remove the lower bell housing cover and remove the special bolts holding the flexplate to the torque converter. To remove, turn the engine crankshaft with a box wrench and bring the bolts into a position appropriate for removal, one at a time. After removing the bolts, push the torque converter toward the transaxle so it doesn't stay on the engine, allowing oil to pour out of the converter hub or cause damage to the converter.

18. Remove the lower transaxle-to-engine bolts and remove the transaxle assembly.

To install:

19. After the torque converter has been mounted on the transaxle, install the transaxle assembly on the engine. Tighten the transaxle-to-engine bolts to 35 ft. lbs. (48 Nm) and tighten the driveplate bolts to 34–38 ft. lbs. (46–53 Nm). Reinstall the bell housing cover.

20. On AWD models, install the transfer case and frame pieces. Reconnect the exhaust pipe using a new gasket.

21. Replace the circlips and install the halfshafts.

22. Reinstall the tie rods and ball joint.

23. Reinstall the transaxle mounting bracket.

24. Reinstall the under-guard.

25. Reinstall the starter.

26. Reconnect the speedometer cable and oil cooler lines.

27. Reconnect the solenoid, neutral safety switch (inhibitor switch), the pulse generator kickdown servo switch and oil temperature sensor.

28. Reinstall the remaining components.

29. Refill with Dexron II, Mopar ATF Plus type 7176, Mitsubishi Plus ATF, or equivalent, automatic transaxle fluid. If the vehicle is equipped with AWD, check and fill the transfer case.

30. Start the engine and allow it to idle for 2 minutes. Apply the parking brake and move the selector through each gear position, ending in N (neutral). Recheck the fluid level and add if necessary. If the vehicle has run for less than 15 minutes but more than one minute, the fluid is considered warm and should be above the ADD mark on the dipstick. Do not add fluid unless the level is at or below the ADD mark.

Clutch

ADJUSTMENTS

Clutch Pedal Free-Play

1. Measure the clutch pedal height from the face of the pedal pad to the firewall.

2. Compare the measured value with the proper distance of 6.93–7.17 in. (176–182mm).

3. Measure the clutch pedal clevis pin play at the face of the pedal pad. Press the pedal lightly until resistance is met, and measure this distance. The clutch pedal clevis pin play should be within 0.04–0.12 in. (1–3mm).

4. If the clutch pedal height or clevis pin play are not within the standard values, adjust as follows:

　a. For vehicles without cruise control, turn and adjust the stop bolt so the pedal height is the standard value, then tighten the locknut.

　b. For vehicles with cruise control, detach the clutch switch connector and turn the switch to obtain the standard clutch pedal height. Then, lock by tightening the locknut.

　c. Turn the pushrod to adjust the clutch pedal clevis pin play to agree with the standard value and secure the pushrod with the locknut.

➡**When adjusting the clutch pedal height or the clutch pedal clevis pin play, be careful not to push the pushrod toward the master cylinder.**

　d. Check that when the clutch pedal is depressed all the way, the interlock switch changes from ON to OFF.

REMOVAL & INSTALLATION

2.0L (VIN F) Engine

1. Be sure to observe all cautions and warnings in the beginning of the section that may be related to this procedure.

2. Remove the transaxle from the vehicle.

3. Unscrew the fittings, then remove the clutch oil tubes.

4. Unfasten the retaining bolt, then remove the clutch oil fluid chamber.

5. Remove the clutch release (slave) cylinder union bolt, the gaskets and the union.

6. Remove the valve plate and valve plate spring.

7. Without disconnecting the fluid line, remove the clutch release (slave) cylinder.

8. Unfasten the pressure plate retaining bolts, slowly and evenly in a crisscross pat-

Slide the release fork in the direction of the arrow to disengage it from the pivot ball

tern, then remove the pressure plate. Remove the clutch disc.

9. Unfasten the return clip, then remove the clutch release bearing.

10. Slide the release fork in the direction of the arrow shown in the accompanying figure, then detach the fulcrum from the clip to remove the release fork. Be careful not to cause damage to the clip by pushing the fork in any other direction or removing it with force.

11. Remove the release fork boot and fulcrum.

To install:

12. Install the fulcrum and the release fork boot.

13. Apply grease to the areas shown on the clutch release fork, then install the fork.

14. Before installation, apply a suitable grease to the areas shown on the clutch release bearing.

15. Install the return clip.

16. Lightly apply multi-purpose grease to the clutch disc splines. Install the clutch disc, using a suitable guide to position the disc on the flywheel.

17. Install the pressure plate.

18. Install the clutch release (slave) cylinder. Tighten the bolts to 13 ft. lbs. (18 Nm).

19. Install the valve plate spring and valve plate.

20. Install the gasket, union, gasket and union bolt on the release cylinder.

21. Install the clutch oil fluid chamber. Uncap or unplug the clutch oil tubes, then attach them and tighten the fittings to 11 ft. lbs. (15 Nm).

22. Install the transaxle assembly.

2.0L (Vin Y) Engine

1. Be sure to observe all cautions and warnings in the beginning of the section that may be related to this procedure.

2. Remove the transaxle from the vehicle.

7922DG15

Lubrication points for the clutch release lever and bearing

7922DG12

Cross-sectional view of proper clutch disc and pressure plate alignment, showing the alignment tool

3. Unscrew the fittings, then remove the clutch oil tube. Plug or cap the ends to prevent contamination from entering the line.

4. Remove the release (slave) cylinder.

5. Unfasten the retaining bolts, then remove the pressure plate and clutch disc.

6. Remove the clutch release bearing.

7. Remove the clutch release lever.

8. Remove the boot.

To install:

9. Install the boot assembly.

10. Apply a suitable grease to the clutch release lever, as shown in the accompanying figure. Install the clutch release lever.

11. Install the clutch release bearing.

12. Lightly apply multi-purpose grease to the clutch disc splines. Install the clutch disc and pressure plate assembly.

13. Install the clutch release (slave) cylinder.

14. Install the clutch oil tube.

15. Install the transaxle in the vehicle.

Hydraulic Clutch System

BLEEDING

→**Do not allow the reservoir to run out of fluid during bleeding, otherwise the entire procedure must be repeated.**

1. Fill the reservoir with clean brake fluid meeting DOT 3 specifications.

2. Attach a hose to the bleeder valve on the slave cylinder with the other end of the hose submerged in a container at least half full of fresh DOT 3 brake fluid from a sealed container.

3. Have an assistant press the clutch pedal to the floor, then loosen the bleed screw on the slave cylinder.

4. Tighten the bleed screw and have your helper release the clutch pedal.

5. Repeat the procedure until the fluid is free of air bubbles.

Transfer Case Assembly

REMOVAL & INSTALLATION

1. Be sure to observe all cautions and warnings in the beginning of the section that may be related to this procedure.

2. Disconnect the battery negative cable.

3. Raise the vehicle and support safely. Drain the transfer oil.

4. Disconnect the front exhaust pipe.

5. Unbolt the transfer case assembly and remove by sliding it off the rear driveshaft. Be careful not to damage the oil seal in the transfer case output housing. Do not let the rear driveshaft hang; suspend it from the body with a piece of wire. Cover the opening in the transaxle and transfer case to keep oil from dripping and to keep dirt out.

To install:

6. Lubricate the driveshaft sleeve yoke and oil seal lip on the transfer extension housing with clean engine oil. Install the transfer case assembly onto the transaxle. Use care when installing the rear driveshaft to the transfer case output shaft.

7. Tighten the transfer case-to-transaxle bolts to 40–43 ft. lbs. (55–60 Nm) on manual transaxle vehicles, or 43–58 ft. lbs. (60–80 Nm) on automatic transaxle vehicles.

**54–59 Nm
40–44 ft.lbs.**

7922DG13

Exploded view of the transfer case assembly mounting—vehicles with manual transaxle shown

8. Install the exhaust pipe, using a new gasket.

9. Refill the transfer case with gear oil of classification GL-4 or higher, SAE 75W-85W or 75W-90. Check the fluid level in the transaxle and add as required.

Halfshaft

REMOVAL & INSTALLATION

Front

1. Be sure to observe all cautions and warnings in the beginning of the section that may be related to this procedure.

✳ WARNING

If the vehicle is going to be rolled while the halfshafts are out of the vehicle, obtain two outer CV-joints or proper equivalent tools and install to the hubs. If the vehicle is rolled without the proper torque applied to the front wheel bearings, the bearings will no longer be usable.

2. Disconnect the negative battery cable.

3. Remove the cotter pin, halfshaft nut and washer.

4. Raise the vehicle and support safely. If removing the right halfshaft, remove the retainer bolt and the speedometer drive from the right extension housing.

5. Using the proper tool, disconnect the tie rod from the knuckle.

6. Disconnect the stabilizer link from the damper fork.

7. Disconnect the damper fork from the lateral lower arm.

8. Remove the lateral lower arm from the knuckle.

✳ WARNING

Use of improper methods of joint separation can result in damage to the joint, leading to possible failure.

9. On halfshafts with an inner shaft (AWD vehicles), remove the center support bearing bracket bolts and washers. Then, remove the halfshaft by setting up a puller on the outside wheel hub and pushing the halfshaft from the front hub. Then, tap the shaft union at the joint case with a plastic hammer to remove the halfshaft and inner shaft from the transaxle.

10. On one piece halfshafts (FWD vehicles), remove the halfshaft from the hub/knuckle by setting up a puller on the outside wheel hub and pushing the halfshaft

from the front hub. After pressing the outer shaft out of the hub, insert a pry-bar between the transaxle case and the half-shaft and pry the shaft from the transaxle.

✳ WARNING

Do not pull on the shaft to dislodge it from the transaxle; doing so damages the inboard joint. Do not insert the prybar too far or the oil seal in the case may be damaged.

To install:

11. Inspect the halfshaft boot for damage or deterioration. Check the ball joints and splines for wear.

12. Replace the circlips on the ends of the halfshafts.

13. Insert the halfshaft into the transaxle. Be sure it is fully seated.

14. Pull the strut assembly outward and install the outer end of the halfshaft into the hub.

15. Reinstall the center bearing bracket bolts and tighten to 33 ft. lbs. (45 Nm), if equipped.

16. Reinstall the washer so the chamfered edge faces outward. Reinstall the half-shaft nut and tighten temporarily.

17. Reinstall the tie rod end and ball joint to the steering knuckle. Tighten the ball joint nut to 21 ft. lbs. (28 Nm) and the tie rod nut to 17–25 ft. lbs. (24–33 Nm).

18. Reinstall the wheel and lower the vehicle to the floor. Tighten the axle nut with the brakes applied. Tighten the nut to 145–188 ft. lbs. (200–260 Nm).

19. Reinstall a new cotter pin and bend to secure.

Rear

1. Be sure to observe all cautions and warnings in the beginning of the section that may be related to this procedure.

2. Raise and safely support the vehicle.

3. Remove the rear wheel(s).

4. If equipped with ABS, remove the wheel speed sensor.

5. Remove the brake caliper and rotor or brake drum.

6. Remove the parking brake shoes (for disc brakes) or the shoe and lever assembly (for drum brakes).

7. Remove the parking brake cable from the backing plate.

8. If equipped with drum brakes, disconnect the brake line from the wheel cylinder.

9. Disconnect the shock absorber from the knuckle.

10. Disconnect the trailing arm and the lower arm from the knuckle.

11. Disconnect the toe control arm from the knuckle.

12. Remove the cotter pin, nut and washer from the axle shaft.

13. Remove the differential mount support.

14. Pull the lower end of the knuckle outward and pry the axle shaft out of the differential housing.

15. Remove the axle shaft from the hub assembly.

To install:

16. Install the axle shaft in the hub assembly.

17. Install a new circlip on the inner shaft, and install the shaft in the differential.

18. Reinstall the differential mount support.

19. Reinstall the washer on the axle shaft in the correct direction.

20. Reinstall the nut and tighten to 145–188 ft. lbs. (196–255 Nm). If the hole for the cotter pin does not line up, tighten the nut up to 188 ft. lbs. (255 Nm) and install the cotter pin in the first hole that lines up.

21. Reconnect the toe control arm, trailing arm and the lower arm to the knuckle. Tighten the nut for the toe control arm to 20 ft. lbs. (28 Nm), trailing arm to 85–99 ft. lbs. (118–137 Nm) and lower arm to 71 ft. lbs. (98 Nm).

22. Reinstall the lower shock mount to the knuckle.

23. Reconnect the brake line to the wheel cylinder, if removed.

24. Reinstall the parking brake cable through the backing plate.

25. Assemble the remaining brake components.

26. Reinstall the ABS wheel speed sensor, if removed.

27. Reinstall the wheel.

28. If equipped with drum brakes, bleed the brake system.

STEERING AND SUSPENSION

Air Bag

✳ CAUTION

Some vehicles are equipped with an air bag system, also known as the Supplemental Inflatable Restraint (SIR) or Supplemental Restraint System (SRS). The system must be dis-

abled before performing service on or around system components, steering column, instrument panel components, wiring and sensors. Failure to follow safety and disabling procedures could result in accidental air bag deployment, possible personal injury and unnecessary system repairs.

PRECAUTIONS

Several precautions must be observed when handling the inflator module to avoid accidental deployment and possible personal injury.

• Never carry the inflator module by the wires or connector on the underside of the module.

• When carrying a live inflator module, hold securely with both hands, and ensure that the bag and trim cover are pointed away from you.

• Place the inflator module on a bench or other surface with the bag and trim cover facing up.

• With the inflator module on the bench, never place anything on or close to the module which may be thrown in the event of an accidental deployment.

DISARMING

1. Position the front wheels in the straight-ahead position and place the ignition key in the **LOCK** position. Remove the key from the ignition lock cylinder.

2. Disconnect the negative battery cable and insulate the cable end with high-quality electrical tape or similar non-conductive wrapping.

3. Wait at least one minute before working on the vehicle. The air bag system is designed to retain enough voltage to deploy the air bag for a short period of time after the battery has been disconnected.

To arm:

4. Reconnect the negative battery cable, turn the ignition switch to the **ON** position and check the air bag warning light for proper operation.

Power Rack and Pinion Steering Gear

REMOVAL & INSTALLATION

1. Be sure to observe all cautions and warnings in the beginning of the section that may be related to this procedure.

A13X0236

1. Brake fluid reservoir assembly
2. A/C compressor
3. Joint assembly and gear box connecting bolt
4. Power steering pipe connection
5. Cotter pin
6. Tie-rod end and knuckle connection
7. Stay (L.H.)
8. Stay (R.H.)
9. Centermember assembly
10. Clamp
11. Gear box assembly
12. Return tube

NOTE
The fasteners marked * should be temporarily tightened before they are finally tightened once the total weight of the engine has been placed on the vehicle body.

7922DG14

Exploded view of the power steering gear assembly mounting, showing related components

2. Disconnect the negative battery cable.

3. Drain the power steering fluid into a suitable container.

4. Raise and safely support the vehicle.

5. Remove the stabilizer bar.

6. For 2.0L non-turbocharged engines, remove the windshield washer fluid reservoir.

7. For 2.0L turbocharged engines, perform the following:

   a. Remove the brake fluid reservoir.

   b. Unbolt the A/C compressor and position aside. DO NOT disconnect the refrigerant lines.

8. Remove the joint assembly and gear body connecting bolt.

9. Disconnect the power steering pipe connection.

10. Use a suitable puller to separate the tie rod end and knuckle connection.

11. Unfasten the retaining bolts, then remove the left and right side stays.

12. Remove the retainers, then remove the center member assembly.

13. Unfasten the retaining clamp, then remove the power steering gear assembly.

To install:

14. Install the power steering gear assembly onto the vehicle, and tighten the mounting bolts to specification as shown.

15. Connect the tie rod ends to the knuckle.

16. Installation is the reverse of the removal procedure.

17. Refill the reservoir with power steering fluid and bleed the system.

18. Check the front end alignment, and adjust if necessary.

Strut

REMOVAL & INSTALLATION

Front

1. Be sure to observe all cautions and warnings in the beginning of the section that may be related to this procedure.

2. Remove the top strut assembly mounting nuts from inside the engine compartment.

3. Raise and safely support the vehicle. Remove the wheel and tire assembly.

4. Remove the stabilizer link mounting nut.

5. Unfasten the strut assembly lower mounting bolts.

1. Stabilizer link mounting nut
2. Shock absorber upper mounting nuts
3. Shock absorber lower mounting bolt
4. Damper fork mounting bolt

5. Damper fork
6. Shock absorber assembly

7922DG23

Exploded view of the front strut mounting

6. Remove the damper fork mounting bolt, then remove the damper fork from the vehicle.

7. Remove the strut assembly by maneuvering it out of the vehicle.

8. Installation is the reverse of the removal procedure. Be sure to tighten the retainers to the specifications shown in the accompanying figure.

Rear

1. Be sure to observe all cautions and warnings in the beginning of the section that may be related to this procedure.

2. Remove the service lid in the luggage compartment.

3. Remove the cap and flange nuts securing the upper mounting bracket to the body. Do not remove the large nut in the center of the strut assembly.

4. Raise and safely support the vehicle.

5. Remove the bolt attaching the lower end of the strut to the knuckle and remove the strut from the vehicle.

To install:

6. Reinstall the upper bracket of the shock to the vehicle. Tighten the mounting nuts to 32 ft. lbs. (44 Nm).

7. Raise the suspension up with a jack or adjustable stand to align the strut lower mounting holes.

8. Reinstall the lower mounting bolt. Tighten the bolt to 71 ft. lbs.

1. Cap
2. Flange nuts
3. Bolt
4. Shock absorber

7922DG26

Exploded view of the rear strut mounting

9. Remove the jack or stand and safely lower the vehicle to the floor.

10. Reinstall the cap and service lid.

OVERHAUL

Front

1. Be sure to observe all cautions and warnings in the beginning of the section that may be related to this procedure.

2. Remove the shock and strut assembly from the vehicle.

> **❊❊ CAUTION**

Do not use air tools to tighten the compressor tool bolt.

3. Use the proper spring compressing tools (MB991237 and MB991239) to compress the coil spring. Be sure to install the tools evenly so the maximum length will be attained within the installation range.

4. While holding the piston rod, remove the self-locking nut.

5. Remove the washer.

6. Remove the upper bushing A, the upper bracket assembly and the upper spring pad.

7. Remove the collar, upper bushing B, cup assembly, rubber bumper and dust cover.

8. Separate the coil spring and strut assemblies.

To assemble:

9. Use the compressor tools to compress the coil spring, then install it to the strut. Align the edge of the coil spring to the stepped portion of the strut spring seat.

10. Install the dust cover, rubber bumper, cup, upper bushing B, collar and upper spring pad.

11. Install the upper bracket assembly, installing it so the position of the three bolts are in the proper orientation with the damper fork, as shown in the accompanying figure.

12. Install the other upper bushing.

13. Install the washer and the self-locking nut. Temporarily tighten the self-locking nut, then remove the spring compressor tools and tighten the nut to 14–18 ft. lbs. (20–25 Nm) using a torque wrench. Do not use air tools to tighten the self-locking nut!

14. Install the strut assembly in the vehicle.

Rear

1. Be sure to observe all cautions and warnings in the beginning of the section that may be related to this procedure.

2. Remove the strut from the vehicle.

3. Use a coil spring compressor to compress the spring.

20 – 25 Nm
14 – 18 ft.lbs.

Disassembly steps
1. Self-locking nut
2. Washer
3. Upper bushing A
4. Upper bracket assembly
5. Upper spring pad
6. Collar

7. Upper bushing B
8. Cup assembly
9. Bump rubber
10. Dust cover
11. Coil spring
12. Shock absorber assembly

7922DG28

Exploded view of the front strut assembly

22 Nm
16 ft.lbs.

Disassembly steps
1. Self-locking nut
2. Washer
3. Upper bushing A
4. Upper bracket assembly
5. Upper spring pad
6. Upper bushing B

7. Collar
8. Cup assembly
9. Dust cover
10. Bump rubber
11. Coil spring
12. Shock absorber assembly

7922DG27

Exploded view of the rear strut assembly

4. While holding the piston rod, remove the self-locking nut.

5. Remove the upper bracket assembly and spring pad.

6. Remove the collar, upper bushing, cup assembly, bump rubber and dust cover.

7. Remove the coil spring from the strut.

To assemble:

8. Align the end of the coil spring with the stepped part of the spring seat and install the compressed coil spring on the strut.

9. Reinstall the dust cover, bump rubber, cup assembly, upper bushing, collar, upper spring pad and bracket assembly on the strut.

10. Reinstall the upper bushing and washer on the piston rod.

11. Install a new self-locking nut on the piston rod. Temporarily tighten the nut.

12. Carefully remove the spring compressor from the spring. Tighten the self-locking nut to 16 ft. lbs. (25 Nm).

13. Install the strut assembly in the vehicle.

Upper Ball Joint

REMOVAL & INSTALLATION

The upper ball joint is an integral part of the upper control arm. If the upper ball joint is to be serviced, the upper control arm will have to be replaced.

Lower Ball Joint

REMOVAL & INSTALLATION

The lower ball joint is an integral part of the lower control arm assembly, and cannot be serviced separately. A worn or damaged ball joint, requires replacement of the lower control arm assembly.

Upper Control Arm

REMOVAL & INSTALLATION

1. Be sure to observe all cautions and warnings in the beginning of the section that may be related to this procedure.

2. Raise and safely support the vehicle.

3. Remove the front wheel(s).

4. Disconnect the upper ball joint from the steering knuckle.

5. Remove the upper shaft mounting nuts from the body.

6. Remove the upper arm.

7. Remove the through-bolts that attach the upper arm to the shafts.

86 Nm
62 ft.lbs.

N 2

4

57 Nm
41 ft.lbs.

57 Nm
41 ft.lbs.

3

1

28 Nm
20 ft.lbs.

N

Removal steps

1. Upper arm ball joint and knuckle connection
2. Upper arm self-locking nut
3. Upper arm assembly
4. Upper arm shaft assembly

9300DG01

Exploded view of the upper control arm and related components

A : 299.9 mm (11.8 in.)
B : 234.0 mm (9.2 in.)

Ball joint case
V groove

9300DG02

Be sure to install the shafts on the control arm at the correct angle

To install:

8. Assemble the upper arm to the shafts at the proper angle. Tighten the through-bolts and nuts to 41 ft. lbs. (57 Nm). The proper angle is 84–86°. After the arm and the shafts are connected at the correct angle, measure dimensions A and B to insure correct assembly.

- A—11.8 in. (299.9mm)
- B—9.2 in. (234.0mm)

9. Install the control arm assembly to the body with new self-locking nuts. Tighten the self-locking nuts to 62 ft. lbs. (86 Nm).

10. Reconnect the upper ball joint to the steering knuckle with a new self-locking nut. Tighten the locking nut to 20 ft. lbs. (28 Nm).

11. Reinstall the front wheel(s).

12. Perform front wheel alignment and adjust if necessary.

13. Safely lower the vehicle to the floor.

Lower Control Arm

REMOVAL & INSTALLATION

Compression Lower Arm

1. Be sure to observe all cautions and warnings in the beginning of the section that may be related to this procedure.

2. Raise and safely support the vehicle.

3. Remove the wheel.

4. Disconnect the compression lower arm ball joint from the steering knuckle.

5. Remove the two mounting bolts and remove the compression lower arm.

To install:

6. Install the compression lower arm. Tighten the two mounting bolts to 60 ft. lbs. (81 Nm).

7. Using a new self-locking nut, connect the ball joint to the knuckle assembly. Tighten the nut to 43–51 ft. lbs. (59–71 Nm).

8. Reinstall the wheel, and lower the vehicle to the floor.

9. Check and adjust the front wheel alignment if necessary.

Lateral Lower Arm

1. Be sure to observe all cautions and warnings in the beginning of the section that may be related to this procedure.

2. Raise and safely support the vehicle.

3. Remove the wheel.

4. Remove the stay (bracket).

5. Remove the strut lower mounting bolts.

6. Disconnect the lateral lower arm from the knuckle assembly.

7. Remove the lateral lower arm mounting bolts and the lateral arm.

To install:

8. Install the lateral lower arm and temporarily install the mounting bolts. Do not tighten the bolt until the vehicle is on the floor at normal riding height.

9. Use a new self-locking nut and connect the ball joint to the knuckle assembly. Tighten the self-locking nut to 43–51 ft. lbs. (59–71 Nm).

10. Reinstall the strut lower mounting bolts, secure with the nut and tighten to 64 ft. lbs. (88 Nm).

11. Reinstall the stay with the bolts and tighten them to 51–58 ft. lbs. (69–78 Nm).

12. Reinstall the wheel assembly and lower the vehicle to the floor.

13. Tighten the lateral lower arm through-bolt and nut to 71–85 ft. lbs. (97–118 Nm).

14. Check and adjust the front wheel alignment if necessary.

Wheel Bearings

ADJUSTMENT

Front

The front wheel bearing is a sealed and not adjustable. If the wheel bearing shows signs of play, the hub assembly must be replaced.

Rear

The wheel bearing play is not adjustable. If the wheel bearing play is not within specifications, the hub assembly must be replaced.

98–118 Nm*
72–87 ft.lbs.*

88 Nm*
65 ft.lbs.*

81 Nm
60 ft.lbs.

81 Nm
60 ft.lbs.

59–71 Nm
43–51 ft.lbs

69–78 Nm
51–58 ft.lbs.

Lateral lower arm

3, 8

Specified grease: MOPAR Multi-mileage Lubricant Part No. 2525035 or equivalent

Compression lower arm assembly removal steps

1. Compression lower arm ball joint and knuckle connection
2. Compression lower arm mounting bolts
3. Compression lower arm assembly

Lateral lower arm assembly removal steps

4. Stay
5. Shock absorber lower mounting bolt
6. Lateral lower arm ball joint and knuckle connection
7. Lateral lower arm mounting bolt
8. Lateral lower arm assembly

Caution
*: Indicates parts which should be temporarilly tightened, and then fully tightened with the vehicle on the ground in the unladen condition.

9300DG03

Exploded view of the lower arms and related component

FWD VEHICLES

1. Release the parking brake and if equipped, remove the brake drum.

2. If equipped with rear disc brakes, remove the caliper assembly and the brake disc (rotor).

3. Place a dial gauge against the hub surface, then move the hub in the axial direction and check whether or not there is end-play. Specification is 0.002 in (0.05mm).

4. To check for rotary sliding resistance, turn the hub a few times to seat the bearing. Wind a rope around the hub bolts and turn the hub by pulling at a 90° angle with a spring scale. Measure to determine whether or not the rotary sliding resistance of the rear hub is at the limit value. Specification is 3.9 lbs. (1.8 kg) or less.

AWD VEHICLES

1. Remove the caliper assembly and the brake disc (rotor).

2. Place a dial gauge against the hub surface, then move the hub in the axial direction and check whether or not there is end-play. Specification is 0.002 in (0.05mm).

REMOVAL & INSTALLATION

Front

➡**The front hub assembly is a sealed unit and should not be disassembled.**

1. Before servicing the vehicle, refer to the precautions in the beginning of this section.

2. Raise and safely support the vehicle.

3. Remove the wheel and tire assembly.

4. Remove and discard the halfshaft nut cotter pin.

5. Remove the halfshaft nut, holding the rotor in place with a suitable tool.

6. If equipped with ABS, remove the front wheel speed sensor.

7. Unbolt the caliper assembly and suspend out of the way with a piece of wire. Do not disconnect the fluid line.

8. Use a suitable puller to separate the upper control arm ball joint from the steering knuckle.

9. Unfasten the retaining bolts, then remove the front hub assembly. Shift the knuckle to the outside in order to keep the clearance between the front hub mounting bolts and halfshaft. Be careful not to damage the ball joint boot. If equipped with ABS, be careful not to damage the rotor.

10. If steering knuckle removal is necessary, proceed with the following substeps:

a. Unfasten the retaining bolts, then remove the dust shield.

b. Remove and discard the cotter pin, then separate the tie rod end from the steering knuckle using a puller.

c. Use a suitable puller to separate the compression and lateral lower control arm ball joints from the steering knuckle.

d. Unfasten the connecting nut and bolt of the damper fork and lateral lower control arm.

e. Remove the steering knuckle from the vehicle.

To install:

11. If the steering knuckle was removed, perform the following substeps:

a. Position the steering knuckle in the vehicle. Install the connecting bolt and nut and secure hand-tight.

b. Attach the lateral and compression lower control arm ball joints into the steering knuckle.

c. Fasten the tie rod end ball joint to the steering knuckle, then install the retaining nut and tighten to 17–25 ft. lbs. (24–33 Nm). Install a new cotter pin.

d. Install the dust shield. Tighten the retaining bolt to 6.5 ft. lbs. (8.5 Nm).

12. Position the front hub assembly, then secure with the retaining bolts. Tighten the bolts to 65 ft. lbs. (88 Nm).

13. Fasten the upper control arm ball joint to the steering knuckle.

14. Install the brake disc (rotor) and caliper.

15. If equipped, install the front wheel speed sensor.

16. Install the halfshaft nut. Hold the rotor in position while tightening the halfshaft nut to 145–188 ft. lbs. (196–255 Nm). If the cotter pin holes do not match, tighten the nut up to 188 ft. lbs. (225 Nm) maxi-

Turn to Section 6 for brake system applications

Removal steps

1. Cotter pin
2. Drive shaft nut
3. Front wheel speed sensor
   <Vehicles with ABS>
4. Caliper assembly
5. Brake disc

6. Upper arm ball joint and knuckle connection
7. Front hub assembly

7922DG25

Exploded view of the front hub assembly

mum. Install a new cotter pin in the first matching holes, then bend it over securely.

17. Install the wheel assembly, then carefully lower the vehicle.

Rear

1. Be sure to observe all cautions and warnings in the beginning of the section that may be related to this procedure.

2. Raise and safely support the vehicle.

3. Remove the wheel and tire assembly.

4. For AWD vehicles, remove the half-shaft.

5. If equipped with ABS, remove the rear wheel speed sensor.

6. If equipped with rear disc brakes, unbolt the caliper and suspend it from the body with a suitable piece of wire. Do not disconnect the fluid line. Remove the rotor.

7. If equipped with drum brakes, remove the brake drum.

8. For FWD vehicles, remove the clip mounting bolt.

9. For AWD vehicles, remove the shoe and lining assembly.

10. For vehicles with disc brakes, remove the parking brake shoe and lining assembly.

11. For AWD vehicles, remove the parking brake cable clip, then detach the cable.

12. Remove the retaining bolts, then remove the rear hub and bearing assembly.

13. For FWD vehicles equipped with ABS, use a suitable inner shaft remover to press off the ABS rotor.

To install:

14. If removed, install the ABS rotor.

15. Install the rear hub and bearing and secure with the mounting bolts.

16. For AWD vehicles, attach the parking brake cable, then install the retaining clip.

17. If equipped with disc brakes, install the parking brake shoe and lining assembly.

18. For AWD vehicles, install the shoe and lining assembly.

19. For FWD vehicles, install the clip mounting bolt.

20. If equipped with drum brakes, install the brake drum.

21. If equipped with disc brakes, install the rotor, then position the caliper and secure with the retaining bolts.

22. If equipped, install the rear wheel speed sensor.

23. For AWD vehicles, install the half-shaft.

24. Install the front wheel assembly, then carefully lower the vehicle.

1. Rear wheel speed sensor
   <Vehicles with ABS>
2. Brake drum
3. Shoe and lever assembly
4. Caliper assembly
5. Brake disc
6. Shoe and lining assembly

7. Clip
8. Parking brake cable
9. Rear hub assembly
10. Brake pipe connection
11. Dust seal

7922DG24

Exploded view of the rear hub assembly

CHRYSLER CORPORATION

Dodge/Plymouth-Neon

15

PRECAUTIONS

Before servicing any vehicle, please be sure to read all of the following precautions, which deal with personal safety, prevention of component damage, and important points to take into consideration when servicing a motor vehicle:

• Never open, service or drain the radiator or cooling system when the engine is hot; serious burns can occur from the steam and hot coolant.

• Observe all applicable safety precautions when working around fuel. Whenever servicing the fuel system, always work in a well ventilated area. Do not allow fuel spray or vapors to come in contact with a spark, open flame, or excessive heat (a hot drop light, for example). Keep a dry chemical fire extinguisher near the work area. Always keep fuel in a container specifically designed for fuel storage; also, always properly seal fuel containers to avoid the possibility of fire or explosion. Refer to the additional fuel system precautions later in this section.

• Fuel injection systems often remain pressurized, even after the engine has been turned **OFF**. The fuel system pressure must be relieved before disconnecting any fuel lines. Failure to do so may result in fire and/or personal injury.

• Brake fluid often contains polyglycol ethers and polyglycols. Avoid contact with the eyes and wash your hands thoroughly after handling brake fluid. If you do get brake fluid in your eyes, flush your eyes with clean, running water for 15 minutes. If eye irritation persists, or if you have taken brake fluid internally, IMMEDIATELY seek medical assistance.

• The EPA warns that prolonged contact with used engine oil may cause a number of skin disorders, including cancer! You should make every effort to minimize your exposure to used engine oil. Protective gloves should be worn when changing oil. Wash your hands and any other exposed skin areas as soon as possible after expo-sure to used engine oil. Soap and water, or waterless hand cleaner should be used.

• All new vehicles are now equipped with an air bag system, often referred to as a Supplemental Restraint System (SRS) or Supplemental Inflatable Restraint (SIR) system. The system must be disabled before performing service on or around system components, steering column, instrument panel components, wiring and sensors. Failure to follow safety and disabling procedures could result in accidental air bag deployment, possible personal injury and unnecessary system repairs.

• Always wear safety goggles when working with, or around, the air bag system. When carrying a non-deployed air bag, be sure the bag and trim cover are pointed away from your body. When placing a non-deployed air bag on a work surface, always face the bag and trim cover upward, away from the surface. This will reduce the motion of the module if it is accidentally deployed. Refer to the additional air bag system precautions later in this section.

• Clean, high quality brake fluid from a sealed container is essential to the safe and proper operation of the brake system. You should always buy the correct type of brake fluid for your vehicle. If the brake fluid becomes contaminated, completely flush the system with new fluid. Never reuse any brake fluid. Any brake fluid that is removed from the system should be discarded. Also, do not allow any brake fluid to come in contact with a painted surface; it will damage the paint.

• Never operate the engine without the proper amount and type of engine oil; doing so WILL result in severe engine damage.

• Timing belt maintenance is extremely important! Many models utilize an interference-type, non-freewheeling engine. If the timing belt breaks, the valves in the cylinder head may strike the pistons, causing potentially serious (also time-consuming and expensive) engine damage. Refer to the maintenance interval charts in the front of this manual for the recommended replacement interval for the timing belt, and to the timing belt section for belt replacement and inspection.

• Disconnecting the negative battery cable on some vehicles may interfere with the functions of the on-board computer system(s) and may require the computer to undergo a relearning process once the negative battery cable is reconnected.

• When servicing drum brakes, only disassemble and assemble one side at a time, leaving the remaining side intact for reference.

• Only an MVAC-trained, EPA-certified automotive technician should service the A/C system or its components.

ENGINE REPAIR

Ignition Timing

ADJUSTMENT

Ignition timing is controlled by the Powertrain Control Module (PCM). No adjustment is necessary or possible.

Engine Assembly

REMOVAL & INSTALLATION

➡**After all components are installed on the engine, a DRB or equivalent scan tool is necessary to perform the camshaft and crankshaft timing relearn procedure.**

1. Before servicing the vehicle, refer to the precautions in the beginning of this section.

2. Properly recover the A/C system refrigerant.

3. Properly relieve the fuel system pressure.

4. Disconnect the negative, then the positive battery cables. Remove the battery and the battery tray. Set the PCM aside.

5. Drain the cooling system into a suitable container.

6. Remove the upper radiator hose, radiator and fan module assembly. Remove the lower radiator hose.

7. If equipped with an automatic transaxle, disconnect and plug the transaxle cooler lines.

8. Disconnect the clutch cable (manual transaxles) and transmission shift linkage.

9. Disconnect the throttle body linkage.

10. Detach the engine wiring harness.

11. Disconnect the heater hoses.

12. Raise and safely support the vehicle, then remove the right inner splash shield.

13. Drain the engine oil.

14. Remove the accessory drive belts.

15. Remove the halfshafts.

16. Disconnect the exhaust pipe from the manifold.

17. Support the engine and transaxle assembly with a suitable jack, then remove the front engine mount.

18. On vehicles equipped with manual transaxle, remove the power hop damper.

19. Carefully lower the vehicle.

20. Remove the air cleaner assembly.

21. Unbolt the power steering pump and reservoir and position them aside.

22. If equipped, remove the A/C compressor.

23. Remove the ground straps from the chassis.

24. Raise the vehicle enough to allow a suitable engine dolly and cradle to be placed under the engine.

25. Loosen the engine support posts in order to allow movement for positioning onto the engine locating holes and flange on the engine bedplate. Carefully lower the vehicle and position the cradle until the engine is resting on the support posts. Tighten the mounts to the cradle frame. This will keep the support posts from moving when removing or installing the engine and transmission.

26. Install safety straps around the engine to the cradle; tighten the straps and lock them into position.

27. Raise the vehicle enough to see if the straps are tight enough to hold the cradle assembly to the engine.

28. Lower the vehicle so the weight of the engine and transaxle ONLY is on the cradle.

29. Remove the engine and transaxle mount through-bolts.

30. Raise the vehicle slowly, it might be necessary to move the engine/transaxle assembly with the cradle to allow removal around the body flanges.

To install:

Installation is the reverse of the removal procedure. Please note the following important steps.

31. Tighten the front engine mount retainers as follows (bolt specifications are on accompanying figure:

a. If the engine mount bracket was removed, tighten bolt 1 to 20 inch lbs. (3 Nm) and bolts 2, 3 and 4 to 80 ft. lbs. (108 Nm).

b. If the engine mount bracket was removed, tighten bolts 5 and 1 to 40 ft. lbs. (54 Nm).

c. Tighten the engine mount bracket-to-insulator assembly through-bolt to 40 ft. lbs. (54 Nm).

d. Tighten the insulator assembly nuts to the lower radiator crossmember to 40 ft. lbs. (54 Nm).

e. Tighten the mass damper bolt to 40 ft. lbs. (54 Nm).

32. Tighten the left engine mount as follows:

a. To 40 ft. lbs. (54 Nm) for (A) fasteners

b. To 80 ft. lbs. (108 Nm) for (B) fasteners.

33. Tighten the right engine mount as follows:

a. Engine mount-to-rail fasteners to 40 ft. lbs. (54 Nm).

b. Engine mount-to-engine bracket to 80 ft. lbs. (108 Nm).

34. If equipped, tighten the power hop damper retainers to 40 ft. lbs. (54 Nm).

35. Fill the engine with fresh engine oil.

36. After all components are installed, perform the camshaft and crankshaft timing relearn procedure as follows:

a. Connect a DRB or equivalent scan tool to the Data Link Connector (located under the instrument panel, near the steering column).

b. Turn the ignition switch **ON**, and access the "miscellaneous" screen.

c. Select "re-learn cam/crank" option and follow the directions on the scan tool screen.

37. If equipped with A/C, recharge the system.

Front engine mount location and bolt identification

Exploded view of the left engine mount

On vehicles with manual transaxles, you must remove the power hop damper

Location of the right engine mount

Water Pump

REMOVAL & INSTALLATION

➡ **After all components are installed on the engine, a DRB scan tool is necessary to perform the camshaft and crankshaft timing relearn procedure.**

1. Before servicing the vehicle, refer to the precautions in the beginning of this section.

2. Disconnect the negative battery cable.

3. Raise and safely support the vehicle. Remove the right inner splash shield.

4. Remove the accessory drive belts and power steering pump.

5. Drain the cooling system into a suitable container.

6. Securely support the engine from the bottom with a jack, then remove the right engine mount.

7. Remove the power steering pump bracket bolts, then set the pump and bracket assembly aside, but the power steering lines do not need to be disconnected.

8. Remove the right engine mount bracket.

9. Remove the timing belt tensioner and timing belt.

10. Remove the camshaft sprocket(s) and inner timing belt cover.

11. Unfasten the water pump-to-engine attaching screws, then remove the water pump from the engine.

12. Remove and discard the water pump O-ring, and thoroughly clean the mating surfaces.

To install:

13. Install a new O-ring gasket in the water pump O-ring groove. Hold the O-ring in place with a few small dabs of suitable silicone sealant.

❋❋ WARNING

Before proceeding, be sure the O-ring gasket is properly seated in the

water pump groove before tightening the screws. An improperly installed O-ring could cause a coolant leak.

14. Position the water pump on the block and install the retainers. Tighten the retainers to 9 ft. lbs. (12 Nm). Use a pressure tester to pressurize the cooling system to 15 psi (103 kPa) and check the water pump shaft seal and O-ring for leaks.

15. Rotate the pump by hand to check for freedom of movement.

16. Install the inner timing belt cover, timing belt and tensioner.

17. Install the right engine mount bracket and engine mount.

18. Refill the cooling system with the proper type and amount of coolant.

19. Install the power steering pump and accessory drive belts.

20. Connect the negative battery cable.

21. Use a DRB or equivalent scan tool to

perform the camshaft and crankshaft timing relearn procedure, as follows:

a. Connect the scan tool to the Data Link Connector (DLC), located under the instrument panel near the steering column.

b. Turn the ignition switch **ON**, and access the "miscellaneous" screen.

c. Select the "re-learn cam/crank" option, then follow the instructions on the scan tool screen.

Cylinder Head

REMOVAL & INSTALLATION

➡ **After all components are installed on the engine, a DRB scan tool is necessary to perform the camshaft and crankshaft timing relearn procedure.**

1. Before servicing the vehicle, refer to the precautions in the beginning of this section.

Be sure the O-ring is seated into its groove before installing the new pump

Exploded view of the cylinder head and valvetrain components—DOHC engine

Exploded view of the cylinder head and valvetrain components—SOHC engine

2. Disconnect the negative battery cable.

3. Properly relieve the fuel system pressure.

4. Drain the cooling system into a suitable container.

5. Remove the air cleaner inlet duct and air cleaner. Tag and disconnect all vacuum lines, electrical wiring and fuel lines from the throttle body.

6. Remove the throttle linkage.

7. Remove the accessory drive belts.

8. Disconnect the power brake vacuum hose from the intake manifold.

9. Raise and safely support the vehicle, then separate the exhaust pipe from the manifold. Carefully lower the vehicle.

10. Unbolt the power steering pump and set it aside. DO NOT disconnect the fluid lines!

11. Detach the ignition coil pack wiring connector, then remove the coil pack and bracket from the engine.

12. Detach the Camshaft Position (CMP) sensor and fuel injector electrical connectors.

13. Remove the intake manifold.

14. For SOHC engines, remove the timing belt and camshaft sprocket.

15. For DOHC engines, remove the timing belt, timing belt tensioner and camshaft sprocket. Remove the inner timing belt cover.

16. Remove the rocker arm (valve) cover.

17. For SOHC engine, remove the rocker arm shaft assemblies.

18. For DOHC engines, remove the camshaft and cam follower assemblies.

19. For SOHC engines, if necessary, remove the oil separator assembly bolts, then remove the oil separator.

20. For SOHC engines, unfasten the hose clamps, then disconnect the heater hoses. Remove any remaining hoses or lines.

21. Use a ratchet to unfasten the cylinder head bolts, working from the center outward, then remove the cylinder head from the engine block.

22. The cylinder head bolts must be inspected before they can be reused. If the threads of bolts are stretched, they must be replaced. Check for thread stretching by holding a scale or other straightedge against the threads. If all the threads do not contact the scale, the bolts must be replaced.

✱✱ WARNING

Use only a plastic scraper to clean the mating surfaces. NEVER use

metal, as this may gouge the surfaces and cause leaks!

23. Cover the combustion chambers, then use a plastic scraper to thoroughly and carefully clean the engine block and cylinder head mating surfaces.

To install:

24. Position a new gasket on the engine block, then place the cylinder head over the gasket.

25. Apply a thin coat of engine oil to the cylinder head bolt threads. The four short bolts 4.33 in. (110mm) are installed in positions 7, 8, 9 and 10, as shown in the accompanying figure.

26. For SOHC engines, tighten the cylinder head bolts, in the sequence shown, to the following specifications:

a. Tighten the bolts to 25 ft. lbs. (34 Nm).

b. Tighten the bolts to 50 ft. lbs. (68 Nm).

c. Loosen, then re-tighten the bolts to 50 ft. lbs. (68 Nm).

d. Tighten all bolts an additional ¼ turn. DO NOT use a torque wrench for this step.

Timing belt service is covered in Section 5 of this manual

Cylinder head tightening sequence—SOHC engine

7922EG08

✳ LOCATION OF 110 mm (4.330 in.) BOLTS

7922EG09

Cylinder head tightening sequence—DOHC engine

27. For DOHC engines, tighten the cylinder head bolts, in the sequence shown, to the following specifications:

   a. Tighten bolts 1–6 to 25 ft. lbs. (34 Nm) and bolts 7–10 to 20 ft. lbs. (28 Nm).

   b. Tighten bolts 1–6 to 50 ft. lbs. (68 Nm) and bolts 7–10 to 20 ft. lbs. (28 Nm).

   c. Loosen, then re-tighten bolts 1–6 to 50 ft. lbs. (68 Nm) and bolts 7–10 to 20 ft. lbs. (28 Nm).

   d. Tighten all bolts an additional ¼ turn. DO NOT use a torque wrench for this step.

28. The remainder of installation is the reverse of the removal procedure.

29. Connect the negative battery cable.

30. Fill the cooling system with the proper amount and type of coolant.

31. Use a DRB or equivalent scan tool to perform the camshaft and crankshaft timing relearn procedure, as follows:

   a. Connect the scan tool to the Data Link Connector (DLC), located under the instrument panel near the steering column.

   b. Turn the ignition switch **ON**, and access the "miscellaneous" screen.

   c. Select the "re-learn cam/crank" option, then follow the instructions on the scan tool screen.

Rocker Arms/Shafts

REMOVAL & INSTALLATION

This procedure applies to SOHC engines only. On DOHC engines, the valves are actuated directly by the camshafts and no rocker arms are used.

1. Before servicing the vehicle, refer to the precautions in the beginning of this section.

2. Disconnect the negative battery cable.

3. Remove the cylinder head cover.

➡ **Be sure to note the installed positions of the rocker arm shaft assemblies before removal.**

4. Loosen the rocker arm shaft attaching fasteners.

5. Remove the rocker arm shaft assembly from the cylinder head.

6. If necessary, disassemble the rocker arm assemblies by removing the attaching bolts from the shaft.

7. Slide the rocker arms and spacers off the shaft. Be sure to keep the spacers and rocker arms in their original locations for installation.

EXHAUST ROCKER ARM ASSEMBLY

ROCKER ARM SHAFT RETAINERS

PLASTIC SHAFT SPACERS

INTAKE ROCKER ARM ASSEMBLY

7922EG10

Be sure to note the rocker arm shaft component positions before disassembling the rocker arm shafts

EXHAUST ROCKER ARM

ROLLER

HYDRAULIC LASH ADJUSTERS

INTAKE ROCKER ARM

7922EG11

Disassembled view of an intake and exhaust rocker arm

8. Inspect the rocker arm for scoring, wear on the roller or damage to the rocker arm; replace any components showing damage. Check the location where the rocker arms mount to the shafts for wear or damage. Replace if damaged or worn. The rocker arm shaft is hollow and is used as a lubrication oil duct. Check the oil holes for clogs with a small piece of wire, and clean as required. Lubricate the rocker arms and spacers. Be sure to install in their original locations.

   To install:

✳✳ WARNING

You MUST set the crankshaft to three notches before TDC before installing the rocker arm shafts, otherwise valvetrain damage may occur when the mounting bolts are tightened.

9. Set the crankshaft sprocket to TDC by aligning the mark on the sprocket with the arrow on the oil pump housing, then back off to three notches before TDC.

10. Install the rocker arm/hydraulic lash adjuster assembly making sure that the adjusters are at least partially full of oil. This is indicated by little or no plunger travel when the lash adjuster is depressed. If there is excessive plunger travel, submerge the rocker arm assembly into clean engine oil and pump the plunger until the lash adjuster travel is taken up. If travel is not reduced, replace the assembly. The hydraulic lash adjuster and rocker arm are serviced as an assembly.

11. Install the rocker arm and shaft assemblies with the NOTCH in the rocker arm shafts pointing up and toward the timing belt side of the engine. Install the retainers in their original positions on the exhaust and intake shafts.

✳✳ WARNING

When installing the intake rocker arm shaft assembly, be sure the plastic spacers do not interfere with the spark plug tubes. If the spacers do interfere, rotate them until they are at the proper angle. To avoid damaging the spark plug tubes, do not try to rotate the spacers by forcing the shaft down.

12. Tighten the bolts to 21 ft. lbs. (28 Nm) in the sequence shown in the accompanying figure.

13. Install the rocker arm (valve) cover.

14. Connect the negative battery cable.

Rocker arm shaft assembly bolt tightening sequence

Be sure the notches in the rocker arm shafts points up and toward the timing belt side of the engine

Intake Manifold

REMOVAL & INSTALLATION

SOHC Engine

1. Before servicing the vehicle, refer to the precautions in the beginning of this section.

2. Disconnect the negative battery cable.

3. Remove the fresh air inlet duct from the air cleaner.

4. Properly relieve the fuel system pressure.

5. Detach the Idle Air Control (IAC) motor and Throttle Position (TP) sensor wiring connectors.

6. Disconnect the vacuum hoses from the throttle body.

7. Disengage the accelerator, kickdown and speed control cables from their bracket and the throttle lever.

8. Remove the throttle body.

9. Remove the clean air duct and upper air filter housing.

10. Wrap towels around the fitting to catch any spilled fuel, then disconnect the fuel supply line quick-connect from the fuel tube assembly.

11. Unfasten the fuel rail attaching screws, then remove the fuel rail from the engine. Be sure to cover the injector openings.

※ WARNING

DO NOT set the fuel injectors on their tips, as this may damage them.

12. Detach the electrical connector(s) from the Manfiold Absolute Pressure (MAP) and Intake Air Temperature (IAT) sensors. On early models there are two sensors, on later models they are combined into one sensor.

13. Unplug the Knock Sensor (KS) electrical connector.

14. Disconnect the wiring from the starter, then unclip the wiring harness and position it out of the way.

15. Remove the EGR tube bolts at the intake manifold, then remove the tube from the manifold. Remove the gasket.

16. Disconnect the brake booster vacuum hose.

17. Disconnect the PCV vapor hose.

18. Unfasten the intake manifold-to-inlet water tube support fastener.

19. Remove and discard the intake manifold retainers. Remove the intake manifold from the vehicle.

20. Remove and discard the gaskets and seals. Thoroughly clean the gasket mating surfaces.

To install:

21. Position new gaskets and seals, then install the intake manifold. Install new retainers and tighten them in the sequence shown in the accompanying figure to 9 ft. lbs. (12 Nm).

22. Install the intake manifold-to-water inlet support fastener and tighten to 9 ft. lbs. (12 Nm).

23. Remove the covering from the fuel injector holes and be sure the holes are clean. Install the fuel rail assembly to the intake manifold and tighten the screws to 17 ft. lbs. (23 Nm).

INTAKE MANIFOLD TO
WATER INLET SUPPORT

7922EG14

Intake manifold retainer tightening sequence—SOHC engines

24. Connect the PCV and brake booster vacuum hoses.

25. Inspect the fuel line quick-connect fittings for damage and replace if necessary. Apply a small amount of clean engine oil to the fuel inlet tube. Connect the fuel supply hose to the fuel rail assembly. Ensure the connection is fastened securely by pulling on the connector.

26. Install the throttle body. Tighten the fastener to 16 ft. lbs. (22 Nm). Install the transmission-to-throttle body support bracket and tighten to 9 ft. lbs. (12 Nm) at the throttle body first. Next, tighten the bracket at the transmission.

27. Attach the MAP and IAT electrical connector(s).

28. Connect the KS and starter motor wiring. Fasten the wiring harness to the intake manifold tab.

29. Attach the IAC motor and TP sensor connectors.

30. Connect the vacuum hoses to the throttle body.

31. Install accelerator, kickdown and speed control cables to their bracket and connect them to the throttle lever.

32. Loosely assemble the EGR tube to the intake manifold finger-tight, then tighten the retainers to 95 inch lbs. (11 Nm).

33. Install the clean air duct to the air filter housing, then tighten the clamp to 30 inch lbs. (3 Nm).

34. Connect the negative battery cable.

35. Attach the fresh air duct to the air cleaner and tighten the wing nut securely.

DOHC Engine

1. Before servicing the vehicle, refer to the precautions in the beginning of this section.

2. Disconnect the negative battery cable.

3. Loosen the wing nut on the intake, then remove the fresh air inlet duct.

4. Properly relieve the fuel system pressure.

5. Wrap towels around the fitting to catch any spilled fuel, then disconnect the fuel supply line quick-connect from the fuel tube assembly.

6. Remove the clean air inlet duct.

7. Detach the Engine Coolant Temperature (ECT) sensor connector.

8. Disconnect the heater hose from the intake manifold and the heater tube from the bottom of the intake manifold.

9. Disconnect the upper radiator and coolant recovery hoses.

✳ WARNING

Do not allow the injectors to rest on their tips, as this may damage them.

10. Unfasten the attaching screws, then remove the fuel rail from the engine. Cover the injector openings with a suitable covering to prevent debris from entering the ports.

11. Remove the accelerator, kickdown and speed control (if equipped) cables from the throttle lever and bracket.

12. Detach the Idle Air Control (IAC) motor and Throttle Position (TP) sensor wiring connectors.

13. Tag and disconnect the vacuum hoses from the throttle body, then remove the throttle body from the vehicle.

14. Detach the Manifold Absolute Pressure (MAP) and Intake Air Temperature (IAT) sensor electrical connector. Disconnect the vapor and brake booster hoses.

15. Detach the Knock Sensor (KS) electrical connector and detach the wiring harness from the tab located on the heater tube.

16. Disconnect the wiring from the starter.

17. Unfasten the EGR tube bolts at the valve and at the intake manifold. Remove the tube from the engine.

18. Remove the intake manifold fasteners, then remove the upper and lower intake manifold assemblies. If necessary, you can separate the upper and lower manifolds.

19. Remove and discard the gaskets, then thoroughly clean all of the gasket mating surfaces.

To install:

20. If separated, along with a new gasket, assemble the lower manifold to the upper manifold. Tighten the retaining bolts to 21 ft. lbs. (28 Nm) in the sequence shown in the accompanying figure.

21. Position a new gasket on the cylinder head, then install the intake manifold on the head. Tighten the fasteners to 21 ft. lbs. (28 Nm).

22. Remove the covering from the fuel injector holes and be sure the holes are clean. Install the fuel rail assembly onto the

INTAKE MANIFOLD BOTTOM VIEW
7922EG15

Lower-to-upper intake manifold bolt tightening sequence—DOHC engines

7922EG16

Be sure to follow the proper sequence when tightening the intake manifold-to-cylinder head retainers

intake manifold, and tighten the screws to 17 ft. lbs. (23 Nm).

23. Connect the PCV and brake booster vacuum hoses.

24. Inspect the fuel line quick-connect fittings for damage and replace if necessary. Apply a small amount of clean engine oil to the fuel inlet tube. Connect the fuel supply hose to the fuel rail assembly. Ensure the connection is fastened securely by pulling on the connector.

25. Connect the heater tube and hose to the intake manifold.

26. Attach the upper radiator hose and coolant recovery reservoir hose.

27. Attach the coolant temperature sensor wiring.

28. Install the throttle body. Tighten the fastener to 16 ft. lbs. (22 Nm).

29. Attach the MAP and IAT electrical connectors.

30. Connect the KS wiring and the wiring at the starter. Fasten the wiring harness to the heater tube tab.

31. Attach the IAC motor and TP sensor wiring connectors.

32. Connect the vacuum hoses to the throttle body.

33. Install accelerator, kickdown and speed control cables to their bracket and connect them to the throttle lever.

34. Loosely assemble the EGR tube to valve and the intake manifold finger-tight. Tighten the tube fasteners to the at the EGR valve first to 95 inch lbs. (11 Nm), then tighten the intake manifold side retainers to 95 inch lbs. (11 Nm).

35. Install the clean air duct to the air filter housing, then tighten the clamp to 25 inch lbs. (3 Nm).

36. Connect the negative battery cable.

37. Attach the fresh air duct to the air cleaner and tighten the wing nut securely.

Exhaust Manifold

REMOVAL & INSTALLATION

1. Before servicing the vehicle, refer to the precautions in the beginning of this section.

2. Disconnect the negative battery cable.

3. Remove the air cleaner assembly and bracket.

4. Unfasten the retainers, then separate the exhaust pipe from the manifold. If Low Emission Vehicle (LEV) equipped, discard the manifold-to-flex joint gasket.

5. Unbolt the power steering pump reservoir and position it aside. DO NOT disconnect the fluid lines.

6. Unfasten the retainers, then remove the exhaust manifold heat shield.

7. Detach the upstream Heated Oxygen (HO2S) sensor connector.

➡ **It may be necessary to loosen the alternator bracket bolt to remove the outer exhaust manifold bolt.**

8. Remove the eight exhaust manifold retaining fasteners, then remove the exhaust manifold and gasket.

9. Discard the gasket, then thoroughly clean the mating surfaces.

To install:

10. Position a new gasket and the exhaust manifold in their proper positions. Apply Mopar stud and bearing mount, or equivalent, to the fasteners. Install the fasteners and tighten to 17 ft. lbs. (23 Nm), starting at the center and working outward in both directions. Repeat this procedure until all fasteners are tightened to specifications.

11. If loosened, tighten the alternator bracket bolt.

12. Install the exhaust manifold heat shield.

13. Place the power steering pump reservoir in position and secure with the mounting bolts.

14. If necessary, attach the upstream HO2S sensor.

15. Install the air cleaner bracket and assembly.

16. If Low Emission Vehicle (LEV) equipped, replace the manifold-to-flex fold gasket.

17. Attach the exhaust pipe to the manifold and tighten to 21 ft. lbs. (28 Nm).

18. Connect the negative battery cable.

Front Crankshaft Seal

REMOVAL & INSTALLATION

1. Before servicing the vehicle, refer to the precautions in the beginning of this section.

2. Disconnect the negative battery cable.

Removing the front crankshaft oil seal

3. Turn the crankshaft clockwise until the engine is at TDC No. 1 cylinder compression stroke (firing position). Remove the timing belt using the recommended procedure.

4. Using a suitable puller, remove the crankshaft pulley and sprocket.

5. Remove the crankshaft oil seal using a suitable puller.

6. Using Seal Puller tool 6771 or equivalent, remove the front crankshaft oil seal. Take care not to damage the seal surface of the cover.

To install:

7. Using tool 6780–1 or equivalent, install a new front crankshaft oil seal.

8. Reinstall the crankshaft timing belt drive pulley and sprocket. Install the timing belt following the recommended procedure. Take care that all timing marks are properly aligned or engine damage will result.

9. Reconnect the negative battery cable.

10. Remove the engine oil pressure sending unit and install an oil pressure gauge. Start and run the engine until the thermostat opens. Curb idle oil pressure should be 4 psi (27.5 kPa) minimum. At 3000 rpm, the oil pressure should be between 25–80 psi (172–551 kPa). If the oil pressure is zero at idle, immediately shut **OFF** the engine and check to see if the pressure relief valve is stuck open. Also

Installing a new seal using Seal Installer 6780–1—proceed with caution if using substitute tools

check for other problems such as oil level, oil type, loose filter, etc..

> ❋❋ **WARNING**

If the oil pressure is zero at idle DO NOT run the engine at 3000 rpm looking for a pressure increase, otherwise the engine will be damaged.

Camshaft and Lifters

REMOVAL & INSTALLATION

SOHC Engine

This engine uses a Single Over Head Camshaft (SOHC) running in an aluminum cylinder head. Rocker arm shafts mount directly to the cylinder head. Care must be taken to ensure all valve timing marks align after cylinder head and valvetrain service. Please note that the cylinder head must be removed from the vehicle to service the camshaft.

➡ **After all components are installed on the engine, a DRB scan tool is necessary to perform the camshaft and crankshaft timing relearn procedure.**

1. Before servicing the vehicle, refer to the precautions in the beginning of this section.

2. Disconnect the negative battery cable.

3. Relieve the fuel system pressure using the recommended procedure.

4. Remove the cylinder head cover.

5. Mark the rocker arm shaft assemblies to identify them for later installation.

6. Remove the rocker arm shaft bolts and remove the rocker arm assemblies from the cylinder head.

7. Remove the timing belt and camshaft sprocket using the recommended procedure.

8. Remove the cylinder head using the recommended procedure.

9. Remove the Camshaft Position (CMP) sensor and remove the camshaft from the rear of the cylinder head.

To install:

➡ **The cylinder head bolts should be checked for stretching before reuse. If the thread area of the bolt is necked down the bolts must be replaced with new. New head bolts are recommended.**

10. Clean all parts well. Inspect the camshaft journals for scoring. Check the oil

feed holes in the head for blockage. Check the camshaft bearing journals for scoring. If light scratches are present, they may be removed with 400 grit abrasive paper. If deep scratches are present, replace the camshaft and check the cylinder head for damage. Replace the cylinder head if worn or damaged.

11. If the camshaft lobes show signs of wear, check the corresponding rocker arm roller for wear or damage. Replace rocker arms/hydraulic lash adjuster if worn or damaged. If the camshaft lobes show signs of pitting on the nose, flank or base circle, replace the camshaft.

12. If the rocker arms and shaft are to be serviced, mark the rocker arms so any that are to be returned to service will be installed in their original locations. Slide the rocker arms off the shaft. Keep the spacers and rocker arms in the same location for reassembly.

a. Inspect the rocker arms for scoring, wear on the roller or damage to the shaft. Replace parts as necessary.

b. The rocker arm shaft is hollow and used as a lubrication oil duct. Check that the shaft is clean inside and out.

c. Check all oil holes for clogging with a small wire and clean as required.

d. To assemble, thoroughly lubricate all rocker arm components and spacers, then install them on the rocker arm shaft in their original locations.

13. If the vehicle exhibited a tappet-like noise, the valve lash adjusters built into the rocker arms should be cleaned and checked. Lash adjusters removed from a rocker arm should be returned to their original locations. Replace worn or defective lash adjusters. To install a lash adjuster, use the following procedure.

a. Lubricate the lash adjuster thoroughly with clean engine oil.

b. Install the adjuster into the rocker arm making sure the adjuster is at least partially filled with oil.

c. Submerge the rocker arm in clean engine oil and pump the plunger until the lash adjuster travel is taken up. If travel is not reduced, replace the adjuster.

d. Install the rocker arm on the rocker arm shaft.

14. Camshaft end-play can be checked, using the following procedure:

a. Oil the camshaft journals and install the camshaft without the rocker arm assemblies.

b. Install the camshaft target magnet on the end of the camshaft. Tighten the

Refer to Section 1 for engine rebuilding specifications

Exploded view of the cylinder head and valvetrain assembly—SOHC engine

Rocker arm shaft identification—SOHC engine

Rocker arm shaft tightening sequence—SOHC engine

Rocker arm shaft notch location—SOHC engine

screw to 30 inch lbs. (3.4 Nm). Be sure to fit the dowels on the magnet in the holes on the camshaft.

c. Install the CMP sensor and tighten the screws to 80 inch lbs. (9 Nm).

d. Setup a dial indicator to touch on the nose of the camshaft.

e. Using a suitable tool, move the camshaft as far rearward as it will go. Be sure the dial indicator probe is in contact with the camshaft.

f. Zero the dial indicator.

g. Move the camshaft as far forward as it will go.

h. Read the end-play on the dial indi-

cator. Specification is 0.005–0.013 inch (0.13–0.33mm).

15. To install the camshaft, lubricate the bearing journals thoroughly. Install the camshaft into the cylinder head carefully. Be sure it turns freely. If the camshaft installation is satisfactory, install the cam sensor and tighten the screws to 85 inch lbs. (9.6 Nm).

16. Reinstall the camshaft seal. The camshaft must be installed before the camshaft seal is installed. The seal should be flush with the cylinder head after installation.

17. Reinstall the camshaft sprocket and tighten to the bolt to 85 ft. lbs. (115 Nm).

18. Reinstall the cylinder head using the recommended procedure.

19. Before installing the rocker arm and shaft assemblies, set the crankshaft to three notches before TDC on the crankshaft sprocket.

20. Reinstall the rocker arm and shaft assemblies with the small notches in the rocker shafts pointing up and toward the timing belt side of the engine. Install the retainers in their original positions on the exhaust and intake shafts. Tighten the bolts to 200 inch lbs. (23 Nm).

21. Reinstall the timing belt using care to align all valve timing marks, using the recommended procedure.

22. Reconnect all electrical, vacuum and fluid connections as required.

23. Refill the cooling system. An oil and filter change are recommended.

24. Reconnect the negative battery cable.

25. Use a DRB or equivalent scan tool to perform the camshaft and crankshaft timing relearn procedure, as follows:

    a. Connect the scan tool to the Data Link Connector (located under the instrument panel, near the steering column).

    b. Turn the ignition switch **ON**, and access the "miscellaneous" screen.

    c. Select the "re-learn cam/crank" option, then follow the instructions on the scan tool screen.

26. Start the engine and check for leaks. Run the engine with the radiator cap off so as the engine warms and the thermostat opens, coolant can be added to the radiator. Test drive vehicle to check for proper operation.

DOHC Engine

This engine is called a Dual Over Head Camshaft (DOHC) engine since it uses two camshafts. Care must be taken to be sure all valve timing marks align after any cylinder head and valvetrain service.

➥**After all components are installed on the engine, a DRB scan tool is necessary to perform the camshaft and crankshaft timing relearn procedure.**

1. Be sure to observe all precautions in the beginning of this section.

2. Disconnect the negative battery cable.

3. Remove the cam cover.

➥**Always rotate the crankshaft in a clockwise direction. Make a mark on the back of the timing belt indicating the direction of rotation so it may be reassembled in the same direction if it is to be reused.**

4. Rotate the crankshaft clockwise and align the timing marks so the No. 1 piston will be at TDC of the compression stroke.

5. Remove the timing belt cover and the timing belt.

6. Remove both camshaft sprockets.

7. Loosen the bearing caps in sequence, 1 camshaft at a time. The bearing caps are identified for location. Remove the outside bearing caps first.

➥**If the bearing caps are difficult to remove, use a plastic hammer to gently tap the rear part of the camshaft.**

8. Remove the intake and exhaust camshafts.

Identifying the camshaft bearing caps— DOHC engine

Bearing cap removal sequence—DOHC engine

9. Remove the cam follower assemblies from the cylinder head. Keep the cam followers in the order they have been removed from the head for reassembly.

10. Mark the lash adjusters for reassembly in their original positions.

11. Check the camshaft end-play. Oil the camshaft journals and install the camshaft **WITHOUT** cam follower assemblies. Install the rear cam caps following the recommended procedure.

12. Using a suitable tool, move the camshaft as far rearward as it will go.

13. Attach a dial indicator and zero it.

14. Move the camshaft as far forward as it will go.

15. Measure and record the end-play. End play specs are: 0.002–0.06 inches (0.05–0.15mm)

✷✷ WARNING

The camshafts and their components are NOT interchangeable. Place an identifying mark on each component. Be sure to keep all parts organized for proper reassembly in their original positions.

To install:

16. Before installation, clean the cylinder head and cover mating surfaces. Make certain that the rails are flat.

17. Reinstall the lash adjuster assembly making sure the adjusters are at least partially full of oil. This is indicated by little or no plunger travel when the adjuster is depressed.

18. Lubricate the cam followers with clean engine oil and install the cam followers in their original positions on the lash adjuster and valve stem.

19. Check the camshaft journals on the cylinder head and the cam bearings for wear or damage. Check the cam lobes and rocker rollers for damage. Also, check the cylinder head oil holes for clogging.

20. Inspect the cam followers for wear or damage. Replace as necessary.

21. Lubricate the camshafts with heavy engine oil and position the camshafts on the cylinder head.

✷✷ WARNING

The pistons should not be at top dead center when installing the camshafts since some valves will be open depending on camshaft position.

22. Be sure the dowel pin on both camshaft sprocket ends are located on the top.

23. Reinstall the bearing caps No. 2 through No. 5 and right No. 6 and tighten the caps in sequence to 9 ft. lbs. (12 Nm). Check the markings on the caps to identify the cap number and intake/exhaust symbol. Be sure the rocker arm is correctly mounted on the lash adjuster and the valve stem end.

24. Apply Mopar Gasket Maker® to the No. 1 and No. 6 bearing caps. Install the bearing caps and tighten the retaining bolts, using the same sequence as when removed, to 215 inch lbs. (24 Nm).

25. Apply a coating of engine oil to the oil seal. Using proper size driver, press-fit the seal into the cylinder head.

To prevent leaking from the bearing cap ends, apply sealant as shown—DOHC engine

---

For engine torque specifications, refer to Section 1 of this manual

Cam cover tightening sequence—DOHC engine

26. Install the cam sprockets. Install the timing belt using care to follow the recommended procedure. Cam timing is critical or engine damage will result. Install the timing belt cover and related components.

27. Apply Mopar® silicone rubber adhesive sealant at the camshaft cap corners and at the top edge of the half round seal.

28. Reinstall the cam cover using a new gasket. Tighten the cam cover retaining bolts in sequence, using a three step torque method:

a. Tighten all bolts, in sequence to 3.3 ft. lbs. (4.5 Nm)

b. Tighten all bolts, in sequence to 6.5 ft. lbs. (9 Nm)

c. Tighten all bolts, in sequence to 9 ft. lbs. (12 Nm)

29. Check the engine oil level. After this type of service, an oil and filter change is recommended. If a camshaft had failed, metal particles may be spread throughout the engine so an oil and filter change should be mandatory.

30. Reconnect the negative battery cable.

31. Use a DRB or equivalent scan tool to perform the camshaft and crankshaft timing relearn procedure, as follows:

a. Connect the scan tool to the Data Link Connector (located under the instrument panel, near the steering column).

b. Turn the ignition switch **ON**, and access the "miscellaneous" screen.

c. Select the "re-learn cam/crank" option, then follow the instructions on the scan tool screen.

32. Start the engine and check for proper operation and leaks.

Valve Lash

ADJUSTMENT

The engines in these vehicles do not require periodic valve lash adjustment.

➡ Refer to the rocker arm removal and installation procedure for additional information.

Oil Pan

REMOVAL & INSTALLATION

1996–97 Vehicles

1. Before servicing the vehicle, refer to the precautions in the beginning of this section.

2. Raise and safely support the vehicle.

3. Drain the engine oil into a suitable container.

4. Remove the transmission bending bracket.

5. Support the engine and transaxle assembly, then remove the front engine mount and bracket.

6. Remove the transmission inspection cover.

7. If equipped with A/C, remove the oil filter and adapter.

8. Unfasten the retainers, then remove the oil pan.

9. Thoroughly clean the gasket mating surfaces.

To install:

10. Apply silicone sealer to the oil pump-to-engine block parting line, as shown in the accompanying figure.

11. Position a new oil pan gasket on the pan.

12. Install the pan, then tighten the retainers to 105 inch lbs. (12 Nm).

13. If removed, install the oil filter and adapter.

14. Install the transmission inspection cover.

15. Install the front engine mount and bracket. Tighten the front engine mount retainers as follows (bolt specifications are on accompanying figure:

a. If the engine mount bracket was removed, tighten bolt 1 to 20 inch lbs. (3 Nm) and bolts 2, 3 and 4 to 80 ft. lbs. (108 Nm).

b. If the engine mount bracket was removed, tighten bolts 5 and 1 to 40 ft. lbs. (54 Nm).

Silicone sealer application locations—oil pan service

Front engine mount location and bolt identification

c. Tighten the engine mount bracket-to-insulator assembly through-bolt to 40 ft. lbs. (54 Nm).

d. Tighten the insulator assembly nuts to the lower radiator crossmember to 40 ft. lbs. (54 Nm).

e. Tighten the mass damper bolt to 40 ft. lbs. (54 Nm).

16. Install the transmission bending bracket.

17. Carefully lower the vehicle. Fill the crankcase with the proper type and amount of engine oil.

18. Start the engine and check for leaks, then recheck the fluid level and add as necessary.

1998–00 Vehicles

1. Before servicing the vehicle, refer to the precautions in the beginning of this section.

2. Raise and safely support the vehicle.

3. Drain the engine oil into a suitable container.

4. Properly support the engine and transaxle assembly, then remove the front engine mount bracket.

5. Remove the powertrain bending strut.

6. Remove the structural collar from the oil pan-to-transaxle.

Exploded view of the structural collar mounting—1998–00 vehicles

7. Remove the transaxle lower dust cover.

8. If equipped with A/C, remove the oil filter and adapter.

9. Unfasten the retaining bolts, then remove the oil pan.

10. Thoroughly clean the gasket mating surfaces.

To install:

11. Apply suitable silicone sealer to the oil pump-to-engine block parting line, as shown in the accompanying figure.

12. Position a new oil pan gasket on the pan.

13. Install the pan, then tighten the retainers to 105 inch lbs. (12 Nm).

14. If removed, install the oil filter and adapter.

15. Install the transaxle lower dust cover.

16. Install the powertrain bending strut.

17. Install the front engine mount and bracket. Tighten the front engine mount retainers as follows (bolt specifications are on accompanying figure:

a. If the engine mount bracket was removed, tighten bolt 1 to 20 inch lbs. (3 Nm) and bolts 2, 3 and 4 to 80 ft. lbs. (108 Nm).

b. If the engine mount bracket was removed, tighten bolts 5 and 1 to 40 ft. lbs. (54 Nm).

c. Tighten the engine mount bracket-to-insulator assembly through-bolt to 40 ft. lbs. (54 Nm).

d. Tighten the insulator assembly nuts to the lower radiator crossmember to 40 ft. lbs. (54 Nm).

e. Tighten the mass damper bolt to 40 ft. lbs. (54 Nm).

❄❄ WARNING

You MUST follow the proper tightening sequence for the structural collar or damage to the collar or oil pan may occur!

18. Install the structural collar, then tighten the retainers as follows:

a. Install the collar-to-oil pan bolts and tighten to 30 inch lbs. (3 Nm).

b. Install the collar-to-transaxle bolts and tighten to 80 ft. lbs. (108 Nm).

c. Final-tighten the collar-to-oil pan bolts to 40 ft. lbs. (54 Nm).

19. Carefully lower the vehicle. Fill the crankcase with the proper type and amount of engine oil.

20. Start the engine and check for leaks, then recheck the fluid level and add as necessary.

Oil Pump

REMOVAL & INSTALLATION

1. Before servicing the vehicle, refer to the precautions in the beginning of this section.

2. Disconnect the negative battery cable.

3. Remove the timing belt.

4. Raise and safely support the vehicle.

5. Drain the engine oil into a suitable container.

6. Remove the oil pan.

7. Remove the crankshaft sprocket using a suitable puller.

8. Remove the oil pick-up tube.

9. Remove the oil pump and the front crankshaft seal.

10. Remove the oil pump cover screws, then lift the cover off.

11. Remove the oil pump rotors.

12. Wash all parts in a suitable solvent,

Exploded view of the oil pump and related component mounting

Exploded view of the oil pump assembly

Use calipers to measure the outer rotor thickness . . .

Use a feeler gauge and straightedge to check the oil pump cover for warpage

. . . and the inner rotor thickness

Measure the outer rotor clearance in the housing

then inspect carefully for damage or wear, as follows:

a. Clean all parts thoroughly. The mating surface of the oil pump should be smooth. Replace the pump cover if it is scratched or grooved.

b. Lay a straightedge across the pump cover surface. If a 0.003 in. (0.076mm) feeler gauge can be inserted between the cover and the straightedge, the cover should be replaced.

c. Measure the thickness and diameter of the outer rotor. If the outer rotor thickness measures 0.301 in. (7.64mm) or less, or if the diameter is 3.148 in. (79.95mm) or less, replace the outer rotor.

d. If the inner rotor measures 0.301 in. (7.64mm) or less, replace the inner rotor.

e. Slide the outer rotor into the pump housing, press to one side with your fingers and measure the clearance between the rotor and the housing. If the measurement is 0.015 in. (0.39mm) or more, replace the housing only if the outer rotor is within specification.

f. Install the inner rotor into the pump housing, If the clearance between the inner and outer rotors is 0.008 in. (0.203mm) or more, replace both rotors.

g. Place a straightedge across the face of the pump housing, between the bolt holes. If a feeler gauge of 0.004 in. (0.102mm) or more can be inserted between the rotors and the straightedge, replace the pump assembly ONLY if the rotors are within specifications.

h. Inspect the oil pressure relief valve plunger for scoring and free operation in its bore. Small marks may be removed with 400 grit wet or dry sandpaper.

i. The relief valve spring has a free length of about 2.39 in. (60.7mm) and should test between 18–19 lbs. (8.1–8.6 kg) when compressed to 1.60 in.

Apply a small amount of gasket maker to the pump body cover mounting surface

(40.6mm). Replace the spring if it falls outside of specifications.

j. If the oil pressure is low and the pump is within specifications, inspect for worn engine bearings or for other reasons for oil pressure loss.

To install:

13. Assemble the pump, using new parts as required. Install the inner rotor with the chamfer facing the cast iron oil pump cover.

14. Apply Mopar or equivalent gasket maker to the oil pump as shown in the accompanying figure. Install the oil ring into the oil pump body discharge passage.

15. Prime the oil pump before installation by filling the rotor cavity with engine oil.

16. Align the oil pump rotor flats with the flats on the crankshaft as you install the oil pump to the block.

✳✳ WARNING

The front crankshaft seal MUST be out of the pump to align, or damage may result.

17. Tighten all of the pump attaching bolts to 21 ft. lbs. (28 Nm).

18. Install a new front crankshaft seal using seal driver tool 6780 or equivalent.

19. Install the crankshaft sprocket using a suitable crankshaft damper installation tool.

20. Install the oil pump pick-up tube and oil pan.

21. Install the timing belt.

22. Carefully lower the vehicle. Fill the crankcase with the proper type and amount of engine oil.

23. Start the engine and check for leaks, then recheck the fluid level and add as necessary.

Rear Main Seal

REMOVAL & INSTALLATION

1. Before servicing the vehicle, refer to the precautions in the beginning of this section.

When prying the seal out, be sure to use the prytool at the proper angle

2. Remove the transaxle and flexplate/flywheel from the vehicle.

3. Insert a ³⁄₁₆ in. flat-bladed tool between the dust lip and the metal case of the crankshaft seal. Angle the tool through the dust lip against the metal case of the seal. Pry out the seal.

❊❊ WARNING

DO NOT let the prytool contact the crankshaft seal surface. Contact of the tool blade against the crankshaft edge (chamfer) is permitted.

To install:

❊❊ WARNING

If the crankshaft edge (chamfer) has any burrs or scratches on the, you can clean it up with 400 grit sand paper to prevent seal damage during installation of the new seal.

➡**No lubrication is necessary when installing the seal.**

4. Place special tool 6926–1, or equivalent on the crankshaft. This is a pilot tool with a magnetic base.

5. Position the seal over the pilot tool. Be sure you can read the words THIS SIDE OUT on the seal. The pilot tool should stay on the crankshaft during installation of the seal. Be sure that the lip of the seal if facing towards the crankcase during installation.

❊❊ WARNING

If the seal is driven in the block past flush, this may cause an oil leak.

6. Drive the seal into the block using special seal installation tools 6926–2 and handle C-4171 until the tool bottoms out against the block.

Place a proper size pilot tool with a magnetic base on the crankshaft

7. Install the flexplate/flywheel. Tighten the bolts in a star pattern to 70 ft. lbs. (95 Nm).

8. Install the transaxle in the vehicle.

FUEL SYSTEM

Fuel System Service Precautions

Safety is an important factor when servicing the fuel system. Failure to conduct maintenance and repairs in a safe manner may result in serious personal injury. Maintenance and testing of the vehicle's fuel system components can be accomplished safely and effectively by adhering to the following rules and guidelines:

• To avoid the possibility of fire and personal injury, always disconnect the negative battery cable unless the repair or test procedure requires that battery voltage be applied.

• Always relieve the fuel system pressure prior to disconnecting any fuel system component (injector, fuel rail, pressure regulator, etc.), fitting or fuel line connection. Exercise extreme caution whenever relieving fuel system pressure to avoid exposing skin, face and eyes to fuel spray. Please be advised that fuel under pressure may penetrate the skin or any part of the body that it contacts.

• Always place a shop towel or cloth around the fitting or connection prior to loosening to absorb any excess fuel due to spillage. Ensure that all fuel spillage is quickly removed from engine surfaces. Ensure that all fuel soaked cloths or towels are deposited into a suitable waste container.

• Always keep a dry chemical (Class B) fire extinguisher near the work area.

• Do not allow fuel spray or fuel vapors to come into contact with a spark or open flame.

• Always use a back-up wrench when loosening and tightening fuel line connection fittings. This will prevent unnecessary stress and torsion to fuel line piping.

• Always replace worn fuel fitting O-rings. Do not substitute fuel hose where fuel pipe is installed.

Fuel System Pressure

RELIEVING

❊❊ CAUTION

You MUST relieve the fuel system pressure before servicing any compo-

nents of the fuel system. Service vehicles in well ventilated areas and avoid ignition sources. NEVER smoke while servicing the vehicle!

1. Before servicing the vehicle, refer to the precautions in the beginning of this section.

2. Disconnect the negative battery cable.

3. Remove the fuel filler cap.

4. Remove the protective cap from the fuel pressure port on the fuel rail.

5. Place the open end of a suitable fuel pressure release hose (tool C-4799–1 or equivalent) into an approved gasoline container. Connect the other end of the hose to the fuel pressure test port. The fuel pressure will bleed off through the hose into the gasoline container.

➡**Fuel pressure gauge kit C-4799-B contains hose C-4799–1.**

6. The vehicle is now safe for servicing.

7. After you are finished working on the fuel system, don't forget to install the fuel filler cap.

Relieve the fuel system, allowing the pressure to bleed off through the hose into the container

Fuel Filter

A combination fuel filter/pressure regulator assembly is used, which is located on the top of the fuel pump module.

REMOVAL & INSTALLATION

❊❊ CAUTION

Do not allow fuel spray or fuel vapors to come in contact with a spark or

open flame. Keep a dry chemical fire extinguisher nearby. Never store fuel in an open container due to risk of fire or explosion.

1. Before servicing the vehicle, refer to the precautions in the beginning of this section.

2. Properly relieve the fuel system pressure.

3. If not done already, disconnect the negative battery cable.

4. Raise and safely support the vehicle.

5. Unfasten the quick-connect fuel supply line from the filter/regulator nipple.

6. Depress the locking spring tab, located on the side of the fuel filter/regulator, then rotate 90° and pull out. Be sure the upper and lower O-rings are still on the filter assembly.

To install:

7. Lightly coat the filter O-rings with clean engine oil. Insert the filter into the opening in the fuel pump module, then align the two hold-down tabs with the flange.

8. While applying downward pressure, rotate the filter clockwise until the spring tab catches in the locating slot.

9. Attach the fuel line to the filter/regulator assembly.

10. Carefully lower the vehicle, then connect the negative battery cable.

Depress the spring tab, then rotate and pull the fuel filter assembly out

Fuel Pump

The fuel pump is integral with the pump module, which also contains the fuel reservoir, level sensor, inlet strainer and fuel pressure regulator. The inlet strainer, fuel pressure regulator and level sensor are the only serviceable items. If the fuel pump requires service, replace the entire fuel pump module.

REMOVAL & INSTALLATION

1. Before servicing the vehicle, refer to the precautions in the beginning of this section.

The fuel module assembly contains the pump, pressure regulator, reservoir, inlet strainer and level sensor

2. Disconnect the negative battery cable.

3. Properly relieve the fuel system pressure.

4. Raise and safely support the vehicle.

5. Drain the fuel tank.

❋ WARNING

The fuel reservoir of the fuel pump module does not empty out when the tank is drained. The fuel in the reservoir will spill out when the module is removed.

6. Disconnect the fuel lines from the fuel pump module by depressing the quick-connect retainers with your thumb and forefinger.

7. Slide the fuel pump module electrical lock to unlock it.

8. Detach the electrical connection from the fuel pump module, by pushing down on the connector retainer and pulling the connector off of the module.

9. Use a transmission jack to safely support the fuel tank, then remove the bolts from the fuel tank straps.

10. Carefully lower the tank slightly for access to the module.

11. Use a ratchet and spanner wrench to remove the fuel pump module locknut.

To loosen the fuel pump module locknut, use a ratchet and spanner wrench

12. Remove the fuel pump and O-ring seal from the tank. Discard the old seal.

To install:

❋ WARNING

Take care to avoid wiping dirt or debris into the fuel tank opening. Such contaminants may clog or damage the new fuel pump.

13. Wipe the fuel pump mounting flange and surrounding area of the tank clean, then place a new O-ring seal in position in the tank opening.

14. Position the fuel pump in the tank. Be sure the alignment tab on the underside of the fuel pump module flange sits in the notch on the fuel tank.

15. Position the locknut over the fuel pump module.

16. Using the ratchet and spanner wrench, tighten the locknut to 41 ft. lbs. (55 Nm).

17. Carefully lower the vehicle, then check for leaks.

18. Connect the negative battery cable.

DRIVE TRAIN

Transaxle Assembly

REMOVAL & INSTALLATION

Manual

1. Before servicing the vehicle, refer to the precautions in the beginning of this section.

2. Disconnect the negative, then the positive battery cables.

3. Pull the Power Distribution Center (PDC) up and out of its holding bracket. Position the PDC aside for working clearance.

4. Remove the battery heat shield, then remove the battery from the vehicle. Remove the battery tray from the engine compartment. If equipped, disconnect the cruise control.

5. Remove the Vehicle Speed Sensor (VSS) wire.

6. Detach the back-up lamp switch wiring from the transaxle.

❋ WARNING

Pry with equal amounts of force on both sides of the shifter cable isola-

tor bushing to avoid damaging the cable isolator bushing.

7. Use two prytools to disconnect both gear shift cable ends from the transaxle shift levers.

8. Remove the clutch housing vent cap, exposing the clutch cable end and clutch release lever. Then, remove the clutch cable from the transaxle bell housing.

9. Unfasten the retaining bolts, then remove the shift cable (linkage) mounting bracket.

Use two prytools to disconnect the gear shift cable ends from the shift levers—manual transaxle

Pull the clutch cable backward, to disconnect the clutch cable from the bell housing—manual transaxle

Remove the clutch cable from the lever—manual transaxle

10. If equipped, remove the accelerator cable shield.

11. Remove the intake manifold support bracket and the upper starter bolt.

12. Remove the upper bell housing bolt.

13. Install a suitable engine bridge fixture and support the engine securely.

14. Raise and safely support the vehicle, then remove the front wheel and tire assemblies.

15. Position a suitable drain pan under the vehicle, then drain the transaxle.

16. Remove both front halfshafts.

❊❊ WARNING

When installing the halfshafts, new retaining clips MUST be used. NEVER reuse the old clips. If you do not use new clips, the inner CV-joints may disengage.

17. Remove the power hop damper and bracket.

18. Remove the lower starter mounting bolt.

19. Remove the transaxle-to-rear lateral bending strut from the engine and transaxle.

Exploded view of the linkage mounting bracket—manual transaxle

Removing the lower starter mounting bolts—manual transaxle

20. Support the transaxle with a suitable jack.

21. Remove the front motor mount through-bolt. Remove the front motor mount bolts from the engine and transaxle.

22. Remove the lower dust shield screw and dust shield.

23. Rotate the crankshaft clockwise in order to access the driveplate-to-modular clutch bolts.

➡ **For installation purposes, matchmark the driveplate and pressure plate before removing any bolts.**

24. Unfasten the four driveplate-to-modular clutch bolts in order to separate the driveplate from the clutch.

25. Push the modular clutch assembly into the transaxle bell housing for easier transaxle removal.

26. Remove the frame rail-to-left transaxle mount through-bolt.

27. Remove the left transaxle mount from the transaxle. Then, push the mount up to get clearance for transaxle removal.

28. Remove the transaxle from the vehicle.

29. Remove the modular clutch assembly from the transaxle input shaft.

Unfasten the two bolts, then remove the bracket (strut) from the engine and transaxle—manual transaxle

Exploded view of the left manual transaxle mount through-bolt

To install:

30. Installation is the reverse of the removal procedure. Please note the following important steps.

31. The following items must be tightened to the specifications listed:
- Dust shield: 9 ft. lbs. (12 Nm)
- Front engine mount-to-transaxle: 80 ft. lbs. (108 Nm)
- Front mount through-bolt: 45 ft. lbs. (61 Nm)
- Front mount-to-engine bolt: 40 ft. lbs. (54 Nm)
- Lateral bending strut bolts: 40 ft. lbs. (54 Nm)
- Left mount through-bolt: 80 ft. lbs. (108 Nm)
- Left mount-to-transaxle bolt: 40 ft. lbs. (54 Nm)
- Power hop damper bolts: 40 ft. lbs. (54 Nm)
- Transaxle-to-engine bolt: 70 ft. lbs. (95 Nm)
- Transaxle-to-engine intake bracket bolts: 70 ft. lbs. (95 Nm)

32. After installing the transaxle, before lowering the vehicle to the floor, fill the transaxle to the bottom of the fill plug hole with Mopar® type M.S. 9417 or equivalent manual transaxle fluid.

33. Be sure the vehicle's back-up lights and speedometer are functioning properly.

34. After installing the transaxle in the vehicle, you must adjust the crossover cable in order to ensure proper shifter adjustment. Adjust as follows:

   a. Remove the floor shift console from the vehicle.

   b. Loosen the adjusting screw on the crossover cable at the shifter.

   c. Pin the transaxle crossover cable in the 3–4 neutral position using a ¼ in. drill bit. Align the hole in the crossover lever with the hole in the boss on the transaxle case. Be sure the drill bit goes

Loosen the adjustment screw on the crossover cable at the shifter—manual transaxle

Insert a ¼ in. diameter drill bit to pin the crossover lever in the 3–4 neutral position—manual transaxle

into the transaxle case at least ½ in. (12mm).

   d. The shifter is spring loaded and self-centering. Allow the shifter to rest in its neutral position. Tighten the adjustment screw to 70 inch lbs. (8 Nm). You must be careful to avoid moving the shift mechanism off-center during screw tightening.

   e. Remove the drill bit from the transaxle case and perform a functional check by shifting the transaxle into all gears.

   f. Reinstall the center shift console. Blouse the boot out around the console. Seat the boot lip on the top of the console.

35. Road test the vehicle to be sure the transaxle is operating properly.

Automatic

The transaxle and torque converter must be removed as an assembly; otherwise the torque converter drive plate, pump bushing or oil seal may be damaged. The drive plate will not support a load; therefore, none of the weight of the transaxle should be allowed to rest on the plate during removal.

1. Before servicing the vehicle, refer to the precautions in the beginning of this section.

2. Disconnect the negative, then the positive battery cables.

3. Pull the Power Distribution Center (PDC) up and out of its holding bracket. Set the PDC aside to gain clearance.

4. Remove the battery heat shield, then remove the battery from the engine compartment. Remove the battery tray from the engine compartment. If equipped, disconnect the cruise control.

5. Remove the Vehicle Speed Sensor (VSS) wiring.

6. Disconnect the neutral safety switch and torque converter control wiring from the transaxle.

Disconnect the gear shift cable end from the transaxle shift lever—automatic transaxle

✳✳ WARNING

Pry up on both sides of the shift cable isolator bushing, evenly, to avoid damaging the cable isolator bushing.

7. Disconnect the gear shift cable end from the transaxle shift lever. Remove the bracket bolt from the transaxle.

8. Remove the throttle pressure control cable from the lever. Then, remove the bracket bolts from the transaxle.

9. Remove the transaxle dipstick tube.

10. Disconnect the transaxle oil cooler lines, and plug them to prevent contamination from entering.

11. Remove the throttle pressure control cable support bracket bolts. Remove the upper bell housing bolts and upper starter bolt.

12. Install a suitable engine bridge fixture, then support the engine.

13. Raise and safely support the vehicle, then remove the front wheel and tire assemblies.

✳✳ WARNING

When installing the halfshafts, new retaining clips must be used. DO NOT reuse the old clips. Failure to use new clips could cause the inner CV-joints to disengage.

14. Remove both front halfshafts.

✳✳ WARNING

On 1998–00 vehicles, the exhaust flex joint must be disconnected from the exhaust manifold anytime the engine is lowered. If the engine is lowered while the flex pipe is attached, damage will occur.

15. On 1998–00 vehicles, remove the bolts securing the exhaust flex joint to the

exhaust manifold. Disconnect the exhaust pipe from the manifold.

16. Unfasten the transaxle-to-rear lateral bending strut from the engine and transaxle.

17. Remove the front engine bracket through-bolt. Remove the front engine bracket bolts.

18. Remove the lower starter bolt.

19. Remove the lower dust shield screw.

20. Rotate the engine clockwise to get access to the converter bolts. Remove the torque converter bolts, then matchmark the converter to the flexplate for alignment during installation.

21. Support the transaxle with a transaxle jack.

22. Remove the left mount through-bolt. Remove the left mount bolts from the transaxle, then remove the left mount.

23. Remove the rear engine bolt from the transaxle.

24. Carefully work the transaxle and torque converter assembly rearward off the engine block dowels. Disengage the converter hub from the end of the crankshaft. Attach a small C-clamp to the edge of the bell housing. This will hold the torque converter in place during transaxle removal. Lower the transaxle and remove the assembly from under the vehicle.

To install:

25. Installation is the reverse of the removal procedure. Please note the following important steps.

26. The following items must be tightened to the specifications listed:
- Bell housing cover bolts: 9 ft. lbs. (12 Nm)
- Transaxle oil cooler line-to-radiator connection: 9 ft. lbs. (12 Nm).
- Transaxle oil cooler line connection: 21 ft. lbs. (28 Nm).
- Flexplate-to-crankshaft bolts: 70 ft. lbs. (95 Nm).
- Flexplate-to-torque converter bolts: 50 ft. lbs. (68 Nm).
- Left motor mount bolts: 40 ft. lbs. (54 Nm).
- Transaxle-to-cylinder block bolt: 70 ft. lbs. (95 Nm).

27. If the torque converter was removed from the transaxle, be sure to align the pump inner gear pilot flats with the torque converter impeller hub flats.

28. Adjust the gearshift and throttle cables.

29. Refill the transaxle.

30. Be sure the vehicle's back-up lights and speedometer are working properly.

Clutch

ADJUSTMENT

The manual transaxle clutch release system has a unique self-adjusting mechanism to compensate for clutch disc wear. This adjuster mechanism is located with the clutch cable assembly. The preload spring maintains tension on the cable. This tension keeps the clutch release bearing continuously loaded against the fingers of the clutch cover assembly. No manual adjustment is obtainable.

When servicing this vehicle or if removing and installing the clutch cable, do not pull on the clutch cable housing to remove it from the dash panel. Damage to the cable self-adjuster may occur.

To check the function of the adjuster mechanism, use the following procedure:

1. With slight pressure, pull the clutch release lever end of the cable to draw the cable taut.

2. Push the clutch cable housing toward the dash panel. With less than 25 pounds of effort the cable housing should move 1.2–2.0 in. (30–50mm). This indicates proper adjuster mechanism function.

3. If the cable does not adjust, determine if the mechanism is properly seated on the bracket.

REMOVAL & INSTALLATION

➡**Vehicles made at the Toluca, Mexico assembly plant have conventional clutch and flywheel assembles. Vehicles made at the Belvidere assembly plant have modular clutch assemblies. If the 11th digit of the VIN code is "D", the vehicle was produced at the Belvidere assembly plant; if the VIN code is "T", the vehicle was produced at the Toluca assembly plant.**

Toluca Built Vehicles

1. Before servicing the vehicle, refer to the precautions in the beginning of this section.

2. Remove the transaxle from the vehicle.

3. Matchmark the position of the clutch cover and flywheel for proper alignment during installation.

4. Install a suitable clutch alignment tool through the clutch disc hub to prevent the clutch disc from falling and damaging the facings.

Exploded view of the conventional clutch components—vehicles built in Toluca

5. Loosen the clutch cover attaching bolts, one or two turns at a time, in a crisscross pattern. This releases the spring pressure gradually, avoiding cover damage.

➡**DO NOT touch the clutch disc facing with oily or dirty hands. Oil or dirt transferred from your hands onto the clutch disc may cause clutch chatter.**

6. Remove the clutch pressure plate, cover assembly and disc from the flywheel. Handle the components carefully to avoid contaminating the friction surfaces.

7. Inspect for oil leakage through the engine rear main bearing oil seal and transaxle input shaft seal. If there is leakage, it should be fixed at this time.

8. The friction faces of the flywheel and pressure plate should not have excessive discoloration, burned areas, cracks, deep grooves or ridges. Replace parts as required.

9. Clean the flywheel face with medium sandpaper, then wipe the surface with mineral spirits. If the surface is severely scored, heat checked, cracked or warped, replace the flywheel.

10. The heavy side of the flywheel is indicated by a white paint mark, near the outside diameter. To minimize the effects of flywheel unbalance, perform the following installation procedure:

a. Loosely assembly the flywheel to the crankshaft. If available, use new flywheel attaching bolts which have sealant on the threads. If new bolts are not available, apply Loctite® sealant to the threads of the original bolts. This sealant is required to prevent engine oil leakage.

b. Rotate the flywheel and crankshaft until the white paint (heavy side) is at the 12 o'clock position.

c. Tighten the flywheel attaching bolts, in a crisscross pattern, to 70 ft. lbs. (95 Nm).

11. The clutch disc should be handled without touching the facings. Replace the disc if the facings show grease or oil soakage, or wear to within less than 0.008 in. (0.20mm) of the rivet heads. The splines on the disc hub and transaxle input shaft should be a snug fit without signs of excessive wear. Metallic portions of the disc assembly should be dry, clean and not discolored from excessive heat. Each of the arched springs between the facings should be tight.

12. Wipe the friction surface of the pressure plate with mineral spirits.

13. Using a straightedge, check the pressure plate for flatness. The pressure plate friction area should be flat to slightly concave, with the inner diameter 0.000–0.0039 in. (0.0–0.1mm) below the outer diameter. It should also be free from discoloration, burned areas, cracks, grooves or ridges.

14. Using a surface plate, test the cover for flatness. All sections around the attaching bolt holes should be in contact with the surface plate within 0.015 in. (0.381mm).

15. The cover should be a snug fit on the flywheel dowels. If the clutch assembly does not meet these requirements, it should be replaced.

To install:

16. Mount the clutch assembly on the flywheel with the disc centered on the alignment tool, being careful to properly align the dowels and the alignment marks made before removal. The flywheel side of the clutch disc is marked for proper installation. If the new clutch or flywheel is installed, align the orange cover balance spot as close as possible to the orange flywheel balance spot. Apply pressure to the alignment tool. Center the tip of the tool into the crankshaft and the sliding cone into the clutch fingers. Tighten the clutch attaching bolts sufficiently to hold the disc in position.

17. To avoid distorting the clutch cover, tighten the bolts gradually, a few turns at a time. Use a crisscross pattern until all bolts are seated. Tighten the bolts to a final torque of 21 ft. lbs. (28 Nm).

18. Remove the clutch alignment tool.

19. Install the transaxle.

Belvidere Built Vehicles

1. Before servicing the vehicle, refer to the precautions in the beginning of this section.

2. Disconnect the negative battery cable.

3. Remove the starter wiring, then remove the starter motor assembly.

The transaxle and modular clutch are removed as an assembly

4. Remove the rear and front transaxle brackets.

5. Unfasten the modular clutch assembly works.

6. Remove the transaxle from the vehicle. The transaxle and modular clutch come out as an assembly.

7. Remove the modular clutch assembly from the transaxle input shaft. Handle the components carefully to avoid contaminating the friction surface.

8. Inspect for oil leakage through the engine rear main bearing oil seal and transaxle input shaft seal. If any leakage is noted, it should be fixed at this time.

To install:

➡**Always use new bolts when mounting the modular clutch assembly to the drive plate.**

9. Mount the modular clutch assembly onto the input shaft. Install the transaxle.

10. To avoid distorting the drive plate, tighten the bolts gradually a few turns at a time. Use a crisscross pattern, until all bolts are seated. Tighten the bolts to a final torque of 55 ft. lbs. (75 Nm).

11. Install the clutch inspection cover.

12. Install the transaxle lower support brackets.

13. Install the starter assembly, then attach the wiring.

14. Connect the negative battery cable.

Halfshafts

REMOVAL & INSTALLATION

1. Before servicing the vehicle, refer to the precautions in the beginning of this section.

2. Remove the cotter pin, locknut and spring washer from the end of the outer CV-joint stub axle. Discard the cotter pin.

3. With the vehicle on the ground and brakes applied, loosen, but do not remove the stub axle-to-hub and bearing retaining

Exploded view of the cotter pin, locknut and washer—halfshaft service

nut. The front hub and driveshaft are splined together and retained by the hub nut.

4. Raise and safely support the vehicle.

5. Remove the front wheel and tire assembly.

6. Unfasten the front caliper-to-steering knuckle bolts.

7. Remove the caliper from the steering knuckle by lifting the bottom of the caliper away from the steering knuckle, then remove the top of the caliper out from under the steering knuckle.

8. Support the caliper out of the way by suspending it with a piece of wire from the strut. DO NOT allow the caliper to hang by the brake hose.

9. Remove the rotor from the hub.

10. Remove the nut attaching the outer tie rod end to the steering knuckle, as follows:

   a. Hold the tie rod end stud with a 11/32 in. socket while loosening and removing the nut.

11. Separate the tie rod end stud from the steering knuckle using a side puller.

12. Remove the nut and bolt holding the ball joint stud into the steering knuckle.

✳✳ WARNING

Be careful when separating the ball joint stud from the steering knuckle, so the ball joint seal does not get damaged.

13. Separate the ball joint stud from the steering knuckle by prying down on the lower control arm.

14. For 1998–00 vehicles, perform the following steps:

   a. Remove the hub and bearing-to-stub axle retaining nut.

   b. Install a suitable puller on the hub and bearing assembly, using the lug nuts to hold it in place.

   c. Install a wheel lug nut on wheel stud to protect the threads on the stud. Install a flat-bladed prytool to keep the hub from turning. Using the puller, force the outer stub axle from the hub and bearing.

❈❈ WARNING

Be careful when separating the inner CV-joint during this operation. Do not let the driveshaft hang by the inner CV-joint, the driveshaft must be supported.

15. Pull the steering knuckle assembly out and away from the outer CV-joint of the driveshaft assembly. Support the outer end of the driveshaft assembly.

16. Insert a prybar between the inner tripod joint and the transaxle case. Pry against the inner tripod joint until the joint retaining snapring is disengaged from the transaxle side gear.

➡ **Inner tripod joint removal is easier if you apply outward pressure on the joint as you hit the punch with a hammer.**

17. Remove the inner tripod joints from the side gears of the transaxle using a punch to dislodge the inner tripod joint retaining ring from the transaxle side gear. If removing the right-side inner tripod joint, position the punch against the inner tripod joint. Hit the punch sharply with a hammer to dislodge the right inner joint from the side gear. If removing the left-side inner tripod joint, position the punch in the groove of the inner tripod joint. Hit the punch sharply with a hammer to dislodge the left inner tripod joint from the side gear.

18. Hold the inner tripod joint and interconnecting shaft of the driveshaft assembly. Remove the inner tripod joint from the transaxle by pulling it straight out of the transaxle side gear and transaxle oil seal. When removing the tripod joint, do not let the spline or snapring drag across the sealing lip of the transaxle-to-tripod joint oil seal.

❈❈ WARNING

The driveshaft, when installed, acts as a bolt which secures the front hub and bearing assembly. If the vehicle is to be supported or moved on its wheels with a driveshaft removed, install a proper-sized bolt and nut through the front hub. Tighten the bolt and nut to 135 ft. lbs. (183 Nm). This will ensure that the hub bearing cannot loosen.

To install:

19. Thoroughly clean the spline and oil seal sealing surface on the tripod joint.

Lightly lubricate the oil seal sealing surface on the tripod joint with fresh, clean transmission fluid.

20. Holding the driveshaft assembly by the tripod joint and interconnecting shaft, install the tripod joint into the transaxle side gear as far as possible by hand.

21. Carefully align the tripod joint with the transaxle side gears. Then, grasp the driveshaft interconnecting shaft and push the tripod joint into the transaxle side gear until fully seated. Be sure the snapring is fully engaged with the side gear by trying to remove the tripod joint from the transaxle by hand. If the snapring is fully seated with the side gear, the tripod joint will not be removable by hand.

22. Clean all debris and moisture out of the steering knuckle.

23. Be sure that the outer CV-joint, which fits into the steering knuckle, has no debris or moisture on it before installing into the steering knuckle.

24. Slide the driveshaft back into the front hub. Install the steering knuckle into the ball joint stud.

25. Install a NEW steering knuckle-to-ball joint stud bolt and nut. Tighten the nut and bolt to 70 ft. lbs. (95 Nm).

26. Insert the tie rod end into the steering knuckle. Start the tie rod end-to-steering knuckle nut onto the stud of the tie rod end. While holding the stud of the tie rod end stationary, tighten the nut. Then, using a crow's foot wrench and 11/32 in socket, tighten the tie rod end nut to 45 ft. lbs. (61 Nm).

27. Install the rotor back onto the hub and bearing assembly.

28. Position the caliper on the steering knuckle. Slide the top of the caliper under the top abutment on the steering knuckle, then install the bottom of the caliper against the bottom abutment of the steering knuckle.

29. Install the caliper-to-knuckle bolts and tighten to 23 ft. lbs. (31 Nm).

30. Clean all foreign matter from the threads of the outer CV-joint stub axle. Install hub nut and washer onto the threads of the stub axle and tighten the nut.

31. With the vehicle's brakes applied to prevent the axle shaft from turning, tighten the hub nut to 135 ft. lbs. (183 Nm).

32. Install the spring washer, locknut and new cotter pin into the outer CV-joint stub axle.

33. Install the front wheel and tire assembly. Install the lug nuts and tighten to 100 ft. lbs. (135 Nm).

34. Check the transaxle fluid level, lowering the vehicle as necessary.

35. If not already done, carefully lower the vehicle.

STEERING AND SUSPENSION

Air Bag

❈❈ CAUTION

Some vehicles are equipped with an air bag system, also known as the Supplemental Restraint System (SRS). The system MUST BE disabled before performing service on or around system components, steering column, instrument panel components, wiring and sensors. Failure to follow safety and disabling procedures could result in accidental air bag deployment, possible personal injury and unnecessary system repairs.

PRECAUTIONS

Several precautions must be observed when handling the inflator module to avoid accidental deployment and possible personal injury.

• Never carry the inflator module by the wires or connector on the underside of the module.

• When carrying a live inflator module, hold securely with both hands, and ensure that the bag and trim cover are pointed away.

• Place the inflator module on a bench or other surface with the bag and trim cover facing up.

• With the inflator module on the bench, never place anything on or close to the module which may be thrown in the event of an accidental deployment.

DISARMING

Proper SRS disarming can be obtained by disconnecting and isolating the negative battery cable. Allow the air bag system capacitor at least two minutes to discharge before removing any air bag system components.

Rack and Pinion Steering Gear

The replacement procedure for both the manual and power steering gears is the same. The only additional steps for power steering gear removal and installation is the disconnection and reconnection of the power steering fluid lines from and to the steering gear.

These vehicles are designed and assembled using NET BUILD front suspension alignment settings. This means that the alignment settings are determined as the vehicle is designed by the location of the front suspension components in relation to the body. This is carried out when building the vehicle, by precisely locating the front crossmember to meter gauge holes located in the underbody of the vehicle. With this method of designing and building a vehicle, it is no longer possible to adjust a vehicle's front suspension alignment settings to the required specifications. As a result, whenever the crossmember is removed from a vehicle, it MUST be replaced in the same location on the body of the vehicle it was removed from. The front suspension toe settings can still be adjusted by the outer tie rod ends.

REMOVAL & INSTALLATION

1. Before servicing the vehicle, refer to the precautions in the beginning of this section.
2. From inside the vehicle, disconnect the steering gear coupler, from the steering column shaft coupler.
3. Raise and safely support the vehicle.
4. Remove both front wheel and tire assemblies.

You must disconnect the steering gear coupler from inside the vehicle

Some vehicles are equipped with a bobble damper which must be removed from the crossmember during steering gear service

5. If equipped, remove the engine/transaxle bobble damper, from the front suspension crossmember. The bobble strut does not have to be removed from the transaxle.
6. Unfasten the nut attaching the outer tie rod end to the steering knuckle. The nut is removed by holding the tie rod end stud with an $^{11}/_{32}$ in. socket while loosening and removing the nut with a wrench.

7. Separate the tie rod ends from the steering knuckles using a side puller, tool MB-991113 or equivalent.
8. If equipped with power steering, perform the following:
   a. Remove the vehicle wiring harness connector from the power steering fluid pressure switch.
   b. Remove the power steering pressure and return hose routing bracket from the front crossmember. The bracket does not have to be removed from the power steering pressure and turn hoses.
   c. Remove the power steering fluid, pressure and return hoses from the power steering gear assembly.

✳✳ WARNING

Before removing the crossmember from the vehicle, the location of the crossmember MUST be scribed or marked on the vehicle, as shown in the accompanying figure. This has to be done so the crossmember can be installed in the exact location from which it was removed. If this is not done, the proper NET BUILD alignment specifications will not be obtained and may lead to handling and/or tire wear problems.

9. Using a paint marker, an awl or equivalent, make a line marking the location where the crossmember is mounted against the body of the vehicle.
10. Place a transmission jack under the center of the crossmember. The jack will be used to lower, support and raise the crossmember when removing the steering gear.
11. Loosen, then remove the front two bolts attaching the crossmember to the frame rails of the vehicle. Then, loosen the

Because of the method used for aligning the vehicle, you MUST matchmark the crossmember installed position prior to steering gear removal

Identification of the rack and pinion steering gear components

two rear bolts attaching the crossmember and lower control arm to the body of the vehicle. Lower the crossmember while loosening the rear bolts.

12. Using the transmission jack, carefully lower the crossmember enough to allow the steering gear to be removed from the crossmember. When lowering the crossmember, do not let the crossmember hang from the lower control arms, the weight should be supported by the jack.

13. Loosen and remove the four bolts

Location of the front crossmember mounting bolts

You must carefully lower the crossmember for access to the steering gear

Unfasten the mounting bolts, then remove the steering gear from the vehicle

securing the steering gear to the crossmember. Then, remove the steering gear assembly from the vehicle.

14. If a new steering gear is being installed, transfer any necessary parts from the old steering gear to the new steering gear.

To install:

15. Position the steering gear on the crossmember. Install the four mounting bolts and tighten to 50 ft. lbs. (68 Nm).

16. Using the transmission jack, raise the crossmember and steering gear against the body and frame rails of the vehicle. Start the two rear bolts into the tapping plates, attaching the crossmember to the body. Then, install the two front bolts, attaching the crossmember to the frame rails of the vehicle. Tighten the four mounting bolts until the crossmember is at the four mounting points. Then, tighten the bolts to 20 inch lbs. (2 Nm) to hold the crossmember in position.

➡ **When the crossmember is reinstalled in the vehicle, it MUST be aligned with the matchmarks made during removal. This MUST be done to maintain NET BUILD front suspension alignment settings.**

17. Using a rubber mallet, tap the crossmember into position, until it is aligned with the two previously scribed positioning marks on the body. When the crossmember is properly positioned, tighten the two rear crossmember/lower control arm bolts to 120 ft. lbs. (163 Nm). Then, tighten the two front bolts to 120 ft. lbs. (163 Nm).

18. If equipped with power steering, perform the following:

  a. Install the power steering fluid pressure and return hoses into the correct fluid ports on the steering gear. Tighten the line-to-steering gear tube nuts to 23 ft. lbs. (31 Nm).

  b. Install the power steering pressure and return hose routing bracket and attaching screw on the crossmember. Tighten the hose routing bracket-to-attaching bolt to 17 ft. lbs. (23 Nm).

  c. Install the vehicle wiring harness connector onto the power steering fluid pressure switch on the steering gear assembly. Be sure the locking tab on the wiring harness connector is securely latched to the pressure switch.

19. Install the tie rod end into the steering knuckle. Start the tie rod end-to-steering knuckle attaching nut onto the stud of the tie rod end. While holding the stud of the tie rod still, tighten the tie rod end-to-steering knuckle attaching nut. Then, using a crow's foot wrench and $^{11}/_{32}$ in. socket, tighten the tie rod end attaching nut to 40 ft. lbs. (55 Nm).

20. If equipped, install the engine/transaxle bobble strut back onto the crossmember bracket. Install and securely tighten the dampener-to-crossmember attaching bolt.

21. Install the wheel and tire assembly and tighten the lug nuts in a crisscross pattern to 100 ft. lbs. (135 Nm).

22. Carefully lower the vehicle.

23. From inside the vehicle, reconnect the steering gear coupler with the steering column shaft coupler. Install the steering gear coupler retaining pinch bolt and tighten to 21 ft. lbs. (28 Nm). Be sure to install the upper-to-lower steering coupler retaining bolt retention pin.

✳✳ WARNING

When filling and bleeding the power steering system, always use the proper type of fluid. NEVER substitute automatic transmission fluid for the specified fluid.

24. If equipped with power steering, fill the power steering pump fluid reservoir to the FULL-COLD level with the proper type and amount of fluid. Bleed the system.

Strut

REMOVAL & INSTALLATION

Front

1. Before servicing the vehicle, refer to the precautions in the beginning of this section.

2. With the vehicle on the ground, loosen the wheel lug nuts.

3. Raise and safely support the vehicle.

4. Remove the wheel and tire assembly.

5. If both strut assemblies are being removed, mark each one right or left, as applicable.

6. Remove the hydraulic brake hose routing bracket and attaching screw from

STRUT ASSEMBLY MOUNTING NUT

STRUT SHAFT NUT

STRUT TOWER

STRUT MOUNT ASSEMBLY

SPRING SEAT AND BEARING ASSEMBLY

JOUNCE BUMPER

DUST SHIELD

COIL SPRING

STRUT DAMPER ASSEMBLY

CLEVIS BRACKET BOLT (2)

STEERING KNUCKLE

BRAKING DISC

TIE ROD END ATTACHING NUT

PINCH BOLT NUT

PINCH BOLT

BALL JOINT SEAL

NUT

LOWER CONTROL ARM

SPACER

TIE ROD END

JAM NUT

LOWER CONTROL ARM PIVOT BOLT

NUT

LOWER CONTROL ARM/CROSSMEMBER ATTACHING BOLT

CROSSMEMBER ATTACHING BOLT

CLAMP

SWAY BAR CLAMP BOLT

STEERING GEAR ASSEMBLY MOUNTING BOLT (4)

STEERING GEAR MOUNTING BRACKET

STEERING GEAR BUSHING

STEERING GEAR INNER BRACKET

STEERING GEAR

FRONT SUSPENSION CROSSMEMBER

SWAY BAR

SWAY BAR BUSHING

SWAY BAR BUSHINGS AND WASHERS (4)

SWAY BAR LINK BOLT

NUT

Exploded view of the front suspension

792E660

the strut damper bracket. If equipped with ABS, the hydraulic hose routing bracket is combined with the speed sensor cable routing bracket.

➡️**The steering knuckle-to-strut assembly attaching bolts are serrated and must not be turned during removal. Remove the nuts while holding the bolts stationary in the steering knuckle.**

7. Hold the bolts in place, then remove the two nuts securing the strut to the steering knuckle.

8. Remove the three nuts attaching the upper mount of the strut to the strut tower of the vehicle. If necessary, partially lower the vehicle for access to the upper mounting nuts.

9. Carefully remove the strut assembly from the vehicle.

To install:

10. Install the strut assembly into the strut tower, aligning the three studs on the upper strut mount into the holes in the shock tower. Install the three upper strut mount retaining nut and washer assemblies. Tighten the three nuts to 23 ft. lbs. (31 Nm).

➡️**The steering knuckle-to-strut assembly attaching bolts are serrated and must not be turned during installation. Install the nuts while holding the bolts stationary in the steering knuckle.**

11. Align the strut assembly with the steering knuckle. Position the arm of the steering knuckle into the strut assembly, aligning the strut assembly to the steering knuckle mounting holes. Install the two strut-to-steering knuckle bolts. The bolts should be installed with the nuts facing the front of the vehicle. Tighten both attaching bolts to 40 ft. lbs. (53 Nm), plus an additional ¼ turn after the specified torque is met.

12. Install the hydraulic brake hose routing bracket and attaching screw onto the strut damper bracket. If the vehicle has ABS, the hydraulic hose routing bracket is combined with the speed sensor cable routing bracket. Tighten the bracket attaching bolts to 10 ft. lbs. (13 Nm).

13. Install the wheel and tire assembly, then tighten the lug nuts hand-tight.

14. Carefully lower the vehicle, then tighten the lug nuts, in a criss-cross pattern, to 100 ft. lbs. (135 Nm).

Rear

1. Before servicing the vehicle, refer to the precautions in the beginning of this section.

2. Raise and safely support the vehicle.

3. Remove the wheel and tire assembly.

4. Unfasten the retainer(s), then remove the hydraulic flex hose bracket from the strut bracket. If equipped with ABS, the wheel speed sensor cable routing clip is also attached to the strut assembly bracket.

5. Support the rear knuckle, suspension and brake components before removing the clevis bracket-to-knuckle attaching bolts. DO NOT allow the weight of the knuckle and related components to hang without support when the strut is removed.

> ❋❋ **WARNING**
>
> **The knuckle-to-strut attaching bolts are serrated and must not be turned during removal. Remove the nuts while holding the bolts stationary in the knuckle.**

6. Hold the bolt with a wrench, then unfasten the two clevis bracket nuts attaching the strut to the knuckle.

7. Carefully lower the vehicle, then open the trunk. Access to the rear upper strut mount-to-strut tower attaching bolts is through the trunk of the vehicle.

8. If necessary, remove the carpet from the top of the strut tower. Then, remove the rubber dust shield from the top of the strut tower for easier access to the upper strut nuts.

9. Loosen, but do not remove the four upper strut mounting nuts. Then, while sup-

Location of the knuckle-to-clevis bracket bolts

porting the strut assembly, fully remove the four strut mount attaching nuts.

10. Remove the strut assembly from the knuckle by sliding the knuckle out of the clevis bracket on the strut, then remove it from the vehicle.

To install:

11. Position the strut back into the vehicle with the four studs on the strut mount assembly through holes in the strut tower of the vehicle. Install the four strut mount-to-body attaching nuts onto the mount studs. Tighten the nuts to 25 ft. lbs. (34 Nm).

12. Install the dust shield into the opening on top of the strut tower. Install the carpeting back on top of the rear strut tower.

13. Raise and safely support the vehicle.

14. Install the knuckle into the clevis bracket on the strut assembly. Install the two clevis bracket-to-knuckle attaching bolts and nuts. Hold the bolts with a wrench while tightening the nuts to 70 ft. lbs. (95 Nm).

15. Install the brake hose bracket to the strut bracket and secure with the retaining bolts. If equipped with ABS, the wheel speed sensor cable routing clip is also attached to the strut bracket.

16. Install the wheel and tire assembly on the vehicle. Tighten the lug nuts evenly, in sequence, to 100 ft. lbs. (135 Nm).

17. Carefully lower the vehicle.

18. Check the alignment and adjust, if necessary.

Coil Spring

REMOVAL & INSTALLATION

Front

1. Before servicing the vehicle, refer to the precautions in the beginning of this section.

2. Remove the strut assembly from the vehicle.

3. Clamp the strut in a suitable vise, in a vertical position. When clamping the strut in the vise, do not clamp the strut using the body of the strut, only by the strut clevis bracket, as shown in the accompanying figure.

4. Mark the coil spring and strut assembly as right or left, according to which side of the vehicle to strut was

FRONT OF CAR

TENSION STRUT NUT

TENSION STRUT RETAINER (SMALL HOLE)

TENSION STRUT BRACKET BOLT

TENSION STRUT RETAINER (LARGE HOLE)

BRAKE SUPPORT PLATE ATTACHING BOLT

BRAKE SUPPORT PLATE

LATERAL ARM BOLT

FRAME

TENSION STRUT BUSHINGS

TENSION STRUT

TENSION STRUT BUSHING

LATERAL ARM WASHER

STRUT TOWER

STRUT SHAFT NUT

WASHER

STRUT MOUNT

WASHER

DUST SHIELD

TENSION STRUT RETAINER (LARGE HOLE)

SPRING ISOLATOR

KNUCKLE

TENSION STRUT BUSHING

TENSION STRUT RETAINER (SMALL HOLE)

STRUT MOUNTING NUT (4)

JOUNCE BUMPER

COIL SPRING

CLEVIS BRACKET BOLT

STRUT DAMPER

CLEVIS BRACKET

CLEVIS BRACKET NUT

TENSION STRUT NUT

LATERAL ARM NUT

LATERAL ARM WASHER

LATERAL ARM NON-ADJUSTABLE

REAR CROSSMEMBER

LATERAL ARM (ADJUSTABLE)

LATERAL ARM WASHER

LATERAL ARM NUT

LARGE BUSHING IN THIS POSITION

ALIGNMENT ADJUSTMENT CAM

LATERAL ARM BOLT

Exploded view of the rear suspension

79225G61

Be sure to clamp the stut in the vise by the lower bracket and not the body of the strut

removed from, and which strut the coil spring was removed from.

✳✳ CAUTION

DO NOT remove the strut rod nut before the strut assembly coil spring is compressed, removing spring tension from the upper spring seat and bearing assembly. When compressing the coil spring for removal from the strut, the first full top and bottom coil of the spring must be held by the jaws of the spring compressor.

5. Carefully compress the strut assembly coil spring, using a suitable spring compressor tool.

6. Install a suitable strut nut socket or an open ended wrench on the strut shaft retaining nut. Then, install a 10mm socket on the hex end of the strut damper shaft. While holding the strut shaft from turning, remove the strut shaft retaining nut.

7. Remove the strut assembly mount/isolator from the strut.

8. Remove the upper spring seat, pivot bearing and dust shield as an assembly from the strut.

9. Remove the jounce bumper from the shaft of the strut assembly.

10. Remove the coil spring from the strut assembly. Mark left and right on the coil springs for their installation back on the correct side of the vehicle.

➡ **If a replacement coil spring is being installed on the strut, then first full top and bottom coil of the spring must be captured by the jaws of the coil spring compressor.**

11. Inspect the strut for any binding of the strut shaft over the full stroke of the shaft.

12. Inspect the strut mount and upper spring seat assembly for any of the following conditions:

• Check the mount for cracks and distortion and the retaining studs for any sign of damage.

• Inspect for severe deterioration of the rubber isolator and binding of the strut pivot bearing. If the pivot bearing is replaced, it is to be installed with the white side of the bearing facing up.

• Inspect the dust shield for rips and/or deterioration.

• Check the jounce bumper for cracks and/or signs of deterioration.

13. Replace any components of the strut assembly found to be worn or defective during the inspection, before assembling the strut.

To install:

14. Clamp the strut, in a vertical position, in a suitable vise. Only clamp the strut by the clevis bracket, NEVER by the body of the strut.

15. Install the compressed coil spring onto the strut. The spring should be installed with the smaller coil down, so the spring properly seats on the strut.

16. Install the jounce bumper on the strut shaft.

17. Install the dust shield, pivot bearing and upper spring seat as an assembly on the strut.

18. Position the upper spring seat alignment notch with the clevis bracket on the strut assembly.

19. Install the strut mount on the strut assembly and the strut mount retaining nut on the shaft of the strut assembly.

✳✳ CAUTION

The following two steps must be completely done before the spring compressor tool can be released from the coil spring.

20. Install strut nut socket or an open end wrench on the strut shaft retaining nut. Then, install a 10mm socket through the center of the socket and on the hex of the strut shaft. While holding the strut shaft from turning, tighten the strut shaft retaining nut to 55 ft. lbs. (75 Nm).

21. Equally loosen both spring compressor tools, until the top coil of the spring is fully seated against the upper spring seat

and strut mount. Then, relieve all tension from the spring compressors and remove the compressors from the strut spring.

22. Install the strut into the vehicle, as outlined earlier.

Rear

1. Before servicing the vehicle, refer to the precautions in the beginning of this section.

2. Remove the strut requiring overhaul from the vehicle.

3. Position the strut in a vise. Using paint or a marker, matchmark the strut unit, lower spring isolator, spring and upper strut mount for installation purposes.

4. Place suitable spring compressor tools (Special tool C-4838) on the strut spring. Compress the coil spring until all load is removed from the upper strut mount.

5. Install a suitable strut nut socket or open ended wrench on the strut shaft retaining nut. Then, install a 10mm socket on the hex end of the strut damper shaft. While holding the strut shaft from turning, remove the strut shaft retaining nut.

6. Remove the washer between the strut shaft nut and the upper strut mount and isolator.

7. Remove the upper strut mount assembly from the strut shaft and spring.

8. Remove the washer from the strut shaft that is between the strut upper mount assembly and dust shield.

9. Remove the coil spring and spring compressor as an assembly from the strut.

10. Remove the dust shield from the strut assembly.

11. Remove the jounce bumper from the strut shaft.

12. Remove the coil spring lower isolator from the strut assembly spring seat.

13. Inspect all of the disassembled components for damage, abnormal wear or failure. Check the strut unit for excessive oil leakage and/or loss of oil charge, as follows:

a. Push the strut shaft into the body of the strut and release, the strut shaft should return to its original position.

b. If the shaft does not return to its original position, replace the strut unit.

To install:

14. Install the isolator on the lower spring seat of the strut.

15. Install the jounce bumper on the strut shaft.

16. Install the dust shield on the strut assembly.

17. Lower the coil spring onto the strut unit. Position the end of the coil spring against the edge of the spring isolator on the lower spring seat of the strut assembly.

18. Install the washer on the strut shaft with the raised edge of the washer facing upward.

19. Place the strut upper mount onto the strut shaft.

20. Install the washer on the strut upper mount. The washer must be installed with the raised edge of the washer facing down.

21. Install the upper strut mount-to-strut shaft retaining nut.

22. Use a strut rod socket or an open ended wrench and a 10mm socket, to prevent the strut shaft from rotating, tighten the strut shaft nut to 45 ft. lbs. (60 Nm).

23. Equally loosen the spring compressors until the spring is seated on the upper strut mount and all tension is relieved from the spring compressors.

24. Install the strut in the vehicle.

25. Have the toe checked and adjusted as necessary.

Lower Ball Joint

REMOVAL & INSTALLATION

The front suspension ball joints operate with no free-play. The ball joints are replaceable ONLY as an assembly. Do not attempt any type of repair on the ball joint assembly. The ball joint is a press fit into the lower control arm with the joint stud retained in the steering knuckle by the clamp bolt. To check the ball joint, with the weight of the vehicle resting on the road wheels, grasp the grease fitting and without using any tools, attempt to move the grease fitting. If the ball joint is worn the grease fitting will move easily. If movement is noted, replacement of the ball joint is recommended.

Wiggle the grease fitting with your fingers—if it moves, the ball joint should be replaced

1. Before servicing the vehicle, refer to the precautions in the beginning of this section.

2. Raise and safely support the vehicle. Remove the wheel and tire assembly.

3. Remove the steering knuckle-to-ball joint ball stud, clamping nut and bolt.

4. Remove the two attaching links connecting the stabilizer bar to the lower control arms.

5. Loosen, but do not remove the bolts holding the stabilizer bar retainers to the crossmember. Then, rotate the stabilizer bar and attaching links away from the lower control arms.

✴✴ WARNING

Pulling the steering knuckle out from the vehicle after releasing the ball joint can separate the inner CV-joint.

6. Use a prybar to separate the steering knuckle from the ball joint stud. Be careful when separating the ball joint stud from the knuckle, so the seal does not become damaged.

7. Remove the front lower control arm bushing-to-crossmember attaching nut and bolt. Remove the rear lower control arm-to-crossmember and frame rail attaching bolt. Then, remove the lower control arm from the crossmember.

8. Carefully pry the seal boot off the ball joint, using a suitable prytool.

9. Using a suitable press remove the ball joint from the lower control arm.

To install:

10. Reinstall the ball joint into the lower control arm with the notch in the ball joint stud facing the front lower control arm bushing.

11. Using a suitable press, press the ball joint into the lower control arm.

12. Reinstall the ball joint boot seal using a suitable driver such as a large socket or suitable sized piece of pipe. Do not use a shop press as was used to install the ball joint as a press exerts too much force.

13. Position the lower control arm into the front crossmember. Install the rear lower control arm-to-crossmember and frame rail attaching bolt. DO NOT tighten the rear bolt at this time. Then, install the front lower control arm-to-crossmember nut and bolt.

14. Tighten the front lower, then the rear control arm nut and bolt to 120 ft. lbs. (163 Nm).

15. Place the ball joint stud into the steering knuckle. Install the steering knuckle-to-ball joint stud clamping bolt and nut. Tighten the bolt to 70 ft. lbs. (95 Nm).

16. Assemble the stabilizer bar-to-lower control arm link assemblies and bushings.

17. Rotate the stabilizer bar into position, installing the stabilizer bar links into the lower control arms. Install the top stabilizer bar link bushings and nuts. DO NOT tighten the link yet.

18. Install the wheel and tire assembly.

19. Carefully lower the vehicle so the suspension is supporting the total weight of the vehicle.

20. Tighten the stabilizer bar-to-lower control arm links to 21 ft. lbs. (28 Nm).

21. Tighten the stabilizer bar bushing retainer-to-crossmember attaching bolts to 21 ft. lbs. (28 Nm).

22. The toe should be checked and adjusted as necessary.

Wheel Bearings

ADJUSTMENT

Neons are equipped with sealed hub and bearing assemblies. The hub and bearing assembly is non-serviceable. If the assembly is damaged, the complete unit must be replaced.

REMOVAL & INSTALLATION

Front

1. Before servicing the vehicle, refer to the precautions in the beginning of this section.

2. Remove the steering knuckle and hub and bearing assembly from the vehicle.

3. Use a suitable C-clamp and adapter, tool 4150A or equivalent to press one wheel lug stud out of the hub flange.

4. Rotate the hub to align the removed lug stud with the notch in the bearing retainer plate. Remove the lug stud from the hub.

5. Rotate the hub so the hole in the hub that the stud was removed from is facing away from the brake caliper lower rail on the steering knuckle. Install one half of a bearing splitter tool, Special tool 1130 or equivalent between the hub and the bearing retainer plate. The threaded hole in this half of the bearing splitter is to be aligned with the caliper rail on the steering knuckle.

Use a proper C-clamp and adapter tool to press out one of the lug studs

Rotate the hub in order to remove the lug stud

Proper installation of the bearing splitter

The steering knuckle must be properly supported for hub and bearing removal

6. Install the remaining pieces of the bearing splitter on the steering knuckle. Hand-tighten the nuts to hold the splitter in place on the knuckle.

7. When the bearing splitter is installed, be sure the three bolts attaching the bearing retainer plate to the knuckle are contacting the bearing splitter. The bearing retainer plate should not support the knuckle or contact the splitter.

8. Place the steering knuckle in a suitable press, supported by the bearing splitter as shown in the accompanying figure.

9. Position a suitable sized driver on the small end of the hub. Using the press, remove the hub from the wheel bearing. The outer bearing race will come out of the wheel bearing when the hub is pressed out of the bearing.

10. Remove the bearing splitter tool from the knuckle.

11. Place the knuckle in a press supported by the press blocks, as shown in the accompanying figure. The blocks must not obstruct the bore in the steering knuckle so the wheel bearing can be pressed out of the knuckle. Place a suitable driver on the outer race of the wheel bearing, then press the bearing out of the knuckle.

12. Install the bearing splitter on the hub. The splitter is to be installed on the hub so it is between the flange of the hub and the bearing race on the hub. Place the hub, bearing race and splitter in a press. Use a driver to press the hub out of the bearing race.

To install:

13. Use clean, dry cloth to wipe and grease or dirt from the bore of the steering knuckle.

14. Clean the rust preventative from the replacement wheel bearing using a clean, dry towel.

15. Place the new wheel bearing into the bore of the steering knuckle. Be sure the bearing is placed squarely into the bore. Place the knuckle in a press with a receiver tool, C-4698–2 supporting the steering knuckle. Place a suitable driver tool on the outer race of the wheel bearing. Press the wheel bearing into the steering knuckle until it is fully bottomed in the bore of the steering knuckle.

➡Only the original or original equipment replacement bolts should be used to mounting the bearing retainer to the

knuckle. If a bolt requires replacement when installing the bearing retainer plate, be sure to get the proper type of replacement.

16. Install the bearing retainer plate on the steering knuckle. Install the 3 bearing retainer mounting bolts. Tighten the bolts to 21 ft. lbs. (28 Nm).

17. Install the removed wheel lug stud into the hub flange.

18. Place the hub, with the lug stud installed, in a suitable press supported by adapter tool C-4698–1 or equivalent. Press the wheel lug stud into the hub flange until it is fully seated against the back side on the hub flange.

19. Place the steering knuckle, with the wheel bearing installed, in a press with special receiver tool MB-990799 supporting the inner race of the wheel bearing. Place the hub in the wheel bearing, making sure it is square with the bearing. Press the hub into the wheel bearing until it is fully bottomed in the wheel bearing.

20. Install the steering knuckle in the vehicle.

21. Install the wheel and tire assembly, then carefully lower the vehicle.

22. Take the vehicle to a reputable repair shop to have the front end alignment checked and the toe adjusted as required.

Rear

1. Before servicing the vehicle, refer to the precautions in the beginning of this section.

2. Raise and safely support the vehicle.

3. Remove the wheel and tire assembly.

4. If equipped with rear drum brakes, remove the brake drum. If equipped with rear disc brakes, remove the caliper and suspend aside with a piece of wire, then remove the rotor. DO NOT allow the caliper to hang by the brake hose.

5. Remove the dust cap from the rear hub/bearing.

6. Remove the retaining nut securing the hub/bearing assembly to the knuckle/spindle. Discard the hub nut and replace with a new one during installation.

7. Remove the hub/bearing from the spindle buy pulling it off the end of the spindle by hand.

To install:

8. Position the hub/bearing assembly on the rear spindle/knuckle. Install a NEW hub nut and tighten to 160 ft. lbs. (217 Nm).

9. Install the dust cap and seat it using a soft face hammer to carefully tap it into place.

10. If equipped with drum brakes, install the brake drum. If equipped with disc brakes, install the rotor.

11. If equipped with disc brakes, install the caliper and two guide pin bolts. Tighten the bolts to 16 ft. lbs. (22 Nm).

12. Install the wheel and tire assembly. Tighten the lug nuts, in a crisscross pattern, to 100 ft. lbs. (135 Nm).

13. Carefully lower the vehicle.

CHRYSLER CORPORATION

16

Chrysler-Cirrus • Sebring Convertible • **Dodge-**Stratus • **Plymouth-**Breeze

PRECAUTIONS

Before servicing any vehicle, please be sure to read all of the following precautions. The following precautions deal with personal safety, preventing of component damage, and important points to take into consideration when servicing a motor vehicle:

• Never open, service or drain the radiator or cooling system when the engine is hot; serious burns can occur from the steam and hot coolant.

• Observe all applicable safety precautions when working around fuel. Whenever servicing the fuel system, always work in a well ventilated area. Do not allow fuel spray or vapors to come in contact with a spark, open flame, or excessive heat (a hot drop light, for example). Keep a dry chemical fire extinguisher near the work area. Always keep fuel in a container specifically designed for fuel storage; also, always properly seal fuel containers to avoid the possibility of fire or explosion. Refer to the additional fuel system precautions later in this section.

• Fuel injection systems often remain pressurized, even after the engine has been turned **OFF**. The fuel system pressure must be relieved before disconnecting any fuel lines. Failure to do so may result in fire and/or personal injury.

• Brake fluid often contains polyglycol ethers and polyglycols. Avoid contact with the eyes and wash your hands thoroughly after handling brake fluid. If you do get brake fluid in your eyes, flush your eyes with clean, running water for 15 minutes. If eye irritation persists, or if you have taken brake fluid internally, IMMEDIATELY seek medical assistance.

• The EPA warns that prolonged contact with used engine oil may cause a number of skin disorders, including cancer! You should make every effort to minimize your exposure

to used engine oil. Protective gloves should be worn when changing the oil. Wash your hands and any other exposed skin areas as soon as possible after exposure to used engine oil. Soap and water, or waterless hand cleaner should be used.

• All vehicles are equipped with an air bag system, often referred to as a Supplemental Restraint System (SRS) or as a Supplemental Inflatable Restraint (SIR) system. The system must be disabled before performing service on or around system components, steering column, instrument panel components, wiring and sensors. Failure to follow safety and disabling procedures could result in accidental air bag deployment, possible personal injury and unnecessary system repairs.

• Always wear safety goggles when working with, or around, the air bag system. When carrying a non-deployed air bag, be sure the bag and trim cover are pointed away from your body. When placing a non-deployed air bag on a work surface, always face the bag and trim cover upward, away from the surface. This will reduce the motion of the module if it is accidentally deployed.

• Clean, high quality brake fluid from a sealed container is essential for the safe and proper operation of the brake system. You should always buy the grade of fluid recommended for your vehicle. If the brake fluid becomes contaminated, drain and flush the system, then refill the master cylinder with new fluid. Never reuse any brake fluid. Any brake fluid that is removed from the system should be discarded. Also, do not allow any brake fluid to come in contact with a painted surface; it will damage the paint.

• Never operate the engine without the proper amount and type of engine oil; doing so WILL result in severe engine damage.

• Timing belt maintenance is extremely important! Many models may utilize an interference-type, non-free-wheeling engine.

If the timing belt breaks, the valves in the cylinder head may strike the pistons, causing potentially serious (also time-consuming and expensive) engine damage. Refer to the maintenance interval charts in the front of this manual for the recommended replacement interval for the timing belt, and to the timing belt section for belt replacement and inspection.

• Disconnecting the negative battery cable on some vehicles may interfere with the functions of the on board computer system(s) and may require the computer to undergo a relearning process once the negative battery cable is reconnected.

• When servicing drum brakes, only disssemble and assemble one side at a time, leaving the remaining side intact for reference.

• Only an MVAC-trained, EPA-certified, automotive technician should service the A/C system or its components.

ENGINE REPAIR

Distributor

REMOVAL

2.5L Engine

The 2.5L engine is equipped with a camshaft driven mechanical distributor. This engine uses a fixed ignition timing system. The basic ignition timing is not adjustable. The Powertrain Control Module (PCM) determines spark advance. The Crankshaft Position (CKP) sensor and Camshaft Position (CMP) sensor are Hall Effect devices. The CKP sensor is mounted remotely from the distributor while the CMP sensor is mounted inside the distributor housing. Both sensors generate pulses that are inputs to the PCM. The PCM determines crankshaft position from these sensors. The PCM calculates injector sequence and ignition timing. There is a resistor built into the distributor cap. An ohmmeter connected between the center button and ignition coil terminal should read 5000 ohms.

1. Before servicing the vehicle, refer to the precautions in the beginning of this section.

2. Disconnect the negative battery cable from the left shock tower. The ground cable is equipped with an insulator grommet which should be placed on the stud to prevent the negative battery cable from accidentally grounding.

3. Remove the bolt attaching the air inlet resonator to the intake manifold.

4. Loosen the clamps holding the air cleaner cover to the air cleaner housing.

5. Remove the PCV make-up air hose from the air inlet tube.

6. Remove the EGR tube.

7. Mark for identification, if necessary, and remove the spark plug wires from the distributor cap.

8. Remove the distributor cap.

9. Mark the rotor position. A scribe mark indicates where to position the rotor when reinstalling the distributor. Remove the rotor.

10. Detach the two electrical harness connections from the distributor.

11. Remove the two distributor hold-down nuts and washers.

12. Remove the spark plug cable mounting bracket.

13. Remove the transaxle dipstick tube.

14. Carefully remove the distributor from the engine.

INSTALLATION

2.5L Engine

TIMING NOT DISTURBED

1. Inspect the rotor for cracks or a burned electrode. Replace if defective. Install the rotor onto the distributor.

2. Inspect the O-ring seal. If nicked or cracked, replace with a new one. Be sure the O-ring is properly seated on the distributor.

3. Carefully engage the distributor drive with the slotted end of the camshaft. When the distributor is installed properly, the rotor will be in line with the previously made mark.

4. Verify proper rotor alignment with mark made at disassembly.

5. Reinstall the distributor hold-down nuts and washers. Tighten the nuts to 9 ft. lbs. (13 Nm).

6. Reinstall the spark plug cable bracket.

7. Reattach the two distributor wiring connectors.

8. Reinstall the distributor cap.

9. Reinstall the spark plug cables following the identification marks made at disassembly.

10. Reinstall the transaxle dipstick tube.

11. Reinstall the EGR tube and tighten the bolts to 95 inch lbs. (11 Nm).

12. Reinstall the PCV hose.

13. Reinstall the air cleaner and tighten the hose clamps.

14. Reinstall the air inlet resonator.

15. Reconnect the negative battery cable.

TIMING DISTURBED

1. Rotate the crankshaft until No. 1 piston is at Top Dead Center (TDC) of the compression stroke.

2. Rotate the rotor to the No. 1 terminal position on the distributor cap.

3. Lower the distributor into place, engaging the distributor drive with the drive on the camshaft. With the distributor fully seated on the engine, the rotor should be under the No. 1 terminal.

4. Reinstall the distributor hold-down nuts and washers. Tighten the nuts to 9 ft. lbs. (13 Nm).

5. Reinstall the spark plug cable bracket.

6. Reattach the two distributor wiring connectors.

7. Reinstall the distributor cap.

8. Reinstall the spark plug cables following the identification marks made at disassembly.

9. Reinstall the transaxle dipstick tube.

10. Reinstall the EGR tube and tighten the bolts to 95 inch lbs. (11 Nm).

11. Reinstall the PCV hose.

12. Reinstall the air cleaner and tighten the hose clamps.

13. Reinstall the air inlet resonator.

14. Reconnect the negative battery cable.

Ignition Timing

ADJUSTMENT

These engines use a fixed ignition system. The Powertrain Control Module (PCM) regulates the ignition timing. Basic ignition timing is not adjustable.

Engine Assembly

REMOVAL & INSTALLATION

1. Before servicing the vehicle, refer to the precautions in the beginning of this section.

2. Relieve the fuel system pressure using the recommended procedure. Disconnect the fuel line quick-connect fitting from the fuel rail by squeezing the retainer tabs together and pulling the fuel tube/quick-connect fitting assembly off the fuel tube nipple.

3. Remove the battery and battery tray according to the following:

a. Be sure the ignition switch is in the **OFF** unlocked position and all vehicle accessories are turned **OFF**.

b. Disconnect the negative battery cable from the left shock tower. The ground cable is equipped with an insulator grommet which should be placed on the stud to prevent the negative battery cable from accidentally grounding.

c. Turn the steering wheel to the extreme left position.

d. Release the shield by twisting the four plastic screws ¼ turn. Remove the shield.

e. Disconnect the battery blanket heater, if equipped.

f. Remove the negative battery cable, then remove the positive battery cable.

g. Remove the bolt securing the battery strap to the battery hold-down bracket. Remove the hold-down bracket bolt.

h. Slide the battery to the rear of the battery tray and lift over the lip. Be careful not to tip the battery or acid will spill out.

i. Remove the battery from the vehicle. Remove the battery blanket heater, if equipped.

j. Remove the battery tray mounting bolts.

k. Remove the battery tray and battery strap.

4. Remove the complete air cleaner and inlet duct assembly.

5. Unbolt the Powertrain Control Module (PCM) and move it aside.

6. Drain and properly contain the coolant from the engine.

7. Remove the upper and lower radiator hose, radiator and cooling fan.

8. Disconnect and plug the automatic transaxle cooler lines, if equipped.

9. Disconnect the clutch cable and transaxle shift linkage, if equipped.

10. Disconnect the throttle body linkage and the engine wiring harness.

11. Disconnect the heater hoses.

12. Recover and properly contain the refrigerant of the A/C system with an R-134a recovery unit.

13. Raise and safely support the vehicle. Remove the front wheels.

14. Drain the engine oil, if necessary.

15. Remove the right side inner splash shield.

16. Remove the accessory drive belts.

17. Remove the right and left halfshaft assemblies.

18. Disconnect the exhaust pipe from the exhaust manifold.

19. Remove the front and rear engine mount brackets from the body.

20. Lower the vehicle.

21. Remove the power steering pump and reservoir; set them aside.

22. Remove the A/C compressor as follows:

a. Disconnect the compressor clutch wire lead.

b. Disconnect and plug the refrigerant lines from the compressor.

c. Remove the compressor mounting bolts.

d. Remove the compressor unit from the vehicle. Be sure to plug all openings in the A/C system to prevent moisture contamination.

23. Disconnect the ground straps from the engine.

24. Raise the vehicle and install an engine dolly under the vehicle and support engine.

Exploded view of the right side engine mount—all engines

Exploded view of the left side engine mount—Type 2

TORQUE	
A	61 N•m (45 ft. lbs.)
B	33 N•m (24 ft. lbs.)

Exploded view of the left side engine mount—Type 1

Exploded view of the rear engine mounting torque bracket—2.0L engine

TORQUE	
A	61 N•m (45 ft. lbs.)
B	110 N•m (80 ft. lbs.)

REAR TORQUE BRACKET

ENGINE

SUPPORT

STARTER WIRING CLIP (2.5L ENGINE)

TRANSMISSION   STRUT

7922FG05

Exploded view of the rear engine mounting torque bracket—2.4L and 2.5L engines

ENGINE

FRONT TORQUE BRACKET

FWD

FRONT MOUNT

STRUT

ENGINE SUPPORT MODULE

FWD

A/C COMPRESSOR

STRUT (SOME MODELS)

7922FG06

Exploded view of the front engine mounting torque bracket—2.0L and 2.4L engines

FRONT TORQUE BRACKET

TORQUE	
A	61 N•m (45 ft. lbs.)
B	110 N•m (80 ft. lbs.)
C	33 N•m (24 ft. lbs.)

FWD

STRUT

SUPPORT

7922FG07

Exploded view of the front engine mounting torque bracket—2.5L engine

25. Remove the transaxle and engine mount through-bolts.

26. Raise the vehicle slowly allowing the engine and transaxle assembly to remain on the dolly.

To install:

27. Position the engine and the transaxle under the vehicle and lower the vehicle onto the engine assembly.

28. Align the engine mounts and install the right and left mount bolts.

29. Reinstall the transaxle mount.

30. Reinstall the right and left halfshaft assemblies.

31. Reinstall the transaxle and engine braces.

32. Reinstall the splash shields.

33. Reconnect the exhaust pipe to the exhaust manifold.

34. Reinstall the power steering pump and reservoir.

35. Reinstall the A/C compressor on the engine as follows:

   a. Position the compressor correctly against the engine.

   b. Reinstall the compressor mounting bolts. Tighten the compressor mounting bolts to 30 ft. lbs. (41 Nm).

   c. Reconnect the A/C refrigerant hoses with new seals.

   d. Reconnect the compressor clutch wire.

36. Reinstall the accessory drive belts and adjust.

37. Reinstall the front engine mount.

38. Reinstall the inner splash shield. Install the front wheels and lug nuts. Tighten the lug nuts, in a star pattern sequence, to 95–100 ft. lbs. (129–135 Nm).

39. If equipped with a manual transaxle, reconnect the clutch cable and linkages.

40. If equipped with an automatic transaxle, reconnect the shifter and kick-down linkages.

41. Reconnect the fuel lines and heater hoses.

42. Reconnect the ground straps.

43. Reattach the throttle body electrical harnesses and connections.

44. Reconnect the throttle body linkage.

45. Reinstall the radiator, cooling fan/shroud assembly and hoses. Reconnect the automatic transaxle cooler lines to the radiator, if equipped.

46. Refill the cooling system with a 50/50 mixture of clean water and ethylene glycol antifreeze.

47. If the engine oil was drained, install fresh oil and a new oil filter.

48. Reinstall the battery tray and the battery as follows:

   a. Reinstall the battery strap and battery tray into the vehicle through the left front fender well.

   b. Reinstall and tighten the battery tray mounting bolts.

   c. Reinstall the battery blanket heater onto the battery, if equipped.

   d. Reinstall the battery onto the battery tray in the proper position.

   e. Reinstall the hold-down bracket bolt and the bolt securing the battery strap to the battery hold-down bracket. Tighten the battery hold-down bracket bolt to 124 inch lbs. (14 Nm).

   f. Reconnect the positive battery cable to the battery, then attach the negative battery cable to the battery. Tighten the battery cables to 150 inch lbs. (17 Nm). DO NOT reattach the negative battery cable remote connection to the left shock tower at this time.

   g. Reconnect the battery blanket heater, if equipped.

   h. Install the shield. Turn the four plastic screws to secure the shield in place.

49. Reinstall the PCM.

50. Reinstall the air cleaner and inlet duct assembly.

51. Reconnect the negative battery cable.

52. Recharge the air conditioning system.

53. Check to be sure all ducts, hoses, fuel lines and wiring connectors have been properly reattached.

54. Start the engine, check for oil pressure, and run until operating temperature is reached.

55. Check for leaks and proper operation.

Water Pump

REMOVAL & INSTALLATION

2.0L and 2.4L Engines

This engine uses a die-cast aluminum body water pump with a stamped steel impeller. The water pump bolts directly to the block. The cylinder block-to-water pump sealing is provided by a large rubber O-ring. The water pump is driven by the timing belt which must be removed to service the water pump.

1. Disconnect the negative battery cable from the left shock tower. The ground cable is equipped with an insulator grommet which should be placed on the stud to prevent the negative battery cable from accidentally grounding.

➡**This procedure requires removing the engine timing belt and the auto-tensioner. The factory specifies that the timing marks should always be aligned before removing the timing belt. Set the engine at TDC on No. 1 compression stroke. This should align all tim-**

Timing belt service is covered in Section 5 of this manual

ing marks on the crankshaft sprocket and both camshaft sprockets.

2. Before servicing the vehicle, refer to the precautions in the beginning of this section.

3. Raise and safely support the vehicle.

4. Remove the right inner splash shield.

5. Remove the accessory drive belts.

6. Place a drain pan under the radiator drain plug. Drain and properly contain the cooling system.

7. Support the engine and remove the right motor mount.

8. Remove the power steering pump mounting bracket bolts and place the pump/bracket assembly off to one side. Do not disconnect the power steering fluid lines.

9. Remove the right engine mount bracket.

10. Remove the timing belt front covers.

11. Loosen the timing belt tensioner screws and remove the belt tensioner and timing belt.

✸✸ WARNING

With the timing belt removed, DO NOT rotate the camshaft or crankshaft or damage to the engine could occur.

12. Remove the camshaft sprockets. With the timing belt removed, remove both camshaft sprocket bolts. Do not allow the camshafts to turn when the camshaft sprockets are being removed.

13. Remove the rear timing belt cover to access the water pump.

14. Remove the water pump attaching bolts.

15. Remove the water pump.

To install:

16. Thoroughly clean all sealing surfaces. Replace the water pump if there are

any cracks, signs of coolant leakage from the shaft seal, loose or rough turning bearings, damaged impeller or sprocket or sprocket flange loose or damaged.

17. Install a new rubber O-ring into the water pump.

✸✸ WARNING

Be sure the O-ring is properly seated in the water pump groove before tightening the screws. An improperly located O-ring may cause damage to the O-ring and cause a coolant leak.

18. Install the water pump and tighten the bolts to 105 inch lbs. (12 Nm).

19. Pressurize the cooling system to 15 psi (103.4 kPa) and check for leaks. If okay, release the pressure and continue the engine assembly process.

20. Reinstall the rear timing belt cover.

21. Reinstall the camshaft sprockets and tighten the attaching bolts to 75 ft. lbs. (101 Nm). DO NOT allow the camshafts to turn while the sprockets bolts are being tightened to maintain timing mark alignment.

✸✸ WARNING

Do not attempt to compress the tensioner plunger with the tensioner assembly installed in the engine. This will cause damage to the tensioner and other related components. The tensioner MUST be compressed in a vise.

22. Reinstall the timing belt tensioner and timing belt. Be sure to properly tension the timing belt.

23. Reinstall the front upper and lower timing belt covers.

24. Reinstall the right engine mount bracket and engine mount.

25. Reinstall the crankshaft damper and tighten the center bolt to 105 ft. lbs. (142 Nm).

26. Reinstall the right inner splash shield.

27. Lower the vehicle.

28. Reinstall the power steering pump bracket and power steering pump. Tighten the bracket mounting bolts to 40 ft. lbs. (54 Nm).

29. Reinstall the drive belts. Properly tension the drive belts.

30. Refill the cooling system using a mixture of 50/50 water and ethylene glycol antifreeze. Bleed the cooling system.

31. Start the engine and check for proper operation.

32. Check and top off cooling system, if necessary.

When installing the water pump, properly install the O-ring to ensure a tight seal—2.0L and 2.4L engines

2.5L Engine

The water pump bolts directly to the engine block using a gasket for pump-to-block sealing. The pump is serviced as a unit. The 2.5L engine uses metal piping beyond the lower radiator hose to route coolant to the suction side of the water pump, located in the "V" of the cylinder banks. These pipes also have connections for thermostat bypass and heater return coolant hoses. The pipes use O-rings for sealing.

The water pump is driven by the timing belt which must be removed to service the water pump. Timing belt covers must be removed to access the timing belt.

1. Before servicing the vehicle, refer to the precautions in the beginning of this section.

2. Disconnect the negative battery cable from the left shock tower. The ground cable is equipped with an insulator grommet which should be placed on the stud to prevent the negative battery cable from accidentally grounding.

3. Drain the engine coolant.

➡**This procedure requires removing the engine timing belt and the auto-tensioner. To help assure proper alignment at assembly, it may be helpful to set the engine at TDC on No. 1 compression stroke. This should align all timing marks on the crankshaft sprocket and both camshaft sprockets.**

4. Remove the accessory drive belts and crankshaft damper.

5. Remove the right engine mount. This requires safely supporting the engine so the mount can be removed.

6. Remove the timing belt covers in this order: upper left cover, upper right cover, lower cover.

7. Remove the timing belt and tensioner.

8. Remove the water pump mounting bolts.

9. Separate the water pump from the water inlet pipe and remove the pump.

To install:

10. Thoroughly clean all sealing surfaces. Inspect the pump for damage or cracks, signs of coolant leakage at the vent and excessive looseness or rough turning bearing. Any problems require a new pump.

11. Install a new O-ring on the water inlet pipe. Wet the O-ring with water to make installation easier. DO NOT use oil or grease on the O-ring.

12. Install a new gasket on the water pump and fit the pump inlet opening over

Exploded view of the water pump mounting—2.5L engine

the water pipe. Press the assembly together to force the pipe into the water pump.

13. Reinstall the water pump-to-engine bolts and tighten to 20 ft. lbs. (27 Nm).

14. Reinstall the timing belt and timing belt tensioner. Set the timing belt tension.

15. Reinstall the timing belt covers. Reinstall the right engine mount.

16. Reinstall the crankshaft damper.

17. Install the accessory drive belts and set to proper tension.

18. Reconnect the negative battery cable.

19. Refill and bleed the engine cooling system.

20. Start the engine and verify proper operation.

Cylinder Head

REMOVAL & INSTALLATION

2.0L Engine

This engine uses a Single Over Head Camshaft (SOHC) 4-valves per cylinder cross flow aluminum cylinder head. Care must be taken to be sure all valve timing marks align after cylinder head service.

1. Before servicing the vehicle, refer to the precautions in the beginning of this section.

2. Relieve the fuel system pressure using the recommended procedure.

3. Disconnect the negative battery cable from the left shock tower. The ground cable is equipped with an insulator grommet which should be placed on the stud to prevent the negative battery cable from accidentally grounding.

4. Remove the air cleaner assembly.

5. Drain the engine coolant.

6. Detach and tag all vacuum hoses and all electrical connections from the throttle body. Detach the fuel line quick-connect fitting from the fuel injectors by squeezing

Exploded view of the cylinder head and valvetrain components—2.0L engine

the retainer tabs together and pulling the fuel tube/quick-connect fitting assembly off the fuel tube nipple.

7. Disconnect the throttle linkage.

8. Remove the accessory drive belt(s).

9. Disconnect the power brake booster vacuum hose from the intake manifold.

10. Raise and safely support the vehicle.

11. Disconnect the exhaust pipe from the exhaust manifold. Lower the vehicle.

12. Remove the power steering pump and move aside.

13. Detach the coil pack wiring connector. Disconnect the spark plug wires from the spark plugs. Remove the ignition coil pack unit from the engine.

14. Remove the cylinder head cover.

15. Disconnect the cam sensor and fuel injector wiring.

16. Remove the intake and exhaust manifolds, if necessary.

17. Remove the timing belt cover, timing belt, camshaft sprocket and rear timing belt cover using the recommended procedure.

18. Remove the rocker arm/rocker arm shaft assemblies.

19. Remove the cylinder head bolts and remove the cylinder head.

To install:

➡The cylinder head bolts should be checked for stretching before reuse. If the thread area of the bolt is necked-down the bolts must be replaced with new. New head bolts are recommended.

20. Thoroughly clean all parts. Clean all sealing surfaces. Use care not to scratch the aluminum cylinder head sealing surface. Check the cylinder head for flatness using a feeler gauge and a straightedge. The cylinder head must be flat within 0.004 in. (0.1mm).

Before reusing old cylinder head bolts, check them for necking (stretching)—2.0L and 2.4L engines

7922FG12

Cylinder head bolt tightening sequence—2.0L engine

21. Check the cylinder head for cracks or other damage.

22. Install a new gasket and the cylinder head to the engine block.

23. Be sure to oil the cylinder head bolt threads with clean engine oil. Install the cylinder head bolts, the 4.330 in. (110mm) short bolts are to be installed in positions 7, 8, 9 and 10. Tighten the bolts in proper sequence.

24. Tighten the bolts in four steps as follows:

   a. All bolts to 25 ft. lbs. (34 Nm).
   b. All bolts to 50 ft. lbs. (68 Nm).
   c. All bolts again to 50 ft. lbs. (68 Nm).
   d. All bolts an additional ¼ turn.

➡**Do not use a torque wrench for the fourth step.**

25. Set the crankshaft to three notches BTDC before installing the rocker arm shafts. Install the rocker arm/rocker arm shaft assemblies.

26. Reinstall the cylinder head cover with a new cylinder head cover gasket. Be sure the cover gasket mating surfaces are clean of any dirt, oil or old gasket material. Tighten the cylinder head cover mounting bolts to 105 inch lbs. (12 Nm).

27. Reinstall the timing belt rear cover and camshaft sprocket. Reinstall the timing belt using the recommended procedure to be sure the timing marks are properly aligned. Failure to do so will cause engine damage.

28. Reinstall the timing belt cover.

29. Reinstall the intake and exhaust manifolds, if removed.

30. Reconnect the cam sensor and the fuel injector wiring.

31. Reinstall the ignition coil pack onto the engine. Reattach the coil pack wiring connector and the spark plug wires to the correct spark plugs.

32. Reinstall the power steering pump.

33. Raise the vehicle and reconnect the exhaust pipe to the exhaust manifold. Lower the vehicle.

34. Reconnect the brake booster vacuum line.

35. Reinstall and adjust the accessory drive belts.

36. Reconnect the throttle linkage.

37. Reattach all vacuum hoses and wiring connectors to the throttle body.

38. Reconnect the fuel line to the fuel injectors.

39. Reinstall the air cleaner assembly.

40. Refill the cooling system with a 50/50 mixture of clean antifreeze and water. A complete oil and filter change is recommended.

41. Reconnect the negative battery cable.

42. Check to be sure all ducts, hoses, fuel lines and wiring connectors have been properly reattached.

43. Start the engine and check for leaks. Run the engine with the radiator cap off so as the engine warms and the thermostat opens, coolant can be added to the radiator. When satisfied that the cooling system is full, shut the engine **OFF**, install the radiator cap and allow the engine to cool.

44. With the engine cool, check all fluid levels. Add coolant and oil as required. Restart the engine and test drive the vehicle to check for proper operation.

2.4L Engine

This engine uses a Dual Over Head Camshaft (DOHC) 4-valves per cylinder cross flow aluminum cylinder head. The valves are actuated by roller cam followers which pivot on stationary hydraulic valve adjusters. Care must be taken to be sure all valve timing marks align after cylinder head and valvetrain service.

1. Before servicing the vehicle, refer to the precautions in the beginning of this section.

2. Disconnect the negative battery cable from the left shock tower. The ground cable is equipped with an insulator grommet which should be placed on the stud to prevent the negative battery cable from accidentally grounding.

3. Relieve the fuel system pressure using the recommended procedure.

4. Drain the cooling system.

5. Remove the air cleaner assembly and disconnect all vacuum lines, electrical wiring and fuel lines from the throttle body.

6. Disconnect the throttle linkage.

7. Remove the accessory drive belts.

8. Disconnect the power brake vacuum hose from the intake manifold.

9. Raise and safely support the vehicle. Disconnect the exhaust pipe from the exhaust manifold.

10. Lower the vehicle as required to remove the power steering pump. Do not disconnect the fluid lines. Set the pump aside.

11. Label the spark plug wires for correct installation. detach the coil pack wiring connector and remove the coil pack and spark plug wires from the engine.

12. Detach the cam sensor and fuel injectors' wiring connectors.

13. Remove the timing belt covers, timing belt and camshaft sprockets using the recommended procedure.

14. Remove the timing belt idler pulley and rear timing belt cover.

15. Remove the cylinder head cover mounting fasteners and cylinder head cover. Remove the ground strap.

16. Identify the camshafts, if they are to be reused, for later installation. The camshafts are not interchangeable. Remove the camshaft bearing cap bolts in sequence and remove the camshafts.

➡**Refer to the camshaft removal and installation procedure for correct bolt removal/installation sequence.**

17. Remove the camshaft followers. Any components that are to be reused must be installed in their original locations. Use care to identify and mark the positions of any removed valvetrain components so they may be reinstalled correctly.

18. Remove the intake and exhaust manifolds.

19. Remove the cylinder head bolts.

20. Remove the cylinder head from the vehicle, using care not to damage the aluminum gasket surfaces.

21. Remove all gasket material from the cylinder head and engine block. Be careful not to gouge or scratch the sealing surface of the aluminum head. The cylinder head should be checked for flatness using a good straightedge and feeler gauges. The cylinder head must be flat within 0.004 in. (0.1mm).

22. Inspect the camshaft bearing oil feed holes in the cylinder head for clogging. Inspect the camshaft bearing journals for wear or scoring. Check the cam surface for abnormal wear and damage. A visible worn groove in the roller path or on the cam lobes is cause for replacement. Valve service may be performed at this time.

To install:

23. Thoroughly clean all parts. Note that the cylinder head bolts are tightened using a new procedure. The cylinder head bolts should be checked carefully BEFORE reuse. If the threads are necked-down the bolts should be replaced with new bolts. Necking can be checked by holding a

steel scale or straightedge against the threads. If all the threads do not contact the scale, the bolt should be replaced. New cylinder head bolts are recommended for any engine rebuild, especially if it is known that the engine has been disassembled before.

24. Thoroughly clean all sealing surfaces. Install a new gasket making sure all holes align with the openings in the engine block. Carefully set the cylinder head in place. A helper may be required.

25. Before installing the bolts the threads should be oiled with clean engine oil. Install the bolts and tighten in sequence in four Steps as follows:

    a. Tighten all bolts to 25 ft. lbs. (34 Nm).

    b. Tighten all bolts to 50 ft. lbs. (68 Nm).

    c. Tighten all bolts again to 50 ft. lbs. (68 Nm).

    d. Tighten all bolts and additional ¼ turn.

➡**Do not use a torque wrench for the fourth step.**

26. Check the camshaft end-play using the recommended procedure, then install the camshaft.

27. Apply Mopar Gasket Maker or equivalent sealer to the No. 1 and No. 6 bearing caps. Install the bearing caps and tighten the M8 fasteners to 250 inch lbs. (28 Nm). The end caps must be installed before the seals may be installed.

28. Apply a light coating of clean engine oil to the lip of the new camshaft seal. Install the camshaft seal until it fits flush with the cylinder head.

29. Reinstall the camshaft sprockets, if removed. Reinstall the rear timing belt cover and timing belt using care to be sure all timing marks are properly aligned, using the recommended procedure. Install timing belt cover.

Cylinder head bolt tightening sequence— 2.4L engine

⁕⁕ WARNING

Verify that all timing marks are correct. If the timing belt or sprockets are incorrectly installed, engine damage will occur. Take time to be sure all timing marks are correctly aligned.

30. Reinstall the intake and exhaust manifolds.

31. Thoroughly clean the cylinder head cover sealing surfaces.

32. Install new cylinder head cover gaskets. Use care. DO NOT allow oil or solvents to contact the timing belt as they can deteriorate the rubber and cause tooth skipping. Apply Mopar Silicone Rubber Adhesive Sealant, or equivalent, at the camshaft cap corners and at the top edge of the ½ round seal.

33. Install the cylinder head cover assembly to the head and tighten the fasteners in sequence using the following three Steps:

    a. Tighten all cylinder head cover fasteners to 40 inch lbs. (4.5 Nm).

    b. Tighten all fasteners to 80 inch lbs. (9 Nm).

    c. Tighten all fasteners to 105 inch lbs. (12 Nm).

34. Reinstall the ground strap.

35. Reinstall the ignition coil pack and reconnect the spark plug wiring.

36. Reconnect the cam sensor and fuel injector wiring.

37. Reinstall the power steering pump assembly.

38. Reconnect the exhaust pipe to the exhaust manifold.

39. Reattach all vacuum lines and remaining wiring. Reconnect the throttle linkage and fuel lines.

40. Reinstall and adjust the accessory drive belts.

41. Refill the cooling system. An oil and filter change is recommended since coolant can enter the oil system when a head is removed.

42. Connect the remaining air ducting. Connect the negative battery cable and test run vehicle. Check for leaks and for proper operation.

2.5L Engine

This engine uses aluminum alloy cylinder heads with 4-valves per cylinder and pressed-in cast iron valve guides. The cylinders are common to either cylinder bank. Two overhead camshafts are supported by four bearing journals which are part of the head with the distributor driven off the right (firewall side) cylinder head. Right and left camshaft drive sprockets are interchangeable. The sprockets and engine water pump are driven by the timing belt. Care must be taken to be sure all valve timing marks align after cylinder head and valvetrain service.

➡**Please note that for camshaft service, the cylinder head must be removed.**

1. Before servicing the vehicle, refer to the precautions in the beginning of this section.

2. Disconnect the negative battery cable from the left shock tower. The ground cable is equipped with an insulator grommet which should be placed on the stud to prevent the negative battery cable from accidentally grounding.

3. Relieve the fuel system pressure using the recommended procedure.

4. Drain the cooling system.

5. Remove the accessory drive belts.

6. Remove the front timing belt covers and timing belt using the recommended procedure. Remove the camshaft sprockets.

7. The intake manifold is a 2-piece unit. The upper part is a large air intake plenum of aluminum alloy. Use care working with light alloy parts. Remove the air intake plenum first, then remove the lower intake manifold.

8. Label, disconnect and set aside the spark plug wires.

9. Remove the cylinder head cover screws and remove the cover.

10. Identify the rocker arm shaft assemblies before removal.

11. Install the Auto Lash Adjuster Retainers MD 998443 or equivalents to keep the auto lash adjusters from falling out of the rocker arms when the rocker arm assembly is removed.

12. Loosen the attaching fasteners and remove the rocker arm shaft assemblies from the cylinder head.

13. Remove the distributor assembly.

14. Remove the exhaust manifold and crossover.

15. Remove the cylinder head bolts and remove the cylinder head from the vehicle.

16. If the camshaft(s) are to be serviced, remove the thrust case from the left head assembly and remove the camshaft from the rear of the head. If not already done, remove the distributor from the right cylinder head

Exploded view of the cylinder head, camshafts and rocker assemblies—2.5L engine

7922FG14

and remove the camshaft from the rear of the head.

17. Valve service may be performed at this time, if required.

To install:

18. Thoroughly clean all parts well. All sealing surfaces on the engine block, cylinder head(s) and both the upper and lower sections of the intake manifold must be clean. Check for cracks, signs of wear in the camshaft bores or other damage. With a straightedge and feeler gauge, check the head for flatness. It should be within 0.0012 in. (0.03mm) along its length. The service limit is 0.008 in. (0.2mm). If the head must be resurfaced, the grinding limit is 0.008 in. (0.2mm). Note that this dimension is a combined total dimension of stock material removal from the cylinder head, if any, and the block top surface is 0.0079 in. (0.2mm).

19. Camshaft end-play can be checked as follows:

   a. Oil the camshaft journals with clean engine oil and install (if removed) the camshaft without the rocker arm assemblies.

   b. Move the camshaft as far rearward as it will go.

   c. Mount a dial indicator to bear on the front of the camshaft.

   d. Zero the indicator.

TIMING BELT END

10 mm ALLEN HEX

CYLINDER HEAD BOLT AND WASHER

Cylinder head bolt tightening sequence—2.5L engine

7922FG15

e. Move the camshaft as far forward as it will go. End-play should be 0.004–0.008 in. (0.1–0.2mm). Maximum allowed end-play is 0.016 in. (0.4mm).

20. If the camshafts were removed, lubricate the camshaft journals and carefully reinstall the camshaft into the cylinder head. Install the thrust case and tighten the thrust case mounting bolts to 9 ft. lbs. (13 Nm).

21. Apply a light coating of engine oil to the lip of the camshaft seal(s). Install the camshaft seal(s). The camshaft must be installed before installing the seal. Reinstall the camshaft sprocket(s) and tighten to 65 ft. lbs. (88 Nm).

22. Reinstall a new head gasket over the locating dowels in the cylinder head. Install the head, using care to locate on top of the dowels. Install the 10mm Allen hex head bolts with washers. New head bolts are recommended. Tighten the head bolts in proper sequence. Tighten gradually, working in two or three steps and finally tighten to 80 ft. lbs. (108 Nm).

23. Reinstall the lower intake manifold using new gaskets.

24. Clean and install the rocker arm assemblies.

25. Reinstall the exhaust manifold and crossover exhaust pipe.

26. Reinstall the timing belt using the recommended procedure. It is very important that all valve timing marks align properly or engine damage will result.

27. Reinstall the timing belt covers.

28. Inspect the spark plug tube seals located on the ends of each tube. These seals slide onto each tube to seal the cylinder head cover to the spark plug tube. If these seals show signs of hardness and/or cracks, they should be replaced.

29. Thoroughly clean all sealing surfaces. Install a new gasket and install the cover. Tighten bolts to 88 inch lbs. (10 Nm).

30. Reinstall the distributor assembly. Reconnect the spark plug wires.

31. Position a new upper intake manifold (plenum) gasket in place and install the upper intake manifold plenum. Tighten the bolts to 13 ft. lbs. (18 Nm). Install the bolts for the plenum support brackets and connect the EGR tube.

32. Reinstall the speed control cable (if equipped) and the throttle cable.

33. Reattach the Throttle Position (TP) sensor and the Idle Air Control (IAC) motor electrical connectors.

34. Reinstall the air cleaner cover, inlet hoses and air inlet resonator. Tighten the air tube connections.

35. Reattach the MAP and Intake Air Temperature (IAT) sensor wiring connectors.

36. Reinstall and adjust the accessory drive belts.

37. Refill the cooling system with a 50/50 mixture of clean antifreeze and water. An oil and filter change is recommended whenever a cylinder head has been removed since coolant can get into the oil system.

38. Reconnect the negative battery cable. Check to be sure all ducts, hoses, fuel lines and wiring connections have all been properly reattached.

39. Start the engine and check for leaks, abnormal noises and vibrations.

Bleed the cooling system.

Rocker Arm/Shaft

REMOVAL & INSTALLATION

The 2.0L and 2.5L engines are equipped with rocker arms/shafts. On the 2.4L engine the camshaft acts directly on the valve, therefore, no rocker arms/shafts are used.

2.0L Engine

This engine uses a Single Over Head Camshaft (SOHC) running in an aluminum cylinder head. Rocker arm shafts mount directly to the cylinder head. Care must be taken to be sure all valve timing marks align after cylinder head and valvetrain service. The Hydraulic Lash Adjusters (HLAs) are located in the valve actuating end of the rocker arm and are serviced as an assembly.

1. Before servicing the vehicle, refer to the precautions in the beginning of this section.

2. Disconnect the negative battery cable from the left shock tower. The ground cable is equipped with an insulator grommet which should be placed on the stud to prevent the negative battery cable from accidentally grounding.

3. Relieve the fuel system pressure using the recommended procedure.

4. Label the spark plug wires to the correct spark plugs. Disconnect the spark plug wires from each spark plug.

5. Remove the inlet duct for the air cleaner.

6. Remove the ignition coil pack.

7. Remove the cylinder head cover retaining bolts and remove the cylinder head cover. Remove and discard any gasket material. Thoroughly clean the cylinder head cover and gasket mating surfaces. Be sure the gasket mating surfaces are flat.

Rocker arm shaft identification—2.0L engine

8. Mark the rocker arm shaft assemblies to identify them for later installation.

9. Remove the rocker arm shaft bolts and remove the rocker arm assemblies from the cylinder head.

10. Mark the rocker arm spacers and retainers to identify them for correct installation. Disassemble the rocker arm/shaft assemblies by removing the attaching bolts from the rocker arm shaft.

11. Slide the rocker arm/HLA assembly and rocker arm spacers off the rocker arm shaft. Be sure the rocker arms and spacers are reassembled in the same positions they are removed from.

To install:

➡ Inspect the rocker arms and shaft for scoring and/or wear on the rollers or damage to the rocker arm. If scoring, wear or damage is present, replace the rocker arm assemblies. The rocker arm shaft is hollow and, therefore, used as an oil lubrication duct. Inspect the oil holes for clogging, using a small wire and clean, if necessary. Inspect the location where the rocker arms mount to the shaft and replace if damaged or worn.

12. If the camshaft lobes show signs of wear, check the corresponding rocker arm roller for wear or damage. Replace rocker arms/HLAs if worn or damaged. If the camshaft lobes show signs of pitting on the nose, flank or base circle replace the camshaft.

13. Inspect the rocker arms for scoring, wear on the roller or damage to the shaft. Replace parts as necessary. Check that the rocker arm shaft is clean inside and out. Check all oil holes for clogging with a small wire and clean and required.

14. Thoroughly lubricate all rocker arm components and spacers and reinstall on the rocker arm shaft in the original locations.

15. If the vehicle exhibited a tappet-like noise, the valve lash adjusters built into the rocker arms should be cleaned and checked. Lash adjusters removed from a rocker arm should be returned to their original locations. Replacement of worn or defective lash adjusters would require the replacement of the rocker arm/HLAs as an assembly. To install a HLA, use the following procedure:

  a. Lubricate the HLA thoroughly with clean engine oil.

  b. Reinstall the HLA into the rocker arm making sure the HLA is at least partially filled with oil.

  c. Place the rocker arm in clean engine oil and pump the plunger until the HLA travel is taken up. If travel is not reduced, replace the adjuster with the rocker arm as an assembly.

  d. Reinstall the rocker arm back on the rocker arm shaft.

16. Before installing the rocker arm and shaft assemblies, set the crankshaft to three notches before TDC on the crankshaft sprocket.

➡**When installing the intake rocker arm/shaft assembly, be sure the plastic rocker arm spacers do not interfere with the spark plug tubes. If there is interference, rotate the plastic spacers until they are at the proper angle. Do not rotate the spacers by forcing down on the shaft assembly or damage to the spark plug tubes will occur.**

17. Reinstall the rocker arm and shaft assemblies with the small notches in the rocker shafts pointing up and toward the timing belt side of the engine. Install the retain-ers in their original positions on the exhaust and intake shafts. Tighten the bolts in proper sequence to 200 inch lbs. (23 Nm).

18. Install new cylinder head cover gasket and cylinder head cover. Tighten the cylinder head cover retaining bolts to 105 inch lbs. (12 Nm).

19. Install the ignition coil pack. Tighten the ignition coil pack mounting fasteners to 200 inch lbs. (23 Nm).

20. Reconnect the spark plug wires to each spark plug.

21. Install the air cleaner inlet duct.

22. Check to be sure all electrical, vacuum and fluid connections are reattached as required.

23. An oil and filter change are recommended.

24. Reconnect the negative battery cable.

25. Start the engine and check for leaks. Test drive the vehicle to check for proper operation.

2.5L Engine

1. Before servicing the vehicle, refer to the precautions in the beginning of this section.

2. Disconnect the negative battery cable from the left shock tower. The ground cable is equipped with an insulator grommet which should be placed on the stud to prevent the negative battery cable from accidentally grounding.

3. Relieve the fuel system pressure using the recommended procedure.

4. If removing the right (firewall) side rocker arm/shaft assembly, Remove the upper intake manifold (air intake plenum), which is a 2-piece unit of aluminum alloy. Use care working with light alloy parts. Remove the air intake plenum using the following procedure:

  a. Verify that the fuel system pressure relief procedure has been performed. Disconnect the fuel supply tube from the fuel rail by squeezing the retainer tabs together and pulling the fuel tube/quick-connect fitting assembly off the fuel tube nipple. Use care handling the quick-connect fittings.

  b. Unplug the electrical connectors from the Manifold Absolute Pressure (MAP) and Intake Air Temperature (IAT) sensors.

  c. Remove the plenum support bracket bolt located rearward of the MAP sensor.

  d. Remove the bolt holding the air inlet resonator to the intake manifold.

  e. Loosen the throttle body air inlet hose clamp. Release the snaps holding the air cleaner housing cover to the

NOTCHES FACING UP AND TOWARD THE TIMING BELT SIDE OF THE ENGINE

7922FG19

Rocker arm shaft notch locations—2.0L engine

EXHAUST ROCKER ARM SHAFT

INTAKE ROCKER ARM SHAFT

7922FG20

Rocker arm shaft tightening sequence—2.0L engine

housing. Remove the air cleaner cover and inlet hoses from the engine.

f. Unplug the Throttle Position (TP) sensor and Idle Air Control (IAC) motor electrical connections.

g. Squeeze the retainer tab on the throttle cable and slide the cable out of the bracket. Slide the speed control cable out of its bracket, if equipped.

h. Remove the EGR tube from the intake manifold.

i. Remove the plenum support bracket bolt located rearward of the EGR tube.

j. Remove the seven bolts holding the upper intake plenum and remove the plenum.

5. Disconnect, label and set aside the spark plug wires.

6. Remove the cylinder head cover screws and remove the cover.

7. Identify the rocker arm shaft assemblies before removal.

8. Install the auto lash adjuster retainers Special Tool MD 998443 or equivalent to keep the auto lash adjusters from falling out of the rocker arms when the rocker arm assembly is removed.

9. Loosen the attaching fasteners and remove the rocker arm shaft assemblies from the cylinder head.

➡ The hydraulic automatic lash adjusters are precision units installed in the machined openings in the rocker arm units. Do not disassemble the auto lash adjusters from the rocker arms.

To install:

10. The rocker arm shafts are hollow and used as a lubrication oil duct. Be sure all valvetrain parts are clean. Check the rocker arm mounting portion of the shafts for wear or damage. Replace if necessary. Check all oil holes for clogging with a small wire and clean as required. If any rockers were removed, lubricate and install on the shafts in their original positions.

11. Install the rocker arm and shaft assemblies with the FLAT in the rocker arm shafts facing toward the timing belt side of the engine for the right cylinder head. For the left cylinder head install the rocker arm and shaft assembly with the FLAT in the rocker arm shaft facing toward the transaxle side of the engine. Install the retainers and spring clips in their original positions on the exhaust and intake shafts. Tighten the retainer bolts to 23 ft. lbs. (31 Nm) working from the center, outward. Remove the valve lash retainer tools that should have been installed at disassembly.

The flats on the rocker arm shaft aids proper orientation—2.5L engine

Rocker arm shaft tightening sequence—2.5L engine

12. Inspect the spark plug tube seals located on the ends of each tube. These seals slide onto each tube to seal the cylinder head cover to the spark plug tube. If these seals show signs of hardness and/or cracking, they should be replaced.

13. Clean the cylinder head and cover mating surfaces. Install a new gasket and install the cover. Tighten bolts to 88 inch lbs. (10 Nm). Reconnect the spark plug wires.

14. Position a new upper intake manifold (plenum) gasket in place and install the upper manifold. Tighten the bolts to 13 ft. lbs. (18 Nm). Install the bolts for the plenum support brackets and connect the EGR tube.

15. Reconnect the throttle and speed control cables.

16. Reattach the TP sensor and IAC motor electrical connectors.

17. Reconnect the MAP and IAT sensors.

18. Install the air inlet resonator, air inlet hose and the air cleaner housing cover.

19. Check to be sure all remaining electrical connectors have been reattached. 20. Tighten the air tube connections.

21. An oil and filter change is recommended.

✳✳ WARNING

Operating the engine without the proper amount and type of engine oil will result in severe engine damage.

22. Connect the negative battery cable. Start the engine and check for leaks, abnormal noises and vibrations.

Intake Manifold

REMOVAL & INSTALLATION

2.0L Engine

The intake manifold is a long branch design made of a molded plastic composition. It is attached to the cylinder head with 10 fasteners. Please note that all seals are to be replaced with new seals and all fasteners are to be replaced with new fasteners. Procure the necessary parts before beginning work.

1. Before servicing the vehicle, refer to the precautions in the beginning of this section.

2. Disconnect the negative battery cable from the left shock tower. The ground cable is equipped with an insulator grommet which should be placed on the stud to prevent the negative battery cable from accidentally grounding.

3. Relieve the fuel system pressure using the recommended procedure.

4. Remove the air inlet resonator as follows:

a. Loosen the screw securing the air inlet resonator to the throttle body.

b. Loosen the clamp holding the air inlet resonator to the air inlet tube. Remove the resonator.

5. Separate the fuel supply line quick-disconnect fitting from the fuel rail by squeezing the retainer tabs together and pulling the fuel tube/quick-disconnect fitting from the fuel tube nipple. The retainer will remain on the fuel tube. Wrap shop towels around the fuel line openings to catch any spilling fuel.

6. Remove the fuel rail attaching screws and remove the fuel rail. Use care when handling the fuel injectors. Do not set them on their tips. Cover the fuel injector openings after fuel rail removal.

7. Remove the accelerator, kickdown and speed control cables from the throttle lever and bracket.

8. Detach the Throttle Position (TP) sensor and the Idle Air Control (IAC) motor electrical connections.

9. Disconnect the vacuum hoses from the throttle body.

10. Detach the connectors from the Manifold Absolute Pressure (MAP) sensor and the Intake Air Temperature (IAT) sensors.

11. Disconnect the vapor and brake booster hoses.

12. Detach the knock sensor electrical connector, starter relay connector and the wiring harness from the tab located on the intake manifold.

13. Remove the transaxle-to-throttle body support bracket fasteners at the throttle body and loosen the fastener at the transaxle end.

14. Remove the throttle body assembly.

15. Remove the EGR tube bolts at the valve and at the intake manifold. Remove the tube from the engine.

16. Remove the intake manifold-to-inlet water tube support fastener.

17. Remove the nine intake manifold screws and washer assemblies and the one nut and washer assembly. Discard the fasteners. At assembly, they should be replaced with new fasteners.

18. Remove the intake manifold from the vehicle.

To install:

19. Clean all sealing surfaces. Check upper and lower manifold gasket surfaces for flatness with a straightedge. Surface must be flat within 0.006 in. (0.15mm) per foot (30 cm).

➡**All seals are to be replaced with new seals and all fasteners are to be replaced with new fasteners.**

20. Install the intake manifold with new O-ring seals. Tighten the fasteners in proper sequence to 105 inch lbs. (12 Nm).

21. Apply a light coating of engine oil to the fuel injector O-rings. Remove the covers from the fuel injector openings and install the fuel injectors into the engine. Seat the injectors in place and tighten the fuel rail bolts to 200 inch lbs. (23 Nm).

22. Reattach the electrical connectors to the fuel injectors.

23. Lubricate the quick-connect fittings with clean 30W engine oil. Connect the fuel supply line to the fuel rail. Check the connection by pulling on the connector to insure it is locked into position.

24. Connect the PCV and the brake booster hoses.

25. Reinstall the throttle body and tighten to 200 inch lbs. (23 Nm). Reinstall the transaxle-to-throttle body support bracket and tighten to 105 inch lbs. (12 Nm) at the throttle body first. Next tighten the bracket at the transaxle.

26. Reattach the MAP sensor and the air temperature sensor wiring connectors.

27. Reattach the knock sensor electrical and starter relay connectors. Reattach the wiring harness to the intake manifold tab.

28. Reattach the IAC and TP sensor wiring connectors.

29. Reconnect the throttle body vacuum hoses.

30. Reinstall the accelerator, kickdown and speed control cables to their bracket and connect them to the throttle lever.

31. Loosely assemble the EGR tube onto the valve and intake manifold finger-tight. Tighten the tube fasteners at the EGR valve first to 95 inch lbs. (11 Nm), then tighten the intake manifold side fasteners to 95 inch lbs. (11 Nm).

32. Reinstall the fresh air duct to the air filter housing.

33. Reinstall the air inlet resonator to the throttle body. Reconnect the air inlet tube to the resonator and tighten the clamps to 20–30 inch lbs. (2–3 Nm).

34. Reconnect the negative battery cable.

2.4L Engine

The intake manifold is a long branch design made of cast aluminum. It is attached to the cylinder head with eight fasteners.

1. Before servicing the vehicle, refer to the precautions in the beginning of this section.

2. Disconnect the negative battery cable from the left shock tower. The ground cable is equipped with an insulator grommet which should be placed on the stud to prevent the negative battery cable from accidentally grounding.

3. Relieve the fuel system pressure using the recommended procedure.

4. Remove the air inlet resonator as follows:

a. Remove the two mounting bolts that secure the air inlet resonator to the intake manifold.

b. Loosen the screw securing the resonator to the throttle body.

c. Loosen the clamp securing the air inlet resonator to the air inlet tube. Remove the resonator.

5. Separate the fuel supply line quick-disconnect at the fuel tube assembly by squeezing the retainer tabs together and pulling the fuel tube/quick-disconnect fitting assembly from the fuel tube nipple. The retainer will remain on the fuel tube. Use shop towels to catch any dripping fuel.

6. Remove the fuel rail assembly attaching screws and remove the fuel rail assembly from the engine. Use care when handling the fuel injectors. Do not set them on their tips. Cover the fuel injector openings after fuel rail removal.

7. Remove the accelerator, kickdown and speed control cables from the throttle lever and bracket.

8. Detach the Idle Air Control (IAC) motor and Throttle Position (TP) sensor wiring connectors.

9. Disconnect the vacuum hoses from the throttle body.

10. Detach the Manifold Absolute Pressure (MAP) and Intake Air Temperature (IAT) electrical connectors. Disconnect the vapor and brake booster hoses.

11. Detach the knock sensor electrical connector and detach the wiring harness from the tab located on the intake manifold.

12. Remove the transaxle-to-throttle body support bracket fasteners at the throttle body and loosen the fastener at the transaxle end. Remove the throttle body from the intake manifold.

13. Remove the EGR tube bolts at the valve end and at the intake manifold. Remove the tube from the engine.

14. Remove the intake manifold support bracket. Remove the eight intake manifold fasteners and washers. Remove the intake manifold from the engine.

INTAKE MANIFOLD TO WATER INLET SUPPORT

7922FG23

Intake manifold torque sequence—2.0L engine

VACUUM SOURCE VAPOR CANISTER

MAP SENSOR

VACUUM SOURCE BRAKE BOOSTER

7922FG25

MAP sensor location—2.4L engine

Intake manifold bolt torque sequence—
2.4L engine

To install:

15. Thoroughly clean all parts. Clean all sealing surfaces

16. Install a new intake manifold gasket and position the manifold on the cylinder head. Tighten the fasteners to 200 inch lbs. (23 Nm) in correct sequence, starting from the center and working out.

17. Remove the covering from the fuel injector openings and be sure the openings are clean. Install the fuel rail assembly to the intake manifold. Tighten the retainer screws to 200 inch lbs. (23 Nm).

18. Connect the PCV and brake booster hoses.

19. Inspect the quick-disconnect fittings for damage and repair as required. Lube the fuel tube with clean 30W engine oil. Reconnect the fuel supply tube hose to the fuel rail assembly. Check the connection by pulling on the connector to insure it is locked in position.

20. Reinstall the throttle body. Tighten the fasteners to 200 inch lbs. (23 Nm). Reinstall the transaxle-to-throttle body support bracket and tighten to 105 inch lbs. (12 Nm) at the throttle body first, then tighten the bracket at the transaxle.

21. Reattach the MAP and IAT wiring connectors.

22. Reconnect the knock sensor and attach the wiring harness to the tab located on the intake manifold.

23. Reattach the IAC motor and TP sensor wiring connectors.

24. Reconnect the remaining vacuum hoses to the throttle body.

25. Reconnect the accelerator, kickdown and speed control cables to the throttle lever and bracket.

26. Loosely assemble the EGR tube onto

the valve and intake manifold finger-tight. Tighten the tube fasteners at the EGR valve first to 95 inch lbs. (11 Nm), then, tighten the intake manifold side fasteners to 95 inch lbs. (11 Nm).

27. Reinstall the air inlet resonator to the throttle body, then install the air inlet tube to the resonator. Tighten the clamps to 20–30 inch lbs. (2.5–3.5 Nm). Tighten the two air inlet resonator-to-intake manifold mounting bolts.

28. Reconnect the negative battery cable.

2.5L Engine

The intake manifold assembly is composed of an upper plenum and lower manifold. This aluminum alloy manifold has long runners to improve airflow inertia. The plenum chamber absorbs air pulsations created during the suction phase of each cylinder. The lower intake manifold is machined for six injectors and the fuel rail mounts.

1. Before servicing the vehicle, refer to the precautions in the beginning of this section.

2. Disconnect the negative battery cable from the left shock tower. The ground cable is equipped with an insulator grommet

Exploded view of the intake/exhaust manifolds and related components—2.5L engine

Please refer to Section 9 for electric cooling fan wiring schematics

which should be placed on the stud to prevent the negative battery cable from accidentally grounding.

3. Relieve the fuel system pressure using the recommended procedure.

4. Disconnect the fuel supply line from the fuel rail. This is a quick-disconnect fitting. Squeeze the fitting retainer tabs together and separate the connection.

✳✳ CAUTION

Wrap shop towels around the connection to catch any gasoline spillage.

➡**It may be helpful to identify and tag each sensor connector as it is being removed. This may save time at assembly.**

5. Detach the connectors from the Manifold Absolute Pressure (MAP) and Intake Air Temperature (IAT) sensors.

6. Remove the plenum support bracket located to the rear of the MAP sensor.

7. Remove the air inlet resonator attaching bolt.

8. Loosen the throttle body air inlet hose clamp.

9. Release the snaps holding the air cleaner housing cover to the housing. Remove the air cleaner cover and inlet hoses from the engine.

10. Detach the Throttle Position (TPS) sensor and the Idle Air Control (IAC) motor electrical connections.

11. Squeeze the retainer tab on the throttle cable and slide the cable out of the bracket.

12. If equipped with speed control, slide the speed control cable out of the bracket.

13. Remove the EGR tube from the engine intake manifold.

14. Remove the plenum support bracket located to the rear of the EGR tube.

15. Remove the seven bolts attaching the upper intake plenum to the intake manifold and remove the plenum.

16. Detach the fuel injector electrical connectors.

17. Remove the four bolts attaching the fuel rail to the intake manifold. Use care. There are spacers under each fuel rail bolt. Remove the fuel rail.

18. Remove the lower intake manifold attaching bolts.

19. Remove the intake manifold and discard the old gaskets.

To install:

20. Clean all sealing surfaces.

21. Check upper and lower manifold gasket surfaces for flatness with a straightedge. Surface must be flat within 0.006 in.

Intake manifold bolt torque sequence—2.5L engine

(0.15mm) per 12 in. (30 cm) of manifold length.

22. Install the lower intake manifold with new gaskets.

23. Tighten the bolts in correct sequence to 185 inch lbs. (21 Nm).

24. Apply a light coating of engine oil to the fuel injector O-rings.

25. Reinstall the fuel injectors into the engine.

26. Seat the injectors in place and tighten the fuel rail bolts to 8 ft. lbs. (12 Nm).

27. Reattach the electrical connectors to the fuel injectors.

28. Reconnect the fuel supply line to the fuel rail.

29. Install the upper intake plenum with new gaskets.

30. Tighten the plenum bolts to 13 ft. lbs. (18 Nm).

31. Reinstall the plenum support brackets and tighten to 13 ft. lbs. (18 Nm).

32. Reinstall the EGR tube and tighten the screws to 95 inch lbs. (11 Nm).

33. Reinstall the throttle cables.

34. Reattach the TP sensor and IAC motor electrical connections.

35. Reattach the MAP sensor and the IAT sensor connectors.

36. Reinstall the air cleaner assembly and tighten the hose clamps to 25 inch lbs. (3 Nm).

37. Reinstall the air inlet resonator attaching bolt.

38. Reconnect the negative battery cable.

39. Start the engine and check for leaks.

Exhaust Manifold

REMOVAL & INSTALLATION

2.0L and 2.4L Engines

1. Before servicing the vehicle, refer to the precautions in the beginning of this section.

2. Disconnect the negative battery cable from the left shock tower. The ground cable is equipped with an insulator grommet

which should be placed on the stud to prevent the negative battery cable from accidentally grounding.

3. Disconnect the exhaust pipe from the exhaust manifold. Apply penetrating oil on the exhaust manifold-to-exhaust pipe flange bolts to aid in removal. It may be necessary to remove the entire exhaust system.

4. Remove the exhaust manifold heat shield.

5. Disconnect the Heated Oxygen (HO2S) sensor, if necessary.

6. Remove the eight manifold attaching bolts and remove the manifold from the vehicle.

To install:

7. Thoroughly clean all parts. Discard the gasket and clean all sealing surfaces of the manifold and cylinder head. Check the manifold gasket surface for flatness with a straightedge and feeler gauge. The surface must be flat within 0.006 in. per foot (0.15mm per 30cm) of manifold length. Inspect the manifold for cracks or distortion. Replace if necessary.

8. Install the manifold into the vehicle with a new gasket. DO NOT APPLY SEALER.

9. Reinstall the eight manifold bolts and tighten starting at the center and working outward in both directions. Tighten to 200 inch lbs. (23 Nm).

Be sure the gasket mating surfaces are clean and flat before installing the exhaust manifold—2.0L engine

Be careful not to damage the oxygen sensor when servicing the manifold—2.4L engine

10. Reconnect the HO2S sensor.

11. Reinstall the heat shield.

12. Reinstall the exhaust pipe and tighten fasteners to 250 inch lbs. (28 Nm).

13. Reconnect the negative battery cable. Start the engine and allow to idle while inspecting the manifold for exhaust leaks.

2.5L Engine

1. Before servicing the vehicle, refer to the precautions in the beginning of this section.

2. Disconnect the negative battery cable from the left shock tower. The ground cable is equipped with an insulator grommet which should be placed on the stud to prevent the negative battery cable from accidentally grounding.

3. Raise and safely support the vehicle.

4. Disconnect the exhaust pipe connection to the rear (cowl side) exhaust manifold at the flex joint.

➡It may be necessary to remove the whole exhaust system.

5. Remove the bolts attaching the crossover pipe to the manifolds and remove the crossover pipe assembly.

6. Disconnect the Heated Oxygen (HO2S) sensor lead wire at the rear manifold. Remove the HO2S sensor at the rear exhaust manifold.

7. Remove the power steering bracket.

8. Remove the rear exhaust manifold heat shield.

9. Remove the rear manifold attaching nuts and remove the rear manifold.

10. Lower the vehicle and detach the front HO2S sensor wiring connector. Remove the front HO2S sensor.

11. Remove the front manifold heat shield.

12. Remove the front manifold securing nuts and remove the front manifold.

To install:

13. Thoroughly clean all parts. Inspect the exhaust manifolds for damage or cracks and check for distortion of the cylinder head sealing surface and exhaust crossover sealing surface with a straightedge and thickness gauge.

14. Install a new front manifold gasket.

15. Install the front manifold and tighten the nuts to 22 ft. lbs. (30 Nm).

16. Reinstall the front exhaust manifold heat shield and tighten the heat shield mounting screws to 115 inch lbs. (13 Nm).

17. Reinstall the front HO2S sensor. Reattach the HO2S sensor wiring connector.

18. Raise and safely support the vehicle.

19. Install a new rear exhaust manifold gasket. Install the rear exhaust manifold.

20. Tighten the manifold nuts to 22 ft. lbs. (30 Nm).

21. Reinstall the power steering bracket.

22. Reinstall the crossover pipe and tighten the nuts to 22 ft. lbs. (30 Nm).

23. Install the rear HO2S sensor. Reconnect the rear HO2S sensor lead.

24. Reconnect the exhaust pipe to the rear manifold. Tighten the exhaust pipe-to-rear exhaust manifold flange mounting bolts to 21 ft. lbs. (28 Nm).

25. Lower the vehicle. Reconnect the negative battery cable. Start the engine and allow the engine to idle while inspecting the vehicle for exhaust leaks at the manifold.

Front Crankshaft Seal

REMOVAL & INSTALLATION

2.0L and 2.4L Engines

The timing belt must be removed for this procedure. Use care that all timing marks are aligned after installation or the engine will be damaged.

1. Before servicing the vehicle, refer to the precautions in the beginning of this section.

2. Disconnect the negative battery cable from the left shock tower. The ground cable is equipped with an insulator grommet which should be placed on the stud to prevent the negative battery cable from accidentally grounding.

3. Remove the accessory drive belts.

4. Raise and safely support the vehicle. Drain the engine oil.

5. Remove the crankshaft damper/pulley using a jaw puller tool.

6. Remove the timing belt.

7. Remove the crankshaft timing belt sprocket using a suitable gear/sprocket puller.

❉❉ CAUTION

Be careful not to nick the seal surface of the crankshaft or the seal bore.

8. Remove the front crankshaft seal using Seal Removal tool No. 6771 or equivalent seal puller. Be careful not to damage the seal contact area of the crankshaft.

To install:

9. Apply a light coating of clean engine oil to the lip of the new oil seal. Install the

new front crankshaft oil seal by using oil seal installer tool No. 6780–1 or equivalent seal tool.

10. Place the new oil seal into the opening with the seal spring facing the inside of the engine. Be sure the oil seal is installed flush with the front cover.

11. Install the crankshaft timing belt sprocket using tool No. 6792.

➡Be sure the word "FRONT" on the timing belt sprocket is facing outward.

12. Reinstall the timing belt and timing belt cover using the recommended procedure.

13. Reinstall the crankshaft damper/pulley onto the crankshaft. Use thrust bearing/washer and 12M-1.75 x 150mm bolt from special tool No. 6792. Install the crankshaft damper/pulley retaining bolt and tighten it to 105 ft. lbs. (142 Nm).

14. Lower the vehicle.

15. Reinstall the accessory drive belts. Adjust the belts to the proper tension.

❉❉ WARNING

Operating the engine without the proper amount and type of engine oil will result in severe engine damage.

16. Refill the engine with the correct amount of clean engine oil.

17. Reconnect the negative battery cable. Start the engine and check for leaks.

2.5L Engine

The timing belt must be removed for this procedure. Use care to be sure all timing marks are aligned after this service or the engine will be damaged.

1. Before servicing the vehicle, refer to the precautions in the beginning of this section.

2. Disconnect the negative battery cable from the left shock tower. The ground cable is equipped with an insulator grommet which should be placed on the stud to prevent the negative battery cable from accidentally grounding.

3. Remove the accessory drive belts.

4. Raise and safely support the vehicle. Drain the engine oil.

5. Remove the right inner splash shield.

6. Remove the crankshaft damper/pulley.

7. Remove the timing belt covers and timing belt using the recommended procedure.

8. Remove the crankshaft timing belt sprocket and key.

9. Remove the front crankshaft seal by prying it out with a flat-tipped prytool. Be sure to cover the end of the prytool tip with a shop towel.

✳✳ CAUTION

Be careful not to nick the seal surface of the crankshaft or the seal bore.

To install:

10. Apply a light coating of clean engine oil to the lip of the new oil seal. Install the new front crankshaft oil seal into the oil pump housing by using Oil Seal Installer MD998717 or equivalent seal installer. Be sure the oil seal is installed flush with the oil pump cover.

11. Reinstall the crankshaft timing belt sprocket and key.

12. Reinstall the timing belt and timing belt covers using the recommended procedure. Verify that all timing marks are correctly aligned or the engine will be damaged.

13. Reinstall the crankshaft damper/pulley onto the crankshaft. Install the crankshaft damper/pulley retaining bolt and tighten to 134 ft. lbs. (182 Nm).

14. Reinstall the right inner splash shield.

15. Lower the vehicle.

16. Reinstall the accessory drive belts. Adjust the belts to the proper tension.

✳✳ WARNING

Operating the engine without the proper amount and type of engine oil will result in severe engine damage.

17. Refill the engine with the correct amount of clean engine oil.

18. Reconnect the negative battery cable, then start the engine and check for leaks.

To prevent damage to the end of the crankshaft, use Oil Seal Installer MD998717 or equivalent, as shown—2.5L engine

Camshaft

REMOVAL & INSTALLATION

2.0L Engine

1. Before servicing the vehicle, refer to the precautions in the beginning of this section.

2. Remove the rocker arm assemblies.

3. Remove the timing belt and camshaft sprocket using the recommended procedure.

4. Remove the cylinder head using the recommended procedure.

5. Remove the Camshaft Position (CMP) sensor and remove the camshaft from the rear of the cylinder head.

To install:

➡**The cylinder head bolts should be checked for stretching before reuse. If the threaded area of the bolt is necked-down the bolts must be replaced with new ones. New head bolts are recommended.**

6. Thoroughly clean all parts. Inspect the camshaft journals for scoring. Check the oil feed holes in the head for blockage. Check the camshaft bearing journals for scoring. If light scratches are present, they may be removed with 400 grit abrasive paper. If deep scratches are present, replace the camshaft and check the cylinder head for damage. Replace the cylinder head if worn or damaged.

7. If the camshaft lobes show signs of wear, check the corresponding rocker arm roller for wear or damage. Replace rocker arms/Hydraulic Lash Adjuster (HLAs) if worn or damaged. If the camshaft lobes show signs of pitting on the nose, flank or base circle, replace the camshaft.

8. If the rocker arms and shaft are to be serviced, mark the rocker arms so any that are to be returned to service will be installed in their original locations.

9. Reinstall the rocker arm back on the rocker arm shaft.

10. To install the camshaft, lubricate the bearing journals thoroughly. Install the camshaft into the cylinder head carefully. Be sure it turns freely. If the camshaft installation is satisfactory, install the cam sensor and tighten the screws to 85 inch lbs. (10 Nm).

11. Camshaft end-play can be checked. Use the following procedure:

a. Oil the camshaft journals and install the camshaft without the rocker arm assemblies. Install the cam sensor

and tighten the screws to 85 inch lbs. (10 Nm).

b. Set up a dial indicator to touch on the nose of the camshaft.

c. Using a suitable prying tool, move the camshaft as far rearward as it will go. Be sure the dial indicator probe is in contact with the camshaft.

d. Zero the dial indicator.

e. Move the camshaft as far forward as it will go.

f. Read the end-play on the dial indicator. Specification is 0.005–0.013 in. (0.13–0.33mm).

12. Install the camshaft seal. The camshaft must be installed before the camshaft seal is installed. The seal should be flush with the cylinder head after installation.

13. Reinstall the camshaft sprocket and tighten the bolt to 85 ft. lbs. (115 Nm).

14. Reinstall the cylinder head using the recommended procedure. Be sure to use new cylinder head mounting bolts.

15. Before installing the rocker arm and shaft assemblies, set the crankshaft to three notches before TDC on the crankshaft sprocket.

16. Reinstall the rocker arm and shaft assemblies.

17. Reinstall the camshaft sprocket and timing belt using the recommended procedure taking care to align all valve timing marks.

2.4L Engine

This engine uses a Dual Over Head Camshaft (DOHC) 4-valves per cylinder crossflow aluminum cylinder head. The valves are actuated by roller cam followers which pivot on stationary hydraulic valve adjusters. Care must be taken to ensure all valve timing marks align after cylinder head and valvetrain service.

1. Before servicing the vehicle, refer to the precautions in the beginning of this section.

2. Disconnect the negative battery cable from the left shock tower. The ground cable is equipped with an insulator grommet which should be placed on the stud to prevent the negative battery cable from accidentally grounding.

3. Relieve the fuel system pressure using the recommended procedure.

4. Label and disconnect the spark plug wires from the spark plugs.

5. Remove the ignition coil pack and spark plug wires.

6. Remove the cylinder head cover retaining fasteners and remove the cylinder

Use special tool 6847 or equivalent to hold the camshaft sprocket while removing or installing the center bolt—2.4L engine

head cover from the cylinder head. Discard the old cylinder head cover gasket.

7. Remove the ground strap.

8. Remove the timing belt covers and timing belt.

9. Remove the camshaft sprockets by holding them with special tool 6847 or equivalent while removing the bolt.

10. Take note that the camshaft bearing caps are numbered for correct location during installation. Remove the outer bearing caps first.

11. Loosen, but do not remove, the camshaft bearing cap retaining fasteners in the correct sequence, inside working out-

Camshaft bearing cap identification—2.4L engine

Camshaft bearing cap bolt removal sequence—2.4L engine

ward. Perform this step on one camshaft at a time.

12. Identify the camshafts, if they are to be reused, for later installation. The camshafts are not interchangeable. Remove the camshaft bearing caps and remove the camshafts.

13. Remove the camshaft followers. Any components that are to be reused must be installed in their original locations. Use care to identify and mark the positions of any removed valvetrain components so they may be reinstalled correctly.

14. Inspect the camshaft bearing oil feed holes in the cylinder head for clogging. Inspect the camshaft bearing journals for wear or scoring. Check the cam surface for abnormal wear and damage. A visible worn groove in the roller path or on the cam lobes is cause for replacement.

To install:

15. Thoroughly clean all camshaft and related parts.

16. The camshaft end-play should be checked using the following procedure:

a. Oil the camshaft journals and install the camshaft **WITHOUT** the cam follower assemblies. Install the rear cam caps and tighten to 250 inch lbs. (28 Nm).

b. Carefully push the camshaft as far rearward as it will go.

c. Set up a dial indicator to bear against the front of the camshaft (the sprocket end). Zero the indicator.

d. Move the camshaft forward as far as it will go. Read the dial indicator. End-play specification is 0.002–0.010 in. (0.05–0.15mm).

e. If excessive end-play is present, inspect the cylinder head and camshaft for wear; replace if necessary.

17. If the fit and condition of the camshafts are acceptable, remove the camshafts for installation of the cam followers.

18. The hydraulic valve lash adjusters are inside the roller cam followers. Be sure they are clean, well-lubricated with clean engine oil and properly positioned. Install the cam followers in their original positions on the hydraulic adjuster and valve stem.

⁂ **WARNING**

Be sure NONE of the pistons are at Top Dead Center (TDC) when installing the camshafts.

19. Lubricate the camshaft bearing journals and cam followers with clean engine oil and install the camshafts. Install right

and left camshaft bearing caps Nos. 2 through 5 and right side No. 6. Tighten the M6 fasteners to 105 inch lbs. (12 Nm) in the correct sequence.

20. Apply Mopar® Gasket Maker or equivalent sealer to the No. 1 and left side No. 6 bearing caps. Install the bearing caps and tighten the M8 fasteners to 250 inch lbs. (28 Nm). The end-caps must be installed before the seals may be installed.

21. Install the camshaft end seals.

22. Reinstall the camshaft sprockets, if removed. Tighten the mounting bolts to 75 ft. lbs. (101 Nm).

23. Install the timing belt using care to be sure all timing marks are properly aligned, using the recommended procedure. Install the timing belt covers.

⁂ **WARNING**

Verify that all timing marks are correct. If the timing belt or sprockets are incorrectly installed, engine damage will occur. Take time to be sure all timing marks are correctly aligned.

24. Clean all sealing surfaces. Make certain the rails are flat.

25. Install new cylinder head cover gaskets. Use care; DO NOT allow oil or solvents to contact the timing belt as they can

Camshaft bearing cap tightening sequence—2.4L engine

FRONT CAM CAP

1.5 mm (.060 in.) DIAMETER BEAD OF MOPAR GASKET MAKER

LEFT REAR CAM CAP

Apply sealer as shown to prevent oil leakage from the camshaft bearing end caps—2.4L engine

Timing belt service is covered in Section 5 of this manual

deteriorate the rubber and cause tooth skipping. Apply Mopar® Silicone Rubber Adhesive Sealant, or equivalent, at the camshaft cap corners and at the top edge of the ½ round seal.

➡**Inspect the spark plug well seals for cracking and/or swelling and replace if necessary.**

26. Install the cylinder head cover assembly to the head and tighten the fasteners in sequence using the following three substeps:

   a. Tighten all cylinder head cover fasteners to 40 inch lbs. (4.5 Nm).

   b. Tighten all fasteners to 80 inch lbs. (9 Nm).

   c. Tighten all fasteners to 105 inch lbs. (12 Nm).

27. Install the ignition coil pack and connect the spark plug wiring to the correct spark plugs. Tighten the coil pack retaining fasteners to 105 inch lbs. (12 Nm).

28. Reconnect the ground strap.

29. Check to be sure all vacuum lines and remaining wiring have been reconnected.

➡**An oil and filter change is recommended.**

30. Reconnect the negative battery cable and test run vehicle. Check for leaks and for proper operation.

2.5L Engine

This engine uses aluminum alloy cylinder heads with 4-valves per cylinder and pressed-in cast iron valve guides. The cylinders are common to either cylinder bank. Two overhead camshafts are supported by four bearing journals which are part of the head with the distributor driven off the right (firewall side) cylinder head. Right and left camshaft drive sprockets are interchangeable. The sprockets and engine water pump are driven by the timing belt. Care must be taken to be sure all valve timing marks align after cylinder head and valvetrain service. Please note that for camshaft service, the cylinder head must be removed.

1. Before servicing the vehicle, refer to the precautions in the beginning of this section.

2. Disconnect the negative battery cable from the left shock tower. The ground cable is equipped with an insulator grommet which should be placed on the stud to prevent the negative battery cable from accidentally grounding.

3. Relieve the fuel system pressure using the recommended procedure.

4. Place a large drain pan under the radiator drain plug. Drain the cooling system.

5. Remove the timing belt covers and the timing belt.

6. Remove the camshaft sprockets by holding them with special tool 6847 or equivalent while removing the bolt.

7. The intake manifold is a two-piece unit. The upper part is a large air intake plenum of aluminum alloy. Use care working with light alloy parts. Remove the air intake plenum first, then remove the lower intake manifold.

8. Disconnect, label and set aside the spark plug wires.

9. Remove the cylinder head cover screws and remove the cover.

10. Identify the rocker arm shaft assemblies before removal.

11. Install the Auto Lash Adjuster Retainers MD 998443 or their equivalents to keep the auto lash adjusters from falling out of the rocker arms when the rocker arm assembly is removed.

12. Loosen the attaching fasteners and remove the rocker arm shaft assemblies from the cylinder head.

13. Remove the distributor assembly.

14. Remove the exhaust manifold and crossover pipe.

15. Remove the cylinder head bolts and remove the cylinder head from the vehicle.

16. Remove the thrust case from the left head assembly and remove the camshaft from the rear of the head. If not already done, remove the distributor from the right cylinder head and remove the camshaft from the rear of the head.

17. Remove and discard the camshaft oil seals.

18. The camshafts should be carefully inspected for scratches or worn areas. If light scratches are seen, they may be removed with 400 grit sandpaper. If there are deep scratches, replace the camshaft and check the cylinder head for damage. Check the oil holes to be sure they are open and free of debris. If the camshaft lobes show signs of wear, check the corresponding rocker arm roller for wear or damage. Replace the rocker arm if worn or damaged. If the camshaft shows signs of wear on the lobes, replace it.

To install:

19. Check camshaft end-play, as follows:

   a. Oil the camshaft journals with clean engine oil and install the camshaft **WITHOUT** the rocker arm assemblies.

   b. Move the camshaft as far rearward as it will go.

   c. Mount a dial indicator to bear on the front of the camshaft.

   d. Zero the indicator.

   e. Move the camshaft as far forward as it will go. End-play should be 0.004–0.008 in. (0.1–0.2mm). Maximum allowed end-play is 0.016 in. (0.4mm).

20. Lubricate the camshaft journals and carefully install the camshaft into the cylinder head. Install the thrust case and tighten the fasteners to 9 ft. lbs. (13 Nm).

21. Apply a light coating of engine oil to the camshaft oil seal lip and install the camshaft seal. The camshaft must be installed before installing the seal. Be sure the seal is installed flush with the cylinder head surface. Install the camshaft sprocket and tighten to 75 ft. lbs. (101 Nm).

22. Install the cylinder head(s).

23. Reinstall the lower intake manifold using new gaskets.

24. The rocker arm shafts are hollow and used as a lubrication oil duct. Be sure all valvetrain parts are clean. Check the rocker arm mounting portion of the shafts for wear or damage. Replace if necessary. Check all oil holes for clogging with a small wire and clean as required. If any rockers were removed, lubricate and install on the shafts in their original positions.

25. Reinstall the rocker arm and shaft assemblies.

26. Reinstall the timing belt using the recommended procedure. It is very important that all valve timing marks align properly or engine damage will result.

27. Inspect the spark plug tube seals located on the ends of each tube. These seals slide onto each tube to seal the cylinder head cover to the spark plug tube. If these seals show signs of hardness and/or cracking, they should be replaced.

28. Clean all sealing surfaces. Install a new gasket and install the cover. Tighten the bolts to 88 inch lbs. (10 Nm). Reconnect the spark plug wires.

29. Position a new upper intake manifold (plenum) gasket in place and install the upper manifold. Tighten the bolts to 13 ft. lbs. (18 Nm). Reinstall the bolts for the plenum support brackets and connect the EGR tube.

30. Reconnect the throttle and speed control cables.

31. Reattach the TP sensor and IAC motor electrical connectors.

32. Reattach the MAP and IAT sensors.

33. Reinstall the air inlet resonator, air inlet hose and the air cleaner housing cover.

34. Check to be sure all remaining electrical connectors have been reattached. Tighten the air tube connections.

35. Refill the cooling system. An oil and filter change is recommended whenever a cylinder head has been removed since coolant can get into the oil system.

❊❊ WARNING

Operating the engine without the proper amount and type of engine oil will result in severe engine damage.

36. Reconnect the negative battery cable. Start the engine and check for leaks, abnormal noises and vibrations. Bleed the cooling system.

Valve Lash

ADJUSTMENT

2.0L and 2.5L Engines

The engines are equipped with Hydraulic Lash Adjusters (HLAs) which are precision units installed in machined openings in the valve actuating ends of the rocker arms. Valve clearance adjustments are not performed.

2.4L Engine

The valves are actuated by roller cam followers which pivot on stationary Hydraulic Lash Adjusters (HLAs). The HLAs are precision units installed in machined openings of the cam follower. Valve clearance adjustments are not performed.

Oil Pan

REMOVAL & INSTALLATION

2.0L Engine

1. Before servicing the vehicle, refer to the precautions in the beginning of this section.
2. Disconnect the negative battery cable from the left shock tower. The ground cable is equipped with an insulator grommet which should be placed on the stud to prevent the negative battery cable from accidentally grounding.
3. Raise and safely support the vehicle.
4. Place a large oil pan under the oil pan drain plug. Drain the oil from the engine.

5. Remove the transaxle bending bracket.
6. Remove the front engine mount and bracket.
7. Remove the transaxle inspection cover.
8. Remove the oil filter and oil filter adapter.
9. Remove the oil pan attaching bolts.
10. Remove the oil pan.
11. Clean the oil pan as well as the oil pan gasket sealing surfaces.

To install:

12. Using a suitable rubber adhesive gasket sealant, apply a ⅛ in. (3mm) bead at the oil pump-to-engine block parting line.
13. Install the new oil pan gasket by positioning it properly onto the oil pan.

➡**If a gasket is not available, use a ⅛ in. (3mm) bead of silicone gasket maker.**

14. Install the oil pan onto the engine.
15. Tighten the oil pan attaching bolts to 105 inch lbs. (12 Nm).
16. Reinstall the oil filter adapter as follows:

  a. Be sure the O-ring seal is seated in the groove on the adapter.

O-RING • OIL FILTER ADAPTER • NIPPLE • O-RING • FILTER • O-RING • OIL PUMP BODY • OIL PICK-UP TUBE • DRAIN PLUG • OIL PAN GASKET • OIL PAN

Exploded view of the oil pan and pump assembly—2.0L engine

Please visit our web site at www.chiltononline.com

b. Align the locating roll pin into the engine block.

c. Tighten the retaining fastener to 60 ft. lbs. (80 Nm).

17. Reinstall a new oil filter as follows:

a. Lubricate the contact surface of the rubber oil filter gasket with a light bead of clean engine oil.

b. Be sure the gasket contact surface on the oil filter adapter is smooth, flat and clean of any debris or old pieces of rubber.

c. Rotate the oil filter clockwise until the gasket contacts the adapter base. Tighten the filter to 15 ft. lbs. (21 Nm).

18. Reinstall the transaxle inspection cover.

19. Reinstall the front engine mount and engine mount bracket.

20. Reinstall the transaxle bending bracket.

21. Reinstall the oil pan drain plug and gasket. Tighten the drain plug to 25 ft. lbs. (34 Nm).

22. Lower the vehicle.

✵✵ WARNING

Operating the engine without the proper amount and type of engine oil will result in severe engine damage.

23. Refill the engine with fresh oil to the proper level.

• With an oil filter change—4.5 qts. (4.25L)

• Without an oil filter change—4.0 qts. (3.8L)

24. Reconnect the negative battery cable. Start the engine and check for leaks.

2.4L Engine

1. Before servicing the vehicle, refer to the precautions in the beginning of this section.

2. Disconnect the negative battery cable from the left shock tower. The ground cable is equipped with an insulator grommet which should be placed on the stud to prevent the negative battery cable from accidentally grounding.

3. Raise and safely support the vehicle.

4. Place a large drain pan under the oil pan drain plug and drain the oil from the engine.

5. If necessary, remove the transaxle bending bracket.

6. Remove the front engine mount and bracket.

7. Remove the oil pan attaching bolts.

8. Remove the oil pan.

To install:

9. Using a suitable gasket sealant apply a ⅛ in. (3mm) bead at the oil pump-to-engine block parting line.

10. Install the new gasket.

➡️**If a gasket is not available, use a ⅛ in. (3mm) bead of silicone gasket maker.**

11. Install the oil pan on the engine.

12. Tighten the oil pan attaching bolts to 105 inch lbs. (12 Nm).

13. Reinstall the front engine mount and engine mount bracket.

14. Reinstall the transaxle bending bracket, if necessary.

15. Install the oil pan drain plug and gasket. Tighten the drain plug to 25 ft. lbs. (34 Nm).

16. Lower the vehicle.

✵✵ WARNING

Operating the engine without the proper amount and type of engine oil will result in severe engine damage.

17. Refill the engine with fresh oil to the proper level. A filter change is recommended.

COLLAR

OIL PAN GASKET WITH WINDAGE TRAY

OIL PAN

DRAIN PLUG

O-RING

OIL PUMP BODY

OIL PICK-UP TUBE

FILTER

7922FG36

Exploded view of the oil pan and pump assembly—2.4L engine

- With oil filter—5.0 qts. (4.7L)
- Without oil filter—4.5 qts. (4.3L)

18. Reconnect the negative battery cable. Start the engine and check for leaks.

2.5L Engine

1. Before servicing the vehicle, refer to the precautions in the beginning of this section.

2. Disconnect the negative battery cable from the left shock tower. The ground cable is equipped with an insulator grommet which should be placed on the stud to prevent the negative battery cable from accidentally grounding.

3. Raise and safely support the vehicle.

4. Place a large drain pan under the oil pan drain plug and drain the oil from the engine.

5. Remove the engine support module as follows:

a. Place a suitable support jack underneath the engine/transaxle assembly at the transaxle to prevent it from rotating.

b. Remove the through-bolt at the rear mount and remove the bolts securing the support module to the crossmember.

c. Remove the upper mounting bolt from the rear support strut bracket.

d. Remove the front mounting bolts from the support module to the lower radiator support member.

e. Support the radiator/cooling fan assembly. Remove the lower radiator support member.

f. Remove the through-bolt at the front engine mount and remove the engine support module.

6. Remove the engine oil dipstick tube and dipstick.

7. Remove the starter motor.

8. Remove the engine-to-transaxle struts.

9. Remove the transaxle inspection cover.

10. Remove the oil pan attaching bolts.

11. Remove the oil pan.

To install:

➡**Oil pan-to-engine block sealing is provided by using MOPAR® Silicone Rubber Adhesive Sealant or equivalent gasket material. The gasket material should be applied in a continuous bead approximately ⁵⁄₃₂ in. (4mm) in diameter with all mounting holes circled. Sealant that is not cured can be removed with a shop towel. Compo-**

157 in (4 mm)
DIAMETER OF SEALANT

7922FG37

To ensure an adequate seal, apply sealer as shown—2.5L engine

nents should be tightened in place while the gasket sealer is still wet to the touch (within a 10 minute period). It is recommended that locating dowels be used during assembly to prevent smearing the gasket material from its location.

12. Apply a continuous ⁵⁄₃₂ in. (4mm) bead of MOPAR® Silicone Adhesive Sealant or equivalent to the oil pan gasket surface. Be sure to circle all mounting bolt holes as well. Install the oil pan within a 10 minute period of applying the gasket material to ensure proper sealing.

13. Install the oil pan on the engine.

14. Tighten the oil pan attaching bolts to 53 inch lbs. (6 Nm).

15. Reinstall the transaxle inspection cover.

16. Reinstall the engine-to-transaxle struts.

17. Reinstall the starter motor.

18. Reinstall the engine oil dipstick tube and dipstick.

19. Reinstall the engine support module as follows:

a. Place the engine support module in the proper position under the engine/transaxle assembly.

b. Reinstall the through-bolt at the front mount. Do not tighten the through-bolt at this time.

c. Reinstall the lower radiator support.

d. Reinstall the mounting bolts from the engine support module to the lower radiator support.

e. Reinstall the upper mounting bolt to the rear support strut bracket.

f. Reinstall the through-bolt to the rear mount and tighten to 45 ft. lbs. (61 Nm).

g. Tighten the through-bolt at the front mount to 45 ft. lbs. (61 Nm).

h. Remove the support jack holding the engine/transaxle assembly in place.

20. Reinstall the oil pan drain plug and gasket. Tighten the drain plug to 29 ft. lbs. (40 Nm).

21. Lower the vehicle.

❄❄ WARNING

Operating the engine without the proper amount and type of engine oil will result in severe engine damage.

22. Refill the engine with fresh oil to the proper level. An oil filter change is recommended.

- With oil filter—4.5 qts. (4.3L)
- Without oil filter—4.0 qts. (3.8L)

23. Reconnect the negative battery cable. Start the engine and check for leaks.

➡**Whenever the vehicle sub-frame is removed or lowered, the wheel alignment should be checked.**

Oil Pump

REMOVAL & INSTALLATION

2.0L and 2.4L Engines

The oil drawn up through the pick-up tube is pressurized by the pump and routed through the full flow filter to the main oil galley running the length of the cylinder block. The oil pick-up, pump and check valve provide oil flow to the main oil gallery. A vertical hole at the number 5 bulkhead routes pressurized oil through a restrictor up past a cylinder head bolt to an oil galley running the length of the cylinder head. The camshaft journals are slotted to allow pressurized oil to pass into the bearing cap cavities. Small holes in the bearing caps direct oil to the camshaft lobes.

It is necessary to remove the oil pan, oil pick-up and oil pump housing to service the oil pump rotors. The oil pump pressure relief valve can be serviced without removing the oil pan and oil pick-up tube.

1. Before servicing the vehicle, refer to the precautions in the beginning of this section.

2. Disconnect the negative battery cable from the left shock tower. The ground cable is equipped with an insulator grommet which should be placed on the stud to prevent the negative battery cable from accidentally grounding.

3. Raise and safely support the vehicle.

4. Drain the engine oil as well as the engine coolant into suitable containers.

Refer to Section 1 for engine rebuilding specifications

5. Remove the oil pan assembly. Remove the oil pump pick-up tube and O-ring.

6. Remove the right inner fender splash shield.

7. Lower the vehicle.

8. Remove the drive belts as required.

9. Using a puller, remove the crankshaft damper from the front of the crankshaft.

10. Take up the weight of the engine with a suitable lift and remove the right engine mount and bracket. Be sure the engine is safely supported.

11. Remove the timing belt cover.

12. Loosen the timing belt tensioner bolts and remove the tensioner and the timing belt.

13. Using a suitable puller, draw the crankshaft sprocket from the front of the crankshaft.

14. Loosen the oil pump bolts and remove. Take note of the location of each bolt for reassembly. Remove the oil pump from the face of the engine block. If necessary, tap lightly with a soft face mallet. Use care working with light alloy parts. Remove and discard the front oil seal.

15. Remove the relief valve from the pump body by removing the threaded plug and gasket and pulling out the spring and relief valve. Note the order of parts removal.

To install:

16. Clean all parts well for inspection. Remove the screws holding the back cover to the pump body. Remove the pump rotors. The mating surface of the oil pump should be smooth. Replace the pump cover if scratched or grooved.

17. The pump should be checked for wear by carefully measuring the components. Use the following procedure:

a. Lay a straightedge across the pump cover surface. If a 0.003 in. (0.076mm) feeler gauge can be inserted between the cover and straightedge, the cover should be replaced.

b. Measure the thickness and diameter of the outer rotor. If the outer rotor thickness measures 0.301 in. (7.6mm) or less, or if the diameter is 3.148 in. (80mm) or less, replace the outer rotor.

c. If the inner rotor measures 0.301 in. (7.6mm) or less, replace the inner rotor.

d. Slide the outer rotor into the pump housing, press to one side with your fingers and measure the clearance between the rotor and housing. If the measurement is 0.015 in. (0.38mm) or more, replace the oil pump housing only if the outer rotor is in specification.

e. Install the inner rotor into the pump housing. If the clearance between the inner and outer rotors is 0.008 in. (0.20mm) or more, replace both rotors.

f. Place a straightedge across the face of the pump housing between the bolt holes. If a feeler gauge of 0.004 in. (0.10mm) or more can be inserted between the rotors and straightedge, replace the pump assembly only if the rotors are within specification.

g. Inspect the oil pressure relief valve plunger for scoring and free operation in its bore. Small marks may be removed with 400 grit wet or dry sandpaper.

h. The relief valve spring has a free-length of approximately 2.39 in. (60.7mm). It should test between 18–19 lbs. (39.6–41.8 kg) when compressed to 1.60 in. (40.6mm). Replace the spring if weak, damaged or fails to meet specifications.

➡**If oil pressure is low and the pump is within specifications, inspect for worn engine bearings, clogged oil filter, pressure relief valve stuck open, damaged or missing oil pick-up tube O-ring, clogged oil pick-up tube screen or other reasons for oil pressure loss.**

18. Clean all oil pump parts in suitable solvent before assembly. Assemble the pump with new parts as required. Install the inner rotor with the chamfer facing the cast iron oil pump cover (back of the pump). Tighten the cover screws to 105 inch lbs. (12 Nm).

19. Reinstall the relief valve first, then the spring, gasket and cover cap into the pump body. Note that installing the spring first will seriously damage the engine. The relief valve goes in first. Tighten the cover cap to 30 ft. lbs. (41 Nm) for 2.0L engine or 40 ft. lbs. (55 Nm) for 2.4L engine.

20. Prime the oil pump before installation by filling the rotor cavity with clean engine oil.

21. Insert a new oil ring seal to the oil pump counterbore on the pump body discharge passage. Apply Mopar Gasket Maker or equivalent anaerobic type gasket sealer to the oil pump body flange. This material cures in the absence of air when squeezed between two flat machined metal surfaces. For this reason, the mating surfaces of both the pump body and the engine block must be spotlessly clean so all air will be expelled when the parts are bolted together and tightened. Install the pump slowly onto the crankshaft aligning the oil pump rotor flats with the flats on the crankshaft until seated to the engine block. Tighten the fasteners to 250 inch lbs. (28 Nm).

22. Install a new front oil seal. Install the seal with the spring side towards the inside of the engine. Tap the seal into place until flush with the cover.

23. Install the crankshaft sprocket. A special tool is used to draw the sprocket onto the end of the crankshaft. Use care if using substitutes.

24. Install the timing belt and covers using the recommended procedures. Use care to be sure all valve timing marks are aligned; this is most important. Failure to properly align the timing marks will result in severe engine damage.

25. Reinstall the crankshaft damper. A special tool making use of a 12mm x 1.75 x 150mm bolt is used to draw the crankshaft damper onto the end of the crankshaft. Use care if using substitutes. Tighten the center bolt to 105 ft. lbs. (142 Nm).

26. Raise and safely support the vehicle.

27. Reinstall the oil pump pick-up tube and O-ring. Tighten the oil pump pick-up tube mounting screw to 21 ft. lbs. (28 Nm).

28. Clean the oil pan well and be sure the gasket rails are in good condition. Use Mopar® Silicone Rubber Adhesive Sealant or equivalent sealer at the oil pump-to-engine block parting line. Use a new oil pan gasket, install the oil pan and tighten the 13 oil pan bolts to 105 inch lbs. (12 Nm).

29. Install a new oil filter.

30. Reinstall the right inner fender splash shield.

31. Lower the vehicle.

32. Reinstall the drive belts and accessories as required. Adjust the accessory drive belts.

33. Reinstall the engine mount and bracket as required.

❊❊ **WARNING**

Operating the engine without the proper amount and type of engine oil will result in severe engine damage.

34. Refill the engine with new, clean engine oil and coolant.

35. Test run the vehicle to check for leaks. An oil pressure gauge should be installed to verify proper engine oil pressure.

2.5L Engine

The oil pump assembly is mounted on the timing belt end of the cylinder block with the inner pump rotor indexed and installed on the crankshaft nose. The oil pump case also retains the crankshaft front oil seal and provides oil pan front end closure.

Oil pressure can be checked with a mechanical oil pressure gauge installed at the oil switch location. Oil pressure should be 6 psi (41.4 kPa) at idle and 35–75 psi (241.3–517.1 kPa) at 3000 rpm with the engine at operating temperature. If an oil pressure problem is suspected or if oil pressure is zero at idle, do not run the engine up to 3000 rpm in an attempt to raise oil pressure or the engine will be severely damaged.

Because the oil pump is driven off the nose of the crankshaft, the timing belt must be removed to access the pump. This is a lengthy process. Use care to properly align all valve timing marks.

1. Before servicing the vehicle, refer to the precautions in the beginning of this section.

2. Disconnect the negative battery cable from the left shock tower. The ground cable is equipped with an insulator grommet which should be placed on the stud to prevent the negative battery cable from accidentally grounding.

3. Remove the drive belts and accessories.

4. Drain the coolant and remove the radiator and cooling fan.

5. Raise and safely support the vehicle. Drain the engine oil.

6. Remove the right inner splash shield.

7. Remove the crankshaft damper.

8. Support the engine and remove the right engine mount and the engine mount bracket

9. Remove the timing belt upper and lower covers.

10. Loosen the timing belt tensioner bolts and remove the timing belt and the tensioner.

11. Using a suitable puller, draw the crankshaft sprocket from the crankshaft.

12. Remove the five bolts that attach the oil pump to the block and remove the oil pump.

13. Inspect the oil pump case for damage and remove the rear cover.

14. Remove the pump rotors and inspect the inside of the case for excessive wear.

15. Check that the oil relief plunger slides smoothly and check for a broken spring.

To install:

16. Clean all parts well. Be sure the block and pump surfaces are clean and free of old sealer.

17. Assemble the pump using new parts as required with clean oil. Align the marks on the inner and outer rotors when assembling.

18. Reinstall the pump back cover and tighten the screws to 88 inch lbs. (10 Nm).

19. Reinstall the pump relief valve, spring, gasket and valve cap. Tighten the valve cap to 30–33 ft. lbs. (41–44 Nm).

20. Prime the pump before installation by filling the rotor cavity with clean engine oil.

21. Apply Mopar® Gasket Maker or equivalent sealer to the pump. Install the O-ring into the counterbore on the pump body discharge passage. Position the pump onto the crankshaft until seated on the block. Tighten the size M8 fasteners to 10 ft. lbs. (14 Nm) and size M10 fasteners to 30 ft. lbs. (41 Nm).

22. Reinstall the timing belt and crankshaft sprocket using the recommended procedure and following all cautions. Valve timing MUST be correct or engine damage will result.

23. Reinstall the timing belt cover.

24. Reinstall the engine mount bracket.

25. Reinstall the right engine mount.

26. Remove the engine support.

Exploded view of the oil pump assembly. Note the different bolt lengths—2.5L engine

Aligning the matchmarks for the inner and outer rotor of the oil pump—2.5L engine

Oil pump mounting bolt locations and dimensions—2.5L engine

For engine torque specifications, refer to Section 1 of this manual

27. Reinstall the crankshaft damper and tighten to 134 ft. lbs. (182 Nm).

28. Reinstall the drive belts and accessories.

29. Reinstall the right inner splash shield.

30. Reinstall the radiator and the cooling fan assembly.

❋❋ WARNING

Operating the engine without the proper amount and type of engine oil will result in severe engine damage.

31. Refill the cooling system. Install a new oil filter and refill the engine with oil.

32. Road test the vehicle. Check for proper operation as well as leaks.

Rear Main Seal

REMOVAL & INSTALLATION

1. Before servicing the vehicle, refer to the precautions in the beginning of this section.

2. Disconnect the negative battery cable from the left shock tower. The ground cable is equipped with an insulator grommet which should be placed on the stud to prevent the negative battery cable from accidentally grounding.

3. Remove the transaxle and flexplate/flywheel.

4. Remove the rear crankshaft oil seal from the oil seal housing using a suitable flat-bladed prying tool.

To install:

➡**When installing the seal there is no need to lubricate the sealing surface.**

5. Install the seal into the housing using a suitable driver or seal installer.

6. Install the flexplate/flywheel bolts and tighten them to 70 ft. lbs. (95 Nm).

7. Reinstall the transaxle.

8. Reconnect the negative battery cable. Start the engine and check for leaks.

FUEL SYSTEM

Fuel System Service Precautions

Safety is the most important factor when performing not only fuel system maintenance but any type of maintenance. Failure to conduct maintenance and repairs in a safe manner may result in serious personal injury or

death. Maintenance and testing of the vehicle's fuel system components can be accomplished safely and effectively by adhering to the following rules and guidelines.

• To avoid the possibility of fire and personal injury, always disconnect the negative battery cable unless the repair or test procedure requires that battery voltage be applied.

• Always relieve the fuel system pressure prior to disconnecting any fuel system component (injector, fuel rail, pressure regulator, etc.), fitting or fuel line connection. Exercise extreme caution whenever relieving fuel system pressure to avoid exposing skin, face and eyes to fuel spray. Please be advised that fuel under pressure may penetrate the skin or any part of the body that it contacts.

• Always place a shop towel or cloth around the fitting or connection prior to loosening to absorb any excess fuel due to spillage. Ensure that all fuel spillage (should it occur) is quickly removed from engine surfaces. Ensure that all fuel soaked cloths or towels are deposited into a suitable waste container.

• Always keep a dry chemical (Class B) fire extinguisher near the work area.

• Do not allow fuel spray or fuel vapors to come into contact with a spark or open flame.

• Always use a back-up wrench when loosening and tightening fuel line connection fittings. This will prevent unnecessary stress and torsion to fuel line piping.

• Always replace worn fuel fitting O-rings with new. Do not substitute fuel hose or equivalent, where fuel pipe is installed.

Fuel System Pressure

RELIEVING

2.0L and 2.4L Engines

1. Before servicing the vehicle, refer to the fuel system precautions and to the precautions in the beginning of this section.

2. Disconnect the negative battery cable from the left shock tower. The ground cable is equipped with an insulator grommet which should be placed on the stud to prevent the negative battery cable from accidentally grounding.

3. Remove the fuel filler cap.

4. Remove the cap on the fuel pressure test port on the fuel rail.

5. Place the open end of Fuel Pressure Release Hose special tool number C-4799–1 or equivalent into an approved gasoline con-

Fuel pressure test port location—2.0L and 2.4L engines

tainer. Connect the other end of hose C-4799–1 or equivalent to the fuel pressure test port. Fuel pressure will bleed off through the hose into the gasoline container.

2.5L Engine

1. Before servicing the vehicle, refer to the fuel system precautions and to the precautions in the beginning of this section.

2. Disconnect the fuel rail electrical harness from the engine harness. This is connector C165, a black plastic connector located at the right rear of the intake manifold.

3. Circuit A142 supplies voltage for the fuel injectors while the Powertrain Control Module (PCM) controls the ground for each injector. Connect a jumper wire to the terminal for Circuit A142 (18 Ga. wire, Dark Green with Orange tracer, from ASD relay).

4. Connect the other end of the jumper wire to a 12 volt power source.

5. Connect one end of a second jumper wire to a ground source.

6. Momentarily ground each of the injectors by connecting the other end of the jumper wire to the injector terminal in the harness connector. Repeat this procedure for two or three injectors.

❋❋ WARNING

Do not attempt to start the engine for several minutes to avoid hydrostatic lock.

Fuel Filter

REMOVAL & INSTALLATION

The fuel delivery system contains a replaceable inline filter. The fuel filter mounts to the frame above the rear of the fuel tank. The fuel tank assembly must be loosened and lowered slightly to access the filter. The inlet and outlet tubes are permanently attached to the filter. Please note that

Be sure the shoulder and locking tabs are visible through the window of the connector when attached

the fuel system pressure must be relieved before servicing fuel system components. In addition, quick-disconnect fittings are used on fuel line connections. When the tubes are fully connected, the locking ears and the fuel tube shoulder are visible in the windows of the connector.

1. Before servicing the vehicle, refer to the precautions in the beginning of this section.

2. Disconnect the negative battery cable from the left shock tower. The ground cable is equipped with an insulator grommet which should be placed on the stud to prevent the negative battery cable from accidentally grounding.

3. Relieve the fuel system pressure using the recommended procedure.

4. From inside the trunk, disconnect the fuel pump module wiring jumper from the main body harness. The 4-pin connector is located under the trunk mat on the left side of the trunk near the base of the shock tower. Locate the body grommet for the jumper near the base of the rear seat. Push the grommet out and feed the jumper completely through the hole in the body.

5. Remove the fuel cap slowly to release tank pressure.

6. Raise and safely support the vehicle.

7. Locate the drain plug on the bottom left of the fuel tank. Place an approved fuel container with a capacity of at least 16 gallons, under the drain plug. Remove the plug and drain the fuel tank. When finished draining, install the plug since there will be one to two gallons of fuel remaining. Tighten the drain plug to 32 inch lbs. (3.6 Nm).

8. Remove the driver's side fuel tank strap. Loosen, but do not remove the passenger's side fuel tank strap. Allow the tank to lower until the fuel tank neck touches the rear suspension crossmember.

❊❊ CAUTION

Wrap shop towels around the fuel hoses to catch any gasoline spillage.

Fuel filter mounting location

9. Detach the fuel lines from the fuel pump module. These are quick-disconnect fittings. Depress the releasing tabs on the fuel filter hose connections and detach the fuel lines.

10. Remove the fuel filter.

To install:

➡**The fuel supply (to filter) tube and the return tube (to fuel pump module) are permanently attached to the fuel filter. The ends of the fuel supply and return tubes have different size quick-disconnect fittings. The large quick-disconnect fitting attaches to the large nipple (supply side) on the fuel pump module. The smaller quick-disconnect fitting attaches the small nipple (return side) on the fuel pump module.**

11. Apply a light coat of clean engine oil to the fuel filter nipples. Install the fuel tubes.

12. Raise the tank into position and install the straps. Tighten the strap bolts to 17 ft. lbs. (23 Nm).

➡**Be sure the fuel pump module electrical harness grommet is installed in the body as the tank is raised into position.**

13. Lower the vehicle and reattach the pump module connector.

14. Refill the tank with fuel.

15. Reconnect the negative battery cable.

Fuel Pump

REMOVAL & INSTALLATION

The in-tank fuel pump module contains the fuel pump and pressure regulator which adjusts fuel system pressure to approximately 49 psi (337.8 kPa). Voltage to the fuel pump is supplied through the fuel pump relay.

The fuel pump is serviced as part of the fuel pump module. The fuel pump module is installed in the top of the fuel tank and contains the electric fuel pump, fuel pump

reservoir, inlet strainer fuel gauge sending unit, fuel supply and return line connections and the pressure regulator. The inlet strainer, fuel pressure regulator and level sensor are the only serviceable items. If the fuel pump requires service, replace the fuel pump module.

1. Before servicing the vehicle, refer to the precautions in the beginning of this section.

2. Disconnect the negative battery cable from the left shock tower. The ground cable is equipped with an insulator grommet which should be placed on the stud to prevent the negative battery cable from accidentally grounding.

3. Remove the fuel filler cap and relieve the fuel system pressure using the recommended procedure.

4. Disconnect the fuel pump harness in the left side of the trunk near the base of the shock tower.

5. Remove the grommet and push the harness through the hole.

6. Raise the vehicle and drain the fuel tank.

7. Detach the fuel tank inlet from the filler hose.

8. Place a jack under the tank and remove the straps. Carefully lower the tank.

9. Clean the top of the tank to remove any loose dirt.

10. Disconnect the fuel lines from the fuel pump module.

11. Using special tool 6856 or an equivalent spanner wrench, remove the fuel pump locknut.

❊❊ CAUTION

The fuel reservoir of the fuel pump module does not empty out when the tank is drained. The fuel in the reservoir may spill out when the module is removed.

Removing the fuel pump module lock ring using special tool 6856

12. Remove the fuel pump and O-ring from the tank. Discard the O-ring.

To install:

13. Thoroughly clean all parts. Wipe the seal area of the tank clean. Place a new O-ring on the ledge between the tank threads and the pump module opening.

14. Position the fuel pump module in the tank. Be sure the alignment tab on the underside of the pump module flange sits in the corresponding notch in the fuel tank.

15. While holding the fuel pump module in place, install the locking ring and tighten to 40–45 ft. lbs. (54–61 Nm) using tool 6856 or a spanner-type tool.

16. Reinstall the fuel tank assembly.

17. Reconnect the negative battery cable.

18. Refill the fuel tank with clean fuel. Turn the ignition switch to the **ON** position to pressurize the system. Check the fuel system for leaks.

DRIVE TRAIN

Transmission Assembly

REMOVAL & INSTALLATION

Manual

✸✸ WARNING

If the vehicle is going to be rolled on its wheels while the transaxle is out of the vehicle, obtain two outer CV-joints to install to the hubs. If the vehicle is rolled without the proper torque applied to the front wheel bearings, the bearings will no longer be usable.

1. Before servicing the vehicle, refer to the precautions in the beginning of this section.

2. Disconnect both battery cables, negative side first. Remove the battery, tray and stay brace.

3. Remove the air cleaner and intake hoses.

4. Drain the transaxle into a suitable waste container.

5. Remove the select and shift cables from the transaxle.

6. Disconnect the back-up light switch harness and position it aside.

7. Disengage the speedometer electrical harness, from the transaxle assembly.

8. Remove the starter motor.

Secure the engine assembly with an appropriate support fixture

9. Using special tool 7137 or C-4852 or equivalent, support the engine assembly.

10. Remove the rear roll stopper mounting bracket.

11. Remove the transaxle mount bracket.

12. Remove the upper transaxle mounting bolts.

13. Raise and safely support the vehicle.

14. Remove the front wheel assemblies.

15. Remove the undercover.

16. Remove the halfshaft assemblies. Plug the halfshaft openings in the transaxle assembly to prevent foreign material from entering.

17. Remove the cover from the transaxle bell housing.

Remove the driveplate clutch bolts—rotate the engine clockwise to advance to the next bolt

Removing the lower engine-to-transaxle mounting bolts

18. Remove the engine front roll stopper through-bolt.

19. Remove the centermember.

20. Support the transaxle, using a transmission jack.

21. Rotate the engine clockwise to gain access to the driveplate clutch bolts. Remove the driveplate clutch bolts.

22. Remove the lower engine-to-transaxle mounting bolts.

23. Slide the transaxle rearward and carefully lower it from the vehicle.

24. To prepare the vehicle for rolling, support the engine with a suitable support or reinstall the front motor mount to the engine. Then, reinstall the ball joints to the steering knuckle and install the retaining bolt. Install the obtained outer CV-joints to the hubs, install the washers and tighten the axle nuts to 180 ft. lbs. (244 Nm). The vehicle may now be safely rolled.

To install:

25. Installation is the reverse of the removal procedure. Please note the following important steps.

26. The following items must be tightened to the specifications listed:

- Transaxle-to-engine mounting bolts—70 ft. lbs. (95 Nm)
- Transaxle bell housing cover bolts—7 ft. lbs. (9 Nm)
- Centermember front mounting bolts—65 ft. lbs. (88 Nm)
- Centermember rear mounting bolt—54 ft. lbs. (73 Nm)
- Front engine roll stopper through-bolt—first, lightly tighten, then once the full weight of the engine is on the mounts, tighten the bolt to 42 ft. lbs. (57 Nm).
- Damper fork-to-lower control arm through-bolt—65 ft. lbs. (88 Nm)
- Stabilizer link-to-damper fork nut—29 ft. lbs. (39 Nm)
- Transaxle mount bracket nuts—32 ft. lbs. (43 Nm)

Be sure to connect the ground cable at the starter

- Transaxle mount through-bolt—51 ft. lbs. (69 Nm)

27. Check to be sure that all fasteners are tightened and connections made.

28. Be sure the vehicle is level, and refill the transaxle.

29. Check the transaxle for proper operation. Be sure the reverse lights come on when in reverse.

Automatic

> ❈❈ **WARNING**

If the vehicle is going to be rolled on its wheels while the transaxle is out of the vehicle, obtain two outer CV-joints to install to the hubs. If the vehicle is rolled without the proper torque applied to the front wheel bearings, the bearings will no longer be usable.

1. Before servicing the vehicle, refer to the precautions in the beginning of this section.

2. Disconnect both battery cables, negative side first.

3. If necessary, drain the coolant and remove the coolant return extension.

7922FG49

Location of the transaxle solenoid assembly 8-way connector and retaining bolt

7922FG50

Removing the shift cable and clamp

4. Remove the air cleaner/inlet duct assembly. Remove the upper bell housing bolts and water tube, where applicable.

5. Label and disengage all electrical connectors, cable linkages, hoses and mounting brackets required for removal of the transaxle assembly.

6. Remove the bolt securing the fluid dipstick tube, to the transaxle. Remove the dipstick and tube from the transaxle.

7. Using special tool 7137 or C-4852 or equivalent, support the engine assembly.

8. Remove the starter motor

9. Drain the transaxle fluid into a suitable waste container.

10. Raise the vehicle and support it safely.

11. Remove the tire and wheel assemblies.

12. Remove the splash shields.

13. Disconnect the exhaust pipe from the exhaust manifold.

14. Remove the halfshaft assemblies. Position a drain pan under the transaxle where the axles enter the differential or extension housing.

15. Unbolt the center bearing and remove the intermediate axle from the transaxle, if equipped.

16. Disconnect and tag the oil cooler lines, at the transaxle.

17. If equipped with Direct Ignition System (DIS), detach the harness connector and remove the Crankshaft Position (CKP) sensor from the transaxle bell housing.

18. Remove the front and rear motor/transaxle mounts.

19. Remove the centermember.

20. Remove the torque converter inspection cover, matchmark the torque converter to the flexplate.

21. Remove the bolts holding the flexplate to the torque converter with a box wrench. Rotate the crankshaft to bring the bolts into a position for removal, one at a time.

22. Support the transaxle using a transmission jack (at the side of the case, NOT at the pan).

23. Remove the lower bell housing bolts.

24. Remove the transaxle mount bolts.

➡**The torque converter can become disengaged from the transaxle. Keep the front of the transaxle slightly raised during removal.**

25. Carefully pry the transaxle from the engine.

26. Slide the transaxle rearward until the dowels disengage from the mating holes in the transaxle case.

27. Pull the transaxle completely away from the engine and remove it from the vehicle.

28. To prepare the vehicle for rolling, support the engine with a suitable support or reinstall the front motor mount to the engine. Then, reinstall the ball joints to the steering knuckle and install the retaining bolt. Install the obtained outer CV-joints to the hubs, install the washers and tighten the axle nuts to 180 ft. lbs. (244 Nm). The vehicle may now be safely rolled.

To install:

29. Installation is the reverse of the removal procedure. Please note the following important steps.

30. Tighten the transaxle-to-engine mounting bolts to 70 ft. lbs. (95 Nm).

31. Tighten the torque converter-to-flexplate bolts to 55 ft. lbs. (74 Nm).

32. Tighten the torque converter inspection cover mounting bolts to 9 ft. lbs. (12 Nm).

33. Tighten the motor mounts to the following specifications:

- Front mount-to-lower radiator support bolts—45 ft. lbs. (61 Nm)

- Rear mount-to-front suspension crossmember—45 ft. lbs. (61 Nm)

- Rear mount through-bolt—45 ft. lbs. (61 Nm)

- Left motor mount-to-frame rail—24 ft. lbs. (33 Nm)

34. Tighten the shifter lever retaining nut to 14 ft. lbs. (19 Nm).

35. Ensure all wiring harness plugs, cable linkages, and hoses have been properly connected during installation.

36. Adjust the gearshift and throttle cables.

37. Reconnect the negative battery cable.

38. Refill the transaxle and the cooling system.

39. Check the transaxle for proper operation. Be sure the car's back-up lights and speedometer are working properly.

Clutch

ADJUSTMENT

Free-Play

The manual transaxle clutch release system has a unique self-adjusting mechanism to compensate for clutch disc wear. This adjuster mechanism is located with the clutch cable assembly. The preload spring maintains tension on the cable. This tension

Clutch cable routing

keeps the clutch release bearing continuously loaded against the fingers of the clutch cover assembly. No manual adjustment is necessary.

When servicing this vehicle or if removing and installing the clutch cable, do not pull on the clutch cable housing to remove it from the dash panel. Damage to the cable self-adjuster may occur.

To check the function of the adjuster mechanism, use the following procedure:

1. With slight pressure, pull the clutch release lever end of the cable to draw the cable taut.

2. Push the clutch cable housing toward the dash panel. With less than 25 lbs. (11 kg) of effort, the cable housing should move 1.2–2.0 in. (30–50mm). This indicates proper adjuster mechanism function.

3. If the cable does not adjust, determine if the mechanism is properly seated on the bracket.

REMOVAL & INSTALLATION

➡ **The transaxle assembly must be removed to service the clutch assembly.**

1. Before servicing the vehicle, refer to the precautions in the beginning of this section.

2. Disconnect the negative battery cable from the left shock tower. The ground cable is equipped with an insulator grommet which should be placed on the stud to prevent the negative battery cable from accidentally grounding.

3. Raise and safely support the vehicle.

4. Disconnect the starter wiring and remove the starter assembly.

5. Remove the rear and front transaxle support brackets.

6. Remove the clutch inspection cover.

7. Remove the bolts attaching the modular clutch to the flywheel.

8. Remove the transaxle assembly with the clutch as an assembly.

9. Remove the clutch assembly from the input shaft of the transaxle.

To install:

10. Clean all parts well. Inspect for oil leakage through the engine rear crankshaft oil seal and transaxle input shaft seal. If leakage is noted, it should be corrected at this time.

11. Examine the throwout or clutch release bearing. It is prelubricated and sealed and should not be washed in solvent. The bearing should turn smoothly when held in the hand with a light thrust load. A light drag caused by the lubricant fill is normal. If the bearing is noisy, rough or dry, replace the complete bearing assembly. In most cases where a clutch is being serviced, the complete clutch assembly and release bearing are usually replaced together.

12. Check the condition of the stud pivot spring clips on the back side of the clutch fork. If the clips are broken or distorted, replace the clutch fork. The pivot ball pocket in the fork is Teflon® coated and should be installed WITHOUT any lubricant such as grease which will break down the Teflon® coating. Be sure the ball stud and fork pocket are clean of contamination and dirt. When assembling the fork to the bearing, the small pegs on the bearing must go over the fork arms.

13. Check the flywheel for cracks, glazing or grooves. If any of these conditions exist, machine (reface) or replace the flywheel to prevent clutch chatter and premature clutch wear.

➡**The manual transaxle is equipped with a reverse brake. It functions as a synchronizer, but only if the vehicle is not moving. When the clutch pedal is depressed to the floor and held for 3 seconds, and the transaxle shifts to reverse, no gear clash should be present. If there is, the input shaft should be checked. When the transaxle is removed for clutch service, check the input clutch shaft, clutch disc splines and release bearing for dry rust. If present, clean rust off and apply a light coat of high temperature bearing grease to the input shaft splines. Apply grease on the input shaft splines only where the clutch disc slides. Verify that the clutch disc slides freely along the input shaft splines.**

14. Install the modular clutch assembly onto the input shaft of the transaxle.

15. Install the transaxle assembly using the recommended procedure.

16. Install new clutch-to-driveplate (flywheel) bolts. Tighten the bolts in a crisscross pattern a few turns at a time to prevent distortion of the flywheel. Tighten the bolts to 55 ft. lbs. (75 Nm).

17. Install the clutch inspection cover.

18. Install the transaxle lower support brackets.

19. Install the starter assembly.

20. Lower the vehicle. Connect the negative battery cable.

21. Road test the vehicle to check for proper clutch operation.

Exploded view of the clutch assembly

Halfshafts

REMOVAL & INSTALLATION

➡ **If the vehicle is going to be rolled while the halfshafts are out of the vehicle, obtain two outer CV-joints or proper equivalent tools and install to the hubs. If the vehicle is rolled without the proper torque applied to the front wheel bearings, the bearings will no longer be usable.**

1. Before servicing the vehicle, refer to the precautions in the beginning of this section.
2. Disconnect the negative battery cable.
3. Remove the cotter pin, nut lock and spring washer.
4. Loosen, but do not remove the halfshaft nut while the vehicle is on the floor with the brakes applied.
5. Raise and safely support the vehicle.
6. Remove the wheel.
7. Remove the brake caliper assembly and support it from the shock coil using a strong piece of wire.
8. Remove the brake rotor.
9. Remove the halfshaft nut and washer.
10. Using Joint Separation tool MB991113 or equivalent, disconnect the tie rod end from the steering knuckle.

❋❋ WARNING

Use of improper methods of joint separation can result in damage to the joint, leading to possible failure.

11. If equipped with ABS, remove the speed sensor cable routing bracket.
12. If necessary, disconnect the sway bar link from the damper fork.
13. Remove the damper fork lower through-bolts and upper pinch bolt. Remove the damper fork assembly.
14. Using a joint separation tool, disconnect the steering knuckle from the lower control arm.
15. Remove the halfshaft from the hub/knuckle by setting up a puller on the outside wheel hub, if necessary, and pushing the halfshaft from the front hub. After pressing the outer shaft, insert a prybar between the transaxle case and the halfshaft and pry the shaft from the transaxle.

❋❋ WARNING

Do not pull on the shaft. Doing so damages the inboard joint. Do not

insert the prybar too far or the oil seal in the case may be damaged.

To install:

16. Inspect the halfshaft boot for damage or deterioration. Check the ball joints and splines for wear.
17. Replace the circlips on the ends of the halfshaft(s).
18. Insert the halfshaft into the transaxle. Be sure it is fully seated.
19. Pull the knuckle assembly outward and install the other end of the halfshaft into the hub.
20. Install the washer so the chamfered edge faces outward. Install the halfshaft nut and tighten temporarily.
21. Connect the control arm to the steering knuckle. Tighten the self-locking nuts to 43–52 ft. lbs. (59–71 Nm).
22. Install the damper fork. Tighten the lower through-bolt/nut to 65 ft. lbs. (88 Nm) and the upper pinch bolt to 76 ft. lbs. (103 Nm).
23. Connect the tie rod end to the steering knuckle. Tighten the retaining nut to 17–25 ft. lbs. (24–33 Nm) and install a new cotter pin.

Carefully remove the outer CV joint from the steering knuckle—be careful NOT to damage the threads or splines on the joint

Inserting the prybar too far may damage the transaxle seal

24. Connect the sway bar link to the damper fork and tighten the link nut to 29 ft. lbs. (39 Nm).
25. Install the lockwasher and axle nut. Tighten the axle nut to 145–188 ft. lbs. (200–260 Nm).

➡ **Before securely tightening the axle nut be sure there is no load on the wheel bearings.**

26. Install the brake rotor and caliper assembly.
27. Install a new cotter pin and bend to secure.
28. Install the wheel.
29. Check the transaxle fluid level and top off, if necessary.
30. Connect the negative battery cable.
31. Test drive the vehicle and check for proper operation.

STEERING AND SUSPENSION

Air Bag

❋❋ CAUTION

Some vehicles are equipped with an air bag system, also known as the Supplemental Inflatable Restraint (SIR) or Supplemental Restraint System (SRS). The system must be disabled before performing service on or around system components, steering column, instrument panel components, wiring and sensors. Failure to follow safety and disabling procedures could result in accidental air bag deployment, possible personal injury and unnecessary system repairs.

PRECAUTIONS

Several precautions must be observed when handling the inflator module to avoid accidental deployment and possible personal injury.

➡ **Before servicing the vehicle, also refer to the precautions in the beginning of this section.**

• Never carry the inflator module by the wires or connector on the underside of the module.

• When carrying a live inflator module, hold securely with both hands, and ensure that the bag and trim cover are pointed away.

• Place the inflator module on a bench or other surface with the bag and trim cover facing up.

• With the inflator module on the bench, never place anything on or close to the module which may be thrown in the event of accidental deployment.

DISARMING

This air bag system is a sensitive, complex, electromechanical unit. Proper SRS (also called Supplemental Inflatable Restraint, or SIR, or air bag system) disarming can be obtained by disconnecting and isolating the negative battery cable (wrapping the battery cable end with electrical tape is a good method for isolating it). Failure to disconnect the battery could result in accidental air bag deployment and possible personal injury. Before beginning service work, allow the system capacitor 2 minutes to discharge after disconnecting and isolating the negative battery cable.

Power Rack and Pinion Steering Gear

REMOVAL & INSTALLATION

1. Before servicing the vehicle, refer to the precautions in the beginning of this section.

2. Disconnect the negative battery cable from the left shock tower. The ground cable is equipped with an insulator grommet which should be placed on the stud to prevent the negative battery cable from accidentally grounding.

➡ **The negative battery is equipped with a insulated grommet that is to be placed on the shock tower connection to prevent accidental grounding.**

3. Remove the retaining pin from the intermediate shaft coupler pin bolt and remove the pin bolt.

4. Raise and safely support the vehicle.

5. Remove the front wheels.

6. Disconnect the tie rod ends by holding the tie rod end stud with a 11/32 in. socket and loosen the retaining nut with a wrench.

7. Separate the tie rod end using a suitable tool.

➡ **Before removing the front suspension crossmember from the vehicle you**

must scribe the front suspension crossmember and the vehicle body. This must be done to retain the proper alignment. The caster and camber are not adjustable.

8. Scribe a line on the body and on the crossmember on all four sides.

9. Disconnect the stabilizer from the body.

10. If equipped with anti-lock brakes remove the three bolts attaching it to the crossmember and tie the anti-lock brake controller to the vehicle body.

11. Disconnect the shock absorber clevis from the lower control arm.

Steering gear rear mounting bolt location

Steering gear front mounting bolt location

Check the condition of the isolator—if worn or oil soaked, replace

12. Remove the two bolts attaching the engine support bracket to the crossmember.

13. Remove the bolt attaching the engine support bracket to the transaxle mounting bracket.

14. Place a suitable lifting device under the front suspension crossmember.

15. Remove the eight bolts attaching the crossmember to the body of the vehicle.

16. Lower the lifting device enough to gain access to the steering rack.

17. Disconnect the power steering lines and drain the fluid if equipped.

18. Disconnect the power steering pressure switch wiring.

19. If equipped with speed proportional steering, disconnect the solenoid control module wiring.

20. Remove the two steering rack isolator attaching bolts.

21. Remove the two steering rack saddle bracket attaching bolts.

22. Remove the steering rack from the vehicle.

To install:

23. Install the steering rack into the crossmember.

24. Reinstall the isolator and saddle bracket bolts. Tighten the bolts to 50 ft. lbs. (68 Nm).

25. If equipped with power steering reinstall the pressure and return lines. Tighten the lines to 275 inch lbs. (31 Nm).

26. Raise the crossmember against the frame rails and install the two rear bolts.

27. Reinstall the two front bolts.

28. Tighten all four bolts until the crossmember contacts the body.

29. Tighten the bolts to 20 inch lbs. (2 Nm).

30. Using a soft faced hammer tap the crossmember into position.

➡ **Be sure to align the scribed marks on the crossmember.**

31. Starting with the rear bolts, tighten the crossmember bolts to 120 ft. lbs. (163 Nm).

32. Reinstall the engine support bracket.

33. Reinstall the engine support bracket bolts to the crossmember.

34. Reinstall the engine support bracket bolt to the transaxle bracket.

35. Tighten the three bolts to 55 ft. lbs. (75 Nm).

36. Reconnect the power steering pressure switch.

37. Reinstall the anti-lock brake control unit.

38. Tighten the anti-lock brake bolts to 21 ft. lbs. (28 Nm).

39. Reinstall the heat shield on the tie rod ends.

40. Reconnect the shock clevis to the lower control arm.

41. Reinstall the tie rod ends and tighten to 45 ft. lbs. (61 Nm).

42. Reinstall and tighten the two stabilizer clamps.

43. Tighten the shock absorber clevis bolt to 68 ft. lbs. (92 Nm).

44. Reinstall the wheels and tighten the lug nuts to 95 ft. lbs. (129 Nm).

45. Lower the vehicle.

46. Reinstall the intermediate shaft pin bolt and retaining pin.

47. Tighten the pin bolt to 240 inch lbs. (27 Nm).

48. Reconnect the negative battery cable.

49. Refill the power steering system to the cold level with approved fluid.

50. Start the engine and allow it to run for a few minutes.

51. Shut **OFF** the engine and check the power steering fluid.

52. Add power steering fluid if necessary.

53. Raise the front wheels off the ground.

54. Start the engine and turn the wheel from stop-to-stop to bleed any air from the system.

55. Check the fluid level and add if necessary.

56. Check and adjust the alignment.

Shock Absorber

REMOVAL & INSTALLATION

Front

1. Before servicing the vehicle, refer to the precautions in the beginning of this section.

2. Raise and safely support the vehicle.

3. Remove the wheel and tire.

4. Remove the steering knuckle.

5. Remove the pin bolt attaching the shock absorber to the shock clevis.

6. Remove the through-bolt attaching the clevis to the lower control arm.

7. Tap the clevis with a brass drift to remove it from the shock.

8. Remove the four bolts attaching the shock to the shock tower.

9. Remove the shock and upper control arm mounting bracket as an assembly.

To install:

10. Install the shock assembly into the shock tower.

11. Reinstall the four upper shock mounting bolts.

Separating the upper ball joint from the steering knuckle

Component view of the front shock mounting

Be sure the orientation tab is situated into the clevis split

12. Tighten the bolts to 23 ft. lbs. (31 Nm).

13. Reinstall the clevis onto the shock with a brass drift until the clevis is fully seated against the locating tab.

14. Reinstall the clevis pin bolt.

15. Reinstall the clevis onto the lower control arm.

16. Reinstall the clevis through-bolt.

17. Reinstall the steering knuckle.

18. Tighten the clevis-to-shock pin bolt to 65 ft. lbs. (88 Nm).

19. Lower the vehicle to support the lower control arm.

20. Tighten the clevis-to-lower control arm mounting bolt 40 ft. lbs. (54 Nm).

21. Reinstall the wheel and tire.

22. Lower the vehicle.

Rear

1. Before servicing the vehicle, refer to the precautions in the beginning of this section.

2. Pull back the carpeting from the rear shock tower.

3. Remove the plastic cover from the top of the shock tower.

4. Remove the two nuts attaching the shock assembly to the body.

5. Raise and safely support the vehicle.

6. Remove the wheel and tire.

7. Remove the bolt attaching the shock to the rear knuckle.

8. Push downward on the rear suspension and tilt the top of the shock outward.

9. Remove the shock from the vehicle.

To install:

10. Install the shock into the vehicle at the rear knuckle.

11. Push downward on the rear suspension and insert the top of the shock into the vehicle.

Access the rear shock upper mounting from inside the trunk

View of the rear shock lower mounting

12. Reinstall the shock-to-rear knuckle attaching bolt.

13. Tighten the bolt to 70 ft. lbs. (95 Nm).

14. Lower the vehicle enough to gain access to the trunk.

15. Reinstall the shock upper mounting nuts and tighten to 25 ft. lbs. (34 Nm).

16. Reinstall the shock top cover.

17. Reinstall the rear wheel and tire and tighten to 95 ft. lbs. (125 Nm).

18. Lower the vehicle and check for proper operation.

Coil Spring

REMOVAL & INSTALLATION

Front

1. Before servicing the vehicle, refer to the precautions in the beginning of this section.

2. Place the shock absorber assembly in a spring compressor (MB991237 and MB991238 or equivalent). Tighten the compressor and compress the spring slowly. Make certain the compressor is properly engaged before tightening.

3. After tension has been removed from the shock absorber assembly and shock absorber plate, remove the piston rod nut and washer from the top of the shock absorber assembly.

4. If the spring is to be replaced, slowly release the tension on the spring compressor. Allow the spring to expand fully. If only the shock absorber is being replaced the spring may remain in the compressor assembly.

5. By hand, remove the upper shock absorber bearing, washer, mount and shock absorber shield. Remove the upper insulator ring, the spring, the bumper and lower insulator from the spring. Take notice to each components location for proper reassembly.

To install:

6. Install the lower insulator, the shock absorber bumper and the uncompressed spring. Install the upper spring insulator, shock absorber shield, mount and washer.

7. Install or align the spring compressor. Make certain the spring is correctly positioned relative to the upper and lower insulator rings. Smoothly compress the spring.

8. Install the washer and piston rod nut. Tighten the nut to 18 ft. lbs. (25 Nm). Install the dust cap.

9. Carefully release the spring compressor, watching the spring position as it seats. When the spring is properly seated, release/remove the compressor tools.

10. Reinstall the shock absorber assembly.

Rear

1. Before servicing the vehicle, refer to the precautions in the beginning of this section.

2. With the shock absorber removed from the vehicle, place the shock absorber assembly in a spring compressor (MB991237 and MB991239 or equivalent) service tool. Tighten the compressor and compress the spring slowly. Make certain the compressor is properly engaged before tightening.

3. After tension has been removed from the shock absorber assembly and shock absorber plate, remove the piston rod nut and washer from the top of the shock absorber assembly.

4. If the spring is to be replaced, slowly release the tension on the spring compressor. Allow the spring to expand fully. If only the shock absorber is being replaced the spring may remain in the compressor assembly.

5. By hand, remove the upper shock absorber bearing, washer, mount and shock absorber shield. Remove the upper insulator ring, the spring, the bumper and lower insulator from the spring. Take notice to each components location for proper reassembly.

To install:

6. Install the lower insulator, the shock absorber bumper and the uncompressed spring. Install the upper spring insulator, shock absorber shield, mount and washer.

7. Install or align the spring compressor. Make certain the spring is correctly positioned relative to the upper and lower insulator rings. Smoothly compress the spring.

8. Install the washer and piston rod nut. Tighten the nut to 16 ft. lbs. (22 Nm). Install the dust cap.

9. Carefully release the spring compressor, watching the spring position as it seats. When the spring is properly seated, release/remove the compressor tools.

10. Reinstall the shock absorber assembly.

Upper Ball Joint

REMOVAL & INSTALLATION

The upper ball joint is an integrated part of the upper control arm assembly, and can not be serviced separately. A worn or damaged ball joint requires replacement of upper control arm assembly.

Upper Control Arm

REMOVAL & INSTALLATION

Front

1. Before servicing the vehicle, refer to the precautions in the beginning of this section.

Front upper control arm component identification

7922FG63

2. Raise and safely support the vehicle.

3. Remove the appropriate wheel.

4. Using the Joint Separation tool, MB991113 or equivalent, disconnect the ball joint stud from the steering knuckle.

5. Inside the engine compartment, at the shock absorber tower, locate the upper control arm mounting nuts. Remove the nuts and using the joint separation tool, separate the upper arm shafts from the shock absorber tower.

6. Remove the control arm assembly.

To install:

7. Align the upper control arm shafts to the shock absorber tower and secure it with the mounting nuts. Tighten the mounting nuts to 62 ft. lbs. (86 Nm).

8. Connect the ball joint to the knuckle and tighten the locking nut to 20 ft. lbs. (28 Nm).

9. Install the wheel and lower the vehicle.

10. Check the wheel alignment and adjust if necessary.

Rear

1. Before servicing the vehicle, refer to the precautions in the beginning of this section.

2. Raise and safely support the vehicle on a frame contact (twin post) lift.

3. Remove both rear wheels.

4. Disconnect both shock absorbers from the knuckles.

5. Remove the muffler hanger from the frame rail.

6. Remove the rear exhaust pipe hanger from the rear crossmember and allow the exhaust system to hang down as far as possible.

7. On the control arm to be replaced, disconnect the ball joint stud from the knuckle.

8. Support the center of the rear crossmember with a jack and a block of wood.

9. If equipped with ABS, unclip the speed sensor wiring from the upper control arms.

10. Remove the four bolts attaching the crossmember to the frame.

✳✳ WARNING

Do not damage the rear brake hoses while lowering the crossmember.

11. Lower the crossmember to access the two upper control arm pivot bar mounting bolts.

A jack with a block of wood should be used to support the rear crossmember

Use a drift to align the rear crossmember to the frame

12. Remove the two bolts and the control arm from the crossmember.

To install:

13. Install the control arm on the crossmember. Be sure to place the flat washers between the crossmember and the pivot bar. Tighten the bolts to 80 ft. lbs. (108 Nm).

14. Raise the crossmember into position and loosely install the four mounting bolts. Using a drift, align the holes in the crossmember with the holes in the frame. Tighten the bolts to 80 ft. lbs. (108 Nm).

15. Remove the jack and install the remaining components using the following torque specifications:

• Ball joint stud nut to 63 ft. lbs. (85 Nm).

• Lower shock absorber bolt to 70 ft. lbs. (95 Nm)

• Wheel mounting nuts to 100 ft. lbs. (135 Nm) using two steps

Turn to Section 6 for brake system applications

Lower Ball Joint

REMOVAL & INSTALLATION

On all vehicles, the ball joint cannot be serviced separately. If the ball joint is defective it will require replacement of the lower control arm.

Lower Control Arm

REMOVAL & INSTALLATION

Front

1. Raise and safely support the vehicle.
2. Remove the front wheels and tires.
3. If equipped with 15 inch wheels, the heat shield will need to be removed before the lower control arm can be separated from the steering knuckle.
4. Remove the ball joint clamping nut.
5. Remove the sway bar attaching bolts from both control arms.
6. Disconnect the shock clevis from the lower control arm.
7. Loosen the sway bar-to-crossmember attaching bolts and rotate the sway bar away from the control arm.
8. Using a prybar separate the lower control arm from the steering knuckle.
9. Remove the two control arm attaching bolts.
10. Remove the control arm.
To install:
11. Install the control arm. Tighten the control arm attaching bolts to 120 ft. lbs. (163 Nm).
12. Reinstall the control arm to the steering knuckle and tighten to 70 ft. lbs. (95 Nm).
13. Rotate the sway bar up to the control arms.
14. Reinstall the shock absorber clevis.
15. Reinstall the sway bar attaching bolts.
16. Tighten the sway bar bolts to 21 ft. lbs. (28 Nm).
17. Tighten the sway bar-to-crossmember attaching bolts 21 ft. lbs. (28 Nm).
18. Reinstall the wheels and tires.

Wheel Bearings

ADJUSTMENT

Front

The front hub wheel bearing is designed for the life of the vehicle and requires no type of adjustment or periodic maintenance. The bearing is a sealed unit with the wheel hub and can only be removed and/or replaced as one unit.

Rear

The rear hub and wheel bearing assembly is designed for the life of the vehicle and requires no type of adjustment or periodic maintenance. The bearing is a sealed unit with the wheel hub and can only be removed and/or replaced as one unit.

The following procedure may be used for evaluation of bearing condition:

1. Raise and safely support the vehicle.
2. Remove the rear wheels and brake drums.
3. Turn the hub flange carefully. Excessive roughness, lateral play or resistance to rotation may indicate dirt intrusion or bearing failure.
4. If the rear wheel bearings exhibit the conditions during inspection, the hub and bearing assembly should be replaced.
5. Damaged bearing seals and resulting excessive grease loss may also require bearing replacement. Moderate grease loss from the bearing is considered normal and should not require replacement of the hub and bearing assembly.

REMOVAL & INSTALLATION

Front

The front wheel bearing used on this vehicle is a bolt-in type wheel bearing.

The wheel bearing is serviced separately from the front steering knuckle and front hub assembly. Retention of the front wheel bearing into the steering knuckle is by means of three bolts installed from the rear of the steering knuckle. The three bolts attach the hub/bearing to the front surface of the steering knuckle. Removal and installation of the hub/bearing assembly from the steering knuckle must be done with the steering knuckle removed from the vehicle.

This vehicle does not use a rubber lip seal as on past front wheel drive vehicles to prevent contamination of the front wheel bearing. On this vehicle the face of the outer CV-joint has a metal bearing shield pressed on it. This design deters direct water splash on the bearing seal while allowing any water that gets in to run out the bottom of the steering knuckle. It is important to thoroughly clean the outer CV-joint and the wheel bearing area in the steering knuckle before it is assembled after servicing the front wheel bearing or driveshaft.

At no time when servicing this vehicle, can a sheet metal screw, bolt or other metal fastener be installed in the shock tower to take the place of an original plastic clip. Also, no holes can be drilled into the front shock tower for the installation of any metal fasteners into the shock tower. Because of the minimum clearance in this area installation of metal fasteners could damage the coil spring's protective coating and lead to

SHOCK ABSORBER CLEVIS

LOWER CONTROL ARM

BALL JOINT CAP

7922FG64

Be sure to pre-load the suspension before final tightening the control arm to the steering knuckle

corrosion failure of the spring. If a plastic clip is missing, lost or broken during servicing a vehicle, replace only with the equivalent part listed in the Mopar parts catalog.

1. Before servicing the vehicle, refer to the precautions in the beginning of this section.

2. Raise and safely support the vehicle.

3. Remove the front tire and wheel.

4. Remove the steering knuckle assembly using the recommended procedure.

5. Remove the three bolts attaching the hub/bearing assembly to the steering knuckle.

6. Remove the hub/bearing assembly out from the front of the steering knuckle. The bolt-in front wheel bearing used on the vehicle is transferable to a replacement steering knuckle is the bearing found in serviceable condition. If the bearing will not come out of the steering knuckle, it can be tapped out using a soft-faced hammer.

To install:

7. Clean all parts well. Thoroughly clean all the hub/bearing assembly mounting surfaces on the steering knuckle.

8. Reinstall the replacement hub/bearing assembly in the steering knuckle aligning the bolt holes in the bearing flange with the holes in the steering knuckle.

9. Reinstall the three attaching bolts and tighten evenly to be sure the bearing is square to the face of the steering knuckle. Tighten the attaching bolts to 80 ft. lbs. (110 Nm).

10. Reinstall the steering knuckle. Install the tire and wheel.

11. Lower the vehicle and check for proper operation.

Rear

All vehicles are equipped with permanently lubricated and sealed for life rear wheel bearings. There is no periodic lubrication or maintenance recommended for these units.

To evaluate the condition of the rear wheel bearings, remove the wheel and brake drum or rotor and rotate the flanged outer ring of the hub. Excessive roughness or resistance to rotation may indicate dirt intrusion or wheel bearing failure. If the rear wheel bearings exhibit these conditions during inspection, the hub and bearing assembly should be replaced. Damaged bearing seals and resulting excessive grease loss may also require bearing replacement. Moderate grease loss from the bearing is considered normal and should not require replacement of the hub and bearing assembly. If service requires removal for inspection or replacement of the rear wheel bearing and hub assembly, use the following procedure.

1. Before servicing the vehicle, refer to the precautions in the beginning of this section.

Independent rear suspension component identification

2. Raise and safely support the vehicle.

3. Remove the wheel and tire assembly.

4. If equipped with drum brakes, remove the brake drum.

5. If equipped with disc brakes, remove the brake caliper and pull the rotor off the wheel studs.

6. Remove the rear hub dust cap.

7. Remove the rear hub retaining nut and discard.

8. Remove the rear hub and bearing assembly by pulling straight off the spindle.

To install:

9. Install the new bearing on the rear spindle.

10. Reinstall the hub and a new retaining nut.

11. Tighten the retaining nut to 185 ft. lbs. (250 Nm). Install the dust cap by tapping on with a soft-faced mallet.

12. Install the brake drum or rotor and caliper.

13. Install the wheel and tire. Tighten the lug nuts in a crisscross pattern using two steps. Final torque of the lug nuts is 95 ft. lbs. (129 Nm).

14. Lower the vehicle.

PRECAUTIONS

Before servicing any vehicle, please be sure to read all of the following precautions, which deal with personal safety, prevention of component damage, and important points to take into consideration when servicing a motor vehicle:

• Never open, service or drain the radiator or cooling system when the engine is hot; serious burns can occur from the steam and hot coolant.

• Observe all applicable safety precautions when working around fuel. Whenever servicing the fuel system, always work in a well ventilated area. Do not allow fuel spray or vapors to come in contact with a spark, open flame, or excessive heat (a hot drop light, for example). Keep a dry chemical fire extinguisher near the work area. Always keep fuel in a container specifically designed for fuel storage; also, always properly seal fuel containers to avoid the possibility of fire or explosion. Refer to the additional fuel system precautions later in this section.

• Fuel injection systems often remain pressurized, even after the engine has been turned **OFF**. The fuel system pressure must be relieved before disconnecting any fuel lines. Failure to do so may result in fire and/or personal injury.

• Brake fluid often contains polyglycol ethers and polyglycols. Avoid contact with the eyes and wash your hands thoroughly after handling brake fluid. If you do get brake fluid in your eyes, flush your eyes with clean, running water for 15 minutes. If eye irritation persists, or if you have taken brake fluid internally, IMMEDIATELY seek medical assistance.

• The EPA warns that prolonged contact with used engine oil may cause a number of skin disorders, including cancer! You should make every effort to minimize your exposure to used engine oil. Protective gloves should be worn when changing oil. Wash your hands and any other exposed skin areas as soon as possible after expo-sure to used engine oil. Soap and water, or waterless hand cleaner should be used.

• All new vehicles are now equipped with an air bag system, often referred to as a Supplemental Restraint System (SRS) or Supplemental Inflatable Restraint (SIR) system. The system must be disabled before performing service on or around system components, steering column, instrument panel components, wiring and sensors. Failure to follow safety and disabling procedures could result in accidental air bag deployment, possible personal injury and unnecessary system repairs.

• Always wear safety goggles when working with, or around, the air bag system. When carrying a non-deployed air bag, be sure the bag and trim cover are pointed away from your body. When placing a non-deployed air bag on a work surface, always face the bag and trim cover upward, away from the surface. This will reduce the motion of the module if it is accidentally deployed. Refer to the additional air bag system precautions later in this section.

• Clean, high quality brake fluid from a sealed container is essential to the safe and proper operation of the brake system. You should always buy the correct type of brake fluid for your vehicle. If the brake fluid becomes contaminated, completely flush the system with new fluid. Never reuse any brake fluid. Any brake fluid that is removed from the system should be discarded. Also, do not allow any brake fluid to come in contact with a painted surface; it will damage the paint.

• Never operate the engine without the proper amount and type of engine oil; doing so WILL result in severe engine damage.

• Timing belt maintenance is extremely important! Many models utilize an interference-type, non-freewheeling engine. If the timing belt breaks, the valves in the cylinder head may strike the pistons, causing potentially serious (also time-consuming and expensive) engine damage. Refer to the maintenance interval charts in the front of this manual for the recommended replace-ment interval for the timing belt, and to the timing belt section for belt replacement and inspection.

• Disconnecting the negative battery cable on some vehicles may interfere with the functions of the on-board computer system(s) and may require the computer to undergo a relearning process once the negative battery cable is reconnected.

• When servicing drum brakes, only disassemble and assemble one side at a time, leaving the remaining side intact for reference.

• Only an MVAC-trained, EPA-certified automotive technician should service the A/C system or its components.

ENGINE REPAIR

Distributor

REMOVAL

1. Before servicing the vehicle, refer to the precautions in the beginning of this section.

2. Disconnect the negative battery cable.

3. Position the No. 1 piston at Top Dead Center (TDC) of the compression stroke.

4. Loosen the distributor cap screws and position the cap to one side.

5. Make a matchmark with a scribe or marker on the distributor base flange and the cylinder head.

6. Mark the position of the rotor on the distributor housing.

7. Disengage the distributor electrical connections.

8. Loosen the distributor hold-down bolts.

9. Remove the distributor from the engine.

10. Inspect the distributor O-ring, if damaged or worn, replace it with a new one.

INSTALLATION

Timing Not Disturbed

➡**When installing the distributor, be sure the offset drive tangs engage the camshaft slots.**

1. Ensure the No. 1 piston is still at TDC on the compression stroke.

2. Install the distributor and align the matchmarks on the distributor base flange and cylinder head. Also be sure that the rotor points toward the mark on the distributor housing made previously. Make certain the rotor is pointing to the No. 1 mark on the distributor base.

3. When all the marks are aligned, install the distributor hold-down bolts and tighten them to 14–19 ft. lbs. (19–25 Nm).

4. Install the cap and tighten the screws.

5. Connect the negative battery cable.

6. Engage the electrical connections.

7. Install the No. 1 spark plug, if removed.

8. Recheck the initial timing, and adjust if necessary.

Timing Disturbed

➡**When installing the distributor, be sure the offset drive tangs engage the camshaft slots.**

1. Ensure the No. 1 piston is still at TDC on the compression stroke.

➡**If the engine was disturbed while the distributor was removed, it will be necessary to remove the No. 1 spark plug and rotate the engine clockwise until the No. 1 piston is on the compression stroke. Align the timing marks.**

2. If installing the old distributor:

a. Install the distributor and align the matchmarks on the distributor base flange and cylinder head. Also be sure that the rotor points toward the mark on the distributor housing made previously. Make certain the rotor is pointing to the No. 1 mark on the distributor base.

3. If installing a new distributor:

a. Install the rotor and cap (with wires still attached) on the distributor, then follow the No. 1 spark plug wire from the plug to the cap; this will be the No. 1 tower on the cap. Mark the location of the tower on the distributor housing, then remove the cap.

b. Install the distributor and be sure the rotor aligns with the No.1 tower mark made on the distributor.

4. When all the marks are aligned, install the distributor hold-down bolts and tighten them to 14–19 ft. lbs. (19–25 Nm).

5. Install the cap and tighten the screws.

6. Connect the negative battery cable.

7. Engage the electrical connections.

8. Install the No. 1 spark plug, if removed.

9. Recheck the initial timing, and adjust if necessary.

Ignition Timing

ADJUSTMENT

1. Before servicing the vehicle, refer to the precautions in the beginning of this section.

2. Start the vehicle and let it reach operating temperature.

3. Turn all accessories OFF.

4. Connect a timing light according to the tool manufacturer's instructions.

5. Check the timing by aiming the light at the timing pointer on the timing belt cover. The yellow timing mark on the crankshaft pulley should line up with the mark on the pointer and should read 10 ° Before Top Dead Center (BTDC).

6. If the timing is incorrect, loosen the distributor hold-down bolts.

7. Rotate the distributor until the desired timing is achieved.

8. Tighten the distributor hold-down bolts to 14–19 ft. lbs. (19–25 Nm).

9. Recheck the timing and if it is still correct, remove the light.

10. If the timing is still incorrect, repeat Steps 5 through 8.

DISTRIBUTOR 12127

CAMSHAFT SLOTS

OFFSET DRIVE TANGS

Distributor

7922GG01

View of the cylinder head and the drive side of the distributor showing the offset drive tangs and the camshaft slots

CRANKSHAFT PULLEY 6A312

WHITE TIMING MARK 10° BTDC

TIMING ANALYZER

7922GG34

Clean the timing marks with a shop rag to help view them with the timing light

Engine Assembly

REMOVAL & INSTALLATION

1. Before servicing the vehicle, refer to the precautions in the beginning of this section.
2. Disconnect the negative battery cable.
3. Relieve the fuel system pressure.
4. Remove the battery and tray.
5. Remove the hood.
6. Remove the air cleaner assembly and hoses.
7. Remove the electric cooling fan and the radiator.
8. Disconnect the accelerator cable from the throttle body.
9. Loosen the accelerator shaft bracket bolts and remove the bracket.
10. Disconnect the speedometer cable from the transaxle.
11. Disconnect the fuel tube hose and tube from the injection supply manifold.
12. Disconnect the hoses from the heater core.
13. Disconnect the power brake booster hose, vacuum modulator hose and governor hose.
14. Tag and disengage all the engine harness electrical connections and grounds.
15. On automatic transaxles, tag and disengage the Park/Neutral safety switch and the kickdown solenoid electrical connections and the transaxle ground.
16. On manual transaxles, tag and disengage the Park/Neutral safety switch electrical connection, the transaxle ground and disconnect the clutch cable.
17. On automatic transaxles, remove the shift-to-manual shaft boot, then disconnect the shift cable and bracket from the transaxle.
18. On manual transaxles, disconnect the transaxle gearshift rod and clevis. Disconnect the gearshift lever stabilizer bar and support from the transaxle.
19. Remove all the drive belts, then tag and disconnect the power steering hydraulic lines from the pump, then remove the pump.
20. Raise the vehicle and safely support it.
21. Drain the engine oil and transaxle fluid.
22. Remove the front wheels and splash shields.
23. Loosen the front suspension lower arm clamp bolts and nuts. Pull the arms downward, separating the arms from the wheel knuckles.

24. Remove the halfshafts from each side and install plugs in the transaxle to avoid leakage or contamination.
25. Loosen the power steering pump bolts and separate the pump from the engine.
26. Remove the A/C compressor.
27. Disconnect the exhaust inlet pipe.
28. Loosen the front and rear transaxle support insulator nuts.
29. Loosen the muffler pipe bracket bolts and remove the bracket.
30. Loosen the transaxle case-to-block front bracket and case rear bracket bolts. Remove the brackets.
31. Loosen the engine rear plate bolt and remove the plate.
32. On automatic transaxles, loosen the flywheel-to-torque converter nuts.
33. Lower the vehicle.
34. Tag and disconnect all vacuum lines.
35. Using an engine hoist and chain, attach lifting hooks to the lifting eyes and remove all slack in the chain.
36. Loosen the engine mount through-bolt and nut.
37. Remove the engine and transaxle from the engine compartment as an assembly.
38. If necessary, loosen the transaxle-to-engine bolts and separate the two components.

FRONT SUSPENSION
LOWER ARM
BALL JOINT BOLT

7922GG02

Use two wrenches (one as a back-up) to loosen the front suspension lower arm clamp bolts and nuts

REAR ENGINE SUPPORT   REAR TRANSAXLE SUPPORT INSULATOR NUTS

FRONT TRANSAXLE SUPPORT INSULATOR NUTS

7922GG03

Location of the front and rear transaxle support insulator nuts

ENGINE LIFTING EYES

7922GG04

To avoid damaging the engine, attach the hoist chain to the lifting eyes as shown

To install:

39. Connect the transaxle to the engine and lower them as an assembly into the engine compartment.
40. Install the engine mount through-bolt and nut. Tighten the bolt to 39–47 ft. lbs. (53–64 Nm).
41. Remove the lifting cables.
42. Connect all vacuum lines.
43. Raise the vehicle and safely support it.
44. On automatic transaxles, install the flywheel-to-torque converter nuts. Tighten the nuts to 25–36 ft. lbs. (34–49 Nm).
45. Install the engine rear plate and bolt. Tighten the bolt to 61–87 inch lbs. (7–10 Nm).
46. Install the transaxle case-to-engine block front bracket and case rear bracket bolts. Tighten the bolts to 27–38 ft. lbs. (37–52 Nm).
47. Install the muffler pipe bracket and bolts. Tighten the bolts to 28–41 ft. lbs. (38–56 Nm).
48. Install the front and rear transaxle support insulator nuts. Tighten the rear nuts to 21–34 ft. lbs. (28–46 Nm) and the front nuts to 27–38 ft. lbs. (37–52 Nm).
49. Install the starter motor and exhaust inlet pipe.
50. Install the A/C compressor.
51. Engage the power steering pump to the engine, install the bolts and tighten them to 27–40 ft. lbs. (36–54 Nm).
52. Remove the plugs from the transaxle and install the halfshafts.

53. Engage the suspension lower arms to the wheel knuckles. Install the clamp nuts and bolts. Tighten the bolts and nuts to 32–40 ft. lbs. (43–54 Nm).

54. Install the splash shields and tires. Tighten the wheel hub bolt to 65–87 ft. lbs. (88–118 Nm).

55. On manual transaxles perform the following:

    a. Connect the transaxle gearshift rod and clevis.

    b. Connect the gearshift lever stabilizer bar and support to the transaxle.

    c. Engage the clutch cable and the starter motor electrical connections.

    d. Engage the Park/Neutral safety switch, back-up lamp switch and the transaxle ground.

56. Lower the vehicle.

57. Connect the power steering lines and install the drive belts.

58. On automatic transaxles, connect the shift cable and bracket. Engage the Park/Neutral safety switch and the kickdown solenoid electrical connections and the transaxle ground.

59. Reattach all of the engine harness electrical connections and grounds.

60. Connect the power brake booster hose, vacuum modulator hose and governor hose.

61. Connect the hoses to the heater core.

62. Connect the fuel tube and hose to the injection supply manifold.

63. Connect the speedometer cable to the transaxle.

64. Install the accelerator shaft bracket and tighten the bolts.

65. Connect the accelerator cable to the throttle body.

66. Install the radiator and electric cooling fan.

67. Install the air cleaner assembly and connect the hoses.

68. Install the hood.

69. Install the battery and tray.

70. Fill and bleed the cooling system.

71. Fill the transaxle with MERCON® automatic transmission fluid.

72. Fill the crankcase with engine oil.

73. Connect the battery cables and check for proper engine operation.

Water Pump

REMOVAL & INSTALLATION

1. Before servicing the vehicle, refer to the precautions in the beginning of this section.

2. Disconnect the negative battery cable.

3. Remove the timing belt.

4. Drain the cooling system into a suitable container.

5. Remove the two bolts attaching the inlet tube to the water pump housing. Remove the inlet tube and gasket.

6. Remove the four water pump-to-cylinder block retaining bolts and remove the water pump.

7. Remove all existing gasket material from the cylinder block and inlet tube gasket surfaces.

To install:

8. Coat both sides of the new water pump and inlet tube gaskets with a suitable water resistant sealer. Apply the gaskets to the engine and inlet tube surfaces. Make certain the gasket holes are aligned with the bolt holes.

9. Position the water pump against the gasket. Be sure the holes in the water pump are aligned with the gasket holes and that the pump does not shift the position of the gasket.

10. Install the four water pump retaining bolts and tighten to 14–19 ft. lbs. (19–26 Nm).

1	Cylinder Block
2	Heater Water Hose
3	Water Inlet Connection
4	Hot Water Heater Elbow Connector Bolt (2 Req'd)
5	Water Pump Inlet Gasket
6	O-Ring
7	Water Pump Bolt (4 Req'd)
8	Water Pump
9	Water Pump Housing Gasket
A	Tighten to 19-30 N·m (14-22 Lb-Ft)
B	Tighten to 19-26 N·m (14-19 Lb-Ft)

7922GG05

Exploded view of the water pump and its related components

11. Position the inlet tube and gasket against the water pump housing and install the attaching bolts. Tighten the bolts to 14–22 ft. lbs. (19–30 Nm).

12. Install the timing belt.

13. Fill the cooling system.

14. Connect the negative battery cable.

15. Start the engine and allow it to reach normal operating temperature. Check for coolant leaks and proper operation.

Cylinder Head

REMOVAL & INSTALLATION

1. Before servicing the vehicle, refer to the precautions in the beginning of this section.

2. Disconnect the negative battery cable.

3. Drain the cooling system.

4. Tag and disconnect the spark plug wires from the plugs.

5. Remove the distributor.

6. Remove the timing belt and the valve cover.

7. Remove the exhaust and intake manifolds.

8. Remove the front and rear engine lift hangers. Disengage the engine block ground wire.

9. Tag and disengage all wiring harness connectors.

10. Use a pair of pliers to compress the upper radiator hose clamp and slide it away from the radiator. Disconnect the upper radiator hose from the radiator.

11. Remove the water bypass tube (or hose) and bracket.

12. Remove the ten cylinder head bolts.

13. Remove the cylinder head and gasket from the engine.

FRONT OF ENGINE

7922GG06

Be sure to position the gasket properly on the engine block before installing the cylinder head to ensure proper sealing

Timing belt service is covered in Section 5 of this manual

Tighten the cylinder head bolts in the order shown to the proper specification

To install:

14. Use a scraper to clean any old gasket material residue from the cylinder head gasket mating surfaces.

➡ **The cylinder head gasket has marks on one of its edges that match the shape of the cylinder head, when the gasket is installed these marks must align properly before cylinder head installation.**

15. Install a new gasket and place the cylinder head in position.

16. Install NEW cylinder head bolts and tighten them with a torque wrench in the sequence illustrated and also in the following order:
 • First pass: 35–40 ft. lbs. (50–60 Nm)
 • Second pass: 56–60 ft. lbs. (75–81 Nm).

17. Install the water bypass tube (or hose) and bracket.

18. Connect the upper radiator hose and engage the clamp.

19. Engage all wiring harness connectors.

20. Engage the engine ground wire, then install the front and rear engine lift hangers.

21. Install the distributor, the intake and exhaust manifolds, the valve cover, and the timing belt.

22. Connect the spark plug wires to the plugs.

23. Fill the cooling system and install the radiator cap.

24. Connect the negative battery cable.

25. When the engine is warmed up, check for leaks.

Rocker Arms/Shafts

REMOVAL & INSTALLATION

1. Before servicing the vehicle, refer to the precautions in the beginning of this section.

2. Disconnect the negative battery cable.

3. Disconnect the accelerator cable from the throttle lever and routing bracket.

4. Remove the PCV valve and the oil separator hose.

5. Remove the air cleaner-to-intake manifold tube.

6. Remove the spark plug wires from the routing clips.

7. Remove the upper timing belt cover.

8. Remove the six valve cover retaining bolts. Remove the valve cover and discard the gasket.

9. Loosen the ten rocker arm shaft retaining bolts in the proper sequence, and remove the bolts and seats from the shafts.

10. Remove the rocker arm/shaft assemblies from the engine. If the shafts are to be disassembled, keep all parts in order so they can be assembled in their correct positions.

To install:

11. Clean all gasket mating surfaces.

12. If disassembled, coat the rocker arms and shafts with clean engine oil and reassemble.

13. The intake rocker arm shaft can be

Exploded view of the rocker arm/shaft assemblies' mounting

Rocker arm and shaft retaining bolt loosening and tightening sequence

Method of identifying the intake and exhaust rocker arm shafts

identified from the exhaust rocker arm shaft by measuring the distance between the oiling holes **A** and **B**.

14. Install the rocker arm/shaft assemblies with the shaft retaining bolts and seats. Tighten the bolts, in sequence, to 16–21 ft. lbs. (22–28 Nm).

15. Install the valve cover with a new gasket. Tighten the six valve cover retaining bolts to 44–79 inch lbs. (5–9 Nm).

16. Install the upper timing belt cover.

17. Install the spark plug wires onto the routing clips.

18. Install the PCV valve and the oil separator hose onto the valve cover.

19. Install the accelerator cable.

20. Install the air cleaner-to-intake manifold tube.

21. Connect the negative battery cable.

22. Run the engine, and check for leaks and proper engine operation.

Intake Manifold

REMOVAL & INSTALLATION

Upper Manifold

1. Before servicing the vehicle, refer to the precautions in the beginning of this section.

2. Disconnect the negative battery cable.

3. Relieve the fuel system pressure.

4. Drain the engine cooling system.

5. Loosen the upper intake manifold support bolts, then remove the support.

6. Disconnect the accelerator cable from the throttle lever.

7. Disconnect the air cleaner-to-intake manifold tube.

8. Tag and disconnect the coolant hoses from the upper manifold.

9. Tag and disconnect all wiring and hoses that will interfere with manifold removal.

10. Loosen the upper intake manifold-to-lower intake manifold bolts.

11. Remove the upper intake manifold and gasket.

12. Insert clean shop rags into the lower manifold passages to prevent dirt or other debris from entering the engine.

To install:

13. Use a scraper to clean any old gasket material residue from the upper and lower manifold mating surfaces.

14. Remove the rags from the lower intake manifold.

15. Install a new gasket and place the upper intake manifold in position.

16. Install the upper intake manifold-to-lower intake manifold bolts. Tighten the bolts to 14–20 ft. lbs. (19–26 Nm).

17. Connect the coolant hoses to the upper manifold.

18. Engage all wiring and hoses that were tagged and disconnected during removal.

19. Connect the air cleaner-to-intake manifold tube.

20. Connect the accelerator cable to the throttle lever.

21. Install the upper intake manifold support, then tighten the bolts to 22–34 ft. lbs. (31–46 Nm).

22. Fill the cooling system and connect the negative battery cable.

23. Start the vehicle and check for proper engine operation.

Lower Manifold

1. Remove the upper intake manifold

2. Tag and disconnect all wiring and hoses that will interfere with lower manifold removal.

3. Loosen the lower intake manifold-to-cylinder head bolts.

➡**You may have to raise the vehicle to unfasten the lower nut on the passenger's side of the manifold.**

4. Remove the intake manifold and gasket.

5. Insert clean shop rags into the cylinder head openings to prevent dirt or other debris from entering the engine.

To install:

6. Use a scraper to clean any old gasket material residue from the cylinder head and intake manifold mating surfaces.

7. Remove the rags from the cylinder head openings.

8. Install a new gasket and place the intake manifold in position.

9. Install the intake manifold-to-cylinder head bolts. Tighten the bolts to 14–20 ft. lbs. (19–26 Nm).

10. Install the intake manifold support, then tighten the bolts to 22–34 ft. lbs. (31–46 Nm).

11. Install the upper intake manifold.

Exhaust Manifold

REMOVAL & INSTALLATION

1. Before servicing the vehicle, refer to the precautions in the beginning of this section.

2. Disconnect the negative battery cable.

3. Raise and safely support the vehicle.

4. Remove the exhaust inlet pipe-to-exhaust manifold nuts and washers.

5. Remove the muffler pipe bracket bolts.

6. Lower the vehicle.

7. Remove the air cleaner-to-intake manifold tube.

8. Remove the exhaust manifold heat shield bolts and the shield.

9. Separate the Oxygen (O2S) sensor wiring connector from the routing bracket and disconnect the electrical connector.

10. Remove the O2S sensor. Inspect the sensor gasket for damage and replace if necessary.

11. Remove the four exhaust manifold retaining bolts and three nuts.

12. Remove the exhaust manifold from the vehicle.

13. Remove the inlet pipe and exhaust manifold gaskets and discard.

During installation, be sure the ignition wires are not pinched between the manifold and cylinder head

To install:

14. Remove all existing gasket material from the exhaust manifold and cylinder head inlet pipe. Clean all threaded surfaces.

15. Apply a new gasket onto the cylinder head studs and position the exhaust manifold onto the gasket. Install the attaching nuts and bolts and tighten to 12–17 ft. lbs. (16–23 Nm).

16. Position a new gasket on the O_2S sensor, if needed, and install it in the exhaust manifold.

17. Position the heat shield and tighten the bolts to 12–17 ft. lbs. (16–23 Nm).

18. Engage the O_2S sensor electrical connector and secure the wiring harness in the routing bracket.

19. Install the air cleaner-to-intake manifold tube.

20. Raise and safely support the vehicle.

21. Position a new muffler inlet pipe gasket over the exhaust manifold studs.

22. Raise the exhaust inlet pipe into position on the exhaust manifold and support by hand. Install the attaching nuts and washers and tighten to 23–34 ft. lbs. (31–46 Nm).

23. Position the muffler pipe bracket and install the bolts. Tighten to 28–47 ft. lbs. (38–56 Nm).

24. Lower the vehicle.

25. Connect the negative battery cable.

26. Start the engine and inspect for exhaust leaks.

Front Crankshaft Seal

REMOVAL & INSTALLATION

The timing belt must be removed for this procedure. The crankshaft seal is located behind the crankshaft sprocket in the oil pump front housing.

1. Before servicing the vehicle, refer to the precautions in the beginning of this section.

2. Disconnect the negative battery cable.

3. Remove the accessory drive belts.

4. Remove the timing belt cover and the timing belt.

5. Remove the crankshaft sprocket and crankshaft key.

6. Using seal remover T92C-6700-CH or equivalent, remove the crankshaft front seal from the oil pump housing.

CRANKSHAFT FRONT SEAL

SEAL REMOVER
T92C-6700-CH

7922GG12

When removing the front crankshaft seal, be careful not to damage the crankshaft threads or the seal bore

To install:

7. Lubricate the lip of the new seal and the crankshaft seal surface with clean engine oil.

8. Using front seal installer T87C-6019-A or equivalent, draw the front crankshaft seal into the oil pump housing.

9. Install the crankshaft sprocket and key.

10. Install the timing belt and timing belt cover.

11. Install the accessory drive belts.

12. Connect the negative battery cable.

13. Run the engine and check for oil leaks and proper engine operation.

Camshaft and Valve Lifters

REMOVAL & INSTALLATION

1. Before servicing the vehicle, refer to the precautions in the beginning of this section.

2. Remove the battery.

3. Remove the timing belt and valve cover.

4. Remove the camshaft sprocket and the distributor.

5. Remove the rocker arm/shaft assemblies.

6. Pull the lash adjuster from the rocker arm.

7. Loosen the camshaft thrust plate bolt and remove the thrust plate.

8. Gently pull the camshaft from the left-hand side of the cylinder head.

To install:

9. Clean the camshaft and cylinder head surface.

➡**Inspect the camshaft oil seal and replace it if necessary.**

10. Coat the surfaces of the camshaft with clean engine oil and gently install the camshaft into the left-hand side of the cylinder head.

11. Install the camshaft thrust plate and bolt. Tighten the bolt to 71–88 inch lbs. (8–10 Nm).

12. Pour clean engine oil into the oil reservoir in the rocker arm and apply engine oil to the lash adjuster.

✳✳ WARNING

Be careful not to damage the O-ring when installing the adjuster.

13. Insert the adjuster into the rocker arm.

14. Install the rocker arm/shaft assemblies and the distributor.

15. Install the camshaft sprocket.

16. Install the valve cover and the timing belt.

17. Adjust the camshaft timing.

18. Install the battery.

19. Start the vehicle and check for proper engine operation.

CYLINDER HEAD

FRONT CAMSHAFT

7922GG35

Lubricate the machined surfaces of the camshaft during installation to prevent premature wear

ROCKER ARM 6564

OIL RESERVOIR

HYDRAULIC LASH ADJUSTER 6C501

7922GG13

The lash adjuster is located in a bore in the underside of the rocker arm

Valve Lash

ADJUSTMENT

No valve lash adjustment is necessary. The hydraulic lash adjuster maintains zero clearance between the camshaft lobes and the valve stems. Inspect lash adjuster operation by pushing down on each rocker arm by hand without the engine running. If a rocker arm moves down with little force, the lash adjuster is collapsed and may need replacing. Check for signs of damage or wear to the valvetrain components.

Oil Pan

REMOVAL & INSTALLATION

1. Before servicing the vehicle, refer to the precautions in the beginning of this section.
2. Raise and safely support the vehicle.
3. Drain the engine oil into a suitable container.
4. Remove the exhaust header pipe.
5. Remove the oil pan-to-cylinder block retaining nuts and bolts. Lower the oil pan and discard the old gasket.

To install:
6. Clean the oil pan and cylinder block sealing surfaces to remove all traces of existing gasket material. Thoroughly clean the oil pan.
7. Apply a suitable oil resistant sealant to the joint lines formed at the cylinder block and front and rear engine covers.
8. Apply a new gasket onto the oil pan.
9. Position the oil pan and gasket against the cylinder block and install the

Apply sealer at these locations to ensure a good seal

7922GG14

retaining nuts and bolts. Tighten the oil pan nuts and bolts in an alternating pattern to 69–78 inch lbs. (8–9 Nm). Do not over-tighten the bolts or the gasket will split.
10. Install the oil pan drain plug and tighten to 22–30 ft. lbs. (29–41 Nm).
11. Lower the vehicle.
12. Install the exhaust header pipe.
13. Fill the crankcase with the proper amount of clean engine oil.
14. Run the engine and check for oil leaks.

Oil Pump

REMOVAL & INSTALLATION

1. Before servicing the vehicle, refer to the precautions in the beginning of this section.
2. Raise and safely support the vehicle.
3. Remove the timing belt covers and the timing belt.
4. Remove the crankshaft sprocket.
5. Drain the engine oil and remove the oil pan.

7922GG15

Exploded view of the oil pump assembly and mounting bolt locations

6. If equipped, remove the Crankshaft Position (CKP) sensor bracket bolt and move the sensor and bracket aside.
7. Remove the six oil pump assembly retaining bolts and remove the oil pump assembly and gasket from the engine. Discard the gasket.
8. Remove the oil pump pick-up tube and screen, if required.
9. Disassemble the oil pump and inspect all components as necessary. Replace the oil pump if needed.

To install:
10. Clean all gasket mating surfaces. If disassembled, clean the oil pump housing and components with a suitable solvent and allow to dry. Reassemble the oil pump, lubricating all components with clean engine oil. Install a new front crankshaft seal using a suitable seal installer.
11. Carefully coat both sides of the new oil pump gasket with a suitable sealant compound. Apply the gasket to the oil pump and remove any excess sealant.

➡**Do not allow the sealant compound to enter the oil pump discharge opening once the gasket is in place. This opening must be free and clear before the oil pump is installed onto the cylinder block.**

12. Position the oil pump on the cylinder block mating surface and install the six retaining bolts. Tighten the bolts to 14–19 ft. lbs. (19–25 Nm).
13. If removed, install a new gasket on the oil pump pick-up tube and screen. Position the oil pump pick-up tube and screen on the oil pump and install the two retaining bolts. Tighten the bolts to 69–95 inch lbs. (8–11 Nm).
14. If removed, install the CKP and tighten the bracket bolt to 25 inch lbs. (3 Nm).
15. Install the oil pan.
16. Install the crankshaft.
17. Install the timing belt and the timing belt covers.
18. Lower the vehicle.

✳✳ WARNING

Operating the engine without the proper amount and type of engine oil will result in severe engine damage.

19. Fill the crankcase to the proper level with engine oil.
20. Run the engine and check for leaks and proper engine operation.

Refer to Section 1 for engine rebuilding specifications

Rear Main Seal

REMOVAL & INSTALLATION

1. Before servicing the vehicle, refer to the precautions in the beginning of this section.

2. Remove the transaxle from the vehicle.

3. Remove the six flywheel retaining bolts and the flywheel from the rear of the engine.

4. Remove the flywheel reinforcing plate bolt and the flywheel reinforcing plate.

5. Remove the rear oil seal using Seal Remover tool T92C-6700-CH, or equivalent.

To install:

6. Clean the sealing surface of the oil seal retainer.

7. Apply clean engine oil to the inside and outside of the new seal. Install the seal with the lip of the seal facing the engine using Seal Replacer T87C-6701-A, or equivalent.

➡**Two flywheel retaining bolts may be used along with the seal replacer tool to install the rear crankshaft seal.**

8. Install the flywheel reinforcing plate and bolt. Tighten the bolt to 71–97 inch lbs. (8–11 Nm).

9. Install the flywheel and tighten the six bolts to 71–76 ft. lbs. (96–103 Nm).

10. Install the transaxle.

When installing a new rear main seal, be sure to use the proper tool, such as Seal Replacer T87C-6701-A

FUEL SYSTEM

Fuel System Service Precautions

Safety is the most important factor when performing not only fuel system maintenance, but any type of maintenance. Failure to conduct maintenance and repairs in a safe manner may result in serious personal injury or death. Work on a vehicle's fuel system components can be accomplished safely and effectively by adhering to the precautions listed in the beginning of this section along with the following rules and guidelines:

• To avoid the possibility of fire and personal injury, always disconnect the negative battery cable unless the repair or test procedure requires that battery voltage by applied.

• Always relieve the fuel system pressure prior to disconnecting any fuel system component (injector, fuel rail, pressure regulator, etc.) fitting or fuel line connection. Exercise extreme caution whenever relieving fuel system pressure to avoid exposing skin, face and eyes to fuel spray. Please be advised that fuel under pressure may penetrate the skin or any part of the body that it contacts.

• Always place a shop towel or cloth around the fitting or connection prior to loosening to absorb any excess fuel due to spillage. Ensure that all fuel spillage is quickly remove from engine surfaces. Ensure that all fuel-soaked cloths or towels are deposited into a flame-proof waste container with a lid.

• Always keep a dry chemical (Class B) fire extinguisher near the work area.

• Do not allow fuel spray or fuel vapors to come into contact with a spark or open flame.

• Always use a second wrench when loosening or tightening fuel line connections fittings. This will prevent unnecessary stress and torsion to fuel piping.

• Always replace worn fuel fitting O-rings with new ones. Do not substitute fuel hose where rigid pipe is installed.

Fuel System Pressure

RELIEVING

1. Before servicing the vehicle, refer to the precautions in the beginning of this section.

2. Remove the fuel tank filler cap.

3. Unplug the fuel pump relay electrical connection, which is located behind the left-hand side of the instrument panel.

4. Turn the engine **ON** and let it idle normally.

5. The engine will stall, when it does, turn the ignition key **OFF** and engage the fuel pump relay electrical connection.

Fuel pump relay location

➡**The fuel system pressure has now been relieved and will remain so until the engine is turned ON.**

Fuel Filter

REMOVAL & INSTALLATION

1. Before servicing the vehicle, refer to the precautions in the beginning of this section.

2. Properly relieve the fuel system pressure.

3. Disconnect the negative battery cable.

4. Loosen the clamp and disconnect the fuel supply line at the inlet of the fuel filter. Plug the end to prevent spillage.

5. Loosen the clamp and disconnect the fuel return line at the fuel filter outlet fitting.

6. Remove the filter bracket attaching bolt and nuts from the fuel filter.

7. Remove the fuel filter from the bracket and properly dispose.

To install:

8. Install the new fuel filter into the bracket. Be sure the filter is positioned in the proper direction of fuel flow.

9. Connect the fuel return line to the fuel filter outlet fitting. Install the fuel filter bracket bolt and nuts and tighten to 71–97 inch lbs. (8–11 Nm).

10. Remove the plug from the fuel supply line and connect it to the fuel filter inlet. Secure it with the clamp.

11. Connect the negative battery cable.

12. Run the engine and check for fuel leaks.

Fuel Pump

REMOVAL & INSTALLATION

1. Before servicing the vehicle, refer to the precautions in the beginning of this section.

2. Properly relieve the fuel system pressure.

Fuel system component identification

When removing the fuel pump housing from the fuel tank, slowly pull it out to prevent fuel from splashing

3. Disconnect the negative battery cable.

4. Remove the rear seat cushion and cover.

5. Remove the three luggage compartment floor cover hold-down pins and fold the luggage compartment floor cover forward until the sending unit access plate is visible.

6. On 2-door vehicles, remove the six inner rear floor filler cover bolts and the two inner rear floor filler cover nuts.

7. Remove the inner rear floor filler cover.

8. Remove the four fuel pump assembly

Remove the mounting screws to separate the fuel pump from the housing during pump replacement

access plate screws, the ground lead, and the sending unit access plate from the chassis.

9. Detach the fuel pump and sending unit electrical connector.

10. On 4-door vehicles, remove the 2-way check valve bolt and the 2-way check valve from the bracket on the fuel pump and sending unit housing.

11. Loosen the two hose clamps and disconnect the two hoses from the fittings on the fuel pump and sending unit housing.

12. Matchmark the fuel pump assembly to the fuel tank.

13. Remove the four screws (2-door) or eight screws (4-door) and lift the fuel pump and sending unit housing from the fuel tank.

14. Detach the fuel tank sending unit electrical connector.

15. Remove the two fuel tank sending unit washers and nuts and the fuel tank sending unit.

16. Remove the fuel pump screw, fuel pump grommet and the fuel pump bracket from the bottom of the fuel pump.

17. Remove the fuel filter bracket, fuel filter and the retainer from the fuel pump.

18. Detach the fuel pump electrical connector.

19. Remove the clamp and the fuel pump from the housing.

To install:

20. Position the fuel pump on the housing and secure with the clamp.

21. Install the fuel tank sender filter, bracket and the retainer on the fuel pump.

22. Clip the fuel tank sender bracket onto the fuel pump.

23. Install the grommet, screw and the bracket onto the bottom of the fuel pump.

24. Position the fuel tank sending unit on the housing and install the sending unit washers and nuts.

25. Connect the fuel tank sending unit electrical connector.

26. Place the fuel pump and sending unit housing into the fuel tank opening, making sure the matchmarks are properly aligned, and install the four screws (2-door) or eight screws (4-door).

27. Install the two fuel hoses on the two sending unit hose fittings and tighten the two hose clamps.

28. On 4-door vehicles, position the 2-way check valve on the fuel pump and sending unit housing and secure with the bolt.

29. Connect the fuel pump and sending unit electrical connector.

30. Connect the negative battery cable.

31. Start the engine and check for leaks at the fuel line connections and proper fuel pump operation. Turn the engine **OFF**.

32. Install the four fuel pump and sending unit access plate screws, the ground lead and the fuel pump and sending unit access plate.

33. Fold the luggage compartment floor cover over the fuel pump and sending unit access plate and install the three hold-down pins.

34. Install the rear seat cushion and cover.

DRIVE TRAIN

➡**For CV-joint replacement procedures, refer to the applicable Unit Repair Section in the beginning of this manual.**

Transaxle Assembly

REMOVAL & INSTALLATION

Manual

1. Before servicing the vehicle, refer to the precautions in the beginning of this section.

2. Disconnect the negative battery cable.

3. Unplug the two back-up light switch wiring connectors.

4. Remove the clutch cable adjusting nut and disengage the cable from the release lever. Pull the cable through the clutch cable bracket.

5. Remove the engine compartment wiring harness ground strap from the transaxle.

6. Remove the starter motor.

7. Loosen the speedometer cable

When removing the gearshift rod and clevis, note the position of the washers

Support the transaxle before removing the transaxle case rear bracket

retainer and disconnect the speedometer cable.

8. Remove the 2 bolts from the top of the clutch housing.

9. Install 3 Bar Engine Support tool D88L-6000-A, or equivalent. Properly secure the engine to the engine support tool.

10. Raise and safely support the vehicle.

11. Remove the halfshafts.

12. Install a Differential Side Gear Plug tool T87C-7025-C, or equivalent, to prevent the side gears from moving.

13. Remove the nut and bolt attaching the shift rod to the input shift rail.

14. Remove the gearshift stabilizer bar nut, lockwasher, and flat washer, and remove the bar from the control rod-to-support bar stud.

15. Remove the three transaxle-to-engine retaining bolts from the transaxle case rear bracket and remove the bracket.

16. Remove the three transaxle-to-engine retaining bolts from the transaxle case front bracket and remove the bracket.

17. Remove the two rear and two front transaxle support insulator nuts from the rear engine support.

18. Remove the four rear engine support rebound insulator bolts and remove the rear engine support.

19. Position a suitable transmission jack under the transaxle and secure it with a safety chain or strap.

20. Remove the four flywheel reinforcing plate bolts.

21. Remove the two remaining transaxle-to-engine block retaining bolts.

22. Carefully separate the transaxle from the engine and lower the transaxle from the vehicle.

To install:
23. Raise the transaxle into position and seat it against the rear of the engine.

24. Install the four flywheel reinforcing plate bolts and tighten to 62–86 inch lbs. (7–10 Nm).

25. Install the two lower transaxle retaining bolts and tighten to 47–66 ft. lbs. (64–89 Nm).

26. Remove the transmission jack.

27. Position the rear engine support. Install the two rear transaxle support insulator nuts and tighten to 21–34 ft. lbs. (28–46 Nm.).

28. Install the two front transaxle support insulator nuts and tighten to 32–38 ft. lbs. (43–52 Nm.).

29. Install the four rear engine support rebound insulator bolts and tighten to 47–66 ft. lbs. (64–89 Nm.).

30. Install the transaxle case-to-cylinder block front and rear brackets and install the

three bolts on each. Tighten the bolts to 27–38 ft. lbs. (37–52 Nm.).

31. Install the washer and the gearshift stabilizer bar on the control rod-to-support bar stud.

32. Install the washer, lockwasher, and gearshift stabilizer bar nut. Tighten the nut to 28–38 ft. lbs. (38–52 Nm.).

33. Position the gearshift rod and clevis on the main shift control shaft, and install the selector shift rod adjustment sleeve. Tighten the nut to 12–17 ft. lbs. (16–23 Nm.).

34. Route the Park/Neutral switch wiring over the rear engine support.

35. Install the halfshaft and joint assemblies.

36. Check and fill the transaxle, if needed.

37. Lower the vehicle and remove the engine support bar.

38. Install two retaining bolts at the top of the clutch housing. The top bolt is installed through the heater pipe bracket. Tighten the bolts to 47–66 ft. lbs. (64–89 Nm).

39. Connect the ground strap to the transaxle case.

40. Connect the speedometer cable onto the sleeve and hand-tighten.

41. Install the starter motor.

42. Attach the Park/Neutral and back-up light switch wiring connectors.

43. Connect the clutch cable to the release lever and adjust the clutch pedal free-play.

44. Connect the negative battery cable.

45. Road test the vehicle and check for proper transaxle operation.

Automatic

1. Before servicing the vehicle, refer to the precautions in the beginning of this section.

2. Disconnect the negative battery cable.

3. From the engine compartment, remove the manual control lever nut and arm.

4. Remove the shift cable and bracket from the transaxle.

5. Disconnect the speedometer cable from the transaxle.

6. Detach the transaxle electrical connectors, located next to the governor.

7. Disconnect the transaxle ground wire. Disconnect the transaxle vacuum hose and vent hose located below the distributor cap.

8. Remove the starter motor.

9. Remove the coolant pipe retaining bracket, located below the distributor cap.

10. Remove the two upper bell housing bolts.

11. Support the engine using Engine Support Bar tool D87L-6000-a or equivalent.

12. Raise and safely support the vehicle.

13. Remove the front wheel and tire assemblies.

14. Drain the transaxle fluid.

15. Remove the front fender splash shield.

16. Remove the front stabilizer bar.

17. Remove the lower arm clamp bolts and nuts. Pull the lower arms downward, separating the lower arms from the knuckles.

➡**Use care not to damage the ball joint dust boots.**

18. Remove the tie rod cotter pin and nut. Disconnect the tie rod end from the knuckle and discard the cotter pin.

19. Remove the halfshafts. Install the Differential Plug tool T87C-7025-C, or equivalent, between the differential side gears to prevent side gear movement.

20. Remove the front and rear transaxle support insulator nuts.

21. Remove the four rear engine support rebound insulator bolts and the transmission support crossmember.

22. Remove the front transaxle support insulator through-bolt and nut. Remove the front transaxle support insulator.

23. Remove the four front transaxle support bracket bolts and the front transaxle support bracket.

24. Remove the two rear transaxle support bracket bolts and the rear transaxle support bracket and insulator.

25. Remove the intake manifold support.

26. Remove the three transaxle-to-engine bolts and remove the transaxle case rear bracket.

27. Remove the three transaxle-to-engine bolts from the transaxle case-to-cylinder block front bracket and remove the bracket.

28. Remove the flywheel cover bolts and cover.

29. Using a wrench, rotate the crankshaft pulley bolt clockwise to gain access to the four torque converter-to-flywheel nuts, and remove all nuts.

30. Make alignment marks between the oil cooler tubes and hoses. Disconnect and plug the oil cooler lines.

31. Position a transmission jack under the transaxle and secure it with a chain or strap.

32. Remove the remaining engine-to-transaxle retaining bolts.

33. Carefully separate and lower the transaxle from the vehicle.

To install:

34. Raise the transaxle into position and install the two engine-to-transaxle bolts. Be sure that the torque converter is in alignment with the flexplate. Tighten to 47–66 ft. lbs. (64–89 Nm).

35. Remove the transaxle jack.

36. Install the starter motor.

37. Install the torque converter bolts and tighten to 26–36 ft. lbs. (34–49 Nm).

38. Install the flywheel cover and tighten the bolts to 71–97 inch lbs. (8–11 Nm).

39. Position the front transaxle-to-engine support and install the three retaining bolts. Tighten the bolts to 27–38 ft. lbs. (37–52 Nm.).

40. Install the intake manifold support and tighten the bolts to 27–38 ft. lbs. (37–52 Nm.).

41. Install the transaxle case rear bracket and three retaining bolts. Tighten the bolts to 27–38 ft. lbs. (37–52 Nm.).

42. Install the front transaxle support insulator bracket and four retaining bolts. Tighten the bolts to 28–37 ft. lbs. (38–51 Nm.).

43. Install the front transaxle support bracket and the through-bolt and nut. Do not tighten the through-bolt and nut until the rear engine support is installed.

44. Position the transmission support crossmember and install the rear engine support rebound insulator bolts. Tighten the rear engine support rebound insulator bolts to 47–66 ft. lbs. (64–89 Nm.).

45. Tighten the front transaxle support bracket through-bolt and nut to 69–83 ft. lbs. (93–113 Nm.).

46. Install the two front transaxle support insulator nuts and tighten them to 32–38 ft. lbs. (43–52 Nm).

47. Install the two rear transaxle support insulator nuts and tighten them to 21–34 ft. lbs. (28–46 Nm).

48. Remove the differential plugs and install the halfshafts.

49. Align the marks made on the oil cooler lines, and install the lines. Install the hose clamps.

50. Connect the tie rod ends to the steering knuckles and tighten the attaching nuts to 26–30 ft. lbs. (35–40 Nm). Install new cotter pins.

51. Attach the lower ball joints to the knuckles. Tighten the lower arm clamp bolt to 40–50 ft. lbs. (54–68 Nm).

52. Install the front stabilizer bar. Tighten the retaining nuts to 43–52 ft. lbs. (43–52 Nm).

53. Install the front fender splash shield and tighten the bolts to 65–95 inch lbs. (8–10 Nm.).

54. Install the front wheel and tire assemblies. Tighten the lug bolts to 65–87 ft. lbs. (88–118 Nm).

55. Lower the vehicle.

56. Remove the engine support tool.

57. Attach the shift cable and bracket to the transaxle. Install the manual control lever arm on the manual control lever. Install the retaining nut and tighten to 34–47 ft. lbs. (44–64 Nm).

✳✳ WARNING

Do not use any type of power wrench to tighten the nut. Damage to the transaxle may result.

58. Install the coolant pipe retaining bracket located below the distributor.

59. Connect the vacuum hose and vent hose located below the distributor cap.

60. Attach the transaxle electrical connectors located next to the governor.

61. Connect the ground wire to the transaxle and tighten the bolt to 65–95 inch lbs. (8–10 Nm.).

62. Connect the speedometer cable.

63. Connect the negative battery cable.

64. Fill the transaxle with Motorcraft MERCON® automatic transmission fluid to the proper level.

➡**Be sure that the gearshift lever position aligns with the manual control lever position exactly before starting the engine.**

65. Start the engine. Check for leaks and proper fluid level.

66. Road test the vehicle and check for proper operation.

Clutch

ADJUSTMENT

Clutch Cable Free-Play

1. Before servicing the vehicle, refer to the precautions in the beginning of this section.

2. Carefully move the clutch pedal back and forth and measure the amount of travel before the pedal activates the clutch. If the clutch pedal free-play is 0.35–0.59 in.

Clutch pedal free-play—specifications

Check the clearance between the release lever and connecting link

Be sure to line up the matchmarks, if re-using the pressure plate

Exploded view of the clutch assembly

(9–15mm), no adjustment is necessary. If the free-play is not within specification, proceed to Step 3.

3. Pull back the transaxle release lever (near the bell housing) and measure the clearance between the lever and the cable connecting link, as shown in the accompanying graphic. Thread the adjuster in or out until the clearance between the connecting link and the release lever is 0.06–0.10 in. (1.5–2.5mm).

4. Check the free-play at the clutch pedal. If it is not within specification, inspect the clutch release components for a problem.

5. After adjusting the clutch, be sure the clutch disengagement height is 2.92 inches (74mm) minimum.

REMOVAL & INSTALLATION

1. Before servicing the vehicle, refer to the precautions in the beginning of this section.

2. Disconnect the negative battery cable.

3. Raise and safely support the vehicle.

4. Remove the transaxle assembly.

➡During the removal procedure, do not allow oil or grease to come in contact with the clutch disc facing if the disc is to be reused. Handle the disc with clean rags wrapped around the edges and do not touch the disc facing. Even a small amount of dirt or grease may cause the clutch to grab or slip.

5. If the pressure plate is to be reused, paint or scribe alignment marks on the pressure plate and flywheel for assembly reference.

6. Install an appropriate locking tool to prevent the flywheel from turning.

7. Install a clutch aligning tool to prevent the clutch plate from dropping when the retaining bolts are removed.

8. Loosen the six pressure plate retaining bolts in a crisscross pattern, one turn at a time. This will relieve the pressure plate spring tension evenly and prevent distortion of the pressure plate. Remove the pressure plate and clutch disc once the retaining bolts are removed.

9. Inspect all clutch components including the clutch release fork and release bearing, and replace as required.

10. Inspect the flywheel for scoring, cracks and heat checks. Resurface or replace the flywheel, as necessary.

11. Inspect the pilot bearing for damage. Be sure the bearing turns easily. If replace-

ment is necessary, remove the flywheel and remove the pilot bearing.

To install:

12. If necessary, install a new pilot bearing using a suitable installation tool. Use only a driver tool that contacts the bearing outer race. A driver tool that contacts the inner race or the bearing area will damage the bearing.

13. If the flywheel was removed, clean the sealant from the flywheel retaining bolts. Coat the bolt threads with a suitable sealer compound.

14. Be sure the crankshaft flange and the back of the flywheel are clean. Position the flywheel on the crankshaft and install the six retaining bolts. Tighten the bolts to 71–76 ft. lbs. (96–103 Nm).

15. Position the clutch disc on the flywheel and install a clutch alignment tool to hold the disc in place.

➡When installing the clutch disc, be sure the disc dampener springs are facing away from the flywheel. A new disc will be stamped FLYWHEEL to indicate the correct installation position.

16. Align the reference marks, if present, and position the pressure plate on the flywheel and install the retaining bolts. Tighten the bolts evenly, in a crisscross pattern and in several steps, to 13–20 ft. lbs. (18–26 Nm). The bolts must be tightened in this manner to prevent distortion of the pressure plate.

17. Remove the clutch alignment tool.

18. Clean the clutch disc splines on the input shaft with a dry rag and coat the spline surfaces with a light film of clutch grease.

19. Install the transaxle.

20. Connect the negative battery cable.

21. Adjust the clutch pedal free-play.

22. Road test the vehicle for proper clutch operation.

Halfshaft

REMOVAL & INSTALLATION

1. Before servicing the vehicle, refer to the precautions in the beginning of this section.

2. Disconnect the negative battery cable.

3. With the vehicle sitting on all four wheels, use a small cape chisel to raise the staked portion of the front wheel hub locknut. Have an assistant apply the brakes, then loosen, but do not remove, the locknut.

4. Raise the vehicle and support it safely.

5. Drain the transaxle fluid.

6. Remove the front wheel and tire assembly.

7. Remove the ball joint clamp bolt and nut from the steering knuckle. Carefully pry the lower control arm down to disconnect the ball joint from the steering knuckle. Be careful not to tear or puncture the dust boot when disconnecting the ball joint.

8. Using a small prybar, separate the halfshaft from the transaxle.

Use a chisel to raise the staked edge of the wheel hub retaining nut, then loosen the nut

To separate the ball joint from the steering knuckle, remove the clamp bolt and nut

Use a small prybar to disengage the inner CV-joint from the transaxle, as shown

➡**The halfshaft must be separated from the transaxle gradually. If the halfshaft is yanked out suddenly, the oil seal may be damaged.**

9. Install Differential Plug tool T87C-7025-C or equivalent, to prevent the differential side gear from moving.

10. Remove and discard the wheel hub locknut.

11. Withdraw the halfshaft from the hub. Be careful not to damage the oil seal. If necessary, use a suitable wheel puller to push the halfshaft out of the hub.

To install:

12. Inspect the differential and wheel hub oil seals for damage and replace as required.

13. Remove the circlip from the inboard halfshaft spline end and replace with a new clip. Lubricate the inboard and outboard halfshaft spline ends with grease.

14. Remove the differential gear holding plug.

15. Position and install the inboard end of the halfshaft into the differential side gear. Be sure the circlip snaps into place and take care not to damage the differential oil seal.

16. Position and install the outboard end of the halfshaft into the wheel hub. Take care not to damage the wheel hub oil seal.

17. Install the wheel hub locknut onto the halfshaft and tighten it by hand.

18. Raise the lower control arm and connect it to the ball joint. Take care not to damage the ball joint dust boot. Install the clamp nut and bolt and tighten the nut to 32–40 ft. lbs. (43–54 Nm).

19. Install the wheel and tire assembly. Tighten the lug bolts to 65–87 ft. lbs. (88–118 Nm).

20. Install and tighten the transaxle drain plug.

21. Lower the vehicle.

22. With the vehicle sitting on all four wheels, have an assistant apply the brakes. Tighten the wheel hub locknut to 116–174 ft. lbs. (157–235 Nm). Stake the nut using a suitable tool.

➡**Do not stake the locking tab with a pointed tool. Be sure the locking tab is depressed at least 0.16 in. (4mm) into the locknut slot to ensure proper locking capability.**

23. Raise and safely support the vehicle.

24. Grasp the wheel hub and pull on it to ensure that the halfshaft is installed properly. Rotate the wheel hub by hand to check

that the hub and halfshaft assembly turns smoothly.

25. Fill the transaxle with MERCON® automatic transmission fluid.

26. Lower the vehicle.

27. Connect the negative battery cable.

28. Road test the vehicle and check for transaxle leaks and proper operation.

STEERING AND SUSPENSION

Air Bag

✳✳ CAUTION

Some vehicles are equipped with the Supplemental Inflatable Restraint (SIR) or air bag system. The SIR system must be disabled before performing service on or around SIR system components, steering column, instrument panel components, wiring and sensors. Failure to follow safety and disabling procedures could result in accidental air bag deployment, possible personal injury and unnecessary SIR system repairs.

PRECAUTIONS

Several precautions must be observed when handling the inflator module to avoid accidental deployment and possible personal injury.

• Never carry the inflator module by the wires or connector on the underside of the module.

• When carrying a live inflator module, hold securely with both hands, and ensure that the bag and trim cover are pointed away.

• Place the inflator module on a bench or other surface with the bag and trim cover facing up.

• With the inflator module on the bench, never place anything on or close to the module which may be thrown in the event of an accidental deployment.

DISARMING

➡Be sure to observe all air bag precautions before commencing with this procedure.

1. Disconnect the negative battery cable.
2. Wait one minute before proceeding with the service procedure. This is the time required for the back-up power supply in the air bag diagnostic monitor to deplete its stored energy.
3. After service is completed, reconnect the negative battery cable.
4. Turn the ignition switch to the **RUN** position. The air bag indicator should light continuously for approximately 6 seconds, then turn OFF. If the indicator flashes, fails to light or remains lit continuously, there is a fault in the air bag system.

Rack and Pinion Steering Gear

REMOVAL & INSTALLATION

Manual

1. Before servicing the vehicle, refer to the precautions in the beginning of this section.
2. Disconnect the negative battery cable.
3. Matchmark the steering column lower universal joint and steering rack pinion for assembly reference. Remove the steering column and intermediate shaft assembly from the vehicle.
4. Remove the floor set plate bolts and the floor set plate.
5. Cut the plastic tie wrap securing the steering column boot to the steering rack.
6. Raise and safely support the vehicle.
7. Remove the front wheel and tire assemblies.
8. Using the proper tool, separate both tie rod ends from the steering knuckles.
9. Remove the catalytic converter.
10. Remove the plastic splash shield from the right inner fender.

✳✳ WARNING

While maneuvering the tie rod boots in and out of the inner fender openings, guide the steering rack assembly carefully to avoid cutting or nicking the boots.

11. Remove the two steering rack mounting bolts and lower the steering rack until it is free of the steering column boot. Slide the rack to the right, through the inner fender opening until the left tie rod is clear of the left inner fender, then lower the left end until the steering rack assembly can be withdrawn from the left side of the vehicle.
12. Remove the steering column intermediate shaft coupling bolt and the coupling from the steering rack.

To install:

13. Install the steering column intermediate shaft coupling and retaining bolts to the steering rack and tighten to 13–20 ft. lbs. (18–26 Nm).
14. Position the steering rack by starting the right side tie rod end through the right inner fender opening far enough to insert the left end of the steering gear assembly into the left front fender opening. Adjust the positioning of the steering rack to the left being careful not to snag the bellows.
15. Align the intermediate shaft coupling with the steering column boot. Raise the steering rack fully into position.
16. Install the left steering rack mounting bolt followed by the right steering rack mounting bolt. Tighten the bolts to 27–38 ft. lbs. (37–52 Nm).
17. Connect the tie rod ends to the steering knuckles. Install and tighten the tie rod end nuts to 31–42 ft. lbs. (42–57 Nm). Install new cotter pins.
18. Attach the right side splash shield on the right inner fender panel.
19. Install the catalytic converter.
20. Install the tire and wheel assemblies. Tighten the lug bolts to 65–87 ft. lbs. (88–118 Nm).
21. Lower the vehicle.

22. Secure the steering column boot to the steering rack housing with a new tie wrap.
23. Install the floor set plate bolts and the floor set plate.
24. Align the matchmarks made on the steering column lower universal joint and the steering rack pinion shaft. Install the steering column when the proper alignment is achieved.
25. Connect the negative battery cable.
26. Check the front end alignment.
27. Road test the vehicle and check for proper steering rack operation.

Power

1. Before servicing the vehicle, refer to the precautions in the beginning of this section.
2. Disconnect the negative battery cable.
3. Remove the steering column tube boot retainer and pry up the boot.
4. Remove the intermediate shaft coupling bolt.
5. Raise and safely support the vehicle.
6. Remove the front tire and wheel assemblies.
7. Remove the power steering hose bracket. Disconnect and plug the high pressure and return lines.

1	Steering Column Gear Input Shaft Coupling
2	Steering Column Tube Boot
3	Steering Gear Bolts
4	Front Wheel Spindle Connecting Rod Bellow
5	Front Wheel Spindle Connecting Rod End Nut
6	Front Wheel Spindle Connecting Rod End Cotter Pin
7	Front Wheel Knuckle
8	Front Wheel Spindle Connecting Rod Or End
9	Front Splash Shield
10	Steering Gear and Linkage

7922GG28

Exploded view of the manual steering gear mounting, showing related components

Item	Description
1	Steering Column Intermediate Shaft Coupling
2	Front Wheel Spindle Tie Rod
3	Tie Rod End Nut (2 Req'd)
4	Power Steering Pressure Hose
5	Power Steering Return Hose
6	Power Steering Hose Clamp Bolt
7	Steering Gear Bracket Bolts (4 Req'd)
8	Power Steering Hose Bracket Bolt
9	Tie Rod End Splash Shield
10	Tie Rod End Splash Shield Bolt (3 Req'd)
11	Steering Gear Mounting Bracket
12	Power Steering Hose Bracket
13	Steering Column Gear Input Shaft Coupling Bolt
A	Tighten to 42–57 N·m (31–42 Lb-Ft)

7922GG38

Exploded view of the power steering gear mounting, showing related components

8. Remove the tie rod end cotter pins and nuts. Using the proper tool, separate both tie rod ends from the steering knuckles. Discard the cotter pins.

9. Remove the front fender splash shield.

➡ **Lowering the exhaust system will ease access to the steering gear.**

10. Remove the three exhaust inlet pipe nuts and two bracket bolts.

11. Remove the muffler inlet pipe hanger posts from the exhaust hanger insulators.

12. Place alignment marks on the right tie rod end to ease installation. Loosen the jam nut and remove the right tie rod end.

13. Remove the steering rack mounting bolts and lower the steering rack until it is free of the steering column boot. Slide the rack to the left and pull the right tie rod through the fender opening. Remove the steering gear by sliding it to the right.

To install:

14. Position the steering rack in its mounting location.

15. With an assistant lifting the steering gear, align the intermediate shaft with the universal joint and install the coupling bolt, but do not tighten it at this time.

16. Install the four steering rack bracket bolts and tighten to 27–38 ft. lbs. (37–52 Nm).

17. Tighten the intermediate shaft coupling bolt to 13–20 ft. lbs. (18–26 Nm).

18. Unplug and connect the high pressure and return lines and install the power steering hose bracket.

19. Install the muffler inlet pipe hanger posts onto the exhaust hanger insulators.

20. Raise the exhaust system and install the three exhaust inlet pipe nuts. Tighten the nuts to 28–38 ft. lbs. (38–53 Nm.).

21. Install the two exhaust inlet pipe bracket bolts.

22. Install the right tie rod end and attach the tie rod ends to the steering knuckles. Install the tie rod end nuts and tighten to 31–42 ft. lbs. (42–57 Nm). Install new cotter pins.

23. Install the small front fender splash shield.

24. Install the front wheel and tire assemblies and tighten the lug bolts to 65–87 ft. lbs. (88–118 Nm).

25. Lower the vehicle.

26. Connect the negative battery cable.

27. Add power steering fluid and allow any air to bleed from the power steering system.

28. Check for leaks.

29. Adjust the toe setting by performing a front end alignment.

30. Road test the vehicle and check for proper operation.

Strut and Spring

REMOVAL & INSTALLATION

Front

1. Before servicing the vehicle, refer to the precautions in the beginning of this section.

2. Raise and safely support the vehicle.

3. Remove the wheel and tire assembly.

4. Remove the brake line clip from the strut lower mounting bracket and disengage the brake line.

5. Remove the two nuts and bolts securing the strut lower bracket to the steering knuckle.

6. Working in the engine compartment, remove the two nuts securing the strut mounting block in the strut tower.

7. Disengage the strut lower bracket from the steering knuckle and lower the strut clear of the wheel well.

8. To separate the coil spring from the strut, install Spring Compressor tool T81P-5310-A or equivalent, and compress the coil spring.

9. Pry out the mounting block cap and remove the strut upper nut and lockwasher.

10. Remove the strut mounting block and spacer plate. Remove the washer, bearing seal and bearing from the strut rod.

11. Remove the upper spring seat, seat insulator and spring. Slide the jounce bumper/shield off the strut.

➡ **If replacing the spring, release the spring compressor progressively to prevent spring arching. Open the compressor jaws wide enough to grip the new spring in the same position and tighten the compressor screws progressively, compressing the spring until the strut can be assembled without interference.**

To install:

12. Check the condition of the jounce bumper and spring seat insulator and replace, as necessary. Be sure the bearing operates smoothly. Check the spring for uniform coil spacing, for nicks or burrs and compare the spring length with a new spring to check for excessive spring set; replace as necessary.

13. Slide the jounce bumper/shield onto the strut rod and over the body. Install the compressed spring, upper spring seat insulator and upper seat, positioning the spring ends against the steps in the seats.

14. Install the bearing, seal and plain washer on the strut rod. Install the strut mounting block with the white alignment spot on the same side of the strut as the steering knuckle mounting bracket.

15. Install the spacer plate. Install the lockwasher and nut and tighten to 40–50 ft. lbs. (54–67 Nm). Release and remove the spring compressor.

16. Place the strut assembly with spacer plate in the strut tower with the white alignment mark facing outward.

17. Install the two upper mounting block stud nuts and tighten to 34–46 ft. lbs. (46–63 Nm).

18. Engage the steering knuckle in the strut tower lower bracket and install the two retaining bolts and nuts. Tighten to 69–86 ft. lbs. (93–117 Nm).

19. Position the brake line into the strut lower mounting bracket cutout and install the retaining clip.

Exploded view of the front strut assembly

20. Install the wheel and tire assembly and tighten the lug bolts to 65–87 ft. lbs. (88–118 Nm).

21. Lower the vehicle.

22. Check the front wheel alignment.

23. Road test the vehicle and check for proper operation.

Rear

Do not attempt to remove both left and right spring and strut assemblies at the same time. Do one side at a time to prevent damage to the rear suspension.

1. Before servicing the vehicle, refer to the precautions in the beginning of this section.

2. From the cargo compartment, remove the side cover.

3. Remove the quarter trim panel as follows:

   a. Remove the luggage compartment cover.

   b. Remove the rear seat.

   c. Remove the screws and push-pins from the package tray. Detach the radio speaker electrical connector.

   d. Remove the rear safety belt anchor bolt.

   e. Remove the push pins and the luggage compartment side cover.

   f. Remove the rear door scuff plate.

   g. Pull the seaming welt away from

the quarter trim panel and remove the panel.

4. Remove the strut cap, jam nut and flanged nut from the strut rod and remove the bushing washer and upper bushing.

5. Raise and safely support the vehicle.

➡ **Raising the vehicle will release any tension left on the coil spring.**

6. Remove the rear wheel and tire assembly.

7. Remove the lower strut mounting bolt from the torsion beam.

8. Remove the strut assembly from the vehicle and separate it from the spring and seat insulator.

9. Inspect the condition of the spring, spring seat insulator and strut. Replace any damaged or deteriorated components, as required.

To install:

10. If the upper spring seat insulator is replaced, install the new insulator on the spring upper end, seating the end of the coil against the step in the insulator. Position the spring on the strut, making sure the end of the coil seats against the step in the strut spring seat.

11. Guide the strut into the upper strut mounting hole through the wheel well.

12. Align the strut lower end with the mounting hole in the torsion beam. Start the mounting bolt in by hand to hold the strut in position.

13. Install the wheel and tire assembly. Tighten the lug bolts to 65–87 ft. lbs. (88–118 Nm).

14. Lower the vehicle.

➡ **Be sure that the coil spring is positioned properly on the spring seat insulator.**

15. From the cargo compartment, install the rod upper end bushing, bushing washer and flanged nut. Tighten the flanged nut to 12–18 ft. lbs. (16–24 Nm). Hold the flanged nut stationary and tighten the locknut.

1. Luggage Compartment Side Cover
2. Rear Strut Dust Boot Cover
3. Rear Spring Anti-Squeak Insert
4. Rear Spring
5. Lower Bushing
6. Rear Strut Dust Boot Seat
7. Rear Strut
8. Strut Mounting Bolt
9. Upper Bushing
10. Bushing Washer
11. Rear Strut Mounting Bushing
12. Jam Nut
13. Strut Cap

Exploded view of the rear strut assembly

16. Install the jam nut and the strut cap.

17. Install the side cover in the cargo compartment.

18. Raise and safely support the vehicle.

19. Tighten the lower strut mounting bolt to 50–60 ft. lbs. (68–81 Nm).

20. Lower the vehicle.

21. Check the rear wheel alignment.

Lower Ball Joints

REMOVAL & INSTALLATION

The lower ball joint is an integral component of the lower control arm. If the lower ball joint is defective, the entire lower control arm must be replaced.

Lower Control Arm

REMOVAL & INSTALLATION

The ball joint is an integral component of the lower control arm and cannot be serviced separately.

1. Before servicing the vehicle, refer to the precautions in the beginning of this section.

2. Raise and safely support the vehicle.

3. Remove the front wheel and tire assembly.

4. Loosen the lower control arm-to-chassis bolt and washer at the frame bracket.

5. Remove the ball joint clamp bolt and nut from the steering knuckle assembly.

6. Remove the cotter pin and stabilizer bar bushing nut from the rear of the control arm.

7. Remove the rear bushing washer and bushing. Discard the cotter pin.

8. Lower the control arm, prying the ball joint stud out of the steering knuckle if necessary.

9. Disengage and remove the control arm from the stabilizer bar end and remove it from the vehicle.

10. If the lower control arm is to be reused, inspect the control arm bushings for damage or excessive wear. Verify that the ball joint swivels freely, but is not loose.

11. Replace the lower control arm as required.

To install:

12. Position the front bushing washer and bushing onto the stabilizer bar end. Engage the lower control arm with the stabilizer bar.

Item	Description
1	Front Suspension Lower Arm-to-Chassis Bolt and Washer
2	Front Suspension Lower Arm Ball Joint Washer and Nut
3	Front Suspension Lower Arm Ball Joint Dust Boot (Part of 3078)
4	Cotter Pin (Part of 5A486)
5	Front Stabilizer Bar Nut (Part of 5A486)
6	Front Stabilizer Bar Washers (2 Req'd) (Part of 5A486)
7	Front Stabilizer Bar Bushings (2 Req'd) (Part of 5A486)
8	Front Suspension Lower Arm

Item	Description
9	Front Suspension Lower Arm Ball Joint Bolt
10	Stabilizer Bar Bracket Washers and Nuts (2 Req'd)
11	Stabilizer Bar Bracket
12	Front Stabilizer Bar
13	Lower Suspension Arm Stabilizer Bar Insulator
14	Front Suspension Lower Arm Mounting Bolt Bushing
A	Tighten to 43-54 N·m (32-40 Lb-Ft)
B	Tighten to 64-77 N·m (47-57 Lb-Ft)
C	Tighten to 54-68 N·m (40-50 Lb-Ft)

7922GG33

Exploded view of the lower control arm assembly

13. Raise the control arm inner end into the pivot bracket on the frame and start the pivot bolt to hold the control arm in place. Do not completely tighten the bolt at this time.

14. Engage the control arm ball joint stud with the clamp bore in the steering knuckle, and install the clamp bolt and nut. Do not tighten it yet.

15. Install the stabilizer bar rear bushing and washer onto the stabilizer bar end with the retaining nut. Tighten the retaining nut to 47–57 ft. lbs. (64–77 Nm). Install a new cotter pin.

16. Tighten the lower arm-to-chassis bolt at the frame bracket to 32–40 ft. lbs. (43–54 Nm).

17. Hold the clamp bolt stationary and tighten the clamp nut to 32–40 ft. lbs. (43–54 Nm).

18. Install the wheel and tire assembly.

19. Check the front wheel alignment.

Wheel Bearings

ADJUSTMENT

Front

The front wheel bearings on this vehicle do not require adjustment, nor is adjustment possible.

Rear

1. Before servicing the vehicle, refer to the precautions in the beginning of this section.

Turn to Section 6 for brake system applications

2. Be sure the parking brake is fully released.

3. Raise and safely support the vehicle.

4. Remove the wheel and tire assembly.

5. Remove the grease cap.

6. Rotate the brake drum to be sure there is no brake drag.

7. Remove the cotter pin, wheel bearing nut cover. Discard the cotter pin.

8. To seat the bearings, tighten the wheel bearing nut to 18–22 ft. lbs. (25–29 Nm). Rotate the brake drum by hand while tightening the nut.

9. Loosen the wheel bearing nut until it can be turned by hand.

10. Before the bearing preload can be set, the amount of seal drag must be measured and added to the required preload.

11. To measure the seal drag proceed as follows:

   a. Install a lug bolt and rotate the brake drum until the stud is in the 12 o'clock position.

   b. Place an inch pound torque wrench onto the bolt to measure the amount of force required to rotate the brake drum.

   c. Pull the torque wrench and record the torque reading when rotation begins.

12. Add the oil seal drag value obtained in Step 10 to the specified value of 0.6–1.9 inch lbs. (2.6–8.5 Nm). This is the standard bearing preload.

13. Loosely tighten the bearing nut and rotate the brake drum until the nut and wheel are at the 12 o' clock position.

14. Position an inch pound torque wrench onto the nut and measure the amount of pull required to rotate the drum.

15. Tighten the wheel bearing nut until the torque shown is within the range previously calculated.

16. Turn the wheel bearing nut slowly to adjust it to the standard bearing preload.

17. Install the nut retaining cap and a new cotter pin.

18. Install the grease cap and the wheel and tire assembly.

19. Lower the vehicle.

20. Road test the vehicle and check for proper operation.

REMOVAL & INSTALLATION

Front

1. Before servicing the vehicle, refer to the precautions in the beginning of this section.

2. With the vehicle sitting on all 4 wheels, use a small chisel to straighten the staked edge of the wheel hub retaining nut.

Use a puller to separate the front wheel bearing hub from the steering knuckle

Take care not to damage the halfshaft threads.

3. Remove and discard the wheel hub retaining nut.

4. Raise and safely support the vehicle.

5. Remove the wheel.

6. Remove the retaining clip securing the brake hose to the strut.

7. If equipped, remove the front brake anti-lock sensor.

8. Remove the cotter pin and tie rod end attaching nut. Discard the cotter pin and set the nut aside. Inspect the nut for damage, and replace if necessary.

9. Using a tie rod end separator tool T85M-3395-A or equivalent, separate the tie rod end from the steering knuckle arm.

10. Without disconnecting the brake hose, remove the brake caliper attaching bolts and lift the caliper assembly from the steering knuckle. Support the caliper by a length of wire attached to the strut. Do not allow the caliper to hang by the brake hose.

11. Loosen the screws and remove the brake rotor.

12. Remove the clamp bolt and nut at the point where the lower control arm ball joint connects to the steering knuckle.

13. With a medium prybar, release the lower ball joint from the steering knuckle by prying downward on the lower control arm.

14. Loosen the two bolts that position the steering knuckle between the strut bracket flanges.

15. Slide the knuckle/hub assembly from the end of the halfshaft. If necessary, use a wheel puller to press the shaft out of the hub and remove from the vehicle.

16. If necessary, use a chisel to separate the disc brake rotor shield from the

Use a bearing pulling attachment, driver and a press to remove the front outer wheel bearing, as shown

knuckle/hub assembly. Discard the shield.

➡ **Shield replacement is not a requirement for normal bearing service.**

17. Using Puller tool T87C-1104-A and Hub/Bearing Remover Adapter T92C-1104-AH, or equivalents, separate the hub from the knuckle.

18. Remove the outer bearing retainer washer.

➡ **The outer bearing retainer washer is pre-selected to yield the correct bearing preload. Save the washer for use during assembly.**

19. Remove the outer bearing from the wheel hub using a bearing pulling attachment, driver and a press.

20. Remove the grease seals from the hub and steering knuckle bore and discard. Remove the inner wheel bearing.

21. Remove the bearing races from the steering knuckle using a suitable puller and slide hammer.

22. Thoroughly clean the hub and knuckle. Inspect the hub and knuckle for wear and/or damage. Replace as necessary.

To install:

23. If the brake rotor shield was removed, install a new one using installation tools T80T-4000-W and T94C-1175-B or equivalents.

24. If the wheel bearings or steering knuckle are being replaced, bearing preload must be checked before assembly as follows:

   a. Install the outer bearing races in the steering knuckle using suitable bearing cup installation tools.

   b. Lubricate the bearing races and bearing with a thin film of clean grease. Install the bearings in the steering knuckle.

   c. Install Spacer Selection tool T87C-

1104-B or equivalent, and clamp the bolt head in a vise.

d. Tighten the center bolt in increments, to 36, 72, 108 and 145 ft. lbs. (49, 98, 147 and 196 Nm). After tightening the center bolt to each specified increment, seat the bearings by rotating the steering knuckle.

e. Remove the tool/steering knuckle from the vise. Remount the assembly in the vise, clamping it where the strut mounts.

f. Measure the amount of torque required to rotate the spacer selector tool, using an inch pound torque wrench. The torque wrench reading must be taken just as the tool starts to rotate.

g. If the torque wrench indicates 2.2–10.4 inch lbs. (0.25–1.80 Nm), the outer bearing retainer washer is the correct thickness. If the torque wrench indicates less than 2.2 inch lbs. (0.25 Nm), a thinner outer bearing retainer washer must be installed. If the torque wrench indicates more than 10.4 inch lbs. (1.8 Nm), a thicker outer bearing retainer washer must be installed.

h. Each outer bearing retainer washer has a numerical code that identifies its thickness, which is stamped onto the outer diameter of the washer. The numbers range from 1 to 21, with 1 being the thinnest washer. If the number stamped on the washer is not legible, measure the

Stamped mark	Thickness
1	6.285 mm (0.2474 in)
2	6.325 mm (0.2490 in)
3	6.365 mm (0.2506 in)
4	6.405 mm (0.2522 in)
5	6.445 mm (0.2538 in)
6	6.485 mm (0.2554 in)
7	6.525 mm (0.2570 in)
8	6.565 mm (0.2586 in)
9	6.605 mm (0.2602 in)
10	6.645 mm (0.2618 in)
11	6.685 mm (0.2634 in)
12	6.725 mm (0.2650 in)
13	6.765 mm (0.2666 in)
14	6.805 mm (0.2682 in)
15	6.845 mm (0.2698 in)
16	6.885 mm (0.2714 in)
17	6.925 mm (0.2730 in)
18	6.965 mm (0.2746 in)
19	7.005 mm (0.2762 in)
20	7.045 mm (0.2778 in)
21	7.085 mm (0.2794 in)

7922GG32

Front outer wheel bearing retainer washer thickness chart

washer with a micrometer and compare it to the thickness chart to determine the number.

Changing the outer bearing retainer washer thickness by 1 number, either higher or lower, will change the bearing preload by 1.7–3.5 inch lbs. (0.2–0.4 Nm).

25. Pack the bearings and the hub area with a suitable high temperature wheel bearing grease. Place the inner wheel bearing into the steering knuckle bore.

26. Lubricate the lip of the new inner grease seal with the bearing grease. Form the lubricant into a strip, concentrated along the edges of the seal lip. Install the bore, using a suitable installation tool.

27. Place the original outer bearing retainer washer, or the outer bearing retainer washer selected from the front wheel bearing adjustment procedure, in the steering knuckle bore. Position the outer wheel bearing in the steering knuckle bore.

28. Lubricate the lip of the new outer grease seal with the bearing grease. Form the lubricant into a strip, concentrated along the edges of the seal lip. Install the outer seal into the bore, using a suitable installation tool.

29. Position the hub in the steering knuckle bore and press it into position using a suitable driver.

30. If the brake rotor shield was removed, install a new one using installation tools T80T-4000-W and T94C-1175-B, or equivalents.

31. Clean the halfshaft spline end and lubricate with a coating of wheel bearing grease. Apply a thin film of clean SAE 30 weight oil to the steering knuckle/hub assembly up to the point where the uppermost arm of the steering knuckle seats into the strut bracket. Guide the steering knuckle/hub assembly onto the halfshaft and the strut.

32. Install the strut-to-steering knuckle bolts and attaching nuts. Tighten the nuts to 69–86 ft. lbs. (93–117 Nm).

33. Position the lower control arm ball joint in the steering knuckle. Install the lower control arm pinch bolt and attaching nut. Tighten the nut to 32–40 ft. lbs. (43–54 Nm).

34. Install the brake rotor.

35. Position the caliper on the steering knuckle and install the attaching bolts. Tighten the bolts to 29–36 ft. lbs. (39–49 Nm).

36. Position the caliper hose in the strut routing bracket and install the retaining clip.

37. If equipped, install the brake anti-lock sensor.

38. Install a new wheel hub retaining nut and tighten by hand.

39. Connect the tie rod end to the steering knuckle and install the attaching nut. Tighten the attaching nut to 22–33 ft. lbs. (29–44 Nm).

40. Install a new cotter pin through the nut and ball stud. If the openings in the nut and the hole in the ball stud are not aligned, tighten the nut to the point of alignment. Never loosen the nut.

41. Install the wheel and tire assembly.

42. Tighten the wheel hub retaining nut to 116–174 ft. lbs. (157–235 Nm). After installation, the wheel hub assembly must rotate freely by hand. Stake the halfshaft attaching nut into the shaft groove.

➡**Do not use a pointed tool to stake the nut. If the nut cracks even slightly during staking, replace it with another new one.**

43. Check the front wheel alignment.

44. Road test the vehicle and check for proper operation.

Rear

1. Before servicing the vehicle, refer to the precautions in the beginning of this section.

2. Be sure the parking brake is fully released.

3. Raise and safely support the vehicle.

4. Remove the wheel and tire assembly.

5. Remove the hub grease cap.

6. Remove the cotter pin, nut cover and the nut. Discard the cotter pin.

7. Pull the brake drum bearings and hub assembly away from the spindle shaft. Take care not to damage the spindle shaft threads.

8. Remove the outer wheel bearing assembly and washer.

9. With a small roll head prybar or equivalent, remove the bearing grease seal from the bearing hub. Discard the seal regardless of condition.

10. Remove the inner wheel bearing assembly from the bearing hub. If the bearings are to be reused, identify and tag each bearing for installation reference.

11. Thoroughly clean the wheel bearings and hub using suitable solvent and allow to dry. Inspect the bearings and bearing races for scoring, pitting, wear or other damage and replace as necessary.

12. If replacing the bearings, the bearing races must also be replaced.

13. Remove the bearing races from the hub using a brass drift.

To install:

14. If replacing the bearing races, install new races in the hub using suitable installation tools.

15. Pack the bearings and the drum hub area with high temperature wheel bearing grease. Do not fill the entire hub with grease.

16. Position the inner bearing in the hub. Install and seat a new grease seal with a suitable driving tool. Lubricate the lip of the seal with wheel bearing grease.

17. Position the brake drum and hub assembly on the spindle. Keep the hub centered during positioning to prevent damage to the new grease seal and the spindle threads.

18. Install the outer wheel bearing, washer and nut.

19. Adjust the bearing preload.

20. Install the wheel bearing nut cover and a new cotter pin.

21. Install the hub grease cap.

22. Install the wheel and tire assembly.

23. Check and adjust the brakes as required.

24. Check for proper brake operation.

Item	Description	Item	Description
1	Axle Torsion Beam	9	Washer
2	Brake Assembly	10	Wheel Bearing Nut
3	Rear Wheel Spindle	11	Wheel Bearing Nut Cover
4	Rear Brake Anti-Lock Sensor (If Equipped)	12	Hub Grease Cap
5	Inner Wheel Bearing Oil Seal	13	Cotter Pin
6	Inner Rear Wheel Bearing	14	Rear Wheel Spindle Nut (4 Req'd)
7	Brake Drum	A	Tighten to 43-61 N·m (31-45 Lb-Ft)
8	Outer Rear Wheel Bearing		

7922GG40

Exploded view of the rear wheel bearing and related components

FORD MOTOR COMPANY

Ford-Probe

18

PRECAUTIONS

Before servicing any vehicle, please be sure to read all of the following precautions, which deal with personal safety, prevention of component damage, and important points to take into consideration when servicing a motor vehicle:

• Never open, service or drain the radiator or cooling system when the engine is hot; serious burns can occur from the steam and hot coolant.

• Observe all applicable safety precautions when working around fuel. Whenever servicing the fuel system, always work in a well ventilated area. Do not allow fuel spray or vapors to come in contact with a spark, open flame, or excessive heat (a hot drop light, for example). Keep a dry chemical fire extinguisher near the work area. Always keep fuel in a container specifically designed for fuel storage; also, always properly seal fuel containers to avoid the possibility of fire or explosion. Refer to the additional fuel system precautions later in this section.

• Fuel injection systems often remain pressurized, even after the engine has been turned **OFF**. The fuel system pressure must be relieved before disconnecting any fuel lines. Failure to do so may result in fire and/or personal injury.

• Brake fluid often contains polyglycol ethers and polyglycols. Avoid contact with the eyes and wash your hands thoroughly after handling brake fluid. If you do get brake fluid in your eyes, flush your eyes with clean, running water for 15 minutes. If eye irritation persists, or if you have taken brake fluid internally, IMMEDIATELY seek medical assistance.

• The EPA warns that prolonged contact with used engine oil may cause a number of skin disorders, including cancer! You should make every effort to minimize your exposure to used engine oil. Protective gloves should be worn when changing oil. Wash your hands and any other exposed skin areas as soon as possible after exposure to used engine oil. Soap and water, or waterless hand cleaner should be used.

• All new vehicles are now equipped with an air bag system, often referred to as a Supplemental Restraint System (SRS) or Supplemental Inflatable Restraint (SIR) system. The system must be disabled before performing service on or around system components, steering column, instrument panel components, wiring and sensors. Failure to follow safety and disabling procedures could result in accidental air bag deployment, possible personal injury and unnecessary system repairs.

• Always wear safety goggles when working with, or around, the air bag system. When carrying a non-deployed air bag, be sure the bag and trim cover are pointed away from your body. When placing a non-deployed air bag on a work surface, always face the bag and trim cover upward, away from the surface. This will reduce the motion of the module if it is accidentally deployed. Refer to the additional air bag system precautions later in this section.

• Clean, high quality brake fluid from a sealed container is essential to the safe and proper operation of the brake system. You should always buy the correct type of brake fluid for your vehicle. If the brake fluid becomes contaminated, completely flush the system with new fluid. Never reuse any brake fluid. Any brake fluid that is removed from the system should be discarded. Also, do not allow any brake fluid to come in contact with a painted surface; it will damage the paint.

• Never operate the engine without the proper amount and type of engine oil; doing so WILL result in severe engine damage.

• Timing belt maintenance is extremely important! Many models utilize an interference-type, non-freewheeling engine. If the timing belt breaks, the valves in the cylinder head may strike the pistons, causing potentially serious (also time-consuming and expensive) engine damage. Refer to the maintenance interval charts in the front of this manual for the recommended replacement interval for the timing belt, and to the timing belt section for belt replacement and inspection.

• Disconnecting the negative battery cable on some vehicles may interfere with the functions of the on-board computer system(s) and may require the computer to undergo a relearning process once the negative battery cable is reconnected.

• When servicing drum brakes, only disemble and assemble one side at a time, leaving the remaining side intact for reference.

• Only an MVAC-trained, EPA-certified automotive technician should service the A/C system or its components.

ENGINE REPAIR

Distributor

REMOVAL

2.0L Engine

1. Before servicing the vehicle, refer to the precautions in the beginning of this section.

2. Disconnect the negative battery cable.

3. Remove the distributor cap and position aside, leaving the spark plug wires connected. Before removing the distributor, mark the position of the distributor cap No. 1 spark plug wire tower on the distributor.

4. Disconnect the distributor electrical harness.

5. Using a wrench on the crankshaft pulley, rotate the crankshaft to position the No. 1 piston at TDC on the compression stroke. The crankshaft pulley notch should align with the timing plate indicator and the distributor rotor should be pointing to the No. 1 spark plug tower position on the distributor cap.

6. Using chalk or paint, mark the position of the distributor housing on the cylinder head.

7. Remove the distributor hold-down bolt and remove the distributor.

8. Inspect the O-ring on the distributor housing and replace it if damaged or worn.

2.5L Engine

1. Before servicing the vehicle, refer to the precautions in the beginning of this section.

2. Disconnect the negative battery cable.

3. Remove the air cleaner intake tube nuts. Loosen the spring clamp at the front of the engine air cleaner assembly and slide it forward. Remove the engine air cleaner intake tube.

4. Loosen the clamp on the front of the Volume Air Flow (VAF) meter and disconnect the air duct. Detach the VAF meter electrical connector at the left side of the air cleaner.

5. Disconnect the evaporative emission canister vacuum hose from the routing clip on the front of the air cleaner.

6. Remove the fuel pressure regulator control solenoid from the air cleaner and position aside.

7. Remove the engine air cleaner nuts and bolt and remove the air cleaner assembly.

8. Tag and disconnect the spark plug wires from the distributor cap. Detach the two electrical connectors from the top of the distributor.

9. Using chalk or paint, mark the position of the distributor housing on the cylinder head. Remove the two distributor hold-down bolts and remove the distributor.

INSTALLATION

2.0L Engine

TIMING NOT DISTURBED

1. Using clean engine oil, lubricate the distributor O-ring.

2. Align the marks on the distributor shaft and the distributor housing.

3. Install the distributor. Be sure the distributor rotor aligns with the No. 1 spark

ALIGNMENT MARKS

7922HG01

Distributor assembly alignment mark locations—2.0L engine

plug tower position on the distributor cap and the distributor housing mark aligns with the cylinder head or cylinder block mark.

➡ **There are existing marks on the distributor shaft and housing, which when aligned, indicate the No. 1 position.**

4. Install the distributor hold-down bolt.

5. Attach the electrical connectors to their original locations. Install the distributor cap.

6. Connect the negative battery cable.

7. Run the engine and check the ignition timing. Adjust the ignition timing if required.

TIMING DISTURBED

1. Using clean engine oil, lubricate the distributor O-ring.

2. Disconnect the spark plug wire from the No. 1 cylinder spark plug. Remove the spark plug from the No. 1 cylinder and press a thumb over the spark plug hole.

3. Using a wrench on the crankshaft pulley, rotate the crankshaft until pressure is felt at the spark plug hole, indicating the piston is approaching TDC on the compression stroke. Continue rotating the crankshaft until the crankshaft pulley mark aligns with the timing cover indicator.

4. Position the distributor rotor so it aligns with the No. 1 spark plug wire tower on the distributor cap.

5. Install the distributor. Align the mark that was made on the distributor housing with the mark that was made on the cylinder block. Loosely tighten the distributor hold-down bolts.

➡ **There are existing marks on the distributor shaft and housing, which when aligned, indicate the No. 1 position.**

6. Attach the electrical connectors to their original locations. Install the distributor cap.

7. Install the spark plug in the No. 1 cylinder and connect the spark plug wire.

8. Connect the negative battery cable.

9. Run the engine and check the ignition timing. Adjust the ignition timing if required.

2.5L Engine

1. Align the distributor shaft with the camshaft end and install the distributor.

➡ **The tangs on the distributor shaft are different sizes, allowing the distributor to be installed in only one position.**

2. Install the distributor hold-down bolts. Align the mark that was made on the distributor housing with the mark that was made on the cylinder head and loosely tighten the bolts.

3. Attach the electrical connectors to the distributor and the spark plug wires to the distributor cap.

4. Install the engine air cleaner assembly and tighten the nuts and bolt to 14–18 ft. lbs. (19–25 Nm).

5. Install the fuel pressure regulator solenoid and connect the evaporative emission canister vacuum hose to the routing clip.

6. Attach the VAF meter electrical connector. Connect the air duct and tighten the clamp.

7. Align the engine air cleaner intake tube and install it to the engine air cleaner assembly. Loosen the spring clamp and slide it into position. Install the engine air cleaner intake tube nuts and tighten to 71–88 inch lbs. (8–10 Nm).

8. Connect the negative battery cable.

9. Run the engine and check the ignition timing. Adjust the ignition timing if required.

Ignition Timing

ADJUSTMENT

2.0L Engine

1. Before servicing the vehicle, refer to the precautions in the beginning of this section.

2. Apply the parking brake.

3. Be sure that the transmission is in NEUTRAL if equipped with a manual transaxle or in **P** (Park) if equipped with an automatic transaxle.

4. Locate the timing marks on the crankshaft pulley and the timing indicator

Location of the SPOUT connector—2.0L engine

Data Link Connector terminal locations—2.5L engine

scale on the engine front cover. If the marks are hard to see, clean them with degreaser and a stiff brush.

5. Start the engine and bring it to normal operating temperature.

6. Be sure all accessories are OFF.

7. Connect a tachometer and timing light to the engine according to the manufacturer's instructions.

8. Remove the shorting bar from the SPOUT connector.

9. Verify that the idle speed is 650–750 rpm; adjust if necessary.

10. Aim the timing light at the timing marks. The mark on the crankshaft pulley should line up with the 10 degrees BTDC (plus or minus 1 degree) timing mark on the timing indicator on the front engine cover.

11. If the timing marks are not aligned (within 1 degree), loosen the distributor hold-down bolts (2) and turn the distributor housing to adjust. When the marks align, tighten the hold-down bolt to 14–19 ft. lbs. (19–25 Nm). Recheck the timing after the bolt has been tightened.

12. Install the shorting bar to the SPOUT connector.

13. Remove all test equipment.

2.5L Engine

1. Before servicing the vehicle, refer to the precautions in the beginning of this section.

2. Apply the parking brake.

3. If equipped with a manual transaxle, place the shift lever in NEUTRAL. If equipped with an automatic transaxle, place the shift lever in **P** (Park).

4. Locate the timing marks on the crankshaft pulley and timing belt cover. If the marks are hard to see, clean them off with some degreasing cleaner and a wire brush.

5. Start the engine and allow it to come to normal operating temperature.

6. Be sure all accessories are OFF.

7. Connect a tachometer and a timing light according to the manufacturer's instructions.

8. Connect terminals **STI (TEN)** and **GND** on the Data Link Connector (DLC) with a jumper wire.

9. Check the idle speed and verify that it is 600–700 rpm. Adjust the idle speed if necessary.

10. Aim the timing light at the timing marks. The mark on the crankshaft pulley should line up with the 10 degrees BTDC (plus or minus 1 degree) timing mark on the timing indicator on the front engine cover.

➡**Do not pinch the ignition coil-to-distributor high tension wiring when turning the distributor.**

11. If the marks are not aligned, loosen the distributor hold-down bolts (2) just enough to turn the distributor housing. While aiming the timing light at the timing marks, turn the distributor until the marks are aligned. Tighten the distributor hold-down bolts to 14–19 ft. lbs. (19–25 Nm) and recheck the timing.

12. Stop the engine.

13. Remove the jumper wire and test equipment.

Engine Assembly

REMOVAL & INSTALLATION

2.0L Engine

WITH AUTOMATIC TRANSAXLE

➡**The engine is lifted from the engine compartment, leaving the transaxle in the vehicle.**

1. Before servicing the vehicle, refer to the precautions in the beginning of this section.

2. Relieve the fuel system pressure using the recommended procedure.

3. Disconnect the battery cables, negative cable first. Remove the battery and battery tray.

4. Mark the position of the hood on its hinges and carefully remove the hood.

5. Drain the cooling system and the engine oil into suitable containers. Reinstall the engine oil pan plug.

6. Remove the air intake system.

7. If equipped, remove the A/C compressor and position aside, leaving the refrigerant lines attached. Support the compressor with suitable wire.

8. Label, disconnect and plug the fuel lines at the fuel rail.

9. Label and detach the electrical connectors from the distributor, Engine Coolant Temperature (ECT) sensor, cooling fan temperature sensor (if equipped), water temperature indicator sender unit, Throttle Position (TP) sensor, Idle Air Control (IAC) valve, idle switch (if equipped), fuel injector harness, EGR solenoid vacuum valve, Oxygen (O_2S) sensor(s) and alternator.

10. Remove the sensor harness tie wrap and retainer clip from the cylinder head cover bracket.

11. Remove the power steering pump and position aside, leaving the hoses connected.

12. Loosen the alternator adjusting bolt and remove the upper lockbolt.

13. Remove the upper and lower radiator hoses. If equipped, disconnect the cruise control vacuum hose from the back right-hand side of the intake manifold.

14. Disconnect the vacuum hose connecting the Evaporative Emission (EVAP) canister to the metal vacuum tube. If equipped, detach the EGR temperature sensor connector.

15. Disconnect the accelerator cable.

16. Disconnect the brake power booster vacuum line from the back left-hand side of the intake manifold.

17. Disconnect the heater hoses at the bulkhead.

18. Raise and safely support the vehicle and remove the splash shields..

19. Remove the intake manifold support bracket.

20. Remove the starter motor. Remove the torque converter access plug.

21. Remove the halfshaft support bearing bracket bolts.

22. Remove the four torque converter-to-flexplate nuts.

23. Remove the three engine-to-transaxle bolts and the two transaxle-to-engine mounting bolts.

Hold the crankshaft using tool T92C-6316-AH or equivalent, while removing the pulley bolt—2.0L engine

24. Remove and discard the exhaust inlet pipe-to-catalytic converter nuts.

25. Remove the exhaust pipe bracket bolts. Remove and discard the exhaust inlet pipe-to-exhaust manifold nuts and remove the exhaust pipe. Support the remaining exhaust system with mechanic's wire.

26. Use Crankshaft Pulley Holder tool T92C-6316-AH or equivalent, to hold the crankshaft pulley and remove the pulley bolt. Remove the crankshaft pulley.

27. Lower the vehicle.

28. Attach an engine sling to the engine lifting eyes and a suitable hoist. Raise the engine slightly and remove the right-hand engine support insulator.

29. Remove the remaining transaxle-to-engine mounting bolts and remove the engine from the vehicle.

30. Remove the flexplate from the crankshaft and mount the engine on a workstand, if required.

To install:

31. Remove the engine from the workstand. Remove the old sealant from the flexplate mounting bolts and bolt holes.

32. If reusing the flexplate bolts, apply silicone sealant to the bolt threads. Install the flexplate and loosely install the bolts.

➡**New flexplate mounting bolts come with sealant already on them.**

33. Tighten the six flexplate bolts in 2–3 steps to 70–75 ft. lbs. (96–103 Nm) in a crisscross pattern.

34. Carefully lower the engine into the vehicle and align it to the transaxle. Be sure that the torque converter studs are aligned with the holes in the flexplate.

35. Install the upper four transaxle-to-engine bolts and tighten mounting bolts marked **A** to 50–73 ft. lbs. (68–99 Nm) for vehicles equipped with the 4EAT transaxle and 66–86 ft. lbs. (90–116 Nm) for vehicles equipped with the CD4E transaxle.

Flexplate bolt torque sequence—2.0L engine

Transaxle and engine mounting bolt identification, 4EAT transaxle—2.0L engine

Transaxle and engine mounting bolt identification, CD4E transaxle—2.0L engine

36. Raise the engine slightly and install the right-hand engine support insulator. Tighten the support insulator through-bolt to 63–86 ft. lbs. (86–116 Nm) and support insulator nuts to 54–75 ft. lbs. (74–103 Nm).

37. Remove the engine lifting equipment.

38. Raise and safely support the vehicle.

39. Install the four torque converter-to-flexplate nuts and tighten to 32–45 ft. lbs. (44–60 Nm). Rotate the flexplate, as necessary, to gain access to all of the nuts. Install the torque converter access plug.

40. Install the remaining transaxle-to-engine mounting bolts. Tighten mounting bolts marked **B** to 50–73 ft. lbs. (68–99 Nm) for vehicles equipped with the 4EAT transaxle and 28–38 ft. lbs. (38–51 Nm) for vehicles equipped with the CD4E transaxle. Tighten mounting bolt **C** to 28–38 ft. lbs. (38–51 Nm) for vehicles equipped with the 4EAT transaxle and 14–18 ft. lbs. (19–25 Nm) for vehicles equipped with the CD4E transaxle. On vehicles equipped with the 4EAT transaxle, install and tighten mounting bolt **D** to 14–18 ft. lbs. (19–25 Nm), **E** to 28–38 ft. lbs. (38–51 Nm) and **F** to 50–73 ft. lbs. (68–99 Nm).

41. Install the alternator and loosely install the through-bolt. Connect the alternator wiring and install the harness bracket to the back of the alternator.

42. Install the starter motor and tighten the bolts to 23–34 ft. lbs. (31–46 Nm). Install the intake manifold support bracket and tighten the bolts to 27–38 ft. lbs. (37–52 Nm).

43. Install the halfshaft bearing bracket bolts and tighten, in sequence, to 32–45 ft. lbs. (43–61 Nm).

44. Connect the fuel injector wiring harness to the bottom of the intake manifold.

45. Attach the oil pressure switch electrical connector. If equipped, install the A/C compressor on the mounting bracket and tighten the bolts to 26 ft. lbs. (35 Nm).

46. Install the crankshaft pulley and hold it with a suitable tool. Tighten the pulley bolt to 116–123 ft. lbs. (157–167 Nm).

47. Install the exhaust pipe to the catalytic converter, and tighten the new nuts to 27–38 ft. lbs. (37–52 Nm). Attach the exhaust pipe support bracket to the engine and tighten the bolts to 27–38 ft. lbs. (37–52 Nm).

Halfshaft bearing bracket bolt torque sequence—2.0L engine with an automatic transaxle

Timing belt service is covered in Section 5 of this manual

48. Install the new exhaust inlet pipe-to-exhaust manifold nuts and tighten to 27–38 ft. lbs. (37–52 Nm). Install the exhaust hanger insulators and remove the mechanic's wire.

49. Attach the O₂S sensor(s) electrical connector.

50. Lower the vehicle.

51. Loosely attach the alternator to the alternator adjuster arm. Install the alternator belt and adjust the tension. Tighten the alternator upper mounting bolt to 14–18 ft. lbs. (19–25 Nm).

52. Raise and safely support the vehicle.

53. Tighten the alternator through-bolt to 27–38 ft. lbs. (37–52 Nm).

54. Install the splash shields.

55. Lower the vehicle.

56. Install the power steering pump support and loosely install the power steering pump through-bolt and lockbolt. Attach the PSP switch electrical connector and install the power steering pump drive belt.

57. Adjust the power steering drive belt tension, then tighten the through-bolt to 27–38 ft. lbs. (37–52 Nm) and the lockbolt to 14–18 ft. lbs. (19–25 Nm).

58. Install the power steering pump belt shield and tighten the bolts to 71–88 inch lbs. (8–10 Nm). Install the power steering hose brackets to the cylinder head cover and tighten the bolts to 71–88 inch lbs. (8–10 Nm).

59. Connect the heater hoses. If equipped, connect the cruise control vacuum line to the back right-hand side of the intake manifold.

60. Connect the vacuum line connecting the EVAP canister to the metal vacuum tube.

61. Connect the power brake booster vacuum line to the back left-hand side of the intake manifold.

62. Unplug and attach the fuel lines to the fuel rail and all remaining electrical connectors.

63. Connect the sensor harness retainer clip to the cylinder head cover and the tie wrap to the water bypass hose.

64. Install the accelerator cable and the upper and lower radiator hoses.

65. Install the air intake system.

66. Carefully install the hood, aligning the marks that were made during removal.

67. Install the battery tray and battery.

68. Connect the battery cables, negative cable first.

69. Fill the engine with the proper type and quantity of oil.

70. Fill and bleed the cooling system.

71. Run the engine and bring to normal operating temperature. Check for leaks and proper engine operation.

WITH MANUAL TRANSAXLE

➡ **The engine and transaxle are lifted from the engine compartment as an assembly.**

1. Before servicing the vehicle, refer to the precautions in the beginning of this section.

2. Relieve the fuel system pressure using the recommended procedure.

3. Disconnect the battery cables, negative cable first. Remove the battery and battery tray.

4. Mark the position of the hood on its hinges and carefully remove the hood.

5. Drain the cooling system and the engine oil into suitable containers. Reinstall the engine oil pan plug.

6. Remove the air intake system.

7. Remove the upper and lower radiator hoses and remove the radiator.

8. If equipped, remove the A/C compressor and position aside, leaving the refrigerant lines attached. Support the compressor with suitable wire.

9. Label, disconnect and plug the fuel lines at the fuel rail and set the fuel lines aside.

10. Label and detach the electrical connectors from the distributor, coil, Engine Coolant Temperature (ECT) sensor, coolant temperature gauge sensor, Throttle Position (TP) sensor, Idle Air Control (IAC) valve, fuel injectors, EGR solenoid vacuum valve, EGR temperature sensor and the alternator.

11. Remove the power steering pump and position aside, leaving the hoses connected.

12. Loosen the alternator adjusting bolt, remove the upper lockbolt.

13. If equipped, disconnect the cruise control vacuum hose from the back right-hand side of the intake manifold.

14. Disconnect the vacuum line connecting the Evaporative Emission (EVAP) canister to the metal vacuum tube. If equipped, detach the EGR temperature sensor connector.

15. Disconnect the accelerator cable. Disconnect the power booster vacuum hose from the back left-hand side of the intake manifold.

16. Disconnect the heater hoses at the bulkhead and remove the upper starter motor mounting bolts. If equipped, detach the speed control electrical connector, remove the two speed control servo mounting nuts and position the speed control servo aside.

17. Remove the ignition coil.

18. Remove the two fuel filter bracket bolts and position the filter and bracket aside.

19. Remove the ignition control module.

20. Remove the ground wire bracket from between the transaxle and rear transaxle support insulator (mount).

21. Remove the rear transaxle support insulator through-bolt and remove the transaxle ground from the top rear of the transaxle.

22. Label and detach the Brake On/Off (BOO) switch and Vehicle Speed Sensor (VSS) electrical connectors from the rear of the transaxle.

23. Disconnect and plug the lower clutch slave cylinder tube fitting at the slave cylinder. Pull the spring clips from the slave cylinder line mounting brackets, then remove the hydraulic clutch hose from the lower clutch slave cylinder tube.

24. Label and detach the park/neutral position switch from the front of the transaxle.

25. Raise and safely support the vehicle.

26. Remove the splash shields and the front wheels.

27. Remove the six crossmember bolts and the crossmember.

28. Remove the two lower transaxle support insulator bolts and the lower transaxle support insulator.

29. Remove the six rear engine support nuts and two bolts and remove the rear engine support.

30. Remove the halfshafts.

31. Install Transaxle Plug tools T88C-7025-AH or equivalent, into the differential side gears.

➡ **If the plugs are not installed, the differential side gears may become misaligned. If the gears are misaligned, the differential may have to be removed to reposition them.**

32. Remove the intake manifold support bolts and the support. Remove the three rear transaxle support bracket bolts and remove the rear transaxle support bracket.

33. Remove the starter.

34. Label and detach the oil pressure switch and Heated Oxygen Sensor (HO₂S) electrical connectors.

35. Remove and discard the exhaust inlet pipe-to-catalytic converter nuts. Remove the exhaust support bolts. Remove and discard the exhaust inlet pipe-to-exhaust manifold nuts and remove the exhaust pipe. Support the exhaust system with mechanics wire.

36. Remove the control rod-to-support bar stud nut, then disengage the bar from the transaxle. Remove the transaxle shift rod adjustment sleeve through-bolt and nut,

then disengage the linkage from the transaxle.

37. Remove the alternator drive belt if not already done. Remove the wiring harness bracket from the rear of the alternator and remove the alternator through-bolt. Label and detach the remaining alternator wiring and remove the alternator.

38. Hold the crankshaft pulley with Crankshaft Pulley Holder T92C-6316-AH or equivalent tool and remove the pulley bolt. Remove the crankshaft pulley.

39. If equipped with A/C, remove the A/C compressor bolts and position the compressor aside by supporting the compressor with mechanics wire. Do not remove the A/C lines.

40. Lower the vehicle.

41. Attach an engine sling to the engine lifting eyes and a suitable hoist to the sling. Raise the engine slightly and remove the right-hand engine support insulator.

42. Remove the left-hand engine support insulator nuts and bolt and through-bolt and remove the left-hand engine support insulator.

43. Carefully raise and remove the engine/transaxle assembly from the vehicle.

44. Remove the transaxle-to-engine bolts and the engine-to-transaxle bolts. Separate the transaxle from the engine.

45. Remove the clutch assembly, flywheel and crankshaft rear cover plate. Mount the engine on a workstand.

To install:

46. Remove the engine from the workstand using an engine sling and hoist. Install the crankshaft rear cover plate and tighten the bolt to 71–88 inch lbs. (8–10 Nm).

47. Install the flywheel and clutch assembly.

48. Install the transaxle on the engine. Install the transaxle-to-engine bolts. Tighten

Transaxle and engine mounting bolt identification, MTX transaxle—2.0L engine

7922HG07

bolts **A** to 66–86 ft. lbs. (90–116 Nm), **B** to 28–38 ft. lbs. (38–51 Nm) and **C** to 14–18 ft. lbs. (19–25 Nm). Install the engine-to-transaxle bolts. Tighten bolt **D** to 28–38 ft. lbs. (38–51 Nm) and bolt **E** to 66–86 ft. lbs. (90–116 Nm).

49. Carefully lower the engine/transaxle assembly into the engine compartment.

50. Install the left-hand transaxle support insulator and tighten the two nuts and one bolt to 50–68 ft. lbs. (67–93 Nm). Tighten the left-hand transaxle support insulator through-bolt to 63–86 ft. lbs. (86–116 Nm).

51. Raise the engine slightly and install the right-hand engine support insulator. Tighten the right-hand engine support insulator through-bolt to 63–86 ft. lbs. (86–116 Nm) and the right-hand engine support insulator nuts to 54–75 ft. lbs. (74–103 Nm). Remove the engine lifting equipment.

52. Raise and safely support the vehicle.

53. Install the alternator and loosely install the alternator through-bolt. Install the alternator drive belt. Connect the alternator wiring and install the wiring harness bracket to the rear of the alternator.

54. Connect the control rod-to-support bar. Tighten the nut to 28–38 ft. lbs. (38–51 Nm).

55. Connect the shift rod adjustment sleeve to the transaxle with the through-bolt and nut. Tighten the through-bolt to 14–18 ft. lbs. (19–25 Nm).

56. Install the exhaust pipe to the catalytic converter and tighten the new nuts to 27–38 ft. lbs. (37–52 Nm). Attach the exhaust pipe support bracket to the engine and tighten the bolts to 27–38 ft. lbs. (37–52 Nm).

57. Install the new exhaust pipe-to-exhaust manifold nuts and tighten to 27–38 ft. lbs. (37–52 Nm).

58. Attach the HO_2S and oil pressure sensor electrical connectors.

59. Install the starter motor and tighten the bolts to 23–34 ft. lbs. (31–46 Nm).

60. Install the rear transaxle support insulator and tighten the three bolts to 50–68 ft. lbs. (67–93 Nm).

61. Install the intake manifold support bracket and tighten the bolts to 27–38 ft. lbs. (38–52 Nm).

62. Remove the plugs from the differential side gears and install the halfshafts.

63. Install the lower transaxle support insulator and tighten the bolts to 41–59 ft. lbs. (55–80 Nm).

64. Install the rear engine support. Tighten bolts and nuts **B** to 50–68 ft. lbs.

(67–93 Nm), nuts **A** to 55–77 ft. lbs. (75–104 Nm) and nuts **C** to 32–44 ft. lbs. (44–60 Nm).

65. Install the crossmember and tighten the six bolts to 68–96 ft. lbs. (94–131 Nm).

66. Install the crankshaft pulley. Hold the crankshaft pulley with a suitable tool. Install the pulley bolt and tighten to 116–123 ft. lbs. (157–167 Nm).

67. If equipped, install the A/C compressor and tighten the bolts to 18–26 ft. lbs. (24–35 Nm).

68. Lower the vehicle.

69. Loosely attach the alternator to the alternator adjuster arm. Adjust the alternator drive belt tension. Tighten the alternator upper mounting bolt to 14–18 ft. lbs. (19–25 Nm).

70. Raise and safely support the vehicle.

71. Tighten the alternator through-bolt to 27–38 ft. lbs. (38–52 Nm).

72. Install the splash shields and the wheels. Tighten the lug nuts to 65–86 ft. lbs. (88–118 Nm).

73. Lower the vehicle.

74. Attach the park/neutral position switch electrical connector.

75. Remove the plug and install the hydraulic clutch hose to the clutch slave cylinder metal tube. Install the clips to the clutch cylinder hose brackets. Install the hydraulic line fitting on the slave cylinder.

76. Attach the VSS and BOO switch electrical connectors at the rear of the transaxle.

77. Install the ground wire bracket between the transaxle and the rear transaxle support insulator. Install the rear transaxle support insulator through-bolt and tighten to 50–68 ft. lbs. (67–93 Nm). Install the transaxle ground at the top rear of the transaxle.

78. Install the ignition control module.

79. Install the fuel filter and bracket and tighten the bolts to 71–97 inch lbs. (8–11 Nm).

80. Install the ignition coil.

81. If equipped, install the speed control servo and tighten the nuts. Attach the speed control servo electrical connector.

82. Install the upper starter motor mounting bolts and tighten to 23–34 ft. lbs. (31–46 Nm).

83. Connect the heater hoses and connect the power brake booster vacuum line to the back left-hand side of the intake manifold.

84. Connect the accelerator cable. Connect the EGR temperature sensor, if equipped.

85. Connect the vacuum line between the EVAP canister and the metal vacuum tube. If equipped, connect the cruise control vacuum line to the back right-hand side of the intake manifold.

86. Loosely install the power steering pump through-bolt and lockbolt. Attach the PSP switch electrical connector and install the power steering drive belt.

87. Adjust the power steering drive belt tension, then tighten the through-bolt to 32–45 ft. lbs. (43–61 Nm) and the lockbolt to 23–34 ft. lbs. (31–46 Nm).

88. Install the power steering pump drive belt pulley shield and tighten the bolts to 61–86 inch lbs. (7–9 Nm). Install the power steering hose brackets to the cylinder head cover and tighten the bolts to 71–88 inch lbs. (8–10 Nm).

89. Attach all remaining electrical connectors.

90. Unplug and connect the fuel lines.

91. Install the radiator and the upper and lower radiator hoses.

92. Install the air intake system.

93. Install the battery tray and battery.

94. Install the hood, aligning the marks that were made during removal.

95. Connect the battery cables, negative cable last.

96. Fill the engine with the proper type and quantity of oil.

97. Fill and bleed the cooling system.

98. Bleed the clutch hydraulic system.

99. Run the engine and bring to normal operating temperature. Check for leaks and proper engine operation.

2.5L Engine

WITH AUTOMATIC TRANSAXLE

➡ **The engine and transaxle are lifted from the engine compartment as an assembly.**

1. Before servicing the vehicle, refer to the precautions in the beginning of this section.

2. Relieve the fuel system pressure using the recommended procedure.

3. Disconnect the battery cables, negative cable first. Remove the battery and battery tray.

4. Mark the position of the hood on its hinges and carefully remove the hood.

5. Drain the cooling system and the engine oil into suitable containers. Reinstall the engine oil pan plug.

6. Remove the engine air intake system.

7. Loosen the A/C and alternator belt tensioner locknut and adjuster bolt and remove the drive belt.

8. Raise and safely support the vehicle.

9. Remove the front wheels and the splash shields.

10. Remove the six crossmember bolts and remove the crossmember.

11. Detach the front and rear Heated Oxygen Sensor (HO2S) electrical connectors. Remove the exhaust inlet pipe-to-exhaust manifold nuts.

12. Detach the oil pressure switch electrical connector, located near the oil filter.

13. Remove the halfshafts.

14. Loosen the power steering and water pump drive belt tensioner locknut and adjuster bolt and remove the drive belt.

15. Remove the three power steering pump mounting bolts through the holes in the pump pulley. Remove the power steering hose bracket-to-power steering pump bolt and the pump rear bracket bolt. Secure the pump aside with mechanics wire, leaving the hoses connected.

16. If equipped, remove the four A/C compressor mounting bolts and secure the compressor aside with mechanics wire, leaving the refrigerant lines attached. Do not let the compressor hang by the refrigerant lines.

17. Lower the vehicle.

18. Remove the upper and lower radiator hoses and overflow hose.

19. Detach the cooling fan electrical connectors. Disconnect and plug the transaxle cooler lines.

20. Remove the two radiator hold-down bolts and remove the radiator and cooling fan assembly.

➡**Use care when lifting the radiator/cooling fan assembly not to damage the radiator and condenser cooling fins.**

21. Label and disconnect the wiring from the alternator and distributor. Remove the two A/C and alternator wiring harness retaining bolts, then disconnect the harness from the engine block.

22. Label and detach the electrical connectors from the fuel injector harness, Vehicle Speed Sensor (VSS), starter motor, Throttle Position (TP) sensor, Knock Sensor (KS), EGR, Idle Air Control (IAC) valve, EGR valve position sensor, neutral safety switch, Engine Coolant Temperature (ECT) sensor, cooling fan engine coolant temperature sensor, temperature gauge sending unit and Crankshaft Position (CKP) sensor, as equipped.

23. Label and disconnect the vacuum hoses from the speed control servo, EGR, throttle body, power brake booster, climate control assembly and fuel pressure regulator.

24. Remove the two heater hoses from the thermostat housing. Remove the wiring harness grounds.

25. If equipped, detach the speed control servo electrical connector. Remove the two nuts from the servo bracket and position the speed control servo and bracket aside.

26. Disconnect the fuel supply and return lines and discard the copper crush washer. Remove the two fuel line retaining bolts from the fuel line bracket.

27. Disconnect the accelerator cable from the throttle body. Remove the two nuts from the fuel filter bracket and position the filter aside, without disconnecting the fuel lines.

28. Remove the spring clip from the shift cable bracket and pull the cable from the switch. Remove the two bolts from the cooling fan relay bracket and position the bracket aside.

29. Raise and safely support the vehicle.

30. Remove the front and rear transaxle support insulator through-bolts.

31. Lower the vehicle.

32. Attach suitable lifting equipment to the engine lifting eyes and remove any slack using an engine hoist attached to the lifting cables.

33. Remove the left-hand transaxle support insulator through-bolt and the right-hand transaxle support insulator through-bolt and two nuts. Remove the right-hand engine support insulator from the vehicle.

Engine-To-Transaxle Bolts

Transaxle-To-Engine Bolts

7922HG08

Engine and automatic transaxle retaining bolt locations—2.5L engine

34. Carefully lift the engine/transaxle assembly from the vehicle.

35. Separate the transaxle from the engine.

36. Remove the flexplate and mount the engine on a suitable engine stand.

To install:

37. Attach suitable lifting cables to the engine lifting eyes and remove any slack on the cables.

38. Remove the engine from the engine stand and install the flexplate. Tighten the flexplate bolts, in 2–3 steps, in sequence to 45–49 ft. lbs. (61–67 Nm).

39. Position the engine to the transaxle and install the retaining bolts. Tighten the engine-to-transaxle bolts and the transaxle-to-engine bolts to 50–73 ft. lbs. (68–99 Nm).

40. Carefully lower the engine/transaxle assembly into position in the engine compartment. Install the right-hand engine support insulator. Tighten the through-bolt to 50–68 ft. lbs. (67–93 Nm) and the three nuts to 54–76 ft. lbs. (74–103 Nm).

41. Install the left-hand transaxle support insulator through-bolt and tighten to 63–86 ft. lbs. (86–116 Nm). Remove the engine lifting equipment.

42. Raise and safely support the vehicle.

43. Install the front and rear transaxle support insulator through-bolts and tighten to 63–86 ft. lbs. (86–116 Nm).

44. Lower the vehicle.

45. Align the cooling fan relay bracket and install the two bolts. Tighten to 88 inch lbs. (10 Nm).

46. Install the shift cable and retain with the spring clip. Align the fuel filter and install the two nuts. Tighten to 71–88 inch lbs. (8–10 Nm).

47. If equipped, connect the vacuum line to the climate control assembly. Connect the vacuum line to the power brake booster.

48. Connect the accelerator cable and vacuum lines to the throttle body. Connect the vacuum line to the fuel pressure regulator.

49. Align the fuel line bracket and install the two bolts. Tighten to 71–88 inch lbs. (8–10 Nm). Connect the fuel supply and return lines, using new copper crush washers. Tighten the supply line bolt to 18–25 ft. lbs. (25–34 Nm).

50. If equipped, align the speed control servo and install the nuts. Attach the speed control servo electrical connector.

51. Install the wiring harness grounds and connect the heater hoses to the thermostat housing.

52. Attach the electrical connectors for the CKP sensor, ECT sensor, cooling fan engine coolant temperature sensor, temperature gauge sending unit, neutral safety switch, EGR valve position sensor, IAC valve, EGR, KS, TP sensor, starter, VSS and fuel injector harness, as equipped.

53. Connect the vacuum hose to the EGR and if equipped, the speed control servo.

54. Align the A/C and alternator wiring harness and install the two bolts. Attach the two electrical connectors to the top of the distributor.

55. Carefully install the radiator and cooling fan assembly and attach the cooling fan electrical connectors. Install the two radiator hold-down bolts and tighten to 71–88 inch lbs. (8–10 Nm).

56. Unplug and connect the transaxle oil cooler lines and install the upper and lower radiator hoses.

57. Raise and safely support the vehicle.

58. If equipped, install the A/C compressor and tighten the bolts to 28–38 ft. lbs. (38–51 Nm).

59. Position the power steering pump and install the rear bracket bolt. Tighten to 24–34 ft. lbs. (32–46 Nm). Install the power steering hose bracket bolt and tighten to 24–34 ft. lbs. (31–46 Nm).

60. Install the three power steering pump bolts through the pulley and tighten to 23–34 ft. lbs. (31–46 Nm). Install the power steering pump drive belt and adjust the tension.

61. Install the halfshafts.

62. Attach the oil pressure switch electrical connector.

63. Install the exhaust inlet pipe to the manifolds and tighten the nuts to 30–41 ft. lbs. (40–55 Nm). Attach the front and rear HO2S electrical connectors.

64. Position the crossmember and install the six bolts. Tighten to 69–93 ft. lbs. (94–126 Nm).

65. Install the splash shields and the wheels. Tighten the lug nuts to 65–87 ft. lbs. (88–118 Nm).

66. Lower the vehicle.

67. Install the alternator drive belt and adjust the tension. Be sure all electrical connectors and vacuum hose are connected.

68. Install the air intake system.

69. Carefully install the hood, aligning the marks that were made during removal.

70. Install the battery tray and battery. Connect the battery cables, negative cable last.

71. Fill the engine with the proper type and quantity of oil.

72. Add transmission fluid to the transaxle if needed.

73. Fill and bleed the cooling system.

74. Run the engine and bring to normal operating temperature. Check for leaks and proper engine operation.

75. Top off all fluids.

WITH MANUAL TRANSAXLE

➡**The engine and transaxle are lifted from the engine compartment as an assembly.**

1. Before servicing the vehicle, refer to the precautions in the beginning of this section.

2. Relieve the fuel system pressure using the recommended procedure.

3. Disconnect the battery cables, negative cable first. Remove the battery and battery tray.

4. Mark the position of the hood on its hinges and carefully remove the hood.

5. Drain the cooling system and the engine oil into suitable containers. Reinstall the engine oil pan plug.

6. Remove the air intake system.

7. Raise and safely support the vehicle.

8. Remove the front wheels and the splash shields.

9. Remove the six crossmember bolts and remove the crossmember.

10. Remove the two bolts and six nuts from the rear engine support and remove the rear engine support.

11. Detach the front and rear Heated Oxygen (HO2S) sensor electrical connectors. Remove the exhaust inlet pipe-to-exhaust manifold nuts.

12. Remove the control rod-to-support bar stud nut, then disengage the bar from the transaxle. Remove the transaxle shift rod adjustment sleeve through-bolt and nut, then disengage the linkage from the transaxle.

13. Detach the A/C and oil pressure switch electrical connectors. Disconnect and plug the hydraulic line at the slave cylinder, then remove the two spring clips from the lower clutch slave cylinder tube.

14. Remove the halfshafts.

15. Remove the three bolts and one through-bolt from the rear transaxle support bracket and remove the rear transaxle support bracket.

Refer to Section 1 for engine rebuilding specifications

16. Loosen the locknut and adjuster bolt on the power steering pump drive belt tensioner and remove the drive belt. Remove the three power steering pump mounting bolts working through the pulley holes.

17. Remove the rear bracket bolt from the power steering pump and secure the pump aside with mechanics wire.

18. If equipped, remove the four A/C compressor mounting bolts and secure the compressor aside with mechanics wire, leaving the refrigerant lines attached. Do not let the compressor hang by the refrigerant lines.

19. Remove the power steering hose bracket from the pump. Loosen the alternator drive belt tensioner locknut and adjuster bolt and remove the drive belt.

20. Remove the upper and lower radiator hoses and overflow hose. Detach the cooling fan electrical connectors.

21. Remove the two radiator hold-down bolts and remove the radiator and the cooling fan as an assembly.

➡ **Use care when lifting the radiator/cooling fan assembly not to damage the radiator and condenser cooling fins.**

22. Label and detach the electrical connectors at the alternator. Remove the two A/C and alternator wiring harness bolts, then disconnect the harness from the engine block.

23. Label and detach the electrical connectors from the distributor, fuel rail, Vehicle Speed Sensor (VSS), starter motor, Throttle Position (TP) sensor, Engine Coolant Temperature (ECT) sensor, cooling fan engine coolant temperature sensor, temperature gauge sending unit, Knock Sensor (KS), Crankshaft Position (CKP) sensor, EGR valve, park/neutral position switch, Idle Air Control (IAC) valve, EGR valve position sensor, if equipped, speed control servo.

24. Label and disconnect the vacuum hoses from the speed control servo, if equipped, EGR valve and fuel pressure regulator.

25. Remove the ground-to-engine bracket bolt located near the starter. If equipped, remove the two nuts from the speed control servo and position aside.

26. Remove the transaxle ground and back-up lamp switch electrical connector from the rear of the transaxle. Remove the starter-to-chassis ground.

27. Disconnect the heater hoses from the engine.

28. Disconnect and plug the fuel supply and return lines. Remove the two fuel line retaining bolts and bracket.

29. Label and disconnect the vacuum lines and the accelerator cable from the throttle body. Label and disconnect the vacuum line from the intake manifold to the climate control assembly and the power brake booster vacuum hose.

30. Remove the two fuel filter mounting nuts and position the filter aside, leaving the fuel lines connected.

31. Attach suitable engine lifting equipment to the engine lifting eyes and take up any slack.

32. Remove the two left-hand transaxle support insulator nuts and through-bolt.

33. Remove the three right-hand engine support insulator nuts and the through-bolt and remove the right-hand engine support insulator.

34. Carefully lift the engine/transaxle assembly from the vehicle.

Engine and manual transaxle mounting bolt locations—2.5L engine

35. Remove the transaxle-to-engine bolts and the engine-to-transaxle bolts. Separate the transaxle from the engine.

36. Remove the clutch assembly, flywheel and crankshaft rear cover plate. Mount the engine on a workstand.

To install:

37. Remove the engine from the workstand using an engine sling and hoist.

38. Install the flywheel and clutch assembly.

39. Align the engine with the transaxle and install the retaining bolts. Tighten the six transaxle-to-engine bolts to 50–73 ft. lbs. (68–99 Nm) and the three engine-to-transaxle bolts to 28–38 ft. lbs. (38–51 Nm).

40. Carefully lower the engine/transaxle assembly into position in the engine compartment.

41. Install the rear transaxle support insulator. Tighten the three nuts to 50–68 ft. lbs. (67–93 Nm) and the through-bolt to 63–86 ft. lbs. (86–116 Nm).

42. Install the left-hand transaxle support insulator. Tighten the two nuts to 55–77 ft. lbs. (75–104 Nm) and the through-bolt to 63–86 ft. lbs. (86–116 Nm).

43. Install the right-hand transaxle support insulator. Tighten the two nuts to 54–77 ft. lbs. (74–104 Nm) and the through-bolt to 50–68 ft. lbs. (67–93 Nm). Remove the engine lifting equipment.

44. Raise and safely support the vehicle.

TIGHTENING TORQUE
A: 75 – 104 N·m (55 – 77 LB-FT)
B: 67 – 93 N·m (50 – 68 LB-FT)
C: 44 – 60 N·m (32 – 44 LB-FT)

Rear engine support mounting nut and bolt locations—2.5L engine

45. Install the power steering pump and tighten the three bolts to 23–34 ft. lbs. (31–46 Nm).

46. Tighten the power steering pump rear bracket bolt to 24–34 ft. lbs. (32–46 Nm). Install the power steering pump drive belt and adjust the tension.

47. If equipped, install the A/C compressor and tighten the four bolts to 28–38 ft. lbs. (38–51 Nm). Install the alternator and A/C drive belt and adjust the tension.

48. Connect the control rod-to-support bar. Tighten the nut to 23–33 ft. lbs. (32–46 Nm).

49. Connect the shift rod adjustment sleeve to the transaxle with the through-bolt and nut. Tighten the through-bolt to 12–16 ft. lbs. (16–22 Nm).

50. Install the halfshafts.

51. Install the rear engine support. Tighten bolts and nuts **B** to 50–68 ft. lbs. (67–93 Nm), nuts **A** to 55–77 ft. lbs. (75–104 Nm) and nuts **C** to 32–44 ft. lbs. (44–60 Nm).

52. Install the exhaust inlet pipe to the exhaust manifolds and tighten the nuts to 30–41 ft. lbs. (40–55 Nm).

53. Attach the HO2S electrical connectors.

54. Install the crossmember and tighten the six bolts to 69–93 ft. lbs. (94–126 Nm).

55. Install the splash shields and the wheels. Tighten the lug nuts to 65–86 ft. lbs. (88–118 Nm).

56. Lower the vehicle.

57. Install the power steering hose bracket bolt to the pump.

58. Attach the electrical connectors to the KS, ECT sensor, cooling fan engine coolant temperature sensor, temperature gauge sending unit, CKP sensor, EGR solenoids, EGR valve position sensor, VSS, starter motor, back-up lamp switch, fuel injectors, TP sensor, distributor and park/neutral position switch.

59. Connect the vacuum hoses to the climate control assembly, located in the right-hand rear of the engine compartment, EGR valve, fuel pressure regulator, if equipped, speed control servo.

60. Install the starter-to-chassis grounds, the transaxle ground and the ground-to-engine bracket bolt.

61. Connect the heater hoses.

62. Unplug and connect the fuel supply and return lines. Tighten the two fuel line bracket bolts to 71–88 inch lbs. (8–10 Nm) and the fuel supply line bolt to 18–25 ft.

lbs. (25–34 Nm). Be sure to use new copper crush washers.

63. Install the fuel filter to the bracket and install the two nuts. Install the speed control servo with the nuts and attach the electrical connector.

64. Connect the vacuum lines to the throttle body and connect the accelerator cable. Connect the power brake booster vacuum hose.

65. Attach the IAC valve, oil pressure switch, A/C compressor and alternator electrical connectors. Connect the A/C and alternator harness bracket to the engine.

66. Connect the hydraulic line to the slave cylinder and install the line bracket spring clips.

67. Carefully install the radiator and cooling fan assembly and install the two radiator hold-down bolts. Tighten the two bolts to 71–88 inch lbs. (8–10 Nm). Attach the cooling fan electrical connectors. Install the upper and lower radiator hoses.

68. Install the air intake system.

69. Check that all vacuum and electrical connectors are installed.

70. Carefully install the hood, aligning the marks that were made during removal.

71. Install the battery tray and the battery. Connect the battery cables, negative cable last.

72. Fill and bleed the cooling system.

73. Fill the engine with the proper type and quantity of oil.

74. Fill the transaxle with the proper type and quantity of oil, if needed.

75. Bleed the clutch hydraulic system.

76. Run the engine and bring to normal operating temperature. Check for leaks and proper operation.

77. Stop the engine and check all fluid levels.

Water Pump

REMOVAL & INSTALLATION

2.0L Engine

1. Before servicing the vehicle, refer to the precautions in the beginning of this section.

2. Disconnect the negative battery cable.

3. Drain the cooling system into a suitable container.

4. Remove the accessory drive belts.

5. Detach the Power Steering Pressure (PSP) switch electrical connector.

Water pump mounting bolt locations— 2.0L engine

7922HG11

6. Remove the power steering pump drive belt idler pulley shield bolts and remove the shield.

7. Remove the power steering pump through-bolt and lockbolt, and position it out of the way.

8. Remove the cylinder head cover.

9. Raise and safely support the vehicle.

10. Remove the water pump pulley using pulley tool T92C-6312-AH, or equivalent, to hold the pulley while the bolts are removed.

11. Remove the splash shields.

12. Remove the timing belt.

13. Remove the power steering pump lower bracket from the water pump.

14. Remove the five water pump mounting bolts and remove the water pump.

To install:

15. Clean all gasket mating surfaces.

16. Install a new gasket on the water pump and install the water pump on the engine. Install the mounting bolts and tighten to 14–19 ft. lbs. (19–25 Nm).

17. Install the power steering pump lower bracket from the water pump.

18. Install the water pump pulley and bolts. Hold the pulley with the tool and tighten the bolts to 71–88 inch lbs. (8–10 Nm).

19. Install the timing belt.

20. Install the splash shields and tighten the bolts to 71–88 inch lbs. (8–10 Nm).

21. Lower the vehicle and install the cylinder head cover. Tighten the bolts in 2–3 steps to 52–69 inch lbs. (6–7 Nm) in the proper sequence.

22. Place the power steering pump in position. Install the through-bolt and tighten to 32–45 ft. lbs. (43–61 Nm). Install the lockbolt and tighten to 23–34 ft. lbs. (31–46 Nm).

23. Attach the PSP switch electrical connector.

24. Install the accessory drive belts and adjust the tension.

25. Install the steering idler pulley shield and tighten the bolts to 61–86 inch lbs. (7–9 Nm).

26. Connect the negative battery cable.

27. Fill and bleed the cooling system.

28. Run the engine and bring to normal operating temperature. Check for leaks.

2.5L Engine

1. Before servicing the vehicle, refer to the precautions in the beginning of this section.

2. Disconnect the negative battery cable.

3. Drain the cooling system into a suitable container.

4. Remove the timing belt covers and the timing belt.

5. Use pulley removal tool T92C-6312-AH or equivalent, to hold the water pump pulley and remove the bolts. Remove the water pump pulley.

6. Position a drain pan under the water pump.

7. Remove the three front engine support insulator mounting bracket bolts.

8. Remove the five water pump mounting bolts and remove the water pump.

To install:

9. Clean the mating surfaces of the water pump and the engine block.

10. Install a new O-ring onto the water pump.

11. Install the water pump and tighten the bolts 14–18 ft. lbs. (19–25 Nm).

12. Install the three engine support mounting bracket bolts.

13. Install the water pump pulley with the bolts. Hold the pulley with the tool and tighten the bolts to 71–88 inch lbs. (8–10 Nm).

14. Install the timing belt and timing belt covers.

15. Connect the negative battery cable.

16. Fill and bleed the cooling system.

17. Run the engine and bring to normal operating temperature. Check for leaks.

Cylinder Head

REMOVAL & INSTALLATION

2.0L Engine

1. Before servicing the vehicle, refer to the precautions in the beginning of this section.

2. Relieve the fuel system pressure using the recommended procedure.

3. Disconnect the negative battery cable.

4. Drain the engine cooling system into a suitable container.

5. Remove the air intake system.

6. Remove the power steering hose bracket bolts from the cylinder head cover.

7. Detach the Power Steering Pressure (PSP) switch.

8. Remove the two power steering pump idler pulley shield bolts and the shield.

9. Remove the accessory drive belts.

10. Remove the power steering pump through-bolt and lockbolt and secure the pump aside with wire, leaving the hoses attached.

11. Remove the exhaust manifold.

12. Label and disconnect the spark plug wires from the spark plugs.

13. Disconnect the hoses from the cylinder head cover and loosen the cover bolts in sequence, in 2–3 steps. Remove the cylinder head cover.

14. Remove the timing belt covers and remove the timing belt.

15. Remove the two intake manifold support bolts and the intake manifold support.

16. Label and detach the wiring from the distributor/coil connectors, Engine Coolant Temperature (ECT) sensor and temperature gauge sensor.

17. Remove the four retaining bolts and the coolant temperature sensor housing from the back of the cylinder head.

18. Disconnect the fuel supply and return lines and tag for reassembly. Plug and position the fuel lines aside.

19. Label, detach and move aside the following electrical connectors:
- Idle switch
- Throttle Position (TP) sensor
- Idle Air Control (IAC) valve
- Fuel injector harness wiring
- EGR solenoid vacuum valve
- Alternator

20. Disconnect the vacuum hose from the vacuum fitting on the right-hand side of the intake manifold, emissions canister and the brake vacuum booster.

21. Disconnect the accelerator cable.

22. Remove the distributor.

23. Remove the camshafts.

24. Loosen the cylinder head bolts in 3 steps in the proper sequence.

25. Remove the cylinder head bolts, the cylinder head and the cylinder head gasket.

26. If necessary, remove the intake manifold from the cylinder head.

27. Clean all gasket mating surfaces. Inspect the cylinder head for damage, cracks, and fluid leakage. Check the head gasket surface for distortion (warpage) using a straight-edge and feeler gauge. Maximum allowable distortion is 0.004 in. (0.10mm).

To install:

28. If removed, install the intake manifold using a new gasket.

29. Position a new cylinder head gasket on the cylinder block and carefully install the cylinder head.

30. Measure the cylinder head bolts to determine if they are reusable or if they are stretched beyond use. If the cylinder head bolt is longer than 4 inches (105.5mm), it is stretched and must be replaced. Measurements are taken from under the shoulder to the end of the threads.

Water pump mounting bolt locations—2.5L engine

Cylinder head cover mounting bolt loosening sequence—2.0L engine

Measuring the cylinder head bolt length to check for excessive stretching—2.0L engine

TIGHTENING SEQUENCE

CYLINDER HEAD BOLTS (10)

FRONT OF ENGINE

CYLINDER HEAD

7922HG14

Cylinder head bolt tightening sequence—2.0L engine

FRONT OF ENGINE

VALVE COVER

VALVE COVER BOLT (11 REQ'D)

7922HG25

Cylinder head cover mounting bolt tightening sequence—2.0L engine

31. Tighten the cylinder head bolts in the proper sequence as follows:

    a. Tighten each bolt to 10 ft. lbs. (13 Nm).

    b. Tighten each bolt again to 16 ft. lbs. (22 Nm).

    c. Paint a mark on the socket or the edge of each cylinder head bolt to use as a reference.

    d. Using the same torque sequence, tighten each bolt 85–95 degrees.

    e. Use the same sequence and tighten each bolt an additional 85–95 degrees.

32. Install the valve lifters, if removed, and the camshafts.

➡ **Be sure that none of the camshaft lobes are located directly on the hydraulic valve lifters when tightening the camshaft cap bolts.**

33. Install the distributor.

34. Connect the brake booster vacuum hose, emissions canister vacuum hose and the vacuum hose to the right-hand side of the intake manifold.

35. Connect the accelerator cable.

36. Attach the following engine wiring connectors:

- Idle switch
- TP sensor
- IAC valve
- Fuel injector harness wiring
- EGR solenoid vacuum valve
- Alternator

37. Connect the fuel supply and return lines.

38. Attach the distributor/coil electrical connectors.

39. Install the timing belt and the timing belt covers.

40. Install the intake manifold support and bolts. Tighten the support bolts to 28–38 ft. lbs. (38–51 Nm).

41. Install a new cylinder head cover gasket on the cover. Apply sealant to the cylinder head surface in the area adjacent to the front camshaft caps, then install the cover. Tighten the bolts in two steps, in sequence, to 52–69 inch lbs. (6–7 Nm).

42. Connect the hoses to the cylinder head cover.

43. Connect the spark plug wires.

44. Install the exhaust manifold.

45. Install the alternator belt and adjust the tension.

46. Loosely install the power steering pump through-bolt and lockbolt.

47. Attach the PSP switch electrical connector.

For complete mechanical specifications, refer to Section 1 of this manual

48. Install the power steering pump drive belt and adjust the tension. Tighten the pump through-bolt to 32–45 ft. lbs. (43–61 Nm) and the lockbolt to 23–34 ft. lbs. (31–46 Nm).

49. Install the power steering pump idler pulley and retaining bolts. Tighten the shield retaining bolts to 61–86 inch lbs. (7–9 Nm).

50. Install the power steering hose brackets to the cylinder head cover. Tighten to 71–88 inch lbs. (8–10 Nm).

51. Install the coolant temperature sensor housing with a new gasket. Tighten the four bolts to 14–18 ft. lbs. (19–25 Nm).

52. Attach the ECT sensor and temperature gauge sensor electrical connectors.

53. Install the air intake system.

54. Connect the negative battery cable.

55. Fill and bleed the cooling system.

56. Run the engine and check for leaks and proper operation.

57. Adjust the ignition timing, if necessary.

2.5L Engine

➡The cylinder head bolts may be replaced with new, or measured and reused if they are not stretched beyond allowable limits. Before beginning this procedure, be sure new cylinder head bolts are available, if needed.

1. Before servicing the vehicle, refer to the precautions in the beginning of this section.

2. Relieve the fuel system pressure using the recommended procedure.

3. Disconnect the negative battery cable.

4. Drain the engine cooling system into a suitable container.

5. Remove the timing belt covers and the timing belt.

6. Remove the intake manifold.

7. Disconnect the ventilation pipe from the left cylinder head cover, remove the bolts and remove both cylinder head covers.

8. Remove the camshafts.

9. Remove the timing belt tensioner and the lower timing belt idler.

10. Remove the two alternator-to-alternator adjusting arm bolts.

11. Remove the three seal plate bolts and the seal plate from the front of the engine.

12. Remove the four coolant elbow bolts and the coolant elbow.

13. Raise and safely support the vehicle.

14. Detach the two Heated Oxygen (HO2S) sensor electrical connectors. Remove the exhaust pipe-to-exhaust manifold nuts and lower the exhaust pipes.

15. If removing the rear cylinder head, remove the Exhaust Gas Recirculation (EGR) tube and bracket from the EGR valve and the cylinder head.

16. Lower the vehicle.

17. Remove the hydraulic lifters. Identify each lifter as it is removed so it can be reinstalled in the same position. If the lifters are to be reused, store them upside down in an oil filled container.

18. Loosen the cylinder head bolts, in 2–3 steps in the reverse order of the tightening sequence.

19. Remove the cylinder head bolts, if equipped, head bolt washers and the cylinder heads.

20. If required, remove the exhaust manifolds, manifold shields and gaskets.

21. Clean all gasket mating surfaces. Inspect the cylinder head(s) for damage, cracks, and water and oil leakage.

22. Check the cylinder head gasket surface for distortion using a straight-edge and feeler gauge. Maximum allowable distortion is 0.004 in. (0.10mm).

To install:

23. If removed, install the exhaust manifolds using new gaskets. Tighten the exhaust manifold nuts and bolts to 14–18 ft. lbs. (19–25 Nm). Tighten the manifold heat shield bolts to 71–88 inch lbs. (8–10 Nm).

24. Position new head gaskets on the cylinder block. The gaskets cannot be interchanged and are marked **R** and **L** for the right and left banks.

25. Carefully position the cylinder heads on the head gaskets.

26. Measure the cylinder head bolts from the shoulder to the end of the threads. If the length of the bolt measures more than 5.217 in. (132.5mm), it has stretched

beyond its service limit and must be replaced. Be sure that the washer is removed when measuring.

27. Apply clean engine oil to the threads of the cylinder head bolts and install the washers.

28. Install the cylinder head bolts.

29. Tighten the cylinder head bolts using the following procedure:

    a. Tighten the cylinder head bolts in sequence to 10 ft. lbs. (13 Nm).

    b. Tighten the bolts again in sequence to 19 ft. lbs. (26 Nm).

    c. Paint a mark on the edge of the socket or each cylinder head bolt to use as a reference.

    d. Turn each bolt, in sequence, 85–95 degrees.

    e. Turn each bolt, in sequence, an additional 85–95 degrees.

30. Apply clean engine oil to the hydraulic lifters and install them in their original positions. Be sure they move freely in the bores.

31. Install the seal plate and the seal plate bolts. Tighten the seal plate bolts to 71–88 inch lbs. (8–10 Nm).

32. Install the coolant elbow. Tighten the four bolts to 14–18 ft. lbs. (19–25 Nm).

33. Install the two alternator-to-adjusting arm bolts. Tighten the bolts to 14–18 ft. lbs. (19–25 Nm).

34. Install the lower timing belt idler and tighten the idler bolt to 28–38 ft. lbs. (38–51 Nm).

35. Install the timing belt tensioner and tighten the Allen head bolt to 27–33 ft. lbs. (37–44 Nm).

36. Install the camshafts.

37. Raise and safely support the vehicle.

38. If installing the rear cylinder head, install the EGR tube and the EGR tube bracket.

39. Connect the exhaust inlet pipes to the manifolds and tighten the nuts to 41 ft. lbs. (55 Nm).

40. Attach the two HO2S sensor electrical connectors.

41. Lower the vehicle.

42. Apply sealant to the cylinder head surface in the area of the front and rear camshaft caps. Install new gaskets and install the cylinder head covers. Tighten the bolts in 2 steps, in sequence, to 43–78 inch lbs. (5–8 Nm).

43. Install the intake manifold.

44. Install the timing belt and timing belt covers.

45. Connect the negative battery cable.

46. Fill and bleed the cooling system.

47. Run the engine and check for leaks and proper engine operation.

7922HG15

Cylinder head bolt tightening sequence (same for both heads)—2.5L engine

Front cylinder head cover torque sequence—2.5L engine

9300HG06

Rear cylinder head cover torque sequence—2.5L engine

9300HG07

Intake Manifold

REMOVAL & INSTALLATION

2.0L Engine

1. Before servicing the vehicle, refer to the precautions in the beginning of this section.

2. Relieve the fuel system pressure using the recommended procedure.

3. Disconnect the negative battery cable.

4. Remove the air ducts and air cleaner assembly.

5. Remove and plug the fuel supply and return lines from the intake manifold.

6. Disconnect the accelerator cable.

7. Disconnect and plug the coolant lines at the Idle Air Control Bypass Air (IAC BPA) valve and the throttle body.

8. Label and disconnect the vacuum lines to the throttle body, the vacuum lines for the brake booster at the left-hand side of the intake manifold and disconnect the vacuum line fitting on the right-hand side of the intake manifold.

9. Label and detach the electrical connectors for the Throttle Position (TP) sensor, EGR temperature sensor, if equipped, and the EGR solenoid vacuum valve.

10. Disconnect the PCV valve from the cylinder head cover.

11. Raise and safely support the vehicle.

12. Remove the intake manifold support bracket and remove the EGR pipe from the intake manifold.

13. Lower the vehicle.

14. Remove the five bolts and two nuts securing the intake manifold and remove the manifold and gasket.

To install:

15. Clean all gasket mating surfaces.

16. Install the intake manifold, using a new gasket. Tighten the nuts and bolts to 14–19 ft. lbs. (19–25 Nm) in the proper sequence.

17. Raise and safely support the vehicle.

18. Attach the EGR pipe to the manifold and install the intake manifold support bracket. Tighten the support bracket bolts to 28–38 ft. lbs. (38–51 Nm).

19. Lower the vehicle.

20. Connect the PCV valve to the cylinder head cover. Attach the electrical connectors to the EGR solenoid vacuum valve, EGR temperature sensor, if equipped, and the TP sensor.

21. Connect the vacuum lines running to the throttle body, the brake booster and the vacuum line fitting on the right-hand side of the intake manifold.

22. Connect the coolant lines to the IAC BPA valve and the throttle body.

23. Connect the accelerator cable and the fuel lines. Install the fuel line mounting bracket and tighten the bolt to 97 inch lbs. (11 Nm).

24. Install the air cleaner assembly and ducts.

25. Connect the negative battery cable.

26. Fill and bleed the cooling system.

27. Run the engine and check for leaks.

Intake manifold fastener torque sequence—2.0L engine

7922HG16

2.5L Engine

1. Before servicing the vehicle, refer to the precautions in the beginning of this section.

2. Relieve the fuel system pressure using the recommended procedure.

3. Disconnect the negative battery cable.

4. Drain the cooling system into a suitable container.

5. Detach the vacuum hoses and electrical connectors from the air cleaner housing. Remove the air cleaner assembly.

6. Detach the Knock Sensor (KS) connector and remove the knock sensor bracket from the intake manifold. Remove the Crankshaft Position (CKP) sensor bracket from the right side of the intake manifold.

7. Remove the right bank (rear) spark plug wires from the spark plugs and the routing clips. Remove the Variable Resonance Induction System (VRIS) solenoid connector bracket from the rear of the intake manifold.

8. Label and disconnect the necessary vacuum hoses from the rear of the intake manifold and EGR valve. Disconnect the PCV valve hose from the intake manifold, near the throttle body.

9. Label and detach the Throttle Position (TP) sensor and fuel rail electrical connectors. Disconnect the accelerator cable from the throttle body and the vacuum hose from the evaporative canister.

10. Disconnect and plug the fuel supply line at the fuel rails and discard the copper crush washers. Disconnect the fuel and vacuum lines from the fuel pressure regulator.

11. Disconnect the EGR breather tube.

12. Remove the intake manifold mounting nuts and bolts in 2–3 steps, then remove the intake manifold.

To install:

13. Clean all gasket mating surfaces.

14. Position new gaskets and install the intake manifold. Tighten the nuts and bolts in 2–3 steps to 14–18 ft. lbs. (19–25 Nm).

15. Connect the EGR breather tube and connect the fuel and vacuum lines to the fuel pressure regulator.

16. Connect the fuel supply line to the fuel rail, using new copper crush washers. Tighten the fuel line fittings to 18–25 ft. lbs. (25–34 Nm).

17. Connect the vacuum hoses to the evaporative canister, intake manifold, throttle body and EGR valve.

18. Attach the TP sensor and fuel rail electrical connectors. Install the VRIS solenoid connector bracket.

Please refer to Section 9 for electric cooling fan wiring schematics

19. Connect the spark plug wires to the spark plugs and routing clips. Install the CKP bracket.

20. Install the KS bracket and attach the KS electrical connector.

21. Install the air cleaner assembly and attach the vacuum hoses and electrical connectors to the air cleaner housing.

22. Connect the negative battery cable.

23. Fill and bleed the cooling system.

24. Run the engine and check for leaks.

Exhaust Manifold

REMOVAL & INSTALLATION

2.0L Engine

1. Before servicing the vehicle, refer to the precautions in the beginning of this section.

2. Disconnect the negative battery cable.

3. Remove the seven exhaust manifold heat shield bolts and the heat shield.

4. Detach the Oxygen (O2S) sensor electrical connector.

5. Raise and safely support the vehicle.

6. Remove and discard the exhaust inlet pipe-to-exhaust manifold nuts. Suspend the exhaust system with wire.

7. Remove the two exhaust inlet pipe bracket bolts.

8. Disconnect the EGR pipe from the exhaust manifold.

9. Lower the vehicle.

10. Remove the two nuts and eight bolts and remove the exhaust manifold. Discard the nuts.

To install:

11. Clean all gasket mating surfaces.

12. Position a new exhaust manifold gasket over the studs and install the exhaust manifold. Tighten the eight mounting bolts to 12–17 ft. lbs. (16–23 Nm).

Exhaust manifold-to-cylinder head mounting bolt and nut locations—2.0L engine

13. Install two new manifold mounting nuts and tighten to 14–21 ft. lbs. (20–28 Nm).

14. Raise and safely support the vehicle.

15. Connect the exhaust pipe to the manifold. Install new nuts and tighten to 27–38 ft. lbs. (37–52 Nm). Attach the oxygen sensor connector.

16. Install the two exhaust inlet pipe bracket bolts.

17. Connect the EGR pipe to the back of the exhaust manifold and tighten to 24–34 ft. lbs. (32–47 Nm).

18. Lower the vehicle.

19. Install the exhaust manifold heat shield and tighten the bolts to 71–88 inch lbs. (8–10 Nm).

20. Connect the negative battery cable. Run the engine and check for exhaust leaks.

2.5L Engine

1. Before servicing the vehicle, refer to the precautions in the beginning of this section.

2. Disconnect the negative battery cable.

3. Raise and safely support the vehicle.

4. Detach the Oxygen (O2S) sensor connectors.

5. Remove the nuts from the front and rear exhaust pipes and lower the exhaust

Right side exhaust manifold-to-cylinder head mounting bolt locations—2.5L engine

Left side exhaust manifold-to-cylinder head mounting bolt locations—2.5L engine

system. Both pipes must be disconnected, even if only one manifold is to be removed.

6. If removing the rear (right side) manifold, disconnect the EGR pipe.

7. Remove the three exhaust manifold shield bolts and remove the shield.

8. Remove the two nuts and five bolts and remove the exhaust manifold(s).

To install:

9. Clean all gasket mating surfaces.

10. Install the exhaust manifold, using a new gasket, and tighten the nuts and bolts to 14–18 ft. lbs. (19–25 Nm).

11. Install the exhaust manifold shield and tighten the bolts to 71–88 inch lbs. (8–10 Nm).

12. If installing the rear (right side) manifold, connect the EGR pipe.

13. Connect the exhaust pipes to the manifolds, using new gaskets and nuts, and tighten the nuts to 30–41 ft. lbs. (40–55 Nm).

14. Attach the O2S sensor connectors and the negative battery cable. Run the engine and check for exhaust leaks.

Front Crankshaft Seal

REMOVAL & INSTALLATION

2.0L Engine

1. Before servicing the vehicle, refer to the precautions in the beginning of this section.

2. Disconnect the negative battery cable.

3. Remove the accessory drive belts.

4. Raise and safely support the vehicle.

5. Remove the front splash shields.

6. Prevent the crankshaft pulley from rotating by installing crankshaft pulley holder T92C-6316-AH or equivalent, and remove the crankshaft pulley bolt.

7. Remove the timing belt.

➡ **Be careful not to turn either the crankshaft or camshaft sprockets after the belt has been removed. This is especially important when removing the crankshaft damper retaining bolt and when using a puller on the crankshaft sprocket.**

8. If necessary, remove the Crankshaft Position (CKP) sensor bolt and position the CKP sensor aside.

9. Remove the crankshaft sprocket, sprocket key and the timing chain guide.

10. Using seal remover T92C-6700-CH or equivalent, remove the front crankshaft seal.

Using the Ford tools to remove the front crankshaft oil seal—2.0L engine

➡ Seal extractor tool T92C-6700-CH is recommended. It hooks the seal from inside and pulls the seal outward. If the special seal extractor recommended by the vehicle manufacturer is not available, remove the oil pump to remove the seal. Be careful not to score the crankshaft or the seal seat.

To install:

11. Lubricate the seal lip with clean engine oil. Using oil seal installation tool T74P-6150-A or equivalent, press or drive the new seal into the oil pump cavity. Install the seal so it is flush with the oil pump body.

12. Install the timing chain guide and crankshaft sprocket.

13. If removed, install the CKP sensor and tighten the mounting bolt to 71–88 inch lbs. (8–10 Nm).

14. Install the timing belt.

15. Install the crankshaft pulley and tighten the crankshaft pulley bolt to 116–123 ft. lbs. (157–166 Nm).

16. Install the front splash shields.

17. Lower the vehicle.

18. Install the accessory drive belts.

19. Connect the negative battery cable.

Using the appropriate tools to install the front crankshaft oil seal—2.0L engine

20. Run the engine and check for oil leaks and proper engine operation.

2.5L Engine

1. Before servicing the vehicle, refer to the precautions in the beginning of this section.

2. Disconnect the negative battery cable.

3. Remove the oil pump.

➡ Protect the oil pump housing with a rag while removing the crankshaft front seal.

4. Using a suitable drift or punch tool protected with a rag, knock out the front crankshaft seal from the oil pump housing.

To install:

5. Clean the oil, dirt and old sealant from all contact surfaces.

6. Lubricate the new front crankshaft seal lip with clean engine oil. Using front seal replacer T74P-6150-A or equivalent, press or drive the new seal into the oil pump housing. Install the seal so it is flush with the edge of the oil pump housing or protrudes no more than 0.021 inch (0.7mm) from the edge of the pump body.

7. Install the oil pump.

Removing the front crankshaft seal—2.5L engine

Press a new front crankshaft seal into the oil pump housing as shown—2.5L engine

8. Connect the negative battery cable.

9. Run the engine and check for leaks and proper engine operation.

Camshaft and Valve Lifters

REMOVAL & INSTALLATION

2.0L Engine

1. Before servicing the vehicle, refer to the precautions in the beginning of this section.

2. Disconnect the negative battery cable.

3. Label and disconnect the spark plug wires and clips from the cylinder head cover. Remove the ignition distributor with wiring and set aside.

4. Remove the power steering hose brackets from the cylinder head cover.

5. Disconnect the breather tube and PCV valve from the cylinder head cover. Remove the cylinder head cover.

6. Remove the accessory drive belts, timing belt covers and timing belt.

7. Remove the camshaft sprockets.

8. Note the location of the numbers on top of the camshaft caps, so the caps can be reinstalled in their original positions.

9. Loosen the camshaft cap bolts in 2 steps, in the reverse order of the tightening sequence. Remove the camshaft caps and the oil seals.

10. Remove the camshafts.

11. If they are to be removed, number each hydraulic lifter (hydraulic lash adjuster) with a paint marker or equivalent during removal.

12. Inspect the camshafts and lifters for wear and/or damage and replace, as necessary.

To install:

13. If removed, apply clean engine oil to the lifters and install. If the original lifters are to be reused, be sure to install them in their original positions.

14. Lubricate the camshaft lobes and journals with clean engine oil and install the camshafts on the cylinder head. Be sure none of the lobes are depressing any of the hydraulic lifters.

15. Apply silicone sealant to the cylinder head on the front camshaft cap mating surface. Do not get sealant on the camshaft journals.

16. Install the camshaft bearing caps in their original locations. Install the bolts and tighten, in sequence, in 3 steps:

TIGHTENING SEQUENCE

CAMSHAFTS

CAMSHAFT BEARING CAPS (10)

7922HG24

Camshaft bearing cap bolt torque sequence—2.0L engine

- Step 1: 35 inch lbs. (4 Nm)
- Step 2: 71 inch lbs. (8 Nm)
- Step 3: 100–126 inch lbs. (12–14 Nm)

17. Apply clean engine oil to the lips of two new camshaft front seals. Install the seals using seal replacer T90P-6256-BH or equivalent.

18. Install the camshaft sprockets, timing belt and timing belt covers.

19. Install the accessory drive belts and adjust the tension.

20. Apply silicone sealant to a new cylinder head cover gasket and install the gasket on the cylinder head cover.

21. Apply silicone sealant to the cylinder head in the area adjacent to the front camshaft caps.

22. Install the cylinder head cover. Tighten the bolts in 2 steps, in sequence, to 52–69 inch lbs. (6–7 Nm).

23. Install the power steering hose brackets and tighten the bolts to 71–88 inch lbs. (8–10 Nm).

24. Connect the breather hose and PCV valve.

25. Install the ignition distributor and connect the spark plug wires and clips.

26. Connect the negative battery cable.

← **FRONT OF ENGINE**

VALVE COVER

VALVE COVER BOLT (11 REQ'D)

7922HG25

Cylinder head cover bolt torque sequence—2.0L engine

27. Run the engine and check for leaks and proper engine operation.

28. Check the ignition timing and adjust if required.

2.5L Engine

1. Before servicing the vehicle, refer to the precautions in the beginning of this section.

2. Disconnect the negative battery cable.

3. Remove the intake manifold.

4. Label and disconnect the spark plug wires from the spark plugs and move aside.

FRONT **REAR**

9300HG04

Camshaft bearing end-cap mounting bolt loosening sequence—2.5L engine

5. Remove the upper timing belt cover bolts. On the left cylinder head cover, disconnect the ventilation pipe from the front of the left side (front) cylinder head cover.

6. Remove the bolts and the cylinder head covers.

7. Remove the timing belt.

8. Hold the camshafts on the hexagonal casting and loosen the sprocket retaining bolts. Remove the camshaft sprockets.

✳✳ WARNING

Do not remove any of the camshaft bearing caps when the camshaft lobes are depressing the valve lifters or damage to the thrust journal support or camshaft may result.

9. Turn the camshafts so the knock pins are aligned with the marks on the camshaft bearing end-caps. This will reduce the pressure on the hydraulic lifters.

10. Note the markings on the camshaft bearing caps prior to removal, so they can be reinstalled in the same positions. The right bank (rear) caps are marked with numbers and the left bank (front) caps are marked with letters.

FRONT

REAR

9300HG05

Camshaft bearing cap loosening sequence for the front and rear cylinder heads—2.5L engine

Camshaft bearing cap tightening sequence for the front and rear cylinder heads—2.5L engine

18. Apply clean engine oil to the camshaft lobes, journals and supports.

19. Install the camshafts so the timing marks align on the camshaft gears.

20. Apply silicone sealant to the cylinder head surface in the area forward of the camshaft gear cavity on both cylinder heads and to the left (front) cylinder head on the rear exhaust camshaft end-cap mating surface.

21. Install the thrust caps. Tighten the thrust cap bolts until the caps are fully seated on the cylinder head.

✵✵ WARNING

Do not install any of the camshaft bearing caps when the camshaft lobes are depressing the valve lifters or damage to the thrust journal support or camshaft may result.

22. Install the remaining camshaft bearing caps and camshaft bearing end-caps in their original positions. Tighten the caps, in sequence, in 5 equal steps, with the final step being 98–123 inch lbs. (11–14 Nm).

➡ **The right bank (rear) camshaft bearing caps are marked with numbers and the left bank (front) camshaft bearing caps are marked with letters.**

23. Apply a light coat of clean engine oil to four new camshaft oil seals and install the seals using a suitable socket and hammer. The camshaft oil seals should be flush with the front of the cylinder head with a maximum protrusion of 0.020 inch (0.5mm).

24. Apply sealant to four new blind caps and install the blind caps using a plastic hammer or equivalent.

25. Install the camshaft sprockets and retaining bolts. Hold the hexagonal casting on the camshafts with a suitable wrench and tighten the retaining bolts to 90–103 ft. lbs. (123–140 Nm).

26. Install the timing belt.

27. Remove any sealant and gasket material from the cylinder head cover contact surfaces.

28. Apply silicone sealant to the cylinder head in the area adjacent to the front and rear camshaft caps. Install a new gasket on the cylinder head.

29. Install the cylinder head cover following the proper torque sequence, as shown earlier in this section, to 43–78 inch lbs. (5–8 Nm).

11. Loosen the camshaft bearing end-cap bolts in sequence, in 5–6 steps. Remove the camshaft bearing end-caps.

12. Remove the blind caps.

13. Remove the remaining camshaft bearing cap bolts, in 5–6 steps, in the proper sequence. Remove the caps, being sure to remove the thrust caps last. Do not damage the cylinder head thrust bearing support.

14. Remove the camshafts and oil seals. Tag the camshafts for identification.

15. If they are to be removed, number each hydraulic lifter (hydraulic lash adjuster) with a paint marker or equivalent during removal.

16. Inspect the camshafts and lifters for wear and/or damage; replace as necessary.

To install:

17. If removed, apply clean engine oil to the hydraulic lifters and install. If the old lifters are to be reused, be sure to install them in their original positions. Be sure that the hydraulic lifters move freely in their bores.

Timing belt service is covered in Section 5 of this manual

30. Tighten the upper timing cover bolts to 71–88 inch lbs. (8–10 Nm). Connect the ventilation pipe to the left side cylinder head cover.

31. Install the intake manifold.

32. Connect the spark plug wires to the spark plugs.

33. Connect the negative battery cable.

34. Run the engine and check for leaks and proper engine operation.

Valve Lash

ADJUSTMENT

The hydraulic lash adjusters cannot be adjusted. When the lash adjusters are removed from the engine, check the friction surfaces for wear or damage. Hold the lash adjuster and try to depress the plunger by hand. If the lash adjuster is worn or damaged, or the plunger can be moved by hand, replace the lash adjuster.

Oil Pan

REMOVAL & INSTALLATION

2.0L Engine

1. Before servicing the vehicle, refer to the precautions in the beginning of this section.

2. Disconnect the negative battery cable.

3. Raise and safely support the vehicle.

4. Remove the right-hand splash shield.

5. Drain the engine oil into a suitable container. Temporarily reinstall the drain plug.

6. Detach the Oxygen (O2S) sensor electrical connector. Remove and discard the exhaust pipe-to-manifold nuts. Move the exhaust pipe aside and support it with a jack.

7. Remove the exhaust clamp from the hold-down bracket.

8. Remove the oil pan bolts and carefully pry the oil pan from the engine stiffener.

To install:

9. Clean the oil pan. Clean all dirt, oil and old sealant from the oil pan, cylinder block and stiffener contact surfaces.

10. Apply a continuous bead of silicone sealant around the oil pan, going on the inside of the bolt holes.

11. Install the oil pan and tighten the bolts to 14–19 ft. lbs. (19–25 Nm).

12. Install a new exhaust clamp and tighten the clamp nuts to 26–34 ft. lbs. (34–47 Nm).

13. Connect the exhaust pipe to the manifold with new nuts. Tighten the nuts to 27–38 ft. lbs. (37–52 Nm).

14. Attach the O2S sensor electrical connector.

15. Install the right-hand splash shield.

16. Tighten the oil pan drain plug to 22–30 ft. lbs. (30–41 Nm).

17. Lower the vehicle.

18. Fill the engine with the proper type and quantity of engine oil.

19. Connect the negative battery cable.

20. Run the engine and check for leaks.

2.5L Engine

1. Before servicing the vehicle, refer to the precautions in the beginning of this section.

2. Disconnect the negative battery cable.

3. Raise and safely support the vehicle.

4. Drain the engine oil into a suitable container and reinstall the drain plug.

5. Detach the two Oxygen (O2S) sensor electrical connectors.

6. Remove the six crossmember bolts and remove the crossmember.

7. Remove the exhaust pipe-to-manifold nuts (3 per side) and lower the exhaust system to gain access to the oil pan bolts.

➡️**The oil pan bolts are different lengths. Identify them as they are removed so they can be reinstalled in their proper locations.**

8. Remove the oil pan bolts and the oil pan.

To install:

9. Clean the oil pan. Clean all dirt, oil and old sealant from the oil pan and cylinder block contact surfaces. Remove the old sealant from the threads of the oil pan bolts and the bolt holes in the block.

Be sure to apply the bead of sealant on the inside of the bolt holes, as shown—2.5L engine

7922HG47

✳✳ WARNING

Failure to remove the old sealant from the bolts and bolt holes may cause the block to crack.

10. Apply a continuous bead of silicone sealant along the inside of the bolt holes, overlapping the ends.

➡️**Once the new silicone sealant is applied, the oil pan must be installed within 5 minutes.**

11. Install the oil pan with the bolts. Tighten the long oil pan bolts to 14–18 ft. lbs. (19–25 Nm) and short bolts to 71–88 inch lbs. (8–10 Nm).

12. Connect the exhaust pipes to the manifolds with new gaskets and tighten the nuts to 30–41 ft. lbs. (40–55 Nm).

13. Attach the two O2S sensor electrical connectors.

14. Install the crossmember and tighten the six retaining bolts to 69–93 ft. lbs. (94–126 Nm).

15. Tighten the oil pan drain plug to 22–30 ft. lbs. (30–41 Nm).

16. Lower the vehicle.

17. Fill the engine with the proper type and quantity of engine oil.

18. Run the engine and check for leaks.

Oil Pump

REMOVAL & INSTALLATION

2.0L Engine

1. Before servicing the vehicle, refer to the precautions in the beginning of this section.

2. Disconnect the negative battery cable.

3. Remove the accessory drive belts.

4. Raise and safely support the vehicle.

Stiffener bolt and nut loosening sequence—2.0L engine

7922HG27

Oil pump mounting bolt locations—2.0L engine

5. Remove the engine oil pan and the oil pump pick-up tube and screen.

6. Remove the two rear main seal housing-to-stiffener nuts and the 12 stiffener bolts in 2 steps, in the proper sequence, and remove the stiffener.

7. Remove the engine front covers, timing belt and crankshaft sprocket.

8. If equipped, remove the A/C compressor and secure it aside, leaving the refrigerant lines attached. Remove the compressor mounting bracket.

9. Remove the seven oil pump bolts and remove the oil pump.

To install:

10. Clean the oil, dirt and old sealant from all contact surfaces.

11. Apply a bead of silicone to the oil pump-to-cylinder block contact surface, along the inside of the bolt holes. Be sure the sealer does not fall into the engine and form plugs that could block oil passages.

12. Install the oil pump and tighten the bolts to 14–19 ft. lbs. (19–25 Nm).

13. Clean the engine block contact area and stiffener. Apply a bead of silicone sealant to the perimeter of the stiffener, going on the inside of the bolt holes. Apply

sealant to the four rear bolt holes. Be sure the sealer does not fall into the engine and form plugs that could block oil passages.

14. Install the stiffener and the mounting bolts. Tighten the bolts in 2 steps, in sequence, to 14–19 ft. lbs. (19–25 Nm). Tighten the rear main seal housing-to-stiffener nuts to 88 inch lbs. (10 Nm).

15. Install a new gasket and the oil pump pick-up tube and screen. Tighten the mounting bolts to 71–88 inch lbs. (8–10 Nm).

16. Install the oil pan.

17. If equipped, install the A/C compressor bracket and tighten the bolts to 38 ft. lbs. (52 Nm). Install the A/C compressor and tighten the bolts to 26 ft. lbs. (35 Nm).

18. Install the crankshaft sprocket, timing belt and the engine front covers.

19. Install the accessory drive belts.

20. Fill the engine with the proper grade and quantity of oil.

21. Connect the negative battery cable.

22. Run the engine; check oil pressure and check for leaks.

2.5L Engine

➡**The oil pump is located behind the crankshaft timing belt sprocket. Oil pump replacement is an in-vehicle service, however it requires that the timing belt covers, timing belt, and oil pan be removed. It is recommended that the front crankshaft seal be replaced whenever the oil pump is removed from the vehicle.**

1. Before servicing the vehicle, refer to the precautions in the beginning of this section.

2. Disconnect the negative battery cable.

3. Remove the accessory drive belts.

4. Remove the engine front covers and the timing belt.

5. Remove the engine oil pan.

6. If equipped, remove the four A/C compressor mounting bolts and support the compressor aside, without disconnecting the refrigerant lines. Remove the five A/C compressor mounting bracket bolts and remove the bracket.

7. Remove the power steering pump and tensioner bolts from the engine block. Remove the pump and tensioner and position aside.

8. Remove the crankshaft sprocket using a suitable puller. Remove the crankshaft sprocket key.

9. Remove the nine oil pump mounting bolts and the two oil strainer-to-oil pump bolts. Remove the oil pump.

Apply sealant to the stiffener in the places indicated—2.0L engine

Stiffener bolt tightening sequence—2.0L engine

➡ **The oil pump mounting bolts are different lengths. Identify them as they are removed so they can be reinstalled in their proper locations.**

10. Remove the oil pump O-ring. If necessary, use a small prybar or punch protected with a rag to knock out the front crankshaft seal from the oil pump housing.

➡ **Protect the oil pump housing with a rag while removing the crankshaft front seal.**

To install:

11. Clean the oil, dirt and old sealant from all contact surfaces.

12. Lubricate the new front crankshaft seal lip with clean engine oil. Using front seal replacer T74P-6150-A or equivalent, press or drive the new seal into the oil pump housing. Install the seal so it is flush with the edge of the oil pump housing or protrudes no more than 0.021 in. (0.7mm) from the edge of the pump body.

13. Install a new O-ring onto the oil pump. Apply a continuous bead of silicone sealant to the oil pump mating surface and install the pump.

14. Install the nine oil pump mounting bolts.

➡ **Be sure that the proper length bolts are placed into the correct positions.**

15. Tighten bolts A and B to 14–18 ft. lbs. (19–25 Nm).

16. Install the crankshaft timing belt sprocket and key.

17. Install the power steering pump and tensioner. Tighten the two power steering belt tensioner upper bolts and the power steering pump rear bracket bolt to 24–33 ft. lbs. (32–46 Nm). Tighten the tensioner lower bolt to 14–18 ft. lbs. (19–25 Nm).

18. If equipped, install the A/C compressor bracket and tighten the bolts to 28–38 ft. lbs. (38–51 Nm). Install the A/C compressor and tighten the bolts to 28–38 ft. lbs. (38–51 Nm).

BOLT A : 40mm (1.57 IN.)
BOLT B : 25mm (0.98 IN.)

7922HG31

Notice the positions of the different length oil pump mounting bolts—2.5L engine

19. Install the two oil strainer-to-oil pump bolts and tighten to 71–88 inch lbs. (8–10 Nm).

20. Install the oil pan, timing belt and the front engine covers.

21. Install the accessory drive belts.

22. Fill the engine with the proper grade and quantity of oil.

23. Connect the negative battery cable.

24. Run the engine; check oil pressure and check for leaks.

FUEL SYSTEM

Fuel System Service Precautions

Safety is the most important factor when performing not only fuel system maintenance but any type of maintenance. Failure to conduct maintenance and repairs in a safe manner may result in serious personal injury or death. Maintenance and testing of the vehicle's fuel system components can be accomplished safely and effectively by adhering to the following rules and guidelines.

• To avoid the possibility of fire and personal injury, always disconnect the negative battery cable unless the repair or test procedure requires that battery voltage be applied.

• Always relieve the fuel system pressure prior to disconnecting any fuel system component (injector, fuel rail, pressure regulator, etc.), fitting or fuel line connection. Exercise extreme caution whenever relieving fuel system pressure to avoid exposing skin, face and eyes to fuel spray. Please be advised that fuel under pressure may penetrate the skin or any part of the body that it contacts.

• Always place a shop towel or cloth around the fitting or connection prior to loosening to absorb any excess fuel due to spillage. Ensure that all fuel spillage (should it occur) is quickly removed from engine surfaces. Ensure that all fuel soaked cloths or towels are deposited into a suitable waste container.

• Always keep a dry chemical (Class B) fire extinguisher near the work area.

• Do not allow fuel spray or fuel vapors to come into contact with a spark or open flame.

• Always use a back-up wrench when loosening and tightening fuel line connection fittings. This will prevent unnecessary stress and torsion to fuel line piping.

• Always replace worn fuel fitting O-rings with new. Do not substitute fuel hose or equivalent, where fuel pipe is installed.

Fuel System Pressure

RELIEVING

1. Before servicing the vehicle, refer to the precautions in the beginning of this section.

Fuel pump relay location in the fuse box

FUEL PUMP RELAY

LH FRONT SPRING AND SHOCK TOWER

BATTERY

7922HG32

2. Start the engine and let it idle.

3. Locate and remove the fuel pump relay from the main fuse junction panel located next to the left-hand front strut tower.

4. After the engine stalls, turn **OFF** the ignition switch.

5. Disconnect the negative battery cable.

6. Install the fuel pump relay.

Fuel Filter

REMOVAL & INSTALLATION

1. Before servicing the vehicle, refer to the precautions in the beginning of this section.

2. Properly relieve the fuel system pressure.

3. Disconnect the negative battery cable.

4. If equipped with cruise control, remove the three speed control servo nuts and position the servo aside.

5. Remove the two fuel filter bracket nuts and remove the fuel tube clamps.

6. Disconnect the fuel lines from both ends of the fuel filter. Plug the lines to prevent leakage.

7. Remove the filter from the mounting bracket.

To install:

8. Position the fuel filter in the mounting bracket.

9. Unplug the fuel lines and place new fuel line clamps onto each fuel line.

10. Install the fuel lines to the fuel filter and position the clamps.

11. Install the two bracket nuts and tighten to 71–97 inch lbs. (8–11 Nm).

12. If equipped with cruise control, position the speed control servo and install the three mounting nuts.

13. Connect the negative battery cable.

14. Run the engine and check for fuel leaks.

Fuel Pump

REMOVAL & INSTALLATION

1. Before servicing the vehicle, refer to the precautions in the beginning of this section.

2. Relieve the fuel system pressure using the recommended procedure.

3. Disconnect the negative battery cable.

4. Remove the fuel tank as follows:

a. Drain the fuel from the tank into a suitable container.

b. Loosen the clamps, then remove the hoses attached to the fuel tank.

c. Detach the fuel pump electrical connector.

d. Remove the fuel tank heat shield.

e. Support the fuel tank and remove the tank support brackets.

f. Slowly, lower the tank out of the vehicle and place it on a work bench.

5. Remove any dirt that has accumulated around the fuel pump retaining flange

so it will not enter the tank during pump removal and installation.

6. Turn the fuel pump locking ring counterclockwise and remove the locking ring.

❊❊ CAUTION

If the locking ring is tapped around, be sure to use a brass drift and mallet to prevent sparks.

7. Remove the fuel pump and fuel level sensor assembly. Remove and discard the seal ring.

To install:

8. Clean the fuel pump mounting flange, fuel tank mounting surface and seal ring groove.

9. Apply a light coating of grease on a new seal ring to hold it in place during assembly and install in the seal ring groove.

10. Install the fuel pump and fuel level sensor assembly carefully to ensure the filter and sensor arm are not damaged. Be sure the locating keys are in the keyways and the seal ring remains in the groove.

11. Hold the pump assembly in place and install the locking ring finger-tight. Be sure all the locking tabs are under the tank lock ring tabs.

12. Rotate the locking ring clockwise until the ring is against the stops.

Exploded view of the fuel filter assembly mounting

FUEL TUBE

FUEL FILTER

FUEL TUBE

7922HG33

FUEL PUMP LOCKING RETAINER RING

Use a brass drift and mallet to prevent sparks when removing the fuel pump lockring

7922HG34

13. Install the fuel tank in the vehicle in the reverse order of the removal steps. Add a minimum of 10 gallons of fuel to the tank and check for leaks.

14. Connect the negative battery cable, start the engine and check for proper system operation and for fuel leaks.

DRIVE TRAIN

Transaxle Assembly

REMOVAL & INSTALLATION

Manual

1. Before servicing the vehicle, refer to the precautions in the beginning of this section.

2. Disconnect the battery cables, negative cable first, and remove the battery and battery tray.

3. Remove the air cleaner intake tube and the engine air cleaner.

4. Label and disengage all connectors and ground straps related to transaxle removal.

5. Disconnect the clutch slave cylinder and position it aside, without disconnecting the hydraulic line.

6. Support the engine with engine support tool 014–00750 or equivalent.

7. Remove the upper transaxle-to-engine mounting bolts.

8. Remove the starter. Remove the fuel filter mounting nuts and position the filter aside, without disconnecting the fuel lines.

9. Remove the two nuts and the through-bolt from the left side engine support insulator.

10. Raise and safely support the vehicle. Remove the front wheels.

11. If equipped with the 2.0L engine, remove the intake manifold support bolts and bracket.

12. Remove the drain plug and drain the transaxle fluid into a suitable container.

13. Remove the halfshafts.

14. Remove the lower splash shields.

15. Remove the crossmember bolts and the crossmember.

16. On vehicles equipped with anti-lock brakes, remove the clips from the left-hand side anti-lock sensor and bracket. Remove the bracket nuts from the anti-lock sensor and bracket harness mount on the left-hand side of the vehicle.

17. Remove the nuts and bolts from the rear engine support and remove the rear engine support.

18. Disconnect the shift rod and control rod from the transaxle.

19. Remove the rear transaxle support bracket bolts.

20. Support the transaxle with a suitable jack.

21. Remove the rear transaxle support insulator bolts and the rear transaxle support insulator.

22. Remove the lower transaxle-to-engine mounting bolts.

23. Separate the transaxle from the engine and carefully lower it from the vehicle.

To install:

24. Place the transaxle on a suitable jack. Apply a thin coating of molybdenum grease, or equivalent, to the input shaft splines. Raise the transaxle into position and align it with the engine.

25. Position the transaxle to the engine and loosely install the lower transaxle-to-engine bolts. Remove the transmission jack.

26. Install the nuts and bolts to the engine support insulator. Tighten the nuts to 32–44 ft. lbs. (44–60 Nm) and the bolts to 63–86 ft. lbs. (86–116 Nm).

27. Install the rear transaxle support insulator with the three bolts. Tighten the bolts to 50–68 ft. lbs. (67–93 Nm).

28. Connect the control rod and shift rod to the transaxle. Tighten the control rod nut to 28–38 ft. lbs. (38–51 Nm) and the shift rod bolt and nut to 14–18 ft. lbs. (19–25 Nm).

29. Install the rear engine support and tighten the bolts and nuts as follows:

• Tighten **A** to 55–77 ft. lbs. (75–104 Nm)

• Tighten **B** to 50–68 ft. lbs. (67–93 Nm)

• Tighten **C** to 32–44 ft. lbs. (44–60 Nm)

Front axle bearing bracket bolt locations and tightening sequence—2.0L engine

30. Install the halfshafts.

31. Pry the lower control arm down and insert the lower ball joint stud into the knuckle. Install the pinch bolt and nut and tighten to 26–41 ft. lbs. (35–56 Nm).

32. If equipped with anti-lock brakes, install the anti-lock sensor harness mounting nuts and tighten to 71–88 inch lbs. (8–10 Nm). Install the sensor harness clips.

33. Install the three halfshaft support bearing bracket bolts. Tighten the bolts, in sequence, to 32–45 ft. lbs. (43–61 Nm).

34. If equipped with the 2.5L engine, connect the exhaust pipes to the manifolds and tighten the new nuts to 30–41 ft. lbs. (40–55 Nm). Attach the two oxygen sensor connectors.

35. Position the crossmember and tighten the six retaining bolts to 69–96 ft. lbs. (94–131 Nm).

36. Install new halfshaft retaining nuts. Have an assistant apply the brakes to lock the hubs, then tighten the nuts to 174–235 ft. lbs. (235–319 Nm). Stake the nuts using a dull chisel or similar tool.

37. Install the wheels and tighten the lug nuts to 65–87 ft. lbs. (88–118 Nm).

38. Install a new washer on the transaxle drain plug. Install and tighten the drain plug to 29–43 ft. lbs. (40–58 Nm).

Front axle bearing bracket bolt locations and tightening sequence—2.5L engine

39. Position the starter motor and tighten the lower retaining bolt to 28–38 ft. lbs. (35–52 Nm). Connect the starter wiring.

40. If equipped with the 2.0L engine, install the intake manifold support bracket and bolts. Tighten the bolts to 27–38 ft. lbs. (37–52 Nm).

41. Install the lower splash shields.

42. If equipped with the 2.0L engine, install the two lower transaxle-to-engine bolts. Tighten bolt **B** to 28–38 ft. lbs. (38–51 Nm) and bolt **C** to 14–18 ft. lbs. (19–25 Nm). Install the two engine-to-transaxle bolts. Tighten bolt **D** to 28–38 ft. lbs. (38–51 Nm) and bolt **E** to 66–86 ft. lbs. (90–116 Nm).

43. If equipped with the 2.5L engine, install and tighten the three lower transaxle-to-engine bolts to 28–38 ft. lbs. (38–51 Nm).

44. Install the three rear transaxle support bracket bolts and tighten to 50–68 ft. lbs. (67–93 Nm).

45. Fill the transaxle with the proper fluid to a level even with the lower edge of the oil level plug port, with the vehicle level. Install the plug, using a new washer, and tighten to 29–43 ft. lbs. (40–58 Nm) if not already done.

46. Lower the vehicle.

47. Position the fuel filter and install the two retaining nuts. Tighten the nuts to 71–88 inch lbs. (8–10 Nm).

48. If equipped with the 2.0L engine, install the four remaining transaxle-to-engine bolts. Tighten the **A** bolts to 66–86 ft. lbs. (90–116 Nm). If equipped with the 2.5L engine, install the seven upper transaxle-to-engine bolts and tighten to 50–73 ft. lbs. (68–99 Nm).

49. Install the two upper starter motor bolts and tighten to 28–38 ft. lbs. (35–51 Nm).

50. Remove the engine support tool.

51. Install the clutch slave cylinder and the two retaining bolts. Tighten the bolts to 12–16 ft. lbs. (16–22 Nm).

52. Attach the back-up lamp switch and vehicle speed sensor electrical connectors and the transaxle ground straps.

53. Install the battery and battery tray.

54. Install the engine air cleaner and the air cleaner intake tube.

55. Connect the battery cables, negative cable last.

56. Run the engine and check for leaks.

57. Check transaxle operation and bleed the clutch hydraulic system if required.

Automatic

4EAT TRANSAXLE

1. Before servicing the vehicle, refer to the precautions in the beginning of this section.

2. Disconnect the battery cables, negative cable first, and remove the battery and battery tray.

3. Remove the engine air cleaner assembly.

4. Pry the shift cable from the manual control shift outer lever. Remove the cable bracket lock-tab retainer, press in on the lock-tabs to release the shift cable and pull the cable through the bracket.

5. Detach the Manual Lever Position (MLP) sensor electrical connector. Detach the two Heated Oxygen (HO$_2$S) sensor electrical connectors and the transaxle electrical connector.

6. Remove the wiring harness bracket from the shift cable bracket.

7. Remove the starter motor wiring and remove the starter motor.

8. Detach the Vehicle Speed Sensor (VSS) electrical connector. Remove the ground wire bracket and the ground wire.

9. Remove the harness support bracket to the alternator, located at the rear engine support insulator bracket.

10. Disconnect and plug the inlet and outlet oil cooler tubes.

Engine-To-Transaxle Bolts

Transaxle-To-Engine Bolts

7922HG08

Engine and transaxle retaining bolt locations—2.5L engine

11. Remove the three transaxle-to-engine mounting bolts.

12. Support the engine from above with engine support tool 014–00750 or equivalent.

13. Remove the two left-hand engine support insulator nuts and bolt and the mount through-bolt.

14. Remove the two fuel filter bracket nuts from the left transaxle mount. Position the filter and bracket aside without disconnecting the fuel lines.

15. Remove the left-hand engine support insulator bracket.

16. Detach the Pulse Signal Generator (PSG) electrical connector.

17. Raise and safely support the vehicle.

18. Remove the front wheels and the splash shields.

19. Remove the six crossmember bolts and the crossmember.

20. Remove the six rear engine support nuts and two bolts and remove the rear engine support.

21. Remove the two lower transaxle support insulator bolts and remove the lower transaxle support insulator.

22. Remove the halfshafts and install transaxle plugs to prevent the differential gears from becoming misaligned.

23. Disconnect the transaxle vent hose and the dipstick tube.

24. Remove the three inspection cover bolts. Use a small prybar to hold the flexplate and remove the four torque converter nuts.

25. Support the transaxle with a suitable transmission jack. Secure the transaxle to the transmission jack to keep it from falling.

26. Remove the two engine-to-transaxle bolts.

27. Remove the three rear transaxle support bracket bolts.

28. Use a small prybar to separate the transaxle from the engine. Slightly tilt the transaxle and engine to ease removal.

29. Carefully remove the transaxle from the engine and lower the transaxle from the vehicle.

To install:

➡ **If the transaxle was rebuilt or replaced, be sure to flush the transmission oil cooler tubes to remove contaminants before installing the oil cooler tubes to the transaxle.**

30. Position the transaxle onto a suitable transmission jack and secure the transaxle to the jack.

1. Battery
2. Battery tray
3. Front fender splash shield
4. LH front wheel driveshaft & joint
5. Cotter pin
6. Wheel & tire
7. Lower transaxle support insulator
8. Rear engine support
9. LH transaxle support insulator
10. Transaxle
11. Oil cooler tubes
12. Front transaxle support insulator
13. Crossmember
14. Halfshaft
15. Starter motor
16. Exhaust inlet pipe
17. RH front wheel driveshaft & joint
18. Stabilizer bar link
19. Flywheel to converter retaining nut
20. Cover plate
21. Transmission shift cable & bracket
22. Rear transaxle support insulator

7922HG49

Exploded view of all transaxle removal/installation related components—4EAT transaxle

31. Raise the transaxle into position. Align the torque converter studs with the flexplate.

32. Install the two engine-to-transaxle bolts and tighten to 50–73 ft. lbs. (68–99 Nm).

33. Install the three rear transaxle support bracket bolts and tighten to 50–68 ft. lbs. (67–93 Nm).

34. Install the four torque converter-to-flexplate nuts and tighten to 32–45 ft. lbs. (44–60 Nm).

35. Install the inspection cover.

36. Connect the transaxle vent hose and install the dipstick tube. Tighten the dipstick tube mounting bolts to 71–88 inch lbs. (8–10 Nm).

37. Remove the transaxle plugs and install the halfshafts.

38. Install the lower transaxle support insulator and tighten the bolts to 41–59 ft. lbs. (55–80 Nm).

39. Remove the transmission jack.

40. Install the rear engine support. Tighten the rear engine support-to-body bolts and nuts to 50–68 ft. lbs. (67–93 Nm). Tighten the rear engine support-to-front mount nuts to 55–77 ft. lbs. (75–104 Nm) and the rear engine support-to-rear mount nuts to 32–44 ft. lbs. (44–60 Nm).

41. Install the crossmember and tighten the six bolts to 68–96 ft. lbs. (94–131 Nm).

42. Install the splash shields and the front wheels. Tighten the lug nuts to 66–86 ft. lbs. (88–118 Nm).

43. Lower the vehicle.

44. Install the three transaxle-to-engine support bolts and tighten to 50–73 ft. lbs. (68–99 Nm).

45. Attach the VSS and the PSG electrical connectors. Install the ground wire bracket and the ground wire.

46. Install the harness support bracket to the engine block located at the left-hand engine support insulator bracket.

47. Install the left-hand engine support insulator and two nuts and one bolt. Tighten the two nuts and bolt to 50–68 ft. lbs. (67–93 Nm). Install the through-bolt and tighten to 63–86 ft. lbs. (86–116 Nm).

48. Remove the engine support tool.

49. Install the fuel filter bracket and tighten the two nuts to 71–88 inch lbs. (8–10 Nm).

50. Unplug and connect the inlet and outlet oil cooler tubes.

51. Install the starter motor and wiring.

52. Attach the transaxle electrical con-

nector and the two HO2S sensor electrical connectors.

53. Insert the shift cable through the cable bracket and pull the cable until the lock-tabs engage. Install the lock-tab retainer. Connect the shift cable to the manual control shift outer lever.

54. Attach the MLP sensor electrical connector. Snap the wiring harness bracket on the cable bracket.

55. Install the air cleaner assembly.

56. Install the battery tray and battery. Connect the battery cables, negative cable last.

57. Fill the transaxle with the proper type and quantity of fluid.

58. Run the engine and check for leaks. Road test and check for proper transaxle operation.

CD4E TRANSAXLE

1. Before servicing the vehicle, refer to the precautions in the beginning of this section.

2. Disconnect the battery cables, negative cable first, and remove the battery and battery tray.

3. Remove the air cleaner assembly.

4. Detach the Manual Lever Position (MLP) sensor electrical connector. Remove the two MLP sensor bolts and the sensor.

5. Remove the ground wire bracket and the ground wire.

6. Remove the shift cable from the cable bracket. Remove the two cable bracket bolts and remove the bracket.

7. Detach the transaxle electrical connector by pushing on the retaining ring and gently pulling up on the connector.

8. Disconnect and plug the oil cooler inlet and outlet hoses.

9. Remove the two upper starter motor bolts.

10. Support the engine from above with engine support tool 014–00750 or equivalent.

11. Remove the top three transaxle-to-engine mounting bolts.

12. Remove the two fuel filter bracket nuts from the left-hand transaxle mount. Position the filter and bracket aside without disconnecting the fuel lines.

13. Remove the two ignition coil nuts and position the ignition coil out of the way.

14. Remove the three speed control servo nuts and position the speed control servo out of the way.

15. Remove the three ignition coil mounting strap bolts.

16. Disconnect the wiring harness clips from the ignition coil mounting straps. Remove the ignition coil mounting straps.

17. Remove the two nut and two bolts from the left-hand engine support insulator. Remove the left-hand support insulator through-bolt. Remove the left-hand support insulator.

18. Raise and safely support the vehicle.

19. Remove the front wheels and the splash shields.

20. Remove the six crossmember bolts and the crossmember.

21. Remove the six rear engine support nuts and two bolts and remove the rear engine support.

22. Remove the halfshafts. Install transaxle plugs into the differential side gears.

23. Remove the intake manifold support bolts and the support.

24. Disconnect the starter motor wiring. Remove the lower starter motor bolt and remove the starter motor.

25. Detach the Transmission Speed Sensor (TSS) connector.

26. Remove the four torque converter-to-flywheel retaining nuts through the starter opening.

27. Remove the front transaxle support insulator through-bolt and remove the front support insulator.

28. Remove the four front transaxle support bracket bolts and remove the support bracket.

29. Remove the rear transaxle support insulator through-bolt.

30. Lower the vehicle.

31. Lower the transaxle by loosening the bolt on the engine support.

32. Raise and safely support the vehicle.

33. Secure the transaxle to a suitable jack using the appropriate adapters.

34. Remove the three engine-to-transaxle bolts.

35. Remove the two remaining transaxle-to-engine bolts.

36. Use a small prybar or similar tool to separate the transaxle from the engine.

37. Partially lower the transaxle from the engine.

38. Detach the Vehicle Speed Sensor (VSS) connector.

39. Finish lowering the transaxle and remove from the vehicle.

To install:

➡**If the transaxle was rebuilt or is being replaced, be sure to flush the transmission oil cooler hoses to**

Transaxle-to-engine mounting bolts—CD4E transaxle

7922HG42

remove contaminants before installing the oil cooler hoses to the transaxle.

40. Place the transaxle on a suitable jack using the appropriate adapters.

41. Raise the transaxle into position. Align the torque converter studs with the flexplate.

42. Install the transaxle-to-engine bolts. Tighten bolts **B** to 28–38 ft. lbs. (38–51 Nm) and bolts **C** to 14–18 ft. lbs. (19–25 Nm).

43. Remove the jack.

44. Install the rear transaxle support insulator through-bolt. Do not tighten it fully at this time.

45. Install the front transaxle support bracket. Tighten the four front transaxle support bracket bolts to 28–38 ft. lbs. (38–51 Nm). Install the front transaxle support insulator and through-bolt. Do not tighten the through-bolt fully at this time.

46. Attach the TSS and VSS connectors.

47. Install the four torque converter-to-flexplate nuts and tighten to 24–30 ft. lbs. (33–40 Nm).

48. Install the torque converter access plug.

49. Lower the vehicle.

50. Install the left-hand engine support insulator and tighten the through-bolt to 63–86 ft. lbs. (86–116 Nm). Install the two left-hand engine support insulator nuts and

two bolts. Do not tighten them fully at this time.

51. Remove the engine support.

52. Raise and safely support the vehicle.

53. Install the rear engine support. Tighten the rear engine support bolts and nuts as follows:

- Tighten **A** to 55–77 ft. lbs. (75–104 Nm)

- Tighten **B** to 50–68 ft. lbs. (67–93 Nm)

- Tighten **C** to 32–44 ft. lbs. (44–60 Nm)

54. Tighten the front and rear transaxle support insulator through-bolts to 63–86 ft. lbs. (86–116 Nm).

55. Install the starter motor and the lower starter motor bolt. Tighten the lower starter motor bolt to 23–34 ft. lbs. (31–46 Nm). Attach the starter motor wiring.

56. Install the intake manifold support and bolts. Tighten the bolts to 27–38 ft. lbs. (37–52 Nm).

57. Remove the transaxle plugs and install the halfshafts.

58. Install the crossmember and six bolts. Tighten the crossmember bolts to 68–96 ft. lbs. (94–131 Nm).

59. Install the splash shields and the wheels. Tighten the lug nuts to 67–86 ft. lbs. (88–118 Nm).

60. Lower the vehicle.

61. Tighten the two left-hand support insulator nuts to 12–17 ft. lbs. (16–23 Nm).

Tighten the two left-hand engine support insulator bolts to 28–38 ft. lbs. (38–51 Nm).

62. Position the ignition coil mounting straps and install the wiring harness clips and the three ignition coil strap bolts.

63. Position the speed control servo and install and tighten the three nuts.

64. Position the ignition coil and install the two nuts. Tighten the ignition coil nuts to 71–88 inch lbs. (8–10 Nm).

65. Install the two fuel filter bracket nuts and tighten to 71–97 inch lbs. (8–11 Nm).

66. Install the two upper starter motor bolts and tighten to 23–34 ft. lbs. (31–46 Nm).

67. Install the three remaining transaxle-to-engine bolts. Tighten the **A** bolts to 66–86 ft. lbs. (89–117 Nm).

68. Install the shift cable bracket and two bolts.

69. Attach the transaxle electrical connector.

70. Install the MLP sensor and the two MLP sensor bolts. Adjust the MLP sensor and tighten the bolts to 96–117 inch lbs. (11–13 Nm). Attach the MLP sensor electrical connector

71. Connect the oil cooler inlet and outlet hoses.

72. Install the air cleaner assembly.

73. Install the battery tray and battery.

74. Install the ground wire bracket and the ground wire.

75. Connect the battery cables, negative cable last.

76. Fill the transaxle with the proper type and quantity of fluid.

77. Run the engine and check for leaks.

78. Road test and check for proper transaxle operation.

Clutch

ADJUSTMENTS

Pedal Height

1. Before servicing the vehicle, refer to the precautions in the beginning of this section.

2. To determine if the clutch pedal height requires an adjustment, measure the distance from the bulkhead to the upper center of the pedal pad. The distance should be 7.32–8.31 in. (186–211mm).

3. If adjustment is required, loosen locknut **A** and turn the adjusting bolt **B** until the desired pedal height is reached.

4. Tighten the locknut to 122–156 inch lbs. (14–17 Nm).

LOCKNUT C

PUSH ROD D

ADJUSTING BOLT B

LOCKNUT A

PEDAL HEIGHT

PEDAL FREE PLAY

DISENGAGEMENT HEIGHT

7922HG39

Clutch pedal adjustments and related components

Pedal Free-Play

1. Before servicing the vehicle, refer to the precautions in the beginning of this section.

2. Measure the clutch pedal height at rest.

3. Depress the clutch pedal by hand and measure the height of the pedal when resistance is felt.

4. The difference should be 0.04–0.12 inch (1–3mm).

5. If adjustment is necessary, proceed as follows:

a. Loosen locknut **C** and turn clutch master cylinder pushrod **D** until the pedal play is within specifications.

b. Measure the distance from the floor to the center of the pedal pad when the pedal is fully depressed. The distance should be 2.64 inches (67mm).

c. Tighten the locknut to 105–147 inch lbs. (12–16 Nm).

REMOVAL & INSTALLATION

1. Before servicing the vehicle, refer to the precautions in the beginning of this section.

2. Disconnect the negative battery cable.

3. Remove the transaxle assembly.

4. Position a suitable clutch alignment tool through the pressure plate, clutch disc and into the pilot bearing; this will keep the assembly from dropping when the bolts are removed.

5. Install flywheel holding tool T74P-6375-A or equivalent, to keep the flywheel from turning.

6. Remove the pressure plate-to-flywheel bolts evenly to relieve the spring pressure.

7. Remove the pressure plate, clutch disc and alignment tool.

8. Inspect the pressure plate and clutch disc for wear and/or damage and replace, as necessary.

9. Inspect the pilot bearing for excessive wear or scoring. Remove it using a suitable puller, only if replacement is necessary.

10. Inspect the flywheel for scoring, cracks, worn or broken teeth, or other damage. Remove the flywheel if machining or replacement is necessary. Use care when removing the last bolt to prevent dropping the flywheel.

11. Remove the release bearing and fork. Inspect them for wear or damage and replace as necessary.

To install:

12. Apply molybdenum grease to the release bearing where it contacts the release fork. Apply molybdenum grease to the release fork at the pivot point and to the area where it contacts the release bearing.

13. Install the release fork and bearing.

14. If removed, install the flywheel. Be sure the crankshaft flange and flywheel mating surfaces are clean. Remove the old sealant from the flywheel bolts and apply stud and bearing mount sealant to them. If the old sealant cannot be removed, replace the bolts.

15. Install the flywheel holding tool. Tighten the flywheel bolts, in sequence, to 71–75 ft. lbs. (97–102 Nm) on the 2.0L engine or 45–49 ft. lbs. (61–67 Nm) on the 2.5L engine.

16. If removed, install a new pilot bearing using a suitable bearing installer. When

2.0L

FLYWHEEL
HOLDING
TOOL
T74P-6375-A

2.5L

FLYWHEEL
HOLDING TOOL
T74P-6375-A

7922HG37

Flywheel bolt tightening sequences

installed, the pilot bearing should be 0–0.016 in. (0–0.4mm) below the surface of the crankshaft flange.

17. Apply a small amount of molybdenum grease to the clutch disc and input shaft splines. Do not let grease get on the clutch face.

18. Install the clutch disc with the spring side of the disc toward the transaxle. Install the alignment tool to hold the disc in place.

19. Install the pressure plate to the flywheel. Install the pressure plate-to-flywheel bolts and tighten evenly until the bolts are seated. Tighten to 13–18 ft. lbs. (18–26 Nm) in the proper sequence.

CLUTCH
PRESSURE PLATE
BOLTS 6 REQ'D
18–26 N·m
(13–18 LB-FT)

FLYWHEEL HOLDING TOOL
T74P-6375-A

FLYWHEEL

7922HG38

Clutch pressure plate bolt tightening sequence

20. Install the transaxle assembly.
21. Connect the negative battery cable.
22. Check for proper clutch operation.

Hydraulic Clutch System

BLEEDING

➡ **The fluid reservoir must be maintained at the ¾ level or higher during air bleeding.**

1. Before servicing the vehicle, refer to the precautions in the beginning of this section.

2. Remove the bleeder cap from the slave cylinder and attach a vinyl hose to the bleeder screw.

3. Place the other end of the hose in a clear container partially filled with brake fluid.

4. Have an assistant slowly pump the clutch pedal several times.

5. With the clutch pedal depressed, loosen the bleeder screw to release the fluid and air.

6. Tighten the bleeder screw. Repeat this procedure until there are no air bubbles in the fluid in the container.

7. When complete, tighten the bleeder screw to 53–78 inch lbs. (6–8 Nm).

8. Check the fluid level and fill as required.

9. Check for leaks and proper clutch operation.

Halfshaft

REMOVAL & INSTALLATION

1. Before servicing the vehicle, refer to the precautions in the beginning of this section.

2. Disconnect the negative battery cable.

3. With the vehicle sitting on all four wheels, use a chisel to raise the staked portion of the hub nut. Have an assistant apply the brakes to lock the wheels, then loosen but do not remove the hub nut.

4. Raise and safely support the vehicle.

5. Remove the wheel and the necessary inner fender splash guards.

6. Remove the stabilizer link assembly from the lower control arm.

7. Remove the ball joint clamp bolt from the lower control arm. Carefully pry the lower control arm downward to separate the ball joint from the steering knuckle.

➡ **If removing the right halfshaft, remove the support bearing bracket from the cylinder block.**

Item	Description
1	Pressure Plate
2	Clutch Disc
3	Pilot Bearing
4	Flywheel
5	Brake Master Cylinder Reservoir
6	Clutch Pedal Position (CPP) Switch
7	Clutch Pedal
8	Clutch Master Cylinder
9	Clutch Release Bearing
10	Clutch Release Fork
11	Slave Cylinder

7922HG48

Hydraulic clutch system component identification

8. Separate the halfshaft from the transaxle by positioning a prybar between the halfshaft and transaxle case. Pry out the halfshaft while pulling out on the steering knuckle. Be careful not to damage the transaxle case, transaxle oil seal, CV-joint or CV-joint boot.

9. Remove and discard the hub nut. Pull the halfshaft out of the wheel hub. If necessary, use a plastic hammer to tap it out or a wheel puller to press it out. Do not use a metal hammer.

10. Support the halfshaft and slide it out of the transaxle.

11. Install transaxle plug T88C-7025-AH or equivalent, into the halfshaft opening of the transaxle case and into the differential side gear; this will keep the differential side gear from falling out of place.

To install:

➡**If replacing a halfshaft and joint on an ABS equipped vehicle, install a new front brake anti-lock sensor indicator.**

12. On the end of the halfshaft, install a new circlip. Start one end of the clip in the groove and work the clip over the stub shaft end and into the groove. This will prevent over-expanding the clip. Be sure the end-gap is positioned at the top of the splines.

13. Remove the transaxle plug and inspect the transaxle oil seal. Replace if necessary.

14. Lubricate the halfshaft splines with a CV-joint grease, align the splines with the differential side gear and push the halfshaft into the differential. Be sure the retaining clip clicks into the differential side gear groove.

15. Position the halfshaft through the wheel hub and install a new attaching nut. Do not tighten the nut at this time.

16. If installing the right halfshaft, install the halfshaft support bearing and tighten the mounting bolts to 31–46 ft. lbs. (42–62 Nm).

➡**The support bearing bolts must be tightened in the proper sequence, as shown earlier in this section.**

17. Position the ball joint in the steering knuckle and install the clamp bolt/nut. Tighten the nut to 25–42 ft. lbs. (34–57 Nm).

18. Install the stabilizer link assembly and tighten the nuts to 27–40 ft. lbs. (36–54 Nm).

19. Install the splash shields and wheel, then lower the vehicle.

20. With the vehicle sitting on all four wheels, have an assistant apply the brakes and tighten the halfshaft attaching nut to 174–235 ft. lbs. (235–319 Nm). Stake the nut using a suitable chisel with a rounded cutting edge.

➡**If the nut splits or cracks after staking, it must be replaced with a new nut.**

21. Connect the negative battery cable.

22. Check the transaxle fluid level. Road test the vehicle and check for leaks.

STEERING AND SUSPENSION

Air Bag

✳ CAUTION

The Supplemental Restraint System (SRS) must be disarmed before removing the air bag module. Failure to do so may cause accidental deployment of the air bag, resulting in unnecessary SRS repairs and/or personal injury.

PRECAUTIONS

Several precautions must be observed when handling the inflator module to avoid accidental deployment and possible personal injury.

• Never carry the inflator module by the wires or connector on the underside of the module.

• When carrying a live inflator module, hold securely with both hands, and ensure that the bag and trim cover are pointed away.

• Place the inflator module on a bench or other surface with the bag and trim cover facing up.

• With the inflator module on the bench, never place anything on or close to the module that may be thrown in the event of an accidental deployment.

DISARMING

1. Before servicing the vehicle, refer to the precautions in the beginning of this section.

2. Position the vehicle with the front wheels in a straight-ahead position.

3. Disconnect the negative battery cable.

4. Disconnect the positive battery cable.

5. Wait at least one minute for the air bag back-up power supply to drain before continuing.

6. Proceed with the repair.

7. Once complete, connect the battery cables, negative cable LAST.

Power Rack and Pinion Steering Gear

REMOVAL & INSTALLATION

1. Before servicing the vehicle, refer to the precautions in the beginning of this section.

2. Disconnect the negative battery cable.

3. Support the engine with engine support tool D88L-6000-A or equivalent.

4. Raise and safely support the vehicle.

5. Remove both front wheels.

6. Remove the cotter pins and castellated nuts from the tie rod ends. Use tool 3290-D or equivalent, to separate the tie rod ends from the steering knuckles.

7. Remove the splash shields. Remove the six crossmember bolts and remove the crossmember.

8. Remove the two bolts and six nuts from the rear engine support and remove the support.

9. If equipped with the 2.5L engine, detach the Oxygen (O_2S) sensor connectors. Remove the exhaust pipe-to-manifold nuts and separate the pipes from the manifolds. Move the front exhaust pipe aside.

10. Disconnect and plug the power steering pressure and return hoses.

11. Remove the steering shaft U-joint shield bolt and shield.

12. Remove the ground wire bracket from the rear transaxle support bracket (4EAT and MTX transaxles only).

13. Remove the three rear transaxle support bracket bolts and the transaxle insulator through-bolt. Remove the transaxle support bracket (4EAT and MTX transaxles only).

14. Remove the four bolts from the two rack and pinion assembly mounting brackets and remove the brackets.

15. Remove the steering column lower yoke-to-power steering gear input shaft and bolt.

16. If equipped with a manual transaxle, remove the control rod-to-support bar stud nut and position the control rod aside.

17. Position a jack under the front sub-frame. Remove the six sub-frame bolts and two nuts.

18. Remove the vent tube attached to the driver's side of the sub-frame.

19. Remove the upper stabilizer bar link nuts.

20. Lower the sub-frame to allow removal of the rack and pinion assembly. Remove the rack and pinion assembly from the driver's side of the vehicle.

2.0L Engine

1	Power Steering Reservoir Pump Hose	4	Steering Gear
2	Power Steering Return Hose	5	Power Steering Pump
3	Power Steering Pressure Hose	6	Power Steering Pump Reservoir
		7	Power Steering Fluid Cooler

Power steering system component identification—2.0L engine

7922HG51

2.5L Engine

1	Power Steering Reservoir Pump Hose	4	Steering Gear
2	Power Steering Return Hose	5	Power Steering Pump
3	Power Steering Pressure Hose	6	Power Steering Pump Reservoir
		7	Power Steering Fluid Cooler

7922HG50

Power steering system component identification—2.5L engine

To install:

➡ **If a new rack and pinion assembly is being installed or if the old assembly was turned, place the assembly into a soft-jawed vise and rotate the steering gear input shaft, counting the number of turns lock-to-lock. Back the steering gear input shaft up one-half of the number of the turns counted to center the rack and pinion. Do not damage the input shaft splines.**

21. Position the rack and pinion assembly in the vehicle.

22. With the aide of an assistant, install the steering column lower yoke-to-power

steering gear input shaft and bolt. Tighten the bolt to 13–20 ft. lbs. (18–26 Nm).

23. Raise the front sub-frame into position. Install the sub-frame mounting bolts and nuts and tighten to 69–97 ft. lbs. (93–131 Nm).

24. Remove the jack.

25. Install the upper stabilizer bar link nuts and tighten to 27–40 ft. lbs. (36–54 Nm). Install the vent tube.

26. Position the two rack and pinion assembly mounting brackets and install the four mounting bolts. Tighten to 28–38 ft. lbs. (38–51 Nm).

27. Position the rear transaxle support insulator and install the through-bolt, if

equipped. Tighten the through-bolt to 63–86 ft. lbs. (85–117 Nm).

28. Install the three rear transaxle support bracket bolts, if equipped, and tighten to 50–68 ft. lbs. (67–93 Nm). Install the ground wire bracket to the rear engine mount.

29. Install the steering shaft U-joint shield and bolt and tighten securely.

30. Remove the plugs and connect the power steering pressure and return lines.

31. If equipped with a manual transaxle, install the control rod to the support bar stud and install the nut. Tighten the nut to 28–38 ft. lbs. (38–51 Nm).

32. If equipped with the 2.5L engine, connect the exhaust pipes to the manifolds and tighten the nuts to 38 ft. lbs. (51 Nm). Attach the O$_2$S sensor connectors.

33. Position the rear engine support and install the six nuts and two bolts. Tighten the rear engine support nuts and bolts as follows:

   a. Tighten **A** to 55–77 ft. lbs. (75–104 Nm).

   b. Tighten **B** to 50–68 ft. lbs. (67–93 Nm).

   c. Tighten **C** to 32–44 ft. lbs. (44–60 Nm).

34. Position the crossmember and install the four crossmember bolts. Tighten to 69–97 ft. lbs. (93–131 Nm).

35. Connect the tie rod ends to the steering knuckles and tighten the castellated nuts to 23–33 ft. lbs. (31–44 Nm). Install new cotter pins.

36. Install the splash shields and the front wheels. Tighten the lug nuts to 65–87 ft. lbs. (88–118 Nm).

37. Lower the vehicle.

38. Remove the engine support tool.

39. Fill the power steering system with the proper fluid.

40. Connect the negative battery cable.

41. Run the engine and check for leaks. Bleed the air from the system.

42. Top off the power steering reservoir when complete.

43. Check the front wheel alignment.

Strut and Spring

REMOVAL & INSTALLATION

Front

1. Before servicing the vehicle, refer to the precautions in the beginning of this section.

2. Disconnect the negative battery cable.

3. Raise and support the vehicle safely.

4. Remove the wheel.

5. If equipped with anti-lock brakes, disconnect the electrical harness and remove the bracket.

6. Remove the U-clip from the brake line hose and slide it out of the strut bracket.

7. Remove the two strut-to-steering knuckle bolts and nuts.

8. Lower the vehicle enough to remove the four upper strut mounting bolts.

9. Remove the strut from the vehicle.

Front strut attaching nut and bolt locations

10. Place the strut assembly in a suitable holding fixture. Loosen, but do not remove the shock mounting nut. Compress the spring with a suitable compressor tool, then remove the shock mounting nut. Gradually release the spring compressor to relieve the spring tension.

11. Remove the strut mounting bracket, thrust bearing, upper spring seat with insulator, dust tube and bumper.

12. Remove the coil spring and the lower spring insulator. Replace components as required.

To install:

➡**Face the direction indicator on the strut mounting bracket towards the rear outboard position during reassembly. Be sure that the notch on the upper spring seat faces towards the outboard position during reassembly.**

Be sure the direction indicator is positioned as shown

13. Compress the coil spring with the compressor and install the spring and the lower insulator onto the strut.

14. Install the bumper, dust tube, upper spring seat with insulator, thrust bearing and the strut mounting bracket.

15. Install the strut mounting nut and tighten to 66–86 ft. lbs. (89–117 Nm).

16. Gradually release the compressor tool and remove it from the strut assembly.

17. Install the strut in the shock tower with the direction indicator facing the rear outboard position. Tighten the four upper strut mounting nuts to 34–46 ft. lbs. (46–63 Nm).

18. Position the strut to the steering knuckle and tighten the nuts and bolts to 68–86 ft. lbs. (93–117 Nm).

19. Install the brake caliper and the brake hose in its bracket. If equipped with anti-lock brakes, install the bracket and harness. Tighten the anti-lock sensor bracket to 13–19 ft. lbs. (18–25 Nm).

20. Install the wheel and tighten the lug nuts to 65–87 ft. lbs. (88–118 Nm).

21. Lower the vehicle.

22. Connect the negative battery cable.

23. Check the wheel alignment.

Rear

1. Before servicing the vehicle, refer to the precautions in the beginning of this section.

2. Raise and safely support the vehicle.

3. Remove the rear wheel.

4. If equipped with anti-lock brakes, remove the speed sensor routing bracket.

5. Remove the brake line U-clip from the strut housing.

6. Remove the two spindle-to-strut mounting nuts and bolts.

7. Remove the trunk side panel to gain access to the strut assembly.

8. Remove the three upper strut attaching nuts and remove the strut.

✳✳ CAUTION

Do not attempt to remove the coil spring from the strut assembly without compressing the coil spring first.

9. Use spring compressor tool D85P-7178-A or equivalent, to compress the coil spring.

10. Remove the mounting nut from the strut and disassemble the strut components.

To install:

11. Assemble the strut, the compressed coil spring and related components.

1. Shock absorber strut mounting nut
2. Rear shock absorber bracket
3. Rear spring anti-squeak insert, upper
4. Shock absorber dust tube
5. Rear shock absorber dust boot
6. Rear spring
7. Rear spring anti-squeak insert, lower
8. Rear shock absorber
A. 66–87 ft. lb. (89–117 Nm)

7922HG45

Exploded view of the rear strut assembly

12. Install the mounting nut and tighten to 66–87 ft. lbs. (89–117 Nm). Release the compressor and remove the strut.

➡**Be sure that the lower coil spring is seated properly.**

13. Position the strut in the vehicle and install the three upper strut nuts. Tighten to 34–46 ft. lbs. (46–63 Nm).
14. Install the trunk side panel.
15. Install the two spindle-to-strut bolts and nuts and tighten to 69–87 ft. lbs. (93–117 Nm).
16. Install the brake line U-clip.
17. Install the wheel speed sensor bracket, if equipped.
18. Install the wheel and tighten the lug nuts to 65–87 ft. lbs. (88–118 Nm).
19. Lower the vehicle.
20. Check the wheel alignment.

Lower Ball Joint

REMOVAL & INSTALLATION

The lower ball joint is an integral part of the lower control arm and cannot be serviced separately. If the lower ball joint is defective, the entire lower control arm must be replaced.

Lower Control Arm

REMOVAL & INSTALLATION

➡**The lower ball joint is an integral part of the lower control arm and cannot be serviced separately. If the lower ball joint is defective, the entire lower control arm must be replaced.**

1. Before servicing the vehicle, refer to the precautions in the beginning of this section.
2. Disconnect the negative battery cable.
3. Raise and safely support the vehicle.
4. Remove the wheel.
5. Remove the ball-joint clamp bolt and nut from the steering knuckle.
6. Remove the stabilizer bar link nut.
7. Using a prybar, press downward to separate the ball joint from the steering knuckle.
8. Remove the two lower control arm rear mounting bolts.
9. Remove the lower control arm front mounting bolt and the lower control arm from the vehicle.

   To install:
10. Position the lower control arm, install the two lower control arm rear mounting bolts and tighten to 69–96 ft. lbs. (93–131 Nm).
11. Install the lower control arm front mounting bolt and tighten to 58–78 ft. lbs. (78–106 Nm).
12. Install the ball joint stud into the steering knuckle and tighten the clamp bolt to 32–40 ft. lbs. (43–54 Nm).
13. Install the stabilizer bar link nut and tighten to 27–40 ft. lbs. (36–54 Nm).
14. Install the wheel and tighten the lug nuts to 65–87 ft. lbs. (88–118 Nm).
15. Lower the vehicle.
16. Check the front suspension and steering for proper operation. Check wheel alignment.

Wheel Bearings

ADJUSTMENT

➡**Wheel bearings are sealed units and are not adjustable or able to be greased. The wheel bearing unit must be replaced for noisy or rough operation or excessive end-play.**

1. Before servicing the vehicle, refer to the precautions in the beginning of this section.

2. Raise and safely support the vehicle.
3. Be sure the parking brake is fully released.
4. Remove the wheel.
5. On disc brakes, remove the disc brake caliper.
6. On rear disc brakes install the lug nuts to hold the rotor in place.
7. Rotate the drum or rotor to be sure there is no brake drag.
8. Position a suitable dial indicator.
9. Check the wheel bearing end-play. End-play should not exceed 0.002 in. (0.05mm).
10. If the end-play exceeds specification, replace the wheel bearing or hub/bearing assembly, as required.
11. When complete, install the calipers if removed.
12. Install the wheel and tighten the lug nuts to 65–87 ft. lbs. (88–118 Nm).

REMOVAL & INSTALLATION

Front

1. Before servicing the vehicle, refer to the precautions in the beginning of this section.
2. Disconnect the negative battery cable.
3. Raise and safely support the vehicle.
4. Remove the front wheel.
5. Using a small cape chisel or similar tool and a hammer, raise the staked portion of the hub retaining nut. With an assistant applying the brakes to prevent the hub from turning, loosen and remove the wheel hub retaining nut. Discard the nut after removal; it must not be reused.
6. If equipped with anti-lock brakes, remove the two anti-lock sensor retaining bolts and the sensor and bracket.
7. At the tie rod end, remove the cotter pin and castellated nut. Using a tie rod end separator tool or equivalent, separate the tie rod end from the steering knuckle.
8. Remove the lower control arm ball joint clamp nut/bolt. Using a prybar, pry the lower control arm downward and separate the ball joint from the steering knuckle.
9. Remove the steering knuckle-to-strut attaching bolts.
10. Remove the front disc brake caliper anchor bracket and suspend the caliper assembly from the coil spring with wire.
11. Remove the disc brake rotor.
12. Pull the steering knuckle/hub assembly off of the halfshaft. If necessary, lightly tap the end of the halfshaft CV-joint with a

Turn to Section 6 for brake system applications

plastic faced hammer or use a wheel puller to press the shaft out of the hub. Support the halfshaft with wire or a stand; do not let the halfshaft hang on the inner CV-joint or the joint could be pulled apart.

13. Remove the steering knuckle, hub and wheel bearing assembly from the vehicle.

14. Using a prybar, pry the grease seal from the knuckle.

15. Position the steering knuckle in a suitable fixture and remove the hub from the knuckle. If the inner race remains on the hub, grind a section of the inner race to approximately 0.020 in. (0.5mm) and use a chisel to remove it. Wear appropriate eye protection.

16. Remove the snapring from the steering knuckle.

➡**Wheel bearings are contained within a sealed unit and are not serviceable.**

17. Position the steering knuckle in a suitable fixture and remove the wheel bearing from the knuckle.

➡**Unless the disc brake rotor dust shield is damaged, it should be left on the steering knuckle; it is pressed on and must be replaced if removed or damaged.**

To install:

18. Inspect the steering knuckle and hub for cracks, wear and scoring. Replace parts as necessary.

19. Position the steering knuckle in a suitable fixture and press in the wheel bearing. Be sure the press tool contacts only the outer bearing race or the bearing will be damaged.

20. Install the snapring.

21. Position the steering knuckle in a suitable fixture and press the hub into the steering knuckle. Be sure the inner bearing race is supported or the bearing will be damaged.

22. Apply grease to the lip of a new seal and press the seal into the knuckle, using a suitable seal installer.

23. Grease the halfshaft splines. Slide the hub/steering knuckle onto the halfshaft and position it into the strut bracket.

24. Install the strut-to-steering knuckle bolts and nuts and tighten to 68–86 ft. lbs. (93–117 Nm).

25. Push the lower control arm ball joint into the steering knuckle. Install the clamp bolt and nut and tighten to 25–42 ft. lbs. (34–57 Nm).

26. Install the disc brake rotor.

27. Position the caliper anchor bracket. Install the caliper anchor bracket-to-steering knuckle bolts and tighten to 58–72 ft. lbs. (78–98 Nm).

28. Connect the tie rod end to the steering knuckle and tighten the castellated nut to 22–33 ft. lbs. (29–44 Nm). Install a new cotter pin.

29. If equipped with anti-lock brakes, install the anti-lock brake sensor and

bracket and tighten the two retaining bolts to 12–17 ft. lbs. (16–23 Nm).

30. Have an assistant apply the brakes. Install a new hub nut and tighten the nut to 174–235 ft. lbs. (235–319 Nm). Stake the hub nut, using a chisel with a rounded cutting edge or similar tool.

31. Install the wheel and tighten the lug nuts to 65–87 ft. lbs. (88–118 Nm).

32. Lower the vehicle.

33. Connect the negative battery cable.

34. Check the front brakes, suspension and steering for proper operation. Check the front wheel alignment.

Rear

➡**The wheel bearing cannot be disassembled from the hub; it must be replaced as an assembly.**

1. Before servicing the vehicle, refer to the precautions in the beginning of this section.

2. Disconnect the negative battery cable.

3. Raise and safely support the vehicle.

4. Remove the rear wheel.

5. Carefully unstake the wheel hub retainer. Have an assistant apply the brakes to lock the hub, then remove the retainer. Discard the nut.

6. On vehicles equipped with rear disc brakes, remove the disc brake caliper and rotor.

7. On vehicles equipped with rear drum brakes, remove the brake drum.

8. Remove the wheel bearing and hub assembly from the wheel spindle.

To install:

9. Install the wheel bearing and hub assembly onto the wheel spindle.

10. On vehicles equipped with rear disc brakes, install the rotor and rear disc brake caliper.

11. On vehicles equipped with rear drum brakes, install the brake drum.

12. Install a new wheel hub retainer. Have an assistant apply the brakes to lock the hub, then tighten the wheel hub retainer to 130–174 ft. lbs. (177–235 Nm).

13. Stake the nut in place using a dull bladed chisel or similar tool.

14. Install the wheel and tighten the lug nuts to 65–87 ft. lbs. (88–118 Nm).

15. Lower the vehicle.

16. Connect the negative battery cable.

17. Pump the brake pedal to position the brakes, prior to moving the vehicle.

1. Retaining ring
2. Front disc brake rotor shield
3. Wheel hub
4. Wheel hub bolt
5. Front wheel bearing
6. Inner wheel bearing oil seal
7. Front wheel knuckle

7922HG44

Exploded view of the front hub and knuckle assembly, showing the wheel bearings

FORD MOTOR COMPANY

19

Ford-Contour • Mercury-Mystique • 1999–00 Cougar

PRECAUTIONS

Before servicing any vehicle, please be sure to read all of the following precautions, which deal with personal safety, prevention of component damage, and important points to take into consideration when servicing a motor vehicle:

• Never open, service or drain the radiator or cooling system when the engine is hot; serious burns can occur from the steam and hot coolant.

• Observe all applicable safety precautions when working around fuel. Whenever servicing the fuel system, always work in a well-ventilated area. Do not allow fuel spray or vapors to come in contact with a spark, open flame, or excessive heat (a hot drop light, for example). Keep a dry chemical fire extinguisher near the work area. Always keep fuel in a container specifically designed for fuel storage; also, always properly seal fuel containers to avoid the possibility of fire or explosion. Refer to the additional fuel system precautions later in this section.

• Fuel injection systems often remain pressurized, even after the engine has been turned **OFF**. The fuel system pressure must be relieved before disconnecting any fuel lines. Failure to do so may result in fire and/or personal injury.

• Brake fluid often contains polyglycol ethers and polyglycols. Avoid contact with the eyes and wash your hands thoroughly after handling brake fluid. If you do get brake fluid in your eyes, flush your eyes with clean, running water for 15 minutes. If eye irritation persists, or if you have taken brake fluid internally, IMMEDIATELY seek medical assistance.

• The EPA warns that prolonged contact with used engine oil may cause a number of skin disorders, including cancer! You should make every effort to minimize your exposure to used engine oil. Protective gloves should be worn when changing oil. Wash your hands and any other exposed skin areas as soon as possible after exposure to used engine oil. Soap and water, or waterless hand cleaner should be used.

• All new vehicles are now equipped with an air bag system, often referred to as a Supplemental Restraint System (SRS) or Supplemental Inflatable Restraint (SIR) system. The system must be disabled before performing service on or around system components, steering column, instrument panel components, wiring and sensors. Failure to follow safety and disabling procedures could result in accidental air bag deployment, possible personal injury and unnecessary system repairs.

• Always wear safety goggles when working with, or around, the air bag system. When carrying a non-deployed air bag, be sure the bag and trim cover are pointed away from your body. When placing a non-deployed air bag on a work surface, always face the bag and trim cover upward, away from the surface. This will reduce the motion of the module if it is accidentally deployed. Refer to the additional air bag system precautions later in this section.

• Clean, high quality brake fluid from a sealed container is essential to the safe and proper operation of the brake system. You should always buy the correct type of brake fluid for your vehicle. If the brake fluid becomes contaminated, completely flush the system with new fluid. Never reuse any brake fluid. Any brake fluid that is removed from the system should be discarded. Also, do not allow any brake fluid to come in contact with a painted surface; it will damage the paint.

• Never operate the engine without the proper amount and type of engine oil; doing so WILL result in severe engine damage.

• Timing belt maintenance is extremely important! Many models utilize an interference-type, non-freewheeling engine. If the timing belt breaks, the valves in the cylinder head may strike the pistons, causing potentially serious (also time-consuming and expensive) engine damage. Refer to the maintenance interval charts in the front of this manual for the recommended replacement interval for the timing belt, and to the timing belt section for belt replacement and inspection.

• Disconnecting the negative battery cable on some vehicles may interfere with the functions of the on-board computer system(s) and may require the computer to undergo a relearning process once the negative battery cable is reconnected.

• When servicing drum brakes, only dissemble and assemble one side at a time, leaving the remaining side intact for reference.

• Only an MVAC-trained, EPA-certified automotive technician should service the A/C system or its components.

ENGINE REPAIR

Ignition Timing

ADJUSTMENT

The ignition timing is set at 10 degrees Before Top Dead Center (BTDC) and is not adjustable.

Engine Assembly

REMOVAL & INSTALLATION

2.0L Engine

1. Before servicing the vehicle, refer to the precautions in the beginning of this section.

2. Disconnect the battery cables, negative cable first.

3. Relieve the fuel system pressure using the recommended procedure.

4. Remove the pinch bolt and disconnect the steering shaft and joint at the cowl, inside the vehicle.

5. Remove the engine air cleaner and the engine air intake resonators.

6. Properly recover the refrigerant from the A/C system.

7. Raise and safely support the vehicle.

8. Remove the front splash shield from between the front subframe and the body.

9. Remove the catalytic converter.

10. Drain the engine cooling system and engine oil.

11. Remove the front wheel and tire assemblies.

12. Separate the left and right stabilizer bar links from the front stabilizer bar.

13. Separate the left and right outer tie rod ends from the front wheel knuckles. Discard the cotter pins.

14. Remove the pinch bolts and separate the front suspension lower control arms from the front wheel knuckles at the ball joints.

15. Remove the left and right wheel hub retainer nuts from the halfshaft ends and remove the halfshafts from the front wheel knuckles.

16. Remove the A/C accumulator retaining screws from the front subframe.

17. Disengage the Vehicle Speed Sensor (VSS) wiring harness at the connector.

18. Disconnect the speedometer drive cable from the transaxle.

19. If the engine is to be separated from the transaxle after removal from the vehicle, and the transaxle is an automatic, remove the right splash shield from the front fender apron.

20. Remove the access plug from the engine rear plate and remove the four torque converter retaining nuts.

21. Push the torque converter into the transaxle front pump support and gear.

22. Disconnect the wiring to the knock sensor and the oil pressure sensor located on the right side of the cylinder block.

23. Lower the vehicle.

24. Secure the radiator and fan shroud assembly to the radiator support, using safety wire or equivalent.

25. Disconnect the accelerator cable and speed control actuator from the throttle body.

26. Remove the accelerator cable bracket.

27. Disengage the wiring to the fuel injectors at the connector located near the fuel pressure regulator.

28. Remove the retaining screws from the engine control wiring at the intake manifold.

29. Remove the power steering pump auxiliary reservoir from the bracket and lay on top of the engine assembly using shop towels to absorb the fluid.

30. Disconnect the return hose from the power steering reservoir and plug the hose.

✷✷ WARNING

Do not allow the power steering fluid to come into contact with the accessory drive belts.

31. Disconnect the power steering return hose from the power steering pump.

32. Disconnect the wiring from the power steering pressure switch located on the power steering pressure hose.

33. Disconnect the wiring from the alternator and the grounding strap from the alternator mounting bracket.

34. Disconnect the vacuum supply hose from the fitting on the rear of the intake manifold.

35. Disconnect the coolant hoses from the radiator coolant recovery reservoir.

36. Disconnect the hoses from the A/C compressor and plug.

37. Disconnect the fuel return and supply lines from the fuel rail and plug.

38. Disconnect the vacuum supply hose to the EGR valve, EGR pressure sensor and the EGR valve-to-exhaust manifold tube.

39. If equipped with automatic transaxle, pry the end of the shift cable from the stud, remove the two retaining bolts and remove shift cable and bracket from the transaxle. Remove the wiring to the transmission range sensor and remove the wire retainers.

40. Disconnect the grounding strap from the transaxle.

41. Disconnect the wiring from the ignition coil and the radio ignition interference capacitor. Move the wiring out of the way.

42. Remove the vacuum supply line from the power brake booster.

43. Disconnect the upper radiator hose from the radiator.

44. Remove the evaporative emission hose from the connector located near the radio ignition interference capacitor.

45. Disconnect the heater hose from the connection located near the EGR valve.

46. Disconnect the positive and negative battery cable retainer from the battery tray.

47. If equipped with manual transaxle, remove the retainer and disconnect the clutch hydraulic line from the clutch actuator pipe at the transaxle case.

48. If equipped, disconnect the block heater power supply wiring from the left side of the radiator support.

49. If equipped with automatic transaxle, remove the transmission oil cooler lines from the transaxle. Remove the oil cooler return line from the bracket on the left-hand side of the transaxle.

50. If equipped with manual transaxle, remove the bolt from the shift rod and the nut from the stabilizer bar and remove from the transaxle.

51. Disconnect the lower radiator hose from the radiator.

52. Remove the four bolts retaining the lower radiator supports to the front subframe. Rotate the radiator supports forward.

53. Disconnect the wiring harness from the A/C compressor.

54. Disconnect the engine wiring from the Heated Oxygen (HO$_2$S) sensor, Engine Coolant Temperature (ECT) sensor and the Crankshaft Position (CKP) sensor.

55. Remove the two screws retaining the bumper cover braces to the left and right sides of the front subframe and rotate the cover braces forward.

56. Disconnect the power steering oil cooler hoses at the right front subframe. Drain the fluid from the hoses.

57. Partially lower the vehicle.

58. Position and secure all lines, hoses and components that will be removed with the engine.

59. Install Powertrain and Subframe Support Bracket 134–00250 or equivalent, with Powertrain Lift (hydraulic lift) 134–00251 or equivalent, to support the powertrain assembly for removal from the vehicle.

➡**Be sure that the powertrain and subframe support bracket and lift are correctly positioned for safe removal of the powertrain assembly.**

60. Remove the four subframe to body retaining bolts.

61. Remove the upper front engine support bracket and the engine and transmission support insulator retaining nuts.

62. With an assistant, carefully lower the powertrain assembly while checking for body interference.

63. With the powertrain assembly lowered from the vehicle, carefully roll the powertrain lift or equivalent away from the vehicle.

64. Using Floor Crane 014–00071 or equivalent, and Floor Crane Positioning Sling 014–00036 or equivalent, support the engine using the engine lifting eyes.

65. Remove the left and the right halfshafts from the transaxle.

66. Remove the left and the right front engine support insulators from the subframe and transaxle.

67. Using the floor crane and sling or equivalent, raise the engine and transaxle assembly and remove from the subframe.

68. Position the transaxle part of the assembly onto Transmission Jack 066–00016 or equivalent.

69. Remove the two starter retaining bolts and remove the starter motor.

70. Remove the battery ground cable from the engine to transaxle retaining stud bolt.

71. Remove the transaxle to engine retaining bolts and separate the engine from the transaxle.

72. If equipped with manual transaxle, remove the six clutch pressure plate retaining bolts and remove the pressure plate and the clutch disc.

73. Remove the eight flywheel retainer bolts and the flywheel from the crankshaft.

74. Remove the engine rear plate.

75. Install the engine to an engine stand for further service.

To install:

76. Remove the engine from the engine stand using the floor crane and sling or equivalent, attached to the engine lifting eyes.

77. Reinstall the engine rear plate and flywheel.

78. Tighten the flywheel retaining bolts in an alternating sequence to 79–86 ft. lbs. (107–117 Nm) for automatic transaxles and 81–89 ft. lbs. (110–120 Nm) for manual transaxles.

79. If equipped with manual transaxle, install the clutch disc and the clutch pressure plate.

80. Tighten the retaining bolts in an alternating sequence to 22 ft. lbs. (30 Nm).

81. Reinstall the engine to the transaxle. If equipped with automatic transaxle, align the torque converter to the flywheel while positioning the engine to the transaxle.

82. Reinstall the engine to transaxle retaining bolts and tighten to 25–34 ft. lbs. (34–46 Nm).

83. If removed, place the subframe onto the powertrain and subframe support bracket and hydraulic lift.

84. Using the floor crane and sling, position the engine and transaxle assembly onto the subframe keeping the crane attached for support.

85. Install Powertrain Alignment Gauge T94P-6000-AH or equivalent, to the left-hand front engine support bracket and subframe. Reinstall the through-bolt. Tighten the retaining bolts and the through-bolt to 20 ft. lbs. (27 Nm).

86. Reinstall the right engine support insulator retaining bolts and through-bolt to the subframe. Leave the bolts finger-tight.

87. Reinstall the battery ground cable to the engine at the transaxle stud bolt. Tighten the retaining nut to 15–22 ft. lbs. (20–30 Nm).

88. Reinstall the starter motor.

89. Reinstall the left and right halfshafts into the transaxle.

90. Install Subframe Alignment Pin Set 94P-2100-AH or equivalent into the subframe.

91. Reinstall the four subframe retaining bolts and tighten to 92–100 ft. lbs. (125–135 Nm).

92. Remove the subframe alignment pins.

➡ **Be sure that the engine and transaxle are firmly seated against the front and rear insulator brackets.**

93. Using new nuts, install the upper front engine support bracket and the transmission support insulator. Tighten the nuts to 74 inch. lbs. (10 Nm).

94. Remove the subframe support bracket and the hydraulic lift.

95. Raise and safely support the vehicle.

96. Tighten the right front engine support insulator to the subframe bolts to 30–41 ft. lbs. (41–55 Nm).

➡ **Check the position of the right front engine support insulator. It must be centered in its bracket and in perfect alignment front-to-rear.**

97. Lower the vehicle.

98. Tighten the front engine support bracket nuts to 52–70 ft. lbs. (70–95 Nm).

99. Tighten the engine and transmission support insulator nuts to 30–41 ft. lbs. (41–55 Nm) for automatic transaxles and 52–70 ft. lbs. (70–95 Nm) for manual transaxles.

100. Tighten the right front engine support insulator through-bolt to 75–102 ft. lbs. (103–137 Nm).

101. Remove the powertrain alignment gauge.

102. Reinstall the left front engine support insulator to the subframe. Tighten the retaining bolts to 84 inch. lbs. (10 Nm).

➡ **Check the position of the left front engine support insulator to ensure perfect front-to-rear alignment.**

103. Retighten the two retaining bolts to 30–41 ft. lbs. (41–55 Nm).

104. Reinstall the left front engine support insulator through-bolt. Tighten the through-bolt to 75–102 ft. lbs. (103–137 Nm).

105. Reconnect the power steering oil cooler hoses at the right side of the subframe. Tighten the hose clamps securely.

106. Reconnect the engine wiring to the HO2S sensor, ECT sensor and the CKP sensor.

107. Reconnect the wiring harness to the A/C compressor.

108. Reinstall the radiator supports to the subframe bolts. Tighten to 71–97 inch lbs. (8–11 Nm).

109. Reconnect the lower radiator hose to the radiator.

110. If equipped with manual transaxle, install the shift rod stabilizer to the transaxle.

111. Tighten the shift rod bolt to 17 ft. lbs. (23 Nm) and the stabilizer nut to 41 ft. lbs. (55 Nm).

112. If equipped with automatic transaxle, install the transmission oil cooler lines and tighten the nuts to 18–22 ft. lbs. (24–31 Nm).

113. Reconnect the heater hose to the heater water tube located under the engine.

114. Lower the vehicle.

115. If equipped, connect the block heater power supply wiring.

116. If equipped with manual transaxle, connect the clutch hydraulic line to the clutch actuator pipe at the transaxle case and install the retainer.

117. Reconnect the positive and negative battery cable retainer to the battery tray.

118. Reinstall the heater hose to the connector tube located near the EGR valve and clamp securely.

119. Reconnect the evaporative emission hose located near the radio ignition interference capacitor.

120. Reconnect the upper radiator hose to the radiator.

121. Reconnect the vacuum supply line to the power brake booster.

122. Reconnect the wiring to the ignition coil and the radio ignition interference capacitor.

123. Reconnect the ground strap to the transaxle case.

124. Reconnect the wiring harness to the transmission range sensor.

125. If equipped with automatic transaxle, install the shift cable and bracket to the transaxle. Tighten the retaining bolts to 15–19 ft. lbs. (20–25 Nm).

126. Reconnect the vacuum hoses from the EGR pressure sensor to the EGR valve to exhaust manifold tube and the vacuum supply hose to the EGR valve.

127. Unplug and connect the fuel supply and return lines to the fuel rail.

128. Unplug and connect the refrigerant hoses to the A/C compressor.

129. Reconnect the coolant hoses to the radiator coolant recovery reservoir.

130. Reconnect the vacuum supply hose for the body to the fitting at the rear of the intake manifold.

131. Reinstall the ground strap on the alternator mounting bracket.

132. Reconnect the wiring harness to the alternator.

133. Reconnect the wiring to the power steering pressure switch located on the power steering pressure hose.

134. Reconnect the power steering return hose to the power steering pump. Clamp the hose securely.

135. Reinstall the power steering pump auxiliary reservoir to its bracket.

136. Reinstall the retainer screws for the engine wiring to the intake manifold.

137. Reattach the wiring to the connector located near the fuel pressure regulator for the fuel injectors.

138. Reconnect the accelerator cable and the speed control actuator to the accelerator cable bracket and the throttle body.

139. Remove the safety wire holding the radiator and fan shroud to the radiator support.

140. Raise and safely support the vehicle.

141. Reconnect the wiring harness to the knock sensor and the oil pressure sensor located on the right side of the cylinder block.

142. If equipped with automatic transaxle, install the torque converter to flywheel retaining nuts. Tighten the retaining nuts in an alternating sequence to 54–64 ft. lbs. (73–87 Nm). Reinstall the access plug into the engine rear plate.

143. Reinstall the right splash shield onto the front fender apron.

144. Reconnect the Vehicle Speed Sensor (VSS).

145. Reinstall the speedometer drive cable to the transaxle.

146. Reinstall the A/C accumulator retaining screws to the subframe.

147. Reinstall the left and right halfshafts.

148. Reinstall the left and right front wheel knuckles into the front suspension lower control arms at the ball joints. Tighten the bolts to 37–43 ft. lbs. (50–58 Nm).

149. Reinstall the left and right tie rod ends to the front wheel knuckles. Install new castellated nuts onto the tie rod end studs. Tighten the castellated nuts to 21 ft. lbs. (28 Nm). Install new cotter pins.

150. Reconnect the left and right front stabilizer bar links to the front stabilizer bar. Tighten the nuts to 35 ft. lbs. (48 Nm).

151. Reinstall the front wheel and tire assemblies. Tighten the lug nuts to 95 ft. lbs. (129 Nm).

152. Reinstall the catalytic converter.

153. Reinstall the splash shield to the front of the subframe and body.

154. Rotate the front bumper cover braces rearward. Reinstall the two screws to the subframe and tighten securely.

155. Lower the vehicle.

156. Reinstall the engine air cleaner and the engine air intake resonators.

157. Reconnect the steering shaft and joint inside the vehicle. Tighten the bolt to 18 ft. lbs. (24 Nm).

158. If equipped with automatic transaxle, fill the transmission with the proper amount and type of fluid.

159. Fill the power steering reservoir with the proper type of fluid.

160. Fill the engine cooling system.

161. Fill the engine with fresh oil.

162. Reconnect the battery cables, negative cable last.

163. Check all fluid levels.

164. Evacuate and recharge the A/C system.

➡ **Whenever the vehicle subframe is removed or lowered, the wheel alignment should be checked.**

165. Start the engine and check for leaks and proper operation.

2.5L Engine

1. Before servicing the vehicle, refer to the precautions in the beginning of this section.

2. Disconnect the battery cables, negative cable first.

3. Relieve the fuel system pressure using the recommended procedure.

4. Remove the water pump pulley shield.

5. Remove the pinch bolt and disconnect the steering shaft and joint at the cowl inside the vehicle.

6. Remove the engine air cleaner.

7. Properly recover the refrigerant from the A/C system.

8. Raise and safely support the vehicle.

9. Remove the exhaust crossover and the catalytic converter.

10. Drain the engine cooling system and engine oil.

11. Remove the front wheel and tire assemblies.

12. Separate the left and right stabilizer bar links from the front stabilizer bar.

13. Separate the left and right outer tie rod ends from the front wheel knuckles. Discard the cotter pins.

14. Remove the pinch bolts and separate the front suspension lower control arms from the front wheel knuckles at the ball joints.

15. Remove the left and right wheel hub retainer nuts from the halfshaft ends and remove the halfshafts from the front wheel knuckles.

16. Remove the A/C accumulator retaining screws from the front subframe.

17. Disconnect the Vehicle Speed Sensor (VSS) wiring.

18. Disconnect the speedometer drive cable from the VSS.

19. If the engine is to be separated from the transaxle after removal from the vehicle, and the transaxle is an automatic, remove the access plug from the engine rear plate and remove the four torque converter retaining nuts.

20. Push the torque converter into the transaxle front pump support and gear.

21. Lower the vehicle.

22. Secure the radiator and fan shroud assembly to the radiator support, using safety wire.

23. Disconnect the accelerator cable and speed control actuator from the throttle body.

24. Remove the accelerator cable bracket from the throttle body.

25. Disengage the three connectors for the engine control wiring from the bracket located on the left-front fender apron and unplug the connectors.

26. Remove the retainer for the engine control wiring from the air cleaner bracket.

27. Remove the Ignition Control Module (ICM) from the bulkhead, if equipped.

Timing belt service is covered in Section 5 of this manual

28. Remove the power steering pump auxiliary reservoir from the bracket and lay on top of the engine assembly using shop towels to absorb the fluid.

29. Disconnect the return hose from the power steering reservoir and plug the hose.

✳✳ WARNING

Do not allow the power steering fluid to come into contact with the accessory drive belts.

30. Disconnect the power steering pressure hose from the power steering pump.

31. Disconnect the power steering pressure hose bracket from the upper front engine support bracket. Lay the hose on top of the engine.

32. Disconnect the wiring from the Powertrain Control Module (PCM) and retainer located on the right side of the dash panel.

33. Remove the ground strap for the engine control wiring at the right fender apron.

34. Disconnect the coolant hoses from the radiator coolant recovery reservoir.

35. Disconnect the fuel return and supply lines from the fuel rail.

36. If equipped with automatic transaxle, pry the end of the shift cable from the stud, remove the two retaining bolts and remove shift cable and bracket from the transaxle. Remove the wiring to the Transmission Range Sensor (TRS) and remove the wire retainers.

37. Disconnect the grounding strap from the transaxle.

38. Remove the vacuum supply line from the power brake booster.

39. Disconnect the upper radiator hose from the radiator.

40. Disconnect the positive and negative battery cable retainer from the battery tray.

41. If equipped with manual transaxle, remove the retainer and disconnect the clutch hydraulic line from the clutch actuator pipe at the transaxle case.

42. Disconnect the block heater power supply wiring from the right side of the radiator support if equipped.

43. Raise and safely support the vehicle.

44. Disconnect the heater hoses from the heater core.

45. Disconnect the A/C suction hose from the A/C condenser core and plug the hose.

46. Disconnect the A/C discharge hose from the A/C accumulator and plug the hose.

47. If equipped with an automatic transaxle, remove the transmission oil cooler lines from the transaxle. Remove the oil cooler return line from the bracket on the left side of the transaxle.

48. If equipped with manual transaxle, remove the bolt from the shift rod and the nut from the stabilizer bar and remove from the transaxle.

49. Disconnect the lower radiator hose from the radiator.

50. Remove the four bolts retaining the lower radiator supports to the front subframe. Rotate the radiator supports forward.

51. Disconnect the wiring harness from the A/C compressor.

52. Remove the two screws retaining the bumper cover braces to the left and right sides of the front subframe and rotate the cover braces forward.

53. Partially lower the vehicle.

54. Position and secure all lines, hoses and components that will be removed with the engine.

55. Install Powertrain and Subframe Support Bracket 134–00250 or equivalent with Powertrain Lift (hydraulic lift) 134–00251 or equivalent to support the powertrain assembly for removal from the vehicle.

➡ **Be sure that the powertrain and subframe support bracket and lift are correctly positioned for safe removal of the powertrain assembly.**

56. Remove the four subframe-to-body retaining bolts.

57. Remove the upper front engine support bracket and the engine and transmission support insulator retaining nuts.

58. With an assistant, carefully lower the powertrain assembly while checking for body interference.

59. With the powertrain assembly lowered from the vehicle, carefully roll the powertrain lift or equivalent away from the vehicle.

60. Using Floor Crane 014–00071 or equivalent, and Floor Crane Positioning Sling 014–00036 or equivalent, support the engine using the engine lifting eyes.

61. Remove the left and the right halfshafts from the transaxle.

62. Remove the left and the right front engine support insulators from the subframe and transaxle.

63. Using the floor crane and sling or equivalent, raise the engine and transaxle assembly and remove from the subframe.

64. Position the transaxle part of the assembly onto Transmission Jack 066–00016 or equivalent.

65. Remove the two starter retaining bolts and remove the starter motor.

66. Unplug the engine control wiring connectors and retaining clips at the transaxle and move aside.

67. Remove the battery ground cable from the engine-to-transaxle retaining stud bolt.

68. Remove the transaxle-to-engine retaining bolts and separate the engine from the transaxle.

69. If equipped with manual transaxle, remove the six clutch pressure plate retaining bolts and remove the pressure plate and the clutch disc.

70. Remove the eight flywheel retainer bolts and the flywheel from the crankshaft.

71. Remove the engine rear plate.

72. Install the engine on an engine stand for further service.

To install:

73. Remove the engine from the engine stand using the floor crane and sling or equivalent, attached to the engine lifting eyes.

74. Reinstall the engine rear plate and flywheel.

75. Tighten the flywheel retaining bolts in an alternating sequence to 79–86 ft. lbs. (107–117 Nm) for automatic transaxles, or 81–89 ft. lbs. (110–120 Nm) for manual transaxles.

76. If equipped with manual transaxle, install the clutch disc and the clutch pressure plate. Tighten the retaining bolts in an alternating sequence to 22 ft. lbs. (30 Nm).

77. Reinstall the engine to the transaxle. If equipped with an automatic transaxle, align the torque converter to the flywheel while positioning the engine to the transaxle.

78. Reinstall the engine-to-transaxle retaining bolts and tighten to 25–34 ft. lbs. (34–46 Nm).

79. If removed, place the subframe onto the powertrain and subframe support bracket and hydraulic lift.

80. Using the floor crane and sling, position the engine and transaxle assembly onto the subframe keeping the crane attached for support.

81. Install Powertrain Alignment Gauge T94P-6000-AH or equivalent, to the left front engine support bracket and subframe. Reinstall the through-bolt. Tighten the retaining bolts and the through-bolt to 20 ft. lbs. (27 Nm).

82. Reinstall the right engine support insulator retaining bolts and through-bolt to the subframe. Leave the bolts finger-tight.

83. Reinstall the battery ground cable to the engine at the transaxle stud bolt. Tighten the retaining nut to 15–22 ft. lbs. (20–30 Nm).

84. Position the engine control wiring

across the transaxle and install the retaining clips.

85. Reinstall the engine control wiring to the transaxle connectors.

86. Reinstall the starter motor.

87. Reinstall the left and right halfshafts into the transaxle.

88. Install Subframe Alignment Pin Set 94P-2100-aH or equivalent into the subframe.

89. Reinstall the four subframe retaining bolts and tighten to 92–100 ft. lbs. (125–135 Nm).

90. Remove the subframe alignment pins.

➡ **Be sure that the engine and transaxle are firmly seated against the front and rear insulator brackets.**

91. Using new nuts, install the upper front engine support bracket and the transmission support insulator. Tighten the nuts to 84 inch. lbs. (10 Nm).

92. Remove the subframe support bracket and the hydraulic lift.

93. Raise and safely support the vehicle.

94. Tighten the right front engine support insulator to the subframe bolts to 30–41 ft. lbs. (41–55 Nm).

➡ **Check the position of the right front engine support insulator. It must be centered in its bracket and in perfect alignment front-to-rear.**

95. Lower the vehicle.

96. Tighten the front engine support bracket nuts to 52–70 ft. lbs. (70–95 Nm).

97. Tighten the engine and transmission support insulator nuts to 30–41 ft. lbs. (41–55 Nm) for automatic transaxles or 52–70 ft. lbs. (70–95 Nm) for manual transaxles.

98. Tighten the right front engine support insulator through-bolt to 75–102 ft. lbs. (103–137 Nm).

99. Remove the powertrain alignment gauge.

100. Reinstall the left front engine support insulator to the subframe. Tighten the retaining bolts to 84 inch. lbs. (10 Nm).

➡ **Check the position of the left front engine support insulator to ensure perfect front-to-rear alignment.**

101. Retighten the two retaining bolts to 30–41 ft. lbs. (41–55 Nm).

102. Reinstall the left front engine support insulator through-bolt. Tighten the through-bolt to 75–102 ft. lbs. (103–137 Nm).

103. Reconnect the wiring harness to the A/C compressor.

104. Reinstall the front bumper cover braces to the left and right side of the subframe.

105. Reinstall the radiator supports to the subframe. Tighten the retaining bolts to 71–97 inch lbs. (8–11 Nm).

106. Reconnect the lower radiator hose to the radiator.

107. If equipped with a manual transaxle, install the shift rod stabilizer to the transaxle. Tighten the shift rod bolt to 17 ft. lbs. (23 Nm) and the stabilizer nut to 41 ft. lbs. (55 Nm).

108. If equipped with an automatic transaxle, install the transmission oil cooler lines and tighten the nuts to 18–22 ft. lbs. (24–31 Nm).

109. Unplug and connect the A/C suction hose to the A/C condenser core.

110. Unplug and connect the A/C discharge hose to the A/C accumulator.

111. Lower the vehicle.

112. If equipped, connect the block heater power supply wiring.

113. If equipped with manual transaxle, connect the clutch hydraulic line to the clutch actuator pipe at the transaxle case and install the retainer.

114. Reconnect the positive and negative battery cable retainer to the battery tray.

115. Reconnect the upper radiator hose to the radiator.

116. Reconnect the vacuum supply line to the power brake booster.

117. Reconnect the ground strap to the transaxle case.

118. If equipped with automatic transaxle, install the shift cable and bracket to the transaxle. Tighten the retaining bolts to 15–19 ft. lbs. (20–25 Nm).

119. Reconnect the fuel supply and return lines to the fuel rail.

120. Reconnect the ground strap for the engine control wiring to the right cylinder head.

121. Reconnect the wiring to the PCM and position the wiring into the retainer bracket.

122. Reconnect the power steering pressure hose to the power steering pump.

123. Reinstall the power steering pressure hose bracket to the upper front engine support bracket.

124. Reinstall the power steering pump auxiliary reservoir to its bracket.

125. Reinstall the ICM and bracket to the bulkhead, if equipped.

126. Reinstall the retainer for the engine control wiring to the air cleaner bracket.

127. Reattach the three engine control connectors and install to the bracket on the left front fender apron.

128. Reinstall the accelerator cable bracket to the throttle body and tighten to the retaining bolts to 71–106 inch lbs. (8–12 Nm).

129. Reconnect the accelerator cable and the speed control actuator to the accelerator cable bracket.

130. Remove the safety wire holding the radiator and fan shroud to the radiator support.

131. Raise and safely support the vehicle.

132. If equipped with an automatic transaxle, push the torque converter into the flywheel pilot and install four torque converter-to-flywheel retaining nuts. Tighten the retaining nuts in an alternating sequence to 54–64 ft. lbs. (73–87 Nm). Reinstall the access plug into the engine rear plate.

133. Reconnect the VSS wiring harness.

134. Reinstall the speedometer drive cable to the VSS.

135. Reinstall the A/C accumulator retaining screws to the subframe.

136. Reinstall the left and right halfshafts into the front wheel knuckles and install the front axle wheel retaining nuts.

137. Reinstall the left and right front wheel knuckles into the front suspension lower control arms at the ball joints. Tighten the bolts to 37–43 ft. lbs. (50–58 Nm).

138. Reinstall the left and right tie rod ends to the front wheel knuckles. Install new castellated nuts onto the tie rod end studs. Tighten the castellated nuts to 21 ft. lbs. (28 Nm). Install new cotter pins.

139. Reconnect the left and right front stabilizer bar links to the front stabilizer bar. Tighten the nuts to 35 ft. lbs. (48 Nm).

140. Reinstall the front wheel and tire assemblies. Tighten the lug nuts to 95 ft. lbs. (129 Nm).

141. Reinstall the exhaust crossover and the three way catalytic converter.

142. Reinstall the splash shield to the front of the subframe and body.

143. Rotate the front bumper cover braces rearward. Reinstall the two screws to the subframe and tighten securely.

144. Lower the vehicle.

145. Reinstall the engine air cleaner.

146. Reconnect the steering shaft and joint inside the vehicle. Tighten the bolt to 18 ft. lbs. (24 Nm).

147. Reinstall the water pump pulley shield.

148. If equipped with automatic transaxle, fill the transmission with the proper amount and type of fluid.

149. Fill the power steering reservoir with the proper type of fluid.

150. Fill the engine cooling system.

✳ WARNING

Operating the engine without the proper amount and type of engine oil will result in severe engine damage.

151. Fill the engine crankcase with clean, fresh oil.

152. Check all fluid levels.

153. Reconnect the battery cables, negative cable last.

154. Evacuate and recharge the A/C system.

➡ Whenever the vehicle subframe is removed or lowered, the wheel alignment should be checked.

155. Start the engine and check for leaks and proper operation.

Water Pump

REMOVAL & INSTALLATION

2.0L Engine

1. Before servicing the vehicle, refer to the precautions in the beginning of this section.

2. Disconnect the negative battery cable.

3. Drain the engine cooling system.

4. Raise and safely support the vehicle.

5. Remove the lower radiator hose from the water pump.

6. Lower the vehicle.

FRONT OF ENGINE

1. Water pump
2. Water pump housing gaskets
3. Cylinder block
4. Oil pump
5. Bolt(4)
A. 12-15 ft. lb.(16-20 Nm)

7922JG01

Exploded view of the water pump mounting—2.0L engine

7. Remove the accessory drive belt.

8. Remove the timing belt covers and the timing belt using the recommended procedure.

9. Remove the four water pump retaining bolts.

10. Remove the water pump.

To install:

11. Thoroughly clean all sealing surfaces.

12. Install a new water pump gasket and the water pump onto the cylinder block.

13. Tighten the retaining bolts to 12–15 ft. lbs. (16–20 Nm).

14. Reinstall the timing belt and the timing belt covers using the recommended procedure.

15. Reinstall the accessory drive belt.

16. Raise and safely support the vehicle.

17. Reinstall the lower radiator hose.

18. Lower the vehicle.

19. Fill the engine cooling system.

20. Reconnect the negative battery cable.

21. Start the engine and top off the coolant as necessary. Check for leaks.

2.5L Engine

➡ Before continuing with this procedure, be sure three new water pump retaining bolts (W701544) are available. Due to their torque-to-yield design, the bolts stretch and cannot be reused.

1. Before servicing the vehicle, refer to the precautions in the beginning of this section.

FRONT OF ENGINE

1. Bolt
2. Water pump drive belt tensioner
3. Water pump
4. Water pump outlet hose
5. LH cylinder head
6. Bolt(3)
A. 71-106 in. lb.(8-12 Nm)
B. 11-13 ft. lb.(15-18 Nm)
   then rotate 85-95°

7922JG02

Exploded view of the water pump mounting—2.5L engine

2. Disconnect the negative battery cable.

3. Drain the engine cooling system.

4. Remove the water pump pulley shield.

5. Remove the water pump drive belt.

6. Remove the water pump inlet and outlet hoses from the water pump.

7. Remove the three water pump-to-left cylinder head retaining bolts.

8. Remove the water pump and water pump housing from the vehicle.

9. Remove the water pump-to-water pump housing retaining bolts and separate the water pump from the water pump housing.

To install:

10. Thoroughly clean all sealing surfaces.

11. Install the water pump to the water pump housing using a new gasket and install the retaining bolts. Tighten the retaining bolts to 16–18 ft. lbs. (22–25 Nm).

12. Position the water pump and water pump housing and install three new torque-to-yield retaining bolts into the left cylinder head.

13. Tighten the new retaining bolts to 11–13 ft. lbs. (15–18 Nm), then rotate the retaining bolts 85–95 degrees.

14. Reinstall the water pump inlet and outlet hoses to the water pump.

15. Reinstall the water pump drive belt.

16. Reinstall the water pump shield.

17. Fill the engine cooling system.

18. Reconnect the negative battery cable.

19. Start the engine and top off the coolant as necessary. Check for leaks.

Cylinder Head

REMOVAL & INSTALLATION

2.0L Engine

➡The cylinder head bolts are a torque-to-yield design and cannot be reused. Be sure new cylinder head bolts are available before beginning this procedure. If the cylinder head bolts are reused, engine damage may occur.

1. Before servicing the vehicle, refer to the precautions in the beginning of this section.

2. Disconnect the negative battery cable.

3. Drain the engine coolant from the radiator and the cylinder block drain plugs.

4. Remove the intake manifold.

5. Remove the exhaust manifold.

6. Remove the camshafts and valve tappets.

7. Support the engine with a wood block between the crankshaft pulley and the front subframe.

8. Remove the Three Bar Engine Support D88L-6000-A or equivalent, previously installed for the timing belt cover removal.

9. Remove the right-hand engine lifting eye retaining bolt and the lifting eye.

10. Remove the support bracket from the power steering pump mounting bracket and cylinder head.

11. Remove the camshaft timing belt tensioner pulley and the engine front cover from the front of the cylinder head.

12. Remove the thermostat housing from the rear of the cylinder head.

13. Remove the ignition coil and bracket from the cylinder head.

14. Remove the spark plugs if not already removed.

15. Remove the cylinder head retaining bolts in the reverse of the installation sequence.

16. Remove the cylinder head and gasket from the engine.

17. If the cylinder head is to be serviced, remove the left-hand engine lifting eye.

To install:

18. Clean the cylinder head and cylinder block gasket surfaces and check for flatness.

19. Install a new cylinder head gasket onto the cylinder block. Be sure the head gasket is properly positioned on the dowels.

✳✳ WARNING

Use care when positioning the cylinder head to prevent damage to the head gasket or dowels.

20. Place a light coating of engine oil onto the threads of the new cylinder head bolts and install.

21. Tighten the cylinder head bolts in sequence and in the following steps:

   a. Tighten all bolts to 15–22 ft. lbs. (20–30 Nm)

   b. Tighten all bolts to 30–37 ft. lbs. (40–50 Nm)

   c. Rotate all bolts 90–120 degrees.

← **FRONT OF ENGINE** →

TIGHTEN BOLTS IN SEQUENCE SHOWN

7922JG03

Cylinder head mounting bolt tightening sequence—2.0L engine

Refer to Section 1 for engine rebuilding specifications

22. Reinstall the ignition coil bracket and the ignition coil.

23. Reinstall the water thermostat housing.

24. Reinstall the engine front cover. Tighten the retaining bolts to 71–97 inch lbs. (8–11 Nm).

25. Reinstall the camshaft timing belt tensioner pulley and retaining bolt onto the front of the cylinder head.

26. Reinstall the support bracket to the power steering pump mounting bracket and the cylinder head.

27. Tighten the support bracket to 29–41 ft. lbs. (39–55 Nm).

28. Reinstall the right engine lifting eye to the cylinder head and the alternator mounting bracket. Tighten the retaining bolts to 30–41 ft. lbs. (41–55, Nm).

29. If removed, install the left-hand engine lifting eye to the cylinder head and tighten to 10–13 ft. lbs. (14–18 Nm).

30. Install the Three Bar Engine Support D88L-6000-A or equivalent to the engine lifting eyes and support the engine.

31. Remove the wood block from between the subframe and the crankshaft pulley.

32. Reinstall the valve tappets and camshaft into their original locations.

33. Reinstall the exhaust manifold.

34. Reinstall the intake manifold.

35. Reinstall the spark plugs.

36. Drain the engine oil and remove the engine oil filter.

37. Reinstall the drain plug and tighten to 15–21 ft. lbs. (21–28 Nm).

38. Reinstall a new engine oil filter and fill the crankcase with the proper amount and grade of oil.

39. Fill the engine cooling system.

40. Reconnect the negative battery cable.

41. Run the engine and check for oil and coolant leaks. Check for proper engine operation.

2.5L Engine

➡ **The cylinder head bolts are a torque-to-yield design and cannot be reused. Be sure new cylinder head bolts are available before beginning this procedure.**

1. Before servicing the vehicle, refer to the precautions in the beginning of this section.

2. Disconnect the negative battery cable.

3. Drain the engine coolant from the radiator and cylinder block drain plugs.

4. Close the radiator petcock and install the drain plugs into the cylinder block.

5. Remove the upper and lower intake manifolds.

6. Drain the engine oil and remove the oil pan.

7. Remove the alternator and the alternator mounting bracket.

8. Remove the heated oxygen sensor from the right cylinder head exhaust manifold.

9. Remove the left cylinder head exhaust manifold.

10. Remove the water pump.

11. Remove the engine front cover.

12. Install the upper front engine mount (support insulator) and the upper front engine support bracket to the front of the engine and the right front fender apron.

13. Remove Three Bar Engine Support D88L-60000-A or equivalent.

14. Remove the camshafts and valve tappets from both cylinder heads.

15. Disconnect the hoses from the EGR pressure sensor at the EGR valve, to the exhaust manifold tube.

16. Disengage the EGR pressure sensor.

17. Disconnect the interior vacuum source hose from the main emission vacuum harness.

18. Disconnect the fuel vapor hose from the PCV valve.

19. Disconnect the EGR transducer.

20. Remove the EGR valve-to-exhaust manifold tube from the right exhaust manifold and remove from the vehicle.

21. Remove the wiring retaining bracket from the EGR transducer bracket.

22. Remove the engine air cleaner.

23. Remove the crankcase ventilation tube from the water crossover and oil separator.

24. Remove the water crossover retaining bolt and stud bolt from the right cylinder head. Set the water crossover aside.

25. Remove the oil level dipstick from the left cylinder head.

26. Remove the cylinder head retaining bolts from the cylinder heads in the reverse of the tightening sequence illustration.

27. Remove the right cylinder head with the exhaust manifold and the EGR transducer bracket attached.

28. If required, remove the exhaust manifold and the EGR transducer bracket from the right cylinder head.

29. Remove the left cylinder head.

30. Inspect the cylinder heads and cylinder block.

To install:

31. Clean the cylinder heads, intake manifolds, valve covers and the cylinder head gasket sealing surfaces on the cylinder block.

➡ **If the cylinder heads were removed for cylinder head gasket replacement, check the flatness of the cylinder heads and the cylinder block gasket sealing surfaces.**

32. If removed, install the right exhaust manifold and EGR transducer bracket to the right cylinder head.

33. Install new cylinder head gaskets onto the dowels of the cylinder block.

34. Position the cylinder heads into their original positions using care not to damage the heads, block or gaskets.

35. Be sure that the cylinder heads are correctly positioned on the dowels.

36. Lightly oil the threads of the new cylinder head retaining bolts and install into the cylinder heads.

37. Tighten the new cylinder head retaining bolts as follows:

   a. Tighten the bolts, in sequence, to 27–32 ft. lbs. (37–43 Nm)

   b. Rotate the bolts, in sequence, 85–95 degrees

   c. Loosen the bolts, in sequence, a minimum of one full turn

   d. Tighten the bolts, in sequence, to 27–32 ft. lbs. (37–43 Nm)

   e. Rotate the bolts, in sequence, 85–95 degrees

   f. Rotate the bolts, in sequence, an additional 85–95 degrees

38. Inspect the water crossover O-rings and replace if required.

39. Reinstall the water crossover to the cylinder heads and tighten the retaining bolts to 71–106 inch lbs. (8–12 Nm).

40. Reinstall the crankcase ventilation tube. Tighten the tube to 44–62 inch lbs. (5–7 Nm).

41. Reinstall the oil level dipstick to the left cylinder head.

LH CYLINDER HEAD

7922JG04

Cylinder head mounting bolt tightening sequence—2.5L engine

42. Reinstall the engine air cleaner.

43. Reinstall the wiring retaining bracket onto the EGR transducer bracket.

44. Reinstall the EGR to exhaust manifold tube onto the right exhaust manifold.

45. Reconnect the EGR transducer and the EGR pressure sensor.

46. Reconnect the fuel vapor hose to the PCV valve.

47. Reconnect the interior vacuum source hoses to the main emission vacuum harness.

48. Reconnect the hoses from the EGR pressure sensor and EGR valve to the exhaust manifold tube.

49. Reinstall the camshafts and valve tappets.

50. Install the Three Bar Engine Support D88L-6000-A or equivalent, to the engine lifting eyes and support the engine.

51. Reinstall the engine front cover.

52. Reinstall the left exhaust manifold.

53. Reinstall the water pump.

54. Reinstall the heated oxygen sensor to the right exhaust manifold.

55. Reinstall the alternator mounting bracket and the alternator.

56. Reinstall the engine oil pan.

57. Reinstall the lower and upper intake manifolds.

58. Replace the engine oil filter.

59. Fill the engine with the proper amount and grade of engine oil.

60. Fill the engine cooling system.

61. Reconnect the negative battery cable.

62. Run the engine and check for oil and coolant leaks. Check for proper engine operation.

Rocker Arms

REMOVAL & INSTALLATION

The 2.0L engine is not equipped with rocker arms, the camshaft directly actuates the valves through a hydraulic lifter.

2.5L Engine

1. Before servicing the vehicle, refer to the precautions in the beginning of this section.

2. Disconnect both battery cables, negative cable first.

3. Remove the valve covers as follows:

a. Remove the ignition wires and spark plugs.

b. Remove the ignition coil from the right valve cover.

c. Remove the crankcase ventilation tubes from both valve covers.

d. Remove the wiring harness and bracket to the fuel injectors and move aside.

e. Remove the retaining nuts and engine wiring from both valve covers and move aside.

f. Remove the valve cover retaining bolts and studs.

g. Remove both valve covers from the engine.

4. Remove the crankshaft pulley retaining bolt.

5. Rotate the crankshaft so that the keyway is at the 11 o'clock position to locate the crankshaft at TDC for No. 1 cylinder.

6. Verify that the alignment arrows on the camshafts are aligned. If not, rotate the crankshaft one complete revolution and recheck.

7. Rotate the crankshaft so that the keyway is at the 3 o'clock position. This positions the right cylinder head camshafts to the neutral position.

8. Remove the accessory drive belts.

9. Remove the battery.

10. Remove the water pump drive pulley from the left intake camshaft using Camshaft Dampener Remover/Replacer T94P-6312-AH or equivalent, along with the shaft protector and screw or equivalent.

11. Remove the camshaft rear oil seal retainer bolts and the camshaft rear oil seal retainer and gasket from the left cylinder head.

➡ **The camshaft journal caps and cylinder heads are numbered to ensure that they are assembled in their original positions. If removed, keep the camshaft journal caps together with the cylinder head that they were removed from.**

12. Remove the right cylinder head camshaft journal thrust cap retaining bolts and thrust caps.

13. Loosen the remaining camshaft journal cap bolts in sequence, releasing the bolts several revolutions at a time by making several passes to allow the camshaft to be raised from the cylinder head evenly. Do not remove the retaining bolts completely.

➡ **If the valve lifters (tappets) and roller rocker arms are to be reused, mark the positions of the valve lifters and rocker arms so that they are reassembled into their original positions.**

14. With the camshafts loose, remove the rocker arms, keeping them in the order that they were removed.

15. If required, remove the valve lifters from the cylinder head.

16. Rotate the crankshaft two revolutions and locate the crankshaft keyway at the 11 o'clock position. This will position the left cylinder head camshafts to their neutral position.

17. Verify that the alignment arrows on the camshafts are aligned.

➡ **The camshaft journal caps and cylinder heads are numbered to ensure that they are assembled in their original positions. If removed, keep the camshaft journal caps together with the cylinder head that they were removed from.**

18. Remove the camshaft journal thrust cap retaining bolts and thrust caps from the left cylinder head.

19. Loosen the remaining camshaft journal cap bolts in sequence, releasing the bolts several revolutions at a time by making several passes to allow the camshaft to be raised from the cylinder head evenly. Do not remove the retaining bolts completely.

➡ **If the valve lifters (tappets) and roller rocker arms are to be reused, mark the positions of the valve lifters and rocker arms so that they are reassembled into their original positions.**

20. With the camshafts loose, remove the rocker arms, keeping them in the order that they were removed.

21. If required, remove the valve lifters from the cylinder head.

22. Inspect the rocker arms and valve lifters for wear and/or damage and replace as necessary.

After the camshaft is loose, the rocker arm/cam follower (arrow) can be removed—2.5L engine

For engine torque specifications, refer to Section 1 of this manual

To install:

23. Be sure that the crankshaft keyway is at the 11 o'clock position.

24. Lubricate the left cylinder head valve lifters with engine assembly lubricant and install into their correct positions in the cylinder head.

25. If the valve lifters are being replaced with new units, soak the lifters in a container of clean engine oil and/or manually pump up the lifters before installing into the cylinder head.

26. Lubricate the left cylinder head rocker arms with engine assembly lubricant and install the left cylinder head rocker arms into their original locations.

➡**Do not install the camshaft journal thrust caps until the camshaft journal caps are secured into position.**

27. Tighten the left cylinder head camshaft journal cap bolts in sequence (see camshaft procedure for sequence) making several passes to pull the camshafts down evenly. Tighten the bolts to 71–106 inch lbs. (8–12 Nm).

28. Reinstall the left-hand cylinder head thrust caps and bolts. Tighten to 71–106 inch lbs. (8–12 Nm).

29. Rotate the crankshaft two revolutions and position the crankshaft keyway to the 3 o'clock location. This will position the right cylinder head camshafts to the neutral position.

30. Lubricate the right cylinder head valve lifters with engine assembly lubricant and install into their original positions in the cylinder head.

31. If the valve lifters are being replaced with new units, soak the lifters in a container of clean engine oil and/or manually pump the lifters up before installing into the cylinder head.

32. Lubricate the right cylinder head rocker arms with engine assembly lubricant and install the right cylinder head rocker arms into their original locations.

➡**Do not install the camshaft journal thrust caps until the camshaft journal caps are secured into position.**

33. Tighten the right cylinder head camshaft journal cap bolts in sequence making several passes to pull the camshafts down evenly. Tighten the bolts to 71–106 inch lbs. (8–12 Nm).

34. Reinstall the right-hand cylinder head thrust caps and bolts. Tighten to 71–106 inch lbs. (8–12 Nm).

35. Reinstall the left cylinder head camshaft rear oil seal and retainer with gasket onto the cylinder head. Tighten the

retaining bolts to 71–106 inch lbs. (8–12 Nm).

36. Reinstall the water pump drive pulley onto the left intake camshaft using Power Steering Pump Pulley Replacer T91P-3A733-A, screw and replacer cup or equivalent.

37. Reinstall the accessory drive belts.

38. Reinstall the battery.

39. Reinstall the crankshaft pulley retaining bolt.

40. Tighten the crankshaft pulley retaining bolt as follows:

    a. Tighten to 89 ft. lbs. (120 Nm).

    b. Loosen the bolt at least one full turn.

    c. Tighten the bolt to 35–39 ft. lbs. (47–53 Nm).

    d. Rotate the bolt 85–95 degrees.

41. Reinstall both valve covers as follows:

    a. Clean the valve cover gasket sealing surfaces.

    b. Install new valve cover gaskets onto the valve covers.

    c. For each valve cover, place a bead of silicone sealant at two places on the valve cover sealing surfaces where the engine front cover and the cylinder heads make contact and at two places on the rear of the cylinder head where the camshaft seal retainer contacts the cylinder head.

    d. Reinstall the valve cover retaining bolts and studs and tighten in sequence to 71–106 inch lbs. (8–12 Nm).

➡**The valve covers must be installed and properly tightened within six minutes of applying the silicone sealant.**

42. Reconnect both battery cables, negative cable last.

43. Run the engine and check for leaks and proper operation.

Intake Manifold

REMOVAL & INSTALLATION

2.0L Engine

1. Before servicing the vehicle, refer to the precautions in the beginning of this section.

2. Disconnect the negative battery cable.

3. Remove the engine air intake resonators.

4. Relieve the fuel system pressure.

5. Remove the accelerator cable and the speed control actuator from the throttle body.

6. Remove the accelerator cable bracket.

7. Disconnect the wiring harness to the fuel injectors and move aside.

8. Disconnect the vacuum line at the fuel pressure regulator.

9. Using the proper spring lock coupling disconnect tools (⅜ inch and ½ inch), remove the fuel supply and return hoses from the fuel injection supply manifold (fuel rail).

10. Remove the fuel supply and return hoses from the retaining bracket on the intake manifold and move aside.

11. Carefully disengage the fuel injection supply manifold with the fuel injectors attached and remove from the engine.

12. Disconnect the wiring for the Engine Coolant Temperature (ECT) sensor and the engine control sensor.

13. Remove the crankcase ventilation tube from the intake manifold fitting.

14. Remove the wiring harness connector at the Camshaft Position (CMP) sensor located on the cylinder head.

15. Remove the CMP sensor retaining screw and remove the sensor.

16. Disconnect the vacuum hose at the Exhaust Gas Recirculation (EGR) valve.

17. Use a 22mm crowfoot wrench to completely loosen the EGR valve to exhaust manifold tube nut.

18. Remove the two EGR valve retaining bolts and remove the EGR valve and gasket.

19. Remove the vacuum supply hoses for the body and brake booster from the bottom of the intake manifold.

20. Remove the retaining bracket screws for the engine control sensor wiring.

➡**The intake manifold can be removed without the removal of the alternator and alternator mounting bracket however their removal will make the job easier.**

21. Remove the retaining bolts and nuts from the intake manifold.

22. Remove the intake manifold and gasket from the cylinder head.

To install:

23. If the intake manifold is to be replaced, remove the throttle body and Idle Air Control (IAC) valve from the old manifold and install on the new one.

24. Clean the gasket sealing surfaces on the intake manifold and the cylinder head.

25. Install the intake manifold using a new gasket to the cylinder head.

26. Reinstall the intake manifold retaining nuts and bolts.

27. Tighten the retaining nuts and bolts in several passes to 12–15 ft. lbs. (16–20

FRONT OF ENGINE

1. Cylinder head
2. Stud (2 req'd)
3. Bolt (8 req'd)
4. Intake manifold gasket
5. Nut (2 req'd)
6. Intake manifold
A. Tighten to 0-10 Nm (0-89 lb. in.)
B. Tighten to 16-20 Nm (12-15 lb. ft.)

7922JG06

Exploded view of the intake manifold mounting—2.0L engine

Nm), starting at the center and working towards the ends of the cylinder head.

28. Reinstall the alternator mounting bracket and alternator, if removed.

29. Reinstall the retaining screws for the engine control wiring sensor retaining bracket.

30. Reinstall the vacuum supply hoses for the body and brake booster to the bottom of the intake manifold.

31. Reinstall the EGR valve using a new gasket and tighten the two retaining bolts.

32. Reinstall the EGR valve-to-exhaust manifold tube nut and tighten to 26–33 ft. lbs. (35–45 Nm).

33. Reinstall the EGR valve vacuum hose.

34. Reinstall the CMP sensor and its retaining screw and tighten to 13–17 ft. lbs. (18–23 Nm).

35. Reconnect the CMP sensor.

36. Reinstall the crankcase ventilation tube to the intake manifold fitting.

37. Reconnect the ECT sensor and the engine control sensor wiring.

38. Carefully position the fuel injection supply manifold with injectors into the intake manifold.

39. Reinstall the fuel supply and return hoses to the fuel injection supply manifold.

40. Reinstall the vacuum line to the fuel pressure regulator.

41. Position the wiring harness for the fuel injectors and install.

42. Reinstall the accelerator cable bracket.

43. Reinstall the speed control actuator and the accelerator cable to the throttle body.

44. Reinstall the air cleaner assembly and the air intake resonators.

45. Reconnect the negative battery cable.

46. Run the engine and check for leaks and proper operation.

2.5L Engine

UPPER AND LOWER INTAKE MANIFOLDS

1. Before servicing the vehicle, refer to the precautions in the beginning of this section.

2. Disconnect the negative battery cable.

3. Relieve the fuel system pressure.

4. Remove the water pump pulley shield.

5. Depress the black retainer with a screwdriver on the upper intake manifold and disconnect the main emission vacuum control and the brake booster vacuum connector from the upper intake manifold.

6. Remove the accelerator cable and speed control actuator from the throttle body.

7. Remove the accelerator cable bracket from the intake manifold and move aside.

8. Remove the Idle Air Control (IAC) valve fresh air supply hose from the fitting on the upper intake manifold.

9. Disconnect the wiring harnesses from the Throttle Position (TP) sensor, IAC valve and the Exhaust Gas Recirculation (EGR) vacuum regulator control.

10. Remove the vacuum supply hose from the upper intake manifold to the PCV valve at the upper intake manifold.

11. Disconnect the vacuum supply hoses to the EGR vacuum regulator control and the EGR valve.

12. Loosen and remove the EGR valve to exhaust manifold tube and move aside.

13. Remove the Intake Manifold Runner Control (IMRC) vacuum solenoid linkage rod by carefully prying with a screwdriver.

For complete mechanical specifications, refer to Section 1 of this manual

14. Remove the upper intake manifold retaining bolts in the reverse of the installation sequence illustration.

➡ **When removing engine components such as manifolds and cylinder heads, always remove the retaining bolts in a reverse order of their tightening sequence to prevent warpage to the component.**

15. Remove the upper intake manifold and gaskets from the engine.

➡ **If only removing the upper intake manifold, stop at this point. The remainder of the procedure is for the lower manifold.**

16. Disconnect the fuel injector wiring harness and move aside.

17. Disconnect the vacuum line to the fuel pressure regulator and the IMRC valve and set aside.

18. Remove the spring lock coupling retainer clips from the fuel supply and return fittings.

19. Use spring lock coupling disconnect tools (⅜ inch and ½ inch) to disconnect the fuel supply and return hoses from the fuel injection supply manifold.

20. Remove the eight lower intake manifold-to-cylinder head retaining bolts in reverse of the tightening sequence illustration.

21. Remove the lower intake manifold and gaskets from the vehicle.

22. If the lower intake manifold is to be replaced or machined, remove the fuel injectors and the IMRC vacuum solenoid.

To install:

23. Install the IMRC vacuum solenoid and fuel injectors onto the lower intake manifold if removed. Use a hand vacuum pump to verify operation of the IMRC vacuum solenoid and plate operation at this time.

24. Thoroughly clean the gasket sealing areas and place two new intake to cylinder head gaskets into position.

25. Carefully install the lower intake manifold and install the intake manifold to cylinder head retaining bolts.

26. Tighten the retaining bolts in sequence to 71–106 inch lbs. (8–12 Nm).

27. Install the fuel supply and return hoses to the fuel supply manifold and

Installation Sequence

● **TIGHTEN BOLTS IN SEQUENCE SHOWN**

* **HOLE LOCATION FOR GASKET LOCATING PINS**

FRONT OF ENGINE

③ **LOCATING PINS (2 EACH PER GASKET)**

VIEW A

1. Bolt (6)
2. Intake manifold, upper
3. Intake manifold upper gasket
4. Intake manifold, lower
5. Isolator (6)
6. 71-106 in. lb. (8-12 Nm)

7922JG08

Upper intake manifold bolt tightening sequence—2.5L engine

Installation Sequence

● **INSTALL BOLTS IN SEQUENCE SHOWN**

LOWER INTAKE MANIFOLD

FRONT OF ENGINE

7922JG07

Lower intake manifold tightening sequence—2.5L engine

ensure that the spring lock couplings are correctly installed.

28. Install the retaining clips onto the spring lock couplings.

29. Reconnect the vacuum line to the fuel pressure regulator and the IMRC vacuum solenoid.

30. Temporarily connect the negative battery cable.

31. Reconnect the fuel pressure gauge to the fuel pressure relief valve located on the fuel injection supply manifold.

32. Cycle the ignition key several times to the **RUN** position to pressurize the fuel system.

33. Watch the fuel pressure gauge for signs of leakage. If the gauge holds pressure, remove the gauge and continue with the installation of the upper intake manifold. If the pressure gauge loses pressure, remove the fuel injection supply manifold and replace the leaking O-ring(s) before continuing.

34. Disconnect the negative battery cable.

35. Reposition and install the fuel injector wiring harness.

➡**If only installing the upper intake manifold, start at this point.**

36. Install the upper intake manifold using two new gaskets onto the lower intake manifold.

37. Install the upper manifold retaining bolts and tighten following the proper sequence to 71–106 inch lbs. (8–12 Nm).

38. Install new bushings for the IMRC linkage rod and install the rod.

39. Reinstall the EGR valve-to-exhaust manifold tube and tighten the nut to 26–33 ft. lbs. (35–45 Nm).

40. Reconnect the vacuum supply hoses to the EGR vacuum regulator control and the EGR valve.

41. Reconnect the TP sensor, IAC valve and the EGR vacuum regulator control.

42. Reinstall the IAC valve fresh air supply hose to the fitting on the upper intake manifold.

43. Reinstall the accelerator cable bracket to the intake manifold.

44. Reinstall the speed control actuator and the accelerator cable to the throttle body.

45. Reinstall the main emission vacuum control connector and the brake booster vacuum connector to the upper intake manifold.

46. Reinstall the water pump pulley shield.

47. Reconnect the negative battery cable.

48. Run the engine and check for leaks.

Exhaust Manifold

REMOVAL & INSTALLATION

2.0L Engine

1. Before servicing the vehicle, refer to the precautions in the beginning of this section.

2. Disconnect the negative battery cable.

3. Remove the engine air intake resonators.

4. Disconnect the Heated Oxygen (HO$_2$S) sensor.

5. Remove the oil level indicator tube.

6. Remove the exhaust manifold heat shield retainers and the exhaust manifold heat shield.

7. Remove the HO$_2$S sensor from the exhaust manifold.

8. Remove the four catalytic converter retaining nuts.

9. Raise and safely support the vehicle.

10. Remove the Exhaust Gas Recirculation (EGR) valve-to-exhaust manifold tube, retaining bracket and clamp.

11. Remove the catalytic converter.

12. Lower the vehicle.

13. Remove the nine exhaust manifold retaining nuts from the cylinder head studs.

← FRONT OF ENGINE →

1	Cylinder Head
2	Exhaust Manifold Gasket
3	Spacer
4	Exhaust Manifold
5	Nut (9 Req'd)
6	Stud (9 Req'd)
A	Tighten to 14-17 N-m (13-16 Lb-Ft)

7922JG09

Exhaust manifold and related components—2.0L engine

14. Remove the exhaust manifold and gasket.

15. Remove the exhaust manifold from the vehicle.

16. Clean all gasket mating surfaces.

To install:

17. Position a new exhaust manifold gasket and the exhaust manifold onto the cylinder head studs.

18. Reinstall the exhaust manifold retaining nuts and tighten to 13–16 ft. lbs. (14–17 Nm).

19. Raise and safely support the vehicle.

20. Reinstall the catalytic converter using a new exhaust converter inlet gasket.

21. Reinstall the EGR valve-to-exhaust manifold tube, retaining bracket and clamp.

22. Tighten the EGR valve-to-exhaust manifold tube nut to 44 ft. lbs. (60 Nm).

23. Lower the vehicle.

24. Reinstall the catalytic converter to exhaust manifold retaining nuts.

25. Reinstall the HO$_2$S sensor to the exhaust manifold and tighten to 44 ft. lbs. (60 Nm).

26. Reinstall the exhaust manifold heat shield and heat shield retainers.

27. Tighten the heat shield retainers to 71–106 inch lbs. (8–11 Nm).

28. Reinstall the oil level indicator tube.

29. Reconnect the HO$_2$S sensor.

30. Reinstall the air intake resonators.

31. Reconnect the negative battery cable.

32. Run the engine and check for leaks and proper operation.

2.5L Engine

RIGHT SIDE

1. Before servicing the vehicle, refer to the precautions in the beginning of this section.

2. Disconnect the negative battery cable.

3. Disconnect the wiring harness from the Oxygen (O$_2$S) sensor.

4. Raise and safely support the vehicle.

5. Remove the alternator and the alternator mounting bracket.

6. Remove the retaining nuts from the outlet flange on the catalytic converter.

7. Remove the muffler and the exhaust converter outlet gasket from the catalytic converter.

8. Remove the catalytic converter retaining nuts and the exhaust pipe flange hold-down springs.

9. Remove the catalytic converter.

10. Remove the halfshaft support bearing retainer bracket from the support bearing and cylinder block.

1	EGR Valve
2	RH Cylinder Head
3	Exhaust Manifold Gasket
4	Stud Bolt (6 Req'd)
5	Nut (6 Req'd)
6	RH Exhaust Manifold
7	Heated Oxygen Sensor
8	EGR Valve to Exhaust Manifold Tube
A	Tighten to 18-22 N·m (13-16 Lb-Ft)
B	Tighten to 35-45 N·m (26-33 Lb-Ft)

7922JG10

Exploded view of the right-side exhaust manifold mounting—2.5L engine

11. Remove the O_2S sensor from the exhaust manifold.

12. Loosen the Exhaust Gas Recirculation (EGR) valve-to-exhaust manifold tube nuts and remove the tube.

13. Remove the exhaust manifold retaining nuts from the cylinder head studs.

14. Remove the exhaust manifold and gasket from the engine.

15. Clean all gasket mating surfaces.

To install:

16. Install the exhaust manifold with a new exhaust manifold gasket.

17. Reinstall the exhaust manifold retaining studs and tighten to 13–16 ft. lbs. (18–22 Nm) in the proper sequence.

18. Reinstall the EGR valve-to-exhaust manifold tube and tighten the nuts to 26–33 ft. lbs. (35–45 Nm).

19. Reinstall the O_2S sensor into the exhaust manifold and tighten to 26–34 ft. lbs. (35–46 Nm).

20. Reinstall the halfshaft support bearing retainer bracket to the support bearing and the cylinder block.

21. Reinstall the catalytic converter using a new exhaust converter inlet gasket.

22. Position the muffler and a new exhaust converter outlet gasket onto the catalytic converter and loosely install the retaining nuts.

23. Align the exhaust system and tighten all nuts and bolts.

24. Tighten the catalytic converter retaining nuts with the exhaust pipe flange hold-down springs to 22–30 ft. lbs. (27.9–40.3 Nm).

25. Tighten the muffler inlet flange nuts to 26–33 ft. lbs. (34–46 Nm).

26. Reinstall the alternator mounting bracket and the alternator.

27. Lower the vehicle.

28. Reconnect the wiring harness to the O_2 sensor.

29. Reconnect the negative battery cable.

30. Run the engine and check for exhaust leaks and proper operation.

LEFT SIDE

1. Before servicing the vehicle, refer to the precautions in the beginning of this section.

2. Disconnect the negative battery cable.

3. Disconnect the Oxygen (O_2S) sensor.

4. Raise and safely support the vehicle.

5. Remove the front and rear exhaust crossover tube flange fasteners from the exhaust manifolds.

6. Remove the stud and nut retainer from the engine oil pan.

7. Remove the two remaining nuts and bolts from the exhaust crossover tubes outlet connection.

8. Remove the exhaust crossover tube.

9. Remove the lower radiator hose tube retaining bracket nuts.

10. Remove the six exhaust manifold retaining nuts from the cylinder head studs.

11. Move the lower radiator hose tube to gain access for removal of the exhaust manifold.

12. Remove the exhaust manifold. If the manifold is being replaced, remove the O_2 sensor.

13. Clean all gasket mating surfaces.

Exhaust manifold mounting bolt tightening sequence—2.5L engine

To install:

14. If removed, install the O2S sensor in the new manifold.

15. Place a new exhaust manifold to cylinder block gasket onto the cylinder head studs.

16. Move the lower radiator hose to allow installing the exhaust manifold.

17. Place the exhaust manifold onto the cylinder head studs and install the six retaining nuts.

18. Tighten the retaining nuts to 13–16 ft. lbs. (18–22 Nm), in sequence.

19. Reinstall the lower radiator hose tube retaining bracket and tighten to 71–106 inch lbs. (8–12 Nm).

20. Reinstall the exhaust crossover tube.

21. Reinstall two nuts and bolts to the exhaust crossover tube outlet connection.

22. Reinstall the stud and nut retainer at the engine oil pan.

23. Reinstall the front and rear exhaust crossover tube flange fasteners at the exhaust manifolds.

24. Lower the vehicle.

25. Reconnect the O2S sensor.

26. Reconnect the negative battery cable.

27. Run the engine and check for exhaust leaks and proper operation.

Front Crankshaft Seal

➡**The front crankshaft seal procedures apply on to engines equipped with timing belts. For the front seals on engines equipped with timing chains or gears, refer to the applicable procedure later in this section.**

REMOVAL & INSTALLATION

2.0L Engine

1. Before servicing the vehicle, refer to the precautions in the beginning of this section.

2. Disconnect the negative battery cable.

3. Remove the camshaft timing belt and the crankshaft sprocket.

4. Using seal remover T92C-6700-CH or equivalent, remove the front crankshaft seal from the oil pump housing.

To install:

5. Clean and inspect the oil pump housing crankshaft front oil seal bore.

6. Lubricate the oil pump crankshaft oil seal bore and crankshaft front seal with engine assembly lubricant.

7. Use oil pump seal replacer T81P-6700-A or equivalent tool, and the crankshaft pulley retaining bolt, install the new crankshaft seal into the oil pump.

8. Reinstall the crankshaft sprocket and the camshaft timing belt.

9. Reconnect the negative battery cable.

10. Run the engine and check for leaks and proper operation.

Be sure not to damage the crankshaft sealing surface while removing the seal—2.0L engine

Camshaft and Valve Lifters

REMOVAL & INSTALLATION

2.0L Engine

1. Before servicing the vehicle, refer to the precautions in the beginning of this section.

2. Disconnect the negative battery cable.

3. Remove the valve cover as follows:
   a. Remove the engine air intake resonators.
   b. Disconnect the crankcase ventilation tube from the valve cover.
   c. Remove the ignition wires from the valve cover and move aside.
   d. Remove the retaining bolt and nut for the power steering pressure hose

retaining bracket and move the hose aside.
   e. Remove the bolts for the upper camshaft timing belt cover and remove the cover.
   f. Remove the valve cover retaining bolts in a standard removal sequence starting from the outside of the valve cover and working toward the inside of the valve cover.
   g. Remove the valve cover and gasket from the engine.

1. Bolt (10)
2. Spacer (10)
3. O-ring (10)
4. Oil filler cap
5. Valve cover gasket
6. Cylinder head
7. Valve cover
A. 53-71 in. lb. (6-8 Nm)

Valve cover and related components—2.0L engine

4. Remove the camshaft timing belt and sprockets.

➡**Mark the camshaft journal caps to the cylinder head for installation. Do not mix the caps between the two camshafts or from another cylinder head.**

5. Loosen all of the camshaft journal cap bolts in pairs and in sequence one turn at a time starting at the rear cap. This will allow the camshaft to raise up from the cylinder head evenly.

➡**Remove the camshaft journal thrust caps last.**

6. Remove all of the camshaft journal caps making sure that they are marked so that they can be reassembled to their original positions.

Remove the bearing cap bolts in pairs using the sequence shown—2.0L engine

7. Remove the intake and exhaust camshafts and the camshaft front seals from the cylinder head.

8. Inspect the camshafts and cylinder head for wear.

➡ **If the valve lifters (tappets) are to be reused, mark their locations to ensure that they will be installed into their correct positions.**

9. If required, remove the valve lifters from the cylinder head.

10. Inspect the valve lifters for wear.

To install:

➡ **Before installing the camshafts, the crankshaft must be positioned so that No. 1 cylinder is at TDC on its compression stroke.**

11. If removed, lubricate the valve lifters with engine assembly lubricant and install into the lifter bores that they were removed from.

12. If the valve lifters are new, soak the lifters in a container of clean engine oil or manually pump up the lifters before installation.

13. Lubricate the camshafts with engine assembly lubricant and place the camshafts into the cylinder head.

➡ **The intake and exhaust camshafts are marked for identification, also the intake camshaft has an extra cam lobe for the Camshaft Position (CMP) sensor.**

14. Loosely install the camshaft journal caps and retaining bolts into their original positions.

15. Install the camshaft journal thrust caps and retaining bolts last. Apply a bead of silicone sealant to the sealing surfaces of the camshaft journal thrust caps.

16. Tighten all of the camshaft journal caps in several steps pulling the camshaft down evenly following the proper sequence.

1. Bolt(20)
2. Camshaft journal cap(8)
3. Cylinder head
4. Camshaft
5. Camshaft journal thrust cap(2)
A. 13–15 ft. lb.(17–21 Nm)

FRONT OF ENGINE

NOTE: APPLY A 3 mm (1/8 INCH) BEAD OF SILICONE GASKET AND SEALANT F1AZ-19562-A OR EQUIVALENT MEETING FORD SPECIFICATION WSE-M4G320-A2 TO SEALING SURFACES OF THE CAMSHAFT JOURNAL THRUST CAPS AS SHOWN.

VIEW A

During assembly, apply sealant to the camshaft journal thrust cap as shown—2.0L engine

17. Once the camshaft journal caps are fully seated, tighten the retaining bolts to 13–15 ft. lbs. (17–21 Nm).

18. Install new camshaft front seals using the Camshaft Seal Replacer T92C-6700-cH or equivalent.

19. Reinstall the camshaft sprockets and the camshaft timing belt.

20. Reinstall the valve cover as follows:
    a. Clean the gasket sealing surfaces.
    b. Inspect the valve cover gasket and O-rings, replace as required.
    c. Reinstall the valve cover retaining bolts and tighten in a standard sequence starting from the center and working

Camshaft journal cap retaining bolt tightening sequence—2.0L engine

towards the outside of the valve cover to 53–71 inch lbs. (6–8 Nm).
    d. Reinstall the upper camshaft timing belt cover and tighten the retaining bolts to 27–44 inch lbs. (3–5 Nm).
    e. Reinstall the power steering hose retaining bracket and the power steering hose.
    f. Reinstall the ignition wires.
    g. Reinstall the crankcase ventilation tube to the valve cover.
    h. Reinstall the engine air intake resonators.

21. Reconnect the negative battery cable.

22. Run the engine and check for leaks and proper operation.

2.5L Engine

1. Before servicing the vehicle, refer to the precautions in the beginning of this section.

2. Disconnect the negative battery cable.

3. Remove both valve covers as follows:
    a. Remove the ignition wires and spark plugs.
    b. Remove the ignition coil from the right valve cover.
    c. Remove the crankcase ventilation tubes from both valve covers.

d. Remove the wiring harness and bracket to the fuel injectors and move aside.

e. Remove the retaining nuts and engine wiring from both valve covers and move aside.

f. Loosen the valve cover retaining bolts and studs, in sequence.

g. Remove both valve covers from the engine.

4. Remove the engine front cover.

5. Remove the timing chains.

※※ WARNING

The camshaft journal thrust caps must be removed first, before loosening the remaining camshaft journal cap bolts, to ensure that the camshaft journal thrust caps are not damaged.

6. Remove the camshaft journal thrust caps.

7. Loosen the camshaft journal cap bolts in sequence, in several passes, to allow the camshaft to raise off of the cylinder head evenly.

Left (front) cylinder head camshaft journal cap retaining bolt loosening sequence—2.5L engine

7922JG18

Right (rear) cylinder head camshaft journal cap retaining bolt loosening sequence—2.5L engine

7922JG19

Camshafts Shown Removed From Cylinder Heads For Clarity

CAUTION: CAMSHAFTS MUST BE IN TIME WITH CRANKSHAFT PRIOR TO INSTALLATION OF ROCKER ARMS

NOTE: VALVE TAPPET MUST BE PUMPED UP PRIOR TO INSTALLATION

FRONT OF ENGINE

CAUTION: REMOVE CYLINDER HEAD JOURNAL THRUST CAPS FIRST. INSTALL CYLINDER HEAD JOURNAL THRUST CAPS LAST.

CAUTION: ROTATE CRANKSHAFT KEYWAY TO 11 O'CLOCK POSITION PRIOR TO INSTALLATION OF LH CAMSHAFT AND ROCKER ARMS. ROTATE CRANKSHAFT KEYWAY TO 3 O'CLOCK POSITION PRIOR TO INSTALLATION OF RH CAMSHAFT AND ROCKER ARMS.

1. Cylinder head
2. Camshaft journal thrust cap(2)
3. Camshaft journal cap(7)
4. Bolt(18)
5. LH intake camshaft
6. Rocker arm(12)
7. Valve tappet(12)
8. LH exhaust camshaft
A. 71-106 in. lb.(8-12 Nm)

7922JG17

Exploded view of camshaft mounting—2.5L engine

Timing belt service is covered in Section 5 of this manual

❄❄ WARNING

The camshaft journal caps and cylinder heads are numbered to ensure that they are assembled in their original positions. Keep the camshaft journal caps from each cylinder head together; do not mix them with caps from another cylinder head. Failure to do so may result in engine damage.

8. Remove the camshaft journal caps with the retaining bolts installed.

9. Remove the camshafts from the cylinder head. If necessary, remove the rocker arms, marking their positions so they can be reinstalled in their original locations.

10. Repeat the procedure for both cylinder heads.

11. Inspect the camshafts and bearing journals for wear or damage.

To install:

❄❄ WARNING

The crankshaft keyway must be at the 11 o'clock position before reassembly. Failure to do so may lead to engine damage.

12. Rotate the crankshaft so that the keyway is at the 11 o'clock position for installation of the camshafts.

13. Reinstall the rocker arms, if removed.

14. Lubricate the camshafts with engine assembly lubricant.

15. Reinstall the camshafts into their correct positions into each cylinder head with the timing marks on the camshaft sprockets aligned.

16. Loosely install the camshaft journal caps and retaining bolts into their correct positions.

➡️ **Do not install the camshaft journal thrust caps until the rocker arms and timing chains have been installed and the camshaft journal caps are secured into position.**

17. Reinstall the rocker arms.

18. Reinstall the timing chains.

19. Tighten the camshaft journal cap bolts, in the opposite order of the removal sequence, to 71–106 inch lbs. (8–12 Nm). Reinstall the thrust caps and tighten the retaining bolts to 71–106 inch lbs. (8–12 Nm).

20. Reinstall the engine front cover.

21. Reinstall both valve covers as follows:

a. Clean the valve cover gasket sealing surfaces.

b. Reinstall new valve cover gaskets onto the valve covers.

c. For each valve cover, place a bead of silicone sealant at the two places on the valve cover sealing surfaces where the engine front cover and the cylinder heads make contact and at two places on the rear of the cylinder head where the camshaft seal retainer contacts the cylinder head.

d. Reinstall the valve cover retaining bolts and studs and tighten in sequence to 71–106 inch lbs. (8–12 Nm).

➡️ **The valve covers must be installed and properly tightened within six minutes of applying the silicone sealant.**

22. Reconnect the negative battery cable.

23. Run the engine and check for leaks and proper engine operation.

Valve Lash

ADJUSTMENT

The lash adjusters (valve tappets), are hydraulic and are not adjustable. It is important that all valve components are in good condition and installed and tightened properly.

Oil Pan

REMOVAL & INSTALLATION

2.0L Engine

1. Before servicing the vehicle, refer to the precautions in the beginning of this section.

2. Disconnect the negative battery cable.

3. Install Three Bar Engine Support D88L-6000-A or similar engine support, to the engine lifting eyes and support the engine.

4. Raise and safely support the vehicle.

5. Remove the catalytic converter system.

6. Disconnect the wiring to the low oil level sensor, if equipped.

7. Remove the heater water bolt from the bottom of the oil pan and position the tube out of the way.

8. Drain the engine oil.

9. Reinstall the oil pan drain plug and tighten to 15–21 ft. lbs. (21–28 Nm).

10. Remove the oil pan retaining bolts from the transaxle housing.

11. Remove the lower engine rear plate.

12. Remove the through-bolt for the left and right support insulators.

13. Lower the vehicle to work on the top side of the engine but keep on the hoist.

➡️ **Mark the location of the upper front engine support bracket before removing from the front engine support bracket.**

14. Remove the upper front engine support bracket retaining nuts from the upper front engine support insulator.

15. Raise the engine to allow room for removal of the engine oil pan, using the Three Bar Engine Support or equivalent engine brace.

16. Raise and safely support the vehicle.

17. Remove the oil pan retaining bolts from the cylinder block, working from the ends of the block toward the center.

18. Loosen and remove the oil pan and gasket.

19. Inspect the oil pump pick-up tube and screen and clean or replace as necessary.

To install:

20. If removed, install the oil pump pick-up tube and screen. Tighten the retaining bolts to 71–97 inch lbs. (8–11 Nm). Install a new self-locking oil pump pick-up tube support nut to the crankshaft main bearing cap retaining stud bolt. Tighten to 13–15 ft. lbs. (17–21 Nm).

21. Clean the gasket sealing surfaces for the oil pan at the cylinder block.

22. Clean the oil pan thoroughly leaving no traces of gasket material, grease or solvents.

23. Apply a bead of silicone gasket sealer to the oil pump parting lines and at the crankshaft rear main seal retainer on the cylinder block.

24. Install the oil pan and a new gasket into position and hold with several oil pan retaining screws.

25. Reinstall the rest of the retaining bolts and push the oil pan flush against the transaxle case before tightening the retaining bolts.

26. Tighten the 10 oil pan retaining bolts, in several passes, to 15–18 ft. lbs. (20–24 Nm), working from the center of the block towards the ends.

27. Reinstall the lower engine rear plate.

28. Reinstall the oil pan-to-transaxle housing retaining bolts.

29. Tighten the retaining bolts to 25–34 ft. lbs. (34–46 Nm).

30. Lower the vehicle but keep on the hoist.

31. Lower the engine into position by adjusting the Three Bar Engine Support or equivalent.

32. Reinstall the upper front engine sup-

FRONT OF ENGINE

NOTE: WHEN OIL PAN IS INSTALLED TO CYLINDER BLOCK SHIMS MAY BE REQUIRED TO ALIGN REAR SURFACES OF OIL PAN TO CYLINDER BLOCK

VIEW A

3 mm (0.25 INCH)

NOTE: APPLY A 3 mm (0.25 INCH) BEAD OF SILICONE GASKET AND SEALANT F1AZ-19562-A OR EQUIVALENT MEETING FORD SPECIFICATION WSE-M4G320-A2

SEALER

VIEW A
TYPICAL FOUR PLACES

1 Oil pan drain plug
2 Bolt (10 req'd)
3 Oil pan
4 Cylinder block
5 Oil pan gasket
6 Oil pan spacer (as req'd)
A Tighten to 21-28 Nm (15-21 lb-ft)
B Tighten to 20-24 Nm (15-18 lb-ft)

7922JG20

Exploded view of the oil pan mounting—2.0L engine

port bracket retaining nuts onto the upper front engine support insulator.

33. Raise and safely support the vehicle.

34. Reinstall the through-bolts for the left and the right insulators.

35. Reconnect the low oil level sensor, if equipped.

36. Position the heater water tube and retaining bolt to the bottom of the oil pan.

37. Reinstall the catalytic converter system.

38. Lower the vehicle.

39. Remove the Three Bar Engine Support or equivalent.

40. Fill the crankcase with the proper amount of engine oil.

41. Reconnect the negative battery cable.

42. Run the engine and check for leaks and proper operation.

2.5L Engine

1. Before servicing the vehicle, refer to the precautions in the beginning of this section.

2. Disconnect the negative battery cable.

3. Remove the water pump pulley shield.

4. Install Three Bar Engine Support D88L-6000-A or equivalent, to the engine lifting eyes and support the engine.

5. Raise and safely support the vehicle.

6. Remove the exhaust crossover and the exhaust retaining bracket located on the right side of the oil pan.

7. Remove the exhaust heat shield retaining nuts and the exhaust heat shields from the left side of the oil pan.

8. Drain the engine oil.

9. Reinstall the oil pan drain plug using a new gasket and tighten to 16–22 ft. lbs. (22–30 Nm).

10. Remove the oil pan retaining bolts from the transaxle housing.

11. If equipped with automatic transaxle, remove the access plug from the engine rear plate.

12. Remove the through-bolt for the left and right front engine support insulators.

13. Partially lower the vehicle on the hoist.

➡**Mark the location of the upper front engine support bracket before it is removed.**

14. Remove the upper front engine support bracket retaining nuts and remove the upper front engine support bracket.

15. Using the three bar engine support or equivalent, raise the engine to allow room for removal of the engine oil pan.

16. Raise and safely support the vehicle.

17. Remove the oil pan retaining bolts and studs from the lower cylinder block following the bolt removal sequence.

18. Remove the oil pan and the oil pan gasket from the vehicle.

To install:

19. Clean the oil pan-to-lower cylinder block gasket sealing surfaces.

20. Thoroughly clean the oil pan.

21. Install a new oil pan gasket into the groove of the oil pan.

22. Apply a bead of silicone sealer to the gasket area where the pan meets the parting lines of the lower cylinder block and the front engine cover.

23. Carefully install the oil pan with gasket to the lower cylinder block.

24. Reinstall the bolts and studs but do not tighten.

25. Push the oil pan against the transaxle case and tighten the oil pan bolts and studs.

26. Reinstall the oil pan-to-transaxle case bolts and tighten to 25–34 ft. lbs. (34–46 Nm).

27. Tighten the oil pan bolts and studs in the proper sequence to 15–22 ft. lbs. (20–30 Nm).

28. If equipped with automatic transaxle, install the access plug into the engine rear plate.

29. Lower the vehicle but keep it on the hoist.

30. Using the three bar engine support or equivalent, lower the engine into its proper position.

31. Reinstall the upper front engine support bracket and its retaining nuts onto the upper front engine support insulator.

32. Raise and safely support the vehicle.

33. Reinstall the through-bolts for the left and right front engine support insulators.

34. Reinstall the exhaust crossover, exhaust retaining bracket and heat shield.

35. Replace the engine oil filter.

36. Lower the vehicle.

37. Remove the three bar engine support or equivalent.

38. Fill the crankcase with the correct amount and grade of engine oil.

39. Reconnect the negative battery cable.

40. Run the engine and check for leaks and proper operation.

Oil Pump

REMOVAL & INSTALLATION

2.0L Engine

1. Before servicing the vehicle, refer to the precautions in the beginning of this section.

2. Disconnect the negative battery cable.

3. Remove the accessory drive belt.

4. Remove the camshaft timing belt

SEALER

NOTE: APPLY 8 mm (0.31 INCH) DIAMETER BEAD OF BLACK SILICONE SEALER AT TWO PLACES AS SHOWN

VIEW A
TYPICAL 2 PLACES

FRONT OF ENGINE

* LOCATION OF STUDS
● TIGHTEN BOLTS/STUDS IN SEQUENCE SHOWN

1 Upper cylinder block
2 Lower cylinder block
3 Oil pan
4 Stud bolt (5 req'd)
5 Bolt (10 req'd)
6 Oil pan gasket
7 Engine front cover
A Tighten to 20-30 Nm (15-22 lb-ft)

Exploded view of the oil pan mounting, showing the mounting bolt and stud tightening sequence—2.5L engine

covers, camshaft timing belt and the crankshaft sprocket.

5. Install Three Bar Engine Support D88L-6000-A or similar engine support, to the engine lifting eyes and support the engine.

6. Raise and safely support the vehicle.

7. Remove the catalytic converter system.

8. Remove the oil pan.

9. Remove the oil pump screen cover and tube retaining nut from the crankshaft main bearing cap stud bolt.

10. Remove the oil pump screen cover and tube retaining bolts from the oil pump and remove from the engine.

11. Remove the engine oil filter.

12. Remove the oil pump retaining bolts.

13. Remove the oil pump and gasket from the cylinder block.

To install:

14. Clean the oil pump gasket sealing surface on the cylinder block and oil pump.

15. Rotate the inner rotor of the oil pump to align with the flats on the crankshaft.

16. Reinstall the oil pump using a new gasket onto the cylinder block.

17. Loosely install the oil pump retaining bolts.

➡**Clearance between the cylinder block oil pan sealing surface to the oil pump oil pan sealing surface should not exceed 0.012–0.031 in. (0.3–0.8mm).**

18. Use a straight-edge to align the oil pump oil pan sealing surface with the cylinder block oil pan sealing surface.

19. Tighten the oil pump retaining bolts to 71–102 inch lbs. (8–11.5 Nm).

20. Install a new engine oil filter.

21. Reinstall the oil pump screen cover and tube using a new gasket to the oil pump. Tighten the retaining bolts to 71–97 inch lbs. (8–11 Nm).

22. Reinstall a new self-locking oil pump screen cover and tube support nut to the crankshaft main bearing cap stud bolt. Tighten the retaining nut to 13–15 ft. lbs. (17–21 Nm).

23. Reinstall the engine oil pan.

24. Reinstall the catalytic converter system.

25. Lower the vehicle.

26. Remove the three bar engine support or equivalent.

27. If required, replace the front crankshaft seal at this time.

28. Reinstall the crankshaft sprocket, camshaft timing belt and the camshaft timing belt covers.

29. Reinstall the accessory drive belt.

30. Fill the crankcase with the proper amount and grade of engine oil.

31. Reconnect the negative battery cable.

32. Run the engine and check for leaks and proper operation.

2.5L Engine

1. Before servicing the vehicle, refer to the precautions in the beginning of this section.

2. Disconnect the negative battery cable.

3. Remove the oil pan and the engine front cover.

4. Remove the timing chains and the crankshaft sprockets.

5. Remove the oil pump screen cover and tube retaining nut from the lower cylinder block stud bolt.

6. Remove the oil pump screen cover and tube retaining bolts from the oil pump and remove the tube from the engine.

7. Remove the four oil pump retaining bolts in reverse of the removal sequence.

8. Remove the oil pump from the vehicle.

To install:

9. Rotate the inner rotor of the oil pump to align with the flats on the crankshaft.

10. Reinstall the oil pump flush to the cylinder block.

11. Reinstall the oil pump retaining bolts and tighten in sequence to 71–106 inch lbs. (8–12 Nm).

Exploded view of the oil pump mounting—2.0L engine

Exploded view of the oil pump mounting, showing the retaining bolt tightening sequence—2.5L engine

Refer to Section 1 for engine rebuilding specifications

12. Inspect the oil pump screen and tube O-ring and replace if needed.

13. Position the oil pump screen and tube with the O-ring to the oil pump. Tighten the retaining bolts to 71–106 inch lbs. (8–12 Nm).

14. Install a new self-locking tube support nut to the lower cylinder block stud. Tighten the nut to 15–22 ft. lbs. (20–30 Nm).

15. Reinstall the crankshaft sprockets and the timing chains.

16. Reinstall the oil pan and the engine front cover.

17. Fill the crankcase with the correct amount of engine oil.

18. Reconnect the negative battery cable.

19. Run the engine and check for leaks and proper operation.

Rear Main Seal

REMOVAL & INSTALLATION

➡ **The following procedure requires a specific Ford design seal remover, or equivalent aftermarket version.**

1. Before servicing the vehicle, refer to the precautions in the beginning of this section.

2. Disconnect the negative battery cable.

3. Remove transaxle and flexplate/flywheel using the recommended procedure.

4. Using a sharp awl, punch a hole in the rear oil seal metal surface between the oil seal lip and the oil seal retainer.

5. Screw the threaded end of a seal remover into the oil seal, then install a slide hammer and remove the seal from the crankshaft oil seal retainer.

To install:

6. Clean all sealing surfaces.

7. Lubricate the crankshaft, oil seal

7922JG24

Thread the oil seal remover into the seal, then withdraw the seal using a slide hammer—2.5L engines

bore and the lip of the seal with Engine Assembly Lubricant D9AZ-19579-D or equivalent meeting Ford specification ESR-M99C80-A.

8. Install the oil seal using an appropriate seal installer. Seat the seal flush to the rear of the crankshaft oil seal retainer.

9. Reinstall the transaxle and flexplate/flywheel using the recommended procedure.

10. Reconnect the negative battery cable.

11. Start the engine and check for leaks.

Timing Chain, Sprockets, Front Cover and Seal

REMOVAL & INSTALLATION

2.5L Engine

1. Before servicing the vehicle, refer to the precautions in the beginning of this section.

2. Disconnect the negative battery cable.

3. Remove the upper intake manifold.

4. Remove the valve covers as follows:

   a. Remove the ignition wires and spark plugs.

   b. Remove the ignition coil from the right valve cover.

   c. Remove the crankcase ventilation tubes from both valve covers.

   d. Remove the wiring harness and bracket to the fuel injectors and move aside.

   e. Remove the retaining nuts and engine wiring from both valve covers and move aside.

   f. Loosen the valve cover retaining bolts and studs following the proper removal sequence.

   g. Remove both valve covers from the engine.

5. Install Three Bar Engine Support D88L-6000-A or equivalent to the engine lifting eyes and support the engine.

6. Remove the power steering pressure hose bracket retainer bolt from the upper front engine support bracket.

7. Disconnect the power steering pressure hose from the power steering pump and position out of the way.

➡ **Mark the position of the upper front engine support bracket before removing.**

8. Remove the upper front engine support bracket retainer nuts and remove the bracket.

9. Disconnect the low coolant level sensor from the wiring harness.

10. Remove the radiator coolant recovery reservoir retainers and move the recovery reservoir aside.

11. Remove the upper front engine insulator.

12. Set the radiator coolant recovery reservoir back into its position but do not secure.

13. Disengage the three wiring harness connectors located at the inline connector bracket at the front of the right cylinder head and set aside.

14. Loosen the power steering pump pulley retaining bolts but do not remove the bolts completely.

15. Remove the accessory drive belt.

16. Finish removing the power steering pump pulley retaining bolts and remove the pulley.

17. Remove the power steering pump and pump support retaining nuts and bolts and remove the power steering pump and pump support.

18. Raise and safely support the vehicle.

19. Remove the right-front wheel and tire assembly.

20. Remove the alternator from its mounting bracket and move aside.

21. Remove the alternator mounting bracket.

22. Remove the crankshaft pulley.

23. Disconnect the wiring from the Crankshaft Position (CKP) sensor and the Camshaft Position (CMP) sensor.

24. Remove the engine oil pan.

25. Loosen the A/C compressor retaining bolts and move the A/C compressor to gain access to the front cover retaining bolt.

26. Partially lower the vehicle.

27. Remove the bracket retainers and the bracket for the engine wiring and the A/C hose at the engine front cover.

➡ **It may be necessary to raise and lower the vehicle several times in order to follow the engine front cover bolt removal sequence.**

28. Remove the engine front cover bolts in reverse of the installation sequence illustration.

29. Remove the engine front cover and gasket from the vehicle.

30. Rotate the crankshaft so that the keyway is at the 11 o'clock position to locate the crankshaft at TDC for No. 1 cylinder.

31. Verify that the alignment arrows on the camshafts are aligned. If not, rotate the crankshaft one complete revolution and recheck.

RH CAMSHAFT TIMING
INDEX MARKS

11 O'CLOCK POSITION
(TDC NO. 1 CYLINDER)

CRANKSHAFT TIMING
INDEX MARK

**∗ NOTE: AT TDC NO. 1 FIRING
POSITION, ARROWS ON BACK
OF CAMSHAFT SPROCKETS
POINT DIRECTLY AT EACH OTHER**

7922JG25

View of the timing chains and gears, showing the right timing chain alignment marks properly positioned—2.5L engine

LH CAMSHAFT TIMING
INDEX MARKS

11 O'CLOCK POSITION
(TDC NO. 1 CYLINDER)

CRANKSHAFT TIMING
INDEX MARK

**∗NOTE: AT TDC NO. 1 FIRING
POSITION, ARROW HEADS ON BACK
OF CAMSHAFT SPROCKETS POINT
DIRECTLY AT EACH OTHER**

7922JG26

Left timing chain alignment mark positioning for servicing the chain—2.5L engine

For engine torque specifications, refer to Section 1 of this manual

32. Rotate the crankshaft so that the keyway is at the 3 o'clock position. This positions the right cylinder head camshafts to the neutral position.

33. Remove the right cylinder head timing chain tensioner retaining bolts and the timing chain tensioner.

➡**The camshaft journal caps and cylinder heads are numbered to ensure that they are assembled in their original positions. If removed, keep the camshaft journal caps together with the cylinder head that they were removed from.**

34. Remove the right cylinder head camshaft journal thrust cap retaining bolts and thrust caps.

35. Loosen the remaining camshaft journal cap bolts in sequence, releasing the bolts several revolutions at a time by making several passes to allow the camshaft to be raised from the cylinder head evenly. Do not remove the retaining bolts completely.

➡**If the valve tappets and roller rocker arms are to be reused, mark the positions of the valve tappets and rocker arms so that they are reassembled into their original positions.**

36. With the camshafts loose, remove the rocker arms, keeping them in the order that they were removed.

➡**If the right cylinder head timing chain tensioner arm and timing chain guide are to be reused, mark the position of the timing chain tensioner arm and the timing chain guide so that they are reassembled into their original positions.**

37. Remove the right cylinder head timing chain tensioner arm and the timing chain.

38. Remove the right cylinder head timing chain guide retaining bolts and the timing chain guide.

39. If worn, replace the timing chain guide.

40. Remove the right crankshaft timing chain sprocket.

41. Remove the right cylinder head camshaft timing chain sprockets if they are to be replaced.

42. Rotate the crankshaft two revolutions and locate the crankshaft keyway at the 11 o'clock position. This will position the left cylinder head camshafts to their neutral position.

43. Verify that the alignment arrows on the camshafts are aligned.

44. Remove the left cylinder head timing chain tensioner retaining bolts and the timing chain tensioner.

➡**The camshaft journal caps and cylinder heads are numbered to ensure that they are assembled in their original positions. If removed, keep the camshaft journal caps together with the cylinder head that they were removed from.**

45. Remove the camshaft journal thrust cap retaining bolts and thrust caps from the left cylinder head.

46. Loosen the remaining camshaft journal cap bolts in sequence, releasing the bolts several revolutions at a time by making several passes to allow the camshaft to be raised from the cylinder head evenly. Do not remove the retaining bolts completely.

➡**If the valve tappets and roller rocker arms are to be reused, mark the positions of the valve tappets and rocker arms so that they are reassembled into their original positions.**

47. With the camshafts loose, remove the rocker arms, keeping them in the order that they were removed.

➡**If the left cylinder head timing chain tensioner arm and timing chain guide are to be reused, mark the position of the timing chain tensioner arm and the timing chain guide so that they are reassembled into their original positions.**

48. Remove the left cylinder head timing chain tensioner arm and the timing chain.

49. Remove the left cylinder head timing chain guide retaining bolts and the timing chain guide.

50. If worn, replace the timing chain guide.

51. Remove the left crankshaft timing chain sprocket.

52. If required, the left cylinder head camshaft sprockets may be removed at this time.

To install:

➡**Inspect the timing chains, tensioners, tensioner arms, guides and sprockets for wear or damage. If any components are to be replaced for premature wear or damage, the camshaft damper should also be replaced.**

53. Reinstall or replace the camshaft sprockets, if removed.

54. Be sure that the crankshaft keyway is still at the 11 o'clock position.

55. Reinstall the left timing chain crankshaft sprocket onto the crankshaft.

56. Reinstall the left timing chain guide and retaining bolts to the engine. Tighten the retaining bolts to 15–22 ft. lbs. (20–30 Nm).

57. Verify that the alignment arrows on the left cylinder head camshafts are aligned before proceeding.

58. Reinstall the left timing chain over the left crankshaft sprocket and the left camshaft sprockets.

59. Align the timing index marks on the left cylinder head timing chain with the timing index marks on the crankshaft sprocket and the camshaft sprockets.

60. Reinstall the left timing chain tensioner arm over the alignment dowel on the left cylinder head.

➡**Before installing the timing chain tensioner, it must be properly compressed and locked.**

61. Using a small prytool, release the timing chain tensioner ratchet/pawl mechanism through the access hole in the timing chain tensioner as follows:

a. Insert a small piece of wire into the top of the piston and gently unseat the oil check ball.

Using a thin prytool, release the timing chain tensioner ratchet/pawl mechanism—2.5L engine

Insert a small piece of wire (such as a paper clip) into the top of the piston and gently unseat the oil check ball—2.5L engine

b. Compress the timing chain tensioner by hand.

c. With the tensioner compressed, install a 0.060 inch (1.5mm) drill bit or wire into the small hole above the ratchet, engaging the lock groove in the rack of the timing chain tensioner.

62. Reinstall the compressed and locked left cylinder head timing chain tensioner and retaining bolts onto the cylinder block. Tighten the retaining bolts to 15–22 ft. lbs. (20–30 Nm).

63. Verify that the timing index marks on the left timing chain are in alignment with the timing index marks on the crankshaft sprocket and the camshaft sprockets.

64. Reinstall or replace the camshaft sprockets if removed.

65. Reinstall the right timing chain crankshaft sprocket onto the crankshaft.

66. Reinstall the right timing chain guide and retaining bolts to the engine. Tighten the retaining bolts to 15–22 ft. lbs. (20–30 Nm).

67. Verify that the alignment arrows on the right cylinder head camshafts are aligned before proceeding.

68. Reinstall the right timing chain over the right crankshaft sprocket and the right camshaft sprockets.

69. Align the timing index marks on the right cylinder head timing chain with the timing index marks on the crankshaft sprocket and the camshaft sprockets.

70. Reinstall the right timing chain tensioner arm over the alignment dowel on the right cylinder head.

➡**Before installing the timing chain tensioner, it must be properly compressed and locked.**

71. Using a small prytool, release the timing chain tensioner ratchet/pawl mechanism through the access hole in the timing chain tensioner as follows:

a. Insert a small wire into the top of the piston and gently unseat the oil check ball.

b. Compress the timing chain tensioner by hand.

c. With the tensioner compressed, install a 0.060 inch (1.5mm) drill bit or wire into the small hole above the ratchet, engaging the lock groove in the rack of the timing chain tensioner.

72. Reinstall the compressed and locked right cylinder head timing chain tensioner and retaining bolts onto the cylinder block.

Tighten the retaining bolts to 15–22 ft. lbs. (20–30 Nm).

73. Verify that the timing index marks on the right timing chain are in alignment with the timing index marks on the crankshaft sprocket and the camshaft sprockets.

74. Be sure that the crankshaft keyway is at the 11 o'clock position.

75. Lubricate the left-side rocker arms with engine assembly lubricant and install the left cylinder head rocker arms into their original locations.

➡**Do not install the camshaft journal thrust caps until the camshaft journal caps are secured into position.**

76. Tighten the left cylinder head camshaft journal cap bolts in sequence making several passes to pull the camshafts down evenly. Tighten the bolts to 71–106 inch lbs. (8–12 Nm).

77. Reinstall the left cylinder head thrust caps and bolts. Tighten to 71–106 inch lbs. (8–12 Nm).

78. Rotate the crankshaft two revolutions and position the crankshaft keyway to the 3

APPLY 3 mm (0.118 INCH) BEAD OF SEALANT

**VIEW A
TYPICAL 6 PLACES**

7922JG29

To prevent oil leakage, apply sealant to the places indicated—2.5L engine

For complete mechanical specifications, refer to Section 1 of this manual

When installing the Crankshaft Position (CKP) sensor pulse ring, be sure to use the correct keyway—2.5L engine

o'clock location. This will position the right cylinder head camshafts to the neutral position.

79. Lubricate the right-side rocker arms with engine assembly lubricant and install the right cylinder head rocker arms into their original locations.

➡ **Do not install the camshaft journal thrust caps until the camshaft journal caps are secured.**

80. Tighten the right cylinder head camshaft journal cap bolts in sequence making several passes to pull the camshafts down evenly. Tighten the bolts to 71–106 inch lbs. (8–12 Nm).

81. Reinstall the right cylinder head thrust caps and bolts. Tighten to 71–106 inch lbs. (8–12 Nm).

82. Remove the lockpins from the timing chain tensioners.

83. Verify that the timing index marks on the timing chains are in alignment with the timing index marks on the crankshaft sprocket and the camshaft sprockets.

84. Install the Crankshaft Position (CKP) sensor pulse ring, be sure to use the keyway for the 2.5L engine as shown.

85. Replace the crankshaft seal in the front cover with a new one. Apply clean engine oil to the seal lip.

86. Clean the engine front and the front cover-to-cylinder block gasket sealing surfaces.

➡ **The front cover must be installed and properly tightened within six minutes of the application of the sealer.**

87. Apply silicone sealer to the six critical areas shown in View **A**, to the cylinder block to prevent oil seepage.

88. Place new front cover gaskets onto the dowel pins on the cylinder block and heads.

89. Place the front cover into position by placing the front cover onto the dowel pins at the cylinder block.

90. Reinstall the six front cover retaining bolts and stud bolts where the silicone sealer was applied.

91. Tighten the bolts and stud bolts until the front cover contacts the cylinder block and heads an, then turn the bolts and stud bolts an additional ¼ turn.

92. Reinstall the remaining front cover retaining bolts and stud bolts.

93. Tighten all of the front cover retaining bolts and stud bolts in proper sequence to 15–22 ft. lbs. (20–30 Nm).

94. Reinstall the bracket and bracket retainers to the front cover. Reinstall the wiring and the A/C hose to the bracket.

95. Raise and safely support the vehicle.

96. Reinstall the A/C compressor and its retaining bolts. Tighten the retaining bolts to 15–22 ft. lbs. (20–30 Nm).

97. If required, replace the crankshaft front seal at this time.

98. Reinstall the engine oil pan.

99. Reconnect the wiring harness to the CKP sensor and the CMP sensor.

100. Reinstall the crankshaft pulley.

101. Reinstall the alternator mounting bracket and the alternator.

102. Reinstall the right-front wheel and

tire assembly. Tighten the lug nuts to 62 ft. lbs. (85 Nm).

103. Lower the vehicle on the hoist.

104. Lower the engine to its correct position.

105. Reinstall the power steering pump support and the power steering pump to the front of the engine.

106. Reinstall the power steering pump pulley. Loosely install the retaining bolts.

107. Reinstall the accessory drive belt.

108. Tighten the power steering retaining bolts to 15–22 ft. lbs. (20–30 Nm).

109. Position and attach the wiring to the three connectors located on the inline connector bracket at the front of the right cylinder head.

110. Reinstall the upper front support insulator and the upper front engine support bracket.

111. Loosen and remove the Three Bar Engine Support or equivalent.

112. Reconnect the power steering pressure hose to the power steering pump.

113. Reconnect the power steering pressure hose bracket and retainer bolt to the upper front engine support bracket.

114. Reinstall both valve covers as follows:

   a. Clean the valve cover gasket sealing surfaces.

   b. Install new valve cover gaskets onto the valve covers.

   c. For each valve cover, place a bead of silicone sealant at two places on the valve cover sealing surfaces where the engine front cover and the cylinder heads make contact and at two places on the rear of the cylinder head where the camshaft seal retainer contacts the cylinder head.

   d. Reinstall the valve cover retaining bolts and studs and tighten in sequence to 71–106 inch lbs. (8–12 Nm).

➡ **The valve covers must be installed and properly tightened within six minutes of applying the silicone sealant.**

115. Reinstall the upper intake manifold.

116. Fill the engine with the proper amount and grade of oil.

117. Replace any lost fluid to the power steering reservoir.

118. Reconnect the negative battery cable.

119. Run the engine and check for leaks and proper operation.

120. Recheck the fluid levels.

✳ LOCATION OF STUDS 8 PLACES

● TIGHTEN BOLTS/STUDS IN SEQUENCE SHOWN

1. Cylinder head, RH
2. Cylinder block
3. Crankshaft
4. Cylinder block
5. Bolt (8 req'd)
6. Bolt
7. Dust cover
8. Drive belt idler pulley
9. Engine front cover
10. Stud bolt (8 req'd)
11. Crankshaft position sensor pulse ring
A. Tighten to 20-30 Nm (15-22 lb. ft.)

7922JG31

Exploded view of the front cover mounting, showing the retaining bolt and nut tightening sequence—2.5L engine

FUEL SYSTEM

Fuel System Service Precautions

Safety is the most important factor when performing not only fuel system maintenance but any type of maintenance. Failure to conduct maintenance and repairs in a safe manner may result in serious personal injury or death. Maintenance and testing of the vehicle's fuel system components can be accomplished safely and effectively by adhering to the following rules and guidelines.

• To avoid the possibility of fire and personal injury, always disconnect the negative battery cable unless the repair or test procedure requires that battery voltage be applied.

• Always relieve the fuel system pressure prior to disconnecting any fuel system component (injector, fuel rail, pressure regulator, etc.), fitting or fuel line connection. Exercise extreme caution whenever relieving fuel system pressure to avoid exposing skin, face and eyes to fuel spray. Please be advised that fuel under pressure may penetrate the skin or any part of the body that it contacts.

• Always place a shop towel or cloth around the fitting or connection prior to loosening to absorb any excess fuel due to spillage. Ensure that all fuel spillage (should it occur) is quickly removed from engine surfaces. Ensure that all fuel soaked cloths or towels are deposited into a suitable waste container.

• Always keep a dry chemical (Class B) fire extinguisher near the work area.

• Do not allow fuel spray or fuel vapors to come into contact with a spark or open flame.

• Always use a back-up wrench when loosening and tightening fuel line connection fittings. This will prevent unnecessary stress and torsion to fuel line piping.

• Always replace worn fuel fitting O-rings with new. Do not substitute fuel hose or equivalent, where fuel pipe is installed.

Before servicing the vehicle, make sure to refer to the precautions in the beginning of this section as well.

Fuel System Pressure

RELIEVING

1. Before servicing the vehicle, refer to the precautions in the beginning of this section.
2. Disconnect the negative battery cable.
3. Remove the engine air cleaner assembly.
4. Loosen the fuel tank filler cap to relieve pressure in the fuel tank.
5. Connect Fuel Pressure Gauge T80L-9974-B or equivalent, to the fuel pressure relief valve located on the fuel rail.
6. Open the manual valve on the fuel pressure gauge and drain the fuel through the drain tube into a suitable container.
7. Remove the fuel pressure gauge.
8. When service on the vehicle is complete, be sure to install the engine air cleaner assembly, tighten the fuel tank filler cap and connect the negative battery cable.

Fuel Filter

REMOVAL & INSTALLATION

1. Before servicing the vehicle, refer to the precautions in the beginning of this section.
2. Disconnect the negative battery cable.
3. Relieve the fuel system pressure using the following procedure:
   a. Remove the air cleaner assembly.
   b. Connect Fuel Pressure Gauge T80L-9974-B or equivalent, to the fuel

Once the retainer clip has been removed from the connector, the fuel line can be removed from the filter

Be sure to install the fuel filter with the arrow pointing in the direction of the fuel flow

pressure relief valve located on the fuel rail.
   c. Open the manual valve on the fuel pressure gauge and drain the fuel through the drain tube into a suitable container.
   d. Remove the fuel pressure gauge and reinstall the air cleaner assembly.
4. Locate the fuel filter near the fuel tank. Clean the area before disassembly.
5. Remove the retainer clips at both ends of the fuel filter in the following manner:
   a. Bend the shipping tab downward so that it will clear the body.
   b. Using hands only, spread the clip legs to disengage the body and push the legs up into the fitting.
   c. Pull on the triangular end of the clip to finish removal.

✳✳ WARNING

Never use any tools to remove the retainer clips as distortion to the fittings may result causing fuel leaks.

6. Prepare for fuel to be released from the fuel filter and fuel lines by placing a shop towel around the area to absorb the fuel being released. Twist and pull the fuel lines from the fuel filter.
7. Check the fuel line fittings for any internal parts that may have been dislodged during removal and correct.
8. Loosen the mounting clamp and remove the fuel filter.
9. Drain, then properly dispose of the fuel filter.

To install:
10. Place the new fuel filter into its mount with the arrow pointed in the direction of flow and tighten the clamp.
11. Install new retainer clips onto the fuel line fittings before placing the lines onto the fuel filter ends.
12. Push the fuel lines onto the fuel filter

until an audible click is heard. Pull on the fitting to verify a good connection.
13. Start the engine and check for fuel leaks and proper operation.

Fuel Pump

REMOVAL & INSTALLATION

1. Before servicing the vehicle, refer to the precautions in the beginning of this section.
2. Disconnect the negative battery cable.
3. Relieve the fuel pressure using the following procedure:
   a. Open the fuel tank filler cap to vent off pressure in the tank.
   b. Remove the air cleaner assembly.
   c. Connect Fuel Pressure Gauge T80L-9974-B or equivalent, to the fuel pressure relief valve located on the fuel rail.
   d. Open the manual valve on the fuel pressure gauge and drain the fuel through the drain tube into a suitable container.
   e. Remove the fuel pressure gauge.
   f. Secure the fuel fill cap and install the air cleaner assembly.
4. Remove the rear seat cushion.
5. Remove the plastic grommet from the floor pan.
6. Disconnect the fuel pump electrical harness.
7. Disconnect the fuel lines from the fuel pump by compressing the tabs on both sides of each nylon push-connect fitting and easing the fuel line off of the fuel pump.
8. Using Fuel Tank Sender Wrench D84P-9275-A or equivalent, turn the fuel pump locking ring counterclockwise to loosen the ring.
9. Remove the fuel pump locking ring.
10. Remove the fuel pump being careful not to damage the fuel gauge sending unit.
11. Place a shop towel over the opening in the fuel tank to prevent dirt from contaminating the fuel.

To install:
12. Remove the shop towel over the opening in the fuel tank and clean the groove for the fuel pump seal. Be careful not to allow dirt to enter the fuel tank.
13. Apply a light coat of grease onto a new O-ring seal and install into the groove of the fuel tank.
14. Carefully install the fuel pump into the tank to prevent damage to the fuel gauge sender or the fuel pick-up filter.

View of fuel pump fittings through the floor pan

Remove the locking ring from the fuel pump sender with a special wrench such as Fuel Tank Sender Wrench D84P-9275-A

➡ **It is recommended that the inline fuel filter be replaced whenever a fuel pump is being replaced.**

15. Ensure that the flange of the fuel pump mounting plate is located properly in its keyway and that the O-ring has not shifted out of position.

16. Keep a light downward pressure on the fuel pump while installing the fuel pump locking retainer ring.

17. Install the ring ensuring that all of the locking tabs are under the fuel tank lock ring tabs. Turn the ring clockwise finger-tight.

18. Install the fuel tank sender wrench or equivalent, over the retainer ring and finish tightening until the retainer ring is resting against its stops.

19. Reconnect the fuel lines to the fuel pump.

20. Reinstall the fuel pump electrical harness connector.

21. Reinstall the plastic grommet into the floor pan.

22. Reinstall the rear seat cushion.

23. Reconnect the negative battery cable.

24. Start the engine and check for leaks and proper operation.

DRIVE TRAIN

Transaxle Assembly

REMOVAL & INSTALLATION

Automatic

1. Before servicing the vehicle, refer to the precautions in the beginning of this section.

2. Disconnect the negative battery cable.

3. Disconnect the positive battery cable and remove the battery.

4. On vehicles equipped with the 2.0L engine, remove the oil level dipstick and the exhaust manifold heat shield.

5. On vehicles equipped with the 2.5L engine, remove the water pump pulley shield.

6. Secure the radiator and fan shroud with safety wire to the radiator support.

7. Remove the air cleaner assembly and mounting bracket.

8. Loosen the left and right upper strut mounting nuts five turns to allow room for removal of the halfshafts. Do not remove the nuts completely.

9. Disconnect the shift cable and remove the two retaining bolts securing the shift cable bracket to the transaxle case.

10. Disconnect the Transmission Range (TR) sensor.

11. Remove the TR sensor.

12. Disconnect the 10-pin harness from the transaxle.

13. Support the engine with Three Bar Engine Support D88L-6000-A or equivalent.

14. Remove the upper transaxle support insulator bracket mounting nuts.

15. Remove the three bolts retaining the upper transaxle support insulator to the inner fenderwell and remove the insulator.

16. Remove the upper bell housing to engine retaining bolts.

17. Raise and safely support the vehicle.

18. Remove the wheel and tire assemblies.

19. Disconnect the steering column from the rack and pinion by removing the pinch bolt.

20. Disconnect the tie rod ends from the steering knuckles. Discard the cotter pins.

21. Remove the ball joint-to-lower control arm pinch bolts and separate the ball joints from the lower control arms.

Turbine Shaft Speed (TSS) sensor location

Transaxle drain plug location

22. Remove the sway bar (stabilizer bar) link nuts and separate the sway bar links from the stabilizer bar.

23. Remove the splash shield at the front of the subframe.

24. Remove the through-bolts retaining the left and right front engine support insulators to the subframe.

25. Disconnect the power steering oil cooler hoses at the right front subframe and drain the power steering system.

26. Remove the two screws retaining the bumper cover braces to the subframe. Rotate the bumper cover braces forward.

27. Remove the radiator air deflector.

28. Remove the four bolts retaining the left and right lower radiator support brackets to the front of the subframe. Rotate the radiator supports forward.

29. Disconnect and remove the exhaust system components necessary for transaxle removal.

30. Remove the two bolts retaining the A/C accumulator to the subframe, located at the drivers side front corner of the vehicle.

31. Remove the bolt retaining the transaxle cooler line bracket to the front of the subframe.

32. Position Powertrain Lift 014–00765 or equivalent with wood blocks approxi-

mately 40 inches (1,016mm) in length secured to the lift under the subframe.

33. Remove the four subframe-to-body retaining bolts. Lower the subframe slightly and disconnect the power steering pressure and return hoses from the rack and pinion.

34. Finish lowering the subframe and set aside.

35. Disconnect the Turbine Shaft Speed (TSS) sensor at the transaxle oil pump.

36. Drain the transaxle oil into a suitable container for recycling.

37. Disconnect the transaxle cooler inlet line at the transaxle case.

38. Remove the transaxle cooler inlet line from the bracket at the transaxle oil pump.

39. Disconnect the transaxle cooler outlet line at the transaxle case.

40. Disconnect the transaxle cooler inlet and outlet lines at the radiator and remove from the vehicle.

41. Remove the left halfshaft and the right halfshaft and intermediate shaft from the vehicle.

42. Remove the speedometer cable and disconnect the Vehicle Speed Sensor (VSS).

43. Remove the inspection cover from the transaxle to engine spacer plate located at the right-rear corner of the engine.

44. Rotate the torque converter to align each of the four torque converter-to-flywheel retaining nuts and remove the nuts.

45. Lower the vehicle.

46. Remove the upper right engine support insulator (engine mount) bracket nuts.

47. Lower the engine and transaxle assembly using the three bar engine support until the transaxle assembly is level with the left frame member.

STRAIGHT EDGE

MINIMUM 10 mm (7/16 IN)

TORQUE CONVERTER

7922JG36

Be sure that the torque converter is properly seated in the transaxle

48. On vehicles equipped with A/C, lower the engine until the A/C compressor is below the right frame member.

49. Raise and safely support the vehicle.

50. Support the transaxle on a transmission jack and secure the transaxle to the jack.

51. Remove the starter motor retaining nuts and remove the starter.

52. Remove the lower transaxle-to-engine retaining bolts.

53. Separate the transaxle from the engine.

➡**Use care when removing the transaxle to prevent the torque converter from falling out.**

54. Carefully lower the transaxle from the vehicle.

To install:

55. Be sure that the torque converter is fully engaged in the transaxle.

56. There should be approximately a ⁷⁄₁₆ inch (10mm) air gap between a straightedge across the bell housing flange and the torque converter.

57. If removed, place the transaxle on the transmission jack and secure.

✳✳ WARNING

Use care not to allow the torque converter to fall out of the transaxle when tilted.

58. Raise the transaxle into position and align with the engine.

59. Align the torque converter studs with the mating holes in the flywheel.

60. Once the transaxle is fitted to the engine, install the lower transaxle to engine retaining bolts. Tighten the retaining bolts to 41–50 ft. lbs. (55–68 Nm).

61. Rotate the torque converter and install the four converter-to-flywheel retaining nuts. Tighten the retaining nuts to 23–39 ft. lbs. (31–53 Nm).

62. Remove the transmission jack.

63. Reinstall the transaxle-to-engine separator plate.

64. Reinstall the electrical connector to the TSS.

65. If removed, place the subframe on the powertrain lift, or equivalent with wood blocks approximately 40 inches (1,016mm) in length secured to the lift under the subframe.

66. Raise the subframe and connect the power steering pressure and return hoses to the rack and pinion.

67. Align the subframe. Route the power steering hoses into position at the rear of the engine.

68. Reinstall the four subframe retaining bolts loosely.

69. Install Subframe Alignment Pin Set T95P-2100-AH or equivalent into the subframe and body alignment holes. After aligning the holes, slightly tighten the four subframe retaining bolts.

70. After the subframe alignment is complete, tighten the four subframe retaining bolts to 81–110 ft. lbs. (110–150 Nm). Remove the alignment tools.

71. Reinstall the A/C accumulator bracket to the subframe and tighten the screws to 48–72 inch. lbs. (6–8 Nm).

72. Reconnect the power steering oil cooler hoses to the right front side of the subframe.

73. Install Powertrain Alignment Gauge T94P-6000-AH or equivalent to the left-front engine support bracket and the subframe. Tighten the two retaining bolts to 20 ft. lbs. (27 Nm) and snug the through-bolt.

74. Reinstall the right engine support insulator with retaining bolts to the subframe and through-bolt. Tighten the two subframe retaining bolts to 30–41 ft. lbs. (41–55 Nm) and the through-bolt to 75–102 ft. lbs. (103–137 Nm).

75. Observe the position of the right engine support insulator. It must be centered in the bracket and in perfect alignment front-to-rear. Remove the powertrain alignment gauge.

76. Reinstall the left engine support insulator to the subframe with two retaining bolts. Tighten the retaining bolts to 84 inch. lbs. (10 Nm).

77. Observe the position of the left engine support insulator to ensure perfect alignment front-to-rear. Retighten the bolts to 30–41 ft. lbs. (41–55 Nm). Reinstall the left engine support insulator through-bolt and tighten to 75–102 ft. lbs. (103–137 Nm).

78. Reinstall the transaxle cooler inlet and outlet lines.

79. Reinstall the lower radiator support brackets to the subframe. Tighten the bolts to 20 ft. lbs. (27 Nm).

80. Reconnect the speedometer cable and the VSS.

81. Reinstall the exhaust system.

82. Reinstall the left halfshaft using a new circlip.

83. Reinstall the intermediate halfshaft and tighten the two retaining nuts to 20 ft. lbs. (27 Nm).

84. Reinstall the right-side halfshaft.

85. Reinstall the left and right lower control arms to the steering knuckles.

86. Install new pinch bolts and nuts. Tighten the pinch bolts to 61 ft. lbs. (83 Nm).

87. Reinstall the sway bar (stabilizer bar) links. Reinstall the retaining nuts and tighten to 35–48 ft. lbs. (47–65 Nm).

88. If equipped, install the ABS wiring loom retainer to the sway bar link stud. Tighten the retaining nuts to 35 ft. lbs. (47 Nm).

89. Reinstall the left and right tie rod ends to the steering knuckles. Tighten the castellated nuts to 23–35 ft. lbs. (31–47 Nm). Install new cotter pins.

90. Reinstall the front bumper cover braces and tighten the bolts securely. Reinstall the splash shield to the subframe.

91. Reinstall the wheel and tire assemblies. Tighten the lug nuts to 62 ft. lbs. (85 Nm).

92. Lower the vehicle.

93. Reconnect the steering yoke to the steering gear shaft. Tighten the steering yoke retaining bolt to 15–20 ft. lbs. (20–27 Nm).

94. Reinstall the upper transaxle to engine retaining bolts. Tighten the retaining bolts to 23–39 ft. lbs. (55–68 Nm).

95. Remove the safety wire securing the radiator and fan shroud to the radiator support.

96. Reinstall all wiring retaining clips that were disturbed during transaxle removal.

97. Raise the engine and transaxle assembly into position using the three bar engine support or similar tool.

98. Reinstall the engine and transmission support insulator to the left front fender apron. Tighten the bolts to 40–55 ft. lbs. (54–75 Nm).

99. Reinstall new locknuts retaining the engine and transmission support insulator to the transaxle. Tighten the locknuts to 40–55 ft. lbs. (54–75 Nm).

100. Reinstall the front engine support insulator.

101. If equipped with 2.5L engine, install the power steering line retaining bracket to the front engine support insulator. Tighten the new locknuts to 56–76 ft. lbs. (77–103 Nm). Reinstall the water pump pulley shield.

102. If equipped with the 2.0L engine, install the exhaust manifold heat shield and oil level dipstick. Tighten the retaining bolts to 71–106 inch lbs. (8–12 Nm).

103. Remove the three bar engine support, or equivalent.

104. Reinstall the TR sensor and adjust.

105. Reattach the 10-pin harness connector to the transaxle.

106. Reinstall the TR sensor electrical connector.

107. Reinstall the starter motor and retaining bolts. Tighten the starter motor retaining bolts to 43–58 ft. lbs. (59–79 Nm) for the 2.5L engine or 15–20 ft. lbs. (20–27 Nm) for the 2.0L engine.

108. Reinstall the shift cable mounting bracket. Tighten the retaining bolts to 15–19 ft. lbs. (20–25 Nm).

109. Reinstall the shift cable to the manual lever by pressing the cable end onto the stud until a click is heard.

110. Reinstall the battery tray, battery and the battery hold-down.

111. Reinstall new upper strut mounting nuts. Tighten the strut mounting nuts to 34 ft. lbs. (46 Nm).

112. Fill the power steering remote oil reservoir.

113. Reconnect the battery cables, negative cable last.

114. Fill the transaxle with the proper type and amount of transmission fluid.

115. Run the engine and check the transaxle for leaks.

116. Recheck the transmission fluid level.

➡ **Whenever the vehicle subframe is removed or lowered, the wheel alignment should be checked.**

117. Check the alignment and adjust if necessary.

118. Road test the vehicle to check for proper transmission operation.

Manual

1. Before servicing the vehicle, refer to the precautions in the beginning of this section.

2. Disconnect the battery cables, negative cable first.

3. Remove the battery.

4. Secure the radiator and fan shroud to the radiator support using safety wire.

5. Loosen the front strut upper retaining nuts a total of five turns to allow room for the removal of the halfshafts. Do not remove the nuts.

6. Remove the Mass Air Flow sensor (MAF) and the air cleaner assembly. Remove the air cleaner lower bracket.

7. Install Three Bar Engine Support D88L-6000-A or equivalent, and support the engine.

8. Disconnect the back-up lamp switch.

9. Remove the bolts securing the ground strap to the transaxle housing.

10. Remove the engine and transmission support insulator (mount).

11. Disconnect the hydraulic line and rubber grommet from the support insulator bracket.

12. Remove the rubber inspection cover from the transaxle clutch housing.

13. Remove the retaining clip and remove the hydraulic line fitting at the clutch slave cylinder.

14. Remove the upper transaxle-to-engine bolt.

15. Remove the two upper starter motor retaining bolts with the ground strap.

To properly align the subframe, install subframe alignment pins such as Subframe Alignment Pin Set T95P-2100-AH—manual and automatic transaxles

7922JG37

16. If equipped with the 2.0L engine, remove the exhaust manifold heat shield and the catalytic converter retaining nuts at the exhaust manifold.

17. Remove the wheel and tire assemblies.

18. Remove the accessory drive belt pulley cover.

19. Raise and safely support the vehicle.

20. If equipped with the 2.0L engine, remove the oil level dipstick. Remove the catalytic converter-to-engine bracket strap and the retaining bolts to the halfshaft bracket.

21. Remove the catalytic converter.

22. If equipped with the 2.5L engine, remove the water pump pulley shield. Remove the front Y-pipe nuts and the rear Y-pipe to catalytic converter nuts and remove the Y-pipe.

23. Disconnect the Vehicle Speed Sensor (VSS).

24. Remove the speedometer cable.

25. Remove the nine screws securing the lower radiator air deflector and remove the deflector.

26. Push the shift rod forward and remove the shift rod pinch bolt.

27. Pull the shift rod back and remove it from the transaxle.

28. Remove the shift control stabilizer bar nut at the stud and remove the stabilizer bar.

29. Remove the shift control stabilizer bar and bracket from the right engine support insulator bracket.

30. Remove the underbody heat shield from under the shift control.

31. Reposition the shift rod and stabilizer bar to allow transaxle removal.

32. Remove the two screws securing the A/C accumulator to the subframe.

33. Remove the halfshafts and the intermediate shaft.

34. Remove the bolts and the right engine support insulator mounting nuts and remove the bracket from the transaxle.

35. Remove the left engine support insulator through-bolt.

36. Lower the vehicle.

37. Adjust the three bar engine support or equivalent, to relieve tension on the right front engine support bracket.

38. Remove the right front engine support bracket through-bolt.

39. Raise and safely support the vehicle.

40. Disconnect the steering column from the steering gear at the pinch bolt.

41. Remove the catalytic converter.

42. Disconnect the tie rod ends from the steering knuckles and discard the cotter pins.

43. Remove the lower control arm to ball joint pinch bolts and separate the lower control arms from the ball joints.

44. Separate the sway bar (stabilizer bar) links from the sway bar.

45. Remove the splash shield at the front of the subframe.

46. Remove the through-bolt from the left front engine support insulator and remove the right front engine support insulator and mounting bracket.

47. Disconnect the power steering oil cooler hoses at the right front of the subframe and drain the power steering fluid.

48. Remove the A/C accumulator retaining bracket screws from the subframe.

49. Remove the four bolts retaining the lower radiator supports to the subframe. Rotate the radiator supports forward.

50. Remove the two screws retaining the bumper cover braces to the left and right sides of the subframe. Rotate the bumper cover braces forward.

51. Position Powertrain Lift 014–00765 or equivalent, with wood blocks approximately 40 in. (1m) in length secured to the lift under the subframe.

52. Remove the four subframe-to-body retaining bolts.

53. Allow the subframe to lower slightly and disconnect the power steering pressure and return hoses from the rack and pinion (steering gear).

54. Finish lowering the subframe and move aside.

55. Lower the vehicle.

56. Loosen the front mount retaining nuts five turns.

57. Place a floor jack and a block of wood under the transaxle and raise the transaxle enough to release the tension on the three bar engine support, or equivalent.

58. Back off on the three bar engine support adjustment to allow downward travel of the transaxle.

59. Slowly lower the transaxle until it reaches the limits of the front engine mount movement.

60. Adjust the three bar engine support or equivalent, to hold the transaxle in this position.

61. Remove the floor jack and wood block.

62. Raise the vehicle and safely support.

63. Position Transmission Jack 014–00210 or equivalent, to the transaxle and secure.

64. Remove the last starter motor retaining bolt and hang the starter off to the side using safety wire.

65. Remove the two bolts retaining the engine oil pan to the transaxle.

66. Remove the remaining bolts.

67. Separate the transaxle from the engine and carefully remove from the vehicle.

To install:

68. If removed, place the transaxle on the transmission jack and secure.

69. Apply a film of grease to the input shaft splines.

70. If removed, install the right engine support insulator bracket to the transaxle case. Tighten the bolts to 62 ft. lbs. (84 Nm).

71. If removed, install the shift stabilizer bar mounting bracket to the right transaxle support insulator bracket stud and transaxle case. Tighten the nut and bolt to 28–38 ft. lbs. (38–51 Nm).

72. Carefully raise the transaxle into position with the engine.

73. If required, use an 18mm socket to rotate the engine to line up the splines on the clutch disc with the input shaft.

74. Reinstall two lower side and two lower transaxle retaining bolts. Tighten the retaining bolts to 30 ft. lbs. (40 Nm).

75. Reinstall the starter motor and the lower bolt. Tighten the starter motor lower bolt to 35 ft. lbs. (48 Nm).

76. Lower the vehicle.

77. Using the floor jack and a block of wood positioned at the engine and transaxle mating area, raise the assembly into position.

78. Adjust the three bar engine support to maintain the engine in the correct position.

79. Remove the floor jack and the block of wood. Reinstall the upper transaxle retaining bolts.

80. Tighten the retaining bolts to 28–38 ft. lbs. (38–51 Nm).

81. Reinstall the nuts retaining the front engine support bracket. Tighten the retaining nuts to 61 ft. lbs. (83 Nm).

82. Reinstall the upper starter motor retaining bolts. Tighten the retaining bolts to 35 ft. lbs. (48 Nm).

83. Reinstall the ground strap to the transaxle retaining bolt.

7922JG38

The Powertrain Alignment Gauge (T94P-6000-AH) tool must be installed in the correct position to ensure proper engine/transaxle orientation

84. Reconnect the back-up lamp switch.

85. Reinstall the engine and transaxle support insulator.

86. Raise and safely support the vehicle.

87. Reinstall the left and right halfshafts and the intermediate shaft.

88. If removed, place the subframe on the powertrain lift, or equivalent with wood blocks approximately 40 in. (1m) in length secured to the lift under the subframe.

89. Raise the subframe and connect the power steering pressure and return hoses to the rack and pinion.

90. Align the subframe to the body. Route the power steering hoses into position at the rear of the engine.

91. Reinstall the four subframe retaining bolts loosely.

92. Reinstall Subframe Alignment Pin Set T95P-2100-AH or equivalent into the subframe and body alignment holes. After aligning the holes, slightly tighten the four subframe retaining bolts.

93. After the subframe alignment is complete, tighten the four subframe retaining bolts to 81–110 ft. lbs. (110–150 Nm). Remove the alignment tools.

94. Reinstall the A/C accumulator bracket to the subframe and tighten the screws to 48–72 inch. lbs. (6–8 Nm).

95. Reconnect the power steering oil cooler hoses to the right front side of the subframe.

96. Install Powertrain Alignment Gauge T94P-6000-AH or equivalent to the left-front engine support bracket and the subframe. Tighten the two retaining bolts to 20 ft. lbs. (27 Nm) and snug the through-bolt.

97. Reinstall the right engine support insulator with retaining bolts to the subframe and through-bolt. Tighten the two retaining bolts to subframe to 30–41 ft. lbs. (41–55 Nm) and the through-bolt to 75–102 ft. lbs. (103–137 Nm).

98. Observe the position of the right engine support insulator. It must be centered in the bracket and in perfect alignment front-to-rear. Remove the powertrain alignment gauge.

99. Reinstall the left engine support insulator to the subframe with two retaining bolts. Tighten the retaining bolts to 84 inch. lbs. (10 Nm).

100. Observe the position of the left engine support insulator to ensure perfect alignment front-to-rear. Retighten the bolts to 30–41 ft. lbs. (41–55 Nm). Reinstall the left engine support insulator through-bolt and tighten to 75–102 ft. lbs. (103–137 Nm).

101. Reinstall the left and right lower control arms to the steering knuckles. Install new pinch bolts and nuts. Tighten the pinch bolts to 61 ft. lbs. (83 Nm).

102. Reconnect the steering yoke to the steering gear shaft. Tighten the steering yoke retaining bolt to 15–20 ft. lbs. (20–27 Nm).

103. Reinstall the sway bar (stabilizer bar) links. Reinstall the retaining nuts and tighten to 35–48 ft. lbs. (47–65 Nm).

104. Reinstall the left and right tie rod ends to the steering knuckles. Tighten the castellated nuts to 23–35 ft. lbs. (31–47 Nm). Install new cotter pins.

105. Reinstall the front bumper cover braces and tighten the bolts securely. Reinstall the splash shield to the subframe.

106. Reinstall the two retaining screws and the A/C accumulator to the subframe.

107. Reinstall the radiator supports to the subframe. Tighten the bolts to 71–97 inch lbs. (8–11 Nm).

108. Reinstall the splash shield at the front of the subframe.

109. Reinstall the front wheel and tire assemblies. Tighten the lug nuts to 62 ft. lbs. (85 Nm).

110. Reinstall the shift rod-to-transaxle gearshift shaft. Reinstall the retaining bolt and tighten to 14–18 ft. lbs. (19–25 Nm).

111. Reinstall the shift control stabilizer bar to its mounting stud. Reinstall the mounting nut and tighten to 28–38 ft. lbs. (38–51 Nm).

112. Reinstall the underbody heat shield under the shift control.

113. Reconnect the VSS.

114. Reinstall the speedometer cable.

115. If equipped with 2.5L engine, install the Y-pipe to the exhaust manifolds and the catalytic converter using new gaskets. Reinstall the water pump pulley shield.

116. If equipped with 2.0L engine, install the catalytic converter between the exhaust manifold and the exhaust pipe using new gaskets. Reinstall the exhaust manifold heat shield and the oil level dipstick. Tighten the retaining bolts to 71–106 inch lbs. (8–11 Nm).

117. Reinstall the support bracket strap to the catalytic converter and engine.

118. Reinstall the bracket to the catalytic converter and the intermediate halfshaft bearing bracket.

119. Reinstall the lower radiator air deflector.

120. Reinstall the belt pulley cover by sliding it up and under the front fender splash shield.

121. Check the transmission fluid level and add fluid as required.

122. Lower the vehicle.

123. Remove the three bar engine support, or equivalent.

124. Reinstall the wire loom retainers removed during the transaxle removal.

125. Reinstall the hydraulic line to the clutch slave cylinder and install the clip.

126. Reinstall the rubber inspection cover to the clutch housing and the hydraulic line to the retaining grommet.

127. Remove the upper strut mounting nuts and replace with new locknuts. Tighten the strut mounting nuts to 34 ft. lbs. (46 Nm).

128. Reinstall the air cleaner lower bracket.

129. Reinstall the MAF sensor and the air cleaner assembly.

130. Remove the wire retaining the radiator and fan shroud to the radiator support.

131. Reinstall the battery and cables, negative cable last.

132. Adjust the shift linkage and bleed the hydraulic clutch system as required.

133. Road test the vehicle and check for proper operation.

Clutch

ADJUSTMENTS

Because the clutch system is hydraulic, the clutch pedal free-play is self-adjusting and requires no additional maintenance.

REMOVAL & INSTALLATION

1. Before servicing the vehicle, refer to the precautions in the beginning of this section.

2. Disconnect the negative battery cable.

3. Raise and safely support the vehicle.

4. Remove the starter motor.

5. Disconnect the hydraulic coupling for the slave cylinder at the transaxle by sliding the sleeve on the tube towards the slave cylinder and applying a slight pulling force to the tube.

6. Remove the transaxle.

7. Mark the assembled position of the clutch and pressure plate to the flywheel if it is to be reinstalled.

➡**The clutch pressure plate is only held in place by the retaining bolts. No dowel pins are used, therefore the pressure plate must be supported when removing the retaining bolts.**

Clutch System

1. Engine rear plate
2. Dowl (flywheel)
3. Bolt(8)
4. Bolt(6)
5. Bolt(3)
6. Clutch slave cylinder
7. Transaxle assy
8. Transaxle mounting bolts
9. Clutch pressure plate
10. Clutch disc
11. Flywheel
12. Dowl bushing (engine plate)

7922JG39

Exploded view of the clutch disc, pressure plate and related component mounting

CLUTCH ALIGNER
T74P-7137-K

CLUTCH DISC

7922JG40

Insert an alignment tool through the clutch disc to ensure that it is centered after the pressure plate is installed

7922JG41

Tighten the pressure plate bolts gradually and in the sequence shown to ensure correct clutch operation

8. Loosen the pressure plate bolts evenly until the pressure plate spring pressure is released, then finish removing the bolts while supporting the clutch and pressure plate assembly.

9. Remove the clutch and pressure plate from the vehicle.

10. Inspect the flywheel, slave cylinder and other components for wear or damage.

To install:

11. Clean the pressure plate and flywheel surfaces.

12. Install the clutch disc using Clutch Aligner T74P-7137-K or equivalent.

➡ **If the clutch disc and pressure plate are being reused, align the marks made during disassembly.**

13. Install Flywheel Holding Tool T74P-6375-A or equivalent, to hold the flywheel.

14. Install the pressure plate and start the retaining bolts.

15. Tighten the retaining bolts evenly and in sequence to 13–18 ft. lbs. (18–26 Nm).

16. Remove the clutch aligner tool.

17. Reinstall the transaxle.

18. Reconnect the slave cylinder tube coupling by pushing the male coupling into the slave cylinder female coupling.

19. Lower the vehicle.

20. Reconnect the negative battery cable.

21. Bleed the hydraulic clutch system, if required.

22. Check the clutch system for proper operation.

Hydraulic Clutch System

BLEEDING

1. Before servicing the vehicle, refer to the precautions in the beginning of this section.

2. Disconnect the negative battery cable.

3. Remove the air cleaner outlet tube and the Mass Air Flow (MAF) sensor.

4. Clean the top of the brake master cylinder fluid reservoir before opening it.

➡ **The brake master cylinder fluid reservoir is also the reservoir for the hydraulic clutch master cylinder.**

5. Be sure that there is adequate fluid in the master cylinder fluid reservoir before attempting to bleed the system. Check the fluid level throughout the bleeding procedure.

Remove the dust cover to gain access to the clutch slave cylinder bleeder valve

6. Remove the rubber inspection cover from the bell housing.

7. Connect a hose to the bleeder valve fitting on the clutch slave cylinder. Submerge the other end of the hose into a container of clean brake fluid.

8. Push the clutch pedal down while opening the bleeder on the clutch slave cylinder. Watch for air bubbles escaping from the hydraulic system.

9. Close the bleeder before releasing the clutch pedal.

10. Repeat the procedure until no more air bubbles are seen.

11. Reinstall the rubber inspection cover to the bell housing.

12. Top off the brake master cylinder fluid reservoir and install the diaphragm and cap securely.

13. Reinstall the MAF sensor and air cleaner outlet tube.

14. Reconnect the negative battery cable.

15. Check the clutch for proper operation.

Halfshaft

REMOVAL & INSTALLATION

➡ **Do not begin this procedure without a new wheel hub retaining nut(s), a new lower control arm to steering knuckle pinch bolt and new retainer circlips for the CV-joints. Once removed, these parts lose their torque holding or retention capabilities and must not be reused.**

Left Side

1. Before servicing the vehicle, refer to the precautions in the beginning of this section.

2. Raise and safely support the vehicle.

Use a puller such as Front Hub Remover/Replacer T81P-1104-C to press the halfshaft out of the hub assembly

If the right halfshaft has been removed, install Differential Rotator T81P-4026-A or equivalent into the differential before removing the left halfshaft

Use a slide hammer with the special adapter to pull the inner CV-joint from the transaxle

3. Remove the left front wheel and tire assembly.

4. Snug two of the lug nuts back onto the rotor.

5. Insert the tapered end of a prybar or steel rod into one of the cooling slots of the disc brake rotor and place the bar against the disc brake anchor plate, to keep the rotor from turning.

6. Loosen and remove the wheel hub retaining nut. Discard the nut.

7. Remove the nut of the stabilizer bar link and separate the stabilizer bar from the strut using a tie rod end removal tool.

8. Remove the cotter pin and castellated nut that secures the tie rod end to the steering knuckle. Discard the cotter pin.

9. Using a tie rod end removal tool, separate the tie rod end from the steering knuckle.

10. Remove the lower control arm to steering knuckle pinch bolt and nut.

11. Using a prybar or similar tool, separate the lower control arm ball joint from the steering knuckle.

✷✷ WARNING

Never use a hammer to separate the halfshaft from the front wheel hub as damage to the threads or internal components may result.

12. Separate the outer CV-joint and halfshaft from the wheel hub using Front Hub Remover/Replacer T81P-1104-C and its associated components, or equivalent.

13. Install CV-joint puller T86P-3514-A1 or equivalent, between the inner CV-joint and the transaxle case.

➡ **If the right halfshaft has already been removed, install Differential Rotator T81P-4026-A or equivalent into the right side of the differential before removing the left shaft to maintain alignment within the differential.**

14. Attach the corresponding extension and slide hammer to the CV-joint puller and remove the halfshaft with both CV-joints as an assembly from the transaxle case.

15. Remove the assembly from the vehicle.

To install:

16. Replace the driveshaft bearing retainer circlip. Start one end of the circlip into the groove and work the circlip over the housing end and into the groove. This will avoid over-expanding the circlip.

17. Carefully align the splines of the inner CV-joint (install the halfshaft and both CV-joints as an assembly) with the splines in the transaxle case and push it into the differential side gear until the circlip is felt to seat.

➡ **A non-metallic mallet may be used to aid in seating the inner CV-joint into the differential side gear of the transaxle case. Only tap on the outboard CV-joint stub shaft.**

Turn to Section 6 for brake system applications

18. Position the outer CV-joint with half-shaft and carefully align the splines of the outer CV-joint with the splines of the wheel hub.

19. Push the CV-joint shaft into the wheel hub as far as possible.

20. Reinstall the front suspension lower control arm ball joint into the steering knuckle.

21. Reinstall a new lower control arm-to-knuckle pinch bolt and nut. Tighten the nut to 54–67 ft. lbs. (74–92 Nm).

22. Insert the tapered end of a prybar into one of the cooling slots in the disc brake rotor and jamb to prevent the rotor from turning.

23. Install a new wheel hub retaining nut onto the exposed threads of the outer CV-joint and manually thread the nut on as far as possible.

24. Finish running the nut up and tighten it to 246 ft. lbs. (340 Nm).

25. Remove the steel rod or prybar.

26. Reinstall the tie rod end on the steering knuckle. Reinstall the castellated nut and tighten it to 20 ft. lbs. (28 Nm). Install a new cotter pin.

27. Reinstall the stabilizer link bar with a new nut. Tighten the nut to 14–23 ft. lbs. (20–32 Nm).

28. Reinstall the wheel and tire assembly. Tighten the lug nuts to 62 ft. lbs. (85 Nm).

29. Lower the vehicle.

30. Road test the vehicle and check for proper operation.

Right Side and Intermediate

1. Before servicing the vehicle, refer to the precautions in the beginning of this section.

2. Raise and safely support the vehicle.

3. Remove the right front wheel and tire assembly.

4. Snug two of the lug nuts back onto the rotor.

5. Insert the tapered end of a prybar into one of the cooling slots of the disc brake rotor and place the bar against the disc brake anchor plate, to prevent the rotor from turning.

6. Loosen and remove the wheel hub retaining nut. Discard the retaining nut.

7. Remove the nut of the stabilizer bar link and separate the stabilizer bar from the strut using a tie rod end removal tool.

8. Remove the cotter pin and castellated nut that secures the tie rod end to the steering knuckle. Discard the cotter pin.

9. Using a tie rod end removal tool, separate the tie rod end from the steering knuckle.

10. Remove the lower control arm-to-wheel spindle pinch bolt and nut.

11. Using a prybar or similar tool, separate the lower control arm ball joint from the steering knuckle.

> **✳✳ WARNING**
>
> **Never use a hammer to separate the halfshaft from the front wheel hub as damage to the threads or internal components may result.**

12. Separate the outer CV-joint and half-shaft from the wheel hub using Front Hub Remover/Replacer T81P-1104-C and its associated components, or an equivalent tool.

13. Install CV-joint puller T86P-3514-A1 or equivalent, between the inner CV-joint and the intermediate halfshaft.

14. Using the extension and slide hammer on the CV-joint puller, separate the right halfshaft with CV-joints from the intermediate halfshaft.

15. Remove the right side halfshaft from the vehicle.

16. If intermediate shaft removal is required, proceed as follows:

   a. Remove the two nuts securing the support bracket.

   b. Remove the intermediate shaft and bearing shield.

   c. On the 2.0L engine, the exhaust clamp and two bolts will need to be removed to allow removal of the intermediate shaft.

   d. Remove the intermediate shaft from the vehicle.

   e. If the intermediate shaft support bracket needs to be removed, locate the three bolts securing the support bracket and remove the bolts.

   f. Remove the support bracket.

To install:

17. If the intermediate shaft was removed, reinstall as follows:

   a. If the support bracket was removed, reinstall with the three bolts and tighten them to 15–23 ft. lbs. (21–32 Nm).

   b. Carefully align the splines of the intermediate shaft with the splines of the differential side gears in the transaxle case.

   c. Push the shaft into the case until it is fully seated. The inner CV-joint is to be installed with the halfshaft and outer CV-joint attached as an assembly.

   d. Reinstall the two nuts onto the intermediate shaft support bracket and bearing shield. Tighten the nuts to 17–22 ft. lbs. (24–30 Nm).

   e. On the 2.0L engine, install the two bolts and the exhaust clamp.

18. Replace the bearing retainer circlip on the intermediate shaft. Start one end of the circlip into the groove and work the circlip over the housing end into the groove. This will prevent over-expanding the circlip.

19. Carefully align the splines of the inner CV-joint with the splines of the intermediate shaft. The inner CV-joint is to be installed as an assembly with the right halfshaft and outer CV-joint.

20. Push the inner CV-joint onto the intermediate shaft until it is fully seated.

21. Carefully align the splines of the outer CV-joint with the wheel hub and push the CV-joint into the hub as far as possible.

22. Reinstall the lower control arm ball joint into the steering knuckle.

23. Reinstall a new lower control arm-to-knuckle pinch bolt and nut. Tighten to 54–67 ft. lbs. (74–92 Nm).

24. Insert the tapered end of a prybar into one of the cooling slots in the front disc brake rotor and jamb the prybar to prevent the rotor from turning.

25. Install a new wheel hub retaining nut onto the exposed threads of the outer CV-joint and manually thread the nut on as far as possible.

26. Tighten the wheel hub retaining nut to 246 ft. lbs. (340 Nm).

27. Remove the prybar.

28. Reinstall the tie rod end into the steering knuckle. Reinstall the castellated nut and tighten to 20 ft. lbs. (28 Nm). Install a new cotter pin.

29. Reinstall the stabilizer link bar and nut. Tighten to 14–23 ft. lbs. (20–32 Nm).

30. Reinstall the right front wheel and tire assembly. Tighten the lug nuts to 62 ft. lbs. (85 Nm).

31. Lower the vehicle.

32. Road test the vehicle and check for proper operation.

STEERING AND SUSPENSION

Air Bag

PRECAUTIONS

Several precautions must be observed when handling the inflator module to avoid accidental deployment and possible personal injury.

- Never carry the inflator module by the wires or connector on the underside of the module.
- When carrying a live inflator module, hold securely with both hands, and ensure that the bag and trim cover are pointed away.
- Place the inflator module on a bench or other surface with the bag and trim cover facing up.
- With the inflator module on the bench, never place anything on or close to the module which may be thrown in the event of an accidental deployment.

Before servicing the vehicle, also be sure to refer to the precautions in the beginning of this section as well.

DISARMING

1. Before servicing the vehicle, refer to the precautions in the beginning of this section.
2. Position the vehicle with the front wheels in a straight ahead position.
3. Disconnect the negative battery cable.
4. Disconnect the positive battery cable.
5. Wait at least one minute for the air bag back-up power supply to drain before continuing.
6. Proceed with the repair.

ARMING

1. Once complete, connect the battery cables, negative cable last.
2. Check the functioning of the air bag system by turning the ignition key to the **RUN** position and visually monitoring the air bag indicator lamp in the instrument cluster. The indicator lamp should illuminate for approximately six seconds, then turn **OFF**. If the indicator lamp does not illuminate, stays on, or flashes at any time, a fault has been detected by the air bag diagnostic monitor.

Power Rack and Pinion Steering Gear

REMOVAL & INSTALLATION

1. Before servicing the vehicle, refer to the precautions in the beginning of this section.
2. Disconnect the negative battery cable.

3. Working inside the vehicle, remove the clamp plate bolt retaining the steering column shaft to the flexible coupling.
4. Rotate the clamp plate to separate it from the shaft of the flexible coupling.
5. Remove the floor seal being careful not to damage the sealing lip.
6. Remove the pinch bolt securing the flexible coupling to the rack and pinion (steering gear) pinion shaft and remove the flexible coupling.
7. Remove as much of the power steering fluid as possible from the power steering auxiliary reservoir using a suction gun or similar method.
8. Disconnect the power steering return hose from the power steering pump auxiliary reservoir.

➡ **The front subframe must be removed in order to allow removal of the rack and pinion (steering gear).**

9. If equipped with the 2.0L engine, remove the oil level dipstick and the exhaust manifold shield.
10. If equipped with the 2.5L engine, remove the water pump pulley shield.
11. Secure the radiator and fan shroud assembly to the radiator support using safety wire.

STEERING COLUMN
SHAFT CLAMP
PLATE

FLEXIBLE
COUPLING

7922JG46

Disconnect the steering column shaft from the flexible coupling

FLEXIBLE
COUPLING

STEERING GEAR
PINION SHAFT

7922JG47

Disengage the flexible coupling from the steering gear pinion shaft

12. Install Three Bar Engine Support D88L-6000-a or equivalent, to the engine lifting eyes and support the engine/transaxle assembly.
13. Raise and safely support the vehicle.
14. Remove the catalytic converter.
15. Remove the front wheel and tire assemblies.
16. Separate the left and right stabilizer bar links from the front stabilizer bar.
17. Separate the left and right outer tie rod ends from the steering knuckles. Discard the cotter pins.
18. Remove the pinch bolts and separate the front suspension lower control arms from the steering knuckles at the ball joints.
19. Remove the splash shield at the front of the subframe.
20. If equipped with an automatic transaxle, remove the retaining through-bolts from the left and right front engine support insulators (engine mounts) to the subframe.
21. If equipped with a manual transaxle, remove the through-bolt from the left front engine support insulator and remove the right front engine support insulator and mounting bracket.
22. Disconnect the power steering oil cooler hoses at the right front of the subframe and drain the power steering system.
23. Remove the A/C accumulator retaining screws from the front subframe.
24. Remove the four bolts retaining the lower radiator supports to the front subframe. Rotate the radiator supports forward.
25. Remove the two screws retaining the bumper cover braces to the left and right sides of the front subframe and rotate the cover braces forward.
26. Position Powertrain Lift (hydraulic lift) 014–00765 or equivalent, and two wood blocks approximately 40 in. (1m) in length attached to the subframe to support the subframe for removal from the vehicle.

➡ **Be sure that the powertrain lift and wood blocks are correctly positioned for safe removal of the subframe.**

27. Remove the four subframe-to-body retaining bolts.
28. Lower the subframe slightly and disconnect the power steering pressure and return hoses from the rack and pinion.
29. Finish lowering the subframe.
30. Remove the six bolts and the steering gear cover plate from the subframe.
31. Disconnect the power steering pressure and return hose unions from the steering gear.

FRONT OF VEHICLE

FRONT SUB-FRAME

SUB-FRAME
ALIGNMENT
PIN SET
T94P-2100-AH

7922JG48

Install alignment pins such as Subframe Alignment Pin Set T94P-2100-AH into the subframe to ensure correct positioning

32. Remove the two bolts retaining the steering gear to the subframe and remove the rack and pinion.

To install:

33. If the rack and pinion (steering gear) is being replaced, remove the inner tie rods and boots from the old unit and install on the new one, if they are in good condition.

34. Install new plastic seals on the power steering pressure and return line fittings as required.

35. Reinstall the rack and pinion to the subframe and install the retaining bolts.

36. Tighten the two rack and pinion retaining bolts to 101 ft. lbs. (137 Nm).

37. Reconnect the power steering and return hose unions to the rack and pinion.

38. Tighten the unions to 23 ft. lbs. (31 Nm).

39. Reinstall the rack and pinion cover plate and install the six retaining bolts.

40. Tighten the retaining bolts to 37 ft. lbs. (50 Nm).

41. If lowered, raise and safely support the vehicle.

42. If removed, position the front subframe onto the powertrain lift and raise.

43. Reinstall the power steering pressure and return hoses to the rack and pinion.

44. Position the front subframe to the body.

45. Route the power steering hoses to their correct positions.

46. Loosely install the four subframe-to-body bolts.

47. Install Subframe Alignment Pin Set T94P-2100-AH or equivalent, into the front subframe-to-body alignment holes.

48. Slightly tighten the four subframe-to-body retaining bolts.

49. Move the subframe to complete the alignment.

50. Tighten the four subframe-to-body retaining bolts to 81–110 ft. lbs. (110–150 Nm).

51. Remove the alignment tools.

52. Reinstall the A/C bracket retaining screw to the subframe and secure.

53. Reconnect the power steering oil cooler hoses to the front of the subframe.

54. Install the Powertrain Alignment Gauge T94P-6000-AH or equivalent, to the left front engine support bracket and the subframe.

55. Tighten the two retaining bolts to 20 ft. lbs. (27 Nm) and snug the through-bolt.

56. Lower the vehicle.

57. Remove the engine support from the top of the engine compartment.

58. Reconnect the power steering return hose to the power steering pump auxiliary reservoir.

59. Working inside the vehicle, install the flexible coupling to the steering gear pinion shaft and install the pinch bolt.

60. Tighten the pinch bolt to 21 ft. lbs. (28 Nm).

61. Reinstall the floor seal.

62. Align the steering column shaft clamp plate with the flexible coupling and install the clamp plate bolt. Tighten the clamp plate bolt to 18 ft. lbs. (24 Nm).

63. Partially raise and safely support the vehicle.

64. Install the right front engine support insulator (engine mount). Tighten the two retaining bolts to 30–41 ft. lbs. (41–55 Nm) and the through-bolt to 75–102 ft. lbs. (103–137 Nm).

65. Check the position of the right front engine mount (support insulator). It must be centered in the transaxle bracket and in perfect front-to-rear alignment.

66. Remove the two retaining bolts and the through-bolt securing the powertrain alignment gauge and remove the powertrain alignment gauge.

67. Reinstall the left front engine mount to the front subframe using the two retaining

1. Front Suspension Steering Ball Dust Seal
2. Front Wheel Spindle Connecting End
3. Steering Gear
4. Power Steering Gear Rack Balance Tube
5. Power Steering Left Turn Pressure Tube
6. Power Steering Right Turn Pressure Tube

7922JG49

Power rack and pinion steering gear assembly component identification

bolts. Tighten the retaining bolts to 84 inch lbs. (10 Nm).

68. Check the position of the left front engine mount to ensure perfect front-to-rear alignment.

69. Retighten the two retaining bolts to 30–40 ft. lbs. (41–55 Nm).

70. Reinstall the left front engine mount through-bolt. Tighten the through-bolt to 75–102 ft. lbs. (103–137 Nm).

71. Reinstall the stabilizer bar link to the front stabilizer bar. Tighten the retaining nuts to 35–48 ft. lbs. (47–65 Nm).

72. Reconnect the left and right lower control arms to the ball joints and install the pinch bolts. Tighten the pinch bolts to 37–43 ft. lbs. (50–58 Nm).

73. Reinstall the catalytic converter.

74. Reinstall both tie rod ends to the steering knuckles. Install new cotter pins.

75. Reinstall the wheel and tire assemblies and tighten the lug nuts to 63 ft. lbs. (85 Nm).

76. Reinstall the front bumper cover braces to both sides of the subframe.

77. Reinstall the radiator supports and the splash shield to the subframe.

78. Lower the vehicle.

79. Remove the safety wire supporting the radiator and fan shroud assembly.

80. If equipped with the 2.0L engine, install the exhaust manifold shield and the oil level dipstick.

81. If equipped with the 2.5L engine, install the water pump pulley shield and secure.

82. Fill the power steering system with the proper fluid.

83. Reconnect the negative battery cable.

84. Run the engine and check for leaks and proper operation.

➡ **Whenever the vehicle subframe is removed or lowered, the wheel alignment should be checked.**

85. Bleed the power steering system, if needed.

Strut and Spring

REMOVAL & INSTALLATION

Front

1. Before servicing the vehicle, refer to the precautions in the beginning of this section.

2. Disconnect the negative battery cable.

3. Raise and safely support the vehicle.

4. Remove the wheel and tire assembly.

5. Lower the vehicle enough to gain access to the strut retaining nut.

7922JG50

Hold the strut piston with an Allen wrench while removing the retaining nut

7922JG51

Properly compress the coil spring assembly before removing the retaining nut

6. From inside the engine compartment, hold the strut piston with an 8mm Allen head wrench while removing the top retaining nut.

7. Raise and safely support the vehicle.

8. Disconnect the stabilizer bar link from the strut.

9. Remove the brake hose and anti-lock wiring from the strut bracket.

10. Remove the steering knuckle-to-strut pinch bolt.

11. Work the strut out of the steering knuckle and lower the strut out of the strut tower.

12. Remove the strut/coil spring assembly from the vehicle.

✳✳ CAUTION

Do not attempt to remove the coil spring from the strut without first compressing the coil spring with the appropriate tool. Personal injury or component damage can occur.

13. Install Spring Compressor 086–00029 or equivalent, to the coil spring and compress the spring until the spring tension is relieved from the spring seat.

14. Remove the thrust bearing retainer nut.

15. Remove the thrust bearing, spring seat and dust shield.

16. Remove the coil spring from the strut.

17. Remove the jounce bumper from the strut.

18. Replace the coil spring or the strut as needed.

To install:

19. Reinstall the jounce bumper to the strut.

20. Position the coil spring on the strut.

21. Compress the coil spring if removed from the spring compressor.

22. Reinstall the dust shield, spring seat and thrust bearing.

23. The coil spring must seat in the notch of the spring seat.

24. Reinstall the thrust bearing retainer nut. Tighten the nut to 44 ft. lbs. (59 Nm).

25. Position the strut/coil spring assembly into the strut tower and fit the lower portion of the strut into the steering knuckle.

26. Reinstall the knuckle-to-strut pinch bolt. Do not tighten the bolt at this time.

27. Partially lower and safely support the vehicle.

28. Reinstall the top strut mounting nut.

29. Use an 8mm Allen head wrench to prevent the strut piston rod from turning

1 Nut
2 Retainer
3 Upper Mount Retainer Nut
4 Upper Mount
5 Bearing
6 Spring Seat
7 Front Coil Spring
8 Front Shock Absorber
9 Jounce Bumper
10 Dust Shield

7922JG52

Exploded view of the strut assembly

while tightening the mounting nut to 34 ft. lbs. (46 Nm).

30. Tighten the knuckle to strut pinch bolt to 40 ft. lbs. (54 Nm).

31. Raise and safely support the vehicle.

32. Reinstall the stabilizer bar link. Be careful not to damage the ball joint seal. Replace the stabilizer bar link if the seal is damaged.

33. Tighten the stabilizer bar link retaining nut to 37 ft. lbs. (50 Nm).

34. Position the brake hose and the anti-lock wiring to the strut bracket.

35. Reinstall the wheel and tire assembly. Tighten the lug nuts to 63 ft. lbs. (85 Nm).

36. Lower the vehicle.

37. Connect the negative battery cable.

38. Check the front wheel alignment.

39. Road test the vehicle and check for proper operation.

Rear

1. Before servicing the vehicle, refer to the precautions in the beginning of this section.

2. Disconnect the negative battery cable.

3. Raise and safely support the vehicle.

4. Remove the wheel and tire assembly.

5. Remove the anti-lock sensor wiring from the strut bracket.

6. Remove the anti-lock sensor mounting bolt and remove the sensor.

7. Disconnect the rear brake hose fitting from the brake tube. Plug the brake lines.

8. Remove the retainer and the rear brake hose from the strut.

9. Remove the tie strap retaining the parking brake rear cable and conduit to the rear suspension tie rod.

10. Disconnect the rear sway bar link and bushings from the rear control arm (suspension arm).

11. Disconnect the rear suspension tie rod from the wheel spindle.

➡ **The front and rear control arms (suspension arms) must be supported prior to the removal of the upper or lower strut attachments.**

12. Position a support under the front and rear control arms.

13. Remove the spindle-to-strut pinch bolt.

14. Separate the spindle from the strut by tapping down on the wheel spindle.

15. Compress the coil spring using Strut Spring Compressor T81P-5310-A or equivalent.

16. Remove the two top retaining bolts and remove the strut assembly.

17. Place the strut assembly on a suitable workbench.

18. Compress the coil spring enough to relieve the tension on the spring seat.

STABILIZER BAR LINK AND BUSHING

FRONT REAR SUSPENSION ARM AND BUSHING

7922JG53

For rear strut removal, disconnect the sway bar link from the control arm . . .

REAR SUSPENSION TIE ROD AND BUSHING

REAR WHEEL SPINDLE

7922JG54

. . . and separate the tie rod from the rear wheel spindle

SHOCK ABSORBER

REAR WHEEL SPINDLE

SPINDLE-TO-SHOCK ABSORBER PINCH BOLT

7922JG55

Remove the rear strut pinch bolt to release the strut assembly from the spindle

1 Rear Spring
2 Strut Spring Compressor
3 Shock Absorber
4 Mounting Nuts

7922JG56

Compress the coil spring, then unthread the two top retaining bolts and remove the strut from the vehicle

1 Rear Shock Absorber Bracket
2 Shock Absorber Mounting Nut
3 Rear Shock Absorber Dust Boot
4 Rear Suspension Jounce Bumper
5 Shock Absorber
6 Rear Spring
7 Spring Seat
8 Shock Absorber Bushing

7922JG57

Exploded view of the rear strut assembly

19. Remove the top mount nut, rear strut bracket, bushing and spring seat.

20. Remove the coil spring and slowly relieve the tension on the spring if it is not to be reinstalled.

21. Remove the dust shield and the jounce bumper if the strut is being replaced.

To install:

22. If removed, install the jounce bumper and dust shield to the strut.

23. Reinstall the coil spring and compress the spring if not already done.

24. Reinstall the spring seat, bushing, rear strut bracket and the top mount nut. Tighten the top mount nut to 30–43 ft. lbs. (41–58 Nm).

25. With the coil spring compressed, install the strut assembly into position.

26. Reinstall the two rear strut bracket mounting bolts. Tighten the rear strut bracket mounting bolts to 17–22 ft. lbs. (23–30 Nm).

27. Position the strut to the wheel spindle.

28. Reinstall the spindle-to-strut pinch bolt. Tighten the pinch bolt to 52–72 ft. lbs. (70–98 Nm).

29. Remove the strut spring compressor.

30. Reinstall the rear suspension tie rod and bushing. Tighten the bolt to 75–102 ft. lbs. (102–138 Nm).

31. Remove the support.

32. Attach the rear brake hose to the strut.

33. Reinstall the rear brake anti-lock sensor and retaining bolt. Tighten the retaining bolt to 84 inch. lbs. (9 Nm).

34. Reinstall the anti-lock wiring to the strut.

35. Secure the parking brake cable and conduit to the rear suspension tie rod with a tie strap.

36. Unplug and connect the rear brake hose fitting to the brake tube. Tighten the fitting securely.

37. Bleed the brake system.

38. Reinstall the wheel and tire assembly. Tighten the lug nuts to 62 ft. lbs. (85 Nm).

39. Lower the vehicle.

40. Connect the negative battery cable.

41. Check the rear wheel alignment.

42. Road test the vehicle and check for proper operation.

Lower Ball Joint

REMOVAL & INSTALLATION

If the lower ball joint requires replacement, the lower control arm and ball joint assembly must be replaced together, as the lower ball joint is not separately serviceable.

Lower Control Arm

REMOVAL & INSTALLATION

Right Side

1. Disconnect the negative battery cable.

2. Raise and safely support the vehicle.

3. Remove the wheel and tire assembly.

4. Remove the lower ball joint to steering knuckle pinch bolt.

5. Separate the lower control arm ball joint from the steering knuckle.

6. Remove the four lower control arm bushing to front subframe nuts and bolts.

7. Remove the right side lower control arm.

To install:

8. Place the right side lower control arm to the front subframe.

9. Reinstall the mounting bolts with the threads pointed down. Tighten the mounting bolts to 96 ft. lbs. (130 Nm).

10. Reinstall the lower ball joint stud to the steering knuckle.

11. Reinstall the lower ball joint to steering knuckle pinch bolt. Tighten the pinch bolt to 40 ft. lbs. (54 Nm).

12. Reinstall the wheel and tire assembly.

13. Lower the vehicle.

14. Connect the negative battery cable.

15. Check the wheel alignment.

16. Road test the vehicle and check for proper operation.

Left Side

1. Disconnect the negative battery cable.

2. Support the radiator and fan shroud using safety wire to the radiator support.

3. If equipped with 2.0L (VIN 3) engine, remove the heat shield and the catalytic converter retaining nuts from the exhaust manifold.

4. Raise and safely support the vehicle.

5. Remove the catalytic converter.

6. Disconnect the steering column lower yoke.

7. If equipped with a manual transaxle, disconnect the gearshift rod and clevis.

8. Remove the front lower radiator cover.

9. Remove the radiator supports.

10. Remove the ball joint to steering knuckle pinch bolt.

11. Separate the lower control arm from the steering knuckle.

12. Disconnect the power steering cooler lines at the right–hand side of the front subframe.

13. Disconnect the stabilizer bar link from the front stabilizer bar.

14. Remove the thru-bolts from the front and rear engine mounts.

15. Position Powertrain Lift 014-00765 (transmission jack) or equivalent, under the front subframe.

16. Remove the subframe mounting bolts.

17. Remove the four lower control arm bushing to front subframe mounting nuts.

18. Lower the front subframe enough to allow removal of the lower control arm mounting bolts.

19. Remove the mounting bolts and remove the lower control arm.

To install:

20. Position the lower control arm into the front subframe.

21. Reinstall the mounting bolts with threads pointed down.

22. Raise the front subframe into position.

23. Reinstall the lower control arm to subframe mounting bolts. tighten the mounting bolts and nuts to 96 ft. lbs. (130 Nm).

24. Reinstall the subframe mounting bolts. Tighten the bolts to 81–110 ft. lbs. (110–150 Nm).

25. Remove the powertrain lift or equivalent.

26. Reinstall the front and rear engine mount thru-bolts. Tighten the thru-bolts to 40–55 ft. lbs. (54–75 Nm).

27. Connect the power steering cooler lines to the right-hand side of the subframe.

28. Position the lower control arm ball joint stud to the steering knuckle.

29. Reinstall the pinch bolt and tighten to 40 ft. lbs. (54 Nm).

30. Connect the stabilizer bar link to the front stabilizer bar. Tighten the bar link to 37 ft. lbs. (50 Nm).

31. Reinstall the radiator support.

32. Reinstall the front lower radiator cover.

33. Reinstall the catalytic converter.

34. Lower the vehicle.

35. If equipped with 2.0L (VIN 3) engine,

Turn to Section 6 for brake system applications

install the heat shield and the catalytic converter retaining nuts.

36. Raise and safely support the vehicle.

37. If equipped with a manual transaxle, install the gearshift rod and clevis.

38. Connect the steering column lower yoke.

39. Reinstall the wheel and tire assembly.

40. Lower the vehicle.

41. Remove the safety wire supporting the radiator.

42. Connect the negative battery cable.

➡ **Whenever the vehicle subframe is removed or lowered, the wheel alignment should be checked.**

43. Check the wheel alignment.

44. Road test the vehicle and check for proper operation.

Wheel Bearings

ADJUSTMENT

Front

The front wheel bearings consist of a cartridge design and are permanently lubricated and sealed requiring no further maintenance. The bearings are preset and cannot be adjusted. If any part of a wheel bearing assembly is defective, the unit must be replaced. It is critical that the wheel hub retainer is properly tightened to 210 ft. lbs. (290 Nm) and that a new wheel hub retainer is always used.

Rear

The rear wheel bearings are not adjustable. If the bearings make noise or become loose, they must be replaced.

REMOVAL & INSTALLATION

Front

➡ **Before proceeding, be sure to have available new pinch bolts for the steering knuckle to lower ball joint and steering knuckle to strut as well as a new wheel hub retaining nut.**

1. Before servicing the vehicle, refer to the precautions in the beginning of this section.

2. Disconnect the negative battery cable.

3. Raise and safely support the vehicle.

4. Remove the wheel and tire assembly.

5. Remove the disc brake caliper and rotor.

6. Support the disc brake caliper with safety wire. Do not let the caliper hang by the brake hose.

7. Remove the anti-lock brake sensor retaining bolt and remove the sensor from the steering knuckle.

8. Remove the outer tie rod end cotter pin and remove the castellated nut. Discard the cotter pin.

9. Separate the outer tie rod end from the steering knuckle using Tie Rod End Remover 3290-D or equivalent.

10. Remove the wheel hub retaining nut. Discard the nut.

11. Separate the halfshaft from the wheel hub using Front Hub Remover/Replacer T81P-1104-C or equivalent, and the related adapters.

12. Once removed, support the end of the halfshaft.

13. Remove the steering knuckle to lower ball joint pinch bolt.

14. Remove the steering knuckle to strut pinch bolt.

15. Work the steering knuckle off of the lower ball joint and out of the lower strut tube.

16. Remove the steering knuckle from the vehicle.

17. Place the steering knuckle assembly onto a suitable workbench.

18. Install Front Hub Remover/Replacer T81P-1104-C or equivalent with the appropriate adapters and separate the hub from the steering knuckle.

The wheel bearing is retained in the knuckle by two snaprings, as shown

19. Remove the inner and outer snap rings securing the wheel bearing.

20. Remove the wheel bearing from the steering knuckle. Drive or press the old wheel bearing out as required.

To install:

21. Install the outer snapring into the steering knuckle.

22. Install the wheel bearing using a hydraulic press with Pinion Bearing Cup Replacer T80T-4000-E or equivalent.

23. Reinstall the inner snapring in the steering knuckle.

24. Reinstall the hub to the steering knuckle using Threaded Drawbar T75T-1176-A or equivalent.

25. Carefully align the splines of the outer CV-joint with the splines in the hub.

26. Position the steering knuckle to the lower ball joint stud.

27. Position the steering knuckle to the lower strut tube.

FRONT HUB REMOVER/REPLACER T81P-1104-C

FRONT WHEEL KNUCKLE

BEARING PULLING ATTACHMENT D79L-4621-A

Use gear or bearing pulling tools to remove the hub from the steering knuckle

28. Install a new steering knuckle to lower ball joint pinch bolt. Tighten the bolt to 55–58 ft. lbs. (75–79 Nm).

29. Install a new steering knuckle-to-strut pinch bolt. Tighten the bolt to 40 ft. lbs. (54 Nm).

30. Reinstall the anti-lock brake sensor and retaining bolt. Tighten the retaining bolt to 84 inch. lbs. (10 Nm).

31. Reinstall the disc brake rotor and caliper assembly.

32. Reinstall a new wheel hub retaining nut. Tighten the retaining nut to 210 ft. lbs. (290 Nm).

➡**Do not use an impact gun to tighten the wheel hub retaining nut or damage to the wheel bearing may result.**

33. Attach the tie rod end to the steering knuckle. Install the castellated nut and tighten the nut to 18–22 ft. lbs. (24–30 Nm). Install a new cotter pin.

34. Reinstall the wheel and tire assembly. Tighten the lug nuts to 62 ft. lbs. (85 Nm).

35. Lower the vehicle.

36. Connect the negative battery cable.

37. Pump the brake pedal several times to position the disc brake pads before attempting to move the vehicle.

Using a press, install the new wheel bearing in the knuckle

Use the special tools shown or a press to install the hub in the knuckle assembly

38. Road test the vehicle and check for proper operation.

Rear

➡**The wheel bearings are contained within the wheel hub and must be replaced as an assembly.**

WITH REAR DISC BRAKES

1. Before servicing the vehicle, refer to the precautions in the beginning of this section.

2. Disconnect the negative battery cable.

3. Raise and safely support the vehicle.

4. Remove the wheel and tire assembly.

5. Remove the anti-lock sensor retaining bolt and remove the sensor.

6. Remove the rear disc brake caliper and rotor.

➡**Do not use an impact gun to remove the hub retainer nut.**

7. Remove the hub retainer nut.

8. Slide the hub and wheel bearing assembly off of the spindle.

9. Remove the disc brake dust shield.

10. Disconnect the rear tie rod and bushing from the spindle.

11. Disconnect the rear control arm (suspension arm) from the spindle. Remove the front control arm (suspension arm) from the spindle.

12. Remove the strut-to-spindle pinch bolt.

13. Separate the spindle from the strut and remove from the vehicle.

To install:

14. Reinstall the spindle to the strut. Tighten the pinch nut to 52–72 ft. lbs. (70–98 Nm).

15. Connect the rear control arm (suspension arm) to the spindle. Connect the front control arm (suspension arm) to the spindle. Install the bolt, but do not fully tighten it at this time.

16. Connect the rear tie rod and bushing to the spindle. Install the bolt, but do not fully tighten it at this time.

17. Reinstall the disc brake dust shield.

18. Reinstall the hub and bearing assembly to the spindle.

19. Reinstall the hub retainer nut. Tighten the hub retainer nut to 170–192 ft. lbs. (230–260 Nm).

➡**Do not use an impact gun to tighten the hub retainer nut.**

20. Reinstall the rear disc brake rotor and caliper.

21. Reinstall the anti-lock sensor. Tighten the retaining bolt for the sensor to 84–96 inch. lbs. (9–11 Nm).

22. Reinstall the wheel and tire assembly. Tighten the wheel nuts to 62 ft. lbs. (85 Nm).

23. Lower the vehicle until the wheels are supporting the vehicle's weight. This will properly load the suspension.

24. Tighten the spindle-to-control arm bolt to 52–79 ft. lbs. (70–98 Nm).

25. Tighten the tie rod-to-spindle bolt to 75–102 ft. lbs. (98 Nm).

26. Finish lowering the vehicle.

27. Road test the vehicle and check for proper operation.

WITH REAR DRUM BRAKES

➡**The wheel bearings are contained within the wheel hub and must be replaced as an assembly.**

1. Before servicing the vehicle, refer to the precautions in the beginning of this section.

2. Disconnect the negative battery cable.

3. Raise and safely support the vehicle.

4. Remove the wheel and tire assembly.

5. Remove the anti-lock sensor retaining bolt and remove the sensor.

6. Remove the brake drum retainer and the brake drum.

➡**Do not use an impact gun to remove the hub retainer nut.**

7. Remove the wheel hub retainer nut.

8. Slide the hub and bearing assembly off of the spindle.

9. Remove the four backing plate bolts and move the backing plate out of the way. Be careful not to damage the brake line to the wheel cylinder.

10. Disconnect the rear tie rod and bushing from the spindle.

11. Disconnect the rear control arm (suspension arm) from the spindle. Remove the front control arm (suspension arm) from the spindle.

12. Remove the strut-to-spindle pinch bolt.

13. Separate the spindle from the strut and remove.

To install:

14. Reinstall the spindle to the strut. Tighten the pinch bolt to 52–72 ft. lbs. (70–98 Nm).

15. Connect the rear control arm (suspension arm) to the spindle. Connect the

front control arm (suspension arm) to the spindle.

16. Connect the rear tie rod and bushing to the spindle. Do not tighten the bolt at this time.

17. Place the backing plate into position. Reinstall the four backing plate bolts and tighten to 33–40 ft. lbs. (45–54 Nm).

18. Reinstall the hub and bearing assembly to the spindle.

19. Reinstall the hub retainer nut. Tighten the retainer nut to 170–192 ft. lbs. (230–260 Nm).

✳✳ WARNING

Do not use an impact gun to tighten the hub retainer nut, otherwise the bearings may be damaged.

20. Reinstall the brake drum.

21. Check the brake shoes for proper adjustment.

22. Reinstall the anti-lock sensor and the retaining bolt. Tighten the retaining bolt to 7–8 ft. lbs. (9–11 Nm).

23. Reinstall the wheel and tire assembly. Tighten the wheel nuts to 62 ft. lbs. (85 Nm).

7922JG62

After removing the spindle nut, use the special tools or a puller to remove the rear hub/bearing assembly—models equipped with rear drum brakes

24. Lower the vehicle until the wheels are supporting the vehicle's weight. This will properly load the suspension.

25. Tighten the spindle-to-control arm bolt to 52–79 ft. lbs. (70–98 Nm).

26. Tighten the tie rod-to-spindle bolt to 75–102 ft. lbs. (98 Nm).

27. Finish lowering the vehicle.

28. Road test the vehicle and check for proper operation.

FORD MOTOR COMPANY

20

Ford-Taurus • Mercury-Sable

PRECAUTIONS

Before servicing any vehicle, please be sure to read all of the following precautions, which deal with personal safety, prevention of component damage, and important points to take into consideration when servicing a motor vehicle:

• Never open, service or drain the radiator or cooling system when the engine is hot; serious burns can occur from the steam and hot coolant.

• Observe all applicable safety precautions when working around fuel. Whenever servicing the fuel system, always work in a well-ventilated area. Do not allow fuel spray or vapors to come in contact with a spark, open flame, or excessive heat (a hot drop light, for example). Keep a dry chemical fire extinguisher near the work area. Always keep fuel in a container specifically designed for fuel storage; also, always properly seal fuel containers to avoid the possibility of fire or explosion. Refer to the additional fuel system precautions later in this section.

• Fuel injection systems often remain pressurized, even after the engine has been turned **OFF**. The fuel system pressure must be relieved before disconnecting any fuel lines. Failure to do so may result in fire and/or personal injury.

• Brake fluid often contains polyglycol ethers and polyglycols. Avoid contact with the eyes and wash your hands thoroughly after handling brake fluid. If you do get brake fluid in your eyes, flush your eyes with clean, running water for 15 minutes. If eye irritation persists, or if you have taken brake fluid internally, IMMEDIATELY seek medical assistance.

• The EPA warns that prolonged contact with used engine oil may cause a number of skin disorders, including cancer! You should make every effort to minimize your exposure to used engine oil. Protective gloves should be worn when changing oil. Wash your hands and any other exposed skin areas as soon as possible after exposure to used engine oil. Soap and water, or waterless hand cleaner should be used.

• All new vehicles are now equipped with an air bag system, often referred to as a Supplemental Restraint System (SRS) or Supplemental Inflatable Restraint (SIR) system. The system must be disabled before performing service on or around system components, steering column, instrument panel components, wiring and sensors. Failure to follow safety and disabling procedures could result in accidental air bag deployment, possible personal injury and unnecessary system repairs.

• Always wear safety goggles when working with, or around, the air bag system. When carrying a non-deployed air bag, be sure the bag and trim cover are pointed away from your body. When placing a non-deployed air bag on a work surface, always face the bag and trim cover upward, away from the surface. This will reduce the motion of the module if it is accidentally deployed. Refer to the additional air bag system precautions later in this section.

• Clean, high quality brake fluid from a sealed container is essential to the safe and proper operation of the brake system. You should always buy the correct type of brake fluid for your vehicle. If the brake fluid becomes contaminated, completely flush the system with new fluid. Never reuse any brake fluid. Any brake fluid that is removed from the system should be discarded. Also, do not allow any brake fluid to come in contact with a painted surface; it will damage the paint.

• Never operate the engine without the proper amount and type of engine oil; doing so WILL result in severe engine damage.

• Timing belt maintenance is extremely important! Many models utilize an interference-type, non-freewheeling engine. If the timing belt breaks, the valves in the cylinder head may strike the pistons, causing potentially serious (also time-consuming and expensive) engine damage. Refer to the maintenance interval charts in the front of this manual for the recommended replacement interval for the timing belt, and to the timing belt section for belt replacement and inspection.

• Disconnecting the negative battery cable on some vehicles may interfere with the functions of the on-board computer system(s) and may require the computer to undergo a relearning process once the negative battery cable is reconnected.

• When servicing drum brakes, only disassemble and assemble one side at a time, leaving the remaining side intact for reference.

ENGINE REPAIR

➡**Disconnecting the negative battery cable on some vehicles may interfere with the functions of the on board computer systems and may require the computer to undergo a relearning process, once the negative battery cable is reconnected.**

Distributor

The 3.0L (OHV), 3.0L (DOHC) and 3.4L (DOHC) engines use Distributorless Ignition Systems (DIS).

Ignition Timing

ADJUSTMENT

The base ignition timing is set at 10 degrees Before Top Dead Center (BTDC) and is not adjustable.

Engine Assembly

REMOVAL & INSTALLATION

1. Before servicing the vehicle, refer to the precautions at the beginning of this section.
2. Disconnect the battery cables, negative cable first.
3. On the 3.0L (DOHC) engine, perform the following:
    a. Remove the cowl extension and windshield wiper.
    b. Disconnect the main emission vacuum control connector from both connectors at the right side of the dash panel.
4. On the 3.4L engine, perform the following:
    a. Remove the battery and the battery tray.
    b. Remove the oil filler cap.
    c. Remove the engine appearance cover.
    d. Remove the cowl top extension and windshield wiper module.

☀ CAUTION

Never open, service or drain the radiator or cooling system when hot; serious burns can occur from the steam and hot coolant.

5. Drain the cooling system.
6. Mark the position of the hood on the hinges and remove the hood.
7. Disconnect the steering coupling at the pinch bolt joint inside the passenger compartment.
8. Disconnect the wiring from the Mass Air Flow (MAF) sensor, and the Intake Air Temperature (IAT) sensor.

➡**Label all electrical connectors and vacuum hoses prior to removal so they can be reinstalled in their proper locations.**

9. Remove the air cleaner outlet tube.
10. Remove the air cleaner retaining bolts at the air cleaner body.

11. Disconnect the engine intake air resonator by pushing in the top and bottom tube surfaces at the engine air cleaner and pulling the air cleaner outward. Lift the air cleaner up and out of the engine compartment.

☀ CAUTION

Observe all applicable safety precautions when working around fuel. Whenever servicing the fuel system, always work in a well ventilated area. Do not allow fuel spray or vapors to come in contact with a spark or open flame. Keep a dry chemical fire extinguisher near the work area. Always keep fuel in a container specifically designed for fuel storage; also, always properly seal fuel containers to avoid the possibility of fire or explosion.

12. Properly relieve the fuel system pressure and disconnect the fuel tube(s) from the fuel injection manifold.
13. Recover the refrigerant from the A/C system using the proper equipment.
14. Disconnect the chassis vacuum supply hose at the connection on the intake manifold. Position the hose aside.
15. Remove the ground straps from the dash panel.
16. Disconnect the control sensor wiring from the Powertrain Control Module (PCM) and position aside.
17. Remove the connectors for the engine control sensor wiring from the retaining bracket on the power brake booster. Disconnect the engine control sensor wiring at the two connectors.
18. Disconnect engine control sensor wiring from the evaporative emission canister purge valve.
19. Disconnect the evaporative emission hose at the crankcase vent connector and hose. Position the hose aside.
20. Remove the shield and disconnect the accelerator cable and the speed control actuator from the throttle body and from the accelerator cable bracket. Position the cables aside.
21. Remove the retaining nut and disconnect the manual control lever from the manual control lever shaft at the Transmission Range (TR) sensor.
22. Remove the connectors for the engine control sensor wiring from the retaining bracket on top of the transaxle.

Disconnect the engine control sensor wiring at the two connectors.
23. Disconnect the wiring connector from the secondary air injection pump relay located on the retaining bracket on top of the transaxle.
24. Disconnect the main emission vacuum control connector at the connection near the fan shroud.
25. Disconnect the oil cooler inlet tube from the transaxle.
26. Disconnect the heater water hose from the water pump and water hose connection.
27. Disconnect the upper radiator hose and degas tube from the water hose connection.
28. Remove the power steering return hose from the power steering oil reservoir and drain.
29. Disconnect the alternator wiring harness from the alternator at the BAT terminal and stator connector plug. Remove the wiring harness retaining clip from the alternator mounting bracket.
30. If necessary, disconnect the retaining clips and the A/C compressor lines from the compressor or the accumulator. Cap all openings to prevent the entrance of dirt or moisture.
31. On the 3.4L engine, loosen the A/C manifold-to-A/C compressor bolt; then, disconnect the A/C pressure cut-off switch from the compressor and position it aside.
32. Raise and safely support the vehicle. Remove the front wheel and tire assemblies.
33. Remove both front stabilizer bar links from the front stabilizer bar.
34. Remove both halfshafts using the procedure in this manual.
35. Remove the splash shield from the radiator support and front bumper.

☀ CAUTION

The EPA warns that prolonged contact with used engine oil may cause a number of skin disorders, including cancer! You should make every effort to minimize your exposure to used engine oil. Protective gloves should be worn when changing the oil. Wash your hands and any other exposed skin areas as soon as possible after exposure to used engine oil. Soap and water, or waterless hand cleaner should be used.

36. Drain the engine oil.

Remove the Heated Oxygen (HO₂S) sensor(s) from the exhaust pipe before removing the Y pipe as damage to the sensor(s) may occur.

37. Remove the converter Y-pipe.

38. Disconnect the power steering pressure hose from the power steering/transaxle oil cooler connection. Position the hose aside.

39. Disconnect the lower radiator hose at the radiator and at the radiator overflow hose.

40. Disconnect the wiring at the starter motor, and remove the starter motor (3.0L OHV engine).

41. Disconnect the lower cooler line from the transaxle.

42. Support the front subframe and engine/transaxle assembly using Powertrain Lift 014-00765 and Universal Powertrain Removal Bracket 014-00766 or equivalents.

43. Remove the four subframe bolts.

44. Lower the engine/transaxle and front subframe from the vehicle.

45. Disconnect the power steering pressure hose from the power steering pump.

46. Disconnect the engine control sensor wiring from the power steering gear.

47. Disconnect engine control sensor wiring from power steering gear.

48. Install suitable engine lifting brackets on the engine and transaxle assembly.

49. Remove the front engine support insulator, rear engine support insulator and engine and transaxle support.

50. Lift the engine and transaxle from the subframe.

51. Lower the engine and transaxle. Support the transaxle on a level, stationary surface for transaxle storage.

52. Remove flywheel-to-torque converter nuts.

53. Remove the transaxle-to-cylinder block mounting bolts and separate the engine from the transaxle/torque converter assembly.

54. Place the engine on a safe suitable workstand.

To install:

55. Install the transaxle/torque converter assembly to the engine. Tighten the mounting bolts to 30–44 ft. lbs. (40–60 Nm) for all except 1999–00 3.0L (DOHC) engines or 25–33 ft. lbs. (33–46 Nm) for 1999–00 3.0L (DOHC) engines. Tighten the torque converter nuts to 20–34 ft. lbs. (27–46 Nm).

56. Remove the engine and transaxle assembly from the workstand and position it on the subframe.

57. Install the front engine support insulator, rear engine support insulator and engine and transaxle support.

58. Connect the power steering pressure hose to the power steering pump.

59. Attach the engine control sensor wiring to the power steering gear.

60. Raise the engine, transaxle and subframe into position using the powertrain lifting tool.

61. Align the front subframe to the body and install the subframe-to-body bolts. Tighten the bolts to 57–76 ft. lbs. (77–103 Nm).

62. Remove the lifting equipment and move aside.

63. Install the remaining components in the reverse order of removal and tighten the following:

• Hub retainer nuts to 170–202 ft. lbs. (230–275 Nm)

• Tie rod end-to-steering knuckle nuts to 35–46 ft. lbs. (47–63 Nm)

• Front suspension lower arm-to-front wheel knuckle nuts to 50–68 ft. lbs. (68–92 Nm)

• Front stabilizer bar link-to-front stabilizer bar nuts to 30–40 ft. lbs. (40–55 Nm)

• Manual control lever-to-manual control lever nut to 12–16 ft. lbs. (16–22 Nm)

Operating the engine without the proper amount and type of engine oil will result in severe engine damage.

64. On the 3.4L engine, perform the following:

a. Connect the A/C pressure cut-off switch to the compressor and tighten the A/C manifold-to-A/C compressor bolt.

b. Install the windshield wiper module and cowl top extension.

c. Install the engine appearance cover.

d. Install the oil filler cap.

e. Install the battery tray and the battery.

65. On the 3.0L (DOHC) engine, perform the following:

a. Connect the main emission vacuum control connector to both connectors at the right side of the dash panel.

b. Install the windshield wiper and cowl extension.

66. Fill the cooling system. Fill the crankcase with the proper type of motor oil to the required level.

67. Connect the battery cables, negative cable last. Run the engine and check for leaks.

68. Evacuate and recharge the air conditioning system.

69. Install and align the hood.

➡**Whenever the vehicles subframe is removed or lowered, the wheel alignment should be checked.**

70. Check the front wheel alignment. Road test the vehicle and check the engine and transaxle for proper operation.

Water Pump

REMOVAL & INSTALLATION

Do not remove the radiator cap or open the cooling system until the engine has cooled. Removing the radiator cap or opening the cooling system prior to the engine cooling could cause severe burns from scalding engine coolant.

3.0L (OHV) Engine

1. Before servicing the vehicle, refer to the precautions at the beginning of this section.

2. Disconnect the negative battery cable. Allow the engine to cool. Remove the radiator cap and drain the cooling system.

3. Loosen the four water pump pulley-to-water pump hub bolts.

4. Remove the accessory drive belts. Remove the idler pulley or automatic tensioner, as required.

5. Disconnect and remove the heater hose from the water pump.

6. Remove the engine control sensor wiring from the locating stud bolt, if equipped.

7. Remove the water pump-to-engine bolts and lift the water pump and pulley up and out of the vehicle.

To install:

8. Clean the gasket surfaces on the water pump and engine front cover. Install a new gasket on the water pump using gasket adhesive.

9. Place the water pump in position on the engine with the pulley and four bolts loosely installed on the hub.

➡**The bolts are of different lengths and must be installed in the correct locations.**

10. Apply pipe sealant to bolt threads. Install the bolts in the water pump housing. Tighten bolts No's. 1, 2, 3, 4, 5, 6, 7, 8, 9 and 15 to 15–22 ft. lbs. (20–30 Nm). Tighten bolts No's. 10, 11, 12, 13 and 14 to 72–106

Fasteners			Torque Specifications	
Fastener And Hole No.	Size	Fastener Application	Nm	Lb-Ft
1A	M8 x 1.25 x 43.5	F/C TO BLOCK	20-30	15-22
2A	M8 x 1.25 x 73	W/P & F/C TO BLOCK	20-30	15-22
3A	M8 x 1.25 x 104.3	W/P & F/C TO BLOCK	20-30	15-22
4A	M8 x 1.25 x 71.3	F/C TO BLOCK	20-30	15-22
5A	M8 x 1.25 x 71.3	W/P & F/C TO BLOCK	20-30	15-22
6A	M8 x 1.25 x 71.3	W/P & F/C TO BLOCK	20-30	15-22
7A	M8 x 1.25 x 104.3	W/P & F/C TO BLOCK	20-30	15-22
8A	M8 x 1.25 x 104.3	W/P & F/C TO BLOCK	20-30	15-22
9A	M8 x 1.25 x 52	F/C TO BLOCK	20-30	15-22
10B	M6 x 1 x 28.5	W/P TO F/C	8-12	71-106 (lb-in)
11B	M6 x 1 x 28.5	W/P TO F/C	8-12	71-106 (lb-in)
12B	M6 x 1 x 28.5	W/P TO F/C	8-12	71-106 (lb-in)
13B	M6 x 1 x 28.5	W/P TO F/C	8-12	71-106 (lb-in)
14B	M6 x 1 x 28.5	W/P TO F/C	8-12	71-106 (lb-in)
15A	M8 x 1.25 x 71.3	W/P & F/C TO BLOCK	20-30	15-22

W/P—Water Pump
F/C—Engine Front Cover

9300KG01

Exploded view of the water pump and timing front cover bolt locations—3.0L (OHV) engine

Timing belt service is covered in Section 5 of this manual

inch lbs. (8–12 Nm). Refer to the accompanying illustration for the bolt locations.

11. Install the remaining components in the reverse order of removal. Tighten the water pump pulley bolts to 15–22 ft. lbs. (20–30 Nm).

12. Fill the cooling system. Connect the negative battery cable.

13. Start the engine and allow it to reach normal operating temperature. Check for leaks and proper operation.

3.0L (DOHC) Engine

1. Before servicing the vehicle, refer to the precautions at the beginning of this section.

2. Disconnect the negative battery cable. Drain the engine cooling system.

3. Remove the water pump drive belt. Remove the radiator and heater hoses from the water pump.

4. Remove the A/C compressor brace-to-water pump bracket.

5. Remove the four water pump-to-engine nuts and remove the water pump.

To install:

6. Clean the water pump-to-engine gasket sealing surfaces.

7. Using a new gasket, install the water pump and torque the four nuts and bracket to 15–22 ft. lbs. (20–30 Nm).

8. Install the remaining components in the reverse order of removal.

9. Fill the engine cooling system, then connect the negative battery cable.

10. Start the engine and allow it to reach normal operating temperature, then check for coolant leaks and proper engine operation.

3.4L Engine

1. Before servicing the vehicle, refer to the precautions at the beginning of this section.

2. Disconnect the negative battery cable. Drain the engine cooling system.

3. Remove the two flange bolts and four

1	Water Outlet Hose	12	Oil Cooler to Water Pump Return Hose
2	Throttle Body to Water Pump Return Hose	13	Drive Belt
3	Water Pump to Throttle Body Supply Hose	14	Bolt
		15	Belt Idler Pulley
4	Bolt (2 Req'd)	16	Water Pump Drive Pulley
5	Water Pump	17	Collar
6	Water Thermostat	18	O-Ring
7	Oil Cooler Return Tube Gasket	19	Water Inlet Hose
8	Water Hose Connection	20	Bolt
9	Bolt (2 Req'd)	A	Tighten to 18-28 N·m (14-20 Lb-Ft)
10	Heater Core to Water Pump Return Hose	B	Tighten to 10-16 N·m (89-141 Lb-In)
11	Stud	C	Tighten to 8-12 N·m (71-106 Lb-In)

7922KG03

Exploded view of the water pump and related components—3.4L engine

cap nuts and remove the engine appearance cover.

4. Remove the battery and battery tray.

5. Remove the water pump drive belt.

6. Disconnect the throttle body return and supply hoses, heater core return hose and the oil cooler return hose from the water pump.

7. Remove the two water hose connection (thermostat housing) bolts and remove the thermostat.

8. Remove the bolts and collar retaining the water pump housing to the left side cylinder head.

9. Disconnect the water outlet and inlet hoses from the water pump and remove the water pump from the engine.

10. Remove the belt idler pulley nut and remove the idler pulley from the water pump.

To install:

11. Clean the water pump-to-engine and housing gasket sealing surfaces.

12. Install the belt idler pulley and bolt and tighten the bolt to 89–141 inch lbs. (10–16 Nm).

13. Apply a silicone lubricant to the water pump inlet and outlet hoses, install them on the water pump housing and clamp securely.

14. Apply a silicone lubricant to the O-ring and install it between the water pump housing and left side cylinder head.

15. Install the water pump housing-to-left side cylinder head bolts. Tighten the two water inlet bolts to 71–106 inch lbs. (8–12 Nm). Tighten the two remaining bolts to 14–20 ft. lbs. (18–28 Nm).

16. Install the water thermostat, oil cooler return tube gasket and water hose connection to the water pump housing and tighten the two bolts to 71–106 inch lbs. (8–12 Nm).

17. Connect the throttle body return and supply hoses, heater core return hose and the oil cooler return hose to the water pump.

18. Install the water pump drive belt and carefully release drive belt tensioner.

19. Tighten the two flange bolts and four cap nuts to 71–106 inch lbs. (8–12 Nm).

20. Install engine appearance cover.

21. Fill the engine cooling system, then connect the negative battery cable.

22. Start the engine and allow it to reach normal operating temperature, then check for coolant leaks and proper engine operation.

Cylinder Head

REMOVAL & INSTALLATION

✳✳ CAUTION

The fuel injection system remains under pressure, even after the engine has been turned OFF. The fuel system pressure must be relieved before disconnecting any fuel lines. Failure to do so may result in fire and/or personal injury.

3.0L (OHV) Engines

1. Before servicing the vehicle, refer to the precautions at the beginning of this section.

2. Rotate the crankshaft until the No. 1 cylinder piston is at Top Dead Center (TDC) of the compression stroke.

3. Disconnect the negative battery cable. Properly relieve the fuel system pressure. Drain the cooling system into a suitable container.

4. Remove the air cleaner outlet hose to throttle body. Label and disconnect the vacuum lines from the throttle body.

5. Disconnect the hoses from the EGR valve. Loosen the lower EGR tube nut and rotate the tube away from the valve.

6. Label and disconnect the wiring from the Intake Air Temperature (IAT) sensor, Throttle Position (TP) sensor, Idle Air Control (IAC) valve and Pressure Feedback EGR (PFE) or Differential Pressure Feedback EGR (DPFE) sensors.

7. Remove the fuel line safety clips and disconnect the fuel lines from the fuel supply manifold.

8. Remove the upper intake manifold and discard the gasket.

9. Label and disconnect the fuel injector harness from the valve cover studs and fuel injectors.

➡**Fuel injectors and fuel injection supply manifold may be removed with lower intake manifold as an assembly.**

10. Remove fuel injection supply manifold and fuel injectors.

11. Remove the ignition coil and bracket from the left (front) cylinder and set aside.

12. Label and disconnect the ignition wires from the spark plugs and the valve

cover studs. Disconnect the upper radiator and heater hoses.

13. Remove Camshaft Position (CMP) sensor and housing.

14. Disconnect the Engine Coolant Temperature (ECT) sensor and temperature sending unit electrical connectors.

15. For the left (front) cylinder head, perform the following:

a. Disconnect the alternator electrical connectors.

b. Rotate the tensioner clockwise and remove the accessory drive belt.

c. Remove the automatic belt tensioner assembly.

d. Remove the alternator.

e. Remove the power steering mounting bracket bolts. Leave the hoses connected and place the pump aside in a position to prevent fluid from leaking out.

f. Remove the engine oil dipstick tube from the exhaust manifold.

16. For the right (rear) cylinder head, perform the following:

a. Remove the alternator belt tensioner bracket.

b. Remove the heater supply tube brackets from the exhaust manifold.

c. Remove the Vehicle Speed Sensor (VSS) cable bolt.

d. Remove the throttle emission control solenoid and bracket.

17. Remove the rocker arm covers. Loosen the rocker arm fulcrum bolts and remove the rocker arms, fulcrums and bolts. Keep the assemblies in order so they can be reinstalled in their original locations.

➡**Regardless of the cylinder head being removed, the No. 3 cylinder intake valve pushrod must be removed to allow removal of the intake manifold.**

18. Remove the pushrods and label their positions. The pushrods must be installed in their original position during reassembly.

19. Remove the intake manifold. Remove the spark plugs. Remove the exhaust manifolds.

20. Remove and discard the cylinder head bolts and remove the cylinder heads from the engine. Remove and discard the old cylinder head gaskets.

➡**Use caution when scraping aluminum surfaces as not to cause leak paths.**

To install:

21. Clean the cylinder head bolts

holes in the block with a tap. Clean the cylinder head, intake manifold, rocker arm cover and cylinder head gasket contact surfaces.

➡️**Place shop cloth in valve tappet valley to catch any dirt or gasket material which could become entrapped with in the engine. Check cylinder head and block surfaces for flatness.**

22. Position new head gaskets on the cylinder block using the dowels in the block for alignment. If the dowels are damaged, they must be replaced.

23. Position the cylinder head on the block. Install new cylinder head bolts.

Install the cylinder head gasket with the "UP" designation on gasket facing the cylinder head—3.0L (OHV) engines

24. On 1996–98 models, tighten the bolts in sequence as follows:

    a. First step: 53–66 ft. lbs. (70–90 Nm).

    b. Second step: back off the bolts one complete turn.

    c. Third step: tighten the bolts, in sequence, to 34–40 ft. lbs. (45–55 Nm).

    d. Final step: tighten the bolts, in sequence, to 63–73 ft. lbs. (85–99 Nm).

25. On 1999–00 models, tighten the bolts in sequence as follows:

    a. First step: 36–39 ft. lbs. (47–53 Nm).

    b. Second step: back off the bolts one complete turn.

    c. Third step: tighten the bolts, in sequence, to 20–24 ft. lbs. (27–33 Nm).

    d. Fourth step: tighten the bolts, in sequence an additional 85–95 degrees.

    e. Final step: repeat step four.

26. Install the intake manifold. Connect the ECT and coolant temperature sending unit connectors.

27. Dip each pushrod end in oil conditioner or heavy engine oil. Install the pushrods in their original position.

28. Before installation, coat the valve tips, rocker arm and fulcrum contact areas with Lubriplate® or equivalent.

29. Rotate the crankshaft until the lifter is on the base circle of the cam (valve closed).

30. Install the rocker arm assemblies and tighten the rocker arm fulcrum bolts to 24 ft. lbs. (32 Nm). Be sure the lifter is on the base circle of the cam for each rocker arm as it is installed.

➡️**The fulcrums must be fully seated in the cylinder head and the pushrods must be seated in the rocker arm sockets prior to the final tightening.**

31. Install the exhaust manifolds. Install lower intake manifold. Install the spark plugs.

32. Position the valve covers on the cylinder head and install the bolts. Note the location of the ignition wire retainer stud bolts.

33. Install the fuel charging wiring to the fuel injectors and inboard valve cover stud bolts.

34. Install the upper intake manifold upper gasket and the upper intake manifold.

35. Install the ignition coil and bracket torque to 30–39 ft. lbs. (40–55 Nm). Connect all sensor electrical connectors.

36. For the left (front) cylinder head, perform the following:

    a. Connect the oil dipstick tube to the exhaust manifold stud and tighten the nut to 13 ft. lbs. (18 Nm).

    b. Install the power steering support bracket and pump. Tighten the bolt to 35 ft. lbs. (48 Nm).

    c. Install the automatic belt tensioner and tighten the nuts/bolt to 35 ft. lbs. (48 Nm).

37. For the right (rear) cylinder head, perform the following:

    a. Install the alternator and tighten the long bolt to 35 ft. lbs. (48 Nm) and belt tensioner bracket short bolt to 27ft. lbs. (37 Nm). Tighten alternator brace bolts and nut to 11 ft. lbs. (15 Nm).

    b. Install the throttle emission control solenoid and bracket. Tighten the bolt to 26 ft. lbs. (35 Nm).

    c. Install the heater supply tube brackets to the exhaust manifold and tighten the nuts to 26 ft. lbs. (35 Nm).

38. Install fuel tubes and fuel tube safety clips.

39. Install the VSS cable bracket.

40. On flexible fuel vehicles, install the CMP sensor.

41. Install the drive belt. Connect the fuel lines.

42. Connect the upper radiator hose and heater hoses. Connect all vacuum lines to pre-marked locations. Change the engine oil and filter.

43. Install the air cleaner outlet tube to throttle body and engine air cleaner. Install crankcase ventilation tube to valve cover.

44. Fill and bleed the cooling system. Connect the negative battery cable. Start the engine and check for coolant, fuel, oil, vacuum and exhaust leaks.

45. Check and if necessary, adjust the cruise control cable and the throttle valve cable.

Cylinder head bolt tightening sequence—3.0L (OHV) engines

3.0L (DOHC) Engines

➡The cylinder head bolts are a torque-to-yield design and cannot be reused. Be sure new cylinder head bolts are available before beginning this procedure.

1. Before servicing the vehicle, refer to the precautions at the beginning of this section.

2. Disconnect the negative battery cable. Drain the engine coolant from the radiator and cylinder block drain plugs.

3. Remove the engine from the vehicle and position on a suitable workstand.

4. If necessary, remove throttle body, EGR vacuum control solenoid and idle control valve.

5. Disconnect engine control sensor wiring.

6. Remove the upper and lower intake manifolds. Remove the exhaust manifolds.

✳✳ WARNING

Do not loosen or bend Intake Manifold Runner Control (IMRC) actuator cable bracket retainer; bracket alignment is critical and potential damage to the intake manifold runner control actuator may occur.

7. Unfasten the bolts retaining both valve covers, in sequence, then remove the valve covers.

8. Disconnect and remove radiator hose tube and bracket from the cylinder head.

9. Release front accessory drive belt tensioner by rotating the pulley clockwise.

10. Remove crankcase ventilation tube nut and crankcase tube from the oil separator and water by-pass tube; loosen clamp remove heater hose, remove by-pass tube from cylinder head.

11. Remove power steering pump, A/C compressor and A/C mounting brackets.

✳✳ WARNING

The A/C compressor mounting bracket uses torque-to-yield bolts; discard old bolts and install new ones.

12. Remove water pump assembly.

✳✳ WARNING

Crankshaft accessory drive pulley shaft has left threads. Rotate pulley shaft clockwise to remove, use a 24mm open end wrench on the inside nut to remove crankshaft accessory drive pulley shaft.

● REMOVE BOLTS/STUDS IN SEQUENCE SHOWN
✳ STUD LOCATION

Left side valve cover bolt removal sequence—3.0L (DOHC) engine

9300KG02

✳ LOCATION OF STUDS
● REMOVE BOLTS/STUDS IN SEQUENCE SHOWN

Right side valve cover bolt removal sequence—3.0L (DOHC) engine

9300KG03

● REMOVE BOLTS IN SEQUENCE SHOWN

Cylinder head bolt removal sequence—right side head shown, left side similar—3.0L (DOHC) engine

9300KG04

13. Drain the engine oil and remove the oil pan. Remove the engine front cover.

14. Remove the timing chains, camshafts and lash adjusters from both cylinder heads.

15. Remove the cylinder head bolts from the cylinder heads in the proper removal sequence. Inspect the cylinder heads and cylinder block.

✳✳ WARNING

Cylinder heads should not be set on cylinder head face; scratches or dents on cylinder head may cause improper sealing.

To install:

16. Clean the cylinder heads, intake manifolds, valve covers and the cylinder head gasket sealing surfaces on the cylinder block.

Cylinder head bolt tightening sequence—3.0L (DOHC) engine

7922KG07

✳ LOCATION OF STUDS
● TIGHTEN BOLTS/STUDS IN SEQUENCE SHOWN

Left side valve cover bolt tightening sequence—3.0L (DOHC) engine

9300KG05

Refer to Section 1 for engine rebuilding specifications

Right side valve cover bolt tightening sequence—3.0L (DOHC) engine

➡**If the cylinder heads were removed for cylinder head gasket replacement, check the flatness of the cylinder heads and the cylinder block gasket sealing surfaces.**

17. Install new cylinder head gaskets onto the dowels of the cylinder block.

➡**Left and right cylinder head gaskets are not interchangeable.**

18. Place the cylinder heads to their original positions using care not to damage the heads, block or gaskets.

19. Be sure the cylinder heads are correctly positioned on the dowels. Lightly oil the threads of the new cylinder head bolts and install into the cylinder heads.

20. Tighten the new cylinder head bolts as follows:

• Tighten the bolts, in sequence, to 27–32 ft. lbs. (37–43 Nm)

• Rotate the bolts, in sequence, 85–95 degrees

• Loosen the bolts, in sequence, a minimum of one full turn

• Tighten the bolts, in sequence, to 27–32 ft. lbs. (37–43 Nm)

• Rotate the bolts, in sequence, 85–95 degrees

• Rotate the bolts, in sequence, an additional 85–95 degrees

21. Install the EGR backpressure transducer and bracket to the rear of the right cylinder head. Tighten the bolts to 71–106 inch lbs. (8–12 Nm).

22. Install the lash adjusters, camshafts and timing chains. Install the engine front cover and oil pan.

23. Refer to Camshaft section for proper installation of camshafts.

24. Install the exhaust manifolds. Install the lower and upper intake manifolds. Replace the engine oil filter.

25. Install valve covers bolts, in sequence, and tighten.

26. Install engine accessories in reverse order.

27. Install the engine assembly into the vehicle. Fill the engine with the proper amount and grade of engine oil. Fill the engine cooling system.

28. Connect the negative battery cable. Run the engine and check for leaks. Road test the vehicle and check for proper engine operation.

3.4L Engines

➡**The cylinder head bolts are torque-to-yield design and cannot be reused. Be sure that new cylinder head bolts are available before beginning this procedure.**

1. Before servicing the vehicle, refer to the precautions at the beginning of this section.

2. Disconnect the negative battery cable. Drain the engine coolant from the radiator and cylinder block drain plugs.

3. Remove the engine from the vehicle and position on a suitable workstand.

4. Remove the upper and lower intake manifolds. Remove the exhaust manifolds.

5. Drain the engine oil and remove the oil pan. Remove the engine front cover.

Cylinder head bolt removal sequence—3.4L (DOHC) engine

RH CYLINDER HEAD   FRONT OF ENGINE   LH CYLINDER HEAD

● TIGHTEN BOLTS IN SEQUENCE SHOWN

7922KG08

Cylinder head bolt tightening sequence—3.4L (DOHC) engine

6. Remove the timing chains and camshafts.

7. Remove the cylinder head bolts from the cylinder heads in the proper removal sequence. Inspect the cylinder heads and cylinder block.

To install:

8. Clean the cylinder heads, intake manifolds, valve covers and the cylinder head gasket sealing surfaces on the cylinder block.

➡**If the cylinder heads were removed, check the flatness of the cylinder heads and the cylinder block gasket sealing surfaces.**

9. Install new cylinder head gaskets onto the dowels of the cylinder block.

➡**Left and right cylinder head gaskets are not interchangeable.**

10. Install the cylinder heads in their original positions using care not to damage the heads, block or gaskets.

11. Be sure the cylinder heads are correctly positioned on the dowels. Lightly oil the threads of the new cylinder head bolts and install into the cylinder heads.

12. Tighten the new cylinder head bolts as follows:

• Tighten the bolts, in sequence, to 20–23 ft. lbs. (27–32 Nm)

• Rotate the bolts, in sequence, 85–95 degrees

13. Refer to camshaft section for proper installation of camshafts.

14. Install the camshafts and timing chains. Install the engine front cover and oil pan.

15. Install the exhaust manifolds. Install the lower and upper intake manifolds. Replace the engine oil filter.

16. Install the engine assembly into the vehicle. Fill the engine with the proper amount and grade of engine oil. Fill the engine cooling system.

17. Connect the negative battery cable. Run the engine and check for leaks. Road test the vehicle and check for proper engine operation.

Rocker Arms/Shafts

REMOVAL & INSTALLATION

3.0L (OHV) Engines

1. Before servicing the vehicle, refer to the precautions at the beginning of this section.

2. Disconnect the negative battery cable. Disconnect and label the spark plug wires.

3. Remove upper intake manifold.

4. Remove the ignition wire/separator assembly from the rocker arm attaching bolt studs.

5. If the left rocker arm cover is being removed, perform the following procedure:

a. Remove the oil fill cap.

b. Disconnect the air cleaner closure system hose.

c. Remove the fuel injector harness from the inboard rocker arm cover studs.

6. If removing the right rocker arm cover, perform the following procedure:

a. Remove the upper intake manifold.

b. Label and disconnect the vacuum hoses at the vacuum tee.

c. Loosen the EGR tube nuts at the EGR valve and exhaust manifold fitting; remove or rotate the tube aside.

d. Remove the PCV valve and the engine sensor wiring harness; move the wiring aside.

e. Remove the alternator brace.

7. Remove the rocker arm cover attaching screws and the covers and gaskets from the vehicle.

8. Remove the rocker arm bolts, fulcrums, rocker arms and fulcrum washers. Keep the parts in order so they can be reinstalled to their original positions.

9. Remove the pushrods, if necessary. Keep them in order so they can be reinstalled in their original positions.

For engine torque specifications, refer to Section 1 of this manual

1 Bolt (12 Req'd)
2 Rocker Arm Seat (12 Req'd)
3 Rocker Arm (12 Req'd)
4 Push Rod (12 Req'd)
5 Cylinder Head (2 Req'd)
6 2.15-4.69 mm (0.085-0.185 inch)
A Tighten in Two Steps:
   7-15 N·m (5-11 Lb-Ft)
   26-38 N·m (19-28 Lb-Ft)

7922KG22

Exploded view of the rocker arms and related components—3.0L (OHV) engines

10. Inspect the rocker arms, fulcrums and pushrods for wear and/or damage. Replace as necessary.

To install:

11. Install the pushrods, if removed, making sure they seat in the lifters.

TIGHTENING SEQUENCE — VALVE COVER

9300KG08

Valve cover tightening sequence—3.0L (OHV) engine

12. Coat the valve and pushrod tips, rocker arm and fulcrum contact areas with Lubriplate® or equivalent. Lightly oil all the bolt and stud threads before installation.

13. Rotate the engine until each lifter is on the base circle of the cam (valve closed).

14. Install the rocker arm and components and tighten the rocker arm fulcrum bolts in two steps: the first to 8 ft. lbs. (11 Nm) and the final to 24 ft. lbs. (32 Nm).

➡ **Be sure the lifter is on the base circle of the cam for each rocker arm as it is installed.**

15. Clean the cylinder head and rocker arm cover sealing surfaces of all dirt and old sealer. If not equipped with integral gaskets, be sure all old gasket material is removed.

16. Apply a bead of silicone sealant at the cylinder head-to-intake manifold

rail step. If not equipped with integral gaskets, install a new rocker arm cover gasket.

17. Install the rocker arm cover and the bolts and studs. Tighten to 89–123 inch lbs. (10–14 Nm) in the proper sequence.

18. Install the remaining components in the reverse order of their removal.

3.0L (DOHC) Engine

1. Before servicing the vehicle, refer to the precautions at the beginning of this section.

2. Disconnect the negative battery cable.

3. Remove upper intake manifold.

4. Remove both cylinder head valve covers.

5. Remove the crankshaft pulley bolt from the front of the crankshaft allowing the keyway to be referenced.

6. Rotate the crankshaft so the keyway is at the 11 o'clock position to locate the crankshaft at Top Dead center (TDC) for No. 1 cylinder.

7. Verify that the alignment arrows on the camshafts are aligned. If not, rotate the crankshaft one complete revolution and recheck camshaft arrows.

8. Rotate the crankshaft so the keyway is at the 3 o'clock position. This positions the right cylinder head camshafts to the neutral position.

CAUTION: CAMSHAFTS MUST BE IN TIME WITH CRANKSHAFT PRIOR TO INSTALLATION OF ROCKER ARMS

Journal Cap

Intake Camshaft

Rocker Arm

Tappet

NOTE: VALVE TAPPET MUST BE PUMPED UP PRIOR TO INSTALLATION

Exhaust Camshaft

Thrust Cap

CAUTION: REMOVE CYLINDER HEAD JOURNAL THRUST CAPS FIRST. INSTALL CYLINDER HEAD JOURNAL THRUST CAPS LAST

CAUTION: ROTATE CRANKSHAFT KEYWAY TO 11 O'CLOCK POSITION PRIOR TO INSTALLATION OF LH CAMSHAFT AND ROCKER ARMS. ROTATE CRANKSHAFT KEYWAY CLOCKWISE TO 3 O'CLOCK POSITION PRIOR TO INSTALLATION OF RH CAMSHAFT AND ROCKER ARMS AND CAMSHAFT JOURNAL THRUST CAPS

7922KG10

Exploded view of camshaft mounting—3.0L (DOHC) engine

➡**Remove the camshaft thrust cap first to prevent damage to the camshaft thrust journal cap.**

9. Remove the right cylinder head camshaft journal thrust cap bolts and thrust caps.

10. Loosen the remaining camshaft journal cap bolts in sequence, releasing the bolts several revolutions at a time by making several passes to allow the camshaft to be raised from the cylinder head evenly. Do not remove the bolts completely.

11. With the camshafts loose, remove the rocker arms, keeping them in the order that they were removed.

12. If required, remove the lash adjusters from the cylinder head.

13. Rotate the crankshaft two revolutions and locate the crankshaft keyway at the 11 o'clock position. This will position the left cylinder head camshafts to their neutral position.

14. Verify that the alignment arrows on the camshafts are aligned.

➡**The camshaft journal caps and cylinder heads are numbered to ensure that they are assembled in their original positions. If removed, keep the camshaft journal caps together with the cylinder head that they were removed from.**

15. Remove the camshaft journal thrust cap bolts and thrust caps from the left cylinder head.

16. Loosen the remaining camshaft journal cap bolts in sequence, releasing the bolts several revolutions at a time by making several passes to allow the camshaft to be raised from the cylinder head evenly. Do not remove the bolts completely.

➡**If the lash adjusters (tappets) and roller rocker arms are to be reused, mark the positions of the lash adjusters and rocker arms so they are reassembled into their original positions.**

17. With the camshafts loose, remove the rocker arms, keeping them in the order that they were removed.

18. If required, remove the lash adjusters from the cylinder head.

19. Inspect the rocker arms and lash adjusters for wear and/or damage and replace as necessary.

To install:

20. Be sure the crankshaft keyway is at the 11 o'clock position.

21. If removed, lubricate the left cylinder head lash adjusters with engine assembly lubricant and install into their correct positions in the cylinder head.

➡**If the lash adjusters are being replaced with new units, soak the adjusters in a container of clean engine oil, then manually pump up the adjusters before installing into the cylinder head.**

22. Lubricate the left cylinder head rocker arms with engine assembly lubricant and install the left cylinder head rocker arms into their original locations.

➡**Do not install the camshaft journal thrust caps until the camshaft journal caps are tightened into position.**

23. Tighten the left cylinder head camshaft journal cap bolts in sequence making several passes to pull the camshafts down evenly. Tighten the bolts to 71–106 inch lbs. (8–12 Nm).

24. Install the left-hand cylinder head thrust caps and bolts. Tighten to 71–106 inch lbs. (8–12 Nm).

25. Rotate the crankshaft two revolutions and position the crankshaft keyway to the 3 o'clock location. This will position the right cylinder head camshafts to the neutral position.

26. Lubricate the right cylinder head lash adjusters with engine assembly lubricant and install into their original positions in the cylinder head.

➡**If the lash adjusters are being replaced with new units, soak the adjusters in a container of clean engine oil and manually pump the adjusters up before installing them into the cylinder head.**

27. Lubricate the right cylinder head rocker arms with engine assembly lubricant and install the right cylinder head rocker arms into their original locations.

➡**Do not install the camshaft journal thrust caps until the camshaft journal caps are tightened into position.**

28. Tighten the right cylinder head camshaft journal cap bolts in sequence making several passes to pull the camshafts down evenly. Tighten the bolts to 71–106 inch lbs. (8–12 Nm).

29. Install the right-hand cylinder head thrust caps and bolts. Tighten to 71–106 inch lbs. (8–12 Nm).

30. Install the crankshaft pulley bolt and tighten as follows:

 a. Tighten to 89 ft. lbs. (120 Nm).

 b. Loosen the bolt at least one full turn.

 c. Tighten the bolt to 35–39 ft. lbs. (47–53 Nm).

 d. Rotate the bolt 85–95 degrees.

31. Install both valve covers as follows:

 a. Clean the valve cover gasket sealing surfaces.

 b. Install new valve cover gaskets onto the valve covers.

 c. For each valve cover, place a bead of silicone sealant at two places on the valve cover sealing surfaces where the engine front cover and the cylinder heads make contact and at two places on the rear of the cylinder head where the

Left cylinder head camshaft journal cap tightening sequence—3.0L (DOHC) left cylinder head

Right cylinder head camshaft journal cap tightening sequence—3.0L (DOHC)

camshaft seal retainer contacts the cylinder head.

d. Install the valve cover bolts and studs and tighten, in sequence, to 71–106 inch lbs. (8–12 Nm).

➡ **The valve covers must be installed and properly tightened within six minutes of applying the silicone sealant.**

32. Connect the negative battery cable.

33. Run the engine and check for leaks and proper operation.

3.4L (DOHC) Engine

The 3.4L (DOHC) engine does not have rocker arms. The camshaft lobes work directly on the valves.

Intake Manifold

REMOVAL & INSTALLATION

✳✳ CAUTION

The fuel injection system remains under pressure, even after the engine has been turned OFF. The fuel system pressure must be relieved before disconnecting any fuel lines. Failure to do so may result in fire and/or personal injury.

3.0L (OHV) Engine

UPPER INTAKE MANIFOLD

1. Before servicing the vehicle, refer to the precautions at the beginning of this section.

2. Disconnect the negative battery cable.

3. Remove the air cleaner outlet tube.

4. Remove the accelerator cable shield from the from the cable bracket.

5. Remove the accelerator cable spring. Disconnect the accelerator and speed control cables from the throttle body.

6. Remove the two accelerator cable bracket bolts from the side of the throttle body and position the cable bracket aside.

7. Label and disconnect the vacuum hose from the fuel pressure regulator.

8. Loosen the EGR tube nut at the EGR valve and disconnect the EGR backpressure transducer hoses from the EGR valve to exhaust manifold tube.

9. Disconnect the PCV hose, aspirator vacuum supply hose and evaporative emission return tube from the fitting under the upper intake manifold.

10. Disconnect the electrical connectors to the Throttle Position (TP) sensor, Idle Air Control (IAC) valve, EGR backpressure transducer and EGR vacuum regulator solenoid.

11. Disconnect the degas tube from the radiator coolant recovery tank and lower intake manifold fitting.

12. Remove the nut and bolts for the upper alternator brace and remove the brace.

13. Remove the sensor wiring bracket from the throttle body stud bolt and position the wiring aside.

14. Remove the intake manifold support from the throttle body and right cylinder head.

15. Remove the upper intake manifold bolts and stud bolts and note their location for installation. Remove the upper intake manifold.

16. Remove the manifold gaskets and discard.

To install:

17. Clean the gasket sealing surfaces and install the new intake manifold gaskets using locating pins as necessary to aid in gasket alignment.

18. Lightly oil all attaching bolt and stud threads before installation.

19. Position the upper intake gasket and

Item	Description
1	Stud Bolt
2	Bolt (2 Req'd)
3	Stud Bolt (2 Req'd)
4	Bolt
5	Upper Intake Manifold
6	Lower Intake Manifold
7	Intake Manifold Upper Gasket
A	Tighten to 20-30 N-m (15-22 Lb-Ft)

9300KG09

Exploded view of the upper intake manifold mounting—3.0L (OHV) engine

manifold on top of the lower intake manifold. Use locating pins to secure the position of gasket between manifolds.

20. Install the bolts and studs in their original locations. Tighten the stud bolts and bolts to 15–22 ft. lbs. (20–30 Nm).

21. Install the alternator brace to the upper intake manifold mounting stud and alternator mounting bracket. Tighten the nut and bolts to 9–15 ft. lbs. (12–20 Nm).

22. Install the intake manifold support to the throttle body and the right cylinder head. Tighten the top bolt to 71–106 inch lbs. (8–12 Nm). Tighten the bottom bolt to 30–40 ft. lbs. (40–55 Nm).

23. Install the engine sensor wiring bracket onto the throttle body stud bolts.

24. Connect the PCV hose, aspirator vacuum supply hose and evaporative emission return tube to the fitting under the upper intake manifold.

25. Install the EGR tube nut to the EGR valve and tighten to 22–28 ft. lbs. (30–40 Nm).

26. Connect the vacuum hose to the fuel pressure regulator.

27. Connect the electrical connectors to the TPS, IAC, EGR backpressure transducer and EGR vacuum regulator solenoid.

28. Install the accelerator cable bracket to the side of the throttle body and install the two bolts. Tighten the bolts to 13 ft. lbs. (17 Nm).

29. Connect the accelerator cable and speed control cable to the throttle body. Install the throttle retracting spring.

30. Install the accelerator cable shield and tighten the bolts to 13 inch lbs. (1.4 Nm).

31. Install the air cleaner outlet tube. Connect the negative battery cable.

32. Fill the cooling system.

33. Start the engine and check for leaks and proper operation.

➡ **Idle adjustment may be necessary if the throttle body was removed or if the throttle plate idle adjustment screw position is changed.**

LOWER INTAKE MANIFOLD

1. Before servicing the vehicle, refer to the precautions at the beginning of this section.

2. Disconnect the negative battery cable. Relieve the fuel system pressure.

3. Drain cooling system.

4. Disconnect the wiring from the Mass Air Flow (MAF) sensor and the Intake Air Temperature (IAT) sensor.

5. Remove the air cleaner outlet tube. Remove the air cleaner bolts at the air cleaner body.

6. Disconnect the engine intake air resonator by pushing in the top and bottom tube surfaces at the engine air cleaner and pulling the air cleaner outward. Lift the air cleaner up and out of the engine compartment.

7. Remove the fuel line safely clips. Disconnect the fuel supply and return lines from the fuel supply manifold using the proper disconnect tools.

8. Disconnect the remaining engine wire connectors from the Camshaft Position (CMP) sensor, Throttle Position (TP) sensor, Idle Air Control (IAC) valve, Engine Coolant Temperature (ECT) sensor, ignition coil, water temperature sensor, EGR backpressure transducer and EGR vacuum regulator solenoid connector.

➡ **Note the position of the CMP sensor electrical connector. Installation requires that the connector be located in the same location.**

9. With suitable pliers, slide back the upper radiator hose clamp and with a twisting motion loosen the hose from the hose connection.

10. Remove the upper intake manifold.

11. Loosen the EGR tube nut and remove the EGR valve to exhaust manifold tube from the EGR valve tube-to-manifold connector.

12. Disconnect the sensor wiring from the valve cover stud bolts. Carefully disconnect the electrical connectors to each fuel injector and position the sensor wiring harness aside.

13. Disconnect the heater water hoses.

14. Label and disconnect the ignition wires.

➡ **Before removing the CMP sensor, position No. 1 cylinder to TDC of its compression stroke.**

15. Remove the screws from the CMP sensor and remove the sensor from the sensor housing.

16. Remove the hold-down clamp and remove the CMP housing from the cylinder block.

17. Remove the cylinder head covers.

18. Remove the ignition coil from the rear of the left cylinder head.

19. Loosen the intake valve rocker arm bolt from cylinder No. 3 and rotate the rocker arm away from the valve stem and pushrod. Remove the pushrod.

➡ **The lower intake manifold may be removed with the fuel injection supply manifold and fuel injectors in place.**

20. Remove the intake manifold attaching bolts using a Torx® head socket. Use a suitable prybar to loosen the intake manifold. Pry upward using the area between the thermostat and transaxle as a leverage point. Remove the manifold and old gaskets and seals.

To install:

21. Clean the gasket mating surfaces of the intake manifold and the cylinder heads. Lay a shop rag in the lifter valley to catch

LOWER INTAKE MANIFOLD

7922KG17

Tighten the lower intake manifold bolts, in two steps, according to the sequence shown—3.0L (OHV) engine

Please refer to Section 9 for electric cooling fan wiring schematics

any gasket material. After scraping, carefully lift the shop rag from the lifter valley, being careful not to let any particles enter the oil drain holes or cylinder head. If necessary, use a suitable solvent to remove old rubber sealant.

22. Lightly oil all the attaching bolts and stud threads before installation.

➡ **When using a silicone rubber sealer, assembly must occur within 15 minutes after the sealer has been applied. After this time, the sealer may start to set-up and its sealing quality may be reduced. In high temperature and/or humidity conditions, the sealant will start to set up in approximately five minutes.**

23. Apply a suitable silicone rubber sealer to the intersection of the cylinder block end rails and cylinder heads. Be careful not to let sealer, that may block oil passages, fall into the engine.

24. Install the front and rear intake manifold end seals in place and secure. Install the intake manifold gaskets, aligning the locking tabs to the provisions on the cylinder head gaskets.

25. Carefully lower the intake manifold into position on the cylinder block and cylinder heads to prevent smearing the silicone sealer and causing gasket voids.

26. Install the bolts No's. 1, 2, 3 and 4 and hand tighten.

27. Install all the remaining bolts and tighten in sequence, starting at the center and working towards the ends. Tighten the bolts in two steps, tighten to 15–22 lbs. (20–30 Nm). Tighten again in sequence to 19–24 ft. lbs. (26–32 Nm).

28. Install the fuel supply manifold and injectors, if removed. Apply a small amount of clean engine oil to the injector holes in the intake manifold and fuel supply manifold prior to injector installation. Install the fuel supply manifold bolts and tighten to 7 ft. lbs. (10 Nm).

✳✳ WARNING

A special Synchro Positioning tool T95T-12200-A or equivalent must be used before installing the CMP sensor. If the special tool is not used, the fuel system will be out of time possibly causing engine damage.

29. Attach the Synchro Position tool T95T-12200-A as follows:

 a. Engage the CMP sensor housing vane into the radial slot of the tool.

 b. Rotate the tool on the CMP sensor housing until the tool boss engages the notch in the CMP sensor housing.

30. Lube the drive gear with clean engine oil and install the CMP sensor housing so the drive gear engagement occurs when the arrow on the locator tool is pointed about 75 degrees counterclockwise from the rear face of the cylinder block. This step will locate the CMP sensor electrical connector in the same position as was noted on removal.

31. Install the hold-down clamp and tighten the bolt to 14–22 ft. lbs. (19–30 Nm).

32. Install the CMP sensor to the housing and tighten the screws to 13–35 inch lbs. (1.5–4.0 Nm).

33. Install the No. 3 cylinder intake valve pushrod. Apply Lubriplate® or equivalent, to the pushrod and valve stem prior to installation. Turn the crankshaft as necessary to position the lifter on the base circle of the camshaft (pushrod all the way down). Tighten the rocker arm bolt in two steps, first to 8 ft. lbs. (11 Nm), then to 24 ft. lbs. (32 Nm).

34. Install the cylinder head covers.

35. Install the fuel injector harness wiring and attach to the injectors.

36. Install the ignition coil to the rear of left cylinder head. Tighten the bolts to 30–40 ft. lbs. (40–55 Nm).

37. Install the wiring harness to the valve cover stud bolts and connect the ignition wires to the spark plugs and ignition coil.

38. Install the upper intake manifold.

39. Install the exhaust manifold tube to the EGR valve on the intake manifold. Tighten the upper EGR tube nut to 26–48 ft. lbs. (35–65 Nm). Tighten the lower (exhaust manifold) tube nut to 26–48 ft. lbs. (35–65 Nm).

40. Install the fuel lines and safety clips.

41. Connect the water bypass hose and the upper radiator hose and properly install the squeeze clamps.

42. Connect the vacuum hoses to their pre-marked positions.

43. Connect the engine sensor wiring to the CMP sensor, IAC valve, TP sensor, ECT sensor, EGR backpressure transducer, EGR vacuum regulator solenoid, ignition coil and water temperature sender.

➡ **Be sure the CMP connector is installed in the same position as it was removed for correct operation.**

44. Install engine air cleaner and air cleaner outlet tube.

45. Connect the negative battery cable.

46. Cycle the ignition switch to the **RUN** position several times without starting the

engine to pressurize the fuel system and check for fuel leaks.

47. Fill the cooling system.

48. Start the engine and check for leaks and proper operation.

3.0L (DOHC) Engine

UPPER INTAKE MANIFOLD

1. Before servicing the vehicle, refer to the precautions at the beginning of this section.

2. Disconnect the negative battery cable. Relieve the fuel system pressure.

3. Remove the windshield wiper, then remove the cowl top inner panels.

4. Remove the accelerator cable shield.

5. Remove the accelerator cable and speed control actuator from the throttle body.

6. Remove the accelerator cable bracket from the intake manifold throttle body and move aside.

7. Remove the Idle Air Control (IAC) valve fresh air supply hose from the fitting on the upper intake manifold.

8. Disconnect the wiring harnesses from the Throttle Position (TP) sensor and the IAC valve.

9. Remove the upper intake manifold-to-PCV valve vacuum supply hose from the upper intake manifold.

10. Disconnect the main emission vacuum control connector from the upper intake manifold.

11. Remove the EGR valve. Disconnect the secondary air injection diverter valve bracket bolts from the upper intake manifold and position the bracket aside.

12. Remove the upper intake manifold bolts in the proper sequence.

✳✳ WARNING

When removing engine components such as manifolds and cylinder heads, always remove the bolts in a reverse order of their tightening sequence to prevent warpage to the component.

13. Remove the upper intake manifold and gaskets from the engine.

To install:

14. Install the upper intake manifold using two new gaskets onto the lower intake manifold. Install the upper manifold bolts and tighten following the proper sequence to 71–106 inch lbs. (8–12 Nm).

15. Tighten the (EGR) valve-to-exhaust manifold tube nut to 25–33 ft. lbs. (35–45 Nm).

Item	Description
1	Bolt (3 Req'd)
2	Bolt (3 Req'd)
3	Isolator (3 Req'd)
4	Isolator (3 Req'd)
5	Upper Intake Manifold
6	Gasket (2 Req'd)
7	Lower Intake Manifold
A	Tighten to 8-12 N·m (71-106 Lb-in)

TIGHTEN BOLTS IN SEQUENCE SHOWN

LOCATING PIN TWO PLACES PER GASKET   VIEW A

9300KG10

Upper intake manifold bolt tightening sequence—3.0L (DOHC) engine

16. Install the remaining components in the reverse order of removal.

17. Connect the negative battery cable. Run the engine and check for leaks and proper engine operation.

LOWER INTAKE MANIFOLD

1. Before servicing the vehicle, refer to the precautions at the beginning of this section.

2. Disconnect the negative battery cable. Relieve the fuel system pressure.

3. Remove the upper intake manifold.

4. Remove the fuel supply and return lines to the fuel injection manifold.

5. Disconnect the fuel injector wiring harness and move aside.

6. Disconnect the vacuum line from the fuel pressure regulator.

7. Disconnect the intake manifold runner actuator control cable from the lower intake manifold.

⁂ WARNING

Be careful not to loosen or bend the cable bracket, alignment is critical and potential damage to the control actuator may occur.

8. Disconnect the ignition wires from the left cylinder head and position the wires aside.

9. Remove the eight lower intake manifold-to-cylinder head bolts in sequence.

10. Remove the lower intake manifold and gaskets from the vehicle.

11. If the lower intake manifold is to be replaced or machined, remove the fuel injector supply manifold (fuel rail) and the fuel injectors.

To install:

12. Install the fuel injectors and the fuel supply manifold onto the lower intake manifold if removed. Verify the operation of the manifold runner control plate.

13. Thoroughly clean the gasket sealing areas and place two new intake manifold-to-cylinder head gaskets into position.

14. Carefully, install the lower intake manifold and install the intake manifold-to-cylinder head bolts. Tighten the bolts, in sequence, to 71–106 inch lbs. (8–12 Nm).

15. Install the fuel supply and return hoses to the fuel supply manifold and ensure that the spring lock couplings are correctly installed.

16. Install the retaining clips onto the spring lock couplings.

17. Connect the vacuum line to the fuel pressure regulator.

18. Temporarily connect the negative battery cable.

19. Connect the fuel pressure gauge to the fuel pressure relief valve located on the fuel injection supply manifold.

20. Cycle the ignition key several times to the **RUN** position to pressurize the fuel system.

21. Watch the fuel pressure gauge for signs of leakage. If the gauge holds pressure, remove the gauge and continue with the installation of the upper intake manifold. If the pressure gauge loses pressure, remove the fuel injection supply manifold and replace the leaking O-ring(s) before continuing.

22. Disconnect the negative battery cable.

23. Reposition and install the fuel injector wiring harness.

24. Connect the ignition wires to the left cylinder head.

25. Connect the intake manifold runner actuator control cable to the intake manifold. Be careful not to loosen or bend the cable bracket, alignment is critical.

26. Install the remaining components.

27. Connect the negative battery cable.

3.4L Engine

UPPER INTAKE MANIFOLD

1. Before servicing the vehicle, refer to the precautions at the beginning of this section.

2. Disconnect the negative battery cable. Relieve the fuel system pressure.

3. Remove the engine appearance cover.

4. Remove the right half of the cowl vent screen.

5. Remove the throttle body.

6. Disconnect the main emission vacuum supply hose from the surge tank vacuum fitting and EGR valve and move out of the way.

7. Disconnect the vacuum tube from the intake manifold vacuum union.

8. Remove the two transducer mounting bracket-to-surge tank bolts and position the bracket aside.

9. Remove the two intake manifold supports from the surge tank and cylinder head.

10. Remove the EGR valve.

11. Remove the retaining bolts and surge tank stay from the front of the surge tank.

12. Remove the bolt, nuts and surge tank stay from the rear of the surge tank.

13. Disconnect the crankcase ventilation tube from the valve cover and surge tank.

14. Disconnect the vacuum tube from the pressure regulator.

15. Disconnect the right side crankcase ventilation hose and move aside.

16. Loosen the intake air connector hose clamps and remove the surge tank from the engine.

17. Remove the radio ignition interference capacitor bracket retaining bolt and

FRONT OF ENGINE

● REMOVE IN SEQUENCE SHOWN

LOWER INTAKE MANIFOLD

9300KG11

Lower intake manifold bolt removal sequence—3.0L (DOHC) engine

FRONT OF ENGINE

LOWER INTAKE MANIFOLD

7922KG16

Lower intake manifold bolt tightening sequence—3.0L (DOHC) engine

Item	Description
1	Bolt (2 Req'd)
2	Transducer Mounting Bracket
3	Stud Bolt (2 Req'd)
4	Bolt (2 Req'd)
5	Intake Manifold Support (2 Req'd)
6	EGR Valve to Exhaust Manifold Tube
7	EGR Valve
A	Tighten to 18-28 N·m (14-20 Lb-Ft)
B	Tighten to 25-35 N·m (19-25 Lb-Ft)

FRONT OF ENGINE

9300KG12

Exploded view of Transducer mounting bracket and intake manifold support with torque specification—3.4L (DOHC) engine

7922KG18

Exploded view of the upper intake manifold mounting—3.4L engine

position the radio ignition interference capacitor aside.

18. Remove the upper intake manifold bolts in the proper sequence.

✳✳ WARNING

When removing engine components such as manifolds and cylinder heads, always remove the bolts in a reverse order of their tightening sequence to prevent warpage to the component.

19. Remove the upper intake manifold and gaskets from the lower intake manifold.

To install:

20. Install the upper intake manifold using new gaskets onto the lower intake manifold. Install the upper manifold bolts and tighten, in sequence, to 14–20 ft. lbs. (18–28 Nm).

21. Install the radio ignition interference capacitor bracket and bolt and tighten to 71–106 inch lbs. (8–12 Nm).

22. Install the surge tank and align and tighten the intake air connector hose clamps.

23. Connect the right side crankcase ventilation hose.

24. Connect the vacuum tube to the pressure regulator.

25. Connect the crankcase ventilation tube to the surge tank and valve cover.

26. Install the rear surge tank stay and tighten the bolts and nuts to 14–20 ft. lbs. (18–28 Nm).

27. Install the front surge tank stay and tighten the bolts and nuts to 14–20 ft. lbs. (18–28 Nm).

28. Install the EGR valve.

29. Install the two intake manifold supports to the surge tank and cylinder head and tighten the bolts to 14–20 ft. lbs. (18–28 Nm).

30. Position the transducer mounting bracket to surge tank and tighten the bolts to 14–20 ft. lbs. (18–28 Nm).

31. Connect the vacuum tube-to-intake manifold vacuum union.

32. Connect the main emission vacuum supply hose to the surge tank vacuum fitting and EGR valve.

33. Install the throttle body.

34. Install the right half of the cowl vent screen.

35. Install the engine appearance cover.

36. Connect the negative battery cable. Run the engine and check for leaks and proper engine operation.

Timing belt service is covered in Section 5 of this manual

LOWER INTAKE MANIFOLD

1. Before servicing the vehicle, refer to the precautions at the beginning of this section.

2. Disconnect the negative battery cable. Relieve the fuel system pressure.

3. Disconnect the fuel injector wiring harness and move aside.

4. Remove the upper intake manifold.

5. Remove the fuel supply and return lines from the fuel injection supply manifold (fuel rail).

6. Disconnect the Intake Manifold Runner Control (IMRC) deactivation cable from the lower intake manifold. Remove the cable from the bracket and position aside.

7. Disconnect the engine control sensor wiring from the fuel injectors and wiring retainers and position the sensor wiring aside.

8. Remove the lower intake manifold-to-cylinder head bolts and remove the intake manifold and gaskets. Discard the gaskets.

To install:

9. Thoroughly clean the gasket sealing areas and place new intake-to-cylinder head gaskets into position.

10. Carefully, install the lower intake manifold and install the intake manifold-to-cylinder head bolts. Tighten the bolts to 14–20 ft. lbs. (18–28 Nm).

11. Connect the engine control sensor wiring to the fuel injectors.

12. Connect the Intake Manifold Runner Control (IMRC) deactivation cable to the lower intake manifold.

13. Install the fuel supply and return lines to the fuel injection supply manifold (fuel rail).

14. Install the upper intake manifold.

15. Connect the fuel injector wiring harness.

16. Connect the negative battery cable.

Exploded view of the lower intake manifold mounting—3.4L engine

Exhaust Manifold

REMOVAL & INSTALLATION

3.0L (DOHC) Engine

1. Before servicing the vehicle, refer to the precautions at the beginning of this section.

2. Disconnect the negative battery cable.

3. For the right side, perform the following procedures:

   a. Remove the upper intake manifold assembly.

   b. Remove the ignition coil assembly.

   c. Loosen the EGR valve-to-exhaust manifold tube nuts and remove the tube.

   d. Disconnect the wiring harness from the Oxygen (O_2S) sensor and remove the sensor if equipped.

4. Remove the secondary air injection manifold tube from the exhaust manifold.

5. Raise and safely support the vehicle.

6. Remove the dual converter Y-pipe nuts from the exhaust manifolds.

7. Remove both bolt and nut retainers from the transaxle.

8. Remove the two remaining nuts and bolts from the dual converter Y-pipe connection. Remove the Y-pipe from the vehicle.

9. Remove the lower exhaust manifold

Right side exhaust manifold mounting bolt tightening sequence—3.0L (DOHC) engine

Left side exhaust manifold mounting bolt tightening sequence—3.0L (DOHC) engine

nuts from the cylinder head studs and lower the vehicle.

10. Remove the upper exhaust manifold nuts from the cylinder head studs.

11. Remove the exhaust manifold and gasket from the engine.

12. Clean all gasket mating surfaces.

To install:

13. Install the exhaust manifold with a new exhaust manifold gasket.

14. Install the exhaust manifold studs and tighten, in sequence, to 13–16 ft. lbs. (18–22 Nm).

15. Raise and safely support the vehicle.

16. Position the Y-pipe assembly using a new flange gasket and install all the nuts and bolts loosely.

17. Starting at the front of the system tighten the Y-pipe-to-exhaust manifold nuts to 26–34 ft. lbs. (34–46 Nm).

18. Tighten the converter-to-transaxle nut and bolt to 30 ft. lbs. (40.3 Nm). Tighten the converter outlet bolts to 26–34 ft. lbs. (34–46 Nm).

19. Lower the vehicle.

20. Install the O_2S sensor and tighten to 26–34 ft. lbs. (35–46 Nm). Connect the electrical connector.

21. Install the secondary air injection manifold tube-to-exhaust manifold and tighten the nut to 28–31 ft. lbs. (38–42 Nm).

22. On the right side, perform the following procedures:

   a. Install the EGR valve-to-exhaust manifold tube and tighten the nuts to 26–33 ft. lbs. (35–45 Nm).

   b. Install the ignition coil assembly.

   c. Install the upper intake manifold assembly.

23. Connect the negative battery cable.

24. Run the engine and check for exhaust leaks and proper operation.

3.0L (OHV) Engine

LEFT SIDE

1. Before servicing the vehicle, refer to the precautions at the beginning of this section.

2. Disconnect the negative battery cable.

3. Remove oil level indicator tube support bracket nut. Remove the oil level indicator tube and move engine control sensor wiring aside.

4. Raise and safely support the vehicle.

5. Remove the exhaust manifold-to-exhaust pipe nuts.

6. Lower the vehicle.

7. Remove the four exhaust manifold bolts and two exhaust manifold stud bolts.

Remove the exhaust manifold from the vehicle.

To install:

8. Clean all mating surfaces and lightly oil all bolt and stud threads prior to installation.

9. Place the exhaust manifold into position on the cylinder head using a new gasket. Tighten the four exhaust manifold bolts and two stud bolts to 15–18 ft. lbs. (20–25 Nm).

10. Install the exhaust pipe-to-exhaust manifold and tighten the exhaust pipe attaching nuts to 25–34 ft. lbs. (34–47 Nm).

11. Install the oil level indicator tube. Tighten the bracket nut to 12–15 ft. lbs. (16–20 Nm). Reposition the engine control sensor wiring.

12. Connect negative battery cable.

13. Run the engine and check for exhaust leaks and proper operation.

RIGHT SIDE

1. Before servicing the vehicle, refer to the precautions at the beginning of this section.

2. Disconnect the negative battery cable.

3. Disconnect the EGR valve hoses. Remove the EGR tube from the exhaust manifold. Use a back-up wrench on the lower adapter.

4. Remove the three bolts from the exhaust manifold heat shield and remove the shield.

5. Raise and safely support the vehicle.

6. Remove the exhaust manifold-to-exhaust pipe nuts and separate the exhaust pipe from the exhaust manifold.

7. Lower the vehicle.

8. Remove the six exhaust manifold bolts and remove the exhaust manifold from the vehicle.

To install:

9. Clean all mating surfaces and lightly oil all bolt threads prior to installation.

10. Place the exhaust manifold into position on the cylinder head. Tighten the six exhaust manifold bolts to 15–18 ft. lbs. (20–25 Nm).

11. Raise and safely support the vehicle.

12. Position the exhaust pipe and install the nuts. Tighten the nuts to 25–34 ft. lbs. (34–47 Nm).

13. Install the exhaust manifold heat shield and install the three bolts. Tighten the bolts to 71–106 inch lbs. (8–12 Nm).

14. Lower the vehicle.

15. Install the EGR tube-to-exhaust manifold and tighten the tube nut to 26–48 ft. lbs. (35–65 Nm). Connect the EGR valve hoses.

16. Connect the negative battery cable.

17. Run the engine and check for exhaust leaks and proper operation.

3.4L Engine

LEFT SIDE

1. Before servicing the vehicle, refer to the precautions at the beginning of this section.

2. Disconnect the negative battery cable.

3. Raise and safely support the vehicle.

4. Remove the dual converter Y-pipe.

5. Remove the two lower exhaust manifold nuts.

6. Lower the vehicle.

7. Remove the secondary air injection manifold tube from the exhaust manifold.

8. Remove the three bolts and exhaust manifold shield from the exhaust manifold.

9. Remove the oil level indicator tube bolt.

10. Remove the four upper exhaust manifold nuts.

11. Remove the left side exhaust manifold and gasket.

To install:

12. Position the exhaust manifold to the engine, using a new gasket.

13. Install the four upper exhaust manifold nuts and tighten to 30–44 ft. lbs. (40–60 Nm).

14. Install the oil level indicator tube bolt.

15. Install the three bolts and exhaust manifold shield to the exhaust manifold and tighten to 12–16 ft. lbs. (16–23 Nm).

16. Install the secondary air injection manifold tube-to-exhaust manifold and tighten the nut to 29–33 ft. lbs. (40–45 Nm).

17. Raise and safely support the vehicle.

18. Install the two lower exhaust manifold nuts and tighten to 30–44 ft. lbs. (40–60 Nm).

19. Install the dual converter Y-pipe.

20. Lower the vehicle.

21. Connect the negative battery cable.

RIGHT SIDE

1. Before servicing the vehicle, refer to the precautions at the beginning of this section.

2. Disconnect the negative battery cable.

3. Remove the secondary air injection manifold tube from the exhaust manifold.

4. Remove the three bolts and exhaust manifold shield from the exhaust manifold.

5. Raise and safely support the vehicle.

6. Remove the EGR valve-to-exhaust manifold tube from the exhaust manifold.

7. Disconnect the EGR valve-to-exhaust manifold tube from the EGR transducer.

8. Remove the dual converter Y-pipe.

9. Remove the two lower exhaust manifold nuts.

10. Lower the vehicle.

11. Remove the four upper exhaust manifold nuts.

12. Raise and safely support the vehicle.

13. Remove the right side exhaust manifold and gasket.

To install:

14. Position the exhaust manifold to the engine, using a new gasket.

15. Install the four upper exhaust manifold nuts and tighten to 30–44 ft. lbs. (40–60 Nm).

16. Raise and safely support the vehicle.

17. Install the two lower exhaust manifold nuts and tighten to 30–44 ft. lbs. (40–60 Nm).

18. Install the dual converter Y-pipe.

19. Connect the EGR valve-to-exhaust manifold tube to the EGR transducer.

20. Install the EGR valve-to-exhaust manifold tube to the exhaust manifold.

21. Lower the vehicle.

22. Install the three bolts and exhaust manifold shield to the exhaust manifold and tighten to 12–16 ft. lbs. (16–23 Nm).

23. Install the secondary air injection manifold tube to the exhaust manifold.

24. Connect the negative battery cable.

Front Crankshaft Seal

REMOVAL & INSTALLATION

➡️**The front crankshaft oil seal procedure is only for timing belt-equipped engines. For engines equipped with timing chains or gears, refer to the procedures in this section.**

Camshaft and Valve Lifters

REMOVAL & INSTALLATION

✳✳ CAUTION

The fuel injection system remains under pressure, even after the engine has been turned OFF. The fuel system pressure must be relieved before disconnecting any fuel lines. Failure to do so may result in fire and/or personal injury.

3.0L (OHV) Engine

1. Before servicing the vehicle, refer to the precautions at the beginning of this section.

2. Disconnect the negative battery cable. Remove the engine from the vehicle and position on a suitable holding fixture.

3. Rotate the crankshaft to Top Dead Center (TDC) for No. 1 cylinder on its compression stroke.

4. Remove the upper intake manifold.

5. Disconnect the engine wiring harness connectors from the cylinder head cover stud bolts. Carefully, disconnect and remove the fuel injector harness connectors from each fuel injector and position aside.

6. Label and disconnect the ignition wires from the spark plugs. Remove the ignition wire separators from the cylinder head cover stud bolts.

7. Remove the Camshaft Position (CMP) sensor housing retainer bolt and washer and remove the CMP sensor housing.

8. Remove the ignition coil from the rear of the left cylinder head.

9. Remove the cylinder head covers.

Tighten the rocker arm nuts according to the position of the camshaft—3.0L (OHV) engine

7922KG30

10. Loosen the intake rocker arm fulcrum nut for No. 3 cylinder and rotate the rocker arm off the pushrod. Remove the pushrod.

11. Remove the accessory drive belt. Remove the drive belt tensioner, alternator and alternator brackets.

12. Remove the lower intake manifold leaving the fuel supply manifold (fuel rail) and fuel injectors in place.

13. Loosen the remaining rocker arm fulcrum nuts enough to allow the rocker arms to be lifted off the pushrods. Remove the remaining pushrods, identifying each pushrod for installation.

14. Remove the valve lifter guide plate retainer bolts and the valve lifter guide plate.

15. Using a suitable magnet or lifter removal tool, remove the hydraulic valve lifters and keep them in order so they can be installed in their original positions. If the valve lifters are stuck in the bores by excessive varnish, use a hydraulic lifter puller to remove the lifters.

16. Remove the crankshaft pulley bolts and the crankshaft pulley.

17. Remove the crankshaft damper bolt and washer. Remove the crankshaft damper using remover T58P-6316-D or equivalent puller and adapter T82L-6316-B or equivalent.

18. Remove the engine oil pan.

19. Remove the engine front cover bolts leaving the water pump attached. Remove the engine front cover.

20. Align the timing marks on the camshaft and crankshaft sprockets. Check the camshaft end-play as follows:

   a. Push the camshaft toward the rear of the engine and install a dial indicator tool, so the indicator point is on the camshaft sprocket attaching screw.

   b. Zero the dial indicator. Position a small prybar or equivalent, between the camshaft sprocket and block.

   c. Pull the camshaft forward and release it. Compare the dial indicator reading with the camshaft end-play service limit specification of 0.005 inch (0.13mm).

   d. If the camshaft end-play is over the amount specified, replace the thrust plate.

21. Remove the camshaft sprocket bolt and washer.

22. Inspect the timing chain for excessive deflection.

23. Grasp the camshaft sprocket and the crankshaft sprocket, then slide the timing chain and sprocket assembly off the engine.

24. Remove the two camshaft thrust plate bolts and the camshaft thrust plate. Discard the thrust plate if it was found to be worn beyond specifications made during the camshaft end-play check.

25. Carefully, remove the camshaft by pulling it toward the front of the engine. Remove it slowly to avoid damaging the bearings, journals and lobes.

26. Inspect the camshaft journals, lobes and bearings for wear and/or damage. Replace as necessary.

➡ **If replacing the camshaft, the valve lifters must also be replaced.**

To install:

27. Clean all gasket mating surfaces. Lubricate the camshaft lobes, journals, drive gear and bearing surfaces with engine assembly lubricant or equivalent. Carefully insert the camshaft through the bearings into the cylinder block.

28. Lubricate the camshaft thrust plate on both sides. Install the thrust plate and the two bolts. Tighten the bolts to 7 ft. lbs. (10 Nm).

➡ **If installing a new camshaft, check the camshaft end-play.**

29. Lubricate the timing chain and sprockets with engine assembly lubricant or equivalent and align the timing marks on the sprockets before installation.

30. Install the timing chain and sprocket assembly. Install the camshaft sprocket bolt. Tighten the camshaft sprocket bolt to 37–51 ft. lbs. (50–70 Nm).

❋❋ WARNING

The camshaft bolt has a drilled oil passage in it for timing chain lubrication. Be sure the passage is clean prior to bolt installation. If the bolt is damaged, do not replace the camshaft bolt with a standard bolt or engine damage will result.

31. Lubricate the valve lifters and lifter bores with engine assembly lubricant or equivalent. Install the valve lifters into their original bores.

32. Align the flat surfaces on the valve lifters and install the valve lifter guide plate. The plate must be installed with the word **UP** and/or a dimple on the plate visible. Install the two bolts and tighten to 8–10 ft. lbs. (10–14 Nm).

33. Install the lower intake manifold. Install the CMP sensor.

34. Lubricate the pushrods and rocker arms with engine assembly lubricant or equivalent. Install the pushrods into their original positions. Position each rocker arm onto its related pushrod.

35. Rotate the crankshaft to set each lifter on its base circle, then tighten the rocker arm bolts in two steps. Tighten the rocker arm bolts first to 5–11 ft. lbs. (7–15 Nm), then to 19–28 ft. lbs. (26–38 Nm).

36. If new valve lifters are being installed, check the collapsed valve lifter gaps. Clearance should be 0.085–0.185 inch (2.15–4.69mm) with the valve lifter installed and the camshaft lobe on its base circle.

37. Install the engine front cover and the engine oil pan.

38. Install the crankshaft damper and pulley. Tighten the crankshaft damper bolt to 93–121 ft. lbs. (125–165 Nm) and the four pulley bolts to 30–40 ft. lbs. (40–55 Nm).

39. Install the alternator and brackets.

40. Install the drive belt tensioner and the accessory drive belt.

41. Install the cylinder head covers.

42. Install the fuel injector harness to each fuel injector. Secure the harness to the cylinder head cover stud bolts.

43. Install the ignition coil to the left cylinder head. Tighten the bolts to 29–41 ft. lbs. (40–55 Nm).

44. Install the upper intake manifold.

45. Install the ignition wiring harness retainers to the cylinder head cover stud bolts and connect the ignition wires to the spark plugs and ignition coil.

46. Install the engine assembly into the vehicle.

47. Fill the engine cooling system.

48. Fill the crankcase with the correct amount and type of engine oil.

49. Connect the negative battery cable.

50. Start the engine and check for leaks and proper engine operation.

51. Check and adjust the ignition timing, if needed.

3.0L (DOHC) Engine

1. Before servicing the vehicle, refer to the precautions at the beginning of this section.

2. Disconnect the negative battery cable. Remove the engine assembly from the vehicle and place on an appropriate engine stand.

3. Remove the upper intake manifold. Remove both cylinder head covers.

To allow the camshaft to raise off the cylinder head evenly, remove the bolts in the sequence shown—3.0L (DOHC) engine

4. Remove the engine front cover.

5. Remove the crankshaft pulley and damper.

6. Remove the timing chains and rocker arms.

✳✳ WARNING

The camshaft journal thrust caps must be removed first, before loosening the remaining camshaft journal cap bolts, to ensure that the camshaft journal thrust caps are not damaged.

7. Loosen the camshaft journal cap bolts in sequence, in several passes, to allow the camshaft to raise off the cylinder head evenly.

✳✳ WARNING

The camshaft journal caps and cylinder heads are numbered to ensure that they are assembled in their original positions. Keep the camshaft journal caps from each cylinder head together. Do not mix with caps from another cylinder head. Failure to do so may result in engine damage.

8. Remove the camshaft journal caps with the bolts installed.

9. Remove the camshafts from the cylinder head, then repeat the procedure for both cylinder heads.

10. Pull the valve lifters out of their bores. Mark them so they can be installed in their original locations.

11. Inspect the camshafts and cylinder heads for wear or damage.

To install:

✳✳ WARNING

The crankshaft keyway must be at the 11 o'clock position before reassembly. Failure to do so may lead to engine damage.

12. Rotate the crankshaft so the keyway is at the 11 o'clock position for installation of the camshafts.

13. Lubricate the camshaft lobes and journals with engine assembly lubricant.

14. Install the valve lifters in their original positions.

15. Install the camshafts into their correct positions into each cylinder head with the timing marks on the camshaft sprockets aligned.

16. Loosely install the camshaft journal caps and bolts into their correct positions.

➡**Do not install the camshaft journal thrust caps until the rocker arms and timing chains have been installed and the camshaft journal caps are tightened into position.**

17. Install the timing chains.

18. Tighten the camshaft journal cap bolts, in sequence, to 71–106 inch lbs. (8–12 Nm). Install the thrust caps and tighten the bolts to 71–106 inch lbs. (8–12 Nm).

19. Install the engine front cover.

20. Install the crankshaft pulley and damper.

21. Install both cylinder head covers, then install the upper intake manifold.

➡**The cylinder head covers must be installed and properly tightened within six minutes of applying the silicone sealant.**

22. Install the engine assembly into the vehicle. Connect the negative battery cable.

23. Run the engine and check for leaks and proper engine operation.

3.4L Engine

1. Before servicing the vehicle, refer to the precautions at the beginning of this section.

✳✳ CAUTION

The fuel injection system remains under pressure, even after the engine has been turned OFF. The fuel system pressure must be relieved before disconnecting any fuel lines. Failure to do so may result in fire and/or personal injury.

2. Disconnect the negative battery cable. Properly relieve the fuel system pressure.

3. Remove the timing chain, sprockets and front cover.

4. Remove the timing chain sprocket tensioners from the cylinder heads.

Camshaft journal bolt tightening sequence—3.0L (DOHC) engine

Camshaft journal thrust cap bolt removal sequence—3.4L engine

Tighten the camshaft journal caps in sequence to avoid warping the camshafts—3.4L engine

5. Remove the camshaft timing chain sprocket tensioners from the cylinder heads.

6. Note the positions for reassembly and remove the cylinder head camshaft journal thrust cap bolts in the proper sequence. Remove thrust caps from the cylinder heads.

❄❄ **WARNING**

The cylinder head camshaft journal caps must be installed in their original positions.

7. Remove the timing chain and camshafts from the cylinder head.

8. Inspect the camshafts for wear and/or damage and replace, as necessary.

To install:

9. Apply a thin coat of clean engine oil to the camshaft bearing surfaces on the cylinder head and camshaft journal caps.

10. Rotate the crankshaft to position the No. 1 piston at Top Dead Center (TDC) by aligning the crankshaft keyway groove with the oil pump mark.

11. Install the timing chain on the intake and exhaust camshafts. Match the sprocket and chain timing marks and install the camshafts into the cylinder heads with the timing marks pointing up.

12. Apply a 0.08–0.11 inch (2–3mm) bead of silicone gasket and sealant to the left side cylinder head camshaft journal cap.

❄❄ **WARNING**

Be sure the camshaft journal caps are installed in their original positions.

13. Loosely install the cylinder head camshaft journal caps and bolts.

14. Tighten the cylinder head camshaft journal caps bolts, in sequence, and in two steps:

   a. First step: Tighten, in sequence, to 62–106 inch lbs. (7–12 Nm).

   b. Second step: Tighten, in sequence, to 12–15 ft. lbs. (16–21 Nm).

15. Install a new camshaft seal with a Cam Seal expander T89P-6256-B or equivalent, and Cam Seal Replacer T89-6256-A or equivalent.

16. Install a Cam Position Tool T96P-6256-AH or equivalent, on the left side intake cam and the right side exhaust cam using the existing cam chain tensioner bolts.

17. Install the timing chain, sprockets and front cover.

18. Connect the negative battery cable.

Valve Lash

ADJUSTMENT

3.0L (DOHC) Engines

The lash adjusters (valve tappets), are hydraulic and are not adjustable. It is important that all valve components are in good condition, installed and tightened properly.

3.0L (OHV) Engines

Hydraulic valve lifters are used and no valve clearance adjustment is available. A clearance check of the rocker arm-to-valve stem gap is required when machining has been done to the cylinder heads, valves, valve seats or cylinder block head gasket surfaces or when new valve train components have been installed. The clearance check is also useful in determining loose, worn or damaged parts when there is a concern with the valve train. Clearance must be checked when the lifter is completely collapsed.

1. Before servicing the vehicle, refer to

the precautions at the beginning of this section.

2. Disconnect the negative battery cable. Remove both rocker arm covers.

3. To check valve clearance, use Lifter Bleed Down Wrench T71P-6513-B or equivalent, to slowly push down on the pushrod end of the rocker arm and bleed the oil from the valve lifter.

4. Once the valve lifter is totally collapsed, insert the appropriate thickness feeler gauge between the rocker arm and valve stem to check the clearance. There should be 0.085–0.185 inch (2.15–4.69mm) clearance between the valve stem and rocker arm.

5. Rotate the crankshaft until the No. 1 cylinder is at Top Dead Center (TDC) of its compression stroke. With the engine in this position, the following valve clearances can be checked:

    a. Intake—1, 2 and 4

    b. Exhaust—1, 3 and 6

6. Rotate the crankshaft 360 degrees and check the following valves in the same manner:

    a. Intake—3, 5 and 6

    b. Exhaust—2, 4 and 5

7. If the clearance is not correct, check for loose, worn or damaged components. If no problems are found, the clearance can be adjusted by the use of shorter or longer pushrods.

3.4L Engine

1. Before servicing the vehicle, refer to the precautions at the beginning of this section.

2. Disconnect the negative battery cable. Remove the valve covers and intake manifold.

➡**The cam lobes must be directed 90 degrees or more away from the lash adjusters (valve tappets). The engine must be COLD to check the valve clearance.**

To measure the valve clearance, slide the feeler gauge between the base circle of the cam and the tappet—3.4L engine

Correct positioning of the tappet compressor and holder tools—3.4L engine

3. Insert a feeler gauge under the camshaft lobe at a 90 degree angle to the camshaft. Clearance for the intake valves should be 0.006–0.010 inch (0.15–0.25mm). Clearance for the exhaust valves should be 0.010–0.014 inch (0.25–0.35mm).

4. If no adjustments are required, install the cylinder head covers.

5. If adjustment is required, install Tappet Compressor T89P-6500-A or equivalent, under the camshaft next to the lobe and rotate the tool downward to depress the valve tappet.

6. Install Tappet Holder T96P-6500-AH or equivalent, and remove the compressor tool.

✻✻ CAUTION

Use eye protection when using compressed air to avoid possible personal injury.

7. Direct a jet of compressed air toward the hole in the face of the valve adjusting spacer to lift the valve adjusting spacer off of the valve tappet.

8. Determine the size of the adjusting spacer by the numbers on the bottom face of the spacer or by measuring with a micrometer.

9. Install the replacement adjusting spacer with the numbers down. Be sure the spacer is properly seated.

10. Release the tappet holder by installing the tappet compressor, then remove the tappet compressor.

11. Repeat the procedure for each valve requiring adjustment by rotating the crankshaft as necessary.

12. Check all adjusting spacers to ensure that they are properly seated.

13. Install the intake manifold and valve covers.

14. Connect the negative battery cable.

Run the engine and check for proper operation.

Oil Pan

REMOVAL & INSTALLATION

3.0L (OHV) Engines

1. Before servicing the vehicle, refer to the precautions at the beginning of this section.

2. Disconnect the negative battery cable. Remove the engine oil level dipstick.

3. Raise and safely support the vehicle. Drain the engine oil.

4. If equipped with a low oil level sensor, remove the retainer clip at the sensor. Disconnect the electrical connector from the sensor.

5. Remove the starter motor and brace.

6. Detach the connector from the Oxygen (O_2S) sensor(s).

7. Remove the catalytic converter and exhaust Y-pipe assembly.

8. Remove the engine rear plate from the torque converter housing.

9. Remove the 16 oil pan bolts and carefully remove the engine oil pan from the cylinder block. Remove the oil pan gasket.

To install:

10. Clean the gasket sealing surfaces on the cylinder block and the engine oil pan. Apply a ¼ inch (6mm) bead of silicone sealer to the junction of the front cover assembly and the cylinder block and to the junction of the rear main bearing cap and cylinder block.

➡**When using a silicone sealer, the assembly process should occur within five minutes after the sealer has been applied. Be sure the sealer does not fall into the engine and form plugs that could block oil passages.**

11. Place the oil pan gasket on the engine oil pan and secure with a suitable contact adhesive.

12. Place the engine oil pan into position on the cylinder block. Install the 16 engine oil pan bolts. Tighten the bolts to 8–10 ft. lbs. (10–14 Nm). Back off all bolts and retighten.

13. Install the remaining components in the reverse order of removal.

14. Connect the negative battery cable. Fill the crankcase with the proper type and quantity of engine oil, then start the engine and check for leaks and proper operation.

3.0L (DOHC) and 3.4L Engines

1. Before servicing the vehicle, refer to the precautions at the beginning of this section.

2. Disconnect the negative battery cable.

3. Raise and safely support the vehicle. Drain the engine oil.

4. Remove the dual catalytic converter Y-pipe nuts from the exhaust manifolds.

5. Remove the bolt and nut retainers from the transaxle.

6. Remove the two remaining nuts and bolts from the dual converter Y-pipe connection. Remove the Y-pipe from the vehicle.

7. Reinstall the oil pan drain plug using a new gasket and tighten to 16–22 ft. lbs. (22–30 Nm).

8. Remove the oil pan bolts from the transaxle housing.

9. Remove the access plug from the engine rear plate.

10. Remove the support bracket from the oil pan and transaxle.

11. Remove the oil pan bolts and studs from the lower cylinder block following the correct bolt removal sequence.

12. Remove the oil pan and the oil pan gasket from the vehicle.

13. If required, remove the oil pump screen and tube assembly from the oil pump.

To install:

14. Clean the oil pan to lower cylinder block gasket sealing surfaces.

15. Thoroughly clean the oil pan and mating surfaces with soap and water and dry completely with compressed air.

16. Clean the mating surfaces with Metal Surface Cleaner F4AZ9A536-RA or equivalent, to remove all the residues that may cause oil leakage.

17. If removed, install the oil pump screen and tube assembly to the oil pump using a new O-ring. Tighten the bolts to 71–106 inch lbs. (8–12 Nm). Install a new self-locking nut and tighten to 71–106 inch lbs. (8–12 Nm).

18. On the 3.0L engine, install a new oil pan gasket into the groove of the oil pan. Apply silicone sealer on the gasket at the places where the engine front cover meets the engine block.

19. On the 3.4L engine, apply a 0.16 inch (4mm) bead of silicone sealer on the entire oil pan sealing surface.

Oil Pan Removal Sequence

Item	Description
1	Upper Cylinder Block
2	Lower Cylinder Block (Part of 6010)
3	Oil Pan
4	Stud Bolt (5 Req'd)
5	Bolt (10 Req'd)
6	Oil Pan Gasket
7	Engine Front Cover

FRONT OF ENGINE

✶ LOCATION OF STUDS

● REMOVE BOLTS/STUDS IN SEQUENCE SHOWN

9300KG14

Remove the oil pan bolts in the sequence illustrated—3.0L (DOHC) engine

BOLT
90119-08229
16 REQ'D TIGHTEN TO
18-28 N·m (14-20 LB-FT)

7922KG39

Oil pan bolt tightening sequence—3.0L (DOHC) and 3.4L SHO engines

For complete mechanical specifications, refer to Section 1 of this manual

APPLY SILICONE GASKET AND SEALANT F6AZ-19562-AA

FRONT OF ENGINE

OIL PAN

7922KG40

Apply silicone sealant to the entire sealing surface of the oil pan—3.0L (DOHC) and 3.4L SHO engines

20. Carefully install the oil pan with gasket to the lower cylinder block. Install the bolts and studs but do not tighten.

21. Push the oil pan against the transaxle case and tighten the oil pan bolts and studs, finger-tight.

22. Tighten the oil pan bolts and studs in the proper sequence to 15–22 ft. lbs. (20–30 Nm).

23. Tighten the oil pan-to-transaxle case bolts to 25–34 ft. lbs. (34–46 Nm).

24. Install the transaxle support bracket to the oil pan stud bolts and transaxle. Tighten the nuts to 71–106 inch lbs. (8–12 Nm). Tighten the bolts to 15–22 ft. lbs. (20–30 Nm).

25. Install the access plug into the engine rear plate.

26. Position the Y-pipe assembly using a new flange gasket and install all of the nuts and bolts loosely.

27. Starting at the front of the system tighten the Y-pipe-to-exhaust manifold nuts to 26–34 ft. lbs. (34–46 Nm). Tighten the converter-to-transaxle nut and bolt to 30 ft. lbs. (40.3 Nm). Tighten the converter outlet bolts to 26–34 ft. lbs. (34–46 Nm).

28. Replace the engine oil filter.

29. Lower the vehicle.

30. Fill the crankcase with the correct amount and grade of engine oil.

❈❈ WARNING

Operating the engine without the proper amount and type of engine oil will result in severe engine damage.

31. Connect the negative battery cable. Run the engine and check for leaks and proper operation.

Oil Pump

REMOVAL & INSTALLATION

3.0L (OHV) Engines

1. Before servicing the vehicle, refer to the precautions at the beginning of this section.

2. Disconnect the negative battery cable.

3. Raise and safely support the vehicle. Drain the engine oil.

4. Remove the engine oil pan.

Oil Pump

FRONT OF ENGINE

Intermediate Shaft

7922KG42

Exploded view of the oil pump mounting—3.0L (OHV) engine

5. Remove the oil pump bolt, the oil pump and the oil pump intermediate shaft from the engine.

6. If replacing the engine oil pump, separate the intermediate shaft from the oil pump.

To install:

7. If replacing the engine oil pump, insert the oil pump intermediate shaft into the new oil pump assembly until the intermediate shaft retaining ring clicks into place.

8. Prime the new oil pump by filling either the inlet or the outlet port with engine oil. Rotate the pump shaft to distribute the oil within the oil pump body cavity.

9. Insert the oil pump intermediate shaft assembly through the hole in the rear main bearing cap and place the oil pump onto the locating pins.

10. Install the oil pump bolt and tighten the bolt to 30–40 ft. lbs. (40–55 Nm).

11. Install the engine oil pan.

12. Lower the vehicle. Fill the crankcase with the proper type and quantity of engine oil.

13. Connect the negative battery cable. Start engine and check for leaks, proper oil pressure and proper engine operation.

3.0L (DOHC) Engine

1. Before servicing the vehicle, refer to the precautions at the beginning of this section.

2. Disconnect the negative battery cable. Remove the engine from the vehicle.

3. Remove the engine oil pan and the engine front cover.

4. Remove the timing chains and the crankshaft sprockets.

5. Remove the oil pump screen cover/tube nut/bolts and the tube from the engine.

6. Remove the four oil pump bolts in sequence. Remove the oil pump from the vehicle.

To install:

7. Rotate the inner rotor of the oil pump to align with the flats on the crankshaft. Install the oil pump flush to the cylinder block.

8. Install the oil pump bolts and tighten in sequence to 71–106 inch lbs. (8–12 Nm).

9. Inspect the oil pump screen and tube O-ring and replace, if necessary.

10. Position the oil pump screen and tube with the O-ring to the oil pump. Tighten the bolts to 71–106 inch lbs. (8–12 Nm).

● REMOVE BOLTS IN SEQUENCE SHOWN

CRANKSHAFT

OIL PUMP

1

2

4

3

BOLT
4 REQ'D

FRONT OF
ENGINE

CYLINDER BLOCK

9300KG15

Oil pump bolts removal sequence—3.0L (DOHC) engine—3.4L SHO engine is similar

CRANKSHAFT

OIL PUMP

4

3

1

2

BOLT
M6 X 1.0 X 33.5
4 REQ'D
TIGHTEN TO
8-12 N·m
(71-106 LB-IN)

FRONT OF ENGINE

CYLINDER BLOCK

7922KG43

Tighten the oil pump bolts in the proper sequence to ensure sealing to the engine block—3.0L (DOHC) engine—3.4L SHO engine is similar

11. Install a new self-locking tube support nut to the lower cylinder block stud. Tighten the nut to 15–22 ft. lbs. (20–30 Nm).

12. Install the crankshaft sprockets and the timing chains.

13. Install the oil pan and the engine front cover.

14. Install the engine in the vehicle. Fill the crankcase with the correct amount of engine oil.

15. Connect the negative battery cable. Run the engine and check for leaks and proper operation.

3.4L Engine

1. Before servicing the vehicle, refer to the precautions at the beginning of this section.

2. Disconnect the negative battery cable. Remove the engine from the vehicle.

3. Remove the engine oil pan and the engine front cover.

4. Remove the timing chains and the crankshaft sprockets.

5. Remove the oil pump screen cover/tube nut/bolts and the tube from the engine.

6. Remove the four oil pump bolts in sequence. Remove the oil pump from the vehicle.

To install:

7. Rotate the inner rotor of the oil pump to align with the flats on the crankshaft. Install the oil pump flush to the cylinder block.

8. Install the oil pump bolts and tighten, in sequence, to 80–115 inch lbs. (9–13 Nm).

9. Inspect the oil pump screen and tube O-ring and replace, if necessary.

10. Position the oil pump screen and tube with the O-ring to the oil pump. Tighten the oil pump tube-to-oil pump nuts to 71–123 inch lbs. (8–14 Nm) and the oil pump tube bracket-to-block nuts to 11–18 ft. lbs. (14–25 Nm).

11. Install the crankshaft sprockets and the timing chains.

12. Install the oil pan and the engine front cover.

13. Install the engine in the vehicle. Fill the crankcase with the correct amount of engine oil.

14. Connect the negative battery cable. Run the engine and check for leaks and proper operation.

Please refer to Section 9 for electric cooling fan wiring schematics

FRONT OF ENGINE

Item	Description
1	Cylinder Block
2	Oil Pan Baffle
3	Nut (5 Req'd)
4	Nut (2 Req'd)
5	Oil Pump Screen Cover and Tube
6	Oil Pump Inlet Tube Gasket
7	Oil Pump
A	Tighten to 14-25 Nm (11-18 Lb-Ft)
B	Tighten to 8-14 Nm (71-123 Lb-In)

9300KG16

Exploded view of the oil pump pick-up tube and screen mounting—3.4L SHO engine—3.0L (DOHC) engine is similar

Rear Main Seal

REMOVAL & INSTALLATION

3.0L (OHV) Engines

1. Before servicing the vehicle, refer to the precautions at the beginning of this section.
2. Disconnect the negative battery cable.
3. Raise and safely support the vehicle.
4. Remove the transaxle assembly.
5. Remove the flywheel.

➡**Use care to avoid damaging the crankshaft oil seal surface.**

6. Using a sharp pick or similar tool, punch a hole in the rear crankshaft seal between the seal lip and the cylinder block.
7. Screw in the threaded end of a jet plug remover or similar tool and remove the rear crankshaft seal.

To install:

8. Inspect the crankshaft seal area for

any damage which may cause the seal to leak. If damage is evident, service or replace the crankshaft as necessary.
9. Coat the crankshaft seal area and the seal lip with clean engine oil.
10. Place the rear crankshaft seal on Seal Replacer T88L-6701-A or equivalent, and position the tool and seal to the rear of the cylinder block with three bolts. Alternately, tighten the bolts to properly seat the seal. The seal must be flush or within 0.020 inch (0.50mm) of the cylinder block surface. Do not bottom the seal.
11. Install the flywheel. Tighten the bolts to 54–64 ft. lbs. (73–87 Nm).
12. Install the transaxle assembly.
13. Lower the vehicle.
14. Connect the negative battery cable.
15. Run the engine and check for leaks.
16. Road test the vehicle and check for proper engine and transaxle operation.

3.0L (DOHC) and 3.4L Engines

1. Before servicing the vehicle, refer to the precautions at the beginning of this section.
2. Disconnect the negative battery cable.
3. Raise and safely support the vehicle.
4. Remove the transaxle assembly.
5. Remove the flywheel.

➡**Use care not to scratch the crankshaft or the crankshaft retainer oil sealing surfaces when removing the rear crankshaft seal.**

6. Use Seal Remover T92C-6700-CH (3.0L) or T95P-6700-EH (3.4L) or equivalent, to remove the rear crankshaft seal.

➡**If the removal tool is going to rest against the back of the crankshaft, place a piece of thin copper or other soft metal 0.010 inch (0.25mm) thick, between the tool and the rear face of the crankshaft to protect the surface of the crankshaft.**

To install:

7. Clean and inspect the rear crankshaft seal sealing surfaces on the crankshaft and the cylinder block.
8. Lubricate the crankshaft flange and the rear crankshaft seal bore with engine assembly lubricant.
9. Install the rear main oil seal using Rear Seal Replacer T82L-6701-A and adapter T91P-6701-A or equivalents.
10. Alternate tightening the bolts to pull the rear crankshaft seal in evenly. Seat the

rear crankshaft seal flush to the rear of the cylinder block.

11. Install the flywheel. Install the flywheel bolts and tighten in a standard sequence to 54–64 ft. lbs. (73–87 Nm).

12. Install the transaxle.

13. Connect the negative battery cable.

14. Run the engine and check for leaks and proper operation.

Timing Chain, Sprockets and Front Cover and Seal

REMOVAL & INSTALLATION

3.0L (OHV) Engine

1. Before servicing the vehicle, refer to the precautions at the beginning of this section.

2. Disconnect the negative battery cable, then drain the engine cooling system.

3. Loosen four water pump pulley bolts while the accessory drive belt is in place.

4. Remove the accessory drive belts. Remove the idler pulley or automatic tensioner, as necessary.

5. Remove the lower radiator hose and the heater hose from the water pump and front cover.

6. Remove the crankshaft pulley and damper.

7. On flexible fuel vehicles, remove the Crankshaft Position (CKP) sensor.

8. Drain the engine oil and remove the oil pan.

9. If necessary, unfasten the water pump pulley bolts, then remove the pulley.

10. Remove the bolts from the timing cover to the cylinder block and remove the timing cover.

11. Tap the seal out of the cover with a seal driver.

12. Remove the crankshaft damper and timing chain front cover.

13. Rotate the crankshaft until the No. 1 piston is at Top Dead Center (TDC) of its compression stroke and the timing marks are aligned.

14. Remove the camshaft sprocket attaching bolt and washer. Slide both sprockets and timing chain forward and remove as an assembly.

15. Check the timing chain and sprockets for excessive wear. Replace if necessary.

To install:

16. Before installation, clean and inspect all parts. Clean the gasket material and dirt from the oil pan, cylinder block and front cover.

17. Slide both sprockets and timing chain onto the camshaft and crankshaft with the timing marks aligned. Install the camshaft bolt and washer and tighten to 46 ft. lbs. (63 Nm). Apply clean engine oil to the timing chain and sprockets after installation.

➡ **The camshaft bolt has a drilled oil passage in it for timing chain lubrication. Prior to installation, clean the passage and be sure it is clear. Never replace the camshaft bolt with a standard bolt.**

18. Lightly oil all bolt and stud threads except bolts 1, 2 and 3 that require a suitable pipe sealant.

19. Install a new seal in the timing cover.

20. Install a new timing cover gasket over the cylinder block dowels.

21. Install the timing cover/water pump assembly onto the cylinder block with the water pump pulley loosely attached to the water pump hub.

22. Apply a non-hardening sealant to bolt numbers 1, 2 and 3 and hand start them along with the rest of the cover bolts. Tighten bolts 1–10 to 19 ft. lbs. (25 Nm) and bolts 11–15 to 84 inch lbs. (10 Nm).

23. Install the engine oil pan. Tighten the bolts to 108 inch lbs. (12 Nm).

24. Hand-tighten the water pump pulley bolts.

25. Install the crankshaft damper and pulley. Tighten the damper bolt to 107 ft. lbs. (145 Nm).

26. On flexible fuel vehicles, install the CKP sensor. Tighten the bolt to 44–61 inch lbs. (5–7 Nm).

27. Install the automatic belt tensioner or idler pulley, as necessary.

28. Install the water pump and accessory drive belts. Tighten the water pump pulley bolts to 16 ft. lbs. (21 Nm).

29. Install the lower radiator hose and the heater hose and tighten the clamps.

30. Fill the crankcase with the correct amount and type of engine oil. Fill and bleed the engine cooling system.

31. Connect the negative battery cable. Start the engine and check for coolant and oil leaks. Road test the vehicle and check for proper operation.

3.0L (DOHC) Engine

1. Before servicing the vehicle, refer to the precautions at the beginning of this section.

2. Disconnect the negative battery cable.

3. Remove the engine from vehicle and position on a suitable workstand.

4. Remove the upper and lower intake manifolds.

5. Remove the cylinder head covers, then remove the drive belt.

6. Remove the wire connector from the water temperature sender.

7. Remove the heater water hose from the bypass tube.

CAMSHAFT SPROCKET

TIMING MARKS MUST BE IN POSITION SHOWN WITH NO. 1 PISTON AT TDC FIRING

TIMING CHAIN

CRANKSHAFT SPROCKET

7922KG47

Be sure the timing marks are facing each other after the chain has been installed—3.0L (OHV) engine

| Fastener And Hole | Fasteners | | Torque Specifications | |
No.	Size	Fastener Application	N·m	LB-FT
1A	M8 x 1.25 x 43.5	F/C TO BLOCK	20-30	15-22
2A	M8 x 1.25 x 43.5	F/C TO BLOCK	20-30	15-22
3A	M8 x 1.25 x 73	W/P & F/C TO BLOCK	20-30	15-22
4A	M8 x 1.25 x 104 3	W/P & F/C TO BLOCK	20-30	15-22
5A	M8 x 1.25 x 73	F/C TO BLOCK	20-30	15-22
6A	M8 x 1.25 x 73	W/P & F/C TO BLOCK	20-30	15-22
7A	M8 x 1.25 x 73	W/P & F/C TO BLOCK	20-30	15-22
8A	M8 x 1 25 x 104.3	W/P & F/C TO BLOCK	20-30	15-22
9A	M8 x 1.25 x 104.3	W/P & F/C TO BLOCK	20-30	15-22
10A	M8 x 1.25 x 52	F/C TO BLOCK	20-30	15-22
11B	M6 x 1 x 28.5	W/P TO F/C	8-12	71-106 (lb-in)
12B	M6 x 1 x 28.5	W/P TO F/C	8-12	71-106 (lb-in)
13B	M6 x 1 x 28.5	W/P TO F/C	8-12	71-106 (lb-in)
14B	M6 x 1 x 28.5	W/P TO F/C	8-12	71-106 (lb-in)
15B	M6 x 1 x 28.5	W/P TO F/C	8-12	71-106 (lb-in)

W/P—Water Pump

F/C—Engine Front Cover

7922KG48

Timing chain front cover bolt location and identification—3.0L (OHV) engine

8. Remove the bypass tube bolts and the tube.

9. Remove the power steering pump bolts and the pump.

10. Remove the A/C compressor bracket-to-water pump brace, the mounting bolts, the compressor and bracket.

➡**The A/C mounting bracket bolts are torque-to-yield bolts and must be replaced when removed.**

11. Remove the alternator and the water pump.

12. Install Flywheel Holding tool T74P-6375-A or equivalent, to keep the crankshaft from rotating.

13. Remove the crankshaft accessory pulley and bracket.

➡**Rotate the pulley shaft clockwise to remove. Use a 24mm open end wrench on the inside nut to remove the pulley.**

14. Remove the crankshaft pulley bolt and washer.

15. Install a suitable damper puller and remove the crankshaft damper from the crankshaft.

16. Remove the flywheel holding tool.

17. Detach the wiring from the Crankshaft Position (CKP) sensor and the Camshaft Position (CMP) sensor connectors.

18. Remove the engine oil pan, remove the bolts in sequence.

19. Remove the engine front cover bolts, in sequence, the front cover and gasket.

20. Rotate the crankshaft so the keyway is at the 11 o'clock position to locate the crankshaft at TDC for No. 1 cylinder.

21. Verify that the alignment arrows on the camshafts are aligned. If not, rotate the

1 RH Exhaust Camshaft	6 Timing Chain Tensioner
2 RH Intake Camshaft	7 Bolt (2 Req'd)
3 RH Timing Chain Crankshaft Sprocket	8 Timing Chain Tensioner Arm
4 RH Timing Chain	9 Timing Chain Guide
5 Bolt (2 Req'd)	10 RH Cylinder Head
	A Tighten to 20-30 N·m (15-22 Lb-Ft)

7922KG49

Exploded view of the right cylinder head timing chain and related components—3.0L (DOHC) engine—left side similar

crankshaft one complete revolution and recheck.

22. Rotate the crankshaft so the keyway is at the 3 o'clock position. This positions the right cylinder head camshafts to the neutral position.

23. Remove the right cylinder head timing chain tensioner bolts and tensioner.

24. Remove the right cylinder head timing chain tensioner arm and the timing chain.

25. Remove the right cylinder head timing chain guide bolts and guide; if worn, replace the timing chain guide.

26. Remove the right crankshaft timing chain sprocket.

27. Remove the right cylinder head camshaft timing chain sprockets, if being replaced.

28. Rotate the crankshaft two revolutions and locate the crankshaft keyway at the 11 o'clock position. This will position the left cylinder head camshafts to their neutral position.

29. Verify that the alignment arrows on the camshafts are aligned.

30. Remove the left cylinder head timing chain tensioner bolts and the timing chain tensioner.

➡ **If the left cylinder head timing chain tensioner arm and timing chain guide are to be reused, mark the position of the timing chain tensioner arm and the timing chain guide so they are reassembled into their original positions.**

31. Remove the left cylinder head timing chain tensioner arm and the timing chain.

32. Remove the left cylinder head timing chain guide bolts and guide; if worn, replace the timing chain guide.

33. Remove the left crankshaft timing chain sprocket.

34. If required, the left cylinder head camshaft sprockets may be removed at this time.

To install:

➡ **Inspect the timing chains, tensioners, tensioner arms, guides and sprockets for wear or damage. If any components are to be replaced for premature wear or damage, the camshaft damper should also be replaced.**

35. Reinstall or replace the camshaft sprockets, if removed.

36. Be sure the crankshaft keyway is still at the 11 o'clock position.

37. Install the left timing chain crankshaft sprocket onto the crankshaft.

38. Install the left timing chain guide and bolts to the engine. Tighten the bolts to 15–22 ft. lbs. (20–30 Nm).

39. Verify that the arrows on the left cylinder head camshafts are aligned.

40. Install the left timing chain over the left crankshaft sprocket and the left camshaft sprockets.

41. Align the timing marks on the left cylinder head timing chain with the timing marks on the crankshaft sprocket and the camshaft sprockets.

42. Install the left timing chain tensioner arm over the alignment dowel on the left cylinder head.

➡ **Before installing the timing chain tensioner, it must be properly compressed and locked.**

43. Using a small prybar, release the timing chain tensioner ratchet/pawl mechanism through the access hole in the timing chain tensioner as follows:

   a. Insert a small piece of wire into the top of the piston and gently unseat the oil check ball.

   b. Compress the timing chain tensioner by hand.

   c. With the tensioner compressed, install a 0.060 inch (1.5mm) drill bit or wire into the small hole above the ratchet, engaging the lock groove in the rack of the timing chain tensioner.

44. Install the compressed and locked left cylinder head timing chain tensioner and bolts onto the cylinder block. Tighten the bolts to 15–22 ft. lbs. (20–30 Nm).

NOTE: UNSEAT CHECK BALL WITH SMALL WIRE. COMPRESS TENSIONER AND INSTALL LOCK PIN PRIOR TO INSTALLATION ON ENGINE.

7922KG50

Be sure to compress the tensioner before installing it on the engine—3.0L (DOHC) engine

Timing belt service is covered in Section 5 of this manual

45. Verify that the timing marks on the left timing chain are in alignment with the timing marks on the crankshaft sprocket and the camshaft sprockets.

46. Reinstall or replace the camshaft sprockets, if removed.

47. Install the right timing chain crankshaft sprocket onto the crankshaft.

48. Install the right timing chain guide and bolts to the engine. Tighten the bolts to 15–22 ft. lbs. (20–30 Nm).

49. Verify that the arrows on the right cylinder head camshafts are aligned.

50. Install the right timing chain over the right crankshaft sprocket and the right camshaft sprockets.

51. Align the timing marks on the right cylinder head timing chain with the timing marks on the crankshaft sprocket and camshaft sprockets.

52. Install the right timing chain tensioner arm over the alignment dowel on the right cylinder head.

➡ **Before installing the timing chain tensioner, it must be properly compressed and locked.**

53. Using a small prybar, release the timing chain tensioner ratchet/pawl mechanism through the access hole in the timing chain tensioner as follows:

　a. Insert a small wire into the top of the piston and gently unseat the oil check ball.

　b. Compress the timing chain tensioner by hand.

　c. With the tensioner compressed, install a 0.060 inch (1.5mm) drill bit or wire into the small hole above the ratchet, engaging the lock groove in the rack of the timing chain tensioner.

54. Install the compressed and locked right cylinder head timing chain tensioner and bolts onto the cylinder block. Tighten the bolts to 15–22 ft. lbs. (20–30 Nm).

55. Verify that the timing marks on the right timing chain are aligned with the timing marks on the crankshaft sprocket and the camshaft sprockets.

56. Be sure the crankshaft keyway is at the 11 o'clock position.

57. Rotate the crankshaft two revolutions and position the crankshaft keyway to the 3 o'clock location. This will position the right cylinder head camshafts to the neutral position.

58. Remove the lock pins from the timing chain tensioners.

59. Verify that the timing marks on the timing chains are aligned with the timing marks on the crankshaft sprocket and camshaft sprockets.

RH CAMSHAFT TIMING INDEX MARKS

11 O'CLOCK POSITION (TDC NO. 1 CYLINDER)

CRANKSHAFT TIMING INDEX MARK

* **NOTE: AT TDC NO. 1 FIRING POSITION, ARROWS ON BACK OF CAMSHAFT SPROCKETS POINT DIRECTLY AT EACH OTHER**

7922KG51

Be sure the timing marks are as shown after the chain has been installed—3.0L (DOHC) engine

FRONT OF ENGINE

* LOCATION OF STUDS FOUR PLACES

● TIGHTEN BOLTS/STUDS IN SEQUENCE SHOWN FINGER-TIGHT

* STUD LOCATIONS

7922KG52

To prevent leaks, tighten the front cover bolts in the sequence shown—3.0L (DOHC) engine

60. Clean the engine front and the front cover-to-cylinder block gasket sealing surfaces.

➡ **The front cover must be installed and properly tightened within six minutes of the application of the sealer.**

61. Apply silicone sealer to the six critical areas of the cylinder block to prevent oil seepage.

62. Place new front cover gaskets onto the dowel pins on the cylinder block and heads.

63. Place the front cover into position by

placing the front cover onto the dowel pins at the cylinder block.

64. Install the six front cover bolts and stud bolts where the silicone sealer was applied.

65. Tighten the bolts and stud bolts until the front cover contacts the cylinder block and heads; then, turn the bolts and stud bolts an additional ¼ turn.

66. Install the remaining front cover bolts and stud bolts. Tighten all of the front cover bolts and stud bolts, in sequence, to 15–22 ft. lbs. (20–30 Nm).

67. If removed, install the belt tensioner onto the right side of the engine front cover. Tighten the bolt to 15–22 ft. lbs. (20–30 Nm).

68. Install a new oil pan gasket and apply a thin bead of silicone sealer where the timing cover meets the cylinder block.

69. Install the oil pan and install the bolts loosely.

70. With the oil pan aligned to the rear of the cylinder block, tighten the oil pan bolts and studs, in sequence, to 15–22 ft. lbs. (20–30 Nm) no more than six minutes after applying the silicone sealer.

71. Connect the wiring to the CKP and CMP sensors.

72. Install Flywheel Holding tool T74P-6375-A or equivalent, to keep the crankshaft from rotating.

73. Install the crankshaft damper using Crankshaft Damper Replacer T74P-6316-B or equivalent.

74. Apply a thin coating of silicone sealer to the front of the crankshaft on the inside diameter of the damper at the keyway before installing the washer and bolt.

75. Install the crankshaft damper pulley washer and bolt and tighten the bolt as follows:

   a. Tighten the bolt to 89 ft. lbs. (120 Nm) and loosen the bolt.

   b. Retighten the bolt to 39 ft. lbs. (53 Nm).

   c. Turn the bolt an additional 90 degrees.

76. Install the accessory drive crankshaft pulley and bracket. Using a 34mm socket, tighten the pulley counterclockwise to 70–77 ft. lbs. (95–105 Nm), tighten the bracket nuts to 15–22 ft. lbs. (20–30 Nm). Remove the flywheel holding tool.

77. Install the water pump and nuts and tighten to 15–22 ft. lbs. (20–30 Nm).

78. Install the alternator and the bolts. Tighten the bolts to 15–22 ft. lbs. (20–30 Nm). Connect the wiring connector.

The A/C compressor mounting bracket must engage in the front cover dowels or an engine vibration may occur. New torque-to-yield bolts must be used.

79. Install the A/C compressor mounting bracket. Tighten the bolts to 18 ft. lbs. (25 Nm); then, tighten an additional 90 degrees.

80. Install the A/C compressor and bolts. Tighten the bolts to 15–22 ft. lbs. (20–30 Nm).

81. Tighten the A/C compressor mounting bracket-to-water pump brace nuts to 15–22 ft. lbs. (20–30 Nm).

82. Replace the water bypass tube O-ring and lubricate with clean coolant. Install the bypass tube onto the right cylinder head and install the stud and bolt. Tighten the stud and bolt to 71–106 inch lbs. (8–12 Nm).

83. Install the heater water hose and position the hose clamp. Install the wire connector to the water temperature sender.

84. Install the power steering pump and tighten the bolts to 71–106 inch lbs. (8–12 Nm).

85. Install both cylinder head covers.

➡ **The cylinder head covers must be installed and properly tightened within six minutes of applying the silicone sealant.**

86. Install the lower and upper intake manifolds.

87. Release the accessory drive belt tension by rotating the tensioner clockwise and installing the drive belt.

88. Install the engine assembly into the vehicle. Restore all fluid levels. Connect the negative battery cable.

89. Run the engine and check for leaks. Road test the vehicle and check for proper operation.

3.4L Engine

EXCEPT FRONT SEAL

1. Before servicing the vehicle, refer to the precautions at the beginning of this section.

2. Disconnect the negative battery cable.

3. Remove the engine from vehicle and position on a suitable workstand.

4. Release the accessory drive belt tension by rotating the tensioner counterclockwise.

5. Remove the A/C compressor mount-

ing bolts from the cylinder blocks and remove the A/C compressor.

6. Release the water pump drive belt tension by rotating the tensioner clockwise and remove the belt.

7. Remove the three water pump drive pulley bolts from the left side camshaft.

8. Disconnect the main emission vacuum supply hose from the surge tank vacuum fitting, secondary air injection diverter valve and EGR valve.

9. Disconnect the engine control sensor wiring from the EGR backpressure transducer, EGR vacuum regulator solenoid and secondary air injection control solenoid vacuum valve.

10. Disconnect the EGR pressure sensor valve hoses from the EGR valve-to-exhaust manifold tube and remove the transducer mounting bracket from the engine.

11. Remove the EGR valve-to-exhaust manifold tube.

12. Remove the two intake manifold supports from the surge tank and cylinder head.

13. Remove the bolts and surge tank stay from the front of the surge tank.

14. Remove the bolt, nuts and surge tank stay from the rear of the surge tank.

15. Loosen the intake air connector hose clamps and remove the surge tank from the engine.

16. Disconnect the engine control sensor wiring connections from the Idle Air Control (IAC) valve and the Throttle Position (TP) sensor.

17. Remove the right and left intake manifolds from the lower intake manifold.

18. Disconnect and tag the engine control sensor wiring connections to components, as necessary.

19. Remove the exhaust air supply tube from the exhaust manifolds and secondary air injection diverter valve.

20. Remove the secondary air injection diverter valve, as necessary.

21. Remove the water pump and hoses.

22. Remove the left and right valve covers.

23. Remove the power steering pump and pump support.

24. Remove the crankshaft pulley.

25. Remove the Camshaft Position (CMP) sensor from the left cylinder head and the Crankshaft Position (CKP) sensor from the engine front cover, as necessary.

26. Drain the engine oil and remove the oil pan.

27. Remove the drive belt idler pulleys from the engine front cover.

28. Remove the engine front cover.

29. Remove the CKP sensor pulse ring from the crankshaft.

30. Rotate the crankshaft to position the No. 1 piston at Top Dead Center (TDC) by aligning the crankshaft keyway groove with the oil pump mark.

31. Verify that the alignment on the camshafts sprockets are on top. If not, rotate the crankshaft one complete revolution and recheck.

32. Remove the timing chain guides, tensioner arm and tensioner bolts and remove the timing chain from the engine.

33. Using a small prybar, release the timing chain tensioner ratchet/pawl mechanism through the access hole in the timing chain tensioner. Compress the timing chain tensioner rack and piston into the tensioner housing by inserting a small wire into the top of the piston and gently unseat the oil check ball. Compress the timing chain tensioner by hand.

❋❋ WARNING

Failure to compress and lock the timing chain tensioner prior to installation may cause damage to the engine.

34. With the tensioner compressed, install a 0.060 inch (1.5mm) drill bit or wire into the small hole above the ratchet, engaging the lock groove in the rack of the timing chain tensioner.

35. Remove the camshaft timing chain sprockets, if being replaced.

To install:

➡ **Inspect the timing chains, tensioners, tensioner arms, guides and sprockets for wear or damage and replace, as necessary.**

36. Rotate the crankshaft to position the No. 1 piston at Top Dead Center (TDC) by aligning the crankshaft keyway groove with the oil pump mark.

❋❋ WARNING

Do not rotate the crankshaft more than 45 degrees counterclockwise or more than 90 degrees clockwise from the previously set No. 1 cylinder TDC position or valve to piston contact could occur.

37. Match the sprocket and chain timing marks and install the timing chain with the crankshaft, camshaft and balance shaft correctly aligned.

38. Reinstall or replace the camshaft sprockets, if removed, and tighten the bolt to 48–70 ft. lbs. (64–95 Nm).

39. Install the compressed timing chain guides, tensioner arm and tensioner. Tighten the timing chain tensioner pivot bolt to 25–39 ft. lbs. (34–53 Nm). Tighten the timing chain tensioner bolts to 14–20 ft. lbs. (18–27 Nm).

40. Verify the timing index marks on the timing chain are in alignment with the index marks on the crankshaft sprocket, camshaft sprocket and balance shaft driven gear.

41. Install the power steering pump and pump support and tighten the three bolts to 14–20 ft. lbs. (18–28 Nm).

42. Install the CKP sensor pulse ring onto the crankshaft aligning the crankshaft key with the keyway on the sensor ring.

43. Clean the engine front and the front cover-to-cylinder block gasket sealing surfaces.

➡ **The front cover must be installed and properly tightened within six minutes of the application of the sealer.**

44. Apply silicone sealer to the 13 critical areas of the cylinder block to prevent oil seepage.

Be sure the timing marks are as shown after the chains have been installed—3.4L engine

7922KG53

45. Place new front cover gaskets onto the dowel pins on the cylinder block and heads.

46. Place the front cover into position by placing the front cover onto the dowel pins at the cylinder block.

47. Install the front cover bolts and stud bolts and tighten to 14–20 ft. lbs. (18–28 Nm).

48. Install a new oil pan gasket and apply a thin bead of silicone sealer where the timing cover meets the cylinder block.

49. Install the oil pan and install the bolts loosely.

50. With the oil pan aligned to the rear of the cylinder block, tighten the oil pan bolts and studs, in sequence, to 14–20 ft. lbs. (18–28 Nm) no more than six minutes after applying the silicone sealer.

51. Install the CMP sensor to the left cylinder head and the CKP sensor to the engine front cover, as necessary and tighten to 71–106 inch lbs. (8–12 Nm).

52. Apply a thin coat of silicone sealer to the front of the crankshaft on the inside diameter of the damper at the keyway before installing the washer and bolt.

53. Install the crankshaft damper pulley washer and bolt and tighten the bolt as follows:

    a. Tighten the bolt to 78–99 ft. lbs. (105–135 Nm), then loosen the bolt one full turn.

    b. Retighten the bolt to 35–39 ft. lbs. (47–53 Nm).

    c. Turn the bolt an additional 85–90 degrees.

54. Install the power steering pump pulley, plain washer, split washer and nut and tighten to 41–50 ft. lbs. (55–69 Nm).

55. Install the drive belt idler pulleys to the engine front cover and tighten to 27–38 ft. lbs. (36–52 Nm).

56. Install both cylinder head covers and tighten to 71–106 inch lbs. (8–12 Nm).

➡**The cylinder head covers must be installed and properly tightened within six minutes of applying the silicone sealant.**

57. Install the water pump and hoses.

58. Install the secondary air injection diverter valve, as necessary.

59. Install the exhaust air supply tube to the exhaust manifolds and secondary air injection diverter valve.

60. Connect the engine control sensor wiring connections to components, as necessary.

61. Install the right and left intake manifolds to the lower intake manifold.

62. Connect the engine control sensor wiring connections to the IAC valve and the TP sensor.

63. Install the surge tank to the engine.

64. Connect the EGR pressure sensor valve hoses, manifold tube and the transducer mounting bracket to the engine.

65. Connect the engine control sensor wiring to the EGR backpressure transducer, EGR vacuum regulator solenoid and secondary air injection control solenoid vacuum valve.

66. Connect the main emission vacuum supply hose to the surge tank vacuum fitting, secondary air injection diverter valve and EGR valve.

67. Tighten the A/C compressor and mounting bolts-to-cylinder blocks to 17–27 ft. lbs. (23–37 Nm).

68. Rotate the drive belt tensioner clockwise and install the belt.

69. Install the engine and connect the negative battery cable.

FRONT SEAL ONLY

1. Before servicing the vehicle, refer to the precautions at the beginning of this section.

2. Disconnect the negative battery cable.

3. Release the belt tensioner and remove the accessory drive belt.

4. Remove the crankshaft pulley attaching bolt from the crankshaft pulley. Using a suitable puller, remove the crankshaft pulley from the crankshaft.

5. Using Locknut Pin Remover T78P-3504-N or equivalent, remove the crankshaft front seal from the engine front cover.

To install:

6. Lubricate the seal bore in the front cover and the seal lip area with clean engine oil.

7. Install the new seal using Crankshaft Seal Replacer/Cover Aligner T88T-6701-A or equivalent. Be sure the seal is installed evenly and straight.

8. Install the crankshaft pulley. Be sure to lubricate the sealing surface of the pulley with clean engine oil prior to installation. Apply a suitable silicone sealer to the crankshaft keyway and tighten the crankshaft damper bolt as follows:

• Tighten the crankshaft pulley bolt to 78–99 ft. lbs. (105–135 Nm).

• Loosen the crankshaft pulley bolt a minimum of one full turn.

Use the special tool or a slide hammer to remove the crankshaft front oil seal—3.4L engine

Install the new crankshaft front oil seal using a suitable seal driver or the special tool—3.4L engine

• Tighten the crankshaft pulley bolt to 35–39 ft. lbs. (47–53 Nm).

• Rotate the crankshaft pulley bolt to an additional 85–95 degrees.

9. Install the accessory drive belt.

10. Connect the negative battery cable.

FUEL SYSTEM

Fuel System Service Precautions

Safety is the most important factor when performing not only fuel system maintenance but any type of maintenance. Failure to conduct maintenance and repairs in a safe manner may result in serious personal injury or death. Maintenance and testing of the vehicle's fuel system components can be accomplished safely and effectively by adhering to the following rules and guidelines.

• To avoid the possibility of fire and personal injury, always disconnect the negative battery cable unless the repair or test procedure requires that battery voltage be applied.

• Always relieve the fuel system pressure prior to disconnecting any fuel system component (injector, fuel rail, pressure regulator, etc.), fitting or fuel line connection. Exercise extreme caution whenever relieving fuel system pressure to avoid exposing skin, face and eyes to fuel spray. Please be advised that fuel under pressure may penetrate the skin or any part of the body that it contacts.

• Always place a shop towel or cloth around the fitting or connection prior to loosening to absorb any excess fuel due to spillage. Ensure that all fuel spillage (should it occur) is quickly removed from engine surfaces. Ensure that all fuel soaked cloths or towels are deposited into a suitable waste container.

• Always keep a dry chemical (Class B) fire extinguisher near the work area.

• Do not allow fuel spray or fuel vapors to come into contact with a spark or open flame.

• Always use a back-up wrench when loosening and tightening fuel line connection fittings. This will prevent unnecessary stress and torsion to fuel line piping. Always follow the proper torque specifications.

• Always replace worn fuel fitting O-rings with new. Do not substitute fuel hose or equivalent, where fuel pipe is installed.

Fuel System Pressure

RELIEVING

1. Before servicing the vehicle, refer to the precautions at the beginning of this section.

❋❋ CAUTION

The fuel injection system remains under pressure, even after the engine has been turned OFF. The fuel system pressure must be relieved before disconnecting any fuel lines. Failure to do so may result in fire and/or personal injury.

2. Disconnect the negative battery cable.

3. Remove the fuel tank fill cap to relieve the pressure in the fuel tank.

4. Remove the cap from the Schrader valve located on the fuel supply manifold (fuel rail).

5. On gasoline engines, attach Fuel Pressure Gauge T80L-9974-A or equivalent, to the valve and drain the fuel through the drain tube into a suitable container.

6. On flex-fuel engines, connect Fuel Pressure Gauge T80L-9974-A or equivalent and Fuel Pressure Test Kit 134-R0035 or equivalent, to the Schrader valve. Drain the fuel through the drain tube into a suitable container.

7. After the fuel system pressure is relieved, remove the fuel pressure gauge and install the cap on the Schrader valve.

8. Install the fuel tank fill cap.

9. Connect the negative battery cable only after system repairs are completed.

Fuel Filter

REMOVAL & INSTALLATION

1. Before servicing the vehicle, refer to the precautions at the beginning of this section.

❋❋ CAUTION

The fuel injection system remains under pressure, even after the engine has been turned OFF. The fuel system pressure must be relieved before disconnecting any fuel lines. Failure to do so may result in fire and/or personal injury.

2. Disconnect the negative battery cable.

3. Properly relieve the fuel system pressure.

4. Raise and safely support the vehicle.

5. If equipped with the push connect type connection, disengage the fuel lines as follows:

a. Push the disconnect tool into the fitting to release the internal locking fingers.

b. Gently separate the fuel line from the connector.

6. If equipped with the hairpin clip type push connect fitting, remove the connection as follows:

a. Inspect the visible internal portion of the fitting for dirt accumulation. If more than a light coating of dust is present, clean the fitting before disassembly.

b. Some adhesion between the seals

Use Fuel Line Disconnect tool (T90T-9550-B) or (T90T-9550-C) or their equivalents to disconnect the push connect type fitting

Exploded view of the hairpin clip type fuel line connection

in the fitting and the filter will occur with time. To separate, twist the fitting on the filter, then push and pull the fitting until it moves freely on the filter.

c. Remove the hairpin clip from the fitting by first bending and breaking the shipping tab. Next, spread the two clip legs by hand about ⅛ inch each, to disengage the body and push the legs into the fitting. Lightly pull the triangular end of the clip and work it clear of the filter and fitting.

➡ **Do not use hand tools to complete this operation.**

d. Grasp the fitting and pull in an axial direction to remove the fitting from the filter. Be careful on 90 degree elbow connectors, as excessive side loading could break the connector body.

e. After disassembly, inspect the inside of the fitting for any internal parts such as O-rings and spacers that may have been dislodged from the fitting. Replace any damaged connector.

7. Loosen the filter retaining clamp and remove the fuel filter. Note the direction of the flow arrow on the filter, so the replacement filter can be reinstalled in the same position.

To install:

8. Install the fuel filter with the flow arrow facing the proper direction and tighten the filter retaining clamp.

9. If equipped, install the rubber insula-

tor rings on the new filter (replace the insulator rings if the filter moves freely after the retainer is installed). Install the filter into the retainer with the flow arrow pointing out the open end of the retainer. Install the retainer on the bracket and tighten the mounting bolts to 15–24 inch lbs. (1.7–2.8 Nm).

10. If equipped with the push connect fitting, insert the fuel line in the fitting until an audible click is heard, then gently try to pull the connection apart to confirm positive engagement.

11. If equipped with the hairpin clip type push connect fittings, connect the fuel lines as follows:

a. Install a new connector if damage was found. Insert a new clip into any two adjacent openings with the triangular portion pointing away from the fitting opening. Install the clip until the legs of the clip are locked on the outside of the body. Piloting with an index finger is necessary.

b. Before installing the fitting on the filter, wipe the filter end with a clean cloth. Inspect the inside of the fitting to be sure it is free of dirt and/or obstructions.

c. Apply a light coating of engine oil to the filter end. Align the fitting and filter axially and push the fitting onto the filter end. When the fitting is engaged, a definite click will be heard. Pull on the fitting to be sure it is fully engaged.

12. Lower the vehicle.

13. Connect the negative battery cable.

14. Start the engine and check for fuel leaks and proper operation.

Fuel Pump

REMOVAL & INSTALLATION

1. Before servicing the vehicle, refer to the precautions at the beginning of this section.

☼☼ CAUTION

The fuel injection system remains under pressure, even after the engine has been turned OFF. The fuel system pressure must be relieved before disconnecting any fuel lines. Failure to do so may result in fire and/or personal injury.

2. Disconnect the negative battery cable. Properly relieve the fuel system pressure.

3. Raise and safely support the vehicle. Remove the fuel tank and place on a suitable work bench.

4. Remove any dirt that has accumulated around the fuel pump retaining flange so it will not enter the tank during pump removal and installation.

5. Turn the fuel pump locking ring counterclockwise and remove the locking ring using Fuel Tank Sender Wrench T74P-9275-A or equivalent.

6. Pull the fuel pump module up and out of the fuel tank until the locking tabs for the fuel pump module are accessible. Squeeze both locking tabs together and remove the fuel pump module from the fuel tank. Remove and discard the O-ring seal.

To install:

7. Clean the fuel pump mounting flange, fuel tank mounting surface and O-ring seal groove.

8. Apply a light coating of grease on a new O-ring seal to hold it in place during assembly and install the O-ring seal.

9. Install the fuel pump module carefully to ensure the filter and hoses and float rod are not damaged.

10. Align the fuel pump module and the fuel tank retainer axially and push the fuel pump module into the fuel tank retainer. When the fuel pump module is properly engaged, a definite click will be heard engaging two locking tabs on the outside of the fuel pump.

11. Pull on the fuel pump module to ensure that both locking tabs are properly engaged.

12. Be sure the locating keys are in the keyways and the seal ring remains in the groove.

13. Hold the fuel pump module in place and install the locking ring finger-tight. Be sure all the locking tabs are under the tank lock ring tabs.

14. Using the sender wrench or equivalent, rotate the locking ring clockwise until the ring is against the stops.

15. Install the fuel tank in the vehicle. Lower the vehicle.

FUEL PUMP MUST BE SNAPPED IN RETAINER TWO PLACES

1   Fuel Pump Locking Retainer Ring
2   Fuel Tank Pressure / Vacuum Transducer
3   Locking Tab
4   Fuel Tank
5   O-Ring Seal
6   Connector
7   Fuel Pump Module

7922KG58

Exploded view of the fuel pump module mounting

16. Add a minimum of 10 gallons (38 liters) of clean fuel to the tank. Connect the negative battery cable.

17. Install a suitable fuel pressure gauge to the Schrader valve on the fuel supply manifold.

18. Cycle the ignition switch from **OFF** to **RUN** for three seconds. Repeat this procedure 5–10 times until the pressure gauge reads at least 30 psi (207 kPa). Check for fuel leaks.

19. Remove the fuel pressure gauge. Start the engine and again, check for fuel leaks. Road test the vehicle and check for proper operation.

DRIVE TRAIN

Transaxle

REMOVAL & INSTALLATION

Automatic

1. Before servicing the vehicle, refer to the precautions at the beginning of this section.

2. Disconnect both battery cables, negative cable first.

3. Remove the battery and battery tray. Remove the engine air cleaner assembly.

4. Detach the transaxle harness and the Transmission Range (TR) sensor connectors.

5. Remove the shift cable actuator fitting (cable clip) and one nut and disconnect the shift cable from the shift cable bracket on the transaxle.

6. Disconnect the transaxle cooler lines.

7. For the 3.0L (OHV) engine, remove the four upper transaxle-to-engine bolts and one transaxle-to-engine stud.

8. For the 3.0L (DOHC) or 3.4L engine, remove five transaxle-to-engine bolts.

9. Install two engine lifting brackets on the engine assembly.

10. Install and secure the engine using Three Bar Engine Support D88L-6000-A or equivalent.

11. Raise and safely support the vehicle.

12. Loosen the transaxle oil pan bolts and drain the transaxle fluid into a suitable container.

13. Remove both front wheel and tire assemblies.

14. Remove both halfshafts.

15. Detach the four Heated Oxygen Sensor (HO2S) electrical connectors.

16. Remove three bolts and seven nuts securing the converter Y-pipe assembly and remove from the vehicle.

17. Detach the two starter motor connectors, then remove the starter.

18. Remove one bolt and one stud securing the starter motor and remove the starter motor from the transaxle.

19. For the OHV engine, remove one bolt and the transaxle housing cover.

20. Support the rack and pinion assembly using wire attached to the strut and spring assembly to hold it in position. Remove two rack and pinion assembly nuts from the subframe.

21. Remove two lower control arm-to-ball joint nuts and separate the lower control arms from the steering knuckles and ball joints.

22. Remove the nuts from the front engine support insulators (mounts) at the subframe.

23. Remove the sway bar (stabilizer bar) link nuts at each end of the sway bar and separate the links from the sway bar.

24. Remove the engine and transaxle support insulator through-bolts from the subframe.

25. Place High Lift Transmission Jack 014-00210 or equivalent, using a suitable subframe adapter under the subframe and support the subframe.

26. Remove the four subframe-to-body bolts. Carefully lower the subframe and set aside.

27. Place High Lift Transmission Jack 014-00210 or equivalent, using Adapter 014-00461 or equivalent, under the transaxle and support the transaxle assembly. Secure the transaxle to the transaxle adapter using a strap or chain.

28. For the OHV engine, remove one lower engine-to-transaxle bolt.

29. For the DOHC engines, remove the four lower engine-to-transaxle bolts.

30. Remove the four flywheel-to-torque converter nuts.

31. Remove three bolts and two nuts securing the rear engine support to the transaxle and remove the rear engine support.

32. Remove one bolt from the right engine mount brace, then slowly lower the transaxle from the vehicle.

To install:

➡**Flush the transaxle cooler lines thoroughly before installing the transaxle assembly.**

33. If removed, place the transaxle assembly on High Lift Transmission Jack 014-00210 or equivalent, using Adapter 014-00461 or equivalent. Secure the transaxle to the transaxle adapter using a strap or chain.

34. Slowly raise the transaxle assembly into place. Align the torque converter studs with the appropriate holes in the flywheel and engage the transaxle housing to the engine dowel pins.

35. Install one bolt in the right engine mount brace and tighten to 39–53 ft. lbs. (53–72 Nm).

36. Install the rear engine support to the transaxle and install three bolts and two nuts. Tighten the bolts and nuts to 39–53 ft. lbs. (53–72 Nm).

37. Install the four flywheel-to-torque converter nuts and tighten to 20–34 ft. lbs. (27–46 Nm).

38. For the OHV engine, install one lower transaxle-to-engine bolt and tighten to 39–53 ft. lbs. (53–72 Nm).

39. For the DOHC engines, install the four lower transaxle-to-engine bolts and tighten to 39–53 ft. lbs. (53–72 Nm).

40. Place the subframe on High Lift Transmission Jack 014-00210 or equivalent, using a suitable subframe adapter and raise the subframe into position.

41. Install the subframe insulators, if removed and loosely install four subframe-to-body bolts.

42. Install a ¾ inch (19mm) outside diameter pipe or similar tool into the front left subframe and body alignment holes and align the holes. Slightly tighten the front left subframe-to-body bolt.

43. Repeat the subframe alignment procedure on the front right subframe and body alignment holes. Slightly tighten the right subframe-to-body bolt.

44. Check the left alignment holes again and adjust, if necessary.

45. After the subframe alignment is complete, tighten all four subframe-to-body bolts to 57–76 ft. lbs. (77–103 Nm).

46. Install the remaining components in the reverse order of removal. Tighten the following:

• Engine and transaxle support insulator-to-subframe bolts to 65–87 ft. lbs. (88–118 Nm)

• Sway bar link-to-sway bushings and nuts to 35–46 ft. lbs. (47–63 Nm)

• Rack and pinion-to-subframe nuts to 84–113 ft. lbs. (113–133 Nm)

• Front engine support insulator-to-subframe nuts to 57–76 ft. lbs. (77–103 Nm)

• Ball joint-to-lower control arm nuts

to 51–67 ft. lbs. (68–92 Nm), using new nuts

• For the OHV engine: transaxle housing cover bolt to 80–106 inch lbs. (9–12 Nm)

• Starter motor bolt and stud to 15–21 ft. lbs. (21–29 Nm)

• Converter Y-pipe three bolts and seven nuts to 26–34 ft. lbs. (34–46 Nm)

• For the OHV engine: four upper transaxle-to-engine bolts and one upper transaxle-to-engine stud to 39–53 ft. lbs. (53–72 Nm)

• For the DOHC engine: five transaxle-to-engine bolts to 39–53 ft. lbs. (53–72 Nm)

• Shift actuator cable fitting nut to 14–19 ft. lbs. (19–26 Nm)

47. Connect both battery cables, negative cable last.

48. If the transaxle is empty of transaxle fluid, add several quarts of MERCON or equivalent transaxle fluid to the transaxle.

49. Start the engine and continue to fill the transaxle until the correct level is reached. Check for leaks and proper operation.

➡**Whenever the vehicles subframe is removed or lowered, the wheel alignment should be checked.**

50. Check the front end alignment.

51. Road test the vehicle and check the transaxle for proper operation.

Halfshaft

REMOVAL & INSTALLATION

➡**DO NOT begin this procedure unless the following parts are available:**

• New hub retainer nut
• New lower control arm-to-steering knuckle bolt and nut
• New stub shaft/link shaft circlip
Once removed, these parts must not be reused during assembly. Their torque holding ability or retention capability is diminished during removal.

1. Before servicing the vehicle, refer to the precautions at the beginning of this section.

2. Remove the wheel cover/hub cover from the wheel and tire assembly. Loosen the hub retainer nut and the lug nuts.

3. Raise the vehicle and support safely.

4. Remove the wheel and tire assembly. Remove the hub retainer nut and washer and discard the hub nut.

5. Remove the nut from the ball joint-to-steering knuckle attaching bolts. Drive the bolt out of the steering knuckle using a punch and hammer. Discard the bolt and nut.

6. If equipped with ABS, remove the anti-lock brake sensor and position aside. If equipped with air suspension, remove the height sensor bracket bolt and wire sensor bracket to inner fender. Position the sensor link aside.

7. Separate the ball joint from the steering knuckle using a suitable prybar. Position the end of the prybar outside of the bushing pocket to avoid damage to the bushing. Use care to prevent damage to the ball joint boot. Remove the stabilizer bar link at the stabilizer bar.

8. Install CV-joint puller tool T86P-3514-A1 or equivalent, between the CV-joint and transaxle case. Turn the steering hub and/or wire the strut assembly aside.

9. Screw extension tool T86P-3514-A2 or equivalent, into the CV-joint puller and hand-tighten. Screw an impact slide hammer onto the extension and remove the CV-joint from the transaxle.

10. Support the end of the shaft by suspending it from a convenient underbody component with a piece of wire. Do not allow the shaft to hang unsupported; damage to the outboard CV-joint may occur.

✳ **WARNING**

Never use a hammer to separate the outer CV-joint stub shaft from the hub. Damage to the CV-joint threads and internal components may result.

11. Separate the outboard CV-joint from the hub using front hub remover tool T81P-1104-C or equivalent, metric adapter tools T83-P-1104-BH, T86P-1104-Al and front hub installer T81P-1104-A or equivalent.

12. Remove the halfshaft assembly from the vehicle.

✳ **WARNING**

Never use a hammer to separate the outboard CV-joint stub shaft from the hub. Damage to the CV-joint threads and internal components may result.

The right side link shaft and halfshaft assembly is removed as a complete unit.

To install:

13. Install a new circlip on the inboard CV-joint stub shaft and/or link shaft. The outboard CV-joint does not have a circlip. When installing the circlip, start one end in the groove and work the circlip over the stub shaft end into the groove. This will avoid over expanding the circlip.

➡**The circlip must not be re-used. A new circlip must be installed each time the inboard CV-joint is installed into the transaxle differential.**

14. Carefully align the splines of the inboard CV-joint stub shaft with the splines in the differential. Exerting some force, push the CV-joint into the differential until the circlip is felt to seat in the differential side gear. Use care to prevent damage to the differential oil seal. If equipped, tighten the link shaft bearing bolts to 16–23 ft. lbs. (21–32 Nm).

➡**A non-metallic mallet may be used to aid in seating the circlip into the differential side gear groove. If a mallet is necessary, tap only on the outboard CV-joint stub shaft.**

15. Carefully align the splines of the outboard CV-joint stub shaft with the splines in the hub and push the shaft into the hub as far as possible.

16. Temporarily fasten the rotor to the hub with washers and two wheel lug nuts. Insert a steel rod into the rotor and rotate clockwise to contact the knuckle to prevent the rotor from turning during the CV-joint installation.

17. Install the hub nut washer and a new hub nut. Manually thread the retainer onto the CV-joint as far as possible.

18. Install the remaining components in the reverse order of removal. Tighten the following:

• Control arm-to-steering knuckle nut and bolt to 50–68 ft. lbs. (68–92 Nm), using a new nut and bolt

• Stabilizer link-to-stabilizer bar/front strut to 57–75 ft. lbs. (77–103 Nm)

• Hub retainer nut to 180–200 ft. lbs. (245–270 Nm)

• Lug nuts to 85–105 ft. lbs. (115–142 Nm)

19. Fill the transaxle to the proper level with the specified fluid.

STEERING AND SUSPENSION

Air Bag

✳✳ CAUTION

Some vehicles are equipped with an air bag system, also known as the Supplemental Inflatable Restraint (SIR) system. The system must be disabled before performing service on or around system components, steering column, instrument panel components, wiring and sensors. Failure to follow safety and disabling procedures could result in accidental air bag deployment, possible personal injury and unnecessary system repairs.

PRECAUTIONS

Several precautions must be observed when handling the inflator module to avoid accidental deployment and possible personal injury.

• Never carry the inflator module by the wires or connector on the underside of the module.

• When carrying a live inflator module, hold securely with both hands, and ensure that the bag and trim cover are pointed away.

• Place the inflator module on a bench or other surface with the bag and trim cover facing up.

• With the inflator module on the bench, never place anything on or close to the module which may be thrown in the event of an accidental deployment.

DISARMING

✳✳ CAUTION

The Supplemental Inflatable Restraint (SIR) system must be disarmed before performing service around SIR system components or SIR system wiring. Failure to do so may cause accidental deployment of the air bag, resulting in unnecessary SIR system repairs and/or personal injury.

1. Disconnect both battery cables from the battery, negative cable first.

2. Wait one minute before proceeding with the service procedure. This is the time required for the back-up power supply in the air bag diagnostic monitor to deplete its stored energy.

3. After service is completed, reconnect the battery cables, negative cable last.

4. Turn the ignition switch to the **RUN** position. The air bag indicator should light continuously for approximately six seconds, then turn OFF. If the indicator fails to light, flashes or remains lit continuously, there is a fault in the air bag system.

Power Rack and Pinion Steering Gear

REMOVAL & INSTALLATION

1. Before servicing the vehicle, refer to the precautions at the beginning of this section.

2. Disconnect the negative battery cable.

3. From inside the vehicle, remove the boot covering the shaft at the cowl panel.

4. Remove the bolts retaining the intermediate shaft to the steering column shaft. Set the weather boot aside.

5. Remove the pinch bolt at the steering gear input shaft and remove the intermediate shaft. Raise the vehicle and support safely.

6. Safely raise and support the vehicle.

7. Remove the front wheels.

8. Remove the exhaust system flex tube, then remove the dual converter Y-pipe from the vehicle.

9. Support the rear end of the front subframe with tall jackstands.

10. Disconnect the tie rod ends from the

JACK STANDS

7922KG60

Support the rear of the subframe with two tall jackstands while removing the steering gear

steering knuckle tie rods. Mark the position of the jam nuts for correct installation.

11. Remove the nuts securing the steering gear to the subframe.

12. Remove the bolts securing the rear of the subframe to the body.

13. Carefully, raise the lift until the subframe separates from the body approximately 4 inches (102mm).

14. Remove the push-pin retainers from the power steering hose bracket, then remove the shield.

15. Remove the left turn pressure hose from the bracket, then remove the bracket.

16. Disconnect the left stabilizer link from the strut assembly.

17. Disconnect the power steering auxiliary actuator.

18. Rotate the steering gear to clear the mounting bolts and move the gear to the left to gain access to the hose fittings.

19. Position a drain pan under the steering gear and disconnect the pressure and return hoses.

20. Remove the steering gear assembly through the left wheel opening.

To install:

21. Install new Teflon® seals on the hydraulic line fittings on the gear assembly. Install the mounting bolts in the steering gear housing, then insert the steering gear through the left fender apron.

22. Install the remaining components in the reverse order of removal.

23. Align the steering gear bolts, install the nuts and tighten to 85–100 ft. lbs. (115–135 Nm). Lower the vehicle.

24. Tighten the hydraulic pressure line and return line to 15–25 ft. lbs. (20–35 Nm).

25. Tighten the tie rod end castle nuts to 35 ft. lbs. (48 Nm). If necessary, tighten the nuts a little bit more to align the slot in the nut for the cotter pin. Install the cotter pin.

26. Fill and bleed the power steering system. Check the system for leaks and proper operation. Adjust the toe setting as necessary.

Strut

REMOVAL & INSTALLATION

Front

➡Be sure new wheel hub retainer nuts, tie rod end castellated nuts, stabilizer bar link nuts and knuckle-to-strut pinch bolt/nuts are available. These parts

lose their torque holding/retention capabilities during removal and must not be reused.

1. Before servicing the vehicle, refer to the precautions at the beginning of this section.

2. Turn the ignition switch to the **OFF** position. Leave the steering column in the UNLOCKED position.

3. With all four wheels on the ground, remove the wheel hub retainer nut. Discard the nut.

4. On the SHO vehicles:

   a. Disconnect the height sensor wiring connector.

   b. Remove the wiring harness from the routing clip on the front shock absorber.

   c. Remove air suspension height sensor from the height sensor ball studs.

5. Loosen the three top mount-to-shock tower nuts, but do not remove the nuts at this time.

6. Raise and safely support the vehicle. Remove the wheel and tire assembly.

➡ **When raising the vehicle, do not lift by using the lower control arms.**

7. Remove the disc brake caliper. Hang the caliper out of the work area with wire to prevent damage to the brake hose.

8. Remove the disc brake rotor.

9. Remove the anti-lock brake sensor wiring harness clip and the mounting screw from the brake hose bracket on the strut

Item	Description
1	Front Coil Spring
2	Front Shock Absorber
3	Tie Rod End
4	Wheel Hub

Item	Description
5	Front Wheel Knuckle
6	Front Suspension Lower Arm
7	Front Stabilizer Bar
8	Stabilizer Bar Link

7922KG61

Front suspension component identification

assembly. Move the anti-lock brake sensor aside.

10. Remove the cotter pin and the castel-lated nut from the tie rod end. Discard the cotter pin and nut.

11. Using Removal tool 3290-D or equivalent, and Adapter tool T81P-3504-W or equivalent, separate the tie rod end from the steering knuckle.

12. On SHO vehicles, remove the vinyl cover from the upper link stud.

13. Remove the sway bar (stabilizer bar) link nut and link from the strut. Discard the link nut.

14. Remove and discard the lower ball joint retaining nut. Using Ball Joint Remover T96P-3010-A or equivalent, separate the ball joint from the lower control arm.

15. Using Spring Compressor 164-R-3571 or equivalent, compress the coil spring until the ball joint clears the lower arm.

16. Remove the pinch bolt and nut from the bottom of the steering knuckle. It may be necessary to use a drift punch to remove the bolt. Discard the pinch bolt and nut.

17. Separate the halfshaft from the wheel hub using Front Hub Remover/Replacer T81P-1104-C or equivalent, and the required adapters.

18. Support the halfshaft with wire in a level position to prevent it from hanging by the inner CV-joint.

Item	Description
1	Rear Stabilizer Bar
2	Rear Spring
3	Shock Absorber
4	Nut
5	Washer
6	Lower Suspension Arm (Rear)
7	Rear Wheel Spindle
8	Nut (4 Req'd)
9	Washer (2 Req'd)

Item	Description
10	Rear Suspension Tie Rod Bushing (4 Req'd)
11	Washer (2 Req'd)
12	Rear Suspension Tension Strut and Bushing (2 Req'd)
13	Rear Suspension Lower Arm (Front)
A	Tighten to 68-92 N·m (50-67 Lb-Ft)
B	Tighten to 46.7-63.3 N·m (35-46 Lb-Ft)

Rear suspension component identification—sedan models

➡**Do not let the halfshaft hang by the inner CV-joint or move too far outward. The internal parts of the tripod CV-joint could be pulled apart.**

19. Remove the three top mount-to-strut tower nuts while supporting the strut. Lower the strut assembly from the vehicle.

To install:

20. Install the strut assembly with the spring compressor installed to the vehicle and install the three top mount-to-strut tower nuts loosely.

➡**Further compress the coil spring if added clearance is required for installation.**

21. Install the steering knuckle and hub assembly to the strut. Install a new pinch bolt and nut. Tighten to 73–97 ft. lbs. (98–132 Nm).

22. Install the halfshaft into the hub using care to align the splines.

23. Install the sway bar link to the strut and install a new sway bar link nut. Tighten to 55–75 ft. lbs. (75–101 Nm).

24. On SHO vehicles, install the vinyl cover-to-upper link stud.

25. Install the tie rod end onto the steering knuckle using a new castellated nut. Tighten the nut to 35–46 ft. lbs. (47–63 Nm). Continue to tighten the nut until a slot lines up with the opening in the tie rod end stud and install a new cotter pin.

26. Install the anti-lock brake sensor wiring routing clip and the brake hose bracket mounting screw and tighten to 11 ft. lbs. (15 Nm).

27. On the SHO vehicles, perform the following:

   a. Install air suspension height sensor-to-height sensor ball studs.

   b. Install the wiring harness to the routing clip on the front shock absorber.

   c. Connect the height sensor wiring connector.

28. Install the disc brake rotor and caliper. Tighten the caliper anchor bracket bolts to 65–87 ft. lbs. (88–118 Nm).

29. Install the wheel and tire assembly. Tighten the lug nuts to 85–105 ft. lbs. (115–142 Nm).

30. Tighten the three top mount-to-shock tower nuts to 22–29 ft. lbs. (30–40 Nm).

31. Lower the vehicle.

32. Install a new wheel hub retainer nut. Tighten the nut to 170–202 ft. lbs. (230–275 Nm).

33. Pump the brake pedal several times prior to moving the vehicle, to position the brake pads.

34. Road test the vehicle and check for proper operation.

Rear

1. Before servicing the vehicle, refer to the precautions at the beginning of this section.

2. Remove the package tray trim panel and loosen the three strut-to-body nuts.

3. Raise the vehicle and remove the rear wheel.

4. Remove the brake load sensor from the rear suspension arm.

5. Remove the brake hose-to-strut clip and position the hose aside.

6. Remove the stabilizer bar bracket from the body.

7. Separate the stabilizer bar from the link.

8. Remove the tension strut from the front of the rear wheel spindle. Pull the spindle back to remove the tension strut.

9. If required, remove the stabilizer link from the strut.

10. Support the spindle with a jack and remove the strut-to-spindle pinchbolt. Do not let the assembly hang by the brake line.

11. Remove the strut-to-body nuts and remove the strut.

To install:

12. If removed, install the stabilizer link on the strut. Tighten the nut to 60–81 inch lbs. (7–9 Nm).

13. Position the strut in the vehicle and install the three upper mounting nuts. Do not tighten the nuts at this time.

14. Install the lower end of the strut in the spindle. Use a new pinch bolt tightened to 50–67 ft. lbs. (68–92 Nm).

15. Pull the spindle back and install the tension strut. Tighten the nut to 35–46 ft. lbs. (68–92 Nm).

16. Connect the link-to-stabilizer bar and tighten the nut to 62–79 inch lbs. (7–9 Nm).

17. Install the stabilizer bar bracket on the body. Tighten the bolts to 25 –33 ft. lbs. (34–46 Nm).

18. Install the brake hose on the strut.

19. Connect the load sensor to the suspension arm.

20. Tighten the three upper mounting nuts to 19–25 ft. lbs. (25–34 Nm).

21. Install the rear wheel and lower the vehicle.

Shock Absorber

REMOVAL & INSTALLATION

Wagons Only

➡**Before continuing, be sure new mounting bolts and nuts and shock absorber insulator bushings are available.**

1. Before servicing the vehicle, refer to the precautions at the beginning of this section.

2. Raise the vehicle enough to allow wheel and tire removal. Safely support the vehicle.

3. Remove the wheel and tire assembly.

❋❋ WARNING

The lower control arm must be supported before removal of the upper or lower shock absorber attachments to prevent injury or damage to attached components.

4. From inside the vehicle, remove the rear compartment access panel.

5. Remove the top shock absorber retaining nut using a crow foot wrench and ratchet while holding the shock absorber shaft stationary with an open-end wrench. Do not grip the shaft of the shock absorber if it is to be reused. Discard the retaining nut.

6. Remove the upper washer and insulator from the shock absorber.

➡**The shock absorbers are gas filled. It will require an effort to collapse the shock to remove it from the lower control arm.**

7. Remove the lower shock absorber mounting nut and bolt.

8. Remove the shock absorber from the vehicle. Discard the nut and bolt.

To install:

9. Install a new washer and insulator on the upper shock absorber rod.

10. Maneuver the upper part of the shock absorber into the shock tower opening in the body. Push slowly on the lower part of the shock absorber until the lower bracket is aligned with the mounting holes in the lower control arm.

11. Install a new retaining bolt and nut; then, tighten to 50–68 ft. lbs. (68–92 Nm).

12. From inside the vehicle, install a new insulator, washer and nut on top of the shock absorber shaft. Tighten the nut to 19–25 ft. lbs. (26–34 Nm).

13. Install the rear compartment access panel.

14. Install the wheel and tire assembly. Remove the jackstand.

15. Lower the vehicle. Road test the vehicle and check for proper operation.

Coil Spring

REMOVAL & INSTALLATION

Front

1. Before servicing the vehicle, refer to the precautions at the beginning of this section.

✳✳ CAUTION

Do not remove the strut rod nut until the spring has been compressed until it comes away from the seat.

10 mm
SIX POINT
DEEPWELL
SOCKET

OXYGEN SENSOR
WRENCH

7922KG64

Hold the strut rod while loosening or tightening the nut

2. Remove the strut from the vehicle.

3. Compress the coil spring using a commercially available spring compressor until the spring comes away from the seat.

4. Remove the large center nut and slowly release the spring compressor.

Item	Description
1	Dust Boot (Part of 18124)
2	Nut (3 Req'd)
3	Washer
4	Nut
5	Front Shock Absorber Mounting Bracket
6	Washer
7	Front Suspension Bearing and Seal
8	Front Spring Insulator (Part of 18124)
9	Front Coil Spring
10	Front Shock Absorber
11	Jounce Bumper (Part of 18124)

7922KG63

Exploded view of the front strut and coil spring assembly

To install:

5. Compress the spring and install it on the strut.

6. Install the lower washer and mounting bracket.

7. Install the upper washer and a new nut. Tighten the nut to 39–53 ft. lbs. (53–72 Nm) while holding the rod with a T-50 size Torx® socket.

8. Install the strut assembly in the vehicle.

Taurus and Sable Wagons

1. Before servicing the vehicle, refer to the precautions at the beginning of this section.

2. Raise and safely support the vehicle. Remove the wheel and tire assembly.

3. Position a floor jack under the lower suspension control arm.

✳✳ WARNING

The lower control arm must be supported before removal of the upper or lower shock absorber mounts to prevent injury or damage to the related components due to tension applied by the coil spring.

4. Perform the following procedures:
   a. Remove the bolt retaining the rear brake hose bracket to the body.
   b. Remove the stabilizer bar and bracket from the lower control arm.
   c. Using the floor jack, slowly raise the lower control arm to normal curb height.
   d. From inside the vehicle, remove the rear compartment access panel.

5. Remove and discard the top shock absorber retaining nut using a crows foot wrench while holding the shaft with and open end wrench.

✳✳ CAUTION

The shock absorbers are gas-filled. It will require an effort to collapse the shock in order to remove the shock from the lower arm.

6. Remove the lower shock mounting nut and bolt and remove the shock absorber.

7. Perform the following procedures:
   a. Install Spring Cage 164-R3555 or equivalent, on the coil spring.
   b. Remove and discard the upper ball joint nut. Separate the upper ball joint from the wheel spindle.

8. Slowly lower the lower control arm using the floor jack until the tension is

relaxed on the coil spring. Remove the coil spring and the upper and lower spring insulators.

To install:

9. Place the lower spring insulator on the lower control arm. Press the insulator downward into place, making certain that the insulator is properly seated.

10. Position the upper insulator on top of the coil spring. Install the coil spring on the lower control arm. Make certain the spring is properly seated.

11. Using the floor jack, slowly raise the lower control arm. Guide the upper spring insulator onto the upper spring seat on the underbody.

12. Position the upper ball joint into the upper control arm. Install a new nut and tighten to 50–68 ft. lbs. (68–92 Nm).

13. Position the shock absorber into the tower opening with a new washer and insulator installed. Push on the lower end of the shock until the lower bracket is aligned with the mounting holes in the lower control arm. Install a new lower bolt and nut. Tighten to 50–68 ft. lbs. (68–92 Nm).

14. From inside the vehicle, install a new upper shock absorber insulator and washer. Tighten the nut to 19–25 ft. lbs. (25–34 Nm).

15. Perform the following procedures:

a. Install the rear compartment access panel.

b. Install the stabilizer bar and bracket to the lower control arm. Tighten to 15–19 ft. lbs. (19–26 Nm).

16. Install the brake hose support bracket to the body and install the bolt. Tighten the bolt to 10 ft. lbs. (12 Nm).

17. Install the wheel and tire assembly. Tighten the lug nuts to 85–105 ft. lbs. (115–142 Nm).

18. Remove the floor jack.

19. Lower the vehicle.

20. Check the rear wheel alignment and adjust, if necessary.

21. Road test the vehicle and check for proper operation.

Lower Ball Joints

REMOVAL & INSTALLATION

The lower ball joint is an integral part of the steering knuckle. If the lower ball joint is found to be defective, the entire steering knuckle must be replaced.

Wheel Bearings

ADJUSTMENT

There is no adjustment for the front or rear wheel bearings due to the nature of their design. These bearings are permanently lubricated and require no periodic maintenance.

REMOVAL & INSTALLATION

Front

➡️ **Be sure new wheel hub retainer nuts, tie rod end castellated nuts, hub-to-knuckle bolts, knuckle-to-strut pinch bolt/nut and inboard halfshaft circlips are available. These parts lose their torque holding/retention capabilities during removal and must not be reused.**

1. Before servicing the vehicle, refer to the precautions at the beginning of this section.

2. Turn the ignition switch to the **OFF** position. Place the steering column in the UNLOCKED position.

3. Remove the wheel hub retainer nut before raising the vehicle off the ground. Discard the wheel hub retainer nut.

4. Raise and safely support the vehicle. Remove the wheel and tire assembly.

➡️ **When raising the vehicle, do not lift by using the lower control arms.**

5. Remove the wheel and tire assembly.

6. Remove the cotter pin and the castellated nut from the tie rod end. Discard the cotter pin and nut.

7. Separate the tie rod end from the steering knuckle using Remover tool 3290-D and adapter T81P-3504-W or equivalents.

8. On SHO vehicles, remove the vinyl cover from the upper link stud.

9. Remove the stabilizer link from the strut. Remove the disc brake caliper and hang it aside.

10. Remove the disc brake rotor.

11. Remove the anti-lock sensor and move it aside.

12. Remove and discard the lower ball joint nut. Using Ball Joint Remover T96P-3010-A or equivalent, separate the ball joint from the lower control arm.

13. Using Rotunda Spring Compressor 164-R-3571 or equivalent, compress the coil spring until the ball joint clears the lower control arm.

14. Remove and discard the steering knuckle-to-strut pinch bolt and nut.

15. Separate the halfshaft from the wheel hub using Front Hub Remover/Replacer T81P-1104-C or equivalent, and adapters.

16. Support the halfshaft with wire in a level position to prevent it from hanging by the inner CV-joint.

➡️ **Do not let the halfshaft hang by the inner CV-joint or move too far outward. The internal parts of the tripod CV-joint could be pulled apart.**

17. Separate the steering knuckle from the strut assembly and place on a suitable workbench.

18. Remove the three hub and bearing retainer bolts from the back of the steering knuckle while using a prybar to steady the assembly. Discard the three hub and bearing retainer bolts.

✳️✳️ WARNING

The wheel hub is not pressed into the front wheel knuckle. DO NOT USE a slide hammer to remove a stuck wheel hub. Do not strike the back of the inner bearing race.

19. Remove the wheel hub from the steering knuckle using a suitable prybar.

20. Inspect all components and replace as necessary. The wheel bearings are not serviceable and must be replaced with a new wheel hub assembly.

To install:

21. Install the disc brake rotor shield using new rivets, if removed.

➡️ **If the hub bearing journal is scored or damaged, replace the steering knuckle. If the wheel hub is damaged or any end-play is detectable, replace the wheel hub.**

22. Remove all foreign material from the knuckle bearing bore and hub bearing journal to ensure correct seating of the new hub.

➡️ **The knuckle must be clean enough to allow the wheel hub to be completely seated by hand. Do not press or draw the wheel hub into place.**

23. Place the wheel hub to the steering knuckle using light oil. Push the wheel hub assembly into the steering knuckle. Install bolts and tighten to 61–78 ft. lbs. (83–107 Nm).

24. Position the steering knuckle assembly to the vehicle.

Turn to Section 6 for brake system applications

25. Install the steering knuckle to the strut and loosely install a new pinch bolt.

26. Install the steering knuckle and hub assembly onto the halfshaft. Be sure the splines are properly aligned.

27. Slowly release Rotunda Spring Compressor 164-R-3571 or equivalent, while guiding the lower ball joint into the lower control arm.

28. Remove the spring compressor.

29. Install a new nut on the lower ball joint stud and tighten to 50–67 ft. lbs. (68–92 Nm).

30. Install a new nut on the steering knuckle-to-strut pinch bolt. Tighten the pinch bolt nut to 72–97 ft. lbs. (98–132 Nm).

31. Position the tie rod end to the steering knuckle. Install a new castellated nut and tighten to 35–46 ft. lbs. (47–63 Nm). Install a new cotter pin.

32. Install the sway bar link and tighten the nut to 57–75 ft. lbs. (77–103 Nm).

33. On SHO vehicles, install the vinyl cover to the upper link stud.

➡ **Use care not to damage the sway bar link boot seals. Do not use power tools to tighten the nuts or seal damage will result.**

34. Install the disc brake rotor and disc brake caliper. Tighten the caliper anchor bracket bolts to 65–87 ft. lbs. (88–118 Nm).

35. Install the wheel and tire assembly.

36. Lower the vehicle.

37. Install a new wheel hub retainer nut. Tighten the nut to 170–202 ft. lbs. (230–275 Nm).

38. Pump the brake pedal several times prior to moving the vehicle, to position the brake pads.

39. Road test the vehicle and check for proper operation.

Rear

1. Before servicing the vehicle, refer to the precautions at the beginning of this section.

2. Raise and safely support the vehicle. Remove the wheel and tire assembly.

3. Remove the bolt retaining the brake hose to the strut bracket. Remove the rear disc/drum brake assembly.

4. Remove the grease cap from the bearing and hub assembly and discard the grease cap.

5. Remove the bearing and hub assembly nut and discard. Remove the bearing and hub assembly from the spindle.

To install:

6. Position the wheel hub and bearing on the rear spindle.

7. Install a new wheel hub retainer nut and tighten to 188–254 ft. lbs. (255–345 Nm).

8. Install a new hub cap grease seal using Shaft Protector T89P-19623-FH or equivalent. Tap on the tool until the hub cap grease seal is fully seated.

9. Install the rear disc/drum brake assembly.

10. Install the wheel and tire assembly. Lower the vehicle.

11. Check the front end alignment. Road test the vehicle and check for proper operation.

FORD MOTOR COMPANY

Lincoln-Continental

PRECAUTIONS

Before servicing any vehicle, please be sure to read all of the following precautions, which deal with personal safety, prevention of component damage, and important points to take into consideration when servicing a motor vehicle:

• Never open, service or drain the radiator or cooling system when the engine is hot; serious burns can occur from the steam and hot coolant.

• Observe all applicable safety precautions when working around fuel. Whenever servicing the fuel system, always work in a well-ventilated area. Do not allow fuel spray or vapors to come in contact with a spark, open flame, or excessive heat (a hot drop light, for example). Keep a dry chemical fire extinguisher near the work area. Always keep fuel in a container specifically designed for fuel storage; also, always properly seal fuel containers to avoid the possibility of fire or explosion. Refer to the additional fuel system precautions later in this section.

• Fuel injection systems often remain pressurized, even after the engine has been turned **OFF**. The fuel system pressure must be relieved before disconnecting any fuel lines. Failure to do so may result in fire and/or personal injury.

• Brake fluid often contains polyglycol ethers and polyglycols. Avoid contact with the eyes and wash your hands thoroughly after handling brake fluid. If you do get brake fluid in your eyes, flush your eyes with clean, running water for 15 minutes. If eye irritation persists, or if you have taken brake fluid internally, IMMEDIATELY seek medical assistance.

• The EPA warns that prolonged contact with used engine oil may cause a number of skin disorders, including cancer! You should make every effort to minimize your exposure to used engine oil. Protective gloves should be worn when changing oil. Wash your hands and any other exposed skin areas as soon as possible after exposure to used engine oil. Soap and water, or waterless hand cleaner should be used.

• All new vehicles are now equipped with an air bag system, often referred to as a Supplemental Restraint System (SRS) or Supplemental Inflatable Restraint (SIR) system. The system must be disabled before performing service on or around system components, steering column, instrument panel components, wiring and sensors. Failure to follow safety and disabling procedures could result in accidental air bag deployment, possible personal injury and unnecessary system repairs.

• Always wear safety goggles when working with, or around, the air bag system. When carrying a non-deployed air bag, be sure the bag and trim cover are pointed away from your body. When placing a non-deployed air bag on a work surface, always face the bag and trim cover upward, away from the surface. This will reduce the motion of the module if it is accidentally deployed. Refer to the additional air bag system precautions later in this section.

• Clean, high quality brake fluid from a sealed container is essential to the safe and proper operation of the brake system. You should always buy the correct type of brake fluid for your vehicle. If the brake fluid becomes contaminated, completely flush the system with new fluid. Never reuse any brake fluid. Any brake fluid that is removed from the system should be discarded. Also, do not allow any brake fluid to come in contact with a painted surface; it will damage the paint.

• Never operate the engine without the proper amount and type of engine oil; doing so WILL result in severe engine damage.

• Timing belt maintenance is extremely important! Many models utilize an interference-type, non-freewheeling engine. If the timing belt breaks, the valves in the cylinder head may strike the pistons, causing potentially serious (also time-consuming and expensive) engine damage. Refer to the maintenance interval charts in the front of this manual for the recommended replacement interval for the timing belt, and to the timing belt section for belt replacement and inspection.

• Disconnecting the negative battery cable on some vehicles may interfere with the functions of the on-board computer system(s) and may require the computer to undergo a relearning process once the negative battery cable is reconnected.

• When servicing drum brakes, only disassemble and assemble one side at a time, leaving the remaining side intact for reference.

ENGINE REPAIR

Ignition Timing

ADJUSTMENT

The base ignition timing is set by the Powertrain Control Module (PCM) and is not adjustable.

Engine Assembly

REMOVAL & INSTALLATION

✳✳ CAUTION

The air suspension switch, located in the left-hand side of the luggage compartment on 1996–97 models or on the right side kick panel for 1998–00 models, must be turned OFF before raising the vehicle. Failure to do so may result in unexpected inflation or deflation of the air springs which may result in shifting of the vehicle during service.

➡Be sure to have available a New Generation Star (NGS) tester or equivalent scan tool with the proper software to properly deflate the air springs before servicing the suspension system. Be sure to have available a new wheel hub retainer nut, lower ball-joint to lower control arm nut and a halfshaft circlip, per side.

1. Before servicing the vehicle, refer to the precautions in the beginning of this section.

2. Place the vehicle over a frame contact hoist. Properly deflate the air springs.

3. Disconnect both battery cables, negative cable first. Drain the engine cooling system.

4. Mark the position of the hood on the hinges and remove the hood.

5. Disconnect the steering coupling at the pinch bolt joint inside the passenger compartment.

6. Remove the engine appearance cover from the engine. Properly relieve the fuel system pressure.

7. Recover the refrigerant from the A/C system using the proper equipment.

➡**Label all electrical connectors and vacuum hoses prior to removal so they can be reinstalled in their proper locations.**

8. Disconnect the engine control sensor wiring from the Intake Air Temperature (IAT) sensor and disconnect the crankcase ventilation tube from air cleaner outlet tube.

9. Loosen the clamps on the air cleaner outlet tube to engine air cleaner and throttle body. Remove the air cleaner outlet tube.

10. Disconnect the chassis vacuum supply hose at the connection on the intake manifold. Position the hose aside.

11. Remove the ground straps from the dash panel.

12. Disconnect the engine control sensor wiring from the Powertrain Control Module (PCM) and position the engine control sensor wiring aside.

13. Remove the connectors for the engine control sensor wiring from the retaining bracket on the power brake booster. Disconnect the engine control sensor wiring at the two connectors.

14. Disconnect engine control sensor wiring from the Mass Air Flow (MAF) sensor.

15. Disconnect engine control sensor wiring from the evaporative emission canister purge valve.

16. Disconnect evaporative emission hose at crankcase vent connector and hose. Position the hose aside.

17. Remove the throttle cable shield and disconnect the accelerator cable and the speed control actuator from the throttle body and from the accelerator cable bracket. Position the cables aside.

18. Remove the retaining nut and disconnect the manual control lever from the manual control lever shaft at the Transmission Range (TR) sensor.

19. Remove the connectors for the engine control sensor wiring from the retaining bracket on top of the transaxle. Disconnect the engine control sensor wiring at the two connectors.

20. Disconnect the wiring connector from the secondary air injection pump relay located on the retaining bracket on top of the transaxle.

21. Disconnect the main emission vacuum control connector at the connection near the fan shroud.

22. Disconnect the oil cooler inlet tube from the transaxle. Remove the oil level dipstick from the indicator tube.

23. Disconnect the heater water hose from the water bypass tube. Disconnect the heater water hose at the rear of the right cylinder head. Disconnect the upper radiator hose at the water bypass tube.

24. Remove the power steering return hose from the power steering oil reservoir and drain.

25. Disconnect the alternator wiring harness from the alternator at the BAT terminal and stator connector plug. Remove the wiring harness retaining clip from the alternator mounting bracket.

26. Partially raise and safely support the vehicle. Remove the front wheel and tire assemblies.

27. Disconnect both ride height sensor links from the lower control arms. Remove both stabilizer bar links from the front stabilizer bar.

28. Separate both lower control arms from the steering knuckles at the ball joints. Separate both tie rod ends from the steering knuckles. Discard the cotter pins.

29. Remove both wheel hub retainer nuts from the halfshaft ends. Remove both halfshafts from the steering knuckles.

30. Raise and safely support the vehicle. Remove the splash shield from the radiator support and subframe.

31. Drain the engine oil. Remove the dual converter Y-pipe.

32. Disconnect the power steering pressure hose from the power steering/transaxle oil cooler connection. Position the hose aside.

33. Disconnect the lower radiator hose at the radiator and thermostat housing and remove the radiator.

34. Disconnect the wiring at the starter, and remove the starter. Disconnect the lower cooler line from the transaxle.

35. Disconnect the retaining clips and the A/C compressor lines from the compressor. Cap all openings to prevent the entrance of dirt or moisture.

36. Support the subframe, engine and transaxle assembly using Powertrain Lift 014–00765 and Universal Powertrain Removal Bracket 014–00766, or equivalents.

37. Remove the four subframe-to-body retaining bolts. Slowly lower the engine, transaxle and subframe from the vehicle as one assembly.

38. Disconnect the power steering pressure hose from the power steering pump.

39. Install suitable engine lifting brackets on the engine and transaxle assembly.

40. Remove the front engine support insulator, rear engine support insulator and engine and transaxle support. Lift the engine and transaxle from the subframe.

41. Lower the engine and transaxle. Support the transaxle on a level, stationary surface for transaxle storage.

42. Remove the transaxle-to-cylinder block mounting bolts and separate the engine from the transaxle/torque converter assembly. Place the engine on a suitable workstand.

To install:

43. Install the transaxle/torque converter assembly to the engine. Tighten the mounting bolts to 30–44 ft. lbs. (40–60 Nm). Tighten the torque converter nuts to 20–34 ft. lbs. (27–46 Nm).

44. Place the engine and transaxle assembly on the subframe. Install the front engine support insulator, rear engine support insulator and engine and transaxle support.

45. Connect the power steering pressure hose from the power steering pump.

46. Raise the engine, transaxle and subframe assembly into position using the powertrain lifting tool. Loosely install the four subframe to body bolts.

47. Align the subframe using a 0.75 inch (19mm) outside diameter pipe or similar tool installed through both alignment holes. Tighten the bolts to 55–75 ft. lbs. (75–102 Nm).

48. Remove the lifting equipment and move aside. Connect the retaining clips and the A/C compressor lines to the compressor.

49. Install the remaining components in the reverse order of removal, then tighten the following:

- Hub retainer nuts to 170–202 ft. lbs. (230–275 Nm)
- Tie rod end-to-steering knuckle castellated nuts to 35–46 ft. lbs. (47–63 Nm)

- Lower control arm-to-steering knuckle nuts to 50–68 ft. lbs. (68–92 Nm)
- Stabilizer bar links-to-stabilizer bar nuts to 30–40 ft. lbs. (40–55 Nm)
- Manual control lever-to-manual control lever shaft nut to 12–16 ft. lbs. (16–22 Nm)
- Air cleaner outlet tube clamps to 12–22 inch lbs. (1.4–2.5 Nm)

50. Install the hood and align as needed. Install the fuel tank fill cap.

51. Fill the cooling system with the proper type and quantity of coolant and fill the crankcase with the proper type of motor oil to the required level. Check the power steering and transaxle fluid levels and fill as needed.

52. Connect both battery cables, negative cable last. Fill the air springs. Run the engine and check for leaks.

53. Evacuate, pressure test and recharge the air conditioning system.

54. Install the engine appearance cover. Tighten the retaining nuts to 61–79 inch lbs. (7–9 Nm).

➡**Whenever the vehicles subframe is removed or lowered, the wheel alignment should be checked.**

55. Check the front wheel alignment. Road test the vehicle and check the engine for proper operation.

Water Pump

REMOVAL & INSTALLATION

1. Before servicing the vehicle, refer to the precautions in the beginning of this section.

2. Disconnect the negative battery cable. Drain the engine cooling system.

3. Remove the coolant recovery reservoir assembly.

4. Loosen the four bolts retaining the water pump pulley to the water pump.

5. Release the drive belt tensioner and remove the drive belt.

6. Remove the four bolts retaining the water pump pulley to the water pump and remove the pulley.

7. Remove the four bolts retaining the water pump to the cylinder block and remove the water pump.

To install:

8. Replace the water pump O-ring and clean the sealing surface of the cylinder block and the water pump.

9. Lubricate the water pump O-ring with fresh coolant and install the water

pump into position. Be sure the water pump is fully seated. Install the four water pump retaining bolts and tighten to 15–22 ft. lbs. (20–30 Nm).

10. Install the water pump pulley on the water pump with the four retaining bolts. Tighten to 15–22 ft. lbs. (20–30 Nm).

11. Install the remaining components in the reverse order of removal.

12. Fill the cooling system to the proper level. Connect the negative battery cable, then start the engine and check for coolant leaks.

Exploded view of the water pump mounting

Cylinder Head

REMOVAL & INSTALLATION

➡**The cylinder head bolts are a torque-to-yield design and cannot be reused. Be sure new cylinder head bolts are available before performing this procedure.**

1. Before servicing the vehicle, refer to the precautions in the beginning of this section.

2. Disconnect the negative battery cable. Remove the engine from the vehicle and position on a suitable workstand.

3. Remove both cylinder head covers. Remove the engine front cover.

4. Remove the intake manifold. Remove the Crankshaft Position (CKP) sensor pulse wheel.

5. Remove the rocker arms. Remove the exhaust manifolds. Drain the coolant from the cylinder block.

6. Rotate the engine to position the piston for No. 1 cylinder to Top Dead Center (TDC) on its compression stroke.

7. Install Camshaft Positioning tool T93P-6256-A or equivalent, in the rear D-slots of the camshafts.

This is not a freewheeling engine. Cam Positioning tool T93P-6256-A or equivalent, must be installed on the camshafts to prevent the camshafts from rotating. Do not rotate the camshafts or crankshaft with the timing chains removed or the valves will contact the pistons.

8. Remove the bolts retaining both primary timing chain tensioners to the cylinder heads and remove the timing chain tensioners.

9. Remove both primary timing chains, timing chain tensioner arms and timing chain guides. Do not loosen the camshaft timing sprocket retaining bolts.

10. Remove the outlet heater water hose retaining bolts from the rear of the right cylinder head.

11. Remove the 10 bolts retaining the cylinder head to the engine block in the opposite order of the installation sequence and remove the cylinder head.

12. Discard the cylinder head bolts. Remove one or both cylinder heads as required.

13. Clean all gasket mating surfaces and bolt holes. Check the cylinder head and cylinder block for flatness. Check the cylinder head for scratches near the coolant passage and combustion chamber that could provide leak paths.

To install:

14. Rotate the crankshaft counterclockwise 45 degrees. The crankshaft keyway should be at the 9 o'clock position as viewed from the front of the engine. This ensures that all pistons are below the top of the cylinder block deck face.

15. Position new head gaskets on the cylinder block.

Turn the crankshaft counterclockwise to the 9 o'clock position before installing the cylinder heads

16. Position the cylinder heads on the engine block dowels, being careful not to score the surface of the head face. Apply clean engine oil to the new cylinder head bolts and install them hand-tight.

17. Tighten the cylinder head bolts as follows:

    a. Tighten the bolts, in sequence, to 27–32 ft. lbs. (37–43 Nm).

    b. Rotate each bolt, in sequence, 85–95 degrees.

    c. Rotate each bolt, in sequence, an additional 85–95 degrees.

18. Position the outlet heater water hose on the right cylinder head. Install and tighten the bolts to 15–22 ft. lbs. (20–30 Nm).

Be sure to tighten the cylinder head bolts in the correct sequence to avoid leakage

19. Install the primary timing chains and set the valve timing. Install the rocker arms.

20. Install the CKP sensor pulse wheel. Install the intake manifold.

➡ **When cleaning the sealing surfaces of the timing chain cover and oil pan-to-cylinder block joints, be careful not to damage the rubber bead of the oil pan gasket. If damaged, the oil pan gasket must be replaced.**

21. Install the engine front cover. Install the cylinder head covers. Install the exhaust manifolds.

22. Install the engine in vehicle. Connect the negative battery cable.

23. Start the engine and bring to normal operating temperature and check for leaks.

24. Check all fluid levels. Road test the vehicle and check for proper engine operation.

Rocker Arms

REMOVAL & INSTALLATION

1. Before servicing the vehicle, refer to the precautions in the beginning of this section.

2. Disconnect the negative battery cable.

3. Remove the camshaft covers.

4. Position the cylinder being serviced at the bottom of it's travel.

➡ **Two different valve spring compressor tools are used for this procedure. Valve Spring Compressor (T91P-6565-A) is used on the exhaust camshaft and Valve Spring Compressor (T93P-6565-A) is used on the intake camshaft.**

5. Compress the valve spring and remove the rocker arm.

To install:

6. Position the cylinder being serviced at the bottom of it's travel.

7. Apply clean engine oil to the rocker arm, valve stem tip and tappet bore.

➡ **Valve tappet should have no more than ¹⁄₁₆ inch (1.5mm) of travel before installing the rocker arm.**

8. Compress the valve spring using the correct tool and install the rocker arm.

VALVE SPRING
COMPRESSOR
T91P-6565-A

Using the proper tool, compress the valve spring and remove the rocker arm

Intake Manifold

REMOVAL & INSTALLATION

1. Before servicing the vehicle, refer to the precautions in the beginning of this section.

2. Disconnect the negative battery cable. Drain the engine cooling system.

3. Remove engine appearance cover. Remove the air cleaner outlet tube.

➡ **Label all electrical connectors and vacuum hoses as they are removed, so they can be reinstalled in their original locations.**

4. Relieve the fuel system pressure. Disconnect the fuel supply and return lines from the fuel injection supply manifold.

5. Remove the 8 retaining nuts on both ignition wire covers and remove the ignition wire covers.

6. Tag and disconnect the ignition wires from the spark plugs with a gentle twist/pull motion on the spark plug boot.

7. Disconnect the ignition wires from the ignition coils.

8. Detach the two center ignition wire separators from the retaining studs.

9. Remove the ignition wires.

10. Disconnect the alternator wiring harness from the alternator at the battery terminal and disconnect the stator connector plug. Remove the wiring harness retaining clip from the alternator mounting bracket.

11. Remove the two bolts and two nuts attaching the alternator mounting bracket to the intake manifold. Remove the mounting bracket.

12. Disconnect the upper radiator hose, the heater water hose and the water bypass tube to water thermostat hose at the water bypass tube.

13. Disconnect the wiring from the Engine Coolant Temperature (ECT) sensor at the water bypass tube.

14. Remove the two retaining nuts and spacers from the water bypass tube hold-down braces to intake manifold studs and remove the water bypass tube.

15. Disconnect the accelerator cable and the speed control actuator from the throttle body and from the accelerator cable bracket. Position the accelerator cable and speed control actuator aside.

16. Disconnect the chassis vacuum supply hose from the intake manifold connector and move it aside.

17. Disconnect the vacuum harness from the fuel pressure regulator, right and left secondary air injection diverter valves, EGR control valve, EGR vacuum regulator control, and secondary air injection vacuum control solenoid and intake manifold connection. Remove the vacuum harness.

18. Disconnect the Intake Manifold Runner Control (IMRC) actuator from the IMRC

Timing belt service is covered in Section 5 of this manual

CRANKCASE VENT CONNECTOR AND HOSE

POSITIVE CRANKCASE VENTILATION VALVE

RH VALVE COVER

THROTTLE BODY

FRONT OF ENGINE

9300LG01

Exploded view of the crankcase vent connector and related components

assemblies at the levers. Remove the IMRC actuator retainers and the IMRC actuator.

19. Disconnect the crankcase vent connector and hose from the throttle body. Remove the PCV valve from the left side cylinder head cover. Move the crankcase vent connector and hose and PCV valve aside.

20. Disconnect the engine wiring harness retaining clips from the intake manifold studs.

21. Disconnect the 8 wiring connectors from the fuel injectors.

22. Disconnect the engine control sensor wiring from the Idle Air Control (IAC) valve, Throttle Position (TP) sensor or TP sensors (if equipped with traction control). Position the wiring harness aside.

23. Remove the two retaining bolts attaching the EGR valve to the intake manifold.

24. Loosen and remove the 20 bolts and studs retaining the intake manifold to the cylinder heads in sequence.

25. Lift the engine control sensor wiring upward for intake manifold removal clearance.

26. Lift the intake manifold off the engine.

27. Remove the four fuel injection supply manifold retaining bolts from the intake manifold. Remove the fuel injection supply manifold from the fuel injectors.

28. Remove the four bolts retaining both lower intake manifolds (IMRC housing assemblies) to the intake manifold and remove both lower intake manifolds.

FRONT OF ENGINE

7922LG05

To prevent warping or cracking the manifold, remove the intake manifold bolts in the sequence shown

➡ **The upper intake manifold gaskets must be replaced when the manifold retaining bolts have been loosened.**

29. Remove the intake manifold upper gaskets and all load limiting spacers from both lower intake manifolds (IMRC assemblies) and discard.

30. Remove the lower intake manifold gaskets from the cylinder heads and discard.

31. Remove the EGR valve gasket and discard. Clean the EGR gasket sealing surface on the EGR valve and the intake manifold.

To install:

32. Clean and inspect all gasket mating surfaces. The upper sealing surfaces of the IMRC housing assemblies and intake manifold mating surfaces should be cleaned with a suitable solvent to remove adhesive residue. Inspect the intake manifold mating surfaces and upper IMRC assembly surfaces to be sure no load limiting spacers (washers) are stuck to the sealing surfaces. The load limiting spacers are part of the intake manifold upper gasket. New load limit spacers will be included with the replacement intake manifold upper gasket as an assembly.

33. If a new intake manifold or IMRC housing assembly is being installed, transfer all necessary components to the new intake manifold or lower intake manifold using new gaskets.

34. Install the upper intake manifold

FRONT OF ENGINE

7922LG06

Tighten the intake manifold bolts in the sequence shown to ensure proper sealing

gasket on the right IMRC housing using the tapered pins at the end bolt locations for proper gasket alignment. Repeat the procedure for the left IMRC housing.

35. Install the IMRC assemblies to the intake manifold and install the four IMRC retaining bolts finger-tight.

36. Install the fuel injection supply manifold to the fuel injectors and install the four retaining bolts. Tighten to 71–106 inch lbs. (8–12 Nm).

37. Position new intake manifold gaskets onto the cylinder heads, using the gaskets integral locating pins to align the gaskets.

38. Place the intake manifold under the engine control sensor wiring and connect the fuel charging wiring to the IAC valve and TP sensor, or sensors, depending upon application.

39. Move the intake manifold into position and install a new EGR valve gasket and the EGR retaining bolts. Finger-tighten the bolts.

40. Install the longer bolts and stud bolts in the outer bolt holes of the intake manifold, but do not tighten yet.

41. Install the shorter bolts and stud bolts in the inner bolt holes of the intake manifold. Hand-tighten all 20 fasteners.

42. Following the sequence shown, tighten fasteners 1 through 20 in numerical sequence as follows:

● = STUD
◼ = BOLT

7922LG07

Tighten the IMRC bolts in alphabetical order for proper sealing

a. No's. 5, 7, 9 and 11—9–11 ft. lbs. (12–15 Nm)

b. All other fasteners—13–16 ft. lbs. (18–22 Nm)

c. Then, tighten all fasteners in numerical sequence, by rotating an additional 85–95 degrees.

43. Tighten the four intake manifold to IMRC housing retaining bolts A through D to 71–89 inch lbs. (8–10 Nm). Tighten fasteners A through D, in sequence, by rotating an additional 85–95 degrees.

44. Tighten the two EGR valve retaining bolts to 15–22 ft. lbs. (20–30 Nm).

45. Connect the wiring to the 8 fuel injectors.

46. Connect the fuel charging wiring harness retaining clips to the intake manifold studs.

47. Connect the crankcase vent connector and hose to the throttle body connection and install the PCV valve into the grommet on the right cylinder head cover.

48. Install the IMRC actuator to the IMRC assemblies at the levers. Position the actuator on the engine and install the retainers. Tighten the retainers to 71–106 inch lbs. (8–12 Nm).

49. Connect the vacuum harness to the fuel pressure regulator, right and left secondary air injection diverter valves, EGR valve, EGR vacuum regulator control and secondary air injectors vacuum control solenoids, and intake manifold vacuum rear connection.

50. Connect the chassis vacuum supply hose and spring clamp to the intake manifold vacuum connection.

51. Connect the accelerator cable and the speed control actuator to the throttle body. Connect the cables to the accelerator cable bracket.

52. Replace all O-rings on the water bypass tube. Clean the O-ring sealing surface on the cylinder heads.

53. Coat all O-rings with clean coolant.

54. Install the water bypass tube support braces over the intake manifold inner studs and install the water bypass tube into position.

55. Install the two water bypass tube spacers and retaining nuts. Tighten the nuts to 71–106 inch lbs. (8–12 Nm).

56. Connect the wiring connector to the ECT sensor.

57. Connect the upper radiator hose, heater water hose and water bypass tube to thermostat housing hose to the water bypass tube.

58. Position the alternator mounting bracket and install the two front retaining bolts and the two rear nuts. Tighten to 71–106 inch lbs. (8–12 Nm).

59. Connect the alternator wiring harness connector plug and battery terminal wire to the alternator. Install the retaining clip to the alternator mounting bracket. Tighten the retaining screw securely.

60. Position the ignition wires and connect the two center ignition wire separators to the retaining studs on the intake manifold.

61. Connect the ignition wires to the ignition coils.

62. Connect the ignition wires to the proper spark plugs.

63. Install the ignition wires into the cylinder head cover slots and install the ignition wire covers. Install the 8 retaining nuts and tighten to 18–35 inch lbs. (2–4 Nm).

64. Connect the fuel supply and return lines to the fuel injection supply manifold.

65. Install the engine air cleaner outlet tube. Tighten the air cleaner outlet tubes clamps to 12–22 inch lbs. (1.4–2.5 Nm).

66. Install the engine appearance cover. Tighten the retaining nuts to 61–79 inch lbs. (7–9 Nm).

67. Install the fuel tank fill cap.

68. Connect the negative battery cable.

69. Fill the cooling system.

70. Start the engine and check for leaks.

71. Road test the vehicle and check for proper operation.

Exhaust Manifold

REMOVAL & INSTALLATION

✲✲ CAUTION

The air suspension switch, located in the left-hand side of the luggage compartment on 1996–97 models or on the right side kick panel for 1998–00 models, must be turned OFF before raising the vehicle. Failure to do so may result in unexpected inflation or deflation of the air springs which may result in shifting of the vehicle during service.

1. Before servicing the vehicle, refer to the precautions in the beginning of this section.

2. Turn the air suspension switch, located in the left side of the luggage compartment, to the **OFF** position.

3. Disconnect the negative battery cable.

4. Raise and safely support the vehicle.

5. For the right side, remove the wiring connectors from the Heated Oxygen Sensors (HO2S).

6. For the left side, remove the splash shield from the lower radiator support and subframe.

7. Remove the dual converter Y-pipe from the exhaust manifolds.

8. For the right side, perform the following procedures:

a. Remove the four exhaust connector retaining bolts and the exhaust connector and muffler gasket from the exhaust manifold.

b. Remove the EGR valve to exhaust manifold tube from the EGR valve tube to manifold connector using a 22mm crowsfoot wrench.

9. Loosen the retaining nut and remove the secondary air injection manifold tube from the exhaust manifold.

10. Remove the 8 exhaust manifold-to-cylinder head retaining nuts.

11. Remove the exhaust manifold and gasket.

➡**For the right side, access may be gained through the right wheel opening area. It may be necessary to remove the EGR valve tube to manifold connector from the right exhaust manifold.**

To install:

12. Clean the mating surfaces of the manifold and the cylinder head.

13. For the right side, if removed, install the EGR valve tube to manifold connector to the right exhaust manifold. Tighten to 33–48 ft. lbs. (45–65 Nm).

14. Position a new exhaust manifold gasket and the exhaust manifold to the cylinder head. Install the 8 retaining nuts. Tighten the nuts in sequence to 13–16 ft. lbs. (18–22 Nm) following the same pattern for both manifolds.

7922LG08

Be sure to tighten the exhaust manifold bolts according to the sequence shown— right side shown, left side similar

15. Connect the secondary air injection manifold tube to the exhaust manifold and tighten the nut to 25–34 ft. lbs. (34–46 Nm).

16. For the right side, perform the following procedures:

a. Connect the EGR valve to exhaust manifold tube to the EGR valve tube to manifold connector. Tighten the nut to 30–33 ft. lbs. (40–45 Nm).

b. Install the exhaust connector with a new inlet pipe gasket.

c. Install the inlet pipe retaining bolts and tighten to:
- 1st—13–17 ft. lbs. (17–23 Nm)
- 2nd—30–40 ft. lbs. (41–54 Nm)

17. Install the dual converter Y-pipe to the exhaust manifolds.

18. For the right side, connect the HO2S wiring connectors.

19. For the left side, install the splash shield to the subframe and lower radiator support.

20. Lower the vehicle.

21. Connect the negative battery cable.

22. Turn the air suspension switch to the ON position.

23. Start the engine and check for exhaust leaks and proper engine operation.

Camshaft and Valve Lifters

REMOVAL & INSTALLATION

1. Before servicing the vehicle, refer to the precautions in the beginning of this section.

2. Disconnect the negative battery cable. Remove the engine from the vehicle and position on a suitable workstand.

3. Remove the cylinder head covers and the engine front cover.

4. Remove the timing chains.

➡**If the rocker arms are to be reused, label them as they are removed so they can be reinstalled in their original locations.**

5. Remove the rocker arms from the cylinder head and the camshaft that is being serviced. If both bank camshafts are to be serviced, all the rocker arms must be removed.

6. Remove the 13 bolts retaining the exhaust camshaft cap cluster assemblies to the cylinder head to remove the exhaust camshaft.

7. Remove the 12 bolts retaining the intake camshaft cap cluster assemblies to the cylinder head to remove the intake camshaft.

8. Tap upward lightly on the camshaft cap clusters and gradually lift the camshaft cap clusters from the cylinder head.

9. Lift the camshaft straight upward to avoid bearing surface damage.

➡**The previous steps will remove only one bank of camshafts. If both banks are being serviced, repeat the removal procedure for the remaining camshafts.**

10. Inspect the camshaft lobes and journals for wear and/or damage. Replace as necessary.

To install:

➡**When cleaning the sealing surfaces of the engine front cover and the oil pan-to-cylinder block joints, use extreme caution not to damage the rubber bead of the oil pan gasket. If damaged, the oil pan gasket must be replaced.**

11. Clean and inspect the cylinder head cover, engine front cover, and cylinder head sealing surfaces.

12. If removed, install the lash adjusters (valve tappets).

13. Apply clean engine oil to the journals and lobes of the camshaft. Install the camshaft to the cylinder head.

14. Install and seat the camshaft cap cluster assemblies. Hand-start the 12 (52mm long) bolts into the intake camshaft caps, seven (52mm long) bolts into the inboard side of the exhaust camshaft and the six (42mm long) bolts into the outboard side of the exhaust camshaft caps.

➡**Each camshaft cap cluster is tightened individually.**

15. Tighten the camshaft cap cluster retaining bolts, in sequence, to 71–106 inch lbs. (8–12 Nm).

16. Loosen the camshaft cap cluster retaining bolts approximately two turns or until the head of the bolt is free.

17. Tighten all bolts again, in sequence, to 71–106 inch lbs. (8–12 Nm).

➡**Once installed, the camshaft should turn freely but with a slight drag.**

18. Check the camshaft end-play using a dial indicator.

19. Install the timing chains.

20. Install Valve Spring Compressor T91P-6565-A or equivalent, under the exhaust camshaft and on top of the exhaust valve spring retainer. Compress the valve spring far enough to install the rocker arm.

21. Install Valve Spring Compressor T93P-6565-A or equivalent, under the intake camshaft and on top of the primary

Tighten the camshaft cap clusters in the order shown to prevent warpage

intake valve spring retainer. Compress the valve spring far enough to install the rocker arm.

22. Install Valve Spring Compressor T93P-6565-A or equivalent, under the intake camshaft and on top of the secondary intake valve spring retainer. Compress the valve spring far enough to install the rocker arm.

➡ **The previous installation steps must be repeated if both banks are being serviced to install the remaining camshafts.**

23. Inspect and replace the crankshaft front seal and timing chain front cover gasket.

24. Install the engine front cover and the cylinder head covers.

25. Remove the engine from the workstand and install in the vehicle.

26. Start the engine and check for leaks.

27. Road test the vehicle and check for proper engine operation.

Valve Lash

ADJUSTMENT

The 4.6L DOHC engine uses hydraulic valve lash adjusters that do not require any maintenance. If the valve train becomes noisy, inspect the camshafts, rocker arms and valves for excessive wear or damage.

Oil Pan

REMOVAL & INSTALLATION

✱✱ CAUTION

The air suspension switch, located in the left-hand side of the luggage compartment on 1996–97 models or on the right side kick panel for 1998–00 models, must be turned OFF before raising the vehicle. Failure to do so may result in unexpected inflation or deflation of the air springs which may result in shifting of the vehicle during service.

1. Before servicing the vehicle, refer to the precautions in the beginning of this section.

2. Turn the air suspension switch, located in the left side of the luggage compartment on 1996–97 models or on the right side kick panel for 1998–00 models to the **OFF** position.

3. Disconnect the negative battery cable.

4. Remove the oil level dipstick.

5. Raise and safely support the vehicle. Drain the engine oil.

6. Remove the dual converter Y-pipe from the exhaust manifolds.

7. Disconnect the wiring from the low oil sensor connector.

8. Remove the power steering pressure hose retainer brackets from the engine front cover studs in two locations. Position the power steering pressure hose aside.

9. Remove the 16 bolts retaining the oil pan to the cylinder block and remove the oil pan and gasket.

To install:

10. Clean the gasket surfaces on the cylinder block, oil pan and front cover with a clean cloth. If scraping is required, only use plastic-tipped scrapers to prevent damage to aluminum surfaces. Thoroughly clean the inside of the oil pan.

11. Apply a bead of silicone sealer to the oil pan flange. Also apply a bead of sealer to the front cover/cylinder block joint and fill the grooves on both sides of the rear main seal cap.

➡ **When using silicone rubber sealer, assembly must occur within 15 minutes after sealer application. Be sure the sealer does not fall into the engine where it may plug oil passages.**

12. Install a new gasket on the oil pan.

13. Carefully install the oil pan using the 16 retaining bolts. Tighten the bolts, in sequence, first to 14 ft. lbs. (20 Nm), then turn the bolts an additional 60 degrees in the same sequence.

14. Install the power steering pressure hose retainer bracket onto the engine front cover studs. Install and tighten the retaining nuts to 71–106 inch lbs. (8–12 Nm).

Tighten the oil pan bolts in sequence to ensure a good seal with the engine block

15. Install the low oil sensor wiring on the sensor connector.

16. Install the dual converter Y-pipe to the exhaust manifolds.

17. Lower the vehicle. Install the oil level dipstick.

Refer to Section 1 for engine rebuilding specifications

⁕⁕ WARNING

Operating the engine without the proper amount and type of engine oil will result in severe engine damage.

18. Fill the crankcase with the correct type and quantity of engine oil.

19. Connect the negative battery cable. Start the engine and check for leaks.

20. Turn the air suspension switch to the **ON** position.

Oil Pump

REMOVAL & INSTALLATION

1. Before servicing the vehicle, refer to the precautions in the beginning of this section.

2. Disconnect the negative battery cable. Remove the engine from the vehicle and position on a suitable workstand.

3. Remove the engine front cover. Remove the engine oil pan.

4. Remove the oil pump screen cover/tube bolts and the tube; discard the O-ring.

5. Remove the timing chains. Remove the crankshaft sprockets.

6. Remove the oil pump-to-cylinder block bolts and the oil pump.

To install:

7. Thoroughly clean the oil pump and cylinder block mounting surfaces and the oil pump screen cover and tube.

8. Turn the inner rotor of the oil pump to align with the flats on the crankshaft and install the oil pump flush with the cylinder block. Install the four retaining bolts and tighten to 71–106 inch lbs. (8–12 Nm).

9. Replace the engine oil filter. Install the crankshaft sprockets. Install both timing chains.

10. Position the oil pump screen cover and tube on the oil pump with a new O-ring and hand-start the two retaining bolts.

Tighten the oil pump mounting bolts in the sequence shown

11. Install the bolt retaining the oil pump screen cover and tube to the main bearing stud spacer finger-tight.

12. Tighten the oil pump screen cover and tube-to-oil pump bolts to 71–106 inch lbs. (8–12 Nm). Tighten the oil pump screen cover and tube-to-main bearing stud spacer bolt to 15–22 ft. lbs. (20–30 Nm).

13. Install the engine oil pan. Install the engine front cover.

14. Remove the engine from the workstand and install in the vehicle.

15. Restore all fluid levels. Connect the negative battery cable.

16. Run the engine and check for leaks and proper oil pressure. Road test the vehicle and check for proper operation.

Rear Main Seal

REMOVAL & INSTALLATION

⁕⁕ CAUTION

The air suspension switch, located in the left-hand side of the luggage compartment on 1996–97 models or on the right side kick panel for 1998–00 models, must be turned OFF before raising the vehicle. Failure to do so may result in unexpected inflation or deflation of the air springs which may result in shifting of the vehicle during service.

1. Before servicing the vehicle, refer to the precautions in the beginning of this section.

2. Turn the air suspension switch, located in the left side of the luggage compartment on 1996–97 models or on the right side kick panel for 1998–00 models to the **OFF** position.

3. Disconnect the negative battery cable.

4. Raise and safely support the vehicle.

5. Properly support the engine.

6. Remove the sub-frame and transaxle from the vehicle.

7. Remove the flywheel from the crankshaft.

8. Remove the rear crankshaft seal retainer bolts and remove the retainer from the cylinder block.

9. Support the seal retainer securely and remove the seal, using a punch or similar tool.

To install:

10. Clean and inspect the retainer and cylinder block mating surfaces.

11. Apply a 0.060 inch (1.5mm) continuous bead of a silicone gasket sealer to the cylinder block.

12. Install the seal retainer and retaining bolts. Tighten the bolts, in sequence, to 71–106 inch lbs. (8–12 Nm).

13. Install a new rear crankshaft seal using Seal Installer T82L-6701-A and adapter T91P-6701-A or equivalents.

14. Install the flywheel to the engine. Install the six retaining bolts and tighten in an alternating sequence to 54–64 ft. lbs. (73–87 Nm).

15. Install the transaxle and sub-frame.

16. Lower the vehicle.

17. Remove the engine support.

18. Connect the negative battery cable.

19. Turn the air suspension switch to the ON position.

20. Start the engine and check for leaks.

➡ **Whenever the vehicles sub-frame is removed or lowered, the wheel alignment should be checked.**

21. Align the front wheels.

22. Road test the vehicle and check for proper operation.

Be sure to tighten the rear main oil seal retainer bolts in the correct sequence

Use the Seal Installer T82L-6701-A and adapter T91P-6701-A or equivalents to install the seal evenly in the retainer

Timing Chain, Sprockets, Front Cover and Seal

REMOVAL & INSTALLATION

❋❋ WARNING

This is an interference engine. When the timing chains are removed and the cylinder heads are installed, the crankshaft and/or camshafts must not be rotated unless as directed in this procedure. Failure to follow these instructions will result in valve and/or piston damage.

1. Before servicing the vehicle, refer to the precautions in the beginning of this section.

2. Disconnect the negative battery cable. Remove the engine from the vehicle and position on a suitable workstand.

3. Remove the support brackets for the engine sensor wiring from the engine front cover.

4. Loosen the water pump pulley bolts. Remove the accessory drive belt.

5. Remove the water pump pulley and lower water pump-to-cylinder block retaining bolt for engine front cover removal clearance.

6. Using Pulley Remover T69L-10300-B or equivalent, remove the power steering pump pulley.

➡ **The front lower bolt on the power steering pump will not come all the way out.**

7. Remove the bolts retaining the power steering pump to the cylinder block and the engine front cover.

8. Position the power steering pump and reservoir aside. Remove the bolts retaining the front cover to the oil pan.

9. Remove the crankshaft pulley retaining bolt and washer from the crankshaft.

10. Install Crankshaft Damper Remover T58P-6316-D or equivalent, on the crankshaft pulley and pull the crankshaft pulley from the crankshaft.

11. Disconnect the engine control wiring from the Camshaft Position (CMP) sensor.

12. Remove the bolt retaining the belt idler pulley and remove the idler pulley.

13. Remove the drive belt tensioner retaining bolt and drive belt tensioner from the engine front cover.

14. Disconnect the Crankshaft Position (CKP) sensor and move the wiring aside.

15. Remove the engine front cover. Remove both cylinder head covers. Remove the CKP sensor tooth wheel.

16. Rotate the crankshaft to place the piston for No. 1 cylinder at Top Dead Center (TDC) on its compression stroke.

❋❋ WARNING

Camshaft Positioning tool T93P-6256-A or equivalent, and Camshaft Holding tool T93P-6256-AH or equivalent, must be installed to prevent accidental rotation of the camshafts and possible engine damage.

17. Install Camshaft Positioning tool T93P-6256-A or equivalent, in the rear D-slots of the camshaft.

❋❋ WARNING

Failure to use Camshaft Holding tool T93P-6256-AH or equivalent, while assembling or disassembling the timing chains will result in damage

Install the camshaft positioning tool on the rear of the camshafts to position both keyways down toward the crankshaft

Install the Camshaft holding tool to secure the camshafts and prevent damage to the Camshaft Positioning Tool

to the D-slots or Camshaft Positioning tool T93P-6256-A.

18. Install Camshaft Holding tool T93P-6256-AH or equivalent, onto the camshafts to keep the camshafts from rotating and to prevent damaging the camshaft positioning tool.

19. Remove the right primary timing chain tensioner bolts and the tensioner.

20. Remove the right tensioner arm bolt and the arm.

➡ **The two bolts retaining the timing chain guide to the cylinder head are longer than the one to the block.**

21. Remove the right timing chain guide bolts and guide. Remove the right primary timing chain.

22. Remove the right crankshaft sprocket. Remove the camshaft sprocket retaining bolts.

❋❋ WARNING

The secondary timing chain tensioner plunger is spring loaded. Care must be taken to prevent the plunger from dropping out of the tensioner during disassembly.

23. Unlock and compress the secondary timing chain tensioners and lock the timing chain tensioner in the compressed position using a paper clip or stiff wire. Remove the secondary timing chains and camshaft sprockets.

24. Remove the left primary timing chain tensioner bolts tensioner.

25. Remove the bolt retaining the left timing chain tensioner arm and remove the left timing chain tensioner arm.

26. Remove the left timing chain guide bolts and the guide. Remove the left primary timing chain. Remove the left crankshaft sprocket.

❋❋ WARNING

Failure to use Camshaft Holding tool T93P-6256-AH or equivalent, while removing or tightening the camshaft bolts may result in damage to the camshaft D-slots or the camshaft positioning tool.

27. Remove the camshaft sprocket retaining bolts.

❋❋ WARNING

The secondary timing chain tensioner plunger is spring loaded. Care must

be taken to prevent the plunger from dropping out of the tensioner during disassembly.

28. Unlock and compress the secondary chain tensioner and lock the chain tensioner in the compressed position using a paper clip or stiff wire. Remove the secondary timing chain and camshaft sprockets.

❋❋ WARNING

Do not rotate the crankshaft and/or camshafts or engine damage may occur.

29. Inspect the friction material on the timing chain tensioner arms and timing chain guides. If worn or damaged, remove and clean the oil pan and replace the oil pump screen cover and tube.

To install:

30. If the engine has jumped time, be sure all service to the necessary engine components and/or valve train has been made.

31. Be sure the primary and secondary timing chain tensioners are in the collapsed position and retained with paper clips or equivalent.

32. Install Camshaft Positioning tool T93P-6256-A or equivalent, into the D-slots on the rear of the camshafts to position both intake and exhaust camshafts with the keyways pointing down towards the crankshaft. Install Camshaft Holding tool T93P-6256-AH or equivalent, on the center of the camshafts and do not remove until all parts are installed and tightened.

33. Install the left secondary timing chain tensioner and tighten the bolts to 70–106 inch lbs. (8–12 Nm).

34. Install the left secondary camshaft sprockets and secondary timing chain as an assembly. Be sure the hubs of the sprocket are facing the proper direction.

35. Install the left primary camshaft

Be sure the copper links colored black on the timing chain align with the marks on the gears and the keyways are positioned 90 degrees from the camshaft cover surface

sprocket and camshaft sprocket spacer on the left camshaft.

36. Install the washers and camshaft sprocket retaining bolts, finger-tight only.

➡ **The secondary camshaft sprockets must be free to turn.**

37. Install Timing Chain Tensioning tool T93P-6256-BH or equivalent, on the left secondary timing chain tensioner.

38. Tighten the camshaft sprocket bolts to 81–95 ft. lbs. (110–130 Nm).

39. Install the right secondary timing chain tensioner and tighten the retaining bolts to 70–106 inch lbs. (8–12 Nm).

40. Install the right secondary camshaft sprockets and secondary timing chain as an assembly. Be sure the hubs of the sprocket are facing the proper direction.

Secondary timing chain tensioning tool installed

41. Install the right primary camshaft sprocket and camshaft sprocket spacer on the right camshaft.

42. Install the washers and camshaft sprocket retaining bolts, finger-tight only.

➡ **The secondary camshaft sprockets must be free to turn.**

43. Install Timing Chain Tensioning tool T93P-6256-BH or equivalent, on the right secondary timing chain tensioner.

Be sure to position the crankshaft sprockets as shown to prevent engine damage

44. Tighten the camshaft sprocket bolts to 81–95 ft. lbs. (110–130 Nm).

45. Install the left crankshaft sprocket, making sure the tapered part of the sprocket faces away from the cylinder block.

46. Install the primary timing chain on the left primary camshaft sprocket. Be sure the copper link of the timing chain aligns with the timing mark on the camshaft sprocket.

➡ **If the copper links of the timing chain are not visible, pull the chain taught until the opposite sides of the chain contact one another and lay it on a flat surface. Mark the links at each end of the chain and use them in place of the copper links.**

47. Install the left primary timing chain on the left crankshaft sprocket. Be sure the copper link of the timing chain aligns with the timing mark on the crankshaft sprocket.

48. Install the right crankshaft sprocket, making sure the tapered part of the sprocket faces toward the cylinder block.

49. Install the primary timing chain on the right primary camshaft sprocket. Be sure the copper link of the timing chain aligns with the timing mark on the camshaft sprocket.

50. Install the right primary timing chain on the right crankshaft sprocket. Be sure the copper link of the timing chain aligns with the timing mark on the crankshaft sprocket.

➡ **The two timing chain guide bolts to the cylinder head are longer than the bolt to the cylinder block.**

51. Install both timing chain guides and tighten the bolts to 71–106 inch lbs. (8–12 Nm).

52. Lubricate the timing chain tensioner arm contact surfaces with clean engine oil. Install both tensioner arms and tighten the bolts to 84–132 inch lbs. (10–15 Nm).

53. Install right and left primary timing chain tensioners and tighten the bolts to 15–22 ft. lbs. (20–30 Nm).

54. Remove the locking pins from the timing chain tensioners and be sure all timing marks are aligned. Remove the camshaft positioning tool and the camshaft holding tool.

➡ **When cleaning the sealing surfaces of the engine front cover and oil pan-to-cylinder block joints, be extremely careful not to damage the rubber bead of the oil pan gasket. If the oil pan gasket is damaged, it must be replaced.**

55. Clean the sealing surfaces of the cylinder block, cylinder heads and engine

Correct alignment of the primary timing chains and sprockets

front cover; remove all traces of oil, dirt and old sealant. Sealing surfaces must be clean and dry before applying sealant.

56. Replace the engine front cover gaskets and the crankshaft front seal. Apply silicone sealant to the proper locations on the cylinder block and heads.

➡**The engine front cover must be rolled into place. DO NOT slide on the oil pan gasket.**

57. Carefully install the front cover to the engine.

58. Install the five studs and 10 bolts retaining the engine front cover to the engine. Tighten, in sequence, to 15–22 ft. lbs. (20–30 Nm). Tighten the stud bolts and bolts numbered 6, 7, 8, 9, 10, and 11 within four minutes after applying the sealer.

To prevent leakage, tighten the front cover mounting bolts in the sequence shown

59. Install the drive belt tensioner and bolt. Tighten the bolt to 15–22 ft. lbs. (20–30 Nm).

60. Install the belt idler pulley and bolt. Tighten the bolt to 15–22 ft. lbs. (20–30 Nm).

61. Connect the engine control sensor wiring to the CKP and CMP sensors. Install the left and the right cylinder head covers.

62. Install the crankshaft pulley on the crankshaft, using Crankshaft Damper Replacer T74P-6316-B or equivalent.

63. Apply silicone sealant in the keyway of the crankshaft pulley.

64. Install the pulley bolt and washer, then tighten as follows:

   a. Tighten the bolt to 89 ft. lbs. (120 Nm), then loosen the bolt.

   b. Retighten the bolt to 39 ft. lbs. (53 Nm).

   c. Turn the retaining bolt an additional 90 degrees.

65. Install the four bolts retaining the engine front cover to the oil pan and tighten to 15–22 ft. lbs. (20–30 Nm), then rotate the bolts in sequence an additional 60 degrees.

66. Position the power steering pump on the engine and install the four retaining bolts. Tighten the bolts to 15–22 ft. lbs. (20–30 Nm).

67. Install the retainer brackets for the engine control sensor wiring to the engine front cover.

68. Using Power Steering Pump Pulley Replacer T91P-3A733-A or equivalent, install the power steering pump pulley.

69. Install the water pump lower bolt removed for engine front cover clearance. Tighten the bolt to 15–22 ft. lbs. (20–30 Nm).

70. Install the water pump pulley with the four bolts. Tighten the bolts to 15–22 ft. lbs. (20–30 Nm).

71. Install the accessory drive belt. Install the engine assembly in the vehicle. Restore all fluid levels.

72. Connect the negative battery cable. Start the engine and check for leaks and proper engine operation.

FUEL SYSTEM

Fuel System Service Precautions

Safety is the most important factor when performing not only fuel system maintenance but any type of maintenance. Failure to conduct maintenance and repairs in a safe manner may result in serious personal injury or death. Maintenance and testing of the vehicle's fuel system components can be accomplished safely and effectively by adhering to the following rules and guidelines.

• To avoid the possibility of fire and personal injury, always disconnect the negative battery cable unless the repair or test procedure requires that battery voltage be applied.

• Always relieve the fuel system pressure prior to disconnecting any fuel system component (injector, fuel rail, pressure regulator, etc.), fitting or fuel line connection. Exercise extreme caution whenever relieving fuel system pressure to avoid exposing skin, face and eyes to fuel spray. Please be advised that fuel under pressure may penetrate the skin or any part of the body that it contacts.

• Always place a shop towel or cloth around the fitting or connection prior to loosening to absorb any excess fuel due to spillage. Ensure that all fuel spillage (should it occur) is quickly removed from engine surfaces. Ensure that all fuel soaked cloths or towels are deposited into a suitable waste container.

• Always keep a dry chemical (Class B) fire extinguisher near the work area.

• Do not allow fuel spray or fuel vapors to come into contact with a spark or open flame.

• Always use a back-up wrench when loosening and tightening fuel line connection fittings. This will prevent unnecessary stress and torsion to fuel line piping. Always follow the proper torque specifications.

• Always replace worn fuel fitting O-rings with new. Do not substitute fuel hose or equivalent, where fuel pipe is installed.

Fuel System Pressure

RELIEVING

1. Before servicing the vehicle, refer to the precautions in the beginning of this section.

2. Disconnect the negative battery cable.

3. Remove the fuel tank fill cap to relieve the pressure in the fuel tank.

4. Remove the cap from the Schrader valve located on the fuel supply manifold (fuel rail).

5. On gasoline engines, attach Fuel Pressure Gauge T80L-9974-A or equivalent, to the valve and drain the fuel through the drain tube into a suitable container.

6. On flex-fuel engines, connect fuel pressure gauge T80L-9974-A or equivalent and fuel pressure test kit 134-R0035 or equivalent, to the Schrader valve. Drain the fuel through the drain tube into a suitable container.

7. After the fuel system pressure is relieved, remove the fuel pressure gauge and install the cap on the Schrader valve.

8. Install the fuel tank fill cap.

9. Connect the negative battery cable only after system repairs are completed.

Fuel Filter

REMOVAL & INSTALLATION

✳✳ CAUTION

The air suspension switch, located in the left-hand side of the luggage compartment on 1996–97 models or on the right side kick panel for 1998–00 models, must be turned OFF before raising the vehicle. Failure to do so may result in unexpected inflation or deflation of the air springs which may result in shifting of the vehicle during service.

1. Before servicing the vehicle, refer to the precautions in the beginning of this section.

2. Turn the air suspension service switch **OFF**.

3. Disconnect the negative battery cable.

4. Properly relieve the fuel system pressure.

5. Raise and safely support the vehicle.

6. Using Fuel Line Disconnect tool T90T-9550-B or T90T-9550-C or equivalent, disconnect the push connect fittings at the fuel filter.

➡**Grasp the fitting and pull in an axial direction to remove the fitting from the fuel filter. Use care, as excessive side loading could break the connector body.**

7. Loosen the fuel filter retaining clamp and remove the fuel filter. Note the direction of the flow arrow on the filter, so the replacement filter can be reinstalled in the same position.

To install:

8. Install the fuel filter with the flow arrow facing the proper direction. Tighten the filter retaining clamp to 15–25 inch lbs. (1.7–2.8 Nm).

9. Apply a light coating of clean engine oil to the fuel filter ends. Align the fittings and filter axially and push the fittings onto the filter ends. When the fittings are prop-

7922LG21

Slide the special tool into the fitting to disengage it—push connect type fitting shown

7922LG22

Remove the hairpin clip and pull the connection apart—hairpin clip type fitting shown

erly engaged, a definite click will be heard. Be sure the fittings are fully engaged.

10. Lower the vehicle.

11. Connect the negative battery cable.

12. Start the engine and check for fuel leaks.

13. Turn the air suspension switch to the ON position.

Fuel Pump

REMOVAL & INSTALLATION

✳✳ CAUTION

The air suspension switch, located in the left-hand side of the luggage compartment on 1996–97 models or on the right side kick panel for 1998–00 models, must be turned OFF before raising the vehicle. Failure to do so may result in unexpected inflation or deflation of the air springs which may result in shifting of the vehicle during service.

1. Before servicing the vehicle, refer to the precautions in the beginning of this section.

2. Turn the air suspension switch, located in the left side of the luggage compartment on 1996–97 models or on the right side kick panel for 1998–00 models, to the **OFF** position.

3. Disconnect the negative battery cable. Properly relieve the fuel system pressure.

4. Raise and safely support the vehicle. Remove the fuel tank and place on a suitable work bench.

5. Remove any dirt that has accumulated around the fuel pump retaining flange so it will not enter the tank during pump removal and installation.

6. Turn the fuel pump locking ring counterclockwise and remove the locking ring using Fuel Tank Sender Wrench T74P-9275-A, or equivalent.

7. Pull the fuel pump module up and out of the fuel tank until the locking tabs for the fuel pump module are accessible. Squeeze both locking tabs together and remove the fuel pump module from the fuel tank. Remove and discard the O-ring seal.

To install:

8. Clean the fuel pump mounting flange, fuel tank mounting surface and O-ring seal groove.

9. Apply a light coating of grease on a new O-ring seal to hold it in place during assembly and install the O-ring seal.

10. Install the fuel pump module carefully to ensure the filter and hoses and float rod are not damaged.

11. Align the fuel pump module and the fuel tank retainer axially and push the fuel pump module into the fuel tank retainer. When the fuel pump module is properly engaged, a definite click will be heard engaging the two locking tabs on the outside of the fuel pump.

12. Pull on the fuel pump module to ensure that both locking tabs are properly engaged.

13. Be sure the locating keys are in the keyways and the seal ring remains in the groove.

14. Hold the fuel pump module in place and install the locking ring finger-tight. Be sure all the locking tabs are under the tank lock ring tabs.

15. Using the sender wrench or equivalent, rotate the locking ring clockwise until the ring is against the stops.

16. Install the fuel tank in the vehicle. Lower the vehicle.

17. Add a minimum of 10 gallons (38 liters) of clean fuel to the tank. Connect the negative battery cable.

18. Turn the air suspension switch to the **ON** position.

19. Install a suitable fuel pressure gauge to the Schrader valve on the fuel supply manifold.

20. Cycle the ignition switch from **OFF** to **ON** for three seconds. Repeat this procedure 5–10 times until the pressure gauge reads at least 30 psi (207 kPa). Check for fuel leaks.

21. Remove the fuel pressure gauge. Start the engine and again, check for fuel leaks. Road test the vehicle and check for proper operation.

7922LG23

To remove the fuel pump, reach into the tank and press the locking tabs inward

DRIVE TRAIN

Transaxle Assembly

REMOVAL & INSTALLATION

❄❄ CAUTION

The air suspension switch, located in the left-hand side of the luggage compartment on 1996–97 models or on the right side kick panel for 1998–00 models, must be turned OFF before raising the vehicle. Failure to do so may result in unexpected inflation or deflation of the air springs which may result in shifting of the vehicle during service.

➡**Be sure to have available new half-shaft circlips and wheel hub retainer nuts.**

1. Before servicing the vehicle, refer to the precautions in the beginning of this section.

2. Properly deflate the air springs.

3. Disconnect both battery cables, negative cable first. Remove the battery and battery tray.

4. Remove the hoses and electrical connectors from the engine air cleaner, and remove the air cleaner assembly.

5. Remove the two screws and the accelerator control splash shield from the throttle body.

6. Disconnect the transaxle harness electrical connector and the Transmission Range (TR) sensor electrical connectors.

7. Remove the nut from shift lever, remove the clip from the cable bracket and lift the cable from the bracket.

8. Disconnect the transaxle oil cooler lines from the transaxle.

9. Remove the four transaxle housing-to-engine bolts from the top of the transaxle.

10. Install the two engine lifting eyes to the front and rear locations of the engine. Install the three Bar Engine Support Bracket Set D88L-6000-A or equivalent, and suitably support the engine.

11. Raise and safely support the vehicle. Remove the front wheel and tire assemblies.

12. Loosen the transaxle oil pan and drain the fluid into a suitable container.

When most of the fluid has drained, install the pan bolts.

13. Disconnect the height sensors.

14. Remove the cotter pins and castellated nuts from both tie rod ends. Separate the tie rod ends from the steering knuckles. Discard the cotter pins.

15. Disconnect the sway bar links from the sway bar.

16. Separate the lower control arms from the steering knuckles.

17. Remove the wheel hub retainer nuts and remove both halfshafts from the vehicle. Discard the nuts.

18. Disconnect the Heated Oxygen Sensor (HO2S) electrical connectors.

19. Remove the dual converter Y-pipe assembly from the vehicle.

20. Remove the starter motor and the dust cover.

21. Support the subframe using Powertrain Lift 014–00765 and Removal Bracket 014–00766, or equivalents.

22. Remove the four subframe-to-body bolts and lower the subframe.

23. Remove the transaxle housing cover from the transaxle.

24. Remove the four torque converter-to-flywheel retaining nuts.

25. Remove the five bolts retaining the rear engine support and remove the support from the transaxle.

26. Support the transaxle with High Lift Transmission Jack 014–00210 and Adapter 014–00461, or equivalents.

27. Remove the two lower engine-to-transaxle bolts.

28. Remove the two bolts and one nut from the right side of engine mount to transaxle case.

29. Carefully separate the transaxle from the engine and slowly lower the transaxle out of the vehicle.

To install:

➡**Verify the transaxle cooler lines are thoroughly cleaned before installing the transaxle assembly.**

30. If removed, place the transaxle on High Lift Transmission Jack 014–00210 and Adapter 014–00461, or equivalents.

31. Slowly raise the transaxle assembly into position until the transaxle housing engages the engine dowel pins. Align the torque converter studs to the flywheel.

32. Install the two lower engine-to-transaxle bolts. Alternately tighten the bolts while making sure the transaxle pulls in

flush with the engine. Tighten the bolts to 80–106 inch lbs. (9–12 Nm).

➡**When installing the transaxle to the engine, verify that the converter-to-transaxle engagement is maintained. Prevent the converter from moving forward and disengaging during installation.**

33. Install the four flywheel-to-torque converter nuts. Tighten to 20–34 ft. lbs. (27–46 Nm).

34. Mount the rear engine/transaxle support to the transaxle. Tighten the five retaining bolts to 44–60 ft. lbs. (60–80 Nm).

35. Install the transaxle housing cover and securely tighten the bolts.

36. Install the two bolts and one nut to the right side of the engine mount to transaxle case.

37. Install the starter motor and tighten the bolt and stud to 15–21 ft. lbs. (21–29 Nm).

38. Connect the electrical connectors to the starter motor.

39. If removed, place the subframe on Powertrain Lift 014–00765 and Removal Bracket 014–00766, or equivalents.

40. Raise the subframe into position.

41. Loosely install the four subframe to body bolts.

42. Align the subframe using a 0.75 inch (19mm) outside diameter pipe or similar tool installed through both alignment holes. Tighten the bolts to 55–75 ft. lbs. (75–102 Nm).

43. Remove the powertrain lift.

44. Install the remaining components in the reverse order of removal. Tighten the following:

- Ball joint stud retaining nuts to 50–68 ft. lbs. (68–92 Nm)
- Sway bar link-to-sway bar nuts to 30–40 ft. lbs. (40–55 Nm)
- Tie rod end-to-steering knuckle nuts to 35–46 ft. lbs. (47–63 Nm)
- Manual control lever nut to 12–16 ft. lbs. (16–22 Nm)

45. Install the battery tray and the battery. Connect both battery cables, negative cable last.

46. Refill the air springs. Install the engine appearance cover. Tighten the retaining nuts to 61–79 inch lbs. (7–9 Nm).

47. Fill the transaxle with the proper type and quantity of fluid. Check the front end alignment.

48. Check the transaxle for leaks and proper shift selector functioning. Road test the vehicle and check for proper operation.

Halfshaft

REMOVAL & INSTALLATION

➡**Do NOT begin this procedure unless the following parts are available:**

- New hub retainer nut
- New lower control arm-to-steering knuckle bolt and nut
- New stub shaft/link shaft circlip

Once removed, these parts must not be reused during assembly. Their torque holding ability or retention capability is diminished during removal.

➡**Be sure to have available a New Generation Star (NGS) tester or equivalent scan tool with the proper software to properly deflate the air springs before servicing the suspension system.**

✳✳ CAUTION

Do not remove an air spring under any circumstances when pressurized. Do not remove any components supporting an air spring without exhausting the air. Failure to follow these instructions may result in unexpected inflation or deflation of the air springs which may result in shifting of the vehicle during service.

1. Before servicing the vehicle, refer to the precautions in the beginning of this section.

2. Place the vehicle over a frame contact hoist.

3. Properly deflate the air springs.

4. Turn the ignition switch to the **OFF** position. Leave the steering column in the UNLOCKED position.

5. Disconnect the negative battery cable.

6. Loosen and remove the wheel hub retainer nut. Discard the nut.

7. Raise and safely support the vehicle. Remove the wheel and tire assembly.

8. Remove the brake anti-lock sensor mounting bolt and the anti-lock sensor from the steering knuckle. Move the sensor aside.

9. Remove the air suspension height sensor at the lower control arm ball stud attachment. Move the sensor aside.

10. Remove the nuts from the sway bar link at the strut. Remove the sway bar link from the strut and move aside.

11. Using Hub Remover/Replacer T81P-1104-C, Stud Adapter T86P-1104-A1, Hub Remover Adapters T83P-1104-BH and Hub Replacer T81P-1104-A or equivalents, push the CV-joint only to the point that the splines are free in the hub.

12. Remove the lower ball joint-to-lower control arm nut. Using Puller T64P-3590-F or equivalent, separate the lower ball joint from the lower control arm. Discard the nut.

13. Pull down on the lower control arm until the lower ball joint clears the lower control arm.

➡**Do not allow the halfshaft to hang unsupported. Damage to the CV-joint or boots may result.**

14. Push the outboard CV-joint stub shaft in while placing a wooden dowel between the frame pocket and steering knuckle. Remove the outer CV-joint from the hub.

15. Assemble CV-Joint Puller Adapter T89P-3415-B, Puller Extension T86P-3514-A2 or equivalents, and a slide hammer.

7922LG24

Place the wooden dowel between the frame and the steering knuckle to keep it out of your way

7922LG25

Use a slide hammer and adapter to remove the halfshaft from the transaxle

Insert the puller adapter behind the inner CV-joint housing at the 4 o'clock position on the left side or at the 5 o'clock position on the right side.

16. Use the slide hammer to release the halfshaft bearing retainer circlip.

17. Carefully remove halfshaft and tools from the vehicle. Discard the circlip.

To install:

18. Install a new circlip on the inner CV-joint stub shaft. When installing the circlip, start one end in the groove and work the circlip over the stub shaft end into the groove. This will avoid over expanding the circlip.

19. Carefully align the splines of the inner CV-joint stub shaft with the splines in the transaxle. Exerting some force, push the CV-joint into the transaxle until the circlip is felt to seat in the differential side gear. Use care to prevent damage to the oil seal.

➡ **A non-metallic (plastic or rawhide) mallet may be used to aid in seating the halfshaft bearing retainer circlip into the differential side gear groove. If a mallet is necessary, tap only on the outer CV-joint.**

20. Remove the wooden dowel and carefully align the splines of the outer CV-joint with the splines in the wheel hub.

21. Carefully push the shaft into the wheel hub as far as possible.

22. Install a new wheel hub retainer nut. Manually thread the hub retainer nut onto the outer CV-joint as far as possible.

23. Install the remaining components in the reverse order of removal:

• Lower ball joint-to-lower control arm, using a new retaining nut, to 39–53 ft. lbs. (53–72 Nm)

• Sway bar link-to-strut nut to 57–75 ft. lbs. (77–107 Nm)

• Anti-lock sensor bolt to 40–60 inch lbs. (4.5–6.8 Nm)

• Hub retainer to 180–200 ft. lbs. (245–270 Nm)

• Lug nuts to 80–105 ft. lbs. (108–144 Nm)

24. Lower the vehicle. Connect the negative battery cable. Refill the air spring.

25. Check the transaxle fluid level and add, as necessary. Road test the vehicle and check for proper operation.

STEERING AND SUSPENSION

Air Bag

✳✳ CAUTION

Some vehicles are equipped with an Air Bag system, also known as the Supplemental Inflatable Restraint (SIR) or Supplemental Restraint System (SRS). The system must be disabled before performing service on or around system components, steering column, instrument panel components, wiring and sensors. Failure to follow safety and disabling procedures could result in accidental Air Bag deployment, possible personal injury and unnecessary system repairs.

PRECAUTIONS

Several precautions must be observed when handling the inflator module to avoid accidental deployment and possible personal injury.

• Never carry the inflator module by the wires or connector on the underside of the module.

• When carrying a live inflator module, hold securely with both hands, and ensure that the bag and trim cover are pointed away.

• Place the inflator module on a bench or other surface with the bag and trim cover facing up.

• With the inflator module on the bench, never place anything on or close to the module which may be thrown in the event of an accidental deployment.

DISARMING

1. Before servicing the vehicle, refer to the precautions in the beginning of this section.

2. Disconnect both battery cables from the battery, negative cable first.

3. Wait one minute before proceeding with the service procedure. This is the time required for the back-up power supply in the air bag diagnostic monitor to deplete its stored energy.

4. After service is completed, reconnect the battery cables, negative cable last.

5. Turn the ignition switch to the **RUN** position. The air bag indicator should light continuously for approximately six seconds, then turn **OFF**. If the indicator fails to light, flashes or remains lit continuously, there is a fault in the air bag system.

Power Rack and Pinion Steering Gear

REMOVAL & INSTALLATION

✳✳ CAUTION

The air suspension switch, located in the left side of the luggage compartment, must be turned OFF before raising the vehicle. Failure to do so may result in unexpected inflation or deflation of the air springs which may result in shifting of the vehicle during service.

1. Before servicing the vehicle, refer to the precautions in the beginning of this section.

2. Turn the air suspension switch, located in the left side of the luggage compartment on 1996–97 models or on the right kick panel for 1998–00 models, to the **OFF** position.

3. Disconnect the negative battery cable.

4. Disconnect the engine control sensor wiring from the Powertrain Control Module (PCM) and position the wiring aside.

5. Directly above the engine control sensor wiring, remove the ground straps from the dash panel.

6. Working from inside the vehicle, remove the nuts retaining the steering shaft weather boot to the dash panel.

7. Remove the two bolts retaining the intermediate shaft to the steering column shaft. Set the weather boot aside.

8. Remove the pinch bolt at the steering gear input shaft and remove the intermediate shaft. Raise the vehicle and support safely.

9. Support the rear of the subframe with Powertrain Lift 014–00765 and Bracket 014–00766 or equivalents.

10. Remove the front wheels.

1 Tie Rod End
2 Nut
3 Front Wheel Spindle Tie Rod (2 Req'd)
4 Front Suspension Steering Ball Stud Dust Seal
5 Power Steering Hose Bracket
6 Bolt (2 Req'd)
7 Screw (2 Req'd)
8 Steering Gear
9 Screw (2 Req'd)
10 Nut (2 Req'd)
11 Front Wheel Knuckle (LH)
12 Crossmember
13 Nut (2 Req'd)
14 Steering Shaft U-Joint Shield
15 Front Wheel Knuckle (RH)
16 Power Steering Gear Input Shaft and Control

7922LG26

Exploded view of the power rack and pinion steering gear mounting

11. Remove the tie rod cotter pins and nuts. Remove the tie rod ends from the spindle. Remove the tie rod ends from the shaft. Mark the position of the jam nut to maintain the alignment.

12. Remove both air suspension and height sensor attachments.

13. Remove the nuts from the gear-to-subframe attaching bolts. Remove both height sensor attachments.

14. Remove the dual converter Y-pipe.

15. Remove the rear subframe-to-body attaching bolts and loosen the front subframe bolts.

16. Lower the subframe until it separates from the body; approximately 4 inches. Remove the heat shield band and fold down the shield.

17. Disconnect the VAPS electrical connector from the actuator assembly.

18. Disconnect the electrical connectors from the auxiliary actuator and the Power Steering Pressure (PSP) switch.

19. Rotate the gear to clear the bolts from the subframe and pull to the left to facilitate line fitting removal.

20. Position a drain pan under the vehicle and remove the line fittings. Remove the O-rings from the fitting connections and replace with new.

21. Remove the steering gear assembly through the left wheel well.

To install:

22. Install new O-rings into the line fittings on the steering gear.

23. Place the gear attachment bolts in the gear housing.

24. Install the steering gear assembly through the left wheel well.

25. Connect and tighten the line fittings to the steering gear assembly.

a. Connect the power steering pressure and return hoses to the fittings on the rack and pinion assembly and tighten to 24–30 ft. lbs. (33–41 Nm).

b. Install the power steering left turn pressure hose and screw. Tighten to 80–106 inch lbs. (9–12 Nm).

26. Connect the PSP switch and auxiliary actuator electrical connectors.

27. Position the steering gear into the subframe. Install the tie rod ends onto the shaft. Install the heat shield band.

28. Attach the tie rod ends onto the spindle. Install the nuts and secure with new cotter pins. Attach the sway bar link.

29. Raise the vehicle until the subframe contacts the body. Install the subframe attaching bolts.

30. Install the gear-to-subframe nuts.

Tighten the nuts to 84–112 ft. lbs. (113–153 Nm).

31. Install the dual converter Y-pipe.

32. Connect the air suspension height sensors.

33. Attach the exhaust pipe to the catalytic converter.

34. Tighten the following items to:

a. Power steering line fittings-to-steering gear: 24–30 ft. lbs. (33–41 Nm)

b. Tie rod ends-to-steering knuckles: 35–46 ft. lbs. (47–63 Nm)

c. Subframe bolts: 100–144 ft. lbs. (135–195 Nm)

d. Intermediate shaft-to-steering gear input shaft bolt: 30–38 ft. lbs. (41–51 Nm)

e. Intermediate shaft-to-steering column shaft nuts: 15–24 ft. lbs. (21–33 Nm)

35. Install the wheel and tire assemblies and lower the vehicle. Fill the power steering system.

36. Working from inside the vehicle, pull the weather boot end out of the vehicle and install it over the valve housing. Install the intermediate shaft to the steering gear input shaft. Install the inner weather boot to the floor pan.

37. Connect engine control sensor wiring to the PCM.

38. Install the screw retaining the ground straps to the dash panel directly above the engine control sensor wiring.

39. Install the intermediate shaft to the steering column shaft. Fill the power steering system.

40. Turn the air suspension switch to the **ON** position.

41. Check the system for leaks and proper operation. Adjust the toe setting as necessary.

Strut

REMOVAL & INSTALLATION

Front

✳✳ CAUTION

Do not remove an air spring under any circumstances when pressurized. Do not remove any components supporting an air spring without exhausting the air. Failure to follow these instructions may result in unexpected inflation or deflation of the air springs which may result in shifting of the vehicle during service.

1. Turn the air suspension switch to the **OFF** position. The switch is located in the trunk on 1996–97 models or on the right kick panel for the 1998–00 models.

2. Turn the ignition switch to the **OFF** position.

➡ **Be sure to leave the steering column in the UNLOCKED position.**

3. Loosen, but do not remove, the three top mount-to-strut tower retaining nuts.

4. Raise and safely support the vehicle. Remove the wheel and tire assembly.

5. Remove the brake line bracket from the strut assembly.

6. Remove the vinyl cover from the upper link stud, if equipped.

7. Remove the stabilizer bar link nut and the link from the strut.

8. If equipped, disconnect the air line from the solenoid valve.

9. Disconnect the electrical connector at the air spring solenoid valve. Disconnect the front spring and strut actuator electrical connector at the body harness connector.

10. Disconnect the air suspension height sensor from the lower height sensor ball stud and position aside.

PUSH DOWN AND HOLD PLASTIC RELEASE RING

SPRING SOLENOID VALVE 5311

DISCONNECT

PULL TO REMOVE NYLON TUBE

APPROXIMATELY 18 mm (0.71 INCH)

CONNECT

PUSH NYLON TUBING IN UNTIL SEATED AGAINST OUTER TUBE

7922LG27

Air line disconnect/connect procedure

※※ CAUTION

Do not fully release the solenoid until the air is completely bled from the air spring.

11. If equipped, remove the solenoid valve as follows:

a. Remove the air spring solenoid retainer.

b. Rotate the solenoid valve counterclockwise to the first stop.

c. Pull the solenoid valve straight out slowly to the second stop to bleed the air from the system.

d. After the air is fully bled from the system, rotate the solenoid valve counterclockwise to the third stop and remove the solenoid valve from the housing.

12. Remove and discard the front suspension arm-to-ball joint nut. Using Tie Rod End Remover tool 3290-D or equivalent, separate the ball joint from the front suspension lower arm.

※※ CAUTION

Do not allow the halfshaft to move outward. This could result in separation of the internal parts of the tripod CV-joint, causing failure of the joint.

13. Remove the strut-to-steering knuckle pinch bolt and nut. Using a large prybar, slightly spread the strut-to steering knuckle pinch joint, if required, for removal.

※※ WARNING

Do not remove the front spring and strut large center nut while the front spring and strut is in the vehicle as this may result in a permanent air leak through the top of the air spring.

14. Remove the three top mount-to-strut tower retaining nuts and remove the strut/air spring assembly from the vehicle.

To install:

15. Install the strut with the three top mount-to-shock tower nuts, leaving the nuts loose.

16. Install the steering knuckle and hub assembly to the strut. Install a new strut-to-steering knuckle pinch bolt and nut. Tighten the bolt to 73–97 ft. lbs. (98–132 Nm). Install a new control arm-to-ball joint nut. Tighten to 50–68 ft. lbs. (68–92 Nm).

---

17. Install the stabilizer bar link to the strut and install a new stabilizer bar link nut. Tighten to 57–75 ft. lbs. (77–101 Nm).

18. Install the height sensor link on the ball stud pin on the control arm.

19. If equipped, install the solenoid valve as follows:

a. Check the solenoid O-ring for abrasions or cuts and replace, as necessary.

b. Lightly grease the solenoid O-ring prior to installation using a suitable silicone dielectric compound.

c. Insert the solenoid O-ring into the air spring end cap and rotate clockwise to the third stop. Push in to the second stop, then rotate clockwise to the first stop.

d. Install the air solenoid valve retainer.

20. Connect the electrical connector to the solenoid valve.

21. Connect the air line to the solenoid valve.

22. Connect the front spring and shock actuator electrical connector.

23. Install the screw and brake hose bracket to the front spring and shock. Tighten the screw to 11 ft. lbs. (15 Nm).

24. Install the front wheels.

25. Lower the vehicle enough to gain access to the three top mount-to-strut tower nuts.

26. Tighten the three top mount-to-strut tower nuts to 23–29 ft. lbs. (30–40 Nm).

27. Lower the vehicle. Turn the air suspension switch to the **ON** position. Road test the vehicle and check for proper operation.

Shock Absorber

REMOVAL & INSTALLATION

Rear

1. Turn the air suspension switch to the **OFF** position. The switch located in the luggage compartment on 1996–97 models or on the right kick panel for the 1998–00 models.

2. Turn the ignition switch to the **OFF** position.

3. Remove the side trim panel in the luggage compartment and remove the mass damper retaining clip.

4. Raise and safely support the vehicle.

5. Remove the rear wheels.

6. If equipped, unplug the wiring connector and retaining clips.

7. Remove the two upper shock absorber mounting bolts.

8. Remove the lower mounting nut and bolt and remove the shock absorber, mounting bracket and mass damper.

To install:

9. Install the mounting bracket and mass damper on the shock absorber.

10. Turn the shock absorber upside down and compress and expand the piston to remove the air from the cylinder.

➡**If equipped, the actuator should face the rear after the shock has been installed.**

11. Insert the top of the shock through the upper mounting hole, then compress the shock and install the lower mounting bolt and nut.

12. Install the two upper mounting bolts. Tighten the bolts to 58–68 ft. lbs. (68–92 Nm).

13. If equipped, connect the wiring to the actuator and install the retaining clips on the lower arm.

14. Install the wheels and lower the vehicle.

15. Turn the air suspension system **ON** and replace the trim panels.

7922LG28

To bleed the air from the shock, turn it upside down, then compress and expand it several times

Air Spring

REMOVAL & INSTALLATION

✳✳ **CAUTION**

Do not remove an air spring under any circumstances when pressurized. Do not remove any components supporting an air spring without exhausting the air. Failure to follow these

instructions may result in unexpected inflation or deflation of the air springs which may result in shifting of the vehicle during service.

1. Properly deflate the air springs using the New Generation Star (NGS) tester or equivalent scan tool.

2. Turn the air suspension switch to the **OFF** position. The switch located in the luggage compartment on 1996–97 models or on the right kick panel for 1998–00 models.

3. Turn the ignition switch to the **OFF** position.

4. Raise and safely support the vehicle. Remove the wheel and tire assembly.

5. Disconnect the air spring solenoid electrical connector and air line.

6. On the 1996–97 models, remove the three bolts securing the air spring to the suspension. On 1998–00 models, depress the plastic tabs while lifting up on the air spring to disengage it from the suspension.

To install:

7. Inspect the O-rings for cuts or abrasions and replace as required.

8. Collapse the air spring until the bottom of the air spring sleeve (black rubber) is within ½ inch (12mm) of the bottom of the tapered piston.

7922LG29

Be sure to unplug the connections to the air spring before removing it

7922LG30

On 1998–00 models, depress the plastic locking tabs to disengage the air spring from the suspension

9. Position the air spring in the vehicle.

10. On 1996–97 models, install the three air spring-to-lower suspension arm bolts. Tighten them to 50–59 ft. lbs. (68–82 Nm). On 1998–00 models, press the plastic tab through the suspension until it clicks into place.

11. Engage the air spring cap to the body bracket.

12. Connect the solenoid air line and the electrical connector.

13. Fill the air spring.

14. Install the wheel and tire assembly. Install and tighten the lug nuts to 80–105 ft. lbs. (108–144 Nm).

15. Lower the vehicle.

16. Turn the air suspension switch to the **ON** position.

17. Road test the vehicle and check for proper operation.

Ball Joint

REMOVAL & INSTALLATION

1. Before servicing the vehicle, refer to the precautions in the beginning of this section.

2. Place the steering column in the unlocked position.

3. Turn the air suspension switch to the **OFF** position. The switch located in the luggage compartment on 1996–97 models or on the right kick panel for 1998–00 models.

4. Raise and safely support the vehicle, then remove the tire and wheel assembly.

5. Remove the brake caliper and rotor.

6. Remove the front axle wheel hub nut.

7. If equipped, disconnect the air suspension height sensor from the front air suspension sensor pin.

8. Remove the tie rod end from the front wheel knuckle.

9. Remove and discard the front suspension lower arm-to-ball joint nut.

✳✳ **CAUTION**

Do not allow the front wheel drive-shaft joint to move outward. Over extension of the front wheel drive-shaft joint will result in separation of the driveshaft internal parts, causing failure of the joint.

➡**Make sure the steering column is in the unlocked position, and do not use a hammer to separate the ball joint from the front suspension lower arm. Use extreme care not to damage the boot seal.**

10. Using a suitable puller, separate the ball joint from the front suspension lower arm.

11. Using a multiple jawed puller, press the front wheel driveshaft joint out of the wheel hub.

12. Remove the pinch bolt and nut from the front wheel knuckle.

13. Remove the front wheel knuckle from the front shock absorber.

14. If necessary, remove the brake disc shield from the front wheel knuckle.

To install:

15. If removed, install the brake disc shield onto the front wheel knuckle.

16. Position the front wheel knuckle onto the front shock absorber and install a new pinch bolt and nut hand-tight into the front wheel knuckle.

17. Install the front wheel driveshaft joint into the wheel hub.

18. Install a new front axle wheel hub nut and tighten to 170–202 ft. lbs. (230–275 Nm).

19. Position the lower ball joint into the front suspension lower arm, install a new front suspension lower arm-to-ball joint nut and tighten to 50–67 ft. lbs. (68–92 Nm).

20. Tighten the front shock absorber to front wheel knuckle pinch bolt to 73–98 ft. lbs. (98–132 Nm).

21. Install the brake disc and caliper.

➡**Place the steering wheel in the straight-ahead position prior to installing the tie rod end.**

22. Position the tie rod end into the front wheel knuckle and tighten the attaching nut to 35–46 ft. lbs. (47–63 Nm).

23. If equipped, connect the air suspension height sensor to the front air suspension sensor pin.

➡**Prior to installing the tire and wheel assembly, inspect the front wheel driveshaft joint to make sure it is fully inserted into the transaxle. Visually inspect the seal at the transaxle. Some polishing is normal due to axial runout. Failure to fully install the front wheel driveshaft joint will cause premature failure of the front wheel driveshaft joint or the transaxle.**

24. Install the tire and wheel assembly.

25. Lower the vehicle.

26. Turn the air suspension switch to the **ON** position.

27. Road test the vehicle and check for proper operation.

Wheel Bearings

ADJUSTMENT

There is no adjustment for the front or rear wheel bearings due to the nature of their design which contains both inner and outer bearings.

REMOVAL & INSTALLATION

Front

✳ CAUTION

Do not remove an air spring under any circumstances when pressurized. Do not remove any components supporting an air spring without exhausting the air. Failure to follow these instructions may result in unexpected inflation or deflation of the air springs which may result in shifting of the vehicle during service.

➡**Be sure to have available a new wheel hub retainer nut, tie rod end castellated nut and cotter pin, lower control arm-to-ball joint nut, steering knuckle-to-strut pinch bolt and nut, stabilizer bar link nut and the three hub and bearing retaining bolts, per side.**

The air suspension switch, located on the left side of the luggage compartment for 1996–97 models or on the right kick panel for 1998–00 models, must be turned **OFF** before raising the vehicle. Failure to do so may result in unexpected inflation or deflation of the air springs which may result in shifting of the vehicle during service.

1. Properly deflate the air springs using the New Generation Star (NGS) tester or equivalent scan tool.

2. Remove and discard the wheel hub retainer nut.

3. Raise and safely support the vehicle. Remove the wheel and tire assembly.

4. Remove the brake caliper and rotor. Wire the caliper aside.

➡**Do not allow the brake caliper to hang by the brake hose or damage to the hose may result.**

5. Remove the brake rotor splash shield, if damaged.

6. Using Front Hub Remover/Replacer T81P-1104-C or equivalent and adapters, press the outer CV-joint from the hub.

MAKE SURE THE HUB REMOVER ADAPTER IS FULLY THREADED ONTO THE HUB STUD AND IS POSITIONED OPPOSITE THE TWO STUD ADAPTER

FRONT HUB REPLACER

METRIC HUB REMOVER ADAPTERS

TWO STUD ADAPTER

FRONT HUB REMOVER/REPLACER

HOLD WRENCH STATIONARY WHILE TURNING OTHER WRENCH

TURN THIS WRENCH COUNTERCLOCKWISE

7922LG32

Use a puller such as the one shown to press the halfshaft through the hub assembly

7. Support the halfshaft with wire to maintain a level position.

8. Remove and discard the three hub and bearing retainer bolts from the steering knuckle.

9. Using a small prybar, slightly spread the strut-to-knuckle pinch joint and remove the knuckle and hub from the strut.

✳ WARNING

The hub and bearing assembly is not pressed into the steering knuckle. DO NOT use a slide hammer to remove a stuck wheel hub. Do not strike the back of inner bearing race.

10. Remove the wheel hub from the steering knuckle.
To install:

➡**If the hub bearing journal is scored or damaged, replace the knuckle. If the wheel hub is damaged or any end-play is detectable, replace the wheel hub and bearing assembly.**

11. Remove all foreign material from the knuckle bearing bore and hub bearing journal to ensure correct seating of the new hub.

➡**The steering knuckle must be clean enough to allow the wheel hub to be completely seated by hand. Do not press or draw the wheel hub into place.**

12. Install the wheel hub and tighten bolts to 61–79 ft. lbs. (83–107 Nm).

Turn to Section 6 for brake system applications

Pry the hub assembly from the knuckle if it is stuck

13. Install a new brake rotor splash shield using new rivets, if necessary.

14. Install a new wheel hub retainer nut and tighten to 170–202 ft. lbs. (230–275 Nm).

15. Install the brake rotor and brake caliper.

16. Fill the air springs. Lower the vehicle.

17. Pump the brake pedal several times prior to moving the vehicle, to position the brake pads to the rotor. Road test the vehicle and check for proper operation.

Rear

✷✷ CAUTION

The air suspension switch, located in the left side of the luggage compartment, must be turned OFF before raising the vehicle. Failure to do so may result in unexpected inflation or deflation of the air springs which may result in shifting of the vehicle during service.

➡ **Be sure to have available a new wheel hub retainer nut.**

1. Turn the air suspension switch, located in the luggage compartment on 1996–97 models or on the right kick panel for 1998–00 models, to the **OFF** position.

2. Raise and safely support the vehicle. Remove the wheel and tire assembly.

3. Remove the brake caliper assembly from the brake adapter. Support the caliper assembly with a length of wire to prevent damage to the brake hose.

4. If equipped, remove the push on nuts that retain the rotor to the hub and remove the rotor.

5. Remove the grease cap from the bearing and hub assembly.

6. Remove the wheel hub retainer nut, then pull the hub assembly from the spindle. Be sure to use a new retainer nut when installing the hub.

➡ **The wheel bearings are permanently sealed and lubricated. If wheel bearing replacement is required, the bearing**

Remove the retaining nut, then pull the hub assembly from the rear wheel spindle

Remove the grease cap to expose the wheel hub retaining nut

and hub must be replaced as an assembly.

To install:

7. Position the wheel hub and bearing on the rear spindle.

✷✷ WARNING

Damage to the bearing assembly may result if power tools are used to install it. Do not back the nut off after reaching the required torque..

8. Install a new wheel hub retainer nut and tighten to 188–254 ft. lbs. (255–345 Nm).

9. Install the rear disc/drum brake assembly.

10. Install the wheel and tire assembly. Lower the vehicle.

11. Turn the air suspension switch to the **ON** position.

12. Pump the brake pedal several times to position the brake pads to the rotor.

13. Road test the vehicle and check for proper operation.

PRECAUTIONS

Before servicing any vehicle, please be sure to read all of the following precautions, which deal with personal safety, prevention of component damage, and important points to take into consideration when servicing a motor vehicle:

• Never open, service or drain the radiator or cooling system when the engine is hot; serious burns can occur from the steam and hot coolant.

• Observe all applicable safety precautions when working around fuel. Whenever servicing the fuel system, always work in a well-ventilated area. Do not allow fuel spray or vapors to come in contact with a spark, open flame, or excessive heat (a hot drop light, for example). Keep a dry chemical fire extinguisher near the work area. Always keep fuel in a container specifically designed for fuel storage; also, always properly seal fuel containers to avoid the possibility of fire or explosion. Refer to the additional fuel system precautions later in this section.

• Fuel injection systems often remain pressurized, even after the engine has been turned **OFF**. The fuel system pressure must be relieved before disconnecting any fuel lines. Failure to do so may result in fire and/or personal injury.

• Brake fluid often contains polyglycol ethers and polyglycols. Avoid contact with the eyes and wash your hands thoroughly after handling brake fluid. If you do get brake fluid in your eyes, flush your eyes with clean, running water for 15 minutes. If eye irritation persists, or if you have taken brake fluid internally, IMMEDIATELY seek medical assistance.

• The EPA warns that prolonged contact with used engine oil may cause a number of skin disorders, including cancer! You should make every effort to minimize your exposure to used engine oil. Protective gloves should be worn when changing oil.

Wash your hands and any other exposed skin areas as soon as possible after exposure to used engine oil. Soap and water, or waterless hand cleaner should be used.

• All new vehicles are now equipped with an air bag system, often referred to as a Supplemental Restraint System (SRS) or Supplemental Inflatable Restraint (SIR) system. The system must be disabled before performing service on or around system components, steering column, instrument panel components, wiring and sensors. Failure to follow safety and disabling procedures could result in accidental air bag deployment, possible personal injury and unnecessary system repairs.

• Always wear safety goggles when working with, or around, the air bag system. When carrying a non-deployed air bag, be sure the bag and trim cover are pointed away from your body. When placing a non-deployed air bag on a work surface, always face the bag and trim cover upward, away from the surface. This will reduce the motion of the module if it is accidentally deployed. Refer to the additional air bag system precautions later in this section.

• Clean, high quality brake fluid from a sealed container is essential to the safe and proper operation of the brake system. You should always buy the correct type of brake fluid for your vehicle. If the brake fluid becomes contaminated, completely flush the system with new fluid. Never reuse any brake fluid. Any brake fluid that is removed from the system should be discarded. Also, do not allow any brake fluid to come in contact with a painted surface; it will damage the paint.

• Never operate the engine without the proper amount and type of engine oil; doing so WILL result in severe engine damage.

• Timing belt maintenance is extremely important! Many models utilize an interference-type, non-freewheeling engine. If the timing belt breaks, the valves in the cylinder head may strike the pistons, causing poten-

tially serious (also time-consuming and expensive) engine damage. Refer to the maintenance interval charts in the front of this manual for the recommended replacement interval for the timing belt, and to the timing belt section for belt replacement and inspection.

• Disconnecting the negative battery cable on some vehicles may interfere with the functions of the on-board computer system(s) and may require the computer to undergo a relearning process once the negative battery cable is reconnected.

• When servicing drum brakes, only disassemble and assemble one side at a time, leaving the remaining side intact for reference.

• Only an MVAC-trained, EPA-certified automotive technician should service the A/C system or its components.

ENGINE REPAIR

Distributor

REMOVAL

1. Before servicing the vehicle, refer to the precautions in the beginning of this section.

2. Disconnect the negative battery cable.

3. Disengage the distributor electrical connector and coil wire at the cap.

4. Remove the distributor cap and rotor.

5. Position it to the side. If the distributor unit is not being replaced, scribe a reference mark across the distributor base flange and the cylinder head.

6. Loosen the distributor mounting bolts and remove the distributor from the engine.

7. If necessary, remove the distributor base gasket from the distributor.

8. If necessary, remove the distributor O-ring.

➡**Do not rotate the engine while the distributor assembly is removed. Do not attempt to disassemble and service the distributor unit. The distributor unit should be replaced as an assembly.**

9. If removed, install a new distributor base gasket.

10. If removed, install a new O-ring on the distributor unit.

INSTALLATION

Engine Not Disturbed

➡**The distributor can only be installed in one direction. Do not force the distributor into position and be sure the drive tangs engage the camshaft slots.**

1. Install the distributor unit into the engine. Make certain the drive tangs engage with the camshaft slots.

2. If installing the old distributor, be

Exploded view of the distributor assembly—1.8L engine

When installing the distributor be sure the drive tangs engage the camshaft slots—1.8L engine

sure the reference marks made during removal are aligned.

3. Tighten the mounting bolts finger-tight.

4. Install the rotor and distributor cap.

5. Engage the distributor electrical connector and coil wire to the cap.

6. Connect the negative battery cable and check ignition timing.

7. If necessary, adjust the ignition timing.

8. Tighten the distributor mounting bolt to 14–19 ft. lbs. (19–25 Nm).

Engine Disturbed

➡**When installing the distributor be sure the offset drive tangs engage the camshaft slots.**

1. Be sure that the engine is still with the No. 1 piston up on TDC of its compression stroke.

➡**If the engine was disturbed while the distributor was removed, it will be necessary to remove the No. 1 spark plug and rotate the engine clockwise until the No. 1 piston is on the compression stroke. Align the timing marks.**

1. Upper intake manifold
2. Lower intake manifold
3. Oil filter
4. Upper engine front cover
5. Timing belt
6. Rear engine support insulator mounting bracket
7. Middle engine front cover
8. Lower engine front cover
9. Crankshaft pulley retaining washer
10. Crankshaft pulley
11. Water pump pulley
12. Engine oil cooler
13. Timing belt tensioner spring
14. Timing belt tensioner
15. Crankshaft sprocket
16. Crankshaft pulley hub
17. Alternator/water pump drive belt
18. Power steering/air conditioning drive belt
19. Timing belt
20. Timing belt idler pulley
21. Camshaft sprockets
22. Oil pressure sender
23. Spark plug
24. Distributor
25. Spark plug wires
26. Fuel injection supply manifold

Exploded view of upper engine component mounting, including the distributor, intake manifold and timing belt covers—1.8L engine

2. If installing the old distributor:

a. Install the distributor and align the marks on the distributor base flange-to-cylinder head and the rotor points toward the mark on the distributor housing made previously. Make certain the rotor is pointing to the No. 1 mark on the distributor base.

3. If installing a new distributor:

a. Install the rotor and cap (with wires still attached) on the distributor, follow the No. 1 spark plug wire from the plug to the cap, this will be the No.1 tower on the cap. Mark the location of the tower on the distributor housing, then remove the cap.

b. Install the distributor and be sure the rotor aligns with the No.1 tower mark made on the distributor.

4. When all the marks are aligned, install the distributor hold-down bolts and tighten them to 14–19 ft. lbs. (19–25 Nm).

5. Install the cap and tighten the screws.

6. Connect the negative battery cable.

7. Engage the electrical connections.

8. Install the No. 1 spark plug, if removed.

9. Recheck the initial timing and adjust if necessary.

Ignition Timing

ADJUSTMENT

1.8L Engine

1. Before servicing the vehicle, refer to the precautions in the beginning of this section.

2. Clean any dirt from around the timing scale on the timing cover and the yellow timing mark on the crankshaft pulley. This will make it easier to see when you are inspecting the timing.

Connect a jumper wire between the ground and ten terminals on the DLC—1.8L engine

Connect the tachometer positive lead to the IG terminal on the DLC—1.8L engine

3. Place the gear selector lever in the **PARK** or **NEUTRAL** position. Apply the parking brake.

4. Turn all accessories and loads **OFF**.

5. Start the engine and allow it to reach operating temperature.

6. Connect an inductive timing light to the engine, following the tool manufacturers instructions.

7. Using a jumper wire, connect the GROUND terminal to the TEN terminal of the Diagnostic Link Connector (DLC).

8. Using Rotunda tachometer 059–00010 or its equivalent, connect the tachometer positive lead to the IG terminal on the DLC and the tachometer negative lead to the battery negative post.

9. Point the timing light at the timing scale.

10. Check the ignition timing. Timing should be 10° BTDC at 700–800 rpm. The mark on the pulley should be aligned with the corresponding mark on the timing scale.

11. If not, loosen the distributor mounting bolt and turn the distributor until the marks are aligned.

12. Tighten the distributor mounting bolt to 14–19 ft. lbs. (19–25 Nm).

13. Check the timing again to be sure it did not change when tightening the distributor mounting bolts

14. Remove the jumper wire, timing light and tachometer.

1.9L Engine

The 1.9L engine is equipped with an Electronic Distributorless Ignition System (EDIS). Ignition timing adjustment is not possible on the EDIS system.

2.0L Engines

The Powertrain Control Module controls ignition timing on these models. No adjustment is necessary or possible.

Engine Assembly

REMOVAL & INSTALLATION

1. Before servicing the vehicle, refer to the precautions in the beginning of this section.

2. On all engines, perform the following basic steps for engine removal.

a. Remove the hood from the vehicle.

b. Properly relieve the fuel system pressure.

c. Disconnect the negative battery cable.

d. If equipped with A/C, have the system discharged.

e. Tag and disconnect all the wires and hoses that would interfere with engine removal.

f. Tag and disconnect all cables such as the accelerator and kickdown cables (etc.) that would interfere with engine removal.

g. Remove the drive belt(s).

h. Drain the cooling system.

i. Drain the engine oil.

3. On 1.8L engines with a automatic transaxle, complete the generic steps for all engines at the start of this procedure, then perform the following steps for removal.

a. Remove the starter motor.

b. Remove the splash shields and the starter motor.

c. Disconnect the transaxle cooling lines from the radiator and plug the lines.

d. Remove the axle bearing bracket.

e. Remove flywheel inspection plate from the oil pan.

f. Place a wrench on the crankshaft pulley and rotate the crankshaft to gain access to the converter nuts, then unfasten the nuts.

g. If equipped, remove the A/C compressor and set it aside with the hoses still attached.

Remove the fuel pressure regulator and High Speed Inlet Air (HSIA) shutter valve actuator—1.8L engine with a automatic transaxle

h. Remove the power steering pump, transaxle-to-engine upper bolts, radiator, vacuum reservoir, fuel pressure regulator and the High Speed Inlet Air (HSIA) shutter valve actuator.

i. Remove the alternator.

j. Connect an engine sling to the lifting eyes on the engine.

k. Using an engine hoist, take up the slack on the sling until the engine is supported.

l. Unfasten the oil pan-to-transaxle bolts and the transaxle-to-engine bolts from the block.

m. Remove the right-hand support insulator and the front support damper.

n. Separate the engine from the transaxle and remove the engine from the vehicle.

4. On 1.8L engines with a manual transaxle, complete the generic steps for all engines at the start of this procedure, then perform the following steps for removal.

a. Remove the battery and tray.

b. Remove the radiator upper support brackets.

c. Remove the splash shields.

d. Remove the clutch cylinder hose bracket with the hose still attached and position the assembly aside.

e. Disconnect the transaxle gearshift rod, clevis and lever stabilizer bar from the transaxle.

f. Unbolt the power steering pump and bracket assembly and set it aside with the hoses still connected.

g. Unbolt the A/C compressor and set it aside, if equipped.

h. Remove the A/C accumulator hoses clip from the crossmember and move the hose away from the work area.

i. Remove the A/C hose routing support clips from the radiator and position the hose aside.

Remove the right-hand support insulator and the front support damper—1.8L engine with a automatic transaxle

j. Disconnect the speedometer cable from the transaxle.

k. Disconnect the exhaust pipe from the manifold.

l. Disconnect the starter motor wiring.

m. Remove the stabilizer bar.

n. Separate the tie-rod ends from the steering knuckles.

o. Remove the halfshafts.

p. Unbolt the transaxle front and rear mount nuts and remove the mount from the support crossmember.

q. Remove the radiator and fan.

r. Connect an engine sling to the lifting eyes on the engine.

s. Using an engine hoist, take up the slack on the sling until the engine is supported.

t. Remove the crankshaft pulley.

u. Remove the front engine support damper nut and nut.

v. Remove the engine insulator mounting bolt and nut.

w. Remove the right-hand engine support insulator-to-engine nuts.

x. Remove the left-hand transaxle insulator and bracket.

y. Remove the engine and transaxle from the vehicle.

z. Separate the transaxle from the engine and place the engine on a suitable stand.

5. On 1.9L engines, complete the generic steps for all engines at the start of this procedure, then perform the following steps for removal.

a. Remove the Idle Air Control (IAC) valve

b. Remove the splash shields.

c. Disconnect the transaxle cooling lines from the radiator and plug the lines.

d. Remove the radiator from the engine compartment.

e. Disconnect the A/C suction manifold and tube from the accumulator/drier.

f. If equipped, disconnect the power steering return hose from the reservoir and the pressure line from the pump.

g. Unbolt the power steering and A/C bracket bolts from the compressor bracket and set the hoses aside.

h. Remove the drive belt tensioner and pulley.

i. Remove the A/C compressor and set it aside with the lines still attached.

j. On models with an automatic transaxle, remove the catalytic converter.

k. On models with an automatic

transaxle, remove the transaxle housing cover, four flywheel-to-converter nuts, crankshaft pulley and the starter motor.

l. On models with an automatic transaxle, unbolt the lower transaxle-to-engine mounting bolts.

m. On models with a manual transaxle, disconnect the transaxle gearshift rod, clevis and lever stabilizer bar from the transaxle.

n. On models with an automatic transaxle, unbolt the upper transaxle-to-engine mounting bolts.

o. On models with a manual transaxle, remove the halfshafts. Install transaxle plugs into the differential side gears to prevent them from becoming malaligned.

p. On models with a manual transaxle, remove the halfshafts.

q. On models with a manual transaxle, unbolt the clutch slave cylinder and with the line still attached, set it aside.

r. On models with a manual transaxle, unbolt the transaxle front, rear and left-hand support insulator bolts.

s. On models with a manual transaxle, remove the engine cooling fan motor.

t. Connect an engine sling to the lifting eyes on the engine.

u. Using an engine hoist, take up the slack on the sling until the engine is supported.

v. On models with a manual transaxle, remove the front engine support damper nut and nut.

w. On models with a manual transaxle, remove the engine insulator mounting bolt and nut.

Remove the transaxle housing cover to access the torque converter-to-flexplate mounting bolts—1.9L engine with an automatic transaxle

Timing belt service is covered in Section 5 of this manual

x. On models with a manual transaxle, remove the right-hand engine support bracket and support insulator bolt.

y. On models with a manual transaxle, remove the right-hand insulator.

z. On models with a manual transaxle, remove the engine and transaxle from the vehicle.

aa. On models with a manual transaxle, separate the transaxle from the engine and place the engine on a suitable stand.

ab. On models with an automatic transaxle, remove the front engine support damper and right-hand engine support insulator, then remove the engine from the vehicle.

6. On 2.0L SOHC engines, complete the generic steps for all engines at the start of this procedure, then perform the following steps for removal.

a. Remove the battery and tray.

b. Remove the air cleaner assembly, then tag and disengage all wiring, hoses, cables and sensors, etc., that would interfere with engine removal.

c. Loosen the power steering pressure hose bracket bolts and set the hose aside.

d. Remove the exhaust manifold heat shield, exhaust manifold-to-catalytic converter nuts and one upper starter motor bolt. Position the starter motor bracket aside.

e. If equipped with an automatic transaxle, disconnect the transaxle cooler lines from the transaxle.

f. Disconnect the A/C manifold tube spring lock coupling at the accumulator/drier and the condenser.

g. Remove the drive belt auto tensioner and, if equipped, the accessory drive belt tensioner.

h. Drain the power steering fluid and disconnect the lines from the reservoir.

i. Remove the splash shield, crossmember and the catalytic converter.

j. Remove the drive shafts and the A/C compressor with the lines still attached. Set the compressor aside.

k. Remove the radiator, fan and shroud.

l. Attach a lifting bracket on the left rear side of the cylinder head.

m. Install a three-bar engine support as illustrated.

n. Remove the transaxle crossmember.

o. Unfasten the transaxle mount nuts and remove the mount.

p. Remove the right-hand engine support insulator through-bolt.

q. Attach a suitable lifting device to the engine.

r. Remove the engine and the transaxle as an assembly.

7. On 2.0L DOHC engines, complete the generic steps for all engines at the start of this procedure, then perform the following steps for removal.

a. Remove the battery and tray.

b. Remove the air cleaner assembly, then tag and disengage all wiring, hoses, cables and sensors that would interfere with engine removal.

c. If equipped with an automatic transaxle, remove the torque converter cover and loosen the converter nuts.

d. Remove the radiator, fan and shroud.

e. Disconnect the power steering return hose and the A/C compressor-to-condenser discharge line.

f. Remove the catalytic converter and the front roll restrictor

g. Remove the halfshafts and disconnect the hydraulic clutch line.

h. Support the engine with a floor jack.

i. Unfasten all bolts that attach the engine to its compartment.

j. Remove the engine and transaxle as an assembly.

To install:

8. Installation is the reverse of removal, but please note the following important steps.

9. On 1.8L engines with automatic transaxles pay special attention to the following torque specifications:

a. Tighten the transaxle-to-engine upper right-hand bolt to 41–59 ft. lbs. (55–80 Nm).

b. Tighten the right-hand insulator bolt to 49–69 ft. lbs. (67–93 Nm).

c. Tighten the front engine support damper nuts and bolt to 41–59 ft. lbs. (55–80 Nm).

d. Tighten the transaxle-to-engine bolts to 41–59 ft. lbs. (55–80 Nm).

e. Tighten the radiator support upper bracket bolts to 69–95 inch lbs. (7.8–11 Nm).

f. Tighten the oil pan-to-transaxle bolts to 27–38 ft. lbs. (37–52 Nm).

g. Tighten the power steering pump bracket bolts to 27–38 ft. lbs. (37–52 Nm).

h. Tighten the A/C accumulator tube support clip nuts to 56–82 inch lbs. (6–9 Nm).

i. Tighten the flywheel-to-converter nuts to 25–36 ft. lbs. (34–49 Nm).

j. Tighten the front axle bearing bracket bolts in the sequence illustrated to 31–46 ft. lbs. (42–62 Nm).

k. Tighten the exhaust inlet pipe-to-exhaust manifold nuts to 23–34 ft. lbs. (31–46 Nm).

l. Tighten the splash shield bolts to 69–95 inch lbs. (7–11Nm).

m. Tighten the throttle cable bracket bolts to 69–95 inch lbs. (7–11Nm).

10. On 1.8L engines with manual transaxles pay special attention to the following torque specifications:

a. Tighten the transaxle-to-engine bolts to 47–66 ft. lbs. (64–89 Nm).

7922MG13

Properly support the engine as shown—2.0L SOHC engines

FRONT AXLE BEARING BRACKET

7922MG14

Tighten the front axle bearing bracket bolts in the sequence illustrated—1.8L engine with an automatic transaxle

INTAKE MANIFOLD SUPPORT

37 – 52 N·m (27 – 38 LB-FT)

19-25 N·m (14-19 LB-FT)

7922MG15

Tighten the intake manifold support bolts to the specifications illustrated

b. Tighten the oil pan-to-transaxle bolts to 27–38 ft. lbs. (37–52 Nm).

c. Tighten the front transaxle support insulator bolts to 27–38 ft. lbs. (37–52 Nm).

d. Tighten the intake manifold bolts to the specification shown. Refer to the accompanying illustration.

e. Tighten the engine mount through-bolt and nut to 49–69 ft. lbs. (67–93 Nm).

f. Tighten the engine mount-to-engine attaching nuts to 54–76 ft. lbs. (74–103 Nm).

g. Tighten the vibration damper bolt and nut to 41–59 ft. lbs. (55–80 Nm).

h. Tighten the transaxle support bracket bolts to 41–59 ft. lbs. (55–80 Nm).

i. Tighten the transaxle upper mount bolts to 32–45 ft. lbs. (43–61 Nm).

j. Tighten the transaxle upper mount nuts to 49–69 ft. lbs. (67–93 Nm).

k. Tighten the radiator mounting bracket nuts to 69–95 inch lbs. (7.8–11 Nm).

l. Tighten the exhaust mounting flange-to-manifold nuts to 23–34 ft. lbs. (31–46 Nm).

m. Tighten the exhaust pipe support bracket bolts to 27–38 ft. lbs. (37–52 Nm).

n. If equipped, tighten the A/C compressor mounting bolts to 15–22 ft. lbs. (20–30 Nm). And the A/C hose-to-crossmember routing bracket bolt to 56–82 inch lbs. (6.4–9.3 Nm).

o. Tighten the power steering mounting bolts to 27–38 ft. lbs. (37–52 Nm).

p. Tighten the shift control rod attaching nut to 12–17 ft. lbs. (16–23 Nm).

q. Tighten the clutch slave cylinder mounting bolts and the routing bracket bolt to 12–17 ft. lbs. (16–23 Nm).

r. Tighten the splash shield bolts to 69–95 inch lbs. (7.8–11 Nm).

11. On 1.9L engines, pay special attention to the following torque specifications:

a. On models with an automatic transaxle, tighten the crankshaft pulley bolt to 81–96 ft. lbs. (110–130 Nm).

b. If equipped, tighten the A/C compressor-to-bracket bolts to 15–20 ft. lbs. (20–30 Nm).

c. On models with an automatic transaxle, tighten the two upper transaxle-to-engine bolts to 40–59 ft. lbs. (55–80 Nm).

d. On models with an automatic transaxle, tighten the five lower transaxle-to-engine bolts to 27–38 ft. lbs. (37–52 Nm).

e. Tighten the engine insulator mounting bolt to 49–69 ft. lbs. (67–93 Nm).

12. On all models, perform the following steps.

a. Engage all wires and hoses.

b. Evacuate and charge the A/C system using approved equipment.

c. Fill the engine with the proper type and quantity of oil.

d. Fill the cooling system with the proper amount and mix of anti-freeze.

e. Install the drive belt(s).

f. Fill the transaxle with the proper type and amount of fluid.

13. On 2.0L SOHC engines pay special attention to the following torque specifications:

a. Tighten the right-hand insulator through-bolt to 50–69 ft. lbs. (67–93 Nm).

b. Tighten the motor mount bolts to 50–69 ft. lbs. (67–93 Nm).

c. Tighten the transaxle support crossmember inner retainers to 28–38 ft. lbs. (38–51 Nm) and the outer retainers to 48–65 ft. lbs. (64–89 Nm).

d. Tighten the A/C compressor mounting bolts to 15–22 ft. lbs.)

e. Tighten the muffler-to-catalytic converter to 30–40 ft. lbs. (40–55 Nm).

f. Install the crossmember and tighten the bolts to 69–97 ft. lbs. (94–131 Nm).

g. Tighten the power steering pressure hose connection to 15–18 ft. lbs. (20–25 Nm).

h. Tighten the A/C line bracket bolt to 15–18 ft. lbs. (20–25 Nm).

i. Tighten the exhaust manifold-to-

catalytic converter nuts to 26–34 ft. lbs. (34–47 Nm).

14. On 2.0L DOHC engines pay special attention to the following torque specifications:

a. Tighten the front isolator nuts and bolts to 50–68 ft. lbs. (67–93 Nm).

b. Tighten the front engine support isolator through-bolt to 50–68 ft. lbs. (67–93 Nm).

c. Tighten the front roll restrictor bolts to 48–65 ft. lbs. (64–89 Nm) and the nuts to 50–69 ft. lbs. (67–93 Nm).

d. Tighten the rear roll restrictor nuts to 28–38 ft. lbs. (38–51 Nm).

e. If equipped with an automatic transaxle, tighten the torque converter nuts to 27 ft. lbs. (37 Nm).

Water Pump

REMOVAL & INSTALLATION

1.8L Engine

1. Before servicing the vehicle, refer to the precautions in the beginning of this section.

2. Disconnect the negative battery cable.

3. Drain the cooling system.

4. Remove the timing belt.

5. Raise and safely support the vehicle.

6. Remove the engine oil dipstick tube bracket bolt(s) from the water pump.

7. Remove the two bolts and the gasket from the water inlet pipe.

8. Remove all but the uppermost water pump mounting bolt.

9. Lower the vehicle.

10. Remove the remaining bolts and the water pump assembly.

11. If the water pump is being reused, remove all gasket material from the water pump.

12. Remove all gasket material from the engine block.

To install:

13. Install a new gasket onto the water pump.

14. Place the water pump into its mounting position, then install the uppermost bolt.

15. Raise and safely support the vehicle.

16. Install the remaining water pump mounting bolts and tighten all bolts to 14–19 ft. lbs. (19–25 Nm).

17. Install a new gasket onto the water inlet pipe.

1. Camshaft sprockets
2. Valve cover
3. Camshaft front seal
4. Water pump
5. Seal plate
6. Water pump housing gasket
7. Cylinder head
8. Camshaft retaining cap
9. Camshafts
10. Hydraulic Lash Adjuster (HLA)
11. Valve spring retainer keys
12. Upper valve spring retainer
13. Valve spring
14. Lower valve spring retainer
15. Valve stem seal
16. Valve guide
17. Cylinder head bolt
18. Engine Coolant Temperature (ECT) sensor
19. Water hose connection
20. Coolant thermostat
21. Water temperature indicator sender unit
22. Cylinder head gasket
23. Valve
24. Engine block
25. Oil pump pick-up
26. Oil pump
27. Crankshaft front seal
28. Crankshaft sprocket
29. Crankshaft key

9300MG08

Exploded view of engine components, including the water pump, oil pump and camshafts—1.8L engine

Exploded view of water pump and related components—1.8L engine

7922MG16

18. Install the two bolts from the water inlet pipe to the water pump and tighten to 14–19 ft. lbs. (19–25 Nm).

19. Install the bolt to the engine oil dipstick tube bracket.

20. Lower the vehicle.

21. Install the timing belt.

22. Fill the cooling system.

23. Connect the negative battery cable.

24. Start the engine and allow it to reach operating temperature. Check for coolant leaks.

25. Check the coolant level and add coolant, as necessary.

1.9L Engine

1. Before servicing the vehicle, refer to the precautions in the beginning of this section.

2. Disconnect the negative battery cable.

3. Drain the cooling system.

4. Remove the timing belt cover and the timing belt.

5. Raise and safely support the vehicle.

6. Remove the lower radiator hose.

7. Remove the heater hose from the water pump.

8. Lower the vehicle and disconnect the heater hose from the water pump.

9. Unfasten the three bolts and one stud from the water pump.

10. Remove the water pump.

To install:

✳✳ WARNING

Do not use any abrasive grinding discs to remove gasket material. Use a plastic manual gasket scraper to remove the gasket residue. Be careful not to scratch or gouge the aluminum sealing surfaces when cleaning them.

11. Clean the gasket surfaces thoroughly until all traces of the old gasket residue are removed. Inspect the gasket mating surfaces, both must be clean and flat.

12. Install a new gasket and the water pump.

13. Install the water pump bolts and stud to 15–22 ft. lbs. (20–30 Nm).

14. Connect the heater hose to the pump.

15. Raise the vehicle.

16. Connect the lower radiator hose to the pump.

17. Install the timing belt tensioner and tighten the bolt to 15–22 ft. lbs. (20–30 Nm).

18. Install the timing belt and lower the vehicle.

19. Fill the cooling system with the proper amount and mixture of coolant.

20. Start the engine and check for leaks.

DOHC ZETEC

1. Before servicing the vehicle, refer to the precautions in the beginning of this section.

2. Disconnect the negative battery cable.

3. Drain and recycle the engine coolant.

4. Raise the vehicle.

5. Unfasten the splash shield bolts and remove the shield.

6. Loosen the water pump pulley retaining bolts, then remove the drive belt.

7. Remove the A/C compressor bolts and move the compressor aside.

8. Unfasten the water pump bolts and remove the pump from the middle timing belt cover.

To install:

9. Install the water pump and tighten the bolts to 17 ft. lbs. (24 Nm).

WATER PUMP BOLT (4)

WATER PUMP

WATER PUMP HOUSING GASKET

FRONT OF ENGINE

7922MG17

Exploded view of water pump mounting—1.9L engine

8. Lower the vehicle.

9. Support the engine with a suitable floor jack.

10. Remove the right engine mount attaching bolts and roll the engine mount aside.

11. Remove the water pump attaching bolts.

12. Using the floor jack, raise the engine enough to provide clearance for removing the water pump.

13. Remove the water pump and the gasket from the engine through the top of the engine compartment.

To install:

14. Be sure the mating surfaces of the cylinder block and water pump are clean and free of gasket material.

15. If the water pump is to be replaced, transfer the timing belt tensioner components to the new water pump.

16. With the engine supported and raised with a suitable floor jack, place the water pump and the gasket on the cylinder block and install the four attaching bolts. Tighten the bolts to 15–22 ft. lbs. (20–30 Nm).

17. Install the timing belt and cover.

18. Roll the engine mount into position

and install the mount bolts. Remove the floor jack.

19. Raise and safely support the vehicle.

20. Install the lower radiator hose and connect the heater hose to the pump.

21. Lower the vehicle.

22. Connect the negative battery cable.

23. Refill the cooling system.

24. Start the engine, allow it to reach normal operating temperature and check for coolant leaks.

25. Check the coolant level and add as necessary.

2.0L Engine

SOHC SPLIT PORT INJECTION (SPI)

1. Before servicing the vehicle, refer to the precautions in the beginning of this section.

2. Disconnect the negative battery cable.

3. Raise the vehicle.

4. Drain and recycle the engine coolant.

5. Remove the timing belt.

6. Unfasten the timing belt tensioner bolt and remove the tensioner.

7. Disconnect the lower radiator hose from the water pump.

Refer to Section 1 for engine rebuilding specifications

1. Water pump housing gasket
2. Water pump
3. Timing belt tensioner
4. Front engine support mounting bracket
5. Oil pressure sensor
6. Knock sensor
7. Engine block
8. Oil pan
9. Oil filter
10. Crankshaft Position (CKP) sensor
11. Camshaft sprocket
12. Crankshaft pulley
13. Outer engine front cover
14. Crankshaft sprocket
15. Timing belt
16. Timing belt guide
17. Crankshaft front seal
18. Oil pump screen cover and tube
19. Oil pump inlet tube gasket
20. Oil pump

9300MG11

Exploded view of the water pump, oil pump and timing belt mounting—2.0L SOHC SPI engine

7922MG18

Location of the water pump (C) mounting bolts (A) and stud (B)—2.0L SOHC engine

7922MG19

Remove the water pump mounting bolts—2.0L Zetec engine

10. Place the A/C compressor in position and tighten the mounting bolts.

11. Install the drive belt and tighten the water pump pulley bolts.

12. Install the splash shield and tighten the bolts.

13. Fill the cooling system with the proper amount and mixture of coolant.

14. Connect the negative battery cable.

15. Start the engine and check for leaks.

Cylinder Head

REMOVAL & INSTALLATION

✲✲ WARNING

To reduce the possibility of cylinder head warpage and/or distortion, do not remove the cylinder head while the engine is warm. Always, allow the engine to cool entirely before disassembly.

1.8L Engine

1. Before servicing the vehicle, refer to the precautions in the beginning of this section.
2. Properly relieve the fuel system pressure.
3. Disconnect the negative battery cable.
4. Drain the cooling system.
5. Unfasten the bolts from the timing belt upper and middle covers, then remove the covers and gaskets.
6. Manually rotate the crankshaft in the direction of normal engine rotation (clockwise) and align the timing marks located on the camshaft pulleys and seal plate.
7. Loosen the timing belt tensioner lockbolt and temporarily secure the tensioner spring in the fully extended position.
8. Remove the timing belt from the camshaft pulleys and secure it aside to prevent damage during the removal and installation of the cylinder head.

✲✲ WARNING

Do not allow the timing belt to become contaminated by oil or grease.

9. Tag and remove the vacuum hoses from the valve head cover.
10. Tag and disconnect the spark plug wires from the spark plugs and position the wires aside.
11. Remove the rocker arm (valve) cover and gasket.
12. Loosen the air cleaner outlet tube clamps and disconnect it from the resonance chamber and throttle body.
13. Disconnect the accelerator cable, if equipped with automatic transaxle, the kickdown cable from the throttle cam. Remove the cable bracket from the intake manifold.
14. Tag and remove all vacuum lines from the intake manifold.

1. Clutch pressure plate
2. Clutch disc
3. Support
4. Flywheel (automatic trans.)
5. Flywheel (manual trans.)
6. PVC valve
7. Oil separator
8. Engine block
9. Knock sensor
10. Oil pressure sensor
11. Oil filter
12. Throttle body
13. Fuel injection supply manifold
14. Idle Air Control (IAC) valve
15. Retainer clip
16. Fuel injector
17. Bracket
18. Water pump housing gasket
19. Water pump
20. Upper timing belt cover
21. Center timing belt cover
22. Water pump pulley
23. Crankshaft pulley
24. Crankshaft sprocket
25. Timing belt guide
26. Timing belt
27. Timing belt idler pulley
28. Oil pump
29. Oil pump housing gasket
30. Intake manifold
31. Oil pump pick-up
32. Crankshaft front seal
33. Lower timing belt cover

9300MG10

Exploded view of peripheral engine component mounting, including water pump, oil pump and intake manifold—2.0L DOHC Zetec engine

For engine torque specifications, refer to Section 1 of this manual

15. Tag and unplug all necessary electrical connectors from the cylinder head, exhaust manifold, intake manifold, and throttle body.

16. Disconnect the ground straps.

17. Loosen the upper radiator hose clamps and remove the hose.

18. Unfasten the transaxle-to-engine block upper-right bolt.

19. If equipped, remove the safety clips from the fuel rail.

20. Disconnect the fuel pressure and return lines, then plug the lines.

21. Disconnect the ignition coil high-tension lead from the distributor.

22. Tag and disengage the necessary hoses connected to the cylinder head and intake manifold.

23. Remove the two bolts from the transaxle vent tube routing brackets.

24. Raise and safely support the vehicle.

25. Remove the bolt from the water pump-to-cylinder head hose bracket.

26. Remove the front exhaust mounting flange and exhaust pipe support bracket from the exhaust manifold.

27. Remove the intake manifold support bracket.

28. Lower the vehicle.

Removal sequence for cylinder head bolts—1.8L engines

29. Remove the cylinder head bolts in the sequence illustrated.

30. Remove the cylinder head assembly, with the intake manifold, exhaust manifold and distributor still attached, from the vehicle.

31. Remove the intake manifold and exhaust manifold.

To install:

32. Remove all dirt, oil and old gasket material from all gasket contact surfaces.

33. Install the intake manifold and exhaust manifold.

34. Install a new head gasket onto the top of the engine block, using the dowel pins for reference.

35. Place the cylinder head into its mounting position on top of the engine block.

36. Lubricate the cylinder head bolts with engine oil and install them finger-tight. Tighten the bolts in the proper sequence (refer to the accompanying illustration) in two or three steps to 56–60 ft. lbs. (76–81 Nm).

37. Install the two bolts to the transaxle vent tube routing brackets.

38. Connect the heater hoses to the cylinder head and tighten the clamps.

39. Connect the ignition coil high-tension lead to the distributor.

40. Connect the fuel pressure and return lines to the fuel supply manifold and install the safety clips.

41. Install the transaxle-to-engine block upper-right bolt. If equipped with a manual transaxle, tighten the bolt to 47–66 ft. lbs. (64–89 Nm). If equipped with an automatic transaxle, tighten the bolt to 41–59 ft. lbs. (55–80 Nm).

42. Install the upper radiator hose and tighten the clamps.

43. Connect the ground straps.

44. Attach the electrical connectors that were unplugged at the cylinder head, exhaust manifold, intake manifold, and throttle body.

45. Connect the vacuum lines to the intake manifold.

46. Install the accelerator and kickdown cable bracket onto the intake manifold and tighten the bolts to 69–95 inch lbs. (7.8–11.0 Nm). Connect the cable(s) to the throttle cam.

47. Install the valve cover and gasket, then connect the hose running from the manifold to the valve cover. Tighten the cover bolts to 43–78 inch lbs. (4.9–8.8 Nm).

48. Install and connect the spark plug wires.

49. Connect the air cleaner outlet tube to

SEAL PLATE
ALIGNMENT MARKS

CAMSHAFT
PULLEY
TIMING
MARKS

TIMING CHAIN/
BELT

Be sure the timing marks on the camshaft pulleys and seal plate are aligned—1.8L engine

Tighten the cylinder head bolts in this sequence to the proper specification—1.8L engine

the resonator and throttle body and tighten the clamps.

50. Connect the hose going from the air duct to the cylinder head cover.

51. Raise and safely support the vehicle.

52. Install the intake manifold support bracket. Tighten the bolts to 27–38 ft. lbs. (37–52 Nm) and the nut to 14–19 ft. lbs. (19–25 Nm).

53. Install the bolt to the water pump-to-cylinder head hose bracket.

54. Install the exhaust front mounting flange with a new gasket to the exhaust manifold. Tighten the flange-to-manifold attaching nuts to 23–34 ft. lbs. (31–46 Nm).

55. Install the exhaust pipe support bracket. Tighten the bracket attaching bolts to 27–38 ft. lbs. (37–52 Nm).

56. Be sure the yellow ignition timing mark on the crankshaft pulley is aligned with the TDC mark on the timing belt cover.

57. Lower the vehicle.

58. Be sure the timing marks on the camshaft pulleys and seal plate are aligned. Install the timing belt so there is no looseness at the idler pulley side or between the two camshaft pulleys.

➡**Do not turn the crankshaft counterclockwise.**

59. Turn the crankshaft two turns clockwise by hand and verify that the yellow ignition timing mark on the crankshaft pulley is aligned with the timing mark on the timing belt cover. Verify that the timing marks on the camshaft pulley and seal plate are aligned.

➡**If the timing marks are not aligned, remove the timing belt and repeat the procedure.**

60. Turn the crankshaft 1 5⁄6 turns clockwise by hand and align the 4th tooth to the right of the **I** and **E** timing marks on the camshaft pulleys with the seal plate alignment marks.

61. Loosen the timing belt tensioner lockbolt and apply tension to the timing belt. Tighten the tensioner lockbolt to 27–38 ft. lbs. (37–52 Nm).

62. Turn the crankshaft 2 1⁄6 (780 degrees) turns clockwise and verify that the timing marks on the camshaft pulleys and the seal plate are aligned.

63. Install new gaskets onto the timing belt upper and middle covers and install the covers. Tighten the mounting bolts to 69–95 inch lbs. (8–11 Nm).

64. Fill the cooling system.

65. Connect the negative battery cable.

66. Start the engine and check for leaks.

1.9L Engine

1. Before servicing the vehicle, refer to the precautions in the beginning of this section.

2. Properly relieve the fuel system pressure.

3. Disconnect the negative battery cable.

4. Drain the cooling system.

5. Remove the air intake duct.

6. Remove the crankcase breather hose from the rocker arm cover and the vacuum hose from the bottom of the throttle body.

7. Remove the power brake supply hose.

8. Tag and unplug the following the electrical connectors:

- Fuel charging harness (right-hand strut tower)
- Alternator harness (back of the alternator)
- Crank Angle Sensor (CAS)
- Oxygen (O_2S) sensor
- Ignition coil
- Radio suppresser (mounted on the coil bracket)
- Engine Coolant Temperature (ECT) sensor, cooling fan sensor and temperature sending unit

9. Remove the ground strap from the stud on the left side of the cylinder head.

10. Disconnect the accelerator and the transaxle kickdown cables from the throttle lever and remove the cable bracket from the intake manifold.

11. Disconnect the heater hose containing the coolant temperature switches at the bulkhead.

12. Remove the upper radiator hose.

13. Disconnect and plug the fuel supply and return lines.

14. Remove the oil level indicator tube mounting nut from the cylinder head stud.

15. Remove the power steering hose and the air conditioner line retainer bracket bolts from the alternator bracket.

16. Remove the accessory drive belt, alternator, and the drive belt automatic tensioner.

17. Raise and safely support the vehicle.

18. Remove the catalytic converter inlet pipe.

19. Remove the starter wiring harness from the retaining clip below the intake manifold.

20. Set the engine No. 1 cylinder on TDC.

21. Lower the vehicle.

22. Remove the timing belt.

23. Remove the heater hose support bracket retaining bolt and the alternator bracket-to-cylinder head mounting bolt.

24. Remove the rocker arm cover.

25. Remove the cylinder head bolts. The old bolts can be used to check the piston squish height before discarding them.

26. Remove the cylinder head with the exhaust and intake manifolds attached.

27. Remove the cylinder head gasket. Keep the gasket to check the piston squish height, then after checking the squish height, discard the gasket

⁂ WARNING

Do not lay the cylinder head flat. Damage to the spark plugs, valves or gasket surfaces may result.

To install:

28. Clean all gasket material from the mating surfaces on the cylinder head and block and clean out the head bolt holes in the block.

29. Check the piston squish height. Refer to the procedure in this section.

⁂ WARNING

No cylinder block deck machining or use of replacement crankshaft, piston or connecting rod causing the assembled squish height to be over or under tolerance specification, is permitted. If no parts other than the head gasket are replaced, the squish height should be within specification. If parts other than the head gasket are replaced, check the squish height. If the squish height is out of specification, replace the parts again and recheck the squish height.

30. Install the dowels in the cylinder block, if removed. Check the dowel height, it should be 0.407–0.40 in. (10.40–11.75mm) above the surface of the block. A dowel that is too long will not allow the cylinder head to sit properly.

31. Position the cylinder head gasket on the cylinder block.

➡**The cylinder head attaching bolts cannot be tightened to the specified torque more than once and must therefore be replaced when installing a cylinder head.**

For complete mechanical specifications, refer to Section 1 of this manual

32. Install the cylinder head and install new bolts and washers in the following order:

a. Apply a light coat of engine oil to the threads of the new cylinder head bolts and install the new bolts into the head.

b. Tighten the cylinder head bolts in sequence (refer to the illustration) to 44 ft. lbs. (60 Nm).

c. Loosen the cylinder head bolts approximately two turns, then tighten them again in the same sequence to 44 ft. lbs. (60 Nm).

d. After bolts have all been tightened, turn the head bolts 90 degrees in sequence and to complete the head bolt installation, turn the head bolts an additional 90 degrees in the same torque sequence.

33. Install the rocker arm cover and the alternator bracket-to-cylinder head bolt.

34. Be sure the timing marks aligned so that the engine is at Top Dead Center (TDC), install the timing belt and the timing belt cover.

35. Raise and safely support the vehicle.

36. Install the starter wiring harness on the retaining clip below the intake manifold.

37. Install the catalytic converter inlet pipe.

38. Lower the vehicle.

39. Install the alternator and the accessory drive belt automatic tensioner. Install the accessory drive belt.

40. Install both the power steering hose and air conditioner line retainer bracket bolts. Install the oil level indicator tube retainer bolt.

41. Connect the fuel supply and return lines.

42. Install the upper radiator hose and connect the heater hose at the engine compartment bulkhead.

43. Install the heater hose support bracket retaining bolt.

44. Install the accelerator cable bracket on the intake manifold and connect the accelerator and kickdown cables to the throttle lever.

45. Install the ground strap at the left side of the cylinder head.

46. Attach all the remaining electrical connectors according to their positions marked during the removal procedure.

47. Connect the power brake supply hose, crankcase breather hose and the vacuum line at the bottom of the throttle body.

48. Install the air intake duct.

49. Connect the negative battery cable.

50. Fill and bleed the cooling system.

51. Start the engine and check for leaks. Stop the engine and check the coolant level. Add fluid as necessary.

2.0L Engine

SOHC SPLIT PORT INJECTION (SPI)

✸✸ WARNING

Never work on aluminum engine parts when the engine is warm.

1. Before servicing the vehicle, refer to the precautions in the beginning of this section.

2. Disconnect the negative battery cable.

3. Properly relieve the fuel system pressure.

4. Remove the timing belt and engine air cleaner intake tube.

5. Tag and disconnect the vacuum hoses from the following components:
- EGR valve
- PCV valve
- Throttle body
- Fuel pressure regulator
- Intake manifold

6. Disconnect the accelerator cable, throttle control lever and if equipped, the speed control cable.

TIGHTENING SEQUENCE CYLINDER HEAD ATTACHING BOLTS

9 3 1 5 7   INTAKE

8 6 2 4 10   EXHAUST

CYLINDER HEAD

CYLINDER HEAD BOLT (10)

7922MG24

Cylinder head bolt tightening sequence— 1.9L engine

INSTALLED TIMING BELT

LOCATION OF KEYWAYS

CAMSHAFT SPROCKET

CYLINDER HEAD TIMING MARK

CAM SPROCKET TIMING POINTER

TENSIONER

CHECK TENSION HERE

TENSIONER ATTACHING BOLT

OIL PUMP TIMING MARK

WATER PUMP SPROCKET

CRANK SPROCKET TIMING POINTER

BELT TIMING

CRANKSHAFT SPROCKET

CRANKSHAFT AT T.D.C. (CRANK SPROCKET TIMING POINTER ALIGNED WITH OIL PUMP TIMING MARK AND CAMSHAFT SPROCKET TIMING POINTER ALIGNED WITH CYLINDER HEAD TIMING MARK).

7922MG25

Be sure the timing marks aligned so that the engine is at Top Dead Center (TDC) before installing the timing belt—1.9L engine

7922MG26

Tighten the cylinder head bolts in the proper sequence in the order specified—2.0L SOHC engines

7. If equipped, remove the speed control cable bracket bolt.

8. Unplug the two fuel charging wiring electrical connections.

9. Unplug the Crankshaft Position (CKP) sensor and Heated Oxygen (HO$_2$S) sensor electrical connections.

10. Using tool D87L-9280-A or its equivalent, disconnect the fuel supply line from the fuel rail.

11. Unfasten the power steering pressure hose bracket bolts, then position the bracket and hose aside.

12. Loosen the alternator lower bolt, unfasten the alternator upper bolt and pivot the alternator forward.

13. Unfasten the engine oil dipstick tube bracket bolt that attaches the tube to the intake manifold.

14. Disconnect the EGR manifold tube located below the EGR valve.

15. Unfasten the exhaust manifold heat shield nuts and remove the heat shield.

16. Unfasten the catalytic converter-to-exhaust manifold nuts and separate the components.

17. Raise the vehicle.

18. Drain the cooling system into a suitable container.

19. Unfasten the right-hand splash shield bolts and remove the shield.

20. Remove the engine oil dipstick tube from the cylinder block.

21. Unplug the A/C compressor electrical connection.

22. Unbolt the A/C compressor retainers and set the compressor aside with the lines still attached.

23. Loosen but do not remove, the four bolts and nut that attach the front engine accessory drive bracket about four turns ⅜ in.

24. Lower the vehicle and unfasten the uppermost front engine accessory drive bracket-to-cylinder head bolt.

25. Unfasten the A/C line bracket-to-front engine accessory drive bracket bolt.

26. Remove the valve cover, then disconnect the upper radiator hose from the thermostat housing water hose connection.

27. Disconnect the heater hose from the thermostat housing.

✳✳ CAUTION

Removal of the cylinder head usually requires two people, doing so without the proper help may cause personal injury and/or damage to the cylinder head should it fall.

28. Unfasten the cylinder head bolts, remove the head and gasket.

➡**Maintain a balanced pressure when removing the cylinder head bolts.**

29. Discard the old bolts and the gasket.
To install:

✳✳ WARNING

Do not use any abrasive grinding discs to remove gasket material. Use a plastic manual gasket scraper to remove the gasket residue. Be careful not to scratch or gouge the aluminum sealing surfaces when cleaning them.

30. Clean the gasket surfaces thoroughly until all traces of the old gasket residue are removed. Inspect the gasket mating surfaces, both must be clean and flat.

31. Install a new head gasket on the cylinder block.

➡**Always use new bolts when installing the cylinder head.**

32. Lubricate the new cylinder bolts when engine oil.

✳✳ CAUTION

Do not attempt to install the cylinder head without the aid of an assistant, it takes two people.

33. Install the cylinder head and tighten the bolts in the sequence illustrated in the following order:

a. Tighten all the bolts in sequence to 30–44 ft. lbs. (40–60 Nm).

b. Back all the bolts off ½ a turn.

c. Retighten all the bolts to 30–44 ft. lbs. (40–60 Nm).

34. Rotate all the bolts in sequence an additional 180 degrees in two steps of 90 degrees.

35. Install and tighten the uppermost accessory drive bracket bolt to 30–40 ft. lbs. (40–55 Nm).

36. Install the A/C line bracket and tighten the bolt to 15–18 ft. lbs. (20–25 Nm).

37. Install the valve cover, then raise the vehicle.

38. Install and tighten the four front engine accessory drive bracket bolts and the nut to 30–40 ft. lbs. (40–55 Nm).

39. Install the A/C compressor and tighten the retaining bolts.

40. Install the right-hand splash shield and tighten its retainers.

41. Install the engine oil dipstick tube and lower the vehicle.

42. Connect the heater and upper radiator hoses.

43. Install the timing belt and alternator.

44. Install the power steering pressure hose.

45. Attach the CKP sensor and two main fuel charging electrical connections

46. Install and tighten the engine oil dipstick tube bolt.

47. Install and tighten the EGR valve manifold tube connection.

48. Connect the EGR valve manifold tube to the exhaust manifold.

49. Connect the fuel supply line to the fuel rail.

50. Connect the catalytic converter to the exhaust manifold using a new gasket and tighten the nuts.

51. Install the heat shield and tighten the nuts.

52. If equipped, install the speed control cable bracket.

53. Connect the throttle control lever, accelerator cable and if equipped, the speed control cable.

Please refer to Section 9 for electric cooling fan wiring schematics

1. EGR valve
2. EGR valve gasket
3. Accelerator cable bracket
4. Throttle body gasket
5. Throttle Position (TP) sensor
6. Idle Air Control (IAC) valve
7. IAC valve gasket
8. Throttle body
9. Fuel injection supply manifold
10. Fuel injector
11. IMRC actuator
12. Oil filler cap
13. Valve cover
14. Cylinder head
15. EGR valve-to-exhaust manifold tube
16. Exhaust manifold gasket
17. Exhaust manifold
18. Exhaust manifold shield
19. Intake manifold gasket
20. Intake Manifold Runner Control (IMRC)
21. Intake manifold upper gasket
22. Intake manifold
23. Intake manifold tube

9300MG13

Exploded view of the cylinder head, exhaust manifold and intake manifold mounting—2.0L SOHC SPI engine

54. Connect the vacuum hoses tagged and removed to the following components:
- EGR valve
- PCV valve
- Throttle body
- Fuel pressure regulator.
- Intake manifold
55. Install the air cleaner outlet tube.
56. Fill the cooling system.
57. Connect the negative battery cable.
58. Start the engine and check for leaks.

DOHC ZETEC

1. Before servicing the vehicle, refer to the precautions in the beginning of this section.
2. Disconnect the negative battery cable.
3. Properly relieve the fuel system pressure.
4. Remove the air cleaner assembly outlet tube.
5. Remove the timing belt.
6. Tag and disconnect the vacuum hoses from the following components:
- PCV valve
- Throttle body
- Fuel pressure sensor
- Intake manifold

7. Disconnect the speed control and accelerator cables from the control lever.
8. Unplug the fuel charging electrical connectors at the main engine connector.
9. Unplug the Crankshaft Position (CKP) sensor and Heated Oxygen (HO_2S) sensor electrical connections.
10. Disconnect the fuel line.
11. Unbolt the power steering pump and bracket, then set them aside with the lines still attached.
12. Remove the alternator and engine oil dipstick tube.
13. Raise the vehicle.
14. Drain the cooling system into a suitable container.
15. Unfasten the splash shield bolts and remove the shield.
16. Unplug the A/C compressor electrical connection.
17. Unbolt the A/C compressor retainers and set the compressor aside with the lines still attached.
18. Lower the car, tag and disconnect the spark plug wires and remove the plugs.
19. Remove the valve cover, then disconnect the upper radiator hose from the

thermostat housing water hose connection.
20. Disconnect the heater hose from the thermostat housing.
21. Remove the camshafts and the ignition coil.
22. Remove the thermostat housing.
23. Unfasten the cylinder head bolts, then remove the head and the gasket.

To install:

✺✺ WARNING

Do not use any abrasive grinding discs to remove gasket material. Use a plastic manual gasket scraper to remove the gasket residue. Be careful not to scratch or gouge the aluminum sealing surfaces when cleaning them.

24. Clean the gasket surfaces thoroughly until all traces of the old gasket residue are removed. Inspect the gasket mating surfaces, both must be clean and flat.
25. Install a new head gasket on the cylinder block.

➡**Always use new bolts when installing the cylinder head.**

26. Lubricate the new cylinder bolts when engine oil.

✺✺ CAUTION

Do not attempt to install the cylinder head without the aid of an assistant, it takes two people.

27. Install the cylinder head and tighten the bolts in the sequence illustrated in the following steps:
- Step 1: Tighten all the bolts in sequence to 12–18 ft. lbs. (15–25 Nm)
- Step 2: Tighten all the bolts to 26–33 ft. lbs. (35–45 Nm)
- Step 3: Tighten the bolts an additional 90 degrees
28. Install the thermostat housing.
29. Install the ignition coil and the camshafts.
30. Connect the heater and upper radiator hoses.
31. Install the valve cover, spark plugs and connect the spark plug wires.
32. Install the A/C compressor and tighten the retaining bolts.
33. Attach the A/c compressor electrical connection.
34. Install the splash shield and tighten its retainers.
35. Install the engine oil dipstick tube.

Tighten the cylinder head bolts in the order specified—2.0L Zetec engines

7922MG27

36. Install the alternator and the power steering reservoir and bracket.

37. Connect the fuel line.

38. Attach the CKP sensor, HO₂S sensor, and two main fuel charging electrical connections

39. Connect accelerator cable and if equipped, the speed control cable to the control lever.

40. Connect the vacuum hoses tagged and removed to the following components:

- PCV valve
- Throttle body
- Fuel pressure sensor
- Intake manifold

41. Install the timing belt.

42. Install the air cleaner outlet tube.

43. Fill the cooling system.

44. Connect the negative battery cable.

45. Start the engine and check for leaks.

PISTON SQUISH HEIGHT

1.9L Engine

Before final installation of the cylinder head to the engine, piston "squish height" must be checked. Squish height is the clearance of the piston dome to the cylinder head dome at piston TDC. No rework of the head gasket surfaces (slabbing) or use of replacement parts (crankshaft, piston and connecting rod) that causes the assembled squish height to be over or under the tolerance specification is permitted.

➡ If no parts other than the head gasket are replaced, the piston squish height should be within specification. If parts other than the head gasket are replaced, check the squish height. If out of specification, replace the parts again and recheck the squish height.

1. Before servicing the vehicle, refer to the precautions in the beginning of this section.

2. Clean all gasket material from the mating surfaces on the cylinder head and engine block.

3. Place a small amount of soft lead solder or lead shot of an appropriate thickness on the piston spherical areas.

4. Rotate the crankshaft to lower the piston in the bore and install the head gasket and cylinder head.

➡ A compressed (used) head gasket is preferred for checking squish height.

5. Install used head bolts and tighten the head bolts to 30–44 ft. lbs. (40–60 Nm) following proper sequence.

6. Rotate the crankshaft to move the piston through its TDC position.

7. Remove the cylinder head and measure the thickness of the compressed solder to determine squish height at TDC. The compressed lead piece should be 0.039–0.070 in. (1.0–1.77mm).

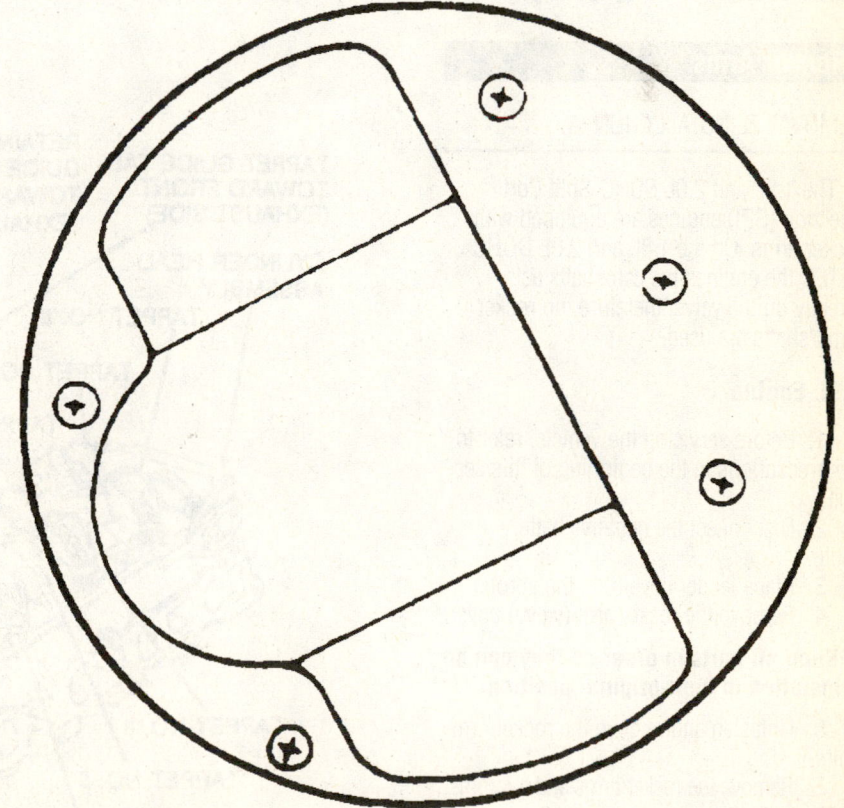

Place the lead shot or solder on the positions illustrated to measure the piston squish height

7922MG28

SQUISH HEIGHT DIMENSION
1.0-1.77MM
(0.039-0.070 INCH)

CYLINDER HEAD

HEAD GASKET

CYLINDER BLOCK

7922MG29

Cross-sectional view of squish height measurements—1.9L engines

8. Rotate the engine until the lifter is on the base circle of the cam (valve closed).

✳✳ WARNING

Be sure to turn the engine only in the normal direction of rotation. Backward rotation will cause the timing belt to slip or lose teeth, altering the valve timing and causing serious engine damage.

9. Install the rocker arm and components and tighten the rocker arm bolts to 17–22 ft. lbs. (23–30 Nm). Be sure the lifter is on the base circle of the cam for each rocker arm as it is installed.
10. Install the rocker arm cover.
11. Connect the negative battery cable.

2.0L Engine

SOHC SPLIT PORT INJECTION (SPI)

➡Refer to the illustration located in the camshaft procedure, earlier in this section, for a view of the rocker arms on this engine.

1. Before servicing the vehicle, refer to the precautions in the beginning of this section.

Rocker Arms

REMOVAL & INSTALLATION

The 1.9L and 2.0L SOHC Split Port Injection (SPI) engines are equipped with rocker arms. On the 1.8L and 2.0L DOHC ZETEC the engines the camshafts acts directly on the valve, therefore, no rocker arms/shafts are used.

1.9L Engine

1. Before servicing the vehicle, refer to the precautions in the beginning of this section.
2. Disconnect the negative battery cable.
3. Place fender covers on the aprons.
4. Remove the rocker arm (valve) cover.

➡**Keep all parts in order so they can be reinstalled in their original position.**

5. Unfasten and remove the rocker arm bolts.
6. Remove the rocker arms and fulcrums.
To install:
7. Before installation, coat the valve tips, rocker arm and fulcrum contact areas with Lubriplate® or equivalent.

FULCRUM

RETAINER TAPPET GUIDE NOTCH TOWARD FRONT (EXHAUST SIDE)

TAPPET GUIDE TAB TOWARD FRONT (EXHAUST SIDE)

CYLINDER HEAD ASSEMBLY

TAPPET NO. 8

TAPPET NO. 7

TAPPET NO. 3

ROCKER ARM

TAPPET ROLLER

TAPPET NO. 6

TAPPET NO. 5

TAPPET NO. 4

TAPPET NO. 2

TAPPET NO. 1

KEY

7922MG30

Exploded view of the upper valvetrain—1.9L engine

2. Disconnect the negative battery cable.
3. Remove the valve cover.
4. Mark the location of the rocker arms, then unfasten the rocker arm bolts.
5. Remove the rocker arms and seats.

To install:

6. Install the seats and rocker arms in their original positions.
7. Install and tighten the rocker arm bolts to 17–22 ft. lbs. (23–30 Nm).
8. Install the valve cover.
9. Connect the negative battery cable.

Intake Manifold

REMOVAL & INSTALLATION

1.8L Engine

UPPER MANIFOLD

➡ **Refer to the illustration located in the distributor procedure, earlier in this section, for a view of the upper intake manifold mounting on this engine.**

1. Before servicing the vehicle, refer to the precautions in the beginning of this section.
2. Properly relieve the fuel system pressure.
3. Disconnect the negative battery cable.
4. Partially drain the cooling system.
5. Remove the air cleaner outlet tube from the throttle body and intake air resonator.
6. Disconnect the throttle cable and throttle valve control actuating cable from the throttle body control lever.
7. Unfasten the accelerator cable throttle valve control actuating cable bracket bolt and remove the bracket from the manifold.
8. Unplug the throttle body electrical connections.
9. Tag and disconnect all necessary vacuum hoses from the upper manifold.
10. Disconnect the air bypass and idle air control hoses from the manifold.
11. Remove the idle air control hose.
12. Unfasten the upper intake manifold upper bolts.
13. Raise and safely support the vehicle.
14. Unfasten the upper intake lower bolts and lower the vehicle.
15. Remove the manifold with the throttle body attached.
16. Remove the upper intake manifold gasket.

To install:

17. Use a gasket scraper to clean the upper intake mounting surfaces.
18. Install a new upper intake manifold gasket.
19. Place the upper intake manifold in position.
20. Install the manifold upper bolts and nuts, then tighten them to 14–19 ft. lbs. (19–25 Nm).
21. Raise the vehicle.
22. Install the manifold lower bolts and nuts, then tighten them to 14–19 ft. lbs. (19–25 Nm) and lower the vehicle.
23. Install the idle air control hose.
24. Connect the air bypass and idle air control hoses to the manifold.
25. Connect all the vacuum hoses to the upper manifold.
26. Engage the throttle body electrical connections.
27. Install the accelerator cable throttle valve control actuating cable bracket and tighten the bolt to 69–95 inch lbs. (7.8–11 Nm).
28. Connect the throttle cable and throttle valve control actuating cable to the throttle body control lever.
29. Install the air cleaner outlet tube.
30. Be sure all wires and hoses are connected.
31. Fill the cooling system
32. Connect the negative battery cable.
33. Start the vehicle and check for proper operation.

LOWER MANIFOLD

➡ **Refer to the illustration located in the distributor procedure, earlier in this section, for a view of the lower intake manifold mounting on this engine.**

1. Before servicing the vehicle, refer to the precautions in the beginning of this section.
2. Properly relieve the fuel system pressure.
3. Disconnect the negative battery cable.
4. Partially drain the cooling system.
5. Tag and disconnect all necessary vacuum hoses from the upper manifold and throttle body.
6. Remove the vacuum reservoir from the upper intake manifold.
7. Tag and disconnect the coolant hoses from the valves.
8. Disconnect the throttle cable and throttle valve control actuating cable from the throttle body control lever.

9. Unfasten the accelerator cable throttle valve control actuating cable bracket bolt and remove the bracket from the manifold.
10. Unplug the throttle body electrical connections.
11. Disconnect the fuel and vapor line spring lock couplings.
12. Disconnect the PCV hose from the upper intake manifold and valve cover.
13. Disconnect the vacuum hose from the fuel pressure regulator.
14. Unplug the fuel charging harness electrical connectors.
15. Unfasten the fuel rail retaining bolts and remove the fuel rail and injectors.
16. Unfasten the transaxle breather tube and separate the tube from the manifold.
17. Unfasten the five uppermost intake manifold-to-cylinder head nuts.
18. Raise the vehicle.
19. Unfasten the bolts attaching the intake manifold support and remove the support.
20. Unfasten the four lowermost intake manifold-to-cylinder block nuts.
21. Lower the vehicle.
22. Remove the lower intake manifold, upper intake manifold and throttle body from the engine compartment as an assembly.
23. Remove the intake manifold gasket.
24. If necessary, separate the upper manifold from the lower manifold.

To install:

25. Use a scraper to clean the manifold mating surfaces.
26. Install a new intake manifold gasket.
27. Install the lower intake manifold, upper intake manifold and throttle body onto the studs.
28. Install the intake manifold-to-cylinder head nuts and tighten them in the sequence illustrated to 14–19 ft. lbs. (19–25 Nm).
29. Raise the vehicle.

7922MG35

Tighten the intake manifold-to-cylinder head nuts as illustrated—1.8L engine

Timing belt service is covered in Section 5 of this manual

Tighten the intake manifold support bolts to the specifications illustrated—1.8L engine

30. Install the intake manifold support and tighten the bolts to the specifications illustrated. Refer to the accompanying illustration.

31. Lower the vehicle.

32. Install the fuel rail and the transaxle breather tube.

33. Install the vacuum reservoir and engage the throttle body electrical connections.

34. Connect all vacuum, coolant and valve hoses

35. Install the accelerator cable throttle valve control actuating cable bracket and tighten the bolt to 69–95 inch lbs. (7.8–11 Nm).

36. Connect the throttle cable and throttle valve control actuating cable to the throttle body control lever.

37. Install the air cleaner outlet tube.

38. Be sure all wires and hoses are connected.

39. Fill the cooling system

40. Connect the negative battery cable.

41. Start the vehicle and check for proper operation.

1.9L Engine

1. Before servicing the vehicle, refer to the precautions in the beginning of this section.

2. Properly relieve the fuel system pressure.

3. Disconnect the negative battery cable.

4. Partially drain the cooling system.

5. Remove the air intake tube.

6. Unplug the fuel injector harness from the engine control harness at the right shock tower.

7. Unplug the Crankshaft Position (CKP) sensor electrical connection.

8. Disconnect and plug the fuel supply and return lines.

9. Unplug the Camshaft Position (CMP) sensor electrical connection.

10. Remove the accelerator cable, if equipped with automatic transaxle, the kickdown cable from the throttle lever.

11. Remove the cable bracket from the intake manifold and position the cables aside.

12. Remove the power brake supply hose, PCV line and the vacuum line from the bottom of the throttle body.

13. Remove the seven attaching nuts from the intake manifold studs.

14. Slide the manifold assembly off of the studs and remove it from the cylinder head.

15. Remove and discard the intake manifold gasket.

To install:

16. Use a scraper to clean and inspect the mounting faces of the intake manifold and cylinder head. Both surfaces must be clean and flat.

17. Clean and oil the manifold studs and position a new gasket over them.

18. Install the intake manifold and the attaching nuts. Tighten the nuts to 12–15 ft. lbs. (16–20 Nm).

19. Install the vacuum line on the bottom of the throttle body, the power brake supply hose and the PCV line.

20. Install the accelerator cable bracket and connect the accelerator cable, if equipped, kickdown cable on the throttle lever.

21. Connect the fuel supply and return lines. Install the fuel line retaining clips.

22. Attach the two fuel injector harness connectors to the engine control harness at the right shock tower.

23. Attach the CKP and CMP sensor electrical connections.

24. Install the air intake tube.

25. Refill the cooling system.

26. Connect the negative battery cable.

27. Start the engine and bring to normal operating temperature, then check for fuel and coolant leaks.

28. Stop the engine and check the coolant level.

2.0L Engine

SOHC SPLIT PORT INJECTION (SPI)

➡ Refer to the illustration located in the cylinder head procedure, earlier in this section, for a view of the intake manifold mounting on this engine.

1. Before servicing the vehicle, refer to the precautions in the beginning of this section.

2. Disconnect the negative battery cable.

Remove the engine oil dipstick tube bracket bolt that attaches the tube to the intake manifold—2.0L SOHC engine

Disconnect the EGR manifold tube located below the EGR valve—2.0L SOHC engine

3. Partially drain the cooling system.

4. Remove the air cleaner outlet tube.

5. Tag and disconnect the vacuum hoses from the following components:
   - EGR valve
   - PCV valve
   - Throttle body
   - Fuel pressure regulator.
   - Intake manifold

6. Disconnect the accelerator cable, throttle control lever and if equipped, the speed control cable.

7. If equipped, remove the speed control cable bracket bolt.

8. Unplug the Idle Air Control (IAC) valve and Throttle Position (TP) sensor electrical connections.

9. Unfasten the engine oil dipstick tube bracket bolt that attaches the tube to the intake manifold.

10. Disconnect the EGR manifold tube located below the EGR valve.

11. Raise the vehicle.

12. Remove the engine oil dipstick tube from the block.

13. Unfasten the intake manifold lower nuts, then lower the vehicle.

14. Unfasten the intake manifold upper nuts and remove the nuts. Discard the manifold gasket.

To install:

> ✳✳ **WARNING**
>
> **Do not use any abrasive grinding discs to remove gasket material. Use a plastic manual gasket scraper to remove the gasket residue. Be careful not to scratch or gouge the aluminum sealing surfaces when cleaning them.**

15. Clean the gasket surfaces thoroughly until all traces of the old gasket residue are removed. Inspect the gasket mating surfaces, both must be clean and flat.

16. Clean and oil the intake manifold mounting studs.

17. Install the intake manifold and hand-tighten the upper nuts.

18. Raise the vehicle.

19. Install the lower manifold nuts and tighten them to 15–22 ft. lbs. (20–30 Nm).

20. Connect the engine oil dipstick tube to the block.

21. Lower the vehicle and tighten the manifold upper nuts to 15–22 ft. lbs. (20–30 Nm).

22. Connect the EGR manifold tube and tighten it to 15–20 ft. lbs. (20–28 Nm).

23. Install and tighten the engine oil dipstick tube bolt to 71–97 inch lbs. (8–11 Nm).

24. Attach the IAC valve and TP sensor electrical connections.

25. If equipped, install and tighten the speed control cable bracket bolt to 71–88 inch lbs. (8–10 Nm).

26. Connect the throttle control lever, accelerator cable and if equipped, the speed control cable.

27. Connect the vacuum hoses tagged and removed to the following components:
- EGR valve
- PCV valve
- Throttle body
- Fuel pressure regulator
- Intake manifold

28. Install the air cleaner outlet tube.

29. Fill the cooling system.

30. Connect the negative battery cable.

31. Start the engine and check for coolant leaks.

DOHC ZETEC

➡ **Refer to the illustration located in the water pump procedure, earlier in this section, for a view of the intake manifold on this engine.**

1. Before servicing the vehicle, refer to the precautions in the beginning of this section.

2. Properly relieve the fuel system pressure.

3. Disconnect the negative battery cable.

4. Remove the air cleaner outlet tube.

5. Unplug the Throttle Position (TP) sensor electrical connection.

6. Raise the vehicle.

7. Drain the cooling system into a suitable container.

8. Remove the bolt that secures the pipe located by the crankshaft pulley, then lower the vehicle.

9. Disconnect the heater hoses from the core.

10. Unplug the main engine control sensor wiring.

11. Remove the connectors from the mounting bracket.

12. Tag and disconnect the vacuum hoses from the intake manifold by squeezing the tabs, twisting the hoses and pulling them away from the manifold.

13. Disconnect the crankcase ventilation hose from the valve cover.

14. Remove the drive belt.

15. Unfasten the alternator mounting bolts and move the alternator aside.

16. Disconnect the fuel lines.

Remove the intake manifold bolts and nuts in this sequence—2.0L Zetec engine

Tighten the manifold bolts and nuts in this sequence—2.0L Zetec

17. Unfasten the intake manifold nuts and bolts in the sequence illustrated.

18. Remove the intake manifold and gasket.

To install:

19. Clean all dirt and gasket residue from the intake manifold mating surfaces.

20. Install a new gasket and place the manifold in position.

21. Install and tighten the manifold bolts and nuts in the sequence illustrated to 10–12 ft. lbs. (14–17 Nm).

22. Connect the fuel lines and install the alternator.

23. Install the drive belt and connect the crankcase ventilation hose to the valve cover.

24. Connect the vacuum hoses to the manifold making sure the tabs are firmly engaged.

25. Install the connectors in the mounting bracket and attach the main engine control sensor wiring.

26. Connect the heater hoses to the heater core.

27. Install the bolt that secures the pipe located by the crankshaft pulley. Tighten the bolt to 71–97 inch lbs. (8–11 Nm).

28. Attach the TP sensor electrical connection.

29. Install the air cleaner outlet tube.

30. Fill the cooling system.

31. Connect the negative battery cable.

Exhaust Manifold

REMOVAL & INSTALLATION

1.8L Engine

1. Before servicing the vehicle, refer to the precautions in the beginning of this section.

2. Disconnect the negative battery cable.

3. Partially drain the cooling system and disconnect the upper radiator hose.

4. Remove the engine intake air resonator (duct).

5. Disconnect the upper radiator hose.

6. Remove the cooling fan motor.

7. Raise and safely support the vehicle.

8. If equipped, remove the engine and transaxle splash shield.

9. Remove the exhaust inlet pipe from the exhaust manifold and remove the gasket.

HEAT SHIELD

EXHAUST MANIFOLD

EXHAUST MANIFOLD GASKET

CATALYTIC CONVERTER

EGO SENSOR

7922MG40

Exploded view of the exhaust manifold assembly—1.8L and 2.0L Zetec engines

10. Remove the two bolts from the exhaust pipe support bracket.

11. Unfasten the cooling fan lower mounting bolts

12. Lower the vehicle.

13. Unplug the Oxygen (O₂S) sensor electrical connector.

14. Unfasten the exhaust manifold heat shield mounting bolts and remove the shield.

15. Unfasten the exhaust manifold mounting nuts and remove the assembly.

16. Using a scraper, remove all gasket material from the cylinder head and exhaust manifold.

To install:

17. Install a new gasket onto the exhaust manifold mounting studs.

18. Place the exhaust manifold onto the mounting studs and install the manifold mounting nuts. Tighten the nuts to 28–34 ft. lbs. (38–46 Nm).

19. Place the heat shield into its mounting position and install the shield mounting bolts. Tighten the bolts to 69–95 inch lbs. (7.8–11.0 Nm).

20. Attach the O₂S sensor electrical connector.

21. Install the cooling fan.

22. Connect the upper radiator hose.

23. Install the intake air duct.

24. Raise and safely support the vehicle.

25. Install the exhaust pipe support bracket.

26. Install a new gasket and attach the exhaust pipe to the exhaust manifold. Tighten the attaching nuts to 23–34 ft. lbs. (31–46 Nm).

27. Install the splash shields and tighten the bolts to 69–95 inch lbs. (7.8–11.0 Nm).

28. Lower the vehicle.

29. Refill the cooling system.

30. Connect the negative battery cable.

1.9L Engine

1. Before servicing the vehicle, refer to the precautions in the beginning of this section.

2. Disconnect the negative battery cable.

3. Remove the accessory drive belt.

4. Remove the alternator.

5. Remove the radiator cooling fan motor and the shroud assembly.

6. Hold the EGR valve tube-to-manifold connector with a wrench and loosen the valve-to-exhaust manifold tube nut.

7. Unfasten the two EGR valve-to- exhaust manifold tube bolts from the ignition coil bracket.

8. Remove the EGR valve tube.

9. remove the exhaust manifold heat shield.

10. Raise and safely support the vehicle.

11. Remove the two catalytic converter inlet pipe-to-exhaust manifold attaching nuts.

12. Lower the vehicle.

13. Remove the eight exhaust manifold attaching nuts and remove the exhaust manifold and gasket.

To install:

14. Use a scraper to clean the cylinder head and exhaust manifold gasket surfaces.

15. Position the new gasket onto the manifold mounting studs.

16. Position the exhaust manifold on the cylinder head and install the attaching nuts. Tighten the nuts to 16–19 ft. lbs. (21–26 Nm).

17. Raise and safely support the vehicle.

18. Install the catalytic converter inlet pipe-to-exhaust manifold attaching nuts. Tighten the nuts to 25–33 ft. lbs. (34–47 Nm).

19. Lower the vehicle.

IGNITION COIL BRACKET

FRONT OF ENGINE

EGR VALVE

EGR VALVE TO EXHAUST MANIFOLD TUBE

EGR VALVE TO EXHAUST MANIFOLD TUBE BOLTS

7922MG41

EGR valve tube-to-exhaust manifold routing—1.9L engine

FRONT OF ENGINE

CYLINDER HEAD ASSEMBLY

EXHAUST MANIFOLD

NUT (8)

7922MG42

Exploded view of the exhaust manifold mounting—1.9L engine

20. Install the exhaust manifold heat shield. Tighten the nuts to 3–5 ft. lbs. (5–7 Nm).

21. Install the EGR valve-to-exhaust manifold tube and tighten the nuts to 18–25 ft. lbs. (25–35 Nm).

22. Install the radiator cooling fan and shroud assembly.

23. Install the alternator and the accessory drive belt.

24. Connect the negative battery cable.

2.0L Engine

SOHC SPLIT PORT INJECTION (SPI)

➡ Refer to the illustration located in the cylinder head procedure, earlier in this section, for a view of the exhaust manifold on this engine.

1. Before servicing the vehicle, refer to the precautions in the beginning of this section.

2. Disconnect the negative battery cable.

3. Remove the drive belt.

4. Unplug the Heated Oxygen (HO_2S) sensor electrical connection which is mounted on the cooling fan shroud.

5. Unfasten the five exhaust manifold heat shield nuts and remove the shield.

6. Unfasten the two EGR tube-to-exhaust manifold nuts studs.

7. Unfasten the power steering pressure hose bracket bolts, then position the bracket and hose aside.

8. Loosen the alternator lower bolt, unfasten the alternator upper bolt and pivot the alternator forward.

9. Unfasten the four exhaust manifold-to-catalytic converter nuts.

✳✳ WARNING

Do not work on aluminum engine components until the engine is cold.

7922MG43

Remove the two EGR tube-to-exhaust manifold stud nuts—2.0L SOHC engine

Refer to Section 1 for engine rebuilding specifications

Remove the exhaust manifold retaining nuts—2.0L SOHC engine

10. Unfasten the eight exhaust manifold nuts and remove the manifold and gasket.

❋❋ WARNING

Do not use any abrasive grinding discs to remove gasket material. Use a plastic manual gasket scraper to remove the gasket residue. Be careful not to scratch or gouge the aluminum sealing surfaces when cleaning them.

11. Clean the gasket surfaces thoroughly until all traces of the old gasket residue are removed. Inspect the gasket mating surfaces, both must be clean and flat.

To install:

12. Install a new gasket and the exhaust manifold.

13. Install and tighten the manifold retaining nuts to 14.7–17.7 ft. lbs.(20–24 Nm).

14. Install and tighten the exhaust manifold-to-catalytic converter nuts to 26–34 ft. lbs. (34–47 Nm).

15. Place the alternator in position and tighten the upper and lower mounting bolts.

16. Place the power steering pressure hose and bracket in position, then tighten the retaining bolts.

17. Tighten the two EGR tube-to-exhaust manifold nuts studs to 44.6–62 inch lbs. (5–7 Nm).

18. Install the exhaust manifold heat shield and tighten the nuts to 45–61 inch lbs. (5–7 Nm).

19. Attach the HO2S sensor electrical connection.

20. Install the drive belt.

21. Connect the negative battery cable.

DOHC ZETEC

1. Before servicing the vehicle, refer to the precautions in the beginning of this section.

2. Disconnect the negative battery cable.

3. Unplug the fan motor electrical connection.

4. Remove the fan shroud.

5. Raise the vehicle.

6. Unplug the Heated Oxygen (O2S) sensor electrical connection.

7. Unfasten the catalytic converter-to-exhaust manifold bolt and nut, then disconnect the converter from the manifold.

8. Lower the vehicle.

❋❋ WARNING

Do not break the threadlock seal on the engine oil dipstick tube. If the seal is broken, relock it to prevent any oil leaks from the block.

9. Unfasten the engine oil dipstick tube bracket bolt.

10. Unfasten the exhaust manifold heat shield bolts and nuts, then remove the shield.

❋❋ WARNING

Do not work on aluminum engine components until the engine is cold.

11. Unfasten the seven exhaust manifold bolts and two studs, then remove the manifold and gasket.

❋❋ WARNING

Do not use any abrasive grinding discs to remove gasket material. Use a plastic manual gasket scraper to remove the gasket residue. Be careful not to scratch or gouge the aluminum sealing surfaces when cleaning them.

12. Clean the gasket surfaces thoroughly until all traces of the old gasket residue are removed. Inspect the gasket mating surfaces, both must be clean and flat.

Remove the exhaust manifold nuts and bolts in the sequence illustrated—2.0L Zetec engine

14-17 Nm (10-12 lb/ft)

7922MG46

Tighten the exhaust manifold nuts and bolts in the sequence illustrated to the proper specification—2.0L Zetec engine

To install:

13. Install a new gasket and the exhaust manifold.

14. Install and tighten the manifold retaining bolts and nuts to 13–16 ft. lbs.(14–17 Nm).

15. Install the exhaust manifold heat shield retainers and tighten them to 71–101 inch lbs. (8–11 Nm).

16. Tighten the engine oil dipstick tube bracket bolt to 71–101 inch lbs. (8–11 Nm).

17. Install and tighten the exhaust manifold-to-catalytic converter bolt and nut.

18. Attach the HO$_2$S sensor electrical connection.

19. Install the fan shroud and attach the fan motor wiring.

20. Connect the negative battery cable.

Front Crankshaft Seal

REMOVAL & INSTALLATION

1.8L Engine

1. Before servicing the vehicle, refer to the precautions in the beginning of this section.

2. Disconnect the negative battery cable.

3. Remove the crankshaft sprocket.

4. If necessary, cut the lip of the front oil seal with a razor to ease removal.

5. Use seal removal tool T92C-6700-CH or its equivalent to remove the seal.

To install:

6. Lubricate the lip of the new oil seal with clean engine oil.

7. Using crankshaft front seal replacer T88C-6701-AH or equivalent tool, install

CRANKSHAFT FRONT SEAL

SEAL REMOVER T92C-6700-CH

7922MG47

Use an appropriate seal removal tool to remove the crankshaft front oil seal—1.8L engine

the seal evenly until it is flush with the edge of the oil pump body.

8. Install the crankshaft sprocket.

9. Connect the negative battery cable.

1.9L Engine

1. Before servicing the vehicle, refer to the precautions in the beginning of this section.

2. Disconnect the negative battery cable.

3. Remove the accessory drive belt.

4. Raise and safely support the vehicle.

5. Remove the right side splash shield.

6. Remove the transmission housing cover.

7. Use a suitable tool to hold the flywheel in place.

8. Remove the crankshaft dampener.

9. Remove the timing belt.

10. Remove the crankshaft sprocket and belt guide.

11. Using a seal removal tool T92C-6700-CH or equivalent, remove the crankshaft seal from the oil pump body.

To install:

12. Install the new seal using seal installation tool T81P-6700-A or equivalent.

13. Install the belt guide and crankshaft sprocket.

14. Install the timing belt.

15. Install the crankshaft dampener.

16. Remove the flywheel holding tool and install the transmission housing cover.

17. Install the right splash shield and lower the vehicle.

18. Install the accessory drive belt.

19. Connect the negative battery cable.

20. Start the engine and check for leaks.

2.0L Engines

1. Before servicing the vehicle, refer to the precautions in the beginning of this section.

2. Remove the timing belt and crankshaft sprocket.

✳✳ WARNING

Be careful not to damage the crankshaft surface when removing the seal.

3. Using seal remover tool T92C-6700-CH or its equivalent, remove the crankshaft front oil seal.

SEAL REMOVER
T92C-6700-CH

7922MG48

Removing the front crankshaft oil seal using tool T92C-6700-CH or equivalent—1.9L engine

To install:

4. Use seal replacer tool T81P-6700-A or its equivalent, install the new seal.

5. Install the crankshaft sprocket and the timing belt.

Camshaft(s) and Valve Lifters

All engines covered in this manual except the 2.0L Zetec engine, employ hydraulic (oil pressurized) valve lifters. These lifters operate more quietly and do not require periodic adjustments.

REMOVAL & INSTALLATION

1.8L Engine

➡**Refer to the illustration located in the water pump procedure, earlier in this section, for a view of the camshaft mounting on this engine.**

1. Before servicing the vehicle, refer to the precautions in the beginning of this section.

2. Disconnect the negative battery cable.

3. Remove the distributor assembly.

4. Remove the camshaft sprockets.

5. Unbolt the seal plate mounting bolts and remove the seal plate.

6. Loosen the camshaft cap bolts in the

correct sequence (see accompanying illustration).

7. Remove the camshaft caps and note their mounting locations for installation reference.

➡**The camshaft caps are numbered and have arrow marks for installation and direction reference.**

8. Remove the camshaft and camshaft oil seal.

To install:

9. Apply clean engine oil to the camshaft journals and bearings.

10. Place the camshaft into its mounting position.

➡**The exhaust camshaft has a groove which must be aligned with the distributor drive gear.**

11. Apply silicone sealant to the required areas (see accompanying illustration).

12. Install the camshaft caps according to the cap numbers and arrow marks.

13. Install the camshaft cap bolts and tighten them in the proper sequence to 100–126 inch lbs. (11.3–14.2 Nm).

14. Apply a small amount of clean engine oil to the lip of a new camshaft oil seal. Using a suitable installation tool,

7922MG50

Camshaft cap bolt loosening sequence—1.8L engines

7922MG51

Apply silicone sealer as shown—1.8L engines

Tighten the cap bolts in the sequence shown—1.8L engines

Use a suitable installation tool to install the new camshaft seal—1.8L engine

install the new seal. Refer to the accompanying illustration.

15. Place the seal plate into its mounting position and install the mounting bolts. Tighten the bolts to 69–95 inch lbs. (7.8–11.0 Nm).

16. Install the camshaft sprockets and the distributor assembly.

17. Connect the negative battery cable.

1.9L Engine

1. Before servicing the vehicle, refer to the precautions in the beginning of this section.

2. Disconnect the negative battery cable.

3. Remove the air cleaner intake duct.

4. Remove the accessory drive belts and the crankshaft pulley.

5. Remove the timing belt cover and the rocker arm cover.

6. Set the engine No. 1 cylinder at TDC prior to removing the timing belt.

➡**Be sure the crankshaft is positioned at TDC. Do not turn the crankshaft until the timing belt is installed.**

7. Remove the rocker arms and lifters.

8. Remove the ignition coil assembly.

9. Remove the timing belt.

10. Remove the camshaft sprocket bolt, sprocket and key.

11. Remove the camshaft thrust plate.

12. Remove the cup plug from the back of the cylinder head.

13. Remove the camshaft through the back of the head toward the transaxle.

14. Remove and discard the camshaft seal.

To install:

15. Thoroughly coat the camshaft bearing journals, cam lobe surfaces and thrust plate groove with a suitable lubricant.

➡**Before installing the camshaft, apply a thin film of lubricant to the lip of the camshaft seal.**

16. Install a new camshaft seal and install the camshaft through the rear of the cylinder head. Rotate the camshaft during installation.

17. Install the camshaft thrust plate. Tighten attaching bolts to 6–9 ft. lbs. (8–13 Nm).

18. Align and install the cam sprocket over the cam key. Install the attaching washer and bolt. While holding the camshaft stationary, tighten the bolt to 70–85 ft. lbs. (95–115 Nm).

19. Install the cup plug using a sealer EOAZ-19554-BA. Use the sealer sparingly, as excess sealer may clog the oil holes in the camshaft.

20. Install the timing belt.

21. Install the timing belt cover.

22. Install the ignition coil assembly.

23. Install a new rocker arm cover gasket, if required.

➡**Be sure the surfaces on the cylinder head and rocker arm cover are clean and free of sealant material.**

24. Install the valve cover.

25. Install the air cleaner intake tube.

26. Connect the negative battery cable.

2.0L Engine

SOHC SPLIT PORT INJECTION (SPI)

1. Before servicing the vehicle, refer to the precautions in the beginning of this section.

2. Disconnect the negative battery cable.

3. Remove the air cleaner and valve cover.

4. Remove the camshaft front seal as follows:

   a. Align the timing marks and remove the timing belt.

   b. Use cam sprocket holding/removing tool T74P-6256-B or its equivalent, and remove the camshaft sprocket.

   c. Unfasten the timing belt tensioner bolt and remove the tensioner.

   d. Remove the inner engine front cover.

   e. Use seal removal tool T92C-6700-CH or its equivalent to remove the camshaft front seal.

5. Remove the ignition coil and bracket.

6. Remove the rocker arms and valve tappets.

7. Unfasten the camshaft thrust plate bolts and remove the plate.

8. Remove and discard the cup plug from the rear of the cylinder head.

9. Carefully remove the camshaft from the rear of the cylinder head.

To install:

➡**Liberally coat the cam bore in the cylinder with clean 5W30 motor oil.**

10. Install the camshaft through the rear of the cylinder head.

11. Install the camshaft thrust plate and the bolts. Tighten the bolts to 71–115 inch lbs. (8–13 Nm).

12. Install a new cup plug and the tappets.

13. Install the rocker arms.

14. Install the ignition coil bracket and coil.

For complete mechanical specifications, refer to Section 1 of this manual

1. Rocker arm
2. Rocker arm seats
3. Camshaft Position (CMP) sensor
4. Valve tappet
5. Valve tappet guide plate
6. Ignition coil
7. Radio interference capacitor
8. Ignition coil bracket
9. Cup plug
10. Camshaft
11. Water hose connection
12. Thermostat
13. Water hose connection gasket

Exploded view of the cylinder head—2.0L SOHC SPI engine

Removing the camshaft front seal—2.0L SOHC engine

Remove and discard the cup plug located at the rear of the cylinder head—2.0L engine

Remove the camshaft thrust plate retaining bolts (A) and the plate (B)—2.0L SOHC engine

0.05-1.0 mm
(0.002-0.04 in)

Use seal Replacer T81P-6292-A or its equivalent, to install the camshaft front seal 0.002-0.04 in. (0.05-1.0mm) below flush with the cylinder head front face—2.0L SOHC engine

15. Install the camshaft front seal as follows:

a. Apply a thin film of 5W30 motor oil to the lip of the seal.

➡**The seal depth should be 0.002-0.04 in. (0.05-1.0mm) below flush with the cylinder head front face.**

b. Use seal replacer T81P-6292-A or its equivalent, to install the camshaft front seal.

c. Install the inner engine front cover.

d. Install the timing belt tensioner. Tighten the tensioner bolt to 15-22 ft. lbs. (20-30 Nm).

e. Install the camshaft sprocket and the timing belt

16. Install the valve cover and the air cleaner assembly.

17. Connect the negative battery cable.

DOHC ZETEC

1. Before servicing the vehicle, refer to the precautions in the beginning of this section.

2. Remove the timing belt, valve cover and camshaft sprockets.

➡**It may be necessary to rotate the oil control solenoid flange 90 degrees prior to removal.**

3. Unfasten the oil control solenoid flange bolts and remove the flange.

➡**Mark the camshaft journal caps with a number to identify their location as they must be replaced in their original position.**

4. Loosen the camshaft journal caps in several passes in the sequence illustrated, then remove the bolts and caps.

5. Remove the camshafts from the cylinder head.

6. Remove the oil control sensor and bushing.

7. Inspect the camshafts for damage and wear.

To install:

8. Be sure the valve clearance is correct.

9. Install the oil control solenoid bushing and flange on the exhaust camshaft.

➡**The front camshaft journal cap must be installed with the bolts tightened to specification within four minutes of applying the sealer.**

10. Coat the surface of the front camshaft journal cap with gasket maker E2AZ-19562-B or its equivalent.

11. Place the camshafts in position and lubricate the bearing surfaces with engine assembly lubricant D9AZ-19579-D or its equivalent.

12. Install new camshaft front oil seals.

13. Apply a thin coat of silicone gasket and sealant F6AZ-19562-AA or its equivalent to the sealing surface of the of the front camshaft journal bearing cap.

14. Install the caps and tighten the bolts in several 2-turn passes in the sequence illustrated to 10–12 ft. lbs. (13–17 Nm).

✳✳ WARNING

The oil control O-ring seals must not fall out of position in the oil control solenoid flange or poor engine performance may occur.

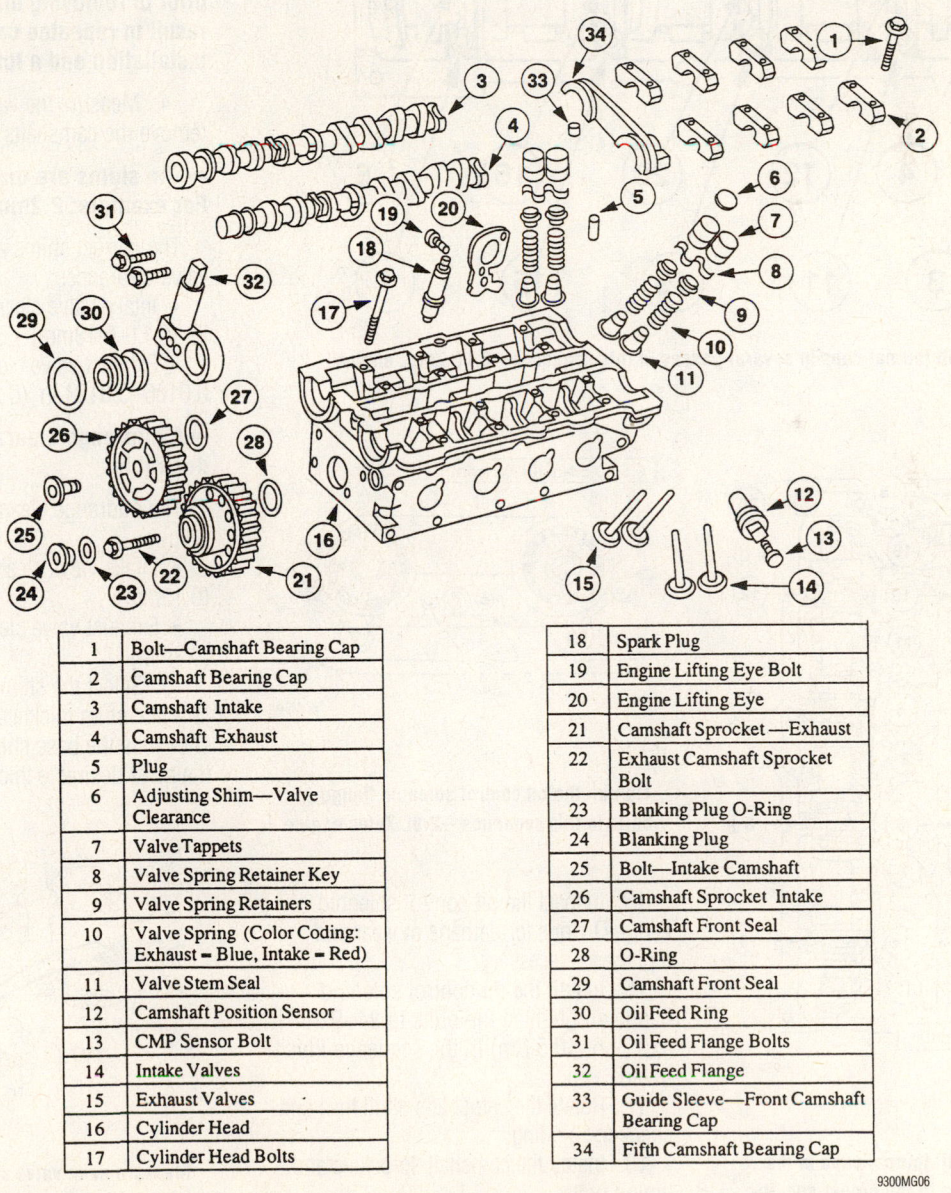

1	Bolt—Camshaft Bearing Cap
2	Camshaft Bearing Cap
3	Camshaft Intake
4	Camshaft Exhaust
5	Plug
6	Adjusting Shim—Valve Clearance
7	Valve Tappets
8	Valve Spring Retainer Key
9	Valve Spring Retainers
10	Valve Spring (Color Coding: Exhaust = Blue, Intake = Red)
11	Valve Stem Seal
12	Camshaft Position Sensor
13	CMP Sensor Bolt
14	Intake Valves
15	Exhaust Valves
16	Cylinder Head
17	Cylinder Head Bolts
18	Spark Plug
19	Engine Lifting Eye Bolt
20	Engine Lifting Eye
21	Camshaft Sprocket —Exhaust
22	Exhaust Camshaft Sprocket Bolt
23	Blanking Plug O-Ring
24	Blanking Plug
25	Bolt—Intake Camshaft
26	Camshaft Sprocket Intake
27	Camshaft Front Seal
28	O-Ring
29	Camshaft Front Seal
30	Oil Feed Ring
31	Oil Feed Flange Bolts
32	Oil Feed Flange
33	Guide Sleeve—Front Camshaft Bearing Cap
34	Fifth Camshaft Bearing Cap

9300MG06

Exploded view of the cylinder head, showing camshaft mounting—2.0L DOHC Zetec engine

Please refer to Section 9 for electric cooling fan wiring schematics

Loosen the camshaft journal caps in several passes in this sequence—2.0L Zetec engine

7922MG58

13-17 Nm (10-12 lb/ft)

7922MG59

Tighten the camshaft journal caps in the sequence illustrated to the proper specification—2.0L Zetec engine

9.5-10.5 Nm (84-92 lb/in)

7922MG60

Tighten the oil control solenoid flange bolts in this sequence—2.0L Zetec engine

15. Inspect the oil control solenoid flange O-rings for damage or wear and replace as necessary.

16. Install the oil control solenoid flange and tighten the bolts to 84–92 inch lbs. (9.5–10.5 Nm) in the sequence illustrated.

17. Rotate the camshafts a full turn and check for binding.

18. Install the camshaft sprockets and timing belt.

19. Install the valve cover.

Valve Lash

ADJUSTMENT

2.0L DOHC Zetec Engine

1. Before servicing the vehicle, refer to the precautions in the beginning of this section.

2. Remove the valve cover.

3. Remove the timing belt.

➡Measure each valve's clearance at the base circle before removing the camshafts. The shims are nit serviceable with the camshafts in place. Failure to measure all valve clearances prior to removing the camshafts, will result in repeated camshaft removal and installation and a lot of wasted time.

4. Measure the valve clearances, then remove the camshafts and shims.

➡The shims are marked for thickness. For example: 2.2mm = 222 on shim.

The correct shims allow the following valve clearances:
• Intake valve clearance: 0.0043–0.0071 in. (0.11–0.18mm)
• Exhaust valve clearance: 0.0106–0.0134 in. (0.27–0.34mm)

➡A midrange clearance is the most desirable.

The midrange clearances should be as follows:
• Intake valve clearance: 0.006 in. (0.15mm)
• Exhaust valve clearance: 0.012 in. (0.3mm)

5. Select the shims using the following formula: shim thickness = measured clearance plus the base shim thickness minus the most desirable thickness.

7922MG61

Measure each valve's clearance at the base circle before removing the camshafts—2.0L Zetec DOHC engine

Example of a valve lifter shim (arrow)— 2.0L Zetec DOHC engine

6. Select the correct shims and mark their installation location (where they are going).

7. Replace the shims and install the camshafts.

8. Check the new valve clearances.

9. Install the timing belt and covers.

10. Install the valve cover.

11. Start the vehicle and check for proper operation.

Oil Pan

REMOVAL & INSTALLATION

1.8L Engine

1. Before servicing the vehicle, refer to the precautions in the beginning of this section.

2. Disconnect the negative battery cable. Remove the oil filler cap.

3. Raise and safely support the vehicle.

4. Remove the drain plug and drain the engine oil into a suitable container.

5. Remove the upper right and lower right and left splash shields.

Use a suitable tool to carefully pry the oil pan away from the engine block and remove the oil pan—1.8L engine

6. Remove the exhaust pipe front mounting flange and exhaust pipe support bracket from the exhaust manifold. Discard the pipe bracket.

7. Unfasten the oil pan-to-transaxle attaching bolts.

8. Place a block of wood on a suitable support and brace the oil pan with the support.

9. Unfasten oil pan-to-engine block attaching bolts.

10. Only at the points of the oil pan illustrated, use a suitable tool to carefully pry the oil pan away from the engine block and remove the oil pan.

✳✳ WARNING

Do not force a prying tool between the engine block and the oil pan contact surface when trying to remove the oil pan. This may damage the oil pan contact surface and cause oil leakage.

11. Use a prytool to remove the oil pan reinforcements away from the block.

12. Remove the front and rear oil pan seals. Remove all sealant material from the engine block and oil pan.

✳✳ WARNING

When removing the oil pan flange reinforcements and sealant material from the oil pan and engine block, be careful not to damage the oil pan and engine block contact surfaces.

To install:

13. Apply a bead of silicone sealant to the oil pan flange reinforcements along the inside of the bolt holes.

14. Install the oil pan flange reinforcements.

After thoroughly cleaning the gasket mating surfaces, apply sealant to the areas shown—1.8L engine

Exploded view of oil pan and related components—1.8L engine

15. Apply sealant to the areas of the end seals as illustrated. Be sure to install the end seals with the projections in the notches.

16. Install the front and rear end seals onto the oil pan.

17. Apply a continuous bead of silicone sealant to the oil pan along the inside of the bolt holes. Overlap the sealant ends.

18. Place the oil pan into its mounting position and install the oil pan-to-engine block attaching bolts. Tighten the bolts to 69–95 inch lbs. (7.8–11.0 Nm).

✳✳ WARNING

If the oil pan attaching bolts are to be reused, the old sealant must be removed from the bolt threads. Tightening the old attaching bolts with old sealant still on them may cause cracking inside the bolt holes.

19. Install the oil pan-to-transaxle attaching bolts and tighten them to 27–38 ft. lbs. (37–52 Nm).

20. Install the oil drain plug and tighten it to 22–30 ft. lbs. (29–41 Nm).

21. Install the front exhaust mounting flange and a new gasket. Tighten the mounting flange-to-exhaust manifold attaching nuts to 23–34 ft. lbs. (31–46 Nm).

22. Install the exhaust pipe support bracket, then tighten the bolts to 27–38 ft. lbs. (37–52 Nm).

23. Install the splash shields. Tighten the bolts to 69–95 inch lbs. (7.8–11.0 Nm).

24. Lower the vehicle.

25. Fill the crankcase with the proper type and quantity of engine oil. Install the filler cap.

26. Connect the negative battery cable.

1.9L Engine

1. Before servicing the vehicle, refer to the precautions in the beginning of this section.

2. Disconnect the negative cable at the battery.

3. Raise the vehicle and support safely.

4. Remove the drain plug and drain the engine oil into a suitable container.

5. Remove the catalytic converter from the exhaust manifold and from the inlet pipe and resonator.

6. Unfasten the two oil pan-to-transaxle bolts.

7. Unfasten the ten oil pan-to-engine bolts.

8. Gently pry the oil pan from the block and remove the oil pan

9. Remove the oil pan gasket and discard.

To install:

10. Use a scraper to clean the oil pan gasket surface and the mating surface on the cylinder block. Wipe the oil pan rail with a solvent-soaked, lint-free cloth to remove all traces of oil.

11. Remove the two oil pump screen cover screws to clean the oil pump pick up tube and screen assembly. Install tube and screen assembly using a new tube gasket. Tighten the screen screws and tube bolts to 7–9 ft. lbs. (10–13 Nm).

➡ **Install the pan within 10 minutes of applying the sealant.**

12. Apply a bead of suitable silicone rubber sealer approximately 0.125 in. (3.0mm) wide at the corners of the block and at the oil pump-to-block and the crankshaft rear oil seal retainer-to-block joints.

13. Install the oil pan gasket in the pan ensuring the press fit tabs are fully engaged in the gasket channel.

14. Install the oil pan and attaching bolts. Tighten the bolts lightly until the two oil pan-to-transaxle bolts can be installed.

➡ **If the oil pan is installed on the engine outside of the vehicle, a transaxle case or equivalent fixture**

Oil pan mounting bolt tightening sequence—1.9L engine

must be bolted to the block to line-up the oil pan flush with the rear face of the block.

15. Tighten the two pan-to-transaxle bolts to 30–40 ft. lbs. (40–54 Nm), then loosen them one half turn.

16. Tighten the oil pan flange-to-cylinder block bolts to 15–22 ft. lbs. (20–30 Nm) in the sequence illustrated.

17. Retighten the two pan-to-transaxle bolts to 30–40 ft. lbs. (40–54 Nm).

18. Install the catalytic converter.

19. Install the oil pan drain plug and tighten it to 15–22 ft. lbs. (20–30 Nm).

Exploded view of oil pan mounting—1.9L engine

20. Lower the vehicle and fill the crankcase.

21. Connect negative battery cable.

22. Start the engine and check for oil leaks.

2.0L Engine

SOHC SPLIT PORT INJECTION (SPI)

1. Before servicing the vehicle, refer to the precautions in the beginning of this section.

2. Raise the vehicle.

3. Remove the catalytic converter.

4. Drain the engine oil.

5. Unfasten the oil pan-to-catalytic converter bracket bolts and remove the bracket.

6. Unfasten the ten oil pan bolts evenly, then remove the oil pan and gasket.

7. Discard the old gasket.

✳✳ WARNING

Do not use any abrasive grinding discs to remove gasket material. Use a plastic manual gasket scraper to remove the gasket residue. Be careful not to scratch or gouge the aluminum sealing surfaces when cleaning them.

8. Clean the gasket surfaces thoroughly until all traces of the old gasket residue are removed. Inspect the gasket mating surfaces, both must be clean, flat and dry.

To install:

➡**Install the oil pan within ten minutes of applying the silicone sealer.**

9. Apply a 0.125 in. (3.0mm) wide bead of silicone sealant F6AZ-19562-AA or its equivalent at the oil pump-to-cylinder block joints and the crankshaft rear oil seal retainer-to-cylinder block joints.

Tighten the oil pan bolts in this sequence to the proper specification—2.0L SOHC engine

➡**Be sure the press fit tabs are fully engaged in the oil pan gasket channel when installing the pan and gasket.**

10. Install the gasket.

11. When installing the oil pan, be sure the rear of the pan is aligned with the cylinder block by using a straight edge as a guide.

12. Install and tighten the oil pan bolts in the sequence illustrated to 15–22 ft. lbs. (20–30 Nm).

13. Install the oil pan-to-catalytic converter bracket and tighten the bolts to 30–40 ft. lbs. (40–55 Nm).

14. Install the catalytic converter and oil pan drain plug. Tighten the drain plug to 15–22 ft. lbs. (20–30 Nm).

15. Lower the vehicle and fill the engine with the proper type and quantity of engine oil.

16. Start the vehicle and check for oil leaks.

DOHC ZETEC

1. Before servicing the vehicle, refer to the precautions in the beginning of this section.

2. Raise the vehicle.

3. Drain the engine oil.

4. Remove the catalytic converter.

5. Unfasten the 17 oil pan bolts evenly, then remove the oil pan.

✳✳ WARNING

Do not use any abrasive grinding discs to remove gasket material. Use a plastic manual gasket scraper to remove the gasket residue. Be careful not to scratch or gouge the aluminum sealing surfaces when cleaning them.

6. Clean the gasket surfaces thoroughly until all traces of the old gasket residue are removed. Inspect the gasket mating surfaces, both must be clean, flat and dry.

To install:

➡**Install the oil pan within four minutes of applying the silicone sealer.**

7. Apply a 0.1in. (3.0mm) wide bead of silicone sealant F6AZ-19562-AA or its equivalent to the oil pan.

8. Install the oil pan and the bolts.

Tighten the oil pan bolts in the proper sequence to the correct torque specification—2.0L Zetec engine

Timing belt service is covered in Section 5 of this manual

Tighten the oil pan bolts in the sequence illustrated to 15–22 ft. lbs. (20–30 Nm).

9. Install the oil pan drain plug.

10. Lower the vehicle and fill the engine with the proper type and quantity of engine oil.

11. Start the vehicle and check for oil leaks.

Oil Pump

REMOVAL & INSTALLATION

1.8L Engine

➡**Refer to the illustration located in the water pump procedure, earlier in this section, for a view of the oil pump on this engine.**

1. Before servicing the vehicle, refer to the precautions in the beginning of this section.

2. Disconnect the negative battery cable.

3. Remove the timing belt and timing belt pulley.

4. Remove the oil pan.

5. Remove the oil pump screen cover and tube.

6. If equipped, remove the A/C compressor mounting bolts and position the compressor so it is free from the work area.

7. Remove the A/C compressor mounting bracket.

8. Unbolt the mounting bolt from the engine oil dipstick tube bracket and the alternator lower mounting bolt.

9. Unfasten all oil pump mounting bolts and remove the oil pump.

10. Use a scraper to remove all gasket material from the oil pump mounting surfaces.

To install:

11. Install a new gasket onto the oil pump.

12. Place the oil pump into its mounting position and install the pump mounting bolts. Tighten the bolts to 14–19 ft. lbs. (19–25 Nm).

13. Place the dipstick tube bracket bolt into its mounting position and install the mounting bolt. Tighten the bolt to 68–95 inch lbs. (7.8–11 Nm).

14. Install the alternator lower mounting bolt and tighten it to 27–38 ft. lbs. (37–52 Nm).

15. Install a new gasket onto the oil strainer, place the strainer into its mounting position and install the mounting bolts. Tighten the bolts to 69–95 inch lbs. (7.8–11.0 Nm).

Exploded view of oil pump mounting—1.8L engine

16. Install the oil pan.

17. If equipped, place the A/C compressor bracket into its mounting position and install the mounting bolts. Tighten the bolts to 30–40 ft. lbs. (40–55 Nm).

18. If equipped, install A/C compressor side bolt. Tighten the bolts to 14–19 ft. lbs. (19–25 Nm).

19. Install the timing belt pulley and timing belt.

20. Connect the negative battery cable.

21. Start the engine and check for oil leaks. Be sure the oil pressure indicator lamp has gone out after a second or two. If the lamp remains on after several seconds, immediately shut off the engine. Determine the cause and correct the condition.

1.9L Engine

1. Before servicing the vehicle, refer to the precautions in the beginning of this section.

2. Be sure the No. 1 cylinder is at TDC.

3. Disconnect the negative battery cable.

4. Remove the accessory drive belt and the automatic tensioner.

5. Support the engine with a suitable floor jack.

6. Remove the right engine mount dampener and remove the right engine mount bolts from the mount bracket.

7. Loosen the mount through-bolt and roll the mount aside.

8. Remove the timing belt cover.

9. Roll the engine mount back into place and install the two mount bolts. Remove the floor jack.

10. Loosen the belt tensioner attaching bolt and pry the tensioner to the rear of the engine. Tighten the attaching bolt.

11. Raise and safely support the vehicle.

12. Remove the right side splash shield.

13. Remove the catalytic converter inlet pipe.

14. Drain and remove the oil pan. Remove the oil filter.

15. Remove the crankshaft dampener and the timing belt.

16. Remove the crankshaft sprocket and the timing belt guide from the crankshaft.

17. Disconnect the Crankshaft Position (CKP) sensor.

18. Unfasten the 6 oil pump-to-engine bolts and remove the oil pump assembly from the engine. Remove and discard the gasket.

19. Remove the crankshaft seal from the pump and discard.

To install:

20. Be sure the pump mating surfaces on the cylinder block and oil pump are clean and free of gasket material.

21. Remove the oil pick-up tube and screen assembly from the pump for cleaning.

22. Lubricate the outside diameter of the crankshaft seal with engine oil and install the seal with a suitable installation

FRONT OF ENGINE

SECTION A
(AFTER ASSEMBLY)

1	Cylinder Block
2	Bottom Sealing Surface
3	0.00 - 1.08mm
4	Oil Pump
5	Oil Pump Screen Cover and Tube
6	Oil Pump Screen Cover and Tube Bolt (2 Req'd)
7	Oil Pump Inlet Tube Gasket
8	Oil Filter Mounting Position
9	Crankshaft Front Seal
10	Oil Pump Bolt (2 Req'd)
11	Oil Pump Bolt (4 Req'd)
12	Oil Pump to Cylinder Block Gasket
13	Cylinder Block
A	Tighten to 10-13 N·m (7-9 Lb-Ft)
B	Tighten to 11-16 N·m (8-12 Lb-Ft)

7922MG71

Exploded view of oil pump mounting, including related components—1.9L engine

tool. Lubricate the seal lip with clean engine oil.

23. Position the oil pump gasket on the cylinder block.

24. Using a suitable tool, position the pump drive gear to allow the pump to pilot over the crankshaft and seat firmly on the cylinder block.

➡**The pump drive gear can be accessed through the oil pick-up hole in the body of the pump. Do not install the oil pump pick-up tube and screen until the pump has been correctly installed on the cylinder block.**

25. Install the six oil pump bolts and tighten to 8–12 ft. lbs. (11–16 Nm).

➡**When the oil pump bolts are tightened, the gasket must not be below the cylinder block sealing surface.**

26. Install the pick-up tube and screen assembly on the oil pump using a new gasket. Tighten the attaching screws to 7–9 ft. lbs. (10–13 Nm).

27. Install the timing belt guide over the end of the crankshaft and install the crankshaft sprocket.

28. Be sure the No. 1 cylinder is at TDC.

29. Position the timing belt over the sprockets.

30. Connect the Crank Angle Sensor (CAS).

31. Install the oil pan and the crankshaft dampener.

32. Install the catalytic converter inlet pipe.

33. Install the splash shield and lower the vehicle.

34. Install the timing belt. Tighten the tensioner attaching bolt to 17–22 ft. lbs. (23–30 Nm).

35. Support the engine with a suitable floor jack.

36. Remove the right engine mount bolts and roll the mount back.

37. Install the timing belt cover.

38. Roll the engine mount back into place and install the attaching bolts. Tighten the mount through-bolt and install the mount dampener.

39. Remove the floor jack.

40. Install the accessory drive belt automatic tensioner and the accessory drive belt.

41. Fill the crankcase with the proper type and amount of engine oil.

42. Connect the negative battery cable, start the engine and check for leaks.

2.0L Engine

SOHC SPLIT PORT INJECTION (SPI)

➡**Refer to the illustration located in the water pump procedure, earlier in this section, for a view of the oil pump on this engine.**

1. Before servicing the vehicle, refer to the precautions in the beginning of this section.

2. Remove the timing belt.

3. Raise the vehicle.

4. Remove the oil pan.

5. Unplug the Crankshaft Position (CKP) sensor electrical connection.

6. Unfasten the oil pump screen cover and tube bolts and remove the cover and tube.

7. Unfasten the six oil pump retaining bolts.

8. Remove the old pump and gasket. Discard the gasket.

To install:

✷✷ WARNING

Do not use any abrasive grinding discs to remove gasket material. Use a plastic manual gasket scraper to remove the gasket residue. Be careful not to scratch or gouge the aluminum sealing surfaces when cleaning them.

9. Clean the gasket surfaces thoroughly until all traces of the old gasket residue are removed. Inspect the gasket mating surfaces, both must be clean, flat and dry.

10. Lubricate the crankshaft front oil seal lip with clean engine oil.

➡**When the oil pan bolts are tightened, the oil pump-to-cylinder block gasket must be below the cylinder block sealing surface.**

11. Install the pump gasket and the pump.

12. Install and tighten the oil pump bolts to 8–12 ft. lbs. (11–16 Nm).

13. Install the oil pump screen cover and tube. Tighten the retaining bolts to 71–97 inch lbs. (8–11 Nm).

14. Attach the CKP sensor electrical connection.

15. Install the oil pan.

16. Lower the vehicle and install the timing belt.

17. Fill the engine with the proper type and quantity of engine oil.

18. Start the vehicle and check for oil leaks.

DOHC ZETEC

➡**Refer to the illustration located in the water pump procedure, earlier in this section, for a view of the oil pump on this engine.**

1. Before servicing the vehicle, refer to the precautions in the beginning of this section.

2. Remove the timing covers and belt.

3. Raise the vehicle.

4. Remove the crankshaft pulley, sprocket and the timing chain guide.

5. Remove the oil pan.

6. Unfasten the oil pump cover and screen bolts and remove the cover and screen.

7. If necessary, remove the lower cylinder block shims.

8. If necessary, remove the lower cylinder block, the gasket and the crankshaft front oil seal.

9. Unfasten the oil pump retaining bolts and remove the pump and gasket.

To install:

※※ WARNING

Do not use any abrasive grinding discs to remove gasket material. Use a plastic manual gasket scraper to remove the gasket residue. Be careful not to scratch or gouge the aluminum sealing surfaces when cleaning them.

10. Clean the gasket surfaces thoroughly until all traces of the old gasket residue are removed. Inspect the gasket mating surfaces, both must be clean, flat and dry.

Remove the oil pump mounting bolts—2.0L Zetec engine

Tighten the lower cylinder block bolts in the sequence illustrated to the proper torque specification—2.0L Zetec engine

➡**The clearance between the lower cylinder block sealing surfaces on the oil pump and the cylinder block cannot exceed 0.012–0.031 in. (0.3–0.8mm).**

11. Install a new oil pump gasket and the pump.

12. Install and tighten the oil pump bolts to 88–97 inch. Lbs. (10–11 Nm).

13. If removed, install the crankshaft front oil seal.

14. If removed, install the lower cylinder block and gasket. Tighten the lower cylinder block bolts to 15–17 ft. lbs. (20–24 Nm) in the sequence illustrated.

15. Install the oil pump screen cover and tube. Tighten the retaining bolts to 71–97 inch lbs. (8–11 Nm).

16. Install the oil pan, timing chain guide, crankshaft sprocket and the pulley.

17. Lower the car, then install the timing belt and covers.

18. Fill the engine with the proper type and quantity of engine oil.

19. Start the vehicle and check for oil leaks.

Rear Main Seal

REMOVAL & INSTALLATION

1.8L engine

1. Before servicing the vehicle, refer to the precautions in the beginning of this section.

2. Remove the flywheel (MT) or flexplate (AT).

3. If necessary, unfasten the rear cover attaching bolts and remove the cover.

4. Using a prytool with a rag over the end (refer to the accompanying illustration) or seal removal tool such as T92C-6700-

CH or its equivalent, pry out the rear oil seal.

To install:

5. If removed install the rear cover and tighten its retaining bolts to 69–95 inch lbs. (7.8–11 Nm).

6. Coat the lip of the new seal wit clean engine oil.

7. Use seal Replacer T87C-6701-A or its equivalent, and tighten the bolts to install the seal. Keep tightening the bolts until the seal is flush with the rear cover.

8. Install the flywheel or flexplate.

Use a suitable prytool and a rag (as shown) or . . .

. . . a seal removal tool such as T92C-6700-CH to remove the rear crankshaft oil seal—1.8L engine

1.9L Engine

1. Before servicing the vehicle, refer to the precautions in the beginning of this section.

2. Remove the flywheel.

3. Remove the engine or transmission housing cover.

※※ WARNING

Use care to avoid damaging the crankshaft surface.

4. Using a seal removal tool such T92C-6700-CH or its equivalent, pry out the rear oil seal.

To install:

5. Inspect the oil seal area for damage. If damage is found, service or replace the crankshaft

6. Coat the lip of the new seal with clean engine oil.

➡**Be sure the rear oil seal is properly aligned and that the edges are not rolled up.**

7. Place crankshaft rear seal pilot T88P-6701-B2 (or equivalent) into the crankshaft rear seal replacer T88P-6701-B1 (or equivalent) and lubricate the pilot replacer with clean engine oil.

8. Slide the rear oil seal over the pilot onto the replacer.

9. Remove the rear seal pilot T88P-6701-B2 (or equivalent) from seal replacer T88P-6701-B1 (or equivalent).

10. Place the rear oil seal and replacer over the crankshaft and install the seal.

11. Remove the seal installer tool and install the flywheel.

Use a seal removal tool such as T92C-6700-CH or its equivalent to pry out the rear oil seal—1.9L engine

7922MG77

Use rear seal pilot T88P-6701-B2 (or equivalent) and crankshaft rear seal replacer T88P-6701-B1 (or equivalent) when installing the seal—1.9L engine

2.0L Engine

1. Before servicing the vehicle, refer to the precautions in the beginning of this section.

2. Remove the transaxle and flywheel.

※※ WARNING

Be careful not to damage the crankshaft surface when removing the seal.

3. Use seal replacer tool T92C-6700-Ch or its equivalent to remove the old seal.

To install:

4. Coat the lip of the new seal with clean 5W30 engine oil.

➡**Be sure the crankshaft rear oil seal is on correctly and that the edges are not rolled over.**

5. Install the new seal using crankshaft rear seal pilot tool T88P-6701-B2 and Rear seal replacer tool T88P-6701-B1 or their equivalents.

6. Install the flywheel and the transaxle.

FUEL SYSTEM

Fuel System Service Precautions

Safety is the most important factor when performing not only fuel system maintenance but any type of maintenance. Failure to conduct maintenance and repairs in a safe manner may result in serious personal injury or death. Maintenance and testing of the vehicle's fuel system components can be accomplished safely and effectively by adhering to the following rules and guidelines.

• To avoid the possibility of fire and personal injury, always disconnect the negative battery cable unless the repair or test procedure requires that battery voltage be applied.

• Always relieve the fuel system pressure prior to disconnecting any fuel system component (injector, fuel rail, pressure regulator, etc.), fitting or fuel line connection. Exercise extreme caution whenever relieving fuel system pressure to avoid exposing skin, face and eyes to fuel spray. Please be advised that fuel under pressure may penetrate the skin or any part of the body that it contacts.

• Always place a shop towel or cloth around the fitting or connection prior to loosening to absorb any excess fuel due to spillage. Ensure that all fuel spillage (should it occur) is quickly removed from engine surfaces. Ensure that all fuel soaked cloths or towels are deposited into a suitable waste container.

• Always keep a dry chemical (Class B) fire extinguisher near the work area.

• Do not allow fuel spray or fuel vapors to come into contact with a spark or open flame.

• Always use a back-up wrench when loosening and tightening fuel line connection fittings. This will prevent unnecessary stress and torsion to fuel line piping.

• Always replace worn fuel fitting O-rings with new. Do not substitute fuel hose or equivalent, where fuel pipe is installed.

Fuel System Pressure

RELIEVING

1996 Models

1. Before servicing the vehicle, refer to the precautions in the beginning of this section.

2. Remove the rear seat cushion to access the fuel pump electrical connector.

3. Start the engine.

4. Disconnect the fuel pump electrical connector.

5. Wait for the engine to stall, then turn the ignition switch **OFF**.

6. Connect the fuel pump electrical connectors.

7. Install the rear seat cushion.

8. Disconnect the negative battery cable.

1997–00 Models

1. Before servicing the vehicle, refer to the precautions in the beginning of this section.

2. Remove the Schrader valve cap at the end of the fuel rail and a attach a fuel pressure gauge.

3. Open the manual relief valve on the fuel pressure gauge slowly to relive the fuel pressure

Fuel Filter

REMOVAL & INSTALLATION

1.8L and 1.9L Engines

The inline fuel filter is located in the engine compartment between the fuel tank and the fuel rail.

1. Before servicing the vehicle, refer to the precautions in the beginning of this section.

2. Properly relieve the fuel system pressure.

3. Disconnect the negative battery cable.

4. Position a suitable container below the fuel filter to collect any excess fuel that may leak from the filter and lines.

5. Remove the retaining clip from the fuel filter upper hose.

6. Disconnect the upper hose from the fuel filter and drain any excess fuel into the container. Plug the hose.

7. Loosen the fuel filter mounting clamp.

8. Raise and safely support the vehicle.

9. Remove the retaining clip from the fuel filter lower hose.

10. Disconnect the lower hose from the fuel filter and drain any excess fuel into the container. Plug the hose.

11. Lower the vehicle.

12. Remove the fuel filter.

To install:

13. Position the fuel filter and tighten the filter mounting clamp.

14. Remove the plug, then connect the upper hose to the filter and install the hose retaining clip.

15. Raise and safely support the vehicle.

16. Remove the plug, connect the lower hose to the filter and install the hose retaining clip.

17. Lower the vehicle.

18. Connect the negative battery cable.

19. Start the engine and check for leaks.

2.0L Engines

The inline fuel filter is located in the engine compartment between the fuel tank and the fuel rail.

1. Before servicing the vehicle, refer to the precautions in the beginning of this section.

2. Properly relieve the fuel system pressure.

3. Disconnect the negative battery cable.

4. Position a suitable container below the fuel filter to collect any excess fuel that may leak from the filter and lines.

5. Loosen the fuel filter mounting clamp.

6. Remove the filter from the mounting bracket.

7. Remove the retaining clips from the upper fuel filter hose.

8. Disconnect the upper hose from the fuel filter and drain any excess fuel into the container. Plug the hose.

9. Remove the retaining clip from the fuel filter lower hose.

10. Disconnect the lower hose from the fuel filter and drain any excess fuel into the container. Plug the hose.

11. Remove the fuel filter.

To install:

12. Remove the plug from the lower hose and connect the hose to the filter, then install the hose retaining clip.

13. Remove the plug from the upper hose and connect the hose to the filter, then install the hose retaining clip.

14. Position the fuel filter and tighten the filter mounting clamp.

15. Connect the negative battery cable.

16. Start the engine and check for leaks.

➡ **On newer model vehicles when the battery is disconnected it may cause some abnormal drive symptoms until the Powertrain Control Module (PCM) relearns its adaptive strategy. The vehicle may need to be driven 10 miles (16 km) or more for the PCM to relearn its strategy.**

Fuel Pump

The fuel pump is located inside the fuel tank.

REMOVAL & INSTALLATION

1996 Models

This procedure will require a new fuel pump gasket for pump installation, so be sure to have one before starting.

1. Before servicing the vehicle, refer to the precautions in the beginning of this section.

2. Relieve the fuel system pressure.

3. Disconnect the negative battery cable.

4. Remove the rear seat cushion and unplug the electrical connector from the fuel pump.

5. Unfasten and remove the four pump cover screws and the ground strap.

6. Unfasten the fuel tube clips and disconnect the tubes from the pump.

7. Use a fuel pump locking ring removal tool or a brass drift and a hammer to unfasten the pump locking retaining ring.

8. Remove the fuel pump and the gasket from the tank.

To detach the upper fuel hose, remove the fuel filter hose retaining clip—1995–96 models

7922MG78

Detach the upper and lower hose clips before disconnecting hoses (1) from the fuel filter

7922MG79

To install:

9. Install a new gasket and place the pump into position in the tank.

10. Install the pump locking retaining ring.

11. Connect the fuel tubes to the pump and install the tube retaining clips.

12. Install the ground strap and fuel pump cover, then tighten the retainers.

13. Attach the electrical connector to the pump.

14. Install the rear seat cushion.

15. Connect the negative battery cable.

16. Start the vehicle and check for proper operation.

1997–00 Models

This procedure will require a new fuel pump gasket for pump installation, so be sure to have one before starting.

1. Before servicing the vehicle, refer to the precautions in the beginning of this section.

2. Relieve the fuel system pressure.

3. Disconnect the negative battery cable.

4. Remove the rear seat cushion and unplug the electrical connectors from the fuel pump.

5. Unfasten the four pump access cover screws and remove the cover.

6. If equipped, unplug the pump electrical connector located under the cover.

7. Unfasten the fuel line clip(s) and disconnect the line(s) from the pump.

8. Use a fuel pump locking ring removal tool or a brass drift and a hammer to unfasten the pump locking retaining ring.

9. Remove the fuel pump and the gasket from the tank.

To install:

10. Install a new gasket and place the pump into position in the tank.

11. Install the pump locking retaining ring.

12. Connect the fuel line(s) to the pump and install the line retaining clip(s).

13. If equipped, attach the fuel pump electrical connection(s).

14. Install access cover, then tighten the retainers.

15. Attach the pump electrical connector(s).

16. Install the rear seat cushion.

17. Connect the negative battery cable.

18. Start the vehicle and check for proper operation.

DRIVE TRAIN

Transaxle Assembly

REMOVAL & INSTALLATION

Manual

1.8L AND 1.9L ENGINES

1. Before servicing the vehicle, refer to the precautions in the beginning of this section.

2. Disconnect both battery cables, negative cable first.

3. Remove the battery and battery tray.

4. Remove the engine air cleaner tube and the air intake resonator.

5. Disconnect the speedometer cable at the transaxle.

6. Remove the slave cylinder line-to-slave cylinder hose retaining clip, then disconnect the slave cylinder line from the slave cylinder hose and plug the hose.

7. Disconnect the ground strap from the transaxle.

8. Remove the tie wrap and unplug the three electrical connectors located above the transaxle.

9. Remove the electrical connector support bracket.

10. Install Engine Support Bar 014–00750 or equivalent, and attach it to the engine lifting eyes with suitable chains or cables.

11. If equipped, remove the three nuts from the left-hand engine support bracket.

12. Loosen the mount pivot nut and rotate the mount out of the way.

13. Remove the three bolts and the left-hand engine support mount.

14. Remove the two upper transaxle-to-engine bolts.

15. Raise and safely support the vehicle.

16. Remove the front wheel and tire assemblies.

17. Remove the inner fender splash shields.

18. Drain the transaxle fluid and install the drain plug.

19. Remove the halfshafts.

20. Install Transaxle Plugs T88C-7025-AH or equivalent, between the differential side gears.

21. If equipped with the 1.8L engine, remove the intake manifold support bolts and the support.

22. Remove the starter motor.

23. Unfasten the gearshift stabilizer bar nut and washers. Remove the stabilizer bar and bracket from the transaxle.

24. Unfasten the shift control rod-to-transaxle bolt and nut and remove the shift control rod from the transaxle.

25. Remove both lower splash shields.

26. Unfasten the transaxle mount-to-crossmember bolts and nuts and remove the lower crossmember (rear engine support).

27. Position and secure a suitable transaxle jack under the transaxle.

28. Remove the front transaxle mount and bracket.

Removing the front transaxle mount and bracket—1.8L and 1.9L engines

Location of the lower engine-to-transaxle bolts—1.8L and 1.9L engines

29. Remove the lower engine-to-transaxle bolts and slowly lower the transaxle out of the vehicle.

To install:

30. Apply a thin coating of suitable grease to the spline of the input shaft.

31. Place the transaxle onto a suitable transaxle jack. Be sure the transaxle is secure.

32. Raise the transaxle into position.

33. Install the lower engine-to-transaxle bolts and tighten to 27–38 ft. lbs. (37–52 Nm).

34. Install the front transaxle mount and bracket. Tighten the bolts to 12–17 ft. lbs. (16–23 Nm).

35. Remove the transaxle jack.

36. Install the lower crossmember. Tighten the support bolts to 47–66 ft. lbs. (64–89 Nm) and the transaxle support insulator-to-rear engine support nuts to 27–38 ft. lbs. (37–52 Nm).

37. Install both lower splash shields.

38. Install the shift control rod bolt and nut and tighten to 12–17 ft. lbs. (16–23 Nm).

39. Install the stabilizer bracket and stabilizer bar with the nut and washers and tighten to 23–34 ft. lbs. (31–46 Nm).

40. Install the starter motor.

41. If equipped with the 1.8L engine, install the intake manifold support and tighten the retaining bolts to 27–38 ft. lbs. (37–52 Nm).

42. Remove the transaxle plugs and install the halfshafts.

43. Install the inner fender splash shields.

44. Install the wheel and tire assemblies.

45. Lower the vehicle.

46. Install the upper engine-to-transaxle bolts and tighten to 47–66 ft. lbs. (64–89 Nm).

47. Install the left-hand engine support mount and tighten 3 bolts to 32–45 ft. lbs. (43–61 Nm) for 1.8L engine or 41–59 ft. lbs. (55–80 Nm) for 1.9L engine.

48. Rotate the left-hand engine support bracket into position and tighten the pivot nut.

49. Install and tighten the left-hand engine support bracket nuts and tighten to 47–66 ft. lbs. (64–89 Nm).

50. Remove the engine support bar.

51. Install the electrical connector support bracket. Attach the electrical connectors and secure with a new tie wrap.

52. Connect the ground strap to the transaxle.

53. Connect the slave cylinder line to the slave cylinder hose and install the retaining clip.

54. Add the proper type and amount of fluid to the transaxle.

55. Connect the speedometer cable.

56. Install the engine air cleaner tube and the air intake resonator.

57. Install the battery tray and the battery.

58. Connect the battery cables, negative cable last.

59. Check for fluid leaks and proper clutch operation.

60. Road test the vehicle and check for proper transaxle operation.

2.0L ENGINES

1. Before servicing the vehicle, refer to the precautions in the beginning of this section.

2. Disconnect both battery cables, negative cable first.

3. Remove the battery and battery tray.

4. Remove the engine air cleaner outlet tube.

5. If necessary, unplug the Constant Control Relay Module (CCRM) electrical connection, loosen its retainers and remove the module and bracket as an assembly.

6. Disconnect the slave cylinder line from the slave cylinder hose and plug the hose.

7. Unfasten the slave cylinder line retaining clip and remove the line from the bracket.

8. Unplug the Heated Oxygen (HO2S) sensor electrical connection.

9. Unplug the back-up light electrical connection.

10. Unfasten the electrical connector bracket bolt and remove the bracket.

11. Unplug the Vehicle Speed Sensor (VSS) electrical connection.

12. Remove the halfshafts.

13. Install Engine Support Bar D88–6000A or equivalent, and attach it to the engine lifting eyes with suitable chains or cables.

14. Remove the insulator nuts from the left-hand engine support bracket.

15. Remove the front and rear upper transaxle-to-engine bolts.

16. Raise and safely support the vehicle.

17. Drain the transaxle fluid and install the drain plug.

18. Disconnect the A/C line from the retainer located on the engine support crossmember.

19. Unfasten the engine support crossmember bolts and nuts, then remove the crossmember.

20. Unfasten the gearshift stabilizer bar-to-transaxle nut, then remove the stabilizer bar and support from the transaxle.

Location of the left-hand engine support bracket nuts—2.0L engines

Loosen the transaxle gearshift bolt and remove the gearshift rod and clevis pin from the input shift shaft—2.0L engines

21. Unfasten the transaxle gearshift rod nut.

22. Unfasten the transaxle gearshift bolt and remove the gearshift rod and clevis pin from the input shift shaft.

23. Remove the starter motor.

24. Disconnect the lower slave cylinder tube and remove the slave cylinder.

25. Unfasten the lower transaxle-to-engine bolts.

26. Position and secure a suitable transaxle jack under the transaxle.

27. Remove the catalytic converter.

28. Unfasten the middle transaxle-to-engine bolts and remove the transaxle from the vehicle.

To install:

29. Apply a thin coating of suitable grease to the spline of the input shaft.

30. Place the transaxle onto a suitable transaxle jack. Be sure the transaxle is secure.

31. Raise the transaxle into position.

32. Install the middle transaxle-to-engine bolts and tighten them to 23–38 ft. lbs. (38–51 Nm).

33. Install the lower engine-to-transaxle bolts and tighten them to 23–38 ft. lbs. (38–51 Nm).

34. Install the clutch slave cylinder and

tighten the nuts to 12–17 ft. Lbs. (16–23 Nm).

35. Connect the lower slave cylinder tube and tighten the fitting to 10–16 ft. Lbs. (13–21 Nm).

36. Install the starter motor.

37. Place the gearshift rod and clevis into position on the input shift shaft, then install gearshift bolt and gearshift rod nut and tighten to 12–17 ft. Lbs. (16–23 Nm).

38. Install the gearshift stabilizer bar and tighten the nut to 23–34 ft. Lbs. (31–46 Nm).

39. Install the halfshafts and the catalytic converter.

40. Install the engine support crossmember. Tighten the crossmember bolts and nuts to 47–65 ft. Lbs. (64–89 Nm) and the insulator nuts to 28–37 ft. Lbs. (38–51 Nm).

41. Install the front and rear upper transaxle-to-engine bolt and tighten it to 28–38 ft. Lbs. (38–51 Nm).

42. Install the left-hand engine support insulator nuts and tighten them to 50–68 ft. lbs. (67–93 Nm).

43. Remove the engine support bar.

44. Install the electrical connector support bracket.

45. Attach all the electrical connectors.

46. Connect the slave cylinder line to the slave cylinder hose and install the retaining clip. Tighten the fitting to 10–16 ft. lbs. (13–21 Nm).

47. Bleed the clutch hydraulic system.

48. Add the proper type and amount of fluid to the transaxle.

49. If removed, install the CCRM and bracket assembly. Tighten the retainers and attach the electrical connection.

50. Install the engine air cleaner tube.

51. Install the battery tray and the battery.

52. Connect the battery cables, negative cable last.

53. Check for fluid leaks and proper clutch operation.

54. Road test the vehicle and check for proper transaxle operation.

Automatic

1.8L AND 1.9L ENGINES

1. Before servicing the vehicle, refer to the precautions in the beginning of this section.

2. Disconnect both battery cables, negative cable first.

3. Remove the battery and battery tray.

4. Disconnect the wiring harness retaining clip from the battery tray.

5. Remove the engine air cleaner assembly.

6. Disconnect the shift control cable from the manual shift lever on the transaxle.

7. Disconnect the speedometer cable from the transaxle by unsnapping the cable at the Vehicle Speed Sensor (VSS).

8. Unplug the transaxle electronic control electrical connectors and separate the harness from the transaxle clips.

9. Remove the Manual Lever Position (MLP) switch wiring brackets and disconnect the ground cables from the top of the transaxle.

10. Remove the starter motor.

11. Unplug the MLP switch wiring connectors.

12. Install Engine Support D88L-6000-A or equivalent, to the engine. The engine must be properly supported for transaxle removal.

13. Disconnect the kickdown cable (also known as the throttle valve cable) at the throttle cam on the throttle body.

14. Place a suitable drain pan under the transaxle and disconnect the transaxle cooler lines at the transaxle.

➡ **In some later models, the upper transaxle cooler line has a spring and a check ball under the fitting.**

15. Remove the left-hand engine mount bolts and the mount.

16. Remove the upper transaxle housing bolts.

17. Unplug the Heated Oxygen (HO2S) sensor electrical connector, the transaxle vent hose and the electrical connector at the VSS.

18. Raise and safely support the vehicle.

19. Separate the halfshafts from both steering knuckles.

20. Remove the three engine/transaxle lower splash shield bolts and the torque converter inspection plate.

21. Remove the four nuts securing the torque converter to the flexplate.

22. Remove the bolts securing the lower transaxle to the engine oil pan.

23. Unfasten the rear engine support-to-vehicle chassis bolt and remove the transaxle support crossmember from the vehicle chassis.

24. Unfasten the rear engine support-to-transaxle mount nuts and remove the transaxle support crossmember from the transaxle mounts.

25. Remove both halfshafts from the transaxle. Install two transaxle plugs T88C-7025-AH or equivalent, into the differential side gears.

❋❋ WARNING

Failure to install the transaxle plugs may cause the differential side gears to become improperly positioned. If the gears become malaligned, the differential will have to be removed from the transaxle to align them.

26. Position a drain pan and remove the drain plug from the transaxle. Drain the fluid from the differential cavity. Remove the transaxle pan and drain the remaining transaxle fluid, then install the pan and drain plug.

27. Position a suitable transaxle jack under the transaxle. Secure the transaxle to the jack.

28. Remove the lower transaxle-to-engine bolts.

29. Slowly lower the transaxle out of the vehicle.

30. Inspect all components including mounts and brackets.

Install the engine support crossmember and tighten the retainers to specification—2.0L engines

To install:

➤A pin is used for securing the throttle control lever in a fixed position on new and rebuilt transaxles. This pin must be removed to allow proper transaxle operation. If the pin is not removed, the throttle lever will remain in a fixed position. After removing the pin, apply sealant to the bolt from the previous transaxle. Install the bolt and tighten to 69–95 inch lbs. (8–11 Nm).

31. If rebuilding or replacing the transaxle, be sure to completely flush the transaxle cooler and cooler lines before installing the transaxle.

32. Remove the pin securing the throttle control lever, if installed.

33. Secure the transaxle on the transaxle jack.

34. Carefully raise the transaxle into position and install the lower transaxle-to-engine bolts. Tighten the bolts to 41–59 ft. lbs. (55–80 Nm).

35. Position the torque converter to the flexplate and install the retaining nuts. Tighten the nuts to 25–36 ft. lbs. (34–49 Nm). Install the torque converter inspection plate.

36. Remove the transaxle plugs and install the halfshafts.

37. Connect the crossmember to the transaxle mounts and the chassis. Tighten the crossmember-to-transaxle mount nuts to 27–38 ft. lbs. (37–52 Nm). Tighten the crossmember-to-chassis nuts and bolts to 47–66 ft. lbs. (64–89 Nm).

38. Install the lower transaxle-to-engine oil pan bolts and tighten to 27–38 ft. lbs. (37–52 Nm). Install the engine/transaxle splash shields.

39. Install the starter motor.

40. Lower the vehicle.

41. Install the upper transaxle-to-engine bolts and tighten to 41–59 ft. lbs. (55–80 Nm).

42. Install the left-hand engine mount and tighten the nuts to 49–69 ft. lbs. (67–93 Nm).

43. Connect the transaxle vent hose, the electrical connector at the VSS, the speedometer cable and the Heated Oxygen (HO₂S) sensor connector.

44. Install the check ball and spring under the cooler line fitting if equipped, then connect the transaxle cooler lines.

45. Connect the kickdown cable at the throttle body.

46. Remove the engine support.

47. Connect the ground wires to the transaxle and connect the MLP switch bracket and wiring connectors.

48. Connect the shift control cable to the manual shift lever on the transaxle. Tighten the selector lever attaching locknut to 33–47 ft. lbs. (44–64 Nm).

✳✳ WARNING

Do not use any type of power wrench to tighten the locknut. Damage to the transaxle may result.

49. Install the battery tray and battery. Connect the wiring harness retaining clip to the battery tray.

50. Install the engine air cleaner assembly.

51. Connect both battery cables, negative cable last.

52. Add the proper type and quantity of transaxle fluid.

53. Check the transaxle for leaks and for proper operation.

54. Check the MLP switch for proper adjustment, as follows:

   a. Remove the air cleaner outlet tube.

   b. Remove the clip that attaches the shift cable and bracket to the manual control shift outer lever.

   c. Remove the manual control shift outer lever from the shift cable and bracket.

   d. Turn the manual control shift lever to neutral position.

   e. Remove the screw from the access hole on the transmission range switch.

   f. Using a 5/64 inch (2.0mm) pin or drill bit shank, insert the pin inside the access hole and align the indentation inside the switch with the access hole.

   g. Tighten the switch retaining bolts to 69–95 inch lbs. (8–11 Nm) and remove the pin.

   h. Install the screw in the access hole on the switch.

   i. Attach the manual control shift outer lever to the shift cable and bracket and install the clip.

   j. Install the air cleaner outlet tube.

55. Road test the vehicle and check for proper operation.

2.0L ENGINES

1. Before servicing the vehicle, refer to the precautions in the beginning of this section.

2. Disconnect both battery cables, negative cable first.

3. Remove the battery and battery tray.

4. Remove the engine air cleaner assembly.

5. Unplug the Computer Control Relay Module (CCRM) electrical connections, unfasten the relay retainers and remove the relay and bracket from the engine.

6. Unfasten the shift control cable and bracket retaining nut from the manual shift lever , remove the shift cable and bracket clip, then set the bracket and cable assembly aside.

7. Tag and disconnect all electrical connections from the transaxle.

8. Remove the starter motor.

9. If equipped, unfasten the throttle valve actuating cable bolts and disconnect the cable from the throttle cam.

10. Install Engine Support D88L-6000-A or equivalent, to the engine. The engine must be properly supported for transaxle removal.

11. Place a suitable drain pan under the transaxle and disconnect the transaxle cooler lines at the transaxle.

12. Remove the left-hand engine mount bolts and the mount.

13. Remove the upper transaxle housing bolts.

14. Raise and safely support the vehicle.

15. If equipped, remove the left-hand splash shields.

16. Remove the transaxle plug and drain the fluid.

17. Remove the halfshafts. Install two transaxle plugs T88C-7025-AH or equivalent, into the differential side gears.

PIN DIAMETER: 4mm
PIN LENGTH: 62mm

PIN 7C492

BOLT 7N279

7922MG87

The pin used for securing the throttle control lever in a fixed position on new and rebuilt transaxles must be removed—1995–96 models

⁂ WARNING

Failure to install the transaxle plugs may cause the differential side gears to become improperly positioned. If the gears become malaligned, the differential will have to be removed from the transaxle to align them.

18. Remove the engine support cross-member and the catalytic converter.

19. Disconnect the A/C line from the retainer located on the engine support crossmember.

20. Unfasten the transaxle support crossmember bolts and nuts, the left-hand engine isolator nuts,, then remove the crossmember.

21. Unfasten the transaxle housing cover bolts and remove the cover.

22. Remove the four flywheel-to-torque converter nuts.

23. Position a suitable transaxle jack under the transaxle. Secure the transaxle to the jack.

24. Remove the remaining transaxle-to-engine bolts.

➡ **The upper front transaxle-to-engine bolt on 1997 models is equipped with a retainer and will remain in the engine block.**

25. On 1997 models, unfasten the upper front transaxle-to-engine bolt.

26. Slowly lower the transaxle out of the vehicle.

27. Inspect all components including mounts and brackets.

To install:

➡ **Prior to installing the transaxle, lubricate the torque converter pilot hub with multi-purpose grease.**

28. Align the torque converter studs to the flywheel.

29. Secure the transaxle on the transaxle jack.

30. Carefully raise the transaxle into position and install the middle and lower transaxle-to-engine bolts. Tighten the bolts to 40–58 ft. lbs. (55–80 Nm).

31. On 1997 models, install the upper front transaxle-to-engine bolt. Tighten the bolt to 40–58 ft. lbs. (55–80 Nm).

32. Install the flywheel-to-converter nuts and tighten them to 26–36 ft. Lbs. (35–49 Nm).

33. Install the transaxle housing cover and tighten the bolts to 40–58 ft. Lbs. (55–80 Nm).

34. Install the engine support crossmember. Tighten the crossmember bolts and nuts to 47–65 ft. Lbs. (64–89 Nm) and the insulator nuts to 28–37 ft. Lbs. (38–51 Nm).

35. Install the front and rear upper transaxle-to-engine bolt and tighten it to 28–38 ft. Lbs. (38–51 Nm).

36. Remove the transaxle plugs and install the halfshafts.

37. Connect the crossmember to the transaxle mounts and the chassis. Tighten the crossmember-to-transaxle mount nuts to 27–38 ft. lbs. (37–52 Nm). Tighten the crossmember-to-chassis nuts and bolts to 47–66 ft. lbs. (64–89 Nm).

38. Install the lower transaxle-to-engine oil pan bolts and tighten to 27–38 ft. lbs. (37–52 Nm).

39. Install the engine/transaxle splash shields.

40. Install the starter motor.

41. Attach all the electrical connections.

42. Lower the vehicle.

43. Install the upper transaxle-to-engine

bolts and tighten to 40–58 ft. lbs. (55–80 Nm).

44. Install the left-hand engine mount and tighten the nuts to 50–68 ft. lbs. (67–93 Nm).

45. If equipped, connect the throttle valve cable at the throttle cam. Adjust the cable as outlined in this section.

46. Remove the engine support.

47. Attach the shift cable and bracket to the manual shift lever, install the shift cable and bracket clip. Tighten the nut to 12–16 ft. Lbs. (16–22 Nm).

48. Install the engine air cleaner assembly. Adjust the cable as outlined in this section.

49. Install the battery tray and battery.

50. Connect both battery cables, negative cable last.

51. Add the proper type and quantity of transaxle fluid.

52. Check the transaxle for leaks and for proper operation.

53. Check the MLP switch for proper adjustment, as follows:

   a. Shift the transaxle into NEUTRAL, then align the marks on the transmission range switch and the manual control lever.

Align the marks on the MLP switch and the manual control lever as shown

Connect the throttle valve cable at the throttle cam (B) and tighten the cable retaining bolts (A)—1997–00 models

Attach an ohmmeter to terminals A and B on the transmission range switch

b. Install and finger-tighten the switch retaining bolts.

c. Attach an ohmmeter between terminals **A** and **B** on the switch as shown in the accompanying illustration.

d. Adjust the switch by rotating the switch housing on the manual control lever until there is no continuity between the terminals.

e. Hold the switch in place, then tighten its retaining bolts to 70–95 inch lbs. (8–11 Nm).

f. Remove the ohmmeter and attach the switch electrical connection.

g. Place the manual control shift outer lever in position and tighten its retaining nut to 33–47 ft. lbs. (44–64 Nm).

54. Road test the vehicle and check for proper operation.

Clutch

ADJUSTMENT

Pedal Free-Play

1996 MODELS

To determine if the clutch pedal free-play needs adjusting, depress the clutch pedal by hand until resistance is felt. Using a ruler, measure the distance between the upper clutch pedal height and where the resistance is felt.

Free-play should be 0.20–0.51 in. (5–13mm). If not, proceed as follows:

1. Before servicing the vehicle, refer to the precautions in the beginning of this section.

2. Loosen the clutch pedal to clutch master cylinder rod locknut.

3. Turn the clutch pedal to clutch master cylinder rod until the free-play is within specification.

4. Check that the disengagement height is within specification. Minimum disengagement height is 1.6 in. (41mm).

5. Tighten the clutch pedal to clutch master cylinder rod locknut to 9–12 ft. lbs. (12–17 Nm).

6. Check clutch pedal free-play to verify proper adjustment.

1997–00 MODELS

1. Before servicing the vehicle, refer to the precautions in the beginning of this section.

2. Depress the clutch pedal until resistance can be felt, and measure the distance between the upper clutch height and where the resistance is felt. The free-play should be 0.0–0.40 in. (5.0–13.9mm).

3. If an adjustment is necessary, turn the locknut and equalizer bar-to-clutch release lever rod.

4. After adjustment, measure the disengagement height from the upper surface of the clutch pedal pad to the carpet. The distance should be 2.3 in. (59mm).

Pedal Height

1996 MODELS

To determine if the pedal height requires adjustment, measure the distance from the bulkhead to the upper center of the pedal pad. The distance should be 7.72–8.03 in. (196–204mm). If adjustment is necessary, proceed as follows:

1. Before servicing the vehicle, refer to the precautions in the beginning of this section.

2. Disconnect the negative battery cable.

3. Unplug the clutch switch electrical connector.

4. Loosen the clutch switch locknut.

5. Turn the clutch switch until the correct height is achieved.

6. Tighten the locknut to 10–13 ft. lbs. (14–18 Nm).

7. Measure the pedal free-play.

8. Attach the electrical connector.

9. Connect the negative battery cable.

1997–00 MODELS

1. Measure the distance from the upper surface of the pedal pad to the carpet. The measurement should be 8.35–8.54 in. (212–217mm).

2. If an adjustment is necessary, turn the locknut and the Clutch Pedal Position (CPP) switch until the pedal height is correct.

REMOVAL & INSTALLATION

1996 Models

1. Before servicing the vehicle, refer to the precautions in the beginning of this section.

2. Disconnect the negative battery cable.

3. Raise and safely support the vehicle.

4. Remove the transaxle assembly.

5. If the clutch assembly is to be reused, matchmark the pressure plate and the flywheel so they can be assembled in the same position.

Clutch pedal measurements and adjustment points

7922MG91

6. Install flywheel holding tool T84P-6375-a or equivalent, in a transaxle mounting hole on the engine and engage the tooth of the holding tool into the flywheel ring gear.

7. Loosen the pressure plate-to-flywheel retaining bolts one turn at a time, in a crisscross pattern, until the spring tension is relieved, to prevent pressure plate cover distortion.

8. Support the pressure plate and unfasten the retaining bolts. Remove the pressure plate and clutch disc from the flywheel.

➡ **If the flywheel shows any signs of overheating (blue discoloration) or if it is badly grooved or scored, it should be refaced or replaced.**

9. Inspect the flywheel, clutch disc, pressure plate, release bearing, pilot bearing and the clutch fork for wear. Replace parts as needed.

To install:

10. If removed, install a new pilot bearing using a suitable installation tool.

11. If removed, install the flywheel. Be sure the flywheel and crankshaft flange mating surfaces are clean. Tighten the flywheel retaining bolts to 71–76 ft. lbs. (96–103 Nm) on the 1.8L engine or 54–67 ft. lbs. (73–91 Nm) on the 1.9L engine.

12. Clean the pressure plate and flywheel surfaces thoroughly. Position the clutch disc and pressure plate into the installed position and support them with a dummy shaft or clutch aligning tool. If the clutch assembly is being reused, align the matchmarks that were made during the removal procedure.

13. Install the pressure plate-to-flywheel retaining bolts. Tighten the bolts in the correct sequence to 13–20 ft. lbs. (18–26 Nm). Remove the alignment tool.

14. If the release bearing was removed, lubricate the release fork where it contacts the bearing and install the bearing in the fork.

15. Install the transaxle assembly.

16. Lower the vehicle.

17. Bleed the hydraulic clutch system, if needed.

18. Connect the negative battery cable.

19. Road test the vehicle and check the clutch for proper operation.

Tighten the pressure plate-to-flywheel retaining bolts in the sequence illustrated to specification—1996 models

1997–00 Models

1. Before servicing the vehicle, refer to the precautions in the beginning of this section.

2. Disconnect the negative battery cable.

3. Raise and safely support the vehicle.

4. Remove the transaxle assembly.

5. If the clutch assembly is to be reused, matchmark the pressure plate and the flywheel so they can be assembled in the same position.

6. Install flywheel holding tool T74P-7337-K or equivalent, in a transaxle mounting hole on the engine and engage the tooth of the holding tool into the flywheel ring gear.

7. Install clutch alignment tool T74P-7137-k or equivalent.

8. Loosen the pressure plate-to-flywheel retaining bolts one turn at a time, in a crisscross pattern, until the spring tension is relieved, to prevent pressure plate damage.

✳✳ WARNING

Do not use any cleaners with a petroleum base and do not immerse the clutch pressure plate in solvent.

CLUTCH PRESSURE PLATE

CLUTCH ALIGNER T74P-7137-K

FLYWHEEL HOLDING TOOL T84P-6375-A

To hold the crankshaft from turning, install a flywheel holding tool in a transaxle mounting hole on the engine and engage the tooth of the tool into the flywheel ring gear—1996 models

Turn to Section 6 for brake system applications

9. Clean the clutch pressure plate with a suitable commercial alcohol base solvent.

10. Inspect the pressure plate surface for burns, scores, flatness or ridges. Reface or replace the pressure plate.

11. Inspect the pressure plate diaphragm fingers for wear. Replace the pressure plate if necessary.

12. Using a slide caliper, measure the depth of the rivet heads. If the rivet head is within 0.012 in. (0.3mm) from the clutch surface, replace the clutch.

❊❊ WARNING

If the clutch disc is saturated with oil, inspect the rear engine crankshaft seal for leakage. If the seal is leaking, it must be replaced before installing the clutch.

➡**Use emery cloth to remove minor imperfections from the clutch disc lining surface.**

13. Inspect the clutch disc for the following:
- Oil or grease saturation
- Worn or loose facings
- Warpage or loose rivets at the hub
- Loose or broken torsion dampening springs
- Wear or rust on the splines.

14. If the clutch disc shows any of these conditions, it should be replaced.

15. Use a dial indicator mounted on a metal base to measure the clutch disc runout. If the run-out exceeds 0.0276 in. (0.700mm), replace the disc.

16. Inspect the clutch release for distortion, cracks, excessive release bearing surface wear or damaged tines and replace as necessary.

To install:

17. Clean the pressure plate and flywheel surfaces thoroughly. Position the clutch disc and pressure plate into the installed position and support them with clutch aligning tool T74P-7137-k or equivalent. If the clutch assembly is being reused, align the matchmarks that were made during the removal procedure.

18. Install the pressure plate-to-flywheel retaining bolts. Tighten the bolts in the correct sequence to 12–24 ft. lbs. (16–32 Nm). Remove the alignment tool.

19. Install the transaxle assembly.

20. Lower the vehicle.

21. Bleed the hydraulic clutch system.

22. Adjust the clutch pedal free-play.

23. Connect the negative battery cable.

24. Road test the vehicle and check the clutch for proper operation.

Hydraulic Clutch System

BLEEDING

1. Before servicing the vehicle, refer to the precautions in the beginning of this section.

2. Check that the brake master cylinder is at least ¾ full during the entire bleeding process.

3. Remove the bleeder screw cap from the clutch slave cylinder and attach a hose to the bleeder screw. Place the other end of the hose into a container to catch the fluid.

4. Have an assistant slowly pump the clutch pedal several times, then hold the clutch pedal down.

5. Loosen the bleeder screw to release the fluid and air. Tighten the bleeder screw.

6. Repeat the bleeding procedure until no more air bubbles are seen in the fluid.

7. Tighten the bleeder screw to 52–78 inch lbs. (6–9 Nm).

8. Top off the brake master cylinder to the full line.

9. Check for proper clutch system operation.

16-32 Nm (12-24 lb/ft)

7922MG95

Tighten the pressure plate-to-flywheel retaining bolts in the sequence illustrated to specification—1997–00 models

Halfshafts

REMOVAL & INSTALLATION

1996 Models

1.8L ENGINE—LEFT SIDE

➡**Before continuing with any halfshaft procedure, be sure to have available, new halfshaft retaining nuts and circlips. Once removed, these parts loose their torque holding ability or retention capability and must not be reused.**

1. Before servicing the vehicle, refer to the precautions in the beginning of this section.

2. Disconnect the negative battery cable.

3. With the vehicle sitting on the ground, carefully raise the staked portion of the halfshaft retaining nut using a suitable small chisel. Loosen the nut.

4. Raise and safely support the vehicle.

5. Remove the wheel and tire assembly.

6. Remove the splash shield.

7. Remove and discard the halfshaft retaining nut.

8. Remove the cotter pin and castellated nut from the tie rod end and separate the tie rod end from the steering knuckle using a suitable removal tool. Discard the cotter pin.

9. Remove the lower ball joint pinch bolt. Carefully pry down on the lower control arm to separate the ball joint stud from the steering knuckle.

10. Pull outward on the steering knuckle/brake assembly. Carefully pull the halfshaft from the hub and position it aside.

11. Removal of the left side halfshaft requires removal of the crossmember to allow access with a prybar as follows:

a. Support the transaxle with a suitable transaxle jack.

b. Remove the four transaxle mount-to-crossmember retaining nuts.

c. Remove the two crossmember retaining nuts at the rear of the crossmember.

d. While supporting the rear of the crossmember, unfasten the two front mounting bolts and remove the crossmember.

12. Position a drain pan under the transaxle.

13. Insert a prybar between the halfshaft and the transaxle case. Gently pry outward to release the halfshaft from the differential side gear. Be careful not to damage the transaxle case, oil seal, CV-joint or CV-joint boot.

14. Remove the halfshaft.

➡Install suitable plugs after removing the halfshafts to prevent the differential side gears from moving out of place. Should the gears become malaligned, the differential will have to be removed from the transaxle to align the gears.

To install:

15. Position a new circlip on the inner CV-joint spline so the circlip gap is at the top. Lubricate the splines lightly with a suitable grease.

16. Remove the plugs that were installed in the differential side gears.

17. Position the halfshaft so the CV-joint splines are aligned with the differential side gear splines. Push the halfshaft into the differential. When seated properly, the circlip can be felt snapping into the differential side gear groove.

18. Pull outward on the steering knuckle/brake assembly and insert the halfshaft into the hub.

19. Pry downward on the lower control arm and position the lower ball joint stud in the steering knuckle.

20. Install the crossmember and the crossmember-to-frame nuts and bolts. Tighten the nuts to 27–38 ft. lbs. (37–52

Nm) and the bolts to 47–66 ft. lbs. (64–89 Nm).

21. Install the four transaxle mount-to-crossmember nuts and tighten to 27–38 ft. lbs. (37–52 Nm).

22. Remove the transaxle jack.

23. Install the lower ball joint pinch bolt and tighten to 32–43 ft. lbs. (43–59 Nm).

24. Attach the tie rod end to the steering knuckle. Install the castellated nut and tighten to 31–42 ft. lbs. (42–57 Nm). Install a new cotter pin.

25. Install the splash shield.

26. Install the wheel and tire assembly.

27. Install a new halfshaft retaining nut and tighten to 174–235 ft. lbs. (235–319 Nm). Stake the halfshaft retaining nut using a suitable chisel with a rounded cutting edge.

➡If the nut splits or cracks after staking, replace it with a new nut.

28. Check and refill the transaxle with the proper type and quantity of fluid.

29. Connect the negative battery cable.

30. Road test the vehicle and check for proper operation.

1.8L ENGINE—RIGHT SIDE

➡The right side halfshaft assembly is a two piece shaft with a bearing support bracket positioned between the two halves. The bearing support bracket is mounted on the cylinder block and must be unbolted if the entire halfshaft assembly is to be removed. If only the CV-joints/boots are to be serviced, the outboard shaft assembly may be removed, leaving the bearing support bracket mounted on the engine cylinder block.

1. Before servicing the vehicle, refer to the precautions in the beginning of this section.

2. Disconnect the negative battery cable.

3. With the vehicle sitting on the ground, carefully raise the staked portion of the halfshaft retaining nut using a suitable small chisel. Loosen the nut.

4. Raise and safely support the vehicle.

5. Remove the right front wheel and tire assembly.

6. Remove the splash shield.

7. Remove and discard the halfshaft retaining nut.

8. Remove the cotter pin and castellated nut from the tie rod end and separate the tie rod end from the steering knuckle using a suitable removal tool. Discard the cotter pin.

9. Remove the lower ball joint pinch bolt. Carefully pry down on the lower control arm to separate the ball joint stud from the steering knuckle.

10. Pull outward on the steering knuckle/brake assembly. Carefully pull the halfshaft from the hub and position it aside.

11. Position a drain pan under the transaxle.

12. Remove the three bearing support bracket mounting bolts.

13. Insert a prybar between the bearing support bracket and the starter bracket. Gently pry outward on the damper until the halfshaft disengages from the differential side gear.

14. Remove the halfshaft assembly. Install an appropriate differential plug in the differential side gear.

To install:

15. Position a new circlip on the inner CV-joint spline so the circlip gap is at the top. Lubricate the splines lightly with a suitable grease.

16. Remove the differential plug from the side gear. Position the halfshaft assembly

1	Front Axle Bearing Bracket (Part of 3A329)	9	Front Wheel Driveshaft Joint (1.8L)
2	Tie Rod End	10	Front Axle Bearing Bracket Bolts (3 Req'd)
3	Front Fender Splash Shield	11	Halfshaft (1.8L)
4	Ball Joint Bolt	A	Tighten to 43-59 N·m (32-43 Lb-Ft)
5	Front Suspension Lower Arm Ball Joint	B	Tighten to 34-46 N·m (25-33 Lb-Ft)
6	Ball Joint Bolt Nut	C	Tighten to 42-62 N·m (31-46 Lb-Ft)
7	Cotter Pin		
8	Tie Rod End Nut		

7922MG96

Exploded view of typical halfshaft positioning—1.8 and 1.9L engines

so the shaft splines are aligned with the differential side gear splines. Push the half-shaft into the differential. When seated properly, the circlip can be felt snapping into the differential side gear groove.

17. Pull outward on the steering knuckle/brake assembly and insert the half-shaft into the hub.

18. Pry downward on the lower control arm and position the lower ball joint stud into the steering knuckle. Install the lower ball joint pinch bolt and tighten to 32–43 ft. lbs. (43–59 Nm).

19. Install the tie rod end to the steering knuckle. Install the castellated nut and tighten to 31–42 ft. lbs. (42–57 Nm). Install a new cotter pin.

20. Position the bearing support bracket and install the three retaining bolts. Tighten the outer bolt first, then the top inner, then the bottom inner. Tighten the bolts to 31–46 ft. lbs. (42–62 Nm).

21. Install the splash shield.

22. Install the wheel and tire assembly.

23. Lower the vehicle.

24. Install a new halfshaft retaining nut and tighten to 174–235 ft. lbs. (235–319 Nm). Stake the retaining nut using a suitable chisel with the cutting edge rounded off.

➡ **If the nut splits or cracks after staking, it must be replaced with a new nut.**

25. Check and refill the transaxle with the proper type and quantity of fluid.

26. Connect the negative battery cable.

27. Road test the vehicle and check for proper operation.

1.9L ENGINE

➡ **Before continuing with any halfshaft procedure, be sure to have available, new halfshaft retaining nuts and cir-clips. Once removed, these parts loose their torque holding ability or retention capability and must not be reused.**

1. Before servicing the vehicle, refer to the precautions in the beginning of this section.

2. Disconnect the negative battery cable.

3. With the vehicle sitting on the ground, carefully raise the staked portion of the halfshaft retaining nut using a suitable small chisel. Loosen the nut.

4. Raise and safely support the vehicle.

5. Remove the wheel and tire assembly.

6. Remove the splash shield.

7. Remove and discard the halfshaft retaining nut.

8. Remove the cotter pin and castellated nut from the tie rod end and separate the tie rod end from the steering knuckle using a suitable removal tool. Discard the cotter pin.

9. Remove the lower ball joint pinch bolt. Carefully pry down on the lower control arm to separate the ball joint stud from the steering knuckle.

10. Pull outward on the steering knuckle/brake assembly. Carefully pull the halfshaft from the hub and position it aside.

11. Removal of the left side halfshaft requires removal of the crossmember to allow access with a prybar as follows:

   a. Support the transaxle with a suitable transaxle jack.

   b. Remove the four transaxle mount-to-crossmember retaining nuts.

   c. Remove the two crossmember retaining nuts at the rear of the cross-member.

   d. While supporting the rear of the crossmember, unfasten the two front mounting bolts and remove the cross-member.

12. Position a drain pan under the transaxle.

13. Insert a prybar between the halfshaft and the transaxle case. Gently pry outward to release the halfshaft from the differential side gear. Be careful not to damage the transaxle case, oil seal, CV-joint or CV-joint boot.

14. Remove the halfshaft.

➡ **Install suitable plugs after removing the halfshafts to prevent the differential side gears from moving out of place. Should the gears become malaligned, the differential will have to be removed from the transaxle to align the gears.**

To install:

15. Position a new circlip on the inner CV-joint spline so the circlip gap is at the top. Lubricate the splines lightly with a suitable grease.

16. Remove the plugs that were installed in the differential side gears.

17. Position the halfshaft so the CV-joint splines are aligned with the differential side gear splines. Push the halfshaft into the differential. When seated properly, the circlip can be felt snapping into the differential side gear groove.

18. Pull outward on the steering knuckle/brake assembly and insert the half-shaft into the hub.

19. Pry downward on the lower control arm and position the lower ball joint stud in the steering knuckle.

20. Install the crossmember and the crossmember-to-frame nuts and bolts. Tighten the nuts to 27–38 ft. lbs. (37–52 Nm) and the bolts to 47–66 ft. lbs. (64–89 Nm).

21. Install the four transaxle mount-to-crossmember nuts and tighten to 27–38 ft. lbs. (37–52 Nm).

22. Remove the transaxle jack.

23. Install the lower ball joint pinch bolt and tighten to 32–43 ft. lbs. (43–59 Nm).

24. Attach the tie rod end to the steering knuckle. Install the castellated nut and tighten to 31–42 ft. lbs. (42–57 Nm). Install a new cotter pin.

25. Install the splash shield.

26. Install the wheel and tire assembly.

27. Install a new halfshaft retaining nut and tighten to 174–235 ft. lbs. (235–319 Nm). Stake the halfshaft retaining nut using a suitable chisel with a rounded cutting edge.

➡ **If the nut splits or cracks after staking, replace it with a new nut.**

28. Check and refill the transaxle with the proper type and quantity of fluid.

29. Connect the negative battery cable.

30. Road test the vehicle and check for proper operation.

1997–00 Models

➡ **Before continuing with any halfshaft procedure, be sure to have available, new halfshaft retaining nuts and cir-clips. Once removed, these parts loose their torque holding ability or retention capability and must not be reused.**

1. Before servicing the vehicle, refer to the precautions in the beginning of this section.

2. Disconnect the negative battery cable.

3. With the vehicle sitting on the ground, carefully raise the staked portion of the halfshaft retaining nut using a suitable small chisel. Loosen the nut.

4. Raise and safely support the vehicle.

5. Remove the wheel and tire assembly.

6. Remove and discard the halfshaft retaining nut.

7. Remove the cotter pin and nut from the tie rod end, then separate the tie rod end from the steering knuckle using a suitable removal tool. Discard the cotter pin.

8. On 1998–00 models, remove the stabilizer bar link as follows:

   a. Unfasten the stabilizer bar end nut (1) and bolt (2).

   b. Remove the stabilizer bar end retainer (3).

   c. Remove the end bushing (4) above the stabilizer bar.

d. Remove the end bushing (5) below the stabilizer bar.

e. Remove the stabilizer bar spacer (6).

f. Remove the stabilizer bar end bushings from above (7) and below (8) the sub-frame

g. Remove the lower stabilizer bar end retainer (9).

h. Remove the stabilizer bar.

9. Remove the ball joint bolt and nut. Carefully pry down on the lower control arm to separate the ball joint stud from the steering knuckle.

10. Pull outward on the steering knuckle/brake assembly. Carefully pull the halfshaft from the hub and position it aside.

➡**Removal of the left side halfshaft requires removal of the crossmember to allow access with a prybar.**

11. Support the transaxle with a suitable transaxle jack.

12. Unfasten the four transaxle crossmember retainers and remove the crossmember.

13. If removing the right side halfshaft, remove the right-hand shield and splash shield.

14. Position a drain pan under the transaxle.

15. Remove the left-hand halfshaft on 1997–99 models and right-hand halfshaft on 1997 models as follows:

a. Insert a prybar between the halfshaft and the transaxle case. Gently pry outward to release the halfshaft from the differential side gear. Be careful not to damage the transaxle case, oil seal, CV-joint or CV-joint boot.

b. Remove the halfshaft.

16. On 1998–00 models, remove the right-hand halfshaft as follows:

a. On models with a manual

transaxle, unfasten the center support bearing bolts.

b. Lower the halfshaft and remove it from the transaxle.

c. Separate the halfshaft from the center support bearing and remove the halfshaft from the vehicle.

d. Inspect the center support bearing for damage and replace as necessary.

➡**Install suitable plugs after removing the halfshafts to prevent the differential side gears from moving out of place. Should the gears become malaligned, the differential will have to be removed from the transaxle to align the gears.**

To install:

17. Position a new circlip on the inner CV-joint spline so the circlip gap is at the top. Lubricate the splines lightly with a suitable grease.

18. Remove the plugs that were installed in the differential side gears.

19. On all models except 1998–00 models wit a manual transaxle, position the halfshaft so the CV-joint splines are aligned with the differential side gear splines. Push the halfshaft into the differential.

➡**When seated properly, the circlip can be felt snapping into the differential side gear groove.**

20. Install the right-hand halfshaft on 1998–00 models with a manual transaxle as follows:

a. Position the halfshaft and joint so that the splines line up with the splines in the halfshaft, and push the halfshaft, joint and halfshaft together with the center support bearing.

b. Install the halfshaft in the transaxle.

21. Place the center support bearing into position and tighten it retaining bolts to 32–46 ft. Lbs. (46–62 Nm).

a. Install the right-hand shield and splash shield.

22. Pull outward on the steering knuckle/brake assembly and insert the halfshaft into the hub.

23. Pry downward on the lower control arm and position the lower ball joint stud in the steering knuckle.

24. Install the crossmember and the crossmember-to-frame bolts. Tighten the bolts to 69–93 ft. lbs. (94–126 Nm).

25. Remove the transaxle jack.

26. Install the steering knuckle and ball joint nut and bolt. Tighten the nut and bolt to 32–43 ft. Lbs. (43–59 Nm).

27. On 1998–99 models, install the stabilizer bar link in reverse order of removal and tighten the bar end nut until the protruding bar end bolt length is 0.67–75 in. (17–19mm).

28. Install the tie rod end to the steering knuckle. Install the nut and tighten to 25–33 ft. Lbs. (34–46 Nm) on 1997 models and 32–41 ft. Lbs. (43–56 Nm) on 1998–00 models. Install a new cotter pin.

29. Install the wheel and tire assembly.

30. Install a new halfshaft retaining nut and tighten to 174–235 ft. lbs. (235–319 Nm). Stake the halfshaft retaining nut using a suitable chisel with a rounded cutting edge.

➡**If the nut splits or cracks after staking, replace it with a new nut.**

31. Check and refill the transaxle with the proper type and quantity of fluid.

32. Connect the negative battery cable.

33. Road test the vehicle and check for proper operation.

STEERING AND SUSPENSION

Air Bag

PRECAUTIONS

Several precautions must be observed when handling the inflator module to avoid accidental deployment and possible personal injury.

• Never carry the inflator module by the wires or connector on the underside of the module.

• When carrying a live inflator module,

On 1998–00 2.0L models with a manual transaxle, unfasten the center support bearing bolts

7922MG97

During assembly, be sure to install a new circlip on the inner CV-joint spline—2.0L engine

7922MGA1

hold securely with both hands, and ensure that the bag and trim cover are pointed away.

• Place the inflator module on a bench or other surface with the bag and trim cover facing up.

• With the inflator module on the bench, never place anything on or close to the module which may be thrown in the event of an accidental deployment.

DISARMING

1. Before servicing the vehicle, refer to the precautions in the beginning of this section.

2. Disconnect both battery cables, negative cable first.

3. Wait at least 1 minute. This allows time for the back-up power supply to deplete its stored energy.

4. Remove the drivers side air bag module, then the passenger side if required.

5. Use caution when carrying live air bags. Always place the air bag with the cover up.

6. If the battery needs to be reconnected while one or both of the air bags are removed from the system, install Air Bag Simulator 105–00010 or equivalent, to the drivers side and/or passenger side air bag harness connectors as required. Before removing either air bag simulator, disconnect both battery cables and wait at least 1 minute before continuing.

ARMING

1. Once service is completed and the air bag modules are back in place, connect the negative battery cable and prove out the air bag system by turning the ignition key to the **RUN** position and visually monitoring the air bag indicator lamp in the instrument cluster. The indicator lamp should illuminate for approximately 6 seconds, then turn OFF. if the indicator lamp does not illuminate, stays ON, or flashes at any time, a fault has been detected by the air bag diagnostic monitor requiring immediate attention.

Rack and Pinion Steering Gear

REMOVAL & INSTALLATION

Manual

1996 MODELS

1. Before servicing the vehicle, refer to the precautions in the beginning of this section.

2. Disconnect the negative battery cable.

3. Working from inside the vehicle, unfasten the five nuts securing the steering column tube boot and remove the boot.

4. Remove the intermediate shaft-to-pinion shaft coupling bolt from inside the vehicle.

5. Raise and safely support the vehicle.

6. Remove the front wheel and tire assemblies.

7. Remove the cotter pins and castellated nuts securing the tie rod ends to the steering knuckles. Separate the tie rod ends from the steering knuckles. Discard the cotter pins.

8. If equipped with a manual transaxle, unfasten the gearshift lever stabilizer bar nut and disconnect the bar and support from the transaxle.

9. Unfasten the nuts securing the rack and pinion (steering gear) mounting brackets to the bulkhead. Remove the mounting brackets.

10. Remove the rack and pinion assembly from the vehicle.

To install:

11. Position the rack and pinion assembly to its mounting position and install the mounting brackets and retaining nuts.

Unfasten the intermediate shaft-to-pinion shaft coupling bolt from inside the vehicle—1996 models with manual rack and pinion steering gears

Tighten the nuts to 27–38 ft. lbs. (37–52 Nm).

12. If equipped with a manual transaxle, connect the gearshift lever stabilizer bar. Tighten the nut to 23–34 ft. lbs. (31–46 Nm).

13. Install the tie rod ends to the steering knuckles. Install the castellated nuts and tighten to specifications. Install new cotter pins.

14. Install the front wheel and tire assemblies.

15. Lower the vehicle.

16. Install the intermediate shaft-to-pin-

Exploded view of the steering rack mounting—1996 models

ion shaft bolt and tighten to 33 ft. lbs. (45 Nm).

17. Install the steering column tube boot and 5 retaining nuts. Tighten to 35 inch lbs. (4 Nm).

18. Connect the negative battery cable.

19. Check the alignment and adjust the toe as required.

20. Road test the vehicle and check the steering system for proper operation.

Power

1996 MODELS

1. Before servicing the vehicle, refer to the precautions in the beginning of this section.

2. Disconnect the negative battery cable.

3. From inside the passenger compartment, remove the steering column tube boot nuts at the base of the column and remove the tube boots.

4. Remove the intermediate shaft-to-pinion shaft bolt.

5. Raise and safely support the vehicle.

6. Remove the front wheel and tire assemblies.

7. Remove the left-hand splash shield.

8. Remove the cotter pins and castellated nuts from the tie rod ends. Using a suitable tool, separate the tie rod ends from the steering knuckles. Discard the cotter pins.

9. Remove the strap that holds the power steering lines to the rack and pinion (steering gear) housing and discard the strap.

10. Disconnect the pressure and return lines from the rack and pinion assembly and plug the lines.

11. If equipped with a manual transaxle, disconnect the gearshift stabilizer bar and shift control rod from the transaxle.

12. Remove the retaining nuts from the rack and pinion mounting brackets.

13. Remove the rack and pinion assembly from the left-hand side of the vehicle.

To install:

14. Place the rack and pinion assembly in its mounting location.

15. Install the rack and pinion mounting brackets. Install the retaining nuts and tighten to 28–38 ft. lbs. (37–57 Nm).

16. If equipped with a manual transaxle, connect the gearshift stabilizer bar and shift control rod. Tighten the gearshift stabilizer bar nut to 23–34 ft. lbs. (31–46 Nm) and the shift control rod nut to 12–17 ft. lbs. (16–23 Nm).

17. Remove the plugs and connect the pressure and return lines to the rack and pinion assembly. Tighten the flare nuts to 22–28 ft. lbs. (29–39 Nm).

18. Install a new strap to hold the power steering lines to the rack and pinion housing.

19. Install the tie rod ends to the steering knuckles and install the castellated nuts. Tighten to specification. Install new cotter pins.

20. Install the left-hand splash shield.

21. Install the wheel and tire assemblies.

22. Lower the vehicle.

23. From inside the vehicle, install the intermediate shaft-to-pinion shaft bolt. Tighten the bolt to 30–36 ft. lbs. (40–50 Nm).

24. Install the steering column tube boot and the five retaining nuts. Tighten the retaining nuts to 35 inch lbs. (4 Nm).

25. Connect the negative battery cable.

26. Fill and bleed the power steering system.

27. Check the alignment and adjust as required.

28. Start the engine and check for leaks.

29. Road test the vehicle and check for proper steering system operation.

1997–00 MODELS

1. Before servicing the vehicle, refer to the precautions in the beginning of this section.

2. Turn the key to the **ACC** position.

3. From inside the passenger compartment, remove the steering column tube boot nuts at the base of the column and remove the tube boots.

4. Remove the steering column input shaft coupling-to-steering gear input shaft pinch bolt.

5. Raise and safely support the vehicle.

6. Remove the front wheel and tire assemblies.

7922MGA4

Unfasten the steering column tube boot nuts at the base of the column and remove the tube boots—1997–00 models

7922MGA5

Unfasten the retaining nuts from the rack and pinion mounting brackets and remove the brackets—1997–00 models

7. Using a suitable tool, separate the tie rod ends from the steering knuckles. Discard the cotter pins.

8. Remove the right-hand lower splash shield.

9. Unfasten the bolts and remove the crossmember.

10. Disconnect the pressure and return lines from the rack and pinion assembly and plug the lines.

11. Remove and discard the strap holding the hoses to the steering gear.

12. If equipped with a manual transaxle, disconnect the gearshift rod and clevis from the transaxle.

13. If equipped with a manual transaxle, unfasten the extension bar nut and disconnect the gearshift lever stabilizer bar and support from the transaxle.

14. Unfasten the retaining nuts from the rack and pinion mounting brackets and remove the brackets.

15. Remove the pushpin and position the right-hand boot aside.

16. Remove the rack and pinion assembly from the right-hand side of the vehicle.

To install:

17. Place the rack and pinion assembly in its mounting location.

18. Align the steering column input shaft coupling and the steering gear input shaft.

19. Install the rack and pinion mounting brackets. Install the retaining nuts and tighten to 28–38 ft. lbs. (37–57 Nm).

20. If equipped with a manual transaxle, connect the gearshift stabilizer bar, support and the gearshift rod and clevis.

➡**Install new Teflon seals on the power steering pressure hose fitting and be sure the threads are clean before connecting the hose.**

21. Remove the plugs and connect the pressure and return lines to the rack and

pinion assembly. Tighten the pressure hose to 21–25 ft. lbs. (28–33 Nm) and the return line fitting to 20–25 ft. lbs. (27.3–33.9 Nm).

22. Install a new strap to hold the power steering lines to the rack and pinion housing.

23. Install the crossmember and tighten the bolts to 69–97 ft. lbs. (94–131 Nm).

24. Place the right-hand boot shield into position and install the push pin.

25. Install the right-hand splash shield.

26. Install the tie rod ends to the steering knuckles and install the castellated nuts. Tighten to specification. Install new cotter pins.

27. Install the wheel and tire assemblies.

28. Lower the vehicle.

29. Install the steering column input shaft coupling-to-steering gear input shaft pinch bolt and tighten the bolt to 30–36 ft. lbs. (40–50 Nm).

30. Install the steering column tube boots and the five retainers. Tighten the retainers to 1852 inch lbs. (2–5.9 Nm).

31. Connect the negative battery cable.

32. Fill and bleed the power steering system.

33. Check the alignment and adjust as required.

34. Start the engine and check for leaks.

35. Road test the vehicle and check for proper steering system operation.

Strut

REMOVAL & INSTALLATION

Front

1. Before servicing the vehicle, refer to the precautions in the beginning of this section.

2. Disconnect the negative battery cable.

3. Raise and safely support the vehicle.

4. Remove the front wheel and tire assembly.

5. Remove the clip securing the brake hose to the strut (spring and shock) assembly. If equipped with anti-lock brakes, remove the anti-lock brake harness cable and clip.

6. Unfasten the two nuts and two bolts securing the strut assembly to the steering knuckle.

7. Unfasten the four upper strut retaining nuts and remove the strut assembly from the vehicle.

1	Front Shock Absorber Upper Mounting Bracket	9	Front Suspension Lower Arm Mounting Bolt Bushing (Rear)
2	Upper Spring Seat (Part of 18198)	10	Front Wheel Spindle Tie Rod
3	Front Brake Hose	11	Front Suspension Lower Arm
4	Disc Brake Caliper	12	Front Suspension Lower Arm Mounting Bolt Bushing (Front)
5	Front Disc Brake Rotor	13	Front Shock Absorber
6	Front Wheel Knuckle	14	Front Coil Spring
7	Tie Rod End		
8	Front Stabilizer Bar		

9300MG04

Identification of the front suspension components

> ✳✳ **CAUTION**
>
> **Never remove the strut piston rod nut unless the coil spring is compressed. Always wear safety glasses when using a spring compressor.**

8. Inspect all components and replace as needed.

To install:

9. Position the strut assembly into the wheel housing. Be sure the direction indicator on the upper mounting bracket faces inboard.

10. Secure the upper mounting bracket to the strut tower with the retaining nuts. Tighten the nuts to 22–30 ft. lbs. (29–40 Nm).

11. Attach the strut assembly to the steering knuckle and install the retaining bolts and nuts. Tighten to 69–93 ft. lbs. (93–127 Nm).

7922MGA6

Remove the two nuts and two bolts securing the strut assembly to the steering knuckle

12. Position the brake hose on the strut assembly and secure it with the brake hose clip. If equipped with anti-lock brakes, install the anti-lock harness cable and clip.

13. Install the front wheel and tire assembly.

14. Lower the vehicle.

15. Connect the negative battery cable.

16. Check the front wheel alignment.

17. Road test the vehicle and check for proper operation.

Rear

1996 MODELS

1. Before servicing the vehicle, refer to the precautions in the beginning of this section.

2. Disconnect the negative battery cable.

3. Raise and safely support the vehicle.

4. Remove the wheel and tire assembly.

5. Remove the clip securing the brake hose to the rear strut assembly.

6. If equipped with anti-lock brakes, remove the ABS harness from the clip on the strut assembly.

7. Remove the nuts and bolts securing the rear strut assembly to the wheel spindle.

8. Partially lower the vehicle.

9. On hatchback and wagon models, remove the quarter trim panel.

10. Unfasten the two upper strut insulator retaining nuts and remove the rear strut assembly from the vehicle.

To install:

11. Position the strut assembly into the vehicle wheel housing.

Identification of the rear suspension components—1996 models

12. Install the two upper strut insulator retaining nuts and tighten to 22–27 ft. lbs. (29–40 Nm).

13. On hatchback and wagon models, install the quarter trim panel.

14. Install the nuts and bolts securing the strut assembly to the rear wheel spindle assembly. Tighten the lower strut bolts and nuts to 69–93 ft. lbs. (93–127 Nm).

15. Install the clip securing the flexible brake hose to the rear strut assembly.

16. If equipped with anti-lock brakes, install the ABS harness to the clip.

17. Install the wheel and tire assembly.

18. Lower the vehicle.

19. Connect the negative battery cable.

20. Check the rear wheel alignment.

21. Road test the vehicle and check for proper operation.

1997–00 MODELS

1. Before servicing the vehicle, refer to the precautions in the beginning of this section.

2. Disconnect the negative battery cable.

3. On sedan and coupe models, remove the package tray trim panel.

4. On wagon models, remove the quarter trim panel

1	Rear Floor Cross Member
2	Rear Shock Absorber Insulator
3	Rear Spring
4	Rear Shock Absorber
5	Rear Wheel Spindle
6	Rear Suspension Tie Rod and Bushing
7	Rear Suspension Arm and Bushing (Rear)
8	Rear Stabilizer Bar
9	Rear Suspension Arm and Bushing (Front)
10	Rear Wheel Brake Hose

Identification of the rear suspension components—1997–00 models

Turn to Section 6 for brake system applications

Location of the two rear strut upper retaining nuts (arrows) inside the vehicle— 1997–00 models

5. Unfasten the two upper strut retaining nuts.

6. Raise and safely support the vehicle.

7. Remove the wheel and tire assembly.

8. Remove the clip securing the brake hose to the rear strut assembly.

9. If equipped with anti-lock brakes, unfasten the ABS sensor bolt.

10. Remove the nuts and bolts securing the rear strut assembly to the wheel spindle.

11. Remove the strut assembly from the vehicle.

To install:

12. Position the strut assembly into the vehicle wheel housing.

13. Install the nuts and bolts securing the strut assembly to the rear wheel spindle assembly. Tighten the lower strut bolts and nuts to 76–100 ft. lbs. (103–136 Nm).

14. If equipped with anti-lock brakes, tighten the ABS sensor bolt.

15. Install the clip securing the flexible brake hose to the rear strut assembly.

16. Install the wheel and tire assembly.

17. Lower the vehicle.

18. Install the two upper strut retaining nuts and tighten to 34–46 ft. lbs. (47–62 Nm).

19. Install the trim panel.

20. Connect the negative battery cable.

21. Check the rear wheel alignment.

22. Road test the vehicle and check for proper operation.

Coil Spring

REMOVAL & INSTALLATION

Front

1996 MODELS

1. Remove the strut assembly.

2. Remove the cap from the top of the strut.

3. Place the strut assembly in a vise,

Exploded view of the strut assembly—1996 models

hold the piston rod in position and loosen the piston rod nut.

✳✳ CAUTION

Always take the necessary precautions when using a spring compressor

4. Install a suitable spring compressor tool onto the coil spring.

5. Compress the spring using the tool.

6. Remove the strut piston rod nut, front mounting block, thrust bearing, upper spring seat, rubber spring seat, coil spring and bound stopper.

To install:

7. Place the bound stopper onto the strut.

8. With coil spring compressed, position the spring onto the strut assembly.

9. Install the rubber spring seat, upper spring seat, thrust bearing, mounting block and piston rod nut. Tighten the piston rod nut to 58–81 ft. lbs. (79–110 Nm).

10. After the piston rod nut has been tightened to specification, carefully remove the compressor tool from the spring while making sure the spring is properly seated in the upper and lower spring seats.

11. Install the cap on top of the strut.

➡**The position indicator on the mounting block faces inboard during installation.**

12. Install the strut assembly in the vehicle.

13. Have the vehicle alignment checked and if necessary, adjusted.

1997–00 MODELS

1. Before servicing the vehicle, refer to the precautions in the beginning of this section.

2. Remove the strut assembly.

3. Place the strut assembly in a vise.

4. Install a suitable spring compressor tool onto the coil spring and compress the spring.

5. Unfasten the piston rod nut and remove the upper mounting bracket.

6. Remove the bound stopper, dust boot, rubber spring seat, spring, upper spring seat and thrust bearing.

To install:

7. Install the thrust bearing, upper spring seat, spring, rubber spring seat, dust boot and the bound stopper.

8. Install the piston rod nut and tighten it to 58–81 ft. lbs. (79–110 Nm).

9. After the piston rod nut has been tightened to specification, carefully remove the compressor tool from the spring while making sure the spring is properly seated in the upper and lower spring seats.

10. Install the strut assembly in the vehicle.

11. Have the vehicle alignment checked and if necessary, adjusted.

Rear

1996 MODELS

1. Position the strut assembly in a vise and secure the assembly at the upper insulator bracket.

2. Remove the cap and loosen the pis-

ton rod nut 1 turn. Do not remove the piston rod nut at this time.

❋❋ CAUTION

Attempting to remove the spring from the strut without first compressing the spring with a tool designed for that purpose could cause bodily injury.

3. Install an appropriate coil spring compressor and compress the coil spring.

4. Remove the piston rod nut, washer, retainer, anti-rattle plate and insulator.

5. Remove the coil spring.

6. Remove the stopper seat and dust boot from the strut piston.

To install:

7. Position the strut assembly in a vise and secure.

8. Install the dust boot and the stopper seat onto the strut piston rod.

9. Compress the coil spring and install on the strut assembly.

10. Install the upper strut insulator, then align the upper strut insulator mounting studs and the lower bracket of the strut assembly.

11. Install the retainer, washer and piston rod nut. Tighten the nut to 41–50 ft. lbs. (55–68 Nm).

12. Be sure the spring is properly aligned and carefully release the spring into the seats of the strut.

13. Remove the spring compressor from the coil spring and install the cap.

1997–00 MODELS

1. Remove the strut assembly.

2. Place the strut assembly in a vise.

❋❋ CAUTION

Always take the necessary precautions when using a spring compressor

3. Install a suitable spring compressor tool onto the coil spring and compress the spring.

4. Remove the rear strut assembly top mounting cover

5. Unfasten the piston rod nut and remove the retainer.

6. Remove the strut insulator.

7. Carefully remove the spring compressor.

8. Remove the rear strut dust boot and stopper seat.

9. Remove the spring and the rear strut insulator.

To install:

10. Place the strut assembly in a vise.

11. Install the strut insulator and spring.

12. Install the stopper seat and dust boot.

13. Use the spring compressor tool to compress the strut spring.

14. Remove the strut insulator and the retainer.

15. Install the piston rod nut and tighten it to 41–49 ft. lbs. (55–67 Nm).

16. Install the top mounting cover.

17. Be sure the spring is properly aligned and carefully release the spring into the seats of the strut.

18. Remove the spring compressor from the coil spring.

19. Install the strut assembly.

Lower Ball Joint

REMOVAL & INSTALLATION

➡**Refer to the illustration located in the strut procedure, earlier in this section, for a view of the front suspension.**

1. Before servicing the vehicle, refer to the precautions in the beginning of this section.

2. Raise and safely support the front of the vehicle.

3. Remove the wheel assembly.

4. Unfasten the nut and bolt attaching the lower ball joint to the steering knuckle.

5. Separate the ball joint from the steering knuckle.

6. Unfasten the lower control arm ball joint nuts and bolt. Remove the ball joint.

To install:

7. Place the ball joint into position on the lower control arm. Install the ball joint-to-lower control arm retainers. Tighten the nuts and bolt to 69–86 ft. lbs. (93–117 Nm).

8. Apply Loctite® 290 thread locking compound or equivalent to the ball joint nut and threads.

9. Attach the ball joint to the steering knuckle and install the nut and bolt. Tighten the nut and bolt to 32–43 ft. lbs. (43–59 Nm).

10. Install the wheel assembly and lower the vehicle.

11. Have the vehicle alignment checked and if necessary, adjusted.

Wheel Bearings

ADJUSTMENT

The bearings on the front and rear wheels are a lone piece cartridge design and cannot be adjusted. Wheel bearing play can be checked with a dial indicator. If wheel bearing play exceeds 0.002 in. (0.05mm) check the wheel hub retainer nut for proper torque. If the torque is correct, replacement of the wheel bearing is required.

REMOVAL & INSTALLATION

Front

➡**Refer to the illustration located in the strut procedure, earlier in this section, for a view of the front suspension.**

1. Before servicing the vehicle, refer to the precautions in the beginning of this section.

2. With the vehicle sitting on the ground, carefully raise the staked portion of the halfshaft retaining nut using a suitable small chisel. Loosen the nut.

3. Raise and safely support the front of the vehicle.

4. Remove the wheel and tire assembly.

➡**Do not disconnect the brake hose from the caliper**

5. Remove the brake caliper and secure it out of the way with a piece of mechanics wire. Do not let the caliper hang on the hose.

6. Remove the brake rotor.

7. Remove the halfshaft retaining nut and discard it.

8. Remove the cotter pin and castellated nut from the tie rod end and separate the tie rod end from the steering knuckle using a suitable removal tool. Discard the cotter pin.

9. Use the appropriate tool to separate the tie rod end from the wheel knuckle.

10. If equipped with an Anti-lock Brake System (ABS), unfasten the ABS sensor bolt and remove the sensor.

11. Remove the strut mounting nuts and the studs which attach the strut assembly to the steering knuckle.

12. Separate the strut from the steering knuckle.

13. Remove the lower ball joint pinch bolt. Carefully pry down on the lower control arm to separate the ball joint stud from the steering knuckle.

14. Remove the wheel hub, knuckle and bearing assembly from the vehicle.

To install:

15. Apply Loctite® 290 thread locking compound or equivalent to the ball joint nut and threads.

16. Install the wheel hub, knuckle and bearing assembly onto the ball joint and tighten the pinch bolt and nut to 32–43 ft. lbs. (43–59 Nm).

17. Install the tie rod end and tighten the nut to 25–33 ft. lbs. (34–46 Nm). Install a new cotter pin.

18. If equipped with an Anti-lock Brake System (ABS), install the ABS sensor and tighten the bolt.

19. Attach the knuckle to the strut assembly and tighten the strut mounting nuts to 69–93 ft. lbs. (93–127 Nm).

20. Install a new halfshaft retaining nut and tighten to 174–235 ft. lbs. (235–319 Nm). Stake the retaining nut using a suitable chisel with the cutting edge rounded off.

➡ **If the nut splits or cracks after staking, it must be replaced with a new nut.**

21. Install the brake rotor and caliper.
22. Install the wheel and tire assembly.
23. Lower the vehicle.
24. Check the front wheel alignment.
25. Road test the vehicle and check for proper operation.

Rear

➡ **The wheel bearings are a cartridge design and are not serviceable. If bear-** ing replacement is required, the bearings and hub must be replaced as an assembly. Do not continue with this procedure without having available a new wheel hub retainer nut. Once removed, the nut looses its torque holding ability or retention capability and must not be reused.

1. Before servicing the vehicle, refer to the precautions in the beginning of this section.

2. Raise and safely support the vehicle.

3. Remove the wheel and tire assembly.

4. Remove the hub grease cap.

5. Remove the brake drum or disc brake caliper and rotor, as necessary.

6. Unstake and remove the wheel hub retainer nut securing the hub to the spindle and remove the hub and bearing assembly. Discard the hub retainer nut.

7. If equipped with disc brakes, remove the disc brake shield retaining bolts and the shield.

8. If equipped with drum brakes, remove the backing plate.

9. Remove the strut-to-spindle retaining bolts and nuts.

10. Remove the trailing arm bolt securing the trailing arm to the spindle.

11. Remove the stabilizer bar link nuts, retainers, bushings, sleeves and bolts.

12. Remove the control arm nut and bolt securing both control arms to the wheel spindle and remove the spindle from the vehicle.

13. Inspect all components. If the wheel spindle is damaged, replace it. Wheel bearings are sealed and must be replaced if damaged with the wheel hub.

To install:

14. Place the wheel spindle in position to the strut and install the retaining bolts and nuts. Tighten to 69–93 ft. lbs. (93–127 Nm).

15. Install the trailing arm to the spindle. Install the retaining bolt and tighten to 69–93 ft. lbs. (93–127 Nm).

16. Place both control arms in position to the spindle and install the retaining bolt and nut. Tighten the nut to 63–86 ft. lbs. (85–117 Nm).

17. Install the stabilizer bar link nuts, retainers, bushings, sleeves and bolts.

18. If equipped with drum brakes, install the brake backing plate.

19. If equipped with disc brakes, install the brake shield and the disc brake shield retaining bolts. Tighten securely.

20. Install the wheel hub and bearing assembly to the wheel spindle.

21. Install a new wheel hub retainer nut and tighten to 130–174 ft. lbs. (177–235 Nm).

22. Stake the wheel hub retainer nut using a cape or round end chisel. Do not use a sharp chisel to stake the hub nut.

23. Install the brake drum or the disc brake rotor and caliper, as equipped.

24. Install the hub grease cap.

25. Install the wheel and tire assembly.

26. Lower the vehicle.

27. Pump the brake pedal several times to position the brake lining before attempting to move the vehicle.

28. Road test the vehicle and check for proper operation.

FORD MOTOR COMPANY

23

Ford-Mustang

PRECAUTIONS

Before servicing any vehicle, please be sure to read all of the following precautions, which deal with personal safety, prevention of component damage, and important points to take into consideration when servicing a motor vehicle:

• Never open, service or drain the radiator or cooling system when the engine is hot; serious burns can occur from the steam and hot coolant.

• Observe all applicable safety precautions when working around fuel. Whenever servicing the fuel system, always work in a well-ventilated area. Do not allow fuel spray or vapors to come in contact with a spark, open flame, or excessive heat (a hot drop light, for example). Keep a dry chemical fire extinguisher near the work area. Always keep fuel in a container specifically designed for fuel storage; also, always properly seal fuel containers to avoid the possibility of fire or explosion. Refer to the additional fuel system precautions later in this section.

• Fuel injection systems often remain pressurized, even after the engine has been turned **OFF**. The fuel system pressure must be relieved before disconnecting any fuel lines. Failure to do so may result in fire and/or personal injury.

• Brake fluid often contains polyglycol ethers and polyglycols. Avoid contact with the eyes and wash your hands thoroughly after handling brake fluid. If you do get brake fluid in your eyes, flush your eyes with clean, running water for 15 minutes. If eye irritation persists, or if you have taken brake fluid internally, IMMEDIATELY seek medical assistance.

• The EPA warns that prolonged contact with used engine oil may cause a number of skin disorders, including cancer! You should make every effort to minimize your exposure to used engine oil. Protective gloves should be worn when changing oil. Wash your hands and any other exposed skin areas as soon as possible after exposure to used engine oil. Soap and water, or waterless hand cleaner should be used.

• All new vehicles are now equipped with an air bag system, often referred to as a Supplemental Restraint System (SRS) or Supplemental Inflatable Restraint (SIR) system. The system must be disabled before performing service on or around system components, steering column, instrument panel components, wiring and sensors. Failure to follow safety and disabling procedures could result in accidental air bag deployment, possible personal injury and unnecessary system repairs.

• Always wear safety goggles when working with, or around, the air bag system. When carrying a non-deployed air bag, be sure the bag and trim cover are pointed away from your body. When placing a non-deployed air bag on a work surface, always face the bag and trim cover upward, away from the surface. This will reduce the motion of the module if it is accidentally deployed. Refer to the additional air bag system precautions later in this section.

• Clean, high quality brake fluid from a sealed container is essential to the safe and proper operation of the brake system. You should always buy the correct type of brake fluid for your vehicle. If the brake fluid becomes contaminated, completely flush the system with new fluid. Never reuse any brake fluid. Any brake fluid that is removed from the system should be discarded. Also, do not allow any brake fluid to come in contact with a painted surface; it will damage the paint.

• Never operate the engine without the proper amount and type of engine oil; doing so WILL result in severe engine damage.

• Timing belt maintenance is extremely important! Many models utilize an interference-type, non-freewheeling engine. If the timing belt breaks, the valves in the cylinder head may strike the pistons, causing potentially serious (also time-consuming and expensive) engine damage. Refer to the maintenance interval charts in the front of this manual for the recommended replacement interval for the timing belt, and to the timing belt section for belt replacement and inspection.

• Disconnecting the negative battery cable on some vehicles may interfere with the functions of the on-board computer system(s) and may require the computer to undergo a relearning process once the negative battery cable is reconnected.

• When servicing drum brakes, only disassemble and assemble one side at a time, leaving the remaining side intact for reference.

• Only an MVAC-trained, EPA-certified automotive technician should service the A/C system or its components.

ENGINE REPAIR

Distributor

➡ **The 3.8L and 4.6L engines use distributorless ignition systems.**

Ignition Timing

ADJUSTMENT

The 3.8L and 4.6L engines utilize the Distributorless Ignition System (DIS). On this system, ignition coil packs fire the spark plugs directly through the spark plug wires. All spark timing and advance is determined by the ignition control module and engine control computer. No ignition timing adjustments are necessary or possible.

Engine Assembly

REMOVAL & INSTALLATION

1. Before servicing the vehicle, refer to the precautions in the beginning of this section.

2. Properly discharge the A/C system.

3. Disconnect the battery cables.

4. Drain the engine cooling system.

5. Remove the cooling fan, radiator and all cooling system hoses.

6. If equipped, remove the Mass Air Flow (MAF) sensor and intake air duct.

7. Label and detach all engine wiring and vacuum hoses which will interfere with engine removal.

8. Remove the hood.

9. If equipped, remove the engine compartment brace from the front fender apron and dash panel.

10. Detach the accelerator and transmission control cables from the throttle body, and the control cable(s) mounting bracket from the engine.

11. Relieve the fuel system pressure, then disconnect the fuel supply and return lines from the engine.

12. Remove the A/C compressor mounting bracket and drive belt tensioner.

13. Raise and safely support the vehicle.

14. Remove the power steering pump and hoses.

15. Drain the engine oil and remove the oil filter.

16. Disconnect the exhaust system from the exhaust manifolds.

17. Label and detach any under vehicle engine wiring which will interfere with engine removal.

18. Remove the transmission.

19. If equipped, remove the transmission oil cooler line retainers from the right-hand, front engine support insulator.

20. Remove the front engine support insulator-to-crossmember fasteners.

21. Remove the starter motor and starter motor wiring from the engine.

22. Partially lower the vehicle and support it with jackstands in this new position.

23. On the 3.8L engine, install Engine Lifting Brackets 014–00791 and Separator Bar 014–00793 or their equivalents.

24. On the 4.6L SOHC engine, install the Engine Lifting Brackets D91P-6001-A, or their equivalents, onto the cylinder heads with M-12 x 1.75 x 20mm bolts.

25. On the 4.6L DOHC engine, install the

Install the engine lifting brackets on both sides of the engine—4.6L SOHC engine shown, other engines similar

lifting eyes from the Rotunda Engine Lift Bracket Set 014–00340, or their equivalents, onto the cylinder heads. Tighten the attaching bolts to 30–36 ft. lbs. (40–50 Nm).

26. Using an engine crane or hoist, lift the engine out of the vehicle. Be sure to lift the engine slowly and check often that nothing (such as wires, hoses, etc.) will cause the engine to hang up on the vehicle.

27. At this point, the engine can be installed on an engine stand.

To install:

➡️**Lightly oil all bolts and stud threads, except those specifying special sealant, prior to installation.**

28. Using the hoist or engine crane, slowly and carefully position the engine in the vehicle; lower the engine onto the front engine support insulators.

29. On the 3.8L engine, tighten the front engine support insulator nuts to 72–98 ft. lbs. (97–133Nm).

30. On the 4.6L engine, install the support through-bolts and tighten them to 15–22 ft. lbs. (20–30 Nm).

31. Detach the engine crane or hoist from the engine, and remove the lifting brackets from the cylinder heads.

32. Install the transmission.

33. The remainder of installation is the reverse of the removal procedure.

34. Fill the crankcase with engine oil.

35. Install the air intake duct assembly.

36. Connect the negative battery cable, then fill and bleed the cooling system.

37. Bring the engine to normal operating temperature, then check for leaks.

38. Stop the engine and check all fluid levels.

39. Install the hood, aligning the marks that were made during removal.

40. If equipped, properly evacuate, charge and leak-test the A/C system.

Water Pump

REMOVAL & INSTALLATION

3.8L Engine

1. Before servicing the vehicle, refer to the precautions in the beginning of this section.

2. Drain the engine cooling system.

3. Remove the electric cooling fan from the radiator.

4. Slightly loosen the water pump pulley bolts before removing the accessory drive belt.

5. Remove the accessory drive belt.

FRONT OF ENGINE

1. Mounting stud
2. Water pump housing gasket
3. Water pump

4. Mounting nuts
5. Short mounting bolts
6. Long mounting bolt
7. Mounting stud bolt

7922NG03

Exploded view of the water pump mounting on the 3.8L engine—during removal, note the original positions of the different length bolts for reassembly

6. Remove the water pump pulley retaining bolts, then separate the pulley from the water pump flange.

7. Remove the ignition coil bracket mounting nuts and bolts, then position the ignition coil (with all wires still attached) aside.

8. Remove the power steering pump pulley.

9. Remove the water pump-to-power steering pump brace.

10. Remove the heater water outlet tube retaining bolts, then separate the outlet tube from the water pump.

11. Detach the lower radiator hose from the water pump.

※※ WARNING

If it is necessary to utilize a prytool to separate the water pump from the engine, use caution not to damage the water pump and engine mating surfaces.

12. Loosen the water pump bolts, then pull the water pump off of the engine. Remove and discard the old water pump gasket.

To install:

➡ Lightly oil all bolt and stud threads prior to assembly, except those specifying sealant, with clean engine oil.

● TIGHTEN IN SEQUENCE SHOWN TO 20-30 N·m (15-22 LB-FT)

○ REFER TO LEGEND

1. Engine front cover
2. Mounting bolts

3. Mounting nuts
4. Water pump

5. Mounting bolt
6. Mounting stud bolt

7. Engine block

7922NG04

When tightening the mounting fasteners, be sure to adhere to the sequence shown for proper sealing—3.8L engine

13. Clean the gasket mating surfaces of the water pump and engine of all old gasket material and dirt.

14. Apply adhesive, such as Ford Gasket and Trim Adhesive F3AZ-19B508-B or equivalent, to the water pump gasket, then position the water pump and the new gasket on the engine.

➡ **The threads of the No. 1 water pump retaining bolt must be coated with a Teflon® sealant, such as Ford Pipe Sealant with Teflon® D8AZ-19554-A or equivalent, prior to installation.**

15. Install the water pump retaining bolts, studs and nuts, then tighten, in the sequence shown in the accompanying illustration, the retaining bolts and studs to 15–22 ft. lbs. (20–30 Nm) and the nuts to 71–106 inch lbs. (8–12 Nm).

16. Inspect the O-ring seal on the heater water outlet tube for damage, and replace it if necessary. Then, install the outlet tube to the water pump. Tighten the retaining bolts to 71–106 inch lbs. (8–12 Nm).

17. Attach the lower radiator hose to the water pump. Ensure that the radiator hose clamps are tightened properly.

18. Install the water pump-to-power steering pump brace.

19. Install the power steering pump pulley.

20. Install the water pump pulley and retaining bolts. Tighten the bolts to 15–21 ft. lbs. (21–29 Nm).

21. Install the accessory drive belt.

22. Install the electric cooling fan.

23. Fill the cooling system with the proper amount and type of coolant.

24. Start the engine and check for coolant leaks.

4.6L Engines

1. Before servicing the vehicle, refer to the precautions in the beginning of this section.

2. Drain the engine cooling system.

3. Remove the electric cooling fan from the radiator.

4. Remove the accessory drive belt.

5. Remove the water pump pulley by loosening the retaining bolts and pulling it off of the water pump flange.

✳✳ WARNING

If it is necessary to utilize a prytool to separate the water pump from the engine, use caution not to damage the water pump and engine mating surfaces.

6. Loosen the water pump bolts, then separate the water pump from the engine.

7. Remove and discard the old water pump O-ring.

To install:

➡ **Lightly oil all bolt and stud threads prior to assembly with clean engine oil.**

8. Clean the mating surfaces of the water pump and engine of all corrosion and dirt.

9. Install a new O-ring in the groove on the water pump, then lubricate the O-ring with coolant, such as Ford Premium Cooling System Fluid E2Fz-19549-AA or equivalent.

10. Position the water pump, along with the new O-ring, on the engine.

11. Install the water pump retaining bolts, then tighten them 15–22 ft. lbs. (20–30 Nm) in a crisscross pattern.

12. Install the water pump pulley and retaining bolts. Tighten the bolts to 15–21 ft. lbs. (21–29 Nm).

13. Install the accessory drive belt.

14. Install the electric cooling fan.

✳✳ WARNING

Use care to prevent engine coolant from spilling on the accessory drive belt, otherwise drive belt squeal and early fatigue will result. If necessary, remove the drive belt and rinse it with clean water to clean off any antifreeze.

15. Fill the cooling system with the proper amount and type of coolant.

16. Start the engine and check for coolant leaks.

Cylinder Head

REMOVAL & INSTALLATION

3.8L Engine

1. Before servicing the vehicle, refer to the precautions in the beginning of this section.

2. Disconnect the negative battery cable.

3. Remove the upper and lower intake manifolds.

4. Remove the valve cover(s) and rocker arms.

➡ **Be sure to label or separate all of the cylinder head components (such as pushrods, rocker arms, etc.) so that they can be installed in their original positions on the cylinder heads.**

5. Remove the exhaust manifolds.

6. Perform the following for left-hand cylinder head removal:

   a. Remove the Power Steering (PS) pump front mounting brace retaining nuts from the water pump.

   b. Remove the alternator.

   c. Remove the idler pulley.

   d. Remove the PS pump/alternator bracket mounting fasteners, then (leaving all PS hoses attached) position the PS pump and bracket aside in a position so that PS fluid does not leak out.

WATER PUMP
HOUSING GASKET

BOLT

WATER PUMP

7922NG05

Exploded view of the water pump mounting on all 4.6L engines

Timing belt service is covered in Section 5 of this manual

1. Engine block
2. Locating pin
3. Long cylinder head mounting bolts
4. Cylinder head
5. Short cylinder head mounting bolts
6. Alignment dowel

● **TIGHTEN BOLTS IN SEQUENCE**

FRONT OF ENGINE

7922NG07

Be sure to tighten the cylinder head mounting bolts in the sequence shown (black numbers) to ensure proper cooling system and combustion chamber sealing—3.8L engine

7. Perform the following for right-hand cylinder head removal:

a. If equipped with A/C, remove the compressor mounting bracket bolts, then (leaving all A/C lines attached) position the compressor aside.

b. If not equipped with A/C, remove the idler pulley.

8. Remove and discard the cylinder head mounting bolts.

9. Lift the cylinder head(s) up and off of the engine block.

10. Remove and discard the old cylinder head gasket(s).

To install:

➡**Lightly oil all bolt and stud threads prior to assembly, except those specifying sealant, with clean engine oil.**

11. Clean the cylinder head, intake manifold and valve cover gasket mating surfaces thoroughly.

12. If a cylinder head was removed for head gasket replacement, inspect the cylinder head for warpage.

➡**If a cylinder head is warped, have it ground by a competent machine shop before installing.**

13. Position the new cylinder head gasket(s) on the engine block, then install the cylinder head(s).

❊❊ WARNING

Always use new cylinder head bolts to ensure a leak-tight seal. Torque values with used cylinder head bolts can vary, which may cause coolant or compression leakage.

14. Tighten the cylinder head bolts in the sequence shown, and in the following steps to the proper values:

a. Tighten the bolts to 15 ft. lbs. (20 Nm).

b. Next, tighten the bolts to 29 ft. lbs. (40 Nm).

c. Then, tighten the bolts to 37 ft. lbs. (50 Nm).

❊❊ WARNING

Do not loosen all of the bolts at the same time in the following step; only work on one bolt at a time, then move on the next bolt in the sequence.

d. Loosen the bolts, one at a time, two or three revolutions, then retighten them as follows:

• Tighten longs bolts to 29–37 ft. lbs.

(40–50 Nm) and the short bolts to 133–221 inch lbs. (15–25 Nm).

• Rotate the bolt an additional 180 degrees.

• Proceed to the next bolt in the sequence.

15. Dip each end of the pushrods in engine assembly lubricant, such as Ford D9AZ-19579-D or equivalent, then install the pushrods in their original positions.

16. Apply engine assembly lube to the rocker arms prior to installation, then install the rocker arms.

17. Install the exhaust manifolds.

18. Install the lower and upper intake manifolds.

19. Install the valve cover(s).

20. Install the spark plugs, if removed. Then, connect the spark plug wires to the plugs.

21. If necessary, install the PS pump and bracket on the engine, then install the alternator.

22. If necessary, install the A/C compressor and bracket on the engine.

23. If not already performed, install the accessory drive belt pulleys and the drive belt.

24. Connect the negative battery cable.

25. Fill the engine with the proper type and amount of coolant.

26. Start the engine and check for coolant leaks.

4.6L SOHC Engine

1. Before servicing the vehicle, refer to the precautions in the beginning of this section.

2. Disconnect the negative battery cable, drain the cooling system and relieve fuel system pressure.

3. Remove the valve cover(s).

4. Remove the throttle body.

5. Remove the intake manifold.

6. Disconnect the exhaust system from the exhaust manifolds.

7. Remove the engine front cover.

8. Remove the timing chains. Be sure to note the positions of the flats on the ends of the two camshafts before removing the cylinder heads.

9. Remove or detach any remaining wires, hoses or cables which will interfere with cylinder head removal.

➡**Do not set the cylinder head down on its engine block mating surface; if any valves are open, they may be damaged.**

10. Remove the cylinder head mounting bolts and lift the cylinder heads off of the engine block. If necessary, at this time the heater water hose can be removed from the left-hand cylinder head.

To install:

➡**Lightly oil all bolt and stud threads prior to assembly with clean engine oil.**

11. Clean the cylinder head, intake manifold and valve cover gasket mating surfaces thoroughly.

12. If a cylinder head was removed for head gasket replacement, inspect the cylinder head for warpage. If a cylinder head is warped, have it ground by a competent machine shop before installing. The following step ensures that all of the pistons are below the top of the engine block deck face.

13. Rotate the crankshaft counterclockwise 45°.

14. Inspect the cylinder head face surface for scratches near the coolant passages and combustion chambers.

15. Rotate the camshaft to a stable position where the valves do not extend below the cylinder head face.

16. Position the new cylinder head gasket(s) on the engine block, then install the cylinder head(s).

✶✶ WARNING

Cylinder head mounting bolts must be replaced with new bolts; do NOT reuse original cylinder head mounting bolts. They are torque-to-yield bolts and cannot be reused; otherwise, engine damage may occur.

17. Apply clean engine oil to the cylinder head mounting bolts spot faces. Then, install the mounting bolts hand-tight.

18. Tighten the cylinder head bolts (starting with the left-hand cylinder head first) in the sequence shown in the accompanying illustration and following these steps:

a. Tighten the bolts to 27–31 ft. lbs. (37–43 Nm).

b. Tighten the bolts an additional 85–95 degrees.

c. Loosen the bolts a minimum of one full revolution (360 degrees).

d. Retighten the bolts to 27–31 ft. lbs. (37–43 Nm).

e. Tighten the bolts an additional 85–95 degrees.

f. Finally, tighten the bolts an additional 85–95 degrees.

RH CYLINDER HEAD   **LH CYLINDER HEAD**

FRONT OF ENGINE

7922NG08

When tightening the cylinder head mounting bolts, be sure to follow the order shown—4.6L SOHC engine

19. Install the heater water hose on the left-hand cylinder head, then tighten the lower mounting bolt to 71–106 inch lbs. (8–12 Nm) and the upper mounting bolt to 15–22 ft. lbs. (20–30 Nm).

20. Using the flats matched at the center of the camshafts, rotate the camshafts until both are in time (the position they were in when the timing chains were removed).

21. Install Ford Cam Positioning Tool Adapters T92P-6256-A and Cam Positioning Tool T91P-6256-A (or their equivalents) on the flats of the camshafts to prevent them from rotating.

❊❊ WARNING

The crankshaft must only be rotated in the clockwise direction and only as far as Top Dead Center (TDC).

22. Rotate the crankshaft clockwise 45°.
23. Install the timing chains.
24. Install the engine front cover.
25. Connect the exhaust system to the exhaust manifolds.
26. Install the intake manifold.
27. Install the throttle body.
28. Install the valve cover(s).
29. Install or attach any remaining wires, hoses or cables which were removed earlier.
30. Connect the negative battery cable and fill the cooling system.
31. Start the engine and check for leaks.

4.6L DOHC Engine

➡**According to the manufacturer, the cylinder heads are not removable with the engine in the vehicle; therefore, this procedure is written with the assumption that the engine is removed from the vehicle.**

1. Before servicing the vehicle, refer to the precautions in the beginning of this section.

2. Remove the engine from the vehicle, as described earlier in this section.

3. Remove the valve covers.
4. Remove the engine front cover.
5. Remove the intake manifolds.
6. Remove the Crankshaft Position (CKP) sensor pulse wheel.
7. Remove the rocker arms.
8. Remove the exhaust manifolds.
9. If not already done, drain the coolant from the engine block.
10. Rotate the engine to Top Dead Center (TDC) as follows:

    a. Remove the spark plugs from the cylinder heads.

    b. Install the crankshaft damper center bolt in the crankshaft.

    c. Position your thumb over the No. 1 cylinder's spark plug hole, so that it seals the hole completely.

➡**Only rotate the crankshaft in the clockwise direction (when looking at the front of the engine).**

    d. Have an assistant rotate the crankshaft using a breaker bar and socket on the crankshaft center bolt until you start to feel air escaping past your thumb (you will not have the strength to keep the cylinder sealed—air will escape).

➡**It may take a couple of tries to get the feeling for the air down. Have patience and take your time, it is vitally important to get the engine at TDC.**

    e. From that point, rotate the crankshaft until the TDC marks are aligned. The timing chain and crankshaft gears' timing marks should be aligned at this point. Also, all four valves should be closed (that is, their camshaft lobes should be pointing away from the valves and springs). If the timing chain gear marks are not aligned and all of the valves are not closed, but the TDC ignition timing marks are aligned, rotate the crankshaft one full revolution (360 degrees).

11. Install Ford Camshaft Positioning Tool T93P-6256-A, or the equivalent, in the rear D-slots of the camshafts.

12. Remove the timing chains and tensioners.

13. Disengage the engine harness wiring from the heater water hose, then remove the three bolts retaining the inlet heater water hose to the rear of the right-hand cylinder head.

14. Remove the outlet heater water hose mounting bolts from the rear of the left-hand cylinder head.

15. Using the removal sequence, shown in the accompanying illustration, remove the cylinder head mounting bolts.

16. Discard all of the old cylinder head mounting bolts.

❊❊ WARNING

Do NOT set the cylinder heads down on their engine block mating surface; otherwise, damage may occur to the valve heads, which may protrude beyond the cylinder head surface.

17. Lift the cylinder heads up and off of the engine block.

18. Remove and discard the old cylinder head gaskets.

CAMSHAFT POSITIONING TOOL

7922NG09

Use a camshaft positioning tool to hold the camshafts from rotating once the timing chains are removed—4.6L DOHC engine

RH CYLINDER HEAD   LH CYLINDER HEAD

FRONT OF ENGINE

7922NG10

Be sure to loosen the cylinder head mounting bolts in the sequence shown—4.6L DOHC engine

RH CYLINDER HEAD   LH CYLINDER HEAD

FRONT OF ENGINE

7922NG11

Tighten the new cylinder head mounting bolts ONLY in the order shown. This will ensure proper cooling system and combustion chamber sealing—4.6L DOHC engine

To install:

➡ **Lightly oil all bolt and stud threads prior to assembly with clean engine oil.**

19. Clean the cylinder head, intake manifold and valve cover gasket mating surfaces thoroughly. Ensure that all bolt holes are clean and dry. Remove all engine coolant residue prior to reassembly.

20. If a cylinder head was removed for head gasket replacement, inspect the cylinder head for warpage. If a cylinder head is warped, have it ground by a competent machine shop before installing.

➡ **The following step ensures that all of the pistons are below the top of the engine block deck face.**

21. Rotate the crankshaft counterclockwise 90 degrees.

22. Inspect the cylinder head face surface for scratches near the coolant passages and combustion chambers.

23. Position the new cylinder head gasket(s) on the engine block, then install the cylinder head(s).

❉❉ WARNING

Cylinder head mounting bolts must be replaced with new bolts; do NOT reuse original cylinder head mounting bolts. They are torque-to-yield bolts and cannot be reused; otherwise, engine damage may occur.

24. Apply clean engine oil to both sides of the cylinder head mounting bolts and both sides of the washer faces.

25. Tighten the left cylinder head bolts in the sequence shown in the accompanying illustration, as follows:

a. Tighten the bolts to 28–31 ft. lbs. (37–43 Nm).

b. Then, tighten the bolts an additional 85–95 degrees.

c. Finally, tighten the bolts an additional 85–95 degrees again.

26. Perform Step 23 for the right-hand cylinder head as well.

27. Install the outlet heater water hose on the left-hand cylinder head. Tighten the upper mounting bolt to 15–22 ft. lbs. (20–30 Nm) and the lower bolt to 71–106 inch lbs. (8–12 Nm).

28. Install the inlet heater water hose on the right-hand cylinder head. Tighten the upper mounting bolt to 15–22 ft. lbs. (20–30 Nm) and the two lower bolts to 71–106 inch lbs. (8–12 Nm).

Refer to Section 1 for engine rebuilding specifications

29. Install the primary timing chains and set valve timing.

30. Install the rocker arms.

31. Install the crankshaft position sensor pulse wheel.

32. Install the intake manifolds.

➡ **When cleaning the sealing surfaces of the engine front cover and the oil pan-to-engine block joints, be careful to avoid damaging the oil pan gasket rubber bead. If a leak develops after reassembly, the oil pan must be removed and the oil pan gasket replaced.**

33. Install the engine front cover.

34. Install the exhaust manifolds.

35. Install the engine in the vehicle.

✳✳ WARNING

It is very important to fill the engine with oil prior to starting it. Excessive engine damage will result if the engine is run without oil.

36. If necessary, fill the engine with the proper type and amount of clean engine oil.

37. Fill the engine cooling system.

38. Connect the positive, then the negative battery cables.

39. Start the engine and check for exhaust, coolant, fuel and oil leaks.

40. Shut the engine **OFF** and check the engine oil level; add oil, if necessary.

Rocker Arms

REMOVAL & INSTALLATION

3.8L Engine

➡ **During this procedure, always keep the parts in order so that they may be reinstalled in their original positions.**

1. Before servicing the vehicle, refer to the precautions in the beginning of this section.

2. Remove the valve cover(s) from the engine.

3. Loosen the rocker arm fulcrum (seat) mounting bolts from the cylinder head, then lift the rocker arms, fulcrums and bolts off of the head.

4. If necessary, the pushrods may be removed from the engine at this time. If removing more than one pushrod at a time, be sure to label them so that they can be installed in their original positions.

To install:

5. If removed, install the pushrods in their original positions, after lubricating

their tips with engine assembly lube (such as Ford D9AZ-19579-D).

6. Lubricate the rocker arms and fulcrums with engine assembly lube prior to installation.

7. Install each rocker arm, one at a time, as follows:

a. Rotate the crankshaft so that the valve lifter (tappet), which corresponds to the rocker arm being installed, rests on the base circle of the camshaft (the camshaft lobe points away from the valve lifter). This position can be found by depressing the pushrod while having an assistant rotate the crankshaft with a socket and ratchet wrench on the crankshaft pulley/damper center bolt; when the pushrod is at its lowest point, the lobe is pointing away from the lifter.

b. Position the rocker arm over the pushrods and mounting bolt holes.

c. Install the rocker arm fulcrum and mounting bolt. Tighten the mounting bolt to a maximum of 44 inch lbs. (5 Nm).

8. Perform Step 4 for each of the rocker arms requiring installation.

➡ **For the final-tightening of the rocker arm mounting bolts, the camshaft can be in any position.**

9. Final-tighten the rocker arm fulcrum bolts to 23–29 ft. lbs. (30–40 Nm).

10. Install the valve cover(s).

4.6L Engines

On this engine, the cam followers (rocker arms) are part of the hydraulic valve lash adjustment assembly. The hydraulic lash adjusters are placed at the fulcrum point of the rocker arms and act in a manner similar to hydraulic lifters in pushrod engines.

➡ **Be sure to keep the rocker arms and valve tappets in order so that they can be installed in their original positions.**

1. Before servicing the vehicle, refer to the precautions in the beginning of this section.

2. Remove the valve covers.

➡ **The only difference between the SOHC and DOHC engines for this procedure is simply that the DOHC engine has twice as many valves, rocker arms and valve tappets. The removal and installation technique is the same, regardless of which valve is being serviced, or which engine is being serviced.**

VALVE SPRING COMPRESSOR

VALVE SPRING SPACER

VIEW A

VALVE SPRING SPACER

VIEW A

7922NG13

To properly depress the valve and spring, use both the valve spring spacer and compressor tools

3. Rotate the crankshaft so that the position of the piston in the cylinder being serviced is at the bottom of its stroke, and the base circle of the camshaft is resting against the rocker arm.

✳✳ WARNING

A valve spring spacer, such as Ford Tool T91P-6565-AH or equivalent, must be used in order to prevent the valve spring retainer from contacting the valve stem seal, which can result in damage to the seal.

4. Install the valve spring spacer between the valve spring coils.

5. Install a valve spring compressor, such as Ford Tool T91P-6565-A or equivalent, under the camshaft and on top of the valve spring retainer.

6. Slowly push down on the compressor tool until the spring is depressed far enough to allow the rocker arm to be removed, then pull the rocker arm out from underneath the camshaft.

7. Remove the valve spring compressor and spacer tools.

8. Repeat Steps 2 through 6 for all of the rocker arms needing removal.

9. If necessary, pull the hydraulic valve tappets out of the cylinder head(s).

10. Thoroughly clean the valve tappets and rocker arms with clean solvent, then wipe them with a lint-free cloth. Do not immerse the valve tappet in solvent.

11. Inspect the valve tappet, and discard it if any part shows signs of pitting, scoring, or excessive wear.

To install:

12. Apply clean engine oil to the valve stems and tips, the rocker arm roller surfaces, the valve tappets, and the valve tappet bores in the cylinder head(s).

➡**The valve tappets must not have more than 0.059 in. (1.5mm) of plunger travel prior to installation.**

13. If removed earlier, insert the tappets in their original bores in the cylinder head(s).

14. Rotate the crankshaft so that the position of the piston in the cylinder being serviced is at the bottom of its stroke, and the base circle of the camshaft is facing where the rocker arm will be installed.

15. Install the valve spring spacer and compressor tools as before.

16. Carefully depress the valve spring with the compressor tool until the rocker

arm can be positioned between the valve stem and valve tappet, and the camshaft.

17. Slowly allow the valve spring to decompress, and ensure that the rocker arm is properly retained.

18. Remove the valve spring compressor and spacer tools.

19. Repeat Steps 13 through 17 for all of the rocker arms.

20. Install the valve covers.

21. Start the engine and check for oil leaks from the valve cover gaskets.

Intake Manifold

The 3.8L and 4.6L DOHC engines covered by this manual utilize an upper and lower intake manifold assembly. If necessary, only the upper intake manifold may be removed by following the intake manifold procedure up to that point. Obviously, installation would also begin at the upper intake steps.

REMOVAL & INSTALLATION

➡**Any time the upper or lower intake manifold has been removed, cover all openings with a rag or a sheet of plastic to prevent dirt, debris or, more importantly, a loose nut from falling into the engine.**

3.8L Engine

1. Before servicing the vehicle, refer to the precautions in the beginning of this section.

2. Remove the air inlet tube from the throttle body.

3. Detach the accelerator cable from the throttle body, then remove the cable bracket bolts and position the cable and bracket aside.

4. If equipped, remove the speed control actuator.

5. Detach and label any necessary engine harness wiring connectors and vacuum lines.

6. If necessary, remove the throttle body at this time.

7. Remove the EGR valve from the Upper Intake Manifold (UIM).

8. Remove the engine support and wiring retainer bracket (located on the front, left-hand side of the engine).

➡**Note the original locations of the UIM mounting bolts/studs for reinstallation.**

9. Remove the UIM mounting bolts/studs.

10. Lift the UIM off of the Lower Intake Manifold (LIM). Remove the old UIM-to-LIM gasket.

➡**If only the UIM is to be serviced, stop at this point (and resume installation at Step 23).**

11. Remove the fuel injectors and fuel supply manifold.

12. Remove the heater water outlet hose from the LIM.

➡**Note the original locations of the LIM mounting bolts/studs for reinstallation.**

13. Remove the LIM mounting bolts/studs.

✳✳ WARNING

The LIM may be sealed at the front and rear with silicone sealant. It may be necessary to use a prytool to loosen the intake manifold. If it is necessary to use a prytool, use care to avoid damaging the manifold, cylinder head and engine block machined surfaces.

14. Lift the LIM up and off of the engine. Remove and discard the old gaskets and end seals.

15. If a new manifold is to be installed, transfer the following components to the new manifold:

- Water hose connection and thermostat
- Engine Coolant Temperature (ECT) sensor
- Coolant outlet elbow
- All vacuum and electrical fittings

To install:

➡**Lightly oil all mounting bolt/stud threads before installation.**

16. Clean the UIM and LIM, cylinder head and engine block gasket surfaces of all old gasket material or dirt. Use Ford Metal Surface Cleaner F4AZ-19A536-RGH or equivalent to clean the gasket surfaces of all residues which may interfere with the new sealant's adhesion.

17. Apply a dab of Ford Gasket and Trim Adhesive D7AZ-19B508-B or equivalent to each cylinder head mating surface, then press the new LIM gasket into place.

➡**When using silicone sealant, assembly must occur within 15 minutes after the sealant is applied, otherwise the sealing ability may be jeopardized.**

FRONT OF ENGINE

LOWER INTAKE MANIFOLD

7922NG16

Be sure to tighten the lower intake manifold mounting bolts in the sequence shown—3.8L engine

FRONT OF ENGINE

Bolt

Stud bolt

Bolt

Upper intake manifold

Gasket

Lower intake manifold

Locating pins

7922NG17

When installing the upper intake manifold, tighten the upper-to-lower manifold attaching bolts in the sequence shown—3.8L engine

18. Apply a 1/8 in. (3–4mm) bead of Ford Silicone Rubber D6AZ-19562-BA or equivalent to each corner where the cylinder head meets the engine block.

19. Install the new front and rear LIM end seals.

20. Carefully lower the LIM onto the cylinder heads and engine block.

21. Install the LIM mounting bolts/studs in their original positions. Tighten the bolts/studs in the sequence shown in the accompanying illustration in the following two steps:

    a. Tighten the bolts/studs to 45 inch lbs. (5 Nm).

    b. Then, tighten the bolts/studs to 71–106 inch lbs. (8–12 Nm).

22. Install the front crankcase ventilation tube so that the retaining bracket is positioned over the LIM stud. Then, install the retaining nut and tighten it to 15–22 ft. lbs. (20–30 Nm).

23. Install the fuel injectors and fuel supply manifold.

24. Position the new UIM-to-LIM gasket on the LIM, then set the UIM on the gasket.

25. Apply a light coating of Ford Pipe Sealant with Teflon• D8AZ-19554-A, or equivalent, to the threads of the UIM mounting bolts/studs.

26. Install the bolts/studs in their original positions. Tighten the bolts/studs in the sequence shown in the accompanying illustration in the following three steps:

    a. Tighten the bolts/studs to 88 inch lbs. (10 Nm).

    b. Then, tighten the bolts/studs to 177 inch lbs. (20 Nm).

    c. Finally, tighten them to 24 ft. lbs. (32 Nm).

27. Install the engine support and wiring retainer bracket. Tighten the mounting bolt to 15–22 ft. lbs. (20–30 Nm) and the nut to 71–97 inch lbs. (8–11 Nm).

28. Install the EGR valve and the throttle body (if removed).

29. Attach all necessary wiring and vacuum lines.

30. Install the accelerator cable bracket and attach the cable to the throttle body. Tighten the bracket mounting bolts to 124–177 inch lbs. (14–20 Nm).

31. If applicable, attach the speed control actuator.

32. Install the air inlet tube.

33. Start the engine and check for leaks.

4.6L SOHC Engine

1. Before servicing the vehicle, refer to the precautions in the beginning of this section.

2. Disconnect the negative battery cable.

3. Drain the engine cooling system and relieve fuel system pressure. Detach the fuel lines from the fuel supply manifold.

4. Remove the air inlet tube.

5. Remove the accessory drive belt.

❋❋ WARNING

When removing the spark plug wires, only pull on the spark plug wire boot. Otherwise, the wire may separate from the connector in the boot, necessitating plug wire replacement.

6. Label and remove all spark plug wires and wire separators.

7. Remove the ignition coils, the alternator and their mounting brackets from the engine.

8. Apply the parking brake and block the rear wheels, then raise and safely support the front of the vehicle.

9. Disconnect all necessary wiring.

10. Disconnect the EGR valve-to-exhaust manifold tube from the right-hand exhaust manifold.

11. Lower the vehicle.

12. Label and disconnect all applicable wiring, vacuum lines, cooling system hoses and throttle body cables from the intake manifold or engine which will interfere with manifold removal.

➡Two water outlet connection retaining bolts also retain the intake manifold.

Be sure to tighten the intake manifold mounting bolts in the sequence shown—4.6 SOHC engine

For complete mechanical specifications, refer to Section 1 of this manual

13. Remove the two bolts retaining the water hose connection to the manifold, then position the upper radiator hose and connection out of the way.

14. Remove the remaining bolts, then lift the manifold up and off of the engine.

15. Remove and discard the old gaskets.

➡ **If a replacement intake manifold is being installed, transfer all necessary components to it from the old manifold.**

To install:

16. Thoroughly clean the cylinder head, engine block and intake manifold gasket surfaces.

17. Position the new intake manifold gaskets on the cylinder heads, then place the intake manifold on the heads.

➡ **After positioning the intake manifold, be sure that the alignment tabs on the intake manifold gasket are aligned with the holes in the cylinder heads.**

18. Install and tighten intake manifold mounting bolts Nos. 1 through 9 one at a time to 15–22 ft. lbs. (20–30 Nm), in the sequence shown.

19. Install a new O-ring on the water hose connection, then position the connection on the intake manifold and install the two mounting bolts to 15–22 ft. lbs. (20–30 Nm).

20. Attach all applicable wiring, vacuum lines, cooling system hoses and throttle body cables which were removed earlier.

21. Apply the parking brake and block the rear wheels, then raise and safely support the front of the vehicle.

22. Connect the EGR valve-to-exhaust manifold tube to the right-hand exhaust manifold; tighten the nut to 26–33 ft. lbs. (35–45 Nm).

23. Attach all applicable wiring, which was disconnected earlier.

24. Lower the vehicle and remove the blocks from the wheels.

25. Install the alternator, the ignition coils and their mounting brackets.

26. Install the spark plug wires, being sure to connect them to their applicable plugs and coil terminal towers.

27. Install the accessory drive belt and the air inlet tube.

28. Attach the fuel supply and return lines to the fuel supply manifold.

29. Connect the negative battery cable.

30. Fill and bleed the engine cooling system.

31. Start the engine and check for leaks.

4.6L DOHC Engine

1. Before servicing the vehicle, refer to the precautions in the beginning of this section.

2. Remove the engine compartment brace.

3. Disconnect the negative battery cable.

4. Remove the air inlet tube.

5. Remove the windshield wiper module.

6. Label and disconnect all applicable wiring, vacuum lines, cooling system hoses and throttle body cables from the intake manifold or engine which will interfere with manifold removal.

7. Remove the EGR valve and gasket from the Upper Intake Manifold (UIM).

8. For Lower Intake Manifold (LIM) removal, relieve fuel system pressure. Detach the fuel lines from the fuel supply manifold.

9. Drain the engine cooling system.

10. Remove the accessory drive belt.

11. Remove the ignition wire covers from the valve covers.

❋❋ WARNING

When removing the spark plug wires, only pull on the spark plug wire boot.

Otherwise, the wire may separate from the connector in the boot, necessitating plug wire replacement.

12. Label and remove all spark plug wires and all wire separators.

13. Remove the alternator and its mounting bracket from the engine.

14. If not already performed, detach the cooling system hoses from the water bypass tube.

15. Remove the two nuts retaining the water bypass tube to the manifold, then lift the bypass tube off of the UIM.

16. If necessary, remove the throttle body and the Idle Air Control (IAC) valve from the UIM.

17. Remove the mounting bolts, then lift the UIM up and off of the engine.

18. Remove and discard the old gaskets.

➡ **If only the UIM is to be serviced, stop at this point (and resume installation at Step 37).**

19. Disconnect the four engine wiring harness retaining clips from the LIM studs.

20. Label and unplug all of the fuel injector wiring connectors, then position the wiring aside.

FRONT OF ENGINE

7922NG19

When removing the lower intake manifold, be sure to loosen the mounting bolts in the order shown—1996–98 4.6L DOHC engine

FRONT OF ENGINE

LOOSEN IN SEQUENCE SHOWN

9300NG01

Loosen the lower intake manifold mounting bolts in the sequence shown—1999–00 4.6L DOHC engine

mating surfaces to ensure that no load limiting spacers (washers) are stuck to the surfaces.

➡️ **Usually, new load limiting spacers are included with the new LIM-to-IMRC manifold gaskets.**

28. Remove the protective paper from the adhesive backing on the IMRC upper gasket, then install it onto the top of the right-hand IMRC manifold using, if necessary, tapered pins at both end bolt hole locations for proper gasket alignment. Repeat this for the left-hand IMRC manifold as well.

29. Assemble the IMRC manifolds to the LIM, and install the four attaching bolts finger-tight.

30. Install the fuel injection supply manifold and fuel injectors. Install the four retaining bolts to 71–106 inch lbs. (8–12 Nm).

31. Position new LIM gaskets on the cylinder heads using the integral locating pins to properly align the gaskets.

32. Attach the fuel charging wiring to the IMRC actuator.

33. Set the LIM/IMRC manifold assembly on the engine. Install the bolts and stud bolts in locations Nos. 7, 8, 9 and 10 (refer

21. Loosen and remove the LIM mounting bolts and stud bolts in the sequence shown in the accompanying illustration.

22. Lift the LIM and the Intake Manifold Runner Control (IMRC) manifolds as one unit. Detach the fuel charging wiring from the IMRC actuator.

23. Disconnect the IMRC actuator cables from the IMRC levers and retaining brackets.

24. Remove the fuel injection supply manifold from the LIM.

25. If necessary, separate the IMRC manifolds from the LIM by removing the attaching bolts. Retain the load limiting spacers from the IMRC manifolds for reassembly.

➡️ **If a new or replacement lower or IMRC manifold is being installed, transfer all applicable components to the new manifold.**

To install:

26. Thoroughly clean all gasket surfaces. The sealing surfaces of the LIM and the IMRC manifolds should be cleaned with a suitable solvent to remove any residual adhesive film, which could adversely affect the sealing ability.

27. Inspect the LIM and IMRC manifold

FRONT OF ENGINE

7922NG20

When installing the lower intake manifold, tighten the mounting bolts only in the order shown—1996–98 4.6L DOHC engine

Please refer to Section 9 for electric cooling fan wiring schematics

Tighten the lower intake manifold mounting bolts in the sequence shown—1999–00 4.6L DOHC engine

Tighten the upper-to-lower intake manifold mounting bolts in the sequence shown—4.6L DOHC engine

to the accompanying torque sequence illustration). DO NOT tighten them yet. Then, install the bolts and stud bolts in positions Nos. 1, 2, 3, 4, 5 and 6. Now hand-tighten all bolts and stud bolts.

34. Following the sequence shown in the accompanying illustration, tighten fasteners 1 through 10 to 15–22 ft. lbs. (20–30 Nm).

35. Tighten the four IMRC-to-LIM attaching bolts to 71–106 inch lbs. (8–12 Nm).

36. Connect the IMRC actuator cables to the retaining brackets and IMRC levers.

37. Reattach all fuel injection wiring to the injectors.

38. Clean the LIM-to-UIM gasket surfaces of all old gasket material and dirt, then install a new UIM-to-LIM gasket on the LIM.

39. Install and tighten the UIM mounting bolts in the sequence shown in the accompanying illustration to 71–106 inch lbs. (8–12 Nm).

40. Install the EGR valve.

41. If necessary, position the accelerator cable bracket on the UIM and install the attaching bolts to 71–106 inch lbs. (8–12 Nm).

42. If applicable, install the throttle body.

43. Install new O-rings on the water bypass tube, then install the bypass tube on the intake manifold as follows:

⁕⁕ WARNING

While installing the water bypass tube, be careful not to accidentally damage the new O-ring. Otherwise, coolant leakage may result.

a. Clean the O-ring sealing surface on the cylinder heads and coat the water bypass tube O-rings with a rubber lubricant (such as Ford ESE-M99B 176-A) or its equivalent.

b. Position the bypass tube support braces over the UIM inner studs and press the bypass tube into position.

c. Install and tighten the two bypass tube retaining nuts to 71–106 inch lbs. (8–12 Nm).

44. Install the alternator and bracket on the engine. Tighten the alternator fasteners to 15–22 ft. lbs. (20–30 Nm) and the alternator bracket fasteners to 71–106 inch lbs. (8–12 Nm).

45. Reattach all necessary wiring (including spark plug wires), vacuum lines, cooling system hoses and throttle body cables, which were detached during intake manifold removal.

46. Install the accessory drive belt.

47. Attach the fuel lines to the fuel supply manifold.

48. Install the air inlet tube.

49. Install the windshield wiper module.

50. Connect the negative battery cable.

51. Fill and bleed the engine cooling system.

52. Start the engine and check for leaks.

Exhaust Manifold

REMOVAL & INSTALLATION

3.8L Engine

1. Before servicing the vehicle, refer to the precautions in the beginning of this section.

2. For the left-hand manifold, remove the oil dipstick tube support bracket.

3. Label and detach the spark plug wires from the spark plugs and the ignition coil.

4. For the left-hand manifold, detach the Oxygen (O_2S) sensor wiring from the engine wiring harness.

5. For the right-hand manifold, disconnect the EGR valve-to-exhaust manifold tube from the exhaust manifold. Loosen the retaining nut, then remove the heater inlet tube and heater water hose.

6. Apply the parking brake and block the rear wheels, then raise and safely support the front of the vehicle.

7. Separate the exhaust system pipe from the exhaust manifold by removing the retaining nuts.

8. For the right-hand manifold, remove the heated O_2S sensor from the exhaust manifold.

9. Lower the vehicle.

10. Remove the exhaust manifold mounting bolts, then lift the manifold up and off of the engine.

11. Remove and discard the old exhaust manifold gasket.

To install:

➡**Lightly oil all bolt and stud threads, except any requiring special sealant, with clean oil prior to installation.**

12. If a new exhaust manifold is being installed, or if a new manifold-to-exhaust pipe stud is needed, install the stud until it is securely seated in the manifold.

13. Clean the gasket surfaces of the exhaust manifold, cylinder head and exhaust pipe.

✳✳ WARNING

Do not allow anti-seize compound to enter the oxygen sensor flutes, otherwise possible damage to the sensor may occur.

14. For the left-hand manifold, apply high-temperature anti-seize compound to the O_2S sensor threads, then install the O_2S sensor in the manifold. Tighten the sensor to 28–33 ft. lbs. (37–45 Nm).

15. Install the exhaust manifold, along with a new gasket, on the cylinder head. Install two new retaining bolts loosely to hold them in place.

➡**According to the manufacturer, if slight warpage of the exhaust manifold causes a misalignment between the bolt holes in the cylinder head and exhaust manifold, the holes in the exhaust manifold should be elongated to provide proper alignment. However, DO NOT elongate the pilot hole (lower rear bolt hole on the No. 2 cylinder).**

16. Start the remaining mounting bolts, then (for the right-hand manifold only) loosely connect the EGR valve-to-exhaust manifold tube.

17. Tighten the exhaust manifold bolts in the sequence shown in the accompanying illustration to 22–26 ft. lbs. (30–36 Nm).

18. Apply the parking brake and block the rear wheels, then raise and safely support the front of the vehicle.

19. Connect the exhaust pipe to the manifold, then tighten the retaining nuts to 16–23 ft. lbs. (21–32 Nm).

✳✳ WARNING

Do not allow anti-seize compound to enter the oxygen sensor flutes, otherwise possible damage to the sensor may occur.

20. For the right-hand exhaust manifold, apply high-temperature anti-seize compound to the O_2S sensor threads, then install the O_2S sensor in the manifold. Tighten the sensor to 28–33 ft. lbs. (37–45 Nm).

21. Lower the vehicle and remove the wheel blocks.

22. For the right-hand exhaust manifold, install the heater inlet tube and the heater water hose. Tighten the retaining nut to 15–22 ft. lbs. (20–30 Nm). Then, tighten the EGR valve-to-exhaust manifold tube nuts to 25–34 ft. lbs. (34–47 Nm).

23. Install the spark plug wires, then start the engine and check for exhaust leaks.

4.6L SOHC Engine

1. Before servicing the vehicle, refer to the precautions in the beginning of this section.

2. Disconnect the negative battery cable.

3. For the left-hand manifold, remove the oil dipstick tube support bracket retaining bolt.

4. Apply the parking brake and block the rear wheels, then raise and safely support the front of the vehicle.

5. Separate the exhaust system pipe from the exhaust manifold by removing the retaining nuts. Support the exhaust system pipe from a crossmember with a piece of strong string or wire.

6. Disconnect the engine wiring from the Heated Oxygen (HO_2S) sensor, installed in the exhaust manifold.

7. For the left-hand exhaust manifold, detach the steering column shaft and position it out of the way.

7922NG24

To prevent possible exhaust leaks, tighten the manifold bolts in the sequence shown—3.8L engine

8. Lower the vehicle.

9. Remove the exhaust manifold retaining nuts, then lift the manifold up and off of the engine.

10. Remove and discard the old exhaust manifold gaskets.

To install:

➡ **Lightly oil all bolt and stud threads, except any requiring special sealant, with clean oil prior to installation.**

11. If a new exhaust manifold is being installed, transfer the EGR valve tube to the new manifold connector. Tighten the tube fastener to 33–47 ft. lbs. (45–65 Nm).

12. Clean the gasket surfaces of the exhaust manifold, cylinder head and exhaust pipe.

13. Install the exhaust manifold, along with a new gasket, on the cylinder head. Install the retaining nuts and tighten them, in sequence, to 159–195 inch lbs. (18–22 Nm).

14. If applicable, reattach the steering column shaft.

➡ **Loosen the line nut on the EGR valve before installing it onto the manifold.**

15. Attach the EGR valve-to-exhaust manifold tube to the left-hand exhaust manifold; tighten the tube nut to 26–33 ft. lbs. (35–45 Nm).

16. Apply the parking brake and block the rear wheels, then raise and safely support the front of the vehicle.

➡ **Ensure that the exhaust system is clear of the No. 3 crossmember; adjust it, as necessary.**

17. Connect the exhaust pipe to the manifold, then tighten the retaining nuts to 20–30 ft. lbs. (27–41 Nm).

18. Attach the engine wiring to the O_2S sensor(s), as necessary.

19. Lower the vehicle and remove the wheel blocks.

20. Connect the negative battery cable, then start the engine and check for exhaust leaks.

4.6L DOHC Engine

RIGHT-HAND MANIFOLD

1. Before servicing the vehicle, refer to the precautions in the beginning of this section.

2. Disconnect the negative battery cable.

7922NG25

When installing the exhaust manifolds, be sure to tighten the retaining nuts in the order shown—4.6L SOHC engine

7922NG26

Tighten the right-hand exhaust manifold retaining nuts in the order shown—4.6L DOHC engine

3. Remove the air inlet tube from the air cleaner housing and the throttle body.

4. Detach the secondary air injection manifold tube from the exhaust manifold.

5. Remove the four retaining nuts from the upper side of the exhaust manifold.

6. Apply the parking brake and block the rear wheels, then raise and safely support the front of the vehicle.

7. Separate the exhaust system pipe from the exhaust manifold by removing the retaining nuts. Support the exhaust system pipe from a crossmember with a piece of strong string or wire.

8. Remove the four retaining nuts from the lower side of the manifold, then remove the manifold from the engine.

9. Remove and discard the old exhaust manifold gasket.

To install:

➡**Lightly oil all bolt and stud threads, except any requiring special sealant, with clean oil prior to installation.**

10. Clean the gasket surfaces of the exhaust manifold, cylinder head and exhaust pipe.

11. Install the exhaust manifold, along with a new gasket, on the cylinder head. Install the eight retaining nuts and tighten

them, in the sequence shown in the accompanying illustration, to 159–195 inch lbs. (18–22 Nm).

12. Connect the exhaust pipe to the manifold, then tighten the retaining nuts to 20–30 ft. lbs. (27–41 Nm).

13. Lower the vehicle and remove the wheel blocks.

14. Reattach the secondary air injection manifold tube to the manifold. Tighten the retaining nut to 28–31 ft. lbs. (38–42 Nm).

15. Install the air inlet tube.

16. Connect the negative battery cable, then start the engine and check for exhaust leaks.

LEFT-HAND MANIFOLD

➡**A Ford Three-Bar Engine Support D88L-6000-A and Engine Lifting Bracket Set 014–00340, or equivalent tools, are necessary for this procedure.**

1. Before servicing the vehicle, refer to the precautions in the beginning of this section.

2. Disconnect the negative battery cable.

3. Install the engine lifting brackets on the engine, then position the three-bar engine support on the engine and attach it to the lifting brackets.

4. Loosen the front wheel lug nuts slightly, then apply the parking brake and block the rear wheels. Raise and safely support the front of the vehicle.

5. Remove the front wheels.

6. Detach the secondary air injection manifold tube and the EGR valve-to-exhaust manifold tube from the exhaust manifold.

7. Remove the front exhaust system pipe.

8. Detach both front suspension lower control arms and outer tie rod ends from the front wheel hub/spindle assemblies.

9. Detach the steering column shaft at the pinch bolt joint and position it out of the way.

10. Support the front sub-frame assembly with a floor jack.

11. Remove the front engine support insulator through-bolts.

12. Remove the front sub-frame bolts.

13. Carefully lower the front sub-frame.

14. Remove the retaining nuts from the exhaust manifold, then remove and discard the old exhaust manifold gasket.

To install:

➡**Lightly oil all bolt and stud threads, except any requiring special sealant, with clean oil prior to installation.**

When installing the left-hand exhaust manifold, be sure to tighten the mounting nuts in the sequence shown—4.6L DOHC engine

Timing belt service is covered in Section 5 of this manual

15. Clean the gasket surfaces of the exhaust manifold, cylinder head and exhaust pipe.

16. Install the exhaust manifold, along with new gaskets, on the cylinder head. Install the eight retaining nuts and tighten them, in the sequence shown in the accompanying illustration, to 159–195 inch lbs. (18–22 Nm).

17. Attach the EGR valve-to-exhaust manifold tube to the exhaust manifold. Tighten the nut to 30–33 ft. lbs. (40–45 Nm).

18. Connect the secondary air injection manifold tube to the exhaust manifold. Tighten the nut to 28–31 ft. lbs. (38–42 Nm).

19. Raise the front sub-frame assembly into position, then install and tighten the sub-frame bolts to 70–96 ft. lbs. (95–131 Nm).

20. Attach the steering column shaft to the pinch bolt joint.

21. Reattach the front suspension control arms and tie rod ends to the spindle/hub assemblies.

22. Install the front exhaust system pipe.

23. Install the wheels, then lower the vehicle and remove the wheel blocks.

24. Remove the three-bar engine support and lifting brackets from the engine.

25. Connect the negative battery cable, then start the engine and check for exhaust leaks.

26. Turn the rear suspension leveler compressor switch ON, then shut the trunk lid.

Camshaft and Valve Lifters

REMOVAL & INSTALLATION

3.8L Engine

VALVE LIFTERS

➡**Before replacing a valve lifter because of noisy operation, ensure that the noise is not caused by improper valve-to-rocker arm clearance, or by worn rocker arms or pushrods.**

1. Before servicing the vehicle, refer to the precautions in the beginning of this section.

2. Remove the valve covers.

3. Remove the upper and lower intake manifolds.

➡**Be sure to label or arrange the rocker arms, pushrods and valve tappets so that they can be reinstalled in their original locations.**

4. Remove the rocker arms and pushrods.

5. Remove the bolts holding the two tappet retainers in place (the bolts are held captive in retainers). Remove the six valve tappet guide plates from adjacent tappets.

6. Using a magnet, remove the tappets from their bores. If the valve tappets are stuck in their bores due to excessive varnish or gum build-up, use a claw-type tappet removal tool or equivalent. When using such a tool, rotate the tappets back and forth to loosen the build-up.

To install:

➡**Lightly oil all bolt and stud threads prior to assembly, except those specifying sealant, with clean engine oil.**

7. Clean the cylinder head and valve cover sealing surfaces of all old gasket material, dirt and oil residue.

8. Lubricate each valve tappet and bore with engine assembly lubricant.

9. Insert each valve tappet into its original bore. If new tappets are being installed, check for a free fit in the bore into which they are to be installed.

10. Align the flats on the sides of the valve tappets, then install the six guide plates between adjacent tappets, making sure that the word **UP** is showing.

11. Install the valve tappet retainers and tighten the mounting bolts to 88–124 inch lbs. (10–14 Nm).

12. Install the pushrods and rocker arms.

13. Install the lower and upper intake manifolds.

14. Install the valve covers.

15. Start the engine and check for leaks.

CAMSHAFT

1. Before servicing the vehicle, refer to the precautions in the beginning of this section.

2. If the vehicle is equipped with A/C, remove the condenser core.

3. Remove the radiator and radiator grille.

4. Remove the Camshaft Position (CMP) sensor and housing.

5. Remove the valve tappets.

6. Remove the engine front cover, timing chain and camshaft sprocket spacer.

7. Remove the oil pan.

8. Remove the mounting bolts, then remove the camshaft thrust plate.

9. Carefully slide the camshaft out of the front of the engine block, making sure not to damage the camshaft bearing surfaces and lobes.

To install:

➡**Lightly oil all bolt and stud threads prior to assembly, except those specifying sealant, with clean engine oil.**

10. Lubricate the camshaft lobes and bearing journals with engine assembly lubricant.

11. Carefully slide the camshaft into the engine block, making sure not to damage the bearing or lobe surfaces.

12. Install the camshaft thrust plate, and tighten the mounting bolts to 71–124 inch lbs. (8–14 Nm).

13. Install the camshaft gear spacer, timing chain and engine front cover.

14. Install the oil pan.

15. Install the valve tappets and related components.

16. Install the upper and lower intake manifolds.

17. Install the valve covers.

18. Install the CMP sensor and housing.

19. Install the radiator grille and radiator.

✳✳ WARNING

It is extremely important to fill the engine with oil prior to starting it, otherwise severe engine damage will occur.

20. Fill the engine with the proper amount and type of clean engine oil.

21. Fill the cooling system.

22. Connect the negative battery cable, then start the engine and check for oil, coolant and fuel leaks.

23. After 3–5 minutes, stop the engine.

24. Wait 10 minutes, then check the oil level with the dipstick. Add more oil, if necessary.

25. If necessary, install the A/C condenser core and the recharge the system.

4.6L Engines

➡**The 4.6L engines do not possess removable camshaft bearings. If the bearing surfaces are damaged, the cylinder head must either be serviced or replaced.**

1. Before servicing the vehicle, refer to the precautions in the beginning of this section.

2. Remove the valve covers.

3. Remove the engine front cover.

4. Remove the timing chains.

✳✳ WARNING

The crankshaft must be positioned so that the keyway is 45 degrees (SOHC

engines) or 90 degrees (DOHC engines) counterclockwise from the 12 o'clock position in order to avoid damaging the valves when the camshafts are rotated.

5. Rotate the crankshaft 45 degrees (SOHC engines) or 90 degrees (DOHC engines) counterclockwise.

6. Rotate the camshaft so that the base circle of the camshaft is positioned against the rocker arm being serviced.

A valve spring spacer, such as Ford Tool T91P-6565-AH or its equivalent, must be used in order to prevent the valve spring retainer from contacting the valve stem seal, which can result in damage to the seal.

7. Install the valve spring spacer between the valve spring coils.

8. Install a valve spring compressor, such as Ford Tool T91P-6565-A or its equivalent, under the camshaft and on top of the valve spring retainer.

9. Slowly push down on the compressor tool until the spring is depressed far enough to allow the rocker arm to be removed, then pull the rocker arm out from underneath the camshaft.

10. Remove the valve spring compressor and spacer tools.

11. Repeat Steps 6 through 10 until all of the rocker arms are removed from the cylinder head(s).

12. If necessary, pull the hydraulic valve tappets out of the cylinder head(s).

➡ On the DOHC engine, note the positions of the bearing cap bolts because they are various lengths.

13. Remove the camshaft bearing cap bolts from the cylinder head(s), then tap upward on the bearing caps at the positions shown in the accompanying illustration. Gradually lift the bearing caps off of the cylinder head(s).

14. Lift the camshaft(s) straight upward to avoid damaging the camshaft bearing surfaces.

15. Thoroughly clean the valve tappets and rocker arms with clean solvent, then wipe them with a lint-free cloth. Do not immerse the valve tappet in solvent.

16. Inspect the valve tappet, and discard it if any part shows signs of pitting, scoring, or excessive wear.

To install:

17. Clean and inspect the valve cover, engine front cover and cylinder head gasket mating surfaces.

18. Apply clean engine oil to the camshaft journals on the cylinder head(s), then gently lay the camshaft(s) on the cylinder head(s).

19. Apply clean engine oil to the camshaft lobes and journals.

On the SOHC engine, rotate the crankshaft 45 degrees counterclockwise before depressing the valve and springs—4.6L SOHC engine

On the DOHC engine, the crankshaft must be rotated 90 degrees counterclockwise to ensure that the valves will not contact the pistons when depressed—4.6L DOHC engine

The bearing cap bolts on DOHC engines should be installed as follows:

• 2 in. (52mm) long bolts—intake camshaft bearing caps and inboard side of the exhaust camshaft bearing caps

• 1.6 in. (42mm) long bolts—outboard side of the exhaust camshaft bearing caps

20. Install and seat the camshaft bearing caps. Install and hand-tighten the bearing cap retaining bolts.

➡**Each camshaft bearing cap is tightened individually.**

21. Tighten the bearing cap bolts, in the sequence shown in the accompanying illustration, to 71–106 inch lbs. (8–12 Nm).

22. Loosen the bearing cap bolts approximately 2 revolutions, or until the head of the bolt turns freely.

➡**The camshaft should spin freely with a slight drag.**

23. Retighten the bearing cap bolts, in sequence, to 71–106 inch lbs. (8–12 Nm).

24. Check camshaft end-play.

25. Apply clean engine oil to the valve stems and tips, the rocker arm roller surfaces, the valve tappets, and the valve tappet bores in the cylinder head(s).

➡**The valve tappets must not have more than 0.059 in. (1.5mm) of plunger travel prior to installation.**

26. If removed earlier, insert the tappets in their original bores in the cylinder head(s).

27. Rotate the crankshaft clockwise 45 degrees (for SOHC engines) or 90 degrees (for DOHC engines)—until the keyway is at the 12 o'clock position.

28. Install the timing chains and the engine front cover.

29. Install the rocker arms, as follows:

a. Rotate the crankshaft so that the position the piston of the cylinder being serviced is at the bottom of its stroke and the base circle of the camshaft is facing where the rocker arm will be installed.

b. Install the valve spring spacer and compressor tools as before.

c. Carefully depress the valve spring with the compressor tool until the rocker arm can be positioned between the valve stem and valve tappet, and the camshaft.

d. Slowly allow the valve spring to decompress, and ensure that the rocker arm is properly retained.

e. Remove the valve spring compressor and spacer tools.

f. Repeat Steps **a** through **e** for all of the rocker arms.

30. Install the valve covers.

31. Start the engine and check for leaks.

To remove the camshaft bearing caps, tap the caps with a rubber or leather mallet where shown—4.6L engines

Tighten the camshaft bearing cap mounting bolts in the sequence indicated—4.6L SOHC engine

INTAKE
CAP ASSY

EXHAUST
CAP ASSY

7922NG32

DOHC engine camshaft bearing cap mounting bolt torque sequence—4.6L DOHC engine

Oil Pan

REMOVAL & INSTALLATION

3.8L Engine

1. Before servicing the vehicle, refer to the precautions in the beginning of this section.

2. Disconnect the negative battery cable.

3. Remove the air inlet tube from the throttle body and air cleaner housing.

4. Remove the upper radiator plastic cover and the hood weather seal.

5. Remove the windshield wiper arms.

6. Remove the left-hand cowl vent screen and the windshield wiper module.

7. Install an engine support tool, such as the Ford Three Bar Engine Support D88L-6000-A. Do not support the weight of the engine yet.

8. Apply the parking brake and block the rear wheels, then raise and safely support the front of the vehicle.

9. Remove the front engine mount through-bolts.

10. Using the engine support tool, raise the engine slightly.

11. Remove the starter motor.

12. If equipped, remove the automatic transmission cooler lines.

13. Drain the engine oil and remove the engine oil filter.

14. Remove the oil pan-to-bell housing bolts and the bolts at the Crankshaft Position (CKP) sensor lower shield.

15. Remove the remaining oil pan mounting bolts.

16. Separate the steering column shaft at the pinch bolt joint.

17. Position a transmission jack under the front sub-frame, then support the front sub-frame with the jack.

18. Matchmark the sub-frame position in relation to the vehicle chassis for reinstallation purposes.

19. Remove the six rear and the two front mounting bolts from the front sub-frame.

20. Remove the lower shock absorber-to-lower control arm bolts and nuts on both sides of the vehicle.

21. Cautiously lower the front sub-frame.

22. Remove the oil pan. Pour any residual oil out of the oil pan.

23. If necessary, remove the oil pump screen and tube retainer bolts, and support bracket nut. Remove the oil pump screen cover and tube. Discard the old oil pump inlet tube gasket.

To install:

24. Install the oil pump screen cover and tube, along with a new gasket. Tighten the retaining bolts to 15–22 ft. lbs. (20–30 Nm) and the bracket nut to 30–40 ft. lbs. (40–55 Nm).

25. Trial fit the oil pan on the engine block to ensure that there is adequate clearance to prevent the new sealer from being scraped off of the engine block by the oil pan.

26. Clean the mating surfaces of the oil pan and engine block of all old sealant and oil residue with Ford Metal Surface Cleaner F4AZ-19A536-RA or equivalent.

➡It is imperative to use the proper solvent when cleaning the engine block-to-oil pan surfaces, otherwise the new sealer may not adhere properly. Also, when using silicone sealer, assembly must be performed within 15 minutes

Refer to Section 1 for engine rebuilding specifications

Be sure to tighten the oil pan mounting bolts in the sequence shown to ensure proper sealing—3.8L engine

of applying the sealer, otherwise the sealer will start to set-up and lose its sealing effectiveness.

27. Apply a bead of silicone sealer, such as Ford Silicone Gasket and Sealant F6AZ-19652-AA, to the oil pan.

28. Install the oil pan, then install all of the oil pan mounting bolts. Tighten the bolts, in the sequence shown in the accompanying illustration, to 80–106 inch lbs. (9–12 Nm).

29. Raise the front sub-frame into position, then install the lower shock absorber mounting bolts and nuts to 103–143 ft. lbs. (140–195 Nm).

30. Install the two front and six rear sub-frame bolts loosely.

31. Adjust the position of the front sub-frame assembly until the matchmarks are correctly aligned. Then, tighten the large sub-frame bolts to 83–113 ft. lbs. (113–153 Nm) and the small bolts to 72–97 ft. lbs. (98–132 Nm).

➡It is important that the front sub-frame be realigned as when removed to ensure proper chassis geometry.

32. Connect the steering column shaft at the pinch bolt joint. Tighten the pinch bolt to 30–42 ft. lbs. (41–57 Nm).

33. Install the starter motor and the automatic transmission cooler lines, when applicable.

34. Install the engine oil drain plug and a new oil filter.

➡When seating the engine on the mounts, set it on the left-hand side mount first.

35. Slowly lower the engine until it is resting on the front engine mounts, then install the mount through-bolts. Tighten them to 35–50 ft. lbs. (47–68 Nm).

36. Lower the vehicle and remove the rear wheel blocks.

37. Remove the engine support tool.

38. Install the wiper module and left-hand cowl vent screen.

39. Install the windshield wiper arms and the hood weather seal.

40. Install the radiator upper plastic cover and the air inlet tube.

41. Fill the engine with oil.

42. Connect the negative battery cable, then start the engine and check for oil leaks.

43. After 3–5 minutes, stop the engine and check the oil level; add more oil if necessary.

4.6L SOHC Engine

1. Before servicing the vehicle, refer to the precautions in the beginning of this section.

2. Properly discharge the A/C system.

3. Disconnect the negative battery cable.

4. Remove the air inlet tube from the throttle body and air cleaner housing.

5. Drain the engine cooling system.

6. Remove the cooling fan assembly.

7. Relieve fuel system pressure, then detach the fuel lines from the engine.

8. Remove the upper radiator hose.

9. Remove the windshield wiper governor and support bracket.

10. Remove the A/C hose-to-right-hand ignition coil bracket retaining bolt.

11. Label and disengage the engine wiring harness 42-pin and 8-pin connectors.

12. Remove the EGR backpressure transducer, and disconnect the heater water hose.

13. Detach the heater water hose from the left-hand cylinder head, then position it aside.

14. Remove the heater blower switch resistor.

15. Remove the right-hand front engine mount-to-front sub-frame bolt.

16. Disconnect the vacuum hose from the EGR valve.

17. Detach the EGR backpressure transducer hoses from the EGR valve-to-exhaust manifold tube.

18. Remove the EGR valve from the throttle body.

19. Apply the parking brake and block the rear wheels, then raise and safely support the front of the vehicle.

20. Drain the engine oil.

21. Remove both front engine mount through-bolts.

22. Remove the EGR valve-to-manifold tube nut from the left-hand exhaust manifold, then remove the tube.

23. Detach the exhaust system pipes from the exhaust manifolds. Suspend the exhaust pipes with strong cord or wire from the crossmember.

24. Position a floor jack and a block of wood beneath the oil pan, just rearward of the oil drain plug, then raise the engine approximately 4 inches (10cm). Insert two wood blocks (approximately 2.5–2.75 in./60–70mm thick) under each front engine mount. Carefully lower the engine onto the wood blocks, once the engine is securely settled, remove the floor jack from beneath the oil pan.

➡It may be necessary to loosen, not remove, the two transmission mount nuts.

25. Using a floor jack (a bottle jack may be necessary because of the lack of clearance), raise the transmission extension housing slightly.

7922NG35

Be sure to tighten the oil pan mounting bolts in the order shown for proper sealing—4.6L SOHC engine

26. Remove the oil pan mounting bolts, then lower the oil pan out of the vehicle.

27. If necessary, the oil pump screen cover and tube may be removed. Remove the old cover and tube gasket.

To install:

28. Clean the oil pan and inspect it for damage; replace it if necessary.

29. Clean the mating surfaces of the oil pan and engine block of all old sealant and oil residue with Ford Metal Surface Cleaner F4AZ-19A536-RA or equivalent.

➥It is imperative to use the proper solvent when cleaning the engine block-to-oil pan surfaces, otherwise the new sealer may not adhere properly.

30. Inspect the oil pump screen cover, tube and O-ring; replace any of them if necessary.

31. If necessary, position the oil pump screen cover and tube on the oil pump. Hand start the mounting bolts. Install the oil pump screen cover and tube-to-main bearing stud spacer retaining bolt hand-tight.

32. Tighten the oil pump screen cover and tube-to-oil pump bolts to 71–106 inch lbs. (8–12 Nm) and the oil pump screen cover and tube-to-main bearing stud spacer bolt to 15–22 ft. lbs. (20–30 Nm).

33. Install a new oil pan gasket on the oil pan.

➥When using silicone sealer, assembly must be performed within four minutes of applying the sealer, otherwise the sealer will start to set-up and lose its sealing effectiveness.

34. Apply a bead of silicone sealer, such as Ford Silicone Gasket and Sealant F6AZ-19652-AA or its equivalent, where the engine front cover, and the crankshaft rear oil seal retainer, meet the engine block.

35. Within four minutes of applying the silicone sealer, install the oil pan and retaining bolts. Tighten the bolts, in the sequence shown in the accompanying illustration, to 177 inch lbs. (20 Nm), then tighten all of the bolts an additional 60 degrees.

36. Position the floor jack under the oil pan and raise the engine to remove the wood blocks.

37. Lower the engine onto the front engine mounts, then remove the floor jack.

38. Install the front engine mounts' through-bolts and tighten them to 15–22 ft. lbs. (20–30 Nm).

➥Prior to installation, loosen the nut at the EGR valve. This will allow adequate movement to align the EGR valve bolts.

39. Install the EGR valve-to-exhaust manifold tube. Tighten the line nut to 26–33 ft. lbs. (35–45 Nm).

40. Attach the exhaust system pipes to the exhaust manifolds.

41. Install a new engine oil filter, and install the oil pan drain plug.

42. Lower the vehicle and remove the rear wheel blocks.

43. Install the right-hand front engine mount-to-front sub-frame retaining bolt and tighten it to 15–22 ft. lbs. (20–30 Nm).

44. Install the EGR valve along with a new gasket.

45. Install the heater blower motor switch resistor.

46. Install the EGR backpressure transducer bracket and heater water hose. Tighten the upper bolts to 15–22 ft. lbs. (20–30 Nm) and the lower bolts to 71–106 inch lbs. (8–12 Nm).

47. Connect the heater water hose.

48. Engage the 42-pin and 8-pin engine wiring harness connectors.

49. Install the upper radiator hose.

50. Connect the fuel lines.

51. Install the windshield wiper governor and retaining bracket.

52. Install the engine cooling fan.

53. Install the air inlet tube.

54. Fill the engine with the proper type and amount of clean engine oil.

55. Connect the negative battery cable, then start the engine and check for oil leaks.

56. After 3–5 minutes, stop the engine and check the oil level; add more oil if necessary.

57. Attach the A/C compressor line and evacuate and recharge the system.

4.6L DOHC Engine

1. Before servicing the vehicle, refer to the precautions in the beginning of this section.

2. Open the trunk lid and turn the suspension leveler compressor switch **OFF**.

3. Disconnect the negative battery cable.

4. Remove the engine oil dipstick.

5. Install an engine support device, such as the Ford Three Bar Engine Support D88L-6000-A or its equivalent, in the engine compartment, and attach it to engine lifting eyes, such as those found in the Rotunda Engine Lift Bracket Set 014-00340 or its equivalent.

6. Slightly loosen the front wheel lug nuts.

For engine torque specifications, refer to Section 1 of this manual

When installing the oil pan, be sure to tighten the mounting bolts in the order shown—4.6L DOHC engine

7. Apply the parking brake and block the rear wheels, then raise and safely support the front of the vehicle.

8. Remove the front wheels.

9. Drain the engine oil and remove the engine oil filter.

10. Detach the front, lower suspension control arms and outer tie rod ends from the front wheel hubs and spindles.

11. Disconnect the steering column shaft at the pinch bolt connection.

12. Matchmark the relationship between the front sub-frame and the vehicle's chassis for reinstallation purposes.

13. Support the front sub-frame with a floor jack and jack stands, then remove through-bolts from the front engine mounts.

14. Detach the front suspension struts from the lower control arms.

15. Remove the sub-frame mounting bolts.

16. Remove the jack stands, then carefully lower the front sub-frame with the floor jack.

17. If equipped, disengage the wiring from the low oil level sensor connector.

18. Detach the wiring from the oil pan rail.

19. Remove the oil pan mounting bolts, then separate the pan from the engine block and front engine cover.

20. If necessary, remove the oil pump screen cover and tube.

To install:

21. Clean the oil pan and inspect it for damage; replace it if necessary.

22. Clean the mating surfaces of the oil pan and engine block of all old sealant and oil residue with Ford Metal Surface Cleaner

F4AZ-19A536-RA or equivalent. If scraping is required, only use a plastic tool.

➡It is imperative to use the proper solvent when cleaning the engine block-to-oil pan surfaces, otherwise the new sealer may not adhere properly.

23. Inspect the oil pump screen cover and tube; replace either of them if necessary.

24. If necessary, position the oil pump screen cover and tube on the oil pump, along with a new gasket. Hand start the mounting bolts. Install the oil pump screen cover and tube-to-main bearing stud spacer retaining bolt hand-tight.

25. Tighten the oil pump screen cover and tube-to-oil pump bolts to 71–106 inch lbs. (8–12 Nm) and the oil pump screen cover and tube-to-main bearing stud spacer bolt to 15–22 ft. lbs. (20–30 Nm).

26. Install a new oil pan gasket on the oil pan.

➡When using silicone sealer, assembly must be performed within four minutes of applying the sealer, otherwise the sealer will start to set-up and lose its sealing effectiveness.

27. Apply a bead of silicone sealer, such as Ford Silicone Gasket and Sealant F6AZ-19652-AA, where the engine front cover, and the crankshaft rear oil seal retainer, meet the engine block.

28. Within four minutes of applying the silicone sealer, install the oil pan and retaining bolts. Tighten the bolts, in the sequence shown in the accompanying illustration, to 15–22 ft. lbs. (20–30 Nm).

29. If equipped, attach the wiring to the low oil level sensor connector, and attach the wiring harness to the oil pan rail.

30. Raise the sub-frame into position, install the front engine mount through-bolts, then install the front sub-frame mounting bolts.

31. Adjust the position of the front sub-frame assembly until the matchmarks are correctly aligned. Then, tighten the large sub-frame bolts to 83–113 ft. lbs. (113–153 Nm) and the small bolts to 72–97 ft. lbs. (98–132 Nm).

➡It is important that the front sub-frame be realigned as when removed to ensure proper chassis geometry.

32. Connect the steering column shaft at the pinch bolt joint. Tighten the pinch bolt to 30–42 ft. lbs. (41–57 Nm).

33. Reconnect the lower control arms and outer tie rod ends to the front wheel hubs and spindles.

34. Install the wheels and tighten the lug nuts until snug.

35. Install the oil pan drain plug to 97–142 inch lbs. (11–16 Nm) and a new engine oil filter hand-tight (follow the oil filter manufacturer's instructions).

36. Lower the vehicle and remove the rear wheel blocks. Fully tighten the lug nuts.

37. Remove the engine support device from the engine and engine compartment. Remove the lifting eye brackets from the engine.

✳✳ WARNING

It is extremely important to fill the engine with oil prior to starting it, otherwise severe engine damage will occur.

38. Fill the engine with the proper amount and type of clean engine oil.

39. Connect the negative battery cable, then start the engine and check for oil leaks.

40. After 3–5 minutes, stop the engine.

41. Wait 10 minutes, then check the oil level with the dipstick. Add more oil, if necessary.

42. Turn the rear suspension leveler compressor switch **ON**, then shut the trunk lid.

Oil Pump

REMOVAL & INSTALLATION

3.8L Engine

1. Before servicing the vehicle, refer to the precautions in the beginning of this section.

2. If necessary, remove the engine oil filter.

3. Remove the oil pump and filter body-to-engine front cover retaining bolts, then separate the oil pump from the front cover.

4. Inspect the oil pump sealing O-ring for damage or distortion.

To install:

5. Position the oil pump on the engine front cover, then install the mounting bolts.

6. Tighten the four large bolts to 17–23 ft. lbs. (23–32 Nm) and the two small bolts to 71–97 inch lbs. (8–11 Nm).

7. If necessary, install a new engine oil filter.

4.6L Engines

1. Before servicing the vehicle, refer to the precautions in the beginning of this section.

2. For the SOHC engine, remove the valve covers.

3. Remove the engine front cover.

4. Remove the oil pan, and oil pump screen cover and pick-up tube.

5. Remove the timing chain(s).

6. For the DOHC engine, remove the crankshaft sprockets.

7. Remove the four oil pump mounting bolts, then separate the oil pump from the engine block.

To install:

8. Rotate the inner rotor of the oil pump to align it with the flats on the crankshaft,

then install the oil pump on the engine block.

9. Install the four mounting bolts and tighten them to 71–106 inch lbs. (8–12 Nm).

10. Install a new engine oil filter.

11. If applicable, install the crankshaft sprockets.

12. Install the timing chain.

13. Install the oil pump screen cover and pick-up tube.

14. Install the oil pan.

15. Install the engine front cover.

16. If applicable, install the valve covers.

17. Fill the engine with oil.

18. Start the engine and check for oil leaks.

19. After 3–5 minutes, stop the engine.

20. Wait 10 minutes, then check the oil level with the dipstick. Add more oil, if necessary.

Rear Main Seal

REMOVAL & INSTALLATION

3.8L Engine

1. Before servicing the vehicle, refer to the precautions in the beginning of this section.

2. Disconnect the negative battery cable for safety.

3. Remove the flywheel or flexplate for access to the rear main seal.

Use extreme caution not to scratch the crankshaft oil seal surface.

4. Carefully punch 2 holes in the crankshaft rear oil seal on opposite sides of the crankshaft, just above the bearing cap-to-cylinder block split line. Install a sheet metal screw in each of the holes or use a small slide hammer to pry the crankshaft rear main oil seal from the block.

To install:

5. Clean the oil seal recess in the cylinder block and main bearing cap.

6. Coat the seal and the seal mounting surfaces with oil.

7. Position the seal on rear main seal installer T82L-6701-A, or equivalent, then position the tool and seal to the rear of the engine.

8. Alternate tightening the seal installer tool bolts until the seal is properly seated. The rear face of the seal must be within 0.020 in. (0.508mm).

9. Install the flywheel or flexplate, as applicable.

10. Connect the negative battery cable.

4.6L Engines

1. Before servicing the vehicle, refer to the precautions in the beginning of this section.

2. Disconnect the negative battery cable for safety.

3. Remove the flywheel or flexplate for access to the rear main seal.

4. Remove the crankshaft rear main oil seal retainer.

Use care to avoid damaging the retainer when removing the oil seal; a damaged retainer may allow oil to leak.

5. Securely support the oil seal retainer, then remove the oil seal from the retainer using a punch and a hammer.

To install:

6. Clean the crankshaft rear oil seal retainer and retainer-to-engine block mating surfaces of all dirt, grime and oil residue. The oil residue should be cleaned from the surfaces with an appropriate metal cleaner, such as Ford Metal Surface Cleaner F4AZ-19A536-RA or its equivalent. Also inspect for any damage.

OIL PUMP

BOLT

TIGHTEN TO
8-12 N·m
(71-106 LB-IN)

FRONT OF
ENGINE

CYLINDER BLOCK

7922NG37

Exploded view of the oil pump mounting on the 4.6L SOHC and DOHC engines

For complete mechanical specifications, refer to Section 1 of this manual

The one piece rear main seal on these engines is installed with a special installation tool—3.8L engine

Apply silicone gasket sealant to the engine block (as shown) to prevent oil leakage from the oil seal retainer

Position the oil seal retainer against the engine block, then install and tighten the mounting bolts in the sequence shown

➡ **Failure to clean the surfaces with the appropriate cleaning solvent can retard the new sealant's ability to adhere to the surfaces.**

7. Apply a continuous 0.06 in. (1.5mm) diameter bead of silicone gasket sealant, such as Ford Sealant F6AZ-19562-A or its equivalent, to the engine block as shown in the accompanying illustration.

8. Install the rear oil seal retainer on the engine block, then tighten the mounting fasteners to 71–106 inch lbs. (8–12 Nm) in the sequence shown.

9. Coat the seal and the seal mounting surfaces with oil.

10. Position the seal on rear main seal installer tool (Ford T82L-6701-A or equivalent) and the adapters (Ford T91P-6701-A or equivalent), then position the tool and seal on the rear of the engine.

11. Tighten the bolts alternately until the seal is properly seated.

12. Install the flywheel or flexplate, as applicable.

13. Connect the negative battery cable.

Timing Chain, Sprockets and Front Cover

REMOVAL & INSTALLATION

3.8L Engine

1. Before servicing the vehicle, refer to the precautions in the beginning of this section.

2. Disconnect the negative battery cable and drain the cooling system.

3. Remove the air cleaner assembly and air intake duct.

4. On non-supercharged engines, remove the fan/clutch assembly and shroud. On supercharged engines, remove the electric cooling fan assembly.

5. Remove the accessory drive belt idlers, drive belts and the water pump pulley.

6. Remove the power steering pump bracket retaining bolts. Leaving the hoses connected, place the pump/bracket assembly aside in a position to prevent fluid from leaking out.

7. If equipped with air conditioning, remove the compressor front support bracket but leave the compressor in place.

8. Disconnect the coolant bypass hose and heater hose at the water pump. Disconnect the upper radiator hose at the thermostat housing.

9. Disconnect the coil wire from the distributor cap and remove the cap with the secondary wires attached.

10. Remove the distributor hold-down clamp and lift the distributor out of the front cover.

11. Raise and safely support the vehicle. Remove the crankshaft damper and pulley using a puller.

➡ **If the crankshaft pulley and vibration damper have to be separated, mark the damper and pulley so they may be reassembled in the same relative position. This is important as the damper and pulley are initially balanced as a unit. If the crankshaft damper is being replaced, check if the original damper has balance pins installed. If so, new balance pins must be installed on the new damper in the same position as the original damper. The crankshaft pulley, new or original, must also be installed in the same relative position as originally installed.**

12. Remove the oil filter. On supercharged engines, remove the oil cooler.

13. Disconnect the lower radiator hose at the water pump. Remove the oil pan.

➡ **The front cover cannot be removed without lowering the oil pan.**

14. Lower the vehicle. Remove the front cover retaining bolts. It is not necessary to remove the water pump.

❋❋ WARNING

Do not overlook the cover retaining bolt located behind the oil filter adapter. The front cover will break if pried on and all retaining bolts are not removed.

15. Remove the front cover and water pump as an assembly. Remove and discard the cover gasket.

➡ **The front cover contains the oil pump and water pump. If a new front cover is to be installed, remove the water pump and oil pump from the old front cover.**

16. Remove the camshaft bolt and washer from the end of the camshaft.

17. Remove the distributor drive gear, camshaft sprocket, crankshaft sprocket and timing chain.

➡ **If the crankshaft sprocket is difficult to remove, pry the sprocket off the shaft using a pair of large prybars positioned on both sides of the sprocket.**

CRANKSHAFT SPROCKET

TIMING CHAIN

CAMSHAFT SPROCKET

POSITIONING OF TIMING MARKS AND KEYWAYS IN CAMSHAFT AND CRANKSHAFT SPROCKETS MUST BE IN LINE AS SHOWN WITH NO. 1 PISTON AT TOP DEAD CENTER FIRING.

7922NG53

Be sure that the timing marks are facing each other after the chain in installed—3.8L engine

To install:

18. Clean all gasket mating surfaces. If reusing the front cover, replace the front cover oil seal.

19. Rotate the crankshaft to position the No. 1 piston at TDC and the crankshaft keyway at the 12 o' clock position.

20. Lubricate the timing chain with engine oil.

21. Install the camshaft sprocket, crankshaft sprocket and timing chain. Be sure the timing marks align.

22. Install the distributor drive gear. Install the bolt and washer assembly on the end of the camshaft and tighten to 30–37 ft. lbs. (40–50 Nm).

23. Position a new gasket on the cylinder block and install the front cover using dowels for proper alignment. Install the front cover retaining bolts and tighten to 15–22 ft. lbs. (20–30 Nm).

24. Raise and safely support the vehicle. Install the oil pan. Connect the lower radiator hose and install the oil filter.

25. Coat the crankshaft damper sealing surface with clean engine oil. Apply a small amount of silicone sealer to the crankshaft keyway.

26. Position the crankshaft pulley key in the crankshaft keyway and install the damper, using a suitable installation tool.

27. Install the damper washer and retain-

ing bolt and tighten to 103–132 ft. lbs. (140–180 Nm). Install the crankshaft pulley and tighten the retaining bolts to 20–28 ft. lbs. (26–38 Nm).

28. Lower the vehicle. Connect the coolant bypass hose.

29. Install the distributor with the rotor pointing at the No. 1 distributor cap tower. Install the distributor cap and coil wire. On supercharged engines, install the camshaft synchronizer.

30. Connect the upper radiator hose at the thermostat housing. Connect the heater hose.

31. If equipped with air conditioning, install the compressor and mounting brackets. Tighten retaining bolts to 30–45 ft. lbs. (41–61 Nm).

32. Install the power steering pump and mounting bracket. Tighten the retaining bolts to 30–45 ft. lbs. (41–61 Nm).

33. Install the water pump pulley. Position the accessory drive belts over the pulleys.

34. Install the fan/clutch assembly and fan shroud. Cross-tighten the fan/clutch assembly retaining bolts to 12–18 ft. lbs. (16–24 Nm).

35. Fill the crankcase with the proper type and quantity of engine oil. Fill and bleed the cooling system.

36. Connect the negative battery cable.

Please refer to Section 9 for electric cooling fan wiring schematics

37. Start the engine and check for leaks. Check the ignition timing and curb idle speed and adjust, as necessary.

4.6L SOHC Engine

➡ **This is not a free wheeling engine. If it has "jumped time" there will be damage to the valves and/or pistons and will require the removal of the cylinder heads.**

1. Before servicing the vehicle, refer to the precautions in the beginning of this section.

2. Disconnect the negative battery cable.

3. Remove the cooling fan and shroud. Loosen the water pump pulley bolts, remove the accessory drive belt and remove the water pump pulley.

4. Raise and safely support the vehicle.

5. Remove the bolts retaining the power steering pump to the engine block and cylinder front cover. The lower front bolt on the power steering pump will not come all the way out. Wire the power steering pump out of the way.

6. Remove the 4 bolts retaining the oil pan to the front cover. Remove the crankshaft damper retaining bolt and washer. Remove the damper using a puller.

7. Lower the vehicle. Remove the bolt retaining the air conditioner high pressure line to the right coil bracket.

8. Remove the front bolts and loosen the remaining bolts on the camshaft covers. Using plastic wedges or similar tools, prop up both camshaft covers. Disconnect both ignition coils and CID sensor.

9. Remove the 3 nuts retaining the right coil bracket to the front cover. Position the power steering hose out of the way.

10. Remove the 4 nuts retaining the left coil bracket to the front cover. Slide both coil brackets and ignition wires off the mounting studs and lay the assembly on top of the engine.

11. Disconnect the High Data Rate (HDR) sensor. Remove the 7 stud bolts and 4 bolts retaining the front cover to the engine and remove the front cover.

12. Remove the High Data Rate (HDR) wheel.

13. Rotate the engine to set the No. 1 piston at TDC on the compression stroke.

14. Install cam positioning tools T91P-6256-A or equivalent, on the flats of the camshaft. This will prevent accidental rotation of the camshafts.

15. Remove the 2 bolts retaining the right tensioner to the cylinder head and remove the tensioner. Remove the right tensioner arm.

16. Remove the 2 bolts retaining the right chain guide to the cylinder head and remove the chain guide. Remove the right chain and right crankshaft sprocket. Remove the right camshaft sprocket retaining bolt, washer, sprocket and spacer.

➡ **Cam positioning tools T91P-6256-A or equivalent, must be installed on the camshaft to prevent the camshaft from rotating.**

17. Remove the 2 bolts retaining the left tensioner to the cylinder head and remove

the tensioner. Remove the left tensioner arm.

18. Remove the 2 bolts retaining the left chain guide to the cylinder head and remove the chain guide. Remove the left chain and left crankshaft sprocket. Remove the left camshaft sprocket retaining bolt, washer, sprocket and spacer.

➡ **Cam positioning tools T91P-6256-A or equivalent, must be installed on the camshaft to prevent the camshaft from rotating.**

1. Cylinder
2. Cylinder
3. Oil pan gasket
4. Gasket
5. Front cover assembly
6a. Bolts
7a. Studs
8. Dowel

7922NG54

Timing chain front cover installation—4.6L SOHC engine

Crankshaft sprocket positioning—4.6L SOHC engine

7922NG55

COPPER
TIMING LINK
RH CHAIN

TIMING MARK
RH CAM GEAR

COPPER
TIMING LINK
LH CHAIN

TDC

CRANKSHAFT
GEAR
KEYWAYS
POSITIONED
AT 315°

TIMING MARK
LH CAM GEAR

CRANKSHAFT GEAR
TIMING MARKS

COPPER TIMING LINKS
RH AND LH CRANKSHAFT
GEARS

7922NG56

Timing chain and sprocket alignment—4.6L SOHC engine

19. Inspect the friction material on the tensioner arms and chain guides. If worn or damaged, remove and clean the oil pan and replace the oil pick-up tube.

➡ **At no time, when the timing chains are removed and the cylinder heads are installed, may the crankshaft and/or camshafts be rotated. Failure to follow these directions will result in valve and/or piston damage.**

To install:
20. Be sure cam positioning tools T91P-6256-A or equivalent, are installed on the camshafts to prevent them from rotating.
21. Position the camshaft spacers and sprockets on the camshafts and install the washers and retaining bolts. Tighten the retaining bolts to 81–96 ft. lbs. (110–130 Nm).
22. Install the left crankshaft sprocket

with the tapered part of the sprocket facing away from the engine block.

➡ **The crankshaft sprockets are identical. They may only be installed one way, with the tapered part of the sprocket facing each other.**

23. Install the left timing chain on the camshaft and crankshaft sprockets. Be sure the copper links of the chain line up with the timing marks of the sprockets.

➡ **If the copper links of the timing chain are not visible, pull the chain taught until the opposite sides of the chain contact one another and lay it on a flat surface. Mark the links at each end of the chain and use them in place of the copper links.**

24. Install the right crankshaft sprocket with the tapered part of the sprocket facing the left crankshaft sprocket.
25. Install the right timing chain on the camshaft and crankshaft sprockets. Be sure the copper links of the chain line up with the timing marks of the sprockets.
26. It is necessary to bleed the timing chain tensioners before installation. Proceed as follows:
   a. Position the timing chain tensioner in a soft-jawed vice.
   b. Using a small pick or similar tool, hold the ratchet lock mechanism away from the ratchet stem and slowly compress the tensioner plunger by rotating the vise handle.

➡ **The tensioner must be compressed slowly or damage to the internal seals will result.**

   c. Once the tensioner plunger bottoms in the tensioner bore, continue to hold the ratchet lock mechanism and push down on the ratchet stem until flush with the tensioner face.
   d. While holding the ratchet stem flush to the tensioner face, release the ratchet lock mechanism and install a paper clip or similar tool in the tensioner body to lock the tensioner in the collapsed position.
   e. The paper clip must not be removed until the timing chain, tensioner, tensioner arm and timing chain guide are completely installed on the engine.
27. Lubricate the tensioner arm contact surfaces with engine oil and install the right and left tensioner arms on their dowels.
28. Install the right and left timing chain

Camshaft positioning tool—4.6L SOHC engine

7922NG57

Timing chain tensioner bleeding procedure—4.6L SOHC engine

7922NG58

NOTE: ENSURE RATCHET STEM IS FLUSH TO TENSIONER BODY FACE PRIOR TO INSTALLING PAPER CLIP

7922NG59

Timing chain tensioner locking procedure—4.6L SOHC engine

tensioners and secure with 2 bolts on each. Tighten the bolts to 15–22 ft. lbs. (20–30 Nm).

29. Install the right and left timing chain guides and secure with 2 bolts on each. Tighten the bolts to 6.0–8.8 ft. lbs. (8–12 Nm).

30. Remove the paper clips from the timing chain tensioners and be sure all timing marks are aligned.

31. Remove the camshaft positioning tools.

32. Inspect and replace the front cover seal as necessary and clean the sealing surfaces of the cylinder block. Apply silicone sealer to the oil pan where it meets the cylinder block and to the points where the cylinder head meets the cylinder block.

33. Install the front cover and the attaching studs and bolts. Tighten to 15–22 ft. lbs. (20–30 Nm). Connect the HDR sensor.

34. Position the coil brackets and ignition wires as an assembly onto the mounting studs. Position the power steering hose and install the 7 nuts retaining the coil brackets to the front cover. Tighten the nuts to 15–22 ft. lbs. (20–30 Nm). Connect both ignition coils and CID sensor.

35. Remove the plastic wedges holding up the camshaft covers. Apply silicone sealer where the front cover meets the cylinder head and be sure the camshaft cover gaskets are properly positioned. Install the front retaining bolts into the camshaft cover and tighten the bolts to 6.0–8.8 ft. lbs. (8–12 Nm).

36. Position the air conditioner high pressure line on the right coil bracket and install the bolt. Raise and safely support the vehicle.

37. Apply a small amount of silicone sealer in the rear of the keyway in the damper. Position the damper on the crankshaft and install, using a suitable installation tool. Install the damper bolt and washer and tighten to 114–121 ft. lbs. (155–165 Nm).

38. Install the 4 bolts retaining the oil pan to the front cover. Tighten to 15–22 ft. lbs. (20–30 Nm).

39. Position the power steering pump on the engine and install the 4 retaining bolts. Tighten to 15–22 ft. lbs. (20–30 Nm). Lower the vehicle.

40. Install the water pump pulley with the 4 bolts. Tighten to 15–22 ft. lbs. (20–30 Nm). Install the accessory drive belt and the cooling fan and shroud.

41. Connect the negative battery cable, start the engine and check for leaks.

4.6L DOHC Engine

✷✷ WARNING

This is not a free-wheeling engine. When the timing chains are removed and the cylinder heads are installed, the crankshaft and/or camshafts must not be rotated unless as directed in this procedure. Failure to follow these instructions will result in valve and/or piston damage.

1. Before servicing the vehicle, refer to the precautions in the beginning of this section.
2. Disconnect the negative battery cable.
3. Remove the windshield wiper module assembly.
4. Remove the engine appearance cover, if equipped.
5. Remove the engine air cleaner outlet tube.
6. Drain the engine cooling system.
7. Remove the water bypass tube and the upper radiator hose.
8. Remove the engine cooling fan motor and shroud assembly.
9. Remove the engine control wiring support bracket and straps from the left-hand center of the engine front cover.
10. Loosen the water pump pulley bolts.
11. If equipped with air injection, disconnect the vacuum and electrical harness connectors. Remove the necessary tube brackets, hoses and gaskets. Remove the air injection diverter valve.
12. Remove the accessory drive belt.
13. Remove the water pump pulley and lower water pump-to-cylinder block retaining bolt for engine front cover removal clearance.
14. Remove the bolts and stud bolt retaining the power steering pump reservoir to the left-hand ignition coil bracket.
15. Raise and safely support the vehicle.
16. Using Pulley Remover T69L-10300-B or equivalent, remove the power steering pump pulley.
17. Remove the bolt retaining the power steering pressure hose to the power steering pump bracket.
18. Remove the bolts retaining the power steering pump to the cylinder block and the engine front cover.

➡ **The front lower bolt on the power steering pump will not come all the way out.**

19. Position the power steering pump and reservoir out of the way.
20. Remove the 4 bolts retaining the oil pan to the engine front cover.
21. Remove the crankshaft pulley retaining bolt and washer from the crankshaft.
22. Install Crankshaft Damper Remover T58P-6316-D or equivalent, on the crankshaft pulley and pull the crankshaft pulley from the crankshaft.
23. Lower the vehicle.
24. Remove both cylinder head covers.
25. Disconnect the engine control wiring from both ignition coils and the Camshaft Position (CMP) sensor.
26. Remove the 3 bolts retaining the right-hand ignition coil bracket to the engine front cover.
27. Remove the 3 nuts and 1 bolt retaining the left-hand ignition coil bracket to the engine front cover.
28. Slide both ignition coil brackets with the ignition wires attached off of the front cover studs and move aside.
29. Remove the bolt retaining the belt idler pulley and remove the idler pulley.
30. Remove the drive belt tensioner retaining bolt and drive belt tensioner from the engine front cover.
31. Disconnect the Crankshaft Position (CKP) sensor and move the wiring out of the way.
32. Remove the stud bolts and bolts retaining the engine front cover to the engine.
33. Remove the engine front cover.
34. Remove the left-hand and right-hand cylinder head covers.
35. Remove the CKP sensor tooth wheel.
36. Rotate the crankshaft to place the piston for No. 1 cylinder at Top Dead Center (TDC) on its compression stroke.

✷✷ WARNING

Camshaft Positioning Tool T93P-6256-A or equivalent, and Camshaft Holding Tool T93P-6256-AH or equivalent, must be installed to prevent accidental rotation of the camshafts and possible engine damage.

37. Install Camshaft Positioning Tool T93P-6256-A or equivalent, in the rear D-slots of the camshaft.

✷✷ WARNING

Failure to use Camshaft Holding Tool T93P-6256-AH or equivalent, while assembling or disassembling the timing chains will result in damage to the D-slots or Camshaft Positioning Tool T93P-6256-A.

38. Install Camshaft Holding Tool T93P-6256-AH or equivalent, onto the camshafts to keep the camshafts from rotating and to prevent damaging the camshaft positioning tool.
39. Remove the 2 bolts retaining the right-hand primary timing chain tensioner to the cylinder head and remove the primary timing chain tensioner.
40. Remove the bolt retaining the right-hand tensioner arm and remove the right-hand tensioner arm.

➡ **The 2 bolts retaining the timing chain guide to the cylinder head are longer than the one to the block.**

41. Remove 3 bolts retaining the right-hand timing chain guide and remove the timing chain guide.
42. Remove the right-hand primary timing chain from the camshaft and crankshaft sprockets.
43. Remove the right-hand crankshaft sprocket.
44. Remove the camshaft sprocket retaining bolts.

✷✷ WARNING

The secondary timing chain tensioner plunger is spring loaded. Care must be taken to prevent the plunger from dropping out of the tensioner during disassembly.

45. Unlock and compress the secondary timing chain tensioners and lock the timing chain tensioner in the compressed position using a paper clip or stiff wire. Remove the secondary timing chains and camshaft sprockets.
46. Remove the 2 bolts retaining the left-hand primary timing chain tensioner to the cylinder head and remove the primary timing chain tensioners.
47. Remove the bolt retaining the left-hand timing chain tensioner arm and remove the left-hand timing chain tensioner arm.
48. Remove the 3 bolts retaining the left-hand timing chain guide and remove the timing chain guide.
49. Remove the left-hand primary timing chain from the camshaft sprocket and crankshaft sprocket.

Timing belt service is covered in Section 5 of this manual

50. Remove the left-hand crankshaft sprocket.

⁂ WARNING

Failure to use Camshaft Holding Tool T93P-6256-AH or equivalent, while removing or tightening the camshaft bolts may result in damage to the camshaft D-slots or the camshaft positioning tool.

51. Remove the camshaft sprocket retaining bolts.

⁂ WARNING

The secondary timing chain tensioner plunger is spring loaded. Care must be taken to prevent the plunger from dropping out of the tensioner during disassembly.

52. Unlock and compress the secondary chain tensioner and lock the chain tensioner in the compressed position using a paper clip or stiff wire. Remove the secondary timing chain and camshaft sprockets.

⁂ WARNING

Do not rotate the crankshaft and/or camshafts or engine damage may occur.

53. Inspect the friction material on the timing chain tensioner arms and timing chain guides. If worn or damaged, remove and clean the oil pan and replace the oil pump screen cover and tube.

To install:

54. If the engine has jumped time, be sure that all service to the necessary engine components and/or valve train have been made.

55. Be sure the primary and secondary timing chain tensioners are in the collapsed position and retained with paper clips or equivalent.

56. If the cylinder heads were removed from the cylinder block, position the crankshaft keyway to 270 degrees (9 o'clock position), before reinstalling the cylinder heads.

➡**The rocker arms must not be installed in the cylinder heads at this time.**

57. Install Camshaft Positioning Tool T93P-6256-A or equivalent, into the D-slots on the rear of the camshafts to position both intake and exhaust camshafts with the keyways pointing down towards the crankshaft. Install Camshaft Holding Tool T93P-6256-AH or equivalent, on the center of the camshafts and do not remove until all parts are installed and tightened.

58. Install the left-hand secondary timing chain tensioner and tighten the retaining bolts to 70–106 inch lbs. (8–12 Nm).

59. Install the left-hand secondary camshaft sprockets and secondary timing chain as an assembly. Be sure the hubs of the sprocket are facing the proper direction.

60. Install the left-hand primary camshaft sprocket and camshaft sprocket spacer on the left-hand camshaft.

61. Install the washers and camshaft sprocket retaining bolts, finger-tight only.

➡**The secondary camshaft sprockets must be free to turn.**

62. Install Timing Chain Tensioning Tool T93P-6256-BH or equivalent, on the left-hand secondary timing chain tensioner.

63. Tighten the camshaft sprocket bolts to 81–95 ft. lbs. (110–130 Nm).

64. Install the right-hand secondary timing chain tensioner and tighten the retaining bolts to 70–106 inch lbs. (8–12 Nm).

65. Install the right-hand secondary camshaft sprockets and secondary timing chain as an assembly. Be sure the hubs of the sprocket are facing the proper direction.

66. Install the right-hand primary camshaft sprocket and camshaft sprocket spacer on the right-hand camshaft.

67. Install the washers and camshaft sprocket retaining bolts, finger-tight only.

➡**The secondary camshaft sprockets must be free to turn.**

68. Install Timing Chain Tensioning Tool T93P-6256-BH or equivalent, on the right-hand secondary timing chain tensioner.

69. Tighten the camshaft sprocket bolts to 81–95 ft. lbs. (110–130 Nm).

70. Install the left-hand crankshaft sprocket, making sure the tapered part of the sprocket faces away from the cylinder block.

71. Install the primary timing chain on the left-hand primary camshaft sprocket. Be sure the copper link of the timing chain aligns with the timing mark on the camshaft sprocket.

➡**If the copper links of the timing chain are not visible, pull the chain taught until the opposite sides of the chain contact one another and lay it on a flat surface. Mark the links at each end of the chain and use them in place of the copper links.**

72. Install the left-hand primary timing chain on the left-hand crankshaft sprocket. Be sure the copper link of the timing chain aligns with the timing mark on the crankshaft sprocket.

73. Install the right-hand crankshaft sprocket, making sure the tapered part of the sprocket faces toward the cylinder block.

74. Install the primary timing chain on the right-hand primary camshaft sprocket. Be sure the copper link of the timing chain aligns with the timing mark on the camshaft sprocket.

75. Install the right-hand primary timing chain on the right-hand crankshaft sprocket. Be sure the copper link of the timing chain aligns with the timing mark on the crankshaft sprocket.

➡**The two timing chain guide bolts to the cylinder head are longer than the bolt to the cylinder block.**

76. Install the right-hand and left-hand timing chain guides and tighten the bolts to 71–106 inch lbs. (8–12 Nm).

77. Lubricate the timing chain tensioner arm contact surfaces with clean engine oil. Install the right-hand and left-hand tensioner arms and tighten the bolts to 84–132 inch lbs. (10–15 Nm).

78. Install right-hand and left-hand primary timing chain tensioners and tighten the bolts to 15–22 ft. lbs. (20–30 Nm).

79. Remove the locking pins from the timing chain tensioners and be sure all timing marks are aligned. Remove the camshaft positioning tool and the camshaft holding tool.

➡**When cleaning the sealing surfaces of the engine front cover and oil pan-to-cylinder block joints, be extremely careful not to damage the rubber bead of the oil pan gasket. If the oil pan gasket is damaged, it must be replaced.**

80. Clean the sealing surfaces of the cylinder block, cylinder heads and engine front cover; remove all traces of oil, dirt and old sealant. Sealing surfaces must be clean and dry before applying sealant.

81. Replace the engine front cover gaskets and the crankshaft front seal.

82. Apply silicone sealant to the proper locations on the cylinder block and heads.

➡**The engine front cover must be rolled into place. DO NOT slide on the oil pan gasket.**

83. Carefully install the front cover to the engine.

84. Install the bolts and stud bolts retaining the front cover to the engine. Tighten in sequence to 15–22 ft. lbs. (20–30 Nm). Tighten the stud bolts and

FRONT OF ENGINE

Front cover bolt torque sequence—4.6L DOHC engine

7922NG60

RH PRIMARY CHAIN

LH PRIMARY CHAIN

30 PLATES RH AND LH

Timing chain alignment to TDC—4.6L DOHC engine

7922NG61

bolts numbered 6, 7, 8, 9, 10, and 11 within 4 minutes after applying the sealer.

85. Install the drive belt tensioner and bolt. Tighten the bolt to 15–22 ft. lbs. (20–30 Nm).

86. Install the belt idler pulley and bolt. Tighten the bolt to 15–22 ft. lbs. (20–30 Nm).

87. Connect the engine control sensor wiring to the CKP sensor.

88. Place the left-hand and right-hand ignition coil brackets in position on the engine front cover. Install all retaining nuts and bolts and tighten to 15–22 ft. lbs. (20–30 Nm).

89. Install the power steering pump reservoir to the left-hand ignition coil bracket. Tighten the retaining bolts to 71–106 inch lbs. (8–12 Nm).

90. Connect the engine control wiring to both ignition coils and the CMP sensor.

91. Install both cylinder head covers.

92. Raise the vehicle.

93. Install the crankshaft pulley on the crankshaft, using Crankshaft Damper Replacer T74P-6316-B or equivalent.

94. Apply silicone sealant in the keyway of the crankshaft pulley.

95. Install the pulley bolt and washer. Tighten the bolt to 114–121 ft. lbs. (155–165 Nm).

96. Install the 4 bolts retaining the oil pan to the engine front cover. Tighten the bolts to 15–22 ft. lbs. (20–30 Nm).

97. Position the power steering pump on the engine and install 4 retaining bolts. Tighten the bolts to 15–22 ft. lbs. (20–30 Nm).

98. Install the retainer bolt for the power steering pressure hose to power steering pump bracket.

99. Install the strap retaining the engine control wiring to the engine front cover.

100. Using Power Steering Pump Pulley Replacer T91P-3A733-A or equivalent, install the power steering pump pulley.

101. Lower the vehicle.

102. Install the lower water pump retaining bolt removed for engine front cover clearance. Tighten the bolt to 15–22 ft. lbs. (20–30 Nm).

103. Install the water pump pulley with 4 bolts. Tighten the bolts to 15–22 ft. lbs. (20–30 Nm).

104. Install the support bracket and retaining bolt for the engine control wiring to the left-hand center of the engine front cover.

Timing chain tensioner installation—4.6L DOHC engine

105. If equipped with air injection, install the air injection diverter valve and retaining nuts. Tighten the nuts to 6–8 ft. lbs. (8–12 Nm). Connect the vacuum and electrical connectors.

106. If equipped with air injection, install the hose to the air injection pump. Connect both tube and gasket assemblies and tighten the fittings to 25–35 ft. lbs. (32–48 Nm). Tighten the tube bracket retaining bolts to 15–22 ft. lbs. (20–30 Nm).

107. Install the engine cooling fan motor and shroud assembly.

108. Install the water bypass tube and the upper radiator hose.

109. Install the accessory drive belt.

110. Restore all fluid levels.

111. Install the windshield wiper module assembly.

112. Connect the engine air cleaner outlet tube.

113. Connect the negative battery cable.

114. Start the engine and check for leaks.

115. Install the engine appearance cover, if equipped.

116. Road test the vehicle and check for proper engine operation.

FUEL SYSTEM

Fuel System Service Precautions

Safety is the most important factor when performing not only fuel system maintenance, but any type of maintenance. Failure to conduct maintenance and repairs in a safe manner may result in serious personal injury or death. Work on a vehicle's fuel system components can be accomplished safely and effectively by adhering to the following rules and guidelines.

• To avoid the possibility of fire and personal injury, always disconnect the negative battery cable unless the repair or test procedure requires that battery voltage be applied.

• Always relieve the fuel system pressure prior to disconnecting any fuel system component (injector, fuel rail, pressure regulator, etc.) fitting or fuel line connection. Exercise extreme caution whenever relieving fuel system pressure to avoid exposing skin, face and eyes to fuel spray. Please be advised that fuel under pressure may penetrate the skin or any part of the body that it contacts.

• Always place a shop towel or cloth around the fitting or connection prior to loosening to absorb any excess fuel due to spillage. Ensure that all fuel spillage is quickly removed from engine surfaces. Ensure that all fuel-soaked cloths or towels are deposited into a flame-proof waste container with a lid.

• Always keep a dry chemical (Class B) fire extinguisher near the work area.

• Do not allow fuel spray or fuel vapors to come into contact with a spark or open flame.

• Always use a second wrench when loosening or tightening fuel line connection fittings. This will prevent unnecessary stress and torsion on fuel piping. Always follow the proper torque specifications.

• Always replace worn fuel fitting O-rings with new ones. Do not substitute fuel hose where rigid pipe is installed.

Fuel System Pressure

RELIEVING

All Sequential Fuel Injection (SFI) engines are equipped with a pressure relief valve located on the fuel supply manifold. Remove the fuel tank cap and attach fuel pressure gauge T80L-9974-B, or equivalent, to the valve on the fuel rail. Place the tube from the tool into a small container and open the valve on the tool to release the fuel pressure. Be sure to drain the fuel into a suitable container and to avoid gasoline spillage. If a pressure gauge is not available, disconnect the vacuum hose from the fuel pressure regulator and attach a hand-held vacuum pump. Apply about 25 in. Hg (84 kPa) of vacuum to the regulator to vent the fuel system pressure into the fuel tank through the fuel return hose.

➡This procedure will remove the fuel pressure from the lines, but not the fuel. Take precautions to avoid the risk of fire and use clean rags to soak up any spilled fuel when the lines are disconnected.

Fuel Filter

REMOVAL & INSTALLATION

1. Before servicing the vehicle, refer to the precautions in the beginning of this section.

2. Disconnect the negative battery cable.

3. Properly relieve the fuel system pressure using a test gauge at the fuel pressure relief valve.

4. Raise and safely support the rear of the vehicle.

5. Detach the fuel lines from both ends of the fuel filter by disengaging both push-connect fittings. Install new retainer clips in each push-connect fitting prior to reassembly.

➡Position a rag below the filter to catch any fuel which may spill as it is disconnected and removed.

6. Remove the fuel filter from the bracket by loosening the worm gear clamp. Note the orientation of the direction-of-flow arrow on the fuel filter, as installed in the bracket, to ensure proper fuel flow through the replacement filter.

To install:

7. Install the fuel filter into the bracket, ensuring the proper direction of flow. Tighten the worm gear clamp to 15–25 inch lbs. (2–3 Nm).

Always use new hairpin clips when assembling connections using them

To disengage the duckbill clip fitting, depress the two tabs until one tube can be pulled from the other

8. Install the push-connect fittings onto the filter ends. Connect the negative battery cable, then start the engine and check for fuel leaks.

✳ CAUTION

Use extreme caution when starting and running an engine which is supported by jackstands. ENSURE that no drive wheels are on the ground. Also, ensure that the wheels which are on the ground are properly blocked so the vehicle cannot move.

9. Lower the vehicle.

Fuel Pump

REMOVAL & INSTALLATION

➡**To gain access to the fuel pump, it is necessary to remove the fuel tank.**

1. Before servicing the vehicle, refer to the precautions in the beginning of this section.

2. Disconnect the negative battery cable.

3. Remove the fuel tank as follows:
   a. Drain the fuel tank.
   b. Raise and safely support the vehicle.
   c. Remove the filler pipe bolt attachment and disconnect the filler pipe hose connections to the fuel tank.
   d. Detach the fuel tank electrical connector.
   e. Disconnect the vapor tube fitting at the left front of the fuel tank.
   f. Disconnect the EVAP canister tube and hose.
   g. Place a safety support under the fuel tank.
   h. Remove the front two bolts from the fuel tank support straps and swing the left-hand strap out of the way.

Exploded view of the electric fuel pump assembly, which is mounted in the fuel tank

i. Remove the right-hand fuel tank support strap bolt and remove the strap.

j. Partially lower the fuel tank and disconnect the fuel line.

✳✳ CAUTION

The filler pipe grommet must be removed prior to removing the fuel tank from the filler pipe or damage to the fill tube check valve will occur.

k. Cut outer edge of pipe-to-tank grommet to facilitate pipe removal and carefully remove the grommet from the fuel tank. Take care to avoid damage to the filler pipe check valve.

4. Remove the tank from the vehicle.

5. Remove any dirt that has accumulated around the fuel pump attaching flange, to prevent it from entering the tank during service.

6. Turn the fuel pump locking ring counterclockwise using a locking ring removal tool, then remove the ring.

7. Remove the fuel pump and bracket assembly.

8. Remove the seal gasket and discard it.

To install:

9. Put a light coating of heavy grease on a new seal ring to hold it in place during assembly. Install it in the fuel tank ring groove.

10. Insert the fuel pump assembly into the fuel tank, then secure it in place with the locking ring. Tighten the ring until secure.

11. Install the fuel tank in the vehicle in the reverse order of removal. Be sure to tighten the mounting straps to 28 ft. lbs. (35 Nm).

12. Add a minimum of 10 gallons of fuel and check for leaks.

13. Install a pressure gauge on the throttle body valve and turn the ignition **ON** for 3 seconds. Turn the key **OFF**, then repeat the key cycle five to ten times until the pressure gauge shows at least 30 psi (207 kPa). Reinspect for leaks at the fittings.

14. Remove the pressure gauge. Start the engine and check for fuel leaks.

DRIVE TRAIN

➡ **For information on driveshaft and U-joint service, refer to the unit repair section.**

Transmission Assembly

REMOVAL & INSTALLATION

1. Before servicing the vehicle, refer to the precautions in the beginning of this section.

2. Disconnect the negative battery cable.

3. On manual transmissions, remove the shifter boot and lever from inside the vehicle.

4. Raise and safely support the vehicle.

5. Disconnect all cables, connectors and fluid lines that may interfere with transmission removal. Tag them if helpful for installation.

6. On automatic transmissions, unbolt the torque converter from the flexplate and disconnect the shift linkage.

7. Place a drain pan under the transmission and drain the fluid.

8. Position a transmission jack under the transmission and safety-chain the case to the jack.

9. Matchmark and remove the driveshaft.

10. Disconnect the exhaust pipe(s) from the manifold(s) and use wire to position the pipe(s) out of the way.

11. Remove the transmission rear mount.

12. Slightly raise the transmission and remove the crossmember.

13. On automatic transmissions, remove the transmission-to-engine block bolts. For manual transmissions, remove the bolts securing the transmission to the bell housing.

✳✳ CAUTION

The torque converter will fall out of the transmission if it is tilted forward. Keep a hand on it while lowering the transmission out of the vehicle.

14. Roll the transmission rearward until the input shaft clears, lower the jack and remove the transmission.

To install:

15. Carefully raise the transmission to the engine or bell housing.

16. Roll the transmission forward and into position.

17. On automatic transmissions tighten the bolts to 28–38 ft. lbs. (38–51 Nm. On manual transmissions, tighten the bolts to 45–65 ft. lbs. (61–68 Nm).

18. Install the crossmember, tighten the bolts to 36–50 ft. lbs. (47–68 Nm).

19. Lower the transmission onto the crossmember and remove the jack.

20. Install the transmission rear insulator and lower retainer. Tighten the nuts to 26–35 ft. lbs. (34–48 Nm).

21. Connect the exhaust pipe(s) to the manifold(s).

22. The rest of the installation is the reverse of removal.

23. Refill the transmission with the correct type and amount of fluid.

Clutch

ADJUSTMENTS

The clutch free-play is adjusted automatically by a built-in clutch control mechanism. This device allows the clutch controls to self-adjust during normal operation.

The system consists of a spring-loaded gear quadrant, a spring-loaded pawl and a clutch cable which is spring-loaded to preload the release lever bearing. This compensates for movement of the release lever, as the clutch disc wears. The pawl, located at the top of the clutch pedal, engages the gear quadrant when the clutch pedal is depressed and pulls the cable through its continuously adjusted stroke. Clutch cable adjustments are not required because of this feature.

REMOVAL & INSTALLATION

1. Before servicing the vehicle, refer to the precautions in the beginning of this section.

2. Disconnect the negative battery cable for safety purposes.

✳✳ WARNING

The clutch release lever cable should never be removed from the clutch and brake pedal pivot shaft with a prying instrument such as a prybar.

3. Lift the clutch pedal to its uppermost position to disengage the pawl and quadrant. Push the quadrant forward, unhook the cable from the quadrant and allow it to slowly swing rearward.

4. Raise and support the vehicle safely using jackstands. Remove the clutch release lever dust shield.

5. Disconnect the cable from the release lever. Remove the retaining clip and remove the clutch cable from the flywheel housing.

6. Remove the starter motor and the bolts holding the engine rear plate to the lower part of the flywheel housing.

FRONT OF ENGINE

Clutch Release
Lever
Cable

Self-adjuster
Quadrant

Support Bracket

Clutch Pedal

**HOLD PEDAL IN FULL "UP"
POSITION WHILE INSTALLING
CLUTCH CABLE IN RELEASE
LEVER. APPROXIMATELY
44 N (10 LBS) LOAD IN
DIRECTION OF ARROW**

Clutch Release
Lever

C-clip

7922NG45

Clutch self-adjusting system component identification—4.6L engine shown, the 3.8L engine is similar

7. Remove the transmission from the vehicle. Remove the bolts attaching the flywheel housing to the engine block, then remove the flywheel housing from the vehicle.

8. Remove the clutch release lever from the housing by pulling it through the window in the housing until the retainer spring is disengaged from the pivot. Remove the release bearing from the release lever.

9. Loosen the pressure plate cover attaching bolts evenly, to release spring tension gradually and avoid distorting the cover. If the same pressure plate and cover are to be reinstalled, matchmark the cover and flywheel so that the pressure plate can be installed in its original position. Remove the pressure plate and clutch disc from the engine.

10. Inspect the flywheel for scoring, cracks or other damage. Machine or replace as necessary. Inspect the pilot bearing for damage and free movement. Replace as necessary.

To install:

11. If removed, install the flywheel. Be sure the mating surfaces of the flywheel and the crankshaft flange are clean prior to installation. Tighten the flywheel bolts to 54–64 ft. lbs. (73–87 Nm).

12. Position the clutch disc and pressure plate assembly on the flywheel. The three dowel pins on the flywheel must be properly aligned with the pressure plate. Bent, damaged or missing dowels must be replaced. Start the pressure plate bolts, but do not tighten them.

13. Align the clutch disc using a disc alignment tool inserted into the pilot bearing. Alternately tighten the bolts a few turns at a time, until they are all tight. Then, tighten all the bolts to 20–28 ft. lbs. (27–39 Nm) for 3.8L engines, 19–24 ft. lbs. (25–33 Nm) for 4.6L engines. Remove the alignment tool.

14. Apply a light coat of multi-purpose grease to the release lever pivot pocket, the release lever fork and the flywheel housing pivot ball. Fill the grease groove of the release bearing hub with the same grease. Clean all excess grease from the inside bore of the bearing hub.

15. Install the release bearing on the release lever and install the lever in the flywheel housing.

16. Install the flywheel housing. Tighten the bolts to 28–38 ft. lbs. (38–52 Nm).

17. Install the remaining components.

18. Remove the jackstands and carefully lower the vehicle.

✸✸ WARNING

The clutch pedal must be lifted to disengage the adjusting mechanism during clutch release lever cable installation. If this is not done, damage to the self-adjuster mechanism will occur.

19. Install the clutch release lever cable by lifting the clutch pedal to disengage the clutch and brake pedal pivot shaft, then push the pivot shaft forward and hook the end of the clutch release cable over the rear of the pivot shaft.

20. Depress and lift the clutch several times to allow the self-adjusting mechanism to properly set the free-play.

21. Connect the negative battery cable, then check for proper clutch operation.

SPRINGS ARE NOT TO BE BENT OR DAMAGED DURING ASSEMBLY

* LUBRICATE BALL AND POCKET

* LUBRICATE WITHIN 63.5-165 mm (2.5-6.5 INCHES) OF REAR SHOULDER

NOTE: INSTALL WITH "FW SIDE" OR "FLYWHEEL SIDE" STAMPED NOTATION FACING FORWARD

* LUBRICATE LEVER CROWN DO NOT DISTURB GREASE DURING ASSEMBLY

SECTION A

* LUBRICATE LEVER CROWN AND SPRING RETENTION CROWN

SPRING MUST BE POSITIONED WITHIN BEARING GROOVE

SECTION A

* PREMIUM LONG-LIFE GREASE XG-1-C OR XG-1-K (ESA-M1C75-B)

1. Rear face of engine block
2. Flywheel-to-clutch cover alignment dowel
3. Pilot bearing
4. Clutch disc
5. Clutch pleasure plate
6. Clutch release lever
7. Clutch release lever stud
8. Lockwasher
9. Flywheel housing
10. Bolt
11. Input shaft
12. Bolt
13. Clutch release lever dust shield
14. Bolt
15. Clutch release bearing
16. Bolt
17. Flywheel housing-to-engine block dowel

7922NG46

Exploded view of the clutch system components used on all Mustang models

STEERING AND SUSPENSION

Air Bag

❊❊ CAUTION

Some vehicles are equipped with an Air Bag system, also known as the Supplemental Inflatable Restraint (SIR) or Supplemental Restraint System (SRS). The system must be disabled before performing service on or around system components, steering column, instrument panel components, wiring and sensors. Failure to follow safety and disabling procedures could result in accidental Air Bag deployment, possible personal injury and unnecessary system repairs.

PRECAUTIONS

• Always wear safety glasses when servicing an air bag vehicle, and when handling an air bag.
• Never attempt to service the steering wheel or steering column on an air bag-equipped vehicle without first properly disarming the air bag system. The air bag system should be properly disarmed whenever ANY service procedure in this manual indicates that you should do so.
• When carrying a live air bag module, always be sure the bag and trim cover are pointed away from your body. In the unlikely event of an accidental deployment, the bag will, then deploy with minimal chance of injury.
• When placing a live air bag on a bench or other surface, always face the bag and trim cover up, away from the surface. This will reduce the motion of the air bag if it is accidentally deployed.
• If you should come in contact with a

deployed air bag, be advised that the air bag surface may contain deposits of sodium hydroxide, which is a product of the gas combustion and is irritating to the skin. Always wear gloves and safety glasses when handling a deployed air bag, and wash your hands with mild soap and water afterwards.

DISARMING THE SYSTEM

1. Before servicing the vehicle, refer to the precautions in the beginning of this section.

2. Disconnect the negative battery cable from the battery.

3. Disconnect the positive battery cable from the battery.

4. Wait one minute. This time is required for the back-up power supply in the air bag diagnostic monitor to completely drain. The system is now disarmed.

If you are disarming the system with the intent of testing the system, do not! The SRS is a sensitive, complex system and specific tools are needed for SRS testing.

After the necessary repairs are completed, re-enable the system as follows:

5. Connect the positive battery cable.

6. Connect the negative battery cable.

7. Stand outside the vehicle and carefully turn the ignition to the **RUN** position. Be sure that no part of your body is in front of the air bag module on the steering wheel, to prevent injury in case of an accidental air bag deployment.

8. Ensure the air bag indicator light turns off after approximately 6 seconds. If the light does not illuminate at all, does not turn off, or starts to flash, have the system tested by a qualified automotive technician. If the light does turn off after 6 seconds and does not flash, the SRS is working properly.

Power Rack and Pinion Steering Gear

REMOVAL & INSTALLATION

1. Before servicing the vehicle, refer to the precautions in the beginning of this section.

2. Disconnect the negative battery cable. Turn the ignition switch to the **RUN** position so that the front wheels can be turned while working on the power rack and pinion.

3. Loosen all of the wheel lug nuts ½ turn to break them free.

4. Raise and support the vehicle safely

1. No. 2 front crossmember
2. Mounting bolt
3. Steering gear mounting bracket
4. Retaining nut
5. Power steering rack and pinion

7922NG47

Power rack and pinion steering gear mounting on the No. 2 crossmember

using jackstands. Position a drain pan to catch the fluid from the power steering lines.

5. Remove the one bolt retaining the steering column shaft flexible coupling to the input shaft.

6. Remove the front wheel and tire assemblies. Remove the cotter pins and nuts from the tie rod ends, then separate the tie rod studs from the spindles.

7. Remove the two nuts, insulator washers and bolts retaining the steering rack to the crossmember. Remove the front rubber insulators.

8. Position the rack to allow access to the hydraulic lines and disconnect the lines.

9. Remove the steering rack from the vehicle.

To install:

10. Install new plastic seals on the hydraulic line fittings.

11. Install the rack on the mounting studs, and connect the hydraulic lines to the rack and pinion. Tighten the fittings to 20–25 ft. lbs. (27–34 Nm). Tighten the nut on the studs to 30–40 ft. lbs. (41–54 Nm).

➡**The hoses are designed to swivel when properly tightened. Do not attempt to eliminate looseness by overtightening the fittings.**

12. Install the front rubber insulators. Be sure all rubber insulators are pushed completely inside the gear housing before installing the mounting bolts.

13. Insert the input shaft into the steering column shaft flexible coupling. Install the mounting bolts, insulator washers and nuts. Tighten the nuts to 20–30 ft. lbs. (28–40 Nm).

14. Connect the tie rod ends to the spindle arms and install the retaining nuts. Tighten the nut to 35–47 ft. lbs. (47–64 Nm). Continue tightening the nut to align the next castellation of the nut with the cotter pin hole in the stud. Install a new cotter pin.

15. Remove the jackstands and carefully lower the vehicle.

16. Turn the ignition switch **OFF** and connect the negative battery cable.

17. Fill the power steering system with the proper type and quantity of fluid.

18. If the tie rod ends were loosened, check the front end alignment.

Strut

REMOVAL & INSTALLATION

Front

✸✸ CAUTION

During this procedure when the strut is detached from the spindle, if the floor jack under the lower control arm is lowered, the coil spring, under a great amount of tension, can

be abruptly released and cause severe physical injury. As a precaution, chain the bottom end of the coil spring to the lower control arm so that it cannot accidentally spring out of its seat.

1. Before servicing the vehicle, refer to the precautions in the beginning of this section.

2. Disconnect the negative battery cable.

3. Place the ignition switch in the unlocked position to permit free movement of the front wheels.

4. Raise the vehicle by the lower control arms until the wheels are just off the ground.

5. From the engine compartment, remove the strut's central upper mount nut. Do not remove the three small retaining nuts around the larger central nut, and NEVER remove the pop rivet holding the camber plate in position. Slide the large washer off of the strut shaft.

6. Continue to raise the front of the vehicle by the lower control arm and position a jackstand under the frame jacking pad, rearward of the front wheel. DO NOT remove the jack from beneath the lower control arm!

7. Remove the wheel and tire assembly, then remove the brake caliper. Support the caliper with a length of wire; do not let the caliper hang by the brake hose.

8. If equipped, remove the brake anti-lock sensor and bracket.

9. Chain the lower end of the coil spring to the lower control arm for safety.

10. Remove the two lower nuts that attach the strut to the spindle, leaving the bolts in place. Carefully remove both spindle-to-strut bolts, then push the bracket free of the spindle and remove the strut.

11. Compress the strut to clear the upper mount of the body mounting pad. If necessary, remove the upper mount and jounce bumper.

➡ **The upper insulator mounts, if damaged and in need of replacement, can be removed after the strut is removed from the vehicle. Pull the upper and lower insulators out of the bracket assembly.**

To install:

12. If removed, install the upper insulators in the bracket assembly.

13. Position the upper strut shaft through the insulator mounts and camber plate, then start the central mounting nut.

14. Compress the strut and position the lower end in the spindle. Install two new lower retaining bolts and hand-start the nuts. Remove the suspension load from the control arm by slowly lowering the floor jack until the arm hangs without any support from the jack. Tighten the lower retaining nuts 141–191 ft. lbs. (190–259 Nm).

15. Raise the suspension control arm (to position the suspension at normal ride height) and tighten the upper mount retaining nut to 55–92 ft. lbs. (75–125 Nm).

16. Remove the safety chain from the lower control arm and coil spring.

17. Install the brake anti-lock sensor bracket, along with the anti-lock sensor, caliper and front wheel.

18. Remove the jackstands and carefully lower the vehicle to the ground.

19. Tighten the wheel lug nuts in a crisscross pattern to 85–105 ft. lbs. (115–142 Nm).

20. Check and adjust the front end alignment, if necessary.

Shock Absorber

REMOVAL & INSTALLATION

Rear

➡ **Some Ford Mustangs use Torx® head bolts to retain the shocks at the lower mounts. Check to be sure you have the proper drivers before beginning this procedure.**

1. Before servicing the vehicle, refer to the precautions in the beginning of this section.

2. Open the luggage compartment (trunk) lid.

3. Remove the trim panels, as necessary, to gain access to the upper shock absorber mount.

4. Remove the shock absorber retaining nut washer and insulator.

5. Raise the vehicle and support it safely using jackstands under the rear axle housing.

6. From under the vehicle, remove the shock absorber bolt, washer and nut at the lower arm and remove the shock absorber.

➡ **These vehicles are equipped with gas pressurized shock absorbers which will extend unassisted.**

To install:

7. Prime the new shock absorber as follows:

   a. With the shock absorber right side up, extend it fully.

NUT
TIGHTEN TO
75-125 Nm (55-92 LB FT)

WASHER
UPPER INSULATOR
BRACKET ASSY
LOWER INSULATOR
JOUNCE CUP
DUST SHIELD
CLAMP
SPACER
INSULATOR ASSY
JOUNCE BUMPER
STRUT ROD ASSY

7922NG48

Exploded view of the front strut upper mounting

1. Insulator nut
2. Shock absorber
3. Mounting bolt
4. Mounting nut
5. Shock absorber lower mount bracket
6. Mounting nut
7. Rear axle housing

7922NG49

Exploded view of the rear shock absorber mounting

b. Turn the shock absorber upside down and fully compress it.

c. Repeat the previous two steps at least three times to be sure any trapped air has been expelled.

8. From under the vehicle, place the inner washer and insulator on the upper retaining stud and position the stud through the shock tower mounting hole.

9. Attach the lower end of the shock absorber with the retaining bolt and nut. Tighten the bolt to 57–75 ft. lbs. (76–103 Nm).

10. Remove the jackstands and carefully lower the vehicle.

11. Install the upper insulator, washer and retaining nut, then tighten the nut to 25–34 ft. lbs. (34–46 Nm).

Coil Spring

REMOVAL & INSTALLATION

Front

1. Before servicing the vehicle, refer to the precautions in the beginning of this section.

2. Loosen the front wheel lug nuts only slightly.

3. Raise and support the vehicle safely using jackstands, but allow the control arms to hang free.

4. Remove the wheel and tire assembly.

5. Remove the brake caliper. Suspend the caliper with a length of wire; DO NOT let the caliper hang by the brake hose.

6. Disconnect the tie rod end from the steering spindle and disconnect the stabilizer link from the lower arm.

7. If necessary, remove the steering gear (rack and pinion) bolts and reposition the gear so the suspension arm-to-No. 2 crossmember mounting bolts can be removed.

8. On models equipped with the 3.8L engine, use a coil spring compressor, such as Ford Coil Spring Compressor T82P-5310-A or its equivalent, and install the upper plate in the spring pocket cavity on the crossmember. The hooks on the plate should be facing toward the center of the vehicle.

9. On Mustangs with the 4.6L engines, use spring compressor tool D78P-5310-A or its equivalent, to install a plate between the coils near the toe of the spring. Mark the location of the upper plate on the coils for installation.

1. Mounting bolt
2. Damper
3. Front coil spring
4. Insulator
5. Front suspension lower arm
6. Nuts

7922NG50

Exploded view of the front coil spring mounting

10. Install the compression rod into the lower arm spring pocket hole, through the coil spring and into the upper plate.

11. Install the lower plate, lower ball nut, thrust washer and bearing, and forcing nut onto the compression rod. Tighten the forcing nut until a drag on the nut is felt.

12. Remove the suspension arm-to-crossmember nuts and bolts. The compressor tool forcing nut may have to be tightened or loosened for easy bolt removal.

13. Pull the lower control arm down and remove the spring from the suspension.

14. Loosen the compression rod forcing nut until spring tension is relieved and remove the forcing nut. Remove the compression rod and coil spring.

To install:

15. Place the insulator on top of the spring. Position the spring into the lower arm pocket. Be sure the spring pigtail is positioned between the two holes in the lower arm spring pocket.

16. Position the spring into the upper spring seat in the crossmember.

17. On Mustangs with the 3.8L engine, insert the compression rod through the control arm and spring, then hook it to the upper plate. The upper plate is installed with the hooks facing the center of the vehicle.

18. On Mustangs with either the 4.6L engines, install the upper plate between the coils in the location marked during removal.

19. Install the lower plate, ball nut, thrust washer and bearing, and forcing nut onto the compression rod.

20. Tighten the forcing nut, position the lower arm into the crossmember and install new lower arm-to-crossmember bolts and nuts. Do not tighten at this time.

21. Remove the spring compressor tool from the vehicle. Raise the suspension arm to a normal attitude position with a jack. With the suspension in the normal ride-height position, tighten the lower arm-to-crossmember attaching nuts to 141–191 ft. lbs. (191–259 Nm). Carefully lower the suspension again and remove the jack.

22. If repositioning, install the steering gear (rack and pinion)-to-crossmember bolts and nuts. Hold the bolts and tighten the nuts to 30–40 ft. lbs. (41–54 Nm).

23. Connect the stabilizer bar link to the lower suspension arm. Tighten the attaching nut to 11–16 ft. lbs. (16–22 Nm).

24. Position the tie rod into the steering spindle and install the retaining nut. Tighten the nut to the specified torque value and continue tightening the nut to align the next castellation with the hole in the stud. Install a new cotter pin.

25. Install the brake caliper.

26. Install the wheel and tire assembly, then remove the jackstands and carefully lower the vehicle.

27. Tighten the wheel lug nuts to the specified torque value.

Rear

➡ **It is easier to replace one spring at a time; otherwise, the axle housing will be disconnected from both lower control arms.**

1. Before servicing the vehicle, refer to the precautions in the beginning of this section.

2. Raise and support the vehicle safely under the frame. Support the body at the rear body crossmember.

3. If equipped, remove the stabilizer bar.

4. Support the axle with a suitable jack.

5. Place another jack under the lower arm axle pivot bolt. Remove and discard the bolt and nut. Lower the jack slowly until the coil spring load is relieved.

6. Remove the coil spring and insulator from the vehicle.

To install:

7. Place the upper spring insulator on top of the spring. Place the lower spring insulator on the lower arm.

8. Position the coil spring on the lower arm spring seat, so the pigtail on the lower arm is at the rear of the vehicle and pointing toward the left side of the vehicle.

9. Slowly raise the jack until the arm is in position. Insert a new rear pivot bolt and nut, with the nut facing outward. Do not tighten them at this time.

10. Raise the axle to curb height. Tighten the lower arm-to-axle pivot bolt to 71–97 ft. lbs. (97–132 Nm).

11. If equipped, install the stabilizer bar.

12. Remove the crossmember supports and carefully lower the vehicle.

Lower Ball Joint

REMOVAL & INSTALLATION

1. Before servicing the vehicle, refer to the precautions in the beginning of this section.

2. Remove the front strut and spindle from the vehicle.

3. Position the lower control arm in a vise so that the ball joint is easy to service.

4. Using a large C-clamp and adapters, such as Ford Tools T74P-4635-C, D89P-3010-A and D84P-3395-A4, or their equivalents, carefully press the old ball joint out of the lower control arm.

To install:

➡ **When installing a new front ball joint, leave the protective cover in place to protect the ball joint seal. It may be necessary to cut off the end of the cover to allow it to pass through the receiving cup adapter tool.**

5. Press the new ball joint into the lower control arm with Ford's Ball Joint Replacer D89P-3010-B, Cup D84P-3395-A4 and C-Frame T74P-4635C, or their

Use the C-clamp, cup and adapters to press the old ball joint out of the lower control arm

7922NG51

equivalents, until it is fully seated in the control arm.

6. Discard the ball joint protective cover and inspect the ball joint to ensure that it is fully seated in its bore and that it is free of cuts or tears.

7. Install the lower control arm in the vehicle.

Lower Control Arm

REMOVAL & INSTALLATION

1. Before servicing the vehicle, refer to the precautions in the beginning of this section.

2. Raise and safely support the vehicle.

3. Remove the wheel and tire assembly.

4. If necessary, remove the brake caliper and suspend it with a length of wire; DO NOT let the caliper hang by the brake hose. Remove the brake rotor and dust shield.

5. Disconnect the tie rod end from the steering spindle. Disconnect the stabilizer bar link from the lower control arm.

6. If necessary for suspension arm mounting bolt removal, remove the steering gear (rack and pinion) bolts and lower the gear out of the way to provide access.

7. Remove the cotter pin and loosen the lower ball joint stud nut 1–2 turns. **Do not completely remove the nut at this time.** Tap the spindle boss sharply with a brass mallet to relieve the stud pressure; the lower control arm and ball joint should "pop" loose from the spindle (leaving the nut on the ball joint prevents the arm from completely disengaging from the spindle, which would allow the coil spring to jump out of the lower arm cup, possibly causing severe personal injury).

8. Install a suitable spring compressor and compress the coil spring until it can be moved freely in the lower control arm seat.

➡**For more information on coil spring compression or removal, refer to the coil spring procedure earlier in this section.**

9. Remove and discard the ball joint nut, then raise the entire strut and spindle assembly up and off of the ball joint stud. Wire the strut/spindle out of the way to obtain working room.

10. Remove and discard the suspension arm-to-crossmember nuts and bolts. Remove the lower control arm and coil spring from the vehicle.

To install:

11. Position the compressed coil spring into the lower arm pocket. Make sure the spring pigtail is positioned between the two holes in the pocket.

12. Position the lower arm ends in the crossmember brackets and install new arm-to-crossmember bolts and nuts. Do not tighten at this time.

13. Remove the retaining wire from the strut/spindle assembly, then position the spindle over the ball joint stud.

14. Raise the control arm with a jack to the normal vehicle resting position, ensuring the ball joint stud is inserted into the spindle hole. Install the ball joint nut loosely.

15. With the jack in place, tighten the lower arm-to-crossmember attaching nuts to 141–191 ft. lbs. (191–259 Nm).

➡**When tightening the ball joint nut, do not loosen the nut to install the cotter pin. Tighten the nut until the next set of grooves are aligned with the stud hole, then install the new cotter pin.**

16. Tighten the ball joint stud nut to 109–149 ft. lbs. (148–202 Nm) and install a new cotter pin; bend the cotter pin ends over. Remove the floor jack.

17. If removed, install the dust shield, rotor and brake caliper.

18. If removed, install the steering gear (rack and pinion)-to-crossmember bolts and nuts. Hold the bolts and tighten the nuts to 30–40 ft. lbs. (41–54 Nm).

➡**When tightening the tie rod end nut, do not loosen the nut to install the cotter pin. Tighten the nut until the next set of grooves are aligned with the stud hole, then install the new cotter pin.**

19. Position the tie rod into the steering spindle and install the retaining nut. Tighten the nut to 35–47 ft. lbs. (47–64 Nm) and continue tightening the nut to align the next castellation with the hole in the stud. Install a new cotter pin and bend its ends over.

20. Connect the stabilizer bar link to the lower control arm. Tighten the retaining nut to 11–16 ft. lbs. (16–22 Nm).

21. Install the wheel and tire assembly, then lower the vehicle.

22. Tighten the wheel lug nuts to 85–105 ft. lbs. (115–142 Nm).

23. Check the front end alignment.

Wheel Bearings

ADJUSTMENT

➡**The wheel bearings are an integral part of the hub assembly. They require no periodic maintenance or adjustment. If the bearings are found to be defective, they must be replaced along with the hub assembly.**

REMOVAL & INSTALLATION

Front

➡**The front wheel bearings, hub and anti-lock sensor ring (where applicable) are one unit and cannot be separately serviced or replaced. Therefore, when the wheel bearings are faulty, the entire assembly must be replaced.**

1. Before servicing the vehicle, refer to the precautions in the beginning of this section.

2. Raise and safely support the vehicle.

3. Using a prytool, remove the plastic hub grease cap and discard it.

4. Remove the brake caliper and suspend it with strong cord or wire from the chassis.

✳✳ WARNING

Do not allow the brake caliper to hang from its brake hose.

5. Remove the front disc brake rotor.

6. Remove the front axle wheel hub retainer and discard it.

7. Pull the wheel hub and bearing assembly off of the spindle. If the assembly cannot be removed by hand, a two or three jaw puller may be used. Take care not to damage the spindle.

To install:

8. Install the hub/bearing assembly on the wheel spindle.

9. Install a new front axle wheel hub retainer and tighten it to 221–295 ft. lbs. (300–400 Nm).

10. Install the front disc brake rotor and new push-on nuts.

11. Install a new front hub grease cap, being cautious to avoid damaging or distorting the grease cap.

12. Install the brake caliper.

Turn to Section 6 for brake system applications

FRONT WHEEL SPINDLE

WHEEL HUB

FRONT DISC BRAKE ROTOR SHIELD

7922NG52

Note that the hub assembly shown here is equipped with an anti-lock brake sensor ring (the serrated disc affixed to the inboard side of the hub assembly)

LOCK BOLT TIGHTEN TO 20-40 N.m (15-30 lb-ft)

DIFFERENTIAL PINION SHAFT

7922NG65

Be sure to tighten the pinion shaft lockbolt as indicated to prevent it from accidentally loosening

13. Install the wheel and tire assembly, and snug the wheel lug nuts.

14. Lower the vehicle and remove the rear wheel blocks.

15. Tighten the wheel lug nuts in a criss-cross pattern to 85–105 ft. lbs. (115–143 Nm).

Rear

1. Before servicing the vehicle, refer to the precautions in the beginning of this section.

2. Raise and support the vehicle.

3. Remove the wheel, then remove the rear brake caliper and rotor.

4. If equipped, remove the anti-lock brake speed sensor.

5. Clean all dirt from the area of the axle housing cover. Drain the axle lubricant by removing the housing cover.

6. Remove the differential pinion shaft lockbolt and pinion shaft.

7. Push the flanged end of the axle shaft toward the center of the vehicle (to create the necessary play and free the C-lock), then remove the C-lock from the button end of the axle shaft.

8. Slowly withdraw the axle shaft from the housing, being careful not to damage the oil seal (unless you are replacing it anyway).

9. If the seal is being replaced (or if you damaged it on the way out) insert a wheel bearing and seal replacement tool, such as T85L-1225-AH or equivalent, in the bore and position it behind the bearing so the tangs on the tool engage the bearing outer race. Remove the bearing and seal as a unit, using an impact slide hammer.

➡ **If only the seal is being replaced, use a seal removal tool to pry ONLY THE SEAL from the axle housing.**

To install:

10. If removed, lubricate the new bearing with rear axle lubricant. Install the bearing into the housing bore with a bearing installer.

11. If removed, install a new axle seal using a seal installer. Essentially, the installation tool is a driver of the right diameter; a smooth socket or piece of pipe can also be used as a driver, just be careful not to damage the seal.

➡ **Check for the presence of an axle shaft O-ring on the spline end of the shaft; install one if none is found.**

12. Carefully slide the axle shaft **STRAIGHT** into the axle housing, without damaging the bearing or seal assembly. Start the splines into the side gear and push firmly until the shaft splines engage. It may be necessary to rotate the axle slightly to align the splines.

13. Install the C-lock, then pull outward slightly on the axle shaft and be sure the C-lock seats in the counterbore of the differential side gear.

14. Insert the differential pinion shaft through the case and pinion gears, aligning the hole in the shaft with the lockbolt hole. Apply a suitable locking compound to the lockbolt and insert it through the case and pinion shaft. Tighten the lockbolt to 15–30 ft. lbs. (20–41 Nm).

15. Cover the inside of the differential case with a shop rag and clean the machined surface of the carrier and cover. Remove the shop rag.

16. Carefully clean the gasket mating surfaces of the cover and axle housing of any remaining gasket or sealer. A putty knife is a good tool to use for this. You may want to cover the differential gears using a rag or piece of plastic to prevent contaminating them with dirt or pieces of the old gasket.

17. Install the rear cover using a new gasket and sealant. Tighten the retaining bolts using a crosswise pattern.

18. Refill the rear axle housing. Install the filler plug.

19. If removed, install the anti-lock speed sensor and tighten the retaining bolt to 40–60 inch lbs. (5–7 Nm).

20. Install the brake caliper and rotor.

21. Install the wheels, then lower the vehicle.

FORD MOTOR COMPANY

24

Lincoln-Mark VIII

PRECAUTIONS

Before servicing any vehicle, please be sure to read all of the following precautions, which deal with personal safety, prevention of component damage, and important points to take into consideration when servicing a motor vehicle:

• Never open, service or drain the radiator or cooling system when the engine is hot; serious burns can occur from the steam and hot coolant.

• Observe all applicable safety precautions when working around fuel. Whenever servicing the fuel system, always work in a well ventilated area. Do not allow fuel spray or vapors to come in contact with a spark, open flame, or excessive heat (a hot drop light, for example). Keep a dry chemical fire extinguisher near the work area. Always keep fuel in a container specifically designed for fuel storage; also, always properly seal fuel containers to avoid the possibility of fire or explosion. Refer to the additional fuel system precautions later in this section.

• Fuel injection systems often remain pressurized, even after the engine has been turned **OFF**. The fuel system pressure must be relieved before disconnecting any fuel lines. Failure to do so may result in fire and/or personal injury.

• Brake fluid often contains polyglycol ethers and polyglycols. Avoid contact with the eyes and wash your hands thoroughly after handling brake fluid. If you do get brake fluid in your eyes, flush your eyes with clean, running water for 15 minutes. If eye irritation persists, or if you have taken brake fluid internally, IMMEDIATELY seek medical assistance.

• The EPA warns that prolonged contact with used engine oil may cause a number of skin disorders, including cancer! You should make every effort to minimize your exposure to used engine oil. Protective gloves should be worn when changing oil. Wash your hands and any other exposed skin areas as soon as possible after exposure to used engine oil. Soap and water, or waterless hand cleaner should be used.

• All new vehicles are now equipped with an air bag system, often referred to as a Supplemental Restraint System (SRS) or Supplemental Inflatable Restraint (SIR) system. The system must be disabled before performing service on or around system components, steering column, instrument panel components, wiring and sensors. Failure to follow safety and disabling procedures could result in accidental air bag deployment, possible personal injury and unnecessary system repairs.

• Always wear safety goggles when working with, or around, the air bag system. When carrying a non-deployed air bag, be sure the bag and trim cover are pointed away from your body. When placing a non-deployed air bag on a work surface, always face the bag and trim cover upward, away from the surface. This will reduce the motion of the module if it is accidentally deployed. Refer to the additional air bag system precautions later in this section.

• Clean, high quality brake fluid from a sealed container is essential to the safe and proper operation of the brake system. You should always buy the correct type of brake fluid for your vehicle. If the brake fluid becomes contaminated, completely flush the system with new fluid. Never reuse any brake fluid. Any brake fluid that is removed from the system should be discarded. Also, do not allow any brake fluid to come in contact with a painted surface; it will damage the paint.

• Never operate the engine without the proper amount and type of engine oil; doing so WILL result in severe engine damage.

• Timing belt maintenance is extremely important! Many models utilize an interference-type, non-freewheeling engine. If the timing belt breaks, the valves in the cylinder head may strike the pistons, causing potentially serious (also time-consuming and expensive) engine damage. Refer to the maintenance interval charts in the front of this manual for the recommended replacement interval for the timing belt, and to the timing belt section for belt replacement and inspection.

• Disconnecting the negative battery cable on some vehicles may interfere with the functions of the on-board computer system(s) and may require the computer to undergo a relearning process once the negative battery cable is reconnected.

• When servicing drum brakes, only dissemble and assemble one side at a time, leaving the remaining side intact for reference.

• Only an MVAC-trained, EPA-certified automotive technician should service the A/C system or its components.

ENGINE REPAIR

Ignition Timing

ADJUSTMENT

The ignition timing is controlled by the Engine Control Module (ECM). No provision is made for timing adjustment.

Engine Assembly

REMOVAL & INSTALLATION

1. Before servicing the vehicle, refer to the precautions in the beginning of this section.

2. Disconnect the negative battery cable. Drain the crankcase and the cooling system.

3. Remove the engine appearance cover.

4. Properly relieve the fuel system pressure and discharge the A/C system.

5. Disconnect the Intake Air Temperature (IAT) sensor and the crankcase vent tube from the air cleaner outlet tube. Loosen the air cleaner outlet-to-throttle body bolt and disconnect the tube.

6. Remove the remaining bolt from support bracket clamp on right valve cover and remove air cleaner outlet tube assembly and resonator assembly.

7. Remove the hush panel to expose the windshield wiper module, remove the screw, lower module and bracket assembly and unplug the electrical connector. Remove the wiper module.

8. Remove the cooling fan and shroud.

9. Disconnect the fuel lines. Remove the 42 pin connector from the retaining bracket on the left fender well. Detach the connector and position aside.

10. Remove the power distribution box and remove the alternator **B+** connector from inside of the box.

11. Detach the engine harness connector from the canister purge solenoid assembly. Disconnect the accelerator and speed control cables from the throttle body and accelerator cable bracket.

12. Disconnect the canister purge vacuum line at the throttle body and chassis vacuum supply hose at the connection on the cowl support.

13. Disconnect the heater supply and return hose at the rear of the right cylinder head and upper radiator hose at the coolant crossover tube.

14. Remove the power steering return and supply hoses from the reservoir and drain the fluid into an appropriate container. Remove the reservoir retaining bolt and stud from the left coil bracket and remove the reservoir.

15. Remove the upper transmission cooler line from the radiator.

16. Install suitable engine lifting eyes. Disconnect and plug the air conditioning compressor lines and disconnect the retaining clips from the pump.

17. Raise and safely support the vehicle. Remove the wheel and tire assemblies.

18. Detach right and left ride height sensor electrical connectors.

19. Remove the right and left caliper bolts and remove the calipers from the rotors. Support calipers with mechanic's wire.

20. Disconnect the right and left upper control arms from the spindles.

21. Remove the Y-pipe from both exhaust manifolds and the resonator. Disconnect the ground strap from the right fender apron.

22. Detach the power steering pressure line from the steering rack at the power steering pump connection.

23. Remove the lower radiator hose. Remove the right and left lower strut-to-control arm bolts and nuts.

24. Disconnect the transmission wiring harness and shift linkage.

25. Disconnect the lower transmission cooler line from the radiator.

26. Index the driveshaft to the rear axle companion flange.

27. Remove the four bolts connecting the driveshaft to the rear axle companion flange. Support the rear axle housing.

28. Remove the two nut and bolt assemblies retaining the front of the differential to the undercarriage. Loosen the rear differential bracket-to-body bolts.

29. Slide the driveshaft rearward until it is free of the transmission extension housing.

30. Remove the two nuts from the bottom front cover studs and remove the starter cable.

31. Detach the low oil level sensor connector and wiring harness from the oil pan. Remove the starter.

32. Support the sub-frame with Rotunda Powertrain Lift 014–00765 and adapter 014–00341, or equivalent. Remove the rear transmission mount bolts.

33. Disconnect the steering shaft coupler at the rag joint. Remove the eight sub-frame bolts.

34. Lower the engine and transmission assembly from the vehicle.

35. Remove the motor mount through-bolts.

36. Install suitable engine lifting equipment on the engine lifting eyes and lift the engine and transmission from the sub-frame.

37. Lower the engine and transmission.

Support the transmission on a level, stationary surface for transmission storage.

38. Remove the transmission-to-cylinder block mounting bolts and separate the engine from the transmission/torque converter assembly. Place the engine on a suitable workstand. Remove the engine lifting equipment.

39. Remove the right and left motor mounts from the block. Drain the coolant and remove the right and left water jacket pipe plugs from the cylinder block. Reinstall the plugs.

40. Detach the EGR-to-exhaust manifold tube from the left exhaust manifold connector, differential pressure feedback EGR hose connections and loosen the EGR tube connector at the EGR control valve. Remove the EGR valve-to-exhaust manifold tube.

41. Remove the exhaust manifolds and discard the gaskets.

To install:

42. Install the exhaust manifolds with new gaskets. Tighten the nuts in sequence to 15–22 ft. lbs. (20–30 Nm).

43. Connect the EGR system.

44. Install the left and right motor mounts to the engine block. Install the engine lifting bracket.

45. Remove the engine from the stand using suitable lifting equipment.

46. Connect the transmission to the cylinder block. Tighten the bolts to 30–44 ft. lbs. (40–60 Nm).

47. Position the engine and transmission on the sub-frame assembly. Install the mount through-bolts and tighten them to 15–22 ft. lbs. (20–30 Nm).

48. Raise the engine, transmission and sub-frame assembly into position.

49. Align the sub-frame-to-body and install the bolts. Tighten them to 73–100 ft. lbs. (95–130 Nm).

50. Connect the steering shaft coupler at the rag joint. Install the rear transmission mount bolt and tighten to 15–22 ft. lbs. (20–30 Nm). Remove the lifting equipment.

51. Install the starter, low oil level sensor and lower engine wiring harness.

52. Install the starter cable and two retaining nuts to the lower front cover studs.

53. Install the driveshaft to the transmission. Lift the rear differential into position. Install the two nut and bolt assemblies retaining the front of the differential to the rear sub-frame and tighten to 72–89 ft. lbs. (98–120 Nm).

54. Tighten the two differential mounts to 75–89 ft. lbs. (102–127 Nm). Align the driveshaft to the companion flange and

install the four bolts. Tighten them to 70–96 ft. lbs. (95–130 Nm).

55. Connect the lower transmission cooler line to the radiator. Connect the transmission wiring harness and shift linkage.

56. Position the lower control arms to the strut and install the bolt. Tighten the bolt to 118–162 ft. lbs. (160–220 Nm).

57. Install the lower radiator hose and power steering pressure line. Connect the ground strap to the right fender apron.

58. Install the exhaust Y-pipe.

59. Connect the upper control arms to the spindles. Tighten the bolt to 50–68 ft. lbs. (68–92 Nm). Connect the right and left ride height sensors.

60. Install the brake calipers. Install the front wheels. Lower the vehicle.

61. Unplug and connect the air conditioning lines. Remove the engine lifting brackets and eyelets.

62. Connect the upper transmission cooler line.

63. Install the power steering reservoir, power steering return line and power steering supply hose.

64. Install the coolant supply hose to the reservoir. Connect the upper radiator hose at the crossover pipe and connect the heater supply and return hoses.

65. Connect the chassis vacuum supply and canister purge vacuum hoses.

66. Connect the accelerator and speed control cables. Connect the engine wiring harness to the canister purge solenoid assembly.

67. Attach the alternator **B+** connector and install the power distribution box. Attach the 42 pin connector to the retaining bracket on the left fender.

68. Connect the fuel lines. Install the cooling fan and shroud.

69. Install the windshield wiper module. Install the engine air cleaner outlet tube assembly and resonator assembly.

70. Connect the IAT sensor and crankcase vent tube.

71. Fill the engine with the proper type and quantity of engine oil. Fill and bleed the cooling system.

72. Fill the power steering system with the proper type and quantity of fluid. Connect the negative battery cable.

73. Start the engine and bring to normal operating temperature. Check for leaks. Check all fluid levels.

74. Leak test, evacuate and charge the air conditioning system. Observe all safety precautions.

75. Install the engine appearance cover.

Water Pump

REMOVAL & INSTALLATION

1. Before servicing the vehicle, refer to the precautions in the beginning of this section.

2. Disconnect the negative battery cable and drain the cooling system.

3. Remove the four bolts retaining the pulley to the water pump shaft.

4. Release belt tensioner and remove the drive belts. Remove the four bolts retaining the water pump pulley and remove the pulley.

5. Remove the four water pump retaining bolts and remove the water pump.

To install:

6. Install a new water pump O-ring seal.

7. Installation is the reverse of the removal procedure. Clean all mating surfaces prior to installation. Tighten the water pump bolts and pulley retaining bolts to 15–22 ft. lbs. (20–30 Nm).

8. Fill and bleed the cooling system. Operate the engine until normal operating temperatures have been reached and check for leaks.

WATER PUMP HOUSING GASKET

BOLT 4 REQ'D TIGHTEN TO 20-30 N·m (15-22 LB-FT)

WATER PUMP

7922PG04

Exploded view of the water pump mounting

Cylinder Head

REMOVAL & INSTALLATION

1. Before servicing the vehicle, refer to the precautions in the beginning of this section.

2. Remove the engine from the vehicle.

3. Remove the valve covers and the engine front cover.

4. Remove the intake manifold.

5. Remove the Crankshaft Position (CKP) sensor and pulse wheel.

6. Remove the rocker arms using the recommended procedure.

7. Remove the exhaust manifolds and drain the coolant.

8. Position the No. 1 cylinder at TDC on the compression stroke. Be sure the timing marks on the camshaft sprockets are on top.

9. Install the Camshaft Positioning tool (T93P-6256-A) into the D-shaped slots at the rear of the camshafts.

10. Remove both left and right primary timing chain tensioners.

11. Remove both primary timing chains, tensioner arms and guides but do not loosen the camshaft sprocket mounting bolts.

12. Remove the one nut and two bolts attaching the inlet heater coolant tube to the rear of the right cylinder head and remove the tube.

13. Remove the outlet heater coolant tube from the rear of the right cylinder head.

14. Loosen the 10 cylinder head bolts in the correct sequence, then remove the head. Discard all cylinder head bolts. New bolts must be used for installation.

✳✳ WARNING

Do not place the bottom of the cylinder head on the workbench or table. Damage to the valves may occur on any that are open.

To install:

15. Clean and dry all cylinder head bolt holes.

16. Turn the crankshaft counterclockwise 90 degrees to the 9 o'clock position. This will position all of the pistons below the deck surface of the engine block.

17. Place new head gaskets on the engine block.

18. Carefully place the cylinder head on the engine block, be sure to align the dowels.

➡**New cylinder head bolts must be used. Cylinder head bolts are of a torque-to-yield design and cannot be reused.**

19. Apply clean engine oil to the new bolt threads and both sides of the bolt washer. Install the cylinder head bolts finger-tight.

➡**The cylinder head bolts should be tightened in three stages using the proper sequence.**

20. Tighten the cylinder head bolts in three steps:

   a. Tighten bolts in sequence to 27–32 ft. lbs. (37–43 Nm).

Be sure to remove the cylinder head bolts in the correct sequence to prevent damage to the head

For proper cylinder sealing, be sure to tighten the cylinder head bolts in the correct sequence

b. Tighten bolts in sequence 85–95 degrees.

c. Tighten bolts in sequence an additional 85–95 degrees.

21. Install the outlet heater coolant tube on the rear of the right cylinder head. Tighten the stud bolts to 15–22 ft. lbs. (20–30 Nm).

22. Install the inlet heater coolant tube on the right cylinder head. Tighten the two bolts and one nut to 71–106 inch lbs. (8–12 Nm).

23. Install the primary timing chains. Be sure the valve timing is correct.

24. Install the rocker arms.

25. Install the CKP sensor and pulse wheel.

26. Install the intake manifold.

27. Install the engine front cover.

28. Install the valve covers.

29. Install the exhaust manifolds.

30. Install the engine assembly in the vehicle.

31. Refill the engine and cooling system with the correct type and amount of fluid.

32. Start the engine and check for leaks.

Rocker Arms

REMOVAL & INSTALLATION

1. Before servicing the vehicle, refer to the precautions in the beginning of this section.

2. Disconnect the negative battery cable.

3. Remove the camshaft covers.

4. Position the cylinder being serviced at the bottom of its stroke.

➡ **Two different valve spring compressor tools are used for this procedure. Valve Spring Compressor (T91P-6565-A) or equivalent is used on the exhaust camshaft and Valve Spring Compressor (T93P-6565-A) or equivalent is used on the intake camshaft.**

5. Compress the valve spring and remove the rocker arm.

To install:

6. Position the cylinder being serviced at the bottom of its stroke.

7. Apply clean engine oil to the rocker arm, valve stem tip and tappet bore.

➡ **Valve tappet should have no more than 1/16 in. (1.5mm) of travel before installing the rocker arm.**

8. Compress the valve spring using the correct tool and install the rocker arm.

Timing belt service is covered in Section 5 of this manual

SECONDARY TENSIONER — 90° — **RH PRIMARY CHAIN** — **SECONDARY TENSIONER** — 90°

TIMING MARK — **TIMING MARK**

LH PRIMARY CHAIN

30 PLATES RH AND LH

7922PG03

The timing marks should be positioned as shown after the primary chains have been installed

VALVE SPRING COMPRESSOR T93P-6565-A

7922PG14

Use the proper tool to compress the valve springs and remove the rocker arms

9. Install the camshaft covers.
10. Connect the negative battery cable.

Intake Manifold

REMOVAL & INSTALLATION

1996 Models

1. Before servicing the vehicle, refer to the precautions in the beginning of this section.

2. Turn the ignition switch to the **ON** position. Turn the wipers ON, then turn the ignition switch **OFF**, to stop the wipers in the mid-wipe position.

3. Disconnect the negative battery cable.

4. Remove the fuel tank fill cap to relieve the pressure in the fuel tank.

5. Remove the cap from the fuel pressure relief valve located on the fuel injection supply manifold.

6. Attach Fuel Pressure Gauge T80L-9974-B or equivalent, to the valve and drain the fuel through the drain tube into a suitable container.

7. After the fuel system pressure is relieved, remove the fuel pressure gauge and install the cap on the fuel pressure relief valve.

8. Install the fuel tank fill cap.

9. Remove the engine appearance cover.

10. Remove the engine and cleaner outlet tube assembly.

11. Remove the hush panel to expose the windshield wiper module, remove screw, lower module and bracket assembly and detach electrical connector. Remove the wiper module.

12. Allow the engine to cool, then drain the cooling system.

13. Disconnect and plug the fuel supply and return lines at the fuel injection supply manifold.

14. Remove the accessory drive belt.

15. Remove air inlet tube support bracket.

16. Remove the left-hand and right-hand ignition wire covers.

17. Label and disconnect the ignition wires from the spark plugs and ignition coils. Detach the center ignition wire separators and remove the ignition wire assembly.

18. Detach the alternator wiring harness at the **B+** terminal and the stator connector plug.

19. Disconnect the wiring harness retaining clip from the alternator support bracket.

20. Remove the two bolts and two studs retaining the support bracket to the alternator and intake manifold.

21. Disconnect the upper radiator hose and coolant bypass hose at the coolant crossover tube.

22. Remove the coolant crossover tube.

23. Remove the alternator assembly.

24. Disconnect the accelerator and speed control cables from the throttle body lever and from the cable mounting bracket.

25. Disconnect the chassis vacuum sup-

ply hose from the intake manifold and position aside.

26. Tag and disconnect the vacuum lines from the fuel pressure regulator, right and left Intake Manifold Runner Control (IMRC) vacuum control, EGR control valve, EGR vacuum regulator control, IMRC vacuum control solenoids and the intake manifold.

27. Disconnect the PCV hose from the throttle body. Remove the PCV valve from the left-hand cylinder head cover and move the PCV tube assembly aside.

28. Disconnect the four engine harness retaining clips from the intake manifold studs and one clip from the fuel regulator bracket.

29. Detach the fuel injector electrical harness connectors.

30. Remove the upper bolt retaining the accelerator cable bracket to the left-hand cylinder head. Loosen the lower bolt and move the bracket against the left-hand cylinder head cover.

31. Remove the two bolts retaining the EGR control valve to the intake manifold, then remove the EGR control valve.

32. Remove the 20 bolts and stud bolts retaining the intake manifold following the proper loosening sequence. Note the locations of the bolts and stud bolts for installation reference.

33. Lift the engine harness upward for intake manifold removal clearance.

34. Lift the front of the intake manifold and IMRC assembly and move the assembly forward to obtain access to the rear of the intake manifold and detach the connectors at the Idle Air Control (IAC), Throttle Position (TP) switch and harness clip at the IAC retaining stud.

35. Remove the intake manifold assembly.

36. Remove the fuel injection supply manifold from the fuel injectors, if required.

37. Remove the right-hand and left-hand IMRC units. Remove the gaskets and load limiting spacers. Discard the gaskets.

38. Remove and discard the EGR and lower intake manifold gaskets.

To install:

39. Clean and inspect all gasket sealing surfaces.

40. Remove the paper from the adhesive backing on a new upper intake manifold gasket. Install the gasket on the top of the right-hand IMRC unit. Use tapered pins at the end bolt hole locations for proper alignment. Repeat the gasket installation for the left-hand IMRC unit.

41. Assemble the IMRC units onto the intake manifold and hand-tighten the four retaining bolts.

42. Install the fuel injection supply manifold onto the fuel injectors and tighten the four retaining screws to 26–45 inch lbs. (3–5 Nm). Install the two fuel pressure regulator retaining bracket screws and tighten to 72–108 inch lbs. (8–12 Nm).

43. Place new IMRC gaskets onto the cylinder heads. Use the gaskets integral location pins to align the gaskets.

44. Place the intake manifold under the engine harness and connect the wiring harness plugs to IAC valve, TP sensor and connect wiring clip to the IAC valve retaining clip.

45. Move the intake manifold into position and install a new EGR valve gasket. Hand-tighten the two retaining bolts.

46. Install the 10 long bolts and stud bolts in the outer holes of the intake manifold. Do not tighten.

47. Install the 10 short bolts and stud bolts in the inner holes of the intake manifold. Hand-tighten all 20 fasteners.

48. Tighten the intake manifold bolts and stud bolts in sequence as follows:

    a. Bolt numbers 5, 7, 9, 11: tighten to 8.8–11 ft. lbs. (12–15 Nm).

    b. All remaining intake manifold bolts: tighten to 13–16 ft. lbs. (18–22 Nm).

    c. Rotate all intake manifold bolts in sequence, 85–95 degrees.

49. Tighten the four IMRC retaining bolts to 6–8 ft. lbs. (8–10 Nm). Tighten, in sequence, 85–95 degrees.

50. Tighten the two EGR retaining bolts to 15–22 ft. lbs. (20–30 Nm).

51. Install the upper retaining bolt into the accelerator cable bracket and tighten both upper and lower bolts to 15–22 ft. lbs. (20–30 Nm).

52. Attach the fuel injector electrical harness connectors.

53. Connect the engine harness clips to the intake manifold studs and connect the harness clip to the fuel pressure regulator bracket. Connect the PCV system.

54. Attach the vacuum harness connectors to the fuel pressure regulator, right and left IMRC vacuum controls, EGR vacuum regulator control, IMRC vacuum control solenoids and intake manifold vacuum at the rear connection.

55. Attach the chassis vacuum supply hose and spring clamp to the intake manifold vacuum at the forward connection.

56. Connect the accelerator and speed control cables to the throttle body lever and to the cable mounting bracket.

57. Replace the O-rings on the coolant crossover tubes, if necessary. Insert the crossover tube support braces over the intake manifold inner studs and press the crossover tube into place. Install the retaining nuts and tighten to 6–9 ft. lbs. (8–12 Nm).

58. Attach the Engine Coolant Temperature (ECT) and temperature gauge sensor electrical harness connectors. Connect the upper radiator hose and coolant bypass hose at the coolant crossover tube.

59. Install the alternator and tighten the two bolts to 15–22 ft. lbs. (20–30 Nm). Install the alternator support bracket and tighten the two bolts and two stud bolts to 6–9 ft. lbs. (8–12 Nm).

60. Attach the alternator wiring harness connector plug and the **B+** terminal wire to the alternator. Connect the wiring harness retaining clip to the support bracket.

61. Install the center ignition wire separators and the ignition wire assembly. Connect the ignition wires to the spark plugs and ignition coils.

62. Install the accessory drive belt.

63. Install the engine air inlet tube support bracket. Tighten the retaining nuts to 6–9 ft. lbs. (8–12 Nm).

FRONT OF ENGINE

7922PG05

Be sure to tighten the intake manifold fasteners in the sequence shown to ensure sealing—1996 models

Install the bolts and studs in the correct locations—1996 models

64. Unplug and connect the fuel supply and return lines at the fuel injection supply manifold.

65. Install the engine air cleaner outlet tube and resonator assembly.

66. Install the windshield wiper module.

67. Fill and bleed the engine cooling system.

68. Connect the negative battery cable.

69. Start the engine and check for fuel, coolant and oil leaks.

70. Install the engine appearance cover.

71. Road test the vehicle and check for proper engine operation.

1997–98 Models

1. Before servicing the vehicle, refer to the precautions in the beginning of this section.

2. Disconnect the negative battery cable.

3. Relieve fuel system pressure as follows.

4. Remove the water bypass tube.

5. Disconnect the accelerator and cruise control cables.

6. Disconnect the evaporator emission hose from the upper intake manifold.

7. Detach the Throttle Position (TP) sensor electrical connector.

8. Disconnect the crankcase ventilation hose from the intake manifold.

9. Detach the Idle Air Control (IAC) valve electrical connector.

10. Loosen the EGR tube nut from the EGR valve.

11. Disconnect the EGR valve vacuum hose.

12. Remove the bolts and remove the upper intake manifold.

13. Remove the fuel injection supply manifold.

14. Remove the bolts and remove the lower intake manifold.

15. Disconnect the right and left Intake Manifold Runner Control (IMRC).

16. Remove the IMRC and the upper and lower gaskets. The lower runner control gaskets are housed within the grooves on the bottom surface of the IMRC. Discard the lower gaskets and use new ones.

To install:

17. Install the right and left IMRC and gaskets and tighten the retaining bolts to 71–89 inch lbs. (8–10 Nm) plus an additional 85–95 degree rotation.

18. Install the lower intake manifold and following the sequence shown, tighten the 10 retaining fasteners to 15–22 ft. lbs. (20–30 Nm).

19. Tighten the two remaining lower intake manifold retaining bolts shown, to 71–88 inch lbs. (8–10 Nm) plus an additional 85–95 degree rotation.

20. Install the fuel injection supply manifold and tighten the retaining bolts to 71–106 inch lbs. (8–12 Nm).

21. Install the upper intake manifold and tighten the retaining bolts to 15–22 ft. lbs. (20–30 Nm).

Tighten the intake manifold bolts according to the sequence shown to prevent leakage—1997–98 models

After tightening the 10 lower intake manifold bolts in sequence, tighten these two remaining bolts to specifications—1997–98 models

22. Tighten the EGR valve tube nut and connect the EGR valve vacuum hose.

23. Attach the IAC valve electrical connector.

24. Connect the crankcase ventilation hose to the intake manifold.

25. Attach the TP sensor electrical connector.

26. Connect the evaporator emission hose to the upper intake manifold.

27. Connect the accelerator and cruise control cables.

28. Install the water bypass tube.

29. Disconnect the negative battery cable.

Exhaust Manifold

REMOVAL & INSTALLATION

1996 Models

RIGHT SIDE

1. Before servicing the vehicle, refer to the precautions in the beginning of this section.

2. Turn the air suspension switch, which is located in the luggage compartment, to the OFF position.

3. Disconnect the negative battery cable.

4. Remove the engine appearance

cover. Detach the Intake Air Temperature (IAT) sensor electrical harness connector and the crankcase vent tube from the engine air cleaner outlet tube.

5. Completely loosen the air cleaner outlet-to-throttle body bolt.

6. Remove the remaining bolt from the support bracket clamp on the right-hand cylinder head cover-to-air cleaner outlet tube assembly and remove the assembly and resonator.

7. Detach the Heated Oxygen (HO2) sensor electrical harness connector and the secondary air injection manifold tube.

8. Raise and safely support the vehicle.

9. Remove the four exhaust manifold-to-cylinder head retaining nuts from the upper side of the exhaust manifold.

10. Disconnect the dual converter Y-pipe from both exhaust manifolds and remove the dual converter Y-pipe assembly.

11. Remove the four lower exhaust manifold-to-cylinder head retaining nuts and remove the manifold. Remove the exhaust manifold gasket and discard it.

To install:

12. If the exhaust manifold is being replaced, transfer the EGR valve tube-to-exhaust manifold connector. Tighten the connector to 24–35 ft. lbs. (32–48 Nm).

13. Clean the exhaust manifold gasket sealing surfaces.

14. Place a new exhaust manifold gasket and the exhaust manifold in position on the right-hand cylinder head.

15. Install the eight upper and lower exhaust manifold retaining nuts and tighten, in sequence, to 14–16 ft. lbs. (18–22 Nm).

16. Install the dual converter Y-pipe assembly to both exhaust manifolds.

17. Lower the vehicle.

18. Attach the HO2 sensor electrical harness connector and the secondary air injection manifold tube.

19. Install the engine air cleaner outlet tube and resonator assembly. Install the outlet tube-to-throttle body bolt and tighten to 16–23 inch lbs. (1.8–2.6 Nm).

20. Install the engine air cleaner outlet tube bracket and tighten to 45–63 inch lbs. (5.1–7.1 Nm). Tighten the air cleaner outlet tube clamp to 15–29 inch lbs. (1.7–3.3 Nm).

21. Attach the IAT sensor electrical harness connector and the crankcase vent tube to the air cleaner outlet tube.

22. Install the engine appearance cover.

23. Turn the air suspension switch to the ON position.

24. Connect the negative battery cable.

25. Start the engine and check for exhaust leaks.

26. Road test the vehicle and check for proper engine operation.

LEFT SIDE

1. Before servicing the vehicle, refer to the precautions in the beginning of this section.

2. Turn the air suspension switch, which is located in the luggage compartment, to the OFF position.

3. Disconnect the negative battery cable.

4. Detach the Heated Oxygen (HO2) sensor electrical harness connector.

5. Disconnect the left-hand secondary air injection manifold tube.

6. Remove the left-hand secondary air injection tube bracket bolt from the exhaust manifold.

7. Install the 3-Bar Engine Support D88L-6000-A or equivalent to the engine compartment and secure to suitable engine lifting brackets on the engine.

8. Raise and safely support the vehicle.

9. Remove the front wheel and tire assemblies.

10. Disconnect the EGR valve-to-exhaust manifold tube at the dual converter Y-pipe.

11. Detach the left-hand and right-hand exhaust manifold connections at the dual converter Y-pipe.

12. Detach the left-hand and right-hand ride height sensor wiring connectors.

13. Remove the right-hand and left-hand disc brake caliper bolts. Remove the brake calipers and support them with mechanic's wire.

14. Disconnect the left-hand and right-hand upper control arms from the wheel spindles.

15. Disconnect the steering shaft coupling at the pinch bolt joint.

16. Remove the power steering line clamp from the sub-frame.

17. Support the sub-frame with a suitable jack.

18. Remove the two front engine support insulator (mount) through-bolts. Remove the left-hand and right-hand lower strut-to-control arm retaining nuts and bolts.

19. Remove the eight sub-frame retaining bolts, then carefully lower the sub-frame.

20. Remove the eight exhaust manifold retaining nuts and remove the left-hand

FRONT OF ENGINE

7922PG10

Tighten the exhaust manifold bolts in the sequence shown—1996 models

Refer to Section 1 for engine rebuilding specifications

exhaust manifold. Remove and discard the gaskets.

To install:

21. If the exhaust manifold is being replaced, transfer the HO2 sensor and the EGR valve tube-to-exhaust manifold connector. Tighten the HO2 sensor to 27–33 ft. lbs. (37–45 Nm) and the EGR tube connector to 24–35 ft. lbs. (32–48 Nm).

22. Clean the left-hand exhaust manifold gasket sealing surfaces.

23. Place new front and rear exhaust manifold gaskets on the cylinder head studs.

24. Place the left-hand exhaust manifold in position and install the eight retaining nuts. Tighten the nuts in the correct sequence, to 14–16 ft. lbs. (18–22 Nm).

25. Connect the EGR valve-to-exhaust manifold tube. Tighten the nuts to 30–33 ft. lbs. (40–45 Nm).

26. Raise the sub-frame into position and install the eight sub-frame retaining bolts Only hand-tighten the bolts at this time.

27. Install a ¾ in. (19mm) outside diameter length of suitable pipe into both the left-hand and right-hand front sub-frame and body alignment holes to align the sub-frame to the body. Tighten one bolt on each corner securely.

28. Remove the alignment tool, then tighten all sub-frame retaining bolts to 57–75 ft. lbs. (77–103 Nm).

29. Install the two front engine support insulator through-bolts.

30. Connect the power steering line clamp to the sub-frame.

31. Connect the left-hand and right-hand upper control arms to the wheel spindles. Tighten the pinch bolt retaining nut to 50–68 ft. lbs. (68–92 Nm).

32. Connect the steering shaft coupling at the pinch bolt joint. Tighten the pinch bolt to 30–42 ft. lbs. (41–57 Nm).

33. Install the disc brake calipers and bolts. Tighten the brake pin retainers to 16–23 ft. lbs. (22–32 Nm).

34. Attach the left-hand and right-hand ride height sensor wiring connectors.

35. Connect the dual converter Y-pipe to the exhaust manifolds.

36. Install the front wheel and tire assemblies. Tighten the lug nuts to 85–105 ft. lbs. (115–142 Nm).

37. Remove the jack.

38. Lower the vehicle.

39. Attach the HO2 sensor electrical harness connector.

40. Install the left-hand secondary air

injection manifold tube to the exhaust manifold and install the secondary air tube bracket bolt. Tighten the bracket bolt to 15–22 ft. lbs. (20–30 Nm) and the tube nuts to 24–35 ft. lbs. (32–48 Nm).

41. Remove the 3-Bar Engine Support or equivalent, from the engine compartment.

42. Connect the negative battery cable.

43. Turn the air suspension switch to the ON position.

44. Start the vehicle and check for exhaust leaks.

➡ **Whenever the vehicle's sub-frame is removed or lowered, the wheel alignment should be checked.**

45. Check the alignment and adjust if not within specification.

46. Road test the vehicle and check for proper engine operation.

1997–98 Models

RIGHT SIDE

1. Before servicing the vehicle, refer to the precautions in the beginning of this section.

2. Turn the air suspension switch, which is located in the luggage compartment, to the OFF position.

3. Disconnect the negative battery cable.

Be sure to tighten the bolts according to the sequence shown to prevent leaks—1997–98 models, right side shown

18-22 Nm (14-16 lb/ft)

7922PG11

Be sure to tighten the bolts according to the sequence shown to prevent leaks—1996–98 models, left side shown

4. Detach the Heated Oxygen (HO2) sensor electrical harness connector and the secondary air injection manifold tube.

5. Raise and safely support the vehicle.

6. Disconnect the dual converter Y-pipe.

7. Disconnect the exhaust air tube from the exhaust manifold.

8. Remove the four exhaust manifold-to-cylinder head retaining nuts from the upper side of the exhaust manifold.

9. Remove the four lower exhaust manifold-to-cylinder head retaining nuts and remove the manifold. Remove the exhaust manifold gasket and discard it.

To install:

10. Clean the exhaust manifold gasket sealing surfaces.

11. Place a new exhaust manifold gasket and the exhaust manifold in position on the right-hand cylinder head.

12. Install the eight upper and lower exhaust manifold retaining nuts and tighten in sequence, to 14–16 ft. lbs. (18–22 Nm).

13. Connect the exhaust air tube to the exhaust manifold.

14. Install the dual converter Y-pipe assembly to both exhaust manifolds.

15. Lower the vehicle.

16. Attach the HO2 sensor electrical harness connector and the secondary air injection manifold tube.

17. Turn the air suspension switch to the ON position.

18. Connect the negative battery cable.

19. Start the engine and check for exhaust leaks.

20. Road test the vehicle and check for proper engine operation.

LEFT SIDE

1. Before servicing the vehicle, refer to

the precautions in the beginning of this section.

2. Turn the air suspension switch, which is located in the luggage compartment, to the OFF position.

3. Disconnect the negative battery cable.

4. Disconnect the left side Heated Oxygen (HO2) sensor.

5. Raise and safely support the vehicle.

6. Disconnect the dual converter Y-pipe.

7. Disconnect the exhaust air tube from the exhaust manifold.

8. Disconnect the EGR valve-to-exhaust manifold tube.

9. Remove the four exhaust manifold-to-cylinder head retaining nuts from the upper side of the exhaust manifold.

10. Remove the four lower exhaust manifold-to-cylinder head retaining nuts and remove the manifold. Remove the exhaust manifold gasket and discard it.

To install:

11. Clean the exhaust manifold gasket sealing surfaces.

12. Place a new exhaust manifold gasket and the exhaust manifold in position on the right-hand cylinder head.

13. Install the eight upper and lower exhaust manifold retaining nuts and tighten in sequence, to 14–16 ft. lbs. (18–22 Nm).

14. Connect the EGR valve-to-exhaust manifold tube. Tighten the nuts to 30–33 ft. lbs. (40–45 Nm).

15. Connect the exhaust air tube from the exhaust manifold.

16. Install the dual converter Y-pipe assembly to both exhaust manifolds.

17. Lower the vehicle.

18. Connect the HO2 sensor.

19. Turn the air suspension switch to the ON position.

20. Connect the negative battery cable.

21. Start the engine and check for exhaust leaks.

22. Road test the vehicle and check for proper engine operation.

Camshaft and Valve Lifters

REMOVAL & INSTALLATION

1. Before servicing the vehicle, refer to the precautions in the beginning of this section.

2. Disconnect the negative battery cable. Remove the engine from the vehicle and position on a suitable workstand.

3. Remove the cylinder head covers and the engine front cover.

4. Remove the timing chains.

➡️ **If the rocker arms are to be reused, label them as they are removed so they can be reinstalled in their original locations.**

5. Remove the rocker arms from the cylinder head and the camshaft that is being serviced. If both bank camshafts are to be serviced, all the rocker arms must be removed.

6. Remove 13 bolts retaining the exhaust camshaft cap cluster assemblies to the cylinder head to remove the exhaust camshaft.

7. Remove 12 bolts retaining the intake camshaft cap cluster assemblies to the cylinder head to remove the intake camshaft.

8. Tap upward lightly on the camshaft cap clusters and gradually lift the camshaft cap clusters from the cylinder head.

9. Lift the camshaft straight upward to avoid bearing surface damage.

10. If required, lift off the rocker arm and pull the lash adjuster (lifter) out of its bore. Be sure to return the lash adjuster and rocker to the same location that it was removed from.

➡️ **The previous steps will remove only one bank of camshafts. If both banks are being serviced, repeat the removal procedure for the remaining camshafts.**

11. Inspect the camshaft lobes and journals for wear and/or damage. Replace as necessary.

To install:

➡️ **When cleaning the sealing surfaces of the engine front cover and the oil pan-to-cylinder block joints, use extreme caution not to damage the rubber bead of the oil pan gasket. If damaged, the oil pan gasket must be replaced.**

12. Clean and inspect the cylinder head cover, engine front cover, and cylinder head sealing surfaces.

13. If removed, install the lash adjusters (lifters) and rocker arms.

14. Apply clean engine oil to the journals and lobes of the camshaft.

Install the camshaft to the cylinder head.

15. Install and seat the camshaft cap cluster assemblies. Hand-start twelve 2 in. (52mm) long bolts into the intake camshaft caps, seven 2 in. (52mm) long bolts into the inboard side of the exhaust camshaft and the six 1 11/16 in. (42mm) long bolts into the outboard side of the exhaust camshaft caps.

➡️ **Each camshaft cap cluster is tightened individually.**

16. Tighten the camshaft cap cluster retaining bolts, in sequence, to 71–106 inch lbs. (8–12 Nm).

17. Loosen the camshaft cap cluster retaining bolts approximately two turns or until the head of the bolt is free.

18. Tighten all bolts again, in sequence, to 71–106 inch lbs. (8–12 Nm).

➡️ **Once installed, the camshaft should turn freely but with a slight drag.**

19. Check the camshaft end-play using a dial indicator.

20. Install the timing chains.

21. Install Valve Spring Compressor T91P-6565-A or equivalent, under the exhaust camshaft and on top of the exhaust valve spring retainer. Compress the valve spring far enough to install the rocker arm.

22. Install Valve Spring Compressor T93P-6565-A or equivalent, under the intake camshaft and on top of the primary intake valve spring retainer. Compress the valve spring far enough to install the rocker arm.

23. Install Valve Spring Compressor T93P-6565-A or equivalent, under the intake camshaft and on top of the secondary intake valve spring retainer. Compress the valve spring far enough to install the rocker arm.

➡️ **The previous installation steps must be repeated if both banks are being serviced to install the remaining camshafts.**

24. Inspect and replace the crankshaft front seal and timing chain front cover gasket.

25. Install the engine front cover and the cylinder head covers.

26. Remove the engine from the workstand and install in the vehicle.

27. Start the engine and check for leaks.

28. Road test the vehicle and check for proper engine operation.

Tighten the camshaft cap clusters in the order shown to prevent camshaft damage

Valve Lash

ADJUSTMENT

The 4.6L DOHC engine uses hydraulic valve lash adjusters that do no require any maintenance. If the valvetrain becomes noisy, inspect the camshaft, rocker arm and valve for excessive wear or damage.

Oil Pan

REMOVAL & INSTALLATION

1. Before servicing the vehicle, refer to the precautions in the beginning of this section.

2. Turn the air suspension switch, located in the luggage compartment, to the OFF position.

3. Disconnect the negative battery cable.

4. Remove the engine appearance cover.

5. Remove the engine oil level dipstick.

6. Install Three Bar Engine Support D88L-6000-A or equivalent, into the engine compartment and attach to the engine using suitable lifting brackets.

7. Raise and safely support the vehicle.

8. Remove the front wheel and tire assemblies.

9. Drain the engine oil.

10. Detach the left-hand and right-hand ride height sensor electrical harness connectors.

11. Remove the right-hand and left-hand disc brake caliper retaining bolts. Remove the brake calipers from the rotors and support with mechanic's wire. Do not allow the brake calipers to hang by the brake hoses.

12. Remove the pinch bolts and nuts and separate the left-hand and right-hand upper control arms from the wheel spindles.

13. Remove the pinch bolt at the steering column coupling joint and separate the coupling.

14. Remove the power steering hose clamp from the sub-frame.

15. Support the sub-frame.

16. Remove the two front engine support insulator (mount) through-bolts.

17. Remove the left-hand and right-hand strut-to-lower control arm retaining nuts. Separate the struts from the lower control arms.

18. Remove the eight sub-frame retaining bolts.

19. Lower the sub-frame enough to access the engine oil pan.

20. Detach the low oil level sensor electrical harness connector and sensor wiring clips from the engine oil pan rail in two places.

21. Remove the 16 engine oil pan bolts and remove the oil pan.

22. If removing the oil pump pick-up tube, remove the two bolts retaining the tube to the oil pump and one nut securing the tube to the main bearing stud. Remove and discard the gasket at the oil pump.

To install:

23. Clean the engine oil pan gasket sealing surfaces and inspect for damage.

24. Clean the oil pump pick-up tube screen, if required.

25. If the oil pump pick-up tube was removed, install the tube to the oil pump housing using a new gasket and install the two retaining bolts. Tighten the bolts to 71–106 inch lbs. (8–12 Nm). Install the nut retaining the tube to the main bearing stud and tighten to 15–22 ft. lbs. (20–30 Nm).

26. Place a new gasket on the engine oil pan.

27. Apply silicone sealer where the engine front cover meets the cylinder block and where the rear crankshaft seal retainer meets the cylinder block.

28. Carefully place the engine oil pan in

position on the cylinder block and install 16 oil pan bolts. Tighten the bolts in sequence, to 15 ft. lbs. (20 Nm), then rotate the bolts an additional 60 degrees.

29. Attach the low oil level sensor electrical harness connector and the sensor wiring clips to the engine oil pan rail.

30. Raise the sub-frame into position and install the eight sub-frame retaining bolts. Only hand-tighten the bolts at this time.

31. Install a ¾ in. (19mm) outside diameter length of suitable pipe into both the left-hand and right-hand front sub-frame and body alignment holes to align the sub-frame to the body. Tighten one bolt on each corner securely.

32. Remove the alignment tools, then tighten all sub-frame retaining bolts to 57–75 ft. lbs. (77–103 Nm).

33. Place the struts into the lower control arms and install the retaining nuts. Tighten the nuts to 83–113 ft. lbs. (113–153 Nm).

34. Install the two front engine support insulator through-bolts.

35. Connect the power steering hose clamp to the sub-frame.

36. Connect the left-hand and right-hand upper control arms to the wheel spindles. Tighten the pinch bolt retaining nut to 50–68 ft. lbs. (68–92 Nm).

37. Connect the steering shaft coupling at the pinch bolt joint. Tighten the pinch bolt to 30–42 ft. lbs. (41–57 Nm).

38. Install the disc brake calipers and bolts. Tighten the brake pin retainers to 16–23 ft. lbs. (22–32 Nm).

39. Attach the left-hand and right-hand ride height sensor electrical harness connectors.

40. Install the front wheel and tire assemblies. Tighten the lug nuts to 85–105 ft. lbs. (115–142 Nm).

41. Remove the jack stands, or equivalent.

42. Lower the vehicle.

43. Remove the 3-Bar Engine Support or equivalent, from the engine compartment.

44. Install the engine oil level dipstick.

45. Fill the crankcase with the proper type and quantity of engine oil.

46. Connect the negative battery cable.

47. Turn the air suspension switch to the ON position.

48. Start the engine and check for oil leaks.

➡**Whenever the vehicle's sub-frame is removed or lowered, the wheel alignment should be checked.**

Oil pan bolt tightening sequence—1996 models

Oil pan bolt tightening sequence— 1997–98 models

49. Check the alignment and adjust if not within specification.

50. Road test the vehicle and check for proper engine operation.

Oil Pump

REMOVAL & INSTALLATION

1. Before servicing the vehicle, refer to the precautions in the beginning of this section.

2. Disconnect the negative battery cable. Remove the engine from the vehicle and position on a suitable workstand.

3. Remove the engine front cover. Remove the engine oil pan.

4. Remove the oil pump screen cover/tube bolts and the tube; discard the O-ring.

5. Remove the timing chains. Remove the crankshaft sprockets.

6. Remove the oil pump-to-cylinder block bolts and the oil pump.

To install:

7. Thoroughly clean the oil pump and cylinder block mounting surfaces and the oil pump screen cover and tube.

8. Turn the inner rotor of the oil pump to align with the flats on the crankshaft and

8-12 Nm
(71-106 lb/in)

Tighten the oil pump mounting bolts in the sequence shown

For complete mechanical specifications, refer to Section 1 of this manual

install the oil pump flush with the cylinder block. Install the four retaining bolts and tighten to 71–106 inch lbs. (8–12 Nm).

9. Replace the engine oil filter. Install the crankshaft sprockets. Install both timing chains.

10. Position the oil pump screen cover and tube on the oil pump with a new O-ring and hand-start the two retaining bolts.

11. Install the bolt retaining the oil pump screen cover and tube to the main bearing stud spacer finger-tight.

12. Tighten the oil pump screen cover and tube-to-oil pump bolts to 71–106 inch lbs. (8–12 Nm). Tighten the oil pump screen cover and tube-to-main bearing stud spacer bolt to 15–22 ft. lbs. (20–30 Nm).

13. Install the engine oil pan. Install the engine front cover.

14. Remove the engine from the workstand and install in the vehicle.

15. Restore all fluid levels. Connect the negative battery cable.

16. Run the engine and check for leaks and proper oil pressure. Road test the vehicle and check for proper operation.

Rear Main Seal

REMOVAL & INSTALLATION

1. Before servicing the vehicle, refer to the precautions in the beginning of this section.

2. Remove the transmission assembly.

3. Remove the flexplate.

4. With a sharp awl, carefully punch a small hole in the metal portion of the seal.

5. Remove the seal using a slide hammer with a sheet metal screw attached.

To install:

6. Lubricate the seal and the crankshaft with clean engine oil.

7. Install the seal with the spring side toward the engine using Rear Crankshaft Seal Replacer (T95P-6701-CH) or equivalent.

8. Remove the installation tool and install the flexplate.

9. Install the transmission assembly.

Timing Chain, Sprockets, Front Cover and Seal

REMOVAL & INSTALLATION

✳✳ WARNING

This is not a free-wheeling engine. When the timing chains are removed and the cylinder heads are installed,

the crankshaft and/or camshafts must not be rotated unless as directed in this procedure. Failure to follow these instructions will result in valve and/or piston damage.

1. Before servicing the vehicle, refer to the precautions in the beginning of this section.

2. Disconnect the negative battery cable.

3. Remove the windshield wiper module assembly.

4. Remove the engine appearance cover, if equipped.

5. Remove the engine air cleaner outlet tube.

6. Drain the engine cooling system.

7. Remove the water bypass tube and the upper radiator hose.

8. Remove the engine cooling fan motor and shroud assembly.

9. Remove the engine control wiring support bracket and straps from the left-hand center of the engine front cover.

10. Loosen the water pump pulley bolts.

11. If equipped with air injection, detach the vacuum and electrical harness connectors. Remove the necessary tube brackets, hoses and gaskets. Remove the air injection diverter valve.

12. Remove the accessory drive belt.

13. Remove the water pump pulley and lower water pump-to-cylinder block retaining bolt for engine front cover removal clearance.

14. Remove the bolts and stud bolt retaining the power steering pump reservoir to the left-hand ignition coil bracket.

15. Raise and safely support the vehicle.

16. Using Pulley Remover T69L-10300-B or equivalent, remove the power steering pump pulley.

17. Remove the bolt retaining the power steering pressure hose to the power steering pump bracket.

18. Remove the bolts retaining the power steering pump to the cylinder block and the engine front cover.

➡ **The front lower bolt on the power steering pump will not come all the way out.**

19. Position the power steering pump and reservoir out of the way.

20. Remove the four bolts retaining the oil pan to the engine front cover.

21. Remove the crankshaft pulley retaining bolt and washer from the crankshaft.

22. Install Crankshaft Damper Remover T58P-6316-D or equivalent, on the crankshaft pulley and pull the crankshaft pulley from the crankshaft.

23. Lower the vehicle.

24. Remove both cylinder head covers.

25. Disconnect the engine control wiring from both ignition coils and the Camshaft Position (CMP) sensor.

26. Remove the three bolts retaining the right-hand ignition coil bracket to the engine front cover.

27. Remove the three nuts and one bolt retaining the left-hand ignition coil bracket to the engine front cover.

28. Slide both ignition coil brackets with the ignition wires attached off of the front cover studs and move aside.

29. Remove the bolt retaining the belt idler pulley and remove the idler pulley.

30. Remove the drive belt tensioner retaining bolt and drive belt tensioner from the engine front cover.

31. Disconnect the Crankshaft Position (CKP) sensor and move the wiring out of the way.

32. Remove the stud bolts and bolts retaining the engine front cover to the engine.

33. Remove the engine front cover.

34. Remove the left-hand and right-hand cylinder head covers.

35. Remove the CKP sensor tooth wheel.

36. Rotate the crankshaft to place the piston for No. 1 cylinder at TDC on its compression stroke.

7922PG18

Install the camshaft holding tool to maintain correct alignment of the camshafts while the chain is removed

✳✳ WARNING

Camshaft Positioning Tool T93P-6256-A or equivalent, and Camshaft Holding Tool T93P-6256-AH or equivalent, must be installed to prevent accidental rotation of the camshafts and possible engine damage.

37. Install Camshaft Positioning Tool T93P-6256-A or equivalent, in the rear D-slots of the camshaft.

❋❋ WARNING

Failure to use Camshaft Holding Tool T93P-6256-AH or equivalent, while assembling or disassembling the timing chains will result in damage to the D-slots or Camshaft Positioning Tool T93P-6256-A.

38. Install Camshaft Holding Tool T93P-6256-AH or equivalent, onto the camshafts to keep the camshafts from rotating and to prevent damaging the camshaft positioning tool.

39. Remove the two bolts retaining the right-hand primary timing chain tensioner to the cylinder head and remove the primary timing chain tensioner.

40. Remove the bolt retaining the right-hand tensioner arm and remove the right-hand tensioner arm.

➡**The two bolts retaining the timing chain guide to the cylinder head are longer than the one to the block.**

41. Remove the three bolts retaining the right-hand timing chain guide and remove the timing chain guide.

42. Remove the right-hand primary timing chain from the camshaft and crankshaft sprockets.

43. Remove the right-hand crankshaft sprocket.

44. Remove the camshaft sprocket retaining bolts.

❋❋ WARNING

The secondary timing chain tensioner plunger is spring loaded. Care must be taken to prevent the plunger from dropping out of the tensioner during disassembly.

45. Unlock and compress the secondary

7922PG20

Release the ratchet lock to compress the chain tensioner

7922PG19

After the secondary tensioner has been compressed, install a pin through the tensioner to

timing chain tensioners and lock the timing chain tensioner in the compressed position using a paper clip or stiff wire. Remove the secondary timing chains and camshaft sprockets.

46. Remove the two bolts retaining the left-hand primary timing chain tensioner to the cylinder head and remove the primary timing chain tensioners.

47. Remove the bolt retaining the left-hand timing chain tensioner arm and remove the left-hand timing chain tensioner arm.

48. Remove the three bolts retaining the left-hand timing chain guide and remove the timing chain guide.

49. Remove the left-hand primary timing chain from the camshaft sprocket and crankshaft sprocket.

50. Remove the left-hand crankshaft sprocket.

❋❋ WARNING

Failure to use Camshaft Holding Tool T93P-6256-AH or equivalent, while removing or tightening the camshaft bolts may result in damage to the camshaft D-slots or the camshaft positioning tool.

51. Remove the camshaft sprocket retaining bolts.

❋❋ WARNING

The secondary timing chain tensioner plunger is spring loaded. Care must be taken to prevent the plunger from dropping out of the tensioner during disassembly.

52. Unlock and compress the secondary chain tensioner and lock the chain tensioner in the compressed position using a paper clip or stiff wire. Remove the secondary timing chain and camshaft sprockets.

❋❋ WARNING

Do not rotate the crankshaft and/or camshafts or engine damage may occur.

53. Inspect the friction material on the timing chain tensioner arms and timing chain guides. If worn or damaged, remove and clean the oil pan and replace the oil pump screen cover and tube.

To install:

54. If the engine has jumped time, be sure that all service to the necessary engine components and/or valvetrain have been made.

55. Be sure the primary and secondary timing chain tensioners are in the collapsed

position and retained with paper clips or equivalent.

56. If the cylinder heads were removed from the cylinder block, position the crankshaft keyway to 270 degrees (9 o'clock position), before reinstalling the cylinder heads.

➡ **The rocker arms must not be installed in the cylinder heads at this time.**

57. Install Camshaft Positioning Tool T93P-6256-A or equivalent, into the D-slots on the rear of the camshafts to position both intake and exhaust camshafts with the keyways pointing down towards the crankshaft. Install Camshaft Holding Tool T93P-6256-AH or equivalent, on the center of the camshafts and do not remove until all parts are installed and tightened.

58. Install the left-hand secondary timing chain tensioner and tighten the retaining bolts to 70–106 inch lbs. (8–12 Nm).

59. Install the left-hand secondary camshaft sprockets and secondary timing chain as an assembly. Be sure the hubs of the sprocket are facing the proper direction.

60. Install the left-hand primary camshaft sprocket and camshaft sprocket spacer on the left-hand camshaft.

61. Install the washers and camshaft sprocket retaining bolts, finger-tight only.

➡ **The secondary camshaft sprockets must be free to turn.**

62. Install Timing Chain Tensioning Tool T93P-6256-BH or equivalent, on the left-hand secondary timing chain tensioner.

63. Tighten the camshaft sprocket bolts to 81–95 ft. lbs. (110–130 Nm).

64. Install the right-hand secondary timing chain tensioner and tighten the retaining bolts to 70–106 inch lbs. (8–12 Nm).

65. Install the right-hand secondary camshaft sprockets and secondary timing chain as an assembly. Be sure the hubs of the sprocket are facing the proper direction.

66. Install the right-hand primary camshaft sprocket and camshaft sprocket spacer on the right-hand camshaft.

67. Install the washers and camshaft sprocket retaining bolts, finger-tight only.

➡ **The secondary camshaft sprockets must be free to turn.**

68. Install Timing Chain Tensioning Tool T93P-6256-BH or equivalent, on the right-hand secondary timing chain tensioner.

69. Tighten the camshaft sprocket bolts to 81–95 ft. lbs. (110–130 Nm).

70. Install the left-hand crankshaft sprocket, making sure the tapered part of the sprocket faces away from the cylinder block.

71. Install the primary timing chain on the left-hand primary camshaft sprocket. Be sure the copper link of the timing chain aligns with the timing mark on the camshaft sprocket.

➡ **If the copper links of the timing chain are not visible, pull the chain tight until the opposite sides of the chain contact one another and lay it on a flat surface. Mark the links at each end of the chain and use them in place of the copper links.**

72. Install the left-hand primary timing chain on the left-hand crankshaft sprocket. Be sure the copper link of the timing chain aligns with the timing mark on the crankshaft sprocket.

73. Install the right-hand crankshaft sprocket, making sure the tapered part of the sprocket faces toward the cylinder block.

74. Install the primary timing chain on the right-hand primary camshaft sprocket. Be sure the copper link of the timing chain aligns with the timing mark on the camshaft sprocket.

75. Install the right-hand primary timing chain on the right-hand crankshaft sprocket. Be sure the copper link of the timing chain aligns with the timing mark on the crankshaft sprocket.

Be sure that the copper links (shown here as the black links) on the timing chains align with the marks on the sprockets

Be sure the crankshaft sprockets are installed correctly as shown

➡ **The two timing chain guide bolts to the cylinder head are longer than the bolt to the cylinder block.**

76. Install the right-hand and left-hand timing chain guides and tighten the bolts to 71–106 inch lbs. (8–12 Nm).

77. Lubricate the timing chain tensioner arm contact surfaces with clean engine oil. Install the right-hand and left-hand tensioner arms and tighten the bolts to 84–132 inch lbs. (10–15 Nm).

78. Install right-hand and left-hand primary timing chain tensioners and tighten the bolts to 15–22 ft. lbs. (20–30 Nm).

79. Remove the locking pins from the timing chain tensioners and be sure all timing marks are aligned. Remove the camshaft positioning tool and the camshaft holding tool.

➡ **When cleaning the sealing surfaces of the engine front cover and oil pan-to-cylinder block joints, be extremely careful not to damage the rubber bead of the oil pan gasket. If the oil pan gasket is damaged, it must be replaced.**

80. Clean the sealing surfaces of the cylinder block, cylinder heads and engine front cover; remove all traces of oil, dirt and old sealant. Sealing surfaces must be clean and dry before applying sealant.

81. Replace the engine front cover gaskets and the crankshaft front seal.

82. Apply silicone sealant to the proper locations on the cylinder block and heads.

➡ **The engine front cover must be rolled into place. DO NOT slide it on the oil pan gasket.**

83. Carefully install the front cover to the engine.

84. Install the bolts and stud bolts retaining the front cover to the engine. Tighten in sequence to 15–22 ft. lbs.

Be sure to apply silicone sealant to the areas on the engine where two components come together and the sealing surface is irregular as shown

Tighten the front cover mounting bolts in the proper sequence to ensure a good seal

(20–30 Nm). Tighten the stud bolts and bolts numbered 6, 7, 8, 9, 10, and 11 within four minutes after applying the sealer.

85. Install the drive belt tensioner and bolt. Tighten the bolt to 15–22 ft. lbs. (20–30 Nm).

86. Install the belt idler pulley and bolt. Tighten the bolt to 15–22 ft. lbs. (20–30 Nm).

87. Connect the engine control sensor wiring to the CKP sensor.

88. Place the left-hand and right-hand ignition coil brackets in position on the engine front cover. Install all retaining nuts and bolts and tighten to 15–22 ft. lbs. (20–30 Nm).

89. Install the power steering pump reservoir to the left-hand ignition coil bracket. Tighten the retaining bolts to 71–106 inch lbs. (8–12 Nm).

90. Connect the engine control wiring to both ignition coils and the CMP sensor.

91. Install both cylinder head covers.

92. Raise the vehicle.

93. Install the crankshaft pulley on the crankshaft, using Crankshaft Damper Replacer T74P-6316-B or equivalent.

94. Apply silicone sealant in the keyway of the crankshaft pulley.

95. Install the pulley bolt and washer. Tighten the bolt to 114–121 ft. lbs. (155–165 Nm).

96. Install the four bolts retaining the oil pan to the engine front cover. Tighten the bolts to 15–22 ft. lbs. (20–30 Nm).

97. Position the power steering pump on the engine and install the four retaining bolts. Tighten the bolts to 15–22 ft. lbs. (20–30 Nm).

98. Install the retainer bolt for the power steering pressure hose to the power steering pump bracket.

99. Install the strap retaining the engine control wiring to the engine front cover.

100. Using Power Steering Pump Pulley Replacer T91P-3A733-A or equivalent, install the power steering pump pulley.

101. Lower the vehicle.

102. Install the lower water pump retaining bolt removed for engine front cover clearance. Tighten the bolt to 15–22 ft. lbs. (20–30 Nm).

103. Install the water pump pulley with the four bolts. Tighten the bolts to 15–22 ft. lbs. (20–30 Nm).

104. Install the support bracket and retaining bolt for the engine control wiring to the left-hand center of the engine front cover.

105. If equipped with air injection, install the air injection diverter valve and retaining nuts. Tighten the nuts to 6–8 ft. lbs. (8–12 Nm). Attach the vacuum and electrical connectors.

106. If equipped with air injection, install the hose to the air injection pump. Connect both tube and gasket assemblies and tighten the fittings to 25–35 ft. lbs. (32–48 Nm). Tighten the tube bracket retaining bolts to 15–22 ft. lbs. (20–30 Nm).

107. Install the engine cooling fan motor and shroud assembly.

108. Install the water bypass tube and the upper radiator hose.

109. Install the accessory drive belt.

110. Restore all fluid levels.

111. Install the windshield wiper module assembly.

112. Connect the engine air cleaner outlet tube.

113. Connect the negative battery cable.

114. Start the engine and check for leaks.

115. Install the engine appearance cover, if equipped.

116. Road test the vehicle and check for proper engine operation.

FUEL SYSTEM

Fuel System Service Precautions

Safety is the most important factor when performing not only fuel system maintenance but any type of maintenance. Failure to conduct maintenance and repairs in a safe manner may result in serious personal injury or death. Maintenance and testing of the vehicle's fuel system components can be accomplished safely and effectively by adhering to the following rules and guidelines.

• To avoid the possibility of fire and personal injury, always disconnect the negative battery cable unless the repair or test procedure requires that battery voltage be applied.

• Always relieve the fuel system pressure prior to disconnecting any fuel system component (injector, fuel rail, pressure regulator, etc.), fitting or fuel line connection. Exercise extreme caution whenever relieving fuel system pressure to avoid exposing skin, face and eyes to fuel spray. Please be advised that fuel under pressure may penetrate the skin or any part of the body that it contacts.

• Always place a shop towel or cloth around the fitting or connection prior to loosening to absorb any excess fuel due to spillage. Ensure that all fuel spillage (should it occur) is quickly removed from engine surfaces. Ensure that all fuel soaked cloths or towels are deposited into a suitable waste container.

• Always keep a dry chemical (Class B) fire extinguisher near the work area.

• Do not allow fuel spray or fuel vapors to come into contact with a spark or open flame.

• Always use a back-up wrench when loosening and tightening fuel line connection fittings. This will prevent unnecessary stress and torsion to fuel line piping.

• Always replace worn fuel fitting O-rings with new. Do not substitute fuel hose or equivalent, where fuel pipe is installed.

Fuel System Pressure

RELIEVING

Fuel supply lines on all fuel injected engines will remain pressurized for some period of time after the engine is shut **OFF**. This pressure must be relieved before servicing the fuel system. Pressure is relieved through the fuel pressure relief valve.

1. Before servicing the vehicle, refer to the precautions in the beginning of this section.

2. Remove the fuel tank cap to relieve pressure in the tank.

3. Remove the cap on the fuel pressure relief valve, located on the fuel rail.

4. Attach fuel pressure gauge T80L-9974-A or equivalent and open the manual valve on the pressure gauge to release the pressure and drain the system through the drain tube into a suitable container.

5. Remove the fuel pressure gauge and replace the cap on the relief valve.

Fuel Filter

REMOVAL & INSTALLATION

1. Before servicing the vehicle, refer to the precautions in the beginning of this section.

2. Disconnect the negative battery cable and relieve the fuel system pressure.

3. Raise and safely support the vehicle.

4. Remove the push connect fittings at both ends of the filter. Install new retainer clips in each push connect fitting.

5. Remove the filter bracket and the filter.
To install:
6. Install the filter on the frame rail, be sure it is in the correct direction.

7. Install the push connect fittings onto the filter ends. Start the engine and check for leaks.

8. Install the fender liner.

9. Lower the vehicle.

Fuel Pump

REMOVAL & INSTALLATION

1996 Models

1. Before servicing the vehicle, refer to the precautions in the beginning of this section.

2. Disconnect the negative battery cable and properly relieve the fuel system pressure.

3. Remove the fuel tank and place it on a bench.

4. Remove any dirt that has accumulated around the fuel pump retaining flange so it will not enter the tank during pump removal and installation.

5. Turn the fuel pump locking ring counterclockwise and remove the locking ring.

6. Remove the fuel pump and bracket assembly. Remove and discard the seal ring.

1	**Front Fuel Supply Return and Vapor Tube**
2	**Fuel Tube Clip**
3	**Fuel Tank Vent Tube**
4	**Body**
5	**Screw (2 Req'd)**
6	**Atmospheric Vapor Line**
7	**Fuel Filter and Base**
8	**Screw**
A	**Tighten to 5.2-7.2 N·m (46-64 Lb-In)**
B	**Tighten to 7.6-10.4 N·m (67-92 Lb-In)**

7922PG24

Fuel filter mounting—1996 models

To install:

7. Clean the fuel pump mounting flange, fuel tank mounting surface and seal ring groove.

8. Apply a light coating of grease on a new seal ring to hold it in place during assembly and install in the seal ring groove.

9. Install the fuel pump and bracket assembly carefully to ensure the filter is not damaged. Be sure the locating keys are in the keyways and the seal ring remains in the groove.

10. Hold the pump assembly in place and install the locking ring finger-tight. Be sure all the locking tabs are under the tank lock-ring tabs.

11. Rotate the locking ring clock-wise until the ring is against the stops.

12. Install the fuel tank in the vehicle. Add a minimum of 10 gallons (38 L) of fuel to the tank and check for leaks.

13. Install a suitable fuel pressure gauge to the valve on the fuel rail.

14. Turn the ignition switch from **OFF** to **ON** for three seconds. Repeat this procedure 5–10 times until the pressure gauge shows at least 35 psi (241 kPa). Check for fuel leaks.

15. Remove the pressure gauge, start the engine and check for leaks.

7922PG25

Fuel filter location, showing the filter mounting bolt (arrow)—1997-98 models

1997–98 Models

1. Before servicing the vehicle, refer to the precautions in the beginning of this section.

2. Disconnect the negative battery cable and properly relieve the fuel system pressure.

3. Remove the fuel tank and place it on a bench.

4. Remove any dirt that has accumulated around the fuel pump retaining flange so it will not enter the tank during pump removal and installation.

Turn the retainer ring counterclockwise to unlock it and remove the pump from the tank.

Squeeze the locking tabs together to release the pump from the tank.

5. Remove the fuel pump retaining bolts and remove the top flange plate.

6. Reach into the tank and squeeze the locking tabs together, then remove the pump.

To install:

7. Clean the fuel pump mounting flange, fuel tank mounting surface.

8. Install the fuel pump in the tank and tighten the mounting screws to 71–88 inch lbs. (8–10 Nm).

9. Install the fuel tank in the vehicle. Add a minimum of 10 gallons (38 L) of fuel to the tank and check for leaks.

DRIVE TRAIN

Transmission Assembly

REMOVAL & INSTALLATION

1. Before servicing the vehicle, refer to the precautions in the beginning of this section.

2. Turn the air suspension switch to the OFF position.

3. Disconnect the negative battery cable.

4. Raise and safely support the vehicle.

5. Drain the fluid from the transmission by removing all of the oil pan bolts except the two at the front of the pan. Loosen the remaining bolts at the front of the pan and slowly lower the oil pan at the rear to allow the fluid to drain into a container. When drained, install a few of the bolts at the rear of the pan to hold it in place.

6. Remove the exhaust system as required for transmission removal.

7. Remove the converter inspection cover and remove the torque converter drain plug to allow the converter to drain. After the torque converter has drained, reinstall the drain plug and tighten.

8. Crank the engine over with a wrench on the crankshaft pulley retaining bolt to access and remove the four torque converter-to-flywheel retaining nuts.

➡ **Never rotate the crankshaft pulley in a counterclockwise direction, as viewed from the front of the engine, to prevent possible engine damage.**

9. Matchmark and remove the driveshaft as follows:

a. Loosen the differential housing assembly rear mounting nuts approximately ¼ inch (6.4mm).

b. Support the front of the differential housing and remove the forward mounting nuts and bushings. Pull the vent tube from the hole in the sub-frame.

c. Lower the front of the differential housing and slide the driveshaft out of the transmission above the axle housing. Let the driveshaft rest on the front driveshaft support and axle assembly.

10. Disconnect and remove the Vehicle Speed Sensor (VSS) from the transmission extension housing.

11. Disconnect the shift cable from the manual control lever.

12. Remove the starter cable and remove the starter motor.

13. Remove the transmission electrical harness connectors.

14. Place a suitable transmission jack under the transmission and raise it slightly.

15. Remove the rear crossmember and transmission support insulator.

16. Lower the transmission allowing it to hang.

17. Place a suitable jack under the front of the engine and raise the engine enough to gain access to the two upper converter housing-to-cylinder block retaining bolts. Do not remove the bolts at this time.

18. Disconnect and plug the transmission cooler lines at the transmission.

19. Remove the lower converter housing-to-cylinder block retaining bolts.

20. Remove the transmission fluid dipstick tube.

21. Secure the transmission to the transmission jack with a safety strap or chain.

22. Remove the two upper converter housing-to-cylinder block retaining bolts.

23. Move the transmission rearward and down from under the vehicle. Hold the converter in place to avoid having it drop from the transmission.

24. Remove the torque converter from the transmission.

To install:

➡ **If overhauling the transmission, be sure to flush the transmission oil cooler**

Install a torque converter holding tool to keep the converter from falling out of the transmission

and the cooler lines of any contaminates before transmission installation.

25. Place the transmission on a suitable transmission jack and secure with a strap or chain.

26. Tighten the torque converter drain plug to 21–22 ft. lbs. (28–30 Nm).

27. Place the torque converter into the converter housing and rotate while pushing in on the torque converter to fully engage the converter drive flats are fully engaged in the pump gear.

28. Raise the transmission assembly and align it with the engine. Rotate the converter until the studs and drain plug are in alignment with the holes in the flywheel. Align the orange balancing marks on the converter stud and flywheel bolt hole, if balancing marks are present.

➡**The torque converter face must rest squarely against the flywheel. This indicates that the converter pilot is not binding in the engine crankshaft. To ensure that the converter is properly seated, grasp a converter stud. It should move freely back and forth in the flywheel hole. If the converter will not move, the transmission must be removed and the converter repositioned so the impeller hub is properly engaged in the pump gear.**

29. Move the transmission forward and install to the cylinder block dowels. Be sure that the torque converter studs are properly aligned with the flywheel.

30. Install the transmission-to-cylinder block retaining bolts. Tighten the bolts to 30–40 ft. lbs. (40–55 Nm).

31. Remove the safety chain or strap from around the transmission.

32. Install the transmission fluid dipstick tube and secure it to the cylinder block with one retaining bolt. Tighten the bolt to 28–38 ft. lbs. (38–51 Nm).

33. Unplug and connect the oil cooler lines to the right-hand side of the transmission case. Tighten the cooler line fittings to 15–19 ft. lbs. (20–26 Nm).

34. Remove the jack supporting the front of the engine.

35. Raise the transmission enough to install the crossmember and support insulator.

40-55 Nm
(30-40 lb/ft)

Transmission mounting bolt location and torque specification

36. Install the transmission support insulator and crossmember assembly.

37. Lower the transmission and remove the jack.

38. Install the transmission support insulator-to-crossmember retaining nut.

39. Install the starter motor.

40. Install the four torque converter-to-flywheel retaining nuts. Tighten the nuts to 20–33 ft. lbs. (27–46 Nm). Install the converter housing cover. Tighten the cover retaining bolts to 12–16 ft. lbs. (16–22 Nm).

41. Install the exhaust system.

42. Install the VSS and connect the wiring.

43. Install the driveshaft, making sure the matchmarks are aligned as follows:

   a. Raise the differential housing with a jack and install the bushings and retaining nuts. Tighten the nuts to 68–100 ft. lbs. (92–136 Nm). Remove the jack stand.

   b. Install the vent tube in the hole of the sub-frame.

   c. Align the driveshaft yoke and companion flange and install the retaining bolts. Tighten the retaining nuts to 70–95 ft. lbs. (95–129 Nm).

44. Safely lower the vehicle.

45. Connect the negative battery cable.

46. Turn the air suspension switch to the ON position.

47. Fill the transmission with the proper type and quantity of fluid.

48. Start the engine and add transmission fluid as needed until the proper fluid level is reached while checking for leaks.

49. Road test the vehicle and check for proper operation.

50. Recheck the transmission fluid level.

Halfshaft

REMOVAL & INSTALLATION

➡**Before continuing with this procedure, be sure to have available one new inboard CV-joint stub shaft pilot bearing housing seal, one shaft bearing retaining clip and one wheel hub retainer nut, per side. Once removed, these parts lose their torque holding ability or retention capability and must not be reused.**

1. Before servicing the vehicle, refer to the precautions in the beginning of this section.

2. With the vehicle sitting on the ground, remove the wheel hub retainer nut.

3. Raise and safely support the vehicle.

4. Remove the wheel and tire assembly.

5. Remove the anti-lock brake speed sensor, if equipped.

6. Use needle-nose pliers or equivalent, to slide the parking brake cable adjusting clip downward until the cable is free.

7. Remove the parking brake cable from the rear disc brake caliper.

8. Remove the upper and lower caliper retaining bolts and remove the caliper. Support the caliper aside with wire, do not allow it to hang from the brake hose.

9. Remove the upper control arm retaining nut and bolt. Wire the upper control arm to the top of the shock absorber.

10. Using a paint marker, matchmark the position of the lower control arm in relation to the knuckle with the lower bushings in the relaxed position.

➡ **Failure to matchmark this relationship will result in bushing wind-up on assembly and incorrect ride height, causing misalignment and premature tire wear.**

11. Use a suitable puller to free the halfshaft from the hub.

12. Remove the lower control arm-to-knuckle retaining nuts. Push the halfshaft through the hub while positioning the CV-joint and knuckle to allow the front lower bolt to clear the CV-joint and remove the bolt. Remove and save the washers.

13. Remove the rear bolt, washer, and knuckle assembly. Be careful not to damage the differential oil seal, differential housing and/or CV-joint boot.

14. Remove the halfshaft from the vehicle.

15. Insert a plug into the differential housing to prevent fluid loss.

To install:

16. Remove the differential plug and install a new differential oil seal.

17. Install a new circlip on the halfshaft. Start the ends in the groove and push the circlip into the groove, to prevent over expanding the circlip.

18. Lightly lubricate the stub shaft splines and carefully align the splines on the shaft with the splines in the differential.

19. Push the halfshaft inward to seat the circlip in the differential side gear groove. Use care not to damage the seal.

20. Engage the hub splines with the outboard CV-joint splines.

21. Install the lower control arm retaining bolts and nuts. Align the paint marks and tighten the bolts to 94–131 ft. lbs. (128–178 Nm).

22. Install a new wheel hub retaining nut and use it to draw the CV-joint into the hub as far as possible by hand.

23. Install the upper arm retaining bolt and nut and tighten to 117–142 ft. lbs. (158–193 Nm).

24. Install the brake caliper assembly to the rotor with the outer brake shoe against the rotor's braking surface. This prevents pinching the piston boot between the inner brake shoe and the piston.

25. Install the upper and lower caliper retaining bolts and tighten to 64–88 ft. lbs. (87–119 Nm).

26. Install the parking brake cable to the brake caliper. Install the cable adjustment clip.

27. Install the anti-lock brake speed sensor, if equipped. Tighten the retaining bolts to 15–19 ft. lbs. (19–27 Nm).

28. Check the inboard CV-joint circlip engagement by attempting to pull the inboard CV-joint from the axle. If the CV-joint circlip is not seated, push the CV-joint in until the circlip is fully engaged in the side gear.

29. Check the axle lubricant level and fill, as necessary.

30. Install the wheel and tire assembly. Tighten the lug nuts to 85–105 ft. lbs. (115–142 Nm).

31. Lower the vehicle.

32. Pump the brake pedal several times to position the brake pads before moving the vehicle.

33. Tighten the wheel hub retainer nut to 250 ft. lbs. (340 Nm).

34. Check the rear alignment and adjust if not within specification.

35. Road test the vehicle and check for proper operation.

Be sure to matchmark the lower control arm and the knuckle assembly to maintain correct alignment

STEERING AND SUSPENSION

Air Bag

⁂ CAUTION

Some vehicles are equipped with an air bag system, also known as the Supplemental Inflatable Restraint (SIR) or Supplemental Restraint System (SRS). The system must be disabled before performing service on or around system components, steering column, instrument panel components, wiring and sensors. Failure to

follow safety and disabling procedures could result in accidental air bag deployment, possible personal injury and unnecessary system repairs.

PRECAUTIONS

Several precautions must be observed when handling the inflator module to avoid accidental deployment and possible personal injury.

• Never carry the inflator module by the wires or connector on the underside of the module.

• When carrying a live inflator module, hold securely with both hands, and ensure that the bag and trim cover are pointed away.

• Place the inflator module on a bench or other surface with the bag and trim cover facing up.

• With the inflator module on the bench, never place anything on or close to the module which may be thrown in the event of an accidental deployment.

DISARMING

1. Before servicing the vehicle, refer to the precautions in the beginning of this section.

2. Disconnect and isolate the negative battery cable. Wait one minute for the back-up power supply in the diagnostic monitor to deplete its stored energy.

3. Remove the four nut and washer assemblies (2 screws on Mark VIII) retaining the driver air bag module to the steering wheel.

✳✳ CAUTION

When carrying a live air bag, be sure the bag and trim cover are pointed away from the body. In the unlikely event of an accidental deployment, the bag will, then deploy with minimal chance of injury. When placing a live air bag on a bench or other surface, always face the bag and trim cover up, away from the surface. This will reduce the motion of the module if it is accidentally deployed.

4. Detach the driver air bag connector. Connect air bag simulator tool 105–00008 or equivalent, to the vehicle harness at the top of the steering wheel.

ENABLING

1. Install the air bag module.
2. Connect the negative battery cable.
3. Turn the ignition **ON** and be sure the air bag warning light does not remain ON.

Power Rack and Pinion Steering Gear

REMOVAL & INSTALLATION

1. Before servicing the vehicle, refer to the precautions in the beginning of this section.

2. Turn the air suspension switch to the OFF position.

3. Disconnect the negative battery cable.

4. Leave the ignition key in the **ON** position to prevent the steering column from locking.

5. Raise and safely support the vehicle.

6. Remove both front wheel and tire assemblies.

7. Remove the cotter pins from both outer tie rod ends and discard.

8. Remove the tie rod end castellated nuts and separate the tie rod ends from the wheel spindles using Tie Rod End Remover T-3290-D, or equivalent.

9. Place a drain pan under the steering rack. Disconnect and plug the pressure and return hoses at the steering rack fittings.

10. Remove the pinch bolt retaining the flexible coupling to the input shaft.

11. Remove the two steering rack-to-crossmember retaining bolts and nuts. The nuts are accessed through the holes in the crossmember.

12. Lower the steering rack enough to disconnect the pressure line inlet tube. Remove the tube and discard the plastic seal on the inlet tube.

13. Cut the tie strap securing the power steering pressure hose to the tube.

14. Remove the steering rack assembly from the vehicle.

To install:

15. If a short steering rack is being installed, reuse the outer tie rod ends and inner tie rod spindle assemblies from the previously removed rack assembly if in good condition, or replace with new.

16. Install a new seal on the pressure line inlet tube.

17. Install the two steering rack mounting insulators, if not equipped.

➡The rubber insulators must be pushed completely inside the gear housing before the installation of the gear housing on the No. 2 crossmember.

18. Place the steering rack in position on the crossmember so that the pressure line inlet tube can be installed and install the inlet tube.

19. Align the steering shaft to allow the steering rack to completely seat on the crossmember.

20. Install the two steering rack-to-crossmember retaining bolts and nuts. Tighten the bolts to 100–143 ft. lbs. (135–195 Nm).

21. Install the steering shaft pinch bolt retaining the flexible coupling to the input shaft. Tighten the pinch bolt to 30–42 ft. lbs. (41–57 Nm).

22. Secure the power steering pressure hose to the tube with a new tie strap.

23. Connect the power steering pressure hose to the steering rack. Tighten the fitting to 42–53 ft. lbs. (57–73 Nm). The design allows the hoses to swivel when tightened properly. Do not attempt to eliminate looseness by overtightening, since this can cause damage to the fittings.

24. Connect the power steering return hose to the steering rack. Tighten the clamp to 12–17 inch lbs. (1.4–2.0 Nm).

25. Place the outer tie rod end studs to the wheel spindles. Install the castellated nuts and tighten to 40–53 ft. lbs. (53–72 Nm). If required, tighten the nuts to the next cotter pin castellation. Install new cotter pins.

26. Install the wheel and tire assemblies. Tighten the lug nuts to 85–105 ft. lbs. (115–142 Nm).

27. Lower the vehicle.

28. Turn the ignition key to the **OFF** position.

29. Connect the negative battery cable.

30. Turn the air suspension switch to the ON position.

31. Fill the power steering pump reservoir.

32. Start the engine and turn the steering wheel slowly from lock-to-lock several times to purge any air from the power steering system while checking for leaks.

33. Check the fluid level and add as required.

34. Check the alignment and adjust if not within specification.

35. Road test the vehicle and check for proper steering system operation.

Item	Part Number	Description
1	N800237-S1050	Nut (2 Req'd)
2	72044-S36	Cotter Key
3	N803972-S150	Nut (2 Req'd)
4	3A130	Tie Rod End
5	N803637-S100	Jam Nut (2 Req'd)
6	3504	Steering Gear
7	N807147-S190	Bolt (2 Req'd)
8	385935-S36	Washer (2 Req'd)
9	3F638	Insulator (2 Req'd)
10	3280	Front Wheel Spindle Tie Rod (2 Req'd)
11	3332	Front Suspension Steering Ball Stud Dust Seal
12	3K576	Insulator (2 Req'd)

7922PG31

Exploded view of the steering gear mounting and related components

Shock Absorber

REMOVAL & INSTALLATION

Front

➡**The front air spring and shock absorber are incorporated into one assembly and are not serviceable separately.**

1. Before servicing the vehicle, refer to the precautions in the beginning of this section.

2. Turn the air suspension switch, located in the luggage compartment, to the OFF position.

3. Raise and safely support the vehicle.

➡**The front suspension system must be allowed to hang at full rebound.**

4. Remove the wheel and tire assembly.

5. Remove the air spring height sensor as follows:

a. Carefully remove the forward section of the front fender splash shield enough to access the height sensor electrical harness connector and the push-in clips.

b. Pull out the height sensor clips.

c. Detach the height sensor electrical harness connector from the wiring harness.

d. Remove the air spring height sensor from its retaining studs by gently pulling back on the height sensor spring clips and removing the height sensor.

6. Detach the air spring solenoid electrical harness connector.

7. Remove the air line from the air spring solenoid valve by pushing down and holding the plastic retaining ring on the valve while pulling on the air line.

Cover

Seal

Shock/Spring

FRONT OF
VEHICLE

7922PG32

**Exploded view of the front shock
absorber/air spring assembly**

8. Remove the air spring solenoid valve
as follows:

a. Remove the solenoid retainer
clip.

b. Rotate the solenoid valve counterclockwise to the 1st stop.

c. Pull the solenoid valve straight out
slowly to the 2nd stop to bleed air from
the system.

➡**Do not fully release the solenoid
until the air is completely bled from the
air spring.**

d. After the air is fully bled from the
system, rotate the solenoid valve counterclockwise to the third stop and remove
the solenoid valve from the solenoid
housing. Remove the large O-ring from
the solenoid housing.

9. Remove the clip retaining the spring
to the lower arm. Push down on the spring
clip on the collar of the air spring and
rotate the collar counterclockwise to
release the spring from the body spring
seat.

10. Remove the shock tower cover from
the engine compartment.

11. Remove three retaining nuts and the
collar securing the air spring to the shock
tower.

➡**Do not remove the large center nut
which may result in a permanent air
leak.**

12. Remove the lower nut and bolt
retaining the air spring and shock assembly
to the lower control arm.

13. Remove the air spring and shock
assembly from the vehicle.

To install:

14. Install the air spring solenoid valve
as follows:

a. Check the solenoid valve O-rings
for cuts or abrasion. Replace the O-rings
as required. Lightly grease the O-ring
area of the solenoid valve and the larger
solenoid housing O-ring with silicone
dielectric compound.

b. Insert the solenoid valve into the
air spring end cap and rotate clockwise
to the third stop, push in to the second
stop, then rotate clockwise to the first
stop.

c. Install the air spring solenoid
retainer clip. Inspect the electrical harness connector and ensure the rubber
gasket is in place at the bottom of the
connector cavity.

15. Place the upper air spring and shock
mounting studs into position and loosely
install the three upper air spring stud retaining nuts and collar at the shock tower.

➡**The solenoid valve socket for either
front air spring should be oriented forward of the air spring.**

16. Place the lower end of the air spring
and shock assembly into position over the
lower control arm support and loosely
install the retaining bolt and nut. Tighten the
three upper retaining nuts over the shock
tower to 17–24 ft. lbs. (23–32 Nm).

17. Install the appearance cover over the
top of the shock tower.

18. Attach the air line and the electrical
harness connector to the air spring solenoid
valve.

19. Install the air spring height sensor as
follows:

a. Snap the height sensor into the
upper and lower ball studs with the
height sensor wiring oriented downward.

b. Install the air spring height sensor
electrical harness connector.

c. Install the two harness wiring
retaining clips into their original locations.

d. Install the front fender splash
shield.

20. Verify that the air suspension switch

is OFF, then connect the negative battery
cable.

21. Fill the air spring as follows:

a. Attach Super Star II Tester
007–0041B or equivalent scan tool to the
Data Link Connector (DLC) located on the
front side of the right-hand shock tower.

b. Install a battery charger to reduce
battery drain.

c. Enter the appropriate function test
to fill the required air spring:

• 212 left-front air spring

• 214 right-front air spring

d. Remove the tester and battery
charger.

➡**Any further inflation should be done
with the vehicle on the ground and the
air suspension switch in the ON position.**

22. Inspect the air spring folds and
creases.

23. Install the wheel and tire assembly.
Tighten the lug nuts to 85–105 ft. lbs.
(115–142 Nm).

24. Lower the vehicle.

25. Turn the air suspension switch to the
ON position.

26. Place the vehicle on an alignment
rack or equivalent, to raise the vehicle off of
the ground but keep the suspension loaded.

27. Neutralize the front suspension
bushings by pushing the front of the vehicle
down several times and allowing the suspension to settle. Tighten the lower air
spring and shock assembly retaining bolt
and nut to 125–170 ft. lbs. (170–230 Nm).

28. Check the alignment and adjust if
not within specification.

29. Road test the vehicle and check for
proper operation.

Rear

⁜ **CAUTION**

**The rear shocks act as the rebound
stops for the rear suspension. When
the rear shocks are removed, the suspension arms must be supported. The
best method for rear shock removal is
to use a drive-on hoist or an alignment pit. Portable vehicle ramps can
be substituted, but be sure the ramps
are secure, the parking brake is set,
and the front wheels are chocked
properly before proceeding.**

1. Before servicing the vehicle, refer to
the precautions in the beginning of this section.

FRONT OF VEHICLE

1 Nut (2 Req'd Each Side)
2 Body Reference
3 Nut
4 Nut
5 Washer
6 Bolt
7 Washer (2 Req'd Each Side)
8 Insulator Mount

7922PG33

Exploded view of the rear shock absorber mounting

2. Place the vehicle on a drive-on hoist or over an alignment pit or equivalent.

3. Turn the air suspension switch, located in the luggage compartment, to the OFF position.

4. From inside the luggage compartment, remove the two upper shock absorber retaining nuts.

5. Remove the lower shock absorber retaining bolt and nut at the lower control arm.

6. Remove the shock absorber and insulator mount from the vehicle.

7. Grasp the flats on the insulator mount upper washer and loosen the insulator retaining nut.

8. Remove the upper washer, insulator mount, retaining nut and lower washer for use on the new shock absorber assembly.

To install:

9. Install the upper insulator lower washer and insulator mount on the shock absorber. Align the upper washer with the flat on the shock absorber rod and install the washer and retaining nut.

10. Grasp the upper washer flats firmly and rotate the insulator mount studs 90 degrees from the upper washer flats.

11. Holding the insulator mount studs in this position, tighten the insulator retaining nut to 53–65 ft. lbs. (72–88 Nm).

12. Properly prime the new shock absorber to remove air from the working cylinder by inverting and compressing, then releasing the shock to its fully extended position at least three times.

13. Install the shock absorber rod and insulator mount studs through the shock tower mounting holes.

14. Compress the shock absorber and align the lower mounting hole with the lower control arm. Install the retaining bolt, washer and nut to the lower control arm. While holding the nut, tighten the bolt to 83–113 ft. lbs. (113–153 Nm).

15. Install the retaining nuts to the upper insulator studs and tighten to 17–23 ft. lbs. (23–31 Nm).

16. Install the luggage compartment panels, if removed.

17. Lower vehicle.

18. Turn the air suspension switch to the ON position.

19. Road test the vehicle and check for proper operation.

Air Spring

REMOVAL & INSTALLATION

Front

The service procedure for the front spring is covered in the front shock absorber procedure located earlier in this section.

Rear

1. Before servicing the vehicle, refer to the precautions in the beginning of this section.

2. Turn the air suspension switch to the OFF position.

3. Disconnect the negative battery cable.

4. Raise and safely support the vehicle.

➡**The rear suspension system must be allowed to hang at full rebound.**

5. Remove the wheel and tire assembly.

6. Detach the air spring solenoid electrical harness connector.

7. Remove the air line from the air spring solenoid valve by pushing down and holding the plastic retaining ring on the valve while pulling on the air line.

8. Remove the air spring solenoid valve as follows:

a. Remove the solenoid retainer clip.

b. Rotate the solenoid valve counterclockwise to the first stop.

c. Pull the solenoid valve straight out slowly to the second stop to bleed air from the system.

➡**Do not fully release the solenoid until the air is completely bled from the air spring.**

d. After the air is fully bled from the system, rotate the solenoid valve counterclockwise to the 3rd stop and remove the solenoid valve from the solenoid housing. Remove the large O-ring from the solenoid housing.

9. Depress the four plastic locking fingers in the bottom of the air spring's piston to disconnect the air spring from the lower control arm.

10. Depress the metal locking tab at the top of the air spring and rotate to disengage the air spring cap from the body bracket.

11. Carefully remove the air spring from the vehicle.

METAL LOCKING TAB
INSTALLATION POSITION
LOCK POSITION
REAR SPRING ASSY

7922PG34

Depress the metal locking tab and rotate the spring, away from the lock position, to remove it from the body

To install:

12. Install the air spring solenoid as follows:

a. Check the solenoid O-rings for cuts or abrasion. Replace the O-rings as required. Lightly grease the O-ring area of the solenoid and the larger solenoid housing O-ring with silicone dielectric compound.

b. Insert the solenoid valve into the air spring end cap and rotate clockwise to the 3rd stop, push in to the 2nd stop, then rotate clockwise to the first stop.

c. Install the air spring solenoid retainer clip. Inspect the wiring harness connector and ensure the rubber gasket is in place at the bottom of the connector cavity.

13. Insert the air spring upper cap into the two stud holes in the body bracket and twist to lock in place.

➡**Rear air springs are the same for left-hand or right-hand installation.**

14. Insert the four plastic locking fingers into the lower control arm and lock them into position.

✳✳ WARNING

Do not inflate the air spring until it is properly installed.

15. Attach the air line and electrical connector to the solenoid.

16. Verify that the air suspension switch is OFF, then connect the negative battery cable.

17. Fill the air spring as follows:

a. Attach the Super Star II Tester 007–0041B or equivalent scan tool to the Data Link Connector (DLC) located on the front side of the right-hand shock tower.

b. Install a battery charger to reduce battery drain.

➡**The following function test numbers are for the Star Tester II only. The Star Tester II is the scan tool used in the Ford dealerships. Follow the instructions included with your scan tool to fill the air spring.**

c. Enter the appropriate function test to fill the required air spring:

- 216 left-rear air spring
- 218 right-rear air spring

d. Remove the tester and battery charger.

➡**Any further inflation should be done with the vehicle on the ground and the air suspension switch in the ON position.**

18. Inspect the air spring folds and creases.

19. Install the wheel and tire assembly. Tighten the lug nuts to 85–105 ft. lbs. (115–142 Nm).

20. Lower the vehicle.

21. Turn the air suspension switch to the ON position.

22. Check the alignment and adjust if not within specification.

23. Road test the vehicle and check for proper operation.

Upper Ball Joint

REMOVAL & INSTALLATION

The ball joint is an integral part of the upper control arm. If the ball joint is defective, the entire upper control arm must be replaced.

Lower Ball Joint

REMOVAL AND INSTALLATION

1. Before servicing the vehicle, refer to the precautions in the beginning of this section.

2. If equipped, turn the air suspension switch to the OFF.

3. Raise and safely support the vehicle.

4. Remove the wheel and tire assembly.

5. Remove the lower control arm assembly.

6. Remove and discard the lower ball joint boot seal.

7. Clamp the lower control arm in a suitable vise.

8. Press out the lower control arm ball joint using Ball Joint Remover D89P-3010-A and Receiving Cup D84P-3395-A4 or equivalents and a suitable U-joint tool or hydraulic press.

To install:

➡**When installing a new lower ball joint, it is advisable that the protective cover be left in place during installa-** tion to protect the ball joint seal. It may be necessary to cut off the end of the cover to allow it to pass through the receiving cup.

9. Install the lower ball joint into the lower control arm using Ball Joint Replacer D89P-3010-B and Receiving Cup D84P-3395-A4 or equivalents and a suitable U-joint tool or hydraulic press.

10. Remove and discard the protective cover. Check the lower ball joint to be sure that it is fully seated in the lower control arm.

11. Inspect the ball joint seal and ensure that it is free of cuts or tears.

12. Install the lower control arm assembly into the vehicle.

13. Install the wheel and tire assembly. Tighten the lug nuts to 85–105 ft. lbs. (115–142 Nm).

14. Lower the vehicle.

15. If equipped, turn the air suspension switch to the ON position.

16. Check the alignment and adjust if not within specification.

17. Road test the vehicle and check for proper operation.

FRONT SUSPENSION LOWER ARM

BALL JOINT REMOVER

U-JOINT TOOL

RECEIVING CUP

7922PG35

The lower ball joint must be pressed out of the control arm using the appropriate tools as shown

Turn to Section 6 for brake system applications

Upper Control Arm

REMOVAL & INSTALLATION

➡ **The following procedure is the same for both the right-hand and left-hand upper control arm assemblies.**

1. Before servicing the vehicle, refer to the precautions in the beginning of this section.

2. Turn the air suspension switch to the OFF position which is located in the luggage compartment.

3. Raise and safely support the vehicle.

4. Remove the wheel and tire assembly.

5. Remove and discard the upper wheel spindle-to-ball joint pinch bolt and nut. Slightly spread the wheel spindle at the slot opening to remove the upper ball joint stud from the wheel spindle.

6. Lower the vehicle enough to gain access to the upper control arm pivot bolts. Support the vehicle in this position.

➡ **A 6-point socket must be used on the bolt due to the fact that the corners of the heads have been shaved off. Discard the nuts and bolts after removing them. Replacement bolts do not require metal flags.**

7. Break off the small metal flags from the upper control arm pivot bolt heads. Remove the bolts and nuts.

8. Remove the upper control arm from the vehicle. Inspect the upper control arm ball joint. If worn the entire upper control arm assembly must be replaced.

To install:

9. Place the upper control arm in position and install new pivot bolts and nuts. Holding the control arm in the horizontal position, tighten the nuts to 65–88 ft. lbs. (88–119 Nm).

➡ **If nuts cannot be torqued due to limited access on some models, tighten the pivot bolts to 82–88 ft. lbs. (110–120 Nm).**

10. Raise and safely support the vehicle.

11. Install the upper control arm ball joint stud to the wheel spindle and install a new pinch bolt and nut, making sure to install the bolt from the front of the vehicle. Tighten the nut to 51–67 ft. lbs. (68–92 Nm).

12. Install the wheel and tire assembly. Using a torque wrench, tighten the lug nuts in a star pattern to 85–105 ft. lbs. (115–142 Nm).

13. Lower the vehicle.

14. If equipped, turn the air suspension switch to the ON position.

15. If required, check the alignment and adjust if not within specification.

16. Road test the vehicle and check for proper operation.

Lower Control Arm

REMOVAL & INSTALLATION

1. Before servicing the vehicle, refer to the precautions in the beginning of this section.

2. Disconnect the negative battery cable.

3. Turn the air suspension switch to the OFF position which is located in the luggage compartment.

4. Raise and safely support the vehicle.

5. Remove the wheel and tire assembly.

6. Remove the air line from the air spring solenoid valve by pushing down and holding the plastic retaining ring on the valve while pulling on the air line.

7. Remove the air spring solenoid valve as follows:

  a. Remove the solenoid retainer clip.

  b. Rotate the solenoid valve counterclockwise to the 1st stop.

  c. Pull the solenoid valve straight out slowly to the 2nd stop to bleed air from the system.

➡ **Do not fully release the solenoid until the air is completely bled from the air spring.**

  d. After the air is fully bled from the system, rotate the solenoid valve counterclockwise to the 3rd stop and remove the solenoid valve from the solenoid housing. Remove the large O-ring from the solenoid housing.

8. Loosen the lower ball joint retaining nut 3 to 4 turns.

9. Rap on the wheel spindle with a hammer to separate the lower ball joint from the wheel spindle. Leave the nut on the lower ball joint stud.

10. Support the wheel spindle by a length of wire or other means to prevent excessive sagging of the upper control arm.

11. Matchmark the position of the camber adjustment cam.

12. Remove the rubber bumper from the lower control arm strut, if equipped.

13. Using a wrench to hold the lower control arm strut, remove the nut retaining the lower control arm strut to the lower control arm and discard the nut.

✳ CAUTION

Do not hold the lower control arm strut with a wrench on any curved surface of the strut. Use only the flat spots, as damage to the tension strut may result.

14. Verify that all air is exhausted from the air spring, then remove the lower air spring/shock assembly retaining bolt and nut.

15. Remove the pivot (camber) bolt and nut.

16. Remove the nut from the lower ball joint stud and remove the lower control arm.

To install:

17. Install the air spring solenoid valve as follows:

  a. Check the solenoid valve O-rings for cuts or abrasion. Replace the O-rings as required. Lightly grease the O-ring area of the solenoid valve and the larger solenoid housing O-ring with silicone dielectric compound.

  b. Insert the solenoid valve into the air spring end cap and rotate clockwise to the 3rd stop, push in to the 2nd stop, then rotate clockwise to the 1st stop.

  c. Install the air spring solenoid retainer clip. Inspect the electrical harness connector and ensure the rubber gasket is in place at the bottom of the connector cavity.

18. Attach the air line and the electrical harness connector to the air spring solenoid valve.

19. Place the lower control arm into the vehicle and loosely install the pivot (camber) bolt and nut.

20. Place the lower control arm strut to the lower control arm and install the washer, bushings and retaining nut. Do not tighten the nut at this time.

21. Install the lower control arm ball joint nut loosely.

22. Install the lower air spring/shock assembly retaining bolt and nut to the lower control arm. Do not tighten at this time.

23. Tighten the lower ball joint retaining nut to 83–113 ft. lbs. (113–153 Nm).

24. Tighten the lower control arm strut retaining nut to 89–118 ft. lbs. (120–160 Nm).

25. Install the rubber bumper to the lower control arm strut, if equipped.

26. Remove the wire or other type of support holding the wheel spindle.

27. Verify that the air suspension switch is OFF, then connect the negative battery cable.

28. Fill the air spring as follows:

a. Attach Super Star II Tester 007-0041B or equivalent, to the Data Link Connector (DLC) located on the front side of the right-hand shock tower.

b. Install a battery charger to reduce battery drain.

c. Enter the appropriate function test to fill the required air spring:

- 212 left-front air spring
- 214 right-front air spring

d. Remove the tester and battery charger.

➡ **Any further inflation should be done with the vehicle on the ground and the air suspension switch in the ON position.**

29. Inspect the air spring folds and creases.

30. Install the wheel and tire assembly. Torque the lug nuts to 85–105 ft. lbs. (115–142 Nm).

31. Lower the vehicle.

32. Turn the air suspension switch to the ON position.

33. Place the vehicle on an alignment rack or equivalent, to raise the vehicle off of the ground but to keep the suspension loaded.

34. Neutralize the front suspension bushings by pushing the front of the vehicle down several times and allowing the suspension to settle. Tighten the lower air spring and shock assembly retaining bolt and nut to 125–170 ft. lbs. (170–230 Nm).

35. Align the camber match marks at the pivot bolt. Using a torque wrench, tighten the retaining nut to 82–114 ft. lbs. (110–155 Nm).

36. Check the alignment and adjust if not within specification.

37. Road test the vehicle and check for proper operation.

Wheel Bearings

ADJUSTMENT

The wheel bearings are not adjustable. If the bearings feel rough or make noise, they must be replaced.

REMOVAL & INSTALLATION

Front

➡ **Before continuing with this procedure, be sure to have available, a new wheel hub retainer nut, two wheel** spindle-to-strut nuts and bolts, one lower ball joint stud nut and one wheel hub grease cap, per side. Once these parts are removed, they lose their torque holding ability or retention capability and must not be reused.

✳✳ CAUTION

The air spring must be completely drained of air before disassembling the suspension components.

1. Before servicing the vehicle, refer to the precautions in the beginning of this section.

2. Raise and safely support the vehicle.

3. Place supports under both frame rails just behind the lower control arms.

4. Remove the wheel and tire assembly.

5. Detach the air spring solenoid electrical harness connector.

6. Remove the air line from the air spring solenoid valve by pushing down and holding the plastic retaining ring on the valve while pulling on the air line.

7. Remove the air spring solenoid valve as follows:

a. Remove the solenoid retainer clip.

b. Rotate the solenoid valve counterclockwise to the first stop.

c. Pull the solenoid valve straight out slowly to the second stop to bleed air from the system.

➡ **Do not fully release the solenoid until the air is completely bled from the air spring.**

d. After the air is fully bled from the system, rotate the solenoid valve counterclockwise to the third stop and remove the solenoid valve from the solenoid housing. Remove the large O-ring from the solenoid housing.

8. Remove the anti-lock speed sensor from the wheel spindle and move aside.

9. Remove and discard the hub cap grease seal.

10. Remove the two bolts from the disc brake caliper and caliper anchor plate and remove as an assembly. Support the assembly with wire. Do not allow the caliper assembly to hang by the brake hose.

11. Matchmark the brake rotor to one of the lug bolts and remove the disc brake rotor.

12. Remove the disc brake rotor dust shield.

13. Remove and discard the wheel hub retainer nut.

➡ **The front wheel bearings are part of the wheel hub and cannot be replaced separately.**

14. Remove the wheel hub and bearing assembly. If necessary, use Front Hub Remover T81P-1104-C or equivalent, to remove the wheel hub from the spindle.

15. Remove the sway bar link retaining nut at the wheel spindle. Separate the sway bar link from the wheel spindle using Ball Joint Remover D88L-3006-A, or equivalent.

16. Remove the tie rod end cotter pin and castellated nut. Separate the tie rod end from the wheel spindle using Tie Rod End Remover T-3290-D, or equivalent.

17. Loosen the lower ball joint retaining nut one or two turns. Do not remove the nut at this time.

18. Tap the wheel spindle boss sharply to separate the lower ball joint stud from the wheel spindle. Remove and discard the lower ball joint retaining nut.

19. Remove and discard the upper control arm-to-wheel spindle pinch bolt and nut.

20. Spread the slot in the wheel spindle slightly and remove the wheel spindle from the upper ball joint stud.

21. Remove the wheel spindle from the vehicle.

To install:

22. Install the air spring solenoid valve as follows:

a. Check the solenoid valve O-rings for cuts or abrasion. Replace the O-rings as required. Lightly grease the O-ring area of the solenoid valve and the larger solenoid housing O-ring with silicone dielectric compound.

b. Insert the solenoid valve into the air spring end cap and rotate clockwise to the 3rd stop, push in to the 2nd stop, then rotate clockwise to the 1st stop.

c. Install the air spring solenoid retainer clip. Inspect the electrical harness connector and ensure the rubber gasket is in place at the bottom of the connector cavity.

23. Attach the air line and the electrical harness connector to the air spring solenoid valve.

24. Place the wheel spindle in position to the lower and upper control arm ball joint studs. Install a new upper ball joint pinch bolt and nut. Tighten the nut to 50–68 ft. lbs. (68–92 Nm). Install a new retaining nut on the lower control arm ball joint stud and tighten to 83–113 ft. lbs. (113–153 Nm).

FRONT WHEEL SPINDLE

HUB AND BEARING ASSY

FRONT DISC BRAKE ROTOR SHIELD

7922PG36

The wheel bearings are an integral part of the front hub assembly

25. Install the disc brake rotor dust shield.

26. Clean the wheel spindle stem, then install the wheel hub and bearing assembly onto the spindle.

➡️**Any time a wheel hub retainer nut is loosened or removed, it must be replaced with a new nut. Do not use an impact tool to install the new nut.**

27. Install a new wheel hub retainer nut and tighten to 188–254 ft. lbs. (255–345 Nm).

28. Install the disc brake rotor. Check the brake rotor run-out to verify proper installation.

29. Install a new hub cap grease seal.

30. Install the disc brake caliper and anchor plate assembly to the wheel spindle. Install the two anchor plate retaining bolts and tighten to 88 ft. lbs. (119 Nm).

31. Install the anti-lock speed sensor and mounting bolt. Tighten the bolt to 40–60 inch lbs. (4.5–6.8 Nm).

32. Connect the sway bar to the wheel spindle and install the retaining nut. Tighten the nut to 39–53 ft. lbs. (53–72 Nm).

33. Attach the tie rod end stud to the wheel spindle. Install the castellated nut and tighten to 39 ft. lbs. (53 Nm). Continue

tightening the nut to align the next castellation with the hole in the stud. Install a new cotter pin.

34. Verify that the air suspension switch if OFF, then connect the negative battery cable.

35. Fill the air spring as follows:

a. Attach Super Star II Tester 007–0041B or equivalent to the data link connector (DLC) located on the front side of the right-hand shock tower.

b. Install a battery charger to reduce battery drain.

c. Enter the appropriate function test to fill the required air spring:
- 212 left-front air spring
- 214 right-front air spring

d. Remove the tester and battery charger.

➡️**Any further inflation should be done with the vehicle on the ground and the air suspension switch in the ON position.**

36. Inspect the air spring folds and creases.

37. Install the wheel and tire assembly. Using a torque wrench, tighten the lug nuts in a star pattern, to 85–105 ft. lbs. (115–142 Nm).

38. Lower the vehicle.

39. Turn the air suspension switch to the ON position.

40. Pump the brake pedal several times to position the brake pads.

41. Check the alignment and adjust if not within specification.

42. Road test the vehicle and check for proper operation.

Rear

➡️**Before continuing with this procedure, be sure to have available, one new wheel hub retainer nut, one inboard halfshaft circlip and one inboard CV-joint stub shaft seal, per side. Once removed, these parts lose their torque holding ability or retention capability and must not be reused.**

1. Before servicing the vehicle, refer to the precautions in the beginning of this section.

2. Turn the air suspension switch, located in the luggage compartment, to the OFF position.

3. Remove the hub cap grease seal.

4. With all wheels on the ground, remove and discard the wheel hub retainer nut.

5. Raise and safely support the vehicle.

6. Remove the wheel and tire assembly.

7. Use needle-nose pliers to slide the parking brake cable adjusting clip downward until the cable is free.

8. Remove the parking brake cable from the rear disc brake caliper.

9. Remove the disc brake caliper from the brake rotor, leaving the brake hose connected. Wire the brake caliper aside. Do not let it hang by the brake hose.

10. Remove the brake rotor.

11. Remove the upper control arm nut and bolt at the wheel knuckle. Wire the upper control arm to the body to prevent damage to the CV-joint boots when the knuckle and hub assembly is removed.

12. Mark the position of the control arm in relation to the knuckle with the bushings in the relaxed position. When the upper control arm bolt is removed from the knuckle, the lower arm bushings will return to the relaxed position.

➡️**Failure to mark the position will cause bushing wind up at assembly resulting in improper ride height. This can cause incorrect alignment and tire wear.**

13. Install Hub Remover/Replacer T81P-1104-C or equivalent to the hub studs and turn the tool shaft until the halfshaft is free in the hub.

14. Remove the lower control arm-to-knuckle retaining bolts and nuts and remove the knuckle assembly from the half-shaft.

15. Remove and save the washers used between the lower control arm bushings and the wheel knuckle for installation.

16. Place the knuckle and hub assembly in a suitable vise.

17. Wire the halfshaft to a suitable location to prevent damage to the CV-joint boot.

18. Place a suitable two or three jaw puller and Step Plate Adapter D80L-630–5 or equivalent, on the rear wheel knuckle and press out the hub from the wheel knuckle and bearing assembly.

19. Remove the disc brake backing plate from the wheel knuckle.

20. Remove the snapring retaining the wheel bearing assembly.

21. Place the wheel knuckle and bearing assembly on a press bed using Hub Support T89P-1104-A and Front Hub Bearing Remover/Replacer T83P-1104-AH2 or

equivalents and press the wheel bearing assembly from the wheel knuckle.

22. Inspect all components for wear and/or damage and replace as needed.

To install:

23. Place the wheel knuckle on the press bed and position the wheel bearing assembly in the wheel knuckle bore. Press the wheel bearing assembly into the knuckle bore using Bearing Replacer T86P-1104-A3 or equivalent. Be sure the bearing assembly is fully seated.

24. Install the wheel bearing retainer snapring.

25. Place the disc brake backing plate in position on the wheel knuckle and install the three retaining bolts. Tighten the bolts to 22–37 ft. lbs. (30–50 Nm).

❊❊ WARNING

Before proceeding with the following step, the wheel bearing must be supported or damage will result.

---

26. Place the wheel knuckle on Hub Support T89P-1104-A or equivalent and place on a suitable press bed plate. Place the wheel hub in position with the wheel bearing and knuckle assembly and press into position using Front Hub Bearing Remover/Replacer T83P-1104-AH2 or equivalent. Be sure the inner bearing race is properly supported or the bearing will be damaged.

27. Using a hammer and chisel, drive the bearing dust seal from the outer CV-joint. Using Axle Seal Replacer T83T-3132-A1 and Bearing Dust Seal Replacer T89P-1249-A or equivalents, install a new dust seal, making sure the seal flange faces out toward the bearing.

28. Remove the wire holding the half-shaft.

29. Engage the wheel knuckle and hub assembly on the halfshaft splines and install the rear lower bolt, washer and nut, finger-tight.

30. Install the washers between the front

2/3-JAW PULLER

STEP PLATE

**DRUM BRAKE SHOWN
DISC BRAKE SIMILAR**

7922PG37

Use a two or three jaw puller to press the bearing out of the hub assembly as shown and rear lower control arm/wheel knuckle locations and install the bolts with the bolt heads facing the rear of the vehicle.

31. Push the halfshaft inward through the hub assembly while placing the wheel knuckle in position to install the front lower bolt, washer and nut.

32. Align the lower control arm to wheel knuckle matchmarks made during removal. If a new wheel knuckle is being installed, set the knuckle at the approximate angle noted during removal. Tighten the lower control arm-to-wheel knuckle retaining bolts to 94–131 ft. lbs. (128–178 Nm) using Holding Tool T93P-5494-A, or equivalent.

33. Install the brake rotor.

34. Install a new wheel hub retainer nut and hand-tighten only.

35. Install the upper control arm retaining bolt and nut. Tighten the nut to 117–142 ft. lbs. (158–193 Nm).

36. Install the disc brake caliper over the brake rotor with the outer brake pad against the brake rotor, to prevent pinching the caliper piston boot between the inner pad and piston. Install the two disc brake caliper retaining bolts and tighten to 64–88 ft. lbs. (87–119 Nm).

37. Connect the parking brake rear cable to the disc brake caliper and install the cable adjustment clip.

38. Install the wheel and tire assembly. Using a torque wrench, tighten the lug nuts to 85–105 ft. lbs. (115–142 Nm).

39. Lower the vehicle.

40. Turn the air suspension switch to the ON position.

41. Apply the parking brake several times and adjust if necessary.

42. With all wheels on the ground, tighten the wheel hub retainer nut to 188–254 ft. lbs. (255–345 Nm).

43. Install the hub cap grease seal.

44. Pump the brake pedal several times to position the brake pads before moving the vehicle.

45. Check the alignment and adjust if not within specification.

46. Road test the vehicle and check for proper operation.

FORD MOTOR COMPANY

Ford-Thunderbird • **Mercury**-Cougar (1996–97)

25

PRECAUTIONS

Before servicing any vehicle, please be sure to read all of the following precautions. The following precautions deal with personal safety, prevention of component damage, and important points to take into consideration when servicing a motor vehicle:

• Never open, service or drain the radiator or cooling system when the engine is hot; serious burns can occur from the steam and hot coolant.

• Observe all applicable safety precautions when working around fuel. Whenever servicing the fuel system, always work in a well ventilated area. Do not allow fuel spray or vapors to come in contact with a spark, open flame, or excessive heat (a hot drop light, for example). Keep a dry chemical fire extinguisher near the work area. Always keep fuel in a container specifically designed for fuel storage; also, always properly seal fuel containers to avoid the possibility of fire or explosion. Refer to the additional fuel system precautions later in this section.

• Fuel injection systems often remain pressurized, even after the engine has been turned **OFF**. The fuel system pressure must be relieved before disconnecting any fuel lines. Failure to do so may result in fire and/or personal injury.

• Brake fluid often contains polyglycol ethers and polyglycols. Avoid contact with the eyes and wash your hands thoroughly after handling brake fluid. If you do get brake fluid in your eyes, flush your eyes with clean, running water for 15 minutes. If eye irritation persists, or if you have taken brake fluid internally, IMMEDIATELY seek medical assistance.

• The EPA warns that prolonged contact with used engine oil may cause a number of skin disorders, including cancer! You should make every effort to minimize your exposure to used engine oil. Protective gloves should be worn when changing the oil. Wash your hands and any other exposed skin areas as soon as possible after exposure to used engine oil. Soap and water, or waterless hand cleaner should be used.

• All vehicles are equipped with an air bag system, often referred to as a Supplemental Restraint System (SRS) or as a Supplemental Inflatable Restraint (SIR) system. The system must be disabled before performing service on or around system components, steering column, instrument panel components, wiring and sensors. Failure to follow safety and disabling procedures could result in accidental air bag deployment, possible personal injury and unnecessary system repairs.

• Always wear safety goggles when working with, or around, the air bag system. When carrying a non-deployed air bag, be sure the bag and trim cover are pointed away from your body. When placing a non-deployed air bag on a work surface, always face the bag and trim cover upward, away from the surface. This will reduce the motion of the module if it is accidentally deployed. Refer to the additional air bag system precautions later in this section.

• Clean, high quality brake fluid from a sealed container is essential to the safe and proper operation of the brake system. You should always buy the correct type of brake fluid for your vehicle. If the brake fluid becomes contaminated, completely flush the system with new fluid. Never reuse any brake fluid. Any brake fluid that is removed from the system should be discarded. Also, do not allow any brake fluid to come in contact with a painted surface; it will damage the paint.

• Never operate the engine without the proper amount and type of engine oil; doing so WILL result in severe engine damage.

• Timing belt maintenance is extremely important! Many models may utilize an interference-type, non-free-wheeling engine. If the timing belt breaks, the valves in the cylinder head may strike the pistons, causing potentially serious (also time-consuming and expensive) engine damage. Refer to the maintenance interval charts in the front of this manual for the recommended replacement interval for the timing belt, and to the timing belt section for belt replacement and inspection.

• Disconnecting the negative battery cable on some vehicles may interfere with the functions of the on board computer system(s) and may require the computer to undergo a relearning process once the negative battery cable is reconnected.

• When servicing drum brakes, only dissemble and assemble one side at a time, leaving the remaining side intact for reference.

• Only an MVAC-trained, EPA-certified, automotive technician should service the A/C system or its components.

ENGINE REPAIR

Ignition Timing

ADJUSTMENT

➡**Always refer to the Vehicle Emission Control Information (VECI) label to verify the timing adjustment procedure.**

The 3.8L and 4.6L engines are equipped with Distributorless Ignition Systems (DIS), and, therefore, the base timing for these engines is set from the factory at 10 degrees BTDC and is not adjustable.

Engine Assembly

REMOVAL & INSTALLATION

3.8L Engine

1. Before servicing the vehicle, refer to the precautions in the beginning of this section.
2. Disconnect the negative battery cable.
3. Drain the crankcase and the cooling system.
4. Relieve the fuel system pressure and discharge the A/C system.
5. Detach the electrical connector to the underhood lamp. Mark the position of the hood on the hinges and remove the hood.
6. Remove the left cowl vent screen and wiper module. disconnect the alternator-to-voltage regulator wiring assembly.
7. Remove the radiator upper sight shield. Release the belt tension and remove the drive and accessory belts. Remove the air cleaner-to-throttle body tube.
8. Remove the fan and shroud.
9. Remove the upper radiator hose and disconnect the heater hoses. If equipped with an automatic transmission, disconnect the oil cooler lines from the radiator.
10. Disconnect the lower radiator hose at the water pump. Remove the radiator.
11. Disconnect the power steering pressure hose assembly. Remove the power steering pump and bracket assembly and position aside.
12. Disconnect the air conditioner compressor clutch wire. Disconnect and plug the refrigerant lines. Remove the compressor.
13. Remove the coolant recovery reservoir and remove the wiring shield. Remove the accelerator cable mounting bracket and position aside.
14. Disconnect the fuel lines from the fuel rail. Tag and disconnect the Engine Control Module (ECM) wiring, engine feed harnesses and vacuum hoses.
15. Disconnect the ground and coil wires.
16. Disconnect the canister purge line.
17. Raise and safely support the vehicle. Remove the oil filter element.
18. Remove the exhaust pipe-to-manifold nuts and remove the left exhaust shield. Disconnect the Oxygen (O_2S) sensors.
19. If equipped with an automatic trans-

mission, remove the inspection plug and remove the torque converter bolts.
20. Remove the engine-to-transmission bolts and remove the engine mount through-bolts.
21. Remove the crankshaft pulley assembly.

➡ If the crankshaft pulley and vibration damper have to be separated, mark the damper and pulley so they may be reassembled in the same relative position. This is important as the damper and pulley are initially balanced as a unit. If the crankshaft damper is being replaced, check if the original damper has balance pins installed. If so, new balance pins must be installed on the new damper in the same position as the original damper.

22. Remove the starter. Remove the ground cable and remove the left and right starter harness retainers.
23. Disconnect the oil level indicator sensor and partially lower the vehicle.
24. Disconnect the oil pressure sending unit gauge assembly.
25. Position a floor jack under the transmission and install suitable engine lifting equipment.
26. Remove the engine from the vehicle and position it on a workstand.

To install:
27. Remove the engine assembly from the workstand and install the engine lifting equipment.
28. Position the engine in the vehicle and install the two engine-to-transmission bolts. Lower the engine onto the mounting seats, left side first, and remove the lifting equipment. Remove the jacks.
29. Tighten the two engine-to-transmission bolts to 40–50 ft. lbs. (55–68 Nm) and connect the oil pressure sending unit gauge assembly. Raise and safely support the vehicle.
30. Install the remaining engine-to-transmission bolts and tighten to 40–50 ft. lbs. (55–68 Nm).
31. Install the torque converter bolts and tighten to 20–34 ft. lbs. (27–46 Nm). Install the inspection plug.
32. Install and tighten the engine mount through-bolts to 35–50 ft. lbs. (47–68 Nm).
33. Install the starter. Install the starter harness retainer, ground cable and transmission oil cooler line bracket. Install the exhaust pipe-to-manifold nuts.

34. Install the crankshaft pulley assembly and tighten the bolts to 20–28 ft. lbs. (26–30 Nm).
35. Connect the O_2S sensors and the oil level indicator sensor. Install a new oil filter and lower the vehicle.
36. Connect the canister purge line.
37. Install the coolant recovery reservoir.
38. Connect the alternator-to-voltage regulator wiring, the ECM wiring assembly and engine feed harnesses. Connect the vacuum hoses.
39. Connect the wiring assembly ground and coil wire.
40. Connect the fuel lines to the fuel rail. Install the accelerator cable mounting bracket and the wiring shield.
41. Install the air conditioning compressor and retaining bolts. Tighten the bolts to 30–45 ft. lbs. (41–61 Nm).
42. Remove the plugs from the air conditioner compressor lines and connect the lines to the compressor. Connect the compressor clutch wire.
43. Install the power steering pump bracket assembly. Connect the power steering hoses.
44. Install the radiator.
45. Connect the lower radiator hose to the water pump and install the heater hoses.
46. If equipped with an automatic transmission, install the oil cooler lines to the radiator.
47. Install the upper radiator hose and the fan and fan shroud.
48. Position the drive belts and the accessory belts. Install the radiator sight shield.
49. Install the cowl vent screen and wiper module. Install the hood, aligning the marks that were made during removal. Connect the underhood lamp wiring.
50. Fill the crankcase with the proper type and quantity of engine oil. Fill and bleed the cooling system.
51. Connect the negative battery cable, start the engine and bring to normal operating temperature. Check for leaks. Check all fluid levels.
52. Leak test, evacuate and charge the air conditioning system. Observe all safety precautions.

4.6L Engine

1. Before servicing the vehicle, refer to the precautions in the beginning of this section.
2. Disconnect the negative battery cable, drain the cooling system and discharge the A/C system.

3. Remove the air cleaner outlet tube and air cleaner assembly.

4. Remove the fan blade and shroud.

5. Relieve the fuel system pressure.

6. Detach the 42-pin and 8-pin connectors and position out of the way.

7. Label all components for reassembly. Detach the accelerator cable, speed control actuator, throttle valve control cable, canister purge electrical connector and vacuum lines.

8. Disconnect the power supply from the power distribution box and starter relay.

9. Disconnect the transmission oil cooler tubes from the transmission, upper radiator hose and heater hoses.

10. Disconnect the engine-to-frame ground straps. Partially raise the vehicle and support safely. Remove the front wheels.

11. Disconnect the right and left front anti-lock sensor and brackets.

12. Remove the right and left disc brake caliper bolts. Remove the calipers and support with wire to a frame member.

13. Disconnect the right and left front suspension upper arms from the spindles.

14. Disconnect the front springs and shocks from the lower arms.

15. Raise the vehicle and support safely.

16. Drain the engine oil.

17. Disconnect the dual converter Y-pipe from the manifolds. Disconnect the transmission shift cable and bracket.

18. Matchmark the driveshaft centering socket yoke to the rear axle universal joint flange.

19. Remove the four bolts connecting the driveshaft centering socket yoke to the rear axle universal joint flange. Support the rear axle assembly.

20. Remove the rear axle assembly to rear sub-frame bolts. Loosen the rear differential bracket-to-body bolts and lower.

21. Slide the driveshaft rearward until it is free of the extension housing.

22. Remove the lower radiator hose, power steering lines and steering oil cooler.

23. Detach the wiring connector at the bulkhead. Support the front sub-frame using Rotunda Powertrain Lift 014–00765 and Adapter 014–00341 or equivalent.

24. Remove the rear engine support insulator bolts and disconnect the steering coupling at the pinch bolt joint.

25. Remove the eight sub-frame bolts and lower the engine/transmission assembly.

26. Label and remove all needed components. Separate the engine from the transmission and place the engine on a suitable workstand.

To install:

27. Install Engine Lifting Brackets 014–00334, or equivalent engine brackets. Install the transmission to the engine. Be sure the torque converter studs align with the holes in the flexplate. Tighten the bell housing retaining bolts to 30–44 ft. lbs. (40–60 Nm). Tighten the torque converter-to-flexplate bolts to 25 ft. lbs. (35 Nm).

28. Install the transmission housing cover, starter motor and transmission-to-engine block brackets.

29. Position the transmission oil cooler tube bracket on the transmission case.

30. Raise the engine/transmission assembly and carefully lower onto the front sub-frame.

31. Install the right and left front engine support insulator through-bolts. Tighten the bolts to 22 ft. lbs. (30 Nm).

32. Install the power steering lines and remove the engine lift brackets from the cylinder heads.

33. Raise the engine/transmission/sub-frame assembly using the Powertrain Lift 014–00765 and Adapter 014–00341 into the vehicle.

34. Align the sub-frame to the body and install the bolts. Tighten the bolts to 100 ft. lbs. (130 Nm).

35. Connect the steering shaft pinch joint and driveshaft. Raise the rear axle assembly into the vehicle and tighten the rear sub-frame bolts to 89 ft. lbs. (120 Nm). Tighten the two rear axle differential insulator nuts to 94 ft. lbs. (127 Nm).

36. Align the driveshaft centering socket yoke to the rear axle universal joint flange and install the four retaining bolts to 162 ft. lbs. (220 Nm).

37. Connect the transmission shift linkage, front suspension arms and lower radiator hose.

38. Adjust the transmission shift linkage as follows:

    a. Position the transmission range selector into the OVERDRIVE position.

    b. Raise and safely support the vehicle.

    c. Loosen the shift cable and bracket-to-cable bracket retaining nut.

    d. Move the transmission manual control lever to the OVERDRIVE position (the third detent position from the full clockwise position).

    e. Tighten the retaining nut to 10–18 ft. lbs. (13–25 Nm).

    f. Check the operation of the transmission in each range.

39. Connect the power steering hoses to steering cooler, ground straps and dual converter Y-pipe.

40. Connect the front suspension upper arms to the spindles and tighten to 98 ft. lbs. (92 Nm).

41. Connect the anti-lock sensor and install the calipers. Install the front wheels.

42. Lower the vehicle and connect the A/C lines, transmission cooler lines and radiator hoses.

43. Attach all remaining hoses, lines, electrical connectors and cables.

44. Install the fan, fan shroud and air cleaner.

45. Refill the cooling system. Evacuate, recharge and leak test the A/C system.

46. Connect the negative battery cable, fill the engine with oil, start the engine and check for leaks.

Water Pump

REMOVAL & INSTALLATION

3.8L Engine

1. Before servicing the vehicle, refer to the precautions in the beginning of this section.

2. Disconnect the negative battery cable and drain the cooling system.

3. Remove the fan/clutch assembly and shroud.

4. Rotate the main accessory drive belt tensioner. Remove the main drive belt and water pump pulley.

5. Remove the power steering pump pulley and remove the water pump-to-power steering pump brace.

6. Disconnect the coolant bypass hose(s) and the heater hose at the water pump.

7. Disconnect the lower radiator hose. Remove the water pump retaining bolts and the pump. If a prybar is used to assist removal, be careful not to damage the mating surfaces.

8. Installation is the reverse of the removal procedure. Clean all gasket mating surfaces prior to installation. Tighten the water pump retaining bolts to 15–22 ft. lbs. (20–30 Nm). Fill and bleed the cooling system. Operate the engine until normal operating temperatures have been reached and check for leaks.

➡ The threads of the No. 1 water pump retaining stud/bolt must be coated with pipe sealant before installing.

TIGHTEN BOLTS IN SEQUENCE

FRONT OF ENGINE

Item	Description
1	Stud (4 Req'd)
2	Water Pump Housing Gasket
3	Water Pump
4	Nut (4 Req'd)
5	Bolt (3 Req'd)
6	Bolt
7	Stud Bolt

93000G01

Exploded view of the water pump mounting—3.8L engine

4.6L Engine

1. Before servicing the vehicle, refer to the precautions in the beginning of this section.

2. Disconnect the negative battery cable and drain the cooling system.

3. Release the drive belt tensioner and remove the belt.

4. Remove the water pump pulley bolts and pulley.

5. Loosen the water pump-to-block bolts, then remove the pump.

6. Installation is the reverse of the removal procedure. Clean all gasket mating surfaces prior to installation. Tighten the water pump bolts and pulley retaining bolts to 15–22 ft. lbs. (20–30 Nm).

7. Fill and bleed the cooling system. Operate the engine until normal operating temperatures have been reached and check for leaks.

COOLING SYSTEM BLEEDING

When the entire cooling system is drained, the following procedure should be used to ensure a complete fill.

1. Install the block drain plug, if removed and close the petcock. On 3.8L engine, remove the vent plug on the intake manifold behind the thermostat housing. With the engine OFF, add a 50/50 mixture of water and anti-freeze to the radiator until it reaches the radiator filler neck seat.

2. Install the radiator cap to the first notch to keep spillage to a minimum. On 3.8L engine, install the vent plug.

3. Start the engine and let it idle until the upper radiator hose is warm. This indicates that the thermostat is open and coolant is flowing through the entire system.

4. Carefully remove the radiator cap and top off the radiator with the water/anti-freeze mixture. Install the cap on the radiator securely.

5. Fill the coolant recovery reservoir to the FULL HOT mark with the water/anti-freeze mixture. Install the reservoir cap.

Cylinder Head

REMOVAL & INSTALLATION

3.8L Engine

➡Before continuing with this procedure, be sure to have available eight

WATER PUMP HOUSING GASKET

BOLT 4 REQ'D TIGHTEN TO 20-30 N·m (15-22 LB-FT)

WATER PUMP

7922QG02

Exploded view of the water pump mounting—4.6L engine

Timing belt service is covered in Section 5 of this manual

new cylinder head retaining bolts, per cylinder head. Once removed, these parts lose their torque holding ability or retention capability and must not be reused.

1. Before servicing the vehicle, refer to the precautions in the beginning of this section.

2. Disconnect the negative battery cable.

3. Properly relieve the fuel system pressure.

4. Allow the engine to cool, then drain the cooling system.

5. Remove the engine air cleaner outlet tube from the throttle body.

6. Remove the accessory drive belts.

7. If removing the left-hand cylinder head, perform the following:

   a. Remove the engine oil fill cap.

   b. Remove the power steering pump front mounting bracket retaining bolts.

   c. Remove the alternator and the drive belt idler pulley.

   d. Remove the alternator/power steering pump bracket retaining bolts. Leaving the hoses connected, place the power steering pump/alternator bracket assembly aside in a position to prevent the fluid from leaking out.

8. If removing the right-hand cylinder head, perform the following:

   a. Remove the accessory drive belt.

   b. If equipped with air conditioning, remove the A/C compressor mounting bracket retaining bolts. Leave the hoses connected and move the A/C compressor aside.

➡ **It is not necessary to drain and evacuate the A/C system since the refrigerant lines do not need to be disconnected.**

   c. If not equipped with air conditioning, remove the idler pulley.

   d. Remove the PCV valve.

9. Remove the upper intake manifold.

10. Remove both cylinder head covers.

11. Disconnect and plug the fuel supply and return lines at the fuel injection supply manifold.

12. Remove the fuel rail and fuel injectors.

13. Remove the lower intake manifold.

14. Remove the exhaust manifolds.

15. Loosen the rocker arm seat retaining bolts enough to allow the rocker arms to be lifted off the pushrods and rotated aside.

16. Remove the pushrods. Identify the position of each rod so that they can be installed in their original positions.

Cylinder head bolt tightening sequence—3.8L engines

17. Remove the eight cylinder head retaining bolts, per head, and discard.

18. Remove the cylinder heads and gaskets.

To install:

19. Clean all gasket sealing surfaces.

20. Check the flatness of the cylinder head gasket surface using a straight-edge and a feeler gauge. The allowable warpage is 0.003 in. (0.08mm) for a 6.0 in. span (152mm). Do not machine the entire head more than 0.010 in. (0.254mm)

21. Lightly oil the new cylinder head bolt threads, except those entering coolant jackets which require pipe sealant applied to the threads.

22. Place the new cylinder head gaskets on the cylinder block using the dowels for alignment.

23. Carefully place the cylinder heads on the cylinder block.

24. Install the new cylinder head bolts and tighten in sequence, as follows:

   a. 15 ft. lbs. (20 Nm)

   b. 29 ft. lbs. (40 Nm)

   c. 37 ft. lbs. (50 Nm)

25. Loosen each cylinder head bolt, one at a time, 2–3 turns, then retighten as follows:

   a. Tighten each long bolt to 11–19 ft. lbs. (15–25 Nm), then rotate an additional 85–95 degrees.

   b. Tighten each short bolt to 7–15 ft. lbs. (10–20 Nm), then rotate an additional 85–95 degrees.

   c. Continue to the next bolt in sequence.

26. Lubricate each pushrod tip with a suitable engine assembly lubricant.

27. Install the pushrods in their original positions and rotate the rocker arms into position.

28. For each valve, rotate the crankshaft until the valve lifter rests on the heel (base circle) of the camshaft lobe (pushrod all the way down), then tighten the rocker arm fulcrum bolt to 44 inch lbs. (5 Nm). The fulcrum must be fully seated and the pushrod must be seated in the rocker arm socket before final tightening.

29. Lubricate the rocker arm assemblies with a suitable engine assembly lubricant. Tighten the rocker arm fulcrum bolts to 19–25 ft. lbs. (25–35 Nm). Final tightening can be done with the camshaft in any position.

➡ **If the original valvetrain components are being installed, a valve lash adjustment is not required. If a component has been replaced, adjust the valve clearance.**

30. Install the exhaust manifolds.

31. Install the lower intake manifold using new gaskets.

32. Install the fuel injection supply manifold and connect the fuel supply and return lines.

33. Install the cylinder head covers using new gaskets. Note the location of ignition wire routing clip stud bolts. Tighten the retaining bolts to 80–106 inch lbs. (9–12 Nm).

34. Install the upper intake manifold.
35. Install the spark plugs, if removed.
36. Connect the ignition wires to the spark plugs.
37. If the left-hand cylinder head is being installed, perform the following:
 a. Install the engine oil filler cap.
 b. Install the alternator/power steering pump mounting bracket.
 c. Install the alternator assembly.
 d. Install the accessory drive belt tensioner.
 e. Install the power steering pump.
 f. Install the power steering pump support bracket. Tighten the retaining bolts to 30–45 ft. lbs. (40–62 Nm).
38. If the right-hand cylinder head is being installed, perform the following:
 a. Install the PCV valve.
 b. If equipped with air conditioning, install the A/C compressor mounting and support brackets. Install the A/C compressor.
 c. If not equipped with air conditioning, install the idler pulley.
39. Install the accessory drive belt.
40. Install the engine air cleaner outlet tube.
41. Connect the negative battery cable.
42. Fill and bleed the engine cooling system.
43. Start the engine and check for coolant, fuel and oil leaks.
44. Road test the vehicle and check for proper operation.

4.6L Engine

1. Before servicing the vehicle, refer to the precautions in the beginning of this section.
2. Disconnect the negative battery cable.
3. Drain the cooling system and remove the cooling fan and shroud.
4. Relieve the fuel system pressure and disconnect the fuel lines.
5. Remove the air inlet tube and the wiper module. Release the belt tensioner and remove the accessory drive belt.
6. Tag and disconnect the ignition wires from the spark plugs. Disconnect the ignition wire brackets from the camshaft cover studs and remove the two bolts retaining the ignition wire tray to the coil brackets.
7. Remove the bolt retaining the air conditioner high pressure line to the right coil bracket. Disconnect both ignition coils and CID sensor.
8. Remove the nuts retaining the coil brackets to the front cover. Slide the ignition coil brackets and ignition wire assembly off the mounting studs and remove from the vehicle.
9. Remove the water pump pulley. Disconnect the generator wiring harness from the junction block, fender apron and generator. Disconnect the bolts retaining the generator to the intake manifold and engine block and remove the generator.
10. Disconnect the positive battery cable at the power distribution box. Remove the retaining bolt from the positive battery cable bracket located on the side of the right cylinder head.
11. Disconnect the vent hose from the canister purge solenoid and position the positive battery cable out of the way. Disconnect the canister purge solenoid vent hose from the PCV valve and remove the PCV valve from the camshaft cover.
12. Remove the 42-pin engine harness connector from the retaining bracket on the brake vacuum booster, disconnect and position out of the way.
13. Detach the Crankshaft Position (CKP) sensor, air conditioning compressor clutch and canister purge solenoid connectors.
14. Raise and safely support the vehicle.
15. Remove the bolts retaining the power steering pump to the engine block and front cover. The front lower bolt on the power steering pump will not come all the way out. Wire the power steering pump out of the way.
16. Remove the four bolts retaining the oil pan to the front cover. Remove the crankshaft damper retaining bolt and remove the damper, using a suitable puller.
17. Disconnect the oil sending unit. Position the oil pressure sending unit harness out of the way.
18. Disconnect the EGR tube from the right exhaust manifold. Disconnect the exhaust pipes from the exhaust manifolds. Lower the exhaust pipes and hang with wire from the crossmember.
19. Remove the bolt retaining the starter wiring harness to the rear of the right cylinder head. Lower the vehicle.
20. Remove the bolts and stud bolts retaining the camshaft covers to the cylinder heads and remove the covers.
21. Disconnect the accelerator, cruise control and throttle valve cables. Remove the accelerator cable bracket from the intake manifold and position out of the way.

22. Disconnect the vacuum hose from the throttle body elbow vacuum port, both Oxygen (O2S) sensors and the heater supply hose.
23. Remove the two bolts retaining the thermostat housing to the intake manifold and position the upper hose and thermostat housing out of the way.

➡ **Two thermostat housing bolts also retain the intake manifold.**

24. Remove the nine bolts retaining the intake manifold to the cylinder heads and remove the intake manifold and gaskets.
25. Remove the seven stud bolts and four bolts retaining the front cover to the engine and remove the front cover.
26. Remove the timing chains.
27. Remove the 10 bolts retaining the left cylinder head to the engine block and remove the head.

➡ **The lower rear bolt cannot be removed due to interference with the brake vacuum booster. Use a rubber band to hold the bolt away from the engine block.**

28. Remove the ground strap, one stud and one bolt retaining the heater return line to the right cylinder head.
29. Remove the 10 bolts retaining the right cylinder head to the engine block and remove the head.

➡ **The lower rear bolt cannot be removed due to interference with the evaporator housing. Use a rubber band to hold the bolt away from the engine block.**

30. Clean all gasket mating surfaces. Check the cylinder head and engine block for flatness. Check the cylinder head for scratches near the coolant passage and

7922QG06

A rubber band should be used to secure the lower rear bolt in the up position—4.6L engine

Cylinder head bolt tightening sequence—4.6L engine

Rotate the crankshaft clockwise 45 degrees, then install the timing chains—4.6L engine

combustion chamber that could provide leak paths. Machine as necessary.

To install:

31. Rotate the crankshaft counterclockwise 45 degrees. The crankshaft keyway should be at the 9 o'clock position viewed from the front of the engine. This ensures that all pistons are below the top of the engine block deck face.

32. Rotate the camshaft to a stable position where the valves do not extend below the head face.

33. Position new head gaskets on the engine block. Install the lower rear bolts on both cylinder heads and retain with rubber bands as explained during the removal procedure.

34. Position the cylinder heads on the engine block dowels, being careful not to score the surface of the head face. Apply clean oil to the head bolts, remove the rubber band from the lower rear bolt and install all bolts hand-tight.

35. Tighten the head bolts as follows:

   a. Tighten the bolts, in sequence, to 15–22 ft. lbs. (20–30 Nm).

   b. Rotate each bolt, in sequence, 85–96 degrees.

   c. Rotate each bolt, in sequence, an additional 85–96 degrees.

36. Position the heater return hose and install the two bolts. Rotate the camshafts using the flats matched at the center of the camshaft until both are in time. Install cam positioning tools T91P-6256-A or equivalent, on the flats of the camshafts to keep them from rotating.

37. Rotate the crankshaft clockwise 45 degrees to position the crankshaft at TDC on No. 1 cylinder.

➡The crankshaft must only be rotated in the clockwise direction and only as far as TDC.

38. Install the timing chains according to the proper procedure.

39. Install a new front cover seal and gasket. Apply silicone sealer to the lower corners of the cover where it meets the junction of the oil pan and cylinder block and to the points where the cover contacts the junction of the cylinder block and cylinder head.

40. Install the front cover and the stud bolts and bolts. Tighten to 15–22 ft. lbs. (20–30 Nm).

41. Position new intake manifold gaskets on the cylinder heads. Be sure the alignment tabs on the gaskets are aligned with the holes in the cylinder heads.

➡Before installing the intake manifold, inspect it for nicks and cuts that could provide leak paths.

42. Position the intake manifold on the cylinder heads and install the retaining bolts. Tighten the bolts, in sequence, to 15–22 ft. lbs. (20–30 Nm).

43. Install the thermostat and O-ring, then position the thermostat housing and install the two bolts. Tighten to 15–22 ft. lbs. (20–30 Nm). Connect the hose to the thermostat housing.

44. Connect the heater supply hose and both O2S sensors. Connect the vacuum hose to the throttle body adapter vacuum port.

45. Connect, if necessary, adjust the throttle valve cable. Install the accelerator cable bracket on the intake manifold and connect the accelerator and cruise control cables to the throttle body.

46. Apply silicone sealer to both places where the front cover meets the cylinder head. Install new gaskets on the camshaft covers.

47. Install the camshaft covers on the cylinder heads. Install the bolts and stud bolts and tighten to 6.0–8.8 ft. lbs. (8–12 Nm).

48. Raise and safely support the vehicle. Position the starter wiring harness to the right cylinder head and install the retaining bolt.

49. Cut the wire and position the exhaust pipes to the exhaust manifolds. Tighten the four nuts to 20–30 ft. lbs. (27–41 Nm).

➡Be sure the exhaust system clears the No. 3 crossmember. Adjust as necessary.

50. Connect the EGR tube to the right exhaust manifold and tighten the line nut to 26–33 ft. lbs. (35–45 Nm). Connect the oil sending unit.

51. Apply a small amount of silicone sealer in the rear of the keyway on the damper. Position the damper on the crankshaft, making sure the crankshaft key and keyway are aligned.

52. Using damper installer T74P-6316-B or equivalent, install the crankshaft damper. Install the damper bolt and washer and tighten to 114–121 ft. lbs. (155–165 Nm).

53. Install the four bolts retaining the oil pan to the front cover and tighten to 15–22 ft. lbs. (20–30 Nm).

54. Position the power steering pump on the engine and install the four retaining bolts. Tighten to 15–22 ft. lbs. (20–30 Nm). Lower the vehicle.

55. Connect the air conditioning compressor, crankshaft position sensor and canister purge solenoid.

56. Attach the 42-pin engine harness and the transmission harness connector. Install the 42-pin connector on the retaining bracket on the vacuum brake booster.

57. Install the PCV valve in the right camshaft cover and connect the canister purge solenoid vent hose.

58. Position the positive battery cable harness on the right cylinder head and install the bolt retaining the cable bracket to

the cylinder head. Connect the positive battery cable at the power distribution box and battery.

59. Position the generator and install the two retaining bolts. Tighten to 15–22 ft. lbs. (20–30 Nm). Install the two bolts retaining the generator brace to the intake manifold and tighten to 53–71 inch lbs. (6–12 Nm).

60. Install the water pump pulley and tighten the bolts to 15–22 ft. lbs. (20–30 Nm).

61. Position the ignition coil brackets and ignition wire assembly onto the mounting studs. Install the seven nuts retaining the coil brackets to the front cover and tighten to 15–22 ft. lbs. (20–30 Nm).

62. Install the two bolts retaining the ignition wire tray to the coil bracket and tighten to 6.0–8.8 ft. lbs. (8–12 Nm). Connect both ignition coils and CID sensor.

63. Position the air conditioner high pressure line on the right coil bracket and install the bolt. Connect the ignition wires to the spark plugs and install the bracket onto the camshaft cover studs.

64. Install the accessory drive belt and the wiper module. Connect the fuel lines and install the cooling fan and shroud. Fill and bleed the cooling system.

65. Install the air inlet tube and connect the negative battery cable. Start the engine and bring to normal operating temperature. Check for leaks. Check all fluid levels.

Rocker Arms

REMOVAL & INSTALLATION

3.8L Engine

1. Before servicing the vehicle, refer to the precautions in the beginning of this section.

2. Disconnect the negative battery cable.

3. Disconnect the spark plug wires from the spark plugs. Remove the spark plug wire routing clips from the rocker arm cover attaching bolt studs.

4. To remove the left rocker arm cover, proceed as follows:

   a. Remove the oil fill cap.

   b. Remove the crankcase vent tube.

5. To remove the right rocker arm cover, proceed as follows:

   a. Remove the PCV valve.

   b. Position the air cleaner assembly aside, if necessary.

6. Remove the rocker arm cover attaching screws and remove the rocker arm covers.

7. Remove the rocker arm, fulcrum and bolt assemblies. Keep each assembly together and identify the assemblies so they may be reinstalled in their original positions.

To install:

8. Clean all gasket mating surfaces on the rocker arm covers and cylinder heads. Clean the rocker arms and fulcrums and inspect for wear or damage. Replace as necessary.

9. Apply grease to the pushrod tips and valve stem tips. Lubricate the fulcrums and rocker arms with heavy engine oil and install them over the pushrods and valve stems.

10. For each valve, rotate the crankshaft until the lifter is on the base circle of the camshaft (NOT on the camshaft lobe!). Install the fulcrum bolt and tighten to 5–11 ft. lbs. (7–15 Nm). Be sure the pushrod and fulcrum are fully seated prior to tightening the fulcrum bolt.

11. Lubricate all rocker arm assemblies with engine oil. Final tighten the fulcrum bolts to 19–25 ft. lbs. (25–35 Nm). When final tightening, the camshaft may be in any position. Be sure the pushrod and fulcrum are fully seated prior to tightening.

12. Position new gaskets on the cylinder heads and install the rocker arm covers. Tighten the attaching bolts to 80–106 inch lbs. (9–12 Nm). Note the location of the spark plug wire routing clip stud bolts prior to installation.

13. After installing the left rocker arm cover, proceed as follows:

   a. Install the oil fill cap.

   b. Install the crankcase vent tube.

14. After installing the right valve cover, proceed as follows:

   a. Install the PCV valve.

   b. Install the air cleaner assembly, if necessary.

15. Install the spark plug wire routing clips and connect the wires to the spark plugs.

16. Connect the negative battery cable, start the engine and check for leaks.

4.6L Engine

1. Before servicing the vehicle, refer to the precautions in the beginning of this section.

2. Disconnect the negative battery cable.

3. Disconnect the necessary hoses from the valve covers and remove the covers.

With the valve spring spacer installed, compress the valve spring and remove the rocker arm (cam follower)—4.6L engine

Refer to Section 1 for engine rebuilding specifications

4. Rotate the camshaft so the base circle of the cam is facing the cam follower to be removed.

5. Install the Valve Spring Spacer T91P-6565-AH or equivalent between the coils of the spring.

6. Using Valve Spring Compressor T93P-6565-A or equivalent, compress the lash adjuster as required and remove the roller follower.

7. Repeat Steps 4 and 5 for followers being removed.

To install:

8. Rotate the camshaft so the base circle of the cam is facing the cam follower to be installed.

9. Compress the exhaust valve spring and install the roller follower.

10. Compress the primary intake valve spring and install the roller follower. Compress the secondary intake valve spring and install the roller follower.

11. Remove the valve spring compressor and spacer. Repeat Steps 7 through 11 until all followers are installed.

12. Install the rocker arm covers and necessary hoses. Connect the negative battery cable, start the engine and check for leaks.

Intake Manifold

REMOVAL & INSTALLATION

3.8L Engine

1. Before servicing the vehicle, refer to the precautions in the beginning of this section.

2. Disconnect the negative battery cable.

3. Drain the cooling system and relieve the fuel system pressure.

4. Remove the air cleaner assembly or air inlet tube.

5. Disconnect the accelerator cable at the throttle body. Disconnect the cruise control cable, if equipped.

6. Remove the retaining bolts from the accelerator cable mounting bracket and position the cables aside.

7. If equipped, disconnect the thermactor air supply hose at the check valve. The valve is located in the Y-pipe assembly.

8. Disconnect the fuel lines.

9. Disconnect the radiator hose at the thermostat housing and the coolant bypass hose at the manifold.

10. Disconnect the heater tube at the intake manifold and remove the tube support bracket retaining nut. Remove the heater hose at the rear of the heater tube. Loosen the hose clamp at the heater elbow and remove the heater tube with the hose attached. Remove the heater tube with the lines attached and set the assembly aside.

11. Tag and disconnect the vacuum lines at the fuel rail assembly and intake manifold. Tag and detach the necessary electrical connectors.

12. If equipped with air conditioning, remove the compressor support bracket. Disconnect the PCV line at the upper intake manifold and at the valve. Remove the 2nd PCV line from the left rocker arm cover.

13. Remove the throttle body assembly. Remove the EGR valve assembly from the upper manifold.

14. Remove the retaining nut and remove the wiring retainer bracket located at the left front of the intake manifold and set aside with the spark plug wires.

15. Remove the upper intake manifold retaining bolts/studs and remove the upper intake manifold.

16. Remove the injectors and fuel rail assembly. Remove the heater water outlet hose.

17. Remove the lower intake manifold

Upper intake manifold bolt tightening sequence—3.8L engines

Lower intake manifold bolt tightening sequence—3.8L engine

retaining bolts/studs and remove the lower intake manifold.

➥ **The manifold is sealed at each end with RTV-type sealer. To break the seal, it may be necessary to pry on the front of the manifold with a small pry-bar. If it is necessary to pry on the manifold, use care to prevent damage to the machined surfaces.**

To install:

18. Clean all gasket mating surfaces. Lightly oil all retaining bolt and stud threads.

19. Apply a dab of gasket adhesive to each cylinder head mating surface. Press new intake manifold gaskets in place, using location pins as necessary to aid in installation.

20. Apply a ⅛ in. (3mm) bead of silicone sealer at each corner where the cylinder head joins the cylinder block. Install the front and rear intake manifold end seals.

21. Carefully lower the intake manifold into place on the cylinder heads and cylinder block. Use the locating pins as necessary to guide the manifold.

22. Install the bolts and stud bolts in their original locations.

23. Connect the rear PCV line to the upper intake tube. Install the front PCV tube so the mounting bracket sits over the lower intake manifold stud. Tighten the nut on the stud to 15–22 ft. lbs. (20–30 Nm).

24. Install the injectors and the fuel rail. Install the upper intake manifold assembly. Install the bolts and stud bolts in their original locations. Tighten the four center bolts, then the end bolts in three steps, 1st to 8 ft. lbs. (10 Nm), then to 15 ft. lbs. (20 Nm), and finally to 24 ft. lbs. (32 Nm).

25. Install the EGR valve. Install the throttle body and cross-tighten the retaining nuts to 15–22 ft. lbs. (20–30 Nm).

26. Connect the rear PCV line at the PCV valve on the upper intake manifold. If equipped with air conditioning, install the compressor support bracket.

27. Attach the necessary electrical connectors and vacuum hoses. Connect the heater tube hose to the heater elbow and position the heater tube support bracket. Tighten the retaining nut to 15–22 ft. lbs. (20–30 Nm).

28. Connect the heater hose to the heater tube, the coolant bypass hose and radiator upper hose.

29. Connect the fuel lines. Position the accelerator cable mounting bracket and tighten the mounting bolts to 15–22 ft. lbs. (20–30 Nm).

30. Connect the transmission linkage at the upper intake manifold. If equipped, connect the cruise control cable.

31. Fill and bleed the cooling system. Connect the negative battery cable, start the engine and check for leaks.

32. Connect the throttle cable and, if equipped, the cruise control cable.

4.6L Engine

1. Before servicing the vehicle, refer to the precautions in the beginning of this section.

2. If equipped with air suspension, the air suspension switch, located on the right-hand side of the luggage compartment, must be turned to the **OFF** position before raising the vehicle.

3. Disconnect the negative battery cable.

4. Drain the engine cooling system.

5. Relieve the fuel system pressure.

6. Disconnect the fuel supply and return lines.

7. Remove the windshield wiper governor (module).

8. Remove the engine air cleaner outlet tube.

9. Release the drive belt tensioner and remove the accessory drive belt.

10. Tag and disconnect the ignition wires from the spark plugs. Disconnect the ignition wire brackets from the cylinder head cover studs.

11. Disconnect the wiring from both ignition coils and the Camshaft Position (CMP) sensor. Tag and disconnect all ignition wires from both ignition coils. Remove the two bolts retaining the ignition wire bracket to the ignition coil brackets and remove the ignition wire assembly.

12. Disconnect the alternator wiring harness from the junction block at the fender apron and alternator. Remove the bolts retaining the alternator brace to the intake manifold and the alternator to the cylinder block and remove the alternator.

13. Raise and safely support the vehicle.

14. Disconnect the oil pressure sensor and power steering control valve actuator wiring and position the wiring harness out of the way.

15. Disconnect the EGR valve-to-exhaust

FRONT OF ENGINE

79220G14

To avoid leakage, tighten the bolts according to the sequence shown—4.6L engine

For engine torque specifications, refer to Section 1 of this manual

manifold tube from the right-hand exhaust manifold.

16. Lower the vehicle.

17. Remove and disconnect the engine/transmission harness connector from the retaining bracket on the power brake booster.

18. Detach the A/C compressor clutch, Crankshaft Position (CKP) sensor and the canister purge solenoid wiring connectors.

19. Remove the PCV valve from the cylinder head cover and disconnect the canister purge vent hose from the PCV valve.

20. Disconnect the accelerator and cruise control cables from the throttle body. Remove the accelerator cable bracket from the intake manifold and position out of the way.

21. Disconnect the vacuum hose from the throttle body adapter port.

22. Disconnect both Heated Oxygen Sensors (HO2S) and the heater water hose.

23. Remove the two bolts retaining the thermostat housing to the intake manifold and position the upper hose and thermostat housing out of the way.

➡The two thermostat housing bolts are also used to retain the intake manifold.

24. Remove the nine bolts retaining the intake manifold to the cylinder heads and remove the intake manifold. Remove and discard the gaskets.

25. If replacing the intake manifold, swap over the necessary parts.

To install:

26. Clean all gasket mating surfaces.

27. Position new intake manifold gaskets on the cylinder heads. Be sure the alignment tabs on the gaskets are aligned with the holes in the cylinder heads.

28. Install the intake manifold and nine retaining bolts. Hand-tighten the right-rear bolt (viewed from the front of the engine) before final tightening, then tighten the bolts, in sequence, to 15–22 ft. lbs. (20–30 Nm).

29. Inspect and, if necessary, replace the O-ring seal on the thermostat housing. Position the housing and upper hose and install the two retaining bolts. Tighten to 15–22 ft. lbs. (20–30 Nm).

30. Connect the heater water hose.

31. Attach both HO2S wiring connectors.

32. Connect the vacuum hose to the throttle body adapter vacuum port.

33. Install the accelerator cable bracket on the intake manifold and connect the accelerator and cruise control cables to the throttle body.

34. Install the PCV valve in the cylinder head cover and connect the canister purge solenoid vent hose. Attach the A/C compressor clutch, CKP sensor and canister purge solenoid wiring connectors.

35. Attach the engine/transmission harness connector. Install the connector on the retaining bracket on the power brake booster.

36. Raise and safely support the vehicle.

37. Connect the EGR valve-to-exhaust manifold tube to the right-hand exhaust manifold. Tighten the tube nut to 26–33 ft. lbs. (35–45 Nm).

38. Attach the power steering control valve actuator and the oil pressure sensor wiring connectors.

39. Lower the vehicle.

40. Position the alternator and install the two retaining bolts. Tighten to 15–22 ft. lbs. (20–30 Nm). Install the two bolts retaining the alternator brace to the intake manifold and tighten them to 71–106 inch lbs. (8–12 Nm).

41. Connect the alternator wiring harness to the alternator, right-hand fender apron and junction block.

42. Position the ignition wire assembly on the engine and install the two bolts retaining the ignition wire bracket to the ignition coil brackets. Tighten the bolts to 71–106 inch lbs. (8–12 Nm).

43. Connect the ignition wires to the ignition coils in their proper positions. Connect the ignition wires to the spark plugs.

44. Connect the ignition wire brackets on the cylinder head cover studs. Attach the wiring connectors to both ignition coils and the CMP sensor.

45. Install the accessory drive belt.

46. Install the engine air cleaner outlet tube.

47. Install the windshield wiper governor.

48. Connect the fuel supply and return lines.

49. Fill and bleed the engine cooling system.

50. Connect the negative battery cable.

51. If equipped with air suspension, turn the air suspension switch to the **ON** position.

52. Start the engine and check for leaks.

53. Road test the vehicle and check for proper operation.

Exhaust Manifold

REMOVAL & INSTALLATION

3.8L Engine

LEFT SIDE

1. Before servicing the vehicle, refer to the precautions in the beginning of this section.

2. Disconnect the negative battery cable. Remove the oil level dipstick tube support bracket.

3. Detach the Oxygen (O2S) sensor at the wiring connector.

4. Tag and disconnect the wires from the spark plugs.

5. Raise and safely support the vehicle.

6. Remove the manifold-to-exhaust pipe attaching nuts.

7. Lower the vehicle.

8. Remove the exhaust manifold attaching bolts and manifold.

9. Installation is the reverse of the removal procedure. Tighten the manifold retaining bolts to 15–22 ft. lbs. (20–30 Nm).

RIGHT SIDE

1. Before servicing the vehicle, refer to the precautions in the beginning of this section.

2. Disconnect the negative battery cable.

3. Remove the spark plugs and the outer heat shield.

4. Raise and safely support the vehicle. Disconnect the EGR tube.

5. If equipped with an automatic transmission, remove the dipstick tube.

6. Remove the manifold-to-exhaust pipe retaining nuts and lower the vehicle.

7. Remove the exhaust manifold retaining bolts and remove the manifold.

8. Installation is the reverse of the removal procedure. Tighten the exhaust manifold retaining bolts to 15–22 ft. lbs. (20–30 Nm).

4.6L Engine

1. Before servicing the vehicle, refer to the precautions in the beginning of this section.

2. Disconnect the battery cables. Remove the air inlet tube.

3. Drain the cooling system and remove the cooling fan and shroud. Relieve the fuel system pressure and disconnect the fuel lines.

4. Remove the upper radiator hose. Remove the wiper module and support bracket.

5. Discharge the A/C system.

6. Disconnect and plug the compressor outlet hose at the compressor and remove the bolt retaining the hose assembly to the right coil bracket. Cap the compressor opening.

7. Remove, then detach the 42-pin engine harness connector from the retaining bracket on the brake vacuum booster.

8. Disconnect the heater outlet hose.

NOTE: ENGINE SHOWN REMOVED FOR CLARITY

NOTE: LH EXHAUST MANIFOLD SHOWN RH EXHAUST MANIFOLD SIMILAR

7922QG15

Exhaust manifold bolt tightening sequence—4.6L engine, left side shown, right side is similar

9. Remove the nut retaining the ground strap to the right cylinder head. Remove the upper stud and lower bolt retaining the heater outlet hose to the right cylinder head and position out of the way.

10. Remove the blower motor resistor and remove the bolt retaining the right engine insulator to the lower engine bracket. Disconnect both Oxygen (O_2S) sensors.

11. Raise and safely support the vehicle. Remove the engine mount through-bolts.

12. Remove the EGR tube line nut from the right exhaust manifold.

13. Disconnect the exhaust pipes from the manifolds. Lower the exhaust system and hang it from the crossmember with wire.

14. To remove the left exhaust manifold, remove the engine mount from the engine block, and remove the eight bolts retaining the exhaust manifold.

15. Position a jack and a block of wood under the oil pan, rearward of the oil drain hole. Raise the engine approximately 4 in. (100mm).

16. Remove the eight bolts retaining the right exhaust manifold and remove the manifold.

To install:

17. If the exhaust manifolds are being replaced, transfer the O_2S sensors and tighten to 27–33 ft. lbs. (37–45 Nm). On the right manifold, transfer the EGR tube connector and tighten to 33–48 ft. lbs. (45–65 Nm).

18. Clean the mating surfaces of the exhaust manifolds and cylinder heads.

19. Position the exhaust manifolds to the cylinder heads and install the retaining bolts. Tighten, in sequence, to 15–22 ft. lbs. (20–30 Nm).

20. Position and connect the EGR valve and tube assembly to the exhaust manifold. Tighten the line nut to 26–33 ft. lbs. (35–45 Nm).

21. Install the left engine mount and tighten the bolts to 15–22 ft. lbs. (20–30 Nm). Lower the engine onto the mounts and remove the jack. Install the engine mount through-bolts and tighten to 15–22 ft. lbs. (20–30 Nm).

22. Cut the wire and position the exhaust system. Tighten the nuts to 20–30 ft. lbs. (27–41 Nm).

➡ **Be sure the exhaust system clears the No. 3 crossmember. Adjust as necessary.**

23. Lower the vehicle. Connect both O_2S sensors and install the bolt retaining the right engine mount to the frame. Tighten to 15–22 ft. lbs. (20–30 Nm).

24. Install the blower motor resistor. Position the heater outlet hoses. Install the upper stud and lower bolt and tighten to 15–22 ft. lbs. (20–30 Nm). Install the ground strap onto the stud and tighten the nut to 15–22 ft. lbs. (20–30 Nm).

25. Connect the heater outlet hose.

26. Attach the 42-pin connector and transmission harness connector. Install the connector to the retaining bracket on the brake vacuum booster.

27. Connect the air conditioning compressor outlet hose to the compressor and install the bolt retaining the hose assembly to the right coil bracket.

28. Install the upper radiator hose and connect the fuel lines. Install the wiper module and retaining bracket.

29. Install the cooling fan and shroud. Install the air inlet tube. Connect the battery cables, start the engine and check for leaks.

30. Leak test, evacuate and charge the air conditioning system according to the proper procedure. Observe all safety precautions.

Camshaft and Valve Lifters

REMOVAL & INSTALLATION

3.8L Engine

1. Before servicing the vehicle, refer to the precautions in the beginning of this section.

2. Disconnect the negative battery cable and drain the cooling system.

3. Relieve the fuel system pressure and discharge the A/C system.

4. Remove the radiator. If equipped with air conditioning, remove the condenser.

5. Remove the grille.

6. Remove the Camshaft Position (CMP) sensor.

7. Remove the upper intake manifold.

8. Remove the valve covers.

9. Remove the lower intake manifold.

10. Loosen each rocker arm enough to remove the pushrods. Remove the pushrods and keep them in order so they can be returned to their original positions.

11. Remove the lifter guide plates.

12. Remove the valve lifters using a magnet, if necessary. Keep them in order so they can be returned to their original positions.

13. Remove the engine front cover, timing chain and camshaft sprocket spacer.

14. Remove the oil pan.

15. Remove the thrust plate. Remove the camshaft, being careful not to damage the bearing surfaces.

To install:

16. Lubricate the cam lobes and journals with heavy engine oil. Install the camshaft, being careful not to damage the bearing surfaces while sliding into position.

17. Install the thrust plate. Tighten the bolts to 71–123 inch lbs. (8–14 Nm).

18. Install the timing chain and sprockets. Install the engine front cover.

19. Install the oil pan.

20. Install the lifters, guide plate and retainers.

21. Install the lower intake manifold.

22. Install the pushrods and tighten the rocker arms.

23. Install the valve cover and the upper intake manifold.

24. Install the CMP sensor.

25. Install the grille. If equipped with air conditioning, install the condenser.

26. Install the radiator. Fill and bleed the cooling system.

27. Connect the negative battery cable. Start the engine and check for leaks.

4.6L Engine

1. Before servicing the vehicle, refer to the precautions in the beginning of this section.

2. Disconnect the negative battery cable and drain the cooling system.

3. Relieve the fuel system pressure.

4. Remove the right and left camshaft covers.

5. Remove the timing chain front cover. Remove the timing chains.

6. Rotate the crankshaft counterclockwise 45 degrees from TDC to be sure all pistons are below the top of the engine block deck face.

> ✳✳ **WARNING**
>
> **The crankshaft must be in this position prior to rotating the camshafts or damage to the pistons and/or valvetrain will result.**

7. Install Valve Spring Compressor T91P-6565-A or equivalent, under the camshaft and on top of the valve spring retainer.

➡ **Valve Spring Spacer T91P-6565-AH or equivalent, must be installed between the spring coils and the camshaft must be at the base circle before compressing the valve spring.**

8. Compress the valve spring far enough to remove the roller follower. Repeat Steps 7 and 8 until all roller followers are removed.

9. Remove the bolts retaining the camshaft cap cluster assemblies to the cylinder heads. Tap upward on the camshaft caps at points near the upper bearing halves and gradually lift the camshaft clusters from the cylinder heads.

10. Lift the camshafts straight upward to avoid bearing damage.

To install:

11. Apply heavy engine oil to the camshaft journals and lobes. Position the camshafts on the cylinder heads.

12. Install and seat the camshaft cap cluster assemblies. Hand start the bolts.

13. Tighten the camshaft cluster retaining bolts in sequence to 71–106 inch lbs. (8–12 Nm).

➡ **Each camshaft cap cluster assembly is tightened individually.**

14. Loosen the camshaft cap cluster retaining bolts approximately two turns or until the heads of the bolts are free. Retighten all bolts, in sequence, to 71–106 inch lbs. (8–12 Nm).

➡ **The camshafts should turn freely with a slight drag.**

15. Install Camshaft Positioner T91P-6256-A or equivalent, on the flats of the camshafts and install the spacers and camshaft sprockets. Install the bolts and washers and tighten to 81–96 ft. lbs. (110–130 Nm).

16. Install Valve Spring Compressor T91P-6565-A or equivalent, under the camshaft and on top of the valve spring retainer.

To remove the rocker arm, install the spacer and compress the valve spring using the special tools—4.6L engine

To avoid damage to the camshaft and related components, tighten the cap cluster bolts in the order shown—4.6L engine

→ **Valve Spring Spacer T91P-6565-AH or equivalent, must be installed between the spring coils, and the camshaft must be at the base circle before compressing the valve spring.**

17. Compress the valve spring far enough to install the roller followers.

18. Repeat Steps 15 and 16 until all roller followers are installed.

19. Rotate the crankshaft clockwise 45 degrees to position the crankshaft at TDC.

→ **The crankshaft must only be rotated in the clockwise direction and only as far as TDC.**

20. Install the timing chains and install the timing chain front cover. Install the camshaft covers.

21. Install the remaining components in the reverse order of removal.

22. Connect the negative battery cable. Start the engine and check for leaks.

Valve Lash

ADJUSTMENT

3.8L Engine

The valve lash is not adjustable. If the collapsed lifter clearance is found to be incorrect, there are replacement pushrods available to compensate for excessive or insufficient clearance. To check the lifter clearance, perform the following:

1. Before servicing the vehicle, refer to the precautions in the beginning of this section.

2. Disconnect the negative battery cable.

ROCKER ARM SEAT AND BOLT MUST BE FULLY SEATED AFTER FINAL TORQUE

CLEARANCE SHOULD BE 2.25-4.79mm (0.09-0.19 INCH) WITH VALVE TAPPET FULLY COLLAPSED ON BASE CIRCLE OF CAMSHAFT AFTER ASSEMBLED.

7922QG17

Collapse the valve lifter before measuring the valve clearance—3.8L engines

3. Remove the valve cover assembly on the side to be checked.

4. Turn the engine until the No. 1 piston is at TDC on the compression stroke.

5. The following valves can be checked with the engine in this position:
- No. 1 intake
- No. 1 exhaust
- No. 2 exhaust
- No. 3 intake
- No. 4 exhaust
- No. 6 intake

6. Rotate the engine 360 degrees and check the following valves:
- No. 2 intake
- No. 3 exhaust
- No. 4 intake
- No. 5 exhaust
- No. 5 intake
- No. 6 exhaust

7. Check each of the lifters by placing Hydraulic Lifter Compressor T71P-6513-B or equivalent, on the rocker arm and slowly applying pressure to the lifter, until the lifter is collapsed.

8. Hold the lifter in this position and check the clearance between the rocker arm and the valve stem tip. The clearance should be 0.09–0.19 in. (2.25–4.79mm).

9. Repeat this operation for each valve to be checked.

10. If the clearance is greater than specification, replace the pushrod with a longer one. If the clearance is less than specified, replace the pushrod with a shorter one.

4.6L Engine

The 4.6L SOHC engine requires no periodic valve adjustment. Hydraulic Lash Adjusters (HLAs) are used in the valve train to compensate for excessive valve lash.

Oil Pan

REMOVAL & INSTALLATION

3.8L Engine

1. Before servicing the vehicle, refer to the precautions in the beginning of this section.

2. Disconnect the negative battery cable and remove the air inlet tube.

3. Remove the two bolts retaining the sight shield and position aside. Remove the hood weather seal.

4. Remove the wipers. Remove the left cowl vent screen and the wiper module.

5. Install Engine Support Fixture D88L-6000-A or equivalent. Raise and safely support the vehicle.

6. Remove the engine mount through-bolts.

7. Partially lower the vehicle and raise the engine with the support fixture.

8. Raise and safely support the vehicle. Remove the starter.

9. Drain the crankcase and remove the oil filter.

10. Remove the wire loom, ground strap and automatic transmission oil cooler lines, if equipped.

11. Remove the oil pan-to-bell housing bolts and the bolts at the Crankshaft Position (CKP) sensor shield, if equipped. Remove the remaining oil pan retaining bolts.

12. Remove the steering shaft pinch bolts and separate the steering shaft. Position a jack under the front of the sub-frame.

13. Remove the six rearward bolts on the front of the sub-frame. Loosen the two front sub-frame bolts.

14. Remove the lower strut-to-control arm bolts and nuts and lower the sub-frame. Remove the oil pan.

To install:

15. Clean the gasket mating surfaces and the oil pan. Apply silicone sealer to the oil pan.

16. Fit the oil pan to the cylinder block. Be sure enough clearance has been provided to allow the oil pan to be installed without sealer being scraped off under the cylinder block.

17. Install the oil pan retaining bolts at the cylinder block and bell housing and install the lower crankshaft sensor shield, if equipped. Tighten the bolts to 80–106 inch lbs. (9–12 Nm).

Please refer to Section 9 for electric cooling fan wiring schematics

18. Raise the sub-frame into position and install the lower strut mount-to-control arm bolts. Tighten to 103–144 ft. lbs. (140–195 Nm).

19. Install the two front sub-frame bolts and the six bolts at the rear of the front sub-frame member. Install a ¾ in. outside diameter pipe or equivalent, into both front left and right sub-frame and body alignment holes. Tighten one bolt at each corner. Remove the alignment tools and tighten the bolts to 70–96 ft. lbs. (95–130 Nm).

20. Connect the steering shaft and install the pinch bolt. Tighten to 30–42 ft. lbs. (41–57 Nm).

21. Install the transmission cooler lines, wire loom and ground strap. Install a new oil filter.

22. Install the starter and partially lower the vehicle.

23. Lower the engine with the support fixture. Seat the left side locating pin before the right. Partially raise the vehicle and support safely.

24. Install the engine mount through-bolts and tighten to 35–50 ft. lbs. (47–68 Nm).

25. Lower the vehicle.

26. Remove the engine support fixture.

27. Install the wiper module and the left cowl vent screen. Install the wipers and the hood weather seal.

28. Install the sight shield and the two retaining bolts. Install the air duct assembly. Fill the crankcase with the proper type and quantity of engine oil.

29. Connect the negative battery cable, start the engine and check for leaks.

4.6L Engine

1. Before servicing the vehicle, refer to the precautions in the beginning of this section.

2. Disconnect the battery cables and remove the air inlet tube.

3. Drain the cooling system and remove the cooling fan and shroud. Relieve the fuel system pressure and disconnect the fuel lines.

4. Remove the upper radiator hose. Remove the wiper module and support bracket.

5. Discharge the A/C system.

6. Disconnect and plug the compressor outlet hose at the compressor and remove the bolt retaining the hose assembly to the right coil bracket. Cap the compressor outlet.

7. Remove the 42-pin engine harness connector from the retaining bracket on the brake vacuum booster and detach the con-

Place wooden blocks between the engine mounts and the frame to allow access to the oil pan—4.6L engine

nector and transmission harness connector.

8. Disconnect the heater outlet hose.

9. Remove the nut retaining the ground strap to the right cylinder head. Remove the upper stud and loosen the lower bolt retaining the heater outlet hose to the right cylinder head and position it out of the way.

10. Remove the blower motor resistor. Remove the bolt retaining the right engine mount to the lower engine bracket.

11. Disconnect the vacuum hoses from the EGR valve and tube. Remove the two bolts retaining the EGR valve to the intake manifold.

12. Raise and safely support the vehicle. Drain the crankcase and remove the engine mount through-bolts.

13. Remove the EGR tube line nut from the right exhaust manifold and remove the EGR valve and tube assembly.

14. Disconnect the exhaust from the exhaust manifolds. Lower the exhaust system and support it with wire from the crossmember.

15. Position a jack and a block of wood under the oil pan, rearward of the oil drain hole. Raise the engine approximately 4 in. (10cm) and insert two wood blocks approximately 2 ½ in. (6.3cm) thick under each engine mount. Lower the engine onto the wood blocks and remove the jack.

16. Remove the 16 bolts retaining the oil pan to the engine block and remove the oil pan.

➡It may be necessary to loosen, but not remove, the two nuts on the rear transmission mount and with a jack, raise the transmission extension housing slightly to remove the pan.

To install:

17. Clean the oil pan and the gasket mating surfaces.

18. Position a new gasket on the oil pan.

Oil pan bolt tightening sequence—4.6L engine

Apply silicone sealer to where the front cover meets the cylinder block and rear seal retainer meets the cylinder block. Position the oil pan on the engine and install the bolts. Tighten the bolts, in sequence, to 15–22 ft. lbs. (20–30 Nm).

19. Position the jack and wood block under the oil pan, rearward of the oil drain hole and raise the engine enough to remove the wood blocks. Lower the engine and remove the jack.

20. Install the engine mount through-bolts and tighten to 15–22 ft. lbs. (20–30 Nm).

21. Position the EGR valve and tube assembly in the vehicle and connect to the exhaust manifold. Tighten the line nut to 26–33 ft. lbs. (35–45 Nm).

➡**Loosen the line nut at the EGR valve prior to installing the assembly into the vehicle. This will allow enough movement to align the EGR valve retaining bolts.**

22. Cut the wire and position the exhaust system to the manifolds. Install the four nuts and tighten to 20–30 ft. lbs. (27–41 Nm). Be sure the exhaust system clears the crossmember. Adjust as necessary.

23. Install a new oil filter and lower the vehicle.

24. Install the bolt retaining the right engine mount to the lower engine bracket. Tighten to 15–22 ft. lbs. (20–30 Nm).

25. Install a new gasket on the EGR valve and position on the intake manifold. Install the two bolts retaining the EGR valve to the intake manifold and tighten to 15–22 ft. lbs. (20–30 Nm). Tighten the EGR tube line nut at the EGR valve to 26–33 ft. lbs. (35–45 Nm). Connect the vacuum hoses to the EGR valve and tube.

26. Install the blower motor resistor. Position the heater outlet hose, install the upper stud and tighten the upper and lower bolts to 15–22 ft. lbs. (20–30 Nm). Install the ground strap on the stud and tighten to 15–22 ft. lbs. (20–30 Nm).

27. Connect the heater outlet hose.

28. Attach the 42-pin connector and transmission harness connector. Install the harness connector on the brake vacuum booster.

29. Connect the air conditioning compressor outlet hose to the compressor and install the bolt retaining the hose to the right coil bracket.

30. Install the upper radiator hose and connect the fuel lines. Install the wiper module and retaining bracket.

31. Install the cooling fan and shroud and fill the cooling system. Fill the crankcase with the proper type and quantity of engine oil.

32. Connect the negative battery cable and install the air inlet tube. Start the engine and check for leaks.

33. Evacuate and recharge the air conditioning system.

Oil Pump

REMOVAL & INSTALLATION

3.8L Engine

➡**The timing chain front cover houses the oil pump on the 3.8L engines. If the oil pump housing is scored, worn or grooved, the entire front cover will have to be replaced.**

1. Before servicing the vehicle, refer to the precautions in the beginning of this section.

2. Disconnect the negative battery cable. Raise and safely support the vehicle.

3. Remove the oil filter.

4. Remove the cover/filter mount assembly.

5. Lift the pump gears from their mounting pocket in the front cover.

6. Clean all gasket mounting surfaces.

7. Inspect the mounting pocket for wear. If excessive wear is present, complete timing cover assembly replacement is necessary.

8. Inspect the cover/filter mount gasket-to-timing cover surface for flatness. Place a straight-edge across the flat and check clearance with a feeler gauge. If the measured clearance exceeds 0.0016 in. (0.04mm), replace the cover/filter mount.

9. Replace the pump gears if wear is excessive.

10. Remove the plug from the end of the pressure relief valve passage using a small drill and slide hammer. Use caution when drilling.

11. Remove the spring and valve from the bore. Clean all dirt and metal chips from the bore and valve. Inspect all parts for wear. Replace as necessary.

To install:

12. Install the valve and spring after lubricating them with engine oil. The end with the smaller diameter goes in first.

13. Install a new plug. The plug can be tapped into the bore using a plastic tipped hammer. Be sure the plug is 0–0.010 in. (0–0.25mm) below the machined surface.

14. Lightly pack the gear pocket with petroleum jelly. Install the gears in the cover pocket, making sure petroleum jelly fills all the voids between the gears and pockets.

➡**Failure to properly coat the oil pump gears may result in failure of the pump to prime when the engine is started.**

15. Position the pump body O-ring seal and install the pump body onto the front cover using alignment dowels on the front cover.

16. Tighten the pump body retaining bolts to 18–22 ft. lbs. (25–30 Nm) for M8 bolts and 30–40 ft. lbs. (40–55 Nm) for M10 bolts.

17. Install a new oil filter. Fill the crankcase with the proper type and quantity of engine oil.

18. Connect the negative battery cable, start the engine and check for leaks and proper oil pressure.

4.6L Engine

1. Before servicing the vehicle, refer to the precautions in the beginning of this section.

2. Disconnect the negative battery cable. Remove the front cover.

3. Remove the oil pan and pick-up tube.

4. Remove primary timing chain only. Remove the crankshaft timing sprockets.

5. Remove four bolts retaining the oil pump to the cylinder block. Remove the oil pump. Clean the mating surfaces and inspect for damage.

To install:

6. Rotate the inner rotor of the oil pump to align with the flats on the crankshaft, and install oil pump flush with cylinder block.

7. Install the four retaining bolts and tighten to 71–106 inch lbs. (8–12 Nm).

8. Replace the oil filter. Install the timing chains.

9. Install the pick-up tube and oil pan.

10. Install the front cover. Fill the crankcase with the proper type and quantity of engine oil.

11. Connect the negative battery cable, start the engine and check for leaks and proper oil pressure.

OIL PUMP

BOLT
4 REQ'D
TIGHTEN TO
8-12 N·m
(71-106 LB-IN)

FRONT OF
ENGINE

CYLINDER BLOCK

7922QG20

Exploded view of the oil pump mounting—4.6L engine

Rear Main Seal

REMOVAL & INSTALLATION

➡**Special tools are available for installing rear main oil seals. In most cases, the seals can be installed using a common seal and bearing driver set.**

1. Before servicing the vehicle, refer to the precautions in the beginning of this section.
2. Remove the transmission assembly.
3. Remove the flexplate or flywheel.
4. With a sharp awl, carefully punch a small hole in the metal portion of the seal.
5. Remove the seal using a slide hammer with a sheet metal screw attached.

To install:
6. Lubricate the seal and the crankshaft with clean engine oil.
7. Install the seal with the spring side toward the engine.
8. Remove the installation tool and install the flexplate or flywheel.
9. Install the transmission assembly.

Timing Chain, Sprockets, Front Cover and Seal

REMOVAL & INSTALLATION

3.8L Engine

1. Before servicing the vehicle, refer to the precautions in the beginning of this section.
2. Disconnect the negative battery cable and drain the cooling system.
3. Remove the air cleaner assembly and air intake duct.
4. Remove the fan/clutch assembly and shroud.
5. Remove the accessory drive belt idlers, drive belts and the water pump pulley.
6. Remove the power steering pump bracket retaining bolts. Leaving the hoses connected, place the pump/bracket assembly aside in a position to prevent fluid from leaking out.
7. If equipped with air conditioning, remove the compressor front support bracket but leave the compressor in place.

8. Disconnect the coolant bypass hose and heater hose at the water pump. Disconnect the upper radiator hose at the thermostat housing.
9. Disconnect the coil wire from the distributor cap and remove the cap with the secondary wires attached.
10. Remove the distributor hold-down clamp and lift the distributor out of the front cover.
11. Raise and safely support the vehicle. Remove the crankshaft damper and pulley using a puller.

➡**If the crankshaft pulley and vibration damper have to be separated, mark the damper and pulley so they may be reassembled in the same relative position. This is important as the damper and pulley are initially balanced as a unit. If the crankshaft damper is being replaced, check if the original damper has balance pins installed. If so, new balance pins must be installed on the new damper in the same position as the original damper. The crankshaft pulley, new or original, must also be installed in the same relative position as originally installed.**

12. Remove the oil filter.
13. Disconnect the lower radiator hose at the water pump. Remove the oil pan.

➡**The front cover cannot be removed without lowering the oil pan.**

14. Lower the vehicle. Remove the front cover retaining bolts. It is not necessary to separate the water pump from the front cover.

➡**Do not overlook the cover retaining bolt located behind the oil filter adapter. The front cover will break if pried on and all retaining bolts are not removed.**

15. Remove the front cover and water pump as an assembly. Drive the crankshaft seal out of the front cover with a suitable seal driver. Remove and discard the cover gasket.

➡**The front cover contains the oil pump, water pump and crankshaft seal. If a new front cover is to be installed, remove the water pump and oil pump from the old front cover and install them on the new cover along with a new crankshaft seal.**

16. Remove the camshaft bolt and washer from the end of the camshaft.

TIMING CHAIN

CAMSHAFT SPROCKET

CRANKSHAFT SPROCKET

POSITIONING OF TIMING MARKS AND KEYWAYS IN CAMSHAFT AND CRANKSHAFT SPROCKETS MUST BE IN LINE AS SHOWN WITH NO. 1 PISTON AT TOP DEAD CENTER FIRING

7922QG21

The timing marks should be facing each other, when the timing chain is installed correctly—3.8L engines

17. Remove the distributor drive gear, camshaft sprocket, crankshaft sprocket and timing chain.

➡**If the crankshaft sprocket is difficult to remove, pry the sprocket off the shaft using a pair of large prybars positioned on both sides of the sprocket.**

To install:

18. Clean all gasket mating surfaces. If reusing the front cover, replace the front cover oil seal.

19. If removed, install the timing chain vibration damper. Tighten the mounting bolts to 71–123 inch lbs. (8–14 Nm).

20. Rotate the crankshaft to position the No. 1 piston at TDC and the crankshaft keyway at the 12 o' clock position.

21. Lubricate the timing chain with engine oil.

22. Install the camshaft sprocket, crankshaft sprocket and timing chain. Be sure the timing marks align.

23. Install the distributor drive gear. Install the bolt and washer assembly on the end of the camshaft and tighten to 30–37 ft. lbs. (40–50 Nm).

24. Install a new crankshaft seal in the front cover and lubricate the seal lip with engine oil.

25. Position a new gasket on the cylinder block and install the front cover using dowels for proper alignment. Install the front cover retaining bolts and tighten to 15–22 ft. lbs. (20–30 Nm).

26. Raise and safely support the vehicle. Install the oil pan. Connect the lower radiator hose and install the oil filter.

27. Coat the crankshaft damper sealing surface with clean engine oil. Apply a small amount of silicone sealer to the crankshaft keyway.

28. Position the crankshaft pulley key in the crankshaft keyway and install the damper, using a suitable installation tool.

29. Install the damper washer and retaining bolt and tighten to 103–132 ft. lbs. (140–180 Nm). Install the crankshaft pulley and tighten the retaining bolts to 20–28 ft. lbs. (26–38 Nm).

30. Lower the vehicle. Connect the coolant bypass hose.

31. Install the distributor with the rotor pointing at the No. 1 distributor cap tower. Install the distributor cap and coil wire.

32. Connect the upper radiator hose at the thermostat housing. Connect the heater hose.

33. If equipped with air conditioning, install the compressor and mounting brackets. Tighten the retaining bolts to 30–45 ft. lbs. (41–61 Nm).

34. Install the power steering pump and mounting bracket. Tighten the retaining bolts to 30–45 ft. lbs. (41–61 Nm).

35. Install the water pump pulley. Position the accessory drive belts over the pulleys.

36. Install the fan/clutch assembly and fan shroud. Cross-tighten the fan/clutch assembly retaining bolts to 12–18 ft. lbs. (16–24 Nm).

37. Fill the crankcase with the proper type and quantity of engine oil. Fill and bleed the cooling system. Connect the negative battery cable.

38. Start the engine and check for leaks. Check the ignition timing and curb idle speed and adjust, as necessary.

4.6L Engine

➡**This is not a free-wheeling engine. If it has "jumped time" there will be damage to the valves and/or pistons and will require the removal of the cylinder heads.**

1. Before servicing the vehicle, refer to the precautions in the beginning of this section.

2. Disconnect the negative battery cable.

3. Remove the cooling fan and shroud. Loosen the water pump pulley bolts, remove the accessory drive belt and remove the water pump pulley.

4. Raise and safely support the vehicle.

5. Remove the bolts retaining the power steering pump to the engine block and cylinder front cover. The lower front bolt on the power steering pump will not come all the way out. Wire the power steering pump out of the way.

6. Remove the four bolts retaining the oil pan to the front cover. Remove the crankshaft damper retaining bolt and washer. Remove the damper using a puller.

7. Lower the vehicle. Remove the bolt retaining the air conditioner high pressure line to the right coil bracket.

8. Remove the front bolts and loosen the remaining bolts on the camshaft covers. Using plastic wedges or similar tools, prop up both camshaft covers. Disconnect both ignition coils and the CID sensor.

Timing belt service is covered in Section 5 of this manual

Install the Camshaft Positioning tools in order to keep the camshaft in the correct position—4.6L engine

9. Remove the three nuts retaining the right coil bracket to the front cover. Position the power steering hose out of the way.

10. Remove the four nuts retaining the left coil bracket to the front cover. Slide both coil brackets and ignition wires off the mounting studs and lay the assembly on top of the engine.

11. Disconnect the Crankshaft Position (CKP) sensor. Remove the seven stud bolts and four bolts retaining the front cover to the engine and remove the front cover. Remove the crankshaft seal with a suitable seal driver.

12. Remove the CKP sensor wheel.

13. Rotate the engine to set the No. 1 piston at TDC on the compression stroke.

14. Install Camshaft Positioning tools T91P-6256-A or equivalent, on the flats of the camshaft. This will prevent accidental rotation of the camshafts.

15. Remove the two bolts retaining the right tensioner to the cylinder head and remove the tensioner. Remove the right tensioner arm.

16. Remove the two bolts retaining the right chain guide to the cylinder head and remove the chain guide. Remove the right chain and right crankshaft sprocket. Remove the right camshaft sprocket retaining bolt, washer, sprocket and spacer.

➡**Camshaft Positioning tools T91P-6256-A or equivalent, must be installed on the camshaft to prevent the camshaft from rotating.**

17. Remove the two bolts retaining the left tensioner to the cylinder head and remove the tensioner. Remove the left tensioner arm.

18. Remove the two bolts retaining the left chain guide to the cylinder head and remove the chain guide. Remove the left chain and left crankshaft sprocket. Remove the left camshaft sprocket retaining bolt, washer, sprocket and spacer.

➡**Camshaft Positioning tools T91P-6256-A or equivalent, must be installed on the camshaft to prevent the camshaft from rotating.**

19. Inspect the friction material on the tensioner arms and chain guides. If worn or damaged, remove and clean the oil pan and replace the oil pick-up tube.

✳✳ WARNING

At no time, when the timing chains are removed and the cylinder heads are installed, may the crankshaft and/or camshafts be rotated. Fail-

Be sure the marks on the sprockets align with the copper colored links on the chain—4.6L engine

INSTALL TOOL OVER FRONT COVER ALIGNMENT DOWEL

CRANKSHAFT HOLDING TOOL T93P-6303-A

NOTE: ALIGN CRANKSHAFT WOODRUFF KEY WITH KEYWAY ON TOOL

79220G25

Install the Crankshaft Holding tool T93P-6303-A or equivalent to maintain crankshaft position while removing the slack from the timing chain—4.6L engine

ure to follow these directions will result in valve and/or piston damage.

To install:

20. Be sure Camshaft Positioners T91P-6256-A or equivalent, are installed on the camshafts to prevent them from rotating.

21. Position the camshaft spacers and sprockets on the camshafts and install the washers and retaining bolts. Tighten the retaining bolts to 81–96 ft. lbs. (110–130 Nm).

22. Install the left crankshaft sprocket with the tapered part of the sprocket facing away from the engine block.

➡**The crankshaft sprockets are identical. They may only be installed one way, with the tapered part of the sprocket facing each other.**

23. Install the left timing chain on the camshaft and crankshaft sprockets. Be sure the copper links of the chain line up with the timing marks of the sprockets.

➡**If the copper links of the timing chain are not visible, pull the chain taught until the opposite sides of the chain**

contact one another and lay it on a flat surface. Mark the links at each end of the chain and use them in place of the copper links.

24. Install the right crankshaft sprocket with the tapered part of the sprocket facing the left crankshaft sprocket.

25. Install the right timing chain on the camshaft and crankshaft sprockets. Be sure the copper links of the chain line up with the timing marks of the sprockets.

26. It is necessary to bleed the timing chain tensioners before installation. Proceed as follows:

a. Position the timing chain tensioner in a soft-jawed vice.

b. Using a small pick or similar tool, hold the ratchet lock mechanism away from the ratchet stem and slowly compress the tensioner plunger by rotating the vise handle.

➡**The tensioner must be compressed slowly or damage to the internal seals will result.**

c. Once the tensioner plunger bottoms in the tensioner bore, continue to hold the ratchet lock mechanism and

push down on the ratchet stem until flush with the tensioner face.

d. While holding the ratchet stem flush to the tensioner face, release the ratchet lock mechanism and install a paper clip or similar tool in the tensioner body to lock the tensioner in the collapsed position.

e. The paper clip must not be removed until the timing chain, tensioner, tensioner arm and timing chain guide are completely installed on the engine.

27. Lubricate the tensioner arm contact surfaces with engine oil and install the right and left tensioner arms on their dowels.

28. Install the right and left timing chain tensioners and secure with two bolts on each. Tighten the bolts to 15–22 ft. lbs. (20–30 Nm).

29. Install the right and left timing chain guides and secure with two bolts on each. Tighten the bolts to 71–106 inch lbs. (8–12 Nm).

30. Install the Crankshaft Holding tool T93P-6303-A or equivalent to the crankshaft and the alignment dowel on the front cover mounting surface.

31. Remove the slack from the timing chain using a suitable C-clamp positioned on the timing chain guide and tensioner arm.

32. Remove the paper clips from the timing chain tensioners and be sure all timing marks are aligned.

33. Remove the camshaft positioning tools.

34. Replace the front cover seal with a new one and clean the sealing surfaces of the cylinder block. Apply silicone sealer to the oil pan where it meets the cylinder block and to the points where the cylinder head meets the cylinder block.

35. Install the front cover and the attaching studs and bolts. Tighten to 1 5–22 ft. lbs. (20–30 Nm). Connect the CKP sensor.

36. Position the coil brackets and ignition wires as an assembly onto the mounting studs. Position the power steering hose and install the seven nuts retaining the coil brackets to the front cover. Tighten the nuts to 15–22 ft. lbs. (20–30 Nm). Connect both ignition coils and CID sensor.

37. Remove the plastic wedges holding up the camshaft covers. Apply silicone sealer where the front cover meets the cylinder head and be sure the camshaft cover gaskets are properly positioned. Install the

NOTE: USE C-CLAMP TO REMOVE SLACK FROM CAMSHAFT TIMING CHAIN

7922QG26

Remove the slack from the timing chain with a C-clamp before removing the pin from the tensioner—4.6L engine

front retaining bolts into the camshaft cover and tighten the bolts to 71–106 inch lbs. (8–12 Nm).

38. Position the air conditioner high pressure line on the right coil bracket and install the bolt. Raise and safely support the vehicle.

39. Apply a small amount of silicone sealer in the rear of the keyway in the damper. Position the damper on the crankshaft and install, using a suitable installation tool. Install the damper bolt and washer and tighten to 114–121 ft. lbs. (155–165 Nm).

40. Install the four bolts retaining the oil pan to the front cover. Tighten to 15–22 ft. lbs. (20–30 Nm).

41. Position the power steering pump on the engine and install the four retaining bolts. Tighten to 15–22 ft. lbs. (20–30 Nm). Lower the vehicle.

42. Install the water pump pulley with the four bolts. Tighten to 15–22 ft. lbs. (20–30 Nm). Install the accessory drive belt and the cooling fan and shroud.

43. Connect the negative battery cable, start the engine and check for leaks.

● **TIGHTEN IN SEQUENCE SHOWN**

7922QG24

Be sure to install the fasteners in the correct position and tighten them in the sequence shown—4.6L engine

FUEL SYSTEM

Fuel System Service Precautions

➡**Be sure to refer to the precautions in the beginning of this section as well as these fuel system-specific precautions.**

Safety is the most important factor when performing not only fuel system maintenance but any type of maintenance. Failure to conduct maintenance and repairs in a safe manner may result in serious personal injury or death. Maintenance and testing of the vehicle's fuel system components can be accomplished safely and effectively by adhering to the following rules and guidelines.

• To avoid the possibility of fire and personal injury, always disconnect the negative battery cable unless the repair or test procedure requires that battery voltage be applied.

• Always relieve the fuel system pressure prior to disconnecting any fuel system component (injector, fuel rail, pressure regulator, etc.), fitting or fuel line connection. Exercise extreme caution whenever relieving fuel system pressure to avoid exposing skin, face and eyes to fuel spray. Please be advised that fuel under pressure may penetrate the skin or any part of the body that it contacts.

• Always place a shop towel or cloth around the fitting or connection prior to loosening to absorb any excess fuel due to spillage. Ensure that all fuel spillage (should it occur) is quickly removed from engine surfaces. Ensure that all fuel soaked cloths or towels are deposited into a suitable waste container.

• Always keep a dry chemical (Class B) fire extinguisher near the work area.

• Do not allow fuel spray or fuel vapors to come into contact with a spark or open flame.

• Always use a back-up wrench when loosening and tightening fuel line connection fittings. This will prevent unnecessary stress and torsion to fuel line piping.

• Always replace worn fuel fitting O-rings with new. Do not substitute fuel hose or equivalent, where fuel pipe is installed.

Fuel System Pressure

RELIEVING

Fuel supply lines on all fuel injected engines will remain pressurized for some period of time after the engine is shut **OFF**. This pressure must be relieved before servicing the fuel system. Pressure is relieved through the fuel pressure relief valve. To relieve the fuel system pressure:

1. Remove the fuel tank cap to relieve pressure in the tank.
2. Remove the cap on the fuel pressure relief valve, located on the fuel rail.
3. Attach Fuel Pressure Gauge T80L-9974-A or equivalent and open the manual valve on the pressure gauge to release the pressure and drain the system through the drain tube into a suitable container.
4. Remove the fuel pressure gauge and replace the cap on the relief valve.

Fuel Filter

REMOVAL & INSTALLATION

1. Before servicing the vehicle, refer to the precautions in the beginning of this section.
2. Disconnect the negative battery cable and relieve the fuel system pressure.
3. Raise and safely support the vehicle.
4. Remove the push-connect fittings at both ends of the filter. Install new retainer clips in each push-connect fitting.
5. Remove the fuel filter from the bracket by loosening the worm gear clamp. Note the direction of the flow arrow as installed in the bracket to ensure proper direction of fuel flow through the replacement filter.

To install:

6. Install the fuel filter into the bracket, ensuring the proper direction of flow. Tighten the worm gear clamp to 15–25 inch lbs. (1.7–2.8 Nm).
7. Install the push-connect fittings onto the filter ends.

FUEL FILTER

7922QG27

Exploded view of the fuel filter mounting

8. Reattach the battery cable.
9. Start the engine and check for leaks.
10. Lower the vehicle.

Fuel Pump

REMOVAL & INSTALLATION

1. Before servicing the vehicle, refer to the precautions in the beginning of this section.
2. Disconnect the negative battery cable and properly relieve the fuel system pressure.
3. Remove the fuel tank, as follows, and place it on a bench.
   a. Drain the fuel from the tank through the filler neck.
   b. Raise and safely support the vehicle.
   c. Remove the exhaust system.
   d. Disconnect the vent and fluid hoses from the tank.
   e. Safely support the fuel tank.
   f. Partially lower the tank, then detach the fuel level sensor and pump electrical connector and any remaining hoses.
   g. Remove the tank from the vehicle.
4. Remove any dirt that has accumulated around the fuel pump retaining flange so it will not enter the tank during pump removal and installation.
5. Turn the fuel pump locking ring counterclockwise and remove the locking ring.
6. Remove the fuel pump and bracket assembly. Remove and discard the seal ring.

To install:

7. Clean the fuel pump mounting flange, fuel tank mounting surface and seal ring groove.
8. Apply a light coating of grease on a new seal ring to hold it in place during assembly and install in the seal ring groove.
9. Install the fuel pump and bracket assembly carefully to ensure the filter is not damaged. Be sure the locating keys are in the keyways and the seal ring remains in the groove.
10. Hold the pump assembly in place and install the locking ring finger-tight. Be sure all the locking tabs are under the tank lock ring tabs.
11. Rotate the locking ring clockwise until the ring is against the stops.
12. Install the fuel tank in the vehicle in the reverse order of removal. Be sure to tighten the fuel tank support bracket retaining bolts to 22–30 ft. lbs. (29–41 Nm). Add a minimum of 10 gallons of fuel to the tank and check for leaks.
13. Install a suitable fuel pressure gauge to the valve on the fuel rail.

To remove the fuel pump, turn the locking ring counter clockwise

14. Turn the ignition switch from **OFF** to **ON** for three seconds. Repeat this procedure 5–10 times until the pressure gauge shows at least 35 psi (241 kPa). Check for fuel leaks.

15. Remove the pressure gauge, start the engine and check for leaks.

DRIVE TRAIN

Transmission Assembly

REMOVAL & INSTALLATION

Manual

1. Before servicing the vehicle, refer to the precautions in the beginning of this section.

2. Disconnect the negative battery cable.

3. Shift the transmission into the **N** position.

4. Remove the shift knob and the console top cover.

5. Remove the two shifter retaining bolts and remove the shifter.

6. Raise and support the vehicle safely.

7. Remove the drain plug and drain the oil from the transmission.

8. Remove the body reinforcement in front of the axle.

9. Disconnect the rear exhaust assembly from the resonator.

10. Remove the four bolts retaining the driveshaft to the companion flange. If the rear driveshaft yoke and companion flange are not marked, mark the position for reassembly.

11. Position an axle stand under the front axle housing and remove the forward retaining nuts and bushings. Loosen the rear retaining nuts to allow the axle to tilt for driveshaft removal.

12. Pull the vent tube from the hole in the sub-frame.

13. Lower the front of the axle housing with the axle stand and slide the driveshaft out of the transmission above the axle housing. Let the driveshaft rest on the front driveshaft support and axle assembly.

14. Remove the catalytic converter.

15. Disconnect the hydraulic clutch line.

16. Detach the electrical connectors and remove the starter.

17. Position a transmission jack under the transmission. Remove the crossmember and the bell housing-to-engine bolts.

18. Move the transmission to the rear until the input shaft clears the flywheel and lower the transmission from the vehicle.

To install:

19. Install guide studs in the engine block and raise the transmission until the input shaft splines are aligned with the clutch disc splines.

20. Slide the transmission forward on the guide studs until it is against the bell housing. Install the bell housing-to-engine retaining bolts to 28–38 ft. lbs. (38–51 Nm).

21. Install the crossmember and tighten the bolts to 35–50 ft. lbs. (47–68 Nm). Remove the transmission jack.

22. Install the starter and attach the electrical connectors. Connect the hydraulic clutch line.

23. Install the catalytic converter assembly.

24. Lubricate the splines with grease and slide the driveshaft into the transmission.

25. Raise the axle housing with the axle stand and install the bushings and retaining nuts. Tighten the retaining nuts to 68–100 ft. lbs. (92–136 Nm) and remove the axle stand.

26. Position the vent tube in the hole of the sub-frame.

27. Align the driveshaft yoke and companion flange and install the retaining bolts. Tighten to 71–96 ft. lbs. (95–129 Nm).

28. Connect the exhaust pipe muffler assembly to the resonator. Lower the vehicle.

29. Position the shifter and install the retaining bolts. Tighten to 18–24 ft. lbs. (24–33 Nm). Install the console top cover and the shifter knob.

30. Connect the negative battery cable. Check transmission operation.

Automatic

1. Before servicing the vehicle, refer to the precautions in the beginning of this section.

2. Disconnect the negative battery cable.

3. Raise and safely support the vehicle.

4. Drain the fluid from the transmission by removing all of the oil pan bolts except the two at the front of the pan. Loosen the bolts and slowly lower the rear of the pan to allow the fluid to drain into a suitable container. When drained, reinstall a few of the bolts to hold the transmission oil pan in place.

5. Remove the inspection cover and remove the torque converter drain plug if equipped, allowing the torque converter to drain. After the converter has drained, reinstall the drain plug and tighten.

6. Crank the engine over with a wrench on the crankshaft pulley retaining bolt to access and remove the four torque converter-to-flywheel retaining nuts.

➡**To prevent possible engine damage, never rotate the crankshaft pulley in a counterclockwise direction as viewed from the front of the engine.**

7. Remove the exhaust system as required for transmission removal.

8. Matchmark and disconnect the driveshaft assembly, proceed as follows:

a. Loosen the differential housing assembly rear mounting nuts approximately ¼ in. (6mm).

b. Position an axle stand under the front of the differential housing and remove the forward mounting nuts and bushings. Pull the vent tube from the hole in the sub-frame.

c. Lower the front of the differential housing with the axle stand and slide the driveshaft out of the transmission above the axle housing. Let the driveshaft rest on the front driveshaft support and axle assembly.

9. Remove the speedometer cable or Vehicle Speed Sensor (VSS) as equipped, from the extension housing.

10. Disconnect the shift cable from the transmission manual control lever.

11. Remove the starter cable and remove the starter motor.

12. Remove the electrical wires and vacuum lines as required from the transmission assembly.

13. Place a suitable transmission jack under the transmission and raise it slightly.

14. Remove the transmission support insulator (mount)-to-crossmember bolts.

15. Remove the crossmember-to-frame side rail retaining bolts. Remove the crossmember and the transmission support insulator.

16. Lower the transmission jack allowing the transmission to hang.

17. Place a suitable jack under the front of the engine and raise the engine slightly to gain access to two upper transmission bell housing-to-cylinder block retaining bolts. Do not remove the bolts at this time.

18. Disconnect and plug the oil cooler lines at the transmission.

19. Remove the lower transmission bell housing-to-cylinder block retaining bolts.

20. Remove the transmission fluid fill tube.

21. Secure the transmission to the transmission jack with a safely chain or strap.

22. Remove the two upper transmission bell housing-to-cylinder block retaining bolts.

23. Carefully move the transmission to the rear of the vehicle disengaging the transmission from the cylinder block dowels and the torque converter from the flywheel.

24. Lower the transmission from the vehicle.

25. Remove the torque converter from the transmission.

To install:

➡**Thoroughly flush the transmission oil cooler and cooler lines of any contaminates before installing the transmission.**

26. Place the transmission on a suitable transmission jack and secure with a safety chain or strap.

27. Tighten the torque converter drain plug to 8–28 ft. lbs. (11–38 Nm).

28. Place the torque converter to the transmission and rotate into position to be sure the drive flats are fully engaged in the pump gear.

29. Raise the converter and transmission assembly into position. Rotate the converter until the studs and drain plug are in alignment with the holes in the flywheel. Align the orange balancing marks on the converter stud and flywheel bolt hole if balancing marks are present.

➡**The torque converter face must rest squarely against the flywheel. This indicates that the converter pilot is not binding in the engine crankshaft. To ensure the converter is properly seated, grasp a converter stud. It should move freely back and forth in**

the flywheel hole. If the converter will not move, the transmission must be removed and the converter repositioned so the impeller hub is properly engaged in the pump gear.

30. Install the transmission bell housing-to-cylinder block retaining bolts. Tighten the bolts to 40–50 ft. lbs. (55–68 Nm)

31. Remove the safety chain or strap from around the transmission.

32. Install a new O-ring on the lower end of the transmission fill tube and install the tube to the transmission case.

33. Unplug and connect the oil cooler lines to the transmission case.

34. Raise the transmission slightly and place the crossmember on the side supports. Position the transmission support insulator on the crossmember and install the retaining bolts and/or nuts to the frame side rails and the transmission extension housing.

35. Lower the transmission jack and remove it from under the vehicle.

36. Install the exhaust system components removed for transmission removal.

37. Connect the speedometer or VSS cable to the transmission extension housing.

38. Install the starter motor and wiring.

39. Connect the shift cable to the manual control lever.

40. Attach all transmission electrical connectors.

41. Install the four torque converter-to-flywheel retaining nuts. Tighten the nuts to 20–34 ft. lbs. (27–46 Nm).

42. Install the transmission inspection cover.

43. Install the driveshaft, making sure the index marks are aligned. Proceed as follows:

a. Raise the differential housing with the axle stand and install the bushings and retaining nuts. Tighten to 68–100 ft. lbs. (92–136 Nm). Remove the axle stand.

b. Install the vent tube in the hole of the sub-frame.

c. Align the driveshaft yoke and companion flange and install the retaining bolts. Tighten to 70–95 ft. lbs. (95–129 Nm).

44. Remove all supports, if applicable, and lower the vehicle.

45. Connect the negative battery cable.

46. Fill the transmission with the proper type and quantity of fluid.

47. Start the engine and check the transmission for leakage.

48. Adjust the transmission shift linkage as follows:

a. Position the transmission range selector into the OVERDRIVE position.

b. Raise and safely support the vehicle.

c. Loosen the shift cable and bracket-to-cable bracket retaining nut.

d. Move the transmission manual control lever to the OVERDRIVE position (the third detent position from the full clockwise position).

e. Tighten the retaining nut to 10–18 ft. lbs. (13–25 Nm).

f. Check the operation of the transmission in each range.

49. Road test the vehicle and check the transmission for proper operation.

Clutch

REMOVAL & INSTALLATION

1. Before servicing the vehicle, refer to the precautions in the beginning of this section.

2. Disconnect the negative battery cable.

3. Disconnect the clutch hydraulic system master cylinder from the clutch pedal.

4. Raise and support the vehicle safely.

5. Remove the starter.

6. Disconnect the hydraulic coupling at the transmission with tool T88T-70522-A or equivalent, by sliding the white plastic sleeve toward the slave cylinder and applying a slight tug on the tube.

7. Remove the transmission.

8. Matchmark the assembled position of the pressure plate to the flywheel.

9. Loosen the pressure plate attaching bolts evenly until the pressure plate springs are expanded, and remove the bolts. Be sure to support the pressure plate before removing the last bolt.

10. Remove the pressure plate and clutch disc from the flywheel.

11. Inspect the flywheel for scoring, cracks or other damage and machine or replace, as necessary. Inspect the pilot bearing for damage and free movement. Replace, as necessary.

To install:

12. If removed, install the flywheel. Be sure the mating surfaces of the flywheel and the crankshaft flange are clean prior to installation. Tighten the flywheel bolts to 54–64 ft. lbs. (73–87 Nm).

13. Position the clutch disc on the flywheel so a suitable alignment tool can enter the clutch pilot bearing and align the disc.

7922QG29

Tighten the pressure plate bolts gradually in the correct sequence

14. If reinstalling the original pressure plate, align the matchmarks. Position the pressure plate on the flywheel and install the retaining bolts hand-tight. Tighten the bolts, in sequence, to 20–28 ft. lbs. (27–39 Nm). Remove the alignment tool.

15. Install the remaining components in the reverse order of removal. Tighten the flywheel housing-to-engine bolts to 40–49 ft. lbs. (54–67 Nm).

➡**Reuse the aluminum washers under the attaching bolts to prevent galvanic corrosion.**

Hydraulic Clutch System

BLEEDING

1. Before servicing the vehicle, refer to the precautions in the beginning of this section.

2. Clean all dirt and grease from the cap to be sure no foreign substances enter the system.

3. Remove the cap and diaphragm and fill the reservoir to the top with the proper fluid.

4. Raise and support the vehicle safely.

5. Attach a hose to the bleeder valve at the slave cylinder.

➡**Keep the clutch fluid reservoir full at all times to prevent air from being pulled into the system.**

6. While the clutch pedal is being depressed, slightly open the bleeder valve and observe air bubbles in the clutch fluid at the end of the hose.

7. Close the bleeder valve before releasing the clutch pedal.

8. Repeat Steps 6 and 7, as necessary, until no air bubbles are observed.

9. Lower the vehicle and fill the reservoir. Road test the vehicle.

Halfshaft

REMOVAL & INSTALLATION

➡**Before continuing with this procedure, be sure to have available one new inboard CV-joint stub shaft pilot bearing housing seal, one shaft bearing retaining clip and one wheel hub retainer nut, per side. Once removed, these parts lose their torque holding ability or retention capability and must not be reused.**

1. Before servicing the vehicle, refer to the precautions in the beginning of this section.

2. With the vehicle sitting on the ground, remove the wheel hub retainer nut.

3. Raise and safely support the vehicle.

4. Remove the wheel and tire assembly.

5. Remove the anti-lock brake speed sensor, if equipped.

6. Use needle-nose pliers or equivalent, to slide the parking brake cable adjusting clip downward until the cable is free.

7. Remove the parking brake cable from the rear disc brake caliper.

8. Remove the upper and lower caliper retaining bolts and remove the caliper. Support the caliper aside with wire, do not allow it to hang from the brake hose.

9. Remove the upper control arm retaining nut and bolt. Wire the upper control arm to the top of the shock absorber.

10. Using a paint marker, matchmark the position of the lower control arm in relation to the knuckle with the lower bushings in the relaxed position.

➡**Failure to matchmark this relationship will result in bushing wind-up on assembly and incorrect ride height, causing misalignment and premature tire wear.**

11. Use a suitable puller to free the halfshaft from the hub.

12. Remove the lower control arm-to-knuckle retaining nuts. Push the halfshaft through the hub while positioning the CV-joint and knuckle to allow the front lower bolt to clear the CV-joint, then remove the bolt. Remove and save the washers.

13. Remove the rear bolt, washer, and knuckle assembly. Be careful not to damage the differential oil seal, differential housing and/or CV-joint boot.

14. Remove the halfshaft from the vehicle.

15. Insert a plug into the differential housing to prevent fluid loss.

To install:

16. Remove the differential plug and install a new differential oil seal.

17. Install a new circlip on the halfshaft. Start the ends in the groove and push the circlip into the groove, to prevent over expanding the circlip.

18. Lightly lubricate the stub shaft splines and carefully align the splines on the shaft with the splines in the differential.

19. Push the halfshaft inward to seat the circlip in the differential side gear groove. Use care not to damage the seal.

20. Engage the hub splines with the outboard CV-joint splines.

21. Install the lower control arm retaining bolts and nuts. Align the paint marks and tighten the bolts to 94–131 ft. lbs. (128–178 Nm).

22. Install a new wheel hub retaining nut

and use it to draw the CV-joint into the hub as far as possible by hand.

23. Install the upper arm retaining bolt and nut and tighten to 117–142 ft. lbs. (158–193 Nm).

24. Install the brake caliper assembly to the rotor with the outer brake shoe against the rotor's braking surface. This prevents pinching the piston boot between the inner brake shoe and the piston.

25. Install the upper and lower caliper retaining bolts and tighten to 64–88 ft. lbs. (87–119 Nm).

26. Install the parking brake cable to the brake caliper. Install the cable adjustment clip.

27. Install the anti-lock brake speed sensor, if equipped. Tighten the retaining bolts to 15–19 ft. lbs. (19–27 Nm).

28. Check the inboard CV-joint circlip engagement by attempting to pull the inboard CV-joint from the axle. If the CV-joint circlip is not seated, push the CV-joint in until the circlip is fully engaged in the side gear.

29. Check the axle lubricant level and fill, if necessary.

30. Install the wheel and tire assembly. Tighten the lug nuts to 85–105 ft. lbs. (115–142 Nm).

31. Lower the vehicle.

32. Pump the brake pedal several times to position the brake pads before moving the vehicle.

33. Tighten the wheel hub retainer nut to 250 ft. lbs. (340 Nm).

34. Check the wheel alignment and adjust if not within specification.

35. Road test the vehicle and check for proper operation.

STEERING AND SUSPENSION

Air Bag

✳✳ CAUTION

Some vehicles are equipped with an air bag system, also known as the Supplemental Inflatable Restraint (SIR) or Supplemental Restraint System (SRS). The system must be disabled before performing service on or around system components, steer-ing column, instrument panel components, wiring and sensors. Failure to follow safety and disabling procedures could result in accidental air bag deployment, possible personal injury and unnecessary system repairs.

PRECAUTIONS

➡**Be sure to refer to the precautions in the beginning of this section as well as these air bag system-specific precautions.**

Several precautions must be observed when handling the inflator module to avoid accidental deployment and possible personal injury.

• Never carry the inflator module by the wires or connector on the underside of the module.

• When carrying a live inflator module, hold securely with both hands, and ensure that the bag and trim cover are pointed away.

• Place the inflator module on a bench or other surface with the bag and trim cover facing up.

• With the inflator module on the bench, never place anything on or close to the module which may be thrown in the event of an accidental deployment.

DISARMING

1. Before servicing the vehicle, refer to the precautions in the beginning of this section.

2. Disconnect the negative, then the positive, battery cables. Wait one minute for the back-up power supply in the diagnostic monitor to deplete its stored energy.

3. Remove the four nut and washer assemblies retaining the driver air bag module to the steering wheel.

✳✳ CAUTION

When carrying a live air bag, be sure the bag and trim cover are pointed away from the body. In the unlikely event of an accidental deployment, the bag will, then deploy with minimal chance of injury. When placing a live air bag on a bench or other surface, always face the bag and trim cover up, away from the surface. This will reduce the motion of the module if it is accidentally deployed.

4. Detach the driver air bag connector. Connect Air Bag Simulator 105–00008 or equivalent, to the vehicle harness at the top of the steering wheel.

After the applicable service is accomplished, re-enable the air bag system as follows:

5. Remove the air bag simulator from the air bag connector.

6. Attach the connector and install the air bag.

7. Connect the positive, then the negative, battery cables.

8. Turn the ignition key **ON** and be sure the air bag light does not stay ON.

Power Rack and Pinion Steering Gear

REMOVAL & INSTALLATION

1. Before servicing the vehicle, refer to the precautions in the beginning of this section.

2. Disconnect the negative battery cable.

3. Turn the ignition key to the **ON** position.

4. Raise and safely support the vehicle.

5. Place a drain pan under the rack and pinion assembly.

6. Remove the bolt retaining the flexible coupling to the rack and pinion input shaft.

7. Remove the cotter pins and castellated nuts from both tie rod ends. Discard the cotter pins.

8. Separate the tie rod end studs from the wheel spindles using Tie Rod End Remover T-3290-D, or equivalent.

9. Remove the two nuts and insulator washers retaining the rack and pinion assembly to the front crossmember.

10. Remove the rubber insulators, if needed.

11. Move the rack and pinion assembly to gain access to the pressure and return lines at the rack.

12. Disconnect the pressure and return lines allowing the power steering fluid to drain into the drain pan.

13. Detach the electrical harness connector at the power steering pressure switch on the rack and pinion assembly, if equipped.

14. Remove the rack and pinion assembly from the vehicle.

15. Remove the inner tie rod spindles and install on the new rack and pinion assembly if they are in good condition.

To install:

16. Install the rack and pinion assembly into the vehicle allowing access for connecting the power steering pressure and return lines to the rack.

17. Install new plastic seals on the power steering line fittings.

18. Be sure that the rubber insulators are fully seated in the rack housing.

19. Place the rack and pinion assembly in position on the mounting bolts.

20. Install the power steering pressure and return lines. Tighten the line fittings to 20–25 ft. lbs. (27–34 Nm).

21. Connect the rack and pinion input shaft with the flexible coupling of the steering column. The design allows the hoses to swivel when tightened properly. Do not attempt to eliminate looseness by overtightening, since this can damage the fittings and cause leaks.

22. Install the two insulator washers and nuts securing the rack and pinion assembly to the crossmember. Tighten the nuts to 30–40 ft. lbs. (41–54 Nm).

23. Install the flexible coupling bolt and tighten to 20–30 ft. lbs. (28–40 Nm).

24. Install the tie rod end studs to the wheel spindles and install the castellated nuts. Tighten the nuts to 35–47 ft. lbs. (48–63 Nm), then continue to tighten until a new cotter pin can be installed. Install new cotter pins.

25. Lower the vehicle.

26. Turn the ignition key to the **OFF** position.

27. Connect the negative battery cable.

28. Fill the power steering pump reservoir.

29. Bleed the power steering system and check for leaks.

30. Check and adjust the wheel alignment.

31. Road test the vehicle and check for proper steering system operation.

Shock Absorber

REMOVAL & INSTALLATION

Front

1. Before servicing the vehicle, refer to the precautions in the beginning of this section.

2. Disconnect the negative battery cable.

3. Remove the plastic cover from the top of the shock assembly in the engine compartment.

4. If equipped with automatic ride control, remove the actuator and actuator mounting washer at top shock mount in the engine compartment.

5. Remove three upper retaining nuts and the housing seal from the mounting studs.

6. Raise and safely support the vehicle.

7. Remove the front wheels.

8. Remove the lower mounting bolt and nut.

9. Remove the nut at the sway (stabilizer) bar link upper mounting stud.

10. Separate the sway bar link from the wheel spindle using Ball Joint Remover D88L-3006-A, or equivalent.

11. Support the lower control arm with a transmission jack or equivalent.

12. Raise the lower control arm and wheel spindle with the jack until the sway bar link can be completely separated from the wheel spindle, then move the sway bar link out of the way.

13. Remove the wheel spindle-to-upper ball joint pinch bolt and nut. Discard the bolt and nut.

14. Lower the jack to separate the wheel spindle from the upper ball joint stud. Do not allow the wheel spindle to hang free, support it with wire or other means.

Steering Gear

Item	Description
1	Nut (2 Req'd)
2	Pin (2 Req'd)
3	Nut (2 Req'd)
4	Tie Rod End (2 Req'd)
5	Steering Gear
6	Bolt and Washer Assy (2 Req'd)

Item	Description
7	Steering Gear Insulator (2 Req'd)
8	Front Suspension Steering Ball Stud Dust Seal
9	Front Wheel Spindle Tie Rod (2 Req'd)

Exploded view of the power rack and pinion steering gear mounting

79220G30

Exploded view of the front shock absorber mounting

15. Remove the jack from under the lower control arm.

16. Remove the shock absorber assembly from the vehicle.

To install:

17. Place the shock assembly over the lower control arm and insert the lower bolt through the shock into the lower control arm.

18. Using a transmission jack or equivalent, raise the lower control arm and shock into position aligning the upper shock mounting studs with the mounting holes.

19. Remove the wire or other support holding the wheel spindle and attach the wheel spindle to the upper ball joint stud. Raise the lower control arm with the jack and install a new wheel spindle-to-upper ball joint stud pinch bolt and nut. Tighten the nut to 51–67 ft. lbs. (68–92 Nm).

20. Place the sway bar link and the wheel spindle assembly into the proper position to install the nut onto the link. Tighten the nut to 30–40 ft. lbs. (40–55 Nm).

21. Remove the jack from under the lower control arm.

22. Install the lower shock nut. Do not tighten at this time.

23. Install the wheel and tire assembly.

Using a torque wrench, tighten the lug nuts in a star pattern to 85–105 ft. lbs. (115–142 Nm).

24. Lower the vehicle.

25. Be sure the upper shock mounting studs are aligned with the mounting holes.

26. Install the housing seal and three upper shock retaining nuts onto the mounting studs. Tighten the nuts to 17–22 ft. lbs. (22–31 Nm).

27. Install the automatic ride actuator, if equipped.

28. Install the plastic shock cover, if equipped.

29. Place the vehicle on a drive-on hoist or alignment rack. Neutralize the lower control arm bushings by pushing down on the front of the vehicle, then releasing it.

30. Connect the negative battery cable.

31. Install the lower shock retaining nut onto the bolt and tighten to 126–169 ft. lbs. (170–230 Nm).

32. Road test the vehicle and check for proper operation.

Rear

✳✳ CAUTION

The rear shock absorbers act as the rebound stops for the rear suspension. When the rear shocks are removed, the suspension arms must be supported. The best method for rear shock removal is to use a drive-on hoist or an alignment pit. Portable vehicle ramps can be substituted, but be sure the ramps are secure, the parking brake is set, and the front wheels are chocked properly before proceeding.

1. Before servicing the vehicle, refer to the precautions in the beginning of this section.

2. Place and safely support the vehicle on a drive-on hoist, alignment pit, or suitable ramps.

3. Remove the side trim panels from inside the luggage compartment.

4. If equipped with Automatic Ride Control:

   a. Detach the actuator wiring connector from the harness connector.

   b. Squeeze the two actuator retaining tabs firmly inward with one hand and lift the actuator off with the other hand.

   c. Using suitable pliers, grasp the mounting bracket and hold firmly.

Loosen the upper shock absorber retaining nut and remove the mounting bracket.

5. With standard shock absorbers, remove the upper retaining nut, washer and insulator.

6. Remove the lower shock absorber-to-lower control arm retaining bolt, washer and nut.

7. Remove the shock absorber from the vehicle.

To install:

8. Properly prime the new shock absorber by inverting and compressing, then releasing the shock absorber to its fully extended position. Repeat this procedure several times.

➡**When replacing a shock absorber on an Automatic Ride Control equipped vehicle, an exact replacement adjustable shock absorber must be used. Failure to do so will result in a vehicle with dangerous handling qualities.**

9. Install the lower washer and insulator on the shock absorber. Place the shock absorber into position in the upper mounting hole.

Exploded view of the rear shock absorber mounting

10. Compress the shock absorber enough to align the lower mounting hole with the lower control arm, then install the retaining bolt, washer and nut. While holding the nut, tighten the lower shock absorber retaining bolt to 95–126 ft. lbs. (128–172 Nm).

11. With the upper shock absorber stud protruding through the shock tower hole into the luggage compartment, install the insulator, washer or actuator mounting bracket and the upper shock absorber retaining nut. Tighten the nut to 27–40 ft. lbs. (37–54 Nm).

12. If equipped with Automatic Ride Control:

   a. Align the flats on the mounting bracket with flats on the shock stud, and install the mounting bracket.

   b. Install the nut onto the stud. Tabs on the mounting bracket must be aligned in a fore and aft direction before tightening the nut.

   c. Using suitable pliers, grasp the mounting bracket firmly and tighten the bracket retaining nut to 27–35 ft. lbs. (27–47 Nm).

   d. Grasp the actuator by the retaining tabs, then install it onto the mounting bracket by pushing down on the retainer tabs, if equipped. The actuator assembly may be difficult to install if the plastic becomes eccentric to the actuator driving shaft. If so, loosen the two mounting screws allowing the actuator to float with respect to the locator, then install it onto the shock absorber, then tighten the screws.

   e. Attach the actuator wiring connector, and harness mating connector. Slide the connector onto the rail and push it into the secured position.

13. Install the luggage compartment panels.

14. Lower vehicle.

15. Road test the vehicle and check for proper operation.

Coil Spring

REMOVAL & INSTALLATION

Front

1. Before servicing the vehicle, refer to the precautions in the beginning of this section.

2. Remove the shock absorber assembly from the vehicle.

3. Support the bottom of the shock assembly in a suitable vise. Mark the posi-

Safely compress the front coil spring in a spring compressor such as Ford tool No. 086–0029B

tion of the coil spring to the shock upper mount with a marker or chalk.

➡ **If the coil spring is not positioned properly, the assembly will not mount into position in the vehicle.**

4. Using Spring Compressor 086–0029B or equivalent, compress the coil spring, then remove the retaining nut, washer and the upper shock mounting bracket.

5. Slowly release the spring compressor and remove the coil spring from the shock.

6. Inspect all components for damage or wear and replace parts as necessary.

   To install:

➡ **When installing a new coil spring or upper mount, transfer the reference (chalk) marks from the old part to the new part. Always work on only one shock and coil spring assembly at a time to avoid possible mixing of parts. Also, if the reference marks are missing the opposite assembly may be used as reference for aligning the coil spring to the upper mount. The right-hand and left-hand upper mount orientations are identical.**

7. Place the coil spring on the shock assembly. Using Spring Compressor

Be sure to install the mounting bracket in the correct orientation—front coil spring

086–0029B or equivalent, compress the coil spring and install the upper mount, aligning the previously made marks. Install the washer and retaining nut and tighten to 37–52 ft. lbs. (50–71 Nm).

8. Release the spring compressor and remove.

9. Verify that the coil spring is seated properly at the top and bottom of the shock assembly.

10. Install the shock absorber assembly into the vehicle.

Rear

1. Before servicing the vehicle, refer to the precautions in the beginning of this section.

2. Raise and safely support the vehicle.

3. Remove the rear wheel and tire assembly.

4. Remove the sway (stabilizer) bar link nuts at both ends of the sway bar. Rotate the sway bar up and out of the way.

5. Disconnect the parking brake cable at the disc brake caliper, if equipped with rear disc brakes.

6. Install three Spring Cages 086–00031 or equivalent, as follows:

   a. Install one spring cage without an adjuster link, to the inboard side (the innermost bend of the spring) of the coil spring.

   b. Install the two more spring cages with adjusters, at 120 degree angles to the previously installed cage.

7. Place a transmission jack or equivalent, under the lower control arm as far outboard as possible.

8. Use a wire or other suitable means to secure the upper control arm to the frame or body. The upper control arm must remain in place when the lower control arm is disconnected from the wheel knuckle.

9. Remove the lower shock absorber mounting bolt, washer and nut.

➡**The lower control arm must not be lowered until the pivot bolts are loose. Do not attempt to remove the plastic cap on the front pivot nut.**

10. Matchmark the toe adjustment cam positioning to the sub-frame with a suitable marker. Loosen both inboard pivot bolts on the lower control arm.

11. Remove the two bolts and nuts retaining the lower control arm to the wheel knuckle.

12. Lower the control arm by carefully lowering the transmission jack, or equivalent. Be sure the spring cages are securely holding the coil spring as the control arm is lowered.

REAR SPRING

REAR SUSPENSION ARM AND BUSHING

TRANSMISSION JACK ASSY

79220G35

Be sure the spring compressor is installed correctly before lowering the control arm—rear coil spring

13. Remove the jack once the coil spring pressure is relieved, then pull the lower control arm down fully by hand and remove the coil spring with the cages in place.

14. Remove the coil spring mounting insulators if necessary.

15. Before removing the cages from the spring:

   a. Measure the length of the coil spring with the cages installed. This dimension is needed for installation.

   b. Install Coil Spring Compressor D78P-5310-A or equivalent, to the coil spring and compress the spring.

   c. Remove the cages, then the spring compressor.

To install:

16. If the cages were removed from the coil spring, use the spring compressor to compress the spring to the dimension measured during removal. If the original dimension is not available, compress the spring to a length of 10.5 in. (267mm) not including the mounting insulators. Install the spring cages and remove the spring compressor.

17. Install the spring mounting insulators, if removed.

18. Place the caged coil spring onto the

upper and lower control arm seats. The cage with no adjuster must face inward and cages must be closer to the bottom of spring. The spring pigtails can be in any position.

19. Place two supports/stands under the front bumper reinforcement of the vehicle. This will prevent the rear of the vehicle from lifting off of the hoist, or equivalent.

20. Place a transmission jack or equivalent, under the lower control arm and carefully raise the arm enough to line up the mounting holes to the wheel knuckle, ensuring that the coil spring is properly seated.

21. Install the two bolts and nuts retaining the lower control arm to the wheel knuckle. Tighten the bolts to 110–148 ft. lbs. (149–201 Nm).

22. Remove the wire or equivalent support holding the upper control arm assembly.

23. Install the lower shock absorber mount bolt, washer and nut. Tighten nut to 83–113 ft. lbs. (113–153 Nm).

24. Remove the transmission jack or equivalent, from under the lower control arm.

25. Remove the stands/supports or equivalent, placed under the front bumper reinforcement.

Turn to Section 6 for brake system applications

26. Remove the spring cages from the coil spring.

27. Connect the parking brake cable to the disc brake caliper, if equipped with rear disc brakes.

28. Place the sway bar in position and connect the sway bar links to the sway bar. Install the retaining nuts and tighten to 35–47 ft. lbs. (47–63 Nm).

29. Install the wheel and tire assembly. Using a torque wrench, tighten the lug nuts in a star pattern, to 85–105 ft. lbs. (115–142 Nm).

30. Lower the vehicle.

31. Place the vehicle on an alignment rack or equivalent, to allow access to the suspension while the suspension is loaded.

32. Set the toe adjustment cam to the match mark made during removal.

33. Tighten the front lower control arm pivot nut at the sub-frame to 166–202 ft. lbs. (225–275 Nm). Tighten the rear lower control arm pivot nut at the sub-frame to 142–191 ft. lbs. (192–259 Nm).

34. Check the vehicles alignment and adjust if not within specifications.

35. Road test the vehicle and check for proper operation.

Upper Ball Joint

REMOVAL & INSTALLATION

The ball joint is an integral part of the upper control arm. If the ball joint is defective, the entire upper control arm must be replaced.

Lower Ball Joint

REMOVAL & INSTALLATION

Front

1. Before servicing the vehicle, refer to the precautions in the beginning of this section.

2. Raise and safely support the vehicle.

3. Remove the wheel and tire assembly.

4. Remove the lower control arm assembly.

5. Remove and discard the lower ball joint boot seal.

6. Clamp the lower control arm in a suitable vise.

7. Press out the lower control arm ball joint using Ball Joint Remover D89P-3010-A and Receiving Cup D84P-3395-A4 or equivalents and a suitable U-joint tool or hydraulic press.

FRONT SUSPENSION LOWER ARM

BALL JOINT REMOVER D89P-3010-A

U-JOINT TOOL T74P-4635-C

RECEIVING CUP D84P-3395-A4

7922QG36

Use a ball joint press and adapters such as Ball Joint Remover D89P-3010-A and Receiving Cup D84P-3395-A4 to remove the ball joint from the control arm

To install:

➡️ When installing a new lower ball joint, it is advisable that the protective cover be left in place during installation to protect the ball joint seal. It may be necessary to cut off the end of the cover to allow it to pass through the receiving cup.

8. Install the lower ball joint into the lower control arm using Ball Joint Replacer D89P-3010-B and Receiving Cup D84P-3395-A4 or equivalents and a suitable U-joint tool or hydraulic press.

9. Remove and discard the protective cover. Check the lower ball joint to be sure that it is fully seated in the lower control arm.

10. Inspect the ball joint seal and ensure that it is free of cuts or tears.

11. Install the lower control arm assembly into the vehicle.

12. Install the wheel and tire assembly. Tighten the lug nuts to 85–105 ft. lbs. (115–142 Nm).

13. Lower the vehicle.

14. Check the alignment and adjust if not within specification.

15. Road test the vehicle and check for proper operation.

Rear

The ball joint is an integral part of the lower control arm. If the ball joint is defective, the entire lower control arm must be replaced.

Upper Control Arm

REMOVAL & INSTALLATION

Front

➡️ The following procedure is the same for both the right-hand and left-hand upper control arm assemblies.

1. Raise and safely support the vehicle.

2. Remove the wheel and tire assembly.

3. Remove and discard the upper wheel spindle-to-ball joint pinch bolt and nut. Slightly spread the wheel spindle at the slot opening to remove the upper ball joint stud from the wheel spindle.

4. Lower the vehicle enough to gain access to the upper control arm pivot bolts. Support the vehicle in this position.

➡️ A 6-point socket must be used on the bolt due to the fact that the corners of the heads have been shaved off. Discard the nuts and bolts after removing them. Replacement bolts do not require metal flags.

5. Break off the small metal flags from the upper control arm pivot bolt heads. Remove the bolts and nuts.

6. Remove the upper control arm from the vehicle. Inspect the upper control arm ball joint. If worn the entire upper control arm assembly must be replaced.

To install:

7. Place the upper control arm in position and install new pivot bolts and nuts. Holding the control arm in the horizontal position, tighten the nuts to 65–88 ft. lbs. (88–119 Nm).

➡**If nuts cannot be tightened due to limited access on some models, Tighten the pivot bolts to 82–88 ft. lbs. (110–120 Nm).**

8. Raise and safely support the vehicle.

9. Install the upper control arm ball joint stud to the wheel spindle and install a new pinch bolt and nut, making sure to install the bolt from the front of the vehicle. Tighten the nut to 51–67 ft. lbs. (68–92 Nm).

10. Install the wheel and tire assembly. Using a torque wrench, tighten the lug nuts in a star pattern to 85–105 ft. lbs. (115–142 Nm).

11. Lower the vehicle.

12. If required, check the alignment and adjust if not within specification.

13. Road test the vehicle and check for proper operation.

Rear

1. Before servicing the vehicle, refer to the precautions in the beginning of this section .

2. Raise and safely support the vehicle.

3. Remove the wheel and tire assembly.

4. Support the wheel knuckle and hub assembly so that it can not swing outward using wire, or equivalent.

5. Remove the inner and outer pivot bolts and nuts from the upper control arm.

➡**Match mark the position of the inner pivot bolt washer, relative to the frame mount, to ensure proper camber alignment upon installation.**

6. Remove the upper control arm from the vehicle.

To install:

➡**Inspect all fasteners for damage, pitting, corrosion, stretching, etc. Replace fasteners as necessary.**

7. Place the upper control arm into position.

8. Install the inner upper control arm pivot bolt and nut. Align the match marks made during removal and tighten to 81–98 ft. lbs. (110–133 Nm). The inner pivot bolt is used for camber adjustment and had a specifically designed washer under the bold head. Make sure that the correct pivot bolt is used.

9. Install the outer pivot bolt and nut. Tighten the nut to 110–148 ft. lbs. (149–201 Nm).

10. Remove the wire or other means of support used to hold the wheel knuckle and hub assembly.

11. Install the wheel and tire assembly. Using a torque wrench, tighten the lug nuts in a star pattern, to 85–105 ft. lbs. (115–142 Nm).

12. Lower the vehicle.

13. Check the alignment and adjust if not within specification.

14. Road test the vehicle and check for proper operation.

Lower Control Arm

REMOVAL & INSTALLATION

Rear

1. Before servicing the vehicle, refer to the precautions in the beginning of this section .

2. Raise and safely support the vehicle.

3. Remove the rear wheel and tire assembly.

4. Remove the sway (stabilizer) bar link nuts at both ends of the sway bar. Rotate the sway bar up and out of the way.

5. Disconnect the parking brake cable at the disc brake caliper, if equipped with rear disc brakes.

6. Install 3 Spring Cages 086–00031 or equivalent, as follows:

  a. Install 1 spring cage without an adjuster link, to the inboard side (the innermost bend of the spring) of the coil spring.

  b. Install 2 more spring cages with adjusters, at 120 degree angles to the previously installed cage.

7. Place a transmission jack or equiva-

lent, under the lower control arm as far outboard as possible.

8. Use a wire or other suitable means to secure the upper control arm to the frame or body. The upper control arm must remain in place when the lower control arm is disconnected from the wheel knuckle.

9. Remove the lower shock absorber mounting bolt, washer and nut.

➡**The lower control arm must not be lowered until the pivot bolts are loose. Do not attempt to remove the plastic cap on the front pivot nut.**

10. Match mark the toe adjustment cam positioning to the sub-frame with a suitable marker. Loosen both inboard pivot bolts on the lower control arm.

11. Remove 2 bolts and nuts retaining the lower control arm to the wheel knuckle.

12. Lower the control arm by carefully lowering the transmission jack, or equivalent. Make sure the spring cages are securely holding the coil spring as the control arm is lowered.

13. Remove the jack once the coil spring pressure is relieved, then pull the lower control arm down fully by hand and remove the coil spring with the cages in place.

14. Remove the lower control arm pivot bolts and nuts at the sub-frame brackets.

15. Remove the lower control arm.

16. Remove the compensator link from the lower control arm.

To install:

17. Inspect the large nut used at the inner front arm attachment for the condition of the plastic cap. Use a new nut if the cap is cracked, loose or missing.

18. Install the compensator link on the lower control arm.

19. Install the lower control arm to the sub-frame brackets and loosely install the pivot bolts and nuts.

20. Tighten the compensator link nut to 110–148 ft. lbs. (149–201 Nm).

21. Place the caged coil spring onto the upper and lower control arm seats. The cage with no adjuster must face inward and cages must be closer to the bottom of spring. The spring pigtails can be in any position.

22. Place 2 jack stands under the front bumper reinforcement of the vehicle. This will prevent the rear of the vehicle from lifting off of the hoist, or equivalent.

23. Place a transmission jack or equivalent, under the lower control arm and care-

fully raise the arm enough to line up the mounting holes to the wheel knuckle, ensuring that the coil spring is properly seated.

24. Install 2 bolts and nuts retaining the lower control arm to the wheel knuckle. Tighten the bolts to 110–148 ft. lbs. (149–201 Nm).

25. Remove the wire or equivalent support holding the upper control arm assembly.

26. Install the lower shock absorber mount bolt, washer and nut. Tighten nut to 83–113 ft. lbs. (113–153 Nm).

27. Remove the transmission jack or equivalent, from under the lower control arm.

28. Remove the jack stands or equivalent, placed under the front bumper reinforcement.

29. Remove the spring cages from the coil spring.

30. Connect the parking brake cable to the disc brake caliper, if equipped with rear disc brakes.

31. Place the sway bar in position and connect the sway bar links to the sway bar. Install the retaining nuts and tighten to 35–47 ft. lbs. (47–63 Nm).

32. Install the wheel and tire assembly. Using a torque wrench, tighten the lug nuts in a star pattern, to 85–105 ft. lbs. (115–142 Nm).

33. Lower the vehicle.

34. Place the vehicle on an alignment rack or equivalent, to allow access to the suspension while the suspension is loaded.

35. Set the toe adjustment cam to the match mark made during removal.

36. Tighten the front lower control arm pivot nut at the sub-frame to 166–202 ft. lbs. (225–275 Nm). Tighten the rear lower control arm pivot nut at the sub-frame to 142–191 ft. lbs. (192–259 Nm).

37. Check the vehicles alignment, specifically the rear toe and adjust if not within specifications.

38. Road test the vehicle and check for proper operation.

Wheel Hub and Bearings

ADJUSTMENT

The front and rear wheel bearings are pregreased, sealed and require no periodic maintenance. The bearings are preset and cannot be adjusted.

REMOVAL & INSTALLATION

Front

➡ Before continuing with this procedure, be sure to have available, one new wheel hub retainer nut, one upper ball joint pinch bolt and nut, one lower ball joint stud nut and one wheel hub grease cap, per side. Once these parts are removed, they lose their torque holding ability or retention capability and must not be reused.

1. Before servicing the vehicle, refer to the precautions in the beginning of this section.

2. Raise and safely support the vehicle.

3. Place supports under both frame rails just behind the lower control arms.

4. Remove the wheel and tire assembly.

5. Remove and discard the hub cap grease seal.

6. Remove the two retaining bolts and the disc brake caliper. Support the brake caliper with wire or equivalent. Do not allow the caliper assembly to hang by the brake hose.

7. Matchmark the disc brake rotor to a lug bolt for proper indexing during reassembly, then remove the brake rotor.

8. Remove the brake rotor dust shield.

9. Remove and discard the wheel hub retainer nut.

➡ The front wheel bearings are part of the wheel hub and cannot be replaced separately.

10. Remove the wheel hub and bearing assembly. If necessary, use Hub Puller T81P-1104-C or equivalent to remove the wheel hub from the spindle.

11. If front spindle removal is necessary, perform the following:

a. If equipped with ABS, remove the speed sensor from the wheel spindle.

b. Remove the outer tie rod end cotter pin and castellated nut. Separate the tie rod end from the wheel spindle using Tie Rod End Remover T-3290-D, or equivalent.

c. Separate the sway bar link from the wheel spindle using Ball Joint Remover D88L-3006-A, or equivalent.

➡ Use care when separating the sway bar link. If the ball joint seal is damaged, a new link must be used.

d. Loosen the lower ball joint nut one or two turns. Do not remove the nut at this time.

e. Tap the wheel spindle boss sharply to separate the lower ball joint stud from the wheel spindle. Remove the lower ball joint nut and discard.

f. Remove and discard the upper ball joint pinch bolt and nut.

WHEEL HUB ASSY

FRONT DISC BRAKE ROTOR SHIELD

FRONT WHEEL SPINDLE

79220G37

The hub/bearing assembly can be pulled from the spindle after removing the retaining nut

g. Spread the slot slightly and separate the wheel spindle from the upper ball joint stud.

h. Separate the wheel spindle from the lower ball joint stud and remove from the vehicle.

To install:

12. If the spindle was removed, perform the following:

a. Place the wheel spindle on the lower ball joint stud. Install a new lower ball joint stud nut and tighten to 83–113 ft. lbs. (113–153 Nm).

b. Place the wheel spindle to the upper ball joint stud and install a new pinch bolt and nut. Tighten the nut to 51–67 ft. lbs. (68–92 Nm).

c. Attach the outer tie rod end to the wheel spindle. Install the castellated nut and tighten to 39–53 ft. lbs. (53–73 Nm). continue to tighten the nut until a slot in the nut lines up with the hole through the stud. Install a new cotter pin.

d. Place the sway bar link to the wheel spindle. Install the retaining nut and tighten to 30–40 ft. lbs. (40–55 Nm).

13. Install the wheel hub and bearing assembly onto the wheel spindle.

14. Install a new wheel hub retainer nut. Tighten the nut to 188–254 ft. lbs. (255–345 Nm).

➡**Any time a wheel hub retainer nut is loosened or removed, it must be replaced with a new nut. Do not use an impact tool to install the new nut.**

15. Install the brake anti-lock speed sensor, if equipped.

16. Install the disc brake rotor splash shield, if removed.

17. Install the brake rotor making sure to align the match marks made during removal. Install new push on nuts, if available.

18. Install a new wheel hub grease cap.

19. Place the disc brake caliper in position on the brake rotor and install the two retaining bolts. Tighten the bolts to 97 ft. lbs. (132 Nm).

20. Install the wheel and tire assembly. Using a torque wrench, tighten the lug nuts in a star pattern, to 85–105 ft. lbs. (115–142 Nm).

21. Remove the safely stands.

22. Lower the vehicle.

23. Pump the brake pedal several times to position the brake pads.

24. Road test the vehicle and check for proper operation.

Rear

➡**Before continuing with this procedure, be sure to have available, one new wheel hub retainer nut, one inboard halfshaft circlip and one inboard CV-joint stub shaft seal, per side. Once removed, these parts lose their torque holding ability or retention capability and must not be reused.**

1. Be sure to observe all precautions in the beginning of this section.

2. Remove the hub cap grease seal.

3. With all wheels on the ground, remove and discard the wheel hub retainer nut.

4. Raise and safely support the vehicle.

5. Remove the wheel and tire assembly.

6. Use needle-nose pliers to slide the parking brake cable adjusting clip downward until the cable is free.

7. If equipped with rear disc brakes, remove the parking brake cable from the brake caliper. Remove the disc brake caliper from the brake rotor, leaving the brake hose connected. Wire the brake caliper aside. Do not let it hang by the brake hose.

Use a two or three jaw puller to press the hub out of the bearing

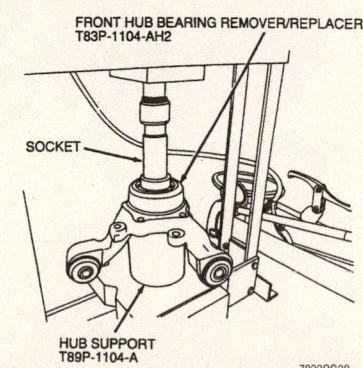

Support the knuckle while removing the bearing assembly with a hydraulic press

8. Remove the brake rotor or brake drum, as equipped.

9. If equipped with disc brakes, remove the brake dust shield.

10. If equipped with drum brakes, disconnect the parking brake cable and remove and plug the brake line at the wheel cylinder.

11. Remove the upper control arm nut and bolt at the wheel knuckle. Wire the upper control arm to the body to prevent damage to the CV-joint boots when the knuckle and hub assembly is removed.

12. Mark the position of the control arm in relation to the knuckle with the bushings in the relaxed position. When the upper control arm bolt is removed from the knuckle, the lower arm bushings will return to the relaxed position.

➡**Failure to mark the position will cause bushing wind up at assembly resulting in improper ride height. This can cause incorrect alignment and tire wear.**

13. Install Hub Remover/Replacer T81P-1104-C or equivalent to the hub studs and turn the tool shaft until the halfshaft is free in the hub.

14. Remove the lower control arm-to-knuckle retaining bolts and nuts and remove the knuckle assembly from the halfshaft.

15. Place the wheel knuckle and hub assembly in a suitable vise.

16. Wire the halfshaft to a suitable location to prevent damage to the CV-joint boot.

17. Place a suitable two or three jaw puller and Step Plate Adapter D80L-630–5 or equivalent, on the rear wheel knuckle and press out the hub from the wheel knuckle and bearing assembly.

18. Remove the disc brake backing plate from the wheel knuckle.

19. Remove the snapring retaining the wheel bearing assembly.

20. Place the wheel knuckle and bearing assembly on a press bed using Hub Support T89P-1104-A and Front Hub Bearing Remover/Replacer T83P-1104-AH2 or equivalents and press the wheel bearing assembly from the wheel knuckle.

21. Inspect all components for wear and/or damage and replace as needed.

To install:

22. Place the wheel knuckle on the press bed and position the wheel bearing assembly in the wheel knuckle bore. Press the wheel bearing assembly into the knuckle bore using Bearing Replacer T86P-1104-A3

or equivalent. Be sure the bearing assembly is fully seated.

23. Install the wheel bearing retainer snapring.

> ### ❋❋ WARNING
>
> **Before proceeding with the following step, the wheel bearing must be supported or damage will result.**

24. Place the wheel knuckle on Hub Support T89P-1104-A or equivalent and place on a suitable press bed plate. Place the wheel hub in position with the wheel bearing and knuckle assembly and press into position using Front Hub Bearing Remover/Replacer T83P-1104-AH2 or equivalent. Be sure the inner bearing race is properly supported or the bearing will be damaged.

25. Using a hammer and chisel, drive the bearing dust seal from the outer CV-joint. Using Axle Seal Replacer T83T-3132-A1 and Bearing Dust Seal Replacer T89P-1249-A or equivalents, install a new dust seal, making sure the seal flange faces out toward the bearing.

26. Remove the wire holding the halfshaft.

27. Engage the wheel knuckle and hub assembly on the halfshaft splines and install the lower control arm-to-wheel knuckle retaining bolts and nuts, finger-tight.

28. Push the halfshaft inward through the hub assembly while placing the wheel knuckle in position to install the front lower bolt, washer and nut.

29. Align the lower control arm to wheel knuckle match marks made during removal. If a new wheel knuckle is being installed, set the knuckle at the approximate angle noted during removal. Tighten the lower control arm-to-wheel knuckle retaining bolts to 94–131 ft. lbs. (128–178 Nm) using Holding Tool T93P-5494-A, or equivalent.

30. Install a new wheel hub retainer nut and hand-tighten only.

31. If equipped with rear disc brakes, place the disc brake backing plate in position on the wheel knuckle and install three retaining bolts. Tighten the bolts to 22–37 ft. lbs. (30–50 Nm).

32. If equipped with drum brakes, install the brake backing plate to the wheel knuckle and install four retaining bolts. Tighten the bolts to 44–59 ft. lbs. (59–80 Nm).

33. Connect the rear parking brake cable.

34. If equipped with drum brakes, connect the brake line to the wheel cylinder.

35. Install the brake rotor or brake drum, as equipped.

36. Install the upper control arm retaining bolt and nut. Tighten the nut to 117–142 ft. lbs. (158–193 Nm).

37. If equipped, install the disc brake caliper over the brake rotor with the outer brake pad against the brake rotor, to prevent pinching the caliper piston boot between the inner pad and piston. Install the two disc brake caliper retaining bolts and tighten to 64–88 ft. lbs. (87–119 Nm).

38. Connect the parking brake rear cable to the disc brake caliper and install the cable adjustment clip.

39. Install the wheel and tire assembly. Using a torque wrench, tighten the lug nuts in a star pattern, to 85–105 ft. lbs. (115–142 Nm).

40. Lower the vehicle.

41. Apply the parking brake several times and adjust if necessary.

42. With all wheels on the ground, tighten the wheel hub retainer nut to 188–254 ft. lbs. (255–345 Nm).

43. Install the hub cap grease seal.

44. Pump the brake pedal several times to position the brake pads before moving the vehicle.

45. Check the alignment and adjust if not within specification.

46. Road test the vehicle and check for proper operation.

FORD MOTOR COMPANY

26

Ford-Crown Victoria • **Lincoln-**Town Car • **Mercury-**Grand Marquis

PRECAUTIONS

Before servicing any vehicle, please be sure to read all of the following precautions, which deal with personal safety, prevention of component damage, and important points to take into consideration when servicing a motor vehicle:

• Never open, service or drain the radiator or cooling system when the engine is hot; serious burns can occur from the steam and hot coolant.

• Observe all applicable safety precautions when working around fuel. Whenever servicing the fuel system, always work in a well-ventilated area. Do not allow fuel spray or vapors to come in contact with a spark, open flame, or excessive heat (a hot drop light, for example). Keep a dry chemical fire extinguisher near the work area. Always keep fuel in a container specifically designed for fuel storage; also, always properly seal fuel containers to avoid the possibility of fire or explosion. Refer to the additional fuel system precautions later in this section.

• Fuel injection systems often remain pressurized, even after the engine has been turned **OFF**. The fuel system pressure must be relieved before disconnecting any fuel lines. Failure to do so may result in fire and/or personal injury.

• Brake fluid often contains polyglycol ethers and polyglycols. Avoid contact with the eyes and wash your hands thoroughly after handling brake fluid. If you do get brake fluid in your eyes, flush your eyes with clean, running water for 15 minutes. If eye irritation persists, or if you have taken brake fluid internally, IMMEDIATELY seek medical assistance.

• The EPA warns that prolonged contact with used engine oil may cause a number of skin disorders, including cancer! You should make every effort to minimize your exposure to used engine oil. Protective gloves should be worn when changing oil. Wash your hands and any other exposed skin areas as soon as possible after exposure to used engine oil. Soap and water, or waterless hand cleaner should be used.

• All new vehicles are now equipped with an air bag system, often referred to as a Supplemental Restraint System (SRS) or Supplemental Inflatable Restraint (SIR) system. The system must be disabled before performing service on or around system components, steering column, instrument panel components, wiring and sensors. Failure to follow safety and disabling procedures could result in accidental air bag deployment, possible personal injury and unnecessary system repairs.

• Always wear safety goggles when working with, or around, the air bag system. When carrying a non-deployed air bag, be sure the bag and trim cover are pointed away from your body. When placing a non-deployed air bag on a work surface, always face the bag and trim cover upward, away from the surface. This will reduce the motion of the module if it is accidentally deployed. Refer to the additional air bag system precautions later in this section.

• Clean, high quality brake fluid from a sealed container is essential to the safe and proper operation of the brake system. You should always buy the correct type of brake fluid for your vehicle. If the brake fluid becomes contaminated, completely flush the system with new fluid. Never reuse any brake fluid. Any brake fluid that is removed from the system should be discarded. Also, do not allow any brake fluid to come in contact with a painted surface; it will damage the paint.

• Never operate the engine without the proper amount and type of engine oil; doing so WILL result in severe engine damage.

• Timing belt maintenance is extremely important! Many models utilize an interference-type, non-freewheeling engine. If the timing belt breaks, the valves in the cylinder head may strike the pistons, causing potentially serious (also time-consuming and expensive) engine damage. Refer to the maintenance interval charts in the front of this manual for the recommended replacement interval for the timing belt, and to the timing belt section for belt replacement and inspection.

• Disconnecting the negative battery cable on some vehicles may interfere with the functions of the on-board computer system(s) and may require the computer to undergo a relearning process once the negative battery cable is reconnected.

• When servicing drum brakes, only disassemble and assemble one side at a time, leaving the remaining side intact for reference.

ENGINE REPAIR

Ignition Timing

ADJUSTMENT

The 4.6L engine used in the Ford Crown Victoria, Lincoln Town vehicle and Mercury Grand Marquis utilizes a Distributorless Ignition System (DIS). The DIS consists of the following components: crankshaft sensor, ignition module, ignition coil packs, the spark angle portion of the ECU and the related wiring.

The DIS eliminates the need for a distributor by using multiple ignition coils. Each coil fires two spark plugs at the same time. The plugs are paired so as one fires during the compression cycle, the other fires during the exhaust stroke. The next time the coil is fired, the plug that was on exhaust will be on compression and the one that was on compression will be on exhaust. The spark in the exhaust cylinder is wasted but little of the coil energy is lost. The ignition coils are mounted together in coil packs. There are two coil packs used, each containing two ignition coils.

The crankshaft sensor is a variable reluctance-type sensor triggered by a 36-minus-1 tooth trigger wheel located inside the front cover. The signal generated by this sensor is called a Variable Reluctance Sensor (VRS) signal. The VRS signal provides engine position and rpm information to the ignition module.

The ignition module is a microprocessor

that receives input from the crankshaft sensor in regards to engine position, base timing and engine speed and input from the ECU pertaining to spark advance. The ignition module uses this information to direct which coil to fire and to calculate the turn **ON** and turn **OFF** times of the coils required to achieve the correct dwell and spark advance.

Base ignition timing is referenced to the position of the crankshaft sensor, and is set at 8–12° Before Top Dead Center (BTDC) and is not adjustable.

Engine Assembly

REMOVAL & INSTALLATION

1. Before servicing the vehicle, refer to the precautions in the beginning of this section.
2. Disconnect both battery cables, negative cable first.
3. Mark the position of the hood on the hinges and remove the hood.
4. Drain the engine cooling system into a suitable container.
5. Recover the refrigerant from the A/C system using approved recovery equipment.
6. Properly relieve the fuel system pressure.
7. Remove the engine cooling fan, shroud and radiator.
8. Remove the windshield wiper governor (module) and support bracket.
9. Remove the engine air cleaner outlet tube.
10. Remove and detach the engine/transmission harness connector from the retaining bracket on the power brake booster and move aside.
11. Disconnect the accelerator and cruise control cables at the throttle body.
12. Detach the electrical connector and vacuum hose from the evaporative emission canister purge valve.
13. Disconnect the positive battery cable from the power distribution box and harness.
14. Disconnect the vacuum supply hose from the throttle body adapter vacuum port.
15. Disconnect both heater hoses.
16. Disconnect the alternator harness from the front fender apron and the power distribution box.
17. Disconnect the A/C hoses from the A/C compressor using the appropriate spring-lock disconnect tools.
18. Detach the power steering control

valve harness connector. Disconnect the body ground strap from the dash panel.
19. Raise and safely support the vehicle.
20. Disconnect the exhaust system from the exhaust manifolds and support with wire hung from the crossmember.
21. Remove the retaining nut from the transmission line bracket and remove the three bolts and one stud retaining the engine to the transmission knee braces.
22. Remove the starter motor.
23. Remove the four bolts retaining the power steering pump to the cylinder block and position aside.
24. Remove the transmission housing cover from the cylinder block to access the torque converter retaining nuts. Rotate the crankshaft until each of the four nuts is accessible and remove the nuts.
25. Remove the six transmission-to-engine retaining bolts.
26. Remove the engine support insulator (mount) through-bolts.
27. Lower the vehicle.
28. Support the transmission with a suitable floor jack and a block of wood.
29. Remove the bolt retaining the right-hand front engine support insulator to the front engine mount insulator support bracket.
30. Install an engine lifting bracket to the front of the left-hand cylinder head and to the rear of the right-hand cylinder head. Connect suitable engine lifting equipment to the lifting brackets.
31. Raise the engine slightly using a suitable floor crane and carefully separate the engine from the transmission. Do not let the torque converter fall out of the transmission.
32. Carefully lift the engine out of the engine compartment and position on a workstand. Remove the engine lifting equipment.

To install:
33. Install the engine lifting brackets. Support the engine using a suitable floor crane installed to the lifting equipment and remove the engine from the workstand.
34. Carefully lower the engine into the engine compartment. Start the converter pilot into the flywheel and align the paint marks on the flywheel and torque converter. Be sure the studs on the torque converter align with the holes in the flywheel.
35. Fully engage the engine to the transmission and lower onto front engine support insulators.
36. Remove the engine lifting equipment and brackets.

37. Install the bolt retaining the right-hand front engine support insulator to the front engine mount insulator support bracket.
38. Raise and safely support the vehicle.
39. Install the six engine-to-transmission retaining bolts and tighten to 30–44 ft. lbs. (40–60 Nm).
40. Install the front engine support insulator through-bolts and tighten to 15–22 ft. lbs. (20–30 Nm).
41. Install the four torque converter retaining nuts and tighten to 22–25 ft. lbs. (20–30 Nm).
42. Install the transmission housing cover to the cylinder block.
43. Position the power steering pump on the cylinder block and install the four retaining nuts. Tighten to 15–22 ft. lbs. (20–30 Nm).
44. Install the starter motor.
45. Position the engine-to-transmission brace and install the three bolts and one stud. Tighten the bolts and stud to 18–31 ft. lbs. (25–43 Nm).
46. Position the transmission line bracket to the brace stud and install one retaining nut. Tighten to 15–22 ft. lbs. (20–30 Nm).
47. Position the exhaust system to the exhaust manifolds. Install the four nuts and tighten to 20–30 ft. lbs. (27–41 Nm). Be sure the exhaust system clears the No. 3 crossmember. Adjust as necessary.
48. Lower the vehicle.
49. Attach the power steering valve harness connector. Reconnect the ground strap to the dash panel.
50. Reconnect the A/C lines to the A/C compressor.
51. Reconnect the alternator harness at the front fender apron and the power distribution box.
52. Reconnect both heater hoses.
53. Reconnect the vacuum supply hose to the throttle body adapter vacuum port.
54. Reconnect the positive battery cable to the power distribution box and harness. Attach the electrical connector and vacuum hose to the evaporative emission canister purge valve.
55. Reconnect the accelerator and cruise control cables at the throttle body.
56. Attach and install the engine/transmission harness connector to the retaining bracket on the power brake booster.
57. Install the windshield wiper governor and support bracket.
58. Reconnect the fuel supply and return lines.

59. Install the radiator, cooling fan and shroud.

60. Install the engine air cleaner outlet tube.

61. If needed, fill the crankcase with the proper type and quantity of engine oil.

62. Fill the cooling system.

63. Reconnect both battery cables, negative cable last.

64. Start the engine and allow to reach normal operating temperature.

65. Check for leaks and proper fluid levels.

66. Properly evacuate and recharge the A/C system.

67. Install the hood, aligning the marks that were made during removal.

68. Road test the vehicle and check the engine and transmission for proper operation.

Water Pump

REMOVAL & INSTALLATION

1. Before servicing the vehicle, refer to the precautions in the beginning of this section.

2. Disconnect the negative battery cable.

3. Drain the cooling system, remove the cooling fan and the shroud.

4. Release the belt tensioner and remove the accessory drive belt.

20-30 Nm
(15-22 lb/ft)

7922RG01

Be sure to tighten the water pump mounting bolts to the specification

5. Remove the four bolts retaining the water pump pulley to the water pump and remove the pulley.

6. Remove the four bolts retaining the water pump to the engine assembly and remove the water pump.

To install:

7. Installation is the reverse of the removal procedure. Be sure to clean the sealing surfaces of the water pump and block and use a new O-ring. Lubricate the O-ring with clean anti-freeze prior to installation.

8. Tighten the water pump-to-engine bolts and the pulley-to-water pump bolts to 15–22 ft. lbs. (20–30 Nm). Fill the cooling system. Operate the engine until normal operating temperatures have been reached and check for leaks.

Cylinder Head

REMOVAL & INSTALLATION

➡**The cylinder head bolts are a torque-to-yield design and cannot be reused. Before beginning this procedure, be sure new cylinder head bolts are available.**

1. Before servicing the vehicle, refer to the precautions in the beginning of this section.

2. If equipped with air suspension, the air suspension switch, located on the right-hand side of the luggage compartment, must be turned to the **OFF** position before raising the vehicle.

3. Disconnect the negative battery cable.

4. Drain the engine cooling system.

5. Remove the cooling fan and shroud assembly.

6. Properly relieve the fuel system pressure.

7. Remove the engine air cleaner outlet tube.

8. Remove the windshield wiper governor (module).

9. Release the drive belt tensioner and remove the accessory drive belt.

10. Tag and disconnect the ignition wires from the spark plugs. Disconnect the ignition wire brackets from the cylinder head cover studs and remove the two bolts retaining the ignition wire tray to the ignition coil brackets.

11. Remove the bolt retaining the A/C pressure line to the right-hand ignition coil bracket.

12. Disconnect the wiring to both ignition coils and the Camshaft Position (CMP) sensor.

13. Remove the nuts retaining the ignition coil brackets to the engine front cover. Slide the ignition coil brackets and ignition wire assemblies off the mounting studs and remove from the vehicle.

14. Remove the water pump pulley.

15. Disconnect the alternator wiring harness from the junction block, fender apron and alternator. Disconnect the bolts retaining the alternator to the intake manifold and cylinder block and remove the alternator.

16. Disconnect the positive battery cable at the power distribution box. Remove the retaining bolt from the positive battery cable bracket located on the side of the right-hand cylinder head.

17. Disconnect the vent hose from the canister purge solenoid and position the positive battery cable out of the way. Disconnect the canister purge solenoid vent hose from the PCV valve and remove the PCV valve from the cylinder head cover.

18. Remove and detach the engine/transmission harness connector from the retaining bracket on the power brake booster.

19. Detach the Crankshaft Position (CKP) sensor, A/C compressor clutch and canister purge solenoid electrical connectors.

20. Raise and safely support the vehicle.

21. Remove the bolts retaining the power steering pump to the cylinder block and engine front cover. The front lower bolt on the power steering pump will not come all the way out. Wire the power steering pump out of the way.

22. Remove the engine oil pan and oil pan gasket.

23. Remove the crankshaft pulley retaining bolt and remove the pulley, using Damper Remover T58P-6316-D, or equivalent.

24. Detach the power steering control

LOWER REAR HEAD BOLT

RUBBER BAND

LH CYLINDER HEAD

7922RG02

Use a rubber band to support the rear cylinder head bolt to ease removal of the head

valve actuator and oil pressure sensor wiring connectors and position out of the way.

25. Disconnect the EGR tube from the right-hand exhaust manifold.

26. Disconnect the exhaust pipes from the exhaust manifolds. Lower the exhaust pipes and hang with wire from the crossmember.

27. Remove the bolt retaining the starter wiring harness to the rear of the right-hand cylinder head.

28. Lower the vehicle.

29. Remove the bolts and stud bolts retaining the cylinder head covers to the cylinder heads and remove the covers.

30. Disconnect the accelerator and cruise control cables. Remove the accelerator cable bracket from the intake manifold and position out of the way.

31. Disconnect the vacuum hose from the throttle body elbow vacuum port, both Heated Oxygen Sensors (HO$_2$S) and the heater water hose.

32. Remove the two bolts retaining the thermostat housing to the intake manifold and position the upper hose and thermostat housing out of the way.

➡**The two thermostat housing bolts also retain the intake manifold.**

33. Remove the nine bolts retaining the intake manifold to the cylinder heads and remove the intake manifold and gaskets.

34. Remove seven stud bolts and the four bolts retaining the engine front cover to the engine and remove the front cover.

35. Remove both timing chains.

❊❊ WARNING

This is an interference engine. (For a definition of an interference engine, please refer to the timing belt unit repair section in the front of this manual). Camshaft Positioning Tools T92P-6256-A or equivalent, must be installed on the camshafts to prevent the camshafts from rotating. Do not rotate the camshafts or crankshaft with the timing chains removed or the valves will contact the pistons.

36. Remove the 10 bolts retaining the left-hand cylinder head to the cylinder block and remove the head. The lower rear cylinder head bolt must stay in the cylinder head until the cylinder head is removed due to lack of clearance for removal in the vehicle. Use a rubber band to secure the cylinder head bolt in the cylinder head during

removal and installation of the cylinder head and to prevent the bolt from damaging the cylinder block or head gasket.

➡**The lower rear cylinder head bolt cannot be removed due to interference with the power brake booster. Use a rubber band to hold the bolt away from the cylinder block.**

37. Remove the ground strap, one stud and one bolt retaining the heater return line to the right-hand cylinder head.

38. Remove the 10 bolts retaining the right-hand cylinder head to the cylinder block and remove the head. The lower rear cylinder head bolt must stay in the cylinder head until the cylinder head is removed due to lack of clearance for removal in the vehicle. Use a rubber band to secure the cylinder head bolt in the cylinder head during removal and installation of the cylinder head and to prevent the bolt from damaging the cylinder block or head gasket.

➡**The lower rear cylinder head bolt cannot be removed due to interference with the evaporator housing. Use a rubber band to hold the bolt away from the cylinder block.**

39. Clean all gasket mating surfaces. Check the cylinder heads and cylinder block for flatness. Check the cylinder heads for scratches near the coolant passages and combustion chambers that could provide leak paths.

To install:

40. Rotate the crankshaft counterclockwise 45 degrees. The crankshaft keyway should be at the 9 o'clock position viewed from the front of the engine. This ensures

that all pistons are below the top of the engine block deck face.

41. Rotate the camshaft to a stable position where the valves do not extend below the head face.

42. Position new head gaskets on the cylinder block. Install new bolts in the lower rear bolt holes on both cylinder heads and retain with rubber bands as explained during the removal procedure.

➡**New cylinder head bolts must be used whenever the cylinder head is removed and reinstalled. The cylinder head bolts are a torque-to-yield design and cannot be reused.**

43. Position the cylinder heads on the cylinder block dowels, being careful not to score the surface of the head face. Apply clean oil to the new cylinder head bolts, remove the rubber bands from the lower rear bolts and install all bolts hand-tight.

44. Tighten the new cylinder head bolts as follows:

   a. Tighten the bolts in sequence, to 28–31 ft. lbs. (37–43 Nm).

   b. Rotate each bolt in sequence 85–95 degrees.

   c. Loosen all bolts at least one full turn.

   d. Tighten the bolts in sequence, to 27–32 ft. lbs. (37–43 Nm).

   e. Rotate each bolt in sequence 85–95 degrees.

   f. Rotate each bolt in sequence an additional 85–95 degrees.

45. Position the heater return hose and install the two retaining bolts.

46. Rotate the camshafts using the flats matched at the center of the camshaft until

RH CYLINDER HEAD ASSY **LH CYLINDER HEAD ASSY**

CYLINDER HEAD TIGHTENING SEQUENCE

7922RG03

Tighten the cylinder head bolts in the proper sequence to prevent damage to the head and possible leaks

Timing belt service is covered in Section 5 of this manual

both are in time. Install Camshaft Positioning Tools T91P-6256-A or equivalent, on the flats of the camshafts to keep them from rotating.

47. Rotate the crankshaft clockwise 45 degrees to position the crankshaft at Top Dead Center (TDC) for the No. 1 cylinder.

➡**The crankshaft must only be rotated in the clockwise direction and only as far as TDC.**

48. Install both timing chains.

49. Install a new engine front cover seal and gasket. Apply silicone sealer to the lower corners of the cover where it meets the junction of the engine oil pan and cylinder block and to the points where the cover contacts the junction of the cylinder block and the cylinder heads.

50. Install the engine front cover and the stud bolts and bolts. Tighten to 15–22 ft. lbs. (20–30 Nm).

51. Position new intake manifold gaskets on the cylinder heads. Be sure the alignment tabs on the gaskets are aligned with the holes in the cylinder heads.

➡**Before installing the intake manifold, inspect it for nicks and cuts that could provide leak paths.**

52. Position the intake manifold on the cylinder heads and install the retaining bolts. Tighten the bolts in sequence, to 15–22 ft. lbs. (20–30 Nm).

53. Install the thermostat and O-ring, then position the thermostat housing and upper hose and install the two retaining bolts. Tighten to 15–22 ft. lbs. (20–30 Nm).

54. Reconnect the heater water hose and both HO$_2$S sensors.

55. Reconnect the vacuum hose to the throttle body adapter vacuum port.

56. Install the accelerator cable bracket on the intake manifold and connect the accelerator and cruise control cables to the throttle body.

57. Apply silicone sealer to both places where the engine front cover meets the cylinder heads. Install new gaskets on the cylinder head covers.

58. Install the cylinder head covers on the cylinder heads. Install the bolts and stud bolts and tighten to 71–106 inch lbs. (8–12 Nm).

59. Raise and safely support the vehicle.

60. Place the starter motor wiring harness to the right-hand cylinder head and install the retaining bolt.

61. Fit the exhaust pipes to the exhaust manifolds. Install and tighten the four nuts to 20–30 ft. lbs. (27–41 Nm).

➡**Be sure the exhaust system clears the No. 3 crossmember. Adjust as necessary.**

62. Reconnect the EGR tube to the right-hand exhaust manifold and tighten the line nut to 26–33 ft. lbs. (35–45 Nm).

63. Attach the power steering control valve actuator and oil pressure sensor electrical connectors.

64. Apply a small amount of silicone sealer in the rear of the keyway on the crankshaft pulley. Position the pulley on the crankshaft, making sure the crankshaft key and keyway are aligned.

65. Using Damper Installer T74P-6316-B or equivalent, install the crankshaft pulley. Install the pulley bolt and washer and tighten to 114–121 ft. lbs. (155–165 Nm).

66. Install the engine oil pan and a new gasket.

67. Place the power steering pump in position on the cylinder block and install the four retaining bolts. Tighten the bolts to 15–22 ft. lbs. (20–30 Nm).

68. Lower the vehicle.

69. Attach the A/C compressor, CKP sensor and canister purge solenoid electrical connectors.

70. Attach the engine/transmission harness connector and install on the retaining bracket on the power brake booster.

71. Install the PCV valve in the right-hand cylinder head cover and connect the canister purge solenoid vent hose.

72. Position the positive battery cable harness on the right-hand cylinder head and install the bolt retaining the cable bracket to the cylinder head. Reconnect the positive battery cable at the power distribution box and battery.

73. Position the alternator and install the two retaining bolts. Tighten the bolts to 15–22 ft. lbs. (20–30 Nm). Install the two bolts retaining the alternator brace to the intake manifold and tighten to 6–8 ft. lbs. (8–12 Nm).

74. Install the water pump pulley and tighten the bolts to 15–22 ft. lbs. (20–30 Nm).

75. Position the ignition coil brackets and ignition wire assemblies onto the mounting studs. Install seven nuts retaining the ignition coil brackets to the engine front cover and tighten to 15–22 ft. lbs. (20–30 Nm).

76. Install the two bolts retaining the ignition wire tray to the ignition coil bracket and tighten to 71–106 inch lbs. (8–12 Nm). Attach both the ignition coil and CMP sensor harness connectors.

77. Place the A/C pressure line on the right-hand ignition coil bracket and install the retaining bolt. Reconnect the ignition wires to the spark plugs and install the bracket onto the cylinder head cover studs.

78. Install the accessory drive belt and the windshield wiper governor.

79. Reconnect the fuel supply and return lines.

80. Install the cooling fan and shroud.

81. Fill the cooling system.

82. Install the engine air cleaner outlet tube.

83. Reconnect the negative battery cable.

84. If equipped with air suspension, turn the air suspension switch to the ON position.

85. Refill the engine with the correct amount of oil and replace the filter.

86. Start the engine and bring to normal operating temperature while checking for leaks.

87. Road test the vehicle and check for proper engine operation.

Rocker Arms

REMOVAL & INSTALLATION

1. Before servicing the vehicle, refer to the precautions in the beginning of this section.

2. Disconnect the negative battery cable.

3. Remove the right camshaft cover as follows:

a. Disconnect the positive battery cable at the battery and at the power distribution box. Remove the retaining bolt from the positive battery cable bracket located on the side of the right cylinder head.

b. Detach the Crankshaft Position (CKP) sensor, air conditioning compressor clutch and canister purge solenoid connectors. Position the harness out of the way.

7922RG04

After installing the spring spacer, compress the valve spring and remove the rocker arm

c. Disconnect the vent hose from the purge solenoid and position the positive battery cable out of the way.

d. Disconnect the ignition wires from the spark plugs. Remove the ignition wire brackets from the camshaft cover studs and position the wires out of the way.

e. Remove the PCV valve from the camshaft cover grommet and position out of the way.

f. Remove the bolts and stud bolts and remove the camshaft cover.

4. Remove the left camshaft cover as follows:

a. Remove the air inlet tube. Relieve the fuel system pressure and disconnect the fuel lines.

b. Raise and safely support the vehicle.

c. Disconnect the EVO sensor and oil pressure sending unit and position the harness out of the way. Lower the vehicle.

d. Remove the 42-pin engine harness connector from the retaining bracket on the brake vacuum booster. Disconnect and position out of the way.

e. Remove the windshield wiper module.

f. Disconnect the ignition wires from the spark plugs. Remove the ignition wire brackets from the studs and position the wires out of the way.

g. Remove the bolts and stud bolts and remove the camshaft cover.

5. Position the piston of the cylinder being serviced at the bottom of its stroke and position the camshaft lobe on the base circle.

6. Install valve spring spacer tool T91P-6565-AH or equivalent, between the spring coils to prevent valve seal damage.

➡**If the valve spring spacer tool is not used, the retainer will hit the valve stem seal and damage the seal.**

7. Install valve spring compressor tool T91P-6565-A or equivalent, under the camshaft and on top of the valve spring retainer.

8. Compress the valve spring and remove the roller follower. Remove the valve spring compressor and spacer.

To install:

9. Apply engine oil to the valve stem and tip and roller follower contact surfaces.

10. Install valve spring spacer tool T91P-6565-AH or equivalent, between the spring coils. Compress the valve spring using valve spring compressor tool T91P-

6565-A or equivalent, and install the roller follower.

➡**The piston must be at the bottom of its stroke and the camshaft at the base circle.**

11. Remove the valve spring compressor and spacer.

12. Clean the sealing surfaces of the camshaft covers and cylinder heads. Apply silicone sealer to the places where the front cover meets the cylinder head.

13. Position new gaskets onto the camshaft covers and install the covers. Install the bolts and stud bolts and tighten to 6.0–8.8 ft. lbs. (8–12 Nm).

14. When installing the right camshaft cover, proceed as follows:

a. Install the PCV into the camshaft cover grommet.

b. Install the ignition wire brackets on the studs and connect the wires to the spark plugs.

c. Position the harness and connect the canister purge solenoid, air conditioning compressor clutch and CKP sensor.

d. Position the positive battery cable harness on the right cylinder head. Install the bolt retaining the cable bracket to the cylinder head.

e. Reconnect the positive battery cable at the power distribution box and the battery.

15. When installing the left camshaft cover, proceed as follows:

a. Install the ignition wire brackets on the studs and connect the wires to the spark plugs.

b. Install the windshield wiper module.

c. Attach the 42-pin and transmission harness connectors. Install the connector on the retaining bracket.

d. Raise and safely support the vehicle. Position and connect the EVO sensor and oil pressure sending unit harness.

e. Lower the vehicle. Reconnect the fuel lines.

16. Reconnect the negative battery cable. Start the engine and check for leaks.

Intake Manifold

REMOVAL & INSTALLATION

1. Before servicing the vehicle, refer to the precautions in the beginning of this section.

2. If equipped with air suspension, the air suspension switch, located on the right-hand side of the luggage compartment, must be turned to the **OFF** position before raising the vehicle.

3. Disconnect the negative battery cable.

4. Drain the engine cooling system.

5. Properly relieve the fuel system pressure.

6. Disconnect the fuel supply and return lines.

7. Remove the windshield wiper governor (module).

8. Remove the engine air cleaner outlet tube.

9. Release the drive belt tensioner and remove the accessory drive belt.

10. Tag and disconnect the ignition wires from the spark plugs. Disconnect the ignition wire brackets from the cylinder head cover studs.

11. Disconnect the wiring from both ignition coils and the Camshaft Position (CMP) sensor. Tag and disconnect all ignition wires from both ignition coils. Remove the two bolts retaining the ignition wire bracket to the ignition coil brackets and remove the ignition wire assembly.

12. Disconnect the alternator wiring harness from the junction block at the fender apron and alternator. Remove the bolts retaining the alternator brace to the intake manifold and the alternator to the cylinder block and remove the alternator.

13. Raise and safely support the vehicle.

14. Disconnect the oil pressure sensor and power steering control valve actuator wiring and position the wiring harness out of the way.

15. Disconnect the EGR valve-to-exhaust manifold tube from the right-hand exhaust manifold.

16. Lower the vehicle.

17. Remove and detach the engine/transmission harness connector from the retaining bracket on the power brake booster.

18. Detach the A/C compressor clutch, Crankshaft Position (CKP) sensor and the canister purge solenoid wiring connectors.

19. Remove the PCV valve from the cylinder head cover and disconnect the canister purge vent hose from the PCV valve.

20. Disconnect the accelerator and cruise control cables from the throttle body. Remove the accelerator cable bracket from the intake manifold and position out of the way.

21. Disconnect the vacuum hose from the throttle body adapter port.

20-30 Nm (15-22 lb/ft)

7922RG06

Tighten the intake manifold in the sequence shown

22. Disconnect both Heated Oxygen (HO2S) sensors and the heater water hose.

23. Remove the two bolts retaining the thermostat housing to the intake manifold and position the upper hose and thermostat housing out of the way.

➡**The two thermostat housing bolts are also used to retain the intake manifold.**

24. Remove the nine bolts retaining the intake manifold to the cylinder heads and remove the intake manifold. Remove and discard the gaskets.

25. If replacing the intake manifold, swap over the necessary parts.

To install:

26. Clean all gasket mating surfaces.

27. Position new intake manifold gaskets on the cylinder heads. Be sure the alignment tabs on the gaskets are aligned with the holes in the cylinder heads.

28. Install the intake manifold and the nine retaining bolts. Hand-tighten the right-rear bolt (viewed from the front of the engine) before final tightening, then tighten the bolts, in sequence, to 15–22 ft. lbs. (20–30 Nm).

29. Inspect and if necessary, replace the O-ring seal on the thermostat housing. Position the housing and upper hose and

install the two retaining bolts. Tighten to 15–22 ft. lbs. (20–30 Nm).

30. Reconnect the heater water hose.

31. Reconnect both HO2S.

32. Reconnect the vacuum hose to the throttle body adapter vacuum port.

33. Install the accelerator cable bracket on the intake manifold and connect the accelerator and cruise control cables to the throttle body.

34. Install the PCV valve in the cylinder head cover and connect the canister purge solenoid vent hose. Attach the A/C compressor clutch, CKP sensor and canister purge solenoid wiring connectors.

35. Attach the engine/transmission harness connector. Install the connector on the retaining bracket on the power brake booster.

36. Raise and safely support the vehicle.

37. Reconnect the EGR valve-to-exhaust manifold tube to the right-hand exhaust manifold. Tighten the tube nut to 26–33 ft. lbs. (35–45 Nm).

38. Attach the power steering control valve actuator and the oil pressure sensor wiring connectors.

39. Lower the vehicle.

40. Position the alternator and install the two retaining bolts. Tighten to 15–22 ft. lbs.

(20–30 Nm). Install the two bolts retaining the alternator brace to the intake manifold and tighten to 71–106 inch lbs. (8–12 Nm).

41. Reconnect the alternator wiring harness to the alternator, right-hand fender apron and junction block.

42. Position the ignition wire assembly on the engine and install the two bolts retaining the ignition wire bracket to the ignition coil brackets. Tighten the bolts to 71–106 inch lbs. (8–12 Nm).

43. Reconnect the ignition wires to the ignition coils in their proper positions. Reconnect the ignition wires to the spark plugs.

44. Reconnect the ignition wire brackets on the cylinder head cover studs. Attach the wiring connectors to both ignition coils and the CMP sensor.

45. Install the accessory drive belt.

46. Install the engine air cleaner outlet tube.

47. Install the windshield wiper governor.

48. Reconnect the fuel supply and return lines.

49. Fill the engine cooling system.

50. Reconnect the negative battery cable.

51. If equipped with air suspension, turn the air suspension switch to the **ON** position.

52. Start the engine and check for leaks.

53. Road test the vehicle and check for proper operation.

Exhaust Manifold

REMOVAL & INSTALLATION

1. Before servicing the vehicle, refer to the precautions in the beginning of this section.

2. Disconnect both battery cables, negative cable first.

3. Remove the engine air inlet tube.

4. Drain the engine cooling system.

5. Remove the cooling fan and shroud assembly.

6. Relieve the fuel system pressure using the recommended procedure.

7. Disconnect the fuel supply and return lines.

8. Remove the upper radiator hose.

9. Remove the windshield wiper governor and support bracket.

10. Discharge the air conditioning system using proper recovery equipment. Disconnect the compressor outlet hose at the compressor and remove the bolt retaining the hose assembly to the right-hand ignition coil bracket. Plug both openings.

11. Remove and detach the engine/trans-

NOTE: ENGINE SHOWN REMOVED FOR CLARITY
NOTE: LH EXHAUST MANIFOLD SHOWN RH EXHAUST MANIFOLD TYPICAL

7922RG07

Tighten the bolts in the correct sequence to prevent possible leaks—1996 models

23-27 Nm (17-20 lb/ft)

7922RG08

To prevent warpage, be sure to tighten the exhaust manifold bolts according to the sequence shown—1997–00 models (left side)

7922RG09

To prevent warpage, be sure to tighten the exhaust manifold bolts according to the sequence shown—1997–00 models (right side)

mission harness connector from the retaining bracket on the power brake booster.

12. Disconnect the heater hose.

13. Remove the nut retaining the ground strap to the right-hand cylinder head.

14. Remove the upper stud and lower bolt retaining the heater hose to the right cylinder head and position out of the way.

15. Remove the heater blower motor switch resistor.

16. Remove the bolt retaining the right-hand front engine support insulator to the sub-frame.

17. Disconnect both Heated Oxygen (HO2S) sensors.

18. Raise and safely support the vehicle.

19. Remove the front engine support insulator through-bolts.

20. Remove the EGR valve-to-exhaust manifold tube nut from the right-hand exhaust manifold.

21. Disconnect the catalytic converter pipes from both exhaust manifolds. Lower the exhaust system and hang it from the crossmember with wire.

22. To remove the left-hand exhaust manifold, remove the front engine support insulator from the cylinder block and remove the eight nuts retaining the exhaust manifold. Remove the left-hand exhaust manifold and the two manifold gaskets.

23. Position an adjustable jackstand and a block of wood under the engine oil pan, rearward of the oil drain hole. Raise the engine approximately 4 inches (100mm).

24. To remove the right-hand exhaust manifold, remove the eight exhaust manifold retaining nuts. Remove the manifold and the manifold gasket.

To install:

25. If the exhaust manifolds are being replaced, transfer the heated oxygen sensors and tighten to 27–33 ft. lbs. (37–45 Nm). On the right-hand exhaust manifold, transfer the EGR tube connector and tighten to 33–48 ft. lbs. (45–65 Nm).

26. Clean the mating surfaces of the exhaust manifolds and cylinder heads.

27. Position the exhaust manifolds to the cylinder heads, using new gaskets and install the retaining bolts. Tighten the bolts in sequence to 15–22 ft. lbs. (20–30 Nm).

28. Reconnect the EGR valve and tube assembly to the exhaust manifold. Tighten the line nut to 26–33 ft. lbs. (35–45 Nm).

29. Install the left-hand front engine support insulator to the cylinder block and tighten the bolts to 15–22 ft. lbs. (20–30 Nm). Lower the engine onto the front engine support insulator and remove the jack.

30. Install the left-hand and right-hand engine support insulator through-bolts and tighten to 15–22 ft. lbs. (20–30 Nm).

31. Reconnect the catalytic converter pipes to both exhaust manifolds. Install the four retaining nuts and tighten to 20–30 ft. lbs. (27–41 Nm).

➡ **Be sure the exhaust system clears the No. 3 crossmember. Adjust as necessary.**

32. Lower the vehicle.

33. Reconnect both HO2S and install the bolt retaining the right-hand front engine support insulator to the sub-frame. Tighten to 15–22 ft. lbs. (20–30 Nm).

34. Install the heater blower motor switch resistor and attach it using the two retaining screws.

35. Place the heater hose in position. Install the upper stud and lower bolt and tighten to 15–22 ft. lbs. (20–30 Nm). Install the ground strap onto the stud and tighten the nut to 15–22 ft. lbs. (20–30 Nm).

36. Reconnect the heater hose.

37. Attach the engine/transmission harness connector. Install the connector to the retaining bracket on the power brake booster.

38. Unplug and connect the air conditioning compressor outlet hose to the compressor and install the bolt retaining the hose assembly to the right-hand ignition coil bracket.

39. Install the upper radiator hose.

40. Reconnect the fuel supply and return lines.

41. Install the windshield wiper governor and retaining bracket.

42. Install the engine cooling fan blade and fan shroud.

43. Fill the cooling system.

44. Install the engine air inlet tube.

45. Reconnect both battery cables, negative cable last.

46. Start the engine and check for leaks.

47. Properly evacuate and charge the air conditioning system.

48. Road test the vehicle and check for proper operation.

Camshaft and Valve Lifters

REMOVAL & INSTALLATION

1. Before servicing the vehicle, refer to the precautions in the beginning of this section.

2. If equipped with air suspension, the air suspension switch, must be turned to the **OFF** position before raising the vehicle.

3. Disconnect the negative battery cable.

4. Properly relieve the fuel system pressure.

5. Remove the fan blade and fan shroud assembly.

6. Disconnect the fuel supply and return lines from the fuel injection supply manifold.

7. Remove the windshield wiper governor (module) assembly from the vehicle.

8. Remove the engine air cleaner outlet tube.

9. Release the drive belt tensioner and remove the accessory drive belt.

10. Tag and disconnect all ignition wires from the spark plugs. Disconnect the ignition wire brackets from the cylinder head cover studs.

11. Remove the two bolts retaining the ignition wire separator to the ignition coil brackets and the bolt retaining the A/C pressure line to the right-hand ignition coil bracket.

12. Detach the electrical connectors from both ignition coils and the Camshaft Position (CMP) sensor.

13. Remove both ignition coils with brackets attached.

14. Detach the electrical connector from the alternator and at the power distribution box.

15. Remove the water pump pulley.

16. Disconnect the positive battery cable at the power distribution box.

17. Remove the bolt from the positive battery cable bracket located on the right-hand cylinder head.

18. Disconnect the fuel vapor hose from the evaporative emission canister purge valve (EVAP canister purge valve) and position the positive battery cable out of the way.

19. Disconnect the PCV valve from the cylinder head cover and position out of the way.

20. Remove and detach the engine/transmission harness connector from the bracket on the power brake booster.

21. Detach the Crankshaft Position (CKP) sensor and A/C clutch harness connectors.

22. Raise and safely support the vehicle.

23. Remove the bolts retaining the power steering pump to the cylinder block and wire the pump out of the way.

➡ **The front lower bolt on the power steering pump will not come all the way out.**

24. Drain the engine oil and remove the oil pan.

25. Remove the crankshaft pulley bolt and washer. Remove the crankshaft pulley using Pulley Remover T58P-6316-D, or equivalent.

26. Remove the engine oil filter.

27. Disconnect the power steering control valve actuator and oil pressure sensor.

28. Remove the oil filter adapter.

29. Lower the vehicle.

30. Remove both cylinder head covers.

31. Remove the engine front cover.

32. Remove the timing chains.

33. Rotate the crankshaft counterclockwise no more than 45 degrees from Top Dead Center (TDC) to ensure that all pistons are below the top of the engine block deck face.

❈❈ WARNING

The crankshaft must be in this position prior to rotating the camshafts or damage to the pistons and/or valve train will result.

34. Install Valve Spring Compressor T91P-6565-A or equivalent, under the camshaft and on top of one of the valve spring retainers.

❈❈ WARNING

Valve Spring Spacer Tool T91P-6565-AH or equivalent, must be installed between the spring coils and the camshaft lobe must be at the base circle before compressing the valve spring for each valve to prevent damage.

35. Install Valve Spring Spacer T91P-6565-AH or equivalent, between the valve spring coils. Be sure that the valve being compressed is on its base circle. Compress the valve spring and remove the rocker arm. Repeat the procedure until all rocker arms are removed.

36. If required, pull the lash adjusters (lifters) out of their bores in the cylinder head. Note their locations, they must be installed in the same bore they were removed from.

➡ **Do not mix the camshaft bearing caps. Note the camshaft bearing cap locations for installation.**

37. To remove each camshaft, remove the 14 bolts retaining the camshaft bearing caps (cluster assemblies) to the cylinder head. Tap upward on the camshaft bearing caps at points near the upper bearing halves and gradually lift the camshaft bearing cap clusters from the cylinder head.

38. Repeat the removal procedure for the opposite cylinder head.

39. Remove the camshaft straight upward to avoid bearing damage.

40. Clean and inspect the camshafts and related components for unusual wear or damage.

To install:

41. Clean and inspect the cylinder head covers, engine front cover and cylinder head sealing surfaces.

42. Apply clean engine oil to the camshaft journals and lobes. Position the camshafts on the cylinder heads.

43. Install and seat the camshaft bearing cap cluster assemblies. Install and hand start the retaining bolts. Tighten the camshaft cluster retaining bolts in sequence to 71–106 inch lbs. (8–12 Nm). Be sure to tighten each camshaft bearing cap cluster individually.

➡️**Each camshaft bearing cap cluster assembly is tightened individually.**

44. Loosen the camshaft bearing cap cluster retaining bolts approximately two turns or until the heads of the bolts are free. Tighten all bolts, again in sequence, to 71–106 inch lbs. (8–12 Nm).

45. Repeat the camshaft bearing cap installation for the opposite cylinder head.

➡️**The camshafts should turn freely but with a slight drag.**

46. Check camshaft end-play as follows:

a. Install a suitable dial indicator on the front of the engine. Position it so the indicator foot is resting on the camshaft sprocket bolt or the front of the camshaft.

b. Push the camshaft toward the rear of the engine and zero the dial indicator.

c. Pull the camshaft forward and release it. Specified end-play is 0.0901–0.006 inch (0.025–0.190mm).

d. If end-play is too tight, check for binding or foreign material in the camshaft thrust bearing. If end-play is excessive, check for worn camshaft thrust plate and replace the cylinder head, as required.

e. Remove the dial indicator.

47. If removed, install the lash adjusters in their original positions.

48. If necessary, install Camshaft Positioning Tools T92P-6256-A or equivalent, on the flats of the camshafts and install the spacers and camshaft sprockets. Install the bolts and washers and tighten to 81–95 ft. lbs. (110–130 Nm).

49. Install Valve Spring Compressor T91P-6565-A or equivalent, under the camshaft and on top of the valve spring retainer.

✳✳ WARNING

Valve Spring Spacer Tool T91P-6565-AH or equivalent, must be installed between the spring coils and the camshaft lobe must be at the base circle before compressing the valve spring for each valve to prevent damage.

50. Install Valve Spring Spacer T91P-6565-AH or equivalent, between the valve spring coils. Be sure that the valve being compressed is on its base circle. Compress the valve spring and install the rocker arm. Repeat the procedure until all rocker arms are installed.

8 -12 Nm (71.4 - 107.1 Lb-In)

7922RG10

Be sure to tighten the camshaft bearing cap cluster bolts in the sequence shown to avoid damage to the camshaft or bearings

51. Rotate the crankshaft clockwise 45 degrees to position the crankshaft at TDC.

➡️**The crankshaft must only be rotated in the clockwise direction and only as far as TDC.**

52. Install the timing chains.

53. Install the engine front cover.

54. Install both cylinder head covers. Tighten the cylinder head cover bolts to 71–106 inch lbs. (8–12 Nm).

55. Raise and safely support the vehicle.

56. Attach the power steering control valve actuator and oil pressure sensor harness connectors.

57. Apply silicone sealer to the crankshaft keyway, and install the crankshaft pulley, using Damper Replacer T74P-6316-B or equivalent. Tighten the crankshaft pulley bolt to 114–121 ft. lbs. (155–165 Nm).

58. Install the engine oil pan.

59. Position the power steering pump on the engine and install the four retaining bolts. Tighten the bolts to 15–22 ft. lbs. (20–30 Nm).

60. Safely lower the vehicle.

61. Attach the A/C clutch, CKP sensor and evaporative emission canister purge valve harness connectors.

62. Attach the engine/transmission harness connectors and install the connectors on the power brake booster retaining bracket.

63. Install the PCV valve to the right-hand cylinder head cover.

64. Install the positive battery cable harness on the right-hand cylinder head.

65. Install the bolt retaining the battery cable bracket to the cylinder head.

66. Reconnect the evaporative emission hose to the canister purge valve.

67. Reconnect the positive battery cable at the power distribution box.

68. Install the water pump pulley and tighten the bolts to 15–22 ft. lbs. (20–30 Nm).

69. Install the ignition coil brackets and ignition wires to the engine front cover. Tighten the retaining nuts to 15–22 ft. lbs. (20–30 Nm).

70. Attach the harness connectors to the ignition coils and the CMP sensor.

71. Position the A/C pressure line on the right-hand ignition coil bracket and install the retaining bolt.

For engine torque specifications, refer to Section 1 of this manual

72. Reconnect the ignition wires to the spark plugs and install the brackets onto the cylinder head cover studs.

73. Release the drive belt tensioner and install the accessory drive belt.

74. Install the windshield wiper governor.

75. Properly connect the fuel supply and return lines.

76. Install the fan and shroud assembly.

77. Fill the engine cooling system to the proper level.

78. Fill the crankcase to the proper level and grade of engine oil.

79. Reconnect the negative battery cable.

80. If equipped with air suspension, turn the air suspension switch to the ON position.

81. Start the engine and check for leaks.

82. Road test the vehicle and check for proper engine operation.

Valve Lash

ADJUSTMENT

The valve lash is not adjustable. If the collapsed lash adjuster clearance is incorrect, check the camshaft, roller follower and valve for wear or damage.

1. Before servicing the vehicle, refer to the precautions in the beginning of this section.

2. Disconnect the negative battery cable.

3. Remove the camshaft covers.

4. Rotate the crankshaft until the camshaft base circle is contacting the roller follower.

5. Use a suitable tool to bleed down the lash adjuster. Slowly compress the lash adjuster until the plunger is bottomed.

6. Use a feeler gauge to check the clearance between the camshaft and the roller follower. The clearance should be 0.018–0.033 inch (0.45–0.85mm).

Oil Pan

REMOVAL & INSTALLATION

1. Before servicing the vehicle, refer to the precautions in the beginning of this section.

2. Disconnect the negative battery cable.

3. Remove the engine air cleaner outlet tube.

4. Relieve the fuel system pressure.

5. Disconnect the fuel supply and return lines at the fuel injection supply manifold.

6. Drain the engine cooling system and remove the cooling fan and fan shroud.

7. Remove the upper radiator hose.

8. Remove the wiper governor and support bracket.

9. Properly discharge the air conditioning system using suitable recovery equipment. Disconnect and plug the compressor outlet hose at the compressor and remove the bolt retaining the hose assembly to the right-hand ignition coil bracket. Cap the compressor outlet.

10. Remove the engine/transmission electrical harness connector from the retaining bracket on the power brake booster and detach.

11. Disconnect the heater water hose.

12. Remove the nut retaining the ground strap to the right-hand cylinder head. Remove the upper stud and loosen the lower bolt retaining the heater outlet hose to the right-hand cylinder head and position out of the way.

13. Remove the heater blower motor switch resistor.

14. Raise and safely support the vehicle.

15. Drain the engine oil and reinstall the oil pan drain plug with a new gasket. Tighten the plug to 8–12 ft. lbs. (11–16 Nm).

16. Remove the bolt retaining the right-hand engine support insulator to the lower front sub-frame.

17. Remove the bolts retaining the left-hand and right-hand front engine support insulators to the engine mount supports.

18. Disconnect the catalytic converter pipes from both exhaust manifolds. Lower the exhaust system and support it with wire from the transmission crossmember.

19. Position a screw-type jack, or equivalent and a block of wood under the oil pan, rearward of the oil drain hole. Raise the engine approximately 4 inches (100mm) and insert two wood blocks approximately 2 ½ –2 ¾ inches (60–70mm) thick under each front engine support insulator. Lower the engine onto the wood blocks and remove the jack.

20. Remove the bolts retaining the oil pan to the cylinder block and remove the oil pan.

➡ It may be necessary to loosen, but not remove, the two nuts on the transmission support insulator and with a suitable jack, raise the transmission extension housing slightly to allow enough clearance to remove the engine oil pan.

To prevent oil leaks, tighten the oil pan bolts in the sequence shown

7922RG11

21. If necessary, remove the two bolts retaining the oil pick-up tube to the oil pump and remove the bolt retaining the pick-up tube to the main bearing stud spacer. Remove the pick-up tube.

To install:

22. Clean the engine oil pan and inspect for damage. Clean the sealing surfaces of the front cover and cylinder block. Clean and inspect the oil pick-up tube and replace the O-ring.

23. If removed, position the oil pick-up tube on the oil pump and hand start the two retaining bolts. Install the bolt retaining the pick-up tube to the main bearing stud spacer hand tight.

24. Tighten the pick-up tube-to-oil pump bolts to 72–108 inch lbs. (8–12 Nm), then tighten the pick-up tube-to-main bearing stud spacer bolt to 15–22 ft. lbs. (20–30 Nm).

25. Position a new gasket on the oil pan. Apply silicone sealer to where the front cover meets the cylinder block and the crankshaft rear oil seal and retainer meets the cylinder block. Position the oil pan to the engine and install the retaining bolts. Tighten the bolts in sequence, to 14 ft. lbs. (20 Nm), then rotate the oil pan retaining bolts, in sequence an additional 60 degrees within four minutes of applying the silicone sealer.

26. Position the jack and wood block under the engine oil pan, rearward of the oil drain hole, and raise the engine enough to remove the wood blocks. Lower the engine and remove the jack.

27. Install the left-hand and right-hand engine support insulator through-bolts and tighten to 15–22 ft. lbs. (20–30 Nm).

28. Install the bolt retaining the right-hand engine support insulator to the lower front sub-frame. Tighten the bolt to 15–22 ft. lbs. (20–30 Nm).

29. Position the exhaust system to the exhaust manifolds. Install the four retaining nuts and tighten to 20–30 ft. lbs. (27–41 Nm). Be sure the exhaust system clears the crossmember. Adjust as necessary.

30. Install a new engine oil filter.

31. Lower the vehicle.

32. Install the heater blower motor switch resistor using the two retaining screws.

33. Position the heater water hose, install the upper stud and tighten the upper and lower bolts to 15–22 ft. lbs. (20–30 Nm). Install the ground strap on the stud and tighten to 15–22 ft. lbs. (20–30 Nm).

34. Reconnect the heater water hose.

35. Reconnect the throttle valve cable, if equipped.

36. Attach the engine/transmission electrical harness connector. Install the harness connector on the power brake booster bracket.

37. Unplug and connect the air conditioning compressor outlet hose to the compressor and install the bolt retaining the hose to the right-hand ignition coil bracket.

38. Install the upper radiator hose.

39. Reconnect the fuel supply and return lines.

40. Install the wiper governor and retaining bracket.

41. Install the engine cooling fan and fan shroud.

42. Fill the cooling system.

43. Fill the engine crankcase with engine oil.

44. Install the engine air cleaner outlet tube.

45. Reconnect the negative battery cable.

46. Start the engine and check for leaks.

47. Properly evacuate and recharge the air conditioning system.

48. Road test the vehicle and check for proper engine operation.

Oil Pump

REMOVAL & INSTALLATION

1. Before servicing the vehicle, refer to the precautions in the beginning of this section.

2. Disconnect the negative battery cable.

3. Remove both cylinder head covers.

4. Remove the engine front cover.

5. Remove the engine oil pan.

6. Remove both timing chains.

7. Remove the two bolts retaining the oil pick-up tube to the oil pump and remove the bolt retaining the oil pick-up tube to the main bearing stud spacer. Remove the pick-up tube.

8. Remove the four bolts retaining the oil pump to the cylinder block and remove the oil pump.

To install:

9. Rotate the inner rotor of the oil pump to align with the flats on the crankshaft and install the oil pump flush with the cylinder block. Install the four retaining bolts and tighten to 72–106 inch lbs. (8–12 Nm).

10. Clean the oil pick-up tube and replace the O-ring.

11. Place the pick-up tube on the oil pump and hand start the two retaining bolts.

The oil pump is mounted on the crankshaft at the front of the engine

Install the bolt retaining the pick-up tube to the main bearing stud spacer hand tight. Tighten the pick-up tube-to-oil pump bolts to 72–106 inch lbs. (8–12 Nm). Tighten the pick-up tube to main bearing stud spacer bolt to 15–22 ft. lbs. (20–30 Nm).

12. Install a new engine oil filter.

13. Install both timing chains.

14. Install the engine oil pan.

15. Install the engine front cover.

16. Install both cylinder head covers.

17. Fill the crankcase with the proper type and quantity of engine oil.

18. Reconnect the negative battery cable.

19. Start the engine and check for leaks and proper engine oil pressure.

20. Road test the vehicle and check for proper engine operation.

Rear Main Seal

REMOVAL & INSTALLATION

➡**Special tools are available for installing rear main oil seals. In most cases, the seals can be installed using a common seal and bearing driver set.**

1. Before servicing the vehicle, refer to the precautions in the beginning of this section.

2. Remove the transmission assembly.

3. Remove the flexplate or flywheel.

4. With a sharp awl, carefully punch a small hole in the metal portion of the seal.

5. Remove the seal using a slide hammer with a sheet metal screw attached.

➡**If the oil leak is coming from around the seal retainer, the retainer must also be removed and resealed.**

To install:

6. If the seal retainer was removed, carefully clean the sealant from the retainer and engine block using a plastic scraper. Remove any oil or grease residue from the sealing surfaces with a solvent.

7. Apply silicone sealant to the back of the retainer and immediately install it on the engine block. Tighten the bolts in the proper sequence to 71–107 inch lbs. (8–12 Nm).

8. Lubricate the seal and the crankshaft with clean engine oil.

9. Install the seal with the spring side toward the engine.

10. Remove the installation tool and install the flexplate or flywheel. Tighten the bolts, in a crisscross pattern, to 54–64 ft. lbs. (73–87 Nm).

11. Install the transmission assembly.

12. Lower the vehicle.

13. Check the engine oil level.

14. Reconnect the negative battery cable.

15. Start the engine and check for leaks.

Timing Chain, Sprockets, Front Cover and Seal

REMOVAL & INSTALLATION

✳✳ WARNING

This is an interference engine. The camshafts and/or crankshaft must never be rotated with any timing chains removed. If the engine has "jumped time", there will be damage to the valves and/or pistons. The cylinder heads must be removed for inspection and repairs.

1. Before servicing the vehicle, refer to the precautions in the beginning of this section.

2. Disconnect the negative battery cable.

3. Remove the cooling fan and shroud.

4. Loosen the water pump pulley bolts, then remove the accessory drive belt.

5. Remove the water pump pulley.

6. Raise and safely support the vehicle.

7. Remove the bolts retaining the power steering pump to the cylinder block and engine front cover. The lower front bolt on the power steering pump will not come all the way out. Wire the power steering pump out of the way.

8. Drain the oil and remove the engine oil pan.

9. Remove the crankshaft pulley retaining bolt and washer.

10. Install Crankshaft Damper Remover T58P-6316-D, or equivalent and remove the crankshaft pulley.

11. Lower the vehicle.

12. Remove the bolt retaining the A/C pressure line to the right-hand ignition coil bracket.

13. Remove both cylinder head covers.

14. Disconnect the wiring at both ignition coils and the Camshaft Position (CMP) sensor.

15. Remove the three bolts retaining the right-hand ignition coil bracket to the engine front cover. Position the power steering hose out of the way.

16. Remove the three nuts retaining the left-hand ignition coil bracket to the engine front cover. Slide both ignition coil brackets and ignition wires off the mounting studs and lay the assembly on top of the engine.

17. Remove the bolts retaining the drive belt idler pulley and remove the pulley.

18. Disconnect the wiring to the Crank-

4 mm (.16 in)

7922RG13

Apply a continuos bead of silicone sealant to the back of the seal retainer before installing it on the engine

8 -12 Nm (71.4 - 107.1 Lb - In)

7922RG14

To avoid leakage, be sure to tighten the crankshaft rear oil seal retainer bolts in the correct sequence

COPPER TIMING LINK RH CHAIN

COPPER TIMING LINK LH CHAIN

TIMING MARK RH CAM GEAR

TDC

CRANKSHAFT GEAR KEYWAYS POSITIONED AT 315°

COPPER TIMING LINKS RH AND LH CRANKSHAFT GEARS

TIMING MARK LH CAM GEAR

CRANKSHAFT GEAR TIMING MARKS

7922RG16

Be sure that the timing marks are aligned when the No. 1 piston is at TDC on compression

shaft Position (CKP) sensor and remove the sensor.

19. If equipped, remove the retainers for the oil cooler from the engine front cover retaining stud bolts and position the oil cooler out of the way.

20. Remove the nine stud bolts and the six standard bolts retaining the engine front cover to the engine and remove the cover.

21. Remove the crankshaft oil seal from the cover using a suitable seal driver.

22. Remove the CKP sensor pulse wheel.

23. Rotate the engine to set the piston for No. 1 to Top Dead Center (TDC) on its compression stroke.

➡**Camshaft Positioning Adapters T92P-6256-A or equivalent, must be installed on the camshafts to prevent the camshafts from rotating.**

24. Install Camshaft Positioning Adapters T92P-6256-A or equivalent, on the flats of both camshafts. This will prevent accidental rotation of the camshafts.

25. Remove the two bolts retaining the tensioner to the right-hand cylinder head and remove the tensioner. Remove the right-hand timing chain tensioner arm.

26. Remove the two bolts retaining the right-hand timing chain guide to the cylinder head and remove the timing chain guide.

27. Remove the right-hand timing chain from the camshaft and crankshaft sprockets.

28. If necessary, remove the right-hand camshaft sprocket retaining bolt, washer, sprocket and spacer.

29. Remove the two bolts retaining the timing chain tensioner to the left-hand cylinder head and remove the timing chain tensioner. Remove the left-hand timing chain tensioner arm.

30. Remove the two bolts retaining the

CAM
POSITIONING
TOOL

7922RG17

Use the special tool to maintain camshaft position while installing the timing chains

INSTALL TOOL OVER FRONT COVER ALIGNMENT DOWEL

CRANKSHAFT POSITIONING TOOL

7922RG18

Install the crankshaft positioning tool to be sure the crankshaft does not turn while installing the timing chains

timing chain guide to the left-hand cylinder head and remove the timing chain guide.

31. Remove the left-hand timing chain from the camshaft and crankshaft sprockets.

32. If necessary, remove the left-hand camshaft sprocket retaining bolt, washer, sprocket and spacer.

33. If necessary, note the position of the crankshaft sprockets and remove the crankshaft sprockets by sliding them off the front of the crankshaft.

34. Inspect the plastic running face on the tensioner arms and chain guides. If worn or damaged, inspect the engine oil pan for contamination and thoroughly clean the oil pan. Replace the oil pick-up tube.

To install:

35. Examine the timing chains, looking for the copper links. If the copper links are not visible, lay the chain on a flat surface and pull the chain taught until the opposite sides of the chain contact one another. Mark the links at each end of the chain and use these marks in place of the copper links.

➡**If the engine jumped time, damage has been done to valves and possibly pistons and/or connecting rods. Any damage must be corrected before installing the timing chains.**

36. Be sure Camshaft Positioning Adapters T92P-6256-A or equivalent, are installed on the flats of the camshafts to prevent them from rotating.

37. Install the left-hand and right-hand timing chain guides and retaining bolts. Tighten the retaining bolts to 71–106 inch lbs. (8–12 Nm).

38. If removed, position the left-hand and right-hand camshaft spacers and sprockets on the camshafts. Install the washers and retaining bolts but do not tighten at this time.

39. If removed, install the left-hand

TIMING MARKS ALIGNED

VIEW A

INCORRECT   CORRECT INSTALLATION

KEYWAYS ALIGNED VIEW A

7922RG19

Be sure to install the crankshaft sprockets with the tapered sides facing each other as shown

crankshaft sprocket with the tapered part of the sprocket facing away from the engine block.

➡**The crankshaft sprockets are identical. They may only be installed one way, with the tapered part of the sprockets facing each other. Ensure that the keyway and timing marks on the crankshaft sprockets are aligned.**

40. Install the left-hand timing chain on the camshaft and crankshaft sprockets. Be sure the copper links of the timing chain line up with the timing marks on both sprockets.

41. If removed, install the right-hand crankshaft sprocket with the tapered part of the sprocket facing the left-hand crankshaft sprocket.

42. Install the right-hand timing chain on the camshaft and crankshaft sprockets. Be sure the copper links of the timing chain line up with the timing marks on both sprockets.

43. It is necessary to bleed the timing chain tensioners before installation. Proceed as follows:

a. Position the timing chain tensioner in a soft-jawed vise.

b. Using a small pick or similar tool, hold the ratchet lock mechanism away from the ratchet stem and slowly compress the tensioner plunger by rotating the vise handle.

✳✳ WARNING

The tensioner must be compressed slowly or damage to the internal seals will result.

c. Once the tensioner plunger bottoms in the tensioner bore, continue to hold the ratchet lock mechanism and push down on the ratchet stem until flush with the tensioner face.

d. While holding the ratchet stem

Please refer to Section 9 for electric cooling fan wiring schematic

Slowly compress the timing chain tensioner while holding the ratchet lock away from the stem with a suitable tool

NOTE: Ensure ratchet stem is flush to tensioner body face prior to installing paper clip.

7922RG21

Install a paper clip or wire into the tensioner to hold the plunger in during

flush to the tensioner face, release the ratchet lock mechanism and install a paper clip or similar tool in the tensioner body to lock the tensioner in the collapsed position.

e. The paper clip must not be removed until the timing chain, tensioner, tensioner arm and timing chain guide are completely installed on the engine.

44. Install the right-hand and left-hand timing chain tensioners and secure with two bolts on each. Tighten the bolts to 15–22 ft. lbs. (20–30 Nm).

45. Install Crankshaft Positioning Tool T93P-6265-A or equivalent, over the crankshaft and the engine front cover alignment dowel to position the crankshaft.

46. Lubricate the timing chain tensioner arm contact surfaces with clean engine oil and install the right-hand and left-hand tensioner arms on their dowel pins.

47. Position a suitable C-clamp around the timing chain tensioner arm and timing chain guide to remove all slack from the timing chain. Use care not to bend the timing chain guide.

48. Remove the locking pins or paper clips from the timing chain tensioners and be sure that all timing marks are aligned.

49. Using Camshaft Positioning

Adapters T92P-6265-A or equivalent to align and hold the camshafts, tighten the camshaft sprocket retaining bolts to 81–95 ft. lbs. (110–130 Nm).

50. Position a suitable dial indicator in the No. 1 cylinder spark plug hole to measure intake valve lift. The intake valve should be at maximum lift when the crankshaft is at 114 degrees after TDC. If the intake valve lift is not at maximum lift, loosen the camshaft sprocket bolt and repeat the steps detailing the installation of the timing chain tensioners to the tightening of the camshaft sprockets.

51. Remove the camshaft and crankshaft positioning tools.

52. Install a new crankshaft seal in the front cover. Apply engine oil to the lip of the seal.

53. Thoroughly clean the sealing surfaces of the front cover, cylinder block and oil pan. Apply silicone sealer to the points where the cylinder head meets the cylinder block.

54. Place the front cover in position using new gaskets. Install the retaining bolts and studs in their proper locations. Tighten in sequence to 15–22 ft. lbs. (20–30 Nm) within four minutes of applying the silicone sealer.

Timing chain front cover bolt tightening sequence

55. If equipped, install the oil cooler to the front cover retaining stud bolts.

56. Install the CKP sensor and attach the harness connector.

57. Install the drive belt idler pulley.

58. Place the ignition coil brackets and ignition wires as an assembly onto the mounting studs. Position the power steering hose and install the nuts retaining the coil brackets to the front cover. Tighten the nuts to 15–22 ft. lbs. (20–30 Nm). Reconnect the wiring to both ignition coils and the CMP sensor.

59. Install both cylinder head covers.

60. Position the A/C pressure line on the right-hand ignition coil bracket and install and tighten the retaining bolt.

61. Raise and safely support the vehicle.

62. Apply a small amount of silicone sealer in the rear of the keyway in the crankshaft pulley. Position the pulley on the crankshaft and install, using Crankshaft Damper Replacer T74P-6316-B or equivalent. Install the crankshaft pulley bolt and washer and tighten to 114–121 ft. lbs. (155–165 Nm).

63. Install the engine oil pan.

64. Place the power steering pump on the engine and install the four retaining bolts. Tighten to 15–22 ft. lbs. (20–30 Nm).

65. Lower the vehicle.

66. Install the water pump pulley with the four retaining bolts. Tighten to 15–22 ft. lbs. (20–30 Nm).

67. Install the accessory drive belt.

68. Install the engine cooling fan and shroud.

69. Fill the engine with the proper type and quantity of engine oil.

70. Reconnect the negative battery cable.

71. Start the engine and check for leaks.

72. Road test the vehicle and check for proper engine operation.

FUEL SYSTEM

Fuel System Service Precautions

Safety is the most important factor when performing not only fuel system maintenance but any type of maintenance. Failure to conduct maintenance and repairs in a safe manner may result in serious personal injury or death. Maintenance and testing of the vehicle's fuel system components can be accomplished safely and effectively by adhering to the following rules and guidelines.

• To avoid the possibility of fire and personal injury, always disconnect the negative battery cable unless the repair or test procedure requires that battery voltage be applied.

• Always relieve the fuel system pressure prior to disconnecting any fuel system component (injector, fuel rail, pressure regulator, etc.), fitting or fuel line connection. Exercise extreme caution whenever relieving fuel system pressure to avoid exposing skin, face and eyes to fuel spray. Please be advised that fuel under pressure may penetrate the skin or any part of the body that it contacts.

• Always place a shop towel or cloth around the fitting or connection prior to loosening to absorb any excess fuel due to spillage. Ensure that all fuel spillage (should it occur) is quickly removed from engine surfaces. Ensure that all fuel soaked cloths or towels are deposited into a suitable waste container.

• Always keep a dry chemical (Class B) fire extinguisher near the work area.

• Do not allow fuel spray or fuel vapors to come into contact with a spark or open flame.

• Always use a back-up wrench when loosening and tightening fuel line connection fittings. This will prevent unnecessary stress and torsion to fuel line piping. Always follow the proper torque specifications.

• Always replace worn fuel fitting O-rings with new. Do not substitute fuel hose or equivalent, where fuel pipe is installed.

Fuel System Pressure

RELIEVING

Fuel supply lines on all fuel injected engines will remain pressurized for some period of time after the engine is shut **OFF**. This pressure must be relieved before servicing the fuel system. Pressure is relieved through the fuel pressure relief valve, located on the fuel rail.

To relieve the fuel system pressure, first remove the fuel tank cap to relieve pressure in the tank, then remove the cap on the fuel pressure relief valve. Attach fuel pressure gauge T80L-9974-a or equivalent, and drain the system through the drain tube into a suitable container. Remove the fuel pressure gauge and replace the cap on the relief valve.

Fuel Filter

REMOVAL & INSTALLATION

1. Before servicing the vehicle, refer to the precautions in the beginning of this section.

2. Disconnect the negative battery cable.

3. Relieve the fuel system pressure.

4. If equipped with air suspension, turn the air suspension switch to the **OFF** position.

5. Raise and safely support the vehicle.

6. Remove the hairpin clip push connect fittings from both ends of the fuel filter as follows:

   a. Inspect the visible internal portion of the fitting for dirt accumulation. If more than a light coating of dust is present, clean the fitting before disassembly.

   b. Some adhesion between the seals in the fitting and the filter will occur with time. To separate, twist the fitting on the filter, then push and pull the fitting until it moves freely on the filter.

   c. Remove the hairpin clip from the fitting by first bending and breaking the shipping tab. Next, spread the two clip legs by hand about 1/8 inch each, to disengage the body and push the legs into the fitting. Lightly pull the triangular end of the clip and work it clear of the filter and fitting.

➡**Do not use hand tools to complete this operation.**

   d. Grasp the fitting and pull in an axial direction to remove the fitting from the filter. Be careful on 90 degree elbow connectors, as excessive side loading could break the connector body.

   e. After disassembly, inspect the

2–3 Nm
(18–26 lb/in)

7922RG22

The fuel filter is located near the center of the vehicle on the frame rail

inside of the fitting for any internal parts such as O-rings and spacers that may have been dislodged from the fitting. Replace any damaged connector.

7. Loosen the filter retaining clamp and remove the fuel filter. Note the direction of the flow arrow on the filter, so the replacement filter can be reinstalled in the same position.

To install:

8. Install the fuel filter with the flow arrow facing the proper direction and tighten the filter retaining clamp.

9. Install the rubber insulator rings on the new filter (replace the insulator rings if the filter moves freely after the retainer is installed). Install the filter into the retainer with the flow arrow pointing out the open end of the retainer. Install the retainer on the bracket and tighten the mounting bolts to 27–44 inch lbs. (3–5 Nm).

10. Install the hairpin clip push connect fittings at both ends of the fuel filter as follows:

   a. Install a new connector if damage was found. Insert a new clip into any two adjacent openings with the triangular portion pointing away from the fitting opening. Install the clip until the legs of the clip are locked on the outside of the body. Piloting with an index finger is necessary.

   b. Before installing the fitting on the filter, wipe the filter end with a clean cloth. Inspect the inside of the fitting to be sure it is free of dirt and/or obstructions.

   c. Apply a light coating of engine oil to the filter end. Align the fitting and filter axially and push the fitting onto the filter end. When the fitting is engaged, a definite click will be heard. Pull on the fitting to be sure it is fully engaged.

11. Lower the vehicle.

12. If equipped with air suspension, turn the air suspension switch to the **ON** position.

13. Reconnect the negative battery cable.

14. Start the engine and check for fuel leaks and proper operation.

Fuel Pump

REMOVAL & INSTALLATION

1. Before servicing the vehicle, refer to the precautions in the beginning of this section.

2. Disconnect the negative battery cable.

3. Relieve the fuel system pressure.

4. Raise and safely support the vehicle.

5. Install a hose into the fuel filler pipe and drain or siphon the fuel into a suitable storage tank designed for fuel storage.

6. Remove any dirt that has accumulated around the fuel pump and fuel lines to prevent the entry of contaminants into the tank during fuel pump removal and installation.

7. Disconnect the fuel supply and return line fittings at the fuel pump using Fuel Line Disconnect Tools T90T-9550-B and T90T-9559-C, or equivalents.

8. Detach the fuel pump module electrical connector.

9. Remove the six retaining bolts around the perimeter of the fuel pump module.

10. Remove the fuel pump module and seal from the fuel tank.

To install:

11. Clean the fuel pump module mounting flange and fuel tank mounting surface.

12. Install a new seal and the fuel pump module using care not to damage the inlet filter and fuel sending unit float arm.

13. Install and tighten the six retaining bolts to 80–107 inch lbs. (9–12 Nm).

14. Attach the fuel pump module electrical connector.

15. Install the fuel supply and return lines to the fuel pump module. Pull on the fuel line fittings to verify engagement.

16. Lower the vehicle.

17. Add a minimum of 10 gallons (38L) of clean fuel to the fuel tank and check for leaks.

18. Install Fuel Pressure Gauge T80L-9974-B or equivalent, to the Schrader valve on the fuel injection supply manifold.

19. Reconnect the negative battery cable.

20. Cycle the ignition switch from the **OFF** to **ON** position 5–10 times for three second intervals or until the fuel pressure gauge shows at least 35 psi (241 kPa).

21. Check for fuel leaks.

22. Remove the fuel pressure gauge.

Tighten the fuel pump mounting bolts to 80–107 inch lbs. (9–12 Nm)

23. Start the engine and recheck for fuel leaks.

24. Road test the vehicle and check for proper operation.

DRIVE TRAIN

Transmission Assembly

REMOVAL & INSTALLATION

1. Before servicing the vehicle, refer to the precautions in the beginning of this section.

2. If equipped with air suspension, the air suspension switch, located on the right-hand side of the luggage compartment, must be turned to the **OFF** position before raising the vehicle.

3. Disconnect the negative battery cable.

4. Raise and safely support the vehicle.

5. Remove the exhaust system as necessary for transmission removal.

6. Drain the fluid from the transmission by removing all oil pan bolts except the two bolts at the front of the pan. Loosen the two remaining bolts and if necessary, gently pry on the opposite end of the pan to lower the pan and allow the fluid to drain into a suitable container. When drained, reinstall a few of the bolts to hold the pan in place.

7. Remove the converter bottom access cover and adapter plate bolts.

8. If equipped, remove the torque converter drain plug, to allow the converter to drain into a suitable container. After the converter has drained, reinstall the drain plug and tighten.

9. Remove the four torque converter-to-flywheel retaining nuts.

➡**Crank the engine over with a wrench on the crankshaft pulley retaining bolt to gain access to each torque converter-to-flywheel retaining bolt. Never turn the crankshaft in a counterclockwise direction, as viewed from the front of the vehicle.**

10. Mark the position of the driveshaft on the rear axle flange and remove the driveshaft. Install a suitable plug in the transmission extension housing to prevent fluid leakage.

11. Disconnect and remove the Vehicle Speed Sensor (VSS) or if equipped, the speedometer cable from the transmission extension housing.

12. Carefully disconnect the shift cable from the transmission manual control lever. If equipped, disconnect the throttle valve cable from the transmission throttle valve lever.

13. Detach all transmission wiring harness connectors.

14. Remove the starter motor retaining bolts and place the starter motor aside.

15. Position a suitable transmission jack under the transmission and raise it enough to allow crossmember removal.

16. Remove the engine rear support-to-crossmember bolts and the crossmember-to-frame side support retaining bolts. Remove the crossmember and transmission support insulator.

17. Lower the transmission jack and allow the transmission to hang.

18. Place a suitable jack to the front of the engine and raise the engine enough to gain access to the two upper transmission-to-cylinder block retaining bolts. Do not remove the bolts at this time.

19. Disconnect the transmission cooler lines at the transmission. Plug all openings to keep dirt out.

20. Remove the lower transmission-to-cylinder block retaining bolts.

21. Remove the transmission fluid fill tube and plug the opening in the transmission.

22. Secure the transmission to the transmission jack with a safety strap or chain.

23. Remove the two upper transmission-to-cylinder block retaining bolts.

24. Carefully move the transmission rearward to disengage it from the dowel pins and the torque converter studs from the flywheel.

25. Lower the transmission from the vehicle.

26. Remove the torque converter to prevent the converter from dropping out of the transmission causing possible damage or personal injury.

27. If the transmission is to be removed for more than a speedy repair, support the rear of the engine with a safety stand and a block of wood.

To install:

➡**Verify the transmission cooler lines are thoroughly cleaned before installing the transmission assembly.**

28. Remove the safety stand and block of wood supporting the rear of the engine, if installed.

29. If equipped, tighten the torque converter drain plug to 21–23 ft. lbs. (28–30 Nm).

30. If removed, position the torque converter on the transmission and rotate into position to be sure the drive flats are fully engaged in the pump gear. When fully seated, the center of the torque converter should be about 7/16–9/16 inch (10.2–14.4mm) below the transmission mounting surface

31. If removed, install the transmission on a suitable transmission jack and secure with a safely strap or chain. Raise the transmission and align with the cylinder block dowel pins.

➡**Do not allow the transmission to get in a nose-down position causing possible torque converter disengagement from the pump gear.**

32. Rotate the converter until the studs and drain plug are in alignment with the holes in the flywheel. Align the orange balancing marks on the converter stud and flywheel bolt hole, if balancing marks are present.

33. Move the transmission assembly forward into position, being careful not to damage the flywheel and converter pilot.

➡**The converter face must rest squarely against the flywheel. This indicates that the converter pilot is not binding in the engine crankshaft. To ensure the converter is properly seated, grasp a converter stud. It should move freely back and forth in the flywheel hole. If the converter will not move, the transmission must be removed and the converter repositioned so the impeller hub is properly engaged in the pump gear.**

34. Install the two transmission housing-to-cylinder block retaining bolts at the engine dowel pin locations. Tighten the bolts to 41–50 ft. lbs. (55–68 Nm).

35. Install the remaining transmission housing-to-cylinder block retaining bolts. Tighten the bolts to 41–50 ft. lbs. (55–68 Nm).

36. Remove the safety strap or chain from around the transmission.

37. Install the transmission fluid fill tube and secure with the retaining bolt. Tighten the bolt to 28–38 ft. lbs. (38–51 Nm).

38. Reconnect the oil cooler lines to the transmission case. Tighten the cooler line fittings to 15–19 ft. lbs. (20–26 Nm).

39. Remove the jack supporting the front of the engine.

40. Using the transmission jack, raise the transmission enough to install the crossmember.

41. Place the crossmember and transmission support insulators in position. Install the engine rear support-to-crossmember retaining bolts and the crossmember-to-frame side support retaining bolts.

42. Remove the transmission jack.

43. Attach all transmission wiring harness connectors.

44. Install the starter motor and wiring.

45. Install the four torque converter-to-flywheel retaining nuts. Tighten to 20–33 ft. lbs. (27–46 Nm).

46. Install the torque converter access cover and cover plate bolts. Tighten the bolts to 12–16 ft. lbs. (16–22 Nm).

47. Install the exhaust system.

48. Install the Vehicle Speed Sensor (VSS) and connect the wiring or if equipped, the speedometer cable to the transmission extension housing.

49. Install the driveshaft aligning the marks that were made during removal.

50. Reconnect the shift cable to the transmission manual control lever. If equipped, connect the throttle valve cable to the transmission throttle valve lever.

DIMENSION A TO BE 10.23-14.43 mm (7/16-9/16 INCH) APPROXIMATELY

7922RG24

To prevent transmission damage, be sure that the torque converter is fully seated in the front pump of the transmission

51. Lower the vehicle.

52. If equipped with air suspension, turn the air suspension switch to the **ON** position.

53. Fill the transmission with the proper type and quantity of fluid.

54. Start the engine and check the transmission for leakage.

55. Road test the vehicle and check for proper transmission operation.

STEERING AND SUSPENSION

Air Bag

PRECAUTIONS

Several precautions must be observed when handling the inflator module to avoid accidental deployment and possible personal injury.

• Never carry the inflator module by the wires or connector on the underside of the module.

• When carrying a live inflator module, hold securely with both hands, and ensure that the bag and trim cover are pointed away.

• Place the inflator module on a bench or other surface with the bag and trim cover facing up.

• With the inflator module on the bench, never place anything on or close to the module which may be thrown in the event of an accidental deployment.

DISARMING

1. Before servicing the vehicle, refer to the precautions in the beginning of this section.

2. Position the vehicle with the front wheels in a straight ahead position.

3. Disconnect both battery cables, negative cable first.

4. Wait at least one minute for the air bag back-up power supply to deplete its stored energy before continuing.

5. Proceed with the repair.

6. Once the repair is complete.

7. Reconnect both battery cables, negative cable last.

8. Prove out the air bag system by turning the ignition key to the **RUN** position and visually monitoring the air bag indicator lamp in the instrument cluster. The indicator lamp should illuminate for approximately six seconds, then turn **OFF**. If the indicator lamp does not illuminate, stays on, or flashes at any time, a fault has been detected by the air bag diagnostic monitor.

Recirculating Ball Power Steering Gear

REMOVAL & INSTALLATION

1. Before servicing the vehicle, refer to the precautions in the beginning of this section.

2. If equipped with air suspension, the air suspension switch must be turned to the **OFF** position before raising the vehicle.

3. Center the steering wheel and turn the key to the locked position.

4. Disconnect the negative battery cable.

5. On the Town Car, separate the two halves and remove the steering gear cover.

6. Remove the bolt and separate the intermediate shaft from the steering gear.

7. Tag the power steering pressure and return lines so they may be reassembled in their original positions.

8. Place a drain pan under the steering gear and disconnect the pressure and return lines. Plug the lines and ports in the gear to prevent the entry of dirt.

9. Raise and safely support the vehicle.

10. Disconnect the Pitman arm from the center link using a suitable puller. It is not necessary to remove the Pitman arm from the steering gear.

11. Support the steering gear and remove the steering gear-to-frame rail retaining bolts.

12. Remove the steering gear from the vehicle.

To install:

13. Position the steering gear on the frame rail. Install the retaining bolts and tighten them to 50–67 ft. lbs. (66–90 Nm).

14. Install the Pitman arm to the center link. Tighten the retaining nut to 52–60 ft. lbs. (70–81 Nm).

15. Lower the vehicle.

16. Unplug and connect the power steering pressure and return lines to the steering gear and tighten the lines to 12–18 ft. lbs. (16–24 Nm).

17. Connect the intermediate shaft to the steering gear. Tighten the bolt to 31–41 ft. lbs. (41–55 Nm).

18. Reconnect the negative battery cable.

19. If equipped with air suspension, turn the air suspension switch to the **ON** position.

20. Fill the reservoir with the correct power steering fluid and turn the steering wheel from stop-to-stop to distribute the fluid. Check the fluid level and add fluid, if necessary.

Remove the bolt and separate the intermediate shaft from the steering gear input shaft

7922RG25

Remove the locknut and separate the Pitman arm from the center link using the appropriate

21. Start the engine and turn the steering wheel from left to right. Check for leaks.

22. On the Town Car, install the steering gear cover.

23. Road test the vehicle and check the steering system for proper operation.

Shock Absorber

REMOVAL & INSTALLATION

Front

1. Before servicing the vehicle, refer to the precautions in the beginning of this section.

2. If equipped with air suspension, the air suspension switch, located on the right-hand side of the luggage compartment, must be turned to the **OFF** position before raising the vehicle.

3. Remove the nut, washer and bushing from the upper end of the shock absorber.

4. Raise and safely support the vehicle.

5. Remove the two bolts retaining the shock absorber to the lower control arm and remove the shock absorber.

To install:

6. Prior to installation, prime the new shock absorber. Fully extend the shock absorber while in the right side up (installed) position. Turn the shock absorber upside down and fully compress it. Repeat the procedure at least three times to purge any air trapped in the shock absorber.

7. Install a new bushing and washer on the stud on the top of the new shock absorber and position the unit inside the front coil spring.

8. Install the two lower retaining bolts and tighten them to 10–12 ft lbs. (13–17 Nm).

9. Lower the vehicle.

10. If equipped with air suspension, turn the air suspension switch to the **ON** position.

11. Place a new bushing and washer on the shock absorber top stud and install a new retaining nut. Tighten the retaining nut to 25–34 ft. lbs. (34–46 Nm).

12. Road test the vehicle and check for proper operation.

Rear

✷✷ WARNING

When removing and installing rear shock absorbers on vehicles with air springs, it is very important that this procedure be followed exactly. Failure to do so may result in damaged shock absorbers.

1. Before servicing the vehicle, refer to the precautions in the beginning of this section.

2. If equipped with air suspension, turn the air suspension service switch **OFF**.

3. Be sure the ignition switch is in the **OFF** position.

4. Raise and safely support the vehicle.

5. Support the rear axle assembly with a jack.

➡ To assist in removing the upper retainer on shock absorbers using a plastic dust tube, place an open end wrench on the hex stamped into the dust tube's metal cap. For shock absorbers with a steel dust tube, simply grasp the tube to prevent stud rotation when loosening the retaining nut.

6. Remove the top retaining nut, washer and bushing.

7. Remove the bottom retaining nut and washer. Remove the shock absorber.

To install:

8. Position the shock absorber so the upper stud enters the hole in the frame. Install the top bushing, washer and retaining nut. Tighten to 26–34 ft. lbs. (34–46 Nm).

9. Extend the shock absorber and place the lower stud through the hole in the bracket. Install the bottom retaining washer and nut. Tighten to 57–75 ft. lbs. (76–103 Nm).

10. Remove the jack from the axle assembly.

11. Safely lower the vehicle to the floor.

12. Turn the air suspension service switch to the **ON** position.

13. Road test the vehicle and check for proper operation.

Coil Spring

REMOVAL & INSTALLATION

Front

1. Before servicing the vehicle, refer to the precautions in the beginning of this section.

2. If equipped with air suspension, turn the air suspension service switch to the **OFF** position before raising the vehicle.

3. Raise and safely support the vehicle.

4. Remove the wheel and tire assembly.

5. Remove the shock absorber.

6. Separate the center link from the Pitman arm using Tie Rod End Remover 3290-D, or equivalent.

7. Using Spring Compressor D78P-5310-A or equivalent, install one plate with the pivot ball seat facing downward into the coils of the spring. Rotate the plate so it is flush with the upper surface of the lower arm.

8. Install the other plate with the pivot ball seat facing upward into the coils of the spring. Insert the upper ball nut through the coils of the spring, so the nut rests in the upper plate.

9. Insert the compression rod into the opening in the lower arm, through the upper and lower plate and upper ball nut. Insert

1 Upper Ball
2 Compression Rod
3 Forcing Nut
4 Thrust Washer
5 Lower Ball Nut
6 Plate
7 Pin

7922RG27

Exploded view of Spring Compressor D78P-5310-A—similar compressors are commercially available that will do the same job

7922RG28

Compress the coil spring until it moves away from it's seat

the securing pin through the upper ball nut and compression rod.

➡**This pin can only be inserted one way into the upper ball nut because of a stepped hole design.**

10. With the upper ball nut secured, turn the upper plate so it walks up the coil until it contacts the upper spring seat. Then, back off ½ turn.

11. Install the lower ball nut and thrust washer on the compression rod and screw on the forcing nut. Tighten the forcing nut until the spring is compressed enough so it is free in its seat.

12. Remove the two lower control arm pivot bolts, disengage the lower arm from the frame crossmember and remove the coil spring.

13. If a new coil spring is to be installed, mark the position of the upper and lower plates on the spring with chalk. With an assistant, compress a new spring for installation and measure the compressed length and the amount of curvature of the old spring.

14. Loosen the forcing nut to relieve the spring tension and remove the tools from the spring.

To install:

15. Assemble the spring compressor and locate in the same position as marked during disassembly.

16. Before compressing the coil spring, be sure the upper ball nut securing the pin is inserted properly.

17. Compress the coil spring until the spring height reaches the dimension measured during disassembly.

18. Position the coil spring assembly into the lower arm and position the lower arm into the frame crossmember.

19. Install both the front and rear lower control arm pivot bolts through the frame and lower arm bushings. Tighten the bolts and nuts to 109–148 ft. lbs. (148–201 Nm).

20. Remove the spring compressor from the coil spring.

21. Install the drag link to the Pitman arm. Tighten the retaining nut to 60 ft. lbs. (80 Nm).

22. Position the shock absorber inside the coil spring and install the retaining bolts.

23. Install the wheel and tire assembly. Tighten the lug nuts in a star pattern to 85–105 ft. lbs. (115–142 Nm).

24. Lower the vehicle.

25. If equipped with air suspension, turn the air suspension switch to the **ON** position.

Fasteners

Lower Arm

7922RG29

Remove the fasteners attaching the lower arm to the frame, then lower the arm and remove the spring with the compressor

26. Place a washer and retaining nut on the shock absorber top stud. Tighten the nut to 25–34 ft. lbs. (34–46 Nm).

27. Check the front end alignment.

28. Road test the vehicle and check for proper operation.

Rear

AIR SPRING

✳✳ CAUTION

Before servicing any air suspension component, disconnect power to the system by turning the air suspension service switch OFF or by disconnecting the negative battery cable. Do not remove an air spring under any circumstances when there is pressure in the air spring. Do not remove any components supporting an air spring without either exhausting the air or providing support for the air spring.

1. Before servicing the vehicle, refer to the precautions in the beginning of this section.

2. Turn the air suspension switch to the **OFF** position.

3. Raise and safely support the vehicle. The suspension must be fully down with no load.

4. Remove the heat shield, as required. Remove the spring retainer clip.

5. Detach the air spring solenoid valve electrical connector, then disconnect the air line.

6. Remove the air spring solenoid retainer.

7. Rotate the solenoid valve counterclockwise to the first stop.

8. Pull the solenoid valve straight out slowly to the second stop to bleed air from the system.

✳✳ CAUTION

Do not fully release the solenoid until the air is completely bled from the air spring or personal injury may result.

9. After the air is fully bled from the system, rotate the solenoid valve counterclockwise to the third stop and remove the solenoid valve from the solenoid housing.

Remove the large O-ring from the solenoid housing.

10. On 1996–97 models, insert Air Spring Removal Tool T90P-5310-A or equivalent, between the axle tube and the spring seat on the forward side of the axle. Position the tool so its flat end rests on the piston knob. Push downward, forcing the piston and retainer clip off the axle spring seat.

11. On 1998–00 models, lift the air spring off of the rear axle.

12. Remove the air spring.

To install:

13. Check the solenoid valve O-rings for cuts or abrasions. Replace the O-rings as required. Lightly grease the O-ring area of the solenoid valve and the larger solenoid housing O-ring with silicone dielectric compound.

14. Insert the solenoid into the air spring end cap and rotate clockwise to the third stop, push in to the second stop, then rotate clockwise to the first stop.

15. Install the air spring solenoid retainer. Inspect the wiring harness connector and ensure the rubber gasket is in

HEAT SHIELD

SPRING RETAINER CLIP

AIR SPRING WITH INTEGRAL SOLENOID

7922RG30

Exploded view of the air spring mounting

place at the bottom of the connector cavity.

16. Install the air spring into the frame (upper) spring seat, taking care to keep the solenoid air and electrical connections clean and free of damage.

17. Reconnect the push-on ring spring retainer clip to the knob of the spring cap from the top side of the frame spring seat.

18. Attach the air line and electrical connector to the solenoid. Install the heat shield to the frame spring seat, if removed.

19. Align the air spring piston-to-axle (lower) seat. Squeeze to increase pressure and push downward on the piston, snapping the piston to the axle seat at rebound and supported by the shock absorber.

✴✴ WARNING

The air springs may be damaged if the suspension is allowed to compress before the spring is inflated.

20. Reconnect the negative battery cable.

21. Refill the air spring as follows:

a. Turn the air suspension switch to the **ON** position. The ignition switch must be **ON** and the engine running or a battery charger must be connected to the battery to reduce battery drain.

b. Fold back or remove the right-hand luggage compartment trim panel and connect Super Star II Tester 007–0041-A or equivalent, to the air suspension Data Link Connector (DLC), which is located near the air suspension switch.

c. Set the tester to EEC-IV/MCU mode. Also set the tester to FAST mode. Release the tester button to the HOLD (up) position and turn the tester **ON**.

d. Depress the tester button to TEST (down) position. A Code 10 will be displayed. Within two minutes a Code 13 will be displayed. After Code 13 is displayed, release the tester button to the HOLD (up) position, wait five seconds and depress the tester button to TEST (down) position. Ignore any codes displayed.

e. Release the tester button to the HOLD (up) position. Wait at least 20 seconds, then depress the tester button to TEST (down) position. Within 10 seconds, the codes will be displayed in the order shown.

f. Within four seconds after Code 26

is displayed, release the tester button to the HOLD (up) position. Waiting longer than four seconds may result in Functional Test 31 being entered. The compressor will fill the air springs with air as long as the tester button is in the HOLD (up) position. To stop filling the air springs, depress the tester button to the TEST (down) position.

➡ **It is possible to overheat the compressor during this operation. If the compressor overheats, the self-resetting circuit breaker in the compressor will open and remain open for about 15 minutes. This allows the compressor to cool down.**

g. To exit Functional Test 26, disconnect the tester and turn the ignition switch to the **OFF** position.

22. Install the luggage trim panel, if removed.

23. Lower the vehicle.

24. Road test the vehicle and check for proper operation.

COIL SPRING

1. Before servicing the vehicle, refer to the precautions in the beginning of this section.

2. Place a hoist under the rear axle housing and raise and safely support the vehicle.

3. Support the frame side rails with two jackstands.

➡ **If the vehicle is raised by the frame rails, place a jack under the rear axle housing.**

4. Remove the rear sway (stabilizer) bar.

5. Disconnect the lower studs of both rear shock absorbers from the mounting brackets on the axle tube.

6. Unsnap the parking brake cable from the upper arm retainer before lowering the axle housing.

7. Lower the axle housing until the coil springs are released. If the axle housing is supported by the hoist, lower the hoist allowing the rear of the vehicle to rest on the jackstands. If the vehicles axle housing is supported by the jackstands, leave the hoist stationary and lower the jackstands or raise the hoist to release the tension on the coil springs.

8. Remove the coil springs and insulators.

To install:

9. Position the coil spring in the upper and lower seats with an insulator between the upper end of the spring and frame seat.

10. Raise the axle housing and connect the lower studs of the shock absorbers to the mounting brackets.

11. Snap the parking cable into the upper arm retainer.

12. Install the sway bar.

13. Remove the jackstands.

14. Lower the vehicle.

15. Road test the vehicle and check for proper operation.

Upper Ball Joint

REMOVAL & INSTALLATION

1. Before servicing the vehicle, refer to the precautions in the beginning of this section.

2. If equipped with air suspension, the air suspension switch to the **OFF** position before raising the vehicle.

3. Raise and safely support the vehicle.

4. Place supports under both sides of the frame just behind the lower control arms.

5. Remove the wheel and tire assembly.

6. Place a floor jack under the lower control arm at the lower ball joint area. The floor jack will support the spring load on the lower control arm.

7. Remove the retaining nut and pinch bolt from the upper ball joint stud.

8. Mark the position of the alignment cams. When replacing the upper ball joint this will approximate the current alignment.

9. Remove the two nuts retaining the upper ball joint to the upper control arm.

10. Separate the upper ball joint from the upper control arm and spread the slot in the wheel spindle with a suitable prybar to remove the ball joint stud from the wheel spindle.

To install:

11. Place the upper ball joint to the upper control arm and insert the ball stud into the wheel spindle.

12. Install the upper ball joint pinch bolt and retaining nut. Tighten to 56–77 ft. lbs. (76–104 Nm).

13. Install the alignment cams to the approximate position at removal. If not marked, install in the neutral positions.

14. Install the two nuts retaining the upper ball joint to the upper control arm. Hold the cams and tighten the nuts to 107–129 ft. lbs. (145–175 Nm).

15. Remove the floor jack from under the lower control arm.

16. Install the wheel and tire assembly.

Tighten the lug nuts in a star pattern to 85–105 ft. lbs. (115–142 Nm).

17. Remove the supports.

18. Lower the vehicle.

19. If equipped with air suspension, turn the air suspension switch to the **ON** position.

20. Check and adjust the front wheel alignment.

21. Road test the vehicle and check for proper operation.

Lower Ball Joint

REMOVAL & INSTALLATION

1. Before servicing the vehicle, refer to the precautions in the beginning of this section.

2. If equipped with air suspension, the air suspension service switch to the **OFF** position before raising the vehicle.

3. Raise and safely support the vehicle.

4. Place supports under both sides of the frame behind the lower control arms.

5. Remove the wheel and tire assembly.

6. Remove the wheel spindle.

7. Remove and discard the ball joint boot seal.

8. Press out the ball joint using U-Joint Tool T74P-4635-C, Ball Joint Remover D89P-3395-A4 and Receiving Cup D84P-3395-A4, or equivalents.

To install:

9. When installing a new ball joint, the protective cover should be left on to protect the ball joint seal during installation. It may be necessary to trim the cover so it can pass through the installation tool.

10. Install the ball joint with Ball Joint Replacer D89P-3010-B, Receiving Cup D84P-3395-A4 and U-Joint Tool T74P-4635-C, or equivalents.

11. Discard the protective cover and be sure the new ball joint is fully seated in the lower control arm. ensure that the ball joint seal is not damaged.

12. Install the wheel spindle.

13. Install the wheel and tire assembly. Tighten the lug nuts in a star pattern to 85–105 ft. lbs. (115–142 Nm).

14. Lower the vehicle.

15. If equipped with air suspension, turn the air suspension service switch to the **ON** position.

16. Check the front end alignment.

17. Road test the vehicle and check for proper operation.

Use a ball joint press such as the one shown to remove the ball joint from the lower control arm

Use a ball joint press such as the one shown to install the new ball joint into the lower control arm

Turn to Section 6 for brake system applications

Wheel Bearings

ADJUSTMENT

The front wheel bearings are of a hub unit design and are pregreased, sealed and require no maintenance. The bearings are preset and cannot be adjusted. No adjustment is possible for the rear axle bearing. If either the front or rear bearings make noise or become loose, replacement is necessary.

REMOVAL & INSTALLATION

Front

➡ **Before continuing with this procedure, be sure that two new caliper mounting bolts, one sway bar link nut, one lower ball joint stud nut and one hub grease cap are available, per side. Once removed, these parts lose their torque holding ability or retention capability and must not be reused.**

1. Before servicing the vehicle, refer to the precautions in the beginning of this section.
2. If equipped, turn the air suspension service switch to the **OFF** position before raising the vehicle.
3. Raise and safely support the vehicle.
4. Remove the front wheel.
5. Remove grease cap from the hub.
6. Remove the disc brake caliper. Suspend the caliper with a length of wire. Do not let it hang from the brake hose. Discard the disc brake caliper mounting bolts.
7. Remove the disc brake rotor. If the factory installed push on nuts are installed, remove them first.
8. Remove the wheel hub retainer nut and discard.
9. Remove the hub and bearing assembly.

➡ **The wheel bearings are permanently greased and sealed. If replacement is necessary, the wheel hub and bearings must be replaced as an assembly.**

To install:

10. Install the hub and bearing assembly. Install a new wheel hub retainer nut and tighten to 189–254 ft. lbs. (255–345 Nm).
11. Install the disc brake rotor and push on nuts, if equipped.
12. Install a new grease cap seal.

Front hub and bearing assembly

13. Install the disc brake caliper using the two new disc brake caliper mounting bolts. Tighten the bolts to 125–170 ft. lbs. (170–230 Nm).
14. Install the wheel and tire assembly. Tighten the lug nuts in a star pattern to 85–104 ft. lbs. (115–142 Nm).
15. Remove the safely stands.
16. Lower the vehicle.
17. If equipped with air suspension, turn the air suspension switch to the **ON** position.
18. Pump the brake pedal several times to position the brake pads prior to moving the vehicle.
19. Check the front end alignment.
20. Road test the vehicle and check for proper operation.

Rear

1. Before servicing the vehicle, refer to the precautions in the beginning of this section.
2. Raise and safely support the vehicle.
3. Remove the wheel and tire assembly.
4. Remove the brake drum or brake rotor.
5. If equipped, remove the anti-lock brake speed sensor.
6. Clean all dirt from the area of the axle housing cover.
7. Place a suitable drain pan under the axle housing. Remove the axle housing cover retaining bolts and the cover, draining the axle lubricant from the housing.
8. Remove the differential pinion shaft lock bolt and the differential pinion shaft.
9. Push the flanged end of the axle shaft being removed toward the center of the vehicle and remove the C-lock from the button end of the axle shaft.
10. Pull the axle shaft from the housing, being careful not to damage the oil seal and anti-lock brake sensor ring, if equipped.
11. Insert Rear Axle Bearing Remover T85L-1225-AH or equivalent, in the axle housing bore and position it behind the wheel bearing so the tangs on the tool engage the bearing outer race. Remove the wheel bearing and seal as an assembly using a suitable impact slide hammer attached to the bearing remover tool.

To install:

12. Lubricate the new wheel bearing with rear axle lubricant. Install the wheel bearing into the axle housing bore using Axle Tube Bearing Replacer T78P-1225-A, or equivalent.

SPEED SENSOR

CALIPER ASSY

DISC BRAKE ADAPTER ASSY

PARKING BRAKE ASSY

SPEED SENSOR RING

AXLE SHAFT ASSY

DISC BRAKE ROTOR

7922RG34

Exploded view of the rear axle shaft assembly

13. Lubricate the lips of a new wheel bearing oil seal with wheel bearing grease.

14. Install the new wheel bearing seal using Axle Tube Seal Replacer T78P-1177-A, or equivalent.

➡**Check for the presence of an axle shaft O-ring on the spline end of the shaft and install, if not present.**

15. Carefully slide the axle shaft into the axle housing without damaging the bearing/seal assembly or anti-lock brake sensor ring, if equipped. Start the splines into the side gear and push firmly until the button end of the axle shaft can be seen in the differential case.

16. Install the C-lock on the button end of the axle shaft splines, then push the shaft outboard until the shaft splines engage and the C-lock seats in the counterbore of the differential side gear.

17. Insert the differential pinion shaft through the case and pinion gears, aligning the hole in the shaft with the lock bolt hole. Apply a suitable thread locking compound to the lock bolt threads and install in the case and pinion shaft. Tighten to 15–30 ft. lbs. (20–41 Nm).

18. Cover the inside of the differential case with a shop rag and clean the sealing surface of the axle housing and the axle housing cover. Remove the shop rag.

19. Apply a ⅛–³⁄₁₆ inch (3.18–4.76mm) wide bead of silicone sealer to the cover and install on the axle housing. Install the retaining bolts and tighten in a crisscross

DIFFERENTIAL PINION SHAFT

7922RG35

Removal of differential pinion shaft

pattern. Final torque the cover retaining bolts to 28–38 ft. lbs. (38–52 Nm).

➡**The axle housing cover must be installed and tightened within 15 min-** utes of applying the silicone sealer to **prevent leakage.**

20. Add the appropriate rear axle lubricant to the axle housing to a level ¼–⁹⁄₁₆

inch (6–14mm) below the bottom of the fill hole. If equipped with a limited slip differential, add 4 oz. (118.3 ml) of the appropriate friction modifier.

21. Install the axle housing fill plug and tighten to 15–30 ft. lbs. (20–41 Nm).

22. Install the anti-lock brake speed sensor, if equipped. Tighten the retaining bolt to 40–60 inch lbs. (4.5–6.8 Nm).

23. Install the brake calipers and rotors or the brake drums, as required.

24. Install the wheel and tire assembly.

25. Lower the vehicle.

26. Road test the vehicle and check for proper operation.

Removing axle shaft C-lock clips

GENERAL MOTORS CORPORATION—A BODY

Buick-Century • **Oldsmobile**-Cutlass Ciera • **Cutlass Cruiser**

PRECAUTIONS

Before servicing any vehicle, please be sure to read all of the following precautions, which deal with personal safety, prevention of component damage, and important points to take into consideration when servicing a motor vehicle:

- Never open, service or drain the radiator or cooling system when the engine is hot; serious burns can occur from the steam and hot coolant.

- Observe all applicable safety precautions when working around fuel. Whenever servicing the fuel system, always work in a well-ventilated area. Do not allow fuel spray or vapors to come in contact with a spark, open flame or excessive heat (a hot drop light, for example). Keep a dry chemical fire extinguisher near the work area. Always keep fuel in a container specifically designed for fuel storage; also, always properly seal fuel containers to avoid the possibility of fire or explosion. Refer to the additional fuel system precautions later in this section.

- Fuel injection systems often remain pressurized, even after the engine has been turned **OFF**. The fuel system pressure must be relieved before disconnecting any fuel lines. Failure to do so may result in fire and/or personal injury.

- Brake fluid often contains polyglycol ethers and polyglycols. Avoid contact with the eyes and wash your hands thoroughly after handling brake fluid. If you do get brake fluid in your eyes, flush your eyes with clean, running water for 15 minutes. If eye irritation persists, or if you have taken brake fluid internally, IMMEDIATELY seek medical assistance.

- The EPA warns that prolonged contact with used engine oil may cause a number of skin disorders, including cancer! You should make every effort to minimize your exposure to used engine oil. Protective gloves should be worn when changing oil. Wash your hands and any other exposed skin areas as soon as possible after exposure to used engine oil. Soap and water, or waterless hand cleaner should be used.

- All new vehicles are now equipped with an air bag system, often referred to as a Supplemental Restraint System (SRS) or Supplemental Inflatable Restraint (SIR) system. The system must be disabled before performing service on or around system components, steering column, instrument panel components, wiring and sensors. Failure to follow safety and disabling procedures could result in accidental air bag deployment, possible personal injury and unnecessary system repairs.

- Always wear safety goggles when working with, or around, the air bag system. When carrying a non-deployed air bag, be sure the bag and trim cover are pointed away from your body. When placing a non-deployed air bag on a work surface, always face the bag and trim cover upward, away from the surface. This will reduce the motion of the module if it is accidentally deployed. Refer to the additional air bag system precautions later in this section.

- Clean, high quality brake fluid from a sealed container is essential to the safe and proper operation of the brake system. You should always buy the correct type of brake fluid for your vehicle. If the brake fluid becomes contaminated, completely flush the system with new fluid. Never reuse any brake fluid. Any brake fluid that is removed from the system should be discarded. Also, do not allow any brake fluid to come in contact with a painted surface; it will damage the paint.

- Never operate the engine without the proper amount and type of engine oil; doing so WILL result in severe engine damage.

- Timing belt maintenance is extremely important! Many models utilize an interference-type, non-freewheeling engine. If the timing belt breaks, the valves in the cylinder head may strike the pistons, causing potentially serious (also time-consuming and expensive) engine damage. Refer to the maintenance interval charts in the front of this manual for the recommended replacement interval for the timing belt, and to the timing belt section for belt replacement and inspection.

- Disconnecting the negative battery cable on some vehicles may interfere with the functions of the on-board computer system(s) and may require the computer to undergo a relearning process once the negative battery cable is reconnected.

- When servicing drum brakes, only disassemble and assemble one side at a time, leaving the remaining side intact for reference.

- Only an MVAC-trained, EPA-certified automotive technician should service the A/C system or its components.

ENGINE REPAIR

Ignition Timing

ADJUSTMENT

The Engine Control Module (ECM) controls the ignition timing on these vehicles, no adjustment is possible or necessary.

Engine Assembly

REMOVAL & INSTALLATION

2.2L Engine

1. Before servicing the vehicle, refer to the precautions in the beginning of this section.
2. Disconnect the negative battery cable.
3. Drain the cooling system.
4. While supporting the hood, disconnect the hydraulic shock from the cowl pan and secure the hood in the fully open position.
5. Remove the air cleaner and air duct assembly.
6. Disconnect the control cables from the throttle body and remove the control cable bracket from the intake manifold and rocker arm cover. Set the assembly out of the way.
7. Disconnect and cap the fuel lines

from the throttle body and manifold mounting bracket.

8. Tag and disconnect any vacuum hoses that will interfere with engine removal.

9. Remove the upper and lower radiator hoses.

10. Disconnect the heater hoses from the intake manifold and water pump and secure out of the way.

11. Remove the torque strut.

12. Disconnect the engine harness connector.

13. Rotate the engine forward.

14. Remove the power steering pump from the engine and support out of the way with the power steering lines attached.

15. Disconnect the electrical connectors from the rear of the engine.

16. Remove the transaxle oil fill tube.

17. Remove the transaxle-to-engine bolts leaving in only the upper two bolts.

18. Rotate the engine to its normal position.

19. Raise and safely support the vehicle.

20. Remove the right front wheel assembly.

21. Remove the right inner fender well splash shield.

22. Disconnect the exhaust pipe from the exhaust manifold.

23. Remove the flywheel cover.

24. Disconnect and remove the starter.

25. Remove the engine mount-to-frame nuts.

26. Remove the torque converter-to-flywheel bolts.

27. Remove the A/C compressor from the mounting bracket and secure out of the way to the side without disconnecting the refrigerant lines.

28. Remove the front pipe support bracket from the transaxle.

29. Remove the transaxle support bracket from the transaxle and frame.

30. Lower the vehicle.

31. Remove the two remaining engine-to-transaxle mounting bolts.

32. Attach a suitable lifting device and slowly remove the engine. While lifting out the engine be sure that no hoses or electrical connectors are still attached.

To install:

33. Lower the engine into the vehicle and connect the engine to the transaxle.

34. Install the two upper engine-to-transaxle bolts. Tighten the bolts only until snug.

35. Raise and safely support the vehicle.

36. Install the transaxle support bracket and tighten the mounting bolts to 38 ft. lbs. (52 Nm).

37. Install the front exhaust pipe-to-transaxle mounting bolt.

38. Install the A/C compressor in the mounting bracket.

39. Install the torque converter-to-flywheel bolts and tighten to 46 ft. lbs. (62 Nm).

40. Install the engine mount-to-frame nuts and tighten to 33 ft. lbs. (45 Nm).

41. Connect and install the starter and tighten the mounting bolts to 33 ft. lbs. (45 Nm).

42. Install the flywheel cover.

43. Connect the exhaust pipe to the exhaust manifold and tighten the mounting bolts to 22 ft. lbs. (30 Nm).

44. Install the right inner fender well splash shield.

45. Install the tire and wheel assembly and tighten the lug nuts to 100 ft. lbs. (136 Nm).

46. Lower the vehicle.

47. Install the remainder of the engine-to-transaxle bolts and tighten all the bolts to 37 ft. lbs. (50 Nm).

48. Install the transaxle fill tube.

49. Connect the electrical connectors to the rear of the engine.

50. Install the power steering pump on the mounting bracket.

51. Connect the engine harness.

52. Install the torque strut and tighten the mounting bolts to 41 ft. lbs. (56 Nm).

53. Connect the heater hoses to the intake manifold and water pump.

54. Install the upper and lower radiator hoses.

55. Connect any vacuum hoses disconnected for engine removal.

56. Connect the fuel lines to the throttle body and fuel line brackets.

57. Install the throttle cable bracket on the intake manifold and rocker arm cover and connect the control cables to the throttle body.

58. Install the air cleaner assembly and air inlet duct work.

59. Connect the hood hydraulic shock to the cowl panel.

✳✳ WARNING

Operating the engine without the proper amount and type of engine oil will result in severe engine damage.

60. Refill the cooling system. An oil and filter change is recommended.

61. Connect the negative battery cable.

62. Start the vehicle and verify no leaks.

3.1L Engine

1. Before servicing the vehicle, refer to the precautions in the beginning of this section.

2. Relieve the fuel system pressure.

3. Disconnect the negative battery cable.

4. Scribe reference marks at the hood supports and remove the hood. Install covers on both fenders.

5. Remove the air cleaner assembly.

6. Drain the cooling system.

7. Remove the radiator hoses from the engine.

8. Remove the engine torque strut.

9. Remove the serpentine belt.

10. Remove the heater hoses.

11. Remove the throttle body bracket and cable.

12. Disconnect the fuel lines.

13. Tag and disconnect electrical connections, from the engine wiring harness and position the harness aside.

14. Tag and disconnect the vacuum lines, from the engine, to non-engine mounted components.

15. Disconnect the power steering lines.

16. Remove the power steering brace.

17. Remove the coolant reservoir.

18. Remove the two A/C compressor upper bolts.

19. Remove the electrical connections from transaxle.

20. Remove the electrical grounds from transaxle mounting bolts.

21. Remove the four transaxle top bolts.

22. Safely raise and support the vehicle.

23. Disconnect the front exhaust pipe from the manifold.

24. Remove the oil drip shield bolts and shield.

25. Remove the flywheel cover bolts and cover.

26. Disconnect and remove the starter motor.

27. Disconnect the electrical connection to the lower engine.

28. Remove the flywheel-to-converter bolts.

29. Remove the A/C compressor, position aside.

➡ Do not disconnect the A/C compressor lines when removing.

30. Remove the transaxle support bracket-to-transaxle bolts.

31. Remove the engine mounts.

32. Remove the two remaining transaxle bolts.

33. Lower the vehicle.

34. Attach a lifting device to the engine.

35. Carefully remove the engine assembly.

To install:

36. Install the engine assembly into vehicle with lifting device.

37. Start two transaxle-to-engine bolts.

38. Remove the lifting device and the transaxle support.

39. Safely raise and support the vehicle.

40. Install the remaining transaxle bolts and tighten them to 37 ft. lbs. (50 Nm).

41. Install the engine mounts.

42. Install the transaxle support bracket-to-transaxle bolts.

43. Properly position the A/C compressor.

44. Install the flywheel-to-converter bolts and tighten them to 47 ft. lbs. (63 Nm).

45. Install the flywheel cover and bolts. Tighten the bolts to 89 inch lbs. (10 Nm).

46. Install the electrical grounds to the transaxle mounting bolts.

47. Connect the lower engine wiring to the engine.

48. Install the oil drip shield and bolts.

49. Connect the front exhaust pipe to the manifold.

50. Safely lower the vehicle.

51. Install the four transaxle top bolts and tighten them to 37 ft. lbs. (50 Nm).

52. Connect the electrical grounds-to-transaxle mounting bolts.

53. Connect the upper engine electrical connections, to the engine.

54. Install the A/C compressor upper bolts.

55. Install the coolant reservoir.

56. Install the power steering brace.

57. Connect the power steering lines.

58. Connect all previously removed vacuum lines to the engine.

59. Connect the fuel lines.

60. Install the throttle body bracket and cable.

61. Install the heater hoses and secure with clamps.

62. Install the serpentine belt.

63. Connect the radiator hoses and secure with clamps.

64. Align the hood-to-hinge mating marks and install the hood.

65. Connect the negative battery cable.

66. Install air cleaner assembly.

✸✸ WARNING

Operating the engine without the proper amount and type of engine oil will result in severe engine damage.

67. Fill the coolant and engine oil.

68. Start the engine and allow it to reach normal operating temperature. Check for leaks and refill the cooling system.

Water Pump

REMOVAL & INSTALLATION

2.2L Engine

1. Before servicing the vehicle, refer to the precautions in the beginning of this section.

2. Disconnect the negative battery cable.

3. Drain the cooling system.

4. Loosen, but do not remove, the water pump pulley bolts.

5. Remove the serpentine belt.

6. Remove the alternator mounting bolts and set the alternator aside.

7. Remove the water pump pulley bolts and remove the water pump pulley.

8. Remove the four water pump mounting bolts, and remove the water pump.

To install:

9. Clean all gasket surfaces completely.

10. Apply a thin bead of sealer around the outer edge of the water pump gasket seating area and place the gasket on the pump.

11. Install the water pump on the engine and tighten the four mounting bolts to 18 ft. lbs. (25 Nm).

12. Install the water pump pulley and tighten the mounting bolts finger-tight.

13. Install the alternator in the mounting bracket.

14. Install the serpentine belt.

15. Tighten the water pump pulley mounting bolts to 22 ft. lbs. (30 Nm).

16. Connect the negative battery cable.

17. Refill and bleed the cooling system.

3.1L Engine

1. Before servicing the vehicle, refer to the precautions in the beginning of this section.

2. Disconnect the negative battery cable.

3. Drain the cooling system into a suitable container.

4. Loosen, but do not remove, the water pump pulley bolts.

5. Remove the serpentine belt.

6. Remove the water pump pulley bolts and remove the water pump pulley.

7. Remove the five water pump mounting bolts and remove the water pump.

1 GASKET, WATER PUMP
2 PUMP ASSEMBLY, WATER
3 BOLT/SCREW, WATER PUMP

7922SG01

Exploded view of the water pump mounting—2.2L engine

1 COVER ASSEMBLY, ENGINE FRONT
2 BOLT/SCREW, WATER PUMP
3 PUMP ASSEMBLY, WATER
4 GASKET, WATER PUMP

7922SG02

Exploded view of the water pump mounting—3.1L engine

To install:

8. Clean all gasket surfaces completely.

9. Apply a thin bead of sealer around the outside edge of the water pump along the gasket sealing area and install the gasket onto the water pump.

10. Install the water pump on the engine and tighten the water pump mounting bolts to 89 inch lbs. (10 Nm).

11. Install the water pump pulley and tighten the pulley bolts finger-tight.

12. Install the serpentine belt.

13. Tighten the water pump pulley bolts to 18 ft. lbs. (25 Nm).

14. Connect the negative battery cable.

15. Refill and bleed the cooling system.

Cylinder Head

REMOVAL & INSTALLATION

2.2L Engine

1. Before servicing the vehicle, refer to the precautions in the beginning of this section.

2. Disconnect the negative battery cable.

3. Relieve fuel system pressure.

4. Drain the cooling system.

5. Remove the air cleaner and air duct assembly.

6. Remove the air inlet resonator upper tie bar.

7. Remove the lower air inlet.

8. Remove the serpentine belt.

9. Remove the alternator.

10. Remove the power steering pump and position it aside without disconnecting the power steering lines.

11. Disconnect the spark plug wires and lay them out of the way.

12. Disconnect the control cables from the throttle body, and remove the cable bracket at the throttle body and rocker arm cover.

➡**Use care when removing valvetrain components. Parts to be reused must be returned to their original locations.**

13. Remove the rocker arm cover, rocker arm nuts, rocker arms and pushrods.

14. Disconnect the electrical connectors from the intake manifold, throttle body and cylinder head.

15. Disconnect the Oxygen (O_2S) sensor connector.

16. Remove the power steering pump

bracket from the intake manifold brace, located under the intake manifold.

17. Remove the torque strut and engine-side torque strut mounting bracket.

18. Remove the alternator rear bracket.

19. Tag and disconnect the vacuum lines at the intake manifold and cylinder head.

20. Disconnect the upper radiator hose from the engine.

21. Raise and safely support the vehicle.

22. Disconnect the exhaust pipe from the exhaust manifold.

23. Lower the vehicle.

24. Disconnect and cap the fuel lines at the quick disconnects.

25. Remove the transaxle fill tube.

26. Remove the cylinder head bolts.

27. Remove the cylinder head with both manifolds. Remove the intake and exhaust manifolds from the cylinder head.

To install:

28. Clean all gasket surfaces completely. Clean the threads on the cylinder head bolts and the block threads.

29. Install the intake and exhaust manifolds on the cylinder head.

30. Place a new cylinder head gasket in position over the dowel pins on the block. Carefully guide the cylinder head into position.

➡**New head bolts are recommended. Install all the cylinder head bolts finger-tight. The long bolts go in bolt positions 1, 4, 5, 8 and 9. The short bolt are in positions 2, 3, 6 and 7. The stud is in position 10.**

31. Install the cylinder head bolts, then tighten them in sequence. The long bolts to 46 ft. lbs. (63 Nm) and the short bolts and stud to 43 ft. lbs. (58 Nm). Make a second pass tightening the long bolts to 46 ft. lbs. (63 Nm) and the short bolts to 43 ft. lbs. (58 Nm). Make a final pass over all bolts tightening each an additional 90 degrees (¼ turn).

32. Install the transaxle fill tube.

33. Connect the fuel lines to the throttle body.

34. Raise and safely support the vehicle.

35. Connect the exhaust pipe to the exhaust manifold. Tighten the mounting bolts to 22 ft. lbs. (30 Nm).

36. Lower the vehicle.

37. Connect the upper radiator hose.

38. Connect the vacuum lines to the intake manifold.

39. Install the engine-side torque strut bracket and torque strut.

40. Install the alternator rear bracket.

41. Install the power steering pump

Timing belt service is covered in Section 5 of this manual

1 Long bolts
2 Short bolts
3 Stud
4 Numbers on gasket indicate torque sequence

7922SG03

Tighten the cylinder head bolts in the sequence shown for proper cylinder sealing and gasket crush—2.2L engine

bracket to the intake manifold brace, located under the intake manifold.

42. Connect the electrical connections at the intake manifold, throttle body and cylinder head.

43. Connect the O2S sensor connector.

44. Install the pushrods, rocker arms and rocker arm nuts and tighten the nuts to 22 ft. lbs. (30 Nm).

45. Install the rocker arm cover.

46. Connect the control cables to the throttle body and install the cable brackets at the throttle body and rocker arm cover.

47. Connect the spark plug wires.

48. Install the power steering pump in the mounting bracket.

49. Install the alternator.

50. Install the serpentine belt.

51. Install the lower air inlet duct.

52. Install the air inlet resonator tie bar.

53. Install the air cleaner and duct assembly.

54. Refill the cooling system.

➡An oil and filter change are recommended since coolant can enter the oil system when the head is being removed.

55. Connect the negative battery cable.

56. Start the vehicle and verify no leaks.

3.1L Engine

LEFT SIDE (FRONT)

1. Before servicing the vehicle, refer to the precautions in the beginning of this section.

2. Disconnect the negative battery cable.

3. Relieve fuel system pressure.

4. Drain the cooling system.

✳✳ CAUTION

When servicing the A/C system the correct tools and procedures must be used. Protective eye covering must be worn. DO NOT smoke or expose the refrigerant to any open flames or sparks.

5. Recover the A/C refrigerant using a refrigerant recovery and recycling station.

6. Remove the rocker arm covers.

7. Remove upper intake plenum and lower intake manifold.

8. Remove the exhaust crossover pipe.

9. Disconnect the spark plug wires from spark plugs and wire looms, and route the wires out of the way.

➡When removing valvetrain components use care to identify any components that will be reused. Valvetrain components must be kept in order for installation in the same locations from which they were removed.

10. Remove the rocker arms nut, rocker arms, balls and pushrods.

11. Remove the oil level indicator tube.

12. Remove any A/C compressor bolts accessible from the top.

13. Raise and safely support the vehicle.

14. Remove the lower A/C compressor mounting bolts.

15. Remove the refrigerant lines from the rear of the compressor.

16. Disconnect the A/C compressor electrical connections and remove the A/C compressor.

17. Remove the A/C compressor lower bracket bolts.

18. Lower the vehicle.

19. Remove the A/C compressor upper bracket bolts.

20. Remove the compressor brackets.

21. Remove the cylinder head bolts evenly.

22. Remove the cylinder head.

To install:

23. Clean all gasket surfaces completely. Clean the threads on the cylinder head bolts and block threads.

24. Place the cylinder head gasket in position over the dowel pins on the cylinder block so the words **THIS SIDE UP** or other gasket identification are showing.

25. Coat the bolt threads with sealer and install finger-tight.

26. Tighten the cylinder head bolts in sequence to 33 ft. lbs. (45 Nm). With all the bolts tightened, make a second pass tightening all the bolts an additional 90 degrees (¼ turn).

27. Install compressor bracket and tighten the upper bracket bolts to 35 ft. lbs. (47 Nm).

28. Raise vehicle and safely support.

29. Install the compressor lower bracket bolts and tighten to 35 ft. lbs. (47 Nm).

30. Connect the electrical connection to the rear of compressor.

31. Install the A/C compressor in the mounting bracket.

32. Connect the A/C lines to the rear of the compressor with NEW seals.

33. Install the compressor lower mounting bolts and tighten to 18 ft. lbs. (25 Nm).

34. Lower the vehicle.

35. Tighten the compressor upper mounting bolts to 18 ft. lbs. (25 Nm).

TIGHTENING SEQUENCE

7922SG04

Tighten the cylinder head bolts in the proper sequence to ensure good cylinder sealing—3.1L engine

36. Install the oil level indicator tube.

37. Install the pushrods, rocker arms, balls and rocker arm nuts. Tighten the rocker arm nuts to 20 ft. lbs. (27 Nm).

38. Connect the wires to the spark plugs and wire looms.

39. Install the exhaust crossover pipe.

40. Install the lower intake manifold and upper intake plenum.

41. Install the rocker arm covers.

42. Refill the cooling system.

43. Evacuate and charge the A/C system.

44. Connect the negative battery cable.

➡**An oil and filter change are recommended since coolant can enter the oil system when the head is being removed.**

45. Start vehicle and verify no leaks.

RIGHT SIDE (REAR)

1. Before servicing the vehicle, refer to the precautions in the beginning of this section.

2. Disconnect the negative battery cable.

3. Relieve fuel system pressure.

4. Drain the cooling system into a suitable container.

5. Remove the rocker arm covers.

6. Remove the upper intake plenum and lower intake manifold.

7. Disconnect the electrical connector from the ignition assembly.

8. Remove the alternator.

9. Remove the exhaust crossover pipe.

10. Disconnect the Oxygen (O$_2$S) sensor connector.

11. Raise and safely support the vehicle.

12. Disconnect the exhaust pipe from the exhaust manifold.

13. Lower the vehicle.

14. Remove the exhaust manifold.

15. Disconnect the spark plug wires from the spark plugs and wire looms, and route the wires out of the way.

➡**When removing valvetrain components use care to identify any components that will be reused. Valvetrain components must be kept in order for installation in the same locations from which they were removed.**

16. Remove the rocker arms nut, rocker arms, balls and pushrods.

17. Remove the cylinder head bolts evenly.

18. Remove the cylinder head.
    To install:

19. Clean all gasket surfaces completely.

Clean the threads on the cylinder head bolts and the bolt holes in the block.

20. Place the cylinder head gasket in position over the dowel pins on the cylinder block so the words **THIS SIDE UP** or other gasket identification is showing.

21. Coat the bolt threads with sealer and install finger-tight.

22. Tighten the cylinder head bolts in sequence to 33 ft. lbs. (45 Nm). With all the bolts tightened make a second pass tightening all the bolts an additional 90 degrees (¼ turn).

23. Install the pushrods, rocker arms, balls and rocker arm nuts. Tighten the rocker arm nuts to 20 ft. lbs. (27 Nm).

24. Install the exhaust manifold.

25. Raise the vehicle and support it safely.

26. Connect the exhaust pipe to the exhaust manifold.

27. Lower the vehicle.

28. Connect the O$_2$S sensor connector.

29. Connect the plug wires to the spark plugs and wire looms.

30. Install the exhaust crossover pipe.

31. Install the alternator.

32. Connect the electrical connector to the ignition assembly.

33. Install the lower intake manifold and upper intake plenum.

34. Install the rocker arm covers.

35. Refill the cooling system.

➡**An oil and filter change are recommended since coolant can enter the oil system when the head is being removed.**

36. Connect the negative battery cable.

37. Start the vehicle and verify that there are no leaks.

Rocker Arms

REMOVAL & INSTALLATION

2.2L Engine

1. Before servicing the vehicle, refer to the precautions in the beginning of this section.

2. Disconnect the negative battery cable.

3. Remove the air cleaner and air duct assembly.

4. Tag and disconnect the wires from the spark plugs, and disconnect the spark plug wire clips from the rocker arm cover and position aside.

5. Disconnect the throttle cables from

1. Bolt
2. Rocker cover
3. Gasket
4. Rocker stud
5. Flange, must be free of oil upon rocker cover gasket installation.
6. Pushrod
7. Rocker arm
8. Ball
9. Nut

7922SG05

The rocker arms are attached to the studs by means of a ball and nut—2.2L engine

the throttle body, and remove the throttle cable bracket from the intake plenum and move aside.

6. Remove the rocker arm cover bolts.

7. Remove the rocker arm cover.

➡**If any valvetrain components are to be reused, keep them in order. They should be installed in the same locations from which they were removed.**

8. Remove the rocker arm nut(s), ball(s) and rocker arms.
    To install:

9. Clean the gasket surfaces completely.

10. Coat the bearing surfaces of the rocker arm(s) and the rocker arm ball(s) with Molykote® or its equivalent.

11. Seat the pushrods in the lifters.

12. Install the rocker arm(s), ball(s) and nut(s) in the same positions from which they were removed, and tighten the rocker arm nut(s) to 22 ft. lbs. (30 Nm).

13. Install a new gasket in the cutout in the rocker arm cover.

14. Install the rocker arm cover on the cylinder head, and tighten the rocker arm cover bolts to 89 inch lbs. (10 Nm).

15. Install the throttle cable bracket on

the intake plenum, and connect the throttle control cables to the throttle body.

16. Connect the spark plug wire clips to the rocker arm cover, and connect the spark plug wires to the spark plugs.

17. Install the air cleaner and air duct assembly.

18. Connect the negative battery cable.

19. Start the engine and verify that there are no oil leaks.

3.1L Engine

1. Before servicing the vehicle, refer to the precautions in the beginning of this section.

2. Disconnect the negative battery cable.

3. For the left-hand cylinder bank, perform the following:

    a. Drain the cooling system to a level below the coolant pipe on the front of the engine.

    b. Remove the coolant bypass hose clamp at the coolant tube.

    c. Remove the two bolts and nut securing the coolant tube to the cylinder head, and position the tube out of the way.

4. For the right-hand cylinder bank, perform the following:

    a. Drain the cooling system into a suitable container.

    b. Remove the serpentine belt.

    c. Remove the alternator.

    d. Remove the alternator mounting bracket.

➡ **If any valvetrain components are to be reused, keep them in order. They should be installed in the same locations from which they were removed.**

5. Remove the four rocker arm cover bolts and remove the rocker arm cover.

6. Remove the rocker arm nut(s), ball(s) and rocker arm(s).

To install:

7. Clean all gasket surfaces completely.

8. Coat all valvetrain components with engine oil prior to installation.

9. Install the rocker arm(s) on the stud(s). Install the rocker arm ball(s) and mounting nuts. Be sure each pushrod is properly seated in its lifter and rocker arm.

10. Tighten the rocker arm nuts to 89 inch lbs. (10 Nm), then an additional 30 degrees.

11. Install the rocker arm cover using a new gasket and tighten the rocker cover bolts to 90 inch lbs. (10 Nm).

12. For the right-hand cylinder bank, perform the following:

    a. Install the alternator mounting bracket.

    b. Install the alternator.

    c. Install the serpentine belt.

13. For the left-hand cylinder bank, perform the following:

    a. Reposition the coolant tube and connect the thermostat bypass hose.

    b. Install the coolant tube mounting nut and bolts. Tighten the screw at the water pump to 106 inch lbs. (12 Nm), the bolt at the corner of the cylinder head to 18 ft. lbs. (25 Nm) and the nut to 18 ft. lbs. (25 Nm).

14. Refill the cooling system.

15. Connect the negative battery cable.

16. Start the vehicle and verify no oil or coolant leaks.

Intake Manifold

REMOVAL & INSTALLATION

2.2L Engine

These vehicles use a two-piece intake manifold. The upper half, sometimes called a plenum, contains the throttle body and control cable connections. The lower half has individual port runners to each intake port on the cylinder head. The lower half of the manifold bolts to the cylinder head and houses the fuel injectors. Note that these pieces are cast aluminum. Care should be exercised when working with any light alloy component.

1. Before servicing the vehicle, refer to the precautions in the beginning of this section.

2. Relieve the fuel system pressure.

3. Disconnect the negative battery cable.

4. Remove the throttle body air intake duct.

5. Drain the cooling system.

6. Identify, tag and disconnect all necessary vacuum lines.

7. Disconnect the control cables from the throttle body lever and remove the control cable bracket from the intake manifold.

8. Remove the serpentine belt.

9. Remove the power steering pump and lay it aside, without disconnecting the fluid lines.

10. Remove the transaxle fluid fill tube.

11. Identify, tag and disconnect the electrical connectors from the Manifold Absolute Pressure (MAP) sensor, Exhaust Gas Recirculation (EGR) solenoid valve, Idle Air Control (IAC) valve, Throttle Position (TP) sensor and fuel injectors.

12. Remove the MAP sensor.

13. Remove the upper intake manifold mounting bolts and the upper intake manifold.

14. Disconnect the fuel lines from the fuel rail.

15. Remove the EGR valve injector.

16. Remove the EGR valve.

1 Pushrod
2 Valve rocker arm stud
3 Valve rocker arm
4 Valve rocker arm pivot ball
5 Valve rocker arm nut

7922SG06

Rocker arms and related components—3.1L engine

INTAKE MANIFOLD NUT
TIGHTENING SEQUENCE

7922SG07

Lower intake manifold bolt tightening sequence—2.2L engine

1 **Bolt**
2 **Stud**
3 **Upper intake manifold assembly**
4 **Gasket**
5 **Lower intake manifold**
6 **EGR valve injector**
A **Upper intake manifold assembly tightening sequence**

7922SG08

Upper intake manifold bolt tightening sequence—2.2L engine

17. Remove the fuel injector retainer bracket, regulator and injectors.
18. Remove the control cable bracket.
19. Remove the six intake manifold nuts.
20. Remove the intake manifold.
To install:
21. Clean the gasket mounting surfaces.
22. Install a new gasket and position the lower intake manifold. Tighten the lower intake manifold nuts in the proper sequence to 24 ft. lbs. (33 Nm).
23. Connect the control cables and cable bracket.
24. Install the EGR valve.
25. Connect the fuel lines to the fuel rail.
26. Install the fuel injectors, regulator and injector retainer bracket and tighten the retaining bolts to 22 inch lbs. (3.5 Nm).
27. Install the EGR valve injector so that the port is facing directly towards the throttle body.
28. Install the upper intake manifold assembly. Tighten the upper intake manifold nuts in the proper sequence to 22 ft. lbs. (30 Nm).
29. Install the MAP sensor.
30. Connect the electrical connectors to the MAP sensor, EGR solenoid valve, IAC valve, TP sensor and the fuel injectors.
31. Install the transaxle fill tube.
32. Install the power steering pump.
33. Install the serpentine belt.
34. Connect the vacuum lines.
35. Install the air intake duct.
36. Connect the negative battery cable.
37. Refill the coolant system.
38. Start the vehicle and verify no coolant or vacuum leaks.

3.1L Engine

These vehicles use a two-piece intake manifold. These pieces are aluminum and care should be exercised when working with these components.
1. Before servicing the vehicle, refer to the precautions in the beginning of this section.
2. Disconnect the negative battery cable.
3. Relieve the fuel system pressure.
4. Remove the air cleaner assembly.
5. Remove the throttle cables from the throttle body and bracket.
6. Remove the fuel line retaining clamp from control cable bracket.
7. Remove the control cable bracket from the manifold.
8. Tag and disconnect the vacuum lines from the upper intake manifold.

Refer to Section 1 for engine rebuilding specifications

1. Manifold, lower intake
2. Gasket, upper intake manifold
3. Manifold, upper intake
4. Stud, upper intake manifold
5. Bolt, upper intake manifold

7922SG09

Exploded view of the upper intake manifold mounting—3.1L engine

1. Apply sealant
2. Head, cylinder
3. Gasket, lower intake manifold
4. Manifold, lower intake
5. Bolt, lower intake manifold
6. Bolt, lower intake manifold

7922SG10

Exploded view of the lower intake manifold mounting—3.1L engine

9. Remove the EGR valve.

10. Position the heater inlet pipe hose clamps out of the way.

11. Remove the rear ignition coil nuts.

12. Remove the front ignition coil bolts.

13. Remove the power steering line clip from the alternator brace.

14. Remove the alternator and brackets.

15. Disconnect the electrical connections from the throttle body.

16. Remove the upper intake manifold bolts and remove upper intake manifold with throttle body.

17. Remove the heater hoses from the upper intake manifold pipes.

18. Remove the fuel rail.

19. Disconnect the coolant hose.

20. Remove the power steering pump.

21. Remove the heater hose from the thermostat housing.

22. Remove the ignition coil.

23. Remove the engine mount strut.

24. Remove the valve covers.

25. Remove the lower intake manifold bolts.

26. Remove the lower intake manifold.

To install :

27. Clean all gasket material from mating surfaces. Then, clean all sealing surfaces with a degreaser product and blow dry with compressed air.

28. Apply a small bead (0.08–0.11 inch) of RTV sealer on each ridge where the intake manifold contacts the engine block.

29. Install the gasket and position the lower intake manifold into place.

30. Apply sealant, GM P/N 12345382 or equivalent to the threads of the manifold bolts.

➡ **When installing the manifold bolts, you must tighten the vertical bolts before the diagonal bolts. Failure to follow this may result in an oil leak.**

31. Tighten the manifold fasteners as follows:

  a. Hand-tighten the vertical bolts.

  b. Hand-tighten the diagonal bolts.

  c. Tighten the vertical bolts to 115 inch lbs. (13 Nm).

  d. Tighten the diagonal bolts to 115 inch lbs. (13 Nm).

32. Install the valve covers.

33. Install the engine mount strut.

34. Install the ignition coil.

35. Install the heater hose to the thermostat housing.

36. Install the upper radiator hose.

37. Install the power steering pump.

38. Install the alternator brackets.

39. Install the fuel rail and lines.

40. Install the gasket on top of the lower

intake manifold and place upper intake manifold into place.

41. Connect the coolant hoses to the manifold pipes.

42. Install the upper intake manifold bolts and tighten them to 18 ft. lbs. (25 Nm).

43. Connect the electrical connections to the throttle body.

44. Install the upper alternator brace and alternator.

45. Install the power steering line clip to the alternator brace.

46. Install the mounting nuts for the coil.

47. Properly position the heater inlet pipe hose clamps.

48. Install the EGR valve.

49. Connect the vacuum lines to the upper intake manifold.

50. Install the control cable bracket and return spring.

51. Install the fuel line retaining clamp to the control cable bracket.

52. Install the throttle control cables to the throttle body and bracket.

53. Install the air cleaner assembly.

54. Refill the coolant system.

55. Connect the negative battery cable.

56. Start the vehicle and verify that there are no leaks.

Exhaust Manifold

REMOVAL & INSTALLATION

2.2L Engine

1. Before servicing the vehicle, refer to the precautions in the beginning of this section.

2. Disconnect the negative battery cable.

3. Remove the air cleaner and air duct assembly.

4. Remove the lower air inlet duct.

5. Remove the engine drive belt.

6. Remove the alternator.

7. Remove the engine torque strut from the engine bracket and radiator support bracket.

8. Remove the torque strut bracket from the cylinder head.

9. Remove the alternator rear support bracket.

10. Raise and safely support the vehicle.

11. Remove the two bolts securing the exhaust pipe to the exhaust manifold.

12. Lower the vehicle.

13. Remove the dipstick tube mounting bolt and dipstick tube and dipstick.

14. Disconnect the electrical connector from the Oxygen (O_2S) sensor.

15. Remove the exhaust manifold mounting bolts.

16. Remove the exhaust manifold.

To install:

17. Clean all gasket surfaces completely.

18. Install the exhaust manifold and tighten the mounting bolts to 116 inch lbs. (13 Nm)—start on the center two ports and work outwards.

19. Connect the O_2S sensor electrical connector.

20. Install the dipstick tube and mounting bolt.

21. Raise and safely support the vehicle.

22. Connect the front exhaust pipe to the exhaust manifold, then tighten the mounting bolts to 18 ft. lbs. (25 Nm).

23. Lower the vehicle.

24. Install the alternator rear support bracket and tighten the three mounting bolts to 74 ft. lbs. (100 Nm).

25. Install the engine torque strut bracket to the engine and tighten the nuts to 41 ft. lbs. (56 Nm) and the bolt to 40 ft. lbs. (55 Nm).

26. Install the torque strut and tighten the through-bolts to 40 ft. lbs. (55 Nm).

27. Install the alternator.

28. Install the drive belt.

29. Install the lower air inlet duct.

30. Install the air inlet resonator to the upper tie bar.

31. Install the air cleaner and duct work.

32. Connect the negative battery cable.

33. Start the vehicle and verify no exhaust leaks.

3.1L Engine

LEFT SIDE (FRONT)

1. Before servicing the vehicle, refer to the precautions in the beginning of this section.

2. Relieve the fuel system pressure.

3. Disconnect the negative battery cable.

4. Drain the engine coolant.

5. Disconnect the electrical connectors and the heater hoses from the throttle body.

6. Remove the throttle body from the intake.

7. Disconnect the fuel lines and position aside.

8. Disconnect the coolant hose from the thermostat housing.

9. Remove the crossover pipe heat shield, then remove the crossover pipe.

10. Remove the engine torque strut.

11. If equipped with air conditioning, perform the following steps:

a. Recover the air conditioning refrigerant, using an approved recovery system.

b. Remove the serpentine belt cover and belt.

c. Remove the compressor front mounting bolts.

d. Remove the two bolts at the top of the compressor mounting bracket.

e. Raise and properly support the vehicle.

f. Disconnect the A/C lines from the rear of the compressor.

g. Disconnect the electrical connector from the compressor.

h. Remove the compressor rear mounting bolts.

i. Remove the compressor assembly from the vehicle.

j. Remove the mounting bracket lower bolts.

k. Remove the compressor mounting bracket.

l. Lower the vehicle.

12. Remove the exhaust manifold retaining nuts and manifold.

To install:

13. Thoroughly clean all gasket material from the manifold and cylinder head mating surfaces.

14. Install the exhaust manifold and retaining nuts. Tighten the retaining nuts to 18 ft. lbs. (25 Nm).

15. If equipped with air conditioning, perform the following steps:

a. Raise and properly support the vehicle.

b. Install the mounting bracket lower bolts and tighten to 35 ft. lbs. (47 Nm).

c. Position the compressor assembly in the mounting bracket.

d. Install the rear compressor mounting bolts and tighten to 18 ft. lbs. (25 Nm).

e. Connect the electrical connector to the compressor.

f. Using new O-rings, connect the A/C lines to the rear of the compressor. Tighten the mounting bolt to 24 ft. lbs. (35 Nm).

g. Lower the vehicle.

h. Install the front compressor mounting bolts and tighten to 37 ft. lbs. (50 Nm).

i. Install the two bolts at the top of the compressor mounting bracket and tighten to 35 ft. lbs. (47 Nm).

j. Install the serpentine belt and belt cover.

16. Install the torque strut and tighten to 39 ft. lbs. (53 Nm).

17. Connect the exhaust crossover pipe to the manifold and tighten the retaining nuts to 18 ft. lbs. (25 Nm).

18. Install the heat shield and tighten the bolts to 89 inch lbs. (10 Nm).

19. Connect the coolant hose to the thermostat housing and secure with retaining clamp.

20. Connect the fuel lines.

21. Install the throttle body to the intake manifold.

22. Connect the coolant hoses and electrical wiring to the throttle body.

23. Refill the engine coolant and bleed the cooling system as required.

24. Following proper procedures, evacuate and recharge the A/C system.

25. Connect the negative battery cable.

26. Start the engine and check for coolant, fuel, refrigerant, and exhaust leaks.

RIGHT SIDE (REAR)

1. Before servicing the vehicle, refer to the precautions in the beginning of this section.

2. Relieve the fuel system pressure.

3. Disconnect the negative battery cable.

4. Drain the engine coolant.

5. Disconnect the electrical connectors and the heater hoses from the throttle body.

6. Remove the throttle body from the intake.

7. Disconnect the fuel lines and position aside.

8. Disconnect the upper radiator hose from the thermostat housing.

9. Disconnect the EGR tube from the manifold.

10. Remove the crossover pipe heat shield, then remove the crossover pipe.

11. Disconnect the Oxygen (O_2S) sensor electrical connector and remove the sensor.

12. Remove the exhaust manifold upper heat shield.

13. Raise and properly support the vehicle.

14. Disconnect the front (converter) exhaust pipe at the manifold.

15. Remove the automatic transaxle dipstick and fill tube from the transaxle.

16. Remove the exhaust manifold lower heat shield.

17. Remove the exhaust manifold retaining nuts and manifold.

To install:

18. Thoroughly clean all gasket material from the manifold and cylinder head mating surfaces.

For engine torque specifications, refer to Section 1 of this manual

19. Install the exhaust manifold and retaining nuts. Tighten the retaining nuts to 18 ft. lbs. (25 Nm).

20. Install the manifold lower heat shield and tighten the bolts to 89 inch lbs. (10 Nm).

21. Install the transaxle fill tube and dipstick.

22. Connect the front exhaust pipe to the manifold assembly and tighten the bolts to 22 ft. lbs. (30 Nm).

23. Lower the vehicle.

24. Install the upper manifold heat shield and tighten the bolts to 89 inch lbs. (10 Nm).

25. Install the O2S sensor and connect the wiring.

26. Connect the exhaust crossover pipe to the manifold and tighten the retaining nuts to 18 ft. lbs. (25 Nm).

27. Install the crossover pipe heat shield and tighten the bolts to 89 inch lbs. (10 Nm).

28. Connect the upper radiator hose to the thermostat housing and secure with retaining clamp.

29. Connect the fuel lines.

30. Connect the EGR tube to the manifold.

31. Install the throttle body to the intake manifold.

32. Connect the coolant hoses and electrical wiring to the throttle body.

33. Refill the engine coolant and bleed the cooling system as required.

34. Connect the negative battery cable.

35. Start the engine and check for coolant, fuel and exhaust leaks.

Camshaft and Valve Lifters

REMOVAL & INSTALLATION

2.2L Engine

➡Please note that the engine must be removed from the vehicle for this procedure. Use care when disassembling valvetrain components. Any part that is to be reused must be returned to its original location. In addition, if the camshaft is being replaced, all new lifters must also be installed. Installing used lifters on a new camshaft will fail the new camshaft.

1. Before servicing the vehicle, refer to the precautions in the beginning of this section.

2. Disconnect the negative battery cable.

3. Relieve the fuel system pressure.

4. Remove the engine assembly from

1 LIFTER, VALVE ROLLER
2 ROD, PUSH
3 BOLT – 11 N·m (97 LBS. IN.)
4 BRACKET, ANTI–ROTATION
5 BLOCK, CYLINDER

7922SG28

Remove the lifters after removing the anti-rotation bracket—2.2L engine

the vehicle using the recommended procedure. Mount the engine assembly on a suitable engine stand.

5. Remove the serpentine belt.

6. Remove the serpentine belt tensioner assembly with the alternator attached.

7. Remove the strut bracket and the rear alternator bracket.

8. Remove the front engine mount bracket.

9. Remove the oil level indicator tube.

10. Drain the engine oil, then remove the oil pan.

11. Remove the crankshaft balancer and front cover.

12. Remove the timing chain and camshaft sprocket.

13. Disconnect the spark plug wires.

14. Remove the Camshaft Position (CMP) sensor.

15. Remove the rocker arm cover.

➡When removing the valvetrain components they must be kept in order for installation in the same locations from which they were removed.

16. Remove the rocker arm nuts, rocker arms, balls and pushrods.

17. Remove the power steering pump pencil brace.

18. Remove the cylinder head with the intake and exhaust manifolds attached.

19. Remove the anti-rotation bracket and the valve lifters. A magnet may be helpful when removing the lifters from the cylinder head. Be sure to keep the lifters in order. They must be returned to their original locations.

20. Remove the camshaft thrust plate mounting bolts and remove the thrust plate.

21. Remove the oil pump drive assembly.

22. Remove the camshaft carefully from the engine.

To install:

23. Coat the camshaft lobes with and bearings with GM Engine Oil Supplement (E.O.S.) part number 1051396 or equivalent camshaft break-in lube and insert the camshaft carefully into the engine.

➡If a new camshaft is being installed, be sure to install new lifters as well.

24. Install the oil pump drive assembly.

25. Install the thrust plate and tighten the mounting bolts to 106 inch lbs. (12 Nm).

26. Install the valve lifters in their original locations.

27. Install the anti-rotation brackets on the lifters. Tighten the bolt to 97 in. lbs. (11 Nm).

28. Install the cylinder head and manifold assemblies.

29. Install the power steering pump pencil brace.

30. Install the pushrods, rocker arms, balls and rocker arm nuts. Tighten the nuts to 22 ft. lbs. (30 Nm).

31. Install the rocker arm cover.

32. Connect the spark plug wires.

33. Install the CMP sensor.

34. Install the timing chain and camshaft sprocket. Verify that the camshaft and crankshaft sprocket timing marks are correctly aligned.

35. Install the timing chain front cover and crankshaft balancer.

36. Install the oil pan.

37. Install the oil level indicator tube.

38. Install the front engine bracket, rear alternator bracket and strut bracket.

39. Install the drive belt tensioner and alternator assembly and install the serpentine belt.

40. Install the engine assembly in the vehicle.

41. Install the oil filter and refill the engine with oil.

☀☀ WARNING

Operating the engine without the proper amount and type of engine oil will result in severe engine damage.

42. Connect the negative battery cable.

43. Refill the crankcase with the recommended engine oil and the cooling system with $^{50}/_{50}$ water/antifreeze mix.

44. Start the vehicle and verify that there are no leaks.

3.1L Engine

➡**Please note that the engine must be removed from the vehicle to perform this procedure. When removing valve-train components, any parts that are to be reused must be returned to their original locations. Lay all parts out in an orderly fashion and mark them for identification. In addition, if the camshaft is being replaced, all of the valve lifters must also be replaced with new parts. Installing used lifters on a new camshaft will quickly wear the camshaft.**

1. Before servicing the vehicle, refer to the precautions in the beginning of this section.

2. Relieve the fuel system pressure following the recommended procedure.

3. Disconnect the negative battery cable.

4. Remove the engine assembly.

5. Remove the intake manifold, valve cover, rocker arms, pushrods and valve lifters.

6. Remove the crankshaft balancer and front cover.

7. Remove the timing chain and sprockets.

8. Remove the oil pump driven gear mounting bolt and remove the oil pump driven gear.

9. Remove the two bolts and remove the camshaft thrust plate.

10. Carefully remove the camshaft. Avoid marring the camshaft bearing surfaces.

To install:

11. Coat the camshaft with lubricant GM part number 1052365 or equivalent camshaft break-in lubricant or quality engine oil supplement, and install the camshaft.

```
A   TIMING ALIGNMENT MARKS
24  SPROCKET, CRANKSHAFT
25  CHAIN, TIMING
50  BOLT, TIMING CHAIN DAMPER
51  DAMPENER, TIMING CHAIN
52  BLOCK, ENGINE
91  BOLT, CAMSHAFT SPROCKET
92  SPROCKET, CAMSHAFT
93  BOLT, THRUST PLATE
94  PLATE, THRUST
```

Exploded view of the camshaft and timing chain mounting—3.1L engine

7922SG29

➡ **If a new camshaft is being installed, be sure to install new lifters as well.**

12. Install the camshaft thrust plate and tighten the mounting bolts to 89 inch lbs. (10 Nm).

13. Install the oil pump driven gear and tighten the mounting bolt to 27 ft. lbs. (36 Nm).

14. Install the timing chain and sprocket.

15. Install the camshaft thrust button and front cover.

16. Install the crankshaft balancer and tighten the bolt to 76 ft. lbs. (103 Nm).

17. Install the intake manifold, valve cover, rocker arms, pushrods and valve lifters. Tighten the rocker arm bolts to 89 inch lbs. (10 Nm) plus 30 degrees.

18. Install the engine assembly.

19. Connect the negative battery cable.

20. Fill the crankcase with fresh oil.

21. Start the engine and verify that there are no oil leaks.

Valve Lash

ADJUSTMENT

The 2.2L and 3.1L engines are equipped with hydraulic lifters that do not require periodic adjustment. If the valves are making noise, inspect the pushrods, rocker arms and valve stem tips for excessive wear.

Oil Pan

REMOVAL & INSTALLATION

2.2L Engine

1. Before servicing the vehicle, refer to the precautions in the beginning of this section.

2. Disconnect the negative terminal from the battery.

3. Remove the air cleaner and air duct assembly.

4. Remove the serpentine belt.

5. Remove the engine torque strut.

6. Install engine support fixture J-28467-A, or a similar engine support fixture.

7. Raise and safely support the vehicle.

8. Remove the right front tire and wheel assembly.

9. Remove the right inner fender well splash shield.

10. Remove the flywheel cover bolts.

1 SEAL
2 BOLT, 10 N•m (89 LB. IN.)
3 OIL PAN
4 NUT, OIL PAN 10 N•m (89 LB. IN.)

7922SG30

Exploded view of the oil pan mounting—2.2L engine

11. Disconnect and remove the starter motor and starter bracket.

12. Remove the flywheel cover.

13. Remove the exhaust pipe and converter.

14. Remove the A/C compressor mounting bolts and set the compressor aside without disconnecting the refrigerant lines.

15. Remove the front engine mount nuts from the frame.

16. Remove the front engine mount bolts from the engine.

17. Lower the vehicle.

18. Raise the engine about 3 inches (76mm) using the support fixture.

19. Raise and safely support the vehicle.

20. Drain the engine oil.

21. Remove the front engine mount bracket.

22. Remove the oil pan mounting nuts and bolts.

23. Remove the oil pan.

To install:

24. Clean all gasket surfaces completely.

25. Apply a thin bead of sealer around the outside edge of the oil pan and on the corners of the end seals.

26. Position the oil pan gasket onto the sealer.

27. Install the oil pan onto the engine and loosely install all the fasteners.

28. Tighten the nuts and bolts to 89 inch lbs. (10 Nm).

29. Install the front engine mount bracket and loosely install the mount-to-engine bolts.

30. Lower the vehicle.

31. Lower the engine into place.

32. Raise and safely support the vehicle.

33. Tighten the front engine mount bolts.

34. Install the engine mount nuts to 33 ft. lbs. (45 Nm).

35. Install the A/C compressor in the mounting bracket and tighten to 37 ft. lbs. (50 Nm).

36. Install the exhaust pipe and converter.

37. Connect the starter and install the starter and support bracket.

38. Install the flywheel cover and cover mounting bolts.

39. Install the right fender well splash shield.

40. Install the right front tire and wheel assembly and tighten to 100 ft. lbs. (136 Nm).

41. Lower the vehicle.

42. Remove the engine support fixture.

43. Install the engine torque strut.
44. Refill the crankcase with oil.
45. Install the serpentine belt.
46. Install the air cleaner and air duct assembly.
47. Connect the negative battery cable.
48. Start the vehicle and verify no leaks.

3.1L Engine

1. Before servicing the vehicle, refer to the precautions in the beginning of this section.
2. Disconnect the negative battery cable.
3. Install engine support fixture J-28467-A or an equivalent engine support fixture.
4. Remove the engine mount strut bolt.
5. Raise and safely support the vehicle.
6. Drain the engine oil.
7. Remove the oil drip shield bolts and shield.
8. Remove the engine mount.
9. Remove the transaxle mount nuts.

10. Disconnect the exhaust pipe from the exhaust manifold.
11. Support the engine with an engine support fixture such as J-28467-A.
12. Lower the vehicle.
13. Place supports under the frame at the front and rear center crossmembers.
14. Loosen the rear frame bolts, but do not remove.
15. Remove the front frame bolts and lower front of frame.
16. Remove the front engine mount bracket bolts, bracket and mount.
17. Disconnect the electrical leads from the starter and remove the starter.
18. Remove the brackets from the oil pan.
19. Remove the oil pan retaining bolts and remove the oil pan.
20. If required, remove the oil deflector.
21. Clean all gasket mating surfaces.

To install:

22. Apply a small amount of RTV sealer on either side of the rear main bearing cap, where the seal surface on the cap meets the cylinder block.
23. If removed, install the oil deflector

and tighten the mounting nuts to 18 ft. lbs. (25 Nm).
24. Install the gasket and oil pan and hand-tighten retaining bolts.
25. After all bolts are hand-tight, tighten to 18 ft. lbs. (25 Nm). Tighten the side bolts to 37 ft. lbs. (50 Nm).
26. Install the electrical brackets to the pan.
27. Install the starter and connect the electrical leads.
28. Install the engine mount bracket and mount.
29. Install the front engine mount bracket bolts.
30. Raise the frame to the proper position. Using new bolts, tighten to 76 ft. lbs. (103 Nm).
31. Remove the supports.
32. Raise and safely support the vehicle.
33. Lower the engine to the correct position.
34. Install the exhaust pipe to the manifold.
35. Install the transaxle mount nuts.
36. Install the engine mount.
37. Install the oil drip shield.
38. Lower the vehicle.
39. Fill the crankcase with new engine oil.
40. Install the engine mount strut bolt.
41. Remove the engine support fixture.
42. Connect the negative battery cable.
43. Start the vehicle and verify no leaks.

Oil Pump

REMOVAL & INSTALLATION

2.2L Engine

1. Before servicing the vehicle, refer to the precautions in the beginning of this section.
2. Disconnect the negative battery cable.
3. Raise and safely support the vehicle.
4. Drain the engine oil.
5. Remove the oil pan-to-engine bolts and the oil pan.
6. Remove the oil pump-to-rear main bearing cap bolt, the oil pump and extension shaft.

To install:

❋❋ WARNING

Heat the extension shaft retainer in hot water prior to assembly. Be sure the retainer does not crack upon installation.

10 PAN, OIL
11 BOLT, OIL PAN SIDE
12 BOLT, OIL PAN RETAINING
52 BLOCK, ENGINE

7922SG31

Exploded view of the oil pan mounting—3.1L engine

Please refer to Section 9 for electric cooling fan wiring schematics

1 BRACKET
2 BOLT
3 OIL PUMP DRIVE ASSEMBLY
4 O-RING
5 SHAFT
6 RETAINER; HEAT AND WATER SOAK
  PRIOR TO INSTALLATION.
7 BOLT
8 OIL PUMP
9 CYLINDER BLOCK

7922SG13

Exploded view of the oil pump mounting—2.2L engine

7. Install the extension shaft, oil pump and pump-to-rear main cap bolt. Tighten the oil pump-to-bearing cap bolt to 32 ft. lbs. (43 Nm) and the upper oil pump drive bolt to 18 ft. lbs. (25 Nm).

> ❄ **WARNING**
>
> **To avoid engine damage, all oil pump cavities must be filled with petroleum jelly before installing the gears into the pump body. This seals the gears, acts like a prime and allows the pump to start drawing oil as soon as the engine begins to crank the first time after pump service. Also, only use original equipment gaskets. Gasket thickness is critical to proper oil pump operation.**

8. Install the oil pan and attaching bolts.
9. Lower the vehicle.
10. Fill the crankcase with clean engine oil.
11. Connect the negative battery cable.
12. Start the engine and check for proper oil pressure and for any leakage.
13. Turn the engine **OFF** and allow to stand. Check oil level, add as necessary.

3.1L Engine

1. Before servicing the vehicle, refer to the precautions in the beginning of this section.
2. Disconnect the negative battery cable.
3. Raise and safely support the vehicle.
4. Drain the engine oil into a suitable container.
5. Remove the oil pan.
6. Remove the crankshaft oil deflector bolts.
7. Remove the crankshaft oil deflector.
8. Remove the oil pump retaining bolts and remove the oil pump and pump driveshaft.

To install:

9. Install the oil pump and pump driveshaft. Tighten the oil pump mounting bolts to 30 ft. lbs. (41 Nm).
10. Install the crankshaft oil deflector and mounting bolts. Tighten the mounting bolts to 18 ft. lbs. (25 Nm).
11. Install the oil pan.
12. Lower the vehicle.

> ❄ **WARNING**
>
> **Operating the engine without the proper amount and type of engine oil will result in severe engine damage.**

14 BOLT/SCREW, OIL PUMP
15 PUMP, OIL
16 DRIVESHAFT, OIL PUMP
18 CAP, REAR CRANKSHAFT BEARING
19 PIN, OIL PUMP
52 BLOCK, ENGINE
240 BOLT/SCREW, OIL PUMP DRIVE
241 CLAMP, OIL PUMP DRIVE
242 SEAL, OIL PUMP DRIVE
243 DRIVE, OIL PUMP

VIEW A

7922SG12

Exploded view of the oil pump and related components—3.1L engine

13. Fill the crankcase to the correct level with oil.

14. Start the engine, check the oil pressure and check for leaks.

Rear Main Seal

REMOVAL & INSTALLATION

2.2L Engine

The transaxle must be removed from the vehicle to perform this service.

1. Before servicing the vehicle, refer to the precautions in the beginning of this section.

2. Disconnect the negative battery cable.

3. Remove the transaxle using the recommended procedure.

4. Remove the flywheel mounting bolts and remove the flywheel and retainer.

5. Remove the crankshaft seal by inserting a suitable pry tool in through the dust lip. Pry out the seal, moving the tool around the seal as required until is removed.

✳ WARNING

Care must be taken not to damage the crankshaft sealing surface with the prytool.

To install:

6. Coat the inside and outside of the new rear main oil seal with engine oil.

7. Install the new seal on tool J-34686 until the seal bottom is squarely against the collar of J-34686.

8. Align the dowel pin of J-34686 with the dowel pin hole in the crankshaft. Tighten the attaching screws to 45 inch lbs. (6 Nm).

DUST LIP

7922SG14

Carefully pry the oil seal from the rear of the block, do not damage the sealing surface of the crankshaft—all engines

9. Turn the handle of the tool until the collar is tight against the case. This will ensure the seal is fully seated.

10. Back the tool off and remove the attaching screws.

11. Install the flywheel and retainer and tighten the flywheel mounting bolts to 55 ft. lbs. (75 Nm).

12. Install the transaxle assembly using the recommended procedure.

13. Connect the negative battery cable.

14. Check the engine oil level and fill as necessary.

3.1L Engine

The transaxle must be removed from the vehicle to perform this service.

1. Before servicing the vehicle, refer to the precautions in the beginning of this section.

2. Disconnect the negative battery cable.

3. Remove the transaxle using the recommended procedure.

4. Remove the flywheel mounting bolts and remove the flywheel and spacer.

5. Using a small prybar, pry the seal from the block.

✳ WARNING

Be careful not to damage the crankshaft sealing surface when removing the oil seal.

6. Clean the seal mounting surface.

To install:

7. Coat the inside and outside of the new rear main oil seal with engine oil.

8. Install the new seal on tool J-34686 until the seal bottom is squarely against the collar of J-34686.

9. Align the dowel pin of J-34686 with the dowel pin hole in the crankshaft. Tighten the attaching screws to 45 inch lbs. (5 Nm).

10. Turn the handle of the tool until the collar is tight against the case. This will ensure the seal is fully seated.

11. Back the tool off and remove the attaching screws.

12. Install the flywheel and spacer. Tighten the flywheel mounting bolts to 61 ft. lbs. (83 Nm).

13. Install the transaxle assembly using the recommended procedure.

14. Connect the negative battery cable.

15. Check the engine oil level and fill as necessary.

Timing Chain, Sprockets, Front Cover and Seal

REMOVAL & INSTALLATION

2.2L Engine

1. Before servicing the vehicle, refer to the precautions in the beginning of this section.

2. Disconnect the negative battery cable.

3. Drain the engine coolant.

4. Remove the serpentine belt.

5. Remove the coolant reservoir.

6. Remove the front alternator mounting bolts.

7. Remove the three mounting bolts from the power steering pump. These bolts can be reached by going through the holes in the drive pulley on the pump. Lay the pump aside without disconnecting the hoses.

8. Remove the four tensioner mounting bolts, and remove the tensioner.

9. Raise and safely support the vehicle.

10. Drain the engine oil.

11. Remove the engine oil pan.

12. Remove the right front tire and wheel assembly.

13. Remove the right inner fender well splash shield.

14. Remove the crankshaft pulley.

15. Remove the crankshaft balancer.

16. Remove the front cover bolts and remove the front cover. If the cover is difficult to remove, use a soft-faced mallet to lightly tap the cover to loosen it.

17. Remove the crankshaft seal from the cover with a suitable seal driver.

18. Rotate the crankshaft until the piston in the No. 1 cylinder is at TDC on the compression stroke (firing position). The marks on the camshaft and crankshaft sprockets should be in alignment.

19. Loosen, but do not remove, the timing chain tensioner nut.

20. Remove the camshaft sprocket bolt and remove the sprocket and chain together. If the sprocket does not slide from the camshaft easily, a light blow with a soft mallet at the lower edge of the sprocket will dislodge it.

21. Use puller tool J-22888 or equivalent, and remove the crankshaft sprocket.

To install:

22. Install the crankshaft sprocket, using installation tool J 5590 or equivalent.

23. Install the timing chain over the camshaft sprocket, then around the crankshaft sprocket. Be sure that the marks on

1 BOLT
2 CAMSHAFT SPROCKET
3 BOLT
4 TENSIONER
5 BOLTS
6 CRANKSHAFT SPROCKET

A ALIGN TABS ON TENSIONER WITH
MARKS ON CAMSHAFT & CRANKSHAFT
SPROCKETS.

Exploded view of the timing chain components with timing mark alignment—2.2L engine

the two sprockets are in alignment. Lubricate the thrust surface with Molykote® or its equivalent.

24. Align the dowel in the camshaft with the dowel hole in the sprocket, then install the sprocket onto the camshaft. Use the mounting bolt to draw the sprocket onto the camshaft, then tighten to 77 ft. lbs. (105 Nm).

25. Lubricate the timing chain with clean engine oil. Tighten the bolts on the chain tensioner to 18 ft. lbs. (24 Nm).

26. Clean all gasket surfaces completely.

27. Install a new seal in the front cover using a suitable seal driver. Apply engine oil to the lip of the seal.

28. Apply a thin layer of sealer to the front cover and install a new gasket onto the cover.

29. Install the cover to the engine making sure the dowel pins line up with the holes in the front cover.

30. Install the cover mounting bolts and tighten them to 97 inch lbs. (11 Nm).

31. Install the crankshaft and pulley and tighten the pulley bolts to 37 ft. lbs. (50 Nm) and the center balancer bolt to 77 ft. lbs. (105 Nm).

32. Install the right side splash shield.

33. Install the tire and wheel assembly.

34. Install the oil pan.

35. Lower the vehicle.

36. Install the belt adjuster and tighten the bolts to 37 ft. lbs. (50 Nm).

37. Install the power steering pump and tighten the mounting bolts to 25 ft. lbs. (34 Nm).

38. Install the alternator mounting bolts, then tighten the upper bolt to 22 ft. lbs. (30 Nm) and tighten the lower to 37 ft. lbs. (50 Nm).

39. Install the coolant reservoir.

40. Install the serpentine belt.

41. Fill the engine crankcase with clean oil.

42. Refill the coolant system.

43. Connect the negative battery cable.

44. Start the vehicle and verify that there are no leaks.

45. Road test the vehicle and ensure proper operation.

3.1L Engine

1. Before servicing the vehicle, refer to the precautions in the beginning of this section.

2. Disconnect the negative battery cable.

3. Drain the cooling system into a suitable container.

4. Remove the right engine mount bracket.

A	TIMING ALIGNMENT MARKS	52	BLOCK, ENGINE
B	LOCATOR HOLE	91	BOLT, CAMSHAFT SPROCKET
24	SPROCKET, CRANKSHAFT	92	SPROCKET, CAMSHAFT
25	CHAIN, TIMING	93	BOLT, THRUST PLATE
50	BOLT, TIMING CHAIN DAMPENER	94	PLATE, THRUST
51	DAMPENER, TIMING CHAIN		

Exploded view of the timing chain mounting—3.1L engine

5. Remove the serpentine belt.

6. Remove the crankshaft balancer as follows:

    a. Raise and safely support the vehicle.

    b. Remove the right front tire and wheel assembly.

    c. Remove the right inner fender well splash shield.

    d. Remove the flywheel cover and install a flywheel holding tool.

    e. Remove the balancer mounting bolt and washer.

    f. Using a suitable puller, J-24420-B or the equivalent remove the balancer from the crankshaft.

7. Remove the serpentine belt tensioner mounting bolt and tensioner.

8. Remove the oil pan following the recommended procedure.

9. Remove coolant bypass pipe from the water pump and the intake manifold.

10. Disconnect the lower radiator hose from the front cover outlet.

11. Remove the front cover mounting bolts and remove the front cover.

12. Rotate the crankshaft until the timing marks on the camshaft and crankshaft sprockets are in alignment at their closest approach.

13. Remove the camshaft sprocket mounting bolt and remove the camshaft sprocket and timing chain.

14. Remove the crankshaft sprocket, using a gear puller J-5825-A or equivalent.

15. Remove the two mounting bolts from the timing chain damper and remove the damper.

To install:

16. Install the timing chain damper and tighten the mounting bolts to 15 ft. lbs. (21 Nm).

17. Install the crankshaft sprocket onto the crankshaft making sure the notch in the sprocket fits over the crankshaft key. Fully seat the sprocket on the crankshaft using J-38612, or an equivalent gear installer.

18. Be sure the timing mark on the crankshaft sprocket is pointing straight up.

19. Install the timing chain over the camshaft sprocket and hold the sprocket in such a way, that the timing mark is pointing down, and the timing chain is hanging down off the sprocket.

20. Loop the timing chain under the crankshaft sprocket and install the camshaft sprocket on the camshaft. The sprocket will only fit on the camshaft if, the dowel on the camshaft lines up with the hole in the sprocket.

21. Verify that the marks are aligned (the camshaft sprocket will be at the 6 o'clock position and the crankshaft sprocket will be in the 12 o'clock position).

22. Tighten the camshaft sprocket mounting bolt to 81 ft. lbs. (110 Nm).

23. Lubricate the timing chain components with engine oil.

24. Clean all gasket surfaces completely.

25. Apply a thin bead of sealer around the gasket sealing area of the front cover. Install a new front cover seal on the front cover.

26. Install the front cover on the engine and install the mounting bolts. Tighten the small bolts to 15 ft. lbs. (21 Nm) and the large bolts to 35 ft. lbs. (47 Nm).

27. Connect the radiator hose to the coolant outlet.

28. Install coolant bypass pipe to the water pump and the intake manifold.

29. Install the oil pan following the recommended procedure.

30. Install crankshaft balancer as follows:

    a. Coat the seal contact surface of the crankshaft balancer with clean engine oil.

    b. Line up the notch in the balancer with the crankshaft key and slide the balancer on until the key is in the balancer.

    c. Using J-29113 or an equivalent puller, seat the balancer on the crankshaft.

    d. Install the balancer mounting bolt and washer and tighten to 76 ft. lbs. (103 Nm).

    e. Install the flywheel cover.

    f. Install the right inner fender well splash shield.

    g. Install the tire and wheel assembly and tighten to 100 ft. lbs. (136 Nm).

31. Install the serpentine belt tensioner and tighten the mounting bolt to 40 ft. lbs. (54 Nm).

32. Install the serpentine belt.

33. Install the right engine mount bracket and tighten the bracket-to-mount bolts to 96 ft. lbs. (130 Nm).

34. Refill the cooling system.

35. Check the engine oil level and top off as necessary.

36. Connect the negative battery cable.

37. Start the vehicle and verify no oil leaks.

FUEL SYSTEM

Fuel System Service Precautions

Safety is the most important factor when performing not only fuel system maintenance but also any type of maintenance. Failure to conduct maintenance and repairs in a safe manner may result in serious personal injury or death. Maintenance and testing of the vehicle's fuel system components can be accomplished safely and effectively by adhering to the following rules and guidelines.

• To avoid the possibility of fire and personal injury, always disconnect the negative battery cable unless the repair or test procedure requires that battery voltage be applied.

• Always relieve the fuel system pressure prior to disconnecting any fuel system component (injector, fuel rail, pressure regulator, etc.), fitting or fuel line connection. Exercise extreme caution whenever relieving fuel system pressure to avoid exposing skin, face and eyes to fuel spray. Please be advised that fuel under pressure may penetrate the skin or any part of the body that it contacts.

• Always place a shop towel or cloth around the fitting or connection prior to loosening to absorb any excess fuel due to spillage. Ensure that all fuel spillage (should it occur) is quickly removed from engine surfaces. Ensure that all fuel soaked cloths or towels are deposited into a suitable waste container.

• Always keep a dry chemical (Class B) fire extinguisher near the work area.

• Do not allow fuel spray or fuel vapors to come into contact with a spark or open flame.

• Always use a back-up wrench when loosening and tightening fuel line connection fittings. This will prevent unnecessary stress and torsion to fuel line piping.

• Always replace worn fuel fitting O-rings with new. Do not substitute fuel hose or equivalent, where fuel pipe is installed.

Before servicing the vehicle, be sure to also refer to the precautions in the beginning of this section as well.

Fuel System Pressure

RELIEVING

1. Before servicing the vehicle, refer to the precautions in the beginning of this section.

2. Disconnect the negative battery cable

to avoid possible fuel discharge if an accidental attempt is made to start the engine.

3. Loosen the fuel filler cap to relieve the tank pressure.

4. Connect a suitable fuel pressure gauge to the fuel pressure test fitting. Wrap a shop towel around the fitting while connecting gauge to avoid spillage.

5. Place the bleed hose in an approved container and open the valve on the pressure gauge to relieve system pressure.

6. Dispose of the discharged liquid fuel promptly.

Fuel Filter

REMOVAL & INSTALLATION

1. Before servicing the vehicle, refer to the precautions in the beginning of this section.

2. Disconnect the negative battery cable.

3. Relieve the fuel system pressure.

4. Raise and safely support the vehicle.

5. Place a pan under the fuel filter.

6. Rotate each of the fuel filter quick-connect fittings ¼ turn to loosen any dirt trapped under the fittings.

7. Squeeze the plastic tabs on the male ends of the quick-connect fittings and disconnect the fuel lines from the filter.

8. Remove the filter bracket mounting bolt.

9. Remove the filter from the vehicle.

To install:

10. Install the filter assembly in position and install the filter bracket mounting bolt.

11. Apply a few drops of clean engine oil to the male ends of the fuel filter assembly and fuel line.

12. Snap the fuel lines onto the fuel filter. The lock tabs on the quick-connect fittings will lock in place. Give each line a light tug to be sure the fittings are tight.

13. Lower the vehicle.

14. Connect the negative battery cable.

15. Pressurize the fuel system and verify that there are no leaks.

Fuel Pump

REMOVAL & INSTALLATION

The fuel pump is located in the fuel tank. The fuel tank must be removed from the vehicle for this procedure. Note that the fuel pump has a strainer attached to reduce sed-

1 **FUEL SENDER**
2 **FUEL TANK**
3 **QUICK CONNECT FITTINGS**
4 **IN-PIPE FUEL FILTER BRACKET**
5 **FILTER BRACKET ATTACHING SCREW**

7922SG17

Typical fuel filter mounting

iment and debris that might enter the pump. These strainers may become clogged on high-mileage vehicles or when the vehicle has had contamination in the tank. A clogged strainer can keep the pump from drawing sufficient fuel to maintain enough fuel pressure to keep the engine running smoothly. Keep this in mind when troubleshooting a driveability and/or low fuel pressure complaint. This strainer should be replaced whenever the tank is removed for any kind of service.

1. Before servicing the vehicle, refer to the precautions in the beginning of this section.

2. Properly relieve the fuel system pressure.

3. Disconnect the negative battery cable.

4. Drain the fuel tank.

5. Disconnect the hoses, pipes and electrical connector from the fuel tank.

6. Support the tank and remove the two rear retaining strap bolts.

7. Remove the fuel tank.

8. Remove the fuel sender assembly locking cam using a spanner wrench, J-24187, or an equivalent.

9. Remove the fuel sender assembly from the fuel tank.

10. Place the sender assembly on a work bench with the fuel strainer facing up.

11. Note the direction the fuel strainer is facing and remove the strainer from the fuel pump by pulling it off the pump.

12. Disconnect the electrical connectors from the fuel pump.

13. Push the fuel pump toward the fuel outlet hose to unseat the pump from the lower mounting bracket. Once the pump is clear of the mounting bracket, tilt the bottom of the pump outward away from the mounting bracket.

14. Remove the plastic clamp on the

1 CAM
2 FUEL TANK
3 O-RING
4 FUEL SENDER

FRT

7922SG18

Fuel pump and sender assembly is located in the fuel tank

outlet line and disconnect the fuel pump from the outlet hose.

To install:

15. Connect the new pump to the outlet hose and install the plastic clamp.

16. Install the rubber insulator on the fuel pump.

17. Push the pump toward the outlet hose until the bottom of the pump can be seated in the mounting bracket.

18. Connect the electrical connectors to the fuel pump.

19. Install a new fuel strainer on the pump making sure the direction the strainer is facing is the same as on the old pump.

20. Install the fuel sender into the fuel tank using a new O-ring on top of the tank. It may help to lubricate the O-ring with silicone grease.

21. Install the locking cam and rotate into the locked position with a spanner wrench, J-24187, or an equivalent.

22. Position the fuel tank on the vehicle and install the retaining straps. Tighten the bolts to 25 ft. lbs. (34 Nm).

23. Connect the hoses, pipes and electrical connectors to the fuel tank.

24. Refill the fuel tank with gasoline.

Never attempt to test run a fuel pump dry, even for a short period of time. It is made to be immersed in fuel for both lubrication and cooling.

25. Connect the negative battery cable.

26. Pressurize the fuel system and verify no fuel leaks. This can be done by rotating the ignition switch to the **ON** position without starting the vehicle.

DRIVE TRAIN

Transaxle Assembly

REMOVAL & INSTALLATION

1. Before servicing the vehicle, refer to the precautions in the beginning of this section.

2. Disconnect the negative battery cable.

3. Remove the air cleaner assembly.

4. Remove the engine torque strut from the engine.

5. Remove the shift control cable bracket from the transaxle case and lever.

6. Disengage the electrical connector from the torque converter clutch solenoid.

7. Disconnect the Throttle Valve (TV) cable from the throttle bracket and transaxle.

8. Remove the upper transaxle bolts, including the grounds.

9. Install Engine Support Fixture J-28467-A or equivalent.

10. Raise and safely support the vehicle.

11. Remove the front tire and wheel assemblies.

12. Remove the engine splash shields.

13. Remove the pinch bolts from the control arms.

14. Remove the pinch bolt from the intermediate steering shaft.

15. Remove the stabilizer shaft bolts and reinforcement plates from the frame.

16. Remove the stabilizer shaft nuts and bracket from the control arm and separate the stabilizer shaft from the control arm.

17. Using a 7/16 in. drill bit, drill through two spot welds located between the front and rear holes of the left front stabilizer shaft mounting to separate the crossmember from the frame.

1 LOCATING DOWEL
2 BOLT/SCREW, TRANSAXLE
3 STUD, TRANSAXLE
4 TRANSAXLE ASSEMBLY

7922SG19

Transaxle-to-engine mounting bolt locations

For complete service labor times order Chilton's Labor Guide Manual

18. Remove the front and rear transaxle mounting nuts.

19. Disconnect the engine wiring harness from the frame.

20. Remove the power steering cooler line bolts.

21. Remove the right frame-to-left frame retaining bolt. Position a support under the frame for stability.

22. Loosen the two right frame mounts and discard the bolts.

23. Remove the two left frame bolts from the frame.

24. Remove the left frame with the aid of an assistant.

25. Disconnect the right lower ball joint from the steering knuckle.

26. Remove the transaxle support bracket bolts from the transaxle.

27. Remove the power steering cooler line support from the transaxle.

28. Remove the torque converter cover.

29. Remove the starter.

30. Remove the torque converter bolts.

31. Remove the transaxle mount bolts from the transaxle case and remove the mount.

32. Disconnect the transaxle range switch electrical connectors.

33. Remove both drive axles from the transaxle.

34. Disconnect the Vehicle Speed Sensor (VSS) from the transaxle.

35. Position transaxle jack under the transaxle.

36. Remove the oil cooler lines and plug openings.

37. Remove the remaining transaxle bolts.

38. Remove the transaxle.

To install:

39. Install the transaxle. Tighten the transaxle-to-engine bolts to 55 ft. lbs. (75 Nm).

40. Install the oil cooler lines.

41. Remove the transaxle jack.

42. Connect the VSS connector to the transaxle.

43. Install the drive axles.

44. Connect the transaxle range switch electrical connector.

45. Install the transaxle mount and mounting bolts to the transaxle case.

46. Install the torque converter bolts and tighten them to 47 ft. lbs. (63 Nm).

47. Install the starter motor.

48. Install the torque converter cover.

49. Install the power steering cooler line support to the transaxle.

50. Install the transaxle brace and the bolts to the transaxle.

51. Install the pinch bolts to the control arms.

52. Install the left frame with the aid of an assistant.

53. Tighten the frame bolts to 40 ft. lbs. (54 Nm).

54. Install the right frame bolts to the body and tighten them to 40 ft. lbs. (54 Nm).

55. Remove the support.

56. Install the right frame to the left frame retaining bolts, and tighten to 40 ft. lbs. (54 Nm).

57. Install the engine wiring harness to the frame.

58. Install the power steering cooler lines.

59. Install the transaxle rear mount nuts to frame and tighten to 39 ft. lbs. (53 Nm).

60. Install the left stabilizer shaft to the control arm.

61. Install the stabilizer shaft bolts and reinforcement plates to frame using support.

62. Install the steering shaft pinch bolt and tighten to 35 ft. lbs. (48 Nm).

63. Install the engine splash shields.

64. Install the front tire and wheel assemblies.

65. Lower the vehicle.

66. Remove the engine support fixture.

67. Install the three upper transaxle bolts and the ground wires to the engine and tighten to 55 ft. lbs. (75 Nm).

68. Connect the TV cable to the transaxle and throttle bracket.

69. Connect the torque converter clutch switch electrical connector.

70. Install the transaxle shift cable, mounting bracket and lever.

71. Install the engine torque strut.

72. Install the air cleaner assembly.

73. Connect the negative battery cable.

74. Start the vehicle and check transaxle oil level.

➡**Whenever the vehicle subframe is removed or lowered, the wheel alignment should be checked.**

75. Check the front end alignment and adjust as required.

76. Road test the vehicle and verify proper operation.

Halfshaft

REMOVAL & INSTALLATION

1. Before servicing the vehicle, refer to the precautions in the beginning of this section.

2. Raise and safely support the vehicle.

3. Remove the tire and wheel assembly.

4. Because the hub nut is torqued so tightly, the halfshaft must be kept from turning while the hub nut is being loosened. Insert a drift punch through the opening in the top of the caliper and down into the brake rotor cooling fins to keep the assembly from turning.

5. Remove the halfshaft nut and washer.

6. Remove the drift punch.

7. Remove the caliper mounting bolts and remove the caliper from the steering knuckle and support out of the way. Hang the caliper on a stiff piece of wire. DO NOT allow the brake hose to support the caliper.

8. Remove the brake rotor.

9. Remove the lower ball joint pinch bolt and separate the ball joint from the steering knuckle.

10. Separate the halfshaft from the hub bearing using J-28733-B, or an equivalent puller.

11. Pull the steering knuckle outward to slip the halfshaft out of the hub bearing.

12. Disconnect the halfshaft from the transaxle using GM Slide Hammer tools J-33008, J-29794 and J-2619–01 or an equivalent slide hammer.

To install:

13. If installing the right side halfshaft, install J-37292-B, or an equivalent halfshaft seal protector over the end of the CV-joint. The handle of the tool should be between 5 and 7 o'clock for ease of removal.

14. Seat the halfshaft into the transaxle until the inner lock ring locks in the transaxle. This can be checked by pulling lightly on the inner CV-joint body, not on the halfshaft, to be sure it stays seated in the transaxle. DO NOT pull on the halfshaft or the inboard joint could come apart, damaging internal components.

15. Remove the halfshaft seal protector by cutting it off and removing all pieces.

16. Seat the halfshaft into the hub bearing assembly. Be sure the splines engage smoothly. If the halfshaft will not engage smoothly, coat the internal splines on the hub bearing with grease.

17. Connect the lower ball joint to the steering knuckle and tighten the pinch bolt to 38 ft. lbs. (52 Nm).

18. Install the washer and halfshaft nut loosely.

19. Install the brake rotor.

20. Install the caliper over the steering knuckle and tighten the caliper mounting bolts to 38 ft. lbs. (52 Nm).

21. Insert a drift punch through the caliper opening and into the brake rotor cooling fins.

Knuckle

Outer CV Joint

Inner CV Joint

FRT

Adapter
Slide Hammer

FRT

7922SG20

A slide hammer with a special adapter is used to remove the halfshaft from the transaxle

22. Tighten the halfshaft nut to 103 ft. lbs. (140 Nm) plus 20 degrees additional rotation.
23. Remove the drift.
24. Install the tire and wheel assembly and tighten the wheel nuts to 100 ft. lbs. (140 Nm).
25. Lower the vehicle.

STEERING AND SUSPENSION

Power Rack and Pinion Steering Gear

REMOVAL & INSTALLATION

Models With 2.2L Engine

1. Before servicing the vehicle, refer to the precautions in the beginning of this section.
2. Disconnect the negative battery cable.

3. Install an Engine Support Fixture J-28467-A, or the equivalent.
4. Raise and safely support the vehicle.
5. Remove the tire and wheel assemblies.
6. Remove the intermediate shaft lower pinch bolt.
7. Disconnect the intermediate shaft from the stub shaft.

✳✳ WARNING

Failure to disconnect the intermediate shaft from the rack and pinion stub shaft can result in damage to the steering gear and/or intermediate shaft. This damage can cause loss of steering control, which could result in personal injury.

8. Remove the exhaust pipe hanger bracket near the rear of the frame, including the brake line retainer and rubber exhaust pipe hangers.
9. Remove the engine and transaxle mount nuts at the subframe.
10. Support the rear of the subframe.
11. Remove the rear subframe bolts and discard.

12. Lower the subframe for access to rack and pinion.

→**Do not lower rear of cradle too far as damage to engine components nearest to the cowl may result.**

13. Remove the cotter pins and castle nuts from the outer tie rod ends and separate the tie rod ends from the steering knuckles using a suitable puller.
14. Disconnect the power steering lines from the steering gear.
15. Remove the rack and pinion mounting bolts and nuts.
16. Remove the rack and pinion through left wheel opening.
To install:
17. Install the rack and pinion through left wheel opening.
18. Install the rack and pinion mounting bolts and nuts and tighten to 66 ft. lbs. (90 Nm).
19. Connect the power steering lines to the rack using new O-rings and tighten the fittings to 13 ft. lbs. (17 Nm) on the return line and 21 ft. lbs. (28 Nm). on the pressure line.
20. Install the power steering line clip to steering gear.

For complete service labor times order Chilton's Labor Guide Manual

1 STEERING GEAR
2 BUSHING
3 BOLT
4 NUT
5 NUT
6 COTTER PIN
7 SLEEVE

7922SG32

Rack and pinion steering gear mounting

21. Connect the tie rod ends to the steering knuckles. Tighten the castle nuts to 31 ft. lbs. (42 Nm). Install new cotter pins.

22. Raise the subframe into position and install new frame mounting bolts. Tighten the bolts to 103 ft. lbs. (140 Nm).

23. Remove the jack.

24. Install the engine mount and transaxle mount nuts and tighten to 39 ft. lbs. (53 Nm).

25. Install the exhaust pipe hanger bracket near the rear of frame, including brake line retainer and rubber exhaust pipe hanger.

26. Connect the intermediate shaft to the stub shaft and tighten the pinch bolt to 29 ft. lbs. (40 Nm).

27. Install the tire and wheel assemblies.

28. Lower the vehicle.

29. Remove the support fixture.

30. Connect the negative battery cable.

31. Refill the power steering reservoir and bleed the system.

➡the wheel alignment should be checked whenever the vehicle subframe is removed or lowered.

32. Check the front end alignment and adjust as necessary.

Models With 3.1L Engine

1. Before servicing the vehicle, refer to the precautions in the beginning of this section.

2. Disconnect the negative battery cable.

3. Remove the engine torque strut from engine.

4. Install Engine Support Fixture J-28467-A, or the equivalent.

5. Raise and safely support the vehicle.

6. Remove the tire and wheel assemblies.

7. Remove the cotter pins and castle nuts from the outer tie rod ends and separate the tie rod ends from the steering knuckles using a suitable puller.

8. Remove the center engine and rear transaxle mounts from the frame.

9. Remove the intermediate shaft lower pinch bolt.

10. Disconnect the intermediate shaft from stub shaft.

✳✳ CAUTION

Failure to disconnect the intermediate shaft from the rack and pinion stub shaft can result in damage to the steering gear and/or intermediate shaft. This damage can cause loss of

steering control, which could result in personal injury.

11. Remove the brace bolts and brace, including brake line brace.

12. Support the rear of the subframe with supports.

13. Remove the rear subframe bolts and discard.

14. Lower the subframe for access to rack and pinion.

15. Remove the steering gear heat shield.

16. Remove the clip holding lines at rack assembly.

17. Disconnect the power steering lines and O-rings.

18. Remove the rack and pinion mounting bolts and nuts.

19. Remove the rack and pinion unit through the left wheel well.

To install:

20. Install the rack and pinion through the left wheel opening.

21. Install the rack and pinion mounting bolts and nuts and tighten the mounting bolts to 66 ft. lbs. (90 Nm).

22. Connect the power steering lines to the rack using new O-rings and tighten the fittings to 13 ft. lbs. (17 Nm) on the return line and 21 ft. lbs. (28 Nm) on the pressure line.

23. Install the power steering line clip to the steering gear.

24. Install the steering gear heat shield.

25. Raise the subframe into position and install new frame mounting bolts. Tighten the bolts to 103 ft. lbs. (140 Nm).

26. Remove the supports.

27. Install the engine mount and transaxle mount nuts and tighten to 39 ft. lbs. (53 Nm).

28. Install the brace and bolts including the brake line brace.

29. Connect the intermediate shaft to the stub shaft and tighten the pinch bolt to 29 ft. lbs. (40 Nm).

30. Connect the tie rod ends to the steering knuckles. Tighten the castle nuts to 31 ft. lbs. (42 Nm). Install new cotter pins.

31. Install the tire and wheel assemblies.

32. Lower the vehicle.

33. Remove the support fixture.

34. Connect the negative battery cable.

35. Refill the power steering reservoir and bleed the system.

➡Whenever the vehicle subframe is removed or lowered, the wheel alignment should be checked.

36. Check the front end alignment and adjust as necessary.

Strut

REMOVAL & INSTALLATION

Front

1. Before servicing the vehicle, refer to the precautions in the beginning of this section.

2. Raise and safely support the vehicle.

3. Remove the tire and wheel assembly.

4. Remove the bolt securing the brake hose bracket to the strut and position the hose out of the way.

5. Matchmark the strut to the steering knuckle to preserve the camber setting when the strut is installed.

6. Remove the lower strut mounting nuts and through-bolts.

7. Remove the upper mounting nuts and remove the strut from the vehicle.

➡ **If the spring is to be removed, make a note of the orientation of the upper spring seat in relation to the strut assembly. When assembled, the seat must be installed in the same position.**

1. Front wheel drive shaft kit
2. Front suspension strut mount washer
3. Front suspension strut mount nut
4. Prevailing torque nut (M 12 x 1.75)
5. Front suspension strut bolt
6. Front suspension strut nut
7. Front suspension strut mount
8. Front spring seat
9. Front suspension strut bumper
10. Front suspension strut shield
11. Front spring upper insulator
12. Front spring

13. Front suspension strut
15. Front suspension strut washer
16. Steering knuckle
17. Front wheel inner bearing seal
18. Front wheel hub
19. Front brake splash shield
20. Front brake splash shield bolt
21. Steering bolt
22. Front wheel drive shaft washer
23. Front wheel drive shaft nut
24. Front brake rotor
25. Wheel bolt
26. Steering knuckle nut
27. Front brake caliper
28. Front caliper bolt

29. Front wheel drive shaft kit
30. Front lower control arm reinforcement
31. Front lower control arm reinforcement bolt
32. Washer flat (M 12.2 x 24 x 3.38)
33. Front lower control arm bolt
34. Front lower control arm
35. Front lower control arm ball stud kit

36. Front stabilizer shaft insulator
37. Front stabilizer shaft insulator clamp
38. Prevailing torque nut
39. Prevailing torque nut
40. Front lower control arm bushing
41. Front stabilizer shaft insulator
42. Front stabilizer shaft
43. Front suspension nut
44. Drivetrain and front suspension frame reinforcement
45. Drivetrain and front suspension frame bolt

Note: Bolt/screws must be installed in direction shown

7922SG33

Exploded view of the front suspension

2	WASHER, FRONT SUSPENSION STRUT	24	ROTOR, FRONT BRAKE
3	NUT, FRONT SUSPENSION STRUT MOUNT	34	ARM, FRONT LOWER CONTROL
5	BOLT, FRONT SUSPENSION STRUT	100	FRAME ASSEMBLY
13	STRUT, FRONT SUSPENSION	101	SHOCK TOWER
15	WASHER, FRONT SUSPENSION STRUT	43	NUT, FRONT SUSPENSION STRUT

7922SG21

Exploded view of the upper and lower strut mounting

7922SG22

Exploded view of the coil spring mounting and related components

8. To remove the spring from the strut, compress the spring using a good quality spring compressor until the spring is approximately ½ in. (13mm) away from the seat.

9. Hold the center shaft with a socket and remove the shaft nut with a line or crow's foot wrench.

10. Remove the bearing assembly, upper spring seat, bumper, shield, upper spring insulator and spring from the strut.

To install:

11. If the spring was removed, position the spring on the lower spring seat. Be sure the end of the spring is against the notch in the lower seat.

12. Install the upper spring insulator, shield, bumper, upper spring seat and bearing assembly.

13. Install the shaft nut on the strut shaft. Tighten the nut to 80 ft. lbs. (108 Nm).

14. Install the strut into the vehicle so the upper plate studs pass through the body. Install the mounting nuts loosely.

15. Install the lower strut bracket through-bolts. Install the mounting nuts and with the matchmarks in alignment tighten the nuts to 122 ft. lbs. (165 Nm).

16. Connect the brake line bracket to the strut and tighten the mounting bolt to 15 ft. lbs. (21 Nm).

17. Install the tire and wheel assembly.

18. Lower the vehicle.

19. Tighten the upper strut plate mounting nuts to 18 ft. lbs. (25 Nm).

20. Check the front end alignment and adjust as necessary.

Shock Absorber

REMOVAL & INSTALLATION

Rear

➡**If the vehicle is equipped with Super Lift® shocks, bleed the air out of the system before disconnecting the air lines.**

1. Before servicing the vehicle, refer to the precautions in the beginning of this section.

2. Raise and safely support the vehicle at a height where the upper shock plate mounting nuts in the trunk can be reached.

3. Support the rear axle with a jack.

4. Pull the trunk side trim away from the rear shock tower.

5. Remove the cap from the top of the shock and remove the two shock plate mounting nuts.

6. Disconnect the air line from the shock absorber, if equipped with Super Lift® shocks.

7. Remove the lower shock through-bolt and nut and remove the shock assembly from the vehicle.

8. Remove the center shock nut and washer, and remove the shock plate from the shock.

To install:

9. Install the shock plate on the new shock absorber and install the washer and mounting nut. Tighten the nut to 21 ft. lbs. (28 Nm).

10. Position the shock absorber in the vehicle so the upper plate studs line up with the holes in the shock tower. Loosely install the mounting nuts.

11. Install the lower shock through-bolt and nut and tighten to 50 ft. lbs. (72 Nm).

12. Remove the jack under the suspension and lower the vehicle.

13. Tighten the shock plate mounting nuts to 18 ft. lbs. (25 Nm).

14. Install the cap on the top of the shock and position the trunk side trim in place.

Coil Spring

REMOVAL & INSTALLATION

Front

Refer to the strut removal and installation procedure for the front coil spring procedure.

Rear

1. Before servicing the vehicle, refer to the precautions in the beginning of this section.

2. Raise and safely support the vehicle.

3. Support the rear axle with a suitable jack.

4. Remove the left and right side brake line bracket attaching screws and allow the brake lines to hang freely.

5. Remove the lower track arm bolt from the suspension and position the bar out of the way.

6. Remove the lower shock absorber mounting bolts.

7. Lower the rear axle.

8. Remove the coil springs and insulators.

10 BOLT/SCREW, REAR SHOCK ABSORBER
11 ABSORBER, REAR SHOCK
13 MOUNT, SHOCK ABSORBER UPPER
14 NUT, REAR SHOCK ABSORBER UPPER MOUNT
15 NUT, REAR SHOCK ABSORBER
28 BODY

7922SG23

Exploded view of the rear shock absorber mounting and related components

Turn to Section 6 for brake system applications

POSITION RIGHT HAND AND LEFT HAND REAR SPRINGS SUCH THAT THE LOWER PIGTAIL (END OF SPRING) IS POINTING TOWARD THE REAR OF VEHICLE.

7922SG24

Proper alignment of the rear springs

To install:

9. Install the springs and insulators in the vehicle and orient the springs so the lower spring ends point toward the rear of the vehicle.

10. Raise the rear axle into place and install the lower shock mounting bolts and nuts. Tighten the nuts to 53 ft. lbs. (72 Nm).

11. Connect the track arm to the suspension and install the mounting nut and bolt and tighten to 53 ft. lbs. (72 Nm).

12. Position the brake line mounting brackets and tighten the mounting bolts.

13. Remove the jack from under the suspension.

14. Lower the vehicle.

Lower Ball Joint

REMOVAL & INSTALLATION

1. Raise and safely support the vehicle under the frame so the control arm is unsupported.

2. Remove the tire and wheel assembly.

3. Remove the nut from the ball joint pinch bolt nut and remove the pinch bolt.

4. Loosen the stabilizer shaft at the lower control arm.

5. Pull the control arm down to disengage the ball joint stud from the steering knuckle.

6. Drill a pilot hole into each of the three ball joint rivets using a ⅛ in. drill bit.

7. Using a ½ in. drill bit, drill off the rivet heads.

8. With a hammer and punch, remove the remaining part of the rivets.

9. Remove the ball joint from the control arm.

To install:

10. Install the ball joint in the control arm and install the mounting nuts and bolts provided with the service kit. Tighten the nuts to the specifications in the service kit.

11. Connect the ball joint to the steering knuckle and install a new pinch bolt and nut. Tighten the nut to 38 ft. lbs. (52 Nm). If the replacement joint is supplied with a grease fitting, lubricate the ball joint with quality chassis grease.

12. Tighten the stabilizer shaft bracket bolts to 32 ft. lbs. (43 Nm).

13. Install the tire and wheel assembly and tighten the wheel nuts to 100 ft. lbs. (136 Nm).

14. Lower the vehicle.

Wheel Bearings

ADJUSTMENT

The front and rear wheel bearings on these vehicles are not adjustable. The wheel bearings are pressed into the hub assembly. If the wheel bearings are noisy or defective, the hub and bearing assembly must be replaced.

REMOVAL & INSTALLATION

Front

The front wheel bearings on these vehicles are not serviced separately. The wheel bearings are pressed into the hub. If the wheel bearings are noisy or defective, the hub and bearing assembly must be replaced.

1. Before servicing the vehicle, refer to the precautions in the beginning of this section.

2. Disconnect the negative battery cable.

3. Raise and safely support the vehicle.

4. Remove the front tire and wheel assembly.

5. Matchmark the lower strut bracket to the steering knuckle.

6. To keep the hub and rotor from turning when removing the axle nut, insert a drift punch through the caliper and into the brake rotor cooling fins to lock the assembly.

7. Remove the axle nut and washer. Remove the drift.

8. Remove the caliper mounting bolts and the caliper from the steering knuckle. support it out of the way. DO NOT allow the caliper to hang unsupported from the brake hose.

9. Remove the brake rotor.

10. Remove the three hub/bearing assembly mounting bolts and the backing plate.

11. If equipped, disengage the ABS speed sensor connector.

12. Using a puller, separate the axle from the hub bearing assembly. Remove the hub bearing assembly.

13. If the steering knuckle must also be removed, continue this procedure. Remove the cotter pin and castle nut from the outer tie rod end and using a steering linkage

1. Front wheel speed sensor connector
2. Front wheel speed sensor
3. Knuckle
4. Hub and bearing assy

7922SG27

Don't forget to disconnect the ABS sensor harness when removing the front hub assembly

puller, separate the tie rod from the steering knuckle.

14. Remove the strut mounting nuts and through-bolts.

15. Remove the ball joint pinch bolt and lift the steering knuckle off of the ball joint.

To install:

16. If removed, install the steering knuckle onto the lower ball joint and install a new pinch bolt and nut and tighten to 38 ft. lbs. (52 Nm).

17. Connect the steering knuckle to the lower strut bracket and install the through-bolts and nuts. With the matchmarks in alignment, tighten the nuts to 122 ft. lbs. (165 Nm).

18. Connect the tie rod end to the steering knuckle and tighten the castle nut to 30 ft. lbs. (41 Nm). If necessary to align the cotter pin holes tighten the castle nut up to 60 degrees additional. Install a new cotter pin.

19. Install the hub bearing onto the steering knuckle and position the backing plate. Be sure the ABS sensor is properly routed.

20. Install the hub bearing mounting bolts and tighten to 63 ft. lbs. (85 Nm).

21. Install the brake rotor.

22. Install the caliper onto the steering knuckle and tighten the mounting bolts to 38 ft. lbs. (52 Nm).

23. Insert a drift punch into the rotor cooling fins. Install the washer and axle nut onto the axle and tighten to 103 ft. lbs. (140 Nm) plus 20 degrees additional rotation.

24. Install the tire and wheel assembly.

25. Lower the vehicle.

26. Connect the negative battery cable.

27. Check the front end alignment and adjust as necessary.

Rear

The rear wheel bearings on this vehicle are not serviced separately. The wheel bearings are pressed into the rear hub. If the wheel bearings are noisy or defective, the hub and bearing assembly must be replaced.

1. Before servicing the vehicle, refer to the precautions in the beginning of this section.

2. Disconnect the negative battery cable.

3. Raise and safely support the vehicle.

4. Remove the tire and wheel assembly.

5. Remove the brake drum.

➡ **the backing plate assembly must be supported when the hub/bearing has been removed from the axle.**

6. Remove the four bolts securing the hub and bearing assembly to the axle.

7. Remove the hub and bearing assembly and support the backing plate.

8. Disconnect the rear ABS sensor.

To install:

9. Connect the ABS speed sensor.

10. Position the hub bearing assembly along with the backing plate onto the axle. Install and tighten the mounting bolts to 60 ft. lbs. (82 Nm).

11. Install the brake drum.

12. Install the tire and wheel assembly.

13. Lower the vehicle.

14. Connect the negative battery cable.

1. Rear sensor electrical connector
2. Sensor retaining bolts (4)
3. Sensor retaining nuts (4)
4. Bolt removal access hole
5. Drum brake assy
6. Rear integral bearing and speed sensor assy

7922SG26

Remove the hub mounting bolts through the large holes in the wheel mounting flange—rear hub assembly shown

For complete service labor times order Chilton's Labor Guide Manual

1 REAR SPRING UPPER INSULATOR
2 REAR SPRING
3 REAR SPRING LOWER INSULATOR
4 BOLT/SCREW, REAR AXLE TIE ROD BRACKET BRACE
6 BRACE, REAR AXLE TIE ROD BRACKET (WAGON)
7 NUT, REAR AXLE TIE ROD BRACKET BRACE
8 ROD, REAR AXLE TIE (TRACK BAR)
9 BOLT/SCREW REAR AXLE TIE ROD
10 BOLT/SCREW, REAR SHOCK ABSORBER
11 ABSORBER, REAR SHOCK
12 BOLT/SCREW, REAR AXLE TIE ROD BRACKET BRACE
13 MOUNT, SHOCK ABSORBER UPPER
14 NUT, REAR SHOCK ABSORBER UPPER MOUNT
15 NUT, REAR SHOCK ABSORBER
16 STUD, WHEEL

17 HUB AND BEARING ASSEMBLY, REAR WHEEL
18 BOLT/SCREW REAR WHEEL HUB AND BEARING
19 PLATE, REAR BRAKE BACKING
20 BUSHING, REAR SUSPENSION CONTROL ARM
21 NUT, REAR SUSPENSION CONTROL ARM BRACKET
22 BOLT/SCREW, REAR SUSPENSION CONTROL ARM BRACKET
23 BRACKET, REAR SUSPENSION CONTROL ARM
24 BOLT/SCREW, REAR SUSPENSION CONTROL ARM
25 AXLE, REAR
26 COVER, REAR SHOCK ABSORBER UPPER
27 BRACKET, REAR AXLE TIE ROD
29 NUT, REAR AXLE TIE ROD
30 DRUM, REAR BRAKE
31 INSULATOR, REAR STABILIZER SHAFT
32 CLAMP, REAR STABILIZER SHAFT INSULATOR

7922SG25

Exploded view of the rear suspension and related components

GENERAL MOTORS CORPORATION—B BODY

28

Buick-Roadmaster • **Cadillac**-Fleetwood • **Chevrolet**-Caprice • Impala SS

PRECAUTIONS

Before servicing any vehicle, please be sure to read all of the following precautions, which deal with personal safety, prevention of component damage, and important points to take into consideration when servicing a motor vehicle:

• Never open, service or drain the radiator or cooling system when the engine is hot; serious burns can occur from the steam and hot coolant.

• Observe all applicable safety precautions when working around fuel. Whenever servicing the fuel system, always work in a well-ventilated area. Do not allow fuel spray or vapors to come in contact with a spark, open flame, or excessive heat (a hot drop light, for example). Keep a dry chemical fire extinguisher near the work area. Always keep fuel in a container specifically designed for fuel storage; also, always properly seal fuel containers to avoid the possibility of fire or explosion. Refer to the additional fuel system precautions later in this section.

• Fuel injection systems often remain pressurized, even after the engine has been turned **OFF**. The fuel system pressure must be relieved before disconnecting any fuel lines. Failure to do so may result in fire and/or personal injury.

• Brake fluid often contains polyglycol ethers and polyglycols. Avoid contact with the eyes and wash your hands thoroughly after handling brake fluid. If you do get brake fluid in your eyes, flush your eyes with clean, running water for 15 minutes. If eye irritation persists, or if you have taken brake fluid internally, IMMEDIATELY seek medical assistance.

• The EPA warns that prolonged contact with used engine oil may cause a number of skin disorders, including cancer! You should make every effort to minimize your exposure to used engine oil. Protective gloves should be worn when changing oil. Wash your hands and any other exposed skin areas as soon as possible after exposure to used engine oil. Soap and water, or waterless hand cleaner should be used.

• All new vehicles are now equipped with an air bag system, often referred to as a Supplemental Restraint System (SRS) or Supplemental Inflatable Restraint (SIR) system. The system must be disabled before performing service on or around system components, steering column, instrument panel components, wiring and sensors. Failure to follow safety and disabling procedures could result in accidental air bag deployment, possible personal injury and unnecessary system repairs.

• Always wear safety goggles when working with, or around, the air bag system. When carrying a non-deployed air bag, be sure the bag and trim cover are pointed away from your body. When placing a non-deployed air bag on a work surface, always face the bag and trim cover upward, away from the surface. This will reduce the motion of the module if it is accidentally deployed. Refer to the additional air bag system precautions later in this section.

• Clean, high quality brake fluid from a sealed container is essential to the safe and proper operation of the brake system. You should always buy the correct type of brake fluid for your vehicle. If the brake fluid becomes contaminated, completely flush the system with new fluid. Never reuse any brake fluid. Any brake fluid that is removed from the system should be discarded. Also, do not allow any brake fluid to come in contact with a painted surface; it will damage the paint.

• Never operate the engine without the proper amount and type of engine oil; doing so WILL result in severe engine damage.

• Timing belt maintenance is extremely important! Many models utilize an interference-type, non-freewheeling engine. If the timing belt breaks, the valves in the cylinder head may strike the pistons, causing potentially serious (also time-consuming and expensive) engine damage. Refer to the maintenance interval charts in the front of this manual for the recommended replacement interval for the timing belt, and to the timing belt section for belt replacement and inspection.

• Disconnecting the negative battery cable on some vehicles may interfere with the functions of the on-board computer system(s) and may require the computer to undergo a relearning process once the negative battery cable is reconnected.

• When servicing drum brakes, only disassemble and assemble one side at a time, leaving the remaining side intact for reference.

• Only an MVAC-trained, EPA-certified automotive technician should service the A/C system or its components.

ENGINE REPAIR

Distributor

All models in this section use a distributor ignition system which was originally developed for use on the Corvette. The system known as the Opti-Spark ignition system consists of a distributor assembly which is mounted on the front engine cover, under the water pump assembly. The system consists of a distributor assembly, control circuitry and an external coil. In the Opti-Spark system, all ignition timing is controlled by the Powertrain Control Module (PCM) based on signals from the distributor's internally mounted optical camshaft position sensor. There is no way to bypass the PCM control or to adjust/set ignition timing on this system.

REMOVAL

1. Before servicing the vehicle, refer to the precautions in the beginning of this section.

2. Be sure the ignition is in the **OFF** or **LOCK** position, then disconnect the negative battery cable.

3 BOLT/SCREW, DISTRIBUTOR
29 BOLT/SCREW, DISTRIBUTOR CAP
30 CAP, DISTRIBUTOR
31 BOLT/SCREW, DISTRIBUTOR ROTOR
32 ROTOR, DISTRIBUTOR
33 COVER
34 SHIELD, DISTRIBUTOR
35 BASE, DISTRIBUTOR

7922TG01

Exploded view of the distributor assembly which is located under the water pump

3. Disengage the wiring harness from the engine cooling fan assembly, then remove the cooling fan from the vehicle.

4. Remove the block drain plug and the knock sensor, then drain the engine cooling system.

5. Remove the air intake duct and the air cleaner assembly.

6. Remove the coolant and heater hoses from the water pump assembly and the throttle body.

7. Unplug the wiring harness from the Engine Coolant Temperature (ECT) sensor, then reposition the ignition coil and bracket.

8. Remove the water pump assembly.

9. Remove the serpentine drive belt from the vehicle.

10. If not done already to remove the pump or the belt, raise and safely support the vehicle for access.

11. Remove the torsional damper bolts, then remove the damper from the crankshaft hub.

12. Disconnect the spark plug wires from the distributor. Be sure to twist each boot ½ turn and pull only on the boot to remove each wire. The wire numbers should be molded into the distributor housing. If

not, be sure to tag the wires before disconnection.

13. Unplug the 4-terminal PCM connector from the distributor.

14. Remove the distributor mounting bolts and pull the distributor forward until the driveshaft disengages from the engine. Mark the top of the shaft for alignment during reassembly.

INSTALLATION

1. Align the mark made on the distributor shaft and install the distributor. Tighten the distributor bolts to 8 ft. lbs. (11 Nm).

2. Install the 4-terminal PCM connector and the spark plug wires to the distributor.

3. Position the crankshaft damper to the hub, then install the damper bolts and tighten to 60 ft. lbs. (81 Nm).

4. Install the serpentine drive belt.

5. Install the water pump assembly and engage the ECT wiring harness.

6. Reposition the ignition coil and bracket, then install the coolant and heater hoses.

7. Install the air cleaner assembly and air intake duct.

8. Install the engine block drain plug and the knock sensor.

9. Install the cooling fan assembly, then connect the wiring harness.

10. Connect the negative battery cable and fill the engine cooling system.

11. Start and run the engine, then check for leaks.

Ignition Timing

ADJUSTMENT

When checking ignition timing NEVER pierce a secondary ignition wire. Use either a timing light with an inductive type pick-up or connect an adapter between the wire and the spark plug. If the secondary wire insulation is pierced, current will eventually arc and cause engine misfiring.

➡ **Some engines incorporate a magnetic timing probe hole for the use with electronic timing equipment. Be sure to consult the tool manufacture's instructions for the use of this equipment.**

On these vehicles, base timing is preset when the engine is manufactured. All timing changes are controlled directly by the Powertrain Control Module (PCM) based on information from the ignition and knock sensor systems. No adjustments are necessary or possible.

Engine Assembly

REMOVAL & INSTALLATION

Except Fleetwood Brougham

1. Before servicing the vehicle, refer to the precautions in the beginning of this section.
2. Disconnect the negative cable, then the positive cable from the battery.
3. Relieve the fuel system, then scribe alignment marks and remove the hood from the vehicle.
4. Remove the air cleaner assembly and drain the engine cooling system into a suitable container.
5. Remove the radiator hoses and upper fan shroud.
6. Remove the engine cooling fan, then remove the radiator from the vehicle.
7. Disconnect the heater hoses at the engine
8. Disconnect the power steering pump and air conditioning compressor brackets and position out of the way. Be careful not to kink or damage the fluid or refrigerant lines.
9. Disconnect the accelerator, Throttle Valve (TV), and cruise control cables.
10. Tag and disconnect all necessary vacuum hoses.
11. Disconnect the Powertrain Control Module (PCM) wiring harness, the engine wiring harness at the engine bulkhead, engine-to-bulkhead ground strap and any remaining wires between body and engine.
12. Remove the distributor assembly from the engine.
13. Remove the windshield wiper motor assembly.
14. Remove the Manifold Absolute Pressure (MAP) sensor.
15. Remove the negative battery cable from the cylinder head.
16. If not done already, remove the brake pipe from the intake manifold.
17. Raise and support the vehicle safely.

✵✵ WARNING

Never raise the engine using a jack under the oil pan, crankshaft pulley or any sheet metal. Because there only is a small clearance between the oil pan and the oil pump screen, if the pan is bent even slightly, damage could occur to the pump screen and pick-up unit.

18. Disconnect the battery positive cable and wires at the starter motor. Be sure to tag the wires for installation purposes.
19. Disconnect the crossover pipe and catalytic converter as an assembly.
20. Remove the flywheel cover and torque converter-to-flywheel bolts.
21. Remove the engine mount through-bolts.
22. Disconnect the front fuel hoses from the front fuel pipes.
23. Disconnect the transmission converter clutch wiring at the transmission and the transmission oil cooler lines at the clip on the oil pan.
24. Disconnect the equalizer rod from the transmission.
25. Remove the transmission-to-engine bolts.
26. Lower the vehicle.
27. Support the transmission and connect a suitable lifting device to the engine.
28. Remove the engine.

To install:

29. With the engine safely supported, lower into position and align with the motor mounts and transmission.
30. Install motor mount through-bolts and the transmission-to-engine bolts. Tighten either the nuts to 59 ft. lbs. (80 Nm) or the through-bolts to 70 ft. lbs. (95 Nm). Tighten the transmission-to-engine bolts to 35 ft. lbs. (47 Nm).
31. Raise and support the vehicle safely.
32. If applicable, connect the Air Injection Reaction (AIR) pipe to the exhaust manifold or the equalizer rod to the transmission.
33. Connect the transmission converter clutch wiring to the transmission and the transmission oil cooler lines to the clip on the oil pan.
34. Connect the front fuel hoses to the front fuel pipes.
35. Install the torque converter-to-flywheel bolts and the flywheel housing cover.
36. Connect the crossover pipe and catalytic converter assembly.
37. Connect the battery positive cable and wires to the starter motor.
38. Lower vehicle.
39. Connect the brake pipe to the intake manifold, then connect the negative battery cable to the cylinder head.
40. As applicable, install the EGR solenoid, the MAP sensor and the windshield wiper motor.
41. Install the distributor assembly.
42. Connect the PCM wiring harness, the engine wiring harness at the engine bulkhead, engine to bulkhead ground straps and all other wires between body and engine.
43. Connect all vacuum hoses as noted during removal.
44. Connect the accelerator, TV and cruise control cables.
45. Connect the power steering pump and air conditioning compressor brackets.
46. Connect the heater hoses to the engine.
47. Install the engine cooling fan.
48. Install the radiator, hoses and fan shroud.
49. Install the air cleaner assembly.
50. Install the hood, aligning the marks made during removal.
51. Connect the negative battery cable, then fill and bleed the engine cooling system.
52. Inspect vehicle fluid levels, specifications and verify there are no fluid leaks.

Fleetwood Brougham

1. Before servicing the vehicle, refer to the precautions in the beginning of this section.
2. Disconnect the battery cables and properly relieve fuel system pressure.
3. Mark the hood hinge outline for proper reassembly alignment and remove the hood. Remove the air cleaner assembly.
4. Drain the cooling system. Disconnect the radiator hoses. Disconnect the heater hose from the radiator. Disconnect and plug the transmission and engine oil cooler lines.
5. Remove the radiator cover and tie struts. Disconnect the fan shroud from the radiator assembly and position it aside. Remove the radiator from the vehicle.
6. Remove the serpentine drive belt. Remove the cooling fan assembly and the fan shroud from the vehicle.
7. Disconnect the heater hose at the rear of the intake manifold. Disconnect and plug the power steering hoses at the power steering gear.
8. Remove the air conditioning compressor and position it aside.
9. Disconnect the accelerator, cruise control and throttle valve cables from their mountings and position out of the way. Remove the vacuum pipe and fuel lines from the throttle body.
10. Remove the generator assembly. Disconnect the fuel line clips at the thermostat housing and air pump. Position the fuel lines aside. As required, remove the air pump assembly.

11. Disconnect and plug all required electrical connectors. Remove the distributor cap. Remove the negative battery cable from the cylinder head.

12. Raise and support the vehicle safely. Disconnect the crossover pipe at both manifolds.

13. Disconnect the starter electrical connectors and the positive battery cable. If necessary, remove the starter retaining bolts and remove the starter from the vehicle.

14. Remove the flywheel cover. Remove the torque converter to flywheel retaining bolts. Remove the motor mount through-bolts.

15. Disconnect the transmission oil cooler lines at the clip on the oil pan. Disconnect the oil pressure, knock and Oxygen (O$_2$S) sensor connectors. Remove the oil cooler hose shield.

16. Remove the ground wires from the rear of the cylinder head at both sides.

17. Remove the transmission-to-engine retaining bolts. Lower the vehicle.

18. Install the lifting equipment to the engine. Support the transmission properly.

19. Raise the engine slightly and pull it forward to disengage it from the transmission. Remove the engine from the vehicle.

To install:

20. Lower the engine assembly into the engine compartment; align the transmission bell housing dowels and motor mounts.

21. Loosely install two transmission-to-engine bolts.

22. Remove the engine and transmission supports.

23. Raise and safely support the vehicle, install the engine mount through-bolts and tighten to 70 ft. lbs. (95 Nm).

24. Route the wiring harness into its original location and reconnect the oil pressure, knock sensor and O$_2$S sensor connectors.

25. Reinstall the oil cooler line bracket and heat shield.

26. Connect the ground straps to the back of the cylinder heads.

27. Install and tighten all transmission-to-engine bolts to 55 ft. lbs. (75 Nm).

28. Install the starter assembly, if removed and/or reconnect the wiring. Clip the transmission cooler lines to the oil pan bracket.

29. Install the flywheel-to-torque converter bolts and tighten the bolts to 45 ft. lbs. (62 Nm). Install the flywheel cover.

30. Reconnect the exhaust and exhaust hangers. Tighten the crossover pipe bolts to 15 ft. lbs. (20 Nm).

31. Lower the vehicle.

32. Install the heater hose to the right rear of the intake manifold. Reconnect the throttle cable brackets and cables.

33. Install the distributor cap and coil wires.

34. Install the generator with wiring, but leave the rear brace disconnected. Connect the negative battery cable at the cylinder head.

35. Unplug and connect the power steering lines at the power steering gear.

36. Route the fuel lines and connect at the throttle body. Install the fuel line clips at the thermostat housing and the Air Injection Reaction (AIR) pump.

37. Connect the rear generator brace. Connect all vacuum hoses to the throttle body. Connect all electrical connections to the intake manifold and the throttle body.

38. Connect the AIR hose from the diverter valve to the converter.

39. Install the fan and fan shroud assembly.

40. Install the radiator assembly. Connect the transmission and oil cooler lines.

41. Connect the heater hose to the radiator tank and the radiator hoses.

42. Install the radiator cover and secure the fan shroud. Install the radiator tie struts.

43. Install the air conditioning compressor and serpentine belt. Install the air cleaner assembly.

44. Fill the cooling system and connect the battery cables.

45. Check all fluid levels, start engine and inspect for leaks.

46. Align the marks made earlier and install the hood assembly.

Water Pump

REMOVAL & INSTALLATION

1. Before servicing the vehicle, refer to the precautions in the beginning of this section.

2. Disconnect the negative battery cable.

3. Disengage the wiring harness from the cooling fan assembly, then remove the assembly from the vehicle.

4. Drain the engine cooling system, removing the block drain plug and the knock sensor to assure proper draining. Reinstall the drain plug and knock sensor, as soon as the system is empty.

5. Disconnect the upper and lower radiator hoses from the water pump assembly.

6. Remove the heater hose assemblies from the water pump and from the throttle body.

7. Disengage the coolant sensor wiring harness, then reposition the ignition coil and bracket assembly.

8. Remove the shorter water pump retaining bolt from the center of each pump

1. Water pump assembly
2. Water pump gasket
3. Shaft coupling
4. Water pump cover bolt, 33 LB FT (45 NM)
5. Water pump bolt, 31 LB FT (42 NM)

Exploded view of the water pump assembly mounting

7922TG02

Timing belt service is covered in Section 5 of this manual

mating flange, then remove the longer pump bolts from either side of the center bolts.

9. Carefully remove the water pump assembly and gaskets along with the pump shaft coupling.

To install:

10. Thoroughly clean the gasket mating surfaces of any remaining gasket material.

11. Install the water pump shaft coupling along with the water pump and gaskets.

12. Install the longer pump bolts and tighten 33 ft. lbs. (45 Nm), then install the shorter bolts and tighten to 31 ft. lbs. (42 Nm).

13. Reposition the ignition coil and bracket assembly.

14. Engage the coolant sensor electrical connector.

15. Install the heater and radiator hoses to the throttle body and water pump, as applicable.

16. Install the air cleaner and intake duct assemblies.

17. Install the engine cooling fan assembly and engage the wiring harness connector.

18. Connect the negative battery cable and properly fill the engine cooling system.

Cylinder Head

REMOVAL & INSTALLATION

Left Side

1. Before servicing the vehicle, refer to the precautions in the beginning of this section.

2. Disconnect the negative battery cable, then raise and support the vehicle safely.

3. Drain the engine cooling system, then disconnect the crossover pipe from the exhaust manifold.

4. Lower the vehicle.

5. Remove the intake manifold assembly.

6. Disconnect the secondary air injection hose from the check valve assembly.

7. Disconnect the coolant air bleed pipe and bolt from the left cylinder head assembly using a back-up wrench on the pipe fitting.

8. Remove the ignition coil assembly.

9. Remove the left exhaust manifold assembly.

10. Remove the spark plug wiring harness assembly from the clips, then disconnect the harness from the spark plugs and remove the plugs from the left cylinder head.

11. Disengage the coolant temperature sensor connector.

12. Remove the left rocker arm cover.

13. Loosen the rocker arm nuts, then remove the arms and pushrods, either tagging or arranging the components to assure installation in their original locations.

14. Remove the cylinder head bolts, then remove the cylinder head and gasket from the block.

To install:

15. Thoroughly clean the gasket mating surfaces of any remaining gasket material, then position a new cylinder head gasket on the block with the yellow tab facing upwards.

16. Install the cylinder head over the locator pins and the new gasket.

17. Coat the cylinder head bolts with a sealing compound, then install the bolts finger-tight.

18. Tighten the bolts using three passes of the proper sequence until all bolts have been tightened to 65 ft. lbs. (88 Nm).

19. Install the pushrods and rocker arms, making sure they are in the proper locations, then adjust the valve lash.

20. Install the left rocker arm cover and tighten the retaining bolts to 100 inch lbs. (11 Nm).

21. Install the spark plugs and tighten to 11 ft. lbs. (15 Nm), then install the wiring harness assembly and secure the assembly to the clips.

22. Install the left exhaust manifold assembly.

23. Install the ignition coil assembly and tighten the bolts to 24 ft. lbs. (33 Nm).

24. Connect the engine coolant air bleed pipe and bolt to the left cylinder head assembly using a back-up wrench on the pipe fitting in order to prevent component damage. Tighten the bolt to 30 ft. lbs. (40 Nm).

25. Install the secondary air injector hose to the check valve assembly.

26. Install the intake manifold assembly.

27. Raise and support the vehicle safely, then connect the crossover pipe to the exhaust manifold.

28. Lower the vehicle and fill the engine cooling system.

29. Connect, then negative battery cable.

Right Side

1. Before servicing the vehicle, refer to the precautions in the beginning of this section.

2. Disconnect the negative battery cable.

3. Raise and support the vehicle safely, then drain the engine cooling system.

4. Remove the serpentine drive belt and the belt tensioner assembly.

5. Remove the transmission fluid level indicator tube assembly bracket from the transmission housing.

6. Remove the air conditioning compressor rear brace bolt from the engine block, then disengage the compressor connector.

7. Remove the front compressor mounting bolts, then position the compressor aside taking care not to kink or damage the lines.

8. Remove the right exhaust manifold assembly.

A. V8 cylinder head
B. V6 cylinder head

7922TG03

Cylinder head bolt torque sequences

9. Lower the vehicle.

10. Remove the alternator assembly.

11. Remove the right rocker arm cover.

12. Remove the intake manifold assembly.

13. Remove the coolant air bleed pipe bolt from the left cylinder head assembly.

14. Disconnect the lower radiator hose and the heater hose from the water pump assembly, then position the hoses aside.

15. Remove the coolant air bleed pipe hose from the radiator.

16. Remove the power steering pump assembly.

17. Remove the engine accessory bracket bolts, then remove the bracket assembly.

18. Disconnect the wiring harness assembly from the spark plugs, then remove the plugs from the right cylinder head.

19. Loosen the rocker arm nuts, then remove the arms and pushrods, either tagging or arranging the components to assure installation in their original locations.

20. Remove the cylinder head bolts, then remove the cylinder head and gasket from the block. If necessary, carefully remove the coolant air bleed pipe bolt and pipe assembly from the cylinder head.

To install:

21. If removed, loosely install the coolant air bleed pipe bolt and pipe to the cylinder head.

22. Thoroughly clean the gasket mating surfaces of any remaining gasket material, then position a new cylinder head gasket on the block with the yellow tab facing upwards.

23. Install the cylinder head over the locator pins and the new gasket.

24. Coat the cylinder head bolts with a sealing compound, then install the bolts finger-tight.

25. Tighten the bolts using three passes of the proper sequence until all bolts have been tightened to 65 ft. lbs. (88 Nm).

26. If loosened, tighten the coolant air bleed pipe bolt to 30 ft. lbs. (40 Nm).

27. Install the pushrods and rocker arms, making sure they are in the proper locations, then adjust the valve lash.

28. Install the spark plugs and tighten to 11 ft. lbs. (15 Nm), then install the wiring harness assembly to the plugs.

29. Install the engine accessory bracket and tighten the retaining bolts to 31 ft. lbs. (42 Nm).

30. Install the right rocker arm cover and tighten the retaining bolts to 100 inch lbs. (11 Nm).

31. Install the alternator assembly.

32. Install the power steering pump assembly.

33. Connect the coolant air bleed pipe hose to the radiator, then connect the heater hose and the lower radiator hose to the water pump.

34. Connect the coolant air bleed pipe bolt to the left cylinder head and tighten to 30 ft. lbs. (41 Nm) while using a back-up wrench to prevent component damage.

35. Install the intake manifold assembly.

36. Raise and support the vehicle safely.

37. Install the right exhaust manifold assembly.

38. Position the compressor and install the front mounting bolts, then engage the electrical connector. Install the rear compressor brace bolt and tighten to 24 ft. lbs. (33 Nm).

39. Install the transmission fluid level indicator tube assembly to the transmission housing.

40. Install the serpentine drive belt, then lower the vehicle.

41. Fill the engine cooling system, then connect the negative battery cable.

Rocker Arms

REMOVAL & INSTALLATION

1. Before servicing the vehicle, refer to the precautions in the beginning of this section.

2. Disconnect the negative battery cable.

3. Remove the left valve cover, as follows:

   a. Remove the brake booster vacuum hose.

   b. Remove the secondary Air Injection Reaction (AIR) injection hose from the pump to check valve assembly.

   c. Remove the valve cover retaining bolts, then remove the cover and gasket.

4. Remove the right valve cover, as follows:

   a. Raise and support the vehicle safely, then remove the serpentine drive belt.

   b. Remove the transmission fluid level indicator tube assembly from the bracket on the transmission housing.

   c. Lower the vehicle, then remove the crankcase vent hose.

27 PUSHROD ASSEMBLY, VALVE
28 STUD, VALVE ROCKER ARM BALL
29 ARM, VALVE ROCKER
30 BALL, VALVE ROCKER ARM
31 NUT, VALVE ROCKER ARM

7922TG04

Exploded view of a typical rocker arm mounting

d. Remove the alternator and rear alternator brace.

e. Remove the valve cover retaining bolts, then remove the cover and gasket.

5. Remove the valve rocker arm nuts and balls, then remove the rocker arms and pushrods. Tag or arrange all valvetrain components to assure installation in their original locations.

To install:

6. Coat the bearing surfaces of the rocker arms, balls and pushrods with pre-lube.

7. Install the pushrods, making sure they are properly seated in the lifter sockets, then install the rocker arms, balls and nuts. If components are being reused, be sure they are installed in their original locations.

8. Adjust the valve lash.

9. Install the valve covers and gaskets, then tighten the retainers to 100 inch lbs. (11 Nm).

10. Install the components which were removed to access the valve covers in the reverse order of removal.

11. Connect the negative battery cable.

Intake Manifold

REMOVAL & INSTALLATION

1. Before servicing the vehicle, refer to the precautions in the beginning of this section.

2. Disconnect the negative battery cable and relieve the fuel system pressure.

3. Drain the engine cooling system into a suitable container.

4. Remove the throttle body air duct.

5. Disengage the wiring harness connectors from the fuel injectors. Disengage and reposition the left and right wiring harnesses.

6. Remove the accelerator cable bracket retainers, then disconnect the cable and bracket assembly from the throttle body.

7. Disconnect the secondary Air Injection Reaction (AIR) diverter valve hoses.

8. Disengage the fuel pipe connectors from the fuel rail assembly.

9. Remove the fuel rail bolts and disconnect the vacuum hose from the fuel pressure regulator.

10. Carefully remove the fuel rail and injector assembly from the manifold and position aside.

11. Disconnect the vacuum and crankcase vent hoses.

12. Remove the Exhaust Gas Recirculation (EGR) solenoid assembly and the fuel EVAP canister solenoid assembly.

13. Remove the EGR valve.

14. Remove the AIR pipe from the intake and the right exhaust manifold.

15. Remove the alternator rear brace.

16. Disconnect the coolant hoses from the throttle body.

17. Remove the throttle body bolts, the throttle body and gasket from the intake.

18. Remove the intake manifold bolts and studs.

19. Remove the intake manifold and discard the old gaskets.

To install:

20. Thoroughly clean the intake manifold bolts and studs. Inspect and clean all gasket mating surfaces.

21. Apply a ³⁄₁₆ in. (5mm) bead of RTV sealer to the front and rear of the cylinder block. Extend the bead ½ in. (13mm) up each cylinder head to seal and retain the gaskets.

22. Position the new gaskets and install the intake manifold.

23. Install the manifold bolts and studs, then tighten them in sequence. First, tighten the bolts/studs to 71 inch lbs. (8 Nm), then tighten them to 35 ft. lbs. (48 Nm).

24. Install the throttle body, gasket and retaining bolts. Tighten the throttle body bolts to 19 ft. lbs. (26 Nm).

25. Connect the coolant hoses to the throttle body, then install the alternator rear brace.

26. Install the accelerator cables and bracket, then tighten the bracket bolts to 90 inch lbs. (10 Nm).

27. Install the secondary AIR pipe. Tighten the exhaust manifold fitting to 25 ft. lbs. (34 Nm) and tighten the flange-to-intake manifold bolts to 19 ft. lbs. (26 Nm).

28. Install the EGR valve, then EGR solenoid and bracket. Tighten valve nuts and the solenoid bracket nut to 16 ft. lbs. (22 Nm).

29. Install the fuel EVAP canister purge solenoid and bracket, then tighten the bolt to 53 inch lbs. (6 Nm).

30. Connect the vacuum and crankcase vent hoses.

31. Install the fuel injector and fuel rail assembly to the intake manifold, connect the fuel pressure regulator vacuum hose and install the fuel rail bolts. Tighten the bolts to 15 ft. lbs. (20 Nm). Engage the fuel pipe connections to the fuel rail assembly.

32. Connect the secondary AIR diverter valve hoses.

33. Position the left and right wiring harnesses, then engage the fuel injector electrical connectors.

34. Install the throttle body air duct.

35. Properly fill the engine cooling system.

36. Connect the negative battery cable.

Exhaust Manifold

REMOVAL & INSTALLATION

Left Side

1. Before servicing the vehicle, refer to the precautions in the beginning of this section.

2. Disconnect the negative battery cable, then raise and support the vehicle safely.

3. Disconnect the exhaust crossover pipe from the manifold, then lower the vehicle.

4. Remove the brake booster vacuum hose.

5. Disconnect the secondary Air Injection Reaction (AIR) pipe fitting from the exhaust manifold.

6. Disengage the Oxygen (O_2S) sensor electrical connector.

7. Remove the exhaust manifold retaining bolts, then remove the heat shields, manifold and gasket.

FRT ▶

INTAKE MANIFOLD ASSEMBLY

7922TG05

Intake manifold bolt tightening sequence

To install:

8. Clean the gasket mating surfaces.

9. Position the gasket, then install the exhaust manifold and heat shields.

10. Install the manifold retaining bolts and tighten to 26 ft. lbs. (35 Nm).

11. Engage the O2S sensor electrical connector.

12. Connect the secondary AIR pipe fitting to the exhaust manifold and tighten to 25 ft. lbs. (34 Nm).

13. Install the brake booster vacuum hose.

14. Raise and support the vehicle safely.

15. Connect the exhaust crossover pipe to the manifold, then lower the vehicle.

16. Connect the negative battery cable.

Right Side

1. Before servicing the vehicle, refer to the precautions in the beginning of this section.

2. Disconnect the negative battery cable, then raise and support the vehicle safely.

3. Remove the exhaust crossover pipe.

4. Remove the serpentine drive belt.

5. Remove the oil level indicator and tube assembly, then disengage the Oxygen (O2S) sensor electrical connector.

6. Remove the three rear exhaust manifold retaining bolts, then lower the vehicle.

7. Disconnect the secondary Air Injection Reaction (AIR) pipe fitting from the exhaust manifold.

8. Remove the alternator rear lower brace.

9. Remove the remaining exhaust manifold retaining bolts, then remove the heat shields, manifold and gasket.

To install:

10. Clean the gasket mating surfaces.

11. Position the gasket, then install the exhaust manifold and heat shields.

12. Install the front three manifold retaining bolts and tighten to 26 ft. lbs. (35 Nm).

13. Install the alternator rear lower brace.

14. Raise and support the vehicle safely.

15. Install the remaining manifold retaining bolts and tighten to 26 ft. lbs. (35 Nm).

16. Engage the O2S sensor electrical connector.

17. Install the oil level indicator and tube assembly.

18. Install the serpentine drive belt.

19. Install the exhaust crossover pipe.

20. Lower the vehicle.

21. Connect the secondary AIR pipe fitting to the exhaust manifold and tighten to 25 ft. lbs. (34 Nm).

22. Connect the negative battery cable.

Camshaft and Valve Lifters

REMOVAL & INSTALLATION

1. Before servicing the vehicle, refer to the precautions in the beginning of this section.

2. Disconnect the negative battery cable.

3. Remove the intake manifold assembly.

4. Remove the rocker arms and pushrods.

5. Remove the bolt retaining the oil pump drive assembly, then lift the drive assembly from the rear of the block.

6. Remove the timing chain front cover, then remove the crankshaft shaft sprocket and timing chain.

7. Remove the valve lifters by pulling them out of their bores. Keep them in order so they can be installed in their original locations.

A TIMING MARKS
B KEYWAY
C PIN
56 BOLT/SCREW, CAMSHAFT SPROCKET
57 SPROCKET, CAMSHAFT
58 BOLT/SCREW, CAMSHAFT RETAINER
59 RETAINER, CAMSHAFT
60 CAMSHAFT ASSEMBLY
61 CHAIN ASSEMBLY, TIMING
62 SPROCKET, CRANKSHAFT
63 DRIVESHAFT ASSEMBLY, WATER PUMP
64 BOLT/SCREW, WATER PUMP DRIVESHAFT BEARING RETAINER

7922TG06

The camshaft is withdrawn through the front of the engine block, after the timing chain and sprocket is removed

Refer to Section 1 for engine rebuilding specifications

➡If valvetrain components are to be reused, be sure they are tagged or arranged in order to assure installation in their original locations.

8. If necessary, properly discharge and recover the refrigerant from the air conditioning system.

9. Remove the air conditioning compressor and condenser hose from the condenser, then remove the receiver and dehydrator hose from the condenser. Plug all of the openings in order to prevent system contamination.

10. Remove the radiator and condenser assembly, then remove the air conditioning condenser support.

11. Remove the camshaft retainer bolts, then remove the camshaft retainer from the front of the block.

12. Install three 5/16–18 x 4 in. bolts or equivalent, in the camshaft bolt holes, then using the bolts to pull and rotate the camshaft, carefully pull the camshaft from the bearings. All camshaft journals are the same diameter and care must be used to avoid damage to the bearings.

To install:

13. If installing a new camshaft, be sure to coat all camshaft lobes with Molykote®

or an equivalent prelube and to replace all lifters in order to assure camshaft durability.

14. Lubricate the camshaft journals with clean engine oil, then carefully insert the camshaft into the engine.

15. Install the camshaft retainer and tighten the bolts to 105 inch lbs. (12 Nm).

16. Install the condenser support, then install the radiator and condenser assembly.

17. Unplug the openings, then connect the condenser refrigerant lines.

18. Install the valve lifters. If reusing the camshaft and lifters, they must be installed into their original bores.

19. Install the camshaft sprocket and timing chain, then install the timing chain front cover.

20. Install the oil pump drive assembly and tighten the retaining bolt to 13 ft. lbs. (18 Nm).

21. Install the rocker arms and pushrods.

22. Install the intake manifold assembly.

23. Connect the negative battery cable, then if necessary, recharge the A/C system.

A   5/16–18 X 4" BOLTS
60   CAMSHAFT ASSEMBLY

7922TG07

Temporarily install three long bolts in the camshaft to use as a handle, then carefully withdraw the camshaft without damaging the bearings

Valve Lash

ADJUSTMENT

These engines do not require any routine valve lash adjustments. However, if the rocker arms are removed, the initial valve lash must be adjusted before the engine is started. Use the following procedure:

1. Before servicing the vehicle, refer to the precautions in the beginning of this section.

2. With the valve covers removed and the rocker arm assemblies loosely installed, position the engine at the No. 1 cylinder Top Dead Center (TDC) on compression stroke position.

3. To determine TDC, slowly turn the engine until the mark on the vibration damper aligns with the center or **0** mark on the timing tab of the front cover. At this point the engine is on the No. 1 firing position or the firing position of its opposite cylinder No. 6.

➡**The firing cylinder may be determined by placing a finger on the No. 1 cylinder valve rocker arms as the mark on the damper comes near the 0 mark on the crankcase front cover. If the valve rocker arms move as the mark comes up to the timing tab, the engine is on the opposite cylinder firing position, No. 6 and should be turned over a complete revolution to reach the No. 1 cylinder firing position. If the engine is in the No. 1 TDC position, the valves for the No. 1 cylinder should remain closed as the timing mark approaches.**

4. With the engine in the No. 1 firing position, adjust the following valves:
- Exhaust—1, 3, 4, 8
- Intake—1, 2, 5, 7

5. Adjust each valve by backing out the adjusting nut until lash (up and down movement) is felt at the pushrod, then tighten the adjusting nut until all lash is removed. This can be determined by rotating the pushrod while turning the adjusting nut. When play has been removed, turn the adjusting nut one full additional turn clockwise. The lifter plunger will now be centered.

6. Turn the engine one revolution until the pointer **0** mark and the vibration damper mark are again in alignment. This is the No. 6 firing position. As the timing mark approaches the pointer, the No. 1 cylinder valves should move.

7. With the engine in this position, adjust the following valves:

- Exhaust—2, 5, 6, 7
- Intake—3, 4, 6, 8

8. Install the rocker arm covers or valve covers.

9. Start the engine and check/adjust the minimum the idle speed, as required.

Oil Pan

REMOVAL & INSTALLATION

1. Before servicing the vehicle, refer to the precautions in the beginning of this section.

2. Disconnect the negative battery cable.

3. Remove the air intake duct.

4. Raise and support the vehicle safely, then drain the engine crankcase of oil.

5. Drain the engine cooling system.

6. Disengage the wiring harness connector from the oil level sensor, then remove the sensor.

7. Disconnect the exhaust crossover pipe from the exhaust manifolds, then remove the pipe hanger bolts and reposition the pipe.

8. If equipped, remove the engine oil cooler hose bracket nut from the oil pan, then remove the oil cooler bolt from the oil cooler assembly. Reposition the engine oil cooler assembly.

9. Remove the transmission fluid cooler lines from the oil pan clip and remove the torque converter cover.

10. Remove the start motor assembly.

11. Remove the engine mount through-bolts, then install a suitable engine jacking fixture and carefully raise the engine, watching the clearance between engine mounted components and the firewall.

✳✳ WARNING

Never raise the engine using a jack under the oil pan, crankshaft pulley or any sheet metal. Because there only is a small clearance between the oil pan and the oil pump screen, if the pan is bent even slightly, damage could occur to the pump screen and pick-up unit.

12. Remove the oil pan bolts, studs and nuts, then lower the oil pan assembly along with the gasket and the pan reinforcements. If necessary, rotate the crankshaft to reposition the counterweights.

To install:

13. Thoroughly clean the gasket mating surfaces of any remaining sealer and/or gasket material.

14. Apply a small amount of RTV sealer, 1052914 or equivalent, to the front cover-cylinder block junction and to the rear seal retainer-cylinder block junction. Continue the bead of sealer for 1 in. (25mm) in either direction of the radius cavity of these junctions.

15. Install the oil pan and gasket assembly, using the reinforcements, nuts, bolts and studs.

16. Tighten the corner oil pan bolts, stud or nuts to 15 ft. lbs. (20 Nm) and the remaining bolts or studs to 100 inch lbs. (11 Nm).

17. Lower the engine, remove the jacking fixture and install the engine mount through-bolts.

18. Install the oil level sensor assembly and tighten to 16 ft. lbs. (22 Nm), then engage the wiring harness connector.

19. Install the starter motor assembly.

20. Install the torque converter cover, then secure the transmission fluid cooler lines with the oil pan clip.

21. If equipped, install the engine oil cooler bolts screw to the cooler assembly and tighten to 24 ft. lbs. (33 Nm), then install the oil cooler hose bracket nut to the oil pan.

22. Install the exhaust pipe hanger bolt, then connect the crossover pipe to the exhaust manifolds.

23. Lower the vehicle and refill the engine crankcase with clean engine oil.

24. Install the air intake duct and connect the negative battery cable.

25. Start the engine and check for leaks.

Oil Pump

REMOVAL & INSTALLATION

1. Before servicing the vehicle, refer to the precautions in the beginning of this section.

A SEALER
53 REINFORCEMENT, OIL PAN
54 PAN ASSEMBLY, OIL
55 GASKET, OIL PAN

7922TG08

Oil pan and related components. Apply RTV sealant to the areas shown

For engine torque specifications, refer to Section 1 of this manual

2. Disconnect the negative battery cable.

3. Remove the oil pan.

4. Remove the bolt(s) attaching the pump to the rear main bearing cap, then remove the pump and driveshaft extension.

5. Remove the oil pump baffle retaining nuts and remove the baffle.

To install:

➡ **The oil pump pick-up should be submerged in oil and the pump primed prior to installation. Failure to prime the pump may result in oil pump failure or internal engine damage. Also, if the pick-up screen and pipe assembly was removed from the pump, they must be replaced to assure a proper interference fit.**

6. If the pick-up screen and pipe was removed, it should be replaced as an assembly with a new part. Using a suitable tool, install a new pick-up screen and pipe to the oil pump

7. Align the slot or hexagon head on the end of the shaft extension with the drive tang or the hexagonal socket on the distributor shaft and position the oil pump on the rear main bearing cap. Do not install the bolt at this time.

8. Position the oil pump baffle before installing the pump retaining bolt.

9. Install the baffle nuts and tighten to 25 ft. lbs. (34 Nm). Tighten the oil pump bolt to 66 ft. lbs. (90 Nm).

10. Install the oil pan assembly to the engine.

11. Connect the negative battery cable, then check the engine oil level and add, as necessary.

12. Start the engine while watch the indicator light or oil pressure gauge to ensure immediate oil pump operation.

Rear Main Seal

REMOVAL & INSTALLATION

The transmission assembly must be removed to perform this service.

1. Before servicing the vehicle, refer to the precautions in the beginning of this section.

2. Disconnect the negative battery cable.

3. Raise and safely support the vehicle.

4. Remove the transmission assembly using the recommended procedure.

5. Remove the flywheel mounting bolts and the flywheel.

6. Remove the rear crankshaft oil seal by

A SEAL REMOVAL NOTCHES
114 HOUSING ASSEMBLY, CRANKSHAFT REAR OIL SEAL

7922TG09

Rear main seal housing and removal notches

prying the seal out of the seal carrier using a suitable tool in the notches provided.

To install:

7. A special tool is used to remove the seal and install it. If not available, use the following procedure.

a. Unbolt the crankshaft rear oil seal housing assembly.

b. Locate the notches in the housing. Using a suitable drift pin, carefully tap the old seal out of the housing.

c. Clean the housing well. Tap in a new seal using care to keep the seal square to the housing.

d. Install the housing and seal back onto the rear of the block and crankshaft. Oil the seal well with clean engine oil to help it slide over the end of the crankshaft.

8. If tool J-35621 or equivalent is available, use the following procedure.

a. Install the seal assembly on tool J-35621 or the equivalent seal installation tool. Tighten the tool retainer screws snugly to ensure the seal will be installed squarely over the end of the crankshaft.

b. Install the rear crankshaft oil seal by tightening the wing nut on the special tool, if used, until the tool bottoms out.

c. Remove J-35621.

9. Install the flywheel and tighten the mounting bolts to 74 ft. lbs. (100 Nm). New replacement bolts are recommended.

10. Install the transmission in the vehicle using the recommended procedure.

11. Lower the vehicle.

12. Check engine oil level.

13. Connect the negative battery cable.

Timing Chain, Sprockets, Front Cover and Seal

REMOVAL & INSTALLATION

1. Before servicing the vehicle, refer to the precautions in the beginning of this section.

2. Disconnect the negative battery cable.

3. Drain the engine oil and coolant into suitable containers.

4. Remove the throttle body air intake duct.

5. Remove the serpentine drive belt.

6. Remove the water pump assembly.

7. Remove the crankshaft balancer and hub.

a. If not done already, raise and support the vehicle safely.

b. Remove the crankshaft balancer

50 COVER ASSEMBLY, ENGINE FRONT
51 GASKET, ENGINE FRONT COVER
52 BOLT/SCREW, ENGINE FRONT COVER
74 PIN, ENGINE FRONT COVER LOCATING

7922TG11

Exploded view of the timing chain front cover mounting—the crankshaft seal is easier to replace while the front cover is off

retaining bolts, then remove the balancer from the hub.

c. Matchmark the crankshaft hub to the engine front cover, then remove the hub bolt and washer.

d. Remove the crankshaft hub using J-39046 or an equivalent hub removal/installation tool. To preserve the relationship between the hub and crankshaft, DO NOT crank the engine over once the hub has been removed. If the hub is not matchmarked and installed in the original position, an engine imbalance could result.

8. Remove the distributor assembly.

9. Remove the oil pan assembly.

10. Remove the engine front cover bolts.

11. Remove the engine front cover and gasket.

12. Remove the crankshaft seal from the front cover with a suitable seal driver.

13. Rotate the crankshaft until the timing marks on the timing chain sprockets are aligned nearest to each other. The camshaft sprocket mark should be at the 6 o'clock position while the mark on the crankshaft sprocket should be at the 12 o'clock position.

14. Remove the camshaft sprocket bolts.

Align the timing marks on the gears before removing the chain

7922TG10

15. Remove the camshaft sprocket and timing chain.

➡ **To prevent piston or valve damage, do not turn the crankshaft after the timing chain has been removed.**

16. Remove the water pump bearing retainer bolts, then remove the driveshaft assembly using J-39243 or equivalent driven gear assembly remover.

17. Remove the crankshaft sprocket using J-5825-A or equivalent crankshaft sprocket remover.

18. If necessary, remove the crankshaft key.

To install:

19. If removed, install the crankshaft key.

20. Install the crankshaft sprocket using J-5590 or an equivalent installation tool.

21. Install the water pump driveshaft assembly using J-39092 or an equivalent installer tool. Install the retainer bolts and tighten to 105 inch lbs. (12 Nm).

22. Align the timing marks and install the camshaft sprocket and timing chain. The gears of the camshaft sprocket and water

pump driveshaft must mesh or damage to the thrust plate retainer could occur.

23. Install the camshaft sprocket bolts and tighten to 21 ft. lbs. (28 Nm).

24. Install a new O-ring to the water pump driven gear shaft using J-39089 or an equivalent seal installation tool.

25. Thoroughly clean the engine front cover and cylinder block gasket mating surfaces. Inspect the engine front cover for damage, replace as necessary. Install a new seal in the front cover.

26. Using J-39087 or equivalent front cover seal protector on the water pump driveshaft, install the gasket and front cover into position over the shafts and guide pins.

27. Install the engine front cover bolts and tighten to 100 inch lbs. (11 Nm).

28. Install the oil pan and gasket.

29. Install the distributor assembly.

30. Install the crankshaft hub and torsional damper assembly, as follows:

a. Align the matchmarks made earlier and install the crankshaft hub using the hub tool. If the engine was cranked and the matchmarks were lost, set the engine to No. 1 TDC, then install the crankshaft hub with the cast arrow in the 12 o'clock position.

b. Install the hub washer and bolt, but do not tighten it at this time.

c. Install the crankshaft balancer to the hub, then tighten the crankshaft hub bolt to 75 ft. lbs. (102 Nm) and the balancer bolts to 60 ft. lbs. (81 Nm).

➡If a new balancer is installed, new balancer weights of the same size must be installed in the same hole locations as the original balancer.

31. Install the water pump assembly.

32. Install the serpentine drive belt.

33. Install the throttle body air duct.

34. Properly fill the engine crankcase with clean engine oil.

35. Properly fill the engine cooling system.

36. Connect the negative battery cable, operate the engine and check for leaks.

FUEL SYSTEM

Fuel System Service Precautions

Safety is the most important factor when performing not only fuel system maintenance but any type of maintenance. Failure to conduct maintenance and repairs in a safe manner may result in serious personal injury or death. Maintenance and testing of the vehicle's fuel system components can be accomplished safely and effectively by adhering to the following rules and guidelines.

• To avoid the possibility of fire and personal injury, always disconnect the negative battery cable unless the repair or test procedure requires that battery voltage be applied.

• Always relieve the fuel system pressure prior to disconnecting any fuel system component (injector, fuel rail, pressure regulator, etc.), fitting or fuel line connection. Exercise extreme caution whenever relieving fuel system pressure to avoid exposing skin, face and eyes to fuel spray. Please be advised that fuel under pressure may penetrate the skin or any part of the body that it contacts.

• Always place a shop towel or cloth around the fitting or connection prior to loosening to absorb any excess fuel due to spillage. Ensure that all fuel spillage (should it occur) is quickly removed from engine surfaces. Ensure that all fuel soaked cloths or towels are deposited into a suitable waste container.

• Always keep a dry chemical (Class B) fire extinguisher near the work area.

• Do not allow fuel spray or fuel vapors to come into contact with a spark or open flame.

• Always use a back-up wrench when loosening and tightening fuel line connection fittings. This will prevent unnecessary stress and torsion to fuel line piping.

• Always replace worn fuel fitting O-rings with new. Do not substitute fuel hose or equivalent, where fuel pipe is installed.

Before servicing the vehicle, also make sure to refer to the precautions in the beginning of this section as well.

Fuel System Pressure

RELIEVING

1. Before servicing the vehicle, refer to the precautions in the beginning of this section.

2. Disconnect the negative battery cable to prevent fuel discharge if the key is accidentally turned to the **RUN** position.

3. Loosen the fuel filler cap to relieve the tank pressure and do not tighten until service has been completed.

4. Connect J-34730–1 fuel pressure gauge or equivalent, to the fuel pressure valve. Wrap a shop cloth around the fitting while connecting the gauge to avoid spillage.

5. Place the end of the bleed hose into a suitable container and open the valve to relieve the fuel system pressure.

Fuel Filter

REMOVAL & INSTALLATION

The fuel injection system uses an inline filter located in the fuel feed line under the hood, attached to the frame rail or on the rear crossmember of the vehicle. The high pressure fuel system used with all fuel injection systems requires special fuel lines to contain the pressure and utilizes nylon lines with quick-connect fittings.

1. Before servicing the vehicle, refer to the precautions in the beginning of this section.

2. Disconnect the negative battery cable and relieve fuel system pressure.

3. Raise and support the vehicle safely.

4. Remove the filter bracket attaching bolt.

5. While grasping the fuel filter and one of the fuel lines, twist the line approximately ¼ turn in each direction to loosen any dirt in the fitting, then use compressed air (and safety glasses) to blow dirt out of the fitting. Squeeze the plastic tabs of the male connector on the fuel lines and the pull connection apart. Repeat for the other fitting.

6. If applicable, remove the fuel feed and return line body harness clips.

7. Remove the filter.

To install:

8. Remove the protective caps from the new filter, then position the fuel filter in the original location with the arrow pointing in the correct direction.

9. Install the new connector retainers on the filter inlet and outlet tubes.

10. Apply a few drops of clean engine oil to the male ends of both fuel lines connectors.

11. Push the fuel line connectors onto the fuel filter tubes until their retaining tabs snap into place.

12. Once installed, pull on both ends of the lines to verify they are secure.

13. Secure the filter and bracket to the frame trapping the return pipe and tighten the attaching bolt to 89 inch lbs. (10 Nm).

14. Lower the vehicle.

15. Reconnect the negative battery cable.

Metal Collar Quick-connect Fitting

Plastic Collar Quick-connect Fitting

Removal

① CAUTION: TO REDUCE THE RISK OF FIRE AND PERSONAL INJURY, RELIEVE FUEL SYSTEM PRESSURE BEFORE DISCONNECTING FUEL PIPE FITTINGS.

② IF EQUIPPED, SLIDE DUST COVER BACK TO ACCESS FITTING

③ *Twist*

④ *Blow*

⑤ J 37088 OR J 39504

OR

⑥

Installation

① OIL

②

③

④ IF EQUIPPED, REPOSITION DUST COVER AFTER SERVICE

7922TG13

Two different types of fuel line connections may be used, use the diagrams too determine which type you have and how to disconnect them

1	**FUEL FEED PIPE**	3	**IN-LINE FUEL FILTER**
2	**FUEL FEED PIPE**	4	**IN-LINE FUEL FILTER ATTACHING BOLT**

7922TG12

Fuel filter is typically located on the rear frame rail near the fuel tank

16. Turn the ignition **ON** for two seconds, **OFF** for 10 seconds, then **ON** again to pressurize the fuel system. Inspect the tank and lines for leaks.

Fuel Pump

REMOVAL & INSTALLATION

1. Before servicing the vehicle, refer to the precautions in the beginning of this section.

2. Disconnect the negative battery cable and relieve the fuel system pressure.

3. Drain the fuel tank using a suitable hand-operated pump, then raise and support the vehicle safely.

4. Remove the fuel tank.

5. Remove the fuel tank sending unit and pump assembly as follows: remove the assembly attaching nuts, retaining flag, assembly and O-ring from the tank. Discard the O-ring.

   To install:

6. Install the fuel sending unit in the fuel tank as follows: position a new O-ring on

1	RETAINING CLIP
2	SPRING
3	FUEL FEED HOSE
4	CLAMP
5	HOUSING COVER
6	FUEL SENDER ASSEMBLY
7	FUEL PUMP
8	FUEL PUMP ISOLATOR
9	FUEL PUMP HOUSING
10	FUEL PUMP STRAINER
11	FUEL LEVER SENSOR ASSEMBLY
12	FUEL SENDER ELECTRICAL CONNECTOR

7922TG14

Exploded view of the fuel pump, showing all related components

the fuel tank. Install the fuel sender assembly, retaining flag, and attaching nuts to the fuel tank. Tighten the attaching nuts to 27 inch lbs. (3 Nm).

7. Install the fuel tank.

8. Lower the vehicle.

9. Turn the ignition **ON** for two seconds, **OFF** for 10 seconds, then **ON** again to pressurize the fuel system. Inspect the fuel system for leaks.

DRIVE TRAIN

Transmission Assembly

REMOVAL & INSTALLATION

1. Before servicing the vehicle, refer to the precautions in the beginning of this section.

2. Disconnect the negative battery cable and remove the air cleaner.

3. Disconnect the Throttle Valve (TV) cable at the throttle lever.

4. Remove the transmission dipstick, then remove the dipstick tube from the transmission.

5. Raise and support the vehicle safely.

6. Remove the driveshaft.

7. Disconnect the shift linkage at the transmission.

8. Disengage all electrical leads at the transmission and any clips that retain the leads to the transmission case.

9. Remove the retaining bolts, then remove the flywheel cover.

10. Matchmark the flywheel and converter for installation purposes.

11. Remove and discard the torque converter-to-flywheel bolts.

12. Remove the catalytic converter support bracket.

13. Support and raise the transmission slightly using a suitable transmission jack.

14. Remove the transmission mount-to-support nut, washer, and bolt.

15. Remove the transmission support-to-frame bolts, nuts, and if used, insulators.

16. Slide the transmission support rearward.

17. Lower the transmission to gain access to the oil cooler lines and TV cable attachments.

18. Disconnect the lines and cap all openings to prevent excessive fluid loss or system contamination, then disconnect the TV cable.

19. Support the engine with a suitable tool, then remove the transmission-to-engine bolts.

20. Install tool J-21366 or equivalent, to the torque converter to hold it in place.

21. Remove the transmission assembly from the vehicle.

To install:

22. Raise the transmission into place and remove tool J-21366.

23. Install the transmission-to-engine bolts and tighten to 35 ft. lbs. (47 Nm).

24. Unplug and install the oil cooler pipes, then connect the TV cable.

25. Install the fluid level tube using a new seal, then tighten tube retaining bolt to 35 ft. lbs. (47 Nm).

26. Install the transmission support-to-frame bolts, nuts and, if applicable, the insulators. Tighten the bolts to 41 ft. lbs. (55 Nm) for Fleetwood Brougham or to 25 ft. lbs. (34 Nm) except for Fleetwood Brougham. Tighten the nuts to 30 ft. lbs. (41 Nm), if equipped.

27. If removed or replaced, install the transmission mount bolts and tighten to 35 ft. lbs. (47 Nm). Install the transmission support nut and washer, then tighten to 30 ft. lbs. (41 Nm).

28. Remove the transmission jack, then position the converter by aligning it to the flywheel in the original position marked. Be sure the weld nuts on the converter are flush with the flywheel. Test the converter or clutch for freedom of movement.

29. Install and finger-tighten three new bolts, then tighten to 35 ft. lbs. (47 Nm) for Fleetwood Brougham or to 46 ft. lbs. (62 Nm) except for Fleetwood Brougham. After tightening all bolts, retighten the first bolt.

30. If removed, install the floor pan reinforcement.

31. Install the catalytic converter support bracket, then install the converter cover and tighten the bolts to 89 inch lbs. (10 Nm).

32. Install the shift linkage, electrical leads, retaining clips, and if equipped, speedometer cable.

33. Install the driveshaft and lower the vehicle.

34. Install the fluid level indicator.

35. Install the air cleaner, then connect the negative battery cable.

36. If necessary, use the following substeps to adjust the shift linkage.

a. Place the control lever in Neutral.

b. Attach a 2–3 lb. weight on the end of the lever to remove play.

c. Raise the vehicle.

d. Loosen the bolt on the swivel so the rod slides freely.

e. Place the selector on the transmission to the neutral position.

f. Tighten the swivel bolt to 21 ft. lbs. (28 Nm).

37. Flush the transmission and cooler system to prevent damage to the system components.

STEERING AND SUSPENSION

Air Bag

✸✸ CAUTION

Some vehicles are equipped with an air bag system, also known as the Supplemental Inflatable Restraint (SIR) or Supplemental Restraint System (SRS). The system must be disabled before performing service on or around system components, steering column, instrument panel components, wiring and sensors. Failure to follow safety and disabling procedures could result in accidental air bag deployment, possible personal injury and unnecessary system repairs.

PRECAUTIONS

Several precautions must be observed when handling the inflator module to avoid accidental deployment and possible personal injury.

• Never carry the inflator module by the wires or connector on the underside of the module.

• When carrying a live inflator module, hold securely with both hands, and ensure that the bag and trim cover are pointed away.

• Place the inflator module on a bench or other surface with the bag and trim cover facing up.

• With the inflator module on the bench, never place anything on or close to the module which may be thrown in the event of an accidental deployment.

Before servicing the vehicle, also make sure to refer to the precautions in the beginning of this section as well.

DISARMING

1. Align the steering wheel so the vehicle wheels are pointing in the straight-ahead position.
2. Turn the ignition switch to the **LOCK** position.
3. Remove the SIR or AIR BAG fuse from the fuse block.
4. Remove the Connector Position Assurance (CPA) device, then disengage the yellow 2-way SIR wiring harness connector at the base of the steering column.

ARMING

After the appropriate repairs have been made, re-enable the air bag system as follows:

1. Turn the ignition switch to the **LOCK** position.
2. Engage the yellow 2-way connector at the base of the steering column, then install the CPA device.
3. Reinstall the SIR or AIR BAG fuse.
4. Turn the ignition switch to the **RUN** position.
5. Verify the SIR indicator light flashes 7–9 times, if not, inspect the system for malfunction.

Reciprocating Ball Power Steering Gear

REMOVAL & INSTALLATION

1. Before servicing the vehicle, refer to the precautions in the beginning of this section.
2. Disconnect the negative battery cable, then lock the steering wheel in the straight-ahead position to prevent damage to the SIR coil assembly.
3. Remove the shield from the steering gear return pipe nut, then remove the bolt from the intermediate shaft-to-gear coupling. Push the intermediate shaft rearward, disengaging the latch from the gear.
4. Remove the valve bracket nut from the gear.
5. Remove the steering linkage relay rod nut from the Pitman arm.
6. Raise and support the vehicle safely.

5 GEAR, POWER STEERING
29 WASHER, STEERING GEAR
30 BOLT/SCREW, STEERING GEAR

7922TG15

The steering gear is mounted on the left frame rail

7. Remove the nut from the Pitman arm, then separate the arm from the steering gear using J-9172 or an equivalent puller.
8. Disconnect the power steering hoses from the gear assembly. Either plug the hoses or raise and secure them to prevent excessive fluid loss.
9. Remove the steering gear mounting bolts, then remove the gear assembly.
To install:
10. Position the gear to the frame and loosely install the mounting bolts.
11. Adjust the gear to align as straight as possible with the intermediate shaft, then hold the gear in position and tighten the mounting bolts to 70 ft. lbs. (95 Nm).
12. Install the power steering hose assemblies to the gear and tighten the fittings to 21 ft. lbs. (28 Nm).
13. Install the Pitman arm to the steering gear using a lockwasher and a new nut. Tighten the nut to 185 ft. lbs. (250 Nm) for Fleetwood Brougham or to 179 ft. lbs. (243 Nm) except for Fleetwood Brougham.
14. Lower the vehicle, then install the steering linkage relay rod nut and tighten to 35 ft. lbs. (47 Nm).
15. Install the valve bracket nut to the gear assembly and tighten to 18 ft. lbs. (24 Nm).
16. Install the intermediate shaft cou-

pling bolt and nut, then tighten to 30 ft. lbs. (40 Nm) for Fleetwood Brougham or to 40 ft. lbs. (54 Nm) except for Fleetwood Brougham.
17. Position the shield, making sure the latch is seated around the gear return pipe nut.
18. Connect the negative battery cable, then properly bleed the steering system.

Shock Absorber

REMOVAL & INSTALLATION

Front

1. Before servicing the vehicle, refer to the precautions in the beginning of this section.
2. Raise and support the vehicle safely.
3. Hold the shock absorber upper stem from turning and remove the upper nut, then remove the retainer and grommet.
4. Remove the two bolts and lockwashers securing the shock to the lower control arm, then lower the shock from the vehicle.
To install:
5. With the lower retainer and grommet in place over the upper stem, install the fully extended shock up through the lower control arm and spring. Be sure the upper

5 NUT, FRONT SHOCK ABSORBER, 11 N•m (97 LB. IN.)
6 RETAINER, FRONT SHOCK ABSORBER
7 INSULATOR, FRONT SHOCK ABSORBER
19 NUT, FRONT SHOCK ABSORBER
34 BOLT/SCREW, FRONT SHOCK ABSORBER, 27 N•m (20 LB. FT.)

7922TG16

One nut and two bolts secure the front shock absorber to the suspension and frame

stem passes through the mounting hole in the frame bracket.

6. Install the upper rubber insulator, retainer and attaching nut over the shock, then tighten the nut to 97 inch lbs. (11 Nm).

7. Install the shock lower pivot to the lower control arm and tighten the two attaching bolts to 20 ft. lbs. (27 Nm).

8. Lower the vehicle.

Rear

1. Before servicing the vehicle, refer to the precautions in the beginning of this section.

2. Raise and safely support the vehicle safely, making sure to properly support the rear axle housing.

3. If equipped with adjustable shocks, disconnect the air line by turning the spring clip 90 degrees and pulling gently on air line housing.

4. Remove the upper nuts and bolts from the shock absorber at the frame.

5. Using a wrench to hold the stud in place, remove the lower nut and washer from the shock at the rear axle housing. The stud must not be allowed to turn during this

operation or damage may result in the bond between the bushing and stud.

6. Remove the shock absorber from the vehicle.

To install:

7. Install the shock absorber and loosely connect the upper frame bolts and nuts.

8. Position the stud into the bracket on the axle housing, then install the nut and washer.

9. Either tighten the upper bolts at the frame to 20 ft. lbs. (27 Nm) or the nuts at the frame to 12 ft. lbs. (16 Nm), whichever is easier. Then, while holding the stud steady with a wrench, tighten the lower shock retaining nut to 65 ft. lbs. (88 Nm) for Fleetwood Brougham or to 50 ft. lbs. (68 Nm) except for Fleetwood Brougham.

10. If equipped, connect the shock air line.

11. Remove the supports and lower the vehicle.

Coil Spring

REMOVAL & INSTALLATION

Front

1. Before servicing the vehicle, refer to the precautions in the beginning of this section.

A BRACKET, REAR AXLE TUBE
20 WASHER, REAR SHOCK ABSORBER
21 NUT, REAR SHOCK ABSORBER, 85 N•m (63 LB. FT.)
22 ABSORBER, REAR SHOCK
23 BOLT/SCREW, REAR SHOCK ABSORBER
25 NUT, REAR SHOCK ABSORBER, 22 N•m (16 LB. FT.)
36 FRAME
39 SHIELD, REAR SHOCK ABSORBER BOOT HEAT (WITH ELC ONLY)

7922TG17

Two upper bolts and one through-bolt secure the rear shock absorber to the frame and axle assembly

FRONT SPRING IS INSTALLED WITH TAPE AT LOWEST POSITION. BOTTOM OF FRONT SPRING IS COILED HELICAL AND THE TOP IS COILED FLAT WITH A GRIPPER NOTCH NEAR END OF WIRE.

AFTER ASSEMBLY, END OF FRONT SPRING MUST COVER ALL OR PART OF ONE INSPECTION DRAIN HOLE. THE OTHER HOLE MUST BE PARTLY EXPOSED OR COMPLETELY UNCOVERED.

FRONT SPRING MUST NEVER BE COMPRESSED TO AN OVERALL DIMENSION OF 244 mm (9.6 INCHES) OR LESS.

7922TG18

Position the front coil spring as shown

2. Raise and support the vehicle safely.

3. Remove the tire and wheel assembly from the vehicle.

4. If equipped, remove the ABS wheel speed sensor and secure aside.

5. Remove shock absorber.

6. Remove the stabilizer bar linkage nut, retainer and linkage from the lower control arm.

7. Remove the cotter pin and castellated nut, then separate the tie rod from the steering knuckle, using a suitable puller tool.

8. Compress the coil spring using a universal spring compressor tool.

9. Support the lower control arm using an adjustable lifting device, then remove the lower control arm-to-frame pivot bolts.

10. Pivot the lower control arm rearward, then carefully remove the compressor and spring.

To install:

11. Position the spring onto the lower control arm making sure the insulator is in position, then install the compressor tool and compress the spring so the control arm may be repositioned.

➡ **When installed, the lower end of the coil spring must cover all or part of one**

of the drain holes in the lower control arm, the other drain hole should remain uncovered.

12. Position the control arm into the frame and install the pivot bolts (install the front bolt first, positioned from the front to the rear), but wait until the suspension is supporting the vehicle's weight before tightening the control arm fasteners to specification at the end of the procedure.

13. Remove the spring compressor tool, then install the tie rod end to the steering knuckle and tighten the nut to 35 ft. lbs. (47 Nm). Tighten the nut additionally, as necessary to align the hole, then install a new cotter pin.

14. Remove the support from the lower control arm and install the stabilizer bar linkage.

15. Install the shock absorber. Tighten the lower attaching bolts to 20 ft. lbs. (27 Nm) and the upper attaching nut to 97 inch lbs. (11 Nm).

16. If equipped, install the ABS wheel speed sensor.

17. Install the wheel and lower the vehicle.

18. Tighten the lower control arm nuts to 92 ft. lbs. (125 Nm).

Rear

➡ **If both springs are to be replaced, only disconnect one control arm at a time in order to prevent the axle from rolling or slipping sideways.**

1. Before servicing the vehicle, refer to the precautions in the beginning of this section.

2. Raise and support the vehicle safely, then place an adjustable support under the axle housing.

3. If equipped, disconnect the ABS rear speed sensor.

4. If equipped, disconnect the height sensor link from the upper control arm by removing the attaching nut and sliding the sensor link stud out of the hole in the upper control arm.

5. Disconnect the brake line fitting bolt at the center of the axle housing. No brake lines need to be disconnected, therefore brake bleeding should not be necessary.

6. Remove the nut and washer from the shock absorber, then disconnect the shock absorber from the axle bracket.

7. Carefully lower the axle housing sufficiently to remove the spring. Be careful not to stretch the brake hose.

8. Remove the spring, upper and lower insulator, as equipped.

A   UNIVERSAL SPRING COMPRESSOR
10   SPRING, FRONT
39   ARM ASSEMBLY, FRONT LOWER CONTROL

7922TG19

Use a coil spring compressor installed through the lower control arm when removing the front coil spring

A FIVE DEGREES MAXIMUM
   REARWARD
B LINE PERPENDICULAR TO CENTER
   LINE OF CHASSIS
C FIFTEEN DEGREES MAXIMUM
   FORWARD
4 INSULATOR, REAR SPRING UPPER
5 SPRING, REAR
36 FRAME ASSEMBLY
40 INSULATOR, REAR SPRING LOWER (WAGON ONLY)

7922TG20

Position the coil spring leg perpendicular to the centerline of the chassis

2 STUD, FRONT UPPER CONTROL ARM BALL
3 ARM, FRONT UPPER CONTROL
16 KNUCKLE, STEERING
17 NUT, STEERING KNUCKLE
   170 N•m (125 LB. FT.)
18 PIN, STEERING KNUCKLE COTTER
63 SERVICE KIT NUT
64 SERVICE KIT BOLT

7922TG21

To install:

9. Install the upper insulator, lower insulator, as equipped, and the rear spring to the bracket on the frame seat. Point the coil leg toward the left side of the vehicle, at a right angle from the centerline of the vehicle within 5 degrees rearward and 15 degrees forward.

➡️**If the spring is being replaced, be sure to position the tape facing the top or spring noises could occur.**

10. Raise the rear axle back into position using the adjustable lifting device.

11. Install the rear shock absorber to the bracket, and tighten the nut to 50 ft. lbs. (68 Nm).

12. Connect the rear brake line fitting bolt and tighten to 20 ft. lbs. (27 Nm).

13. If equipped, connect the height sensor link to the upper control arm and tighten the nut to 27 inch lbs. (3 Nm).

14. Remove the adjustable support from under the rear axle assembly.

15. If equipped, connect the ABS rear axle speed sensor.

16. Lower the vehicle and, if necessary, adjust the height sensor.

Upper Ball Joint

REMOVAL & INSTALLATION

1. Before servicing the vehicle, refer to the precautions in the beginning of this section.

2. Raise and safely support the vehicle; place supports under the lower control arm between the spring seats and the ball joints.

➡️**Leave the jack under the spring seat during removal and installation, in order to retain the coil spring and relieve spring tension from the upper control arm. The weight of the vehicle is used to relieve spring tension on the upper control arm.**

3. Remove the wheel.

4. Remove the cotter pin and nut from the upper ball joint.

5. Using a ball joint separator tool, break the stud loose and pull the stud out of the knuckle. Support the steering knuckle to prevent damage to the brake line.

6. With the control arm in a raised

The replacement kit comes with nuts and bolts to mount the ball joint in the control arm

position, use a 1/8 in. diameter bit and drill into each of the four rivet heads to a depth of 1/4 in. (6mm).

7. Drill off the rivet heads with a 1/2 in. diameter bit.

8. Punch out the rivets using a suitable driver or punch, then remove the ball joint.

To install:

9. Place the new ball joint in the upper control arm and secure it with four bolts and nuts in place of rivets. Tighten the nuts to specifications provided with the ball joint kit.

10. Connect the ball joint to the steering knuckle. Tighten the nut to 61 ft. lbs. (83 Nm), then insert a new cotter pin. Do not back off the specified torque in order to install the cotter pin.

➡️**When replacing the ball joints, use only high-quality replacement parts; bolts and nuts specified to be strong enough to endure the stress.**

11. Attach the grease fitting and lubricate until grease appears at the seal.

12. Install the wheel and road test the vehicle.

Turn to Section 6 for brake system applications

Lower Ball Joint

REMOVAL & INSTALLATION

1. Before servicing the vehicle, refer to the precautions in the beginning of this section.

2. Raise the vehicle and support the frame safely.

3. Remove the tire and wheel assembly.

4. Place a support under the control arm spring seat.

➡**Leave the support under the spring seat during removal and installation, in order to keep the spring and control arm positioned.**

5. Remove the cotter pin and nut from the ball joint stud, then using a ball joint separator, remove the ball joint stud from the steering knuckle.

6. Guide the control arm down, past the brake shield (backing plate) with a flat-bladed tool.

7. Block the steering knuckle aside using a block of wood between the frame and the upper control arm.

8. Remove the grease fittings.

9. Using a suitable ball joint remover, drive the lower ball joint from the control arm.

14 SHIELD, FRONT BRAKE

Guide the lower control arm over the brake shield

To install:

10. Using a ball joint installer, press in a new ball joint until it bottoms on the lower control arm.

➡**Be sure the grease purge on the seal faces away from the brakes.**

11. Assemble the suspension and tighten the lower ball joint nut to 83 ft. lbs. (113 Nm) for Fleetwood Brougham or to 125 ft. lbs. (170 Nm) except for Fleetwood Brougham. Install the cotter pin and bend it to the side, not over the top of the nut.

12. Install the ball joint fitting and grease the new ball joint.

13. Install the tire and wheel assembly.

14. Check and adjust the wheel alignment, as necessary.

15. Lower and road test the vehicle.

Wheel Bearings

ADJUSTMENT

Front

1. Before servicing the vehicle, refer to the precautions in the beginning of this section.

2. Raise the vehicle so the wheel can spin freely.

3. Remove the wheel cover, dust cap, cotter pin and loosen the adjusting nut.

4. Tighten the adjusting nut to 12 ft. lbs. (16 Nm) while turning the wheel, this will seat the bearings and remove any grease or burrs which could cause play later.

5. Back off the nut until it is just loose.

6. Finger-tighten the nut and install the cotter pin through the retaining ring or castle nut.

➡**If the cotter pin cannot be installed, back off the nut until the slot aligns with the serrations on the nut. Do not back off the nut more than ¼ of a turn.**

7. Once adjusted, the front wheel bearings should have 0.001–0.005 in. (0.03–0.13mm) end-play.

8. When adjusted properly cut off any extra length from the cotter pin to prevent interference, then install the dust cap and wheel cover.

9. Lower the vehicle.

Rear

The rear axle bearings are not adjustable. If the bearings become loose or make noise, they must be replaced.

REMOVAL & INSTALLATION

Front

1. Before servicing the vehicle, refer to the precautions in the beginning of this section.

2. Raise and support the vehicle safely.

3. Remove the tire and wheel assembly.

4. Remove the rotor and hub assembly.

5. Pry the inner bearing seal from the hub, then remove the inner roller bearing assembly.

6. If necessary, remove the inner and outer bearing races using tool J-29117-A or a suitable brass punch inserted behind the races.

J 9519-30

J 9519-16

J 21474-13

A special tool is needed to remove and install the lower ball joint in the control arm

A SPINDLE
14 SHIELD, FRONT BRAKE
15 GASKET, FRONT BRAKE SHIELD
16 KNUCKLE, STEERING
24 SEAL, FRONT WHEEL HUB
25 BEARING, FRONT WHEEL INNER
27 ROTOR, FRONT BRAKE
28 BEARING, FRONT WHEEL OUTER
29 WASHER, FRONT WHEEL BEARING
30 CAP, FRONT WHEEL BEARING LUBRICANT
31 NUT, FRONT WHEEL BEARING, 16 N•m (12 LB. FT.)
55 PIN, STEERING KNUCKLE   COTTER
56 RACE, FRONT WHEEL INNER
57 RACE, FRONT WHEEL OUTER

Exploded view of the front wheel bearings

To install:

7. Using fresh solvent, clean all old grease from hub, spindle and bearing.

8. If the inner and outer races were removed, press or drive the races into the hub using a suitable sized driver.

9. Pack the bearings with a high temperature wheel bearing grease and reassemble the hub. Do not mix greases.

10. Install a new inner bearing seal using a flat plate to assure the seal is flush with the rotor.

11. Apply a thin coat of grease to the spindle, then install the rotor and hub assembly on the steering knuckle.

12. Adjust the wheel bearings, install a new cotter pin and replace the dust cap.

13. Install the caliper assembly.

14. Install the tire and wheel assembly.

15. Lower the vehicle.

Rear

1. Before servicing the vehicle, refer to the precautions in the beginning of this section.

2. Raise and support the vehicle safely.

3. Remove the tire and wheel assembly, then remove the brake drum.

4. Clean all dirt from the rear carrier cover, then loosen the bolts and remove the cover while draining the gear oil. Discard the old gasket.

5. Remove the shaft lock bolt from the differential case located in the housing, then withdraw the pinion gear shaft.

6. Push the flanged end of the axle shaft toward center of the vehicle, then

3 GEAR, DIFFERENTIAL RING
7 CASE, DIFFERENTIAL
28 BOLT/SCREW, DIFFERENTIAL BEARING CAP, 75 N•m
     (55 LB. FT.)
29 CAP, DIFFERENTIAL BEARING
37 HOUSING, REAR AXLE
38 LOCK, REAR AXLE SHAFT

Differential component identification

30 NUT, REAR BRAKE BACKING PLATE, 48 N•m (35 LB. FT.)
32 PLATE, REAR BRAKE BACKING
33 BOLT/SCREW, REAR BRAKE BACKING PLATE
34 SEAL, REAR AXLE SHAFT BEARING
35 BEARING, REAR AXLE SHAFT
37 HOUSING, REAR AXLE
39 SHAFT, REAR AXLE

7922TG27

Cut-away view of the rear axle bearing and seal

remove C-lock from the end of the shaft located in the housing.

➡ **Try not to turn the differential unit too much when one or both of the axle shafts are removed because the spider gears can fall out of the unit, creating more work and frustration.**

7. Remove axle shaft from the housing. If replacement of the oil seal is not planned, be very careful not to damage the seal.

8. Remove the brake backing plate.

9. Remove seal from housing using a prybar behind the seal's steel case, being careful not to damage housing.

10. Insert an appropriately-sized bearing remover into the bore and position it behind the bearing so tangs on tool engage bearing

outer race. Remove the bearing, using a slide hammer.

To install:

11. Lubricate the new bearing with gear lubricant and install the bearing using a suitable driver so the tool bottoms against the shoulder in the housing.

12. Lubricate seal lips with gear lubricant, then position the seal on a suitably sized driver and position seal into housing bore. Tap seal into place so it is flush with axle tube.

13. If removed, install the brake backing plate.

14. Insert the axle into place while engaging the splines on the end of the shaft with the splines of the rear axle side gear. Be careful when inserting the axle not to damage the seal.

15. Install the C-lock in the groove on the end of the axle shaft and push the shaft outward so the lock seats in the counterbore of the rear axle side gear.

16. Install the rear axle pinion gear shaft through the differential case, thrust washers and pinions, align the hole in the shaft with the lock bolt hole. Install the lock bolt and tighten to 24 ft. lbs. (31 Nm) for 7½ in. ring gears or 20 ft. lbs. (27 Nm) for 8½ in. ring gear.

17. Position a new gasket, then install the carrier cover and tighten the bolt to 22 ft. lbs. (30 Nm) using a crosswise pattern.

18. Fill the rear assembly with the proper grade and type gear oil.

19. Install the brake drum, then install the tire and wheel assembly.

20. Lower the vehicle.

GENERAL MOTORS CORPORATION—C & H BODIES

29

Buick-Le Sabre • Park Ave. • Oldsmobile-Eighty Eight • Eighty Eight LS • LSS • Regency • Pontiac-Bonneville

PRECAUTIONS

Before servicing any vehicle, please be sure to read all of the following precautions, which deal with personal safety, prevention of component damage, and important points to take into consideration when servicing a motor vehicle:

• Never open, service or drain the radiator or cooling system when the engine is hot; serious burns can occur from the steam and hot coolant.

• Observe all applicable safety precautions when working around fuel. Whenever servicing the fuel system, always work in a well-ventilated area. Do not allow fuel spray or vapors to come in contact with a spark, open flame, or excessive heat (a hot drop light, for example). Keep a dry chemical fire extinguisher near the work area. Always keep fuel in a container specifically designed for fuel storage; also, always properly seal fuel containers to avoid the possibility of fire or explosion. Refer to the additional fuel system precautions later in this section.

• Fuel injection systems often remain pressurized, even after the engine has been turned **OFF**. The fuel system pressure must be relieved before disconnecting any fuel lines. Failure to do so may result in fire and/or personal injury.

• Brake fluid often contains polyglycol ethers and polyglycols. Avoid contact with the eyes and wash your hands thoroughly after handling brake fluid. If you do get brake fluid in your eyes, flush your eyes with clean, running water for 15 minutes. If eye irritation persists, or if you have taken brake fluid internally, IMMEDIATELY seek medical assistance.

• The EPA warns that prolonged contact with used engine oil may cause a number of skin disorders, including cancer! You should make every effort to minimize your exposure to used engine oil.

Protective gloves should be worn when changing oil. Wash your hands and any other exposed skin areas as soon as possible after exposure to used engine oil. Soap and water, or waterless hand cleaner should be used.

• All new vehicles are now equipped with an air bag system, often referred to as a Supplemental Restraint System (SRS) or Supplemental Inflatable Restraint (SIR) system. The system must be disabled before performing service on or around system components, steering column, instrument panel components, wiring and sensors. Failure to follow safety and disabling procedures could result in accidental air bag deployment, possible personal injury and unnecessary system repairs.

• Always wear safety goggles when working with, or around, the air bag system. When carrying a non-deployed air bag, be sure the bag and trim cover are pointed away from your body. When placing a non-deployed air bag on a work surface, always face the bag and trim cover upward, away from the surface. This will reduce the motion of the module if it is accidentally deployed. Refer to the additional air bag system precautions later in this section.

• Clean, high quality brake fluid from a sealed container is essential to the safe and proper operation of the brake system. You should always buy the correct type of brake fluid for your vehicle. If the brake fluid becomes contaminated, completely flush the system with new fluid. Never reuse any brake fluid. Any brake fluid that is removed from the system should be discarded. Also, do not allow any brake fluid to come in contact with a painted surface; it will damage the paint.

• Never operate the engine without the proper amount and type of engine oil; doing so WILL result in severe engine damage.

• Timing belt maintenance is extremely important! Many models utilize an interfer-

ence-type, non-freewheeling engine. If the timing belt breaks, the valves in the cylinder head may strike the pistons, causing potentially serious (also time-consuming and expensive) engine damage. Refer to the maintenance interval charts in the front of this manual for the recommended replacement interval for the timing belt, and to the timing belt section for belt replacement and inspection.

• Disconnecting the negative battery cable on some vehicles may interfere with the functions of the on-board computer system(s) and may require the computer to undergo a relearning process once the negative battery cable is reconnected.

• When servicing drum brakes, only disassemble and assemble one side at a time, leaving the remaining side intact for reference.

• Only an MVAC-trained, EPA-certified automotive technician should service the A/C system or its components.

ENGINE REPAIR

Ignition Timing

The 3.8L (VIN K and 1) engines utilizes a Distributorless Ignition System (DIS). This system uses three twin tower coils which fire two spark plugs simultaneously. One spark plug is located in a cylinder on the compression stroke and the other in a cylinder on the exhaust stroke. This is known as the waste spark method of distribution.

ADJUSTMENT

The ignition timing is not adjustable, and is set according to engine demand electronically. The Powertrain Control Module (PCM) controls the ignition timing for all driving conditions.

Engine Assembly

REMOVAL & INSTALLATION

1. Before servicing the vehicle, refer to the precautions in the beginning of this section.
2. Disconnect the negative battery cable.
3. Mark the position of the hood hinges, for installation reference, and remove the hood from the vehicle.
4. Relieve the fuel system pressure using the recommended procedure.
5. Drain the engine coolant and engine oil.
6. Remove the radiator and heater supply hoses.
7. Remove the negative battery cable from the engine block.
8. Disconnect the engine harness at the bulkhead.
9. Remove the drive belts.
10. Remove the power steering pump and set aside.
11. Remove the air flow duct.
12. Remove the throttle cable from the throttle mounting bracket and other applicable cables.
13. Disconnect the following sensors:
   • Manifold Air Temperature (MAT) sensor
   • Throttle Position (TP) sensor
   • Idle Air Control valve (IAC)
   • Oxygen (O2S) sensor
   • Oil pressure switch
   • Power Steering cutoff switch
   • Vehicle Speed Sensor (VSS)
   • Low oil level sensor
14. Remove the ignition assembly ground strap from the fender inner panel attaching screws.
15. Remove the fuel feed and return lines from the fuel rail and fuel pressure regulator.
16. Remove the emission control canister hoses from the throttle body connections.
17. Remove the brake booster and heater control hoses from the engine vacuum connections.
18. Disconnect the vacuum hoses at the cruise control servo assembly.
19. Raise and safely support the vehicle.
20. Remove the exhaust pipe from the right manifold.
21. Remove the A/C compressor and tie back the compressor away from the engine. Do not disconnect the refrigerant lines.

22. Remove the right front engine-to-transaxle bracket.
23. Remove the flexplate cover.
24. Remove the starter motor.
25. Remove the torque converter-to-flexplate bolts.

➡ **Use a scribe to mark the flexplate-to-torque converter relationship for reassembly.**

26. Lower the vehicle.
27. Attach a suitable lifting hook and chain to the engine lifting brackets. Raise the engine slightly to take the weight off the engine mounts.
28. Remove the engine torque axis engine mount.
29. Support the transaxle and remove the engine-to-transaxle bolts.
30. Separate the engine from the transaxle, raise the engine and remove from the vehicle.

To install:

31. Lower the engine assembly into the vehicle.
32. Install and tighten the engine-to-transaxle bolts to 55 ft. lbs. (75 Nm).
33. Install and tighten the torque axis engine mount bolts to 52 ft. lbs. (87 Nm).
34. Raise and safely support the vehicle.
35. Align the torque converter and flexplate with the marks made during removal.
36. Install and tighten the converter to flexplate bolts to 46 ft. lbs. (62 Nm).
37. Install the starter motor.
38. Install the flexplate cover.
39. Install the engine to transaxle bracket.
40. Remount the A/C compressor.
41. Connect the exhaust pipe to the manifold.
42. Lower the vehicle.
43. Connect the brake booster and heater control hoses to the engine vacuum connections.
44. Connect the vacuum hoses to the cruise control servo assembly.
45. Connect the emission control canister hoses to the throttle body connections.
46. Connect the fuel feed and return lines from the fuel rail and fuel pressure regulator.
47. Connect the ignition assembly ground strap to the fender inner panel attaching screws.
48. Connect the following sensors:
   • MAT sensor
   • TP sensor
   • IAC valve
   • O2S sensor

   • Oil pressure switch
   • Power Steering cutoff switch
   • VSS
   • Low oil level sensor
49. Connect the throttle cable to the throttle mounting bracket and connect other applicable cables.
50. Install the air flow duct.
51. Install the power steering pump.
52. Install the drive belts.
53. Connect the engine harness at the bulkhead.
54. Install the negative battery cable to the engine block.
55. Connect the radiator and heater supply hoses.
56. Refill engine oil.
57. Refill and bleed the engine cooling system following the recommended procedure.
58. Install the hood, aligning the marks made during removal.
59. Connect the negative battery cable.
60. Start the engine and check for leaks.
61. Road test the vehicle and check operation.

Water Pump

REMOVAL & INSTALLATION

3.8L (VIN K) Engine

1. Before servicing the vehicle, refer to the precautions in the beginning of this section.
2. Disconnect the negative battery cable.
3. Drain the cooling system into an approved container.
4. Remove the accessory drive belt following the procedure in the belt removal section.
5. Disconnect the coolant hoses from the water pump.
6. Remove the water pump pulley bolts. (The long bolt can be removed by lining the head of the bolt up with the hole in the frame rail). Remove the pulley.
7. Remove the water pump mounting bolts and remove the water pump.

To install:

8. Clean all the sealing surfaces.
9. Apply a thin bead of sealer around the outside edge of the water pump and install the gasket on the pump.
10. Install the water pump on the engine. Tighten the water pump-to-engine block bolts to 22 ft. lbs. (30 Nm) and the water

1. Coolant pump
2. Engine front cover
3. Gasket
4. 11 ft. lb. (15 Nm)
5. 22 ft. lb. (30 Nm)

7922UG01

Exploded view of the water pump mounting—3.8L (VIN K and 1) engines shown

pump-to-front cover bolts to 11 ft. lbs. (15 Nm) plus an additional 80 degree turn.

11. Install the water pump pulley. Tighten the water pump pulley bolts to 115 inch lbs. (13 Nm).

12. Connect the coolant hoses to the water pump and secure clamps.

13. Install the drive belt following the procedure in the belt section.

14. Refill and bleed the cooling system following proper procedures.

15. Run the engine and check for leaks.

16. Recheck the coolant level when the engine has cooled.

3.8L (VIN 1) Engine

1. Before servicing the vehicle, refer to the precautions in the beginning of this section.

2. Disconnect the negative battery cable.

3. Drain the cooling system into an approved container.

4. Remove the A/C compressor splash shield.

5. Remove the supercharger and accessory drive belts.

6. Remove the coil pack and position out of the way.

7. Remove the supercharger belt tensioner.

8. Support the engine using engine support fixture J 28467-A or equivalent, and remove the front engine mount.

9. Remove the power steering pump.

10. Remove the engine mount bracket and the idler pulley.

11. Remove the water pump pulley.

12. Remove the water pump mounting bolts and remove the water pump.

To install:

13. Clean all sealing surfaces.

14. Apply a thin bead of sealer around the outside edge of the water pump and install a new gasket on the pump.

15. Install the water pump on the engine and tighten the short bolts to 11 ft. lbs. (15 Nm). Tighten the long bolts to 22 ft. lbs. (30 Nm).

16. Install the water pump pulley and tighten bolts to 115 inch lbs. (13 Nm).

17. Install the engine mount bracket and the idler pulley.

18. Install the power steering pump.

19. Install the front engine mount.

20. Install the supercharger belt tensioner.

21. Install the ignition coil pack assembly.

22. Install the supercharger and accessory drive belts.

23. Install the A/C compressor splash shield.

24. Connect the negative battery cable.

25. Fill and bleed the cooling system following the proper procedure.

26. Run the engine and check for leaks.

27. Recheck the coolant level when the engine has cooled.

Cylinder Head

REMOVAL & INSTALLATION

1. Before servicing the vehicle, refer to the precautions in the beginning of this section.

2. Disconnect the negative battery cable.

3. Relieve the fuel system pressure using the recommended procedure.

4. Drain the cooling system.

5. Remove the supercharger assembly (VIN 1 only).

6. Remove the intake manifold (VIN K only).

7. Remove the valve covers.

8. Tag and disconnect the ignition wires and remove the ignition coil/ module assembly.

9. Remove the alternator front mounting bracket.

10. Remove the one bolt securing the A/C bracket to the cylinder head.

11. Remove the power steering pump and set to the side. Complete removal of the steering pump is not needed.

12. Remove the accessory drive belt tensioner. For VIN 1 engines, remove the supercharger belt tensioner.

13. Remove the fuel pipe heat shield.

14. Remove the rocker arm assemblies and take note of their original position.

15. Remove the pushrods.

16. Remove the cylinder head bolts and discard.

17. Remove the cylinder head gaskets.

18. Clean all sealing surfaces and the cylinder head bolt holes in the block.

To install:

19. Place the cylinder head gasket on the engine block dowels with the note **THIS SIDE UP** facing the cylinder head and the arrow facing the front of the engine. Position the cylinder head on the engine block.

❋❋❋ WARNING

In order to prevent damage to the gasket when installing the cylinder head, do not slide the cylinder head on the gasket. Head gaskets are not interchangeable. Failure to install

with arrow pointing to the front will cause gasket failure and possible engine damage. Gaskets are identified by either an L or an R stamped on it next to the arrow.

20. Install the cylinder head bolts and tighten them as follows:

➡This engine uses special torque-to-yield head bolts. The procedure must be followed carefully and new bolts must be used whenever the head is removed. Total bolt torque should not exceed 60 ft. lbs. (81 Nm).

   a. Tighten the cylinder head bolts, in the proper sequence, to 37 ft. lbs. (50 Nm).

   b. Rotate each bolt 130 degrees, in sequence.

   c. Rotate the center four bolts an additional 30 degrees, in sequence.

21. Install the pushrods and guide plate.

22. Install the rocker arm assemblies into their original location.(Apply approved thread lock compound to the rocker arm pedestal bolts before assembly).

23. Install the valve covers.

24. Install the fuel pipe heat shield.

25. Install the accessory drive belt tensioner. For VIN 1 engines, install the supercharger belt tensioner.

26. Install the power steering pump.

27. Install the A/C compressor bracket bolt, and tighten to 52 ft. lbs. (70 Nm).

28. Install the alternator front mounting bracket.

29. Install the ignition coil/ module assembly. Install the spark plug wires.

30. Install the supercharger assembly. (VIN 1 ONLY).

31. Install the intake manifold. (VIN K ONLY).

32. Fill and bleed the cooling system following the proper procedure.

33. Connect the negative battery cable.

34. Start the engine and check for leaks and proper operation.

Rocker Arms

REMOVAL & INSTALLATION

➡When removing valvetrain components, it is very important that they are marked for installation reference, so that they can be reinstalled in the same location from which they were removed.

1. Before servicing the vehicle, refer to the precautions in the beginning of this section.

2. Disconnect the negative battery cable.

3. If removing the left (front) rocker arm cover, proceed as follows:

   a. Disconnect the spark plug wires from the spark plugs and position the wires aside, out of the way.

   b. Remove the rocker arm cover bolts and pull off valve cover.

4. If removing the right (rear) rocker arm cover, proceed as follows:

   a. Disconnect the spark plug wires from the spark plugs and position the wires aside, out of the way.

5. Remove the rocker arm cover bolts and the rocker arm cover.

6. Remove the rocker arm pedestal bolts and remove the rocker arm and pedestal assembly. Keep all parts in order so they can be reinstalled in their original locations.

7. Inspect the rocker arms and pedestals for wear and/or damage; replace as necessary.

8. Remove the pushrods. Keep them in order so they can be reinstalled in their original locations.

9. Inspect the pushrod tips for wear and/or damage. Roll the pushrods on a flat surface to check for a bent condition. Replace any pushrod that is bent and/or damaged.

10. Clean all parts and all sealing surfaces. Be sure all thread adhesive is removed from the rocker arm pedestal bolts and rocker arm cover bolts.

To install:

11. Lubricate the pushrod tips with assembly lubricant and install them in their proper locations.

12. Lubricate the rocker arms and pedestals with assembly lubricant and install. Be sure the pushrod tips are properly seated in the rocker arms.

13. Apply suitable thread locking compound to the rocker arm pedestal bolt threads and install. Tighten the bolts to 11 ft. lbs. (15 Nm) plus an additional 90 degree turn.

14. Install the rocker arm cover using a new gasket. Apply suitable thread locking compound to the rocker arm cover bolts and install. Tighten to 89 inch lbs. (10 Nm).

15. Reposition the spark plug wires and connect them to the spark plugs.

16. Reinstall the power steering pump and/or alternator brace, as required.

17. Install the accessory drive belt(s).

18. Connect the negative battery cable.

19. Run the engine and check for leaks and proper engine operation.

Supercharger

REMOVAL & INSTALLATION

➡A small amount of oil seepage through the front seal, behind the pulley, of the supercharger is normal. This

To avoid leakage and to prevent damage to the cylinder head, always tighten the bolts according to the sequence shown—3.8L (VIN K and 1) engines

7922UG02

1. Dowel pin
2. Head gasket
3. Valve lifter
4. Pivot retainer
5. Rocker arm
6. Pushrod
7. Lifter guide
8. Bolt
9. Bolt
10. Head bolt

7922UG03

Exploded view of the rocker arms and related component mounting—3.8L engines

Timing belt service is covered in Section 5 of this manual

Legend

(1) Fuel Injection Rail
(2) Fuel Injector Sight Shield Bracket
(3) MAP Sensor Bracket Bolt
(4) MAP Sensor Bolt
(5) MAP Sensor
(6) MAP Sensor Bracket
(7) Bypass Valve
(8) Throttle Body
(9) Water Outlet Bolt
(10) Accelerator Cable Control Bracket
(11) Accelerator Cable Control Bracket Bolt
(12) Water Outlet
(13) Water Outlet Gasket
(14) Thermostat
(15) Supercharger Gasket
(16) Engine Coolant Manifold Bolt
(17) Engine Coolant Manifold
(18) Engine Coolant Manifold Gasket
(19) Coolant Temperature Sensor
(20) Lower Intake Manifold Gasket

(21) Lower Intake Manifold Seal
(22) Heater Inlet Pipe With Seal
(23) Exhaust Manifold Gasket
(24) Exhaust Manifold (Right)
(25) Lower Intake Manifold
(26) Lower Intake Manifold Bolt
(27) Supercharger
(28) Supercharger Bolt
(29) Heated Oxygen Sensor
(30) Exhaust Manifold Bolt/Stud (Right)
(31) EGR Valve Adapter Bolt
(32) EGR Valve Outlet Pipe
(33) EGR Valve Outlet Pipe Bolt
(34) EGR Valve Outlet Pipe Nut
(35) EGR Valve Nut
(36) EGR Valve
(37) EGR Valve Gasket
(38) EGR Valve Adapter
(39) Fuel Injection Rail Nut

Exploded view of the supercharger and related components—VIN 1 engine

9300UG01

seepage is caused by minute traces of oil escaping around the seal due to normal pressure build up in the oil cavity within the supercharger. A build up of dust can stick to the thin oil film, which causes the oil seepage to appear worse than it really is. The supercharger should not be replaced for this seepage, however, if supercharger oil is visually dripping from the supercharger front seal, the supercharger will need to be replaced. The supercharger oil level should be checked every 30,000 miles or every 36 months.

1. Before servicing the vehicle, refer to the precautions in the beginning of this section.

2. Disconnect the negative battery cable.

3. Relieve the fuel system pressure using the recommended procedure.

4. Drain the cooling system.

5. Remove the drive belt from the supercharger pulley.

6. Remove the engine dress up cover.

7. Remove the air duct from the throttle body.

8. Label and disconnect the right side spark plug wires from the ignition module and set aside.

9. Remove the alternator brace with purge solenoid.

10. Remove EGR wiring harness and shield.

11. Disconnect the fuel injectors.

12. Remove the Manifold Absolute Pressure (MAP) sensor bracket.

13. Disconnect and cap the fuel lines from the fuel rail.

14. Remove the fuel rail mounting bolts and remove the fuel rail.

15. Remove the boost control solenoid.

16. Remove the throttle body nuts and remove the throttle body.

17. Remove the bolts from the supercharger assembly.

18. Remove the supercharger.

To install:

19. Thoroughly clean the supercharger and intake manifold sealing surfaces.

20. Install a new supercharger-to-intake manifold gasket. Do not use any sealer on this gasket.

21. Install the supercharger with the mounting bolts. Tighten the bolts, gradually and evenly, to 17 ft. lbs. (23 Nm).

22. Install the MAP sensor bracket.

23. Install the throttle body to the supercharger. Tighten the nuts to 89 inch lbs. (10 Nm).

24. Install the boost control solenoid. Tighten the nut to 72 inch lbs. (8 Nm).

25. Install the fuel rail and connect the fuel lines.

26. Attach the electrical connectors to the fuel injectors.

27. Install the alternator brace with purge solenoid.

28. Install the EGR wiring harness and shield.

29. Connect the right side spark plug wires to the ignition module.

30. Install the supercharger belt.

31. Install the air duct to the throttle body.

32. Install the engine dress up cover.

33. Connect the negative battery cable.

34. Fill and bleed the cooling system using the recommended procedure.

35. Run the engine and check for leaks and proper engine operation.

Intake Manifold

REMOVAL & INSTALLATION

3.8L (VIN K) Engine

1. Before servicing the vehicle, refer to the precautions in the beginning of this section.

2. Disconnect the negative battery cable.

3. Relieve the fuel system pressure using the recommended procedure.

4. Remove the fuel injector sight shield and air inlet duct.

5. Disconnect the spark plug wires from the right side spark plugs and route the wires out of the way.

6. Label and disconnect the vacuum lines from the intake manifold.

7. Disconnect the fuel lines, vacuum lines and electrical connectors from the fuel rail.

8. Remove the fuel rail mounting bolts and remove the fuel rail from the intake manifold.

9. Remove the EGR heat shield.

10. Remove the throttle cable bracket from the cylinder head mounting bracket and disconnect the cables from the throttle body lever.

11. Remove the throttle body support bracket.

12. Remove the upper intake plenum mounting bolts and remove the plenum and gasket.

13. Drain the cooling system.

14. Disconnect the upper radiator hose from the thermostat housing.

15. Remove the serpentine belt and the alternator.

16. Remove the four bolts and remove the drive belt tensioner assembly.

17. Disconnect the EGR valve outlet pipe, if necessary.

18. Remove the lower intake manifold mounting bolts and remove the intake manifold and gaskets.

To install:

19. Thoroughly clean all of the sealing surfaces.

20. Install the intake manifold using new manifold gaskets and install the intake manifold bolts finger-tight. With all the bolts in place, tighten the bolts in sequence to 11 ft. lbs. (15 Nm). With all bolts tightened, make a second pass and tighten each bolt again to 11 ft. lbs. (15 Nm).

21. Connect the EGR valve outlet pipe, if necessary.

22. Install the drive belt tensioner assembly and tighten the tensioner bolts to 37 ft. lbs. (50 Nm).

23. Install the alternator and serpentine belt.

24. Connect the upper radiator hose to the thermostat housing.

25. Install the upper intake plenum and mounting bolts. Tighten the intake plenum bolts to 11 ft. lbs. (15 Nm).

26. Install the throttle body support bracket.

27. Install the throttle cable bracket to the cylinder head mounting bracket and connect the cables to the throttle body lever.

28. Install the EGR heat shield.

29. Install the fuel rail and the mounting bolts on the intake manifold. Tighten the fuel rail bolts to 88 inch. lbs. (10 Nm).

30. Connect the fuel lines, vacuum lines and electrical connectors to the fuel rail.

31. Connect the vacuum lines to the intake manifold.

32. Connect the spark plug wires to the right side spark plugs and route the wires.

33. Install the fuel injector sight shield and air inlet duct.

34. Connect the negative battery cable.

35. Turn the ignition **ON**, to pressurize the fuel system, and check for leaks.

36. Refill and bleed the cooling system using the recommended procedure.

37. Run the engine and check for leaks and proper engine operation.

Legend

(1) Fuel Injector Sight Shield Bracket
(2) Vacuum Source Manifold
(3) Accelerator Cable Control Bracket
(4) Throttle Body Support Bolt
(5) Throttle Body
(6) Water Outlet Bolt
(7) Water Outlet
(8) Exhaust Manifold Gasket
(9) Water Outlet Gasket
(10) Thermostat
(11) Lower Intake Manifold
(12) Intake Manifold Seal
(13) Heater Water Inlet Pipe
(14) Lower Intake Manifold Gasket
(15) Coolant Temperature Sensor
(16) Engine Coolant Manifold Bolt
(17) Engine Coolant Manifold
(18) Engine Coolant Manifold Gasket
(19) Lower Intake Manifold Bolt
(20) Exhaust Manifold (Right)
(21) Exhaust Manifold Bolt/Stud
(22) Exhaust Oxygen Sensor
(23) EGR Valve Adapter Bolt
(24) EGR Valve Outlet Pipe
(25) EGR Valve Outlet Pipe Bolt
(26) EGR Valve Outlet Pipe Nut
(27) EGR Valve Adapter
(28) EGR Valve Gasket
(29) EGR Valve
(30) EGR Valve Nut
(31) Upper Intake Manifold
(32) ICM
(33) Fuel Injection Rail
(34) Fuel Injector Rail Nut
(35) Upper Intake Manifold Bolt

Exploded view of the intake manifold and related components—VIN K engine

9300UG02

Be sure to tighten the lower intake manifold mounting bolts in the correct sequence—3.8L (VIN K) engine

15. Clean all old sealant from the intake manifold bolts and bolt holes.

16. Install new gaskets and manifold seals. Apply sealant to the ends of the manifold seals.

17. Install the intake manifold.

18. Install the intake manifold bolts and tighten, in sequence, to 11 ft. lbs. (15 Nm).

19. Install the electrical connector to the ECT sensor.

20. Install the EGR tube to the intake manifold.

21. Install the thermostat housing.

22. Install the supercharger assembly.

23. Connect the negative battery cable.

24. Fill and bleed the cooling system using the recommended procedure.

25. Run the engine and check for leaks and proper engine operation.

Exhaust Manifold

REMOVAL & INSTALLATION

Left Side (Front) Manifold

1. Before servicing the vehicle, refer to the precautions in the beginning of this section.

2. Disconnect the negative battery cable.

3. Remove the two bolts attaching the left exhaust manifold to the right exhaust manifold.

4. Label and disconnect the spark plug wires from the spark plugs and position out of the way.

5. Remove the engine oil dipstick and tube.

6. Remove the manifold mounting bolts and studs and remove the exhaust manifold.

To install:

7. Be sure that the manifold and cylinder head sealing surfaces are clean and free

Upper intake manifold mounting bolt torque sequence—3.8L (VIN K) engine

7. Reinstall the front splash shield.

8. Lower the vehicle.

9. Remove the supercharger assembly.

10. Remove the thermostat housing.

11. Disconnect the EGR tube at the intake manifold.

12. Disconnect the Engine Coolant Temperature (ECT) sensor.

13. Remove the intake manifold.

To install:

14. Thoroughly clean all sealing surfaces.

3.8L (VIN 1) Engine

1. Before servicing the vehicle, refer to the precautions in the beginning of this section.

2. Disconnect the negative battery cable.

3. Relieve the fuel system pressure using the recommended procedure.

4. Raise and safely support vehicle.

5. Remove the front splash shield.

6. Drain the radiator coolant into a suitable container. Close radiator drain.

Tighten the lower intake manifold mounting bolts in the correct sequence to prevent warping the manifold—3.8L (VIN 1) engine

Refer to Section 1 for engine rebuilding specifications

Exploded view of the left exhaust manifold mounting

7922UG31

of any debris that might cause an exhaust leak.

8. Install the manifold to the cylinder head.

9. Tighten the studs and bolts, gradually and evenly, to 22 ft. lbs. (30 Nm).

10. Install the engine oil dipstick and tube.

11. Connect the spark plug wires to the spark plugs.

12. Install the two bolts attaching the left exhaust manifold to the right exhaust manifold. Tighten the bolts to 15 ft. lbs. (20 Nm).

13. Connect the negative battery cable.

14. Run the engine and check for exhaust leaks.

Right Side (Rear) Manifold

1. Before servicing the vehicle, refer to the precautions in the beginning of this section.

2. Disconnect the negative battery cable.

3. Label and disconnect the spark plug wires from the spark plugs.

4. Remove the transaxle fluid dipstick and tube.

5. Disconnect the Oxygen (O2S) sensor.

6. Remove the two bolts attaching the right exhaust manifold to the crossover pipe.

7. Raise and safely support the vehicle.

8. Remove the front exhaust pipe-to-exhaust manifold nuts and disconnect the exhaust pipe from the manifold.

9. Lower the vehicle.

10. Remove the engine lift bracket.

11. Remove the exhaust manifold mounting studs and bolts and remove the exhaust manifold.

12. Remove and discard the manifold-to-crossover pipe gasket and manifold-to-front exhaust pipe gasket.

To install:

13. Be sure that the manifold, cylinder head and crossover pipe sealing surfaces

are clean and free of any debris that might cause an exhaust leak.

14. Install the manifold to the cylinder head and crossover pipe using a new manifold-to-crossover pipe gasket.

15. Install the manifold mounting studs and bolts. Tighten the studs and bolts, gradually and evenly, to 22 ft. lbs. (30 Nm), beginning at the center of the manifold and working towards the ends.

16. Install the engine lift bracket.

17. Raise and safely support the vehicle.

18. Connect the exhaust pipe from the manifold and install the front exhaust pipe-to-manifold nuts. Tighten the nuts to 18 ft. lbs. (25 Nm).

19. Lower the vehicle.

20. Install the two bolts attaching the right exhaust manifold to the crossover pipe. Tighten the manifold-to-crossover pipe bolts and tighten to 15 ft. lbs. (20 Nm).

21. Attach the O2S sensor electrical connector.

22. Install the transaxle fluid dipstick and tube.

23. Connect the spark plug wires to the spark plugs.

24. Connect the negative battery cable.

25. Run the engine and check for exhaust leaks.

Camshaft and Valve Lifters

REMOVAL & INSTALLATION

1. Before servicing the vehicle, refer to the precautions in the beginning of this section.

2. Disconnect the negative battery cable.

3. Relieve the fuel system pressure using the recommended procedure.

4. Remove the engine assembly from the vehicle and mount on a suitable engine stand.

5. If equipped, remove the supercharger.

TIMING MARKS

TIMING MARKS

BALANCE SHAFT GEAR TO BALANCE SHAFT DRIVE GEAR

CAMSHAFT SPROCKET TO CRANKSHAFT SPROCKET

7922UG09

The timing marks should face each other when the chain and gears are installed properly

6. Remove the intake manifold.

7. Remove the rocker arm covers.

8. Remove the rocker arm assemblies, pushrods and lifters. A magnet may be helpful when pulling the lifters out of their bores. Identify all parts as they are removed, so they can be reinstalled in their original locations.

9. Remove the crankshaft balancer center bolt, using a suitable puller, remove the balancer from the crankshaft.

10. Remove the timing chain front cover.

11. Set the engine to Top Dead Center (TDC) No. 1 cylinder (firing position) to align the timing marks, before disassembling the timing chain and sprockets.

✳✳ WARNING

Align the timing marks of the camshaft and crankshaft sprockets to avoid burring the camshaft journals by the crankshaft.

12. Remove the camshaft sprocket and timing chain.

13. Remove the camshaft thrust plate bolts and remove the thrust plate.

14. Carefully remove the camshaft from the engine block.

15. Inspect the camshaft lobes and journals for wear and/or damage; replace as necessary.

✳✳ WARNING

If the camshaft was replaced the lifters must also be replaced. The old lifters have developed a wear pattern and will cause the new camshaft to wear prematurely.

To install:

16. Coat the camshaft lobes and bearings with lubricant GM part number 1052365 or equivalent camshaft break-in prelube prior to installation.

17. Carefully install the camshaft into the engine.

18. Install the camshaft thrust plate and tighten the mounting bolts to 10 ft. lbs. (14 Nm).

19. Install the camshaft sprocket and timing chain. Be sure the timing marks are aligned. Tighten the camshaft sprocket retaining bolt to 74 ft. lbs. (100 Nm) plus an additional 90 degree (1/4) turn.

20. Install the timing chain front cover.

21. Install the crankshaft balancer and tighten the mounting bolt to 111 ft. lbs. (150 Nm) plus an additional 76 degree turn.

22. Coat the valve lifters with camshaft prelube and install the lifters in the lifter bores.

23. Install the lifter guides and lifter guide retainer. Tighten the retainer mounting bolts to 22 ft. lbs. (30 Nm).

24. Install the pushrods and rocker arms and tighten the rocker arm bolts to 11 ft. lbs. (15 Nm) plus an additional 90 degree turn.

25. Install the rocker arm covers.

26. Install the intake manifold.

27. If equipped, install the supercharger.

28. Install the engine in the vehicle.

29. Connect the negative battery cable.

30. Verify that all fluid levels are full and correct.

31. Start the engine and check for leaks. Check engine operation.

Valve Lash

ADJUSTMENT

The valve clearance cannot be adjusted on these engines. The hydraulic lifters function to maintain a zero clearance when the valves are opening and closing. Any clearance is instantaneously taken up by the hydraulic action. "Valve lifter noise" complaints may require cleaning of sludge coated or varnished valve lifters, or replacement.

Oil Pan

REMOVAL & INSTALLATION

✳ WARNING

The oil level sensor, located in the oil pan, must be removed prior to removal of the oil pan. If the oil pan is removed first, damage to the oil level sensor may occur.

If equipped, be sure to remove the oil level sensor before removing the pan

1. Disconnect the negative battery cable.

2. Before servicing the vehicle, refer to the precautions in the beginning of this section.

3. Raise and safely support the vehicle.

4. Remove the oil drain plug and drain the engine oil into a suitable container.

5. Remove the flexplate cover.

6. Disconnect the oil level sensor and remove the sensor.

7. Remove the oil filter.

8. Remove the oil pan mounting bolts and remove the oil pan.

To install:

✳ WARNING

The oil level sensor, located in the oil pan, must be installed after the oil pan has been installed. If the oil level sensor is installed first, damage to the sensor may occur.

9. Clean all sealing surfaces completely. Thoroughly clean the inside of the oil pan.

10. Install the oil pan with a new gasket and tighten the mounting bolts to 125 inch lbs. (14 Nm).

11. If necessary, install a new oil filter and the flexplate cover.

12. Install the oil level sensor and attach the connector.

13. Install the oil drain plug and tighten to 30 ft. lbs. (40 Nm).

14. Lower the vehicle.

15. Refill the crankcase with the proper type and quantity of engine oil.

16. Connect the negative battery cable.

17. Run the engine and check for leaks.

Oil Pump

REMOVAL & INSTALLATION

1. Before servicing the vehicle, refer to the precautions in the beginning of this section.

2. Disconnect the negative battery cable.

3. Remove the engine drive belts and tensioner assembly.

4. Remove the drive belt idler pulley and bracket, if necessary.

5. Raise and safely support the vehicle.

6. Support the engine using engine support fixture J 28467 or equivalent, and remove the torque axis mount and bracket assembly.

7. Remove the engine front cover assembly.

The oil pump is located inside the front engine cover—VIN K and 1 engines

For engine torque specifications, refer to Section 1 of this manual

8. Remove the four bolts securing the oil filter adapter to the front cover assembly and remove the adapter, pressure regulator valve and spring.

9. Remove the four oil pump cover, on the inside of the front cover, attaching screws and remove the cover.

10. Remove the inner and outer pump gears and inspect.

To install:

11. Lubricate the oil pump gears with petroleum jelly and install the gears into the housing.

12. Pack the gear cavity with petroleum jelly after the gears have been installed in the housing.

➡ **Petroleum jelly seals the pump and acts like a "prime" so oil will begin to be drawn from the oil pan as soon as the engine begins to turn. DO NOT neglect this step. DO NOT use any type of grease. Petroleum jelly has a low melting point and will correctly dissipate when oil begins to flow and it is no longer needed.**

13. Install the oil pump cover and screws and tighten to 97 inch lbs. (11 Nm).

14. Install the oil filter adapter with new gasket, pressure regulator valve and spring. Apply sealant to the bolt threads and tighten the mounting bolts to 24 ft. lbs. (33 Nm).

15. Install the front cover assembly.

16. Install the tensioner assembly.

17. Install the drive belt idler pulley and bracket, if removed.

18. Install the drive belts.

19. Install the torque axis mount assembly and remove the engine support fixture.

20. Verify the correct engine oil level. A new oil filter is recommended.

21. Connect the negative battery cable.

22. Start the vehicle and verify no leaks and proper oil pressure.

Rear Main Seal

REMOVAL & INSTALLATION

1. Before servicing the vehicle, refer to the precautions in the beginning of this section.

2. Remove the transaxle assembly.

3. Remove the flexplate from the crankshaft.

4. Carefully pry the old seal out of the engine block. Do not damage or scratch the sealing surface of the crankshaft or the seal bore.

7922UG32

Rear main oil seal and rear cover

To install:

5. Lubricate the lip and the outer edge of the new seal with clean engine oil.

6. Slide the oil seal on the mandrel until the back of the seal is seated squarely against the collar of the tool.

7. Attach Seal Installer J-38196 or equivalent to the rear of the crankshaft with the two mounting bolts, then turn the T-handle until the oil seal is fully seated into the rear of the engine.

8. Loosen the T-handle of the tool completely.

9. Remove the two attaching bolts and remove the tool

10. Install the flexplate. Tighten the bolts to 11 ft. lbs. (15 Nm), then turn the bolts an additional 50 degrees.

11. Install the transaxle using the recommended procedure.

Timing Chain, Sprockets, Front Cover and Seal

REMOVAL & INSTALLATION

1. Before servicing the vehicle, refer to the precautions in the beginning of this section.

2. Disconnect the negative battery cable.

3. Drain the cooling system.

4. Disconnect the coolant hoses from the timing chain front cover.

5. Support the engine using support fixture J 28467-A or equivalent, and remove the engine mount.

6. Remove the drive belt(s).

7. Raise and safely support the vehicle.

8. Remove the right front wheel.

9. Remove the right inner fender access panel.

10. Remove the drive belt idler pulley and bracket. (VIN 1).

11. Remove the drive belt tensioner.

12. Keep the flexplate from turning using holder tool J 37096 or equivalent. Remove the crankshaft balancer retaining bolt, then use puller tool J 38197 or equivalent, to remove the balancer from the crankshaft.

BOLT   OIL SEAL   STUD   COVER   GASKET

7922UG12

Timing chain front cover—VIN K and 1) engines

13. Remove the Crankshaft Position (CKP) sensor shield and the CKP sensor.

14. Remove the oil pan-to-front cover bolts.

15. Remove the front cover attaching bolts and remove the timing chain front cover.

16. Align the timing marks on the camshaft and crankshaft sprockets so they are as close together as possible.

17. Remove the timing chain damper.

18. Remove the camshaft sprocket retaining bolt and remove the camshaft sprocket and timing chain.

19. Remove the crankshaft sprocket.

➡**Do not rotate the camshaft or crankshaft while the timing chain and sprockets are removed.**

20. Thoroughly clean all sealing surfaces.

To install:

21. Assemble the timing chain and sprockets with the timing marks aligned.

22. Install the timing chain and sprockets to the crankshaft first,, then to the camshaft.

23. Install the camshaft sprocket bolt and tighten to 74 ft. lbs. (100 Nm) plus an additional 90 degree turn. Recheck the camshaft and crankshaft sprocket timing marks to be sure they are still aligned.

24. Install the timing chain damper and tighten the bolt to 16 ft. lbs. (22 Nm).

✳✳ WARNING

The oil pump is built into the front cover. When the cover is removed, oil drains from the pump. Since the pump "loses its prime" it may not establish oil pressure as soon as the engine starts. Therefore, it is important to remove the oil pump cover from the back of the timing chain front cover and pack the space around the oil pump gears completely full of petroleum jelly. If this is not done, the oil pump may not pump engine oil when the engine is started, resulting in severe engine damage.

25. Remove the screws and the oil pump cover from the back of the timing chain front cover. Pack the space around the oil pump gears completely full of petroleum jelly. There must be no air space left inside the pump.

26. Reinstall the pump cover and tighten the screws to 97 inch lbs. (11 Nm).

BALANCE SHAFT GEAR TO BALANCE SHAFT DRIVE GEAR

CAMSHAFT SPROCKET TO CRANKSHAFT SPROCKET

7922UG09

Timing chain sprocket and balance shaft gear alignment—VIN K and 1 engines

27. Using new gaskets, install the timing chain front cover to the block. Tighten the front cover-to-engine block bolts to 11 ft. lbs. (15 Nm) plus an additional 40 degrees.

28. Install the oil pan-to-front cover bolts and tighten the bolts to 125 inch lbs. (14 Nm).

29. Install the CKP sensor and tighten the bolts to 14–28 ft. lbs. (20–40 Nm). Install the CKP sensor shield.

30. Keep the flexplate from turning using holder tool J 37096 or equivalent. Install the crankshaft balancer and tighten the bolt to 111 ft. lbs. (150 Nm) plus an additional 76 degree turn.

31. Install the drive belt tensioner assembly.

32. Install the drive belt idler pulley. (VIN 1).

33. Install the right inner fender access panel and the right front wheel.

34. Lower the vehicle.

35. Install the drive belt(s).

36. Install the engine mount and remove the engine support fixture.

37. Connect the coolant hoses.

38. Connect the negative battery cable.

39. Fill and bleed the cooling system using the recommended procedure.

40. Start the vehicle and check for leaks and proper engine operation.

FUEL SYSTEM

Fuel System Service Precautions

Safety is the most important factor when performing not only fuel system maintenance but any type of maintenance. Failure to conduct maintenance and repairs in a safe manner may result in serious personal injury or death. Maintenance and testing of the vehicle's fuel system components can be accomplished safely and effectively by adhering to the following rules and guidelines.

• To avoid the possibility of fire and personal injury, always disconnect the negative battery cable unless the repair or test procedure requires that battery voltage be applied.

• Always relieve the fuel system pressure prior to disconnecting any fuel system component (injector, fuel rail, pressure regulator, etc.), fitting or fuel line connection. Exercise extreme caution whenever relieving fuel system pressure to avoid exposing skin, face and eyes to fuel spray. Please be advised that fuel under pressure may penetrate the skin or any part of the body that it contacts.

• Always place a shop towel or cloth around the fitting or connection prior to loosening to absorb any excess fuel due to spillage. Ensure that all fuel spillage (should it occur) is quickly removed from engine surfaces. Ensure that all fuel soaked cloths or towels are deposited into a suitable waste container.

• Always keep a dry chemical (Class B) fire extinguisher near the work area.

• Do not allow fuel spray or fuel vapors to come into contact with a spark or open flame.

• Always use a back-up wrench when loosening and tightening the fuel line connection fittings. This will prevent unnecessary stress and torsion to fuel line piping.

• Always replace worn fuel fitting O-rings with new. Do not substitute fuel hose or equivalent, where fuel pipe is installed.

Fuel System Pressure

RELIEVING

1. Disconnect the negative battery cable to avoid possible fuel discharge if an accidental attempt is made to start the engine.

2. Remove the fuel tank cap to relieve tank pressure. Do not tighten until service procedure has been completed.

3. Connect a suitable fuel pressure gauge with bleed valve such as J-34730–1 or equivalent, to the fuel pressure test port. Wrap a shop towel around the fitting while connecting the gauge to catch any spilled fuel.

4. Install the bleed hose into an approved container and open the valve to bleed off the fuel system pressure.

5. Drain any fuel remaining in the gauge into an approved container.

✛ CAUTION

There may still be residual fuel in the system, and a small amount of fuel may be released when servicing fuel lines or connections. In order to reduce the chance of personal injury, cover the fuel line fittings with a shop towel before disconnecting to catch any fuel that may leak out.

Fuel Filter

REMOVAL & INSTALLATION

1996 Models

1. Before servicing the vehicle, refer to the precautions in the beginning of this section.

2. Disconnect the negative battery cable.

3. Relieve the fuel system pressure using the recommended procedure.

4. Raise and safely support the vehicle.

5. Detach the inlet and outlet quick connect fuel lines from the filter following these steps:

a. Twist quick connector ¼ turn in each direction to loosen ant dirt that may have accumulated in the connector.

b. Use compressed air to remove any dirt in the connector.

c. Squeeze plastic tabs of male connector and pull apart.

6. Remove the filter bracket mounting bolt and remove the fuel filter from the vehicle.

To install:

7. Position the fuel filter in the mounting bracket, making sure it is facing in the proper direction.

8. Attach the inlet and outlet quick connect lines to the fuel filter following these steps:

a. Be sure the connectors are clean and that new plastic retainers are used on the filter.

b. Apply a couple of drops of engine oil to the male pipe ends of filter.

c. Push the fuel lines onto the fuel filter until the plastic retainer snaps into place.

d. Check that the connectors are locked into place by trying to pull the connector from the filter.

9. Install the filter bracket mounting bolt and tighten to 10 ft. lbs. (14 Nm).

10. Lower the vehicle.

11. Connect the negative battery cable.

12. Pressurize the fuel system by turning the ignition switch to the **ON** position, then check for leaks.

1997–00 Models

1. Disconnect the negative battery cable.

2. Relieve the fuel system pressure using the recommended procedure.

3. Raise and safely support the vehicle.

4. Detach the quick connect fuel line from the filter following these steps:

a. Twist quick connector ¼ turn in each direction to loosen ant dirt that may have accumulated in the connector.

b. Use compressed air to remove any dirt in the connector.

c. Squeeze the plastic tabs of the male connector and pull apart.

5. Remove the threaded connection from the inlet side of the filter.

6. Remove the filter.

To install:

7. Position the fuel filter, making sure it is facing in the proper direction.

8. Attach the outlet quick connect line to the fuel filter following these steps:

a. Be sure the connector is clean and that a new plastic retainer is used on the filter.

b. Apply a couple of drops of engine oil to the male pipe end of filter.

c. Push the fuel line onto the fuel filter until the plastic retainer snaps into place.

d. Check that the connector is locked into place by trying to pull the connector from the filter.

Common fuel filter mounting location

9. Install the threaded connection to the inlet side of filter.

10. Lower the vehicle.

11. Connect the negative battery cable.

12. Pressurize the fuel system by turning the ignition switch to the **ON** position, then check for leaks.

Fuel Pump

REMOVAL & INSTALLATION

Except 1997–00 Park Avenue

1. Before servicing the vehicle, refer to the precautions in the beginning of this section.

2. Disconnect the negative battery cable.

3. Relieve the fuel system pressure using the recommended procedure.

4. Raise and safely support the vehicle.

5. Remove the fuel tank from the vehicle following these steps:

    a. Drain the fuel tank with a hand operated pumping device.

    b. Remove the fuel tank filler pipe and the EVAP pipe from the tank.

    c. Remove the quick connect fuel lines from the fuel tank.

    d. Remove the rubber exhaust hangers in the rear to allow room to lower the fuel tank.

    e. Use a jacking device, such as a transmission jack, to support the fuel tank.

    f. Remove the fuel tank strap retaining bolts and let the straps hang freely.

    g. Lower the fuel tank enough to remove fuel sender connector.

    h. Remove the fuel tank and place on a suitable workbench.

6. Clean the fuel tank in the area of the fuel sender assembly, to prevent dirt and debris from entering the tank when the fuel sender is removed.

7. Rotate the lock ring on top of the tank counterclockwise using a fuel sender spanner wrench and remove the fuel sender assembly from the tank.

8. Note the direction the strainer is pointing and remove the strainer from the pump by pulling it down and twisting.

9. Disconnect the pump electrical wires and hoses.

10. Pull the pump assembly out of the rubber connectors.

To install:

11. Transfer any insulators and grommets from the old pump to the new one.

12. Connect the pump to the fuel hose and tilt the bottom of the pump into the mounting bracket.

13. Install a new strainer on the pump so it points in the same direction as noted during removal.

14. Attach the electrical connectors and fuel lines to the pump.

15. Install a new O-ring on top of the fuel tank and install the fuel sender assembly carefully into the tank.

16. Install the lock ring and rotate it clockwise until the tabs are against the stops.

17. Install the fuel tank in the vehicle following these sub-steps:

    a. Raise the fuel tank into position.

    b. Attach the fuel sender electrical connector to the sender.

    c. Place the fuel tank straps into position and install the retaining bolts. Tighten the retaining bolts to 25 ft. lbs. (34 Nm).

    d. Remove the support.

    e. Install the rubber exhaust hangers to rear exhaust.

    f. Install the quick connect lines onto the fuel tank.

    g. Install the fuel tank EVAP pipe to the tank and tighten the hose clamp to 25 inch lbs. (2.8 Nm).

Fuel pump and level sender assembly

7922UG34

    h. Install the fuel tank filler pipe to the tank and tighten the hose clamp to 25 inch lbs. (2.8 Nm).

18. Lower the vehicle.

19. Connect the negative battery cable.

20. Refill the fuel tank.

21. Turn the ignition switch to the **ON** position, to pressurize the fuel system, and check for leaks.

22. Run the engine and check for leaks and proper engine operation.

1997–00 Park Avenue

1. Before servicing the vehicle, refer to the precautions in the beginning of this section.

2. Disconnect the negative battery cable.

3. Relieve the fuel system pressure using the recommended procedure.

4. Drain the fuel tank with a hand operated pumping device to at least a ¼ of tank of fuel.

5. Open trunk and remove the spare tire cover, jack and spare tire.

6. Pull back the trunk lining to access the fuel sender access panel.

7. Remove the retaining screws in the sender access panel and remove.

8. Clean the area around the connection before removing sender.

9. Remove the quick connect fittings from the sender.

10. Remove the electrical connector from the sender and position harness and hoses aside.

✳✳ CAUTION

When removing the fuel sender from the tank, the reservoir bucket is full of fuel. Use caution in containing the fuel with some shop towels.

11. Remove the sender retaining ring with a fuel sender spanner wrench.

12. Remove the sender and take note of it's removal position.

13. Remove and discard fuel sender O-ring.

14. Note the direction the strainer is pointing and remove the strainer from the pump by pulling it down and twisting.

15. Disconnect the pump electrical wires and hoses.

16. Pull the pump assembly out of the rubber connectors.

To install:

17. Transfer any insulators and grommets from the old pump to the new one.

18. Connect the pump to the fuel hose and tilt the bottom of the pump into the mounting bracket.

The fuel pump service cover is located in the luggage compartment under the spare tire—1997–00 Park Avenue

7922UG13

19. Install a new strainer on the pump so it points in the same direction as noted during removal.

20. Attach the electrical connectors and fuel lines to the pump.

21. Install a new O-ring on top of the fuel tank and install the fuel sender assembly carefully into the tank.

22. Install the lock ring and rotate clockwise until the tabs are against the stops.

23. Attach the fuel line quick connectors and the sender electrical connector.

24. Install the fuel sender access cover.

25. Reposition trunk liner and install the spare tire, jack and spare tire cover.

26. Fill with fuel and check for leaks.

DRIVE TRAIN

Transaxle Assembly

REMOVAL & INSTALLATION

1. Before servicing the vehicle, refer to the precautions in the beginning of this section.

2. Raise the hood and place protective covers over the fenders.

3. Disconnect the negative battery cable.

4. Loosen the cross brace assembly through-bolts and remove the inboard strut retaining nuts.

5. Remove the cross brace.

6. Reinstall the inboard strut retaining nuts.

7. Remove the air intake duct.

8. Remove the cruise control cable at throttle body.

9. Remove the shift control linkage and mounting bracket at the transaxle.

10. Detach the wiring connectors at the following switches:

• Transaxle park/neutral position switch

• Back-up light switch

• Transaxle electrical connector

• Vehicle Speed Sensor (VSS)

11. Remove the fuel pipe retainers.

12. Remove the three top transaxle-to-engine bolts.

13. Install special tool J 28467 A or equivalent engine support fixture.

14. Load the engine support fixture by tightening the wing nuts several turns to relieve tension on the frame and mounts.

15. Turn the steering wheel to the full left position.

16. Raise and safely support the vehicle.

17. Remove both front wheels.

18. Remove the right and left front ball joint nuts.

19. Separate the right and left control arms from the steering knuckle.

20. Remove the right halfshaft from the transaxle only. Do not remove the halfshaft from the steering knuckle assembly.

21. Remove the left halfshaft from both the transaxle and steering knuckle assembly.

22. Support the transaxle with a suitable jack.

23. Remove the left front transaxle mount.

24. Remove the torque strut bracket from the transaxle.

25. Remove the left rear transaxle mount-to-transaxle bolts.

26. Remove the transaxle brace from the engine bracket.

27. Remove the stabilizer shaft link-to-control arm bolt.

28. Remove the flexplate cover bolts and the flexplate cover.

29. Mark the flexplate to the converter with a reference line and remove the flexplate-to-converter bolts.

30. Remove the bolts attaching the rear frame member to the front dog leg.

31. Remove the front left frame-to-body attaching bolts.

32. Remove the frame assembly by swinging it aside and supporting with a suitable stand.

33. Remove the oil cooler lines from the transaxle.

34. Remove the remaining lower transaxle-to-engine block bolts.

➡ One transaxle bolt is located between the transaxle case and the engine block and is installed in the opposite direction.

35. Remove the transaxle assembly and lower it away from the vehicle.

To install:

36. Install the transaxle into the vehicle.

37. Support the transaxle with a suitable jack.

38. Install the lower transaxle-to-engine block bolts and tighten to 55 ft. lbs. (76 Nm).

39. Connect the cooler lines at the transaxle.

40. Raise the frame assembly into place and tighten the frame-to-body bolts to 83 ft. lbs. (112 Nm).

41. Install and tighten the front frame dog leg-to-right frame member bolts.

42. Install the left frame-to-body attaching bolts and tighten to 83 ft. lbs. (112 Nm).

43. Install the bolts attaching the rear frame member to the front frame dog leg.

44. Install the flexplate-to-converter bolts, aligning the marks made during removal, and tighten to 46 ft. lbs. (62 Nm).

45. Install the oil cooler lines to the transaxle.

46. Install the flexplate cover bolts and the flexplate cover.

47. Install the stabilizer shaft link-to-control arm bolt.

48. Install the transaxle brace to the engine bracket. Tighten the transaxle brace-to-engine bracket bolts to 70 ft. lbs.(95Nm).

49. Install the left rear transaxle mount-to-transaxle bolts.

50. Install the torque strut bracket to the transaxle.

51. Install the left front transaxle mount.

52. Install the left halfshaft to both the transaxle and steering knuckle assembly.

53. Install the right halfshaft to the transaxle.

54. Connect the right and left control arms to the steering knuckle.

55. Install the right and left front ball joint nuts.

56. Install both front wheels.

57. Lower the vehicle.

58. Turn the steering wheel to the straight ahead position.

59. Remove the support fixture from the engine.

60. Install the three top transaxle-to-engine bolts. Tighten the bolts to 55 ft. lbs. (76 Nm).

61. Install the fuel pipe retainers.

62. Attach the wiring connectors at the following switches:
- Transaxle park/neutral position switch.
- Back-up light switch.
- Transaxle electrical connector.
- VSS

63. Install the shift control linkage and mounting bracket at the transaxle.

64. Install the cruise control cable at throttle body.

65. Install the air intake duct.

66. Remove the inboard strut retaining nuts.

67. Install the cross brace.

68. Install the cross brace assembly through-bolts and remove the inboard strut retaining nuts.

69. Connect the negative battery cable.

70. Check the transaxle fluid level.

71. Start the engine and check for leaks.

72. Adjust the transaxle shifter cable, as necessary.

73. Road test the vehicle.

Halfshaft

REMOVAL & INSTALLATION

✳✳ WARNING

Use care when removing the halfshaft to prevent the inner CV-joint from becoming over-extended. Over-extension of the joint could result in separation of internal components and possible joint failure.

1. Before servicing the vehicle, refer to the precautions in the beginning of this section.

2. Raise and safely support the vehicle.

3. Remove the front wheel. Mark the position of the wheel to the wheel stud, prior to removal, for installation reference.

4. Install J-34754 boot protector, or equivalent on the outer CV-joint boot.

5. If necessary, loosen and remove the stabilizer shaft link assembly bolt.

6. Remove the ball joint cotter pin and nut. Loosen the joint using tool J-36226 or equivalent. The grease fitting may have to be removed from ball joint for tool access.

7. If removing the right halfshaft, turn the wheel to the left. If removing the left halfshaft, turn the wheel to the right.

8. Use a suitable prybar between the suspension support and the lower control arm to separate the joint.

9. Remove the hub nut. A large amount of torque is required to loosen the hub nut. Insert a drift pin or punch through the opening in the caliper into the ventilation openings in the brake rotor to keep the rotor from turning as the nut is loosened. Discard the hub nut; it must not be reused.

10. Partially install the hub nut to protect the threads, then remove the halfshaft from the hub using tool J-28733-B or equivalent.

11. Move the strut and knuckle rearward.

12. Remove the halfshaft from the transaxle using special tools J-33008 and J-2619–01 or their equivalents.

✳✳ WARNING

If equipped with anti-lock brakes, care must be used to prevent damage to the toothed sensor ring on the halfshaft and the wheel speed sensor on the steering knuckle.

To install:

13. If installing the right side halfshaft, install J-37292-B seal protector tool or equivalent, so that it can be pulled out after the halfshaft is installed.

14. Install the halfshaft into the transaxle by placing a drift pin or punch into the groove on the joint housing and tapping lightly until seated. Verify that the halfshaft is seated by grasping the inner joint housing and pulling. DO NOT pull on the halfshaft.

15. Install the halfshaft into the hub and

Use a slide hammer with the special adapter J-3308 or equivalent to remove the halfshaft from the transaxle

Insert the seal protector in the transaxle to prevent seal damage while the halfshaft is being installed

bearing assembly. Loosely install a new hub nut.

16. Install the ball joint into the steering knuckle.

17. Install the castle nut and tighten the nut to 88 inch lbs. (10 Nm), then tighten an additional 120 degrees (⅓ turn) during which a torque of 41 ft. lbs. (55 Nm) must be obtained.

➡**If necessary to install the cotter pin, the nut can be tightened up to 20 degrees additional. NEVER loosen the castle nut to install the cotter pin.**

18. Insert a drift in the brake rotor cooling fins to keep the rotor from turning and tighten the nut to 107 ft. lbs. (145 Nm), unless equipped the J55 brake option, in which case the torque is 130 ft. lbs. (177 Nm).

19. If removed, install the stabilizer shaft link assembly. Tighten the nut to 14 ft. lbs. (17 Nm).

20. If J-37292-B seal protector was installed, remove it by pulling in line with the handle.

21. Install the wheel, aligning the marks made during removal.

22. Lower the vehicle and road test for proper operation.

accidental deployment and possible personal injury.

• Never carry the inflator module by the wires or connector on the underside of the module.

• When carrying a live inflator module, hold securely with both hands, and ensure that the bag and trim cover are pointed away.

• Place the inflator module on a bench or other surface with the bag and trim cover facing up.

• With the inflator module on the bench, never place anything on or close to the module which may be thrown in the event of an accidental deployment.

DISARMING

✳✳ CAUTION

The Supplemental Restraint System (SRS) must be disarmed before performing service around the air bag or SRS wiring. Failure to do so may cause accidental deployment of the air bag, resulting in unnecessary SRS repairs and/or personal injury.

1. Turn the steering wheel so the front wheels are in the straight ahead position.

2. Turn the ignition switch to the **LOCK** position.

3. Disconnect the negative battery cable.

4. Remove the Air Bag fuse from the fuse panel.

➡**The position of the fuse on the panel varies according to model and year. Consult the vehicle owner's manual for fuse location.**

5. Remove the left-hand sound insulator (trim panel under the instrument panel).

6. Remove the Connector Position Assurance (CPA) clip and detach the yellow 2-way connector at the base of the steering column.

7. Remove the CPA and detach the passenger side yellow 2-way connector, if equipped. Positions for the connector vary from behind the glove box to removing the right side sound insulator and finding the yellow connector.

ARMING

After the necessary repairs have been made, re-enable the air bag system as follows:

1. Turn the steering wheel so the front wheels are in the straight ahead position.

STEERING AND SUSPENSION

Air Bag

✳✳ CAUTION

Some vehicles are equipped with an air bag system, also known as the Supplemental Inflatable Restraint (SIR) or Supplemental Restraint System (SRS). The system must be disabled before performing service on or around system components, steering column, instrument panel components, wiring and sensors. Failure to follow safety and disabling procedures could result in accidental air bag deployment, possible personal injury and unnecessary system repairs.

PRECAUTIONS

Several precautions must be observed when handling the inflator module to avoid

1 CONNECTOR, SIR
2 BRACKET, MULTIUSE MODULE
3 CONNECTOR POSITION ASSURANCE (CPA)
4 CONNECTOR, STEERING COLUMN WIRING HARNESS

7922UG35

Drivers side air bag connector

1 MODULE, INFLATOR
2 BRACKET, MULTIUSE
3 CONNECTOR, SIR

7922UG36

Passenger's side air bag connector

2. Turn the ignition switch to the **LOCK** position.

3. Disconnect the negative battery cable.

4. Attach the yellow 2-way connector at the base of the steering column and install the CPA.

5. Install the left-hand sound insulator.

6. Attach the yellow 2-way connector on the right side and install the CPA, if equipped. Install the sound insulator and/or glove box.

7. Install the air bag fuse.

8. Connect the negative battery cable.

9. Turn the ignition switch to the **RUN** position. Verify that the INFLATABLE RESTRAINT indicator lamp flashes 7–9 times, then remains OFF. If the lamp does not function as specified, there is a malfunction in the air bag system.

Power Rack and Pinion Steering Gear

REMOVAL & INSTALLATION

❋❋ WARNING

The wheels of the vehicle must be

straight ahead and the steering column in the LOCK position before disconnecting the steering column or intermediate shaft from the steering gear. Failure to do so will cause the Supplemental Inflatable Restraint (SIR) coil assembly in the steering column to become uncentered which will cause damage to the coil assembly.

1. Before servicing the vehicle, refer to the precautions in the beginning of this section.

2. Disconnect the negative battery cable.

3. Raise and safely support the vehicle.

4. Remove both front wheels.

5. Remove the pinch bolt from the intermediate shaft at the rack and pinion assembly and separate the shaft from the rack.

❋❋ CAUTION

Failure to disconnect the intermediate shaft from the rack and pinion stub shaft can result in damage to the steering gear and/or intermediate

shaft. This damage can cause loss of steering control which could result in personal injury.

6. Remove the cotter pins and castle nuts from the tie rod ends and separate the tie rods from the steering knuckles using special tool J 24319–01 or equivalent.

7. Remove the power steering line retainers and retaining clips.

8. Disconnect the power steering lines from the rack and pinion unit.

9. Support the rear of the subframe with a suitable jack. Loosen the front frame bolts and remove the rear bolts, then lower the frame about 3 in. (76mm) for clearance purposes.

❋❋ WARNING

Do not lower rear of frame too far as damage to engine components nearest to the cowl may result. Lower the rear of the frame no more than 3 in. (76mm).

10. Remove the rack and pinion mounting bolts.

11. Remove the rack and pinion through the left wheel opening.

To install:

12. Install the rack and pinion through the left wheel opening.

13. Raise the rear of the frame.

14. Apply Loctite® or equivalent, to the threads of the rack and pinion mounting bolts. Install the rack and pinion mounting bolts and tighten, in sequence, to 50 ft. lbs. (68 Nm).

15. Raise the subframe into position and install the mounting bolts. Tighten to 76 ft. lbs. (103 Nm).

16. Remove the jack.

17. Connect the power steering hoses and tighten the fittings to 20 ft. lbs. (27 Nm).

18. Connect the power steering lines to the retainers.

19. Connect the tie rod ends to the steering knuckles and tighten the castle nuts to 35 ft. lbs. (47 Nm). If necessary to align the holes for the cotter pin, tighten the nuts up to 60 degrees additional. NEVER loosen the castle nuts to align the holes.

20. Connect the intermediate shaft to the rack and pinion and tighten the pinch bolt to 35 ft. lbs. (47 Nm).

21. Install the wheels and tighten the lug nuts to 100 ft. lbs. (140 Nm).

VIEW A

1 BOLT; 68 N•m (50 LB. FT.).
   TIGHTEN IN SEQUENCE A THRU E.
2 STEERING GEAR
3 NUT; 47 N•m (35 LB. FT.). MAXIMUM
   PERMISSIBLE TORQUE TO ALIGN COTTER
   PIN SLOT IS 70 N•m (52 LB. FT.).
4 WASHER
5 STEERING KNUCKLE

7922UG16

Be sure to tighten the steering gear mounting bolts in the sequence shown

22. Lower the vehicle.
23. Connect the negative battery cable.
24. Fill the reservoir with fluid and bleed the air from the system.
25. Start the engine, check for leaks and proper steering operation.
26. Check the wheel alignment.

Strut

REMOVAL & INSTALLATION

Front

✳✳ WARNING

The steering knuckle must be retained after the strut-to-steering knuckle bolts have been removed. Failure to observe this may cause ball joint and/or halfshaft damage.

1. Before servicing the vehicle, refer to the precautions in the beginning of this section.
2. Loosen the strut housing tie bar through-bolts on both ends of the tie bar.
3. If equipped with electronic ride control option, detach the electrical connection.
4. Remove the three strut-to-body nuts at the strut mount.
5. Raise and safely support the vehicle, allowing the control arms to hang free.
6. Disconnect the ABS front wheel speed sensor.
7. Remove the wheel speed sensor bracket from the strut.

8. Remove the brake line bracket from the strut.
9. Remove the strut-to-steering knuckle bolts and remove the strut from the vehicle.
10. Install the strut assembly into compressor tool J 34013-B or equivalent, to compress the coil spring.
11. Compress spring slightly.
12. Hold the strut shaft from turning using a number 50 Torx® socket and remove the 24mm nut on the top end of the strut.
13. Install rod J 34013–38 or equivalent, to help guide the strut shaft out of the upper mount assembly.
14. Loosen the spring compressor tool until the coil spring and mount can be removed as an assembly. Remove the lower spring insulator, if equipped.
   To install:
15. Install the strut into spring compressor tool J 34013-B or equivalent. Install the lower insulator, coil spring and upper mount.
16. Compress the coil spring while guiding the strut shaft through the upper mount, using tool J 34013–38 or equivalent.
17. Install and tighten the upper nut to 55 ft. lbs. (75 Nm) while holding the strut shaft with a socket.
18. Remove the strut assembly from the spring compressor.
19. Install the strut in the vehicle.
20. Install and tighten the three strut mount nuts to 18 ft. lbs. (24 Nm).
21. Attach the electronic ride control option electrical connector, if removed.
22. Install the strut-to-knuckle bolts and tighten to 140 ft. lbs. (190 Nm).
23. Install the brake line bracket to the strut.
24. Install the wheel speed sensor bracket from the strut.
25. Attach the ABS front wheel speed sensor connector.
26. Install the front wheel, aligning the marks made during removal, and tighten the lug nuts to 100 ft. lbs. (140 Nm).
27. Lower the vehicle.
28. Check and adjust the wheel alignment.

Rear

1. Remove the trunk side cover or the rear seat cushion and seat back, as required, to gain access to the upper strut mounting nuts.
2. Raise and safely support the vehicle so the rear wheels are just off the ground.

1 NUTS, 47 N·m (35 LB. FT.)
2 WASHER
3 NUTS, 185 N·m (136 LB. FT.)
4 KNUCKLE
5 BOLT
6 STRUT

The strut assembly is mounted between the steering knuckle and the body—front strut shown

Use a Torx® socket to keep the piston rod from turning while removing the upper nut—front strut shown

Install the strut assembly into a suitable compressor such as compressor tool J 34013-B to safely remove the strut from the coil spring—front strut shown

Install rod J 34013–38 or equivalent, to help guide the strut shaft out of the upper mount assembly—front strut shown

3. Remove the rear wheel.
4. Using a suitable floor jack and a block of wood, support the lower control arm.
5. Remove the two upper strut mounting nuts.
6. If equipped with Electronic Leveling Control (ELC), disconnect the air tube from the strut.
7. Remove the lower strut bracket-to-knuckle bolts.
8. If equipped with Computer Control

Ride (CCR), lower the strut and separate the electrical connector.
9. Remove the strut from the vehicle.
To install:
10. If equipped with CCR, attach the electrical connector. As the strut is positioned, be sure the CCR wiring is routed properly.
11. Position the strut in the vehicle and loosely install the upper strut mounting nuts.
12. Install the sway bar bracket and the lower strut bracket-to-knuckle bolts.

13. Tighten the upper strut mounting nuts to 30 ft. lbs. (41 Nm).
14. Tighten the strut bracket-to-knuckle bolts to 140 ft. lbs. (190 Nm).
15. If equipped with ELC, connect the air tube.
16. For ELC equipped vehicles, lightly pressurize the ELC system by momentarily grounding terminal B at the height sensor connector before lowering the vehicle.

7922UG22

Exploded view of the lower strut mounting to the knuckle assembly—rear strut shown

7922UG21

Remove the cover to gain access to the upper strut mounting components—rear strut shown

17. Install the wheel and tighten the lug nuts to 100 ft. lbs. (140 Nm).

18. Remove the jack from under the control arm.

19. Lower the vehicle.

20. Check, if necessary, adjust the wheel alignment.

Coil Spring

REMOVAL & INSTALLATION

✳✳ CAUTION

The coil springs are under a considerable amount of tension. Be very careful when removing or installing them; they can exert enough force to cause very serious injury.

Front

For front coil spring service, please refer to the front strut procedure.

Rear

1. Before servicing the vehicle, refer to the precautions in the beginning of this section.

2. Raise and safely support the vehicle.

3. Remove the rear wheel.

4. If removing the right side coil spring, disconnect the height sensor link from the right control arm, if equipped with Electronic Leveling Control (ELC).

5. If removing the left side coil spring,

7922UG23

Exploded view of the rear coil spring mounting—H body

J 23028 – 01

7922UG24

Use a support bracket such as tool J-23028–01 mounted on a jack to support the rear lower control arm—H body

disconnect the parking brake cable retaining clip from the left control arm.

6. If equipped, remove the rear sway bar link from the bracket on the knuckle.

7. Mount tool J-23028–01 or an equivalent control arm support adapter, on a transmission jack and position to cradle the control arm bushings.

❊❊ CAUTION

Tool J-23028–01 or equivalent, must be secured to the jack or personal injury could result.

8. Place a chain around the spring and through the control arm as a safety measure.

9. Raise the jack to remove tension from the control arm pivot bolts.

10. Remove the rear nut and through-bolt.

11. Slowly maneuver the jack to relieve tension from the front control arm bolt.

12. Remove the front nut and through-bolt.

➥**Do not apply force to the control arm and/or ball joint to remove the spring. Proper maneuvering of the spring will allow for easy removal.**

13. Lower the jack to pivot the control arm downward. When all compression is removed from the spring, remove the safety chain, spring and insulators.

14. Inspect the spring insulators and replace them if they are cut or torn. If the vehicle has been driven more than 50,000 miles, replace them regardless of condition.

To install:

15. Snap the upper insulator onto the spring.

16. Position the lower insulator and spring in the vehicle.

17. Using the jack and J-23028–01 or equivalent, raise the control arm into place.

18. Slowly maneuver the jack to permit

installation of the control arm bolts and nuts.

➥**DO NOT tighten the nuts until the weight of the vehicle is on the suspension.**

19. If equipped, connect the rear sway bar to the knuckle bracket with the link assembly. Do not tighten the link bolt yet.

20. Connect the height sensor link to the right control arm or connect the parking brake cable retaining clip to the left control arm, as required.

21. Install the rear wheel and tighten the lug nuts to 100 ft. lbs. (140 Nm).

22. Lower the vehicle.

23. With the vehicle resting on its wheels, tighten the control arm through-bolt nuts to 85 ft. lbs. (115 Nm).

24. Tighten the sway bar link bolt to 13 ft. lbs. (17 Nm).

25. Check, if necessary, adjust the rear wheel alignment.

26. Road test the vehicle for proper operation.

Turn to Section 6 for brake system applications

Lower Ball Joint

REMOVAL & INSTALLATION

Front

EXCEPT PARK AVENUE

> ※※ **WARNING**
>
> **If the ball joint is separated for related suspension/drive line service, the ball joint seal should be inspected for damage. A damaged seal will cause ball joint failure. The ball joint should be replaced if seal damage is found.**

1. Before servicing the vehicle, refer to the precautions in the beginning of this section.

2. Raise and safely support the vehicle, allowing the control arms to hang free.

3. Remove the front wheel.

4. Remove the cotter pin from the lower ball joint and loosen the nut.

5. Using separator tool J 36226 or equivalent, separate the ball joint from the steering knuckle.

6. Remove the stabilizer shaft link assembly.

7. Drill out the three rivets retaining the lower ball joint to the lower control arm.

8. Remove the lower ball joint from the steering knuckle and control arm.

To install:

9. Install the lower ball joint to the steering knuckle and align the holes with the holes in the lower control arm.

10. Attach the ball joint to the lower control arm with bolts and nuts, making sure the bolts face down. Tighten the nuts to 50 ft. lbs. (68 Nm).

11. Install the stabilizer shaft link assembly. Tighten the nut to 13 ft. lbs. (17 Nm).

12. Tighten the lower ball joint nut to 88 inch lbs. (10 Nm). Then, tighten an additional 120 degree turn, during which a torque of 41 ft. lbs. (55 Nm) must be obtained.

13. Install the cotter pin to the lower ball joint. To align the slot in the nut with the hole in the lower ball joint stud, Tighten the ball joint nut up to one more flat. Never loosen the nut to align the slot.

14. Install the wheel and tighten the lug nuts to 100 ft. lbs. (140 Nm).

15. Lower the vehicle.

16. Check and adjust the wheel alignment.

1 PIN
2 NUT, BALL JOINT TO KNUCKLE; TIGHTEN TO 10 Nm (88 LB. IN.) THEN TIGHTEN 2 FLATS TO 55 Nm (41 LB. FT), MIN.
3 KNUCKLE
4 BALL JOINT MOUNTING BOLTS MUST FACE DOWN
5 CONTROL ARM
6 BALL JOINT MOUNTING NUTS 68 Nm (59 LB. FT.)
7 SERVICE BALL JOINT

7922UG25

The replacement ball joint should be attached to the control arm using three bolts and nuts—except Park Avenue

PARK AVENUE

The ball joint on the Park Avenue must be replaced with the lower control arm as an assembly.

Rear

1. Before servicing the vehicle, refer to the precautions in the beginning of this section.

2. Raise the vehicle and remove the rear wheel assembly.

3. If equipped with Electronic Level Control (ELC), remove the height sensor link from the right control arm.

4. Remove the parking brake cable retaining clip from the left control arm.

5. Remove the adjustment link from the knuckle using the appropriate puller.

6. Support the control arm with a jack, then remove the cotter pin and nut from the ball joint stud. Reinstall the nut on the stud with the flat side of the nut facing up. Do not tighten the nut.

> ※※ **WARNING**
>
> **Use only the recommended tools to remove the ball joint stud from the knuckle or damage to the ball joint or seal can occur.**

7. Using tool J 34505 or equivalent ball joint separator, remove the stud from the knuckle. Remove the slotted hex nut from the ball joint stud.

8. Press the ball joint out of the control arm using a suitable ball joint press such as tools J 9519–18, J 9519–7 and J 9519–17.

To install:

9. Press the new ball joint into the control arm using a ball joint press such as tools J 9519–16, J 9519–17, J 9519–18 and J 9519–23.

10. Install the ball joint stud into the knuckle and secure it with the slotted hex nut. Tighten the nut to 88 inch lbs. (10 Nm), then tighten the nut an additional four flats. The minimum torque on the nut should be 40 ft. lbs. (55 Nm).

11. Install a new cotter pin to secure the nut in position. The nut may be tightened up to one more flat in order to align the slot with the hole in the stud.

12. Install the adjustment link to the knuckle. Tighten the slotted nut to 33 ft. lbs. (45 Nm).

13. Install a new cotter pin to secure the nut. The nut must only be tightened to align the cotter pin hole with the slot in the nut.

14. If equipped with ELC, connect the height sensor link to the right control arm.

7922UG26

Use the ball joint press to remove the ball joint from the lower control arm—except Park Avenue

7922UG27

Use the ball joint press to install the ball joint into the lower control arm—except Park Avenue

15. Install the parking brake cable retainer to the left control arm.

16. Install the rear wheel assembly and lower the vehicle to the floor.

Lower Control Arm

REMOVAL & INSTALLATION

✳✳ WARNING

If the ball joint is separated for related suspension/drive line service, the ball joint seal should be inspected for damage. A damaged seal will cause ball joint failure. The ball joint should be replaced if seal damage is found.

1. Before servicing the vehicle, refer to the precautions in the beginning of this section.

2. Raise and safely support the vehicle, allowing the control arms to hang free.

3. Remove the front wheel.

4. Remove the stabilizer shaft link assembly from the control arm.

5. Remove the cotter pin from the lower ball joint and remove the nut.

6. Using separator tool J 36226 or equivalent, remove the ball joint from the steering knuckle.

7. Remove the lower control arm mounting bolts, then remove the lower control arm from the frame.

   To install:

8. Install the lower control arm to the frame with the attaching bolts, washers and nuts.

➡**Do not tighten the lower control arm nuts at this time. The weight of the vehicle must be supported by the control arms such that the vehicle design**

trim heights are obtained before tightening the lower control arm mounting nuts.

9. Connect the ball joint stud to the steering knuckle and torque the lower ball joint nut to 88 inch lbs. (10 Nm). Then tighten an additional 120 degree turn, during which a torque of 41 ft. lbs. (55 Nm) must be obtained.

10. Install the cotter pin to the lower ball joint. To align the slot in the nut with the hole in the lower ball joint stud, Tighten the ball joint nut up to one more flat. Never loosen the nut to align the slot.

11. Install the stabilizer shaft link assembly and torque the nuts to 13 ft. lbs. (17 Nm).

12. Install the wheel and torque the lug nuts to 100 ft. lbs. (140 Nm).

13. Lower the vehicle.

14. Torque the front lower control arm mounting nut to 140 ft. lbs. (190 Nm), then torque the rear lower control arm nut to 91 ft. lbs. (123 Nm).

15. Check and adjust wheel alignment.

Lower control arm mounting—Park Avenue

7922UG37

Wheel Bearings

ADJUSTMENT

The wheel bearings are not adjustable. If a wheel bearing is out of specifications, it must be replaced. Using a dial indicator, check for looseness. If play exceeds 0.005 in. (0.127mm) the bearing wear is excessive and the hub and bearing should be replaced.

REMOVAL & INSTALLATION

Front

1. Before servicing the vehicle, refer to the precautions in the beginning of this section.

2. Raise and safely support the vehicle.

3. Remove the front wheel.

4. Insert a drift punch through the caliper and into the rotor cooling fins to prevent the rotor from turning.

5. Remove the axle nut and washer.

6. Remove the caliper mounting bolts. Remove the caliper from the steering knuckle and support out of the way.

7922UG28

Exploded view of the front hub and wheel bearing assembly

For complete service labor times order Chilton's Labor Guide Manual

J 28733 – B

7922UG29

Use a puller such as J 2873-B to push the axle shaft out of the hub assembly

✳✳ WARNING

DO NOT allow the brake hose to support the weight of the caliper.

7. Remove the brake rotor.

8. Disconnect the ABS speed sensor and unclip from the dust shield.

9. Remove the three hub and bearing bolts and remove the dust shield.

10. Place the transaxle selector in the **P** detent.

11. Install J-28733 or an equivalent puller, and separate the hub and bearing from the drive axle.

12. Remove the hub and bearing assembly from the steering knuckle.

To install:

➡**The hub and bearing are replaced only as an assembly.**

13. Install the hub and bearing over the half shaft splines. Be sure the splines engage smoothly.

14. Apply a light coating of grease to the steering knuckle bore.

15. Slide the hub assembly onto the axle as far as possible. If the hub will not bottom out on the axle, install the hub mounting bolts and use the axle nut to draw the hub onto the axle.

16. Once the hub is flush with the steering knuckle, remove the mounting bolts and install the dust shield.

17. Reinstall the mounting bolts and tighten to 70 ft. lbs. (95 Nm).

18. Place the transaxle in **N**.

19. Attach the ABS front wheel speed sensor connector and clip to the dust shield.

20. Install the brake rotor.

7922UG30

Exploded view of the rear hub/wheel bearing assembly

21. Install the caliper and tighten the mounting bolts to 38 ft. lbs. (51 Nm).

22. Insert a drift punch through the rotor to prevent the axle from turning.

23. Tighten the drive axle shaft nut to 107 ft. lbs. (145 Nm).

24. Remove the drift punch.

25. Install the wheels and tighten the lug nuts to 100 ft. lbs. (140 Nm).

26. Lower the vehicle.

27. Road test the vehicle.

Rear

1. Before servicing the vehicle, refer to the precautions in the beginning of this section.

2. Raise and safely support the vehicle.

3. Remove the rear wheel.

4. Remove the brake drum.

5. Disconnect the ABS sensor wire, if equipped.

✳✳ WARNING

The hub assembly mounting bolts also secure the backing plate

assembly. Once the bolts are removed, the backing plate must be supported with wire or other means. Do not let the brake line or ABS electrical wire support the brake assembly.

6. Remove the four hub and bearing mounting bolts and remove the hub assembly.

To install:

7. Install hub and bearing assembly onto the rear knuckle.

8. Install the four mounting bolts and tighten to 52 ft. lbs. (70 Nm).

9. Attach the ABS sensor connector, if equipped.

10. Install the brake drum.

11. Install the wheel and tighten the nuts to 100 ft. lbs. (140 Nm).

12. Lower the vehicle and road test for proper operation.

PRECAUTIONS

Before servicing any vehicle, please be sure to read all of the following precautions, which deal with personal safety, prevention of component damage, and important points to take into consideration when servicing a motor vehicle:

• Never open, service or drain the radiator or cooling system when the engine is hot; serious burns can occur from the steam and hot coolant.

• Observe all applicable safety precautions when working around fuel. Whenever servicing the fuel system, always work in a well-ventilated area. Do not allow fuel spray or vapors to come in contact with a spark, open flame, or excessive heat (a hot drop light, for example). Keep a dry chemical fire extinguisher near the work area. Always keep fuel in a container specifically designed for fuel storage; also, always properly seal fuel containers to avoid the possibility of fire or explosion. Refer to the additional fuel system precautions later in this section.

• Fuel injection systems often remain pressurized, even after the engine has been turned **OFF**. The fuel system pressure must be relieved before disconnecting any fuel lines. Failure to do so may result in fire and/or personal injury.

• Brake fluid often contains polyglycol ethers and polyglycols. Avoid contact with the eyes and wash your hands thoroughly after handling brake fluid. If you do get brake fluid in your eyes, flush your eyes with clean, running water for 15 minutes. If eye irritation persists, or if you have taken brake fluid internally, IMMEDIATELY seek medical assistance.

• The EPA warns that prolonged contact with used engine oil may cause a number of skin disorders, including cancer! You should make every effort to minimize your exposure to used engine oil. Protective gloves should be worn when changing oil. Wash your hands and any other exposed skin areas as soon as possible after exposure to used engine oil. Soap and water, or waterless hand cleaner should be used.

• All new vehicles are now equipped with an air bag system, often referred to as a Supplemental Restraint System (SRS) or Supplemental Inflatable Restraint (SIR) system. The system must be disabled before performing service on or around system components, steering column, instrument panel components, wiring and sensors. Failure to follow safety and disabling procedures could result in accidental air bag deployment, possible personal injury and unnecessary system repairs.

• Always wear safety goggles when working with, or around, the air bag system. When carrying a non-deployed air bag, be sure the bag and trim cover are pointed away from your body. When placing a non-deployed air bag on a work surface, always face the bag and trim cover upward, away from the surface. This will reduce the motion of the module if it is accidentally deployed. Refer to the additional air bag system precautions later in this section.

• Clean, high quality brake fluid from a sealed container is essential to the safe and proper operation of the brake system. You should always buy the correct type of brake fluid for your vehicle. If the brake fluid becomes contaminated, completely flush the system with new fluid. Never reuse any brake fluid. Any brake fluid that is removed from the system should be discarded. Also, do not allow any brake fluid to come in contact with a painted surface; it will damage the paint.

• Never operate the engine without the proper amount and type of engine oil; doing so WILL result in severe engine damage.

• Timing belt maintenance is extremely important! Many models utilize an interference-type, non-freewheeling engine. If the timing belt breaks, the valves in the cylinder head may strike the pistons, causing potentially serious (also time-consuming and expensive) engine damage. Refer to the maintenance interval charts in the front of this manual for the recommended replacement interval for the timing belt, and to the timing belt section for belt replacement and inspection.

• Disconnecting the negative battery cable on some vehicles may interfere with the functions of the on-board computer system(s) and may require the computer to undergo a relearning process once the negative battery cable is reconnected.

• When servicing drum brakes, only disassemble and assemble one side at a time, leaving the remaining side intact for reference.

• Only an MVAC-trained, EPA-certified automotive technician should service the A/C system or its components.

ENGINE REPAIR

Ignition Timing

ADJUSTMENT

The 4.6L Northstar engine is equipped with a Distributorless Ignition System (DIS). The system consists of two Crankshaft Position (CKP) sensors, crankshaft reluctor ring, Camshaft Position (CMP) sensor, ignition control module, four ignition coils, eight plug wires and spark plugs, knock sensor and the Powertrain Control Module (PCM).

The base ignition timing is determined by the relationship of the CKP sensors to the crankshaft reluctor ring. This relationship is not adjustable. Base ignition timing is 10 degrees Before Top Dead Center (BTDC).

The PCM controls spark advance under all driving conditions. The PCM incorporates a permanent spark control override, which electronically lowers the base timing if spark knock (detonation) is encountered during normal operation due to the use of low octane fuel.

Engine Assembly

REMOVAL & INSTALLATION

1. Before servicing the vehicle, refer to the precautions in the beginning of this section.

2. Relieve the fuel system pressure.

3. Remove the air cleaner assembly.

4. Remove the left and right torque struts. Install the left front strut bolt back into the bracket.

5. Disconnect the radiator hoses at the water crossover.

6. Remove both cooling fans from the engine.

7. Properly remove the refrigerant from the A/C system.

8. Detach the cruise control servo connections.

9. Detach the Idle Speed Control (ISC) motor connectors.

10. Disconnect the throttle cable from the throttle body cam. Disconnect the shift cable from the park/neutral switch. Remove the cable bracket at the transaxle.

11. Remove the park/neutral switch connector and detach the power brake vacuum hose.

12. Disconnect the fuel inlet and fuel return lines using special tool J37088 or equivalent.

13. Remove the fuel line retainer at the transaxle case.

14. Disconnect the hoses from the coolant reservoir. Remove the reservoir.

15. Disconnect the heater hoses from the front of the right cylinder head. Disconnect the temperature switch.

16. Remove the starter.

17. Disconnect the power steering pump pressure and return lines at the cooler. Remove power steering line retainer from the right front of the crankcase.

18. Detach the engine harness connectors at the PCM.

19. From under the hood, remove the wiring harness retainer screws at the cowl and pull the engine harness through.

20. Disconnect the refrigerant high temperature switch.

21. To remove the engine harness on the left wheel housing, remove one screw holding the connector halves together and separate. The engine portion of the harness will be removed with the engine.

22. Remove the serpentine drive belt.

23. Raise and safely support the vehicle.

24. Remove both front wheels.

25. Disconnect the oil cooler lines at the oil filter adapter.

26. Disconnect the exhaust Y-pipe.

27. Disconnect the coupling between the steering rack and the column.

28. Disconnect the speed sensitive steering solenoid and the knock sensor.

29. Disconnect the power steering switch.

30. Separate the lower ball joints and stabilizer links (the struts will stay in the vehicle).

31. Disconnect the A/C hoses from the accumulator and the condenser.

32. Move powertrain dolly J-36295 or equivalent, into position and lower the vehicle onto the table.

33. Remove the six engine cradle mounting bolts and remove the powertrain assembly by lifting the vehicle or lowering the table.

34. Remove the torque converter splash shield and remove the four converter-to-flywheel bolts.

35. Separate the engine and transaxle assemblies.

To install:

36. Install the engine to the transaxle and tighten the bolts to 55 ft. lbs. (75 Nm).

37. Install the exhaust manifolds and tighten to 18 ft. lbs. (25 Nm).

38. Install the exhaust system Y-pipe and the transaxle to oil pan brace.

39. With the powertrain on the dolly, move the assembly into approximate position under the vehicle.

40. Lower the vehicle onto the powertrain.

41. Align the engine cradle to the body and install the six engine cradle mounting bolts. Tighten the bolts to 75 ft. lbs. (100 Nm).

42. Raise the vehicle and remove the dolly.

43. Connect the oil cooler lines at the oil filter adapter.

44. Install the exhaust Y-pipe.

45. Connect the coupling between the steering rack and the column.

46. Connect the speed sensitive steering solenoid and the knock sensor.

47. Connect the power steering switch.

48. Install the A/C hoses to the accumulator and the condenser.

49. Connect the lower ball joint and the stabilizer shaft link.

50. Position the ABS/TCS assembly to the engine cradle.

51. Lower the vehicle.

52. Attach the engine harness connectors at the PCM.

53. Connect the refrigerant high temperature switch.

54. Position the engine harness connector on the left wheel housing and install the one screw holding the connector halves together.

55. Connect or install the remaining components.

56. Install the right and left torque struts and tighten the retainer bolts as follows:

➡ **It is important during installation that the engine torque struts are not preloaded in their installed position. Adjustment is provided at the point the strut fastens to the core support bracket. Be sure this bolt is loose during assembly. Tighten to 45 ft. lbs. (60 Nm) as the final step of assembly.**

   a. Tighten the strut bracket to cylinder head (M10) bolt: 35 ft. lbs. (50 Nm).

   b. Tighten the strut bracket to cylinder head (M10) stud: 35 ft. lbs. (50 Nm).

   c. Tighten the strut bracket to water manifold (M8) bolts: 20 ft. lbs. (25 Nm).

   d. Tighten the strut bracket to cylinder head (M10) bolt: 35 ft. lbs. (50 Nm).

   e. Tighten the strut to core support bracket bolt: 45 ft. lbs. (60 Nm).

57. Connect the negative battery cable.

58. Evacuate and recharge the A/C system.

59. Install the air cleaner.

60. Refill the cooling system and engine crankcase.

61. Run the engine and check for leaks and proper vehicle operation.

➡ **A wheel alignment is recommended after the removal of the sub-frame assembly.**

Water Pump

REMOVAL & INSTALLATION

➡ **On 4.6L engines, there was a design change to the water pump inlet housing. If it is a black plastic housing, the housing must be replaced. There are no seals available for the plastic housings. The new housings are made of aluminum. When ordering parts, be sure to ask for a water pump, water pump seal, inlet housing seal and housing if needed.**

1. Before servicing the vehicle, refer to the precautions in the beginning of this section.

2. Disconnect the negative battery cable.

3. Drain the coolant into a suitable container.

1 WATER PUMP ASSEMBLY
2 O-RING SEAL
3 WATER PUMP HOUSING ASSEMBLY

7922VG01

To ensure proper operation, be sure to install a new O-ring

4. Remove the accessory drive belt. Remove the water pump pulley.

5. Remove the air cleaner.

6. Remove the lower radiator hose and the thermostat bypass hose from the coolant inlet housing.

7. Remove the water pump from the vehicle by rotating clockwise with tool J-38816-A or equivalent. Remove the O-ring and clean out the groove.

To install:

8. Clean all gasket mating surfaces.

9. Install the O-ring seal into the groove, then install the water pump, turning it counterclockwise until it stops, using tool J-38816-A or equivalent.

10. Install the water pump housing and tighten the bolts to 88 inch lbs. (10 Nm).

11. Install the water pump on the engine and tighten the mounting bolts.

12. Install the water pump pulley. Install the pulley bolts finger-tight.

13. Install the accessory drive belt.

14. Tighten the water pump pulley bolts to 115 inch lbs. (13 Nm).

15. Install the air cleaner.

16. Connect the negative battery cable.

17. Refill and bleed the cooling system.

18. Run the engine and check for leaks.

Cylinder Head

REMOVAL & INSTALLATION

➡ **The manufacturer recommends that the entire powertrain be removed from the vehicle before removing the cylinder heads.**

1. Before servicing the vehicle, refer to the precautions in the beginning of this section.

2. Disconnect the negative battery cable.

3. Properly relieve the fuel system pressure.

4. Drain the cooling system into a suitable container.

5. Remove the powertrain assembly.

6. Remove the intake manifold, cam covers, harmonic balancer, timing chain front cover and oil pump.

✷✷ WARNING

Align all timing marks before performing the next step.

7. Remove the chain tensioner from the timing chain.

8. Remove the cam sprockets. The timing chain remains in the chain case.

7922VG02

Left cylinder head bolt tightening sequence

7922VG03

Right cylinder head bolt tightening sequence

9. Removing the timing chain guides. Access for the retaining screws is through the plugs at the front of the cylinder head.

10. Remove the water crossover.

11. Remove the exhaust manifold.

12. Remove the cylinder head bolts, a little at a time, in the reverse order of the tightening sequence.

13. Remove the cylinder head and gasket.

✳✳ WARNING

With the camshafts remaining in the cylinder head, some valves will be open at all times. Do not rest the cylinder head on a flat service with

the cylinder face down, or valve damage will result.

14. Clean all gasket mating surfaces. Clean the head bolt holes in the crankcase with compressed air.

✳✳ WARNING

Be careful when cleaning aluminum gasket surfaces to prevent damage to the sealing surfaces. Use only plastic, wood or "dull" gasket scrapers. Chemical agents to dissolve gasket materials can also be used by following the manufacturers directions.

7922VG04

Minimum head resurface dimension

15. Check the cylinder head for warpage using a straightedge and feeler gauge. Measure along each edge, at the center and across both ends.

16. If warpage is less than 0.002 in. (0.05mm), the cylinder head surface is usable. If warpage is 0.002–0.008 in. (0.05–0.2mm), the cylinder head must be resurfaced. After resurfacing, the dimension between the combustion chamber gauge pad and the deck surface must be at least 10.5mm.

To install:

17. Using a new cylinder head gasket, install the cylinder head and the M11 and M6 head bolts. Lube the washer and the underside of the bolt head with engine oil prior to installation.

18. Tighten the M11 bolts, in sequence, to 22 ft. lbs. (30 Nm) plus 60 degrees. Repeat the sequence twice, turning each bolt an additional 60 degrees (total 180 degrees). Tighten the M6 bolts to 106 inch lbs. (12 Nm).

19. Install the camshafts and set the camshaft timing.

20. Install the camshaft guide bolt access hole plugs in the cylinder heads. The plugs should be seated and snug.

21. Install the intake cam covers, oil pump, timing chain front cover, harmonic balancer, intake manifold and water crossover.

22. Install the exhaust manifold. Tighten the nuts to 22 ft. lbs. (30 Nm) or the bolts to 18 ft. lbs. (25 Nm).

23. Install the powertrain assembly.

24. Connect the negative battery cable.

25. Fill the cooling system and check all fluid levels.

26. Properly charge the A/C system.

27. Run the engine and check for leaks and proper engine performance.

➡ **A wheel alignment is recommended after removal of the sub-frame assembly.**

Intake Manifold

REMOVAL & INSTALLATION

1. Before servicing the vehicle, refer to the precautions in the beginning of this section.

2. Disconnect the negative battery cable.

3. Remove the dress-up cover by removing the four nuts.

Timing belt service is covered in Section 5 of this manual

4. Relieve the fuel system pressure.

5. Drain the cooling system into a suitable container.

6. Remove the intake duct from the throttle body.

7. Remove the transaxle vent hose and the transaxle shift cable at the bracket.

8. Remove the Throttle Position (TP) sensor and the Idle Air Control (IAC) valve connectors.

9. Disconnect the throttle cable and the cruise control cable at the throttle body.

10. Remove the throttle body coolant hoses and the surge tank pipe.

11. Remove the EGR pipe and the crankcase ventilation pipe at the throttle body spacer.

12. Remove the brake booster vacuum hose at the intake manifold.

13. Remove the fuel rail ground wire at the rear cylinder head.

14. Remove the quick-disconnect fuel rail fittings using tool J-37088-A or equivalent, insert the tool into the female connector and push inward to release the locking tabs and pull the connection apart.

15. Disconnect the fuel rail bracket at the EGR valve.

16. Disconnect the PCV hose at the intake manifold.

17. Detach the main injector harness connector.

18. Remove the six bolts and the four studs in the intake manifold.

➡**The intake manifold carrier gaskets are attached to the intake manifold**

Exploded view of the intake manifold mounting—4.6L engine

7922VG05

through a snap-lock feature. When removing the intake manifold, the carrier gaskets will remain attached to the intake manifold. DO NOT replace the intake manifold gaskets after the intake manifold removal. The gaskets are reusable. The gaskets should only be replaced if the plastic housing or the rubber seals are damaged.

To install:

19. Install the intake manifold to the engine assembly.

20. Install the six bolts and four studs in their proper locations. Tighten the bolts and studs to 89 inch lbs. (10 Nm). When tightening the intake manifold bolts and studs, start at the center of the manifold and work outward in a circular pattern. DO NOT tighten the intake manifold bolts when the engine is HOT or at operating temperature. This repair should only be done on a cool engine.

21. Connect the injector main wiring harness.

22. Install the PCV hose to the intake manifold.

23. Install the fuel bracket at the EGR valve.

24. Install the fuel lines to the intake manifold. Apply a few drops of clean engine oil to the male ends of the fuel rail inlet and outlet tubes prior to assembly. When installed, pull outward to ensure a good connection.

25. Install the removed ground wire to the rear cylinder head.

26. Install the brake booster vacuum hose to the intake manifold vacuum fitting.

27. Install the EGR pipe and the crankcase ventilation pipe at the throttle body spacer. Tighten the EGR pipe bolt to 21 ft. lbs. (28 Nm).

28. Install the remaining components.

29. Connect the negative battery cable.

30. Turn the ignition switch to **RUN** and inspect for any fuel leaks. If there are no leaks, install the engine dress-up cover and tighten the cover nuts to 89 inch lbs. (10 Nm).

31. Fill and bleed the cooling system.

32. Road test the vehicle for proper operation.

Exhaust Manifold

REMOVAL & INSTALLATION

Left Side

1. Before servicing the vehicle, refer to the precautions in the beginning of this section.

2. Disconnect the negative battery cable.

3. Remove the radiator cover panel.

4. Remove the air cleaner assembly.

5. Disconnect the left and right engine torque struts and position out of the way.

6. Remove the engine cooling fans.

7. Support the engine using engine support fixture J-28467-A or equivalent.

8. Raise and safely support the vehicle.

9. Remove the nuts securing the engine mount to the engine cradle.

10. Remove the bolts securing the engine mount bracket to the crankcase.

11. Remove the bolts securing the engine mount bracket to the cylinder head.

12. Remove the nuts securing the engine mount to the mount bracket.

13. Disconnect the Y-pipe from the front of the catalytic converter and position the converter out of the way.

14. Lower the vehicle.

15. Raise the engine by adjusting the engine support fixture.

16. Remove the engine mount and bracket.

17. Raise and safely support the vehicle.

18. Remove the rear alternator bracket.

19. Remove the bolts at the manifold outlet flange.

20. Disconnect the Oxygen (O_2S) sensor.

21. Remove the exhaust manifold from the cylinder head, then remove the manifold from the vehicle.

22. Remove the gasket. Thoroughly clean the cylinder head and exhaust manifold mating surfaces.

To install:

23. Position the exhaust manifold by inserting the outlet pipe partially into the exhaust crossover pipe and moving the manifold into position.

24. Install a new gasket to the manifold. Insert two bolts to hold the gasket in place.

25. Install the remainder of the bolts and tighten all the bolts to 18 ft. lbs. (25 Nm).

9300VG03

Exploded view of the left exhaust manifold

26. Coat the O$_2$S sensor threads with high temperature anti-seize compound and install. Tighten the sensor to 30 ft. lbs. (40 Nm). Connect the O$_2$S sensor harness.

27. Install the rear alternator bracket. Tighten the crankcase bolts to 40 ft. lbs. (60 Nm) and the alternator bolts to 25 ft. lbs. (30 Nm).

28. Install two new bolts at the manifold outlet flange and tighten them to 25 ft. lbs. (30 Nm).

29. Position the engine mount and bracket.

30. Loosely install the two nuts securing the mount to the bracket.

31. Lower the vehicle.

32. Loosely install the two bolts securing the mount bracket at the cylinder head.

33. Lower the engine into position guiding the engine mount studs in the cradle holes.

34. Raise and safely support the vehicle.

35. Loosely install the two nuts to the bottom of the engine mount.

36. Loosely install the two bolts securing the mount bracket to the crankcase.

37. Tighten the two nuts securing the mount to the bracket, the two nuts at the bottom of the engine mount, and the two bolts securing the mount bracket to the crankcase to 22 ft. lbs. (30 Nm).

38. Install the two bolts at the converter-to-exhaust Y-pipe and tighten to 20 ft. lbs. (25 Nm).

39. Lower the vehicle.

40. Remove the engine support fixture.

41. Tighten the two bolts securing the mount bracket to the cylinder head to 22 ft. lbs. (30 Nm).

42. Install the engine cooling fans.

43. Install the air cleaner assembly.

44. Connect the left and right engine torque struts. Be sure to tighten the bolts that attach the struts to the core support bracket last, and tighten them to 44 ft. lbs. (60 Nm).

45. Install the radiator trim panel.

46. Connect the negative battery cable.

47. Run the engine and check for exhaust leaks.

Right Side

1. Before servicing the vehicle, refer to the precautions in the beginning of this section.

2. Disconnect the negative battery cable.

3. Disconnect the Oxygen (O$_2$S) sensor at the rear of the right cam cover. Disconnect the harness clip.

4. Raise and safely support the vehicle.

5. Disconnect the Y-pipe from the front of the catalytic converter.

6. Disconnect the suspension position sensor at the lower control arm from both sides.

7. Disconnect the intermediate shaft from the steering gear.

8. Place a support below the rear crossmember of the engine cradle and remove the four cradle to body bolts.

9. Lower the rear of the engine cradle and disconnect the Y-pipe from the exhaust crossover and from the manifold.

10. Remove the manifold nuts and manifold.

11. Remove the gasket from the manifold.

12. Thoroughly clean all cylinder head and exhaust manifold contact surfaces.

To install:

13. Coat the O$_2$S sensor threads with hi-temperature anti-seize compound. Tighten the sensor to 30 ft. lbs. (40 Nm).

14. Install the gasket, manifold and nuts. Tighten the nuts to 25 ft. lbs. (30 Nm).

15. Install the exhaust Y-pipe and install four new bolts. Tighten the M10 bolts to 35 ft. lbs. (50 Nm) and the M8 bolts to 25 ft. lbs. (30 Nm).

16. Raise the engine cradle into position and tighten the bolts to 75 ft. lbs. (100 Nm).

17. Connect the intermediate shaft to the steering gear and tighten to 35 ft. lbs. (50 Nm).

18. Connect the exhaust Y-pipe to the catalytic converter and tighten the bolts to 35 ft. lbs. (50 Nm).

19. Connect the suspension position sensors to the lower control arms.

20. Lower the vehicle and connect the O$_2$S sensor. Install the harness retainer.

21. Connect the negative battery cable.

9300VG04

Exploded view of the right exhaust manifold

22. Run the engine and check for exhaust leaks.

Camshaft and Valve Lifters

REMOVAL & INSTALLATION

Left Side

1. Before servicing the vehicle, refer to the precautions in the beginning of this section.

2. Disconnect the negative battery cable.

3. Drain the coolant from the radiator.

4. Disconnect the upper radiator hose at the water crossover.

5. Label and disconnect the spark plug wires.

6. Remove the right-side fan.

7. Disconnect the battery cable at the alternator. Disconnect the cable harness at the cam cover and move out of the way.

8. Disconnect the PCV fresh air tube from the cam cover.

9. Remove the right and left torque struts.

10. Disconnect the water pump drive belt and pulley.

11. Remove the camshaft seal retainer screws and remove the seal.

12. Remove the cam cover screws and remove the cam cover by moving the cam drive end of the cover up, then pivot the entire cover around the water pump drive shaft. Continue moving the cover upward and pivoting so that the edge of the cover closely follows the left edge of the intake manifold cover.

13. Discard the cam cover seal if it is damaged. The spark plug seals may be reused if undamaged.

14. Secure the cam sprocket to the timing chain by installing tie-wraps through the cam sprocket holes. Use four tie-wraps per sprocket.

➡**The sprocket/chain relationship must be maintained throughout this procedure or camshaft timing will be lost and require further engine disassembly to retime.**

15. Working from behind the sprockets, install cam chain holder J-38222 so that it is positioned between the chain tensioner and chain guide. Apply tension to the tool by tightening the tension adjusting screw.

16. Remove both cam sprocket bolts. Note the relative location of the cam drive pins in the end of the camshafts.

9300VG01

Use the camshaft chain holder tool J-38822 or equivalent to keep the chain in position while removing the camshafts

7922VG06

Left cylinder head camshaft bearing cap tightening sequence

17. Work the sprockets off the cams using play in the chain.

18. Alternately loosen the cam bearing cap screws a few turns at a time until all valve spring pressure has been released. Remove the bolts and caps.

19. Remove the camshaft.

20. Remove the valve lifters. Store the lifters on their camshaft face so that the residual oil is retained.

➡ **Retain the valve lifters in order so that they can be installed in the same bores.**

21. Inspect the lifters for wear and/or damage; replace as necessary.

22. Inspect the camshaft for excessive lobe wear. Check the bearing journals, making sure they are not scored or burned. Replace the camshaft, as necessary.

To install:

23. Install the valve lifters in the same bore from which they were removed.

24. Lubricate the camshaft lobes with camshaft prelube 1052365 or equivalent. Lubricate the camshaft journals with clean engine oil.

25. Install the camshaft.

26. Position the cam bearing caps to the cylinder head.

➡ **Each cap is identified for position and direction. The arrow points towards the front of the engine. An "E" indicates a cap for the exhaust cam. An "I" indicates a cap for the intake cam. Position No. 1 is towards the front of the engine.**

27. Loosely install the cam bearing cap bolts.

28. Alternately tighten the cam bearing cap bolts a few turns at a time against valve spring pressure until all the bolts are snug. Tighten the bolts to 106 inch lbs. (12 Nm).

29. Using the hex cast into the camshaft, rotate the cams until the drive pins are in position to engage the cam sprockets over the cams, and install the retaining bolts.

30. Attach the cam sprockets and install the retaining bolts. Tighten the bolts to 90 ft. lbs. (120 Nm).

31. Remove the chain holder J-38222.

32. Remove the tie-wraps from the cam sprockets.

33. Install the remaining components.

34. Install the cam cover screws and tighten to 89 inch lbs. (10 Nm).

35. Connect the battery cable retainer to the front of the cam cover.

36. Connect the battery cable at the alternator.

37. Lubricate the seal lips and install the

camshaft seal to the end of the intake cam. Seal the screw threads with sealer.

38. Install the water pump pulley with tool J-38825 or equivalent, the install the drive belt.

39. Install the right and left torque struts and tighten the retaining bolts as follows:

➡ **It is important during installation that the engine torque struts are not preloaded in their installed position. Adjustment is provided at the point the strut fastens to the core support bracket. Be sure this bolt is loose during assembly. Tighten to 45 ft. lbs. (60 Nm) as the final step of assembly.**

    a. Tighten the strut bracket to cylinder head (M10) bolt: 35 ft. lbs. (50 Nm).

    b. Tighten the strut bracket to cylinder head (M10) stud: 35 ft. lbs. (50 Nm).

    c. Tighten the strut bracket to water manifold (M8) bolts: 20 ft. lbs. (25 Nm).

    d. Tighten the strut bracket to cylinder head (M10) bolt: 35 ft. lbs. (50 Nm).

    e. Tighten the strut to core support bracket bolt: 45 ft. lbs. (60 Nm) (see note above).

40. Connect the PCV fresh air tube to the cam cover.

41. Install the right-side fan.

42. Connect the spark plug wires.

43. Connect the upper radiator hose to the water crossover.

44. Fill the cooling system.

45. Connect the negative battery cable.

46. Run the engine and check for leaks and proper engine operation.

Right Side

1. Before servicing the vehicle, refer to the precautions in the beginning of this section.

2. Disconnect the negative battery cable.

3. Raise and support the vehicle safely.

4. Disconnect the exhaust Y-pipe at the converter. Position the converter out of the way.

5. Lower the vehicle.

6. Remove the tower-to-tower brace.

7. Disconnect the ICM wiring harnesses and mounting bolts.

8. Remove the ICM and the spark plug wires on the right bank. Tag wires for installation reference.

9. Disconnect the PCV valve.

10. Remove the purge canister solenoid from the rear of the cover.

11. Remove the three screws retaining the wiring harness to the cover.

12. Remove the cam cover screws.

13. Support the front of the engine cradle and remove the mounting screws at the front of the cradle.

14. Remove the right and left torque struts.

15. Lower the engine cradle (or raise the vehicle) to provide clearance at the rear of the engine compartment.

16. Remove the cam cover.

17. Discard the cover seal if damaged. The spark plug seals may be reused if undamaged.

18. Secure the cam sprocket to the timing chain by installing tie-wraps through the cam sprocket holes. Use four tie-wraps per sprocket.

➡ **The sprocket/chain relationship must be maintained throughout this procedure or camshaft timing will be lost and require further engine disassembly to retime.**

19. Working from behind the sprockets, install cam chain holder J-38222 so that it is positioned between the chain tensioner and chain guide. Apply tension to the tool by tightening the tension adjusting screw.

20. Remove both cam sprocket bolts. Note the relative location of the cam drive pins in the end of the camshafts.

21. Work the sprockets off the cams.

22. Alternately loosen the cam bearing cap screws a few turns at a time until all valve spring pressure has been released. Remove the bolts and caps.

23. Remove the camshaft.

24. Inspect the camshaft for excessive lobe wear. Check the bearing journals, making sure they are not scored or burned. Replace the camshaft, as necessary.

To install:

25. Lubricate the camshaft lobes with camshaft prelube 1052365 or equivalent. Lubricate the camshaft journals with clean engine oil.

26. Install the camshaft.

27. Position the cam bearing caps to the cylinder head.

➡ **Each cap is identified for position and direction. The arrow points towards the front of the engine. An "E" indicates a cap for the exhaust cam. An "I" indicates a cap for the intake cam. Position No. 1 is towards the front of the engine.**

Right cylinder head camshaft bearing cap tightening sequence

7922VG07

Refer to Section 1 for engine rebuilding specifications

28. Loosely install the cam bearing cap bolts.

29. Alternately tighten the cam bearing cap bolts a few turns at a time against valve spring pressure until all the bolts are snug. Tighten the bolts to 106 inch lbs. (12 Nm).

30. Using the hex cast into the camshaft, rotate the cams until the drive pins are in position to engage the cam sprockets over the cams and install the retaining bolts.

31. Attach the cam sprockets and install the retaining bolts. Tighten the bolts to 90 ft. lbs. (120 Nm).

32. Remove the chain holder J-38222.

33. Remove the tie-wraps from the cam sprockets.

34. Install spark plug and cam cover seals, as required.

35. Install the cam cover and tighten the screws to 7 ft. lbs. (10 Nm).

36. Raise the engine cradle into position. Install and tighten the two mounting bolts to 75 ft. lbs. (100 Nm).

37. Install the right and left torque struts and tighten the retaining bolts as follows:

➡ **It is important during installation that the engine torque struts are not pre-loaded in their installed position. Adjustment is provided at the point the strut fastens to the core support bracket. Be sure this bolt is loose during assembly. Tighten to 45 ft. lbs. (60 Nm) as the final step of assembly.**

a. Tighten the strut bracket to cylinder head (M10) bolt: 35 ft. lbs. (50 Nm).

b. Tighten the strut bracket to cylinder head (M10) stud: 35 ft. lbs. (50 Nm).

c. Tighten the strut to core support bracket bolt: 45 ft. lbs. (60 Nm) (see note above).

38. Install the remaining components.

39. Connect the negative battery cable.

40. Run the engine and check for leaks and proper engine operation.

Valve Lash

ADJUSTMENT

The valve clearance cannot be adjusted. The hydraulic lifters function to maintain a zero clearance when the valves are opening and closing. Any clearance is instantaneously taken up by the hydraulic action. The hydraulic lifter consists of 3 main parts: the body, plunger and valve. Oil under pressure from the engine lubricating system passes through the check valve and forces the plunger upwards in the body of the lifter and takes up any excess clearance. "Valve lifter noise" complaints may require cleaning of sludged or varnished valve lifters, or replacement of the lifters.

Oil Pan

REMOVAL & INSTALLATION

1. Before servicing the vehicle, refer to the precautions in the beginning of this section.

2. Disconnect the negative battery cable.

3. Raise and safely support the vehicle.

4. Remove the oil pan drain plug and drain the engine oil into a suitable container.

5. Disconnect the oil level indicator harness, if equipped.

6. Remove the exhaust Y-pipe, if needed.

7. Remove the transaxle assembly from the vehicle.

✳✳ WARNING

Attempting to remove the oil pan without first dropping the oil pump will result in breaking the oil pump housing.

FRT

Oil pan bolt tightening sequence

8. Remove the oil pan mounting bolts and remove the oil pan.

To install:

➡**The oil pan gasket is reusable unless it is damaged. Do not remove the gasket from the oil pan groove unless gasket replacement is required.**

9. Thoroughly clean the inside of the oil pan and the cylinder block contact surface. If the oil pan gasket is being reused, be careful not to damage it. Do not expose the gasket to cleaning solvents.

10. If a new gasket is being installed, start the gasket into the oil pan groove and work the gasket into the groove in both directions. Once the gasket is exposed to oil, it will expand and no longer stay in the groove without wrinkles. If this condition exists, replace the gasket.

11. Install the oil pan and secure using the mounting bolts. Tighten, in sequence, to 89 inch lbs. (10 Nm).

12. Connect the oil level indicator connector, if removed.

13. Install the transaxle assembly, if removed.

14. Install the Y-pipe, if removed.

15. Install the flywheel cover, if removed.

16. Install the oil pan drain plug and tighten.

17. Lower the vehicle.

18. Refill the crankcase with the proper type and quantity of engine oil.

19. Connect the negative battery cable.

20. Run the engine and check for leaks.

Oil Pump

REMOVAL & INSTALLATION

1. Before servicing the vehicle, refer to the precautions in the beginning of this section.

2. Disconnect the negative battery cable.

3. Remove the drive belt.

4. Remove the bolt securing the power steering hose.

5. Raise and safely support the vehicle.

6. Remove the right front wheel.

7. Remove the two splash shields from the wheel well.

8. Remove the brace between the engine oil pan and transaxle case.

9. Install flywheel holder tool J-39411 or equivalent, to keep the crankshaft from turning.

10. Remove the crankshaft balancer bolt.

1. Gerotor assembly
2. Outer gear
3. Inner gear
4. Housing
5. Drive spacer
6. Relief valve
7. Cover

7922VG09

Exploded view of the oil pump

11. Support the engine cradle with a screw type jack and remove the three right-side engine cradle bolts.

12. Disconnect the RSS sensor from the right lower control arm.

13. Lower the cradle to gain access for the crankshaft balancer puller.

14. Using puller tool J-38416 or equivalent, remove the crankshaft balancer.

15. Remove the accessory drive belt tensioner and idler pulley.

16. Remove the front cover bolts and remove the front cover and gasket.

➡**The front cover gasket is reusable as long as it is not damaged.**

17. Remove the three oil pump mounting bolts and remove the oil pump and drive spacer.

18. If necessary, disassemble and inspect the pump as follows:

 a. Remove the drive spacer from the pump housing.

 b. Remove the two screws holding the pump housing halves together.

 c. Remove the inner (drive) and outer (driven) rotors from the housing. Indicate the mating surfaces (dimples).

 d. Remove the pressure relief valve.

 e. Inspect the pump housing for nicks, burrs, chips or debris that might cause a leak or binding condition in the rotor pocket.

 f. Inspect the drive and driven rotors for nicks or burrs.

 g. Check the pump cover and interior surface for excessive wear or score marks. Check for flatness.

 h. If any components show signs of excessive wear or damage, replace the pump assembly.

To install:

19. If the pump was disassembled, reassemble as follows:

 a. Install the inner and outer rotors to the pump cover in the same orientation as removed.

 b. Install the pressure relief valve seat, spring and pilot in the pump housing.

 c. Pack the pump housing halves with Amojell® ; or white petroleum grease to ensure pump priming.

 d. Assemble the housing and cover over the locating dowel.

 e. Insert a 9mm drill in the pump

mounting hole on the opposite side to aid alignment of the housing and cover. Install the two screws and tighten to 108 inch lbs. (12 Nm).

20. Install the oil pump drive spacer into the oil pump from the rear so the drive flat engages the pump rotor.

21. Install the oil pump over the crankshaft and loosely install the mounting bolts.

22. Hold the pump in its furthest up position and tighten the mounting bolts (1, 2 and 3) in sequence, in 2 Steps. First tighten in sequence to 89 inch lbs. (10 Nm), then tighten in sequence to 20 ft. lbs. (26 Nm).

23. Place a small amount of RTV sealant at the split line of the upper and lower crankcases.

24. Install the front cover gasket on the dowel pins on the block.

25. Install the front cover on the dowel pins and install the front cover mounting bolts. Tighten the bolts to 89 inch lbs. (10 Nm).

26. Install the drive belt idler pulley and tighten the mounting bolt to 37 ft. lbs. (50 Nm).

27. Install the drive belt tensioner and tighten the tensioner mounting bolt to 37 ft. lbs. (50 Nm).

28. Install the crankshaft balancer using tool J-39344 or equivalent.

29. Apply engine oil to the balancer bolt threads and tighten the bolt to 37 ft. lbs. (50 Nm) plus an additional 120 degrees

30. Raise the screw jack until the three cradle bolts can be installed. Tighten the bolts to 75 ft. lbs. (100 Nm).

31. Connect the RSS sensor.

32. Remove the flywheel holding tool and install the oil pan-to-transaxle brace. Tighten the bolts to 37 ft. lbs. (50 Nm).

33. Install the wheel well splash shields and the front wheel.

34. Lower the vehicle.

35. Install the power steering hose retainer.

36. Install the accessory drive belt.

37. Connect the negative battery cable.

38. Run the engine and check for proper engine oil pressure. Check for leaks.

Rear Main Seal

REMOVAL & INSTALLATION

1. Before servicing the vehicle, refer to the precautions in the beginning of this section.

2. Remove the transaxle.

3. Remove the flywheel.

Exploded view of the rear main oil seal

➡**Now is the time to confirm that the rear seal is leaking.**

4. Insert a suitable prytool in through the dust lip and pry out the seal by moving the tool around the seal until it is removed.

❋❋ WARNING

Use care not to damage the crankshaft seal surface with a prytool.

To install:

5. Before installing, lubricate the seal bore to seal surface with clean engine oil.

6. Install the new seal using Seal Installer tool J-38817 or an equivalent rear main seal installation tool.

7. Slide the new seal over the mandrel until the dust lip bottoms squarely against the tool collar.

8. Thread the tool into the crankshaft flange and install the seal by turning the T-handle until the tool bottoms against the crankcase.

9. Loosen and remove the tool from the crankshaft.

➡**Check to see that the seal is squarely seated in the bore.**

10. Install the flywheel and tighten the

bolts to 11 ft. lbs. (15 Nm) plus 50 degrees, then install the transaxle.

11. Start the engine and check for leaks.

Timing Chain, Sprockets, Front Cover And Seal

REMOVAL & INSTALLATION

The left and right-side secondary timing chains can be removed with the engine in the vehicle. If the primary timing chain or intermediate shaft sprocket need to be replaced, the engine must be removed from the vehicle and supported on an engine stand.

➡**Setting the camshaft timing is necessary whenever the cam drive system has been disturbed, meaning the relationship between any chain and sprocket has been lost. Correct timing exists when the crankshaft and intermediate shaft sprocket timing marks are in alignment and all four camshaft drive pins are perpendicular (90 degrees) to the cylinder head surface.**

1. Before servicing the vehicle, refer to the precautions in the beginning of this section.

9300VG02

Correct timing chain alignment

2. Disconnect the negative battery cable.

3. Remove the drive belt.

4. Remove the bolt securing the power steering hose.

5. Raise and safely support the vehicle.

6. For the left side secondary chain and sprocket, perform the following:

a. Remove the right front wheel.

b. Remove the two splash shields from the wheel well.

c. Remove the flywheel cover and install a suitable flywheel holder.

d. Remove the crankshaft balancer bolt.

e. Support the engine cradle with a screw type jack and remove the three right-side engine cradle bolts.

f. Disconnect the RSS sensor from the right control arm.

g. Lower the cradle to gain access for the crankshaft damper puller.

h. Using puller J-38416 or equivalent, remove the crankshaft damper.

i. Remove the drive belt tensioner.

j. Remove the drive belt idler pulley.

k. Remove the front cover bolts.

7. Remove the front cover and gasket.

➡**The front cover gasket is reusable as long as it is not damaged.**

a. Partially drain the coolant from the radiator.

b. Disconnect the upper radiator hose at the water crossover.

c. Label and disconnect the spark plug wires.

d. Remove the right side fan.

e. Disconnect the battery cable at the alternator and disconnect the cable harness at the cam cover.

f. Disconnect the PCV fresh air tube from the cam cover.

g. Remove the right and left torque struts.

h. Remove the water pump pulley with tool J-38825 or equivalent.

i. Remove the camshaft seal retainer screws and remove the seal.

j. Disconnect the battery cable retainer at the front of the cam cover.

k. Remove the cam cover screws and remove the cam cover by pivoting the entire cover around the water pump drive shaft. Continue moving the cover upward and pivoting so that the edge of the cover

closely follows the left edge of the intake manifold cover.

➡**The cam cover gasket is reusable as long as it is not damaged.**

l. Remove the left side secondary chain tensioner.

m. Remove the left side chain guide. Access the upper chain guide mounting bolt through the hole in the cylinder head capped with the plastic plug.

n. Remove the left side cam sprocket bolts and sprockets.

o. Remove the secondary drive chain.

8. For the right side secondary chain and sprocket, perform the following:

a. Disconnect the exhaust Y-pipe at the converter.

b. Lower the vehicle.

c. Remove the tower-to-tower brace.

d. Detach the ICM wiring connectors and mounting bolts.

e. Remove the ICM and the plug wires on the right bank.

f. Disconnect the PCV valve.

g. Remove the purge canister solenoid from the rear of the cover.

h. Remove the cam cover screws.

i. Safely support the front of the engine cradle and remove the two mounting bolts at the front of the cradle.

j. Remove the right and left torque struts.

k. Lower the engine cradle (or raise the vehicle) to provide clearance at the rear of the engine compartment.

l. Remove the cam cover.

➡**The cam cover gasket is reusable as long as it is not damaged.**

m. Remove the right side secondary chain tensioner.

n. Remove the right side chain guide. Access the upper chain guide mounting bolt through the hole in the cylinder head capped with the plastic plug.

o. Remove the right side cam sprocket bolts and cam sprockets.

9. Remove the secondary drive chain.

10. If only servicing the secondary chains, proceed to Step 20 of the installation procedure.

11. Remove the engine.

12. Remove the intermediate shaft sprocket-to-intermediate shaft bolt, then remove the sprocket.

13. Slide the primary timing sprockets and primary chain off the engine.

For complete mechanical specifications, refer to Section 1 of this manual

1 INTERMEDIATE SHAFT
2 PRIMARY CHAIN
3 INTERMEDIATE SHAFT SPROCKET
4 CRANKSHAFT SPROCKET KEY
5 SPROCKET

7922VG10

Primary drive chain components

To install:

➡**The following procedure must be followed to set the camshaft timing on the vehicle.**

14. Install the primary and secondary chain guide.

15. Rotate the crankshaft until the sprocket drive key is at the 1 o'clock position. Use tool J-39946 or the equivalent, to rotate the crankshaft.

16. Install the crankshaft sprocket and intermediate shaft sprocket in the primary timing chain so the timing marks are aligned. Install the assembly in position on the engine. The crankshaft sprocket key way will have to slide over the key on the crankshaft. If it is necessary to turn the crankshaft sprocket, the intermediate shaft sprocket will also have to be turned so the timing mark still lines up with the crankshaft sprocket.

17. Install the intermediate shaft sprocket-to-intermediate shaft bolt and tighten to 45 ft. lbs. (61 Nm).

18. Install the primary timing chain tensioner. Tighten the tensioner mounting bolts to 20 ft. lbs. (27 Nm).

19. Install a suitable flywheel holder to lock the crankshaft in position.

20. Install the secondary timing chain over the inner row of teeth on the intermediate shaft sprocket. Route the chain over the chain guide and install the exhaust cam sprocket so the **RE** (Right Head Exhaust) pin engages the sprocket notch. There should be no slack in the lower section of the timing chain and the cam drive pin **must** be perpendicular to the cylinder head face.

21. Install the intake cam sprocket into the chain so the sprocket notch **RI** (Right Head Intake) engages the cam and the camshaft drive pin remains perpendicular to the cylinder head face. A hex is cast into the camshafts behind the lobes for cylinder No.

7922VG11

Rotating tensioner release lever

1, so an open end wrench may be used to provide minor repositioning of the cams.

22. Loosely install the exhaust cam sprocket bolt and intake sprocket bolt.

23. Install the chain tensioner and tighten the mounting bolts to 20 ft. lbs. (27 Nm).

24. Tighten the camshaft sprocket bolts to 90 ft. lbs. (120 Nm).

25. Route the secondary timing chain for the left side over the outer row of intermediate sprocket teeth.

26. Install the secondary timing chain over the inner row of teeth on the intermediate shaft sprocket. Route the chain over the chain guide and install the exhaust cam sprocket so the **LE** (Left Head Exhaust) pin engages the sprocket notch. There should be no slack in the lower section of the timing chain and the cam drive pin **must** be perpendicular to the cylinder head face.

27. Install the intake cam sprocket into the chain so the sprocket notch **LI** (Left Head Intake) engages the cam and the camshaft drive pin remains perpendicular to the cylinder head face. A hex is cast into the camshafts behind the lobes for cylinder No. 2, so an open end wrench may be used to provide minor repositioning of the cams.

1 RELEASE TO FIRST CLICK
2 INSTALL LOCK PIN

7922VG12

Locking the tensioner in the collapsed position

28. Loosely install the exhaust cam sprocket bolt and intake sprocket bolt.

29. Install the chain tensioner and tighten the mounting bolts to 20 ft. lbs. (27 Nm).

30. Tighten the camshaft sprocket bolts to 90 ft. lbs. (120 Nm).

➡**The RE cam sprocket must contain the Camshaft Position (CMP) sensor pick-up.**

31. Install the front cover gasket on the dowel pins on the block.

32. Install the front cover on the dowel pins and install the front cover mounting bolts. Tighten the bolts to 89 inch lbs. (10 Nm). Apply a dab of RTV to the split line between the upper and lower crankcase assemblies.

33. Install the drive belt idler pulley and tighten the mounting bolt to 35 ft. lbs. (47 Nm).

34. Install the drive belt tensioner and tighten the tensioner mounting nut to 35 ft. lbs. (47 Nm).

35. Install the crankshaft balancer using tool J-39344 or the equivalent.

36. Apply engine oil to the balancer bolt threads and tighten the bolt to 44 ft. lbs. (60 Nm) plus an additional 120 degree turn.

37. Raise the screw jack until the three cradle bolts can be installed. Tighten the bolts to 75 ft. lbs. (102 Nm).

38. Connect the RSS sensor.

39. Remove the flywheel holding tool and install the flywheel cover.

40. Install the wheel well splash shields.

41. Install the left cam cover as follows:

a. Install the spark plugs and cam cover seals.

b. Insert the intake cam through the hole in the cam cover and using fingers, guide the cam cover up over the edge of the cylinder head.

⁂ WARNING

Use care to prevent the exposed section of the cam cover seal from being damaged by the edge of the cylinder head casting.

c. Work the cover into position by allowing the top edge of the cover to follow the left side edge of the intake manifold.

d. Install the cam cover screws and tighten to 7 ft. lbs. (10 Nm).

e. Connect the battery cable retainer to the front of the cam cover.

f. Connect the battery cable at the alternator.

g. Lubricate the seal lips and install the camshaft seal to the end of the intake cam. Seal the screw threads with sealer.

h. Install the water pump pulley with tool J-38825 or equivalent.

i. Connect the PCV fresh air tube to the cam cover.

j. Install the right side fan.

k. Connect the spark plug wires.

l. Connect the upper radiator hose to the water crossover.

m. Refill the cooling system.

42. Install the right cam cover as follows:

a. Install spark plug and cam cover seals.

b. Install the cam cover and tighten the screws to 7 ft. lbs. (10 Nm).

c. Raise the engine cradle into position and install and tighten the two mounting bolts to 75 ft. lbs. (100 Nm).

d. Install the right and left torque struts and tighten the retaining bolts as follows:

➡**It is important during installation that the engine torque struts are not pre-loaded in their installed position. Adjustment is provided at the point the strut fastens to the core support bracket. Be sure this bolt is loose during assembly. Tighten to 45 ft. lbs. (60 Nm) as the final step of assembly.**

e. Tighten the strut bracket to cylinder head (M10) bolt: 35 ft. lbs. (50 Nm).

f. Tighten the strut bracket to cylinder head (M10) stud: 35 ft. lbs. (50 Nm).

g. Tighten the strut bracket to water manifold (M8) bolts: 20 ft. lbs. (25 Nm).

h. Tighten the strut bracket to cylinder head (M10) bolt: 35 ft. lbs. (50 Nm).

i. Tighten the strut to core support bracket bolt: 45 ft. lbs. (60 Nm) (see note above).

j. Install the screws retaining wiring harness to the cover.

k. Install the purge canister solenoid to the rear of the cover.

l. Connect the PCV valve.

m. Install the ICM and the spark plug wires on the right-bank.

n. Attach the ICM wiring connectors.

o. Install the tower-to-tower brace.

p. Raise and support the vehicle safely. Connect the exhaust Y-pipe to the converter and tighten the bolts to 20 ft. lbs. (25 Nm).

43. Connect the negative battery cable.

44. Start the engine. Check for leaks and inspect for proper operation.

Please refer to Section 9 for electric cooling fan wiring schematics

FUEL SYSTEM

Fuel System Service Precautions

Safety is the most important factor when performing not only fuel system maintenance but any type of maintenance. Failure to conduct maintenance and repairs in a safe manner may result in serious personal injury or death. Maintenance and testing of the vehicle's fuel system components can be accomplished safely and effectively by adhering to the following rules and guidelines.

• To avoid the possibility of fire and personal injury, always disconnect the negative battery cable unless the repair or test procedure requires that battery voltage be applied.

• Always relieve the fuel system pressure prior to disconnecting any fuel system component (injector, fuel rail, pressure regulator, etc.), fitting or fuel line connection. Exercise extreme caution whenever relieving fuel system pressure to avoid exposing skin, face and eyes to fuel spray. Please be advised that fuel under pressure may penetrate the skin or any part of the body that it contacts.

• Always place a shop towel or cloth around the fitting or connection prior to loosening to absorb any excess fuel due to spillage. Ensure that all fuel spillage (should it occur) is quickly removed from engine surfaces. Ensure that all fuel soaked cloths or towels are deposited into a suitable waste container.

• Always keep a dry chemical (Class B) fire extinguisher near the work area.

• Do not allow fuel spray or fuel vapors to come into contact with a spark or open flame.

• Always use a back-up wrench when loosening and tightening fuel line connection fittings. This will prevent unnecessary stress and torsion to fuel line piping.

• Always replace worn fuel fitting O-rings with new. Do not substitute fuel hose or equivalent, where fuel pipe is installed.

Fuel System Pressure

RELIEVING

✳✳ CAUTION

The fuel injection system remains under pressure, even when the engine has been turned OFF. The fuel system pressure must be relieved before disconnecting any fuel lines. Failure to do so may result in fire and/or personal injury.

1. Loosen the fuel filler cap to relieve tank vapor pressure.

✳✳ CAUTION

Observe all applicable safety precautions when working around fuel. Whenever servicing the fuel system, always work in a well ventilated area. Do not allow fuel spray or vapors to come in contact with a spark or open flame. Keep a dry chemical fire extinguisher near the work area. Always keep fuel in a container specifically designed for fuel storage; also, always properly seal fuel containers to avoid the possibility of fire or explosion.

2. Be sure the ignition switch is in the **OFF** position.
3. Disconnect the negative battery cable.
4. Remove the engine dress-up cover.

✳✳ CAUTION

There may still be residual fuel in the system, and a small amount of fuel

1. Cartridge regulator ASM - fuel pressure
2. Rail ASM - fuel
3. Cap - fuel pressure connector
4. Core ASM - fuel pressure port
5. Clip - MFI fuel injector retainer
6. O-ring - MFI fuel injector upper
7. Injector ASM - MFI fuel
8. O-ring - MFI fuel injector lower

7922VG13

View of the fuel rail assembly showing fuel system service port location

may be released when servicing fuel lines or connections. In order to reduce the chance of personal injury, cover the fuel line fittings with a shop towel before disconnecting to catch any fuel that may leak out.

5. Install a fuel pressure gauge with a drain hose attached, J-34730–1 or equivalent. Wrap a shop towel around the fitting while connecting the gauge to avoid spillage.

6. Install the drain hose into an approved container and open the valve to drain the system pressure. Fuel connections are now safe for servicing.

7. Drain any remaining fuel from inside the gauge into the approved container.

Fuel Filter

REMOVAL & INSTALLATION

1. Before servicing the vehicle, refer to the precautions in the beginning of this section.

2. Properly relieve the fuel system pressure.

3. Disconnect the negative battery cable.

1. FUEL FILTER   3. BOLT/SCREW
2. QUICK CONNECTOR   4. FUEL FILTER BRACKET

7922VG14

Exploded view of the fuel filter mounting

4. Release the locking tabs on the fuel filter retainer.

5. Disconnect the fuel lines from the fuel filter by releasing the locking tabs on the fuel filter quick-connects. Wrap a shop towel around the fitting when removing to catch excess fuel leaking out of the filter.

6. Remove the fuel filter.

To install:

7. Apply a few drops of engine oil to the tips of the fuel filter and install the fuel filter in the mounting bracket.

8. Connect the fuel lines to the fuel fil-

ter and snap the quick-connects into place. Be sure the tabs on the quick-connects lock into place.

9. Engage the locking tabs on the fuel filter retainer.

10. Connect the negative battery cable.

11. Turn the ignition key **ON** for 2 seconds, then **OFF** for 5 seconds. Again turn the ignition key **ON** and check for fuel leaks.

Fuel Pump

REMOVAL & INSTALLATION

➡ **The modular fuel sender assembly must be disassembled in the exact order described.**

1. Before servicing the vehicle, refer to the precautions in the beginning of this section.

2. Disconnect the negative battery cable.

3. Relieve the fuel system pressure.

4. Remove the fuel tank from the vehicle and position it on a suitable workbench.

5. Clean the fuel tank in the area of the modular fuel sender assembly.

6. Remove the locking nut by turning

STEP 1	STEP 2	STEP 3
1. Locking tab 1	2. Locking tab 2	3. Locking tab 3

7922VG15

Modular fuel sender disassembly

counterclockwise using tool J-39348 or equivalent.

7. Remove the modular fuel sender assembly from the fuel tank.

✷✷ CAUTION

The modular fuel sender assembly may spring up from its position. When removing the assembly, be aware that the reservoir bucket is full of fuel. Tip the assembly slightly during removal to avoid damaging the float. Have a shop towel ready to absorb any leakage.

8. Slide the fuel sender seal downward, past the reservoir and carefully over the float arm assembly. Discard the seal.

9. Remove the Connector Position Assurance (CPA) clip from the wiring harness under the modular fuel sender assembly cover. Depress the black connector tabs to remove the electrical connector from the cover.

10. Locate the curved side of the modular unit's reservoir. Beginning at locking tab 1, squeeze the reservoir to release the first locking tab.

11. Moving clockwise to locking tab 2, apply gentle pressure to the guide rod to release the second locking tab.

12. At locking tab 3, gently twist and squeeze to release the reservoir from the retainer.

13. Remove the cover and the retainer from the reservoir. Be careful not to damage the crossover tube; the unit will still be attached by the convoluted fuel pipe and the crossover tube.

14. Remove the external strainer by carefully prying the strainer ferrule off the reservoir. Excessive force may dislodge the jet pump. Note the position of the strainer for installation reference. Discard the strainer.

15. Remove the rubber bumper pad and discard. The fuel pump and the sleeve assembly are attached to the retainer when pulled from the reservoir. Depress the flex member on the pump sleeve and rotate the sleeve counterclockwise to remove the fuel pump from the retainer. Note the orientation of the pump to the retainer.

16. Slide the lower connector assembly out of the retainer to remove the fuel pulse dampener from the lower connector. Note the orientation of the seal (the modular unit is now held together by the crossover tube only). Discard the fuel pulse dampener.

To install:

17. Install the fuel pulse dampener. Always use a new dampener when installing a new fuel pump.

18. Slide the lower connector into the retainer.

19. Push the pump outlet tube into the fuel pulse dampener and rotate the flex member back to its original position. Line up the pump outlet tube into the retainer opening. All three sleeve tabs should protrude through the retainer before rotating. Rotate the pump clockwise until a click is heard, be sure fit is snug before rotating. Place the fuel pump back into its reservoir. The crossover tube must be placed in its proper slot.

20. Install a new rubber bumper pad. Insert the drain tube into the proper retainer and bumper pad slots.

21. Install a new strainer, being careful not to dislodge the jet pump.

22. Install the fuel pump wire connector, the undercover wiring harness connector and the CPA clip.

23. Install a new lip seal on the modular fuel sender assembly. Always use a new seal when servicing the modular fuel sender assembly. Lightly lubricate the inside diameter of the lip seal with clean engine oil. The lip seal should be positioned over the float arm assembly, moved up over the reservoir and half-way up the guide posts.

24. Install the modular fuel assembly into the tank. Seat the lip seal into the tank opening.

25. Align the arrows on top of the fuel tank to the arrow on the modular assembly.

26. Slowly apply pressure to the top of the spring loaded sender until the lip seal is flush between the fuel tank and the modular cover.

27. Install the locking nut, and tighten to 37 ft. lbs. (50 Nm).

28. Install the fuel tank in the vehicle.

29. Replace the fuel that was drained before removal.

30. Connect the negative battery cable.

31. Pressurize the fuel system and verify there are no fuel leaks.

DRIVE TRAIN

Transaxle Assembly

REMOVAL & INSTALLATION

1. Before servicing the vehicle, refer to the precautions in the beginning of this section.

2. Disconnect the negative battery cable.

3. Remove the headlight housing upper filler panel and diagonal brace.

4. Remove the air cleaner assembly.

5. Disconnect the shift control cable and bracket at the transaxle.

6. Remove the torque struts.

7. Disconnect the oil cooler lines at the cooler and the oil sending line at the transaxle.

8. Remove the two upper transaxle-to-engine bolts.

9. Disconnect the power steering return hose at the auxiliary cooler. Plug the cooler and return hose to prevent leakage.

10. Support the engine with engine support fixture J-28467 or equivalent. Tighten the wing nuts several turns to take the weight of the powertrain off of the mounts and frame.

11. Raise and safely support the vehicle. Remove the front wheels.

12. Remove the splash shields from both front wheel wells.

13. Disconnect both front suspension position sensors from the lower control arms and position aside.

14. Remove both stabilizer links from the struts.

15. Separate the tie rod ends from the steering knuckles.

16. Separate the lower ball joints from the steering knuckles.

17. Remove the halfshafts.

18. Remove the power steering filter at the cradle and the A/C splash shield from the frame.

19. Remove the ABS modulator from the bracket and support. Remove the engine oil pan-to-transaxle bracket.

20. Remove the torque converter cover, then remove the torque converter-to-flexplate bolts. Prior to bolt removal, mark the torque converter position in relation to the flexplate so they can be reassembled in the same position.

21. Remove the powertrain mount nuts from the cradle.

22. Rotate the intermediate steering shaft until the steering gear stub shaft clamp bolt is accessible from the left wheel well. Remove the clamp bolt and disconnect the intermediate steering shaft from the steering gear.

✷✷ CAUTION

If the intermediate steering shaft is not disconnected from the steering gear stub shaft, damage to the steering gear and/or intermediate shaft may result. This damage can cause loss of steering control which could result in personal injury.

1 NUT
2 THROUGH-BOLTS
3 STUD, STRUT INBOARD
4 BAR, CROSS BRACE

7922VG16

Exploded view of the crossbrace-to-strut towers mounting

※※ **WARNING**

Do not turn the steering wheel or move the position of the steering gear once the intermediate steering shaft is disconnected as this will uncenter the air bag coil in the steering column. If the air bag coil becomes uncentered, it may be damaged during vehicle operation.

23. Remove the electrical harness and connector from the front of the cradle.

24. Support the rear of the cradle with a suitable jack, then remove the four rear cradle bolts.

25. Lower the jack a few inches to gain access to the power steering gear heat shield and return line fitting. Remove the heat shield and disconnect the return line. Plug the line and the opening in the gear to prevent fluid leakage.

26. Detach the power steering electrical connector.

27. Raise the jack and reinstall one rear cradle bolt on each side finger-tight to support the cradle. Remove the jack.

28. Support the frame with a suitable jack and remove the six frame mount bolts. Lower the frame and/or raise the vehicle with the steering gear attached.

LOCATING PIN

A

VIEW A

1 75 N·m (55 LB. FT.)
2 LOCATING PIN (NO BOLT AT THIS POSITION)
3 TIGHTEN BOLTS TWICE IN SEQUENCE TO 62 N·m (46 LB. FT.)

7922VG17

Exploded view of the engine-to-transaxle attachments

For complete service labor times order Chilton's Labor Guide Manual

29. Label and detach the electrical connectors to the transaxle, Vehicle Speed Sensor (VSS) and ground. Remove the transaxle harness from the transaxle clip.

30. Remove the fuel line bundle from the transaxle.

31. Remove the left and right transaxle mount and bracket from the transaxle.

32. Support the transaxle with a suitable jack.

33. Remove the engine-to-transaxle heat shield and bracket and the remaining transaxle-to-engine bolts. Lower the transaxle.

34. Remove the manual shaft linkage and neutral safety switch. Remove the VSS and oil return line.

To install:

35. Install the oil return line and the VSS.

36. Install the neutral safety switch and tighten the bolts to 106 inch lbs. (12 Nm).

37. Install the manual shaft linkage and tighten the manual shaft nut to 15 ft. lbs. (20 Nm).

38. Raise the transaxle into position and install the two lower transaxle-to-engine bolts. Tighten to 35 ft. lbs. (47 Nm).

39. Install the engine-to-transaxle bracket and heat shield. Tighten the bolts to 35 ft. lbs. (47 Nm).

40. Remove the transaxle jack.

41. Install the right and left transaxle bracket and mount to the transaxle. Tighten the bolts and nuts to 35 ft. lbs. (47 Nm).

42. Install the fuel line bundle to the transaxle.

43. Attach the electrical connectors to the transaxle, VSS and ground. Install the transaxle harness to the transaxle clip.

44. Raise the frame and/or lower the vehicle while locating the engine and transaxle mount studs into the frame, harnesses at the cradle, and frame mount bolt holes to the underbody.

45. Install two front and two rear cradle bolts finger-tight to support the cradle, then remove the cradle support.

46. Support the rear of the cradle with a suitable jack and remove the two rear cradle bolts.

47. Lower the jack a few inches to gain access to the power steering gear. Connect the hose at the steering gear and tighten the fitting to 20 ft. lbs. (27 Nm). Attach the power steering gear electrical connector and install the steering gear heat shield.

48. Raise the cradle with the jack. Install the six frame mount bolts beginning with the No. 2 mount bolt into the body, followed by the No. 1 mount bolt into the body, followed by the remaining frame mount bolts. Tighten the bolts to 74 ft. lbs. (100 Nm).

49. Install the electrical harness to the front of the cradle.

50. Connect the intermediate steering shaft to the steering gear and install the clamp bolt. Tighten the bolt to 35 ft. lbs. (47 Nm).

✷✷ WARNING

Do not turn the steering wheel or move the position of the steering gear while the intermediate steering shaft is disconnected as this will uncenter the air bag coil in the steering column. If the air bag coil becomes uncentered, it may be damaged during vehicle operation.

51. Install the left and right transaxle mount nuts and right engine mount nuts at the frame. Tighten the nuts to 35 ft. lbs. (47 Nm).

52. Align the flexplate and torque converter using the marks made during the removal procedure. Install the flexplate-to-converter bolts and tighten to 35 ft. lbs. (47 Nm).

53. Install the torque converter cover and tighten the bolts to 106 inch lbs. (12 Nm).

54. Install the engine oil pan-to-transaxle bracket and tighten the bolts to 35 ft. lbs. (47 Nm).

55. Install the ABS modulator to the bracket and install the A/C splash shield at the frame.

56. Install the halfshafts. Tighten the halfshaft nuts to 110 ft. lbs. (145 Nm).

57. Install the lower ball joints into the steering knuckles and install the nuts.

58. Install new cotter pins.

59. Install the tie rod ends into the steering knuckles and install the nuts.

60. Install new cotter pins.

61. Connect the stabilizer links to the struts and tighten the nuts to 49 ft. lbs. (65 Nm).

62. Install both front suspension position sensors to the lower control arms.

63. Install the power steering filter to the cradle and install the splash shields in the wheel wells.

64. Install the wheels and lower the vehicle. Remove the engine support fixture.

65. Connect the power steering hose at the auxiliary cooler.

66. Install the remaining transaxle-to-engine bolts and tighten to 35 ft. lbs. (47 Nm).

67. Flush the transaxle oil cooler using flushing tool J-35944 and flushing solution J-35944–20. The transaxle oil cooler and lines should be flushed before the oil cooler lines are connected to the transaxle.

68. Connect the transaxle oil cooler lines to the transaxle. Start the fittings by hand, then tighten the fittings to 16 ft. lbs. (22 Nm).

69. Install the torque struts.

70. Adjust the neutral safety switch.

71. Install the shift control cable and bracket to the transaxle and tighten the bracket bolts to 106 inch lbs. (12 Nm). Adjust the shift control cable.

72. Install the air cleaner assembly. Install the headlight housing upper filler panel and diagonal brace.

73. Connect the negative battery cable.

74. Fill the transaxle with the proper type and quantity of transaxle fluid. Bleed the power steering system.

75. Check the front suspension alignment and adjust as necessary.

76. The Powertrain Control Module (PCM) maintains three types of transaxle adapt parameters which are used to modify transaxle line pressure. The line pressure is modified to maintain shift quality regardless of wear or tolerance variations within the transaxle. Whenever the transaxle is replaced, the transaxle adapts must be reset as follows:

a. Turn the ignition key **ON**. Enter the self-diagnostic system.

b. Select Powertrain Control Module (PCM) override PS13 (TP SENSOR LEARN).

c. Press the WARMER button. The Driver Information Center (DIC) should display 09, indicating that the Garage Shift Adapt value has been reset.

d. Select PCM override PS14 (TRAN ADAPT).

e. Press the COOLER button. The DIC should display 90, indicating the Upshift Adapt (UA) value has been reset.

f. Press the WARMER button. The DIC should display 09, indicating the Steady State Adapt (SSA) value has been reset.

➡**The PCM maintains a value for transaxle oil life. This value indicates the percentage of oil life remaining and is calculated based on transaxle temperature and speed. When the vehicle is new, the transaxle oil life value is 100 As the vehicle operates, the percentage will decrease. Whenever the transaxle is replaced, the transaxle oil life indicator should be reset to 100 as follows:**

g. Turn the ignition key ON , but leave the engine OFF.

h. Press and hold the OFF and REAR DEFOG buttons on the DIC until the message TRANSAXLE OIL LIFE RESET is displayed on the DIC.

Halfshaft

REMOVAL & INSTALLATION

✳✳ WARNING

Use care when removing the half-shaft to prevent the inner CV-joint from becoming over-extended. Over-extension of the joint could result in separation of internal components and possible joint failure.

1. Before servicing the vehicle, refer to the precautions in the beginning of this section.

2. Raise and safely support the vehicle.

3. Remove the front wheel. Mark the position of the wheel to the wheel studs, prior to removal, for installation reference.

4. Install J-34754 boot protector, or the equivalent, on the outer CV-joint boot.

5. Remove the hub nut. To prevent the rotor from turning insert a drift punch in the rotor cooling fins. Discard the hub nut; it must not be reused.

6. Disconnect the stabilizer link, if necessary.

7. Remove the ball joint cotter pin and nut. Loosen the ball joint in the knuckle using tool J-36226 or equivalent, being careful not to damage the ball joint and grease seal. If removing the right halfshaft, turn the wheel to the left. If removing the left halfshaft, turn the wheel to the right.

8. Using a suitable prybar between the suspension support and the lower control arm, separate the ball joint from the steering knuckle.

9. Partially install the hub nut to protect the threads, then remove the halfshaft from the hub using tool J-28733-B or equivalent.

10. Move the strut and knuckle rearward.

11. Remove the halfshaft from the transaxle using a suitable prying tool and a wood block fulcrum to protect the transaxle case.

➡ **If equipped with anti-lock brakes, care must be used to prevent damage to the toothed sensor ring on the half-shaft and the wheel speed sensor on the steering knuckle.**

To install:

12. If installing the right-side halfshaft, install tool J-37292-B or equivalent, so it

Removing the halfshaft from the hub

can be pulled out after the halfshaft is installed.

13. Install the halfshaft into the transaxle. To verify the halfshaft is properly seated, grasp the inner CV-joint housing and pull it outward. DO NOT pull on the halfshaft. If the CV-joint is properly seated, the halfshaft will not pull back out.

14. Install the halfshaft into the hub and bearing assembly. Loosely install a new hub nut.

15. Install the ball joint into the steering knuckle.

Exploded view of the removal of the halfshaft from the transaxle

16. Install the castle nut and tighten to 84 inch lbs. plus 120 degrees (⅓ turn). A minimum of 37 ft. lbs. (51 Nm) of torque must be attained. If necessary to install the cotter pin, the nut can be tightened up to 20 degrees additional. NEVER loosen the castle nut to install the cotter pin.

17. With a drift in the brake rotor cooling fins to keep the rotor from turning, tighten the nut to 110 ft. lbs. (149 Nm) on all models, except DeVille with J55 brake option, in which case the torque is 130 ft. lbs. (177 Nm).

18. Connect the stabilizer link, if removed.

19. Remove the boot protector.

20. If tool J-37292-B was installed, remove it by pulling in line with the handle.

21. Install the wheel, aligning the marks made during removal.

22. Lower the vehicle.

23. Road test and check vehicle operation.

STEERING AND SUSPENSION

Air Bag

❊❊ CAUTION

Some vehicles are equipped with an air bag system, also known as the Supplemental Inflatable Restraint (SIR) or Supplemental Restraint System (SRS). The system must be disabled before performing service on or round system components, steering column, instrument panel components, wiring and sensors. Failure to follow safety and disabling procedures could result in accidental air bag deployment, possible personal injury and unnecessary system repairs.

PRECAUTIONS

Several precautions must be observed when handling the inflator module to avoid accidental deployment and possible personal injury.

• Never carry the inflator module by the wires or connector on the underside of the module.

• When carrying a live inflator module, hold securely with both hands, and ensure that the bag and trim cover are pointed away.

• Place the inflator module on a bench or other surface with the bag and trim cover facing up.

• With the inflator module on the bench, never place anything on or close to the module which may be thrown in the event of an accidental deployment.

DISARMING

❊❊ CAUTION

The air bag system must be disarmed before performing service procedures around the air bag or wiring. Failure to do so may cause accidental deployment, resulting in unnecessary repairs and/or personal injury.

1. Before servicing the vehicle, refer to the precautions in the beginning of this section.

2. Disconnect the negative battery cable.

3. Turn the steering wheel so that the vehicle's wheels are pointing straight ahead.

4. Turn the ignition switch to the **LOCK** position and remove the key.

5. Remove the **AIR BAG** fuse from the fuse block.

6. Remove the left sound insulator.

7. Remove the Connector Position Assurance (CPA) clip from the yellow 2-way connector at the base of the steering column, and detach the harness. If equipped with a passenger's side air bag, remove the CPA and detach the yellow 2-way connector from the passenger air bag lead.

1. Steering column
2. Connector, SRS (yellow)

7922VG20

Detach the SRS yellow 2-way connector

ARMING

After the applicable service is concluded, enable the air bag system as follows:

1. Turn the ignition switch to the **LOCK** position and remove the key.

2. Attach the yellow 2-way connector at the base of steering column and secure it with the CPA clip. If equipped with a passenger's side air bag, attach the yellow 2-way connector at the passenger air bag lead and secure it with the CPA clip.

3. Install the left sound insulator.

4. Install the **AIR BAG** fuse in the fuse block.

5. Turn the ignition switch to the **RUN** position and verify that the **AIR BAG** warning lamp flashes seven times, then turns OFF.

6. Connect the negative battery cable.

Power Rack and Pinion Steering Gear

REMOVAL & INSTALLATION

❊❊ CAUTION

Failure to disconnect the intermediate shaft from the rack and pinion stub shaft can result in damage to the steering gear and/or intermediate shaft. This damage can cause loss of steering control which could result in personal injury.

1. Disconnect the negative battery cable.

❊❊ WARNING

The wheels of the vehicle must be straight ahead and the steering column in the LOCK position before disconnecting the steering column or intermediate shaft from the steering gear. Failure to do so will cause the coil assembly in the steering column to become uncentered which will cause damage to the coil assembly.

2. Before servicing the vehicle, refer to the precautions in the beginning of this section.

3. Raise and safely support the vehicle.

4. Remove the front wheels.

5. Remove the bolt holding the intermediate shaft to the steering shaft. Disconnect the intermediate shaft lower coupling.

6. Disconnect the Road Sensing Suspension (RSS) sensor from the lower control arm.

7. Remove the cotter pin and castle nuts from both outer tie rods and using tool J-24319 or the equivalent, separate the outer tie rod ends from the steering knuckles.

STEERING KNUCKLE

RACK AND PINION STEERING GEAR

BOLT

WASHER

TIE ROD END

COTTER PIN

TIE ROD END NUT

FRONT OF CAR

7922VG21

Exploded view of the power steering rack components

8. Disconnect the Y-pipe from the catalytic converter.

9. Support the rear of the subframe with a screw jack.

10. Remove the rear subframe bolts.

11. Slowly lower the subframe to gain access.

12. Remove the heat shield.

13. Remove the power steering line retainer.

14. Place a catch pan under the power steering rack and the line fittings.

15. Disconnect the power steering pressure and return lines from the rack and pinion unit.

16. Detach the Speed Sensitive Steering (SSS) solenoid valve connector.

17. Remove the five power steering rack-to-subframe bolts.

18. Slide the rack and pinion unit out the left wheel well.

To install:

19. Install the rack and pinion through the left wheel well and into position on the subframe.

20. Install the five mounting bolts and tighten to 50 ft. lbs. (68 Nm).

21. Attach the Speed Sensitive Steering (SSS) solenoid valve connector.

22. Connect the power steering pressure and return hoses and tighten the fittings to 20 ft. lbs. (27 Nm).

23. Install the power steering line retainer.

24. Install the heat shield.

25. Raise the subframe into position and install the subframe mounting bolts. Tighten to 76 ft. lbs. (103 Nm).

26. Connect the Y-pipe to the catalytic converter.

27. Connect the outer tie rod ends to the steering knuckle. Install the castle nuts and tighten. Install the cotter pins.

28. Connect the RSS sensor to the lower control arm.

29. Connect the intermediate shaft and install the intermediate shaft-to-steering shaft bolt. Tighten the bolt to 30 ft. lbs. (41 Nm).

30. Install the front wheels.

31. Lower the vehicle.

32. Connect the negative battery cable.

33. Refill the power steering reservoir and bleed the power steering system.

34. Check the wheel alignment. Road test the vehicle.

Strut

REMOVAL & INSTALLATION

Front

✳✳ WARNING

When working near the halfshafts, use care to prevent the inner Tripot CV-joint from being overextended. If the joint is overextended, the internal joint components could separate, resulting in CV-joint failure.

1. Before servicing the vehicle, refer to the precautions in the beginning of this section.

2. Disconnect the negative battery cable.

3. Raise and safely support the vehicle.

4. Remove the front wheel.

5. If equipped, detach the electrical connector from the top of the strut.

6. Remove the upper strut mounting nuts.

7. Remove the Road Sensing Suspen-

Exploded view of the strut mounting

sion (RSS) position sensor from the lower control arm, if equipped.

8. Disconnect the ABS wheel speed sensor, if equipped.

9. Remove the wheel speed sensor from the bracket on the strut, if equipped.

10. Remove the brake line bracket from the strut.

11. Remove the stabilizer link from the strut.

12. Scribe a mark on the strut referencing the lower strut bracket to the steering knuckle.

13. Remove the nuts and through-bolts from the lower strut bracket and remove the strut from the vehicle.

To install:

14. Install the strut assembly into the vehicle. Install the strut-to-knuckle bolts and nuts, but do not tighten yet.

15. Connect the stabilizer link to the strut assembly, but do not tighten the nuts yet.

16. Connect the brake line bracket to the strut.

17. Install the speed sensor bracket on the strut, if equipped.

18. Connect the ABS sensor, if equipped.

19. Install the RSS sensor to the lower control arm, if equipped.

20. Install the upper strut mounting nuts. If equipped, attach the electrical connector to the top of the strut.

21. Tighten the upper strut mounting nuts to 18 ft. lbs. (24 Nm). Tighten the stabilizer link nuts to 48 ft. lbs. (65 Nm). Align the marks made during removal and tighten the strut-to-knuckle bolt nuts to 140 ft. lbs. (190 Nm).

22. Install the front wheel and lower the vehicle.

23. Check the wheel alignment.

Shock Absorber

REMOVAL & INSTALLATION

Rear

1. Before servicing the vehicle, refer to the precautions in the beginning of this section.

2. Disconnect the negative battery cable.

3. Raise and safely support the vehicle.

4. Remove the rear wheel.

5. If equipped, detach the shock absorber electrical connector from the rear suspension support.

6. Support the lower control arm with a

Exploded view of the rear shock absorber mounting

jack to relieve the tension on the shock absorber.

7. Remove the lower shock absorber mounting bolt and nut.

8. Remove the upper mounting nut, retainer, and insulator.

9. Compress the shock absorber by hand and remove through the upper control arm.

To install:

10. Position the top of the shock absorber with the insulator attached into the suspension support.

11. Install the upper shock insulator, retainer and nut.

12. Install the shock absorber lower mounting nut and bolt.

13. Tighten the upper nut to 55 ft. lbs. (74 Nm) and the lower nut to 75 ft. lbs. (102 Nm).

14. If equipped, attach the shock absorber electrical connector to the rear suspension support.

15. Install the rear wheel and lower the vehicle.

16. Connect the negative battery cable.

Coil Spring

REMOVAL & INSTALLATION

Front

1. Before servicing the vehicle, refer to the precautions in the beginning of this section.

2. Remove the strut from the vehicle.

※ WARNING

Be careful not to scratch or crack the protective coating on the coil spring, as damage may cause premature spring failure.

3. Mount the strut assembly in strut compressor tool J-34013 or equivalent strut compressor.

4. Turn the compressor forcing screw until the spring compresses slightly.

5. Use a T-50 Torx® bit to keep the strut shaft from turning, then remove the nut on the top of the strut shaft.

6. Loosen the compressor screw while guiding the strut shaft out of the assembly. Continue loosening the compressor screw until the strut and spring can be removed.

To install:

7. Mount the strut in the compressor tool. Use clamping tool J-34013–20 or the equivalent, to hold the strut shaft in place.

1	NUT, STRUT TO MOUNT
2	STRUT MOUNT
3	FRONT SPRING SEAT
4	FRONT SPRING UPPER INSULATOR
5	JOUNCE BUMPER
6	DUST SHIELD
7	SPRING
8	FRONT SPRING LOWER INSULATOR
9	FRONT STRUT

7922VG23

Disassembled view of strut

8. Install the spring over the strut. The flat on the upper spring seat must face out from the centerline of the vehicle, or when mounted in the strut compressor, the spring seat must face the same direction as the steering knuckle mounting flange.

➡ **If the bearing was removed from the upper spring seat, it must be reinstalled in the spring seat in the same position before attaching to the strut mount.**

9. Turn the compressor screw to compress the spring, while guiding the strut shaft through the top of the strut assembly. If necessary, use tool J-34013–38 or equivalent, to guide the shaft.

10. When the strut shaft threads are visible through the top of the strut assembly, install the nut.

11. Remove clamping tool J-34013–20 from the strut shaft.

12. Tighten the strut shaft nut to 55 ft. lbs. (75 Nm) while holding the strut shaft with a T-50 Torx® bit.

13. Remove the strut assembly from the compressor tool, then install the strut into the vehicle.

Rear

1. Before servicing the vehicle, refer to the precautions in the beginning of this section.

2. Raise and safely support the vehicle.

3. Remove the rear wheel.

4. Support the inboard end of the lower control arm with a transmission jack.

5. Remove the sway bar link lower mounting bolt.

6. Remove the shock absorber lower mounting bolt and push the shock up and out of the way.

7. Remove the lower control arm inner mounting nuts and bolts.

8. Slowly lower the transmission jack until the spring tension has been released.

9. Remove the coil spring.

To install:

10. Install the coil spring and spring insulators.

11. Raise the control arm with the transmission jack until the lower control arm bolts can be installed.

12. Install the mounting nuts. Do not tighten at this time.

13. Remove the transmission jack.

14. Extend the shock absorber and install the mounting nuts. Tighten the nut to 75 ft. lbs. (102 Nm).

15. Install the link kit and tighten the nut to 44 ft. lbs. (60 Nm).

1. Suspension support
2. Lower control arm
3. Lower control arm inner nut - 102 Nm (75 lb. ft.)
4. Lower control arm inner bolt

7922VG24

Exploded view of the lower control arm mounting

16. Install the rear wheel and lower the vehicle.

17. Tighten the lower control arm inner bolts to 75 ft. lbs. (102 Nm).

18. Check the alignment and adjust, as necessary.

Lower Ball Joint

REMOVAL & INSTALLATION

1. Before servicing the vehicle, refer to the precautions in the beginning of this section.

2. Raise and safely support the vehicle, allowing the front suspension to hang free.

3. Remove the front wheel.

❊❊ CAUTION

Be careful when working in the area of the CV-boot. Damage to the boot could result in eventual joint failure. Install CV-boot protector tool J-34754 or take equivalent precautions to protect the soft boot.

4. If equipped, remove the Road Sensing Suspension (RSS) position sensor from the lower control arm.

5. Separate the ball joint from the steering knuckle.

6. Drill out the three rivets retaining the ball joint to the lower control arm and remove the ball joint.

To install:

7. Attach the new ball joint to the lower control arm with three mounting bolts and nuts. The bolts must be installed from the bottom of the control arm. Tighten the nuts to 50 ft. lbs. (68 Nm).

Exploded view of the lower ball joint mounting

8. Connect the ball joint to the steering knuckle and install the castellated nut.

9. Tighten the ball joint nut to 84 inch lbs. (10 Nm), then tighten the nut an additional 120 degrees during which a minimum torque of 37 ft. lbs. (50 Nm) must be obtained. If the minimum torque is not obtained, check for stripped threads. If the threads are okay, replace the ball joint and knuckle.

10. Install a new cotter pin. If the cotter pin cannot be installed because the hole in the stud does not align with a nut slot, tighten the nut up to an additional 60 degrees to allow for installation. NEVER loosen the nut to provide for cotter pin installation.

11. If equipped, install the RSS position sensor to the lower control arm.

12. If used, remove the CV-Joint boot protector tool.

13. Install the front wheel and lower the vehicle.

14. Check the wheel alignment.

Wheel Bearings

ADJUSTMENT

The wheel bearings are not adjustable. If a wheel bearing is out of specifications, it must be replaced. Using a dial indicator, check for looseness. If play exceeds 0.005 in. (0.127mm) the bearing wear is excessive and the hub and bearing should be replaced.

REMOVAL & INSTALLATION

Front

1. Before servicing the vehicle, refer to the precautions in the beginning of this section.

2. Raise and safely support the vehicle.

3. Remove the front wheel.

4. Insert a drift punch through the caliper and into the rotor cooling fins to prevent the rotor from turning.

5. Remove the axle nut and washer.

6. Remove the caliper mounting bolts. Remove the caliper from the steering knuckle and support out of the way. DO NOT allow the brake hose to support the weight of the caliper.

7. Remove the brake rotor.

8. Detach the ABS speed sensor connector and unclip from the dust shield.

WHEEL BEARING LOOSENESS DIAGNOSIS

DRUM BRAKE

Mount dial indicator. Grasp bearing flange; using a push-pull movement, note indicator readings.

If looseness exceeds 0.1270 mm (0.005 inch), replace hub and bearing assembly.

J 8001

MOUNTING DIAL
INDICATOR
WITH DRUM BRAKES

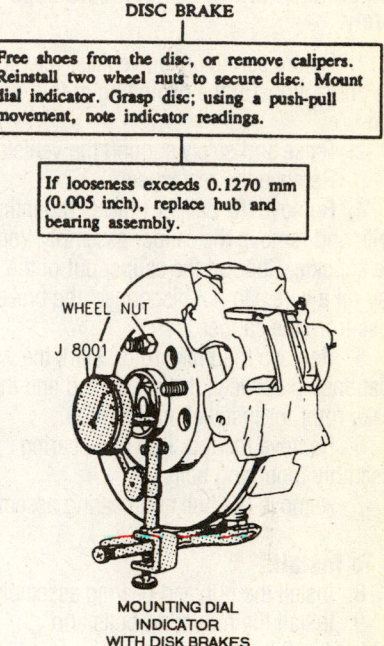

DISC BRAKE

Free shoes from the disc, or remove calipers. Reinstall two wheel nuts to secure disc. Mount dial indicator. Grasp disc; using a push-pull movement, note indicator readings.

If looseness exceeds 0.1270 mm (0.005 inch), replace hub and bearing assembly.

WHEEL NUT

J 8001

MOUNTING DIAL
INDICATOR
WITH DISK BRAKES

7922VG33

Inspect the wheel bearings for play with a dial indicator

9. Remove the three hub and bearing bolts and remove the dust shield.

10. Place the transaxle selector in the **P** detent.

11. Install J-28733 or an equivalent puller, and separate the hub and bearing from the drive axle.

12. Remove the hub and bearing assembly from the steering knuckle.

To install:

13. Install the hub and bearing over the half shaft splines. Be sure the splines engage smoothly.

7922VG26

Exploded view of the front wheel bearing mounting

14. Apply a light coating of grease to the steering knuckle bore.

15. Slide the hub assembly onto the axle as far as possible. If the hub will not bottom out on the axle, install the hub mounting bolts and use the axle nut to draw the hub onto the axle.

16. Once the hub is flush with the steering knuckle, remove the mounting bolts and install the dust shield. Reinstall the mounting bolts and tighten to 70 ft. lbs. (95 Nm).

17. Place the transaxle in **N**.

18. Attach the ABS front wheel speed sensor connector and clip to the dust shield.

19. Install the brake rotor.

20. Install the caliper and tighten the mounting bolts to 38 ft. lbs. (51 Nm).

21. Insert a drift punch through the rotor to prevent the axle from turning.

22. Tighten the drive axle shaft nut to 107 ft. lbs. (145 Nm).

23. Remove the drift punch.

24. Install the wheel and lower the vehicle.

25. Road test for proper operation.

Turn to Section 6 for brake system applications

Rear

➤ **The wheel bearing and hub are serviced as an assembly. The individual components are not serviceable separately.**

1. Before servicing the vehicle, refer to the precautions in the beginning of this section.

2. Raise and safely support the vehicle.

3. Remove the rear wheel.

4. Remove the caliper bracket mounting bolts and remove the caliper assembly from the knuckle. Support the caliper out of the way on a wire. Do not disconnect the brake hose from the caliper.

5. Remove the brake rotor. Mark the relationship between the wheel stud and the brake rotor for installation reference.

6. Remove the four hub and bearing assembly mounting bolts.

7. Remove the hub and bearing assembly.

To install:

8. Install the hub and bearing assembly.

9. Install the mounting bolts and tighten to 52 ft. lbs. (70 Nm).

Exploded view of the rear wheel bearing hub mounting

7922VG27

10. Install the brake rotor, aligning the marks made during removal.

11. Install the caliper and new caliper bracket mounting bolts. Tighten to 83 ft. lbs. (113 Nm).

12. Install the wheel and lower the vehicle.

13. Road test the vehicle for proper operation.

GENERAL MOTORS CORPORATION—F BODY

31

Chevrolet-Camaro • **Z28** • **Pontiac**-Firebird • **Trans Am**

PRECAUTIONS

Before servicing any vehicle, please be sure to read all of the following precautions, which deal with personal safety, prevention of component damage, and important points to take into consideration when servicing a motor vehicle:

- Never open, service or drain the radiator or cooling system when the engine is hot; serious burns can occur from the steam and hot coolant.
- Observe all applicable safety precautions when working around fuel. Whenever servicing the fuel system, always work in a well-ventilated area. Do not allow fuel spray or vapors to come in contact with a spark, open flame, or excessive heat (a hot drop light, for example). Keep a dry chemical fire extinguisher near the work area. Always keep fuel in a container specifically designed for fuel storage; also, always properly seal fuel containers to avoid the possibility of fire or explosion. Refer to the additional fuel system precautions later in this section.
- Fuel injection systems often remain pressurized, even after the engine has been turned **OFF**. The fuel system pressure must be relieved before disconnecting any fuel lines. Failure to do so may result in fire and/or personal injury.
- Brake fluid often contains polyglycol ethers and polyglycols. Avoid contact with the eyes and wash your hands thoroughly after handling brake fluid. If you do get brake fluid in your eyes, flush your eyes with clean, running water for 15 minutes. If eye irritation persists, or if you have taken brake fluid internally, IMMEDIATELY seek medical assistance.
- The EPA warns that prolonged contact with used engine oil may cause a number of skin disorders, including cancer! You should make every effort to minimize your exposure to used engine oil. Protective gloves should be worn when changing oil. Wash your hands and any other exposed skin areas as soon as possible after exposure to used engine oil. Soap and water, or waterless hand cleaner should be used.
- All new vehicles are now equipped with an air bag system, often referred to as a Supplemental Restraint System (SRS) or Supplemental Inflatable Restraint (SIR) system. The system must be disabled before performing service on or around system components, steering column, instrument panel components, wiring and sensors. Failure to follow safety and disabling procedures could result in accidental air bag deployment, possible personal injury and unnecessary system repairs.
- Always wear safety goggles when working with, or around, the air bag system. When carrying a non-deployed air bag, be sure the bag and trim cover are pointed away from your body. When placing a non-deployed air bag on a work surface, always face the bag and trim cover upward, away from the surface. This will reduce the motion of the module if it is accidentally deployed. Refer to the additional air bag system precautions later in this section.
- Clean, high quality brake fluid from a sealed container is essential to the safe and proper operation of the brake system. You should always buy the correct type of brake fluid for your vehicle. If the brake fluid becomes contaminated, completely flush the system with new fluid. Never reuse any brake fluid. Any brake fluid that is removed from the system should be discarded. Also, do not allow any brake fluid to come in contact with a painted surface; it will damage the paint.
- Never operate the engine without the proper amount and type of engine oil; doing so WILL result in severe engine damage.
- Timing belt maintenance is extremely important! Many models utilize an interference-type, non-freewheeling engine. If the timing belt breaks, the valves in the cylinder head may strike the pistons, causing potentially serious (also time-consuming and expensive) engine damage. Refer to the maintenance interval charts in the front of this manual for the recommended replacement interval for the timing belt, and to the timing belt section for belt replacement and inspection.
- Disconnecting the negative battery cable on some vehicles may interfere with the functions of the on-board computer system(s) and may require the computer to undergo a relearning process once the negative battery cable is reconnected.
- When servicing drum brakes, only dissemble and assemble one side at a time, leaving the remaining side intact for reference.
- Only an MVAC-trained, EPA-certified automotive technician should service the A/C system or its components.

ENGINE REPAIR

Distributor

All 1998–00 5.7L (VIN G) engines use a direct ignition system. This system eliminates the need for a distributor and has several advantages. Some of the advantages are, no moving parts, no load on the engine, more coil cool down time between firing and increased coil saturation time which produces a stronger spark.

The direct ignition system consists of
- Eight ignition coils and modules (one for each cylinder)
- Eight ignition control circuits
- Camshaft Position (CMP) sensor
- 1X Camshaft reluctor wheel
- 24X Crankshaft reluctor wheel
- Crankshaft Position (CKP) sensor
- Powertrain Control Module (PCM)

The 24X crankshaft position sensor is the most critical part of the system, if it is damaged, the engine will not start. Ignition timing is controlled by the PCM. There are no timing marks on the crankshaft balancer or timing chain cover.

REMOVAL

➡**This procedure is for 5.7L VIN P engines only. The 3.8L VIN K and the 5.7 VIN G engines do not utilize a distributor.**

1. Before servicing the vehicle, refer to the precautions in the beginning of this section.

2. Be sure the ignition is in the **OFF** or **LOCK** position. Disconnect the negative battery cable.

3. Remove the water pump and crankshaft balancer.

❊❊ WARNING

To prevent wire damage, the spark plug wire boots should be twisted ½ turn in each direction while removing. Do not pull on the wires to remove them from the spark plugs. Pull on the boots or use a tool specifically designed for this purpose.

4. Remove the spark plug wiring harnesses from the distributor, as follows:
   a. Raise and safely support the vehicle.
   b. Remove the power steering pump.
   c. Unfasten the spark plug wiring harness from the wiring harness clips.
   d. Remove the spark plug wiring harness from the distributor.

5. Unplug the 4-terminal electrical connector from the distributor.

6. If equipped, disconnect the distributor vacuum harness from the distributor.

7. Loosen and remove the distributor attaching bolts.

8. Pull the distributor assembly forward until the driveshaft disengages from the end of the camshaft.

9. Before servicing the vehicle, refer to the precautions in the beginning of this section.

10. Mark the top surface of the driveshaft for proper alignment during installation.

To install:

➡**Replace the O-rings on the coupling shaft, otherwise ignition system performance may suffer. Lubricate the O-rings and the end of the camshaft.**

❊❊ WARNING

Don't try to fully seat the distributor using the distributor retainers. If the distributor will not seat by hand, it's not properly aligned with the camshaft. Rotate the crankshaft until the engine is at the number 1 cylinder TDC (camshaft sprocket pin at the 9 o'clock position). Rotate the distributor coupling until the camshaft sprocket pin slot aligns with the distributor base timing mark. Install the distributor using hand pressure to fully seat the distributor.

11. Install the distributor assembly into position with the driveshaft in the end of the camshaft. Rotate the distributor coupling until the camshaft sprocket pin slot aligns with the camshaft sprocket pin. Slide the distributor onto the end of the camshaft until fully seated on the engine front cover.

12. Install the distributor mounting bolts. Tighten to 97–106 inch lbs. (11–12 Nm).

13. Engage all electrical connections and/or vacuum hoses on the distributor that were unplugged earlier.

14. Install the crankshaft balancer and water pump.

15. Connect the negative battery cable.

Ignition Timing

ADJUSTMENT

When checking ignition timing NEVER pierce a secondary ignition wire. Use either a timing light with an inductive pick-up or connect an adapter between the wire and the spark plug. If the secondary wire insulation is pierced, current will eventually arc and cause engine misfiring.

➡**Some engines incorporate a magnetic timing probe hole for use with electronic timing equipment. Be sure to consult the tool manufacture's instructions for the use of this equipment.**

On these vehicles, base timing is preset when the engine is manufactured. All timing changes are, then controlled directly by the PCM based on information from the ignition and knock sensor systems. No adjustments are necessary or possible.

Engine Assembly

REMOVAL & INSTALLATION

➡**The engine, transmission and suspension assembly is removed from the bottom of the vehicle. After the assem-**

A	CAMSHAFT PIN
B	CAMSHAFT PIN SLOT
C	DISTRIBUTOR BASE TIMING MARK
24	DISTRIBUTOR VACUUM HARNESS
47	BOLT/SCREW DISTRIBUTOR
49	DISTRIBUTOR

Exploded view of the distributor assembly mounting (located under the water pump)—5.7L (VIN P) engine bly is removed, separate the engine from the transmission and frame.

1. Before servicing the vehicle, refer to the precautions in the beginning of this section.
2. Discharge the A/C system.
3. Disconnect the negative and positive battery cables.
4. Raise and safely support the vehicle.
5. Remove the front wheels.
6. Drain the coolant and engine oil.
7. Relieve the fuel system pressure.
8. Remove the exhaust pipes front exhaust pipe from the engine.
9. Remove the front fascia lower deflectors.
10. Remove the stabilizer bar.
11. Remove the drive belt.
12. If equipped, disconnect the transmission cooler lines from the radiator.
13. Remove the radiator and heater hoses.
14. Unplug all electrical connections from the engine and wheel speed sensors.
15. Disconnect the right front brake line from the caliper brake hose.
16. Unplug the wiring harness from the transmission assembly.
17. Disconnect the shift linkage from the transmission.
18. Remove the driveshaft from the vehicle after matchmarking.
19. Remove the torque arm from the transmission assembly.
20. Remove the intermediate steering shaft from the rack and pinion assembly.
21. Disconnect the ground straps from the left side frame rail.
22. Lower the vehicle.
23. Remove the air intake duct.
24. Disconnect the fuel pipes from the engine.
25. Disconnect the throttle and cruise control cables from the throttle body.
26. Unplug the radiator fan electrical connections and remove the fan.
27. Disconnect the brake booster vacuum hose.
28. If equipped, remove the "Y" brace from the right side exhaust manifold.
29. Remove the alternator and air conditioning compressor bracket, then reposition out of the way.
30. Remove the brake master cylinder and reposition it out of the way.
31. Detach both upper strut assemblies from the body.
32. Remove the right front brake line from the modulator valve assembly and clips.
33. Raise and safely support the vehicle.

34. Position a lift table under the engine and engine frame assembly.
35. Remove the engine frame and transmission support screws.
36. Raise the vehicle from the engine, transmission and engine frame assemblies.
37. Secure the strut assemblies to the engine frame.
38. Remove the transmission assembly from the engine.

To install:
39. If removed, install the engine assembly onto the frame. Tighten the through-bolt to 70 ft. lbs. (95 Nm).
40. Install the transmission assembly.
41. Install the engine, transmission, and frame assembly.
42. Install the frame and transmission support bolts.
43. Remove the engine lift table.
44. Lower the vehicle.
45. Install the bolts and nuts to the upper strut assemblies.
46. Connect the right front brake line to the modulator valve assembly and clips.
47. Install the brake master cylinder.
48. Engage the engine wiring harness connectors.
49. Install the alternator and compressor bracket.
50. If removed, install the "Y" brace to the right exhaust manifold assembly.
51. Connect the brake booster vacuum line.
52. Install the radiator fan assembly.
53. Install the lower and upper radiator hoses.
54. Connect the cruise control and accelerator cables to the throttle body.
55. Connect the engine fuel pipes.
56. Raise and suitably support the vehicle.
57. Install the intermediate steering shaft to the rack and pinion assembly.
58. Install the torque arm to the transmission assembly.

59. Install the driveshaft.
60. Connect the wiring and shift linkage to the transmission assembly.
61. Connect the right front brake line to the caliper brake hose.
62. Engage all electrical connectors that were unplugged for engine removal.
63. Connect the heater hoses to the engine.
64. If equipped, connect the transmission fluid cooler lines to the radiator.
65. Install the drive belt.
66. Install the stabilizer bar.
67. Install the front fascia lower deflectors.
68. If removed, install the catalytic converter on A/T cars.
69. Install the front exhaust pipe(s).
70. Install the wheels.
71. Lower the vehicle.
72. Refill the engine with motor oil.
73. Refill radiator with coolant.
74. Connect the negative battery cable.
75. Bleed the brake system.
76. Bleed the power steering system.
77. Install the air intake duct.
78. Wheel alignment must be performed.

Water Pump

REMOVAL & INSTALLATION

3.8L Engine

1. Before servicing the vehicle, refer to the precautions in the beginning of this section.
2. Disconnect the negative battery cable.
3. Drain the cooling system into a suitable container.
4. Remove the serpentine belt.
5. Disconnect the radiator inlet hose from the water pump.

Exploded view of the water pump mounting—3.8L engine

7922WG03

6. Unfasten the water pump pulley bolts and remove the pulley.

7. Remove the water pump pulley retaining bolts, then remove the pump from the vehicle.

8. Remove and discard the gasket and thoroughly clean the gasket mating surfaces.

To install:

9. Position a new water pump gasket, then install the pump. Secure using the water pump retaining bolts and tighten to 11 ft. lbs. (15 Nm), plus an additional 80 degree rotation.

10. Install the water pump pulley and retaining bolts. Tighten to 115 inch lbs. (13 Nm).

11. Install the serpentine drive belt.

12. Connect the radiator inlet hose to the water pump.

13. Connect the negative battery cable.

14. Fill the cooling system. Start the engine and check for leaks.

5.7L Engines

1. Before servicing the vehicle, refer to the precautions in the beginning of this section.

2. Unplug the electrical connector from the cooling fan.

3. Remove both cooling fan assemblies.

4. Place a suitable drain pan under the vehicle, then remove the block coolant drain plug and the knock sensor. Drain the radiator.

5. Install the drain plug and knock sensor.

6. Remove the air intake duct and air cleaner.

7. Disconnect the upper and lower radiator hoses from the water pump.

8. Remove the heater hoses from the water pump and throttle body.

9. Unplug the electrical connector from the Engine Coolant Temperature (ECT) sensor.

10. Unfasten the retainers and reposition the ignition coil and bracket.

11. If equipped, remove the air pump and bracket.

12. Unfasten the water pump attaching bolts, then remove the water pump and discard the gasket. Remove the shaft coupling and water pump driveshaft seals, if necessary.

13. Thoroughly clean the gasket mating surfaces

To install:

14. If removed, install the shaft coupling and water pump driveshaft using J 39089 or equivalent water pump driveshaft O-ring installer.

15. Install the water pump with a new gasket. Tighten the bolts to 30–32 ft. lbs. (41–43 Nm).

16. If equipped, install the air pump and bracket.

17. Reposition and secure the ignition coil and bracket.

18. Attach the ECT sensor connector.

19. Connect the heater hoses to the water pump and throttle body.

20. Connect the upper and lower radiator hoses to the water pump.

21. Install the air cleaner and air inlet duct.

22. Install the electric cooling fan(s), then attach the electrical connector.

23. Refill the cooling system.

24. Connect the negative battery cable, then start the engine and check for leaks.

VIEW A

A   SHAFT, WATER PUMP
B   TAB ON GASKET
37 PUMP ASSEMBLY, WATER
38 GASKET, WATER PUMP
39 COUPLING, WATER PUMP DRIVESHAFT
40 BOLT/SCREW, WATER PUMP
41 BOLT/SCREW, WATER PUMP
63 DRIVESHAFT ASSEMBLY, WATER PUMP
156 SEAL, WATER PUMP DRIVESHAFT

7922WG04

Exploded view of the water pump mounting and related components—5.7L engines

Timing belt service is covered in Section 5 of this manual

Cylinder Head

REMOVAL & INSTALLATION

✷✷ WARNING

When servicing the engine, be absolutely sure to mark or tag vacuum hoses and wiring so that these items may be properly reconnected during installation. Also, when disconnecting fittings of metal lines (fuel, power brake vacuum), always use a back-up wrench to prevent damage to the line.

3.8L Engine

LEFT SIDE

1. Before servicing the vehicle, refer to the precautions in the beginning of this section.

2. Disconnect the negative battery cable. Properly relieve the fuel system pressure.

3. Disconnect the fuel lines from the fuel rail.

4. Drain the cooling system into a suitable container.

5. Remove the upper and lower intake manifolds.

6. Tag and detach the spark plug wires, then remove the spark plugs.

7. Remove the left exhaust manifold.

8. Remove the rocker arm (valve) cover and the rocker arms and pushrods.

9. Unfasten the cylinder head retaining bolts, then remove the cylinder head. Remove and discard the gasket and bolts. The cylinder head should be properly cleaned and inspected before installation. Clean the gasket mating surfaces of all components. Be careful not to nick or scratch any surfaces as this will allow leak paths. Clean the bolt threads in the cylinder block and on the head bolts. Dirt will affect bolt torque.

To install:

10. Place a new cylinder head gasket on the engine with the arrow pointing to the front of the engine.

11. Position the cylinder head on top of the gasket, and secure with NEW head bolts. Tighten the bolts as follows:

   a. Tighten, in sequence, to 37 ft. lbs. (50 Nm).

   b. Rotate the bolts 130 degrees, in sequence, using tool J 36660 or equivalent torque angle meter.

   c. Rotate the center four bolts an additional 30 degrees, in sequence, using tool J 36660.

12. Install the rocker arms and pushrods, then install the valve cover.

13. Install the left exhaust manifold.

14. Install the spark plugs, tighten to 20 ft. lbs. (27 Nm) and connect the spark plugs as tagged during removal.

15. Install the lower and upper intake manifolds.

16. Fill the cooling system with the proper type and amount of coolant. Connect the negative battery cable.

17. Start the engine and check for leaks.

RIGHT SIDE

1. Before servicing the vehicle, refer to the precautions in the beginning of this section.

2. Disconnect the negative battery cable.

3. Properly relieve the fuel system pressure.

4. Disconnect the fuel lines from the fuel rail.

5. Drain the cooling system into a suitable container.

6. Remove the upper and lower intake manifolds.

A TIGHTENING SEQUENCE
89 BOLT/SCREW, CYLINDER HEAD
90 HEAD, CYLINDER
91 GASKET, CYLINDER HEAD
92 LOCATOR PINS

7922WG06

Exploded view of the cylinder head mounting (showing the bolt torque sequence)—3.8L engine

7. Tag and detach the spark plug wires, then remove the spark plugs.

8. Remove the right exhaust manifold.

9. Remove the rocker arm (valve) cover and the rocker arms and pushrods.

10. Remove the serpentine drive belt tensioner.

11. Remove the rear alternator brace.

12. Unfasten the cylinder head retaining bolts, then remove the cylinder head. Remove and discard the gasket and bolts. The cylinder head should be properly cleaned and inspected before installation. Clean the gasket mating surfaces of all components. Be careful not to nick or scratch any surfaces as this will allow leak paths. Clean the bolt threads in the cylinder block and on the head bolts. Dirt will affect bolt torque.

To install:

13. Place a new cylinder head gasket on the engine with the arrow pointing to the front of the engine.

14. Position the cylinder head on top of the gasket, and secure with NEW head bolts. Tighten the bolts as follows:

   a. Tighten, in sequence, to 37 ft. lbs. (50 Nm).

   b. Rotate the bolts 130 degrees, in sequence, using tool J 36660 or equivalent torque angle meter.

   c. Rotate the center four bolts an additional 30 degrees, in sequence, using tool J 36660.

15. Install the rocker arms and pushrods, then install the valve cover.

16. Install the right exhaust manifold.

17. Install the spark plugs, tighten to 20 ft. lbs. (27 Nm) and connect the spark plugs as tagged during removal.

18. Install the lower and upper intake manifolds.

19. Fill the cooling system with the proper type and amount of coolant. Connect the negative battery cable.

20. Start the engine and check for leaks.

5.7L Engines

LEFT SIDE

1. Before servicing the vehicle, refer to the precautions in the beginning of this section.

2. Disconnect the negative battery cable.

3. Raise and safely support the vehicle.

4. Place a suitable pan under the vehicle and drain the cooling system.

5. Remove the catalytic converter.

6. Carefully lower the vehicle.

7. Remove the intake manifold.

8. Disconnect the secondary air injection hose from the check valve.

9. Using a back-up wrench on the pipe fitting, remove the engine coolant bleed pipe bolt from the left cylinder head.

10. Unfasten the ignition coil bolts, then remove the coil.

11. Remove the left exhaust manifold.

12. Detach the spark plug wiring harness from the clips, then tag and disconnect the spark plug wiring harness from the plugs. Remove the spark plugs.

13. Detach the Engine Coolant Temperature (ECT) sensor electrical connector.

14. Remove the rocker arm (valve) cover. Remove the rocker arm nuts, rocker arms and pushrods.

15. Unfasten the cylinder head bolts, then remove the cylinder head and gasket. Discard the gasket.

The cylinder head should be properly cleaned and inspected before installation. Clean the gasket mating surfaces of all components. Be careful not to nick or scratch any surfaces as this will allow leak paths. Clean the bolt threads in the cylinder block and on the head bolts. Dirt will affect bolt torque.

To install:

16. Position a new cylinder head gasket with the yellow tab facing up on the engine block. Place the cylinder head over the locator pins and head gasket.

➡ Before installing the head bolts, be sure to mark the short bolts so the correct tightening specifications are used.

17. Coat the threads of the head bolts with GM 1052080 or equivalent, then install the bolts finger-tight.

```
  17 O  9 O  1 O  6 O  14
O  13 O  5 O  2 O  10
  16 12  8  4  3  7  11 15
```

◀FRT

◀FRT

A GASKET TAB (YELLOW SIDE UP)
B BOLT TIGHTENING SEQUENCE
34 HEAD, CYLINDER
67 BLOCK, ENGINE
81 BOLT/SCREW, CYLINDER HEAD
82 GASKET, CYLINDER HEAD

34
81
81
82
A
67

Exploded view of the cylinder head mounting (showing the bolt torque sequence)—5.7L engine

7922WG07

18. Tighten the cylinder head bolts in sequence to 22 ft. lbs. (30 Nm), then tighten the long and medium length bolts an additional 80 degrees and the short bolts an additional 67 degrees.

19. Install the pushrods and rocker arms. Install the rocker arm (valve) cover. Tighten the retaining bolts to 106 inch lbs. (12 Nm).

20. Attach the Engine Coolant Temperature (ECT) sensor electrical connector.

21. Install the spark plugs to 15 ft. lbs. (20 Nm). Connect the spark plug wiring harness to the spark plugs. Fasten the harness to the retaining clips.

22. Install the left exhaust manifold.

23. Install the ignition coil and secure with the retaining bolts/studs. Tighten to 30 ft. lbs. (40 Nm).

24. Install the engine coolant air bleed pipe and bolt to the left cylinder head, using a back-up wrench on the pipe fitting. Tighten to 30 ft. lbs. (40 Nm).

25. Connect the secondary air injection hose to the check valve.

26. Install the intake manifold.

27. Raise and safely support the vehicle.

28. Install the catalytic converter, then carefully lower the vehicle.

29. Fill the cooling system with the proper type and amount of coolant. Connect the negative battery cable.

30. Start the engine and check for leaks.

RIGHT SIDE

1. Before servicing the vehicle, refer to the precautions in the beginning of this section.

2. Disconnect the negative battery cable.

3. Raise and safely support the vehicle.

4. Place a suitable pan under the vehicle and drain the cooling system.

5. Remove the serpentine drive belt and belt tensioner.

6. If equipped, remove the automatic transmission fluid level indicator tube bracket from the transmission housing.

7. If equipped, remove the A/C compressor rear brace bolt from the engine block. Detach the compressor electrical connector. Remove the A/C compressor front mounting bolts, then position the compressor aside. DO NOT disconnect the refrigerant lines.

8. Remove the right exhaust manifold.

9. Carefully lower the vehicle.

10. Remove the alternator.

11. Remove the right side rocker arm (valve) cover.

12. Remove the intake manifold.

13. Using a back-up wrench on the pipe fitting, remove the engine coolant bleed pipe bolt from the left cylinder head.

14. Disconnect the lower radiator hose and the heater hose from the water pump and place them out of the way.

15. Disconnect the engine coolant air bleed pipe hose from the radiator.

16. Remove the power steering pump. If possible, unfasten the mounting bolts and position aside without disconnecting the lines.

17. Remove the alternator bracket bolts and alternator and A/C compressor and power steering pump bracket.

18. Tag and disconnect the spark plug wiring harness from the plugs. Remove the spark plugs.

19. Remove the rocker arms and pushrods.

20. Unfasten the cylinder head bolts, then remove the cylinder head and gasket. Discard the gasket.

21. Using a back-up wrench on the pipe fitting, remove the engine coolant air bleed pipe bolt, and the nut and fitting from the cylinder head.

To install:

22. Install the engine coolant air bleed pipe, nut and bolt, using a back-up wrench on the pipe fitting, to the cylinder head hand-tight.

23. Position a new cylinder head gasket with the yellow tab facing up. Place the cylinder head over the locator pins and head gasket.

➡**When installing the head bolts, be sure the mark the short bolts to ensure the correct tightening specifications are achieved.**

24. Coat the threads of the head bolts with GM 1052080 or equivalent, then install the bolts finger-tight.

25. Tighten the cylinder head bolts in sequence to 22 ft. lbs. (30 Nm), then tighten the long and medium length bolts an additional 80 degrees and the short bolts an additional 67 degrees.

26. Tighten the engine coolant air bleed pipe bolt to 30 ft. lbs. (40 Nm) and the nut to 13 ft. lbs. (17 Nm).

27. Install the pushrods and rocker arms.

28. Install the spark plugs, tighten to 15 ft. lbs. (20 Nm) and attach the spark plug wiring harness to the spark plugs.

29. Install the alternator, A/C compressor and power steering pump bracket(s) and secure with the retaining bolts. Tighten to 30 ft. lbs. (40 Nm).

30. Install the right side valve cover.

31. Install the alternator and power steering pump.

32. Attach the engine coolant air bleed pipe hose to the radiator.

33. Connect the heater and the lower radiator hoses to the water pump.

34. Fasten the air bleed pipe bolt to the left cylinder head using a back-up wrench. Tighten to 30 ft. lbs. (40 Nm).

35. Install the intake manifold.

36. Raise and safely support the vehicle.

37. Install the right exhaust manifold.

38. Install the A/C compressor front mounting bolts. Attach the compressor electrical connector, then fasten the rear brace bolt to the engine block. Tighten to 24 ft. lbs. (33 Nm).

39. If equipped, install the automatic transmission fluid level indicator tube bracket to the transmission housing.

40. Install the serpentine drive belt and tensioner.

41. Carefully lower the vehicle.

42. Fill the cooling system with the proper type and amount of coolant. Connect the negative battery cable.

43. Start the engine and check for leaks.

Rocker Arms

REMOVAL & INSTALLATION

Be sure to keep all the components in the exact order of removal so they may be installed in their original locations; adjust the valve lash after replacing the rocker arms. Coat the replacement rocker arm and ball with engine oil before installation. Rocker arm studs that have damaged threads or are loose in the cylinder heads may be replaced by reaming the bore and installing oversize studs. available oversizes are 0.003 in. (0.076mm) and 0.013 in. (0.33mm). The bore may also be tapped and screw-in studs installed. Several aftermarket companies produce complete rocker arm stud kits with installation tools.

➡**The 5.7L engines use press-fit studs.**

1. Before servicing the vehicle, refer to the precautions in the beginning of this section.

2. Disconnect the negative battery cable.

3. Remove the rocker arm cover.

4. Remove the rocker arm nuts, balls and rocker arms. Place components in a rack so they can be reinstalled in the same locations.

To install:

5. Coat the bearing surfaces with a thin coating of Molykote® or equivalent assembly lube.

LOCKS
CAP
SEAL
SHIELD

7922WG08

Exploded view of common rocker arm components and valve spring retainer

6. Install the pushrods and be sure the rod is in the lifter seat.

7. Install the rocker arm, balls and nut. Tighten the nut until all lash is eliminated.

8. The engine must be on the No. 1 firing position before proceeding. This may be determined by placing your fingers on the No. 1 rocker arms as the mark crankshaft damper is rotated towards the "0" on the timing tab. If the arms did not move, it is in the No. 1 firing position. If they did move, turn the crankshaft one full revolution to reach the No. 1 position. Remember, the mark on the crankshaft balancer must be aligned with the "0" on the timing tab.

9. Adjust the valves as follows:

V6 Engine:

With the engine on the number 1 firing position, exhaust valves 1, 2 and 3 and intake valves 1, 5 and 6 may be adjusted. Back out the adjusting nut until lash is felt at the pushrod. Tighten the adjusting nut until all lash is removed, then tighten the nut an additional 1 ½ turns to center the lifter plunger. Turn the engine one revolution until the "0" timing mark is once again aligned. Exhaust valves 4, 5 and 6 and intake valves 2, 3 and 4 may be adjusted.

V8 Engines:

With the engine on the number 1 firing position, exhaust valves 1, 3, 4 and 8, intake valves 1, 2, 5 and 7 may be adjusted. Back out the adjusting nut until lash is felt at the pushrod. Tighten the adjusting nut until all lash is removed, then tighten an additional 1 turn to center the lifter plunger. Turn the engine one revolution until the 0 timing mark is once again aligned. Exhaust valves 2, 5, 6 and 7, intake valves 3, 4, 6 and 8 may be adjusted.

10. Install the rocker arm cover.

11. Connect the negative battery cable.

Intake Manifold

REMOVAL & INSTALLATION

3.8L Engine

UPPER MANIFOLD

1. Before servicing the vehicle, refer to the precautions in the beginning of this section.

2. Disconnect the negative battery cable.

3. Relieve the fuel system pressure.

4. Drain the coolant into a suitable container.

5. Remove the serpentine drive belt.

6. If necessary, remove the transmission fluid level indicator.

7. Remove the alternator and the serpentine drive belt tensioner.

8. Remove the Manifold Absolute Pressure (MAP) sensor and vacuum source from the upper intake manifold.

9. Remove the evaporative emission canister purge solenoid valve.

10. Remove the fuel pressure regulator and canister purge harness.

11. Remove the Idle Air Control (IAC) valve from the upper intake manifold.

12. Disconnect the fuel lines from the fuel rail.

13. Remove the accelerator control cable bracket bolts, bracket and accelerator control cables from the throttle body.

14. Remove the ignition coil pack/control module assembly.

15. Disconnect the brake booster hose from the upper manifold.

16. Remove the alternator brace from the upper manifold.

17. Detach the electrical connectors from the Idle Air Control (IAC), Throttle Position (TP), Mass Air Flow (MAF) and Intake Air Temperature (IAT) sensors.

18. Unfasten the wiring harness from the rosebud clips at the fuel rail.

19. Remove the air cleaner, outlet rear duct and resonator duct.

20. If necessary, remove the throttle body from the upper intake manifold.

21. Remove the EGR valve outlet pipe.

➡**The thermostat must be removed to get to the "hidden" bolt located under the housing. This bolt retains the upper and lower manifolds.**

22. Remove the thermostat and thermostat housing.

23. Detach the electrical connectors from the fuel injectors. Clean the fuel injector bores using compressed air.

24. Unfasten the fuel rail nuts, then remove the fuel rail.

25. Unfasten the upper intake manifold retaining bolts, then remove the upper manifold and gasket. Discard the gasket and clean the mating surfaces and bolt threads.

To install:

26. Position a new gasket, then install the upper intake manifold. Tighten the bolts as follows:

a. Tighten the ten vertical intake manifold bolts 1–10 to 11 ft. lbs. (15 Nm) using the sequence in the accompanying figure.

b. Tighten the two coolant outlet bolts to 20 ft. lbs. (27 Nm).

c. Tighten the side bolts to 22 ft. lbs. (30 Nm).

27. Install the fuel rail:

a. Lightly lubricate the fuel injector O-rings using clean engine oil.

b. Install the injectors into the bores of the manifold.

c. Carefully press the fuel rail with the palms of your hands until the injectors are properly seated.

28. Install the fuel rail nuts and tighten them to 89 inch lbs. (10 Nm). Attach the fuel injector electrical connectors.

29. Install the thermostat and thermostat housing.

30. Install the EGR valve outlet pipe.

31. If necessary, install the throttle body to the intake manifold.

32. Install the air cleaner, resonator duct and air cleaner outlet duct.

33. Fasten the wiring harness to the rosebud clips at the fuel rail.

34. Attach the electrical connectors to the IAC, TP, MAF and IAT sensors.

35. Install the alternator brace.

36. Connect the brake booster hose to the upper intake manifold.

37. Install the ignition control module.

38. Install the accelerator cable bracket, bolts and accelerator control cables to the throttle body. Tighten the bracket bolts to 89 inch lbs. (10 Nm).

39. Connect the fuel lines to the fuel rail.

40. Install the IAC valve to the upper intake manifold.

41. Install the fuel pressure regulator and the canister purge harness. Install the evaporative emissions canister purge solenoid valve.

42. Install the MAP sensor and vacuum source to the upper intake manifold.

43. Install the serpentine drive belt tensioner.

44. Install the alternator.

45. If necessary, install the transmission level indicator.

46. Install the serpentine drive belt.

47. Fill the coolant system.

48. Connect the negative battery cable, then start the engine and check for leaks.

LOWER MANIFOLD

1. Before servicing the vehicle, refer to the precautions in the beginning of this section.

2. Disconnect the negative battery cable.

➡**There are two bolts which are hidden under the upper manifold. They are located in the front and left rear corners of the lower manifold. It is necessary to remove the upper manifold to service the lower manifold.**

3. Remove the upper intake manifold.

4. Remove the rocker arm (valve) covers.

5. Remove the Engine Coolant Temperature (ECT) sensor.

6. Unfasten the lower intake manifold bolts, then remove the manifold, gaskets and seals. Discard the gaskets and seals.

7. Thoroughly clean the gasket mating surfaces.

To install:

8. Install new gaskets and seals. Apply GM part no. 12345336 or equivalent to the front and rear manifold seals. Coat the bolt threads with GM part no. 12345493, or equivalent.

9. Position the lower manifold and install the retaining bolts. The two lower intake manifold bolts are located under the upper intake manifold (right front and left rear corners) and must be installed before upper manifold installation. Tighten the manifold bolts, in sequence, to 11 ft. lbs. (15 Nm).

10. Install the ECT sensor.

11. Install the valve covers and the upper intake manifold.

12. Connect the negative battery cable.

5.7L Engines

1. Before servicing the vehicle, refer to the precautions in the beginning of this section.

2. Disconnect the negative battery cable.

3. Relieve the fuel system pressure.

4. Remove the air duct.

5. Drain the coolant system.

6. Unplug the connectors from the fuel injectors. Lay the wiring harnesses aside.

7. Disconnect the control cables from the throttle body.

8. Remove the secondary air injection diverter valve hoses.

9. Detach the fuel pipe connectors from the fuel rail. Remove the fuel rail bolts.

10. Detach the fuel pressure regulator vacuum tube.

11. Remove the fuel rail from the intake manifold and position aside.

12. Disconnect the vacuum and crankcase vent hoses.

13. Remove the EGR valve control valve relay nut and control valve relay.

14. Remove the emission canister purge solenoid bracket nut and solenoid.

15. Remove the EGR nuts, then remove the valve. Remove the EGR valve pipe nuts and studs.

16. Remove the secondary air injection pipe fitting, nuts and pipe from the intake and right exhaust manifold.

17. Remove the alternator rear brace.

18. Unplug the hoses and electrical connections from the throttle body. Remove the throttle body and gasket.

19. Remove the manifold bolt and studs. Remove the intake manifold and gaskets. Discard the gaskets and thoroughly clean the gasket mating surfaces, bolt and stud threads.

To install:

20. Be sure the sealing surfaces are clean.

21. Apply a 3/16 in. (5mm) bead of RTV sealant on the front and rear ridge of the cylinder block.

22. Install the new gaskets on the cylinder heads. Hold the gaskets in place by extending the RTV bead up onto the gasket ends.

Intake manifold bolt tightening sequence—5.7L engines

7922WG10

23. Install the intake manifold along with the intake manifold bolts. Tighten bolts in sequence to 71 inch lbs. (8 Nm) on the first pass and 35 ft. lbs. (48 Nm) on the second pass.

24. Install the throttle body, tightening the throttle body bolts to 18 ft. lbs. (26 Nm). Engage all cable, hose and wiring connections on the throttle body.

25. Install the alternator rear brace.

26. If equipped, install the accelerator control/cruise control servo cable adjuster. Install the accelerator cable bracket and tightening the retaining screws to 90 inch lbs. (10 Nm). Connect the cables.

27. Install the secondary air injection pipe and nuts. Tighten the exhaust manifold fitting to 41 ft. lbs. (55 Nm).

28. Install the EGR valve pipe studs and nuts. Install the EGR valve and nuts and the control valve relay and nuts. Tighten as follows:

   a. EGR valve pipe studs to 53 inch lbs. (6 Nm).

   b. EGR valve pipe nuts, valve nuts and control valve relay nut to 18 ft. lbs. (25 Nm).

29. Install the emission canister purge solenoid and bracket bolt. Tighten to 53 inch lbs. (6 Nm).

30. Connect the vacuum and crankcase vent hoses.

31. Install the fuel rail, fuel pressure regulator vacuum tube, and fuel rail bolts. Tighten to 15 ft. lbs. (20 Nm). Attach the fuel pipe connectors to the fuel rail.

32. Connect the secondary air injection diverter valve hoses.

33. Install the left and right wiring harnesses and engage the wiring harness connectors.

34. Install the air duct. Connect the negative battery cable. Fill the cooling system.

Exhaust Manifold

REMOVAL & INSTALLATION

3.8L Engine

LEFT SIDE

1. Before servicing the vehicle, refer to the precautions in the beginning of this section.

2. Disconnect the negative battery cable.

3. Remove the EGR valve adapter from the exhaust manifold.

4. Remove the oil level dipstick and tube.

5. Unfasten the retaining nuts, then remove the exhaust manifold heat shields.

6. Raise and safely support the vehicle.

7. Remove the exhaust catalytic converter pipe.

8. Detach the Oxygen (O_2S) sensor electrical connector.

9. Tag and disconnect the spark plug wires from the plugs.

10. Carefully lower the vehicle.

11. Unfasten the bolt and the studs, then remove the exhaust manifold and gasket from the vehicle.

12. Clean the exhaust manifold and cylinder head mating surfaces.

To install:

13. Position the exhaust manifold gasket on the cylinder head, then install the exhaust manifold and heat shields. Tighten the studs to 106 inch lbs. (12 Nm).

14. Install the retaining bolt and tighten to 106 inch lbs. (12 Nm).

15. Raise and safely support the vehicle.

16. Attach the O_2S sensor electrical connector.

17. Install the exhaust catalytic converter pipe.

18. Connect the wires to the spark plugs, as tagged during removal.

19. Carefully lower the vehicle.

20. Install the exhaust manifold heat shields and tighten the retaining nuts to 80 inch lbs. (9 Nm).

21. Install the oil level dipstick and tube.

22. Install the EGR valve adapter to the exhaust manifold. Tighten the retaining bolt to 18 ft. lbs. (25 Nm).

23. Connect the negative battery cable.

RIGHT SIDE

1. Before servicing the vehicle, refer to the precautions in the beginning of this section.

2. Disconnect the negative battery cable.

3. Unfasten the retaining nuts, then remove the exhaust manifold heat shields.

4. Raise and safely support the vehicle.

5. Remove the exhaust catalytic converter pipe.

6. Detach the Oxygen (O_2S) sensor electrical connector.

7. Tag and disconnect the spark plug wires from the plugs.

8. Carefully lower the vehicle.

9. Unfasten the bolt and the studs, then remove the exhaust manifold and gasket from the vehicle.

10. Clean the exhaust manifold and cylinder head mating surfaces.

To install:

11. Position the exhaust manifold gasket on the cylinder head, then install the exhaust manifold and heat shields. Tighten the fasteners to 106 inch lbs. (12 Nm).

12. Raise and safely support the vehicle.

13. Attach the O_2S sensor electrical connector.

14. Install the exhaust catalytic converter pipe.

15. Connect the wires to the spark plugs, as tagged during removal.

16. Carefully lower the vehicle.

17. Install the exhaust manifold heat shields and tighten the retaining nuts to 80 inch lbs. (9 Nm).

18. Connect the negative battery cable.

5.7L Engines

LEFT SIDE

1. Before servicing the vehicle, refer to the precautions in the beginning of this section.

2. Disconnect the negative battery cable.

3. Raise and safely support the vehicle.

4. Remove the catalytic converter.

5. Disconnect the brake booster vacuum hose.

6. Remove the secondary air injection pipe fitting from the exhaust manifold.

7. If equipped, remove the accelerator control/cruise control servo cable adjuster.

8. Detach the Oxygen (O_2S) sensor electrical connector.

9. Unfasten the exhaust manifold retaining bolts, then remove the manifold from the vehicle.

10. Remove and inspect the manifold gasket for damage and replace if necessary. Clean the exhaust manifold and cylinder head mating surfaces.

To install:

11. Position the exhaust manifold gasket and manifold. Secure with the retaining bolts and tighten to 30 ft. lbs. (40 Nm).

12. Attach the O_2S sensor electrical connector.

13. If equipped, install the accelerator control/cruise control servo cable adjuster.

25	MANIFOLD, UPPER INTAKE
46	MANIFOLD, LEFT EXHAUST
116	BOLT/SCREW, EGR VALVE OUTLET PIPE
117	PIPE, EGR VALVE OUTLET
118	NUT, EGR VALVE OUTLET PIPE
119	ADAPTER, EGR VALVE
120	NUT, EGR VALVE ADAPTER
121	STUD, EGR VALVE ADAPTER
122	BOLT/SCREW, EGR VALVE ADAPTER
123	BRACKET, ENGINE LIFT

9300WG01

Exploded view of the EGR valve adapter and outlet pipe—3.8L engine

A CYLINDER HEAD
46 MANIFOLD, LEFT EXHAUST
50 MANIFOLD, RIGHT EXHAUST
51 GASKET, EXHAUST MANIFOLD
52 BOLT/SCREW, EXHAUST MANIFOLD
53 STUD, EXHAUST MANIFOLD

9300WG02

Exploded view of the right and left exhaust manifold mounting—3.8L engine

For complete mechanical specifications, refer to Section 1 of this manual

16 MANIFOLD, EXHAUST
17 GASKET, EXHAUST MANIFOLD
18 GASKET, EXHAUST MANIFOLD
19 MANIFOLD, EXHAUST
20 STUD, EXHAUST MANIFOLD
21 BOLT/SCREW, EXHAUST MANIFOLD
26 SPACER, EXHAUST MANIFOLD BOLT

7922WG36

Exploded view of right and left exhaust manifold mounting—5.7L engines

14. Fasten the secondary air injection pipe fitting from the exhaust manifold. Tighten the fitting to 41 ft. lbs. (55 Nm).

15. Connect the brake booster vacuum hose.

16. Raise and safely support the vehicle.

17. Install the catalytic converter, then carefully lower the vehicle.

18. Connect the negative battery cable.

RIGHT SIDE

1. Before servicing the vehicle, refer to the precautions in the beginning of this section.

2. Disconnect the negative battery cable.

3. Raise and safely support the vehicle.

4. Remove the catalytic converter.

5. Remove the serpentine drive belt.

6. Remove the oil level dipstick and tube assembly.

7. Detach the Oxygen (O_2S) sensor electrical connector.

8. Remove the three rear exhaust manifold bolts.

9. Carefully lower the vehicle.

10. Remove the secondary air injection pipe fitting from the exhaust manifold.

11. Remove the EGR valve pipe.

12. Remove the alternator and rear lower brace.

13. Remove the remaining exhaust manifold mounting studs and bolt.

14. Remove the exhaust manifold and gasket from the vehicle.

15. Inspect the manifold gasket for damage and replace if necessary. Clean the

exhaust manifold and cylinder head mating surfaces.

To install:

16. Position the exhaust manifold gasket, then install the exhaust manifold. Secure with the front three studs and bolt screw.

17. Install the alternator and the rear lower brace.

18. Raise and safely support the vehicle.

19. Install the remaining exhaust manifold bolts. Tighten to 30 ft. lbs. (40 Nm).

20. Attach the O_2S sensor electrical connector.

21. Install the oil level dipstick and tube assembly.

22. Install the serpentine drive belt.

23. Install the catalytic converter.

24. Carefully lower the vehicle.

25. Install the EGR valve pipe.

26. Fasten the secondary air injection pipe fitting to 41 ft. lbs. (55 Nm).

27. Connect the negative battery cable.

Camshaft and Valve Lifters

REMOVAL & INSTALLATION

3.8L Engine

1. Before servicing the vehicle, refer to the precautions in the beginning of this section.

2. Discharge the A/C system using an approved method.

3. Disconnect the negative battery cable.

4. Remove the radiator with the A/C condenser assembly.

5. Remove the valve lifters.

6. Remove the timing chain (engine) front cover.

7. Remove the camshaft sprocket and timing chain.

8. Remove the camshaft thrust plate bolts, then remove the thrust plate.

9. Remove the camshaft assembly, as follows:

   a. Install three 5⁄16–18 x 4-inch bolts in the camshaft bolt holes.

   b. Carefully rotate and pull the camshaft assembly out of the bearings.

10. Inspect the camshaft for damage and replace if necessary.

To install:

11. Coat the camshaft with prelube 12345501 or equivalent, then install the camshaft.

12. Install the thrust plate and secure with the retaining bolts. Tighten to 11 ft. lbs. (15 Nm).

13. Install the timing chain (front) cover.

14. Install the valve lifters.

15. Install the radiator with the A/C condenser.

16. Connect the negative battery cable.

17. Evacuate and charge the A/C system.

18. Refill the cooling system.

19. Start the engine and check for leaks.

5.7L Engines

1. Discharge the A/C system using an approved method.

90 DRIVE ASSEMBLY, OIL PUMP
91 BOLT/SCREW, OIL PUMP DRIVE CLAMP
92 CLAMP, OIL PUMP DRIVE

7922WG12

Unfasten the retaining bolt and clamp, then remove the oil pump drive

A BOLTS
100 CAMSHAFT ASSEMBLY

7922WG11

Thread three bolts into the camshaft to facilitate removal and installation

2. Disconnect the negative battery cable.

3. Remove the upper intake manifold assembly.

4. Remove the rocker arms and pushrod assemblies.

5. Remove the lower intake manifold assembly.

6. Unfasten the bolt, clamp and oil pump drive assembly.

7. Remove the timing chain (front) cover assembly.

8. Remove the camshaft sprocket.

9. Remove the valve lifters.

10. Disconnect the A/C compressor and condenser hose from the condenser.

11. Disconnect the A/C receiver and dehydrator hose from the condenser.

12. Remove the radiator with the condenser. Remove the A/C condenser support assembly.

➡ **All camshaft journals are the same diameter so care must be used when removing the camshaft to avoid damaging the bearings.**

13. Remove the camshaft assembly, as follows:

a. Install three 5/16–18 x 4-inch bolts in the camshaft bolt holes.

b. Carefully rotate and pull the camshaft assembly out of the bearings.

To install:

14. When installing a new camshaft assembly, coat the camshaft lobes with "Molykote" or equivalent. When installing a new camshaft, replace all valve lifters to ensure durability of the camshaft lobes and lifters.

15. Lubricate all camshaft journals with engine oil, then install the camshaft assembly.

16. Install the A/C condenser support assembly.

17. Install the radiator with the A/C condenser.

18. Connect the A/C receiver and dehydrator hose to the condenser. Attach the A/C compressor and condenser hose to the condenser.

19. Install the valve lifters.

20. Install the camshaft sprocket.

21. Install the timing chain (front) cover.

22. Lubricate the oil pump drive gear with prelube 1052365 and coat the assembly with engine oil, then install the oil pump drive assembly, clamp and bolt. Tighten the bolt to 25 ft. lbs. (34 Nm).

23. Install the lower intake manifold.

Please refer to Section 9 for electric cooling fan wiring schematics

24. Install the pushrods and rocker arms.

25. Install the upper intake manifold.

26. Connect the negative battery cable.

27. Recharge the A/C system.

Valve Lash

ADJUSTMENT

➡ **The engines in this section utilize hydraulic valve lifters which do not require periodic adjustment, however, if the rocker arms have been removed use the following procedure for initial adjustment.**

1. Install the pushrods and be sure the rod is in the lifter seat.

2. Install the rocker arm, balls and nut. Tighten the nut until all lash is eliminated.

3. The engine must be on the No. 1 firing position before proceeding. This may be determined by placing your fingers on the No. 1 rocker arms as the mark crankshaft damper is rotated towards the "0" on the timing tab. If the arms did not move, it is in the No. 1 firing position. If they did move, turn the crankshaft one full revolution to reach the No. 1 position. Remember, the mark on the crankshaft balancer must be aligned with the "0" on the timing tab.

4. Adjust the valves as follows:

V6 Engines:

With the engine on the number 1 firing position, exhaust valves 1, 2 and 3 and intake valves 1, 5 and 6 may be adjusted. Back out the adjusting nut until lash is felt at the pushrod. Tighten the adjusting nut until all lash is removed, then tighten the nut an additional 1 ½ turns to center the lifter plunger. Turn the engine one revolution until the "0" timing mark is once again aligned. Exhaust valves 4, 5 and 6 and intake valves 2, 3 and 4 may be adjusted.

V8 Engines:

With the engine on the number 1 firing position, exhaust valves 1, 3, 4 and 8, intake valves 1, 2, 5 and 7 may be adjusted. Back out the adjusting nut until lash is felt at the pushrod. Tighten the adjusting nut until all lash is removed, then tighten an additional 1 turn to center the lifter plunger. Turn the engine one revolution until the 0 timing mark is once again aligned. Exhaust valves 2, 5, 6 and 7, intake valves 3, 4, 6 and 8 may be adjusted.

5. Install the rocker arm cover.

6. Connect the negative battery cable.

Oil Pan

REMOVAL & INSTALLATION

3.8L Engine

1. Before servicing the vehicle, refer to the precautions in the beginning of this section.

2. Disconnect the negative battery cable.

3. Remove the alternator.

4. Remove the ignition coil.

5. Raise and safely support the vehicle.

6. Disconnect the exhaust catalytic converter pipe.

7. If equipped with an automatic transmission, remove the converter cover.

8. Unfasten the engine mount through-bolts and nuts.

9. Raise the engine using tools J 28467 and J 41044.

❊❊ WARNING

The oil level switch, located in the oil pan, must be removed before removing the pan. If the pan is removed first, the switch may be damaged.

59	COVER, FRONT
93	PAN, OIL
94	BOLT/SCREW, OIL PAN
95	GASKET, OIL PAN

7922WG14

Exploded view of the oil pan and gasket—3.8L engine

10. Detach the oil level indicator switch electrical connector, then remove the switch.

11. Unfasten the oil pan retaining bolts, then remove the oil pan and gasket. Lower the rear of the oil pan while rotating outward.

12. Clean all of the old RTV sealant or gasket from the oil pan and engine block. Be sure the mating surfaces are clean.

To install:

13. Position the oil pan gasket, then install the oil pan. Tighten the retainers to 125 inch lbs. (14 Nm).

14. Install the oil level switch and attach the switch electrical connector.

15. Carefully lower the engine. Install the engine mount through-bolts.

16. If equipped, install the automatic transmission converter cover.

17. Connect the exhaust catalytic converter pipe.

18. Carefully lower the vehicle.

19. Install the ignition coil.

20. Install the alternator.

21. Connect the negative battery cable.

22. Fill the crankcase with the proper type and amount of engine oil.

23. Start the engine and check for leaks.

5.7L Engines

1. Before servicing the vehicle, refer to the precautions in the beginning of this section.

2. Disconnect the negative battery cable. Remove the air intake duct.

3. Raise the vehicle and support it safely.

4. Drain the engine oil into a suitable container.

5. Detach the oil level sensor connector, then remove the sensor.

✳✳ CAUTION

Be sure that the exhaust system is cool before proceeding.

6. Remove the catalytic converter.

7. Remove the exhaust pipe hanger bolt and reposition the pipe.

8. If equipped with an automatic transmission, detach the cooler lines from the clip at the oil pan.

9. Remove the starter motor.

10. If equipped with an automatic transmission, unfasten the converter cover bolts, then remove the cover.

11. Remove the engine mount through-bolts.

12. Use a suitable jacking fixture to raise the engine enough to provide sufficient clearance for oil pan removal.

➡️**If the front crankshaft throw prohibits removal of the pan, turn the crankshaft to position the throw horizontally.**

13. Unfasten the oil pan bolts, studs and nuts. If necessary, rotate the crankshaft to reposition the counterweights.

14. Clean all of the old RTV sealant or gasket from the oil pan and engine block. Be sure the mating surfaces are clean.

To install:

15. Apply a small amount of RTV sealer to the front cover and engine block junction and to the rear oil seal housing and engine block junction. Apply sealer 1 in. (25mm) in either direction of the radius cavity of these junctions.

16. Position the oil pan gasket, then install the oil pan and secure with the retainers.

17. Tighten the corner oil and bolts or stud and nuts to 15 ft. lbs. (20 Nm) and the remaining oil pan bolts and studs to 106 inch lbs. (12 Nm).

18. Carefully lower the engine.

19. Install the engine mount through-bolts. Tighten to 70 ft. lbs. (95 Nm).

20. Install the oil level sensor. Tighten to 16 ft. lbs. (22 Nm).

21. If equipped, install the converter cover and secure with the retaining bolts. Tighten to 89 inch lbs. (10 Nm).

22. Install the starter motor.

23. If equipped, fasten the transmission fluid cooler lines to the clip at the oil pan.

24. Install the exhaust pipe hanger bolt.

25. Install the catalytic converter.

26. Attach the oil level sensor electrical connector.

27. Carefully lower the vehicle. Install the air cleaner duct.

28. Connect the negative battery cable.

29. Fill the crankcase with the proper type and amount of engine oil.

30. Start the engine and check for leaks.

A SEALER
53 REINFORCEMENT, OIL PAN
54 PAN, OIL
55 GASKET, OIL PAN

Oil pan sealer and gasket location—5.7L engines

7922WG13

Oil Pump

REMOVAL & INSTALLATION

3.8L Engine

1. Before servicing the vehicle, refer to the precautions in the beginning of this section.

2. Disconnect the negative battery cable.

3. Remove the engine front cover.

4. Remove the oil filter adapter, pressure valve and spring.

5. Remove the oil pump cover attaching bolts and cover.

6. Remove the oil pump gear set.

To install:

7. Lubricate the gear set with petroleum jelly.

8. Position the oil pump gear set into the front cover.

9. Pack the gear cavity with petroleum jelly after the gear set has been installed.

10. Install the oil pump cover and secure with the retaining bolts.

11. Install the oil filter adapter, pressure valve and spring.

12. Install the engine front cover.

13. Connect the negative battery cable.

89 DRIVESHAFT, OIL PUMP
95 RETAINER, OIL PUMP DRIVESHAFT
118 PUMP, OIL
119 DEFLECTOR, CRANKSHAFT OIL
120 BOLT/SCREW, OIL PUMP

7922WG17

Exploded view of the oil pump and driveshaft mounting—5.7L engine

59 COVER, FRONT
96 BOLT/SCREW, OIL PUMP COVER
97 COVER, OIL PUMP
98 GEAR SET, OIL PUMP

7922WG16

Exploded view of the oil pump gear set—3.8L engine

5.7L Engines

1. Before servicing the vehicle, refer to the precautions in the beginning of this section.

2. Drain and remove the oil pan.

3. Remove the oil pan deflector/baffle nuts.

4. Remove the oil pump-to-rear main bearing cap bolt. Remove the oil pump and the driveshaft.

To install

5. Install the oil pump and driveshaft. Align the slot on the end of the intermediate shaft with the drive tang on the oil pump drive.

6. Install the oil pan deflector/baffle.

7. Install the bolt attaching the oil pump to the rear crankshaft bearing cap. Tighten the bolt to 66 ft. lbs. (90 Nm) and the oil pan baffle nuts to 30 ft. lbs. (40 Nm).

8. Install the oil pan and fill the crankcase with engine oil.

Rear Main Seal

REMOVAL & INSTALLATION

➡**The rear main seal is a one piece unit. It can be removed or installed without removing the oil pan or crankshaft.**

DUST LIP

7922WG18

When prying the rear main seal out, be careful not to damage the crankshaft sealing surface or the seal bore

1. Before servicing the vehicle, refer to the precautions in the beginning of this section.
2. Raise and safely support the vehicle.
3. Remove the transmission.
4. If equipped with a manual transmission, remove the clutch and pressure plate.
5. Remove the flywheel assembly.
6. Using a suitable prytool, carefully pry the old seal out.
7. Inspect the crankshaft for nicks or burrs, correct as required.

To install:

8. Clean the area and coat the seal with engine oil. Install the seal onto tool J-41349 for 3.8L engines or J-35621 for the 5.7L engines.
9. Install the tool (with the seal mounted to it) onto the rear of the crankshaft. Tighten the screws snugly to be sure the seal will be installed squarely over the crankshaft.
10. Tighten the wing nut on the installation tool until it bottoms out.
11. Remove the tool from the crankshaft or rear oil seal housing, as applicable.
12. Install the flywheel.
13. If equipped with a manual transmission, install the clutch and pressure plate.
14. Install the transmission.
15. Check the fluid levels, start the engine and check for leaks.

Timing Chain, Sprockets, Front Cover and Seal

REMOVAL & INSTALLATION

3.8L Engine

1. Before servicing the vehicle, refer to the precautions in the beginning of this section.
2. Disconnect the negative battery cable.
3. Remove the air cleaner and intake air duct.
4. Remove the radiator hose from the front cover.
5. Raise and safely support the vehicle.
6. Remove the crankshaft balancer.
7. Remove the oil pan-to-front cover bolts and lower the vehicle.
8. Remove the Crankshaft Position (CKP) sensor shield.
9. Remove the water pump.
10. Remove the timing chain (front) cover.
11. Remove the crankshaft seal from the cover using a suitable seal driver.
12. Align the timing marks on the sprockets so they are as close together as possible, as shown in the accompanying figure.

13. Remove the timing chain damper.
14. Unfasten the camshaft sprocket retaining bolt, then pull the timing chain and sprocket from the camshaft.
15. If necessary, remove the crankshaft sprocket. If the sprocket does not come off easily, a light blow on the edge of the sprocket with a plastic mallet should dislodge it.
16. Clean the chain and sprockets. Inspect all components for damage, and replace as necessary.

To install:

17. If the crankshaft has been turned in the engine, perform the following:
    a. Turn the crankshaft so the No. 1 piston is at Top Dead Center (TDC).
    b. Turn the camshaft so that, with the sprocket temporarily installed, the timing mark is straight down.
18. Assemble the timing chain on the sprockets with the timing marks aligned. Install the timing chain and sprockets.
19. Install the camshaft sprocket retaining bolt and tighten to 74 ft. lbs. (100 Nm) plus an additional 90 degrees using tool J 36660 or equivalent torque angle meter.
20. Install the timing chain damper and tighten the retaining bolt to 16 ft. lbs. (22 Nm).
21. Rotate the engine two revolutions, then check to be sure the timing marks are aligned.

➤**It may be necessary to loosen the oil pan bolts to provide clearance for the front cover.**

22. Install the timing chain (front) cover. Tighten the fasteners to 11 ft. lbs. (15 Nm) plus 40 degrees using a torque angle meter.
23. Install the water pump.
24. Install the CKP sensor shield.
25. Raise and safely support the vehicle.
26. Install the oil pan-to-front cover bolts. Tighten the bolts to 125 in. lbs. (14 Nm).
27. Install the crankshaft balancer.
28. Lower the vehicle to the floor.
29. Connect the radiator hose to the front cover.
30. Install the serpentine belt and air cleaner assembly.
31. Refill the engine with coolant.
32. Connect the negative battery cable.
33. Start the engine and check for leaks.

Timing belt service is covered in Section 5 of this manual

62 CHAIN, TIMING
63 BOLT/SCREW, CAMSHAFT SPROCKET
64 SPROCKET, CAMSHAFT
65 GEAR, BALANCE SHAFT DRIVEN
66 SPROCKET, CRANKSHAFT
67 DAMPENER, TIMING CHAIN
68 BOLT/SCREW, BALANCE SHAFT GEAR
69 GEAR, BALANCE SHAFT

7922WG20

Exploded view of the timing chain and sprockets and timing mark alignment—3.8L engine

68 BOLT/SCREW, BALANCE SHAFT GEAR
69 GEAR, BALANCE SHAFT
70 BOLT/SCREW, BALANCE SHAFT RETAINER
71 RETAINER, BALANCE SHAFT
72 BUSHING, BALANCE SHAFT REAR
73 SHAFT, BALANCE

9300WG03

Exploded view of the balance shaft assembly—3.8L engine

A LOCATOR PINS
B STUDS
C BOLTS/SCREWS
40 SEAL, CRANKSHAFT FRONT OIL
54 BOLT/SCREW, CRANKSHAFT BALANCER
58 GASKET, FRONT COVER
59 COVER, FRONT
60 STUD, FRONT COVER
61 BOLT/SCREW, FRONT COVER

7922WG37

Exploded view of the front cover mounting and bolt locations—3.8L engine

5.7L Engines

1. Before servicing the vehicle, refer to the precautions in the beginning of this section.

2. Disconnect the negative battery cable.

3. Drain the engine oil and coolant.

4. Remove the throttle body air intake duct.

5. Remove the serpentine drive belt.

6. Remove the water pump assembly.

7. Remove the crankshaft balancer and hub.

   a. If not done already, raise and support the vehicle safely.

   b. Remove the crankshaft balancer retaining bolts, then remove the balancer from the hub.

   c. Matchmark the crankshaft hub to the engine front cover, then remove the hub bolt and washer.

   d. Remove the crankshaft hub using J-39046, or an equivalent hub removal/installation tool. To preserve the relationship between the hub and crankshaft, DO NOT crank the engine over once the hub has been removed. If the hub is not matchmarked and installed in the original position, an engine imbalance could result.

8. Remove the distributor assembly.

9. Remove the oil pan assembly.

10. Remove the engine front cover bolts.

11. Remove the engine front cover and gasket.

12. Remove the crankshaft seal from the front cover using a suitable seal driver.

13. Rotate the crankshaft until the timing marks punched on the crankshaft and camshaft sprockets are aligned as shown in the accompanying figure.

14. Unfasten the camshaft sprocket bolts, then remove the camshaft sprocket and timing chain.

When assembled, be sure the marks on the gears are facing each other—5.7L engine

7922WG21

❋❋ WARNING

Do not turn the crankshaft after the timing chain has been removed to prevent damage to the pistons or valves.

15. Remove the water pump bearing retainer bolts, then remove the water pump driveshaft assembly using tool J 39243 or equivalent driven gear remover. Remove and discard the O-ring from the driveshaft.

16. Remove the crankshaft sprocket using gear remover J 5825-A, or equivalent.

17. If necessary, remove the crankshaft sprocket key.

18. Clean the chain and sprockets. Inspect all components for damage, and replace as necessary.

To install:

19. If removed, install the crankshaft sprocket key.

20. Install the crankshaft sprocket using gear installer J 5590 or equivalent.

21. Install the water pump driveshaft assembly using driven gear installer J 39092, or equivalent.

22. Install the water pump bearing retaining bolts and tighten to 105 inch lbs. (12 Nm).

23. Install the camshaft sprocket and timing chain assembly. The camshaft sprocket and water pump driveshaft gears must mesh, or damage to the camshaft retainer may occur.

Use a gear puller to remove, and a large socket to install, the crankshaft sprocket—5.7L engine shown

7922WG22

---

24. Install the camshaft retaining bolts. Be sure the camshaft and crankshaft timing marks align properly. Tighten the camshaft sprocket bolts to 18 ft. lbs. (25 Nm).

25. Install a new O-ring to the water pump driveshaft using seal installer J 39089 or equivalent.

26. Thoroughly clean the engine front cover and cylinder block gasket mating surfaces. Inspect the engine front cover for damage, replace as necessary.

27. Install a new crankshaft seal in the front cover.

28. Using J-39087 or equivalent front cover seal protector on the water pump driveshaft, install the gasket and front cover into position over the shafts and guide pins.

29. Install the engine front cover bolts and tighten to 100 inch lbs. (11 Nm).

30. Install the oil pan and gasket.

31. Install the distributor assembly.

32. Install the crankshaft hub and torsional damper assembly.

   a. Align the matchmarks made earlier and install the crankshaft hub using the hub tool. If the engine was cranked and the matchmarks were lost, set the engine to No. 1 TDC, then install the crankshaft hub with the cast arrow in the 12 o'clock position.

   b. Install the hub washer and bolt, but do not torque at this time.

   c. Install the crankshaft balancer to the hub, then tighten the crankshaft hub bolt to 75 ft. lbs. (102 Nm) and the balancer bolts to 60 ft. lbs. (81 Nm).

➡**If a new balancer is installed, new balancer weights of the same size must be installed in the same hole locations as the original balancer.**

33. Install the water pump assembly.

34. Install the serpentine drive belt.

35. Install the throttle body air duct.

36. Properly fill the engine crankcase with clean engine oil.

37. Properly fill the engine cooling system.

38. Connect the negative battery cable, operate the engine and check for leaks.

FUEL SYSTEM

Fuel System Service Precautions

Safety is the most important factor when performing not only fuel system maintenance but any type of maintenance. Failure to conduct maintenance and repairs in a safe manner may result in serious personal injury or death. Maintenance and testing of the vehicle's fuel system components can be accomplished safely and effectively by adhering to the following rules and guidelines.

• To avoid the possibility of fire and personal injury, always disconnect the negative battery cable unless the repair or test procedure requires that battery voltage be applied.

• Always relieve the fuel system pressure prior to disconnecting any fuel system component (injector, fuel rail, pressure regulator, etc.), fitting or fuel line connection. Exercise extreme caution whenever relieving fuel system pressure to avoid exposing skin, face and eyes to fuel spray. Please be advised that fuel under pressure may penetrate the skin or any part of the body that it contacts.

• Always place a shop towel or cloth around the fitting or connection prior to loosening to absorb any excess fuel due to spillage. Ensure that all fuel spillage (should it occur) is quickly removed from engine surfaces. Ensure that all fuel soaked cloths or towels are deposited into a suitable waste container.

• Always keep a dry chemical (Class B) fire extinguisher near the work area.

• Do not allow fuel spray or fuel vapors to come into contact with a spark or open flame.

• Always use a back-up wrench when loosening and tightening fuel line connection fittings. This will prevent unnecessary stress and torsion to fuel line piping.

• Always replace worn fuel fitting O-rings with new. Do not substitute fuel hose or equivalent, where fuel pipe is installed.

Fuel System Pressure

RELIEVING

1. Before servicing the vehicle, refer to the precautions in the beginning of this section.

2. Disconnect the negative battery cable to prevent fuel discharge if the key is accidentally turned to the **RUN** position.

3. Loosen the fuel filler cap to relieve the tank pressure and do not tighten until service has been completed.

4. Connect J-34730–1 fuel pressure gauge or equivalent, to the fuel pressure valve. Wrap a shop cloth around the fitting while connecting the gauge to avoid spillage.

5. Place the end of the bleed hose into a suitable container and open the valve to relieve the fuel system pressure.

Fuel Filter

REMOVAL & INSTALLATION

The inline fuel filter is located on the fuel feed pipe before the fuel injection system, and mounted directly in front of the rear axle. The filter housing is constructed of steel with quick-connect inlet and threaded outlet fittings. The threaded fitting is sealed with an O-ring. In order to disengage quick-connect fittings, a fuel line quick-connect separator tool set, such as J-37088-A or equivalent, is required. There is no service interval for fuel filter replacement. We suggest replacing the filter every 30–40 thousand miles.

1. Before servicing the vehicle, refer to the precautions in the beginning of this section.

2. Relieve the fuel system pressure.

3. Raise and safely support the vehicle.

4. Clean both the inlet and the outlet fittings on the fuel filter.

5. Disengage the quick-connect fittings at the fuel filter inlet as follows:

a. Slide the dust covers from the quick-connect fittings, if equipped.

1	THREADED FITTING
2	IN-LINE FUEL FILTER
3	QUICK-CONNECT FITTING
4	IN-LINE FUEL FILTER BRACKET

7922WG23

The inline fuel filter is mounted in a bracket located under the vehicle, directly in front of the rear axle

b. Grasp both sides of the fitting. Twist female connector ¼ turn in each direction to loosen any dirt within the fitting. Using compressed air and safety glasses, blow dirt out of fitting.

c. If equipped with the plastic hand releasable fitting, squeeze the plastic retainer release tabs and pull the connection apart.

d. If equipped with metal fitting, choose correct size tool from tool set J-37088-A. Insert tool into female connector, then push inward to release locking tabs. Pull the connector apart.

e. Use a clean lint free rag to clean male pipe ends. Inspect both ends of the fitting for dirt and burrs. Clean or replace components as required. If it is necessary to remove rust or burrs from the fuel pipe, use emery cloth in a radial motion with the pipe end to prevent damage to the O-ring sealing surface.

6. Remove the threaded outlet fitting from the chassis fuel pipe. Slide the fuel filter from the bracket.

7. Inspect the fuel pipe O-ring for cuts, nicks, swelling or distortion. Replace if necessary.

To install:

8. Slide the fuel filter into the bracket. Thread the outlet fitting to the chassis fuel pipe.

9. Tighten the inline fitting to 20 ft. lbs. (27 Nm).

10. Engage the quick-connect inlet fitting as follows:

a. Apply a few drops of clean engine oil to the male pipe end. This will ensure proper reconnection and prevent a possible fuel leak.

b. Push both sides of the fitting together to cause the retainer tabs to snap in place. Once installed, pull on both sides of the fitting to ensure connection is secure.

c. Reposition dust cover over the quick-connect fitting, if equipped.

11. Lower the vehicle. Tighten the fuel filler cap.

12. Confirm that the ignition is in the **OFF** position. Connect the negative battery cable.

13. Pressurize the fuel system by cycling the ignition without attempting to start the engine. Turn the ignition switch to the **ON** position for two seconds, then turn to the **OFF** position for ten seconds. Again, turn to the **ON** position and check for fuel leaks.

Fuel Pump

REMOVAL & INSTALLATION

The fuel pump is part of the fuel sender assembly located inside the fuel tank.

1. Before servicing the vehicle, refer to the precautions in the beginning of this section.

2. Release the fuel system pressure and disconnect the negative battery cable.

3. Drain the fuel tank, then raise and safely support the vehicle.

4. Remove the fuel tank from the vehicle.

5. Clean the area surrounding the sender assembly to prevent contamination of the fuel system.

6. To remove the fuel sender from the tank, remove the fuel sender assembly nuts and retaining ring. Carefully remove the sending unit from the fuel tank. Discard the O-rings.

7. If necessary, separate the fuel pump from the sending unit assembly.

To install:

8. If removed, install the fuel pump to the sending unit. If the strainer was

removed, it must be replaced with a new one.

9. Inspect and clean the O-ring mating surfaces.

10. Install a new O-ring in the groove around the tank opening. If applicable, install a new O-ring on the fuel sender feed tube.

11. Install the fuel sender assembly as follows:

a. The fuel pump strainer must be in a horizontal position, and when installed, must not block the travel of the float arm. Gently fold the strainer over itself and slowly position the sending assembly in the tank so the strainer is not damaged or trapped by the sump walls.

12. Install the retaining ring and nuts, then tighten the nuts to 63 inch lbs. (7 Nm).

13. Install the fuel tank assembly.

14. Lower the vehicle.

15. Fill the fuel tank, tighten the fuel filler cap and connect the negative battery cable.

16. Turn the ignition switch to the **ON** position for 2 seconds, **OFF** for 10 seconds, then back to the **ON** position. Check for fuel leaks.

DRIVE TRAIN

Transmission

REMOVAL & INSTALLATION

1. Before servicing the vehicle, refer to the precautions in the beginning of this section.

2. Disconnect the negative battery cable.

3. On manual transmissions, remove the shift lever boot and the shift lever from inside the vehicle before raising the vehicle.

4. Raise the vehicle and support it safely.

✳✳ WARNING

Disconnect the clutch master cylinder pushrod before disconnecting the actuator cylinder. If not disconnected, permanent damage to the actuator cylinder will occur if the clutch pedal is depressed while the actuator is disconnected.

1   SENDER – FUEL

2   FUEL PUMP AND RESERVOIR ASSEMBLY
A   VAPOR VENT HOSE
B   FUEL PUMP FLEX PIPE AND QUICK – CONNECT FITTING
C   FUEL RETURN HOSE

3   STRAINER – FUEL PUMP

Fuel sender/pump assembly component identification

7922WG24

5. On manual transmissions, disconnect the clutch actuator line from the actuator.

6. Position a suitable pan under the vehicle, then drain the lubricant from the transmission.

7. On automatic transmissions, disconnect the fluid cooler lines, throttle valve cable and remove the dipstick tube.

8. Support the rear axle.

9. Matchmark and remove the driveshaft.

10. Remove the rear axle torque arm from the vehicle.

11. Remove the catalytic converter hanger.

12. Detach all electrical connectors from the transmission and position them out of the way.

13. On manual transmissions, disengage the clutch fork from the release bearing. The fork MUST be detached from the release bearing to prevent damage to the clutch system.

14. On automatic transmissions, remove the starter, then remove the bolts securing the torque converter to the flexplate. Push the torque converter away from the flexplate into the transmission.

15. Support the engine and the transmission.

16. Remove the transmission rear crossmember.

17. On automatic transmissions, remove the bolts securing the transmission to the engine. On manual transmissions, remove the bolts securing the transmission to the bell housing. Pull the transmission rearward and carefully lower the assembly away from the vehicle. Place the transmission in a suitable holding fixture.

18. Installation is the reverse of the removal procedure. Please note the following important steps:

19. On manual transmissions, position the splined input shaft into the clutch disc hub and pilot bearing.

20. For the 5-speed manual transmission, tighten the transmission mounting bolts to 55 ft. lbs. (75 Nm) and the transmission control assembly bolts to 15 ft. lbs. (20 Nm).

21. For the 6-speed manual transmission, tighten the transmission mounting bolts to 26 ft. lbs. (35 Nm). Tighten the actuator cylinder nuts to 15 ft. lbs. (25 Nm).

22. On manual transmissions, when connecting the actuator line, be sure it is not twisted or kinked and will not rub against any other components. Also, the

quick-connect fitting must be pushed on, then pulled back to be sure of proper engagement.

23. For 3.8L engines, tighten the transmission mounting bolts to 70 ft. lbs. (95 Nm).

24. For 5.7L engine, tighten the transmission mounting bolts to 35 ft. lbs. (47 Nm).

25. Fill the transmission with the proper type and amount of fluid. For manual transmissions, bleed the clutch system if any hydraulic clutch components were removed.

Clutch

REMOVAL & INSTALLATION

1. Before servicing the vehicle, refer to the precautions in the beginning of this section.

2. Disconnect the negative battery cable.

3. Remove the instrument panel knee bolster assembly.

4. Disconnect the clutch master cylinder pushrod from the clutch pedal.

5. Raise and safely support the vehicle.

6. Remove the transmission assembly.

7. Remove the clutch actuator cylinder nuts.

✳✳ WARNING

Do NOT let the actuator cylinder hang by the fluid lines, as this could damage them.

8. Remove the clutch actuator cylinder and position aside, supporting with a suitable piece of wire.

9. Unfasten the transmission brace nut and bolt, then remove the brace.

10. Remove the flywheel housing cover retaining bolts, then remove the cover.

11. Unfasten the flywheel housing bolts, then remove the housing.

12. Install a clutch disc alignment tool through the center of the disc and into the pilot bearing to prevent the disc from falling when the pressure plate is removed.

13. Remove the pressure plate retaining bolts.

14. Remove the pressure plate with clutch disc from the flywheel.

15. Inspect the pressure plate and driven disc for damage and replace if necessary. Inspect the flywheel for damage also.

Exploded view of the clutch disc, pressure plate and related components—5-speed transmission shown

7922WG25

For complete service labor times order Chilton's Labor Guide Manual

To install:

16. Position the driven plate to the flywheel.

17. Install the clutch pressure plate (with the cover) and install the retaining bolts finger-tight.

18. Align the clutch driven plate with the pilot bearing and clutch pressure plate (with the cover) using tool J 33169 or equivalent alignment arbor.

19. Tighten the clutch pressure plate and cover bolts, in a star pattern, as follows:

   a. For 5-speed transmissions, tighten to 15 ft. lbs. (20 Nm), plus an additional 45 degrees using J 36660 or equivalent torque angle meter.

   b. For 6-speed transmissions, tighten to 22 ft. lbs. (30 Nm).

20. Position the flywheel housing assembly and secure with the retaining bolts. Tighten to 55 ft. lbs. (75 Nm) for 5-speeds or 35 ft. lbs. (47 Nm) for 6-speed transmissions.

➡**Check for proper clutch fork-to-clutch release bearing engagement.**

21. Install the flywheel housing cover and retain with the bolts. Tighten to 75 inch lbs. (8.5 Nm).

22. Position the transmission brace, install the retaining nut and bolt, then tighten to 37 ft. lbs. (50 Nm).

23. Install the clutch actuator cylinder and secure with retaining nuts. Tighten the nuts to 15 ft. lbs. (20 Nm).

24. Install the transmission assembly.

25. Carefully lower the vehicle.

26. Connect the clutch master cylinder pushrod to the clutch pedal.

27. Install the instrument panel knee bolster.

28. Connect the negative battery cable.

Hydraulic Clutch System

BLEEDING

Bleeding air from the hydraulic clutch system is necessary whenever any part of the system has been disconnected or the fluid level (in the reservoir) has been allowed to fall so low that air has been drawn into the master cylinder.

✳✳ WARNING

NEVER use fluid that has been bled from a clutch system to fill the master cylinder reservoir, as it may be aerated, contain excessive moisture and/or be contaminated in some other way.

5-SPEED TRANSMISSIONS

1. Before servicing the vehicle, refer to the precautions in the beginning of this section.

2. Raise and safely support the vehicle.

3. Attach a hose to the bleeder on the clutch actuator and submerge the other end of the hose in a container of hydraulic clutch fluid.

4. Have an assistant slowly depress and hold the clutch pedal.

5. Loosen the bleeder to purge air.

6. Tighten the bleeder.

7. Repeat the above 2 steps until all air is completely purged from the system.

8. Fill the clutch master cylinder reservoir with the proper type and amount of fluid.

6-Speed Transmissions

1. Before servicing the vehicle, refer to the precautions in the beginning of this section.

2. Loosen the master cylinder nuts to the end of the threads on the U-bolt.

3. Use a shop towel to clean the dirt and grease from the reservoir cap to avoid getting and foreign debris in the system.

4. Remove the reservoir cap and diaphragm.

5. Wrap a suitable piece of wire around the left-hand hood strut bracket, making sure the wire can be accessed from under the vehicle.

6. Raise and safely support the vehicle.

7. Remove the actuator cylinder nuts, then remove the actuator cylinder. Secure the actuator cylinder in the engine compartment using the wire previously installed.

8. Carefully lower the vehicle.

9. Grasp the actuator cylinder and depress the actuator cylinder pushrod about 0.0787 in. (20mm) into the cylinder bore and hold.

10. Have an assistant install the diaphragm and reservoir cap while holding the actuator pushrod in. Release the pushrod.

11. Hold the actuator cylinder lower than the master cylinder, vertically with the pushrod end facing down.

12. Press the pushrod into the actuator cylinder bore with short 0.0390 in. (10mm) strokes. Check the master cylinder reservoir for bubbles.

13. Continue until bubbles are not longer entering the reservoir.

14. Raise and safely support the vehicle.

15. Remove the actuator cylinder from the wire.

16. Install the actuator cylinder and secure with the retaining nuts. Tighten to 15 ft. lbs. (20 Nm).

17. Carefully lower the vehicle, then remove the wire from the hood strut.

18. Fill the clutch master cylinder reservoir with the proper type and amount of fluid.

STEERING AND SUSPENSION

Air Bag

✳✳ CAUTION

Some vehicles are equipped with an air bag system, also known as the Supplemental Inflatable Restraint (SIR) or Supplemental Restraint System (SRS). The system must be disabled before performing service on or around system components, steering column, instrument panel components, wiring and sensors. Failure to follow safety and disabling procedures could result in accidental air bag deployment, possible personal injury and unnecessary system repairs.

PRECAUTIONS

Several precautions must be observed when handling the inflator module to avoid accidental deployment and possible personal injury.

• Never carry the inflator module by the wires or connector on the underside of the module.

• When carrying a live inflator module, hold securely with both hands, and ensure that the bag and trim cover are pointed away.

• Place the inflator module on a bench or other surface with the bag and trim cover facing up.

• With the inflator module on the bench, never place anything on or close to the module which may be thrown in the event of an accidental deployment.

DISARMING

1. Align the steering wheel so the vehicle wheels are pointing in the straight-ahead position.

2. Turn the ignition switch to the **LOCK** position.

3. Remove the SIR or AIR BAG fuse from the fuse block.

4. Remove the Connector Position Assurance (CPA) device, then disengage the yellow 2-way SIR wiring harness connector at the base of the steering column.

ARMING

1. Turn the ignition switch to the **LOCK** position.

2. Engage the yellow 2-way connector at the base of the steering column, then install the CPA device.

3. Reinstall the SIR or AIR BAG fuse.

4. Turn the ignition switch to the **RUN** position.

5. Verify the SIR indicator light flashes 7–9 times, if not, inspect system for malfunction.

Power Rack and Pinion Steering Gear

REMOVAL & INSTALLATION

1. Before servicing the vehicle, refer to the precautions in the beginning of this section.

2. Raise and safely support the vehicle.

3. Remove the wheel and tire assemblies.

4. Place a drain pan under the steering gear unit.

5. Disconnect the inlet and outlet hoses from the steering gear.

6. Separate the outer tie rod ends from the knuckles.

7. Remove the steering gear coupling shaft from the steering gear.

8. Remove the steering gear mounting nuts and bolts, then remove the steering gear from the vehicle.

To install:

9. Position the steering gear to the crossmember. Adjust the steering gear so it aligns as straight as possible with the steering gear coupling shaft.

10. Hand-start the retaining bolts and nuts. Using a back-up wrench on the nuts, tighten the bolts to 63 ft. lbs. (85 Nm).

11. Position the steering gear to the coupling shaft.

12. Fasten the outer tie rod ends to the steering knuckle.

13. Connect the inlet and outlet hoses to the steering gear.

14. Install the tire and wheel assemblies.

15. Carefully lower the vehicle, then bleed the power steering system.

Shock Absorber

While each shock absorber can be replaced individually, it is recommended that they be changed as a pair (both front or both rear) to maintain equal response on both sides of the vehicle.

REMOVAL & INSTALLATION

Front

The following GM tools, or their equivalents, will be needed for coil spring/shock absorber disassembly.

• J 34013-B Strut Spring Compressor

• J 34013–114 Modular Shock Compressor Adapter

• J 34013–88 Strut Compressor Adapter

• J 39642 Modular Shock Nut Removal Set 0.60 in. (15mm)

• J 34013–115 Modular Alignment Rod

1. Before servicing the vehicle, refer to the precautions in the beginning of this section.

2. If removing the driver's side spring and shock assembly, unbolt the brake master cylinder from the booster and position it aside, but do not disconnect the brake lines.

3. Remove the upper spring/shock mounting bolts (15) and nuts (14).

4. Raise the vehicle.

5. Remove the wheel and tire assembly.

6. Disconnect the stabilizer bar (shaft link) from the control arm.

7. Using paint or chalk (do not scribe!), carefully matchmark the relationship of the lower coil spring mount location to the upper coil spring mount location before removing the shock absorber from the vehicle.

8. Remove the lower shock absorber nuts (11) and bolts (9).

9. Separate the lower ball joint stud (8) from the steering knuckle (5).

10. Remove the spring/shock absorber unit (12 & 13) from the vehicle.

11. To remove the spring from the shock absorber assembly perform the following steps.

➡**If using other than a GM spring compressor, follow the manufacturers instructions regarding the use of the specific tool you are using.**

a. Assemble J 34013-B and J 34013–114 on the spring unit. Use the wing nuts to secure the tool to mounting holes **C-H** (lower left corner) and **P** (upper right corner) for the driver's side shock and to mounting holes **A-X-P** (upper left) and **C-H** (lower right) for the passenger's side shock.

12. Install J 34013–114 and J 34013–88.

➡**Make certain that J 34013–114 and J 34013–88 are aligned so that they can open and close together. If not properly aligned, they will not function.**

13. Attach the shock unit to the tools.

➡**Make certain that the top of the shock is flat against J 34013–114!**

Exploded view of the power steering gear mounting

Steering Gear

FRT

7922WG26

1 ARM ASSEMBLY, FRONT UPPER CONTROL
2 STUD ASSEMBLY, FRONT UPPER CONTROL ARM BALL
3 PIN, FRONT UPPER CONTROL ARM COTTER
4 NUT, FRONT UPPER CONTROL ARM, 53 N•m (39 LB. FT.)
5 KNUCKLE ASSEMBLY, STEERING
6 NUT, FRONT LOWER CONTROL ARM,
   110 N•m (81 LB. FT.)
7 PIN, FRONT LOWER CONTROL ARM COTTER
8 STUD ASSEMBLY, FRONT LOWER CONTROL ARM BALL
9 BOLT/SCREW, FRONT SHOCK ABSORBER,
   65 N•m (48 LB. FT.)
10 ARM ASSEMBLY, FRONT LOWER CONTROL
11 NUT, FRONT SHOCK ABSORBER LOWER BRACKET,
   65 N•m (48 LB. FT.)
12 SPRING ASSEMBLY, FRONT
13 ABSORBER ASSEMBLY, FRONT SHOCK
14 NUT, FRONT SHOCK ABSORBER UPPER MOUNT,
   43 N•m (32 LB. FT.)
15 BOLT/SCREW, FRONT SHOCK ABSORBER UPPER
   MOUNT, 50 N•m (37 LB. FT.)
16 HUB ASSEMBLY, FRONT WHEEL
17 MOUNT ASSEMBLY, FRONT UPPER SHOCK ABSORBER
18 SUPPORT, FRONT UPPER CONTROL ARM

7922WG27

Exploded view of the shock absorber unit and related suspension components

14. Close the tools and install the locking pin.

➡ **Make certain that the mounting ears of the shock are facing downward toward the rear of J 34013-B, otherwise the shock will not align properly.**

15. Turn the screw of J 34013-B counterclockwise to raise the shock up to J 34013–114. Be sure that the studs go through the guide holes in J 34013–114 and the top of the shock is flat against the tool.

✻✻ CAUTION

Do not over-compress the spring! Over-compression can cause tool failure, resulting in severe bodily injury!

16. Compress the spring approximately ½ in. (13mm), or 3–4 complete turns of the screw on J 34013–114.
17. Insert J 39642–1 on the shock nut, then insert J 39642–2 through J 39642–1 to hold the shock absorber rod in place.
18. Remove the shock absorber nut with J 39642–1, while holding the shock rod from rotating with J 39642–2.
19. Discard the shock absorber nut.
20. Turn J 34013-B clockwise to fully relieve spring pressure and remove the spring from the shock.
   To install:
21. Assemble J 34013-B spring compressor and J 34013–114 adapter on the spring unit. Use wing nuts to secure the tool to mounting holes **C-H** (lower left corner and **P** (upper right corner) for the driver's side shock and to mounting holes **A-X-P** (upper left) and **C-H** (lower right) for the passenger's side shock.
22. Install J 34013–114 and J 34013–88.
23. Attach the shock unit to the tools.

➡ **Make certain that the mounting ears of the shock are facing downward towards the rear of J 34013-B!**

24. Close the tools and install the locking pin.
25. Be sure that the spring seats are positioned properly.

➡ **Make certain that the top of the shock is flat against J 34013–114!**

26. Turn the screws of J 34013-B counterclockwise to raise the shock up to J-34013–114. Be sure that the studs go through the guide holes in J 34013–114 and the top of the shock is flat against the tool.

Shock absorber compressor mounting hole locations

Install the strut compressor adapter on the spring compressor

➡ **Turn the screw only enough to secure the shock. DO NOT compress the spring.**

27. Place J 34013–115 down through the top of J 34013–B, through the top of the shock absorber and onto the rod.

➡ **Make certain that J 34013–115 is straight with the shock.**

※※ CAUTION

Do not over-compress the spring! Over-compression can cause tool failure, resulting in severe bodily injury!

28. Turn the operating screw clockwise to compress the spring until the threaded portion of the rod is through the top of the shock. Remove J 34013–115.

29. Install a NEW shock absorber nut.

30. Install J 39642–1 on the nut, insert J 39642–2 through J 39642–1 and tighten the nut while holding J 39642–2.

31. Remove the spring and shock assembly from the tool.

32. Position the unit on the lower control arm.

33. Install the lower mounting nuts and bolts, then tighten them to 48 ft. lbs. (65 Nm).

34. Attach the lower ball joint to the steering knuckle.

35. Install the stabilizer shaft link.

36. Install the wheel and tire assembly, then lower the vehicle.

37. Install the upper shock and spring assembly bolts and nuts. Tighten the bolts to 37 ft. lbs. (50 Nm) and the nuts to 32 ft. lbs. (43 Nm).

38. Reposition the master cylinder, then install the retaining nuts and tighten them securely.

Rear

1. Before servicing the vehicle, refer to the precautions in the beginning of this section.

2. Fold down the rear seatback.

3. Remove the quarter panel trim assembly.

4. Fold back the carpet.

5. Raise the vehicle. Place a support under the rear axle. The rear axle must be supported before removing the upper mounting nut to avoid any possible damage to the brake hose lines, tie rod and driveshaft.

FRONT
SPRING ASSEMBLY

J 34013-114

J 34013-88

FRONT SHOCK
ABSORBER ASSEMBLY

J 34013-B

7922WG30

Installing the shock absorber on the compressor

J 34013-115

J 34013-B

J 34013-114

FRONT SHOCK
ABSORBER ROD

FRONT SHOCK
ABSORBER ASSEMBLY

FRONT SPRING
ASSEMBLY

7922WG31

Inserting the shock assembly alignment rod

6. Unfasten the upper shock attaching nut. Remove the retainer and upper insulator.

7. Remove the retainer and lower insulator.

8. Remove the lower shock-to-rear axle mounting nut.

9. Remove the shock absorber from the vehicle.

To install:

10. Place the shock in position.

11. Install the lower shock-to-axle mounting nut and tighten to 66 ft. lbs. (90 Nm).

12. Install the lower insulator and retainer to the shock absorber.

13. Position the shock absorber through the underbody pan and seat the insulator.

14. Place the upper insulator and retainer to the shock absorber. Hand-start the upper retaining nut.

➡ **Turning the shock absorber while tightening the nut could damage the shock. To prevent damage, keep the shock absorber stationary when tightening the nut.**

15. Tighten the upper nut to 13 ft. lbs. (17 Nm).

16. Remove the rear axle support, then carefully lower the vehicle.

17. Reposition the carpet.

18. Install the quarter panel trim assembly.

19. Raise the rear seat seatback.

Coil Spring

REMOVAL & INSTALLATION

Front

Refer to the shock absorber procedure for front spring service.

Rear

1. Before servicing the vehicle, refer to the precautions in the beginning of this section.

2. Raise and support the vehicle by the frame so that the rear axle can be independently raised and lowered.

3. Support the rear axle with an adjustable support.

4. If equipped with brake hose attaching brackets, disconnect the brackets allowing the hoses to hang free. Do not disconnect the hoses. Perform this step only if the hoses would otherwise be

A

A Typical rear shock absorber assembly installation (right-hand shown)
B Underbody pan assembly
1 Rear axle assembly
2 Rear shock absorber nut 17 Nm (13 lb. ft.)
3 Rear shock absorber upper insulator retainer
4 Rear shock absorber upper insulator
5 Rear shock absorber lower insulator
6 Rear shock absorber assembly
7 Rear shock absorber nut 90 Nm (66 lb. ft.)

7922WG32

Exploded view of the rear shock absorber mounting

stretched and damaged when the axle is lowered.

5. Remove the lower shock absorber bolts, then carefully lower the rear axle. Be sure the axle is supported securely on the floor jack and that there is no chance of the axle slipping after the shock absorbers are disconnected.

➡**Be sure that the brake hoses are not stretched.**

6. Lower the axle and remove the upper insulator.

7. Remove the spring assembly.

➡**The springs are painted with a protective coating. Take care to avoid damaging this coating. If the coating is chipped or damaged, paint the exposed spring to prevent rust.**

To install:

8. Position the spring on the axle with the open lower end facing forward.

9. Install the upper insulator.

10. Raise the rear axle and install the lower shock absorber bolts.

11. Connect the brake hose attaching brackets, if removed.

12. Remove the support from the rear axle.

13. Carefully lower the vehicle.

Upper Ball Joint

REMOVAL & INSTALLATION

1. Before servicing the vehicle, refer to the precautions in the beginning of this section.

2. Raise and safely support the vehicle, then remove the wheel and tire assembly.

3. Position a floor jack under the shock mounting location on the lower control arm for support.

✳✳ CAUTION

The jack must remain in place for the entire duration of the procedure to hold the spring and lower control arm in proper position.

4. Remove the cotter pin and loosen, then remove the ball stud nut. Discard the cotter pin.

5. Support the steering knuckle with a stand.

6. Separate the ball joint from the upper control arm using tool J 39549 or equivalent separator tool.

7. With the upper control arm still in the raised position, use a 1/8 in. (3.175mm) bit to drill the four rivets about 0.25 in. (6mm) deep. Now use a 1/2 in. (12.7mm) bit to drill off the rivet heads.

8. Use a small drift to punch out the rivets, then remove upper ball joint from the lower control arm.

To install:

9. Position the new upper ball joint on the control arm, then secure using the nuts and bolts supplied with the kit. Be sure to follow the specifications given in the replacement kit.

10. Remove the stand from under the knuckle and connect the ball joint to the steering knuckle.

11. Hand-start the nut, then tighten to 39 ft. lbs. (53 Nm). Advance the nut to align the nearest cotter pin hole. NEVER back off the nut to align a hole! Install a new cotter pin.

12. Remove the floor jack from under the lower control arm shock mounting point.

13. Install the wheel and tire assembly, then carefully lower the vehicle.

Turn to Section 6 for brake system applications

1 Front upper control arm assembly
2 Front upper control ball stud assembly
3 Front upper control arm cotter pin
4 Front upper control arm nut 53 Nm (39 lb. ft.)
5 Steering knuckle assembly
6 Service kit bolt/screw
7 Service kit nut

7922WG33

Position the new upper ball joint (stud) in the control arm and secure with the replacement nuts and bolts

Lower Ball Joint

REMOVAL & INSTALLATION

➡ **To prevent component damage, an on-car ball joint press, such as Kent-Moore tool J-9519-23 should be used.**

1. Before servicing the vehicle, refer to the precautions in the beginning of this section.
2. Raise the vehicle.
3. Remove the wheel and tire assembly.
4. Position a support under the shock mounting location on the lower control arm.

✳✳ CAUTION

The support must remain in place for the entire duration of the procedure to hold the spring and lower control arm in proper position.

5. Remove and discard the lower ball joint cotter pin, then loosen the lower ball joint nut.
6. Separate the lower ball joint from the steering knuckle using J 39549 or an equivalent separator.

Ball Joint Removal

Ball Joint Installation

7922WG34

Lower ball joint replacement requires the use of special tools, such as the ones shown

7. Press the lower ball joint out of the lower control arm using tools J 9519–7, J 9519–18 and 9518–23.

To install:

8. Position a new lower ball joint into the lower control arm, and press in using tools J 9519–7, J 9519–18 and 9518–23. The ball joint must firmly press into the lower control arm. If it doesn't the lower control arm must be replaced.

9. Attach the ball joint (stud) to the steering knuckle.

10. Hand-start the lower control arm nut, then tighten to 81 ft. lbs. (110 Nm). Continue to tighten the nut just until the cotter pin holes align, then install a new pin. NEVER back off the nut to align the holes.

11. Remove the floor jack from under the control arm shock absorber mounting location.

12. Install the tire and wheel assembly, then carefully lower the vehicle.

13. Take the vehicle to a reputable repair shop to have the alignment checked.

Wheel Bearings

ADJUSTMENT

The front wheel bearing assembly used on these vehicles is a sealed, non-service-able unit. No wheel bearing adjustments (front or rear bearings) are necessary or possible.

REMOVAL & INSTALLATION

Front

1. Before servicing the vehicle, refer to the precautions in the beginning of this section.

2. Raise and safely support the vehicle.

3. Remove the wheel and tire assembly.

4. Remove the brake caliper and rotor.

5. Detach the wheel speed sensor electrical connector and position it aside.

6. Unfasten the hub retaining bolts, then pull the hub and bearing assembly from the spindle.

To install:

7. Position the hub and bearing assembly on the spindle. Install the retaining bolts and tighten to 63 ft. lbs. (86 Nm).

1 Steering knuckle assembly
2 Front brake rotor assembly
3 Front brake caliper assembly
4 Front brake caliper bolt/screw
5 Front wheel bolt/screw 86 Nm (63 lb. ft.)
6 Wheel speed sensor wire bracket
7 Front wheel hub assembly

7922WG35

Exploded view of the wheel hub/bearing unit mounting

8. Attach the wheel speed sensor electrical connector.

✹✹ WARNING

Be sure the wheel speed sensor electrical connector is reattached to the sensor wire bracket and sensor or the wires could be damaged.

9. Install the brake rotor and caliper.

10. Install the tire and wheel assembly, then carefully lower the vehicle.

Rear

1. Before servicing the vehicle, refer to the precautions in the beginning of this section.

2. Raise and support the vehicle safely.

3. Remove the rear tire and wheel assembly.

4. Remove the brake rotor or the brake drum and components, as equipped.

5. Clean the carrier cover and surrounding area to prevent dirt or contamination from entering the housing, then remove the carrier cover and drain the gear oil into a suitable container.

6. Install J-39446, or an equivalent ABS tone ring protector kit.

7. Remove the rear axle pinion shaft lockscrew and pinion shaft.

8. Push the flanged end of the axle shaft into the axle housing and remove the C-clip shaft lock from the differential case end of the shaft.

9. Remove the axle shaft from the axle housing.

10. If necessary to service the seal or bearing, use a small suitable prytool to remove the oil seal from the axle housing. Be careful not to score or damage the housing.

11. If necessary, install tool J-22813-01 or equivalent axle bearing remover, into the bore of the axle housing and position it behind the bearing, ensure the tangs of the tool engage the outer race. Remove the bearing using a slide hammer.

To install:

12. If removed, lubricate the new bearing and sealing lips with gear lubricant and install the bearing with a suitable driver so the tool bottoms against the shoulder in axle housing.

16 HOUSING, REAR AXLE
22 CAP, DIFFERENTIAL CARRIER BEARING
26 BOLT/SCREW, DIFFERENTIAL BEARING CAP
29 BOLT/SCREW, DIFFERENTIAL PINION GEAR SHAFT
   LOCK
39 WHEEL, REAR WHEEL SPEED SENSOR RELUCTOR
54 LOCK, REAR AXLE SHAFT

7922WG38

Differential component identification

16 HOUSING, REAR AXLE
44 BEARING, REAR AXLE SHAFT
49 SEAL, REAR AXLE SHAFT BEARING
63 SHAFT, REAR AXLE (DRUM BRAKE ASSEMBLY)
70 SHAFT, REAR AXLE (DISC BRAKE ASSEMBLY)

7922WG39

Cut-away view of the rear axle bearing and seal

13. If removed, Position seal on suitable seal installer, then insert the seal into the housing bore. Position the seal flush with the axle tube.

14. Taking care not to damage the seal, slide the axle shaft into place so the splines engage with the splines of the side gear.

15. Insert the shaft C-lock into the bottom end of the axle shaft and push the shaft outward so the lock seats in the counterbore of the rear axle side gear.

16. Insert the rear axle pinion gear shaft through the differential case, thrust washer and pinion gears. Align the hole in the shaft with the lockscrew hole.

17. Install the lockscrew and tighten to 27 ft. lbs. (36 Nm).

18. Clean the cover gasket mating surfaces of any remaining gasket or old sealant.

19. Install the gasket onto the carrier cover, then install the carrier cover and tighten the bolts in a crosswise pattern to 22 ft. lbs. (30 Nm).

➡**When refilling a limited slip differential rear axle with gear oil, 4 oz (118ml) of limited slip additive should be added.**

20. Fill the differential carrier with SAE 80–90W GL-5 gear lubricant or equivalent, then install the plug.

21. Install the rear brake assemblies and rear wheels. Lower the vehicle.

GENERAL MOTORS CORPORATION—G BODY

Buick-Riviera • **Oldsmobile**-Aurora

32

PRECAUTIONS

Before servicing any vehicle, please be sure to read all of the following precautions, which deal with personal safety, prevention of component damage, and important points to take into consideration when servicing a motor vehicle:

• Never open, service or drain the radiator or cooling system when the engine is hot; serious burns can occur from the steam and hot coolant.

• Observe all applicable safety precautions when working around fuel. Whenever servicing the fuel system, always work in a well-ventilated area. Do not allow fuel spray or vapors to come in contact with a spark, open flame, or excessive heat (a hot drop light, for example). Keep a dry chemical fire extinguisher near the work area. Always keep fuel in a container specifically designed for fuel storage; also, always properly seal fuel containers to avoid the possibility of fire or explosion. Refer to the additional fuel system precautions later in this section.

• Fuel injection systems often remain pressurized, even after the engine has been turned **OFF**. The fuel system pressure must be relieved before disconnecting any fuel lines. Failure to do so may result in fire and/or personal injury.

• Brake fluid often contains polyglycol ethers and polyglycols. Avoid contact with the eyes and wash your hands thoroughly after handling brake fluid. If you do get brake fluid in your eyes, flush your eyes with clean, running water for 15 minutes. If eye irritation persists, or if you have taken brake fluid internally, IMMEDIATELY seek medical assistance.

• The EPA warns that prolonged contact with used engine oil may cause a number of skin disorders, including cancer! You should make every effort to minimize your exposure to used engine oil. Protective gloves should be worn when changing oil.

Wash your hands and any other exposed skin areas as soon as possible after exposure to used engine oil. Soap and water, or waterless hand cleaner should be used.

• All new vehicles are now equipped with an air bag system, often referred to as a Supplemental Restraint System (SRS) or Supplemental Inflatable Restraint (SIR) system. The system must be disabled before performing service on or around system components, steering column, instrument panel components, wiring and sensors. Failure to follow safety and disabling procedures could result in accidental air bag deployment, possible personal injury and unnecessary system repairs.

• Always wear safety goggles when working with, or around, the air bag system. When carrying a non-deployed air bag, be sure the bag and trim cover are pointed away from your body. When placing a non-deployed air bag on a work surface, always face the bag and trim cover upward, away from the surface. This will reduce the motion of the module if it is accidentally deployed. Refer to the additional air bag system precautions later in this section.

• Clean, high quality brake fluid from a sealed container is essential to the safe and proper operation of the brake system. You should always buy the correct type of brake fluid for your vehicle. If the brake fluid becomes contaminated, completely flush the system with new fluid. Never reuse any brake fluid. Any brake fluid that is removed from the system should be discarded. Also, do not allow any brake fluid to come in contact with a painted surface; it will damage the paint.

• Never operate the engine without the proper amount and type of engine oil; doing so WILL result in severe engine damage.

• Timing belt maintenance is extremely important! Many models utilize an interference-type, non-freewheeling engine. If the timing belt breaks, the valves in the cylinder head may strike the pistons, causing potentially serious (also time-consuming and

expensive) engine damage. Refer to the maintenance interval charts in the front of this manual for the recommended replacement interval for the timing belt, and to the timing belt section for belt replacement and inspection.

• Disconnecting the negative battery cable on some vehicles may interfere with the functions of the on-board computer system(s) and may require the computer to undergo a relearning process once the negative battery cable is reconnected.

• When servicing drum brakes, only dissemble and assemble one side at a time, leaving the remaining side intact for reference.

• Only an MVAC-trained, EPA-certified automotive technician should service the A/C system or its components.

ENGINE REPAIR

Ignition Timing

ADJUSTMENT

The 3.8L and 4.0L engines are equipped with a Distributorless Ignition System (DIS). The system consists of two Crankshaft Position (CKP) sensors, crankshaft reluctor ring, Camshaft Position (CMP) sensor, ignition control module, four ignition coils, eight plug wires and spark plugs, Knock Sensor (KS) and the Powertrain Control Module (PCM).

The base ignition timing is determined by the relationship of the crankshaft position sensors to the crankshaft reluctor ring. This relationship is not adjustable. Base ignition timing is 10 degrees Before Top Dead Center (BTDC).

The PCM controls spark advance under all driving conditions. The PCM incorporates a permanent spark control override, which electronically lowers the base timing if spark knock (detonation) is encountered during normal operation due to the use of low octane fuel.

Engine Assembly

REMOVAL & INSTALLATION

3.8L (VIN 1 and K) Engines

1. Before servicing the vehicle, refer to the precautions in the beginning of this section.
2. Relieve the fuel system pressure using the recommended procedure.
3. Disconnect the negative battery cable.
4. Matchmark the hood to the hood hinges and remove the hood.
5. Drain the cooling system.
6. Remove the radiator hoses and disconnect the heater hoses from the heater core.
7. Disconnect the negative battery cable from the engine block.
8. Detach the engine harness connector at the bulkhead.
9. Remove the serpentine belt(s).
10. Remove the power steering pump from the mounting bracket and position the pump aside. DO NOT disconnect the power steering lines from the pump.
11. Remove the air inlet duct.
12. Disconnect the throttle cables from the linkage mounting bracket and disconnect all the cables from the throttle body lever.
13. Detach the following wiring connectors from their related components:
- Manifold Air Temperature (MAT) sensor
- Throttle Position (TP) sensor
- Idle Air Control (IAC) valve
- Oxygen (O2S) sensor
- A/C compressor
- Oil pressure switch
- Power steering cutout switch
- Vehicle Speed Sensor (VSS)
- Low oil level sensor
14. Remove the screws securing the ignition assembly ground strap to the inner fender panel.
15. Disconnect and cap the fuel feed and sender lines from the fuel rail and pressure regulator.
16. Disconnect the EVAP canister hoses from the throttle body.
17. Disconnect the vacuum lines from the power brake booster and heater control hoses.

18. Disconnect and remove the cruise control servo.
19. Raise and safely support the vehicle.
20. Drain the engine oil.
21. Disconnect the exhaust pipe from the right side exhaust manifold.
22. Remove the A/C compressor from the mounting bracket and support the compressor out of the way. DO NOT disconnect the refrigerant lines from the compressor.
23. Remove the right front engine-to-transaxle brace.
24. Remove the flywheel cover mounting screws and remove the cover.
25. Disconnect and remove the starter.
26. Matchmark the flywheel to the converter. Remove the torque converter-to-flywheel bolts.
27. Lower the vehicle.
28. Install a suitable engine lifting device and slightly raise the engine to take the weight off the front engine mount.
29. Remove the torque axis mount.
30. Support the transaxle with a floor jack. Remove the engine-to-transaxle bolts.
31. Carefully remove the engine from the vehicle. Be sure as the engine is being raised that there are no electrical or vacuum connections still attached.

To install:

32. Lower the engine into the vehicle. Guide the engine into position against the transaxle and be sure the alignment dowels are correctly seated in the transaxle.
33. Reinstall the engine-to-transaxle bolts and tighten to 55 ft. lbs. (75 Nm).
34. Reinstall the torque axis mount. Tighten the mount-to-frame bolts to 64 ft. lbs. (87 Nm), the engine side through-bolt to 65 ft. lbs. (87 Nm) and the frame side through-bolt to 52 ft. lbs. (70 Nm).
35. Remove the engine lifting assembly and floor jack.
36. Raise and safely support the vehicle.
37. Line up the matchmarks on the torque converter and flywheel and install the mounting bolts. Tighten the mounting bolts to 46 ft. lbs. (62 Nm).
38. Reconnect and install the starter.
39. Reinstall the flywheel cover and tighten the mounting screws to 88 inch lbs. (10 Nm).
40. Reinstall the right side engine-to-transaxle bracket.
41. Position the A/C compressor in the mounting bracket and tighten the front mounting bolts to 44 ft. lbs. (60 Nm), the rear mounting bolts to 18 ft. lbs. (25 Nm) and the rear mounting nut to 18 ft. lbs. (25 Nm).

42. Reconnect the exhaust pipe to the rear exhaust manifold and tighten the mounting nuts to 18 ft. lbs. (25 Nm).
43. Lower the vehicle.
44. Reinstall the cruise control servo and connect the vacuum lines.
45. Reconnect the vacuum lines to the power brake booster and heater control hoses.
46. Reconnect the EVAP canister hoses to the throttle body.
47. Reconnect the fuel feed and return lines to the fuel rail and pressure regulator.
48. Reconnect the ignition assembly ground strap to the inner fender well mounting screw.
49. Reconnect the following wiring connectors to their related components:
- MAT sensor
- TP sensor
- IAC valve
- O2S sensor
- A/C compressor
- Oil pressure switch
- Power steering cutout switch
- VSS
- Low oil level sensor
50. Reconnect the control cables to the throttle body lever and connect the throttle cable to the mounting bracket.
51. Reinstall the air inlet duct.
52. Reinstall the power steering pump in the mounting bracket.
53. Reinstall the serpentine belt(s).
54. Reconnect the main engine harness at the bulkhead connector.
55. Reconnect the negative battery cable to the engine block.
56. Reconnect the heater hoses to the heater core and install the upper and lower radiator hoses.
57. Refill the crankcase with engine oil.
58. Reconnect the negative battery cable.
59. Reinstall the hood on the vehicle.
60. Pressurize the fuel system and verify no leaks.
61. Refill and bleed the cooling system.

4.0L Engine

On this vehicle, some engine-related service procedures require that the entire Powertrain Assembly be removed from the vehicle. The requires specialized lifts and supports to lower the powertrain as the vehicle body is lifted up and off of the powertrain support cradle. Use care during this operation.

1. Before servicing the vehicle, refer to the precautions in the beginning of this section.

2. Relieve the fuel system pressure using the recommended procedure.

3. Disconnect the negative battery cable.

4. Remove the air inlet duct.

5. Drain the cooling system.

6. Drain the engine oil.

7. Recover the refrigerant from the A/C system.

8. Disconnect and cap the fuel feed and return lines from the fuel rail.

9. Disconnect the vacuum harness from the rear of the intake manifold.

10. Disconnect the throttle cables from the throttle body lever and bracket, then position them out of the way.

11. Detach the engine harness connector at the bulkhead.

12. Disconnect the coolant hoses from the radiator surge tank.

13. Disconnect the upper radiator hose from the coolant crossover.

14. Disconnect the lower radiator hose from the thermostat housing.

15. Disconnect and cap the upper transaxle cooler line from the radiator and the lower cooler line from the transaxle.

16. Disconnect the heater hoses from the engine compartment heater pipes.

17. Disconnect the vacuum supply line from the power booster.

18. Disconnect the shift lever from the transaxle manual shift lever and remove the transaxle cable bracket and position the cable assembly out of the way.

19. Remove the vacuum reservoir.

20. Detach the electrical connectors and vacuum lines from the cruise control servo.

21. Install an engine support fixture, J-28467-A, or the equivalent.

22. Disconnect the positive battery cable at the junction block.

23. Remove the through-bolt from the torque axis mount.

24. Remove the front engine mount bolts from the torque axis mount bracket and set the mount aside.

25. Disconnect the negative battery cable from the engine block.

26. Raise and safely support the vehicle.

27. Remove both front wheels.

28. Remove the left and right inner fender well splash shields.

29. Detach the electrical connector from the power steering rack.

30. Remove the cotter pins and castle nuts from the lower ball joints and separate the ball joints from the steering knuckles using J-36226, or an equivalent puller.

31. Remove the cotter pins and castle nuts from the outer tie rod ends and separate the ends from the steering knuckles using J-36226, or the equivalent.

32. Remove the axle nuts and separate the halfshafts from the wheel bearing and hub assemblies.

33. Remove the pinch bolt from the power steering rack at the intermediate shaft.

34. Remove the complete exhaust system.

35. Disconnect the engine oil cooler lines at the adapter.

36. Remove the engine-to-transaxle brace located at the oil pan, right cylinder bank in the rear of the engine and the left bank on the front of the engine.

37. Remove the flywheel cover.

38. Matchmark the converter to the flywheel and remove the mounting bolts.

39. Remove the oil cooler adapter from the engine.

40. Disconnect the A/C hose and muffler from the rear of the A/C compressor.

41. Position a frame support table under the powertrain assembly.

42. Remove the left transaxle mount.

43. Remove the subframe mounting bolts.

44. Release the engine support fixture.

45. Raise the vehicle off of the engine table slowly and verify no electrical or vacuum connections are still hooked to the engine.

46. Remove the transaxle-to-engine.

47. Using a suitable engine lift, separate the engine from the transaxle and subframe assembly.

To install:

48. Position the engine assembly onto the subframe. Line up the engine dowels with the holes in the transaxle and install the mounting bolts. Tighten the bolts to 55 ft. lbs. (75 Nm).

49. Remove the engine lift and position the powertrain assembly under the vehicle.

50. Lower the vehicle and line up the subframe with the vehicle and install the mounting bolts and tighten to 142 ft. lbs. (192 Nm).

51. Reinstall the engine support fixture.

52. Raise the vehicle and remove the engine dolly.

53. Reinstall the left side transaxle mount.

54. Reconnect the A/C hose and muffler to the A/C compressor.

55. Reinstall the oil filter adapter to the engine block and tighten the mounting bolts to 12 ft. lbs. (16 Nm).

56. With the converter-to-flywheel matchmarks in alignment, tighten the mounting bolts to 35 ft. lbs. (47 Nm).

57. Reinstall the rear engine-to-transaxle brace and tighten the mounting bolts to 44 ft. lbs. (60 Nm).

58. Reinstall the front engine-to-transaxle brace and tighten the mounting bolts to 44 ft. lbs. (60 Nm).

59. Reinstall the oil pan brace and tighten the mounting bolts to 37 ft. lbs. (50 Nm).

60. Reinstall the flywheel cover.

61. Reconnect the oil cooler hoses to the adapter and tighten the fittings to 12 ft. lbs. (18 Nm).

62. Reinstall the exhaust system.

63. Reconnect the halfshafts to the hub bearing assemblies and tighten the axle nuts to 107 ft. lbs. (148 Nm).

64. Reconnect the tie rod ends to the steering knuckle and tighten the castle nuts to 41 ft. lbs. (55 Nm). If necessary tighten the castle nuts up to 60 degrees additional to align the cotter pin holes. NEVER loosen the castle nut and DO NOT exceed 52 ft. lbs. (70 Nm) to make the holes align. Install new cotter pins.

65. Reconnect the ball joints to the steering knuckles and tighten the castle nuts to 88 inch lbs. (10 Nm) plus 120 degrees additional. If necessary tighten the castle nuts up to 60 degrees additional to align the cotter pin holes. NEVER loosen the castle nuts to make the holes align. Install new cotter pins.

66. Reconnect the intermediate shaft to the rack and pinion and tighten the pinch bolt to 35 ft. lbs. (47 Nm).

67. Reconnect the electrical connector to the rack and pinion assembly.

68. Reinstall the left and right inner fender splash shields.

69. Reinstall the front tire and wheel assemblies and tighten the wheel nuts to 100 ft. lbs. (140 Nm).

70. Lower the vehicle.

71. Reconnect the negative battery cable to the engine block.

72. Reinstall the front engine mount bracket-to-torque axis mount bolts.

73. Reinstall the torque axis mount through-bolt.

74. Reconnect the positive battery cable to the junction block.

75. Remove the engine support fixture.

76. Reconnect the electrical and vacuum connectors to the cruise control servo.

77. Install the vacuum reservoir.

78. Reconnect the shift cable to the transaxle manual shift lever and install the cable mounting bracket.

79. Reconnect the vacuum hose to the power booster.

80. Reconnect the heater hoses at the rear of the engine.

81. Reconnect the transaxle cooler lines.

82. Reconnect the lower radiator hose to the thermostat housing.

83. Reconnect the upper radiator hose to the coolant crossover.

84. Reconnect the hoses to the coolant surge tank.

85. Reconnect the main engine harness to the bulkhead connector.

86. Reconnect the throttle cables to the throttle body lever and install the intake manifold bracket.

87. Reconnect the vacuum hoses to the rear of the intake manifold.

88. Reconnect the fuel feed and return lines.

89. Refill the cooling system, engine crankcase and recharge the A/C system.

90. Reinstall the air inlet duct.

✸✸ WARNING

Operating the engine without the proper amount and type of engine oil will result in severe engine damage.

91. Refill the crankcase with engine oil.

92. Reconnect the negative battery cable.

93. Start the vehicle and verify no leaks.

Water Pump

REMOVAL & INSTALLATION

3.8L (VIN 1 and K) Engines

1. Before servicing the vehicle, refer to the precautions in the beginning of this section.

2. Disconnect the negative battery cable.

3. Drain the cooling system into a suitable container.

4. Remove the serpentine belt.

5. Disconnect the heater and bypass hoses from the water pump.

6. Remove the water pump pulley bolts. The long bolt can be removed by lining the head of the bolt up with the hole in the frame rail. Remove the pulley.

7. Install an engine support fixture and remove the torque axis mount.

8. Remove the water pump mounting bolts and remove the water pump.

To install:

9. Thoroughly clean all the sealing surfaces.

10. Apply a thin bead of sealer around the outside edge of the water pump and install the gasket on the pump.

11. Install the water pump on the engine and tighten the water pump bolts on the sides of the water inlet and outlet to 29 ft. lbs. (39 Nm) and the remainder of the bolts to 97 inch lbs. (11 Nm).

12. Reinstall the torque axis mount and remove the support fixture.

13. Reinstall the water pump pulley and tighten the bolts finger-tight.

14. Reconnect the hoses to the water pump.

1. Water pump
2. Engine front cover assembly
3. Gasket
4. 11 N·m (97 lbs. in.)
5. 39 N·m (29 lbs. ft.)

7922XG01

Exploded view of the water pump and mounting bolt locations—3.8L engines

Timing belt service is covered in Section 5 of this manual

1 WATER PUMP ASM.

2 O-RING SEAL

3 WATER PUMP HOUSING ASM.

7922XG02

Exploded view of the water pump housing and water pump—4.0L engine

15. Reinstall the serpentine belt.

16. Tighten the water pump pulley bolts to 115 inch lbs. (13 Nm).

17. Refill the cooling system.

18. Reconnect the negative battery cable.

19. Start the vehicle and check for proper operation.

4.0L Engine

1. Before servicing the vehicle, refer to the precautions in the beginning of this section.

2. Disconnect the negative battery cable.

3. Drain the cooling system.

4. Remove the air inlet duct.

5. Remove the water pump drive belt cover.

6. Remove the water pump drive belt and set aside.

7. Disconnect the lower radiator hose and bypass hose.

8. Remove the thermostat housing from the water pump housing.

9. Remove the water pump from the water pump housing by rotating turning the locking ring with J-38816, or an equivalent water pump remover/installer.

To install:

10. Install the water pump and seat the locking ring using J-38816.

11. Reinstall the thermostat housing to the water pump housing.

12. Reconnect the lower radiator hose and coolant bypass hose.

13. Reinstall the drive belt and drive belt cover.

14. Reinstall the air inlet duct.

15. Reconnect the negative battery cable.

16. Refill and bleed the cooling system.

Cylinder Head

REMOVAL & INSTALLATION

3.8L (VIN 1 and K) Engines

✳✳ WARNING

Head gaskets are not interchangeable. Failure to install them with the arrow pointing to the front, will cause gasket failure and possible engine

failure. The left-hand gasket can be identified with the letter "L" punched in it (next to the arrow).

LEFT SIDE (FRONT)

1. Before servicing the vehicle, refer to the precautions in the beginning of this section.

2. Disconnect the negative battery cable.

3. Relieve the fuel system pressure using the recommended procedure.

4. Drain the cooling system and remove the intake manifold.

5. Remove the left exhaust manifold.

6. Remove the valve covers, the rocker arm assemblies and pushrods, keeping everything in order for reinstallation.

7. Tag and disconnect the ignition wires and remove the spark plugs.

8. Remove the alternator front mounting bracket and the ignition module with bracket.

9. Remove the one bolt securing the A/C bracket to the cylinder head.

10. Remove the power steering pump.

11. Remove the drive belt tensioner.

12. Remove the cylinder head bolts in the reverse order of installation, and remove the cylinder head.

13. Thoroughly clean all sealing surfaces and the cylinder head bolt holes in the block.

To install:

14. Place the cylinder head gasket on the engine block dowels with the note

7922XG03

Cylinder head bolt tightening sequence—3.8L (VIN 1 and K) engines

Legend

(1) Oil Fill Cap
(2) Valve Rocker Arm Cover Bolt
(3) ICM Bracket Nut
(4) ICM
(5) ICM Bracket Bolt
(6) Exhaust Crossover Pipe
(7) Exhaust Crossover Bolt
(8) Exhaust Manifold
(9) Exhaust Manifold Stud
(10) Exhaust Manifold Bolt
(11) Exhaust Manifold Gasket
(12) Valve Stem Key
(13) Valve Stem Cap
(14) Valve Spring
(15) Valve Seal
(16) Spark Plug
(17) Intake Valve

(18) Cylinder Head Gasket
(19) Cylinder Head
(20) Valve Rocker Arm
(21) Valve Rocker Arm Bolt
(22) Generator Brace Bolt
(23) Generator Brace
(24) Idler Pulley Bracket Bolt
(25) Idler Pulley
(26) Drive Belt Tensioner
(27) Drive Belt Tensioner Bracket Bolt
(28) Drive Belt Tensioner Bracket Stud
(29) Drive Belt Tensioner Bracket
(30) Valve Lifter
(31) Valve Lifter Guide
(32) Pushrod
(33) Valve Rocker Arm Cover Gasket
(34) Valve Rocker Arm Cover

9300XG03

Exploded view of the cylinder head and related components—3.8L (VIN 1) engine

THIS SIDE UP facing the cylinder head and the arrow facing the front of the engine. Position the cylinder head on the engine block.

❊❊ WARNING

To prevent damage to the gasket when installing the cylinder head, do not slide the cylinder head on the gasket.

15. Install the cylinder head bolts and tighten as follows:

➡ **This engine uses special torque-to-yield head bolts. The procedure must be followed carefully and NEW BOLTS MUST BE USED WHENEVER THE HEAD IS REMOVED. Total bolt torque should not exceed 60 ft. lbs. (81 Nm).**

   a. Tighten the cylinder head bolts, in sequence, to 35 ft. lbs. (47 Nm).
   b. Rotate each bolt 130 degrees, in sequence.
   c. Rotate the center four bolts an additional 30 degrees, in sequence.
16. Reinstall the pushrods, rocker arm assemblies and valve covers.
17. Reinstall the intake and exhaust manifolds.
18. Reinstall the alternator front mount bracket and ignition module with bracket.
19. Reinstall the spark plugs and wires.
20. Reinstall the power steering pump.
21. Reinstall the drive belt tensioner
22. Reinstall the A/C compressor bracket bolt, and tighten to 52 ft. lbs. (70 Nm).
23. Refill the cooling system and reconnect the negative battery cable.

RIGHT SIDE (REAR)

1. Before servicing the vehicle, refer to the precautions in the beginning of this section.
2. Disconnect the negative battery cable.
3. Relieve the fuel system pressure using the recommended procedure.
4. Drain the cooling system and disconnect the exhaust crossover pipe.
5. Remove the intake manifold.
6. Remove the right side exhaust manifold.
7. Remove the valve covers.
8. Remove the serpentine drive belt.
9. Remove the belt tensioner pulley.
10. Remove the power steering pump mounting bracket and lay the pump aside.
11. Remove the fuel line heat shield.
12. Tag and disconnect the ignition wires and remove the spark plugs.

13. Remove the rocker arm assemblies and pushrods, keeping everything in order for reinstallation.
14. Remove the cylinder head bolts in reverse order of installation and remove the cylinder head.
15. Thoroughly clean all sealing surfaces and the cylinder head bolt holes in the block.

   To install:
16. Place the cylinder head gasket on the engine block dowels with the note **THIS SIDE UP** facing the cylinder head and the arrow facing the front of the engine. Position the cylinder head on the engine block.

❊❊ WARNING

In order to prevent damage to the gasket, when installing the cylinder head, do not slide the cylinder head on the gasket.

17. Install the cylinder head bolts and tighten as follows:

➡ **This engine uses special torque-to-yield head bolts. The procedure must be followed carefully and NEW BOLTS MUST BE USED WHENEVER THE HEAD IS REMOVED. Total bolt torque should not exceed 60 ft. lbs. (81 Nm).**

   a. Tighten the cylinder head bolts, in sequence, to 35 ft. lbs. (47 Nm).
   b. Rotate each bolt 130 degrees, in sequence.
   c. Rotate the center four bolts an additional 30 degrees, in sequence.
18. Reinstall the exhaust manifold and intake manifold.
19. Reinstall the pushrods and rocker arm assemblies.
20. Reinstall the valve cover(s).
21. Reinstall the spark plugs and wires.
22. Reinstall the power steering pump bracket and tighten the bolts to 35 ft. lbs. (47 Nm).
23. Reinstall the belt tensioner pulley and serpentine belt.
24. Reinstall the exhaust crossover pipe.
25. Refill the cooling system and connect the negative battery cable.

4.0L Engine

➡ **The manufacturer recommends that the entire powertrain be removed from the vehicle before removing the cylinder heads.**

1. Before servicing the vehicle, refer to the precautions in the beginning of this section.

2. Disconnect the negative battery cable.
3. Relieve the fuel system pressure using the recommended procedure.
4. Drain the cooling system into a suitable container.
5. Remove the powertrain assembly.
6. Remove the intake manifold, cam covers, harmonic balancer, timing chain front cover and oil pump.

➡ **Align all timing marks before performing the next step.**

7. Remove the chain tensioner from the timing chain for the cylinder head being removed.
8. Remove the cam sprockets from the head being removed. The timing chain remains in the chain case.
9. Removing the timing chain guides. Access for the retaining screws is through the plugs at the front of the cylinder head.
10. Remove the water crossover.
11. Remove the exhaust manifold.
12. Remove the cylinder head bolts, a little at a time, in the reverse order of the tightening sequence.
13. Remove the cylinder head and gasket.

❊❊ WARNING

With the camshafts remaining in the cylinder head, some valves will be open at all times. Do not rest the cylinder head on a flat service with the cylinder face down, or valve damage will result.

14. Clean all gasket sealing surfaces. Clean the head bolt holes in the crankcase with compressed air and clean the head bolt bosses in the cylinder head.

❊❊ WARNING

Be careful when cleaning aluminum gasket surfaces to prevent damage to the sealing surfaces. Use only plastic, wood or "dull" gasket scrapers. Chemical agents to dissolve gasket materials can also be used by following the manufacturers directions.

15. Check the cylinder head for warpage using a straightedge and feeler gauge. Measure along each edge, at the center and across both ends.
16. If warpage is less than 0.002 in. (0.05mm), the cylinder head surface is usable. If warpage is 0.002–0.008 in. (0.05–0.2mm), the cylinder head must be resurfaced. After resurfacing, the dimension between the combustion chamber gauge

FRONT

Cylinder head bolt tightening sequence—4.0L engine

7922XG04

pad and the deck surface must be at least 10.5mm.

To install:

17. Using a new cylinder head gasket, install the cylinder head and the ten M11 and three M6 head bolts. Lube the washer and the underside of the bolt head with engine oil prior to installation. New replacement head bolts are recommended.

18. Tighten the ten M11 bolts, in sequence, to 22 ft. lbs. (30 Nm) plus 90 degrees (¼ turn). Repeat the sequence, turning each bolt an additional 75 degrees (total 165 degrees). Tighten the three M6 bolts to 10 ft. lbs. (12 Nm).

19. Reinstall the camshafts and set the camshaft timing.

20. Reinstall the camshaft guide bolt access hole plugs in the cylinder heads. The plugs should be seated and snug.

21. Reinstall the intake cam covers, oil pump, timing chain front cover, harmonic balancer, intake manifold and water crossover.

22. Reinstall the exhaust manifold. Tighten the nuts to 22 ft. lbs. (30 Nm) or the bolts to 18 ft. lbs. (25 Nm).

23. Reinstall the powertrain assembly into the vehicle.

24. Reconnect the negative battery cable.

25. Refill the cooling system and check all fluid levels.

26. Properly charge the A/C system.

27. Run the engine and check for leaks and proper engine performance.

Rocker Arms

REMOVAL & INSTALLATION

➡ **All valvetrain components should be kept in the order that they were removed, so that they can be reinstalled in the their original position.**

3.8L (VIN 1 and K) Engines

LEFT SIDE (FRONT)

1. Before servicing the vehicle, refer to the precautions in the beginning of this section.

2. Disconnect the negative battery cable.

3. Disconnect the spark plug wires from the plugs and route the wires out of the way.

4. Remove the rocker arm cover bolts and remove the rocker arm cover.

5. Remove the rocker arm mounting bolt and remove the pedestal and rocker arm.

6. Remove the pushrod.

To install:

7. Install the pushrod into the lifter and install the rocker arm and pedestal. Tighten

the mounting bolt to 19 ft. lbs. (25 Nm) plus 70 degrees additional rotation.

8. Reinstall the rocker arm cover with a new gasket and tighten the mounting bolt to 88 ft. lbs. (10 Nm).

9. Reconnect the spark plug wires to the front plugs.

10. Reconnect the negative battery cable.

RIGHT SIDE (REAR)

1. Before servicing the vehicle, refer to the precautions in the beginning of this section.

2. Disconnect the negative battery cable.

3. Remove the serpentine belt.

4. Remove the alternator rear brace.

5. Disconnect the spark plug wires from the plugs and route the wires out of the way.

6. Remove the rocker arm cover bolts and remove the rocker arm cover.

7. Remove the rocker arm mounting bolt and remove the pedestal and rocker arm.

8. Remove the pushrod.

To install:

9. Install the pushrod into the lifter and install the rocker arm and pedestal. Tighten the mounting bolt to 19 ft. lbs. (25 Nm) plus 70 degrees additional rotation.

Refer to Section 1 for engine rebuilding specifications

10. Reinstall the rocker arm cover with a new gasket and tighten the mounting bolt to 88 ft. lbs. (10 Nm).

11. Reconnect the spark plug wires to the front plugs.

12. Reinstall the alternator rear brace.

13. Reinstall the serpentine belt.

14. Reconnect the negative battery cable.

4.0L Engine

The 4.0L engine is not equipped with rocker arms. The camshaft directly actuates the valves.

Supercharger

REMOVAL & INSTALLATION

3.8L (VIN 1) Engine

1996 MODELS

The supercharger oil level should be checked every 30,000 miles or 36 months.

Remove the oil only when the engine is cold. The oil level should be maintained to the bottom of the threads in the inspection hole. Do not use petroleum based oil. Use only GM 12345982 synthetic oil or equivalent 5W-30 synthetic oil. Use of the wrong oil can cause the supercharger to fail.

1. Before servicing the vehicle, refer to the precautions in the beginning of this section.

2. Relieve the fuel system pressure.

3. Disconnect the negative battery cable.

4. Remove the drive belt from the supercharger pulley. It is not necessary to remove the drive belt from the remainder of the pulleys.

5. Remove the plastic fuel injector shield.

6. Disconnect and cap the fuel lines from the fuel rail.

7. Disconnect the vacuum lines from the supercharger.

8. Detach the electrical connectors from the fuel injector.

9. Remove the electrical harness shield from the front of the supercharger and detach the electrical connector from the supercharger.

10. Remove the fuel rail mounting bolts and remove the fuel rail.

11. Detach the following electrical connectors and lay the harness aside:
- Idle Air Control (IAC) valve
- Throttle Position (TP) sensor
- Manifold Absolute Pressure (MAP) sensor
- Mass Air Flow (MAF) sensor
- Exhaust Gas Recirculation (EGR) valve
- Boost control solenoid
- Engine Coolant Temperature (ECT) sensor

12. Disconnect the air intake duct from the throttle body.

13. Disconnect the EGR pipe from the supercharger.

14. Disconnect the control cables from the throttle body.

15. Remove the boost pressure manifold and vacuum block.

16. Remove the control cable bracket.

17. Remove the tensioner bracket-to-supercharger mounting stud.

➡**The stud must be removed or the supercharger can not be lifted off the lower intake manifold mounting dowels.**

18. Disconnect the throttle body from the supercharger.

19. Remove the supercharger-to-intake manifold bolts.

20. Remove the supercharger, gasket and coolant passage O-rings.

To install:

21. Install new coolant passage O-rings and new supercharger-to-intake manifold gasket.

1 Supercharger
2 Supercharger gasket
3 Lower intake manifold
4 Supercharger bolts (8)
5 Locator pins
6 Coolant passage o-rings (2)
7 Tensioner bracket to supercharger stud

Exploded view of the supercharger mounting—3.8L (VIN 1) Engine

7922XG05

22. Install the supercharger and the mounting bolts. Only tighten the bolts finger-tight.

23. Install the tensioner bracket-to-supercharger stud and tighten to 88 inch lbs. (10 Nm).

24. Tighten the supercharger mounting bolts to 19 ft. lbs. (26 Nm).

25. Install the tensioner bracket nut and tighten to 37 ft. lbs. (50 Nm).

26. Install the throttle body and tighten the mounting nuts to 11 ft. lbs. (15 Nm).

27. Install the boost pressure manifold.

28. Install the vacuum block with a new gasket and tighten the mounting bolt to 62 inch lbs. (7 Nm).

29. Install the control cable bracket.

30. Reconnect the control cables to the throttle body.

31. Reconnect the EGR pipe to the supercharger.

32. Install the air intake duct.

33. Reconnect the electrical connectors to the following components:
- IAC valve
- TP sensor
- MAP sensor
- MAF sensor
- EGR valve
- Boost control solenoid
- ECT sensor

34. Install the fuel rail and mounting bolts.

35. Reconnect the electrical connectors to the fuel injectors.

36. Reconnect the vacuum hoses to the supercharger.

37. Reconnect the harness to the front of the supercharger and install the harness shield.

38. Install the drive belt.

39. Reconnect the negative battery cable.

40. Start the vehicle and verify no leaks.

41. Install the fuel injector sight shield.

1997–00 MODELS

1. Before servicing the vehicle, refer to the precautions in the beginning of this section.

2. Disconnect the negative battery cable.

3. Remove the engine cover.

4. Relieve the fuel system pressure using the recommended procedure.

5. Remove the drive belt from the supercharger pulley. It is not necessary to remove the drive belt from the remainder of the pulleys.

6. Disconnect the right side spark plug wires from the ignition module and set aside.

7. Remove the alternator brace.

8. Detach the electrical connectors from the fuel injectors.

9. Remove the Manifold Absolute Pressure (MAP) sensor bracket.

10. Remove the fuel rail mounting bolts and the fuel rail with the injectors.

11. Remove the boost control solenoid.

12. Remove the throttle body nuts and the supercharger.

To install:

13. Clean all sealing surfaces.

14. Install the supercharger with the intake gasket. Tighten the bolts to 17 ft. lbs. (23 Nm).

15. Reinstall the MAP sensor bracket.

16. Reinstall the throttle body to the supercharger.

17. Reinstall the boost control solenoid.

18. Reinstall the fuel rail and reconnect the lines.

19. Reinstall the alternator brace.

24	DOWEL PIN
143	HEAD GASKET
149	VALVE LIFTER
150	PIVOT RETAINER
151	ROCKER ARM
154	PUSHROD
155	LIFTER GUIDE
201	BOLT
202	BOLT
203	HEAD BOLT

Exploded view of the cylinder head and valvetrain components—3.8L (VIN 1 and K) engines

For engine torque specifications, refer to Section 1 of this manual

7922XG28

20. Reconnect the right side spark plug wires to the ignition module.

21. Reinstall the supercharger belt.

22. Reinstall the engine cover.

23. Reconnect the negative battery cable.

24. Start the engine and check for proper operation and no leaks.

Camshaft and Valve Lifters

REMOVAL & INSTALLATION

➡ All valvetrain components should be kept in the order that they were removed, so that they can be reinstalled in the their original position.

3.8L (VIN 1 and K) Engines

1. Before servicing the vehicle, refer to the precautions in the beginning of this section.

2. Relieve the fuel system pressure using the recommended procedure.

3. Disconnect the negative battery cable.

4. Remove the engine from the vehicle and mount the engine on a suitable engine stand.

5. Remove the intake manifold.

6. Remove the rocker arm covers.

7. Remove the rocker arm assemblies, and pushrods.

8. Remove the lifter guide retainer mounting bolts and retainer.

9. Remove the lifter guides.

10. Remove the lifters from their bores.

11. Remove the crankshaft balancer center bolt and using a puller remove the balancer from the crankshaft.

12. Remove the Crankshaft Position (CKP) sensor cover and disconnect the CKP sensor.

13. Remove the timing chain front cover.

☀ WARNING

Align the timing marks of the camshaft and crankshaft sprockets to avoid burring the camshaft journals by the crankshaft.

14. Remove the camshaft sprocket and timing chain.

15. Remove the camshaft thrust plate bolts and remove the thrust plate.

16. Carefully remove the camshaft.

To install:

17. Coat the camshaft lobes and bearings with prelube prior to installation.

18. Install the camshaft into the engine.

19. Reinstall the camshaft thrust plate and tighten the mounting bolts to 10 ft. lbs. (14 Nm).

20. Reinstall the camshaft sprocket and timing chain.

21. Reinstall the front timing chain cover.

22. Reconnect the CKP sensor and install the CKP sensor cover.

23. Reinstall the crankshaft balancer and tighten the mounting bolt to 111 ft. lbs. (150 Nm) plus 76 degrees additional rotation.

☀☀ WARNING

If the camshaft was replaced the lifters must also be replaced. The old lifters have developed a wear pattern and will cause the new camshaft to wear prematurely. New lifters MUST be installed with a new camshaft.

24. Coat the valve lifters with prelube and install the lifters in the lifter bores.

25. Reinstall the lifter guides and lifter guide retainer. Tighten the retainer mounting bolts to 27 ft. lbs. (37 Nm).

26. Reinstall the pushrods and rocker arms and tighten the rocker arm bolts to 28 ft. lbs. (38 Nm).

27. Reinstall the rocker arm covers.

28. Reinstall the intake manifold.

29. Reinstall the engine in the vehicle.

30. Reconnect the negative battery cable, start the engine and check for leaks.

4.0L Engine

LEFT SIDE (FRONT)

1. Before servicing the vehicle, refer to the precautions in the beginning of this section.

2. Disconnect the negative battery cable.

3. Remove the intake manifold sight shield.

4. Raise and safely support the vehicle.

5. Partially drain the cooling system to a level below the water pump assembly.

6. Remove the oil level indicator tube.

7. Lower the vehicle.

8. Disconnect the upper radiator hose from the thermostat housing.

9. Disconnect the spark plug wires from the front plugs and route the wires out of the way.

10. Remove the upper radiator support assembly.

11. Disconnect the PCV fresh air tube from the left side camshaft cover.

12. Remove the air inlet duct.

13. Disconnect the EGR outlet pipe.

14. Remove the water pump drive belt shield.

15. Remove the water pump drive belt and drive belt tensioner.

J 38822

Camshaft chain holding tool J38822—4.0L engine

9300XG05

16. Remove the coolant pump pulley using J-38825, or an equivalent pulley remover.

17. Remove the camshaft seal retainer screws and remove the camshaft seal.

18. Remove the camshaft cover bolts.

19. Remove the camshaft cover by pivoting up the intake manifold side of the cover 10 inches. Lift up the exhaust manifold side of the cover 2 inches. Swing the oil fill cap end of the cover up over the intake manifold and slide the cover over the camshafts.

20. Secure the cam sprocket to the timing chain by installing tie-wraps through the cam sprocket holes. Use four tie-wraps per sprocket.

➡**The sprocket/chain relationship must be maintained throughout this procedure or camshaft timing will be lost and require further engine disassembly to retime.**

21. Working from behind the sprockets, install cam chain holder J 38822 so that it is positioned between the chain tensioner and chain guide. Apply tension to the tool by tightening the tension adjusting screw.

22. Remove both cam sprocket bolts. Note the relative location of the cam drive pins in the end of the camshafts.

23. Work the sprockets off the cams using play in the chain.

24. Alternately loosen the cam bearing cap screws a few turns at a time until all valve spring pressure has been released. Remove the bolts and caps.

25. Remove the camshaft.

26. Inspect the camshaft for excessive lobe wear such as the evidence of grooves, scoring or flaking. Check the bearing journals, making sure they are not scored or burned. Replace the camshaft, as necessary.

To install:

27. Lubricate the camshaft lobes with camshaft prelube 1052365 or equivalent. Lubricate the camshaft journals with clean engine oil.

28. Install the camshaft.

29. Position the cam bearing caps to the cylinder head.

➡**Each cap is identified for position and direction. The arrow points towards the front of the engine. An "E" indicates a cap for the exhaust cam. An "I" indicates a cap for the intake cam.**

Position No. 1 is towards the front of the engine.

30. Loosely install the cam bearing cap bolts.

31. Alternately tighten the cam bearing cap bolts a few turns at a time against valve spring pressure until all the bolts are snug. Tighten the bolts to 9 ft. lbs. (12 Nm).

32. Using the hex cast into the camshaft, rotate the cams until the drive pins are in position to engage the cam sprockets over the cams and install the retaining bolts.

33. Work the cam sprockets over cams and install the retaining bolts. Tighten the bolts to 90 ft. lbs. (120 Nm).

34. Remove the chain holder J 38822.

35. Remove the tie-wraps from the cam sprockets.

36. Install a new camshaft cover gasket and spark plug seals in the camshaft cover.

37. Reinstall the back end of the camshaft cover first while keeping the front end of the cover high. Pivot the oil fill end of the cover into place once the back edge of the cover is clear of the tensioner assembly. Hold the seal in place and position the cover so it is square with the cylinder head. Slide the cover left and down onto the cylinder head.

38. Install the camshaft cover bolts and tighten to 89 inch lbs. (10 Nm).

39. Lubricate the seal lip with petroleum jelly and install the camshaft seal retainer over the end of the intake camshaft. Install the mounting bolts and tighten to 10 inch lbs. (1.1 Nm).

40. Reinstall the water pump pulley using J-38823, or an equivalent pulley installer.

41. Reinstall the drive belt tensioner and drive belt.

42. Reinstall the water pump belt shield.

43. Reconnect the EGR outlet pipe.

44. Reconnect the upper radiator hose to the thermostat housing.

45. Reconnect the PCV hose to the camshaft cover.

46. Reinstall the air inlet duct.

47. Reconnect the spark plug wires to the front plugs.

48. Reinstall the upper radiator support.

49. Raise and safely support the vehicle.

50. Reinstall the oil level indicator tube.

51. Lower the vehicle.

Left cylinder head camshaft bearing cap tightening sequence—4.0L (VIN C) engine

7922XG06

For complete mechanical specifications, refer to Section 1 of this manual

52. Refill the cooling system.

53. Reinstall the intake manifold sight shield.

54. Reconnect the negative battery cable.

55. Run the engine and check for leaks and proper engine operation.

RIGHT SIDE (REAR)

1. Before servicing the vehicle, refer to the precautions in the beginning of this section.

2. Disconnect the negative battery cable.

3. Remove the intake manifold sight shield.

4. Remove the vacuum reservoir.

5. Remove the cruise control servo from its mount and position out of the way.

6. Detach the ignition assembly electrical connectors.

7. Disconnect the spark plug wires from the right side plugs and remove the ignition assembly from its mount and position out of the way.

8. Remove the PCV valve from the camshaft cover.

9. Remove the EVAP canister solenoid from the right camshaft cover.

10. Raise and safely support the vehicle.

11. Disconnect the Knock Sensor (KS), Vehicle Speed Sensor (VSS) and Power Steering (PS) pressure switch.

12. Lower the vehicle.

13. Disconnect the wiring harness retainers from the cover.

14. Remove the camshaft cover bolts and remove the camshaft cover.

15. Secure the cam sprocket to the timing chain by installing tie-wraps through the cam sprocket holes. Use four tie-wraps per sprocket.

➡ **The sprocket/chain relationship must be maintained throughout this procedure or camshaft timing will be lost and require further engine disassembly to retime.**

16. Working from behind the sprockets, install cam chain holder J 38815 so that it is positioned between the chain tensioner and chain guide. Apply tension to the tool by tightening the tension adjusting screw.

17. Remove both cam sprocket bolts. Note the relative location of the cam drive pins in the end of the camshafts.

18. Work the sprockets off the cams using play in the chain.

19. Alternately loosen the cam bearing

cap screws a few turns at a time until all valve spring pressure has been released. Remove the bolts and caps.

20. Remove the camshaft.

21. Inspect the camshaft for excessive lobe wear such as the evidence of grooves, scoring or flaking. Check the bearing journals, making sure they are not scored or burned. Replace the camshaft, as necessary.

To install:

22. Lubricate the camshaft lobes with camshaft prelube 1052365 or equivalent. Lubricate the camshaft journals with clean engine oil.

23. Install the camshaft.

24. Position the cam bearing caps to the cylinder head.

➡ **Each cap is identified for position and direction. The arrow points towards the front of the engine. An "E" indicates a cap for the exhaust cam. An "I" indicates a cap for the intake cam. Position No. 1 is towards the front of the engine.**

25. Loosely install the cam bearing cap bolts.

26. Alternately tighten the cam bearing cap bolts a few turns at a time against valve spring pressure until all the bolts are snug. Tighten the bolts to 9 ft. lbs. (12 Nm).

27. Using the hex cast into the camshaft, rotate the cams until the drive pins are in position to engage the cam sprockets over the cams and install the retaining bolts.

28. Work the cam sprockets over cams and install the retaining bolts. Tighten the bolts to 90 ft. lbs. (120 Nm).

29. Remove the chain holder special tool J 38815.

30. Remove the tie-wraps from the cam sprockets.

31. Install a new camshaft cover gasket and spark plug seals in the camshaft cover.

32. Reinstall the camshaft cover on the cylinder head and tighten the mounting bolts to 89 inch lbs. (10 Nm).

33. Reconnect the wiring harness retainers to the camshaft cover.

34. Raise and safely support the vehicle.

35. Reconnect the KS, VSS and PS pressure switch.

36. Lower the vehicle.

37. Reinstall the EVAP canister solenoid on the right side camshaft cover.

38. Reinstall the PCV valve.

39. Reinstall the ignition assembly on the right side cover and connect the spark

7922XG07

Right cylinder head camshaft bearing cap tightening sequence—4.0L engine

plugs wires to the plugs and attach the electrical connector to the ignition assembly.

40. Reinstall the cruise control servo.

41. Reinstall the vacuum reservoir.

42. Reinstall the intake manifold sight shield.

43. Reconnect the negative battery cable.

44. Run the engine and check for leaks and proper engine operation.

Intake Manifold

REMOVAL & INSTALLATION

3.8L (VIN 1) Engine

1. Before servicing the vehicle, refer to the precautions in the beginning of this section.

2. Relieve the fuel system pressure using the recommended procedure.

3. Disconnect the negative battery cable.

4. Raise and safely support the vehicle.

5. Remove the front splash shield and drain the cooling system.

6. Close the drain cock, reinstall the splash shield and lower the vehicle.

7. Remove the supercharger using the recommended procedure.

8. Remove the thermostat housing.

9. Remove the EGR tube at the intake manifold.

10. Detach the electrical connection at the temperature sensor.

11. Remove the intake manifold mounting bolts and the intake manifold and gaskets.

To install:

12. Thoroughly clean all sealing surfaces.

13. Install the intake manifold using new manifold gaskets and install the intake manifold bolts finger-tight. With all the bolts in place tighten the bolts in sequence to 11 ft. lbs. (15 Nm). With all the bolts tightened, make a second pass tightening each bolt to 11 ft. lbs. (15 Nm).

14. Reinstall the electrical connector at the temperature sensor.

15. Reinstall the EGR tube to the intake manifold.

16. Reinstall the thermostat housing.

17. Reinstall the supercharger assembly using the recommended procedure.

18. Reconnect the negative battery cable, start the vehicle and check for proper operation.

19. Pressurize the fuel system, refill and bleed the cooling system.

20. Start the vehicle, check for proper operation and no leaks.

3.8L (VIN K) Engine

➡The 3.8L (VIN K) engine has two bolts which are hidden beneath the upper intake manifold. These bolts are located in the right front and left rear corners of the lower intake manifold. It is necessary to remove the upper intake manifold to service the lower intake manifold.

A TWO HIDDEN INTAKE MANIFOLD BOLT/SCREWS
B APPLY GM P/N 9985675 TO BOTH ENDS OF SEAL
C SEAL, LOWER INTAKE MANIFOLD AND GASKET
24 BOLT/SCREW, UPPER INTAKE MANIFOLD
25 MANIFOLD, UPPER INTAKE
26 GASKET, UPPER INTAKE MAINFOLD
27 MANIFOLD, LOWER INTAKE
33 BOLT/SCREW, LOWER INTAKE MANIFOLD
35 GASKET, LOWER INTAKE MANIFOLD GASKET
36 SEAL, INTAKE MANIFOLD
☐ NUMBER IN BOX IDENTIFY TIGHTENING SEQUENCE

9300XG01

Exploded view of the upper intake plenum showing the torque sequence—3.8L (VIN K) engine

7922XG10

Lower intake manifold mounting bolt tightening sequence—3.8L (VIN 1 and K) engines

Please refer to Section 9 for electric cooling fan wiring schematics

21 NUT, FUEL RAIL MOUNTING
22 RAIL, FUEL
23 INJECTOR, FUEL

9300XG02

Fuel supply rail mounting points—3.8L engine

1. Relieve the fuel system pressure using the recommended procedure.
2. Disconnect the negative battery cable.
3. Remove the fuel injector sight shield and air inlet duct.
4. Remove the air intake duct.
5. Disconnect the spark plug wires from the right side of the engine and set aside.
6. Remove the manifold vacuum source.
7. Remove the fuel rail and the EGR heat shield.
8. Remove the throttle cable bracket from the cylinder head mounting bracket and disconnect the cables from the throttle body lever.
9. Remove the throttle body support bracket.
10. Remove the upper intake plenum mounting bolts and remove the plenum and gasket.
11. Drain the cooling system.
12. Disconnect the upper radiator hose from the thermostat housing.
13. Remove the alternator.
14. Remove the four bolts and remove the drive belt tensioner assembly.
15. Disconnect the EGR valve outlet pipe.
16. Remove the lower intake manifold mounting bolts and remove the intake manifold and gaskets.

To install:

17. Thoroughly clean all sealing surfaces.
18. Install the intake manifold using new manifold gaskets and install the intake manifold bolts finger-tight. With all the bolts in place tighten the bolts in sequence to 11 ft. lbs. (15 Nm). With all the bolts tightened, make a second pass tightening each bolt to 11 ft. lbs. (15 Nm).
19. Reconnect the EGR valve outlet pipe.
20. Reinstall the drive belt tensioner and tighten the mounting bolts to 37 ft. lbs. (50 Nm).
21. Reinstall the alternator and serpentine belt.
22. Reconnect the upper radiator hose to the thermostat housing.
23. Reinstall the intake plenum on the lower intake manifold using a new gasket. Install the mounting bolts and with all the bolts in place, tighten in sequence to 89 inch lbs. (10 Nm).
24. Reinstall the throttle body support bracket and connect the throttle cables to the throttle body lever.
25. Reinstall the EGR heat shield.
26. Reinstall the fuel rail assembly and tighten the mounting bolts to 7 ft. lbs. (10 Nm). Reconnect the vacuum lines, fuel lines and electrical connectors.
27. Reconnect the vacuum lines to the intake manifold.
28. Reconnect the spark plug wires to the rear bank of plugs.
29. Reinstall the air inlet duct and fuel injector sight shield.
30. Reconnect the negative battery cable.
31. Pressurize the fuel system and verify no leaks.
32. Refill and bleed the cooling system.

4.0L Engine

1. Before servicing the vehicle, refer to the precautions in the beginning of this section.
2. Relieve the fuel system pressure using the recommended procedure.
3. Disconnect the negative battery cable.
4. Remove the four cap nut and washers and remove the intake manifold sight shield.
5. Disconnect the PCV hose from the intake manifold.
6. Disconnect the front spark plug wires and route them out of the way.
7. Disconnect the main fuel injector harness.

1	NUT, ATTACHING COVER
2	GROMMET, COVER
3	WASHER, COVER GROMMET
4	COVER, INTAKE MANIFOLD
5	WIRING HARNESS ASM
6	SCREW, ISC BRACKET ASM ATTACHING
7	BRACKET ASM, IDLE SPEED CONTROL (ISC)
8	NUT, HEX
9	WASHER, LOCK
10	ACTUATOR ASM, IDLE SPEED CONTROL (ISC)
11	BODY ASM, THROTTLE
12	TUBE, COOLANT OUTLET
13	BOLT, THROTTLE BODY ATTACHING
14	TUBE, COOLANT INLET
15	SENSOR, THROTTLE POSITION (TP)
16	SCREW ASM, TP SENSOR ATTACHING
17	GASKET, INTAKE MANIFOLD
18	HOUSING ASM, INTAKE MANIFOLD
19	BOLT, INTAKE MANIFOLD ATTACHING
20	SEAL, EGR TRANSFER SPACER TO INTAKE MANIFOLD
21	SEAL, THROTTLE BODY TO EGR TRANSFER SPACER
22	SPACER, EGR TRANSFER
23	RAIL ASM, FUEL
24	CARTRIDGE REGULATOR ASM, FUEL PRESSURE
25	CAP, FUEL PRESSURE CONNECTION
26	CORE ASM, FUEL PRESSURE CONNECTION VALVE
27	O-RING, MFI FUEL INJECTOR UPPER
28	CLIP, MFI FUEL INJECTOR RETAINER
29	INJECTOR ASM, MFI FUEL
30	O-RING, MFI FUEL INJECTOR LOWER
31	SPACER, INTAKE MANIFOLD
32	O-RING, PRESSURE RELIEF VALVE
33	STUD, INTAKE MANIFOLD/COVER ATTACHING
34	VALVE ASM, PRESSURE RELIEF

7922XG11

Exploded view of the intake manifold and related components —4.0L engine

8. Detach the electrical connectors from the Idle Speed Control (ISC) motor, Throttle Position (TP) sensor and the Manifold Absolute Pressure (MAP) sensor.

9. Disconnect the fuel rail ground wires from the right cylinder head.

10. Disconnect the vacuum hoses from the power brake booster and throttle body.

11. Disconnect the crankcase vent hose at the air inlet duct.

12. Disconnect the EGR outlet tube.

13. Disconnect and cap the fuel lines from the fuel rail and remove the line retaining bolt near the throttle body.

14. Remove the air inlet duct.

15. Disconnect and cap the throttle body coolant hoses.

16. Disconnect the control cables from the throttle body lever.

17. Take note of the positions of the four studs and remove the six intake manifold mounting bolts and four mounting studs.

18. Remove the intake manifold.

To install:

19. Install a new intake manifold gasket and position the manifold in place and install the six mounting bolts and four studs. With all the bolts in place tighten the bolts to 89 inch lbs. (10 Nm) starting in the center and working in a circular pattern.

20. Reconnect the control cables to the throttle body lever.

21. Reconnect the throttle body coolant hoses and add coolant as necessary.

22. Reinstall the air inlet duct.

For complete service labor times order Chilton's Labor Guide Manual

23. Reconnect the fuel lines to the fuel rail and install the line retaining bolt near the throttle body.

24. Reconnect the EGR outlet pipe.

25. Reconnect the crankcase vent pipe to the air inlet duct.

26. Reconnect the vacuum hoses to the power booster and throttle body.

27. Reconnect the fuel rail ground wires to the right cylinder head.

28. Reconnect the electrical connectors to the ISC motor, the TP sensor and the MAP sensor.

29. Reconnect the main fuel injector harness.

30. Reconnect the spark plug wires to the front plugs.

31. Reconnect the PCV hose to the intake manifold.

32. Reconnect the negative battery cable.

33. Pressurize the fuel system and verify no leaks.

34. Reinstall the intake manifold sight shield.

Exhaust Manifold

REMOVAL & INSTALLATION

3.8L (VIN 1 and K) Engines

LEFT SIDE (FRONT)

1. Before servicing the vehicle, refer to the precautions in the beginning of this section.

2. Disconnect the negative battery cable.

3. Remove the two bolts attaching the left exhaust manifold to the crossover pipe.

4. Disconnect the spark plug wires from the plugs and position out of the way.

5. Remove the oil level indicator tube.

6. Remove the exhaust manifold bolts and the exhaust manifold.

To install:

7. Install the exhaust manifold with a new gasket and loosely install the mounting bolts.

8. Reinstall the oil level indicator tube.

9. Tighten the exhaust manifold mounting bolts to 22 ft. lbs. (30 Nm).

10. Reconnect the spark plug wires to the plugs.

11. Reinstall the bolts connecting the left exhaust manifold to the crossover pipe and tighten to 15 ft. lbs. (20 Nm).

12. Reconnect the negative battery cable.

13. Start the vehicle and verify no leaks.

1 LEFT (FRONT) EXHAUST MANIFOLD
2 STUD 30 N•m (22 LB. FT.)
3 BOLT 30 N•m (22 LB. FT.)

7922XG30

Exploded view of the left exhaust manifold mounting—3.8L (VIN 1 and K) engines

1 EXHAUST CROSSOVER PIPE
2 BOLT 20 N•m (15 LB. FT.)
3 STUD 20 N•m (15 LB. FT.)
4 SEAL

7922XG31

Exploded view of the crossover pipe mounting—3.8L (VIN 1 and K) engines

RIGHT SIDE (REAR)

1. Before servicing the vehicle, refer to the precautions in the beginning of this section.

2. Disconnect the negative battery cable.

3. Disconnect the spark plug wires from the plugs and position out of the way.

4. Remove the transaxle level indicator tube.

5. Detach the Oxygen (O$_2$S) sensor electrical connector.

1   RIGHT (REAR) EXHAUST MANIFOLD
2   STUD 30 N•m (22 LB. FT.)

7922XG29

Exploded view of the right exhaust manifold mounting—3.8L (VIN 1 and K) engines

6. Remove the two bolts connecting the right exhaust manifold to the crossover pipe.

7. Remove the plastic vacuum tank mounted on the cowl.

8. Raise and safely support the vehicle.

9. Remove the converter heat shield and pipe hanger.

10. Disconnect the exhaust pipe from the manifold.

11. Lower the vehicle.

12. Remove the rear engine lift bracket.

13. Remove the exhaust manifold bolts.

14. Remove the exhaust manifold.

To install:

15. Install the exhaust manifold with a new gasket and tighten the exhaust manifold mounting bolts to 22 ft. lbs. (30 Nm).

16. Reinstall the rear engine lift bracket.

17. Raise and safely support the vehicle.

18. Reconnect the front pipe to the manifold and tighten the mounting bolts to 15 ft. lbs. (20 Nm).

19. Reinstall the exhaust hanger and converter heat shield.

20. Lower the vehicle.

21. Reinstall the vacuum tank on the cowl.

22. Reinstall the bolts connecting the right exhaust manifold to the crossover pipe and tighten the bolts to 15 ft. lbs. (20 Nm).

23. Reinstall the transaxle level indicator tube.

24. Reconnect the O_2S sensor electrical connector.

25. Reconnect the spark plug wires to the plugs.

26. Reconnect the negative battery cable.

27. Start the vehicle and verify no leaks.

4.0L Engine

LEFT SIDE (FRONT)

1. Before servicing the vehicle, refer to the precautions in the beginning of this section.

2. Disconnect the negative battery cable.

3. Release the tension on the serpentine belt and remove the belt from the power steering and alternator pulleys.

4. Remove the alternator upper mounting bolt.

5. Raise and safely support the vehicle.

6. Remove the right inner fender well splash shield.

7. Remove the lower center air deflector.

8. Remove the alternator rear bracket.

9. Remove the lower alternator mounting bolt and position the alternator aside.

10. Remove the exhaust manifold-to-exhaust crossover pipe bolts.

11. Detach the electrical connector from the Oxygen (O_2S) sensor.

12. Remove the bolts securing the power steering line retainers.

13. Remove the exhaust manifold nuts and remove the exhaust manifold.

14. If the manifold is being replaced, remove the O_2S sensor.

To install:

15. Thoroughly clean all sealing surfaces.

16. Coat the O_2S sensor threads with high temperature anti-seize and install the sensor in the manifold and tighten to 30 ft. lbs. (40 Nm).

17. Reinstall the exhaust manifold gasket over the cylinder head studs.

18. Insert the outlet pipe on the manifold partially into the crossover pipe and position the manifold over the cylinder head studs. Tighten the mounting nuts starting in the center and working outward to 18 ft. lbs. (24 Nm).

19. Reconnect the electrical connector to the O_2S sensor.

20. Reinstall the power steering line retainers and tighten the mounting bolts to 10 ft. lbs. (14 Nm).

21. Position the alternator and loosely reinstall the lower retaining bolt and the rear mounting bracket. Tighten the bolts to 35 ft. lbs. (47 Nm) and the nuts to 28 ft. lbs. (38 Nm).

22. Reinstall the crossover pipe mounting bolts and tighten to 37 ft. lbs. (50 Nm).

23. Reinstall the lower center air deflector.

24. Reinstall the right inner fender well splash shield.

25. Lower the vehicle.

26. Reinstall the upper alternator retaining bolt and tighten to 35 ft. lbs. (47 Nm).

27. Reinstall the serpentine belt around the alternator and power steering pulleys.

28. Reconnect the negative battery cable.

29. Start the vehicle and verify no leaks.

RIGHT SIDE (REAR)

1. Before servicing the vehicle, refer to the precautions in the beginning of this section.

2. Disconnect the negative battery cable.

Timing belt service is covered in Section 5 of this manual

1 LEFT EXHAUST MANIFOLD
2 RIGHT EXHAUST MANIFOLD
3 CROSSOVER EXHAUST PIPE
4 EXHAUST MANIFOLD REAR PIPE
5 CONVERTER
6 BLOCK FASTENER FITTING
7 EGR FITTING
8 CYLINDER HEAD FASTENER FITTING
9 OXYGEN SENSOR

7922XG32

Exhaust system component identification—4.0L engine

3. Raise and safely support the vehicle.

4. Remove the exhaust system.

5. Remove the bolts securing the connector pipe to the exhaust manifold and crossover pipe.

6. Remove the heat shield from the Knock Sensor (KS).

7. Detach the electrical connector from the Oxygen (O_2S) sensor.

8. Remove the exhaust manifold nuts and remove the exhaust manifold.

9. If the manifold is being replaced, remove the O_2S sensor.

To install:

10. Thoroughly clean all sealing surfaces.

11. Coat the O_2S sensor threads with high temperature anti-seize and install the sensor in the manifold and tighten to 30 ft. lbs. (40 Nm).

12. Reinstall the exhaust manifold gasket over the cylinder head studs.

13. Position the manifold over the cylinder head studs. Tighten the mounting nuts starting in the center and working outward to 18 ft. lbs. (24 Nm).

14. Reinstall the KS heat shield.

15. Reconnect the electrical connector to the O_2S sensor.

16. Reinstall the connector pipe and

install the mounting bolts connecting it to the exhaust manifold and crossover pipe. Tighten the mounting bolts to 30 ft. lbs. (40 Nm).

17. Reinstall the exhaust system and tighten the spring loaded nuts to 18 ft. lbs. (25 Nm).

18. Lower the vehicle.

19. Reconnect the negative battery cable.

20. Start the vehicle and verify no leaks.

Oil Pan

REMOVAL & INSTALLATION

3.8L (VIN 1 and K) Engines

1. Before servicing the vehicle, refer to the precautions in the beginning of this section.

2. Disconnect the negative battery cable.

3. Raise and safely support the vehicle.

4. Drain the engine oil.

5. Detach the oil level indicator connector.

6. Remove the oil pan mounting bolts and remove the oil pan.

To install:

7. Clean all the gasket surfaces completely.

8. Install the oil pan with a new gasket and tighten the mounting bolts to 10 ft. lbs. (14 Nm).

9. Reconnect the oil level indicator connector.

10. Lower the vehicle.

11. Refill the crankcase with engine oil.

12. Reconnect the negative battery cable.

13. Start the vehicle and verify no oil leaks.

4.0L Engine

On the 4.0L engine, remove the transaxle assembly, not the engine, for engine oil pan removal.

1. Before servicing the vehicle, refer to the precautions in the beginning of this section.

2. Disconnect the negative battery cable. The battery is located under the passenger side of the rear seat cushion. Raise the rear seat cushion to access the battery.

3. Raise and safely support the vehicle.

4. Remove the oil pan drain plug and drain the engine oil into a suitable container.

5. If necessary, remove the exhaust crossover pipe retaining bolts from the left exhaust manifold flange and the exhaust manifold rear pipe.

6. Remove the transaxle assembly.

7. Remove the oil pan bolts and remove the oil pan from the vehicle.

➡**The oil pan gasket is reusable unless it is damaged. Do not remove the gasket from the oil pan groove unless gasket replacement is required.**

To install:

8. Install the oil pan and seal in the vehicle.

9. Reinstall the oil pan mounting bolts and tighten in sequence to 108 inch. lbs. (13 Nm).

10. Reinstall the transaxle assembly.

11. Reinstall the exhaust crossover pipe retaining bolts on the left exhaust manifold flange and the exhaust manifold rear pipe if removed.

12. Reinstall the oil pan drain plug and tighten to 15 ft. lbs. (20 Nm).

13. Lower the vehicle.

14. Refill the crankcase with the proper type and quantity of engine oil.

15. Reconnect the negative battery cable.

Oil Pump

REMOVAL & INSTALLATION

3.8L (VIN 1 and K) Engines

1. Before servicing the vehicle, refer to the precautions in the beginning of this section.

2. Disconnect the negative battery cable.

3. Raise and safely support the vehicle.

4. Drain the engine oil.

5. Remove the front cover assembly.

6. Remove the four bolts securing the oil filter adapter to the front cover assembly and oil filter adapter, pressure regulator valve and spring.

7. Remove the four oil pump cover attaching screws and remove the cover.

8. Remove the inner and outer pump gears.

9. Make the following measurements and replace any components not within specification:

a. Gear pocket depth: 0.461–0.4265 in. (11.71–11.75mm)

b. Gear pocket diameter: 3.508–3.512 in. (89.10–89.20mm)

c. Inner gear tip clearance: 0.006 in. (0.152mm)

d. Outer gear diameter clearance: 0.008–0.015 in. (0.203–0.381mm)

32 GASKET, OIL PAN SCREEN
33 SCREEN, OIL PAN
34 BOLT/SCREW, OIL PAN SCREEN
40 SENSOR, ENGINE OIL LEVEL
44 GASKET, OIL PAN (INCLUDES BAFFLE)
47 PAN, OIL
49 BOLT/SCREW, OIL PAN
50 GASKET, OIL PAN DRAIN PLUG
51 PLUG, OIL PAN DRAIN

7922XG33

Exploded view of the oil pan mounting and related components—3.8L (VIN 1 and K) engines

7922XG12

Oil pan bolt tightening sequence—4.0L engine

1. 97 inch lbs. (11 Nm)
2. Oil pump cover
3. Pump outer gear
4. Pump inner gear
5. Front cover

7922XG13

Exploded view of the oil pump assembly—3.8L (VIN 1 and K) engines

e. Gear end clearance: 0.001–0.0035 in. (0.025–0.089mm)

10. If measurement **A** or **B** is out of specification the front cover assembly must be replaced. If measurement **C**, **D** or **E** is out of specification replace the gears.

To install:

11. Lubricate the gears with petroleum jelly and install the gears into the housing.

12. Pack the gear cavity with petroleum jelly after the gears have been installed in the housing. This seals the gears and acts as a prime to allow the oil pump to draw oil as soon as it starts to turn as the engine is cranked. Do not overlook this step. DO NOT use chassis grease. Use only petroleum jelly since its low-temperature nature means it will dissolve as the engine warms up.

13. Reinstall the oil pump cover and screws and tighten to 97 inch lbs. (11 Nm).

14. Reinstall the oil filter adapter with new gasket, pressure regulator valve and spring. Tighten the mounting bolts to 24 ft. lbs. (33 Nm).

15. Reinstall the front cover assembly.

16. Refill the crankcase with clean engine oil.

17. Reconnect the negative battery cable.

18. Start the vehicle and verify no leaks and proper oil pressure.

4.0L Engine

1. Before servicing the vehicle, refer to the precautions in the beginning of this section.

2. Disconnect the negative battery cable.

3. Install an engine support fixture J-28467-A or the equivalent.

4. Remove the engine mount-to-body through-bolt nut and through-bolt.

5. Remove the through-bolt nut and bolt from the engine side of the mount.

6. Raise and safely support the vehicle.

7. Remove the front tire and wheel assembly.

8. Remove the right inner fender well splash shield.

9. Remove the lower center air deflector.

10. Remove the left transaxle mount-to-frame through-bolt.

11. Remove the lower retaining bolt and nut from the engine mount bracket.

12. Remove the bolt and disconnect the power steering line retainer from the bracket.

13. Lower the vehicle.

14. Remove the upper retaining nut and bolt from the engine mount bracket.

15. Remove the serpentine belt from the power steering pump pulley.

16. Remove the fuel plastic sight shield on the intake manifold.

17. Remove the power steering pump from the mounting bracket and set aside. DO NOT disconnect the power steering lines from the pump.

18. Raise the engine using the support fixture.

19. Remove the engine mount bracket from the engine.

20. Remove the torque axis mount from the frame rail.

21. Lower the engine using the support fixture until clearance for J-38416-B, or an equivalent puller is attained.

22. Raise and safely support the vehicle.

23. Remove the crankshaft balancer retaining bolt.

24. Remove the crankshaft balancer using J-38416-B.

25. Remove the serpentine belt tensioner.

26. Remove the serpentine belt idler pulley.

27. Remove the front cover bolts and remove the cover and gasket. DO NOT discard the gasket, if it is undamaged it can be re-used.

28. Remove the three oil pump mounting bolts and remove the oil pump and drive spacer.

29. If necessary, disassemble and inspect the pump as follows:

a. Remove the drive spacer from the pump housing.

b. Remove the two screws holding the pump housing halves together.

c. Remove the inner (drive) and outer (driven) rotors from the housing. Indicate the mating surfaces (dimples).

d. Remove the pressure relief valve.

e. Inspect the pump housing for nicks, burrs, chips or debris that might cause a leak or binding condition in the rotor pocket.

f. Inspect the drive and driven rotors for nicks or burrs.

g. Check the pump cover and interior surface for excessive wear or score marks. Check for flatness.

h. If any components show signs of excessive wear or damage, replace the pump assembly.

To install:

30. If the pump was disassembled, reassemble as follows:

a. Reinstall the inner and outer rotors to the pump cover in the same orientation as removed.

b. Reinstall the pressure relief valve seat, spring and pilot in the pump housing.

c. Pack the pump housing halves

FRONT OF ENGINE

1. Gerotor assembly
2. Outer gear
3. Inner gear
4. Housing
5. Drive spacer
6. Relief valve
7. Cover

7922XG14

Exploded view of the oil pump—4.0L engine

with Amojell® or white petroleum grease to ensure pump priming.

   d. Assemble the housing and cover over the locating dowel.

   e. Insert a 9mm drill in the pump mounting hole on the opposite side to aid alignment of the housing and cover. Install the two screws and tighten to 108 inch lbs. (12 Nm).

31. Reinstall the oil pump drive spacer into the oil pump from the rear so the drive flat engages the pump rotor.

32. Install the oil pump over the crankshaft and loosely install the mounting bolts.

33. Hold the pump in its furthest up position and tighten the mounting bolts to 89 inch lbs. (10 Nm) plus 35 degrees additional rotation.

34. Place a small amount of RTV sealant at the split line of the upper and lower crankcases.

35. Reinstall the front cover gasket over the dowel pins on the block.

36. Reinstall the front cover on the engine and tighten the mounting bolts to 89 inch lbs. (10 Nm).

37. Reinstall the serpentine belt idler pulley and tighten the mounting bolt to 37 ft. lbs. (50 Nm).

38. Reinstall the serpentine belt ten-

PCM

POWER

REMOVE THIS CONNECTOR FOR CRANKING WITHOUT STARTING

FRT

CAMSHAFT POSITION SENSOR WITH SPROCKET

ICM WITH COILS

2 8 5 3 1 4 7 6

TO SPARK PLUGS

CRANKSHAFT POSITION SENSORS WITH RELUCTOR RING

7922XG15

Remove the connector shown to disable the ignition system—4.0L engine

Refer to Section 1 for engine rebuilding specifications

sioner and tighten the mounting bolt to 37 ft. lbs. (50 Nm).

39. Coat the seal contact area on the balancer with engine oil and install the balancer onto the end of the crankshaft with the notch lined up with the crankshaft key. Using J-39344 or the equivalent push the balancer into place.

40. Install the balancer center bolt and tighten to 44 ft. lbs. (60 Nm) plus 120 degrees (⅔ turn) additional rotation.

41. Lower the vehicle.

42. Raise the engine with the support fixture.

43. Reinstall the torque axis mount on the body.

44. Reinstall the engine mount bracket on the engine and loosely install the mounting nuts and bolts. With all the fasteners in place tighten the nuts to 30 ft. lbs. (40 Nm) and the bolts to 41 ft. lbs. (55 Nm).

45. Lower the engine support fixture until the engine is at its normal height.

46. Reinstall the power steering pump in the mounting bracket.

47. Reinstall the serpentine belt.

48. Reconnect the power steering line retainer to the engine mount bracket and install the mounting bolt.

49. Raise and safely support the vehicle.

50. Reinstall the left transaxle mount-to-frame through-bolt and tighten to 63 ft. lbs. (85 Nm).

51. Reinstall the lower center air deflector.

52. Reinstall the right inner fender well splash shield.

53. Reinstall the tire and wheel assembly and tighten the wheel nuts to 100 ft. lbs. (140 Nm).

54. Lower the vehicle.

55. Reinstall the torque axis mount-to-engine mount bracket through-bolt and nut and tighten the bolt to 70 ft. lbs. (95 Nm).

56. Reinstall the torque axis mount-to-frame through-bolt and nut and tighten the through-bolt to 37 ft. lbs. (50 Nm).

57. Remove the engine support fixture.

58. Reconnect the negative battery cable.

59. Run the engine and check for leaks and proper engine operation.

ENGINE LUBRICATION SYSTEM PRIMING PROCEDURE

➡**After completing service to an Aurora 4.0L (VIN C) engine requiring engine oil pump removal, the following priming procedures MUST be performed before engine start-up.**

The factory recommends a coat of GM Prelube No. 1052367 be applied to all bearing surfaces and crankshaft journals (cover completely) whenever servicing connecting rod and/or main crankshaft bearings. Also perform the following when servicing the internal components of an Aurora engine. These steps will aid in priming the lubrication system: Store the valve lifters (also called tappets or lash adjusters) with the camshaft contact surface down, so engine oil will not drain from the lifters; Apply liberal amounts of GM Camshaft Prelube, No. 1052365 to the camshaft lobes, bearing caps and lifter surfaces; Piston rings and pistons should be completely covered with proper specification motor oil during installation.

To perform the factory-required Engine Lubrication System Priming Procedure, use the following procedures.

1. Thoroughly pack the oil pump with white petroleum jelly during reassembly and fill the oil filter with correct specification engine oil before installation.

2. Verify engine oil is at the proper level. System capacity is 7 quarts with the oil filter full. Fill to proper level if necessary.

3. Detach the right front connector (power lead) from the Distributorless Ignition System (DIS) module and crank the engine for 30 seconds.

4. Connect the power lead to the DIS and start the engine. Check the Driver Information Center (DIC) for **Low Oil Pressure** message and listen for any audible noise such as lifters "ticking".

5. If engine noises persist, stop the engine and remove the oil pressure switch from the oil filter adapter and install a mechanical oil pressure gauge. **Be careful not to damage the threads in the adapter.** It is made of soft magnesium and is easily damaged. Also note that the ports are sealed with O-rings which must be in place and in good condition to seal properly. The bypass valves in the adapter are non-serviceable.

6. If oil is indicated on the gauge and no unusual sounds are heard, oil pressure is present and both the oil pump and engine lubrication system are primed. If no oil pressure is recorded, repeat Step 3 of this procedure, then proceed to Step 7.

7. If no oil pressure is recorded after repeating the process given above, remove the Oil Filter Adapter and force engine oil under pressure (using shop air) in the engine block outlet port (the port closest to the front of the engine). Reinstall the Oil Filter Adapter with the mechanical oil pressure gauge installed in the sender port and start the engine.

8. If oil pressure is obtained, stop the engine and reinstall the Oil Pressure Switch in the Oil Filter Adapter. Once connected, check the instrument display for no oil pressure or **Low Oil Pressure** message. If that message is present, check the switch connection or begin low oil pressure complaint troubleshooting.

Rear Main Seal

REMOVAL & INSTALLATION

1. Before servicing the vehicle, refer to the precautions in the beginning of this section.

2. Disconnect the negative battery cable.

3. Remove the transaxle and flexplate using the recommended procedure.

4. Carefully pry the oil seal from the housing using a suitable prying tool taking care not to damage the housing or the crankshaft sealing surface.

➡**Extreme care must be taken in order to avoid damage to the crankshaft sealing surface.**

To install:

5. On 4.0L engines place a small amount of GM Gasket Maker® or equivalent at the top of the crankcase split line across the end of the upper/lower crankcase seal.

6. Apply clean engine oil to the inside and outside diameter of the oil seal.

7. Install the seal into the housing using tool J-38196 for 3.8L engines or tool J-38817 for 4.0L engines or equivalent.

8. Reinstall the flexplate and transaxle using the recommended procedure.

9. Reconnect the negative battery cable, start the engine and check for leaks.

Timing Chain, Sprockets, Front Cover and Seal

REMOVAL & INSTALLATION

3.8L (VIN 1 and K) Engines

1. Before servicing the vehicle, refer to the precautions in the beginning of this section.

2. Disconnect the negative battery cable.

3. Drain the coolant into a suitable container.

4. Remove the vacuum reservoir.

5. Install an engine support fixture, J-28467-A or equivalent.

6. Raise the engine so that the weight is removed from the torque axis mount.

Legend

(1) Flywheel Bolt
(2) Flywheel
(3) Crankshaft Rear Oil Seal
(4) Oil Pan Gasket (Includes Baffle)
(5) Engine Oil Pan
(6) Oil Level Sensor
(7) Oil Pan Bolt
(8) Oil Pan Drain Plug
(9) Oil Pan Drain Gasket
(10) Crankshaft Position Sensor Shield
(11) Crankshaft Balancer
(12) Crankshaft Balancer Washer
(13) Crankshaft Balancer Bolt
(14) Water Pump Pulley Bolt
(15) Water Pump Pulley
(16) Water Pump
(17) Water Pump Gasket

(18) Engine Front Cover
(19) Engine Front Cover Gasket
(20) Oil Pump Cover Bolt
(21) Engine Crankshaft
(22) Crankshaft Balancer Key
(23) Crankshaft Upper Bearing
(24) Side Main Bolt
(25) Crankshaft Main Bearing Cap Bolt
(26) Crankshaft Lower Bearing
(27) Crankshaft Main Bearing Cap
(28) Oil Pump Cover
(29) Oil Pump Gear Set
(30) Crankshaft Position Sensor
(31) Crankshaft Front Oil Seal
(32) Camshaft Position Sensor
(33) Camshaft Position Sensor Bolt
(34) Water Pump Bolt

9300XG04

Exploded view of lower engine components—3.8L (VIN 1 and K) engines

For engine torque specifications, refer to Section 1 of this manual

7. Remove the two lower torque axis-to-frame bolts.

8. Remove the torque axis mount.

9. Remove the serpentine belt(s).

10. Remove the water pump on vehicles equipped with supercharger.

11. Raise the engine with the support fixture and remove the engine mount bracket bolts and bracket.

12. Remove the alternator and the three bolts securing the drive belt tensioner and remove the tensioner.

13. Remove the crankshaft balancer.

14. Remove the Crankshaft Position (CKP) sensor shield.

15. Detach the electrical connector from the CKP sensor.

16. Remove the front oil pan-to-front cover bolts.

17. Remove the front cover bolts and remove the front cover.

18. Using the appropriate seal driver, remove the seal from the front cover.

19. Rotate the crankshaft until the timing mark on the camshaft sprocket is lined up with the crankshaft sprocket timing mark.

20. Remove timing chain damper mounting bolt and remove the chain damper assembly.

21. Remove camshaft sprocket bolt.

22. Remove camshaft sprocket along with the timing chain.

23. Using a suitable gear puller remove the crankshaft sprocket from the crankshaft.

To install:

24. Line up the notch in the crankshaft sprocket with the crankshaft key and slide the gear on the crankshaft. It may be necessary to use a gear installer to fully seat the gear. Be sure the timing mark on the crankshaft gear is pointing straight up.

25. Insert the camshaft gear into the timing chain. Hold the sprocket with the timing mark straight down and with the chain hanging down off of the sprocket.

26. Loop the chain under the crankshaft sprocket.

27. Install the camshaft sprocket onto the camshaft so the notch in the sprocket fits over the camshaft key.

28. The camshaft and crankshaft timing marks should be in line.

29. If the marks are not in alignment perform the following:

   a. Remove the camshaft sprocket and timing chain.

   b. Install the camshaft sprocket onto the camshaft and rotate the camshaft until the camshaft and crankshaft marks are aligned.

   c. Remove the camshaft sprocket.

   d. Repeat Steps 9 to 11.

30. Reinstall the camshaft sprocket bolt and tighten the bolt to 74 ft. lbs. (100 Nm) plus 90 degrees (¼ turn) additional rotation.

31. Reinstall the timing chain damper and tighten the mounting bolts to 16 ft. lbs. (22 Nm).

32. Thoroughly clean all sealing surfaces.

33. Using the appropriate seal driver, install the seal into the front cover and lubricate the lip of the seal.

Exploded view of the timing chain and sprockets—3.8L (VIN 1 and K) engines

7922XG16

Balance shaft-to-camshaft and camshaft-to-crankshaft timing mark alignment—3.8L (VIN 1 and K) engines

7922XG17

34. Reinstall the front cover onto the engine using a new gasket. Reinstall the mounting bolts and tighten them to 22 ft. lbs. (30 Nm).

35. Reinstall the oil pan-to-front cover bolts and tighten them to 125 inch lbs. (14 Nm).

36. Reinstall the belt tensioner and tighten the bolts to 37 ft. lbs. (50 Nm).

37. Reinstall the alternator.

38. Reconnect the CKP sensor electrical connector.

39. Reinstall the CKP sensor shield.

40. Reinstall the crankshaft balancer onto the crankshaft.

41. Reinstall the crankshaft balancer bolt and draw the balancer into position. Tighten the bolt to 111 ft. lbs. (150 Nm) plus an additional 75 degrees.

42. Reinstall the engine mount bracket and tighten the mounting bolts to 65 ft. lbs. (87 Nm).

43. Reinstall the power steering pump and belt(s).

44. Position the torque axis mount in the vehicle so the lower mounting bracket slips around the two mounting bolts in the frame.

45. Reinstall the two torque axis mount through-bolts and nuts.

46. Tighten the torque axis mount-to-frame bolts to 52 ft. lbs. (70 Nm) and tighten the through-bolts to 65 ft. lbs. (87 Nm).

47. Remove the engine support fixture.

48. Reinstall the vacuum reservoir.

49. Reconnect the negative battery cable.

50. Refill the coolant system.

51. Start the vehicle and verify no leaks.

52. Road test the vehicle and ensure proper operation.

4.0L Engine

The following procedure covers removal and installation of the crankshaft sprocket, intermediate shaft sprocket, primary timing chain, left side secondary timing chain, right side secondary timing chain, left side cam sprockets, right side cam sprockets, primary timing chain tensioner, both secondary timing chain tensioners, and both timing chain guides.

The left and right side secondary timing chains can be removed with the engine in the vehicle. If the primary timing chain or intermediate shaft sprocket need to be replaced, the engine must be removed from the vehicle and supported on an engine stand.

➡**Setting the camshaft timing is neces-**sary whenever the cam drive system has been disturbed, meaning the relationship between any chain and sprocket has been lost. Correct timing exists when the crankshaft and intermediate shaft sprocket timing marks are in alignment and all four camshaft drive pins are perpendicular (90 degrees) to the cylinder head surface.

1. Before servicing the vehicle, refer to the precautions in the beginning of this section.

2. Disconnect the negative battery cable.

3. Remove the drive belt.

4. Remove the bolt securing the power steering hose.

5. Raise and safely support the vehicle.

6. For the left side secondary chain and sprocket, perform the following:

   a. Remove the right front wheel.

   b. Remove the two splash shields from the wheel well.

   c. Remove the flywheel cover and install a suitable flywheel holder.

   d. Remove the crankshaft balancer bolt.

   e. Support the engine cradle with a screw type jack and remove the three right-side engine cradle bolts.

   f. Disconnect the RSS sensor from the right control arm.

   g. Lower the cradle to gain access for the crankshaft damper puller.

   h. Using puller J-38416 or equivalent, remove the crankshaft damper.

   i. Remove the drive belt tensioner.

   j. Remove the drive belt idler pulley.

   k. Remove the front cover bolts.

7. Remove the front cover and gasket.

➡**The front cover gasket is reusable as long as it is not damaged.**

   a. Partially drain the coolant from the radiator.

   b. Disconnect the upper radiator hose at the water crossover.

   c. Label and disconnect the spark plug wires.

   d. Remove the right side fan.

   e. Disconnect the battery cable at the alternator and disconnect the cable harness at the cam cover.

   f. Disconnect the PCV fresh air tube from the cam cover.

   g. Remove the right and left torque struts.

   h. Remove the water pump pulley with tool J-38825 or equivalent.

   i. Remove the camshaft seal retainer screws and remove the seal.

   j. Disconnect the battery cable retainer at the front of the cam cover.

   k. Remove the cam cover screws and remove the cam cover by pivoting the entire cover around the water pump drive shaft. Continue moving the cover upward and pivoting so that the edge of the cover closely follows the left edge of the intake manifold cover.

➡**The cam cover gasket is reusable as long as it is not damaged.**

   l. Remove the left side secondary chain tensioner.

   m. Remove the left side chain guide. Access the upper chain guide mounting bolt through the hole in the cylinder head capped with the plastic plug.

   n. Remove the left side cam sprocket bolts and sprockets.

   o. Remove the secondary drive chain.

8. For the right side secondary chain and sprocket, perform the following:

   a. Disconnect the exhaust Y-pipe at the converter.

   b. Lower the vehicle.

   c. Remove the tower-to-tower brace.

   d. Detach the ICM wiring connectors and mounting bolts.

   e. Remove the ICM and the plug wires on the right bank.

   f. Disconnect the PCV valve.

   g. Remove the purge canister solenoid from the rear of the cover.

   h. Remove the cam cover screws.

   i. Safely support the front of the engine cradle and remove the two mounting bolts at the front of the cradle.

   j. Remove the right and left torque struts.

   k. Lower the engine cradle (or raise the vehicle) to provide clearance at the rear of the engine compartment.

   l. Remove the cam cover.

➡**The cam cover gasket is reusable as long as it is not damaged.**

   m. Remove the right side secondary chain tensioner.

   n. Remove the right side chain guide. Access the upper chain guide mounting bolt through the hole in the cylinder head capped with the plastic plug.

   o. Remove the right side cam sprocket bolts and cam sprockets.

9. Remove the secondary drive chain.

10. If only servicing the secondary

chains, proceed to Step 19 of the installation procedure.

11. Remove the engine.

12. Remove the intermediate shaft sprocket-to-intermediate shaft bolt, then remove the sprocket.

13. Slide the primary timing sprockets and primary chain off the engine.

To install:

➡**The following procedure must be followed to set the camshaft timing on the vehicle.**

14. Install the primary and secondary chain guide.

15. Rotate the crankshaft until the sprocket drive key is at the 1 o'clock position. Use tool J-39946 or the equivalent, to rotate the crankshaft.

16. Install the crankshaft sprocket and intermediate shaft sprocket in the primary timing chain so the timing marks are aligned. Install the assembly in position on the engine. The crankshaft sprocket key way will have to slide over the key on the crankshaft. If it is necessary to turn the crankshaft sprocket, the intermediate shaft sprocket will also have to be turned so the timing mark still lines up with the crankshaft sprocket.

17. Install the intermediate shaft sprocket-to-intermediate shaft bolt and tighten to 45 ft. lbs. (61 Nm).

18. Install the primary timing chain tensioner. Tighten the tensioner mounting bolts to 20 ft. lbs. (27 Nm).

19. Install a suitable flywheel holder to lock the crankshaft in position.

20. Install the secondary timing chain over the inner row of teeth on the intermediate shaft sprocket. Route the chain over the chain guide and install the exhaust cam sprocket so the **RE** (Right Head Exhaust) pin engages the sprocket notch. There should be no slack in the lower section of the timing chain and the cam drive pin **must** be perpendicular to the cylinder head face.

21. Install the intake cam sprocket into the chain so the sprocket notch **RI** (Right Head Intake) engages the cam and the camshaft drive pin remains perpendicular to the cylinder head face. A hex is cast into the camshafts behind the lobes for cylinder No. 1, so an open end wrench may be used to provide minor repositioning of the cams.

22. Loosely install the exhaust cam sprocket bolt and intake sprocket bolt.

23. Install the chain tensioner and tighten the mounting bolts to 20 ft. lbs. (27 Nm).

24. Tighten the camshaft sprocket bolts to 90 ft. lbs. (120 Nm).

25. Route the secondary timing chain for the left side over the outer row of intermediate sprocket teeth.

26. Install the secondary timing chain over the inner row of teeth on the intermediate shaft sprocket. Route the chain over the chain guide and install the exhaust cam sprocket so the **LE** (Left Head Exhaust) pin engages the sprocket notch. There should be no slack in the lower section of the timing chain and the cam drive pin **must** be perpendicular to the cylinder head face.

27. Install the intake cam sprocket into the chain so the sprocket notch **LI** (Left Head Intake) engages the cam and the camshaft drive pin remains perpendicular to the cylinder head face. A hex is cast into the camshafts behind the lobes for cylinder No. 2, so an open end wrench may be used to provide minor repositioning of the cams.

28. Loosely install the exhaust cam sprocket bolt and intake sprocket bolt.

29. Install the chain tensioner and tighten the mounting bolts to 20 ft. lbs. (27 Nm).

30. Tighten the camshaft sprocket bolts to 90 ft. lbs. (120 Nm).

➡**The RE cam sprocket must contain the Camshaft Position (CMP) sensor pick-up.**

1 **INTERMEDIATE SHAFT**
2 **PRIMARY CHAIN**
3 **INTERMEDIATE SHAFT SPROCKET**
4 **CRANKSHAFT SPROCKET KEY**
5 **SPROCKET**

Primary drive chain components—4.0L (VIN C) engine

7922XG25

31. Install the front cover gasket on the dowel pins on the block.

32. Install the front cover on the dowel pins and install the front cover mounting bolts. Tighten the bolts to 89 inch lbs. (10 Nm). Apply a dab of RTV to the split line between the upper and lower crankcase assemblies.

33. Install the drive belt idler pulley and tighten the mounting bolt to 35 ft. lbs. (47 Nm).

34. Install the drive belt tensioner and tighten the tensioner mounting nut to 35 ft. lbs. (47 Nm).

35. Install the crankshaft balancer using tool J-39344 or the equivalent.

36. Apply engine oil to the balancer bolt threads and tighten the bolt to 44 ft. lbs. (60 Nm) plus an additional 120 degree turn.

37. Raise the screw jack until the three cradle bolts can be installed. Tighten the bolts to 75 ft. lbs. (102 Nm).

38. Connect the RSS sensor.

39. Remove the flywheel holding tool and install the flywheel cover.

40. Install the wheel well splash shields.

41. Install the left cam cover as follows:

   a. Install the spark plugs and cam cover seals.

   b. Insert the intake cam through the hole in the cam cover and using fingers, guide the cam cover up over the edge of the cylinder head.

※※ WARNING

Use care to prevent the exposed section of the cam cover seal from being damaged by the edge of the cylinder head casting.

   c. Work the cover into position by allowing the top edge of the cover to follow the left side edge of the intake manifold.

   d. Install the cam cover screws and tighten to 7 ft. lbs. (10 Nm).

   e. Connect the battery cable retainer to the front of the cam cover.

   f. Connect the battery cable at the alternator.

   g. Lubricate the seal lips and install the camshaft seal to the end of the intake cam. Seal the screw threads with sealer.

   h. Install the water pump pulley with tool J-38825 or equivalent.

   i. Connect the PCV fresh air tube to the cam cover.

1 INTAKE POSITION
2 EXHAUST POSITION
3 TIMING MARKS

VIEW A

VIEW B

7922XG18

Primary and secondary timing mark alignment—4.0L (VIN C) engine

Please refer to Section 9 for electric cooling fan wiring schematics

j. Install the right side fan.

k. Connect the spark plug wires.

l. Connect the upper radiator hose to the water crossover.

m. Refill the cooling system.

42. Install the right cam cover as follows:

a. Install spark plug and cam cover seals.

b. Install the cam cover and tighten the screws to 7 ft. lbs. (10 Nm).

c. Raise the engine cradle into position and install and tighten the two mounting bolts to 75 ft. lbs. (100 Nm).

d. Install the right and left torque struts and tighten the retaining bolts as follows:

➡ **It is important during installation that the engine torque struts are not pre-loaded in their installed position. Adjustment is provided at the point the strut fastens to the core support bracket. Be sure this bolt is loose during assembly. Tighten to 45 ft. lbs. (60 Nm) as the final step of assembly.**

e. Tighten the strut bracket to cylinder head (M10) bolt: 35 ft. lbs. (50 Nm).

f. Tighten the strut bracket to cylinder head (M10) stud: 35 ft. lbs. (50 Nm).

Rotating tensioner release lever—4.0L (VIN C) engine

7922XG26

1 RELEASE TO FIRST CLICK
2 INSTALL LOCK PIN

7922XG27

Locking the tensioner into position—4.0L (VIN C) engine

g. Tighten the strut bracket to water manifold (M8) bolts: 20 ft. lbs. (25 Nm).

h. Tighten the strut bracket to cylinder head (M10) bolt: 35 ft. lbs. (50 Nm).

i. Tighten the strut to core support bracket bolt: 45 ft. lbs. (60 Nm) (see note above).

j. Install the screws retaining wiring harness to the cover.

k. Install the purge canister solenoid to the rear of the cover.

l. Connect the PCV valve.

m. Install the ICM and the spark plug wires on the right-bank.

n. Attach the ICM wiring connectors.

o. Install the tower-to-tower brace.

p. Raise and support the vehicle safely. Connect the exhaust Y-pipe to the converter and tighten the bolts to 20 ft. lbs. (25 Nm).

43. Connect the negative battery cable.

44. Start the engine. Check for leaks and inspect for proper operation.

FUEL SYSTEM

Fuel System Service Precautions

Safety is the most important factor when performing not only fuel system maintenance but any type of maintenance. Failure to conduct maintenance and repairs in a safe manner may result in serious personal injury or death. Maintenance and testing of the vehicle's fuel system components can be accomplished safely and effectively by adhering to the following rules and guidelines.

• To avoid the possibility of fire and personal injury, always disconnect the negative battery cable unless the repair or test procedure requires that battery voltage be applied.

• Always relieve the fuel system pressure prior to disconnecting any fuel system component (injector, fuel rail, pressure regulator, etc.), fitting or fuel line connection. Exercise extreme caution whenever relieving fuel system pressure to avoid exposing skin, face and eyes to fuel spray. Please be advised that fuel under pressure may penetrate the skin or any part of the body that it contacts.

• Always place a shop towel or cloth around the fitting or connection prior to loosening to absorb any excess fuel due to spillage. Ensure that all fuel spillage (should it occur) is quickly removed from engine surfaces. Ensure that all fuel soaked cloths or towels are deposited into a suitable waste container.

• Always keep a dry chemical (Class B) fire extinguisher near the work area.

• Do not allow fuel spray or fuel vapors to come into contact with a spark or open flame.

• Always use a back-up wrench when loosening and tightening fuel line connection fittings. This will prevent unnecessary stress and torsion to fuel line piping.

• Always replace worn fuel fitting O-rings with new. Do not substitute fuel hose or equivalent, where fuel pipe is installed.

Fuel System Pressure

RELIEVING

1. Before servicing the vehicle, refer to the precautions in the beginning of this section.

2. Disconnect the negative battery cable.

3. Remove the fuel filler cap from the filler neck.

4. Connect J-34730-1, or an equivalent fuel pressure gauge to the fuel pressure test port. Wrap a shop towel around the fitting while connecting the gauge to prevent fuel spillage.

5. Install the gauge bleed hose into a suitable container and open the valve to bleed the system.

6. Drain any remaining fuel from the gauge into the container and remove the gauge from the test port.

Fuel Filter

REMOVAL & INSTALLATION

1. Before servicing the vehicle, refer to the precautions in the beginning of this section.

2. Relieve the fuel system pressure using the recommended procedure.

3. Disconnect the negative battery cable.

4. Raise and safely support the vehicle.

5. Detach the quick connect fitting at the fuel filter inlet.

6. Disconnect the fuel filter outlet fitting from the fuel filter while holding the filter fitting with a back-up wrench.

7. Remove the fuel filter from the vehicle.

To install:

8. Install a new plastic retainer on the fuel inlet line.

9. Apply a drop of oil on the fuel filter inlet fitting and snap the fitting onto the fuel filter.

1. Fuel Feed Pipe
2. In-Line Fuel Filter
3. Fuel Return Pipe
4. Fuel Pump Flex Pipe
5. Integral Reservoir
6. Fuel Pipe Shut-off Adapters
7. Fuel Pressure Gauge
8. Fuel Pressure Connection
9. Fuel Rail
10. Fuel Pressure Regulator

9300XG07

Fuel system circuit showing the pressure test port on the supply rail—4.0L engine

10. Reconnect the fuel outlet line to the filter and while holding the filter with a back-up wrench tighten the line fitting to 22 ft. lbs. (30 Nm).

11. Lower the vehicle.

12. Pressurize the fuel system and verify no leaks.

Fuel Pump

REMOVAL & INSTALLATION

1. Before servicing the vehicle, refer to the precautions in the beginning of this section.

2. Relieve the fuel system pressure using the recommended procedure.

3. Disconnect the negative battery cable.

4. Drain the fuel tank with a hand held siphon until the level is less than ¼ full.

5. Working in the trunk, remove the spare tire cover, jack and spare tire.

6. Pull back the floor trunk liner.

7. Remove the cover from the fuel sender access cover.

8. Detach the quick connect fittings from the fuel sender assembly.

9. Detach the electrical connector from the fuel sender assembly.

✳✳ WARNING

When the lock-ring is removed from the fuel sender the sender assembly will spring up. Downward pressure should be kept on the assembly and slowly released to ensure the sender assembly does not get damaged.

10. Remove lock-ring from the fuel sender using J-39765, or an equivalent spanner wrench.

11. Slowly release the spring pressure on the sender.

✳✳ CAUTION

The reservoir bucket on the fuel sender assembly will be full of fuel

when it is removed from the tank. Be sure to have a catch pan nearby to drain the sender into.

12. Remove the sender assembly from the tank. It will have to be tilted slightly about half way out to be sure the fuel level float clears the side of the tank.

To install:

13. Install a new O-ring on top of the tank and carefully install the sender assembly into the tank.

14. Reinstall the retainer on top of the tank and compress the sender until the retainer can be engaged.

15. Lock the sender in place with J-39765, or the equivalent.

16. Reconnect the quick connect fittings to the fuel sender assembly.

17. Reconnect the electrical connector to the sender assembly.

18. Reconnect the negative battery cable.

19. Pressurize the fuel system and verify no leaks.

1 SUPPORT ASSEMBLY – FUEL SENDER
2 COVER ASSEMBLY – FUEL SENDER
3 FUEL PIPES (ABOVE COVER)
4 RESERVOIR – FUEL PUMP FUEL
5 SENSOR ASSEMBLY – FUEL LEVEL

7922XG19

Fuel pump and sending unit module assembly

20. Reinstall the fuel sender access panel.
21. Reposition the trunk liner.
22. Reinstall the spare tire, jack and spare tire cover.
23. Refill the fuel tank.

DRIVE TRAIN

Transaxle Assembly

REMOVAL & INSTALLATION

Riviera

1. Before servicing the vehicle, refer to the precautions in the beginning of this section.
2. Disconnect the negative battery cable.
3. Remove the air intake duct.
4. Disconnect the cruise control cable from the throttle body lever, disconnect the vacuum hose at the control servo and remove the servo from the engine.
5. Remove the nut from the shift linkage at the manual shaft on the transaxle. Remove the two linkage bracket bolts and remove the cable and bracket from the transaxle and position out of the way.

6. Disconnect the vacuum line from the modulator.
7. Detach the electrical connectors from the Park Neutral (P/N) switch, back-up light switch, transaxle harness and Vehicle Speed Sensor (VSS).
8. Remove the left-to-right exhaust manifold bolts.
9. Remove the vacuum reservoir.
10. Remove the heater hose retainer bracket.
11. Detach the Oxygen (O_2S) sensor connector.
12. Install an engine support fixture, J-28467-A, or the equivalent. Be sure the support fixture is tight and the weight of the powertrain is removed from the mounts.
13. Remove the upper transaxle-to-engine bolts.
14. Raise and safely support the vehicle.
15. Remove the front tire and wheel assemblies.
16. Remove the left side power steering rack mounting bolts.
17. Remove the left front splash shield.
18. Remove the cotter pins and castle nuts from the lower ball joints and using a suitable ball joint separator, disconnect the ball joints from the steering knuckles.
19. Remove the front lower air deflector.
20. Remove the power steering line retaining clamp from the frame.
21. Remove the remaining rack mounting bolt and raise the rack off its frame mount and support.
22. Remove the left and right transaxle mount through-bolts.
23. Remove the complete exhaust system.
24. Support the subframe assembly.
25. Remove the subframe mounting bolts and remove the subframe assembly.
26. Remove the torque converter cover mounting screws and remove the cover.
27. Matchmark the converter to the flywheel and remove the three converter mounting bolts.
28. Disconnect the starter.
29. Remove the starter.
30. Remove the halfshafts.
31. Support the transaxle with a suitable jack.
32. Remove the rear transaxle mount-to-bracket retaining nuts and remove the rear transaxle mount bracket from the vehicle.
33. Disconnect the rear spark plug wires from the plugs and route them out of the way.
34. Remove the transaxle filler tube.
35. Remove the right side exhaust manifold.
36. Remove the lower transaxle-to-engine mounting bolts.

37. Disconnect and cap the transaxle oil cooler lines from the transaxle.
38. Lower the transaxle from the vehicle.
To install:
39. Raise the transaxle assembly into the vehicle and guide the transaxle onto the engine alignment dowels.
40. Reconnect the upper and lower transaxle oil cooler lines.
41. Reinstall the transaxle-to-engine bolts and with all the bolts in place tighten them alternately an evenly to 55 ft. lbs. (75 Nm).
42. Reinstall the right side exhaust manifold and tighten the mounting bolts to 38 ft. lbs. (52 Nm).
43. Reinstall the transaxle filler tube.
44. Reconnect the spark plug wires to the rear plugs.
45. Reinstall the rear transaxle mount to the body and tighten the mounting bolts to 37 ft. lbs. (50 Nm), the transaxle mount-to-transaxle bolts to 55 ft. lbs. (75 Nm) and the mount-to-transaxle bracket nuts to 29 ft. lbs. (40 Nm).
46. Remove the transaxle jack.
47. Reinstall the halfshafts.
48. Reinstall the starter and attach the electrical connectors.
49. Be sure the matchmarks on the converter and flywheel are in alignment. Install the converter mounting bolts and tighten to 44 ft. lbs. (60 Nm).
50. Reinstall the flywheel cover and cover mounting bolts.
51. Raise the subframe into position and tighten the mounting bolts to 142 ft. lbs. (192 Nm).
52. Reinstall the exhaust system.
53. Reinstall the left transaxle mount-to-frame bolt and tighten to 63 ft. lbs. (85 Nm).
54. Reinstall the right transaxle mount-to-transaxle bolt and tighten to 75 ft. lbs. (102 Nm).
55. Lower the steering rack into position and install the through-bolt on the right side of the rack.
56. Reinstall the power steering line retaining bracket to the subframe.
57. Reconnect the ball joints to the steering knuckles and tighten the castle nuts to 41 ft. lbs. (55 Nm). If necessary tighten the nuts up to 60 degrees (⅙ turn) additional to align the cotter pin holes. NEVER loosen the nuts to make the holes align.
58. Reinstall the left side splash shield.
59. Reinstall the left side rack and pinion mounting bolts.
60. Reinstall the front tire and wheel assemblies and tighten the wheel nuts to 100 ft. lbs. (140 Nm).
61. Lower the vehicle.
62. Remove the engine support fixture.

63. Reconnect the O₂S sensor electrical connector.

64. Reinstall the heater hose retainer bracket.

65. Reinstall the vacuum reservoir.

66. Reinstall the right-to-left exhaust manifold mounting bolts.

67. Reconnect the electrical connectors to the P/N switch, back-up light switch, transaxle harness and Vehicle Speed Sensor (VSS).

68. Reconnect the vacuum line to the modulator.

69. Reconnect the shift cable to the manual shaft and install the cable mounting bracket. Tighten the manual shaft nut to 15 ft. lbs. (20 Nm).

70. Reinstall the cruise control servo, connect the vacuum line and linkage.

71. Reinstall the air inlet duct.

72. Reconnect the negative battery cable.

73. Refill the transaxle with fluid. Start the vehicle and check the fluid level again and top off as necessary.

74. Road test the vehicle and verify proper transaxle operation and no fluid leaks.

Aurora

1. Before servicing the vehicle, refer to the precautions in the beginning of this section.

2. Disconnect the negative battery cable.

3. Remove the nut from the shift linkage at the manual shaft on the transaxle. Remove the two linkage bracket bolts and remove the cable and bracket from the transaxle and position out of the way.

4. Detach the electrical connectors from the Park/Neutral (P/N) switch.

5. Install an engine support fixture, J-28467-A, or the equivalent. Be sure the support fixture is tight and the weight of the powertrain is removed from the mounts.

6. Drain the cooling system.

7. Disconnect the vacuum line at the brake booster.

8. Disconnect the transaxle vent hose.

9. Detach the Vehicle Speed Sensor (VSS) connector and power steering gear connector.

10. Disconnect and cap the upper transaxle oil cooler line from the radiator.

11. Disconnect and cap the lower transaxle oil cooler line from the transaxle.

12. Remove the retaining bracket nut for the cooler lines at the transaxle.

13. Disconnect the coolant bypass pipe from the thermostat housing and position out of the way.

14. Remove the left and right transaxle mount bolts.

15. Raise and safely support the vehicle.

16. Remove the left front tire and wheel assembly.

17. Remove the left front splash shield.

18. Remove the cotter pins and castle nuts from the outer tie rod end and using a suitable ball joint separator, disconnect the tie rod ends from the steering knuckles.

19. Remove the cotter pins and castle nuts from the lower ball joints and using a suitable ball joint separator, disconnect the ball joints from the steering knuckles.

20. Remove the halfshafts.

21. Remove the engine oil pan-to-transaxle bracket.

22. Remove the torque converter cover mounting screws and remove the cover.

23. Matchmark the converter to the flywheel and remove the three converter mounting bolts.

24. Remove the complete exhaust system.

25. Remove the exhaust manifold rear pipe.

26. Remove the steering rack-to-right transaxle mount bolts.

27. Remove the bolt from the right transaxle mount.

28. Remove the frame-to-right transaxle mount and remove the right side mount.

29. Remove the power steering line retaining clamp from the frame.

30. Remove the remaining rack mounting bolt and raise the rack off its frame mount and support.

31. Support the subframe assembly.

32. Remove the Knock Sensor (KS) shield.

33. Remove the engine-to-transaxle brace.

34. Remove the rear transaxle mount-to-bracket retaining nuts and remove the rear transaxle mount bracket from the vehicle.

35. Remove the right and left lower transaxle-to-engine bolts.

36. Remove the subframe mounting bolts and remove the subframe assembly.

37. Support the transaxle with a suitable jack.

38. Remove the remainder of the transaxle-to-engine bolts.

39. Lower the transaxle from the vehicle.

To install:

40. Raise the transaxle assembly into the vehicle and guide the transaxle onto the engine alignment dowels.

41. Reinstall the transaxle-to-engine bolts and with all the bolts in place tighten them alternately an evenly to 55 ft. lbs. (75 Nm).

42. Reinstall the rear transaxle mount to the body and tighten the mounting bolts to 37 ft. lbs. (50 Nm).

43. Reinstall the rear transaxle mount bracket to the transaxle and tighten the mounting bolts to 43 ft. lbs. (58 Nm).

44. Reinstall the engine-to-transaxle brace and tighten the brace mounting bolts to 35 ft. lbs. (47 Nm).

45. Reinstall the KS shield.

46. Reconnect the electrical connectors to the VSS and KS.

47. Be sure the matchmarks on the converter and flywheel are in alignment. Install the converter mounting bolts and tighten to 44 ft. lbs. (60 Nm).

48. Reinstall the flywheel cover and cover mounting bolts.

49. Reinstall the transaxle-to-oil pan brace.

50. Raise the subframe into position and tighten the mounting bolts to 142 ft. lbs. (192 Nm).

51. Reinstall the left transaxle mount-to-frame bolt and tighten to 63 ft. lbs. (85 Nm).

52. Lower the steering rack into position and install the through-bolt on the right side of the rack.

53. Reinstall the power steering line retaining bracket to the subframe.

54. Reinstall the right transaxle mount to the frame and tighten the mounting bolts to 54 ft. lbs. (73 Nm).

55. Reinstall the right transaxle mount-to-transaxle bolt and tighten to 81 ft. lbs. (110 Nm).

56. Reinstall the rear exhaust manifold pipe.

57. Reinstall the exhaust system.

58. Reinstall the halfshafts.

59. Reconnect the ball joints to the steering knuckles and tighten the castle nuts to 41 ft. lbs. (55 Nm). If necessary tighten the nuts up to 60 degrees (⅙ turn) additional to align the cotter pin holes. NEVER loosen the nuts to make the holes align.

60. Reconnect the tie rod ends to the steering knuckles and tighten the castle nuts to 52 ft. lbs. (70 Nm). If necessary tighten the nuts up to 60 degrees (⅙ turn) additional to align the cotter pin holes. NEVER loosen the nuts to make the holes align.

61. Reinstall the left side splash shield.

62. Reinstall the front tire and wheel assemblies and tighten the wheel nuts to 100 ft. lbs. (140 Nm).

63. Lower the vehicle.

64. Remove the engine support fixture.

65. Reconnect the coolant bypass pipe to the thermostat housing.

66. Reinstall the transaxle oil cooler line bracket and mounting bolt.

67. Reconnect the upper and lower transaxle oil cooler lines.

68. Reconnect the shift cable to the manual shaft and install the cable mounting bracket. Tighten the manual shaft nut to 15 ft. lbs. (20 Nm).

69. Reconnect the vacuum line to the brake booster.

70. Reconnect the transaxle vent.

71. Refill the cooling system.

72. Reconnect the negative battery cable.

73. Refill the transaxle with fluid. Start the vehicle and check the fluid level again and top off as necessary. Service this vehicle with DEXRON® II or DEXRON® IIE automatic transmission fluid.

74. Road test the vehicle and verify proper transaxle operation and no fluid leaks.

Halfshaft

REMOVAL & INSTALLATION

1. Before servicing the vehicle, refer to the precautions in the beginning of this section.

2. Raise and safely support the vehicle.

3. Remove the tire and wheel assembly.

4. Remove the sway bar link kit.

5. Remove the cotter pin and castle nut from the lower ball joint. Using a suitable ball joint separator, J-36226 or the equivalent, disconnect the ball stud from the steering knuckle.

6. If removing the right halfshaft turn the wheel to the left and if removing the left halfshaft turn the wheel to the right.

7. Using a suitable prying tool, pry the lower control arm down away from the steering knuckle.

8. Insert a drift punch through the caliper and into the rotor cooling fins. Remove the hub nut from the end of the halfshaft.

9. Separate the halfshaft from the hub using J-28733-B, or an equivalent puller. Once the halfshaft is clear of the knuckle assembly, swing the strut assembly toward the rear of the vehicle.

10. Separate the halfshaft from the transaxle using J-33008 and J-2619–01, or an equivalent slide hammer and adapter.

11. Remove the halfshaft.

To install:

12. If installing the right side halfshaft, install J-37292-B, or an equivalent tear away axle seal protector over the seal.

13. Install the halfshaft into the transaxle and seat in place by inserting a suitable

1 TRANSAXLE
2 RH DRIVE AXLE

5 TO 7 O'CLOCK HANDLE POSITION

7922XG20

Installing the right side axle with the tear away seal protector

prybar in the groove in the inboard joint and tapping the joint into place. Be sure the joint is properly seated by grasping the inboard joint and making sure it wont pull out of the transaxle. DO NOT pull on the shaft itself or the inboard joint can become damaged.

14. Insert the halfshaft through the hub and install the washer and mounting nut. Insert a drift through the caliper and into the rotor cooling fins and tighten the mounting nut to 107 ft. lbs. (145 Nm).

15. Reconnect the ball joint to the steering knuckle and tighten the castle nut to 41 ft. lbs. (55 Nm). If necessary to align the cotter pin holes rotate the nut up to 60 degrees (⅙ turn) additional. NEVER loosen the nut to align the holes.

16. Install a new cotter pin.

17. Install the sway bar link kit and tighten the bolt to 13 ft. lbs. (17 Nm).

18. Remove the tear away seal protector. Be sure no pieces of the tool remain in the transaxle.

19. Install the tire and wheel assembly and tighten the wheel nuts to 100 ft. lbs. (140 Nm).

20. Lower the vehicle.

STEERING AND SUSPENSION

Air Bag

✳✳ CAUTION

Some vehicles are equipped with the Supplemental Inflatable Restraint (SIR) or air bag system. The SIR system must be disabled before performing service on or around SIR system components, steering column, instrument panel components, wiring and sensors. Failure to follow safety and disabling procedures could result in

FRT

1 CONNECTOR, SIR
2 BRACKET, MULTIUSE MODULE
3 CONNECTOR POSITION ASSURANCE (CPA)
4 CONNECTOR, STEERING COLUMN WIRING HARNESS

7922XG21

SRS 2-way connector location—driver's side

accidental air bag deployment, possible personal injury and unnecessary SIR system repairs.

PRECAUTIONS

Several precautions must be observed when handling the inflator module to avoid accidental deployment and possible personal injury.

• Never carry the inflator module by the wires or connector on the underside of the module.

• When carrying a live inflator module, hold securely with both hands, and ensure that the bag and trim cover are pointed away.

• Place the inflator module on a bench or other surface with the bag and trim cover facing up.

• With the inflator module on the bench, never place anything on or close to the module which may be thrown in the event of an accidental deployment.

DISARMING

1. Turn the steering wheel so the vehicle wheels are pointing straight ahead.
2. Turn the ignition key to the **LOCK** position and remove the key.
3. Remove the AIR BAG fuse from the fuse block.

4. Remove the left side sound insulator.
5. Detach the Connector Position Assurance (CPA) and yellow 2-way SIR connector at the multi-use bracket near the base of the steering column. The driver's side air bag is now disabled.
6. Remove the right side sound insulator.
7. Detach the Connector Position Assurance (CPA) and yellow 2-way SIR connector at the DERM mounting bracket. The passenger's side air bag is now disabled.

ARMING

After the necessary repairs are made, re-enable the air bag system as follows:

1. Be sure the ignition is locked and the key is removed.
2. Attach the yellow 2-way SIR connector and Connector Position Assurance (CPA) at the DERM mounting bracket.
3. Install the right side sound insulator.
4. Attach the yellow 2-way SIR connector and Connector Position Assurance (CPA) at the multi-use bracket at the base of the column.
5. Install the left side sound insulator.
6. Install the AIR BAG fuse.
7. Turn the ignition switch to the **RUN** position and verify the AIR BAG light flashes 7 times, then shuts off.

1 MODULE, INFLATOR
2 BRACKET, MULTIUSE
3 CONNECTOR, SIR

7922XG22

SRS 2-way connector location—passenger's side

Power Rack and Pinion Steering Gear

REMOVAL & INSTALLATION

1. Before servicing the vehicle, refer to the precautions in the beginning of this section.
2. Lock the steering wheel in the straight ahead position.
3. Raise and safely support the vehicle.
4. Remove the tire and wheel assembly.
5. Remove the cotter pin and castle nut from the outer tie rod end ball stud.
6. Back off the inner tie rod jam nut ½ turn.
7. Using a suitable puller, J-24319–01 or the equivalent, separate the outer tie rod end from the steering knuckle.
8. Disconnect the exhaust pipe from the rear manifold and remove the intermediate pipe hangers. Lower the exhaust system to provide clearance.
9. Remove the wheel well fasteners and fold back the inner wheel well panel to provide clearance for rack and pinion removal.
10. Remove the pinch bolt from the intermediate shaft at the rack and pinion unit and separate the shaft from the stub shaft on the rack and pinion unit.
11. Unsnap and remove the power steering unit heat shield.
12. Detach the Magnasteer® electrical connector.
13. Disconnect and cap the power steering lines from the rack and pinion unit.
14. Remove the rack and pinion mounting bolts.
15. Support the rear of the subframe. Remove the two rear subframe mounting bolts and lower the frame assembly. Only lower the frame enough to remove the rack and pinion assembly.
16. Remove the rack and pinion assembly through the right side wheel well.

To install:

17. Install the rack and pinion unit through the right side wheel well.
18. Loosely install the three mounting bolts.
19. Raise the subframe into position and tighten the frame mounting bolts to 142 ft. lbs. (192 Nm). Remove the support.
20. Tighten the rack and pinion mounting bolts in sequence to 48 ft. lbs. (65 Nm). Start with the vertically installed bolt closest to the pinion housing and work toward the passenger side of the vehicle.

21. Reconnect the power steering hoses to the rack and pinion unit and tighten the fittings to 20 ft. lbs. (27 Nm).

22. Reconnect the Magnasteer® electrical connector.

23. Reinstall the rack and pinion heat shield.

24. Reconnect the intermediate shaft to the rack and pinion stub shaft and tighten the pinch bolt to 35 ft. lbs. (47 Nm).

25. Reconnect the tie rod end to the steering knuckle and tighten the castle nut to 35 ft. lbs. (47 Nm). If necessary to align the cotter pin holes, tighten the nut up to 60 degrees additional rotation. NEVER loosen the castle nut to align the cotter pin holes.

26. Install a new cotter pin.

27. Reconnect the exhaust pipe to the exhaust manifold and connect the intermediate pipe hangers.

28. Reinstall the wheel well molding.

29. Reinstall the tire and wheel assembly and tighten the wheel nuts to 100 ft. lbs. (140 Nm).

30. Lower the vehicle.

➡ **Whenever the vehicle sub-frame is removed or lowered, the front wheel alignment should be checked.**

31. Refill and bleed the power steering system. Verify no leaks.

32. Check the front end alignment and adjust as necessary.

Strut

REMOVAL & INSTALLATION

Front

1. Before servicing the vehicle, refer to the precautions in the beginning of this section.

2. Disconnect the negative battery cable.

3. Raise and safely support the vehicle.

4. Remove the tire and wheel assembly.

5. Disconnect the ABS wheel speed sensor.

6. Remove the ABS speed sensor bracket from the strut.

7. If removing the left side strut, disconnect the brake line bracket from the strut.

8. Support the steering knuckle so when the strut is disconnected the brake line does not get stretched.

9. Scribe a mark on the strut referenc-

1 NUTS, 47 N•m (35 LB. FT.)
2 WASHER
3 NUTS, 185 N•m (136 LB. FT.)
4 KNUCKLE
5 BOLT
6 STRUT

7922XG23

Exploded view of the upper and lower strut mounting components

ing the lower strut bracket to the steering knuckle.

10. Remove the nut and through-bolts from the lower strut bracket.

11. From under the hood, remove the three upper strut plate mounting nuts and washers,

12. Remove the strut from the vehicle.

13. Place the strut in an approved fixture to disassemble the coil spring from the strut. With the spring compressed, hold the strut shaft from turning using a socket and remove the 24mm strut shaft nut. Relieve the pressure on the spring and separate the front coil spring from the strut.

To install:

14. If the spring and strut were disassembled, assemble using an approved fixture.

15. Position the strut in the vehicle guiding the upper strut plate studs into the body and loosely install the nuts.

16. Reinstall the lower strut through-bolts. With the matchmarks in alignment, tighten the nuts to 136 ft. lbs. (185 Nm).

17. Remove the support from the steering knuckle.

18. Reconnect the brake line to the strut, if removed.

19. Install the speed sensor bracket on the strut.

20. Reconnect the ABS sensor.

21. Reinstall the tire and wheel assembly and tighten the wheel nuts to 100 ft. lbs. (140 Nm).

22. Lower the vehicle.

23. Tighten the upper strut plate mounting nuts to 35 ft. lbs. (47 Nm).

24. Check the front end alignment and adjust as necessary.

25. Reconnect the negative battery cable.

Shock Absorber

REMOVAL & INSTALLATION

Rear

1. Before servicing the vehicle, refer to the precautions in the beginning of this section.

2. Raise and safely support the vehicle.

3. Remove the rear tire and wheel assembly.

4. Support the lower control arm at such a height that the upper shock bolts will still be accessible.

5. Disconnect the Electronic Level Control (ELC) air tube from the shock.

6. Remove the two bolts from under the control arm securing the lower shock mount.

7. From inside the trunk, remove the trunk trim panel to access the upper shock mount bolts.

8. Remove the upper shock cap.

9. Remove the two nuts from the upper shock mount and remove the reinforcement.

10. Remove the shock from the vehicle.

To install:

11. Install the shock in the vehicle.

12. Reinstall the reinforcement and upper shock mounting nuts. Tighten the mounting nuts to 15 ft. lbs. (20 Nm).

13. Reinstall the upper shock cap and reposition the inner trunk trim.

14. Extend the shock and install the lower shock mounting bolts and tighten to 18 ft. lbs. (24 Nm).

15. Reconnect the ELC air tube to the shock.

16. Raise the vehicle off the support or jack, and remove the support/jack.

17. Reinstall the tire and wheel assembly and tighten the wheel nuts to 100 ft. lbs. (140 Nm).

18. Lower the vehicle.

VIEW A

1	SHOCK
2	U–NUTS
3	CONTROL ARM
4	BOLTS 24 N•m (18 LB. FT.)
5	COVER
6	NUTS 20 N•m (15 LB. FT.)
7	REINFORCEMENT
8	MOUNT, UPPER

7922XG34

Exploded view of the rear shock mounting

Coil Spring

REMOVAL & INSTALLATION

Front

For front coil spring removal and installation, please refer to the front strut procedure.

Rear

1. Before servicing the vehicle, refer to the precautions in the beginning of this section.

2. Raise and safely support the vehicle.

3. Remove the rear tire and wheel assembly.

4. Support the lower control arm with a suitable screw type jack.

5. Disconnect the ELC air tube from the shock absorber.

6. Remove the two lower shock absorber-to-control arm bolts.

7. Remove the cotter pin and castle nut from the adjustment link outer ball stud.

8. Using J-24319-B, or an equivalent ball joint separator, disconnect the ball stud from the knuckle.

9. Lower the control arm until the arm bottoms out on the rear suspension support.

10. Using a suitable prying tool, pry under the lower spring insulator to unseat it from the control arm and remove the insulator and coil spring.

11. Remove the upper spring insulator if needed.

To install:

12. Reinstall the upper spring insulator if removed, and engage the retainer on the back of the insulator in the upper mount hole.

13. Install the coil spring and lower insulator in the vehicle and seat the lower insulator in the control arm hole.

14. Raise the control arm until the shock bolts can be installed. Tighten the two bolts to 18 ft. lbs. (24 Nm).

15. Remove the jack.

16. Reconnect the adjustment link ball stud to the knuckle and tighten the castle nut to 88 inch lbs. (10 Nm) plus 180 degrees (½ turn) additional rotation. If necessary to align the cotter pin holes tighten the nut up to 60 degrees (⅙ turn) more. NEVER loosen the castle nut to align the cotter pin holes.

17. Install a new cotter pin.

18. Reconnect the ELC air tube to the shock absorber.

19. Reinstall the tire and wheel assembly and tighten the wheel nuts to 100 ft. lbs. (140 Nm).

20. Lower the vehicle.

1 JOUNCE BUMPER
2 SPRING
3 LOWER SPRING INSULATOR
4 CONTROL ARM
5 RETAINER

7922XG35

Exploded view of the rear coil spring and related components

Lower Ball Joint

REMOVAL & INSTALLATION

Ball joints must be replaced if any looseness is detected in the joint or if the ball joint seal is cut. To inspect the ball joints, raise the front of the vehicle allowing the suspension to hang free. Grasp the tire at the top and bottom and move the top of the tire in an in-and-out motion. Check for any horizontal movement of the knuckle relative to the control arm. If movement is in the wheel bearing, the bearing and hub must be replaced. If the ball joint stud is disconnected from the knuckle and looseness can be detected or if the ball stud can be twisted in its socket using finger pressure, replace the ball joint.

Ball joint tightness in the knuckle boss should also be checked. This may be done by shaking the wheel and feeling for movement of the stud end or nut at the knuckle boss. Worn or damaged ball joints and knuckles must be replaced.

1. Before servicing the vehicle, refer to the precautions in the beginning of this section.

2. Raise and safely support the vehicle.

3. Remove the front tire and wheel assembly.

4. Remove the sway bar link kit. Take note of the positions of the washers and insulators for installation purposes.

5. Remove the cotter pin and castle nut from the lower ball joint and using a suitable ball joint separator, J-36226 or the equivalent separate the ball joint from the steering knuckle.

6. Using a ½ in. drill bit, drill the heads off of the three rivets securing the lower ball joint to the control arm. With the rivet heads removed, drive the bodies of the rivets out of the control arm using a suitable punch.

7. Remove the ball joint.

To install:

8. Position the lower ball joint on the control arm and install the three mounting bolts so the bolt threads point down. Install the mounting nuts and tighten to 50 ft. lbs. (68 Nm).

9. Reconnect the lower ball joint to the steering knuckle and tighten the castle nut to 41 ft. lbs. (55 Nm). If necessary tighten the castle nut up to 60 degrees (⅙ turn) additional rotation to align the cotter pin holes. NEVER loosen the nut to make the alignment. Install a new cotter pin.

1 PIN
2 NUT, BALL JOINT TO KNUCKLE; TIGHTEN TO 10 N·m (88 LB. IN.) THEN TIGHTEN 2 FLATS TO 55 N·m (41 LB. FT.), MIN.
3 KNUCKLE
4 BALL JOINT MOUNTING BOLTS MUST FACE DOWN
5 CONTROL ARM
6 BALL JOINT MOUNTING NUTS 68 N·m (50 LB. FT.)
7 SERVICE BALL JOINT

7922XG24

Exploded view the lower ball joint and replacement mounting bolts and nuts

10. Install the sway bar link kit and tighten the mounting nut to 13 ft. lbs. (17 Nm).

11. Install the tire and wheel assembly and tighten the wheel nuts to 100 ft. lbs. (140 Nm).

12. Lower the vehicle.

Wheel Bearings

ADJUSTMENT

The wheel bearings are not adjustable. If the wheel bearings are defective, the hub and bearing assembly must be replaced.

REMOVAL & INSTALLATION

Front

The front wheel bearings are not serviced separately. If the front wheel bearings are defective, the hub and bearing assembly must be replaced.

1. Before servicing the vehicle, refer to the precautions in the beginning of this section.

2. Disconnect the negative battery cable.

3. Raise and safely support the vehicle.

4. Remove the tire and wheel assembly.

5. Lubricate the threads on the drive axle with clean engine oil.

6. Install a drift punch through the caliper and into the brake rotor cooling fins. This keeps the hub from turning when removing the hub nut. Remove the hub nut from the drive axle.

7. Remove the caliper mounting bolts and remove the caliper from the steering knuckle. Support the caliper out of the way. DO NOT allow the brake hose to support the weight of the caliper.

8. Remove the brake rotor.

9. Disconnect the ABS sensor and unclip the sensor from the backing plate.

10. Remove the three hub and bearing mounting bolts and remove the backing plate.

11. Using axle puller J-28733 or equivalent hub puller, separate the hub and bearing assembly from the halfshaft.

12. Remove the hub and bearing assembly.

13. If the steering knuckle is also to be removed, remove the cotter pin and castle

nut from the outer tie rod end. Using a puller J-24319-B or equivalent, separate the tie rod end from the steering knuckle.

14. Scribe matchmarks on the steering knuckle and strut for reference on installation.

15. Remove the cotter pin and castle nut from the lower ball joint and separate the ball joint from the steering knuckle using J-36226, or the equivalent.

16. Remove the two strut through-bolt nuts and remove the through-bolts.

17. Lift the steering knuckle off of the lower ball joint.

To install:

18. Install the steering knuckle onto the lower ball joint and tighten the castle nut to 41 ft. lbs. (55 Nm). If necessary to align the cotter pin holes tighten the nut up to 60 degrees additional. NEVER loosen the nut to align the holes. Install a new cotter pin.

19. Line up the lower strut bracket with the steering knuckle and install the through-bolts and nuts. With the matchmarks in alignment tighten the strut through-bolts to 136 ft. lbs. (185 Nm).

20. Reconnect the outer tie rod end to the steering knuckle and tighten the castle nut to 35 ft. lbs. (48 Nm). If necessary to align the cotter pin holes tighten the nut up to 60 degrees (⅙ turn) additional rotation. NEVER loosen the nut to align the holes. Install a new cotter pin.

21. Insert the ABS sensor wire through the opening in the steering knuckle and slide the axle shaft into the splined opening of the hub and bearing assembly.

22. Install a new axle nut and draw the hub and bearing assembly in to place.

23. Reinstall the backing plate and install the three mounting bolts. Tighten the bolts alternately and evenly to 70 ft. lbs. (95 Nm).

24. Reconnect the ABS sensor to the backing plate and attach the wiring harness connector.

25. Reinstall the brake rotor.

26. Reinstall the caliper on the steering knuckle and tighten the mounting bolts to 38 ft. lbs. (51 Nm).

27. Insert a drift punch through the caliper and into the brake rotor cooling fins and tighten the axle nut to 107 ft. lbs. (145 Nm).

28. Reinstall the tire and wheel assembly and tighten the wheel nuts to 100 ft. lbs. (140 Nm).

29. Lower the vehicle.

1	DUST SHIELD	4	HUB AND BEARING
2	WHEEL SPEED SENSOR CONNECTOR	5	NUT, DRIVE AXLE, 145 N•m (107 LB. FT.)
3	STEERING KNUCKLE	6	RETAINING BOLT, 95 N•m (75 LB. FT.)

7922XG36

Exploded view of the front hub mounting and related components

Turn to Section 6 for brake system applications

30. Pump the brakes to obtain a firm pedal before attempting to move the vehicle.

31. Check the front end alignment and adjust as necessary.

32. Reconnect the negative battery cable.

Rear

The rear wheel bearings are not serviced separately. If the rear wheel bearings are defective, the hub and bearing assembly must be replaced.

1. Before servicing the vehicle, refer to the precautions in the beginning of this section.

2. Disconnect the negative battery cable.

3. Raise and safely support the vehicle.

4. Remove the tire and wheel assembly.

5. Remove the caliper mounting bracket bolts and remove the caliper and bracket assembly from the brake rotor. Support the assembly out of the way. DO NOT allow the brake hose to support the weight of the caliper and bracket.

6. Remove the brake rotor.

7. Detach the ABS sensor electrical connector.

8. Remove the four hub assembly mounting bolts and remove the hub and bearing assembly along with the backing plate from the rear control arm.

To install:

9. Install the hub and bearing assembly along with the backing plate onto the control arm and loosely install the mounting bolts.

1 BOLT
2 HUB & BEARING
3 BRAKE SHIELD
4 REAR SUSPENSION SUPPORT ASSEMBLY
5 CONTROL ARM

7922XG37

Exploded view of the rear hub mounting and related components

10. Be sure the ABS sensor is properly routed and connect the ABS sensor harness.

11. Tighten the hub and bearing mounting bolts alternately and evenly to 52 ft. lbs. (70 Nm).

12. Reinstall the brake rotor.

13. Reinstall the caliper and bracket assembly and tighten the bracket bolts to 35 ft. lbs. (48 Nm).

14. Reinstall the tire and wheel assembly and tighten the wheel nuts to 100 ft. lbs. (140 Nm).

15. Lower the vehicle.

16. Reconnect the negative battery cable.

GENERAL MOTORS CORPORATION—J BODY

Chevrolet-Cavalier • **Pontiac**-Sunfire

33

PRECAUTIONS

Before servicing any vehicle, please be sure to read all of the following precautions, which deal with personal safety, prevention of component damage, and important points to take into consideration when servicing a motor vehicle:

• Never open, service or drain the radiator or cooling system when the engine is hot; serious burns can occur from the steam and hot coolant.

• Observe all applicable safety precautions when working around fuel. Whenever servicing the fuel system, always work in a well-ventilated area. Do not allow fuel spray or vapors to come in contact with a spark, open flame, or excessive heat (a hot drop light, for example). Keep a dry chemical fire extinguisher near the work area. Always keep fuel in a container specifically designed for fuel storage; also, always properly seal fuel containers to avoid the possibility of fire or explosion. Refer to the additional fuel system precautions later in this section.

• Fuel injection systems often remain pressurized, even after the engine has been turned **OFF**. The fuel system pressure must be relieved before disconnecting any fuel lines. Failure to do so may result in fire and/or personal injury.

• Brake fluid often contains polyglycol ethers and polyglycols. Avoid contact with the eyes and wash your hands thoroughly after handling brake fluid. If you do get brake fluid in your eyes, flush your eyes with clean, running water for 15 minutes. If eye irritation persists, or if you have taken brake fluid internally, IMMEDIATELY seek medical assistance.

• The EPA warns that prolonged contact with used engine oil may cause a number of skin disorders, including cancer! You should make every effort to minimize your exposure to used engine oil. Protective gloves should be worn when changing oil.

Wash your hands and any other exposed skin areas as soon as possible after exposure to used engine oil. Soap and water, or waterless hand cleaner should be used.

• All new vehicles are now equipped with an air bag system, often referred to as a Supplemental Restraint System (SRS) or Supplemental Inflatable Restraint (SIR) system. The system must be disabled before performing service on or around system components, steering column, instrument panel components, wiring and sensors. Failure to follow safety and disabling procedures could result in accidental air bag deployment, possible personal injury and unnecessary system repairs.

• Always wear safety goggles when working with, or around, the air bag system. When carrying a non-deployed air bag, be sure the bag and trim cover are pointed away from your body. When placing a non-deployed air bag on a work surface, always face the bag and trim cover upward, away from the surface. This will reduce the motion of the module if it is accidentally deployed. Refer to the additional air bag system precautions later in this section.

• Clean, high quality brake fluid from a sealed container is essential to the safe and proper operation of the brake system. You should always buy the correct type of brake fluid for your vehicle. If the brake fluid becomes contaminated, completely flush the system with new fluid. Never reuse any brake fluid. Any brake fluid that is removed from the system should be discarded. Also, do not allow any brake fluid to come in contact with a painted surface; it will damage the paint.

• Never operate the engine without the proper amount and type of engine oil; doing so WILL result in severe engine damage.

• Timing belt maintenance is extremely important! Many models utilize an interference-type, non-freewheeling engine. If the timing belt breaks, the valves in the cylinder head may strike the pistons, causing potentially serious (also time-consuming and

expensive) engine damage. Refer to the maintenance interval charts in the front of this manual for the recommended replacement interval for the timing belt, and to the timing belt section for belt replacement and inspection.

• Disconnecting the negative battery cable on some vehicles may interfere with the functions of the on-board computer system(s) and may require the computer to undergo a relearning process once the negative battery cable is reconnected.

• When servicing drum brakes, only dissemble and assemble one side at a time, leaving the remaining side intact for reference.

• Only an MVAC-trained, EPA-certified automotive technician should service the A/C system or its components.

ENGINE REPAIR

Ignition Timing

ADJUSTMENT

Ignition timing is controlled by the PCM. No adjustment is necessary or possible.

Engine Assembly

REMOVAL & INSTALLATION

2.2L Engine

1. Before servicing the vehicle, refer to the precautions in the beginning of this section.
2. Relieve the fuel system pressure.
3. Disconnect the negative, then the positive battery cables.
4. Drain the cooling system into a suitable container.

9300YG01

Exploded view of the upper engine mount—2.2L engine

5. Remove the throttle body air inlet duct.

6. Remove the battery from the vehicle.

7. Remove the air cleaner assembly.

8. Remove the upper radiator.

9. Disconnect the vacuum hose from power brake booster.

10. Remove the alternator upper brace and disconnect the wiring from the alternator.

11. Tag and disconnect the electrical wiring from the following components:

• Oxygen (O2S) sensor
• Fuel injector harness
• Idle Air Control (IAC)
• Throttle Position (TP) sensor
• Engine Coolant Temperature (ECT) sender
• Park/Neutral (P/N) switch
• TCC solenoid
• Transaxle shift solenoid
• Transaxle ground
• Manifold Absolute Pressure (MAP) sensor
• Exhaust Gas Recirculation (EGR) valve
• Cooling fan

12. If equipped, properly discharge and recover the refrigerant from the A/C system.

13. Disconnect the compressor-to-condenser and accumulator lines.

14. Remove the slave cylinder from the transaxle, if equipped with a manual transaxle.

15. Disconnect and cap the fuel lines.

16. Disconnect the shift linkage from the transaxle bracket.

17. Disconnect the control cables from the throttle body lever and remove the cable bracket from the rocker arm cover and intake manifold.

18. Disconnect and cap the power steering lines.

19. Install an engine support fixture, J-28467, or the equivalent.

20. Safely raise and support the vehicle.

21. Drain the engine oil.

22. Remove the front tire and wheel assemblies.

23. Remove the right and left inner fender splash shields.

24. Disconnect the front exhaust pipe from manifold and remove the front exhaust pipe.

25. Tag and detach the following electrical connectors from the lower engine components:

• Ignition assembly
• Starter
• Vehicle Speed Sensor (VSS)
• Transaxle ground wire

26. Remove the flywheel cover.

27. Remove the lower radiator hose.

28. Disconnect the heater hoses from the heater core pipes.

29. Disconnect the transaxle cooler lines at the radiator.

30. Remove the mounting bolt from the lower engine strut at the suspension crossmember.

31. Detach both front ABS wheel sensor connectors and unfasten the harnesses from the suspension crossmember.

32. Remove the cotter pins and castle nuts from the lower ball joints, then separate the joints from the steering knuckles.

33. Remove the suspension crossmembers.

34. Disconnect the halfshafts from the transaxle and support out of the way.

35. Position a suitable table under the engine and transaxle assembly.

36. Lower the vehicle until the powertrain assembly is on the table.

37. Remove the transaxle-to-frame mount bolts.

38. Remove the intermediate bracket from the right engine mount support bracket.

39. Remove the engine support fixture.

40. Raise the vehicle, leaving the powertrain assembly on the table. When raising the vehicle, take it up slowly and verify that no lines are still connected to the powertrain assembly.

41. Remove the torque converter-to-flywheel bolts and transaxle-to-engine mounting bolts and remove the transaxle from the engine.

To install:

42. Install the transaxle on the engine and tighten the mounting bolts to 68 ft. lbs. (93 Nm).

43. Install flywheel-to-converter bolts and tighten to 46 ft. lbs. (62 Nm).

44. Position the engine on the table and lower the vehicle until the engine is in the engine bay.

45. Install an engine support fixture, J-28467, or the equivalent.

46. Raise and safely support the vehicle and remove the engine table.

47. Connect the transaxle cooler lines to the radiator.

48. Attach the heater hoses to the heater core outlet pipes.

49. Install the lower radiator hose.

9300YG02

Exploded view of the lower engine mount and strut—2.2L engine

Legend

(1) Cylinder Block
(2) Flywheel
(3) Flywheel Retainer
(4) Flywheel Bolt
(5) Clutch Pressure Plate Bolt
(6) Clutch Pressure Plate Washer
(7) Clutch Pressure Plate
(8) Clutch Disc
(9) Oil Pump Drive Bolt
(10) Oil Pump Drive
(11) Oil Pump Drive Shaft
(12) Oil Pump Drive Shaft Retainer
(13) Oil Pump
(14) Crankshaft Rear Oil Seal
(15) Crankshaft
(16) Crankshaft Bearing
(17) Crankshaft Thrust Bearing
(18) Main Bearing Cap
(19) Main Bearing Cap
(20) Crankshaft Bearing Cap Bolt
(21) Oil Pan Stud
(22) Connecting Rod Nut
(23) Oil Pan Bolt
(24) Connecting Rod Nut

(25) Oil Pan Drain Plug Gasket
(26) Oil Pan Drain Plug
(27) Oil Pan Nut
(28) Oil Pan
(29) Oil Pan Rear Seal
(30) Crankshaft Pulley Bolt
(31) Crankshaft Pulley Hub Bolt
(32) Crankshaft Pulley Hub Bolt Washer
(33) Crankshaft Pulley
(34) Bracket Bolt
(35) Starter Motor Bracket Nut
(36) Starter Motor Bracket Nut
(37) Starter Motor Bracket
(38) Starter Motor
(39) Starter Motor Shim
(40) Starter Motor Bolt
(41) Starter Motor Bolt
(42) Crankshaft Pulley Hub
(43) Crankshaft Front Oil Seal
(44) Crankcase Front Cover Bolt
(45) Crankcase Front Cover
(46) Timing Chain
(47) Crankshaft Sprocket
(48) Camshaft Sprocket

Exploded view of the crankshaft and related components—2.2L engine

9300YG06

50. Connect the engine mount support bracket to the intermediate bracket and tighten the bolts to 96 ft. lbs. (103 Nm).

51. Install the transaxle mount-to-body bolts and tighten to 40 ft. lbs. (54 Nm).

52. Connect the halfshafts to the transaxle.

53. Install the suspension crossmembers and control arms in the vehicle and tighten the mounting bolts to 89 ft. lbs. (120 Nm).

54. Connect the lower ball joints to the steering knuckles and tighten the mounting bolts to 48 ft. lbs. (65 Nm) and install 2 new cotter pins.

55. Attach the front ABS wheel speed sensors to the harness connector and the subframe clips.

56. Connect the engine strut to the suspension support and tighten the mounting bolt to 89 ft. lbs. (120 Nm).

57. Install the transaxle cover.

58. Attach the following electrical connectors to the lower engine components:
- Ignition assembly
- Starter
- Vehicle Speed Sensor (VSS)
- Transaxle ground wire

59. Install the front exhaust pipe and tighten the pipe-to-manifold bolts to 22 ft. lbs. (30 Nm).

60. Install the left and right inner fender splash shields.

61. Install the front tire and wheel assemblies and tighten to 100 ft. lbs. (140 Nm).

62. Lower the vehicle.

63. Attach the power steering lines to the pump.

64. Connect the control cables to the throttle body lever and mounting bracket.

65. Attach the shift linkage to the transaxle and mounting bracket.

66. Connect the fuel lines.

67. Install the clutch slave cylinder, if equipped.

68. Connect the A/C compressor-to-accumulator and condenser lines.

69. Recharge the A/C system.

70. Connect the electrical wiring to the following components:
- O₂S sensor
- Fuel injector harness
- IAC
- TP sensor
- ECT sender
- P/N switch
- TCC solenoid
- Transaxle shift solenoid
- Transaxle ground

- MAP sensor
- EGR valve
- Cooling fan

71. Install the alternator upper mounting bracket and connect the alternator wiring.

72. Connect the vacuum hose to the power brake booster.

73. Install the upper radiator hoses.

74. Install the air cleaner.

75. Install the battery cable and connect the positive cable.

76. Install the throttle body air inlet duct.

77. Connect the negative battery cable.

78. Fill the engine with the correct amounts and types of coolant and engine oil.

79. Refill and bleed the power steering system.

80. Start the vehicle and verify no leaks.

➡**Whenever the vehicle sub-frame is removed or lowered, the wheel alignment should be checked.**

2.4L Engine

1. Before servicing the vehicle, refer to the precautions in the beginning of this section.

2. If equipped with A/C, properly recover the refrigerant.

3. Disconnect the negative battery.

4. Properly drain the cooling system into an approved container.

5. Relieve the fuel system pressure.

6. Remove the left sound insulator, then disconnect the clutch pushrod from the pedal assembly.

7. Disconnect the heater hose at the thermostat assembly, then detach the radiator inlet (upper) hose.

8. Remove the air cleaner assembly and the coolant fan.

9. If equipped with A/C, disconnect the

9300YG03

Exploded view of the upper engine mount—2.4L engine

compressor/condenser hose assembly at the compressor, then discard the O-rings.

10. Disconnect the 2 vacuum hoses from the front of the engine.

11. Tag and detach the following electrical connectors:
- Alternator
- A/C compressor (if equipped)
- Fuel injector harness
- Idle Air Control (IAC) and Throttle Position (TP) sensor at the throttle body
- Manifold Absolute Pressure (MAP) sensor
- Intake Air Temperature (IAT) sensor
- EVAP canister purge solenoid
- Starter solenoid
- Ground connections
- Negative battery cable from the transaxle
- Electronic ignition coil and module assembly
- Engine Coolant Temperature (ECT) sensor(s)
- Oil pressure sensor/switch
- Oxygen (O₂S) sensor
- Crankshaft Position (CKP) sensor
- Back-up lamp switch, then position the harness aside

12. Disconnect the power brake vacuum hose from the throttle body. Detach the power brake vacuum tube-to-check valve hose from the tube.

13. Remove the throttle cable and bracket.

14. Unfasten the power steering pump rear bracket, then remove the bracket and vacuum tube as an assembly.

15. Unfasten the power steering pivot bolt, then remove the pump and drive belt. Position the pump aside, with the lines still attached.

16. Carefully disconnect the fuel lines.

17. Disconnect the shift cables. Detach the clutch actuator line.

18. Remove the exhaust manifold and heat shield.

19. Disconnect the radiator outlet (lower) hose from the radiator.

20. Install J-28467-A or equivalent engine support fixture.

21. Unfasten the bolt attaching the coolant recovery/surge tank, then position the tank aside with the hoses still connected.

22. Remove the engine mount assembly.

23. Raise and safely support the vehicle, then remove the front wheel and tire assemblies. Remove the right splash shield.

24. Drain and recycle the engine oil.

9300YG04

Exploded view of the lower engine mount and strut—2.4L engine

25. Remove the radiator air deflector.

26. Tag and detach the following electrical connections:

- Vehicle Speed Sensor (VSS)
- Knock Sensor (KS)
- Starter solenoid
- If equipped, both front ABS wheel speed sensors

27. Remove the engine mount strut and the transaxle mount.

28. Separate the ball joints from the steering knuckles.

29. Remove the suspension supports, crossmember, and stabilizer shaft as an assembly.

30. Disconnect the heater outlet hose from the radiator outlet pipe.

31. Remove the axle shaft from the transaxle and intermediate shaft, then position aside.

32. If equipped, disconnect the A/C lines from the oil pan.

33. Remove the flywheel housing cover.

34. Position a suitable support below the engine, then carefully lower the vehicle onto the support.

35. Matchmark the threads on the support fixture hooks so the setting can be duplicated when reinstalling the engine. Remove the engine support fixture J-hooks.

36. Raise the vehicle slowly off the engine and transaxle assembly. If may be necessary to move the engine/transaxle assembly rearward to clear the intake manifold.

37. Noting the position of the bolts, separate the engine from the transaxle.

To install:

⁂ WARNING

Be sure the retaining bolts are in their correct locations. If not, engine damage may occur.

38. Assemble the engine to the transaxle.

39. Position the engine and transaxle assembly under the engine compartment, then slowly lower the vehicle over the assembly until the transaxle mount is indexed, then install the retaining bolt.

40. Install engine support fixture J-28467-A or equivalent, making sure to adjust it to the previous setting.

41. Install the engine mount assembly and transaxle mount.

42. Carefully raise the vehicle off the support.

43. Attach the axle shafts to the transaxle.

44. Connect the heater outlet hose to the radiator outlet pipe.

45. Install the suspension supports, crossmember and stabilizer shaft assembly.

46. Attach the ball joints to the steering knuckles, then secure with the nuts.

47. Install the engine strut mount.

48. If equipped, connect the A/C line to the oil pan.

49. Attach the following electrical connectors, as tagged during removal:

- Vehicle Speed Sensor (VSS)
- Knock Sensor (KS)
- Starter solenoid
- If equipped, both front ABS wheel speed sensors

50. Install the flywheel housing cover.

51. Fasten the radiator air deflector.

52. Connect the lower radiator hose.

53. Install the right splash shield, then the front wheel and tire assemblies.

54. Carefully lower the vehicle, then remove the engine support fixture.

55. Install the coolant recovery/surge tank, then secure using the retaining bolt.

56. Attach the following electrical connections, as tagged during removal:

- Alternator
- A/C compressor (if equipped)
- Fuel injector harness
- IAC and TP sensor at the throttle body
- MAP sensor
- IAT sensor
- EVAP canister purge solenoid
- Starter solenoid
- Ground connections
- Negative battery cable to the transaxle
- Electronic ignition coil and module assembly
- ECT sensor(s)
- Oil pressure sensor/switch
- O_2S sensor
- CKP sensor
- Back-up lamp switch

57. Attach the vacuum hoses.

58. If equipped with A/C, attach the compressor/condenser hose assembly to the compressor.

59. Fasten the clutch actuator line.

60. Install the exhaust manifold and heat shield.

61. Connect the fuel lines.

62. Connect the positive battery cable.

63. Fasten the power steering pump pivot-to-block bolt. Install the power steering pump rear bracket and tension belt.

64. Connect the vacuum hoses to the intake manifold and to the tube from the brake booster.

65. Install the throttle cable and bracket.

66. Install the coolant fan and air cleaner assembly.

Legend

(1) Balance Shaft Chain Cover Bolt
(2) Balance Shaft Chain Cover
(3) Balance Shaft Guide Adjuster Nut
(4) Balance Shaft Chain Guide Adjuster Bolt
(5) Balance Shaft Chain Adjuster Guide
(6) Stud
(7) Balance Shaft Upper Housing
(8) Balance Shaft Thrust Plate Retainer Bolt
(9) Balance Shaft Bearings
(10) Balance Shaft Thrust Plate Retainer
(11) Balance Shaft Drive
(12) Balance Shaft Driven
(13) Balance Shaft Drive Chain
(14) Driven Sprocket Bolt-Note: Left Hand Thread
(15) Balance Shaft Driven Sprocket
(16) Balance Shaft Lower Housing

(17) Balance Shaft Housing Bolt
(18) Balance Shaft Housing to Block Bolt
(19) Balance Shaft Housing to Block Bolt
(20) Balance Shaft Housing to Block Bolt
(21) Balance Shaft Housing Bolt
(22) Oil Pan Bolt
(23) Oil Pan
(24) Oil Pan Gasket
(25) Dowel Pin
(26) Oil Pump Body
(27) Gerotor
(28) Oil Pump Cover
(29) Oil Pump Cover to Body Bolt
(30) Relief Valve Pin
(31) Relief Valve Spring Guide
(32) Relief Valve Spring
(33) Relief Valve
(34) Pickup Screen

Exploded view of the balance shafts and related components—2.4L engine

9300YG09

67. Attach the radiator outlet (upper) hose. Fill the cooling system with the proper type and quantity of coolant.

68. Connect the clutch pushrod to the pedal assembly, then install the left sound insulator.

69. Attach the heater hose at the thermostat housing.

70. Fill the transaxle with fluid, then fill the crankcase with oil.

71. Connect the negative battery cable.

72. If equipped with A/C, evacuate, charge and leak test the system.

73. Start the engine and check the fluid levels, proper operation of the engine and/or fluid leakage.

Water Pump

REMOVAL & INSTALLATION

2.2L Engine

> **※※ WARNING**
>
> **When adding coolant, it is important that you use GM Goodwrench DEX-COOL® coolant meeting GM Specification 6277M.**

1. Before servicing the vehicle, refer to the precautions in the beginning of this section.

2. Disconnect the negative battery cable.

3. Drain the cooling system into a suitable container.

4. Loosen, but do not remove, the water pump pulley bolts.

5. Remove the serpentine belt.

6. Remove the alternator mounting bolts and set the alternator aside.

7. Remove the water pump pulley bolts, then remove the pulley.

8. Remove the 4 water pump mounting bolts, then remove the water pump.

To install:

9. Clean all the gasket surfaces completely.

10. Apply a thin bead of sealer around the outer edge of the water pump gasket seating area and place he gasket on the pump.

11. Install the water pump on the engine and tighten the 4 mounting bolts to 18 ft. lbs. (25 Nm).

12. Install the water pump pulley and tighten the mounting bolts finger-tight.

13. Install the alternator in the mounting bracket.

14. Install the serpentine belt.

15. Tighten the water pump pulley mounting bolts to 22 ft. lbs. (30 Nm).

16. Connect the negative battery cable.

17. Refill and bleed the cooling system.

2.4L Engine

1. Before servicing the vehicle, refer to the precautions in the beginning of this section.

2. Disconnect the negative battery cable

3. Detach the Oxygen (O_2S) sensor connector.

4. Properly drain the engine coolant into a suitable container. Remove the heater hose from the thermostat housing for more complete coolant drain.

5. Remove upper exhaust manifold heat shield.

6. Remove the bolt that attaches the exhaust manifold brace to the manifold.

7. Remove the lower exhaust manifold heat shield.

8. Break loose the manifold to exhaust pipe spring loaded bolts using a 13mm box wrench.

9. Raise and safely support the vehicle.

> **※※ WARNING**
>
> **It is necessary to relieve the spring pressure from 1 bolt prior to removing the second bolt. If the spring pressure is not relieved, it will cause the exhaust pipe to twist and bind up the bolt as it is removed.**

10. Unfasten the two radiator outlet pipe-to-water pump cover bolts.

11. Remove the manifold to exhaust pipe bolts from the exhaust pipe flange as follows:

   a. Unscrew either bolt clockwise 4 turns.

   b. Remove the other bolt.

   c. Remove the first bolt.

> **※※ WARNING**
>
> **DO NOT rotate the flex coupling more than 4 degrees or damage may occur.**

12. Pull down and back on the exhaust pipe to disengage it from the exhaust manifold bolts.

13. Remove the radiator outlet pipe from the oil pan and transaxle. If equipped with a manual transaxle, remove the exhaust manifold brace. Leave the lower radiator hose attached and pull down on the outlet pipe to remove it from the water pump. Leave the radiator outlet pipe hang.

14. Carefully lower the vehicle.

1   BOLT — 25 N·m (18 LBS. FT.)

7922YG01

Exploded view of the water pump mounting—2.2L engine

1 TIMING CHAIN HOUSING
2 GASKET, TIMING CHAIN
   HOUSING TO WATER PUMP COVER
3 NUT (3)
4 WATER PUMP BODY ASM.
5 GASKET, WATER PUMP BODY
   TO WATER PUMP COVER
6 WATER PUMP COVER
7 BOLT (M6 X 1 X 65) – 3
   LOWER POSITIONS
8 BOLT (M6 X 1 X 25)
9 BOLT (M6 X 1 X 90)
10 GASKET, WATER PUMP
   COVER TO BLOCK
11 BOLTS, WATER PUMP COVER
   TO BLOCK (2)

7922YG02

Exploded view of the water pump mounting and related components—2.4L engine

15. Unfasten the exhaust manifold-to-cylinder head retaining nuts, then remove the exhaust manifold, seals and gaskets.

16. Remove the front timing chain cover and the chain tensioner.

17. Unfasten the water pump-to-cylinder block bolts. Remove the water pump-to-timing chain housing nuts. Remove the water pump and cover mounting bolts and nuts. Remove the water pump and cover as an assembly, then separate the 2 pieces.

To install:

18. Thoroughly clean and dry all mounting surfaces, bolts and bolt holes. Using a new gasket, install the water pump to the cover and tighten the bolts finger-tight.

19. Lubricate the splines of the water pump with clean grease and install the assembly to the engine using new gaskets. Install the mounting bolts and nuts finger-tight.

20. Lubricate the radiator outlet pipe O-ring with antifreeze and slid the pipe onto the water pump cover. Install the bolts finger-tight.

21. With all gaps closed, tighten the bolts, in the following sequence, to the proper values:

    a. Pump assembly-to-chain housing nuts—19 ft. lbs. (26 Nm).

    b. Pump cover-to-pump assembly—106 inch lbs. (12 Nm).

    c. Cover-to-block, bottom bolt first—19 ft. lbs. (26 Nm).

    d. Radiator outlet pipe assembly-to-pump cover—125 inch lbs. (14 Nm).

22. Using new gaskets, install the exhaust manifold.

23. Raise and safely support the vehicle.

24. Index the exhaust manifold bolts into the exhaust pipe flange.

25. Connect the exhaust pipe to the manifold. Install the exhaust pipe flange bolts evenly and gradually to avoid binding.

Turn the bolts in until fully seated.

26. Connect the radiator outlet pipe to the transaxle and oil pan. Install the exhaust manifold brace, if removed.

27. Install the timing chain tensioner and front cover.

28. Install the lower heat shield.

29. Carefully lower the vehicle.

30. Fasten the bolt that attaches the exhaust manifold brace to the manifold.

31. Tighten the manifold-to-exhaust pipe nuts to 26 ft. lbs. (35 Nm).

32. Install the upper heat shield.

33. Attach the O_2S sensor connector.

34. Fill the radiator with coolant until it comes out the heater hose outlet at the thermostat housing. Then, connect the heater hose. Leave the radiator cap off.

35. Connect the negative battery cable, then start the engine. Run the vehicle until the thermostat opens, fill the radiator and recovery tank to their proper levels, then turn the engine **OFF**.

36. Once the vehicle has cooled, recheck the coolant level.

Cylinder Head

REMOVAL & INSTALLATION

2.2L Engine

1. Before servicing the vehicle, refer to the precautions in the beginning of this section.

2. Relieve fuel system pressure using the recommended procedure.

3. Disconnect negative battery cable.

4. Remove air cleaner outlet duct assembly.

5. Label and disconnect vacuum lines.

6. Disconnect and tag for identification the electrical connections on the Engine

Coolant Temperature (ECT) sensor, Oxygen (O_2S) sensor, Idle Air Control (IAC), Throttle Position (TP) sensor, Manifold Absolute Pressure (MAP) sensor, EVAP Canister Purge Solenoid and the fuel injector harness.

7. Remove accelerator control, cruise and TV cables from accelerator control bracket.

8. Remove accelerator control cable bracket.

9. Raise and safely support vehicle.

10. Remove exhaust pipe from exhaust manifold.

11. Drain and recover coolant into a suitable container.

12. Lower vehicle.

13. Remove serpentine drive belt.

14. Remove the alternator.

15. Remove the power steering pump and position aside with lines attached.

16. Remove power steering pump bracket.

17. Install engine support fixture J-28467-A or equivalent.

18. Remove serpentine drive belt tensioner bracket.

19. Tag and disconnect the spark plug wires.

20. Disconnect EVAP canister purge line, from under manifold.

21. Remove upper hose from coolant outlet.

22. Remove heater hose from coolant outlet.

23. Remove attaching nut holding automatic transaxle filler tube from intake manifold, if equipped.

24. Disconnect fuel lines.

25. Remove valve cover.

➡**Whenever valvetrain components are removed for service, they should be kept in order. They should be installed in the same locations and with the same mating surfaces as when removed.**

26. Remove rocker arms and pushrods.

27. Remove cylinder head bolts. Two sizes of bolts are used. Note the location of each. These bolts are called "torque-to-yield." This means that, at assembly, after the bolts are tightened to a specific torque, they are tightened another quarter turn. This stretches the bolts slightly. Therefore, new cylinder head bolts are recommended.

28. Remove cylinder head with both manifolds attached.

29. Remove the intake and exhaust manifolds from the cylinder head.

1. Long bolts
2. Short bolts
3. Stud
4. Numbers on gasket
   indicate torque sequence

7922YG03

Cylinder head tightening sequence—2.2L engine

To install:

30. Clean all the gasket surfaces completely. Clean the threads on cylinder head bolts and be sure all bolt holes are clean and free of foreign material. It is good practice to clean all internally threaded openings with the proper size thread cutting tap. This removes rust, dirt and old sealer build-up that can prevent getting a proper torque reading when tightening bolts.

31. Inspect cylinder head and block surface for cracks, nicks, heavy scratches and flatness.

32. Install exhaust and intake manifolds on cylinder head prior to installing cylinder head.

33. Place a new cylinder head gasket in position over the dowel pins on the engine block. Carefully guide the cylinder head into position.

34. Install cylinder head bolts finger-tight. New cylinder head bolts are recommended.

35. Tighten bolts in sequence, tighten the long bolts to 46 ft. lbs. (63 Nm) plus 90 degrees. Tighten the short bolts to 43 ft. lbs. (58 Nm) plus 90 degrees.

36. Install pushrods and rocker arms and rocker arm nuts. Tighten nuts to 22 ft. lbs. (30 Nm).

37. Install valve cover and tighten bolts to 89 inch lbs. (10 Nm).

38. Connect fuel lines.

39. Install transaxle filler tube nut and tighten to 20 ft. lbs. (27 Nm).

40. Install heater hose to coolant outlet.

41. Install upper radiator hose to coolant.

42. Connect EVAP canister purge line.

43. Attach the ignition wires to spark plugs, as tagged during removal.

44. Install serpentine drive belt tensioner bracket and bolts. Tighten bolts to 37 ft. lbs. (27 Nm).

45. Remove engine support fixture.

46. Install power steering pump bracket and power steering pump.

47. Install alternator and brace.

48. Install serpentine drive belt.

49. Raise and safely support the vehicle.

50. Connect the exhaust pipe to the exhaust manifold.

51. Lower the vehicle.

52. Install the accelerator control cable bracket and bolts. Tighten bolts to 18 inch lbs. (25 Nm).

53. Connect the accelerator control, cruise and TV cables to control bracket.

54. Attach all of the electrical connections for the sensors.

55. Connect the vacuum lines.

56. Install air cleaner outlet duct assembly.

57. Refill the coolant system.

58. Connect negative battery cable.

59. Start vehicle and inspect for leaks.

60. Bleed air from coolant system as follows:

    a. Loosen the engine coolant air bleed screw, (located on the top side of the engine coolant outlet) and add coolant until all of the air is evacuated through the air bleed. Tighten the air bleed screw.

    b. When filling the coolant system, use coolant meeting GM specifications.

2.4L Engine

1. Before servicing the vehicle, refer to the precautions in the beginning of this section.

2. Relieve the fuel system pressure.

3. Disconnect the negative battery cable.

4. Drain and recover the coolant into a suitable container.

5. Disconnect the heater inlet and throttle body heater hoses from water outlet.

6. Remove the exhaust manifold.

7. Remove the intake camshaft housing and lifters, then remove the exhaust camshaft housing and lifters.

8. Remove the oil fill tube.

9. Remove the throttle body-to-air cleaner duct.

10. Disconnect the power brake vacuum hose from throttle body.

11. Remove the throttle cable bracket.

12. Remove the throttle body from intake manifold, with electrical harness and throttle cable attached. Position it aside.

13. Disconnect the Manifold Absolute Pressure (MAP) sensor vacuum hose from intake manifold.

14. Remove the intake manifold brace.

15. Disconnect electrical connections from the following sensors: MAP sensor, Intake Air Temperature (IAT) sensor and EVAP canister purge solenoid.

16. Disconnect the upper radiator hose from water outlet.

17. Detach the Engine Coolant Temperature (ECT) sensors connectors.

18. Unfasten the cylinder head bolt, then remove cylinder head and gasket.

To install:

19. This is an aluminum cylinder head and must be treated with care. Do not use abrasive pads to clean the cylinder head or block surfaces. An abrasive pad may damage the cylinder head and block. GM says

that abrasive pads should not be used for the following reasons:

    a. Abrasive pads will produce a fine grit that the oil filter will not be able to remove from the oil. This grit is abrasive and has been known to cause internal engine damage.

    b. Abrasive pads can easily remove enough metal to round cylinder head edges. This has been known to affect the gasket's ability to seal, especially in the narrow areas between the combustion chambers and coolant jackets. The cylinder head gasket is likely to leak if these edges are rounded.

    c. Abrasive pads can also remove enough metal to affect cylinder head flatness. It takes only about 15 seconds to remove 0.008 in. (0.20mm) of metal from the cylinder head with an abrasive pad. If the cylinder head flatness is out of specification, the gasket will not be able to seal and the gasket will leak.

20. Use a razor blade gasket scraper to clean the cylinder head and cylinder block gasket surfaces. Be careful not to gouge or scratch the gasket surfaces. Do not gouge or scrape the combustion chamber surfaces. Use a new razor blade for each cylinder head. Hold the scraper so the razor blade is as parallel to the gasket surface as possible. Do not use any other method or technique to clean these gasket surfaces. In addition, GM warns not to use a tap to clean cylinder head bolt holes.

21. When working on an aluminum head, do not remove spark plugs from an aluminum cylinder head until the cylinder head has cooled. Always clean all dirt and debris from the spark plug recess area. If the spark plug opening threads are damaged and NOT restorable with a Thread Chaser, replace the cylinder head. GM **DOES NOT** approve of the installation of thread inserts into the spark plug openings on this engine. If threads are installed into the spark plug openings, severe engine damage will occur.

22. Clean all the gasket surfaces completely. Clean the threads on cylinder head bolts and be sure all bolt holes are clean and free of debris. New bolts are recommended.

23. Inspect the cylinder head and block surface for cracks, nicks, heavy scratches and flatness.

24. Place a new cylinder head gasket on the block. Do not use any sealing material.

25. Carefully place the cylinder head on dowel pins, being careful not to disturb the gasket.

26. Apply a small amount of clean engine oil to the threads of the cylinder head bolts, and install finger-tight.

27. Tighten head bolts in sequence. Tighten bolts 1 through 8 to 40 ft. lbs. (65 Nm), then tighten bolts 9 and 10 to 30 ft. lbs. (40 Nm). Turn all 10 bolts an additional 90 degrees (¼ turn) in sequence.

28. Attach the ECT sensor connections.

29. Connect upper radiator hose to coolant outlet.

30. Install manifold brace and tighten to 19 ft. lbs. (26 Nm).

31. Attach all sensor connections.

32. Connect the MAP sensor vacuum hose to intake manifold.

SPARINGLY APPLY CLEAN ENGINE OIL HERE

◀FRT

A. Tighten the bolts to the following N.m (lb. ft.) specification in sequence:
    bolts 1 through 8: 65 N·m (40 ft. lb.)
    bolts 9 and 10: 40 N·m (30 ft. lb.)
B. Then turn all 10 bolts an additional 90 degrees in sequence

7922YG04

Head bolt torque sequence—2.4L engine

BOLT- CAMSHAFT HOUSING TO CYLINDER HEAD 15 N·m (11 lbs. ft.) PLUS TURN 90°

BOLT - CAMSHAFT HOUSING COVER TO CAMSHAFT HOUSING 15 N·m (11 lbs. ft.) PLUS TURN 30°

COVER - CAMSHAFT

SEALS - CAMSHAFT HOUSING TO CAMSHAFT

CAMSHAFT HOUSING (INTAKE SHOWN)

DOWEL PIN (2)

GASKET - CAMSHAFT HOUSING TO CYLINDER HEAD

7922YG05

Exploded view of the camshaft housing cover mounting—2.4L engine

For engine torque specifications, refer to Section 1 of this manual

33. Install the throttle body onto the intake manifold, using a new gasket.

34. Install accelerator control cable bracket to the throttle body, and tighten the bolts to 106 inch lbs. (12 Nm). Tighten the nut to 19 ft. lbs. (26 Nm).

35. Install the throttle body-to-air cleaner duct.

36. Install oil fill tube, tighten attaching bolt to 71 inch lbs. (8 Nm).

37. Install the lifters and camshaft housing.

38. Install the exhaust manifold, then tighten the exhaust nuts to 26 ft. lbs. (35 Nm).

39. Connect negative battery.

40. Fill coolant system and bleed off air from system. An oil and filter change is recommended.

41. Check and verify that vehicle has no coolant or vacuum leaks.

Rocker Arms

REMOVAL & INSTALLATION

➡**Place the components in a rack in order to be sure they are installed at the same location and with the same mating surface as when removed.**

1. Before servicing the vehicle, refer to the precautions in the beginning of this section.

2. Disconnect the negative battery cable.

3. Remove the rocker (valve) arm cover(s).

4. Unfasten the rocker arm nuts.

5. Remove the rocker arm pivot ball(s).

6. Remove the rocker arm(s).

7. Remove the pushrods.

To install:

8. Install the pushrods. Be sure to install the pushrods in the correct positions, and be sure they seat properly in the lifters.

9. Coat the bearing surfaces of the rocker arms and pivot balls with camshaft and lifter prelube GM specification 1052365 or equivalent. Install the rocker arm(s).

10. Install the rocker arm pivot ball(s).

11. Install the rocker arm nuts, and tighten them to 22 ft. lbs. (30 Nm).

12. Install the rocker arm covers.

13. Connect the negative battery cable.

Intake Manifold

REMOVAL & INSTALLATION

2.2L Engine

1996–97 MODELS

These vehicles use a two-piece intake manifold. The upper half, sometimes called a plenum, contains the throttle body and the control cable connections. The lower half has individual port runners to each intake port on the cylinder head. The lower half of the manifold bolts to the cylinder head and houses the fuel injectors. Note that these pieces are cast aluminum. Care should be exercised when working with any light alloy component.

1. Before servicing the vehicle, refer to the precautions in the beginning of this section.

2. Properly relieve the fuel system pressure.

3. Disconnect the negative battery cable.

4. Remove the throttle body air intake duct.

5. Drain the cooling system into an approved container.

6. Identify, tag and disconnect all necessary vacuum lines.

7. Disconnect the control cables from the throttle body lever and remove the control cable bracket from the intake manifold.

8. Remove the serpentine belt.

9. Remove the power steering pump and lay it aside with the fluid lines attached.

10. Remove the transaxle fill tube.

11. Tag and disconnect the following electrical wires:

- Idle Air Control (IAC) valve
- Throttle Position (TP) sensor
- Manifold Absolute Pressure (MAP) sensor
- EVAP Emission solenoid
- Fuel injector harness
- Exhaust Gas Recirculation (EGR) valve

12. Remove the MAP sensor.

13. Unfasten the upper intake manifold mounting bolts, then remove the upper intake manifold.

14. Disconnect the fuel lines from the fuel rail.

15. Remove the EGR valve injector, then remove the EGR valve.

16. Remove the fuel injector retainer bracket, regulator and injectors.

17. Unfasten and remove the control cable bracket.

18. If necessary for access, raise and safely support the vehicle.

19. Unfasten the 6 intake manifold nuts, then remove the manifold.

20. Clean the gasket mounting surfaces.

To install:

21. Install a new gasket, then position the lower intake manifold. Tighten the lower intake manifold nuts in the proper sequence to 24 ft. lbs. (33 Nm).

22. Connect the control cables and cable bracket.

23. Install the EGR valve.

24. Attach the fuel lines to the fuel rail.

25. Install the fuel injectors, regulator and injector retainer bracket, then tighten the retaining bolts to 22 inch lbs. (3.5 Nm).

26. Install the EGR valve injector that the port is facing directly towards the throttle body.

1	STUD
2	GASKET
3	INTAKE MANIFOLD
4	NUT
5	CLIP

INTAKE MANIFOLD NUT TIGHTENING SEQUENCE

Lower intake manifold tightening sequence—2.2L engine

7922YG06

Intake manifold tightening sequence—1998–00 2.2L engine

27. Install the upper intake manifold assembly. Tighten the upper intake manifold nuts in the proper sequence to 22 ft. lbs. (30 Nm).

28. Install the MAP sensor.

29. Attach the electrical connectors to the MAP sensor, EGR solenoid valve, IAC valve, TP sensor, and the fuel injectors.

30. Install the transaxle fill tube.

31. Install the power steering pump, then install the serpentine belt.

32. Connect the vacuum lines, as tagged during removal.

33. Install the air intake duct.

34. Refill the coolant system.

35. Connect the negative battery cable, then start the engine and check for leaks.

1998–00 MODELS

1. Disconnect the negative battery cable.

2. Properly relieve the fuel system pressure.

3. Remove the air cleaner inlet duct.

4. Remove the air inlet resonator and bracket.

5. Remove the throttle and cruise control cable from the throttle body.

6. Label and detach the following electrical connectors:

• Manifold Absolute Pressure (MAP) sensor

• Throttle Position (TP) sensor

• Idle Air Control (IAC) valve

7. Unbolt and remove the throttle body.

8. Disconnect the fuel supply line and the fuel inlet pipe.

9. Remove the intake manifold mounting nuts/bolts, then remove the manifold from the engine.

10. Clean the gasket mating surfaces on the cylinder head, intake manifold and throttle body. Inspect the manifold for cracks, broken flanges, and gasket surface damage.

To install:

11. Install the intake manifold using a new gasket.

12. Tighten the mounting bolts/nuts, in sequence, to 17 ft. lbs. (24 Nm).

13. Install the throttle body and tighten the mounting bolts to 89 inch lbs. (10 Nm).

14. Mount the fuel pipe and connect the fuel supply line.

15. Attach the MAP sensor, TP sensor, and the IAC valve electrical connectors.

16. Connect the cruise control and throttle cables to the throttle body.

17. Install the air inlet resonator bracket and resonator.

18. Install the air cleaner inlet duct.

19. Connect the negative battery cable.

2.4L Engine

1. Before servicing the vehicle, refer to the precautions in the beginning of this section.

2. Properly relieve the fuel system pressure.

3. Disconnect the negative battery cable, then properly drain the cooling system.

4. Tag and detach the following electrical connectors:

• Manifold Absolute Pressure (MAP) sensor

• Intake Air Temperature (IAT) sensor

• EVAP canister purge solenoid

• Fuel injector harness

5. Label and disconnect the vacuum hoses from the fuel regulator and EVAP canister purge solenoid to canister.

6. Unfasten the air cleaner duct.

7. Remove the accelerator control cable bracket.

8. Remove the stud-ended alternator

1. STUD – 12 N•M (100 LB. IN.)
2. INTAKE MANIFOLD GASKET
3. INTAKE MANIFOLD
4. BOLT – 24 N•M (17 LB. FT.)
5. NUT – 24 N•M (17 LB. FT.)

Exploded view of the intake manifold, showing the torque sequence—2.4L engine

For complete mechanical specifications, refer to Section 1 of this manual

mount bolt, then detach the EGR pipe from the EGR adapter.

9. Remove the fill tube out the top, rotating as necessary to gain clearance for the oil/air separator nipple between the intake tubes and fuel rail electrical harness.

10. Raise and safely support the vehicle.

11. Remove the intake manifold support brace.

12. If raised, carefully lower the vehicle.

13. Unfasten the manifold retaining nuts and bolts, then remove the intake manifold from the engine.

➡ **If installing a new intake manifold, transfer all necessary parts from the old manifold to the new one.**

14. Using a suitable scraping tool, clean the old gasket material from the intake manifold mating surfaces. Do not let any debris fall into the engine!

To install:

15. Install the manifold with a new gasket.

➡ **Be sure the numbers stamped on the gasket are facing towards the manifold surface.**

16. Follow the tightening sequence in the accompanying figure, then tighten the bolts/nuts to 18 ft. lbs. (24 Nm).

17. Raise and safely support the vehicle.

18. Install the intake manifold brace and retainers.

19. If raised, carefully lower the vehicle.

20. If removed, position the oil fill tube in its cylinder block opening. Align the fill tube so it is in about its proper position. Place the palm of your hand over the oil fill opening and press straight down to seat the fill tube and O-ring into the cylinder block.

21. If necessary, connect the oil/air separator hose to the oil fill tube. You can lubricate the hose as necessary to ease installation. Install the oil fill tube bolt/screw. Fasten the cap.

22. Attach the EGR pipe to the adapter; tighten the fasteners to 19 ft. lbs. (26 Nm). Install the stud-ended alternator bolt.

23. Install the accelerator control cable bracket.

24. Connect the vacuum hoses to the fuel regulator and EVAP canister purge solenoid.

25. Attach all electrical connectors, as tagged during removal.

26. Install the air cleaner duct.

27. Refill the coolant to it's proper level.

28. Connect the negative battery cable, then start the engine and inspect for leaks.

Exhaust Manifold

REMOVAL & INSTALLATION

2.2L Engine

1. Before servicing the vehicle, refer to the precautions in the beginning of this section.

2. Disconnect the negative battery cable.

3. Detach the Oxygen (O_2S) sensor wire.

4. Remove the serpentine belt or alternator drive belt.

5. Remove the alternator-to-bracket bolts, then support the alternator (with the wires attached) out of the way.

6. Raise and support the vehicle safely.

7. Unfasten the exhaust pipe-to-exhaust manifold bolts, then carefully lower the vehicle.

8. If necessary for access to remove the manifold, remove the oil fill tube and disconnect the heater outlet hose assembly nut from the exhaust manifold.

9. Remove the exhaust manifold-to-cylinder head bolts.

10. Detach the exhaust manifold from the exhaust pipe flange.

11. Unfasten the retaining nuts, then remove the exhaust manifold from the vehicle. Remove and discard the gasket(s).

To install:

12. Using a gasket scraper, carefully clean the gasket mounting surfaces.

13. To install, use new gaskets and reverse the removal procedures. Tighten the exhaust manifold-to-cylinder head nuts to 3–12 ft. lbs. (4–16 Nm) and the bolts to 6–13 ft. lbs. (8–18 Nm).

14. Start the engine and check for exhaust leaks.

2.4L Engine

1. Before servicing the vehicle, refer to the precautions in the beginning of this section.

2. Disconnect the negative battery cable

3. Detach the Oxygen (O_2S) sensor connector.

4. Raise and safely support the vehicle.

5. Unfasten the exhaust manifold brace-to-manifold bolt and the oil pan nuts, if necessary.

➡ **Do not bend the exhaust flex coupler more than necessary to remove it. Excessive movement will damage the flex coupler.**

6. Remove the manifold-to-exhaust flex coupler fasteners.

7. Pull down and back on the exhaust

1. STUD, EXHAUST MANIFOLD
2. GASKET, EXHAUST MANIFOLD
3. MANIFOLD, EXHAUST
4. NUT, EXHAUST MANIFOLD, MUST BE TIGHTENED IN SEQUENCE SHOWN TO 12.5 N•m (110 LB. IN.)

7922YG11

Exploded view of the exhaust manifold, showing the torque sequence—2.4L engine

pipe to disengage it from the exhaust manifold bolts.

8. Carefully lower the vehicle.

9. Remove the exhaust manifold-to-cylinder head retaining nuts/bolts, then remove the manifold. Remove and discard the gaskets and/or seals. Clean the mating surfaces.

To install:

10. Install gaskets, then position the exhaust manifold on the cylinder head. Tighten the retaining nuts to 110 inch lbs. (12.5 Nm), in sequence.

11. Raise and safely support the vehicle.

12. Install the heat shield. Tighten the bolts to 124 inch lbs. (14 Nm).

13. Fasten the exhaust manifold brace-to-manifold bolt and the oil pan nuts. Tighten the bolts to 41 ft. lbs. (56 Nm) and the nuts to 19 ft. lbs. (26 Nm).

14. Install the manifold-to-flex coupler fasteners. Tighten the bolts to 26 ft. lbs. (35 Nm).

15. Carefully lower the vehicle.

16. Attach the O_2S connector. Coat the threads of the sensor with anti-seize compound 5613695 or equivalent.

17. Connect the negative battery cable and check for leaks.

Camshaft and Valve Lifters

REMOVAL & INSTALLATION

2.2L Engine

1. Before servicing the vehicle, refer to the precautions in the beginning of this section.

2. Remove the engine and place it on a suitable engine stand.

3. Remove the cylinder head cover, pivot the rocker arms to the sides, and remove the pushrods, keeping them in order. Remove the valve lifters, keeping them in order. There are special tools which make lifter removal easier.

4. Remove the front cover.

5. If necessary, remove the oil pump drive.

6. Remove the fuel pump and it's pushrod.

7. Remove the timing chain and sprocket.

8. Carefully pull the camshaft from the block, being sure the camshaft lobes do not contact the bearings.

To install:

9. To install, lubricate the camshaft journals with clean engine oil. Lubricate the lobes with Molykote® or the equivalent.

10. Install the camshaft into the engine, being extremely careful not to contact the bearings with the cam lobes.

11. Install the timing chain and sprocket. Install the fuel pump and pushrod. Install the timing cover.

12. Install the valve lifters. If a new camshaft has been installed, new lifters should be used to ensure durability of the cam lobes.

13. Install the pushrods and rocker arms and the intake manifold. Adjust the valve lash after installing the engine. Install the cylinder head cover.

2.4L Engine

INTAKE CAMSHAFT

➡ **Any time the camshaft housing-to-cylinder head bolts are loosened or removed, the camshaft housing to cylinder head gasket must be replaced.**

1. Before servicing the vehicle, refer to the precautions in the beginning of this section.

2. Relieve the fuel system pressure. Disconnect the negative battery cable.

3. Label and detach the ignition coil and module assembly electrical connections.

4. Unfasten the ignition coil and module assembly to camshaft housing bolts, then remove the assembly by pulling straight up. Use a special spark plug boot wire remover tool to remove connector assemblies, if they have stuck to the spark plugs.

5. If equipped, remove the idle speed power steering pressure switch connector.

6. Loosen the 3 power steering pump pivot bolts and remove drive belt.

7. Disconnect the 2 rear power steering pump bracket-to-transaxle bolts.

8. Remove the front power steering pump bracket to cylinder block bolt.

9. Disconnect the power steering pump assembly, then position it aside.

10. Using the special tool, remove the power steering pump drive pulley from the intake camshaft.

11. Remove oil/air separator bolts and hoses. Leave the hoses attached to the separator, disconnect from the oil fill, chain housing and intake manifold. Remove as an assembly.

12. Remove vacuum line from fuel pressure regulator and detach the fuel injector harness connector.

13. Disconnect fuel line attaching clamp

from bracket on top of intake camshaft housing.

14. Unfasten the fuel rail-to-camshaft housing attaching bolts, then remove the fuel rail from the cylinder head. Cover or plug injector openings in cylinder head and the injector nozzles. Leave the fuel lines attached, then position fuel rail aside.

15. Disconnect the timing chain and housing, but DO NOT remove from the engine.

16. Remove the intake camshaft housing cover-to-camshaft housing attaching bolts.

17. Unfasten the intake camshaft housing-to-cylinder head attaching bolts. Use the reverse of the tightening sequence when loosening the bolts. Leave 2 of the bolts loosely in place to hold the camshaft housing while separating the camshaft cover from housing.

18. Push the cover off the housing by threading 4 of the housing-to-head attaching bolts into the tapped holes in the cam housing cover. Tighten the bolts evenly so the cover does not bind on the dowel pins.

19. Remove the 2 loosely installed camshaft housing to head bolts and remove the cover. Discard the gaskets.

20. Note the position of the chain sprocket dowel pin for reassembly.

21. Remove intake camshaft oil seal from camshaft and discard seal. This seal must be replaced any time the housing and cover are separated.

22. Remove the camshaft carrier from the cylinder head and remove the gasket. Discard the gasket.

To install:

23. Thoroughly clean the mating surfaces of the camshaft carrier and the cylinder head, bolts and bolt holes. Install a new gasket and place the housing on the head. Install one bolt loosely to hold it in place.

24. Install the lifters into their bores. If the camshaft is being replaced, the lifters must also be replaced. Lubricate camshaft lobes, journals and lifters with camshaft and lifter prelube. The camshaft lobes and journals must be adequately lubricated or engine damage could occur upon start up.

25. Install the camshaft in the same position as when removed. The timing chain sprocket dowel pin should be straight up and align with the centerline of the lifter bores.

26. Install new camshaft housing to camshaft housing cover seals into cover; do not use sealer. Be sure the correct color seal is placed in each groove. Install the cover to the housing.

Please refer to Section 9 for electric cooling fan wiring schematics

27. Apply thread locking compound to the camshaft housing and cover attaching bolt threads.

28. Install the bolts, then tighten to 11 ft. lbs. (15 Nm). Rotate the bolts (except the 2 rear bolts that hold the fuel pipe to the camshaft housing) an additional 75 degrees, in sequence. Tighten the 2 rear bolts to 16 ft. lbs. (15 Nm), then rotate an additional 25 degrees.

29. Install the timing chain housing and the timing chain.

30. Uncover fuel injectors, then install new fuel injector O-ring seals lubricated with oil. Install the fuel rail.

31. Fasten the fuel line attaching clamp and retainer to bracket on top of the intake camshaft housing.

32. Connect the vacuum line to the fuel pressure regulator.

33. Attach the fuel injectors harness connector.

34. Install the oil/air separator assembly.

35. Lubricate the inner sealing surface of the intake camshaft seal with oil and install the seal to the housing.

36. Install the power steering pump pulley onto the intake camshaft.

37. Install the power steering pump assembly and drive belt.

38. Attach the idle speed power steering pressure switch connector.

39. Clean any loose lubricant that is present on the ignition coil and module assembly to camshaft housing bolts. Apply Loctite® 592 or equivalent, onto the ignition coil and module assembly to camshaft housing bolts. Install the bolts and tighten to 13 ft. lbs. (18 Nm).

40. Attach the electrical connectors to ignition coil and module assembly.

41. Connect the negative battery cable, then start the engine and check for leaks.

EXHAUST CAMSHAFT

➡ **Any time the camshaft housing-to-cylinder head bolts are loosened or removed, the camshaft housing to cylinder head gasket must be replaced.**

1. Before servicing the vehicle, refer to the precautions in the beginning of this section.

2. Relieve the fuel system pressure. Disconnect the negative battery cable.

3. Label and disconnect the ignition coil and module assembly electrical connections.

4. Unfasten the ignition coil and module assembly-to-camshaft housing bolts, then remove the assembly by pulling straight up. Use a special tool to remove connector assemblies if they have stuck to the spark plugs.

5. If equipped, remove the idle speed power steering pressure switch connector.

6. Remove the transaxle fluid level indicator tube assembly from exhaust camshaft cover and position aside.

7. Remove exhaust camshaft cover and gasket.

8. Disconnect the timing chain and housing but do not remove from the engine.

9. Remove exhaust camshaft housing to cylinder head bolts. Use the reverse of the tightening procedure when loosening camshaft housing while separating camshaft cover from housing.

10. Push the cover off the housing by threading 4 of the housing to head attaching bolts into the tapped holes in the camshaft cover. When threading the bolt, tighten them evenly so the cover does not bind on the dowel pins.

11. Remove the 2 loosely installed camshaft housing to cylinder head bolts and remove cover, discard gaskets.

12. Loosely reinstall one camshaft housing to cylinder head bolt to retain the housing during camshaft and lifter removal.

13. Note the position of the chain sprocket dowel pin for reassembly. Remove camshaft being careful not to damage the camshaft or journals.

81   SEALS – CAMSHAFT HOUSING TO CAMSHAFT
82A   BOLT – CAMSHAFT HOUSING TO CYLINDER
        HEAD – 15 N·m (11 LBS. FT.) PLUS TURN 90°
82B   BOLT – CAMSHAFT HOUSING COVER TO
        CAMSHAFT HOUSING – 15 N·m (11 LBS. FT.)
        PLUS TURN 30°
83   COVER – CAMSHAFT
90   CAMSHAFT HOUSING (INTAKE SHOWN)
91   GASKET – CAMSHAFT HOUSING TO CYLINDER
        HEAD
117   DOWEL PIN (2)

7922YG31

Exploded view of the camshaft housing, cover and gaskets—2.4L engine

14. Remove the camshaft carrier from the cylinder head and remove the gasket. Discard the gasket.

To install:

15. Thoroughly clean the mating surfaces of the camshaft carrier and the cylinder head, bolts and bolt holes. Install a new gasket and place the housing on the head. Install 1 bolt loosely to hold in place.

16. Install the lifters into their bores. If the camshaft is being replaced, the lifters must also be replaced. Lubricate camshaft lobes, journals and lifters with camshaft and lifter prelube. The camshaft lobes and journals must be adequately lubricated or engine damage could occur upon start up.

17. Install camshaft in same position as when removed. The timing chain sprocket dowel pin should be straight up and align with the centerline of the lifter bores.

18. Install new camshaft housing-to-camshaft housing cover seals into the cover; do not use sealer. Be sure the correct color seal is placed in each groove. Install the cover to the housing.

19. Apply thread locking compound to the camshaft housing and cover attaching bolt threads.

20. Install bolts, then tighten, in sequence, to 11 ft. lbs. (15 Nm). Then, rotate the bolts an additional 75 degrees, in sequence.

21. Install timing chain housing and timing chain.

22. Install the transaxle fluid level indicator tube assembly to the exhaust camshaft cover.

23. Attach the idle speed power steering pressure switch connector.

24. Clean any loose lubricant that is present on the ignition coil and module assembly to camshaft housing bolts. Apply Loctite® 592 or equivalent, onto the ignition coil and module assembly to camshaft housing bolts. Install the bolts and tighten to 13 ft. lbs. (18 Nm).

25. Attach the electrical connectors to ignition coil and module assembly.

26. Connect the negative battery cable, then start the engine and check for leaks.

Valve Lash

ADJUSTMENT

All of the engines are equipped with hydraulic valve lifters that do not require periodic valve lash adjustment. Adjustment is maintained automatically by hydraulic pressure in the lifters. Also, the rocker arm retaining nuts are tightened to a specific torque value (refer to the rocker arm procedure) to provide proper rocker arm placement.

Oil Pan

REMOVAL & INSTALLATION

2.2L Engine

1. Before servicing the vehicle, refer to the precautions in the beginning of this section.

2. Disconnect the negative terminal from the battery.

3. Raise and safely support the vehicle.

4. Drain the engine oil.

5. Remove the right front tire and wheel assembly.

6. Remove the right inner fender well splash shield.

7. Remove the starter and starter bracket.

8. Remove the flywheel cover bolts and flywheel cover.

9. Remove the engine support strut and support strut bracket.

10. Disconnect the oil level sensor.

11. Unfasten the oil pan mounting nuts and bolts, then remove the oil pan.

To install:

12. Clean all the gasket surfaces completely.

13. Place a 2mm bead of GM 1052914 or equivalent RTV sealer to the oil pan sealing surface except at the rear seal mounting surface. Using a new oil pan rear seal, apply a thin coat RTV sealer on the end down to the ears. Position the oil pan into place and install the fasteners.

14. Install the oil pan onto the engine and loosely install all the fasteners.

15. Tighten the nuts and bolts to 89 inch lbs. (10 Nm).

16. connect the oil level sensor.

17. Install the engine mount strut bracket and engine mount strut.

18. Connect the starter and install the starter and support bracket.

19. Install the flywheel cover and cover mounting bolts.

20. Install the right fender well splash shield.

21. Install the right front wheel. Tighten the nuts to 100 ft. lbs. (140 Nm).

22. Lower the vehicle.

1 SEAL
2 BOLT, 10 N•m (89 LB. IN.)
3 OIL PAN
4 NUT, OIL PAN 10 N•m (89 LB. IN.)

7922YG32

Exploded view of the oil pan mounting and related components—2.2L engine

23. Refill the crankcase with oil.
24. Connect the negative battery cable.
25. Start the vehicle and verify no leaks.

2.4L Engine

➡ The oil pan is die cast aluminum and must be handled with care to avoid damage. The oil pan includes an attachment to the transaxle to provide additional structural support.

1. Before servicing the vehicle, refer to the precautions in the beginning of this section.
2. Disconnect the negative battery cable.
3. Raise and safely support the vehicle.
4. Drain the engine oil.
5. Drain the engine coolant into a suitable container.
6. Remove the flywheel/converter cover.
7. Remove right wheel and tire assembly.
8. Remove the serpentine drive belt.
9. Remove the A/C compressor from the mounting bracket, lay it aside leaving the hoses attached.
10. Remove the engine mount strut bracket.
11. Remove the radiator outlet pipe bolts.
12. Remove the air conditioning and radiator outlet pipes from the oil pan.
13. Remove the exhaust manifold brace.
14. Remove the oil pan-to-flywheel cover bolt and nut.
15. Remove the flywheel cover stud for clearance.
16. Disconnect the radiator outlet pipe from the lower radiator hose and oil pan.
17. Detach the oil level sensor connector.
18. Remove the oil pan bolts and remove the oil pan.

To install:
19. Inspect the oil pan gasket for damage. The oil pan gasket is reusable, if it is not damaged.

20. With the gasket in place, position the pan to the engine and install oil pan bolts.
21. Install the flywheel cover stud, spacer and nut. Tighten this nut to 19 ft. lbs. (26 Nm).
22. Attach the oil level sensor connector.
23. Connect the radiator outlet pipe to lower radiator hose and oil pan.
24. Install the exhaust manifold brace.
25. Install the air conditioning and radiator outlet pipes to the oil pan.
26. Install the radiator outlet pipe bolts and tighten them to 124 inch lbs. (14 Nm).
27. Install the engine mount strut bracket and tighten bolts to 55 ft. lbs. (75 Nm).
28. Install the A/C compressor into the mounting bracket.
29. Install the serpentine drive belt.
30. Install the right splash shield.
31. Install the right front wheel and tire assembly.
32. Install the flywheel/converter cover.
33. Lower the vehicle.
34. Fill the crankcase with clean oil.
35. Fill the coolant system.
36. Connect the negative battery cable.
37. Start the vehicle and verify no leaks.

Oil Pump

REMOVAL & INSTALLATION

2.2L Engine

1. Before servicing the vehicle, refer to the precautions in the beginning of this section.
2. Disconnect the negative battery cable.
3. Raise and safely support the vehicle.
4. Drain the engine oil into a suitable container.
5. Remove the oil pan-to-engine bolts and the oil pan.
6. Remove the oil pump-to-rear main bearing cap bolt, the oil pump and extension shaft.

1 Bracket
2 Bolt
3 Oil pump drive assembly
4 O-ring
5 Shaft
6 Retainer: Heat and water soak prior to installation
7 Bolt
8 Oil pump
9 Cylinder block

7922YG13

Exploded view of the oil pump mounting to engine block—2.2L engine

To install:

❊❊ WARNING

A plastic sleeve called the extension shaft retainer connects the oil pump drive shaft to the oil pump. Heat the extension shaft retainer in hot water prior to assembly. Be sure the retainer does not crack upon installation.

7. Install the extension shaft, oil pump and pump-to-rear main cap bolt. Tighten the oil pump-to-bearing cap bolt to 32 ft. lbs. (43 Nm) and the upper oil pump drive bolt to 18 ft. lbs. (25 Nm).

❊❊ WARNING

To avoid engine damage, all oil pump cavities must be filled with petroleum jelly before installing the gears into the pump body. Also, use only original equipment gaskets. Gasket thickness is critical to proper oil pump operation.

8. Install the oil pan and attaching bolts.
9. Lower the vehicle.
10. Fill the crankcase with clean engine oil.
11. It is good practice to install a reliable

OIL PAN BOLT
(M8 × 1.25 × 22)
24 Nm (18 LB.FT.)

OIL PAN BOLT
(M8 × 1.25 × 80)
24 Nm (18 LB.FT.)

OIL PAN

◀FRT

OIL PAN BOLT
(M6 × 1.00 × 25)
12 Nm (106 LB.IN.)

OIL PAN BOLT
(M6 × 1.00 × 25)
12 Nm (106 LB.IN.)

OIL PAN BOLT
(M8 × 1.25 × 22)
24 Nm (18 LB.FT.)

OIL PAN BOLT
(M8 × 1.25 × 22)
24 Nm (18 LB.FT.)

STUD END OIL
PAN BOLT
26 Nm (19 LB.FT.)

7922YG12

Oil pan fastener torque specifications—2.4L engine

mechanical oil pressure gauge so actual pump pressure can be read after startup. If no oil pressure is seen within a short time of startup, shut down the engine to determine why there is no oil pressure.

12. Connect the negative battery cable.

13. Start the engine and check oil pressure and check for leaks.

14. Turn the engine **OFF** and allow to stand. Check oil level, add as necessary.

2.4L Engine

➡**The transaxle must be removed from the vehicle to service the oil pump.**

1. Before servicing the vehicle, refer to the precautions in the beginning of this section.

2. Disconnect the negative battery cable.

3. Install engine support fixture J-28467-A or equivalent.

4. Drain the engine oil.

5. Remove the oil pan.

6. Remove the transaxle.

7. Remove the flywheel.

8. Remove the balance shaft chain cover and guide.

9. Remove the oil pump bolts, then remove the oil pump cover.

10. Pull the housing to disconnect the pump gear from the balance shaft. Remove the housing assembly from the balance shaft assembly.

11. Disassemble the oil pump gerotor from the oil pump housing.

12. Disassemble the oil pump from the balance shaft housing.

13. Disassemble the pressure relief valve.

14. Remove the roll pin (drive it out with a small punch).

To install:

15. Clean all of the parts in suitable cleaning solvent. Remove all varnish, sludge and dirt.

16. Inspect the pump cover and housing for cracks and excessive wear, replace as necessary.

17. Lubricate the gears with clean engine oil.

18. Assemble the gerotor gear into the housing.

➡**Fill oil pump cavities with petroleum jelly prior to installation. This will ensure that there is oil pressure immediately on start-up and will prevent engine damage.**

19. Install the pressure relief valve, use a 9/16 in. deep well socket to seat the valve.

1 mm (0.04") BRASS FEELER GAUGE

APPLY 3 LBS. OF PRESSURE AGAINST GUIDE

7922YG14

Using a feeler gauge to check the chain tension—2.4L engine

20. Install the roll pin.

21. Install the pump housing to the balance shaft assembly.

22. Install the pump cover to the oil pump housing.

23. Install the oil pump to block bolts and tighten 40 ft. lbs. (54 Nm).

24. Install the balance shaft chain guide and chain. Adjust the chain tension by inserting a 0.40 in. (1mm) brass feeler, between the chain guide and the chain.

➡**A brass feeler gauge must be used to ensure that correct measurements are obtained. If a steel gauge is used, it will not bend to conform to the guide and will allow for incorrect measurements.**

25. Before servicing the vehicle, refer to the precautions in the beginning of this section.

26. Press the guide against the chain using about 3 pounds of force.

27. Tighten the chain tensioner fastener to 115 inch lbs. (13 Nm).

28. Install the balance shaft chain cover and tighten the nut and bolt to 115 inch lbs. (13 Nm).

29. Install the flywheel. Tighten the flywheel bolts to 22 ft. lbs. (30 Nm) plus an additional 45 degrees.

30. Install the transaxle.

31. Install the oil pan.

32. Lower the vehicle.

33. Fill the crankcase with clean oil.

34. Remove the engine support fixture.

35. Connect the negative battery cable.

36. Start the vehicle and verify oil pressure and no leaks.

Timing Chain, Sprockets, Front Cover and Seal

REMOVAL & INSTALLATION

2.2L Engine

➡**The following procedure requires the use of a special centering tool (J-23042).**

1. Before servicing the vehicle, refer to the precautions in the beginning of this section.

2. Disconnect the negative battery cable.

3. Remove the serpentine belt and tensioner.

➡**Although not absolutely necessary, removal of the right front inner fender splash shield will facilitate access to the front cover.**

4. Install engine support fixture J-28467-A or equivalent.

5. Remove the engine mount assembly.

6. Remove the alternator rear brace, then remove the alternator.

7. Remove the power steering pump, then position it aside with the lines still attached.

8. Raise and safely support the vehicle.

9. Remove the oil pan.

1 Balance shaft sub assembly
2 Bolt 12 Nm (106 lb. in.)
3 Oil pump sub assembly

7922YG15

Exploded view of the oil pump assembly mounting—2.4L engine

Timing belt service is covered in Section 5 of this manual

Exploded view of the serpentine belt tensioner mounting—2.2L engine

10. Unscrew the center bolt from the crankshaft pulley and slide the pulley and hub from the crankshaft.

11. Unfasten the front cover-to-block bolts, then remove the front cover. If the cover is difficult to remove, use a plastic mallet to carefully loosen the cover.

12. Using a suitable seal driver, tap the oil seal out of the front cover.

13. Place the No. 1 piston at TDC of the compression stroke that the marks on the camshaft and crankshaft sprockets are in alignment.

14. Loosen the timing chain tensioner nut as far as possible without actually removing it.

15. Remove the camshaft sprocket bolts and remove the sprocket and chain together. If the sprocket does not slide from the camshaft easily, a light blow with a soft mallet at the lower edge of the sprocket will dislodge it.

16. Use J-2288–8–20 or equivalent gear puller, and remove the crankshaft sprocket.

To install:

17. Press the crankshaft sprocket back onto the crankshaft.

18. Install the timing chain over the camshaft sprocket, then around the crankshaft sprocket. Be sure the marks on the 2 sprockets are in alignment. Lubricate the thrust surface with Molykote® or equivalent.

19. Align the dowel in the camshaft with the dowel hole in the sprocket, then install the sprocket onto the camshaft. Use the mounting bolts draw the sprocket onto the camshaft, then tighten to 66–68 ft. lbs. (89–92 Nm).

20. Lubricate the timing chain with clean engine oil. Tighten the chain tensioner.

21. Using a suitable seal installer, tap the new seal into the front cover and lubricate the lip of the seal.

22. The surfaces of the block and front cover must be clean and free of oil. Install a new gasket, then position the front cover on the block using a centering tool (J-23042). Tighten the retaining bolts to 6–9 ft. lbs. (8–12 Nm).

23. Installation of the remaining components is the reverse of the removal procedure.

24. Connect the negative battery cable.

2.4L Engine

⁎⁑ WARNING

The timing chain on the 1996–97 2.4L DOHC engine is NOT to be replaced with a timing chain from any other model year. The timing sprockets are different on these engines and the shape of the links matches the sprockets. Engine damage may result if the wrong timing chain is used.

1. Before servicing the vehicle, refer to the precautions in the beginning of this section.

2. Disconnect the negative battery cable.

3. Remove the coolant recovery reservoir.

4. Remove the serpentine belt, using a 13mm wrench that is at least 24 in. (61cm) long.

5. Install tool J-28467–400 onto the alternator stud-ended bolt, and attach the fixture.

6. Remove the upper cover fasteners.

7. Detach the cover vent hose.

8. Remove the right engine mount and the engine mount bracket or bracket adapter. Whenever the engine mounting bracket adapter is removed, the bolts must be replaced.

9. Raise and safely support the vehicle.

10. Remove the right front wheel and tire assembly and the splash shield.

11. Remove the crankshaft balancer assembly.

➡**Do not install an automatic transaxle equipped engine balancer on a manual transaxle equipped engine or vice-versa.**

12. Remove the lower cover fasteners.

13. Carefully lower the vehicle.

14. Remove the front cover and gasket. Inspect the gasket for damage and replace if necessary.

1. Camshaft sprocket
2. Crankshaft sprocket
3. Timing chain tensioner
A. Line up timing marks on sprockets with tabs on timing chain tensioner
B. Remove pin after timing chain is installed

Align the sprocket timing marks with the alignment tabs on the tensioner during timing chain installation—2.2L engine

A Camshaft timing alignment pin location
B Crankshaft gear timing mark
1 Shoe assembly timing chain tensioner
2 Timing chain
3 R.H. timing chain guide
4 L.H. timing chain guide
5 Upper timing chain guide
6 Exhaust camshaft sprocket
7 Intake camshaft sprocket

7922YG17

After installation the chain must be in the "timed" position—2.4L engine

15. Using a suitable seal driver, tap the oil seal out of the front cover.

16. Rotate the crankshaft clockwise, as viewed from the front of engine/normal rotation, until the camshaft sprocket timing dowel pin holes line up with the holes in the timing chain housing. The crankshaft sprocket keyway should point upwards and line up with the centerline of the cylinder bores; this is the "timed" position.

17. Remove the timing chain guides.

18. Raise and safely support the vehicle.

19. Be sure all of the slack in the timing chain is above the tensioner assembly, then remove the tensioner. The timing chain must be disengaged from any wear grooves in the tensioner shoe in order to remove the shoe. Slide a suitable prytool under the timing chain while pulling the shoe outward.

※ WARNING

Do NOT attempt to pry the socket off the camshaft or damage to the sprocket or chain housing could occur.

20. If difficulty is encountered in removing the chain tensioner shoe, remove the intake camshaft sprocket, as follows:

a. Carefully lower the vehicle.

b. Hold the intake camshaft sprocket with tool J-39579, or equivalent, and remove the sprocket bolt and washer.

c. Remove the washer from the bolts and thread the bolt back into the camshaft by hand. The bolt provides a surface to push against.

d. Remove the camshaft sprocket using a three-jaw puller in the 3 relief holes in the sprocket.

21. Unfasten the tensioner assembly retaining bolts, then remove the tensioner.

※ WARNING

The timing chain and crankshaft sprocket MUST be marked before removal. If the chain or sprocket is installed with the wear pattern in the opposite direction, noise and increased wear may occur.

22. Mark the crankshaft sprocket and timing chain outer surface for reassembly, then remove the chain.

23. Clean the old sealant off the bolt with a wire brush. Clean the threaded hole in the camshaft with a round nylon brush.

Inspect the parts for wear and replace as necessary. Note that some scoring of the chain shoe and guides is normal.

To install:

※ WARNING

Failure to follow this procedure may result in severe engine damage.

24. Position the intake camshaft sprocket onto the camshaft with the surface marked during removal showing.

25. Install the intake camshaft sprocket retaining bolt and washer, tighten to 52 ft. lbs. (70 Nm) while holding the sprocket with tool J-39579, if removed. Use sealant 12345493 or equivalent on the camshaft sprocket bolt.

26. Place tool J-36008, or equivalent camshaft aligning pins, through the holes in the camshaft sprockets into the holes in the timing chain housing. This positions the cams for correct timing.

27. If the camshafts are out of position and must be rotated more than ⅛ turn in order to install the alignment dowel pins, proceed as follows:

a. The crankshaft MUST be rotated 90 degrees clockwise off TDC in order to give the valves adequate clearance to open.

b. Once the camshafts are in position and the dowels installed, rotate the crankshaft counterclockwise back to TDC.

※ WARNING

Do not rotate the crankshaft clockwise to TDC; valve or piston damage could result.

28. Place the timing chain over the exhaust camshaft sprockets, around the idler sprocket and around the camshaft sprocket.

29. Set the camshafts at the timed position and install the timing chain. Remove the alignment dowel pin from the intake camshaft. Using tool J-39579, rotate the intake camshaft sprocket counterclockwise enough to slide the timing chain over the intake camshaft sprocket. Release the camshaft sprocket wrench J-39579. The length of the chain between the 2 camshaft sprockets will tighten. If properly timed, the intake camshaft alignment dowel pin should slide in easily. If the dowel pin does not fully index, the camshafts are NOT timed correctly and the procedure must be repeated.

30. Leave the alignment dowel pins

Exploded view of the serpentine belt tensioner mounting—2.4L engine

Exploded view of the serpentine belt idler pulley mounting—2.4L engine

installed. Raise and safely support the vehicle.

31. With the slack removed from the chain between the intake camshaft sprocket and the crankshaft sprocket, the timing marks on the crankshaft and cylinder block should be aligned. If the marks are not aligned, move the chain one tooth forward or rearward, remove the slack and recheck the marks.

32. Reload the timing chain tensioner assembly to it "zero" position as follows:

a. Form a keeper from a piece of heavy gauge wire.

b. Apply slight force on the tensioner blade to compress the plunger.

c. Insert a small prytool into the reset access hole, and pry the ratchet pawl away from the ratchet teeth while forcing the plunger completely in the hole.

d. Install the keeper between the access hole and the blade.

33. Install the tensioner assembly to the timing chain housing. Recheck the plunger assembly installation, it is correctly installed when the long end is toward the crankshaft. Install the tensioner retaining bolts; tighten to 89 inch lbs. (10 Nm).

34. Carefully lower the vehicle enough to reach and remove the alignment dowel pins.

✳✳ WARNING

Severe engine damage could result if the engine is not properly timed.

35. Rotate the crankshaft clockwise (normal rotation) 2 full rotations. Align the crankshaft keyway with the mark on the cylinder block and reinstall the alignment dowel pins. The pins will slide in easily if the engine of correctly timed.

36. Using a suitable seal installer, tap the new seal into the front cover and lubricate the lip of the seal.

37. Install the timing chain guides, then install the front (timing chain) cover. Tighten the timing chain cover fasteners to 106 inch lbs. (12 Nm). Tighten the balancer attaching bolt to 74 ft. lbs. (100 Nm).

38. Installation is the reverse of the removal procedure.

39. Connect the negative battery cable.

FUEL SYSTEM

Fuel System Service Precautions

Safety is the most important factor when performing not only fuel system maintenance but any type of maintenance. Failure to conduct maintenance and repairs in a safe manner may result in serious personal injury or death. Maintenance and testing of the vehicle's fuel system components can be accomplished safely and effectively by adhering to the following rules and guidelines.

• To avoid the possibility of fire and personal injury, always disconnect the negative battery cable unless the repair or test procedure requires that battery voltage be applied.

• Always relieve the fuel system pressure prior to disconnecting any fuel system component (injector, fuel rail, pressure regulator, etc.), fitting or fuel line connection. Exercise extreme caution whenever relieving fuel system pressure to avoid exposing skin, face and eyes to fuel spray. Please be advised that fuel under pressure may penetrate the skin or any part of the body that it contacts.

• Always place a shop towel or cloth around the fitting or connection prior to loosening to absorb any excess fuel due to spillage. Ensure that all fuel spillage (should it occur) is quickly removed from engine surfaces. Ensure that all fuel soaked cloths or towels are deposited into a suitable waste container.

• Always keep a dry chemical (Class B) fire extinguisher near the work area.

• Do not allow fuel spray or fuel vapors to come into contact with a spark or open flame.

• Always use a back-up wrench when loosening and tightening fuel line connection fittings. This will prevent unnecessary stress and torsion to fuel line piping.

• Always replace worn fuel fitting O-rings with new. Do not substitute fuel hose or equivalent, where fuel pipe is installed.

Fuel System Pressure

RELIEVING

1. Before servicing the vehicle, refer to the precautions in the beginning of this section.

2. Loosen the fuel filler cap in order to relieve the pressure in the tank (do not tighten at this time).

3. Raise and safely support the vehicle.

4. Detach the fuel pump electrical connector.

5. Start and run the vehicle until it stalls, the engage the starter for an additional 3 seconds to ensure the relief of any remaining pressure.

6. Disconnect the negative battery cable.

7. Once the tests or repairs are completed, reattach the fuel pump electrical connector.

8. Connect the negative battery cable.

9. Lower the vehicle.

10. Tighten the fuel filler cap.

11. Prime the fuel system by cycling the ignition switch **ON** for 2 seconds, **OFF** for 10 seconds, then **ON** again. Repeat, if necessary to build system pressure.

Fuel Filter

REMOVAL & INSTALLATION

The fuel filter is located under the rear of the vehicle, rearward of the fuel tank. Note that there is an additional filter/strainer inside the fuel tank attached to the fuel pump/sending unit assembly.

1. Before servicing the vehicle, refer to the precautions in the beginning of this section.

2. Relieve the fuel system pressure using the recommended procedure.

3. Disconnect the negative battery cable.

4. Raise and safely support the vehicle.

5. Using a back-up wrench on the fuel filter, disconnect the fuel line from the filter.

➡ **If a nylon fuel line becomes kinked and cannot be straightened, replace it.**

6. Grasp the filter and nylon connection line fitting. Twist the quick-connect fitting ¼ turn in each direction to loosen any dirt within the fitting. Disconnect the quick-connect fitting from the fuel filter by compressing the tabs while pulling outward on the line. GM also has available special tool J-38778, that is placed between the fuel filter and quick-connect fitting release mechanism to force the 2 apart.

7. Remove the fuel filter from the mounting bracket.

To install:

8. Before installing a new filter, always apply a few drops of clean engine oil to the male tube end of the filter and to the fuel sending unit assembly connection. This will help ensure proper connection and prevent possible fuel leaks. During normal operation, the O-rings located in the female connector will swell and may prevent proper connection if not lubricated.

9. Install the fuel filter in the mounting bracket.

10. Connect the quick-connect fitting to the fuel filter using the following procedure:

a. Apply a few drops of clean engine oil to the male ends of the filter and the fuel sender assembly.

b. Push the connectors together to cause the retaining tabs/fingers to snap into place.

c. Once installed, pull on both ends of each connection to be sure they are secure.

11. Using a new O-ring, tighten the fuel line using a back-up wrench on the fuel filter. Tighten the fuel line fitting to 20 ft. lbs. (27 Nm).

12. Lower the vehicle.

13. Connect the negative battery cable.

14. Pressurize the fuel system and verify no leaks.

Fuel Pump

REMOVAL & INSTALLATION

1. Before servicing the vehicle, refer to the precautions in the beginning of this section.

2. Relieve the fuel system pressure using the recommended procedure.

3. Disconnect the negative battery cable.

4. Drain the fuel tank, then remove the fuel tank from the vehicle.

5. While holding the modular fuel sender assembly down, remove the snapring from the designated slots located on the retainer.

❄ **WARNING**

The modular fuel sender assembly may spring up from its position. When removing the modular fuel sender from the tank, be aware that the reservoir bucket is full of fuel. It must be tipped slightly during removal to avoid damage to the float.

6. Remove the external fuel strainer.

7. Detach the Connector Position Assurance (CPA) piece from the electrical connector and detach the fuel pump electrical connector.

8. Gently release the tabs on the sides of the fuel sender at the cover assembly. Begin by squeezing the sides of the reservoir and releasing the tab opposite the fuel level sensor. Move clockwise to release the second and third tabs in the same manner.

9. Lift the cover assembly out far enough to detach the fuel pump electrical connection.

10. Rotate the fuel pump baffle counterclockwise and remove the baffle and pump assembly from the retainer.

11. Slide the fuel pump outlet out of slot, then remove the fuel pump outlet seal.

To install:

12. Install the fuel pump outlet seal, then slide the fuel pump outlet in the slots of reservoir cover.

13. Install the fuel pump and baffle assembly onto the reservoir retainer and rotate clockwise until seated.

14. Install the lower retainer assembly partially into the reservoir. Line up all 3 sleeve tabs. Press the retainer onto the reservoir making sure all 3 tabs are firmly seated.

➡ **Gently pull on the fuel pump reservoir to assure a secure fastening to the retainer. If not secure, replace the entire fuel sender.**

15. Attach the fuel pump connector.

16. Fasten the CPA connector to the fuel sender cover.

17. Install a new external fuel strainer.

1 SUPPORT ASSEMBLY, FUEL SENDER
2 COVER ASSEMBLY
3 FUEL PIPES (ABOVE COVER)
4 RESERVOIR
5 RUBBER PAD
6 STRAINER ASSEMBLY, FUEL LEVEL FUEL
7 SENSOR ASSEMBLY, FUEL LEVEL

7922YG33

Modular fuel pump component identification

18. Install the modular fuel sender.
19. Install the fuel tank in the vehicle.
20. Connect the negative battery cable.
21. Pressurize the fuel system and verify no leaks.

DRIVE TRAIN

Transaxle Assembly

REMOVAL & INSTALLATION

Manual

1. Before servicing the vehicle, refer to the precautions in the beginning of this section.
2. Disconnect the negative battery cable.
3. Install tool J-28467-A or equivalent, and raise the engine enough to take the pressure off the transaxle mounts.
4. Remove the left side hush panel.
5. Disconnect the clutch master cylinder pushrod from the clutch pedal.
6. Remove the air cleaner and duct assembly from the throttle body.
7. Remove the wiring harness from the mount bracket.
8. Remove the upper transaxle mount-to-transaxle bolts.
9. Remove the clutch master cylinder from the clutch actuator.
10. Disconnect the ground cables from the transaxle mounting studs.
11. Detach the back-up light switch connector.
12. Disconnect the transaxle vent tube.
13. Remove the rear transaxle-to-engine bolts.
14. Lower the engine support fixture enough to ease removal and installation of the transaxle.
15. Raise and safely support the vehicle.
16. Drain the transaxle into a suitable container.
17. Remove the tire and wheel assemblies.
18. Remove the left side splash shield.
19. Disconnect both front ABS wheel speed sensor harness and move out of the way.
20. Remove the flywheel cover.
21. Disconnect the Vehicle Speed Sensor (VSS) at the transaxle.
22. Remove the left and right ball joint nuts and separate them from the steering knuckle.
23. Remove the left stabilizer link pin.

24. Remove the left side U-bolt from the stabilizer bar.
25. Remove the left side suspension support attaching bolts.
26. Remove the drive axles from the transaxle.
27. Remove the front lower transaxle mount.
28. Position a suitable jack under the transaxle.
29. Remove the transaxle-to-engine mounting bolts (noting their location).
30. Remove the transaxle away from the engine by carefully lowering the jack.

To install:

31. Position the transaxle on the jack and move it into place.
32. Install the transaxle-to-engine mounting bolts and tighten them to 55 ft. lbs. (75 Nm).
33. Install the front transaxle mount.
34. Install the flywheel cover.
35. Install the drive axles into the transaxle assembly.
36. Install the left side suspension support and attaching bolts.
37. Install the left side U-bolt to the stabilizer bar.
38. Connect the ball joints to the steering knuckle and install the nuts, tighten to 48 ft. lbs. (65 Nm).
39. Install the left side stabilizer link pin assembly.
40. Route the left side ABS wheel speed sensor wiring harness and connect both front wheel speed sensor connectors.
41. Install the inner splash shield.
42. Connect the VSS to the transaxle.
43. Install both tire and wheel assemblies.
44. Lower the vehicle.
45. Install the ground cables to the transaxle mounting studs.
46. Install the vent tube to the transaxle.
47. Attach the back-up light switch connector.
48. Install the upper transaxle mounting bolts and tighten to 55 ft. lbs. (75 Nm).
49. Install the clutch master cylinder to clutch actuator cylinder.
50. Install the rear transaxle mount. Tighten the bolts to 55 ft. lbs. (75 Nm).
51. Clip the wiring harness to the mount bracket.
52. Remove the engine support fixture.
53. Connect the shift cables clamp and nut. Tighten the nut to 89 inch lbs. (10 Nm).
54. Install the air cleaner and duct assembly to the throttle body.
55. Connect the pushrod to the clutch pedal.
56. Install the left side hush panel.
57. Connect the negative battery cable.

58. Fill the transaxle with Synchromesh® Transaxle Fluid.
59. Road test the vehicle and verify proper operation.

Automatic

1. Before servicing the vehicle, refer to the precautions in the beginning of this section.
2. Disconnect the negative battery cable.
3. Remove the air intake duct.
4. Disconnect the TV cable, shift cable and bracket.
5. Disconnect the vacuum lines.
6. Tag and detach all necessary electrical connections.
7. Remove the power steering pump and set it aside (leaving the hoses attached).
8. Remove the filler tube.
9. Attach engine support fixture J-28467-A or equivalent.
10. Remove the top engine to transaxle bolts.
11. Raise and safely support the vehicle.
12. Remove both front tire and wheel assemblies.
13. Remove the left side splash shield.
14. Disconnect both front ABS wheel speed sensors and harness from left suspension support.
15. Disconnect both lower ball joints.
16. Disconnect the stabilizer shaft links.
17. Remove the front air deflector.
18. Remove the left suspension support.
19. Remove both drive axles (halfshafts).
20. Remove the engine to transaxle brace.
21. Remove the transaxle converter cover.
22. Remove the starter motor.
23. Remove the converter bolts.
24. Disconnect the transaxle cooler lines and remove brace.
25. Disconnect the ground wires going to transaxle.
26. Remove the exhaust brace.
27. Remove the bolts from engine and transaxle mount.
28. Support transaxle with a jack and remove transaxle mount-to-body bolts.
29. Disconnect heater core hose brace from transaxle.
30. Remove the remaining engine to transaxle bolts, then remove the transaxle assembly.

To install:

31. Be sure to properly seat the torque converter in the oil pump.
32. Install the transaxle into position with jack while installing right drive axle.

33. Install the lower engine-to-transaxle bolts and tighten to 71 ft. lbs. (96 Nm).

34. Install the transaxle mount-to-body bolts.

35. Install the engine and transaxle mount bolts.

36. Install the exhaust brace.

37. Install the cooler line brace.

38. Attach the ground wires to transaxle bolt.

39. Connect the cooler lines.

40. Install and tighten the converter bolts to 46 ft. lbs. (62 Nm).

41. Install the transaxle converter cover.

42. Install the starter.

43. Install the engine-to-transaxle brace and tighten the bolts to 32 ft. lbs. (43 Nm).

44. Install the drive axles.

45. Install the left suspension support.

46. Install the front air deflector.

47. Install the stabilizer links.

48. Connect the lower ball joints.

49. Connect both ABS wheel speed sensors.

50. Install the left splash shield.

51. Install the heater core pipe brace nut and bolt.

52. Install the front wheel and tire assemblies.

53. Lower the vehicle.

54. Install the top engine-to-transaxle bolts and tighten to 71 ft. lbs. (96 Nm).

55. Remove the engine support fixture.

56. Install the filler tube.

57. Install the power steering pump assembly.

58. Attach the electrical connections, as tagged during removal.

59. Connect the vacuum lines.

60. Attach the shift cable and bracket.

61. Attach the TV cable and adjust as necessary.

62. Install the intake air duct.

63. Connect the negative battery cable.

64. Fill transaxle and start vehicle, verify that there are no leaks.

65. Road test the vehicle.

Clutch

REMOVAL & INSTALLATION

The manual transaxle assembly must be removed from the vehicle to service the clutch assembly.

➡**Prior to any vehicle service that requires the removal of the actuator cylinder, the master cylinder pushrod must be disconnected from the clutch pedal. If not disconnected, permanent damage to the actuator cylinder will occur if the clutch pedal is depressed while the actuator cylinder is disconnected.**

1. Before servicing the vehicle, refer to the precautions in the beginning of this section.

2. Disconnect the negative battery cable.

3. Remove the clutch master cylinder pushrod from the clutch pedal.

4. Remove the transaxle.

5. If any of the parts are to be reused, mark the pressure plate assembly and the flywheel so they can be assembled in the same position. They were balanced as an assembly at the factory.

6. Loosen the attaching bolts one turn at a time until spring tension is relieved.

7. Support the pressure plate and remove the bolts. Remove the pressure plate and clutch disc. Do not disassemble the pressure plate assembly. Replace it if defective.

8. Inspect the flywheel, clutch disc, pressure plate, throwout bearing and the clutch fork and pivot shaft assembly for wear. Replace the parts as required. If the flywheel shows any signs of overheating or if it is badly grooved or scored, it should be resurfaced or replaced.

9. Clean the pressure plate and flywheel mating surfaces thoroughly.

To install:

10. Clean all parts well. Apply a small amount of high temperature grease to the pilot bearing inside the end of the crankshaft.

11. Position the clutch disc and pressure plate into the installed position, and support with clutch aligning tool J-29074 or equivalent. The clutch plate is assembled with the damper springs offset toward the transaxle. One side of the factory supplied clutch disc should be stamped "Flywheel Side."

12. Install the pressure plate-to-flywheel bolts. Tighten them gradually in a cross pattern as follows:
   a. Install and lightly seat all bolts.
   b. Tighten bolts 1, 2, 3, then 4, 5, and 6 to 12 ft. lbs. (16 Nm).
   c. Final torque bolts 1, 2, 3, then 4, 5, 6 to 15 ft. lbs. (20 Nm).

13. Lubricate the outside groove and the inside recess of the release bearing with high temperature grease. Wipe off any excess. Install the release bearing.
   a. On the NVG-T550 transaxle, lubricate the inside diameter of the bearing with clutch bearing lubricant.

   b. On the Isuzu transaxle, pack the inside recess of the release bearing completely full of chassis grease.

➡**On the Isuzu transaxle, be sure the bearing pads are located on the fork ends and both spring ends are in the fork holes with the spring completely seated in bearing groove.**

14. Install the transaxle.

15. Install clutch master cylinder pushrod to the clutch pedal and install the retaining clip.

16. If equipped with cruise control, check switch adjustment at clutch pedal bracket.

✳✳ WARNING

When adjusting the cruise control switch, do not exert an upward force on the clutch pedal pad of more than 20 ft. lbs. (27 Nm) or damage to the master cylinder pushrod retaining ring can result.

17. Connect the negative battery cable.

18. Bleed clutch system as necessary and road test vehicle.

7922YG18

Clutch cover bolt tightening sequence

Hydraulic Clutch System

BLEEDING

Do not use fluid which has been bled from a system to fill the reservoir as it may be aerated, have too much moisture content or possibly be contaminated. Clean the dirt and grease from the cap to ensure that no foreign substances enter the system. It is also important to maintain the fluid level in the clutch reservoir to the top step with hydraulic clutch fluid GM part number 12345347 or equivalent.

1. Before servicing the vehicle, refer to the precautions in the beginning of this section.

2. Attach a hose to the bleeder screw on the clutch actuator assembly and submerge the other end of the hose in a container of hydraulic clutch fluid.

3. Depress the clutch pedal slowly and hold.

4. Loosen the bleeder screw to purge air.

5. Tighten the bleeder screw to 18 inch lbs. (2 Nm).

6. Let up on the clutch pedal.

7. Repeat Steps 2 through 5 until all air is purged from the system.

8. Fill the reservoir to the top step with hydraulic clutch fluid.

9. Repeat this bleeding procedure if there is a grinding noise during the clutch spin down procedure.

Halfshaft

REMOVAL & INSTALLATION

Some manual transaxle applications may also use an intermediate shaft.

1. Before servicing the vehicle, refer to the precautions in the beginning of this section.

2. Disconnect the negative battery cable.

3. With the weight of the vehicle still on the wheels, loosen, but do not remove the front hub nut. This may require an assistant holding the brakes to keep the front halfshaft from turning. It is good practice to wire-brush the exposed threads on the outer CV-joint stub shaft and apply a generous amount of penetrating oil before attempting to loosen the hub nut.

4. Raise and safely support the vehicle.

5. Remove the tire and wheel assembly.

6. Remove the hub nut and washer.

7. Install the axle boot seal protector J-33162 or the equivalent on the right-hand inner boot, if equipped.

8. Remove and support the brake caliper.

9. Remove the brake rotor.

10. Remove the lower ball joint cotter pin and nut and loosen the joint. If removing the right halfshaft, turn the wheel to the left. If removing the left halfshaft turn the wheel to the right.

11. Disconnect the ABS sensor, if equipped.

12. Disconnect the stabilizer bar link.

13. Separate the lower ball joint from the steering knuckle.

14. Disengage the halfshaft stub end from the front wheel bearing and hub assembly using a suitable press-type tool, pressing until the halfshaft splines are just loose.

15. Separate the hub and bearing assembly from the halfshaft. Move the strut and knuckle assembly rearward.

16. Separate the inner joint from the transaxle using the proper puller tools such as J-33008 and J-29764 or their equivalents.

17. Remove the halfshaft from the transaxle. Do not pull the halfshaft by the CV-joint boot or on the joint itself.

To install:

18. Prior to installation, cover all sharp edges in the area of the halfshaft with shop towels so the CV-joint boots will be protected from damage. When a halfshaft is removed for any reason, the transaxle (the halfshaft male and female shank) and knuckle sealing surfaces should be inspected for debris and corrosion. If debris or corrosion are present, clean with 320 grit crocus cloth or equivalent. Transmission fluid may be used to clean off any remaining debris. The surface should be wiped clean and dry before attempting to install the halfshaft.

1 RIGHT DRIVE AXLE
2 LEFT DRIVE AXLE
3 J 28468 OR J 33008
4 J 29794
5 J2619-01

FRT

7922YG34

To prevent damaging the transaxle or halfshaft, use the tools as shown to remove the halfshafts

19. Install the halfshaft into the transaxle (or intermediate shaft, if equipped) by placing a brass drift pin into the groove on the joint housing and tapping until seated. Be careful not to damage the axle seal or dislodge the seal garter spring when installing the axle.

➡**Be sure the halfshaft is fully engaged in the transaxle. Verify that the halfshaft is seated by grasping the inner joint housing and pulling outward. Do not pull on the shaft or the boot, but on the inner joint housing only.**

20. Install the drive axle into the hub and bearing assembly.

21. Install the lower ball joint to the steering knuckle. Tighten the ball joint-to-steering knuckle nut to 41–48 ft. lbs. (55–65 Nm) to install the cotter pin. Do not loosen the nut at any time during installation. Install a new cotter pin.

22. Install the washer and a new hub nut. To keep the hub from turning while the hub nut is being torqued, insert a drift pin through the caliper opening into one of the ventilation openings in the brake rotor. This should lock the assembly together. Tighten the hub nut to 185 ft. lbs. (260 Nm).

23. Install the tire and wheel assembly.

24. Lower the vehicle.

25. Test drive vehicle to verify no front drive noise.

STEERING AND SUSPENSION

Air Bag

❋❋ CAUTION

Some vehicles are equipped with an air bag system, also known as the Supplemental Inflatable Restraint (SIR) system. The system must be disabled before performing service on or around system components, steering column, instrument panel components, wiring and sensors. Failure to follow safety and disabling procedures could result in accidental air bag deployment, possible personal injury and unnecessary system repairs.

5 RETAINER, BEARING
6 LOCK, SHAFT
7 CAM ASM, T/SIG CANCEL
8 SPRING, UPPER BEARING
9 SPACER, UPPER BEARING

9300YG12

Exploded view of the upper steering column components

12 ACTUATOR ASM, IGNITION LOCK
14 SPRING, LOCK PRE-LOAD
15 STRAP, GROUND
21 BOLT ASM, LOCK
22 BRACKET, LOCK BOLT SUPPORT
23 SCREW, TAPPING

9300YG11

Exploded view of the ignition lock cylinder and related components

1-NUT, FLANGED PREVAIL TORQUE
2-RING, RETAINING
3-COIL ASM, SIR
4-WASHER, WAVE
5-RETAINER, BEARING
6-LOCK, SHAFT
7-CAM ASM, T/SIG CANCEL
8-SPRING, UPPER BEARING
9-SEAT, UPPER BEARING INNER RACE
10-RACE, INNER
11-HOUSING ASM, BRG &
12-ACTUATOR ASM, IGNITION LOCK
14-SPRING, LOCK PRE-LOAD
15-STRAP, GROUND
19-SWITCH ASM, IGNITION
20-SCREW, TAPPING
21-BOLT ASM, IGNITION

22-BRACKET, LOCK BOLT SUPPORT
23-SCREW, TAPPING
26-SHAFT ASM, RACE & UPPER
27-SPHERE, CENTERING
28-SPRING, JOINT PRELOAD
29-SHAFT ASM, LOWER
45-SCREW, SUPPORT
46-GUIDE, SPRING
47-SPRING, WHEEL TILT
48-PIN, PIVOT
49-SUPPORT ASM, STRG COL
50-RETAINER, SPRING
51-CLIP, WIRE RESTRAINT
53-JACKET ASM, STRG COL
54-BEARING ASM, ADAPTER &
55-SEAT, LOWER BEARING
56-SPRING, LOWER BEARING
57-RETAINER, LOWER SPRING

9300YG10

Exploded view of the cavalier steering column with tilt wheel

PRECAUTIONS

Several precautions must be observed when handling the inflator module to avoid accidental deployment and possible personal injury.

• Never carry the inflator module by the wires or connector on the underside of the module.

• When carrying a live inflator module, hold securely with both hands, and ensure that the bag and trim cover are pointed away.

• Place the inflator module on a bench or other surface with the bag and trim cover facing up.

• With the inflator module on the bench, never place anything on or close to the module which may be thrown in the event of an accidental deployment.

DISARMING

✳✳ CAUTION

The Supplemental Inflatable Restraint (SIR) system must be disarmed before performing many in-vehicle service procedures. Failure to do so may cause accidental deployment of the air bag, resulting in unnecessary SIR system repairs and/or personal injury.

1. Turn the steering wheel so the vehicle's wheels are pointing straight ahead.
2. Turn the ignition switch to the **LOCK** position and remove the key.
3. Remove the AIR BAG fuse from the instrument panel fuse block.
4. Remove the left-hand sound insulator.
5. Detach the Connector Position Assurance (CPA) and yellow 2-way connector at the base of the steering column.

1. Steering column
2. Connector, sir(yellow)

7922YG19

Driver's side Yellow 2-way air bag CPA connector location

6. If equipped with passenger side air bags, remove the right-hand sound insulator, then disconnect the CPA and yellow 2-way connector from the passenger inflator module pigtail.

ARMING

1. Turn the ignition switch to the **LOCK** position and remove the key.
2. If equipped with passenger side air bags, connect the yellow 2-way connector and CPA to the passenger inflator module pigtail, then install the right-hand sound insulator.
3. Attach the yellow 2-way connector and CPA at the base of the steering column. After installing the CPA, clip the connector to flange on the steering column support.
4. Install the left-hand insulator.
5. Install the AIR BAG fuse into the instrument panel fuse block.
6. Turn the ignition switch to the **RUN** position and verify that the AIR BAG warning lamp flashes 7–9 times, then the light turns OFF.

1. I/P compartment
2. Connector,sir(yellow)

7922YG20

Passenger's side Yellow 2-way air bag CPA connector location

Rack and Pinion Steering Gear

REMOVAL & INSTALLATION

1. Before servicing the vehicle, refer to the precautions in the beginning of this section.
2. Disconnect the negative battery cable.
3. Remove the left side sound insulator.
4. Remove the upper pinch bolt on the inter-shaft assembly.
5. Remove the line retainer, if applicable.
6. Raise and safely support the vehicle.
7. Remove the left front tire and wheel assembly.
8. Disconnect the tie rod ends from the struts using tool J-2431–01 or equivalent.
9. Remove the left and right mounting bolts.
10. Disconnect the gear inlet and outlet hose assemblies from the rack and pinion.
11. Remove the lower pinch bolt from the flange inter-shaft assembly.
12. Remove the inter-shaft assembly.
13. Loosen the crossmember bolts to gain additional clearance for removal.
14. Remove the rack and pinion through the wheel opening.

To install:
15. Install the rack and pinion through the left wheel opening.
16. Install the crossmember bolts as follows:
   a. Tighten the left rear outboard 1st to 96 ft. lbs. (130 Nm).
   b. Tighten the right rear outboard 2nd to 96 ft. lbs. (130 Nm).
   c. Tighten the front upper bolts to 96 ft. lbs. (130 Nm).
   d. Tighten the rear inboard bolts last to 96 ft. lbs. (130 Nm).
17. Install the lower pinch bolt (flange to inter-shaft bolt) and tighten to 30 ft. lbs. (41 Nm).
18. Connect the gear inlet and outlet pipes to the rack and pinion and tighten to 20 ft. lbs. (27 Nm).
19. Hand start bolts and nuts. Tighten left side bolt to 89 ft. lbs. (120 Nm), then tighten right side to 89 ft. lbs. (120 Nm).
20. Connect the tie rod ends to the struts and tighten to 44 ft. lbs. (60 Nm) and install new cotter pins.
21. Install left tire and wheel assembly.
22. Install line retainer, if applicable.
23. Lower the vehicle.

1 RACK AND PINION
2 CROSSMEMBER, SUSPENSION
3 BOLTS, STEERING GEAR
4 CAGE NUT
5 WELD NUTS
6 BUSHING AND SLEEVE
7 TIE ROD

7922YG21

Exploded view of the rack and pinion steering gear mounting

24. Install the upper pinch bolt and tighten to 30 ft. lbs. (41 Nm).
25. Install the left side sound insulator.
26. Connect the negative battery cable.
27. Fill with fluid and bleed air from system.
28. Check toe setting and adjust as required.
29. Road test vehicle and verify no leaks.

Strut

REMOVAL & INSTALLATION

Front

1. Before servicing the vehicle, refer to the precautions in the beginning of this section.
2. From inside the engine compartment, pry off the cover on the strut tower, if equipped, then unfasten the upper strut-to-body nuts and/or bolts.
3. Loosen the wheel lug nuts, then raise and safely support the vehicle.
4. Place jackstands under the front crossmember. Lower the vehicle slightly so the weight of the vehicle rests on the jackstands and NOT the control arms.
5. Remove the wheel and tire assembly.
6. Before removing front suspension components, their positions should be marked so they may assemble correctly.

✳ WARNING

Whenever working near the drive axles, use care to prevent damage from over-extension of the drive shaft joints. When either end of the shaft is disconnected, over-extension of the joint could result in separation of the internal components and possible joint failure.

7. Install a drive axle joint protective cover (modified), such as J-34754 or equivalent.
8. If necessary, remove the brake line bracket.
9. Remove the cotter pin and nut, then press the tie rod out of the strut bracket using J-24319–01 or equivalent two-armed puller. Discard the cotter pin.
10. Unfasten and remove the strut-to-steering knuckle bolts and carefully lift out the strut.

✳ WARNING

The steering knuckle MUST be supported to prevent axle joint over-extension.

11. Remove the strut assembly from the vehicle. Be careful to avoid chipping or cracking the spring coating when handling the front suspension coil spring assembly.

To install:

12. Move the strut into position, then install the nuts and/or bolts connecting the strut assembly to the body.
13. Align the steering knuckle with the strut flange scribe mark made during removal, then install the bolts and nuts. Tighten to 133 ft. lbs. (180 Nm).
14. Position the tie rod end into the strut assembly, then secure with the tie rod end bolt and new cotter pin. Tighten the tie rod end bolt to 44 ft. lbs. (60 Nm).
15. Tighten the nuts and/or bolts attaching the top of the strut to the body to 18–20 ft. lbs. (25–27 Nm).
16. Install the brake line bracket.
17. Slightly raise the vehicle, then remove the jackstands from under the suspension supports.
18. Install the tire and wheel assembly.
19. Carefully lower the vehicle, then final tighten the lug nuts to 100 ft. lbs. (140 Nm).

Rear

✳ WARNING

Do not remove both struts at one time. Suspending the rear axle at full length could result in damage to brake lines and/or hoses.

1. Before servicing the vehicle, refer to the precautions in the beginning of this section.
2. Open the deck lid.
3. Remove the strut attaching nut.
4. Raise and safely support the vehicle. Support the rear axle with safety stands.
5. Remove the bolts from the strut upper mount.
6. Remove strut mounting bolt. Remove the strut assembly.

To install:

7. Install strut assembly at the lower attachment. Install the bolt hand-tight.
8. Install bolts to the strut mount.
9. Lower the vehicle.
10. Install the strut upper mount attaching nut.

Legend
- (1) Bolt
- (2) Clamp, Stabilizer Shaft
- (3) Stabilizer Shaft
- (4) Nut, Stabilizer Link
- (5) Washer
- (6) Insulator, Stabilizer Link
- (7) Spacer Stabilizer Link
- (8) Bushing, Vertical
- (9) Bolt, Vertical Bushing
- (10) Ball Joint
- (11) Bolt, Stabilizer Link
- (12) Control Arm
- (13) Bushing, Control Arm
- (14) Lower Spring Insulator
- (15) Suspension Support
- (16) Insulator, Stabilizer Shaft
- (17) Cover, Strut Mount
- (18) Nut
- (19) Nut, Strut Dampener Shaft
- (20) Strut Mount and Rate Washer Assembly
- (21) Spring Seat
- (22) Upper Spring Insulator
- (23) Strut Bumper and Shield
- (24) Spring
- (25) Lower Spring Insulator
- (26) Strut
- (27) Nut
- (28) Washer
- (29) Bolt
- (30) Hub and Bearing Assembly
- (31) Seal (Part of 5)
- (32) Steering Knuckle
- (33) Nut, Ball Joint
- (34) Cotter Pin
- (35) Bolt
- (36) Bolt

7922YG22

Exploded view of the front suspension

11. Tighten the lower mounting bolt to 125 ft. lbs. (170 Nm).

12. Tighten the strut upper mount bolts to 21 ft. lbs. (28 Nm).

13. Remove the safety stands and lower the vehicle.

14. Tighten the upper strut mounting nut to 15 ft. lbs. (20 Nm).

15. Road test the vehicle.

Coil Spring

REMOVAL & INSTALLATION

Front and Rear

1. Remove the strut assembly from the vehicle, as outlined earlier in this section.

2. Mount the strut compressor J-34013 in holding fixture J-3289–20.

3. Mount the strut assembly into the compressor. Note that the strut compressor has strut mounting holes drilled for specific vehicle lines.

4. Compress the strut approximately ½ its height after initial contact with the top cap.

Turn to Section 6 for brake system applications

◀FRT

1 SHOCK, COIL−OVER
2 NUT
3 BOLT, UPPER STRUT (2)
4 BOLT, AXLE
5 ADAPTER

7922YG23

Exploded view of the rear strut mounting

1 WRENCH
2 SOCKET
3 STRUT ASSEMBLY

7922YG25

Use a socket and a wrench to remove the dampener shaft nut spring cap while compressing the spring

1 STRUT MOUNT NUT
2 STRUT MOUNT
3 RATE WASHER
4 SPRING SEAT
5 SPRING UPPER INSULATOR
6 JOUNCE BUMPER
7 STRUT DUST SHIELD
8 SPRING
9 SPRING LOWER INSULATOR
10 STRUT

7922YG27

Exploded view of the front strut assembly

---

1 STRUT ASSEMBLY
2 INSTALL LOCKING PINS THROUGH STRUT ASSEMBLY
3 TIGHTEN NUTS UNTIL FLUSH WITH STRUT COMPRESSOR
4 COMPRESSOR FORCING SCREW

7922YG24

View of a typical strut assembly mounted in a compressor

1 STRUT COMPRESSOR
2 STRUT ASSEMBLY

7922YG26

Install the rod to guide the dampener shaft straight down through the spring cap while compressing the spring

Never bottom the spring or dampener rod!

5. Remove the nut from the strut dampener shaft and place alignment/guiding rod J-34013−27 on top of the dampener shaft. Use the rod to guide the dampener shaft straight down through the spring cap while compressing the spring. Remove the components.

Be careful to avoid chipping or cracking the spring coating when handling the front suspension coil spring assembly.

To install:
6. Install the bearing cap into the strut compressor if previously removed.
7. Mount the strut assembly in strut compressor, using bottom locking pin only. Extend the dampener shaft and install clamp J-34013−20 on the dampener shaft.
8. Install the spring over the dampener and swing the assembly up so the upper locking pin can be installed.
9. Install all shields, bumpers and insulators on the spring seat. Install the

spring seat on top of the spring. Be sure the flat on the upper spring seat is facing in the proper direction. The spring seat flat should be facing the same direction as the centerline of the strut assembly spindle.

10. Install the guiding rod and turn the forcing screw while the guiding rod centers the assembly. When the threads on the dampener shaft are visible, remove the guiding rod and install the nut. tighten the nut to 52 ft. lbs. (70 Nm). Use a crow's foot line wrench while holding the dampener shaft with a socket.

11. Remove the clamp.

Lower Ball Joint

REMOVAL & INSTALLATION

1. Before servicing the vehicle, refer to the precautions in the beginning of this section.

2. Raise and safely support the vehicle.

3. If suspension contact hoist is used, place safety stands under the crossmember. Lower the vehicle slightly so the weight of the vehicle rests on the crossmember.

4. Remove the tire and wheel assembly.

✳✳ WARNING

Care must be exercised to prevent the axle shaft joints from being overextended. When either end of the shaft is disconnected, over-extension of the joint could result in separation of internal components and possible joint failure. Failure to observe this can result in interior joint or boot damage and possible joint failure.

5. Remove the cotter pin and nut from the ball joint.

6. Separate the ball joint from the steering knuckle using tool J-38892 or equivalent.

7. Drill out the 3 rivets retaining ball joint to the lower control arm. Use an 1⁄8 in. (3mm) drill bit to make a pilot hole through the rivets. Finish drilling rivets with a 1⁄2 in. (13mm) drill bit.

8. Remove the nut attaching link to the stabilizer shaft.

9. Remove the ball joint from the steering knuckle and control arm.

To install:

10. Install ball joint into the control arm.

11. Install 3 new bolts and nuts (supplied with new ball joint) and tighten.

12. Position ball joint stud through the steering knuckle and tighten nut to 50 ft. lbs. (65 Nm) and install cotter pin.

13. Connect stabilizer link to stabilizer shaft and tighten nut to 13 ft. lbs. (17 Nm).

14. Install tire and wheel assembly.

15. Lower the vehicle.

16. Check front wheel alignment and adjust, if necessary.

Wheel Bearings

ADJUSTMENT

These vehicles are equipped with sealed hub and bearing assemblies. The hub and bearing assemblies are non-serviceable. If the assembly is damaged, the complete unit must be replaced.

REMOVAL & INSTALLATION

Front

1. Before servicing the vehicle, refer to the precautions in the beginning of this section.

2. Raise and safely support the vehicle.

3. Remove the tire and wheel assembly.

4. Remove the drive axle nut.

5. Remove the brake caliper bolts and support the brake caliper to the side.

6. Remove the brake rotor.

7. Remove the 3 bolts that go through the steering knuckle from the back of the knuckle. Rust buildup may require a generous application of penetrating oil where the hub fits into the knuckle. Remove the hub and bearing assembly from the steering knuckle.

8. Remove the hub and bearing assembly from the vehicle.

To install:

9. Install hub and bearing assembly to steering knuckle.

10. Install hub and bearing bolts and tighten to 70 ft. lbs. (95 Nm).

11. Install the brake rotor.

12. Install the brake caliper and bolts.

13. Install the drive axle through hub assembly and tighten nut to 192 ft. lbs. (260 Nm).

14. Install the tire and wheel assembly.

15. Lower the vehicle.

16. Road test the vehicle and verify proper operation.

```
1   SERVICE BALL JOINT
2   BALL JOINT MOUNTING BOLTS
3   NUT
4   LOWER CONTROL ARM
5   STEERING KNUCKLE
6   NUT — 55 N·m (41 LBS. FT.) MINIMUM TORQUE
        65 N·m (48 LBS. FT.) MAXIMUM TORQUE
        TO INSTALL PIN
7   PIN
```

7922YG28

Exploded view of the ball joint mounting

1 HUB AND BEARING ASSEMBLY
2 STEERING KNUCKLE
3 WASHER
4 DRIVE AXLE NUT – 260 N·m (192 LBS. FT.)
5 HUB AND BEARING RETAINING BOLT
6 WASHER

7922YG29

Exploded view of the front hub and bearing assembly

1 NUT
2 REAR AXLE ASSEMBLY
3 BACKING PLATE
4 HUB AND BEARING ASSEMBLY
5 BOLT

7922YG30

Exploded view of the rear hub and bearing assembly

Rear

A single-unit hub and bearing assembly is bolted to both ends of the rear axle assembly or rear knuckle assembly. This hub and bearing is a sealed unit which is supposed to eliminate the need for wheel bearing adjustments and does not require periodic maintenance.

1. Before servicing the vehicle, refer to the precautions in the beginning of this section.
2. Raise and safely support vehicle.
3. Remove the wheel and tire assembly.
4. Remove the brake drum.
5. Remove the hub and bearing assembly mounting bolts. The top rear mounting bolt will not clear the brake shoe when removing the hub and bearing assembly. Partially remove the hub and bearing assembly prior to removing this bolt.
6. Detach the ABS wheel speed sensor wire connector.
7. Remove the hub and bearing assembly from the axle.

To install:

8. Attach the rear ABS wheel speed sensor wire connector.
9. Install the hub and bearing assembly. Position the top rear mounting bolt in the hub and bearing assembly prior to installation to the axle housing.
10. Tighten the mounting bolts to 44 ft. lbs. (60 Nm).
11. Install the brake drum.
12. Install the wheel and tire assembly.
13. Lower the vehicle.
14. Road test the vehicle.

GENERAL MOTORS CORPORATION—L BODY

34

Chevrolet-Beretta • Corsica

PRECAUTIONS

Before servicing any vehicle, please be sure to read all of the following precautions, which deal with personal safety, prevention of component damage, and important points to take into consideration when servicing a motor vehicle:

• Never open, service or drain the radiator or cooling system when the engine is hot; serious burns can occur from the steam and hot coolant.

• Observe all applicable safety precautions when working around fuel. Whenever servicing the fuel system, always work in a well-ventilated area. Do not allow fuel spray or vapors to come in contact with a spark, open flame, or excessive heat (a hot drop light, for example). Keep a dry chemical fire extinguisher near the work area. Always keep fuel in a container specifically designed for fuel storage; also, always properly seal fuel containers to avoid the possibility of fire or explosion. Refer to the additional fuel system precautions later in this section.

• Fuel injection systems often remain pressurized, even after the engine has been turned **OFF**. The fuel system pressure must be relieved before disconnecting any fuel lines. Failure to do so may result in fire and/or personal injury.

• Brake fluid often contains polyglycol ethers and polyglycols. Avoid contact with the eyes and wash your hands thoroughly after handling brake fluid. If you do get brake fluid in your eyes, flush your eyes with clean, running water for 15 minutes. If eye irritation persists, or if you have taken brake fluid internally, IMMEDIATELY seek medical assistance.

• The EPA warns that prolonged contact with used engine oil may cause a number of skin disorders, including cancer! You should make every effort to minimize your exposure to used engine oil. Protective gloves should be worn when changing oil. Wash your hands and any other exposed skin areas as soon as possible after exposure to used engine oil. Soap and water, or waterless hand cleaner should be used.

• All new vehicles are now equipped with an air bag system, often referred to as a Supplemental Restraint System (SRS) or Supplemental Inflatable Restraint (SIR) system. The system must be disabled before performing service on or around system components, steering column, instrument panel components, wiring and sensors. Failure to follow safety and disabling procedures could result in accidental air bag deployment, possible personal injury and unnecessary system repairs.

• Always wear safety goggles when working with, or around, the air bag system. When carrying a non-deployed air bag, be sure the bag and trim cover are pointed away from your body. When placing a non-deployed air bag on a work surface, always face the bag and trim cover upward, away from the surface. This will reduce the motion of the module if it is accidentally deployed. Refer to the additional air bag system precautions later in this section.

• Clean, high quality brake fluid from a sealed container is essential to the safe and proper operation of the brake system. You should always buy the correct type of brake fluid for your vehicle. If the brake fluid becomes contaminated, completely flush the system with new fluid. Never reuse any brake fluid. Any brake fluid that is removed from the system should be discarded. Also, do not allow any brake fluid to come in contact with a painted surface; it will damage the paint.

• Never operate the engine without the proper amount and type of engine oil; doing so WILL result in severe engine damage.

• Timing belt maintenance is extremely important! Many models utilize an interference-type, non-freewheeling engine. If the timing belt breaks, the valves in the cylinder head may strike the pistons, causing potentially serious (also time-consuming and expensive) engine damage. Refer to the maintenance interval charts in the front of this manual for the recommended replacement interval for the timing belt, and to the timing belt section for belt replacement and inspection.

• Disconnecting the negative battery cable on some vehicles may interfere with the functions of the on-board computer system(s) and may require the computer to undergo a relearning process once the negative battery cable is reconnected.

• When servicing drum brakes, only disassemble and assemble one side at a time, leaving the remaining side intact for reference.

• Only an MVAC-trained, EPA-certified automotive technician should service the A/C system or its components.

ENGINE REPAIR

Distributor

The 2.2L and 3.1L engines utilize the Direct Ignition System (DIS), which is called the Electronic Ignition (EI) system in later model years, and is designed with a distributorless ignition.

Ignition Timing

ADJUSTMENT

The vehicles covered in this section are equipped with distributorless ignition systems. Accordingly, ignition timing is controlled by the Engine/Powertrain Control Module (ECM/PCM) and is not adjustable.

Engine Assembly

REMOVAL & INSTALLATION

2.2L Engine

➡ **The following procedure is for removing the engine and transaxle assemblies together, which is recommended by the manufacturer.**

1. Before servicing the vehicle, refer to the precautions in the beginning of this section.
2. Disconnect the battery.
3. Drain the cooling system.
4. Relieve the fuel system pressure.
5. Disconnect the hood lamp wiring, if so equipped and remove the hood.
6. Disconnect the throttle body intake duct.
7. Remove the rear sight shields.
8. Disconnect the upper radiator hose.
9. Disconnect the brake booster vacuum hose.
10. Disconnect the alternator top brace and wiring.

11. Disconnect and tag the upper engine harness from the engine.
12. Properly discharge the A/C system.
13. Disconnect the A/C compressor-to-condenser and accumulator lines.
14. Raise and support the vehicle safely.
15. Drain and recycle the engine oil.
16. Remove the left splash shield.
17. Disconnect the exhaust system.
18. Disconnect and tag the lower engine wiring.
19. Remove the flywheel inspection cover.
20. Remove the front wheels.
21. Disconnect the lower radiator hose.
22. Disconnect the heater hoses from the heater core.
23. Remove the brake calipers from the steering knuckle and wire up out of the way.
24. Disconnect the tie rods from the struts.
25. Carefully lower the vehicle.
26. Remove the clutch slave cylinder.
27. With the fuel system pressure released, place an absorbent shop towel around the connections and disconnect the fuel lines.
28. Disconnect the transaxle linkage at the transaxle.
29. Disconnect the accelerator cables from the Throttle Body Injection (TBI) unit.

1 MOUNT ASSEMBLY
2 BOLT – 66 N·m (49 LBS. FT.)(TIGHTEN FIRST)
3 BOLT – 66 N·m (49 LBS. FT.) (TIGHTEN SECOND)
4 NUT – 42 N·m (31 LBS. FT.) (TIGHTEN LAST) .
5 BOLT
6 BOLTS – 170 N·m (125 LBS. FT.)
7 BOLT – 42 N·m (31 LBS. FT.)

9300Z201

Exploded view of the front engine mount—2.2L engine

Exploded view of the engine mount strut—2.2L engine

1 BOLTS – 66 N·m (49 LBS. FT.)
2 ENGINE MOUNT STRUT BRACKET
3 ENGINE MOUNT STRUT
4 BOLT – 120 N·m (89 LBS. FT.)
5 BOLT – 75 N·m (55 LBS. FT.)

USE HOLE "A" FOR AUTOMATIC TRANSAXLE, HOLE "M" FOR MANUAL

VIEW A

9300Z202

1. BOLTS, TORQUE FIRST 43 N•m (32 LB. FT.)
2. BOLTS, TORQUE SECOND 43 N•m (32 LB. FT.)
3. BRACKET, TRANSAXLE TO ENGINE
4. ENGINE
5. TRANSAXLE

9300Z203

Exploded view of the transaxle-to-engine bracket—2.2L engine

1. BOLT, TORQUE FIRST 50 N•m (37 LB. FT.)
2. BOLT, TORQUE SECOND 50 N•m (37 LB. FT.)
3. NUT, TORQUE THIRD 50 N•m (37 LB. FT.)
4. ENGINE
5. TRANSAXLE
6. BRACE, ENGINE TO TRANSAXLE
7. POWER STEERING PUMP

9300Z204

Exploded view of the transaxle-to-engine brace—2.2L engine

30. Disconnect the cruise control cables from the TBI unit.

31. Disconnect the throttle valve cables from the TBI, on vehicles equipped with an automatic transaxle.

32. Disconnect the automatic transaxle cooling lines.

33. Disconnect the power steering hoses from the power steering pump.

34. Remove the center suspension support bolts.

35. Align Engine/Transaxle Frame Handler tool No. J 36295 under the suspension supports, engine and transaxle; lower vehicle to dolly and add support under the engine.

36. Safely support the rear of the vehicle.

37. Disconnect the upper transaxle mount.

38. Remove the upper strut bolts and nuts.

39. Disconnect the front engine mount.

40. Disconnect the rear engine mount.

41. Remove the suspension support bolts.

42. Raise the vehicle and remove the engine and transaxle assembly on tool No. J 36295.

43. Remove the engine from the transaxle as required.

To install:

44. If removed, attach the transaxle to the engine.

45. Carefully lower the vehicle and install the engine and transaxle assembly using tool No. J 36295.

46. Install the suspension supports bolts and tighten them to 89 ft. lbs. (120 Nm).

47. Install the transaxle mount but do not tighten.

48. Install the rear engine mount but do not tighten.

49. Install the front engine mount but do not tighten.

50. Tighten the manual transaxle mounting bolts as follows:

a. Front transaxle strut-to-body bolts to 40 ft. lbs. (54 Nm).

b. Rear transaxle mount-to-body bolts to 23 ft. lbs. (31 Nm).

51. Tighten the automatic transaxle mount bolts to 22 ft. lbs. (30 Nm).

52. Tighten the front and rear engine mount bolts.

➡All engine mount bolts that have been removed must be cleaned and a new thread-locking compound applied to the threads before reinstallation.

53. Install the power steering hoses.

54. Connect the accelerator, cruise control and TV cables to the TBI.

55. Connect the transaxle cooling lines to the automatic transaxle.

56. Connect the transaxle linkage.

57. Reconnect the fuel lines.

58. Reconnect the clutch slave cylinder.

59. Raise and support the vehicle safely.

60. Install the tie rods.

61. Install the calipers to the steering knuckle.

62. Attach the heater hoses to the heater core.

63. Connect the lower radiator hose.

64. Install the A/C compressor.

65. Install the flywheel inspection cover.

66. Install the engine splash shield.

67. Install the front wheel and tighten the wheel stud nuts to 100 ft. lbs. (136 Nm).

68. Lower the vehicle.

69. Install the upper engine wiring.

70. Install the compressor to condenser and accumulator lines.

71. Connect the brake booster vacuum hose.

72. Attach the upper radiator hose.

73. Raise and support the vehicle safely.

74. Install the lower engine wiring.

75. Reconnect the exhaust system.

76. Lower the vehicle.

77. Connect the TBI wiring.

78. Install the air cleaner assembly.

79. Close the radiator cock and refill the cooling system.

80. Fill the crankcase with oil.

81. Recharge the A/C system.

82. Check and adjust the wheel alignment.

83. Install the hood and connect the positive, then the negative battery cables.

3.1L Engine

1. Before servicing the vehicle, refer to the precautions in the beginning of this section.

2. Relieve the fuel pressure. Disconnect the negative, then the positive battery cables. Remove the battery from the vehicle.

3. Remove the air cleaner, the air inlet hose and the Mass Air Flow (MAF) sensor.

4. Drain the cooling system. Remove the exhaust manifold crossover assembly

bolts and separate the assembly from the exhaust manifolds.

5. Remove the serpentine belt tensioner and the drive belt. Remove the power steering pump-to-bracket bolts and support the pump aside.

6. Disconnect the radiator hose from the engine.

7. Disconnect the TV and accelerator cables from the throttle valve bracket on the plenum.

8. Detach the electrical connectors. Remove the alternator-to-bracket bolts and the alternator. Label and disconnect the electrical wiring harness from the engine.

9. Disconnect and plug the fuel hoses. Remove the coolant overflow and bypass hoses from the engine.

10. From the charcoal canister, disconnect the purge hose. Label and disconnect all the necessary vacuum hoses.

11. Using an engine holding fixture tool, support the engine.

12. Raise and safely support the vehicle.

13. Drain the engine oil.

14. Remove the right inner fender splash shield. Remove the crankshaft pul-

VIEW A

1 BOLT – 66 N·m (49 LBS. FT.)(TIGHTEN FIRST)
2 BOLT – 66 N·m (49 LBS. FT.)(TIGHTEN SECOND)
3 NUT – 42 N·m (31 LBS. FT.)(TIGHTEN LAST)
4 BOLT – 130 N·m (96 LBS. FT.)
5 RIGHT HAND SIDE OF CHASSIS
6 ENGINE ASSEMBLY
7 RIGHT ENGINE MOUNT

9300Z205

Front engine mount assembly—3.1L engine

Timing belt service is covered in Section 5 of this manual

1. BOLT – 60 N·m (44 LBS. FT.) +90°
2. BOLT – 75 N·m (55 LBS. FT.)
3. BOLT – 120 N·m (89 LBS. FT.)
4. FRONT SUSPENSION SUPPORT
5. ENGINE MOUNT STRUT
6. ENGINE MOUNT STRUT BRACKET
7. ENGINE ASSEMBLY
8. BOLT – 115 N·m (85 LBS. FT.)

9300Z206

Engine mount strut assembly—3.1L engine

ley-to-crankshaft bolt. Using a wheel puller, press the crankshaft pulley from the crankshaft.

15. Remove the flywheel cover. Label and disconnect the starter wires. Remove the starter-to-engine bolts and the starter.

16. Disconnect the wires from the oil pressure sending unit.

17. Remove the air conditioning compressor-to-bracket bolts and the bracket-to-engine bolts. Support the compressor so it will not interfere with the engine; do not disconnect the refrigerant lines.

18. Disconnect the exhaust pipe from the rear of the exhaust manifold.

19. If equipped with an automatic transaxle, remove the torque converter-to-flywheel bolts and push the converter into the transaxle.

20. Remove the front and rear engine mount bolts along with the mount brackets.

21. Remove the intermediate shaft bracket from the engine.

22. Disconnect the shifter cable from the transaxle.

23. Remove the lower engine-to-transaxle bolts and lower the vehicle.

24. Disconnect the heater hoses from the engine.

25. Using a vertical engine lift, install it

to the engine and lift it slightly. Remove the engine holding fixture. Using a floor jack, support the transaxle.

26. Remove the upper engine-to-transaxle bolts. Remove the front engine mount bolts and transaxle mounting bracket.

27. Remove the engine from the vehicle.

To install:

28. Secure the engine on an engine suitable lifting device.

29. Carefully lower the engine into the vehicle, aligning it to the transaxle.

30. Install the upper engine-to-transaxle bolts. Tighten bolts to 55 ft. lbs. (75 Nm).

31. Install the transaxle mount bracket and front engine mount attaching bolts. Tighten the bolts to 65 ft. lbs. (88 Nm).

32. Using a floor jack, support the transaxle and remove the engine lifting device from the engine.

33. Install the lower engine-to-transaxle.

34. Connect the heater hoses to the engine.

35. Connect the shifter cable to the transaxle.

36. Install the intermediate shaft bracket to the engine.

37. Install the front and rear engine

mount bolts along with the mount brackets.

38. Lower the jack and remove it from the transaxle.

39. Raise the vehicle and support it safely.

40. If equipped with an automatic transaxle, install the torque converter-to-flywheel bolts.

41. Install the flywheel cover and attaching bolts.

42. Connect the exhaust pipe to the exhaust manifold and install the attaching bolts.

43. Lower the vehicle.

44. Position the A/C compressor, with the lines attached, in place and install the compressor-to-bracket bolts.

45. Install the compressor bracket-to-engine bolts.

46. Connect the wires to the oil pressure sending unit.

47. Connect the starter wires. Position the starter in place and install the starter-to-engine bolts.

48. Install the crankshaft pulley and install the pulley-to-crankshaft bolt. Install the right inner fender splash shield.

49. Connect the purge hose to the charcoal canister. Connect all the necessary vacuum hoses.

50. Connect the coolant overflow and bypass hoses to the engine.

51. Connect the fuel delivery hoses to the engine.

52. Position the alternator in place and install the alternator-to-bracket bolts. Connect the electrical connectors to the alternator.

53. Connect all electrical wiring harnesses to the engine.

54. Connect the TV and accelerator cables to the throttle valve bracket on the plenum.

55. Connect the radiator hoses to the engine.

56. Install the serpentine belt tensioner and the drive belt.

57. Position the P/S pump in place and install the power steering pump-to-bracket bolts.

58. Connect the crossover pipe to the exhaust manifold and install the attaching bolts.

59. Install the air cleaner, air inlet hose and the MAF sensor.

60. Close the radiator cock and refill the cooling system.

61. Fill the crankcase with oil.

62. Install the battery and secure it in place. Connect the battery cables (the negative cable last).

63. Start the engine, allow it to reach normal operating temperatures and check for leaks.

Water Pump

REMOVAL & INSTALLATION

2.2L and 3.1L Engines

1. Before servicing the vehicle, refer to the precautions in the beginning of this section.

2. Disconnect the negative battery cable. Drain the cooling system.

3. Loosen, but do not remove, the water pump pulley bolts.

4. Remove the serpentine belt.

5. Remove the alternator mounting bolts and set the alternator aside.

6. Remove the water pump pulley bolts and remove the water pump pulley.

7. Remove the four water pump mounting bolts, and remove the water pump.

To install:

8. Clean the gasket surfaces completely.

9. Apply a thin bead of sealer around the outer edge of the water pump gasket seating area and place the gasket on the pump.

10. Install the water pump on the engine

1   BOLT – 25 N·m (18 LBS. FT.)

79Z2Z120

Exploded view of the water pump mounting—2.2L engine

1   COOLANT PUMP
2   GASKET
3   BOLT – 10 N·m (89 LBS. IN.)
4   LOCATOR (MUST BE VERTICAL)

79Z2Z121

Exploded view of the water pump mounting—3.1L engine

and tighten the mounting bolts to 18 ft. lbs. (25 Nm) for the 2.2L engine or to 89 inch lbs. (10 Nm) on the 3.1L engine.

11. Install the remaining components in the reverse order of removal. Tighten the water pump pulley mounting bolts to 22 ft. lbs. (30 Nm) for the 2.2L engine or to 18 ft. lbs. (25 Nm) on the 3.1L engine.

12. Connect the negative battery cable. Refill the cooling system with the proper coolant. Bleed the cooling system and check for leaks with the engine running at idle.

Cylinder Head

REMOVAL & INSTALLATION

➡ **When removing the valvetrain components, they must be kept in order for installation in the same locations from which they were removed.**

2.2L Engine

1. Before servicing the vehicle, refer to the precautions in the beginning of this section.

2. Relieve the fuel system pressure. Disconnect the negative battery cable. Drain the cooling system.

3. Remove the air inlet duct.

4. Tag and disconnect the vacuum lines at the intake manifold and cylinder head.

5. Tag and disconnect the following electrical connectors:
- Engine Coolant Temperature (ECT) sensor
- Oxygen (O_2S) sensor
- Idle Air Control (IAC)
- Throttle Position (TP) sensor
- Manifold Absolute Pressure (MAP) sensor
- EVAP canister purge solenoid
- Fuel injector harness.

6. Disconnect the control cables from the throttle body and remove the cable bracket at the throttle body and rocker arm cover.

7. Remove the coolant reservoir, if necessary.

8. Install an engine support fixture, J-28467-a, or the equivalent.

9. Remove the right engine mount, if necessary.

10. Remove the serpentine belt.

11. Remove the alternator and alternator mounting bracket.

12. Disconnect and cap the power steering lines from the power steering pump and remove the power steering pump.

13. Remove the serpentine belt tensioner assembly.

14. Remove the right engine mount bracket.

15. Disconnect the spark plug wires and lay them aside.

16. Disconnect the EVAP canister purge line under the intake manifold.

17. Disconnect the upper radiator hose from the engine.

18. Disconnect the coolant inlet pipe brackets at the exhaust manifold and transaxle.

19. Remove the intake manifold brace from the power steering bracket.

20. Disconnect and cap the fuel lines at the quick disconnects.

21. Remove the rocker arm cover, rocker arm nuts, rocker arms and pushrods.

22. Remove the ignition wire bracket.

23. Remove the engine lift bracket.

24. Raise and safely support the vehicle.

1 LONG BOLTS
2 SHORT BOLTS
3 STUD
4 NUMBERS ON GASKET INDICATE TORQUE SEQUENCE

CYLINDER HEAD BOLT TORQUE PROCEDURE

1 TIGHTEN BOLTS IN SEQUENCE (ITEM 4) TO:
LONG BOLTS: 63 N·m (46 LBS. FT.)
SHORT BOLTS: 58 N·m (43 LBS. FT.)

2 TIGHTEN ALL BOLTS AN ADDITIONAL ANGLE OF 90° IN SEQUENCE (ITEM 4) USING J 36660 OR EQUIVALENT

7922Z101

Cylinder head bolt tightening sequence—2.2L engine

Disconnect the exhaust pipe from the exhaust manifold.

25. Lower the vehicle.

26. Remove the transaxle fill tube.

27. Remove the cylinder head bolts.

28. Remove the cylinder head with both manifolds. Remove the intake and exhaust manifolds from the cylinder head.

To install:

29. Clean all gasket surfaces completely. Clean the threads on the cylinder head bolts and the block threads.

30. Install the intake and exhaust manifolds on the cylinder head.

31. Place a new cylinder head gasket in position over the dowel pins on the block. Carefully guide the cylinder head into position.

32. Install all the cylinder head bolts finger-tight. The long bolts go in bolt positions 1, 4, 5, 8 and 9. The short bolts in positions 2, 3, 6 and 7. The stud is in position 10.

33. Tighten the bolts in sequence. The long bolts to 23 ft. lbs. (32 Nm) and the short bolts and stud to 22 ft. lbs. (29 Nm). Make second pass tightening the long bolts to 46 ft. lbs. (63 Nm) and the short bolts to 43 ft. lbs. (58 Nm). Make a final pass over all bolts tightening each an additional 90 degrees.

34. Install the engine lift bracket.

35. Install the ignition wire bracket.

36. Install the transaxle fill tube.

37. Install the pushrods, rocker arms and rocker arm nuts and tighten the nuts to 22 ft. lbs. (30 Nm).

38. Install the rocker arm cover.

39. Connect the control cables to the throttle body and install the cable brackets at the throttle body and rocker arm cover.

40. Connect the fuel lines to the throttle body. Connect the upper radiator hose.

41. Install the intake manifold brace to the power steering pump bracket.

42. Connect the spark plug wires.

43. Install the remaining components in the reverse order of removal. Tighten the serpentine belt tensioner mounting bolts to 37 ft. lbs. (50 Nm) and the exhaust pipe-to-exhaust manifold bolts to 22 ft. lbs. (30 Nm).

44. Refill the cooling system.

45. Connect the negative battery cable. Start the vehicle and verify no leaks.

3.1L Engine

LEFT (FRONT) CYLINDER HEAD

1. Before servicing the vehicle, refer to the precautions in the beginning of this section.

2. Relieve the fuel system pressure.

3. Disconnect the negative battery cable.

4. Drain the cooling system.

5. Remove the top half of the air cleaner assembly and remove the throttle body air inlet duct.

6. Remove the exhaust crossover pipe heat shield and crossover pipe.

7. Disconnect the spark plug wires from spark plugs and wire looms and route the wires aside.

8. Remove the rocker arm covers.

9. Remove upper intake plenum and lower intake manifold.

10. Remove the left side exhaust manifold.

11. Remove oil level indicator tube.

12. Remove rocker arms nut, rocker arms, balls and pushrods.

13. Remove the cylinder head bolts evenly. Remove the cylinder head.

To install:

14. Clean all gasket surfaces completely. Clean the threads on the cylinder head bolts and block threads.

15. Place the cylinder head gasket in position over the dowel pins on the cylinder block so the words **THIS SIDE UP** is showing.

16. Coat the bolt threads with sealer and install finger-tight.

17. Tighten the cylinder head bolts in sequence to 33 ft. lbs. (45 Nm). With all bolts tightened make a second pass tightening all the bolts an additional 90 degrees (¼ turn).

18. Install the pushrods, rocker arms, balls and rocker arm nuts. Tighten the rocker arm nuts to 18 ft. lbs. (25 Nm).

19. Install the lower intake manifold and upper intake plenum.

20. Install the rocker arm covers.

21. Install the oil level indicator tube.

22. Connect the spark plug wires to spark plugs and wire looms.

23. Install the left side exhaust manifold.

24. Install the exhaust crossover pipe and crossover pipe heat shield.

25. Refill the cooling system.

26. Install the top half of the air cleaner assembly and the throttle body air inlet duct.

27. Connect negative battery cable.

28. Start vehicle and verify no leaks.

RIGHT (REAR) CYLINDER HEAD

1. Before servicing the vehicle, refer to the precautions in the beginning of this section.

2. Properly relieve the fuel system pressure.

1 COAT THREADS WITH SEALER TIGHTEN IN PROPER SEQUENCE TO 45 N·m (33 LBS. FT.). TURN AN ADDITIONAL 90° WITH J 36660
2 CYLINDER HEAD
3 GASKET
4 CYLINDER BLOCK

FRT

TIGHTENING SEQUENCE

6 2 30 7
5 10 40 8

79222102

Exploded view of the cylinder head mounting, showing the bolt tightening sequence—3.1L engine

Refer to Section 1 for engine rebuilding specifications

3. Disconnect the negative battery cable.

4. Drain the cooling system.

5. Remove the top half of the air cleaner assembly and remove the throttle body air inlet duct.

6. Remove the exhaust crossover pipe heat shield and crossover pipe.

7. Raise and safely support the vehicle.

8. Disconnect the Oxygen (O2S) sensor connector.

9. Disconnect the exhaust pipe from the exhaust manifold.

10. Remove the right side exhaust manifold. Lower the vehicle.

11. Disconnect the spark plug wires from spark plugs and wire looms and route the wires aside.

12. Remove the rocker arm covers.

13. Remove upper intake plenum and lower intake manifold.

14. Remove rocker arms nut, rocker arms, balls and pushrods.

15. Remove the cylinder head bolts evenly.

16. Remove the cylinder head.

To install:

17. Clean all gasket surfaces completely. Clean the threads on the cylinder head bolts and block threads.

18. Place the cylinder head gasket in position over the dowel pins on the cylinder block so the words **THIS SIDE UP** are showing.

19. Coat the bolt threads with sealer and install finger-tight.

20. Tighten the cylinder head bolts in sequence to 33 ft. lbs. (45 Nm). With all bolts tightened, make a second pass tightening all the bolts an additional 90 degrees (¼ turn).

21. Install the pushrods, rocker arms, balls and rocker arm nuts. Tighten the rocker arm nuts to 18 ft. lbs. (25 Nm).

22. Install the lower intake manifold and upper intake plenum.

23. Install the rocker arm covers.

24. Connect the spark plug wires to the plugs and install them in the wire looms.

25. Raise vehicle and safely support.

26. Install the exhaust manifold.

27. Connect the exhaust pipe to the exhaust manifold.

28. Lower the vehicle.

29. Connect the O2S sensor connector.

30. Install the exhaust crossover pipe and heat shield.

31. Refill the cooling system.

32. Install the top half of the air cleaner assembly and the throttle body air inlet duct.

33. Connect negative battery cable.

34. Start vehicle and verify no leaks.

Rocker Arms

REMOVAL & INSTALLATION

2.2L Engine

This engine uses a simple ball pivot-type rocker arm. Motion is transmitted from the camshaft through the hydraulic roller lifters and pushrod to the rocker arm. The rocker arm pivots on its ball and transmits the camshaft motion to the valve. The rocker arm ball is located on a stud threaded onto the head and is retained by a nut. The pushrod is located by a guide plate held under the rocker arm stud.

1. Before servicing the vehicle, refer to the precautions in the beginning of this section.

2. Disconnect the negative battery cable. Disconnect the air intake hose from the air cleaner and throttle body.

3. Remove the control cable bracket from the rocker arm cover.

4. Disconnect the PCV hose.

5. Remove the rocker arm cover bolts, then remove the cover.

➡**Place the removed components in a rack so they can be kept in order. These parts must be installed in the same locations from which they were removed.**

```
1  BOLT
2  ROCKER COVER
3  GASKET
4  ROCKER STUD
5  FLANGE, MUST BE FREE OF OIL UPON
   ROCKER COVER GASKET INSTALLATION.
6  PUSHROD
7  ROCKER ARM
8  BALL
9  NUT
10 SUPPORT, SPARK PLUG WIRE
```
7922Z122

Exploded view of the valve cover and rocker arm mounting—2.2L engine

6. Remove the rocker arm nut(s), ball(s) and rocker arms. Pushrods may be removed by simply pulling out of the block.

To install:

7. Clean the gasket surfaces completely.

8. Coat the bearing surfaces of the rocker arm(s) and the rocker arm ball(s) with Molykote®, engine assembly lube or equivalent.

9. Seat the pushrods in the lifters.

10. Install the rocker arm(s), ball(s) and nut(s) in the same positions they were removed from and tighten the rocker arm nut(s) to 22 ft. lbs. (30 Nm). Valve lash adjustment is not required.

11. Install a new gasket in the cut out of the rocker arm cover.

12. Install the rocker arm cover on the cylinder head and tighten the rocker arm cover bolts to 89 inch lbs. (10 Nm).

13. Install the remaining components in the reverse order of removal.

14. Connect the negative battery cable. Start the engine and verify no oil leaks.

3.1L Engine

1. Before servicing the vehicle, refer to the precautions in the beginning of this section.

2. Disconnect the negative battery cable.

3. For the left side rocker arms (front), perform the following procedures:

   a. Drain the cooling system to a level below the coolant pipe on the front of the engine.

   b. Remove the coolant bypass hose clamp at the coolant tube.

   c. Remove the two bolts and nut securing the coolant tube to the cylinder head and position the tube aside.

   d. Disconnect the PCV valve from the rocker arm cover.

4. For the right side rocker arms (rear), perform the following procedures:

   a. Disconnect the spark plug wires from the spark plugs and upper intake plenum wire retainer and position aside.

```
1  Pushrod
2  Valve rocker arm stud
3  Valve rocker arm
4  Valve rocker arm pivot ball
5  Valve rocker arm nut
```
7922Z103

Rocker arm component identification— 3.1L engine

b. Disconnect the power brake booster vacuum pipe from the intake plenum.

c. Remove the serpentine belt.

d. Remove the alternator.

e. Disconnect and remove the ignition assembly and EVAP canister purge solenoid as an assembly.

5. Remove the four rocker arm cover bolts and remove the rocker arm cover.

6. Remove the rocker arm nuts, balls, rocker arms and pushrods.

To install:

7. Clean all gasket surfaces completely.

8. Coat all the valvetrain components with engine oil prior to installation.

9. Install the pushrods and install the rocker arms on the studs. Install the rocker arm balls and mounting nuts. Be sure the pushrods are properly seated in the lifter and rocker arm. Tighten the mounting nuts to 18 ft. lbs. (24 Nm).

10. Install the rocker arm cover using a new gasket and bolt grommet, tighten the rocker cover bolts to 90 inch lbs. (10 Nm).

11. For the left side rocker arms (front), perform the following procedures:

a. Connect the PCV valve to the rocker arm cover.

b. Position the coolant tube and connect the thermostat bypass hose.

c. Install the coolant tube mounting nut and bolts. Tighten the screw at the water pump to 106 inch lbs. (12 Nm), the bolt at the corner of the cylinder head to 18 ft. lbs. (25 Nm) and the nut to 18 ft. lbs. (25 Nm).

12. For the right side rocker arms (rear), perform the following procedures:

a. Install the alternator.

b. Install the serpentine belt.

c. Connect the power brake booster vacuum pipe to the plenum.

d. Install the EVAP solenoid and ignition assembly.

e. Connect the spark plug wires to the wire retainers on the plenum and the spark plugs.

13. Refill the cooling system.

14. Connect the negative battery cable. Start the engine and verify that there are no leaks.

Intake Manifold

REMOVAL & INSTALLATION

2.2L Engine

1. Before servicing the vehicle, refer to the precautions in the beginning of this section.

1 BOLT
2 STUD
3 UPPER INTAKE MANIFOLD ASSEMBLY
4 GASKET
5 LOWER INTAKE MANIFOLD
6 EGR VALVE INJECTOR

Exploded view of the upper intake manifold mounting, showing the bolt tightening sequence—2.2L engines

1 STUD
2 GASKET
3 INTAKE MANIFOLD
4 NUT
5 CLIP

INTAKE MANIFOLD NUT TIGHTENING SEQUENCE

Exploded view of the lower intake manifold mounting, showing the bolt tightening sequence—2.2L engines

2. Relieve the fuel system pressure.

3. Disconnect the negative battery cable.

4. Remove the air intake duct.

5. Drain the cooling system.

6. Tag and disconnect all necessary vacuum lines and wires.

7. Disconnect the throttle linkage.

8. Remove the serpentine drive belt.

9. Unbolt the power steering pump, then position it aside without disconnecting the fluid lines.

10. Remove the transaxle fluid level indicator and fill tube.

11. Detach the electrical connectors from the following components:

a. Manifold Absolute Pressure (MAP) sensor

b. Exhaust Gas Recirculation (EGR) solenoid valve

c. Idle Air Control (IAC) valve

d. Throttle Position (TP) sensor

e. Fuel injector wiring harness

12. Remove the MAP sensor and EGR solenoid valve.

13. Remove the upper intake manifold assembly.

For engine torque specifications, refer to Section 1 of this manual

14. Remove the EGR valve injector.

15. Remove the fuel injector retainer bracket, regulator and injectors.

16. Disconnect the accelerator and Throttle Valve (TV) cables, then remove the cable bracket.

17. Remove the EGR valve pipe.

18. Remove the lower intake manifold-to-cylinder head retaining nuts and studs, then remove the lower intake manifold from the vehicle.

19. Remove and discard the gasket. Use a suitable gasket to carefully and thoroughly clean the mating surfaces on the manifold and cylinder head.

To install:

20. Position a new intake manifold gasket on the cylinder, then place the lower intake manifold over the new gasket. Install the retaining nuts and studs. Tighten the studs to 89 inch lbs. (10 Nm) and the nuts, in sequence, to 24 ft. lbs. (33 Nm).

21. Install the EGR valve pipe.

22. Connect the fuel lines.

23. Install the fuel injectors, regulator and injector retainer bracket and tighten the retaining bolts to 22 inch lbs. (3.5 Nm).

24. Install the cable bracket, then connect the accelerator and TV cables.

25. Install the EGR valve injector so that the port is facing directly towards the throttle body.

26. Install the upper intake manifold assembly. Tighten the upper intake manifold nuts in the proper sequence to 22 ft. lbs. (30 Nm).

27. Install the MAP sensor and EGR solenoid valve.

28. Install the serpentine drive belt.

29. Install the accelerator cable bracket and throttle linkage. Tighten the cable bracket bolts to 18 ft. lbs. (25 Nm).

30. Connect the vacuum lines and wires as tagged during removal.

31. Attach the air intake duct.

32. Position the power steering pump and secure with retaining bolts.

33. Install the transaxle dipstick and tube assembly.

34. Connect the negative battery cable.

35. Fill the engine cooling system with the proper type and amount of coolant.

3.1L Engine

These vehicles use a two-piece intake manifold. Note that these pieces are cast aluminum. Use care when working with light alloy components.

1. Before servicing the vehicle, refer to the precautions in the beginning of this section.

A	APPLY SEALANT
121	HEAD ASSEMBLY, CYLINDER
143	GASKET, LOWER INTAKE MANIFOLD
144	BOLT, LOWER INTAKE
145	BOLT, LOWER INTAKE MANIFOLD
146	BOLT, LOWER INTAKE MANIFOLD

144	MANIFOLD, LOWER INTAKE
181	GASKET, UPPER INTAKE MANIFOLD
182	MANIFOLD, UPPER INTAKE
183	STUD, UPPER INTAKE MANIFOLD
184	BOLT, UPPER INTAKE MANIFOLD

Exploded view of the upper and lower intake manifolds—3.1L engine

2. Disconnect the negative battery cable. Relieve the fuel system pressure.

3. Remove the top half of the air cleaner assembly and throttle body duct.

4. Drain the cooling system.

5. Remove the EGR pipe from exhaust manifold.

6. Remove the serpentine belt.

7. Remove the brake vacuum pipe at the intake plenum.

8. Disconnect the control cables from the throttle body and intake plenum mounting bracket.

9. Remove the power steering lines at the alternator bracket.

10. Remove the alternator.

11. Disconnect the spark plug wires from the spark plugs and wire retainers on the intake plenum.

12. Remove the ignition assembly and the EVAP canister purge solenoid together.

13. Detach the connectors from the following components:
- Throttle Position (TP) sensor
- Idle Air Control (IAC)
- Fuel Injectors
- Coolant temperature sensor
- Manifold Absolute Pressure (MAP) sensor
- Camshaft Position (CMP) sensor

14. Detach the vacuum lines from the vacuum modulator, fuel pressure regulator, and the PCV valve.

15. Remove the MAP sensor from upper intake manifold.

16. Remove the upper intake plenum mounting bolts and remove the plenum.

17. Disconnect the fuel lines from the fuel rail and fuel line bracket.

18. Install engine support fixture special tool J-28467-A or an equivalent.

19. Remove the right side engine mount.

20. Remove the power steering mounting bolts and support the pump aside without disconnecting the power steering lines.

21. Disconnect the coolant inlet pipe from coolant outlet housing.

22. Remove the coolant bypass hose from the water pump and the cylinder head.

23. Disconnect the upper radiator hose at thermostat housing.

24. Remove the thermostat housing.

25. Remove both rocker arm covers.

26. Remove the lower intake manifold bolts. Be sure the washers on the four center bolts are installed in their original locations.

➡ **When removing the valvetrain components they should be kept in order for installation the original locations.**

27. Remove the rocker arm retaining nuts and remove the rocker arms and pushrods.

28. Remove the intake manifold from the engine.

To install:

29. Clean gasket material from all mating surfaces. Remove all excess RTV sealant from front and rear ridges of cylinder block.

30. Place a 3mm bead of RTV, on each ridge, where the front and rear of the intake manifold contact the block.

31. Using a new gasket, install the intake manifold to the engine.

32. Install the pushrods, rocker arms and mounting nuts. Be sure the pushrods are properly seated in the valve lifters and rocker arms.

33. Install rocker arm nuts and tighten the rocker arm nuts to 18 ft. lbs. (24 Nm).

34. Install lower the intake manifold attaching bolts. Apply sealant PN 12345739 or equivalent to the threads of bolts, and tighten bolts to 115 inch lbs. (13 Nm).

35. Install the front rocker arm cover.

36. Install the thermostat housing.

37. Connect the upper radiator hose to the thermostat housing.

38. Install the coolant inlet pipe to thermostat housing.

39. Install coolant bypass pipe at the water pump and cylinder head.

40. Install the power steering pump in the mounting bracket.

41. Connect the right side engine mount. Remove the special engine support tool.

42. Connect the fuel lines to fuel rail and bracket.

43. Install the upper intake manifold and tighten the mounting bolts to 18 ft. lbs. (25 Nm).

44. Install the remaining components in the reverse order of removal.

45. Fill the cooling system. An engine oil and filter change is recommended.

46. Connect the negative battery cable. Start the vehicle and verify no leaks.

Exhaust Manifold

REMOVAL & INSTALLATION

2.2L Engine

1. Before servicing the vehicle, refer to the precautions in the beginning of this section.

2. Disconnect the negative battery

1 STUD
2 GASKET
3 EXHAUST MANIFOLD
4 NUT

79222Z123

Exploded view of the exhaust manifold mounting—2.2L engine

cable. Detach the Oxygen (O$_2$S) sensor connector.

3. Remove the serpentine drive belt. Remove the alternator.

4. Raise and support the vehicle safely. Remove the retainers and separate the exhaust pipe from the manifold.

5. Lower the vehicle.

6. Remove the bolt securing the oil fill tube to the engine block and pull the tube from the engine.

7. If the coolant inlet pipe interferes with removal, disconnect the mounting bracket from the transaxle stud.

8. Remove the manifold retaining nuts, then remove the manifold from the cylinder head. Remove and discard the gasket from the mating surfaces.

To install:

9. Install the manifold to the cylinder head using a new gasket. Tighten the retaining nuts to 115 inch lbs. (13 Nm).

10. Raise and support the vehicle safely, then install the exhaust pipe to the manifold. Tighten the retaining nuts to 18 ft. lbs. (25 Nm), then lower the vehicle.

11. Install the alternator and the serpentine drive belt.

12. Connect the coolant inlet pipe, if disconnected.

13. Lubricate the oil fill tube seal and install the oil fill tube.

14. Connect the wiring harness to the O$_2$S sensor.

15. Connect the negative battery cable. Start the engine and check for exhaust leaks.

3.1L Engine

LEFT (FRONT) SIDE MANIFOLD

1. Before servicing the vehicle, refer to the precautions in the beginning of this section.

2. Disconnect the negative battery cable.

3. Remove the top half of the air cleaner assembly and throttle cable duct.

4. Partially drain the cooling system. Remove the radiator hose from the thermostat housing.

5. Remove the coolant bypass hose at

111 SCREW, LH HEAT SHIELD
112 SHIELD, LH HEAT
113 NUT, LH EXHAUST MANIFOLD
114 STUD, LH EXHAUST MANIFOLD
115 MANIFOLD, LH EXHAUST
117 GASKET, LH EXHAUST MANIFOLD
121 HEAD ASSEMBLY, CYLINDER
153 SHIELD, RH LOWER HEAT
154 SCREW, RH LOWER HEAT SHIELD
155 STUD, RH EXHAUST MANIFOLD
156 NUT, RH EXHAUST MANIFOLD
157 MANIFOLD, RH EXHAUST
158 SHIELD, RH UPPER HEAT
159 SCREW, RH UPPER HEAT SHIELD
160 GASKET, RH EXHAUST MANIFOLD

79222124

Exploded view of the exhaust manifold mounting—3.1L engine

the coolant pump and from the exhaust manifold.

6. Remove the exhaust crossover heat shield. Remove the exhaust crossover pipe from the manifold.

7. Tag and disconnect the spark plug wires.

8. Remove the exhaust manifold heat shield. Remove the exhaust manifold retaining nuts.

9. Remove the exhaust manifold.

To install:

10. Clean the mating surfaces at the cylinder head and manifold.

11. Install the exhaust manifold gasket and the exhaust manifold. Tighten the manifold mounting nuts to 12 ft. lbs. (16 Nm).

12. Install the remaining components in the reverse order of removal.

13. Connect the negative battery cable. Start the engine and check for leaks.

RIGHT (REAR) SIDE MANIFOLD

1. Before servicing the vehicle, refer to the precautions in the beginning of this section.

2. Disconnect the negative battery cable. Remove the top half of the air cleaner assembly and throttle cable duct.

3. Remove the exhaust crossover heat shield. Remove the exhaust crossover pipe from the manifold.

4. Remove the Heated Oxygen (HO$_2$S) sensor. Remove the EGR pipe from the exhaust manifold.

5. Raise and safely support the vehicle.

6. Remove the transaxle oil fill tube and lever indicator assembly.

7. Disconnect the front exhaust pipe from the exhaust manifold.

8. Disconnect the exhaust pipe from the converter flange and support the converter.

9. Remove the converter heat shield from the body.

10. Remove the exhaust manifold heat shield.

11. Remove the exhaust manifold nuts. Remove the exhaust manifold from the bottom of vehicle.

To install:

12. Clean mating surfaces at the cylinder head and manifold.

13. Install the exhaust manifold gasket.

14. Install the exhaust manifold loosely and install heat shield at this time.

15. Install the manifold nuts and tighten to 12 ft. lbs. (16 Nm).

16. Install the remaining components in the reverse order of removal.

17. Connect the negative battery cable, then start the engine and check for leaks.

Camshaft and Valve Lifter

REMOVAL & INSTALLATION

2.2L Engine

Please note that the engine must be removed from the vehicle for camshaft service.

1. Before servicing the vehicle, refer to the precautions in the beginning of this section.
2. Disconnect the negative battery cable.
3. Remove the engine assembly from the vehicle and install on a suitable engine stand.
4. Remove the serpentine belt.
5. Remove the alternator and lower mounting bracket.
6. Remove the power steering pump. Remove the serpentine belt tensioner assembly.
7. Remove the water pump pulley.
8. Remove the engine oil filter.
9. Remove the crankshaft pulley from the crankshaft hub.
10. Remove the rocker arm cover.

➡When removing the valvetrain components they must be kept in order for installation in the same locations they were removed from. In addition, a new camshaft requires that new lifters be installed.

11. Remove the rocker arm nuts, rocker arms, balls and pushrods.
12. Remove the cylinder head with the intake and exhaust manifolds attached.
13. Remove the valve lifters.
14. Remove the timing chain front cover. Remove the timing chain, tensioner and camshaft sprocket.
15. Remove the oil pump drive assembly.
16. Remove the camshaft thrust plate mounting bolts and remove the thrust plate.
17. Remove the camshaft carefully from the engine.

To install:

18. Coat the camshaft lobes with and bearings with GM Engine Oil Supplement (E.O.S.) 1051396 or equivalent camshaft lubricant and insert the camshaft carefully into the engine.
19. Install the thrust plate and tighten the mounting bolts to 106 inch lbs. (12 Nm).
20. Install the timing chain, tensioner and camshaft sprocket.

21. Install the timing chain front cover.

➡If the camshaft was replaced with a new one, the valve lifters MUST also be replaced. The lifters have already developed a wear pattern from the old camshaft and installing them on a new camshaft can cause the new camshaft to wear prematurely.

22. Install the valve lifters.
23. Install the cylinder head and manifold assemblies.
24. Install the oil pump drive assembly.
25. Install the pushrods, rocker arms, balls and rocker arm nuts. Tighten the nuts to 22 ft. lbs. (30 Nm).
26. Install the rocker arm cover.
27. Install the crankshaft pulley hub and tighten the mounting bolt to 77 ft. lbs. (105 Nm).
28. Install the crankshaft pulley and tighten the mounting bolts to 37 ft. lbs. (50 Nm).
29. Install the water pump pulley and tighten the mounting bolts to 15 ft. lbs. (21 Nm).
30. Install the drive belt tensioner and tighten the mounting bolts to 37 ft. lbs. (50 Nm).
31. Install the power steering pump. Install the alternator mounting bracket and alternator.
32. Install the engine assembly in the vehicle.
33. Coat the seal on the oil filter with clean engine oil and install the oil filter on the engine.
34. Refill the engine with oil.
35. Connect the negative battery cable. Refill the cooling system.
36. Start the vehicle and verify no leaks.

3.1L Engine

If the camshaft is being replaced, all of the valve lifters must also be replaced with new parts. Installing used lifters on a new camshaft will quickly wear the camshaft.

1. Before servicing the vehicle, refer to the precautions in the beginning of this section.
2. Relieve the fuel system pressure. Disconnect the negative battery cable.
3. Remove the engine assembly from the vehicle, and mount on a suitable engine stand.
4. Remove the intake manifold, valve cover, rocker arms, pushrods and valve lifters.

CAMSHAFT SPROCKET

BOLT

BOLT

CRANKSHAFT SPROCKET

BOLTS TENSIONER

ALIGN TABS ON TENSIONER WITH MARKS ON CAMSHAFT AND CRANKSHAFT SPROCKETS

7922Z107

Camshaft and timing chain components—2.2L engine

Please refer to Section 9 for electric cooling fan wiring schematics

5. Remove the using a puller to draw the crankshaft balancer from the crankshaft nose.

6. Remove the timing chain front cover, timing chain and sprockets.

7. Remove the oil pump driven gear mounting bolt and hold-down. Remove the oil pump driven gear so the camshaft can be pulled out.

8. Remove the two bolts and remove the camshaft thrust plate.

9. Carefully remove the camshaft. Avoid marring the camshaft bearing surfaces.

To install:

10. Coat the camshaft with lubricant GM part No. 1052365 or equivalent camshaft break-in lubricant or quality engine oil supplement, and install the camshaft.

11. Install the camshaft thrust plate and tighten the mounting bolts to 89 inch lbs. (10 Nm).

12. Install the oil pump driven gear and tighten the mounting bolt to 27 ft. lbs. (36 Nm).

13. Install the timing chain and sprocket.

14. Verify that all timing marks are aligned. It is good practice to turn the crankshaft several complete rotations to be sure the timing marks still align when the crankshaft is returned to Top Dead Center (TDC) No. 1 cylinder compression stroke (firing position). This is most important. If the valvetrain is not correctly timed, the engine will be damaged on start-up. When satisfied that all marks are correctly aligned, install the camshaft thrust button and front cover.

15. Install the crankshaft balancer and tighten the bolt to 75 ft. lbs. (103 Nm).

16. Install the intake manifold, valve cover, rocker arms, pushrods and valve lifters.

17. Install the engine assembly.

18. Connect the negative battery cable.

19. Verify that all fluid levels (coolant, engine oil, etc.) are full and correct. An oil and filter change is recommended.

20. Adjust the valves, as required.

21. Start the engine and verify no oil leaks.

Valve Lash

ADJUSTMENT

These vehicles are originally equipped with hydraulic valve lifters and do not require adjustment. Please note that if they are removed for service, they must be kept in order so they may be reinstalled in their original positions.

Oil Pan

REMOVAL & INSTALLATION

2.2L Engine

1. Before servicing the vehicle, refer to the precautions in the beginning of this section.

2. Disconnect the negative battery cable.

3. Raise and safely support the vehicle.

4. Remove the right front tire and wheel assembly, then remove the right engine splash shield.

5. Position a suitable drain pan under the oil pan, then drain the engine oil. Don't forget to install the drain plug after the oil is drained.

6. If equipped, remove the A/C brace.

7. Remove the starter bracket from the block, then remove the starter motor and position it out of the way.

8. Remove the transaxle converter cover or flywheel housing cover.

9. Remove the engine mount strut bracket. Remove the oil level sensor.

10. Remove the oil pan nuts and bolts, then lower the oil pan and remove it from the vehicle.

➡**Before installing the oil pan, be sure the sealing surfaces on the pan, cylinder block and front cover are clean and free of oil. If installing the old pan, be sure that all old RTV has been removed.**

1 SEAL
2 BOLT, 10 N•m (89 LB. IN.)
3 OIL PAN
4 NUT, OIL PAN 10 N•m (89 LB. IN.)

79222Z109

Exploded view of the oil pan and seal mounting—2.2L engine

To install:

11. Apply a ¹⁄₁₀ in. (2mm) wide bead of RTV sealant to the oil pan sealing surface, except for at the rear seal mounting surface. Apply a thin coat of RTV sealer on a new oil pan rear seal, on the ends down to the ears, then install the pan against the case and install bolts. Tighten the bolts to 71–89 inch lbs. (8–10 Nm).

12. Install the oil level sensor and the engine mount strut bracket.

13. If removed, raise the right support into position, then secure using the four retaining bolts.

14. Install the starter motor and bracket.

15. Install the transaxle converter cover or flywheel housing cover.

16. If equipped, remove the A/C brace.

17. If removed, install the right front engine shield, and the right front wheel and tire assembly.

18. Carefully lower the vehicle.

19. Fill the crankcase with the proper type and amount of engine oil.

20. Connect the negative battery cable, then start the engine and check for leaks. Recheck the oil level and add if necessary.

3.1L Engine

1. Before servicing the vehicle, refer to the precautions in the beginning of this section.

2. Disconnect the negative battery cable.

3. Remove the serpentine drive belt.

4. If equipped, loosen but do not remove the upper A/C compressor.

5. Raise and safely support the vehicle.

6. Drain the engine oil.

7. Remove the right front wheel and tire assembly, then remove the splash shield.

8. Remove the engine mount strut from the suspension support.

9. Detach the right front ABS wheel speed sensor harness from the right suspension support.

10. Remove the right front ball joint.

11. Remove the right side stabilizer link. Remove the right side suspension support.

12. If equipped, remove the lower A/C compressor bolts, then position the compressor aside and support. DO NOT disconnect the refrigerant lines.

13. Remove the engine mount strut bracket.

14. Remove the engine-to-transaxle brace.

15. Remove the oil filter and the oil filter adapter, if equipped.

16. Remove the starter motor from the vehicle.

17. Remove the flywheel inspection cover.

10 PAN, OIL
11 BOLT, OIL PAN SIDE
12 BOLT, OIL PAN RETAINING
52 BLOCK, ENGINE

7922Z110

Exploded view of the oil pan mounting—3.1L engine

18. Detach the oil level sensor electrical connector.

19. Remove and discard the oil pan gasket. Thoroughly clean the oil pan flanges, rail, front cover, rear main bearing cap and the threaded bolt holes.

To install:

20. Position a new gasket in the groove on the oil pan. If the rear main bearing cap is being installed, then GM sealant 1052080 or equivalent, must be placed on the oil pan gasket tabs that insert into the gasket groove of the outer surface on the rear main bearing cap.

21. Position the oil pan and secure with the retaining bolts. Tighten the retaining bolts to 18 ft. lbs. (25 Nm).

22. Install the oil pan side bolts, then tighten to 37 ft. lbs. (50 Nm).

23. Attach the oil level sensor electrical connector.

24. Install the transaxle converter cover.

25. Install the starter motor.

26. Install the oil filter.

27. Install the engine-to-transaxle brace.

28. Install the engine mount strut bracket.

29. Loosely assembly the A/C compressor spacer and upper bolts, then secure in place.

30. Install the A/C compressor to the engine.

31. Install the right side suspension support. Install the right side stabilizer bar.

32. Install the right side ball joint.

33. Attach the right front ABS wheel speed sensor wiring harness.

34. Install the engine mount strut to the suspension support.

35. Install the right splash shield, then install the wheel and tire assembly.

36. Carefully lower the vehicle.

37. Install the serpentine drive belt.

38. Fill the crankcase with the proper type and amount of engine oil. Connect the negative battery cable, then start the engine and check for leaks.

39. Turn the engine off and allow it to stand. Check the fluid levels and add as necessary to obtain the proper levels.

Oil Pump

REMOVAL & INSTALLATION

2.2L Engine

1. Before servicing the vehicle, refer to the precautions in the beginning of this section.

2. Remove the engine oil pan.

3. Remove the pump-to-rear bearing cap bolt, then remove the pump and extension shaft.

4. Remove the extension shaft and retainer, being careful not to crack the retainer.

To install:

5. Heat the retainer in hot water prior to assembling the extension shaft.

6. Install the extension to the oil pump.

➡**Be sure the retainer does not crack upon installation.**

7. Install the pump-to-rear bearing cap bolt and tighten to 32 ft. lbs. (43 Nm).

8. Install the oil pan.

3.1L Engine

1. Before servicing the vehicle, refer to the precautions in the beginning of this section.

2. Raise and safely support the vehicle.

3. Remove the oil pan.

4. Unfasten and remove the oil pump and driveshaft extension.

To install:

5. Install the oil pump and driveshaft extension.

6. Engage the driveshaft extension into the drive gear.

7. Install the pump-to-rear bearing cap bolt and tighten to 30 ft. lbs. (41 Nm).

8. Install the oil pan, then carefully lower the vehicle.

9. Fill the crankcase with the proper type and amount of engine oil. Connect the negative battery cable, then start the engine and check for leaks.

10. Turn the engine off and allow it to

1 BOLT, 43 N•m (32 LBS. FT.)
2 PUMP ASSEMBLY, OIL
3 RETAINER, OIL PUMP SHAFT
   THE RETAINER MUST BE HEATED AND SOAKED
   IN WATER PRIOR TO INSTALLATION. THE
   RETAINER MUST NOT HAVE ANY SPLITS IN IT
   AFTER INSTALLATION.
4 SHAFT, OIL PUMP DRIVE

7922Z111

Exploded view of the oil pump assembly mounting—2.2L engine

1 BOLT, 25 N·m (18 LBS. FT.)
2 SUPPORT
3 DRIVE ASSEMBLY, OIL PUMP

79Z2Z112

The oil pump drive is mounted to the top of the engine—2.2L engine

1 34 N·m (25 LBS. FT.)
2 OIL PUMP DRIVE
3 OIL PUMP
4 41 N·m (30 LBS. FT.)

79Z2Z113

Exploded view of the oil pump and drive mounting—3.1L engine

stand. Check the oil level, then add as necessary.

Rear Main Seal

REMOVAL & INSTALLATION

2.2L Engine

The transaxle must be removed from the vehicle to perform this service.

1. Before servicing the vehicle, refer to the precautions in the beginning of this section.
2. Disconnect the negative battery cable.

3. Remove the transaxle.
4. Remove the flywheel mounting bolts and remove the flywheel and retainer.
5. Remove crankshaft seal by inserting a suitable prying tool in through the dust lip. Pry out seal moving tool around seal as required until is removed.

✳✳ WARNING

Care must be taken not to damage crankshaft seal surface with prytool.

To install:
6. Coat the inside and outside of the new seal with engine oil.

7. Install the new seal on tool J-34686 until the seal bottom is squarely against the collar of J-34686.
8. Align the dowel pin of J-34686 with the dowel pin hole in the crankshaft. Tighten the attaching screws to 45 inch lbs. (6 Nm).
9. Turn the handle of the tool until the collar is tight against the case. This will ensure the seal is fully seated.
10. Back the tool off and remove the attaching screws.
11. Install the flywheel and retainer and tighten the flywheel mounting bolts to 55 ft. lbs. (75 Nm).
12. Install the transaxle assembly using the recommended procedure.
13. Connect the negative battery cable.
14. Check the engine oil level and fill as necessary.

3.1L Engine

The transaxle must be removed from the vehicle to perform this service.

1. Before servicing the vehicle, refer to the precautions in the beginning of this section.
2. Disconnect the negative battery cable.
3. Remove the transaxle using the recommended procedure.
4. Remove the flywheel mounting bolts and remove the flywheel and spacer.
5. Using a small prybar, pry the seal from the block.

✳✳ WARNING

Be careful not to damage the crankshaft sealing surface when removing the oil seal.

6. Clean the seal mounting surface.
To install:
7. Coat the inside and outside of the new rear main oil seal with engine oil.
8. Install the new seal on tool J-34686

DUST LIP

79Z2Z114

When removing the rear main seal, be sure not to damage the bore with the prytool—all engines

1	ALIGNMENT HOLE
2	DUST LIP
3	DOWEL PIN
4	COLLAR
5	MANDRIL
6	ATTACHING SCREWS
7	SEAL

7922Z115A

Rear main seal installation—all engines

until the seal bottom is squarely against the collar of J-34686.

9. Align the dowel pin of J-34686 with the dowel pin hole in the crankshaft. Tighten the attaching screws to 45 inch lbs. (5 Nm).

10. Turn the handle of the tool until the collar is tight against the case. This will ensure the seal is fully seated.

11. Back the tool off and remove the attaching screws.

12. Install the flywheel and spacer and tighten the flywheel mounting bolts to 61 ft. lbs. (83 Nm).

13. Install the transaxle assembly using the recommended procedure.

14. Connect the negative battery cable.

15. Check the engine oil level and fill as necessary.

FUEL SYSTEM

Fuel System Service Precautions

Safety is the most important factor when performing not only fuel system mainte-nance but any type of maintenance. Failure to conduct maintenance and repairs in a safe manner may result in serious personal injury or death. Maintenance and testing of the vehicle's fuel system components can be accomplished safely and effectively by adhering to the following rules and guide-lines.

• To avoid the possibility of fire and per-sonal injury, always disconnect the negative battery cable unless the repair or test proce-dure requires that battery voltage be applied.

• Always relieve the fuel system pres-sure prior to disconnecting any fuel system component (injector, fuel rail, pressure reg-ulator, etc.), fitting or fuel line connection. Exercise extreme caution whenever relieving fuel system pressure to avoid exposing skin, face and eyes to fuel spray. Please be advised that fuel under pressure may pene-trate the skin or any part of the body that it contacts.

• Always place a shop towel or cloth around the fitting or connection prior to loosening to absorb any excess fuel due to spillage. Ensure that all fuel spillage (should it occur) is quickly removed from engine surfaces. Ensure that all fuel soaked cloths or towels are deposited into a suit-able waste container.

• Always keep a dry chemical (Class B) fire extinguisher near the work area.

• Do not allow fuel spray or fuel vapors to come into contact with a spark or open flame.

• Always use a back-up wrench when loosening and tightening fuel line con-nection fittings. This will prevent unnec-essary stress and torsion to fuel line piping.

• Always replace worn fuel fitting O-rings with new. Do not substitute fuel hose or equivalent, where fuel pipe is installed.

Fuel System Pressure

RELIEVING

1. Before servicing the vehicle, refer to the precautions in the beginning of this sec-tion.

2. Disconnect the negative battery cable. Remove the fuel filler cap to relieve tank vapor pressure.

3. Connect a fuel gauge to the fuel pres-sure test fitting.

➡**Be sure to wrap a shop rag around the fuel line fitting when connecting the fuel gauge tool to the fuel pressure connector.**

4. Place the bleeder hose in an approved fuel container. Open the pressure valve to bleed the fuel pressure from the system.

5. After the fuel pressure is bled, retighten the fuel pressure valve.

Fuel Filter

REMOVAL & INSTALLATION

1. Before servicing the vehicle, refer to the precautions in the beginning of this sec-tion.

2. Relieve the fuel system pressure. Disconnect the negative battery cable.

3. Raise and safely support the vehicle.

4. Disconnect the fuel inlet line from the fuel filter using a back-up wrench on the filter to prevent damaging the fuel line or fil-ter.

5. Disconnect the fuel line quick-con-

nect from the filter outlet by squeezing the tabs together and pulling the line off the filter.

6. Remove the fuel filter from the bracket.

To install:

7. Install the fuel filter in the mounting bracket.

8. Connect the quick-connect to the fuel filter. Be sure the tabs lock in place and the line cannot be pulled off the filter.

9. Connect the outlet line to the filter using a back-up wrench on the filter body to prevent damaging the fuel line or filter. Tighten the line fitting to 20 ft. lbs. (27 Nm).

10. Lower the vehicle.

11. Connect the negative battery cable. Pressurize the fuel system and verify no leaks.

Fuel Pump

REMOVAL & INSTALLATION

1. Before servicing the vehicle, refer to the precautions in the beginning of this section.

2. Relieve the fuel system pressure. Disconnect the negative battery cable.

3. Drain, then remove the fuel tank from the vehicle.

4. While holding the modular fuel sender assembly down, remove the snapring from the designated slots located on the retainer.

➡**The modular fuel sender assembly may spring up from its position. When removing the modular fuel sender from the tank, be aware that the reservoir bucket is full of fuel. It must be tipped slightly during removal to avoid damage to the float.**

5. Remove the external fuel strainer.

6. Disconnect the Connector Position Assurance (CPA) piece from the electrical connector and disconnect the fuel pump electrical connector.

7. Gently release the tabs on the sides of the fuel sender at the cover assembly. Begin by squeezing the sides of the reservoir and releasing the tab opposite the fuel level sensor. Move clockwise to release the second and third tab in the same manner.

8. Lift the cover assembly out far enough to disconnect the fuel pump electrical connection.

9. Rotate the fuel pump baffle counterclockwise and remove the baffle and pump assembly from the retainer.

10. Slide the fuel pump outlet out of slot. Remove the fuel pump outlet seal.

To install:

11. Install the fuel pump outlet seal. Slide the fuel pump outlet in the slots of reservoir cover.

12. Install the fuel pump and baffle assembly onto the reservoir retainer and rotate clockwise until seated.

13. Install the lower retainer assembly partially into the reservoir. Line up all three sleeve tabs. Press the retainer onto the reservoir making sure all three tabs are firmly seated.

14. Gently pull the fuel pump reservoir from the retainer to assure a secure fastening. If not secure, replace the entire fuel sender.

15. Connect the fuel pump connector. Attach the CPA connector to the fuel sender cover.

16. Install a new external fuel strainer.

17. Install the modular fuel sender.

18. Install the fuel tank in the vehicle.

19. Connect the negative battery cable. Pressurize the fuel system and check for leaks.

1 CHECK VALVE
2 FUEL FLOW TO ENGINE
3 RETURN FUEL FROM ENGINE
4 ANTI-SIPHON HOLE
5 PUMP ASSEMBLY (JET PUMP ASSEMBLY)–
   FUEL PUMP RESERVOIR
6 STRAINER – JET PUMP
7 UMBRELLA VALVE – PRIMARY
8 STRAINER (EXTERNAL) – FUEL SENDER
9 STRAINER – FUEL PUMP FUEL (ROLLERVANE)
10 UMBRELLA VALVE – SECONDARY
11 PUMP ASSEMBLY (ROLLERVANE) – FUEL
12 RESERVOIR

7922Z125

Cut-away view of the modular sender—showing fuel flow

DRIVE TRAIN

Transaxle Assembly

REMOVAL & INSTALLATION

Manual

1. Before servicing the vehicle, refer to the precautions in the beginning of this section.

2. Disconnect the negative terminal from the battery.

3. Using the Engine Support Fixture tool No. J-28467 or equivalent and Adapter tool No. J-35953 or equivalent, raise the engine enough to take the engine weight off of the engine mounts.

4. Remove the left side sound insulator.

5. Disconnect the clutch master cylinder pushrod from the clutch pedal.

6. Disconnect the clutch slave cylinder-to-transaxle support bolts and position the cylinder aside.

7. Remove the wiring harness from the transaxle mount bracket and the shift wire electrical connector.

8. Remove the transaxle-to-mount bolts and the transaxle mount bracket-to-chassis nuts/bolts.

9. Disconnect the shift cables and remove the retaining clamp from the transaxle. Remove the ground cables from the transaxle mounting studs.

10. Raise and support the front of the vehicle.

11. Remove the left front tire assembly and the left side inner splash shield.

12. Remove the transaxle front strut and bracket.

13. Remove the clutch housing cover bolts. Disconnect the speedometer wire connector.

14. From the left suspension support and control arm, disconnect the stabilizer shaft.

15. Remove the left suspension support mounting bolts and move the support aside.

16. Disconnect both halfshafts from the transaxle and remove the left halfshaft from the vehicle.

17. Drain the transaxle.

18. Support the transaxle using a transmission jack.

19. Remove the transaxle-to-engine bolts.

20. Slide the transaxle away from the engine, lower it and remove the right side halfshaft.

A. Transaxle assembly
1. Transaxle mount
2. Bracket (part of body assembly)
3. Bolt (33 ft. lbs. plus 120 degree turn)

Transaxle mount-to-body attachment—all vehicles

1. Mount
2. Bolt (55 ft. lbs.)

Front transaxle mount-to-transaxle attachment and bolt torque values

1. Bolts
2. Transaxle assembly
3. Stud
4. Bracket
5. Engine assembly

Transaxle-to-engine attachment—all vehicles

To install:

21. When installing, guide the right side halfshaft into the transaxle while it is being installed in the vehicle.

22. Install and tighten the transaxle-to-engine bolts to 55 ft. lbs. (75 Nm)

23. Install the left halfshaft into its bore at the transaxle, then seat both halfshafts at the transaxle.

24. Install the left suspension support mounting bolts.

25. Connect the stabilizer shaft to the left suspension support and control arm.

26. Connect the speedometer wire.

27. Connect the clutch housing cover bolts and tighten to 89 inch lbs. (10 Nm).

28. Install the transaxle strut and bracket. Tighten the transaxle strut-to-body bolt to 40 ft. lbs. (54 Nm) and the transaxle strut to transaxle to 50 ft. lbs. (68 Nm). See applicable illustration.

29. Install the left front tire assembly and the left side inner splash shield.

30. Lower the vehicle.
31. Install the ground cables at the transaxle mounting studs.
32. Install the wires for the shift light.
33. Install the slave cylinder to the transaxle bracket aligning the pushrod into the pocket of the clutch release lever and installing the retaining nuts and tighten evenly.
34. Install the transaxle mount bracket. Tighten the rear mount bracket-to-transaxle to 40 ft. lbs. (54 Nm).
35. Install the transaxle mount-to-side frame and tighten to 23 ft. lbs. (30 Nm).
36. Install the wiring harness at the mount bracket.
37. Install the bolt attaching the mount to the transaxle bracket and tighten to 88 ft. lbs. (120 Nm).
38. Remove the engine support.
39. Install the shift cables.
40. Connect the negative cable at the battery.

Automatic

WITH 2.2L ENGINE

1. Before servicing the vehicle, refer to the precautions in the beginning of this section.
2. Disconnect the negative terminal from the battery. Remove the air cleaner and air intake assembly.
3. Disconnect the Throttle Valve (TV) cable from the throttle lever and the transaxle.
4. Remove the fluid level indicator (dipstick) and the filler tube.
5. Install Engine Support Fixture tool No. J-28467 or equivalent and the Adapter tool No. J-35953 or equivalent, on the engine.
6. Remove the wiring harness-to-transaxle nut.
7. Label and disconnect the electrical connectors for the speed sensor, Torque Converter Clutch (TCC) connector and the neutral safety/back-up light switch.
8. Disconnect the shift linkage from the transaxle.
9. Remove the top two transaxle-to-engine bolts, the transaxle mount and bracket assembly.
10. Disconnect the rubber hose that runs from the transaxle to the vent pipe.
11. Raise and support the front of the vehicle.
12. Remove the front wheels.
13. Disconnect the shift linkage and bracket from the transaxle.
14. Remove the left side splash shield.
15. Using a modified Drive Axle Seal Protector tool No. J-34754 or equivalent,

install one on each drive axle to protect the seal from damage and the joint from possible failure.
16. Using care not to damage the half-shaft boots, disconnect the halfshafts from the transaxle.
17. Remove the transaxle strut. Remove the left side stabilizer link pin bolt and bushing clamp nuts from the support.
18. Remove the left frame support bolts and move it aside.
19. Disconnect the speedometer wire from the transaxle.
20. Remove the transaxle converter cover and matchmark the torque converter-to-flywheel for reassembly.
21. Disconnect and plug the transaxle cooler pipes.
22. Remove the transaxle-to-engine support.
23. Using a transmission jack, position and secure the jack to the transaxle. Remove the remaining transaxle-to-engine bolts.
24. Remove the transaxle from the vehicle. Use care not to let the torque converter fall from the front of the transaxle.

➡ The transaxle cooler and lines should be flushed any time the transaxle is removed for overhaul or replacement of the pump, case or converter.

To install:
25. Put a small amount of grease on the pilot hub of the converter and be sure the converter is properly engaged with the pump.
26. Raise the transaxle to the engine while guiding the right side halfshaft into the transaxle.
27. Install the lower transaxle mounting bolts and remove the jack.
28. Align the converter with the marks made previously on the flywheel and install the bolts hand-tight.
29. Tighten the converter bolts to 45 ft. lbs. (61 Nm). Retighten the first bolt after the others have been tightened.
30. Install the transaxle converter cover. Attach the speedometer wire connector.
31. Position the LH halfshaft into the transaxle. Install the left frame support assembly.
32. Install the left stabilizer shaft frame bushing nuts. Install the left stabilizer bar link pin bolt.
33. Install the transaxle strut.
34. Seat the drive axles in the transaxle. Remove the drive axle seal protectors.
35. Install the remaining components in the reverse order of removal.

36. Install the negative battery cable.
37. Fill with automatic transmission fluid and check for leaks.

WITH 3.1L ENGINE

1. Before servicing the vehicle, refer to the precautions in the beginning of this section.
2. Disconnect the negative terminal from the battery.
3. Remove the air cleaner, bracket, Mass Air Flow (MAF) sensor and air tube as an assembly.
4. Disconnect the exhaust crossover from the right side manifold and remove the left side exhaust manifold. Raise and support the manifold/crossover assembly.
5. Disconnect the Throttle Valve (TV) cable from the throttle lever and the transaxle.
6. Remove the vent hose and the shift cable from the transaxle.
7. Remove the fluid level indicator and the filler tube.
8. Using the Engine Support Fixture tool No. J-28467 or equivalent and Adapter tool No. J-35953 or equivalent, install them on the engine. Use care to be sure the engine is safely supported and that the engine support fixture does not damage any bodywork.
9. Remove the wiring harness-to-transaxle nut.
10. Label and disconnect the wires for the speed sensor, Torque Converter Clutch (TCC) connector and the neutral safety/back-up light switch.
11. Remove the upper transaxle-to-engine bolts.
12. Remove the transaxle-to-mount through-bolt, the transaxle mount bracket and the mount.
13. Raise and safely support the vehicle. Remove the front wheels.
14. Disconnect the shift cable bracket from the transaxle.
15. Remove the left side splash shield.
16. Using a modified Drive Axle Seal Protector tool No. J-34754 or equivalent, install one on each drive axle to protect the seal from damage and the joint from possible failure.
17. Using care not to damage the half-shaft boots, disconnect the halfshafts from the transaxle.
18. Remove the torsional and lateral strut from the transaxle. Remove the left side stabilizer link pin bolt.
19. Remove the left frame support bolts and move it aside.
20. Disconnect the speedometer wire from the transaxle.

21. Remove the transaxle converter cover and matchmark the converter-to-flywheel for assembly.

22. Disconnect and plug the transaxle cooler pipes.

23. Remove the transaxle-to-engine support.

24. Using a transmission jack, position and secure it to the transaxle. Remove the remaining transaxle-to-engine bolts.

25. Remove the transaxle from the vehicle using care to be sure the torque converter does not fall out.

To install:

26. Put a small amount of grease on the pilot hub of the converter and be sure the converter is properly engaged with the pump.

27. Raise the transaxle to the engine while guiding the right side halfshaft into the transaxle.

28. Install the lower transaxle mounting bolts and remove the jack.

29. Install the cooler lines at the transmission.

30. Position the left side halfshaft into the transaxle.

31. Install the left frame support bolts.

32. Install the left stabilizer shaft bushing clamp nuts at the support.

33. Install the left stabilizer bar link pin bolt.

34. Seat the drive axles in the transaxle. Remove the drive axle seal protectors.

35. Install the shift linkage bracket to the transaxle.

36. Install the speedometer wire connector.

37. Install the transaxle brace bolts. Install the transaxle lateral strut.

38. Install the transaxle torsional strut.

39. Align the converter with the marks made previously on the flywheel and install the bolts hand-tight.

40. Tighten the converter bolts to 45 ft. lbs. Retighten the first bolt after the others have been tightened.

41. Install the transaxle converter cover. Install the splash shield.

42. Install both front wheels.

43. Lower the vehicle.

44. Install the transaxle mount.

45. Install the transaxle mount through-bolt.

46. Install the wiring harness and nut securing it to the transaxle.

47. Remove the engine support fixture.

48. Install the fluid level indicator and fill tube.

49. Install the neutral start and TCC connectors.

50. Install the shift cable.

51. Install the TV cable at the transaxle and throttle lever.

52. Install the rubber hoses to the transaxle vent pipe.

53. Install the left side exhaust manifold bolts and exhaust crossover bolts.

54. Install the air cleaner mounting bracket, MAF sensor and air tube as an assembly.

55. Install the negative battery cable.

56. Fill transaxle with automatic transmission fluid and check for leaks.

Clutch

REMOVAL & INSTALLATION

1. Before servicing the vehicle, refer to the precautions in the beginning of this section.

2. Disconnect the negative battery cable.

3. From inside the vehicle, remove the hush panel.

4. Disconnect the clutch master cylinder pushrod from the clutch pedal.

5. With the transaxle removed, matchmark the pressure plate and flywheel assembly to insure proper balance during reassembly.

6. Loosen the pressure plate-to-flywheel bolts (one turn at a time) until the spring pressure is removed.

7. Support the pressure plate and remove the bolts.

8. Remove the pressure plate and disc assembly; be sure to note the flywheel side of the clutch disc.

9. Clean and inspect the clutch assembly, flywheel, release bearing, clutch fork and pivot shaft for signs of wear. Replace any necessary parts.

To install:

10. Position the clutch disc and pressure plate in the appropriate position, align the "Heavy Side" of the flywheel assembly stamped with an **X** with the clutch cover "Light Side" marked with paint. Support the assembly with Alignment tool No. J-290742 or equivalent.

➡**The clutch disc is installed with the damper springs offset towards the transaxle. Stamped letters on the clutch disc identify "Flywheel Side". Be sure the clutch disc is facing the same direction it was when removed. If the same pressure plate is being reused, align the marks made during the removal.**

Tighten the clutch cover bolts in the proper sequence

▶ **FRONT OF ENGINE**

7922Z118

11. Install the pressure plate-to-flywheel retaining bolts.

12. Tighten the flywheel-to-pressure plate bolts as follows:

    a. Install and lightly seat bolts 1, 2, 3, then 4, 5, 6.

    b. Tighten bolts 1, 2, 3 to 12 ft. lbs. (16 Nm).

    c. Tighten bolts 4, 5, 6 to 12 ft. lbs. (16 Nm).

    d. Tighten bolts 1, 2, 3, then 4, 5, 6 to 15 ft. lbs. (20mm) plus 30 degree rotation.

13. Remove the alignment tool.

14. Lightly lubricate the clutch fork ends. Fill the recess ends of the release bearing with grease. Lubricate the input shaft with a light coat of grease.

15. To complete the installation, reverse the removal procedures.

❊❊ WARNING

The clutch lever must not be moved toward the flywheel until the transaxle is bolted to the engine. Damage to the transaxle, release bearing and clutch fork could occur if this is not followed.

16. Bleed the clutch system and check the clutch operation when finished.

Hydraulic Clutch System

BLEEDING

1. Before servicing the vehicle, refer to the precautions in the beginning of this section.

2. Remove any dirt or grease around the reservoir cap so dirt cannot enter the system. Fill the reservoir with an approved DOT 3 brake fluid. Maintain the fluid level while bleeding the system.

3. Attach a hose to the bleeder screw on the clutch actuator assembly and submerge the other end of the hose in a container of hydraulic clutch fluid GM P/N 12345347 or equivalent DOT 3 brake fluid.

4. Depress the clutch pedal slowly and hold. Loosen the bleeder screw to purge air.

5. Tighten the bleeder screw to 18 inch lbs. (2 Nm).

6. Repeat the bleeding process until all the air is purged from the system.

7. Fill the master cylinder to the proper level.

8. To test the system, start the engine and push the clutch pedal to the floor. Wait 10 seconds and select reverse gear. There should be no gear clash. If clash is present, air may still be present in the system. Repeat bleeding procedure.

Halfshaft

REMOVAL & INSTALLATION

1. Before servicing the vehicle, refer to the precautions in the beginning of this section.

2. Raise and safely support vehicle. Remove the wheel and tire assembly.

3. Install drive seal protector J-34754 or equivalent, on the outer joint.

4. Insert a drift pin through the opening in the caliper and into the ventilation openings in the brake rotor to prevent the rotor from turning.

5. Remove the drive shaft hub nut and washer.

6. Remove the lower ball joint cotter pin and nut and loosen the joint using tool J-38892 or equivalent. If removing the right axle, turn the wheel to the left. If removing the left axle, turn the wheel to the right.

7. Separate the joint, with a prybar between the suspension support.

8. Disengage the axle from the hub and bearing using J-28733-A or equivalent puller.

1   RIGHT DRIVE AXLE
2   LEFT DRIVE AXLE
3   J 28468 OR J 33008
4   J 29794
5   J2619-01

◀FRT

7922Z126

Use the tools as shown to prevent damaging the transaxle or halfshaft

9. Separate the hub and bearing assembly from the drive axle and move the strut and knuckle assembly rearward.

10. Disconnect the inner joint from the transaxle using tool J-28468 or J-33008 attached to J-29794 and J-2619–01 or from the intermediate shaft, if equipped.

To install:

11. Install the axle seal protector J-37292-A into the transaxle.

12. Insert the drive axle into the transaxle or intermediate shaft, if equipped, by placing a suitable tool into the groove on the joint housing and tapping until seated.

❋❋ CAUTION

Be careful not to damage the axle seal or dislodge the transaxle seal garter spring when installing the axle.

13. Verify that the drive axle is seated into the transaxle by grasping on the housing and pulling outward.

14. Install the drive axle into the hub and bearing assembly.

15. Install the lower ball joint to the knuckle. Tighten the ball joint to steering knuckle nut to 41 ft. lbs. (55 Nm) and install the cotter pin.

16. Install the washer and new drive shaft nut. Again insert a drift pin into the caliper and rotor to prevent the rotor from turning and tighten the drive shaft nut to 185 ft. lbs. (260 Nm). Install the brake caliper.

17. Remove both J-37292-B and J-34754 seal protectors.

18. Install the tire and wheel assembly. Lower the vehicle.

STEERING AND SUSPENSION

Air Bag

❋❋ CAUTION

Some vehicles are equipped with an air bag system, also known as the Supplemental Inflatable Restraint (SIR). The system must be disabled before performing service on or around system components, steering column, instrument panel compo-
nents, wiring and sensors. Failure to follow safety and disabling procedures could result in accidental air bag deployment, possible personal injury and unnecessary system repairs.**

PRECAUTIONS

Several precautions must be observed when handling the inflator module to avoid accidental deployment and possible personal injury.

• Never carry the inflator module by the wires or connector on the underside of the module.

• When carrying a live inflator module, hold securely with both hands, and ensure that the bag and trim cover are pointed away.

• Place the inflator module on a bench or other surface with the bag and trim cover facing up.

• With the inflator module on the bench, never place anything on or close to the

1 CONNECTOR POSITION ASSURANCE (CPA)
2 YELLOW TWO–WAY SIR HARNESS CONNECTOR

79222127

Air bag module connector location

module which may be thrown in the event of an accidental deployment.

Before servicing the vehicle, be sure to refer to the precautions in the beginning of this section as well.

DISARMING

✳✳ CAUTION

The Supplemental Inflatable Restraint (SIR) system must be disarmed before performing many service functions. Failure to do so may cause accidental deployment of the air bag, resulting in unnecessary SIR system repairs and/or personal injury.

1. Before servicing the vehicle, refer to the precautions in the beginning of this section.

2. Turn the steering wheel so the vehicle's wheels are pointing straight ahead. This helps protect the clockspring mechanism under the steering wheel hub which powers the air bag module.

3. Turn the ignition switch to **LOCK** and remove the key.

4. Remove the AIR BAG fuse from the instrument panel fuse block.

5. Remove the left side sound insulator.

6. Remove the air bag connector CPA and disconnect the yellow 2-way SIR harness connector located near the base of the steering column.

➡**With the AIR BAG fuse removed, and if for some reason, the negative battery cable should be connected and the ignition switch turned ON (not recommended), the air bag warning lamp in the instrument cluster will be ON. This is normal operation and does not indicate a SIR system malfunction.**

REARMING

1. Turn the ignition switch to the **LOCK** position and remove the key.

2. At the base of the steering column, connect the yellow 2-way connector and install the CPA bar to verify that the connection is complete and tight.

3. Install the left side sound insulator.

4. Install the AIR BAG fuse into the instrument panel fuse block.

5. Turn the ignition switch to the **RUN** position and verify that AIR BAG warning lamp flashes 7 times and turns OFF. If it does not operate as described, perform SIR Diagnostic System Check.

Power Rack and Pinion Steering Gear

REMOVAL & INSTALLATION

✳✳ WARNING

The wheels of the vehicle must be straight ahead and the ignition switch must be in the LOCK position, before disconnecting the flange and coupling assembly from the steering column. Failure to do so may cause the supplemental inflatable restraint (SIR coil assembly to become off centered, which will damage the SIR coil assembly.

1. Before servicing the vehicle, refer to the precautions in the beginning of this section.

2. Remove the left side sound insulator.

3. Remove the upper pinch bolt on the coupling assembly.

4. Remove the line retainer (if applicable).

5. Remove the power brake assembly away from the cowl wall, leaving the master cylinder attached.

6. Raise and safely support the vehicle. Remove the front tire and wheel assemblies.

7. Disconnect the tie rod ends from the struts using tool J-24319–01 or equivalent.

8. Lower the vehicle.

9. Remove the left and right mounting clamps.

10. Disconnect the gear inlet and outlet pipes from the rack and pinion steering gear.

11. Move the rack and pinion assembly forward and remove the lower pinch bolt from flange on the coupling assembly.

12. Disconnect the coupling from the rack and pinion assembly.

13. Remove the dash seal from the rack and pinion assembly.

14. Remove the rack and pinion assembly through the left wheel opening.

➡**If the studs were removed with the mounting clamps, apply some thread-locking compound on them and reinstall the studs into the cowl panel and tighten until the studs are fully seated against the dash panel. The torque should not exceed 13 ft. lbs. (18 Nm).**

To install:

15. Install the rack and pinion assembly into the vehicle through the left wheel opening.

16. Attach the dash seal onto the rack and pinion assembly.

17. Move the rack and pinion assembly forward and install the coupling onto the rack and pinion.

18. Install the flange and coupling lower pinch bolt. Tighten this bolt to 30 ft. lbs. (41 Nm).

19. Connect the gear inlet and outlet pipes to the rack and pinion assembly and tighten them to 20 ft. lbs. (27 Nm).

20. Install the mounting clamp nuts and tighten (left side first) to 22 ft. lbs. (30 Nm).

21. Raise the vehicle.

22. Connect the tie rods to the struts and tighten to 44 ft. lbs. (60 Nm) and install the cotter pins through the nuts.

23. Install the tire and wheel assemblies.

24. Install the line retainer (if applicable). Lower the vehicle.

25. Install the steering column pinch bolt and tighten to 30 ft. lbs. (41 Nm).

26. Install the left side sound insulator.

27. Fill the reservoir with power steering fluid and bleed air from the system.

28. Check the toe setting and adjust if necessary.

29. Road test the vehicle and verify that there are no leaks and that the steering functions properly.

Strut

REMOVAL & INSTALLATION

Front

1. Before servicing the vehicle, refer to the precautions in the beginning of this section.

2. Raise and safely support the vehicle.

3. Remove the front tire and wheel assembly.

4. Place a support under the lower control arm and raise the jack until the weight of suspension is taken up.

5. Remove the cotter pin and castle nut from the outer tie rod end and using a suitable puller, separate the tie rod end from the strut steering arm.

6. Scribe matching marks on the lower strut mounting bracket and steering knuckle for reference during installation.

7. If the suspension is equipped with a direct acting stabilizer system remove the link to strut mounting nut.

8. Remove the lower strut mounting through-bolts and nuts.

9. Remove the upper strut plate mounting nuts and mounting bolt.

10. Remove the strut from the vehicle.

11. If the coil spring or strut is to be replaced, a strut compressor J-34013 or

VIEW A-A

1 - GROMMET, MOUNTING
2 - LINE ASM, CYLINDER (LT)
3 - ANNULUS ASM, BEARING
5 - SEAL, STUB SHAFT
7 - RING, RETAINING
8 - SEAL, DASH
10 - BOLT, PINCH
11 - COUPLING, FLANGE & STEERING
12 - LINE ASM, CYLINDER (RT)
13 - NUT, ADJUSTER PLUG LOCK
15 - SEAL, O-RING
16 - HOUSING, RACK & PINION
17 - COVER, DUST
18 - COVER, HOUSING END
19 - GROMMET, MOUNTING
20 - CLAMP, BOOT
21 - BUSHING, BOOT RETAINING

22 - BOOT, RACK & PINION
23 - WASHER, CENTER HOUSING COVER (PART OF 22)
24 - BUSHING, BOOT RETAINING
25 - CLAMP, BOOT
26 - ASSEMBLY, INNER TIE ROD
27 - BOLT, PINCH
28 - ASSEMBLY, OUTER TIE ROD
30 - SEAL, TIE ROD
31 - NUT, HEX SLOTTED
32 - PIN, COTTER
33 - ADJUSTER, TIE ROD
35 - BUSHING, INNER PIVOT
36 - PLATE, BOLT SUPPORT
37 - BOLT, INNER TIE ROD
38 - PLATE, LOCK
40 - ASSEMBLY, OUTER TIE ROD
41 - ASSEMBLY, INNER TIE ROD

7922Z128

Exploded view of the rack and pinion steering gear

1   BOLT
2   BOLT – 25 N·m (18 LBS. FT.)
3   NUT – 25 N·m (18 LBS. FT.)
4   STRUT ASSEMBLY

7922Z129

Exploded view of the front strut mounting

equivalent must be used for that procedure.

12. Mount the strut compressor in the holding fixture J-3289–20 or equivalent.

✳✳ WARNING

To prevent possible spring damage, never compress the spring to the point where the coils are touching. Compress the spring only enough to make safe removal possible.

13. Mount the strut into the compressor and compress the spring approximately ½ its height after initial contact with the top cap.

14. Remove the nut from the strut dampener shaft and place the guiding rod tool J-34013–27 or equivalent onto the top of the damper shaft. Use this rod tool to guide the dampener shaft down through the bearing cap while decompressing the spring.

15. Remove the strut and any components that are necessary.

To install:

16. Install the bearing cap into the strut compressor if previously installed.

17. Mount the strut into the compressor using the bottom locking pin only. Extend

the dampener shaft and install clamp J-34013–20 or equivalent on the shaft to hold it in a extended position.

18. Install the spring over the dampener and swing the assembly up so the upper locking pin can be installed.

19. Install the upper insulator, shield, bumper, and upper spring seat. Be sure the flat on the upper spring seat is facing in the proper direction. the spring seat flat should be facing the same direction as the centerline of the strut assembly.

20. Compress the coil spring while guiding the dampener shaft through the upper insulator with the guiding rod tool until the threads on the dampener shaft are visible.

21. Install the shaft nut and tighten to 52 ft. lbs. (70 Nm) while holding the shaft from turning.

22. Remove the clamp and remove the strut assembly from the compressor tool.

23. Install the strut in the vehicle and loosely install the upper mounting nuts and bolts.

24. Connect the lower strut mounting bracket to the steering knuckle and insert the through-bolts. The bolts should point toward the rear of the vehicle.

25. Install the stabilizer link to the strut

bracket if equipped with direct acting suspension. Install the mounting nut and tighten to 70 ft. lbs. (95 Nm).

26. Install the through-bolt nuts loosely. Position the strut so the matching marks are aligned and tighten the nuts to 133 ft. lbs. (180 Nm).

27. Connect the tie rod end to the strut steering arm and tighten the castle nut to 44 ft. lbs. (60 Nm). If necessary tighten the nut up to 60 degrees (⅙ turn) additional rotation to align the cotter pin holes. NEVER loosen the nut to make the holes align.

28. Remove the support jack from under the suspension.

29. Install the tire and wheel assembly and tighten the mounting nuts to 100 ft. lbs. (140 Nm).

30. Lower the vehicle.

31. Tighten the upper strut mounting nuts and bolt and tighten to 18 ft. lbs. (25 Nm).

32. Check the front end alignment and adjust as necessary.

Shock Absorber

REMOVAL & INSTALLATION

Rear

1. Before servicing the vehicle, refer to the precautions in the beginning of this section.

2. Open the deck lid.

3. Remove the shock absorber upper cover and remove the upper mounting nut.

✳✳ WARNING

If both shocks are to be replaced. Remove one shock absorber at a time. This will ensure that the axle assembly will not be suspended by the brake hoses.

4. Raise and safely support the vehicle.

5. Support the rear axle with supports. When lifting the vehicle with a body hoist, it will be necessary to use adjustable safety stands.

6. Remove the shock absorber nut and the shock absorber.

To install:

7. Install the shock absorber at the lower attachment. Install the nut hand-tight.

8. Lower the vehicle enough to guide the upper stud through the body opening and install the upper shock mounting nut.

NOTE: COVER MUST BE INSTALLED SO THAT
ARROW POINTS TO LEFT SIDE OF VEHICLE

1 COVER (MUST BE INSTALLED
WITH ARROW POINTING TO
LEFT OF VEHICLE)
2 NUT
3 REINFORCEMENT
4 UPPER SHOCK ABSORBER
MOUNT
5 SHOCK ABSORBER
6 WASHER
7 WASHER
8 NUT
9 NUT
10 REAR AXLE; SPRING-ON-CENTER TYPE
11 INSULATOR, COIL SPRING
12 COIL SPRING

79222Z130

Exploded view of the rear shock mounting

9. Tighten the lower shock absorber mounting nuts to 35 ft. lbs. (47 Nm).

10. Remove the axle support and lower the vehicle all the way, then tighten the shock absorber upper nut to 21 ft. lbs. (29 Nm).

11. Install the shock absorber upper cover.

Coil Spring

REMOVAL & INSTALLATION

Front

1. Before servicing the vehicle, refer to the precautions in the beginning of this section.

2. Raise and safely support the vehicle. Remove the tire and wheel assembly.

3. Remove the strut assembly.

4. Place the strut assembly into strut compressor tool J-34013-A or equivalent.

5. With the strut firmly mounted in the strut compressor tool, compress the spring and remove the center nut for strut plate. Carefully back off the strut compressor tool, after tension is fully relieved remove the coil spring from its mounting.

To install:

6. Place the coil spring into its mounting perch.

7. Place the strut mounting plate on top of the spring and attach the strut compressor.

8. Compress the coil spring enough so the mounting nut can be installed. Tighten this nut to 52 ft. lbs. (70 Nm).

9. Carefully back off the tension from the strut compressor tool and remove the strut assembly.

10. Install the strut assembly into the vehicle.

11. Install the tire and wheel assembly. Lower the vehicle.

12. Check wheel alignment and road test vehicle.

Rear

※※ CAUTION

When removing rear springs do not use a twin-post type hoist. When certain fasteners are removed from the rear axle assembly, the axle may have a tendency to cause the hoist to slip, which may cause personal injury. Perform operation on the floor if necessary.

1. Before servicing the vehicle, refer to the precautions in the beginning of this section.

2. Raise and safely support the vehicle. Use supports to support the rear axle.

3. Remove the tire and wheel assemblies.

4. Remove the right and left brake line bracket attaching screws from the body and allow brake line to hang free.

5. Remove the lower mounting bolts from the shock absorbers.

※※ WARNING

Do not suspend the rear axle by the brake hoses. Damage to hoses could result.

6. Lower the rear axle and remove the spring(s).

To install:

7. Position the coil spring in its mounting perch and raise the axle. The end of the lower coil spring must be positioned in the spring seat and within 7/16 in. (15mm) of the spring stop.

8. Connect the shock absorbers to the

Turn to Section 6 for brake system applications

rear axle. Tighten the nuts to 35 ft. lbs. (47 Nm).

9. Install the brake line brackets to the body and tighten screws to 97 inch lbs. (11 Nm).

10. Install the tire and wheel assemblies. Remove the supports and lower the vehicle.

Lower Ball Joint

REMOVAL & INSTALLATION

1. Before servicing the vehicle, refer to the precautions in the beginning of this section.

2. Raise and safely support the vehicle.

3. If suspension contact hoist is used, place supports under the crossmember. Lower the vehicle slightly so the weight of the vehicle rests on the crossmember.

4. Remove the tire and wheel assembly.

✳✳ WARNING

Care must be exercised to prevent the halfshaft joints from being over-extended. When either end of the shaft is disconnected, over-extension of the joint could result in sepa-ration of internal components and possible joint failure. Failure to observe this can result in interior joint or boot damage and possible joint failure.

5. Remove the cotter pin and nut from the ball joint.

6. Separate the ball joint from the steering knuckle using tool J-38892 or equivalent.

7. Drill out the three rivets retaining ball joint to the lower control arm. Use an ⅛ in. (3mm) drill bit to make a pilot hole through the rivets. Finish drilling rivets with a ½ in. (13mm) drill bit.

8. Remove the nut attaching link to the stabilizer shaft.

9. Remove the ball joint from the steering knuckle and control arm.

To install:

10. Install the ball joint into the control arm.

11. Install three new bolts and nuts (supplied with new ball joint). Check the ball joint service kit for an instruction sheet listing bolt torque. If none is supplied, tighten the bolts to 40 ft. lbs. (55 Nm).

12. Position the ball joint stud through the steering knuckle and tighten the nut to 50 ft. lbs. (65 Nm) and install the cotter pin.

13. Connect the stabilizer link to the stabilizer shaft and tighten nut to 13 ft. lbs. (17 Nm).

14. Install the tire and wheel assembly.

15. Check the front wheel alignment and adjust if necessary.

Wheel Bearings

ADJUSTMENT

Front and Rear

The wheel bearings are not adjustable. If a wheel bearing is out of specifications, it must be replaced. Using a dial indicator, check for looseness. If it exceeds 0.005 in. (0.1270mm) on drum or disc brakes the bearing wear is excessive and the hub and bearing should be replaced.

REMOVAL & INSTALLATION

Front

The front wheel bearings on these vehicles should not be disassembled and are not serviced separately. The wheel bearings are pressed into the hub. If the wheel bearings are noisy or defective, the hub and bearing assembly must be replaced.

1. Before servicing the vehicle, refer to the precautions in the beginning of this section.

2. Loosen the axle hub nut.

3. Raise and safely support the vehicle. Remove the tire and wheel assembly.

4. Install Special Boot Cover J-33162 or equivalent on the 2.2L engine vehicles with automatic transaxle only. This is to protect the soft CV-joint boot.

5. Remove the axle hub nut.

6. Remove the brake caliper and rotor.

7. Remove the three hub and bearing mounting bolts.

8. Remove the splash shield.

✳✳ WARNING

If the hub and bearing assembly is to be reused, mark the attaching bolt and corresponding hole for installation in the same position. Use of a hammer or direct heat on the half-shaft should be avoided during removal, as this could result in internal bearing damage.

9. Install special tool J-28733 or equivalent hub puller and turn the bolt to press

1 SERVICE BALL JOINT
2 BALL JOINT MOUNTING BOLTS
3 NUT
4 LOWER CONTROL ARM
5 STEERING KNUCKLE
6 NUT − 55 N·m (41 LBS. FT.) MINIMUM TORQUE
   65 N·m (48 LBS. FT.) MAXIMUM TORQUE
   TO INSTALL PIN
7 PIN

79222119

Exploded view of the replacement ball joint assembly mounting

1 HUB AND BEARING ASSEMBLY
2 STEERING KNUCKLE
3 WASHER
4 DRIVE AXLE NUT – 260 N·m (192 LBS. FT.)
5 HUB AND BEARING RETAINING BOLT
6 WASHER

79222131

Exploded view of the front wheel bearing mounting

the hub and bearing assembly off the end of the drive axle (halfshaft).

10. Disconnect the stabilizer link bolt at the lower control arm.

11. Separate the lower ball joint using special tool J-29330 or equivalent.

12. Remove the drive axle from the steering knuckle and support it aside.

13. If removing the steering knuckle use the following procedure:

a. Using a sharp tool, scribe the outline of the strut onto the steering knuckle.

b. Remove the cotter pin and castle nut from the outer tie rod end and using a steering linkage puller, separate the tie rod from the steering knuckle.

c. Remove the bolts attaching the strut to the steering knuckle and remove the knuckle.

d. Using a grinder or file, elongate the lower strut-to-knuckle hole for camber alignment adjustment.

To install:

14. Clean and inspect the hub and bearing surfaces and the steering knuckle bore.

15. If the steering knuckle was removed, use the following procedure:

a. Install the steering knuckle onto

the lower ball joint and tighten the ball joint nut to 48 ft. lbs. (65 Nm).

b. Connect the steering knuckle to the lower strut bracket and install the through-bolts and nuts. With the match-marks in alignment, tighten the nuts to 122 ft. lbs. (165 Nm).

c. Connect the stabilizer link bolt at the lower control arm and tighten the nut to 22 ft. lbs. (30 Nm).

16. Install the hub and bearing assembly and tighten the three attaching bolts to 70 ft. lbs. (90 Nm).

17. If removed, connect the tie rod end to the steering knuckle and tighten the castle nut to 30 ft. lbs. (41 Nm). If necessary to align the cotter pin holes tighten the castle nut up to 60 degrees (⅙ turn) additional. Install a new cotter pin.

18. Install the drive axle (halfshaft) to the hub and bearing assembly being careful to align the axle splines to the hub and not to damage the seal.

19. Install a new hub and bearing nut on the drive axle and apply a partial torque of 75 ft. lbs. (100 Nm).

20. Install the rotor and caliper assembly.

21. Install the wheel and tire assembly.

1 BOLT
2 REAR AXLE ASSEMBLY
3 BACKING PLATE
4 HUB AND BEARING ASSEMBLY
5 LOCKNUT

79222132

Exploded view of the rear wheel bearing

22. Safely lower the vehicle and apply a final torque to the axle hub nut to 190 ft. lbs. (260 Nm).

23. Perform a front-end alignment check, and adjust if required. Road test vehicle.

Rear

1. Before servicing the vehicle, refer to the precautions in the beginning of this section.

2. Raise and safely support the vehicle. Remove the tire and wheel assembly.

3. Remove the brake drum.

4. Remove the nuts from the hub bearing mounting bolts. With the nuts removed, push the mounting bolts out of the hub bearing assembly. The top rear bolt will not clear the brake shoe and has to be left in the hub flange when removing the hub assembly.

5. Remove the rear ABS wheel speed sensor wiring harness.

6. Remove the bearing assembly.

To install:

7. Connect the rear ABS wheel speed sensor wire connector.

8. Install the bearing assembly onto the backing plate with the top rear bolt already installed through the bearing bolt hole.

9. Install the remainder of the mounting bolts.

10. Install the mounting nuts and tighten to 44 ft. lbs. (60 Nm).

11. Install the brake drum.

12. Install the tire and wheel assembly and tighten the wheel nuts to 100 ft. lbs. (140 Nm).

13. Lower the vehicle.

GENERAL MOTORS CORPORATION—L/N BODY

35

Chevrolet-Malibu • Oldsmobile-Cutlass

PRECAUTIONS

Before servicing any vehicle, please be sure to read all of the following precautions, which deal with personal safety, prevention of component damage, and important points to take into consideration when servicing a motor vehicle:

• Never open, service or drain the radiator or cooling system when the engine is hot; serious burns can occur from the steam and hot coolant.

• Observe all applicable safety precautions when working around fuel. Whenever servicing the fuel system, always work in a well ventilated area. Do not allow fuel spray or vapors to come in contact with a spark, open flame, or excessive heat (a hot drop light, for example). Keep a dry chemical fire extinguisher near the work area. Always keep fuel in a container specifically designed for fuel storage; also, always properly seal fuel containers to avoid the possibility of fire or explosion. Refer to the additional fuel system precautions later in this section.

• Fuel injection systems often remain pressurized, even after the engine has been turned **OFF**. The fuel system pressure must be relieved before disconnecting any fuel lines. Failure to do so may result in fire and/or personal injury.

• Brake fluid often contains polyglycol ethers and polyglycols. Avoid contact with the eyes and wash your hands thoroughly after handling brake fluid. If you do get brake fluid in your eyes, flush your eyes with clean, running water for 15 minutes. If eye irritation persists, or if you have taken brake fluid internally, IMMEDIATELY seek medical assistance.

• The EPA warns that prolonged contact with used engine oil may cause a number of skin disorders, including cancer! You should make every effort to minimize your exposure to used engine oil. Protective gloves should be worn when changing oil. Wash your hands and any other exposed skin areas as soon as possible after exposure to used engine oil. Soap and water, or waterless hand cleaner should be used.

• All new vehicles are now equipped with an air bag system, often referred to as a Supplemental Restraint System (SRS) or Supplemental Inflatable Restraint (SIR) system. The system must be disabled before performing service on or around system components, steering column, instrument panel components, wiring and sensors. Failure to follow safety and disabling procedures could result in accidental air bag deployment, possible personal injury and unnecessary system repairs.

• Always wear safety goggles when working with, or around, the air bag system. When carrying a non-deployed air bag, be sure the bag and trim cover are pointed away from your body. When placing a non-deployed air bag on a work surface, always face the bag and trim cover upward, away from the surface. This will reduce the motion of the module if it is accidentally deployed. Refer to the additional air bag system precautions later in this section.

• Clean, high quality brake fluid from a sealed container is essential to the safe and proper operation of the brake system. You should always buy the correct type of brake fluid for your vehicle. If the brake fluid becomes contaminated, completely flush the system with new fluid. Never reuse any brake fluid. Any brake fluid that is removed from the system should be discarded. Also, do not allow any brake fluid to come in contact with a painted surface; it will damage the paint.

• Never operate the engine without the proper amount and type of engine oil; doing so WILL result in severe engine damage.

• Timing belt maintenance is extremely important! Many models utilize an interference-type, non-freewheeling engine. If the timing belt breaks, the valves in the cylinder head may strike the pistons, causing potentially serious (also time-consuming and expensive) engine damage. Refer to the maintenance interval charts in the front of this manual for the recommended replacement interval for the timing belt, and to the timing belt section for belt replacement and inspection.

• Disconnecting the negative battery cable on some vehicles may interfere with the functions of the on-board computer system(s) and may require the computer to undergo a relearning process once the negative battery cable is reconnected.

• When servicing drum brakes, only disassemble and assemble one side at a time, leaving the remaining side intact for reference.

ENGINE REPAIR

Ignition Timing

ADJUSTMENT

Ignition timing is controlled by the Powertrain Control Module (PCM). No adjustment is necessary or possible.

Engine Assembly

REMOVAL & INSTALLATION

2.4L Engine

1. Before servicing the vehicle, refer to the precautions in the beginning of this section.

2. If equipped with A/C, properly recover the refrigerant.

3. Disconnect the negative battery cable.

4. Properly drain the cooling system into an approved container.

5. Relieve the fuel system pressure.

6. Remove the left sound insulator, then disconnect the clutch pushrod from the pedal assembly.

7. Disconnect the heater hose at the thermostat assembly, then detach the radiator inlet (upper) hose.

8. Remove the air cleaner assembly and the coolant fan.

9. If equipped with A/C, disconnect the compressor/condenser hose assembly at the compressor, then discard the O-rings.

10. Disconnect the two vacuum hoses from the front of the engine.

11. Tag and detach the following electrical connectors:
- Alternator
- A/C compressor (if equipped)
- Fuel injector harness
- Idle Air Control (IAC) and Throttle Position (TP) sensor at the throttle body
- Manifold Absolute Pressure (MAP) sensor
- Intake Air Temperature (IAT) sensor
- EVAP canister purge solenoid
- Starter solenoid
- Ground connections
- Negative battery cable from the transaxle
- Electronic ignition coil and module assembly
- Engine Coolant Temperature (ECT) sensor(s)
- Oil pressure sensor/switch
- Oxygen (O2S) sensor
- Crankshaft Position (CKP) sensor
- Back-up lamp switch, then position the harness aside

12. Disconnect the power brake vacuum hose from the throttle body. Detach the power brake vacuum tube-to-check valve hose from the tube.

13. Remove the throttle cable and bracket.

14. Unfasten the power steering pump rear bracket, then remove the bracket and vacuum tube as an assembly.

15. Unfasten the power steering pivot bolt, then remove the pump and drive belt. Position the pump aside, with the lines still attached.

16. Carefully disconnect the fuel lines.

17. Disconnect the shift cables. Detach the clutch actuator line.

18. Remove the exhaust manifold and heat shield.

19. Disconnect the radiator outlet (lower) hose from the radiator.

20. Install J-28467-A or equivalent engine support fixture.

21. Unfasten the bolt attaching the coolant recovery/surge tank, then position the tank aside with the hoses still connected.

22. Remove the engine mount assembly.

23. Raise and safely support the vehicle, then remove the front wheel and tire assemblies. Remove the right splash shield.

24. Drain and recycle the engine oil.

25. Remove the radiator air deflector.

26. Tag and detach the following electrical connections:
- Vehicle Speed Sensor (VSS)

- Knock (KS) sensor
- Starter solenoid
- If equipped, both front ABS wheel speed sensors

27. Remove the engine mount strut and the transaxle mount.

28. Separate the ball joints from the steering knuckles.

29. Remove the suspension supports, crossmember, and stabilizer shaft as an assembly.

30. Disconnect the heater outlet hose from the radiator outlet pipe.

31. Remove the axle shaft from the transaxle and intermediate shaft, then position aside.

32. If equipped, disconnect the A/C lines from the oil pan.

33. Remove the flywheel housing cover.

34. Position a suitable support below the engine, then carefully lower the vehicle onto the support.

35. Matchmark the threads on the support fixture hooks so the setting can be duplicated when reinstalling the engine. Remove the engine support fixture J-hooks.

36. Raise the vehicle slowly off the engine and transaxle assembly. If may be necessary to move the engine/transaxle assembly rearward to clear the intake manifold.

37. Noting the position of the bolts, separate the engine from the transaxle.

To install:

✳✳ WARNING

Be sure the retaining bolts are in their correct locations. If not, engine damage may occur.

38. Assemble the engine to the transaxle.

39. Position the engine and transaxle assembly under the engine compartment, then slowly lower the vehicle over the assembly until the transaxle mount is indexed, then install the retaining bolt.

40. Install engine support fixture J-28467-A or equivalent, making sure to adjust it to the previous setting.

41. Install the engine mount assembly and transaxle mount.

42. Carefully raise the vehicle off the support.

43. Attach the axle shafts to the transaxle.

44. Connect the heater outlet hose to the radiator outlet pipe.

45. Install the suspension supports, crossmember and stabilizer shaft assembly.

46. Attach the ball joints to the steering knuckles, then secure with the nuts.

47. Install the engine strut mount.

48. If equipped, connect the A/C line to the oil pan.

49. Attach the following electrical connectors, as tagged during removal:
- VSS
- KS sensor
- Starter solenoid
- If equipped, both front ABS wheel speed sensors

50. Install the flywheel housing cover.

51. Fasten the radiator air deflector.

52. Connect the lower radiator hose.

53. Install the right splash shield, then the front wheel and tire assemblies.

54. Carefully lower the vehicle, then remove the engine support fixture.

55. Install the coolant recovery/surge tank, then secure using the retaining bolt.

56. Attach the following electrical connections, as tagged during removal:
- Alternator
- A/C compressor (if equipped)
- Fuel injector harness
- IAC and TP sensors
- MAP sensor
- IAT sensor
- EVAP canister purge solenoid
- Starter solenoid
- Ground connections
- Negative battery cable to the transaxle
- Electronic ignition coil and module assembly
- ECT sensor(s)
- Oil pressure sensor/switch
- O2S sensor
- CKP sensor
- Back-up lamp switch

57. Attach the vacuum hoses.

58. If equipped with A/C, attach the compressor/condenser hose assembly to the compressor.

59. Fasten the clutch actuator line.

60. Install the exhaust manifold and heat shield.

61. Connect the fuel lines.

62. Connect the positive battery cable.

63. Fasten the power steering pump pivot-to-block bolt. Install the power steering pump rear bracket and tension belt.

64. Connect the vacuum hoses to the intake manifold and to the tube from the brake booster.

65. Install the throttle cable and bracket.

66. Install the coolant fan and air cleaner assembly.

67. Attach the radiator outlet (upper)

hose. Fill the cooling system with the proper type and quantity of coolant.

68. Connect the clutch pushrod to the pedal assembly, then install the left sound insulator.

69. Attach the heater hose at the thermostat housing.

❄❄ WARNING

Operating the engine without the proper amount and type of engine oil will result in severe engine damage.

70. Fill the transaxle with fluid, then fill the crankcase with oil.

71. Connect the negative battery cable.

72. If equipped with A/C, evacuate, charge and leak test the system.

73. Start the engine and check the fluid levels, proper operation of the engine and/or fluid leakage.

3.1L Engine

Please note that the engine and transaxle are removed as an assembly from under the vehicle.

1. Before servicing the vehicle, refer to the precautions in the beginning of this section.

2. Relieve the fuel system pressure. Disconnect the negative battery cable.

3. Remove the top half of the air cleaner assembly and the throttle body inlet duct. Drain the cooling system.

4. Remove the upper and lower radiator hoses. Disconnect the coolant inlet line from the coolant surge tank.

5. Disconnect the vacuum hoses from the EVAP canister purge valve, vacuum modulator and power brake booster.

6. Disconnect the heater outlet hose from the water pump. Remove the serpentine drive belt.

7. Disconnect the control cables from the throttle body lever and intake manifold bracket and position the cables aside.

8. Label and detach the electrical connectors from the necessary components.

9. Remove the alternator. Disconnect and cap the power steering lines from the power steering pump.

10. Disconnect and cap the fuel lines from the fuel rail. Remove the cooling fan assembly.

11. Disconnect the shift control cable from the transaxle shift lever and cable bracket. Disconnect the transaxle vent tube from the transaxle.

12. Disconnect the vacuum hose from the vacuum reservoir. Install an engine support fixture, J-28467-A, or the equivalent.

13. Loosen, but do not remove the top two A/C compressor mounting bolts. Raise and safely support the vehicle.

14. Remove the front tire and wheel assemblies. Remove the right and left inner fender splash shields.

15. Drain and recycle the engine oil.

16. Remove the engine mount strut. Disconnect the ABS sensor wires from the wheel sensors and suspension member supports, if equipped.

17. Remove the cotter pins and castle nuts from the lower ball joints. Using a suitable tool, separate the lower ball joints from the steering knuckles.

18. Remove the lower suspension support assemblies with the lower control arms attached. Disconnect the halfshafts from the transaxle and support aside.

19. Remove the oil filter and oil filter adapter. Remove the flywheel cover. Remove the starter. Disconnect the heater hoses from the heater core.

20. Remove the A/C compressor lower mounting bolts and remove the compressor from the mounting bracket and position aside. DO NOT disconnect the refrigerant lines from the compressor or allow the lines top support the weight of the compressor.

21. Remove the vacuum reservoir tank. Disconnect the exhaust pipe from the exhaust manifold and position the pipe aside.

22. Remove the engine mount strut bracket from the engine. Disconnect the transaxle cooler lines from the radiator.

23. Remove the transaxle oil fill tube. Lower the vehicle until the power train assembly is resting on a suitable engine table.

24. Remove the transaxle mount-to-body bolts, and the intermediate bracket from the right engine mount.

25. Remove the engine support fixture. Raise the vehicle leaving the powertrain assembly on the engine table.

26. Separate the engine and transaxle assemblies.

To install:

27. Connect the transaxle to the engine and tighten the mounting bolts to 55 ft. lbs. (75 Nm).

28. Position the powertrain assembly under the vehicle and lower the vehicle into position. Loosely install the serpentine belt.

29. Complete the installation by reversing the removal procedures.

30. Tighten the following items to:
• Engine strut bracket-to-engine bolts: 44 ft. lbs. (60 Nm)
• Exhaust pipe-to-exhaust manifold bolts: 18 ft. lbs. (25 Nm)

• Ball joints-to-steering knuckle nuts: 41 ft. lbs. (55 Nm)

31. Connect the negative battery cable. Check and fill all the engine fluids as necessary. Start the vehicle and bleed the power steering system.

Water Pump

REMOVAL & INSTALLATION

2.4L Engine

1. Before servicing the vehicle, refer to the precautions in the beginning of this section.

2. Disconnect the negative battery cable.

3. Drain the cooling system.

4. Detach the Oxygen (O$_2$S) sensor electrical connector.

5. Remove the upper and lower exhaust manifold heat shields.

6. Raise and safely support the vehicle.

7. Remove the exhaust manifold brace-to-manifold bolt.

8. Loosen the exhaust pipe-to-manifold spring loaded nuts.

9. Remove the radiator outlet pipe-to-water pump cover bolts.

10. Raise and safely support the vehicle.

11. Disconnect the exhaust pipe from the manifold.

12. Disconnect the radiator outlet pipe from the oil pan and transaxle.

13. If equipped with a manual transaxle, remove the exhaust manifold brace. If equipped with an automatic transaxle, leave the lower radiator hose attached and pull down on the radiator pipe to disconnect it from the water pump.

14. Lower the vehicle.

15. Remove the exhaust manifold.

16. Remove the water pump cover-to-engine bolts.

17. Remove the three water pump-to-timing chain housing nuts.

18. Remove the water pump and cover assembly.

19. Remove the five water pump cover-to-pump bolts and remove the cover.

To install:

20. Install the water pump-to-engine components and tighten the bolts finger-tight.

21. Lubricate the splines of the water pump drive with chassis grease.

22. To complete the installation, reverse the removal procedures.

23. With all the bolts in place tighten in the following sequence:

1. TIMING CHAIN HOUSING
2. GASKET, TIMING CHAIN HOUSING TO WATER PUMP
3. NUT (3)
4. WATER PUMP BODY ASM.
5. GASKET, WATER PUMP BODY TO WATER PUMP COVER
6. WATER PUMP COVER
7. BOLT (M6 x 1 x 55) – 3 LOWER POSITIONS
8. BOLT (M6 x 1 x 25)
9. BOLT (M6 x 1 x 90)
10. GASKET, WATER PUMP COVER TO BLOCK

VIEW A

7922Z201

Exploded view of the water pump mounting—2.4L engine

• Water pump-to-timing chain housing: 19 ft. lbs. (26 Nm)
• Water pump cover-to-water pump: 106–124 inch lbs. (12–14 Nm)
• Water pump cover-to-engine block (bottom first): 19 ft. lbs. (26 Nm)
• Radiator outlet pipe-to-pump cover: 10 ft. lbs. (14 Nm).

24. Refill the cooling system. Connect the negative battery cable. Start the vehicle and verify no leaks.

3.1L Engine

1. Before servicing the vehicle, refer to the precautions in the beginning of this section.
2. Disconnect the negative battery cable. Drain the cooling system into a suitable container.
3. Loosen, but do not remove, the water pump pulley bolts. Remove the serpentine belt.
4. Remove the water pump pulley bolts and pulley. Remove the five water pump mounting bolts and pump.

To install:

5. Clean all the gasket surfaces completely. Apply a thin bead of sealer around the outside edge of the water pump along the gasket sealing area and install the gasket onto the water pump.
6. Install the water pump and tighten the bolts to 89 inch lbs. (10 Nm).
7. Install the water pump pulley and

Timing belt service is covered in Section 5 of this manual

1 COOLANT PUMP
2 GASKET
3 BOLT – 10 N·m (89 LBS. IN.)
4 LOCATOR (MUST BE VERTICAL)

79222Z202

Exploded view of the water pump mounting—3.1L engine

tighten the pulley bolts finger-tight. Install the serpentine belt.

8. Tighten the water pump pulley bolts to 18 ft. lbs. (25 Nm). Connect the negative battery cable.

9. Refill and bleed the cooling system. Test run the engine and check for leaks.

Cylinder Head

REMOVAL & INSTALLATION

2.4L Engine

1. Before servicing the vehicle, refer to the precautions in the beginning of this section.

2. Disconnect the negative battery cable. Drain the cooling system.

3. Disconnect the heater inlet and throttle body heater hoses from water outlet. Remove the power brake vacuum hose from the throttle body.

4. Disconnect and tag for identification, if necessary, the electrical connections from the following components:
- Manifold Absolute Pressure (MAP) sensor
- Intake Air Temperature (IAT) sensor
- EVAP purge solenoid
- Camshaft Position (CMP) sensor

5. Remove the stud-ended bolt from the alternator. Remove the intake manifold brace. Remove the intake manifold.

6. Install the stud-ended alternator bolt back into the engine. Install engine support fixtures J-28467–400 and J-28467-A or equivalent.

7. Remove the exhaust manifold.

8. Remove the ignition coil and module assembly.

9. Disconnect the camshaft position sensor. Remove the power steering pump.

10. Disconnect the vacuum line from the fuel pressure regulator, fuel injector and fuel injector wiring harness.

11. Disconnect the fuel line clamp from the bracket on top of the intake camshaft housing. Remove the fuel line rail and position it aside (leaving the fuel lines attached).

12. Disconnect the timing chain housing at the intake camshaft housing, but do not remove from the vehicle.

13. Remove the electrical connection from the oil switch.

14. If equipped with an automatic transaxle, remove the transaxle fluid level indicator tube assembly from the exhaust camshaft cover and position it aside.

➡ **Any time the camshaft housing-to-**

cylinder head bolts are loosened or removed, the camshaft housing to cylinder head gasket must be replaced.

15. Remove the intake camshaft housing bolts, the housing and gasket.

✳✳ WARNING

Turn the camshaft housing upside down as soon as it is removed from the cylinder head. The lifters will fall out of the camshaft housing if it is not turned upside down. The lifters can be damaged if they fall out and hit a hard surface.

16. Remove the exhaust camshaft housing from the cylinder head (remove the bolts in reverse of the tightening sequence).

17. Remove the radiator inlet (upper) hose from the coolant outlet. Disconnect the coolant temperature sensor electrical connections.

18. Remove the cylinder head bolts (in reverse of the tightening sequence), the cylinder head and gasket.

✳✳ WARNING

Do not use abrasive pads to clean the cylinder head or block surfaces. An abrasive pad may damage the cylinder head and block. Use a razor or scraper to clean the gasket surfaces.

To install:

19. Clean all gasket surfaces completely. Be sure the threaded holes in the engine block for the cylinder head bolts are clean.

20. Install a new cylinder head gasket on the cylinder block and carefully position the cylinder head in place.

21. New replacement head bolts are recommended. Coat the cylinder head bolt threads with clean engine oil and allow the oil to drain off before installing.

22. Install the cylinder head bolts and tighten, in sequence, as follows:
  a. No's 1 through 8: 40 ft. lbs. (65 Nm)

79222Z203

Cylinder head bolt tightening sequence— 2.4L engine

b. No's 9 and 10: 30 ft. lbs. (40 Nm).

c. All 10 bolts: an additional 90 degrees (¼ turn).

23. Install the intake and exhaust camshaft housings. Tighten the long bolts to 11 ft. lbs. (15 Nm) plus an additional 90 degrees (¼ turn). Tighten the short bolts to 11 ft. lbs. (15 Nm) plus an additional 30 degrees (⅙ turn).

24. Install the timing chain and timing chain housing. Connect the upper radiator hose to the water outlet.

25. Connect the two coolant sensor connections. Install the fuel rail on the intake manifold and the intake manifold brace.

26. Connect the electrical connections to the following components:
- MAP sensor
- IAT sensor
- EVAP purge solenoid
- Camshaft position sensor

27. Connect the MAP sensor vacuum hose to the intake manifold. Install the power steering pump.

28. Install the throttle body and the throttle cable bracket. Connect the throttle body air intake duct.

29. Lubricate the O-ring on the oil fill tube with engine oil. Install oil fill tube into the block and the mounting.

30. Install the ignition coil and module assembly. Attach the injector harness electrical connector.

31. Remove the engine support fixture. Install the exhaust manifold.

32. Fill all fluids to their proper levels. An oil and filter change is recommended.

33. Connect the negative battery cable. Start the vehicle and verify no leaks.

3.1L Engine

LEFT (FRONT) CYLINDER HEAD

1. Before servicing the vehicle, refer to the precautions in the beginning of this section.

2. Relieve the fuel system pressure. Disconnect the negative battery cable. Drain the cooling system.

3. Remove the top half of the air cleaner assembly and the throttle body air inlet duct.

4. Remove the exhaust crossover pipe heat shield and crossover pipe.

5. Disconnect the spark plug wires from the spark plugs and wire looms and route the wires aside. Remove the rocker arm covers.

6. Remove the intake plenum and lower intake manifold. Remove the left side exhaust manifold and oil level indicator tube.

➡**When removing the valvetrain components they must be kept in order for installation in the same locations they were removed from.**

7. Remove rocker arms nut, rocker arms, balls and pushrods.

8. Remove the cylinder head bolts evenly and the cylinder head.

To install:

9. Clean all the gasket surfaces completely. Clean the threads on the cylinder head bolts and block threads.

10. Place the cylinder head gasket in position over the dowel pins on the cylinder block so the words **THIS SIDE UP** are showing.

11. Coat the bolt threads with sealer and install finger-tight.

12. On 1996–97 models, tighten the cylinder head bolts in sequence to 33 ft. lbs. (45 Nm). With all the bolts tightened make a second pass tightening all the bolts an additional 90 degrees (¼ turn).

13. On 1998–00 models, tighten the cylinder head bolts in sequence to 37 ft. lbs. (50 Nm). With all the bolts tightened make a second pass tightening all the bolts an additional 90 degrees (¼ turn).

14. Install the pushrods, rocker arms, balls and rocker arm nuts. Tighten the rocker arm nuts to 18 ft. lbs. (25 Nm).

15. Install the lower intake manifold, intake plenum and the rocker arm covers.

16. Install the oil level indicator tube. Connect the spark plug wires to spark plugs and wire looms.

17. Install the left side exhaust manifold. Install the exhaust crossover pipe and crossover pipe heat shield.

18. Refill the cooling system. Drain the engine oil and refill with the proper type of engine oil. A filter change is recommended.

Cylinder head bolt tightening sequence— 3.1L engine

19. Install the top half of the air cleaner assembly and the throttle body air inlet duct.

20. Connect negative battery cable. Start the engine and verify no leaks.

RIGHT (REAR) CYLINDER HEAD

1. Before servicing the vehicle, refer to the precautions in the beginning of this section.

2. Relieve the fuel system pressure. Disconnect the negative battery cable. Drain the cooling system.

3. Remove the top half of the air cleaner assembly and remove the throttle body air inlet duct.

4. Remove the exhaust crossover pipe heat shield and crossover pipe. Raise and safely support the vehicle.

5. Disconnect the Oxygen (O$_2$S) sensor. Disconnect the exhaust pipe from the exhaust manifold.

6. Remove the right side exhaust manifold. Lower the vehicle.

7. Disconnect the spark plug wires from spark plugs and wire looms and route the wires aside.

8. Remove the rocker arm covers, upper intake plenum and lower intake manifold.

➡**When removing the valvetrain components they must be kept in order for installation in the same locations they were removed from.**

9. Remove rocker arms nut, rocker arms, balls and pushrods.

10. Remove the cylinder head bolts evenly, then remove the cylinder head.

To install:

11. Clean all the gasket surfaces completely. Clean the threads on the cylinder head bolts and block threads.

12. Place the cylinder head gasket in position over the dowel pins on the cylinder block so the words **THIS SIDE UP** are showing.

13. Coat the bolt threads with sealer and install finger-tight.

14. On 1996–97 models, tighten the cylinder head bolts in sequence to 33 ft. lbs. (45 Nm). With all the bolts tightened make a second pass tightening all the bolts an additional 90 degrees (¼ turn).

15. On 1998–00 models, tighten the cylinder head bolts in sequence to 37 ft. lbs. (50 Nm). With all the bolts tightened make a second pass tightening all the bolts an additional 90 degrees (¼ turn).

16. Install the pushrods, rocker arms, balls and rocker arm nuts. Tighten the rocker arm nuts to 18 ft. lbs. (25 Nm).

17. Install the lower intake manifold and upper intake plenum. Install the rocker arm covers.

18. Connect the spark plug wires to spark plugs and wire looms. Raise vehicle and safely support.

19. Install the exhaust manifold. Connect the exhaust pipe to the exhaust manifold.

20. Lower the vehicle. Connect the Oxygen (O₂S) sensor.

21. Install the exhaust crossover pipe and heat shield. Refill the cooling system.

22. Drain the engine oil and refill with the proper type of engine oil. A filter change is recommended.

23. Install the top half of the air cleaner assembly and the throttle body air inlet duct.

24. Connect negative battery cable. Start the engine and verify no leaks.

Rocker Arms

REMOVAL & INSTALLATION

2.4L Engine

The 2.4L engine is not equipped with rocker arms. The camshafts directly actuate the valves.

3.1L Engine

1. Before servicing the vehicle, refer to the precautions in the beginning of this section.

2. Disconnect the negative battery cable.

3. For the left side (front), perform the following procedures:

a. Drain the cooling system to a level below the coolant pipe on the front of the engine.

b. Remove the coolant bypass hose clamp at the coolant tube.

c. Remove the two bolts and nut securing the coolant tube to the cylinder head and position the tube aside.

d. Disconnect the PCV valve from the rocker arm cover.

4. For the right side (rear), perform the following procedures:

a. Disconnect the spark plug wires from the spark plugs and upper intake plenum wire retainer and position aside.

b. Disconnect the power brake booster vacuum pipe from the intake plenum.

c. Remove the serpentine belt.

d. Remove the alternator.

e. Disconnect and remove the ignition

```
129   PUSHROD
131   ARM, ROLLER ROCKER
133   BOLT
```
79222Z205

Rocker arm components—3.1L engine

assembly and EVAP canister purge solenoid as an assembly.

5. Remove the four rocker arm cover bolts and remove the rocker arm cover.

6. Remove the rocker arm nuts, balls, rocker arms and pushrods.

To install:

7. Clean all the gasket surfaces completely.

8. Coat all the valvetrain components with engine oil prior to installation.

9. Install the pushrods and install the rocker arms on the studs. Install the rocker arm balls and mounting nuts. Be sure the pushrods are properly seated in the lifter and rocker arm. Tighten the mounting nuts to 89 inch lbs. (10 Nm) plus an additional 30 degrees.

10. Install the rocker arm cover using a new gasket and tighten the rocker cover bolts to 90 inch lbs. (10 Nm).

11. For the left side (front), perform the following procedures:

a. Connect the PCV valve to the rocker arm cover.

b. Position the coolant tube and connect the thermostat bypass hose.

c. Install the coolant tube mounting nut and bolts. Tighten the screw at the water pump to 106 inch lbs. (12 Nm), the

bolt at the corner of the cylinder head to 18 ft. lbs. (25 Nm) and the nut to 18 ft. lbs. (25 Nm).

12. For the right side (rear), perform the following procedures:

a. Install the alternator.

b. Install the serpentine belt.

c. Connect the power brake booster vacuum pipe to the plenum.

d. Install the EVAP solenoid and ignition assembly.

e. Connect the spark plug wires to the wire retainers on the plenum and the spark plugs.

13. Refill the cooling system.

14. Connect the negative battery cable.

15. Start the vehicle and verify no leaks.

Intake Manifold

REMOVAL & INSTALLATION

2.4L Engine

1. Before servicing the vehicle, refer to the precautions in the beginning of this section.

2. Relieve the fuel system pressure. Disconnect the negative battery cable.

3. Drain the cooling system to a level

(1) Fuel Return Line	(27) Manifold Absolute Pressure Sensor
(2) Fuel Pressure Regulator Vacuum Harness	(28) MAP Sensor Vacuum Line
(3) Fuel Line	(29) Fuel Rail Bracket
(4) Fuel Rail (with Injectors)	(30) Bolt, Intake Manifold to Cylinder Head
(5) Fuel Injector Harness	(31) Nut, Intake Manifold to Cylinder Head
(6) Bolt, Fuel Rail to Cylinder Head	(32) Intake Manifold
(7) Bolt, Fuel Line Retainer	(33) EGR Pipe
(8) Fuel Line Retainer	(34) Bolt, Oil/Air Separator to Engine Block
(9) Fuel Line Seal	(35) Oil/Air Separator
(10) Fuel Line Retainer	(36) Oil/Air Separator Foul Air Tube
(11) Bolt, Fuel Line Retainer	(37) Stud, Intake Manifold to Cylinder Head
(12) Gasket, EGR Adapter	(38) Clamp, Oil/Air Separator Tube
(13) EGR Passage Cover (Export Only)	(39) Cylinder Head
(14) Bolt, EGR Valve	(40) Nut, Exhaust Manifold Brace to Oil Pan Stud
(15) EGR Valve	(41) Exhaust Manifold Brace
(16) Gasket, EGR Valve	(42) Gasket, Exhaust Manifold
(17) Bolt, EGR Valve Adapter to Cylinder Head	(43) Bolt, Exhaust Manifold Brace to Exhaust Manifold
(18) Bolt, EGR Passage Cover (Export Only)	(44) Nut, Exhaust Manifold to Cylinder Head
(19) EGR Adapter	(45) Stud, Exhaust Manifold to Cylinder Head
(20) Oil/Air Separator Fresh Air Tube	(46) Exhaust Manifold Heat Shield
(21) Bolt, EGR Tube to Intake Manifold	(47) Bolt, Exhaust Manifold Heat Shield to Exhaust Manifold
(22) Bolt, EGR Tube to EGR Adapter	(48) Exhaust Manifold
(23) Throttle Cable Bracket	(49) Oxygen Sensor
(24) Bolt, Throttle Body to Intake Manifold	
(25) Throttle Body	
(26) Bolt, Throttle Body to Intake Manifold	

7922Z206

Exploded view of the intake and exhaust manifolds—2.4L engine

Refer to Section 1 for engine rebuilding specifications

below the intake manifold. Disconnect the vacuum hose from the Manifold Absolute Pressure (MAP) sensor.

4. Detach the following electrical connectors from the MAP sensor, Intake Air Temperature (IAT) sensor, EVAP canister purge solenoid and fuel injectors.

5. Disconnect the vacuum hoses from the intake manifold, fuel pressure regulator and EVAP canister purge solenoid to the canister.

6. Remove the air cleaner duct. Remove the vent tube-to-air cleaner duct. Remove the control cable mounting bracket from the intake manifold.

7. Disconnect the power brake vacuum line from the intake manifold and remove the vacuum line mounting bracket at the power steering pump.

8. Disconnect the coolant lines from the throttle body. Remove the crankcase air/oil separator mounting bolts from the intake manifold.

9. Disconnect the hoses from the separator and the separator. Remove the oil fill tube.

10. Remove the intake manifold support brace, the intake manifold nuts/bolts and discard the old gasket.

To install:

11. Clean all the gasket surfaces completely. Install the intake manifold gasket and intake manifold.

12. Tighten the intake manifold fasteners in sequence, to 18 ft. lbs. (25 Nm).

13. Install the intake manifold brace and tighten the mounting bolts to 19 ft. lbs. (26 Nm). The brace-to-block bolts must be tightened first, then the brace-to-manifold bolt.

14. Complete the installation by reversing the removal procedures.

15. Lubricate a new oil fill tube O-ring seal with engine oil and install tube between No. 1 and 2 intake tubes. Rotate as necessary to gain clearance for the oil/air separator nipple on fill tube.

16. Refill the cooling system.

17. Connect the negative battery cable.

3.1L Engine

These vehicles use a two-piece intake manifold. Note that these pieces are cast aluminum. Use care when working with light alloy components.

(1) Upper Intake Manifold Bolt	(19) Exhaust Crossover Upper Heat Shield
(2) Thermostat Bypass Pipe	(20) Upper Intake Manifold Gasket
(3) Thermostat Bypass Pipe Nut	(21) Upper Intake Manifold Gasket
(4) Thermostat Bypass Pipe Bolt	(22) EVAP Canister Purge Valve Bracket Stud
(5) Thermostat Bypass Pipe Screw	(23) EVAP Canister Purge Valve Bracket Stud
(6) Thermostat Bypass Hose Clamp	(24) EVAP Canister Purge Valve Bracket
(7) Thermostat Bypass Hose	(25) EVAP Canister Purge Valve
(8) Thermostat Bypass Hose Clamp	(26) Spark Plug Wire Support
(9) Coolant Outlet Bolt	(27) Electronic Ignition System Nut
(10) Coolant Outlet Assembly	(28) Electronic Ignition System
(11) Thermostat	(29) Electronic Ignition System Bolt
(12) PCV Valve	(30) Electronic Ignition System Bolt
(13) PCV Valve Grommet	(31) EGR Valve Pipe Assembly
(14) Oil Fill Cap	(32) EGR Valve Pipe Gasket
(15) Rocker Arm Cover Bolt	(33) EGR Valve Gasket
(16) Rocker Arm Cover	(34) EGR Valve Assembly Bolt
(17) Exhaust Crossover Nut	(35) EGR Valve Assembly
(18) Exhaust Crossover Pipe	(36) Upper Intake Manifold Stud
	(37) Upper Intake Manifold

7922Z207

Exploded view of the upper and lower intake—3.1L engine

1. Before servicing the vehicle, refer to the precautions in the beginning of this section.

2. Disconnect the negative battery cable. Relieve the fuel system pressure.

3. Remove the top half of the air cleaner assembly and throttle body duct. Drain and recover the cooling system.

4. Remove the EGR pipe from exhaust manifold. Remove the serpentine belt.

5. Remove the brake vacuum pipe at the intake plenum. Disconnect the control cables from the throttle body and intake plenum mounting bracket.

6. Remove the power steering lines at the alternator bracket. Remove the alternator.

7. Disconnect the spark plug wires from the spark plugs and wire retainers on the intake plenum.

8. Remove the Ignition assembly and the EVAP canister purge solenoid together.

9. Detach the upper engine wiring harness connectors from the Throttle Position (TP) sensor, Idle Air Control (IAC), fuel Injectors, Engine Coolant Temperature (ECT) sensor, Manifold Absolute Pressure (MAP) sensor and Camshaft Position (CMP) sensor.

10. Disconnect the vacuum lines from the vacuum modulator, fuel pressure regulator and PCV valve.

11. Remove the MAP sensor from upper intake manifold. Remove the upper intake plenum mounting bolts and the plenum.

12. Disconnect the fuel lines from the fuel rail and fuel line bracket. Install engine support fixture special tool J-28467-A or an equivalent.

13. Remove the right side engine mount. Remove the power steering mounting bolts and support the pump aside without disconnecting the power steering lines.

14. Disconnect the coolant inlet pipe from coolant outlet housing. Remove the coolant bypass hose from the water pump and the cylinder head.

15. Disconnect the upper radiator hose at thermostat housing.

16. Remove the thermostat housing. Remove both rocker arm covers.

17. Remove the lower intake manifold bolts. Be sure the washers on the four center bolts are installed in their original locations.

➡**When removing the valvetrain components they should be kept in order for installation the original locations.**

Lower intake manifold tightening sequence—3.1L engine

18. Remove the rocker arm nuts, rocker arms and pushrods. Remove the intake manifold from the engine.

To install:

19. Clean the gasket material from all mating surfaces. Remove all excess RTV sealant from front and rear ridges of cylinder block.

20. Place a 3mm bead of RTV on each ridge, where the front and rear of the intake manifold contact the block.

21. Using a new gasket, install the intake manifold.

22. Install the pushrods, rocker arms and mounting nuts. Be sure the pushrods are properly seated in the valve lifters and rocker arms.

23. Install rocker arm nuts and tighten them to 18 ft. lbs. (24 Nm).

24. Install the lower intake manifold. Apply sealant PN 12345739 or equivalent to the threads of the bolts, and tighten bolts to 115 inch lbs. (13 Nm).

25. Complete the installation by reversing the removal procedures.

26. Install the upper intake manifold and tighten the mounting bolts to 18 ft. lbs. (25 Nm).

27. Fill the cooling system. An engine oil and filter change is recommended.

28. Connect the negative battery cable. Start the vehicle and verify no leaks.

Exhaust Manifold

REMOVAL & INSTALLATION

2.4L Engine

1. Before servicing the vehicle, refer to the precautions in the beginning of this section.

2. Disconnect the negative battery cable. Disconnect the Oxygen (O_2S) sensor. Raise and safely support the vehicle.

3. Remove the bolt that attaches the exhaust manifold brace to the manifold.

4. Remove the manifold to exhaust pipe spring loaded bolts using a 13mm box wrench. The nuts should be loosened alternately and evenly to prevent the pipe from binding the nuts.

5. Pull down and back on the exhaust pipe to disengage it from the exhaust manifold bolts.

✳✳ WARNING

Do not bend the exhaust flex coupler more than 3 degrees in any direction. Movement of more than 3 degrees will damage the flex coupler.

6. Lower the vehicle. Remove the exhaust manifold mounting nuts and manifold.

To install:

7. Clean all the gasket surfaces completely. Install the exhaust manifold and new gaskets.

8. Install the exhaust manifold-to-cylinder head retaining nuts and tighten in sequence to 110 inch lbs. (13 Nm).

9. Raise and safely support the vehicle. Install the heat shields. Install exhaust manifold brace to the manifold bolt.

10. Install the manifold-to-exhaust pipe nuts and tighten evenly to 26 ft. lbs. (35 Nm).

11. Lower the vehicle. Connect the Oxygen (O$_2$S) sensor.

12. Connect the negative battery cable. Start the vehicle and verify no exhaust leaks.

Exploded view of the exhaust manifold—2.4L engine

Exhaust manifold tightening sequence—2.4L engine

3.1L Engine

1. Before servicing the vehicle, refer to the precautions in the beginning of this section.

2. Disconnect the negative battery cable. Remove the top half of the air cleaner assembly and throttle cable duct.

3. On the left side (front), perform the following procedures:

   a. Partially drain the cooling system.

   b. Remove the radiator hose from the thermostat housing.

   c. Remove the coolant bypass hose at the coolant pump and from the exhaust manifold.

4. Remove the exhaust crossover heat shield. Remove the exhaust crossover pipe from the manifold.

5. On the right side (rear), perform the following procedures:

   a. Remove the Heated Oxygen (HO$_2$S) sensor.

   b. Remove the EGR pipe from the exhaust manifold.

   c. Raise and safely support the vehicle.

   d. Remove the transaxle oil fill tube and lever indicator assembly.

   e. Disconnect the front exhaust pipe from the exhaust manifold.

   f. Disconnect the exhaust pipe from the converter flange and support the converter.

   g. Remove the converter heat shield from the body.

6. Tag and disconnect the secondary ignition wires from the spark plugs.

7. Remove the exhaust manifold heat shield. Remove the exhaust manifold retaining nuts and manifold.

To install:

8. Clean mating surfaces at the cylinder head and manifold.

9. Install the exhaust manifold gasket and the exhaust manifold. Tighten the manifold mounting nuts to 12 ft. lbs. (16 Nm).

10. Install the exhaust manifold heat shield. Install the exhaust crossover pipe to the manifold.

11. On the right side (rear), install the converter heat shield to the body.

12. Install the exhaust crossover pipe heat shield.

13. On the left side (front), perform the following procedures:

   a. Connect the secondary ignition wires to the appropriate spark plug.

   b. Connect the coolant bypass pipe to the coolant pump and exhaust manifold.

   c. Install the radiator hose to the coolant outlet housing.

14. On the right side (rear), perform the following procedures:

   a. Connect the exhaust pipe to the exhaust manifold.

   b. Install the transaxle oil level indicator and fill tube assembly.

   c. Safely lower the vehicle.

   d. Connect the heated oxygen sensor.

   e. Connect the EGR pipe to exhaust manifold.

15. Install the top half of the air cleaner and the throttle body duct. Connect the negative battery cable.

Camshaft and Valve Lifters

REMOVAL & INSTALLATION

2.4L Engine

➡ **Anytime the camshaft housing-to-cylinder head bolts are loosened or removed, the camshaft housing-to-cylinder head gasket must be replaced.**

1. Before servicing the vehicle, refer to the precautions in the beginning of this section.

2. Disconnect the negative battery cable.

111 SCREW, LH EXHAUST MANIFOLD HEAT SHIELD
112 SHIELD LH EXHAUST MANIFOLD
113 NUT, LH EXHAUST MANIFOLD
114 STUD, LH EXHAUST MANIFOLD
115 MANIFOLD, LH EXHAUST
117 GASKET, LH EXHAUST MANIFOLD
121 HEAD, LH CYLINDER

Exploded view of the left-hand exhaust manifold—3.1L engine

115 MANIFOLD, LEFT HAND EXHAUST
116 STUD, EXHAUST CROSSOVER
157 MANIFOLD, RIGHT HAND EXHAUST
166 CROSSOVER PIPE, EXHAUST
167 SHIELD, EXHAUST CROSSOVER UPPER HEAT
168 NUT, EXHAUST CROSSOVER
312 BOLT/SCREW, EXHAUST CROSSOVER
      UPPER HEAT SHIELD

Exploded view of the exhaust crossover pipe—3.1L engine

3. Detach the 11-pin connector from the ignition assembly cover.

4. Remove the four ignition assembly cover-to-camshaft housing bolts and remove assembly by pulling straight up. Use a spark plug boot wire remover to remove connector assemblies.

5. Perform the following procedures on the intake camshaft side:

  a. Remove the throttle lever actuator power steering pressure switch connector.

  b. Loosen the power steering pump adjusting stud bolt. Loosen the power steering pump pivot bolts and remove drive belt.

  c. Remove the two power steering pump bracket-to-transaxle bolts.

  d. Remove the front power steering pump bracket-to-engine block bolt.

  e. Remove the power steering pump assembly from the engine and position it aside. DO NOT disconnect the power steering lines from the pump.

6. On the intake camshaft side, if equipped, perform the following procedures:

  a. Remove the oil/air separator bolts and hoses. Leave the hoses attached to the separator but disconnect from the oil fill tube, timing chain housing and intake manifold.

  b. Disconnect the vacuum line from fuel pressure regulator and disconnect the fuel injector wiring harness.

  c. Remove the two bolts securing the fuel line clamps to the intake camshaft housing.

  d. Remove fuel rail-to-camshaft housing mounting bolts.

  e. Remove the fuel rail from the cylinder head leaving the fuel lines attached and position the fuel rail aside.

7. Remove the timing chain and camshaft sprockets.

8. Remove the timing chain housing bolts but do not remove from the engine.

9. Remove camshaft housing cover-to-camshaft housing attaching bolts.

10. Remove the camshaft housing-to-cylinder head attaching bolts. Use the reverse of the tightening sequence when loosening camshaft housing-to-cylinder head attaching bolts. Leave two bolts loosely in place to hold the camshaft housing while separating camshaft cover from housing.

11. Push the cover off the housing by threading four of the housing-to-cylinder head bolts into the tapped holes in the cam

For complete mechanical specifications, refer to Section 1 of this manual

121 HEAD, CYLINDER
153 SHIELD, RH LOWER HEAT
154 SCREW, RH LOWER HEAT SHIELD
155 STUD, RH EXHAUST MANIFOLD
156 NUT, RH EXHAUST MANIFOLD
157 MANIFOLD, RIGHT HAND EXHAUST
158 SHIELD, RH UPPER HEAT
159 SCREW, RH UPPER HEAT SHIELD
160 GASKET, RH EXHAUST MANIFOLD

79222213

Exploded view of the right-hand exhaust manifold—3.1L engine

housing cover. Tighten the bolts in evenly so the cover does not bind on the dowel pins.

12. Remove the two loosely installed camshaft housing-to-cylinder head bolts and remove the cover. Discard the gaskets.

13. Note the position of the chain sprocket dowel pin for reassembly. Remove the camshaft carefully; do not damage the camshaft oil seal.

14. Remove camshaft oil seal from camshaft and discard seal. This seal must be replaced any time the housing and cover are separated.

➡**The valve lifters must be kept in order for installation in the same locations they were removed from.**

15. Remove the valve lifters from the camshaft housing.

16. Remove the camshaft carrier from the cylinder head and remove the gasket.

To install:

17. Clean all the gasket surfaces completely.

18. Install a new gasket on the cylinder head and install the camshaft housing over the dowel pins. Install one bolt loosely to hold the housing in place.

➡**If the camshaft was replaced the valve lifters must also be replaced.**

19. Install the lifters into their original bores.

20. Lubricate the camshaft lobes, journals and lifters with camshaft and lifter pre-lube. The camshaft lobes and journals must be adequately lubricated or engine damage could occur upon start up.

21. Install the camshaft in the same position it was in prior to removal. The timing chain sprocket dowel pin should be straight up and align with the center line of the lifter bores.

22. Install new camshaft housing-to-camshaft housing cover seals into the cover.

➡**The seals for the intake and exhaust covers are different and the correct seals must be used.**

23. Remove the bolt holding the housing in place.

24. Apply thread locking compound to the camshaft housing and cover attaching bolt threads.

25. Install the camshaft housing cover.

26. Install all the mounting bolts finger-tight. With all the bolts in place tighten the bolts in sequence to 11 ft. lbs. (15 Nm) plus

75 degrees additional rotation (Long bolts) and 16 ft. lbs. (21 Nm) plus 25 degrees additional rotation (Short bolts).

27. Install the timing chain housing mounting bolts.

28. Install the timing chain and sprockets.

29. Install new fuel injector O-ring seals lubricated with oil and install the fuel rail. Tighten the mounting bolts to 19 ft. lbs. (26 Nm).

30. On the intake camshaft side, if equipped, perform the following procedures:

   a. Install the fuel line clamp mounting bolts on top of the intake camshaft housing.

   b. Connect the vacuum line to the fuel pressure regulator.

   c. Attach the fuel injector harness connector.

   d. Install the oil/air separator assembly and connect the hoses to the oil fill tube, timing chain housing and intake manifold.

31. Lubricate the inner sealing surface of the intake camshaft seal with oil and install the seal to the housing using J-36009, or an equivalent seal installer.

32. On the intake camshaft side, if equipped, perform the following procedures:

79222Z214

Camshaft housing bolt tightening sequence—2.4L engine

a. Install the power steering pump pulley onto the intake camshaft using J-36015, or an equivalent pulley installer.

b. Install the power steering pump and drive belt.

c. Attach the throttle lever actuator power steering pressure switch connector.

33. On the exhaust camshaft side, perform the following procedures:

a. Install the transaxle fill tube.

b. Connect the oil pressure switch.

34. Install the ignition assembly on the camshaft housing and tighten the mounting bolts to 13 ft. lbs. (18 Nm).

35. Attach the 11-pin connector to ignition assembly.

36. Connect the negative battery cable.

37. Start the vehicle and verify proper operation and no leaks.

3.1L Engine

1. Before servicing the vehicle, refer to the precautions in the beginning of this section.

2. Relieve the fuel system pressure. Disconnect the negative battery cable. Remove the engine assembly.

➡**When removing valvetrain components they must be marked for installation in the same location they are removed from. When the camshaft is** being replaced the valve lifters should also be replaced.

3. Remove the rocker arm covers and the intake manifold.

4. Remove the rocker arm retaining nuts, rocker arm balls, rocker arms and pushrods.

5. Remove the guide bolts from the lifter guide and remove the guide.

6. Remove the valve lifter(s) from the lifter bores.

7. Remove the crankshaft balancer and front cover. Remove the timing chain and sprockets.

8. Remove the oil pump driven gear bolt and gear. Remove the bolts and camshaft thrust plate.

9. Carefully remove the camshaft. Avoid marring the camshaft bearing surfaces.

To install:

10. Coat the camshaft with lubricant 1052365 or equivalent, and install the camshaft.

11. Install the camshaft thrust plate and tighten bolts to 89 inch lbs. (10 Nm).

12. Install the oil pump driven gear and tighten bolt to 27 ft. lbs. (36 Nm).

13. Install the timing chain and sprocket.

14. Install the camshaft thrust button and front cover. Install the crankshaft balancer.

15. Lubricate the bearing surfaces with Molykote® or equivalent.

➡**Installation of a new camshaft or a wear pattern on the old valve lifter will require the replacement of the camshaft and lifters together. If camshaft replacement is not necessary, be sure to install the used valve lifters in their original position upon reinstallation.**

16. Install the lifters in their original locations.

17. Install the lifter guide and lifter guide bolts and tighten the guide bolts to 89 inch lbs. (10 Nm).

18. Install the pushrods, rocker arms, rocker balls and rocker arm nuts.

19. Tighten the rocker arm nuts to 89 inch lbs. (10 Nm) plus an additional 30 degrees.

20. Install the intake manifold and rocker arm covers.

21. Install the engine assembly. Connect the negative battery cable.

22. Adjust the valves, as required. Start the engine and verify no oil leaks.

Valve Lash

ADJUSTMENT

2.4L Engine

The 2.4L engine is equipped with hydraulic valve lifters that do not require periodic valve lash adjustment. Adjustment is maintained automatically by hydraulic pressure in the lifters. Also, the rocker arm retaining nuts are tightened to a specific torque value (refer to the rocker arm procedure) to provide proper rocker arm placement.

3.1L Engine

➡**These engines come from the factory with non-adjustable valve lash, BUT if the valves and the valve seats are reconditioned, adjustable rocker arm studs must be installed. The adjustment procedure is ONLY for adjustable rocker arm studs.**

The engines are originally equipped with hydraulic valve lifters. Hydraulic valve lifters are not adjustable. The replacement rocker arm stud is adjustable and the adjustment can be performed as listed below. If valve system noise is present, check the torque on the rocker arm nuts. The correct torque is 14–20 ft. lbs. (19–27 Nm). If noise is still present, check the condition of the camshaft, lifters, rocker arms, pushrods and valves.

1. Before servicing the vehicle, refer to the precautions in the beginning of this section.

2. Install the rocker arms, balls and nuts. Tighten the rocker arm nuts until all of the lash (free-play) is eliminated.

3. Adjust the valves when the lifter is on the base circle of a camshaft lobe as follows:

a. Place the engine in the No. 1 firing position. This can be determined by placing a finger on the No. 1 rocker arm as the engine alignment mark on the front face of the of the torsional dampener pulley aligns with the arrow on the front cover. If the valves don't move freely, the engine is in the No. 1 firing position. If the valves move freely, the engine is in the No. 4 firing position and the engine should be rotated one full rotation to reach the No. 1 position.

b. With the engine in the No. 1 firing order, adjust the following valves:

- Exhaust—1, 2, 3
- Intake—1, 5, 6

c. Loosen the adjusting nut several turns backwards, then tighten until all lash (free-play) is removed. After all of the valve lash is removed turn the nut an additional 1 ½ turns, this will center the lifter plunger.

d. Turn the engine one complete revolution until the timing tab and the alignment mark are again aligned, this will place the engine in the No. 4 firing position.

e. With the engine in the No. 4 firing order, adjust the following valves:
- Exhaust—4, 5, 6
- Intake—2, 3, 4

Oil Pan

REMOVAL & INSTALLATION

2.4L Engine

1. Before servicing the vehicle, refer to the precautions in the beginning of this section.
2. Disconnect the negative battery cable. Raise and safely support the vehicle.
3. Properly drain the engine oil and cooling system. Remove the flywheel inspection cover.
4. Remove the right front wheel and tire assembly. Remove the right inner fender splash shield.
5. Remove the serpentine belt. Disconnect the engine mount strut from the engine mount strut bracket.
6. Remove the A/C compressor from the mounting bracket and support it aside. DO NOT disconnect the refrigerant lines.
7. Unfasten the engine mount strut bracket bolts, then remove the bracket. Remove the radiator outlet pipe bolts.
8. Disconnect the radiator and A/C outlet pipes from the suspension supports. Remove the exhaust manifold brace.
9. Remove the oil pan-to-flywheel cover bolt and nut and remove the flywheel cover stud and spacer.
10. Disconnect the radiator outlet pipe from the lower radiator hose and oil pan.
11. If equipped, detach the oil level sensor wire. Unfasten the oil pan bolts, then remove the oil pan.

To install:

12. Install a new gasket, the oil pan and bolts. Tighten the chain housing and carrier seal bolts to 106 inch lbs. (12 Nm). Tighten the oil pan-to-block bolts to 17 ft. lbs. (23 Nm).

13. Install the flywheel cover spacer, stud nut and bolt. Tighten the nut to 41 ft. lbs. (56 Nm), the stud to 115 inch lbs. (13 Nm) and the bolt to 41 ft. lbs. (56 Nm).
14. Install the oil pan-to-transaxle nut and tighten to 41 ft. lbs. (56 Nm).
15. Complete the installation by reversing the removal procedures.
16. Install the engine mount strut bracket and tighten bolts to 49 ft. lbs. (66 Nm).
17. Fill the crankcase with oil. A filter change is recommended.
18. Fill the cooling system. Connect the negative battery cable, then start the engine and check for leaks.

3.1L Engine

1. Before servicing the vehicle, refer to the precautions in the beginning of this section.
2. Disconnect the negative battery cable. Remove the serpentine belt.
3. If equipped, remove the upper A/C compressor bolts. Raise and safely support the vehicle.
4. Properly drain the engine oil. Remove the right front wheel and tire assembly.
5. Remove the engine mount strut from the suspension support.
6. Remove the cotter pin and castle nut from the lower ball joint, then separate the ball joint from the steering knuckle.
7. Remove the right side sway bar link. Detach the ABS sensor from the right subframe.
8. Remove the right side subframe bolts and the right side subframe and control arm as an assembly.
9. If equipped, remove the lower A/C compressor bolts and position the compressor aside. DO NOT disconnect the refrigerant lines or allow the compressor to hang unsupported.
10. Remove the engine mount strut bracket from the engine. Remove the oil filter, the starter and the flywheel cover.
11. Remove the oil pan flange bolts, the oil pan side bolts and the oil pan.

To install:

12. Clean the gasket mating surfaces. Install a new gasket on the oil pan. Apply silicone sealer to the portion of the pan that contacts the rear of the block.
13. Position the oil pan, then install the mounting bolts finger-tight.
14. With all the bolts in place, tighten the oil pan flange bolts to 18 ft. lbs. (25 Nm) and the oil pan side bolts to 34 ft. lbs. (50 Nm).

1 **Oil pan**
2 **Oil pan bolt (M8 x 1.25 x 80)**
 24 Nm (18 lb. ft.)
3 **Oil pan bolt (M8 x 1.25 x 22)**
 24 Nm (18 lb. ft.)
4 **Oil pan bolt (M6 x 1.00 x 25)**
 12 Nm (106 lb. in.)
5 **Stud end oil pan bolt**
 26 Nm (19 lb. ft.)

7922Z215

Oil pan mounting bolt locations—2.4L engine

79222216

Exploded view of the oil pan mounting—3.1L engine

15. Complete the installation by reversing the removal procedures.

16. Tighten the following items to:
   a. Engine-to-transaxle brace, bolts to 68 ft. lbs. (93 Nm)
   b. Engine mount strut bracket-to-engine bolts to 85 ft. lbs. (115 Nm)
   c. Right side subframe/control arm assembly bolts to 89 ft. lbs. (120 Nm)
   d. Right side sway bar line bolt to 22 ft. lbs. (30 Nm)
   e. Ball joint-to-steering knuckle nut to 48 ft. lbs. (60 Nm). Install a new cotter pin.
   f. Engine mount strut bracket bolt-to-frame bolt to 89 ft. lbs. (120 Nm)

17. Fill the crankcase to the correct level. A filter change is recommended. Connect the negative battery cable, then start the engine and check for leaks.

➡ **Whenever the vehicle subframe is removed or lowered, the wheel alignment should be checked.**

18. Check the front end alignment and adjust as required.

Oil Pump

REMOVAL & INSTALLATION

2.4L Engine

➡ **Please note that the transaxle must be removed from the vehicle to service the oil pump.**

1. Before servicing the vehicle, refer to the precautions in the beginning of this section.

2. Disconnect the negative battery cable. Install engine support fixture J-28467-A or equivalent.

3. Properly drain the engine oil, then remove the oil pan. Remove the transaxle and the flywheel.

4. Remove the balance shaft chain cover and chain guide. Remove the oil pump bolts and the oil pump cover.

5. Pull the housing to disconnect the pump gear from the balance shaft. Remove the housing assembly from the balance shaft assembly.

To install:

6. Clean all of the parts in suitable cleaning solvent. Remove all varnish sludge and dirt.

7. Lubricate the gears with clean engine oil. Assemble the geroter gear into the housing.

➡ **Fill oil pump cavities with petroleum jelly prior to installation. This seals the pump and acts like a "prime" so the pump will draw oil as soon as the engine begins to turn. This will ensure that there is oil pressure immediately on start-up and will prevent engine damage.**

8. Install the pump housing to the balance shaft assembly, the pump cover to the oil pump housing.

9. Install the oil pump-to-block bolts and tighten to 40 ft. lbs. (54 Nm).

10. Install the balance shaft chain guide and chain. Adjust the chain tension inserting a 0.40 in. (1mm) brass feeler, between the chain guide and the chain.

➡ **A brass feeler gauge must be used to ensure that correct measurements are obtained. If a steel gauge is used, it will not bend to conform to the guide and will allow for incorrect measurements.**

11. Press the guide against the chain using about 3 lbs. of force. Tighten the chain tensioner fastener to 115 inch lbs. (13 Nm).

12. Install the balance shaft chain cover and tighten the nut and bolt to 115 inch lbs. (13 Nm).

13. Install the flywheel and the transaxle. Install the oil pan, then carefully lower the vehicle.

14. Fill the crankcase with clean engine oil. A filter change is recommended.

15. Remove the engine support fixture. Connect the negative battery cable, then

79222217

Exploded view of the oil pump components—2.4L engine

start the engine and verify oil pressure and no leaks.

3.1L Engine

1. Before servicing the vehicle, refer to the precautions in the beginning of this section.
2. Disconnect the negative battery cable.
3. Raise and safely support the vehicle.
4. Drain the engine oil. Remove the oil pan.
5. Remove the crankshaft oil deflector bolts and deflector.
6. Remove the oil pump bolts, the oil pump and pump driveshaft.

To install:

7. Install the oil pump and pump driveshaft. Tighten the oil pump mounting bolts to 30 ft. lbs. (41 Nm).
8. Install the crankshaft oil deflector and tighten the nuts to 18 ft. lbs. (25 Nm).
9. Install the oil pan, then carefully lower the vehicle.
10. Fill the crankcase to the correct level with oil. An filter change is recommended.
11. Connect the negative battery cable.
12. Start the engine, check the oil pressure and check for leaks.

Exploded view of the oil pump mounting— 3.1L engine

Rear Main Seal

REMOVAL & INSTALLATION

2.4L Engine

1. Before servicing the vehicle, refer to the precautions in the beginning of this section.
2. Disconnect the negative battery cable.
3. Remove the transaxle assembly.
4. If equipped with a manual transaxle, remove the pressure plate and clutch disc.
5. Unfasten the flywheel-to-crankshaft bolts, then remove the flywheel.
6. Disconnect the oil pan-to-seal housing bolts
7. Unfasten the seal housing-to-block bolts, then remove the seal housing and gasket.
8. To support the seal housing for seal removal, place two blocks of wood or metal of equal thickness on a flat surface, position the seal housing and blocks so the transaxle side of the seal housing is supported across the dowel pin and center bolt holes on both sides of the seal opening.

➡**The seal housing could be damaged if not properly supported during seal removal.**

9. Drive the seal evenly out the transaxle side of the seal housing using a small prytool in the relief grooves on the crankshaft side of the seal housing. Discard the seal.

✳✳ WARNING

Be careful not to damage the seal housing sealing surface. If damaged, it may result in an oil leak.

To install:

10. Press a new seal into the housing using tool J 36005 or equivalent seal installation tool.
11. Inspect the oil pan gasket inner silicone bead for damage and repair using a silicone sealant, if necessary.
12. Position a new seal housing-to-block gasket over the alignment. The gasket is reversible.
13. Lubricate the lip of the seal with clean engine oil.
14. Install the housing assembly, then tighten the housing-to-block bolts to 106 inch lbs. (12 Nm).
15. Install the oil pan-to-seal housing bolts, then tighten to 106 inch lbs. (12 Nm).

16. Install the flywheel as outlined later in this section.
17. For vehicles equipped with a manual transaxle, install the clutch, pressure plate and clutch cover assembly.
18. Install the transaxle assembly.
19. Connect the negative battery cable, then start the engine and check for leaks.

3.1L Engine

1. Before servicing the vehicle, refer to the precautions in the beginning of this section.
2. Support the engine with J-28467 engine support or equivalent.
3. Remove the transaxle.
4. Remove the flywheel.
5. Insert a suitable prytool in through the dust lip and pry out the seal by moving the tool around the seal until it is removed.

✳✳ WARNING

Use care not to damage the crankshaft seal surface with a prytool.

To install:

6. Before installing, lubricate the seal bore to seal surface with engine oil.
7. Install the new seal using tool J-34686.
8. Slide the new seal over the mandrel until the dust lip bottoms squarely against the tool collar.
9. Align the dowel pin of the tool with the dowel pin hole in the crankshaft and attach the tool to the crankshaft. Tighten the attaching screws to 2–5 ft. lbs. (2.7–6.8 Nm).
10. Tighten the T-handle of the tool to push the seal into the bore. Continue until the tool collar is flush against the block.
11. Loosen the T-handle completely. Remove the attaching screws and the tool.

➡**Check to see that the seal is squarely seated in the bore.**

12. Install the flywheel and transaxle.
13. Start the engine and check for leaks.

Timing Chain, Sprockets, Front Cover and Seal

REMOVAL & INSTALLATION

2.4L Engine

➡**It is recommended that the entire procedure be reviewed before attempting to service the timing chain.**

1. Before servicing the vehicle, refer to the precautions in the beginning of this section.

2. Disconnect the negative battery cable. Drain the cooling system into a suitable container. Remove the coolant surge tank.

3. Remove the serpentine drive belt using a 13mm wrench that is at least 24 in. (61cm) long.

4. Disconnect and remove the alternator from the mounting bracket.

5. Install a suitable engine support, J-28467-A or the equivalent.

6. Remove the upper cover fasteners. Disconnect the upper cover vent hose.

7. Remove the right engine mount and bracket. Raise and safely support the vehicle.

8. Remove the right front tire and wheel assembly. Remove the right lower splash shield from the right wheel house.

9. Remove the crankshaft balancer assembly using the following procedure:

   a. Remove the torsional damper mounting bolt and washer while holding the crankshaft in place using J-38122, or the equivalent.

   b. Remove the balancer using a suitable puller, J-24420-B or the equivalent.

10. Remove the lower cover fasteners. Lower the vehicle.

11. Remove the front cover and gaskets. Remove the crankshaft oil slinger.

12. Using a suitable seal driver, tap seal out of the front cover.

13. Rotate the crankshaft clockwise, as viewed from front of engine (normal rotation) until the camshaft sprocket's timing dowel pin holes align with the holes in the timing chain housing. The mark on the crankshaft sprocket should align with the mark on the cylinder block. The crankshaft sprocket keyway should point upwards and align with the center line of the cylinder bores. This is the normal timed position.

14. Remove the timing chain guides. Raise and safely support the vehicle.

15. Gently pry off the timing chain tensioner spring retainer and remove the spring.

➡**Two styles of tensioner are used. Early production engines will have a spring post and late production ones will not. Both styles are identical in operation and are interchangeable.**

16. Remove the timing chain tensioner shoe retainer.

17. Be sure all the slack in the timing chain is above the tensioner assembly; remove the chain tensioner shoe. The timing chain must be disengaged from the wear grooves in the tensioner shoe in order to remove the shoe. Slide a prybar under the timing chain while pulling shoe outward.

18. If difficulty is encountered removing chain tensioner shoe, proceed as follows:

   a. Lower the vehicle.

   b. Hold the intake camshaft sprocket with a holding tool and remove the sprocket bolt and washer.

   c. Remove the washer from the bolt and partially install the bolt back into the camshaft by hand, the bolt provides a surface to push against.

   d. Remove intake camshaft sprocket using a 3-jaw puller in the three relief holes in the sprocket. Do not attempt to pry the sprocket off the camshaft or damage to the sprocket or chain housing could occur.

19. Remove the tensioner assembly attaching bolts and the tensioner.

✳✳ CAUTION

The tensioner piston is spring loaded and could fly out causing personal injury.

20. Remove the chain housing-to-block stud, which is actually the timing chain tensioner shoe pivot.

21. Remove the timing chain.

To install:

22. Tighten the intake camshaft sprocket attaching bolt and washer, while holding the sprocket with tool J36013, if removed.

23. Install the special tool through holes in camshaft sprockets into holes in timing chain housing. This positions the camshafts for correct timing.

24. If the camshafts are out of position and must be rotated more than ⅛ turn in order to install the alignment dowel pins:

   a. The crankshaft must be rotated 90 degrees clockwise off Top Dead Center (TDC) in order to give the valves adequate clearance to open.

   b. Once the camshafts are in position and the dowels installed, rotate the crankshaft counterclockwise back to TDC. Do not rotate the crankshaft clockwise to TDC or valve and piston damage could occur.

25. Install the timing chain over the exhaust camshaft sprocket, around the idler sprocket and around the crankshaft sprocket.

26. Remove the alignment dowel pin from the intake camshaft. Using a dowel pin remover tool, rotate the intake camshaft sprocket counterclockwise enough to slide the timing chain over the intake camshaft sprocket. Release the camshaft sprocket wrench. The length of chain between the two camshaft sprockets will tighten. If properly timed, the intake camshaft alignment dowel pin should slide in easily. If the dowel pin does not fully index, the camshafts are not timed correctly and the procedure must be repeated.

27. Leave the alignment dowel pins installed.

28. With slack removed from chain between intake camshaft sprocket and crankshaft sprocket, the timing marks on the crankshaft and the cylinder block should be aligned. If marks are not aligned, move the chain one tooth forward or rearward, remove slack and recheck marks.

29. Tighten the chain housing-to-block stud. The stud is installed under the timing chain. Tighten to 19 ft. lbs. (26 Nm).

30. Reload timing chain tensioner assembly to its 0 position as follows:

   a. Assemble restraint cylinder, spring and nylon plug into plunger. Index slot in restraint cylinder with peg in plunger. While rotating the restraint cylinder clockwise, push the restraint cylinder into the plunger until it bottoms. Keep rotating the restraint cylinder clockwise but allow the spring to push it out of the plunger. The pin in the plunger will lock the restraint in the loaded position.

   b. Install tool J36589 or equivalent, onto plunger assembly.

   c. Install plunger assembly into tensioner body with the long end toward the crankshaft when installed.

31. Install the tensioner assembly to the chain housing. Recheck plunger assembly installation. It is correctly installed when the long end is toward the crankshaft.

32. Install and tighten timing chain tensioner bolts and tighten to 10 ft. lbs. (14 Nm).

33. Install the tensioner shoe and tensioner shoe retainer. Remove special tool J36589 and squeeze plunger assembly into the tensioner body to unload the plunger assembly.

34. Lower vehicle and remove the alignment dowel pins. Rotate crankshaft clockwise two full rotations. Align crankshaft

Timing belt service is covered in Section 5 of this manual

timing mark with mark on cylinder block and reinstall alignment dowel pins. Alignment dowel pins will slide in easily if engine is timed correctly.

✳✳ WARNING

Severe engine damage could occur if the engine is not correctly timed.

35. Install the timing chain guides and crankshaft oil slinger.

36. Install a new seal using a suitable seal driver and lubricate the inner lip of the seal with engine oil.

37. Install the front cover and gaskets on the engine and tighten the mounting nuts and bolts to 106 inch lbs. (12 Nm).

38. Install the torsional damper as follows:

  a. Coat the seal contact area on the crankshaft damper with clean engine oil.

  b. Line up the damper on the crankshaft so the notch in the damper lines up with the crankshaft key.

  c. Tap the balancer into place using a rubber mallet.

  d. Install the damper mounting bolt and washer and tighten the bolt to 129 ft. lbs. (175 Nm) plus 90 degrees rotation.

39. Install the right front lower splash shield. Install the tire and wheel assembly and tighten to specification.

40. Safely lower the vehicle. Install the right engine mount bracket.

41. Install the right engine mount. Connect the upper cover vent hose.

42. Remove the engine support. Install the alternator and attach the electrical connectors.

43. Install the serpentine belt. Install the coolant surge tank.

44. Refill the cooling system. Connect the negative battery cable and check for leaks.

3.1L Engine

1. Before servicing the vehicle, refer to the precautions in the beginning of this section.

2. Disconnect the negative battery cable. Drain the cooling system into a suitable container.

3. Remove the right engine mount bracket. Remove the serpentine belt.

4. Remove the crankshaft balancer as follows:

  a. Raise and safely support the vehicle.

  b. Remove the right front tire and wheel assembly.

  c. Remove the right inner fender well splash shield.

  d. Remove the flywheel cover and install a flywheel holding tool.

  e. Remove the balancer mounting bolt and washer.

  f. Using a suitable puller, J-24420-B or the equivalent remove the balancer from the crankshaft.

5. Remove the serpentine belt tensioner mounting bolt and tensioner. Remove the oil pan.

6. Remove coolant bypass pipe from the water pump and the intake manifold.

7. Disconnect the lower radiator hose from the front cover outlet. Remove the front cover bolts and cover.

8. Using a suitable seal driver, tap seal out of the front cover.

9. Rotate the crankshaft until the timing marks on the camshaft and crankshaft sprockets are in alignment at their closest approach.

10. Remove the camshaft sprocket bolt, sprocket and timing chain.

11. Remove the crankshaft sprocket, using a gear puller J-5825-A or equivalent. Remove the timing chain damper bolts and damper.

To install:

12. Install the timing chain damper and tighten the mounting bolts to 15 ft. lbs. (21 Nm).

13. Install the crankshaft sprocket onto the crankshaft making sure the notch in the sprocket fits over the crankshaft key. Fully seat the sprocket on the crankshaft using J-38612, or an equivalent gear installer.

7922Z219

Timing chain and sprocket alignment positions—2.4L DOHC engine

7922Z220

Timing chain and sprocket timing mark alignment—3.1L engine

14. Be sure the timing mark on the crankshaft sprocket is pointing straight up.

15. Install the timing chain over the camshaft sprocket and hold the sprocket in such a way, that the timing mark is pointing down, and the timing chain is hanging down off the sprocket.

16. Loop the timing chain under the crankshaft sprocket and install the camshaft sprocket on the camshaft. The sprocket will only fit on the camshaft if the dowel on the camshaft lines up with the hole in the sprocket.

17. Verify that the marks are aligned (the camshaft sprocket will be at the 6 o'clock position and the crankshaft sprocket will be in the 12 o'clock position).

18. Tighten the camshaft sprocket mounting bolt to 81 ft. lbs. (110 Nm).

19. Lubricate the timing chain components with engine oil. Clean all gasket surfaces completely.

20. Apply a thin bead of sealer around the gasket sealing area of the front cover. Install a new front cover seal on the front cover.

21. Install a new seal using a suitable seal driver and lubricate the inner lip of the seal with engine oil.

22. Install the front cover on the engine and install the mounting bolts. Tighten the small bolts to 15 ft. lbs. (21 Nm) and the large bolts to 35 ft. lbs. (47 Nm).

23. Connect the radiator hose to the coolant outlet.

24. Install coolant bypass pipe to the water pump and the intake manifold. Install the oil pan.

25. Install crankshaft balancer as follows:

a. Coat the seal contact surface of the crankshaft balancer with clean engine oil.

b. Line up the notch in the balancer with the crankshaft key and slide the balancer on until the key is in the balancer.

c. Using J-29113 or an equivalent puller, seat the balancer on the crankshaft.

d. Install the balancer mounting bolt and washer and tighten to 76 ft. lbs. (103 Nm).

e. Install the flywheel cover.

f. Install the right inner fender well splash shield.

g. Install the tire and wheel assembly and tighten to specification.

26. Install the serpentine belt tensioner and tighten the mounting bolt to 40 ft. lbs. (54 Nm). Install the serpentine belt.

27. Install the right engine mount bracket and tighten the bracket-to-mount bolts to 96 ft. lbs. (130 Nm).

28. Refill the cooling system with the correct amount and type of coolant. Check the engine oil level. An oil and filter change is recommended.

29. Connect the negative battery cable. Start the engine and verify that there are no leaks.

FUEL SYSTEM

Fuel System Service Precautions

Safety is the most important factor when performing not only fuel system maintenance but any type of maintenance. Failure to conduct maintenance and repairs in a safe manner may result in serious personal injury or death. Maintenance and testing of the vehicle's fuel system components can be accomplished safely and effectively by adhering to the following rules and guidelines.

• To avoid the possibility of fire and personal injury, always disconnect the negative battery cable unless the repair or test procedure requires that battery voltage be applied.

• Always relieve the fuel system pressure prior to disconnecting any fuel system component (injector, fuel rail, pressure regulator, etc.), fitting or fuel line connection. Exercise extreme caution whenever relieving fuel system pressure to avoid exposing skin, face and eyes to fuel spray. Please be advised that fuel under pressure may penetrate the skin or any part of the body that it contacts.

• Always place a shop towel or cloth around the fitting or connection prior to loosening to absorb any excess fuel due to spillage. Ensure that all fuel spillage (should it occur) is quickly removed from engine surfaces. Ensure that all fuel soaked cloths or towels are deposited into a suitable waste container.

• Always keep a dry chemical (Class B) fire extinguisher near the work area.

• Do not allow fuel spray or fuel vapors to come into contact with a spark or open flame.

• Always use a back-up wrench when loosening and tightening fuel line connection fittings. This will prevent unnecessary stress and torsion to fuel line piping.

Always follow the proper torque specifications.

• Always replace worn fuel fitting O-rings with new. Do not substitute fuel hose or equivalent, where fuel pipe is installed.

Fuel System Pressure

RELIEVING

2.4L Engine

1. Before servicing the vehicle, refer to the precautions in the beginning of this section.

2. Loosen the fuel filler cap in order to relieve the pressure in the tank (do not tighten at this time).

3. Raise and safely support the vehicle.

4. Detach the fuel pump electrical connector.

5. Start and run the vehicle until it stalls, then engage the starter for an additional three seconds to ensure the relief of any remaining pressure.

6. Disconnect the negative battery cable.

7. Once the tests or repairs are completed, reattach the fuel pump electrical connector.

8. Connect the negative battery cable.

9. Lower the vehicle.

10. Tighten the fuel filler cap.

11. Prime the fuel system by cycling the ignition switch **ON** for 2 seconds, **OFF** for 10 seconds, then **ON** again. Repeat, if necessary to build system pressure.

3.1L Engine

1. Before servicing the vehicle, refer to the precautions in the beginning of this section.

2. Disconnect the negative battery cable in order to avoid possible fuel discharge if an accidental attempt is made to start the engine.

3. Loosen the fuel tank filler cap in order to relieve fuel tank pressure.

4. Connect tool J-34730-A or an equivalent fuel pressure gauge to the fuel pressure test port connection. Wrap a towel around the fuel pressure connection when installing the fuel pressure gauge in order to avoid fuel spillage.

5. Install the bleed hose into an approved container and open the valve in order to bleed the fuel system pressure. The fuel pipe connections are now safe for servicing.

6. Drain any fuel remaining in the fuel pressure gauge into an approved container.

Fuel Filter

REMOVAL & INSTALLATION

All Engines

1. Before servicing the vehicle, refer to the precautions in the beginning of this section.

1 BODY
2 FUEL FILTER BRACKET
3 FUEL FILTER
4 SCREW – FULLY DRIVEN, SEATED
   AND NOT STRIPPED

Exploded view of the fuel filter mounting

2. Relieve the fuel system pressure.
3. Disconnect the negative battery cable.
4. Raise and safely support the vehicle.
5. Using a back-up wrench on the fuel filter, disconnect the fuel line from the filter.
6. Disconnect the quick-connect fitting from the fuel filter by compressing the tabs while pulling outward on the line.
7. Remove the fuel filter from the mounting bracket.
   To install:
8. Install the fuel filter in the mounting bracket.
9. Using a back-up wrench on the fuel filter, tighten the fuel line fitting to 20 ft. lbs. (27 Nm).
10. Connect the quick-connect fitting to the fuel filter.
11. Lower the vehicle.
12. Connect the negative battery cable.
13. Pressurize the fuel system and verify no leaks.

Fuel Pump

REMOVAL & INSTALLATION

All Engines

1. Relieve the fuel system pressure. Disconnect the negative battery cable.

2. Drain fuel tank. Remove the fuel tank from the vehicle.
3. While holding the modular fuel sender assembly down, remove the snapring from the designated slots located on the retainer.

➡**The modular fuel sender assembly may spring up from its position. When removing the modular fuel sender from the tank, be aware that the reservoir bucket is full of fuel. It must be tipped slightly during removal to avoid damage to the float.**

4. Remove the external fuel strainer.
5. Detach the Connector Position Assurance (CPA) piece from the wiring harness and disconnect the fuel pump.
6. Gently release the tabs on the sides of the fuel sender at the cover assembly. Begin by squeezing the sides of the reservoir and releasing the tab opposite the fuel level sensor. Move clockwise to release the second and third tab in the same manner.
7. Lift the cover assembly out far enough to disconnect the fuel pump electrical connection.
8. Rotate the fuel pump baffle counterclockwise and remove the baffle and pump assembly from the retainer.
9. Slide the fuel pump outlet out of the slots. Remove the fuel pump outlet seal.

1 HOSE, PART OF FUEL SENDER
2 FUEL VAPOR PIPE
3 FUEL RETURN PIPE
4 FUEL FEED PIPE
5 FUEL FEED PIPE NUT
   27 N•m (20 LBS. FT.)
6 HOSE, PART OF FUEL SENDER
7 ABS AND FUEL SENDER HARNESS

Fuel filter mounting location and component identification

To install:

10. Install the fuel pump outlet seal. Slide the fuel pump outlet in the slots of reservoir cover.

11. Install the fuel pump and baffle assembly onto the reservoir retainer and rotate clockwise until seated.

12. Install the lower retainer assembly partially into the reservoir. Line up all three sleeve tabs. Press the retainer onto the reservoir making sure all three tabs are firmly seated.

13. Gently pull the fuel pump reservoir from the retainer to assure a secure fastening. If not secure replace entire fuel sender.

14. Complete the installation by reverse the removal procedures.

15. Connect the negative battery cable. Pressurize the fuel system and verify no leaks.

DRIVE TRAIN

Transaxle

REMOVAL & INSTALLATION

1. Before servicing the vehicle, refer to the precautions in the beginning of this section.

1 SNAP RING
2 COVER – TAB
3 MODULAR UNIT
4 WIRE HARNESS – ABOVE COVER
5 FUEL TANK
6 TANK ISOLATION STRIPS (3)
7 RUBBER ISOLATOR

79227223

Exploded view of the fuel sender assembly mounting to the tank

1   HARNESS ASSEMBLY (ABOVE COVER) – FUEL
    PUMP AND FUEL SENDER WIRING
2   CONNECTOR ASSEMBLY – FUEL SENDER WIRING
3   FUEL PIPES (3)
4   COVER ASSEMBLY – FUEL SENDER
5   SEAL – FUEL PUMP OUTLET
6   SUPPORT ASSEMBLY (THREE HOLLOW SUPPORT OR
    GUIDE PIPES) – FUEL PUMP RESERVOIR
7   RETAINER – FUEL PUMP RESERVOIR
8   CONNECTOR POSITION ASSURANCE (CPA)
9   HARNESS ASSEMBLY (BELOW COVER) – FUEL PUMP
10 HARNESS ASSEMBLY (BELOW COVER) – FUEL
    LEVEL SENDER
11 RESERVOIR – FUEL PUMP FUEL
12 SENSOR ASSEMBLY – FUEL LEVEL
13 PUMP ASSEMBLY (JET PUMP ASSEMBLY) –
    FUEL PUMP RESERVOIR
14 STRAINER (EXTERNAL) – FUEL SENDER
15 PAD (BUMPER) – FUEL SENDER
16 VALVE (SECONDARY UMBRELLA VALVE) –
    FUEL PUMP RESERVOIR INLET CHECK
17 STRAINER – FUEL PUMP FUEL
18 BAFFLE (ISOLATOR CUP) – FUEL PUMP
19 PUMP ASSEMBLY (ROLLERVANE) – FUEL
20 OUTLET – FUEL PUMP

79222224

Exploded view of the fuel pump assembly

2. Disconnect the negative battery cable.

3. Remove the air cleaner assembly.

4. Disconnect the shift linkage from the transaxle.

5. Detach the wiring harness connection from the transaxle.

6. Install the Engine Support Fixture J 28467–360 or the equivalent.

7. Disconnect the upper transaxle-to-engine mounting bolts.

8. Raise and safely support the vehicle, then remove the front wheels.

9. Remove the left and right splash shields.

10. Disconnect the ABS wheel speed sensors and electrical harnesses from the suspension supports.

11. Disconnect the outer tie rod ends and the ball joints from the steering knuckle.

12. Remove the front suspension support brace.

13. Support the suspension support assembly, then remove the attaching bolts.

14. Slowly lower the suspension support assembly enough to disconnect the steering coupling and the power steering fluid lines.

15. Disconnect the halfshafts from the transaxle.

16. Remove the engine-to-transaxle brace.

17. Disconnect the shift cable bracket, then remove the starter.

18. Remove the transaxle torque converter cover.

19. Matchmark the flywheel-to-torque converter for reassembly.

20. Remove the torque converter-to-flywheel attaching bolts.

21. Disconnect the transaxle fluid cooling lines.

22. Disconnect the brake hose bracket from the body.

23. Disconnect the transaxle mount pipe expansion bolt.

24. Remove the transaxle-to-body mounting bolts.

25. Lower the vehicle enough to access the engine support fixture.

26. Lower the transaxle/engine, utilizing the engine support fixture, enough to remove the transaxle.

27. Raise and safely support the vehicle.

28. Position transaxle jack under transaxle. Remove the transaxle mount to body bolts.

29. Remove the remaining engine to transaxle bolts. Remove the transaxle.

❋❋ WARNING

Transaxle cooler and lines should be flushed whenever the transaxle has been removed for overhaul or replacement.

To install:

30. Apply a thin film of grease on the torque converter pilot hub.

❋❋ WARNING

Be sure to properly seat the torque converter in the pump.

31. Position the transaxle into the vehicle. Install the lower transaxle to engine bolts and tighten to 66 ft. lbs. (90 Nm).

32. Lower the vehicle enough to access the engine support fixture.

33. Raise the transaxle/engine to the proper position.

34. Raise and safely support the vehicle.

35. Install the transaxle-to-body mounting bolts.

36. Install the brake hose bracket to the body.

37. Connect the transaxle fluid cooling lines.

38. Align the matchmarks on the flywheel and torque converter, then install the bolts and tighten to 46 ft. lbs. (62 Nm).

39. Install the transaxle torque converter cover.

40. Install the starter.

41. Install the shift cable bracket and tighten the bolt to 18 ft. lbs. (24 Nm) and the nut to 37 ft. lbs. (50 Nm).

42. Install the engine-to-transaxle support brace.

43. Connect the halfshafts to the transaxle.

44. Raise the suspension support assembly enough to connect the steering coupling and the power steering fluid lines.

45. Raise the suspension support assembly, install the bolts and tighten to 71 ft. lbs. (110 Nm) plus 90 degrees.

46. Install the front suspension support brace.

47. Connect the ball joints and outer tie rod ends to the steering knuckle.

48. Connect the front ABS wheel speed sensors and harnesses to the suspension support.

49. Install the left and right splash shields.

50. Install the front wheels, then lower the vehicle.

51. Install the upper transaxle-to-engine mounting bolts and tighten to 66 ft. lbs. (90 Nm).

52. Remove the engine support fixture.

53. Attach the wiring harness to the transaxle.

54. Connect the shift linkage to the transaxle.

55. Install the air cleaner assembly, then connect the negative battery cable.

56. Fill the transaxle with Dexron® III or equivalent.

57. Apply the brakes, start the engine and shift the transaxle from reverse to drive, then recheck the fluid level.

58. Install the transaxle mount pipe expansion bolt.

Halfshaft

REMOVAL & INSTALLATION

1. Before servicing the vehicle, refer to the precautions in the beginning of this section.

2. Raise and safely support vehicle. Remove the wheel and tire assembly.

3. Disconnect the tie rod from the steering knuckle.

4. Insert a drift pin through the opening in the caliper and into the ventilation openings in the brake rotor to prevent the rotor from turning.

5. Remove the drive shaft hub nut and washer.

6. Remove the lower ball joint cotter pin and nut and loosen the joint using tool J-38892 or equivalent. If removing the right axle, turn the wheel to the left. If

(1) Drive Axle, Right Side
(2) Drive Axle, Left Side
(3) J 28468 or J 33008
(4) J 29794
(5) J 2619-01

7922Z225

Removing the left and right halfshafts

removing the left axle, turn the wheel to the right.

7. Disconnect the stabilizer link.

8. Separate the joint, with a prybar between the suspension support.

9. Disengage the axle from the hub and bearing using J-28733-A or equivalent puller.

10. Separate the hub and bearing assembly from the drive axle and move the strut and knuckle assembly rearward.

11. Disconnect the inner joint from the transaxle using tool J-28468 or J-33008 attached to J-29794 and J-2619–01 or their equivalents.

To install:

12. Insert the drive axle into the transaxle, by placing a suitable tool into the groove on the joint housing and tapping until seated.

✳✳ WARNING

Be careful not to damage the axle seal or dislodge the transaxle seal garter spring when installing the axle.

13. Verify that the drive axle is seated into the transaxle by grasping on the housing and pulling outward.

14. Connect the tie rod to the steering

knuckle and tighten the nut to 89 inch lbs. (10 Nm) plus 210 degrees.

15. Install the drive axle into the hub and bearing assembly.

16. Install the lower ball joint to the knuckle. Tighten the ball joint to steering knuckle nut to 89 inch lbs. (10 Nm) plus 180 degrees, then install the cotter pin.

17. Install the washer and new drive shaft nut. Again insert a drift pin into the caliper and rotor to prevent the rotor from turning and tighten the drive shaft nut to 30 ft. lbs. (40 Nm) plus 235 degrees.

18. Install the tire and wheel assembly. Lower the vehicle.

(1) J 28733A
(2) Forcing Screw
(3) Turn Box Wrench
(4) Hold Wrench

7922Z226

Removing the halfshaft from the hub utilizing the appropriate tools

STEERING AND SUSPENSION

Air Bag

❊❊ CAUTION

Some vehicles are equipped with an air bag system, also known as the Supplemental Inflatable Restraint (SIR) or Supplemental Restraint System (SRS). The system must be disabled before performing service on or around system components, steering column, instrument panel components, wiring and sensors. Failure to follow safety and disabling procedures could result in accidental air bag deployment, possible personal injury and unnecessary system repairs.

PRECAUTIONS

Several precautions must be observed when handling the inflator module to avoid accidental deployment and possible personal injury.

• Never carry the inflator module by the wires or connector on the underside of the module.

• When carrying a live inflator module, hold securely with both hands, and ensure that the bag and trim cover are pointed away.

• Place the inflator module on a bench or other surface with the bag and trim cover facing up.

• With the inflator module on the bench, never place anything on or close to the module which may be thrown in the event of an accidental deployment.

DISARMING

❊❊ CAUTION

The Supplemental Restraint System (SRS) must be disarmed before performing service procedures around the air bag or SRS wiring. Failure to do so may cause accidental deployment of the air bag, resulting in unnecessary SRS repairs and/or personal injury.

1. Disconnect the negative battery cable.

2. Turn the steering wheel so the vehicle's wheels are pointing straight ahead.

3. Turn the ignition switch to the **LOCK** position and remove the key.

4. Remove the **AIR BAG** fuse from the fuse block.

5. Remove the left sound insulator.

6. Remove the Connector Position Assurance (CPA) clip from the yellow 2-way connector at the base of the steering column, and detach the connector. If equipped with a passenger's side air bag, remove the CPA and detach the yellow 2-way connector from the passenger air bag lead.

REARMING

1. Turn the ignition switch to the **LOCK** position and remove the key.

2. Attach the yellow 2-way connector at the base of steering column and secure it with the Connector Position Assurance (CPA) clip. If equipped with a passenger's side air bag, attach the yellow 2-way connector at the passenger air bag lead and secure it with the CPA clip.

3. Install the left sound insulator.

4. Install the **AIR BAG** fuse in the fuse block.

5. Turn the ignition switch to the **RUN** position and verify that the **AIR BAG** warning lamp flashes 7 times, then turns **OFF**.

6. Connect the negative battery cable.

Power Rack and Pinion Steering Gear

REMOVAL & INSTALLATION

1. Before servicing the vehicle, refer to the precautions in the beginning of this section.

2. Disconnect the negative battery cable.

3. Siphon the power steering fluid from the reservoir.

4. Raise and safely support the vehicle, and remove the left front wheel.

5. Remove the lower pinch bolt on the intermediate shaft assembly and push the shaft up toward the steering column.

6. Remove the tie rods from the steering knuckle.

(1) Gear Assembly, Power Steering
(2) Tie Rod
(3) Shaft, Front Stabilizer
(4) Frame Assembly, Drivetrain and Front Crossmember
(5) Bolt, Power Steering Gear Assembly

7922Z227

Exploded view of the power rack and pinion steering gear mounting

7. Remove the steering gear mounting bolts.

8. Remove the transaxle-to-crossmember mounting bolt.

9. Remove the rear crossmember-to-body mounting bolts in order to provide clearance to remove the power steering pipes/hoses.

10. Loosen the front crossmember bolts.

11. Disconnect the power steering pipes from the steering gear.

12. Remove the steering gear through the left wheel opening.

To install:

13. Install the steering gear through the left wheel opening.

14. Connect the power steering pipes to the steering gear.

15. Tighten the front crossmember bolts to 71 ft. lbs. (110 Nm) plus 90 degrees.

16. Install and tighten the rear cross-member-to-body bolts to 71 ft. lbs. (110 Nm) plus 90 degrees.

17. Install the transmission mount-to-crossmember bolt and tighten to 49 ft. lbs. (66 Nm).

18. Install the steering gear mounting bolts and tighten to 89 ft. lbs. (120 Nm).

19. Connect the tie rod ends to the steering knuckle and tighten to the tie rod nut to 15 ft. lbs. (20 Nm) plus 180 degrees.

20. Install the lower pinch bolt on the intermediate shaft and tighten to 16 ft. lbs. (22 Nm).

21. Install the left front wheel, then lower the vehicle.

22. Connect the negative battery cable.

23. Refill and bleed the power steering system. Check the front end alignment and adjust as necessary.

Strut

REMOVAL & INSTALLATION

Front

1. Before servicing the vehicle, refer to the precautions in the beginning of this section.

2. Raise and safely support the vehicle. Remove the front tire and wheel assembly.

3. Remove the cotter pin and castle nut from the outer tie rod end and separate the ball stud from the strut arm using J-24319–01, or an equivalent tie rod puller.

4. Remove the bolt from the brake line bracket and separate the bracket from the strut.

(1) **Bearing, Strut Mount**
(2) **Nuts, Strut Mount**
(3) **Knuckle**
(4) **Arm, Control**
(5) **Crossmember**
(6) **Bolts, Strut Mount**
(7) **Spring, Strut Coil**

7922Z228

Exploded view and component identification of the front strut

5. Scribe reference marks on the front strut and steering knuckle for installation purposes.

6. Remove the strut lower mounting bracket nut and through-bolts.

7. Lower the vehicle until the upper strut plate mounting bolts are accessible.

8. Support the lower control arm.

9. Hold the strut and remove the strut plate mounting nuts and bolt. Remove the strut from the vehicle.

✳✳ CAUTION

If the strut is being replaced, a spring compressor must be used to remove the coil spring from the strut assembly. Failure to use a spring compressor can result in personal injury.

To install:

10. Install the strut assembly into the vehicle and install the upper strut plate mounting nuts.

11. Connect the lower strut bracket to the steering knuckle and install the through-bolts.

12. Raise the vehicle.

13. Install the through-bolt nuts and tighten to 133 ft. lbs. (180 Nm) with the reference marks in alignment.

14. Connect the tie rod end to the strut arm and tighten the castle nut to 15 ft. lbs. (20 Nm) plus 90 degrees.

15. Connect the brake line bracket to the strut and tighten the bolt to 10 ft. lbs. (14 Nm).

(1) Mount, Strut Upper
(2) Bolt, Strut Mount
(3) Spring, Coil
(4) Nut

7922Z229

Exploded view of the upper strut mounting

(1) Mount, Strut Upper
(2) Spring, Coil
(3) Nuts, Strut Bolt
(4) Knuckle
(5) Bolt, Strut Mount

7922Z230

Exploded view of the lower strut mounting

Turn to Section 6 for brake system applications

J 34013

J 3289-20

1 STRUT ASSEMBLY
2 INSTALL LOCKING PINS THROUGH
   STRUT ASSEMBLY
3 TIGHTEN NUTS UNTIL FLUSH WITH
   STRUT COMPRESSOR
4 COMPRESSOR FORCING SCREW

7922Z231

View of the strut assembly mounted in a compressor

(1) Cap
(2) Nut, Strut Mount
(3) Bearing, Strut Mount
(4) Insulator, Spring (Upper)
(5) Spring, Strut Coil
(6) Insulator, Spring (Lower)
(7) Strut
(8) Bumper, Jounce
(9) Shield, Strut Dust

7922Z233

Exploded view of the front strut

J 34013

1 WRENCH

2 SOCKET

3 STRUT ASSEMBLY

7922Z232

Use a socket and a wrench to remove the dampener shaft nut spring cap while compressing the spring

16. Install the tire and wheel assembly. Lower the vehicle.

17. Tighten the upper strut plate mounting nuts and bolt to 18 ft. lbs. (25 Nm).

18. Check the front end alignment and adjust as necessary.

Rear

1. Raise and safely support the vehicle and remove the rear wheels.

2. Matchmark the strut-to-knuckle position.

3. Remove the upper strut mounting nuts from in the trunk area.

4. Remove the upper strut mounting bolts from inside the fender well.

5. Remove the strut-to-knuckle mounting bolts, then remove the strut from the vehicle.

To install:

6. Install the strut to the vehicle, and loosely install the strut-to-knuckle mounting bolts.

7. Install the strut-to-body bolts inside the fender well.

➡**Align the matchmarks to ensure proper alignment.**

8. Install the strut mount-to-body nuts in the trunk area.

9. Tighten the strut-to-knuckle mounting bolts to 89 ft. lbs. (120 Nm).

10. Install the rear wheels, then lower the vehicle.

11. Check the alignment.

(1) Strut
(2) Dust Shield, Strut
(3) Spring, Strut Coil
(4) Mount, Strut Upper
(5) Washer
(6) Nut

7922Z234

Exploded view of the rear strut

Coil Spring

REMOVAL & INSTALLATION

Front and Rear

1. Remove the strut assembly from the vehicle, as outlined earlier in this section.

2. Mount the strut compressor J-34013 in holding fixture J-3289–20.

3. Mount the strut assembly into the compressor. Note that the strut compressor has strut mounting holes drilled for specific vehicle lines.

4. Compress the strut approximately ½ of its height after initial contact with the top cap.

✳✳ WARNING

Never bottom the spring or dampener rod.

5. Remove the nut from the strut dampener shaft and place alignment/guiding rod J-34013–27 on top of the dampener shaft. Use the rod to guide the dampener shaft straight down through the spring cap while compressing the spring. Remove the components.

✳✳ WARNING

Avoid chipping or cracking the spring coating when handling the front suspension coil spring assembly.

To install:

6. Install the bearing cap into the strut compressor if previously removed.

7. Mount the strut assembly in strut compressor, using bottom locking pin only. Extend the dampener shaft and install clamp J-34013–20 on the dampener shaft.

8. Install the spring over the dampener and swing the assembly up so the upper locking pin can be installed.

9. Install all shields, bumpers and insulators on the spring seat. Install the spring seat on top of the spring. Be sure the flat on the upper spring seat is facing in the proper direction. The spring seat flat should be facing the same direction as the centerline of the strut assembly spindle.

10. Install the guiding rod and turn the forcing screw while the guiding rod centers the assembly. When the threads on the dampener shaft are visible, remove the guiding rod and install the nut. Tighten the

nut to 52 ft. lbs. (70 Nm). Use a crow's foot line wrench while holding the dampener shaft with a socket.

11. Remove the clamp.

Lower Ball Joint

REMOVAL & INSTALLATION

1. Before servicing the vehicle, refer to the precautions in the beginning of this section.

2. Raise and safely support the vehicle.

3. If a suspension contact hoist is used, place safety stands under the crossmember. Lower the vehicle slightly so the weight of the vehicle rests on the crossmember.

4. Remove the tire and wheel assembly.

➡**Care must be exercised to prevent the axle shaft joints from being over-extended. When either end of the shaft is disconnected, over-extension of the joint could result in separation of internal components and possible joint failure. Failure to observe this can result in interior joint or boot damage and possible joint failure.**

5. Remove the cotter pin and nut from the ball joint.

6. Separate the ball joint from the steering knuckle using tool J-38892 or equivalent.

7. Drill out the 3 rivets retaining ball joint to the lower control arm. Use an ⅛ in. (3mm) drill bit to make a pilot hole through the rivets. Finish drilling the rivets with a ½ in. (13mm) drill bit.

8. Remove the nut attaching link to the stabilizer shaft.

9. Remove the ball joint from the steering knuckle and control arm.

To install:

10. Install the ball joint into the control arm.

11. Install 3 new bolts and nuts (supplied with new ball joint) and tighten.

12. Position the ball joint stud through the steering knuckle and tighten nut to 50 ft. lbs. (65 Nm) and install the cotter pin.

13. Connect the stabilizer link to the stabilizer shaft and the tighten nut to 13 ft. lbs. (17 Nm).

14. Install the tire and wheel assembly.

1 PIN
2 NUT – 55 N·m (41 LBS. FT.) MINIMUM TORQUE
   65 N·m (48 LBS. FT.) MAXIMUM TORQUE TO
   INSTALL PIN
3 LOWER BALL JOINT

79222235

Exploded view of the ball joint-to-knuckle mounting

1 SERVICE BALL JOINT
2 BALL JOINT MOUNTING BOLTS
3 NUT
4 LOWER CONTROL ARM
5 STEERING KNUCKLE
6 NUT – 55 N·m (41 LBS. FT.) MINIMUM TORQUE
        65 N·m (48 LBS. FT.) MAXIMUM TORQUE
        TO INSTALL PIN
7 PIN

Exploded view of the ball joint mounting

5. Remove the caliper mounting bolts and remove the caliper from the steering knuckle. Support the caliper aside. DO NOT allow the caliper to hang unsupported from the brake hose.
6. Remove the brake rotor.
7. Remove the three bolts securing the hub bearing to the steering knuckle. Remove the backing plate.
8. Using J-28733-A, or an equivalent front hub remover, separate the halfshaft from the hub bearing assembly.
9. Remove the hub bearing assembly.

To install:
10. Install the hub bearing assembly over the end of the axle making sure the splines engage smoothly.
11. Install the backing plate and the three hub bearing mounting bolts. Tighten the bolts to 70 ft. lbs. (95 Nm).
12. Install the brake rotor.
13. Install the caliper onto the steering knuckle and tighten the caliper mounting bolts to 38 ft. lbs. (51 Nm).
14. Install a drift punch into the rotor cooling fins. This keeps the assembly from turning while the axle nut is being tightened. Tighten the axle nut to 192 ft. lbs. (260 Nm).

15. Lower the vehicle.
16. Check the front wheel alignment and adjust, if necessary.

Wheel Bearings

ADJUSTMENT

These vehicles are equipped with sealed hub and bearing assemblies. The hub and bearing assemblies are non-serviceable. If the assembly is damaged, the complete unit must be replaced.

REMOVAL & INSTALLATION

Front

1. Before servicing the vehicle, refer to the precautions in the beginning of this section.
2. Raise and safely support the vehicle. Remove the front tire and wheel assembly.
3. Insert a drift punch through the caliper and into the rotor cooling fins. This keeps the assembly from turning while the axle nut is being loosened.
4. Remove the axle nut and washer. Remove the punch.

1 HUB AND BEARING ASSEMBLY
2 STEERING KNUCKLE
3 WASHER
4 DRIVE AXLE NUT – 260 N·m (192 LBS. FT.)
5 HUB AND BEARING RETAINING BOLT
6 WASHER

Exploded view of the front hub and bearing assembly

Turn to Section 6 for brake system applications

15. Install the front tire and wheel assembly and tighten the wheel nuts to 100 ft. lbs. (140 Nm). Lower the vehicle.

Rear

1. Before servicing the vehicle, refer to the precautions in the beginning of this section.

2. Raise and safely support the vehicle. Remove the wheel and tire assembly. Remove the brake drum.

3. Remove the four hub bearing assembly mounting nuts from behind the backing plate while holding the bolts from the front. The mounting bolts can be removed from the backing plate once the nuts have been removed. The top rear bolt will not clear the brake shoes and must be removed with the bearing assembly.

4. Disconnect the ABS speed sensor wire from the hub bearing assembly. Remove the hub bearing assembly.

To install:

5. Position the hub bearing assembly on the backing plate and insert the four mounting bolts. Connect the ABS wheel speed sensor, if equipped.

6. Install the hub bearing mounting nuts from behind the backing plate and tighten the nuts to 38 ft. lbs. (52 Nm) while holding the bolts.

7. Install the brake drum.

8. Install the tire and wheel assembly and tighten the wheel bolts to 100 ft. lbs. (140 Nm). Lower the vehicle.

(1) Nut
(2) Knuckle, Rear
(3) Brake Assembly
(4) Hub and Bearing Assembly
(5) Bolt

7922Z238

Hub and bearing components

GENERAL MOTORS CORPORATION—N BODY

Buick-Skylark • **Oldsmobile**-Achieva • Alero • **Pontiac**-Grand Am

PRECAUTIONS

Before servicing any vehicle, please be sure to read all of the following precautions, which deal with personal safety, prevention of component damage, and important points to take into consideration when servicing a motor vehicle:

• Never open, service or drain the radiator or cooling system when the engine is hot; serious burns can occur from the steam and hot coolant.

• Observe all applicable safety precautions when working around fuel. Whenever servicing the fuel system, always work in a well ventilated area. Do not allow fuel spray or vapors to come in contact with a spark, open flame, or excessive heat (a hot drop light, for example). Keep a dry chemical fire extinguisher near the work area. Always keep fuel in a container specifically designed for fuel storage; also, always properly seal fuel containers to avoid the possibility of fire or explosion. Refer to the additional fuel system precautions later in this section.

• Fuel injection systems often remain pressurized, even after the engine has been turned **OFF**. The fuel system pressure must be relieved before disconnecting any fuel lines. Failure to do so may result in fire and/or personal injury.

• Brake fluid often contains polyglycol ethers and polyglycols. Avoid contact with the eyes and wash your hands thoroughly after handling brake fluid. If you do get brake fluid in your eyes, flush your eyes with clean, running water for 15 minutes. If eye irritation persists, or if you have taken brake fluid internally, IMMEDIATELY seek medical assistance.

• The EPA warns that prolonged contact with used engine oil may cause a number of skin disorders, including cancer! You should make every effort to minimize your exposure to used engine oil. Protective gloves should be worn when changing oil. Wash your hands and any other exposed skin areas as soon as possible after exposure to used engine oil. Soap and water, or waterless hand cleaner should be used.

• All new vehicles are now equipped with an air bag system, often referred to as a Supplemental Restraint System (SRS) or Supplemental Inflatable Restraint (SIR) system. The system must be disabled before performing service on or around system components, steering column, instrument panel components, wiring and sensors. Failure to follow safety and disabling procedures could result in accidental air bag deployment, possible personal injury and unnecessary system repairs.

• Always wear safety goggles when working with, or around, the air bag system. When carrying a non-deployed air bag, be sure the bag and trim cover are pointed away from your body. When placing a non-deployed air bag on a work surface, always face the bag and trim cover upward, away from the surface. This will reduce the motion of the module if it is accidentally deployed. Refer to the additional air bag system precautions later in this section.

• Clean, high quality brake fluid from a sealed container is essential to the safe and proper operation of the brake system. You should always buy the correct type of brake fluid for your vehicle. If the brake fluid becomes contaminated, completely flush the system with new fluid. Never reuse any brake fluid. Any brake fluid that is removed from the system should be discarded. Also, do not allow any brake fluid to come in contact with a painted surface; it will damage the paint.

• Never operate the engine without the proper amount and type of engine oil; doing so WILL result in severe engine damage.

• Timing belt maintenance is extremely important! Many models utilize an interference-type, non-freewheeling engine. If the timing belt breaks, the valves in the cylinder head may strike the pistons, causing potentially serious (also time-consuming and expensive) engine damage. Refer to the maintenance interval charts in the front of this manual for the recommended replacement interval for the timing belt, and to the timing belt section for belt replacement and inspection.

• Disconnecting the negative battery cable on some vehicles may interfere with the functions of the on-board computer system(s) and may require the computer to undergo a relearning process once the negative battery cable is reconnected.

• When servicing drum brakes, only dissemble and assemble one side at a time, leaving the remaining side intact for reference.

ENGINE REPAIR

Ignition Timing

ADJUSTMENT

The ignition timing is not adjustable, and is set electronically according to engine demand. The Powertrain Control Module (PCM) controls the ignition timing for all driving conditions. The PCM monitors input signals from the following components Engine Coolant Temperature (ECT) sensor, Intake Air Temperature (IAT) sensor, Mass Air Flow (MAF) sensor, park/neutral switch, Throttle Position (TP) sensor and the Vehicle Speed Sensor (VSS).

Engine Assembly

REMOVAL & INSTALLATION

2.4L Engine

The engine and transaxle are removed as a unit from under the vehicle.

1. Before servicing the vehicle, refer to the precautions in the beginning of this section.

2. Relieve the fuel system pressure. Disconnect the negative battery cable.

3. Drain the cooling system into a suitable container. If equipped with A/C, recover the refrigerant.

4. Remove the left sound insulator and disconnect the clutch pushrod from the pedal assembly (manual transaxle only).

5. Disconnect the heater hose and upper radiator hose from the thermostat housing. Remove the air cleaner-to-throttle body duct, the upper radiator support and cooling fan assembly.

6. If equipped with A/C, disconnect the refrigerant line and discard the O-rings.

7. Disconnect the vacuum hoses from the front of the engine. Label and detach the electrical connectors from the necessary components.

8. Disconnect the power brake booster vacuum lines. Disconnect the throttle cables; remove the cable bracket and position aside.

9. Remove the power steering pump rear bracket and pump; position the pump aside with the lines attached.

10. Disconnect the fuel lines from the fuel rail and cap the lines.

11. Disconnect the shift cable from the transaxle and the Throttle Valve (TV) cable on automatic transaxles.

12. Remove the exhaust manifold and heat shield.

13. Remove the lower radiator hose. Remove the coolant recovery tank and position it aside leaving the hoses attached.

14. Install an engine support fixture, J-28467-A or equivalent. Remove the right engine mount.

15. Raise and safely support the vehicle. Drain the engine crankcase into a suitable container.

16. Remove the front tire and wheel assemblies. Remove the right lower splash shield.

17. Disconnect the electrical connections from the ABS wheel speed sensors. Disconnect the ground connections from the transaxle.

18. Remove the cotter pins and castle nuts from the lower ball joints and separate the ball joints from the steering knuckles.

19. Support the suspension crossmembers, then remove the mounting bolts and crossmembers.

20. Disconnect the heater outlet hose from the radiator outlet pipe.

21. Disconnect the halfshafts from the transaxle. If equipped with a manual transaxle, disconnect the intermediate shaft.

22. Position a suitable engine table under the powertrain and lower the vehicle until the powertrain is resting on the table.

23. Remove the engine strut and transaxle mount bolts. Remove the engine support fixture.

24. Raise the vehicle until it is clear of the engine. Separate the transaxle from the engine.

To install:

25. Install the transaxle onto the engine and tighten the bolts to 55 ft. lbs. (75 Nm). Position the powertrain assembly and the engine table under the vehicle.

26. Lower the vehicle and install the engine support fixture. Install the engine strut and transaxle mounts.

27. Raise the vehicle and remove the engine table. Connect the halfshafts and intermediate shaft to the transaxle.

28. Complete the installation by reversing the removal procedures.

29. Tighten the ball joint-to-steering knuckle nuts to 41 ft. lbs. (55 Nm). Install new cotter pins.

30. Refill the cooling system, the crankcase and fill the remainder of the underhood fluids.

31. Connect the negative battery cable. Recharge the A/C system. Start the vehicle and verify no leaks.

➡ **Whenever the vehicle sub-frame is removed or lowered, the wheel alignment should be checked.**

3.1L Engine

Please note that the engine and transaxle are removed as an assembly from under the vehicle.

1. Before servicing the vehicle, refer to the precautions in the beginning of this section.

2. Relieve the fuel system pressure. Disconnect the negative battery cable.

3. Remove the top half of the air cleaner assembly and the throttle body inlet duct. Drain the cooling system.

4. Remove the upper and lower radiator hoses. Disconnect the coolant inlet line from the coolant surge tank.

5. Disconnect the vacuum hoses from the EVAP canister purge valve, vacuum modulator and power brake booster.

6. Disconnect the heater outlet hose from the water pump. Remove the serpentine drive belt.

7. Disconnect the control cables from the throttle body lever and intake manifold bracket, then position the cables aside.

8. Label and detach the electrical connectors from the necessary components.

9. Remove the alternator. Disconnect the power steering lines from the power steering pump and cap the lines.

10. Disconnect and cap the fuel lines from the fuel rail. Remove the cooling fan assembly.

11. Disconnect the shift control cable from the transaxle shift lever and cable bracket. Disconnect the transaxle vent tube from the transaxle.

12. Disconnect the vacuum hose from the vacuum reservoir. Install engine support fixture, J-28467-A, or the equivalent.

13. Loosen, but do not remove the top two A/C compressor mounting bolts. Raise and safely support the vehicle.

14. Drain the engine crankcase into a suitable container.

15. Remove the front tire and wheel assemblies. Remove the right and left inner fender splash shields.

16. Remove the engine mount strut. Disconnect the ABS sensor wires from the wheel sensors and suspension member supports, if equipped.

17. Remove the cotter pins and castle nuts from the lower ball joints. Using a suitable tool, separate the lower ball joints from the steering knuckles.

18. Remove the lower suspension support assemblies with the lower control arms attached. Disconnect the halfshafts from the transaxle and support aside.

19. Remove the oil filter and oil filter adapter. Remove the flywheel cover. Remove the starter. Disconnect the heater hoses from the heater core.

20. Remove the A/C compressor lower mounting bolts and remove the compressor from the mounting bracket and position aside. DO NOT disconnect the refrigerant lines from the compressor or allow the lines top support the weight of the compressor.

21. Remove the vacuum reservoir tank. Disconnect the exhaust pipe from the exhaust manifold and position the pipe aside.

22. Remove the engine mount strut bracket from the engine. Disconnect the transaxle cooler lines from the radiator.

23. Remove the transaxle oil fill tube. Lower the vehicle until the powertrain assembly is resting on a suitable engine table.

24. Remove the transaxle mount-to-body bolts, and the intermediate bracket from the right engine mount.

25. Remove the engine support fixture. Raise the vehicle leaving the powertrain assembly on the engine table.

26. Separate the engine and transaxle assemblies.

To install:

27. Connect the transaxle to the engine and tighten the mounting bolts to 55 ft. lbs. (75 Nm).

28. Position the powertrain assembly under the vehicle and lower the vehicle into position. Loosely install the serpentine belt.

29. Complete the installation by reversing the removal procedures.

30. Tighten the following items to:
- Engine strut bracket-to-engine bolts: 44 ft. lbs. (60 Nm)
- Exhaust pipe-to-exhaust manifold bolts: 18 ft. lbs. (25 Nm)
- Ball joint-to-steering knuckle nuts: 41 ft. lbs. (55 Nm)

✸✸ WARNING

Operating the engine without the proper amount and type of engine oil will result in severe engine damage.

31. Connect the negative battery cable. Check and fill all the engine fluids as necessary. Start the vehicle and bleed the power steering system.

3.4L Engine

1. Before servicing the vehicle, refer to the precautions in the beginning of this section.

2. Disconnect the negative battery cable.

3. Drain the engine coolant.

4. Remove the air cleaner assembly.

5. Remove the hood.

6. Remove the drive belt.

7. Disconnect the hoses from the surge tank.

8. Remove the cruise control module.

9. Remove the upper wiring harness from the components on the top of the engine and position it out of the way.

10. Disconnect the throttle and cruise control cables.

11. Raise and safely support the vehicle.

12. Remove the starter motor assembly.

13. Remove the A/C compressor with the lines attached. Position the compressor aside.

14. Disconnect the lower wiring harness from the components on the engine and position it out of the way.

15. Remove the catalytic converter from the rear exhaust manifold.

16. Remove the torque converter cover, then remove the flexplate-to-torque converter bolts.

17. Remove the engine splash shields.

18. Remove the transaxle-to-engine brace and the two outer transaxle mounting bolts.

19. Remove the upper and lower radiator hoses.

20. Lower the vehicle to the floor.

21. Disconnect the fuel lines from the engine.

22. Remove the vacuum hose from the power brake booster.

23. Disconnect the heater hoses from the vehicle.

24. Install an engine support fixture and raise the engine slightly.

25. Remove the engine mount and adapter.

26. Remove the power steering pump.

27. Install an engine hoist and remove the engine support fixture.

28. Remove the transaxle-to-engine bolts.

29. Carefully raise the engine out of the vehicle.

To install:

30. Position the engine in the vehicle and align it with the transaxle.

31. Install the upper transaxle-to-engine bolts. Tighten the bolts to 66 ft. lbs. (90 Nm).

32. Install the engine support fixture and remove the engine hoist.

33. Raise and safely support the vehicle.

34. Install the power steering pump on the engine front cover.

35. Install the engine mount bracket and the mount. Tighten the bracket bolts to 43 ft. lbs. (58 Nm).

36. Connect the power steering lines to the pump.

37. Install the upper and lower radiator hoses.

38. Install the two outer transaxle-to-engine bolts. Tighten the bolts to 66 ft. lbs. (90 Nm).

39. Install the transaxle to engine brace. Tighten the bolts to 32 ft. lbs. (43 Nm).

40. Install the right splash shield.

41. Install the flexplate-to-torque converter bolts. Tighten the bolts to 46 ft. lbs. (62 Nm).

42. Install the torque converter cover.

43. Install the A/C compressor.

44. Install the starter.

45. Install the engine mount nuts. Tighten them to 35 ft. lbs. (47 Nm).

46. Connect the catalytic converter to the exhaust manifold.

47. Install a new oil filter and connect the lower wiring harness to the correct components. Be sure to position the harness in the retainers.

48. Lower the vehicle to the floor.

49. Connect the upper wiring harness to the correct components and place the harness in the original retainers.

50. Connect the vacuum hoses.

✸✸ CAUTION

To avoid personal injury and/or damage to the vehicle, replace the throttle cable with a new one any time the engine has been removed from the vehicle.

51. Connect the cruise control cable and replace the throttle cable.

52. Install the cruise control module.

53. Connect the fuel lines at the engine.

54. Install the drive belt.

55. Connect the hoses to the surge tank.

56. Install the hood.

57. Install the air cleaner assembly.

58. Refill the engine with Dex-Cool® coolant.

59. Fill the crankcase to the proper level with the recommended oil.

60. Turn the ignition **ON** and inspect for fuel leaks. Start the engine and inspect for coolant and/or oil leaks.

61. Stop the engine and recheck the fluid levels after the engine has cooled.

Water Pump

REMOVAL & INSTALLATION

2.4L Engine

1. Before servicing the vehicle, refer to the precautions in the beginning of this section.

2. Disconnect the negative battery cable.

3. Drain the cooling system.

4. Detach the Oxygen (O2S) sensor electrical connector.

5. Remove the upper and lower exhaust manifold heat shields.

6. Raise and safely support the vehicle.

7. Remove the exhaust manifold brace-to-manifold bolt.

8. Loosen the exhaust pipe-to-manifold spring loaded nuts.

9. Remove the radiator outlet pipe-to-water pump cover bolts.

10. Raise and safely support the vehicle.

11. Disconnect the exhaust pipe from the manifold.

12. Disconnect the radiator outlet pipe from the oil pan and transaxle.

13. If equipped with a manual transaxle, remove the exhaust manifold brace. If equipped with an automatic transaxle, leave

47	HOUSING, TIMING CHAIN
350	BODY ASM., COOLANT PUMP
350A	NUT
351	COVER ASM., COOLANT PUMP
351A	BOLT – M6 X 1 X 90
351B	BOLT – M6 X 1 X 25
351C	BOLT – M6 X 1 X 55
351D	BOLT – M8 X 1.25 X 30
352	GASKET, COOLANT PUMP TO COVER
353	GASKET, COOLANT PUMP TO TIMING CHAIN HOUSING
354	GASKET, COOLANT PUMP COVER TO CYLINDER BLOCK

7922Z302

Exploded view of the water pump mounting—2.4L engine

the lower radiator hose attached and pull down on the radiator pipe to disconnect it from the water pump.

14. Lower the vehicle.

15. Remove the exhaust manifold.

16. Remove the water pump cover-to-engine bolts.

17. Remove the three water pump-to-timing chain housing nuts.

18. Remove the water pump and cover assembly.

19. Remove the five water pump cover-to-pump bolts and remove the cover.

To install:

20. Install the water pump-to-engine components and tighten the bolts finger-tight.

21. Lubricate the splines of the water pump drive with chassis grease.

22. To complete the installation, reverse the removal procedures.

23. With all the bolts in place tighten in the following sequence:

• Water pump-to-timing chain housing: 19 ft. lbs. (26 Nm)

• Water pump cover-to-water pump: 106–124 inch lbs. (12–14 Nm)

• Water pump cover-to-engine block (bottom first): 19 ft. lbs. (26 Nm)

• Radiator outlet pipe-to-pump cover: 10 ft. lbs. (14 Nm).

24. Refill the cooling system. Connect the negative battery cable. Start the vehicle and verify no leaks.

3.1L and 3.4L Engines

1. Before servicing the vehicle, refer to the precautions in the beginning of this section.

2. Disconnect the negative battery cable. Drain the cooling system into a suitable container.

3. Loosen, but do not remove, the water pump pulley bolts. Remove the serpentine belt.

1	COOLANT PUMP
2	GASKET
3	BOLT – 10 N·m (89 LBS. IN.)
4	LOCATOR (MUST BE VERTICAL)

7922Z303

Exploded view of the water pump mounting—3.1L and 3.4L engines

4. Remove the water pump pulley bolts and pulley. Remove the five water pump mounting bolts and pump.

To install:

5. Clean all the gasket surfaces completely. Apply a thin bead of sealer around the outside edge of the water pump along the gasket sealing area and install the gasket onto the water pump.

Timing belt service is covered in Section 5 of this manual

6. Install the water pump and tighten the bolts to 89 inch lbs. (10 Nm).

7. Install the water pump pulley and tighten the pulley bolts finger-tight. Install the serpentine belt.

8. Tighten the water pump pulley bolts to 18 ft. lbs. (25 Nm). Connect the negative battery cable.

9. Refill and bleed the cooling system. Test run the engine and check for leaks.

Cylinder Head

REMOVAL & INSTALLATION

2.4L Engine

1. Before servicing the vehicle, refer to the precautions in the beginning of this section.

2. Disconnect the negative battery cable. Drain the cooling system.

3. Disconnect the heater inlet and throttle body heater hoses from water outlet. Remove the power brake vacuum hose from the throttle body.

4. Disconnect and tag for identification, if necessary, the electrical connections from the following components:
- Manifold Absolute Pressure (MAP) sensor
- Intake Air Temperature (IAT) sensor
- EVAP purge solenoid
- Camshaft Position (CMP) sensor

5. Remove the stud-ended bolt from the alternator. Remove the intake manifold brace. Remove the intake manifold.

6. Install the stud-ended alternator bolt back into the engine. Install engine support fixtures J-28467–400 and J-28467-A or equivalent.

7. Remove the exhaust manifold. Remove the ignition coil and module assembly.

8. Disconnect the CMP sensor. Remove the power steering pump.

9. Disconnect the vacuum line from the fuel pressure regulator, fuel injector and fuel injector wiring harness.

10. Disconnect the fuel line clamp from the bracket on top of the intake camshaft housing. Remove the fuel line rail and position it aside (leaving the fuel lines attached).

11. Disconnect the timing chain housing at the intake camshaft housing, but do not remove from the vehicle.

12. Remove the electrical connection from the oil switch.

13. If equipped with an automatic transaxle, remove the transaxle fluid level indicator tube assembly from the exhaust camshaft cover and position it aside.

➡ Any time the camshaft housing-to-cylinder head bolts are loosened or removed, the camshaft housing-to-cylinder head gasket must be replaced.

14. Remove the intake camshaft housing bolts, the housing and gasket.

➡ Turn the camshaft housing upside down as soon as it is removed from the cylinder head. The lifters will fall out of the camshaft housing if it is not turned upside down. The lifters can be damaged if they fall out and hit a hard surface.

15. Remove the exhaust camshaft housing from the cylinder head (remove the bolts in reverse of the tightening sequence).

16. Remove the radiator inlet (upper) hose from the coolant outlet. Disconnect the Engine Coolant Temperature (ECT) sensor electrical connections.

17. Remove the cylinder head bolts (in reverse of the tightening sequence).

18. Remove the cylinder head and gasket.

➡ Do not use abrasive pads to clean the cylinder head or block surfaces. An abrasive pad may damage the cylinder head and block. Use a razor or scraper to clean the gasket surfaces.

To install:

19. Clean all gasket surfaces completely. Be sure the threaded holes in the engine block for the cylinder head bolts are clean.

20. Install a new cylinder head gasket on the cylinder block and carefully position the cylinder head in place.

21. New replacement head bolts are recommended. Coat the cylinder head bolt threads with clean engine oil and allow the oil to drain off before installing.

22. Install the cylinder head bolts and tighten, in sequence, as follows:
   a. No's 1 through 8: 40 ft. lbs. (65 Nm)
   b. No's 9 and 10: 30 ft. lbs. (40 Nm)
   c. All 10 bolts: an additional 90 degrees (¼ turn).

23. Install the intake and exhaust camshaft housings. Tighten the long bolts to 11 ft. lbs. (15 Nm) plus an additional 90 degrees (¼ turn). Tighten the short bolts to 11 ft. lbs. (15 Nm) plus an additional 30 degrees (⅙ turn).

24. Install the timing chain and timing chain housing. Connect the upper radiator hose to the water outlet.

25. Connect the two coolant sensor connections. Install the fuel rail on the intake manifold and the intake manifold brace.

26. Connect the electrical connections to the following components:
- MAP sensor
- IAT sensor
- EVAP purge solenoid
- Camshaft position sensor

27. Connect the MAP sensor vacuum hose to the intake manifold. Install the power steering pump.

28. Install the throttle body and the throttle cable bracket. Connect the throttle body air intake duct.

29. Lubricate the O-ring on the oil fill tube with engine oil. Install oil fill tube into the block and the mounting.

30. Install the ignition coil and module assembly. Attach the injector harness electrical connector.

31. Remove the engine support fixture. Install the exhaust manifold.

32. Fill all fluids to their proper levels. An oil and filter change is recommended.

33. Connect the negative battery cable. Start the vehicle and verify no leaks.

3.1L And 3.4L Engines

LEFT (FRONT) CYLINDER HEAD

1. Before servicing the vehicle, refer to the precautions in the beginning of this section.

2. Relieve the fuel system pressure.

Cylinder head bolt tightening sequence—2.4L engine

7922Z305

Disconnect the negative battery cable. Drain the cooling system.

3. Remove the top half of the air cleaner assembly and the throttle body air inlet duct.

4. Remove the exhaust crossover pipe heat shield and crossover pipe.

5. Disconnect the spark plug wires from the spark plugs and wire looms and route the wires aside. Remove the rocker arm covers.

6. Remove the upper intake plenum and lower intake manifold. Remove the left side exhaust manifold and oil level indicator tube.

➡ **When removing the valvetrain components they must be kept in order for installation in the same locations they were removed from.**

7. Remove rocker arms nut, rocker arms, balls and pushrods.

8. Remove the cylinder head bolts evenly and the cylinder head.

To install:

9. Clean all the gasket surfaces completely. Clean the threads on the cylinder head bolts and block threads.

10. Place the cylinder head gasket in position over the dowel pins on the cylinder block so the words **THIS SIDE UP** are showing.

11. Coat the bolt threads with sealer and install finger-tight.

12. On 1996–97 models, tighten the cylinder head bolts in sequence to 33 ft. lbs. (45 Nm). With all the bolts tightened make a second pass tightening all the bolts an additional 90 degrees (¼ turn).

13. On 1998–00 3.1L engines, tighten the cylinder head bolts in sequence to 37 ft. lbs. (50 Nm). On 1999–00 3.4L engines, tighten the cylinder head bolts in sequence to 33 ft. lbs. (45 Nm). With all the bolts tightened make a second pass tightening all the bolts an additional 90 degrees (¼ turn).

14. Install the pushrods, rocker arms, balls and rocker arm nuts. Tighten the rocker arm nuts to 18 ft. lbs. (25 Nm).

15. Install the lower intake manifold, upper intake plenum and the rocker arm covers.

16. Install the oil level indicator tube. Connect the spark the plug wires to spark plugs and wire looms.

17. Install the left side exhaust manifold. Install the exhaust crossover pipe and crossover pipe heat shield.

18. Refill the cooling system. Drain the engine oil and refill with the proper type of engine oil. A filter change is recommended.

19. Install the top half of the air cleaner assembly and the throttle body air inlet duct.

20. Connect the negative battery cable. Start the engine and verify no leaks.

RIGHT (REAR) CYLINDER HEAD

1. Relieve the fuel system pressure. Disconnect the negative battery cable. Drain the cooling system.

2. Remove the top half of the air cleaner assembly and remove the throttle body air inlet duct.

3. Remove the exhaust crossover pipe heat shield and crossover pipe. Raise and safely support the vehicle.

4. Disconnect the Oxygen (O_2S) sensor. Disconnect the exhaust pipe from the exhaust manifold.

5. Remove the right side exhaust manifold. Lower the vehicle.

6. Disconnect the spark plug wires from the spark plugs and wire looms and route the wires aside.

7. Remove the rocker arm covers, upper intake plenum and lower intake manifold.

➡ **When removing the valvetrain components they must be kept in order for installation in the same locations they were removed from.**

8. Remove rocker arms nut, rocker arms, balls and pushrods.

9. Remove the cylinder head bolts evenly and the cylinder head.

To install:

10. Clean all the gasket surfaces completely. Clean the threads on the cylinder head bolts and block threads.

11. Place the cylinder head gasket in position over the dowel pins on the cylinder block so the words **THIS SIDE UP** are showing.

12. Coat the bolt threads with sealer and install finger-tight.

13. On 1996–97 models, tighten the cylinder head bolts in sequence to 33 ft. lbs. (45 Nm). With all the bolts tightened make a second pass tightening all the bolts an additional 90 degrees (¼ turn).

14. On 1998–00 3.1L engines, tighten the cylinder head bolts in sequence to 37 ft. lbs. (50 Nm). On 1999–00 3.4L engines, tighten the cylinder head bolts in sequence to 33 ft. lbs. (45 Nm). With all the bolts tightened make a second pass tightening all the bolts an additional 90 degrees (¼ turn).

1 COAT THREADS WITH SEALER TIGHTEN IN PROPER SEQUENCE TO 45 N·m (33 LBS. FT.). TURN AN ADDITIONAL 90° WITH J 36660
2 CYLINDER HEAD
3 GASKET
4 CYLINDER BLOCK

TIGHTENING SEQUENCE

Cylinder head bolt tightening sequence—3.1L and 3.4L engines

15. Install the pushrods, rocker arms, balls and rocker arm nuts. Tighten the rocker arm nuts to 18 ft. lbs. (25 Nm).

16. Install the lower intake manifold and upper intake plenum. Install the rocker arm covers.

17. Connect the spark plug wires to the spark plugs and wire looms. Raise vehicle and safely support.

18. Install the exhaust manifold. Connect the exhaust pipe to the exhaust manifold.

19. Lower the vehicle. Connect the Oxygen (O$_2$S) sensor.

20. Install the exhaust crossover pipe and heat shield. Refill the cooling system.

21. Drain the engine oil and refill with the proper type of engine oil. A filter change is recommended.

22. Install the top half of the air cleaner assembly and the throttle body air inlet duct.

23. Connect negative battery cable. Start the engine and verify no leaks.

Rocker Arms

REMOVAL & INSTALLATION

2.4L Engine

The 2.4L engine is not equipped with rocker arms. The camshafts directly actuate the valves.

3.1L and 3.4L Engines

1. Before servicing the vehicle, refer to the precautions in the beginning of this section.

2. Disconnect the negative battery cable.

3. For the left side (front), perform the following procedures:

    a. Drain the cooling system to a level below the coolant pipe on the front of the engine.

    b. Remove the coolant bypass hose clamp at the coolant tube.

    c. Remove the two bolts and nut securing the coolant tube to the cylinder head and position the tube aside.

    d. Disconnect the PCV valve from the rocker arm cover.

4. For the right side (rear), perform the following procedures:

    a. Disconnect the spark plug wires from the spark plugs and upper intake plenum wire retainer and position aside.

    b. Disconnect the power brake booster vacuum pipe from the intake plenum.

    c. Remove the serpentine belt.

    d. Remove the alternator.

1 Pushrod
2 Valve rocker arm stud
3 Valve rocker arm
4 Valve rocker arm pivot ball
5 Valve rocker arm nut

79222307

Rocker arm components—3.1L and 3.4L engines

    e. Disconnect and remove the ignition assembly and EVAP canister purge solenoid as an assembly.

5. Remove the four rocker arm cover bolts and remove the rocker arm cover.

➡ Keep the pushrods in order. Intake pushrods are 5¾ inches long and exhaust pushrods are 6 inches long.

6. Remove the rocker arm nuts, balls, rocker arms and pushrods.

To install:

7. Clean all the gasket surfaces completely.

8. Coat all the valvetrain components with engine oil prior to installation.

9. Install the pushrods and install the rocker arms on the studs. Install the rocker arm balls and mounting nuts. Be sure the pushrods are properly seated in the lifter and rocker arm. Tighten the mounting nuts to 89 inch lbs. (10 Nm) plus an additional 30 degrees.

10. Install the rocker arm cover using a new gasket and tighten the rocker cover bolts to 90 inch lbs. (10 Nm).

11. For the left side (front), perform the following procedures:

    a. Connect the PCV valve to the rocker arm cover.

    b. Position the coolant tube and connect the thermostat bypass hose.

    c. Install the coolant tube mounting nut and bolts. Tighten the screw at the water pump to 106 inch lbs. (12 Nm), the bolt at the corner of the cylinder head to 18 ft. lbs. (25 Nm) and the nut to 18 ft. lbs. (25 Nm).

12. For the right side (rear), perform the following procedures:

    a. Install the alternator.

    b. Install the serpentine belt.

    c. Connect the power brake booster vacuum pipe to the plenum.

    d. Install the EVAP solenoid and ignition assembly.

    e. Connect the spark plug wires to the wire retainers on the plenum and the spark plugs.

13. Refill the cooling system.

14. Connect the negative battery cable.

15. Start the vehicle and verify no leaks.

Intake Manifold

REMOVAL & INSTALLATION

Starting with the 1996 Model Year, these vehicles were filled at the factory with a new type of antifreeze/coolant called GM Goodwrench DEX-COOL®. When adding coolant to vehicles, it is important that you use GM Goodwrench DEX-COOL (orange-colored, silicate-free) coolant. **Propylene glycol is not recommended for use in GM vehicles**. A 50/50 mixture of DEX-COOL and clean water will provide all the recommended protection. **DO NOT mix DEX-COOL with any other type of antifreeze.**

2.4L Engine

1. Before servicing the vehicle, refer to the precautions in the beginning of this section.

2. Relieve the fuel system pressure. Disconnect the negative battery cable.

3. Drain the cooling system to a level below the intake manifold. Disconnect the vacuum hose from the Manifold Absolute Pressure (MAP) sensor.

4. Detach the following electrical connectors from the MAP sensor, Intake Air Temperature (IAT) sensor, EVAP canister purge solenoid and fuel injectors.

5. Disconnect the vacuum hoses from the intake manifold, fuel pressure regulator and EVAP canister purge solenoid to the canister.

6. Remove the air cleaner duct. Remove the vent tube-to-air cleaner duct. Remove the control cable mounting bracket from the intake manifold.

7. Disconnect the power brake vacuum line from the intake manifold and remove the vacuum line mounting bracket at the power steering pump.

8. Disconnect the coolant lines from the throttle body. Remove the crankcase air/oil separator mounting bolts from the intake manifold.

9. Disconnect the hoses from the separator and the separator. Remove the oil fill tube.

10. Remove the intake manifold support brace, the intake manifold nuts/bolts and discard the old gasket.

To install:

11. Clean all the gasket surfaces completely. Install the intake manifold gasket and intake manifold.

12. Tighten the intake manifold fasteners in sequence, to 18 ft. lbs. (25 Nm).

13. Install the intake manifold brace and tighten the mounting bolts to 19 ft. lbs. (26

400 INTAKE MANIFOLD BRACE
401 BOLTS, 26 N•m (19 LB. FT.)
A FINGER START ALL BOLTS
B PUSH BRACE AGAINST MANIFOLD WITH FINGERS
C TIGHTEN BOLTS "A" TO SPECIFICATION
D TIGHTEN BOLTS "B" TO SPECIFICATION

7922Z309

Exploded view of the intake manifold brace mounting—2.4L engine

Nm). The brace-to-block bolts must be tightened first, then the brace-to-manifold bolt.

14. Complete the installation by reversing the removal procedures.

15. Lubricate a new oil fill tube O-ring seal with engine oil and install the tube between No. 1 and 2 intake tubes. Rotate as necessary to gain clearance for the oil/air separator nipple on the fill tube.

16. Refill the cooling system. Connect the negative battery cable.

3.1L and 3.4L Engines

These vehicles use a two-piece intake manifold. Note that these pieces are cast aluminum. Use care when working with light alloy components.

1. Before servicing the vehicle, refer to the precautions in the beginning of this section.

2. Disconnect the negative battery cable. Relieve the fuel system pressure.

3. Remove the top half of the air cleaner assembly and throttle body duct. Drain and recover the cooling system.

4. Remove the EGR pipe from exhaust manifold. Remove the serpentine belt.

5. Remove the brake vacuum pipe at the intake plenum. Disconnect the control cables from the throttle body and intake plenum mounting bracket.

6. Remove the power steering lines at the alternator bracket. Remove the alternator.

7. Disconnect the spark plug wires from the spark plugs and wire retainers on the intake plenum.

8. Remove the Ignition assembly and the EVAP canister purge solenoid together.

9. Detach the upper engine wiring harness connectors from the Throttle Position (TP) sensor (TPS), Idle Air Control (IAC), fuel Injectors, Engine Coolant Temperature (ECT) sensor, Manifold Absolute Pressure

TIGHTENING SEQUENCE

99 STUD – 11 N·m (96 LBS. IN.)
100 INTAKE MANIFOLD GASKET
103 INTAKE MANIFOLD
104 BOLT – 26 N·m (19 LBS. FT.)
105 NUT – 26 N·m (19 LBS. FT.)

7922Z308

Exploded view and bolt tightening sequence for the intake manifold—2.4L engine

Refer to Section 1 for engine rebuilding specifications

A	APPLY SEALANT	**144**	MANIFOLD, LOWER INTAKE
121	HEAD ASSEMBLY, CYLINDER	**181**	GASKET, UPPER INTAKE MANIFOLD
143	GASKET, LOWER INTAKE MANIFOLD	**182**	MANIFOLD, UPPER INTAKE
144	BOLT, LOWER INTAKE	**183**	STUD, UPPER INTAKE MANIFOLD
145	BOLT, LOWER INTAKE MANIFOLD	**184**	BOLT, UPPER INTAKE MANIFOLD
146	BOLT, LOWER INTAKE MANIFOLD		

7922Z310

Exploded view of the upper and lower intake—3.1L and 3.4L engines

(MAP) sensor and Camshaft Position (CMP) sensor.

10. Disconnect the vacuum lines from the vacuum modulator, fuel pressure regulator and PCV valve.

11. Remove the MAP sensor from upper intake manifold. Remove the upper intake plenum mounting bolts and the plenum.

12. Disconnect the fuel lines from the fuel rail and fuel line bracket. Install engine support fixture special tool J-28467-A or an equivalent.

13. Remove the right side engine mount. Remove the power steering mounting bolts and support the pump aside without disconnecting the power steering lines.

14. Disconnect the coolant inlet pipe from coolant outlet housing. Remove the coolant bypass hose from the water pump and the cylinder head.

15. Disconnect the upper radiator hose at thermostat housing.

7922Z311

Lower intake manifold tightening sequence—3.1L and 3.4L engines

16. Remove the thermostat housing. Remove both rocker arm covers.

17. Remove the lower intake manifold bolts. Be sure the washers on the four center bolts are installed in their original locations.

➡ **When removing the valvetrain components they should be kept in order for installation the original locations.**

18. Remove the rocker arm nuts, rocker arms and pushrods. Remove the intake manifold from the engine.

To install:

19. Clean gasket material from all mating surfaces. Remove all excess RTV sealant from front and rear ridges of cylinder block.

20. Place a 3mm bead of RTV, on each ridge, where the front and rear of the intake manifold contact the block.

21. Using a new gasket, install the intake manifold to the engine.

22. Install the pushrods, rocker arms and mounting nuts. Be sure the pushrods are properly seated in the valve lifters and rocker arms.

23. Install the rocker arm nuts and tighten the rocker arm nuts to 18 ft. lbs. (24 Nm).

✳✳ WARNING

In order to prevent oil leaks, tighten the vertical bolts before the diagonal bolts.

24. Install the lower intake manifold attaching bolts. Apply sealant PN 12345739 or equivalent to the threads of bolts, and tighten bolts to 115 inch lbs. (13 Nm).

25. Complete the installation by reversing the removal procedures.

26. Install the upper intake manifold and tighten the mounting bolts to 18 ft. lbs. (25 Nm).

27. Fill the cooling system. An engine oil and filter change is recommended.

28. Connect the negative battery cable. Start the vehicle and verify no leaks.

Exhaust Manifold

REMOVAL & INSTALLATION

2.4L Engine

➡ **There are two different exhaust manifolds used on the Quad 4 engine. While the manifolds vary greatly in appearance, the removal and installation procedures are the same. The cast iron manifold is a single outlet design and the sheet metal manifold is a tubular construction with a dual outlet flange.**

1. Before servicing the vehicle, refer to the precautions in the beginning of this section.

2. Disconnect the negative battery cable. Disconnect the Oxygen (O₂S) sensor. Raise and safely support the vehicle.

3. Remove the bolt that attaches the exhaust manifold brace to the manifold.

4. Remove the manifold-to-exhaust pipe spring loaded bolts using a 13mm box wrench. The nuts should be loosened alternately and evenly to prevent the pipe from binding the nuts.

5. Pull down and back on the exhaust pipe to disengage it from the exhaust manifold bolts.

➡ **Do not bend the exhaust flex coupler more than 3 degrees in any direction. Movement of more than 3 degrees will damage the flex coupler.**

6. Lower the vehicle. Remove the exhaust manifold mounting nuts and manifold.

To install:

7. Clean all the gasket surfaces completely. Install the exhaust manifold and new gaskets.

8. Install the exhaust manifold-to-cylinder head retaining nuts and tighten in sequence to 110 inch lbs. (13 Nm).

9. Raise and safely support the vehicle. Install the heat shields. Install exhaust manifold brace to the manifold bolt.

10. Install the manifold-to-exhaust pipe nuts and tighten evenly to 26 ft. lbs. (35 Nm).

11. Lower the vehicle. Connect the O₂S sensor.

12. Connect the negative battery cable. Start the vehicle and verify no exhaust leaks.

3.1L and 3.4L Engines

1. Before servicing the vehicle, refer to the precautions in the beginning of this section.

2. Disconnect the negative battery cable. Remove the top half of the air cleaner assembly and throttle cable duct.

3. On the left side (front), perform the following procedures:

TIGHTENING SEQUENCE

1. **Stud - 100 in. lbs. (12Nm)**
2. **Intake manifold gasket**
3. **Intake manifold**
4. **Bolt - 17 ft. lbs. (24 Nm)**
5. **Nut - 17 ft. lbs. (24 Nm)**

79227313

Exploded view of the exhaust manifold assembly mounting—2.4L engine

For engine torque specifications, refer to Section 1 of this manual

a. Partially drain the cooling system.

b. Remove the radiator hose from the thermostat housing.

c. Remove the coolant bypass hose at the coolant pump and from the exhaust manifold.

4. Remove the exhaust crossover heat shield. Remove the exhaust crossover pipe from the manifold.

5. On the right side (rear), perform the following procedures:

a. Remove the Heated Oxygen (HO2S) sensor.

b. Remove the EGR pipe from the exhaust manifold.

c. Raise and safely support the vehicle.

d. Remove the transaxle oil fill tube and lever indicator assembly.

e. Disconnect the front exhaust pipe from the exhaust manifold.

f. Disconnect the exhaust pipe from the converter flange and support the converter.

g. Remove the converter heat shield from the body.

6. Tag and disconnect the secondary ignition wires from the spark plugs.

7. Remove the exhaust manifold heat shield. Remove the exhaust manifold retaining nuts and manifold.

To install:

8. Clean mating surfaces at the cylinder head and manifold.

9. Install the exhaust manifold gasket and the exhaust manifold. Tighten the manifold mounting nuts to 12 ft. lbs. (16 Nm).

10. Install the exhaust manifold heat shield. Install the exhaust crossover pipe to the manifold.

11. On the right side (rear), install the converter heat shield to the body.

12. Install the exhaust crossover pipe heat shield.

13. On the left side (front), perform the following procedures:

a. Connect the secondary ignition wires to the appropriate spark plug.

b. Connect the coolant bypass pipe to the coolant pump and exhaust manifold.

c. Install the radiator hose to the coolant outlet housing.

14. On the right side (rear), perform the following procedures:

a. Connect the exhaust pipe to the exhaust manifold.

b. Install the transaxle oil level indicator and fill tube assembly.

c. Safely lower the vehicle.

d. Connect the heated oxygen sensor.

e. Connect the EGR pipe to exhaust manifold.

15. Install the top half of the air cleaner and the throttle body duct. Connect the negative battery cable.

Camshaft and Valve Lifters

REMOVAL & INSTALLATION

2.4L Engine

➡Anytime the camshaft housing-to-cylinder head bolts are loosened or removed, the camshaft housing-to-cylinder head gasket must be replaced.

1. Before servicing the vehicle, refer to the precautions in the beginning of this section.

2. Disconnect the negative battery cable.

3. Detach the 11-pin connector from the ignition assembly cover.

4. Remove the four ignition assembly cover-to-camshaft housing bolts and remove assembly by pulling straight up.

111 SCREW, LH HEAT SHIELD
112 SHIELD, LH HEAT
113 NUT, LH EXHAUST MANIFOLD
114 STUD, LH EXHAUST MANIFOLD
115 MANIFOLD, LH EXHAUST
117 GASKET, LH EXHAUST MANIFOLD
121 HEAD ASSEMBLY, CYLINDER
153 SHIELD, RH LOWER HEAT
154 SCREW, RH LOWER HEAT SHIELD
155 STUD, RH EXHAUST MANIFOLD
156 NUT, RH EXHAUST MANIFOLD
157 MANIFOLD, RH EXHAUST
158 SHIELD, RH UPPER HEAT
159 SCREW, RH UPPER HEAT SHIELD
160 GASKET, RH EXHAUST MANIFOLD

7922Z314

Exploded view of the exhaust manifold mounting—3.1L and 3.4L engines

Use a spark plug boot wire remover to remove connector assemblies.

5. On the intake camshaft side, if equipped, perform the following procedures:

a. Remove the throttle lever actuator power steering pressure switch connector.

b. Loosen the power steering pump adjusting stud bolt. Loosen the power steering pump pivot bolts and remove the drive belt.

c. Remove the two power steering pump bracket-to-transaxle bolts.

d. Remove the front power steering pump bracket-to-engine block bolt.

e. Remove the power steering pump assembly from the engine and position it aside. DO NOT disconnect the power steering lines from the pump.

6. On the intake camshaft side, if equipped, perform the following procedures:

a. Remove the oil/air separator bolts and hoses. Leave the hoses attached to the separator but disconnect from the oil fill tube, timing chain housing and intake manifold.

b. Disconnect the vacuum line from fuel pressure regulator and disconnect the fuel injector wiring harness.

c. Remove the two bolts securing the fuel line clamps to the intake camshaft housing.

d. Remove fuel rail-to-camshaft housing mounting bolts.

e. Remove the fuel rail from the cylinder head leaving the fuel lines attached and position the fuel rail aside.

7. Remove the timing chain and camshaft sprockets.

8. Remove the timing chain housing bolts but do not remove from the engine.

9. Remove camshaft housing cover-to-camshaft housing attaching bolts.

10. Remove the camshaft housing-to-cylinder head attaching bolts. Use the reverse of the tightening sequence when loosening the camshaft housing-to-cylinder head attaching bolts. Leave two bolts loosely in place to hold the camshaft housing while separating the camshaft cover from housing.

11. Push the cover off the housing by threading four of the housing-to-cylinder head bolts into the tapped holes in the cam housing cover. Tighten the bolts in evenly so the cover does not bind on the dowel pins.

12. Remove the two loosely installed camshaft housing-to-cylinder head bolts and remove the cover. Discard the gaskets.

13. Note the position of the chain sprocket dowel pin for reassembly. Remove the camshaft carefully; do not damage the camshaft oil seal.

14. Remove camshaft oil seal from camshaft and discard seal. This seal must be replaced any time the housing and cover are separated.

➡ **The valve lifters must be kept in order so that they can be installed in the same locations they were removed from.**

15. Remove the valve lifters from the camshaft housing.

16. Remove the camshaft carrier from the cylinder head and remove the gasket.

To install:

17. Clean all the gasket surfaces completely.

18. Install a new gasket on the cylinder head and install the camshaft housing over the dowel pins. Install one bolt loosely to hold the housing in place.

➡ **If the camshaft was replaced the valve lifters must also be replaced.**

19. Install the lifters into their original bores.

20. Lubricate the camshaft lobes, journals and lifters with camshaft and lifter prelube. The camshaft lobes and journals must be adequately lubricated or engine damage could occur upon start up.

21. Install the camshaft in the same position it was in prior to removal. The timing chain sprocket dowel pin should be straight up and align with the center line of the lifter bores.

22. Install new camshaft housing-to-camshaft housing cover seals into the cover.

➡ **The seals for the intake and exhaust covers are different and the correct seals must be used.**

23. Remove the bolt holding the housing in place.

24. Apply thread locking compound to the camshaft housing and cover attaching bolt threads.

25. Install the camshaft housing cover.

26. Install all the mounting bolts finger-tight. With all the bolts in place tighten the bolts in sequence to 11 ft. lbs. (15 Nm) plus 75 degrees additional rotation (long bolts) and 16 ft. lbs. (21 Nm) plus 25 degrees additional rotation (short bolts).

27. Install the timing chain housing mounting bolts.

28. Install the timing chain and sprockets.

29. Install new fuel injector O-ring seals lubricated with oil and install the fuel rail and tighten the mounting bolts to 19 ft. lbs. (26 Nm).

30. On the intake camshaft side, if equipped, perform the following procedures:

a. Install the fuel line clamp mounting bolts on top of the intake camshaft housing.

b. Connect the vacuum line to the fuel pressure regulator.

c. Attach the fuel injector harness connector.

d. Install the oil/air separator assembly and connect the hoses to the oil fill tube, timing chain housing and intake manifold.

31. Lubricate the inner sealing surface of the intake camshaft seal with oil and install the seal to the housing using J-36009, or an equivalent seal installer.

32. On the intake camshaft side, if equipped, perform the following procedures:

a. Install the power steering pump pulley onto the intake camshaft using J-36015, or an equivalent pulley installer.

b. Install the power steering pump and install the drive belt.

c. Attach the throttle lever actuator power steering pressure switch connector.

33. On the exhaust camshaft side, perform the following procedures:

a. Install the transaxle fill tube.

b. Connect the oil pressure switch.

34. Install the ignition assembly on the

Camshaft housing bolt tightening sequence—2.4L engine

For complete mechanical specifications, refer to Section 1 of this manual

camshaft housing and tighten the mounting bolts to 13 ft. lbs. (18 Nm).

35. Attach the 11-pin connector to ignition assembly.

36. Connect the negative battery cable.

37. Start the vehicle and verify proper operation and no leaks.

3.1L and 3.4L Engines

1. Before servicing the vehicle, refer to the precautions in the beginning of this section.

2. Relieve the fuel system pressure. Disconnect the negative battery cable. Remove the engine assembly.

❄❄ WARNING

When removing valvetrain components they must be marked for installation in the same location they are removed from. When the camshaft is being replaced, the valve lifters must also be replaced.

3. Remove the rocker arm covers and the intake manifold.

4. Remove the rocker arm retaining nuts, rocker arm balls, rocker arms and pushrods.

5. Remove the guide bolts from the lifter guide and remove the guide.

6. Remove the valve lifter(s) from the lifter bores.

7. Remove the crankshaft balancer and front cover. Remove the timing chain and sprockets.

8. Remove the oil pump driven gear bolt and gear. Remove the bolts and camshaft thrust plate.

9. Carefully remove the camshaft. Avoid damaging the camshaft bearing surfaces.

To install:

10. Coat the camshaft with lubricant 1052365 or equivalent, and install the camshaft.

11. Install the camshaft thrust plate and tighten bolts to 89 inch lbs. (10 Nm).

12. Install the oil pump driven gear and tighten bolt to 27 ft. lbs. (36 Nm).

13. Install the timing chain and sprocket.

14. Install the camshaft thrust button and front cover. Install the crankshaft balancer.

15. Lubricate the bearing surfaces with Molykote® or equivalent.

➡**Installation of a new camshaft or a wear pattern on the old valve lifter will require the replacement of the camshaft and lifters together. If camshaft replacement is not necessary, be sure to install the used valve lifters in their original position upon reinstallation.**

16. Install the lifters in their original locations.

17. Install the lifter guide and lifter guide bolts and tighten the guide bolts to 89 inch lbs. (10 Nm).

18. Install the pushrods, rocker arms, rocker balls and rocker arm nuts.

19. Tighten the rocker arm nuts to 89 inch lbs. (10 Nm) plus an additional 30 degrees.

20. Install the intake manifold and rocker arm covers.

21. Install the engine assembly. Connect the negative battery cable.

22. Adjust the valves, as required. Start the engine and verify no oil leaks.

Valve Lash

ADJUSTMENT

2.4L Engine

The 2.4L engines are equipped with hydraulic valve lifters that do not require periodic valve lash adjustment. Adjustment to zero lash is maintained automatically by hydraulic pressure in the lifters.

3.1L and 3.4L Engines

➡**These engines come from the factory with non-adjustable valve lash, BUT if the valves and the valve seats are reconditioned, adjustable rocker arm studs must be installed. The adjustment procedure is ONLY for adjustable rocker arm studs.**

The engines are originally equipped with hydraulic valve lifters. Hydraulic valve lifters are not adjustable. The replacement rocker arm stud is adjustable and the adjustment can be performed as listed below. If valve system noise is present, check the tightness on the rocker arm nuts. The correct torque is 14–20 ft. lbs. (19–27 Nm). If noise is still present, check the condition of the camshaft, lifters, rocker arms, pushrods and valves.

1. Install the rocker arms, balls and nuts. Tighten the rocker arm nuts until all of the lash (free-play) is eliminated.

2. Adjust the valves when the lifter is on the base circle of a camshaft lobe as follows:

a. Place the engine in the No. 1 firing position. This can be determined by placing a finger on the No. 1 rocker arm as the engine alignment mark on the front face of the of the torsional dampener pulley aligns with the arrow on the front cover. If the valves don't move freely, the engine is in the No. 1 firing

position. If the valves move freely, the engine is in the No. 4 firing position and the engine should be rotated one full rotation to reach the No. 1 position.

b. With the engine in the No. 1 firing order, adjust the following valves:

- Exhaust—1, 2, 3
- Intake—1, 5, 6

c. Loosen the adjusting nut several turns backwards, then tighten until all lash (free-play) is removed. After all of the valve lash is removed turn the nut an additional 1 ½ turns, this will center the lifter plunger.

d. Turn the engine one complete revolution until the timing tab and the alignment mark are again aligned, this will place the engine in the No. 4 firing position.

e. With the engine in the No. 4 firing order, adjust the following valves:

- Exhaust—4, 5, 6
- Intake—2, 3, 4

Oil Pan

REMOVAL & INSTALLATION

2.4L Engine

1. Before servicing the vehicle, refer to the precautions in the beginning of this section.

2. Disconnect the negative battery cable. Raise and safely support the vehicle.

3. Properly drain the engine oil and cooling system. Remove the flywheel inspection cover.

4. Remove the right front wheel and tire assembly. Remove the right inner fender splash shield.

5. Remove the serpentine belt. Disconnect the engine mount strut from the engine mount strut bracket.

6. Remove the A/C compressor from the mounting bracket and support it aside. DO NOT disconnect the refrigerant lines.

7. Unfasten the engine mount strut bracket bolts, then remove the bracket. Remove the radiator outlet pipe bolts.

8. Disconnect the radiator and A/C outlet pipes from the suspension supports. Remove the exhaust manifold brace.

9. Remove the oil pan-to-flywheel cover bolt and nut and remove the flywheel cover stud and spacer.

10. Disconnect the radiator outlet pipe from the lower radiator hose and oil pan.

11. If equipped, detach the oil level sensor wire. Unfasten the oil pan bolts, then remove the oil pan.

◀FRT

38 OIL PAN
39A BOLT, OIL PAN (M8 X 1.25 X 80)
    24 N•m (18 LB. FT.)
39B BOLT, OIL PAN (M8 X 1.25 X 22)
    24 N•m (18 LB. FT.)
39C BOLT, OIL PAN (M6 X 1.00 X 25)
    12 N•m (106 LB. IN.)
39D BOLT, STUD END OIL PAN
    26 N•m (19 LB. FT.)

7922Z316

Oil pan mounting bolt locations—2.4L engine

10 PAN, OIL
11 BOLT, OIL PAN SIDE
12 BOLT, OIL PAN RETAINING
52 BLOCK, ENGINE

7922Z317

Exploded view of the oil pan mounting—
3.1L engine

To install:

12. Install a new gasket, the oil pan and bolts. Tighten the chain housing and carrier seal bolts to 106 inch lbs. (12 Nm). Tighten the oil pan-to-block bolts to 17 ft. lbs. (23 Nm).

13. Install the flywheel cover spacer, stud nut and bolt. Tighten the nut to 41 ft. lbs. (56 Nm), the stud to 115 inch lbs. (13 Nm) and the bolt to 41 ft. lbs. (56 Nm).

14. Install the oil pan-to-transaxle nut and tighten to 41 ft. lbs. (56 Nm).

15. Complete the installation by reversing the removal procedures.

16. Install the engine mount strut bracket and tighten bolts to 49 ft. lbs. (66 Nm).

17. Fill the crankcase with oil. A filter change is recommended.

18. Fill the cooling system. Connect the negative battery cable, then start the engine and check for leaks.

3.1L and 3.4L Engine

1. Before servicing the vehicle, refer to the precautions in the beginning of this section.

2. Disconnect the negative battery cable. Remove the serpentine belt.

3. If equipped, remove the upper A/C compressor bolts. Raise and safely support the vehicle.

4. Properly drain the engine oil. Remove the right front wheel and tire assembly.

5. Remove the engine mount strut from the suspension support.

6. Remove the cotter pin and castle nut from the lower ball joint, then separate the ball joint from the steering knuckle.

7. Remove the right side sway bar link. Detach the ABS sensor from the right sub-frame.

8. Remove the right side subframe bolts and the right side subframe and control arm as an assembly.

9. If equipped, remove the lower A/C compressor bolts and position the compressor aside. DO NOT disconnect the refrigerant lines or allow the compressor to hang unsupported.

10. Remove the engine mount strut bracket from the engine. Remove the oil filter, the starter and the flywheel cover.

11. Remove the oil pan flange bolts, the oil pan side bolts and the oil pan.

To install:

12. Clean the gasket mating surfaces. Install a new gasket on the oil pan. Apply silicone sealer to the portion of the pan that contacts the rear of the block.

13. Position the oil pan, then install the mounting bolts finger-tight.

14. With all the bolts in place, tighten the oil pan flange bolts to 18 ft. lbs. (25 Nm) and the oil pan side bolts to 34 ft. lbs. (50 Nm).

15. Complete the installation by reversing the removal procedures.

16. Tighten the following item to:
   a. Engine-to-transaxle brace, bolts to 68 ft. lbs. (93 Nm)
   b. Engine mount strut bracket-to-engine bolts to 85 ft. lbs. (115 Nm)
   c. Right side subframe/control arm assembly bolts to 89 ft. lbs. (120 Nm)
   d. Right side sway bar line bolt to 22 ft. lbs. (30 Nm)
   e. Ball joint-to-steering knuckle nut to 48 ft. lbs. (60 Nm). Install a new cotter pin.
   f. Engine mount strut bracket bolt-to-frame bolt to 89 ft. lbs. (120 Nm)

17. Fill the crankcase to the correct level. A filter change is recommended. Connect the negative battery cable, then start the engine and check for leaks.

➡**Whenever the vehicle subframe is removed or lowered, the wheel alignment should be checked.**

18. Check the front end alignment and adjust as required.

Please refer to Section 9 for electric cooling fan wiring schematics

Oil Pump

REMOVAL & INSTALLATION

2.4L Engine

➡️**Please note that the transaxle must be removed from the vehicle to service the oil pump.**

1. Before servicing the vehicle, refer to the precautions in the beginning of this section.

2. Disconnect the negative battery cable. Install engine support fixture J-28467-A or equivalent.

3. Properly drain the engine oil, then remove the oil pan. Remove the transaxle and the flywheel.

4. Remove the balance shaft chain cover and chain guide. Remove the oil pump bolts and the oil pump cover.

5. Pull the housing to disconnect the pump gear from the balance shaft. Remove the housing assembly from the balance shaft assembly.

To install:

6. Clean all of the parts in suitable cleaning solvent. Remove all varnish sludge and dirt.

7. Lubricate the gears with clean engine oil. Assemble the geroter gear into the housing.

➡️**Fill oil pump cavities with petroleum jelly prior to installation. This seals the pump and acts like a "prime" so the pump will draw oil as soon as the engine begins to turn. This will ensure that there is oil pressure immediately on start-up and will prevent engine damage.**

8. Install the pump housing to the balance shaft assembly and the pump cover to the oil pump housing.

9. Install the oil pump-to-block bolts and tighten to 40 ft. lbs. (54 Nm).

10. Install the balance shaft chain guide and chain. Adjust the chain tension inserting a 0.40 in. (1mm) brass feeler, between the chain guide and the chain.

➡️**A brass feeler gauge must be used to ensure that correct measurements are obtained. If a steel gauge is used, it will not bend to conform to the guide and will allow for incorrect measurements.**

11. Press the guide against the chain using about 3 lbs. of force. Tighten the

chain tensioner fastener to 115 inch lbs. (13 Nm).

12. Install the balance shaft chain cover and tighten the nut and bolt to 115 inch lbs. (13 Nm).

13. Install the flywheel and the transaxle. Install the oil pan, then carefully lower the vehicle.

14. Fill the crankcase with clean engine oil. A filter change is recommended.

15. Remove the engine support fixture. Connect the negative battery cable, then start the engine and verify oil pressure and no leaks.

3.1L and 3.4L Engines

1. Before servicing the vehicle, refer to the precautions in the beginning of this section.

2. Disconnect the negative battery cable.

3. Raise and safely support the vehicle.

4. Drain the engine oil into a suitable container. Remove the oil pan.

5. Remove the crankshaft oil deflector bolts and deflector.

6. Remove the oil pump bolts, the oil pump and pump driveshaft.

143 PIN, RELIEF VALVE
144 COVER, OIL PUMP
145 GEROTOR
146 BODY, OIL PUMP
149 GUIDE, RELIEF VALVE SPRING
150 SPRING, RELIEF VALVE
151 VALVE, RELIEF VALVE

7922Z318

Exploded view of the oil pump components—2.4L engine

1   34 N·m (25 LBS. FT.)
2   OIL PUMP DRIVE
3   OIL PUMP
4   41 N·m (30 LBS. FT.)

79222319

Exploded view of the oil pump mounting—3.1L and 3.4L engines

To install:

7. Install the oil pump and pump driveshaft. Be sure the drive shaft engages the oil pump drive. Tighten the oil pump mounting bolts to 30 ft. lbs. (41 Nm).

8. Install the crankshaft oil deflector and tighten the nuts to 18 ft. lbs. (25 Nm).

9. Install the oil pan, then carefully lower the vehicle.

10. Fill the crankcase to the correct level with oil. A filter change is recommended.

11. Connect the negative battery cable, then start the engine, check the oil pressure and check for leaks.

Rear Main Seal

REMOVAL & INSTALLATION

2.4L Engine

1. Before servicing the vehicle, refer to the precautions in the beginning of this section.

2. Disconnect the negative battery cable.

3. Remove the transaxle assembly.

4. If equipped with a manual transaxle, remove the pressure plate and clutch disc.

5. Unfasten the flywheel-to-crankshaft bolts, then remove the flywheel.

6. Disconnect the oil pan-to-seal housing bolts

7. Unfasten the seal housing-to-block bolts, then remove the seal housing and gasket.

8. To support the seal housing for seal removal, place two blocks of wood or metal of equal thickness on a flat surface, position the seal housing and blocks so the transaxle side of the seal housing is supported across the dowel pin and center bolt holes on both sides of the seal opening.

➡**The seal housing could be damaged if not properly supported during seal removal.**

9. Drive the seal evenly out the transaxle side of the seal housing using a small prytool in the relief grooves on the crankshaft side of the seal housing. Discard the seal.

✳✳ WARNING

Be careful not to damage the seal housing sealing surface. If damaged, it may result in an oil leak.

To install:

10. Press a new seal into the housing using tool J 36005 or equivalent seal installation tool.

11. Inspect the oil pan gasket inner silicone bead for damage and repair using a silicone sealant, if necessary.

12. Position a new seal housing-to-block gasket over the alignment. The gasket is reversible.

13. Lubricate the lip of the seal with clean engine oil.

14. Install the housing assembly, then tighten the housing-to-block bolts to 106 inch lbs. (12 Nm).

15. Install the oil pan-to-seal housing bolts, then tighten to 106 inch lbs. (12 Nm).

16. Install the flywheel as outlined later in this section.

17. For vehicles equipped with a manual transaxle, install the clutch, pressure plate and clutch cover assembly.

18. Install the transaxle assembly.

19. Connect the negative battery cable, then start the engine and check for leaks.

3.1L and 3.4L Engines

1. Support the engine with J-28467 engine support or equivalent.

2. Remove the transaxle.

3. Remove the flywheel.

4. Insert a suitable prytool in through the dust lip and pry out the seal by moving the tool around the seal until it is removed.

✳✳ WARNING

Use care not to damage the crankshaft seal surface with a prytool.

To install:

5. Before installing, lubricate the seal bore to seal surface with engine oil.

6. Install the new seal using tool J-34686.

7. Slide the new seal over the mandrel until the dust lip bottoms squarely against the tool collar.

8. Align the dowel pin of the tool with the dowel pin hole in the crankshaft and attach the tool to the crankshaft. Tighten the attaching screws to 2–5 ft. lbs. (2.7–6.8 Nm).

9. Tighten the T-handle of the tool to push the seal into the bore. Continue until the tool collar is flush against the block.

10. Loosen the T-handle completely. Remove the attaching screws and the tool.

➡**Check to see that the seal is squarely seated in the bore.**

11. Install the flywheel and transaxle. Tighten the flexplate bolts to 52 ft. lbs. (71 Nm).

12. Start the engine and check for leaks.

Timing Chain, Sprockets, Front Cover and Seal

REMOVAL & INSTALLATION

2.4L Engine

➡ It is recommended that the entire procedure be reviewed before attempting to service the timing chain.

1. Before servicing the vehicle, refer to the precautions in the beginning of this section.

2. Disconnect the negative battery cable. Drain the cooling system into a suitable container. Remove the coolant surge tank.

3. Remove the serpentine drive belt using a 13mm wrench that is at least 24 in. (61cm) long.

4. Disconnect and remove the alternator from the mounting bracket.

5. Install a suitable engine support, J-28467-A or the equivalent.

6. Remove the upper cover fasteners. Disconnect the upper cover vent hose.

7. Remove the right engine mount and bracket. Raise and safely support the vehicle.

8. Remove the right front tire and wheel assembly. Remove the right lower splash shield from the right wheel housing.

9. Remove the crankshaft balancer assembly using the following procedure:

a. Remove the torsional damper mounting bolt and washer while holding the crankshaft in place using J-38122, or the equivalent.

b. Remove the balancer using a suitable puller, J-24420-B or the equivalent.

10. Remove the lower cover fasteners. Lower the vehicle.

11. Remove the front cover and gaskets. Remove the crankshaft oil slinger.

12. Using a suitable seal driver, tap the oil seal out of the front cover.

13. Rotate the crankshaft clockwise, as viewed from front of engine (normal rotation) until the camshaft sprocket's timing dowel pin holes align with the holes in the timing chain housing. The mark on the crankshaft sprocket should align with the mark on the cylinder block. The crankshaft sprocket keyway should point upwards and align with the center line of the cylinder bores. This is the normal timed position.

14. Remove the timing chain guides. Raise and safely support the vehicle.

15. Gently pry off timing chain tensioner spring retainer and remove spring.

➡ Two styles of tensioners are used. Early production engines will have a spring post and late production ones will not. Both styles are identical in operation and are interchangeable.

16. Remove the timing chain tensioner shoe retainer.

17. Be sure all the slack in the timing chain is above the tensioner assembly; remove the chain tensioner shoe. The timing chain must be disengaged from the wear grooves in the tensioner shoe in order to remove the shoe. Slide a prybar under the timing chain while pulling shoe outward.

18. If difficulty is encountered removing chain tensioner shoe, proceed as follows:

a. Lower the vehicle.

b. Hold the intake camshaft sprocket with a holding tool and remove the sprocket bolt and washer.

c. Remove the washer from the bolt and thread the bolt back into the camshaft by hand, the bolt provides a surface to push against.

d. Remove intake camshaft sprocket using a 3-jaw puller in the three relief holes in the sprocket. Do not attempt to pry the sprocket off the camshaft or damage to the sprocket or chain housing could occur.

19. Remove the tensioner assembly attaching bolts and the tensioner.

❊❊ CAUTION

The tensioner piston is spring loaded and could fly out causing personal injury.

20. Remove the chain housing-to-block stud, which is actually the timing chain tensioner shoe pivot.

21. Remove the timing chain.

To install:

22. Tighten intake camshaft sprocket attaching bolt and washer, while holding the sprocket with tool J36013, if removed.

23. Install the special tool through holes in camshaft sprockets into holes in timing chain housing. This positions the camshafts for correct timing.

24. If the camshafts are out of position and must be rotated more than ⅛ turn in order to install the alignment dowel pins:

a. The crankshaft must be rotated 90 degrees clockwise off Top Dead Center (TDC) in order to give the valves adequate clearance to open.

b. Once the camshafts are in position and the dowels installed, rotate the crank-

shaft counterclockwise back to TDC. Do not rotate the crankshaft clockwise to TDC or valve and piston damage could occur.

25. Install the timing chain over the exhaust camshaft sprocket, around the idler sprocket and around the crankshaft sprocket.

26. Remove the alignment dowel pin from the intake camshaft. Using a dowel pin remover tool, rotate the intake camshaft sprocket counterclockwise enough to slide the timing chain over the intake camshaft sprocket. Release the camshaft sprocket wrench. The length of chain between the two camshaft sprockets will tighten. If properly timed, the intake camshaft alignment dowel pin should slide in easily. If the dowel pin does not fully index, the camshafts are not timed correctly and the procedure must be repeated.

27. Leave the alignment dowel pins installed.

28. With slack removed from chain between intake camshaft sprocket and crankshaft sprocket, the timing marks on the crankshaft and the cylinder block should be aligned. If marks are not aligned, move the chain one tooth forward or rearward, remove slack and recheck marks.

29. Tighten the chain housing to block stud. The stud is installed under the timing chain. Tighten to 19 ft. lbs. (26 Nm).

30. Reload timing chain tensioner assembly to its 0 position as follows:

a. Assemble restraint cylinder, spring and nylon plug into plunger. Index the slot in the restraint cylinder with the peg in the plunger. While rotating the restraint cylinder clockwise, push the restraint cylinder into the plunger until it bottoms. Keep rotating the restraint cylinder clockwise but allow the spring to push it out of the plunger. The pin in the plunger will lock the restraint in the loaded position.

b. Install tool J36589 or equivalent, onto plunger assembly.

c. Install plunger assembly into tensioner body with the long end toward the crankshaft when installed.

31. Install the tensioner assembly to the chain housing. Recheck plunger assembly installation. It is correctly installed when the long end is toward the crankshaft.

32. Install and tighten timing chain tensioner bolts and tighten to 10 ft. lbs. (14 Nm).

33. Install the tensioner shoe and tensioner shoe retainer. Remove special tool J36589 and squeeze plunger assembly into the tensioner body to unload the plunger assembly.

34. Lower vehicle and remove the alignment dowel pins. Rotate crankshaft clockwise two full rotations. Align crankshaft timing mark with mark on cylinder block

and reinstall alignment dowel pins. Alignment dowel pins will slide in easily if engine is timed correctly.

✳✳ WARNING

If the engine is not correctly timed, severe engine damage could occur.

35. Install the timing chain guides and crankshaft oil slinger.

36. Using a suitable seal installer, tap the new seal into the front cover and lubricate the lip of the seal.

37. Install the front cover and gaskets on the engine and tighten the mounting nuts and bolts to 106 inch lbs. (12 Nm).

38. Install the torsional damper as follows:

a. Coat the seal contact area on the crankshaft damper with clean engine oil.

b. Line up the damper on the crankshaft so the notch in the damper lines up with the crankshaft key.

c. Tap the balancer into place using a rubber mallet.

d. Install the damper mounting bolt and washer and tighten the bolt to 129 ft. lbs. (175 Nm) plus 90 degrees rotation.

39. Install the right front lower splash shield. Install the tire and wheel assembly and tighten to 100 ft. lbs. (140 Nm).

40. Safely lower the vehicle. Install the right engine mount bracket.

A. Camshaft timing alignment pin locations
B. Crankshaft gear timing marks
1. Shoe asm. timing chain tensioner
2. Timing chain
3. Timing chain tensioner
4. R.H. timing chain guide
5. L.H. timing chain guide
6. Upper timing chain guide
7. Exhaust camshaft sprocket
8. Intake camshaft sprocket

7922Z321

Timing chain and sprocket alignment positions—2.4L DOHC engine

41. Install the right engine mount. Connect the upper cover vent hose.

42. Remove the engine support. Install the alternator and attach the electrical connectors.

43. Install the serpentine belt. Install the coolant surge tank.

44. Refill the cooling system. Connect the negative battery cable and check for leaks.

3.1L and 3.4L Engines

1. Before servicing the vehicle, refer to the precautions in the beginning of this section.

2. Disconnect the negative battery cable. Drain the cooling system into a suitable container.

3. Recover the refrigerant into an approved recovery station.

4. Install an engine support fixture and remove the front engine mount assembly and bracket.

5. Remove the serpentine belt.

6. Remove the air cleaner assembly and the air intake duct.

7. Remove the power steering pump.

8. Loosen the two upper A/C compressor mounting bolts.

9. Remove the generator and mounting bracket.

10. Raise and safely support the vehicle.

11. Remove the right front wheel and splash shield.

12. Remove the flywheel inspection cover so the ring gear can be held while removing the crankshaft balancer bolt.

13. Remove the crankshaft balancer.

14. Remove the drive belt tensioner.

15. Disconnect the right wheel speed sensor harness at the suspension support.

16. Disconnect the ball joint.

17. Remove the stabilizer bar from the control arm and suspension support.

18. Remove the suspension support.

19. Remove the A/C compressor-to-oil pan bolts.

20. Remove the oil filter and adapter.

21. Drain the oil.

22. Remove the starter and the oil pan.

23. Remove the Crankshaft Position (CKP) sensor.

24. Remove the lower front cover bolts and lower the vehicle.

25. Remove the coolant hoses and the remaining front cover bolts.

26. Remove the engine front cover.

27. Using a suitable seal driver, tap the oil seal out of the front cover.

28. Using the flywheel and a flywheel

turning tool, rotate the crankshaft until the timing marks on the camshaft and crankshaft sprockets are in alignment (facing each other).

29. Remove the camshaft sprocket bolt, sprocket and timing chain.

30. Remove the crankshaft sprocket, using a gear puller J-5825-A or equivalent. If necessary, remove the timing chain damper bolts and damper.

To install:

31. If removed, install the timing chain damper and tighten the mounting bolts to 15 ft. lbs. (21 Nm).

32. Install the crankshaft sprocket onto the crankshaft making sure the notch in the sprocket fits over the crankshaft key. Fully seat the sprocket on the crankshaft using J-38612, or an equivalent gear installer.

33. Be sure the timing mark on the crankshaft sprocket is pointing toward the mark on the chain dampener.

34. Install the timing chain over the camshaft sprocket and hold the sprocket in such a way, that the timing mark is pointing down, and the timing chain is hanging down off the sprocket.

35. Loop the timing chain under the crankshaft sprocket and install the camshaft sprocket on the camshaft. The sprocket will only fit on the camshaft if the dowel on the camshaft lines up with the hole in the sprocket.

36. Verify that the marks are aligned (the

9300Z301

Be sure to align the dampener mark (1) with the crankshaft mark (2) and the dampener mark (3) with the camshaft sprocket mark (4)—3.1L and 3.4L engines

Timing belt service is covered in Section 5 of this manual

camshaft sprocket will be at the 6 o'clock position and the crankshaft sprocket will be in the 12 o'clock position).

➡ **The No. 1 piston will be at Top Dead Center (TDC) and the No. 4 piston will also be at TDC but on the compression stroke.**

37. Tighten the camshaft sprocket bolt to 103 ft. lbs. (140 Nm).

38. Lubricate the timing chain components with engine oil. Clean all gasket surfaces completely.

39. Install a new front cover seal on the front cover. Apply a thin bead of sealer around the gasket sealing area of the front cover.

40. Install the front cover and gasket on the engine and install the two upper mounting bolts. Tighten the bolts to 15 ft. lbs. (21 Nm).

41. Install the coolant hoses.

42. Raise and safely support the vehicle.

43. Install the remaining front cover bolts. Tighten the small bolts to 15 ft. lbs. (21 Nm), and the large bolts to 35 ft. lbs. (47 Nm).

44. Install the CKP sensor, oil pan, starter motor, oil filter adapter and filter.

45. Install the A/C compressor-to-oil pan bolts.

46. Assemble the suspension and connect the speed sensor wiring harness.

47. Install the drive belt tensioner and the crankshaft balancer using the proper balancer installer.

✳✳ WARNING

Do not hammer the balancer on the crankshaft.

48. Install the remaining components in the reverse of the removal sequence. Be sure to tighten the 8mm engine mount bolts to 15 ft. lbs. (20 Nm) and the 12mm bolts to 30 ft. lbs. (40 Nm).

49. Refill the fluids.

50. Connect the negative battery cable.

51. Start the engine and check for leaks.

FUEL SYSTEM

Fuel System Service Precautions

Safety is the most important factor when performing not only fuel system maintenance but any type of maintenance. Failure to conduct maintenance and repairs in a safe man-

ner may result in serious personal injury or death. Maintenance and testing of the vehicle's fuel system components can be accomplished safely and effectively by adhering to the following rules and guidelines.

• To avoid the possibility of fire and personal injury, always disconnect the negative battery cable unless the repair or test procedure requires that battery voltage be applied.

• Always relieve the fuel system pressure prior to disconnecting any fuel system component (injector, fuel rail, pressure regulator, etc.), fitting or fuel line connection. Exercise extreme caution whenever relieving fuel system pressure to avoid exposing skin, face and eyes to fuel spray. Please be advised that fuel under pressure may penetrate the skin or any part of the body that it contacts.

• Always place a shop towel or cloth around the fitting or connection prior to loosening to absorb any excess fuel due to spillage. Ensure that all fuel spillage (should it occur) is quickly removed from engine surfaces. Ensure that all fuel soaked cloths or towels are deposited into a suitable waste container.

• Always keep a dry chemical (Class B) fire extinguisher near the work area.

• Do not allow fuel spray or fuel vapors to come into contact with a spark or open flame.

• Always use a back-up wrench when loosening and tightening fuel line connection fittings. This will prevent unnecessary stress and torsion to fuel line piping. Always follow the proper torque specifications.

• Always replace worn fuel fitting O-rings with new. Do not substitute fuel hose or equivalent, where fuel pipe is installed.

Fuel System Pressure

RELIEVING

2.4L Engine

1. Before servicing the vehicle, refer to the precautions in the beginning of this section.

2. Loosen the fuel filler cap in order to relieve the pressure in the tank (do not tighten at this time).

3. Raise and safely support the vehicle.

4. Detach the fuel pump electrical connector.

5. Start and run the vehicle until it stalls, the engage the starter for an additional three seconds to ensure the relief of any remaining pressure.

6. Disconnect the negative battery cable.

7. Once the tests or repairs are com-

pleted, reattach the fuel pump electrical connector.

8. Connect the negative battery cable.

9. Lower the vehicle.

10. Tighten the fuel filler cap.

11. Prime the fuel system by cycling the ignition switch **ON** for 2 seconds, **OFF** for 10 seconds, then **ON** again. Repeat, if necessary to build system pressure.

3.1L and 3.4L Engines

1. Before servicing the vehicle, refer to the precautions in the beginning of this section.

2. Disconnect the negative battery cable in order to avoid possible fuel discharge if an accidental attempt is made to start the engine.

3. Loosen the fuel tank filler cap in order to relieve fuel tank pressure.

4. Connect tool J-34730-A or equivalent fuel pressure gauge (with bleed hose) to the fuel pressure test port connection. Wrap a towel around the fuel pressure connection when installing the fuel pressure gauge in order to avoid fuel spillage.

5. Install the bleed hose into an approved container and open the valve in order to bleed the fuel system pressure. The fuel pipe connections are now safe for servicing.

6. Drain any fuel remaining in the fuel pressure gauge into an approved container.

Fuel Filter

REMOVAL & INSTALLATION

All Engines

1. Before servicing the vehicle, refer to the precautions in the beginning of this section.

2. Relieve the fuel system pressure.

3. Disconnect the negative battery cable.

4. Raise and safely support the vehicle.

5. Using a back-up wrench on the fuel filter, disconnect the fuel line from the filter.

6. Disconnect the quick-connect fitting from the fuel filter by compressing the tabs while pulling outward on the line.

7. Remove the fuel filter from the mounting bracket.

To install:

8. Install the fuel filter in the mounting bracket.

9. Using a back-up wrench on the fuel filter, tighten the fuel line fitting to 20 ft. lbs. (27 Nm).

10. Connect the quick-connect fitting to the fuel filter.

11. Lower the vehicle.

1 BODY
2 FUEL FILTER BRACKET
3 FUEL FILTER
4 SCREW – FULLY DRIVEN, SEATED
  AND NOT STRIPPED

7922Z323

Exploded view of the fuel filter mounting

1 HOSE, PART OF FUEL SENDER
2 FUEL VAPOR PIPE
3 FUEL RETURN PIPE
4 FUEL FEED PIPE
5 FUEL FEED PIPE NUT
  27 N•m (20 LBS. FT.)
6 HOSE, PART OF FUEL SENDER
7 ABS AND FUEL SENDER HARNESS

7922Z324

Fuel filter mounting location and component identification

12. Connect the negative battery cable.
13. Pressurize the fuel system and verify no leaks.

Fuel Pump

REMOVAL & INSTALLATION

All Engines

1. Before servicing the vehicle, refer to the precautions in the beginning of this section.

2. Relieve the fuel system pressure. Disconnect the negative battery cable.

3. Drain fuel tank. Remove the fuel tank from the vehicle.

4. While holding the modular fuel sender assembly down, remove the snapring from the designated slots located on the retainer.

1 SNAP RING
2 COVER – TAB
3 MODULAR UNIT
4 WIRE HARNESS – ABOVE COVER
5 FUEL TANK
6 TANK ISOLATION STRIPS (3)
7 RUBBER ISOLATOR

7922Z325

Exploded view of the fuel sender assembly mounting to the tank

1 HARNESS ASSEMBLY (ABOVE COVER) – FUEL
  PUMP AND FUEL SENDER WIRING
2 CONNECTOR ASSEMBLY – FUEL SENDER WIRING
3 FUEL PIPES (3)
4 COVER ASSEMBLY – FUEL SENDER
5 SEAL – FUEL PUMP OUTLET
6 SUPPORT ASSEMBLY (THREE HOLLOW SUPPORT OR
  GUIDE PIPES) – FUEL PUMP RESERVOIR
7 RETAINER – FUEL PUMP RESERVOIR
8 CONNECTOR POSITION ASSURANCE (CPA)
9 HARNESS ASSEMBLY (BELOW COVER) – FUEL PUMP
10 HARNESS ASSEMBLY (BELOW COVER) – FUEL
   LEVEL SENDER
11 RESERVOIR – FUEL PUMP FUEL
12 SENSOR ASSEMBLY – FUEL LEVEL
13 PUMP ASSEMBLY (JET PUMP ASSEMBLY) –
   FUEL PUMP RESERVOIR
14 STRAINER (EXTERNAL) – FUEL SENDER
15 PAD (BUMPER) – FUEL SENDER
16 VALVE (SECONDARY UMBRELLA VALVE) –
   FUEL PUMP RESERVOIR INLET CHECK
17 STRAINER – FUEL PUMP FUEL
18 BAFFLE (ISOLATOR CUP) – FUEL PUMP
19 PUMP ASSEMBLY (ROLLERVANE) – FUEL
20 OUTLET – FUEL PUMP

7922Z326

Exploded view of the fuel pump assembly

➡ **The modular fuel sender assembly may spring up from its position. When removing the modular fuel sender from the tank, be aware that the reservoir bucket is full of fuel. It must be tipped slightly during removal to avoid damage to the float.**

5. Remove the external fuel strainer.

6. Detach the Connector Position Assurance (CPA) piece from the wiring harness and disconnect the fuel pump.

7. Gently release the tabs on the sides of the fuel sender at the cover assembly. Begin by squeezing the sides of the reservoir and releasing the tab opposite the fuel level sensor. Move clockwise to release the second and third tab in the same manner.

8. Lift the cover assembly out far enough to disconnect the fuel pump electrical connection.

9. Rotate the fuel pump baffle counterclockwise and remove the baffle and pump assembly from the retainer.

10. Slide the fuel pump outlet out of slot. Remove the fuel pump outlet seal.

To install:

11. Install the fuel pump outlet seal. Slide the fuel pump outlet in the slots of reservoir cover.

12. Install the fuel pump and baffle assembly onto the reservoir retainer and rotate clockwise until seated.

13. Install the lower retainer assembly partially into the reservoir. Line up all three sleeve tabs. Press the retainer onto the reservoir making sure all three tabs are firmly seated.

➡ **Gently pull on the fuel pump reservoir from retainer to assure a secure fastening. If not secure, replace the entire fuel sender.**

14. Complete the installation by reverse the removal procedures.

15. Connect the negative battery cable. Pressurize the fuel system and verify no leaks.

DRIVE TRAIN

Transaxle

REMOVAL & INSTALLATION

Manual

1. Disconnect the negative battery cable. Install an engine support fixture, J-28467-A, or the equivalent.

2. Use the fixture to take the weight off the engine mounts. Remove the left side sound insulator from under the dash board.

3. Disconnect the clutch master cylinder pushrod from the clutch pedal stud. Remove the air cleaner and duct work from the throttle body.

4. Disconnect the shift cable from the manual shift lever on the transaxle. Disconnect the wiring harness from the transaxle mount bracket.

5. Remove the upper transaxle mount-to-transaxle bolts. Disconnect the clutch master cylinder from the slave cylinder.

6. Detach the ground wires from the transaxle mounting studs, and the back-up light switch connector.

7. Disconnect the transaxle vent tube. Remove the upper transaxle-to-engine bolts.

8. Lower the powertrain assembly with the support fixture. Raise and safely support the vehicle.

9. Drain the transaxle fluid. Remove the front tire and wheel assemblies.

10. Remove the left inner fender well splash shield. Detach the front ABS sensor connectors and unroute the left side sensor wiring.

11. Remove the flywheel housing cover bolts. Disconnect the Vehicle Speed Sensor (VSS) from the transaxle.

12. Remove the cotter pins and castle nuts and using a suitable ball joint separator, disconnect the ball joints from the steering knuckles.

13. Remove the left side link kit. Remove the left side U-bolt from the sway bar.

14. Remove the left side suspension support bolts and remove the suspension support.

15. Disconnect the halfshafts from the transaxle. Remove the front lower transaxle mount.

16. Support the transaxle with a suitable jack. Remove the remainder of the engine-to-transaxle bolts.

17. Carefully slide the transaxle away from the engine. Once there is sufficient clearance, lower the transaxle from the vehicle.

To install:

18. Raise the transaxle into position with the jack and install the mounting bolts loosely. DO NOT tighten the bolts until at least four of the bolts are in place. Tighten the lower bolts to 55 ft. lbs. (75 Nm).

19. Install the front transaxle mount and tighten the bolts to 55 ft. lbs. (75 Nm).

20. Complete the installation by reversing the removal procedures.

21. Install the upper transaxle-to-engine bolts and tighten to 55 ft. lbs. (75 Nm).

22. Install the rear transaxle mount and tighten the bolts to 55 ft. lbs. (75 Nm) on Isuzu transaxle or 96 ft. lbs. (130 Nm) on NVG transaxle.

23. Connect the negative battery cable. Refill the transaxle with Synchromesh Transaxle Fluid.

Automatic

1996–98 MODELS

1. Disconnect the negative battery cable. Remove the air intake duct.

2. For 3T40 transaxle, remove the cable control cover.

3. For 4T60-E transaxle, disconnect the shift linkage from the transaxle.

4. Disconnect the vacuum modulator line from the modulator.

5. For 3T40 transaxle, disconnect the throttle cable from the throttle body.

6. Detach the electrical connectors from the TCC, Park/Neutral position switch and shift solenoid.

7. For 3T40 transaxle, remove the power steering pump and set it aside leaving the hoses attached.

❋❋ CAUTION

When servicing requires that the "T" latch type wiring connector be detached from the switch, use care to ensure proper reassembly of both the connector and the "T" latch. Failure to do so may result in intermittent loss of switch functions.

8. For 3T40 transaxle, remove the oil fill tube.

9. Install engine support fixture J-28467-A or equivalent. Remove the top (2) transaxle-to-engine bolts.

10. For 4T60-E transaxle, disconnect the rubber hose from the transaxle vent pipe.

11. Remove the remaining upper transaxle-to-engine bolts. Raise and safely support the vehicle.

12. Remove both front tire and wheel assemblies. Remove right and left engine splash shields.

13. Detach the ABS Wheel Speed Sensor (WSS) connectors and remove the harness from the left side suspension support.

14. Separate both ball joints from the control arms. Remove the left side stabilizer shaft link pin bolt.

15. Remove the left side stabilizer shaft frame bushing clamp nuts. Remove the left side suspension support assembly.

16. Remove both halfshaft. Remove the engine-to-transaxle brace.

17. Remove the starter motor. Remove the transaxle converter cover.

1. Flywheel bolts
2. Transaxle assy
3. Flywheel
4. Net slot

VIEW A

7922Z327

Flywheel net slot view—vehicles with the 4T60-E transaxle

18. Remove the heater core hose pipe brace-to-transaxle nut and bolt. Remove the torque converter to flywheel bolts.

➡**Using a scribe mark the flywheel-to-torque converter relationship to assure proper reassembly.**

19. For 4T60-E transaxle, remove the oil level indicator and fill tube.
20. Disconnect the transaxle cooler lines and plug openings to prevent excess oil leakage.
21. For 4T60-E transaxle, disconnect the Vehicle Speed sensor (VSS) and remove the vacuum reservoir tank.
22. Position transaxle jack under transaxle. Remove the transaxle mount-to-body bolts.
23. Remove the remaining engine-to-transaxle bolts. Remove the transaxle.

➡**Transaxle cooler and lines should be flushed with J-35944 or equivalent whenever the transaxle has been removed for overhaul or replacement.**

To install:

24. Apply a thin film of grease on the torque converter pilot hub.

➡**Be sure to properly seat the torque converter in the pump.**

25. Position the transaxle into the vehicle. Install the lower transaxle-to-engine bolts.
26. Install the transaxle mount-to-body bolts and tighten to 66 ft. lbs. (90 Nm). Install the transaxle cooler lines.

27. Install the torque converter-to-flywheel bolts and tighten the bolts to 46 ft. (62 Nm).

➡**For 4T60-E transaxle, note that the flywheel has one oval shaped bolt opening. This is for the so-called "net slot bolt." Hand start and tighten the net slot bolt first, then tighten the remaining bolts.**

28. Install the oil level indicator and fill tube.
29. For 4T60-E transaxle, install the vacuum reserve tank.
30. Install the starter. Install the transaxle converter cover.
31. For 4T60-E transaxle, attach the electrical connector to the VSS.
32. Install the halfshafts. Install the left side suspension support assembly.
33. Install the left stabilizer shaft frame bushing nuts. Install the stabilizer shaft link pin bolt.
34. Install the engine-to-transaxle brace. Connect the ball joints to the control arms.
35. Attach the ABS WSS harness and connectors. Install the right and left side splash shields.
36. Install the heater core pipe brace-to-transaxle nut and bolt. Install the tire/wheel assemblies. Lower the vehicle.
37. Install the upper transaxle-to-engine bolts and tighten to 66 ft. lbs. (90 Nm). Connect the shift linkage to the transaxle.
38. Attach the electrical connector to the torque converter clutch.
39. Attach the electrical connector to the park/neutral and back-up lamp switch.
40. For 4T60-E transaxle, install the wiring harness and nut securing it to the transaxle.
41. For 3T40 transaxle, install the throttle cable to the throttle body.
42. Remove the engine support fixture.
43. For 4T60-E transaxle, connect the rubber hose to the vent pipe.
44. Connect the vacuum line to the modulator. Install the air intake duct.
45. Connect the negative battery cable. Fill the transaxle with clean transaxle fluid.
46. Verify proper shift linkage adjustment. Start the engine and check for leaks.
47. Road test the vehicle verify proper operation and check the transaxle fluid level.

➡**Whenever the vehicle sub-frame is removed or lowered, the wheel alignment should be checked.**

1999–00 MODELS

1. Before servicing the vehicle, refer to the precautions in the beginning of this section.
2. Use a scan tool to perform the ABS brake modulator gear tension relief procedure.
3. Disconnect the negative battery cable.
4. Install an engine support fixture.
5. Remove the front transmission mount bolts.
6. Remove the splash shield.
7. Remove the air cleaner and duct assembly.
8. Detach the wiring harness from the upper transaxle mount bracket.
9. Remove the upper transaxle mount.
10. Detach the shifter cable from the transaxle.
11. Secure the radiator and condenser to the upper radiator support.
12. Detach the ground cables from the engine.
13. Detach the park neutral position switch connectors from the transaxle.
14. Raise and safely support the vehicle.
15. Support the vehicle with a safety stand.
16. Drain the transaxle fluid.
17. Remove the front wheels and splash shields.
18. Remove the lower radiator and condenser support.
19. Remove the front transaxle mount and bracket.
20. Disconnect the both front ABS Wheel Speed Sensors (WSS) at the wheels.
21. Remove the speed sensor wiring harness from the body clips.
22. Lower the vehicle and remove the battery and tray.
23. Remove the radiator inlet hose.
24. Disconnect the wiring from the ABS modulator assembly.
25. Remove the two hydraulic lines at the ABS modulator from the master cylinder.
26. Remove the three hydraulic lines at the ABS modulator that go out to the wheels.
27. Remove the mounting nut at the bottom of the modulator and remove it from the vehicle.
28. Detach the connector from the Vehicle Speed Sensor (VSS) on the transaxle.
29. Remove the torque converter bolts.
30. Separate the ball joints from the control arms and remove the axle shafts.
31. Remove the front transaxle mount.

32. Remove the ABS brake control module.

33. Separate the tie rod ends from the steering knuckles.

34. Remove the power steering pressure line from the steering rack.

35. Remove the brake lines from the retainer under the steering rack.

36. Disconnect the steering column intermediate shaft from the steering gear.

37. Place a jack under the transaxle.

✳✳ CAUTION

The torque converter may fall out of the transaxle if it is tilted downward.

38. Remove the transaxle-to-engine bolts, pull the transaxle away from the engine and lower it out of the vehicle.

To install:

39. Position the transaxle on the engine and install the mounting bolts. Tighten the bolts to 66 ft. lbs. (90 Nm).

40. Remove the jack from the transaxle.

41. Connect the intermediate shaft to the steering gear.

42. Install the brake lines in the retainer under the steering gear.

43. Connect the power steering pressure line to the steering gear.

44. Install the tie rod ends to the steering knuckles.

45. Install the ABS control module.

46. Install the front transaxle mount.

47. Install the axle shafts and assembly the suspension.

48. Install the torque converter bolts. Tighten the bolts to 46 ft. lbs. (62 Nm).

49. Connect the VSS wiring.

50. Install the ABS modulator assembly. Tighten the nut to 22 ft. lbs. (30 Nm) and the fluid lines to 18 ft. lbs. (24 Nm).

51. Connect the front WSS and install the wiring in the original body clips.

52. Install the front transaxle mount bracket.

53. Install the lower radiator and condenser support.

54. Install the transaxle fluid pan.

55. Install the splash shields and the front wheels.

56. Lower the vehicle and connect the wiring to the transaxle (PNP switch).

57. Install the ground wiring on the engine.

58. Install the shifter cable and the upper transaxle mount. Attach the wiring harness to the mount bracket.

59. Install the air cleaner and duct assembly.

60. Install the splash shield and front transaxle mount bolts.

61. Remove the engine support fixture.

62. Connect the negative battery cable.

63. Refill the transaxle with fluid and bleed the brakes.

Clutch

REMOVAL & INSTALLATION

1. Disconnect the negative battery cable.

2. If necessary, disconnect the hydraulic line from the clutch actuator (slave cylinder).

3. Remove the transaxle from the vehicle.

4. If any clutch components are to be reused, use the following procedure:

   a. Matchmark (dots of paint or marks made with a center punch) the clutch pressure plate to the flywheel. This is to retain the balance of the original parts. If all parts are to be replaced with new, this step is not necessary.

   b. If the pressure plate is to be reused, loosen the pressure plate mounting bolts by turning each bolt one full turn until all the spring pressure is

1 FLYWHEEL
2 CLUTCH DISC
3 CLUTCH COVER
4 WASHER
5 BOLT
6 FLYWHEEL "HEAVY SIDE" IDENTIFICATION
7 CLUTCH COVER "LIGHT SIDE" IDENTIFICATION
8 ALIGN IDENTIFICATION MARKS ON ASSEMBLY

Exploded view of the clutch components—showing the clutch disk alignment tool

7922Z328

79222329

Clutch cover tightening sequence

removed. This helps avoid warping the pressure plate.

   c. Remove the bolts the remainder of the way and remove the clutch disc and pressure plate.

To install:

5. Apply a small amount of high-temperature grease to the pilot bearing as well as the tip of the transaxle input shaft and the clutch splines.

6. Install J-29074, or an equivalent clutch alignment tool into the flywheel and install the clutch disc onto the tool. Be sure the clutch is installed in the correct direction. The light side of the disc should be visible. Many replacement discs will also be marked "Flywheel Side" as an aid in getting the disc correctly positioned.

7. Install the pressure plate and loosely install the mounting bolts. New replacement bolts are recommended.

8. Make a first pass tightening the bolts in sequence to 12 ft. lbs. (16 Nm). With all the bolts tight make a second pass tightening each bolt to 15 ft. lbs. (20 Nm). Make a third pass tightening the bolts 30 degrees additional if equipped with a 3.1L engine and 45 degrees additional if equipped with the 2.4L engine.

9. Remove the clutch alignment tool.

10. Lubricate the inside diameter of the actuator (slave cylinder/throwout bearing) with clutch bearing lubricant.

11. Install the transaxle assembly into the vehicle.

12. If necessary, connect the clutch master cylinder hydraulic line to the actuator (slave cylinder).

13. Bleed the clutch hydraulic system.

14. Connect the negative battery cable. Road test the vehicle to verify correct operation and easy shifting.

Hydraulic Clutch System

BLEEDING

With Bleeder Screw

1. Be sure the reservoir is full of DOT 3 fluid and is kept topped off throughout this procedure.

2. Loosen the bleed screw, located on the actuator cylinder body next to the inlet connection.

3. When a steady stream of fluid comes out the bleeder, tighten it to 17 inch lbs. (2 Nm).

4. Refill the fluid reservoir.

5. To check the system, start the engine and wait 10 seconds.

6. Depress the clutch pedal and shift into **R**. If there is any gear clash, air may still be present.

Without Bleeder Screw

1. Remove the actuator cylinder from the transaxle.

2. Loosen the master cylinder attaching nuts to the ends of the studs.

3. Remove the reservoir cap and diaphragm.

4. Depress the actuator cylinder pushrod about ¾ in. into its bore and hold the position.

5. Install the reservoir diaphragm and cap while holding the actuator pushrod.

6. Release the pushrod when the diaphragm and cap are properly installed.

7. With the actuator lower than the master cylinder, hold the actuator vertically with the pushrod end facing the ground.

8. Press the actuator pushrod into its bore with ½ in. strokes. Check the reservoir for bubbles. Continue until no bubbles enter the reservoir.

9. Install the master cylinder and actuator. Refill the fluid reservoir.

10. To check the system, start the engine and wait 10 seconds.

11. Depress the clutch pedal and shift into reverse. If there is any gear clash, air may still be present.

Halfshaft

REMOVAL & INSTALLATION

Left and Right Halfshafts

1. Before servicing the vehicle, refer to the precautions in the beginning of this section.

2. Disconnect the negative battery cable. Raise and safely support the vehicle. Remove the wheel assembly.

3. Insert a drift or a punch through the caliper and into the rotor cooling fins to keep the axle from turning.

4. Remove the hub nut and washer and remove the drift.

5. Remove the cotter pin and castle nut from the lower ball joint. Using a suitable ball joint separator, disconnect the ball joint from the steering knuckle.

6. Disconnect the ABS sensor wire. Remove the sway bar link kit.

7. Unseat the halfshaft from the hub bearing assembly using a suitable puller, J-28733-A, or the equivalent.

8. Pivot the strut and knuckle assembly off the halfshaft and position it aside.

9. Place a pan under the transaxle.

10. Disconnect the inner joint from the transaxle using axle puller, J-28468 or J-33008 in conjunction with J-29794 and J-2619–01 or their equivalents.

To install:

11. Insert the halfshaft into the transaxle and using a non-ferrous drift positioned in the groove in the inboard joint, tap the joint in until it is seated in the transaxle.

12. Verify the joint is seated properly by grasping the inboard joint and pulling on it firmly. DO NOT pull on the axle shaft or damage to the inner joint will result.

13. Position the strut and knuckle assembly and guide the axle into the hub assembly.

14. Connect the lower ball joint to the steering knuckle and tighten the castle nut to 41 ft. lbs. (55 Nm). If necessary, tighten the nut up to 60 degrees (⅙ turn) additional rotation to align the cotter pins. NEVER loosen the nut to make the holes align. Install a new cotter pin.

15. Install the washer and hub nut.

16. Insert a drift punch through the caliper and into the rotor cooling fins. On 1996–98 models, tighten the hub nut to 185 ft. lbs. (260 Nm). On 1999–00 models, tighten the hub nut to 284 ft. lbs. (385 Nm).

17. Remove the drift. Install the link kit and tighten the mounting nut to 13 ft. lbs. (17 Nm).

18. Install the tire and wheel assembly and tighten the wheel nuts to 100 ft. lbs. (140 Nm).

19. Lower the vehicle. Connect the negative battery cable. Check the transaxle fluid level and top off as necessary.

Intermediate Shaft

1. Before servicing the vehicle, refer to the precautions in the beginning of this section.

2. Install an engine support fixture J-28467-A or equivalent. Raise and safely support the vehicle.

3. Remove the right side wheel assembly. Remove the sway bar link kit.

4. Remove the cotter pin and castle nut from the lower ball joint. Using a suitable ball joint separator, disconnect the ball joint from the steering knuckle.

5. Separate the inner joint from the intermediate shaft using an axle puller, J-33008 in conjunction with J-29794 and J-2619–01 or their equivalents.

6. Remove the rear engine mount through-bolt. Remove the intermediate shaft support bracket-to-engine bolts.

7. Place a pan under the transaxle. Carefully disconnect the intermediate shaft from the transaxle and remove the assembly from the vehicle.

To install:

8. Insert the intermediate shaft assembly into the transaxle and position the shaft

1 TRANSAXLE
2 INTERMEDIATE SHAFT SUPPORT BRACKET
3 BOLT
4 INTERMEDIATE SHAFT

7922Z330

Intermediate shaft components

bracket so the mounting bolts can be installed finger-tight.

9. With all the bolts installed tighten them to 49 ft. lbs. (66 Nm). Coat the splines of the intermediate shaft with chassis grease.

10. Connect the halfshaft to the intermediate shaft. Install the rear engine mount through-bolt.

11. Connect the lower ball joint to the steering knuckle and tighten the castle nut to 41 ft. lbs. (55 Nm). If necessary, tighten the nut up to 60 degrees (⅙ turn) additional rotation to align the cotter pins. NEVER loosen the nut to make the holes align. Install a new cotter pin.

12. Install the link kit and tighten the mounting nut to 13 ft. lbs. (17 Nm).

13. Install the tire and wheel assembly and tighten the wheel nuts to 100 ft. lbs. (140 Nm).

14. Lower the vehicle. Remove the engine support fixture.

15. Connect the negative battery cable. Check the transaxle fluid level and top off as necessary.

STEERING AND SUSPENSION

Air Bag

✳✳ CAUTION

Some vehicles are equipped with an air bag system, also known as the

Supplemental Inflatable Restraint (SIR) or Supplemental Restraint System (SRS). The system must be disabled before performing service on or around system components, steering column, instrument panel components, wiring and sensors. Failure to follow safety and disabling procedures could result in accidental air bag deployment, possible personal injury and unnecessary system repairs.

PRECAUTIONS

Several precautions must be observed when handling the inflator module to avoid accidental deployment and possible personal injury.

• Never carry the inflator module by the wires or connector on the underside of the module.

• When carrying a live inflator module, hold securely with both hands, and ensure that the bag and trim cover are pointed away.

• Place the inflator module on a bench or other surface with the bag and trim cover facing up.

• With the inflator module on the bench, never place anything on or close to the module which may be thrown in the event of an accidental deployment.

DISARMING

✳✳ CAUTION

The Supplemental Restraint System (SRS) must be disarmed before performing service procedures around the air bag or SRS wiring. Failure to do so may cause accidental deployment of the air bag, resulting in unnecessary SRS repairs and/or personal injury.

1. Disconnect the negative battery cable.

2. Turn the steering wheel so the vehicle's wheels are pointing straight ahead.

3. Turn the ignition switch to the **LOCK** position and remove the key.

4. Remove the **AIR BAG** fuse from the fuse block.

5. Remove the left sound insulator.

6. Remove the Connector Position Assurance (CPA) clip from the yellow 2-way connector at the base of the steering column, and detach the connector. If equipped with a passenger's side air bag, remove the CPA and detach the yellow 2-way connector from the passenger air bag lead.

REARMING

1. Turn the ignition switch to the **LOCK** position and remove the key.

2. Attach the yellow 2-way connector at the base of steering column and secure it with the Connector Position Assurance (CPA) clip. If equipped with a passenger's side air bag, attach the yellow 2-way connector at the passenger air bag lead and secure it with the CPA clip.

3. Install the left sound insulator.

4. Install the **AIR BAG** fuse in the fuse block.

5. Turn the ignition switch to the **RUN** position and verify that the **AIR BAG** warning lamp flashes 7 times, then turns **OFF**.

6. Connect the negative battery cable.

Power Rack and Pinion Steering Gear

REMOVAL & INSTALLATION

1996–98 Models

1. Before servicing the vehicle, refer to the precautions in the beginning of this section.

2. Remove the left sound insulator from under the dashboard. Remove the upper pinch bolt from the steering shaft coupling assembly.

3. Remove the power steering line retainer, if equipped. Remove the power brake booster mounting nuts and disconnect the brake pedal pushrod from the pedal stud.

4. Pull the booster away from the firewall and position away from the rack and pinion mounting clamp. DO NOT remove the master cylinder or allow the brake lines to kink.

5. Raise and safely support the vehicle. Remove the left tire and wheel assembly.

6. Remove the cotter pins and castle nuts from the outer tie rod ends and separate the tie rod ends from the strut arms using J-24319–01, or an equivalent tie rod puller.

7. Remove the four clamp mounting bolts and the two rack and pinion mounting clamps. Disconnect and cap the power steering lines from the rack and pinion unit.

8. Pull the rack away from the firewall and remove the lower steering shaft pinch bolt and separate the steering shaft from the rack and pinion stub shaft.

9. Remove the dash seal from the rack

1 RACK AND PINION
2 L.H. CLAMP – HORIZONTAL SLOT AT TOP
3 R.H. CLAMP – HORIZONTAL SLOT AT TOP
4 NUT – 30 N·m (22 LBS.FT.) – HAND START ALL NUTS. TIGHTEN LEFT HAND SIDE CLAMP NUTS FIRST, THEN TIGHTEN RIGHT SIDE NUTS.
5 STUD – 18 N·m (13 LBS. FT.) – AFTER SECOND REUSE OF STUD, THREAD LOCKING KIT NO. 1052624 MUST BE USED.
6 NUT – 60 N·m (44 LBS. FT.)
7 COTTER PIN

7922Z331

Rack and pinion mounting components–1996–98 models

and pinion housing. Remove the rack and pinion unit out through the hood.

10. If when removing the rack and pinion mounting clamp nuts the studs came out, remove the nuts from the studs and install the studs back into the firewall. Tighten the studs to 15 ft. lbs. (20 Nm).

To install:

11. Install the rack and pinion assembly through the engine compartment and position it on the firewall. Install the dash seal on the firewall.

12. Connect the steering shaft coupling to the stub shaft and tighten the pinch bolt to 30 ft. lbs. (41 Nm).

13. Connect the power steering lines to the rack and pinion assembly and tighten the fittings to 20 ft. lbs. (27 Nm).

14. Install the rack and pinion clamps and loosely install the mounting nuts. Tighten the left side clamps first, then the right to 22 ft. lbs. (30 Nm).

15. Install the power booster on the firewall. Raise and safely support the vehicle.

16. Connect the tie rod ends to the strut arms and tighten the castle nuts. Install the left front tire and wheel assembly.

17. Connect the booster pushrod to the

brake pedal and tighten the booster mounting nuts to 22 ft. lbs. (30 Nm). Install the power steering line retainer.

18. Install the steering column upper pinch bolt and tighten to 30 ft. lbs. (41 Nm). Install the left side sound insulator.

19. Refill and bleed the power steering system. Check the front end alignment and adjust as necessary.

1999–00 Models

1. Before servicing the vehicle, refer to the precautions in the beginning of this section.

2. Disconnect the negative battery cable.

3. Raise and safely support the vehicle.

4. Remove both front wheels.

5. Remove the stabilizer shaft links from the control arms.

6. Remove the tie rod ends from the steering knuckles.

7. Remove the intermediate shaft lower pinch bolt from the power steering gear.

8. Remove the through-bolt from the rear transmission mount.

9. Remove the power steering line bracket from the crossmember.

Power steering gear mounting—1999–00 models

10. Remove the stabilizer shaft brackets from the crossmember.

11. Support the rear of the sub-frame with jacks.

12. Remove the rear sub-frame mounting bolts and loosen the front ones.

13. Lower the sub-frame about three inches using the jacks and remove the stabilizer bar.

14. Remove the hoses from the steering gear.

15. Remove the steering gear mounting bolts and the steering gear from the vehicle through the left wheel opening.

To install:

16. Install the steering gear. Tighten the bolts to 89 ft. lbs. (120 Nm).

17. Install the hoses to the steering gear.

18. Install the stabilizer bar.

19. Raise the sub-frame into position and install the bolts. Tighten the bolts in the following order; left rear, right rear, left front, right front to 71 ft. lbs. (110 Nm).

20. Tighten the stabilizer bar bracket bolts to 49 ft. lbs. (66 Nm).

21. Install the intermediate shaft pinch bolt. Tighten the bolt to 16 ft. lbs. (22 Nm).

22. Install the tie rod ends and the stabilizer bar links.

23. Verify all steering hose fittings are tight.

24. Install the front wheels and lower the vehicle to the floor.

25. Fill the steering reservoir to the FULL COLD level.

26. Install adapter cap J 43485 or equivalent on the fluid reservoir with a vacuum pump attached to it.

27. Apply about 20 inches of vacuum to the system and wait five minutes. Typical vacuum drop is 2–3 inches. If the vacuum drop is greater, there may be a leak in the system allowing air to enter.

28. Remove the tools and install the reservoir cap.

29. Start the engine and allow it to idle.

30. Turn the engine **OFF** and check the fluid level. Do this until the fluid level stabilizes.

31. Start the engine and allow it to idle.

32. Turn the steering wheel in both directions 180–360 degrees five times.

33. Turn the engine **OFF** and check the fluid level.

34. Install adapter cap J 43485 or equivalent on the fluid reservoir with a vacuum pump attached to it once again.

35. Apply about 20 inches of vacuum to the system and wait five minutes.

36. Remove the tools and check the fluid level. Install the cap.

Strut

REMOVAL & INSTALLATION

Front

1. Before servicing the vehicle, refer to the precautions in the beginning of this section.

2. Raise and safely support the vehicle. Remove the front tire and wheel assembly.

3. Remove the cotter pin and castle nut from the outer tie rod end and separate the ball stud from the strut arm using J-24319–01, or an equivalent tie rod puller.

4. Remove the bolt from the brake line bracket and separate the bracket from the strut.

J 43485 **J 35555**

Install the special tools as shown on the steering fluid reservoir when bleeding the system

5. Scribe reference marks on the front strut and steering knuckle for installation purposes.

6. Remove the strut lower mounting bracket nut and through-bolts.

7. Lower the vehicle until the upper strut plate mounting bolts are accessible.

8. Support the lower control arm.

9. Hold the strut and remove the strut plate mounting nuts and bolt. Remove the strut from the vehicle.

✸✸ WARNING

If the strut is being replaced, a strut compressor tool J-34013-A or equivalent must be used to remove the coil spring from the strut assembly. Failure to use a spring compressing tool can result in personal injury and/or part damage.

To install:

10. Install the strut assembly into the vehicle and install the upper strut plate mounting nuts.

11. Connect the lower strut bracket to the steering knuckle and install the through-bolts.

1 CLAMP, STABILIZER SHAFT	20 STEERING KNUCKLE
2 INSULATOR, STABILIZER SHAFT	21 NUT, BALL JOINT
3 NUT	22 COTTER PIN
4 STABILIZER SHAFT	23 NUT
5 BOLT	24 BALL JOINT
6 NUT	25 BOLT
7 NUT, STRUT DAMPENER SHAFT	26 INSULATOR, STABILIZER LINK
8 RATE WASHER	27 WASHER, STABILIZER LINK
9 STRUT MOUNT	28 BOLT, STABILIZER LINK
10 UPPER SPRING SEAT	29 CONTROL ARM
11 UPPER SPRING INSULATOR	30 BOLT
12 DUST TUBE ASSEMBLY	31 BUSHING, CONTROL ARM
13 SPRING	32 BOLT
14 LOWER SPRING INSULATOR	33 BOLT
15 STRUT	34 SUSPENSION SUPPORT
16 NUT	35 NUT
17 WASHER	36 WASHER
18 BOLT	37 BOLT
19 HUB AND BEARING ASSEMBLY	38 SPACER, STABILIZER LINK

7922Z332

Exploded view of the front suspension

12. Raise the vehicle.

13. Install the through-bolt nuts and tighten to 133 ft. lbs. (180 Nm) with the reference marks in alignment.

14. Connect the tie rod end to the strut arm and tighten the castle nut to 44 ft. lbs. (60 Nm). If necessary tighten the nut up to 60 degrees (⅙ turn) additional to align the cotter pin holes. NEVER loosen the nut to make the holes align. Install a new cotter pin.

15. Connect the brake line bracket to the strut and tighten the bolt to 10 ft. lbs. (14 Nm).

16. Install the tire and wheel assembly. Lower the vehicle.

17. Tighten the upper strut plate mounting nuts and bolt to 18 ft. lbs. (25 Nm).

18. Check the front end alignment and adjust as necessary.

Rear

1. Before servicing the vehicle, refer to the precautions in the beginning of this section.

2. Raise and safely support the vehicle.

3. Remove the rear wheel assembly.

4. Scribe a mark indicating the position of the strut on the knuckle.

5. Remove the mounting nuts from inside the trunk.

6. Remove the mounting bolts from the wheel well area.

7. Remove the to strut-to-knuckle bolts.

8. Remove the strut from the vehicle.

✳✳ WARNING

If the strut is being replaced, a spring compressor tool J-34013-A or equivalent must be used to remove the coil spring from the strut assembly. Failure to use a spring compressing tool can result in personal injury and/or part damage.

To install:

9. Install the strut loosely in the vehicle using the upper mounting bolts and nuts.

10. Tighten the nuts to 18 ft. lbs. (25 Nm).

11. Align the scribe mark made earlier and install the strut on the knuckle. Tighten the bolts to 89 ft. lbs. (120 Nm).

12. Install the wheel and lower the vehicle to the floor.

13. Check the wheel alignment and adjust if necessary.

Shock Absorber

REMOVAL & INSTALLATION

➡ **Only 1996–98 models use a rear shock absorber. The 1999–00 models use a strut for the rear suspension.**

✳✳ WARNING

When doing this procedure, if both shocks are to be replaced, only remove one shock at a time or damage can occur to the axle assembly and/or personal injury.

1. Before servicing the vehicle, refer to the precautions in the beginning of this section.

2. Raise and safely support the vehicle with the wheel about 6 in. off the ground. Support the rear axle assembly with a safety stand or hydraulic floor jack.

3. From inside the trunk, remove the cap from the upper shock mounting plate. Remove the two shock plate mounting nuts and remove the reinforcement from the shock tower.

4. From under the suspension, remove the lower shock mounting nut. Compress the shock and remove it from the vehicle.

NOTE: COVER MUST BE INSTALLED SO THAT ARROW POINTS TO LEFT SIDE OF VEHICLE

1 COVER (MUST BE INSTALLED WITH ARROW POINTING TO LEFT OF VEHICLE)
2 NUT
3 REINFORCEMENT
4 UPPER SHOCK ABSORBER MOUNT
5 SHOCK ABSORBER
6 WASHER
7 WASHER
8 NUT
9 NUT
10 REAR AXLE; SPRING-ON-CENTER TYPE
11 INSULATOR, COIL SPRING
12 COIL SPRING

Exploded view of the rear suspension—1996–98 models

7922Z333

5. If the shock is being replaced, remove the upper shock insulator, washer and mount.

To install:

6. Install the mount, washer and insulator on the shock and tighten the mounting nut to 21 ft. lbs. (29 Nm).

7. Install the shock assembly into the vehicle. Be sure the alignment tab on the lower mount is pointing toward the rear of the vehicle.

8. Install the mounting nut and tighten to 35 ft. lbs. (47 Nm).

9. Install the reinforcement and upper shock plate mounting nuts and tighten to 18 ft. lbs. (24 Nm). Install the cap over the mounting plate.

10. Remove the safety stand or hydraulic floor jack from under the axle. Lower the vehicle.

Coil Spring

REMOVAL & INSTALLATION

Rear

EXCEPT 1996–98 MODELS

1. Before servicing the vehicle, refer to the precautions in the beginning of this section.

2. Remove the strut assembly from the vehicle.

3. Mount the strut compressor J-34013 in holding fixture J-3289–20.

4. Mount the strut assembly into the compressor. Note that the strut compressor has strut mounting holes drilled for specific vehicle lines.

5. Compress the strut approximately ½ its height after initial contact with the top cap.

✳✳ WARNING

Never bottom the spring or dampener rod!

6. Remove the nut from the strut dampener shaft and place alignment/guiding rod J-34013–27 on top of the dampener shaft. Use the rod to guide the dampener shaft straight down through the spring cap while compressing the spring. Remove the components.

➡ **Be careful to avoid chipping or cracking the spring coating when handling the front suspension coil spring assembly.**

1	STRUT ASSEMBLY
2	INSTALL LOCKING PINS THROUGH STRUT ASSEMBLY
3	TIGHTEN NUTS UNTIL FLUSH WITH STRUT COMPRESSOR
4	COMPRESSOR FORCING SCREW

7922Z334

View of the strut assembly mounted in a compressor

1	WRENCH
2	SOCKET
3	STRUT ASSEMBLY

7922Z335

Use a socket and a wrench to remove the dampener shaft nut spring cap while compressing the spring

To install:

7. Install the bearing cap into the strut compressor if previously removed.

8. Mount the strut assembly in strut compressor, using bottom locking pin only. Extend the dampener shaft and install clamp J-34013–20 on the dampener shaft.

9. Install the spring over the dampener

1	STRUT COMPRESSOR
2	STRUT ASSEMBLY

7922Z336

Install the rod to guide the dampener shaft straight down through the spring cap while compressing the spring

1	STRUT MOUNT NUT
2	STRUT MOUNT
3	RATE WASHER
4	SPRING SEAT
5	SPRING UPPER INSULATOR
6	JOUNCE BUMPER
7	STRUT DUST SHIELD
8	SPRING
9	SPRING LOWER INSULATOR
10	STRUT

7922Z337

Exploded view of the front strut assembly

and swing the assembly up so the upper locking pin can be installed.

10. Install all shields, bumpers and insulators on the spring seat. Install the spring seat on top of the spring. Be sure

Turn to Section 6 for brake system applications

the flat on the upper spring seat is facing in the proper direction. The spring seat flat should be facing the same direction as the centerline of the strut assembly spindle.

11. Install the guiding rod and turn the forcing screw while the guiding rod centers the assembly. When the threads on the dampener shaft are visible, remove the guiding rod and install the nut. Tighten the nut to 52 ft. lbs. (70 Nm). Use a crow's foot line wrench while holding the dampener shaft with a socket.

12. Remove the clamp.

1996–98 MODELS

1. Before servicing the vehicle, refer to the precautions in the beginning of this section.

2. Raise and safely support the vehicle. Support the rear axle with a suitable screw type jack.

3. Remove the lower shock absorber mounting nuts. Remove the right and left brake line mounting bolts from the floor of the vehicle.

4. Slowly lower the rear axle assembly until the tension is removed from the coil springs. Remove the coil springs and insulators.

To install:

5. Install the springs and insulator into the vehicle. The ends of the lowest coil must be within 9/16 of the spring stop.

6. Raise the rear axle assembly until the lower shock nuts can be installed. Tighten the nuts to 35 ft. lbs. (47 Nm).

7. Connect the brake line brackets to the frame and tighten the mounting bolts to 97 inch lbs. (11 Nm).

8. Remove the jack. Lower the vehicle.

Lower Ball Joint

REMOVAL & INSTALLATION

1. Before servicing the vehicle, refer to the precautions in the beginning of this section.

2. Raise and safely support the vehicle. Remove the tire and wheel assembly.

3. Remove the cotter pin and castle nut from the outer ball joint.

4. Separate the ball joint stud from the steering knuckle using J-29330, or an equivalent ball joint separator.

5. Drill a 1/8 in. pilot hole in the center of each of the three ball joint mounting rivets.

6. Using a 1/2 in. drill bit, drill the heads off the rivets.

1   PIN
2   NUT – 55 N·m (41 LBS. FT.) MINIMUM TORQUE
    65 N·m (48 LBS. FT.) MAXIMUM TORQUE TO
    INSTALL PIN
3   LOWER BALL JOINT

79222339

Exploded view of the ball joint-to-knuckle mounting

1   SERVICE BALL JOINT
2   BALL JOINT MOUNTING BOLTS
3   NUT
4   LOWER CONTROL ARM
5   STEERING KNUCKLE
6   NUT – 55 N·m (41 LBS. FT.) MINIMUM TORQUE
    65 N·m (48 LBS. FT.) MAXIMUM TORQUE
    TO INSTALL PIN
7   PIN

79222338

Exploded view of the replacement ball joint mounting

7. With a hammer and punch, knock the rivets out of the control arm. Remove the sway bar link kit.

8. Pull the control arm down so the ball stud clears the steering knuckle. Slide the ball joint out of the control arm.

To install:

9. Position the ball joint into the lower control arm and install the bolts. The nuts must be on top of the control arm. Tighten the mounting bolts to the specification provided with the ball joint service kit.

10. Connect the ball joint to the steering knuckle and tighten the castle nut to 41 ft. lbs. (55 Nm). If necessary to align the cotter pin holes tighten the nut up to 60 degrees (⅙ turn) additional rotation. NEVER loosen the nut to make the holes align. Install a new cotter pin.

11. Install the link kit and tighten the nut to 22 ft. lbs. (30 Nm).

12. Install the tire and wheel assembly and tighten the wheel nuts to 100 ft. lbs. (140 Nm).

13. Lower the vehicle.

Wheel Bearings

ADJUSTMENT

These vehicles are equipped with sealed hub and bearing assemblies. The hub and bearing assemblies are non-serviceable. If the assembly is damaged, the complete unit must be replaced.

REMOVAL & INSTALLATION

Front

1. Before servicing the vehicle, refer to the precautions in the beginning of this section.

2. Raise and safely support the vehicle. Remove the front tire and wheel assembly.

3. Insert a drift punch through the caliper and into the rotor cooling fins. This keeps the assembly from turning while the axle nut is being loosened.

4. Remove the axle nut and washer. Remove the punch.

5. Remove the caliper mounting bolts and remove the caliper from the steering knuckle. Support the caliper aside. DO NOT allow the caliper to hang unsupported from the brake hose.

6. Remove the brake rotor.

1 HUB AND BEARING ASSEMBLY
2 STEERING KNUCKLE
3 WASHER
4 DRIVE AXLE NUT – 260 N·m (192 LBS. FT.)
5 HUB AND BEARING RETAINING BOLT
6 WASHER

79222340

Exploded view of the front hub and bearing assembly

7. Remove the three bolts securing the hub bearing to the steering knuckle. Remove the backing plate.

8. Using J-28733-A, or an equivalent front hub remover, separate the halfshaft from the hub bearing assembly.

9. Remove the hub bearing assembly.

To install:

10. Install the hub bearing assembly over the end of the axle making sure the splines engage smoothly.

11. Install the backing plate and the three hub bearing mounting bolts. Tighten the bolts to 70 ft. lbs. (95 Nm).

12. Install the brake rotor.

13. Install the caliper onto the steering knuckle and tighten the caliper mounting bolts to 38 ft. lbs. (51 Nm).

14. Install a drift punch into the rotor cooling fins. This keeps the assembly from turning while the axle nut is being tightened. Tighten the axle nut to 192 ft. lbs. (260 Nm).

15. Install the front tire and wheel assembly and tighten the wheel nuts to 100 ft. lbs. (140 Nm). Lower the vehicle.

Rear

DRUM BRAKE

1. Before servicing the vehicle, refer to the precautions in the beginning of this section.

2. Raise and safely support the vehicle. Remove the wheel and tire assembly.

1 BOLT
2 REAR AXLE ASSEMBLY
3 BACKING PLATE
4 HUB AND BEARING ASSEMBLY
5 LOCKNUT

79222341

Hub and bearing components

3. Remove the brake drum.

4. Remove the four hub bearing assembly mounting nuts from behind the backing plate while holding the bolts from the front. The mounting bolts can be removed from the backing plate once the nuts have been removed. The top rear bolt will not clear the brake shoes and must be removed with the bearing assembly.

5. Disconnect the ABS speed sensor wire from the hub bearing assembly. Remove the hub bearing assembly.

To install:

6. Position the hub bearing assembly on the backing plate and insert the four mounting bolts. Connect the ABS wheel speed sensor, if equipped.

7. Install the hub bearing mounting nuts from behind the backing plate and tighten the nuts to 38 ft. lbs. (52 Nm) while holding the bolts.

8. Install the brake drum.

9. Install the tire and wheel assembly and tighten the wheel bolts to 100 ft. lbs. (140 Nm). Lower the vehicle.

DISC BRAKE

1. Before servicing the vehicle, refer to the precautions in the beginning of this section.

2. Raise and safely support the vehicle.

3. Remove the wheel assembly.

4. Remove the brake rotor.

5. Detach the parking brake cable from the lever.

6. Disconnect the Wheel Speed Sensor (WSS).

7. Remove the wheel hub assembly bolts and the hub from the knuckle.

8. Remove the Torx® bolts from the rear of the hub assembly and remove the hub from the backing plate.

To install:

9. Install the hub to the backing plate. Tighten the Torx® bolts to 90 inch lbs. (10 Nm).

Rear wheel bearing assembly with disc brakes—1999–00 models

10. Install the hub assembly on the knuckle. Tighten the bolts to 70 ft. lbs. (95 Nm).

11. Connect the WSS and the parking brake cable.

12. Install the brake rotor.

13. Install the wheel assembly.

14. Lower the vehicle to the floor.

PRECAUTIONS

Before servicing any vehicle, please be sure to read all of the following precautions, which deal with personal safety, prevention of component damage, and important points to take into consideration when servicing a motor vehicle:

• Never open, service or drain the radiator or cooling system when the engine is hot; serious burns can occur from the steam and hot coolant.

• Observe all applicable safety precautions when working around fuel. Whenever servicing the fuel system, always work in a well ventilated area. Do not allow fuel spray or vapors to come in contact with a spark, open flame, or excessive heat (a hot drop light, for example). Keep a dry chemical fire extinguisher near the work area. Always keep fuel in a container specifically designed for fuel storage; also, always properly seal fuel containers to avoid the possibility of fire or explosion. Refer to the additional fuel system precautions later in this section.

• Fuel injection systems often remain pressurized, even after the engine has been turned **OFF**. The fuel system pressure must be relieved before disconnecting any fuel lines. Failure to do so may result in fire and/or personal injury.

• Brake fluid often contains polyglycol ethers and polyglycols. Avoid contact with the eyes and wash your hands thoroughly after handling brake fluid. If you do get brake fluid in your eyes, flush your eyes with clean, running water for 15 minutes. If eye irritation persists, or if you have taken brake fluid internally, seek medical assistance IMMEDIATELY.

• The EPA warns that prolonged contact with used engine oil may cause a number of skin disorders, including cancer! You should make every effort to minimize your exposure to used engine oil. Protective gloves should be worn when changing oil. Wash your hands and any other exposed skin areas as soon as possible after exposure to used engine oil. Soap and water, or waterless hand cleaner should be used.

• All new vehicles are now equipped with an air bag system, often referred to as a Supplemental Restraint System (SRS) or Supplemental Inflatable Restraint (SIR) system. The system must be disabled before performing service on or around system components, steering column, instrument panel components, wiring and sensors. Failure to follow safety and disabling procedures could result in accidental air bag deployment, possible personal injury and unnecessary system repairs.

• Always wear safety goggles when working with, or around, the air bag system. When carrying a non-deployed air bag, be sure the bag and trim cover are pointed away from your body. When placing a non-deployed air bag on a work surface, always face the bag and trim cover upward, away from the surface. This will reduce the motion of the module if it is accidentally deployed. Refer to the additional air bag system precautions later in this section.

• Clean, high quality brake fluid from a sealed container is essential to the safe and proper operation of the brake system. You should always buy the correct type of brake fluid for your vehicle. If the brake fluid becomes contaminated, completely flush the system with new fluid. Never reuse any brake fluid. Any brake fluid that is removed from the system should be discarded. Also, do not allow any brake fluid to come in contact with a painted surface; it will damage the paint.

• Never operate the engine without the proper amount and type of engine oil; doing so WILL result in severe engine damage.

• Timing belt maintenance is extremely important! Many models utilize an interference-type, non-freewheeling engine. If the timing belt breaks, the valves in the cylinder head may strike the pistons, causing potentially serious (also time-consuming and expensive) engine damage. Refer to the maintenance interval charts in the front of this manual for the recommended replacement interval for the timing belt, and to the timing belt section for belt replacement and inspection.

• Disconnecting the negative battery cable on some vehicles may interfere with the functions of the on-board computer system(s) and may require the computer to undergo a relearning process once the negative battery cable is reconnected.

• When servicing drum brakes, only disassemble and assemble one side at a time, leaving the remaining side intact for reference.

ENGINE REPAIR

Ignition Timing

ADJUSTMENT

➡The 3.0L DOHC engine used in the Catera utilizes a Distributorless Ignition System (DIS). The ignition timing is determined by inputs from the Knock (KS) sensor, Oxygen (O_2S) sensor and Engine Coolant Temperature (ECT) sensors. No ignition timing adjustment is possible.

Engine Assembly

REMOVAL & INSTALLATION

1. Before servicing the vehicle, refer to the precautions in the beginning of this section.
2. Disconnect the negative battery cable.
3. Drain the engine coolant into a suitable container.
4. Remove the left and right air inlet grilles.
5. Matchmark the relationship of the hinges to the hood, then remove the hood.
6. Remove the battery.
7. Properly discharge and recover the A/C refrigerant using an approved recycling station.
8. Detach the black wiring harness connector.
9. Tag and remove the ground wire from the negative battery cable.

10. Remove the four power supply wires from the positive battery cable.

11. Siphon the power steering fluid from the reservoir, then disconnect the hoses from the pump.

12. Remove the threaded fitting for the power brake booster vacuum pipe from the intake plenum.

13. Tag the hoses and connectors, then remove the switch-over valve from the intake plenum.

14. Remove the Engine Control Module (ECM).

15. Remove the relays, then remove the wiring harness from the electrical center box.

16. Detach the blue and white wiring harness connectors.

17. Disconnect the accelerator and cruise control cables from the throttle body.

18. Properly relieve the fuel system pressure.

19. Disconnect the fuel lines from the fuel rail. Be sure to use a back-up wrench to prevent damage to the fuel rail.

20. Tag and disconnect the following hoses:
- Coolant hose from the throttle body
- Vacuum hose from the purge valve on the engine ventilation chamber
- Vacuum hose from the heater control valve
- Coolant reservoir hose from the coolant inlet pipe
- Coolant hoses from the heater core
- Heater hose quick-disconnects

21. Remove the resonance chamber and the radiator.

22. Remove the A/C hose bracket and position it out of the way.

23. Disconnect the refrigerant line from the A/C compressor. Be sure to cap all open lines to prevent moisture from entering the system.

24. Attach an engine support fixture to support the engine. The two silicone engine mounts are not strong enough to support the engine after the transmission has been removed.

25. Raise and safely support the vehicle.

26. Remove the splash shield.

27. Detach the A/C compressor electrical connector.

28. Remove the transmission from the vehicle.

29. Lower the vehicle and attach a hoist to the engine assembly. Attach the hoist to the three engine lifting shackles. Raise the engine slightly and remove the engine support fixture.

30. Remove the engine mount nuts and lift the engine out of the vehicle. Raise the engine slowly after being certain all wiring, cables and hoses have been removed.

To install:

31. Position the engine in the vehicle. Install the engine mount nuts and tighten them to 41 ft. lbs. (55 Nm).

32. Install the engine support fixture and remove the chain hoist.

33. Raise and safely support the vehicle.

34. Install the transmission assembly.

35. Connect the wiring to the A/C compressor.

36. Install the splash shield. Tighten the bolts until they are fully seated. Be careful not to strip them.

37. Lower the vehicle and remove the engine support fixture.

38. Connect the A/C compressor and install the hose bracket. Tighten the bracket bolts to 71 inch lbs. (8 Nm).

39. Install the radiator and resonance chamber.

40. Connect all coolant, vacuum and fuel lines. Tighten the fuel supply and return lines to 11 ft. lbs. (15 Nm).

41. Connect the accelerator and cruise control cables to the throttle body.

42. Attach the blue and white wiring harness connectors.

43. Install the wiring harness to the electrical center box, then install the relays.

44. Install the ECM.

45. Install the switch-over valve on the intake plenum. Tighten the bolts to 71 inch lbs. (8 Nm).

46. Connect the hoses to the power steering pump. Tighten the discharge hose to 21 ft. lbs. (28 Nm).

47. Install the power brake booster threaded fitting in the intake plenum until it is just seated. Be certain not to strip the threads by over-tightening.

48. Connect the four power supply wires to the positive battery cable and the ground wire to the negative battery cable.

49. Attach the black wiring harness connector.

50. Install the battery and the hood.

51. Install the air inlet grills and the wiper arms.

52. Reprogram all applicable accessories.

53. Fill the bleed the cooling system. Use only GM DEX-COOL® or equivalent coolant. When refilling the cooling system, add two crushed engine coolant supplement sealant pellets PN 3634621 or equivalent into the coolant reservoir.

54. Fill the power steering reservoir with Dexron III® automatic transmission fluid and bleed the system.

55. Recharge the A/C system and check for leaks.

Water Pump

REMOVAL & INSTALLATION

1. Before servicing the vehicle, refer to the precautions in the beginning of this section.

2. Disconnect the negative battery cable.

3. Drain the coolant into a suitable container.

4. Remove the resonance chamber.

5. Remove the front timing belt cover.

6. Remove the water pump.

To install:

7. Clean the water pump mounting surface on the engine block.

8. Apply silicone grease to the water pump O-ring and install the water pump on the engine block. Tighten the mounting bolts to 18 ft. lbs. (21 Nm).

9300Z401

Exploded view of the water pump mounting

9. Install the front timing belt cover.
10. Install the resonance chamber.
11. Connect the negative battery cable.
12. Refill the cooling system through the reservoir tank. The cooling system will bleed automatically during warm-up. Use only GM DEX-COOL® or equivalent coolant. When refilling the cooling system, add two crushed engine coolant supplement sealant pellets PN 3634621 or equivalent into the coolant reservoir.
13. Check the coolant level in the reservoir after the engine has cooled and add coolant as needed.

Cylinder Head

REMOVAL & INSTALLATION

1. Before servicing the vehicle, refer to the precautions in the beginning of this section.
2. Disconnect the negative battery cable.
3. Drain the engine coolant and relieve the fuel system pressure.
4. Remove the intake plenum.
5. Remove the resonance chamber.
6. Remove the intake manifold and spacer.
7. Remove the coolant bridge.
8. Remove the left valve cover and front timing belt cover.
9. Position the crankshaft 60 degrees Before Top Dead Center (BTDC) to avoid contact between the valves and the pistons when the cylinder head is installed.
10. Remove the timing belt.
11. Remove the timing belt tensioner bracket.
12. Install the camshaft gear holding tools Nos. J 42069–1 and J42069–2 or their equivalents, on the camshaft sprockets, then remove the sprocket mounting bolts and sprockets.
13. Remove the water pump.
14. Remove the rear timing belt cover.
15. Disconnect the Camshaft Position (CMP) sensor.
16. Remove the bolt attaching the coolant pipe/engine lift bracket to the cylinder head.
17. Remove the dipstick tube by pulling it up firmly.
18. Remove the upper radiator hose from the coolant pipe, then remove the pipe by twisting it.
19. Separate the exhaust manifold from the cylinder head.
20. If working on the left cylinder head, disconnect the wiring to the ignition coil pack.

(1) Idle Air Control (IAC) Inlet Hose
(2) Resonance Chamber Guide Pin
(3) Resonance Chamber Nut
(4) Mass Air Flow (MAF) Sensor
(5) Intake Air Temperature (IAT) Sensor
(6) Resonance Chamber Air Intake Hose
(7) Intake Plenum Air Inlet Hose

79222406

Resonance chamber and related components

21. Gradually remove the cylinder head bolts in stages using the reverse of the tightening sequence. Then, remove the cylinder head and gasket.
22. If working on the left cylinder head, remove the ignition coil pack and bracket from the cylinder head.
To install:
23. Clean the surface of the engine block and the bottom of the cylinder head.
24. Place a new gasket on the engine with "OBEN/TOP" facing up and towards the front for the left side or towards the rear for the right side of the engine.

➡**Be sure to use new cylinder head bolts when installing the cylinder head. The old bolts have been stretched by the method used to install them and are not reusable.**

25. Be sure nothing is in the way and carefully install the cylinder head on the engine.
26. Using the proper sequence, tighten the bolts to 18 ft. lbs. (25 Nm).
27. Using a torque angle meter, tighten the bolts in sequence using four stages:
   • 90 degrees
   • 90 degrees

Before removing the timing belt, be sure to turn the crankshaft 60° BTDC to avoid valve-to-piston contact and subsequent engine damage

Tighten the cylinder head bolts according the sequence shown

Proper head gasket installation position— left cylinder head

- 90 degrees
- 15 degrees

28. Connect the ignition coil pack.

29. Using a new gasket, install the exhaust manifold.

Proper head gasket installation position— right cylinder head

30. Install the coolant pipe with new O-rings, then connect the upper radiator hose to the coolant pipe.

31. Install the dipstick tube, coolant pipe and engine hanger bracket. Tighten the bolt to 15 ft. lbs. (20 Nm).

32. Install the exhaust camshaft, then connect the CMP sensor.

33. Install the rear timing belt cover and water pump.

34. Install the camshaft sprockets and the timing belt tensioner.

35. Install the timing belt and cover.

36. Using new O-rings and gaskets, install the valve cover. Tighten the bolts to 71 inch lbs. (8 Nm).

37. Install the coolant bridge, intake manifold spacer and the intake manifold.

38. Install the resonance chamber and intake plenum.

39. Connect the negative battery cable.

40. Drain and refill the engine oil, then replace the filter.

41. Refill the cooling system.

42. Inspect the engine compartment to be sure everything has been assembled.

43. Start the engine and check for leaks.

Intake Manifold Assembly

REMOVAL & INSTALLATION

Intake Plenum

1. Before servicing the vehicle, refer to the precautions in the beginning of this section.

2. Disconnect the negative battery cable.

3. Remove the air intake ducts and the Idle Air Control (IAC) hose from the throttle body assembly.

4. Disconnect the accelerator and cruise control cables from the throttle body, then remove the cables with the bracket.

5. Disconnect the Throttle Position (TP) sensor wiring.

6. Remove the threaded brake booster vacuum hose connection from the intake plenum.

7. Remove the wiper arms, them remove the air inlet grilles

8. Remove the wiring harness (channel) from the intake plenum.

9. Disconnect the wiring and vacuum hose from the switch-over valve solenoid.

10. Disconnect the vacuum hose from the fuel pressure regulator.

11. Remove the throttle body.

12. Remove the caps and bolts attaching the intake plenum to the intake manifold, then remove the plenum. and O-rings.

13. Place masking tape over the openings on the intake manifold to prevent foreign objects from falling into the engine.

Intake plenum mounting bolt locations

Timing belt service is covered in Section 5 of this manual

To install:

14. Remove the masking tape and position new O-rings on the intake manifold.

15. Be sure the guide pins are aligned and install the intake plenum. Tighten the bolts to 71 inch lbs. (8 Nm). Install the caps on the bolt heads.

16. Install the throttle body. Tighten the bolts to 71 inch lbs. (8 Nm).

17. Connect the vacuum hose to the fuel pressure regulator and the switch-over valve solenoid.

18. Attach the electrical connector to the switch-over valve solenoid.

19. Position the wiring harness on the plenum and install the two bolts. Tighten the bolts to 71 inch lbs. (8 Nm).

20. Connect the vacuum hoses and crankcase vent hose to the intake plenum.

21. Install the air inlet grilles and the wiper arms.

22. Connect the brake booster hose. Tighten the fitting just until seated.

23. Connect the TP sensor wiring.

24. Install the accelerator and cruise control cables with bracket. Tighten the bracket bolts to 71 inch lbs. (8 Nm).

25. Install the air inlet ducts and the IAC hose.

26. Connect the negative battery cable.

27. Start the engine and check for proper performance.

Intake Manifold

➡ The fuel injector connectors are numbered. Be sure to attach the correct connector to the proper fuel injector when installing the intake manifold.

1. Before servicing the vehicle, refer to the precautions in the beginning of this section.

2. Disconnect the negative battery cable.

3. Remove the intake plenum.

4. Properly relieve the fuel system pressure.

5. Disconnect the fuel lines from the fuel delivery rail assembly.

6. Detach the connectors from the fuel injectors.

7. Remove the intake manifold mounting bolts and the intake manifold.

8. Place masking tape over the openings on the intake spacer to prevent foreign objects from falling into the engine.

To install:

9. Remove the masking tape and position new gaskets (if equipped) on the intake spacer.

10. Install the intake manifold. tighten the bolts to 15 ft. lbs. (20 Nm).

11. Connect the fuel injectors and the fuel lines. Tighten the fuel lines to 11 ft. lbs. (15 Nm).

12. Install the intake plenum.

13. Connect the negative battery cable.

Exhaust Manifold

REMOVAL & INSTALLATION

Left Side

1. Before servicing the vehicle, refer to the precautions in the beginning of this section.

2. Remove the engine assembly.

3. Remove the heat shields from the left exhaust manifold.

4. Remove the AIR injection pipe from the manifold to allow access to the exhaust manifold mounting bolts.

5. Remove the coolant pipe and the engine lifting bracket.

6. Remove the dipstick tube.

7. Remove the exhaust manifold mounting nuts and the manifold with gasket.

8. Clean the cylinder head and exhaust manifold mating surfaces.

To install:

9. Install the exhaust manifold. Tighten the nuts to 15 ft. lbs. (20 Nm).

10. Install the dipstick tube. Tighten the bolt to 15 ft. lbs. (20 Nm).

11. Install the engine lifting bracket and coolant pipe. Tighten the bolt to 15 ft. lbs. (20 Nm).

12. Coat the AIR injection pipe mounting bolts with high temperature anti-seize compound, then install the pipe to the manifold. Tighten the bolts to 15 ft. lbs. (20 Nm).

13. Coat the heat shield mounting bolts with high temperature anti-seize compound and install the heat shield on the manifold. Tighten the bolts to 71 inch lbs. (8 Nm).

14. Install the engine assembly in the vehicle.

Right Side

1. Before servicing the vehicle, refer to the precautions in the beginning of this section.

2. Remove the transmission assembly.

3. Disconnect the radiator hose, then remove the coolant intake pipe from the right side of the engine.

4. Raise and safely support the vehicle.

5. Remove the exhaust manifold lower heat shield and the catalytic converter hanger bolt.

6. Remove the two lower rear exhaust manifold mounting nuts.

7. Lower the vehicle to the floor.

8. Remove the two lower front exhaust manifold mounting nuts.

9. Remove the bolts attaching the upper heat shield to the manifold and leave the shield in place.

7922Z408

Intake manifold mounting bolt locations

10. Remove the AIR injection pipe from the manifold to allow access to the exhaust manifold mounting bolts.

11. Remove the upper nuts from the exhaust manifold and remove the manifold.

12. Clean the cylinder head and exhaust manifold mating surfaces.

To install:

13. Install the exhaust manifold with the three upper nuts. Tighten the nuts to 15 ft. lbs. (20 Nm).

14. Coat the AIR injection pipe mounting bolts with high temperature anti-seize compound, then install the pipe to the manifold. Tighten the bolts to 15 ft. lbs. (20 Nm).

15. Coat the upper heat shield mounting bolts with high temperature anti-seize compound and install the upper heat shield on the manifold. Tighten the bolts to 71 inch lbs. (8 Nm).

16. Install the two lower front exhaust manifold mounting nuts. Tighten the nuts to 15 ft. lbs. (20 Nm).

17. Raise and safely support the vehicle.

18. Install the two lower rear exhaust manifold mounting bolts. Tighten the nuts to 15 ft. lbs. (20 Nm).

19. Install the catalytic converter hanger bolt. Tighten the bolt to 15 ft. lbs. (20 Nm).

20. Install the lower exhaust manifold lower heat shield. Tighten the bolts to 71 inch lbs. (8 Nm).

21. Lower the vehicle to the floor and install the coolant intake pipe.

22. Install the transmission assembly.

Camshaft

REMOVAL & INSTALLATION

1. Before servicing the vehicle, refer to the precautions in the beginning of this section.

2. Disconnect the negative battery cable.

3. Remove the intake plenum.

4. Remove the resonance chamber.

5. Remove the valve cover.

6. Remove the front timing belt cover.

7. Position the crankshaft 60 degrees Before Top Dead Center (BTDC) to avoid contact between the valves and the pistons when the camshaft is installed.

8. Remove the timing belt.

9. Install a tool, such as J 42069–1 or its equivalent, to hold the camshaft gear. Be sure the camshaft is not under load from the lifters and remove the camshaft gear.

J 42069 – 1   J 42069 – 2

7922Z409

Camshaft gear holding tools must be installed before attempting to remove the gears from the camshafts

7922Z410

The camshaft bearing caps have identification marks stamped on the side

10. Gradually loosen the camshaft bearing caps bolt sequentially, starting in the center and working outward in a spiral. Note the identification marks on the caps.

11. Remove the camshaft from the cylinder head.

To install:

12. Lubricate the camshaft lobes and lifters with PN 1234501 or equivalent. Lubricate the camshaft bearing journals with assembly fluid PN 1052367 or equivalent.

L8   L7   L6   L5

L4   L3   L2   L1

7922Z411

Camshaft bearing cap locations—right cylinder head

❊❊ WARNING

The bearing caps must be installed in their original positions.

13. Place a small amount of Locktite® 572 or equivalent on the edge of the front bearing cap to ensure a good seal between the cap and surface of the cylinder head. Don't let the sealer get into the oil journal of the cap.

14. Be sure the pin on the front of the camshaft is at the 1 o'clock position for the right exhaust; 11 o'clock for the right intake;

Camshaft bearing cap locations—left cylinder head

Be sure to apply sealant to the areas shown prior to installing the oil pan housing

Oil pump mounting bolt locations

12 o'clock for the left exhaust or 7 o'clock for the left intake camshaft to reduce the lifter load and install the camshaft on the head. Tighten the bolts in sequence starting in the center and working outwards to 71 inch lbs. (8 Nm).

15. Coat the lip of a new camshaft seal with chassis grease and install the seal using J 35268-A or equivalent seal driver.

16. Install the camshaft gear. Tighten the bolt to 37 ft. lbs. (50 Nm) + 60 degrees + 15 degrees using a torque angle meter.

17. Rotate the crankshaft clockwise back to Top Dead Center (TDC).

18. Install the timing belt.

19. Install the timing belt cover.

20. Install the valve cover.

21. Install the intake plenum.

22. Connect the negative battery cable.

Valve Lash

ADJUSTMENT

➡**Valve lash is automatically adjusted by the valve lifters. No adjustment is possible.**

Oil Pan

REMOVAL & INSTALLATION

1. Before servicing the vehicle, refer to the precautions in the beginning of this section.

2. Disconnect the negative battery cable.

3. Raise and safely support the vehicle.

4. Remove the splash shield.

5. Drain the engine oil.

6. Disconnect the oil level sensor wiring and detach the connector from the C-clip.

7. Remove the oil pan bolts and the oil pan.

8. If necessary, remove the oil level sensor from the oil pan.

To install:

9. Clean the oil pan and housing sealing surfaces.

10. If removed, install the oil level sensor on the oil pan. Tighten the bolts just until seated.

11. Install a new O-ring on the oil level sensor connector.

12. Place the new gasket on the pan, then position the pan near the housing and attach the oil level sensor connector.

13. Apply sealant PN 12345997 or equivalent to the rear main bearing cap area and to the area where the oil pump and engine block meet.

14. Install the oil pan and tighten the bolts to 71 inch lbs. (8 Nm).

15. Install the splash shield.

16. Lower the vehicle to the floor.

17. Refill the engine with the correct amount of oil.

18. Connect the negative battery cable and reprogram the necessary accessories.

Oil Pump

REMOVAL & INSTALLATION

1. Disconnect the negative battery cable.

2. Drain the engine coolant.

3. Remove the resonance chamber.

4. Remove the timing belt cover and the timing belt.

5. Remove the rear timing belt cover.

6. Remove the crankshaft drive gear.

7. Remove the lower generator mounting bolt.

8. Remove the oil pan and housing.

9. Remove the oil pump mounting bolts and the oil pump.

To install:

10. Clean the back of the oil pump and the engine block mounting surface. Be sure to remove all old gasket material.

11. Using a new gasket, install the oil pump. Tighten the bolts to 53 inch lbs. (6 Nm).

12. Apply sealant PN 12345997 or equivalent to the area where the oil pump and engine block meet and also to the rear main bearing cap area as shown.

13. Install the oil pan housing. Tighten the bolts to 11 ft. lbs. (15 Nm).

14. Install the lower generator mounting bolt. Tighten the bolt to 30 ft. lbs. (40 Nm).

15. Using a new bolt, install the crankshaft drive gear. Tighten the bolt to 184 ft. lbs. (250 Nm), then using a torque angle meter, tighten the bolt another 45 degrees and lastly, tighten the bolt an additional 15 degrees. Use tool No. J 42065 to hold the crankshaft drive gear from turning.

16. Install the rear timing belt cover, timing belt and front timing belt cover.

17. Install the resonance chamber.

18. Connect the negative battery cable.

19. Refill the cooling system with the correct type and amount of coolant. Use DEX-COOL® or equivalent coolant only.

Rear Main Seal

REMOVAL & INSTALLATION

1. Before servicing the vehicle, refer to the precautions in the beginning of this section.

2. Disconnect the negative battery cable.

3. Remove the transmission and flexplate.

4. Punch a small hole in the oil seal housing and install a sheet metal screw into the hole. Use pliers to remove the oil seal.

To install:

5. Coat the lip of the new seal with chassis grease.

6. Install the seal using Seal Installer No. J 42067 or an equivalent threaded seal installer to push the seal into position.

7. Install the flexplate using new bolts. Tighten the bolts to 48 ft. lbs. (65 Nm), then

Thread a sheet metal screw into the metal part of the seal and remove the seal with pliers

Press the rear main seal into position using a threaded seal installer like J 42067

using a torque angle meter, tighten the bolts another 30 degrees and lastly, tighten the bolts an additional 15 degrees.

8. Install the transmission assembly.
9. Connect the negative battery cable.

FUEL SYSTEM

Fuel System Service Precautions

Safety is the most important factor when performing not only fuel system maintenance but any type of maintenance. Failure to conduct maintenance and repairs in a safe manner may result in serious personal injury or death. Maintenance and testing of the vehicle's fuel system components can be accomplished safely and effectively by adhering to the following rules and guidelines.

• To avoid the possibility of fire and personal injury, always disconnect the negative battery cable unless the repair or test procedure requires that battery voltage be applied.

• Always relieve the fuel system pressure prior to disconnecting any fuel system component (injector, fuel rail, pressure regulator, etc.), fitting or fuel line connection. Exercise extreme caution whenever relieving fuel system pressure to avoid exposing skin, face and eyes to fuel spray. Please be advised that fuel under pressure may penetrate the skin or any part of the body that it contacts.

• Always place a shop towel or cloth around the fitting or connection prior to loosening to absorb any excess fuel due to spillage. Ensure that all fuel spillage (should it occur) is quickly removed from engine surfaces. Ensure that all fuel soaked cloths or towels are deposited into a suitable waste container.

• Always keep a dry chemical (Class B) fire extinguisher near the work area.

• Do not allow fuel spray or fuel vapors to come into contact with a spark or open flame.

• Always use a back-up wrench when loosening and tightening fuel line connection fittings. This will prevent unnecessary stress and torsion to fuel line piping. Always follow the proper torque specifications.

• Always replace worn fuel fitting O-rings with new. Do not substitute fuel hose or equivalent, where fuel pipe is installed.

Fuel System Pressure

RELIEVING

1. Before servicing the vehicle, refer to the precautions in the beginning of this section.
2. Disconnect the negative battery cable.
3. Loosen the fuel filler cap to relieve the tank pressure.
4. Wrap a shop towel around the fuel pressure valve fitting (located on the side or end of the fuel rail assembly) to catch any fuel spray and connect J-34730–1 or an equivalent fuel gauge.
5. Place the bleed hose into a suitable container, then open the valve to bleed the fuel system pressure.
6. Close the valve and disconnect the fuel gauge. Drain any remaining fuel from the gauge into the bleed container.

Fuel Filter

REMOVAL & INSTALLATION

1. Before servicing the vehicle, refer to the precautions in the beginning of this section.

(1) Fuel feed line
(2) Fuel tank
(3) Fuel filter
(4) EVAP Vapor line
(5) Fuel Return line
(6) EVAP Vapor line
(7) Right rear axle shaft

Fuel line and filter identification

2. Remove the fuel tank cap to relieve the pressure in the tank.

3. Properly relieve the fuel system pressure.

4. Hold the filter firmly and remove both fuel line attaching bolts.

To install:

6. Clean the bolts and fittings on bolt fuel lines.

7. Install the lines to the filter. Be sure the filter is in the proper direction.

8. Install the fuel filter in the bracket.

9. Tighten the fuel tank cap.

10. Crank the engine for a few seconds, if the engine starts, turn it **OFF**.

11. Check for fuel leaks and repair if necessary.

Fuel Pump

REMOVAL & INSTALLATION

1. Before servicing the vehicle, refer to the precautions in the beginning of this section.

2. Disconnect the negative battery cable.

3. Properly relieve the fuel system pressure.

4. Raise and safely support the vehicle.

5. Drain, then remove the fuel tank.

6. Remove the spring loaded clamp from the fuel tank boot.

7. Detach the wiring connector from the fuel pump assembly.

8. Remove the locking ring using tool No. J 42219 or equivalent.

9. Remove the fuel pump from the tank. Tilt the assembly slightly to prevent damaging the float arm.

➡ **The reservoir on the fuel pump assembly still contains fuel. Drain the fuel into a container after removing the pump.**

(1) Fuel pump
(2) Fuel gauge float arm
(3) Fuel reservoir

7922Z419

Fuel pump module components

10. Remove the seal from the fuel pump module. The seal must pass over the reservoir and over the float arm.

To install:

11. Lubricate the inside diameter of a new seal with engine oil and install it on the fuel pump module.

12. Install the pump module in the tank. Be sure to align the hole on the module with the mark on the fuel tank. Tighten the locking ring to 37 ft. lbs. (50 Nm).

13. Attach the wiring harness connector.

14. Install the spring loaded clamp on the fuel tank boot.

15. Install the fuel tank in the vehicle.

16. Connect the negative battery cable.

DRIVE TRAIN

Transmission Assembly

REMOVAL & INSTALLATION

1. Before servicing the vehicle, refer to the precautions in the beginning of this section.

2. Disconnect the negative battery cable.

3. Raise and safely support the vehicle.

4. Disconnect the shift lever rod from the transmission.

5. Remove the three bolts attaching the driveshaft to the flange on the rear of the transmission. Use a flat bladed to pry the driveshaft away from the flange. Position the driveshaft out of the way.

6. Remove the two hole plugs from the oil pan and bell housing.

7. Matchmark the torque converter to the flexplate, then remove the flexplate-to-torque converter bolts.

8. Disconnect the fluid cooler hoses from the center pipes.

9. Disconnect the Oxygen (O_2S) sensor wiring and remove the catalytic converters.

10. Remove the four transmission housing-to-oil pan bolts.

11. Position a transmission jack under the transmission.

12. Remove the two nuts securing the transmission mount to the center of the crossmember.

13. Raise the transmission slightly and remove the crossmember.

14. Lower the transmission in order to gain access to the remaining transmission-

to-engine mounting bolts and electrical connectors.

15. Detach the electrical connectors and remove the vent hose from the transmission.

16. Support the engine with a block of wood and a jack.

17. Remove the remaining transmission-to-engine mounting bolts and remove the transmission from the vehicle.

To install:

✳✳ WARNING

The transmission fluid cooler and lines must be flushed out prior to installing a new or reconditioned transmission.

18. Clean the bolt holes in the engine block with a 12 x 1.75mm tap.

19. Apply thread locking compound to the transmission-to-engine mounting bolts.

20. Position the transmission on the rear of the engine block and install the mounting bolts. Tighten the bolts to 44 ft. lbs. (60 Nm).

21. Remove the jack from the engine.

22. Attach the electrical connectors and vent hose to the transmission.

23. Raise the transmission into position and install the crossmember. Tighten the crossmember-to-body bolts to 33 ft. lbs. (45 Nm). Lower the transmission onto the crossmember. Tighten the transmission mount-to-crossmember nuts to 15 ft. lbs. (20 Nm). Remove the transmission jack.

24. Install the catalytic converters and connect the O_2S sensor wiring.

25. Connect the fluid cooler hoses to the center pipes.

26. Align the matchmarks made earlier on the flexplate and torque converter. Install new flexplate-to-torque converter bolts. Be sure to remove the sealing compound from the firs three threads. Tighten the bolts to 22 ft. lbs. (30 Nm).

27. Install the two access hose plugs.

28. Install the driveshaft to the drive flange. Tighten the bolts to 70 ft. lbs. (95 Nm).

29. Connect the shift lever rod to the transmission. Adjust the rod as follows:

a. Place the shift control lever in **PARK**

b. Loosen the adjusting bolt on the rod

c. Hold the selector lever on the transmission toward the rear stop to eliminate any free-play

d. Tighten the adjusting bolt to 71 inch lbs. (8 Nm)

30. Fill the transmission pan with DEXRON® III to the lower edge of the fill plug. Tighten the plug to 33 ft. lbs. (45 Nm).

31. Lower the vehicle to the floor.

32. Connect the negative battery cable.

33. Start the vehicle and check for leaks. Be sure the vehicle will only start in the **PARK** and **NEUTRAL** positions.

Halfshaft

REMOVAL & INSTALLATION

1. Before servicing the vehicle, refer to the precautions in the beginning of this section.

2. Place the gear selector in **NEUTRAL**.

3. Raise and safely support the vehicle.

4. Remove the rear wheel.

5. Install a tool such as Hub Holding tool No. J 42066 or equivalent, on the outer hub.

6. Remove the bolts attaching the halfshaft outer flange to the hub assembly, then pry the halfshaft away from the hub.

7. Separate the inner side of the halfshaft from the differential using tool No.

Prevent the outer hub from turning by installing a tool such as Hub Holding tool **J 42066**

Pry the halfshaft out of the differential using tool **J 42071** or equivalent

J 42071 or equivalent. Once the initial connection is broken, the halfshaft can be removed by hand.

To install:

8. Lubricate the splined portion of the halfshaft with differential oil.

9. Install the halfshaft into the differential by tapping on the outer end of the shaft with a rubber/plastic hammer until the halfshaft is seated in the differential.

10. Install the outer end of the halfshaft on the hub assembly. Tighten the bolts to 37 ft. lbs. (50 Nm), then using a torque angle meter, tighten the bolts an additional 67 degrees while holding the hub stationary.

11. Install the rear wheel.

12. Lower the vehicle to the floor.

STEERING AND SUSPENSION

Air Bag

✳✳ CAUTION

These vehicles are equipped with an air bag system, also known as the Supplemental Inflatable Restraint (SIR) or Supplemental Restraint System (SRS). The system must be disabled before performing service on or around system components, steering column, instrument panel components, wiring and sensors. Failure to follow safety and disabling procedures could result in accidental air bag deployment, possible personal injury and unnecessary system repairs.

PRECAUTIONS

Several precautions must be observed when handling the inflator module to avoid accidental deployment and possible personal injury.

• Never carry the inflator module by the wires or connector on the underside of the module.

• When carrying a live inflator module, hold securely with both hands, and ensure that the bag and trim cover are pointed away.

• Place the inflator module on a bench or other surface with the bag and trim cover facing up.

• With the inflator module on the bench,

never place anything on or close to the module which may be thrown in the event of an accidental deployment.

DISARMING

1. Turn the steering wheel to align the wheels in the straight-ahead position.

2. Turn the ignition switch to the **LOCK** position and remove the key.

3. Wait one minute until the capacitors in the Sensing and Diagnostic Module (SDM) discharge.

4. Disconnect the negative battery cable.

REARMING

1. Turn the ignition switch to the **LOCK** position and remove the key.

2. Reconnect the negative battery cable.

3. Wait at least one minute for the capacitors to recharge.

4. While staying away from the inflator modules, turn the key to the **RUN** position. The air bag warning lamp should turn on for 3–4 seconds, then turn off.

Recirculating Ball Power Steering Gear

REMOVAL & INSTALLATION

1. Before servicing the vehicle, refer to the precautions in the beginning of this section.

2. Center the front wheels, then turn the ignition key to the **LOCK** position.

3. Disconnect the negative battery cable.

4. Remove the windshield wiper assembly.

5. Detach the three body harness electrical connectors.

6. Remove the Electronic Control Module (ECM) from electrical box.

7. Drain the engine coolant.

8. Remove the radiator hose.

9. Properly discharge and recover the A/C refrigerant using an approved recycling station.

10. Remove the A/C evaporator line extension bolt.

11. Siphon the power steering fluid from the reservoir, then remove the mounting bolt and position the reservoir out of the way.

12. Disconnect the brake booster vacuum hose from the plenum.

13. Siphon the brake fluid from the reservoir, then remove the brake lines from the master cylinder.

Body harness electrical connector locations (1)

Matchmark the coupler to the steering gear before removing the coupler bolts (1)

Steering gear mounting bolt locations

14. Disconnect the brake fluid level sensor from the master cylinder cap.

15. Remove the driver's side sound insulator panel.

16. Matchmark the steering coupler and input shaft of the steering gear.

17. Remove the coupler bolts, then spread the clamp and pull the steering shaft upward and away from the steering gear.

18. Remove the brake booster pushrod from the brake pedal.

19. Remove the knee bolster from the lower instrument panel.

20. Remove the fuse and relay panel mounting screws and position the panels out of the way of the brake booster mounting nuts.

21. Remove the nuts, then remove the brake booster with the master cylinder attached.

22. Disconnect the A/C evaporator line quick-connect fitting.

23. Remove the power steering hoses from the steering gear and remove the Electronic Brake Traction Control Module/Brake Pressure Modulator Valve (EBTCM/BPMV) assembly.

24. Remove the upper heat shield mounting bolt.

25. Raise and safely support the vehicle.

26. Matchmark the Pitman arm position

on the steering gear cross-shaft and remove the Pitman arm using a suitable puller.

27. Remove the lower heat shield mounting nuts.

28. Remove the three lower mounting bolts from the steering gear.

29. Lower the vehicle to the floor and remove the heat shield.

30. Disconnect the power steering fluid flow control actuator.

31. Remove the upper mounting bolt and the steering gear.

To install:

32. Find the center of travel of the steering gear by turning the stubshaft and counting the number of turns from lock-to-lock. Divide the total number in half and turn the stub shaft from either lock position by this amount. Finally align the mark on the stub shaft to the "V" mark on the steering gear.

33. Position the steering gear on the frame and install the shims and upper mounting bolt. Do not tighten the bolt at this time.

34. Connect the power steering fluid flow control actuator.

35. Install the heat shield with the upper mounting bolt. Tighten the bolt to 71 ft. lbs. (8 Nm).

36. Raise and safely support the vehicle.

37. Install the steering gear lower mounting bolts. Tighten all mounting bolts to 30 ft. lbs. (40 Nm).

38. Install the lower heat shield mounting nuts. Tighten the nuts to 11 ft. lbs. (15 Nm).

39. Be sure the rubber steering gear shaft protector is in place, then install the Pitman arm. Tighten the nut to 118 ft. lbs. (160 Nm).

40. Lower the vehicle to the floor.

41. Install the EBTCM/BPMV assembly.

42. Connect the fluid lines to the steering gear. Tighten the fittings to 21 ft. lbs. (28 Nm).

43. Install new O-rings on the A/C evaporator line. Lubricate the O-rings with mineral oil of 525 viscosity and attach the quick-connect.

44. Install the brake booster assembly. Tighten the nuts to 15 ft. lbs. (20 Nm).

45. Install the fuse and relay panel, then install the knee bolster.

46. Connect the brake booster pushrod to the brake pedal.

47. Align the matchmarks and connect the steering shaft to the steering gear. Tighten the bolts to 16 ft. lbs. (22 Nm).

48. Install the sound insulator.

49. Connect the brake lines to the master cylinder. Tighten the fittings to 12 ft. lbs. (16 Nm).

50. Connect the brake fluid level sensor.

Align the mark on the stub shaft with the "V" mark on the steering gear mounting bolt locations

51. Install the power steering fluid reservoir. Tighten the clamp bolt to 62 inch lbs. (7 Nm).

52. Install new O-rings on the A/C evaporator-to-cowl connection. Lubricate the O-rings with mineral oil of 525 viscosity and connect the fitting. Tighten the bolt to 15 ft. lbs. (20 Nm).

53. Install the upper radiator hose and install the ECM.

54. Install the windshield wiper assembly.

55. Connect the negative battery cable.

56. Refill the cooling system.

57. Refill the power steering system and bleed the system using the following substeps:

    a. Turn the ignition switch **OFF**

    b. Raise the front wheels off the ground.

    c. Turn the steering wheel to the full left position.

    d. Fill the reservoir to the **FULL COLD** level.

    e. Have an assistant monitor the fluid level and condition while turning the steering wheel from lock-to-lock at least 20 times or until no air bubbles are present. Refill the reservoir as needed.

    f. Start the engine and allow it to run for two minutes.

    g. Turn the front wheels to the center position and lower the vehicle to the floor.

    h. Turn the steering wheel from lock-to-lock and verify smooth operation.

58. Recharge and leak test the A/C system.

59. Bleed the brake system if necessary.

Strut

REMOVAL & INSTALLATION

Front

1. Before servicing the vehicle, refer to the precautions in the beginning of this section.

2. Raise and safely support the vehicle.

3. Remove the front wheel.

4. Detach the ABS speed sensor and break wear indicator wires from the strut.

5. Remove the brake hose from the strut.

6. Remove the brake caliper and suspend it out of the way with wire.

7. Remove the stabilizer bar link from the strut.

8. Mark the location of the strut on the knuckle and remove the lower strut mounting bolts.

9. Lower the vehicle to gain access to the upper strut mounting.

10. Remove the upper support plate protective cap and nut, then remove the strut from the vehicle.

To install:

11. Position the strut assembly in the strut tower.

12. Install the upper support plate and nut. Tighten the nut to 41 ft. lbs. (55 Nm).

13. Install the protective cap and raise the vehicle.

14. Using new bolts, install the strut on the knuckle. Be sure to align the matchmarks and install the bolts from the front. Tighten the bolts to 66 ft. lbs. (90 Nm), then using a torque angle meter, tighten the bolts an additional 52 degrees.

15. Connect the stabilizer bar link to the strut. Tighten the nut to 48 ft. lbs. (65 Nm).

16. Clean out the brake caliper mounting bolt holes with a M12 x 1.5mm tap. Apply Locktite® 272 or equivalent thread locker to the bolts and install the caliper on the knuckle. Tighten the bolts to 70 ft. lbs. (95 Nm), then using a torque angle meter, tighten the bolts an additional 37 degrees.

17. Install the brake hose, ABS sensor and brake wear indicator wires to the strut assembly.

18. Install the front wheel.

19. Lower the vehicle to the floor.

20. Check and adjust the front wheel alignment if necessary.

Shock Absorber

REMOVAL & INSTALLATION

Rear

1. Before servicing the vehicle, refer to the precautions in the beginning of this section.

2. Position the rear seat backs forward to allow access to the upper shock absorber mounting.

3. Remove the protective cap, nut, washer and grommet.

4. Raise and safely support the vehicle.

5. Detach the Automatic Level Control (ALC) air line from the shock absorber.

6. Remove the lower shock absorber mounting bolt and the shock absorber.

Air line connection to the shock absorber for Automatic Level Control (ALC)

To install:

7. If installing a new shock absorber, remove the cap from the air line connection.

8. Lower the vehicle and install the shock absorber upper mounting. Tighten the nut to 15 ft. lbs. (20 Nm). Install the protective cap.

9. Place the rear seats into the proper position.

10. Raise and safely support the vehicle.

11. Install the shock absorber to the control arm. Tighten the bolt to 81 ft. lbs. (110 Nm).

12. Connect the ALC air line to the shock absorber.

13. Lower the vehicle to the floor.

Coil Spring

REMOVAL & INSTALLATION

Front

1. Before servicing the vehicle, refer to the precautions in the beginning of this section.

2. Remove the strut assembly.

3. Compress the coil spring using a suitable coil spring compressor.

4. Remove the upper bearing support nut, bearing and plate assembly.

5. Decompress and remove the spring.

To install:

6. Compress the spring and position it on the strut. Be sure the spring is properly positioned between the upper and lower insulators.

7. Install the bearing and plate assembly. Tighten the nut to 52 ft. lbs. (70 Nm).

8. Slowly decompress the spring.

9. Install the strut assembly.

Rear

1. Before servicing the vehicle, refer to the precautions in the beginning of this section.

2. Raise and safely support the vehicle.

3. Remove the brake lines from the lower control arm without opening the brake system.

4. Disconnect the stabilizer link from the lower control arm.

5. Support the exhaust system with a jack, then remove the rubber hangers and lower the exhaust system out of the way.

6. Disconnect the wiring from the rear ABS wheel speed sensors.

7. Support the lower control arm with a jack. Raise the jack slightly to remove the pressure exerted by the spring on the shock absorber, then remove the lower shock absorber mounting bolt and remove the jack.

8. Support the differential with a jack and remove the rear axle cradle mount-to-body bolts.

9. Lower the rear axle cradle and remove the springs with the seats attached.

10. Remove the seat from the spring.

To install:

11. Install the seat on the spring.

12. Position the spring on the lower control arm. Be sure the spring is located properly on the seat.

13. Raise the differential and install the rear axle cradle mounting bolts. Tighten the bolts to 48 ft. lbs. (65 Nm).

(1) Upper Support Plate Nut
(2) Upper Support Plate
(3) Upper Bearing Support Nut
(4) Bearing and Bearing Plate Assembly
(5) Upper Spring Support Plate
(6) Upper Insulator
(7) Strut Bumper
(8) Strut Cover
(9) Strut
(10) Lower Insulator
(11) Spring

Exploded view of the strut assembly

Be sure to compress the coil spring before removing the upper bearing support nut

Drill out the rivets to remove the ball joint from the lower control arm

The replacement ball joint will be bolted to the lower control arm with the bolts supplied in the kit

14. Remove the jack and place it under the lower control arm. Raise the control arm enough to install the lower shock absorber mounting bolt. Install the bolt and tighten it to 81 ft. lbs. (110 Nm).

15. Connect the ABS wheel speed sensor wiring.

16. Raise the exhaust system into position and install the rubber hangers.

17. Connect the stabilizer link to the lower control arm. Tighten the bolts to 15 ft. lbs. (20 Nm).

18. Install the brake lines on the lower control arms with the retainers.

19. Lower the vehicle to the floor and check the wheel alignment.

Lower Ball Joint

REMOVAL & INSTALLATION

1. Before servicing the vehicle, refer to the precautions in the beginning of this section.

2. Raise and safely support the vehicle.

3. Remove the front wheel.

4. Remove the brake pad wear indicator rubber sleeve from the strut assembly.

5. Remove the ABS wheel speed sensor.

6. Detach the brake hose from the strut.

7. Remove the brake caliper from the knuckle and support it with a piece of wire.

8. Disconnect the tie rod end from the knuckle.

9. Disconnect the stabilizer link from the stabilizer bar.

10. Matchmark the position of the strut on the knuckle and remove the bolts attaching the strut to the knuckle.

11. Remove the pinch bolt securing the ball joint stud to the knuckle.

12. Loosen the lower control arm horizontal and vertical bolts. Remove the horizontal bolt and rotate the control arm from the support bracket.

13. Remove the vertical control arm mounting bolt and the control arm.

14. Drill out the rivets attaching the ball joint to the lower control arm and remove the ball joint.

To install:

15. Install the new ball joint on the lower control arm. Be sure to install the bolts from the top of the control arm. Tighten the bolts to 26 ft. lbs. (35 Nm).

➡ **New bolts must be used to reinstall the lower control arm on the body.**

16. Install the lower control arm vertical bolt. Do not tighten the bolt at this time.

17. Position the front of the control arm in the support bracket. Install the bolt from the rear of the vehicle. Hold the control arm horizontal and tighten both bolts to 103 ft. lbs. (140 Nm).

18. Install the ball joint stud to the knuckle using a new bolt. Tighten the bolt to 74 ft. lbs. (100 Nm)

19. Using new bolts, install the strut on the knuckle. Be sure to align the matchmarks and install the bolts from the front. Tighten the bolts to 66 ft. lbs. (90 Nm), then using a torque angle meter, tighten the bolts an additional 52 degrees.

20. Connect the stabilizer link to the stabilizer bar. Tighten the nut to 48 ft. lbs. (65 Nm) while holding the link with a 17mm wrench.

21. Connect the tie rod end to the knuckle with a new self-locking nut. Tighten the nut to 44 ft. lbs. (60 Nm).

22. Clean out the brake caliper mounting bolt holes with a M12 x 1.5mm tap. Apply Locktite® 272 or equivalent thread locker to the bolts and install the caliper on the knuckle. Tighten the bolts to 70 ft. lbs. (95 Nm) , then using a torque angle meter, tighten the bolts an additional 37 degrees.

23. Install the brake hose, ABS sensor and brake wear indicator wires to the strut assembly.

24. Install the wheel speed sensor. Tighten the bolts to 71 inch lbs. (8 Nm).

25. Install the front wheel.

26. Lower the vehicle to the floor.

27. Check and adjust the front wheel alignment if necessary.

Wheel Bearings

ADJUSTMENT

The wheel bearings used by the Catera are not adjustable.

REMOVAL & INSTALLATION

Front

1. Before servicing the vehicle, refer to the precautions in the beginning of this section.

2. Raise and safely support the vehicle.

3. Remove the front wheel.

Cut-away view of the hub/wheel bearing assembly and steering knuckle

Turn to Section 6 for brake system applications

4. Remove the brake pad wear indicator wire from the strut assembly.

5. Detach the brake hose from the strut.

6. Remove the brake caliper from the knuckle and support it with a piece of wire.

7. Remove the set screw, then the brake rotor.

8. Remove the wheel hub dust cap.

9. Remove the spindle nut and the wheel bearing assembly.

To install:

10. Install the wheel bearing assembly onto the spindle. Use a socket to press the outer bearing ring into the hub if necessary. Tighten the nut to 236 ft. lbs. (320 Nm).

11. Install the brake rotor. Tighten the set screw to 35 inch lbs. (4 Nm).

12. Clean out the brake caliper mounting bolt holes with a M12 x 1.5mm tap. Apply Locktite® 272 or equivalent thread locker to the bolts and install the caliper on the knuckle. Tighten the bolts to 70 ft. lbs. (95 Nm) , then using a torque angle meter, tighten the bolts an additional 37 degrees.

13. Install the brake hose and the ABS sensor wire to the strut assembly.

14. Install the front wheel.

15. Lower the vehicle to the floor.

Rear

➡**Several special tools are necessary to remove the rear wheel bearing from the knuckle. The tools required are as follows:**

- J 36660 Torque Angle Meter
- J 42066 Holding tool
- J 42094–1 Holding Fixture
- J 42094–2 Spacer
- J 42094–3 Threaded Driver
- J 42094–4 Threaded Arbor
- J 42094–5 Ball Head
- J 42094–6 Bearing Remover
- J 42094–7 Threaded Spacer Pin
- J 42094–8 Bearing Installer
- J 42094–9 Hub Installer
- J 42094–10 Thrust Bearing
- J 42072 Triple Hex Head (10mm) deep socket

The tool numbers mentioned are Kent-Moore tools used by GM. Equivalent tools may be available from other sources.

1. Before servicing the vehicle, refer to the precautions in the beginning of this section.

2. Raise and safely support the vehicle.

3. Remove the rear wheel.

4. Remove the halfshaft from the wheel hub and suspend it out of the way with wire.

J 42094 – 1
J 42094 – 2
J 42094 – 3
J 42094 – 4
J 42094 – 5
J 42094 – 6
J 42094 – 7
J 42094 – 8
J 42094 – 9
J 42094 – 10

7922Z432

Several tools make up the J 42094 tool kit for rear wheel bearing removal and installation

7922Z433

Attach the Spacer and Holding Fixture to the flange before removing the hub retaining nut

5. Remove the brake hose from the clip on the lower control arm, them remove the caliper and suspend it out of the way with wire.

6. Remove the set screw, then the brake rotor.

7. Using socket, J 42072 or its equivalent, back out three of the four brake backing plate bolts about nine turns to allow for installation of the wheel hub puller pins. The pins will screw into the same holes from the other side.

8. Attach spacer, J 42094–2 and hold-

ing fixture, J 42094–1 or their equivalents, to the flange on the inside of the hub. Half-shaft bolts may be used if necessary.

9. Remove the wheel hub nut.

10. Attach the threaded arbor, J 42094–4 or its equivalent, to the holding fixture with three supplied bolts using thrust bearing, J 42094–10 or its equivalent, as a spacer. Thread driver, J 42094–3 or its equivalent, into the threaded arbor, J 42094–4 or its equivalent. Place the ball head, J 42094–5 or its equivalent, onto J 42094–3 or its equivalent, once sufficiently installed.

11. Turn the threaded driver to remove the flange.

12. Screw three spacer pins, J 42094–7 or its equivalent, into the backing plate.

13. Attach holding fixture J 42094–1 or its equivalent, with the stem pointed upward to the spacer pins with nuts and press out the wheel hub with the threaded driver.

14. Remove the wheel bearing retainer with snap ring pliers.

15. Attach bearing remover J 42094–6 or its equivalent, to the end of the threaded driver and remove the wheel bearing by turning the driver clockwise.

1
2
J 43094 – 10
J 42094 – 5
J 42094 – 3
3
J 42094 – 2
J 42094 – 4
J 42094 – 1

7922Z434

Set up the special tools as shown to remove the flange

Set up the special tools as shown to remove the hub

Wheel Bearing

Set up the special tools as shown to remove the bearing assembly

Set up the special tools as shown to install the bearing assembly

For complete service labor times order Chilton's Labor Guide Manual

Set up the special tools as shown to pull the hub into the bearing assembly

Set up the special tools as shown to install the flange on the hub

To install:

16. Assembly wheel bearing installer J 42094–8 or its equivalent, through the bearing.

17. Thread J 42094–8 into the threaded driver J 42094–3 or its equivalent.

18. Turn J 42094–3 or its equivalent, until the bearing is fully seated.

19. Install the wheel bearing retainer.

20. Insert rear wheel hub installer, J 42094–9 or its equivalent, on the shaft of the threaded driver, J 42094–3 or its equiv-alent, and attach holding fixture, J 42094–1 or its equivalent, to the threaded spacer pins, J 42094–7 or its equivalent.

21. Thread the rear wheel hub into the threaded driver, J 42094–3 or its equivalent. Be sure the threaded driver is centered in the bearing to prevent binding of the hub as it is drawn into the bearing.

22. Hold the threaded driver, J 42094–3 or its equivalent, and turn the arbor, J 42094–4 or its equivalent, clockwise to pull the hub into the bearing.

23. Remove the tools from the vehicle.

24. Connect the threaded arbor, J 42094–4, threaded driver, J 42094–3, holding fixture, J 42094–1, spacer, J 42094–2, and thrust bearing, J 42094–10 or their equivalents, to the wheel flange with the halfshaft mounting bolts.

25. Align the splines and position the flange on the hub.

26. Press the flange onto the hub by turning the threaded arbor, J 42094–4 or its equivalent, clockwise while counter-holding with the threaded driver, J 42094–3 or its equivalent.

27. Remove the threaded arbor, J 42094–4, threaded driver, J 42094–3 or their equivalents, and the thrust bearing from the wheel flange. Leave the holding fixture and spacer, J 42094–2 or their equivalents, attached.

28. Tighten the hub nut to 221 ft. lbs. (300 Nm). Remove the holding fixture and spacer, then pry the retaining washer over one side of the nut to lock it in place.

29. Install the brake backing plate mounting bolts. Tighten them to 37 ft. lbs. (50 Nm), then using a torque angle meter, tighten the bolts an additional 40 degrees.

30. Install the brake rotor. Tighten the set screw to 35 inch lbs. (4 Nm).

31. Install the caliper. Tighten the bolts to 59 ft. lbs. (80 Nm).

32. Install the brake line on the control arm with the retainer.

33. Install the halfshaft. Tighten the bolts to 37 ft. lbs. (50 Nm), then using a torque angle meter, tighten the bolts an additional 70°.

34. Install the rear wheel.

35. Lower the vehicle to the floor.

GENERAL MOTORS CORPORATION—W BODY

38

Buick-Century • Regal • **Chevrolet-**Lumina • Monte Carlo
Oldsmobile-Cutlass Supreme • Intrigue • **Pontiac-**Grand Prix

PRECAUTIONS

Before servicing any vehicle, please be sure to read all of the following precautions, which deal with personal safety, prevention of component damage, and important points to take into consideration when servicing a motor vehicle:

• Never open, service or drain the radiator or cooling system when the engine is hot; serious burns can occur from the steam and hot coolant.

• Observe all applicable safety precautions when working around fuel. Whenever servicing the fuel system, always work in a well ventilated area. Do not allow fuel spray or vapors to come in contact with a spark, open flame, or excessive heat (a hot drop light, for example). Keep a dry chemical fire extinguisher near the work area. Always keep fuel in a container specifically designed for fuel storage; also, always properly seal fuel containers to avoid the possibility of fire or explosion. Refer to the additional fuel system precautions later in this section.

• Fuel injection systems often remain pressurized, even after the engine has been turned **OFF**. The fuel system pressure must be relieved before disconnecting any fuel lines. Failure to do so may result in fire and/or personal injury.

• Brake fluid often contains polyglycol ethers and polyglycols. Avoid contact with the eyes and wash your hands thoroughly after handling brake fluid. If you do get brake fluid in your eyes, flush your eyes with clean, running water for 15 minutes. If eye irritation persists, or if you have taken brake fluid internally, seek medical assistance IMMEDIATELY.

• The EPA warns that prolonged contact with used engine oil may cause a number of skin disorders, including cancer! You should make every effort to minimize your exposure to used engine oil. Protective gloves should be worn when changing oil. Wash your hands and any other exposed skin areas as soon as possible after expo-sure to used engine oil. Soap and water, or waterless hand cleaner should be used.

• All new vehicles are now equipped with an air bag system, often referred to as a Supplemental Restraint System (SRS) or Supplemental Inflatable Restraint (SIR) system. The system must be disabled before performing service on or around system components, steering column, instrument panel components, wiring and sensors. Failure to follow safety and disabling procedures could result in accidental air bag deployment, possible personal injury and unnecessary system repairs.

• Always wear safety goggles when working with, or around, the air bag system. When carrying a non-deployed air bag, be sure the bag and trim cover are pointed away from your body. When placing a non-deployed air bag on a work surface, always face the bag and trim cover upward, away from the surface. This will reduce the motion of the module if it is accidentally deployed. Refer to the additional air bag system precautions later in this section.

• Clean, high quality brake fluid from a sealed container is essential to the safe and proper operation of the brake system. You should always buy the correct type of brake fluid for your vehicle. If the brake fluid becomes contaminated, completely flush the system with new fluid. Never reuse any brake fluid. Any brake fluid that is removed from the system should be discarded. Also, do not allow any brake fluid to come in contact with a painted surface; it will damage the paint.

• Never operate the engine without the proper amount and type of engine oil; doing so WILL result in severe engine damage.

• Timing belt maintenance is extremely important! Many models utilize an interference-type, non-freewheeling engine. If the timing belt breaks, the valves in the cylinder head may strike the pistons, causing potentially serious (also time-consuming and expensive) engine damage. Refer to the maintenance interval charts in the front of this manual for the recommended replacement interval for the timing belt, and to the timing belt section for belt replacement and inspection.

• Disconnecting the negative battery cable on some vehicles may interfere with the functions of the on-board computer system(s) and may require the computer to undergo a relearning process once the negative battery cable is reconnected.

• When servicing drum brakes, only disassemble and assemble one side at a time, leaving the remaining side intact for reference.

ENGINE REPAIR

Distributor

The 3.1L, 3.4L, 3.5L and 3.8L engines all utilize a Distributorless Ignition System (DIS). This system uses three twin tower coils which fire two spark plugs simultaneously. One spark plug is located in a cylinder on the compression stroke and the other in a cylinder on the exhaust stroke. This is known as the waste spark method of distribution.

Ignition Timing

ADJUSTMENT

The ignition timing is not adjustable and is set electronically according to the inputs received from various sensors. The Powertrain Control Module (PCM) controls the ignition timing for all driving conditions.

Engine Assembly

REMOVAL & INSTALLATION

3.1L Engine

1. Before servicing the vehicle, refer to the precautions in the beginning of this section.

2. Disconnect the negative battery cable. With the aid of an assistant, remove the hood.

3. Drain the engine coolant.

4. Remove the air cleaner and duct assembly.

5. Disconnect the transaxle fluid filler tube assembly.

6. Remove the engine mount strut brackets.

7. Raise and safely support the vehicle. Drain the engine oil.

8. Remove the front exhaust pipe and exhaust manifold heat shield.

9. Remove the lower the rear transaxle bolts.

10. Disconnect the electrical connector from the Vehicle Speed Sensor (VSS).

11. Remove the engine mount frame side nuts.

12. Remove the flywheel inspection cover and the starter assembly.

13. Remove the torque converter bolts.

14. Remove the transaxle mount assembly. Safely lower the vehicle.

15. Remove the coolant reservoir recovery assembly.

16. Remove the serpentine belt.

17. Remove the accelerator control cable bracket and move the cables assemblies aside.

18. Remove the power brake booster vacuum hose from the upper intake manifold assembly.

19. Remove the plastic cover from the shock tower.

20. Remove the alternator front and rear braces.

21. Remove the alternator assembly from the vehicle.

22. Disconnect the fuel feed and return pipe assemblies.

23. Remove the tie straps around the ignition wiring harness assembly, engine mount strut and air conditioning compressor bracket.

24. Remove the power steering pump pulley assembly.

25. Remove the power steering pump bolts/screws and move the power steering pump aside.

26. Remove the heater outlet and inlet hose assemblies.

27. Remove the upper radiator hose assembly from the engine.

28. Remove the lower radiator hose assembly from the water pump.

29. Remove the engine mount strut and air conditioning compressor bracket bolts and move the compressor assembly aside.

30. Remove the automatic transaxle vacuum modulator pipe assembly.

31. Disconnect the electrical connectors from the Knock Sensor (KS), Oxygen Sensor (O₂S), Engine Coolant Temperature (ECT) sensor, Camshaft Position (CMP) sensor, Crankshaft Position (CKP) sensor and Wheel Speed Sensors (WSS).

32. Disconnect the electrical connectors from the ignition coil assembly.

33. Disconnect the electrical connectors from the idle air control valve and throttle position sensor.

34. Remove the vacuum hoses from the upper intake manifold assembly.

35. Remove the attaching transaxle bolts.

36. Install a safety bolt between the alternator bracket and the engine lift bracket assemblies.

37. Suitably support the transaxle assembly with floor stands.

38. Attach a suitable engine lifting device to the engine.

39. Remove the engine assembly from the vehicle.

To install:

40. Install the engine into the vehicle using a suitable engine lifting device.

41. Remove the engine lifting device. Remove the floor stands from the transaxle.

42. Remove the safety bolt from the alternator bracket and front engine lift bracket assemblies.

43. Install the transaxle bolts.

44. Install the remaining components in the reverse order of removal. Tighten the following:

• Torque converter bolts to 46 ft. lbs. (63 Nm)

• Engine mount frame side nuts-to-drive train bolts to 32 ft. lbs. (43 Nm)

45. Refill the engine with clean oil.

46. Install the engine mount strut brackets.

47. Install the transaxle fluid filler tube assembly.

48. Install the air cleaner and duct assembly. Install the hood panel.

49. Refill the engine coolant and add two engine coolant sealant pellets GM 3634621 or equivalent.

50. Bleed the cooling system using the recommended procedure.

51. Start the engine and verify correct idle and performance.

3.4L Engine

1. Before servicing the vehicle, refer to the precautions in the beginning of this section.

2. Remove the air cleaner assembly.

3. Remove the hood assembly with the help of an assistant.

4. Drain the cooling system. Remove the coolant recovery reservoir.

5. Remove the heater hoses from the engine. Remove the engine torque strut bracket and strut.

6. Remove the cooling fans.

7. Remove the radiator hoses from the engine. Detach the transaxle cooler lines.

8. Remove the radiator and attaching hoses.

9. Remove the control cables from the bracket and throttle body.

10. Remove the exhaust crossover.

11. Remove the ground straps from the bell housing.

12. Remove the fuel injector cover.

13. Remove the power steering lines at the pump and front cover.

14. Remove the serpentine drive belt. Remove the upper A/C compressor bolts.

15. Safely raise and support the vehicle. Remove the right front tire and wheel assembly.

16. Remove the right front splash shield.

17. Remove the lower A/C compressor bolts and reposition the compressor.

18. Remove the flywheel inspection cover. Remove the engine oil filter.

19. Remove the starter assembly.

20. Remove the front exhaust pipe and converter.

21. Remove the motor mount nuts from the subframe.

22. Tag and disconnect the electrical connections from the rear of engine.

23. Remove the right ball joint nut and separate the ball joint from the control arm.

24. Remove the outer tie rod.

25. Remove the drive axle assembly.

26. Remove the transaxle shield.

27. Suitably support the transaxle with an appropriate jacking fixture.

28. Remove the motor mount bracket to the transaxle bolts and nuts.

29. Remove the transaxle support and safely lower the vehicle.

30. Remove the plastic cover from the shock tower.

31. Detach the electrical quick connectors from the Powertrain Control Module (PCM).

32. Disconnect all necessary vacuum lines.

33. Support the transaxle.

34. Install a suitable engine lifting device.

35. Remove the engine assembly from

vehicle after disconnecting the alternator connections.

To install:

36. Install the engine assembly into the vehicle with a suitable engine lifting device.

37. Connect the electrical connections to the alternator.

38. Remove the engine lifting device. Remove the support from the transaxle.

39. Install the bell housing bolts.

40. Connect all necessary vacuum lines.

41. Attach the quick connects near the PCM.

42. Install the plastic cover to the shock tower.

43. Safely raise and support the vehicle. Safely support the transaxle with a jacking fixture.

44. Install the motor mount bracket to transaxle attaching nuts and tighten nuts to 43 ft. lbs. (58 Nm).

45. Install the remaining components in the reverse order of removal. Tighten the following:

- Ball joint-to-control arm nuts to 63 ft. lbs. (85 Nm)
- Torque converter bolts to 46 ft. lbs. (63 Nm)

46. Refill the engine with clean oil.

47. Refill the cooling system.

48. Refill the power steering fluid.

49. Check and refill the transaxle fluid. Install the hood assembly.

50. Install the air cleaner assembly.

51. Connect the negative battery cable. Start the engine and check all fluids for proper level and leaks.

52. Bleed the cooling system and power steering system using the recommended procedure.

3.5L Engine

1. Before servicing the vehicle, refer to the precautions in the beginning of this section.

2. Disconnect the negative battery cable.

3. Remove the sight shield from the fuel injectors.

4. Remove the air intake duct from the throttle body.

5. Remove the engine mount strut from the bracket.

6. Detach the fuel lines from the fuel supply rail.

7. Disconnect the fuel vapor line.

8. Disconnect the throttle and cruise control cables with the bracket from the throttle body.

9. Detach the range selector cable from the Park Neutral Position (PNP) switch.

10. Detach the vacuum booster hose from the engine.

11. Disconnect the A/C vacuum hose from the engine.

12. Disconnect the wiring harness from the engine and transaxle.

13. Drain the engine coolant.

14. Disconnect the radiator inlet hose from the engine.

15. Disconnect the transaxle fluid cooler lines from the radiator.

16. Disconnect the surge tank inlet hose.

17. Remove the heater hoses from the engine.

18. Raise and safely support the vehicle.

19. Drain the engine oil.

20. Remove the lower radiator air deflector.

21. Disconnect the AIR pipe from the AIR inlet valve.

22. Remove the battery cables from the retainers.

23. Remove the radiator outlet hose from the engine.

24. Remove the A/C compressor without disconnecting the lines. Secure the compressor to the frame.

25. Remove the torque converter cover.

26. Remove the starter motor assembly.

27. Matchmark the flexplate to the torque converter and remove the flexplate-to-torque converter bolts.

28. Remove the catalytic converter from the rear exhaust manifold.

29. Remove the lower transaxle-to-engine bolts.

30. Remove the front wheels and splash shields.

31. Disconnect the harness connectors from the fog lamps.

32. Remove the drive axles.

33. Disconnect the intermediate shaft from the steering rack.

✳✳ WARNING

Secure the front of the vehicle to the lift. The vehicle may become unstable as the engine/transaxle assembly is removed from the vehicle.

34. Position a frame table such as J 39580 or its equivalent, under the vehicle.

35. Lower the vehicle so the frame is resting on the frame table.

36. Remove the frame-to-body bolts.

✳✳ WARNING

Do not damage the A/C compressor or lines when removing the frame from the vehicle.

37. Careful raise the vehicle away from the engine/transaxle assembly.

38. Remove the transaxle from the engine as needed.

To install:

39. Install the transaxle on the engine. Tighten the bolts to 55 ft. lbs. (75 Nm).

40. Install the transaxle brace. Tighten the bolts to 32 ft. lbs. (43 Nm).

41. Install engine mount bracket on the front of the engine. Tighten the bolts in sequence to 43 ft. lbs. (58 Nm).

42. Position the engine/transaxle assembly under the vehicle.

43. Coat the sub-frame bushings with rubber lubricant P/N 1051717 or equivalent.

44. Lower the vehicle onto the assembly. Align the sub-frame on the vehicle using two bolts or drill bits, ¾ inches thick by eight inches long through the alignment holes on the right side of the frame.

45. Install new frame-to-body bolts. Tighten the bolts to 133 ft. lbs. (180 Nm) starting with the rear bolts and then the front bolts.

46. Raise the vehicle and remove the frame table.

47. Connect the intermediate shaft to the steering rack. Be sure the shaft is fully seated on the stub before installing the pinch bolt. Tighten the bolts to 35 ft. lbs. (48 Nm).

48. Install the drive axles and assembly the suspension.

49. Install the splash shields and connect the fog lamps.

50. Install the front wheels.

51. If not already done, install the lower transaxle-to-engine bolts. Tighten the bolts to 55 ft. lbs. (75 Nm).

52. Connect the catalytic converter to the rear exhaust manifold.

53. Align the matchmark and install the flexplate-to-torque converter bolts. Tighten the bolts to 47 ft. lbs. (63 Nm).

Engine mount bracket bolt tightening sequence—3.5L engine

9300Z501

54. Install the starter and torque converter cover.

55. Install the A/C compressor. Tighten the nuts and bolts to 37 ft. lbs. (50 Nm).

56. Connect the lower radiator hose to the engine.

57. Install the battery cables in the retainers.

58. Connect the AIR pipe.

59. Install the lower radiator air deflector.

60. Lower the vehicle.

61. Install the heater hoses.

62. Connect the hose to the surge tank.

63. Connect the transaxle fluid cooler lines to the radiator.

64. Install the upper radiator hose to the engine.

65. Connect the wiring harness connectors to the engine and transaxle.

66. Connect the A/C vacuum hose to the engine.

67. Connect the brake booster hose to the engine.

68. Connect the shifter cable to the PNP switch on the transaxle.

➡️**Always us a new throttle cable when replacing the engine assembly.**

69. Remove the trim panel under the left instrument panel and detach the throttle cable from the top of the pedal them squeeze the retainer and push the cable through the bulkhead to remove it.

70. Install a new throttle cable.

71. Connect the cruise and throttle cables to the throttle body.

72. Connect the fuel vapor line.

73. Connect the fuel lines to the supply rail.

74. Install the engine mount strut.

75. Install the air duct to the throttle body.

76. Install the fuel injector shield.

77. Connect the negative battery cable.

78. Refill the cooling system with DEX-COOL® coolant.

79. Install a new oil filter and install the engine oil.

80. Start the engine and check for leaks.

3.8L Engine

1. Before servicing the vehicle, refer to the precautions in the beginning of this section.

2. Relieve the fuel system pressure. Disconnect the negative battery cable.

3. Remove the hood from the vehicle. Remove the air cleaner assembly.

4. Disconnect and cap the fuel lines from the fuel rail and mounting brackets.

5. Drain the engine coolant and remove the recovery bottle.

6. Remove the inner fender electrical cover and the fuel injector sight cover.

7. Disconnect the throttle and cruise control (if equipped) cables from the throttle body and mounting bracket.

8. Remove the rear heat shield from the crossover pipe.

9. Remove the throttle cable mounting bracket and disconnect any vacuum lines from the bracket.

10. Disconnect the exhaust crossover from the manifolds.

11. Remove the torque strut mounting bolt and disconnect the strut from the engine bracket.

12. Remove the right side engine cooling fan.

13. Disconnect the vacuum line from the transaxle module.

14. Remove the serpentine belt.

15. Remove the power steering pump and alternator assemblies.

16. Tag and disconnect all electrical connections from the engine.

17. Disconnect the upper and lower radiator hoses as well as the heater hoses from the engine.

18. Remove the transaxle-to-engine bolts and disconnect the ground wires.

19. Raise and support the vehicle safely. Remove the right front wheel and inner splash shield.

20. Remove the flywheel cover, scribe a mark on the torque converter and flywheel and remove the flywheel-to-torque converter bolts.

21. Disconnect the wiring harness clamps from the frame near the radiator.

22. Remove the A/C compressor from the bracket, lay aside and secure to the frame.

23. Remove the starter.

24. Support the transaxle with a jack and remove the transaxle-to-engine bolt, through the wheel well, using a long extension.

25. Attach a lifting device and remove the engine mount-to-frame nuts.

26. Drain the engine oil and remove the oil filter.

27. Disconnect the oil cooler pipes from the hose connections.

28. Disconnect the exhaust pipe from the manifold.

29. Lower the vehicle and remove the engine assembly from the vehicle.

To install:

30. With the help of an assistant, install a lifting device onto the engine and position the engine into the vehicle.

31. Support the transaxle, install the transaxle-to-engine bolts and ground wiring harness and tighten to 46 ft. lbs. (62 Nm).

32. Install the heater and upper and lower radiator hoses to the engine.

33. Install all electrical connections to the engine.

34. Install the alternator, power steering pump and serpentine belt.

35. Install the vacuum line to the transaxle module.

36. Install the engine torque strut and bolt and tighten to 41 ft. lbs. (56 Nm).

37. Install the exhaust crossover pipe.

38. Install the throttle cable mounting bracket and vacuum lines.

39. Install the heat shield to the crossover pipe and the throttle cables to the throttle body and mounting bracket.

40. Install the inner fender electrical cover and the coolant recovery bottle.

41. Install the fuel hoses to the fuel rail and mounting brackets.

42. Raise and support the vehicle safely.

43. Connect the front exhaust pipe to the manifold.

44. Install the oil filter and oil cooler pipes.

45. Install the engine mount nuts to the frame and tighten to 32 ft. lbs. (43 Nm).

46. Install the transaxle to engine bolt through the wheel well and tighten to 46 ft. lbs. (62 Nm).

47. Install the starter motor assembly and connect the electrical connectors.

48. Install the air conditioner compressor to the bracket.

49. Install the wiring harness clamps to the frame near the radiator.

50. Align the scribe marks, install the torque converter to flywheel bolts and tighten to 46 ft. lbs. (62 Nm).

51. Install the flywheel cover and the inner fender splash shield.

52. Install the right front wheel assembly and lower the vehicle.

53. Refill the cooling system and bleed the power steering system.

54. Install the right side cooling fan.

55. Install the fuel injector sight shield and the air cleaner assembly.

56. Connect the negative battery cable and install the hood.

57. Check and add fluids as required. Test drive vehicle and recheck for leaks and correct levels.

Timing belt service is covered in Section 5 of this manual

Water Pump

REMOVAL & INSTALLATION

3.1L and 3.4L Engines

1. Disconnect the negative battery cable. Drain the cooling system.
2. Remove the coolant reservoir and lay aside.
3. Remove the serpentine belt guard, bolts and nuts.
4. Loosen the water pump pulley bolts. Remove the serpentine belt.
5. Remove the water pulley bolts and pulley.
6. Remove the water pump attaching bolts, then remove the water pump and gasket.

To install:

7. Clean all pump mating surfaces.
8. Inspect the pump. There should be a locator tab to identify the top of the pump. This locator must be in the vertical position when the pump is installed. Install the water pump and gasket. Tighten the attaching bolts to 89 inch lbs. (10 Nm).
9. Install the remaining components in the reverse order of removal. Tighten the pulley bolts to 18 ft. lbs. (25 Nm).

LOCATOR — MUST BE IN VERTICAL POSITION

FRT

GASKET

FRONT COVER

10 N·m (89 LB. IN.) COOLANT PUMP

Water pump, gasket and mounting bolts—3.4L (VIN X) engine

10. Connect the negative battery cable. Install the air cleaner assembly.
11. Refill the cooling system with the proper coolant. Bleed the cooling system and check for leaks with the engine running at idle.

3.5L Engine

1. Before servicing the vehicle, refer to the precautions in the beginning of this section.
2. Partially drain the cooling system.
3. Loosen the bolts on the water pump pulley.
4. Remove the drive belt.
5. Remove the idler pulley.
6. Remove the water pump pulley.

➡ **The water pump is attached to the engine with both long and short bolts, be sure to note their locations.**

7. Remove the water pump mounting bolts. Note the locations of the five long bolts.

1 COVER ASSEMBLY, ENGINE FRONT
2 BOLT/SCREW, WATER PUMP
3 PUMP ASSEMBLY, WATER
4 GASKET, WATER PUMP

Exploded view of the water pump mounting—3.1L (VIN M) engine

Be sure to install the five long water pump bolts in the correct locations—3.5L engine

Water pump mounting—3.5L engine

8. Remove the water pump and gasket.

9. Clean the water pump mounting surface.

To install:

10. Install the water pump with a new gasket. Be sure to install the five long bolts in the proper locations. Tighten the bolts to 124 inch lbs. (14 Nm).

11. Install the water pump pulley.

12. Install the idler pulley. Tighten the bolt to 37 ft. lbs. (50 Nm).

13. Install the drive belt.

14. Fill the cooling system with DEX-COOL® coolant.

15. Start the engine and check for leaks.

3.8L Engines

VIN K MODELS

1. Before servicing the vehicle, refer to the precautions in the beginning of this section.

2. Disconnect the negative battery cable. Drain the cooling system.

3. Remove the coolant recovery reservoir.

4. Remove the serpentine belt. If additional access is needed, remove the inner fender electrical cover.

5. Remove the power steering pump pulley using pulley remover J 25034-B or the equivalent.

6. Remove the water pump pulley.

7. Remove the water pump attaching bolts. Note that there are different length bolts. Use care to keep them organized for proper assembly. Remove the water pump from the vehicle.

To install:

8. Clean the water pump mating surfaces. Install the water pump using a new gasket.

9. Clean the pump bolt threads well. Install the attaching water pump bolts using care to install the proper bolts in the proper locations. Tighten long bolts to 22 ft. lbs.

1. Coolant pump
2. Front cover
3. Gasket
4. 13 ft. lbs.(18 Nm)
5. 22 ft. lbs.(30 Nm)

Exploded view of the water pump assembly mounting—3.8L (VIN K) engines

(30 Nm) and short bolts to 13 ft. lbs. (18 Nm), then using a torque angle meter, tighten the bolts an additional 80 degrees.

10. Install the water pump pulley and tighten the bolts to 115 inch lbs. (13 Nm).

11. For VIN L engines, install the serpentine belt tensioner pulley, then install the alternator.

12. For VIN K engines, install the power steering pump pulley using J 25033-B or the equivalent to press the pulley onto the shaft.

13. Install the serpentine belt.

14. Install the coolant recovery reservoir.

15. Refill the cooling system with the correct amount and type of coolant.

16. Connect the negative battery cable. Start the engine and bleed the cooling system using the recommended procedure.

VIN 1 MODELS

1. Before servicing the vehicle, refer to the precautions in the beginning of this section.

2. Disconnect the negative battery cable.

3. Drain the cooling system into an approved container.

4. Remove the accessory drive and supercharger belts.

5. Remove the alternator and brace.

6. Disconnect the hoses and pipes from the water pump.

Exploded view of the water pump assembly mounting—3.8L (VIN 1) engines

7. Remove the pulley bracket assembly.

8. Raise and safely support the vehicle.

9. Remove the power steering pump and lines.

10. Lower the vehicle.

11. Support the engine using engine support fixture J 28467-A or equivalent, and remove the front engine mount.

12. Remove the water pump pulley.

13. Remove the water pump mounting bolts and remove the water pump from the vehicle.

To install:

14. Clean all sealing surfaces.

15. Apply a thin bead of sealant to the gasket mating surface of the water pump and install a new gasket to the pump.

16. Install the water pump on the engine. Tighten the pump-to-front cover bolts to 11 ft. lbs. (15 Nm), then using a torque angle meter, tighten the bolts an additional 80 degrees.

17. Install the water pump pulley and tighten the bolts to 9.5 ft. lbs. (13 Nm).

18. Install the front engine mount.

19. Raise and safely support the vehicle.

20. Install the power steering pump and lines following the proper procedure.

21. Lower the vehicle.

22. Install the pulley bracket assembly.

23. Connect the hoses and pipes from the water pump.

24. Install the alternator and brace.

25. Install the supercharger and accessory drive and belts.

26. Connect the negative battery cable.

27. Fill and bleed the cooling system following the proper procedure.

28. Run the engine and check for leaks.

29. Recheck the coolant level when the engine has cooled.

Cylinder Head

REMOVAL & INSTALLATION

3.1L Engine

LEFT (FRONT) CYLINDER HEAD

1. Before servicing the vehicle, refer to the precautions in the beginning of this section.

2. Disconnect the negative battery cable. Relieve the fuel system pressure.

3. Drain the cooling system into a suitable container.

4. Remove the rocker arm covers.

5. Remove upper intake plenum and lower intake manifold.

7922Z505

Tighten the cylinder head bolts in the order shown to prevent damaging the head—3.1L (VIN M) engine

6. Remove the exhaust crossover pipe.

7. Disconnect the spark plug wires from spark plugs and wire looms and route the wires out of the way.

➡**When removing the valvetrain components use care to identify any components that will be reused. Valvetrain components must be kept in order for installation in the same locations from which they were removed.**

8. Remove rocker arms nut, rocker arms, balls and pushrods.

9. Remove oil level indicator tube.

10. Remove any A/C compressor bolts accessible from the top.

11. Raise and safely support the vehicle. Remove the lower A/C compressor mounting bolts.

12. Disconnect the A/C compressor electrical connections and reposition the A/C compressor.

13. Remove the A/C compressor lower bracket bolts.

14. Lower the vehicle.

15. Remove the A/C compressor upper bracket bolts.

16. Remove the compressor brackets.

17. Remove the cylinder head bolts evenly.

18. Remove the cylinder head.

To install:

19. Clean all the gasket surfaces completely. Clean the threads on the cylinder head bolts and block threads. New replacement head bolts are recommended.

20. Place the cylinder head gasket in position over the dowel pins on the cylinder block so the words **THIS SIDE UP** or other gasket identification are showing.

21. Coat the bolt threads with sealer and install finger-tight.

22. Tighten the cylinder head bolts in sequence to 33 ft. lbs. (45 Nm). With all the bolts tightened make a second pass tightening all the bolts an additional 90 degrees (¼ turn).

23. Install the remaining components in the reverse order of removal. Tighten the following:

• A/C compressor bracket bolts to 35 ft. lbs. (47 Nm)

• A/C compressor mounting bolts to 18 ft. lbs. (25 Nm)

• Rocker arm nuts to 20 ft. lbs. (27 Nm)

24. Refill the cooling system.

25. Connect negative battery cable.

26. An oil and filter change are recommended since coolant can enter the oil system when the head is being removed.

27. Start vehicle and verify no leaks.

RIGHT (REAR) CYLINDER HEAD

1. Before servicing the vehicle, refer to the precautions in the beginning of this section.

2. Disconnect the negative battery cable. Relieve the fuel system pressure.

3. Drain the cooling system into a suitable container.

4. Remove the rocker arm covers.

5. Remove upper intake plenum and lower intake manifold.

6. Disconnect the electrical connector from the ignition assembly.

7. Remove the alternator.

8. Remove the exhaust crossover pipe. Detach the Oxygen (O_2S) sensor connector.

9. Raise and safely support the vehicle. Disconnect the exhaust pipe from the exhaust manifold.

10. Lower the vehicle.

11. Remove the exhaust manifold.

12. Disconnect the spark plug wires from spark plugs and wire looms and route the wires out of the way.

➡**When removing the valvetrain components use care to identify any components that will be reused. Valvetrain components must be kept in order for installation in the same locations from which they were removed.**

13. Remove rocker arms nut, rocker arms, balls and pushrods.

14. Remove the cylinder head bolts evenly. Remove the cylinder head.

To install:

15. Clean all the gasket surfaces completely. Clean the threads on the cylinder head bolts and block threads. New replacement head bolts are recommended.

16. Place the cylinder head gasket in position over the dowel pins on the cylinder block so the words **THIS SIDE UP** or other gasket identification is showing.

17. Coat the bolt threads with sealer and install finger-tight.

18. Tighten the cylinder head bolts in sequence to 33 ft. lbs. (45 Nm). With all the bolts tightened make a second pass

tightening all the bolts an additional 90 degrees.

19. Install the pushrods, rocker arms, balls and rocker arm nuts. Tighten the rocker arm nuts to 20 ft. lbs. (27 Nm).

20. Install the remaining components in the reverse order of removal.

21. Refill the cooling system.

22. An oil and filter change are recommended since coolant can enter the oil system when the head is being removed.

23. Connect negative battery cable.

24. Start vehicle and verify no leaks.

3.4L Engine

LEFT (FRONT) CYLINDER HEAD

1. Before servicing the vehicle, refer to the precautions in the beginning of this section.

2. Relieve the fuel system pressure. Remove the air cleaner and duct assembly.

3. Disconnect the negative battery cable. Drain the cooling system.

4. Remove the upper and lower intake manifold components.

5. Remove the left side cam carrier cover using the following procedure.

　a. Disconnect oil/air breather hose from cam carrier cover.

　b. Disconnect the spark plug wires from the front spark plugs.

　c. Disconnect the rear spark plug wires from the clips on the front camshaft cover.

　d. Remove the four camshaft cover mounting bolts.

　e. Remove the camshaft cover and discard the old gaskets and O-rings.

6. Remove the left side cam carrier using the following procedure.

　a. Remove the camshaft timing belt.

　b. Remove the exhaust crossover pipe and reposition aside.

　c. Remove the engine torque strut.

　d. Remove the front engine lift bracket.

　e. Install six, six-inch sections of fuel line hose under camshaft and between lifters. This will hold lifters in the carrier. For this procedure use a ³⁄₁₆ in. (8mm) vacuum/fuel line hose for the exhaust valves and a ⁵⁄₃₂ in. (5.5mm) vacuum/fuel line hose for the intake valves.

　f. Remove the camshaft carrier bolts and remove the carrier. Discard the gasket.

7. Remove the front exhaust manifold.

8. Remove the oil level indicator tube mounting bolt and remove the tube assembly.

9. Detach the Engine Coolant Temperature (ECT) sensor electrical connector.

10. Remove the cylinder head mounting bolts and remove cylinder head. Discard the gasket.

To install:

11. Clean all parts well. Be sure the mating surfaces on the head and block are clean. Clean the engine block threaded holes and be sure all oil is removed from the bolt holes. Inspect the cylinder head bolt threads and be sure they are clean. New replacement head bolts are recommended. If the cylinder head is being replaced with a new head, transfer the manifold studs and temperature sensor.

12. Install a new cylinder head gasket on the engine block with the metal tabs (factory type gasket) between the cylinders facing **UP**.

13. Install the cylinder head on the engine block with the dowel pins lined up. Install the mounting bolts finger-tight.

14. With all the bolts in place tighten the mounting bolts in sequence to 44 ft. lbs. (60 Nm) for 1996–97 vehicles. Make a second pass over each bolt in sequence and tighten an additional 90 degrees (¼ turn) rotation using a torque angle meter.

15. Connect the electrical connector to the coolant temperature sender.

16. Install the oil level tube assembly and tighten the mounting bolt to 89 inch lbs. (10 Nm).

17. Install the front exhaust manifold and tighten the attaching nuts to 18 ft. lbs. (25 Nm).

18. Clean any oil from the cam carrier to cylinder head bolt holes (bolt holes closest to the exhaust manifold).

19. Install the special camshaft holding tool J38613-A or equivalent and tighten the mounting bolt to 22 ft. lbs. (30 Nm).

➡ **The use of petroleum jelly (never chassis grease) in the lifter bores along with the use of the lifter hold down hoses will help keep the lifters in place.**

20. Install a new camshaft carrier gasket on the cylinder head and install the camshaft carrier on the cylinder head.

21. Install the camshaft carrier mounting bolts and tighten to 20 ft. lbs. (27 Nm).

22. Remove the lifter hold down hoses.

23. Install the upper and lower intake manifold assembly. If the thermostat housing was removed, install with a new gasket.

24. Install the front engine lift bracket.

25. Install the engine torque strut and tighten the bolt to 39 ft. lbs. (53 Nm).

26. Install the exhaust manifold crossover pipe.

27. Install the camshaft sprockets, if removed. Install the timing belt using great care to align all timing marks.

❋❋ CAUTION

While installing the camshaft sprockets and timing belt, the cam timing must be set observing all timing marks. Failure to properly set the camshaft timing will result in serious engine damage.

28. Remove the special tools J-38613 camshaft holding clamps, if used.

29. Install the front engine coolant pipe. Connect the heater hose pipe to the intake plenum.

30. Connect the upper radiator hose.

31. Install the new O-rings and gasket on the camshaft carrier cover.

➡ **Before tightening the cover mounting bolts, fully seat the bolt insulators in the camshaft cover.**

32. Install the cover on the camshaft carrier and tighten the mounting bolts to 97 inch lbs. (11 Nm).

33. Connect the rear spark plug wires to the camshaft cover.

34. Connect the front spark plug wires to the spark plugs.

35. Connect the oil/air breather hose to the camshaft cover.

36. Drain the engine oil since coolant can contaminate the oil when a cylinder head is removed. Refill with the proper quantity and quality engine oil. A filter change is recommended.

37. Connect the negative battery cable. Install the air cleaner and air duct assembly.

38. Refill the cooling system.

39. Start the vehicle and verify no oil or coolant leaks. Bleed the cooling system as required.

RIGHT (REAR) CYLINDER HEAD

1. Before servicing the vehicle, refer to the precautions in the beginning of this section.

2. Relieve the fuel system pressure. Remove the air cleaner and duct assembly.

3. Disconnect the negative battery cable. Drain the cooling system.

4. Remove the upper intake manifold. Remove the right timing belt cover.

5. Remove the right rear spark plug wires. Disconnect oil/air breather hose from cam carrier cover.

6. Remove the four camshaft cover mounting bolts.

7. Remove the camshaft cover and discard the old gaskets and O-rings.

8. Remove the camshaft timing belt.

9. Install six, six inch sections of fuel line hose under camshaft and between lifters. This will hold lifters in the carrier. For this procedure use a ³⁄₁₆ in. (8mm) vacuum/fuel line hose for exhaust the valves and a ⁵⁄₃₂ in. (5.5mm) vacuum/fuel line hose for the intake valves.

10. Remove the lower intake manifold.

11. Remove the right camshaft carrier mounting bolts.

12. Remove the right camshaft carrier and gasket from the engine.

13. Remove the exhaust crossover pipe from the engine.

14. Raise and safely support the vehicle. Disconnect the front exhaust pipe at the manifold.

15. Lower the vehicle.

16. Disconnect the electrical connector from the Oxygen (O2S) sensor.

17. Remove the rear timing belt tensioner bracket.

18. Remove the cylinder head mounting bolts and remove cylinder head and gasket.

1	HEAD BOLT
2	CYLINDER HEAD
3	GASKET
4	PIN
5	ENGINE BLOCK

TIGHTENING SEQUENCE

Exploded view of the cylinder head mounting and bolt tightening sequence—3.4L (VIN X) engines

Refer to Section 1 for engine rebuilding specifications

To install:

19. Clean all parts well. Be sure the mating surfaces on the head and block are clean. Clean the engine block threaded holes and be sure all oil is removed from the bolt holes. Inspect the cylinder head bolt threads and be sure they are clean. New replacement head bolts are recommended. If the cylinder head is being replaced with a new head, transfer the manifold studs and temperature sensor.

20. Install a new cylinder head gasket on the engine block with the metal tabs (factory type gasket) between the cylinders facing **UP**.

21. Install the cylinder head on the engine block, with attached exhaust manifold, with the dowel pins lined up. Install the mounting bolts finger-tight. With all the bolts in place tighten the mounting bolts in sequence to 44 ft. lbs. (60 Nm) for 1996–97 vehicles. Make a second pass over each bolt in sequence and tighten an additional 90 degrees (¼ turn) rotation using special tool J 36660 or equivalent angle measuring equipment.

22. Install the rear timing belt tensioner bracket.

23. Connect the electrical connector to the O₂S sensor.

24. Raise and safely support the vehicle.

25. Connect the front exhaust pipe to the exhaust manifold.

26. Lower the vehicle.

27. Install the exhaust crossover pipe.

➡ **Remove oil from the cam hold down tool hole in the camshaft carrier before installing and tightening the bolt.**

28. Install the special camshaft hold down tool J 38613 A or equivalent and tighten to 22 ft. lbs. (30 Nm).

➡ **The use of petroleum jelly (never chassis grease) in the lifter bores along with the use of the lifter hold down hoses, will help keep the lifters in place.**

29. Install a new camshaft carrier gasket on the cylinder head and install the camshaft carrier on the cylinder head.

30. Install the mounting bolts and tighten to 20 ft. lbs. (27 Nm).

31. Remove the lifter hold down hoses.

32. Install the camshaft sprockets and timing belt.

❋❋ CAUTION

After installing the camshaft sprockets and timing belt the cam timing must be set. Failure to properly set the camshaft timing will result in serious engine damage.

33. Remove the camshaft hold down tool J-38613 or equivalent.

34. Install the lower intake manifold.

35. Install the new O-rings and gasket on the cam carrier cover.

➡ **Before tightening the cover mounting bolts, fully seat the bolt insulators in the camshaft cover.**

36. Install the cover on the camshaft carrier and tighten the mounting bolts to 97 inch lbs. (11 Nm).

37. Connect the oil/air breather hose to the camshaft cover.

38. Connect the rear spark plug wires to the camshaft cover and spark plugs.

39. Install the right timing belt cover. Install the upper intake manifold.

40. Connect the negative battery cable. Install the air cleaner and air duct assembly.

41. Drain the engine oil since coolant can contaminate the oil when a cylinder head is removed. Refill with the proper quantity and quality engine oil. A filter change is recommended.

42. Refill the cooling system.

43. Start the vehicle and verify no leaks.

3.5L Engine

FRONT

1. Before servicing the vehicle, refer to the precautions in the beginning of this section.

2. Disconnect the negative battery cable.

3. Remove the intake manifold.

4. Remove the water outlet housing.

5. Remove the engine mount strut bracket.

6. Remove the coolant crossover pipe.

7. Remove the front exhaust manifold.

Cylinder head bolt tightening sequence—3.5L engine

9300Z505

Camshaft holding fixture J 42038—3.5L engine

8. Remove the camshaft covers.

9. Install J 42038 or equivalent on the camshafts to hold them in position.

10. Remove the camshaft primary chain.

11. Remove the camshafts from the front cylinder head.

12. Remove the rocker arms and valve lifters. Be sure to keep them in order so they can be installed the their original locations.

13. Remove the M6 bolts from the front of the cylinder head. Note the location of the longer bolt.

14. Remove the M11 cylinder head bolts. DO NOT reuse the bolts.

15. Remove the cylinder head from the engine.

16. Clean the cylinder head mounting surfaces.

To install:

17. Be sure the dowels are securely mounted in the engine block.

18. Install a new gasket on the locating dowels.

19. Place the cylinder head in position on the locating dowels.

20. Install new M11 bolts and the M6 bolts in the front of the cylinder head.

21. Tighten the M11 bolts in sequence using the following sub-steps;

  a. Tighten each bolt in sequence to 22 ft. lbs. (30 Nm).

  b. Tighten each bolt in sequence an additional 60 degrees.

  c. Tighten each bolt in sequence an additional 60 degrees.

  d. Tighten each bolt in sequence an additional 60 degrees to a total of 180 degrees.

22. Tighten the long M6 bolt to 22 ft. lbs. (30 Nm).

23. Tighten the two shorter M6 bolts to 106 inch lbs. (12 Nm).

24. Install the lifters and rocker arms in their original positions.

25. Install the camshafts, primary chain and covers.

26. Install the exhaust manifold.

27. Install the coolant crossover pipe.
28. Install the engine mount strut bracket.
29. Install the water outlet housing.
30. Install the intake manifold.
31. Change the engine oil and filter.
32. Refill the engine with DEX-COOL® coolant.
33. Connect the negative battery cable.
34. Start the engine and check for leaks.

REAR

1. Before servicing the vehicle, refer to the precautions in the beginning of this section.
2. Disconnect the negative battery cable.
3. Remove the intake manifold.
4. Remove the coolant crossover pipe.

➡**Do not remove the rear exhaust manifold. Detach it from the cylinder head and connection from the front manifold and position it aside.**

5. Remove the rear exhaust manifold from the cylinder head and front manifold.
6. Remove the camshaft covers.
7. Install J 42038 or equivalent on the camshafts to hold them in position.
8. Remove the primary camshaft chain.
9. Remove the camshafts, rocker arms and lifters. Keep them in order so they can be installed in their original positions.
10. Remove the Engine Coolant Temperature (ECT) sensor from the cylinder head.
11. Remove the M6 bolts from the front of the cylinder head. Note the location of the longer bolt.
12. Remove the M11 cylinder head bolts. DO NOT reuse the bolts.
13. Remove the cylinder head from the engine.
14. Clean the cylinder head mounting surfaces.

To install:
15. Be sure the dowels are securely mounted in the engine block.
16. Install a new gasket on the locating dowels.
17. Place the cylinder head in position on the locating dowels.
18. Install new M11 bolts and the M6 bolts in the front of the cylinder head.
19. Tighten the M11 bolts in sequence using the following sub-steps;
    a. Tighten each bolt in sequence to 22 ft. lbs. (30 Nm).
    b. Tighten each bolt in sequence an additional 60 degrees.
    c. Tighten each bolt in sequence an additional 60 degrees.

d. Tighten each bolt in sequence an additional 60 degrees to a total of 180 degrees.
20. Tighten the long M6 bolt to 22 ft. lbs. (30 Nm).
21. Tighten the two shorter M6 bolts to 106 inch lbs. (12 Nm).
22. Install the ECT sensor. Tighten the sensor to 15 ft. lbs. (20 Nm).
23. Install the lifters and rocker arms in their original positions.
24. Install the camshafts and primary chain.
25. Remove the camshaft holding fixture.
26. Install the camshaft covers.
27. Install the exhaust manifold on the cylinder head.
28. Install the coolant crossover pipe.
29. Change the engine oil and filter.
30. Refill the engine with DEX-COOL® coolant.
31. Connect the negative battery cable.
32. Start the engine and check for leaks.

3.8L Engines

LEFT (FRONT) CYLINDER HEAD

1. Before servicing the vehicle, refer to the precautions in the beginning of this section.
2. Remove the air cleaner assembly. Disconnect the negative battery cable.
3. Following proper procedures, relieve the fuel system pressure.
4. Drain the cooling system and remove the intake manifold.
5. Remove the valve covers and remove the rocker arm assemblies, pedestals, valve guide plates and pushrods, keeping everything in order for reinstallation.
6. Tag and disconnect the ignition wires and remove the spark plugs.
7. Remove the engine torque strut from the attaching bracket.
8. Remove the vacuum line from the transaxle module.
9. Remove the left exhaust manifold.
10. Remove the spark plugs.
11. Remove the alternator front mount bracket and ignition module with the mount bracket. Lay the ignition module aside.
12. Remove the cylinder head bolts and discard. Remove the cylinder head from the vehicle.
13. Clean all gasket mating surfaces and the cylinder head bolt holes in the block.

To install:
14. Clean all parts well. If the cylinder head is being replaced with a new one,

Cylinder head bolt tightening sequence—3.8L engines

transfer the torque strut bracket and exhaust support bracket with the transaxle vacuum line. If the cylinder head is to be serviced, these parts must be removed, after servicing, installed.
15. Inspect the head gasket and mating surfaces for leaks, corrosion and blow-by.
16. **The factory specifies new replacement cylinder head bolts** when removing and installing a cylinder head. Clean the remains of sealer from all threaded openings. The cylinder block bolt holes should be cleaned using a 7/16 14 tap.
17. Place the cylinder head gasket on the engine block dowels with the note **THIS SIDE UP** facing the cylinder head and the arrow facing the front of the engine. Position the cylinder head on the engine block.

❊❊ CAUTION

To prevent damage to the gasket, when installing the cylinder head, do not slide the cylinder head on the gasket.

18. Install the new replacement cylinder head bolts and tighten as follows:
    a. Tighten the cylinder head bolts, in sequence, to 37 ft. lbs. (50 Nm).
    b. Rotate each bolt 120 degrees (1/3 turn) in sequence using special tool J 36660 or equivalent.
    c. Rotate the center 4 bolts an additional 30 degrees (1/12 turn) in sequence using special tool J 36660 or equivalent.
19. Install the pushrods, rocker arm assemblies, valve guide retainers and the valve covers.
20. Install the exhaust manifold and tighten manifold studs to 32 ft. lbs. (48 Nm).
21. Install the intake manifold using the recommended procedure.
22. Install the alternator front mount bracket and ignition module with bracket.
23. Install the spark plugs and wires.

For engine torque specifications, refer to Section 1 of this manual

24. Install the engine torque strut and tighten bolt to 32 ft. lbs. (53 Nm).

25. Refill the cooling system.

26. It is recommended that the engine oil be drained and crankcase refilled with clean engine oil since coolant and debris will get into the oil pan when removing a cylinder head. A filter change is also recommended.

27. Connect the negative battery cable.

28. Install the air cleaner assembly.

29. Start the engine check for proper operation. Verify no leaks.

RIGHT (REAR) CYLINDER HEAD

1. Before servicing the vehicle, refer to the precautions in the beginning of this section.

2. Remove the air cleaner assembly. Disconnect the negative battery cable.

3. Relieve the fuel system pressure.

4. Drain the cooling system and disconnect the exhaust crossover pipe.

5. Remove the intake manifold.

6. Raise and safely support the vehicle.

7. Remove the right side exhaust pipe from the manifold.

8. Safely lower the vehicle.

9. Remove the right rear valve cover. Remove the serpentine drive belt.

10. Remove the belt tensioner pulley. Remove the heater hose from the engine.

11. Remove the power steering pump mounting bracket and lay the pump aside.

12. Tag and disconnect the ignition wires and remove the spark plugs.

13. Remove the exhaust manifold from the cylinder head only.

14. Disconnect the electrical connection from the Oxygen (O_2S) sensor.

15. Remove the rocker arm assemblies, pedestals, valve guide retainers and pushrods, keeping everything in order for reinstallation.

16. Remove the cylinder head bolts in reverse order of installation and remove the cylinder head. Discard the cylinder head bolts.

To install:

17. Clean all parts well. Inspect the head gasket and mating surfaces for leaks, corrosion and blow-by.

18. **The factory specifies new head bolts** be used when removing and installing a cylinder head. Clean the remains of sealer from all threaded openings. The cylinder block bolt holes should be cleaned using a $7/16$ 14 tap.

19. Place the cylinder head gasket on the engine block dowels with the note **THIS SIDE UP** facing the cylinder head and the arrow facing the front of the engine. Position the cylinder head on the engine block.

✳✳ CAUTION

To prevent damage to the gasket, when installing the cylinder head, do not slide the cylinder head on the gasket.

20. Install the new cylinder head bolts and tighten as follows:

a. Tighten the cylinder head bolts, in sequence, to 37 ft. lbs. (50 Nm).

b. Rotate each bolt 120 degrees ($1/3$ turn) in sequence using special tool J 36660 or equivalent.

c. Rotate the center 4 bolts an additional 30 degrees ($1/12$ turn) in sequence using special tool J 36660 or equivalent.

21. Connect the electrical connector to the O_2S sensor.

22. Install the exhaust manifold and intake manifold.

23. Install the pushrods, valve guide retainers and rocker arm assemblies.

24. Install the right rear valve cover. Install the spark plugs and wires in the proper order.

25. Install the power steering pump bracket and tighten the bolts to 35 ft. lbs. (47 Nm).

26. Install the belt tensioner pulley and serpentine belt.

27. Install the exhaust crossover pipe. Raise and safely support the vehicle.

28. Install the front exhaust pipe to the manifold.

29. Refill the cooling system.

30. It is recommended that the engine oil be drained and crankcase refilled with clean engine oil since coolant and debris will get into the oil pan when removing a cylinder head. A filter change is also recommended.

31. Connect the negative battery cable. Install the air cleaner.

32. Start the engine check for proper operation. Verify no leaks.

Rocker Arms

REMOVAL & INSTALLATION

3.1L Engine

1. Before servicing the vehicle, refer to the precautions in the beginning of this section.

2. Remove the rocker arm cover and gasket.

3. Remove the rocker arm bolts and the rocker arms.

Rocker arm mounting—3.1L engine

➡The exhaust pushrods are approximately $1/4$ in. (6.35mm) longer than the intake pushrods. Place all valvetrain components in a rack so they can be reinstalled in the same location from which they were removed.

4. Remove the pushrod assemblies.

➡Use care when removing pushrods so they do not fall down into the lifter valley.

To install:

5. Clean all the gasket surfaces completely.

6. Coat the bearing surface of the rocker arms, rocker arm bolts and pushrods with prelube No. 1052365 or equivalent prior to installation.

➡Be sure to install all valvetrain components in their original locations.

✳✳ WARNING

If the cylinder head has been milled as part of an overhaul, shims may be necessary under the rocker arm pedestals.

7. Install the rocker arms. Tighten the bolts to 89 inch lbs. (10 Nm), then using a torque angle meter, tighten the bolts an additional 30 degrees.

8. Apply a new gasket to the valve rocker arm cover. Apply sealant GM 12345739 or equivalent at the cylinder head to lower manifold joint. Install the attaching rocker arm cover bolts to 89 inch lbs. (10 Nm).

9. Install the remaining components in the reverse order of removal.

3.4L Engine

The overhead camshaft design of the 3.4L engine uses only hydraulic lifters between the camshaft and the valves. No rocker arm assemblies are used.

3.5L Engine

Refer to the camshaft removal and installation procedure for rocker arm service.

3.8L Engine

✳✳ WARNING

The rocker arm bolts have been permanently stretched during installation. New original type bolts must be used each time the rocker arm assemblies have been removed for any reason.

LEFT SIDE (FRONT) ROCKER ARMS

1. Before servicing the vehicle, refer to the precautions in the beginning of this section.
2. Disconnect the negative battery cable.
3. Remove the engine lift bracket from the exhaust manifold studs.
4. Remove the fuel injector sight shield.
5. Remove the serpentine belt.
6. Remove the alternator-to-brace bolt (lower bolt).
7. Remove the nut and remove the alternator brace from the intake manifold.
8. Disconnect the spark plug wires from the spark plugs. Disconnect the spark plug wire cover from the rocker arm cover and position aside.
9. Remove the rocker arm cover bolt and remove the cover.

➡**The rocker arms, pushrods, pedestals and bolts must be kept in order for installation in the same locations they were removed from.**

10. Remove the rocker arm bolt(s), pedestal(s), rocker arm(s) and pushrod(s).
To install:
11. Clean all gasket surfaces completely.
12. Apply thread lock compound to the rocker arm bolt(s).
13. Seat the pushrod in the lifter and install the rocker arm, pedestal and mounting bolt. Tighten the mounting bolt to 11 ft. lbs. (15 Nm), then using a torque angle meter, tighten the bolts an additional 90 degrees.
14. Install the rocker arm cover with a new gasket and tighten the mounting bolts to 89 inch lbs. (10 Nm).
15. Installation of the remaining components is the reverse of the removal procedure.
16. Connect the negative battery cable. Start the vehicle and verify no oil leaks.

RIGHT SIDE (REAR) ROCKER ARMS

1. Before servicing the vehicle, refer to the precautions in the beginning of this section.

2. Disconnect the negative battery cable. Remove the coolant recovery bottle.
3. Remove the serpentine belt.
4. Remove the power steering pump mounting bolts and pull the power steering pump forward.
5. Remove the fuel injector sight shield. Remove the canister purge valve from the bracket.
6. Remove the power steering pump support braces.
7. Remove the engine lift bracket from the exhaust manifold studs.
8. Disconnect the spark plug wires from the spark plugs. Disconnect the spark plug wire cover from the rocker arm cover and position aside.
9. Remove the rocker arm cover bolt and remove the cover.

➡**The rocker arms, pushrods, pedestals and bolts must be kept in order for installation in the same locations they were removed from.**

10. Remove the rocker arm bolt(s), pedestal(s), rocker arm(s) and pushrod(s).
To install:
11. Clean all gasket surfaces completely.
12. Apply thread lock compound to the rocker arm bolt(s).
13. Seat the pushrod in the lifter and install the rocker arm, pedestal and mounting bolt. Tighten the mounting bolt to 11 ft. lbs. (15 Nm), then using a torque angle meter, tighten the bolts an additional 90 degrees.
14. Install the remaining components in the reverse order of removal. Tighten the rocker arm cover bolts to 89 inch lbs. (10 Nm) and the engine lift bracket bolt to 41 ft. lbs. (55 Nm).

79222Z509

Exploded view of the rocker arm, pushrod and pushrod guide plate assembly—3.8L engine

15. Connect the negative battery cable.
16. Start the vehicle and verify no oil leaks.

Intake Manifold

REMOVAL & INSTALLATION

3.1L Engine

1. Before servicing the vehicle, refer to the precautions in the beginning of this section.
2. Disconnect the negative battery cable.
3. Drain the engine coolant. Remove the coolant recovery bottle.
4. Remove the air cleaner and duct assembly.
5. Remove the serpentine belt.
6. Disconnect the throttle and cruise control cables from the throttle body. Remove retaining brackets and set cable assemblies aside.
7. Disconnect the automatic transaxle vacuum modulator pipe. Disconnect the power brake booster vacuum hose from the manifold assembly.
8. Identify and tag for identification any remaining vacuum lines and disconnect from the intake manifold.

➡**On some vehicles it will be necessary to remove the torque strut-to-engine bracket bolts, swing the torque struts aside and rotate the engine forward using tool J 41131 for clearance.**

9. Disconnect the electrical connectors from the ignition coil assembly.
10. Remove the front and rear alternator braces.
11. Disconnect any remaining electrical connectors from the intake manifold. Remove the MAP sensor.
12. Remove the spark plug wires from the spark plugs.
13. Remove the electronic ignition system and the EVAP canister purge valve mounting bracket mounting bracket.
14. Remove the EGR tube assembly from the right exhaust manifold.
15. Remove the thermostat bypass pipe nut from the upper intake manifold.
16. Remove the upper intake manifold studs and bolts, then remove the upper intake manifold and gaskets.
17. If the lower intake manifold needs to be removed, remove the fuel injector rail

For complete mechanical specifications, refer to Section 1 of this manual

bolts and remove the fuel injector rail assembly.

18. Remove the heater inlet pipe assembly, upper radiator hose and tie straps retaining the heater outlet pipe and ignition wiring assembly. Disconnect the heater pipe from the heater core to the coolant pump.

19. Remove the power steering pump bolts and pump.

20. Remove the rocker arm covers.

21. Remove the lower intake manifold retaining bolts and remove the lower intake manifold and gasket.

To install:

22. Clean all parts well. Use care in cleaning old gasket material from the machined aluminum surfaces on the plenum and manifold as sharp tools may damage sealing surfaces.

23. Clean the mating surfaces to the intake manifold and engine block. Remove any loose pieces of RTV sealer.

24. Apply sealant GM 12345739 or equivalent at the engine block to manifold mating surface. The bead should be 3.0mm wide and 5.0mm thick.

25. Install the lower intake manifold and retaining bolts. Apply sealant GM 12345382 or equivalent to the threads of the bolts. Tighten the bolts in sequence to 115 inch lbs. (13 Nm).

26. Install the valve rocker covers.

27. Connect the heater pipe from the heater core to the coolant pump. Install new tie straps around the heater outlet pipe and ignition harness assembly. Connect the upper radiator hose to the engine and the heater inlet pipe to the manifold assembly.

28. Install the power steering pump and pulley.

29. Remove the injector O-ring seals from both the spray tip ends and the fuel rail end of each injector. Discard the seals. With the spray tip end O-ring removed, the O-ring back-up piece may slip off of the

79222510

Be sure to tighten the lower intake manifold bolts in the sequence shown—3.1L engine

injector. Be sure to retain the O-ring back-up for reuse. Be sure that the O-ring back-up piece is in place on the spray tip end of the injector before installing a new O-ring. Lubricate new injector O-ring seals with clean engine oil and install on the injector assembly.

30. Install the fuel rail assembly to the intake manifold. Tilt the rail assembly to install the injectors. Install the fuel rail attaching bolts and tighten to 89 inch lbs. (10 Nm).

31. Connect the injector electrical connectors.

32. Install new O-rings on the fuel lines and install the fuel feed and return pipes. Tighten the fuel rail nuts to 13 ft. lbs. (17 Nm). Use a back-up wrench on the fittings to prevent them from turning.

33. Using new gaskets, install the intake manifold plenum. Be sure to route the Manifold Absolute Pressure (MAP) sensor electrical connector to the outside of the plenum gasket. Tighten the bolts to 18 ft. lbs. (25 Nm).

34. Install the serpentine drive belt. Install the coolant recovery tank.

35. Install the MAP sensor, braces to the alternator, ignition coil front bolts and the EGR to plenum bolts. Connect the vacuum lines as noted during removal.

36. If the throttle body was removed from the upper intake manifold, inspect the throttle body before installation. Throttle body bore and valve deposits may be cleaned using carburetor cleaner and a parts cleaning brush. DO NOT use a cleaner that contains Methyl Ethyl Ketone (MEK), an extremely strong solvent and not necessary for this type of deposit. The Throttle Position (TP) sensor and Intake Air Control (IAC) valve should NOT come into contact with solvents or cleaners as they may be damaged. Verify that the gasket surfaces are clean, using a new flange gasket, install the throttle body. Tighten the fasteners to 18 ft. lbs. (25 Nm).

37. Return the engine to its original location and install the torque strut.

38. Connect the throttle and cruise control cables.

39. Connect the IAC valve and TP sensor electrical connectors. Connect the air inlet duct. Check that the accelerator pedal is free by depressing the pedal to the floor and releasing.

40. Connect all remaining electrical connections and vacuum lines. Be sure the alternator braces are secure.

41. Refill the cooling system.

42. Since coolant can get into the engine's oil system when the intake mani-

fold is removed, change the engine oil and filter.

43. Connect the negative battery cable.

44. Turn the key to the **ON** position several times to pressurize the fuel system and check for fuel leaks.

45. After the engine is running, bleed the cooling system and check for proper idle quality.

3.4L Engine

1. Before servicing the vehicle, refer to the precautions in the beginning of this section.

2. Relieve the fuel system pressure. Remove the air cleaner and duct work.

3. Disconnect the negative battery cable. Drain the cooling system.

4. Disconnect the control cables from the throttle body lever and the intake plenum mounting bracket.

5. Remove the fuel rail cover bolts and remove the fuel rail cover.

6. Disconnect and cap the fuel lines from the fuel rail.

7. Remove the emission control purge solenoid and bracket.

8. Tag and disconnect the spark plug wires.

9. Remove the control module mounting bolts, then remove the module.

10. Tag and disconnect the vacuum hoses from the plenum.

11. If necessary, remove the wiring loom bracket for the rear spark plug wires.

12. Remove the plenum support bracket nuts, then remove the plenum mounting bolts and remove the intake plenum.

13. Disconnect the vacuum line at the pressure regulator.

14. Remove the fuel rail assembly mounting bolts.

15. Disconnect the fuel injector electrical connectors.

16. Remove the fuel rail assembly.

17. Disconnect the radiator hose from thermostat housing.

18. Remove the heater pipe nut from the throttle body.

19. Remove the intake manifold mounting bolts and remove the intake manifold.

To install:

20. Clean all the gasket surfaces completely.

21. Install the intake manifold gasket and intake manifold.

22. Install the M8 x 50mm bolts with the washer to the vertical holes in the intake manifold. Tighten these bolts to 62 inch lbs. (7 Nm). Install the lower intake manifold mounting bolts. Insert the rubber insulator

fully into the manifold flange before tightening any fasteners. Tighten the bolts as outlined in the following sub-steps:

    a. Draw the lower manifold into place by tightening the bolts gradually, starting with the middle bolts and working in a circular pattern. DO NOT tighten one side more than the other.

    b. Tighten these bolts to 116 inch lbs. (13 Nm).

    c. Remove the 2 bolts in the vertical holes of the intake manifold.

23. Install the remaining components in the reverse order of removal. Tighten the following:

- Fuel rail bolts to 89 inch lbs. (10 Nm)
- Intake plenum and plenum support bracket nuts, starting in the center and working outwards in a circular pattern, to the mounting bolts to 18 ft. lbs. (25 Nm)

24. Fill and bleed the cooling system using the recommended procedure.

25. Connect the negative battery cable.

26. Install the air cleaner assembly.

27. Pressurize the fuel system and verify no leaks.

3.5L Engine

1. Before servicing the vehicle, refer to the precautions in the beginning of this section.

2. Disconnect the negative battery cable.

3. Remove the air duct from the throttle body.

4. Partially drain the engine coolant.

5. Remove the fuel injector cover.

6. Disconnect the cruise control and accelerator cables from the throttle body and bracket.

7. Disconnect the coolant hoses from the throttle body.

Intake manifold assembly—3.5L engine

8. Disconnect the fuel lines from the fuel supply rail.

9. Disconnect the fuel vapor line from the EVAP canister purge solenoid.

10. Disconnect the brake booster vacuum hose.

11. Disconnect the A/C vacuum hose from the engine.

12. Detach the surge tank inlet pipe retainer from the fuel supply rail.

13. Disconnect the connectors from the fuel injectors.

14. Disconnect the following components;

- Throttle Position (TP) sensor
- Idle Air Control (IAC) valve
- EVAP canister purge solenoid
- Manifold absolute pressure (MAP) sensor

15. Remove the wiring harness channel bolts from the camshaft covers and position the channels with harness out of the way.

16. Remove the vacuum tube from the fuel pressure regulator and throttle body.

17. Remove the PCV tubes from both camshaft covers and intake manifold.

18. Remove the EGR valve outlet pipe.

19. Remove the fuel supply rail with injectors. Disengage the snap-lock retainers by pushing toward the camshaft covers and lifting.

20. Remove the intake manifold mounting bolts and the intake manifold.

➡️**The manifold-to-cylinder head seals are reusable unless cut or damaged.**

21. Inspect the intake manifold-to-cylinder head seals for damage or cuts.

22. Clean the intake manifold and cylinder head mating surfaces.

To install:

23. If the throttle body was removed from the manifold, install it using a new gasket and tighten the nuts to 106 inch lbs. (12 Nm).

24. Place the intake manifold-to-cylinder head seals on the engine and install the intake manifold. Tighten the bolts in a circular pattern starting from the center to 62 inch lbs. (7 Nm).

❊❊❊ WARNING

Do not apply excessive pressure to the fuel supply rail assembly. If the assembly is hard to install, check for misalignment of a fuel injector(s).

25. Inspect the o-rings on the fuel injectors and replace them if necessary. Install

the fuel supply rail with injectors. Press the snap-lock retainers in until they lock in place.

26. Install the EGR pipe. Tighten the intake manifold bolt to 89 inch lbs. (10 Nm) and the coolant crossover bolt to 18 ft. lbs. (24 Nm).

27. Install the PCV valve and related tubing.

28. Connect the brake booster and fuel pressure regulator vacuum hoses.

29. Connect the A/C vacuum hose to the intake manifold.

30. Install the engine wiring harness with channel to the camshaft covers. Tighten the bolts to 89 inch lbs. (10 Nm).

31. Install the surge tank pipe retainer to the fuel supply rail.

32. Connect the wiring harness connectors to the TP, IAC, EVAP solenoid and MAP sensor.

33. Connect the fuel injector connectors to the injectors.

34. Connect the coolant hoses to the throttle body.

35. Connect the cruise control and accelerator cables to the throttle body.

36. Connect the fuel lines to the fuel supply rail.

37. Attach the vapor line to the purge solenoid.

38. Install the fuel injector cover and the air duct to the throttle body.

39. Fill the cooling system with DEX-COOL® coolant.

40. Connect the negative battery cable.

41. Start the engine and check for leaks.

3.8L (VIN L) Engine

1. Relieve the fuel system pressure. Disconnect the negative battery cable.

2. Remove the air cleaner assembly and fuel injector sight shield.

3. Disconnect the throttle cables from the throttle body lever and intake manifold bracket.

4. Remove the coolant recovery reservoir.

5. Remove the electrical cover from the right inner fender.

6. Remove the exhaust heat shield.

7. Disconnect the EGR adapter from the upper intake manifold pipe.

8. Disconnect and cap the fuel lines from the fuel rail and remove the lines from the manifold bracket.

9. Remove the serpentine belt.

10. Remove the alternator and rear alternator brace from the intake manifold.

11. Remove the throttle body cable bracket from the intake manifold.

12. Disconnect the electrical connectors from the throttle body.

13. Disconnect the fuel injector electrical connectors.

14. Disconnect the vacuum hoses from the canister purge solenoid, transaxle module and intake manifold connections.

15. Disconnect the vacuum hose quick connect at the upper intake manifold.

16. Remove the power steering pump mounting bolts and pull the pump forward.

17. Remove the serpentine belt tensioner pulley from the mounting bracket.

18. Remove the power steering pump support bracket.

19. Tag and disconnect the spark plug wires from the coil assembly and position them out of the way.

20. Drain the cooling system.

21. Disconnect the coolant bypass from the intake manifold.

22. Disconnect the heater pipes from the intake manifold and front cover.

23. Remove the solenoid valve mounting bracket and power steering pump brace from the intake manifold.

24. Disconnect the upper radiator hose from the thermostat housing.

25. Remove the thermostat housing and thermostat from the intake manifold.

26. Disconnect the electrical connector from the Engine Coolant Temperature (ECT) sensor and remove the sensor from the intake manifold.

27. Remove the intake manifold mounting bolts and remove the intake manifold.

To install:

28. Clean all the gasket surfaces completely. Be sure all threaded opening are clean of dirt and old sealer. A thread-cutting tap can be used to clean threaded bolt holes.

29. Install the intake manifold with new gaskets.

30. Apply thread lock compound to the intake bolts and install the mounting bolts and tighten to 88 inch lbs. (10 Nm). Make a second pass to verify all bolts are tightened to 88 inch lbs. (10 Nm). Do not overtighten or the light alloy manifold will be damaged.

31. Install the remaining components in the reverse order of removal:

• Thermostat housing bolts to 20 ft. lbs. (27 Nm)

• Power steering pump support bracket bolts to 37 ft. lbs. (50 Nm)

• Serpentine belt pulley bolt to 33 ft. lbs. (45 Nm)

32. Refill the cooling system. An oil and filter change is recommended.

33. Install the air cleaner assembly and the fuel injector sight shield.

34. Connect the negative battery cable.

35. Pressurize the fuel system by turn the ignition switch to the **ON** position to start the fuel pump and verify no fuel leaks.

36. Start the vehicle and verify no oil, vacuum or coolant leaks.

3.8L (VIN K) Engine

1. Before servicing the vehicle, refer to the precautions in the beginning of this section.

2. Disconnect the negative battery cable.

3. Remove the plastic engine cover clipped to the fuel rail.

4. Remove the air cleaner and duct assembly. Tag and remove the spark plug wires.

5. Properly relieve the fuel system pressure. Detach the fuel injection wiring harness.

6. Remove the canister purge electrical connector.

7. Remove the fuel rail. Remove the EGR adapter to the upper intake pipe.

Always tighten the lower intake manifold bolts in the sequence shown—3.8L (VIN 1 and K) engines

Upper intake manifold bolt tightening sequence—3.8L (VIN K) engine

8. Remove the throttle body assembly.

9. Remove the upper manifold mounting bolts and remove the manifold from the vehicle.

10. Remove the inner fender electrical cover.

11. Remove the exhaust shield.

12. Remove the alternator and the brace. Remove the control cable bracket.

13. Disconnect the control cables, vacuum lines and electrical connectors from the throttle body and intake manifold.

14. Remove the vacuum lines from the canister purge and the transaxle module at the intake connection.

15. Remove the power steering pump and move forward.

16. Remove the belt tensioner mounting bracket.

17. Remove the steering pump support bracket.

18. Remove the coolant bypass hose. Remove the heater pipes from the intake and the front cover.

19. Remove the alternator support brace.

20. Remove the upper radiator hose from the thermostat housing.

21. Detach the connector from the Engine Coolant Temperature (ECT) sensor electrical connection.

22. Remove the lower manifold mounting bolts and remove the lower manifold.

23. Remove the old sealing gaskets and clean the surfaces correctly.

To install:

24. Install the new lower intake gaskets and apply sealer to the corners of the end seals. Be sure to coat the threads of the intake bolts with P/N 12345336 or the equivalent. Tighten the bolts to 89 inch lbs. (10 Nm) using the proper sequence.

25. Install the remaining components in the reverse order of removal. Tighten the upper manifold bolts, in sequence, to 11 ft. lbs. (15 Nm).

26. Fill and bleed the cooling system using the recommended procedure.

27. Install the air cleaner and duct assembly. Connect the negative battery cable.

28. Cycle the ignition key several times to ensure there are no fuel leaks before starting the vehicle.

29. Verify the proper idle quality and be sure there is no oil or coolant leaks.

3.8L (VIN 1) Engine

1. Before servicing the vehicle, refer to the precautions in the beginning of this section.

2. Disconnect the negative battery cable.

3. Relieve the fuel system pressure using the recommended procedure.

4. Raise and safely support vehicle.

5. Remove the front splash shield.

6. Drain the radiator coolant into a suitable container. Close the radiator drain.

7. Reinstall the front splash shield.

8. Lower the vehicle.

9. Remove the supercharger assembly.

10. Remove the thermostat housing.

11. Disconnect the EGR tube at the intake manifold.

12. Disconnect the Engine Coolant Temperature (ECT) sensor electrical connection.

13. Remove the intake manifold.

To install:

14. Thoroughly clean all sealing surfaces.

15. Clean all old sealant from the intake manifold bolts and bolt holes.

16. Install new gaskets and manifold seals. Apply sealant to the ends of the manifold seals.

17. Install the intake manifold.

18. Install the intake manifold bolts and tighten, in sequence, to 11 ft. lbs. (15 Nm).

19. Install the electrical connector to the temperature sensor.

20. Install the EGR tube to the intake manifold.

21. Install the thermostat housing.

22. Install the supercharger assembly.

23. Connect the negative battery cable.

24. Fill and bleed the cooling system using the recommended procedure.

25. Run the engine and check for leaks and proper engine operation.

Exhaust Manifold

REMOVAL & INSTALLATION

3.1L Engine

LEFT SIDE (FRONT) MANIFOLD

1. Before servicing the vehicle, refer to the precautions in the beginning of this section.

2. Disconnect the negative battery cable. Remove the air cleaner and duct assembly.

3. Remove the coolant recovery bottle.

➡For some vehicles, it will be necessary to rotate the engine forward by removing the torque strut and installing tool J 41131 or equivalent, then rotate the engine assembly forward.

✳✳ WARNING

To prevent shearing of the rubber bushing, loosen the bolts on the engine strut before swinging the struts.

---

4. Relieve the accessory drive belt tension and remove the belt.

5. Disconnect the upper and lower radiator hoses from the engine assembly.

6. Remove the tie straps securing the heater outlet hose and the ignition wiring harness in position.

7. Remove the transaxle modulator vacuum pipe assembly.

8. Disconnect the heater pipe running from the water pump to the heater core.

9. Remove the heat shield and crossover pipe at the manifold.

10. Remove the engine mount strut.

11. Remove the air conditioning compressor bracket.

12. Remove the exhaust manifold mounting bolts and remove the manifold.

To install:

13. Clean the gasket mounting surfaces. Install the exhaust manifold to the engine, loosely install the mounting nuts.

14. Install the exhaust crossover pipe. Tighten the exhaust manifold nuts to 12 ft. lbs. (16 Nm) and the crossover pipe bolts to 18 ft. lbs. (25 Nm).

15. Install the exhaust manifold shield and tighten to 89 inch lbs. (10 Nm).

16. Install the engine mount strut and A/C compressor bracket.

17. Connect the heater pipe at the water pump and the heater core.

18. Connect the transaxle modulator vacuum pipe assembly.

19. Using new tie straps, secure the

Exploded view of the left exhaust manifold mounting—3.1L engine

heater outlet pipe and ignition wiring harness in position.

20. Connect the upper and lower radiator hoses to the engine.

21. Install the serpentine belt.

22. Install the coolant recovery bottle and refill the cooling system. Properly bleed the cooling system.

23. Install the air cleaner and duct assembly.

24. Connect the negative battery cable. Start the engine and check for exhaust leaks.

RIGHT SIDE (REAR) MANIFOLD

1. Before servicing the vehicle, refer to the precautions in the beginning of this section.

2. Disconnect the negative battery cable. Remove the air cleaner and duct assembly.

3. Remove the coolant recovery bottle.

4. Disconnect the upper radiator hose from the engine.

5. Remove the tie straps securing the heater outlet hose and the ignition wiring harness in position.

6. Remove the transaxle modulator vacuum pipe assembly.

7. Disconnect the heater pipe running from the water pump to the heater core.

8. Remove the heat shield and crossover pipe at the manifold.

9. Disconnect the Oxygen (O₂S) sensor electrical connector(s).

➡For some vehicles, it will be necessary to rotate the engine forward by removing the torque strut and installing tool J 41131 or equivalent, then rotate the engine assembly forward.

✳✳ WARNING

To prevent shearing of the rubber bushing, loosen the bolts on the engine strut before swinging the struts.

---

10. Raise and properly support the vehicle.

11. While supporting the rear or the engine carrier assembly, remove the rear mounting bolts and lower the rear portion of the carrier assembly.

12. Disconnect the front exhaust pipe from the manifold.

13. Disconnect the EGR tube from the manifold assembly.

14. Remove the O₂S sensor.

15. Remove the automatic transaxle dipstick and filler tube from the transaxle.

16. Remove the exhaust manifold heat shields and mounting bolts. Remove the manifold assembly from the vehicle.

To install:

17. Clean the gasket mounting surfaces.

18. Install the exhaust manifold to the engine and tighten the mounting nuts to 12 ft. lbs. (16 Nm).

19. Install the automatic transaxle dipstick and filler tube from the transaxle.

20. Install the O_2S sensor and connect the EGR tube the manifold.

21. Raise the rear engine carrier assembly into position. Install the mounting bolts and tighten to 107 ft. lbs. (145 Nm).

22. Lower the vehicle.

23. Install the exhaust crossover pipe and tighten the crossover pipe bolts to 18 ft. lbs. (25 Nm)

24. Connect the heater pipe at the water pump and the heater core.

25. Connect the transaxle modulator vacuum pipe assembly.

26. Using new tie straps, secure the heater outlet pipe and ignition wiring harness in position.

27. Connect the upper radiator hose to the engine.

28. Install the coolant recovery bottle and refill the cooling system. Properly bleed the cooling system.

29. Install the air cleaner and duct assembly.

30. Connect the negative battery cable.

31. Start the engine and check for exhaust leaks.

3.4L Engine

LEFT SIDE (FRONT) MANIFOLD

1. Before servicing the vehicle, refer to the precautions in the beginning of this section.

2. Remove the air cleaner assembly. Disconnect the negative battery cable.

3. Remove the exhaust crossover pipe. remove the cooling fans.

4. If equipped with a manual transaxle, disconnect the AIR hose from the AIR pipe on the exhaust manifold.

5. Remove the exhaust manifold nuts, then remove the exhaust manifold, gasket and heat shield.

To install:

6. Clean all gasket mating surfaces completely. Install a new exhaust manifold gasket.

7. Install the exhaust manifold and heat shield and tighten the mounting nuts to 115 inch lbs. (13 Nm).

8. Install the remaining components in the reverse order of removal. Tighten the exhaust crossover bolts to 18 ft. lbs. (25 Nm).

9. Connect the negative battery cable. Start the engine and check for exhaust leaks.

RIGHT SIDE (REAR) MANIFOLD

1. Before servicing the vehicle, refer to the precautions in the beginning of this section.

2. Remove the air cleaner and duct assembly.

3. Disconnect the negative battery cable. Remove the exhaust crossover pipe.

4. Remove the EGR tube from the exhaust manifold.

5. Raise and safely support the vehicle. Remove the front exhaust pipe and converter assembly.

6. Remove the Oxygen (O_2S) sensor.

7. Remove the exhaust pipe front heat shield.

8. Remove the rear alternator brace. Remove the transmission dipstick tube.

9. Remove the intermediate shaft from the steering gear.

10. Remove the exhaust manifold attaching nuts.

11. Install a jacking fixture to support the rear cradle.

12. Remove the rear cradle bolts.

13. Safely lower the engine cradle.

14. Remove the steering gear heat shield.

15. Remove the exhaust manifold and heat shield and attaching gasket.

To install:

16. Clean all gasket surfaces completely.

17. Install the exhaust manifold gasket, manifold and heat shields.

18. Install exhaust mounting manifold nuts and tighten to 115 inch lbs. (13 Nm).

Exploded view of the right exhaust manifold mounting—3.1L engine

79222514

19. Install the remaining components in the reverse order of removal. Tighten the following:

• Rear cradle bolts to 125 ft. lbs. (170 Nm)

• Intermediate shaft-to-steering gear pinch bolt to 35 ft. lbs. (47 Nm)

• Exhaust crossover pipe and tighten the nuts to 18 ft. lbs. (25 Nm)

20. Connect the negative battery cable. Install the air cleaner and duct assembly.

21. Start the engine and check for exhaust leaks.

➡**Whenever the vehicle sub-frame is removed or lowered, the wheel alignment should be checked.**

3.5L Engine

LEFT

1. Before servicing the vehicle, refer to the precautions in the beginning of this section.

2. Disconnect the negative battery cable.

3. Remove the fuel injector cover.

4. Remove the engine mount strut and bracket.

5. Remove the cooling fans.

6. Drain the engine coolant.

7. Remove the radiator hoses.

8. Detach the transaxle fluid lines from the radiator.

9. Remove the radiator.

10. Remove the generator.

11. Remove the heat shield from the manifold.

12. Remove the dipstick and tube.

13. Remove the AIR control valve assembly from the engine mount strut bracket.

14. Loosen the exhaust manifold mounting bolts.

15. Remove the studs attaching the exhaust manifold to the crossover pipe.

16. Remove the exhaust manifold.

To install:

17. Install the manifold to the crossover pipe using a new gasket. Tighten the studs to 18 ft. lbs. (25 Nm).

18. Position a new gasket between the cylinder head and manifold, then install the mounting bolts. Tighten the bolts to 18 ft. lbs. (25 Nm).

19. Install the AIR valve. Tighten the pipe nut to 44 ft. lbs. (60 Nm) and the mounting bolt to 80 inch lbs. (9 Nm).

20. Install the dipstick and tube.

21. Install the heat shield on the manifold.

22. Install the generator and radiator.

23. Install the cooling fans and the engine mount strut.

24. Install the fuel injector cover.

25. Connect the negative battery cable.

RIGHT

1. Before servicing the vehicle, refer to the precautions in the beginning of this section.

2. Disconnect the negative battery cable.

3. Remove the fuel injector cover.

4. Remove the air intake duct.

5. Remove the engine mount strut.

6. Properly relieve the fuel system pressure.

7. Disconnect the fuel lines from the supply rail.

8. Disconnect the cruise control and accelerator cables from the throttle body.

9. Disconnect the transaxle selector range cable and remove the cable brackets.

10. Remove the transaxle shift cable from the shift module.

11. Disconnect the brake booster vacuum hose from the engine.

12. Disconnect the wiring harness connectors from the engine and transaxle.

13. Drain the engine coolant.

14. Remove the upper radiator hose.

15. Disconnect the transaxle fluid cooler lines from the radiator.

16. Detach the surge tank inlet hose.

17. Remove the heater hoses from the engine.

18. Raise and safely support the vehicle.

19. Remove the lower radiator air deflector.

20. Remove the battery cables from the retainers.

21. Remove the lower radiator hose.

22. Without disconnecting the lines, remove the A/C compressor and position it aside.

23. Disconnect the wiring from the starter.

24. Remove the catalytic converter from the manifold.

25. Remove the front wheels and splash shields.

26. Remove the wheel speed sensor wiring from the lower control arms.

27. Detach the tie rod ends from the steering knuckles.

28. Disconnect the lower ball joints from the knuckles.

29. Remove the drive axles.

30. Disconnect the intermediate shaft from the steering rack.

31. Secure the vehicle to the lift in preparation for engine removal.

32. Position an engine/frame support table under the vehicle and lower the vehicle to meet the table.

33. Remove the frame-to-body bolts and raise the vehicle.

34. Disconnect the crossover pipe from the front manifold.

35. Remove the EGR pipe from the crossover pipe.

36. Remove the right exhaust manifold from the engine.

To install:

37. Install the right exhaust manifold on the engine with a new gasket. Tighten the bolts to 18 ft. lbs. (25 Nm).

38. Connect the crossover pipe to the front exhaust manifold.

39. Connect the EGR pipe to the crossover pipe. Tighten the pipe nut to 44 ft. lbs. (60 Nm).

40. Position the engine/transaxle assembly under the vehicle.

41. Coat the sub-frame bushings with rubber lubricant P/N 1051717 or equivalent.

42. Lower the vehicle onto the assembly. Align the sub-frame on the vehicle using two bolts or drill bits, ¾ inches thick by eight inches long through the alignment holes on the right side of the frame.

43. Install new frame-to-body bolts. Tighten the bolts to 133 ft. lbs. (180 Nm) starting with the rear bolts and then the front bolts.

44. Raise the vehicle and remove the frame table.

45. Connect the intermediate shaft to the steering rack. Be sure the shaft is fully seated on the stub before installing the pinch bolt. Tighten the bolts to 35 ft. lbs. (48 Nm).

46. Install the drive axles and assembly the suspension.

Exploded view of the right exhaust manifold—3.5L engine

47. Install the splash shields and front wheels.

48. Install the catalytic converter. Tighten the nuts to 53 inch lbs. (6 Nm).

49. Connect the wiring to the starter.

50. Install the A/C compressor.

51. Install the lower radiator hose.

52. Install the battery cables in their retainers.

53. Install the lower radiator air deflector.

54. Remove the straps securing the vehicle to the lift.

55. Lower the vehicle and connect the heater hoses.

56. Connect the surge tank hose.

57. Connect the transaxle cooler lines to the radiator.

58. Install the upper radiator hose.

59. Connect the wiring harness connectors to the engine and transaxle.

60. Connect the transaxle shift cable to the shift module and install the bracket.

61. Connect the transaxle selector range cable.

62. Connect the cruise control and accelerator cables to the throttle body.

63. Connect the fuel lines to the supply rail.

64. Install the engine mount strut.

65. Install the intake air duct.

66. Install the fuel injector cover.

67. Refill the cooling system with DEX-COOL coolant.

68. Connect the negative battery cable.

69. Start the engine and check for leaks.

3.8L Engine

LEFT SIDE (FRONT) MANIFOLD

1. Before servicing the vehicle, refer to the precautions in the beginning of this section.

2. Remove the air cleaner and air duct assembly.

3. Disconnect the negative battery cable. Remove the torque struts.

4. Remove the right engine cooling fan.

5. Remove the heat shield from the crossover pipe and disconnect the crossover pipe at the rear manifold.

6. Drain the cooling system.

7. Disconnect the upper radiator hose from the thermostat housing.

8. Remove the fuel rail sight cover.

9. Disconnect the EGR adapter-to-intake manifold pipe.

10. Remove the EGR valve.

11. Remove the front engine lift hook.

Timing belt service is covered in Section 5 of this manual

Exploded view of the left exhaust manifold mounting—3.8L engine

Exploded view of the right exhaust manifold mounting—3.8L engine

12. Remove the torque strut bracket from the left cylinder head.

13. Remove the oil level indicator tube.

14. Disconnect the spark plug wires from the rocker arm cover and spark plugs and position out of the way.

15. Remove the A/C compressor support brace from the exhaust manifold stud.

16. Remove the manifold mounting bolts and remove the exhaust manifold.

To install:

17. Clean all the gasket surfaces completely.

18. Install the exhaust manifold and loosely install the mounting bolts. Starting with the center bolts and working outward tighten the bolts to 38 ft. lbs. (52 Nm).

19. Install the spark plugs and tighten to 11 ft. lbs. (15 Nm).

20. Install the remaining components in the reverse order of removal. Tighten the following:

• Engine lift hook nut to 22 ft. lbs. (30 Nm)

• Crossover pipe-to-rear exhaust manifold bolts to 22 ft. lbs. (30 Nm)

• Tighten the strut mounting nuts to 41 ft. lbs. (56 Nm)

21. Connect the negative battery cable. Install the air cleaner and duct assembly.

22. Start the vehicle and verify no leaks.

RIGHT SIDE (REAR) MANIFOLD

1. Before servicing the vehicle, refer to the precautions in the beginning of this section.

2. Remove the air cleaner and air duct assembly.

3. Remove the fuel rail sight cover.

4. Disconnect the negative battery cable. Remove the coolant recovery bottle.

5. Remove the heat shield from the crossover pipe and disconnect the crossover pipe at the rear manifold.

6. Remove the transaxle oil level indicator tube.

7. Disconnect the spark plug wires from the rocker arm cover and spark plugs and position out of the way.

8. Disconnect the Oxygen (O_2S) sensor electrical connector.

9. Remove the torque struts.

10. Remove the rear engine lift hook. Remove the spark plugs.

11. Raise and safely support the vehicle. Remove the front exhaust pipe and converter assembly.

12. Remove the rear engine mount-to-frame nuts.

13. Lower the vehicle.

14. Using a floor jack raise the right rear corner of the engine to provide clearance.

15. Remove the manifold mounting bolts and remove the exhaust manifold.

To install:

16. Clean all the gasket surfaces completely.

17. Install the exhaust manifold and loosely install the mounting bolts. Starting with the center bolts and working outward tighten the bolts to 38 ft. lbs. (52 Nm).

18. Connect the crossover pipe to the rear exhaust manifold and tighten the mounting bolts to 22 ft. lbs. (30 Nm).

19. Install the remaining components in the reverse order of removal. Tighten the following:

• Rear engine mount nuts to 50 ft. lbs. (68 Nm)

• Engine lift hook nut to 22 ft. lbs. (30 Nm)

• Spark plugs to 11 ft. lbs. (15 Nm)

• Torque the strut mounting nuts to 41 ft. lbs. (56 Nm)

20. Connect the negative battery cable. Install the air cleaner and duct assembly.

21. Start the vehicle and verify no leaks.

Camshaft and Valve Lifters

REMOVAL & INSTALLATION

3.1L Engine

1. Before servicing the vehicle, refer to the precautions in the beginning of this section.

2. Relieve the fuel system pressure. Disconnect the negative battery cable.

3. Remove the engine assembly from the vehicle using the recommended procedure, and mount on a suitable engine stand.

➡**When removing valvetrain components they must be marked for installation in the same location they are removed from. When the camshaft is being replaced the valve lifters should also be replaced.**

4. Remove the intake manifold, valve cover, rocker arms, pushrods and valve lifters.

5. Remove the crankshaft balancer using a puller to draw the crankshaft balancer from the crankshaft nose.

6. Remove the timing chain front cover.

7. It is good practice to set the engine to Top Dead Center (TDC) No. 1 cylinder (firing position) before disassembling the timing chain and sprockets. This should align all the timing marks and serve as a point of reference for later work. Remove the timing chain and sprockets.

✲✲ CAUTION

If the camshaft was replaced the valve liters must also be replaced. The old lifters have already developed a wear pattern from the old camshaft and if installed on the new camshaft they will cause premature wear of the camshaft lobes.

8. Remove the oil pump driven gear so the camshaft can be pulled out in Step 10.

9. Remove the two bolts and remove the camshaft thrust plate.

10. Carefully remove the camshaft. Avoid marring the camshaft bearing surfaces.

To install:

11. Coat the camshaft with lubricant GM part number 1052365 or equivalent camshaft break-in lubricant or quality engine oil supplement, and install the camshaft.

12. Install the camshaft thrust plate and tighten the mounting bolts to 89 inch lbs. (10 Nm).

13. Install the oil pump driven gear and tighten the mounting bolt to 27 ft. lbs. (36 Nm).

14. Install the timing chain and sprocket.

15. Verify that all timing marks are aligned. It is good practice to turn the crankshaft several complete rotations to be sure the timing marks still align when the crankshaft is returned to TDC No. 1 cylinder compression stroke (firing position). This is most important. If the valvetrain is not correctly timed, the engine will be damaged on start-up. When satisfied that all marks are correctly aligned, install the camshaft thrust button and front cover.

16. Install the crankshaft balancer and tighten the bolt to 75 ft. lbs. (103 Nm).

17. Install the intake manifold, valve cover, rocker arms, pushrods and valve lifters.

18. Install the engine assembly into the vehicle using the recommended procedure.

19. Connect the negative battery cable.

20. Verify that all fluid levels (coolant, engine oil, etc.) are full and correct. An oil and filter change is recommended.

➡**The only time valve adjustment in needed is if there was a valve job performed or the rocker studs have been replaced with an adjustable rocker arm stud. The rocker arm stud installed from the factory should be shouldered and not need any adjustment.**

21. Adjust the valves, as required.

22. Start the engine and verify no oil leaks.

3.4L Engine

The 3.4L VIN X engine has aluminum cam carriers which house the camshafts with the actual aluminum of the carrier serving as the camshaft bearing surfaces. Use care when working with these light alloy parts. They can be damaged or broken if carelessly handled.

Dual Overhead Camshaft (DOHC) engines have numerous valvetrain timing marks which must be aligned or serious engine damage will result. It may be helpful to set the engine to Top Dead Center (TDC), compression stroke of No. 1 cylinder (firing position) before beginning work. This gives a known point-of-reference. In this way as the work progresses, timing marks can be observed and noted which should save time at assembly. In addition, note the routing of the timing belt so that it can eventually be properly installed.

LEFT SIDE CAMSHAFT

1. Before servicing the vehicle, refer to the precautions in the beginning of this section.

2. Remove the air cleaner and duct assembly.

3. Disconnect the negative battery cable. Drain the cooling system.

4. Remove the left side camshaft cover. Remove the timing belt assembly.

5. Install six, six inch sections of vacuum/fuel line hose under camshaft and between lifters. This will hold lifters in the carrier. For this procedure use ⁵⁄₁₆ in. (8mm) vacuum/fuel line hose for exhaust valves and ⁷⁄₃₂ in. (5.5mm) vacuum/fuel line hose for the intake valves.

6. Remove the exhaust crossover pipe. Remove the upper radiator hose.

7. Disconnect the heater pipe hose from the intake plenum.

8. Remove the front exhaust manifold.

9. Disconnect the engine front coolant pipe and position out of the way.

10. Remove the camshaft carrier mounting bolts.

11. Remove the camshaft carrier and gasket from the engine.

12. Place the camshaft carrier on a suitable work surface.

13. Remove the hoses securing the lifters and remove the lifters from the camshaft carrier.

14. Clean the oil out of the camshaft hold down tool mounting hole and install J-38613, or an equivalent camshaft hold down tool. Tighten the tool mounting bolt to 22 ft. lbs. (30 Nm).

15. Remove the camshaft sprocket bolts and washers, while holding the camshaft from turning using J-38614, or an equivalent camshaft sprocket holding tool.

16. Using a suitable sprocket puller, J-38616, or the equivalent, remove the camshaft sprockets.

17. Remove the six thrust plate cover screws and remove the cover and gasket.

18. Remove the two camshaft thrust plate bolts and remove the thrust plate.

19. Remove tool J-38613.

❋❋ CAUTION

The camshaft bearing journals are all the same diameter and care must be used when removing the camshaft to prevent damage to the camshaft and/or camshaft carrier.

20. Remove the camshaft by carefully sliding it out the back of the camshaft carrier.

21. Remove the camshaft oil seal using a suitable prying tool. Do not allow the prying tool to scratch the camshaft carrier.

To install:

22. Coat the lips of the camshaft seals with clean engine oil and using J-38619, or an equivalent seal installer, seat the seals in their recesses.

23. Coat the camshaft journals and lobes with engine lube, GM 1052637 or the equivalent.

24. Carefully install the camshaft into the camshaft carrier. Be sure the camshaft does not distort the camshaft seal during installation.

25. Install the thrust plate and tighten the two mounting bolts to 89 inch lbs. (10 Nm).

26. Install the thrust plate cover and gasket and tighten the six mounting bolts to 89 inch lbs. (10 Nm).

27. Install the camshaft holding tool and tighten the mounting bolt to 22 ft. lbs. (30 Nm).

28. Install a new camshaft carrier gasket on the cylinder head and install the camshaft carrier on the cylinder head.

29. Install the mounting bolts and tighten to 18 ft. lbs. (25 Nm).

30. Install the lifters under the camshafts. Install the camshaft sprockets and timing belt.

❋❋ CAUTION

After installing the camshaft sprockets and timing belt the cam timing must be set. Failure to properly set the camshaft timing will result in serious engine damage.

31. Remove tool J-38613.

32. Install the front engine coolant pipe. Install the front exhaust manifold.

33. Connect the heater hose pipe to the intake plenum.

34. Connect the upper radiator hose.

35. Install the exhaust crossover pipe. Install the camshaft cover.

➡**Before tightening the cover mounting bolts, fully seat the bolt insulators in the camshaft cover.**

36. Connect the negative battery cable. Install the air cleaner and air duct assembly.

37. Refill the cooling system.

38. Start the vehicle and verify no leaks and proper engine performance.

RIGHT SIDE CAMSHAFT

1. Before servicing the vehicle, refer to the precautions in the beginning of this section.

2. Remove the air cleaner and duct assembly.

3. Disconnect the negative battery cable. Drain the cooling system.

4. Remove the right side camshaft cover.

5. Remove the timing belt.

6. Install six, six inch sections of vacuum/fuel line hose under camshaft and between lifters. This will hold lifters in the carrier. For this procedure use ⁵⁄₁₆ in. (8mm) fuel line hose for exhaust valves and ⁷⁄₃₂ in. (5.5mm) vacuum/fuel line hose for the intake valves.

7. Remove the front and rear engine lift brackets.

8. Remove the camshaft carrier mounting bolts, then remove the carrier and gasket from the engine.

9. Place the camshaft carrier on a suitable work surface.

10. Remove the hoses securing the lifters and remove the lifters from the camshaft carrier.

11. Clean the oil out of the camshaft hold down tool mounting hole and install J-38613, or an equivalent camshaft hold down tool. Tighten the tool mounting bolt to 22 ft. lbs. (30 Nm).

12. Remove the camshaft sprocket bolts and washers, while holding the camshaft from turning using J-38614, or an equivalent camshaft sprocket holding tool.

13. Using a suitable sprocket puller, J-38616, or the equivalent, remove the camshaft sprockets.

14. Remove the six thrust plate cover screws and remove the cover and gasket.

15. Remove the two camshaft thrust plate bolts and remove the thrust plate.

16. Remove tool J-38613.

✳✳ CAUTION

The camshaft bearing journals are all the same diameter and care must be used when removing the camshaft to prevent damage to the camshaft and/or camshaft carrier.

17. Remove the camshaft by carefully sliding it out the back of the camshaft carrier.

18. Remove the camshaft oil seal using a suitable prying tool. Do not allow the prying tool to scratch the camshaft carrier.

To install:

19. Coat the lips of the camshaft seals with clean engine oil and using J-38619, or an equivalent seal installer, seat the seals in their recesses.

20. Coat the camshaft journals and lobes with engine lube, GM 1052637 or the equivalent.

21. Carefully install the camshaft into the camshaft carrier. Be sure the camshaft does not distort the camshaft seal during installation.

22. Install the thrust plate and tighten the two mounting bolts to 89 inch lbs. (10 Nm).

23. Install the thrust plate cover and gasket and tighten the six mounting bolts to 89 inch lbs. (10 Nm).

24. Install the camshaft holding tool and tighten the mounting bolt to 22 ft. lbs. (30 Nm).

25. Install a new camshaft carrier gasket on the cylinder head and install the camshaft carrier on the cylinder head.

26. Install the mounting bolts and tighten to 18 ft. lbs. (25 Nm).

27. Install the lifters under the camshafts.

28. Install the camshaft sprockets and timing belt.

✳✳ CAUTION

After installing the camshaft sprockets and timing belt the Cam Timing must be set. Failure to properly set the camshaft timing will result in serious engine damage.

29. Remove tool J-38613.

30. Install the front and rear engine lift brackets.

31. Install the camshaft cover.

➡**Before tightening the cover mounting bolts, fully seat the bolt insulators in the camshaft cover.**

32. Connect the negative battery cable. Install the air cleaner and air duct assembly.

33. Fill and bleed the cooling system using the recommended procedure.

34. Start the vehicle and verify no leaks and proper engine performance.

3.5L Engine

1. Before servicing the vehicle, refer to the precautions in the beginning of this section.

2. Disconnect the negative battery cable.

3. If removing the front (left) camshafts, partially drain the engine coolant and remove the thermostat housing for clearance when installing camshaft holding fixture J 42038 or equivalent.

4. Remove the front camshaft cover.

5. Rotate the crankshaft so the camshaft flats are parallel to the sealing surface of the camshaft, then install camshaft holding fixture J 42038 or equivalent to prevent camshaft rotation.

6. Remove the camshaft sprocket bolts.

7. Install the timing chain/sprocket holding fixture J 42042 or equivalent.

8. Evenly slide the camshaft sprocket and chain from the camshafts onto the holding tool.

➡**The camshaft bearing caps are marked. Be sure the raised portion of the cap faces the outside of the engine. They must always be installed in their original positions.**

9. Remove the camshaft bearing caps.

10. Remove J 42038 from the camshafts.

11. Remove the camshafts from the cylinder head.

✳✳ WARNING

The camshafts and rocker arms must be returned to their original positions when installed.

Camshaft holding fixture J 42038 installed on the camshafts—3.5L engine

Timing chain/sprocket holding fixture J 42042 installed on the cylinder head—3.5L engine

1. Left intake
2. Left exhaust
3. Right intake
4. Right exhaust

9300Z511

Camshaft identification—3.5L engine

12. Remove the rocker arms from the cylinder head as required.

To install:

13. Coat the rocker arms with engine oil and place them in their original positions on the cylinder head. Be sure to install the rounded end on the lash adjuster and the flat end on the tip of the valve.

J 42038

9300Z509

Use the flats on the camshaft if rotation is necessary for installation of the holding tool—3.5L engine

9300Z510

Before installation, compress the tensioner and lock it in place with a piece of wire—3.5L engine

14. Clean the camshaft carriers and journals with a lint free cloth.

15. Apply clean engine oil to the camshaft and position them on the cylinder head with the notch for the sprocket drive pins at the top of their rotation.

16. Loosely install the bearing caps in their original positions and directions. Tighten the bearing cap bolts to 44 inch lbs. (5 Nm). Now tighten each bolt an additional 30 degrees with a torque angle meter.

17. Install J 42038 on the camshafts at the rear of the cylinder head. Use the flats on the camshaft if turning is needed. Be sure the tool is fully seated on the camshafts.

18. Compress the secondary timing chain tensioner by hand and insert a wire into the access hole to lock it in place.

19. Slide the camshaft sprockets and chain off the tool and onto the camshafts. Be sure to align the drive pins.

20. Remove the timing chain/sprocket holder from the front of the cylinder head. Tighten the sprocket bolts to 18 ft. lbs. (25 Nm), then using a torque angle meter, tighten the bolts an additional 45 degrees.

21. Remove the wire from the chain tensioner and allow the tensioner to apply pressure to the chain.

22. Remove the camshaft holding fixture.

23. Install the camshaft cover.

24. If removed, install the thermostat housing.

25. Refill the cooling if necessary with DEX-COOL® coolant.

26. Connect the negative battery cable.

3.8L Engine

1. Before servicing the vehicle, refer to the precautions in the beginning of this section.

2. Disconnect the negative battery cable.

3. Relieve the fuel system pressure using the recommended procedure.

4. Remove the engine assembly from the vehicle and mount on a suitable engine stand.

5. If equipped, remove the supercharger.

6. Remove the intake manifold.

7. Remove the rocker arm covers.

8. Remove the rocker arm assemblies, pushrods and lifters. Identify all parts as they are removed, so they can be reinstalled in their original locations.

9. Remove the crankshaft balancer center bolt, using a suitable puller, remove the balancer from the crankshaft.

10. Remove the timing chain front cover.

11. Set the engine to Top Dead Center (TDC) No. 1 cylinder (firing position) to align the timing marks, before disassembling the timing chain and sprockets.

➡ **Align the timing marks of the camshaft and crankshaft sprockets to avoid burring the camshaft journals by the crankshaft.**

12. Remove the camshaft sprocket and timing chain.

13. Remove the camshaft thrust plate bolts and remove the thrust plate.

14. Carefully remove the camshaft from the engine block.

15. Inspect the camshaft lobes and journals for wear and/or damage; replace as necessary.

➡ **If the camshaft was replaced the lifters must also be replaced. The old lifters have developed a wear pattern and will cause the new camshaft to wear prematurely.**

To install:

16. Coat the camshaft lobes and bearings with lubricant GM part number 1052365 or equivalent camshaft break-in prelube prior to installation.

17. Carefully install the camshaft into the engine.

18. Install the camshaft thrust plate and tighten the mounting bolts to 11 ft. lbs. (15 Nm).

19. Install the camshaft sprocket and timing chain. Be sure the timing marks are aligned. Tighten the camshaft sprocket retaining bolt to 74 ft. lbs. (100 Nm) plus an additional 90 degree (¼) turn.

20. Install the timing chain front cover.

21. Install the crankshaft balancer and tighten the mounting bolt to 111 ft. lbs. (150 Nm) plus an additional 76 degree turn.

Refer to Section 1 for engine rebuilding specifications

The timing marks should face each other if the chain and gears are installed properly—3.8L engine

22. Coat the valve lifters with camshaft prelube and install the lifters in the lifter bores.

23. Install the lifter guides and lifter guide retainer. Tighten the retainer mounting bolts to 22 ft. lbs. (30 Nm).

24. Install the pushrods and rocker arms and tighten the rocker arm bolts to 11 ft. lbs. (15 Nm) plus an additional 90 degree turn.

25. Install the rocker arm covers.

26. Install the intake manifold.

27. If equipped, install the supercharger.

28. Install the engine in the vehicle.

29. Connect the negative battery cable.

30. Verify that all fluid levels are full and correct.

31. Start the engine and check for leaks. Check engine operation.

Valve Lash

ADJUSTMENT

The valve clearance cannot be adjusted on these engines. The hydraulic lifters function to maintain zero clearance. Any clearance is instantaneously taken up by the hydraulic action of the lifters. Lifter noise complaints may require cleaning of sludge coated or varnished valve lifters, or replacement.

Oil Pan

REMOVAL & INSTALLATION

3.1L Engine

1. Before servicing the vehicle, refer to the precautions in the beginning of this section.

2. Disconnect the negative battery cable. Remove the hood.

3. Remove the torque struts and A/C compressor/torque strut mounting bracket.

4. Remove the cooling fan assemblies.

5. Install an engine support fixture, J-28467-A, or the equivalent.

6. Raise and safely support the vehicle.

7. Disconnect the front pipe from the exhaust manifold.

8. Remove the pinch bolt from the intermediate steering shaft and disconnect the steering shaft from the rack and pinion unit.

9. Drain the engine oil.

10. Disconnect and remove the oil level indicator.

11. Remove the engine splash shield.

12. Support the frame assembly with suitable floor stands.

13. Remove the transaxle-to-frame nuts and the engine mount-to-frame nuts.

14. Remove the frame mounting bolts and lower the fame slightly.

15. Remove the front engine mount and engine bracket.

16. Remove the flywheel cover.

17. Remove the starter.

18. Remove the transaxle mount from the oil pan.

19. Remove the oil pan mounting bolts and remove the oil pan.

To install:

20. Clean all gasket surfaces completely. Install the oil pan in position with new gaskets.

21. Tighten the oil pan rail bolts to 18 ft. lbs. (25 Nm) and the oil pan side bolts to 37 ft. lbs. (50 Nm).

22. Install the remaining components in the reverse order of removal. Tighten the frame mounting bolts to 103 ft. lbs. (140 Nm) and the intermediate shaft-to-rack and pinion unit pinch bolt to 35 ft. lbs. (47 Nm).

23. Refill the crankcase with oil and the power steering if disconnecting the pressure lines for clearance.

24. Connect the negative battery cable. Start the vehicle and verify no oil leaks.

➡**Whenever the vehicle sub-frame is removed or lowered, the wheel alignment should be checked.**

3.4L Engine

1. Before servicing the vehicle, refer to the precautions in the beginning of this section.

2. Remove the air cleaner assembly. Disconnect the negative battery cable. Drain the cooling system.

3. Remove the coolant recovery tank.

4. Install an engine support fixture J-28467-A, J-28467-90, J-36462, or their equivalents.

5. Raise and safely support the vehicle. Remove the front tire and wheel assemblies.

6. Drain the engine oil.

7. Remove the steering rack and pinion gear assembly retaining bolts and hang the steering gear from the body.

8. Remove the cotter pins and castle nuts from the lower ball joints and separate the lower ball joints from the lower control arms.

9. Remove the power steering cooler line clamps at the frame.

10. Remove the engine mount nuts at the frame.

11. Support the frame with a suitable jack and remove the frame mounting bolts and remove the frame assembly.

12. Remove the oil filter.

13. Remove the engine oil cooler as follows:

   a. Disconnect the oil pressure sender and Crankshaft Position (CKP) sensor electrical connectors.

   b. Disconnect the outlet hose and position aside.

   c. Disconnect the inlet hose and position aside.

   d. Remove the mounting bolts.

   e. Remove the oil cooler.

14. Remove the starter.

15. Remove the flywheel cover.

16. Remove the oil pan retaining nuts and bolts.

17. Remove the oil pan and gasket.

To install:

18. Clean all the gasket surfaces completely. Install a new oil pan gasket and apply sealer to the gasket near the rear main bearing cap.

19. Install the oil pan and fasteners and tighten as follows:

- Oil pan nuts: 97 inch lbs. (11 Nm).

Exploded view of the oil pan mounting—3.4L engine

• Rear mounting bolts: 20 ft. lbs. (27 Nm).

• Remainder of bolts: 97 inch lbs. (11 Nm).

20. Install the remaining components in the reverse order of removal. Tighten the following:

• Engine oil cooler bolts to 24 ft. lbs. (33 Nm)

• Frame mounting bolts to 103 ft. lbs. (140 Nm)

• Ball joint-to-control arm castle nuts to 63 ft. lbs. (85 Nm)

• Steering gear mounting bolts 59 ft. lbs. (80 Nm)

21. Install the coolant recovery tank. Refill the crankcase with oil.

22. Fill and bleed the cooling system. Connect the negative battery cable.

23. Install the air cleaner assembly.

24. Start the vehicle and verify no oil leaks.

➡**Whenever the vehicle sub-frame is removed or lowered, the wheel alignment should be checked.**

25. Check the front end alignment and correct if necessary.

3.5L Engine

1. Before servicing the vehicle, refer to the precautions in the beginning of this section.

2. Raise and safely support the vehicle.

3. Drain the engine oil.

4. Remove the oil filter cap and filter.

5. Disconnect the oil level sensor harness connector.

6. Remove the transaxle brace.

7. Remove the oil pan mounting bolts and the oil pan.

8. Clean the gasket surface carefully to avoid gouging the aluminum.

To install:

9. If removed, install the oil level sensor. Tighten the bolt to 80 inch lbs. (9 Nm).

10. Install the oil pan using a new gasket. DO NOT tighten the bolts at this time.

11. Install the transaxle brace on the engine block only. Tighten the bolts to 18 ft. lbs. (25 Nm).

12. Loosely install the brace-to-oil pan bolts.

13. Align the rear of the oil pan flush with the rear of the engine block. Use a straight edge for reference.

14. Press the front of the oil pan against the transaxle brace and tighten the brace-to-

93002512

Exploded view of the oil pan—3.5L engine

Oil pan

Straight edge

93002513

Use a straight edge to align the rear of the oil pan to the rear of the engine—3.5L engine

93002514

Oil pan mounting bolt tightening sequence—3.5L engine

oil pan bolts to 18 ft. lbs. (25 Nm). Be sure to keep the rear of the pan flush with the rear of the engine.

15. Tighten the oil pan bolts in sequence to 18 ft. lbs. (25 Nm).

16. Tighten the brace-to-transaxle bolts to 32 ft. lbs. (43 Nm).

17. Connect the oil level sensor connector.

18. Install the drain plug and tighten it to 15 ft. lbs. (20 m).

19. Install a new oil filter and tighten the cap to 18 ft. lbs. (25 Nm).

20. Lower the vehicle and install the correct amount of engine oil.

21. Start the engine and inspect for leaks.

22. Stop the engine and verify the oil level.

3.8L Engine

1. Before servicing the vehicle, refer to the precautions in the beginning of this section.

2. Disconnect the negative battery cable. Remove the torque struts.

3. Raise and safely support the vehicle.

4. Disconnect the front exhaust pipe from the exhaust manifold.

5. Remove the right front tire and wheel assembly.

6. Remove the right inner fender well splash shield.

7. Drain the engine oil.

8. Disconnect and cap the engine oil cooler pipes.

9. Safely support the weight of the engine since the engine mounts will be disconnected. Use a suitable lifting/holding device.

10. Remove the engine mount-to-frame nuts from both front engine mounts.

11. Remove the flywheel inspection cover.

12. Raise the powertrain assembly at the transaxle to provide clearance using a suitable transmission jack.

➡**The oil level sensor should be removed before removing the oil pan or damage to the oil level sensor may occur.**

13. Remove the oil level sensor.

14. Remove the oil pan mounting bolts.

15. Lower the oil pan and disconnect the oil pump screen assembly and lower it into the oil pan.

16. Remove the oil pan and pump screen together.

To install:

17. Clean all parts well, especially the gasket sealing flanges on the engine block and the oil pan.

18. Install a new oil pan gasket onto the oil pan.

19. Place the oil pump screen in the oil pan and position the pan under the engine.

20. Mount the screen on the oil pump and tighten the mounting bolt to 10 ft. lbs. (14 Nm).

21. Raise the oil pan into position and tighten the mounting bolts to 10 ft. lbs. (14 Nm).

22. Install the oil level sensor.

23. Install the remaining components in the reverse order of removal. Tighten the following:

- Engine mount nuts to 50 ft. lbs. (68 Nm)
- Tighten the strut mounting bolts to 41 ft. lbs. (56 Nm)

✴✴ WARNING

Operating the engine without the proper amount and type of engine oil will result in severe engine damage.

24. Refill the crankcase with clean engine oil.

25. Connect the negative battery cable. Start the vehicle and verify no oil leaks.

Oil Pump

REMOVAL & INSTALLATION

3.1L Engine

1. Before servicing the vehicle, refer to the precautions in the beginning of this section.

2. Disconnect the negative battery cable. Raise and safely support the vehicle.

3. Drain the engine oil, then remove the oil pan.

4. Remove the crankshaft oil deflector bolts, then remove the deflector.

5. Remove the oil pump retaining bolts and remove the oil pump and pump driveshaft.

To install:

6. Install the oil pump and pump driveshaft. Tighten the oil pump mounting bolts to 30 ft. lbs. (41 Nm).

7. Install the crankshaft oil deflector and mounting bolts. Tighten the mounting bolts to 18 ft. lbs. (25 Nm).

8. Install the oil pan.

9. Lower the vehicle.

10. Fill the crankcase to the correct level with oil.

11. It is good practice to install a reliable mechanical oil pressure gauge so that actual pump pressure can be read after startup. If no oil pressure is seen within a short time of startup, shut down the engine to determine why there is no oil pressure.

12. Start the engine, check the oil pressure and check for leaks.

3.4L Engine

1. Before servicing the vehicle, refer to the precautions in the beginning of this section.

2. Disconnect the negative battery cable. Drain the engine oil.

3. Remove the oil pan.

4. Remove the eight oil pan baffle mounting nuts and remove the oil pan baffle.

5. Remove the oil pump retaining bolt.

6. Remove the oil pump with pick-up and drive shaft extension.

To install:

7. Clean all parts well. Clean the inside of the oil pan, the gasket flanges on pan and gasket rail on the block.

8. Install the oil pump with the driveshaft extension and pick-up assembly onto the rear main bearing cap making sure the driveshaft extension engages in the oil pump drive.

9. Install the oil pump retaining bolt and tighten to 40 ft. lbs. 54 (Nm).

10. Install the oil pan baffle and tighten the mounting nuts to 18 ft. lbs. (25 Nm).

11. Install the oil pan following the recommended procedure.

12. Refill the crankcase with oil.

13. Connect the negative battery cable.

14. Start the vehicle and verify proper oil pressure, 15 lbs. minimum @ 1100 rpm at normal operating temperature.

3.5L Engine

1. Before servicing the vehicle, refer to the precautions in the beginning of this section.

2. Remove the engine front cover as described in the timing chain procedure.

3. Remove the camshaft covers.

4. Install camshaft holding fixtures such as J 42038 on both sets of camshafts. Turn the hex portion of the camshaft to align them for tool installation. When installed, the flats on the rear of the camshafts will be parallel with the camshaft cover sealing surface.

5. Remove the primary chain tensioner and remove the chain from the drive sprocket.

6. Remove the four oil pump mounting bolts and slide the oil pump with the sprocket off of the crankshaft.

➡The internal parts of the oil pump are not serviced separately. The oil pump may be opened for inspection. If damage or wear is noted, replace the entire pump as an assembly.

OIL PUMP BOLT

◀FRT

OIL PUMP DRIVE ROD

OIL PUMP

MAIN BEARING CAP

ENGINE BLOCK

79222519

Oil pump and driveshaft components—3.1L engine

1	BOLT
2	OIL PUMP
3	SHAFT WITH WHITE PAINT ID
4	LOCATING PIN
5	REAR MAIN CAP
6	ENGINE BLOCK
7	BOLT
8	CLAMP
9	OIL PUMP DRIVE
10	GREASE

VIEW A

7922Z520

Oil pump and drivegear assembly—3.4L engine

To install:

7. Pack the oil pump housing with white petroleum jelly to insure priming. Tighten the housing bolts to 97 inch lbs. (11 Nm).

8. Align the splines and install the sprocket in the oil pump.

9. Align the sprocket with the crankshaft and install the pump on the engine until a positive stop is felt. When installed properly, the sprocket will protrude slightly from the oil pump and the face of the sprocket will be behind the machined step in the crankshaft.

10. Align the pump with the mounting holes and install the bolts. Tighten them to 18 ft. lbs. (25 Nm).

11. Install the primary chain on the sprocket. Be sure to maintain correct timing.

12. Install the chain tensioner.

13. Remove the camshaft holding tools.

14. Install the crankshaft covers.

15. Install the engine front cover and remaining components.

3.8L Engines

1. Before servicing the vehicle, refer to the precautions in the beginning of this section.

2. Disconnect the negative battery cable.

3. Remove the engine drive belts and tensioner assembly.

4. Remove the drive belt idler pulley and bracket, if necessary.

5. Raise and safely support the vehicle.

6. Support the engine using engine support fixture J 28467 or equivalent, and remove the torque axis mount and bracket assembly.

7. Remove the engine front cover assembly.

8. Remove the four bolts securing the oil filter adapter to the front cover assembly and oil filter adapter, pressure regulator valve and spring.

9300Z515

The oil pump is mounting on the front of the engine and driven by the crankshaft—3.5L engine

9300Z516

Correct position of the crankshaft sprocket when the oil pump is installed correctly—3.5L engine

For complete mechanical specifications, refer to Section 1 of this manual

1. 97 inch lbs. (11 Nm)
2. Oil pump cover
3. Pump outer gear
4. Pump inner gear
5. Front cover

79222521

Oil pump assembly—3.8L engine

9. Remove the four oil pump cover attaching screws and remove the cover.

10. Remove the inner and outer pump gears and inspect.

To install:

11. Lubricate the oil pump gears with petroleum jelly and install the gears into the housing.

12. Pack the gear cavity with petroleum jelly after the gears have been installed in the housing. This seals the pump and acts like a "prime" so oil will begin to drawn from the oil pan as soon as the engine begins to turn. Do not neglect this step. DO NOT use any type of grease. Petroleum jelly has a low melting point and will correctly dissipate when oil begins to flow and it is no longer needed.

13. Install the oil pump cover and screws and tighten to 97 inch lbs. (11 Nm).

14. Install the oil filter adapter with new gasket, pressure regulator valve and spring. Tighten the mounting bolts to 24 ft. lbs. (33 Nm). Apply sealant to the bolt threads.

15. Install the front cover assembly.

16. Install the tensioner assembly.

17. Install the drive belt idler pulley and bracket, if removed.

18. Install the torque axis mount assembly and remove the engine support fixture.

19. Verify the correct engine oil level. A new oil filter is recommended.

20. Connect the negative battery cable.

21. Start the vehicle and verify no leaks and proper oil pressure.

Rear Main Seal

REMOVAL & INSTALLATION

3.5L Engine

1. Remove the engine/transaxle assembly.

2. Remove the transaxle from the engine.

3. Remove the flexplate.

4. Place seal removal tool J 42841 or equivalent onto the crankshaft.

5. Install eight one-inch self starting screws through the guide holes of the tool and into the seal. A variable speed drill will be helpful for installing the screws.

6. Tighten the center screw of the tool to remove the seal.

7. Clean out the drain at the bottom of the seal bore with a piece of wire or pipe cleaner.

To install:

8. Apply a small amount of gasket maker 1052942 or equivalent at the crankcase split line across the end of the upper/lower crankcase seal.

9. Coat the outer diameter of the cylinder block rear crankshaft seal area with engine oil.

10. Wipe the outer diameter of the crankshaft flexplate flange with a lint-free cloth.

11. Lubricate the outer rubber surface of the seal with clean engine oil. DO NOT apply any oil to the green coating pre-applied to the inner diameter of the seal.

12. Loosen the center bolt of the seal installer J 42842 until the center hub protrudes about ½ inch past the outer plate.

13. Thread the three mounting bolts into the crankshaft flange until the tool is firmly mounted on the crankshaft.

14. Install the seal by tightening the center bolt until the tool bottoms against the crankshaft.

15. Remove the tool and verify that the seal is installed evenly.

16. Install the flexplate. Tighten the bolts to 11 ft. lbs. (15 Nm), then using a torque angle meter, tighten the bolts an additional 50 degrees.

17. Install the transaxle, then install the assembly in the vehicle.

J 42841

9300Z517

Use the guide holes in tool J 42841 to install the screws in the seal—3.5L engine

J 42842

9300Z518

Use rear main seal installer J 42842 to install the seal—3.5L engine

Except 3.5L Engine

1. Before servicing the vehicle, refer to the precautions in the beginning of this section.

2. Remove the transaxle assembly.

3. Remove the flexplate from the crankshaft.

4. Carefully pry the old seal out of the engine block. Do not damage or scratch the sealing surface of the crankshaft or the seal bore.

To install:

5. Lubricate the lip and the outer edge of the new seal with clean engine oil.

7922Z522

Carefully pry the seal from the bore without scratching the crankshaft seal surface

7922Z523

The rear main seal should be pressed into place using a threaded installation tool

6. Slide the oil seal on the mandrel until the back of the seal is seated squarely against the collar of the tool.

7. Attach Seal Installer J 34686 or equivalent for the 3.1L and 3.4L engines or J-38196 or equivalent for the 3.8L engine to the rear of the crankshaft with the two mounting bolts, then turn the T-handle until the oil seal is fully seated into the rear of the engine.

8. Loosen the T-handle of the tool completely.

9. Remove the two attaching bolts and remove the tool

10. Install the flexplate.

11. Install the transaxle using the recommended procedure.

Timing Chain, Sprockets And Front Cover

REMOVAL & INSTALLATION

3.1L Engines

To remove the timing chain front cover from the 3.1L (VIN M) engine in these vehicle applications, the engine oil pan must be removed. This means the engine/drive train and front suspension frame must be lowered from the body assembly during this procedure. This is an involved process requiring lifts, engine support fixtures and jacking devices as various engine and transmission mounts are loosened and/or removed.

1. Before servicing the vehicle, refer to the precautions in the beginning of this section.

2. Disconnect the negative battery cable. Drain the engine coolant.

3. Remove the serpentine drive belt.

4. Remove the hood assembly. An assistant may be required to avoid damage to vehicle's paint work.

➡ **Do not allow the hood to fold back onto the windshield. Glass and paint damage may result from improper handling of the hood.**

5. Remove the engine mount strut and air conditioning compressor bracket and engine mount strut bracket.

6. Remove the electric engine coolant fan assemblies.

7. Install a suitable lifting fixture that will safely support the engine with the vehicle both on the floor or raised on a lift.

8. Raise and safely support vehicle. Disconnect the front exhaust manifold pipe.

9. Remove the intermediate steering shaft bolt/screw and move the cover aside.

10. Drain the engine oil. Remove the engine splash shield.

11. Remove the engine crankshaft balancer. Use the following procedure:

➡ **The inertia weight section of the crankshaft balancer is assembled to the hub with a rubber sleeve. The removal and installation procedures, with the proper tools MUST be followed or movement of the inertia weight section on the hub will destroy the tuning of the torsional damper.**

   a. Remove the right engine splash shield.

   b. Remove the crankshaft balancer center bolt and washer.

   c. Draw the balancer off the crankshaft using the appropriate puller.

12. Support the drive train and front suspension frame assembly with floor stands.

13. Remove the transaxle mount frame side bracket nuts from the drive train and suspension frame assembly. Use the following procedure:

   a. With the vehicle safely supported, remove the left front tire and wheel assembly.

   b. Remove the left front bumper fascia splash shield assembly.

   c. Suitably support the transaxle assembly with floor stands.

   d. Remove the transaxle mount side bracket nuts.

14. Remove the engine mount frame side nuts from the drive train and front suspension frame assembly.

15. Remove the rear drive train and front suspension frame bolts and screws.

16. Lower the drive train and front suspension frame assembly.

17. Remove the engine mount assembly. Remove the flywheel inspection cover.

18. Remove the starter motor assembly. Note any shims between the starter and the engine block so they can be reused at assembly.

19. Remove the transaxle mount assembly from the engine oil pan assembly.

20. Disconnect the oil level sensor. Remove the engine oil pan assembly. Do not miss the bolt going through the side of the pan and threads into the front main bearing cap.

21. Once the pan has been removed, raise the drive train and front suspension frame assembly back into place and install the bolts as required to temporarily secure the frame assembly. Lower the vehicle.

22. Remove the coolant recovery reservoir assembly.

23. Remove the serpentine drive belt shield.

24. Remove the power steering pump pulley, using special tools. Disconnect the ignition control wiring harness, then remove the pump mounting bolts and position the pump aside.

25. Remove the thermostat bypass pipe clip nut from the upper intake manifold. Remove the pipe from the water pump.

26. Remove the coolant pump pulley assembly. Remove the lower radiator outlet hose from the water pump.

27. Remove the serpentine drive belt tensioner.

28. If the front cover is only going to be removed and not replaced with a new cover, the 24X Crankshaft Position (CKP) sensor can be left in place on the front cover. Just disconnect the wiring harness. If the cover is going to be replaced due to damage, remove the sensor from the front cover.

➡ **Note that this engine uses two CKP sensors; one, called the 3X CKP sensor, is in the side of the block to read off the crankshaft. The other sensor is called the 24X CKP sensor and it is mounted to the bottom of the front cover. Only the 24X CKP sensor needs to be removed if the front cover is to be replaced.**

29. Remove the bolts from the front cover, noting their locations, and separate the cover from the engine block. If the cover is being replaced, transfer the water pump to the new cover, making sure the locator on the top of the pump is installed at the top (12 o'clock) position.

30. Rotate the crankshaft until the timing marks on the camshaft and crankshaft sprockets are in alignment at their closest approach.

31. Remove the camshaft sprocket mounting bolt and remove the camshaft sprocket and timing chain.

32. Remove the crankshaft sprocket, using a gear puller J-5825-A or equivalent.

33. Remove the two mounting bolts from the timing chain damper and remove the damper.

To install:

34. Clean all parts and gasket mating surfaces well. Note that the oil pan bolts may have small O-rings under the bolt head flange which should be inspected carefully. A damaged seal will cause an oil leak.

35. Install the timing chain damper and tighten the mounting bolts to 15 ft. lbs. (21 Nm).

36. Install the crankshaft sprocket onto the crankshaft making sure the notch in the sprocket fits over the crankshaft key. Fully seat the sprocket on the crankshaft using J-38612, or equivalent.

37. Be sure the timing mark on the crankshaft sprocket is pointing straight up.

38. Install the timing chain over the camshaft sprocket and hold the sprocket in such a way, that the timing mark is pointing down, and the timing chain is hanging down off the sprocket.

39. Loop the timing chain under the crankshaft sprocket and install the camshaft sprocket on the camshaft. The sprocket will only fit on the camshaft if, the dowel on the camshaft lines up with the hole in the sprocket.

40. Verify that the marks are aligned (the camshaft sprocket will be at the 6 o'clock position and the crankshaft sprocket will be in the 12 o'clock position).

41. Tighten the camshaft sprocket mounting bolt to 81 ft. lbs. (110 Nm).

42. Lubricate the timing chain components with engine oil.

43. The crankshaft front seal should be carefully removed and a replacement installed with the seal lip facing the engine. With the front cover removed, the timing chain and sprockets may be inspected. If the timing chain and sprockets are to be replaced, turn the engine crankshaft until the timing marks on the crankshaft sprocket and camshaft sprocket are aligned. There should also be timing marks on the engine block and the timing chain damper (guide). Remove the camshaft sprocket center bolt and lift off the sprocket and chain. Use a puller to remove the crankshaft sprocket. Replace the chain and sprockets as a set, using care to align all timing marks as before.

44. If the cover is being replaced with a service part or if the coolant pump is being changed out to a service replacement pump, install the coolant pump, using a new gasket, to the front cover taking care that the locator on the top of the pump is installed at the top (12 o'clock) position.

45. Coat both sides of the lower tabs of a new front cover gasket with sealer. Install the front cover assembly. Tighten the large bolts to 35 ft. lbs. (47 Nm) and the small bolts to 15 ft. lbs. (21 Nm).

46. If removed, install the 24X CKP sensor to the front cover and connect the wiring harness.

47. Install the serpentine drive belt tensioner. Tighten the attaching bolt to 37 ft. lbs. (50 Nm).

48. Connect the lower radiator outlet hose assembly to the coolant pump assembly. Install the pulley on the coolant pump.

49. Connect the thermostat bypass pipe to the coolant pump assembly with the pipe clip nut.

50. Position the power steering pump and install the bolts. Tighten the bolts to 25 ft. lbs. (34 Nm). Using the proper tools, install the pulley onto the power steering pump. The face of the pulley hub MUST be flush with the pump drive shaft. DO NOT use an arbor press to install the pulley.

51. Install the serpentine drive belt shield.

52. Install the coolant reservoir. Lube the reservoir hose with clean water and route it through the hole in the ECM heat shield and

NOTE - ALIGN TIMING MARKS ON CAM & CRANK SPROCKETS USING ALIGNMENT MARKS ON DAMPER STAMPING OR CAST ALIGNMENT MARKS ON CYL & CASE

1. Damper
2. Alignment marks
3. Timing chain
4. Crank sprocket
5. 28 Nm (21 lb. ft.)
6. Camshaft sprocket
7. 21 Nm (15 lb. ft.)

VIEW A

#1 CYLINDER AT T.D.C.

NOTE - CAMSHAFT SPROCKET MARK AT 6 O'CLOCK CRANKSHAFT SPROCKET MARK AT 12 O'CLOCK

Timing chain and sprocket timing mark alignment—3.1L engines

79227524

up to the radiator overflow fitting until the hose end butts against the filler neck.

53. Raise and safely support vehicle. Support the drive train and front suspension frame assembly with suitable floor stands.

54. Remove the rear drive train and front suspension frame bolts. Lower the drive train and front suspension frame assembly. This should give clearance for oil pan installation.

55. Apply a small amount of sealer on either side of the rear main bearing cap, where the seal surface on the cap meets the cylinder block (2 locations). Using a new gasket, install the oil pan and retaining bolts. Tighten the oil pan retaining bolts to 18 ft. lbs. (25 Nm). Install the oil pan side bolts to 37 ft. lbs. (50 Nm).

56. Install the transaxle mount assembly to the engine oil pan assembly.

57. Install the starter motor. Tighten the bolts to 32 ft. lbs. (43 Nm). Install the flywheel inspection cover.

➡**Before attaching the electrical leads, tighten the inner nuts on the solenoid terminals. If the nuts are not tight, the solenoid cap may be damaged during installation of the leads. Tighten the inner nut of BAT terminal to 84 inch lbs. (9.5 Nm).**

58. Install the engine mount.

59. Raise the drive train and front suspension frame assembly and install the retainer bolts. Install the engine mount frame side nuts. Tighten the nuts to 32 ft. lbs. (43 Nm). Remove the floor stands from the drive train and front suspension frame assembly.

60. Lubricate the front cover crankshaft seal with clean engine oil. Apply a small amount of sealant to the keyway of the balancer assembly. Install the harmonic balancer using the proper tool to pull the balancer onto the crankshaft. Install the center bolt and tighten to 76 ft. lbs. (103 Nm).

➡**The inertia weight section of the crankshaft balancer is assembled to the hub with a rubber sleeve. The removal and installation procedures, with the proper tools MUST be followed or movement of the inertia weight section on the hub will destroy the tuning of the torsional damper.**

61. Install the engine splash shield.

62. Connect the intermediate steering shaft bolt. Tighten to 35 ft. lbs. (48 Nm). Install the cover shield.

63. Connect the front exhaust manifold pipe. Lower vehicle.

64. Remove the engine support fixtures.

65. Install the electric cooling fan assemblies.

66. Install the engine mount strut and air conditioning compressor bracket and engine mount strut bracket.

67. Install the hood panel assembly.

➡**Use care when working around the hood. Glass and paint damage may result from improper handling of the hood.**

68. Install the right engine splash shield and the front wheel assemblies.

69. Install the serpentine drive belt.

70. Refill the crankcase with engine oil and refill the cooling system. Connect the negative battery cable.

71. Locate the bleeder screw on the thermostat neck. Be sure it is closed but DO NOT overtighten. The air bleeder screw is made of soft brass. Start engine and allow to warm up. Open the bleeder screw as necessary to remove air from the system. Watch for oil or coolant leaks.

➡**The low coolant indicator lamp may come on after this procedure. After operating the vehicle so that the engine heats up and cools down three times, if the low coolant indicator lamp does NOT go out, or fails to come on at ignition check and coolant is at proper level (engine cold, coolant is level to the base of the radiator neck), electrical troubleshooting of the system is required. If at any time the TEMP warning indicator comes on, immediate action is required.**

72. Road test the vehicle.

➡**Whenever the vehicle sub-frame is removed or lowered, the wheel alignment should be checked.**

3.5L Engine

PRIMARY CHAIN

1. Before servicing the vehicle, refer to the precautions in the beginning of this section.

2. Disconnect the negative battery cable.

3. Remove the camshaft covers.

4. Rotate the crankshaft so the No. 1 piston is at Top Dead Center (TDC) and the flats on the rear of the camshafts will be parallel with the camshaft cover sealing surface.

5. Install camshaft holding fixtures such as J 42038 on both sets of camshafts. Turn the hex portion of the camshaft to align them for tool installation. When installed, the flats on the rear of the camshafts will be parallel with the camshaft cover sealing surface.

6. Drain the engine coolant.

7. Remove the front diagonal brace.

8. Remove the battery and tray.

9. Remove the washer and coolant reservoirs.

10. Move the underhood accessory wiring junction block out of the way.

11. Remove the drive belt.

12. Remove the power steering pump pulley.

13. Remove the idler pulley and belt tensioner.

14. Remove the water pump. Clean the gasket material with a plastic scraper.

15. Support the engine cradle and remove the right side mounting bolts.

16. Lower the cradle and remove the crankshaft balancer.

17. Remove the coolant drain plug from the front cover and drain the coolant from the engine.

18. Remove the ten bolts securing the front cover and remove the cover. Clean the gasket material with a plastic scraper.

19. Remove the lift bracket on the front of the engine.

20. Remove the Camshaft Position (CMP) sensor.

21. Remove the sprocket bolt from the exhaust camshaft on the right cylinder head to allow for clearance of the chain guide.

22. Remove the four chain guide access plugs from the cylinder heads. Note that each plug has an O-ring on it.

23. Loosen the two primary chain tensioner bolts, then remove the lower bolt allowing the tensioner to swing down and expand. Remove the tensioner completely.

24. Remove the primary chain tensioner shoe by removing the bolt, the pushing the guide downward slightly and pulling it up through the cylinder head.

25. Remove the primary chain from the right camshaft and allow it to fall into the oil pump area.

26. Remove the primary chain from the engine.

To install:

27. Rotate the crankshaft so the No. 1 piston is at TDC and the mark on the crankshaft is at the four o'clock position.

28. Rotate the balance shaft so the timing mark is at the five o'clock position.

Primary timing chain alignment marks—3.5L engine

➡ **Be sure the painted links are facing the front of the engine.**

29. Install the timing chain on the sprockets. Turn the camshaft with a wrench on the hex to assist when lining up the links with the marks on the sprockets. Be sure the marks are aligned as shown in the diagram.

30. Center the mark on the left intake camshaft sprocket between the two painted links.

31. Make a wire hook to feed down through the right cylinder head and lift the chain onto the right intake camshaft sprocket. While doing this, align the marks

on the balance shaft and crankshaft sprockets with the painted marks on the chain.

32. Verify that all of the timing marks are aligned.

33. Install the primary chain tensioner shoe. Tighten the bolt to 22 ft. lbs. (30 Nm).

34. Compress the primary chain tensioner using the following sub-steps;
   a. Rotate the ratchet release lever counterclockwise and hold it.
   b. Press the tensioner shoe in and hold it.
   c. Release the ratchet lever and slowly release the pressure on the shoe.
   d. Insert a pin through the hole in the lever as the lever moves to the first click. The ratchet should hold the shoe in the compressed position.

➡ **Be sure the lever on the tensioner is facing toward you when installed.**

35. Install the primary chain tensioner. Tighten the bolts to 22 ft. lbs. (30 Nm).

36. Remove the pin from the chain tensioner.

37. Install the four chain guide access plugs. Tighten the plugs to 44 inch lbs. (5 Nm).

Compressing the primary chain tensioner—3.5L engine

Apply RTV sealant to the three areas indicated before installing the front cover and gasket—3.5L engine

38. Install the front engine lift bracket. Tighten the hex head bolt to 37 ft. lbs. (50 Nm) and the internal drive bolt to 18 ft. lbs. (25 Nm).

39. Install the CMP sensor. Tighten the bolts to 80 inch lbs. (9 Nm).

40. Remove the camshaft holding tools and install the camshaft covers.

41. Place a small bead of RTV sealant on the three areas indicated in the diagram.

42. Position a new gasket on the front cover. Use two of the cover bolts to hold it in position.

43. Install the cover on the engine. Tighten the bolts to 124 inch lbs. (14 Nm). Tighten the coolant drain plug to 89 inch lbs. (10 Nm).

44. Install the crankshaft balancer. Tighten the bolt to 37 ft. lbs. (50 Nm), then using a torque angle meter, tighten the bolts an additional 120 degrees.

45. Raise the engine cradle and install the bolts.

46. Coat the sub-frame bushings with rubber lubricant P/N 1051717 or equivalent.

47. Lower the vehicle onto the assembly. Align the sub-frame on the vehicle using two bolts or drill bits, ¾ inches thick by eight inches long through the alignment holes on the right side of the frame.

48. Install new frame-to-body bolts. Tighten the bolts to 133 ft. lbs. (180 Nm).

49. Install the remaining components.

50. Refill the engine with DEX-COOL® coolant.

51. Install the proper amount of oil.

52. Connect the negative battery cable.

53. Start the engine and verify no leaks.

SECONDARY TIMING CHAIN

1. Before servicing the vehicle, refer to the precautions in the beginning of this section.

2. Disconnect the negative battery cable.

3. For the front cylinder head, partially drain the cooling system and remove the thermostat housing for clearance to install tool J 42042 or equivalent.

4. Remove the camshaft cover and install camshaft holding fixture J 42038 or equivalent.

5. Remove the camshaft sprocket bolts and install the timing chain/sprocket holding fixture on the cylinder head.

6. Evenly slide the sprockets and chain onto the tool.

Correct sprocket alignment for secondary timing chain—3.5L engine

7. Remove the secondary timing sprocket and chain.

To install:

8. Install the secondary timing chain on the sprockets. Be sure the drive pins are at the 12 o'clock positions.

9. Slide the sprockets and chain assembly onto the camshafts. Be sure the chain is properly aligned on the tensioner.

10. Remove the sprocket holding fixture from the cylinder head and install the sprocket bolts. Tighten the bolts to 18 ft. lbs. (25 Nm), then using a torque angle meter, tighten the bolts an additional 45 degrees.

11. Remove the camshaft holding fixture.

12. Install the camshaft cover.

13. If removed, install the thermostat housing and fill the cooling system with the correct amount of DEX-COOL® coolant.

14. Connect the negative battery cable.

3.8L Engine

1. Before servicing the vehicle, refer to the precautions in the beginning of this section.

2. Disconnect the negative battery cable. Drain the cooling system.

3. Disconnect the coolant hoses from the timing chain front cover.

4. Support the engine using support fixture J 28467-A or equivalent, then remove the engine mount.

5. Remove the drive belt(s) and belt tensioner.

6. Raise and safely support the vehicle. Remove the right front wheel. Remove the right inner fender access panel.

7. Detach the connectors at the Camshaft Position (CMP) sensor, Crankshaft Position (CKP) sensor and the oil pressure sensor.

8. Keep the flywheel from turning using J 37096 or equivalent. Remove the crankshaft balancer retaining bolts, then use puller tool J 38197 or equivalent, to remove the balancer from the crankshaft.

9. Remove the CMP sensor shield and the CKP sensor.

10. Remove the oil pan-to-front cover bolts.

11. Remove the front cover attaching bolts, then remove the cover.

12. Align the timing marks on the camshaft and crankshaft sprockets so they are as close together as possible.

13. Remove the timing chain damper.

14. Remove the crankshaft sprocket retaining bolts, then remove the sprocket and timing chain.

15. Remove the crankshaft sprocket.

➡ Do NOT rotate the camshaft or crankshaft while the timing chain and sprockets are removed.

16. Thoroughly clean all gasket mating surfaces.

To install:

17. Assembly the timing chain and sprockets with the timing marks aligned. Install the timing chain and sprockets to the camshaft and crankshaft.

18. Install the camshaft sprocket bolt and tighten to 74 ft. lbs. (100 Nm) plus an additional 90 degree turn. Recheck the camshaft and crankshaft sprocket timing marks to be sure they are still aligned.

19. Install the timing chain damper and tighten to 14 ft. lbs. (19 Nm).

20. Remove the screws and the oil pump cover from the back of the timing chain front cover. Pack the space around the oil pump gears completely full of petroleum jelly. There must be no air space left inside the pump. Reinstall the pump cover and tighten the screws to 97 inch lbs. (11 Nm).

21. Using new gaskets, install the timing chain front cover to the block. Tighten the bolts to 11 ft. lbs. (15 Nm) plus an additional 40 degree turn. Tighten the oil pan-to-front cover bolts to 125 inch lbs. (14 Nm).

22. Install the CKP sensor and tighten the bolts to 14–28 ft. lbs. (20–40 Nm). Install the CKP sensor shield.

23. Keep the flywheel from turning using

Timing belt service is covered in Section 5 of this manual

79222525

Install the timing chain and sprockets with the timing marks aligned and close together—3.8L engine

holder tool J 37096 or equivalent. Install the crankshaft balancer and tighten the bolt to 111 ft. lbs. (150 Nm) plus an additional 76 degree turn.

24. Attach the connectors to the CMP sensor, CKP sensor and oil pressure sensor.

25. Install the right inner fender access panel and the right front wheel.

26. Lower the vehicle.

27. Install the tensioner assembly.

28. Install the drive belt(s).

29. Install the engine mount and remove the engine support fixture.

30. Connect the coolant hoses.

31. Connect the negative battery cable. Fill and bleed the cooling system.

32. Start the vehicle and check for leaks and proper engine operation.

FUEL SYSTEM

Fuel System Pressure

RELIEVING

1. Before servicing the vehicle, refer to the precautions in the beginning of this section.

2. Disconnect the negative battery cable to prevent possible discharge of fuel if an accidental attempt is made to start the engine.

3. Loosen the fuel filler cap to relieve tank pressure.

4. This procedure calls for GM special tool J 34730–1A or equivalent. It is a fuel pressure test gauge with a line equipped with a fitting to connect to the to the fuel

pressure test connection and another hose to discharge into an approved gasoline container. Wrap a shop towel around the pressure test fitting connection while connecting gauge to avoid spillage.

5. Install the bleed hose into an approved container and open the valve to bleed fuel system pressure. The fuel connections are now safe for servicing.

6. Drain any fuel remaining in the gauge into an approved container.

7. Reconnect the negative battery cable unless addition service work is being performed.

Fuel Filter

REMOVAL & INSTALLATION

1. Before servicing the vehicle, refer to the precautions in the beginning of this section.

2. Disconnect the negative battery cable. Relieve the fuel system pressure.

3. Raise and safely support the vehicle.

4. Note that one side of the fuel filter uses a quick-connect fitting. Special handling is required. To remove, grasp both sides of the fitting. Twist the female connector ¼ turn in each direction to loosen any dirt within the fitting.

✳✳ CAUTION

Safety glasses must be worn when using compressed air, as flying dirt particles may cause eye injury.

5. Using compressed air, blow dirt out of the fitting.

6. If equipped with a plastic fitting, squeeze the plastic retainer release tabs and pull the connection apart.

7. If equipped with a metal fitting, choose the correct special tool J 37088 A, J 39504 or equivalent tool set for the correct size fitting. Insert tool into the female connector, then push/pull inward to release the locking tabs. Carefully pull the connection apart.

8. Remove the fuel feed pipe nut to the outlet side of the fuel filter.

9. Remove the fuel filter from the holder.

To install:

10. Install the fuel filter into the holder.

11. Use a back-up wrench on the inlet fitting while tightening the fuel filter outlet nut to 22 ft. lbs. (30 Nm).

12. Apply a few drops of clean engine oil to the male pipe end.

13. Push both sides of the fitting

1 BODY
2 FUEL FILTER BRACKET
3 FUEL FILTER
4 SCREW – FULLY DRIVEN, SEATED AND NOT STRIPPED

79222526

Common fuel filter mounting

together to cause the retaining tabs/fingers to snap into place.

14. Once installed, pull on both sides of the fitting to be sure the connection is secure.

15. Safely lower the vehicle.

16. Tighten the fuel filler cap.

17. Turn the ignition switch to the **ON** position to pressurize the fuel system to check for leaks.

Fuel Pump

REMOVAL & INSTALLATION

1. Relieve the fuel system pressure. Disconnect the negative battery cable.

2. On the Lumina, Monte Carlo, 1996 Buick, Oldsmobile and Pontiac vehicles, drain and remove the fuel tank using the recommended procedure. On all others, remove the spare tire, then remove the fuel pump access panel.

3. Disconnect the quick connects from the fuel sender assembly and remove the fuel lines.

4. Using J-35731, or an equivalent spanner wrench, remove the fuel sender lock ring.

5. Lift the sender assembly carefully out of the fuel tank.

6. Remove the sender O-ring from the top of the tank and discard.

✳✳ WARNING

DO NOT run the fuel pump unless it is submerged in fuel. Running the pump dry will cause serious damage to the fuel pump and may cause the pump to explode due to the oxygen in the air.

7. Note position of fuel pump strainer on fuel pump and while supporting the pump assembly in one hand twist the fuel

Fuel pump access panel—1997–00 Buick, Olds and Pontiac models

Remove the fuel pump from the tank after removing the locking ring

strainer off the pump and discard the strainer.

8. Disconnect the fuel pump electrical connector.

9. Remove the clamp from the fuel line at the top of the pump.

10. Hold the fuel sender upside down on a work bench and pull the fuel pump out of the lower mounting bracket. Once the pump is clear of the lower mounting bracket tilt the pump outward and disconnect the pump from the sender assembly.

To install:

11. Install the rubber bumper and insulator on the fuel pump.

12. Hold the fuel sender upside down and install the fuel pump between fuel pulse dampener and mounting bracket.

13. Connect the fuel pump electrical connector.

14. Install the clamp on the fuel line.

15. Install a new fuel pump strainer on outer edge of ferrule until fully seated. The strainer must be facing in the same direction as prior to removal.

16. Install a new O-ring on top of the fuel tank and install the sender assembly.

17. Install the lock ring and using J-35731, or an equivalent spanner wrench.

18. On the Lumina, Monte Carlo, 1996 Buick, Oldsmobile and Pontiac vehicles, install and refill the fuel tank. On all others, install the fuel pump access panel. Tighten the nuts to 8 ft. lbs. (11 Nm) and install the spare tire and cover.

19. Connect the negative battery cable. Turn the ignition switch to the **ON** position to pressurize the fuel system and check for leaks.

DRIVE TRAIN

For information on CV-joint boot replacement, please refer to the unit repair section.

Transaxle Assembly

REMOVAL & INSTALLATION

➡ **These transaxles were used in a variety of General Motors vehicles. Due to model year, vehicle model and installed options, the removal and installation procedures may vary slightly. The procedures given here should suffice for most all vehicles using these transaxles.**

Intrigue

Refer to the engine removal and installation procedure for transaxle removal.

Except Intrigue 3T40 3-Speed Automatic Transaxles

1. Remove the air cleaner assembly.

2. Disconnect the negative battery cable.

3. Remove the coolant recovery reservoir.

4. Remove the shift control and Throttle Valve (TV) cables at the transaxle.

5. Remove the throttle cable bracket and brake booster hose if equipped.

6. Remove both torque struts at the engine.

7. Remove the left torque strut bracket.

8. Remove the transaxle oil cooler lines at the transaxle and plug lines.

9. Install engine support special tools J 28467-A, J 28467 90 and J 36462 or equivalent.

10. Safely raise the vehicle.

11. Remove the tire and wheel assembly.

12. Remove the caliper bracket assemblies and rotors.

13. Remove both lower engine splash shields.

14. Remove the axle assemblies.

15. Remove the tie rods and ball joints.

16. Remove the rack and pinion heat shield and electrical connector.

17. Remove the bolts holding the main engine harness to the transaxle case.

18. Wire the rack and pinion assembly to the exhaust and remove the rack and pinion bolts from the frame.

19. Remove the bolts holding the power steering lines to the frame.

20. Remove the engine and transaxle mounts from the frame.

21. Support the frame with jackstands at each end.

22. Remove the frame bolts.

23. With an assistant, remove the frame and jackstands.

24. Remove the flywheel cover.

25. Remove the torque converter bolts.

26. Remove the starter and hang with mechanics wire.

27. Remove the ground cable at the transaxle.

28. Remove the transaxle fill tube bolt.

29. Remove the transaxle mount bracket.

30. Remove the transaxle-to-engine brace.

31. Safely lower the vehicle.

32. Remove the electrical connector to the transaxle.

33. Remove the transaxle fill tube.

34. Using special tool J 28467-A or equivalent, lower the left side of the engine approximately four inches.

35. Safely raise the vehicle.

36. Remove the fuel line bracket from the transaxle.

37. Remove the transaxle-to-engine bolts.

38. Remove the transaxle from the vehicle.

To install:

39. Apply a small amount of multi-purpose grease on the torque converter pilot hub.

40. Position the transaxle in the vehicle.

41. Install the transaxle-to-engine bolts and tighten to 55 ft. lbs. (75 Nm). Remove the transaxle jack.

42. Install the fuel line bracket to the transaxle.

43. Safely lower the vehicle.

44. Using special tool J 28467-a or

equivalent, raise the engine to its proper position.

45. Install the transaxle oil fill tube.

46. Connect the electrical connector to the transaxle.

47. Safely raise the vehicle.

48. Install and tighten the transaxle engine brace to 35 ft. lbs. (47 Nm).

49. Install the transaxle mount bracket.

50. Install the transaxle oil fill tube bolt.

51. With an assistant, position and support the frame under the vehicle.

52. Install new frame-to-body bolts and tighten bolts to 125 ft. lbs. (170 Nm).

53. Remove the frame supports.

54. Safely lower the vehicle and position engine and transaxle mount to the frame.

55. Safely raise the vehicle.

56. Install and tighten the torque converter-to-flywheel bolts to 46 ft. lbs. (63 Nm).

57. Install the flywheel cover.

58. Install the starter assembly.

59. Install the ground cable to the transaxle.

60. Install the ball joints and tie rod rods.

61. Install the axle assemblies.

62. Install the rotors and caliper bracket assemblies.

63. Install the rack and pinion with attaching lines to the frame.

64. Install the rack and pinion electrical connector and heat shields.

65. Install both lower engine splash shields.

66. Install the main engine harness to the transaxle case.

67. Install the tire and wheel assemblies.

68. Safely lower the vehicle.

69. Remove the engine support tools.

70. Install the throttle cable bracket and brake booster line, if equipped.

71. Install the torque strut bracket.

72. Install the transaxle oil cooler lines to the transaxle.

73. Install the torque struts.

74. Install the shift control and TV cables to the transaxle.

75. Install the coolant recovery reservoir.

76. Connect the negative battery cable.

77. Install the air cleaner assembly.

78. Adjust the shift linkage and TV cables.

79. Start engine and check engine and transaxle oil level. Add oil as necessary.

Except Intrigue 4T60-E And 4T65 4-Speed Automatic Transaxles

1. Remove the hood assembly, scribe a mark at the hinge area for installation reference.

2. Remove the transaxle fluid level indicator (dipstick) assembly.

3. Remove the engine mount strut brackets.

4. Remove the electric engine cooling fan assemblies.

5. Install engine support tools J 28467-A, J 28467–90 and J 36462 or the equivalent.

6. Remove the air intake duct assembly.

7. Disconnect the electrical connections from the transaxle assembly.

8. Remove the upper transaxle-to-engine bolts.

9. Safely raise and support the vehicle.

10. Remove the tire and wheel assembly. Mark the position of the wheel to the wheel studs, prior to removal, for installation reference.

11. Remove the left front bumper fascia splash shield assembly.

12. Remove the front exhaust manifold pipe.

13. Remove the steering gear heat shield assembly.

14. Remove the steering gear bolts.

15. Remove the front lower control arm assemblies from the front suspension strut assemblies.

16. Remove the power steering fluid cooling pipe assembly.

17. Safely support the drive train and front suspension frame assembly with safety stands.

18. Remove the transaxle mount side bracket nuts.

19. Remove the engine mount frame side nuts.

20. Remove the transaxle brace.

21. Remove the drive train and front suspension frame assembly.

22. Disconnect the electrical connector from the Vehicle Speed Sensor (VSS).

23. Remove the front wheel driveshaft assemblies from the transaxle.

24. Remove the transaxle converter cover assembly.

25. Remove the starter assembly.

26. Remove the transaxle torque converter bolts.

27. Remove the transaxle oil cooler upper and lower pipe assemblies.

28. Install a transaxle jack.

29. Remove the transaxle mount assembly from the engine assembly.

30. Remove the transaxle fluid filler tube assembly.

31. Remove the transaxle assembly from the vehicle.

32. Remove the transaxle torque converter assembly from the transaxle assembly.

33. Remove the transaxle assembly from the transaxle jack.

To install:

34. Install the transaxle assembly on the transaxle jack.

35. If removed, install the torque converter in the transaxle assembly.

36. Install the transaxle assembly to the engine. Tighten the lower rear transaxle-to-engine bolts to 55 ft. lbs. (75 Nm).

37. Install the dipstick tube assembly.

38. Install the transaxle mount to engine assembly and tighten bolts to 43 ft. lbs. (58 Nm).

39. Remove the safety stand from the transaxle assembly.

40. Install the transaxle oil cooler upper and lower pipe assemblies.

41. Install and tighten the transaxle torque converter bolts to 46 ft. lbs. (63 Nm).

42. Install the starter motor assembly.

43. Install the transaxle converter cover assembly.

44. Install and tighten the transaxle converter cover bolts to 89 inch lbs. (10 Nm).

45. Install the front wheel drive shaft assemblies to the transaxle.

46. Install and tighten the drive train and front suspension frame bolts to 107 ft. lbs. (145 Nm).

47. Install the transaxle brace and bracket. Tighten the attaching bolts to 39 ft. lbs. (53 Nm).

48. Remove the safety stands from the drive train and front suspension frame assembly.

49. Install the power steering fluid cooling pipe assembly.

50. Install the lower control arm assemblies to the front suspension strut assemblies.

51. Install the steering gear bolts and heat shield assembly.

52. Install the front exhaust manifold pipe to the engine.

53. Install the left front bumper fascia splash shield assembly.

54. Install the tire and wheel assembly, aligning the marks made on the removal.

55. Safely lower the vehicle.

56. Install and tighten the upper transaxle to engine bolts to 55 ft. lbs. (75 Nm).

57. Install the transaxle range selector assembly to the transaxle assembly.

58. Attach the electrical connectors to the transaxle assembly.

59. Install the air intake duct assembly.

60. Remove the engine support fixture tools.

61. Install the engine cooling fan assemblies.

62. Install the engine mount strut brackets.

63. Install the transaxle fluid level indicator assembly.

64. Install the hood panel assembly.

65. Start the engine and check for leaks.

66. Check the fluid level in the transaxle and adjust the shift linkage.

67. Road test to verify proper transaxle shifting and smooth operation.

Halfshaft

REMOVAL & INSTALLATION

Intrigue

1. Before servicing the vehicle, refer to the precautions in the beginning of this section.

2. Raise and safely support the vehicle.

3. Remove the front wheel.

4. Disconnect the stabilizer shaft link.

5. Remove the drive shaft nut by inserting a drift into the rotor to prevent it from turning.

6. Disconnect the tie rod end and the ball joint from the steering knuckle.

7. Press the axle shaft through the hub using a tool such as J 28733-B.

❈❈ WARNING

To prevent damage to the inner CV joint, do not pull on the axle shaft to remove it from the transaxle.

8. Place a drain pan under the transaxle to catch any transaxle fluid that leaks out when the axle shaft is removed.

9. Remove the axle shaft from the transaxle by prying between the transaxle and the inner CV joint housing.

To install:

10. Install the axle shaft in the transaxle. Verify that it is seated by pulling on the housing.

11. Install the axle shaft through the hub/bearing assembly.

12. Connect the ball joint and the tie rod end to the steering knuckle.

13. Install a new nut on the axle shaft. Tighten the nut to 118 ft. lbs. (160 Nm).

14. Install the stabilizer shaft link.

15. Install the front wheel and lower the vehicle.

16. Check the transaxle fluid level.

Except Intrigue

➡**If vehicle is equipped with ABS brakes, use care to avoid damage to**

Use a puller to press the axle shaft through the hub/bearing assembly—Intrigue

the ABS toothed ring. Damage to the ring may cause the self-diagnostic feature of the ABS system to set a system fault code.

1. Disconnect the negative battery cable.

2. Raise and safely support the vehicle. Remove the wheel and tire assembly.

3. Remove the front wheel drive axle nut.

4. Remove the brake calipers, bracket assemblies and hang caliper with mechanic's wire from the strut.

5. Remove the brake rotors.

6. Remove the four hub/bearing retaining bolts and hub.

7. Remove the ABS sensor mounting bolt and position the sensor out of the way, if equipped with ABS brakes.

8. Place a drain pan under the transaxle.

➡**Use care when removing the halfshaft. Tripot joints can be damaged if the drive axle is over-extended. It is important to handle the halfshaft in a manner to prevent over-extending.**

9. Remove the halfshaft from the vehicle using the appropriate procedure for each side and transmission model:

   a. To remove the right side halfshaft, use special tool J 33008, J 29794 and J 2619–01 or equivalent. Separate the halfshaft from the transaxle.

   b. To remove the left side halfshaft on a 3T40 transaxle, use special tools J 33008, J 29794 and J 2619–01 or equivalent. Separate the axle from the transaxle.

   c. To remove the left side halfshaft, using the frame for leverage, separate the halfshaft from the transaxle with a suitable prying tool in the groove provided on the inner joint.

10. Remove the halfshaft/bearing assembly through the knuckle.

To install:

11. Install the halfshaft/bearing assembly through the knuckle and into the transaxle. Remove special tool J 37292-a or equivalent and discard.

12. Properly position the ABS sensor and install the mounting bolt, if removed.

13. Loosely secure the bearing to the knuckle bolts.

14. Seat the halfshaft into the transaxle, using a suitable prying tool in the groove provided on the inner joint. Carefully pry against the frame or the lower control arm to seat the halfshaft.

15. Verify that the snapring is seated by tapping on the inner groove with a suitable prying tool. Grasp the inner housing of the axle shaft and pull outboard. Do not pull on the axle shaft. If the snapring is properly seated, the axle will remain in place.

16. Install the hub and bearing assembly to the axle with a new nut and washer. Tighten the bolts to 60 ft. lbs. (80 Nm).

17. Install the brake rotor.

18. Install the brake caliper and attaching bracket.

19. Install the wheel and tire assembly.

20. Safely lower the vehicle.

➡**Do not reuse the front wheel drive axle nut. Always use a new front wheel drive axle nut of similar design when installing the nut. Do not use a Nylock or free spinning style nut.**

21. Install the front wheel drive axle nut and tighten to 150 ft. lbs. (205 Nm).

22. Connect the negative battery cable.

STEERING AND SUSPENSION

Air Bag

❈❈ CAUTION

These vehicles are equipped with an air bag system, also known as the Supplemental Inflatable Restraint (SIR) or Supplemental Restraint System (SRS). The system must be disabled before performing service on or around system components, steering column, instrument panel compo-

nents, wiring and sensors. Failure to follow safety and disabling procedures could result in accidental air bag deployment, possible personal injury and unnecessary system repairs.

PRECAUTIONS

Several precautions must be observed when handling the inflator module to avoid accidental deployment and possible personal injury.

- Never carry the inflator module by the wires or connector on the underside of the module.
- When carrying a live inflator module, hold securely with both hands, and ensure that the bag and trim cover are pointed away.
- Place the inflator module on a bench or other surface with the bag and trim cover facing up.
- With the inflator module on the bench, never place anything on or close to the module which may be thrown in the event of an accidental deployment.

DISARMING

✳✳ CAUTION

The Supplemental Restraint System (SRS) must be disarmed before performing service around the air bag or SRS wiring. Failure to do so may cause accidental deployment of the air bag, resulting in unnecessary SRS repairs and/or personal injury.

1. Turn the steering wheel so the front wheels are in the straight ahead position.
2. Turn the ignition switch to the **LOCK** position.
3. Disconnect the negative battery cable.
4. Remove the Air Bag fuse from the fuse panel.

➡ **The position of the fuse on the panel varies according to model and year. Consult the vehicle owner's manual for fuse location.**

5. Remove the left-hand sound insulator (trim panel under the instrument panel).
6. Remove the Connector Position Assurance (CPA) clip and detach the yellow 2-way connector at the base of the steering column.
7. Remove the CPA and detach the passenger side yellow 2-way connector, if equipped. Positions for the connector vary from behind the glove box to removing the right side sound insulator and finding the yellow connector.

ARMING

1. Turn the steering wheel so the front wheels are in the straight ahead position.
2. Turn the ignition switch to the **LOCK** position.
3. Disconnect the negative battery cable.
4. Attach the yellow 2-way connector at the base of the steering column and install the Connector Position Assurance (CPA).
5. Install the left-hand sound insulator.
6. Attach the yellow 2-way connector on the right side and install the CPA, if equipped. Install the sound insulator and/or glove box.
7. Install the air bag fuse.
8. Connect the negative battery cable.
9. Turn the ignition switch to the **RUN** position. Verify that the INFLATABLE RESTRAINT indicator lamp flashes 7–9 times, then remains OFF. If the lamp does not function as specified, there is a malfunction in the air bag system.

Power Rack and Pinion Steering Gear

REMOVAL & INSTALLATION

3.4L Engine

1. Before servicing the vehicle, refer to the precautions in the beginning of this section.
2. Disconnect the negative battery cable. Remove the air cleaner and duct assembly.
3. Install the engine support fixtures J 28467-A, J 28467 90 and J 36462 or equivalent.
4. Raise and safely support the vehicle.
5. Remove the left front wheel.
6. Loosen the right side engine splash shield.
7. Remove both left and right tie rod nuts and tie rods from the steering knuckles.
8. Remove the intermediate shaft pinch bolt at the steering gear and disconnect the intermediate shaft from the rack an pinion unit.

✳✳ CAUTION

Failure to disconnect the intermediate shaft from the rack and pinion stub shaft may result in damage to the steering gear. This damage may cause a loss of steering control and may cause personal injury.

➡ **Set the steering shaft so that the block tooth on the upper steering shaft is at the 12 o'clock position. The wheels should be straight ahead. Set the ignition key lock to the LOCK position. Failure to follow these procedures could result in damage to the SIR coil assembly.**

9. Remove the electrical connection from the steering gear pressure switch.
10. Remove the exhaust pipe and catalytic converter assembly.
11. Support frame at the center rear using safety stands.

➡ **DO NOT lower the frame too far. Engine components near the firewall may be damaged.**

12. Remove the rear frame bolts and lower the rear of the frame up to 3 in. (76.mm).
13. Remove the heat shield, power steering line retaining clip and the fluid lines from the rack assembly. Use flare nut wrenches to remove the fluid pipes.
14. Remove the rack and pinion mounting bolts and nuts.
15. Remove the rack and pinion assembly out through the wheel opening.
16. Replace the stub shaft seals.
To install:
17. Install the rack and pinion assembly through the wheel opening.
18. Install the mounting bolts and nuts and tighten to 59 ft. lbs. (80 Nm).
19. Connect the power steering lines with new O-rings to the rack and pinion assembly. Tighten the fittings to 20 ft. lbs. (27 Nm).
20. Install the power steering line retaining clips and heat shield.
21. Raise the frame and align the steering gear stub shaft to the intermediate steering shaft. Install the rear bolts and tighten to 103 ft. lbs. (140 Nm).
22. Remove the safety stands at the frame center rear location.
23. Install the exhaust pipe and catalytic converter assembly.
24. Connect the electrical connection from the steering gear pressure switch.

✳✳ CAUTION

When installing the intermediate shaft be sure the shaft is seated prior to the pinch bolt installation. If the pinch bolt is inserted into the coupling before the intermediate shaft installation, the two mating surfaces may disengage resulting in loss of steering.

1 TIE ROD END
2 JAM NUT
3 TIE ROD INNER
4 BUSHING
5 STUB SHAFT
6 STEERING GEAR
7 FRAME
8 MOUNT
9 BOLT
10 NUT
11 SLEEVE
12 NUT
13 COTTER PIN
14 KNUCKLE STRUT ASSEMBLY
15 BOLT, STEERING GEAR HEAT SHIELD
16 SHIELD, STEERING GEAR HEAT

VIEW A
3.4L ONLY

79222529

Common rack and pinion steering gear mounting—1997–00 models shown

25. Connect the intermediate shaft-to-stub shaft and tighten the lower pinch bolt to 35 ft. lbs. (47 Nm).

26. Connect the tie rod ends to the steering knuckles and tighten the castle nuts to 40 ft. lbs. (54 Nm). Additional tightening is permissible if necessary to align the cotter pin holes. NEVER loosen the nuts to align the holes.

27. Install the right side engine splash shield.

28. Install the left front wheel.

29. Lower the vehicle.

30. Remove the engine support fixtures.

31. Connect the negative battery cable. Install the air cleaner and duct assembly.

32. Refill and bleed the power steering system.

➡ Whenever the vehicle sub-frame is removed or lowered, the wheel alignment should be checked.

33. Check the front end alignment and adjust as necessary.

Except 3.4L Engine

1. Before servicing the vehicle, refer to the precautions in the beginning of this section.

2. Disconnect the negative battery cable.

3. Raise and safely support the vehicle.

4. Remove the front wheels.

5. Remove the electrical connection from the steering gear pressure switch.

6. On the Intrigue, remove the stabilizer shaft through the left wheel opening.

7. Remove the intermediate shaft pinch bolt at the steering gear and disconnect the intermediate shaft from the rack an pinion unit.

Please visit our web site at www.chiltononline.com

✳✳ CAUTION

Failure to disconnect the intermediate shaft from the rack and pinion stub shaft may result in damage to the steering gear. This damage may cause a loss of steering control and may cause personal injury.

8. Set the steering shaft so the block tooth on the upper steering shaft is at the 12 o'clock position. The wheels should be straight ahead. Set the ignition key lock to the **LOCK** position. Failure to follow these procedures could result in damage to the SIR coil assembly.

9. Remove the cotter pins and castle nuts from the outer tire rod ends and separate the tie rods from the steering knuckles using a tie rod puller J 35917 or the equivalent.

10. Support the rear of the subframe with a suitable adjustable jack.

➡**DO NOT lower the frame too far. Engine components near the firewall may be damaged.**

11. Remove the rear frame bolts and lower the rear of the frame up to 5 in. (128mm).

12. Remove the heat shield, pipe retaining clip and the fluid pipes from the rack assembly. Use flare nut wrenches to remove the fluid pipes.

13. Remove the rack mounting bolts and nuts.

14. Remove the rack assembly out through the left wheel opening.

To install:

15. Install the rack assembly through the left wheel opening.

16. Install the mounting bolts and nuts and tighten to 59 ft. lbs. (80 Nm).

17. Connect the power steering fluid lines with new O-rings to the rack and pinion assembly. Tighten the fittings to 20 ft. lbs. (27 Nm).

18. Install the pipe retaining clips and heat shield.

19. Raise the frame and install the rear bolts and tighten to 103 ft. lbs. (140 Nm).

20. Connect the tie rod ends to the steering knuckles and tighten the castle nuts to 40 ft. lbs. (54 Nm). If necessary to align the cotter pin holes, tighten the nuts slightly until the cotter pins can be installed. NEVER loosen the nuts to align the holes.

21. Connect the intermediate shaft-to-stub shaft and tighten the lower pinch bolt to 35–40 ft. lbs. (47–54 Nm).

22. Install the front wheels and tighten to specifications.

23. Lower the vehicle.

24. Connect the negative battery cable.

25. Refill and bleed the power steering system.

➡**Whenever the vehicle sub-frame is removed or lowered, the wheel alignment should be checked.**

26. Check the wheel alignment and adjust if required.

Strut

REMOVAL & INSTALLATION

Front

EXCEPT 1997–00 CENTURY, GRAND PRIX, INTRIGUE AND REGAL— STRUT ASSEMBLY

The strut tube is welded to a stamped steel knuckle with the lower ball joint riveted to the lower end of the knuckle.

1. Before servicing the vehicle, refer to the precautions in the beginning of this section.

2. Scribe the strut cover plate for proper reinstallation.

3. Loosen the three cover plate nuts.

4. Safely raise and support the vehicle.

5. Remove the tire and wheel assembly.

6. Remove the brake caliper and bracket assembly. Support the caliper from the suspension.

7. Remove the brake rotor.

8. Remove the hub and bearing to the knuckle attaching bolts.

9. Remove the ABS sensor mounting bolt and position the ABS sensor aside to prevent damage, if equipped with ABS.

10. Separate the axle from the transaxle and remove the axle.

11. Remove the tie rod to steering knuckle attaching nut.

➡**Use only the recommended tools (a ball joint press or puller, not a "pickle fork") for separating the ball joints. Failure to use recommended tools may cause damage to the ball joint and seal.**

12. Using special tool J 35917 or equivalent, separate the tie rod from the knuckle assembly.

13. Remove the lower ball joint to steering knuckle attaching nut.

14. Using special tool J 35917 or equivalent, separate ball joint from the lower control arm.

15. Remove the ball joint heat joint heat shield retaining bolts and heat shield assembly.

16. Remove the strut cover plate nuts.

17. Remove the steering knuckle and strut assembly.

To install:

18. Install the knuckle and strut assembly into the vehicle.

19. Install the strut mount cover plate and upper strut mount to body attaching nuts Tighten the nuts after lowering the vehicle.

20. Install the ball joint heat shield and tighten retaining bolts to 89 inch lbs. (10 Nm).

21. Install lower joint to the control arm attaching nut. Tighten ball joint nut to 63 ft. lbs. (85 Nm) with a new cotter pin. Tighten the ball joint nut to the next slot in the nut with the cotter pin hole in the stud. Do not tighten the nut more than 60 degrees to align with hole.

22. Install the tie rod to the steering knuckle and tighten the attaching nut with a new cotter pin to 40 ft. lbs. (54 Nm).

23. Carefully install the drive axle assembly through the opening in the steering knuckle.

24. Install and tighten the hub and bearing to knuckle attaching bolts to 60 ft. lbs. (80 Nm).

25. Position the ABS sensor and install the mounting bolts, if removed.

26. Install the brake rotor.

27. Install the brake caliper and bracket assembly. Tighten the slide bolts to 80 ft. lbs. (108 Nm).

28. Install the tire and wheel assembly.

29. Safely lower the vehicle.

30. Tighten the strut cover plate nuts to 18 ft. lbs. (24 Nm) after aligning the scribe marks.

31. Road test the vehicle.

EXCEPT 1997–00 CENTURY, GRAND PRIX, INTRIGUE AND REGAL— STRUT CARTRIDGE

➡**The Lumina, Monte Carlo, 1996 Century, Regal, Grand Prix, 1996–97 Cutlass Supreme models utilize a replaceable cartridge within the strut assembly. This cartridge can be replaced without removing the strut assembly from the vehicle.**

✳✳ CAUTION

DO NOT service the strut cartridge unless the weight of the vehicle is on the suspension. The weight of the vehicle keeps the coil spring com-

pressed. Otherwise the released coil spring could result in personal injury.

1. Before servicing the vehicle, refer to the precautions in the beginning of this section.

2. Disconnect the negative battery cable.

3. Scribe the strut cover to body to assure proper camber adjustment.

4. Remove the strut cover by removing the cover nuts.

5. Remove the strut shaft nut by using a No. 50 Torx® bit and J 35668 or the equivalent.

6. Remove the strut mount insulator by prying with a flat bladed tool. Use J 35668 or the equivalent to apply pressure on the strut as necessary to relieve the side load (compression) on the bushing.

7. Remove the bumper by attaching J 35668 or the equivalent to the strut and pulling out the bumper.

8. Install J 38844 or the equivalent in the correct position and compress the strut down into the cartridge.

9. Remove the strut closure nut by unscrewing the closure nut using J 35671 or the equivalent.

10. Remove the cartridge and remove the oil in the strut housing using a suction pump to remove all the oil.

To install:

11. Install the self contained replacement cartridge into the strut housing.

12. Install the strut cartridge closure nut using J 35671 or the equivalent and tighten the nut to 82 ft. lbs. (110 Nm).

13. Install J 35668 or the equivalent and compress the shaft down into the cartridge.

14. Remove J 38844 or the equivalent strut alignment tool.

Strut shaft nut removal—except 1997–00 Century, Grand Prix, Intrigue and Regal

79222537

Strut closure nut removal

79222532

Strut closure nut removal—except 1997–00 Century, Grand Prix, Intrigue and Regal

15. Install the strut bumper and raise the strut and remove J 35668 or the equivalent.

16. Install the strut mount insulator as follows:

a. Use a soap solution to lubricate the bushing for ease of installation.

b. If necessary, install J 35668 or the equivalent after the bushing is partially installed and position the strut as required to assist in the bushing installation.

(1) Front Suspension Strut Mount Retainer
(2) Front Spring Upper Insulator
(3) Front Spring
(4) Front Spring Seat
(5) Front Suspension Strut Bumper

79222531

Knuckle and strut assembly with replaceable strut cartridge

(1) Front Stabilizer Shaft Insulator Clamp Bolt/screw
(2) Front Stabilizer Shaft Link Nut
(3) Front Suspension Strut Mount Nut
(4) Front Suspension Spring
(5) Front Suspension Strut
(6) Strut To Knuckle Nut
(7) Front Steering Knuckle
(8) Strut To Knuckle Bolt/screw
(9) Front Stabilizer Shaft Link]
(10) Front Lower Control Arm
(11) Front Lower Control Arm Bolt/screw
(12) Front Lower Cotrol Arm Nut
(13) Frame
(14) Front Stabilizer Shaft Insulator
(15) Front Stabilizer Shaft
(16) Front Stabilizer Shaft Clamp

79222530

Exploded view of the front suspension without replaceable strut cartridge

Turn to Section 6 for brake system applications

17. Install the strut shaft nut using the No. 50 Torx® bit and J 35669 or the equivalent and tighten the nut to 59 ft. lbs. (80 Nm).

18. Install the strut cover mount and aligning the scribe marks, then tighten the bolts to 24 ft. lbs. (33 Nm).

19. A four wheel alignment is recommended after any steering/suspension repairs are performed.

1997–00 CENTURY, GRAND PRIX, INTRIGUE AND REGAL

1. Before servicing the vehicle, refer to the precautions in the beginning of this section.

2. Remove the three strut-to-body nuts.

3. Raise and safely support the vehicle allowing the control arms to hang free.

4. Remove the front wheel.

5. Matchmark the position of the strut on the steering knuckle for reference when installing the strut.

✳✳ WARNING

To prevent damage to the ball joint or halfshaft, support the knuckle assembly when removing the strut.

6. Remove the bolts securing the strut assembly to the knuckle and remove the strut.

To install:

7. Position the strut in the body and install the three retaining nuts. Tighten the nuts to 30 ft. lbs. (41 Nm).

8. Attach the lower end of the strut to the knuckle assembly. Install the bolts from the front and tighten the nuts to 90 ft. lbs. (123 Nm).

Front strut mounting—1997–00 Century, Grand Prix, Intrigue and Regal

79222536

9. Install the front wheel.

10. Lower the vehicle to the floor.

Rear

1996 REGAL, CUTLASS SUPREME AND GRAND PRIX

1. Before servicing the vehicle, refer to the precautions in the beginning of this section.

2. Raise and safely support the vehicle.

3. Remove the tire and wheel assembly. Mark the position of the wheel to the wheel studs, prior to removal, for installation reference.

4. Scribe a reference line from the strut to the knuckle.

5. Remove the jack pad.

6. Remove the exhaust system, if equipped with dual exhausts.

7. Install special tool J 35778 or equivalent. This Y-shaped tool spans the width of the fiberglass transverse leaf spring. Fully compress the special tool to take tension off the outboard suspension components. **DO NOT** remove the spring or retention plates. Just relieve the tension so the strut can be removed.

➡**Do not use corrosive cleaning agents, silicone lubricants, engine degreasers, solvents, etc. on or near the fiberglass rear transverse spring. These materials could cause extensive damage to the spring.**

J 35778

J 35778

79222534

Special tool J 35778 is used to compress the fiberglass transverse rear spring during rear suspension service—1996 Regal, Cutlass Supreme and Grand Prix

8. Remove the brake hose bracket at the strut assembly.

9. Remove the strut to body bolts.

10. Remove the strut/stabilizer shaft bracket from the knuckle assembly.

To install:

11. Install the strut assembly to the body bolts. Tighten the bolts to 34 ft. lbs. (46 Nm).

12. Install the strut/stabilizer shaft bracket to the knuckle. Align the scribe marks to ensure proper alignment. Tighten the attaching bolts to 122 ft. lbs. (165 Nm).

13. Install the brake hose bracket.

14. Remove the special tool J 35778 or equivalent, if used, from the transverse leaf spring.

15. Install the exhaust system, if removed.

16. Install the jack pad and tighten the attaching bolts 18 ft. lbs. (25 Nm).

17. Install the tire and wheel assembly, aligning up the marks made during the removal.

18. Safely lower the vehicle.

19. A four wheel alignment is recommended after any steering/suspension repairs are performed.

EXCEPT 1996 REGAL, CUTLASS SUPREME AND GRAND PRIX

These vehicles use direct double-acting struts which are attached to the body and to the rear wheel knuckle assembly. Please note that strut service requires special tools to compress and hold the components during removal and installation. This procedure calls out the GM-recommended special tool numbers. Use care if using substitutes.

1. Before servicing the vehicle, refer to the precautions in the beginning of this section.

2. Disconnect the negative battery cable. Raise and safely support the vehicle.

3. Remove the rear wheel assembly. Mark the position of the wheel to the wheel studs, prior to removal, for installation reference.

4. Make a scribe mark to the strut-to-knuckle for proper installation.

5. Remove the brake hose bracket at the strut.

6. Remove the exhaust system as required to access the strut assemblies.

7. Remove the strut mount to body nuts.

8. On the Intrigue, remove the stabilizer link from the strut. On all others, remove the strut stabilizer shaft bracket from the knuckle.

Rear suspension components—except 1996 Regal, Cutlass Supreme and Grand Prix

9. Remove the strut from the vehicle.
To install:
10. Install and tighten the strut mount to body nuts to 34 ft. lbs. (46 Nm).
11. Install the strut to the steering knuckle. On the Intrigue, tighten the bolts to 90 ft. lbs. (122 Nm). On all others, install the strut stabilizer shaft bracket to steering knuckle, then tighten nuts to 122 ft. lbs. (165 Nm).
12. Install the brake hose bracket.
13. If removed, install the exhaust system.
14. Install the tire and wheel assembly, aligning the marks made on the removal.
15. Safely lower the vehicle.
16. Four wheel alignment is recommended after any steering/suspension repairs are performed.

Coil Spring

REMOVAL & INSTALLATION

1. Remove the strut assembly from the vehicle.

✳✳ CAUTION

Do not over compress the coil spring. Only compress the spring until it comes away from the seat.

2. Compress the coil spring using a suitable spring compressor.
3. Remove the strut rod nut.
4. Remove the upper spring seat and coil spring.

To install:
5. Carefully compress the coil spring and place it on the strut assembly in the same orientation as the original spring.
6. Install the upper spring seat. On front struts with the replaceable cartridge, tighten the nut to 81 ft. lbs. (110 Nm). On all other models, tighten the nut to 63 ft. lbs. (85 Nm). Tighten the nut on all rear strut assemblies to 55 ft. lbs. (75 Nm).
7. Install the strut in the vehicle.

Lower Ball Joint

REMOVAL & INSTALLATION

Except 1997–00 Century, Grand Prix, Intrigue and Regal

1. Raise and safely support the vehicle. Remove the tire and wheel assembly.
2. Remove the ball joint heat shield.
3. Remove the lower ball joint cotter pin and nut.
4. Loosen, but do not remove the stabilizer shaft bushing assembly bolts.
5. Remove the ball joint front the lower control arm using special tool J 35917 or equivalent ball joint press tool.
6. Drill out the four rivets retaining the ball joint to the steering knuckle. Use an ⅛ in. drill bit to make a pilot hole through the rivets. Finish drilling the rivets using a ½ in. drill bit.

➡**Do not damage the drive axle boots when drilling out the ball joint rivets.**

7. Remove the ball joint from the steering knuckle assembly.
To install:
8. Install the ball joint in the steering knuckle assembly.
9. Install four new ball joints bolts and nuts.
10. Install the ball joint to the lower control arm and tighten the nut to 63 ft. lbs. (85 Nm). Tighten the nut to align slot in the ball joint nut with the cotter pin opening in the stud. Do not tighten the ball joint nut more than 60 degrees (one flat, or ⅙ turn) to align the hole and never loosen the nut anytime during installation. When ball joint nut installation is satisfactory, install a new cotter pin.
11. Install the ball joint heat shield.
12. Install the tire and wheel assembly.
13. Safely lower, then road test the vehicle.

➡**A four wheel alignment is recommended after any steering/suspension repairs are performed.**

1997–00 Century, Grand Prix, Intrigue and Regal

1. Raise and safely support the vehicle.
2. Remove the front wheel.
3. Disconnect the tie rod end from the knuckle.
4. Remove the stabilizer bar link from the lower control arm.
5. Remove the halfshaft outer retaining nut and remove the halfshaft.
6. Remove the ABS speed sensor jumper harness.
7. Remove the control arm mounting bolts.
8. Disconnect the ball joint stud from the knuckle.
9. Drill out or grind of the heads of the rivets and remove the ball joint from the control arm.
To install:
10. Install the new ball joint of the control arm. Be sure to install the bolts from the top of the control arm. Tighten the nuts to 50 ft. lbs. (68 Nm).
11. Install the control arm on the frame but do not tighten the fasteners at this time.
12. Install the ball joint stud to the knuckle. Tighten the nut to 40 ft. lbs. (55 Nm). Tighten the nut slightly if necessary to align the cotter pin holes and install the cotter pin.

13. Connect the stabilizer bar link to the control arm. Tighten the nut to 17 ft. lbs. (23 Nm).

14. Install the ABS speed sensor jumper harness.

15. Install the halfshaft.

16. Place a jack under the lower control arm, raise the jack to support the weight of the vehicle and tighten the control arm nuts to 83 ft. lbs. (113 Nm). Remove the jack.

17. Install the front wheel and lower the vehicle to the floor.

Wheel Bearings

ADJUSTMENT

The wheel bearings are not adjustable. If a wheel bearing is out of specification, it must be replaced. Using a dial indicator, check for looseness. If it exceeds 0.005 in. (0.1270mm) on drum or disc brakes the bearing wear is excessive and the hub and bearing should be replaced.

REMOVAL & INSTALLATION

Front

➡**Do not remove the drive axle nut at this time. Failure to follow the proper sequence of removal steps may cause permanent bearing damage.**

1. Loosen the hub nut one full turn. Do not remove.

2. Raise and safely support the vehicle. Remove the tire and wheel assembly.

3. Remove the caliper mounting bracket-to-steering knuckle mounting bolts and remove the caliper and bracket assembly and support the assembly out of the

way. DO NOT disconnect the brake hose from the caliper or allow the hose to support the weight of the caliper.

4. Remove the brake rotor.

5. Remove the hub nut and washer.

6. Using special tool J 28733-a or an equivalent hub puller, push the halfshaft out of the hub assembly about an inch.

7. Remove the hub assembly-to-knuckle attaching bolts.

8. If equipped, remove the ABS sensor mounting bolt and position the ABS sensor out of the way.

9. Remove the hub and bearing assembly from the vehicle.

To install:

10. Clean all parts well. Install the hub and bearing assembly onto the axle shaft splines. Be sure the splines engage smoothly. DO NOT force the hub over the axle splines or the splines will be damaged.

11. Seat the hub and bearing assembly against the steering knuckle and install the mounting bolts. Tighten the bolts alternately and evenly to 52 ft. lbs. (70 Nm) on the 1996–97 Cutlass Supreme, Lumina and Monte Carlo, 96 ft. lbs. (130 Nm) on Century, Grand Prix, Intrigue and Regal.

12. Be sure the ABS sensor is clean. The small magnet in its end will attract rust and metal chips that can degrade its performance. Install the ABS sensor and tighten the mounting bolt.

13. Install the brake rotor.

14. Install the caliper and bracket assembly on the steering knuckle and tighten the caliper bracket mounting bolts to 79 ft. lbs. (107 Nm).

15. Install the tire and wheel assembly. Lower the vehicle.

16. Install a new drive axle nut and washer.

Rear

The rear suspension uses a non-serviceable hub/bearing assembly with integral wheel speed sensor that is bolted to the rear suspension knuckle. This hub/bearing assembly is a sealed, maintenance free unit. If the hub/bearing is damaged, the complete assembly must be replaced.

1. Raise and safely support the vehicle.

2. Remove the rear wheel.

3. Remove the brake hose bracket and the brake drum or caliper.

4. If equipped, detach the ABS electrical connector.

5. Remove the hub and bearing mounting bolts and remove the bearing assembly.

To install:

6. Install the hub and bearing assembly, tighten the bolt to 55 ft. lbs. (75 Nm).

7. If equipped, attach the ABS connector.

8. Install the brake caliper or drum and the brake hose bracket.

9. Install the rear wheel.

10. Safely lower the vehicle to the floor.

11. A four wheel alignment is recommended after any steering/suspension repairs have been performed.

1 KNUCKLE ASSEMBLY, REAR SUSPENSION
2 HUB AND BEARING ASSEMBLY
3 BOLT/SCREW, WHEEL

79222535

The rear hub/bearing assembly is bolted to the knuckle

GENERAL MOTORS CORPORATION—Y BODY

Chevrolet-Corvette

39

PRECAUTIONS

Before servicing any vehicle, please be sure to read all of the following precautions, which deal with personal safety, prevention of component damage, and important points to take into consideration when servicing a motor vehicle:

• Never open, service or drain the radiator or cooling system when the engine is hot; serious burns can occur from the steam and hot coolant.

• Observe all applicable safety precautions when working around fuel. Whenever servicing the fuel system, always work in a well ventilated area. Do not allow fuel spray or vapors to come in contact with a spark, open flame, or excessive heat (a hot drop light, for example). Keep a dry chemical fire extinguisher near the work area. Always keep fuel in a container specifically designed for fuel storage; also, always properly seal fuel containers to avoid the possibility of fire or explosion. Refer to the additional fuel system precautions later in this section.

• Fuel injection systems often remain pressurized, even after the engine has been turned **OFF**. The fuel system pressure must be relieved before disconnecting any fuel lines. Failure to do so may result in fire and/or personal injury.

• Brake fluid often contains polyglycol ethers and polyglycols. Avoid contact with the eyes and wash your hands thoroughly after handling brake fluid. If you do get brake fluid in your eyes, flush your eyes with clean, running water for 15 minutes. If eye irritation persists, or if you have taken brake fluid internally, seek medical assistance IMMEDIATELY.

• The EPA warns that prolonged contact with used engine oil may cause a number of skin disorders, including cancer! You should make every effort to minimize your exposure to used engine oil. Protective gloves should be worn when changing oil. Wash your hands and any other exposed skin areas as soon as possible after exposure to used engine oil. Soap and water, or waterless hand cleaner should be used.

• All new vehicles are now equipped with an air bag system, often referred to as a Supplemental Restraint System (SRS) or Supplemental Inflatable Restraint (SIR) system. The system must be disabled before performing service on or around system components, steering column, instrument panel components, wiring and sensors. Failure to follow safety and disabling procedures could result in accidental air bag deployment, possible personal injury and unnecessary system repairs.

• Always wear safety goggles when working with, or around, the air bag system. When carrying a non-deployed air bag, be sure the bag and trim cover are pointed away from your body. When placing a non-deployed air bag on a work surface, always face the bag and trim cover upward, away from the surface. This will reduce the motion of the module if it is accidentally deployed. Refer to the additional air bag system precautions later in this section.

• Clean, high quality brake fluid from a sealed container is essential to the safe and proper operation of the brake system. You should always buy the correct type of brake fluid for your vehicle. If the brake fluid becomes contaminated, completely flush the system with new fluid. Never reuse any brake fluid. Any brake fluid that is removed from the system should be discarded. Also,

do not allow any brake fluid to come in contact with a painted surface; it will damage the paint.

• Never operate the engine without the proper amount and type of engine oil; doing so WILL result in severe engine damage.

• Timing belt maintenance is extremely important! Many models utilize an interference-type, non-freewheeling engine. If the timing belt breaks, the valves in the cylinder head may strike the pistons, causing potentially serious (also time-consuming and expensive) engine damage. Refer to the maintenance interval charts in the front of this manual for the recommended replacement interval for the timing belt, and to the timing belt section for belt replacement and inspection.

• Disconnecting the negative battery cable on some vehicles may interfere with the functions of the on-board computer system(s) and may require the computer to undergo a relearning process once the negative battery cable is reconnected.

• When servicing drum brakes, only disassemble and assemble one side at a time, leaving the remaining side intact for reference.

ENGINE REPAIR

Distributor

All 1997–00 5.7L (VIN G) engines use a direct ignition system. This system eliminates the need for a distributor and has several advantages. Some of the advantages are, no moving parts, no load on the engine, more coil cool down time between firing and increased coil saturation time which produces a stronger spark.

The direct ignition system consists of

- Eight ignition coils and modules (one for each cylinder)
- Eight ignition control circuits
- Camshaft Position (CMP) sensor
- 1X Camshaft reluctor wheel
- 24X Crankshaft reluctor wheel
- Crankshaft Position (CKP) sensor
- Powertrain Control Module (PCM)

The 24X CKP sensor is the most critical part of the system, if it is damaged, the engine will not start. Ignition timing is controlled by the PCM. There are no timing marks on the crankshaft balancer or timing chain cover.

REMOVAL & INSTALLATION

➥This procedure is for 5.7L (VIN P and 5) engines only. The 5.7 (VIN G) engines do not utilize a distributor.

The 5.7L (VIN P and 5) engines utilize a distributor which is driven off the front of the camshaft and is mounted flush to the front of the engine, behind the water pump.

1. Before servicing the vehicle, refer to the precautions in the beginning of this section.

2. Be sure the ignition is in the **OFF** or **LOCK** position. Disconnect the negative battery cable.

3. Disconnect the Intake Air Temperature (IAT) sensor.

4. Remove the intake air duct.

5. Remove the accessory drive belt.

6. Drain the engine coolant.

7. Disconnect the Engine Coolant Temperature (ECT) sensor.

8. Remove the water pump and crankshaft balancer.

9. Remove the drive belt tensioner.

➥The spark plug wire boots should be twisted ½ turn in each direction while removing. Do not pull on the wires to remove them from the spark plugs. Pull on the boots or use a tool specifically designed for this purpose.

10. Remove the spark plug wiring harnesses from the distributor.

11. Unplug the 4-terminal electrical connector from the distributor.

12. Disconnect the distributor vacuum harness from the distributor.

13. Loosen and remove the distributor attaching bolts.

14. Pull the distributor assembly forward until the driveshaft disengages from the end of the camshaft.

15. Mark the top surface of the driveshaft to assure ease of alignment during installation.

To install:

➥Replace the O-rings on the coupling shaft or ignition system performance may suffer. Lubricate the O-rings and the end of the camshaft.

✳ WARNING

Don't try to fully seat the distributor using the distributor retainers. If the distributor will not seat by hand, it's not properly aligned with the camshaft. Rotate the crankshaft until the engine is at the No. 1 cylinder Top Dead Center (TDC) (camshaft sprocket pin at the 9 o'clock position). Rotate the distributor coupling until the camshaft sprocket pin slot aligns with the distributor base timing mark. Install the distributor using hand pressure to fully seat the distributor.

16. Install the distributor assembly into position with the driveshaft in the end of the camshaft. Rotate the distributor coupling until the camshaft sprocket pin slot aligns with the camshaft sprocket pin. Slide the distributor onto the end of the camshaft until fully seated on the engine front cover.

17. Install the distributor mounting bolts. Tighten to 97–106 inch lbs. (11–12 Nm).

18. Engage all electrical connections and vacuum hoses on the distributor that were unplugged during removal.

19. Install the drive belt tensioner.

20. Install the crankshaft balancer and water pump.

21. Connect the ECT sensor.

22. Install the drive belt.

23. Install the air duct.

24. Connect the IAT sensor.

25. Refill the cooling system.

26. Connect the negative battery cable.

Ignition Timing

ADJUSTMENT

On these vehicles, base timing is preset when the engine is manufactured. All timing

The distributor is located under the water pump assembly—5.7L (VIN P and 5) engines

79222601

changes are, then controlled directly by the Powertain Control Module (PCM) based on information from the ignition and Knock (KS) sensor systems. No adjustments are necessary or possible.

Engine Assembly

REMOVAL & INSTALLATION

5.7L (VIN P and 5) Engines

1. Before servicing the vehicle, refer to the precautions in the beginning of this section.

2. Disconnect the negative battery cable and properly relieve fuel system pressure.

3. Drain the coolant into a suitable container.

4. Remove the air intake duct.

5. Unplug the electrical harness and vacuum connections from the top of the engine.

6. Disconnect the upper radiator, radiator hose and heater hoses from the pump, then remove the throttle body coolant hose from the radiator tee and from the right side of the throttle body.

7. Remove the power steering pump and support aside.

8. Remove the alternator and support aside.

9. Remove the left wheel well center panel. Remove the serpentine drive belt.

10. Remove the air conditioning compressor from the bracket and position aside.

11. Unplug the electrical connector and remove the cover from the wiper motor.

12. Disconnect the AIR diverter valve hose.

13. Disconnect and plug the fuel lines at the fuel rail.

14. Remove the hoses from the power steering fluid reservoir. Plug the openings to prevent system contamination or excessive fluid loss.

15. Disconnect the accelerator cable from the throttle body.

16. Raise and support the vehicle safely.

17. Remove the starter motor.

18. Remove the left and right catalytic converters, then remove the exhaust pipe and muffler assembly.

19. Remove the transmission.

20. If equipped with a manual transmission, remove the clutch cover and plate, then remove the flywheel.

21. Remove the ground leads from the rear of the engine, then disengage the electrical connectors from the oil level sensor, Knock (KS) sensor, oil temperature sensor

and Engine Coolant Temperature (ECT) sensor.

22. Remove the nuts from the engine mount studs, then lower the vehicle.

23. Install a suitable lifting device and carefully remove the engine from the vehicle.

To install:

24. Lower the engine into position in the vehicle.

25. Remove the lifting device from the engine, then raise and support the vehicle safely.

26. Install the nuts on the engine mount studs.

27. Engage the sensor electrical connectors, then connect the ground leads to the rear of the engine.

28. If equipped with a manual transmission, install the flywheel, then install the clutch cover and plate.

29. Install the transmission.

30. Install the right and left catalytic converters, then install the exhaust pipe and muffler assembly.

31. Install the starter and lower the vehicle.

32. Connect the accelerator cable to the throttle body, then unplug the openings and install the hose to the power steering reservoir.

33. Unplug and connect the fuel lines to the fuel rail.

34. Connect the AIR diverter valve hose.

35. Install the electrical connector and cover to the wiper motor.

36. Install the air conditioning compressor.

37. Install the serpentine drive belt, then install the left wheel well center panel.

38. Install the alternator and the power steering pump.

39. Connect the coolant hose to the right side of the throttle body and connect the throttle body hose to the radiator tee. Connect the heater and radiator hoses.

40. Engage the electrical harness and all vacuum connections to the top of the engine.

41. Install the air intake duct and properly fill the engine cooling system.

42. Check all fluid levels, connect the negative battery cable and tighten the fuel filler cap.

43. Reset the CHANGE OIL indicator:

   a. Turn the ignition **ON** but do not start the engine.

   b. Depress the ENG MET button on the trip monitor, then within 5 seconds, depress the button a 2nd time. Within another 5 seconds, depress and hold the GAUGES button.

   c. While holding the GAUGES button, watch the CHANGE OIL light, it should begin to flash. Continue to hold the gauges button until the flashing stops and the light goes out indicating that the indicator is reset.

   d. If the indicator does not reset, turn the ignition **OFF** and restart the procedure.

44. Check and adjust the ASR control cables, as necessary.

45. Start the engine and check for leaks, then bleed the power steering system.

5.7L (VIN G) Engine

1. Before servicing the vehicle, refer to the precautions in the beginning of this section.

The following tools will be required in addition to the basic hand tools:

- Transverse leaf spring compressor and adapters
- Ball joint separator
- Engine support table
- Driveshaft support strap
- Fuel pressure gauge

2. Disconnect the negative battery cable.

3. Properly discharge and recover the air conditioning system.

4. Raise and safely support the vehicle and drain the coolant, then lower the vehicle.

5. Disconnect the wiring from the Intake Air Temperature (IAT) and Mass Air Flow (MAF) sensors.

6. Remove the fuel pressure regulator purge line from the intake air duct.

7. Remove the air cleaner assembly.

8. Remove the accessory drive belts.

9. Remove the fuel rail covers.

10. Relieve the fuel system pressure.

11. Disconnect and cap the fuel lines from the fuel rail.

12. Remove the coolant hoses from the water pump.

13. Disconnect the wiring harness from the following:

- Fuel injectors
- Ignition coil
- EVAP solenoid
- Electric throttle motor
- Throttle Position (TP) sensor
- Engine Coolant Temperature (ECT) sensor
- A/C compressor

14. Disconnect the wiring from the generator.

15. Remove the generator rear bracket, then remove the generator.

16. Disconnect the vacuum hose from the brake booster.

17. Disconnect the intermediate shaft from the steering rack and position it on the left frame rail.

18. Disconnect the AIR hose from the left exhaust manifold.

➡ **Do not remove the bell housing-to-driveshaft support bolts until specified in the procedure.**

19. Raise and safely support the vehicle.
20. Remove the front wheels.
21. Remove the intermediate exhaust pipe.

22. Remove the under covers.
23. Remove the ground wires from the right side of the engine block.
24. Remove the starter.
25. Disconnect the oil level sensor, Crankshaft Position (CKP) sensor and the right front Oxygen (O_2S) sensor.
26. Remove the refrigerant lines from the rear of the compressor.
27. Disconnect the engine oil temperature sensor and all ground wires from the left side of the engine.
28. Disconnect the left front O_2S sensor.

29. Remove the front stabilizer bar from the cradle.
30. Remove both cooling fans.
31. Compress the front transverse spring using tool J 33432-A or equivalent spring compressor.
32. Disconnect the tie rod ends from the steering knuckles.
33. If equipped, detach the ABS, Real Time Damping (RTD) and Electronic Variable Orifice (EVO) connectors at the cradle.
34. Remove the lower shock absorber mounting bolts.

J 33432 – A

79222602

Use a compressor such as J 33432-A to compress the front transverse spring—5.7L (VIN G) engine

Timing belt service is covered in Section 5 of this manual

On A/T vehicles, remove the plugs from the driveshaft support assembly and install two M10 X 1.5 bolts into the plug holes—5.7L (VIN G) engine

35. Separate the lower ball joints from the knuckles.

36. Remove the spring compressor from the spring.

37. If equipped, disconnect the transmission fluid cooler lines from the radiator and at the junction near the bell housing.

38. On vehicles with automatic transmissions, remove the two plugs from the driveshaft support assembly and install two M10 X 1.5 bolts into the plug holes. The bolts must be at least 55mm in length or longer. Tighten the bolts to 26 ft. lbs. (35 Nm).

39. On vehicles with automatic transmission, remove the bell housing inspection cover, then turn the flywheel hub collar to access the bolt and loosen it.

✳✳ CAUTION

Never use J 42203 or equivalent to support the weight of the engine assembly.

40. Install J 42203 or equivalent to the under cover flange and support the engine assembly with a lift such as J 39580.

41. Remove the front cradle nuts BY HAND and lower the engine assembly slightly.

42. Disconnect the wiring harness from

the following and remove the harness from the retainers on the bell housing:

- Engine oil pressure gauge
- Camshaft Position (CMP) sensor
- Manifold Absolute Pressure (MAP) sensor
- Knock (KS) sensor
- Ground wire on the rear of the left cylinder
- Any remaining connectors

43. Remove the front driveshaft support assembly bolts.

44. Move the engine assembly forward to clear the driveshaft.

45. Carefully raise the vehicle off of the engine and cradle assembly.

✳✳ WARNING

Do not disconnect the power steering lines when removing the steering components from the engine. Remove them from the engine and fasten them to the cradle.

46. Remove the engine from the cradle.

To install:

47. Install the engine on the cradle. Tighten the nuts to 40 ft. lbs. (54 Nm).

48. Install the power steering pump and

Loosen the bolt on the flywheel hub collar after turning it for access—5.7L (VIN G) engine

J 42203

79222605

Install bracket J 42203 or equivalent to the under cover flange—5.7L (VIN G) engine

reservoir on the engine. Tighten the mounting bolts to 18 ft. lbs. (25 Nm).

49. Position the assembly under the vehicle, then partially lower the vehicle on the engine and attach the connectors and wiring harness.

⁂ **WARNING**

Do not force the driveshaft into the engine assembly.

50. Move the assembly rearward onto the driveshaft and install the bolts. Tighten the bolts to 37 ft. lbs. (50 Nm).

51. Lower the vehicle onto the cradle and install the mounting nuts BY HAND. Tighten them to 81 ft. lbs. (110 Nm).

52. Raise the vehicle and remove bracket J 42203 or equivalent.

53. Install the spring compressor and compress the spring.

54. Assemble the suspension and attach the connectors. Tighten the shock absorber bolts to 20 ft. lbs. (28 Nm) and the ball joint nut to 55 ft. lbs. (75 Nm). Tighten the tie rod end nuts to 33 ft. lbs. (45 Nm).

55. Remove the spring compressor.

56. On vehicles with automatic transmissions, remove the two M10 X 1.5 bolts and

install the plugs. Tighten the plugs to 37 ft. lbs. (50 Nm).

57. If equipped, install the transmission fluid cooler lines.

58. Install the cooling fans.

59. Install the stabilizer bar. Tighten the bolt to 40 ft. lbs. (54 Nm).

60. Attach the connectors and grounds on the left side of the engine.

61. Connect the lines to the rear of the A/C compressor. Tighten the bolt to 26 ft. lbs. (35 Nm).

62. Attach the connectors and grounds on the right side of the engine.

63. Install the starter and tighten the bolts to 37 ft. lbs. (50 Nm).

64. Install the under covers and the front wheels. Tighten the wheel nuts to 100 ft. lbs. (140 Nm).

65. Connect the AIR hose to the exhaust manifold.

66. Install the intermediate shaft to the steering gear.

67. Connect the vacuum hose to the brake booster.

68. Install the generator and brackets.

69. Reposition the harness and attach all electrical connectors on the engine.

70. Connect the coolant hoses to the water pump.

71. Connect the fuel lines.

72. Install the fuel rail covers and drive belts.

73. Install the intake air duct and regulator purge line.

74. Connect the wiring harness to the IAT and MAF sensors.

75. Connect the negative battery cable.

76. Recharge the A/C system and refill all fluids to the proper level.

77. On vehicles with automatic transmissions, start the vehicle and allow it to reach normal operating temperature. Turn the engine **OFF**. Allow the engine to cool to ambient temperature, then tighten the flywheel hub collar bolt to 96 ft. lbs. (130 Nm).

Water Pump

REMOVAL & INSTALLATION

5.7L (VIN P and 5) Engines

1. Before servicing the vehicle, refer to the precautions in the beginning of this section.

2. Disconnect the negative battery cable.

3. Unplug the Intake Air Temperature (IAT) sensor electrical connection.

4. Remove the air cleaner and air intake duct assembly.

5. Drain the cooling system into a suitable container. Remove the Knock (KS) sensors from the lower left and right side of the block to assure proper draining.

6. Remove the upper and lower radiator hoses and the heater hose from the water pump. Remove the throttle body hose from the tee fitting.

7. Unplug the Engine Coolant Temperature (ECT) sensor electrical connection and remove the sensor wiring harness from the retainer on the front of the coolant pump.

8. Use a box wrench or socket on the tensioner pulley bolt to rotate the tensioner and relieve belt tension, then remove the serpentine drive belt from the alternator pulley. This should create sufficient room to work, if additional room is necessary, the belt can be completely removed.

9. Remove the 6 bolts securing the water pump flanges to the engine block, then remove the water pump from the vehicle.

10. Remove and discard the old gaskets from the mating surfaces.

11. If replacing the pump, remove the ECT sensor from the old pump.

To install:

12. If replacing the pump, install the ECT sensor on the new pump and tighten to 17 ft. lbs. (23 Nm).

13. Thoroughly clean all gasket mating surfaces and apply a light coat of grease to the seals and splines before assembling the coupling to the water pump. The white band on the coupling should be positioned towards the engine.

14. Install the new gaskets with the tabs up, the coolant pump with the drive coupling and the mounting bolts. Tighten the bolts to 30 ft. lbs. (41 Nm).

15. Install the serpentine drive belt.

16. Install the ECT sensor wiring harness to the retainer on the front of the pump, then engage the sensor electrical connection.

17. Connect the heater hose and the upper and lower radiator hoses to the water pump.

18. Install the throttle body hose at the tee.

19. If removed, install the KS sensors.

20. Open the bleed valves on the thermostat housing and the throttle body. Fill the cooling system through the radiator surge tank until a solid stream of coolant comes out of the bleeds.

21. Close all bleeds and continue to fill the surge tank until the coolant is level at the base of the surge tank neck.

22. Install the radiator pressure cap and check the coolant recovery reservoir for the proper level of coolant, add as necessary.

23. Install the air cleaner and intake duct assembly.

24. Engage the IAT sensor electrical con-

VIEW A

1. Coolant pump
2. O-Ring seal
3. Coolant pump
4. Coupling
5. White band (toward engine)
6. Driven gear shaft
7. Timing chain front cover
8. Bolts retainer plate
9. Gasket (install tab up)
10. Bolt (short)
11. Coolant sensor
12. Bolt (long)
13. Thermostat
14. Seal (install taper up)
15. Thermostat housing

Exploded view of the water pump mounting—5.7L (VIN P and 5) engines

79222606

nection and clean any excess coolant from the engine compartment.

25. Connect the negative battery cable, start the engine and check for leaks.

26. If the low coolant indicator lamp is lit, the engine must be cycled from cold to normal operating temperature and back to cold 3 times. If the lamp does not go out after this and coolant is at the proper level, the indicator system must be repaired.

5.7L (VIN G) Engine

1. Before servicing the vehicle, refer to the precautions in the beginning of this section.

2. Disconnect the negative battery cable.

3. Disconnect the wiring harness from the Intake Air Temperature (IAT) and Mass Air Flow (MAF) sensors.

4. Remove the fuel pressure regulator purge line from the intake air duct.

5. Remove the air cleaner assembly.

6. Remove the accessory drive belts.

7. Disconnect the radiator and heater hoses from the water pump.

8. Remove the water pump pulley.

9. Remove the six mounting bolts and the water pump assembly.

To install:

10. Clean the sealing surfaces on the water pump and engine block.

11. Be sure the tabs on the new gaskets are pointing up and install the water pump on the engine. Tighten the mounting bolts to 30 ft. lbs. (41 Nm).

12. Install the water pump pulley. Tighten the bolts first to 89 inch lbs. (10 Nm), then to 18 ft. lbs. (25 Nm).

13. Connect the radiator and heater hoses.

14. Install the drive belts.

15. Install the intake air duct and fuel regulator purge line.

16. Attach the IAT and MAF sensor connectors.

17. Refill the cooling system with the proper type of coolant.

18. Connect the negative battery cable.

19. Start the engine and inspect for leakage.

Cylinder Head

REMOVAL & INSTALLATION

5.7L (VIN P and 5) Engines

RIGHT SIDE

1. Before servicing the vehicle, refer to the precautions in the beginning of this section.

2. Disconnect the negative battery cable and properly relieve the fuel system pressure.

3. Raise and support the vehicle safely.

4. Disconnect the catalytic converter.

5. Drain the engine cooling system, then lower the vehicle.

6. Remove the lower radiator and heater hoses from the water pump.

7. Disconnect the power steering pump reservoir from the cylinder head and reposition aside.

8. Remove the coil and bracket assembly.

9. Remove the intake manifold.

10. Remove the spark plug wires from the clips, then remove the front wire bracket.

11. Remove the oil level indicator tube.

12. Disconnect the spark plug wires from the plugs, then remove the spark plugs from the cylinder head.

13. Remove the right exhaust manifold.

14. Using a back-up wrench on the pipe fitting, disconnect the coolant air bleed pipe from the left cylinder head.

15. Remove the right valve rocker cover, then remove the rocker arm and pushrod assemblies.

16. Remove the cylinder head bolts.

17. Remove the cylinder head along with the coolant air bleed pipe, then remove the head gasket.

18. If necessary, remove the coolant air bleed pipe from the cylinder head.

To install:

19. Thoroughly clean the cylinder head and cylinder case mating surfaces. Be sure both surfaces are free of any foreign matter, nicks or scratches. The threads in both the bolts holes and on the bolts must be clean and free of old sealer.

20. If removed, install the coolant air bleed pipe to the cylinder head, finger-tight.

21. Position the new gasket in place on the cylinder case with the yellow tab facing up. Install the cylinder head over the dowel pins and gasket.

22. Coat the bolts with 1052080, or an equivalent sealant. Install and tighten the cylinder head bolts, using 3 passes of the proper sequence, to 65 ft. lbs. (88 Nm).

23. Install the rocker arm and pushrod assemblies.

24. Install the valve rocker cover and tighten the bolts to 100 inch lbs. (11 Nm).

25. Connect the coolant air bleed pipe to the left cylinder head and tighten the pipe to both cylinder heads. Using a back-up wrench, tighten the coolant air bleed pipe to 30 ft. lbs. (41 Nm).

26. Install the right exhaust manifold.

Water pump assembly mounting—5.7L (VIN G) engine

79222Z608

Refer to Section 1 for engine rebuilding specifications

27. Install the spark plugs and tighten to 11 ft. lbs. (15 Nm).

28. Connect the spark plug wires to the plugs, then install the oil level indicator tube.

29. Install the front wire bracket, then connect the spark plug wiring harness assembly to the wire bracket.

30. Install the intake manifold.

31. Install the coil and bracket assembly.

32. Position and secure the power steering pump reservoir.

33. Install the lower radiator and heater hoses to the water pump.

34. Raise and support the vehicle safely.

35. Connect the catalytic converter, then lower the vehicle.

36. Properly fill the cooling system.

37. Tighten the fuel filler cap and connect the negative battery cable.

LEFT SIDE

1. Before servicing the vehicle, refer to the precautions in the beginning of this section.

2. Disconnect the negative battery cable and properly relieve the fuel system pressure.

3. Raise and support the vehicle safely.

4. Disconnect the catalytic converter.

5. Drain the engine cooling system, then lower the vehicle.

6. Remove the upper radiator hose.

7. Remove the serpentine drive belt.

8. Remove the intake manifold.

9. Remove the left wheel well lower center panel.

10. Disconnect the air conditioning compressor from the bracket and position aside. Use care not to kink or damage the refrigerant lines. Remove the compressor and alternator brace.

11. Remove the spark plug wire bracket, disconnect the wires from the spark plugs and remove the spark plugs from the cylinder head.

12. Remove the left exhaust manifold.

13. Remove the remaining alternator brace, then remove the alternator.

14. Disconnect the AIR diverter valve hose.

15. Remove the left valve rocker cover.

16. Remove the drive belt idler pulley, then remove the drive belt tensioner.

17. Disconnect the power steering lines from the pump, then remove the pump. Plug the openings to prevent system contamination or excessive fluid loss.

18. Remove the spark plug and coil wires from the distributor.

19. Remove the accessory mounting bracket.

20. Remove the rocker arm and pushrod assemblies.

21. Disconnect the coolant air bleed pipe from the cylinder head.

22. Remove the cylinder head bolts, then remove the cylinder head and gasket.

To install:

23. Thoroughly clean the cylinder head and cylinder case mating surfaces. Be sure both surfaces are free of any foreign matter, nicks or scratches. The threads in both the bolts holes and on the bolts must be clean and free of old sealer.

24. Position the new gasket in place on the cylinder case with the yellow tab facing up. Install the cylinder head over the dowel pins and gasket.

25. Coat the bolts with 1052080, or an equivalent sealant. Install and tighten the cylinder head bolts, using 3 passes of the proper sequence, to 65 ft. lbs. (88 Nm).

26. Connect the coolant air bleed pipe to the cylinder head and tighten to 30 ft. lbs. (41 Nm).

27. Install the rocker arm and pushrod assemblies.

28. Install the accessory mounting bracket and bolts. Tighten the bolts to 31 ft. lbs. (42 Nm).

29. Connect the spark plug and coil wires to the distributor.

30. Install the power steering pump, then remove the plugs from the openings and connect the lines.

31. Install the drive belt tensioner, then install the idler pulley. Tighten the tensioner and pulley bolts to 24 ft. lbs. (33 Nm).

32. Install the left valve rocker cover and bolts. Tighten the bolts to 100 inch lbs. (11 Nm).

33. Connect the AIR diverter valve hose and install the alternator lower brace.

34. Install the left exhaust manifold.

35. Install the spark plugs and tighten to 11 ft. lbs. (15 Nm). Connect the spark plug wires to the plugs and insert the wires into the brackets.

36. Install the air conditioning compressor and alternator brace, then install the compressor.

37. Install the left wheel well lower center panel.

38. Install the intake manifold.

39. Install the serpentine drive belt and the upper radiator hose.

40. Raise and safely support the vehicle, then connect the catalytic converter and lower the vehicle.

41. Properly fill the engine cooling system.

42. Tighten the fuel filler cap and connect the negative battery cable.

43. Bleed the power steering system.

5.7L (VIN G) Engine

1. Before servicing the vehicle, refer to the precautions in the beginning of this section.

2. Disconnect the negative battery cable.

3. Drain the engine coolant.

4. Relieve the fuel system pressure.

5. Remove the drive belts.

6. Remove the cylinder head covers.

Cylinder head bolt torque sequence—5.7L (VIN P and 5) engines

79222Z609

7. Remove the rocker arms, pedestals and pushrods. Be sure to keep them in order so they can be installed in their original positions.

8. Remove the exhaust manifolds.

➡ **The intake manifold, throttle body, fuel rail and injectors can be removed as an assembly.**

9. Remove the intake manifold.
10. Remove the vapor vent pipe.
11. Remove the spark plugs.
12. For the left cylinder head remove the power steering pump by first removing the pulley. Then, remove the lower accessory mounting bracket and the ground wire from the back of the cylinder head.

13. Remove the cylinder head bolts and the head assembly. Be sure to place the cylinder head on wooden blocks to prevent damage.

To install:

➡ **New M11 cylinder head bolts must be used when installing the cylinder head assembly.**

14. Clean and degrease the deck of the engine block and the bottom of the cylinder head assembly. Clean the bolt holes with compressed air.

➡ **The tab on the edge of the head gasket will be closer to the front of the engine when properly installed.**

15. Position the new gaskets on the engine block.

16. Carefully place the cylinder head on the engine and install the bolts finger-tight.

17. Tighten the M11 bolts in sequence to 22 ft. lbs. (30 Nm).

18. Tighten the M11 bolts in sequence again 76 degrees using a torque angle wrench.

19. Tighten the M11 bolts (1–8) in sequence 76 degrees, and bolts 9–10 in sequence 34 degrees using a torque angle wrench.

20. Tighten the M8 bolts (11–15) to 22 ft. lbs. (30 Nm) starting at the center bolt and alternately working outward until all of the bolts have been tightened.

21. For the left cylinder head, install the ground wire, lower accessory mounting bracket and the power steering pump.

22. Install the spark plugs. If using new plugs, tighten them to 15 ft. lbs. (20 Nm). Tighten used plugs to 11 ft. lbs. (15 Nm).

23. Install the vapor vent pipe.
24. Install the intake manifold assembly.
25. Install the exhaust manifolds.
26. Use new gaskets and install the cylinder head covers. Tighten the bolts to 106 inch lbs. (12 Nm).

27. Install the drive belts.
28. Connect the negative battery cable.
29. Refill the cooling system.
30. Start the engine and inspect for leaks.

Be sure the tab on the edge of the gasket is closer to the front of the engine when installed—5.7L (VIN G) engine

Always tighten the cylinder head bolts according to the sequence shown to prevent damaging the head and causing leaks—5.7L (VIN G) engine

Rocker Arms

REMOVAL & INSTALLATION

5.7L (VIN P and 5) Engines

1. Before servicing the vehicle, refer to the precautions in the beginning of this section.

2. Disconnect the negative battery cable.

3. Remove the right valve rocker cover as follows:

　a. Remove the fuel rail cover and the fuel rail bolts.

　b. Disconnect the fuel pressure regulator vacuum hose.

　c. Remove the fuel injector and rail

For engine torque specifications, refer to Section 1 of this manual

assembly from the manifold and reposition.

d. Remove the fuel rail cover studs and position the wiring harness aside.

e. Remove the AIR pipe and check valve from the intake and exhaust manifolds.

f. Disconnect the crankcase vent hose.

g. Remove the valve rocker cover bolts, cover and gasket. Replace the gasket as necessary.

4. Remove the left rocker arm cover as follows:

a. If not done already, remove the fuel rail cover.

b. Remove the alternator brace bolts, then remove the brace.

c. Remove the remaining alternator bolts and position the alternator aside.

d. Disconnect the AIR diverter valve hose from the check valve.

e. Position the wiring harness aside.

f. Remove the valve rocker cover bolts, cover and gasket. Replace the gasket as necessary.

5. Remove the rocker arm nuts, rocker arm balls, rocker arms and pushrods. If the valvetrain components are to be reused, mark or arrange the assemblies in a rack to assure installation in their original locations.

To install:

6. Coat the bearing surfaces of the rocker arms and rocker arm balls with 1052365 or equivalent pre-lube, prior to installation.

7. Install the pushrods making certain they seat in the lifter sockets.

8. Install the rocker arms, rocker arm balls and rocker arm nuts in their original positions.

9. Tighten the rocker arm nuts until all lash is eliminated.

10. Adjust the valve lash.

11. Thoroughly clean the gasket mating surfaces and install the valve rocker arm covers in the reverse order of removal. Tighten the valve rocker cover bolts to 100 inch lbs. (11 Nm). For the right valve cover, be sure to tighten the AIR pipe-to-exhaust manifold fitting to 25 ft. lbs. (34 Nm).

12. Connect the battery negative cable, start the engine and inspect for leaks.

5.7L (VIN G) Engine

LEFT SIDE

➡ **Always keep the rocker arms and pushrods in order so they can be installed in their original positions.**

1. Before servicing the vehicle, refer to the precautions in the beginning of this section.

2. Disconnect the negative battery cable.

3. Remove the fuel rail cover.

4. Relieve the fuel system pressure.

5. Disconnect the fuel lines from the fuel rail assembly.

6. Remove the generator rear bracket.

7. Disconnect the generator and Engine Coolant Temperature (ECT) sensor wiring.

8. Disconnect the vacuum hose from the brake booster.

9. Remove the PCV hose from the rocker arm cover.

10. Remove the Secondary Air Injection (SAI) hose from the check valve.

11. Remove the spark plug wires from the coils.

12. Detach the main ignition coil connector.

13. Disconnect the lines from the EVAP purge solenoid and remove the solenoid.

14. Remove the mounting bolts and the rocker arm cover.

15. Remove the rocker arm bolt and the rocker arm. If removing more than one rocker arm, be sure to keep them in order. They must be installed in their original positions.

To install:

16. If removed, install the rocker arm pivot support.

17. Lubricate the rocker arms and pushrods with clean engine oil.

18. Lubricate the flange and washer surface of the bolt rocker arm mounting bolts.

19. Install the pushrod. Be sure it is seated in the lifter socket.

20. Install the rocker arms but do not tighten the bolts at this time.

21. Rotate the crankshaft so the No. 1 piston is at Top Dead Center (TDC) on compression.

➡ **The engine firing order is 1, 8, 7, 2, 6, 5, 4, 3. The cylinders are numbered 1, 3, 5 and 7 on the left bank and 2, 4, 6 and 8 on the right bank.**

22. With the engine in this position, tighten the exhaust valve rocker arm bolts on cylinders 1, 2, 7 and 8. Then, tighten the intake valve rocker arm bolts on cylinders 1, 3, 4 and 5. Tighten the bolts to 22 ft. lbs. 30 Nm).

23. Rotate the crankshaft one revolution (360°).

24. With the engine in this position, tighten the exhaust valve rocker arm bolts on cylinders 3, 4, 5 and 6. Then, tighten the intake valve rocker arm bolts on cylinders 2,

6, 7 and 8. Tighten the bolts to 22 ft. lbs. 30 Nm).

25. Install the rocker arm using a new gasket. Tighten the bolts to 106 inch lbs. (12 Nm).

26. Install the EVAP purge solenoid.

27. Attach the ignition coil connector.

28. Connect the spark plug wires.

29. Connect the SAI hose to the check valve.

30. Install the PCV hose.

31. Connect the vacuum hose to the brake booster.

32. Connect the generator and ECT sensor wiring.

33. Install the generator rear bracket.

34. Connect the fuel lines.

35. Install the fuel rail cover.

36. Connect the negative battery cable.

RIGHT SIDE

➡ **If the oil fill tube is removed from the rocker arm cover, a new tube must be installed during assembly.**

1. Before servicing the vehicle, refer to the precautions in the beginning of this section.

2. Disconnect the negative battery cable.

3. Remove the rocker arm cover bolts.

4. Remove the rocker arm cover.

➡ **Always keep the rocker arms and pushrods in order so they can be installed in their original positions.**

5. Remove the rocker arm bolt and the rocker arm. If removing more than one rocker arm, be sure to keep them in order. They must be installed in their original positions.

To install:

6. If removed, install the rocker arm pivot support.

7. Lubricate the rocker arms and pushrods with clean engine oil.

8. Lubricate the flange and washer surface of the bolt rocker arm mounting bolts.

9. Install the pushrod. Be sure it is seated in the lifter socket.

10. Install the rocker arms but do not tighten the bolts at this time.

11. Rotate the crankshaft so the No. 1 piston is at Top Dead Center (TDC) on compression.

➡ **The engine firing order is 1, 8, 7, 2, 6, 5, 4, 3. The cylinders are numbered 2, 4, 6 and 8 on the right bank.**

12. With the engine in this position, tighten the exhaust valve rocker arm bolts on cylinders 2 and 8. Then, tighten the

intake valve rocker arm bolts on cylinder No. 4. Tighten the bolts to 22 ft. lbs. 30 Nm).

13. Rotate the crankshaft one revolution (360°).

14. With the engine in this position, tighten the exhaust valve rocker arm bolts on cylinders 4 and 6. Then, tighten the intake valve rocker arm bolts on cylinders 2, 6 and 8. Tighten the bolts to 22 ft. lbs. 30 Nm).

15. Install the rocker arm using a new gasket. Tighten the bolts to 106 inch lbs. (12 Nm).

Intake Manifold

REMOVAL & INSTALLATION

5.7L (VIN P and 5) Engines

1. Before servicing the vehicle, refer to the precautions in the beginning of this section.
2. Disconnect the negative battery cable.
3. Drain engine coolant into a suitable container.
4. Remove the throttle body air duct.
5. Remove the fuel rail covers.
6. Disengage the wiring harness connectors from the fuel injectors. Disengage and reposition the left and right wiring harnesses.
7. Remove the accelerator cable bracket, then disconnect the cables from the throttle body.

8. Disconnect the AIR diverter valve hoses.
9. Remove the electrical ground strap from the intake manifold.
10. Remove the fuel rail bolts and disconnect the vacuum hose from the fuel pressure regulator.
11. Carefully remove the fuel rail and injector assembly from the manifold and position aside. Be careful not to damage the fuel lines.
12. Disconnect the vacuum and crankcase vent hoses.
13. Remove the EGR solenoid assembly and the fuel EVAP canister solenoid assembly.
14. Remove the EGR valve.
15. Remove the AIR pipe from the intake and the right exhaust manifold.
16. Remove the alternator brace.
17. Disconnect the coolant hoses from the throttle body.
18. Remove the throttle body bolts, the throttle body and gasket.
19. Remove the intake manifold bolts and studs.
20. Remove the intake manifold and gaskets.

To install:

21. Thoroughly clean the intake manifold bolts and studs. Inspect and clean all gasket mating surfaces.
22. Apply a ³⁄₁₆ in. (5mm) bead of RTV sealer to the front and rear of the cylinder block. Extend the bead ½ in. (13mm) up each cylinder head to seal and retain the gaskets.

23. Position the new gaskets and install the intake manifold.
24. Install the manifold bolts and studs, then tighten using 2 passes of the proper sequence. First, tighten the bolts/studs to 71 inch lbs. (8 Nm), then tighten them to 35 ft. lbs. (48 Nm).
25. Install the throttle body, gasket and retaining bolts. Tighten the throttle body bolts to 19 ft. lbs. (26 Nm).
26. Connect the coolant hoses to the throttle body.
27. Install the alternator brace.
28. Install the accelerator cables and bracket. Tighten the bracket bolts to 90 inch lbs. (10 Nm).
29. Install the AIR pipe. Tighten the exhaust manifold fitting and the bracket-to-cylinder head bolt to 25 ft. lbs. (34 Nm) and tighten the flange-to-intake manifold bolts to 19 ft. lbs. (26 Nm).
30. Install the EGR valve, then EGR solenoid and bracket. Tighten valve bolts to 16 ft. lbs. (22 Nm) and the solenoid bracket nut to 25 ft. lbs. (34 Nm).
31. Install the fuel EVAP canister purge solenoid and bracket, then tighten the nut to 15 ft. lbs. (20 Nm).
32. Connect the vacuum and crankcase vent hoses.
33. Install the fuel injector and fuel rail assembly to the intake manifold, connect the fuel pressure regulator vacuum hose and install the fuel rail bolts. Tighten the bolts to 15 ft. lbs. (20 Nm).
34. Connect the electrical ground strap to the intake manifold.
35. Connect the AIR diverter valve hoses.
36. Position the left and right wiring harnesses, then engage the fuel injector electrical connectors.
37. Install the throttle body air duct.
38. Install the fuel rail covers.
39. Properly fill the engine cooling system.
40. Connect the negative battery cable, then adjust the ASR accelerator and cruise control cables, as necessary.

5.7L (VIN G) Engine

➡The intake manifold, throttle body, fuel injectors and rail may be removed from the engine as an assembly.

1. Before servicing the vehicle, refer to the precautions in the beginning of this section.
2. Disconnect the negative battery cable.

INTAKE MANIFOLD   ⬆FRT

79222615

Intake manifold bolt torque sequence—5.7L (VIN P and 5) engines

3. Drain the cooling system.

4. Detach the Intake Air Temperature (IAT) sensor connector.

5. Detach the Mass Air Flow (MAF) sensor connector.

6. Disconnect the fuel regulator purge line from the intake air duct and remove the air cleaner assembly.

7. Remove the fuel rail covers and relieve the fuel system pressure.

8. Disconnect the fuel lines from the fuel rail.

9. Remove the vacuum and crankcase vent hoses.

10. Remove the coolant hose from the throttle body.

11. Disconnect the wiring from the fuel injectors.

12. Detach any remaining electrical connections on the intake manifold.

13. Remove the vapor vent pipe clamp and hose from the throttle body.

14. Remove the Manifold Absolute Pressure (MAP) sensor from the grommet on the intake manifold.

15. Remove the intake manifold mounting bolts and fuel rail stop bracket.

16. Remove the intake manifold from the engine.

17. Remove and discard the gaskets.

To install:

18. Install new gaskets on the cylinder heads and engine.

19. Position the intake manifold on the engine.

20. Apply a 0.20 in. (5mm) band of threadlocker PN 12345383 or equivalent to the threads of the intake manifold bolts.

✳✳ CAUTION

The fuel rail stop bracket must be installed on the intake manifold in its original position. Failure to reinstall this part may result in fuel spray causing personal injury during a crash.

21. Install the fuel stop bracket and the intake manifold bolts. Tighten the bolts first to 44 inch lbs. (5 Nm) in the sequence shown. Then, make a second pass and tighten the bolts to 89 inch lbs. (8 Nm) using the same sequence.

22. Lubricate the grommet with engine oil and install the MAP sensor.

23. Install the vapor vent pipe and clamp.

24. Attach the fuel injector and remaining electrical connectors.

Be sure to reinstall the fuel stop bracket when installing the intake manifold—5.7L (VIN G) engine

To avoid damage to the intake manifold, tighten the bolts in the sequence shown—5.7L (VIN G) engine

25. Connect the coolant hose to the throttle body.

26. Install the crankcase vent and vacuum hoses.

27. Connect the fuel lines.

28. Install the fuel rail covers.

29. Install the air cleaner assembly and fuel regulator purge line.

30. Connect the wiring harness to the MAF and IAT sensors.

31. Connect the negative battery cable.

❋❋ WARNING

Use only DEX-COOL® or equivalent coolant when refilling the cooling system. If silicate coolant is used, premature corrosion may develop in the engine, heater core and radiator.

32. Refill and bleed the cooling system.

33. Start the engine and check for leaks.

Exhaust Manifold

REMOVAL & INSTALLATION

5.7L (VINS P and 5) Engine

RIGHT SIDE

1. Before servicing the vehicle, refer to the precautions in the beginning of this section.

2. Disconnect the negative battery cable.

3. Raise and support the vehicle safely.

4. For convertibles, if necessary for access, remove the underbody crossbrace.

5. Remove the nuts and disconnect the catalytic converter from the exhaust manifold. It may be necessary to loosen and remove the entire exhaust assembly.

6. Lower the vehicle.

7. Remove the fuel rail covers and disengage the fuel injector electrical connectors.

8. Remove the vacuum hose from the fuel pressure regulator.

9. Remove the fuel rail bolts, then remove the fuel injector/rail assembly from the intake manifold and position aside. Be careful not to damage the fuel lines.

10. Disconnect the spark plug wires from the plugs, then disconnect the wire clips from the supports. If necessary for clearance, or to prevent the possibility of breakage during manifold removal, remove the spark plugs.

11. Remove the front spark plug bracket and bolt.

12. Remove the oil level indicator and guide tube.

13. Remove the AIR pipe, gasket and check valve as an assembly from the intake manifold, exhaust manifolds and the cylinder head.

14. Remove the exhaust manifold studs and bolts.

15. Remove the heat shields, exhaust manifold and gasket.

To install:

16. Thoroughly clean the manifold and cylinder head gasket mating surfaces.

17. Install the exhaust manifold gasket, manifold and heat shields.

18. Install the exhaust manifold studs and bolts. Tighten the fasteners to 26 ft. lbs. (35 Nm).

19. Install the AIR pipe, gasket and check valve assembly with the retaining bolts. Tighten the AIR pipe-to-exhaust manifold fitting and the bracket bolt to 25 ft. lbs. (34 Nm) and tighten the pipe flange bolts to 19 ft. lbs. (26 Nm).

20. Apply 1052080 or equivalent, sealer to the oil level indicator guide tube ½ in. (13mm) below the bead. Install the level indicator and guide tube into the block.

21. Install the front spark plug bracket and bolt. Tighten to 108 inch lbs. (12 Nm).

22. If removed, install the spark plugs and tighten to 11 ft. lbs. (15 Nm).

23. Install the spark plug wires and clips.

24. Install the fuel injectors and fuel rail assembly to the intake manifold. Tighten the fuel rail bolts to 15 ft. lbs. (20 Nm).

25. Connect the fuel pressure regulator vacuum hose.

26. Engage the wiring harness connectors to the fuel injectors.

27. Install the fuel rail covers.

28. Raise and support the vehicle safely.

29. If removed, install the exhaust assembly.

30. Connect the catalytic converter and nuts to the exhaust manifold.

31. Tighten catalytic converter nuts to 15 ft. lbs. (21 Nm).

32. If removed on a convertible, install the underbody crossbrace.

33. Lower the vehicle.

34. Connect the negative battery cable.

LEFT SIDE

1. Before servicing the vehicle, refer to the precautions in the beginning of this section.

2. Disconnect the negative battery cable.

3. Raise and support the vehicle safely.

4. For convertibles, if necessary for access, remove the underbody crossbrace.

5. Remove the nuts and disconnect the catalytic converter from the exhaust manifold. It may be necessary to loosen and remove the entire exhaust assembly.

6. Lower the vehicle.

7. Remove the air intake duct and the serpentine drive belt.

8. Remove the ASR adjuster assembly from the wheel well center panel and reposition out of the way.

9. Remove the mounting bolts and reposition the alternator and the A/C compressor.

10. Remove the AIR pipe, check valve and hose as an assembly from the exhaust manifold.

11. Remove the spark plug wires from the plugs and the clips from the supports, then position the wires aside.

12. Remove the spark plug wire supports. If necessary for clearance, or to prevent the possibility of breakage during manifold removal, remove the spark plugs.

13. Remove the exhaust manifold studs and bolts.

14. Remove the heat shields, exhaust manifold and gasket.

To install:

15. Thoroughly clean the manifold and cylinder head gasket mating surfaces.

16. Install the exhaust manifold gasket, manifold and heat shields.

17. Install the exhaust manifold studs and bolts. Tighten the fasteners to 26 ft. lbs. (35 Nm).

18. Install the spark plug wire supports and tighten to 108 inch lbs. (12 Nm).

19. If removed, install the spark plugs and tighten to 11 ft. lbs. (15 Nm).

20. Connect the spark plug wires and clips.

21. Install the AIR pipe, check valve and hose assembly. Tighten the AIR pipe-to-exhaust manifold fitting and the bracket bolt to 25 ft. lbs. (34 Nm).

22. Reposition and the install the air conditioning compressor and alternator.

23. Install the serpentine drive belt and the air intake duct.

24. Install the ASR adjuster assembly, then check and adjust the control cable, as necessary.

25. Raise and support the vehicle safely.

26. If removed, install the exhaust assembly.

Please refer to Section 9 for electric cooling fan wiring schematics

27. Connect the catalytic converter and nuts to the exhaust manifold.

28. Tighten catalytic converter nuts to 15 ft. lbs. (21 Nm).

29. If removed on a convertible, install the underbody crossbrace.

30. Lower the vehicle.

31. Connect the negative battery cable.

5.7L (VIN G) Engine

LEFT SIDE

1. Before servicing the vehicle, refer to the precautions in the beginning of this section.

2. Disconnect the negative battery cable.

3. Raise and safely support the vehicle.

4. Disconnect the intermediate pipe from the exhaust manifold flange.

5. Disconnect the wiring from the Oxygen (O_2S) sensor.

6. Lower the vehicle to the floor.

7. Remove the left fuel rail cover.

8. Relieve the fuel system pressure.

9. Disconnect the fuel line from the fuel rail.

10. Remove the rear generator bracket.

11. Remove the drive belt from the generator, then remove the generator.

12. Remove the Secondary Air Injection (SAI) hose from the pipe on the exhaust manifold.

13. Remove the SAI pipe from the exhaust manifold.

14. Remove the spark plug wires from the plugs and remove the spark plugs.

15. Remove the No. 5 ignition coil bolts and position the coil aside.

16. Remove the exhaust manifold mounting bolts and the manifold. Discard the gasket.

To install:

17. Clean the bolt holes and the mounting surface of the cylinder head.

18. Apply threadlocker PN 12345493 or equivalent to the threads of the bolts. Do not apply it to the first three threads.

19. Install the exhaust manifold using a new gasket.

20. Beginning with the center two bolts, tighten the bolts to 11 ft. lbs. (15 Nm) alternating from side-to-side until all the bolts are tight. Then, tighten the bolts again in the same sequence to 18 ft. lbs. (25 Nm).

21. Bend over the exposed portion of the gasket at the rear of the cylinder head.

22. Install the AIR pipe using a new gasket. Tighten the bolts to 15 ft. lbs. (20 Nm).

23. If removed, install the O_2S sensor in the manifold, tighten it to 30 ft. lbs. (42 Nm).

24. Connect the air hose to the SAI pipe.

25. Install the No. 5 ignition coil.

26. Install the spark plugs and wires.

27. Install the generator, rear bracket and drive belt.

28. Connect the fuel lines.

29. Install the fuel rail cover.

30. Install the intermediate pipe to the manifold using a new gasket. Tighten the nuts to 15 ft. lbs. (20 Nm)

31. Connect the negative battery cable.

RIGHT SIDE

1. Before servicing the vehicle, refer to the precautions in the beginning of this section.

2. Disconnect the negative battery cable.

3. Raise the vehicle and disconnect the intermediate pipe from the exhaust manifold.

4. Disconnect the wiring from the Oxygen (O_2S) sensor.

5. Lower the vehicle and remove the AIR pipe with check valve from the manifold.

6. Disconnect the spark plug wires from the spark plugs.

7. Remove the exhaust manifold mounting bolts and the manifold.

To install:

8. Clean the bolt holes and the mounting surface of the cylinder head.

9. Apply threadlocker PN 12345493 or equivalent to the threads of the bolts. Do not apply it to the first three threads.

10. Install the exhaust manifold using a new gasket.

11. Beginning with the center two bolts, tighten the bolts to 11 ft. lbs. (15 Nm) alternating from side-to-side until all the bolts are tight. Then, tighten the bolts again in the same sequence to 18 ft. lbs. (25 Nm).

12. Bend over the exposed portion of the gasket at the rear of the cylinder head.

13. Install the AIR pipe using a new gasket. Tighten the bolts to 15 ft. lbs. (20 Nm).

14. If removed, install the O_2S sensor in the manifold, tighten it to 30 ft. lbs. (42 Nm).

15. Connect the spark plug wires to the plugs.

16. Install the intermediate pipe to the manifold using a new gasket. Tighten the nuts to 15 ft. lbs. (20 Nm)

17. Connect the negative battery cable.

Camshaft

REMOVAL & INSTALLATION

5.7L (VINS P and 5) Engine

1. Before servicing the vehicle, refer to the precautions in the beginning of this section.

2. Disconnect battery negative cable and remove the air cleaner assembly.

3. Remove the timing chain front cover.

4. Remove the intake manifold.

5. Remove the retaining bolt and lift the oil pump driveshaft assembly from the rear of the lifter valley.

6. Remove the rocker arm and pushrod assemblies.

7. Remove the camshaft sprocket from the engine.

8. Remove the valve lifters.

9. Remove the high fill reservoir hose from the radiator.

10. Remove the relay bracket from the left side of the radiator support.

11. Remove the AIR pump intake duct and bolts, then reposition the AIR pump.

12. Remove the retaining nuts and screws, then remove the upper radiator support.

13. Remove the radiator.

14. Raise and support the vehicle safely.

15. Unplug the cooling fan electrical connector.

16. Remove the lower fan shroud bolts and lower the vehicle.

17. Remove the fan shroud and fan assembly.

18. Disconnect the A/C condenser line bracket at the front crossmember.

19. Raise the front of the engine with a suitable lifting device.

➡**When raising and supporting the engine, NEVER place a jack under the oil pan, crankshaft pulley or any sheet metal. There is a minimal clearance between the oil pan and the pump screen. Jacking against the pan could cause sufficient deformation to damage the oil pick-up unit.**

20. Remove the camshaft retainer bolts and retainer.

21. Install three $\frac{5}{16}$ –18 x 4 in. bolts into the camshaft bolt holes.

22. Using the bolts, carefully rotate the camshaft and pull from the bearings. All camshaft journals are the same diameter so

A. Timing marks
B. Keyway
1. Bolt
2. Sprocket
3. Bolt
4. Retainer
5. Camshaft
6. Timing chain
7. Sprocket
8. Driven gear
9. Bolts

Exploded view of the camshaft mounting and the valve timing marks—5.7L (VINS P and 5) engines

care must be used to avoid damaging the bearings. Remove the camshaft from the vehicle.

To install:

23. Inspect the camshaft and bearings, replace as necessary.

24. If installing a new camshaft, coat the lobes with Molykote® or equivalent pre-lube and be sure to replace all lifters to assure camshaft durability.

25. Lubricate all camshaft journals with clean engine oil and carefully insert the camshaft into the engine block.

26. Install the camshaft retainer and tighten the bolts to 108 inch lbs. (12 Nm).

27. Lower the front of the engine and connect the A/C condenser line bracket to the front crossmember.

28. Install the fan and shroud assembly.

29. Raise and support the vehicle safely, then install the lower fan shroud bolts.

30. Engage the cooling fan electrical connections and lower the vehicle.

31. Install the radiator, followed by the upper radiator support, nuts and screws.

32. Install the AIR pump, bolts and intake duct.

33. Install the relay bracket to the left side of the radiator support.

34. Connect the high fill reservoir hose to the radiator.

35. Install the valve lifters.

36. Install the camshaft sprocket.

37. Install the valve rocker arm and pushrod assemblies.

38. Install the oil pump driveshaft assembly and bolt. Tighten the bolt to 13 ft. lbs. (18 Nm).

39. Install the intake manifold.

40. Install the timing chain front cover.

41. Install the air cleaner assembly and connect the negative battery cable.

5.7L (VIN G) Engine

1. Before servicing the vehicle, refer to the precautions in the beginning of this section.

2. Disconnect the negative battery cable.

3. Drain the cooling system.

4. Relieve the fuel system pressure, then disconnect the lines from the fuel rail assembly.

5. Remove the cylinder head covers.

6. Remove the rocker arms and

Install three M8–1.25 x 100mm long bolts into the camshaft to use as a handle

pushrods. Keep them in order so they can be installed in their original positions.

7. Remove the cylinder heads and the valve lifters.

8. Remove the radiator assembly.

9. Remove the engine front cover.

10. Remove the oil pump.

11. Remove the camshaft sprocket and timing chain.

12. Remove the Camshaft Position (CMP) sensor bolt and sensor from the engine.

13. Remove the camshaft retainer plate.

❉❉ WARNING

All camshaft bearings are the same diameter, extreme care must be taken during camshaft removal or installation to avoid damaging them.

14. Install three M8–1.25 x 100mm long bolts in the front of the camshaft to use as a handle.

15. Carefully withdraw the camshaft from the engine, be sure not to damage the camshaft bearings.

To install:

16. Lubricate the camshaft with clean engine oil.

17. Install three M8–1.25 x 100mm long bolts in the front of the camshaft to use as a handle.

18. Carefully install the camshaft into the engine and remove the three bolts.

19. Install the camshaft retainer using a new gasket. Tighten the bolts to 18 ft. lbs. (25 Nm).

20. Install the CMP sensor. Use a new O-ring if the old one is damaged. Tighten the bolt to 18 ft. lbs. (25 Nm).

21. Install the timing chain. Be sure the valve timing marks are facing each other.

22. Install the oil pump.

23. Install the front cover.

24. Install the radiator assembly.

25. Install the cylinder heads, valve lifters, pushrods and rocker arms.

26. Install all remaining components.

27. Connect the negative battery cable.

28. Refill the cooling system with DEX-COOL® or equivalent coolant.

29. Start the engine and check for leaks.

Valve Lash

ADJUSTMENT

5.7L (VIN P and 5) Engines

The valve lash on the VIN P and 5 engine is adjusted whenever the rocker arm assemblies have been removed.

➡**The 5.7L (VIN P) engine utilize hydraulic lifters which normally require very little maintenance or adjustment. These components are simple in design and are best maintained through regular, scheduled engine oil changes. If the engine is running well and no audible clicking sounds are heard from the valvetrain, there is no need to remove or disassemble the valve lifters.**

1. Before servicing the vehicle, refer to the precautions in the beginning of this section.

2. Disconnect the negative battery cable.

3. Remove the valve rocker covers.

4. Tighten the nuts slowly until all lash is eliminated.

5. Adjust the valves when the lifter is on the base circle of the camshaft lobe. Slowly turn or crank the engine until the mark on the vibration damper is in the 12 o'clock position (aligned with the timing cover mark, if equipped) and the engine is in the No. 1 firing position.

➡**The No. 1 firing position may be determined by watching the No. 1 cylinder valves as the mark on the damper approaches the 12 o'clock position. If both the intake and exhaust valves are closed as the mark comes up to the timing tab, the engine is in the No. 1 firing position. If either valve opens as the timing mark approaches the top of its travel, the engine is in No. 6 firing position and should be turned over 1 full revolution in order to reach the No. 1 firing position.**

6. With the engine in the No. 1 firing position, adjust the following valves:
- Exhaust—1, 3, 4, 8
- Intake—1, 2, 5, 7

7. Back out the rocker arm adjusting nut until lash is felt at the pushrod, then turn the adjusting nut inward until all lash is removed. This can be determined by rotating pushrod while turning the adjusting nut. When play has been removed, the pushrod will not turn. Then, tighten the adjusting nut 1 full additional turn.

8. Slowly turn or crank the engine 1 revolution until the vibration damper mark is at 12 o'clock again and the No. 1 cylinder valves open. This is the No. 6 firing position.

9. With the engine in this position, adjust the following valves:
- Exhaust—2, 5, 6, 7
- Intake—3, 4, 6, 8

10. Install the valve rocker arm covers.

11. Connect the battery negative cable.

5.7L (VIN G) Engine

The 5.7L (VIN G) engine uses rocker arms, pushrods and hydraulic lifters which are similar to the other pushrod motors in this section (VIN P and 5). The lifters maintain correct valve lash so that no periodic adjustment is necessary or possible. But, unlike the other pushrod motors which use adjustment nuts to retain the rocker arms (and therefore must be adjusted during installation), the rocker arms on the 5.7L (VIN G) are bolted into position so that no initial adjustment is possible either. If the valves are noisy, suspect low oil pressure or worn valvetrain components.

Oil Pan

REMOVAL & INSTALLATION

5.7L (VIN P) Engine

1. Before servicing the vehicle, refer to the precautions in the beginning of this section.

2. Disconnect the negative battery cable.

3. Raise and support the vehicle safely, then drain the engine oil.

4. Disengage the oil level sensor electrical connector and remove the sensor assembly from the side of the oil pan.

5. Remove the oil filter, then remove the oil filter adapter bolts and the adapter assembly.

6. Remove the starter motor assembly.

7. Remove the left catalytic converter.

8. Remove the flywheel cover.

9. Remove the Knock (KS) sensor retaining nuts and shields.

10. Remove the oil pan bolts, nuts and studs. Be sure to note the location of stud bolts.

11. Remove the oil pan, reinforcements and gasket.

To install:

12. Thoroughly clean all gasket mating surfaces and apply a small amount of 1052914 or equivalent sealer, to the front cover and cylinder block junction and the rear seal retainer and cylinder block junction. Extend the bead of sealer approximately 1 in. (25mm) in either direction of these junctions.

13. Install the gasket onto the oil pan and reinforcements.

14. Install the gasket, pan and reinforcement assembly to the cylinder block with the bolts, studs and nuts.

15. Tighten the corner bolts or stud and nuts to 15 ft. lbs. (20 Nm). Tighten the remainder of the bolts and studs to 8 ft. lbs. (11 Nm).

16. Install the oil level sensor and tighten to 16 ft. lbs. (22 Nm).

17. Install the knock sensor shields and nuts. Tighten the nuts to 75 inch lbs. (8.5 Nm).

18. Install the flywheel cover.

19. Install the left catalytic converter.

20. Install the starter motor assembly.

21. Engage the wiring harness to the oil level sensor terminal.

22. Install the oil filter adapter and tighten the retainers to 17 ft. lbs. (23 Nm), then install the oil filter.

23. Lower the vehicle and properly fill the crankcase with clean engine oil.

24. Connect the negative battery cable.

25. Reset the CHANGE OIL indicator:

a. Turn the ignition **ON** but do not start the engine.

b. Depress the ENG MET button on the trip monitor, then within 5 seconds, depress the button a 2nd time. Within another 5 seconds, depress and hold the GAUGES button.

c. While holding the GAUGES button and watch the CHANGE OIL light, it should begin to flash. Continue to hold the gauges button until the flashing stops and the light goes out indicating that the indicator is reset.

d. If the indicator does not reset, turn the ignition **OFF** and restart the procedure.

5.7L (VIN G) Engine

1. Before servicing the vehicle, refer to the precautions in the beginning of this section.

2. Disconnect the negative battery cable.

3. Remove the generator.

4. Support the engine with a suitable support fixture such as engine support fixture J 41803.

5. Raise and safely support the vehicle.

6. Remove the front wheels.

7. Matchmark the adjustment, then remove the tie rod ends from the steering knuckles.

8. Remove the stabilizer bar brackets from the cradle.

9. Remove the power steering fluid cooler tube from the cradle and position it upward.

10. Remove the steering rack assembly mounting bolts and position the rack upward.

11. Install spring compressor J 33432 or equivalent and compress the spring.

12. Remove the lower shock absorber mounting bolts.

13. Remove the lower ball joint nut, then disconnect the ball joint from the knuckle.

14. Remove the spring compressor.

15. Detach all electrical connectors at the front crossmember.

16. Remove the motor mount-to-front crossmember nuts.

17. Remove the front crossmember.

18. Drain the engine oil.

19. Remove the oil filter.

20. If equipped with automatic transmission, remove the fluid cooler line bracket near the oil pan.

21. Remove the flywheel housing to oil pan bolts.

22. Remove the flywheel housing cover.

23. Remove the engine oil level sensor.

24. Disconnect the engine oil temperature sensor.

25. Remove the left and right closeout covers.

26. Remove the oil pan mounting bolts and the oil pan.

To install:

27. Apply a 0.20 in. (5mm) bead of sealant PN 12378190 or equivalent directly on the tabs of the front and rear cover gaskets that extend onto the oil pan mounting surface.

28. Position a new gasket on the oil pan. It is not necessary to rivet the new gasket on the oil pan.

29. Install the oil pan on the engine but do not tighten the bolts.

30. Install the flywheel housing-to-oil pan bolts. Tighten the bolts to 37 ft. lbs. (50 Nm).

31. Tighten the oil pan-to-block and oil pan-to-front cover bolts to 18 ft. lbs. (25 Nm). Tighten the oil pan-to-rear cover bolts to 106 inch lbs. (12 Nm).

32. If removed, install the oil level sensor, tighten the sensor to 26 ft. lbs. (35 Nm).

33. Install the left and right closeout covers. Tighten the bolts to 106 inch lbs. (12 Nm).

34. Connect the oil temperature sensor.

35. Install the transmission fluid cooler line bracket.

79222629

Apply sealant to the areas where the front and rear covers attach to the engine block—5.7L (VIN G) engine

Timing belt service is covered in Section 5 of this manual

Exploded view of the oil pan mounting—5.7L (VIN G) engine

79222630

36. Install a new oil filter.

37. Install the front crossmember. Tighten the nuts to 81 ft. lbs. (110 Nm).

38. Install the motor mount on the crossmember. Tighten the nuts to 40 ft. lbs. (54 Nm).

39. Attach the electrical connectors.

40. Install spring compressor J 33432 or equivalent and compress the spring.

41. Install the lower shock absorber mounting bolts. Tighten them to 20 ft. lbs. (28 Nm).

42. Install the lower ball joints to the steering knuckles.

43. Install the power steering gear and fluid cooling tube.

44. Install the stabilizer bar brackets to the cradle. Tighten the bolts to 40 ft. lbs. (54 Nm).

45. Connect the tie rod ends to the knuckles. Tighten the nuts to 33 ft. lbs. (45 Nm).

46. Install the front wheels. Tighten the nuts to 100 ft. lbs. (140 Nm).

47. Lower the vehicle to the floor and remove the engine support fixture.

48. Install the generator.

49. Connect the negative battery cable.

50. Refill the engine with the proper type of engine oil.

51. Start the engine and check for leaks.

52. Check the front wheel alignment and adjust as needed.

Oil Pump

REMOVAL & INSTALLATION

5.7L (VIN P and 5) Engines

1. Before servicing the vehicle, refer to the precautions in the beginning of this section.

2. Disconnect the negative battery cable.

3. Raise and support the vehicle safely.

4. Drain the engine oil and remove the oil pan.

5. Remove the oil pan baffle nuts.

6. Support the oil pump by hand and remove the bolt attaching the oil pump to the main bearing cap.

7. Carefully remove the baffle, the oil pump assembly, driveshaft and retainer.

To install:

➡**The oil pump pick-up should be submerged in oil and the pump primed prior to installation. Failure to prime the pump may result in oil pump failure or internal engine damage. Also, if the pick-up screen and pipe assembly was removed from the pump, they must be replaced to assure a proper interference fit.**

8. Install the oil pump assembly, shaft and retainer, aligning the slot on the top of the pump driveshaft with the drive tang on the lower end of the distributor driveshaft.

9. Install the oil pan baffle, then install the bolt to the main bearing cap, followed by the baffle nuts. Tighten the retaining bolt to 65 ft. lbs. (88 Nm) and the baffle nuts to 25 ft. lbs. (34 Nm).

10. Install the oil pan and lower the vehicle.

11. Properly fill the engine crankcase with clean engine oil.

12. Connect the negative battery cable.

13. If equipped, reset the CHANGE OIL indicator:

  a. Turn the ignition **ON** but do not start the engine.

  b. Depress the ENG MET button on the trip monitor, then within 5 seconds, depress the button a 2nd time. Within another 5 seconds, depress and hold the GAUGES button.

  c. While holding the GAUGES button and watch the CHANGE OIL light, it should begin to flash. Continue to hold the gauges button until the flashing stops and the light goes out indicating that the indicator is reset.

  d. If the indicator does not reset, turn the ignition **OFF** and restart the procedure.

5.7L (VIN G) Engine

1. Disconnect the negative battery cable.

2. Drain the engine oil and coolant.

3. Remove the engine front cover.

4. Remove the oil pan.

Be sure to seat the tube into the pump before installing the bolt—5.7L (VIN G) engine

Oil pump assembly mounting—5.7L (VIN G) engine

5. Remove the oil pump pick-up and O-ring.

6. Remove the oil pump mounting bolts.

7. Remove the oil pump.

To install:

8. Inspect the oil passages in the pump and on the mounting surface. Be sure they are clean and free of debris.

9. Align the splined surface of the crankshaft sprocket and the oil pump drive gear. Install the oil pump. Tighten the bolts to 18 ft. lbs. (25 Nm).

10. Install a new O-ring on the pick-up tube and install it into the pump by hand. Don't use the bolt to force the tube into the pump. After the tube is seated in the oil pump, tighten the bolt to 106 inch lbs. (12 Nm). Tighten the nut to 18 ft. lbs. (25 Nm).

11. Install the oil pan.

12. Install the front cover.

13. Refill the cooling system and the engine oil with the correct type and amount of fluids.

14. Connect the negative battery cable.

15. Start the engine and check for leaks.

Rear Main Seal

REMOVAL & INSTALLATION

➡The rear main seal is a one piece unit. It can be removed or installed without removing the oil pan or crankshaft.

1. Raise and safely support the vehicle.

2. On 1996 models, remove the transmission. On 1997–00 models, remove the driveshaft support and bell housing.

3. If equipped with a manual transmission, remove the clutch and pressure plate.

4. Remove the flywheel assembly.

5. Using a suitable prytool, carefully pry the old seal out.

6. Inspect the crankshaft for nicks or burrs, correct as required.

To install:

7. Clean the area and coat the seal and crankshaft with engine oil. Install the seal using a suitable seal installer.

8. Install the flywheel.

9. If equipped with a manual transmission, install the clutch and pressure plate.

10. Install the transmission or bell housing and driveshaft support.

11. Check the fluid levels, start the engine and check for leaks.

Use a suitable seal installer to press the seal on the crankshaft—5.7L (VIN G) engine shown, other engines are similar

Timing Chain, Sprockets, Front Cover and Seal

REMOVAL & INSTALLATION

5.7L (VIN P and 5) Engines

1. Before servicing the vehicle, refer to the precautions in the beginning of this section.
2. Disconnect the negative battery cable.
3. Drain the engine oil and coolant into suitable containers.
4. Remove the throttle body air intake duct.
5. Remove the serpentine drive belt.
6. Remove the water pump assembly.
7. Remove the crankshaft balancer and hub.

   a. If not done already, raise and support the vehicle safely, then remove the motor mount nuts.

   b. Remove the power steering fluid cooler, then raise the engine sufficiently for tool access to the crankshaft balancer.

➡When raising and supporting the engine, NEVER place a jack under the oil pan, crankshaft pulley or any sheet metal. There is a minimal clearance between the oil pan and the pump screen. Jacking against the pan could cause sufficient deformation to damage the oil pick-up unit.

   c. Remove the balancer bolts, then remove the balancer from the hub.

   d. Disconnect the power steering line from the steering gear.

   e. Matchmark the crankshaft hub to the engine front cover, then remove the hub bolt and washer.

   f. Remove the crankshaft hub using J-39046, or an equivalent hub removal/installation tool. To preserve the relationship between the hub and crankshaft, DO NOT crank the engine over once the hub has been removed. If the hub is not matchmarked and installed in the original position, an engine imbalance could result.

8. Remove the distributor assembly.
9. Remove the oil pan assembly.
10. Remove the engine front cover bolts.
11. Remove the engine front cover and gasket.
12. Rotate the crankshaft until the timing marks on the timing chain sprockets are aligned nearest each other. The camshaft sprocket mark should be at the 6 o'clock position while the mark on the crankshaft sprocket should be at the 12 o'clock position.
13. Remove the camshaft sprocket bolts.
14. Remove the camshaft sprocket and timing chain.

➡To prevent piston or valve damage, do not turn the crankshaft after the timing chain has been removed.

15. Remove the water pump bearing retainer bolts, then remove the driveshaft assembly using J-39243 or equivalent driven gear assembly remover.
16. Remove the crankshaft sprocket using J-5825-A or equivalent crankshaft sprocket remover.
17. If necessary, remove the crankshaft key.

To install:

18. If removed, install the crankshaft key.
19. Install the crankshaft sprocket using a suitable installation tool.
20. Install the water pump driveshaft assembly using a suitable tool. Install the retainer bolts and tighten to 108 inch lbs. (12 Nm).
21. Align the timing marks and install the camshaft sprocket and timing chain. The gears of the camshaft sprocket and water pump driveshaft must mesh or damage to the thrust plate retainer could occur.
22. Install the camshaft sprocket bolts and tighten to 21 ft. lbs. (28 Nm).
23. Install a new O-ring to the water pump driven gear shaft using a suitable seal installation tool.
24. Thoroughly clean the engine front cover and cylinder block gasket mating surfaces. Inspect the engine front cover and seals for damage, replace as necessary.
25. Using J-39087 or equivalent shaft gear front cover seal protector, on the water pump driveshaft, install the gasket and front cover into position over the shafts and guide pins.
26. Install the engine front cover bolts and tighten to 100 inch lbs. (11 Nm).
27. Install the oil pan and gasket.
28. Install the distributor assembly.
29. Install and connect all remaining components.
30. Connect the negative battery cable.
31. Refill the cooling system, start the engine and check for leaks.

5.7L (VIN G) Engine

1. Before servicing the vehicle, refer to the precautions in the beginning of this section.
2. Remove the oil pump.

A. Timing marks
B. Keyway
1. Bolt
2. Sprocket
3. Bolt
4. Retainer
5. Camshaft
6. Timing chain
7. Sprocket
8. Driven gear
9. Bolts

FRT

Exploded view of the timing chain and gear assembly—5.7L (VIN P and 5) engines

3. Rotate the crankshaft until the timing marks are aligned. The marks should face each other.

4. Remove the camshaft sprocket bolts.

5. Remove the camshaft sprocket and timing chain assembly.

6. Use a puller such as J 8433–1 and adapters to remove the crankshaft sprocket if necessary.

To install:

7. If the crankshaft sprocket has been removed, install it using tool No. J 41665–1 or equivalent.

8. Be sure the timing mark on the crankshaft sprocket is at the 12 O'clock position. If not rotate the crankshaft to the correct position.

9. Position the chain on the camshaft sprocket. Install the chain and sprocket assembly so the timing marks are aligned. Tighten the camshaft sprocket bolts to 18 ft. lbs. (25 Nm).

10. Install the oil pump, front cover and remaining components.

J 41558

J 41816 – 2

J 8433 – 1

A puller is needed to remove the crankshaft sprocket—5.7L (VIN G) engine

Refer to Section 1 for engine rebuilding specifications

J 41665 – 1

79222Z639

Be sure to install the crankshaft sprocket properly—5.7L (VIN G) engine

FUEL SYSTEM

Fuel System Service Precautions

Safety is the most important factor when performing not only fuel system maintenance but any type of maintenance. Failure to conduct maintenance and repairs in a safe manner may result in serious personal injury or death. Maintenance and testing of the vehicle's fuel system components can be accomplished safely and effectively by adhering to the following rules and guidelines.

• To avoid the possibility of fire and personal injury, always disconnect the negative battery cable unless the repair or test procedure requires that battery voltage be applied.

• Always relieve the fuel system pressure prior to disconnecting any fuel system component (injector, fuel rail, pressure regulator, etc.), fitting or fuel line connection. Exercise extreme caution whenever relieving fuel system pressure to avoid exposing skin, face and eyes to fuel spray. Please be advised that fuel under pressure may penetrate the skin or any part of the body that it contacts.

• Always place a shop towel or cloth around the fitting or connection prior to loosening to absorb any excess fuel due to spillage. Ensure that all fuel spillage (should it occur) is quickly removed from engine surfaces. Ensure that all fuel soaked cloths or towels are deposited into a suitable waste container.

• Always keep a dry chemical (Class B) fire extinguisher near the work area.

• Do not allow fuel spray or fuel vapors to come into contact with a spark or open flame.

• Always use a back-up wrench when loosening and tightening fuel line connection fittings. This will prevent unnecessary stress and torsion to fuel line piping. Always follow the proper torque specifications.

• Always replace worn fuel fitting O-rings with new. Do not substitute fuel hose or equivalent, where fuel pipe is installed.

Fuel System Pressure

RELIEVING

1. Before servicing the vehicle, refer to the precautions in the beginning of this section.

2. Disconnect the negative battery cable.

3. Loosen the fuel filler cap to relieve the tank pressure.

4. Wrap a shop towel around the fuel pressure valve fitting (located on the side or end of the fuel rail assembly) to catch any fuel spray and connect J-34730–1 or an equivalent fuel gauge.

5. Place the bleed hose into a suitable container, then open the valve to bleed the fuel system pressure.

6. Close the valve and disconnect the fuel gauge. Drain any remaining fuel from the gauge into the bleed container.

Fuel Filter

REMOVAL & INSTALLATION

1996 Models

1. Disconnect the battery negative cable and properly relieve the fuel system pressure.

2. Remove the fuel pipe retaining nut from the evaporator case.

3. Raise and support the vehicle safely.

4. For convertibles, remove the underbody brace.

5. Remove the three nuts retaining the fuel pipes to the chassis.

6. Clean the filter connections and surrounding areas to prevent fuel system contamination.

7. Disconnect the inlet pipe from the filter, drain any remaining fuel from the line and reposition the line for access to the filter.

8. Hold the pipe outlet nut and remove the filter by turning to unthread it from the fitting.

To install:

9. Check the fuel pipe O-rings for cuts, nicks, swelling or distortion and replace if damaged.

10. Install the fuel filter onto the fuel outlet pipe nut.

11. Connect the fuel inlet pipe to the filter and tighten the fitting to 20 ft. lbs. (27 Nm).

12. Install the 3 chassis-to-fuel pipe retaining nuts.

13. For convertibles, install the underbody brace, tighten the retaining nuts to 20 ft. lbs. (27 Nm) and the retaining bolts to 47 ft. lbs. (63 Nm).

14. Lower the vehicle and install the fuel pipe retaining nut to the evaporator case.

15. Tighten the fuel filler cap and connect the negative battery cable.

16. Turn the ignition **ON** for 2 seconds,

OFF for 10 seconds, then ON again and inspect the system for leaks.

1997–00 Models

1. Before servicing the vehicle, refer to the precautions in the beginning of this section.
2. Disconnect the negative battery cable.
3. Relieve the fuel system pressure.
4. Raise and safely support the vehicle.
5. On vehicles with automatic transmissions, remove the stabilizer bar from the rear cradle and detach the intermediate pipe from the muffler.
6. Clean the filter connections, then depress the locking tabs and detach the quick-connect fittings from the filter.
7. Remove the fuel filter and bracket.

To install:

8. Remove the protective caps from the new filter.
9. Install the new plastic connector retainers on the ends of the filter.
10. Install the filter into the bracket. Apply a few drops of oil to the male end of the fitting and attach the fuel lines.
11. Install the filter and bracket on the mounting stud. Tighten the nut to 40 inch lbs. (4.5 Nm).
12. On vehicles with automatic transmissions, connect the exhaust pipe to the muffler and install the stabilizer bar.
13. Lower the vehicle to the floor.
14. Connect the negative battery cable.
15. Turn the ignition switch ON for two seconds, then OFF for 10 seconds. Turn the ignition switch back ON and inspect for leaks.

Fuel Pump

REMOVAL & INSTALLATION

1996 Models

1. Before servicing the vehicle, refer to the precautions in the beginning of this section.
2. Disconnect the negative battery cable.
3. Properly relieve the fuel system pressure and drain the fuel tank.
4. Remove the 4 filler door bezel attaching screws, then remove the filler door bezel.
5. Lift the fuel tank filler neck housing and disconnect the drain hose from the nipple. Remove filler neck housing.

6. Clean the area around all fuel fittings to prevent system contamination, then disconnect and plug the fuel pipes and fuel vapor pipe.
7. Unplug the sending unit electrical connector, remove the attaching bolts and remove the sending unit assembly from the vehicle.
8. If equipped with the VIN P or 5 engine, service the sender assembly, as necessary:
   a. Note the position of the fuel strainer on the pump.
   b. Support the pump with one hand and grasp the strainer with the other. Turn the strainer in one direction, pull the strainer off the pump and discard it.
   c. Unplug the fuel pump electrical connection.
   d. Place the fuel sender assembly upside down on a flat bench.
   e. Pull the fuel pump downward to remove it from the mounting bracket, then tilt the pump outward and remove it from the pulse dampener.
   f. Note the position of the dampener on the inlet tube, then remove the dampener from the tube. Shake the dampener and listen for fuel, if fuel is heard inside the dampener, it must be replaced.

To install:

9. Assemble the sender for installation, as necessary:
   a. Install the fuel pulse dampener in the same position as noted during disassembly.
   b. Assemble the rear bumper and insulator onto the fuel pump.
   c. Position the fuel sender assembly upside down on a flat bench and install the fuel pump between the fuel pulse dampener and mounting bracket.
   d. Engage the pump electrical connector.
   e. Install the new fuel strainer into the same position as noted during disassembly. Push on the outer edge of ferrule until fully seated.
10. Position a new gasket on the fuel tank with the notch facing forward in the right corner of the fuel tank.
11. Carefully fold the strainer to allow it to fit through the opening in the tank. Be sure the strainer unfolds in the tank and lower the fuel sender assembly into position.
12. Install the fuel sender assembly attaching screws and tighten alternately and evenly to 45 inch lbs. (5 Nm).

13. Engage the fuel sender assembly electrical connector.
14. Connect all sender assembly fuel and vapor hoses.
15. Connect the fuel drain hose to the nipple on the rubber filler neck housing, then position the housing around the fuel tank filler neck.
16. Install the filler door bezel with the attaching screws.
17. Add fuel, tighten the filler cap and connect the negative battery cable.
18. Turn the ignition ON for 2 seconds, OFF for 10 seconds, then ON again and inspect the system for leaks.

1997–00 Models

1997–00 models have two fuel tanks (right and left). The fuel pump is part of the fuel sender assembly in the left fuel tank. The right fuel tank contains a fuel sender assembly with a siphon jet pump which supplies fuel to the left tank through the fuel sender feed pipe.

1. Before servicing the vehicle, refer to the precautions in the beginning of this section.
2. Disconnect the negative battery cable.
3. Properly relieve the fuel system pressure and drain the fuel tank.
4. Raise and safely support the vehicle.
5. Remove the rear wheel.
6. Clean the area around the fuel sender assembly.
7. Mark each fuel line to help identify them during installation.
8. Detach the fuel lines and electrical connector.
9. Support the fuel tank and remove the tank shield.
10. Remove the fuel sender mounting bolts, lift out the sender slightly and remove the float arm retaining clip and float arm.
11. Remove the fuel sender assembly and gasket.

To install:

RIGHT SIDE

➡ **Always install a new fuel strainer before installing the fuel sender assembly. A strainer that has been exposed to fuel will not unfold completely and may interfere with the full travel of the float arm.**

1. Before servicing the vehicle, refer to the precautions in the beginning of this section.

2. Install new fuel strainers on the siphon jet pump. The small strainer goes on the float side. Secure the strainers with a small tie wrap through the tab opening.

3. Install the new gasket on the fuel sender assembly using the new bolts to hold it in place.

✳✳ WARNING

Do not damage the float arm during installation.

4. Fold the long strainer in half on itself, then squeeze both strainers upward toward each other. Insert the fuel sender in the tank. It may be necessary to turn the sender assembly to ease installation. Look into the opening to ensure that the long strainer is about one inch from the opening, if not, rotate the sender assembly back-and-forth until the strainer is visible.

✳✳ WARNING

The mounting bolts break easily. Do not overtighten them.

5. Install the float arm and clip.

6. Using a torque wrench, tighten the mounting bolts to 27 inch lbs. (3 Nm).

7. Connect the fuel lines and attach the electrical connector.

8. Install the fuel tank shield. Tighten the bolts to in sequence to 19 ft. lbs. (25 Nm).

9. Install the wheel.

10. Lower the vehicle to the floor.

11. Refill the fuel tank.

12. Connect the negative battery cable.

13. Turn the ignition **ON** for 2 seconds, **OFF** for 10 seconds, then **ON** again and inspect the system for leaks.

LEFT SIDE

➡ **Always install a new fuel strainer before installing the fuel pump assembly. A strainer that has been exposed to fuel will not unfold completely and may interfere with the full travel of the float arm.**

1. Before servicing the vehicle, refer to the precautions in the beginning of this section.

2. Install a new fuel strainer on the pump.

3. Install the new gasket on the fuel pump using the new bolts to hold it in place.

✳✳ WARNING

Do not damage the float arm during installation.

4. Fold the strainer three times so the strainer is about the same size as the opening in the tank. Insert the fuel pump in the tank. It may be necessary to turn the fuel pump to ease installation. Look into the opening to ensure that the long strainer is

about one inch from the opening, if not, rotate the pump assembly back-and-forth until the strainer is visible.

5. Install the float arm and retaining clip.

Tighten the fuel pump mounting bolts in the sequence shown—1997–00 5.7L (VIN G) engine

Fold the strainer on itself three times so it will fit into the opening in the fuel tank—1997–00 5.7L (VIN G) engine

※※ **WARNING**

The mounting bolts break easily. Do not overtighten them.

6. Using a torque wrench, tighten the mounting bolts in sequence to 27 inch lbs. (3 Nm).

7. Connect the fuel lines and attach the electrical connector.

8. Install the fuel tank shield. Tighten the bolts to 19 ft. lbs. (25 Nm).

9. Install the wheel.

10. Lower the vehicle to the floor.

11. Refill the fuel tank.

12. Connect the negative battery cable.

13. Turn the ignition **ON** for 2 seconds, **OFF** for 10 seconds, then **ON** again and inspect the system for leaks.

DRIVE TRAIN

Automatic Transmission Assembly

REMOVAL & INSTALLATION

1996 Models

The engine must be supported before removing the transmission assembly in order to prevent the vapor blow pipe located across the rear of the engine from contacting the dash panel.

1. Before servicing the vehicle, refer to the precautions in the beginning of this section.

2. Disconnect the negative battery cable and remove the transmission fluid level indicator.

3. Disconnect the Throttle Valve (TV) cable at the throttle lever or the adjuster assembly.

4. Raise and support the vehicle safely.

5. If equipped, remove the upper and lower underbody braces.

6. Remove the complete exhaust system.

7. Support the transmission with a suitable jack.

8. Remove the driveline support beam.

9. Matchmark and remove the driveshaft.

10. Disengage the speedometer electrical connector, then disconnect the shift control cable and the remaining electrical leads from the transmission.

11. Remove the torque converter cover and mark the relationship of the converter to the flywheel, then remove the converter-to-flywheel bolts.

12. Disconnect the oil cooler pipes at the transmission. Plug the openings to prevent system contamination or excessive fluid loss.

13. Disconnect the TV cable at the transmission.

14. Remove the transmission-to-engine mounting bolts and fasten the torque converter to the transmission using a converter restraining tool or a length of wire.

15. Carefully move the transmission rearward, downward and out from under the vehicle. If interference is encountered with cables, cooler lines, etc., remove the component(s) before finally lowering the transmission.

To install:

16. Flush the transmission oil cooler lines using J-35944 or an equivalent transmission cooler and line flushing tool.

17. Install a converter restraint tool to hold the torque converter in place.

18. Support the transmission with a suitable jack, then raise the transmission into position and remove the torque converter holding tool.

19. Install and tighten the transmission-to-engine bolts to 35 ft. lbs. (47 Nm).

20. Connect the TV cable to the transmission.

21. Remove the plugs, then connect the oil cooler pipes to the transmission.

22. Align the marks made during removal and start the torque converter-to-flywheel bolts by hand. Tighten the bolts to 46 ft. lbs. (62 Nm).

23. Install converter cover and tighten screws to 89 inch lbs. (10 Nm).

24. Engage the electrical connectors to the transmission.

25. Connect the shift control cable.

26. Engage the speedometer electrical connector.

27. Align the marks made earlier and install the driveshaft, then the driveline support beam.

28. Install the exhaust system, if equipped, the underbody braces.

29. Lower the vehicle and install the oil level indicator.

Remove the inspection plug, then remove the flexplate-to-torque converter bolts—1997–00 A/T models

79222642

30. Connect the TV cable to the throttle lever or to the adjuster assembly.

31. Connect the negative battery cable.

32. Check and add the proper type and amount of transmission fluid.

33. Because the driveline support beam was removed, check clearance between the air intake duct and the throttle body. If the air duct becomes dislodged from the throttle body, a driveability problem could occur.

1997–00 Models

1. Before servicing the vehicle, refer to the precautions in the beginning of this section.

2. Disconnect the negative battery cable.

3. Shift the transmission into **Neutral**.

4. Raise and safely support the vehicle.

5. Remove the rear wheels.

6. Remove the intermediate exhaust pipe.

7. Tie the left muffler out of the way and remove the right muffler.

8. Remove the driveshaft tunnel undercover.

9. Remove the bell housing inspection plug using a flat bladed tool.

10. Matchmark the torque converter to the flexplate, them remove the attaching bolts.

11. Remove the two plug bolts from the front of the driveshaft support assembly. Install two M10 x 1.5 x 55mm or longer bolts into the bolt holes. Tighten the bolts to 26 ft. lbs. (35 Nm). These bolts must remain installed until instructed to remove them in order to maintain the position of the input shaft bearing.

12. Rotate the flywheel to gain access to the driveshaft clamp bolt, then loosen it.

13. Shift the transmission into **PARK**, then remove the shifter cable bracket at the transmission. Detach the cable from the transmission linkage.

14. Remove the Electronic Brake Traction

Remove the plugs and install two M10 x 1.5 x 55mm or longer bolts into the bolt holes to secure the bearing—1997–00 A/T models

7922Z643

Rotate the flywheel to gain access to the clamp bolt, then loosen it—1997–00 A/T models

Control Module (EBTCM) and position it out of the way.

15. Remove the rear transverse spring.

16. Support the control arm with a jack. Remove the lower shock absorber mounting from the control arm and the tie rod end and ball joint from the knuckle. Remove the jack. Do this for both control arms.

17. Support the transmission securely with a transmission jack.

18. Remove the transmission-to-differential lower nut.

19. Remove the rear suspension crossmember. Be sure to remove the nuts by hand.

20. Remove the transaxle mount and bracket.

21. Remove the halfshafts from the differential and secure them out of the way.

22. Remove the wiring harness from the driveshaft support. Lower the assembly slightly to gain access to the connectors and detach them.

23. Remove the wiring harness from the differential housing.

✳✳ WARNING

Do not lower the top rear portion of the differential past the bottom of the storage compartment or the PCV pipe will hit the dash panel possibly causing damage.

24. Lower the transmission assembly enough to remove the wiring harness from the top of the assembly.

25. Disconnect the transmission fluid cooler lines at the junction near the bell housing.

26. Support the engine with a block of wood and a jack.

27. Remove the driveshaft support-to-flexplate housing bolts. It may be necessary to bend the wiring harness bracket toward the tunnel wall for greater clearance when removing the driveshaft assembly.

28. Pry the front driveshaft support out of the flexplate housing while an assistant moves the assembly rearward.

29. Carefully lower the assembly away from the vehicle while simultaneously adjusting the angle.

30. Attach a chain hoist to the assembly, then remove it from the jack and place it on a workbench.

31. Remove the driveshaft-to-transmission mounting bolts. Carefully pry the driveshaft assembly away from the transmission.

32. Remove the transmission-to-differential mounting bolts and separate the differential from the transmission. Be careful not to damage the output shaft seal on the differential plate.

To install:

33. If removed, install the differential plate on the transmission. Be sure to position the square-lip seal flush with the transmission case.

34. Install the differential on the transmission. Tighten the bolts and nuts to 37 ft. lbs. (50 Nm).

35. Install the driveshaft support assembly on the transmission. Tighten the fasteners to 37 ft. lbs. (50 Nm).

36. Using a chain hoist, place the assembly on a transmission jack.

37. Carefully raise the assembly into the vehicle while placing the wiring harness loosely into the harness retaining slots.

38. Align the assembly for installation into the engine. The driveshaft will slide into the rear of the engine as long as the angles are the same. Install the driveshaft assembly in the engine. Reposition the wiring harness bracket to align with the appropriate hole in the driveshaft assembly. Tighten the bolts to 37 ft. lbs. (50 Nm).

39. Install the wiring harness on the top of the driveshaft assembly.

40. Connect the fluid cooling lines. Tighten the fittings to 20 ft. lbs. (27 Nm).

41. Install the wiring harness to the left side of the transmission. Reattach the connectors.

42. Raise the transmission to installed height and remove the jack from the engine.

43. Install the suspension crossmember. Tighten the nuts to 81 ft. lbs. (110 Nm).

44. Install the transmission mount to the crossmember. Tighten the nuts to 37 ft. lbs. (50 Nm).

45. Install the transmission-to-differential lower nut. Tighten the nut to 37 ft. lbs. (50 Nm).

46. Assemble the suspension.

47. Install the rear spring.

48. Install the EBTCM in the proper position. Tighten the bracket mounting bolts to 37 ft. lbs. (50 Nm).

49. Install the shifter cable and bracket.

50. Align the matchmarks and install the flexplate-to-torque converter bolts. Tighten the bolts to 47 ft. lbs. (63 Nm). Install the inspection plug.

51. Hand-tighten the driveshaft hub clamp bolt.

52. Remove the two M10 x 1.5 x 55mm long bolts and install the plugs. Tighten the plugs to 37 ft. lbs. (50 Nm).

53. Install the tunnel undercover.

Transmission-to-differential mounting bolt locations—1997–00 A/T models

54. Assemble the exhaust system.

55. Install the rear wheels.

56. Connect the negative battery cable.

57. Start the vehicle and allow it to reach normal operating temperature. Turn the engine **OFF**. Allow the engine to cool to ambient temperature, then tighten the flywheel hub collar bolt to 96 ft. lbs. (130 Nm).

58. Install the bell housing inspection plug.

59. Flush the automatic transmission fluid cooler.

Manual Transmission Assembly

REMOVAL & INSTALLATION

1996 Models

1. Before servicing the vehicle, refer to the precautions in the beginning of this section.

2. Disconnect the negative battery cable.

3. Remove the shifter button, retainer, shift knob, set screw and reverse inhibitor.

4. Remove the rear trim plate screws and the screw located underneath the cup holder mat.

5. Disengage the instrument panel harness connectors from the lighter and rear compartment lid release switch, then unclip the accessory plug harness.

6. Pry the locking tabs on the underside of the boot from the shaft groove, then remove the console trim plate and boot from the shaft.

7. Raise and support the vehicle safely.

8. Remove the complete exhaust assembly.

9. Remove the bolts retaining the driveline torque beam, then slide the beam outboard to gain access to the driveshaft.

10. Remove the parking brake cable clip, then remove the bolts retaining the support bracket.

11. To maintain drive train balance, matchmark the relationship between the driveshaft and the differential carrier yoke, then remove the bolts attaching the driveshaft to the yoke.

12. Slide the driveline torque beam rearward until it make contact with the rear exhaust hanger.

13. Support the transmission using an adjustable transmission jack.

14. Disengage the electrical connectors from the speed sensor, back-up lamp switch and the computer aided shift solenoid.

15. Remove the transmission to clutch housing attaching bolts.

16. Carefully lower the transmission and remove the transmission assembly from the vehicle.

To install:

17. Install transmission assembly into the vehicle.

18. Install and tighten the transmission to clutch housing bolts to 37 ft. lbs. (50 Nm). Be sure to tighten the bolts using the proper crisscross sequence, starting at the top right bolt.

19. Engage the wiring harness connectors to the speed sensor, back-up lamp switch and shift solenoid.

20. Slide the driveline torque beam forward and onto the transmission extension housing.

21. Install the driveshaft, aligning the matchmarks made on the shaft and yoke during removal. Tighten the shaft-to-yoke retaining bolts to 18 ft. lbs. (24 Nm).

22. Install the bolts retaining the support bracket and tighten to 18 ft. lbs. (25 Nm).

23. Check transmission oil level and add if necessary.

➡ **In a horizontal position, the transmission should be filled to the point of overflow.**

24. Install the parking brake cable clip.

25. Align the torque beam and install the retaining bolts. Tighten the beam-to-differential carrier bolt to 60 ft. lbs. (80 Nm) and the beam-to-transmission bolt to 37 ft. lbs. (50 Nm).

26. Install the complete exhaust system assembly.

27. Lower the vehicle.

28. Install the console trim plate and boot assembly.

29. Connect the negative battery cable.

1997–00 Models

1. Before servicing the vehicle, refer to the precautions in the beginning of this section.

2. Disconnect the negative battery cable.

3. Remove the console assembly.

4. Pry out the shift control knob button.

5. Pry out the shift control knob retainer.

6. Unscrew and remove the knob.

7. Remove the boot by grabbing both sides and pulling it in toward the lever.

8. Remove the instrument panel accessory trim plate.

9. Remove the shift control closeout boot, then remove the shift control assembly.

10. Remove the left lower instrument panel trim.

11. Remove the clutch master cylinder pushrod retainer and the pushrod from the pedal.

12. Raise and safely support the vehicle.

13. Detach the clutch hydraulic line from the rear of the engine, then disconnect the hose.

14. Remove the rear wheels.

15. Remove the intermediate pipe and secure the mufflers out of the way.

16. Remove the driveshaft tunnel undercover.

17. Remove the Electronic Brake Traction

Control Module (EBTCM) and position it out of the way.

18. Remove the rear spring.

19. Disconnect the lower shock absorber, tie rod end and lower ball joint.

20. Remove the wiring harness and brake lines from the suspension crossmember.

21. Place a transmission jack under the transmission.

22. Remove the transmission-to-differential lower nut.

23. Remove the transmission mount from the crossmember.

24. Place a jack under the suspension crossmember, remove the mounting nuts and the crossmember.

25. Remove the mount from the differential.

26. Remove the halfshafts from the differential and position them out of the way.

27. Remove the wiring harness from the driveshaft support assembly. Lower the assembly to gain access to the connectors.

28. Remove the harness clip from the top of the differential.

29. Detach the electrical connectors from the transmission.

30. Insert a putty knife or other flat bladed tool between the edge of the shifter bracket and the brake line retainer on the side of the driveshaft tunnel.

✳✳ WARNING

Do not lower the top rear portion of the differential past the bottom of the storage compartment or the PCV pipe will hit the dash panel possibly causing damage.

31. Lower the transmission assembly enough to remove the wiring harness from the top of the assembly.

32. Support the engine with a block of wood and a jack.

33. Remove the driveshaft support-to-bell housing bolts. It may be necessary to bend the wiring harness bracket toward the tunnel wall for greater clearance when removing the driveshaft assembly.

34. Pry the front driveshaft support out of the bell housing while an assistant moves the assembly rearward.

35. Carefully lower the assembly away from the vehicle while simultaneously adjusting the angle.

36. Attach a chain hoist to the assembly, then remove it from the jack and place it on a workbench.

37. Remove the driveshaft-to-transmission mounting bolts. Carefully pry the driveshaft assembly away from the transmission while guiding the shift rod through the opening in the driveshaft support.

38. Remove the roll pin to detach the shift rod from the transmission.

39. Remove the transmission-to-differential mounting bolts and separate the differential from the transmission.

To install:

40. Install the differential on the transmission. Tighten the bolts to 37 ft. lbs. (50 Nm).

41. Install the driveshaft support to the transmission. Tighten the bolts to 37 ft. lbs. (50 Nm).

42. To help connect the shift rod to the shift control assembly, place a rubber band on the shift rod just behind the clamp, then tape the rod to the driveshaft support with masking tape.

43. Place the assembly on the transmission jack with the chain hoist.

44. Begin to raise the assembly into the vehicle while loosely installing the wiring harness along the driveshaft assembly retaining slots.

45. Have an assistant guide the front of the driveshaft to the bell housing.

46. Insert a putty knife or other flat bladed tool between the edge of the shifter bracket and the brake line retainer on the side of the driveshaft tunnel.

47. Be sure the driveshaft assembly is at the same angle as the engine before trying to install it. Carefully push the driveshaft splines into the clutch disc. Turn the shaft with a screwdriver if needed to align the splines. Tighten the bolts to 37 ft. lbs. (50 Nm).

48. Reposition the wiring harness bracket to align with the appropriate hole in the driveshaft assembly.

49. Install the wiring harness to the retainer on the top of the transmission and attach the connectors.

50. Raise the transmission to the installed position. Remove the putty knife and the jack from under the engine.

51. Install the halfshafts in the differential.

52. If removed, install the transmission

79222646

Insert a flat bladed tool between the shifter bracket and brake liner retainer before lowering the transmission assembly—5.7L (VIN G) engine

Driveshaft support-to-transmission mounting—5.7L (VIN G) engine

79222Z647

Place a rubber band on the shift rod, then tape the rod to the driveshaft support assembly—5.7L (VIN G) engine

79222Z648

mount on differential. Tighten the bolts to 37 ft. lbs. (50 Nm).

53. Install the suspension crossmember. Tighten the nuts to 81 ft. lbs. (110 Nm) and remove the jacks. Tighten the transmission mount nuts and the transmission-to-differential lower nut to 37 ft. lbs. (50 Nm).

54. Install the wiring harness and brake line retainers to the suspension crossmember.

55. Assemble the suspension and install the spring.

56. Install the EBTCM in the correct position. Tighten the mounting bracket bolts to 37 ft. lbs. (50 Nm).

57. Ensure that the wiring harness is pulled into the retaining slots along the driveshaft support assembly.

58. Connect the clutch hydraulic line and secure it in the retainer.

59. Install the driveshaft tunnel undercover.

60. Assemble the exhaust system.

Pull the shift rod up to break the tape and hook the rubber band on the rear stud—5.7L (VIN G) engine

79222Z649

61. Install the rear wheels and lower the vehicle.

62. Connect the master cylinder pushrod to the pedal and install the instrument panel trim panel.

63. Pull up the shift rod to break the tape and hook the rubber band on the rear stud on the top of the driveshaft tunnel.

64. Install the shift control assembly. Break the rubber band to remove it.

65. Install the closeout boot. Tighten the nuts to 106 inch lbs. (12 Nm).

66. Install the instrument panel accessory trim plate.

67. Install the boot, knob and retainer and button on the shift lever.

68. Install the console.

69. Connect the negative battery cable.

70. Bleed the clutch system.

Clutch

ADJUSTMENT

1996 Models

The hydraulic clutch system on these models requires no periodic adjustment.

1997–00 Models

1. Before servicing the vehicle, refer to the precautions in the beginning of this section.

2. Raise and safely support the vehicle.

3. Remove the flywheel inspection cover.

4. Have an assistant depress the clutch pedal until the tension is released from the stepped adjusting ring.

5. Using two screwdrivers, rotate the stepped adjusting ring counterclockwise until fully adjusted out.

6. Continue to hold them in this position and have the assistant release the clutch pedal.

Clutch cover assembly torque sequence

7. Remove the screwdrivers.

8. Install the inspection cover and lower the vehicle.

REMOVAL & INSTALLATION

1996 Models

1. Before servicing the vehicle, refer to the precautions in the beginning of this section.

2. Disconnect the negative battery cable, then raise and support the vehicle safely.

3. Remove the complete exhaust system.

4. Remove the transmission assembly.

5. Disconnect the ground wire attached to the left clutch housing stud.

6. Remove the nuts attaching the clutch slave cylinder to the housing and support the cylinder to the side. Do not allow the cylinder to hang freely.

7. Remove the clutch housing cover.

8. Remove the bolts retaining the housing to the engine block.

9. Remove the housing by aligning the fork onto the 2 flats of the release bearing and push the fork away from the bearing with a twisting motion. Remove the clutch housing and the aluminum spacers.

➡**Excessive clutch wear may require removal of the ball stud locking screw and loosening of the ball stud to disengage the fork and housing.**

10. Mark the alignment of the clutch cover and flywheel for installation purposes.

11. Loosen the clutch cover bolts evenly, one turn at a time until spring pressure is released. Failure to properly release spring pressure may result in damage to the clutch cover assembly and the flywheel.

12. Remove the clutch plate and disc assembly.

To install:

13. Inspect flywheel, clutch plate and disc for heat stress, cracks or worn parts and replace as necessary.

14. Install the clutch assembly using a suitable universal clutch disc alignment tool.

15. Be sure the marks made earlier are in alignment, then install the cover assembly-to-flywheel bolts. Tighten the bolts in the proper sequence, one turn at a time, until spring pressure is properly attained and the bolts are tightened to 30 ft. lbs. (41 Nm).

16. Position the clutch housing to the engine block and engage the fork onto the release bearing. If equipped, be sure the aluminum spacer is in position.

17. Verify the housing is properly positioned on the 2 engine dowel pins.

18. Tighten the clutch housing bolts to 37 ft. lbs. (50 Nm) and the ball stud to 33 ft. lbs. (45 Nm). Tighten the ball stud locking screw to 11 ft. lbs. (15 Nm).

19. If equipped, install the ground harness connection to the housing.

20. Install the housing cover and tighten the bolts to 80 inch lbs. (9 Nm).

21. Install the clutch slave cylinder and tighten the retaining nuts to 19 ft. lbs. (25 Nm).

22. Install the transmission assembly.

23. Install the exhaust system and lower the vehicle.

24. Connect the battery negative cable and check clutch for proper operation.

1997–00 Models

1. Before servicing the vehicle, refer to the precautions in the beginning of this section.

2. Disconnect the negative battery cable.

3. Raise and safely support the vehicle.

4. Remove the exhaust system.

5. Remove the driveshaft support and transmission as an assembly.

6. Remove the inspection cover.

7. Remove the pressure plate bolts. It will be necessary to rotate the flywheel to access all the bolts.

8. Remove the pressure plate and disc.

To install:

9. Adjust the pressure plate using the following sub-steps:

   a. Place the pressure plate assembly on a press.

   b. Compress the diaphragm fingers until the tension is released from the stepped adjusting ring.

   c. Using two screwdrivers, rotate the stepped adjusting ring counterclockwise until fully adjusted out.

   d. Continue to hold them in this position and releasing the press.

   e. Remove the screwdrivers.

Spring stop   **Spring stops**

There are three stepped adjusting ring tension spring stops on the pressure plate assembly— 1997–00 models

Turn to Section 6 for brake system applications

Rotate the stepped adjusting ring counterclockwise to compress the springs—1997–00 models

79222652

10. Position the clutch disc and pressure plate on the flywheel.

11. Install the clutch disc alignment tool through the disc to keep it in place.

12. Install the pressure plate bolts finger-tight. Turn the flywheel to access all the bolt holes.

13. Tighten the bolts evenly using three steps to 37 ft. lbs. (50 Nm).

14. Remove the alignment tool and install the inspection cover.

15. Install the driveshaft support and transmission assembly.

16. Install the exhaust system.

17. Connect the negative battery cable.

18. Bleed the clutch system.

Hydraulic Clutch System

BLEEDING

1996 Models

1. Before servicing the vehicle, refer to the precautions in the beginning of this section.

2. Disconnect the negative battery cable

and remove the Electronic Control Module (ECM) from the mounting bracket to access the master cylinder for filling. Fill the master cylinder reservoir with the proper grade and type of fresh brake fluid or hydraulic clutch fluid.

3. Prior to bleeding the actuator, most of the air can be removed as follows:

   a. Remove the master cylinder cap and moisture barrier.

   b. Install the master cylinder cover.

   c. Lightly stroke the clutch pedal to release trapped air through the master cylinder.

   d. Remove the master cylinder cap and install the moisture barrier.

   e. Install the master cylinder cap.

4. Raise and support the vehicle safely.

5. Remove the actuator cylinder attaching stud nuts.

6. Remove the pushrod and actuator cylinder from the clutch housing and the hydraulic line from the retaining clip.

7. Lower cylinder slightly for access and disconnect the hydraulic hose fitting from the actuator cylinder.

8. Remove the bleed screw dust cap.

9. Position a drain pan or attach a clear plastic hose.

10. Support the slave cylinder in a hori-

zontal position, with the bleeder screw vertical.

11. Fully depress the clutch pedal and open the bleeder screw.

12. Close the bleed screw and release the clutch pedal.

13. Repeat Steps 11 and 12 until all the air is expelled from the system. Check the fluid reservoir and replenish, as required during the procedure. Be sure the reservoir is kept sufficiently full to prevent air from being drawn into the system.

14. Tighten the bleeder screw and install the dust cover.

15. Install the hydraulic line into the retaining clip, position the actuator cylinder and tighten the stud nuts to 19 ft. lbs. (25 Nm).

16. Lower the vehicle.

17. Install the ECM and connect the negative battery cable.

1997–00 Models

1. Before servicing the vehicle, refer to the precautions in the beginning of this section.

2. Fill the clutch master cylinder with clutch hydraulic fluid PN12345347 or equivalent.

3. Raise and safely support the vehicle with an assistant in it.

4. Remove the intermediate exhaust pipe.

5. Remove the driveshaft tunnel undercover.

6. Have the assistant depress and hold the clutch pedal down.

7. Loosen the bleeder screw on the actuator cylinder to release the air, then tighten the screw. Do not allow the clutch pedal to be released until the bleeder screw is closed or air will be drawn into the system.

8. Repeat steps 6 and 7 until the air has been purged from the system. Check the master cylinder fluid level often and refill as needed during the procedure.

9. Install the driveshaft tunnel undercover.

10. Install the intermediate exhaust pipe.

11. Lower the vehicle to the floor.

Halfshaft

REMOVAL & INSTALLATION

1996 Models

1. Before servicing the vehicle, refer to the precautions in the beginning of this section.

2. Raise and safely support the vehicle.

3. Remove the rear transverse spring from the knuckle.

4. Remove the tie rod end from the knuckle.

5. Remove the spindle rod mounting bracket from the differential.

6. Matchmark the U-joint to the yokes, then remove the halfshaft universal joint retainers at both ends of the shaft.

7. Push the wheel assembly outward while supporting the halfshaft, then remove the shaft.

To install:

8. Hold the wheel assembly outward and place the shaft in position. Be sure to align the marks made earlier. Tighten the retaining bolts to 26 ft. lbs. (35 Nm).

9. Install the spindle rod bracket on the differential carrier. Tighten the bolts to 59 ft. lbs. (80 Nm).

10. Connect the tie rod end to the knuckle. Tighten the nut to 33 ft. lbs. (45 Nm).

11. Install the spring to the knuckle. Tighten the nut until the slot in the nut aligns with the hole in the bolt, then insert the cotter pin.

12. Lower the vehicle to the floor.

1997–00 Models

1. Before servicing the vehicle, refer to the precautions in the beginning of this section.

2. Shift the transmission into **PARK** or **NEUTRAL** for manual transmissions.

3. Apply the parking brake and raise the vehicle.

4. Remove the rear wheel.

5. Insert a large drift through the brake rotor cooling fins to prevent the hub assembly from turning, then remove the axle nut.

6. Release the parking brake.

7. Remove the rear leaf spring.

8. Disconnect the outer tie rod end from the knuckle and position it to the rear.

9. Disconnect the ABS wheel speed sensor.

10. Disconnect the parking brake cable from the lever and bracket.

➡ **Be sure to support the halfshaft until it is removed. Don't let it hang by the Constant Velocity (CV) joint.**

11. Attach a puller such as J 42129 on the wheel studs and start to push the axle shaft into the hub assembly. This will provide clearance for the ball joint to be separated from the knuckle assembly.

Insert a large drift through the cooling fins to keep the hub assembly from turning while removing the retaining nut—1997–00 models

Exploded view of the halfshaft mounting—1997–00 models

Disconnect the ball joint from the knuckle, then continue to disengage the axle shaft from the hub assembly.

12. Support the knuckle and upper control arm while positioning it toward the front.

13. Disengage the halfshaft assembly from the differential by inserting a suitable tool between the CV joint and differential and prying them apart.

To install:

14. Install the halfshaft on the differential output shaft. Use light force to be sure it is fully seated.

15. Begin to install the halfshaft through the hub assembly but do not install completely. This will provide clearance for installing the ball joint.

16. Install the ball joint to the knuckle and insert the halfshaft through the hub assembly completely.

17. Install the parking brake cable and connect the ABS wheel speed sensor.

18. Connect the tie rod end to the knuckle.

19. Install the rear spring.

20. Install the halfshaft retaining nut. Tighten the nut to 118 ft. lbs. (160 Nm).

21. Install the rear wheel and lower the vehicle to the floor.

STEERING AND SUSPENSION

Air Bag

❊❊ CAUTION

All vehicles are equipped with an air bag system, also known as the Supplemental Inflatable Restraint (SIR) or Supplemental Restraint System (SRS). The system must be disabled before performing service on or around system components, steering column, instrument panel components, wiring and sensors. Failure to follow safety and disabling procedures could result in accidental air bag deployment, possible personal injury and unnecessary system repairs.

PRECAUTIONS

Several precautions must be observed when handling the inflator module to avoid accidental deployment and possible personal injury.

• Never carry the inflator module by the wires or connector on the underside of the module.

• When carrying a live inflator module, hold securely with both hands, and ensure that the bag and trim cover are pointed away.

• Place the inflator module on a bench or other surface with the bag and trim cover facing up.

• With the inflator module on the bench, never place anything on or close to the module which may be thrown in the event of an accidental deployment.

DISARMING

1. Before servicing the vehicle, refer to the precautions in the beginning of this section.

2. Turn the steering wheel to align the wheels in the straight-ahead position.

3. Turn the ignition switch to the **LOCK** position.

4. Remove the AIR BAG fuse from the fuse block.

5. Remove the left side lower trim panel, then unplug the Connector Position Assurance (CPA) device and the yellow 2-way SIR harness wire connector at the base of the steering column.

After the necessary repairs have been made, re-enable the air bag system as follows:

6. Turn the ignition switch to the **LOCK** position.

7. Engage the yellow 2-way connector and the CPA device at the base of the steering column.

8. Install the left side lower trim panel, then install the SIR fuse to the fuse block.

9. Turn the ignition switch to the **RUN** position.

10. Verify the SIR indicator light flashes 7–9 times, then turns OFF. If not, inspect system for malfunction.

Power Rack and Pinion Steering Gear

REMOVAL & INSTALLATION

1996 Models

1. Before servicing the vehicle, refer to the precautions in the beginning of this section.

2. Disconnect the negative battery cable and position a drain pan under the vehicle to catch fluid.

3. For VIN P engine, remove the air intake duct, then remove the serpentine drive belt and the drive belt idler pulley.

4. Remove the power steering gear inlet hose assembly from the steering gear.

5. Remove the power steering gear outlet hose assembly from the steering gear.

➡ **If equipped with a power steering fluid cooling pipe, disconnect fluid cooling pipe outlet hose from the fluid cooling pipe.**

6. Remove the steering gear coupling shield.

7. Disconnect the intermediate shaft from the power steering gear and lower steering shaft, then position aside.

8. Raise and support the vehicle safely.

9. Remove the front tire and wheel assemblies.

10. Remove both outer tie rods from the knuckles using a suitable puller.

11. If equipped, remove the power steering cooler assembly.

12. Remove the stabilizer shaft.

13. Remove the steering gear to frame attaching clamp nuts, then remove the bolts and clamp from the vehicle.

14. Remove the power steering gear attaching nut and bolt.

15. Remove the power steering gear from the vehicle.

16. If necessary, remove the outer tie rods, rack and pinion boots, and the inner tie rods from the power steering gear.

To install:

17. If removed, install the inner tie rods, boots and outer tie rods.

18. Install the power steering gear, nuts and bolts. Tighten the attaching nut to 30 ft. lbs. (40 Nm). Tighten the steering gear clamp nuts to 18 ft. lbs. (25 Nm).

19. Install the stabilizer shaft, if applicable, the power steering cooler assembly.

20. Install both outer tie rods to the steering knuckle.

21. Install tire and wheel assemblies, then lower the vehicle.

22. Install the intermediate shaft and the steering gear coupling shield.

23. Install the power steering gear outlet and inlet hose assemblies to the power steering gear. Tighten fittings to 21 ft. lbs. (28 Nm).

24. For VIN P engine, install the drive belt idler pulley and the serpentine drive belt, then install the air intake duct.

25. Remove the drain and fill the power steering reservoir.

26. Connect the negative battery cable, bleed the system and check for proper operation.

1997–00 Models

1. Before servicing the vehicle, refer to the precautions in the beginning of this section.
2. Disconnect the negative battery cable.
3. Drain the power steering fluid into a suitable container.
4. Remove the intermediate shaft cover.
5. Disconnect the inlet hose from the steering gear.
6. Remove the steering fluid cooler tube from the steering gear.
7. Remove the lower steering coupling from the steering gear input shaft.
8. Raise and safely support the vehicle.
9. Remove the front wheels and disconnect the tie rod ends from the knuckles.
10. Detach the magnasteer electrical connector.
11. Remove the stabilizer bar.
12. Remove the steering gear mounting bolt and the steering gear through the left wheel opening.

To install:

13. Install the steering gear to the crossmember. Tighten the nuts to 74 ft. lbs. (100 Nm).
14. Install the stabilizer bar.
15. Connect the tie rods to the knuckles. Tighten the nuts to 33 ft. lbs. (45 Nm).
16. Connect the lower steering coupling to the steering gear input shaft.
17. Attach the magnasteer electrical connector.
18. Install the fluid cooler on the steering gear. Tighten the fitting to 20 ft. lbs. (27 Nm).
19. Connect the inlet hose to the steering gear. Hold the hose against the steering gear while tightening the fitting to 20 ft. lbs. (27 Nm).
20. Install the intermediate shaft cover.
21. Install the front wheels.
22. Lower the vehicle to the floor.
23. Connect the negative battery cable.
24. Refill and bleed the power steering system.
25. Check the toe angle of the front wheels and adjust them if necessary.

Shock Absorber

REMOVAL & INSTALLATION

Front

WITHOUT SELECTIVE RIDE CONTROL

1. Before servicing the vehicle, refer to the precautions in the beginning of this section.
2. Raise and support the vehicle safely.
3. Remove the tire and wheel assemblies.
4. Disconnect the shock absorber from the lower control arm and the shock tower. If necessary, remove the front wheelhousing lower center panel to access the upper mount nut.
5. Remove the insulator and retainers from the shock absorber and the shock absorber from the vehicle.
6. Installation is the reverse of the removal procedure. Tighten the upper and lower mount nuts to 19 ft. lbs. (26 Nm).

WITH SELECTIVE RIDE CONTROL

1. Before servicing the vehicle, refer to the precautions in the beginning of this section.
2. Disconnect the negative battery cable.
3. Raise and safely support vehicle, then remove the tire and wheel assemblies.
4. Safely support the lower control arm with a jackstand.
5. Remove the actuator retaining clip, then remove the actuator from the cup retainer. Note the position of the actuator electrical leads for installation purposes.
6. Remove the shock absorber upper mounting nuts.
7. Remove the cup retainer, then the upper insulator retainer and insulator.
8. Remove the shock absorber lower mounting bolts, nuts, then compress the shock absorber and remove it from the vehicle. If necessary, remove the lower insulator from the shock.

To install:

9. If removed, install the lower insulator to the shock absorber, compress the shock and install into the vehicle.
10. Install the shock absorber lower mounting nuts and bolts, then tighten the bolts to 19 ft. lbs. (26 Nm).
11. Install the upper insulator and retainer, then install the cup assembly retainer.
12. Install the upper mounting nut and tighten the 31 ft. lbs. (42 Nm). The selector gear should be at least 0.178 in. (4.5mm) above the top of the cup assembly retainer.
13. Install and properly seat the actuator retaining clip onto the cup assembly retainer. Be sure the ends of the actuator clip protrude outward from the retainer.
14. Install the actuator onto the cup assembly retainer with the electrical leads in the same position as noted earlier. Verify that there is at least 0.315 in. (8mm) of clearance between the front wheelhousing lower center panel and the actuator electrical leads.

79222655

Exploded view of the power steering gear mounting—1997–00 models

Exploded view of the front shock absorber mounting—1997–00 models

➤**Very little effort is required to snap the actuator onto the retainer, do not force it into position.**

15. Remove the jackstand, then install the tire and wheel assembly.

16. Lower the vehicle and connect the negative battery cable.

Rear

WITHOUT SELECTIVE RIDE CONTROL

1. Before servicing the vehicle, refer to the precautions in the beginning of this section.

2. Raise and support the vehicle safely. Support the knuckle with a jackstand.

3. Remove the shock absorber lower mounting nut and washer.

4. Remove the shock absorber upper bracket mounting bolt.

5. Disconnect the shock absorber from the lower mounting stud.

6. If necessary, remove the shock absorber upper bracket retaining nut and remove the bracket assembly.

7. Installation is the reverse of the removal procedure.

8. Tighten the upper bracket retaining nut, if removed, to 19 ft. lbs. (26 Nm). With the suspension at proper trim height, tighten the upper bracket mounting bolts to 22 ft. lbs. (30 Nm) and the lower mounting nut to 61 ft. lbs. (83 Nm).

WITH SELECTIVE RIDE CONTROL

1. Before servicing the vehicle, refer to the precautions in the beginning of this section.

2. Disconnect the negative battery cable.

3. Raise and support the vehicle safely.

4. Support the rear knuckle with a jackstand.

5. Disconnect the shock absorber lower mounting nut and washer.

6. Remove the shock absorber upper bracket mounting bolt.

7. Disconnect the shock absorber from the mounting stud and support. Do not allow the shock to hang from the actuator harness.

8. Remove the actuator retaining clip and remove the actuator from the shock.

9. Remove the shock absorber from the vehicle.

To install:

10. Install and properly seat the actuator retaining clip onto the cup assembly. The ends of the clip should protrude from the cup.

11. Install the shock absorber electrical actuator into the cup assembly retainer. The actuator should be snapped, not be forced into position.

12. Verify that a minimum of 0.178 in. (4.5mm) of clearance exists between the selector gear and the top of the cup assembly retainer.

13. Position the shock absorber into the frame and onto the lower mounting stud.

14. Install the shock absorber upper bracket mounting bolt.

15. With the suspension held at the proper trim height. Tighten the upper bracket mounting bolts to 22 ft. lbs. (30 Nm) and the lower mounting nut to 61 ft. lbs. (83 Nm).

16. Lower the vehicle to the floor.

17. Connect the negative battery cable.

Upper Ball Joint

REMOVAL & INSTALLATION

1996 Models

1. Before servicing the vehicle, refer to the precautions in the beginning of this section.

2. Raise and support the vehicle safely.

3. Safely support the lower control arm with a jackstand.

4. Remove the tire and wheel assemblies.

5. Using J-33436 or equivalent ball joint removal tool, separate the ball joint from the knuckle.

6. Remove the upper ball joint from the control arm as follows:

    a. Center punch the rivet.

    b. Drill a pilot hole, then drill the rivet head.

    c. Punch out the rivet.

To install:

7. Install a new ball joint into the upper control arm and position so the cotter pin can be installed from the rear to the front of the vehicle.

8. Install and tighten the mounting nuts to 13 ft. lbs. (18 Nm).

9. Position the ball stud into the steering knuckle, then install the upper ball joint stud washer and nut. Tighten the upper control arm ball stud nut to 33 ft. lbs. (45 Nm). Tighten the nut additionally as necessary to insert the cotter pin but do not exceed 63 ft. lbs. (85 Nm).

10. Install a new cotter pin from the rear to the front of the vehicle.

11. Remove the jackstand and lubricate the ball joint.

12. Install the tire and wheel assembly, then lower the vehicle.

1997–00 Models

The upper ball joint is a part of the steering knuckle assembly and must be replaced as a complete unit. Refer to the steering knuckle procedure.

Steering Knuckle

REMOVAL & INSTALLATION

1. Before servicing the vehicle, refer to the precautions in the beginning of this section.

2. Raise and safely support the vehicle.

3. Remove the front wheel.

4. Remove the brake caliper and rotor.

5. Detach the wheel speed sensor electrical connector.

6. Support the lower control arm using a jack.

7. Disconnect the tie rod end from the steering knuckle using a ball joint separator.

8. Separate the upper ball joint stud from the upper control arm with a ball joint separator.

9. Separate the lower ball joint stud from the steering knuckle.

Exploded view of the steering knuckle removal—1997–00 models

10. Remove the knuckle from the vehicle.

To install:

11. Install the knuckle on the lower control arm ball joint stud. Tighten the nut to 55 ft. lbs. (75 Nm).

12. Install the upper ball joint stud in the upper control arm. Tighten the nut to 44 ft. lbs. (60 Nm).

13. Remove the jack from the lower control arm.

14. Connect the tie rod end to the steering knuckle. Tighten the nut to 33 ft. lbs. (45 Nm).

15. Attach the wheel speed sensor electrical connector.

16. Install the brake rotor and caliper.

17. Install the front wheel and lower the vehicle to the floor.

18. Check and adjust the wheel alignment if necessary.

Lower Ball Joint

REMOVAL & INSTALLATION

1996 Models

1. Before servicing the vehicle, refer to the precautions in the beginning of this section.

2. Raise and support the vehicle safely.

3. Safely support the lower control arm with a jackstand.

4. Remove the tire and wheel assembly.

5. Using J-33436 or equivalent ball joint removal tool, separate the ball joint from the knuckle.

6. Press the upper ball joint from the control arm using tool J-9519-E or an equivalent removal tool.

To install:

7. Position the ball stud so the cotter pin may be installed from the rear to the front of the vehicle and press into the control arm using J-9519-E or equivalent.

8. Position the ball joint into the steering knuckle, then install the washer and nut. Tighten the lower control arm ball stud nut to 50 ft. lbs. (68 Nm). Tighten the ball stud nut additionally, as necessary to insert a cotter pin, but do not exceed 88 ft. lbs. (120 Nm) to align the cotter pin holes.

9. Install a new cotter pin from the rear to the front of the vehicle.

10. Remove the jackstand and lubricate the ball joint.

11. Install the tire and wheel assembly, then lower the vehicle.

Spring compressor mounted on the transverse spring—1997–00 models

1997–00 Models

The lower ball joint is an integral part of the lower control arm. If the ball joint is bad, a new lower control arm must be installed.

Lower Control Arm

REMOVAL & INSTALLATION

1. Before servicing the vehicle, refer to the precautions in the beginning of this section.

2. Raise and safely support the vehicle.

3. Remove the front wheel.

4. Install a transverse leaf spring compressor on the front spring and compress the spring.

5. Support the control arm with a jack and remove the lower shock absorber mounting bolts from the control arm to be replaced.

6. Remove the stabilizer bar link from the control arm to be replaced.

7. Separate the lower control arm ball joint stud from the knuckle.

8. Mark the position of the cam bolts attaching the lower control arm to the frame for reference when installing the control arm.

9. Remove the cam bolts and the lower control arm.

To install:

10. Install the control arm to the frame. Align the marks made during removal but do not tighten the cam bolts completely at this time.

Lower control arm mounting bolts— 1997–00 models

11. Install the ball joint stud to the steering knuckle. Tighten the nut to 44 ft. lbs. (60 Nm).

12. Support the control arm with a jack and install the lower shock absorber mounting bolts. Tighten the nuts to 21 ft. lbs. (28 Nm).

13. Install the stabilizer link to the control arm. Tighten the nut to 55 ft. lbs. (75 Nm).

14. Remove the spring compressor from the transverse spring.

15. Install the front wheel and remove the jack from under the control arm.

16. Perform a front wheel alignment. Tighten the lower control arm nuts to 125 ft. lbs. (170 Nm).

Wheel Bearings

ADJUSTMENT

No periodic wheel bearing adjustment is necessary. The wheel bearings are a sealed unit which must be replaced if loosed or noisy.

REMOVAL & INSTALLATION

Front

1. Before servicing the vehicle, refer to the precautions in the beginning of this section.

2. Disconnect the negative battery cable, then raise and support the vehicle safely.

3. Remove the tire and wheel assembly.

4. Remove the caliper and support it aside, then remove the rotor.

5. Disengage the ABS speed sensor electrical connector.

6. Remove the ABS speed sensor cable bracket.

Exploded view of the front hub/wheel bearing and knuckle assembly—1997–00 models

79222Z657

7. Remove the wheel hub/bearing/speed sensor assembly.

To install:

8. Install the hub/bearing/speed sensor assembly onto the vehicle. Be sure the speed sensor cable connection is facing rearward.

9. Tighten the assembly mounting nuts to 46 ft. lbs. (62 Nm).

10. Engage the ABS electrical connector and install the cable bracket.

11. Install the brake rotor and caliper.

12. Install the tire and wheel assembly, then lower the vehicle.

13. Connect the negative battery cable. The bearings do not require adjustment.

Rear

1996 MODELS

1. Before servicing the vehicle, refer to the precautions in the beginning of this section.

2. Disconnect the negative battery cable, then raise and support the vehicle safely.

3. Remove the tire and wheel assembly.

4. Remove the wheel speed sensor.

5. Remove the brake caliper and parking brake assembly, then remove the rotor.

6. Remove the wheel hub mounting bolts.

7. Remove the cotter pin, wheel nut retainer, spindle nut and washer.

8. Remove the wheel hub and bearing, caliper mounting plate and wheel spindle washer from the vehicle.

To install:

9. Inspect the wheel hub and bearing seal, replace if necessary. Also inspect the wheel spindle washer and replace, if damaged or excessively worn.

10. Install the wheel hub and bearing, caliper mounting plate and the wheel spindle washer. The washer flat should firmly seat against the shoulder of the wheel spindle. The lip of the washer should face the wheel spindle splines prior to hub and bearing installation.

11. Install the wheel hub mounting bolts and tighten to 66 ft. lbs. (90 Nm).

12. Install the washer and spindle nut, then tighten the nut to 164 ft. lbs. (223 Nm). The vehicle should not rest on the tires or move until the spindle nut is tightened.

13. Install the wheel retainer and a new cotter pin.

14. Install the brake rotor, then install the caliper and parking brake assembly.

15. Install the wheel speed sensor, then install the wheel and tire assembly.

16. Lower the vehicle and connect the negative battery cable.

1997–00 MODELS

1. Before servicing the vehicle, refer to the precautions in the beginning of this section.

2. Raise and safely support the vehicle.

3. Remove the rear wheel.

4. Disconnect the wheel speed sensor.

5. Remove the brake caliper and rotor.

6. Disconnect the tie rod end from the knuckle.

7. Remove the halfshaft retaining nut and washer.

8. Disconnect the knuckle from the upper and lower control arms and remove the knuckle.

9. Remove the hub mounting bolts and remove the bearing assembly from the knuckle.

To install:

10. Install the bearing assembly on the knuckle. Tighten the mounting bolts to 70 ft. lbs. (95 Nm).

11. Install the knuckle assembly to the upper and lower control arms.

12. Install the halfshaft retaining nut.

13. Connect the tie rod end to the knuckle.

14. Install the brake rotor and caliper.

15. Connect the wheel speed sensor and install the rear wheel.

16. Lower the vehicle to the floor.

Exploded view of the rear hub/wheel bearing and knuckle assembly—1997–00 models

79222Z658

GEO/CHEVROLET

Geo/Chevrolet-Metro • Prizm

40

PRECAUTIONS

Before servicing any vehicle, please be sure to read all of the following precautions, which deal with personal safety, prevention of component damage, and important points to take into consideration when servicing a motor vehicle:

• Never open, service or drain the radiator or cooling system when the engine is hot; serious burns can occur from the steam and hot coolant.

• Observe all applicable safety precautions when working around fuel. Whenever servicing the fuel system, always work in a well-ventilated area. Do not allow fuel spray or vapors to come in contact with a spark, open flame, or excessive heat (a hot drop light, for example). Keep a dry chemical fire extinguisher near the work area. Always keep fuel in a container specifically designed for fuel storage; also, always properly seal fuel containers to avoid the possibility of fire or explosion. Refer to the additional fuel system precautions later in this section.

• Fuel injection systems often remain pressurized, even after the engine has been turned **OFF**. The fuel system pressure must be relieved before disconnecting any fuel lines. Failure to do so may result in fire and/or personal injury.

• Brake fluid often contains polyglycol ethers and polyglycols. Avoid contact with the eyes and wash your hands thoroughly after handling brake fluid. If you do get brake fluid in your eyes, flush your eyes with clean, running water for 15 minutes. If eye irritation persists, or if you have taken brake fluid internally, IMMEDIATELY seek medical assistance.

• The EPA warns that prolonged contact with used engine oil may cause a number of skin disorders, including cancer! You

should make every effort to minimize your exposure to used engine oil. Protective gloves should be worn when changing oil. Wash your hands and any other exposed skin areas as soon as possible after exposure to used engine oil. Soap and water, or waterless hand cleaner should be used.

• All new vehicles are now equipped with an air bag system, often referred to as a Supplemental Restraint System (SRS) or Supplemental Inflatable Restraint (SIR) system. The system must be disabled before performing service on or around system components, steering column, instrument panel components, wiring and sensors. Failure to follow safety and disabling procedures could result in accidental air bag deployment, possible personal injury and unnecessary system repairs.

• Always wear safety goggles when working with, or around, the air bag system. When carrying a non-deployed air bag, be sure the bag and trim cover are pointed away from your body. When placing a non-deployed air bag on a work surface, always face the bag and trim cover upward, away from the surface. This will reduce the motion of the module if it is accidentally deployed. Refer to the additional air bag system precautions later in this section.

• Clean, high quality brake fluid from a sealed container is essential to the safe and proper operation of the brake system. You should always buy the correct type of brake fluid for your vehicle. If the brake fluid becomes contaminated, completely flush the system with new fluid. Never reuse any brake fluid. Any brake fluid that is removed from the system should be discarded. Also, do not allow any brake fluid to come in contact with a painted surface; it will damage the paint.

• Never operate the engine without the proper amount and type of engine oil; doing so WILL result in severe engine damage.

• Timing belt maintenance is extremely important! Many models utilize an interference-type, non-freewheeling engine. If the timing belt breaks, the valves in the cylinder head may strike the pistons, causing potentially serious (also time-consuming and expensive) engine damage. Refer to the maintenance interval charts in the front of this manual for the recommended replacement interval for the timing belt, and to the timing belt section for belt replacement and inspection.

• Disconnecting the negative battery cable on some vehicles may interfere with the functions of the on-board computer system(s) and may require the computer to undergo a relearning process once the negative battery cable is reconnected.

• When servicing drum brakes, only dissemble and assemble one side at a time, leaving the remaining side intact for reference.

ENGINE REPAIR

Distributor

REMOVAL

1. Before servicing the vehicle, refer to the precautions in the beginning of this section.

2. Disconnect the negative battery cable.

3. Tag and disconnect the spark plug wires, wiring harness and vacuum line at the distributor, if equipped.

4. Remove the distributor cap.

5. Mark the position of the distributor rotor in relation to the distributor body. Mark the position of the distributor body in relation to the cylinder head.

6. Mark the distributor position on the housing and engine. Remove the hold-down bolt(s) and the distributor from the cylinder head. Do not rotate the engine after the distributor has been removed.

7. Remove the distributor from the engine and remove the O-ring from the distributor shaft.

8. Inspect all components of the assembly, including the cap and rotor, for cracks, terminal corrosion or wear and replace, if necessary.

INSTALLATION

Timing Not Disturbed

1. Align the reference marks made during removal. Position carefully and be sure the drive gear engages properly within the slot. Install the hold-down bolts but do not tighten.

2. Reconnect the wiring and the plug wires. Connect vacuum hoses, if equipped.

3. Install the distributor cap. Connect the battery negative cable. Check and/or adjust the ignition timing.

4. Tighten the distributor hold-down bolt(s).

Timing Disturbed

1. Remove the No. 1 spark plug.

2. Place a thumb over the spark plug hole. Have someone rotate the engine by hand, using a wrench on the crankshaft pulley, until compression is felt.

3. Align the timing mark on the crankshaft pulley with the **0** degrees mark on the timing scale attached to the front of the engine. This places the engine at Top Dead Center (TDC) on the compression stroke.

4. Turn the distributor shaft until the rotor points to the No. 1 spark plug tower on the cap.

1. Distributor
2. Distributor mounting bolts

7922Z701

Be sure to tighten the distributor mounting bolts to prevent the timing from changing—Prizm

5. Install the distributor to the cylinder head, aligning the distributor housing-to-cylinder head marks made during the removal procedure.

6. Connect the spark plug wires, electrical wires and vacuum advance hose, if equipped.

7. Install the distributor cap.

8. Reconnect the negative battery cable.

9. Check and/or adjust ignition timing.

10. Tighten the distributor hold-down bolt.

Ignition Timing

ADJUSTMENT

➡ **The ignition timing on the Prizm models is not adjustable.**

Metro

1. Before servicing the vehicle, refer to the precautions in the beginning of this section.

2. Run the engine until it reaches normal operating temperature. Stop the engine, but keep the ignition switch in the **ON** position for approximately 5 seconds. Start the engine again.

3. Run the engine at 2000 RPM for approximately 5 minutes. After 5 minutes, allow it to run at idle speed.

4. Be sure all accessories are turned **OFF**.

A. Blank (cavity 1)
B. Diagnostic request terminal (cavity 2)
C. Diagnostic output terminal (cavity 3)
D. Ground terminal(cavity 4)
E. Test switch terminal(cavity 5)
F. Duty check terminal(cavity 6)
1. Duty check DLC
2. Jumper

7922Z702

Jumping terminals in the six terminal Data Link Connector (DLC)—Metro models

5. Fully engage the parking brake.

6. Be sure the shift lever is placed in the **NEUTRAL** or **PARK** depending on transaxle type.

7. Connect a tachometer to the negative terminal of the ignition coil for 1.0L and 1.3L engines, or to the **IG** terminal in the Data Link Connector (DLC), located next to the left strut tower for 1.6L and 1.8L engines. Connect a timing light to the No. 1 spark plug wire. Check the engine idle speed and adjust if needed.

8. Refer to the underhood vehicle emission control information label for ignition timing specifications.

9. Remove the cap from the diagnostic check connector, located next to the ignition coil or left side strut tower, and insert a fused jumper wire between appropriate the terminals.

10. For 1.0L and 1.3L engines, proceed as follows:

a. On four terminal connectors, hold the connector with the locking tab at the top and jump the lower two terminals (**C** and **D**).

b. On six terminal connectors, hold the connector with the locking tab at the top and jump the two terminals at the lower left (**D** and **E**).

11. For 1.6L and 1.8L engines, proceed as follows:

a. Using a fused jumper wire, connect terminals **E1** and **TE1** together at the DLC.

12. Aim the timing light at the timing marks.

13. Loosen the distributor hold-down bolt and rotate the distributor until the correct timing marks are aligned.

14. Tighten the distributor hold-down bolt to 11–15 ft. lbs. (15–20 Nm) and recheck the timing. Be sure the timing advances according to engine speed.

15. Remove the diagnostic check jumper. Remove the timing light and tachometer.

Prizm

➡ **If the ignition timing is out of specification, a possible engine electrical failure may have occurred. The following procedure may be used to check the timing:**

1. Before servicing the vehicle, refer to the precautions in the beginning of this section.

2. Warm the engine to normal operating temperature. Turn all electrical accessories OFF.

+B	**SYSTEM VOLTAGE**
E1	**GROUND TERMINAL**
FP	**FUEL PUMP TERMINAL**
TE1	**DIAGNOSTIC REQUEST TERMINAL**
W	**MALFUNCTION INDICATOR LAMP (MIL) TERMINAL**
600	**DATA LINK CONNECTOR (DLC) (UNDER HOOD)**

79222Z703

DLC pin locations—Prizm models

3. Connect a tachometer or engine scan tool and check the engine idle speed and be sure it is 650–750 rpm.

4. Connect a timing light. Remove the cap on the Data Link Connector (DLC). Using a fused jumper wire, connect terminals **E1** and **TE1**.

5. Start the engine and check timing. With the jumper wire connected, the timing should be at 10 degrees BTDC.

6. Remove the jumper wire from the DLC and reinstall the cap.

7. Shut the engine **OFF** and disconnect all test equipment.

Engine Assembly

REMOVAL & INSTALLATION

Metro

1. Before servicing the vehicle, refer to the precautions in the beginning of this section.

2. Properly relieve the fuel system pressure. Disconnect the negative battery cable.

3. Scribe a hood hinge-to-hood outline, then, with the aid of an assistant remove the hood.

4. Drain the cooling system.

5. Remove the air cleaner. Remove the radiator and cooling fan.

6. Label and unplug the engine electrical connections and vacuum lines.

7. Disconnect and plug the fuel return and feed lines.

8. Disconnect the heater inlet and outlet hoses.

9. Disconnect the following cables:

   a. Accelerator cable from the throttle body.

   b. Clutch cable from manual transaxle vehicles.

   c. The gear select and the oil pressure control cable from automatic transaxle vehicles.

   d. The speedometer cable from the transaxle.

10. Using Engine Support Assembly tool J-28467-A and J-28467–89 or equivalents, support the engine.

11. Raise and safely support the vehicle.

12. Disconnect the exhaust pipe from the manifold.

13. Disconnect the gear shift control shaft and extension from manual transaxle vehicles.

14. Drain the engine and transaxle oil.

15. Remove the left and right halfshafts. It is not necessary to remove the halfshaft from the knuckles.

16. Remove the A/C compressor and belt. Position the compressor aside, leaving the hoses connected.

17. Disconnect and plug the power steering hoses from the pump, if equipped.

18. Remove the engine rear torque rod bracket from automatic transaxle vehicles.

19. Lower the vehicle.

20. Attach suitable lifting equipment to the engine.

21. Remove the right side engine mount from the bracket.

22. On automatic transaxles, remove the transaxle rear mounting nut.

23. On manual transaxles, remove the transaxle rear mount from the body.

24. Remove the transaxle left side mounting bracket.

25. Lift the engine and transaxle assembly out of the vehicle.

To install:

26. Install the engine and transaxle assembly into the vehicle and leave the hoist connected.

27. On automatic transaxles, install the transaxle rear mounting nut.

28. On manual transaxles, install the transaxle rear mount to the body.

29. Install the transaxle left side mounting bracket. Tighten the bolts to 41 ft. lbs. (55 Nm).

30. Install the transaxle right side engine mount and bracket. Tighten the bolts to 41 ft. lbs. (55 Nm).

31. Remove the lifting device and support the engine assembly with tool J-28467-A and J-28467–89 or equivalents.

32. Raise and safely support the vehicle.

33. Install the rear engine torque rod bracket to the transaxle, if equipped.

34. Connect the left and right halfshafts.

35. Connect the gear shift control shaft and the extension to the transaxle, if equipped with a manual transaxle.

36. Connect the exhaust pipe to the manifold. Tighten the to 37 ft. lbs. (50 Nm).

37. Install the A/C compressor and belt. Tighten the compressor-to-mounting bracket bolts to 21 ft. lbs. (28 Nm).

38. Reconnect the power steering hoses to the power steering pump, if equipped.

39. Lower the vehicle.

40. Install the remaining components.

41. Install the hood. Tighten the hood mounting bolts to 20 ft. lbs. (27 Nm).

42. Adjust the clutch pedal free-play, gear select cable and accelerator cable play.

43. Refill the engine, transaxle and power steering pump, if equipped with the proper type and quantity of oil. Refill and bleed the cooling system.

✶✶ WARNING

Operating the engine without the proper amount and type of engine oil will result in severe engine damage.

44. Reconnect the negative battery cable. Start the engine and check for leaks. Make any necessary adjustments.

Prizm

1. Before servicing the vehicle, refer to the precautions in the beginning of this section.

2. Properly relieve the fuel system pressure.

3. Disconnect the battery cables, negative cable first. Remove the battery.

4. Scribe a hood hinge-to-hood outline. Disconnect the windshield washer fluid lines from the hood. Support the hood and remove the hood hinge bolts and remove the hood.

5. Raise and safely support the vehicle.

6. Drain the engine oil and cooling system.

7. Remove the left and right splash shields.

8. Drain the transaxle fluid into a suitable container.

9. Lower the vehicle.

10. Disconnect the accelerator cable from the throttle lever. If equipped with an automatic transaxle, disconnect the throttle cable from the bracket.

11. Remove the radiator and cooling fan.

12. Remove the air cleaner.

13. Remove coolant reservoir support bracket.

14. Remove the windshield washer reservoir.

15. If equipped, remove the cruise control actuator and bracket as follows:

    a. Unclip the actuator cover and remove.

    b. Disconnect the accelerator cable from the actuator.

    c. Remove the three bolts and actuator.

    d. Remove the bolts and actuator bracket.

16. Label and disconnect the Manifold Absolute Pressure (MAP) sensor hose, brake booster hose and A/C solenoid vacuum valve hose.

17. Disconnect the A/C Solenoid Vacuum (SV) valve, MAP sensor, Data Link Connector (DLC) and A/C pressure switch wiring harnesses. Also disconnect the ground wires from the intake manifold and fenders.

18. Remove the bolts, then disconnect the four wiring connectors and remove the fuse and relay box.

19. Disconnect the hose from the evaporative emission canister. Loosen the canister bracket bolt and remove the canister.

20. Loosen the hose clamps and disconnect the heater hoses from the thermostat housing.

21. Disconnect the fuel feed line from the fuel rail. Discard the gaskets.

22. Disconnect the fuel return hose from fuel pressure regulator.

23. If equipped with a manual transaxle, remove the clutch slave cylinder, and disconnect the shift select and shift control cables from the transaxle.

24. If equipped with an automatic transaxle, disconnect the shift select cable from the transaxle.

25. Remove the left and right side sill plates.

26. Remove the knee bolster, glove box, center console trim bezel, and center console.

27. Remove the radio.

28. Remove the retaining bolt and set aside the left side floor carpet bracket.

29. If equipped, remove the two bolts from the cruise control module.

30. Disconnect the Powertrain Control Module (PCM) harnesses.

31. From the engine compartment, pull the wiring harness and grommet through the bulkhead.

32. If equipped, disconnect the A/C compressor belt and harness. Remove the compressor and suspend.

33. If equipped, remove the power steering and suspend without disconnecting the hoses.

34. Raise and safely support the vehicle.

35. Disconnect the Oxygen (O_2S) sensor harness, then remove the front exhaust pipe.

36. Remove the left and right halfshafts. It is not necessary to remove the halfshafts from the steering knuckles.

37. Attach a suitable engine hoist to the engine/transaxle assembly.

38. Remove the front and rear transaxle mounts.

39. Lower the vehicle.

40. Remove the left transaxle mount.

41. Carefully lift the engine/transaxle assembly from the vehicle.

42. Remove the starter.

To install:

43. Install the starter.

44. Lower the engine/transaxle assembly into the vehicle.

45. Install the left transaxle mounts. Tighten the mounting bracket bolts to 41 ft. lbs. (56 Nm), the through-bolt to 64 ft. lbs. (87 Nm) and the reinforcement bolts to 15 ft. lbs. (21 Nm).

46. Raise and safely support vehicle.

47. Install the front and rear transaxle mounts. Tighten the front mount bolts to 47 ft. lbs. (64 Nm) and the through-bolt to 64 ft. lbs. (87 Nm). Tighten the rear transaxle nuts to 42 ft. lbs. (52 Nm) and the through-bolt to 64 ft. lbs. (87 Nm).

48. Remove the engine hoist.

49. Raise and safely support the vehicle.

50. Install the left and right halfshafts.

51. Install the front exhaust pipe and connect the O_2S sensor.

52. If equipped, install the power steering pump and drive belt.

53. Lower the vehicle.

54. If equipped, install the A/C compressor and drive belt.

55. Insert the wiring harness through the bulkhead into the passenger compartment and install the grommet to the bulkhead.

56. Connect the wiring to the PCM.

57. If equipped, position the cruise control module and tighten the bolts to 44 inch lbs. (5 Nm).

58. Position the left side floor carpet bracket and tighten the bolt to 44 inch lbs. (5 Nm).

59. Install the radio, knee bolster, glove box, center console and trim bezel.

60. Install the left and right sill plates.

61. Connect the shift cable(s) to the transaxle.

62. If equipped with manual transaxle, install the clutch slave cylinder.

63. Connect the fuel return hose to the fuel pressure regulator.

64. Connect the fuel feed pipe to the fuel rail, using new gaskets. Tighten the bolt to 22 ft. lbs. (29 Nm).

65. Connect the heater hoses to the thermostat housing.

66. Install the EVAP canister to the bracket and tighten the bolt to 89 inch lbs. (10 Nm). Connect the hose to the canister.

67. Install the fuse and relay box. Connect the wiring connectors and tighten the bolts to 89 inch lbs. (10 Nm).

68. Connect the engine ground wires to the intake manifold and fenders. Connect the A/C pressure switch, DLC, MAP sensor and A/C SV valve wiring harnesses.

69. Connect the hoses to the A/C SV valve (if equipped), brake booster and MAP sensor.

70. If equipped, install the cruise control actuator and bracket as follows:

    a. Install the actuator bracket and tighten the bolts to 18 ft. lbs. (25 Nm).

    b. Install the actuator and tighten the bolts to 89 inch lbs. (10 Nm).

    c. Connect the accelerator cable to the actuator.

    d. Clip the actuator cover in place.

71. Install the windshield washer reservoir and secure with bolt. Connect the wiring harness and hose.

72. Install the coolant reservoir and tighten the bolts to 11 ft. lbs. (15 Nm).

73. Install the remaining components.

74. Install the battery and cables. Connect the positive cable first.

75. Install the hood.

✳✳ WARNING

Operating the engine without the proper amount and type of engine oil will result in severe engine damage.

76. Fill the engine with the proper type and quantity of oil.

77. Fill and bleed the cooling system.

78. Run the engine and check for leaks and proper operation.

Timing belt service is covered in Section 5 of this manual

Water Pump

REMOVAL & INSTALLATION

Metro

1. Before servicing the vehicle, refer to the precautions in the beginning of this section.

2. Disconnect the negative battery cable.

3. Drain the cooling system.

4. Remove the air cleaner.

5. Remove the suction pipe bracket for the A/C compressor, if equipped.

6. Loosen but do not remove the four water pump pulley bolts.

7. Raise and safely support the vehicle.

8. Remove the lower splash shield.

9. Remove the A/C compressor drive belt, if equipped.

10. Remove the alternator drive belt.

11. Remove the crankshaft and water pump pulleys.

12. Remove the timing belt.

13. Remove the oil level dipstick and tube.

14. Remove the alternator adjusting bracket from the water pump.

15. Remove the water pump rubber seals.

16. Remove the water pump mounting bolts and nuts and remove the water pump from the engine.

To install:

17. Clean the gasket mating surfaces thoroughly.

18. Check the water pump by hand for smooth operation. If the pump does not operate smoothly or is noisy, replace it.

19. Install the pump using a new gasket. Tighten the bolts to 115 inch lbs. (13 Nm).

20. Install new rubber seals.

21. Install the upper alternator adjusting bracket and tighten the bolt to 17 ft. lbs. (23 Nm).

1 WATER PUMP

7922Z704

To ensure a tight seal, be sure gasket surfaces are properly prepared—Metro

22. Install the oil level dipstick and tube.

23. Install the timing belt.

24. Install the water pump and crankshaft pulleys. Leave the water pump pulley bolts hand-tight.

25. Install the alternator drive belt.

26. Install the lower alternator cover plate and tighten the bolts to 89 inch lbs. (10 Nm).

27. Install the A/C compressor drive belt, if equipped.

28. Install the lower splash shield and lower the vehicle.

29. Tighten the water pump pulley mounting bolts to 18 ft. lbs. (24 Nm).

30. Adjust the water pump drive belt tension and tighten the alternator adjustment bolt to 17 ft. lbs. (23 Nm).

31. Install the suction pipe bracket for the A/C compressor, if equipped.

32. Install the air cleaner.

33. Refill the cooling system.

34. Connect the negative battery cable.

35. Start the engine and check for leaks.

Prizm

1. Before servicing the vehicle, refer to the precautions in the beginning of this section.

2. Disconnect the negative battery cable.

3. Drain the engine coolant into a suitable container.

4. Support the engine using a lifting device.

5. Remove the right engine mount and insulator.

6. Remove the upper and middle timing belt covers.

7. If equipped with power steering, proceed as follows:

   a. Raise and safely support the vehicle.

   b. Remove the plastic cover from the front transaxle mount.

   c. Remove the two mount-to-chassis bolts.

   d. Remove the nut and through-bolt, then remove the front transaxle mount from the vehicle.

   e. Lower the vehicle.

   f. Remove the coolant reservoir.

   g. Disconnect the upper hose from the radiator.

   h. Unclip the wiring connectors from the shroud.

   i. Remove the cooling fan assembly.

8. Remove the two nuts, one bolt and the engine wiring harness retainer.

9. If equipped, unclip the Crankshaft Position (CKP) sensor electrical connector from the dipstick tube.

10. Remove the dipstick tube and dipstick. Immediately plug the hole in the block.

11. Disconnect the cooling fan switch electrical connector.

12. Remove the two nuts securing the engine coolant inlet pipe to the cylinder block.

13. Loosen the hose clamps and remove the coolant inlet pipe from the water pump.

14. Loosen the hose clamp and remove the coolant inlet hose from the water pump.

15. Remove the water pump bolts and remove the assembly. Discard the O-ring.

To install:

16. Install a new O-ring. Install the water pump, and tighten the retaining bolts evenly to 10 ft. lbs. (14 Nm).

17. Connect the coolant hose to the water pump and secure the clamp.

18. Install the engine coolant inlet pipe. Secure to the hose with clamps and nuts. Tighten the nuts to 11 ft. lbs. (15 Nm).

19. Connect the cooling fan switch electrical connector.

20. Install the dipstick and tube. Tighten the retaining bolt to 84 inch lbs. (9 Nm). If equipped, clip the CKP sensor electrical connector to the dipstick tube.

21. Install the engine wiring harness retainer and tighten the nuts and bolt to 89 inch lbs. (10 Nm).

22. If equipped with power steering, proceed as follows:

   a. Install the cooling fan assembly and tighten the bolts to 52 inch lbs. (6 Nm).

   b. Attach the wiring connectors to the shroud.

   c. Connect the upper hose to the radiator.

   d. Install the coolant reservoir.

   e. Raise and safely support the vehicle.

   f. Install the front transaxle mount

7922Z705

Remove the coolant inlet pipe from the block, then the pump—Prizm

and tighten the through-bolt nut to 64 ft. lbs. (87 Nm).

g. Install the mount-to-chassis bolts and tighten to 47 ft. lbs. (64 Nm).

h. Install the plastic cover to the front transaxle mount.

i. Lower the vehicle.

23. Install the upper and middle timing belt covers.

24. Support the engine using a lifting device. Install the right engine mount and insulator.

25. Remove the engine lifting equipment.

26. Connect the negative battery cable.

27. Fill the cooling system. Start the engine and check for leaks.

Cylinder Head

REMOVAL & INSTALLATION

Metro

1. Before servicing the vehicle, refer to the precautions in the beginning of this section.

2. Properly relieve the fuel system pressure.

3. Disconnect the negative battery cable.

4. Drain the cooling system.

5. Remove the intake and exhaust manifolds.

6. Remove the timing belt.

7. Disconnect and label the spark plug wires. Be sure to pull firmly on the wire boot, not the plug wire.

8. Remove the distributor and case from the cylinder head.

9. Remove the cylinder head cover.

10. Loosen and remove the cylinder head bolts by reversing the tightening sequence.

11. Remove the cylinder head from the engine. Discard the cylinder head gasket and rubber seal.

A. Camshaft pulley side
B. Distributor side

7922Z707

Cylinder head bolt torque sequence—1.3L engine

12. Clean all gasket mating surfaces.

13. Check the cylinder head flatness using a straightedge and feeler gauge. Check the surface across the combustion chambers, on each side of the combustion chambers, and diagonally. If distortion exceeds 0.002 in. (0.05mm) at any location, the cylinder head should be resurfaced.

To install:

14. Install the cylinder head gasket with the TOP indicator facing upward and toward the crankshaft pulley.

15. Install the cylinder head. Lubricate the cylinder head bolts with clean engine oil and install them finger-tight.

1. Cylinder head gasket
2. Cylinder block

7922Z799

Cylinder head gasket positioning—1.3L engine

CYLINDER HEAD
RUBBER SEAL
WATER PUMP

7922Z706

Install the rubber seal as shown—Metro

A CRANKSHAFT PULLEY SIDE
6053 CYLINDER HEAD GASKET

7922Z708

Cylinder head gasket positioning—1.0L engine

Cylinder head bolt torque sequence—1.0L engine

16. Tighten the cylinder head bolts in three even stages, following the tightening sequence, to 54 ft. lbs. (73 Nm).

17. Install the rubber seal between the water pump and the cylinder head.

18. Install the cylinder head cover and secure with nuts and new seal washers. Tighten nuts to 44 inch lbs. (5 Nm).

19. Install the timing belt.

20. Install the distributor.

21. Connect the spark plug wires.

22. Install the intake manifold, using a new gasket.

23. Install the exhaust manifold using a new gasket.

24. Refill the cooling system.

25. Connect the negative battery cable.

26. Start the engine and allow it to reach normal operating temperature. Check for leaks and adjust the ignition timing, if necessary.

Prizm

1. Before servicing the vehicle, refer to the precautions in the beginning of this section.

2. Properly relieve the fuel system pressure.

3. Disconnect the negative battery cable.

4. Drain the engine coolant into a suitable container.

5. Raise and safely support the vehicle.

6. Remove the right side engine splash shield.

7. Lower the vehicle.

8. Remove the accelerator cable from the bracket and throttle body.

9. Disconnect the vacuum hose from the evaporative emissions canister.

10. Unfasten the Intake Air Temperature (IAT) sensor harness from the air cleaner cap. Loosen the air cleaner hose clamp and disconnect four clips to remove the cover.

11. Remove the alternator.

12. Disconnect the spark plug wires and remove the distributor case.

13. Disconnect the Oxygen (O_2S) sensor harness, then detach the bolts and nuts and remove the front exhaust pipe.

14. Remove the exhaust manifold.

15. Remove the thermostat housing.

16. Unfasten the ground strap connector.

17. Disconnect the Manifold Absolute Pressure (MAP) sensor harness and A/C pressure switch harness, if equipped.

18. Remove the engine wiring harness from the right side fender.

19. Label and disconnect all of the hoses from the intake chamber.

A CRANKSHAFT PULLEY END

Cylinder head bolt torque sequence—Prizm

20. If equipped, label and unfasten the A/C solenoid vacuum valve electrical connector.

21. Disconnect the hoses and harnesses from the EGR Switching Valve (SV) and vacuum modulator, then remove.

22. Remove the engine wire clamp and the intake manifold brace.

23. Disconnect the fuel return line from the pressure regulator. Remove the air pipe from the intake manifold.

24. Remove the air pipe and EGR valve.

25. Remove the throttle body assembly.

26. Label and disconnect the PCV hoses from the cylinder head cover.

27. Label and disconnect the vacuum hose from the pressure regulator. Remove the intake chamber cover.

28. Disconnect the fuel line from the fuel rail. Label and disconnect the electrical harness from the fuel injectors. Remove the fuel rail with the injectors attached.

29. Label and disconnect the A/C compressor electrical harness, if equipped. Label and disconnect the oil pressure switch, Crankshaft Position (CKP) sensor and fan thermostat electrical harness. Remove the engine wiring harness cover. Disconnect the engine ground strap and remove the engine wiring harness retainer.

30. Remove the intake manifold.

31. If equipped with cruise control, remove the actuator cover, actuator mounting bolts and actuator bracket.

32. Support the engine using a suitable jack.

33. Remove the two nuts from the right-hand engine mount studs.

34. If equipped, remove the 2-piece A/C line bracket from the engine mount.

35. Remove the engine mount reinforcement bracket and mount, if equipped.

✳✳ WARNING

It may be necessary to lower the engine to gain clearance for engine mount removal. If equipped, be careful not to bend the A/C line too much or a leak may develop.

36. Remove the timing belt.

37. Remove the alternator mounting bracket.

38. Remove the oil level dipstick and tube.

39. Remove the coolant inlet pipe.

40. Remove the camshafts.

41. Uniformly loosen and remove the 10 cylinder head bolts in several passes, in reverse order of tightening.

✳✳ WARNING

Cylinder head warpage or cracking could result from removing the bolts in the incorrect order.

42. Lift off the cylinder head assembly from the dowels.

To install:

43. Clean all gasket mating surfaces, using care not to damage the aluminum components.

44. Check the engine block and cylinder head mating surfaces, using a feeler gauge and straightedge. Check along all four edges and diagonally across. If distortion exceeds 0.002 in. (0.05mm) at any location, resurface the cylinder head.

45. Install a new gasket, then lower the cylinder head to the block. Be sure the dowel pins are aligned.

46. Coat the cylinder head bolt threads and the underside of each bolt head with clean engine oil and install finger-tight.

➡ **The cylinder head bolts are in lengths of 3.54 in. (90mm) and 4.25 in. (108mm). The 3.54 in. (90mm) bolts are to be installed in the intake side of the cylinder head. The 4.25 in. (108mm) bolts are to be installed in the exhaust manifold side of the cylinder head.**

47. Tighten the cylinder head bolts, in sequence, to 22 ft. lbs. (29 Nm).

48. Turn each bolt, in sequence, an additional 90 degrees. Again turn each bolt, in sequence, an additional 90 degrees.

49. Install the camshafts.

50. Install the coolant inlet pipe. Tighten the nuts to 11 ft. lbs. (15 Nm).

51. Install the engine oil level dipstick tube and tighten the bolt to 84 inch lbs. (9.5 Nm).

52. Install the alternator bracket and tighten the bolts to 19 ft. lbs. (26 Nm).

53. Install the timing belt.

54. Position the engine mount, and locate the A/C pipe, if equipped. Tighten the bolts closet to the mount to 47 ft. lbs. (64 Nm), and the bolts farthest away from the mount to 18 ft. lbs. (25 Nm).

55. Install the rubber insulator to the mount and tighten the bolt to 18 ft. lbs. (25 Nm).

56. Install the reinforcement bracket and tighten the nut and bolt to 18 ft. lbs. (25 Nm).

57. Attach the A/C pipe bracket, if equipped, to the engine mount and tighten the bolt to 89 inch lbs. (10 Nm).

58. Install the nuts to the engine mount studs and tighten to 38 ft. lbs. (52 Nm).

59. If equipped, install the cruise control actuator bracket, actuator and cover.

60. Install the intake manifold and ground strap.

61. Install the engine wiring harness with the retainer and tighten the bolts and nuts to 89 inch lbs. (10 Nm). Secure the ground strap with the bolt, and tighten to 89 inch lbs. (10 Nm). Connect the fan thermostat, oil pressure switch, if equipped, A/C compressor harnesses. Install the engine wire cover and tighten the bolts to 89 inch lbs. (10 Nm).

62. Install the fuel rail and injectors. Tighten the fuel rail bolts to 11 ft. lbs. (15 Nm) and connect the fuel injector electrical connectors.

63. Connect the fuel line to the fuel rail, using new gaskets. Tighten the union bolt to 22 ft. lbs. (29 Nm).

64. Install the intake chamber cover using a new gasket. Tighten the nuts and bolts to 14 ft. lbs. (19 Nm). Connect the vacuum hose to the pressure regulator.

65. Connect the PCV hoses to the cylinder head cover.

66. Install the throttle body assembly, using a new gasket. Tighten the bolts and nuts to 16 ft. lbs. (22 Nm). Connect the Throttle Position (TP) sensor harness. Install the accelerator cable bracket and tighten the bolts to 98 inch lbs. (11 Nm).

67. Install the EGR valve, using a new gasket. Tighten the nuts to 115 inch lbs. (13 Nm).

68. Connect the fuel return hose to the pressure regulator.

69. Install the intake manifold brace. Tighten the 12mm bolts to 14 ft. lbs. (19 Nm) and the 14mm bolts to 29 ft. lbs. (39 Nm).

70. Install the engine wire clamp and the EGR SV valve and vacuum modulator. Tighten the EGR SV valve bolt to 115 inch lbs. (13 Nm). Connect the hose to the EGR SV valve pipe and connect the electrical connector.

71. Install the remaining components.

72. Connect the negative battery cable.

73. Fill and bleed cooling system.

74. Run the engine and check for leaks. Check the ignition timing. Road test and check for proper operation.

Refer to Section 1 for engine rebuilding specifications

Rocker Arms/Shafts

REMOVAL & INSTALLATION

All engines except the 1.3L do not use rocker arms/shafts, the camshaft directly actuates the valves.

1.3L Engine

1. Before servicing the vehicle, refer to the precautions in the beginning of this section.

2. Disconnect the negative battery cable.

3. If equipped, remove the A/C compressor drive belt, then the remove the compressor and mounting bracket. Place off to the side.

4. Disconnect the spark plug wires at the plugs.

5. Remove the air cleaner and cylinder head cover.

6. Remove the rocker shaft retaining bolts. Lift out the exhaust and intake rocker arm shafts, with the springs and rocker arms attached.

7. If necessary, remove the rocker arms, washers and springs from the rocker shafts. Note the order in which the components are removed; they must be re-assembled in the same order and position.

➡ **The intake and exhaust rocker arm shafts are NOT the same. The two can be distinguished by looking at the ends of the shafts, which are different. Install the intake rocker arm shaft with the stepped end toward the distributor side.**

8. Inspect the rockers arms, shafts and lash adjusters for wear and/or damage; replace as necessary.

To install:

9. If disassembled earlier, assemble the springs, washers and rocker arms on to the rocker shafts.

10. Lubricate the rocker arms and shafts with clean engine oil. Position the intake

Rocker arm shaft retaining bolts tightening sequence—1.3L engines

79222712

and exhaust rocker arm shafts in their original positions. Secure with the retaining bolts. Tighten the shaft bolts, in the correct sequence, to 97 inch lbs. (11 Nm).

11. Apply a small amount of silicone sealer to the corners of the cylinder head cover gasket mating surface. Install a new head cover gasket and position the cylinder head cover to the head.

12. Install new seal washers and the nuts. Tighten the head cover nuts to 44 inch lbs. (5 Nm).

13. Install the remaining components.

14. Reconnect the negative battery cable. Run the engine and check for leaks and proper engine operation.

Intake Manifold

REMOVAL & INSTALLATION

Metro

1. Before servicing the vehicle, refer to the precautions in the beginning of this section.

2. Relieve the fuel system pressure.

3. Disconnect the negative battery cable.

4. Drain the cooling system.

5. Remove the air cleaner.

6. Disconnect the electrical harnesses to the intake manifold.

7. Disconnect the fuel return and feed hoses from the throttle body.

8. Disconnect the water hoses from the throttle body and the intake manifold.

9. Disconnect all vacuum hoses to the intake manifold.

10. Disconnect the PCV hose from the valve cover.

11. Disconnect the accelerator cable from the throttle body.

12. Remove the intake manifold fasteners and remove with the throttle body attached.

13. Remove and discard the intake manifold gasket. Clean all gasket mating surfaces.

To install:

14. Install the intake manifold to the cylinder head, using a new gasket. Install the fasteners and tighten evenly, to 17 ft. lbs. (23 Nm), starting in the center working towards the ends.

15. Connect the PCV hose to the valve cover.

16. Connect the vacuum and coolant hoses.

17. Install the fuel feed and return hoses.

18. Reconnect the electrical harnesses to the proper locations.

19. Install the accelerator cable and adjust as follows:

a. Be sure the cable locknut and adjusting nut are loose.

b. Adjust the cable end-play to 0.4–0.6 in. (10–15mm), then tighten the lock and adjusting nuts.

c. If equipped with an automatic transaxle, loosen the cable locknut and adjusting nut at the cable retaining bracket on the transaxle. Adjust the cable end-play to 0.4–0.6 in. (10–15mm), then tighten the locknut and adjusting nut.

20. Install the air cleaner.

21. Refill the cooling system and reconnect the negative battery cable.

22. Start the engine. Check for leaks.

Prizm

1. Before servicing the vehicle, refer to the precautions in the beginning of this section.

2. Relieve the fuel system pressure.

3. Disconnect the negative battery cable.

4. Label and disconnect the following hoses:

a. Vacuum sensor hose from the fuel filter.

b. Brake booster vacuum hose.

c. If equipped, A/C vacuum hoses.

5. If equipped, disconnect the A/C actuator electrical connector.

6. If equipped with an EGR Switching Valve (SV), proceed as follows:

a. Disconnect the EGR SV electrical connector and EGR temperature sensor.

b. Disconnect the vacuum hose from the EGR valve.

c. Remove bolt and EGR SV valve.

7. Remove the engine wire clamp.

8. Remove the intake manifold brace.

9. Disconnect the fuel return hose from the pressure regulator.

10. Remove the mounting bolt and nut and the air pipe from the intake manifold.

11. Remove the throttle body as follows:

a. Disconnect the Throttle Position (TP) sensor harness.

b. Loosen the locknut and adjusting nut, then remove the accelerator cable from the throttle lever.

c. If equipped with an automatic transaxle, loosen the locknut and adjusting nut and remove the throttle cable from the bracket.

d. Remove the two bolts and the accelerator bracket.

e. Remove the two bolts, two nuts and the throttle body with the gasket.

12. Remove the fuel inlet hose clamp bolt, intake chamber brace and gasket.

13. Disconnect the PCV hoses from the valve cover.

14. Disconnect the vacuum hose from the fuel pressure regulator.

15. Remove the bolts, nuts and the intake chamber cover with gasket.

16. Remove the union bolt and gaskets and disconnect the fuel inlet pipe from the fuel rail.

17. Disconnect the fuel injector harnesses.

18. Remove the bolts and remove the fuel rail with the injectors attached.

❊❊ WARNING

Be careful not to drop the fuel injectors when removing the fuel rail. Damage could result.

19. Remove the insulators and spacers from the cylinder head.

20. Remove the nuts and bolt and the engine wiring harness retainer.

21. Remove the bolts, ground strap and nuts. Remove the intake manifold and gasket.

22. Clean all gasket mating surfaces.

To install:

23. Install the intake manifold using a new gasket.

24. Install the nuts, bolts and ground strap. Tighten the nuts and bolts to 9 ft. lbs. (13 Nm) and bolts to 14 ft. lbs. (19 Nm).

25. Install the engine wiring harness retainer, and tighten the nuts and bolts to 89 inch lbs. (10 Nm).

26. Install new insulators and spacers to the cylinder head.

27. Install the fuel rail with the injectors. Loosely install the retaining bolts.

➡ **Check the fuel injectors for smooth rotation. If the injectors do not rotate smoothly, replace the O-rings and recheck. Be sure the electrical connector is pointed upward.**

28. Tighten the fuel rail retaining bolts to 11 ft. lbs. (15 Nm).

29. Connect the injector harnesses.

30. Connect the fuel inlet pipe to the fuel rail with the union bolt. Use new gaskets. Tighten the union bolt to 22 ft. lbs. (29 Nm).

31. Install the intake chamber cover using a new gasket. Tighten the nuts and bolts to 14 ft. lbs. (19 Nm).

32. Connect the vacuum hose to the pressure regulator. Connect the PCV hoses to the valve cover.

33. Install the intake chamber brace with a new gasket. Tighten the bolt to 21 ft. lbs. (28 Nm).

34. Install the fuel inlet hose clamp bolt and tighten to 89 inch lbs. (10 Nm).

35. Install the throttle body using a new gasket. Tighten the nuts and bolts to 17 ft. lbs. (23 Nm).

36. Install the accelerator cable bracket and tighten the bolts to 11 ft. lbs. (15 Nm).

37. Connect the throttle cable, if equipped, and accelerator cable. Tighten the locknut and adjusting nut to 11 ft. lbs. (15 Nm).

38. If equipped, install the EGR valve, vacuum modulator and vacuum hose assembly, using new gaskets. Tighten the EGR valve-to-intake manifold bolts and nuts to 115 inch lbs. (13 Nm) and tighten the EGR valve-to-EGR pipe bolts and nuts to 43 ft. lbs. (59 Nm). Connect the two vacuum hoses.

39. Connect the fuel return hose to the pressure regulator.

40. Install the intake manifold brace and engine wire clamps.

41. If equipped, install the EGR SV valve and tighten the bolt to 115 inch lbs. (13 Nm). Connect the EGR SV valve and EGR TP sensors. Connect the vacuum hose to the EGR valve.

42. Connect the remaining components.

43. Connect the negative battery cable.

44. Run the engine and check for leaks.

Exhaust Manifold

REMOVAL & INSTALLATION

Metro

1. Before servicing the vehicle, refer to the precautions in the beginning of this section.

2. Disconnect the negative battery cable.

3. Raise and safely support the vehicle.

4. Disconnect the front pipe/catalytic converter from the exhaust manifold.

5. Lower the vehicle.

6. Disconnect the Oxygen (O_2S) sensor harness.

7. Remove the exhaust manifold heat shield.

8. Remove the manifold retaining bolts and engine hanger. Remove the manifold and gasket from the cylinder head.

9. Clean all gasket mating surfaces.

To install:

10. Install a new gasket, followed by the exhaust manifold, and engine hanger. Install the exhaust manifold bolts and nuts, tighten evenly, to 17 ft. lbs. (23 Nm), working from the center towards the ends.

11. Install the manifold heat shield and tighten the retaining bolts to 11 ft. lbs. (15 Nm).

12. Raise and safely support the vehicle.

13. Connect the exhaust pipe to the manifold with a new seal. Tighten the bolts to 30–43 ft. lbs. (40–60 Nm).

14. Lower the vehicle.

15. Reconnect the O_2S sensor harness.

16. Reconnect the negative battery cable. Start the engine and check for leaks.

Prizm

1. Before servicing the vehicle, refer to the precautions in the beginning of this section.

2. Disconnect the negative battery cable.

3. Disconnect the Oxygen (O_2S) sensor, if equipped, sub-oxygen sensor connectors.

4. Disconnect the exhaust pipe from the exhaust manifold or, if equipped, from the Warm Up Three Way Catalytic Converter (WU TWC).

5. Remove the five bolts and the upper heat shield.

6. Remove the bolts and the exhaust manifold brace.

7. Remove the nuts, then the exhaust manifold and gasket. If equipped, remove the manifold with the WU TWC attached.

8. Remove the three bolts and the lower heat insulator from the exhaust manifold.

9. If equipped, remove the four nuts and two WU TWC heat insulators.

10. If equipped, remove the two bolts, two nuts and WU TWC from the exhaust manifold.

To install:

11. Clean all gasket mating surfaces.

12. If equipped, install the bolts, nuts and WU TWC to the exhaust manifold. Tighten the bolts and nuts to 80 inch lbs. (9 Nm).

13. If equipped, install the nuts and WU TWC heat insulators. Tighten the nuts to 80 inch lbs. (9 Nm).

14. Install the three bolts and the lower heat insulator to the manifold and tighten to 80 inch lbs. (9 Nm).

15. Install a new gasket and the exhaust manifold to the cylinder head. Tighten the

For engine torque specifications, refer to Section 1 of this manual

nuts evenly, to 25 ft. lbs. (34 Nm), working from the center towards the ends.

16. Install the exhaust manifold brace and tighten the bolts to 29 ft. lbs. (39 Nm).

17. Install the upper heat insulator and tighten the bolts to 80 inch lbs. (9 Nm).

18. Using a new gasket, connect the exhaust pipe to the exhaust manifold or WU TWC, as required. Install the nuts and tighten to 32 ft. lbs. (43 Nm).

19. Connect the O$_2$S sensor harness, if equipped, sub-oxygen sensor connector.

20. Connect the negative battery cable. Run the engine and check for exhaust leaks.

Front Crankshaft Seal

REMOVAL & INSTALLATION

Metro

1. Before servicing the vehicle, refer to the precautions in the beginning of this section.

2. Disconnect the negative battery cable.

3. Raise and safely support the vehicle.

4. Drain the engine oil.

5. Remove the timing belt and crankshaft sprocket.

6. Remove the oil pan and strainer.

7. Remove the oil pump bolts and pump assembly. Identify the bolts so they can be reinstalled in their proper locations.

8. Remove the crankshaft oil seal from the oil pump using a suitable removal tool.

To install:

9. Install a new crankshaft oil seal into the oil pump body using a suitable seal installer tool. Lubricate the lip of the new seal with clean engine oil.

10. Using new gaskets, install the oil

To prevent damage to the lip of the seal use an oil seal protector as shown—Metro

pump on the engine. Use Oil Seal Protector tool J-34853 to aid installation of the oil seal over the crankshaft without damaging the seal. The lip of the seal must **NOT** be turned out.

➡ **Take care not to damage the front seal on the crankshaft snout.**

11. Apply Loctite® pipe sealant or equivalent to the pump bolts and install. Tighten to 97 inch lbs. (11 Nm).

➡ **After tightening, the oil pump gasket may bulge out. Trim the edge with a knife, making sure the edge is smooth with the cylinder block.**

12. Install the rubber seal between the oil and coolant pumps.

13. Install the crankshaft sprocket. With the crankshaft locked, tighten the bolt to 81 ft. lbs. (110 Nm).

14. Install the oil strainer and pan.

15. Install the timing belt.

16. Lower the vehicle and fill the engine with clean engine oil.

✳✳ WARNING

Operating the engine without the proper amount and type of engine oil will result in severe engine damage.

17. Connect the negative battery cable, start the engine and check for leaks.

Prizm

1. Before servicing the vehicle, refer to the precautions in the beginning of this section.

2. Disconnect the negative battery cable.

3. Remove the timing belt and crankshaft sprocket.

4. Cut off the oil seal lip.

✳✳ WARNING

When removing the oil seal, be careful not to damage the crankshaft or the oil pump housing.

5. Carefully pry out the oil seal from the pump housing.

To install:

6. Apply clean engine oil to the new oil seal and lubricate the lip of the new oil seal with multi-purpose grease.

7. Install the new oil seal to the oil pump using a suitable seal driver.

8. Install the timing belt and crankshaft sprocket.

9. Connect the negative battery cable. Check the engine oil level.

10. Run the engine and check for leaks.

Camshaft

REMOVAL & INSTALLATION

Metro

1. Before servicing the vehicle, refer to the precautions in the beginning of this section.

2. Disconnect the negative battery cable.

3. Remove the A/C compressor and bracket, if equipped, and position aside.

4. Remove the air cleaner.

5. Disconnect the spark plug wires. Remove the cylinder head cover.

6. Remove the distributor.

7. Remove the timing belt.

8. Remove the camshaft timing belt sprocket. Lock the camshaft with a 0.39 in. (10mm) rod inserted into the hole in the camshaft, before loosening the sprocket retaining bolt.

✳✳ WARNING

The mating surface of the cylinder head and cover must not be damaged during this procedure. Place a clean shop cloth between the rod and mating surfaces and use care not to bump the rod when loosening.

9. On 1.3L engines, remove the rocker arms and shafts from the cylinder head. Keep all parts in order so they can be reinstalled in their original locations. The intake and exhaust rocker arm shafts are different. Be sure to identify them as they are removed.

10. Turn the crankshaft until the crankshaft sprocket timing mark is 60 degrees to the left of the arrow mark on the oil pump case.

11. Remove the camshaft caps from the cylinder head.

Position the crankshaft as shown before removing the camshaft—Metro with 1.0L engines

A - Indicates position from
    timing belt

B - Indicates direction to
    timing belt

79222715

**Directional markings for the camshaft
bearing caps—Metro with 1.0L engine**

79222716

**Torque sequence for the camshaft bearing
cap bolts—Metro with 1.0L engine**

12. Remove the camshaft from the cylinder head.

13. On 1.3L engines remove the camshaft from the cylinder head by removing it from the flywheel end.

14. Inspect the camshaft journals and lobes for wear and/or damage and replace, as necessary.

15. Using a micrometer, measure the camshaft lobe height. If the camshaft lobe height is below the minimum limit, replace the camshaft. The minimum camshaft specifications are as follows:

• **Metro XFi**—1.5562 in. (39.528mm)
• **Metro Standard and LSi**—1.5872 in. (40.315mm)

16. On 1.3L engines, inspect the camshaft for excessive wear or scoring and replace, if necessary. Using a micrometer, measure the cam lobe height; if it is less than 1.49575 in. (38.036mm), replace the camshaft.

To install:

17. Fill the oil passage in the cylinder head with clean engine oil. Pour engine oil through the camshaft journal oil holes and check that engine oil comes out from the oil holes in the Hydraulic Valve Lash (HVL) adjuster bores.

18. Install the camshaft to the cylinder head. After applying engine oil to the camshaft journal and all around the cam,

position the camshaft so the camshaft timing sprocket pin hole in the camshaft is at the lower position.

19. On 1.0L engines, install the camshaft bearing caps to the camshaft and the cylinder head as follows:

a. Apply clean engine oil to the sliding surface of each bearing cap against the camshaft journal.

b. Apply silicone sealant to the mating surface of the No. 1 and No. 3 bearing cap which will mate with the cylinder head.

c. There are marks provided on each camshaft bearing cap indicating the position and direction for installation. Install the bearing cap as indicated by the marks.

d. Camshaft bearing cap No. 1 is installed first. It retains the camshaft in the proper position and thrust direction. Apply clean engine oil to the retaining bolts and install, but do not tighten fully.

e. Install the remaining camshaft bearing caps and bolts.

f. Tighten the bolts evenly, repeating the tightening sequence 3–4 times. Tightened to 8 ft. lbs. (11 Nm).

➡ **On 1.3L engines, exhaust and intake rocker shafts are different. To distinguish between the two, the end dimensions are different. Install the intake rocker arm shaft with the stepped end facing the distributor side.**

20. On 1.3L engines, install the intake rocker arm shaft and arms. Tighten the rocker arm shaft retaining bolts to 97 inch lbs. (11 Nm).

21. On 1.3L engines, install the exhaust rocker arm shaft and arms. Tighten the rocker arm shaft retaining bolts to 97 inch lbs. (11 Nm).

22. Install the camshaft oil seal. After applying engine oil to the seal lip, press-fit the camshaft oil seal until the seal surface until flush with the housing.

23. Install the camshaft timing belt sprocket after installing the dowel pin. Tighten the retaining bolt to 44 ft. lbs. (60 Nm).

24. Using a new valve cover gasket, apply a small amount of silicone sealant to the corners of the cylinder gasket, install the valve cover the cover nuts. Tighten the cylinder head cover nuts to 44 inch lbs. (5 Nm).

25. Install the timing belt.

26. Install the distributor to the cylinder head. Connect the spark plug wires.

27. Install the A/C compressor and bracket, if equipped.

28. Install the air cleaner and connect the negative battery cable.

29. Start the engine and check the ignition timing. Adjust the timing as necessary.

➡ **When the engine is started, if air is trapped in the HVL adjuster, the valve may make a tapping sound when the engine is operated after the HVL adjuster is installed. In such a case, run the engine at 2000 rpm until the air is purged and the tapping sound ceases.**

Prizm

1. Before servicing the vehicle, refer to the precautions in the beginning of this section.

2. Disconnect the negative battery cable.

✼✼ CAUTION

You must wait at least 90 seconds from the time the ignition switch is turned to the LOCK position and the negative battery cable is disconnected before starting work.

3. Disconnect the spark plug wires.

4. Remove the valve cover.

5. Remove the timing belt.

6. Set the exhaust camshaft so the knock pin is slightly above the cylinder head (10 o'clock position). This angle allows the No. 1 and No. 3 cylinder cam lobes of the intake camshaft to push the lash adjusters evenly.

7. Remove the two bolts and the front bearing cap of the intake camshaft.

8. Secure the intake camshaft end gear to the sub gear with a service bolt. The service bolt should match the following specifications:

• Thread diameter: 6.0mm
• Thread pitch: 1.0mm
• Bolt length: 16mm

9. Uniformly loosen each intake camshaft bearing cap bolt in several passes in the proper sequence.

✼✼ WARNING

The camshaft must be held level while it is being removed. If not, the portion of the cylinder head receiving the thrust may become damaged. This could cause the camshaft to bind or break.

For complete mechanical specifications, refer to Section 1 of this manual

1. M6X1.0X 16 - 20 mm service bolt
2. Intake camshaft sub-gear
3. Intake camshaft main gear

7922Z717

Fastening the sub-gear to the main gear—Prizm

1. Exhaust camshaft

7922Z719

Exhaust camshaft bearing cap removal sequence—Prizm

1. Exhaust camshaft

7922Z721

Exhaust camshaft bearing cap tightening sequence—Prizm

1. Intake camshaft

7922Z718

Intake camshaft bearing cap removal sequence—Prizm

1. Exhaust camshaft key
2. Exhaust camshaft

7922Z720

Positioning the exhaust camshaft for removal—Prizm

A   INSTALLATION MARKS
B   TIMING MARKS
C   EXHAUST CAMSHAFT KEY
D   INTAKE CAMSHAFT SERVICE BOLT

7922Z722

Engaging the intake camshaft with the exhaust camshaft—Prizm

1. Intake camshaft

7922Z723

Intake camshaft gearing cap tightening sequence—Prizm

10. Remove the bearing caps and intake camshaft.

➡ **If the camshaft cannot be removed straight and level, install and retighten the No. 3 bearing cap. Alternately loosen the bolts on the bearing cap a little at a time while pulling upwards on the camshaft gear. DO NOT attempt to pry or force the cam loose.**

11. Turn the exhaust camshaft approximately 105 degrees, so the guide pin is just past the 5 o'clock position. This angle allows the No. 1 and the No. 3 cylinder cam

lobes of the exhaust camshaft to push the lash adjusters evenly.

12. Loosen the exhaust camshaft bearing cap bolts uniformly in several passes in sequence.

13. Remove the bearing caps and exhaust camshaft.

➡ **If the camshaft cannot be removed straight and level, install and retighten the No. 3 bearing cap. Alternately loosen the bolts on the bearing cap a little at a time while pulling upwards on the camshaft gear. DO NOT attempt to pry or force the cam loose.**

To install:

14. Apply multi-purpose grease to the thrust portion of the camshaft.

15. Place the exhaust camshaft on the cylinder head so the cam lobes press evenly on the lash adjusters for cylinders Nos. 1 and 3. This will place the guide pin on the camshaft slightly counter clockwise at about 5 o'clock.

16. Apply a light coat of clean engine oil to the camshaft bearing cap bolts. Install the five bearing caps in position according to the number cast into the cap. The arrow should point towards the pulley end of the motor.

17. Tighten the bearing cap bolts uniformly and in several passes in the proper sequence to 9 ft. lbs. (13 Nm)

18. Apply multi-purpose grease to a new exhaust camshaft oil seal.

19. Install the exhaust camshaft seal using a seal driver. Be very careful not to install the seal on a slant.

20. Set the intake camshaft so the guide pin is slightly above the cylinder head.

21. Apply multi-purpose grease to the thrust portion of the intake camshaft.

22. Hold the intake camshaft next to the exhaust camshaft and engage the gears by matching the alignment marks.

➡ **DO NOT use the TDC timing marks for the timing belt.**

23. Keeping the gears engaged, roll the intake camshaft down and into the bearing journals. This angle allows the No. 1 and the No. 3 cylinder cam lobes of the camshaft to push the lash adjusters evenly.

24. Apply a light coat of clean engine oil to the camshaft bearing cap bolts and install the bearing caps. Observe the numbers on each cap and make certain the arrows point to the pulley end of the motor.

25. Uniformly tighten each of the bearing cap bolts in several passes in the proper

sequence. Tighten each bolt to 9 ft. lbs. (13 Nm)

➡ **If the No. 1 bearing cap does not fit properly, push the camshaft gear backwards by prying apart the cylinder head and camshaft gear with a suitable tool.**

26. Turn the exhaust camshaft clockwise, and set it with the guide pin facing upward. Check that the timing marks of the camshaft gears are aligned. The camshaft assembly installation marks should now be in the 12 o'clock position.

27. Secure the exhaust camshaft and install the timing belt pulley. Tighten the bolt to 43 ft. lbs. (59 Nm).

28. Install the timing belt.

29. Install the spark plug wires and connect the negative battery cable.

30. Start the engine, check for leaks. Check the ignition timing.

Valve Lash

ADJUSTMENT

Metro

Hydraulic Valve Lash (HVL) adjusters, located between the camshaft and valve stems, are used to adjust the valve clearance to zero lash automatically at all times. Adjustment is not required.

Prizm

➡ **The following tools and part are needed for this procedure; Valve clearance adjustment tool set J-39871 or equivalent, a feeler gauge, a 0–1 inch micrometer and a selection of valve adjustment shims. Check and adjust the valve clearance with the engine cold.**

1. Before servicing the vehicle, refer to the precautions in the beginning of this section.

2. Disconnect the negative battery cable.

3. Disconnect the ignition wires, then remove the spark plugs.

4. Remove the retaining nuts and remove the cylinder head cover.

5. Turn the crankshaft until the piston in No. 1 cylinder is at Top Dead Center (TDC) on the compression stroke. Align the groove in the crankshaft pulley with the **0** mark on the timing belt cover. Be sure No. 1 cylinder lash adjusters are loose and those on No. 4 are tight. If not, turn the crankshaft

pulley one full revolution (360 degrees) and again align the mark on the crankshaft pulley.

6. The intake valve clearance should be 0.006–0.010 in. (0.15–0.25mm) and the exhaust valve clearance should be 0.010–0.014 in. (0.25–0.35mm).

7. Using a feeler gauge, measure the clearance between the camshaft and valve lifter shim at the No. 1 cylinder intake and exhaust valves, the No. 2 cylinder intake valves and the No. 3 cylinder exhaust valves. Record the clearance measurements for all valves that are not within specification, in order to determine the required replacement shims.

8. Rotate the crankshaft pulley one full turn (360 degrees) and check the clearance at the No. 2 cylinder exhaust valves, the No. 3 cylinder intake valves and the No. 4 cylinder intake and exhaust valves. Record the clearance measurements for all valves that are not within specification, in order to determine the required replacement shims.

9. For valves requiring adjustment, proceed as follows:

   a. Be sure the base of the camshaft lobe is directly over the valve (camshaft lobe pointing away from the valve).

   b. Insert tool J-3987–1 or equivalent, between the camshaft and lifter adjustment shim, to compress the valve spring and push the lifter down.

   c. Insert tool J-39871–2 or equivalent, between the camshaft and the lifter, to hold the lifter away from the camshaft. Position the bottom edge of the tool on the lifter.

   d. Using a small screwdriver and a magnet, remove the adjustment shim from the top of the lifter.

   e. Use the micrometer to measure the thickness of the removed shim. Determine the thickness of the new shim

using the formula below. For the purposes of the following formula, T = Thickness of the shim removed; A = Valve clearance measured; N = Thickness of the required new shim.

• For the intake camshaft valves: N = T + A—0.008 in. (0.20mm))

• For the exhaust camshaft valves: N = T + A—0.010 in. (0.25mm))

   f. Select a shim closest to the calculated thickness. Shims are available in 16 sizes, in increments of 0.002 in. (0.050mm), from 0.1004 in. (2.55mm) to 0.1299 in. (3.30mm).

   g. Install the shim on the valve lifter and remove tool J-39871–2 or equivalent. Recheck the valve clearance.

10. After all valve clearances have been checked and/or adjusted, reinstall the cylinder head cover, using a new gasket. Tighten the nuts to 53 inch lbs. (6 Nm).

11. Install the spark plugs and connect the ignition wires.

12. Connect the negative battery cable.

13. Run the engine and check operation.

Oil Pan

REMOVAL & INSTALLATION

1. Before servicing the vehicle, refer to the precautions in the beginning of this section.

2. Disconnect the negative battery cable.

3. Raise and safely support the vehicle.

4. Drain the engine oil.

5. Remove the flywheel dust cover.

6. On Prizm models, remove the splash shields.

7. Separate the support hanger from the catalytic converter. Remove the front exhaust pipe between the exhaust manifold and the resonator/tail pipe assembly.

8. On Prizm models, perform the following:

   a. Remove the bolts and lower the front end of the center support.

   b. Remove the lower engine reinforcement brace-to-engine bolts and remove the brace.

9. Remove the crankshaft position sensor.

10. On Prizm models, remove the three brace-to-transaxle bolts. Remove the 14 bolts from the powertrain reinforcement brace. Remove the six Torx® bolts and powertrain reinforcement brace from the vehicle.

Using the valve clearance adjustment tool set to hold the lifter—Prizm

Please refer to Section 9 for electric cooling fan wiring schematics

SECTION A-A   SECTION B-B   SECTION C-C

D   6.0 mm (0.24")
E   SILICONE SEALER
669   OIL PAN

79222725

To ensure a leak-free seal, apply sealer as shown—Prizm 1.8L engine

SECTION B-B   SECTION C-C

A   SILICONE SEALER
669   OIL PAN

79222726

To ensure a leak-free seal, apply sealer as shown—Prizm 1.6L engine

➡ **When removing the powertrain reinforcement brace, do not pry on the oil pump body or the rear main seal retainer. Be careful not to damage the contact surfaces of the powertrain reinforcement brace, cylinder block, oil pump or the rear main seal retainer.**

11. Remove the oil pan bolts, nuts and oil pan from the vehicle.

12. Remove the oil pump strainer.

13. Clean all gasket material from the mating surfaces.

To install:

14. Install the oil pump strainer with a new seal. Secure with bolt and tighten to 97 inch lbs. (11 Nm).

15. Apply a continuous bead of RTV sealant to the engine oil pan and install.

Tighten the bolts and nuts to 97 inch lbs. (11 Nm) starting in the center and working outward.

16. Install the exhaust pipe with a new seal to the manifold and secure with bolts. Do not fully tighten the bolts.

17. On Prizm models, apply GM 1050026 gasket paste or equivalent, to the powertrain reinforcement brace-to-cylinder block mating surface.

18. Install the powertrain reinforcement brace. Tighten the Torx® bolts to 12 ft. lbs. (16 Nm). Tighten the remaining bolts to 69 inch lbs. (7.8 Nm). Install the three brace-to-transaxle bolts and tighten to 17 ft. lbs. (23 Nm).

19. On Prizm models, perform the following:

   a. Install the lower engine reinforcement brace to the vehicle and tighten the bolts to 47 ft. lbs. (64 Nm).

   b. Install the center support and tighten the bolts to 45 ft. lbs. (61 Nm).

20. Install the front pipe to the resonator/muffler/tail pipe assembly using a new gasket and secure with nuts.

21. Install the support hanger to the catalytic converter. If equipped, tighten the hanger bolts to 11 ft. lbs. (15 Nm).

22. Tighten the front exhaust pipe-to-exhaust manifold bolts to 37 ft. lbs. (50 Nm). Tighten the front exhaust pipe-to-resonator/muffler/tail pipe assembly nuts to 26 ft. lbs. (35 Nm).

23. Install the flywheel dust cover.

24. Lower the vehicle and fill the engine with oil.

25. Reconnect the negative battery cable, start the engine and check for leaks.

Oil Pump

REMOVAL & INSTALLATION

1. Before servicing the vehicle, refer to the precautions in the beginning of this section.

2. Disconnect the negative battery cable.

3. Raise and safely support the vehicle.

4. Drain the engine oil.

5. Remove the water pump belt and pulley, alternator belt, body and bracket.

6. Remove the air conditioning compressor and mounting bracket, if equipped.

7. On Prizm models, if equipped, unclip the Crankshaft Position (CKP) sensor electrical connector from the dipstick tube. Remove the bolt and the dipstick tube from the oil pump. Remove the dipstick tube O-ring from the oil pump.

Short Bolts   Short Bolts

Long Bolts   Long Bolts

79222727

Oil pump mounting bolt identification—Metro

8. Remove the timing belt and crankshaft pulley.

9. Disconnect the engine oil level gauge.

10. Remove the crankshaft timing belt sprocket.

11. Remove the oil pan and strainer assembly.

12. Remove the oil pump bolts and the oil pump assembly. Identify the bolts so they can be reinstalled in their proper locations. If necessary, gently tap on the back side of the oil pump with a plastic or rubber faced hammer to free it from the cylinder block.

13. Remove the crankshaft oil seal from the oil pump.

14. Remove the pump rotor plate pins from the oil pump. Clean the gasket mating surfaces thoroughly.

To install:

15. Install the pump rotor plate pins into the pump body.

16. Install a new crankshaft oil seal using an oil/grease seal installer tool.

17. Lubricate the oil pump with fresh engine oil.

18. Using new gaskets, install the oil pump. Install the crankshaft seal.

19. Apply Loctite® pipe sealant or equivalent to the oil pump bolts and install. On Metro models, tighten the bolts to 97 inch lbs. (11 Nm) or on Prizm models, tighten the bolts to 16 ft. lbs. (21 Nm).

➡ **After tightening, the oil pump gasket may bulge. Trim the edge with a knife, making sure the edge is smooth with the cylinder block.**

20. Install the rubber seal between the oil and coolant pump.

21. Install the crankshaft belt gear and guide. Tighten the pulley bolt to 81 ft. lbs. (110 Nm).

22. On Prizm models, install a new dip-

stick tube O-ring to the oil pump. Install the dipstick tube and secure. Tighten the bolt to 84 inch lbs. (9.5 Nm). If equipped, clip the CKP sensor electrical connector to the dipstick tube.

23. Install the engine oil level gauge.
24. Install the oil strainer and oil pan.
25. Install the timing belt.
26. Install the remaining components.
27. Lower the vehicle and fill the engine with clean engine oil.
28. Connect the negative battery cable. Start the engine and check for leaks.

Rear Main Seal

REMOVAL & INSTALLATION

Metro

1. Before servicing the vehicle, refer to the precautions in the beginning of this section.
2. Disconnect the negative battery cable.
3. Raise and safely support the vehicle.
4. Remove the transaxle from the vehicle.
5. On manual transaxle equipped vehicles, remove the pressure plate assembly and clutch disc.
6. Mark the flywheel-to-engine position.
7. Remove the flywheel retaining bolts and flywheel from the crankshaft.
8. Remove the rear crankshaft seal housing attaching bolts and remove the seal housing.
9. Remove the rear crankshaft seal from the housing.

To install:
10. Lubricate the inside and outside edges of the rear crankshaft seal and install the seal in the housing.
11. Install the seal housing on the block and tighten the mounting bolts to 9 ft. lbs. (12 Nm).
12. Apply Loctite® sealant, or equivalent, to the flywheel retaining bolt threads.
13. Install the flywheel and secure with retaining bolts. Tighten the bolts to 45–52 ft. lbs. (61–70 Nm).
14. On manual transaxle equipped vehicles, install the pressure plate and clutch disc.
15. Install the transaxle into the vehicle.
16. Lower the vehicle.
17. Reconnect the negative battery cable.
18. Check the engine oil level.
19. Run the engine and check for leaks.

Prizm

1. Before servicing the vehicle, refer to the precautions in the beginning of this section.
2. Disconnect the negative battery cable.
3. Raise and safely support the vehicle.
4. Remove the transaxle from the vehicle.
5. If equipped with a manual transaxle, perform the following procedures:
   a. Matchmark the pressure plate and flywheel.
   b. Remove the pressure plate and clutch assembly.
   c. Unbolt and remove the flywheel. Be careful not to damage the flywheel.
6. If equipped with an automatic transaxle, perform the following procedures:
   a. Matchmark the torque converter flexplate and crankshaft.
   b. Unbolt and remove the torque converter flexplate.
7. Remove the bolts holding the rear end plate to the engine and the remove the rear end plate.
8. Loosen the rear oil seal retainer bolts in a crisscross pattern. Loosen and remove the two bolts securing the oil pan to the rear oil seal retainer, then remove the rear oil seal retainer.
9. Using a small prybar, pry the rear oil seal retainer from the mating surfaces. Don't pry around the crankshaft, or it may be damaged. Be sure not to damage any of the oil seal retainer surfaces. If necessary, wrap a cloth around the edge of the prybar.
10. Using a hammer and small punch or a seal driver, drive the oil seal from the rear bearing retainer.

To install:
11. Clean the gasket mounting surfaces. The contact surfaces must be completely free of oil and foreign matter.
12. Clean the oil seal mounting surface.
13. Using multi-purpose grease, lubricate the lip of the new seal.
14. Use a properly sized seal installation driver to tap the new oil seal straight into the retainer. When properly installed, the oil seal should be flush with the surface of the seal retainer.
15. Position a new gasket on the retainer and coat it lightly with gasket sealer. Fit the seal retainer into place on the engine; be careful when installing the oil seal over the crankshaft.

16. Install the retaining bolts and tighten them to 7 ft. lbs. (10 Nm) in a crisscross pattern.
17. Install the rear end plate. Tighten the bolts to 7 ft. lbs. (10 Nm).
18. Install either the flexplate (automatic transaxle) or the flywheel (manual transaxle), carefully observing the matchmarks made earlier. The front flexplate spacer should be installed so that its chamfered internal edge is facing the crankshaft. The rear flexplate spacer should be installed with its curved side facing out. Apply a small amount of thread locking compound to the first 2–3 threads of each flexplate/flywheel bolt before installation.
19. Tighten the flexplate (automatic transaxle) or the flywheel (manual transaxle) bolts to the correct torque specification following a two-step crisscross pattern as follows:
   • Vehicles with manual transaxles: 58 ft. lbs. (78 Nm)
   • Vehicles with automatic transaxles: 47 ft. lbs. (64 Nm).
20. Install the clutch disc and pressure plate, if equipped with manual transaxle.
21. Install the transaxle.
22. Lower the vehicle.
23. Reconnect the negative battery cable.
24. Check the engine oil level and add oil as necessary.
25. Start the engine and check for leaks.

FUEL SYSTEM

Fuel System Service Precautions

Fuel System Pressure

RELIEVING

1. Before servicing the vehicle, refer to the precautions in the beginning of this section.
2. Remove the fuel filler cap.
3. On Metro models, perform the following:
   a. Remove the control relay box cover from the relay box.
   b. Disconnect the fuel pump relay from the relay box connector.
4. On Prizm models, perform the following:

629 RELAY BOX
630 FUEL PUMP RELAY

7922Z728

View of the relay box showing the location of the fuel pump relay—Metro

7922Z729

Leave the circuit opening relay unplugged during fuel system servicing—Prizm

a. Remove the center trim bezel from the center console by gently prying around the edges.

b. Remove the radio from the center console.

c. Disconnect the circuit opening relay, located in the center console.

5. Attempt to start the engine, if it starts, let it run until the engine stalls due to lack of fuel.

6. Engage the starter for a few seconds to assure relief of remaining fuel pressure.

7. Disconnect the negative battery cable.

8. Continue with the required service procedure(s).

Fuel Filter

REMOVAL & INSTALLATION

Metro

1. Before servicing the vehicle, refer to the precautions in the beginning of this section.

---

1. Fuel Feed Outlet Hose
2. Fuel Filter
3. Fuel Filter Mounting Bolts
4. Parking Brake Cable Bracket Bolt
5. Fuel Feed Inlet Hose
6. Fuel Filter Mounting Bracket to Fuel Filter Bolt

7922Z730

Component view of the fuel filter mounting—Metro

2. Properly relieve the fuel system pressure.

3. Disconnect the negative battery cable.

4. Raise and safely support the vehicle.

5. Remove the bolt securing the parking brake cable bracket from the underbody.

6. Disconnect the fuel feed hose from the fuel filter.

7. Remove the two fuel filter mounting bracket bolts, and remove the fuel filter from the frame.

8. Disconnect the outlet hose from the fuel filter.

9. Remove the fuel filter from the bracket by removing the mounting bolt.

To install:

10. Install the fuel filter on the bracket. Install the mounting bolt and tighten to 11 ft. lbs. (15 Nm).

➡ **Be sure the matchmarks between the fuel filter and the mounting bracket are aligned before tightening the bolt.**

11. Connect the fuel feed outlet hose to the fuel filter. Secure with a new clamp.

12. Install the fuel filter on the frame and install the two bracket bolts. Tighten the bracket bolts to 11 ft. lbs. (15 Nm).

13. Connect the fuel inlet hose to the fuel filter. Secure with a new clamp.

14. Position the brake cable bracket and install the bolt. Tighten the cable bracket bolt to 11 ft. lbs. (15 Nm).

15. Lower the vehicle.

16. Reconnect the negative battery cable.

17. Turn the ignition switch to **ON**, then back to **LOCK** to pressurize the fuel system. Check for leaks and correct as necessary.

Prizm

1. Before servicing the vehicle, refer to the precautions in the beginning of this section.

---

1. Fuel Filter Bracket Bolt
2. Fuel Filter
3. Fuel Filter Bracket

7922Z731

To remove the filter from a Prizm, detach the fuel lines and remove the two bracket bolts, then slide the filter out of the bracket—be sure to check for fuel leaks after replacing the filter

2. Properly relieve the fuel system pressure.

3. Disconnect the negative battery cable.

4. Disconnect the Intake Air Temperature (IAT) sensor.

5. Loosen the air cleaner clamp and release the four air cleaner housing cover clips. Remove the hose and air cleaner cover.

6. Disconnect the hoses from the Evaporative Emissions (EVAP) canister. Remove the bolt and canister from the bracket.

7. Remove the bolt and disconnect the fuel outlet hose from the top of the fuel filter. Discard the gaskets.

8. Remove the two bolts and remove the fuel filter from the bracket.

9. Remove the nut and fuel inlet pipe from the bottom of the fuel filter.

To install:

10. Install the fuel filter to the bracket and tighten the bolts to 43 inch lbs. (5 Nm).

11. Connect the fuel inlet pipe to the bottom of the fuel filter and tighten the nut to 22 ft. lbs. (30 Nm).

12. Install the fuel outlet hose to the top of the fuel filter, using new gaskets. Install the bolt and tighten to 21 ft. lbs. (29 Nm).

13. Install the EVAP canister to the bracket and tighten the bolt to 21 ft. lbs. (29 Nm). Connect the hoses to the canister.

14. Install the air cleaner cover and secure with the clips. Connect the air cleaner hose.

15. Connect the IAT sensor.

16. Connect the negative battery cable. Turn the ignition switch **ON** to pressurize the fuel system. Check for fuel leaks.

Fuel Pump

REMOVAL & INSTALLATION

Metro

1. Before servicing the vehicle, refer to the precautions in the beginning of this section.

2. Properly relieve the fuel system pressure.

3. Disconnect the negative battery cable.

4. Remove the filler cap. Drain the fuel tank by pumping the fuel out through the filler neck into a suitable container.

5. Reinstall the fuel filler cap.

6. Raise and safely support the vehicle.

7. Remove the fuel tank from the vehicle. Clean all dirt from the fuel pump area, to prevent fuel system contamination.

8. Remove the fuel feed and return clamps and hoses from the pump assembly.

9. Remove the screws from the pump assembly and remove with the gasket from the fuel tank.

10. Remove the screws from the pump motor assembly. Remove the fuel pump motor connectors and detach the pump motor from the pump assembly.

To install:

11. Install the two pump motor connectors. Install the pump motor on the pump assembly and tighten the screw.

12. Install the assembly with the gasket on the fuel tank. Install the screws and tighten.

13. Install the fuel feed and return hoses and clamps on the fuel pump assembly.

14. Install the fuel tank in the vehicle.

15. Lower the vehicle and reconnect the negative battery cable.

PULL

FUEL PUMP
FUEL PUMP HOSE
CONNECTION FUEL
PUMP
ELECTRICAL CONNECTOR

79222732

Remove the fuel pump and the sender assembly from the fuel tank slowly to keep from splashing fuel—Prizm

16. Refill the fuel tank. Turn the ignition key **ON** and allow the fuel system to pressurize. Check for leaks.

17. Start the engine and check for leaks.

Prizm

1. Before servicing the vehicle, refer to the precautions in the beginning of this section.

2. Properly relieve the fuel system pressure.

3. Use a pump to drain the fuel through the filler neck.

4. Remove the rear seat cushion to gain access to the service panel.

5. Remove the four screws, then the service access panel.

6. Disconnect the fuel pump and sending wiring.

7. Remove the nut and fuel feed hose from the sender.

8. Remove the clamp and fuel return hose from the sender.

9. Remove the bolts and remove the sender assembly from the tank.

10. Remove the pump from the bracket by pulling off the lower side of the pump from the bracket.

11. Disconnect the fuel pump electrical connector.

12. Remove the rubber cushion from the fuel pump.

13. Remove the clamp and disconnect the strainer from the pump.

To install:

14. Install the clamp and connect the strainer to the pump.

15. Install the rubber cushion to the pump.

16. Connect the fuel pump electrical connector.

17. Install the pump to the bracket.

18. Install the fuel sender assembly to the tank, using a new gasket. Secure with the bolts, tightened to 35 inch lbs. (4 Nm).

19. Install the clamp and fuel return hose to the sender.

20. Install the nut and fuel feed hose to the sender. Tighten the nut to 22 ft. lbs. (30 Nm).

21. Connect the fuel pump electrical connector.

22. Refill the fuel tank.

23. Connect the negative battery cable. Turn the ignition **ON** to pressurize the fuel system. Check for fuel leaks.

24. Install the service access panel and rear seat cushion.

DRIVE TRAIN

Transaxle Assembly

REMOVAL & INSTALLATION

Manual

METRO

1. Before servicing the vehicle, refer to the precautions in the beginning of this section.

2. Disconnect the negative battery cable and ground strap at the transaxle.

3. Loosen the clutch cable adjusting nuts, then remove the cable from the bracket.

4. Disconnect the wiring harness attached to the transaxle.

5. Remove the speedometer cable boot, case clip and cable from the transaxle.

6. Remove the transaxle retaining bolts.

7. Remove the starter.

8. Remove the vacuum hose from the pressure sensor.

9. Install a suitable engine support.

10. Raise and safely support the vehicle. Drain the transaxle oil.

11. Remove the gear shift control shaft bolt and nut, then detach the control shaft from the gear shift shaft.

12. Remove the extension rod nut and rod with washers.

13. Remove the exhaust pipe front and rear flange bolts.

14. Remove the clutch housing lower plate.

15. Remove the wheels.

16. Remove both the tie rod ends.

17. Remove both halfshafts at the transaxle.

18. Support the transaxle with a suitable jack and remove the transaxle retaining bolts and nuts.

19. Remove the two rear engine mounting bolts.

20. Remove the bolts and nuts from the transaxle left-hand bracket and remove.

21. Lower the transaxle with the engine attached. Carefully pull the transaxle straight out toward the left side to disconnect the input shaft from the clutch cover. Lower and remove the transaxle assembly.

To install:

22. While the transaxle is being raised into the correct position, install the right side halfshaft.

23. Install the transaxle to the engine block using the retainer nuts and bolts. Install the left side bracket with the bolts and nuts. Tighten them to 37 ft. lbs. (50 Nm).

24. Install the rear engine mounting nuts and tighten to 37 ft. lbs. (50 Nm).

25. Lower the transaxle supporting jack. Tighten the transaxle to engine bolt and nut to 37 ft. lbs. (50 Nm).

26. Install the left halfshaft to the transaxle.

27. Install both tie rod ends.

28. Install the front wheels.

29. Install the clutch housing lower plate.

30. Install the exhaust pipe front and rear flange nuts.

31. Install the extension rod nut and washers. Tighten the nut to 24 ft. lbs. (33 Nm).

32. Install the control shaft to gear shift and the gear shift control shaft bolt and nut. Tighten the gear shaft bolt and nut to 13–15 ft. lbs. (18–20 Nm).

33. Refill the transaxle.

34. Lower the vehicle.

35. Remove the engine support fixture.

36. Install the vacuum hose to the pressure sensor.

37. Install the starter motor.

38. Install the transaxle retaining bolts. Tighten the retaining bolts to 37 ft. lbs. (50 Nm).

39. Install the speedometer cable, case clip and speedometer cable boot.

40. Install the clutch cable into the bracket, Adjust the cable free-play.

41. Connect the negative battery cable and ground strap to the transaxle.

PRIZM

1. Before servicing the vehicle, refer to the precautions in the beginning of this section.

2. Install Engine Support Fixture J-28467 or equivalent.

3. Disconnect the battery cables, negative cable first. Remove the battery and tray.

4. Remove the air cleaner.

5. Disconnect the reverse light and ground strap at the transaxle.

6. Remove the actuator mounting bolts and actuator line bracket.

7. Remove the shift cable retainers and end clips.

8. Remove the shift cables and place out of the way.

9. Remove the left transaxle mount cover and bracket. Remove the through-bolt from the mount.

10. Remove the two upper transaxle-to-engine bolts.

11. Remove the upper starter bolt. Remove the speedometer cable or disconnect the Vehicle Speed Sensor (VSS), as applicable.

12. Raise and safely support the vehicle.

13. Remove the splash shields. Drain the transaxle oil.

14. Disconnect the starter wires. Remove the bottom starter bolt and starter.

15. Remove both halfshafts.

16. Remove the bolts holding the center crossmember to the radiator support.

17. Remove the bolts holding the center crossmember to the radiator support.

18. Remove the front mount shield.

19. Remove the front mounting bolts and rear mounting nuts.

20. Remove the exhaust pipe support bolts.

21. Support the main crossmember. Remove the bolts holding the main crossmember to the body.

22. Remove the bolts holding the lower control arm brackets to the body.

✷✷ CAUTION

The crossmembers are loose and free to fall. Be sure they are properly supported.

23. Slowly lower the main crossmember while holding onto the center crossmember.

24. Remove the through-bolt and mount, at the front transaxle mount

25. Remove the front mounting bracket from the transaxle.

26. Remove the center mount from the transaxle.

27. Remove the inspection cover bolt.

28. Remove the two lower transaxle bracket-to-transaxle bolts.

29. Lower the vehicle.

30. Remove the transaxle mount.

31. Raise and safely support the vehicle.

32. Support the transaxle with a suitable jack.

33. Remove the lower front and rear bolts holding the transaxle to the engine.

34. Remove the transaxle assembly from the engine and carefully lower it from the vehicle.

To install:

35. Raise the transaxle into position, making sure the input shaft aligns with the clutch splines.

36. Install the lower front and rear bolts holding the transaxle to the engine. Do not tighten them fully.

37. Remove the jack from under the transaxle.

38. Install the starter and wiring.

39. Lower the vehicle.

40. Install the left transaxle mounting bolts.

41. Raise the transaxle and install the through-bolt. Tighten the through-bolt to 64 ft. lbs. (87 Nm). Tighten the transaxle mounting bolts to 45 ft. lbs. (61 Nm).

42. Install the mount cover and bracket. Tighten the cover bolts to 45 ft. lbs. (61 Nm).

43. Install the upper transaxle to engine bolts and tighten them to 34 ft. lbs. (46 Nm).

44. Connect the speedometer cable or VSS connector.

45. Position the shift cables into the brackets and connect the cable retainers and end clips.

46. Install the two actuator mounting bolts, then install the actuator line bracket and bolt. Tighten the line and mounting bolts to 15 ft. lbs. (20 Nm).

47. Connect the ground strap and reverse lights harnesses.

48. Install the air cleaner.

49. Raise and safely support the vehicle.

50. Tighten the lower transaxle mount bolts to 45 ft. lbs. (61 Nm).

51. Install the center mount and bolts. Tighten them to 45 ft. lbs. (61 Nm). Install the inspection cover bolt and tighten it to 45 ft. lbs. (61 Nm).

52. Install the front mount bracket on the transaxle.

53. Install the front mount and through-bolt loosely.

➡ When installing the front mount, the weight on the mount must go toward the transaxle.

54. Position the central crossmember over the center and rear transaxle mount studs. Secure with nuts.

55. Loosely install the bolts holding the center crossmember to the radiator support.

56. Loosely install the front mount bolts.

57. Raise the main crossmember into position over the rear mount studs and align the bolts. Install the rear mount nuts loosely. Install the main crossmember to underbody bolts loosely.

58. Install the lower control arm bracket bolts loosely.

59. Loosely install the bolts holding the center crossmember to the main crossmember.

60. Install the exhaust hanger bracket and hardware.

61. Tighten the components below to the correct torque specification:

   a. Main crossmember to underbody bolts: 152 ft. lbs. (206 Nm).

   b. Lower control arm bolts to 161 ft. lbs. (218 Nm).

   c. Center crossmember to radiator support bolts: 45 ft. lbs. (61 Nm).

   d. Front, center and rear mount bolts: 45 ft. lbs. (61 Nm).

   e. Exhaust bracket bolts: 115 inch lbs. (13 Nm).

   f. Front mount through-bolt: 64 ft. lbs. (87 Nm).

62. Install the remaining components.

63. Install the halfshafts.

64. Install the battery tray and battery.

65. Connect the battery cables to the battery, negative cable last.

Automatic

METRO

1. Before servicing the vehicle, refer to the precautions in the beginning of this section.

2. Disconnect the negative battery cable from the battery and transaxle.

3. Disconnect the throttle valve cable adjustment cover and the cable from top of the transaxle.

4. Disconnect the shift cable from the manual select joint on the transaxle. Remove the retaining clip and cable from the bracket on the transaxle assembly. Loosen the adjustment nuts.

5. Remove the accelerator cable from the bracket on top of the transaxle. Remove the engine harness bracket from the rear of the transaxle.

6. Disconnect the harnesses to the Vehicle Speed Sensor (VSS), shift solenoid and Transaxle Range Switch (TRS).

7. Remove the speedometer cable from the gear case.

8. Disconnect and plug the inlet and outlet fluid cooler lines.

9. Remove the starter motor. Drain the transaxle fluid.

10. Remove the rear transaxle/engine mount. Remove the upper transaxle-to-engine mount bolts from the transaxle.

11. Support the engine from the top using engine support tool J-28467-A and support fixture adapters J-28467–89 or equivalents.

12. Raise and support the vehicle safely. Remove the right and left splash shields.

13. Separate both ball joints from the steering knuckles.

14. Remove the right and left halfshaft assemblies. Remove the rear engine torque rod/engine mount from the transaxle case.

➡ **Make alignment marks on the torque converter and drive plate for assembly reference.**

15. Remove the flywheel cover from the transaxle case. Lock the flywheel in place and remove the flywheel-to-torque converter bolts.

16. Remove the muffler mounting from the rear engine exhaust hanger.

17. Lower the engine slightly.

18. Support the transaxle and remove the transaxle-to-engine bolts. Slide the transaxle off the engine and lower it from the vehicle.

To install:

19. Use grease to lubricate the cup around the center of the torque converter.

20. Measure the distance between the torque converter and the edge of the transaxle housing; it should be at least 0.85 in. (21.4mm). If the distance is less than specified, the torque converter is improperly installed. Remove and reinstall it.

21. Position the transaxle to the engine. Install the lower transaxle-to-engine retaining bolt and tighten to 40 ft. lbs. (55 Nm).

22. Install the left transaxle mount and secure with the bracket bolts and nuts. Tighten the bolts and nuts to 40 ft. lbs. (55 Nm).

23. Remove the transaxle support jack.

24. Raise the engine assembly slightly.

25. Install the rear engine mount bracket to the transaxle. Install the bracket bolts and nuts and tighten to 40 ft. lbs. (55 Nm). Install the rear engine mount-to-bulkhead bolt and tighten to 40 ft. lbs. (55 Nm).

26. Install the muffler mounting to the rear exhaust hanger.

27. Install the flywheel-to-torque converter bolts. Lock the flywheel in place and tighten the flywheel-to-torque converter bolts to 14 ft. lbs. (19 Nm).

28. Install the flywheel inspection cover to the transaxle and tighten the bolts to 89 inch lbs. (10 Nm).

29. Install the rear engine torque rod assembly and tighten the bolts to 40 ft. lbs. (55 Nm).

30. Install the right and left side halfshaft assemblies.

31. Install the ball joints to the steering knuckles.

32. Install the right and left splash shields.

33. Remove the engine support fixture from the vehicle.

34. Install the upper transaxle-to-engine mounting bolts and tighten to 40 ft. lbs. (55 Nm).

35. Install the through-bolt and nut to the rear engine mount and tighten to 40 ft. lbs. (55 Nm).

36. Install the upper rear transaxle mount-to-bulkhead bolt and tighten to 40 ft. lbs. (55 Nm).

37. Install the starter motor.

38. Connect the inlet and outlet fluid cooler lines using new hose clamps.

39. Install the speedometer cable into the gear case.

40. Connect the harness to the VSS, shift solenoid and TRS.

41. Install the remaining components.

42. Connect the negative battery cable to the transaxle and battery.

43. Refill and check the transaxle fluid level.

PRIZM

1. Before servicing the vehicle, refer to the precautions in the beginning of this section.

2. Disconnect both battery cables, negative cable first, then remove the battery.

3. Disconnect the Intake Air Temperature (IAT) sensor, Park Neutral Position (PNP) switch, Vehicle Speed Sensor (VSS) and solenoid wiring harness, if equipped with a 4-speed transaxle.

4. Remove the air cleaner housing cover and filter, then remove the housing from the vehicle.

5. Disconnect the ground wire from the transaxle.

6. Remove the Throttle Valve (TV) cable from the throttle linkage and bracket.

7. Disconnect the VSS harness.

8. Remove the nut and disconnect the shift select cable from the manual lever. Remove the E-clip and disconnect the cable from the cable bracket.

9. Remove the bolt and the TV cable guide bracket from the transaxle case.

10. Remove the upper transaxle-to-engine bolts. Remove the starter motor.

11. Install engine/transaxle support fixture J-28467-A or equivalent.

12. Remove the bolts and left mounting bracket.

13. Raise and safely support the vehicle.

14. Drain the transaxle fluid.

15. On 3-speed transaxles, remove the differential filler plug at the rear of the transaxle and drain the differential fluid.

16. Remove the right and left splash shields.

17. Disconnect the fluid cooler hoses from the lines at the transaxle.

18. Remove the front wheels.

19. Remove the right and left halfshafts.

20. Remove the bolts from the exhaust pipe support. Remove the nut and exhaust pipe support from the center crossmember.

21. Disconnect the Oxygen (O_2S) sensor harness. Remove the front exhaust pipe from the vehicle.

22. Remove the plastic cover from the front transaxle mounting cavity in the center crossmember.

23. Remove the bolts/nuts from the front and rear transaxle mounts.

24. Remove the bolts and nuts, then remove the front suspension and center crossmembers.

25. Support the transaxle with a suitable jack.

26. On 3-speed transaxles, remove the bolts and the lower engine reinforcement brace.

27. Remove the flywheel access cover from the rear of the engine.

28. Remove the six flywheel-to-torque converter bolts.

29. Remove the drain pan from underneath the transaxle fluid pan.

30. Remove the lower transaxle-to-engine bolts from the transaxle.

31. Remove the transaxle by carefully moving the transaxle away from the engine toward the left side of the engine compartment and slowly lowering the jack.

To install:

32. Before installing the transaxle assembly, perform the following:

a. Apply grease around the pilot shaft at the center of the torque converter.

b. Measure the distance between the outside edge of the torque converter housing and the torque converter lug. The distance should be more than 0.906 in. (23mm). If it is less than 0.906 in. (23mm), the torque converter is improperly installed. Remove and properly seat on the input shaft.

33. Install the transaxle to the engine.

34. Install the lower transaxle-to-engine bolts and tighten to 47 ft. lbs. (64 Nm).

35. Install the flywheel-to-torque converter bolts. Tighten the bolts to 14 ft. lbs. (19 Nm).

36. Install the flywheel access cover.

37. On 3-speed transaxles, install the lower engine reinforcement brace and tighten the bolts to 47 ft. lbs. (64 Nm).

38. Remove the jack from under the transaxle.

39. Install the front suspension and center crossmembers. Tighten the front suspension crossmember bolts to 152 ft. lbs. (206 Nm) and the center crossmember bolts to 45 ft. lbs. (61 Nm).

40. Install the front and rear transaxle mount nuts. Tighten the rear nuts to 42 ft. lbs. (57 Nm), and the front to 47 ft. lbs. (64 Nm).

41. Install the plastic access cover to the center crossmember.

42. Install the front exhaust pipe and connect the O_2S sensor harness.

43. Install the halfshafts and the front wheels.

44. Install the bolts to the left transaxle bracket and tighten to 35 ft. lbs. (48 Nm).

45. Connect the fluid cooler hoses to the lines at the transaxle; secure with hose clamps.

46. Install the splash shields.

47. Install the starter.

✳✳ WARNING

The differential portion of the 3-speed transaxle is separated from the rest of the transaxle and must be drained and refilled separately. The differential cannot be drained or refilled through the transaxle drain plug or filler tube. If the differential portion is drained and not refilled as outlined in this procedure, damage to the differential due to lack of lubrication will result.

48. On 3-speed transaxle, refill the differential with 1 ½ qts. (1.4 L) of Dexron® III automatic transmission fluid, into the differential filler plug hole. The fluid level should be even with the bottom of the differential filler plug hole. Install the filler plug and tighten to 29 ft. lbs. (39 Nm).

49. Lower the vehicle.

50. Install the left transaxle bracket reinforcement and tighten the bolts to 15 ft. lbs. (21 Nm).

51. Remove the engine/transaxle support fixture.

52. Install the upper transaxle-to-engine bolts and tighten to 47 ft. lbs. (64 Nm).

53. Install the TV guide cable bracket onto the transaxle and tighten the bolt to 71 inch lbs. (8 Nm).

54. Install the shift select cable into the bracket at the transaxle and secure with clip.

55. Install the shift select cable to the manual lever and secure with the nut and lockwasher. Adjust the shift select cable.

56. Connect the wiring connector to the VSS.

57. Install the TV cable to the throttle linkage. Adjust the cable as follows:

a. Be sure the throttle valve is fully closed.

b. Measure the distance between the end of the outer cable boot and the end of the TV cable stopper, it should be 0–0.04 in. (0–1mm).

c. If the distance is greater than specified, loosen the TV cable locknut and tighten the adjust nut until within specification.

d. If the distance is less than specified, loosen the TV cable adjust nut and tighten the locknut within specification.

e. After adjustment is completed, tighten the locknut and adjust nuts to 71 inch lbs. (8 Nm).

58. Connect the ground strap to the transaxle and tighten the bolt to 115 inch lbs. (13 Nm).

59. Connect the PNP switch, IAT sensor and solenoid harness if equipped with a 4-speed transaxle.

60. Install the air cleaner and filter. Tighten the bolts to 106 inch lbs. (12 Nm). Tighten the air cleaner intake tube clamp.

61. Install the battery and connect the cables, negative cable last.

62. Refill the transaxle with the proper amount of Dexron® III automatic transmission fluid.

63. Operate the vehicle and check for leaks.

Clutch

ADJUSTMENT

These vehicles are equipped with a hydraulic clutch actuating system that is self-adjusting.

REMOVAL & INSTALLATION

1. Before servicing the vehicle, refer to the precautions in the beginning of this section.

2. Disconnect the negative battery cable.

3. Raise and safely support the vehicle.

4. Remove the transaxle assembly.

5. Install a clutch pilot tool into the pilot bearing to support the clutch.

6. Matchmark the clutch cover and flywheel.

7. On Prizm models, unfasten the release fork bearing clips. Withdraw the release bearing hub and release bearing. Remove the release fork and support.

8. Loosen the clutch cover-to-flywheel

Exploded view of the clutch assembly—Metro

710 CLUTCH RELEASE SHAFT
730 CLUTCH RELEASE SHAFT FORK
731 CLUTCH RELEASE SHAFT RETURN SPRING
732 CLUTCH RELEASE SHAFT COVER
733 CLUTCH RELEASE SHAFT SEAL
734 CLUTCH RELEASE SHAFT UPPER BUSHING
735 CLUTCH RELEASE SHAFT LOWER BUSHING
736 CLUTCH RELEASE BEARING
737 CLUTCH RELEASE BEARING PIN
742 CLUTCH PRESSURE PLATE COVER BOLTS
743 CLUTCH DISC
746 FLYWHEEL
749 CLUTCH PRESSURE PLATE COVER

13. Inspect the disc, pressure plate and flywheel for damage and wear using a caliper to measure depth and width and a dial indicator to measure run-out.

  a. The minimum clutch disc rivet head depth is 0.012 in. (0.3mm):

  b. The maximum clutch disc run-out is 0.031 in. (0.8mm).

  c. The maximum pressure plate spring depth is 0.024 in. (0.6mm).

  d. The maximum pressure plate spring width is 0.197 in. (5.0mm).

  e. The maximum flywheel run-out is 0.004 in. (0.1mm).

14. When reassembling, apply a thin coating of multi-purpose grease to the release bearing hub and release fork contact points. Also, pack the groove inside the clutch hub with multi-purpose grease and lubricate the pivot points of the release fork.

15. Position the clutch disc and clutch cover with the matchmarks aligned and support with pilot tool.

16. Install the clutch cover bolts and tighten evenly to 17 ft. lbs. (23 Nm) for Metro models, or 14 ft. lbs. (19 Nm) for Prizm models, in a crisscross pattern. Remove the pilot tool.

17. On Prizm models, install the release bearing, fork, and the boot.

18. Lightly lubricate the splines, pilot bearing surface of the input shaft and release bearing with grease.

19. Install the transaxle.

20. Adjust the clutch cable.

bolts evenly, using a crisscross pattern, until the spring pressure is released.

9. Remove the clutch disc and clutch cover.

To install:

10. Clean the flywheel mating surfaces of all oil, grease and metal deposits.

11. Check the diaphragm spring and pressure plate for wear or damage. If the spring or plate is excessively worn, replace the clutch cover assembly.

12. Check the pilot bearing for smooth operation. If the bearing does not spin freely, replace it.

1 FLYWHEEL
2 DRIVEN PLATE
3 CLUTCH COVER
4 CLUTCH COVER BOLTS
5 RELEASE BEARING
6 CLUTCH FORK
7 CLUTCH FORK BALL STUD
8 FORK BOOT

Exploded view of the clutch assembly—Prizm

21. Connect the negative battery cable. Check clutch operation.

Hydraulic Clutch System

BLEEDING

➡ **If any maintenance on the clutch system was performed or the system is suspected of containing air, bleed the system.**

1. Fill the clutch reservoir with brake fluid. Check the reservoir level frequently and add fluid as needed.

2. Connect one end of a vinyl tube to the bleeder plug on the slave cylinder and submerge the other end into a clear container half-filled with clean brake fluid.

3. Slowly pump the clutch pedal several times.

4. Repeat Steps 2 and 3 until all of the air bubbles are removed from the system.

5. Tighten the bleeder plug when no more air bubbles emerge from the tube.

6. Refill the master cylinder to the proper level.

7. Check the system for leaks.

Halfshaft

REMOVAL & INSTALLATION

Metro

1. Before servicing the vehicle, refer to the precautions in the beginning of this section.

2. Disconnect the negative battery cable.

3. Unstake and remove the halfshaft nut with the vehicle's weight on the ground.

4. Raise and safely support the vehicle.

5. Remove the front wheel.

6. If equipped with ABS, remove the wheel speed sensor.

7. Remove the ball joint from the steering knuckle.

8. Drain the transaxle fluid.

➡ **On 4-door sedan vehicles, the right side halfshaft is stabilized by a center support bearing between the transaxle and the inner tripod joint. It is not necessary to remove the right inner drive axle and center support bearing assembly. The right side halfshaft assembly can be separated from the center support bearing by lightly tapping with a plastic mallet.**

9. Using a suitable prytool, pry on the inboard joints of the halfshaft to detach the snapring lock in the differential. On 4-door

403	DIFFERENTIAL-SIDE JOINT HOUSING
405	RIGHT INNER DRIVE AXLE SHAFT
406	RIGHT INNER DRIVE AXLE SUPPORT ARBOR
417	RIGHT DRIVE AXLE ASSEMBLY

79222735

Tapping out the right inner halfshaft from the transaxle—4-door models

sedans, separate the right side halfshaft assembly from the center support bearing by tapping lightly with a plastic mallet.

10. Remove the stabilizer bar mounting bracket bolts.

11. Pull the halfshaft out of the transaxle, then from the steering knuckle.

To install:

12. Inspect the CV-joint boots for tears or deterioration and replace, if necessary.

13. Snap the halfshaft into the transaxle first, then into the steering knuckle.

14. Install the ball joint to the steering knuckle.

15. Install the stabilizer bar, if necessary.

16. Install the halfshaft nut and washer. Tighten the halfshaft nut to 148 ft. lbs. (200 Nm).

17. Stake the drive axle nut with a hammer and punch.

18. If equipped with ABS, install the ABS speed sensor.

19. Install the front wheel.

20. Lower the vehicle to the ground.

21. Refill the transaxle with clean transaxle fluid.

22. Connect the negative battery cable.

23. Road test the vehicle.

Prizm

✳✳ WARNING

Care must be exercised to prevent the differential-side CV-joint from being over-extended. Over-extension of the differential-side CV-joint could result in separation of internal components and possible joint failure. If the vehicle is to be lowered and moved, the front wheel bearings must be supported using a 9/16 in. (14mm) bolt, 1 3/4 in. (44.45mm) washer, 2 in. (50.8mm) washer, and a 9/16 in. (14mm) nut assembled through the shaft opening in the hub. Tighten the nut and bolt to 40 ft. lbs. (54 Nm). If equipped with Anti-lock Brake Systems (ABS), use caution not to damage the ABS speed sensor ring on the wheel-side CV-joint. DO NOT pry against the ring with metal tools. If the serration's on the speed sensor ring appear damaged, replace the wheel-side CV-joint.

1. Before servicing the vehicle, refer to the precautions in the beginning of this section.

2. Disconnect the negative battery cable.

403 DIFFERENTIAL-SIDE JOINT HOUSING
418 TRANSAXLE ASSEMBLY

7922Z736

Prying out the inner halfshaft from the transaxle—Prizm

3. Raise and safely support the vehicle.
4. Remove the front wheel.
5. Remove the six bolts and splash shield from the vehicle.
6. If equipped with ABS, remove the speed sensor.
7. Remove the cotter pin and lock cap and nut from the halfshaft.
8. Separate the tie rod end from the steering knuckle.
9. Separate the ball joint from the control arm.
10. Remove the wheel-side CV-joint from the steering knuckle.
11. Remove the differential-side CV-joint from the transaxle by gently prying the joint out of the transaxle.
12. Remove the halfshaft from the vehicle.
To install:
13. Inspect the CV-joint boots for tears or deterioration. Replace as necessary.
14. Inspect the front wheel bearing inner and outer oil seals for damage or deterioration. Replace as necessary.
15. Inspect the halfshaft fluid seal at the transaxle for leakage or damage. Replace as necessary.
16. Install the differential-side CV-joint into the transaxle.
17. Install the wheel-side CV-joint into the steering knuckle.
18. Install the ball joint to the control arm.
19. Install the tie rod end.
20. Install the nut onto the halfshaft and tighten to 167 ft. lbs. (228 Nm).
21. Install the lock cap onto the halfshaft and secure with a new cotter pin.
22. Install the front wheel.
23. If equipped, install the ABS speed sensor.

24. Install the splash shield and secure with the six bolts. Tighten the splash shield bolts to 71 inch lbs. (8 Nm). Lower the vehicle.
25. Connect the negative battery cable.
26. Check the wheel alignment.

STEERING AND SUSPENSION

Air Bag

✳✳ CAUTION

All vehicles are equipped with an Air Bag system, also known as the Supplemental Inflatable Restraint (SIR) or Supplemental Restraint System (SRS). The system must be disabled before performing service on or around system components, steering column, instrument panel components, wiring and sensors. Failure to follow safety and disabling procedures could result in accidental Air Bag deployment, possible personal injury and unnecessary system repairs.

PRECAUTIONS

Several precautions must be observed when handling the inflator module to avoid accidental deployment and possible personal injury.
• Never carry the inflator module by the wires or connector on the underside of the module.
• When carrying a live inflator module, hold securely with both hands, and ensure that the bag and trim cover are pointed away.
• Place the inflator module on a bench or other surface with the bag and trim cover facing up.
• With the inflator module on the bench, never place anything on or close to the module which may be thrown in the event of an accidental deployment.

DISARMING

Metro

1. Before servicing the vehicle, refer to the precautions in the beginning of this section.

1 Inflator module housing
2 Steering wheel
3 Rear plastic access cover
4 SIR harness connector
5 Connector position assurance (CPA)

7922Z737

Location of the SIR harness connector—Metro

2. Disconnect the negative battery cable.
3. Turn the steering wheel so the wheels are pointing straight ahead.
4. Turn the ignition switch to the **LOCK** position and remove the key.
5. Remove the **AIR BAG-IG** fuse from the Air Bag fuse box located near the junction/fuse box.
6. Remove the left side steering wheel side cap and disconnect the yellow connector for the driver side Air Bag (inflator) module.
7. Pull out the glove box while pushing in on the stoppers from the left and the right sides. Disconnect the yellow connector for the passenger Air Bag (inflator) module.
To arm:
8. Connect the negative battery cable.
9. Turn the ignition switch to the **LOCK** position and remove the key.
10. Connect the yellow connector for the passenger side Air Bag (inflator) module and the yellow connector for the driver air bag (inflator) module. Be sure to lock each connector with the lock lever.
11. Install the glove box assembly.
12. Install the left side steering wheel side cover.
13. Install the **AIR BAG-IG** fuse to the Air Bag fuse box.
14. Turn the ignition **ON** and verify that the **AIR BAG** warning lamp flashes seven times, then turns off. If the system does

not operate as described, diagnosis and repairs to the air bag system are necessary.

Prizm

➡ **The center sensor assembly can maintain sufficient voltage to cause deployment for up to 2 minutes after the ignition switch is turned to the LOCK position or the battery is disconnected.**

1. Before servicing the vehicle, refer to the precautions in the beginning of this section.

2. Disconnect the negative battery cable.

3. Turn the steering wheel so the front wheels are in the straight-ahead position.

4. Turn the ignition switch to **LOCK**.

5. Remove the **IGN** fuse and **CIG** and **RADIO** fuse from junction block 1.

6. Remove the Connector Position Assurance (CPA) and disconnect the yellow 2-way connector at the base of the steering column.

To arm:

7. Connect the negative battery cable.

8. Turn the ignition switch to the **LOCK** position and remove the key.

9. Attach the yellow connector for the driver air bag (inflator) module. Be sure to lock the connector with the lock lever.

10. Install the **IGN** fuse and **CIG** and **RADIO** fuse from junction block 1.

1. Junction block 1
2. ECU-B fuse
3. CIG & radio fuse
4. IGN fuse

79222738

Connector view and terminal identification of junction block 1—Prizm

11. Turn the ignition **ON** and verify that the **AIR BAG** warning lamp flashes seven times, then turns off. If the system does not operate as described, diagnosis and repairs to the air bag system are necessary.

Rack and Pinion Steering Gear

REMOVAL & INSTALLATION

Manual

METRO

1. Before servicing the vehicle, refer to the precautions in the beginning of this section.

2. Disconnect the negative battery cable.

3. Slide the driver's seat back as far as possible and pull off the front part of the floor mat on the driver's side and remove the steering shaft joint cover.

4. Loosen the steering shaft upper joint bolt, but do not remove. Remove the steering shaft lower joint bolt and disconnect the lower joint from the pinion.

5. Raise and safely support the vehicle. Remove the front wheels.

6. Remove the tie rod ends from the steering knuckles.

7. Remove the rack and pinion mounting bolts, brackets and the rack from the vehicle.

To install:

8. Install the rack, brackets and mounting bolts into the vehicle at the bulkhead. Be sure to align the pinion shaft through the floor opening. Tighten the bolts to 18 ft. lbs. (25 Nm).

9. Install the right and left tie rod ends to the steering knuckles.

10. Install the front wheels. Lower the vehicle.

11. Connect the steering shaft to the steering gear. Install the lower steering shaft-to-steering gear clinch bolt and tighten to 18 ft. lbs. (25 Nm). Tighten the steering shaft upper joint bolt to 18 ft. lbs. (25 Nm).

12. Install the steering joint cover.

13. Place the driver's side floor mat back into position.

14. Check and adjust the front wheel alignment.

PRIZM

1. Before servicing the vehicle, refer to the precautions in the beginning of this section.

2. Disconnect the negative battery cable.

3. Remove the cover from the intermediate shaft.

4. Loosen the upper pinch bolt. Remove the lower pinch bolt at the pinion shaft.

5. Raise and safely support the vehicle. Remove both front wheels.

6. Install an engine support and tension the engine without raising it.

7. Remove the bolts holding the center crossmember to the radiator support.

8. Remove the covers from the front and center mount bolts.

9. Remove the front mount bolts, and the center mount bolts.

10. Support the crossmember and remove the rear mount bolts.

11. Remove the bolts holding the center crossmember to the main crossmember.

12. Use a floor jack and piece of wood to support the main crossmember.

13. Remove the bolts holding the main crossmember to the body.

✷✷ CAUTION

When the fasteners are removed, be sure the crossmembers are properly supported.

14. Remove the bolts holding the lower control arm brackets to the body.

15. Slowly lower the main crossmember while holding onto the center crossmember.

16. Remove both tie rod joints from the steering knuckles.

17. Remove the nuts and bolts attaching the steering rack to the body.

18. Remove the rack through the right side wheel well.

To install:

19. Place the rack in position through the right side wheel well. Tighten the bracket bolts to 45 ft. lbs. (61 Nm).

20. Attach the tie rods to the steering knuckles.

21. Position the center crossmember over the center and rear transaxle mount studs; start the two nuts on the center mount.

22. Loosely install the bolts holding the center crossmember to the radiator support.

23. Loosely install the front mounting bolts.

24. Raise the main crossmember into position over the rear mount studs and align the underbody bolts. Install the two rear mount nuts loosely.

25. Install the main crossmember to underbody bolts loosely.

26. Install the lower control arm bracket bolts loosely.

27. Loosely install the bolts holding the center crossmember to the main crossmember.

28. Tighten the fasteners as follows:
• Main crossmember-to-underbody bolts: 152 ft. lbs. (206 Nm)
• Center crossmember-to-radiator support bolts: 45 ft. lbs. (61 Nm)
• Lower A-frame-to-center bolts: 161 ft. lbs. (218 Nm)
• Lower A-frame-to-outer bolts: 109 ft. lbs. (147 Nm)
• Front, center and rear mount bolts: 45 ft. lbs. (61 Nm)

29. Install the covers on the front and center mount bolts.

30. Install the front wheels. Lower the vehicle.

31. Connect the yoke to the pinion and tighten both the upper and lower bolts to 26 ft. lbs.

32. Install the yoke cover.

33. Check and adjust the front end alignment as necessary. Check steering operation.

Power

METRO

1. Before servicing the vehicle, refer to the precautions in the beginning of this section.

2. Disconnect the negative battery cable.

3. Slide the driver's seat back. Pull off the front part of the floor mat on the driver's side and remove the steering shaft joint cover.

4. Loosen the steering shaft upper joint bolt, but do not remove. Remove the steering shaft lower joint bolt and disconnect the lower joint from the pinion.

5. Raise and safely support the vehicle. Remove the front wheels.

6. Remove the tie rod ends.

7. Disconnect the exhaust pipe at the manifold.

8. If equipped with manual transaxle, separate the shift linkage and extension rod from the transaxle.

9. If equipped with automatic transaxle, remove the engine rear torque rod with the bracket from the transaxle.

10. Disconnect the power steering lines from the rack and pinion assembly. Plug the openings to prevent system contamination.

11. Remove the rack and pinion mounting bolts, brackets and the rack from the vehicle.

To install:

12. Install the rack, brackets and mounting bolts into the vehicle at the bulkhead. Be sure to align the pinion shaft through the floor opening. Tighten bolts to 18 ft. lbs. (25 Nm).

13. Unplug and reconnect the power steering lines to the rack and pinion assembly. Tighten the inlet and outlet fluid lines to 25 ft. lbs. (35 Nm). Tighten the remaining lines to 18 ft. lbs. (25 Nm).

14. If equipped, install the shift linkage and extension rod to the manual transaxle.

15. If equipped, install the engine rear torque rod with torque rod bracket to the automatic transaxle.

16. Connect the front exhaust pipe to the manifold using a new seal, and secure with bolts. Tighten the bolts to 37 ft. lbs. (50 Nm).

17. Install the tie rod ends to the steering knuckles.

18. Install the front wheels. Lower the vehicle.

19. Connect the steering shaft to the steering gear. Install the lower steering shaft-to-steering gear bolts and tighten to 18 ft. lbs. (25 Nm). Tighten the steering shaft upper joint bolt to 18 ft. lbs. (25 Nm).

20. Install the steering joint cover.

21. Place the driver's side floor mat back into the original position.

22. Bleed the system.

23. Check and adjust the front wheel alignment.

PRIZM

1. Before servicing the vehicle, refer to the precautions in the beginning of this section.

2. Disconnect the negative battery cable.

3. Place a drain pan under the steering rack and pinion unit.

4. Remove the cover from the intermediate shaft.

5. Loosen the upper pinch bolt. Remove the lower pinch bolt at the pinion shaft.

6. Raise and safely support the vehicle.

7. Remove both front wheels.

8. Install an engine support and tension the engine without raising it.

9. Remove the bolts holding the center crossmember to the radiator support.

10. Remove the covers from the front and center mount bolts.

11. Remove the front mount bolts, then the center mount bolts, then the rear mount bolts.

12. Remove the bolts holding the center crossmember to the main crossmember.

13. Use a floor jack and piece of wood to support the main crossmember.

14. Remove the bolts holding the main crossmember to the body.

15. Remove the bolts holding the lower control arm brackets to the body.

✷✷ CAUTION

Be sure the crossmembers are properly supported.

16. Slowly lower the main crossmember while holding onto the center crossmember.

17. Remove the tie rods.

18. Remove both ball joints.

19. Disconnect the fluid pressure and return lines from the rack.

20. Remove the nuts and bolts attaching the steering rack to the body.

21. Remove the rack and pinion unit through the right side wheel well.

To install:

22. Place the rack and pinion unit in position through the right wheel well and tighten the bracket bolts to 44 ft. lbs. (59 Nm).

23. Connect the fluid lines to the rack and tighten to 33 ft. lbs. (45 Nm). Make certain the fittings are correctly threaded before tightening.

24. Attach the tie rod ends.

25. Position the center crossmember and rear transaxle mount over the studs. Start the nuts on the center mount.

26. Loosely install the bolts holding the center crossmember to the radiator support.

27. Loosely install the front mount bolts.

28. Raise the main crossmember into position over the rear mount studs and align the underbody bolts. Install the rear mount nuts loosely.

29. Install the main crossmember-to-underbody bolts loosely.

30. Install the lower control arm bracket bolts loosely.

31. Tighten the components in the

order listed to the following torque specification:

- Main crossmember-to-underbody bolts: 152 ft. lbs. (205 Nm).
- Center crossmember-to-radiator support bolts: 45 ft. lbs. (61 Nm)
- Lower A-frame-to-center bolts: 161 ft. lbs. (218 Nm)
- Lower A-frame-to-outer bolts: 109 ft. lbs. (147 Nm)
- Front, center and rear mount bolts: 45 ft. lbs. (61 Nm)

32. Install the covers on the front and center mount bolts.

33. Install the front wheels. Lower the vehicle to the ground.

34. Connect the yoke to the pinion and tighten both the upper and lower bolts to 26 ft. lbs.

35. Install the yoke cover.

36. Add power steering fluid to the reservoir and bleed the system.

37. Check and adjust the front end alignment, as necessary.

Strut

REMOVAL & INSTALLATION

Front

1. Before servicing the vehicle, refer to the precautions in the beginning of this section.

2. Disconnect the negative battery cable.

#		#	
1	DUST CAP	14	LOWER CONTROL ARM RETAINING BRACKET
2	STRUT ROD PISTON NUT	15	LOWER CONTROL ARM RETAINING BRACKET BOLTS
3	STRUT SUPPORT	16	COTTER PIN
4	DUST SEAL	17	BALL JOINT
5	SPRING SEAT	18	BALL JOINT CASTLE NUT
6	UPPER INSULATOR	19	BALL JOINT MOUNTING NUT AND BOLT
7	COIL SPRING	20	CONTROL ARM
8	SPRING BUMPER	21	CROSSMEMBER MOUNTING BOLTS
9	LOWER INSULATOR	22	CROSSMEMBER-TO-CONTROL ARM BOLT
10	STRUT	23	CROSSMEMBER MOUNTING NUTS
11	BRAKE LINE GASKETS	24	CROSSMEMBER MOUNTING BOLTS
12	BRAKE LINE-TO-CALIPER BOLT	25	SUSPENSION CROSSMEMBER
13	STRUT MOUNTING NUT AND BOLT		

7922Z739

Exploded view of the front suspension assembly—Prizm

1 VEHICLE BODY
2 STRUT ASSEMBLY
3 STEERING KNUCKLE
4 CONTROL ARM
5 BALL STUD
6 WHEEL BEARING
7 HUB
8 WHEEL
9 SWAY BAR
10 SWAY BAR LINK
11 SWAY BAR BRACKET

7922Z744

Cut-away view of the front suspension—Metro

3. Remove the upper strut support nuts from the engine compartment.

4. Raise and safely support the vehicle.

5. Remove the front wheel.

6. If equipped with ABS, remove the speed sensor.

7. Remove the brake hose clip, then the hose from the strut.

8. Support the lower control arm with a floor jack.

9. Remove the strut-to-steering knuckle bolts, then remove the strut assembly from the vehicle.

To install:

10. Install the strut assembly onto the vehicle. Install the upper support nuts loosely.

11. Install the strut-to-steering knuckle bolts and tighten to 59 ft. lbs. (80 Nm) for Metro models and 203 ft. Lbs. (275 Nm) for Prizm models.

12. Tighten the upper strut support nuts to 24 ft. lbs. (34 Nm) for Metro models and 29 ft. Lbs. (39 Nm) for Prizm models.

13. Install the brake hose and brake hose clip. Be sure the brake hose is not twisted when installing.

14. If equipped with ABS, attach the wheel speed sensor.

15. Install the front wheels. Lower the vehicle.

16. Connect the negative battery cable. Check front wheel alignment.

Rear

PRIZM

1. Before servicing the vehicle, refer to the precautions in the beginning of this section.

2. Raise and safely support the vehicle.

3. Remove the wheel.

4. Disconnect the brake line from the wheel cylinder (at the backing plate). Plug the lines to prevent leakage.

5. Remove the clip from the brake hose and remove the hose from the strut bracket.

6. Disconnect the sway bar link from the strut.

7. Remove the strut mounting bolts from the rear knuckle.

8. Remove the seat back side cushion (Sedan) or the rear sill side panel (Hatchback) to gain access to the upper strut mount.

9. Remove the nuts holding the upper strut mount to the body. Do not loosen the center strut piston nut.

10. Remove the strut assembly from the vehicle.

To install:

11. Place the strut in position on the vehicle and install the three upper retaining nuts, tightening them to 29 ft. lbs. (39 Nm).

12. Reinstall the seat back side cushion or the rear sill side panel.

13. Install the strut into the rear knuckle assembly; install the bolts and nuts and tighten them to 105 ft. lbs. (142 Nm).

14. Reconnect the sway bar link to the strut. Tighten the bolts to 32 ft. lbs. (44 Nm).

15. Connect the brake hose into the bracket and install the clip.

16. Connect the metal line to the wheel cylinder. Make certain the fittings are properly threaded before tightening them.

17. Bleed the brake system.

18. Install the wheel. Lower the vehicle.

19. Check the wheel alignment.

Turn to Section 6 for brake system applications

1   FUEL TANK BAND
2   STRUT TOWER COVER
3   STRUT ROD PISTON NUT
4   STRUT ASSEMBLY
5   REAR LATERAL LINK
6   BRAKE PIPE
7   BRAKE DRUM

8   HUB ASSEMBLY
9   BRAKE ASSEMBLY
10 TRAILING ARM
11 FRONT LATERAL LINK
12 STABILIZER SHAFT BRACKET
13 BUSHING
14 STABILIZER SHAFT JOINT
15 STABILIZER SHAFT

7922Z740

Exploded view of the rear strut assembly—Prizm

Shock Absorber

REMOVAL & INSTALLATION

Rear

METRO

1. Before servicing the vehicle, refer to the precautions in the beginning of this section.

2. Open the vehicle hatchback or deck lid.

3. Raise and safely support the vehicle just high enough so the top and the bottom of the shock can be accessed. Remove the wheels.

4. Place a floor jack under the suspension arm for support.

5. Remove the lower shock-to-knuckle bolt.

➡ **Do not open the knuckle slit wider than necessary. Do not lower the jack more than necessary during the strut removal or the coil spring may become unseated.**

6. Remove the trim cover from the upper shock tower and remove the upper support nuts.

7. Remove the shock from the knuckle. Compress the shock and remove. If the shock is hard to remove, open the slit of the knuckle by inserting a wedge.

   To install:

8. Install the shock into the vehicle. Position the bottom of the alignment projection inside the knuckle opening.

9. Install the upper support nuts and tighten to 24 ft. lbs. (30 Nm). Install the trim cover to the upper shock tower.

10. Install the shock-to-knuckle bolt and

1	COIL SPRING	**14**	SUSPENSION KNUCKLE CONTROL ROD STUD (CONTROL ROD NOT SHOWN)
2	COIL SPRING UPPER SEAT	**15**	SUSPENSION KNUCKLE
3	STRUT UPPER CAP	**16**	WHEEL SPINDLE
4	STRUT UPPER SUPPORT NUT	**17**	SUSPENSION ARM-TO-KNUCKLE BOLT
5	STRUT TOP NUT	**18**	SUSPENSION ARM
6	STRUT UPPER SEAT	**19**	SUSPENSION ARM FRONT BRACKET
7	STRUT UPPER SUPPORT	**20**	BRACKET BOLT
8	STRUT LOWER SEAT	**21**	SUSPENSION ARM FRONT BUSHING
9	STRUT DUST COVER	**22**	FRONT BUSHING NUT
10	BUMPER STOPPER CAP	**23**	SUSPENSION ARM REAR MOUNTING BOLT
11	BUMPER STOPPER	**24**	SUSPENSION ARM REAR MOUNTING NUT
12	STRUT (SHOCK ABSORBER)		
13	SUSPENSION ARM-TO-KNUCKLE NUT		

7922Z741

Exploded view of the rear suspension—Metro

For complete service labor times order Chilton's Labor Guide Manual

| 1 | STRUT ALIGNMENT PROJECTION |
| 2 | KNUCKLE |

79222742

Be sure to verify the shock-to-knuckle alignment—Metro

tighten to 44 ft. lbs. (60 Nm). Remove the floor jack.

11. Install the rear wheels. Lower the vehicle.

12. Check the wheel alignment.

Coil Spring

REMOVAL & INSTALLATION

Rear

METRO

1. Before servicing the vehicle, refer to the precautions in the beginning of this section.

2. Raise and safely support the vehicle. Remove the rear wheel.

➡ **To facilitate the toe-in adjustment after reinstallation, note or mark which of the lines stamped on the washer is in the closest alignment with the stamped line on the control rod. If not marked, add the alignment marks.**

3. Remove the brake hose from the bracket on the control rod.

4. Remove the control rod inside bolt (body center side) and outside (wheel side) stud bolts.

A	SCRIBE MARK HERE
1	CONTROL ROD
2	ECCENTRIC CAM
3	VEHICLE BODY

79222743

Be sure to matchmark the eccentric cam—Metro

➡ **The control rods are not interchangeable. Be sure the control rods are installed on the same side from which they were removed and in the same direction.**

5. If equipped with ABS, disconnect the speed sensor.

6. Remove the stabilizer link from the control arm, if equipped. Support the control arm with a floor jack.

7. Remove the control arm-to-knuckle bolt and nut.

8. Manually pull down the control arm from the knuckle assembly.

9. Lower the floor jack slowly, lowering the control arm and coil spring.

10. Remove the coil spring and seat. Inspect the coil spring and seat for excessive wear, cracks or deterioration and replace, as necessary.

To install:

➡ **The coil spring is larger in diameter at the bottom end of the spring. Be sure it is not installed upside down.**

11. Install the coil spring on the spring seat, then raise the control arm. When seating the coil spring, mate the spring end with the stepped part of the control arm spring seat.

12. Raise the floor jack under the control arm until it is level with the suspension knuckle. Be sure to align the bolt holes.

13. Install the lower knuckle mount bolt.

14. If equipped with ABS, fasten the speed sensor.

15. If equipped, install the stabilizer link to the control arm.

16. Remove the jack from under the control arm.

17. Install the control rod. Install the inside and outside control rod bolts, Align the marks on the eccentric cam and body that were made before removal. Tighten the control rod inside and outside nuts to 59 ft. lbs. (80 Nm).

18. Install the brake hose to the control rod bracket and secure with the E-clip.

19. Remove the floor jack.

20. Install the rear wheels. Lower the vehicle.

Lower Ball Joints

REMOVAL & INSTALLATION

Metro

The lower ball joint is an integral part of the lower control arm assembly and is not serviceable as an individual component. If the lower ball joint is defective, the entire lower control arm must be replaced.

1. Before servicing the vehicle, refer to the precautions in the beginning of this section.

2. Raise and safely support the vehicle. Remove the front wheels.

3. Remove the stabilizer bar link nut, washer and insulator from the control arm, if equipped.

4. Separate the ball joint from the knuckle.

5. Remove the control arm front mounting bracket bolts.

6. Remove the bolts and control arm rear mounting bracket.

7. Remove the control arm and the front bracket from the vehicle.

To install:

8. Install the control arm on the vehicle and secure with bolts. Do not fully tighten the bolts at this time.

9. Install the ball joint.

10. If equipped, install the stabilizer link insulator, washer and nut to the lower control arm. Do not fully tighten the nut.

11. Tighten the control arm rear mounting bolts to 32 ft. lbs. (43 Nm); front mounting bolts to 66 ft. lbs. (90 Nm) and stabilizer link nut to 20 ft. lbs. (28 Nm).

12. Install the front wheels. Lower the vehicle.

13. Check the front wheel alignment.

Prizm

➡ **A ball joint separator is required to complete this procedure. It is a commonly available tool which prevents damage to the joint and knuckle. Do not attempt to separate the joint without it.**

1. Raise and safely support the vehicle.

❊❊ WARNING

Do not allow the halfshaft joints to over-extend or the CV-joints may become disconnected.

2. Before servicing the vehicle, refer to the precautions in the beginning of this section.

3. Remove the wheel.

4. Remove the cotter pin from the ball joint nut.

5. Loosen the castle nut but do not remove it. Unscrew it just to the top of the threads and install ball joint separator tool 34754 or equivalent.

6. Use the separator to loosen the ball joint from the steering knuckle.

7. Remove the nuts and bolt holding the ball joint to the control arm.

8. Remove the ball joint from the control arm and steering knuckle.

To install:

9. Install the ball joint to the control arm and tighten the bolts and nut to 105 ft. lbs. (142 Nm).

10. Carefully install the ball joint on the steering knuckle. Use a new castle nut and tighten it to 94 ft. lbs. (128 Nm).

11. Install the cotter pin. If the holes are not in alignment, tighten the nut enough so the cotter pin can be installed. NEVER loosen the castle nut to install a cotter pin.

12. Install the wheel.

13. Lower the vehicle.

14. Check the front wheel alignment.

Wheel Bearings

ADJUSTMENT

Front

The front wheel bearings on all models cannot be adjusted. To check for a loose wheel bearing, proceed as follows:

1. Before servicing the vehicle, refer to the precautions in the beginning of this section.

2. Raise and safely support the vehicle.

3. Remove the front wheel.

4. Compress the caliper piston to free the caliper assembly.

5. Mount a suitable dial indicator to the knuckle or strut, with the indicator foot contacting the center of the hub next to the nut.

6. Push and pull the brake rotor by hand. If rotor movement exceeds 0.016 in. (0.04mm) for Metro or 0.020 in. (0.05mm) for Prizm, replace the wheel bearings.

7. Install the wheel and lower the vehicle.

8. Apply the brakes several times before moving the vehicle, to seat the caliper piston.

Rear

The rear wheel bearings cannot be adjusted. To check for a loose wheel bearing, proceed as follows:

1. Raise and safely support the vehicle.

2. Remove the rear wheel.

3. Mount a suitable dial indicator to the knuckle or strut, with the indicator foot contacting the center of the hub next to the hub nut.

4. Push and pull the brake drum/hub assembly by hand. If hub movement exceeds 0.012 in. (0.03mm) on Metro models or 0.020 in. (0.05mm) on Prizm models, replace the wheel bearings.

5. Install the wheel and lower the vehicle.

REMOVAL & INSTALLATION

Front

METRO

1. Before servicing the vehicle, refer to the precautions in the beginning of this section.

2. Raise and safely support the vehicle.

3. Remove the front wheel.

4. Remove the brake caliper and carrier and rotor. Do not let the caliper hang from the brake hose.

5. If equipped, disconnect the ABS wheel speed sensor.

6. Unstake and remove the hub nut and washer. Discard the nut.

7. Remove the hub from the steering knuckle using tools J-2619–01 and J-34866 or equivalent.

8. Separate the tie rod end from the steering knuckle.

9. Separate the ball joint from the steering knuckle.

10. Remove the strut-to-steering knuckle bolts and remove the steering knuckle from the vehicle. Support the halfshaft to prevent damage to the CV-joint.

11. Remove the inner and outer oil seals using removal tools J-26941 and J-2619–01 or equivalent.

12. Remove the inner bearing race and bearing from the steering knuckle.

13. Remove the inner wheel bearing oil seal using special tools J-26941 and J-2619–01, or equivalent.

14. Remove the snapring from the outer side of the steering knuckle.

15. Remove the outer wheel bearing from the steering knuckle.

16. Remove the outer bearing race from the hub using split plate bearing removal tool J-22912–01, hub race puller pilot tool J-38424 or equivalents, and a press.

17. Support the steering knuckle using support tool J-41392 or equivalent, and remove the wheel bearing assembly from the steering knuckle using wheel bearing removal tool J-41391 and driver handle J-7079–2 or equivalents.

18. Inspect the wheel bearings for excessive wear, corrosion or contamination by dirt or water; replace as necessary.

To install:

19. Support the steering knuckle using support tool J-41392 or equivalent.

20. Install the wheel bearing assembly into the steering knuckle using the wheel bearing race/outer seal installer tool J-39722 and driver handle J-7079–2 or equivalents.

21. Install the outer bearing into the steering knuckle.

22. Install the snapring into the outer side of the steering knuckle.

23. Install the inner wheel bearing and inner bearing race into the steering knuckle.

24. Install the outer bearing race onto the wheel hub using wheel hub race installer tool J-36050 or equivalent, and a press.

25. Apply a coating of wheel bearing grease to the lip of the inner oil seal.

26. If equipped with ABS, be sure to align the hole in the seal to the hole in the steering knuckle for the wheel speed sensor.

27. Install the inner oil seal to the inner side of the steering knuckle using installer tool J-41392 and driver handle J-7079–2 or equivalents.

28. Install the outer oil seal to the outer side of the steering knuckle using installer tool J-39722 and driver handle J-7079–2 or equivalents.

29. Apply a light coat of wheel bearing grease to the outside of the hub shaft.

30. Install the wheel hub and outer bearing race to the steering knuckle using a press.

31. Install the steering knuckle on the vehicle, inserting the CV-joint into the hub, and secure with the strut-to-steering knuckle bolts. Tighten the strut-to-steering knuckle bolts to 59 ft. lbs. (80 Nm).

32. Install the ball joint ball. Connect the tie rod end to the steering knuckle with the castle nut. Install a new cotter pin.

33. Install a new hub nut and washer. Tighten the hub nut to 129 ft. lbs. (175 Nm). Using a hammer and dull punch, stake the nut.

34. Install the brake rotor, brake caliper carrier and caliper.

35. If equipped, install the ABS wheel speed sensor. Connect the sensor electrical connector.

36. Install the front wheel and lug nuts.

37. Lower the vehicle. Check the wheel alignment.

PRIZM

1. Before servicing the vehicle, refer to the precautions in the beginning of this section.

2. Raise and safely support the vehicle. Remove the wheel.

3. Disconnect the ABS speed sensor, if equipped.

4. Remove the halfshaft nut.

5. Remove the brake caliper and support it out of the way. Remove the disc brake rotor.

6. Separate the tie rod end from the knuckle.

7. Separate the ball joint from the knuckle.

8. Remove the two nuts and bolts securing the steering knuckle to the strut.

9. Remove the steering knuckle and hub assembly.

10. Clamp the knuckle in a vise with protected jaws.

11. Remove the dust deflector.

12. Use a slide hammer and extractor tool J-26941 or equivalent, to remove the inner oil seal.

13. Remove the snapring.

14. Using hub puller tools J-25287 and J-35378 or equivalents, remove the hub from the knuckle.

15. Remove the brake splash shield.

16. Using a split plate bearing remover, puller pilot and a shop press, remove the inside and outside inner bearing races from the hub.

17. Remove the outer oil seal.

18. Position the steering knuckle on support tool J-35379 or equivalent. Remove the bearing from the knuckle using a plastic hammer and remover tool J-35399 or equivalent, and driver handle J-8092 or equivalent.

To install:

19. Clean and inspect the hub and knuckle for cracks, wear or other damage; replace as necessary.

20. Press a new bearing into the steering knuckle using installation tool J-37777 or equivalent, and driver handle J-8092 or equivalent.

21. Install a new snapring into the steering knuckle.

22. Install a new inner oil seal onto the steering knuckle using seal installer J-35737–2 or equivalent.

23. Insert the side lip of a new outer oil seal into seal installer J-35737–01 or equivalent, and drive the outer oil seal into the steering knuckle.

24. Apply multi-purpose grease to the outer oil seal lip.

25. Install the brake splash shield and tighten the bolts to 73 inch lbs. (8.3 Nm).

26. Place new inside and outside inner races on the hub bearing. Press the hub into the knuckle using installer J-35399 or equivalent, and driver handle J-8092 or equivalent.

27. Apply GM lubricant 1050109 or equivalent, to the contact surfaces of the inner oil seal lip and drive axle.

28. Drive a new dust deflector into the steering knuckle using a hammer and dull chisel.

29. Place the steering knuckle and hub assembly onto the halfshaft and install the knuckle-to-strut bolts and nuts.

30. Attach the ball joint to the control arm.

31. Attach the tie rod end to the knuckle.

32. Install the disc brake rotor and the brake caliper.

33. Install the ABS sensor, if equipped.

34. Install the nut on the end of the half-shaft.

35. Install the wheel and lower the vehicle.

36. Check the wheel alignment.

Rear

METRO WITHOUT ABS

1. Before servicing the vehicle, refer to the precautions in the beginning of this section.

2. Raise and safely support the vehicle.

3. Remove the rear wheel.

4. Pry off the dust cap.

5. Unstake and remove the spindle nut and washer. Discard the spindle nut; it must not be reused.

6. Gently tap on the brake drum/hub assembly with a hammer to break loose and remove the drum/hub assembly from the spindle.

7. Place the brake drum/hub assembly on wooden blocks on a workbench.

8. Drive the inner bearing out from the drum/hub assembly using a hammer and punch. The bearing spacer can be moved from side to side to enable placement of the punch. Work around the perimeter of the inner bearing by moving this spacer.

9. Remove the bearing spacer.

10. Drive the outer bearing out from the inboard side of the drum/hub assembly using the same method.

11. Inspect the wheel bearings for wear, corrosion or contamination and replace, as necessary.

To install:

➡ **The outer bearings is smaller in diameter than the inner one.**

12. Install the outer bearing in the drum/hub assembly using installation tools J-34842 and J-7079–2 or equivalents.

13. Install the bearing spacer in the brake drum hub with the inner lip toward the outer bearing.

➡ **Be sure the bearing spacer is properly installed. The assembly will not fit on the spindle if the spacer lip is toward the inner bearing.**

14. Install the inner bearing in the drum/hub assembly using installation tools J-34842 and J-7079–2 or equivalents.

15. Install the brake drum/hub assembly on the spindle.

16. Install the washer and a new spindle nut.

17. Tighten the spindle nut to 74 ft. lbs. (100 Nm).

18. Stake the spindle nut.

19. Install the dust cap.

20. Install the wheel. Lower the vehicle.

METRO WITH ABS

1. Before servicing the vehicle, refer to the precautions in the beginning of this section.

2. Raise and safely support the vehicle.

3. Remove the rear wheel.

4. Remove the two screws and remove the brake drum.

5. Pry off the dust cap.

6. Unstake and remove the spindle nut and washer.

7. Remove the hub assembly from the spindle.

To install:

8. Install the hub assembly on the spindle.

9. Install the washer and spindle nut.

10. Tighten the spindle nut to 120 ft. lbs. (170 Nm).

11. Stake the spindle nut.

12. Install the dust cap.

13. Install the wheel. Tighten the lug nuts, in a cross sequence, to 44 ft. lbs. (60 Nm).

14. Lower the vehicle.

PRIZM

1. Before servicing the vehicle, refer to the precautions in the beginning of this section.

2. Raise and safely support the vehicle.

3. Remove the wheel.

4. Remove the brake drum or rotor.

5. Check bearing end-play using a dial indicator. If end-play exceeds 0.002 in. (0.05mm), the hub must be replaced.

6. Disconnect and remove the ABS wheel speed sensor, if equipped.

7. Remove the four bolts securing the hub to the knuckle and remove the hub.

8. Remove the O-ring from the backing plate.

To install:

9. Install a new O-ring onto the backing plate.

10. Install the hub to the knuckle with the mounting bolts and tighten to 59 ft. lbs. (80 Nm).

11. Install the wheel speed sensor, if equipped.

12. Install the brake drum or rotor.

13. Install the wheel and lower the vehicle.

14. Check the rear wheel alignment.

PRECAUTIONS

Before servicing any vehicle, please be sure to read all of the following precautions, which deal with personal safety, prevention of component damage, and important points to take into consideration when servicing a motor vehicle:

• Never open, service or drain the radiator or cooling system when the engine is hot; serious burns can occur from the steam and hot coolant.

• Observe all applicable safety precautions when working around fuel. Whenever servicing the fuel system, always work in a well-ventilated area. Do not allow fuel spray or vapors to come in contact with a spark, open flame, or excessive heat (a hot drop light, for example). Keep a dry chemical fire extinguisher near the work area. Always keep fuel in a container specifically designed for fuel storage; also, always properly seal fuel containers to avoid the possibility of fire or explosion. Refer to the additional fuel system precautions later in this section.

• Fuel injection systems often remain pressurized, even after the engine has been turned **OFF**. The fuel system pressure must be relieved before disconnecting any fuel lines. Failure to do so may result in fire and/or personal injury.

• Brake fluid often contains polyglycol ethers and polyglycols. Avoid contact with the eyes and wash your hands thoroughly after handling brake fluid. If you do get brake fluid in your eyes, flush your eyes with clean, running water for 15 minutes. If eye irritation persists, or if you have taken brake fluid internally, IMMEDIATELY seek medical assistance.

• The EPA warns that prolonged contact with used engine oil may cause a number of skin disorders, including cancer! You should make every effort to minimize your exposure to used engine oil. Protective gloves should be worn when changing oil. Wash your hands and any other exposed skin areas as soon as possible after exposure to used engine oil. Soap and water, or waterless hand cleaner should be used.

• All new vehicles are now equipped with an air bag system, often referred to as a Supplemental Restraint System (SRS) or Supplemental Inflatable Restraint (SIR) system. The system must be disabled before performing service on or around system components, steering column, instrument panel components, wiring and sensors. Failure to follow safety and disabling procedures could result in accidental air bag deployment, possible personal injury and unnecessary system repairs.

• Always wear safety goggles when working with, or around, the air bag system. When carrying a non-deployed air bag, be sure the bag and trim cover are pointed away from your body. When placing a non-deployed air bag on a work surface, always face the bag and trim cover upward, away from the surface. This will reduce the motion of the module if it is accidentally deployed. Refer to the additional air bag system precautions later in this section.

• Clean, high quality brake fluid from a sealed container is essential to the safe and proper operation of the brake system. You should always buy the correct type of brake fluid for your vehicle. If the brake fluid becomes contaminated, completely flush the system with new fluid. Never reuse any brake fluid. Any brake fluid that is removed from the system should be discarded. Also, do not allow any brake fluid to come in contact with a painted surface; it will damage the paint.

• Never operate the engine without the proper amount and type of engine oil; doing so WILL result in severe engine damage.

• Timing belt maintenance is extremely important! Many models utilize an interference-type, non-freewheeling engine. If the timing belt breaks, the valves in the cylinder head may strike the pistons, causing potentially serious (also time-consuming and expensive) engine damage. Refer to the maintenance interval charts in the front of this manual for the recommended replacement interval for the timing belt, and to the timing belt section for belt replacement and inspection.

• Disconnecting the negative battery cable on some vehicles may interfere with the functions of the on-board computer system(s) and may require the computer to undergo a relearning process once the negative battery cable is reconnected.

• When servicing drum brakes, only disassemble and assemble one side at a time, leaving the remaining side intact for reference.

• Only an MVAC-trained, EPA-certified automotive technician should service the A/C system or its components.

ENGINE REPAIR

Ignition Timing

ADJUSTMENT

The 1.9L engines utilize a Distributorless Ignition System (DIS). This system uses three twin tower coils which fire two spark plugs simultaneously. One spark plug is located in a cylinder on the compression stroke and the other in a cylinder on the exhaust stroke. This is known as the waste spark method of distribution. The Powertrain Control Module (PCM) controls the ignition timing, no adjustment is necessary or possible.

Engine Assembly

REMOVAL & INSTALLATION

➡ **The manufacturer recommends that the engine and transaxle be removed as a complete unit. Disconnect the cradle and lower the entire assembly** instead of lifting the assembly out of the vehicle. Both the SOHC and DOHC engines are removed or installed in the same manner. We have found that it is often possible, however, to remove the engine or transaxle alone on some models with automatic transaxles by raising it up and out of the engine compartment.

1. Before servicing the vehicle, refer to the precautions in the beginning of this section.

2. Properly disable the SIR system. Disconnect the negative, then the positive battery cable.

3. Drain the engine coolant from the radiator and engine block.

4. Properly relieve the fuel system pressure.

5. Remove the complete air cleaner/intake duct assembly, as applicable.

6. Disconnect and label all the electrical plugs and vacuum lines, as applicable for engine removal.

7. Disengage all connectors from the automatic or manual transaxle. If access is difficult, wait until the vehicle is safely raised and supported, then unplug the connections from under the vehicle.

8. Disconnect the accelerator cable assembly.

9. Separate the fuel supply and return lines at their connectors. Plug the lines to prevent fuel contamination or loss. The lines may be tied to the master cylinder lines to help prevent fuel spillage and to keep them out of the way.

10. Disconnect the upper radiator hose, the cylinder head outlet and the de-aeration hose at the engine.

11. Remove the serpentine drive belt and, if equipped, remove the air conditioning compressor from its brackets—with the hoses attached. Support the compressor from the front crossbar.

➡It is not necessary to discharge the A/C compressor during engine removal, but be careful not to kink, damage or rupture the refrigerant lines.

12. If equipped, disconnect the automatic transaxle cooler lines at the transaxle by pinching the plastic connector tabs and carefully pulling back on the lines. Plug the openings to prevent fluid loss or contamination.

13. Disconnect the automatic transaxle shifter cable or the manual shifter cables from the transaxle.

14. If equipped with a manual transaxle, remove the two hydraulic slave cylinder retaining nuts from the clutch housing studs, then slide the cylinder and bracket assembly from the studs. Rotate the clutch actuator ¼ turn counterclockwise while pushing toward the housing to disengage the bayonet connector and remove it from the clutch housing. Support the clutch hydraulic system to the battery tray, being sure not to kink or pinch the hydraulic lines.

15. Using a length of an appropriate wire, tie the radiator, condenser and fan to the front crossbar. Route the wire around the two fan shroud supports and the crossbar.

16. Raise and support the vehicle safely.

17. Remove the front wheels and remove the fasteners connecting the side and front fender shields to the cradle.

18. Remove the brake caliper bracket attaching bolts (2 on each side) and hang the caliper assemblies from the shock tower springs using wire. Do not hang the assembly by the brake hose or damage to the brake hydraulic system may occur. The springs and shocks will remain with the body when the powertrain is lowered.

19. Disconnect the struts from the knuckles on each side of the vehicle (2 bolts per side). This will allow the knuckle and hub assembly to remain with the powertrain cradle when lowered. The stabilizer bar will remain attached to the cradle and the lower control arms.

20. Using a suitable hose clamp tool, disconnect the lower radiator and heater return hoses from the engine. Disconnect the heater inlet hose at the front of the dash or the engine.

21. Disconnect the steering shaft and pressure switch connectors at the gear, as applicable.

22. Disconnect the front exhaust pipe at the manifold, catalytic converter and powertrain stiffening bracket.

23. Remove the flywheel cover and torque converter bolts, if equipped.

24. Remove the alternator and starter shields.

25. Unclip the brake lines from the rear side of the cradle.

26. Carefully remove the electrical harness from the engine and transaxle, then lay the electrical harness on top of the underhood junction block and battery cover.

27. Place a 1 x 1 x 2 in. long block of wood between the torque strut and cradle to ease removal and installation of the torque engine mount. Remove the three right side

upper engine torque axis to front cover nuts and the two mount-to-midrail bracket nuts, allowing the powertrain to rest on the block of wood.

➡Placing a block of wood under the torque axis mount prior to removing the upper mount will allow the engine to rest on the wood, thus preventing the engine from shifting. If the engine is not to be removed from the cradle, this will allow you to install the engine and the upper mount without jacking or raising the engine.

28. Place a powertrain support dolly under the cradle. Use two 4 x 4 x 36 in. pieces of wood to support the cradle on the dolly.

29. Remove the two right side front engine mount torque strut brackets-to-cradle nuts.

30. Remove the four cradle attaching bolts and carefully lower the complete powertrain assembly from the vehicle. Verify that all necessary components are disconnected and free before complete removal.

31. Attach the two washers located between the cradle and body, to the cradle. They must be repositioned and installed during cradle installation.

32. Disconnect the spark plug wires at the ignition module.

33. If applicable, remove the power steering pump and bracket. Support the assembly, in an upright position, from the cradle or the steering gear.

34. Install a suitable engine lifting device to the service support brackets.

35. Remove the front mount assembly and disconnect the motion restrictor bracket, if applicable.

36. Place a ½ x 1 x 3 in. block of wood under the axle shaft and remove the starter support bracket bolt, intake manifold support brace (on DOHC engines), and three axle shaft bracket support bolts. Allow the bracket to rotate rearward. Lift the engine slightly for clearance, as necessary.

37. Place a 4 x 4 x 6 in. block of wood under the transaxle housing for support.

38. Remove the engine strut bracket and torque strut from the front of the engine as an assembly. Lift the engine slightly as necessary for removal.

39. Remove the four transaxle attaching bolts/studs and separate the assembly. Manual transaxles will require the engine to be moved about 4 inches (100mm) forward in the cradle to disengage the input shaft.

40. Carefully lift the engine off the cradle.

To install:

41. If removed, install the transaxle on the engine.

42. Tighten the front engine mount-to-engine bolts to 41 ft. lbs. (55 Nm).

43. Tighten the engine mount torque strut-to-cradle bracket fasteners to 52 ft. lbs. (70 Nm). Hand-tighten the cradle fasteners, but do not torque until the upper midrail mount is installed.

44. Tighten the axle shaft bracket fasteners to 41 ft. lbs. (55 Nm) and the starter bracket to 80 inch lbs. (9 Nm).

45. Carefully lift the powertrain and cradle into position. Be sure the radiator grommets are correctly aligned and that the two washers are reinstalled between the cradle and body at each rear cradle attachment position. If necessary, use two 3/16 in. x 18 in. long guide pins in the forward cradle holes (located next to the attaching holes) to help align the cradle. Tighten the cradle-to-body fasteners to 151 ft. lbs. (205 Nm).

46. Tighten the steering shaft U-joint bolt to 35 ft. lbs. (47 Nm).

47. Tighten the starter solenoid connector to 44 inch lbs. (5 Nm).

48. Tighten the alternator and starter battery connectors to 89 inch lbs. (10 Nm).

49. Install the following components, if previously removed:

   a. Tighten the oil pressure sensor to 26 ft. lbs. (35 Nm).

   b. Tighten the knock sensor to 133 inch lbs. (15 Nm).

   c. Tighten the Crankshaft Position (CKP) sensor mounting fastener(s) to 80 inch lbs. (9 Nm).

   d. Tighten canister purge valve mounting screw to 22 ft. lbs. (30 Nm).

50. Connect the wiring harness PCM ground and tighten to 89 inch lbs. (10 Nm).

51. Connect the wiring harness to the transaxle case/engine block and tighten to 18 ft. lbs. (25 Nm).

52. Tighten the engine stiffening bracket bolts to 35 ft. lbs. (47 Nm).

53. Tighten the exhaust pipe-to-intake manifold fasteners to 23 ft. lbs. (31 Nm), the pipe-to-stiffener bracket fasteners to 35 ft. lbs. (47 Nm), the pipe-to-support bracket fasteners to 23 ft. lbs. (31 Nm) and the pipe-to-catalytic converter fasteners to 18 ft. lbs. (25 Nm).

54. Tighten the cylinder block drain plug to 27 ft. lbs. (36 Nm), then close the radiator drain.

55. Tighten the steering knuckle-to-strut attachment bolts to 148 ft. lbs. (200 Nm).

56. Tighten the brake caliper assembly bolts to 81 ft. lbs. (110 Nm).

57. If equipped with a manual transaxle, tighten the hydraulic clutch slave cylinder fasteners to 19 ft. lbs. (25 Nm).

58. Tighten the A/C compressor-to-front bracket bolts to 40 ft. lbs. (54 Nm) and the compressor-to-rear bracket bolts to 22 ft. lbs. (30 Nm).

59. Tighten the two engine mounts-to-midrail bracket nuts to 37 ft. lbs. (50 Nm). Tighten the torque axis mount-to-front cover nuts uniformly to 37 ft. lbs. (50 Nm).

60. Tighten the strut bracket-to-cradle nuts to 37 ft. lbs. (50 Nm).

61. If equipped with an automatic transaxle, tighten the torque converter-to-flexplate bolts to 52 ft. lbs. (70 Nm). Tighten the dust cover fasteners to 89 inch lbs. (10 Nm).

62. Tighten the wheel lug nuts in a crisscross pattern to 103 ft. lbs. (140 Nm).

63. Lower the vehicle to the ground.

64. Apply a drop of clean engine oil on the male ends of the fuel line connectors and attach the line quick-connect fittings. Be sure the lines are not kinked or damaged.

➡**Check the upper cooling module grommets for binding or misalignment. The module retaining pins must be centered in the grommets supported by the brackets. If the grommets are pinched, loosen the brackets and reposition them. It is extremely important that the cooling module be able to move freely.**

65. Thoroughly inspect the transaxle and engine compartment area to be sure that all wires, hoses and lines have been connected. Also ensure all components and fasteners have been properly installed.

66. Connect the positive, then the negative battery cables.

❋❋ WARNING

Be sure to fill the engine with the proper type and amount of clean engine oil, because running the engine without adequate oil will cause damage.

67. Fill the engine cooling system, then check all engine and transaxle fluids, add or fill as necessary.

68. Prime the fuel system by cycling the ignition **ON** for 5 seconds and **OFF** for 10 seconds a few times without cranking the engine. Start the engine and check for leaks.

69. Perform a short road test and check the engine again for leaks. Be sure the cooling system is filled to the surge tank FULL COLD line.

Water Pump

REMOVAL & INSTALLATION

1. Before servicing the vehicle, refer to the precautions in the beginning of this section.

2. Allow a sufficient amount of time for the engine to cool down.

3. Disconnect the negative battery cable. Drain the engine coolant from the radiator and block drains into a suitable clean container.

4. Remove the serpentine drive belt.

5. Raise and support the vehicle safely. Remove the right front tire and inner wheel well splash shield.

6. If access to the water pump is desired from underhood, remove the air conditioning compressor bolts and position the compressor aside with the refrigerant lines intact.

7. Spray the water pump hub with penetrating oil to loosen any rust or corrosion that might bind the pulley and damage it during removal.

8. Remove the water pump pulley bolts and allow the pulley to hang freely on the hub. A one in. (25.4mm) block of wood or a hammer handle may be wedged between the pump and crankshaft pulleys to hold the assembly while loosening the retaining bolts.

9. Move the pulley outward or remove as necessary for access and remove the 6 water pump flange bolts. Carefully pull the pump and pulley assembly away from the engine and remove the assembly from the vehicle. If necessary, a gasket scraper may be inserted under the flange, but be careful not to damage the machined aluminum block sealing surface.

To install:

10. Thoroughly clean the gasket mating surfaces of all old gasket material. Apply a small amount of gasket sealant at the outer edges of the bolt holes to hold the gasket in place, then install the gasket onto the water pump assembly.

11. Install the pump assembly with the small bump located next to one of the attaching bolts in the 11 o'clock position. Install and tighten the bolts in a crisscross sequence as shown to 22 ft. lbs. (30 Nm).

12. Install or reposition the pump pulley, as applicable and tighten the bolts to 19 ft. lbs. (25 Nm). If the pump hub exposed through the pulley is rusty, clean it with a wire brush and apply a thin coat of primer to prevent the pulley from rusting onto the hub.

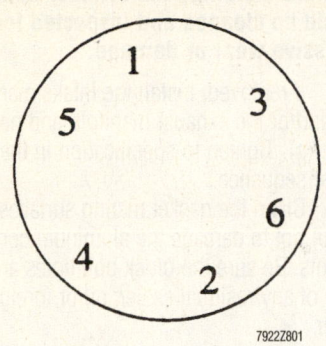

79222Z801

Water pump bolt torque sequence

13. Install the serpentine drive belt, the right splash shield and right tire assembly.

14. If repositioned, install the air conditioning compressor.

15. Close the radiator drain plug and install the cylinder block drain plug. Tighten the block plug to 26 ft. lbs. (35 Nm).

16. Connect the negative battery cable and properly fill the engine cooling system.

17. Operate the engine and check for coolant leaks.

Cylinder Head

REMOVAL & INSTALLATION

✳✳ WARNING

Only remove the cylinder head when the engine is cold. Warpage may result if the cylinder head is removed while the engine is hot.

1. Before servicing the vehicle, refer to the precautions in the beginning of this section.

2. Disconnect the negative battery cable and remove the coolant bottle cap. Drain the engine coolant from the radiator and block drains into a suitable clean container.

3. Remove the air cleaner/inlet duct assembly. Disconnect the PCV valve and fresh air hose from the camshaft cover.

4. Disconnect the accelerator cable from the throttle body and the bracket from the intake manifold.

5. Properly relieve the fuel system pressure.

6. Label and disengage the vacuum hoses and electrical connectors from the cylinder head assembly and components, as applicable. Long nose pliers are necessary to disconnect the coolant temperature connectors. When disconnected, position the electrical harness over the underhood junction block and battery cover.

7. Disconnect the upper radiator hose at the cylinder head outlet, the de-aeration hose at the intake manifold, or the heater hose at the intake manifold or front of dash.

8. Remove the bolt which retains the fuel lines to the intake manifold assembly. Disconnect the fuel feed and return lines from the fuel supply rail.

9. Unclip the lower splash shield for access. Place a 1 x 1 x 2 in. (25.4 x 25.4 x 51mm) block of wood between the torque strut and cradle to ease removal and installation of the torque engine mount. Remove the three right side upper engine torque axis-to-front cover nuts and the two mount to midrail bracket nuts, allowing the powertrain to rest on the block of wood.

➡ **Placing a block of wood under the torque axis mount prior to removing the upper mount will allow the engine to rest on the wood, thus preventing the engine from shifting. This will allow you to install the mount during assembly without jacking or raising the engine.**

10. Remove the serpentine drive belt and belt tensioner. It is not necessary to remove the water pump pulley, however, it will be necessary to remove the idler pulley to access the engine front cover.

11. For SOHC engines, disconnect the de-aeration line at the cylinder head water outlet and from the support bracket.

12. Remove the fasteners and the camshaft cover, then inspect the cover's silicone insulators for cracks or deterioration and replace, as necessary. Be sure to cover the valvetrain area to prevent dirt and debris from entering the engine.

13. Remove the power steering pump bracket attaching bolts (3 for the SOHC engine or 5 for the DOHC engine) and position the assembly next to the right side front of the dash panel away from the intake manifold and cylinder head. It is not necessary to remove the water pump pulley.

14. If equipped, remove the three air conditioning compressor front bracket bolts attached to the cylinder head and block, then remove the rear bracket bolts from the compressor or engine. Do not discharge the system or disconnect the refrigerant lines. Support the compressor out of the way, from the vehicle front support bar.

15. Raise and support the front of the vehicle safely.

16. Drain the engine oil into a suitable drain pan.

17. Remove the right side tire and splash shield.

18. For DOHC engines, remove the intake manifold support brace bolt attached to the intake manifold next to the alternator.

19. Remove the crankshaft damper/pulley assembly. Use a strap wrench or a block of wood wedged between the pulley spoke and the rear lower side of the front cover to hold the assembly while removing the bolt. Then, use a 3-jaw puller on the jaw slots cast into the pulley to remove the assembly.

20. Disconnect the exhaust pipe from the manifold, then remove and discard the gasket.

21. Install a crankshaft sprocket retainer tool, such as SA9104E or equivalent, with the flat side toward the sprocket. Properly remove the engine front/timing chain cover.

✳✳ WARNING

Be sure to properly install the crankshaft sprocket retainer tool. Failure to hold the crankshaft timing sprocket in place will cause timing chain damage.

22. Rotate the crankshaft clockwise to the position 90 degrees from Top Dead Center (TDC) so the timing mark and keyway align with the main bearing cap split line. This will ensure pistons will not contact the valves upon assembly.

23. Remove the timing chain, tensioner, guides, camshaft sprocket(s) and chain. Use a ⅞ in. (21mm) wrench to hold the camshaft when removing the sprocket bolts.

24. Use a 6-point socket to remove the 10 cylinder head bolts in several passes of the proper sequence. Failure to follow the proper sequence or removal of the head when hot could result in head warpage or cracking. Also, the use of a 12 point socket

79222Z802

Crankshaft gear retaining and oil pan removal tool shown—be sure to install the crankshaft tool with the flat side toward the gear

Timing belt service is covered in Section 5 of this manual

Gradually remove the cylinder head bolts in the sequence shown to prevent warping the head

on the cylinder head bolts may round the bolt heads.

25. Lift the cylinder head from the dowels, if necessary use a small prybar for leverage between the cylinder head and block bosses. Be careful not to damage the sealing surfaces if prying is necessary to remove the head from the block.

26. If necessary, remove the intake manifold or the exhaust manifold by loosening the mounting nuts in the proper sequence. If any cylinder head studs back out, the threads should be cleaned, the studs carefully installed, then tightened to 106 inch lbs. (12 Nm).

To install:

Rotate the crankshaft clockwise to 90 degrees past TDC (the crankshaft sprocket timing mark will be at three o'clock) to prevent valve damage during assembly

➡**Before installing the cylinder head, it should be cleaned and inspected for excessive wear or damage.**

27. If removed, install the intake manifold and/or the exhaust manifold and new gasket(s). Tighten to specification in the proper sequence.

28. Clean the gasket mating surfaces. Be careful not to damage the aluminum components. Be sure the block bolt holes are clean of any residual sealer, oil or foreign matter.

29. Using a dial gauge at four points around each cylinder, check that the cylinder liners are flush or do not deviate more than 0.0005 in. (0.013mm).

30. Be sure the crankshaft is still 90 degrees past TDC and that the camshaft(s) are properly positioned with the dowel pin(s) at the 12 o'clock position to prevent valve damage. Install the cylinder head gasket and carefully guide the head into place over the dowels.

31. If the head bolts and/or the block were replaced, install the bolts and tighten in sequence to 48 ft. lbs. (65 Nm) to insure proper clamp load, then remove the bolts.

32. Coat the cylinder head bolts with clean engine oil and thread the bolts by hand until finger-tight. Tighten the bolts in sequence to 22 ft. lbs. (30 Nm).

33. Tighten the cylinder head bolts again, in sequence to 33 ft. lbs. (45 Nm) for SOHC engines or to 37 ft. lbs. (50 Nm) for DOHC engines. Install a torque angle gauge tool and calibrate the tool to zero. In sequence, tighten each cylinder head bolt an additional 90 degrees.

34. Install the timing chain, sprockets, guides and tensioner. Then, install the front cover assembly. Refer to the appropriate procedures in this section.

35. Position a new gasket, then connect the exhaust pipe to the manifold. Install and tighten the fasteners to 23 ft. lbs. (31 Nm).

36. If not already done, remove the crankshaft sprocket retainer tool. Apply a thin film of RTV sealant to the damper/pulley assembly flange and washer only. Install the crankshaft damper/pulley assembly and tighten the bolt to 158 ft. lbs. (214 Nm) while holding the pulley with a strap wrench or block of wood.

37. For DOHC vehicles, install the intake manifold support brace bolts next to the alternator, then tighten the block bolt to 33 ft. lbs. (45 Nm) and tighten the manifold bolt to 22 ft. lbs. (30 Nm).

38. Apply a small drop of RTV across the cylinder head and front cover T-joints.

Tighten the cylinder head bolts in the correct sequence to promote good cylinder sealing and to prevent leaks

Inspect the old camshaft cover gasket and replace if damaged. Install the gasket and the camshaft cover. Tighten the fasteners uniformly to 22 ft. lbs. (30 Nm) for SOHC vehicles or in proper sequence to 89 inch lbs. (10 Nm) for DOHC vehicles.

39. Install the idler pulley and tighten the fasteners to 20 ft. lbs. (27 Nm).

40. If not done during removal, drain the engine oil and change the filter, then install the drain plug and tighten it to 26 ft. lbs. (35 Nm).

41. If removed, verify the gaps on all spark plugs and install them to 20 ft. lbs. (27 Nm).

42. Install the power steering pump assembly to the bracket, then tighten the bolts to 22 ft. lbs. (30 Nm).

43. If equipped, install the air conditioning compressor and bolts. Tighten the rear bracket bolts to 19 ft. lbs. (25 Nm), then tighten the front bracket bolts to 35 ft. lbs. (47 Nm).

44. Install the accessory drive belt, making sure the belt is properly aligned on the pulley.

45. Install the two mount-to-midrail bracket nuts and tighten to 37 ft. lbs. (50 Nm). Install the three upper mount-to-engine front cover nuts and tighten them uniformly to 37 ft. lbs. (50 Nm). Remove the

support block of wood after the assembly is installed.

46. Install the splash shield, then install the tire and wheel assembly. Tighten the lug nuts, in a crisscross pattern, to 103 ft. lbs. (140 Nm).

47. Reconnect all applicable vacuum hoses disconnected during removal.

48. Position the wiring harness and install all applicable wire connectors removed during disassembly.

49. Install the throttle cable bracket and tighten the fastener to 19 ft. lbs. (25 Nm). Connect the cable, then verify that it is properly routed and not binding.

50. Connect the upper radiator hose at the cylinder head outlet, the de-aeration hose at the intake manifold, or the heater hose to the intake manifold or front of the dash.

51. Apply a few drops of clean engine oil to the male fuel line fittings. Connect any fuel line fittings and install the feed/return lines.

52. Tighten the fuel rail and pressure regulator fittings to 133 inch lbs. (15 Nm), as applicable. Install and tighten the fuel bracket retaining bolt.

53. Install the air cleaner and intake duct assembly.

54. Add engine oil and properly fill the engine cooling system.

55. Thoroughly inspect the engine compartment area, especially the cylinder head, to be sure that all wires, hoses and lines have been connected. Also inspect to be sure that all components and fasteners have been properly installed.

56. Connect the negative battery cable.

57. Prime the fuel system by cycling the ignition a few times without cranking the engine, then start the engine and check for leaks.

58. Operate the engine at idle for 3–5 minutes and listen for unusual noises. If the lifters are noisy or the cylinders are misfiring, warm the engine to normal operating temperature running at less than 2000 rpm. Once the engine is warm and the thermostat has opened, cycle the engine between idle and 3000 rpm for 10 minutes or drive the vehicle at least 5 miles to purge air from the lifters. If air cannot be purged, the faulty lifters must be replaced.

59. Verify proper coolant level. Add coolant, if necessary, after the engine has cooled.

Rocker Arms/Shafts

Only the SOHC engine has a cylinder head that uses rocker arms in its valvetrain.

REMOVAL & INSTALLATION

1. Before servicing the vehicle, refer to the precautions in the beginning of this section.

2. Disconnect the negative battery cable.

3. Remove the rocker arm cover, then inspect the cover silicone isolators for cracks or deterioration and replace, as necessary.

4. Uniformly remove the rocker arm assembly bolts, then carefully remove the two shaft and rocker arm assemblies. The shafts may be unsnapped from the lifter guide plates leaving the lifters and plates in the cylinder head. If this cannot be accomplished, remove the guide plates and lifters, but be sure to reposition the lifters in the same bores and guide plates during installation.

5. If necessary, remove the rocker arms from the shafts.

To install:

6. If removed, oil the shafts and install the rocker arms into position on the shafts.

7. Snap one end of each lifter guide plate retaining spring onto the rocker arm shaft between the No. 1 and No. 2 cylinder rocker arms and between the No. 3 and No. 4 cylinder rocker arms.

Exploded view of the rocker arms, shafts and lifter guide plate

The rocker arm tangs or slots must be properly positioned on the plungers and the springs must be positioned on the guide plate slots to prevent valve or piston damage

8. Install the rocker arm shaft assemblies. To prevent valve or piston damage, be sure the rocker arm tangs are squarely seated on the lifter plungers and the retaining springs are positioned in the guide plate slots.

➡ **If difficulty is encountered aligning the rocker arms on the valves and lifters, use a flat piece of wood, cardboard or an extension bar of suitable length on top of the shafts and rocker arms to hold both assemblies in position.**

9. Tighten the 5 rocker arm bolts on each shaft in a uniform sequence to 18 ft. lbs. (25 Nm). Verify the proper position and seating of all rocker components.

10. Apply a small drop of RTV to each cylinder head and front cover T-joint. Inspect the rocker arm cover gasket and replace if necessary. Install the gasket and rocker arm cover, then tighten the fasteners uniformly to 22 ft. lbs. (30 Nm). Be sure all cover hoses and components are reconnected after installation.

11. Connect the negative battery cable, start the engine and check for leaks.

Intake Manifold

REMOVAL & INSTALLATION

SOHC Engine

1. Before servicing the vehicle, refer to the precautions in the beginning of this section.

2. Disconnect the negative battery cable and drain the engine coolant from the radiator and engine block, into a suitable container.

3. Remove the air cleaner, disconnecting the fresh air tube at the valve cover. Remove the PCV tube and hose.

4. Properly relieve the fuel system pressure at the test port.

5. Remove the retaining screw from the fuel line retaining bracket.

6. Disconnect the fuel line(s) at the quick-connect fitting(s) by compressing the two tangs of the retainer and pulling.

7. Plug the line(s) to prevent fuel contamination or loss.

8. Disconnect the throttle cable from the throttle body, then remove the throttle cable bracket attaching nuts and position the assembly aside.

9. Label and disconnect the wiring from the intake manifold, throttle body and valve cover components, as follows:

　a. The fuel injectors.
　b. Idle Air Control (IAC) valve.
　c. Throttle Position (TP) sensor.
　d. Exhaust Gas Recirculation (EGR) solenoid.
　e. Manifold Absolute Pressure (MAP) sensor.

10. Remove the wiring tube and lay the harness away from the manifold onto the Under Hood Junction Block (UHJB).

11. Label and disconnect all vacuum hoses from the throttle body unit. Disconnect the vacuum line from the brake booster.

12. Disconnect the heater hose from the intake manifold and the de-aeration line fitting at the cylinder head coolant outlet. Remove the two clamps and lay the line onto the coolant bottle.

13. Remove the intake manifold support bracket bolt located next to the starter. If necessary, the bolt can be removed from below the vehicle.

14. Remove the serpentine drive belt, then remove the power steering pump and support the pump next to the right side dash panel sufficiently away from the intake manifold and cylinder head.

15. Remove the manifold retaining nuts, then remove the manifold and throttle body

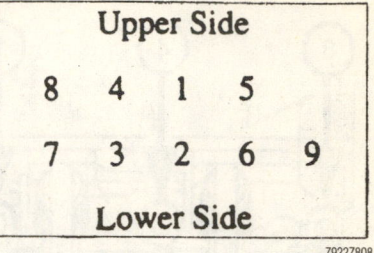

Intake manifold bolt torque sequence— SOHC engine

assembly. It may be much easier to access the lower manifold nuts from under the vehicle. Remove and discard the old gasket from the mating surfaces.

To install:

16. Thoroughly clean all gasket mating surfaces. Be careful not to damage or score the aluminum surface. If replaced, use Loctite® 290 or equivalent to seal the new PCV valve inlet tube into the manifold.

17. Position the new gasket, then install the manifold and retaining nuts. Tighten the nuts in sequence to 22 ft. lbs. (30 Nm).

18. Install the power steering pump and tighten the fasteners to 27 ft. lbs. (38 Nm).

19. Install the serpentine drive belt.

20. Connect the coolant hose, the de-aeration line and clamps, then install the manifold support bracket bolt. Tighten the bolt to 22 ft. lbs. (30 Nm).

21. Lubricate the male ends of the fuel lines with a few drops of clean engine oil, then connect the fuel supply and return lines.

22. Secure the fuel line(s) in the retaining bracket and tighten the mounting screw to 36 inch lbs. (4 Nm).

23. Reposition the wiring harness and connect the wiring and vacuum hoses to their original locations. The harness leads to the TP sensor and EGR solenoid must be routed between the intake manifold runners.

24. Inspect the air cleaner/throttle body unit gasket and replace, if necessary. Install the air cleaner and fresh air tubes, then install the PCV valve hose.

25. Connect the negative battery cable, close the radiator drain and install the engine block drain plug. Tighten the block drain plug to 26 ft. lbs. (35 Nm). Fill the engine cooling system.

26. Prime the fuel system by cycling the ignition switch **ON** for 5 seconds, then **OFF** for 10 seconds and repeating two times. Start the engine and check for leaks.

DOHC Engine

1. Before servicing the vehicle, refer to the precautions in the beginning of this section.

2. Disconnect the negative battery cable and drain the engine coolant from the radiator and engine block, into a suitable container.

3. Remove the air inlet tube, disconnecting the fresh air tube at the camshaft cover. Lift the resonator upward to disengage it from the engine service support bracket. Remove the PCV valve and hose.

4. Properly relieve the fuel system pressure at the test port.

5. Remove the retaining screw from the fuel line retaining bracket.

6. Disconnect the fuel line(s) at the quick-connect fitting(s) by compressing the two tangs of the retainer and pulling.

7. Plug the line(s) to prevent fuel contamination or loss.

8. Disconnect the throttle cable from the throttle body, then remove the throttle cable bracket attaching nuts and position the assembly aside.

9. Label and disconnect the wiring from the intake manifold and surrounding components, as follows:
   a. The fuel injectors.
   b. Idle Air Control (IAC) valve.
   c. Throttle Position (TP) sensor.
   d. Manifold Absolute Pressure (MAP) sensor.

10. Disconnect the heater and de-aeration hoses from the intake manifold outlets. The heater hose may be removed at the firewall, if necessary. Disconnect the EGR solenoid vacuum hose.

11. Position the wiring harness over the brake master cylinder, then remove the intake manifold support bracket bolt attached to the manifold next to the brake master cylinder.

12. Remove the serpentine drive belt. Remove the power steering pump assembly with the support bracket, then remove the upper pump bracket attachment bolts and position the pump away from the manifold and cylinder head, near the right dash panel.

13. Remove the three upper intake manifold attachment nuts, then raise and support the vehicle safely.

14. Remove the lower power steering unit support bracket. Remove the intake manifold support bracket bolt located next to the alternator, then the lower bracket bolt and remove from the vehicle.

15. Disconnect the canister purge solenoid and brake booster vacuum hoses.

16. Remove the intake manifold attaching stud, remove the supports and lower the vehicle.

17. Remove the remaining fasteners and the intake manifold assembly, then remove and discard the old gasket.

To install:

18. Thoroughly clean the gasket mating surfaces. Be careful not to score or damage the aluminum sealing surfaces. If installing a new coolant de-aeration tube elbow into the manifold use Loctite® 290 or equivalent to achieve a proper seal.

19. Position the new gasket, then install the intake manifold and retaining nuts. Tighten the nuts in sequence to 22 ft. lbs. (30 Nm).

20. Install the power steering pump and brackets. Tighten the fasteners to 28 ft. lbs. (38 Nm).

21. Install the serpentine drive belt making sure the belt is properly aligned on the pulleys.

22. Connect the heater hose and de-aeration line to the manifold.

23. Position the manifold support brackets and install the bolts. Tighten the right block bolt to 41 ft. lbs. (55 Nm), then tighten the left block bolt and the support bracket-to-intake manifold bolts to 22 ft. lbs. (30 Nm).

24. Lubricate the male ends of the fuel lines with a few drops of clean engine oil, then connect the fuel supply and return lines.

25. Secure the fuel line(s) in the retaining bracket and tighten the mounting screw to 36 inch lbs. (4 Nm).

26. Connect the throttle cable to the throttle body and install the support bracket. Tighten the bracket retaining bolts to 19 ft. lbs. (25 Nm). Verify that the cable locking tangs are fully engaged when assembled.

27. Position the wiring harness and connect all electrical connectors and vacuum hoses in their original locations.

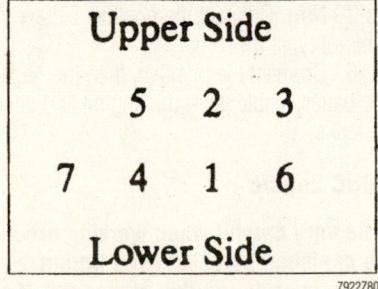

Upper Side

5 2 3

7 4 1 6

Lower Side

79222809

Intake manifold bolt torque sequence—DOHC engine

28. Install the PCV hose, the air inlet tube and resonator.

29. Connect the negative battery cable, close the radiator drain and install the engine block drain plug. Tighten the block drain plug to 26 ft. lbs. (35 Nm). Fill the engine cooling system.

30. Prime the fuel system by cycling the ignition switch **ON** for 5 seconds, then **OFF** for 10 seconds and repeating two times. Start the engine and check for leaks.

Exhaust Manifold

REMOVAL & INSTALLATION

1. Before servicing the vehicle, refer to the precautions in the beginning of this section.

2. Disconnect the negative battery cable, then raise and support the vehicle safely.

3. If equipped, remove the two front exhaust pipe-to-engine support bracket mounting fasteners.

4. Remove the pipe-to-manifold nuts and lower the pipe.

5. Remove the supports and lower the vehicle.

➡**When performing the next step, DO NOT disconnect the refrigerant lines.**

6. If equipped, remove the air conditioning compressor and bracket from the engine, which will first require the removal of the serpentine belt, then position them aside.

7. Disconnect the Oxygen (O₂S) sensor connector. If necessary, use a 19mm, 6-point crow's foot wrench to remove the O₂S sensor from the manifold.

8. Remove the manifold retaining nuts and remove the manifold from the cylinder head. Remove and discard the old gaskets from the mating surfaces.

To install:

9. Thoroughly clean the gasket mating surfaces, being careful not to score or damage the aluminum surface.

10. Install the new gasket with the smooth side facing the manifold, then install the manifold and attaching nuts. Tighten the nuts in sequence to 16 ft. lbs. (22 Nm) for the SOHC engine or to 23 ft. lbs. (31 Nm) for the DOHC engine.

11. If replacing the O₂S sensor, coat the threads with nickel-based anti-seize compound and tighten to 33 ft. lbs. (45 Nm). Connect the O₂S sensor electrical connector.

Refer to Section 1 for engine rebuilding specifications

Upper Side

8	4	1	5
7	3	2	6

Lower Side

7922Z810

Exhaust manifold bolt torque sequence—SOHC engine

Upper Side

	2	3
4	1	5

Lower Side

7922Z811

Exhaust manifold bolt torque sequence—DOHC engine

12. Install the air conditioning compressor and brackets. Tighten all fasteners except the front bracket-to-compressor fasteners to 19 ft. lbs. (25 Nm). Tighten the front bracket-to-compressor fasteners to 40 ft. lbs. (54 Nm).

13. Raise and support the vehicle safely, then install a new gasket onto the studs between the pipe and manifold.

14. Connect the pipe and manifold, then tighten the fasteners in a crosswise pattern to 23 ft. lbs. (31 Nm).

15. If necessary, position the exhaust pipe-to-engine support bracket in place and install the two mounting fasteners. Tighten the mounting fasteners to 23 ft. lbs. (31 Nm).

16. Lower the vehicle.

17. Connect the negative battery cable, start the engine and check for exhaust leaks.

Front Crankshaft Seal

REPLACEMENT

The front crankshaft seal is located in the timing chain front cover. Refer to the timing chain procedure for information about removing the front cover and replacing the seal.

Camshaft and Lifters

REMOVAL & INSTALLATION

SOHC Engine

1. Before servicing the vehicle, refer to the precautions in the beginning of this section.

2. Disconnect the negative, then the positive battery cable. Remove the battery cover and battery from the vehicle.

3. Remove the timing chain front cover.

4. Remove the timing chain and camshaft sprocket.

5. Remove the rocker arm/shaft assemblies.

6. Remove the lifters, and label or position them for assembly in their original locations.

7. Drive the camshaft plug inward, then remove it from the cylinder head with a magnet.

8. Carefully pull the camshaft from the rear of the cylinder head through the oversized camshaft plug hole. Turn the camshaft back and forth slowly while withdrawing to help prevent journal or bearing damage.

To install:

9. Clean and inspect all parts prior to installation. Lubricate the camshaft and carefully insert it through the hole at the rear of the cylinder head.

10. Coat a new rear cylinder head plug with Loctite® 242 or equivalent and install it using a standard bushing driver.

11. Install the valve lifters into their original bores, or if the camshaft has been replaced, install new lifters.

12. Install the rocker arm/shaft assemblies.

13. Install the timing chain and camshaft sprocket.

14. Install the timing chain front cover.

15. Install the battery and tighten the battery hold-down nut and screw to 80 inch lbs. (9 Nm). Connect the positive battery cable only, at this time.

16. Connect the positive, then the negative battery cable, start the engine and check for leaks.

DOHC Engine

➡**Be very careful when working around the camshaft sprockets and timing chain cover during this procedure. If a bolt or washer is accidentally dropped between the front cover and engine assembly, the cover will have to be removed for retrieval.**

1. Before servicing the vehicle, refer to the precautions in the beginning of this section.

2. Disconnect the negative battery cable and remove the serpentine drive belt.

3. Disconnect the spark plug wires from the plugs, remove the EGR valve solenoid attachment screw and remove the PCV fresh air hose.

4. Remove the camshaft cover, then inspect the cover's silicone insulators for cracks or deterioration, and replace, as necessary.

5. Turn the crankshaft clockwise until the mark on the crankshaft pulley is in alignment with the pointer on the front cover and the No. 1 cylinder is at Top Dead Center (TDC) of the compression stroke. Both camshaft dowel pins will be at the 12 o'clock position and the timing pin holes will be aligned when the No. 1 cylinder is at TDC. If necessary, the right wheel and splash shield can be removed to help observe the timing marks.

6. Carefully remove each camshaft sprocket's retaining bolt. Use a ⅞ in. (21mm) open end wrench to hold the camshaft from turning while removing the bolts.

7. Position a front angled support fixture in front of the camshaft sprockets.

8. Attach the camshaft sprocket adapters to the end of each camshaft using the pilot bolts, but do not tighten the bolts. The front angled support should come between the sprocket adapters and camshaft sprockets.

9. Remove the upper timing chain guide and both front camshaft bearing caps.

10. Secure the support fixture using ⅞ in. bolts/blocks and align the two holes in each camshaft sprocket, adapter and the front support fixture. Install the four nuts, but do not tighten. The steel blocks should be installed against the rearward side of the camshaft sprocket. Tighten the sprocket pilot bolts to 19 ft. lbs. (25 Nm) while holding the camshafts from turning with an open end wrench.

11. Move each camshaft sprocket off the end of the camshaft by rocking the sprocket forward or by carefully prying between the end of the camshaft and the sprocket. Then, tighten the four nuts and bolts with blocks from the side of the support fixture to 19 ft. lbs. (25 Nm).

12. Install the two bolts retaining the support fixture to the engine front cover and tighten the bolts to 89 inch lbs. (10 Nm). Then, remove each camshaft sprocket pilot bolt while holding the camshafts with a wrench.

13. Carefully pry between the sprocket

Camshaft cover bolt tightening
sequence—DOHC engine

Install the camshaft support fixture to securely hold the camshafts in position—DOHC engine

**Hold the camshaft with a wrench while
tightening the sprocket bolts—DOHC
engine shown**

and the end of the camshaft to move the camshaft rearward. Pry only enough to remove its end from inside the sprocket pilot otherwise camshaft or lifter damage may occur.

14. Uniformly loosen and remove the remaining camshaft bearing cap bolts. To prevent bolt/cap damage, do not use power tools and make several passes. Then, remove each camshaft. Position the bearing caps for installation in their original locations.

15. Pull the lifters out to remove them, always place them in the order in which they were removed and with the camshaft side facing down. Oil will drain out of the lifter if it is placed valve side down.

To install:

16. Install the lifters in their original locations.

17. Clean and inspect all parts prior to installation. Oil the camshaft and install with the **IN** camshaft on the intake side and **EX** camshaft on the exhaust side.

➡**The dowel pin in each camshaft must be located at the 12 o'clock position during installation to prevent valve and piston damage.**

18. Install all bearing caps, except for the forward pair, in their original positions, making sure the arrows on the caps are pointing forward toward the camshaft sprockets. Lightly oil each of the cap bolts, then install and uniformly tighten the bolts to 124 inch lbs. (14 Nm).

19. Install one camshaft sprocket pilot bolt in each camshaft and tighten to 124 inch lbs. (14 Nm) in order to pull the camshaft fully forward and align the sprocket support for installation of the sprocket onto the camshaft.

20. Remove the four sprocket support bolt/blocks and nuts.

21. Verify that the camshafts are fully positioned forward and install the two forward bearing caps and the upper chain guide. The caps are marked **E1** or **I1** for exhaust or intake and must be positioned with their arrows pointing towards the sprockets. Tighten the cap bolts to 124 inch lbs. (14 Nm).

22. Be sure the camshaft dowel pin aligns with the slot in each camshaft sprocket. If necessary, rotate the camshaft slightly (1–2 degrees) and move each sprocket from the adapter onto the end of

the camshaft. Fully seat each sprocket on the end of each camshaft.

23. Remove the two sprocket pilot bolts and adapters while using a wrench on the camshaft flats to assure the camshaft cannot move.

24. Remove the support angled fixture.

25. Install the camshaft sprocket retaining bolts and washers. Hold the camshafts and tighten the bolts to 76 ft. lbs. (103 Nm).

26. Verify all visible timing marks and holes are in alignment. Turn the crankshaft clockwise until the mark on the crankshaft pulley aligns with the mark on the front cover. Check timing by inserting ³⁄₁₆ in. drill bits through the camshaft sprocket alignment holes, into the cylinder head. If the alignment pins cannot be inserted, turn the crankshaft 360 degrees clockwise and repeat. If the pins cannot be inserted within 1–2 degrees of either TDC position, the camshafts are not properly timed. Do not start the engine until the camshafts are timed.

27. Apply a small drop of RTV across the cylinder head and front cover T-joints. Inspect the old camshaft cover gasket and replace if damaged. Install the gasket and the camshaft cover. Tighten the fasteners in proper sequence to 89 inch lbs. (10 Nm).

28. Install the right splash shield and wheel, if removed to observe the timing marks.

29. Install the PCV and fresh air hoses, the EGR valve solenoid attaching screw and the spark plug wires.

30. Install the serpentine drive belt and connect the negative battery cable.

31. Start the engine and check for leaks.

Valve Lash

ADJUSTMENT

Both the SOHC and DOHC engines utilize hydraulic lash adjusters which do not require any adjustment. There is no provision for adjusting the valve lash.

Oil Pan

REMOVAL & INSTALLATION

1. Before servicing the vehicle, refer to the precautions in the beginning of this section.

2. Raise the vehicle and support it safely. Remove the plug and drain the engine oil from the pan and crankcase.

3. Disconnect the fasteners from the exhaust manifold flange and the pipe rear flange, then remove the front exhaust pipe and gaskets from the vehicle.

4. Remove the engine stiffening bracket and the flywheel cover.

5. Remove the right wheel and splash shield, then loosen the four front motor mount bolts. Back the bolts out about ½ in. (12mm).

6. Remove all the oil pan bolts. For vehicles with a manual transaxle, an 8mm flex socket may be used to access the rear oil pan bolts located next to the flywheel.

7. Using SA9123E, or an equivalent RTV cutter tool, separate the oil pan from the engine. Drive the tool around the pan to shear the RTV seam, then tap the pan sideways with a rubber mallet to loosen.

8. Pry the engine mount away from the engine as necessary and remove the oil pan. Be careful not to damage or score component surfaces when prying.

To install:

9. Carefully clean the gasket mating surfaces with a scraper and solvent.

10. Apply a 0.16 in. (4mm) bead of RTV sealer to the pan flange. Be sure the RTV is applied to the inner side of the flange from the bolt holes as shown.

11. Install the oil pan within three minutes of RTV application and tighten the bolts to 80 inch lbs. (9 Nm).

79222814

Apply a 0.16 in (4mm) bead of RTV to the oil pan flange to the inner side of the bolt holes, as shown

12. Tighten the front mount bolts to 37 ft. lbs. (50 Nm).

13. Install the right splash shield and wheel.

14. Install the engine stiffening bracket and the flywheel cover.

15. Install the exhaust pipe. Tighten the pipe-to-manifold nuts in a crosswise pattern to 23 ft. lbs. (31 Nm) and the pipe to converter bolts to 33 ft. lbs. (45 Nm).

16. Carefully lower the vehicle, then fill the engine crankcase with clean engine oil immediately in order to prevent an attempt to start the engine without oil.

17. Start the engine and check for leaks.

Oil Pump

REMOVAL & INSTALLATION

1. Before servicing the vehicle, refer to the precautions in the beginning of this section.

2. Disconnect the negative battery cable and drain the engine oil.

3. Remove the timing chain front cover which contains the oil pump assembly.

4. Remove the oil pump cover Torx® bolts using a suitable impact driver. Because the pump cover screws are coated with a sealant to prevent oil leakage, they must be replaced when removed.

5. Remove the drive rotor and driven rotor.

6. If necessary, remove the relief valve using tool SA9103E or equivalent, to pull the valve from the bore. Because the puller jaws will damage the relief valve sealing seat, the valve cannot be used again when removed.

79222815

Exploded view of the oil pump assembly

79222816

If replacement is necessary, only use SA9103E or an equivalent puller to remove the relief valve

To install:

7. If removed, install a new relief valve into the cover bore. Coat the valve with clean engine oil and tap it into the bore using a hammer and SA9103E or an equivalent installer tool.

➡**Whenever the oil pump is installed, the assembly must be packed with petroleum jelly in order to prime the pump.**

8. Install the drive and driven rotors into the pump with the chamfer toward the front oil seal.

9. Make sure the front cover bolt holes are clean, then install the pump body cover and secure using new bolts that are coated with sealant to prevent oil leakage. Tighten the bolts to 97 inch lbs. (11 Nm).

10. Install the timing chain cover and oil pump assembly on the front of the engine.

11. Properly fill the engine crankcase, then start the engine and check for leaks.

Rear Main Seal

REMOVAL & INSTALLATION

Both engines use a one-piece round seal mounted in a seal carrier.

1. Before servicing the vehicle, refer to

Exploded view of the rear main seal installation

the precautions in the beginning of this section.

2. Disconnect the negative battery cable.

3. Remove the transaxle assembly from the vehicle.

4. As applicable, remove the clutch and flywheel assembly or the flexplate.

5. Use the prying tangs provided in the carrier to remove the seal with a small suitable prybar and hammer. Be careful not to damage the crankshaft oil seal lip contact surface.

To install:

6. Clean the carrier and crankshaft with solvent and a rag to prevent seal lip damage during installation. Check for scores or damage to the sealing surfaces.

7. Apply a light coat of clean engine oil to the seal lip and the carrier inner diameter. Install using SA9121E or an equivalent seal installer. The tool is designed to prevent the seal lip from rolling during installation and will seat the seal 0.04 in. (1mm) lower than the factory seal. Never tap on the seal or seal installer with a hammer.

8. Install the flywheel or flexplate assembly.

9. Install the transaxle assembly into the vehicle.

10. Connect the negative battery cable, start the engine and check for leaks.

Timing Chain, Sprockets, Front Cover and Seal

REMOVAL & INSTALLATION

SOHC Engine

1. Before servicing the vehicle, refer to the precautions in the beginning of this section.

2. Disconnect the negative battery

cable, then raise and support the vehicle sufficiently to work both under the vehicle and under the hood.

3. Remove the plug from the oil pan and drain the engine oil into a suitable container. Remove the right wheel and splash shield.

4. Place a 1 in. **x** 1 in. **x** 2 in. long block of wood between the torque strut and cradle to ease removal and installation of the torque engine mount. Remove the three right side upper engine torque axis to front cover nuts and the two mount to midrail bracket nuts, allowing the powertrain to rest on the block of wood.

➡**Placing a block of wood under the torque axis mount prior to removing the upper mount will allow the engine to rest on the wood, thus preventing the engine from shifting. This will allow you to install the mount during assembly without jacking or raising the engine.**

5. Remove the serpentine drive belt, belt tensioner and idler pulley.

6. Remove the power steering pump attaching bolts and support the assembly aside with the lines attached. If equipped, and if necessary for access to the front cover bolts, separate the A/C compressor from the bracket and support the assembly aside. Again, keep the compressor lines attached and do not discharge the system.

7. Remove the camshaft cover. Cover the valvetrain assemblies to protect them from foreign debris or dirt.

8. Using a strap wrench or a piece of wood wedged between the damper spoke and the lower side of the engine front cover, hold the damper and remove the bolt. With a suitable 3-jaw puller and the slots cast into the damper, pull the crankshaft damper/pulley assembly from the crankshaft.

9. Install the special oil seal replacement tool SA9104E or equivalent, to be sure the front crankshaft timing sprocket is held firmly in place and prevent guide damage. Install with the flat side towards the crankshaft sprocket.

10. Remove the front four oil pan bolts, then using a suitable RTV cutting tool, cut the front seal away from the front cover.

11. Spray the two dowel pin holes with penetrating oil to facilitate front cover removal from the dowel pins.

12. Remove the front cover bolts. One bolt is located above the serpentine drive belt pulley, under the torque axis mount flange.

Place a 1 x 1 x 2 in. (25 x 25 x 51mm) piece of wood between the torque strut and cradle before removal of the torque engine mount—SOHC engine

13. Using a small suitable tool, carefully pry the cover away from the cylinder block at the pry location tabs which are provided. Remove the cover from under the hood or through the wheel well. Be sure to cover the front of the engine to prevent debris or dirt from entering the oil galley openings and oil pan. If necessary, pry the front cover oil seal from the cover for replacement.

➡**During timing chain and sprocket removal, position the crankshaft 90 degrees past Top Dead Center (TDC), to be sure the pistons will not contact the valves upon assembly.**

14. Carefully rotate the crankshaft clockwise so the timing mark on the crankshaft sprocket and keyway align with the main bearing cap split line (90 degrees past TDC).

15. Remove bolts, then remove the timing guides and tensioner.

16. Remove the camshaft sprocket bolt, using a ⅞ in. (21mm) wrench to hold the camshaft. Then, remove the timing chain and camshaft sprocket. Remove the crankshaft sprocket, if necessary.

To install:

17. Inspect the chain for wear and damage. Check the inside diameter of the chain, it should be no more than 16.77 in. (426mm). Inspect the chain guides for wear or cracks and the timing sprockets for teeth or key wear. Replace components as necessary.

18. Verify that the crankshaft keyway is positioned 90 degrees clockwise past TDC (keyway at three o'clock). The keyway should align with the split between the bearing cap and engine block.

19. Bring the camshaft up to No. 1 TDC by loosely installing the sprocket and rotating the sprocket until the timing pin can be inserted. The camshaft contains wrench flats

to assist in turning the shaft. The dowel pin should be at 12 o'clock when the camshaft is at TDC and a timing pin (³/₁₆ in. drill bit) should, then insert at about the 8 o'clock position.

20. If removed, install the crankshaft sprocket, then rotate the crankshaft counter-clockwise 90 degrees up to No. 1 TDC (keyway at 12 o'clock).

21. Position the chain under the crankshaft sprocket and over the camshaft sprocket. If necessary remove the camshaft sprocket, then slide the camshaft sprocket into position with the chain already engaged. The timing chain should be positioned so that one silver link plate aligns with the reference mark on the camshaft sprocket and the other aligns with the downward tooth (at the 6 o'clock position) on the crankshaft sprocket. The letters FRT on the camshaft sprocket must face forward, away from the cylinder head and excess chain slack should be located on the tensioner side of the block.

22. Temporarily install a timing pin to verify proper alignment of the camshaft and sprocket, then install and tighten the sprocket bolt to 75 ft. lbs. (102 Nm). Again, use a wrench on the camshaft flats to hold the shaft in position while tightening the bolt. Do not allow the camshaft retaining bolt to torque against the timing pin or cylinder head damage will result.

23. Install the chain guides with the words FRONT facing out. Install the fixed guide first and verify the chain is snug against the guide, then install the pivot guide. Tighten the bolts to 19 ft. lbs. (26 Nm) and verify that the pivot guide moves freely.

24. Retract the tensioner plunger and pin the ratchet lever using a ⅛ in. No. 31 drill bit inserted in the alignment hole at the bottom front of the component. Install the tensioner and tighten the bolts to 14 ft. lbs. (19 Nm), then remove the drill bit.

25. Make one final check to verify all components are properly timed, then remove all timing pins.

26. Be sure the oil galleys are clear. Carefully clean the gasket mating surfaces with a scraper or wire brush and carburetor solvent, brake clean or alcohol. Use a ³/₁₆ in. drill bit and tap handle to clean the front cover holes. If removed, seat a new front cover oil seal using the installation tool with a suitable press, or wait until the cover is installed, then use a threaded installation tool and the crankshaft's threads to pull the seal into position.

Apply a 0.08 in. (2mm) bead of RTV sealer along the vertical sealing surfaces of the front cover—SOHC engine

➡️**If the engine front cover casting or assembly is replaced, the three torque axis mount studs should also be replaced. Tighten the new studs to 19 ft. lbs. (25 Nm).**

27. Apply a 0.08 in. (2mm) bead of RTV sealer along the vertical sealing surfaces of the front cover to the inside of the bolt holes and to the front of the oil pan. Extra sealer is necessary at the oil pan and cylinder head joints. Be sure to assemble the front cover to the engine within three minutes of RTV application.

28. If removed, install the crankshaft sprocket retaining tool to align the oil pump and crankshaft during cover installation. Position the front cover to the engine and install the bolts. Tighten the perimeter bolts starting at the center and working outwards on both sides to 19 ft. lbs. (25 Nm).

29. Install and tighten the front cover center or inner bolts to 89 inch lbs. (10 Nm) except for the upper inside bolt which should be tightened to 22 ft. lbs. (30 Nm). Install the four oil pan front bolts and tighten to 80 inch lbs. (9 Nm).

30. After front cover installation, spray 6–12 squirts of oil through the front oil seal drain back hole to verify that it is not plugged.

31. Apply a thin film of RTV between the damper/pulley assembly flange and washer only; the washer and bolt head flange are designed to prevent oil leakage.

32. Remove the crankshaft retaining tool and position the crankshaft damper/pulley assembly, then secure using the wood or strap wrench (as accomplished during removal) and tighten the bolt to 159 ft. lbs. (215 Nm).

33. Apply a small drop of RTV across the cylinder head and front cover T-joints. Inspect the old camshaft cover gasket and replace if damaged. Install the gasket and the camshaft cover. Tighten the fasteners uniformly to 22 ft. lbs. (30 Nm).

34. Position and install the A/C compressor assembly and/or the power steering pump assembly, as applicable.

35. Install the idler pulley if removed, then install the belt tensioner and the serpentine drive belt.

36. Install the two engine mounts-to-midrail bracket nuts and tighten to 37 ft. lbs. (50 Nm). Next install the three mount-to-front cover nuts, tighten them uniformly to 37 ft. lbs. (50 Nm) in order to prevent front cover damage. Then, remove the block of wood from under the torque strut.

37. Install the splash shield and the wheel assembly, then carefully lower the vehicle.

38. Immediately fill the engine crankcase with clean engine oil and connect the negative battery cable.

39. Start the engine and check for leaks.

At 90 degrees past TDC, the crankshaft sprocket keyway will align with the main bearing cap split line

Insert a timing pin to ensure that the camshaft is at No. 1 TDC—SOHC engine

When the camshaft is at TDC, rotate the crankshaft counterclockwise 90 degrees to achieve TDC

DOHC Engine

1. Before servicing the vehicle, refer to the precautions in the beginning of this section.

2. Disconnect the negative battery cable, then raise and support the vehicle sufficiently to work both under the vehicle and under the hood.

3. Remove the plug from the oil pan and drain the engine oil into a suitable container. Remove the right wheel and splash shield.

4. Place a 1 x 1 x 2 in. (25 x 25 x 51mm) block of wood between the torque strut and cradle to ease removal and installation of the torque engine mount. Remove the three right side upper engine torque axis-to-front cover nuts and the two mount-to-midrail bracket nuts, allowing the powertrain to rest on the block of wood.

➡ **Placing a block of wood under the torque axis mount prior to removing the upper mount will allow the engine to rest on the wood, thus preventing the engine from shifting. This will allow you to install the mount during assembly without jacking or raising the engine.**

5. Remove the serpentine drive belt, belt tensioner and idler pulley.

6. Remove the power steering pump attaching bolts and support the assembly aside with the lines attached. If equipped, and if necessary for access to the front cover bolts, separate the A/C compressor from the bracket and support the assembly aside. Again, keep the compressor lines attached and do not discharge the system.

7. Remove the camshaft cover. Cover the valvetrain assemblies to protect them from foreign debris or dirt.

8. Using a strap wrench or a piece of wood wedged between the damper spoke and the lower side of the engine front cover, hold the damper and remove the bolt. With a suitable 3-jaw puller and the slots cast into the damper, pull the crankshaft damper/pulley assembly from the crankshaft.

9. Install the special oil seal replacement tool SA9104E or equivalent, to be sure the front crankshaft timing sprocket is held firmly in place and prevent guide damage. Install with the flat side towards the crankshaft sprocket.

10. Remove the front four oil pan bolts, then using a suitable RTV cutting tool, cut the front seal away from the front cover.

11. Spray the two dowel pin holes with penetrating oil to facilitate front cover removal from the dowel pins.

12. Remove the front cover bolts. One bolt is located above the serpentine drive belt pulley, under the torque axis mount flange.

13. Using a small suitable tool, carefully pry the cover away from the cylinder block at the pry location tabs which are provided. Remove the cover from under the hood or through the wheel well. Be sure to cover the front of the engine to prevent debris or dirt from entering the oil galley openings and oil pan. If necessary, pry the front cover oil seal from the cover for replacement.

➡ **During timing chain and sprocket removal, position the crankshaft clockwise 90 degrees past Top Dead Center (TDC) to be sure the pistons will not contact the valves upon assembly.**

14. Carefully rotate the crankshaft clockwise so the timing mark on the crankshaft sprocket and keyway align with the main bearing cap split line.

15. Remove the bolts, then remove the timing guides and tensioner.

16. Remove the camshaft sprocket bolts, using a ⅞ in. (21mm) wrench to hold the camshaft. Then, remove the timing chain and camshaft sprocket. Remove the crankshaft sprocket, if necessary.

To install:

17. Inspect the chain for wear and damage. Check the inside diameter of the chain, it should be no more than 23.15 in. (588mm). Inspect the chain guides for wear or cracks and the timing sprockets for teeth or key wear. Replace components as necessary.

18. Verify that the crankshaft is positioned 90 degrees clockwise past TDC. The crankshaft keyway should be at three o'clock aligned with the main bearing cap split line to prevent piston and valve damage.

19. Install the camshaft sprockets, retaining bolts and washers. Be sure the letters FRT on the sprockets face forward, away from the cylinder block. Use the wrench flats provided on the camshafts to hold the shaft and tighten the bolts to 75 ft. lbs. (102 Nm).

20. Bring the camshafts up to No. 1 TDC by rotating the camshafts and sprocket until the dowel pins are at 12 o'clock. Install a ⅛ in. drill bit into the hole in the sprocket at about 9 o'clock.

21. If removed, install the crankshaft

Apply a 0.08 in. (2mm) bead of RTV sealer along the vertical sealing surfaces of the front cover and the front of the oil pan—DOHC engine

Please refer to Section 9 for electric cooling fan wiring schematics

Use drill bits as timing pins to verify that the camshafts are at TDC—DOHC engine

sprocket, then rotate the crankshaft counter-clockwise 90 degree up to No. 1 TDC (keyway and sprocket timing mark at 12 o'clock, in alignment with the block timing mark).

22. Position the timing chain under the crankshaft sprocket and over the camshaft sprockets so two silver link plates align with the reference marks on the camshaft sprockets and another two plates align with the downward tooth (at 6 o'clock position) on the crankshaft sprocket. Excess chain slack should be located on the tensioner side of the cylinder block.

23. Verify that the crankshaft reference mark aligns with the cylinder block mark at 12 o'clock and that the timing pins are installed in the holes at about the 9 o'clock position. Remove the timing pins from the camshaft sprockets.

24. Install the timing chain fixed guide to the right of the block face toward the water pump. Tighten the bolts to 21 ft. lbs. (28 Nm) and verify the chain is snug against the guide.

25. Install the pivoting chain guide and check for clearance between the block and head. Tighten the bolt to 19 ft. lbs. (26 Nm) and verify the guide pivots freely.

26. Install the two forward camshaft bearing caps and the upper timing chain guide, then tighten the retaining bolts to 124 inch lbs. (14 Nm).

27. Retract the tensioner plunger and pin the ratchet lever using a 1/8 in. No. 31 drill bit inserted in the alignment hole at the lower front of the component. Install the tensioner and tighten the bolts to 14 ft. lbs. (19 Nm), then remove the drill bit.

28. Make one final check to verify all components are properly timed, then remove all timing pins.

29. Be sure the oil galleys are clear. Carefully clean the gasket mating surfaces with a scraper or wire brush and carburetor solvent, brake clean or alcohol. Use a 3/16 in. drill bit and tap handle to clean the front cover holes. If removed, seat a new front cover oil seal using the installation tool with a suitable press, or wait until the cover is installed, then use a threaded installation tool and the crankshaft's threads to pull the seal into position.

➡️ **If the engine front cover casting or assembly is replaced, the three torque axis mount studs should also be replaced. Tighten the new studs to 19 ft. lbs. (25 Nm).**

30. Apply a 0.08 in. (2mm) bead of RTV sealer along the vertical sealing surfaces of the front cover to the inside of the bolt holes and to the front of the oil pan. Extra sealer is necessary at the oil pan and cylinder head joints. Apply a thin bead around the two inner cover bolt holes. Be sure to assemble the front cover to the engine within three minutes of RTV application.

31. If removed, install the crankshaft sprocket retaining tool to align the oil pump and crankshaft during cover installation. Position the front cover to the engine and install the bolts. Tighten the perimeter bolts starting at the center and working outwards on both sides to 22 ft. lbs. (30 Nm).

32. Install and tighten the front cover center or inner bolts to 89 inch lbs. (10 Nm) except for the upper inside bolt which should be tightened to 22 ft. lbs. (30 Nm). Install the four oil pan front bolts and tighten to 80 inch lbs. (9 Nm).

33. After front cover installation, spray 6–12 squirts of oil through the front oil seal drain back hole to verify that it is not plugged.

34. Apply a thin film of RTV between the damper/pulley assembly flange and washer only; the washer and bolt head flange are designed to prevent oil leakage.

35. Remove the crankshaft retaining tool and position the crankshaft damper/pulley assembly, then secure using the wood or strap wrench (as accomplished during removal) and tighten the bolt to 159 ft. lbs. (215 Nm).

36. Apply a small drop of RTV across the cylinder head and front cover T-joints. Inspect the old camshaft cover gasket and replace if damaged. Install the gasket and the camshaft cover. Tighten the fasteners uniformly to 22 ft. lbs. (30 Nm) for SOHC vehicles or in proper sequence to 89 inch lbs. (10 Nm) for DOHC vehicles.

37. Position and install the A/C compressor assembly and/or the power steering pump assembly, as applicable.

38. Install the idler pulley if removed,

Be sure that the silver link plates and reference marks are all in alignment as shown—DOHC engine

then install the belt tensioner and the serpentine drive belt.

39. Install the two engine mounts to midrail bracket nuts and tighten to 37 ft. lbs. (50 Nm). Next install the three mount to front cover nuts, tighten them uniformly to 37 ft. lbs. (50 Nm) in order to prevent front cover damage. Then, remove the block of wood from under the torque strut.

40. Install the splash shield and the wheel assembly, then carefully lower the vehicle.

41. Immediately fill the engine crankcase with clean engine oil and connect the negative battery cable.

42. Start the engine and check for leaks.

FUEL SYSTEM

Fuel System Service Precautions

Safety is the most important factor when performing not only fuel system maintenance but any type of maintenance. Failure to conduct maintenance and repairs in a safe manner may result in serious personal injury or death. Maintenance and testing of the vehicle's fuel system components can be accomplished safely and effectively by adhering to the following rules and guidelines.

• To avoid the possibility of fire and personal injury, always disconnect the negative battery cable unless the repair or test procedure requires that battery voltage be applied.

• Always relieve the fuel system pressure prior to disconnecting any fuel system component (injector, fuel rail, pressure regulator, etc.), fitting or fuel line connection. Exercise extreme caution whenever relieving fuel system pressure to avoid exposing skin, face and eyes to fuel spray. Please be advised that fuel under pressure may penetrate the skin or any part of the body that it contacts.

• Always place a shop towel or cloth around the fitting or connection prior to loosening to absorb any excess fuel due to spillage. Ensure that all fuel spillage (should it occur) is quickly removed from engine surfaces. Ensure that all fuel soaked cloths or towels are deposited into a suitable waste container.

• Always keep a dry chemical (Class B) fire extinguisher near the work area.

• Do not allow fuel spray or fuel vapors to come into contact with a spark or open flame.

• Always use a back-up wrench when loosening and tightening fuel line connection fittings. This will prevent unnecessary stress and torsion to fuel line piping.

• Always replace worn fuel fitting O-rings with new. Do not substitute fuel hose or equivalent, where fuel pipe is installed.

Fuel System Pressure

RELIEVING

1. Before servicing the vehicle, refer to the precautions in the beginning of this section.

2. Unless battery voltage is necessary for testing, disconnect the negative battery cable. This will prevent the fuel pump from running and causing a fuel spill through the disconnected components if the ignition key is accidentally turned **ON**.

3. Remove the air cleaner assembly, for access.

4. Wrap a shop rag around the fuel test port fitting, located at the lower rear of the engine, then remove the cap and connect the fuel pressure gauge tool SA9127E or equivalent.

5. Install the bleed hose from the pressure gauge into an approved container and open the valve to bleed the system pressure.

6. After the pressure is bled, remove the gauge from the test port and recap it.

7. Install the air cleaner assembly.

8. After servicing the vehicle, connect the negative battery cable and prime the fuel system as follows:

a. Turn the ignition **ON** for 5 seconds, then **OFF** for 10 seconds.

b. Repeat the **ON/OFF** cycle two more times.

c. Crank the engine until it starts.

d. If the engine does not readily start, repeat Substeps a thru c.

9. Run the engine and check for leaks.

Fuel Filter

On 1996–97 models, the fuel filter is attached to the vehicle frame in the lower left portion of the engine compartment. On 1998–00 models, the fuel filter and fuel pressure regulator are one integral component of the new returnless fuel injection system, and is located underneath the vehicle at the forward edge of the left side of the fuel tank.

REMOVAL & INSTALLATION

1996–97 Models

1. Before servicing the vehicle, refer to the precautions in the beginning of this section.

2. Disconnect the negative battery cable from the battery.

3. Remove the fresh air intake hose from the camshaft or rocker cover and remove the air inlet tube.

4. Properly relieve the fuel system pressure.

5. Clean the female end of the quick-connect fitting by spraying it with penetrating oil, then detach the large underhood fuel line connection located near the intake manifold support brace on the left side of the vehicle using the tool supplied with the replacement filter, SA9157E or equivalent.

6. Raise and support the vehicle safely.

7. Disengage the quick-connect fitting at the fuel filter inlet (rear of the filter) by pinching the two plastic tangs together and pulling on the supply line.

8. Loosen the fuel filter band clamp nut, but do not completely remove.

9. Carefully push or pull the filter out of the assembly and discard the filter in an appropriate container.

To install:

10. If the band clamp was removed, clip the fuel return and vapor lines in place and install two new band clamp nuts. Be sure all lines are in place and will not interfere with, or be damaged by, filter installation, then tighten the bracket nuts to 27 inch lbs. (3 Nm).

11. Clean the female end of the filter inlet quick-connect fitting by holding the line facing downward and spraying penetrating oil up into the fitting. Be careful not to bend or kink the line.

12. If not already installed, insert a new snap-lock retainer into the female end of the filter inlet quick-connect fitting.

13. Route the filter's nylon outlet line through the band clamp and insert the filter far enough into the band clamp to connect the outlet line to the engine's fuel line attachment. Lubricate the male end of the connector with clean engine oil, snap the connector together and pull on the line to verify proper fitting.

14. Position the filter in the band clamp assembly with the filter's forward edge located ¼ in. (6.35mm) from the front of the band clamp.

15. Lubricate the male end of the fuel

supply line with clean engine oil. Snap the line into the fuel filter and pull back to verify that the fitting is secure. Tighten the band clamp nut to 89 inch lbs. (10 Nm).

16. Lower the vehicle and install the air cleaner or intake duct, as applicable. Connect the air inlet tube and fresh air hose.

17. Connect the negative battery cable, then prime the fuel system as follows:

a. Turn the ignition **ON** for 5 seconds, then **OFF** for 10 seconds.

b. Repeat the **ON/OFF** cycle two more times.

c. Crank the engine until it starts.

d. If it does not start, repeat Substeps a thru c.

18. Run the engine and check for leaks.

1998–00 Models

1. Before servicing the vehicle, refer to the precautions in the beginning of this section.

2. Disconnect the negative battery cable from the battery.

3. Properly relieve the fuel system pressure.

4. Raise and support the vehicle safely.

5. Loosen the fuel filter/pressure regulator bracket retaining screws.

❊❊ WARNING

Exercise extreme care when opening the retaining clip. The fuel lines must be retained in this clip; if damaged, the fuel tank assembly must be replaced, since the fitting is not serviced separately.

6. Disengage the quick-connect fitting on the left side of the fuel tank by pinching the two plastic tangs together and pulling on the supply line.

7. Disengage the EVAP purge line at the 90° quick-connect fitting.

8. Slide the outlet of the fuel filter/regulator out of the support on the fuel tank bracket and disengage the fuel feed line at the 90° quick-connect fitting.

9. Pivot the fuel filter/regulator down while moving the leg of the mounting bracket out from under the parking brake lines.

➡**It is not necessary to separate the fuel filter/regulator from the mounting bracket, since both items are serviced as an assembly.**

10. Disengage the fuel feed and return line quick-connect fittings on the fuel filter/regulator. Discard the filter in an appropriate container.

79222827

The fuel filter/regulator bracket is held to the frame with two bolts—1998–00 models

To install:

11. Install new fuel line retainers (3) into the female portion of the quick-connect fuel line fittings.

12. To ease installation, lubricate the male ends of the fuel filter/regulator with clean engine oil.

13. Install the fuel feed and return lines onto the fuel filter/regulator and snap them closed. Pull back to verify that the fittings are secure.

14. Install the fuel feed, return, and EVAP purge lines into the fuel tank's retaining clip.

15. Slide the leg of the fuel filter/regulator mounting bracket under the parking brake lines and pivot upward.

❊❊ WARNING

Be sure to route the chassis fuel feed and purge lines above the parking brake cable. The parking brake cable must be firmly secured to the underbody to support the fuel and purge lines.

16. Install the 90° fuel feed line quick-connect fitting onto the fuel filter/regulator outlet and snap it closed. Pull back to verify that the fitting is secure.

17. Install the 90° EVAP purge line quick-connect fitting to the purge line and snap it closed. Pull back to verify that the fitting is secure.

18. Install the fuel feed outlet pipe of the fuel filter/regulator into the retaining clip on the fuel tank bracket.

19. Install the fuel filter/regulator bracket mounting screws. Tighten the bracket mounting screws to 71 inch lbs. (8 Nm).

20. Lower the vehicle and install the air cleaner or intake duct, as applicable. Connect the air inlet tube and fresh air hose.

21. Connect the negative battery cable, then prime the fuel system as follows:

a. Turn the ignition **ON** for 5 seconds, then **OFF** for 10 seconds.

b. Repeat the **ON/OFF** cycle two more times.

c. Crank the engine until it starts.

d. If it does not start, repeat Substeps a thru c.

22. Run the engine and check for leaks.

Fuel Pump

REMOVAL & INSTALLATION

1996–97 Models

To prevent excessive fuel spillage, whenever the tank is removed from the vehicle, it should be no more than ¾ full. Removal of the fuel pump module assembly requires removal of the fuel tank.

1. Before servicing the vehicle, refer to the precautions in the beginning of this section.

2. Disconnect the negative battery cable, then properly relieve the fuel system pressure. Refer to the procedure in this section.

3. Remove the fuel filler cap, then raise and support the vehicle safely, with the rear of the vehicle approximately 28 in. (711mm) higher than the front (to keep any fuel in the tank forward and away from the fill hose).

4. Clean the area surrounding the filler neck to avoid fuel system contamination, then position a container with a minimum 12 in. (30 cm) diameter opening under the filler neck to catch any escaping fuel. Loosen the filler neck clamp at the rear of the fuel tank, wrap a shop rag around the neck tube and carefully remove the tube from the tank.

5. Remove the filler neck, then siphon the fuel from the tank into an approved gasoline container.

6. Remove the filler neck bracket fastener at the left side of the rear frame rail, then loosen the fuel vent hose retaining clamp at the tank.

➡**It is easier to remove hoses from the tank than to pull them from the steel vent and fill tubes.**

7. Disconnect the fuel pressure and return line quick-connect fittings by pinching the two plastic tangs together, then grasp both ends of one fuel line connection and twist ¼ turn in each direction while pulling them apart. Disconnect the fuel vent hose by holding the line and by pushing on the rubber connector with a small open end wrench.

➡**Do not allow the fuel tank retaining straps to become bent during tank**

removal, otherwise strap damage and/or breakage may occur. Always utilize an assistant when removing the fuel tank to prevent damage.

8. With the aid of an assistant, remove the two support strap fasteners at the rear of the tank, then lower the tank and support panel approximately 8 in. (203mm). Reach upward and unplug the electrical connector from the top of the tank, then remove the tank and support panel from the vehicle.

9. Clean the area surrounding the fuel pump module and spray the cam lockring tangs with a suitable penetrating oil to loosen the fitting.

10. Using SA9156E, or an equivalent fuel module lockring removal tool, and a ½ in. breaker bar of approximately 18 in. (457mm) length, remove the pump unit locking ring from the tank. Attempting to use a 12 in. or shorter breaker bar may cause lockring damage.

11. Lift and tilt the unit out at a 45 degree angle, being careful not to bend the sending unit float arm. Remove and discard the unit-to-tank O-ring.

12. The sending unit is the only portion of the module that may be serviced. The filter may be cleaned with mineral spirits, but must be replaced as an assembly with the module if damaged. If necessary, remove the sending unit from the module as follows:

a. Unplug the two electrical connections using needlenose pliers or by pressing down the locking tab and pulling the connectors from the terminal.

b. Using a small suitable tool, push in on the sender assembly attaching tang, then lift upward and remove the sender.

To install:

13. If removed, install the sender on the fuel pump module by positioning the tang in the locator slot and snapping the unit into place. Attach the two sending unit electrical connectors to their terminals.

14. Install a new O-ring to the opening in the top of the fuel tank, then carefully insert the pump module into the tank at a 45 degree angle to prevent sending unit and float damage. The filter and flow arm must be directed toward the front of the tank.

15. Align the pump locator tabs with the fuel tank slots, then install the cam lockring using the ring service tool.

16. With the aid of an assistant, position the tank and support panel so the wires can be connected to the module, install the

Use the special tool to remove the fuel module lockring—1996–97 models shown

Press the sender toward the top of the module to release the bottom attachment tang and remove the sender—1996–97 models shown

module electrical connector, then secure the tank in place using the retaining straps. Tighten the strap bolts to 35 ft. lbs. (47 Nm).

17. Loosely install the filler tube, vent lines and clamps. Align the filler neck and tank so the fender will not be deflected or pushed outward by the hose. When everything is properly positioned, install the fill neck tube and bracket fastener. Vent lines should be installed into the rubber boot until the tube white marks align with the side of the boot.

18. Tighten the clamps to 18 inch lbs. (2 Nm) and tighten the fill neck bracket fastener to 53 inch lbs. (6 Nm). If the clamps must be replaced, original equipment or equivalent parts must be used, because the original parts are designed to prevent hose damage.

19. Lubricate the male ends of the fuel supply and return quick-connect fittings with a few drops of clean engine oil. Push the connectors together until the retaining tabs snap into place, then pull on opposite ends of each connection to verify that the connection is secure.

20. Carefully lower the vehicle, then

install the fuel filler cap and connect the negative battery cable.

21. Prime the fuel system and check for leaks:

a. Turn the ignition **ON** for 5 seconds, then **OFF** for 10 seconds.

b. Repeat the **ON/OFF** cycle two more times.

c. Crank the engine until it starts.

d. If the engine does not readily start, repeat Substeps a thru e.

22. Run the engine and check for leaks.

1998—00 Models

To prevent excessive fuel spillage, whenever the tank is removed from the vehicle it should be no more than ½ full. Removal of the fuel pump module assembly requires the removal of the fuel tank.

1. Before servicing the vehicle, refer to the precautions in the beginning of this section.

2. Disconnect the negative battery cable, then properly relieve the fuel system pressure. Refer to the procedure in this section.

3. Remove the fuel filler cap and rubber closeout grommet (inside fuel filler door). Remove the mounting fastener (using a T-30 Torx® bit) at the upper end of the fuel tank filler pipe.

4. Raise and support the vehicle safely, with the rear of the vehicle at a comfortable working height.

5. Remove the wheel house inner fender liner.

6. Disengage the wiring harness connector from the EVAP canister vent solenoid.

7. Remove the fuel tank filler pipe lower bracket mounting fastener located at the underbody left side rail.

8. Disconnect the EVAP canister vent tube at the ⅝ in. quick-connect fitting.

9. Loosen the fuel tank filler pipe hose clamp located closest to the tank.

10. Disconnect the filler pipe hose from the fuel tank, making sure that it is as straight and level as possible so as to prevent it from falling into the fuel tank. Remove the filler pipe from the vehicle. Be careful when disconnecting the filler hose as a residual amount of fuel may be left sitting in the filler pipe due to the inlet check valve on the fuel tank.

11. If there is more than three gallons of fuel in the tank, insert a siphon hose into the filler neck and drain into an approved gasoline container.

❋❋ CAUTION

Whenever fuel line fittings are loosened or disconnected, always wrap a shop towel around the fitting and have a suitable container available to catch any fuel spill.

12. Disengage the fuel feed line from the outlet tube of the filter/pressure regulator.

13. Disengage the fuel vapor/canister purge line at the fitting adjacent to the filter/pressure regulator.

14. Remove the fuel filter/pressure regulator bracket from under the brake lines.

15. With the aid of an assistant, remove the two fuel tank retaining strap mounting bolts. Lower the tank just enough to disengage the two electrical connectors from the fuel pump and pressure sensor.

16. Carefully remove the fuel tank from the vehicle.

17. If fuel pump module replacement/service is necessary:

18. Clean the area surrounding the fuel pump module and spray the cam lockring tangs with a suitable penetrating oil to loosen the fitting.

19. Using SA9156E, or an equivalent fuel module lockring removal tool, and a ½ in. breaker bar of approximately 18 in. (457mm) length, remove the pump unit locking ring from the tank. Attempting to use a 12 in. or shorter breaker bar may cause lockring damage.

20. Lift and tilt the unit out at a 45 degree angle, being careful not to bend the sending unit float arm. Remove and discard the unit to tank O-ring.

21. The sending unit is the only portion of the module that may be serviced. The filter may be cleaned with mineral spirits, but must be replaced as an assembly with the module if damaged. If necessary, remove the sending unit from the module as follows:

a. Unplug the electrical connector from the fuel level sending unit by disengaging the locking tab and pulling the connector from the terminal.

b. Holding the fuel pump module in both hands, and applying firm upward pressure at the bottom of the fuel sending unit using both thumbs, push the sender toward the top of the module to disengage the bottom attachment clip.

To install:

22. Install the sending unit to the pump module by positioning the attachment clip in the locator slot and snapping the component into place. Verify that the sending unit float arm has the correct relationship to the fuel pump module by holding the component up on a flat, horizontal surface and measuring. Using a ⁵⁄₃₂ in. diameter drill bit, it must easily pass between the float and the horizontal surface with no more than ¹⁄₁₆ in. clearance. If bending the float arm is required to meet the clearance specification, it must be performed at the 90° bend near the level sender while supporting the short section of the arm.

23. Connect the wiring harness from the fuel pump module to the sending unit. Press firmly to engage.

24. Install the fuel pump assembly as follows:

25. Before installing the pump module, inspect the fuel tank and clean the seal groove of any debris or foreign matter.

➡ **The correct fuel pump module O-ring seal is green in color. It is incorrect to use the older black seal.**

26. Install a new O-ring seal to the opening in the top of the fuel tank, then carefully insert the pump module into the tank at a 45 degree angle to prevent sending unit and float damage.

27. Align the pump locator tabs with the fuel tank slots by rotating the module 90° counterclockwise. The lines from the pump unit should face the 10 o'clock position.

28. Install the cam lockring using the ring service tool.

29. Connect the fuel pump vapor line to the tank vent pipe.

30. Connect the feed and return lines to the fuel filter/pressure regulator.

31. Place the feed, return and EVAP canister purge lines into the fuel tank retaining clip and snap closed.

32. Install the loose retainer clip around the fuel feed, return and purge lines and snap shut.

33. With the aid of an assistant, position the fuel tank so the wires can be connected to the pump module and pressure sensor.

34. Properly install the fuel tank under the vehicle by making certain that the small white locator button on the left side of the tank is positioned tightly against the left side rail.

35. Install the retaining straps and shield. Tighten the strap bolts to 35 ft. lbs. (47 Nm).

36. Place the fuel filter/pressure regulator in position and install the mounting screws in the bracket. Tighten the mounting screws to 71 inch lbs. (8 Nm).

37. Install a new retainer into the female portion of the 90° quick-connect fitting of the underbody fuel line.

38. Lubricate the outlet end of the filter/pressure regulator with clean engine oil and connect to the underbody fuel feed line.

39. Be sure that the fuel filler check valve is in correct position at the end of the filler pipe. Using plain water, lightly wipe the outside of the fuel tank inlet connector.

40. Position the fuel tank filler pipe into the wheel opening with the top of the pipe protruding out of the fender/filler door opening.

41. Insert the filler pipe into the fuel tank opening and loosely install the lower bracket attachment screw. Be sure that the EVAP vent solenoid pipe is installed in the correct position on the filler pipe bracket.

42. Lower the vehicle and install the fuel tank filler pipe upper bracket mounting fastener. Tighten the mounting fastener to 31–35 inch lbs. (3.5–4.5 Nm).

43. Install the rubber closeout grommet to the filler pipe and install the fuel cap.

44. Raise the vehicle to a comfortable working height.

45. The fuel pipe connecting hose should be installed to within ¼ in. (6mm) of the stops on the fuel tank inlet connector and the hose clamp should be positioned within ³⁄₁₆ in. (4mm) of the end of the connecting hose. Tighten the hose clamp to 35 inch lbs. (4 Nm).

46. Connect the EVAP canister vent pipe to the canister vent hose.

47. Tighten the lower mounting screw on the filler pipe to the underbody. Tighten the mounting screw to 71 inch lbs. (8 Nm).

48. Engage the wiring harness connector to the EVAP vent solenoid.

49. Install the wheel house inner fender liner.

50. Carefully lower the vehicle, then install the fuel filler cap and connect the negative battery cable.

51. Prime the fuel system and check for leaks:

a. Turn the ignition **ON** for 5 seconds, then **OFF** for 10 seconds.

Use a ⁵⁄₃₂ in. diameter drill bit to measure float arm clearance—1998–00 models

b. Repeat the **ON/OFF** cycle two more times.

c. Crank the engine until it starts.

d. If the engine does not readily start, repeat Substeps a thru c.

52. Run the engine and check for leaks.

DRIVE TRAIN

Transaxle Assembly

REMOVAL & INSTALLATION

1. Before servicing the vehicle, refer to the precautions in the beginning of this section.

2. Properly disable the SIR system and disconnect the negative battery cable.

3. Remove the two air inlet duct fasteners, disengage the air temperature sensor connector and remove the air inlet duct. For the DOHC engine, loosen the flex tube to air box clamp, remove the three air box fasteners and remove the air box.

4. Remove the transaxle strut-to-cradle bracket through-bolt located on the radiator side of the transaxle.

5. Disengage the wiring harness connectors from the vehicle and turbine speed sensor, transaxle temperature sensor, selector switch and actuator connector from the transaxle.

6. On automatic transaxles, remove the two ground terminals from the top two converter housing studs.

7. Remove the ground wire from the neutral (selector) switch and unclip the oxygen sensor wire retainer.

8. Remove the top two transaxle housing studs.

9. Remove the four Electronic Ignition (EI) coil-to-converter housing bolts, then wire the coil to the cylinder head coolant outlet. Discard the old coil retaining bolts and replace with new bolts upon installation.

10. For manual transaxles, remove the shifter cables from the shift arms and clutch housing, taking care not to damage the cable boot.

✳✳ WARNING

On vehicles with manual transaxles, do not use power tools when loosening and removing the slave cylinder.

The use of a power tool to remove the slave cylinder could result in breaking off the hydraulic line.

11. Wire the radiator to the upper radiator support in order to hold the assembly in place when the cradle is removed.

12. Install SA9105E or an equivalent engine support bar assembly.

13. Raise and support the vehicle safely.

14. On manual transaxles, remove the drain plug from the transaxle housing and drain the transaxle fluid. The drain plug is on the lower cowl side of the housing and is inserted from the engine side of the vehicle.

15. Remove the front wheels and engine splash shields from the vehicle. For coupes, remove the left and right lower fascia braces.

16. Remove the front engine strut cradle bracket-to-cradle nuts from below the cradle.

17. Remove the transaxle mount-to-cradle nut from under the cradle.

18. Remove and discard the cotter pin from the lower ball joints. Loosen the ball joint nut until the top of the nut is even with the top of the threads.

19. Use tool SA9132S to separate the lower control arm ball joint from the steering knuckle, then remove the nut. Do not use a wedge tool or seal damage may occur.

➡**The outer CV-joint for vehicles equipped with ABS contains a speed sensor ring. Use of an incorrect tool to separate the control arm from the knuckle may result in damage and loss of the ABS system.**

20. Remove the front exhaust pipe nuts at the manifold, then disconnect the pipe from the support bracket.

21. Remove the front pipe-to-catalytic converter bolts and lower the pipe from the vehicle.

22. Remove the engine-to-transaxle stiffening bracket bolts and remove the bracket.

23. Remove the steering rack-to-cradle bolts and wire the gear for support when the cradle is removed.

24. Remove the brake line from the retainer at the rear of the cradle.

25. On manual transaxles, remove the clutch housing dust cover.

26. On automatic transaxles, remove the torque converter dust cover, then remove the converter-to-flywheel bolts.

27. Position two 4 x 4 x 36 in. (10 x 10 x 91 cm) pieces of wood onto a powertrain support dolly and position the dolly under the vehicle.

28. Remove the four cradle-to-body bolts and carefully lower the cradle from the vehicle with the support dolly. Tape or wire the two large washers from the rear cradle-to-body attachments in position to prevent loss.

29. On automatic transaxles, squeeze the plastic tabs at the transaxle cooler line connectors and pull the lines out of the connectors. The plastic retainer should remain on the lines. Connect one end of a ⅜ in. rubber hose over each cooler line to prevent fluid contamination or loss.

30. If necessary for the transaxle to clear the body, lower the vehicle enough to adjust the engine support assembly and lower the transaxle side of the assembly until the valve body cover clears the frame.

31. Raise and support the vehicle safely, then support the transaxle securely with a suitable jack.

32. Use a prybar to separate the left side axle from the transaxle. Remove the axle sufficiently to install SA91112T or an equivalent seal protector around the axle and into the seal to prevent the seal from being cut by the shaft spline.

33. On automatic transaxles, remove the two bottom converter housing-to-engine bolts and lower the transaxle sufficiently to reach the shifter cable.

34. On manual transaxles, remove the two bottom clutch housing-to-engine bolts and install a guide bolt into the bottom rear clutch housing bolt hole from the side of the engine block.

35. Separate the transaxle only sufficiently enough to install an axle seal protector on the remaining engaged axle.

36. On automatic transaxles, disconnect the transaxle shifter cable, then squeeze the retaining tabs to release the cable from the converter housing.

37. Carefully lower the transaxle from the vehicle. Use SA9165T or an equivalent transaxle cooler cleaning tool to clean the cooler and lines.

To install:

38. Place the transaxle assembly securely onto the jack and position under the vehicle. Install axle seal protectors into seals on both sides.

39. On automatic transaxles, raise the transaxle sufficiently, then connect the shifter cable to the gear selector lever and to the converter housing.

40. Raise the transaxle into the vehicle and verify that the intermediate shaft splines line up with the differential side gear

splines, then install the two lower transaxle housing-to-engine bolts and tighten the bolts to 96 ft. lbs. (130 Nm). The bolts should not be used to draw the transaxle to the engine.

41. Be sure the axle seal protectors are installed into the transaxle. Carefully install the axles to the transaxle. After the splines clear the seal, but before the axle snaps into place, remove the seal protector. Push the axle all of the way into the transaxle and install the snapring. Remove the transaxle jack.

42. Clean and lubricate the ball joint threads, then raise the cradle up on the support dolly and place the ball joints into the knuckles. Verify the correct positioning of the lower control arm bar studs to the knuckles, the cooling module support bushings, the engine strut bracket and the transaxle mount.

43. Insert ⁷⁄₁₆ in. round steel rods into the cradle-to-body alignment holes near the front cradle to body fastener holes. Guide the cradle into position making sure all mount studs are properly guided into their holes.

44. Be sure the washers are in place, then install the two rear cradle to body bolts. Verify proper cradle positioning and install the two front cradle bolts, then tighten the four cradle bolts to 151 ft. lbs. (205 Nm).

45. Remove the support dolly and lower the vehicle sufficiently for underhood access. Remove the engine support bar assembly.

46. Install the transaxle strut-to-cradle bracket through-bolt and nut, then tighten the fasteners to 52 ft. lbs. (70 Nm). If removed, install the strut cradle bracket-to-cradle bolt and also tighten to 52 ft. lbs. (70 Nm).

47. On manual transaxles, connect the shift control cables to the shift arms and the clutch housing, then install the cable retainers.

48. Remove the radiator assembly support wire.

49. Use a 6 x 1.0mm tap to clean the sealant from the ignition module mounting holes in the transaxle. Install the ignition module, then secure using the new bolts with sealant. Use extreme caution to assure proper bolt installation. Tighten the bolts to 71 inch lbs. (8 Nm) and verify that the bolt heads are properly seated on the ignition module.

50. Install the two top transaxle housing-to-engine studs and tighten to 66 ft. lbs. (90 Nm). Connect the two ground terminals to the studs and tighten to 19 ft. lbs. (25 Nm).

51. Engage the actuator circuit connector

and tighten to 22 inch lbs. (2.5 Nm). Engage the wiring harness connectors to the vehicle and turbine speed sensors, the transaxle oil temperature sensor and the selector switch connectors.

52. Connect the ground wire to the neutral (selector) switch and clip the oxygen sensor wire to the converter housing.

53. On automatic transaxles, unplug the transaxle cooler lines and press them into the transaxle connectors until they bottom out.

54. On automatic transaxles, adjust the shifter cable, then for DOHC vehicles, install the air box and tighten the fasteners to 89 inch lbs. (10 Nm). Connect the flex tube to the air box, align the arrows and tighten the clamp to 18 inch lbs. (2 Nm).

55. Install the air inlet duct and fasteners, then engage the air temperature sensor electrical connector.

56. Raise and support the vehicle safely.

57. Install the transaxle mount-to-cradle nut and the transaxle strut cradle bracket-to-cradle nut, then tighten the nuts to 52 ft. lbs. (70 Nm).

58. Install the two engine strut cradle bracket-to-cradle fasteners from under the cradle and tighten to 52 ft. lbs. (72 Nm).

59. If applicable, install the nuts to the front transaxle-to-cradle studs and tighten to 35 ft. lbs. (48 Nm).

60. Remove the steering gear support wire and position the gear to the cradle. Install the gear bolts and nuts, then tighten the fasteners to 40 ft. lbs. (54 Nm).

61. Connect the brake line to the cradle retainer.

62. On automatic transaxles, install the torque converter-to-flexplate bolts and tighten the bolts to 52 ft. lbs. (70 Nm). Install the converter housing dust cover and tighten the bolts to 89 inch lbs. (10 Nm).

63. Install the powertrain stiffening bracket and tighten the bracket bolts to 35 ft. lbs. (47 Nm).

64. Position the exhaust manifold front pipe into the vehicle, then install the gasket and manifold retaining nuts. Tighten the nuts in a crosswise pattern to 23 ft. lbs. (31 Nm). Install the front pipe to the catalytic converter and tighten the bolts to 33 ft. lbs. (45 Nm). Finally, install the front pipe to the transaxle support bracket and tighten the fasteners to 23 ft. lbs. (31 Nm).

65. On manual transaxles, install the transaxle drain plug and tighten to 40 ft. lbs. (45 Nm).

➡ **If the torque converter flange threads (automatic only) are damaged use the Saturn 21010753 converter fastener kit**

in place of the self tapping screws in order to provide proper clamp load and prevent exhaust leaks.

66. Install the nuts onto the ball joint studs and tighten to 55 ft. lbs. (75 Nm). Continue to tighten the nuts as necessary and install a new cotter pin.

67. Install the center and both wheel splash shields.

68. For coupes, install the right left lower fascia braces and J-nuts. Tighten the fasteners to 89 inch lbs. (10 Nm).

69. Install the tire and wheel assemblies, then lower the vehicle.

70. Connect the negative battery cable and fill the transaxle with the proper type and amount of fluid.

71. Properly enable the SIR system.

72. Warm the engine and check the transaxle fluid. Check and adjust vehicle alignment, as necessary.

Clutch

ADJUSTMENT

The hydraulic clutch system is self-adjusting; therefore, no manual clutch pedal adjustments are necessary nor possible.

REMOVAL & INSTALLATION

1. Before servicing the vehicle, refer to the precautions in the beginning of this section.

2. Properly disable the SIR system and disconnect the negative battery cable.

3. Remove the transaxle from the vehicle.

4. Unsnap the release fork from the ball stud, then remove the fork and bearing from the vehicle. Slide the bearing from the fork. The bearing should be checked for excessive play and for minimal bearing drag. It should be replaced if no/little drag or excessive play is found.

➡ **The release bearing is packed with grease and should not be washed with solvent.**

5. Using a feeler gauge, measure the distance between the pressure plate and flywheel surfaces in order to determine clutch face thickness. Replace the clutch disc if it is not within 0.205–0.287 in. (5.2–7.3mm).

6. Remove the pressure plate-to-flywheel bolts in a progressive crisscross pattern to prevent warping the cover, then remove the pressure plate and clutch disc.

7. Inspect the pressure plate, as follows:

a. Check for excessive wear, chatter

Flywheel mounting bolt tightening sequence

Use a proper clutch alignment tool before tightening the pressure plate retaining bolts

marks, cracks or overheating (indicated by a blue discoloration). Black random spots on the friction surface of the pressure plate is normal.

b. Check the plate for warpage using a straightedge and a feeler gauge; the maximum allowable warpage is 0.006 in. (0.15mm).

c. Replace the plate, if necessary.

8. Inspect the clutch disc, as follows:

a. Check the disc face for oil or burnt spots.

b. Check the disc for loose damper springs, hub or rivets.

c. Replace the disc, if necessary.

9. Check the flywheel, as follows:

a. Check the ring gear for wear or damage.

b. Check the friction surface for excessive wear, chatter marks, cracks or overheating (indicated by a blue discoloration). Black random spots on the friction surface of the pressure plate is normal.

c. Check flywheel thickness; the minimum allowable is 1.102 in. (28mm).

d. Measure flywheel run-out using a dial indicator, positioned for at least two flywheel revolutions. Push the crankshaft forward to take up thrust bearing clearance. Maximum flywheel run-out is 0.006 in. (0.15mm).

e. Check the flywheel for warpage using a straightedge and a feeler gauge; the maximum allowable warpage is 0.006 in. (0.15mm).

f. Replace the flywheel, if necessary.

10. If necessary, remove the flywheel retaining bolts and remove the flywheel from the crankshaft.

To install:

11. If removed, install the flywheel and tighten the bolts in a crisscross sequence to 59 ft. lbs. (80 Nm).

12. Install the clutch disc and pressure plate with the yellow dot on the pressure plate aligned as close as possible to the mark on the flywheel. The clutch disc is labeled FLYWHEEL SIDE in order to help correctly position the disc. Start the pressure plate bolts.

13. Install clutch alignment tool SA9145T or equivalent in the clutch disc, and push in until it bottoms out in the crankshaft.

14. Tighten the pressure plate bolts using multiple passes of a crisscross sequence to 18 ft. lbs. (25 Nm) and remove the alignment tool.

15. Lubricate the fork pivot point with high temperature grease and install the release bearing to the fork. Do not lubricate the release bearing or bearing quill.

16. Snap the release bearing and fork onto the ball stud.

17. Lubricate the splines of the input shaft lightly with a high temperature grease.

18. Install the transaxle assembly.

19. Connect the negative battery cable and properly enable the SIR system.

Hydraulic Clutch System

BLEEDING

The clutch hydraulic assembly has been filled with fluid and bled of air at the factory. Do not attempt to bleed the hydraulic system. While the unit does not require periodic checking, it must be serviced, when necessary, as a complete assembly. The system is full when the reservoir is half full.

Only DOT 3 brake fluid should be added to the system. If the fluid level drops, inspect the system, including the slave cylinder, for leakage. A slight wetting of the slave cylinder surface is normal. Fill the clutch master cylinder reservoir with brake fluid. Be careful not to spill brake fluid on the painted surface of the vehicle.

Halfshafts

REMOVAL & INSTALLATION

1. Before servicing the vehicle, refer to the precautions in the beginning of this section.

2. Remove the wheel cover or the center cap for access to the halfshaft nut. Have an assistant depress the brake pedal and loosen the front halfshaft nut.

3. Raise the vehicle and support it safely, then remove the corresponding wheel and splash shield.

4. If removing the left side halfshaft or right side intermediate shaft, loosen the plug and drain the transaxle fluid into a clean container.

5. Remove the halfshaft nut and washer.

6. Remove and discard the cotter pin from the lower control arm ball joints. Back off the ball joint nut until the top of the nut is even with the top of the threads.

7. Use tool SA9132S or equivalent to loosen the lower control arm ball joint in the steering knuckle, then remove the nut. Do not use a wedge tool or seal damage may occur. The ball joint will be completely removed from the knuckle after the tie rod ball joint is separated.

✳✳ WARNING

The outer CV-joint for vehicles equipped with ABS contains a speed sensor ring. Use of an incorrect tool to separate the control arm from the knuckle may result in damage and loss of the ABS system.

8. Remove the tie rod cotter pin and loosen the castle nut, then separate the tie rod end from the knuckle using Tie Rod Separator SA91100C or equivalent. Once loosened sufficiently, remove the castle nut and separate the components completely. Do not use a wedge-type tool or the seal may be damaged.

9. You may wish to place a cloth over the sway bar to protect the surface, then use a prybar to leverage the knuckle and separate the lower control arm ball joint. Position a cloth at the prybar contact point with the cradle, then push down on the bar and separate the ball joint from the knuckle. Be

sure the knuckle does not contact and damage the ball stud seal.

10. While pulling the knuckle/strut assembly away from the halfshaft, pull the end of the halfshaft from the wheel hub. If difficulty is encountered, tap on the end of the halfshaft using a block of wood and a hammer. Support the halfshaft assembly using a length of mechanic's wire or with a stand.

11. If removing the right halfshaft, disconnect the halfshaft from the intermediate shaft by tapping the inner joint with a hammer and a block of wood. Remove the halfshaft from the vehicle.

12. If removing the left halfshaft, disconnect the halfshaft by inserting a large prybar into the space between the inner joint and transaxle. Pry the halfshaft from the transaxle, being careful not to contact and damage the transaxle oil seal. Remove the halfshaft from the vehicle.

To install:

13. If installing the left side halfshaft, install SA91112T or equivalent transaxle seal protector. Install the halfshaft into the transaxle; after the splines have safely passed the transaxle oil seal, remove the seal protector and fully seat the halfshaft.

14. If installing the right side halfshaft, insert the shaft onto the intermediate shaft and push firmly to engage the circlip. Install the shaft assembly into the transaxle.

15. Insert the outer end of the halfshaft into the wheel hub. Be careful not to damage the CV-joint boot.

16. Thoroughly clean and lubricate the ball joint stud threads of the lower control arm and tie rod end.

17. Install the lower control arm ball stud to the steering knuckle, then install the nut, but do not tighten at this time.

18. Attach the tie rod end to the steering knuckle, then install the nut. Tighten the nut to 33 ft. lbs. (45 Nm) and install a new cotter pin. If necessary, tighten the nut additionally, but do not back it off to insert the cotter pin.

19. Tighten the lower control arm ball stud nut to 55 ft. lbs. (75 Nm); tighten additionally if necessary to align the holes, then install a new cotter pin.

20. Install the washer and a new halfshaft nut, then tighten the nut to 148 ft. lbs. (200 Nm).

21. If equipped with ABS, inspect the wheel speed sensor signal for proper operation.

22. Install the inner splash shield and wheel.

23. Lower the vehicle and properly fill the transaxle.

24. Check and adjust the front end alignment as necessary.

SEAL PROTECTOR
79227833

Failure to use a seal protector may allow the halfshaft splines to damage the transaxle seal

STEERING AND SUSPENSION

Air Bag

✱✱ CAUTION

All vehicles are equipped with an air bag system, also known as the Supplemental Inflatable Restraint (SIR) or Supplemental Restraint System (SRS). The system must be disabled before performing service on or around system components, steering column, instrument panel components, wiring and sensors. Failure to follow safety and disabling procedures could result in accidental air bag deployment, possible personal injury and unnecessary system repairs.

PRECAUTIONS

Several precautions must be observed when handling the inflator module to avoid accidental deployment and possible personal injury.

• Never carry the inflator module by the wires or connector on the underside of the module.

• When carrying a live inflator module, hold securely with both hands, and ensure that the bag and trim cover are pointed away.

• Place the inflator module on a bench or other surface with the bag and trim cover facing up.

• With the inflator module on the bench, never place anything on or close to the module which may be thrown in the event of an accidental deployment.

DISARMING

1. Before servicing the vehicle, refer to the precautions in the beginning of this section.

2. Align the steering wheel so the vehicle wheels are pointing in the straight-ahead position.

3. Turn the ignition switch to the **LOCK** position.

4. Remove the SIR or AIR BAG fuse from the fuse block.

5. Remove the Connector Position Assurance (CPA) device, then disengage the yellow 2-way SIR wiring harness connector at the base of the steering column.

ARMING

After the repairs, enable the system as follows:

1. Turn the ignition switch to the **LOCK** position.

2. Engage the yellow 2-way connector at the base of the steering column, then install the CPA device.

3. Reinstall the SIR or AIR BAG fuse.

4. Turn the ignition switch to the **RUN** position.

5. Verify the SIR indicator light flashes 7–9 times, if not, inspect the system for malfunction.

Rack and Pinion Steering Gear

REMOVAL & INSTALLATION

1. Before servicing the vehicle, refer to the precautions in the beginning of this section.

2. Disconnect the negative battery cable, then raise and support the vehicle safely.

3. Remove both front tires and the left inner splash shield.

4. Remove and discard the tie rod cotter pins, then remove the castle nuts. Disconnect the tie rod ends using SA91100C or an equivalent separator tool. Do not use a wedge-type tool or seal damage may occur.

5. Loosen the intermediate shaft cover

The pinch bolt is located under the intermediate shaft cover

Remove the steering gear-to-cradle fasteners, then remove the gear through the left fenderwell

from the steering gear and move up enough to access the pinch bolt. Remove the pinch bolt.

6. On vehicles with power steering, place a suitable container under the steering assembly. Disconnect the pressure and return lines at the steering gear and allow the system to drain.

7. Remove the steering gear-to-cradle fasteners, then remove the gear through the left fenderwell.

To install:

8. Install the steering gear and tighten the steering gear fasteners to 37 ft. lbs. (50 Nm). Be sure to use new nuts because the torque retention of the old nuts may be insufficient.

9. Position the intermediate steering shaft to the gear and tighten the pinch bolt to 35 ft. lbs. (47 Nm).

10. On vehicles with power steering, connect the pressure and return hoses, then tighten the fittings to 20 ft. lbs. (28 Nm).

11. Thoroughly clean and lubricate the threads of the tie rod ends, then install the ends into the steering knuckles. Install the castle nuts and tighten to 33 ft. lbs. (45 Nm), then install new cotter pins. If necessary, tighten the nut additionally to install the pin, do not back off.

12. Install the left inner splash shield and install the front wheels.

13. Lower the vehicle and connect the negative battery cable.

14. Check alignment and adjust vehicle toe, as necessary.

15. On vehicles with power steering, bleed the power steering system.

POWER STEERING SYSTEM BLEEDING

1. Fill the P/S fluid reservoir.

2. Raise the front of the vehicle just sufficiently so that the drive wheels are off the ground, then safely support the vehicle.

3. Bleed the system by turning the wheels from side-to-side without hitting the stops. It may take several cycles to bleed the system.

➡**Maintain the reservoir at the FULL mark during this procedure.**

4. Lower the vehicle.

5. Start the engine and, with the transaxle in **P** (A/T) or **N** (M/T), check the fluid level with the engine idling. If necessary, add fluid to bring the level to the FULL mark.

6. Road test the vehicle and check for proper operation. Recheck the fluid level and make sure it is at or slightly above the FULL mark after the system has stabilized at normal operating temperature.

Strut

REMOVAL & INSTALLATION

Front

✳✳ CAUTION

The MacPherson strut is under extreme spring pressure. Do not remove the strut shaft center nut at the top without using an approved spring compressor. Personal injury may result if this precaution is not followed.

1. Before servicing the vehicle, refer to the precautions in the beginning of this section.

2. If equipped with an Anti-lock Brake System (ABS), disconnect the negative battery cable, then raise and support the vehicle safely. Be sure the vehicle is at a height where underhood access is still possible.

3. Remove the front wheel.

Remove the three nuts to detach the top of the strut from the body

4. If equipped, unplug and disconnect the ABS wire from the strut wiring bracket. Note the wiring position for assembly purposes, then place the ABS wiring out of the way to prevent damage. If the strut is being replaced, drill the rivet head retaining the ABS wiring bracket to the strut and remove the bracket.

5. Loosen the two steering knuckle-to-strut housing bolts, but do not remove them at this time. For reassembly purposes, matchmark the strut position to the steering knuckle.

6. Remove and discard the three upper strut-to-body nuts.

7. Place a rag over the CV-joint seal to protect it from damage, then remove the two steering knuckle-to-strut housing bolts.

8. Remove the strut assembly from the vehicle.

To install:

9. Position the strut in the vehicle and install three new upper mount nuts. New nuts must be used because the torque retention of the old nut may be insufficient. Tighten the nuts to 21 ft. lbs. (29 Nm).

10. Install the knuckle bolts, also using new nuts. Push the bottom of the strut inward while tightening the fasteners to 126 ft. lbs. (170 Nm).

11. If equipped with ABS and the strut was replaced, install the ABS wiring bracket to the strut using a new rivet. Connect the ABS wiring to the bracket and install the wiring to the speed sensor connector. Be sure the wiring is positioned as noted during removal.

12. Install the wheel assembly, remove the supports and lower the vehicle.

13. Connect the negative battery cable, then check and adjust the alignment as necessary.

Matchmark, then remove the two bolts that secure the strut to the knuckle assembly

Rear

> **⁕⁕ CAUTION**
>
> **The MacPherson strut is under extreme spring pressure. Do not remove the strut shaft support nut at the top center of the assembly without using an approved spring compressor. Personal injury may result if this precaution is not followed.**

1. Before servicing the vehicle, refer to the precautions in the beginning of this section.

2. On coupes, remove the rear seat cushion bottom, left or right rocker panel interior moldings and the left or right rear sail interior panels.

3. On sedans, remove the left or right C-pillar interior molding.

4. Fold down the rear seat backs and remove the rear seat side bolsters from the vehicle, if equipped.

5. On coupes, remove the rear deck package shelf retainers that attach the shelf to the side of the cargo area.

6. If equipped, remove the speaker grill fasteners and grills from the shelf, then remove the seat belt bezel and separate the seat belts from the shelf. Remove the rear package shelf cover.

7. If equipped with an Anti-lock Brake System (ABS), disconnect the negative battery cable.

8. Raise the rear of the vehicle and support it safely, then remove the appropriate rear wheel.

9. If equipped, disconnect the ABS wiring from the strut wiring bracket. If the strut is being replaced, drill out the rivet head, if required, retaining the ABS wiring bracket to the strut and remove the bracket. In either case, note the position of the wiring and move the wiring to prevent damage. If necessary, unplug the wheel speed sensor connector.

10. For reassembly purposes, match-mark the strut position to the knuckle. Then, loosen, but do not remove at this time, the two strut-to-knuckle bolts.

11. Position a jack under the rear knuckle, then raise the jack only enough to support the knuckle. If a 2nd jack is not available, position a suitable stand under the knuckle to support the strut.

12. Remove the three strut-to-body mounting nuts.

13. Slowly raise the vehicle using another jack, lowering the strut from the body. If another jack is not available, lower the jack holding the strut, but do so carefully.

14. Unfasten the strut-to-knuckle bolts and remove the strut assembly from the vehicle.

To install:

15. Install three new strut-to-upper mount nuts and tighten the nuts to 21 ft. lbs. (29 Nm).

> **⁕⁕ WARNING**
>
> **New nuts must be used, because the torque retention of the old fasteners may not be sufficient.**

16. Install the knuckle bolts with new nuts, then push the bottom of the strut inward, aligning the marks made earlier. Tighten the fasteners to 126 ft. lbs. (170 Nm).

17. If the strut was replaced, install the ABS wiring bracket to the strut using a new rivet if necessary. Connect the ABS wiring to the bracket, if unplugged, connect the wiring harness to the speed sensor. Be sure the wiring is positioned as noted during removal to prevent damage.

18. Install the wheel assembly, remove the supports and lower the vehicle.

19. Install the interior components.

20. Connect the negative battery cable, then check and adjust the rear alignment as necessary.

Coil Spring

REMOVAL & INSTALLATION

Front

1. Before servicing the vehicle, refer to the precautions in the beginning of this section.

2. Remove the strut assembly from the vehicle.

3. Mount the strut in a bench vise, then attach a suitable spring compressor/holding

Remove the strut shaft nut while the coil spring is compressed to unload the upper strut mount

fixture; be sure that the strut component is firmly secured.

4. Compress the spring sufficiently to completely unload the upper strut mount.

5. Remove the strut shaft nut while holding the strut stationary with a Torx® head socket wrench.

6. Remove the upper spring support and inspect the rubber for cracks or deterioration.

7. Remove the spring from the strut and inspect the spring for damage.

8. Remove the dust shield assembly and inspect for cracks or deterioration.

9. Remove the strut from the vise or applicable holding fixture and retract the strut shaft, checking for smooth, even resistance.

10. If replacing the coil spring, carefully release the spring compressor.

To install:

11. Secure the strut in the bench vise, or applicable holding fixture.

12. Extend the strut shaft to the limit of its travel.

13. Install the dust shield assembly onto the strut, then install the spring with the compressor tool installed.

14. Install the spring isolator and the strut mount to the top of the assembly.

15. Guide the strut shaft through the upper strut mount assembly. Compress the coil until the washer and shaft nut can be installed to the end of the shaft, but do not overcompress and damage the spring.

16. Tighten the shaft to the nut using a Torx® head socket wrench and a torque wrench, while holding the nut steady with an open end wrench. Tighten the fastener to 37 ft. lbs. (50 Nm).

17. Release the spring compressor tool and remove the strut from the fixture.

18. Install the strut assembly in the vehicle.

Rear

1. Before servicing the vehicle, refer to the precautions in the beginning of this section.

2. Remove the strut assembly from the vehicle.

3. Mount the strut in a bench vise, then attach a suitable spring compressor/holding fixture; be sure that the strut component is firmly secured.

4. Compress the spring sufficiently to completely unload the upper strut mount.

5. Remove the strut shaft nut while holding the strut stationary with a Torx® head socket wrench.

6. Remove the upper spring support and inspect the rubber for cracks or deterioration.

7. Remove the spring from the strut and inspect the spring for damage.

8. Remove the dust shield assembly and inspect for cracks or deterioration.

9. Remove the strut from the vise or applicable holding fixture and retract the strut shaft, checking for smooth, even resistance.

10. If replacing the coil spring, carefully release the spring compressor.

To assemble:

11. Secure the strut in the bench vise, or applicable holding fixture.

12. Extend the strut shaft to the limit of its travel.

13. Install the dust shield assembly onto the strut, then install the spring with the compressor tool installed.

14. Install the spring isolator and the strut mount to the top of the assembly.

15. Guide the strut shaft through the upper strut mount assembly. Compress the coil until the washer and shaft nut can be installed to the end of the shaft, but do not overcompress and damage the spring.

16. Tighten the shaft to the nut using a Torx® head socket wrench and a torque wrench, while holding the nut steady with an open end wrench. Tighten the fastener to 37 ft. lbs. (50 Nm).

17. Release the spring compressor tool and remove the strut from the fixture.

18. Install the strut using the procedure in this manual.

Wheel Bearings

ADJUSTMENT

All Saturn wheel bearing assemblies are an integral component of the wheel hub assembly. They are sealed at the factory and do not require any adjustment or maintenance.

REMOVAL & INSTALLATION

Front

1. Before servicing the vehicle, refer to the precautions in the beginning of this section.

2. If equipped with ABS, disconnect the negative battery cable.

3. Loosen the front halfshaft nut, while an assistant depresses the brake pedal, then raise and support the vehicle safely.

4. Remove the wheel assembly.

5. Remove the brake caliper mounting bracket bolts and suspend the assembly from the strut spring with wire.

6. Loosen the strut-to-knuckle bolts, but do not remove at this time.

7. Remove the rotor, axle nut and washer.

8. Remove and discard the cotter pin from the lower control arm ball joint. Back the ball joint nut until the top of the nut is even with the top of the threads.

9. Use tool SA9132S to separate the lower control arm ball joint from the steering knuckle, then remove the nut. Do not use a wedge tool or seal damage may occur.

➡**The outer CV-joint for vehicles equipped with ABS contains a speed**

Tighten the hub driver screw to remove the hub while the assembly is held firmly in a vise

Remove the bearing retainer snapring before pressing out the bearing

sensor ring. Use of an incorrect tool to separate the control arm from the knuckle may result in damage and loss of the ABS system.

10. Remove the tie rod cotter pin and castle nut, then separate the tie rod end from the knuckle using a tie rod separator SA91100C or equivalent. Do not use a wedge-type tool.

11. If equipped, disengage the ABS wheel speed sensor electrical connector.

12. Suspend the halfshaft from the body with wire, then remove the two knuckle-to-strut fasteners and remove the knuckle/hub assembly from the vehicle. If difficulty is encountered, position a block of wood on the end of the halfshaft and tap on the wood with a hammer to free the hub assembly.

13. If necessary, disassemble the knuckle hub assembly as follows:

  a. If equipped, remove the ABS wheel speed sensor from the knuckle.

➡**Any time the hub or bearing is separated from the steering knuckle, a new bearing must be used upon assembly.**

Carefully press the bearing out of the knuckle after removing the snapring

7922Z842

Exploded view of the rear hub/bearing assembly—drum brake set-up shown

b. Install wheel bearing removing tools SA9159S or equivalent, to the knuckle and secure the assembly in a vice.

c. Hold the hub driver with a wrench and tighten the hub driver screw to remove the hub. If the inner bearing race is pulled out with the hub, remove the race with a bearing race remover.

d. Remove the assembly from the vice and separate the wheel hub removal tool from the knuckle.

e. Remove the bearing retainer snapring.

f. Position the knuckle in a shop press on a knuckle support tube and press the bearing from the knuckle with a suitable small driver.

To install:

14. If necessary, assemble the knuckle hub assembly as follows:

a. Use a suitable large driver and press in the new bearing until seated.

b. Use the small driver and the knuckle support tube to press in the hub assembly. The small driver must be used to support the bearing inner race with its small (pilot) side facing towards the press and away from the bearing.

c. Install the bearing retainer snapring.

d. If equipped, install the ABS wheel speed sensor into the knuckle and tighten the fastener to 6 ft. lbs. (8 Nm).

➡**Service knuckles may not have holes for brake dust shield mounting. The dust shield is no longer required and does not have to be reinstalled. Also, should the shield become damaged, it may be removed; there is no need to repair or replace it. But, should a shield be removed and discarded, the shield should also be removed from the opposite side to maintain balance/symmetry.**

15. Thoroughly clean and lubricate the ball joint stud threads of the lower control arm and tie rod end. Install the knuckle/hub assembly onto the axle shaft. Then, install the washer with a new nut, but do not tighten the nut at this time.

16. Install the lower control arm ball stud through the knuckle bore and install the nut, but do not tighten at this time.

17. Install the steering knuckle-to-strut fasteners, but do not tighten at this time.

18. Install the tie rod end and nut, then tighten the nut to 33 ft. lbs. (45 Nm) and install a new cotter pin. If necessary, tighten the nut additionally, do not back off to insert the cotter pin.

19. Push inward on the bottom of the strut and tighten the knuckle fasteners to 148 ft. lbs. (200 Nm).

20. Tighten the lower control arm ball stud nut to 55 ft. lbs. (75 Nm), tighten additionally, if necessary, and install a new cotter pin.

21. Install the rotor onto the hub, then

install the caliper mount bracket onto the knuckle. Tighten the mount bracket assembly bolts to 81 ft. lbs. (110 Nm).

22. If equipped, engage the ABS electrical connector to the wheel speed sensor.

23. While an assistant depresses the brake pedal, tighten the halfshaft nut to 148 ft. lbs. (200 Nm).

24. Install the wheel assembly and lower the vehicle.

25. Connect the negative battery cable, check and adjust the alignment, as necessary.

Rear

Unlike the front wheel bearings, which may be removed from the hub for replacement, the rear wheel hub and bearing assembly is not serviceable. If damaged or worn, the hub and bearing assembly must be replaced as a unit.

1. Before servicing the vehicle, refer to the precautions in the beginning of this section.

2. If equipped with ABS, disconnect the negative battery cable.

3. Raise and support the vehicle safely, then remove the rear wheel.

4. If equipped, unplug the ABS speed sensor connector.

5. On disc brake equipped models, remove the caliper assembly-to-knuckle mounting bolts and support it with a wire from the strut, then remove the rotor.

6. On drum brake equipped models, remove the brake drum.

7. Remove the four hub/bearing-to-knuckle bolts, then remove the assembly from the vehicle.

To install:

8. Install the brake backing plate, hub/bearing assembly and retaining bolts. Tighten the bolts to 63 ft. lbs. (85 Nm).

9. Install the brake drum or rotor and caliper assembly. If applicable, tighten the caliper retaining bolts to 63 ft. lbs. (85 Nm).

10. If equipped, engage the ABS speed sensor connector.

11. Install the wheel assembly and lower the vehicle. If applicable, connect the negative battery cable.